W9-ANB-747

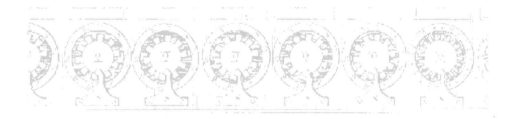

2nd edition

ENCYCLOPEDIA OF
PHILOSOPHY

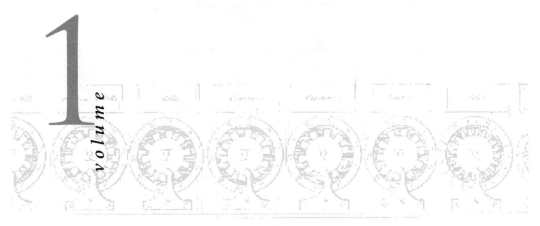

volume

1

2nd edition

ENCYCLOPEDIA OF
PHILOSOPHY

DONALD M. BORCHERT

Editor in Chief

MACMILLAN REFERENCE USA
An imprint of Thomson Gale, a part of The Thomson Corporation

THOMSON

GALE

Detroit • New York • San Francisco • San Diego • New Haven, Conn. • Waterville, Maine • London • Munich

Encyclopedia of Philosophy, Second Edition

Donald M. Borchert, Editor in Chief

For permission to use material from this product, submit your request via Web at http://www.gale-edit.com/permissions, or you may download our Permissions Request form and submit your request by fax or mail to:

Permissions
Thomson Gale
27500 Drake Rd.
Farmington Hills, MI 48331-3535
Permissions Hotline:
248-699-8006 or 800-877-4253 ext. 8006
Fax: 248-699-8074 or 800-762-4058

Since this page cannot legibly accommodate all copyright notices, the acknowledgments constitute an extension of the copyright notice.

While every effort has been made to ensure the reliability of the information presented in this publication, Thomson Gale does not guarantee the accuracy of the data contained herein. Thomson Gale accepts no payment for listing; and inclusion in the publication of any organization, agency, institution, publication, service, or individual does not imply endorsement of the editors or publisher. Errors brought to the attention of the publisher and verified to the satisfaction of the publisher will be corrected in future editions.

LIBRARY OF CONGRESS CATALOGING-IN-PUBLICATION DATA

Encyclopedia of philosophy / Donald M. Borchert, editor in chief.—2nd ed.
    p. cm.
        Includes bibliographical references and index.
        ISBN 0-02-865780-2 (set hardcover : alk. paper)—
        ISBN 0-02-865781-0 (vol 1)—ISBN 0-02-865782-9 (vol 2)—
        ISBN 0-02-865783-7 (vol 3)—ISBN 0-02-865784-5 (vol 4)—
        ISBN 0-02-865785-3 (vol 5)—ISBN 0-02-865786-1 (vol 6)—
        ISBN 0-02-865787-X (vol 7)—ISBN 0-02-865788-8 (vol 8)—
        ISBN 0-02-865789-6 (vol 9)—ISBN 0-02-865790-X (vol 10)
        1. Philosophy–Encyclopedias. I. Borchert, Donald M., 1934-

B51.E53 2005
103–dc22

2005018573

This title is also available as an e-book.
ISBN 0-02-866072-2
Contact your Thomson Gale representative for ordering information.

Printed in the United States of America
10 9 8 7 6 5 4 3 2 1

contents

volume 1
PREFACE TO 2ND EDITION
INTRODUCTION TO 1ST EDITION
LIST OF CONTRIBUTORS
LIST OF ARTICLES

ENCYCLOPEDIA OF
PHILOSOPHY
2nd edition

Abbagnano–Byzantine Philosophy

volume 2
Cabanis–Destutt de Tracy

volume 3
Determinables–Fuzzy Logic

volume 4
Gadamer–Just War Theory

volume 5
Kabbalah–Marxist Philosophy

volume 6
Masaryk–Nussbaum

volume 7
Oakeshott–Presupposition

volume 8
Price–Sextus Empiricus

volume 9
Shaftesbury–Zubiri

volume 10
APPENDIX: ADDITIONAL ARTICLES
THEMATIC OUTLINE
BIBLIOGRAPHIES
INDEX

editorial and production staff

executive vice president and publisher

Frank Menchaca

director, new product development

Hélène Potter

project editors

Jane A. Malonis
Carol A. Schwartz

contributing editors

Erin Bealmear, Deirdre S. Blanchfield, Steve Cusack, Angela Doolin, Susan Doty, Jason Everett, Alan Hedblad, Monica Hubbard, Lynn Koch, Melissa McDade, Bradley J. Morgan, Scot Peacock, Drew Silver, Ken Wachsberger

editorial technical support

Josh Kondek, Andrew Malonis, Mark Mikula, Mark Springer

manuscript editors

Robert A. Arlt, Dorothy Bauhoff, Sharon R. Gunton, William Kaufman, Eric Lagergren, Steven M. Long, Gina Misiroglu, Marie L. Thompson, Alan Thwaits, Amy Unterburger

proofreaders

Archie Hobson, John Krol, Amy Unterburger

bibliographic researcher

Michael Farmer

translators

Names of translators appear throughout the body of the *Encyclopedia*, at the end of each article that has been rendered into English.

indexer

Coughlin Indexing Services

product design

Kate Scheible

graphic art

Argosy Publishing

composition

Evi Seoud

manufacturing

Wendy Blurton

preface to the second edition

Nearly four decades ago, in 1967, Macmillan published its eight-volume *Encyclopedia of Philosophy*. With Paul Edwards as its exceptionally able editor in chief, the *Encyclopedia* became a highly respected, premier reference work consulted by countless professors and students as they pursued the examined life. Indeed, it would be safe to say that most if not all of the scholars who have contributed to the new Second Edition of the *Encyclopedia* leaned on the First Edition for philosophical insight during their formative years as young academicians. For them to be able to participate in reshaping a reference resource that figured importantly in their intellectual development has been a unique opportunity and a privilege.

When Macmillan invited me to serve as editor in chief for the new ten-volume Second Edition, the task appeared daunting because of its magnitude. But it also seemed manageable because backing me up was a valuable learning experience I had as the editor in chief for Macmillan's single-volume *Supplement*, published in 1996, that updated the *Encyclopedia*. Among the insights I gained from that experience three were especially important.

First, it seemed that the *Encyclopedia* had gained the respect of academicians because its articles provided substantive discussions by exceptionally competent scholars and its coverage embraced a wide range of topics in philosophy broadly construed. That was a winning formula: substantive articles by talented scholars exploring the full spectrum of philosophical topics. It would also guide the Second Edition.

Second, while that winning formula involved in-depth and broad coverage, nevertheless it did not and could not aspire to exhaustive coverage of all philosophical topics given the constraints imposed by the limited print space available. Whether the space available was the eight volumes of the First Edition or the one volume of the *Supplement* or the ten volumes of the Second Edition, a policy of selectivity had to be pursued with the unavoidable exclusion of some material that could have been, and perhaps should have been, included.

Third, to maintain the tradition of excellence established by the First Edition, an editor in chief needs to be surrounded by a group of distinguished philosophers who represent expertise in diverse subfields and who are willing to commit considerable time and effort to serve on an editorial board. I was fortunate indeed to have the support of an editorial team for the *Supplement* consisting of K. Danner Clouser, Paul Horwich, Jaegwon Kim, Joseph J. Kockelmans, Helen E. Longino, Vann McGee, Louis Pojman, Ernest Sosa, and Michael Tooley. Because of them, and the highly competent authors they helped to recruit, the *Supplement* continued Macmillan's tradition of publishing highly regarded reference works.

EDITORIAL BOARD FORMATION

Upon accepting the role of editor in chief for the Second Edition, I immediately turned to three of my former editorial colleagues—Jaegwon Kim, Michael Tooley, and Ernest Sosa—and invited them to become the core of a new Board of Associate Editors that would assist me in planning the new edition. The guidance provided by these three colleagues has been astute, seasoned, and truly indispensable from the early planning stages until the day of publication. With their assistance we were able to recruit Don Garrett, Barry Loewer, Doug MacLean, and Susan Wolf to join the Board of Associate Editors. Then we constituted a Board of Consulting Editors that would add expertise in specific subfields of philosophy not already covered by the specializations of the associate editors. The result was the impressive editorial team of distinguished philosophers listed below. Their areas of editorial oversight are noted after their names.

The Board of Associate Editors

Don Garrett—Modern Philosophy

Jaegwon Kim—Philosophy of Mind

Barry Loewer—Philosophy of Science

Doug MacLean—Ethics and Applied Ethics

Ernest Sosa—Epistemology

Michael Tooley—Metaphysics

Susan Wolf—Ethics and Applied Ethics

The Board of Consulting Editors

Louise Antony—Feminist Philosophy

John Burgess—Logic, Philosophy of Logic, Philosophy of Mathematics

Victor Caston—Ancient Philosophy, Medieval Philosophy

Richard P. Hayes—Buddhist Philosophy

Jeffrey King—Philosophy of Language

Oliver Leaman—Islamic Philosophy, Judaic Philosophy

Vladimir Marchenkov—Russian Philosophy

Thomas Nenon—Continental Philosophy

Karl H. Potter—Indian Philosophy

Philip Quinn—Philosophy of Religion

Jenefer Robinson—Aesthetics, Philosophy of Art

Kwong-loi Shun—Chinese Philosophy

James Sterba—Social and Political Philosophy

Charles Taliaferro—Philosophy of Religion

From the very beginning, our project's goal was not to replace the First Edition and the *Supplement* but to build the Second Edition on the foundation of their outstanding scholarly work. Accordingly, the task set before each editor was to analyze all the entries in the First Edition and the *Supplement* that were pertinent to his or her domain in order to determine which entries should be retained "as is" in the Second Edition with perhaps only a bibliographical update, which entries should be retained but needed an updating addendum, and which entries should be replaced by entirely new ones. In addition, all editors were given the opportunity to commission entirely new entries in their subfields. Each editor also had the responsibility to review and assess all new material appearing in his or her subfield. This generic description of the work of our subfield editors for the Second Edition masks all too easily the many hours of painstaking effort devoted to this project by these scholars.

In early autumn of 2004, regrettably, our editorial colleague Phil Quinn passed away after a brief struggle with esophageal cancer. Prior to his death, however, Phil had overseen his domain with an extraordinarily watchful and skilled eye. He had analyzed in detail every entry relating to the philosophy of religion in the First Edition and the *Supplement*, and sent me copious notes and recommendations for either improving, retaining, or replacing those entries. He also made specific recommendations for new entries to be commissioned and wrote detailed scope descriptions for those entries. When his illness forced him to withdraw from his teaching at the University of Notre Dame, he continued to work on the Second Edition, which provided concrete purpose for the day at hand. Phil worked carefully, deliberately, and had his eye on the prize of excellence. His fine work made it relatively easy for our colleague Charles Taliaferro to assume Phil's responsibilities on the editorial team.

If the Second Edition continues the tradition of excellence initiated by the First Edition, as I believe it will, that accomplishment will be due in no small measure to the exceptionally high quality work provided by our editors who, like Phil, have given of their time and talent to enhance the work of philosophy.

DEVELOPMENT OF THE SECOND EDITION'S CONTENT

Our strategy of building the Second Edition on the foundation of the First Edition and the *Supplement* requires a few additional comments.

Carefully and judiciously our editorial team selected those entries from the First Edition and the *Supplement* that were so well done that they merited retention. To virtually all of these entries we added bibliographical updates and to many of them we added substantive addenda. We prized these entries because, appearing together with the new entries, they enabled the reader to view high quality philosophizing over the course of almost a half century thereby adding a measure of historical *gravitas* to our project.

Notwithstanding our respect for the First Edition and the *Supplement,* we added 450 entries on new topics, and nearly 300 completely fresh and newly authored treatments of important topics that were originally covered within the First Edition or Supplement. The presence of all of this new material is a clear indication of the vigorous and innovative philosophical activity that has occurred within the discipline since the *Encyclopedia* made its debut almost four decades ago. Entirely new subfields have appeared such as feminist philosophy, the philosophy of sex and love, and applied ethics. New important topics in virtually every subfield have been explored ranging from artificial intelligence to animal rights. New scholars, whose distinctive contributions to the discipline needed description in substantive personal entries, have appeared on the philosophical landscape. Among such individuals are Karl-Otto Apel, Mohammed Arkoun, Nancy Cartwright, Daniel Dennett, Fred Dretske, Ronald Dworkin, John Earman, Hassan Hanafi, Virginia Held, Julia Kristeva, Jacques Lacan, John McDowell, Ruth Millikan, Richard Montague, Thomas Nagel, Seyyed Hossein Nasr, Martha Nussbaum, Derek Parfit, Hilary Putnam, Peter Singer, Gregory Vlastos, Richard Wollheim, and many, many more.

We also added updates to 90 articles, with those updates provided by their original authors. Additionally, 150 scholarly updates to existing articles have been included by means of "addenda," with each addendum compiled by an author other than the original writer, thus allowing for a fresh perspective that augments discussion of the topic at hand. Approximately 430 of the almost 1,200 classic First Edition or *Supplement* articles that appear in the Second Edition have been strengthened further by the inclusion of new bibliographic citations. Classic articles from the First Edition and *Supplement* are clearly identifiable via specific dates in the author bylines that follow each article. Author bylines followed by "(1967)" indicate that the article originally appeared in the First Edition, while bylines followed by "(1996)" indicate first publication within the *Supplement.* The designation "(2005)" denotes first publication within the Second Edition.

We have modified and expanded the philosophical inclusiveness of the First Edition in several ways. Both the analytic and continental philosophical traditions are well represented in the new topics and new personal entries, as well as in the style of presentation offered by our authors. In addition, enhanced cultural diversity is evident in the major space we have provided for topics relating to Buddhist philosophy, Chinese philosophy, Islamic philosophy, and Indian philosophy. Because of space limitations a number of First Edition entries devoted to national philosophies (such as American, British, and German) were not retained. The major figures from those countries and their contributions to philosophy have, however, been included in the Second Edition via personal and topical entries. Importantly, we have retained and expanded the entries on Japanese philosophy, Latin American philosophy, and Russian philosophy, and have added entries on African philosophy and Korean philosophy.

To preserve and enhance the detailed record of philosophical bibliographies, dictionaries, encyclopedias, and journals contained in the First Edition entries devoted exclusively to these topics, we moved these articles to the last volume of the Second Edition and increased substantially the space that had been allocated to them in the First Edition. The very large number of new philosophical bibliographies, dictionaries, encyclopedias, and journals that have been published in a multitude of languages during the last half century testifies not only to the vitality of philosophy but also to the increasing cultural diversity on its landscape.

A FEW FINAL POINTS

Several additional features of our editorial practices are important to note. In retaining entries from the First Edition, we have studiously avoided changing the text of those entries in the interest of preserving the philosophical and authorial integrity of those entries. Some of the authors, however, of those First Edition entries were available and wished to revise their entries. We, of course, welcomed their modifications. On some occasions, without compromising the integrity of an entry, we made some minor changes in the retained First Edition entries, such as inserting the year of death in the biographical part of a personal entry.

The entries in the Second Edition vary in readability level. Many entries will be readily accessible to the general public. Others will require some familiarity with the specialized vocabulary of philosophers. Still other entries will presuppose some acquaintance with logic. All the entries, it would be safe to say, require the kind of careful reading that is customary in the humanities and that helps to fashion liberally educated persons.

A good number of entries—such as those dealing with ancient, Buddhist, Chinese, Islamic, Judaic, and Russian philosophies—use non-English language words that required transliteration and the use of diacritical marks. In our transliterations and use of diacritical marks we have tried to follow the standard practice adopted by the contemporary leading scholars and the leading journals in the particular subfield to which the entry belongs.

The bibliographies that accompany the entries are selective rather than exhaustive. They provide the references to the works of the scholars cited in the text of an entry. The bibliographical entries in the tenth volume, however, which provide a record of philosophical bibliographies, dictionaries, encyclopedias, and journals, are much more extensive but are not exhaustive.

Volume 10 fulfills at least three important purposes. First, it houses the Appendix, which enabled us to include in the *Encyclopedia* a number of entries that, for a number of reasons, did not move through the editorial process in time to be included in the main alphabetical arrangement of the entries. For example, a few of our contributors encountered unexpected delays in completing their entries because of illness, and a few needed extra time because of other demanding professional commitments. Second, it provided a discrete location where the three lengthy comprehensive bibliographical entries on philosophical dictionaries and encyclopedias, journals, and bibliographies could be bundled together so that they would not distract from the topical and personal entries listed alphabetically in the main body of the set. Third, it contains the Index, a critical access tool for the book's readers.

SPECIAL ACKNOWLEDGMENTS

As editor in chief of this large project I owe a debt of gratitude to many people. I begin with my colleagues at Ohio University. The members of the Philosophy Department were a reservoir of philosophical expertise, good will, and seasoned professional advice. The Philosophy Department's Administrative Assistant, Penny Schall, helped to lighten my tasks, especially with her computer skills. Michael Farmer, the Head of Monographic Cataloging at Ohio University's Alden Library, devoted many painstaking hours to updating the bibliographies of scores of First Edition entries being retained in the Second Edition. The College of Arts and Sciences provided me a professional leave at a crucial juncture in the project so that I could work on the *Encyclopedia* without the standard professorial demands on my time.

Also, I wish to note with appreciation the role played by LinDa L. Grams, the Administrative Assistant in the Philosophy Department at the University of Notre Dame, who graciously served as a conduit of communication between Phil Quinn and me during his all too brief service as the editor overseeing the philosophy of religion.

In addition, there are four groups of people to whom all of us who use the Second Edition owe an expression of appreciation. The first group is the staff of Macmillan Reference and Thomson Gale. Frank Menchaca, Executive Vice President and Publisher, gave the support and encouragement of upper management to the Second Edition to ensure that it would go to press in 2005 and that it would continue the tradition of excellence that has been the hallmark of the reference works published by Macmillan through the years. Hélène Potter, Director of New Product Development, aided by her associates in the New York office, initiated the project and ever so adroitly assisted the editorial team to plan the structure and content of the new edition, and to operationalize those plans in each editor's domain of oversight. The five-person editorial team at Macmillan in Farmington Hills, Michigan, has exhibited seemingly untiring energy to bring the project to press at the targeted time. The core team consisted of Carol Schwartz, Senior Editor and Project Manager, who quarterbacked the team; Jane Malonis, Senior Editor and Project Manager; Brad Morgan, Senior Editor; Deirdre S. Blanchfield, Editor; and Lynn Koch, Associate Editor. This editorial team demonstrated the capacity to multi-task with incredible patience, resilience, diplomacy, and creativeness under many stressful conditions.

The second group to whom we owe words of gratitude consists of the hundreds of scholars who have contributed the multitude of articles that are the substance of the Second Edition. The extraordinarily fine entries that constitute the Second Edition were prepared by scholars with recognized expertise in the topics on which they have written. That fact should assure the reader that forays into the new edition of the *Encyclopedia* will prove to be always educationally valuable. We are deeply grateful for the intellectual heft that these distinguished authors have contributed to the Second Edition.

The third group that merits our appreciation is one that is almost invisible. I refer to the friends and families of our contributors who stood by patiently waiting for our contributors to complete their commitments to our project. Their patience is appreciated. The important contribution to learning that will be made by the new

Second Edition will ensure that the patience of these friends and family members will not have been in vain.

The fourth and final group that deserves appreciation is the team of associate and consulting editors who served on the *Encyclopedia*'s board. They are all very busy, very talented, and very distinguished philosophers. I am amazed and delighted that they were able to find the time to do the tasks that Macmillan and I laid on them. I daresay, however, that they had a special reward accruing from the many hours they devoted to the project. Each of them was asked to assess the new entries in their subfields as those entries were submitted by the authors to Macmillan. The editors were asked to indicate on a review sheet

if, in their judgment, the entry at hand should be approved as is, if the entry needed revision, or if the entry should be rejected. As I reviewed the editors' assessments, I marveled at how often editors would characterize the entries as "superb" or "excellent" or "outstanding," and I could almost feel the editor's delight as those words were written on the review sheets. Occasionally, I even saw the words "the finest piece of this length on this topic that has yet been written." Those words exuded the joy and intellectual excitement which are truly the abiding rewards that the editors, and hopefully all readers, will receive from this project.

Donald M. Borchert, 2005

introduction to the first edition, 1967

The last and, in fact, the only previous major philosophical reference work in the English language, J. M. Baldwin's *Dictionary of Psychology and Philosophy*, appeared in 1901. While it was in many ways an admirable work (it numbered among its contributors men of such caliber as Charles Peirce and G. E. Moore), the scope of Baldwin's *Dictionary* was quite limited. The great majority of articles were exceedingly brief, providing concise definitions of technical terms sometimes accompanied by additional information of a historical nature. There were articles about individual philosophers, but these usually amounted to no more than a few lines. Baldwin himself insisted that his work was primarily a dictionary and not an encyclopedia, but he did feature several articles of "encyclopedic character" dealing with important movements in the history of philosophy and the general divisions of philosophy. Some of these "special" articles, as Baldwin called them, were of the highest quality and have become justly famous. Even they, however, were relatively brief—according to Baldwin's own estimate, they varied in length from 1,000 to 5,000 words—and many important questions were entirely neglected or treated in a very cursory fashion. In Baldwin's own day there was undoubtedly room for a philosophical reference work of more ambitious scope. Since then, especially in the light of the revolutionary developments in philosophy and related fields, the need for a truly encyclopedic presentation of philosophical theories and concepts has become increasingly acute.

The present encyclopedia is intended to fill this need. It has been our aim to cover the whole of philosophy as well as many of the points of contact between philosophy and other disciplines. The *Encyclopedia* treats Eastern and Western philosophy; it deals with ancient, medieval, and modern philosophy; and it discusses the theories of mathematicians, physicists, biologists, sociologists, psychologists, moral reformers, and religious thinkers where these have had an impact on philosophy. The *Encyclopedia* contains nearly 1,500 articles of ample length which can be of value to the specialist, while most of them are sufficiently explicit to be read with pleasure and profit by the intelligent nonspecialist. Some of the longer articles, such as those dealing with the history of the various fields of philosophical investigation or the work of the most influential philosophers, are in effect small books, and even the shorter articles are usually long enough to allow a reasonably comprehensive treatment of the subject under discussion. We believe that there is no philosophical concept or theory of any importance that is not identified and discussed in the *Encyclopedia*, although not every concept or theory has a separate article devoted to it. In apportioning the space at our disposal, we were guided by the thought that the majority of readers would derive more benefit from a smaller number of long and integrated articles than from a multitude of shorter entries.

Throughout we have aimed at presentations which are authoritative, clear, comprehensive, and interesting.

Reference works have a reputation, not altogether undeserved, for being deadly dull. There are notable exceptions to this rule, but by and large it is true that the articles in both general and specialized encyclopedias are written in the most colorless prose and shy away from controversial issues. The authors frequently adopt a pose of complete neutrality and Olympian superiority to the conflicts of warring schools of thought, but in practice this usually amounts to an endorsement of safe positions and to neglect or even misrepresentation of radical thinkers, especially if they are contemporaries. Whatever else may be said about it, we do not believe that the present work will be condemned as either dull or timid. Radical movements and thinkers are given their full due, and the most controversial contemporary issues are discussed at great length. Moreover, the authors of the relevant articles were free and welcome to express their own views and in some instances to propose new solutions. It should be added that our contributors were not required to be serious and solemn at all costs, and some of our articles are certain to offend those who believe that philosophy and laughter are incompatible. As a consequence of our approach, the present work may in some respects have a greater resemblance to Dr. Johnson's *Dictionary* and even to Diderot's *Encyclopedia* than to the uncontroversial reference works to which the public has become accustomed in more recent times.

I have no doubt that in years to come a number of the articles in the *Encyclopedia* will be regarded as original contributions to philosophy. This comment refers in particular to articles which deal with controversial philosophical issues, but many of our historical articles also embody original research and in some instances treat topics which have not previously been the subject of thorough scholarly investigations. We have also made it a special point to rescue from obscurity unjustly neglected figures, and in such cases, where the reader would find it almost impossible to obtain reliable information in standard histories or in general encyclopedias, we have been particularly generous in our space allotments. In addition, the reader will find a number of articles on unexpected subjects—such as "Greek Drama," "If," "Nothing," and "Popular Arguments for the Existence of God"—that we considered sufficiently intriguing to be given individual attention.

In the attempt to make the articles interesting, we did not, however, lose sight of the basic goal of any reference work—to supply information in a clear and authoritative fashion. We have been fortunate in obtaining the collaboration of a large number of the foremost philosophers in the world, representing all shades of opinion. It is notorious that philosophy differs from the natural sciences in having no body of generally accepted conclusions. There are, for example, no answers to the problem of causation or the mind-body problem which have the endorsement of all competent students of the subjects; and the same is true of all or nearly all other philosophical problems. However, it is possible to provide an authoritative account of the nature of philosophical problems and of the various attempts to answer them. As far as exposition is concerned, the articles in the *Encyclopedia* are meant to be authoritative: although our contributors were free to express their own opinions, this was never done at the expense of providing the necessary information. To the attentive reader it will always be clear where a writer's exposition ends and the statement of his personal position begins.

Something should perhaps be said at this stage about the question of editorial bias, a subject on which there exists a great deal of confusion. It is important to distinguish two very different varieties of bias. The first is what we may call "polemical" bias—the kind that is operative in political campaigns, in the lower forms of journalism, and wherever fanatics of any kind discuss the views of their opponents. The stock in trade of this kind of partisanship is familiar: where the writer does not resort to deliberate forgery, he nevertheless frequently distorts his opponent's position by quoting out of context and in general by making him look as foolish as possible. Regrettably, philosophers, including some very great ones, have not been above employing such weapons, but in this *Encyclopedia* the use of such techniques has not been allowed. There is, however, another kind of bias which cannot be totally eliminated. No matter how fair and equitable an editor may try to be, his personal views and commitments are bound to affect the organization of the work, the space allotted to different subjects, and the criteria employed in judging the quality of contributions. If this kind of bias cannot be eliminated, its influence can at least be restricted, and it also can and should be openly acknowledged. One method that was used to limit the influence of editorial opinions was to assign articles, wherever possible, to authors who were to some considerable extent sympathetic to the theory or the figure they were to discuss. This rule was adhered to in most, though not in all, cases. It was not applied when there was a serious conflict with other criteria which were also relevant to the selection of contributors. If, for example, an author was in our opinion far superior to all other available writers in such qualifications as intellectual incisiveness and capacity for clear statement, he was chosen even if his sympathies for the subject of the article were limited. This happened in a few cases, but for the most part we succeeded in finding contributors who met all of our criteria.

It would, nevertheless, be idle to pretend that this *Encyclopedia* is free from bias and that my own ideological commitments have not significantly influenced its content. Like the majority of my closest advisers, I have been raised in the empirical and analytic tradition of Anglo-Saxon philosophy. There can be no doubt that if the *Encyclopedia* had been edited by a follower of Hegel or by a phenomenologist, assuming him to make every effort to be fair and equitable to other viewpoints, it would have looked very different. The topics chosen for separate articles would not have been the same, the space allotments would probably have been appreciably different, and there would undoubtedly have been a significantly different list of contributors. I doubt that an editor with such a background would have featured such articles as "Any and All," "Paradigm-case Argument," and "Proper Names and Descriptions," to give just a few illustrations, or that he would have devoted the same space to logic or to the philosophy of language. I am not here concerned with arguing that what we have done is right and that what other editors, with different commitments, would have done is wrong. I merely wish to remind the reader that in producing an encyclopedia one has to make a vast number of decisions and that one is not in the fortunate position of copying a pre-existing heavenly original. The decisions may be more or less justifiable, but in the last resort they always reflect the beliefs and sympathies of the editors.

We are presenting more than 900 articles on individual thinkers, and any responsible editor, no matter what his viewpoint, would have decided to include articles on the great majority of these. On the other hand, some figures have been omitted who, in the opinion of competent judges, have as good a claim to a separate article as some of those now included. We may as well here and now offer our apologies to all whose lists would have been different and who find that their favorites do not receive adequate attention. Some of these omissions can fairly be blamed on editorial judgment, but others are the result of accidental circumstances. For a number of relatively minor figures even the most diligent search failed to locate a contributor who could write an authoritative and readable article. In such cases it was decided that the space could be put to better use. Fortunately, these omissions are very few, and the ideas of most of the philosophers about whom we should have had separate articles are covered in various of our survey articles on the history of philosophy in different countries, in the articles on philosophical schools and movements, and sometimes also in those dealing with the history of the branches of philosophy. Nevertheless, there are some regrettable gaps, and we can only plead that if one works with over 500 contributors living in every corner of the globe, it is almost impossible that all one's plans should materialize.

One of the most difficult problems confronting the editor of any reference work is that of avoiding duplication without destroying the sense and continuity of individual articles. To be sure, not all duplication is undesirable, especially in a subject in which there is so much disagreement as in philosophy; and in the present work we have not tried to prevent discussions of the same topic in different contexts and from different viewpoints. To give one example, Zeno's paradoxes are discussed in the article bearing the philosopher's name and in the article "Infinity in Mathematics and Logic." The former article critically analyzes the paradoxes considered in the wider context of Greek thought, while in the latter the paradoxes are examined in order to cast light on problems concerning mathematical infinity. We have done our best, however, to avoid all duplication that would not serve a useful purpose. To achieve this end, it was necessary to be extremely flexible in the relative space provisions for various articles. It seemed unwise, for example, to have a lengthy review of the theories of Husserl once in the article bearing his name and then again in the article on phenomenology. In this particular instance we decided to feature a short article under "Husserl" but a very long one under "Phenomenology." This need for flexibility in order to use the available space to maximum advantage will account for many apparent disproportions in our space allotments. The articles on Marx and Engels, to give another illustration, are quite brief—much briefer than those on thinkers who have been far less influential; but this does not mean that Marxism has been neglected in the *Encyclopedia*. For, in addition to the biographical articles on Marx and Engels (and other Marxist thinkers), the *Encyclopedia* contains the very comprehensive articles "Dialectical Materialism," "Historical Materialism," and "Marxist Philosophy," as well as several shorter pieces, in all of which the theories of Marx and Engels are discussed. Our very elaborate index, prepared by a staff of specialists, and our system of cross references have made it possible to avoid a good deal of duplication.

The *Encyclopedia* is primarily the creation of the contributors, and I wish here to record our gratitude to the many fine scholars who have given so much of their time and energy to this enterprise. A certain type of reader drawn to philosophy is not happy unless he finds a plentiful supply of obscure and high-flown phraseology. Such readers will be disappointed by the present work. Those, on the other hand, who prefer simple and unpretentious language will (we hope) find our *Encyclopedia* to their liking. Nothing can make philosophy into an easy subject, but by taking very great pains it is possible to offer a lucid presentation even of extremely difficult and abstruse philosophical theories. If the majority of our articles are entirely intelligible to most educated readers, this is due to the special care taken by our contributors.

It should also be mentioned that although we were, unfortunately, compelled to reject a number of articles, this in no way reflects on their quality. Many of them were excellent studies and were excluded only for reasons pertaining to problems of space, duplication of material, or other technical considerations. The understanding and patience of all contributors as well as of all whose articles could not be used is greatly appreciated.

We are also very much indebted to the members of the editorial board, whose advice was constantly sought and always readily given. They aided us in a great many ways at all stages—they helped in mapping out the table of contents, in locating suitable contributors, and in evaluating manuscripts. When in the spring and summer of 1965 some absolutely indispensable articles had not arrived, it was chiefly through the intervention of members of the editorial board that outstanding scholars agreed to write the missing articles within the space of a few months. We would like to thank the following contributors for coming to our rescue at the last moment: William P. Alston, Stephen Barker, Thomas G. Bergin, George Boas, Vernon J. Bourke, Wing-tsit Chan, Arthur C. Danto, Phillip H. De Lacy, Ronald Grimsley, Philip P. Hallie, Peter L. Heath, John Hick, Paul O. Kristeller, Hugh R. MacCallum, James E. McClellan, Alasdair MacIntyre, John Macquarrie, F. S. Northedge, Robert G. Olson, John Passmore, Bede Rundle, Colin Smith, W. H. Walsh, and Edward Wasiolek. We are particularly grateful to Professor G. B. Kerferd for writing the article on Aristotle at incredibly short notice. That our extremely detailed and exhaustive article on the history of logic was completed in time is in large measure due to the tireless efforts of Professor A. N. Prior, who was wonderfully helpful in a great many other ways as well.

It would be impossible to praise too highly the performance of the members of the editorial staff. The best testimony to their skill and devotion is the fact that a work of this scope could be completed in a relatively short time by such a small group of people. Ann Trabulsi had the very difficult task of coordinating the work of contributors, editors, copy editors, and the production staff. Her admirable calm and self-possession resolved many a potentially explosive situation, while her tact and firmness worked wonders with even the most reluctant contributors. Philip Cummings, Donald Levy, Sandra Litt, and Margaret Miner were the four full-time editors. Their high standards of scholarship and accuracy, their fine feeling for language, and their unfailing good sense again and again evoked admiring comments and expressions of gratitude from our contributors. Their enthusiasm and their delightful and contagious sense of humor made my own share of the work not only less burdensome but frequently a great deal of fun. Dr. Albert Blumberg joined the editorial staff on a part-time basis early in 1964. It is largely owing to his rich knowledge and painstaking labors that our articles on logic and foundations of mathematics are, as we believe, of an exceedingly high quality. Alix Shulman assisted us during the last year in dealing with various tricky editorial problems, and we are most grateful to her for the excellence of her work. Dr. Murray Greene and Sheila Meyer worked for extended periods in the very onerous position of managing editor, and to both of them I wish to express my appreciation of their valuable contributions. I should also like to thank Mr. Sidney Solomon, who designed the *Encyclopedia* and who was involved in the project from the beginning, for giving valuable advice and assistance on many occasions. Finally, we are all indebted to our editorial secretary, Eunice Dean, whose careful management of our vast and complicated records and correspondence has been an indispensable aid to the production of the *Encyclopedia*.

I have left to the last obligations of a more personal nature. Four of my own articles—"Atheism," "Life, Meaning and Value of," "'My Death,'" and "Why" were written during the academic year 1964/1985 while I held a John Simon Guggenheim Foundation Research Fellowship. The award of this fellowship made it possible for me to take a leave of absence from my teaching duties, and I wish to thank the Guggenheim Memorial Foundation for its generous aid. I should also like to thank the following friends and colleagues for reading one or more of my own articles and for offering criticism and suggestions: Reuben Abel, F. M. Barnard, Sandra Bartky, Milič Čapek, Gertrude Ezorsky, Antony Flew, Peter Heath, Martin Lean, Ruth Barcan Marcus, C. Douglas McGee, Sidney Morgenbesser, Mary Mothersill, Ernest Nagel, Andrew Oldenquist, Robert Olson, Richard Popkin, Bertrand Russell, J. B. Schneewind, Elmer Sprague, and Carl Wellman. In connection with the difficult article about Wilhelm Reich I am especially grateful for advice and comments to Mr. A. S. Neill, Drs. Allan Cott and Ola Raknes (all of whom knew Reich well), and to Sir Karl Popper, Alasdair MacIntyre, Sidney Hook, and Michael Scriven. Needless to say, none of those who kindly helped me with my articles is responsible for any of the views expressed in them. To my dear friend and teacher, Ernest Nagel, I am deeply grateful for his unfailing encouragement and moral support ever since I began to edit the *Encyclopedia*. In spite of his many obligations he always found time to listen to our problems and to offer suggestions based on his immense erudition and his acquaintance with scholars in the most diverse fields.

Paul Edwards, Brooklyn College, March 1966

list of contributors

Contributors to the encyclopedia are listed below in alphabetic order followed by their academic affiliations and the article(s) they contributed. Articles reprinted from the first edition and supplement are indicated respectively by (1967) or (1996) following the article name. Affiliations provided for the authors of these articles were their 1967 or 1996 affiliations. New or updated articles are indicated by (2005) and include the current affiliation for the author.

Nicola Abbagnano
Professor, History of Philosophy, University of Turin
ALIOTTA, ANTONIO (1967)
ARDIGÒ, ROBERTO (1967)
FERRI, LUIGI (1967)
LEONARDO DA VINCI (1967)
POSITIVISM (1967)
PSYCHOLOGISM (1967)
RENSI, GIUSEPPE (1967)
RIGNANO, EUGENIO (1967)

Reuben Abel
Adjunct Associate Professor of Philosophy, Graduate Faculty, New School for Social Research, and Chairman of the Division of Humanities
SCHILLER, FERDINAND CANNING SCOTT (1967)

Francine F. Abeles
Mathematics, Kean University
LOGIC, HISTORY OF: MODERN LOGIC: THE BOOLEAN PERIOD: CARROLL (2005)

Raziel Abelson
Associate Professor and Chairman, Philosophy, University College, New York University
DEFINITION (1967)
ETHICS, HISTORY OF (1967)

Peter Achinstein
Professor of Philosophy, Johns Hopkins University
BRAITHWAITE, RICHARD BEVAN (1967, 2005)

Alparslan Açıkgenç
Professor, Philosophy, Fatih University, Istanbul
CAUSATION IN ISLAMIC PHILOSOPHY (2005)

H. B. Acton
Professor of Moral Philosophy, University of Edinburgh; Editor of Philosophy
ABSOLUTE, THE (1967)
BERKELEY, GEORGE (1967)
BOSANQUET, BERNARD (1967)
BRADLEY, FRANCIS HERBERT (1967)
DIALECTICAL MATERIALISM (1967)
HEGEL, GEORG WILHELM FRIEDRICH (1967)
HISTORICAL MATERIALISM (1967)
IDEALISM (1967)

David Adams
Professor of Philosophy, California State Polytechnic University, Pomona
PHILOSOPHY OF LAW, HISTORY OF [ADDENDUM] (2005)

E. M. Adams
Professor of Philosophy, University of North Carolina
LEWIS, CLARENCE IRVING (1967)

Robert M. Adams
Yale University
PHILOSOPHY OF RELIGION (1996)

Alfred Owen Aldridge
Head of Department of Comparative Literature, University of Maryland
PAINE, THOMAS (1967)

Peter Alexander
Reader in Philosophy, University of Bristol
DUHEM, PIERRE MAURICE MARIE (1967)
HERTZ, HEINRICH RUDOLF (1967)
PEARSON, KARL (1967)
POINCARÉ, JULES HENRI (1967)
SENSATIONALISM (1967)

W. M. Alexander
Associate Professor of Religion and Philosophy, St. Andrews College
HAMANN, JOHANN GEORG (1967)

Edwin Allaire
Professor of Philosophy, University of Texas at Austin
BERGMANN, GUSTAV (2005)

James Allen
Professor, Philosophy, University of Pittsburgh
ANCIENT SKEPTICISM (2005)
ANTIOCHUS OF ASCALON (2005)
ARCESILAUS (2005)
CARNEADES (2005)
PHILO OF LARISSA (2005)

Felix Alluntis O.F.M.
Ordinary Professor of Philosophy, Catholic University of America
VITORIA, FRANCISCO DE (1967)

Robert Almeder
McCullough Professor of Philosophy, Hamilton College, Clinton, NY
RESCHER, NICHOLAS (2005)

William P. Alston
Professor of Philosophy, University of Michigan
PHILOSOPHY OF RELIGION, PROBLEMS OF (1967)
PLEASURE (1967)
PSYCHOANALYTIC THEORIES, LOGICAL STATUS OF (1967)
RELIGION (1967)
RELIGION, NATURALISTIC RECONSTRUCTIONS OF (1967)
RELIGION, PSYCHOLOGICAL EXPLANATIONS OF (1967)
RELIGIOUS LANGUAGE (1967)
TELEOLOGICAL ARGUMENT FOR THE EXISTENCE OF GOD (1967)
TILLICH, PAUL (1967)

Andrew Altman
Professor of Philosophy; Director, Jean Beer Blumenfeld Center for Ethics, Georgia State University
DWORKIN, RONALD (2005)

Robert Anchor
Instructor of History, Yale University
RICKERT, HEINRICH (1967)
RITSCHL, ALBRECHT BENJAMIN (1967)

C. Anthony Anderson
Professor, Philosophy, University of California, Santa Barbara
CHURCH, ALONZO (2005)

Stephen C. Angle
Associate Professor of Philosophy, Wesleyan University
ZHU XI (CHU HSI) (2005)

Aldo Antonelli
Professor of Logic and Philosophy of Science, University of California, Irvine
FEMINIST PHILOSOPHY (2005)
INNATE IDEAS, NATIVISM (2005)
NON-MONOTONIC LOGIC (2005)
SEXISM (2005)

Roger Ariew
Professor and Chair, Philosophy, University of South Florida
CLAUBERG, JOHANNES (2005)
CORDEMOY, GÉRAUD DE (2005)

David M. Armstrong
University of Syndey
LAWS OF NATURE (1996)

Douglas Arner
Professor of Philosophy, Arizona State University
MCCOSH, JAMES (1967)

John Arthur
Professor of Philosophy; Director, Program in Philosophy, Politics and Law, Binghamton University
STATE [ADDENDUM] (2005)

Robert J. Arway, C.M.
Associate Professor of Philosophy, St. John's University
GODFREY OF FONTAINES (1967)

R. W. Ashby
Lecturer in Philosophy, King's College, University of London
BASIC STATEMENTS (1967)
VERIFIABILITY PRINCIPLE (1967)

Margaret Atherton
Professor of Philosophy, University of Wisconsin–Milwaukee
ASTELL, MARY (2005)
CAVENDISH, MARGARET (2005)
COCKBURN, CATHARINE TROTTER (2005)
SHEPHERD, MARY (2005)

Samuel Atlas
Professor, Philosophy, Hebrew Union College, New York
JACOBI, FRIEDRICH HEINRICH (1967)
SCHULZE, GOTTLOB ERNST (1967)

Robert Audi
Professor of Philosophy and David E. Gallo Chair in Ethics, University of Notre Dame
PHILOSOPHY (2005)

Bruce A. Aune
Emeritus Professor of Philosophy, University of Massachusetts, Amherst
CAN (1967)
POSSIBILITY (1967, 2005)
SELLARS, WILFRID (1996, 2005)
THINKING (1967)

Franz Austeda
Councilor of the School Board of Vienna
AVENARIUS, RICHARD (1967)
FISCHER, KUNO (1967)
JODL, FRIEDRICH (1967)
PETZOLDT, JOSEPH (1967)
RORETZ, KARL (1967)
STÖHR, ADOLF (1967)
WAHLE, RICHARD (1967)
ZIEHEN, THEODOR (1967)

Kent Bach
Professor of Philosophy, San Francisco State University
PERFORMATIVE UTTERANCES (2005)

Keith Michael Baker
Assistant Professor of History, University of Chicago
CONDORCET, MARQUIS DE (1967)

Edward G. Ballard
Professor of Philosophy, Tulane University
LACHELIER, JULES (1967)

Han Baltussen
Lecturer, Classics, University of Adelaide, South Australia
THEOPHRASTUS (2005)

Renford Bambrough
Fellow, Dean and Director, Studies in Moral Sciences, St. John's College
DEMIURGE (1967)
GREEK DRAMA (1967)

Julian Barbour
Director, The Leibniz Institute, Oxfordshire, U.K.
MACH, ERNST (2005)

Yehoshua Bar-Hillel
Professor of Logic and Philosophy of Science, Hebrew University of Jerusalem
BOLZANO, BERNARD (1967)
LOGIC, HISTORY OF: PRECURSORS OF MODERN LOGIC: BOLZANO (1967)

SYNTACTICAL AND SEMANTICAL
CATEGORIES (1967)

Frederick M. Barnard
*Associate Professor, Political
Science, University of Saskatchewan*
BACHOFEN, JOHANN JAKOB
(1967)
MORGAN, LEWIS HENRY (1967)
REINHOLD, KARL LEONHARD
(1967)
SPINOZISM (1967)
SUMNER, WILLIAM GRAHAM
(1967)
WEBER, ALFRED (1967)

Rachel Barney
*Canada Research Chair in Classical
Philosophy; Associate Professor,
Departments of Classics and
Philosophy, University of Toronto*
GORGIAS OF LEONTINI (2005)
NOMOS AND PHUSIS (2005)
SOPHISTS (2005)

Jeffrey A. Barrett
*Professor, Logic and Philosophy of
Science, University of California
Irvine*
MANY WORLDS/MANY MINDS
INTERPRETATION OF QUANTUM
MECHANICS (2005)

Jean-Pierre Barricelli
*Associate Professor of Romance
Languages and Comparative
Literature; Chair, Department of
French and Italian, University of
California, Riverside*
LEOPARDI, COUNT GIACOMO
(1967)

Irving H. Bartlett
*Professor and Chair, Philosophy,
Duke University*
CHANNING, WILLIAM ELLERY
(1967)
PARKER, THEODORE (1967)

Heather D. Battaly
*Assistant Professor, Philosophy,
California State University,
Fullerton*
ALSTON, WILLIAM P. (2005)

Robert Batterman
*Rotman Canada Research Chair in
Philosophy of Science, University of
Western Ontario*
REDUCTION (2005)

Margaret Pabst Battin
*Distinguished Professor, Philosophy,
and Adjunct Professor, Internal
Medicine, Division of Medical
Ethics, University of Utah, Salt
Lake City*
SUICIDE (2005)

Charles A. Baylis
*Professor and Chair, Philosophy,
Duke University*
CONSCIENCE (1967)

Ken Baynes
*Professor, Philosophy, Syracuse
University*
APEL, KARL-OTTO (2005)

George Bealer
University of Colorado, Boulder
INTUITION [ADDENDUM 1]
(1996)

Monroe C. Beardsley
*Professor and Acting Chairman,
Philosophy, Swarthmore College*
AESTHETICS, HISTORY OF (1967)

Tom L. Beauchamp
Georgetown University
APPLIED ETHICS (1996)

Lewis White Beck
*Burbank Professor of Intellectual
and Moral Philolosphy, University
of Rochester*
NEO-KANTIANISM (1967)
STERN, LOUIS WILLIAM (1967)

Morton O. Beckner
*Associate Professor of Philosophy,
Pomona College*
DARWINISM (1967)
ORGANISMIC BIOLOGY (1967)
TELEOLOGY (1967)
VITALISM (1967)

Jason BeDuhn
*Associate Professor of Religious
Studies, Humanities, Arts, and
Religion, Northern Arizona
University*
MANI AND MANICHAEISM
[BIBLIOGRAPHY] (2005)

Gordon Belot
*Associate Professor of Philosophy,
University of Pittsburgh*
CONSERVATION PRINCIPLE (2005)

John W. Bender
*Professor of Philosophy, Ohio
University*
ART, EXPRESSION IN (1996, 2005)
COHERENTISM (1996)

Stanley I. Benn
*Senior Fellow in Philosophy,
Australian National University*
DEMOCRACY (1967)
EQUALITY, MORAL AND SOCIAL
(1967)
NATIONALISM (1967)
POWER (1967)
PROPERTY (1967)
PUNISHMENT (1967)
SOCIETY (1967)
SOVEREIGNTY (1967)
STATE (1967)

Carlton W. Berenda
*Professor of Philosophy, University
of Oklahoma*
WEYL, (CLAUS HUGO) HERMANN
(1967)

Thomas Goddard Bergin
*Sterling Professor of Romance
Languages and Mast of Timothy
Dwight College, Yale University*
DANTE ALIGHIERI (1967)

Robert Bernasconi
*Moss Professor of Philosophy,
University of Memphis*
ALTERITY (2005)
DERRIDA, JACQUES (1996, 2005)
PHILOSOPHY OF LANGUAGE IN
CONTINENTAL PHILOSOPHY
(2005)

Paul Bernays
*Retired Professor, Swiss Federal
Institute of Technology (Zurich)*
HILBERT, DAVID (1967)

Arthur Berndston
*Professor, Chair, Philosophy,
University of Missouri*
DEUSTUA, ALEJANDRO O. (1967)
CASO, ANTONIO (1967)
INGENIEROS, JOSÉ (1967)
KORN, ALEJANDRO (1967)
ROMERO, FRANCISCO (1967)
VASCONCELOS, JOSÉ (1967)
VAZ FERREIRA, CARLOS (1967)

Richard J. Bernstein
*Chair, Philosophy, Haverford
College*
DEWEY, JOHN (1967)

Sylvia Berryman
Assistant Professor, Philosophy,
University of British Columbia
PNEUMA (2005)
STRATO AND STRATONISM (2005)

Peter A. Bertocci
Bowne Professor of Philosophy,
Brown University (Emeritus)
BOWNE, BORDEN PARKER (1967)
HOWISON, GEORGE HOLMES
  (1967)

Gábor Betegh
Associate Professor, Philosophy,
Central European University,
Budapest
DIOGENES OF APOLLONIA (2005)
MOIRA/TYCHÉ/ANANKÊ (2005)
ORPHISM [ADDENDUM] (2005)

Joël Biard
Professeur des Universités, Centre
d'Études Supérieures de la
Renaissance, Université de Tours
ALBERT OF SAXONY (2005)

Cristina Bicchieri
Carol and Michael Lowenstein
Endowed Term Professor; Director,
Philosophy, Politics and Economics
Program; Professor of Philosophy,
University of Pennsylvania
GAME THEORY (2005)

John Bickle
Professor, Philosophy and
Neuroscience Graduate Program,
University of Cincinnati
NEUROSCIENCE (2005)

John Bigelow
Professor, School of Philosophy and
Bioethics, Monash University,
Australia
NUMBER (2005)

Robert Bird
Assistant Professor, Slavic
Languages and Literatures,
University of Chicago
IVANOV, VIACHESLAV IVANOVICH
  (2005)
ROZANOV, VASILII VASIL'EVICH
  [ADDENDUM] (2005)

Robert Bishop
Lecturer, Faculty of Philosophy,
University of Oxford
DETERMINISM AND
  INDETERMINISM (2005)

Michel Bitbol
Directeur de recherche au CNRS;
Chargé de cours à l'Université Paris
I, Centre de Recherches en
Epistémologie Appliquée,
(CREA/Ecole Polytechnique)
SCHRÖDINGER, ERWIN (2005)

Max Black
Professor, Philosophy, Cornell
University
INDUCTION (1967)
RAMSEY, FRANK PLUMPTON
  (1967)

Simon Blackburn
University of North Carolina,
Chapel Hill
ERROR THEORY OF ETHICS (1996)
RULE FOLLOWING (1996)

Robert Blanché
Professor of Philosophy, Faculty of
Letters and Humane Sciences,
University of Toulouse
COUTURAT, LOUIS (1967)
GOD, CONCEPTS OF (1967)
MEYERSON, ÉMILE (1967)
MILHAUD, GASTON (1967)
ROUGIER, LOUIS (1967)
WHEWELL, WILLIAM (1967)

Brand Blanshard
Sterling Professor Emeritus, Yale
University
WISDOM (1967)

J. L. Blau
Professor, Religion, Columbia
University
ALBO, JOSEPH (1967)
BAHYA BEN JOSEPH IBN PAQUDA
  (1967)
CORDOVERO, MOSES BEN JACOB
  (1967)
HICKOK, LAURENS PERSEUS
  (1967)
IBN ZADDIK, JOSEPH BEN JACOB
  (1967)
ISRAELI, ISAAC BEN SOLOMON
  (1967)
JAMES, HENRY (1967)
KABBALAH (1967)
MATHER, COTTON (1967)
MUQAMMIS, DAVID BEN MERWAN
  AL- (1967)
PORTER, NOAH (1967)
SELLARS, ROY WOOD (1967)
WAYLAND, FRANCIS (1967)

Ned Block
Massachusetts Institute of
Technology
FUNCTIONALISM (1996)

H. Gene Blocker
Professor, Philosophy, Ohio
University
CHINESE PHILOSOPHY: SOCIAL
  AND POLITICAL THOUGHT
  (2005)
JAPANESE PHILOSOPHY (2005)

Mary K. Bloodsworth-Lugo
Associate Professor, Philosophy,
Washington State University,
Pullman
CIXOUS, HÉLÈNE (2005)

Philip Blosser
Professor of Philosophy, School of
History, Philosophy, and Religion,
Lenoir-Rhyne College
SCHELER, MAX (2005)

William T. Bluhm
Associate Professor of Political
Science, University of Rochester
HARRINGTON, JAMES (1967)

Lawrence A. Blum
Professor of Philosophy,
Distinguished Professor of Liberal
Arts and Education, University of
Massachusetts, Boston
ETHICS AND MORALITY (2005)
MURDOCH, IRIS (2005)

James Blumenthal
Associate Professor, Philosophy,
Oregon State University, Corvallis
BUDDHISM—SCHOOLS: DGE-LUGS
  (2005)

George Boas
Professor Emeritus of the History of
Philosophy, Johns Hopkins
University
BONALD, LOUIS GABRIEL
  AMBROISE, VICOMTE DE (1967)
BURTHOGGE, RICHARD (1967)
CHATEAUBRIAND, FRANÇOIS RENÉ
  DE (1967)
COUSIN, VICTOR (1967)
DESTUTT DE TRACY, ANTOINE
  LOUIS CLAUDE, COMTE (1967)
JOUFFROY, THÉODORE SIMON
  (1967)
LAMENNAIS, HUGUES FÉLICITÉ
  ROBERT DE (1967)
LAROMIGUIÈRE, PIERRE (1967)

LOVE (1967)
LOVEJOY, ARTHUR ONCKEN
  (1967)
MAISTRE, COMTE JOSEPH DE
  (1967)
RAVAISSON-MOLLIEN, JEAN
  GASPARD FÉLIX (1967)
RENOUVIER, CHARLES BERNARD
  (1967)
ROYER-COLLARD, PIERRE PAUL
  (1967)
STAËL-HOLSTEIN, ANNE LOUISE
  GERMAINE NECKER, BARONNE DE
  (1967)
TRADITIONALISM (1967)

Susanne Bobzien
*Professor, Philosophy, Yale
University*
LOGIC, HISTORY OF: ANCIENT
  LOGIC (2005)

Margaret Boden
*Research Professor of Cognitive
Science, Centre for Cognitive
Science, University of Sussex*
ARTIFICIAL INTELLIGENCE (1996,
  2005)
COGNITIVE SCIENCE (1996,
  2005)

István M. Bodnár
*Philosophy, Central European
University*
ALEXANDER OF APHRODISIAS
  (2005)

Hermann Boeschenstein
*Head, Department of German,
University of Toronto*
OKEN, LORENZ (1967)

Paul Artin Boghossian
New York University
ANALYTICITY (1996)

Bernadine M. Bonansea, O.F.M
*Ordinary Professor of Philsophy,
Catholic University of America*
CAMPANELLA, TOMMASO (1967)
SCOTISM (1967)
TELESIO, BERNARDINO (1967)

David Boonin
*Associate Professor, Philosophy,
University of Colorado, Boulder*
ABORTION [BIBLIOGRAPHY]
  (2005)

Vernon J. Bourke
*Professor, Philosophy, St. Louis
University; President of the World*

*Union of Catholic Philosophical
Societies*
BÁÑEZ, DOMINIC (1967)
BELLARMINE, ST. ROBERT (1967)
BIEL, GABRIEL (1967)
CAPREOLUS, JOHN (1967)
FONSECA, PETER (1967)
JOHN OF ST. THOMAS (1967)
MARIANA, JUAN DE (1967)
SOTO, DOMINIC DE (1967)
SYLVESTER OF FERRARA, FRANCIS
  (1967)
THOMAS AQUINAS, ST. (1967)
TOLETUS, FRANCIS (1967)
VASQUEZ, GABRIEL (1967)

Bernard R. Boxill
*Pardue Professor, Philosophy,
University of North Carolina at
Chapel Hill*
AFFIRMATIVE ACTION (2005)
KING, MARTIN LUTHER (2005)

Michael Boylan
*John J. McDonnell Jr. Chair in
Ethics, Marymount University*
JEFFERSON, THOMAS (2005)
MACHIAVELLI, NICCOLÒ
  [ADDENDUM] (2005)
MARSILIUS OF PADUA
  [ADDENDUM] (2005)
OAKESHOTT, MICHAEL (2005)

G. R. Boys-Stones
*Senior Lecturer in Classics,
Department of Classics and Ancient
History, Durham University*
CLEMENT OF ALEXANDRIA
  [BIBLIOGRAPHY] (2005)
NUMENIUS OF APAMEA
  [BIBLIOGRAPHY] (2005)

Germaine Brée
*Vilas Professor, Institute for
Research in the Humanities,
Madison, WI*
MALRAUX, GEORGES-ANDRÉ
  (1967)
WEIL, SIMONE (1967)

Ignatius Brady, O.F.M
*Prefect, Theological Comission,
Collegio di S. Bonaventura,
Franciscan International College of
Research, Quaracchi, Italy*
ALEXANDER OF HALES (1967)
JOHN OF LA ROCHELLE (1967)
PETER LOMBARD (1967)

Craig Brandist
*Reader in Cultural Theory and
Intellectual History, Bakhtin Centre*

*and Department of Russian and
Slavonic Studies, University of
Sheffield*
BAKHTIN CIRCLE, THE (2005)

Frithhiof Brandt
*Professor of Philosophy (Emeritus),
University of Copenhagen*
HØFFDING, HARALD (1967)

Richard B. Brandt
*Professor, Philosophy, University of
Michigan*
EPISTEMOLOGY AND ETHICS,
  PARALLEL BETWEEN (1967)
ETHICAL RELATIVISM (1967)
HEDONISM (1967)

Johan Brännmark
*Philosophy, Lund University,
Sweden*
GOOD, THE (2005)

David Braun
*Professor, Philosophy, University of
Rochester*
DEMONSTRATIVES (2005)

Samantha Brennan
*Associate Professor, Philosophy, The
University of Western Ontario*
CARD, CLAUDIA (2005)
HELD, VIRGINIA (2005)

Phillip Bricker
*University of Massachusetts,
Amherst*
IDENTITY (1996)
PROPERTIES (1996)

Harvey H. Brimmer II
*Assistant Professor, Philosophy,
University of Maine*
LEQUIER, (JOSEPH LOUIS) JULES
  (1967)

Crane Brinton
*McLean Professor of Ancient and
Modern History, Harvard
University*
ROMANTICISM (1967)

Susan J. Brison
*Associate Professor, Philosophy,
Dartmouth College*
BEAUVOIR, SIMONE DE (1996,
  2005)

Justin Broackes
Brown University
COLORS (1996)

EXTRINSIC AND INTRINSIC
PROPERTIES (1996)

Dan W. Brock
Brown University
INFORMED CONSENT (1996)

Boruch A. Brody
Fulbright Fellow, Oxford University
LOGICAL TERMS, GLOSSARY OF
(1967)

Sylvain Bromberger
*Massachusetts Institute of
Technology*
PHONOLOGY (1996)

Andrew Brook
*Professor of Philosophy, Director,
Institute of Cognitive Science;
Member, Canadian Psychoanalytic
Society*
DENNETT, DANIEL CLEMENT
(2005)

Charlotte R. Brown
*Associate Professor, Philosophy,
Illinois Wesleyan University*
ALTRUISM (2005)
SHAFTESBURY, THIRD EARL OF
(ANTHONY ASHLEY COOPER)
(2005)
WOLLASTON, WILLIAM (2005)

Eric Brown
*Associate Professor, Philosophy,
Washington University in St. Louis*
EPICTETUS (2005)
MARCUS AURELIUS ANTONINUS
(2005)
PANAETIUS OF RHODES (2005)

Robert Brown
*Senior Fellow, Philosophy, Institute
of Advanced Studies, Australian
National University*
BROAD, CHARLIE DUNBAR (1967)

Stephen F. Brown
*Director of the Institute of Medieval
Philosophy and Theology; Professor,
Theology, Boston College*
GODFREY OF FONTAINES
[BIBLIOGRAPHY] (2005)
GREGORY OF RIMINI
[BIBLIOGRAPHY] (2005)

Anthony Brueckner
*Professor, Philosophy, University of
California, Santa Barbara*
SKEPTICISM, CONTEMPORARY
(1996, 2005)

Leendert Brummel
*Professor, Library Science,
University of Amsterdam*
HEMSTERHUIS, FRANS (1967)

Alexander Brungs
*Research Fellow, Philosophy,
Universität Zürich, Switzerland*
INNER SENSES (2005)

Ronald Bruzina
*Professor, Philosophy, University of
Kentucky, Lexington*
FINK, EUGEN (2005)

Jeffrey Bub
*Chair, Committee for Philosophy
and the Sciences, Philosophy
Department, University of
Maryland, College Park*
COPENHAGEN INTERPRETATION
(2005)
QUANTUM COMPUTING AND
TELEPORTATION (2005)

Allen Buchanan
*James B. Duke Professor of
Philosophy and Public Policy
Studies, Duke University*
APPLIED ETHICS (2005)

Gerd Buchdahl
*Lecturer in Philosophy of Science;
Head, History and Philosophy of
Science, Cambridge University*
CAMPBELL, NORMAN ROBERT
(1967)

Malcolm Budd
*Emeritus Grote Professor of
Philosophy of Mind and Logic,
University College London*
WOLLHEIM, RICHARD (2005)

Otávio Bueno
*Associate Professor, Philosophy,
University of South Carolina*
VAN FRAASSEN, BAS (2005)

John P. Burgess
*Professor, Philosophy, Princeton
University*
KRIPKE, SAUL (1996, 2005)
LOGIC, HISTORY OF: MODERN
LOGIC: SINCE GÖDEL
[OVERVIEW] (2005)
QUANTIFIERS IN FORMAL LOGIC
(2005)

Keith Burgess-Jackson
*Associate Professor, Philosophy, The
University of Texas at Arlington*
FEINBERG, JOEL (2005)

Charles Burnett
*Professor of the History of
Arabic/Islamic Influence in Europe,
Warburg Institute, University of
London*
HERMETICISM [ADDENDUM]
(2005)

David Burrell, C.S.C.
*Hesburgh Professor in Philosophy
and Theology, University of Notre
Dame*
AL-GHAZĀLI, MUHAMMAD
[ADDENDUM] (2005)
ETERNITY [ADDENDUM 2] (2005)

Sam Butchart
*Research Fellow, School of
Philosophy and Bioethics, Monash
University, Australia*
NUMBER (2005)

Alex Byrne
*Associate Professor, Philosophy,
Massachusetts Institute of
Technology*
PRIVATE LANGUAGE PROBLEM
[ADDENDUM] (2005)

Duane L. Cady
Hamline University
VIOLENCE (1996)

Steven M. Cahn
*Doctoral Candidate, Columbia
University*
CHANCE (1967)

Craig Callender
*Associate Professor of Philosophy,
University of California, San Diego*
TIME IN PHYSICS (2005)

Massimo Campanini
*Reader in Arab Culture and
Civilization, Faculty of Letters and
Philosophy, University of Milan*
HANAFI, HASSAN (2005)

A. H. Campbell
*Regius Professor of Public Law,
University of Edinburgh*
DEL VECCHIO, GIORGIO (1967)

Keith Campbell
Emeritus Professor of Philosophy, University of Sydney
MACKIE, JOHN LESLIE (1996, 2005)
MATERIALISM (1967, 2005)
NATURALISM (2005)
ONTOLOGY (2005)
SMART, JOHN JAMIESON CARSWELL (1996, 2005)

Mariano Campo
Professor Emeritus of the History of Philosophy, University of Trieste
LIEBMANN, OTTO (1967)
RIEHL, ALOIS (1967)

Kenneth L. Caneva
Professor, History, University of North Carolina at Greensboro
KUHN, THOMAS (2005)

Walter F. Cannon
Curator of Astronomy and Physics; Curator in Charge of Division of Physical Sciences, Smithsonian Institution
HERSCHEL, JOHN (1967)

Milič Čapek
Professor of Philosophy, Boston University
AMPÉRE, ANDRÉ MARIE (1967)
ETERNAL RETURN (1967)
OSTWALD, WILHELM (1967)
RIBOT, THÉODULE ARMAND (1967)
TAINE, HIPPOLYTE-ADOLPHE (1967)

Ben Caplan
Associate Professor, Philosophy, University of Manitoba
KAPLAN, DAVID (2005)

A. Robert Caponigri
Professor, Philosophy, University of Notre Dame
GIOBERTI, VINCENZO (1967)
MARTINETTI, PIERO (1967)
ROSMINI-SERBATI, ANTONIO (1967)
SCIACCA, MICHELE FEDERICO (1967)
STEFANINI, LUIGI (1967)

George Cardona
Professor Emeritus of Linguistics, University of Pennsylvania, Philadelphia
PHILOSOPHY OF LANGUAGE IN INDIA (2005)

Stefano Caroti
Professore Ordinario di Storia della Filosofia Medievale, Dipartimento di Filosofia, Università degli Studi di Parma
ORESME, NICOLE (2005)

Brian Carr
Honorary University Fellow, University of Exeter
CAUSATION IN INDIAN PHILOSOPHY (2005)

David Carr
Charles Howard Candler Professor of Philosophy, Emory University
PHILOSOPHY OF HISTORY (2005)

Meyrick H. Carré
Reader in Philosophy at University of Bristol (retired)
PHYSICOTHEOLOGY (1967)

John Carroll
Professor of Philosophy, Department of Philosophy and Religion, North Carolina State University, Raleigh
LAWS OF NATURE [ADDENDUM] (2005)

Noel Carroll
Professor, Philosophy, University of Wisconsin, Madison
ART, DEFINITIONS OF (2005)
ART, INTERPRETATION OF (2005)
ART, TRUTH IN (2005)

Scott Carson
Ohio University
ALBERT THE GREAT (2005)
EUDAIMONIA (2005)
PHRONÊSIS (2005)
SOPHIA (2005)
SÔPHROSUNÊ (2005)
VALENTINUS AND VALENTINIANISM (2005)
XENOPHON [ADDENDUM] (2005)

Thomas Carson
Professor of Philosophy, Loyola University Chicago
METAETHICS (2005)

Robyn Carston
Professor of Linguistics, Department of Phonetics and Linguistics, University College
PRAGMATICS [ADDENDUM] (2005)

Benjamin Carter
Special Lecturer, Historical Studies, University of Bristol
PANNENBERG, WOLFHART (2005)

Andre Carus
Graduate Student, Philosophy, University of Chicago
CARNAP, RUDOLF (2005)
POSITIVISM [BIBLIOGRAPHY] (2005)

John Carvalho
Associate Professor, Philosophy, Villanova University
BARTHES, ROLAND (2005)

Héctor-Ner Castannñeda
Professor of Philosophy, Wayne State University
PRIVATE LANGUAGE PROBLEM (1967)

Albert Casullo
Professor, Philosophy, University of Nebraska-Lincoln
KNOWLEDGE, A PRIORI (2005)
KNOWLEDGE AND MODALITY (1996, 2005)

Walter Cerf
Visiting Professor, Philosophy, University of Wisconsin; Professor, Philosophy, City University of New York, Brooklyn College
HARTMANN, NICOLAI (1967)

Henry Chadwick
Regius Professor of Divinity at Oxford University
LESSING, GOTTHOLD EPHRAIM (1967)

Arindam Chakrabarti
Professor, Philosophy, University of Hawaii at Manoa
UNIVERSAL PROPERTIES IN INDIAN PHILOSOPHICAL TRADITIONS (2005)

Alan Chan
Professor, Philosophy, National University of Singapore
GUO XIANG (2005)
WANG BI (2005)

Wing-Tsit Chan
Professor of Chinese Culture and Philosophy, Dartmouth College; Adjunct Professor of Chinese Thought, Columbia University

CHENG HAO (1967)
CHENG YI (1967)
CHINESE PHILOSOPHY [OVERVIEW] (1967)
ZHUANGZI (1967)

Carsun Chang
President, Institute of Political Science, Shanghai (retired)
LU XIANGSHAN (1967)

Christopher K. Chapple
Professor, Theological Studies, Loyola Marymount University
MEDITATION IN INDIAN PHILOSOPHY (2005)

Louis Charland
Associate Professor, Philosophy, University of Western Ontario
EMOTION (2005)

Sebastien Charles
Associate Professor, Philosophy, Université de Sherbrooke
VOLTAIRE, FRANÇOIS-MARIE AROUET DE (2005)

Jo-shui Chen
Research Fellow, Institute of History and Philology, Academia Sinica, Taiwan
HAN YU (2005)
LI AO (2005)
WANG CHONG (2005)

Chung-ying Cheng
Professor of Philosophy, University of Hawaii at Manoa
DAI ZHEN (2005)
ZHANG ZAI (2005)

(John) Hsueh-li Cheng
Professor, Philosophy and Religious Studies, University of Hawaii at Hilo
CHINESE PHILOSOPHY: BUDDHISM (2005)

Roderick M. Chisholm
Romeo Elton Professor of Natural Theology and Professor of Philosophy, Brown University
BRENTANO, FRANZ (1967)
INTENTIONALITY (1967)
MARTY, ANTON (1967)
MEINONG, ALEXIUS (1967)

William Chittick
Professor, Asian and Asian-American Studies, Stony Brook University
IBN AL-ʿARABI (2005)

Peter Cholak
Professor, Mathematics, University of Notre Dame
LOGIC, HISTORY OF: MODERN LOGIC: SINCE GÖDEL: FRIEDMAN AND REVERSE (2005)
REVERSE MATHEMATICS (2005)

Edith Clowes
Professor, Slavic Languages and Literatures, University of Kansas, Lawrence
SHESTOV, LEV ISAAKOVICH [ADDENDUM] (2005)

Duane L. Cody
Hamline University
PACIFISM (1996)

Carl Cohen
Professor of Philosophy, The University of Michigan, Ann Arbor
DEMOCRACY [ADDENDUM] (2005)

L. J. Cohen
Queen's College, Oxford University, England
PRIOR, ARTHUR NORMAN (1996)

Robert S. Cohen
Professor and Chair, Physics, Boston University
NEURATH, OTTO (1967)

Ted Cohen
Professor, Philosophy, University of Chicago
AESTHETIC JUDGMENT (2005)
ART, FORMALISM IN (2005)

Margaret Cole
President, Fabian Society, Vice-Chairman of the Further and Higher Education Committee of the Inner London Education Authority
SOCIALISM (1967)

R. L. Cole
Professor, History and English, University of Iowa
ARMINIUS AND ARMINIANISM (1967)

Jules L. Coleman
Wesley Newcomb Hohfeld Professor of Jurisprudence, Yale Law School, Professor of Philosophy, Yale University
ANALYTIC JURISPRUDENCE (2005)
LEGAL POSITIVISM: ANGLO-AMERICAN LEGAL POSITIVISM SINCE H. L. A. HART (2005)

James Collins
Professor, Philosophy, St. Louis University
NEWMAN, JOHN HENRY (1967)

Juan Comesaña
Assistant Professor, Philosophy, University of Wisconsin-Madison
PYRRHONIAN PROBLEMATIC, THE (2005)

Earl Conee
Professor of Philosophy, University of Rochester, NY
EPISTEMOLOGY (1996, 2005)
EVIDENTIALISM (1996)

James I. Conway
Chair, Philosophy, Fordham University, New York, NY (retired)
MARÉCHAL, JOSEPH (1967)

Roy T. Cook
Visiting Professor, Philosophy; Villanova University, and Associate Research Fellow, Arché: The AHRC Centre for the Philosophy of Logic, Language, Mathematics, and Mind, University of St. Andrews
INFINITY IN MATHEMATICS AND LOGIC (2005)

John M. Cooper
Stuart Professor of Philosophy, Princeton University
OWEN, G. E. L. (2005)

David Copp
University of California, Davis
MORAL SKEPTICISM (1996)

Henry Corbin
Professor of Islamism at the École des Hautes Études, University of Paris at the Sorbonne; Director of the Department of Iranology, Institut franco-iranien (Tehran)
AL-GHAZĀLĪ, MUHAMMAD (1967)
IBN BĀJJA (1967)
IBN ṬUFAYL (1967)

SUHRAWARDĪ, SHIHĀB AL-DĪN
YAḤYĀ (1967)

John Corcoran
*Professor of Philosophy, University
of Buffalo, State University of New
York at Buffalo*
BOOLE, GEORGE (2005)
LOGIC, HISTORY OF: MODERN
LOGIC: THE BOOLEAN PERIOD:
BOOLE (2005)

Michael Corrado
*Allen Professor of Law and
Professor of Philosophy, University
of North Carolina at Chapel*
POSNER, RICHARD (2005)

Gerald R. Cragg
*Professor of Church History,
Andover Newton Theological
School*
LAW, WILLIAM (1967)
MELANCHTHON, PHILIPP (1967)

William Lane Craig
*Research Professor of Philosophy,
Talbot School of Theology, Biola
University*
COSMOLOGICAL ARGUMENT FOR
THE EXISTENCE OF GOD (2005)

Maurice Cranston
*Reader in Political Science,
University of London*
BURKE, EDMUND (1967)
FASCISM (1967)
LIBERALISM (1967)
MONTESQUIEU, BARON DE (1967)
TOLERATION (1967)

Richard Creath
Arizona State University
VERIFIABILITY PRINCIPLE
[ADDENDUM] (1996)

M. J. Cresswell
*Professor of Philosophy, The
University of Auckland and Texas
A&M University*
SEMANTICS, HISTORY OF
[ADDENDUM] (2005)

Stephen D. Crites
*Assistant Professor of Religion,
Wesleyan University*
BAUER, BRUNO (1967)
MEGARIANS (2005)
ROSENKRANZ, JOHANN KARL
FRIEDRICH (1967)

L. G. Crocker
*Dean, Graduate School, and W. G.
Leutner Distinguised Professor of
Romance Languages, Western
Reserve University*
BONNET, CHARLES (1967)
CABANIS, PIERRE-JEAN GEORGES
(1967)
NAIGEON, JACQUES-ANDRÉ
(1967)
ROBINET, JEAN-BAPTISTE-RENÉ
(1967)
SAINT-HYACINTHE, THÉMISEUL DE
(1967)
VAUVENARGUES, LUC DE CLAPIERS,
MARQUIS DE (1967)
VOLNEY, CONSTANTIN-FRANÇOIS
DE CHASSEBOEUF, COMTE DE
(1967)

Richard Cross
*Fellow and Tutor in Theology, Oriel
College, University of Oxford*
DUNS SCOTUS, JOHN
[ADDENDUM] (2005)

Troy Cross
*Assistant Professor of Philosophy,
Yale University*
DETERMINABLES AND
DETERMINATES [ADDENDUM]
(2005)

Antonio S. Cua
*Professor Emeritus, Philosophy,
Catholic University of America*
WANG YANG-MING (2005)
XUNZI (2005)

Ann E. Cudd
*Professor of Philosophy and
Women's Studies, Director of
Women's Studies, University of
Kansas, Lawrence*
ANALYTIC FEMINISM (1996,
2005)
FRYE, MARILYN (2005)

Philip W. Cummings
*Lecturer in Philosophy at City
University of New York, Hunter
College*
KÖHLER, WOLFGANG (1967)
POLITICAL PHILOSOPHY, HISTORY
OF (1967)
RACISM (1967)

Phillip D. Cummins
*Assistant Professor, Philosophy,
University of Iowa*
LE CLERC, JEAN (1967)

Patricia Curd
*Professor of Philosophy, Purdue
University*
PARMENIDES OF ELEA
[ADDENDUM] (2005)

Edwin Curley
*James B. and Grace J. Nelson
Professor of Philosophy, University
of Michigan, Ann Arbor*
DESCARTES, RENÉ (2005)
SPINOZA, BENEDICT (BARUCH) DE
(2005)

Randall Curren
*Professor of Philosophy and
Professor of Education, University
of Rochester*
PHILOSOPHY OF EDUCATION,
HISTORY OF: CONTEMPORARY
ISSUES: ETHICAL AND POLITICAL
(2005)

Haskell B. Curry
*Evan Pugh Research Professor,
University of Pennsylvania*
COMBINATORY LOGIC (1967)

Fred D'Agostino
*University of New England,
Armidale, Australia*
CHOMSKY, NOAM (1996)

Daniel O. Dahlstrom
*Professor of Philosophy, Boston
University*
SCHILLER, FRIEDRICH (2005)
SCHLEGEL, FRIEDRICH VON
(2005)

Hans Daiber
*Universitätsprofessor und Direktor
des Orientalischen Seminars,
Universität Frankfurt, Germany*
PYTHAGORAS AND
PYTHAGOREANISM
[ADDENDUM 2] (2005)

Richard C. Dales
*Associate Professor, History,
University of Southern California*
GROSSETESTE, ROBERT (1967)
PSEUDO-GROSSETESTE (1967)
THOMAS OF YORK (1967)

Arleen B. Dallery
La Salle University
FEMINIST PHILOSOPHY OF
SCIENCE (1996)

Jonathan Dancy
Professor of Philosophy, The University of Reading, U.K., and The University of Texas at Austin
INTUITIONISM, ETHICAL (2005)

Arthur C. Danto
Associate Professor of History, Columbia University
PHILOSOPHY OF SCIENCE, PROBLEMS OF (1967)

B. A. Dar
Director, Iqbal Academy (Karachi), Managing Editor of the Pakistan Philosophical Journal
IQBAL, MUHAMMAD (1967)

Stephen Darwall
University of Michigan, Ann Arbor
RATIONALISM IN ETHICS (PRACTICAL-REASON APPROACHES) (1996)

Joseph W. Dauben
Distinguished Professor of History and History of Science, Department of History, Herbert H. Lehman College, City University of New York (CUNY), and PhD Program in History, The Graduate Center, CUNY
CANTOR, GEORG (2005)

George E. Davie
Reader in Logic and Metapysics, Philosophy, University of Edinburgh
BAIN, ALEXANDER (1967)
FERRIER, JAMES FREDERICK (1967)
HODGSON, SHADWORTH HOLLOWAY (1967)
MANSEL, HENRY LONGUEVILLE (1967)

David Davies
Associate Professor of Philosophy, McGill University
ART, STYLE AND GENRE IN (2005)

Martin Davies
Professor of Philosophy, Research School of Social Sciences, Australian National University
EVANS, GARETH (2005)
LANGUAGE AND THOUGHT (1996)
LANGUAGE OF THOUGHT (1996)
MEANING (1996)

Stephen Davies
Associate Professor, Philosophy, University of Auckland
ART, PERFORMANCE IN (2005)

Martin Davis
New York University
INFINITESIMALS (1996)

Michael Davis
Professor of Philosophy, Humanties Department; Senior Fellow, Center for the Study of Ethics in the Professions, Illinois Institute of Technology
PUNISHMENT [ADDENDUM] (2005)

P. H. DeLacy
Professor, Classics, Cornell University
CICERO, MARCUS TULLIUS (1967)
EPICUREANISM AND THE EPICUREAN SCHOOL (1967)

Alain de Libera
Professoresseur ordinaire, Philosophie médiévale, Université de Genève; Directeur d'études, Histoire des théologies chrétiennes dans l'Occident médiéval, École pratique des Hautes Études, Section des sciences religieuses, Paris
AVERROISM [BIBLIOGRAPHY] (2005)

Julien Deonna
Assistant Professor, Philosophy, University of Lausanne
SYMPATHY AND EMPATHY (2005)

Michael DePaul
Professor, Philosophy, University of Notre Dame
MORAL EPISTEMOLOGY (1996, 2005)
REFLECTIVE EQUILIBRIUM (2005)

William H. Desmonde
Research Staff Member of the IBM Corp.; Lecturer, New School for Social Research
MEAD, GEORGE HERBERT (1967)

Penelope Deutscher
Associate Professor, Philosophy, Northwestern University
IRIGARAY, LUCE (2005)

Mary Devereaux
Ethicist, Research Ethics Program, University of California, San Diego
BEAUTY [BIBLIOGRAPHY] (2005)
UGLINESS [BIBLIOGRAPHY] (2005)

Garrett DeWeese
Associate Professor of Philosophy, Biola University
IMMORTALITY [ADDENDUM] (2005)

P. Diamandopoulos
Dean of Faculty and Associate Professor, Philosophy, Brandeis University
ANAXIMENES (1967)

Cora A. Diamond
University of Virginia, Charlottesville
ANSCOMBE, GERTRUDE ELIZABETH MARGARET (1996, 2005)
WITTGENSTEIN, LUDWIG JOSEF JOHANN [ADDENDUM 1] (1996)

George Dickie
Professor Emeritus, Philosophy, University of Illinois, Chicago
BEARDSLEY, MONROE C. (2005)

Alfred Di Lascia
Associate Professor, Philosopy, Manhattan College
STURZO, LUIGI (1967)

Frank B. Dilley
Emeritus Professor, Philosophy, University of Delaware, Newark
PARAPSYCHOLOGY (2005)

John Dillon
Regius Professor of Greek, School of Classics, Trinity College, Dublin
ALCINOUS (2005)
IAMBLICHUS (2005)

Martin Dillon
Professor of Philosophy, Binghamton University, State University of New York
MERLEAU-PONTY, MAURICE (2005)

Robin S. Dillon
Associate Professor, Philosophy, Lehigh University
RESPECT (2005)

John Dilworth
Professor, Philosophy, Western Michigan University
LANGER, SUSANNE K. (2005)

John Divers
Professor of Philosophy, University of Sheffield
FICTIONALISM (2005)

Zoltan Domotor
Professor of Philosophy, Biochemistry and Biophysics, University of Pennsylvania
MEASUREMENT AND MEASUREMENT THEORY (2005)

Alan Donagan
Professor, Philosophy, University of Illinois
COLLINGWOOD, ROBIN GEORGE (1967)

Thomas Donaldson
Mark O. Winkelman Professor, The Wharton School, and Professor of Philosophy, University of Pennsylvania
BUSINESS ETHICS (2005)

Willis Doney
Associate Professor, Philosophy, Dartmouth College
CARTESIANISM (1967)
GEULINCX, ARNOLD (1967)

Keith S. Donnelan
Associate Professor, Philosophy, Cornell University
PARADIGM-CASE ARGUMENT (1967)

Gerald Doppelt
Professor of Philosophy and Sciences Studies, University of California, San Diego
NATIONALISM [ADDENDUM] (2005)
SCIENTIFIC REVOLUTIONS (2005)

Douglas F. Dowd
Professor and Chair, Economics, Cornell University
VEBLEN, THORSTEIN BUNDE (1967)

Stillman Drake
Municipal Finance Consultant, San Francisco
GALILEO GALILEI (1967)

William H. Dray
Professor, Philosophy, University of Toronto
DETERMINISM IN HISTORY (1967)
HOLISM AND INDIVIDUALISM IN HISTORY AND SOCIAL SCIENCE (1967)
SPENGLER, OSWALD (1967)

James Dreier
Brown University
PROJECTIVISM (1996)

John Driscoll
Former Lecturer in Philosophy, San Francisco State University
OUSIA (2005)

Julia Driver
Professor, Philosophy, Dartmouth College
MORAL PSYCHOLOGY (2005)

John Drummond
Professor, Philosophy, Fordham University
HUSSERL, EDMUND (2005)

James Duerlinger
Professor of Philosophy, University of Iowa
VASUBANDHU (2005)

Timothy J. Duggan
Associate Professor and Chair, Philosophy, Dartmouth College
HAMILTON, WILLIAM (1967)

Daniel Dumouchel
Associate Professor, Philosophy, Université de Montréal
BATTEUX, ABBÉ CHARLES (2005)
BOILEAU, NICOLAS (2005)
DUBOS, ABBE JEAN BAPTISTE (2005)
GOTTSCHED, JOHANN CHRISTOPH (2005)

Harold B. Dunkel
Professor, Education, University of Chicago
HERBART, JOHANN FRIEDRICH (1967)

John D. Dunne
Assistant Professor, Languages and Cultures of Asia, University of Wisconsin, Madison
BUDDHIST EPISTEMOLOGY (2005)

John Dupré
Professor of Philosophy of Science and Director, ESRC Centre for Genomics in Society, University of Exeter
CARTWRIGHT, NANCY (2005)
NATURAL KINDS (2005)

Detlef Durr
Mathematisches Institut, Ludwig-Maximilians-Universität, München
BELL, JOHN, AND BELL'S THEOREM (2005)
BOHM, DAVID (2005)
BOHMIAN MECHANICS (2005)

Gerald Dworkin
Professor of Philosophy, University of California, Davis
LIBERTY (1996)
PATERNALISM [BIBLIOGRAPHY] (2005)

William James Earle
Instructor, Philosophy, Long Island University
JAMES, WILLIAM (1967)

Lloyd Easton
Professor and Chair, Philosophy, Ohio Wesleyan University
HARRIS, WILLIAM TORREY (1967)

A. W. Eaton
Assistant Professor, Philosophy, University of Illinois, Chicago
FEMINIST AESTHETICS AND CRITICISM (2005)

Marcia Muelder Eaton
Professor, Philosophy, University of Minnesota
AESTHETIC EXPERIENCE (2005)

Julius Ebbinghaus
Professor ordinarius Emeritus, University of Marburg
COHEN, HERMANN (1967)

Gary Ebbs
Professor, Philosophy, University of Illinois at Urbana-Champaign
RULE FOLLOWING [ADDENDUM] (2005)

Christopher J. Eberle
Associate Professor, Philosophy, United States Naval Academy
RELIGION AND POLITICS (2005)

Theodor Ebert
Professor, Philosophy, Universität Erlangen-Nürnberg
DIODORUS CRONUS (2005)
PHILO OF MEGARA (2005)

Ludwig Edelstein
Professor of the History of Science and Philsophy, The Rockefeller Institute
POSIDONIUS (1967)

Paul Edwards
Associate Professor, Philosophy, City University of New York, Brooklyn College; Lecturer, Philosophy, New School for Social Research
ATHEISM (1967)
ATHEISMUSSTREIT (1967)
COMMON CONSENT ARGUMENTS FOR THE EXISTENCE OF GOD (1967)
LIFE, MEANING AND VALUE OF (1967)
PANPSYCHISM (1967)
POPPER-LYNKEUS, JOSEF (1967)
REICH, WILHELM (1967)
WHY (1967)

Frances Egan
Associate Professor, Philosophy and Center for Cognitive Science, Rutgers University
COMPUTATIONALISM (2005)

Philip Ehrlich
Professor, Philosophy, Ohio University
CONTINUITY (2005)

Nader El-Bizri
Research Associate in Philosophy, Institute of Ismaili Studies, London; Affiliated Research Scholar, History and Philosophy of Science, University of Cambridge
IKHWĀN AL-ṢAFĀʾ (2005)

Richard Eldridge
Charles and Harriett Cox McDowell Professor of Philosophy and Religion, Swarthmore College
HÖLDERLIN, JOHANN CHRISTIAN FRIEDRICH (2005)

Bernard Elevitch
Assistant Professor, Philosophy, University of Massachusetts, Boston
BRUNSCHVICG, LÉON (1967)

Catherine Elgin
Professor of the Philosophy of Education, Graduate School of Education, Harvard University
GOODMAN, NELSON [ADDENDUM] (1996, 2005)

Mircea Eliade
Sewell L. Avery Distinguished Service Professor of History of Religions and Professor of the Committee on Social Thought, University of Chicago
IONESCU, NAE (1967)
RĂDULESCU-MOTRU, CONSTANTIN (1967)

Charles Elkan
University of California, San Diego
FUZZY LOGIC (1996)

George F. R. Ellis
Professor Emeritus, Mathematics, University of Cape Town, Cape Town
COSMOLOGY [ADDENDUM] (2005)

Reinaldo Elugardo
Professor, Philosophy, University of Oklahoma, Norman
BAKER, LYNNE RUDDER (2005)

Lester Embree
William F. Dietrich Eminent Scholar in Philosophy, Florida Atlantic University; and President, the Center for Advanced Research in Phenomenology, Inc.
CAIRNS, DORION (2005)

Caryl Emerson
A. Watson Armour III University Professor of Slavic Languages and Literatures, Princeton University
BAKHTIN, MIKHAIL MIKHAILOVICH [ADDENDUM] (2005)

Steven M. Emmanuel
Virginia Wesleyan College
KIERKEGAARD, SØREN AABYE [ADDENDUM] (1996)

James Antony Emmen, O.F.M.
Member of the Theological Section, Collegio di S. Bonaventura, Franciscan International College of Research, Quaracchi, Italy
MATTHEW OF ACQUASPARTA (1967)
PETER AUREOL (1967)

Dorothy M. Emmet
Sir Samuel Hall Professor of Philosophy, University of Manchester
ALEXANDER, SAMUEL (1967)
FUNCTIONALISM IN SOCIOLOGY (1967)
WHITEHEAD, ALFRED NORTH (1967)

Herbert B. Enderton
Adjunct Professor, Mathematics, University of California, Los Angeles
COMPUTABILITY THEORY (2005)
LOGIC, HISTORY OF: MODERN LOGIC: SINCE GÖDEL: TURING AND COMPUTABILITY THEORY (2005)

Ronald Endicott
Department of Philosophy and Religion, Program Director for Cognitive Science, North Carolina State University, Raleigh
MULTIPLE REALIZABILITY (1996, 2005)

Edward Erwin
Professor of Philosophy, University of Miami
PSYCHOANALYSIS (2005)

Michael Esfeld
Full Professor of Epistemology and Philosophy of Science, University of Lausanne
HOLISM AND INDIVIDUALISM IN HISTORY AND SOCIAL SCIENCE [ADDENDUM] (2005)

Girard J. Etzkorn
Professor Emeritus, The Franciscan Institute, St. Bonaventure University
CHATTON, WALTER (2005)
MARSTON, ROGER (1967, 2005)
PECKHAM, JOHN (1967, 2005)
RICHARD OF MEDIAVILLA (1967)

Joseph W. Evans
Associate Professor, Philosophy, University of Notre Dame
MARITAIN, JACQUES (1967)

R. E. Ewin
Emeritus Professor of Philosophy, University of Western Australia
HOBBES, THOMAS [ADDENDUM] (1996, 2005)

Gertrude Ezorsky
Assistant Professor, Philosophy, City University of New York, Brooklyn College
PERFORMATIVE THEORY OF TRUTH (1967)

Rick Fairbanks
Philosophy, St. Olaf College
DEATH [ADDENDUM] (2005)

Eugene R. Fairweather
Keble Professor of Divinity, Trinity College, University of Toronto
CAROLINGIAN RENAISSANCE (1967)
DAVID OF DINANT (1967)
HENRY OF GHENT (1967)
ISAAC OF STELLA (1967)
PETER DAMIAN (1967)
WILLIAM OF MOERBEKE (1967)

Cynthia Farrar
Lecturer, Political Science, Yale University
THUCYDIDES (2005)

Sidney B. Fay
Professor Emeritus, Harvard University
MEINECKE, FRIEDRICH (1967)

Susan L. Feagin
Editor, The Journal of Aesthetics and Art Criticism; Research Professor, Department of Philosophy, Temple University
VISUAL ARTS, THEORY OF THE (2005)

Anita Feferman
Biographer, Independent scholar
TARSKI, ALFRED [ADDENDUM] (2005)

Solomon Feferman
Professor of Mathematics and Philosophy, Stanford University
PROOF THEORY (1996)
TARSKI, ALFRED [ADDENDUM] (2005)

Herbert Feigl
Director, Minnesota Center for Philosophy of Science, and Professor of Philosophy, University of Minnesota
MILLER, DICKINSON S. (1967)

Joel Feinberg
University of Arizona, Tucson
PATERNALISM (1996)

Richard Feldman
Professor of Philosophy, University of Rochester
EPISTEMOLOGY (1996, 2005)
EVIDENTIALISM (1996)

Otis Fellows
Professor of French Literature and Chair of Italian Department, Columbia University
BUFFON, GEORGES-LOUIS LECLERC, COMTE DE (1967)
CYRANO DE BERGERAC, SAVINIEN DE (1967)
FONTENELLE, BERNARD LE BOVIER DE (1967)
MAILLET, BENOÎT DE (1967)

M. Jamie Ferreira
Carolyn M. Barbour Chair of Religious Studies, University of Virginia, Charlottesville
NEWMAN, JOHN HENRY [ADDENDUM] (2005)

James H. Fetzer
Distinguished McKnight University Professor, Department of Philosophy, University of Minnesota, Duluth
FRAME PROBLEM (2005)
HEMPEL, CARL GUSTAV (2005)

Paul K. Feyerabend
Professor, Philosophy, University of California, Berkeley
HEISENBERG, WERNER (1967)
PLANCK, MAX (1967)
SCHULTZ, JULIUS (1967)

James Fieser
Professor, Philosophy, University of Tennessee at Martin
BEATTIE, JAMES (2005)

Vladimir Filipović
Professor and Head, Philosophy, Facuty of Arts, University of Zagreb
MARULIĆ, MARKO (1967)

Arthur Fine
Professor of Philosophy, University of Washington, Seattle
EINSTEIN, ALBERT (2005)

Stephen Finlay
Assistant Professor of Philosophy, University of Southern California
EMOTIVE THEORY OF ETHICS (2005)

Kai von Fintel
Associate Professor of Lingustics, Department of Linguistics and Philosophy, Massachusetts Institute of Technology
MODALITY AND LANGUAGE (2005)

John Fischer
Professor, Philosophy, University of California, Riverside
FRANKFURT, HARRY (2005)

Alden L. Fisher
Professor, Philosophy, St. Louis University
MERCIER, DÉSIRÉ JOSEPH (1967)

Sterling Fishman
Assistant Professor, Department of History and Educational Policy Studies, University of Wisconsin
LASSALLE, FERDINAND (1967)

Anthony Flew
Professor, Philosophy, University of Keele
IMMORTALITY (1967)
MALTHUS, THOMAS ROBERT (1967)
MIDDLETON, CONYERS (1967)
MIRACLES (1967)
PRECOGNITION (1967)

Sten G. Flygt
Professor of German, Vanderbilt University
BAHRDT, CARL FRIEDRICH (1967)
HEBBEL, CHRISTIAN FRIEDRICH (1967)

Thomas R. Flynn
Samuel Candler Dobbs Professor of Philosophy, Emory University
BAD FAITH (1996)
CONSCIOUSNESS IN PHENOMENOLOGY (2005)
EXISTENTIALISM [ADDENDUM] (1996)
EXISTENTIAL PSYCHOANALYSIS [ADDENDUM] (1996)
SARTRE, JEAN-PAUL (2005)

Robert J. Fogelin
Associate Professor, Philosophy,
Pomona College
BLANSHARD, BRAND (1967)

Richard Foley
Professor of Philosophy; Ehrenkranz
Dean of the Faculty of Arts and
Science, New York University
CHISHOLM, RODERICK (1996, 2005)
SUBJECTIVIST EPISTEMOLOGY (1996)

Graeme Forbes
Celia Scott Weatherhead
Distinguished Professor of
Philosophy, Tulane University
INTENSIONAL TRANSITIVE VERBS (2005)

Peter Forrest
Professor of Philosophy, University
of New England, Armidale,
Australia
RELIGION, NATURALISTIC
RECONSTRUCTIONS OF
[ADDENDUM] (2005)

Michael Forster
Professor, Philosophy, University of
Chicago
HERDER, JOHANN GOTTFRIED (2005)

Alan Fox
Associate Professor, Philosophy,
University of Delaware
BUDDHISM—SCHOOLS: HUA YAN (2005)

Eli Franco
Professor, Institute for Indology and
Central Asian Studies, University of
Leipzig
KNOWLEDGE IN INDIAN
PHILOSOPHY (2005)

Daniel H. Frank
Professor of Philosophy and
Director of the Jewish Studies
Program, Purdue University
MAIMONIDES [ADDENDUM] (2005)
PHILO JUDAEUS [ADDENDUM] (2005)
SAADYA (1967)
SAADYA [ADDENDUM] (2005)

Charles Frankel
Assistant U.S. Secretary of State for
Educational and Cultural Affairs;
Chair, Committee on Professional
Ethics, American Association of
University Professors
PROGRESS, THE IDEA OF (1967)

Lois Frankel
Ewing, New Jersey
CONWAY, ANNE (1996)

William K. Frankena
Professor, Philosophy, University of
Michigan
VALUE AND VALUATION (1967)

Harry G. Frankfurt
Associate Professor, Rockefeller
University
DOUBT (1967)

Gad Freudenthal
Permanent Senior Research Fellow,
Centre National de la Recherche
Scientifique (CNRS), Paris
GERSONIDES [ADDENDUM] (2005)

Gideon Freudenthal
Professor of Philosophy and History
of Science, Cohn Institute for the
History and Philosophy of Science
and Ideas, Tel-Aviv University
MAIMON, SALOMON (2005)

R. G. Frey
Bowling Green University
SPECIESISM (1996)

Elizabeth Fricker
University Lecturer in Philosophy
and Fellow, Magdalen College,
Oxford University
TESTIMONY (1996, 2005)

Russell L. Friedman
Associate Professor, Philosophy,
Catholic University of Leuven
DURANDUS OF SAINT-POURÇAIN
[BIBLIOGRAPHY] (2005)
PETER AUREOL [ADDENDUM] (2005)

Wolfgang Friedman
Barrister at Law, Middle Temple,
England; Professor of Law and
Director of International Legal
Research, Columbia University
GROTIUS, HUGO (1967)

RADBRUCH, GUSTAV (1967)
STAMMLER, RUDOLF (1967)

Horace L. Friess
Buttenwieser Professor of Human
Relations; Member of the
Departments of Philosophy and
Religion at Columbia University
STEINER, RUDOLF (1967)

Robert Frodeman
Associate Professor and Chair,
Philosophy and Religion Studies,
University of North Texas
SCIENCE POLICY (2005)

Karin Fry
Assistant Professor, Philosophy,
University of Wisconsin, Stevens
Point
LYOTARD, JEAN FRANÇOIS (2005)

Northrop Frye
Principal of Victoria College,
University of Toronto
BLAKE, WILLIAM (1967)

Alan Fuchs
Professor of Philosophy, College of
William & Mary
RAWLS, JOHN (1996, 2005)

Richard Fumerton
F. Wendell Miller Professor of
Philosophy, University of Iowa
CLASSICAL FOUNDATIONALISM (1996, 2005)
SOLIPSISM (2005)

David J. Furley
Reader in Greek and Latin,
University College, University of
London
HOMER (1967)
MELISSUS OF SAMOS (1967)
PARMENIDES OF ELEA (1967)

Michael Gagarin
James R. Dougherty, Jr. Centennial
Professor of Classics, The University
of Texas at Austin
ANTIPHON (2005)
DIKÉ (2005)

Piama Gaidenko
Russian Academy of Sciences,
Institute of Philosophy
SOLOV'ÉV (SOLOVYOV), VLADIMIR
SERGEEVICH (2005)
TRUBETSKOI, SERGEI NIKOLAEVICH (2005)

Elizabeth Cameron Galbraith
Associate Professor of Philosophy and Religion, St. Olaf College
RAHNER, KARL (2005)

Laura L. Garcia
Adjunct Assistant Professor, Philosophy, Boston College
TELEOLOGICAL ARGUMENT FOR THE EXISTENCE OF GOD [ADDENDUM] (2005)

Patrick Gardiner
Fellow and Tutor in Philosophy, Magdalen College, Oxford University
BUCKLE, HENRY THOMAS (1967)
BURCKHARDT, JAKOB (1967)
IRRATIONALISM (1967)
SAINT-SIMON, CLAUDE-HENRI DE ROUVROY, COMTE DE (1967)
SCHOPENHAUER, ARTHUR (1967)
TOYNBEE, ARNOLD JOSEPH (1967)

Martin Gardner
Editor and Writer, Mathematical Games Department of Scientific American
LOGIC DIAGRAMS (1967)
LOGIC MACHINES (1967)

Sebastian Gardner
Professor of Philosophy, University College, London
ROMANTICISM [ADDENDUM] (2005)

Jay Garfield
Doris Silbert Professor in the Humanities and Professor of Philosophy, Smith College; Professor of Philosophy, University of Melbourne; Adjunct Professor of Philosophy, Central Institute of Higher Tibetan Studies
NĀGĀRJUNA (2005)

Eugenio Garin
Ordinary Professor of the History of Philosophy, Faculty of Letters and Philosophy, University of Florence
BANFI, ANTONIO (1967)
BONATELLI, FRANCESCO (1967)
GALLUPPI, PASQUALE (1967)
GENOVESI, ANTONIO (1967)
PASTORE, VALENTINO ANNIBALE (1967)
ROMAGNOSI, GIAN DOMENICO (1967)
VANINI, GIULIO CESARE (1967)

Richard T. Garner
Professor of Philosophy, Ohio State University
NONCOGNITIVISM (1996)
STEVENSON, CHARLES L. (1996, 2005)

Aaron Garrett
Associate Professor, Philosophy, Boston University
FERGUSON, ADAM (2005)

James W. Garson
Professor, Philosophy, University of Houston
MODALITY AND QUANTIFICATION (2005)

Newton Garver
State University of New York Distinguished Service Professor, University at Buffalo
BLACK, MAX (1967, 2005)
SUBJECT AND PREDICATE (1967)

Stephen Gaukroger
Professor of History of Philosophy and History of Science, University of Sydney
BACON, FRANCIS (2005)

Deno J. Geanakoplos
Professor of Medieval and Byzantine History, University of Illinois; Coeditor, Greek, Roman, Byzantine Studies
PLETHO, GIORGIUS GEMISTUS (1967)

R. Douglas Geivett
Professor of Philosophy, Talbot Department of Philosophy, Biola University
MIRACLES [ADDENDUM] (2005)

Hester Goodenough Gelber
Associate Professor, Religious Studies, Stanford University
HOLKOT, ROBERT (2005)

Tamar Szabo Gendler
Associate Professor of Philosophy, Cornell University
IMAGINATION [ADDENDUM] (2005)
THOUGHT EXPERIMENTS IN SCIENCE (2005)

Charles Genequand
Professor, Faculté des lettres, University of Geneva

ALEXANDER OF APHRODISIAS [ADDENDUM] (2005)

Jean-François Genest
Chercheur au Centre National de la Recherche Scientifique, Institut de Recherche et d'Histoire des Textes, Paris
BRADWARDINE, THOMAS (2005)

William Gerber
Economist, U.S. Department of Labor; Associate Professor, Philosophy, University of Maryland
TAGORE, RABINDRANATH (1967)

Hanna-Barbara Gerl-Falkovitz
Chair, Philosophy of Religion and Comparative Religious Studies, Technical University of Dresden
STEIN, EDITH (2005)

B. A. Gerrish
Associate Professor of Historical Theology, Divinity School, University of Chicago
LUTHER, MARTIN (1967)
REFORMATION (1967)

Stephen E. Gersh
Professor, Medieval Institute, and Concurrent Professor, Philosophy, University of Notre Dame
PLATONISM AND THE PLATONIC TRADITION (2005)

Bernard Gert
Stone Professor of Intellectual and Moral Philosophy, Dartmouth College; Adjunct Professor of Psychiatry, Dartmouth Medical School
BAIER, KURT (2005)
EUTHANASIA (1996, 2005)
IMPARTIALITY (1996, 2005)

Brie Gertler
Philosophy, University of Virginia
KNOWLEDGE ARGUMENT (2005)

Alan Gewirth
Professor, Philosophy, University of Chicago
MARSILIUS OF PADUA (1967)

John Gibbons
Assistant Professor of Philosophy, University of Nebraska–Lincoln
KNOWLEDGE, THE PRIORITY OF (2005)

Roger F. Gibson
Washington University, St. Louis
QUINE, WILLARD VAN ORMAN
[ADDENDUM] (1996)

Ronald Giere
Professor of Philosophy, University of Minnesota, Twin Cities
NATURALIZED PHILOSOPHY OF
SCIENCE (2005)

Felix Gilbert
Professor, School of Historical Studies, Institute for Advanced Study, Princeton, NJ
MACHIAVELLI, NICCOLÒ (1967)

Neal W. Gilbert
Professor, School of Historical Studies, Institute for Advanced Study, Princeton, NJ
JUNGIUS, JOACHIM (1967)
MAJOR, JOHN (1967)
RENAISSANCE (1967)
VALLA, LORENZO (1967)
VIVES, JUAN LUIS (1967)

Thomas Gilby, O.P.
S.T.M., PhD, Blackfriars, Cambridge University
THOMISM (1967)

Carl Gillett
Associate Professor, Philosophy, Illinois Wesleyan University
SPECIAL SCIENCES (2005)

Brendan S. Gillon
Associate Professor, Linguistics, McGill University
LOGIC, HISTORY OF: LOGIC AND
INFERENCE IN INDIAN
PHILOSOPHY (2005)
PLURALS AND PLURALITY (2005)

Richard C. Gilman
President, Occidental College, Los Angeles
HOCKING, WILLIAM ERNEST
(1967)

Carl Ginet
Professor of Philosophy Emeritus, Cornell University
VOLITION (2005)

James Ginther
Associate Professor of Medieval Theology, St. Louis University
GROSSETESTE, ROBERT
[ADDENDUM] (2005)

Michael Glanzberg
Associate Professor of Philosophy, University of California, Davis
QUANTIFIERS IN NATURAL
LANGUAGE (2005)

Nahum Norbert Glatzer
Professor of Jewish History, Chair, Near Eastern and Judaic Studies, Brandeis University
ROSENZWEIG, FRANZ (1967)

Lydia Goehr
Professor of Philosophy, Columbia University
ADORNO, THEODOR
WIESENGRUND (2005)
BENJAMIN, WALTER (2005)

Ludmila Gogotishvili
Senior Research Associate, Russian Academy of Sciences, Institute of Philosophy
BAKHTIN, MIKHAIL MIKHAILOVICH
(2005)

Sanford Goldberg
Associate Professor of Philosophy and Director of Cognitive Science, University of Kentucky
PROPOSITIONAL ATTITUDES:
ISSUES IN PHILOSOPHY OF MIND
AND PSYCHOLOGY (2005)

Joshua L. Golding
Associate Professor of Philosophy, Bellarmine University
FAITH [ADDENDUM] (2005)

M. P. Golding
Associate Professor, Philosophy, Columbia University
PHILOSOPHY OF LAW, HISTORY OF
(1967)

Alan H. Goldman
William R. Kenan, Jr. Professor of Humanities, Department of Philosophy, College of William & Mary
AESTHETIC QUALITIES (2005)
CAUSAL OR CONDITIONAL OR
EXPLANATORY-RELATION
ACCOUNTS (1996)

Alvin Goldman
Board of Governors Professor, Department of Philosophy, Rutgers, The State University of New Jersey
SIMULATION THEORY (2005)

Sheldon Goldstein
Professor of Mathematics, Rutgers University
BELL, JOHN, AND BELL'S THEOREM
(2005)
BOHM, DAVID (2005)
BOHMIAN MECHANICS (2005)

Herman H. Goldstine
Director of Scientific Development, Data Processing Division, IBM
NEUMANN, JOHN VON (1967)

Michael F. Goodman
Professor, Philosophy, Humboldt State University
PERSONS (2005)

Russell B. Goodman
Professor of Philosophy, University of New Mexico, Albuquerque
NEW ENGLAND
TRANSCENDENTALISM
[ADDENDUM] (2005)

Robert M. Gordon
Research Professor in Philosophy of Mind and Cognitive Science, University of Missouri, St. Louis
EMOTION (2005)

Eva Gossman
Lecturer in Philosophy, Goucher College (Towson, MD)
FRANK, ERICH (1967)

Rubin Gotesky
Lecturer, Philosophy, Goucher College (Towson, MD)
CARUS, CARL GUSTAV (1967)
EUCKEN, RUDOLF CHRISTOPH
(1967)
LOTZE, RUDOLF HERMANN (1967)

Roger S. Gottlieb
Professor of Philosophy, Department of Humanities and Arts, Worcester Polytechnic Institute
MARXIST PHILOSOPHY
[ADDENDUM] (1996, 2005)

T. A. Goudge
Chair, Philosophy, University of Toronto; Fellow of the Royal Society of Canada
BERGSON, HENRI (1967)
BERTALANFFY, LUDWIG VON
(1967)
BUTLER, SAMUEL (1967)
DARWIN, CHARLES ROBERT (1967)
DARWIN, ERASMUS (1967)

GRAY, ASA (1967)
HUXLEY, THOMAS HENRY (1967)
LAMARCK, CHEVALIER DE (1967)
MORGAN, C. LLOYD (1967)
SMUTS, JAN CHRISTIAAN (1967)
TEILHARD DE CHARDIN, PIERRE (1967)
WALLACE, ALFRED RUSSEL (1967)
WOODGER, JOSEPH HENRY (1967)

Josiah B. Gould Jr.
Assistant Professor and Chair, Philosophy, Claremont Graduate School (Claremont, CA)
CHRYSIPPUS (1967)

Jorge Gracia
Samuel P. Capen Chair and State University of New York Distinguished Professor, Philosophy, State University of New York at Buffalo
HISTORY AND HISTORIOGRAPHY OF PHILOSOPHY (2005)
LATIN AMERICAN PHILOSOPHY (2005)

A. C. Graham
Lecturer in Chinese, School of Oriental and African Studies, University of London
LOGIC, HISTORY OF: CHINESE LOGIC (1967)

Daniel W. Graham
Abraham Owen Smoot Professor of Philosophy, Brigham Young University
ANAXAGORAS OF CLAZOMENAE (2005)
ARCHÉ (2005)
LOGOS (2005)

Gordon Graham
Henry Luce III Professor of Philosophy and the Arts, Princeton Theological Seminary
ART, VALUE IN (2005)

Richard E. Grandy
McManis Professor, Philosophy and Cognitive Sciences, Rice University
GRICE, HERBERT PAUL (1996, 2005)

Herbert Granger
Professor, Philosophy, Wayne State University
HERACLITUS OF EPHESUS (2005)

Robert M. Grant
Professor of New Testament and Early Christianity, Divinity School, University of Chicago
APOLOGISTS (1967)
CELSUS (1967)
EUSEBIUS (1967)
NEMESIUS OF EMESA (1967)
ORIGEN (1967)
PATRISTIC PHILOSOPHY (1967)
TERTULLIAN, QUINTUS SEPTIMIUS FLORENS (1967)

S. A. Grave
Professor of Philosophy, University of Western Australia
BROWN, THOMAS (1967) (1967)
COMMON SENSE (1967)

Margaret Graver
Associate Professor, Classics, Dartmouth College
SENECA, LUCIUS ANNAEUS (2005)

Joseph Grcic
Associate Professor, Philosophy, Indiana State University
LIBERALISM [ADDENDUM] (2005)

John Greco
Associate Professor, Philosophy, Fordham University
INTERNALISM VERSUS EXTERNALISM (1996, 2005)
VIRTUE EPISTEMOLOGY (1996, 2005)

Karen Green
Head of School, School of Philosophy & Bioethics, Monash University
LLOYD, GENEVIEVE (2005)

Michael Griffin
Visiting Assistant Professor, Department of Philosophy, Central European University
MOLINA, LUIS DE (2005)

A. Phillips Griffiths
Professor of Philosophy, University of Warwick
MORAL PRINCIPLES: THEIR JUSTIFICATION (1967)

Ronald Grimsley
Professor, French, University of Bristol
ROUSSEAU, JEAN-JACQUES (1967)

Peter Groff
Assistant Professor of Philosophy, Bucknell University
DIALECTIC IN ISLAMIC AND JEWISH PHILOSOPHY (2005)

Adolf Grünbaum
Andrew Mellon Professor of Philosophy of Science, Research Professor of Psychiatry, Chairman, Center for Philosophy of Science, University of Pittsburgh
FREUD, SIGMUND (2005)

Anil Gupta
Indiana University, Bloomington
LIAR PARADOX, THE (1996)

Bina Gupta
Curators' Professor, Professor of Philosophy; Director, South Asian Studies Program, University of Missouri
BRAHMAN (2005)

W. K. C. Guthrie
Laurence Professor of Ancient Philosophy and Master of Downing College, Cambridge University
PRE-SOCRATIC PHILOSOPHY (1967)
PYTHAGORAS AND PYTHAGOREANISM (1967)

Paul Guyer
Florence R. C. Murray Professor in the Humanities, University of Pennsylvania
AESTHETICS, HISTORY OF [ADDENDUM] (2005)
BULLOUGH, EDWARD (2005)
CATEGORICAL IMPERATIVE (2005)
MORITZ, KARL PHILIPP (2005)

Susan Haack
University of Miami
PRAGMATISM [ADDENDUM] (1996)
PRAGMATIST EPISTEMOLOGY (1996)

Alexander Haardt
Professor and Doctor of Philosophy, Institute of Philosophy (Department of Philosophy of Modern Times), Ruhr Universität Bochum, Germany
SHPET, GUSTAV GUSTAVOVICH (2005)

Jeremiah Hackett
Professor and Chair, Philosophy, University of South Carolina, Columbia
BACON, ROGER [ADDENDUM] (2005)

Adrian Haddock
Lecturer, Philosophy, University of Stirling
NATURAL KINDS (2005)

Garry Hagberg
James H. Ottaway Jr. Professor of Philosophy and Aesthetics, Bard College
WITTGENSTEIN, LUDWIG JOSEF JOHANN [ADDENDUM 2] (2005)

Alan Hájek
Professor of Philosophy, Research School of the Social Sciences, Australian National University
CHANCE (2005)

Roland Hall
Lecturer, Philosophy, University of St. Andrews; Assistant Editor, Philosophical Quarterly
DIALECTIC (1967)
MONISM AND PLURALISM (1967)

Morris Halle
Massachusetts Institute of Technology
PHONOLOGY (1996)

Philip P. Hallie
Griffin Professor and Chair, Philosophy, Wesleyan University
MAINE DE BIRAN (1967)

Stephen Halliwell
Professor of Greek, School of Classics, University of St Andrews
KATHARSIS (2005)
MIMESIS (2005)

G. M. Hamburg
Otho M. Behr Professor of History, Claremont McKenna College
CHICHERIN, BORIS NIKOLAEVICH [ADDENDUM] (2005)

D. W. Hamlyn
Professor of Philosophy, Birkbeck College, University of London
ANALYTIC AND SYNTHETIC STATEMENTS (1967)
A PRIORI AND A POSTERIORI (1967)

EMPIRICISM (1967)
EPISTEMOLOGY, HISTORY OF (1967)

Hassan Hanafi
Professor of Philosophy, Cairo University
LAROUI, ABDULLAH (2005)

Roger Hancock
Assistant Professor, Philosophy, University of Missouri
METAPHYSICS, HISTORY OF (1967)

Michael Hand
Professor of Philosophy, Texas A&M University
DUMMETT, MICHAEL ANTHONY EARDLEY (1996, 2005)

Rollo Handy
Professor and Chair, Philosophy; Chair, Division of Philosophy and the Social Sciences, State University of New York, Buffalo
HAECKEL, ERNST HEINRICH (1967)
MOLESCHOTT, JACOB (1967)
VAIHINGER, HANS (1967)

R. J. Hankinson
Professor of Philosophy and Classics, University of Texas at Austin
AENESIDEMUS (2005)
AGRIPPA (2005)
AITIA (2005)
HIPPOCRATES AND THE HIPPOCRATIC CORPUS (2005)
IMPETUS (2005)
PYRRHO (2005)
SEXTUS EMPIRICUS (2005)
TIMON OF PHLIUS (2005)

Peter Hanks
Assistant Professor, Philosophy, University of Minnesota, Twin Cities
PROPOSITIONS [ADDENDUM] (2005)
QUESTIONS (2005)

Chad Hansen
Chair Professor of Chinese Philosophy, Department of Philosophy, University of Hong Kong
CHINESE PHILOSOPHY: DAOISM (2005)

Norwood Russell Hanson
Professor, Philosophy, Yale University
COPERNICUS, NICOLAS (1967)

Valerie Gray Hardcastle
Associate Dean, College of Liberal Arts and Human Sciences; Professor and Head, Department of Science and Technology in Society, Virginia Tech
ELIMINATIVE MATERIALISM, ELIMINATIVISM (1996)
PAIN (2005)

Stevan Harnad
Canada Research Chair in Cognitives Sciences, Université du Québec à Montréal
CHINESE ROOM ARGUMENT (2005)

Robert M. Harnish
Professor of Philosophy and Linguistics and Research; Professor of Cognitive Science, University of Arizona Tuscon
SEARLE, JOHN (2005)

Vicki Harper
Assistant Professor of Philosophy, St. Olaf College
IONESCU, NAE [BIBLIOGRAPHY] (2005)
STRAWSON, PETER FREDERICK [BIBLIOGRAPHY] (2005)

William L. Harper
Professor, Philosophy, University of Western Ontario
NEWTON, ISAAC (2005)
SCIENTIFIC METHOD (2005)

R. Harre
Fellow of Linacre College, Oxford University, and University Lecturer, Philosophy of Science
LAPLACE, PIERRE SIMON DE (1967)

Karsten Harries
Assistant Professor, Philosophy, Yale University
KEYSERLING, HERMANN ALEXANDER, GRAF VON (1967)
KLEIST, HEINRICH VON (1967)
NOVALIS (1967)
SOLGER, KARL WILHELM FERDINAND (1967)

H. S. Harris
Professor, Philosophy, Glendom College, York University, Toronto
CROCE, BENEDETTO (1967)
GENTILE, GIOVANNI (1967)
SPAVENTA, BERTRANDO (1967)
SPIRITO, UGO (1967)

Jonathan Harrison
Professor, Philosophy, Glendom College, York University
ETHICAL NATURALISM (1967)
ETHICAL SUBJECTIVISM (1967)

H. L. A. Hart
Professor of Jurisprudence, Oxford University
LEGAL POSITIVISM (1967)
PHILOSOPHY OF LAW, PROBLEMS OF (1967)

Klaus Hartmann
Docent, Bonn University
EHRENFELS, CHRISTIAN FREIHERR VON (1967)
SCHUPPE, ERNST JULIUS WILHELM (1967)

William Hasker
Professor Emeritus of Philosophy, Huntington College
EPISTEMOLOGY, RELIGIOUS (1996)
EPISTEMOLOGY, RELIGIOUS [ADDENDUM] (2005)

William H. Hay
Professor, Philosophy, University of Wisconsin
CARUS, PAUL (1967)
MURPHY, ARTHUR EDWARD (1967)

Richard P. Hayes
Assistant Professor, Philosophy, University of New Mexico
BUDDHISM (2005)
NIRVĀṆA (2005)

Allen P. Hazen
Lecturer, Philosophy, University of Melbourne
TYPE THEORY (2005)

P. L. Heath
Professor, Philosophy, University of Virginia
BALFOUR, ARTHUR JAMES (1967)
CARROLL, LEWIS (1967)
DE MORGAN, AUGUSTUS (1967)
EXPERIENCE (1967)
JEVONS, WILLIAM STANLEY (1967)
LOGIC, HISTORY OF: MODERN LOGIC: THE BOOLEAN PERIOD: VENN; DE MORGAN; HAMILTON; JEVONS (1967)
NOTHING (1967)
VENN, JOHN (1967)

Michael Heidelberger
Chair for Logic and Science Theory, Philosophisches Seminar, Universität Tübingen
EXPERIMENTATION AND INSTRUMENTATION (2005)

Steven Heine
Professor and Director of Asian Studies, Florida International University
DŌGEN (2005)

Susan Hekman
Professor of Political Science and Director of Graduate Humanities, University of Texas at Arlington
FEMINISM AND CONTINENTAL PHILOSOPHY (2005)

Lisa Heldke
Professor, Philosophy, Gustavus Adolphus College
FEMINISM AND PRAGMATISM (2005)

Geoffrey Hellman
Professor of Philosophy, University of Minnesota, Minneapolis
STRUCTURALISM, MATHEMATICAL (2005)

Robin F. Hendry
Senior Lecturer in Philosophy, Department of Philosophy, University of Durham
LAVOISIER, ANTOINE (2005)
PAULING, LINUS (2005)

Desmond Paul Henry
Senior Lecturer in Philosophy, University of Manchester
MEDIEVAL PHILOSOPHY (1967)

Grete Henry-Hermann
Professor, Pädagogischen Hocschule, Bremen, Germany
NELSON, LEONARD (1967)

Ronald W. Hepburn
Professor of Philosophy, University of Edinburgh
AGNOSTICISM (1967)
BULTMANN, RUDOLF (1967)
MORAL ARGUMENTS FOR THE EXISTENCE OF GOD (1967)
MYSTICISM, NATURE AND ASSESSMENT OF (1967)
NATURE, PHILOSOPHICAL IDEAS OF (1967)
RELIGIOUS EXPERIENCE, ARGUMENT FOR THE EXISTENCE OF GOD (1967)

Jennifer Herdt
Associate Professor of Theology, University of Notre Dame
CAMBRIDGE PLATONISTS (2005)
CUDWORTH, RALPH (2005)

Ulrike Heuer
Lecturer, School of Philosophy, University of Leeds
INTERNALISM AND EXTERNALISM IN ETHICS (2005)

Joh's Erich Heyde
Ordinary Professor of Philosophy, Technical University of Berlin
REHMKE, JOHANNES (1967)

John Hick
Lecturer in Philosophy of Religion, University of Cambridge
CHRISTIANITY (1967)
EVIL, THE PROBLEM OF (1967)
FAITH (1967)
OMAN, JOHN WOOD (1967)
ONTOLOGICAL ARGUMENT FOR THE EXISTENCE OF GOD (1967)
RELIGIOUS PLURALISM (1996)
REVELATION (1967)
TENNANT, FREDERICK ROBERT (1967)

Pamela Hieronymi
Assistant Professor, Philosophy, University of California, Los Angeles
FORGIVENESS (2005)

James Higginbotham
Somerville College, Oxford University
SYNTAX (1996)

Jocelyn Nigel Hillgarth
Lecturer in History, Harvard University
LULL, RAMÓN (1967)

David Hills
Acting Assistant Professor, Philosophy, Stanford University
ART, REPRESENTATION IN (2005)
METAPHOR [ADDENDUM] (2005)

Iwao Hirose
Donnelley Junior Research Fellow, University College, Oxford
SEN, AMARTYA K. (2005)

R. J. Hirst
Professor and Head, Logic, Glasgow University
ILLUSIONS (1967)
PERCEPTION (1967)
PHENOMENALISM (1967)
PRIMARY AND SECONDARY QUALITIES (1967)
REALISM (1967)
SENSA (1967)

Christopher R. Hitchcock
Professor of Philosophy, Division of Humanities and Social Sciences, California Institute of Technology
CAUSATION: PHILOSOPHY OF SCIENCE (2005)

Henry Hiż
Professor of Linguistics, University of Pennsylvania
CHWISTEK, LEON (1967)

Joshua P. Hochschild
Assistant Professor, Philosophy, Mount St. Mary's University
CAJETAN, CARDINAL (2005)

Andrew Hodges
Lecturer in Mathmatics, Wadham College, University of Oxford
TURING, ALAN M. (2005)

Wilfrid Hodges
Professor of Mathematics, Queen Mary, University of London
FIRST-ORDER LOGIC (2005)
LOGIC, HISTORY OF: MODERN LOGIC: SINCE GÖDEL: DECIDABLE AND UNDECIDABLE THEORIES; MODEL THEORY: ROBINSON; MODEL THEORY: TARSKI (2005)
MODEL THEORY (2005)

Carl Hoefer
Research Professor at ICREA and the Autonomous University of Barcelona
CHANCE (2005)
CONVENTIONALISM (2005)
HOLE ARGUMENT (2005)

Frank J. Hoffman
Associate Professor, Philosophy, West Chester University

MIND AND MENTAL STATES IN BUDDHIST PHILOSOPHY (2005)

Robert Holmes
Professor, Philosophy, University of Rochester
PEACE, WAR, AND PHILOSOPHY [ADDENDUM] (2005)

Nancy Holmstrom
Chair, Associate Professor, Philosophy, Rutgers University, Newark
FEMINIST SOCIAL AND POLITICAL PHILOSOPHY (2005)

Tze-ki Hon
Associate Professor, History, State University of New York–Geneseo
ZHOU DUNYI (2005)

Ted Honderich
Grote Professor Emeritus, University College London
DETERMINISM AND FREEDOM (1996, 2005)

Bradford W. Hooker
Professor of Moral Philosophy, University of Reading
MORAL RULES AND PRINCIPLES (2005)
UTILITARIANISM [ADDENDUM] (2005)

Vincent Hope
Former Fellow of the School of Philosophy, Psychology and Language Sciences, University of Edinburgh
STEWART, DUGALD (2005)

Burt C. Hopkins
Professor, Philosophy, Seattle University
LANDGREBE, LUDWIG (2005)

Patrick D. Hopkins
Associate Professor, Philosophy, Millsaps College
HETEROSEXISM (2005)
NATURAL LAW (2005)

Terence E. Horgan
University of Memphis
CONNECTIONISM (1996)

Irving Louis Horowitz
Professor of Sociology, Washington University
DE SANCTIS, FRANCESCO (1967)

Sergey Horujy
Director of the Institute of Synergetic Anthropology; Professor of the Institute of Philosophy of Russian Academy of Sciences; Honorary Professor of UNESCO (the Chair of Comparative Studies of Religious Traditions)
FLORENSKII, PAVEL ALEKSANDROVICH (2005)
FLOROVSKII, GEORGII VASIL'EVICH (2005)
KARSAVIN, LEV PLATONOVICH (2005)
TRUBETSKOI, EVGENII NIKOLAEVICH (2005)

Nathan Houser
Indiana University, Purdue University
PEIRCE, CHARLES SANDERS [ADDENDUM] (1996)

Daniel Howard-Snyder
Professor of Philosophy, Western Washington University
HIDDENNESS OF GOD (2005)

Bruce W. Hozeski
Chair, Department of English, Ball State University
HILDEGARD OF BINGEN (2005)

Pamela M. Huby
Reader in Philosophy (Retired), University of Liverpool
AGENT INTELLECT (2005)

Carl A. Huffman
Professor of Classics, DePauw University
ALCMAEON OF CROTON (2005)
ARCHYTAS OF TARENTUM (2005)
PHILOLAUS OF CROTON (2005)

Nicholas Huggett
Associate Professor of Philosophy, University of Illinois at Chicago
BLACK HOLES (2005)
FIELDS AND PARTICLES (2005)
SPACE IN PHYSICAL THEORIES (2005)

Namjin Huh
Professor, Philosophy, Seoul National University
KOREAN PHILOSOPHY (2005)

Paul Humphreys
Professor, Corcoran Department of Philosophy, University of Virginia

EMERGENCE (2005)
SALMON, WESLEY (2005)
SUPPES, PATRICK (2005)

David P. Hunt
Professor, Philosophy, Whittier College
FOREKNOWLEDGE AND FREEDOM, THEOLOGICAL PROBLEM OF (2005)

Bruce Hunter
Professor and Head, Logic, Glasgow University
CRITERIOLOGY (1996)

Thomas Hurka
Jackman Distinguished Chair in Philosophical Studies, Philosophy, University of Toronto
INTRINSIC VALUE (2005)
MOORE, GEORGE EDWARD [ADDENDUM] (2005)
TELEOLOGICAL ETHICS (2005)

Rosalind Hursthouse
Professor of Philosophy, University of Auckland
VIRTUE ETHICS [BIBLIOGRAPHY] (2005)

Katerina Ierodiakonou
Associate Professor, Ancient Philosophy, Department of the Philosophy and History of Science, University of Athens
BYZANTINE PHILOSOPHY (2005)
PLETHO, GIORGIUS GEMISTUS [BIBLIOGRAPHY] (2005)

Shams Inati
Professor, Islamic Studies, Villanova University
DETERMINISM, THEOLOGICAL (2005)

David B. Ingram
Professor of Philosophy, Loyola University, Chicago
ARENDT, HANNAH (1996, 2005)
POSTMODERNISM (2005)

Brad Inwood
Professor of Classics and Philosophy, University of Toronto
CLEANTHES (2005)
HELLENISTIC THOUGHT (2005)
STOICISM (2005)

Anna Maria Ioppolo
Full Professor, Ancient Philosophy, Dipartimento di Scienze Filosofiche ed Epistemologiche, Università di Roma "La Sapienza"
ARISTO OF CHIOS (2005)

Michela Ippolito
Assistant Professor of Linguistics, Department of Modern Foreign Languages and Literatures, Boston University
TENSE (2005)

Howard Isham
Associate Professor, Humanities, San Francisco State College
HUMBOLDT, WILHELM VON (1967)

Frank C. Jackson
Director, Research, School of Social Sciences, Australian National University
ARMSTRONG, DAVID M. (1996, 2005)

Pierre Jacob
Director of Institut Jean Nicod, CNRS/EHESS/ENS, Paris
INTENTIONALITY [ADDENDUM] (2005)

Theordore E. James
Associate Professor, Philosophy, Manhattan College
IBN GABIROL, SOLOMON BEN JUDAH (1967)

Dale Jamieson
Professor of Environmental Studies and Philosophy, New York University, Steinhardt School, HMSS
SINGER, PETER (2005)

M. Jammer
Head, Physics; Professor of Physicas and Philosophy of Science, Bar-Ilan University, Israel
ENERGY (1967)
FORCE (1967)
MASS (1967)
MOTION, A HISTORICAL SURVEY (1967)

Richard Janko
Professor and Chair, Classical Studies, Rackham Graduate School, University of Michigan
HOMER [BIBLIOGRAPHY] (2005)

Joyce L. Jenkins
Associate Professor, Philosophy Department, University of Manitoba
SELF-INTEREST (2005)

Robert Johnson
Associate Professor of Philosophy, University of Missouri
PRACTICAL REASON (2005)

Hans Jonas
Professor, Philosophy, Graduate Faculty of Political and Social Science, New School for Social Research
GNOSTICISM (1967)

Alexander Jones
Professor, Classics and the History and Philosophy of Science and Technology, University of Toronto
HELLENISTIC THOUGHT (2005)

Charles Jones
Associate Professor, Political Science, University of Western Ontario
COSMOPOLITANISM (2005)

Karen Jones
Lecturer, Philosophy, The University of Melbourne
BAIER, ANNETTE (2005)
FEMINIST EPISTEMOLOGY (2005)

Inge Jonsson
Docent, History of Literature, University of Stockholm
SWEDENBORG, EMANUEL (1967)

Z. A. Jordan
Lecturer, Philosophy of Science, University of Reading
KOTARBIŃSKI, TADEUSZ (1967)

Lawrence J. Jost
Professor of Philosophy, University of Cincinnati
VIRTUE AND VICE (2005)

James Joyce
Associate Professor of Philosophy, University of Michigan
DECISION THEORY (2005)
SAVAGE, LEONARD (2005)

Eric T. Juengst
Associate Professor of Bioethics, School of Medicine, Case Western Reserve University

GENETICS AND REPRODUCTIVE
TECHNOLOGIES [ADDENDUM]
(2005)

Béla Juhos
*Professor of Theological Philosophy,
University of Vienna*
SCHLICK, MORITZ (1967)

Elzbieta Jung
*Professor, Philosophy, University of
Lodz*
KILVINGTON, RICHARD (2005)

Guy Kahane
*Research Associate, Uehiro Centre
for Practical Ethics, Faculty of
Philosophy, Oxford University*
PAIN, ETHICAL SIGNIFICANCE OF
(2005)

Russell Kahl
*Associate Professor, Philosophy, San
Francisco State College*
HELMHOLTZ, HERMANN LUDWIG
VON (1967)

Charles H. Kahn
*Professor of Philosophy, University
of Pennsylvania*
ANAXIMANDER (1967)
EMPEDOCLES (1967)
PLATO (2005)

Irene Kajon
*Ordinary Professor, Dipartimento
di Ricerche Storico-filosofiche e
Pedagogiche, Università di Roma
"La Sapienza"*
COHEN, HERMANN [ADDENDUM]
(2005)

Ibrahim Kalin
*Assistant Professor of Islamic
Studies, Department of Religious
Studies, College of the Holy Cross*
CORBIN, HENRY (2005)
EPISTEMOLOGY, HISTORY OF
[ADDENDUM] (2005)
MULLĀ ṢADRĀ [ADDENDUM]
(2005)
NASR, SEYYED HOSSEIN (2005)

Paul Kalligas
*Assistant Professor, Philosophy and
History of Science, University of
Athens*
PLOTINUS [BIBLIOGRAPHY]
(2005)

Akihiro Kanamori
*Professor, Mathematics, Boston
University*
SET THEORY (2005)

David Kaplan
*Assistant Professor of Philosophy,
Department of Philosophy and
Religion Studies, University of
North Texas*
RICOEUR, PAUL (2005)

Elizabeth Karger
Chargée de Recherche, CNRS, Paris
WODEHAM, ADAM (2005)

George Kateb
*William Nelson Cromwell Professor
of Politics, Emeritus, Princeton
University*
UTOPIAS AND UTOPIANISM (1967,
2005)

Arnold S. Kaufman
*Professor, Philosophy, Princeton
University*
RESPONSIBILITY, MORAL AND
LEGAL (1967)

Asaf Kedar
*Doctoral Student, Political Science,
University of California, Berkeley*
HISTORICISM [ADDENDUM]
(2005)

Samuel McMurray Keen
*Associate Professor of Philosophy
and Christian Faith, Louisville
Presbyterian Seminary*
MARCEL, GABRIEL (1967)

Morris Keeton
*Professor of Philosophy and
Religion; Dean of the Faculty,
Antioch College*
MONTGOMERY, EDMUND DUNCAN
(1967)

John Kekes
*Research Professor, University at
Albany, State University of New
York*
CONSERVATISM (2005)

Birgit Kellner
*Institute for South Asian, Tibetan
and Buddhist Studies*
NEGATION IN INDIAN PHILOSOPHY
(2005)

Douglas Kellner
*Professor and George F. Kneller
Philosophy of Education Chair,
Graduate School of Education,
University of California, Los
Angeles*
BAUDRILLARD, JEAN (2005)
HORKHEIMER, MAX (2005)

W. E. Kennick
*Professor, Philosophy, Amherst
College*
APPEARANCE AND REALITY (1967)

G. B. Kerferd
*Professor, Classics, University
College of Swansea, University of
Wales*
APEIRON/PERAS (1967)
CRATYLUS (1967)
HEN/POLLA (1967)
HIPPIAS OF ELIS (1967)
PERIPATETICS (1967)
PRODICUS OF CEOS (1967)
PROTAÊORAS OF ABDERA (1967)
PSYCHÊ (1967)

Ralph Ketchum
*Professor of Political Science and
American Studies, Syracuse
University*
FRANKLIN, BENJAMIN (1967)

Jeffrey Ketland
*Lecturer, Philosophy, University of
Edinburgh*
CRAIG'S THEOREM (2005)
SECOND-ORDER LOGIC (2005)

I. G. Kidd
*Senior Lecturer, Greek, University
of St. Andrews*
ANTISTHENES (1967)
CYNICS (1967)
DIOGENES OF SINOPE (1967)
GREEK ACADEMY (1967)

Kihyeon Kim
*Associate Professor, Philosophy,
Seoul National University*
KOREAN PHILOSOPHY (2005)

Jeffrey C. King
*Professor of Philosophy, University
of Southern California*
ANAPHORA [ADDENDUM] (2005)
SEMANTICS (2005)

Peter King
*Professor of Philosophy and of
Mediaeval Studies, University of
Toronto*
ANSELM, ST. (2005)
AUGUSTINE, ST. [ADDENDUM1]
(1996)
WILLIAM OF CHAMPEAUX (2005)

John Kinnaird
*Assistant Professor, English,
University of Maryland*
HAZLITT, WILLIAM (1967)

Eva F. Kittay
*State University of New York at
Stony Brook*
METAPHOR (1996)

Peter Kivy
*Board of Governors Professor of
Philosophy, Rutgers University*
HUTCHESON, FRANCIS
[ADDENDUM] (2005)
MUSIC, PHILOSOPHY OF (2005)
SIBLEY, FRANK (2005)
SMITH, ADAM [ADDENDUM]
(2005)

Pauline Kleingeld
*Professor of Philosophy, Leiden
University*
PATRIOTISM (2005)

Gyula Klima
*Professor, Philosophy, Fordham
University*
OCKHAMISM [BIBLIOGRAPHY]
(2005)

George L. Kline
*Professor, Philosophy, Bryn Mawr
College*
CHICHERIN, BORIS NIKOLAEVICH
(1967)
FRANK, SEMËN LIUDVIGOVICH
(1967)
HERZEN, ALEKSANDR IVANOVICH
(1967)
KAREEV, NIKOLAI IVANOVICH
(1967)
KAVELIN, KONSTANTIN
DMITRIEVICH (1967)
LUNACHARSKII, ANATOLII
VASIL'EVICH (1967)
PISAREV, DMITRI IVANOVICH
(1967)
SHESTOV, LEV ISAAKOVICH (1967)
SKOVORODA, HRYHORII SAVYCH
(GRIGORII SAVVICH) (1967)
VOLSKI, STANISLAV (1967)

Boris C. A. Kment
Princeton University
CONDITIONALS (2005)

William C. Kneale
*White's Professor of Moral
Philosophy, University of Oxford*
ETERNITY (1967)

David Knowles
*Honorary Fellow of Peterhouse and
Christ's College, Cambridge
University*
BERNARD OF CLAIRVAUX, ST.
(1967)
BOETHIUS, ANICIUS MANLIUS
SEVERINUS (1967)
GERBERT OF AURILLAC (1967)
JOHN OF SALISBURY (1967)

Noretta Koertge
*Professor Emeritus, History &
Philosophy of Science, Indiana
University*
SCIENCE STUDIES (2005)

Peter Koestenbaum
*Professor of Philosophy, San Jose
State College*
JASPERS, KARL (1967)
UNAMUNO Y JUGO, MIGUEL DE
(1967)

Arthur Koestler
*Novelist, Essayist, Man of Letters,
Fellow, Royal Society of Literature*
KEPLER, JOHANNES (1967)

Barry S. Kogan
*Efroymson Professor of Philosophy
and Jewish Religious Thought,
Hebrew Union College–Jewish
Institute of Religion, Cincinnati,
Ohio*
HALEVI, YEHUDA (2005)

Eckehart Köhler
*Member of Phlilosophisches
Seminar II, University of Munich,
MA Candidate, New York
University*
SCHOLZ, HEINRICH (1967)

Niko Kolodny
*Assistant Professor, Philosophy,
University of California, Berkeley*
LOVE [ADDENDUM] (2005)
OBJECTIVITY IN ETHICS (2005)

David Konstan
*John Rowe Workman Distinguished
Professor of Classics and Professor
of Comparative Literature, Brown
University*
LUCIAN OF SAMOSATA (2005)
LUCRETIUS (2005)

Milton R. Konvitz
*Professor of Law and Professor of
Industrial and Labor Relations,
Cornell University*
HISTORICAL SCHOOL OF
JURISPRUDENCE (1967)
SAVIGNY, FRIEDRICH KARL VON
(1967)

Hilary Kornblith
*Professor, Philosophy, University of
Massachusetts*
GOLDMAN, ALVIN (2005)

Stephan Körner
*Head, Physics; Professor of Physicas
and Philosophy of Science, Bar-Ilan
University,*
CASSIRER, ERNST (1967)
CONTINUITY (1967)
LAWS OF THOUGHT (1967)

Viacheslav Koshelev
*Professor, Novgorod State
University named after Yaroslav
Mudryi, Member of the
International Academy of Higher
Education*
CHAADAEV, PËTR IAKOVLEVICH
(2005)
KHOMIAKOV, ALEKSEI
STEPANOVICH (2005)

Kathrin Koslicki
*Assistant Professor, Philosophy,
Tufts University*
NOUNS, MASS AND COUNT (2005)

Janet A. Kourany
*Associate Professor, Philosophy,
University of Notre Dame*
FEMINIST PHILOSOPHY OF
SCIENCE: CONTEMPORARY
PERSPECTIVES (2005)

Julius Kovesi
*Lecturer in Philosophy, University
of Western Australia*
PALÁGYI, MENYHERT (1967)
PAULER, AKOS (1967)

A. J. Krailsheimer
University Lecturer and College Tutor in French, Christ Church, Oxford University
BOSSUET, JACQUES BÉNIGNE (1967)
FÉNELON, FRANÇOIS DE SALIGNAC DE LA MOTHE (1967)
LA BRUYÈRE, JEAN DE (1967)
LA ROCHEFOUCAULD, DUC FRANÇOIS DE (1967)

Jill Kraye
Professor of the History of Renaissance, Philosophy, Warburg Institute, University of London
HUMANISM (2005)

Norman Kretzmann
Associate Professor, Philosophy, Cornell University
SEMANTICS, HISTORY OF (1967)
WILLIAM OF SHERWOOD (1967)

Yervant H. Krikorian
Professor Emeritus, Philosophy, City University of New York, City College
COHEN, MORRIS RAPHAEL (1967)

Paul Oskar Kristellar
Professor, Philosophy, Columbia University
FICINO, MARSILIO (1967)
FLORENTINE ACADEMY (1967)
PETRARCH (1967)
PICO DELLA MIRANDOLA, COUNT GIOVANNI (1967)
POMPONAZZI, PIETRO (1967)

George Krzywicki-Herburt
Associate Professor, Philosophy, City University of New York, Queens College
TWARDOWSKI, KAZIMIERZ (1967)

Taneli Kukkonen
Canada Research Chair in the Aristotelian Tradition, University of Victoria
ARISTOTELIANISM (2005)

Rahul Kumar
Associate Professor of Philosophy, Queen's University, Kingston, Canada
CONTRACTUALISM (2005)

Joel J. Kupperman
Professor of Philosophy, University of Connecticut
VALUE AND VALUATION [ADDENDUM] (2005)

Paul Kurtz
Professor, Philosophy, State University of New York at Buffalo
PALMER, ELIHU (1967)

Roxanne Marie Kurtz
Assistant Professor, Philosophy, University of Illinois, Springfield
PERSISTENCE (2005)

Douglas Kutach
Assistant Professor, Philosophy, Brown University
COUNTERFACTUALS IN SCIENCE (2005)

Jonathan Kvanvig
Professor and Chair, Philosophy, University of Missouri, Columbia
KNOWLEDGE AND TRUTH, THE VALUE OF (2005)

Kai Man Kwan
Associate Professor, Religion and Philosophy, Hong Kong Baptist University
MORAL ARGUMENTS FOR THE EXISTENCE OF GOD [ADDENDUM] (2005)
MYSTICISM, NATURE AND ASSESSMENT OF [ADDENDUM] (2005)

Will Kymlicka
Canada Research Chair in Political Philosophy, Queen's University
COMMUNITARIANISM (1996, 2005)

Hugh Lacey
Senior Research Scholar/Scheuer Family Professor Emeritus of Philosophy, Swarthmore College; Visiting Professor Universidade de São Paulo; Lecturer, University of Pennsylvania
SKINNER, B. F. (2005)

John Ladd
Professor, Philosophy, Brown University; Secretary-Treasurer of the American Society for Political and Legal Science
LOYALTY (1967)

James Ladyman
Reader in Philosophy, University of Bristol
THEORIES AND THEORETICAL TERMS (2005)

Henrik Lagerlund
Associate Professor in Philosophy, Uppsala University; Research Associate at CRASSH, University of Cambridge
KILWARDBY, ROBERT (2005)

Sterling P. Lamprecht
Professor Emeritus of Philosophy, Amherst College
WOODBRIDGE, FREDERICK JAMES EUGENE (1967)

Irene Lancaster
Honorary Research Fellow, Centre for Jewish Studies, University of Manchester
KABBALAH [ADDENDUM] (2005)

Marc Lange
Professor, Philosophy, University of North Carolina at Chapel Hill
CLASSICAL MECHANICS, PHILOSOPHY OF (2005)
ENERGY [ADDENDUM] (2005)
LAWS, SCIENTIFIC (2005)

Peter Laslett
Fellow of Trinity College, Cambridge, and Lecturer in History, University of Cambridge, Cofounder of the Cambridge Group for the History of Population and Social Structure
FILMER, ROBERT (1967)
POLITICAL PHILOSOPHY, HISTORY OF (1967)
SOCIAL CONTRACT (1967)

John H. Lavely
Professor and Chair, Philosophy, Boston University; Editor of the Philosophical Forum
BRIGHTMAN, EDGAR SHEFFIELD (1967)
PERSONALISM (1967)

James M. Lawler
Philosophy Department, State University of New York at Buffalo
COMMUNISM (2005)
DIALECTICAL MATERIALISM [ADDENDUM] (2005)

Krista Lawlor
Assistant Professor, Philosophy, Stanford University
MILLIKAN, RUTH (2005)

Leonard Lawlor
Faudree-Hardin University Professor of Philosophy; Graduate Admissions Coordinator, Philosophy Department; At Large Member of the Society for Phenomenology and Existential Philosophy, The University of Memphis
HYPPOLITE, JEAN (2005)
TIME IN CONTINENTAL PHILOSOPHY (2005)

Oliver Leaman
Professor of Philosophy, University of Kentucky
AL-FĀRĀBĪ [ADDENDUM] (2005)
AL-KINDĪ, ABŪ-YŪSUF YAʿQŪB IBN ISḤĀQ [ADDENDUM] (2005)
ARKOUN, MOHAMMED (2005)
AVERROES [ADDENDUM] (2005)
AVERROISM IN MODERN ISLAMIC PHILOSOPHY (2005)
AVICENNA [ADDENDUM] (2005)
BAḤYA BEN JOSEPH IBN PAQUDA [ADDENDUM] (2005)
CODOVERO, MOSES BEN JACOB [BIBLIOGRAPHY] (2005)
COSTA, URIEL DA [BIBLIOGRAPHY] (2005)
CRESCAS, HASDAI [ADDENDUM] (2005)
EMANATIONISM [ADDENDUM] (2005)
ENLIGHTENMENT, ISLAMIC (2005)
ENLIGHTENMENT, JEWISH (2005)
ESSENCE AND EXISTENCE [ADDENDUM] (2005)
HOLOCAUST (2005)
IBN BĀJJA [ADDENDUM] (2005)
IBN GABIROL, SOLOMON BEN JUDAH [BIBLIOGRAPHY] (2005)
IBN KHALDŪN [ADDENDUM] (2005)
IBN ṬUFAYL [ADDENDUM] (2005)
IBN ZADDIK, JOSEPH BEN JACOB [BIBLIOGRAPHY] (2005)
ISLAMIC PHILOSOPHY [ADDENDUM] (2005)
ISRAELI, ISAAC BEN SOLOMON [BIBLIOGRAPHY] (2005)
JEWISH AVERROISM (2005)
JEWISH PHILOSOPHY [ADDENDUM] (2005)
MENASSEH (MANASSEH) BEN ISRAEL [BIBLIOGRAPHY] (2005)
MENDELSSOHN, MOSES [BIBLIOGRAPHY] (2005)
MUQAMMIṢ, DAVID BEN MERWAN AL- [BIBLIOGRAPHY] (2005)
NEOPLATONISM [ADDENDUM] (2005)
SHARIATI, ALI (2005)

Mark LeBar
Associate Professor of Philosophy, Ohio University
KANTIAN ETHICS (2005)

Grace Ledbetter
Associate Professor of Classics and Philosophy, Swarthmore College
GREEK DRAMA [BIBLIOGRAPHY] (2005)

Callan Ledsham
Hoger Instituut voor Wijsbegeerte, Katholieke Universiteit Leuven
MARSILIUS OF INGHEN (2005)

Stephen Leeds
Professor of Philosophy, University of Wisconsin, Milwaukee
FIELD, HARTRY (2005)

Gordon Leff
Reader in Medieval History, University of York
AILLY, PIERRE D' (1967)
GILES OF ROME (1967)
GREGORY OF RIMINI (1967)

Brian Leftow
Nolloth Professor of the Philosophy of the Christian Religion, Oxford University
ETERNITY [ADDENDUM 1] (2005)
GOD, CONCEPTS OF [ADDENDUM] (2005)

Czeslaw Lejewski
Senior Lecturer in Philosophy, University of Manchester
LOGIC, HISTORY OF: MODERN LOGIC: FROM FREGE TO GÖDEL [OVERVIEW] (1967)
ŁUKASIEWICZ, JAN (1967)

Karl-Heinz Lembeck
Universitätsprofessor, Institut für Philosophie, Bayerische Julius-Maximilians-Universität Würzburg
NATORP, PAUL (2005)

Noah M. Lemos
Professor, The College of William and Mary
EPISTEMOLOGY, CIRCULARITY IN (2005)

James Lennox
Professor of History and Philosophy of Science, University of Pittsburgh
PHILOSOPHY OF BIOLOGY (2005)

Maria Lucrezia Leone
Postdoctoral Research Fellow, Philosophy, University of Bari (Italy) and Catholic University of Leuven (Belgium)
HENRY OF GHENT [BIBLIOGRAPHY AND ADDENDUM] (2005)

Ernest Lepore
Director, Center for Cognitive Science, Rutgers University
ANALYTIC AND SYNTHETIC STATEMENTS [ADDENDUM] (2005)
PHILOSOPHY OF LANGUAGE (2005)

Joseph Levine
Philosophy, Ohio State University
QUALIA (1996, 2005)
SUBJECTIVITY (1996, 2005)

Jerrold Levinson
University of Maryland at College Park
ART, AUTHENTICITY IN (1996)

Donald Levy
Faculty Member, New School for Social Research
MACROCOSM AND MICROCOSM (1967)

H. D. Lewis
Head, Department of History and Philosophy of Religion, King's College, University of London, and Fellow of King' College; Dean of the Faculty of Theology, University of London; President of the Society for the Study of Theology, Chairman of the Council of the Royal Institute of Philosophy
GUILT (1967)
PHILOSOPHY OF RELIGION, HISTORY OF (1967)

Neil T. Lewis
Associate Professor, Philosophy, Georgetown University
GROSSETESTE, ROBERT [BIBLIOGRAPHY] (2005)
WILLIAM OF AUVERGNE (2005)

Leonard Lewisohn
Iran Heritage Foundation Fellow in Classical Persian and Sufi Literature, The Institute of Arab and Islamic Studies, University of Exeter, England
AL-GHAZĀLI, AHMAD (2005)
SUFISM (2005)

Anatoly Liberman
Professor, German, Scandinavian and Dutch, University of Minnesota, Minneapolis
TRUBETSKOI, NIKOLAI SERGEEVICH (2005)

David Liggins
ANALYSIS Student, Faculty of Philosophy, University of Cambridge
FICTIONALISM (2005)

Leonard Linsky
Professor of Philosophy, University of Illinois
SYNONYMITY (1967)

Peter Lipton
Kings College, Cambridge University
INFERENCE TO THE BEST EXPLANATION (1996, 2005)

Iurii Lisitsa
Professor of Mathematical Analysis and Function Theory Department, Russian University of Peoples' Friendship; Head of Faculty of Religion, Russian Orthodox Saint Tikhon Humanistic University, Moscow
IL'IN, IVAN ALEKSANDROVICH (2005)

Jeeloo Liu
Assistant Professor, California State University, Fullerton
WANG FUZHI (2005)

Shu-hsien Liu
Adjunct Research Fellow, Institute of Chinese Literature and Philosophy, Academia Sinica, Taipei; Tuan-mu Kai Chair; Professor, Soochow University, Taipei; Emeritus Professor of Philosophy The Chinese University of Hong Kong
CHINESE PHILOSOPHY: CONTEMPORARY (2005)
HUANG ZONGXI (2005)

Wu-chi Liu
Professor of Chinese; Chair of Department of East Asian Languages and Literature, Indiana University
DONG ZHONGSHU (1967)

Paisley Livingston
Professor, Philosophy, Lingnan University, Hong Kong
CREATIVITY (2005)
VALÉRY, PAUL (2005)

A. C. Lloyd
Professor, Philosophy, University of Liverpool
ALEXANDER OF APHRODISIAS (1967)
PORPHYRY (1967)

G. E. R. Lloyd
University Assistant Lecturer in Classics and Fellow of King's College, Cambridge University
LEUCIPPUS AND DEMOCRITUS (1967)

L. E. Loemker
Charles Howard Candler Professor of Philosophy, Emory University
DEUSSEN, PAUL (1967)
HARTMANN, EDUARD VON (1967)
LIEBERT, ARTHUR (1967)
MONAD AND MONADOLOGY (1967)
PAULSEN, FRIEDRICH (1967)
PESSIMISM AND OPTIMISM (1967)
RINTELEN, FRITZ-JOACHIM VON (1967)
SPRANGER, (FRANZ ERNST) EDUARD (2005)

Barry Loewer
Professor II, Philosophy, Rutgers University
CONTENT, MENTAL (1996, 2005)
PHILOSOPHY OF PHYSICS (2005)

Charles Lohr
Professor Emeritus, History of Medieval Theology, Universität Freiburg
LULL, RAMÓN [BIBLIOGRAPHY] (2005)

Lawrence Brian Lombard
Wayne State University
EVENT THEORY (1996)

Franco Lombardi
Ordinary Professor of Moral Philosophy, University of Rome; Director of De Homine
BLOCH, ERNST (1967)

John L. Longeway
Associate Professor, Philosophy, University of Wisconsin at Parkside
HEYTESBURY, WILLIAM (2005)

Robert B. Louden
University of Southern Maine
VIRTUE ETHICS (1996)

Andrew Louth
Professor of Patristic and Byzantine Studies, University of Durham
JOHN OF DAMASCUS (2005)
PSEUDO-DIONYSIUS [BIBLIOGRAPHY] (2005)

Michael Loux
Schuster Professor of Philosophy, University of Notre Dame
METAPHYSICS, HISTORY OF [ADDENDUM] (2005)

E. J. Lowe
Professor, Philosophy, University of Durham
AGENT CAUSATION (2005)
BENNETT, JONATHAN (2005)

Thomas Luckmann
Professor, University of Frankfurt; Visiting Professor, Graduate Faculty, New School for Social Research
PLESSNER, HELMUT (1967)

Peter Ludlow
State University of New York at Stony Brook
PRESUPPOSITION (1996)

Kirk Ludwig
Professor, Philosophy, University of Florida, Gainesville
BELIEF (2005)

Rossella Lupacchini
Philosophy Department, University of Bologna
COMPUTING MACHINES (2005)

David Luscombe
Fellow and Director of Studies in History, Churchill College, Cambridge University
BERNARD, CLAUDE (1967)
BERNARD OF CHARTRES (1967)
BERNARD OF TOURS (1967)
CHARTRES, SCHOOL OF (1967)
GILBERT OF POITIERS (1967)
SAINT VICTOR, SCHOOL OF (1967)
THEODORIC OF CHARTRES (1967)
WILLIAM OF CONCHES (1967)

Dan Lusthaus
Visiting Professor, Boston University
BUDDHISM—SCHOOLS: YOGACĀRĀ (2005)

J. Rebecca Lyman
Samuel Garrett Professor of Church History Emerita, Church Divinity School of the Pacific
ARIUS AND ARIANISM (2005)

Michael Lynch
Associate Professor of Philosophy, University of Connecticut
RORTY, RICHARD (2005)

William Lyons
University of Dublin, Ireland
INTROSPECTION (1996)

Danielle Macbeth
Professor, Philosophy, Haverford College
MCDOWELL, JOHN (2005)

H. R. MacCallum
Associate Professor, English, University of Toronto
MILTON, JOHN (1967)

Stuart MacClintock
U.S. Government, Department of Defense
AVERROES (1967)
AVERROISM (1967)
JOHN OF JANDUN (1967)

Cynthia MacDonald
Professor of Philosophy, Queen's University Belfast
ANOMALOUS MONISM (1996)
PHYSICALISM (1996, 2005)
SHOEMAKER, SYDNEY (2005)

C. A. Mace
Emeritus Professor, University of London
PSYCHOLOGY (1967)
STOUT, GEORGE FREDERICK (1967)

Tibor Machan
R. C. Hoiles Professor of Business Ethics, Argyros School of Business & Economics, Chapman University
POLITICAL PHILOSOPHY, HISTORY OF [ADDENDUM] (2005)
PROPERTY [ADDENDUM] (2005)

Alasdair MacIntyre
Professor, Sociology, University of Essex
BEING (1967)
BRUNNER, EMIL (1967)
EGOISM AND ALTRUISM (1967)
ESSENCE AND EXISTENCE (1967)
EXISTENTIALISM (1967)
JUNG, CARL GUSTAV (1967)
KIERKEGAARD, SØREN AABYE (1967)
MYTH (1967)
ONTOLOGY, HISTORY OF (1967)
PANTHEISM (1967)

J. L. Mackie
Professor of Philosophy, University of York
FALLACIES (1967)
MILL'S METHODS OF INDUCTION (1967)
WESTERMARCK, EDWARD ALEXANDER (1967)

Ruth Macklin
Bronx, New York
GENETICS AND REPRODUCTIVE TECHNOLOGIES (1996)

John MacQuarrie
Professor of Systematic Theology, Union Theological Seminary
BLONDEL, MAURICE (1967)
GOGARTEN, FRIEDRICH (1967)
HARNACK, CARL GUSTAV ADOLF VON (1967)
HEIM, KARL (1967)
INGE, WILLIAM RALPH (1967)
LABERTHONNIÈRE, LUCIEN (1967)
PIETISM (1967)
TAYLOR, ALFRED EDWARD (1967)
VARISCO, BERNARDINO (1967)

Edward H. Madden
Professor of Philosophy, State University of New York at Buffalo; General Editor of Source Books in the History of Science (Harvard University Press)
WRIGHT, CHAUNCEY (1967)

Patrick Maher
Professor, Philosophy, University of Illinois at Urbana-Champaign
CONFIRMATION THEORY (2005)

James Edwin Mahon
Assistant Professor, Philosophy, Washington and Lee University
LYING (2005)

Rudolf Makkreel
Charles Howard Candler Professor of Philosophy, Emory University
DILTHEY, WILHELM (2005)

Norman Malcolm
Susan Linn Sage Professor of Philosophy and Chair of the Department of Philosophy, Cornell University; Managing Editor of the Philosophical Review
WITTGENSTEIN, LUDWIG JOSEF JOHANN (1967)

Paolo Mancosu
Associate Professor of Philosophy, University of California, Berkeley
HILBERT, DAVID [ADDENDUM] (2005)

Maurice Mandelbaum
Professor, Philosophy, Johns Hopkins University
HISTORICISM (1967)

Jon Mandle
Associate Professor of Philosophy, University at Albany (State University of New York)
GENERAL WILL, THE (2005)

William E. Mann
Marsh Professor of Intellectual and Moral Philosophy, University of Vermont
PATRISTIC PHILOSOPHY [BIBLIOGRAPHY] (2005)

A. R. Manser
Senior Lecturer, Philosophy, University of Southampton
DREAMS (1967)
IMAGES (1967)
IMAGINATION (1967)

Vladimir Marchenkov
Assistant Professor of Aesthetics, Ohio University
BAKUNIN, MIKHAIL ALEKSANDROVICH [BIBLIOGRAPHY] (2005)
BELINSKII, VISSARION GRIGOR'EVICH [BIBLIOGRAPHY] (2005)
BULGAKOV, SERGEI NIKOLAEVICH [BIBLIOGRAPHY] (2005)
CHERNYSHEVSKII, NIKOLAI GAVRILOVICH [BIBLIOGRAPHY] (2005)
FRANK, SEMĒN LIUDVIGOVICH [BIBLIOGRAPHY] (2005)

HERZEN, ALEKSANDR IVANOVICH [BIBLIOGRAPHY] (2005)
KAREEV, NIKOLAI IVANOVICH [BIBLIOGRAPHY] (2005)
KAVELIN, KONSTANTIN DMITRIEVICH [BIBLIOGRAPHY] (2005)
KOZLOV, ALEKSEI ALEKSANDROVICH [BIBLIOGRAPHY] (2005)
KROPOTKIN, PËTR ALEKSEEVICH [BIBLIOGRAPHY] (2005)
LAPSHIN, IVAN IVANOVICH [BIBLIOGRAPHY] (2005)
LAVROV, PËTR LAVROVICH [BIBLIOGRAPHY] (2005)
LOPATIN, LEV MIKHAILOVICH [BIBLIOGRAPHY] (2005)
LOSEV, ALEKSEI FËDOROVICH (2005)
LUNACHARSKII, ANATOLII VASIL'EVICH [BIBLIOGRAPHY] (2005)
MIKHAILOVSKII, NIKOLAI KONSTANTINOVICH [BIBLIOGRAPHY] (2005)
PAVLOV, IVAN PETROVICH [BIBLIOGRAPHY] (2005)
PLEKHANOV, GEORGII VALENTINOVICH [BIBLIOGRAPHY] (2005)
RUSSIAN PHILOSOPHY (2005)
VYSHESLAVTSEV, BORIS PETROVICH [BIBLIOGRAPHY] (2005)

John Marenbon
Senior Research Fellow, Trinity College, Cambridge University
ABELARD, PETER (2005)

Adam Margoshes
Assistant Professor of Psychology, Shippensburg State College
BAADER, FRANZ XAVIER VON (1967)
SCHELLING, FRIEDRICH WILHELM JOSEPH VON (1967)

Jacqueline Mariña
Associate Professor of Philosophy; Chair, Religious Studies Program, Purdue University
SCHLEIERMACHER, FRIEDRICH DANIEL ERNST [ADDENDUM] (2005)

R. A. Markus
Senior Lecturer in Medieval History, University of Liverpool
AUGUSTINE, ST. (1967)
ILLUMINATION (1967)

Michael E. Marmura
Associate Professor in the Department of Islamic Studies, University of Toronto
AVICENNA (1967)

Donald Marquis
University of Kansas, Lawrence
ABORTION (1996)

Christopher J. Martin
Associate Professor, Philosophy, University of Auckland
BOETHIUS, ANICIUS MANLIUS SEVERINUS [ADDENDUM] (2005)
LOGIC, HISTORY OF: MEDIEVAL (EUROPEAN) LOGIC (2005)
ROSCELIN (2005)

Rex Martin
Professor of Philosophy, University of Kansas; Honorary Professor, School of European Studies, Cardiff University
PHILOSOPHY OF LAW, PROBLEMS OF [ADDENDUM] (2005)

Wayne M. Martin
Reader in Philosophy, Essex University
HEGELIANISM (2005)

Martin E. Marty
Fairfax M. Cone Distinguished Service Professor Emeritus, The University of Chicago
BONHOEFFER, DIETRICH (1967, 2005)

Elinor Mason
Lecturer, Philosophy, University of Edinburgh
CONSEQUENTIALISM [BIBLIOGRAPHY] (2005)

Kelby Mason
PhD candidate, Philosophy, Rutgers University
EVOLUTIONARY PSYCHOLOGY (2005)

Michelle Mason
Assistant Professor, Philosophy, University of Minnesota
MORAL SENTIMENTS (2005)

Heath Massey
Assistant Professor of Philosophy, Beloit College

TIME IN CONTINENTAL PHILOSOPHY (2005)

Wallace Matson
Professor of Philosophy, Emeritus, University of California, Berkeley
ARISTIPPUS OF CYRENE (2005)
CYRENAICS (2005)

Gareth B. Matthews
Professor of Philosophy, University of Massachusetts, Amherst
AUGUSTINIANISM [BIBLIOGRAPHY] (2005)

Robert Matthews
Rutgers University
MENTAL REPRESENTATION (1996)

Tim Maudlin
Professor, Philosophy, Rutgers University
GAUGE THEORY (2005)
NON-LOCALITY (2005)
QUANTUM LOGIC AND PROBABILITY (2005)
QUANTUM MECHANICS (2005)
RELATIVITY THEORY (2005)

Armand A. Maurer
Professor of Philosophy, Pontifical Institute of Medieval Studies and University of Toronto
BOETIUS OF DACIA (1967)
BROWNSON, ORESTES AUGUSTUS (1967)
EDWARDS, JONATHAN (1967)
HENRY OF HARCLAY (1967)
NICHOLAS OF CUSA (1967)

Wolfe Mays
Senior Lecturer in Philosophy, University of Manchester; Visiting Professor of Philosophy, Northwestern University
PIAGET, JEAN (1967)

Bruce Mazlish
Professor, History, Massachusetts Institute of Technology
COMTE, AUGUSTE (1967)

William L. McBride
Arthur G. Hansen Distinguished Professor of Philosophy, Purdue University
IDEOLOGY (2005)
SOCIETY [ADDENDUM] (2005)

Edwin McCann
Professor of Philosophy, University of Southern California
LOCKE, JOHN (2005)

Hugh J. McCann
Professor of Philosophy, Texas A&M University
CREATION AND CONSERVATION, RELIGIOUS DOCTRINE OF (2005)

Thomas McCarthy
Northwestern University
CRITICAL THEORY (1996)
DISCOURSE ETHICS (1996)
HABERMAS, JÜRGEN (1996)

James E. McClellan Jr.
Director, Foundations of Education Department and the General Education Program for Teachers; Professor of Education, Temple University
PHILOSOPHY OF EDUCATION, INFLUENCE OF MODERN PSYCHOLOGY ON (1967)

John J. McDermott
Distinguished Professor of Philosophy and Humanities, Texas A&M University
DEWEY, JOHN [BIBLIOGRAPHY AND ADDENDUM] (1996)
JAMES, WILLIAM [ADDENDUM] (1996, 2005)

Vann McGee
Professor, Linguistics and Philosophy, Massachusetts Institute of Technology
GÖDEL'S INCOMPLETENESS THEOREMS (2005)
LOGICAL PARADOXES (2005)

Sarah McGrath
Assistant Professor, Philosophy, College of the Holy Cross
THOMSON, JUDITH JARVIS (2005)

Ralph McInerny
Michael P. Grace Professor of Medieval Studies, University of Notre Dame
MARITAIN, JACQUES [ADDENDUM] (2005)

Neil McInnes
Special writer in Paris for Barron's Financial Weekly and the Wall Street Journal
ENGELS, FRIEDRICH (1967)

GRACIÁN Y MORALES, BALTASAR (1967)
GRAMSCI, ANTONIO (1967)
LABRIOLA, ANTONIO (1967)
LUKÁCS, GEORG (1967)
MARÍAS, JULIÁN (1967)
MARXIST PHILOSOPHY (1967)
ORTEGA Y GASSET, JOSÉ (1967)
SOREL, GEORGES (1967)
ZUBIRI, XAVIER (1967)

Sean McKeever
Assistant Professor, Philosophy, Davidson College
ETHICS, HISTORY OF: OTHER DEVELOPMENTS IN TWENTIETH-CENTURY ETHICS (2005)

William McKenna
Chair, Department of Philosophy, Miami University of Ohio
GURWITSCH, ARON (2005)

Robert J. McKim
Professor in the Program for the Study of Religion and Professor of Philosophy, University of Illinois at Urbana-Champaign
BERKELEY, GEORGE [ADDENDUM] (1996, 2005)

Richard McKirahan
E.C. Norton Professor of Classics and Professor of Philosophy, Pomona College
MELISSUS OF SAMOS [BIBLIOGRAPHY] (2005)
XENOPHANES OF COLOPHON (2005)
ZENO OF ELEA (2005)

Brian McLaughlin
Professor of Philosophy, Rutgers University
MENTAL CAUSATION (1996, 2005)
MIND-BODY PROBLEM (2005)
SELF-KNOWLEDGE (2005)
SUPERVENIENCE (1996, 2005)

Y. P. Mei
Professor, Chair, Chinese and Oriental Studies; Director of the Center for Far Eastern Studies, University of Iowa
MOZI (1967)

Jørgen Mejer
Director, Danish Institute; Reader in Classical Philology, University of Copenhagen, Institute for Greek and Latin
DIOGENES LAERTIUS (2005)

Alfred R. Mele
William H. and Lucyle T. Werkmeister Professor of Philosophy, Florida State University
ACTION (1996, 2005)
INTENTION (2005)
WEAKNESS OF THE WILL (2005)

Henry Mendell
California State University, Los Angeles
COSMOS (2005)

Eduardo Mendieta
Associate Professor, Philosophy, Stony Brook University, State University of New York
POSTCOLONIALISM (2005)

Stephen Menn
Associate Professor, Philosophy, McGill University
ARISTOTLE (2005)

Christia Mercer
Gustave M. Berne Professor; Philosophy, Columbia University; North American Editor, Archiv für Geschichte der Philosophie
LEIBNIZ, GOTTFRIED WILHELM (2005)

Philip Merlan
Professor of German Philosophy and Literature, Scripps College and Claremont Graduate School, CA
EMANATIONISM (1967)
PLOTINUS (1967)

Pierre Mesnard
Professor of Philosophy; Faculty of Letters, University of Orléans-Tours; Director of Centre d'Études Supérieures de la Renaissance de Tours
BODIN, JEAN (1967)

Algis Mickunas
Philosophy, Ohio University
LANDGREBE, LUDWIG (2005)

Leland Miles
Dean of the College of Arts and Sciences, University of Bridgeport
COLET, JOHN (1967)

T. R. Miles
Professor of Psychology, University College of North Wales, Bangor
GESTALT THEORY (1967)
KOFFKA, KURT (1967)

Elizabeth Millán-Zaibert
*Assistant Professor of Philosophy,
DePaul University*
LATIN AMERICAN PHILOSOPHY
(2005)

Robert G. Miller, C.S.B.
*Chairman of the Department of
Philosophy, St. John Fisher College*
GILSON, ÉTIENNE HENRY (1967)

Peter Milne
*Reader, School of Philosophy,
Psychology and Language Sciences
of the University of Edinburgh*
DE FINETTI, BRUNO (2005)

Edward H. Minar
*Associate Professor of Philosophy,
University of Arkansas, Fayetteville*
CAVELL, STANLEY (2005)

Robert C. Miner
*Associate Professor of Philosophy in
the Honors College, Baylor
University*
VICO, GIAMBATTISTA (2005)

Carl Mitcham
*Professor, Liberal Arts and
International Studies, Colorado
School of Mines*
PHILOSOPHY OF TECHNOLOGY
(1996, 2005)
SCIENCE POLICY (2005)
SOCIAL CONSTRUCTIONISM
(2005)

Phillip Mitsis
*A.S. Onassis Professor of Hellenic
Studies, New York University*
EPICURUS (2005)

Marc A. Moffett
*Assistant Professor of Philosophy,
University of Wyoming*
SYNONYMITY [ADDENDUM]
(2005)

Jitendra N. Mohanty
Temple University
PHENOMENOLOGY [ADDENDUM]
(1996)

Michel Mohr
*Lecturer, Institute for Language and
Culture, Doshisha University*
BUDDHISM—SCHOOLS: CHAN AND
ZEN (2005)

D. H. Monro
*Professor of Philosophy, Monash
University*
GODWIN, WILLIAM (1967)
HUMOR (1967)
SHELLEY, PERCY BYSSHE (1967)

Josep Puig Montada
*Professor, Arabic and Islamic
Studies, Universidad Complutense,
Madrid*
AL-JABIRI, ʿABD (2005)

Michelle Montague
*Assistant Professor, Philosophy,
University of California, Irvine*
COUNTERFACTUALS (2005)

Ernest A. Moody
*Professor of Philosophy, University
of California, Los Angeles*
LOGIC, HISTORY OF: MEDIEVAL
(EUROPEAN) LOGIC (1967)
OCKHAMISM (1967)
WILLIAM OF OCKHAM (1967)

James H. Moor
*Professor, Philosophy, Dartmouth
College*
COMPUTER ETHICS (1996, 2005)
MACHINE INTELLIGENCE (2005)

Kevin Moore
*PhD candidate, Joint Program at
University of Denver and Iliff
School of Theology*
HERMETICISM [BIBLIOGRAPHY]
(2005)

Merritt Hadden Moore
*Professor and Head of the
Department of Philosophy,
University of Tennessee*
COURNOT, ANTOINE AUGUSTIN
(1967)

Nancy J. Moore
*Professor of Law and Nancy Barton
Scholar, Boston University School of
Law*
INFORMED CONSENT IN THE
PRACTICE OF LAW (2005)

Michael Moran
*Lecturer in Philosophy, School of
European Studies, University of
Sussex*
CARLYLE, THOMAS (1967)
COLERIDGE, SAMUEL TAYLOR
(1967)
EMERSON, RALPH WALDO (1967)

NEW ENGLAND
TRANSCENDENTALISM (1967)
THOREAU, HENRY DAVID (1967)

Parviz Morewedge
*Director, Global Scholarly
Publications, New York; Honorary
Professor, National University,
Bishkek, Kyrgyz Republic; Adjunct
Professor, Philosophy, Fordham
University; Instructor, Philosophy
and Religion, Rutgers University*
NAṢÎR AL-DÎN AL-ṬÛSÎ (2005)
SCHOOL OF QOM, THE (2005)

John Morreall
*Professor, Religious Studies, College
of William and Mary*
HUMOR [ADDENDUM] (2005)

Herbert Morris
*Professor of Philosophy and Law at
University of California, Los
Angeles*
AUSTIN, JOHN (1967)

John Morrison
*President of University College,
Cambridge University*
ORPHISM (1967)

Paul Moser
*Professor and Chair of Philosophy,
Loyola University of Chicago*
PHILOSOPHY OF RELIGION
[ADDENDUM] (2005)
PROPOSITIONAL KNOWLEDGE,
DEFINITION OF (1996)
RATIONALITY (1996)

Albert G. Mosley
*Professor of Philosophy, Smith
College*
AFRICAN PHILOSOPHY (2005)
PLURALISM (1996)
RACISM [ADDENDUM] (1996,
2005)

Ernest Campbell Mossner
*Professor of English, University of
Texas, Austin; Joint Editor of
"Texas Studies in Literature and
Language"*
ANNET, PETER (1967)
BLOUNT, CHARLES (1967)
BOLINGBROKE, HENRY ST. JOHN
(1967)
CHUBB, THOMAS (1967)
COLLINS, ANTHONY (1967)
DEISM (1967)
GIBBON, EDWARD (1967)

JOHNSON, SAMUEL (1967)
MORGAN, THOMAS (1967)
POPE, ALEXANDER (1967)
SWIFT, JONATHAN (1967)
TINDAL, MATTHEW (1967)
TOLAND, JOHN (1967)
WOOLSTON, THOMAS (1967)

Andrzej Mostowski
Professor of Mathematics,
University of Warsaw;
Corresponding Member of the
Polish Academy of Sciences
TARSKI, ALFRED (1967)

Mary Mothersill
Professor and Chair, Philosophy,
Barnard College
DUTY (1967)

Nelia Motroshilova
Head of Department of the History
of Philosophy, Institute of
Philosophy, Russian Academy of
Sciences
MAMARDASHVILI, MERAB
  KONSTANTINOVICH (2005)

Bo Mou
CHINESE PHILOSOPHY: LANGUAGE
  AND LOGIC (2005)
GONGSUN LONG (2005)
HUI SHI (2005)

John A. Mourant
Professor of Philosophy,
Pennsylvania State University
AUGUSTINIANISM (1967)
SCIENTIA MEDIA AND MOLINISM
  (1967)
SUÁREZ, FRANCISCO (1967)

Alexander P. D. Mourelatos
Assistant Professor of Philosophy,
University of Texas at Austin
FRIES, JAKOB FRIEDRICH (2005)
PRE-SOCRATIC PHILOSOPHY
  [BIBLIOGRAPHY] (2005)

Charles Muller
Faculty of Humanities, Toyo
Gakuen University
JINUL (2005)

C. W. K. Mundle
Head, Philosophy Department,
University College of North Wales,
University of Wales
TIME, CONSCIOUSNESS OF (1967)

Milton K. Muntiz
Professor of Philosophy, New York
University
COSMOLOGY (1967)

Peter Munz
Associate Professor of Philosophy,
University of Wellington
HOOKER, RICHARD (1967)

Murray G. Murphey
Associate Professor of American
Civilization, University of
Pennsylvania
PEIRCE, CHARLES SANDERS (1967)

Jeffrie G. Murphy
Regents' Professor of Law,
Philosophy, and Religious Studies,
Arizona State University
SHAME (2005)

Mark C. Murphy
Professor of Philosophy,
Georgetown University
AUTHORITY (2005)
MACINTYRE, ALASDAIR (2005)

Mauro Murzi
Società Filosofica Italiana
REICHENBACH, HANS (2005)

Herbert Musurillo, S.J.
Professor of Classics, Fordham
University
GREGORY OF NAZIANZUS (1967)
GREGORY OF NYSSA (1967)

Mechthild Nagel
Associate Professor of Philosophy,
State University of New York,
Cortland
FERGUSON, ANN (2005)

Thomas Nagel
University Professor, Professor of
Philosophy, and Professor of Law,
New York University
ETHICS (2005)
WILLIAMS, BERNARD (2005)

Jan Narveson
University of Waterloo, Canada
ETHICAL EGOISM (1996)

Seyyed Hossein Nasr
Professor of the History of Science
and Philosophy, Tehran University
MULLĀ ṢADRĀ (1967)

Stephen Nathanson
Professor of Philosophy,
Northeastern University
CIVIL DISOBEDIENCE (2005)

Stephen Neale
University of California, Berkeley
ANAPHORA (1996)

Karen Neander
Professor of Philosophy, University
of California, Davis
EVOLUTIONARY THEORY (2005)
TELEOLOGY [ADDENDUM] (2005)

Jacob Needleman
Associate Professor of Philosophy,
San Francisco State College
BINSWANGER, LUDWIG (1967)
EXISTENTIAL PSYCHOANALYSIS
  (1967)

Alex Neill
Senior Lecturer in Philosophy,
University of Southampton
TRAGEDY (2005)

Susan Neiman
Director, Einstein Forum, Potsdam,
Germany
EVIL (2005)

John O. Nelson
Professor of Philosophy, University
of Colorado
INNATE IDEAS (1967)
MOORE, GEORGE EDWARD (1967)

Lynn Hankinson Nelson
Professor of Philosophy, University
of Washington
CODE, LORRAINE (2005)
HARDING, SANDRA (2005)

Thomas Nenon
Professor of Philosophy, University
of Memphis
ABBAGNANO, NICOLA
  [BIBLIOGRAPHY] (2005)
BINSWANGER, LUDWIG
  [BIBLIOGRAPHY] (2005)
BRUNSCHVICG, LÉON
  [BIBLIOGRAPHY] (2005)
CAMUS, ALBERT [BIBLIOGRAPHY]
  (2005)
CASSIRER, ERNST [BIBLIOGRAPHY]
  (2005)
CONSCIOUSNESS IN
  PHENOMENOLOGY (2005)
CONTINENTAL PHILOSOPHY
  (2005)

EXISTENTIAL PSYCHOANALYSIS
[BIBLIOGRAPHY] (2005)
GEISTESWISSENSCHAFTEN (2005)
HARTMANN, NICOLAI
[BIBLIOGRAPHY] (2005)
INGARDEN, ROMAN
[BIBLIOGRAPHY] (2005)
JASPERS, KARL [BIBLIOGRAPHY]
(2005)
KIERKEGAARD, SØREN AABYE
[ADDENDUM] [BIBLIOGRAPHY]
(2005)
LAVELLE, LOUIS [BIBLIOGRAPHY]
(2005)
LUKÁCS, GEORG [BIBLIOGRAPHY]
(2005)
MARCEL, GABRIEL
[BIBLIOGRAPHY] (2005)
MOUNIER, EMMANUEL
[BIBLIOGRAPHY] (2005)
SCHELLING, FRIEDRICH WILHELM
JOSEPH VON [BIBLIOGRAPHY]
(2005)
UNAMUNO Y JUGO, MIGUEL DE
[BIBLIOGRAPHY] (2005)
WEIL, SIMONE [BIBLIOGRAPHY]
(2005)
ZUBIRI, XAVIER [BIBLIOGRAPHY]
(2005)

G. C. Nerlich
*Senior Lecturer in Philosophy,
University of Sydney*
EDDINGTON, ARTHUR STANLEY
(1967)
JEANS, JAMES HOPWOOD (1967)
POPULAR ARGUMENTS FOR THE
EXISTENCE OF GOD (1967)
STEBBING, LIZZIE SUSAN (1967)

Ram Neta
*Assistant Professor of Philosophy,
University of North Carolina,
Chapel Hill*
CONTEXTUALISM (2005)

Richard R. Niebuhr
*Florence Corliss Lamont Professor
of Divinity, Harvard Divinity
School, Harvard University*
SCHLEIERMACHER, FRIEDRICH
DANIEL ERNST (1967)

Kai Nielsen
*Unversity of Calgary (Emeritus);
Concordia University, Montreal
(Canada)*
SOCIALISM [ADDENDUM] (2005)

Robert Niklaus
*Professor of French and Italian and
Deputy Vice-Chancellor, University*

*of Exeter; Member of the Executive
Committees of the Modern
Humanities Research Association
and the Society for French Studies*
BOULAINVILLIERS, HENRI, COMTE
DE (1967)
CLANDESTINE PHILOSOPHICAL
LITERATURE IN FRANCE (1967)

Daniel Nolan
*Professor of Theoretical Philosophy,
Departments of Philosophy,
University of St. Andrews*
LEWIS, DAVID (2005)

Harold Noonan
*Professor, Philosophy, University of
Nottingham*
PERSONAL IDENTITY [ADDENDUM]
(1996, 2005)
WIGGINS, DAVID (2005)

Calvin G. Normore
*Professor of Philosophy, University
of California, Los Angeles*
SCOTISM (2005)

F. S. Northedge
*Reader in International Relations,
London School of Economics and
Political Science, University of
London*
PEACE, WAR, AND PHILOSOPHY
(1967)

Vivian Nutton
*Professor, History of Medicine,
University College London*
GALEN (2005)

Michael Nylan
*Professor, History, University of
California, Berkeley*
YANG XIONG (2005)

Thomas C. O'Brien, O.P.
*Dominican House of Studies,
Washington, DC*
GARRIGOU-LAGRANGE, RÉGINALD
MARIE (1967)

D. J. O'Connor
*Professor of Philosophy, University
of Exeter*
AYER, ALFRED JULES (1967)
SUBSTANCE AND ATTRIBUTE
(1967)

Graham Oddie
*Professor, Philosophy, University of
Colorado at Boulder*

METAPHYSICS (2005)
TRUTHLIKENESS (1996)

Frederick A. Olafson
*Professor of Education and
Philosophy, Harvard Graduate
School of Education, Harvard
University*
CAMUS, ALBERT (1967)
SANTAYANA, GEORGE (1967)

Andrew Oldenquist
*Associate Professor of Philosophy,
Ohio State University*
FISKE, JOHN (1967)
SELF-PREDICTION (1967)

Kelly Oliver
*W. Alton Jones Professor,
Philosophy, Vanderbilt University*
KRISTEVA, JULIA (2005)

Robert G. Olson
*Associate Professor and Chairman
of the Department of Philosophy,
University College, Rutgers
University*
DEATH (1967)
NIHILISM (1967)

Eileen O'Neill
*University of Massachusetts,
Amherst*
GOURNAY, MARIE LE JARS DE
(1996)
WOMEN IN THE HISTORY OF
PHILOSOPHY (1996)

William G. O'Neill
*Associate Professor of Philosophy,
Iona College, New Rochelle, NY*
CONSCIENCE [BIBLIOGRAPHY]
(2005)

Walter J. Ong, S.J.
*Professor of English, St. Louis
University*
RAMUS, PETER (1967)

Jan Opsomer
*Associate Professor, Philosophy,
University of Cologne*
PLUTARCH OF CHAERONEA (2005)

Leslie E. Orgel
*Professor, Salk Institute for
Biological Studies*
LIFE, ORIGIN OF (2005)

E. F. Osborn
*Professor of Biblical Studies,
Queen's College, University of
Melbourne; Editor of the Australian
Biblical Review*
CLEMENT OF ALEXANDRIA (1967)
PSEUDO-DIONYSIUS (1967)

Jennifer Ottman
*Visiting Assistant Professor, History,
Wake Forest University*
RUFUS, RICHARD (2005)

H. P. Owen
*Reader in the Philosophy of
Religion, University of London*
DOGMA (1967)
ESCHATOLOGY (1967)
INFINITY IN THEOLOGY AND
   METAPHYSICS (1967)
PERFECTION (1967)
PROVIDENCE (1967)

G. Michael Pace
*Assistant Professor, Philosophy,
Chapman University*
PERCEPTION, CONTEMPORARY
   VIEWS (2005)

Alan G. Padgett
*Professor of Systematic Theology,
Luther Seminary, St. Paul, MN;
Editor, Journal for Christian
Theological Research*
BARTH, KARL [ADDENDUM]
   (2005)
LUTHER, MARTIN [ADDENDUM]
   (2005)
RELIGION AND THE PHYSICAL
   SCIENCES (2005)

David A. Pailin
*Emeritus, University of Manchester,
School of Middle Eastern Studies &
Theology*
HERBERT OF CHERBURY (2005)

Richard E. Palmer
MacMurray College
GADAMER, HANS-GEORG (1996)

Claude Panaccio
*Canada Research Chair in the
Theory of Knowledge, Philosophy,
University of Quebec at Montreal*
WILLIAM OF OCKHAM
   [BIBLIOGRAPHY] (2005)

David Papineau
*Professor of Philosophy, King's
College London*

CAUSAL CLOSURE OF THE
   PHYSICAL DOMAIN (2005)

John N. Pappas
*Professor of French, Department of
Romance Languages, University of
Pennsylvania*
ALEMBERT, JEAN LE ROND D'
   (1967)

H. O. Pappé
*Member if the Faculty of the School
of Social Sciences, University of
Sussex*
GEHLEN, ARNOLD (1967)
JÜNGER, ERNST (1967)
PHILOSOPHICAL ANTHROPOLOGY
   (1967)
SOMBART, WERNER (1967)

Charles Parsons
*Edgar Pierce Professor of
Philosophy, Emeritus, Harvard
University*
BROUWER, LUITZEN EGBERTUS JAN
   (1967)
MATHEMATICS, FOUNDATIONS OF
   (1967, 2005)

P. H. Partridge
*Director of the Research School of
Social Sciences and Professor of
Social Philosophy, Australian
National University*
FREEDOM (1967)
MOSCA, GAETANO (1967)

John Passmore
*Professor of Philosophy, Institute of
Advanced Studies, Australian
National University*
ANDERSON, JOHN (1967)
BOYLE, ROBERT (1967)
COLLIER, ARTHUR (1967)
CULVERWEL, NATHANAEL (1967)
CUMBERLAND, RICHARD (1967)
FLUDD, ROBERT (1967)
HARVEY, WILLIAM (1967)
LOGICAL POSITIVISM (1967)
MORE, HENRY (1967)
NORRIS, JOHN (1967)
PRIESTLEY, JOSEPH (1967)
SMITH, JOHN (1967)
WHICHCOTE, BENJAMIN (1967)

Stanley L. Paulson
*William Gardiner Hammond
Professor of Law, and Professor of
Philosophy, Washington University
School of Law, St. Louis, MO*
KELSEN, HANS (2005)

Vuko Pavićević
*Professor of Ethics and Sociology,
University of Belgrade*
PETROVIĆ-NJEGOŠ, PETAR (1967)

Francis Jeffry Pelletier
*Canada Research Chair in
Cognitive Science, Professor of
Philosophy, Professor of Linguistics,
Simon Fraser University*
GENERICS (2005)

Terence Penelhum
*Professor Emeritus of Religious
Studies, University of Calgary*
BUTLER, JOSEPH (2005)
PERSONAL IDENTITY (1967)

Adriaan Peperzak
Loyola University of Chicago
LEVINAS, EMMANUEL (1996)

Derk Pereboom
*Professor, Philosophy, University of
Vermont*
NONREDUCTIVE PHYSICALISM
   (2005)

Alan Perreiah
University of Kentucky
PAUL OF VENICE (2005)

Roy W. Perrett
*Professor of Philosophy, University
of Hawaii at Manoa*
ATOMIC THEORY IN INDIAN
   PHILOSOPHY (2005)

John Perry
Stanford University
INDEXICALS (1996)
SELF (1996)

R. S. Peters
*Professor of the Philosophy of
Education, University of London
Institute of Education*
HOBBES, THOMAS (1967)
PSYCHOLOGY (1967)

Gajo Petrović
*Associate Professor of Philosophy,
University of Zagreb; President of
the Yugoslav Philosophical
Association*
ALIENATION (1967)
PLEKHANOV, GEORGII
   VALENTINOVICH (1967)

Philip Pettit
*L. S. Rockefeller University
Professor of Politics and Human
Values, Princeton University*
PHILOSOPHY OF SOCIAL SCIENCES
(1996)
RESPONSE-DEPENDENCE THEORIES
(2005)

Stephen H. Phillips
*Professor, Philosophy, University of
Texas at Austin*
TRUTH AND FALSITY IN INDIAN
PHILOSOPHY (2005)

Charles R. Pidgen
University of Otago, New Zealand
HARE, RICHARD M. (1996)

Paul M. Pietroski
*Professor of Philosophy, Professor of
Linguistics, University of
Maryland, College Park*
EVENTS IN SEMANTIC THEORY
(2005)
LOGICAL FORM (2005)

Kirk Pillow
*Associate Dean of the Faculty,
Associate Professor of Philosophy,
Hamilton College, Clinton, NY*
SUBLIME, THE (2005)

Shlomo Pines
*Professor of General and Jewish
Philosophy, Hebrew University of
Jerusalem*
JEWISH PHILOSOPHY (1967)
MAIMONIDES (1967)

Gino K. Piovesana, S.J.
*Director of the Board of Regents
and Professor of Philosophy, Sophia
University, Japan*
ANDŌ SHŌEKI (1967)
HATANO SEIICHI (1967)
HAYASHI RAZAN (1967)
ITŌ JINSAI (1967)
KAIBARA EKKEN (1967)
KUMAZAWA BANZAN (1967)
MIKI KIYOSHI (1967)
MINAGAWA KIEN (1967)
MIURA BAIEN (1967)
MURO KYŪSŌ (1967)
NAKAE TŌJU (1967)
NISHI AMANE (1967)
OGYŪ SORAI (1967)
WATSUJI TETSURŌ (1967)
YAMAGA SOKŌ (1967)
YAMAZAKI ANSAI (1967)

Robert B. Pippin
University of Chicago
HEGEL, GEORG WILHELM
FRIEDRICH [ADDENDUM]
(1996)

Fabienne Pironet
*Professeure agrégée, Université de
Montréal, Faculté des arts et des
science, Département de
philosophie*
SIGER OF BRABANT (2005)

Alvin Plantinga
*Professor of Philosophy, Calvin
College*
MALCOLM, NORMAN (1967)

Thomas Pogge
*Professorial Research, Fellow,
Centre for Applied Philosophy and
Public Ethics, Australian National
University*
JUSTICE [BIBLIOGRAPHY] (2005)

Richard H. Popkin
*Professor of Philosophy, University
of California, Los Angeles*
AGRIPPA VON NETTESHEIM,
HENRICUS CORNELIUS (1967)
BAYLE, PIERRE (1967, 2005)
CHARRON, PIERRE (1967, 2005)
COSTA, URIEL DA (1967)
ERASMUS, DESIDERIUS (1967,
2005)
FIDEISM (1967)
GASSENDI, PIERRE (1967, 2005)
GLANVILL, JOSEPH (1967, 2005)
HUET, PIERRE-DANIEL (1967,
2005)
LA MOTHE LE VAYER, FRANÇOIS DE
(1967, 2005)
LA PEYRÈRE, ISAAC (1967, 2005)
MENASSEH (MANASSEH) BEN
ISRAEL (1967)
MERSENNE, MARIN (1967, 2005)
MONTAIGNE, MICHEL EYQUEM DE
(1967, 2005)
OROBIO DE CASTRO, ISAAC (1967,
2005)
PASCAL, BLAISE (1967, 2005)
PICO DELLA MIRANDOLA,
GIANFRANCESCO (2005)
SANCHES, FRANCISCO (1967,
2005)
SIMON, RICHARD (1967, 2005)
SKEPTICISM, HISTORY OF (1967,
2005)

Peter E. Pormann
*Frances A. Yates Long-Term
Research Fellow, Warburg Institute,*

*School of Advanced Studies,
University of London*
GALEN [ADDENDUM] (2005)

Amanda Porter
*PhD candidate, Philosophy,
University of Western Ontario*
CARD, CLAUDIA (2005)
HELD, VIRGINIA (2005)

Karl H. Potter
*Professor Emeritus, University of
Washington, Seattle*
INDIAN PHILOSOPHY (2005)

C. F. Presley
*Head of the Department of
Philosophy, University of the
Queensland (Australia)*
QUINE, WILLARD VAN ORMAN
(1967)

Kingsley Price
*Professor of Philosophy, Johns
Hopkins University*
PHILOSOPHY OF EDUCATION,
HISTORY OF (1967)

Graham Priest
*Boyce Gibson Professor of
Philosophy, University of
Melbourne; Arche Professorial
Fellow, Department of Logic and
Metaphysics, University of St.
Andrews*
LOGIC, HISTORY OF: MODERN
LOGIC: SINCE GÖDEL: THE
PROLIFERATION OF
NONCLASSICAL (2005)
LOGIC, NON-CLASSICAL (2005)
MANY-VALUED LOGICS (2005)
MOTION (2005)
PARACONSISTENT LOGICS (2005)
RELEVANCE (RELEVANT) LOGICS
(2005)

Jesse Prinz
*Associate Professor, Philosophy,
University of North Carolina at
Chapel Hill*
CONCEPTS (2005)

A. N. Prior
*Professor of Philosophy, University
of Manchester; Coeditor of the
Journal of Symbolic Logic; Fellow of
the British Academy*
CORRESPONCENCE THEORY OF
TRUTH (1967)
EXISTENCE (1967)

LOGIC, HISTORY OF: MODERN
LOGIC: THE BOOLEAN PERIOD
[OVERVIEW]; JOHNSON; KEYNES;
PEIRCE; THE HERITAGE OF KANT
AND MILL (1967)
LOGIC, HISTORY OF: PRECURSORS
OF MODERN LOGIC [OVERVIEW]
(1967)
LOGIC, TRADITIONAL (1967)
NEGATION (1967)
RUSSELL, BERTRAND ARTHUR
WILLIAM (1967)

Mary Prior
*Co-author (with A. N. Prior),
"Erotetic Logic," Philosophical
Review (Vol. 64)*
WHATELY, RICHARD (1967)

Duncan Pritchard
*Reader in Philosophy, University of
Stirling*
RELEVANT ALTERNATIVES (2005)

Benjamin S. Pryor
*Assistant Professor, Philosophy; Co-
Director of the Program in Law and
Social Thought, University of
Toledo;*
FOUCAULT, MICHEL (2005)

Stathis Psillos
*Associate Professor, Philosophy and
History of Science, University of
Athens*
PHILOSOPHY OF SCIENCE, HISTORY
OF (2005)
SCIENTIFIC REALISM (2005)
UNDERDETERMINATION THESIS,
DUHEM-QUINE THESIS (2005)

Joseph Pucci
*Associate Professor of Classics and
in the Program in Medieval
Studies; Associate Professor of
Comparative Literature, Brown
University*
CAROLINGIAN RENAISSANCE
[BIBLIOGRAPHY] (2005)

Richard Purtill
Western Washington University
DIVINE COMMAND THEORIES OF
ETHICS (2005)
LEWIS, C. S. (CLIVE STAPLES)
(2005)
PHILOSOPHY OF RELIGION,
HISTORY OF [ADDENDUM]
(2005)
RELIGION AND MORALITY (2005)
THEISM, ARGUMENTS FOR AND
AGAINST (1996)

Anthony Quinton
*University Lecturer in Philosophy
and Fellow of New College, Oxford
University*
KNOWLEDGE AND BELIEF (1967)
POPPER, KARL RAIMUND (1967)

Michael R. Rackett
Cary, NC
PELAGIUS AND PELAGIANISM
(2005)

Diana Raffman
*Professor, Philosophy, University of
Toronto*
MARCUS, RUTH BARCAN (1996)

Fazl-Ur- Rahman
*Director of the Central Institute of
Islamic Research (Karachi)*
ISLAMIC PHILOSOPHY (1967)

Bjørn T. Ramberg
Universitetet i Oslo
DAVIDSON, DONALD (1996, 2005)

Albert G. Ramsperger
*Professor of Philosophy, University
of Wisconsin*
CRITICAL REALISM (1967)

David M. Rasmussen
*Professor, Philosophy, Boston
College; Editor in Chief, Philosophy
and Social Criticism*
HABERMAS, JÜRGEN (2005)

Michael Rea
*Associate Professor, Philosophy,
University of Notre Dame*
PLANTINGA, ALVIN (2005)

Miklós Rédei
Eötvös Loránd Tudományegyetem
COMMON CAUSE PRINCIPLE
(2005)

Joan Wynn Reeves
*Reader in Psychology, Bedford
College, University of London*
BINET, ALFRED (1967)

Marjorie E. Reeves
*Vice-Principal and Fellow of St.
Anne's College and University
Lecturer, Oxford University*
JOACHIM OF FIORE (1967)

Thomas Regan
*Emeritus Professor of Philosophy,
North Carolina State University*

ANIMAL RIGHTS AND WELFARE
(1996, 2005)

David A. Reidy
*Assistant Professor, Philosophy,
University of Tennessee, Knoxville*
PHILOSOPHY OF LAW, PROBLEMS
OF [ADDENDUM] (2005)

Nicholas Rescher
*Professor of Philosophy and
Associate Director of the Center for
Philosophy of Science, University of
Pittsburgh*
LOGIC, HISTORY OF: LOGIC IN THE
ISLAMIC WORLD (1967)

David Resnik
*Bioethicist, National Institute of
Environmental Health Sciences,
National Institutes of Health*
SCIENCE, RESEARCH ETHICS OF
(2005)

Georges Rey
*Professor, Philosophy, University of
Maryland, College Park*
BEHAVIORISM (2005)
FODOR, JERRY A. (2005)

Gretchen A. Reydams-Schils
*Associate Professor, Program of
Liberal Studies and Department of
Philosophy, University of Notre
Dame*
MUSONIUS RUFUS (2005)

Nicholas V. Riasanovsky
*Professor of History, University of
California, Berkeley*
FOURIER, FRANÇOIS MARIE
CHARLES (1967)

Mark Richard
*Professor and Chair, Philosophy,
Tufts University*
BELIEF ATTRIBUTIONS (1996)
NON-TRUTH-CONDITIONAL
MEANING (2005)
PROPOSITIONS (1996)

Henry Richardson
*Professor, Philosophy, Georgetown
University*
DEONTOLOGICAL ETHICS (2005)

Aaron Ridley
*Professor of Philosophy, University
of Southampton*
WILDE, OSCAR FINGAL
O'FLAHERTIE WILLS (2005)

Miles Rind
Independent scholar
ADDISON, JOSEPH (2005)
LONGINUS (PSEUDO)

Fritz-Joachim von Rintelen
Professor of Philosophy, University of Mainz
GEYSER, JOSEPH (1967)

Carolyn Ristau
Adjunct Associate Professor, Psychology, Barnard College
ANIMAL MIND (2005)

David B. Robinson
Lecturer in Greek, University of Edinburgh
XENOPHON (1967)

Jenefer Robinson
Professor of Philosophy, University of Cincinnati
AESTHETICS, PROBLEMS OF (2005)

Thomas Robischon
Associate Professor and Chair, Philosophy, Tuskegee Institute
HOLT, EDWIN BISSELL (1967)
MCGILVARY, EVANDER BRADLEY (1967)
MONTAGUE, WILLIAM PEPPERELL (1967)
NEW REALISM (1967)
PERRY, RALPH BARTON (1967)

Heiner Roetz
Professor for Chinese History and Philosophy, Faculty of East Asian Studies, Ruhr-University, Bochum, Germany
CONFUCIUS (2005)

Yosal Rogat
Associate Professor, Political Science, University of Chicago
LEGAL REALISM (1967)

Robin Rollinger
Research Editor, Katholieke Universiteit Leuven
LIPPS, THEODOR (2005)
PFÄNDER, ALEXANDER (2005)

Mark Rollins
Associate Professor and Chair, Philosophy, Washington University in St. Louis
IMAGERY, MENTAL (2005)

Patrick Romanell
H. Y. Benedict Professor of Philosophy, University of Texas, El Paso
ABBAGNANO, NICOLA (1967)

Grace G. Roosevelt
New York University
ROUSSEAU, JEAN-JACQUES [ADDENDUM] (1996)

Richard M. Rorty
Associate Professor of Philosophy, Princeton University
INTUITION (1967)
RELATIONS, INTERNAL AND EXTERNAL (1967)

Connie Rosati
Associate Professor, Philosophy, University of Arizona
BRANDT, R. B. (2005)

Philipp W. Rosemann
Associate Professor of Philosophy, University of Dallas
PETER LOMBARD [ADDENDUM] (2005)

Gideon Rosen
Professor of Philosophy, Princeton University
NOMINALISM, MODERN (2005)
REALISM [ADDENDUM] (1996)

Roger D. Rosenkrantz
Independent scholar
FISHER, R. A. (2005)
INFORMATION THEORY (2005)
STATISTICS, FOUNDATIONS OF (2005)

David M. Rosenthal
Professor of Philosophy and Coordinator of Cognitive Science, Graduate Center, The City University of New York
CONSCIOUSNESS (2005)

Adina Roskies
Assistant Professor, Philosophy, Dartmouth College
KITCHER, PATRICIA (2005)

James F. Ross
Professor of Philosophy and Law, Philosophy Department, University of Pennsylvania
ANALOGY IN THEOLOGY (2005)

Stephanie Ross
Professor, Philosophy, University of Missouri, St. Louis
ENVIRONMENTAL AESTHETICS (2005)

Ferruccio Rossi-Landi
Research Member of the Staff of the State University of Milan
CALDERONI, MARIO (1967)
CATTANEO, CARLO (1967)
DINGLER, HUGO (1967)
PEANO, GIUSEPPE (1967)
VAILATI, GIOVANNI (1967)

Christopher J. Rowe
Professor of Greek, Durham University
KALON (2005)

William L. Rowe
Professor of Philosophy, Purdue University
EVIL, THE PROBLEM OF [ADDENDUM] (1996, 2005)

Anthony Rudd
Visiting Assistant Professor of Philosophy, St. Olaf College
CALVIN, JOHN [ADDENDUM] (2005)

Richard S. Rudner
Professor and Chairman of the Department of Philosophy, Washington University (St. Louis); Editor in Chief of Philosophy of Science
GOODMAN, NELSON (1967)

Laura Ruetsche
Associate Professor, Philosophy, University of Pittsburgh
EARMAN, JOHN (2005)
STRING THEORY (2005)

T. S. Rukmani
Professor and Chair in Hindu Studies, Concordia University, Montreal, Canada
GOD IN INDIAN PHILOSOPHY (2005)

Bede Rundle
Fellow and Lecturer in Philosophy, Trinity College, Oxford University
LOGIC, HISTORY OF: MODERN LOGIC: FROM FREGE TO GÖDEL: BROUWER AND INTUITIONISM; FREGE; GÖDEL; HERBRAND (1967); HILBERT AND

FORMALISM (2005);
LÖWENHEIM; PEANO; POST;
RAMSEY; SKOLEM (1967);
WHITEHEAD AND RUSSELL
(2005)
LOGIC, HISTORY OF: MODERN
LOGIC: SINCE GÖDEL: CHURCH;
GENTZEN (1967)

Joseph Runzo
*Professor, Philosophy and Religious
Studies, Chapman University; Life
Member, Clare Hall, University of
Cambridge*
LIFE, MEANING AND VALUE OF
[ADDENDUM] (2005)

Michael Ruse
*Lucyle T. Werkmeister Professor of
Philosophy; Director of the
Program in the History and
Philosophy of Science, Department
of Philosophy, Florida State
University*
EVOLUTIONARY ETHICS (1996,
2005)
HUMAN GENOME PROJECT (2005)
RELIGION AND THE BIOLOGICAL
SCIENCES (2005)
WILSON, EDWARD O. (2005)

Bruce Russell
*Professor and Chair of Philosophy,
Wayne State University*
INTUITION [ADDENDUM 2]
(2005)

Cheyney Ryan
*Professor, Philosophy Department,
University of Oregon*
BERLIN, ISAIAH (2005)

Todd Ryan
*Assistant Professor, Trinity College,
Hartford, CT*
LE CLERC, JEAN [ADDENDUM]
(2005)

Martin Ryder
*Adjunct Professor, Information and
Learning Technologies, University
of Colorado, Denver*
SOCIAL CONSTRUCTIONISM
(2005)

Daniel Rynhold
*Lecturer in Judaism, Department of
Theology and Religious Studies,
King's College, London*
ALBO, JOSEPH [ADDENDUM]
(2005)

David Rynin
*Professor of Philosophy, University
of California, Berkeley*
JOHNSON, ALEXANDER BRYAN
(1967)

Hassan Saab
*Professor, Lebanese Unviersity and
St. Joseph University of Beirut*
IBN KHALDŪN (1967)

Marcelo Sabatés
*Associate Professor and Head,
Philosophy Department, Kansas
State University, Manhattan*
KIM, JAEGWON (2005)
REDUCTIONISM IN THE
PHILOSOPHY OF MIND (2005)

Nathan Salmon
*Professor, Philosophy, University of
California, Santa Barbara*
PROPER NAMES AND
DESCRIPTIONS (2005)

Norbert Samuelson
*Grossman Chair in Jewish Studies,
Philosophy Department, Arizona
State University*
ROSENZWEIG, FRANZ
[ADDENDUM] (2005)

David Sanford
*Instructor in Philosophy,
Dartmouth College*
DEGREES OF PERFECTION,
ARGUMENT FOR THE EXISTENCE
OF GOD [BIBLIOGRAPHY]
(1967)

Jonathan J. Sanford
*Department of Philosophy,
Franciscan University of
Steubenville*
PETER DAMIAN (2005)

Antonio Santucci
*University Professor of the History
of Modern and Contemporary
Philosophy; Extraordinary Professor
of the History of Philosophy,
Faculty of Education, University of
Bologna*
PAPINI, GIOVANNI (1967)

Virginia Sapiro
University of Wisconsin, Madison
WOLLSTONECRAFT, MARY (1996)

Jennifer M. Saul
*Professor of Philosophy, University
of Sheffield*
CONVERSATIONAL IMPLICATURE
(2005)

Jason L. Saunders
*Professor of Philosophy, University
of California, San Diego*
LIPSIUS, JUSTUS (1967)
PATRIZI, FRANCESCO (1967)

James P. Scanlan
*Emeritus, Philosophy, Ohio State
University*
BELINSKII, VISSARION
GRIGOR'EVICH (1967)
BULGAKOV, SERGEI NIKOLAEVICH
(1967)
CHERNYSHEVSKII, NIKOLAI
GAVRILOVICH (1967)
DOSTOEVSKY, FYODOR
MIKHAILOVICH (2005)
KOZLOV, ALEKSEI
ALEKSANDROVICH (1967)
LAPSHIN, IVAN IVANOVICH (1967)
LAVROV, PËTR LAVROVICH (1967)
LENIN, VLADIMIR IL'ICH (1967,
2005)
LOPATIN, LEV MIKHAILOVICH
(1967)
MIKHAILOVSKII, NIKOLAI
KONSTANTINOVICH (1967)
RADISHCHEV, ALEKSANDR
NIKOLAEVICH (1967)
ROZANOV, VASILII VASIL'EVICH
(1967)
TOLSTOY, LEV (LEO) NIKOLAEVICH
(2005)
VYSHESLAVTSEV, BORIS PETROVICH
(1967)

Eva Schaper
*Lecturer in Logic and Aesthetic
Philosophy, University of Glasgow*
KAUFMANN, WALTER ARNOLD
(2005)
PATER, WALTER HORATIO (1967)
TROELTSCH, ERNST (1967)

Kevin Schilbrack
*Associate Professor of Religious
Studies, Wesleyan College, Macon,
GA*
MYTH [ADDENDUM] (2005)

G. Schlesinger
*Professor of Philosophy, University
of North Carolina*
BRIDGMAN, PERCY WILLIAM
(1967)
OPERATIONALISM (1967)

Antonia Ruth Schlette
University of Munich
CHAMBERLAIN, HOUSTON
STEWART (1967)

Tad M. Schmaltz
*Professor of Philosophy, Duke
University*
ARNAULD, ANTOINE (2005)
CARTESIANISM [ADDENDUM]
(2005)
CONDILLAC, ÉTIENNE BONNOT DE
(2005)
DESGABETS, ROBERT (2005)
JANSENISM (2005)
MALEBRANCHE, NICOLAS (2005)
NICOLE, PIERRE (2005)
REGIUS, HENRICUS (HENRY DE
ROY)

Dennis Schmidt
*Professor of Philosophy,
Comparative Literature, and
German, Pennsylvania State
University*
GADAMER, HANS-GEORG (2005)
HERMENEUTICS (2005)

James Schmidt
*Professor of History and Political
Science, Boston University*
ENLIGHTENMENT (2005)

David Schmidtz
*Professor of Philosophy, Joint
Professor of Economics; Director,
Program in Philosophy of Freedom,
University of Arizona*
ETHICAL EGOISM
[BIBLIOGRAPHY](2005)
NOZICK, ROBERT (2005)
PHILOSOPHY OF ECONOMICS
(2005)

Frederick F. Schmitt
*Professor of Philosophy, Indiana
University*
NATURALIZED EPISTEMOLOGY
(2005)

Richard Schmitt
*Associate Professor of Philosophy,
Brown University*
PHENOMENOLOGY (1967)

J. B. Schneewind
*Associate Professor of Philosophy,
University of Pittsburgh*
ELIOT, GEORGE (1967)
GROTE, JOHN (1967)
MARTINEAU, JAMES (1967)

MCTAGGART, JOHN MCTAGGART
ELLIS (1967)
MILL, JOHN STUART (1967)
SIDGWICK, HENRY (1967)
STEPHEN, LESLIE (1967)

Malcolm Schofield
*Professor of Ancient Philosophy,
Faculty of Classics, University of
Cambridge*
ZENO OF CITIUM (2005)

Philip Schofield
*Professor of the History of Legal
and Political Thought, Faculty of
Law, University College London*
BENTHAM, JEREMY (2005)

Martin Schönfeld
*Associate Professor, Philosophy,
Core Faculty, Environmental
Science and Policy, University of
South Florida*
WOLFF, CHRISTIAN (2005)

Alan D. Schrift
*Professor of Philosophy; Director,
Center for the Humanities, Grinnell
College*
DECONSTRUCTION (2005)
NIETZSCHE, FRIEDRICH (2005)
STRUCTURALISM AND POST-
STRUCTURALISM (1996, 2005)

Mark Schroeder
*Assistant Professor of Philosophy,
University of Maryland, College
Park*
ETHICAL NATURALISM
[ADDENDUM] (2005)

Oliver Schulte
*Associate Professor, Philosophy,
Simon Fraser University*
SCIENTIFIC METHOD (2005)

R. Barton Schultz
*Fellow and Lecturer, Division of the
Humanities, University of Chicago*
NUSSBAUM, MARTHA (2005)
SIDGWICK, HENRY [ADDENDUM]
(1996, 2005)

George Schumm
*Associate Professor, Philosophy,
Ohio State University*
MARCUS, RUTH BARCAN (1996)

Joachim Schummer
*Editor, HYLE: International
Journal for Philosophy of*

*Chemistry; Heisenberg-Fellow,
Philosophy, University of
Darmstadt; Adjunct Professor,
Philosophy, University of South
Carolina*
CHEMISTRY, PHILOSOPHY OF
(2005)

Charles E. Scott
*Distinguished Professor of
Philosophy and Director of the
Vanderbilt Center for Ethics,
Vanderbilt University*
HEIDEGGER, MARTIN (2005)

Dion Scott-Kakures
*Professor of Philosophy, Scripps
College*
FOLK PSYCHOLOGY (1996, 2005)
SELF-DECEPTION (2005)

William Seager
*Professor of Philosophy, University
of Toronto at Scarborough*
DRETSKE, FRED (2005)

John Searle
*Slusser Professor of Philosophy,
University of California, Berkeley*
DETERMINABLES AND
DETERMINATES (1967)
STRAWSON, PETER FREDERICK
(1967)

Krister Segerberg
*Visiting Professor of Philosophy,
Stanford University*
MODAL LOGIC (2005)
WRIGHT, GEORG HENRIK VON
(1996, 2005)

Svetlana Semënova
*Professor, Institute of World
Literature, Moscow*
FËDOROV, NIKOLAI FËDOROVICH
(2005)

Mikhail Yu. Sergeev
*Adjunct Associate Professor,
Religion, University of the Arts,
Philadelphia*
LOSSKII, NIKOLAI ONUFRIEVICH
(2005)
ZEN'KOVSKII, VASILII VASIL'EVICH
(2005)

Bogdan Šešić
*Ordinary Professor of Logic,
University of Belgrade*
PETRONIEVIĆ, BRANISLAV (1967)

Russ Shafer-Landau
Professor of Philosophy, University of Wisconsin, Madison
RATIONALISM IN ETHICS [ADDENDUM] (2005)

Scott A. Shalkowski
Lecturer, Philosophy, University of Leeds
MODALITY, PHILOSOPHY AND METAPHYSICS OF (2005)

Brian Shanley
Catholic University of America
THOMISM [ADDENDUM] (2005)

Lisa Shapiro
Associate Professor of Philosophy, Simon Fraser University
ELISABETH, PRINCESS OF BOHEMIA (2005)

Stewart Shapiro
O'Donnell Professor of Philosophy, The Ohio State University; Arché Professorial Fellow, University of St. Andrews
REALISM AND NATURALISM, MATHEMATICAL (2005)

Arvind Sharma
Birks Professor of Comparative Religion, McGill University
SELF IN INDIAN PHILOSOPHY (2005)

Vincent Shen
Lee Chair in Chinese Thought and Culture, Department of Philosophy and Department of East Asian Studies, University of Toronto
CHINESE PHILOSOPHY: METAPHYSICS AND EPISTEMOLOGY (2005)
YANG ZHU (2005)

Anne D. R. Sheppard
Senior Lecturer, Classics, Royal Holloway, University of London
ANCIENT AESTHETICS (2005)
PHANTASIA (2005)

Gila Sher
University of California, San Diego
LOGICAL TERMS (1996)

Nancy Sherman
University Professor in Philosophy, Adjunct Professor in Law, Georgetown University
FRIENDSHIP (2005)

Michael Shermer
Founding Publisher of Skeptic magazine; Director of the Skeptics Society; Columnist for Scientific American; Host of the Skeptics Distinguished Science Lecture Series, California Institute of Technology
SCIENCE AND PSEUDOSCIENCE (2005)

Sanford Shieh
Wesleyan University
LOGICAL KNOWLEDGE (1996)

Vincent Y. C. Shih
Professor of Chinese Philosophy and Literature, University of Washington
HU SHI (1967)

J. M Shorter
Professor of Philosophy, University of Canterbury (New Zealand)
OTHER MINDS (1967)

Kwong-loi Shun
Professor, Philosophy and East Asian Studies, University of Toronto
CHINESE PHILOSOPHY: CONFUCIANISM (2005)
MENCIUS (2005)

Alan Sidelle
University of Wisconsin, Madison
CONSTRUCTIVISM AND CONVENTIONALISM (1996)

David Sider
Professor of Classics, New York University
SIMPLICIUS (2005)

Mark Siderits
Professor, Philosophy, Illinois State University, Normal
BUDDHISM—SCHOOLS: MADHYAMAKA (2005)

Wilfried Sieg
Professor, Philosophy, Carnegie Mellon University
COMPUTING MACHINES (2005)

Harvey Siegel
Professor, Philosophy, University of Miami
PHILOSOPHY OF EDUCATION, HISTORY OF: CONTEMPORARY ISSUES: EPISTEMOLOGICAL (2005)

Hugh J. Silverman
State University of New York at Stony Brook
MODERNISM AND POSTMODERNISM (1996)

Anita Silvers
Professor, Philosophy, San Francisco State University
DANTO, ARTHUR (2005)

Keith Simmons
Professor of Philosophy, University of North Carolina at Chapel Hill
TRUTH (2005)

Lawrence H. Simon
Associate Professor, Philosophy and Environmental Studies, Bowdoin College
MARX, KARL (2005)

W. M. Simon
Professor of History, University of Keele
FOUILLÉE, ALFRED (1967)
LAAS, ERNST (1967)
LITTRÉ, ÉMILE (1967)
RENAN, JOSEPH ERNEST (1967)

Peter Simons
Professor of Philosophy, School of Philosophy, University of Leeds
LEŚNIEWSKI, STANISŁAW (2005)
MEREOLOGY (1996)

Marcus G. Singer
Professor and Chair, Department of Philosophy, University of Wisconsin; Chair of the Department of Philosophy of the University of Wisconsin Center System
GOLDEN RULE (1967)

Georgette Sinkler
University of Illinois at Chicago
HEYTESBURY, WILLIAM (2005)

Walter Sinnott-Armstrong
Professor of Philosophy, Hardy Professor of Legal Studies, Dartmouth College
MORAL DILEMMAS (2005)

John Sisko
Assistant Professor, Philosophy, The College of New Jersey

NOUS (2005)

Lawrence Sklar
Carl G. Hempel and William K. Frankena Distinguished University Professor of Philosophy, University of Michigan, Ann Arbor
BOLTZMANN, LUDWIG (2005)
GIBBS, JOSIAH (2005)
PHILOSOPHY OF STATISTICAL MECHANICS (2005)
PHYSICS AND THE DIRECTION OF TIME (1996, 2005)

Henryk Skolimowski
Associate Professor of Philosophy, University of Southern California
INGARDEN, ROMAN (1967)

J. J. C. Smart
Emeritus Professor, Australian National University
SPACE (1967)
TIME (1967, 2005)
UTILITARIANISM (1967)

Ninian Smart
H. G. Wood Professor of Theology, University of Birmingham
BARTH, KARL (1967)
BOEHME, JAKOB (1967)
ECKHART, MEISTER (1967)
HÜGEL, BARON FRIEDRICH VON (1967)
JOHN OF THE CROSS, ST. (1967)
KARMA (1967)
MYSTICISM, HISTORY OF (1967)
REINCARNATION (1967)
RUYSBROECK, JAN VAN (1967)
SUSO, HEINRICH (1967)
TAULER, JOHANNES (1967)
TERESA OF ÁVILA, ST. (1967)
THOMAS À KEMPIS (1967)
ZABARELLA, JACOPO (1967)
ZOROASTRIANISM (1967)

Andrew Smith
Professor of Classics, University College Dublin
PORPHYRY [BIBLIOGRAPHY] (2005)

Barry C. Smith
University of of London, England
LANGUAGE (1996)

Brent Smith
Claremont Graduate University
ASCETICISM [BIBLIOGRAPHY] (2005)

Colin Smith
Reader in French, University of London
BACHELARD, GASTON (1967)
HAMELIN, OCTAVE (1967)
JANKÉLÉVITCH, VLADIMIR (1967)
LALANDE, ANDRÉ (1967)
LE ROY, ÉDOUARD (1967)
LE SENNE, RENÉ (1967)
LOISY, ALFRED (1967)
MODERNISM (1967)
MOUNIER, EMMANUEL (1967)

Daniel W. Smith
Associate Professor, Philosophy, Purdue University
DELEUZE, GILLES (2005)

James Ward Smith
Professor of Philosophy, Princeton University
STACE, WALTER TERENCE (1967)

John E. Smith
Professor of Philosophy, Yale University; General Editor of the Yale Edition of Works of Jonathan Edwards
ROYCE, JOSIAH (1967)

Murray Smith
Professor of Film Studies, University of Kent
PHILOSOPHY OF FILM (2005)

Nicholas D. Smith
James F. Miller Professor of Humanities, Lewis and Clark College
LEHRER, KEITH (2005)

Quentin Smith
Western Michigan University
TIME, BEING, AND BECOMING (1996, 2005)

Howard E. Smokler
Visiting Associate Professor of Philosophy, Stanford University
CLIFFORD, WILLIAM KINGDON (1967)

Paul F. Snowdon
Grote Professor of Mind and Logic, University College London
RYLE, GILBERT [ADDENDUM] (2005)

Scott Soames
Professor, School of Philosophy, University of Southern California
ANALYSIS, PHILOSOPHICAL (2005)
ENTAILMENT, PRESUPPOSITION, AND IMPLICATURE (2005)
PROPOSITIONAL ATTITUDES: ISSUES IN SEMANTICS (2005)

Alan Soble
Professor of Philosophy and University Research Professor, University of New Orleans
PHILOSOPHY OF SEX (2005)

Miriam Solomon
Professor of Philosophy; Director of Graduate Studies, Temple University
LOGIC, HISTORY OF: MODERN LOGIC: SINCE GÖDEL: FRIEDMAN AND REVERSE (2005)
REVERSE MATHEMATICS (2005)
SOCIAL EPISTEMOLOGY (1996, 2005)

Mary Sommers
Director, Center for Thomistic Studies, University of St. Thomas, Houston, TX
BURLEY, WALTER (2005)

Roy Sorensen
Professor, Philosophy, Dartmouth College
KNOWLEDGE AND VAGUENESS (2005)
VAGUENESS (1996, 2005)

David Sosa
Associate Professor of Philosophy, University of Texas at Austin
HARMAN, GILBERT (2005)

Elmer Sprague
Associate Professor of Philosophy, City University of New York, Brooklyn College
BALGUY, JOHN (1967)
GAY, JOHN (1967)
HARTLEY, DAVID (1967)
HOME, HENRY (1967)
HUTCHESON, FRANCIS (1967)
MANDEVILLE, BERNARD (1967)
MORAL SENSE (1967)
PALEY, WILLIAM (1967)
PRICE, RICHARD (1967)
SMITH, ADAM (1967)

Joke Spruyt
Senior University Lecturer, Faculty of Arts and Culture, Maastricht University
PETER OF SPAIN (2005)

Ilja Srubar
Full Professor, Sociology, University of Erlangen
SCHUTZ, ALFRED (2005)

J. F. Staal
Professor of General and Comparative Philosophy and Director of the Instituut voor Filosofie, University of Amsterdam
LOGIC, HISTORY OF [OVERVIEW] (1967)

Werner Stark
Professor of Sociology, Fordham University
MANNHEIM, KARL (1967)
SOCIOLOGY OF KNOWLEDGE (1967)

Robert Stecker
Professor of Philosophy, Central Michigan University
ART, ONTOLOGY OF (2005)
LITERATURE, PHILOSOPHY OF (2005)

Carlos Steel
Professor, Philosophy, Catholic University of Leuven
DAMASCIUS (2005)
ERIGENA, JOHN SCOTUS (2005)
NEOPLATONISM (2005)
PROCLUS (2005)

Warren E. Steinkraus
Professor of Philosophy, State University of New York at Oswego
CREIGHTON, JAMES EDWIN (1967)

James P. Sterba
Professor of Philosophy, University of Notre Dame
DISTANT PEOPLES AND FUTURE GENERATIONS (1996)
GEWIRTH, ALAN (2005)
JUST WAR THEORY (2005)
LIBERTARIANISM (2005)
SOCIAL AND POLITICAL PHILOSOPHY (1996, 2005)
SOCIAL CONTRACT [ADDENDUM] (2005)
TERRORISM (2005)

J. P. Stern
Fellow and Tutor of St. John's College and University Lecturer in German, Cambridge University
BENN, GOTTFRIED (1967)
KAFKA, FRANZ (1967)
RILKE, RAINER MARIA (RENÉ) (1967)

Matthias Steup
Professor of Philosophy, St. Cloud State University
RELIABILISM (2005)
SOSA, ERNEST (2005)

Leslie Stevenson
Honorary Reader in Philosophy, University of St. Andrews
HUMAN NATURE (2005)

M. A. Stewart
Senior Research Fellow, Harris Manchester College, Oxford, U.K
STILLINGFLEET, EDWARD (2005)

Anfinn Stigen
Docent, Institute of Philosophy and History of Ideas, University of Oslo
TRESCHOW, NIELS (1967)

Allan Stoekl
Professor of French and Comparative Literature, Pennsylvania State University
BATAILLE, GEORGES (2005)
BLANCHOT, MAURICE (2005)
EXISTENTIALISM [ADDENDUM] (2005)

Andrija Stojković
Professor of Philosophy, University of Belgrade
MARKOVIĆ, SVETOZAR (1967)

Daniel Stoljar
Senior Fellow, Philosophy Program, Research School of Social Sciences (RSSS), Australian National University
MENTAL-PHYSICAL DISTINCTION (2005)

Jerome Stolnitz
Professor of Philosophy, University of Rochester
BEAUTY (1967)
UGLINESS (1967)

Leonid Stolovich
Professor Emeritus of Tartu University (Estonia)
LOTMAN, IURII MIKHAILOVICH (2005)

A. K. Stout
Professor Emeritus and Fellow of the Senate, University of Sydney
CAIRD, EDWARD (1967)
HOBHOUSE, LEONARD TRELAWNEY (1967)

PRINGLE-PATTISON, ANDREW SETH (1967)
RASHDALL, HASTINGS (1967)
ROSS, WILLIAM DAVID (1967)

D. Stove
Senior Lecturer, University of Sydney
KEYNES, JOHN MAYNARD (1967)

Michael W. Strasser
Associate Professor of Philosophy, Duquesne University
LIBER DE CAUSIS (1967)

Tony Street
Assistant Director of Research in Islamic Studies, Faculty of Divinity, University of Cambridge
LOGIC, HISTORY OF: LOGIC IN THE ISLAMIC WORLD [ADDENDUM] (2005)

Michael Strevens
Associate Professor, Philosophy, New York University
BAYES, BAYES' THEOREM, BAYESIAN APPROACH TO PHILOSOPHY OF SCIENCE (2005)
CHAOS THEORY (2005)
EXPLANATION (2005)
PROBABILITY AND CHANCE (2005)

Avrum Stroll
Professor of Philosophy, University of California, San Diego
PRESUPPOSING (1967)

Fred Gillette Sturm
Professor of Philosophy, Western College for Women (Ohio); Visiting Professor of Philosophy, Eastern Indiana Center of Indiana University
FARIAS BRITO, RAIMUNDO DE (1967)
MOLINA GARMENDIA, ENRIQUE (1967)
REALE, MIGUEL (1967)
VARONA Y PERA, ENRIQUE JOSÉ (1967)

Kathleen M. Sullivan
Stanford University
CENSORSHIP (1996)

L. W. Sumner
University Professor, Philosophy, University of Toronto
HAPPINESS (2005)

Edward Surtz, S.J.
Professor of English, Loyola University
MORE, THOMAS (1967)

John Sutton
Associate Professor, Philosophy, Macquarie University
MEMORY (2005)

Edith D. Sylla
Professor of History, North Carolina State University, Raleigh
SWINESHEAD, RICHARD (2005)

Zoltan G. Szabo
Associate Professor, Philosophy, Cornell University
COMPOSITIONALITY (2005)
SYNTACTICAL AND SEMANTICAL CATEGORIES [ADDENDUM] (2005)

Charles Taliaferro
Professor of Philosophy, St. Olaf College
DEATH [ADDENDUM] (2005)
IDEAL OBSERVER THEORIES OF ETHICS (2005)
NAGEL, THOMAS (2005)

Frank Talmage
Assistant Professor of Hebrew Studies, University of Wisconsin
CRESCAS, HASDAI (1967)
GERSONIDES (1967)

Scott Tanona
Assistant Professor, Philosophy, Kansas State University
BOHR, NIELS (2005)

C. C. W. Taylor
Emeritus Professor of Philosophy, Oxford University, and Emeritus Fellow of Corpus Christi College
LEUCIPPUS AND DEMOCRITUS [BIBLIOGRAPHY] (2005)
SOCRATES (2005)

Richard Taylor
Professor of Philosophy, University of Rochester
DETERMINISM, A HISTORICAL SURVEY (1967)
VOLUNTARISM (1967)

Paul Teller
Professor, University of California, Davis

UNITY AND DISUNITY OF SCIENCE (2005)

Larry S. Temkin
Professor of Philosophy, Rutgers, the State University of New Jersey
EQUALITY, MORAL AND SOCIAL [ADDENDUM] (2005)
PARFIT, DEREK (2005)

Roland J. Teske
Professor of Philosophy, Marquette University
HERVAEUS NATALIS (2005)

Paul Thagard
Professor, University Research Chair, Philosophy, University of Waterloo
PSYCHOLOGY [ADDENDUM] (2005)

Irving Thalberg
Assistant Professor of Philosophy, University of Illinois
ERROR (1967)

Peter Thielke
Assistant Professor, Philosophy, Pomona College
MAIMON, SALOMON (2005)
NAGEL, ERNEST (1967)
PRAGMATISM (1967)

Johannes M. M. H. Thijssen
Professor of Ancient and Medieval Philosophy, Radboud University Nijmegen
NICOLAS OF AUTRECOURT [ADDENDUM] (2005)

Paul Thom
Professor; Executive Dean, Faculty of Arts, Southern Cross University
AUGUSTINE, ST. [ADDENDUM 2] (2005)
PLOTINUS [ADDENDUM] (2005)

Ivo Thomas
Visiting Professor, Notre Dame University and Ohio State University
LOGIC, HISTORY OF: MODERN LOGIC: FROM FREGE TO GÖDEL: NINETEENTH-CENTURY MATHEMATICS (2005)
LOGIC, HISTORY OF: PRECURSORS OF MODERN LOGIC: EULER (1967)
LOGIC, HISTORY OF: PRECURSORS OF MODERN LOGIC: LAMBERT AND PLOUCQUET (1967)

LOGIC, HISTORY OF: PRECURSORS OF MODERN LOGIC: LEIBNIZ (1967)
LOGIC, HISTORY OF: THE INTERREGNUM (BETWEEN MEDIEVAL AND MODERN) (1967)

Richmond Thomason
University of Michigan
ARTIFICIAL AND NATURAL LANGUAGES (2005)
MONTAGUE, RICHARD (2005)

Manley Thompson
Professor and Chair, Philosophy, University of Chicago
CATEGORIES (1967)

Judith Jarvis Thomson
Associate Professor of Philosophy, Massachusetts Institute of Technology
WISDOM, (ARTHUR) JOHN TERENCE DIBBEN (1967)

S. Harrison Thomson
Professor Emeritus of History, University of Colorado
HUS, JOHN (1967)
SCOT, MICHAEL (1967)
WYCLYF, JOHN (1967)

Mark Timmons
University of Memphis
CONSTRUCTIVISM, MORAL (1996)

Robert B. Todd
Professor of Classics, University of British Columbia
THEMISTIUS (2005)

Vincent Tomas
Professor of Philosophy, Brown University
DUCASSE, CURT JOHN (1967)

Giorgio Tonelli
Professor of History of German Literature and History of Modern Philosophy, University of Pisa
BASEDOW, JOHANN BERNHARD (1967)
BAUMGARTEN, ALEXANDER GOTTLIEB (1967)
BILFINGER, GEORG BERNHARD (1967)
BUDDE, JOHANN FRANZ (1967)
CRUSIUS, CHRISTIAN AUGUST (1967)
EBERHARD, JOHANN AUGUST (1967)

GARVE, CHRISTIAN (1967)
KNUTZEN, MARTIN (1967)
LAMBERT, JOHANN HEINRICH (1967)
LAVATER, JOHANN KASPAR (1967)
MEIER, GEORG FRIEDRICH (1967)
MENDELSSOHN, MOSES (1967)
NICOLAI, CHRISTIAN FRIEDRICH (1967)
PLOUCQUET, GOTTFRIED (1967)
REIMARUS, HERMANN SAMUEL (1967)
RÜDIGER, ANDREAS (1967)
SULZER, JOHANN GEORG (1967)
TETENS, JOHANN NICOLAUS (1967)
THOMASIUS, CHRISTIAN (1967)
THÜMMIG, LUDWIG PHILIPP (1967)
TSCHIRNHAUS, EHRENFRIED WALTER VON (1967)
WINCKELMANN, JOHANN JOACHIM (1967)

Michael Tooley
Professor of Philosophy, University of Colorado, Boulder
CAUSAL APPROACHES TO THE DIRECTION OF TIME (2005)
CAUSATION: METAPHYSICAL ISSUES (1996, 2005)
METAPHYSICS, NATURE OF [ADDENDUM] (2005)

Roberto Torretti
Professor Emeritus, Philosophy, Universidad de Puerto Rico en Río Piedras
GEOMETRY (2005)

Norman L. Torrey
Emeritus Professor of French, Columbia University
DIDEROT, DENIS (1967)

Stephen E. Toulmin
Professor of History of Ideas and Philosophy, Brandeis University
MATTER (1967)

Dabney Townsend
Professor of Philosophy, Armstrong Atlantic State University
ALISON, ARCHIBALD (2005)
GERARD, ALEXANDER (2005)

Knut Erik Tranöy
Professor of Philosophy, University of Bergen (Norway)
STEFFENS, HENRICH (1967)

Charles Travis
Sterling University, Scotland
PUTNAM, HILARY (1996)

Simon Trépanier
Lecturer, Classics, School of History and Classics, University of Edinburgh
EMPEDOCLES [ADDENDUM] (2005)

Voula Tsouna
Associate Professor of Philosophy, University of California, Santa Barbara
PHILODEMUS (2005)

Nancy Tuana
Director, Rock Ethics Institute, Pennsylvania State University
FEMINISM AND THE HISTORY OF PHILOSOPHY (2005)

Roderich Tumulka
Wissenschaftlicher Assistent, Mathematics, Eberhard-Karls-Universität, Tübingen, Germany
BELL, JOHN, AND BELL'S THEOREM (2005)
BOHM, DAVID (2005)
BOHMIAN MECHANICS (2005)

Paul Turner
Lecturer in English and Fellow of Linacre College, Oxford University of London; Professor of English, Ankara University
LUCIAN OF SAMOSATA (1967)

Anna-Teresa Tymieniecka
Diplôme d'Études Supérieures (University of Paris, Sorbonne)
LAVELLE, LOUIS (1967)

Shizuteru Ueda
Professor Emeritus, Kyoto University
NISHIDA, KITARŌ (2005)

Robert Ulich
Professor of Education, Emeritus, Harvard University
APPERCEPTION (1967)
COMENIUS, JOHN AMOS (1967)
FROEBEL, FRIEDRICH (1967)
PESTALOZZI, JOHANN HEINRICH (1967)

Mark T. Unno
Associate Professor of East Asian Religions, Department of Religious

Studies, University of Oregon, Eugene
SHINRAN (2005)

James O. Urmson
Fellow of Corpus Christi College, Oxford University
AUSTIN, JOHN LANGSHAW (1967)
IDEAS (1967)
RYLE, GILBERT (1967)

John Douglas Uytman
Senior Lecturer, Department of Psychiatry and Lecturer in Medical Psychology, St. Andrews University
ADLER, ALFRED (1967)
MCDOUGALL, WILLIAM (1967)
PAVLOV, IVAN PETROVICH (1967)

Jouko Väänänen
Professor, Mathematics, University of Helsinki
HINTIKKA, JAAKKO (2005)

Ezio Vailati
Professor, Philosophy, Southern Illinois University, Edwardsville
CLARKE, SAMUEL (2005)

Mark van Atten
Institut d'Histoire et de Philosophie des Sciences et des Techniques (CNRS/Paris 1/ENS)
BROUWER, LUITZEN EGBERTUS JAN [ADDENDUM] (2005)

James Van Cleve
Brown University
REID, THOMAS (2005)

Dirk van Dalen
Professor, Philosophy, Utrecht University
INTUITIONISM AND INTUITIONISTIC LOGIC (2005)

Philippe van Haute
Full Professor in Philosphical Anthropology, Radboud University (The Netherlands); Psychoanalyst (private practice), Leuven, Belgium
LACAN, JACQUES (2005)

Peter van Inwagen
John Cardinal O'Hara Professor of Philosophy, The University of Notre Dame
ONTOLOGICAL ARGUMENT FOR THE EXISTENCE OF GOD [ADDENDUM] (2005)

Andrew G. M. Van Melsen
Professor of Philosophy, University of Nijmegen
ATOMISM (1967)

Linda Van Norden
Professor of English, University of California, Davis
PARACELSUS (1967)

Mark van Roojen
University of Nebraska, Lincoln
ETHICAL SUBJECTIVISM
[BIBLIOGRAPHY] (2005)

Aram Vartanian
Professor of French, New York University
HELVÉTIUS, CLAUDE-ADRIEN (1967)
HOLBACH, PAUL-HENRI THIRY, BARON D' (1967)
LA METTRIE, JULIEN OFFRAY DE (1967)
MAUPERTUIS, PIERRE-LOUIS MOREAU DE (1967)
MESLIER, JEAN (1967)
STAHL, GEORG ERNST (1967)

Pekka Vayrynen
Assistant Professor, Philosophy, University of California, Davis
MORAL REALISM (2005)

Theo Verbeek
Professor, History of Modern Philosophy, Utrecht University
GEULINCX, ARNOLD [ADDENDUM] (2005)

Rineke Verbrugge
University of Göteborg, Sweden
PROVABILITY LOGIC (1996)

Pieter Vermaas
Researcher, Philosophy, Delft University of Technology
MODAL INTERPRETATION OF QUANTUM MECHANICS (2005)

G. N. A. Vesey
Reader in Philosophy, University of London; Honorary Director of The Royal Institute of Philosophy
SOUND (1967)
TOUCH (1967)

Olga Volkogonova
Professor, Moscow State University
BERDYAEV, NIKOLAI ALEKSANDROVICH (2005)

KIREEVSKII, IVAN VASIL'EVICH (2005)

Georg Henrik von Wright
Professor-at-Large, Cornell University
LICHTENBERG, GEORG CHRISTOPH (1967)

Henry Vyverberg
Associate Professor of History, University of Akron
TURGOT, ANNE ROBERT JACQUES, BARON DE L'AULNE (1967)

William J. Wainwright
University of Wisconsin, Milwaukee
OTTO, RUDOLF (1967)
RELIGIOUS EXPERIENCE (1996)

Mary Ellen Waithe
Professor, Philosophy, Cleveland State University
HYPATIA (1996, 2005)

Rebecca L. Walker
Assistant Professor, Social Medicine; Adjunct Assistant Professor, Philosophy, University of North Carolina, Chapel Hill
BIOETHICS (2005)

R. Jay Wallace
Professor of Philosophy, University of California, Berkeley
PROMISES (2005)

Jerry L. Walls
Professor of Philosophy of Religion, Asbury Seminary, Wilmore, KY
HEAVEN AND HELL, DOCTRINES OF (2005)

W. H. Walsh
Professor of Logic and Metaphysics, University of Edinburgh
GREEN, THOMAS HILL (1967)
KANT, IMMANUEL (1967)
METAPHYSICS, NATURE OF (1967)

Kendall Walton
Charles L. Stevenson Collegiate Professor of Philosophy, University of Michigan
NONEXISTENT OBJECT, NONBEING (1996, 2005)

W. J. Waluchow
Professor, Philosophy, McMaster University

HART, HERBERT LIONEL ADOLPHUS (2005)

Richard Walzer
Honorary Professor and Reader, Oxford University
AL-KINDĪ, ABŪ-YŪSUF YAʿQŪB IBN ISḤĀQ (1967)

Richard Warner
Professor of Law, Chicago-Kent College of Law, Illinois Institute of Technology; Professor and Chair of American and Comparative Law, Catholic University of Lublin, Poland
GRICE, HERBERT PAUL (1996, 2005)

G. J. Warnock
Fellow and Tutor of Philosophy, Magdalen College, Oxford University
REASON (1967)

James Warren
University Lecturer in Classics, Corpus Christi College, Cambridge
EPICUREANISM AND THE EPICUREAN SCHOOL [BIBLIOGRAPHY] (2005)

Gary Watson
Professor of Philosophy, University of California, Riverside
FOOT, PHILIPPA (2005)

Richard A. Watson
Philosophy Professor Emeritus, Washington University; Philosophy Faculty Affiliate, University of Montana
FOUCHER, SIMON (1967, 2005)
RÉGIS, PIERRE-SYLVAIN (1967, 2005)
ROHAULT, JACQUES (1967, 2005)

W. Montgomery Watt
Professor and Head, Department of Islamic Studies, University of Edinburgh
AL-FĀRĀBĪ (1967)

Wayne Waxman
Independent scholar
HUME, DAVID (2005)

A. Wedberg
Professor of Philosophy, University of Stockholm

BOSTRÖM, CHRISTOPHER JACOB (1967)
HÄGERSTRÖM, AXEL (1967)

Laura Weed

Associate Professor of Philosophy, The College of St. Rose

RELIGION, PSYCHOLOGICAL EXPLANATIONS OF [ADDENDUM] (2005)

Kai F. Wehmeier

Associate Professor, Logic & Philosophy of Science, University of California, Irvine

FREGE, GOTTLOB (2005)

Vivian Weil

Professor of Ethics; Director, Center for the Study of Ethics in the Professions, Illinois Institute of Technology

ENGINEERING ETHICS (2005)

Gerson Weiler

Research Fellow, Philosophy, Institute of Advanced Studies, Australian National University

MAXWELL, JAMES CLERK (1967)

Julius R. Weinberg

Vilas Professor of Philosophy; Member of the Institute of Research in the Humanities, University of Wisconsin

NICOLAS OF AUTRECOURT (1967)

Kurt Weinberg

Professor of French, and Comparative Literature, University of Rochester

PANTHEISMUSSTREIT (1967)

Rudolph H. Weingartner

Associate Professor and Chair, Philosophy, San Francisco State College

SIMMEL, GEORG (1967)

James A. Weisheipl, O.P.

Professor of Medieval Thought, School of Philosophy, Aquinas Institute (River Forest, IL)

DURANDUS OF SAINT-POURÇAIN (1967)
JOHN OF PARIS (1967)
ULRICH (ENGELBERT) OF STRASBOURG (1967)

John Weiss

Associate Professor of History, Wayne State University

HESS, MOSES (1967)
KAUTSKY, KARL (1967)
SABATIER, AUGUSTE (1967)

Paul Weithman

Professor, Philosophy, University of Notre Dame

REPUBLICANISM (2005)
SOVEREIGNTY [ADDENDUM] (2005)

Morris Weitz

Professor of Philosophy, Ohio State University

PROUST, MARCEL (1967)

Albert Wellek

Professor and Director, Department of Psychology, University of Mainz

KRUEGER, FELIX (1967)
WUNDT, WILHELM (1967)

René Wellek

Sterling Professor and Chair, Department of Comparative Literature, Yale

MASARYK, TOMÁŠ GARRIGUE (1967)

Carl Wellman

Professor Emeritus, Washington University, St. Louis

ASCETICISM (1967)
RIGHTS (2005)

Peter Wenz

Emeritus Professor of Philosophy, University of Illinios at Springfield

ENVIRONMENTAL ETHICS (1996, 2005)

William Werkmeister

Director of the School of Philosophy, University of Southern California

DRIESCH, HANS ADOLF EDUARD (1967)

Karel Werner

Honorary Professorial Associate, Department of the Study of Religions, School of Oriental and African Studies, University of London

LIBERATION IN INDIAN PHILOSOPHY (2005)

Charles C. West

Professor Emeritus of Christian Ethics, Princeton Theological Seminary

CONSEQUENTIALISM (1996)
LIBERATION THEOLOGY (1996, 2005)

Henry R. West

Professor of Philosophy, Macalester College

MILL, JAMES [BIBLIOGRAPHY] (2005)
MILL, JOHN STUART [ADDENDUM] (1996, 2005)

Robin L. West

Professor of Law, Georgetown University Law Center

FEMINIST LEGAL THEORY (1996, 2005)

Willem. G. Weststeijn

Professor of Slavic Literatures, University of Amsterdam

EURASIANISM (2005)
LEONT'EV, KONSTANTIN NIKOLAEVICH (2005)

Rebecca Whisnant

Assistant Professor, Philosophy, University of Dayton

FEMINIST ETHICS (2005)

Alan R. White

Professor of Philosophy, University of Hull; Honorary Secretary of the Mind Association

COHERENCE THEORY OF TRUTH (1967)

Hayden V. White

Professor of History, University of Rochester

FEUERBACH, LUDWIG ANDREAS (1967)
GOBINEAU, COMTE JOSEPH ARTHUR DE (1967)
STRAUSS, DAVID FRIEDRICH (1967)
WINDELBAND, WILHELM (1967)

Roger White

Assistant Professor, Philosophy, New York University

ANTHROPIC PRINCIPLE, THE (2005)

Stephen A. White

Professor, Classics and Philosophy, University of Texas at Austin

CICERO, MARCUS TULLIUS
[BIBLIOGRAPHY] (2005)
POSIDONIUS [ADDENDUM] (2005)
THALES OF MILETUS (2005)

Jacques J. Whitfield
Doctor of Law, Doctor of Economics, University of Würzburg, and other degrees; Author of articles on Michael Servetus and on the economic history of the 18th century
FRANCK, SEBASTIAN (1967)

Lancelot Law Whyte
Author, Next Development in Man; Unconscious Before Freud; Internal Factors in Evolution; Unitary Principle in Physics and Biology; Focus and Diversions; Accent on Form
BOSCOVICH, ROGER JOSEPH (1967)
UNCONSCIOUS (1967)

Henry Nelson Wieman
Professor Emeritus, University of Chicago; Distinguished Visiting Professor, Southern Illinois University
NIEBUHR, REINHOLD (1967)

Christian Wildberg
Professor of Classics, Princeton University
ANAXIMANDER [BIBLIOGRAPHY] (2005)
PHILOPONUS, JOHN (2005)

Bernard Williams
Professor of Philosophy, University of London
HAMPSHIRE, STUART NEWTON (1967)
RATIONALISM (1967)

George Hunston Williams
Professor of Divinity, Divinity School, Harvard University; Director of the Foundation for Reformation Research; Past President of the American Society of Church History
SERVETUS, MICHAEL (1967)
SOCINIANISM (1967)

Raymond Williams
Lecturer in English, Cambridge University, and Director of English Studies, Jesus College, Cambridge University

Arnold, MATTHEW (1967)
ELIOT, THOMAS STEARNS (1967)
RUSKIN, JOHN (1967)

Thomas Williams
Associate Professor of Philosophy, The University of Iowa
GAUNILO (2005)

Timothy Williamson
The University of Edinburgh, Scotland
REFERENCE (1996)
SENSE (1996)

Arthur M. Wilson
Daniel Webster Professor, Professor of Government and of Biology, Dartmouth College; Fellow of the Royal Historical Society (London)
ENCYCLOPÉDIE (1967)

Deirdre Wilson
University College London
PRAGMATICS (1996)

Jessica Wilson
Assistant Professor, Philosophy, University of Toronto
FORCE [ADDENDUM] (2005)

R. McL. Wilson
Senior Lecturer in New Testament Language and Literature, St. Mary's College, St. Andrews University
MANI AND MANICHAEISM (1967)
MARCION (1967)
NUMENIUS OF APAMEA (1967)
SIMON MAGUS (1967)

Peter Winch
Reader in Philosophy, University of London
DURKHEIM, ÉMILE (1967)
LÉVY-BRUHL, LUCIEN (1967)
PARETO, VILFREDO (1967)
SPANN, OTHMAR (1967)
WEBER, MAX (1967)

John Wippel
Theodore Basselin Professor of Philosophy, Catholic University of America
GILES OF ROME (2005)

Gene Witmer
Associate Professor, Philosophy, University of Florida
PHILOSOPHY OF MIND (2005)

Charlotte Witt
Professor of Philosophy and Humanities, University of New Hampshire
FEMINIST METAPHYSICS (2005)

Gerd Wolandt
Docent in Philosophy, University of Bonn
HÖNIGSWALD, RICHARD (1967)

Erik Wolf
Professor of Law, Director of Philosophy of Law Seminar, University of Freiburg im Briesgau
ALTHUSIUS, JOHANNES (1967)
PUFENDORF, SAMUEL VON (1967)

Marvin E. Wolfgang
Professor and Graduate Chair, Sociology, University of Pennsylvania; Codirector of the Center of Criminal Research, University of Pennsylvania; President of the Pennsylvania Prison Society
BECCARIA, CESARE BONESANA (1967)

Harry A. Wolfson
Nathan Littauer Professor Emeritus of Hebrew Literature and Philosophy, Harvard University
PHILO JUDAEUS (1967)

Allan B. Wolter, O.F.M.
Ordinary Professor of Philosophy, Catholic University of America; Editor of Quincy College Publications
BACON, ROGER (1967)
BONAVENTURE, ST. (1967)
DUNS SCOTUS, JOHN (1967)

Nicholas Wolterstorff
Professor of Philosophy, Calvin College
CALVIN, JOHN (1967)

David Wong
Professor of Philosophy, Duke University
CHINESE PHILOSOPHY: ETHICS (2005)
ETHICAL RELATIVISM [ADDENDUM] (2005)

Rega Wood
Research Professor, Philosophy, Stanford University
RUFUS, RICHARD (2005)

George Woodcock
Assistant Professor of English, University of Washington; Associate Professor of English, University of British Columbia
ANARCHISM (1967)
BAKUNIN, MIKHAIL ALEKSANDROVICH (1967)
KROPOTKIN, PËTR ALEKSEEVICH (1967)
PROUDHON, PIERRE-JOSEPH (1967)
STIRNER, MAX (1967)

Arthur E. Woodruff
Assistant Professor, Mathematics and Science Education, Belfer Graduate School of Science, Yeshiva University
FARADAY, MICHAEL (1967)

Paul Woodruff
Darrell K. Royal Professor in Ethics and American Society, Department of Philosophy, The University of Texas at Austin
ARETĒ/AGATHON/KAKON (2005)
HIPPIAS OF ELIS [BIBLIOGRAPHY] (2005)
PRODICUS OF CEOS [BIBLIOGRAPHY] (2005)
PROTAGORAS OF ABDERA [BIBLIOGRAPHY] (2005)
VLASTOS, GREGORY (2005)

A. D. Woozley
Professor of Moral Philosophy, St. Andrews University
UNIVERSALS, A HISTORICAL SURVEY (1967)

John Worrall
Professor of Philosophy of Science; Co-Director, Centre for Philosophy of Natural and Social Sciences, London School of Economics and Political Science, University of London
LAKATOS, IMRE (2005)

Don J. Wyatt
Professor, History, Middlebury College
SHAO YONG (2005)

Michael Wyschogrod
Assistant Professor of Philosophy, City University of New York, City College
BUBER, MARTIN (1967)
HALEVI, YEHUDA (1967)

Liu Xiaogan
Professor, Philosophy, The Chinese University of Hong Kong
LAOZI (2005)

Keith E. Yandell
Julius R. Weinberg Professor of Philosophy, University of Wisconsin, Madison
RELIGIOUS LANGUAGE [ADDENDUM] (2005)

Frances A. Yates
Reader in the History of Renaissance, University of London; Fellow of the Royal Society of Literature
BRUNO, GIORDANO (1967)
HERMETICISM (1967)

Lee Yearley
Walter Y. Evans-Wentz Professor, Religious Studies, Stanford University
CHINESE PHILOSOPHY: RELIGION (2005)

Palle Yourgrau
Associate Professor of Philosophy, Brandeis University
GÖDEL, KURT (1996, 2005)

Mikko Yrjönsuuri
Academy Researcher, Philosophy, University of Jyväskylä
GERSON, JEAN DE (2005)
JOHN OF MIRECOURT (2005)
OLIVI, PETER JOHN (2005)

Naomi Zack
Professor of Philosophy, University of Oregon, Eugene
MULTICULTURALISM (2005)

Taras Zakydalsky
Editor, Russian Studies in Philosophy
SKOVORODA, HRYHORII SAVYCH (GRIGORII SAVVICH) [ADDENDUM] (2005)

Nino Zanghi
Associate Professor, Theoretical Physics, University of Genova, Italy
BELL, JOHN, AND BELL'S THEOREM (2005)
BOHM, DAVID (2005)
BOHMIAN MECHANICS (2005)

Mary-Barbara Zeldin
Associate Professor of Philosophy, Hollins College
SPIR, AFRIKAN ALEXANDROVICH (1967)

Nai Z. Zia
Editor of Christian Classics Series; Former Professor at Lingnan University and the University of Nanking
HAN FEI (1967)

Hossein Ziai
Professor of Iranian and Islamic Studies, Director of Iranian Studies, Department of Near Eastern Languages and Cultures, University of California, Los Angeles
ILLUMINATIONISM (2005)
SUHRAWARDĪ, SHIHĀB AL-DĪN YAḤYĀ [ADDENDUM] (2005)

Dean Zimmerman
Associate Professor, Philosophy, Rutgers University
DUALISM IN THE PHILOSOPHY OF MIND (2005)

Günter Zöller
Professor of Philosophy, University of Munich
FICHTE, JOHANN GOTTLIEB (2005)
KANT, IMMANUEL [ADDENDUM] (1996, 2005)
SCHOPENHAUER, ARTHUR [BIBLIOGRAPHY] (2005)

Arthur Zucker
Associate Professor and Chair; Department of Philosophy; Director, Institute for Applied and Professional Ethics, Ohio University
MEDICAL ETHICS (2005)
PHILOSOPHY OF MEDICINE (1996, 2005)

Jack Zupko
Associate Professor of Philosophy, Emory University
BURIDAN, JOHN (2005)

Arnulf Zweig
Assistant Professor of Philosophy, University of Oregon
BECK, JAKOB SIGISMUND (1967)
BENEKE, FRIEDRICH EDUARD (1967)
DÜHRING, EUGEN KARL (1967)
FECHNER, GUSTAV THEODOR (1967)

GOETHE, JOHANN WOLFGANG VON
 (1967)
KRAUSE, KARL CHRISTIAN
 FRIEDRICH (1967)
KÜLPE, OSWALD (1967)
LANGE, FRIEDRICH ALBERT (1967)
SIGWART, CHRISTOPH (1967)
STUMPF, KARL (1967)

ENCYCLOPEDIA OF PHILOSOPHY
2nd edition

list of articles

A

Abbagnano, Nicola
Abelard, Peter
Abortion
Absolute, The
Action
Addison, Joseph
Adler, Alfred
Adorno, Theodor Wiesengrund
Aenesidemus
Aesthetic Experience
Aesthetic Judgment
Aesthetic Qualities
Aesthetics, History of
Aesthetics, History of [addendum]
Aesthetics, Problems of
Affirmative Action
African Philosophy
Agent Causation
Agent Intellect
Agnosticism
Agrippa
Agrippa von Nettesheim, Henricus
  Cornelius
Ailly, Pierre d'
Aitia
Albert of Saxony
Albert the Great
Albo, Joseph

Albo, Joseph [addendum]
Alcinous
Alcmaeon of Croton
Alembert, Jean Le Rond d'
Alexander, Samuel
Alexander of Aphrodisias
Alexander of Aphrodisias
  [addendum]
Alexander of Hales
al-Fārābī
al-Fārābī [addendum]
al-Ghazālī, Ahmad
al-Ghazālī, Muhammad
al-Ghazālī, Muhammad
  [addendum]
Alienation
Aliotta, Antonio
Alison, Archibald
al-Jabiri, ʿAbd
al-Kindī, Abū-Yūsuf Yaʿqūb ibn
  Isḥāq
al-Kindī, Abū-Yūsuf Yaʿqūb ibn
  Isḥāq [addendum]
Alston, William P.
Alterity
Althusius, Johannes
Altruism
Ampère, André Marie
Analogy in Theology
Analysis, Philosophical

Analytic and Synthetic Statements
Analytic and Synthetic Statements
  [addendum]
Analytic Feminism
Analyticity
Analytic Jurisprudence
Anaphora
Anaphora [addendum]
Anarchism
Anaxagoras of Clazomenae
Anaximander
Anaximenes
Ancient Aesthetics
Ancient Skepticism
Anderson, John
Andō Shōeki
Animal Mind
Animal Rights and Welfare
Annet, Peter
Anomalous Monism
Anscombe, Gertrude Elizabeth
  Margaret
Anselm, St.
Anthropic Principle, The
Antiochus of Ascalon
Antiphon
Antisthenes
Apeiron/Peras
Apel, Karl-Otto
Apologists

Appearance and Reality
Apperception
Applied Ethics
A Priori and A Posteriori
Arcesilaus
Archē
Archytas of Tarentum
Ardigò, Roberto
Arendt, Hannah
Aretē/Agathon/Kakon
Aristippus of Cyrene
Aristo of Chios
Aristotelianism
Aristotle
Arius and Arianism
Arkoun, Mohammed
Arminius and Arminianism
Armstrong, David M.
Arnauld, Antoine
Arnold, Matthew
Art, Authenticity in
Art, Definitions of
Art, Expression in
Art, Formalism in
Art, Interpretation of
Art, Ontology of
Art, Performance in
Art, Representation in
Art, Style and Genre in
Art, Truth in
Art, Value in
Artificial and Natural Languages
Artificial Intelligence
Asceticism
Astell, Mary
Atheism
Atheismusstreit
Atomic Theory in Indian Philosophy
Atomism
Augustine, St.
Augustine, St. [addendum1]
Augustine, St. [addendum2]
Augustinianism
Austin, John
Austin, John Langshaw
Authority
Avenarius, Richard
Averroes
Averroes [addendum]
Averroism
Averroism in Modern Islamic
    Philosophy
Avicenna

Avicenna [addendum]
Ayer, Alfred Jules

B

Baader, Franz Xavier von
Bachelard, Gaston
Bachofen, Johann Jakob
Bacon, Francis
Bacon, Roger
Bacon, Roger [addendum]
Bad Faith
Bahrdt, Carl Friedrich
Baḥyā ben Joseph ibn Paqūda
Baḥyā ben Joseph ibn Paqūda
    [addendum]
Baier, Annette
Baier, Kurt
Bain, Alexander
Baker, Lynne Rudder
Bakhtin, Mikhail Mikhailovich
Bakhtin, Mikhail Mikhailovich
    [addendum]
Bakhtin Circle, The
Bakunin, Mikhail Aleksandrovich
Balfour, Arthur James
Balguy, John
Báñez, Dominic
Banfi, Antonio
Barth, Karl
Barth, Karl [addendum]
Barthes, Roland
Basedow, Johann Bernhard
Basic Statements
Bataille, Georges
Batteux, Abbé Charles
Baudrillard, Jean
Bauer, Bruno
Baumgarten, Alexander Gottlieb
Bayes, Bayes' Theorem, Bayesian
    Approach to Philosophy of Science
Bayle, Pierre
Beardsley, Monroe C.
Beattie, James
Beauty
Beauvoir, Simone de
Beccaria, Cesare Bonesana
Beck, Jakob Sigismund
Behaviorism
Being
Belief
Belief Attributions

Belinskii, Vissarion Grigor'evich
Bell, John, and Bell's Theorem
Bellarmine, St. Robert
Beneke, Friedrich Eduard
Benjamin, Walter
Benn, Gottfried
Bennett, Jonathan
Bentham, Jeremy
Berdyaev, Nikolai Aleksandrovich
Bergmann, Gustav
Bergson, Henri
Berkeley, George
Berkeley, George [addendum]
Berlin, Isaiah
Bernard, Claude
Bernard of Chartres
Bernard of Clairvaux, St.
Bernard of Tours
Bertalanffy, Ludwig von
Biel, Gabriel
Bilfinger, Georg Bernhard
Binet, Alfred
Binswanger, Ludwig
Bioethics
Black, Max
Black Holes
Blake, William
Blanchot, Maurice
Blanshard, Brand
Bloch, Ernst
Blondel, Maurice
Blount, Charles
Bodin, Jean
Boehme, Jakob
Boethius, Anicius Manlius Severinus
Boethius, Anicius Manlius Severinus
    [addendum]
Boetius of Dacia
Bohm, David
Bohmian Mechanics
Bohr, Niels
Boileau, Nicolas
Bolingbroke, Henry St. John
Boltzmann, Ludwig
Bolzano, Bernard
Bonald, Louis Gabriel Ambroise,
    Vicomte de
Bonatelli, Francesco
Bonaventure, St.
Bonhoeffer, Dietrich
Bonnet, Charles
Boole, George
Bosanquet, Bernard

Boscovich, Roger Joseph
Bossuet, Jacques Bénigne
Boström, Christopher Jacob
Boulainvilliers, Henri, Comte de
Bowne, Borden Parker
Boyle, Robert
Bradley, Francis Herbert
Bradwardine, Thomas
Brahman
Braithwaite, Richard Bevan
Brandt, R. B.
Brentano, Franz
Bridgman, Percy William
Brightman, Edgar Sheffield
Broad, Charlie Dunbar
Brouwer, Luitzen Egbertus Jan
Brouwer, Luitzen Egbertus Jan
    [addendum]
Brown, Thomas
Brownson, Orestes Augustus
Brunner, Emil
Bruno, Giordano
Brunschvicg, Léon
Buber, Martin
Buckle, Henry Thomas
Budde, Johann Franz
Buddhism
Buddhism—Schools
    Chan and Zen
    Dge-lugs
    Hua yan
    Madhyamaka
    Yogācāra
Buddhist Epistemology
Buffon, Georges-Louis Leclerc,
    Comte de
Bulgakov, Sergei Nikolaevich
Bullough, Edward
Bultmann, Rudolf
Burckhardt, Jakob
Buridan, John
Burke, Edmund
Burley, Walter
Burthogge, Richard
Business Ethics
Butler, Joseph
Butler, Samuel
Byzantine Philosophy

C

Cabanis, Pierre-Jean Georges

Caird, Edward
Cairns, Dorion
Cajetan, Cardinal
Calderoni, Mario
Calvin, John
Calvin, John [addendum]
Cambridge Platonists
Campanella, Tommaso
Campbell, Norman Robert
Camus, Albert
Can
Cantor, Georg
Capreolus, John
Card, Claudia
Carlyle, Thomas
Carnap, Rudolf
Carneades
Carolingian Renaissance
Carroll, Lewis
Carroll, Lewis [addendum]
Cartesianism
Cartesianism [addendum]
Cartwright, Nancy
Carus, Carl Gustav
Carus, Paul
Caso, Antonio
Cassirer, Ernst
Categorical Imperative
Categories
Cattaneo, Carlo
Causal Approaches to the Direction
    of Time
Causal Closure of the Physical
    Domain
Causal or Conditional or
    Explanatory-Relation Accounts
Causation: Metaphysical Issues
Causation: Philosophy of Science
Causation in Indian Philosophy
Causation in Islamic Philosophy
Cavell, Stanley
Cavendish, Margaret
Celsus
Censorship
Chaadaev, Pëtr Iakovlevich
Chamberlain, Houston Stewart
Chance
Channing, William Ellery
Chaos Theory
Charron, Pierre
Chartres, School of
Chateaubriand, François René de
Chatton, Walter

Chemistry, Philosophy of
Cheng Hao
Cheng Yi
Chernyshevskii, Nikolai Gavrilovich
Chicherin, Boris Nikolaevich
Chicherin, Boris Nikolaevich
    [addendum]
Chinese Philosophy
    Overview
    Buddhism
    Confucianism
    Contemporary
    Daoism
    Ethics
    Language and Logic
    Metaphysics and Epistemology
    Religion
    Social and Political Thought
Chinese Room Argument
Chisholm, Roderick
Chomsky, Noam
Christianity
Chrysippus
Chubb, Thomas
Church, Alonzo
Chwistek, Leon
Cicero, Marcus Tullius
Civil Disobedience
Cixous, Hélène
Clandestine Philosophical Literature
    in France
Clarke, Samuel
Classical Foundationalism
Classical Mechanics, Philosophy of
Clauberg, Johannes
Cleanthes
Clement of Alexandria
Clifford, William Kingdon
Cockburn, Catharine Trotter
Code, Lorraine
Cognitive Science
Cohen, Hermann
Cohen, Hermann [addendum]
Cohen, Morris Raphael
Coherence Theory of Truth
Coherentism
Coleridge, Samuel Taylor
Colet, John
Collier, Arthur
Collingwood, Robin George
Collins, Anthony
Colors
Combinatory Logic

Comenius, John Amos
Common Cause Principle
Common Consent Arguments for the
    Existence of God
Common Sense
Communism
Communitarianism
Compositionality
Computability Theory
Computationalism
Computer Ethics
Computing Machines
Comte, Auguste
Concepts
Condillac, Étienne Bonnot de
Conditionals
Condorcet, Marquis de
Confirmation Theory
Confucius
Connectionism
Conscience
Consciousness
Consciousness in Phenomenology
Consequentialism
Conservation Principle
Conservatism
Constructivism, Moral
Constructivism and Conventionalism
Content, Mental
Contextualism
Continental Philosophy
Continuity
Contractualism
Conventionalism
Conversational Implicature
Conway, Anne
Copenhagen Interpretation
Copernicus, Nicolas
Corbin, Henry
Cordemoy, Géraud de
Cordovero, Moses ben Jacob
Corresponcence Theory of Truth
Cosmological Argument for the
    Existence of God
Cosmology
Cosmology [addendum]
Cosmopolitanism
Cosmos
Costa, Uriel da
Counterfactuals
Counterfactuals in Science
Cournot, Antoine Augustin
Cousin, Victor

Couturat, Louis
Craig's Theorem
Cratylus
Creation and Conservation, Religious
    Doctrine of
Creativity
Creighton, James Edwin
Crescas, Hasdai
Crescas, Hasdai [addendum]
Criteriology
Critical Realism
Critical Theory
Croce, Benedetto
Crusius, Christian August
Cudworth, Ralph
Culverwel, Nathanael
Cumberland, Richard
Cynics
Cyrano de Bergerac, Savinien de
Cyrenaics

D

Dai Zhen
Damascius
Dante Alighieri
Danto, Arthur
Darwin, Charles Robert
Darwin, Erasmus
Darwinism
David of Dinant
Davidson, Donald
Death
Death [addendum]
Decision Theory
Deconstruction
de Finetti, Bruno
Definition
Degrees of Perfection, Argument for
    the Existence of God
Deism
Deleuze, Gilles
Del Vecchio, Giorgio
Demiurge
Democracy
Democracy [addendum]
Demonstratives
De Morgan, Augustus
Dennett, Daniel Clement
Deontological Ethics
Derrida, Jacques
De Sanctis, Francesco

Descartes, René
Desgabets, Robert
Destutt de Tracy, Antoine Louis
    Claude, Comte
Determinables and Determinates
Determinables and Determinates
    [addendum]
Determinism, A Historical Survey
Determinism, Theological
Determinism and Freedom
Determinism and Indeterminism
Determinism in History
Deussen, Paul
Deustua, Alejandro O.
Dewey, John
Dewey, John [addendum]
Dialectic
Dialectical Materialism
Dialectical Materialism [addendum]
Dialectic in Islamic and Jewish
    Philosophy
Diderot, Denis
Dikē
Dilthey, Wilhelm
Dingler, Hugo
Diodorus Cronus
Diogenes Laertius
Diogenes of Apollonia
Diogenes of Sinope
Discourse Ethics
Distant Peoples and Future
    Generations
Divine Command Theories of Ethics
Dōgen
Dogma
Dong Zhongshu
Dostoevsky, Fyodor Mikhailovich
Doubt
Dreams
Dretske, Fred
Driesch, Hans Adolf Eduard
Dualism in the Philosophy of Mind
DuBos, Abbe Jean Baptiste
Ducasse, Curt John
Duhem, Pierre Maurice Marie
Dühring, Eugen Karl
Dummett, Michael Anthony Eardley
Duns Scotus, John
Duns Scotus, John [addendum]
Durandus of Saint-Pourçain
Durkheim, Émile
Duty
Dworkin, Ronald

E

Earman, John
Eberhard, Johann August
Eckhart, Meister
Eddington, Arthur Stanley
Edwards, Jonathan
Egoism and Altruism
Ehrenfels, Christian Freiherr von
Einstein, Albert
Eliminative Materialism,
  Eliminativism
Eliot, George
Eliot, Thomas Stearns
Elisabeth, Princess of Bohemia
Emanationism
Emanationism [addendum]
Emergence
Emerson, Ralph Waldo
Emotion
Emotive Theory of Ethics
Empedocles
Empedocles [addendum]
Empiricism
Encyclopédie
Energy
Energy [addendum]
Engels, Friedrich
Engineering Ethics
Enlightenment
Enlightenment, Islamic
Enlightenment, Jewish
Entailment, Presupposition, and
  Implicature
Environmental Aesthetics
Environmental Ethics
Epictetus
Epicureanism and the Epicurean
  School
Epicurus
Epistemology
Epistemology, Circularity in
Epistemology, History of
Epistemology, History of
  [addendum]
Epistemology, Religious
Epistemology, Religious [addendum]
Epistemology and Ethics, Parallel
  Between
Equality, Moral and Social
Equality, Moral and Social
  [addendum]
Erasmus, Desiderius

Erigena, John Scotus
Error
Error Theory of Ethics
Eschatology
Essence and Existence
Essence and Existence [addendum]
Eternal Return
Eternity
Eternity [addendum 1]
Eternity [addendum 2]
Ethical Egoism
Ethical Naturalism
Ethical Naturalism [addendum]
Ethical Relativism
Ethical Relativism [addendum]
Ethical Subjectivism
Ethics
Ethics, History of
Ethcs, History of: Other
  Developments in Twentieth-
  Century Ethics
Ethics and Economics
Ethics and Morality
Eucken, Rudolf Christoph
Eudaimonia
Eurasianism
Eusebius
Euthanasia
Evans, Gareth
Events in Semantic Theory
Event Theory
Evidentialism
Evil
Evil, The Problem of
Evil, The Problem of [addendum]
Evolutionary Ethics
Evolutionary Psychology
Evolutionary Theory
Existence
Existentialism
Existentialism [addendum]
Existential Psychoanalysis
Existential Psychoanalysis
  [addendum]
Experience
Experimentation and
  Instrumentation
Explanation
Extrinsic and Intrinsic Properties

F

Faith
Faith [addendum]
Fallacies
Faraday, Michael
Farias Brito, Raimundo de
Fascism
Fechner, Gustav Theodor
Fëdorov, Nikolai Fëdorovich
Feinberg, Joel
Feminism and Continental
  Philosophy
Feminism and Pragmatism
Feminism and the History of
  Philosophy
Feminist Aesthetics and Criticism
Feminist Epistemology
Feminist Ethics
Feminist Legal Theory
Feminist Metaphysics
Feminist Philosophy
Feminist Philosophy of Science
Feminist Philosophy of Science:
  Contemporary Perspectives
Feminist Social and Political
  Philosophy
Fénelon, François de Salignac de la
  Mothe
Ferguson, Adam
Ferguson, Ann
Ferri, Luigi
Ferrier, James Frederick
Feuerbach, Ludwig Andreas
Fichte, Johann Gottlieb
Ficino, Marsilio
Fictionalism
Fideism
Field, Hartry
Fields and Particles
Filmer, Robert
Fink, Eugen
First-Order Logic
Fischer, Kuno
Fisher, R. A.
Fiske, John
Florenskii, Pavel Aleksandrovich
Florentine Academy
Florovskii, Georgii Vasil'evich
Fludd, Robert
Fodor, Jerry A.
Folk Psychology
Fonseca, Peter

Fontenelle, Bernard Le Bovier de
Foot, Philippa
Force
Force [addendum]
Foreknowledge and Freedom,
    Theological Problem of
Forgiveness
Foucault, Michel
Foucher, Simon
Fouillée, Alfred
Fourier, François Marie Charles
Frame Problem
Franck, Sebastian
Frank, Erich
Frank, Semën Liudvigovich
Frankfurt, Harry
Franklin, Benjamin
Freedom
Frege, Gottlob
Freud, Sigmund
Friendship
Fries, Jakob Friedrich
Froebel, Friedrich
Frye, Marilyn
Functionalism
Functionalism in Sociology
Fuzzy Logic

G

Gadamer, Hans-Georg
Galen
Galen [addendum]
Galileo Galilei
Galluppi, Pasquale
Game Theory
Garrigou-Lagrange, Réginald Marie
Garve, Christian
Gassendi, Pierre
Gauge Theory
Gaunilo
Gay, John
Gehlen, Arnold
Geisteswissenschaften
General Will, The
Generics
Genetics and Reproductive
    Technologies
Genetics and Reproductive
    Technologies [addendum]
Genovesi, Antonio
Gentile, Giovanni

Geometry
Gerard, Alexander
Gerbert of Aurillac
Gerson, Jean de
Gersonides
Gersonides [addendum]
Gestalt Theory
Geulincx, Arnold
Geulincx, Arnold [addendum]
Gewirth, Alan
Geyser, Joseph
Gibbon, Edward
Gibbs, Josiah
Gilbert of Poitiers
Giles of Rome
Gilson, Étienne Henry
Gioberti, Vincenzo
Glanvill, Joseph
Gnosticism
Gobineau, Comte Joseph Arthur de
God, Concepts of
God, Concepts of [addendum]
Gödel, Kurt
Gödel's Incompleteness Theorems
Godfrey of Fontaines
God/Isvara in Indian Philosophy
Godwin, William
Goethe, Johann Wolfgang von
Gogarten, Friedrich
Golden Rule
Goldman, Alvin
Gongsun Long
Good, The
Goodman, Nelson
Goodman, Nelson [addendum]
Gorgias of Leontini
Gottsched, Johann Christoph
Gournay, Marie le Jars de
Gracián y Morales, Baltasar
Gramsci, Antonio
Gray, Asa
Greek Academy
Greek Drama
Green, Thomas Hill
Gregory of Nazianzus
Gregory of Nyssa
Gregory of Rimini
Grice, Herbert Paul
Grosseteste, Robert
Grosseteste, Robert [addendum]
Grote, John
Grotius, Hugo
Guilt

Guo Xiang
Gurwitsch, Aron

H

Habermas, Jürgen
Haeckel, Ernst Heinrich
Hägerström, Axel
Halevi, Yehuda
Hamann, Johann Georg
Hamelin, Octave
Hamilton, William
Hampshire, Stuart Newton
Hanafi, Hassan
Han Fei
Han Yu
Happiness
Harding, Sandra
Hare, Richard M.
Harman, Gilbert
Harnack, Carl Gustav Adolf von
Harrington, James
Harris, William Torrey
Hart, Herbert Lionel Adolphus
Hartley, David
Hartmann, Eduard von
Hartmann, Nicolai
Harvey, William
Hatano Seiichi
Hayashi Razan
Hazlitt, William
Heaven and Hell, Doctrines of
Hebbel, Christian Friedrich
Hedonism
Hegel, Georg Wilhelm Friedrich
Hegel, Georg Wilhelm Friedrich
    [addendum]
Hegelianism
Heidegger, Martin
Heim, Karl
Heisenberg, Werner
Held, Virginia
Hellenistic Thought
Helmholtz, Hermann Ludwig von
Helvétius, Claude-Adrien
Hempel, Carl Gustav
Hemsterhuis, Frans
Hen/Polla
Henry of Ghent
Henry of Ghent [addendum]
Henry of Harclay
Heraclitus of Ephesus

Herbart, Johann Friedrich
Herbert of Cherbury
Herder, Johann Gottfried
Hermeneutics
Hermeticism
Hermeticism [addendum]
Herschel, John
Hertz, Heinrich Rudolf
Hervaeus Natalis
Herzen, Aleksandr Ivanovich
Hess, Moses
Heterosexism
Heytesbury, William
Hickok, Laurens Perseus
Hiddenness of God
Hilbert, David
Hilbert, David [addendum]
Hildegard of Bingen
Hintikka, Jaakko
Hippias of Elis
Hippocrates and the Hippocratic
  Corpus
Historical Materialism
Historical School of Jurisprudence
Historicism
Historicism [addendum]
History and Historiography of
  Philosophy
Hobbes, Thomas
Hobbes, Thomas [addendum]
Hobhouse, Leonard Trelawney
Hocking, William Ernest
Hodgson, Shadworth Holloway
Høffding, Harald
Holbach, Paul-Henri Thiry, Baron d'
Hölderlin, Johann Christian
  Friedrich
Hole Argument
Holism and Individualism in History
  and Social Science
Holism and Individualism in History
  and Social Science [addendum]
Holkot, Robert
Holocaust
Holt, Edwin Bissell
Home, Henry
Homer
Hönigswald, Richard
Hooker, Richard
Horkheimer, Max
Howison, George Holmes
Huang Zongxi
Huet, Pierre-Daniel

Hügel, Baron Friedrich von
Hui Shi
Human Genome Project
Humanism
Human Nature
Humboldt, Wilhelm von
Hume, David
Humor
Humor [addendum]
Hus, John
Hu Shi
Husserl, Edmund
Hutcheson, Francis
Hutcheson, Francis [addendum]
Huxley, Thomas Henry
Hypatia
Hyppolite, Jean

I

Iamblichus
Ibn al-'Arabī
Ibn Bājja
Ibn Bājja [addendum]
Ibn Gabirol, Solomon ben Judah
Ibn Khaldūn
Ibn Khaldūn [addendum]
Ibn Ṭufayl
Ibn Ṭufayl [addendum]
Ibn Zaddik, Joseph ben Jacob
Idealism
Ideal Observer Theories of Ethics
Ideas
Identity
Ideology
Ikhwān al-Ṣafā'
Il'in, Ivan Aleksandrovich
Illumination
Illuminationism
Illusions
Imagery, Mental
Images
Imagination
Imagination [addendum]
Immortality
Immortality [addendum]
Impartiality
Impetus
Indexicals
Indian Philosophy
Induction
Inference to the Best Explanation

Infinitesimals
Infinity in Mathematics and Logic
Infinity in Theology and Metaphysics
Information Theory
Informed Consent
Informed Consent in the Practice of
  Law
Ingarden, Roman
Inge, William Ralph
Ingenieros, José
Innate Ideas
Innate Ideas, Nativism
Inner Senses
Intensional Transitive Verbs
Intention
Intentionality
Intentionality [addendum]
Internalism and Externalism in
  Ethics
Internalism versus Externalism
Intrinsic Value
Introspection
Intuition
Intuition [addendum1]
Intuition [addendum2]
Intuitionism, Ethical
Intuitionism and Intuitionistic Logic
Ionescu, Nae
Iqbal, Muhammad
Irigaray, Luce
Irrationalism
Isaac of Stella
Islamic Philosophy
Islamic Philosophy [addendum]
Israeli, Isaac ben Solomon
Itō Jinsai
Ivanov, Viacheslav Ivanovich

J

Jacobi, Friedrich Heinrich
James, Henry
James, William
James, William [addendum]
Jankélévitch, Vladimir
Jansenism
Japanese Philosophy
Jaspers, Karl
Jeans, James Hopwood
Jefferson, Thomas
Jevons, William Stanley
Jewish Averroism

Jewish Philosophy
Jewish Philosophy [addendum]
Jinul
Joachim of Fiore
Jodl, Friedrich
John of Damascus
John of Jandun
John of La Rochelle
John of Mirecourt
John of Paris
John of St. Thomas
John of Salisbury
John of the Cross, St.
Johnson, Alexander Bryan
Johnson, Samuel
Johnson, Samuel
Jouffroy, Théodore Simon
Jung, Carl Gustav
Jünger, Ernst
Jungius, Joachim
Justice
Just War Theory

K

Kabbalah
Kabbalah [addendum]
Kafka, Franz
Kaibara Ekken
Kalon
Kant, Immanuel
Kant, Immanuel [addendum]
Kantian Ethics
Kaplan, David
Kareev, Nikolai Ivanovich
Karma
Karsavin, Lev Platonovich
Katharsis
Kaufmann, Walter Arnold
Kautsky, Karl
Kavelin, Konstantin Dmitrievich
Kelsen, Hans
Kepler, Johannes
Keynes, John Maynard
Keyserling, Hermann Alexander, Graf
   von
Khomiakov, Aleksei Stepanovich
Kierkegaard, Søren Aabye
Kierkegaard, Søren Aabye
   [addendum]
Kilvington, Richard
Kilwardby, Robert

Kim, Jaegwon
King, Martin Luther
Kireevskii, Ivan Vasil'evich
Kitcher, Patricia
Klages, Ludwig
Kleist, Heinrich von
Knowledge, A Priori
Knowledge, The Priority of
Knowledge and Belief
Knowledge and Modality
Knowledge and Truth, The Value of
Knowledge and Vagueness
Knowledge Argument
Knowledge in Indian Philosophy
Knutzen, Martin
Koffka, Kurt
Köhler, Wolfgang
Korean Philosophy
Korn, Alejandro
Kotarbiński, Tadeusz
Kozlov, Aleksei Aleksandrovich
Krause, Karl Christian Friedrich
Kripke, Saul
Kristeva, Julia
Kropotkin, Pëtr Alekseevich
Krueger, Felix
Kuhn, Thomas
Külpe, Oswald
Kumazawa Banzan

L

Laas, Ernst
Laberthonnière, Lucien
Labriola, Antonio
La Bruyère, Jean de
Lacan, Jacques
Lachelier, Jules
Lakatos, Imre
Lalande, André
Lamarck, Chevalier de
Lambert, Johann Heinrich
Lamennais, Hugues Félicité Robert
   de
La Mettrie, Julien Offray de
La Mothe Le Vayer, François de
Landgrebe, Ludwig
Lange, Friedrich Albert
Langer, Susanne K.
Language
Language and Thought
Language of Thought

Laozi
La Peyrère, Isaac
Laplace, Pierre Simon de
Lapshin, Ivan Ivanovich
La Rochefoucauld, Duc François de
Laromiguière, Pierre
Laroui, Abdullah
Lassalle, Ferdinand
Latin American Philosophy
Lavater, Johann Kaspar
Lavelle, Louis
Lavoisier, Antoine
Lavrov, Pëtr Lavrovich
Law, William
Laws, Scientific
Laws of Nature
Laws of Nature [addendum]
Laws of Thought
Le Clerc, Jean
Le Clerc, Jean [addendum]
Legal Positivism
Legal Positivism: Anglo-American
   Legal Positivism since H. L. A. Hart
Legal Realism
Lehrer, Keith
Leibniz, Gottfried Wilhelm
Lenin, Vladimir Il'ich
Leonardo da Vinci
Leont'ev, Konstantin Nikolaevich
Leopardi, Count Giacomo
Lequier, (Joseph Louis) Jules
Le Roy, Édouard
Le Senne, René
Leśniewski, Stanisław
Lessing, Gotthold Ephraim
Leucippus and Democritus
Levinas, Emmanuel
Lévy-Bruhl, Lucien
Lewis, Clarence Irving
Lewis, C. S. (Clive Staples)
Lewis, David
Li Ao
Liar Paradox, The
Liberalism
Liberalism [addendum]
Liberation in Indian Philosophy
Liberation Theology
Liber de Causis
Libertarianism
Liberty
Lichtenberg, Georg Christoph
Liebert, Arthur
Liebmann, Otto

Life, Meaning and Value of
Life, Meaning and Value of
   [addendum]
Life, Origin of
Lipps, Theodor
Lipsius, Justus
Literature, Philosophy of
Littré, Émile
Lloyd, Genevieve
Locke, John
Locke, John [addendum]
Logic, History of
   Overview
   Ancient Logic
   Logic and Inference in Indian
     Philosophy
   Chinese Logic
   Logic in the Islamic World
   Logic in the Islamic World
     [addendum]
   Medieval (European) Logic
   The Interregnum (between
     Medieval and Modern)
   Precursors of Modern Logic
     [overview]
   Precursors of Modern Logic:
     Leibniz
   Precursors of Modern Logic:
     Euler
   Precursors of Modern Logic:
     Lambert and Ploucquet
   Precursors of Modern Logic:
     Bolzano
   Modern Logic: The Boolean
     Period [overview]
   Modern Logic: The Boolean
     Period: Hamilton
   Modern Logic: The Boolean
     Period: De Morgan
   Modern Logic: The Boolean
     Period: Boole
   Modern Logic: The Boolean
     Period: Jevons
   Modern Logic: The Boolean
     Period: Venn
   Modern Logic: The Boolean
     Period: Carroll
   Modern Logic: The Boolean
     Period: Peirce
   Modern Logic: The Boolean
     Period: The Heritage of Kant
     and Mill
   Modern Logic: The Boolean
     Period: Keynes

   Modern Logic: The Boolean
     Period: Johnson
   Modern Logic: From Frege to
     Gödel [overview]
   Modern Logic: From Frege to
     Gödel: Nineteenth-Century
     Mathematics
   Modern Logic: From Frege to
     Gödel: Frege
   Modern Logic: From Frege to
     Gödel: Peano
   Modern Logic: From Frege to
     Gödel: Whitehead and Russell
   Modern Logic: From Frege to
     Gödel: Post
   Modern Logic: From Frege to
     Gödel: Ramsey
   Modern Logic: From Frege to
     Gödel: Brouwer and Intu-
     itionism
   Modern Logic: From Frege to
     Gödel: Hilbert and Formalism
   Modern Logic: From Frege to
     Gödel: Löwenheim
   Modern Logic: From Frege to
     Gödel: Skolem
   Modern Logic: From Frege to
     Gödel: Herbrand
   Modern Logic: From Frege to
     Gödel: Gödel
   Modern Logic: Since Gödel
     [overview]
   Modern Logic: Since Gödel:
     Gentzen
   Modern Logic: Since Gödel:
     Church
   Modern Logic: Since Gödel: Tur-
     ing and Computability The-
     ory
   Modern Logic: Since Gödel:
     Decidable and Undecidable
     Theories
   Modern Logic: Since Gödel:
     Model Theory: Tarski
   Modern Logic: Since Gödel:
     Model Theory: Robinson
   Modern Logic: Since Gödel: The
     Proliferation of Nonclassical
     Logics
   Modern Logic: Since Gödel:
     Friedman and Reverse Mathe-
     matics
Logic, Non-Classical
Logic, Traditional
Logical Form

Logical Knowledge
Logical Paradoxes
Logical Positivism
Logical Terms
Logical Terms, Glossary of
Logic Diagrams
Logic Machines
Logos
Loisy, Alfred
Longinus (Pseudo)
Lopatin, Lev Mikhailovich
Losev, Aleksei Fëdorovich
Losskii, Nikolai Onufrievich
Lotman, Iurii Mikhailovich
Lotze, Rudolf Hermann
Love
Love [addendum]
Lovejoy, Arthur Oncken
Loyalty
Lucian of Samosata
Lucretius
Lukács, Georg
Łukasiewicz, Jan
Lull, Ramón
Lunacharskii, Anatolii Vasil'evich
Luther, Martin
Luther, Martin [addendum]
Lu Xiangshan
Lying
Lyotard, Jean François

M

Mach, Ernst
Machiavelli, Niccolò
Machiavelli, Niccolò [addendum]
Machine Intelligence
MacIntyre, Alasdair
Mackie, John Leslie
Macrocosm and Microcosm
Maillet, Benoît De
Maimon, Salomon
Maimonides
Maimonides [addendum]
Maine de Biran
Maistre, Comte Joseph de
Major, John
Malcolm, Norman
Malebranche, Nicolas
Malraux, Georges-André
Malthus, Thomas Robert

Mamardashvili, Merab Konstantinovich
Mandeville, Bernard
Mani and Manichaeism
Mannheim, Karl
Mansel, Henry Longueville
Many-Valued Logics
Many Worlds/Many Minds Interpretation of Quantum Mechanics
Marcel, Gabriel
Marcion
Marcus, Ruth Barcan
Marcus Aurelius Antoninus
Maréchal, Joseph
Mariana, Juan de
Marías, Julián
Maritain, Jacques
Maritain, Jacques [addendum]
Marković, Svetozar
Marsilius of Inghen
Marsilius of Padua
Marsilius of Padua [addendum]
Marston, Roger
Martineau, James
Martinetti, Piero
Marty, Anton
Marulić, Marko
Marx, Karl
Marxist Philosophy
Marxist Philosophy [addendum]
Masaryk, Tomáš Garrigue
Mass
Materialism
Mathematics, Foundations of
Mather, Cotton
Matter
Matthew of Acquasparta
Maupertuis, Pierre-Louis Moreau de
Maxwell, James Clerk
McCosh, James
McDougall, William
McDowell, John
McGilvary, Evander Bradley
McTaggart, John McTaggart Ellis
Mead, George Herbert
Meaning
Measurement and Measurement Theory
Medical Ethics
Medieval Philosophy
Meditation in Indian Philosophy
Megarians

Meier, Georg Friedrich
Meinecke, Friedrich
Meinong, Alexius
Melanchthon, Philipp
Melissus of Samos
Memory
Menasseh (Manasseh) ben Israel
Mencius
Mendelssohn, Moses
Mental Causation
Mental-Physical Distinction
Mental Representation
Mercier, Désiré Joseph
Mereology
Merleau-Ponty, Maurice
Mersenne, Marin
Meslier, Jean
Metaethics
Metaphor
Metaphor [addendum]
Metaphysics
Metaphysics, History of
Metaphysics, History of [addendum]
Metaphysics, Nature of
Metaphysics, Nature of [addendum]
Meyerson, Émile
Middleton, Conyers
Mikhailovskii, Nikolai Konstantinovich
Miki Kiyoshi
Milhaud, Gaston
Mill, James
Mill, John Stuart
Mill, John Stuart [addendum]
Miller, Dickinson S.
Millikan, Ruth
Mill's Methods of Induction
Milton, John
Mimesis
Minagawa Kien
Mind and Mental States in Buddhist Philosophy
Mind-Body Problem
Miracles
Miracles [addendum]
Miura Baien
Modal Interpretation of Quantum Mechanics
Modality, Philosophy and Metaphysics of
Modality and Language
Modality and Quantification
Modal Logic

Model Theory
Modernism
Modernism and Postmodernism
Moira/Tychē/Anankē
Moleschott, Jacob
Molina, Luis de
Molina Garmendia, Enrique
Monad and Monadology
Monism and Pluralism
Montague, Richard
Montague, William Pepperell
Montaigne, Michel Eyquem De
Montesquieu, Baron de
Montgomery, Edmund Duncan
Moore, George Edward
Moore, George Edward [addendum]
Moral Arguments for the Existence of God
Moral Arguments for the Existence of God [addendum]
Moral Dilemmas
Moral Epistemology
Moral Principles: Their Justification
Moral Psychology
Moral Realism
Moral Rules and Principles
Moral Sense
Moral Sentiments
Moral Skepticism
More, Henry
More, Thomas
Morgan, C. Lloyd
Morgan, Lewis Henry
Morgan, Thomas
Moritz, Karl Philipp
Mosca, Gaetano
Motion
Motion, A Historical Survey
Mounier, Emmanuel
Mozi
Mullā Ṣadrā
Mullā Ṣadrā [addendum]
Multiculturalism
Multiple Realizability
Muqammiṣ, David ben Merwan al-
Murdoch, Iris
Muro Kyūsō
Murphy, Arthur Edward
Music, Philosophy of
Musonius Rufus
Mysticism, History of
Mysticism, Nature and Assessment of

Mysticism, Nature and Assessment of
    [addendum]
Myth
Myth [addendum]

N

Nāgārjuna
Nagel, Ernest
Nagel, Thomas
Naigeon, Jacques-André
Nakae Tōju
Naṣīr al-Dīn al-Ṭūsī
Nasr, Seyyed Hossein
Nationalism
Nationalism [addendum]
Natorp, Paul
Naturalism
Naturalized Epistemology
Naturalized Philosophy of Science
Natural Kinds
Natural Law
Nature, Philosophical Ideas of
Negation
Negation in Indian Philosophy
Nelson, Leonard
Nemesius of Emesa
Neo-Kantianism
Neoplatonism
Neoplatonism [addendum]
Neumann, John von
Neurath, Otto
Neuroscience
New England Transcendentalism
New England Transcendentalism
    [addendum]
Newman, John Henry
Newman, John Henry [addendum]
New Realism
Newton, Isaac
Nicholas of Cusa
Nicolai, Christian Friedrich
Nicolas of Autrecourt
Nicolas of Autrecourt [addendum]
Nicole, Pierre
Niebuhr, Reinhold
Nietzsche, Friedrich
Nihilism
Nirvāṇa
Nishi Amane
Nishida, Kitarō
Nominalism, Modern

Nomos and Phusis
Noncognitivism
Nonexistent Object, Nonbeing
Non-locality
Non-Monotonic Logic
Nonreductive Physicalism
Non-Truth-Conditional Meaning
Norris, John
Nothing
Nouns, Mass and Count
Nous
Novalis
Nozick, Robert
Number
Numenius of Apamea
Nussbaum, Martha

O

Oakeshott, Michael
Objectivity in Ethics
Ockhamism
Ogyū Sorai
Oken, Lorenz
Olivi, Peter John
Oman, John Wood
Ontological Argument for the
    Existence of God
Ontological Argument for the
    Existence of God [addendum]
Ontology
Ontology, History of
Operationalism
Oresme, Nicole
Organismic Biology
Origen
Orobio de Castro, Isaac
Orphism
Orphism [addendum]
Ortega Y Gasset, José
Ostwald, Wilhelm
Other Minds
Otto, Rudolf
Ousia
Owen, G. E. L.

P

Pacifism
Pain
Pain, Ethical Significance of

Paine, Thomas
Palágyi, Menyhert
Paley, William
Palmer, Elihu
Panaetius of Rhodes
Pannenberg, Wolfhart
Panpsychism
Pantheism
Pantheismusstreit
Papini, Giovanni
Paracelsus
Paraconsistent Logics
Paradigm-Case Argument
Parapsychology
Pareto, Vilfredo
Parfit, Derek
Parker, Theodore
Parmenides of Elea
Parmenides of Elea [addendum]
Pascal, Blaise
Pastore, Valentino Annibale
Pater, Walter Horatio
Paternalism
Patriotism
Patristic Philosophy
Patrizi, Francesco
Pauler, Akos
Pauling, Linus
Paul of Venice
Paulsen, Friedrich
Pavlov, Ivan Petrovich
Peace, War, and Philosophy
Peace, War, and Philosophy
    [addendum]
Peano, Giuseppe
Pearson, Karl
Peckham, John
Peirce, Charles Sanders
Peirce, Charles Sanders [addendum]
Pelagius and Pelagianism
Perception
Perception, Contemporary Views
Perfection
Performative Theory of Truth
Performative Utterances
Peripatetics
Perry, Ralph Barton
Persistence
Personal Identity
Personal Identity [addendum]
Personalism
Persons
Pessimism and Optimism

Pestalozzi, Johann Heinrich
Peter Aureol
Peter Aureol [addendum]
Peter Damian
Peter Lombard
Peter Lombard [addendum]
Peter of Spain
Petrarch
Petroniević, Branislav
Petrović-Njegoš, Petar
Petzoldt, Joseph
Pfänder, Alexander
Phantasia
Phenomenalism
Phenomenological Psychology
Phenomenology
Phenomenology [addendum]
Philodemus
Philo Judaeus
Philo Judaeus [addendum]
Philolaus of Croton
Philo of Larissa
Philo of Megara
Philoponus, John
Philosophical Anthropology
Philosophy
Philosophy of Biology
Philosophy of Economics
Philosophy of Education,
    Epistemological Issues in
Philosophy of Education, Ethical and
    Political Issues in
Philosophy of Education, History of
Philosophy of Film
Philosophy of History
Philosophy of Language
Philosophy of Language in
    Continental Philosophy
Philosophy of Language in India
Philosophy of Law, History of
Philosophy of Law, History of
    [addendum]
Philosophy of Law, Problems of
Philosophy of Law, Problems of
    [addendum]
Philosophy of Medicine
Philosophy of Mind
Philosophy of Physics
Philosophy of Religion
Philosophy of Religion [addendum]
Philosophy of Religion, History of
Philosophy of Religion, History of
    [addendum]

Philosophy of Religion, Problems of
Philosophy of Science, History of
Philosophy of Science, Problems of
Philosophy of Sex
Philosophy of Social Sciences
Philosophy of Statistical Mechanics
Philosophy of Technology
Phonology
Phronêsis
Physicalism
Physicotheology
Physics and the Direction of Time
Piaget, Jean
Pico della Mirandola, Count
    Giovanni
Pico della Mirandola, Gianfrancesco
Pietism
Pisarev, Dmitri Ivanovich
Planck, Max
Plantinga, Alvin
Plato
Platonism and the Platonic Tradition
Pleasure
Plekhanov, Georgii Valentinovich
Plessner, Helmut
Pletho, Giorgius Gemistus
Plotinus
Plotinus [addendum]
Ploucquet, Gottfried
Pluralism
Plurals and Plurality
Plutarch of Chaeronea
Pneuma
Poincaré, Jules Henri
Political Philosophy, History of
Political Philosophy, History of
    [addendum]
Pomponazzi, Pietro
Pope, Alexander
Popper, Karl Raimund
Popper-Lynkeus, Josef
Popular Arguments for the Existence
    of God
Porphyry
Porter, Noah
Posidonius
Posidonius [addendum]
Positivism
Posner, Richard
Possibility
Postcolonialism
Postmodernism
Power

Practical Reason
Pragmatics
Pragmatics [addendum]
Pragmatism
Pragmatism [addendum]
Pragmatist Epistemology
Precognition
Pre-Socratic Philosophy
Presupposing
Presupposition
Price, Richard
Priestley, Joseph
Primary and Secondary Qualities
Pringle-Pattison, Andrew Seth
Prior, Arthur Norman
Private Language Problem
Private Language Problem
    [addendum]
Probability and Chance
Proclus
Prodicus of Ceos
Progress, The Idea of
Projectivism
Promises
Proof Theory
Proper Names and Descriptions
Properties
Property
Property [addendum]
Propositional Attitudes: Issues in
    Philosophy of Mind and
    Psychology
Propositional Attitudes: Issues in
    Semantics
Propositional Knowledge, Definition
    of
Propositions
Propositions [addendum]
Protagoras of Abdera
Proudhon, Pierre-Joseph
Proust, Marcel
Provability Logic
Providence
Pseudo-Dionysius
Pseudo-Grosseteste
Psychē
Psychoanalysis
Psychoanalytic Theories, Logical
    Status of
Psychologism
Psychology
Psychology [addendum]
Pufendorf, Samuel von

Punishment
Punishment [addendum]
Putnam, Hilary
Pyrrho
Pyrrhonian Problematic, The
Pythagoras and Pythagoreanism
Pythagoras and Pythagoreanism
    [addendum 1]
Pythagoras and Pythagoreanism
    [addendum 2]

Q

Qualia
Quantifiers in Formal Logic
Quantifiers in Natural Language
Quantum Computing and
    Teleportation
Quantum Logic and Probability
Quantum Mechanics
Questions
Quine, Willard Van Orman
Quine, Willard Van Orman
    [addendum]

R

Racism
Racism [addendum]
Radbruch, Gustav
Radishchev, Aleksandr Nikolaevich
Rădulescu-Motru, Constantin
Rahner, Karl
Ramsey, Frank Plumpton
Ramus, Peter
Rashdall, Hastings
Rationalism
Rationalism in Ethics (Practical-
    Reason Approaches)
Rationalism in Ethics [addendum]
Rationality
Ravaisson-Mollien, Jean Gaspard
    Félix
Rawls, John
Reale, Miguel
Realism
Realism [addendum]
Realism and Naturalism,
    Mathematical
Reason
Reduction

Reductionism in the Philosophy of
    Mind
Reference
Reflective Equilibrium
Reformation
Régis, Pierre-Sylvain
Regius, Henricus (Henry de Roy)
Rehmke, Johannes
Reich, Wilhelm
Reichenbach, Hans
Reid, Thomas
Reimarus, Hermann Samuel
Reincarnation
Reinhold, Karl Leonhard
Relations, Internal and External
Relativity Theory
Relevance (Relevant) Logics
Relevant Alternatives
Reliabilism
Religion
Religion, Naturalistic
    Reconstructions of
Religion, Naturalistic
    Reconstructions of [addendum]
Religion, Psychological Explanations
    of
Religion, Psychological Explanations
    of [addendum]
Religion and Morality
Religion and Politics
Religion and the Biological Sciences
Religion and the Physical Sciences
Religious Experience
Religious Experience, Argument for
    the Existence of God
Religious Language
Religious Language [addendum]
Religious Pluralism
Renaissance
Renan, Joseph Ernest
Renouvier, Charles Bernard
Rensi, Giuseppe
Republicanism
Rescher, Nicholas
Respect
Response-Dependence Theories
Responsibility, Moral and Legal
Revelation
Reverse Mathematics
Ribot, Théodule Armand
Richard of Mediavilla
Rickert, Heinrich
Ricoeur, Paul

Riehl, Alois
Rights
Rignano, Eugenio
Rilke, Rainer Maria (René)
Rintelen, Fritz-Joachim von
Ritschl, Albrecht Benjamin
Robinet, Jean-Baptiste-René
Rohault, Jacques
Romagnosi, Gian Domenico
Romanticism
Romanticism [addendum]
Romero, Francisco
Roretz, Karl
Rorty, Richard
Roscelin
Rosenkranz, Johann Karl Friedrich
Rosenzweig, Franz
Rosenzweig, Franz [addendum]
Rosmini-Serbati, Antonio
Ross, William David
Rougier, Louis
Rousseau, Jean-Jacques
Rousseau, Jean-Jacques [addendum]
Royce, Josiah
Royer-Collard, Pierre Paul
Rozanov, Vasilii Vasil'evich
Rozanov, Vasilii Vasil'evich
    [addendum]
Rüdiger, Andreas
Rufus, Richard
Rule Following
Rule Following [addendum]
Ruskin, John
Russell, Bertrand Arthur William
Russian Philosophy
Ruysbroeck, Jan van
Ryle, Gilbert
Ryle, Gilbert [addendum]

S

Saadya
Saadya [addendum]
Sabatier, Auguste
Saint-Hyacinthe, Thémiseul de
Saint-Simon, Claude-Henri de
    Rouvroy, Comte de
Saint Victor, School of
Salmon, Wesley
Sanches, Francisco
Santayana, George
Sartre, Jean-Paul

Savage, Leonard
Savigny, Friedrich Karl von
Scheler, Max
Schelling, Friedrich Wilhelm Joseph von
Schiller, Ferdinand Canning Scott
Schiller, Friedrich
Schlegel, Friedrich von
Schleiermacher, Friedrich Daniel Ernst
Schleiermacher, Friedrich Daniel Ernst [addendum]
Schlick, Moritz
Scholz, Heinrich
School of Qom, The
Schopenhauer, Arthur
Schrödinger, Erwin
Schultz, Julius
Schulze, Gottlob Ernst
Schuppe, Ernst Julius Wilhelm
Schutz, Alfred
Sciacca, Michele Federico
Science, Research Ethics of
Science and Pseudoscience
Science Policy
Science Studies
Scientia Media and Molinism
Scientific Method
Scientific Realism
Scientific Revolutions
Scot, Michael
Scotism
Searle, John
Second-Order Logic
Self
Self-Deception
Self in Indian Philosophy
Self-Interest
Self-Knowledge
Self-Prediction
Sellars, Roy Wood
Sellars, Wilfrid
Semantics
Semantics, History of
Semantics, History of [addendum]
Sen, Amartya K.
Seneca, Lucius Annaeus
Sensa
Sensationalism
Sense
Servetus, Michael
Set Theory
Sexism

Sextus Empiricus
Shaftesbury, Third Earl of (Anthony Ashley Cooper)
Shame
Shao Yong
Shariati, Ali
Shelley, Percy Bysshe
Shepherd, Mary
Shestov, Lev Isaakovich
Shestov, Lev Isaakovich [addendum]
Shinran
Shoemaker, Sydney
Shpet, Gustav Gustavovich
Sibley, Frank
Sidgwick, Henry
Sidgwick, Henry [addendum]
Siger of Brabant
Sigwart, Christoph
Simmel, Georg
Simon, Richard
Simon Magus
Simplicius
Simulation Theory
Singer, Peter
Skepticism, Contemporary
Skepticism, History of
Skinner, B. F.
Skovoroda, Hryhorii Savych (Grigorii Savvich)
Skovoroda, Hryhorii Savych (Grigorii Savvich) [addendum]
Smart, John Jamieson Carswell
Smith, Adam
Smith, Adam [addendum]
Smith, John
Smuts, Jan Christiaan
Social and Political Philosophy
Social Contract
Social Contract [addendum]
Social Constructionism
Social Epistemology
Socialism
Socialism [addendum]
Society
Society [addendum]
Socinianism
Sociology of Knowledge
Socrates
Solger, Karl Wilhelm Ferdinand
Solipsism
Solov'ëv (Solovyov), Vladimir Sergeevich
Sombart, Werner

Sophia
Sophists
Sôphrosunê
Sorel, Georges
Sosa, Ernest
Soto, Dominic de
Sound
Sovereignty
Sovereignty [addendum]
Space
Space in Physical Theories
Spann, Othmar
Spaventa, Bertrando
Special Sciences
Speciesism
Spengler, Oswald
Spinoza, Benedict (Baruch) de
Spinozism
Spir, Afrikan Alexandrovich
Spirito, Ugo
Spranger, (Franz Ernst) Eduard
Stace, Walter Terence
Staël-Holstein, Anne Louise Germaine Necker, Baronne de
Stahl, Georg Ernst
Stammler, Rudolf
State
State [addendum]
Statistics, Foundations of
Stebbing, Lizzie Susan
Stefanini, Luigi
Steffens, Henrich
Stein, Edith
Steiner, Rudolf
Stephen, Leslie
Stern, Louis William
Stevenson, Charles L.
Stewart, Dugald
Stillingfleet, Edward
Stirner, Max
Stöhr, Adolf
Stoicism
Stout, George Frederick
Strato and Stratonism
Strauss, David Friedrich
Strawson, Peter Frederick
String Theory
Structuralism, Mathematical
Structuralism and Post-structuralism
Stumpf, Karl
Sturzo, Luigi
Suárez, Francisco
Subject and Predicate

Subjectivist Epistemology
Subjectivity
Sublime, The
Substance and Attribute
Sufism
Suhrawardī, Shihāb al-Dīn Yaḥyā
Suhrawardī, Shihāb al-Dīn Yaḥyā
    [addendum]
Suicide
Sulzer, Johann Georg
Sumner, William Graham
Supervenience
Suppes, Patrick
Suso, Heinrich
Swedenborg, Emanuel
Swift, Jonathan
Swineshead, Richard
Sylvester of Ferrara, Francis
Sympathy and Empathy
Synonymity
Synonymity [addendum]
Syntactical and Semantical Categories
Syntactical and Semantical Categories
    [addendum]
Syntax

T

Tagore, Rabindranath
Taine, Hippolyte-Adolphe
Tarski, Alfred
Tarski, Alfred [addendum]
Tauler, Johannes
Taylor, Alfred Edward
Teilhard de Chardin, Pierre
Teleological Argument for the
    Existence of God
Teleological Argument for the
    Existence of God [addendum]
Teleological Ethics
Teleology
Teleology [addendum]
Telesio, Bernardino
Tennant, Frederick Robert
Tense
Teresa of Ávila, St.
Terrorism
Tertullian, Quintus Septimius Florens
Testimony
Tetens, Johann Nicolaus
Thales of Miletus
Theism, Arguments For and Against

Themistius
Theodoric of Chartres
Theophrastus
Theories and Theoretical Terms
Thinking
Thomas à Kempis
Thomas Aquinas, St.
Thomasius, Christian
Thomas of York
Thomism
Thomism [addendum]
Thomson, Judith Jarvis
Thoreau, Henry David
Thought Experiments in Science
Thucydides
Thümmig, Ludwig Philipp
Tillich, Paul
Time
Time, Consciousness of
Time, Being, and Becoming
Time in Continental Philosophy
Time in Physics
Timon of Phlius
Tindal, Matthew
Toland, John
Toleration
Toletus, Francis
Tolstoy, Lev (Leo) Nikolaevich
Touch
Toynbee, Arnold Joseph
Traditionalism
Tragedy
Treschow, Niels
Troeltsch, Ernst
Trubetskoi, Evgenii Nikolaevich
Trubetskoi, Nikolai Sergeevich
Trubetskoi, Sergei Nikolaevich
Truth
Truth and Falsity in Indian
    Philosophy
Truthlikeness
Tschirnhaus, Ehrenfried Walter von
Turgot, Anne Robert Jacques, Baron
    de L'Aulne
Turing, Alan M.
Twardowski, Kazimierz
Type Theory

U

Ugliness
Ulrich (Engelbert) of Strasbourg

Unamuno y Jugo, Miguel de
Unconscious
Underdetermination Thesis, Duhem-
    Quine Thesis
Unity and Disunity of Science
Universal Properties in Indian
    Philosophical Traditions
Universals, A Historical Survey
Utilitarianism
Utilitarianism [addendum]
Utopias and Utopianism

V

Vagueness
Vaihinger, Hans
Vailati, Giovanni
Valentinus and Valentinianism
Valéry, Paul
Valla, Lorenzo
Value and Valuation
Value and Valuation [addendum]
Van Fraassen, Bas
Vanini, Giulio Cesare
Varisco, Bernardino
Varona y Pera, Enrique José
Vasconcelos, José
Vasquez, Gabriel
Vasubandhu
Vauvenargues, Luc de Clapiers,
    Marquis de
Vaz Ferreira, Carlos
Veblen, Thorstein Bunde
Venn, John
Verifiability Principle
Verifiability Principle [addendum]
Vico, Giambattista
Violence
Virtue and Vice
Virtue Epistemology
Virtue Ethics
Visual Arts, Theory of the
Vitalism
Vitoria, Francisco de
Vives, Juan Luis
Vlastos, Gregory
Volition
Volney, Constantin-François de
    Chasseboeuf, Comte de
Volski, Stanislav
Voltaire, François-Marie Arouet de

Voluntarism
Vysheslavtsev, Boris Petrovich

W

Wahle, Richard
Wallace, Alfred Russel
Wang Bi
Wang Chong
Wang Fuzhi
Wang Yang-ming
Watsuji Tetsurō
Wayland, Francis
Weakness of the Will
Weber, Alfred
Weber, Max
Weil, Simone
Westermarck, Edward Alexander
Weyl, (Claus Hugo) Hermann
Whately, Richard
Whewell, William
Whichcote, Benjamin
Whitehead, Alfred North
Why
Wiggins, David
Wilde, Oscar Fingal O'Flahertie Wills
William of Auvergne
William of Champeaux

William of Conches
William of Moerbeke
William of Ockham
William of Sherwood
Williams, Bernard
Wilson, Edward O.
Winckelmann, Johann Joachim
Windelband, Wilhelm
Wisdom
Wisdom, (Arthur) John Terence
   Dibben
Wittgenstein, Ludwig Josef Johann
Wittgenstein, Ludwig Josef Johann
   [addendum1]
Wittgenstein, Ludwig Josef Johann
   [addendum2]
Wodeham, Adam
Wolff, Christian
Wollaston, William
Wollheim, Richard
Wollstonecraft, Mary
Women in the History of Philosophy
Woodbridge, Frederick James Eugene
Woodger, Joseph Henry
Woolston, Thomas
Wright, Chauncey
Wright, Georg Henrik von
Wundt, Wilhelm
Wyclyf, John

X

Xenophanes of Colophon
Xenophon
Xenophon [addendum]
Xunzi

Y

Yamaga Sokō
Yamazaki Ansai
Yang Xiong
Yang Zhu

Z

Zabarella, Jacopo
Zen'kovskii, Vasilii Vasil'evich
Zeno of Citium
Zeno of Elea
Zhang Zai
Zhou Dunyi
Zhuangzi
Zhu Xi (Chu Hsi)
Ziehen, Theodor
Zoroastrianism
Zubiri, Xavier

ABBAGNANO, NICOLA

(1901–1990)

Nicola Abbagnano, born in Salerno, was the chief exponent of Italian existentialism, which he defined as a militant and rational "philosophy of the possible." Originally a pupil of Antonio Aliotta at the University of Naples, Abbagnano began teaching at the University of Turin in 1936, where he also for years had been coediting the influential *Rivista di filosofia*. Practically since his first book, *Le sorgenti irrazionali del pensiero* (Naples, 1923), Abbagnano had been advocating a change of philosophical horizon suitable to the problematic nature of human life. This advocacy is reflected in a notable series of historical studies, culminating in the monumental three-volume work *Storia della filosofia* (Turin, 1946–1950; 2nd ed., 1963).

Reacting against the prevailing neo-Hegelianism of Benedetto Croce and Giovanni Gentile in Italy, Abbagnano was influenced, in turn, by Edmund Husserl's phenomenology and, later, by Søren Kierkegaard, Martin Heidegger, and Karl Jaspers; but he revealed in his first attempt at existentialism, *La struttura dell'esistenza* (Turin, 1939), that he was no mere expositor or disciple of German existentialism. In that work he took a stand against Heidegger and Jaspers; and in subsequent writings his polemic was sharpened and extended to French existentialism, including Jean-Paul Sartre on the one hand and Gabriel Marcel, Louis Lavelle, René Le Senne on the other. He groups Sartre with Kierkegaard under German existentialism, and the others under "theological or ontological existentialism."

According to Abbagnano, all forms of existentialism in vogue since Kierkegaard have been self-defeating, since they lead, on examination, to the negation of what is basic to their whole interpretation of human existence: "the primacy of possibility." He discerns two principal directions within the contemporary existentialist movement. One (the left wing) is associated with the early Heidegger, Jaspers, and Sartre; the other (the right wing), with Marcel, Lavelle, and Le Senne. The first group of existentialists negates existence as possibility by reducing human possibilities to *impossibilities*, with everything projected by finite man inevitably foredoomed to fail; the second group negates existence by "surreptitiously" transforming human possibilities into *potentialities*, necessarily destined to succeed in the end.

Even though for Abbagnano the left and the right wings of the existentialist movement are founded, technically, on opposite principles—"the impossibility of the possible" and "the necessity of the possible," respectively—they at least share a common negative ground because each of them, in one way or another, ultimately makes possibility itself impossible. The only valid alternative to "negative existentialism," which for polemical reasons Abbagnano calls "positive existentialism," takes as its guiding principle "the possibility of the possible" or, in Kantian terminology, "transcendental possibility." In this view, an authentic possibility in human life is one that, once it has been chosen or realized, remains open to further choice or realization; that is, continues to be possible. In short, Abbagnano's alternative constitutes an *open possibilism*.

This alternative calls for a clarification and coherent use of the fundamental category of all existentialism: the modal category of possibility. It is perhaps here that Abbagnano made his greatest contribution to the entire existentialist movement, especially since in contemporary logic, as he himself observes, the concept of modality has not been given sufficient "analytic elaboration."

Ever since Aristotle, Abbagnano maintains, there has been confusion concerning the modal categories, particularly with respect to the meaning of the term *possible*. The possible in the empirical sense of what may be has been distinguished from the possible in the purely logical sense of the noncontradictory. But, unfortunately, it has been confused with the "potential" in Aristotle's sense and with the "contingent" in Avicenna's. Since potentiality signifies "*pre*-determination" of the actual, the potential excludes the possible, ex hypothesi. Aristotle did concede that not all potentialities are actualized, but this concession on his part was only introduced "surreptitiously." For, if the potential means what is destined to occur anyway, there is no room for possibility as such. As for Avicenna's concept of the contingent, there is no doubt about its necessitarian character. For he makes the contingent into a species of the necessary—the contingent being, by his own definition, whatever is necessary through another. Hence, it follows that the modal status of the potential and the contingent is not that of possibility, of what may be; but that of necessity, of what must be. Abbagnano concludes that those who think in such terms, including existentialists, are necessitarians in disguise.

Historically, Abbagnano sees his own version of existentialism as an attempt to relate Immanuel Kant and Kierkegaard in a complementary way. In Kant's Table of Categories three pairs of categories are listed under modality: possibility-impossibility, existence-nonexistence, and necessity-contingency. Abbagnano virtually reduces Kant's three pairs of modality categories to one primary pair: the necessary and the nonnecessary. The reason he gives for doing so is that necessity and contingency are not really opposites. Neither are possibility and impossibility. For impossibility is the negative of necessity, not the negative of possibility; what *can't* be at all being the opposite of what *must* be of necessity.

As an existential possibilist, Abbagnano defines existence as possibility, and nonexistence as "non-possibility," not as impossibility. While the nonnecessary excludes the necessary and the impossible, it includes the possible and the nonpossible. This means that man can neither be sure of realizing his conflicting possibilities, nor be sure of the impossibility of their realization. It also means that every concrete possibility open to man has two aspects, a promising (positive) prospect and an inauspicious (negative) aspect. To illustrate, the possibility of knowledge implies the possibility of error. Errors are not "impossible," since we do in fact make them, but they are "non-possible" in the sense that they are unverifiable when put to test. Thus, a double-aspect theory of possibility lies at the heart of Abbagnano's "positive existentialism."

Another distinctive feature of Italian existentialism in general and of Abbagnano's philosophy in particular is the deliberate focus on a problem that was originally foreign to German existentialism; to wit, the problem of value.

Starting with the assumption that the problem of value is the problem of what man *ought to be*, Abbagnano argues in effect that, since the *ought-to-be* is the possible in the normative sense, it is therefore the moral equivalent of the *may-be*, which is the possible in the empirical sense. As a consequence, the logic of possibility coincides with the ethics of possibility, and these two phases of the same problem come together in Abbagnano's possibilistic interpretation of human conduct. This interpretation stresses the "normativity" of human existence, which involves the problem of freedom in all its dimensions. Thus, Abbagnano's existentialism logically unites the complementary categories of possibility and freedom, as is clear from his important volume *Possibilità e libertà* (Turin, 1956).

In the mid-twentieth century, Abbagnano came to characterize the "New Enlightenment," of contemporary philosophy and openly declared his affinities with the neopositivistic and neonaturalistic movements in the Anglo American world. As a result, he developed the empirical and naturalistic strains in his existentialism, emphasizing the methodological connections between possibility as a generic criterion of existence and verifiability as a specific criterion in scientific inquiry. This "transfiguration" of existentialism into scientific methodology is clearly evident in the article on existentialism in *Dizionario di filosofia* (Turin, 1961). However, Abbagnano thought that the romantic "myth of security" in Auguste Comte's positivism, typical of the nineteenth-century mentality, still survives in the scientific utopianism of the Vienna Circle; and although he sympathizes with the later Ludwig Wittgenstein's thesis that the meaning of words depends on their use, he contends that the leader of the analytic movement failed to give a philosophical analysis of the notion of "use" itself. Abbagnano's sympathies with North American naturalism are reflected in his writings on John Dewey and in his review of P. Romanell's volume *Toward a Critical Naturalism* (*Rivista di filosofia* 50 [1959]: 108–109).

See also Aristotle; Avicenna; Comte, Auguste; Croce, Benedetto; Dewey, John; Existentialism; Gentile, Giovanni; Heidegger, Martin; Jaspers, Karl; Kant, Immanuel; Kierkegaard, Søren Aabye; Lavelle, Louis; Le Senne, René; Logical Positivism; Marcel, Gabriel; Naturalism; Possibility; Sartre, Jean-Paul; Scientific Method; Value and Valuation; Wittgenstein, Ludwig Josef Johann.

Bibliography

ADDITIONAL WORKS BY ABBAGNANO

Historical

Il nuovo idealismo inglese e americano. Naples, 1927.
La filosofia di E. Meyerson e la logica dell'identità. Naples: Perrella, 1929.
Guglielmo di Ockham. Lanciano: Carabba, 1931.
La nozione del tempo secondo Aristotele. Lanciano, 1933.
Bernardino Telesio. Milan: Fratelli Bocca, 1941.

Systematic

Introduzione all'esistenzialismo. Milan, 1942.
Filosofia, religione, scienza. Turin: Taylor, 1947.
Esistenzialismo positivo. Turin: Taylor, 1948.
"Contemporary Science and Freedom." *Review of Metaphysics* 5 (3) (1952): 361–378.
Problemi di sociologia. Turin: Taylor, 1959.
"Existentialism in Italy." *Cesare Barbieri Courier* 3 (2) (1961): 12–18.
Critical Existentialism Translated with an introduction by Nino Langiulli. New York: Doubleday, 1969.
Fra il tutto e il nulla. Milan: Rizzoli, 1973.
La saggezza della vita. Milan: Rusconi, 1985.
Scritti esistenzialisti. Turin: UTET, 1988.
Scritti neoilluministici (1948–1965). Turin: UTET, 2001.
The Human Project—The Year 2000. Translated by Bruno Martini e Nino Langiulli. Vol. 119 of the "Value Inquiry Book Series." Amsterdam/New York: Rodopi, 2002.

WORKS ON ABBAGNANO

Bruno Maiorca. *Bibliografia degli scritti di Nicola Abbagnano 1922–1992.* Bari: Laterza, 1993.
Giannini, G. *L'esistenzialismo positivo di N. Abbagnano.* Brescia, 1956.
Langiulli, Nino. *Possibility, Necessity and Existence: Abbagnano and His Predecessors.* Philadelphia: Temple University Press, 1992.
Santucci, Antonio. *Esistenzialismo e filosofia italiana.* Bologna: Mulino, 1959.
Simona, Maria Angela. *La notion de liberté dans l'existentialisme positif de Nicola Abbagnano.* Fribourg, Switzerland: Editions Universitaires, 1962.

Patrick Romanell **(1967)**
Bibliography updated by Thomas Nenon (2005)

ABELARD, PETER
(1079–1142)

Peter Abelard has been famous since the fourteenth century for his exchange of love letters with Héloïse, his former wife, written when he was a monk and she a nun. Nineteenth-century historians saw him as a rationalist critic of traditional Christian doctrine and a forerunner of modernity. More recently, Abelard's originality and power as a philosopher have come to be appreciated.

Abelard's working life splits into two main, slightly overlapping periods. From about 1100 until about 1125, his activity as a thinker and teacher revolved around the ancient logical texts available in Latin at that time—the so-called *logica vetus* ("Old Logic"). But from about 1120, Abelard started to become strongly interested in questions about Christian doctrine, to which he gradually came to give an increasingly ethical emphasis. The important works of the first phase of his career were thus the *Dialectica* (c. 1113–1116), a logical textbook, and the *Logica Ingredientibus* (c. 1119), commentaries on ancient logical texts (along with a shorter logical commentary, the *Logica Nostrorum Petitioni Sociorum*, from the mid-1120s). To the second phase belong his *Theologia*, mainly a philosophical investigation of the Trinity, which exists in three different, much altered versions: *Theologia Summi Boni* (1121), *Theologia Christiana* (c. 1125), *Theologia Scholarium* (c. 1133–1134); biblical commentaries, and a set of *Sentences* (c. 1134), which record his lectures on a wide range of theological topics; the *Collationes* (Comparisons), an imaginary dialogue between a Philosopher, a Jew, and a Christian (probably c. 1130); and the *Scito teipsum* (Know yourself!) or, as it is sometimes called, Abelard's *Ethics* (1138).

Although the division of his career into two phases was partly occasioned by his castration in 1117 (at the hands of ruffians hired by Héloïse's uncle, the canon of Notre-Dame), which put a violent end to his marriage, and his subsequent decision to become a monk of Saint-Denis, Abelard remained a teacher for most of his life. After studying with two of the most celebrated logicians of the time, Roscelin of Compiègne and William of Champeaux, both of whom later considered him an enemy, Abelard set up his own school and finally became the schoolmaster in Paris. He continued to teach as a monk of Saint-Denis and later, when he left that monastery to set up his own hermetic-monastic community. After a period as an unsuccessful reforming abbot of a remote Breton monastery, Abelard returned to the now numerous and flourishing Paris schools in the 1130s. He spent his final years at Cluny and its dependency, after his activity as a teacher was ended by his condemnation at the Council of Sens (1140).

LOGIC

The *logica vetus* included just two texts by Aristotle himself, the *Categories and On Interpretation*, along with the *Isagoge* (Introduction) to the *Categories* by Porphyry (c. 232–305 CE), and texts by Boethius (c. 475–c. 524 CE) on categorical and hypothetical syllogism, division, and topical inference. From this unpromising set of authorities, Abelard was able not merely to explore areas of formal logic untouched by Aristotle, but also to elaborate a whole metaphysics and semantics.

Ancient and medieval logicians worked in natural language, rather than devising a special logical symbolism. One of the hallmarks of Abelard's approach to logic was his awareness of the ambiguities in many ordinary sentences and the need to distinguish them carefully when constructing a logical argument. Abelard was not the first medieval logician to notice this point (Anselm of Canterbury, for instance, was an eleventh-century forerunner), but he placed an emphasis on it that would be taken up by many of his medieval successors. Consider, for instance, a sentence such as "Possibly the standing man sits." Abelard is quick to observe that it can be read in a composite sense (*This is possible: that the man is standing-and-sitting*) or in a divided sense (*The man is standing, and it is possible that he is sitting*). Although this distinction is made by Aristotle in his *Sophistical Refutations*, Abelard had already used it very widely in his *Dialectica* before he read it in the Aristotelian text.

Moreover, Abelard used this approach as the basis for devising—as Christopher Martin has shown—a gen-

uinely propositional logic, to complement the term logic of Aristotelian syllogistic. In antiquity, the Stoics developed a propositional logic, and traces of their theory are found in Boethius's writings on topical argument and hypothetical syllogisms. Boethius, however, clearly neither developed a propositional logic nor understood it. His hypothetical syllogisms (for instance, "If it is day, it is light. It is day. So it is light") look like arguments in propositional logic, but Boethius takes them as being based on the relation between the terms *day* and *light*; and he cannot grasp the negation of a conditional such as, "If it is day, it is light," except as the negation of one of the terms ("If it is day, it is not light"). By contrast, Abelard has a clear notion of propositional negation (It is not the case that: If it is day, it is light), and it governs his reconstruction of the theory of topical argument. For Boethius the theory of topics is a sort of logic for constructing real arguments on the basis of commonly accepted maxims, which range from basic logical principles to (fairly dubious) rules of thumb, such as "What the experts think about something is true." Abelard retains only those maxims which underwrite conditionals that are not just logically necessary, but where the sense of the consequent is contained in that of the antecedent (for example, Abelard accepts "Whatever is predicated of the species is predicated of the genus," on which is based, for instance, "If it is a man, it is an animal"). The resulting system of propositional logic turns out to be more like some modern connexive logics than classical modern propositional calculus.

METAPHYSICS AND SEMANTICS

Aristotle's *Categories* provided Abelard and his contemporaries with a basic metaphysics. It proposes that the items that make up the world are either substances, which exist independently, or non-substances, which exist only in dependence on substances; and that they are either particular or universal. For example, John Marenbon is a particular substance and man (in general) a universal one; the whiteness of John's skin and his rationality are individual non-substances, and whiteness and rationality (in general) are universal non-substances. Abelard, however, is a nominalist. Following, but exploring in more depth, a lead given by others, including Roscelin, he contended that everything which exists is a particular. There are no universal things, he argued, because to be universal a thing would have to be both one and shared between many in a way that is impossible. Abelard had, then, to show how the basic structure of the universe can be explained solely in terms of particular substance and non-substances.

Unlike many more recent nominalists, Abelard accepted that the best scientific description (Aristotle's, he thought) cuts nature at the joints: It is a fundamental truth, he believed, that some things are human beings and others dogs, and that human beings are human because they are mortal, rational animals. To be a mortal, rational animal, indeed, is to have the "status" of man, Abelard said. But, he quickly added, a status is not a thing. Every human, then, is alike in having his or her own particular rationality, mortality, and animality. But what about these particular non-substance things? They are, in Abelard's view, real items on an ontological checklist because, he says, it might have been the case that the particularity rationality R1 by which John is rational was the rationality by which William—who is in fact rational by rationality R^2—is rational, and vice versa; and so R^1 cannot be explained away as just being John insofar as he is rational. The non-substance particulars are dependent, however, because they cannot exist except in some substance or other, and they cannot exist in one substance and then afterward in another. Just as Abelard has to explain what it is that makes John and William both human beings, he must explain too what it is that makes R^1 and R^2 both rationalities. But he does not, as might be expected, try to speak of a status of being rational—analyzing rationality into certain patterns of behavior, for instance. Rather, he seems to admit, in all but name, that there is a universal rationality.

Abelard's nominalism also poses a semantic problem with regard to universal words. It is important to grasp that this problem is *not* one about reference. Once a kind-word is first imposed, it automatically refers to every particular which is really of that kind, even if the impositor himself has merely a vague or inaccurate idea of the internal structure which characterizes the species in question. (This feature, as Peter King [1982] has pointed out, brings Abelard's semantics uncannily close to the thought of contemporary philosophers such as Kripke.) By contrast, a word's signification is, for medieval authors in general, a causal, psychological notion: a word w signifies x by causing a thought of x in the listener's mind. The signification of "human being" in "John is a human being" is clearly universal: the x of which it causes a thought is a universal human being, not a particular one. But how can there be such an x, if every thing is particular? Abelard's answer is to say that universal words cause a mental image, a confused conception of, for instance, what humans have in common, which is not the image of any particular man. Such confused conceptions are not things, and it is these conceptions which universal words signify. The conceptions are not things, because they are not thoughts themselves (which Abelard would class as particular non-substance things), but the contents of thoughts—objects in the world envisaged, to use an anachronistic expression, under a certain mode of presentation.

Abelard also had a theory about the semantics of sentences. A sentence signifies neither the things to which its component words refer, nor the thought they produce, but rather its *dictum* (meaning "what it says"). At first sight, Abelard seems to mean by *dictum* what modern philosophers call a proposition, and he does indeed characterize those logical connections that he understands propositionally—as, for example, between the antecedent and consequent of a conditional—as holding between *dicta*. But it is not quite clear whether *dicta* are truth-bearers or rather, like facts, truth-makers. Moreover, Abelard insists that *dicta*—along with statuses and common conceptions—are not things. But whether he can coherently deny the reality of *dicta*, while at the same time using them to underpin his account of the workings of the universe, remains doubtful. Nonetheless, Abelard's metaphysics is bold and original, and it ranges into many areas other than those discussed here, such as parts and wholes, relations, the physical constitution of objects and their sensible properties, and the laws of nature.

ETHICS

Like any Christian thinker, Abelard held that every detail of world history is providentially ordained. Unlike the great theologians of the thirteenth century, such as Thomas Aquinas and John Duns Scotus, he did not accept that God has any freedom in choosing what the course of providence should be: God, he argues, must choose whatever is best to happen, and that, he believes, leaves no space for alternatives. Yet there is room, Abelard thought (contradicting the Platonizing tradition of Augustine and Anselm) for the existence of genuinely evil things, because—as he explains, citing the distinction between things and *dicta*—it is good that there is evil.

If God ordains the universe so that every human action, good or evil, contributes to the best providence, it is clear that ethical judgment cannot be based on consequences. Abelard is very often seen as a moral theorist who, rather, concentrates entirely on intentions, and subscribes to a subjective view of morality. Both aspects of this characterization need qualification. Following Augustine's lead, almost all medieval thinkers based moral judgment on intentions. For instance, Abelard's immediate predecessors and contemporaries saw sinning as a stage-by-stage process of intending—a person begins to sin once he entertains a temptation to perform a forbidden act; as he thinks about it with pleasure and plans how to put it into effect, the sin becomes graver, and it is more serious still when he actually performs the act. By contrast, for Abelard someone is guilty of sinning when, and only when, he consents to the sin—when he is ready to perform it and will do so unless thwarted. Up until that moment, he is not guilty, and, once that moment is reached, his guilt is complete: performing the act will not increase it.

Abelard's account of what determines whether an action is sinful or not seems at first sight to be subjective. A person sins, he says, by showing contempt for God. It sounds, from this definition, as if it is the mere subjective state of someone's mind, and not what he does or plans to do, that makes him a sinner. But, for Abelard, one shows contempt for God precisely by consenting to an action one knows is divinely forbidden. Sinners do not usually want to perform a forbidden action because it is forbidden; rather, they perform it in spite of the fact that God forbids it, and very often with the fervent wish that it were licit. Moreover, he does not think that it is a matter of guesswork to decide which acts God forbids. Christians and Jews have scriptural revelation to guide them; but, in any case, Abelard believed, all people in all places and in all times, apart from children and the mentally incapable, are able to grasp natural law, which teaches them the fundamental rules for behavior ordained by God. Abelard would not hesitate, therefore, to say that, for example, it is and was always wrong for a mentally normal adult to commit adultery (unless, in some way, he is unaware that it is in this case adultery) because he could not fail to know that adultery is divinely forbidden and that, therefore, it shows contempt to God to perform it.

Abelard's account of acting well is less fully developed than his treatment of sinning. He takes over a list of four virtues (ultimately from Plato's *Republic*) from Cicero: prudence, justice, courage, and temperance. He does not, however, use these virtues to provide a view of the good life for human beings. Rather, he sees justice as the central virtue, by which a person acts in accord with God's commands as known through revelation or natural law. Prudence is a precondition for being just, but not a virtue itself. Courage and temperance are props of justice. A person may be deflected from just action by fear or by desire for pleasure; courage makes him stand firm,

despite what threatens him; temperance makes him resist the blandishments of pleasure.

As this description suggests, Abelard tends to think of morally good action as a hard-won victory over sinning, which is usually the easier or the more pleasant choice. Yet he also wants to insist that there is something deficient in goodness about actions which, although carried out from excellent motives, fail to achieve their intended good effect; as, for example, if a person works hard in order to provide for the poor or the sick, but his plans are never realized. Abelard's ethical theory is further complicated by a somewhat unexpected twist. He believes that judgments made by human judges should be based on a utilitarian evaluation of the punishments given. A woman who entirely unintentionally smothers her baby (whom she was trying to keep warm) should be punished severely, although she has committed no sin, so as to discourage others from making the same mistake.

PHILOSOPHY OF RELIGION

Modern interpreters of Abelard tend to play down any tension between his rationalism and Christian belief: He used the tools of his logic, they say, to analyse Christian doctrines and criticize heretical distortions of them, but he was fully willing to accept the ultimate mysteriousness of doctrines such as the Trinity. Yet there is good reason to see Abelard's main project in the works of his last decade as being the presentation of a rationalized Christianity, which in important ways did not accord with the accepted beliefs of his time.

Abelard's conception of a universal natural law was not merely a foundation for his ethical theory. People at all times and in all places, he believed, have been able to grasp the fact the God exists, and that God is triune. Supposedly pagan sources, such as Plato, the Sibylls, and the writings attributed to Hermes Trismegistus, provide better testimony, he believes, to the Trinity than anything in the Old or even the New Testament. Although Abelard—under pressure to conform to an orthodoxy which, as it turned out, he was in any case accused of infringing—might accept a certain element of inexplicable mystery in the doctrine of divine triunity, he elaborated in the different versions of his *Theologia* a complex theory of sameness and difference, which seems to have been designed to explain in terms of logic how something can be three and yet one. And he considered that God's triune nature emerged just from thinking about the attributes an omniperfect being must have: "For God to be three persons—Father, Son and Holy Spirit—is," he explains at the beginning of the *Theologia Summi Boni*, "as if we were to say that the divine substance is powerful, wise and benign. ...." This attitude was part of Abelard's general, though nuanced, rejection of there being anything praiseworthy in the acceptance by faith of truths that are not understood, and of the limited function he gives to revelation. For most of his contemporaries, the Jews, to whom the Old Law had been revealed, were far closer to a grasp of the truth than the ancient pagans. For Abelard, the pagan philosophers, without revelation but using natural law, were able to live highly virtuous lives and to reach a better understanding of God than most of the Jews.

Abelard did not, however, think that every important theological truth could be grasped by reason, without revelation. In particular, only by revelation can people know of Christ's life and his death, and without this knowledge, he thought, no one can be saved. But Abelard went on to argue that God would reveal what was necessary for salvation to anyone who lived well, and also to give a rationalistic explanation of why it was necessary to know about Christ's crucifixion—because it set an example of love, indispensable for being able to overcome temptations. Similarly, while Abelard broadly accepted the biblical accounts of heaven and hell, he was one of the few medieval thinkers to insist that they should not be interpreted literally.

AFTER ABELARD

One of the schools of later twelfth-century philosophy, the *nominales*, probably consisted of Abelard's followers. But, apart from his letters to Héloïse, Abelard was not one of the authors who was much read after 1200. Elements of his approach to logic were absorbed into the developing medieval curriculum, although many of his subtlest ideas seem never to have been used. The type of doctrinal problems raised by him influenced the *Sentences*, written by Peter Lombard in the 1150s, and through this work, which became the standard textbook, the whole tradition of later medieval theology. Abelard's effect on the positions and arguments they developed was very limited, however, because the university theologians had their outlook formed by a reading of the whole range of Aristotle's philosophy and the Arabic commentary tradition. In many ways, however, Abelard's approach to metaphysics and the philosophy of religion, with its basis in logical and linguistic analysis, is closer to today's philosophical tastes than the grand systems of the thirteenth and early fourteenth-century philosophers.

See also Aristotelianism; Logic, History of: Ancient Logic; Logic, History of: Medieval (European) Logic; William of Champeaux.

Bibliography

WORKS BY ABELARD

Selected Latin Texts

Petri Abaelardi Dialectica, edited by Lambertus M. de Rijk. 2nd ed. Assen: Van Gorcum, 1970.

Petri Abaelardi opera theologica I–III, edited by Eligius Buytaert (and Constant J. Mews, vol. III). Turnhout: Brepols, 1967. Corpus christianorum, continuatio mediaeualis 13 (including the *Theologia* in its different versions).

Peter Abaelards philosophische Schriften, I. 3, edited by Bernhard Geyer. Münster: Aschendorff, 1927 (Beiträge zur Geschichte der Philosophie und Theologie des Mittlalters 21). Logical commentaries.

Sententiae magistri Petri Abaelardi (Sententie Hermanni), edited by Sandro Buzzetti. Florence: La nuova Italia, 1983.

English Translations

Five Texts on the Mediaeval Problem of Universals: Porphyry, Boethius, Abelard, Duns Scotus, Ockham, edited by Paul V. Spade. Indianapolis and Cambridge: Hackett, 1994. Extract from *Logica Ingredientibus*.

Peter Abelard's "Collationes," edited by J. Marenbon and G. Orlandi. Oxford: Oxford University Press, 2001. Latin and English.

Peter Abelard's "Ethics," edited by David E. Luscombe. Oxford: Oxford University Press, 1971. Latin and English.

WORKS ABOUT ABELARD

Brower, Jeffrey E., and Kevin Guilfoy, eds. *The Cambridge Companion to Abelard*. Cambridge, U.K., and New York: Cambridge University Press, 2004.

Clanchy, Michael. *Abelard: A Medieval Life*. Oxford: Blackwell, 1997.

De Rijk, Lambertus M. "Peter Abelard's Semantics and his Doctrine of Being." *Vivarium* 24 (1986): 85–128.

King, Peter O. "Peter Abailard and the Problem of Universals." PhD diss. Princeton University, 1982.

Marenbon, John. *The Philosophy of Peter Abelard*. Cambridge, U.K.: Cambridge University Press, 1997.

Martin, Christopher J. "Embarrassing Arguments and Surprising Conclusions in the Development of Theories of the Conditional in the Twelfth Century." In *Gilbert de Poitiers et ses contemporains*, edited by Jean Jolivet and Alain De Libera, 377–400. Naples: Bibliopolis, 1987.

Martin, Christopher J. "Logic." In *The Cambridge Companion to Abelard*, edited by Jeffrey E. Brower and Kevin Guilfoy, 158–199. Cambridge, U.K., and New York: Cambridge University Press, 2004.

Mews, Constant J. *Abelard and Heloise*. Oxford: Oxford University Press, 2005.

Mews, Constant J. *Peter Abelard*. Aldershot: Variorum, 1995.

Tweedale, Martin. *Abailard on Universals*. Amsterdam and New York: North Holland, 1976.

John Marenbon (2005)

ABORTION

The claims to which partisans on both sides of the "abortion" issue appeal seem, if one is not thinking of the abortion issue, close to self-evident, or they appear to be easily defensible. The case against abortion (Beckwith 1993) rests on the proposition that there is a very strong presumption that ending another human life is seriously wrong. Almost everyone who is not thinking about the abortion issue would agree. There are good arguments for the view that fetuses are both living and human. ("Fetus" is generally used in the philosophical literature on abortion to refer to a human organism from the time of conception to the time of birth.) Thus, it is easy for those opposed to abortion to think that only the morally depraved or the seriously confused could disagree with them.

Standard pro-choice views appeal either to the proposition that women have the right to make decisions concerning their own bodies or to the proposition that fetuses are not yet persons. Both of these propositions seem either to be platitudes or to be straightforwardly defensible. Thus, it is easy for pro-choicers to believe that only religious fanatics or dogmatic conservatives could disagree. This explains, at least in part, why the abortion issue has created so much controversy. The philosophical debate regarding abortion has been concerned largely with subjecting these apparently obvious claims to the analytical scrutiny philosophers ought to give to them.

Consider first the standard argument against abortion. One frequent objection to the claim that fetuses are both human and alive is that we do not know when life begins. The reply to this objection is that fetuses both grow and metabolize and whatever grows and metabolizes is alive. Some argue that the beginning of life should be defined in terms of the appearance of brain function, because death is now defined in terms of the absence of brain function (Brody 1975). This would permit abortion within at least eight weeks after conception. However, because death is, strictly speaking, defined in terms of the irreversible loss of brain function, the mere absence of brain function is not a sufficient condition for the absence of life. Accordingly, the claim that the presence of brain function is a necessary condition for the presence of life is left unsupported. Also, the standard antiabortion argument is criticized on the ground that we do not know when the soul enters the body. However, such a criticism is plainly irrelevant to the standard, apparently secular, antiabortion argument we are considering.

The Thomistic premise that it is always wrong intentionally to end an innocent human life is used by the Vatican to generate the prohibition of abortion. This premise is often attacked for presupposing "absolutism." This Vatican principle seems to render immoral active euthanasia, even when a patient is in excruciating, unrelievable pain or in persistent coma; it even seems to render immoral ending the life of a human cancer-cell culture. In none of these cases is the individual whose life is ended victimized. Thus, the Vatican principle seems most implausible.

Opponents of abortion are better off appealing to the weaker proposition that there is a very strong presumption against ending a human life (Beckwith 1993). Because this presumption can be overridden when the victim has no interest in continued life, use of this premise provides a way of dealing with the above counterexamples. However, this tactic provides room for another objection to the antiabortion argument. Some pro-choicers have argued that insentient fetuses have no interest in continued life. Because what is insentient does not care about what is done to it and because what does not care about what is done to it cannot have interests, insentient fetuses cannot have an interest in living. Therefore, abortion of insentient fetuses is not wrong (Steinbock 1992, Sumner 1981, and Warren 1987).

If this argument were sound, then it would also show that patients who are in temporary coma, and therefore insentient, do not have an interest in living. M. A. Warren (1987) attempts to avoid this counterexample by making the neurological capacity for sentience a necessary condition for having any interests at all and, therefore, for having an interest in living. This move does not solve the problem, however. Because the argument in favor of permitting the abortion of insentient fetuses generated an untenable conclusion, that argument must be rejected. Because the argument rests on an equivocation between what one takes an interest in and what is in one's interest, there are even better reasons for rejecting it. Accordingly, this objection to the standard antiabortion argument is unsupported.

The classic antiabortion argument is subject to a major theoretical difficulty. Antiabortionists have tried vigorously to avoid the charge that they are trying to force their religious views upon persons who do not share them. However, the moral rule to which the standard antiabortion argument appeals obtains its particular force in the abortion dispute because it singles out members of the species *Homo sapiens* (rather than persons or sentient beings or beings with a future like ours, for example). It is difficult to imagine how the *Homo sapiens* rule could be defended against its competitors without relying upon the standard theological exegesis of the Sixth Commandment and upon the divine-command theory on which its moral standing rests. This leads to two problems. First, arguments against divine-command ethical theory seem compelling. Second, when arguments based on divine-command theory are transported into the Constitutional realm, First Amendment problems arise.

The philosophical literature contains two major kinds of pro-choice strategies. The personhood strategy appeals to the proposition that no fetuses are persons. If this is so, then, because a woman plainly has the right to control her own body if she does not directly harm another person, abortion is morally permissible. However, Judith Thomson (1971) has argued that a woman's right to control her own body can justify the right to an abortion in some situations even if fetuses are persons. This second strategy rests on the claim that no one's right to life entails the right to a life-support system provided by another's body even if use of that life-support system is the only way to save one's life. Thus, even if opponents of abortion are successful in establishing that fetuses have the right to life, they have not thereby established that any fetus has the right to anyone else's uterus.

It is widely believed that Thomson's strategy can justify abortion in cases of rape and in cases where the life of a pregnant woman is threatened by pregnancy (Warren 1973). There is much less unanimity concerning other cases, because it is generally believed that, if we create a predicament for others, we have special obligations to help them in their predicament. Furthermore, let us grant that A's right to life does not entail A's right to B's body even when A needs B's body to sustain life. Presumably, by parity of reasoning, B's right to B's body does not entail B's right to take A's life even if A's continuing to live severely restricts B's choices. Thus, we have a standoff, and the winner from the moral point of view will be that individual with the strongest right. Although Thomson's strategy has been widely discussed and raises interesting questions about the duty of beneficence, questions both about its philosophical underpinnings and about its scope suggest that philosophically inclined pro-choicers would be better off with a personhood strategy.

No doubt, this is why personhood strategies have dominated the pro-choice philosophical literature. Such strategies come in many varieties (Engelhardt 1986; Feinberg 1986; Tooley 1972, 1983, and 1994; and Warren 1973, 1987). Warren's 1973 version is most famous. She argued that reflection on our concept of person suggests

that in order to be a person one must possess at least more than one of the following five characteristics: consciousness, rationality, self-motivated activity, the capacity to communicate, and the presence of a concept of self. Since no fetus possesses any of these characteristics, no fetus is a person. If only persons have full moral rights, then fetuses lack the full right to life. Therefore, abortion may never be forbidden for the sake of a fetus.

One might object to such a strategy on the ground that, since fetuses are potential persons, the moral importance of personhood guarantees them a full place in the moral community. The best reply to such an objection is that the claim that X's have a right to Y does not entail that potential X's have a right to Y (think of potential voters and potential presidents; Feinberg 1986).

Although personhood theorists (like antiabortionists) tend to say little about the moral theories on which their views rest (Engelhardt 1986 is an interesting exception), presumably most personhood theorists will turn out to be, when driven to the wall, social-contract theorists. Such theories, according to which morality is a self-interested agreement concerning rules of conduct among rational agents, tend to have problems accounting for the moral standing of those who are not rational agents—beings such as animals, young children, the retarded, the psychotic, and the senile. Thus, the personhood defense of the pro-choice position tends to have problems that are the inverse of those of the classic antiabortion argument.

Both standard antiabortion and personhood accounts appeal, in the final analysis, to the characteristics fetuses manifest at the time they are fetuses as a basis for their arguments concerning the ethics of abortion. This appeal may be a mistake both defenses share. My premature death would be a great misfortune to me because it would deprive me of a future of value. This is both generalizable and arguably the basis for the presumptive wrongness of ending human life. Such a view seems to imply that abortion is seriously immoral, seems to have a defensible intuitive basis, and seems to avoid the counterexamples that threaten alternative views (Marquis 1989). However, this view is subject to two major objections. One could argue that the difference between the relation of fetuses to their futures and the relation of adults to their futures would explain why adults are wronged by losing their futures but fetuses are not (McInerney 1990). One might also argue that because human sperm and ova have valuable futures like ours, the valuable future criterion for the wrongness of killing is too broad (Norcross 1990). Not everyone believes these objections are conclusive.

See also Animal Rights and Welfare; Bioethics; Rights.

Bibliography

Beckwith, Francis J. *Politically Correct Death: Answering Arguments for Abortion Rights*. Grand Rapids, MI: Baker, 1993.

Boonin, David. *A Defense of Abortion*. Cambridge, U.K.: Cambridge University Press, 2003.

Brody, Baruch. *Abortion and the Sanctity of Human Life: A Philosophical View*. Cambridge, MA: MIT Press, 1975.

Burgess, J. A., and S. A. Tawia. "When Did You First Begin to Feel It? Locating the Beginning of Human Consciousness." *Bioethics* 10 (1) (1996): 1–26. An extremely useful discussion for sentience-based views.

Davis, Nancy. "Abortion and Self-Defense." In *Abortion: Moral and Legal Perspectives*, edited by Jay L. Garfield and Patricia Hennessey, pp. 186–210. Amherst: The University of Massachusetts Press, 1984.

Dworkin, Ronald. *Life's Dominion: An Argument about Abortion, Euthanasia, and Individual Freedom*. New York: Knopf, 1993.

Engelhardt, H. Tristam, Jr. *The Foundations of Bioethics*. New York: Oxford University Press, 1986. An attempt to place the personhood strategy in the context of an ethical theory and other issues in bioethics.

English, Jane. "Abortion and the Concept of a Person" (1975). In *Arguing about Abortion*, edited by Lewis M. Schwartz, pp. 159–198. Belmont, CA: Wadsworth, 1993.

Feinberg, J. "Abortion." In *Matters of Life and Death: New Introductory Essays in Moral Philosophy*. 2nd ed., edited by Tom Regan. New York: Random House, 1986. The best account of the personhood strategy in a single essay.

Ford, Norman M. *When Did I begin? Conception of the Human Individual in History, Philosophy and Science*. Cambridge, U.K.: Cambridge University Press, 1988. An excellent discussion of issues relevant to the moral status of the early embryo.

Hare, R. M. "Abortion and the Golden Rule" (1975). In his *Essays on Bioethics*, pp. 147–167. Oxford: Clarendon, 1993.

Hare, R. M. "A Kantian Approach to Abortion" (revised version, 1989). In his *Essays on Bioethics*, pp. 168–184. Oxford: Clarendon, 1993.

Hursthouse, Rosalind. "Virtue Theory and Abortion." *Philosophy and Public Affairs* 20 (3) (Summer 1991): 223–246.

Kamm, F. M. *Creation and Abortion: A Study in Moral and Legal Philosophy*. New York: Oxford University Press, 1992. A defense of Thomson's strategy.

Lee, Patrick. *Abortion and Unborn Human Life*. Washington, DC: The Catholic University of America Press, 1996. One of the best book-length cases against abortion.

Marquis, Donald. "Why Abortion Is Immoral." *Journal of Philosophy* 86 (1989): 183–202.

McInerney, Peter. "Does a Fetus Already Have a Future-Like-Ours?" *Journal of Philosophy* 87 (1990): 265–268.

McDonagh, Eileen L. *Breaking the Abortion Deadlock: From Choice to Consent*. Oxford: Oxford University Press, 1996. Defends a self-defense variant of Thomson's strategy.

Norcross, A. "Killing, Abortion, and Contraception: A Reply to Marquis." *Journal of Philosophy* 87 (1990): 268–277.

Pojman, Louis J., and Francis J. Beckwith, eds. *The Abortion Controversy: 25 Years after* Roe v. Wade: *A Reader*. 2nd ed. Belmont, CA: Wadsworth, 1998. An excellent anthology.

Quinn, Warren. "Abortion: Identity and Loss." In his *Morality and Action*, pp. 20–51. Cambridge, U.K.: Cambridge University Press, 1993.

Schwarz, Stephen. *The Moral Question of Abortion*. Chicago: Loyola University Press, 1990. A useful book-length argument against abortion.

Steinbock, Bonnie. *Life before Birth: The Moral and Legal Status of Embryos and Fetuses*. New York: Oxford University Press, 1992. A sentience strategy.

Stone, Jim. "Why Potentiality Matters." *Canadian Journal of Philosophy* 17 (4) (December 1987): 815–830.

Sumner, L. W. *Abortion and Moral Theory*. Princeton, NJ: Princeton University Press, 1981. A sentience strategy.

Thomson, Judith Jarvis. "A Defense of Abortion." *Philosophy and Public Affairs* 1 (1971): 47–66. A classic paper.

Tooley, M. "Abortion and Infanticide." *Philosophy and Public Affairs* 2 (1972): 37–65. A classic paper.

Tooley, M. *Abortion and Infanticide*. New York: Oxford University Press, 1983.

Tooley, M. "In Defense of Abortion and Infanticide." In *The Abortion Controversy: A Reader*, edited by L. P. Poman and F. J. Beckwith. Boston: Jones and Bartlett, 1994.

Warren, Mary Anne. "The Abortion Issue." In *Health Care Ethics: An Introduction*, edited by D. VanDeVeer and T. Regan. Philadelphia: Temple University Press, 1987. A sentience strategy combined with a personhood strategy.

Warren, Mary Anne. "On the Moral and Legal Status of Abortion." *Monist* 57 (1973): 43–61. A classic paper.

Don Marquis (1996)

Bibliography updated by David Boonin (2005)

ABSOLUTE, THE

"The Absolute" is a term used by philosophers to signify the ultimate reality regarded as one and yet as the source of variety; as complete, or perfect, and yet as not divorced from the finite, imperfect world. The term was introduced into the philosophical vocabulary at the very end of the eighteenth century by Friedrich Wilhelm Joseph von Schelling and Georg Wilhelm Friedrich Hegel and was naturalized into English by Samuel Taylor Coleridge as early as 1809–1810 in *The Friend*. Later in the century it was an important term in the writings of such Idealist philosophers as James Frederick Ferrier, Francis Herbert Bradley, Bernard Bosanquet, and Josiah Royce.

INTRODUCTION OF THE TERM

One of the sources of the philosophy of the Absolute is the literature about Benedict (Baruch) de Spinoza commencing with Moses Mendelssohn's *Morgenstunden* (1785) and F. H. Jacobi's *Ueber die Lehre des Spinoza in Briefen an den Herrn Moses Mendelssohn* (1785). The expression "the Absolute" does not appear in these books, but there is a discussion of Spinoza's view that God does not transcend the world but is the sole infinite substance in which everything has its being. In the second edition of his book (1789), Jacobi printed as an appendix passages from Giordano Bruno's *De la causa, principio et uno* (1584) in order to call attention to a defense of pantheism that had, in Jacobi's view, influenced both Spinoza and Gottfried Wilhelm Leibniz.

Another source of the philosophy of the Absolute is Immanuel Kant's doctrine of the Reason as the faculty that aims at unified knowledge of the Unconditioned— "to find for the conditioned knowledge of the Understanding the Unconditioned that completes its unity" (*Critique of Pure Reason*, A307). In the Fourth Antinomy (A453) Kant writes of "an absolutely necessary being" (*ein Absolutnotwendiges*), and in the *Critique of Judgment*, in his account of the sublime, Kant distinguishes between what is great merely by comparison with something smaller (*comparative magnum*) and what is absolutely, not merely comparatively, great (*absolute magnum*). The former is a sensible concept, the latter is a concept of the Reason that "conducts the notion of nature to a supersensible substratum (underlying both nature and our faculty of thought) which is great beyond every standard of the senses" §26). Kant, of course, warned against supposing that these concepts of absolute unity and the absolutely unconditioned were more than Ideas that direct and regulate the search for empirical knowledge. But he himself, in the *Critique of Practical Reason* (1788), claimed to show that the reality of an unconditioned cause, and hence of freedom, could be *proved* "by means of an apodeictic law of the practical reason, and becomes the keystone of the whole edifice of a system of pure, even of speculative reason" (Preface). Thus Kant himself went some way toward repairing the destruction he had wrought upon "the edifice of speculative reason," and during his last years Johann Gottlieb Fichte and Schelling carried this work further in ways he by no means approved.

We have seen that Kant said that the Practical Reason provided proof of something Unconditioned, namely, of free, uncaused activity. Fichte, in his *Grundlage der gesammten Wissenschaftslehre* (1794), developed this aspect of Kant's teaching, arguing that a nonempirical, free, and active self must be regarded not merely as a condition of human knowledge, but also as the source and essence of all that is. (It is "All my I," as Coleridge derisively parodies it in the *Biographia Literaria*.) Thus the Transcendental Ego, which in Kant's philosophy was a logical or epistemological conception, was transformed by Fichte into the "absolute ego," a being that he later described as "the creator of all phenomena, including phenomenal individuals." Schelling's earliest writings were reinforcements of Fichte's views and shared his philosophical vocabulary.

By 1800, however, Schelling was moving toward a position of his own, and in his *System des transzendentalen Idealismus* of that year he writes of "an Absolute," and even, once or twice, of "the Absolute." In his *Darstellung meines Systems der Philosophie* (1801) he writes that "there is no philosophy except from the standpoint of the Absolute," and "Reason is the Absolute." In Hegel's *Differenz des Fichtischen und Schellingschen Systems der Philosophie* (1801) the Absolute is constantly referred to. Hegel writes, for example: "Division and conflict [*Entzweiung*] is the source of the need for philosophy, and in the form of the culture of the age, is its unfree, merely given aspect. What is merely an appearance of the Absolute has isolated itself from the Absolute and set itself up as independent." It will be noticed that in this passage the Absolute is contrasted with appearances and with what is "unfree," and that there is a further contrast between appearances that are falsely regarded as independent and appearances viewed in relation to the Absolute.

In 1803, there appeared the second edition of the essay by Schelling titled *Ideen zu einer Philosophie der Natur*, which had first appeared in 1797. In an appendix written for this new edition, Schelling argues that philosophy, as concerned with first principles, must be "an absolute science," that it is therefore concerned with what is absolute, and that, since all things (*Dinge*) are conditioned (*bedingt*), philosophy must be concerned with the activity of knowing rather than with things or objects. "Philosophy," he writes, "is the science of the Absolute," and the Absolute is the identity of the act of knowledge and of what is known. Schelling gives the name "Absolute Idealism" to the philosophy in which this identity is recognized. The exponent of Absolute Idealism, he argues, seeks out the intelligence that is necessarily embodied in nature, and he achieves by means of "intellectual intuition" a grasp of the identity between knower and known.

"The Absolute" was now well established in the vocabulary of Idealist philosophy.

SOME VIEWS ABOUT THE NATURE OF THE ABSOLUTE

We have seen that Schelling regarded the Absolute as that which intellectual intuition revealed as the identity of the knower and the known. He argued, furthermore, that knowledge is inseparable from will, so that the ultimate whole is active and free. The Absolute is manifested not only in nature but also in human history, which is a progress toward self-consciousness. An important thesis of Schelling's philosophy of the Absolute is that whereas in nature the Absolute is embodied in an unconscious way, in works of art it is consciously embodied, so that through his productions the artistic genius reveals the Absolute to humankind. In *Philosophie und Religion* (1804) Schelling tried to show how the finite, phenomenal world is related to the Absolute. He here had recourse to the notion of a fall that is a consequence of freedom and is yet, like the Absolute itself, outside time. He recognized that his view might be regarded as pantheistic (it was so regarded by Coleridge), and he attempted to show that human selves are, although finite, divine by nature. Thus the philosophy of the Absolute is developed as a sort of theology with some kinship to the speculations of Nicholas of Cusa.

It is well known that in his *Phenomenology of Mind* (1807) Hegel, by his characterization, "a night in which all cows are black," insinuated that Schelling's Absolute had no positive ascertainable features. Schelling, for his part, regarded Hegel's Absolute as "panlogistical"; that is, as nothing but an array of abstract categories. In his *Encyclopedia* Hegel presents various "definitions" of the Absolute in ascending order of complexity and adequacy. It is Being, he says, as Parmenides had held, but this is the least that can be said about it. It is also the self-identical, and, at a higher level, it is inference (*Schluss*—Wallace translates it "syllogism"). These definitions, from the *Logic,* appear to confirm Schelling's criticisms; but when Hegel comes to the *Philosophy of Mind,* the third part of the *Encyclopedia,* he writes that "the Absolute is mind: this is the highest definition of the Absolute." In his account of mind, Hegel shows how it develops as society moves toward higher levels of freedom in the course of human history, and how it reaches its fullest expression in the self-consciousness of the philosopher. Hegel's intention was to describe the Absolute in such a way that it would be seen to be infinite and yet comprise the finite within itself, and to be real and yet contain the apparent.

But this intention was so ambitious that the result is ambiguity, and the Hegelian Absolute has been regarded by some, including Andrew Seth (later Pringle-Pattison), as "a single self" in which finite selves are lost, and by others, such as J. McT. E. McTaggart, as a society of individual, nontemporal selves. The ambiguity is also reflected in divergent interpretations of the religious significance of Hegel's Absolute, the majority of interpreters regarding it as equivalent to God, with others, for example, Bruno Bauer and Kojève, taking the view that "the Absolute" is Hegel's designation for man as a progressing historical individual.

In the nineteenth century and the early twentieth century, Absolutism became an important influence in the philosophy of Great Britain and the United States. J. S. Ferrier, who had written a life of Schelling and who had studied Coleridge and was aware of Schelling's influence on him, expounded, in his *Institutes of Metaphysics* (1854), a pluralistic Absolutism according to which there is a plurality of contingent "Absolute Existences" that are "minds-together-with-that-which-they-apprehend," and one "Absolute Existence which is strictly *necessary* … a supreme, infinite and everlasting Mind in synthesis with all things." But the most influential version of Absolute Idealism to be published in English was Bradley's *Appearance and Reality* (1893). In this book Bradley argued that mere appearances are conflicting and self-contradictory and that reality or the Absolute must therefore be harmonious and consistent. The self-contradictory character of appearances is due to their relatedness, and therefore the Absolute must not contain relations. Bradley maintained that the nature and possibility of a harmonious nonrelational whole is adumbrated in "immediate experience," the prereflective experience from which the world of distinct and related things emerges as we learn to talk and to judge. In this prereflective experience, subject and object are not yet differentiated, and there is diversity without numerical plurality. "From such an experience of unity below relations," Bradley writes, "we can rise to the idea of a superior unity above them." In this view, the Absolute is a suprarelational, differentiated harmony of experience. It is not a self, and it is not God, for "short of the Absolute, God cannot rest, and having reached that goal, he is lost and religion with him." Some have thought that this view of the Absolute is less open to the charge of panlogism than is that of Hegel. Before the publication of *Appearance and Reality,* Andrew Seth had, from within the Idealist school, criticized the line of thought that submerged individual selves in an impersonal or suprapersonal Absolute. McTaggart, we have seen, did not interpret Hegel in this way, and endeavored on his own account to show that the unreality of the phenomenal world is consistent with the absolute existence of individual selves. Josiah Royce's solidly and persuasively argued *The World and the Individual* (1904) is another attempt to rescue individual minds from absorption in the Absolute.

CRITICAL COMMENTS

It is remarkable that a line of philosophical argument that set out to defend the reality of mind and of freedom should end up with minds that are self-contradictory appearances and an Absolute that alone is free. The Absolute was to have been the seat of freedom, reality, truth, and harmony; yet if Bradley was right, harmony and reality shut out the possibility of truth and freedom. Like Spinoza he tried to meet the difficulty with a doctrine of degrees of truth and freedom; and the comparison is revealing, for Spinoza is often regarded as a determinist. What went wrong? Coleridge, although greatly impressed by Schelling, argued in *The Friend* that Schelling's view, like that of Spinoza, was pantheistic. We may agree that Schelling sought for truth and freedom in the universe at large instead of in the limited beings to which they really belong. Schelling continued Kant's error of locating freedom outside the only world in which it is of importance, the world in which individual men decide and act. The view of Absolute Idealists is, however, that this world is merely phenomenal and must be contrasted with an infinite reality that contains it. The critic will ask whether this infinite reality must exist or whether it is only a projection from the finite. In adopting the former view, Absolutists have used arguments analogous to the Ontological Argument and to the Argument from the Contingency of the World. It would be self-contradictory, that is, to suppose that the Perfect could fail to exist; and in any case contingent being could not *be* unless there were a Necessary Being. Pierre Gassendi, Kant, and others have brought forward arguments against these so-called proofs, but it will not do merely to move forward these "disproofs" in opposition to Absolute Idealism. For the defenders of the Absolute do not allow that the distinctions made in these objections, between thought and reality or between concepts and things, are tenable just as they stand. Absolute Idealists cannot be refuted by arguments in which commonsense distinctions or the terms of an opposed philosophical tradition are uncritically presupposed. It is true that the conceptual adventurousness of Absolute Idealism was the occasion for the extreme conceptual conservatism of G. E. Moore and of those philosophers who insist on the essential rightness of ordinary language. But in the course of philosophical argument it has emerged that facts and concepts, the world and the ways in which it is thought about, cannot be isolated from one another as dogmatic common sense says they can be. On this matter the Absolutists' prejudice in favor of unity seems to have caused them to look in the right direction and to see how closely associated with one another are our conceptual framework and the world it is used to describe and classify.

See also Bosanquet, Bernard; Bradley, Francis Herbert; Bruno, Giordano; Coleridge, Samuel Taylor; Ferrier, James Frederick; Fichte, Johann Gottlieb; Gassendi, Pierre; Hegel, Georg Wilhelm Friedrich; Jacobi, Friedrich Heinrich; Kant, Immanuel; Leibniz, Gottfried Wilhelm; McTaggart, John McTaggart Ellis; Mendelssohn, Moses; Moore, George Edward; Ontological Argument for the Existence of God; Practical Reason; Pringle-Pattison, Andrew Seth; Reason; Royce, Josiah; Schelling, Friedrich Wilhelm Joseph von; Spinoza, Benedict (Baruch) de.

Bibliography

Historians of philosophy do not seem to say much about the introduction of the term "the Absolute." Information can be obtained from Richard Kroner, *Von Kant bis Hegel*, 2nd ed. (Tübingen: Mohr, 1961) and from Frederick Copleston, S.J., *A History of Philosophy*, Vol. VII, *Fichte to Nietzsche* (London: Search Press, 1963).

On various views about the nature of the Absolute, see, in addition to the books mentioned in the text: Bruno Bauer, *Die Posaune des jüngsten Gerichts wider Hegel, den Atheisten und Antichristen* (Leipzig, 1841); Andrew Seth (later Pringle-Pattison), *Hegelianism and Personality* (London and Edinburgh: Blackwood, 1887); J. McT. E. McTaggart, *Studies in Hegelian Cosmology* (Cambridge: University Press, 1901); A. Kojève, *Introduction à la lecture de Hegel* (Paris: Editions Gallimard, 1947).

For criticisms of Absolutism, see: William James, *A Pluralistic Universe* (New York and London: Longmans, Green, 1909), Chs. II and III; G. E. Moore, *Some Main Problems of Philosophy* (London: Allen and Unwin, 1953), Chs. VIII–XII; A. C. Ewing, *Idealism, a Critical Survey* (London: Methuen, 1934). In Ewing, Ch. VIII, §3 is headed "The Absolute" and contains a brief discussion of the views of Bradley and Bosanquet.

H. B. Acton (1967)

ABUBACER

See *Ibn Ṭufayl*

ACADEMY

See *Florentine Academy; Greek Academy*

ACOSTA, GABRIEL

See *Costa, Uriel da*

ACTION

People speak not only of the actions of human beings and other intelligent animals but also of the actions of inanimate objects such as acids and waves. The philosophy of action, however, is not directly concerned with the actions of inanimate objects. Its primary subject matter is intentional action. Two questions are central in the philosophy of action: What are intentional actions? And how are intentional actions to be explained? An adequate answer to the first question would enable one to see how intentional actions differ from everything else—including the actions of acids and waves, nonactions, and unintentional actions. A successful answer to the second question would provide one with the theoretical machinery to use in explaining why you are reading this entry and why the author wrote it.

INTENTIONAL ACTION AND INDIVIDUATION

According to an attractive causal theory, intentional actions are, in one important respect, like money. The piece of paper with which Ann just purchased her drink is a genuine U.S. dollar bill partly in virtue of its having been produced (in the right way) by the U.S. Treasury Department. A duplicate bill produced with plates and paper stolen from the Treasury Department is a counterfeit bill, not a genuine one. Similarly, according to one kind of causal theory of intentional action, a certain event is Ann's buying a drink—an intentional action—partly in virtue of its having been produced in the right way by certain mental items. An event someone else covertly produces by remote control—one including visually indistinguishable bodily motions not appropriately produced by Ann's intentions or decisions (nor by physical states or events that realize the mental items)—is not Ann's intentional action, even if she feels as though she is in charge. (This view does not identify intentional actions with nonactional events—or nonintentional actions—caused in the right way. That would be analogous to identifying genuine U.S. dollar bills with pieces of printed paper that are not genuine U.S. dollar bills and are produced in the right way by the U.S. Treasury Department, which is absurd.)

The question "What are intentional actions?" directly raises two other questions. "How do intentional actions differ from everything else?" and, "How do intentional actions differ from one another?" A crude sketch of one answer to the first question about differences has just been provided. Intentional actions differ from other events in their causal history. Events that are intentional actions are produced in a certain way by mental items (or physical states and events that realize these items); events that are not intentional actions lack such a causal history (a topic picked up again in section 2.) Alternative conceptions of intentional action include (1) an internalist view, according to which intentional actions differ experientially from other events in a way that is essentially independent of how, or whether, they are caused; (2) a conception of intentional actions as composites of nonactional mental events or states (e.g., intentions) and pertinent nonactional effects (e.g., an arm's rising); and (3) views identifying an intentional action with the causing of a suitable nonactional product by appropriate nonactional mental events or states—or, instead, by an agent.

A debate over the second question about differences—the question of action individuation—has produced a collection of relatively precise alternatives: a coarse-grained view, a fine-grained view, and componential views. Donald Davidson writes, "I flip the switch, turn on the light, and illuminate the room. Unbeknownst to me I also alert a prowler to the fact that I am home" (1980, p. 4). How many actions does the agent, Don, perform? Davidson's coarse-grained answer is one action "of which four descriptions have been given" (p. 4). The action is intentional under certain descriptions (e.g., "I flip the switch"), and unintentional under others (e.g., "I alert the prowler"). A fine-grained alternative view treats *A* and *B* as different actions if, in performing them, the agent exemplifies different action properties. In this view, Don has performed at least four actions (only some of which are intentional), because the action properties at issue are distinct. An agent may exemplify any of these action properties without exemplifying any of the others. One may even turn on a light in a room without illuminating the room (the light may be painted black). Componential views represent Don's illuminating the room as an intentional action having various components, including—but not necessarily limited to—his moving his arm, his flipping the switch, and the light's going on. Where proponents of the coarse-grained and fine-grained theories find, respectively, a single action under different descriptions and a collection of intimately related actions, advocates of the various componential views locate a larger action having smaller actions among its parts.

Davidson and Jennifer Hornsby hold that every action is intentional under some description. Proponents of alternative theories of action individuation may make an analogous claim: in every case of action something is done intentionally; when nothing is done intentionally, no action is performed. Where Davidson and Hornsby seek to distinguish descriptions under which an action is intentional from descriptions under which it is not, other philosophers may seek to distinguish intentional from unintentional actions in the same case of action. Either way, intentional actions are of primary importance.

This entry proceeds in a neutral way regarding the leading contending theories of individuation. Readers may treat the action variable A as a variable either for actions themselves (construed componentially or in a more fine-grained way) or for actions under A-descriptions, depending on their preferred mode of action individuation. The same goes for the term *action*.

CAUSALISM: BACKGROUND AND A CHALLENGE

One approach to understanding both the nature of intentional action and the explanation of intentional actions emphasizes causation. The conjunction of the following two theses may be termed *standard causalism*: (1) An event's being an intentional action depends on how it was caused; and (2) Proper explanations of intentional actions are causal explanations. Familiar causal theories feature as causes such psychological or mental items as beliefs, desires, intentions, and such related events as acquiring an intention to A.

Causalism typically is embraced as part of a naturalistic stand on agency, according to which mental items that play causal/explanatory roles in intentional action are in some way dependent on or realized in physical states and events. A range of options is open. Indeed, any viable solution to the mind-body problem that supports the idea that the mental has a significant causal/explanatory role in intentional action would, in principle, be welcomed by causalists.

Aristotle endorses the idea that intentional actions are to be explained, causally, in terms of mental states or events in his assertion that "the origin of action—its efficient, not its final cause—is choice, and that of choice is

desire and reasoning with a view to an end" (Aristotle 1984, 1139a31–32). Davidson, in an influential article, "Actions, Reasons, and Causes," rebuts arguments against causalism, develops a positive causalist view, and presents noncausalists with what has proved to be a difficult challenge. Addressed to philosophers who hold that when people act intentionally they act for reasons, the challenge is to provide an account of the reasons for which people act that does not treat (people's having) those reasons as figuring in the causation of the relevant behavior (or, one might add, as realized in physical causes of the behavior). The challenge is acute when an agent has more than one reason for A-ing but A-s only for only one of them. Imagine that Al has a pair of reasons for mowing his lawn this morning. First, he wants to mow it this week and he believes that this morning is the most convenient time. Second, he has an urge to repay his neighbor for the rude awakening Al suffered recently when the neighbor turned on her mower at the crack of dawn; he believes that his mowing his lawn this morning would repay her. As it happens, Al mows his lawn this morning only for one of these reasons. In virtue of what is it true that he mowed his lawn for this reason, and not the other, if not that this reason—or his having this reason or what realizes either this reason or his having it—and not the other, played a suitable causal role in his mowing his lawn? Alfred Mele rebuts detailed noncausalist attempts to answer this challenge in chapter two of *Motivation and Agency*. Space constraints preclude pursuing the issue here.

TWO ALLEGED PROBLEMS FOR CAUSALISM

Two alleged problems for causalism that continue to be lively topics of debate are causal deviance and vanishing agents.

CAUSAL DEVIANCE. Deviant causal chains raise difficulties for causal analyses of action itself and of doing something intentionally. The alleged problem is that whatever psychological causes are claimed to be both necessary and sufficient for a resultant event's being an action, or for an action's being intentional, cases can be described in which, owing to a deviant causal connection between the favored psychological antecedents—for example, events of intention acquisition—and a resultant event, that event is not an action, or a pertinent resultant action is not done intentionally.

The most common examples of deviance divide into two types: (1) Examples of primary deviance, which raise a problem about a relatively direct connection between mental antecedents and resultant bodily motion; and (2) examples of secondary deviance, which highlight behavioral consequences of intentional actions and the connection between these actions and their consequences. In Davidson's well-known example of primary deviance, "A climber ... want[s] to rid himself of the weight and danger of holding another man on a rope, and he ... know[s] that by loosening his hold on the rope he [can] rid himself of the weight and danger. This belief and want ... so unnerve him as to cause him to loosen his hold" unintentionally (1980, p. 79). In his equally well-known example of secondary deviance, "A man [tries] to kill someone by shooting at him. [He] misses his victim by a mile, but the shot stampedes a herd of wild pigs that trample the intended victim to death" (p. 78).

Instructive attempts to resolve the problems examples such as these pose highlight four points:

((1)) An event is an intentional action only if it is an action, and in many cases of deviance the pertinent event seems not to be an action. For example, the climber's "loosening his hold" is more aptly described as the rope's slipping from his trembling fingers.

((2)) An analysis of intentional action may preclude there being a gap between an action's psychological causal initiator and the beginning of the action. If, for example, every intentional action has the acquisition of a proximal intention—that is, an intention to A now or an intention to A, beginning now—as a proximate cause, there is no room between cause and the beginning of action for primary deviance. ("*Proximate* cause" may be defined as follows: x is a proximate cause of y if and only if x is a cause of y and there is nothing z such that x is a cause of z and z is a cause of y.)

((3)) Intention (or one's preferred psychological item) has a continuous guiding function in the development of intentional action.

((4)) An action's being intentional depends on its fitting the agent's conception or representation of the manner in which it will be performed—a condition violated in Davidson's shooting scenario.

George Wilson challenges point 2. Sometimes, Wilson observes, "intentions cause states of nervous agitation that positively *enable* the agent to perform the type of action intended" (1989, p. 252). He offers the example of a weightlifter whose "intention to lift the weight then caused a rush of nervous excitement that was, in fact, necessary for him to budge the great weight even slightly

from off the floor" (1989, p. 252). However, this observation and example arguably leave the requirement of proximate causation unscathed. What is required is not that intention-inspired nervousness, agitation, and the like, play no role in the production of intentional actions, but rather that they not fill a gap between the acquisition of a pertinent proximal intention and action in such a way that intention acquisition figures only indirectly in the production of the corresponding action. In Wilson's example, one may contend, there is no gap between intention acquisition and the beginning of the lifting that is filled by nervousness. Rather, one may argue that intention acquisition proximately initiates the lifting—which action, according to some causalists, begins with a relevant brain event prior to the weight's rising—while also producing nervousness that is required for the agent's even budging the weight.

Proximal intentions typically are not momentary states, and the intention to lift the weight in the present case is at work as long as the lifting continues. Even if nervousness were somehow required for the occurrence of the agent's muscular movements themselves, a nervousness producing proximal intention to lift the weight whose acquisition plays a causal role in the production of a corresponding intentional lift would, in conjunction with the resultant nervousness, figure in the proximate initiation of those movements. If, alternatively, the causal role of an intention to lift the weight were exhausted by the intention's issuing in nervousness, and the nervousness were somehow to result in the upward movement of limbs and weight independently of any pertinent intention present at the time, the weightlifting would not be intentional. The case—aside from its failure to provide an intuitively appealing mechanistic explanation of the focal occurrence—would then be on par with familiar examples of nonintentional occurrences caused by intention-inspired nervousness (e.g., the climber's case).

The point about the continued functioning of proximal intentions blunts an objection John Bishop (1989) raises to Myles Brand's position on primary deviance. Bishop observes that deviance can break in after intention acquisition has (properly) initiated a causal chain—but before bodily movement occurs—and strip agents of control over their motions. In such cases, although agents' motions may accord with their intentions, they do not act intentionally. On Brand's view, however, the proximal intentions that initiate intentional actions also sustain and guide them: "Given that intention is in part guidance ... of activity, the intention continues as long as guidance … continues" (1984, p. 175). In a case of the kind Bishop imagines, guidance is absent.

Some causal theorists who have assessed cases of primary deviance as attempted counterexamples to a causal account of what it is for an action to be intentional have dismissed them on the grounds that they are not cases of action at all. If this diagnosis is correct, primary deviance poses an apparent problem for the project of constructing a causal analysis of action. Can causalists identify something of a causal nature in virtue of which it is false that the climber performed the action of loosening his grip on the rope?

In a discussion of primary deviance, Alvin Goldman remarks: "A complete explanation of how wants and beliefs lead to intentional acts would require extensive neurophysiological information, and I do not think it is fair to demand of a philosophical analysis that it provide this information.… A detailed delineation of the causal process that is characteristic of intentional action is a problem mainly for the special sciences" (1970, p. 62). This remark may strike some readers as evasive, but Goldman has a point. A deviant causal connection between an X and a Y is deviant relative to normal causal connections between X-s and Y-s. Moreover, what counts as normal in this context is perspective-relative. From the point of view of physics, for example, there is nothing abnormal about Davidson's examples of deviance. And, for beings of a particular kind, the normal route from intention to action may be best articulated partly in neurophysiological terms.

One way around the problem posed by incomplete neuroscientific knowledge is to design (in imagination, of course) an agent's motor control system. Knowing the biological being's design in that sphere, there is then a partial basis for distinguishing causal chains associated with overt action—that is, action essentially involving peripheral bodily motion—from deviant motion-producing chains. If one can distinguish deviant from nondeviant causal chains in designed agents—that is, chains not appropriate to action from action-producing chains—then the same may also be done for normal human beings, if much more than is currently known about the human body is discovered. (This line of thought is pursued in Mele 2003, ch. 2).

VANISHING AGENTS. Some philosophers claim that causalism precludes there being any actions at all and therefore makes agents vanish. According to Thomas Nagel, "The essential source of the problem is a view of persons and their actions as part of the order of nature.…

That conception, if pressed, leads to the feeling that we are not agents at all.… *My doing* of an act—or the doing of an act by someone else—seems to disappear when we think of the world objectively. There seems no room for agency in [such] a world.… There is only what happens" (1986, pp. 110–111).

Nagel's worry is not worrisome. Cats and dogs are part of the natural order. If radical skeptical hypotheses are set aside—for example, the hypotheses that everything is a dream and that all biological entities are brains in vats—it is plain that cats and dogs act. They fight, eat, and play. When they do these things they are acting. The same is true of humans, even if people are part of the natural order. Supernatural beings (e.g., gods and ghosts) are not part of the natural order. That a being needs to be supernatural in order to act is an interesting proposition, but it is difficult to take that proposition seriously in the absence of a powerful argument for it.

J. David Velleman voices a variant of Nagel's worry. He contends that standard causal accounts of intentional action do not capture what "distinguishes human action from other animal behavior" and do not accommodate "human action par excellence" (2000, p. 124). He also reports that his objection to what he calls "the standard story of human action" (p. 123), a causal story, "is not that it mentions mental occurrences in the agent instead of the agent himself [but] that the occurrences it mentions in the agent are no more than occurrences in him, because their involvement in an action does not add up to the agent's being involved" (p. 125). Velleman says that this problem would remain even if the mind-body problem were solved, and, like Nagel, he regards the problem as "distinct from the problem of free-will" (p. 127).

Here, Velleman runs together two separate issues. Human agents may be involved in some of their actions in ways that cats and dogs are involved in many of their actions. Human agents do not vanish in such actions. Scenarios in which human agents vanish are one thing; scenarios in which actions of human agents do not come up to the level of human action par excellence, whatever that may be, are another.

Causalists are entitled to complain that Velleman has been unfair to them. His description of the standard story of human action is apparently a description of the sort of thing found in the work of causalists looking for what is common to all (overt) intentional actions, or all (overt) actions done for reasons, and for what distinguishes actions of these broad kinds from everything else. If some nonhuman animals act intentionally and for reasons, a story with that topic definitely should apply to them.

Also, human action par excellence may be intentional action and action done for a reason in virtue of its having the properties identified in standard causal analyses of these things. That the analyses do not provide sufficient conditions for—or a story about—human action par excellence is not a flaw in the analyses, given their targets. If Velleman were to believe that causalism lacks the resources for accommodating human action par excellence, he may attack the standard story on that front, arguing that it cannot be extended to handle such action. But Velleman himself is a causalist. Moreover, causalists have offered accounts of kinds of action—for example, free or autonomous action and action exhibiting self-control (the contrary of weakness of will)—that exceed minimal requirements for intentional action or action done for a reason. Their story about minimally sufficient conditions for action of the latter kinds is not their entire story about human actions.

REASONS, DESIRES, AND INTENTIONS

Reasons, desires, and intentions are featured in many theories about how intentional actions are to be explained. According to Davidson's influential view, reasons for action are complexes of beliefs and desires. Some philosophers claim that Davidsonian reasons for action really are not reasons at all. T. M. Scanlon, for example, argues that "desires almost never provide reasons for action in the way described by the standard desire model" (1998, p. 43).

Philosophical work on reasons for action tends to be guided primarily either by a concern with the explanation of intentional actions or by a concern with the evaluation of intentional actions or their agents. In work dominated by the former concern, reasons for action tend to be understood as states of mind, along broadly Davidsonian lines. Philosophers with the latter concern may be sympathetic or unsympathetic to this construal, depending on their views about standards for evaluating actions or agents. For example, a theorist whose evaluative concern is with rational action and who holds that the pertinent notion of rationality is subjective—in the sense that a proper verdict about the rationality or irrationality of an agent's intentional action is to be made from the perspective of the agent's own desires, beliefs, principles, and the like, rather than from some external, or partly external, perspective—may be happy to understand reasons for action as states of mind. A theorist with a more objective conception of rational action or rational agency also is likely to have a more objective conception of reasons for action. Such a theorist may find it natural to insist that

many or all reasons for action are facts about the agent-external world. Consider Bob's starting a new diet after his doctor informs him that his cholesterol is dangerously high. Theorists with a subjective conception of rationality tend to regard Bob's reasons for starting the new diet as constituted by desires and beliefs (e.g., his desire to improve his health and his belief that the new diet will help him do that), whereas theorists with an objective conception of rationality tend to regard his reasons as objective facts (e.g., the diet will improve his health, or it is likely to do so). Alleged reasons of these two types may be termed, respectively, *agent-internal* and *agent-external* justificatory reasons.

COMBINING AGENT-INTERNAL AND AGENT-EXTERNAL REASONS. If there are agent-external justificatory reasons for action, it may be that intentional actions are to be relatively directly explained at least partially in terms of Davidsonian reasons, and that when agent-external justificatory reasons—for example, the new diet is likely to improve Bob's health—contribute to explanations of intentional actions, they do so less directly, by way of a causal contribution made by an agent's *apprehending* such a reason. For example, Bob's apprehension of the likelihood that the new diet will improve his health might, along with his desire for improved health, enter into a true causal explanation of Bob's starting the new diet. An exploration of the possibility of agent-external justificatory reasons and of their compatibility with the existence of Davidsonian reasons quickly takes one well beyond the philosophy of action into moral philosophy and value theory. Further discussion of this topic is beyond the scope of the present entry, but is discussed in chapters three through six of Mele's *Motivation and Agency* (2003).

DESIRES. There is a related controversy about the nature of desires. Scanlon's critique of what he calls "the standard desire model" (1998, p. 43) is framed partly in terms of his own account of "what is usually called desire" (p. 65). He contends that something's seeming to an agent to be a reason for A-ing is "the central element in what is usually called [a] desire" to A (p. 65). Seemings of this kind do important motivational work, according to Scanlon. He claims that in a thirsty man with a desire to drink, "the motivational work seems to be done by" the agent's taking "the pleasure to be obtained by drinking … to count in favor of drinking" (p. 38).

Scanlon's account of what is usually called a desire is overly intellectualized. Toddlers and pretoddlers are commonly thought to desire to do things—for example, to drink some juice or to hug a teddy bear. This common thought is not that although these little agents have desires to act, they lack what is usually called a desire. The thought is that they have desires in a usual sense of the term. But because it is unlikely that toddlers have the concept of a reason for action (or of something's counting in favor of a course of action), it is unlikely that things seem to them to be reasons for action (or to count in favor of actions). There is good evidence that younger three-year-olds tend not to have the concept—or a proper concept—of belief and that the concept of desire normally does not emerge until around the age of two. Presumably, even if the concept of a reason for action were to have no conceptual ties to the concepts of belief and desire, it would be sufficiently sophisticated to be out of reach of children too young to have proper concepts of belief and desire. Even so, it is commonly and plausibly thought that such children act intentionally and for reasons. (They also have desires and beliefs, on the assumption that having such attitudes does not require possessing proper concepts of these attitudes.) In thirsty toddlers or pretoddlers, desires to drink—rather than any taking of the pleasure to be obtained by drinking to be a reason for drinking—seem to do the work of motivating drinking.

Thirsty toddlers are attracted by cups of juice, and not in the way moths are attracted by light. Toddlers are flexible in their approach to getting drinks: they try alternative means. Moths behave tropistically. Even though it is unlikely that thirsty toddlers have the conceptual wherewithal to take features—including anticipated consequences—of drinking to be reasons for (or count in favor of) drinking, they are attracted by cups of juice in a way characteristic of desiring agents. Being attracted to cups of juice owing to a sensitivity to certain of their features is distinguishable from being attracted to cups of juice owing to the agent's taking those features to be reasons. An agent's behavior may be sensitive to attractive features of things without the agent's taking those features to be reasons. If this were not so, a radically new theory of animal behavior would be required, one entailing either that only members of the most conceptually sophisticated species ever act intentionally (perhaps just human beings) or that many nonhuman species are much more conceptually sophisticated than anyone has thought.

When ordinary thirsty adults drink (intentionally, and in ordinary scenarios), they presumably are motivated at least partly by a desire to drink. The strength of the desire may sometimes be explained partly by their believing that drinking would be pleasant, or, more fully,

by that belief together with a desire for pleasure. A toddler's desire to drink water and an adult's desire to drink water may admit of the same analysis. Just as something's seeming to be a reason for drinking is not a constituent of the toddler's desire, it may not be a constituent of the adult's desire either. If a seeming of this kind sometimes is at work in thirsty adults, it may function as a partial cause of the desire's strength or of the desire itself.

INTENTIONS. Next on the agenda are intentions, states of mind commonly regarded as being closely linked to desires and beliefs. Intention has a motivational dimension, and the word *desire* (like the word *want*) is often used in the literature as a generic term for motivation. Intention also is widely regarded as involving a belief condition of some sort. Few people are inclined to say that gamblers who believe that their chances of winning today's lottery are about one in a million intend to win the lottery. However, philosophers disagree about the tightness of the connection between intentions, on the one hand, and desires and beliefs, on the other. Some—attracted, perhaps, by the idea that desire and belief are the most fundamental representational states of mind—argue that intentions are reducible to combinations of desires and beliefs, whereas others argue that attempts at such reduction are doomed to failure.

The central issue is whether the settledness that intention encompasses can be articulated in terms of beliefs and desires. Ann wants to go to a 7:00 movie and she wants to attend a 7:00 lecture. She knows that she can do either but not both. Although Ann wants to see the movie more than she wants to attend the lecture and believes that, given what she usually does in such situations, she will probably go to the movie, she is unsettled about what to do. After further deliberation, Ann settles matters for herself by deciding to attend the lecture. In so deciding, she forms an intention to attend it. To intend to A is, at least in part, to be settled (but not necessarily irrevocably) on A-ing. Wanting or desiring to A—even when the desire is stronger than its competitors, and even when it is accompanied by a belief that one probably will A—is compatible with being unsettled about whether to A.

Functions plausibly attributed to intentions include initiating and sustaining intentional actions, guiding intentional actions, helping to coordinate agents' behavior over time and their interaction with others, and prompting and appropriately terminating practical reasoning. Some philosophers have advanced nonreductive accounts of intention designed to accommodate many or all of these functions. According to a representative account of this kind, intentions are executive attitudes toward plans. Plans—which range from simple representations of simple actions to complex strategies for achieving remote goals—constitute the representational contents of intentions. What distinguishes intentions from other practical attitudes (e.g., desires to act), in this account, is their executive nature. The settledness on A-ing that is encompassed in an intention to A is a psychological commitment to executing the intention-embedded plan of action, a commitment of a kind arguably constituted exclusively by intentions.

ANALYZING INTENTIONAL ACTION: DIFFICULTIES

Attention to a trio of problems for the following pair of protoanalyses of intentional action sheds light on what the difficult project of analyzing intentional action encompasses:

> A1. S intentionally A-ed if and only if S A-ed in the way that S intended to A.
>
> A2. S intentionally A-ed if and only if S A-ed for a reason.

SIDE EFFECTS. Gilbert Harman discusses a scenario in which "In firing his gun," a sniper who is trying to kill a soldier, "knowingly alerts the enemy to his presence" (1997, p. 151). Harman claims that although the sniper "does not intend to alert the enemy," he intentionally alerts the enemy, "thinking that the gain is worth the possible cost." If Harman is right, both A1 and A2 are false. The sniper does not intend to alert the enemy, and he does not alert them for a reason either (even if his alerting them is part of some larger action that he does for a reason).

Because Harman's sniper does not unknowingly or accidentally alert the enemy, many people will deny that the sniper unintentionally alerted them. But the truth of that denial is consistent with the action's not being intentional, if there is a middle ground between intentional and unintentional action. Arguably, actions that an agent in no way aims at performing but that are not performed unknowingly or accidentally are properly located on that middle ground. They may be nonintentional, as opposed to unintentional. Of course, it also is arguable that Harman correctly assesses the sniper's case and that A1 and A2 are far too simple to be true.

BELIEF CONSTRAINTS. Some putative belief constraints on intentions or on rational intentions also pose problems for A1. Michael Bratman argues that intention has a

normative side that requires that an agent's intentions be internally consistent (individually and collectively), consistent with the agent's beliefs, and means-end coherent. Rational intentions, he maintains, satisfy those requirements, and he contends that agents rationally intend to A only if, "other things being equal," they do "not have beliefs inconsistent with the belief that [they] will A" (1987, p. 116).

The normative demands figure prominently in an argument Bratman advances against what he calls "the Simple View"—the thesis that intentionally A-ing entails intending to A. The argument revolves around an example involving a pair of video games and an ambidextrous player who shall be called Vic. Vic's task is to hit targets with missiles. In the main case, he simultaneously plays two games, each with its own target and firing mechanism, and he knows that the machines are "so linked that it is impossible to hit both targets" (Bratman 1987, p. 114). (He knows that hitting a target ends both games, and that "if both targets are about to be hit simultaneously," both machines shut down before the targets can be hit.) Vic tries to hit the target on machine 1 while also trying to hit the target on machine 2. He succeeds in hitting the former—"in just the way that [he] was trying to hit it, and in a way which depends heavily on [his] considerable skill"—but, of course, he misses the latter.

If Vic hit target 1 intentionally, fans of the Simple View must say that he intended to hit it. Because Vic's attitude toward hitting that target is not relevantly different from his attitude toward hitting target 2, Simple View fans apparently must also say that he intended to hit target 2. Bratman contends that having both intentions, given what Vic knows—namely, that he cannot hit both targets—would be irrational. Yet, it seems perfectly rational of Vic to have proceeded as he did. So given the point about the symmetry of Vic's attitudes toward the targets, Bratman concludes that he did not have either intention. And if Vic hit target 1 intentionally in the absence of an intention to hit it, the Simple View and A1 are false.

Some critics of the Simple View, including Bratman and Harman, also reject the idea that intentions are reducible to complexes of beliefs and desires; Hugh McCann argues that they are in danger of having to settle for an unwanted reductive analysis of intention (1998). Bratman, who suggests that a "guiding desire" (e.g., to hit target 1) can play the role of an intention (Bratman 1987, p. 137), is McCann's main target. McCann notes that once it is conceded that desires can stand in for intentions, reductionists will justifiably ask what need there is for a notion of intention that is irreducible to desire and belief. However, philosophers who reject the Simple View need not follow Bratman in appealing to guiding desires. For example, it may be argued that intentions to try to *A* can stand in for intentions to *A*, and, of course, intentions to try to *A* are intentions. Presumably, Vic intends to try to hit target 1 while also intending to try to hit target 2.

LUCK. Instances of lucky success pose problems for *A1* and *A2*. Beth, who has never fired a gun, mistakenly thinks that modern technology makes target shooting fool proof, and she intends to hit the bull's-eye on a distant target by aiming and firing at it. She luckily hits it in just the way she intended, but was her hitting it an intentional action? Suppose that Beth has no natural talent with firearms: she fires hundreds of additional rounds at the target and does not even come close. Here philosophers' intuitions differ. According to Christopher Peacocke (1985), an agent who makes a successful attempt "to hit a croquet ball through a distant hoop" intentionally hits the ball through the hoop (p. 69). But Brian O'Shaughnessy (1980) maintains that a novice who similarly succeeds in hitting the bull's-eye on a dart board does not intentionally hit the bull's-eye. Readers inclined to regard Beth's hitting the bull's-eye as an intentional action should consider her brother Bob. He wants to save his town by disarming a bomb, and he believes that his punching in any ten-digit sequence of numbers will disarm it. In fact, only one ten-digit code will work. Bob intends to disarm the bomb by entering ten digits. If he luckily punches in the right code, thereby disarming the bomb, is his disarming it an intentional action? Or was his chance of success too low for that action to count as intentional? If the correct answer to the latter question is yes, *A1* is false.

Protoanalysis *A2* also is threatened by stories such as these. Probably, many people would happily (but perhaps mistakenly) say that Bob's disarming the bomb—that action—was done for a reason. After all, he wanted to save the town and knew that he must disarm the bomb to do so, and this helps to explain why he entered ten digits. But, again, was Bob's chance of success too low for the disarming to count as an intentional action?

Recall the two central questions identified in the introduction to this entry: What are intentional actions? And how are intentional actions to be explained? Depending on how nuanced a satisfactory answer to the first question is, philosophers of action working on the second question may do well to focus their efforts on core instances of intentional action. If the sniper's alerting the

enemy is an intentional action, it is intentional in a different way than his firing his gun is. He fires his gun as a means to an end, but this is not true of his alerting the enemy. He also intends to fire his gun and fires it for a reason, but he does not intend to alert the enemy and does not alert them for a reason. One approach in looking for core instances of intentional action is to look for interesting properties that all cases of intentional action have in common, even if not all intentional actions have them. It may be discovered that there are no cases of intentional action in which the agent does not perform any intended intentional actions. (Even if Vic lacks an intention to hit target 1 in the video games example, he intends to fire at it and he intentionally fires at it.) If so, it may be fruitful for philosophers of action to focus primarily on intended intentional actions in developing their theories about how intentional actions are to be explained—theories in light of which it can explained why the author wrote this entry and why you are reading it, and explain how those actions are produced. Possibly, theories of this kind can then be augmented to cover all intentional actions.

See also Agent Causation; Weakness of the Will.

Bibliography

Aristotle. *Nicomachean Ethics*. In *The Complete Works of Aristotle*, edited by Jonathan Barnes. Princeton, NJ: Princeton University Press, 1984.

Audi, Robert. *Action, Intention, and Reason*. Ithaca, NY: Cornell University Press, 1993.

Bishop, John. *Natural Agency*. Cambridge, U.K.: Cambridge University Press, 1989.

Brand, Myles. *Intending and Acting*. Cambridge, MA: MIT Press, 1984.

Bratman, Michael. *Intention, Plans, and Practical Reason*. Cambridge, MA: Harvard University Press, 1987.

Bratman, Michael. *Faces of Intention*. Cambridge, U.K.: Cambridge University Press, 1999.

Davidson, Donald. "Actions, Reasons, and Causes." *Journal of Philosophy* 60 (1963): 685–700. Reprinted in Davidson 1980.

Davidson, Donald. *Essays on Actions and Events*. Oxford: Clarendon Press, 1980.

Frankfurt, Harry. *The Importance of What We Care About*. Cambridge, U.K.: Cambridge University Press, 1988.

Ginet, Carl. *On Action*. Cambridge, U.K.: Cambridge University Press, 1990.

Goldman, Alvin. *A Theory of Human Action*. Englewood Cliffs, NJ: Prentice-Hall, 1970.

Harman, Gilbert. "Practical Reasoning." In *The Philosophy of Action*, edited by Alfred Mele. Oxford: Oxford University Press, 1997.

Hornsby, Jennifer. *Actions*. London: Routledge, 1980.

McCann, Hugh. *The Works of Agency*. Ithaca, NY: Cornell University Press, 1998.

Mele, Alfred. *Motivation and Agency*. New York: Oxford University Press, 2003.

Nagel, Thomas. *The View from Nowhere*. New York: Oxford University Press, 1986.

O'Shaughnessy, Brian. *The Will*. Cambridge, U.K.: Cambridge University Press, 1980.

Peacocke, Christopher. "Intention and Akrasia." In *Essays on Davidson*, edited by Bruce Vermazen and Merrill Hintikka. Oxford: Clarendon Press, 1985.

Ruben, David-Hillel. *Action and Its Explanation*. Oxford: Clarendon Press, 2003.

Scanlon, T. M. *What We Owe to Each Other*. Cambridge, MA: Harvard University Press, 1998.

Schueler, G. F. *Reasons and Purposes*. Oxford: Clarendon Press, 2003.

Searle, J. *Intentionality*. Cambridge, U.K.: Cambridge University Press, 1983.

Velleman, J. David. *The Possibility of Practical Reason*. Oxford: Clarendon Press, 2000.

Wilson, George. *The Intentionality of Human Action*. Stanford, CA: Stanford University Press, 1989.

Alfred R. Mele (1996, 2005)

ADDISON, JOSEPH
(1672–1719)

Joseph Addison—Oxford scholar, poet, playwright, essayist, and politician—figures in the history of philosophy chiefly on the strength of his *Essay on the Pleasures of the Imagination*, published in 1712 as numbers 411 through 421 of his and Richard Steele's journal *The Spectator*.

Addison defines "pleasures of the imagination" as "such [pleasures] as arise from visible objects" (no. 411). He calls "primary" those derived from things present to vision, "secondary" those derived from things merely called to mind. There are three qualities of objects from which the primary pleasures may arise: greatness, novelty, and beauty. Greatness is an extensiveness that throws the viewer into "a pleasing astonishment," as in, for example, the sight of a mountain range. Novelty includes what is new or unfamiliar to the viewer, as a fresh meadow in spring may be, as well as what continually changes its appearance, for example, a waterfall. Beauty includes, on the one hand, whatever appearances effect sexual attraction, and on the other, "the gaiety or variety of colors," "the symmetry and proportion of parts," and "the arrangement and disposition of bodies" (no. 412).

Addison's account of the secondary pleasures is more complex. Such pleasures may be produced by mere spontaneous imaginings, or by representational artifacts, such as sculptures, paintings, some pieces of music, and descriptions. In these cases, we derive pleasure not merely from the object imagined, but also from the comparison of that object with that which represents it (no. 416). Addison also invokes comparison to explain the pleasure that we take in fictional descriptions of terrible things and events: our pleasure derives from our awareness that we ourselves are not actually threatened by the evils about which we read (no. 418).

Addison's *Essay* has been taken to mark the beginning of modern aesthetics. There are several grounds for such a claim. Addison, in contrast to previous writers on his various topics, investigates pleasures that can be derived from art and nature equally, treats the beautiful as merely one among several pleasing visual qualities, and centers his account on the mental activity of the onlooker rather than on the character of the object viewed. In all these respects, his *Essay* sets the direction for subsequent work in aesthetics.

At the same time, there are considerable differences of purview between Addison's investigation and later aesthetic thought. The sources of the pleasures of the imagination include works of art only so far as these either please the eye or awaken visual images; they do not include nonprogrammatic music, or even the nonimagistic aspects of literature. Further, for Addison, works of history, natural philosophy, travel narrative, and even criticism, morals, and speculative philosophy (so far as these use visual figures of speech) may be sources of the pleasures of the imagination just as much as works of fiction (nos. 420–421). Thus, for all the concerns and assumptions that Addison shares with subsequent writers on taste and the fine arts, the scope of his inquiry is distinctively his own.

See also Aesthetics, History of.

Bibliography

Addison, Joseph, and Richard Steele. *The Spectator*. 5 vols, edited by Donald F. Bond. Oxford: Clarendon Press, 1965. Nos. 411–421 are in vol. 3.

Hipple, Walter John, Jr. *The Beautiful, the Sublime, and the Picturesque in Eighteenth-Century British Aesthetic Theory*. Carbondale: Southern Illinois University Press, 1957. Chapter 1 is an exposition of Addison's *Essay*.

Rind, Miles. "The Concept of Disinterestedness in Eighteenth-Century British Aesthetics." *Journal of the History of Philosophy* 40 (2002): 67–87. A critique of Jerome Stolnitz's historiography of aesthetics.

Stolnitz, Jerome. "On the Origins of 'Aesthetic Disinterestedness.'" *Journal of Aesthetics and Art Criticism* 20 (1961): 131–144. A highly influential study that credits Addison with originating the concept of "aesthetic perception."

Walker, William. "Ideology and Addison's Essays on the Pleasures of the Imagination." *Eighteenth-Century Life* 24 (2000): 65–84. A critique of the widely held view that Addison's *Essay* is a work of "bourgeois ideology."

Miles Rind (2005)

ADLER, ALFRED
(1870–1937)

Alfred Adler, the medical psychologist and founder of Individual Psychology, was born in Vienna of Hungarian-Jewish parents. He received his MD from the University of Vienna in 1895 and practiced general medicine before turning to psychiatry. His soundest scientific works were written before World War I and largely prepared during his ambivalent association with the early Freudian group. After serving in the Austrian army he became concerned with child guidance as a method of preventive medical psychology, and gaining favor with the new Austrian government, opened child-guidance centers in Vienna, Berlin, and Munich schools. Family-guidance interviews in public, with general discussion periods, disseminated his methods and theories, particularly among educators. He became an international lecturer in Europe and the United States and was America's first professor of medical psychology, at Long Island Medical School. In the 1930s his efforts to spread his doctrine of "social interest" in the face of Europe's totalitarian nationalisms marked him as preacher rather than scientist, and his later published work served to promulgate a faith rather than to report scientific work. He died in Aberdeen, Scotland, during a lecture tour.

Adler's first psychologically important work, the *Study in Organ Inferiority and Its Psychical Compensation* (1907), was "a contribution to clinical medicine" in constitutional pathology. In it Adler explored constitutional defects of structure and function and their physiopathological compensation and also described "psychical" compensatory changes in disposition and way of life; overcompensation could produce not only "genius," like the deaf Ludwig van Beethoven, but also neurotic or psychotic responses, like hysteria or paranoia. Adler gave a causal-deterministic exposition of development as dependent upon constitutional endowments, innate biological drives, and environmental pressures. His papers of 1908 described as innate an "aggression drive" (to subdue the environment) and a "need for affection." Both concepts were then rejected by Sigmund Freud's group but reappeared in later psychoanalytic theories.

Adler himself modified both concepts and reformulated his whole psychology in *The Neurotic Constitution* (1912). He repudiated drive psychology and causal determinism. He viewed inferiority (vis-à-vis adults) and consequent "inferiority feeling" as experiences common to every child. The child responds as a whole individual with a "striving for superiority" (the former "aggression drive") directed toward a "fictive goal" of manly strength and dominance, which is pursued through a "guiding fiction," or life plan, modified by the "antifiction" of social demands. Goal and fiction are subjective creations of the individual's making, but unrealistic, rigid, neurotic patterns may be favored by organ inferiority, pampering, or neglect in childhood, or the child's age-ranking in the family. To Adler the Nietzschean "will to power" was this kind of neurotic pattern, not a universal human trait. He also described an opposite but equally effective response to increased insecurity:

> It is one of the triumphs of human wit to put through the guiding fiction by adapting it to the anti-fiction, ... to conquer by humility and submissiveness ... to cause pain to others by one's own suffering, to strive to attain the goal of manly force by effeminate means, to make oneself small in order to appear great. Of such sort ... are often the expedients of neurotics.

In contrast to the neurotic, the psychotic character attempts to shape reality to the fiction, while the normal character adapts itself to the environment.

Adler's later works reiterated, renamed, elaborated, and finally, simplified and broadened the concepts on which he had founded Individual Psychology in 1912 after breaking with Freud. The basis of character was the response of the whole individual to a universal infantile inferiority feeling. Accentuated inferiority feeling became the celebrated "inferiority complex," and a pathological striving for superiority was a "superiority complex." The guiding fiction was renamed the "life style," usually unconscious or "not understood," which Adlerian analysis endeavored to illuminate with insight. The antifiction and the early "need for affection" fused in the important concept of social interest. Adler first diverged from psychoanalysis over Freud's emphasis on sexual instincts. Ultimately, where Freud saw animal instincts humanized through repression, Adler described inborn trends—social interest and striving for superiority—whose full development perfected the personality. In summary, "Heredity only endows [the individual] with certain abilities. Environment only gives him certain impressions ... it is his individual way of using these bricks, ... his attitude toward life, which determines [his] relationship to the outside world."

Despite their differences, Adler always acknowledged his debt to Freud's psychogenetic theory of neurosis. He acknowledged Pierre Janet's *sentiment d'incomplétitude*, a predecessor of the inferiority feeling. Adler's formulation of personality somewhat resembled the "psychic structure" and "attitudes" of Wilhelm Dilthey's psychology, but direct influence is unlikely: Adler never mentioned Dilthey, although he did cite a work of Dilthey's contemporary Hans Vaihinger, the *Philosophy of "As If"* (New York, 1924), for the theory of fictions. Individual psychology had a brushfire success in continental Europe and the United States, rather less in Britain; everywhere it found more acceptance among educators, psychologists, even writers than among physicians and psychiatrists.

Adler's work has been largely absorbed into practice and thought without retaining a separate identity despite the familiar phrases—"overcompensation," "inferiority complex," "organ jargon"—which enrich a conversational rather than a psychological vocabulary. Individual Psychology still has its own centers, schools, and work groups, but Adler's influence has permeated other psychologies. His "aggression drive" reappeared in the ego psychology of orthodox psychoanalysis; other Adlerian echoes are found in Karen Horney, Harry Stack Sullivan, and Franz Alexander, and in Ian Suttie's mother-relationship theories, which surely influenced the contemporary mother-need ethological school. Child-guidance practice is non-Adlerian, and his name is not now invoked in progressive pedagogy, but those who try to see the backward child, the delinquent, the psychopath, or the psychiatric patient as a whole person are sharing Adler's viewpoint.

Adler's approach to psychology, normal and abnormal, was speculative rather than scientific. From 1912 on, he sought the elegantly economical theory rather than the proven fact. At first he recognized his theory as a fiction in Vaihinger's nonpejorative sense; a person behaves "as if" compensating for inferiority feeling. Later this step was omitted—these things *were* so. Adler often illustrated his theory with case material, but this was invariably anecdotal and in excerpts, never statistically organized. He openly despised statistics. It is uncertain how many patients Adler treated in continuity, apart from single consultations to advise physicians or teachers. The same case histories appear as examples through many books over many years, with no systematic follow-up. He made no use of normal "controls," an omission he justified by his insistence upon the uniqueness of the individual, but this left unsolved the problem of why one creative self chose neurosis, another not. Adler never experimented, never firmly predicted, never attempted systematically to verify a hypothesis. He had great intuitive insight, the greater, perhaps, for having grown up as a second son and a sickly rachitic child of a Hungarian-Jewish family in the Austrian imperial capital. His intuitions and their formulations, if not so close to reality as he believed, remain as valuable guiding fictions.

See also Dilthey, Wilhelm; Freud, Sigmund; Psychoanalysis; Psychology; Unconscious; Vaihinger, Hans.

Bibliography

WORKS BY ADLER

Studie über die Minderwertigkeit von Organen. Vienna: Urban and Schwarzenberg, 1907. Translated by Smith Ely Jelliffe as *Inferiority and Its Psychical Compensation*. New York: Nervous and Mental Diseases Publishing, 1917.

Über den nervösen Charakter. Wiesbaden: Bergmann, 1912. Translated by Bernard Glueck and John E. Lind as *The Neurotic Constitution*. New York, 1926.

Praxis und Theorie der Individualpsychologie. Munich: Bergmann, 1920. Translated by P. Radin as *Practice and Theory of Individual Psychology*. New York: Harcourt Brace, 1924.

Menschenkenntnis. Leipzig: Hirzel, 1927. Translated by W. Béran Wolfe as *Understanding Human Nature*. London: Allen and Unwin, 1927.

Understanding Life: An Introduction to the Psychology of Alfred Adler (1927).Edited by Colin Brett.Oxford; Rockport, MA: Oneworld, 1997.

The Education of Children (1930). Chicago: Regnery, 1970.

Der Sinn des Lebens. Vienna: Rolf Passer, 1933. Translated by John Winton and Richard Vaughan as *Social Interest; a Challenge to Mankind*. London: Faber, 1938.

Superiority and Social Interest: A Collection of Letter Writings. Routledge & K. Paul, 1965.

With Ernst Jahn. *Religion und Individualpsychologie: Eine prinzipielle Auseinandersetzung über Menschenführung*. Frankfurt am Main: Fischer-Taschenbuch-Verlag, 1975,

Kindererziehung. Frankfurt am Main: Fischer Taschenbuch, 1976.

Das Problem der homosexualitat und sexueller Pervessionen: Erotisches Training und erotischer Rückzug. Edited by Wolfgang Metzger. Frankfurt am Main: Fischer Taschenbuch Verlag, 1977.

Co-operation between the Sexes: Writings on Women, Love and Marriage, Sexuality, and Its Disorders. Edited and translated by Heinz Ludwig Ansbacher and Rowena R. Ansbacher. Garden City, NY: Anchor Books, 1978.

Journal Articles:, 1910–1913: Elaborating on the Basic Principles of Individual Psychology. Edited by Gerald L. Liebenau, and Henry T. Stein. San Francisco: Classical Adlerian Translation Project, Alfred Adler Institute of San Francisco, 2003.

WORKS ON ADLER

Ansbacher, Heinz, and Rowena Ansbacher, eds. *The Individual Psychology of Alfred Adler*. New York: Basic, 1956. Extracts, full bibliography, and critical annotations, including evaluation of Adler's proclaimed finalistic subjectivism as approximating William James's "soft determinism."

Orgler, Hertha. *Alfred Adler, the Man and His Work*. London: Daniel, 1939; 3rd ed., London: Sidgwick and Jackson, 1963.

J. D. Uytman (1967)
Bibliography updated by Michael J. Farmer (2005)

ADORNO, THEODOR WIESENGRUND
(1903–1969)

Theodor Wiesengrund Adorno, philosopher, composer, sociologist, and aesthetic theorist, was born September 11, 1903, in Frankfurt am Main and died August 6, 1969. His last days were beset by the "emergencies in democracy" prompted by the student movement of the 1960s; the students simultaneously treated him as friend and foe.

LIFE AND WORK

Studying in Frankfurt in the 1920s, but increasingly unable to secure employment in the first years of Nazi Germany, Adorno moved to England in 1934. Four years later, with his new wife, Margarethe ("Gretel") Karplus (1902–1993), he moved to the United States, first to New York and then to Los Angeles. In 1949 they returned to Frankfurt where Adorno worked both as professor at the university and as public intellectual, participating in radio and television programs on philosophy, society, education, and the arts.

Born into a comfortable bourgeois home, he was the only son of a Protestant wine merchant of Jewish descent, Oscar Wiesengrund, and of a Catholic singer, Maria Calvelli-Adorno. Before his move to the United States he was known by his father's name and after by his mother's. However, though "Wiesengrund" was abbreviated to a middle initial, the name was honored in Thomas Mann's *Doctor Faustus* (1947), the exemplary novel on the fate of musical modernism to which Adorno significantly contributed. The Beethovenian tones of the *Wiesengrund—* meadow-ground—expressed an early promise of happiness for the bourgeois age that would eventually be shattered, leaving the ill-fated dodecaphonic composer Adrian Leverkühn no choice but to complete his life with a melancholic requiem composed to the former greatness of German art.

Adorno wrote broadly on metaphysics, epistemology, political philosophy, ethics, the history of philosophy, and the philosophy of history. He is most widely known for his attempt to reveal the intricate historical and dialectical relationships between philosophy, society and the arts, or between philosophy, sociology, and aesthetic theory.

PHILOSOPHY AND MUSIC

In the 1920s, Adorno worked as a music critic reflecting upon contemporary developments in both the high and popular forms of the arts. Following his graduation in 1924 with a critical dissertation on Husserl's phenomenology he moved to Vienna to study composition with Alban Berg, a member alongside Arnold Schoenberg and Anton Webern of the Second Viennese School. Torn initially between philosophy and music he finally chose both, in this way furthering a tradition that had its beginnings with Plato. Following Schopenhauer, Kierkegaard, and Nietzsche (and knowledgeable of his contemporary Ernst Bloch), Adorno gave pride of place to music in his philosophical thinking and to philosophy in his musical thinking. However, he never aimed to reduce one to the other. He aimed neither to produce a philosophy *of* music nor, indeed, a philosophy *of* anything else, as if, by this use of "of," philosophy was assumed to be the master method to which all other disciplines were subject(ed). Philosophy, rather, was one of many nonreducible modes of thinking, and music was another, through which truth might be approached. Like music, philosophy was to be treated critically and self-reflectively; neither offered a guarantee regarding the good, the true, or the beautiful. Both were conditioned by what was going on in history and society. Yet both at best challenged the terms of that conditioning: philosophy by means of reason and music by means of expression.

Philosophy and music stood in an antagonistic but intimate relation. Because music was the exemplary language of pure expression but of no concept, and philosophy that of pure concept but no expression, each yearned, as if seeking a (Goethean) affinity, for what the other had—rational articulation for the one, and expression for the other. In their productive but troubled yearning they jointly tracked the historical course of modernity. Adorno focused predominantly on German philosophy and German music as both consummate and cautionary of enlightenment.

COLLABORATIVE PROJECTS

Temperamentally allied to the solitary thinkers and lonely composers of modernity, Adorno's thinking was shaped by notions of exile, otherness, and alienation. However, this did not render him merely an isolated or esoteric thinker; much of his work was produced collaboratively and often under the auspices of publicly sponsored research projects.

A leading member of the Frankfurt-based Institute of Social Research, he worked most closely with its founder Max Horkheimer, but so too with other members like Herbert Marcuse and Leo Löwenthal. In his early years he was in close contact with Walter Benjamin and Siegfried Kracauer. In New York he worked, albeit with difficulty, under the leadership of the Austrian exiled sociologist Paul Lazarsfeld on the Princeton Radio Project. He worked specifically on the empirical testing (a method of which he was highly critical) of listening habits, opinions, and tastes shaped by the then new means of technological production. A significant proportion of his writing on the arts was devoted to the mass media, to the radio, record player, television, and film, and particularly to the changes in modes of reception each instigated. Generally Adorno showed more interest in developing a critical, sociological aesthetic of the ear than of the eye. He did, however, think about the prohibition of the image and then about the adaptation of that prohibition to word and tone within an increasingly censorious society.

In Los Angeles he collaborated with Horkheimer in research on authoritarianism, fascism, anti-Semitism, and prejudice. To their results they linked descriptions of what came to be called the culture or mass entertainment industry, an industry of cultural production and propaganda devoted to "administering" public opinion and taste. In relation to philosophy, society, and the arts they traced the tendencies they took to be equally prevalent in Germany and America, although in different degrees and modes of advancement. They traced the tendencies toward mass consumerism and standardization, toward conformism and adaptation (as part of their critique of *identity thinking*), and toward domestication and normalization, as if, they argued, that which was being sold to the public as "the good, the true and the beautiful" was nothing but obviously "authentic," "natural," or "self-evident." They picked out these latter terms just because they were the ones most often used in public discourse, where the understanding was that to declare something self-evident, for example, rendered any further justification or reasoning unnecessary. In general, their work aimed to disassemble the philosophical illusions and aesthetic appearances that sustained a modern society of self-evidence. The work culminated in their jointly authored *Dialectic of Enlightenment. Philosophical Fragments* (1944), Adorno's *Philosophy of New Music* (1948), and Horkheimer's *The Eclipse of Reason* (1947).

In tandem with the work he did with Horkheimer, Adorno argued against the false rationalizations offered on behalf of mainstream social and aesthetic forms: the *pseudo-individualization* associated with the mainstream production of jazz and popular music, the *pseudo-ritualization* of some of Igor Stravinsky's music, and the pseudo-naturalism of some of John Cage's. He objected to contemporary appeals made on behalf of particular arts to return to ritual, nature, or the individual, as if these things had not suffered what society in general had suffered. All had suffered the consequences of an ideology of progress or of enlightenment ideals gone wrong. Adorno wanted the contemporary forms of art to take account of what had historically occurred and not assume that good-sounding ideas and ideals remained guiltlessly in place.

While working with Horkheimer and Mann, Adorno also collaborated with the composer Hanns Eisler, a student of Schoenberg and collaborator also with Bertolt Brecht, all of whom were contemporaneously resident in Los Angeles. With Eisler, Adorno furthered his sociological aesthetic of listening. Together they wrote a primer (1947) for the composition of a progressive or new music for the film. They framed their recommendations by a sustained critique of the increasingly dominant Hollywood film industry.

CRITICAL THEORY

Adorno contributed significantly to the development of critical theory, a dialectical, historical approach to both thinking and writing that unrelentingly aimed to expose the errors of the dominant scientistic, empiricist, and positivist methods of the day. In 1961, in Tübingen, he engaged in the so-called positivist dispute with, among others, Karl Popper and Jürgen Habermas. What he argued was just a continuation of his life-long double-pronged critique of a reductionist or eliminativist method, on the one hand, and an overly grounded or too securely founded totalizing metaphysics, on the other. (With the latter he usually associated the work of Heidegger and the postwar Heideggerians.) His work in aesthetic theory mirrored the same double-pronged critical aim.

Influenced by Goethe, Kant, Beethoven, and Hegel at the one end of modernity, and by the post- Marxists and Freudians, Lukacs, Kracauer, and Benjamin at the other, Adorno traced the convergences between philosophy, society, and the arts, or the dialectical movement of reason and irrationality that reached its inconceivable extreme in the Nazi concentration camps. Reversing Hegel's dictum that "the true is the whole"—where the whole is the positive and absolute completion of the dialectical movement of *Geist*—Adorno described the complex tendencies that had historically led toward untruth in its varying regressive and progressive concrete arrangements. He encapsulated his entire philosophical, sociological, and aesthetic reflections in the thought that there is no life—and thus no thought, no art, and no action—that is lived rightly when the whole is false.

Adorno focused on the major thinkers and artists of his times, for example: on Husserl and Heidegger in philosophy, on Schoenberg, Berg, Stravinsky, and Cage in music, and on Brecht, Kafka and Beckett in literature and drama. He did so partially to assess their historical relation to their great predecessors: Goethe, Schiller, Kant, Hegel, Beethoven, Kierkegaard, Wagner, Balzac, Valéry, George, and Proust, to name only a very few of the many writers who absorbed Adorno's indefatigable attention. He explored the tense relation between ideas of tradition, establishment, the accepted, and the expected, on the one hand, and ideas of the new, the unfamiliar, the unexpected, the explosive, and the shocking, on the other. (He particularly liked to work with an analogy between the artwork and the firework.) When he spoke of the old and the new, he most often thought, with Goethe, about how the new comes to suffer from its own aging. In other terms, his aesthetic reflections were also reflections constitutive of a *Geschichtsphilosophie*: a philosophy of history that would attempt to resist either falling into the safety of conservative, nostalgic, or utopian pastures, on the one hand, or reaching absolute or positive end points on a road that had no end, on the other. Most of his thinking aimed to invert the movement of Hegelian spirit in the light of the concrete social changes that had occurred between Hegel's time and his own.

TENDENCIES AND CATEGORIES

Adorno approached history by describing how the general social tendencies toward regression and progression were always mediated by concrete or particular instances. Though he had a rhetorical tendency to make it seem as if all the many thinkers, artists, and composers about whom he wrote would duly be lined up on the side of "the

good" or of "the bad," his more subtle aim was to show how particular thoughts, works, or genres were constellations of contradictory tendencies. Indeed, to show them as such was to counter the very tendency to which his rhetorical tendency pointed, namely, the extreme polarization into which modern, administered society had placed its products and its persons.

Adorno focused on categorization, on the social dynamics of organization that included the stereotying and pigeonholing of persons, the social classification and marketing of the arts, as well as the construction and use of philosophical concepts. In his work on listening, he produced a taxonomy of listeners, to show less the type of which he approved (although his own tastes and preferences were always explicit in his critique), and more the types of listening that had developed in relation to the production of modern, "high" and "low" forms of music. Labels designating one sort of music as "serious," "elite," "esoteric," "difficult" or "incomprehensible" maintained a dialectical relation to those that designated another sort of music as "popular" and "authentic." On either side, the labels deflected the listener's attention from the music itself and refocused it in terms of what best suited the listener as consumer. Concepts of the high and low were not "givens" of aesthetic practice; they were sociological categories used to encourage musicians to produce musics of perfect fit, equally "hit tunes" or "difficult works."

AESTHETIC THEORY AND NEGATIVE DIALECTICS

Adorno may be read through his many essays and books amounting to more than 20 volumes. Or he may be read through his two masterworks, his *Negative Dialectics* of 1966 and his unfinished and posthumously published *Aesthetic Theory* of 1970. More specifically, whether one reads his early *Kierkegaard: Construction of the Aesthetic* or his exemplary essay on the "Social Situation of Music," or one of his monographs on Richard Wagner, Gustav Mahler, or Alban Berg, or whether, rather, one reads only his last works, one sees immediately that his primary interest in music never confined him to this particular art. Music was the model through which to access the entire domain of the aesthetic if not also society. He pursued most of the traditional problems of classical, romantic and modernist aesthetic theory: judgment and experience; the sublime and the beautiful; form, content, and material; genre, movement, and style (naturalism, realism, expressionism, and surrealism); the fateful, tragic, and the comic; art's relation to nature, to time, temporality, history and movement, and to society, politics, and propaganda. He drew upon many concepts unfamiliar to us today as well as upon concepts that at the time had become overly standardized through long term (mis)use, notably: mimesis, autonomy, expression, remembrance, comportment, commitment, and convergence.

Central to his aesthetic theory were two dialectical relationships, first, between the concept of art and that of the work of art; second, between the articulated and the hidden, concealed, or unexpressed dimensions of meaning. To regard a work of art as a constellation of contradictory impulses was to regard it as suspended between historical, social, and aesthetic demands: for example, following Kant, between the demand that the work be a product of labor and construction and the demand that it be a product of genius and thus appear as if natural, spontaneous, and free; or, following Schiller, that the work embody the mutually antagonistic drives toward form and sensuousness; or, following Hegel, that a work tremble between freedom and necessity, or between form and content, or between the demands of the traditional and the new, or between the repetition of the same and the shock of the different, or, finally, between acceptance and exemplarity.

To the extent that a work maintained the tension between conflicting demands, the work, so Adorno argued, was truthful. To resolve the tension in any given direction tended to result in an ideologically, theory-laden, or aesthetically compromised product. Thus, the more autonomous, or the more philosophically and socially truthful a work, the more it failed to conceal its inherent tensions or contradictions behind the illusion of perfect order, the more it refused not to show the untruth of its times. The failure and refusal prompted Adorno to speak of a negative autonomy or of a negative dialectics. Following an old Platonic anxiety, art had the ability to expose the lie of appearance or the untruth of society at the same time that it was able to serve as the primary means (of appearance) by which to encourage and sustain the lie. Its double-sided character and dependence on appearance rendered it exemplary both as a means and as an object of critique.

For Adorno, artworks were social formations set at an aesthetic remove; as such they exhibited a drive toward order, harmony, and internal coherence. This drive was dominant in the very concept of a work, a concept coincident with the dialectical course of enlightenment. And precisely what this drive aimed to do was suppress its opposing drive, the drive that would itself attempt to flout the conditions or possibility of order in a work by

mimetically conveying as residue the non-expressed expression implicit to the concept of art. Just as the one drive toward order couldn't do without the drive toward free expression, so, under the condition of modernity, the concept of a work couldn't do without the concept of art, despite the antagonism they displayed toward one another. Yet in this antagonism resided all that was most productive and exemplary in the world of art. Hence, the more autonomous a work, the more the work exhibited the mimetic tension between silence and expression, between what it brought to expression under the concept of the work and what was concealed or excluded of the concept of art thereby. That Adorno often pursued an analogy between the artwork and the person was not without relevance for the truth art could indirectly reveal about society as a whole. The greater society's untruth, the more reified or fetishized the work's or the person's relation to society. The greater society's untruth the more the work was inclined to show the achievement of workhood as consumer product. The work, like a person, could show the achievement in two ways, either by adapting to or by resisting the social situation.

AFTER CATASTROPHE

When Adorno returned to Germany in 1949 he was confronted with the fact of having survived the catastrophe. He asked what it meant for (West) Germany to become a democracy given what he understood to be a continuation of social injustice and prejudice. He used his experiences in America partially as a model of both the promise and the curse of democracy. While convinced that neither the philosopher nor the artist could assume an ahistorical vantage point from which to view society, Adorno was nonetheless convinced that by describing the dominant tendencies toward philosophical, social, and aesthetic untruth, one would thereby show by dialectical negation what remained as the residue or remainder of truth. With Walter Benjamin, he did not think that truth could be found or established in a sustained method of philosophical argument; he rather looked in the cracks of such arguments, in what was not said, in what had historically come to be concealed by dominant patterns, be they philosophical theories, social formations, or artistic movements.

After the war, Adorno wrote that "to still write a poem after Auschwitz is barbaric," a claim he later somewhat modified (1992, vol. 2, p. 87). However, in the claim he asked a question of despair, whether and how continuation in art or thought was possible in a society that now lived "metaphysically"—as he used that term in concluding his *Negative Dialectic,*—under the condition of death. His *Aesthetic Theory* had, however, opened with the same claim, that it "is self-evident that nothing concerning art is self-evident any more, not its inner life, not its relation to the world, not even its right to exist" (1997, p. 1). Here, the point was to use the concept of self-evidence to begin a critique of its social, philosophical and aesthetic forms, where self-evidence found its subjective side in the formation of public opinion and its objective side in the production of ordered-appearances (say, in works of art). His preoccupation with how art and philosophy could continue in modern times had begun around 1930 when he asked after their "*actuality.*" Later, he posed the question again but now even more concretely against the background of the compromise the university and the concert hall had made under national socialism.

Adorno experimented with the essay form, as is shown in his exemplary essay in his *Notes to Literature* on the essay as form. He wrote his aesthetic theory conscious of aesthetic figuration, sometimes in aphorisms or fragments, sometimes in figures of montage, even if this text often reads as a single paragraph without end. He wrote in such a way as to show his interest both in the techniques of high modernism and in the use and mutilation of language (his own use included), be that language one of communication, speech, gesture, or expression. He often expressed his thoughts as catch-phrases articulated as statements of a negative dialectic: for example, only for the sake of happiness and beauty are happiness and beauty renounced; only in memory and longing is pleasure now possible in art; the old only has refuge in the new; dissonance is the truth about harmony. Adorno was an aesthetic thinker of exemplary modernist form; he mediated that thinking within a dialectical and materialist history of society.

See also Aesthetics, History of; Aesthetics, Problems of; Beauty; Benjamin, Walter; Bloch, Ernst; Critical Theory; Dialectical Materialism; Enlightenment; Goethe, Johann Wolfgang von; Habermas, Jürgen; Hegel, Georg Wilhelm Friedrich; Heidegger, Martin; Horkheimer, Max; Husserl, Edmund; Kant, Immanuel; Kierkegaard, Søren Aabye; Lukács, Georg; Nietzsche, Friedrich; Popper, Karl Raimund; Proust, Marcel; Schiller, Friedrich; Schopenhauer, Arthur.

Bibliography

WORKS BY THEODOR W. ADORNO

Composing for the Films. With Hanns Eisler. New York: Oxford University Press, 1947.

Gesammelte Schriften, edited by Rolf Tiedemann. 20 vols. Frankfurt am Main: Suhrkamp, 1970–1986.

Negative Dialectics. Translated by E. B. Ashton. New York: Seabury Press, 1973.

Minima Moralia: Reflections from Damaged Life. Translated by E. F. N. Jephcott. London: Verso, 1974.

Introduction to the Sociology of Music. Translated by E. B. Ashton. New York: Seabury Press, 1976.

"The Actuality of Philosophy." *Telos* 31 (Spring 1977): 120–133.

In Search of Wagner. Translated by Rodney Livingstone. London: New Left Books, 1981.

Positivist Dispute in German Sociology. Aldershot, Hampshire: Ashgate Press, 1981.

Prisms. Translated by Samuel and Shierry Weber. Cambridge, MA: MIT Press, 1981.

Kierkegaard: Construction of the Aesthetic. Translated by Robert Hullot-Kentor. Minneapolis: University of Minnesota Press, 1989.

Alban Berg: Master of the Smallest Link. Translated by Juliane Brand and Christopher Hailey. Cambridge, U.K.: Cambridge University Press, 1991.

The Culture Industry: Selected Essays on Mass Culture, edited by J. M. Bernstein. London: Routledge, 1991.

Notes to Literature. Translated by Shierry Weber Nicholsen. 2 vols. New York: Columbia University Press, 1991–1992.

Mahler: A Musical Physiognomy. Translated by Edmund Jephcott. Chicago: University of Chicago Press, 1992.

Nachgelassene Schriften, edited by Rolf Tiedemann et al. Frankfurt am Main: Suhrkamp, 1993–.

Aesthetic Theory. Edited by Gretel Adorno and Rolf Tiedemann. Translated by Robert Hullot-Kentor. Minneapolis: University of Minnesota Press, 1997.

Beethoven: The Philosophy of Music, edited by Rolf Tiedemann. Translated by Edmund Jephcott. Stanford, CA: Stanford University Press, 1998.

Sound Figures. Translated by Rodney Livingstone. Stanford, CA: Stanford University Press, 1999.

The Dialectic of Enlightenment. With Max Horkheimer, edited by Gunzelin Schmid Noerr. Translated by Edmund Jephcott. Stanford, CA: Stanford University Press, 2002.

Critical Models: Interventions and Catchwords. Translated and with a preface by Henry W. Pickford, Introduction by Lydia Goehr, New York: Columbia University Press, 2005.

Philosophy of New Music. Translated and with an introduction by Robert Hullot-Kentor. Minneapolis: University or Minnesota Press, 2006.

WORKS ABOUT THEODOR W. ADORNO

Arato, A., and E. Gebhardt. *The Essential Frankfurt School Reader.* New York: Continuum, 1982.

Benjamin, Andrew, ed. *The Problems of Modernity: Adorno and Benjamin.* London and New York: Routledge, 1989.

Bernstein, J. M., ed. *The Culture Industry.* London: Routledge, 2001.

Bernstein, J. M. *The Fate of Art: Aesthetic Alienation from Kant to Derrida and Adorno.* University Park: Pennsylvania State University Press, 1992.

Buck-Morss, Susan. *The Origin of Negative Dialectics: Theodor W. Adorno, Walter Benjamin, and the Frankfurt Institute.* New York: Free Press, 1977.

de Nora, Tia. *After Adorno. Rethinking Music Sociology.* Cambridge, U.K.: Cambridge University Press, 2003.

Hohendahl, Peter Uwe. *Prismatic Thought: Theodor W. Adorno.* Lincoln and London: University of Nebraska Press, 1995.

Huhn, T., ed. *The Cambridge Companion to Adorno,* Cambridge, U.K.: Cambridge University Press, 2004.

Huhn, T., and L. Zuidervaart, eds. *The Semblance of Subjectivity: Essays in Adorno's Aesthetic Theory.* Cambridge, MA: MIT Press, 1997.

Jameson, Fredric. *Late Marxism: Adorno, or the Persistence of the Dialectic.* London and New York: Verso, 1990.

Jarvis, Simon. *Adorno: A Critical Introduction.* Cambridge, U.K.: Polity Press, 1998.

Jay, Martin. *Adorno.* London: Fontana, 1984.

Leppert, Richard, ed. *Essays on Music: Theodor W. Adorno.* Selected, with introduction, commentary, and notes by Richard Leppert. Translated by Susan H. Gillespie. Berkeley: University of California Press, 2002.

O'Connor, B. ed. *The Adorno Reader.* Oxford: Blackwell, 2000.

Paddison, Max. *Adorno, Modernism and Mass Culture. Essays in Critical Theory and Music.* London: Kahn and Averill, 1996.

Paddison, Max. *Adorno's Aesthetics of Music.* Cambridge, U.K.: Cambridge University Press, 1997.

Pensky, Max, ed. *The Actuality of Adorno: Critical Essays on Adorno and the Postmodern* New York: SUNY Press, 1997.

Reijen, Willem van. *Adorno: An Introduction.* Philadelphia: Pennbridge Books, 1992.

Rose, Gillian. *The Melancholy Science: An Introduction to the Thought of Theodor W. Adorno.* London: Macmillan, 1978.

Weber Nicholsen, Shierry. *Exact Imagination, Late Idyll: Adorno's Aesthetics.* Cambridge, MA: MIT Press, 1997.

Zuidervaart, Lambert. *Adorno's Aesthetic Theory: The Redemption of Illusion.* Cambridge, MA: MIT Press, 1991.

Lydia Goehr (2005)

AEGIDIUS COLONNA ROMANUS

See *Giles of Rome*

AENESIDEMUS

(1st century BCE)

Very little is known about Aenesidemus's life. He was associated with the Athenian Academy around the time of its collapse in 87 BCE; and he was party to the dispute between Philo of Larissa, who advocated a mild form of skepticism in the form of an externalist, coherentist epistemology, and Antiochus of Ascalon, whose epistemology was basically that of Stoic foundationalism. The Academy had been for two centuries the home of epistemological skepticism, directed largely against the optimistic epistemology of the Stoics, who posited "apprehensive impressions" (*phantasiai kataleptikai*), which carried their own guarantee of truth. Aenesidemus saw Philo and Antiochus as betraying that heritage, as "Stoics fighting with Stoics" (Photius, *Library Catalogue* 212), and resolved to "philosophize after the fashion of Pyrrho."

Aenesidemus wrote eight books of *Pyrrhonian Discourses*, which Photius summarized: "the whole aim of the book is to ground the view that there is no ground for apprehension, whether through perception or thought." The main burden of the *Discourses*, Photius says, is to establish that nobody really grasps anything. However, only Pyrrhonian skeptics are aware of this ignorance, while everyone else falsely considers themselves to be in possession of secure knowledge. This false conviction, and the inevitable disputes that follow from the evident fact that different people hold different and incompatible beliefs, leads the Dogmatists ("belief-holders," as skeptics styled their opponents) into "ceaseless torments." Skeptics, having no beliefs, avoid these torments; indeed they "are happy … in the wisdom of knowing that they have firm apprehension of nothing." "Apprehension" (*katalepsis*) is the Stoic technical term for sure and unshakable knowledge based on apprehensive impressions. When Aenesidemus claims that Pyrrhonists have no apprehension of anything, he is careful not to say that they have *apprehension* of that second-order fact. Yet they may still be aware of it, since it is evident to them introspectively that they are not certain of anything (thus skeptics seek to avoid the charge that their position is self-refuting).

Moreover, "even in regard to what he knows [this is Photius's language; and he may well be less careful than Aenesidemus in avoiding apparent self-refutation], he takes care to assent no more to its affirmation than to its denial." "Assent" (*sunkatathesis*) is another Stoic term, denoting unwavering commitment to the truth of some proposition (positive or negative); and no skeptic will claim that sort of cognitive security, even in regard to his own claims: a skeptic's "positions" (insofar as he really has any) are invariably provisional. In the same vein, "no more" (*ou mallon*) is a skeptical slogan: things may appear to be thus and so, but in themselves they are no more one way rather than the other. Diogenes Laertius (DL 9.106) reports Aenesidemus as saying that appearances are the criterion for action; thus he seeks to evade the common charge brought against skeptics (most famously by Hume) that their refusal to hold beliefs renders life impossible (it is a further, difficult question how far this notion of appearance can really be divorced from some concept of belief).

In the first *Pyrrhonian Discourse*, according to Photius, Aenesidemus distanced himself from the Academics, since they "posit some things with confidence and deny others unambiguously, while Pyrrhonists are aporetic and devoid of dogma; they say neither that all things are inapprehensible, nor that they are apprehensible, but that they are no more so than not so, or sometimes so and sometimes not so, or so for one person but not for another." The Academics are negative dogmatists, positively affirming that nothing can be apprehended according to the Stoic criterion; Pyrrhonists, by contrast, will say that they do not seem to apprehend anything, but will not reject the possibility of there being apprehension. Crucially, "the Pyrrhonist determines absolutely nothing, not even this very proposition, that nothing is determined." That this is the authentic skeptical attitude is confirmed by Sextus Empiricus, *Outlines of Pyrrhonism* (PH) 1.187–209; and Sextus probably relies heavily upon Aenesidemus in that work.

The second *Pyrrhonian Discourse* casts doubt upon "truth, causes, effects, motion, generation and destruction," while the third "was also about motion and sense perception … working carefully through a similar set of contradictions, he puts them too beyond our grasp." These arguments about perception no doubt included the material of the so-called "Ten Modes of Aenesidemus," arguments designed to undermine the Dogmatists' truth-claims, and hence to induce *epochê*, or suspension of judgment, "which the skeptics say is the goal (*telos*), upon which tranquility follows like a shadow, according to Aenesidemus and Timon" (DL 9.107; cf. PH 1.25–30). Thus "Pyrrhonian discourse is a kind of recollection of appearances … , on the basis of which they are all brought into confrontation with one another, and when compared are found to cause much disparity and confusion; so says Aenesidemus in the summary of his *Pyrrhonics*" (DL 9.78).

The Ten Modes are attributed to Aenesidemus by Sextus (*Against the Professors* [M] 7.345); Aristocles ascribes nine Modes to him, and we know the number of the Modes to have been fluid (our earliest source, Philo of Alexandria, records only eight). Neither Sextus in his extant treatment of the Modes (PH 1.31–163), nor Diogenes in his shorter summary (DL 9.79–88) father them on Aenesidemus; but it is still likely that he was responsible for this organization of earlier skeptical material. The Modes share a common form, involving conflicting appearances: *x* appears *F* in conditions *C*, or to observer *O*, not-*F* in conditions *C**, or to observer *O**; there is no non-question-begging way of privileging either of *C* or

C*, *O* or *O**; so we should suspend judgment as to whether *x* is *F*. The Modes are differentiated by different fillers for *C* or *O*; thus the first (in Sextus's ordering) compares the different sensory representations of different animals, the second collects cases of dissonant judgment between different humans, the third conflicts in the deliverances of different sense-modalities, and the fourth includes discrepant reports from the same sense at different times. Other Modes collect cases of ethical or social discrepancy (the tenth), and point to the ways in which differing conditions of the perceiver may affect what they seem to perceive.

The upshot is that we cannot in any case say how things really are, but only how they seem in particular circumstances. Things are judged relatively to the perceiver and their circumstances. Sextus is careful not to draw relativistic conclusions (although the facts of relativity figure both as a particular Mode, the eighth, and in general in the articulation of all the Modes): He does not positively *assert* that things are for the observer as they appear. By contrast, Aenesidemus, judging from Photius's summary, is quite happy to accept the relative judgments as such, since they do not (cannot) count as Dogmatic.

In the fourth *Discourse*, Aenesidemus discussed signs. Sign-theory and its associated epistemology was of overwhelming importance in post-Aristotelian philosophy. The Stoics (along with various Dogmatic medical schools) held that it was possible to infer directly from the phenomena to the underlying structural conditions responsible for them. Skeptics (and Empiricist doctors) denied the validity of such inferences, allowing only that memories of past conjunctions of phenomena might allow us to expect (although fallibly) similar conjunctions in the future. Aenesidemus advanced the following paradigmatically skeptical argument: If apparent things appear alike to all in a similar condition, then signs should appear alike to all in a similar condition; but they do not; hence signs are not apparent (M 8.215). That is, it is not unequivocal what they are signs of—different doctors, for example, draw radically different conclusions from the same symptoms (M 8.219–220).

In the fifth *Discourse* Aenesidemus turned to causes; again Sextus retails some of his arguments (M 8.218–226)yes; crucial to them is the idea that a cause should operate from its own resources; but if it does, then, since it requires nothing else in order to exercise its causal power, it should do so invariably and continuously. More impressive are the Eight Modes against the Aetiologists, mentioned in Photius and ascribed to Aenesidemus by Sextus at PH 1.180–185. These are eight general arguments against the possibility of inferring from evident phenomena to the hidden structures of things that are supposedly causally responsible for those phenomena, in the manner of Dogmatist philosophers and scientists (notably Epicureans, but also Peripatetics and Stoics). Aenesidemus's basic claim foreshadows the modern maxim that theories are invariably underdetermined by the available data. No amount of evidence can ever entail that any particular theory must be true: There are always many ways in principle of accounting for the same set of phenomena (1.181–182). Moreover (and here Aenesidemus turns from general methodological issues to castigating particular recurrent theoretical foibles), theorists sometimes offer piecemeal, unrelated explanations for what are evidently related sets of phenomena; and they tend to suppose, without justification, that the structure of the hidden, subperceptual realm will mirror in all important respects that of the phenomenal world (1.182; this point is particularly well-taken against Epicurean physics).

Furthermore, Aenesidemus notes (and this too is a staple of contemporary philosophy of science) that researchers are inclined to favor explanations that concur with their own prejudices (1.183), and indeed on occasion to prefer explanations that not only conflict with the facts, but also with their own theories (1.184). Finally, he notes that Dogmatists "frequently … seek to explain doubtful things on the basis of things equally doubtful" (1.184). Taken together, the eight Modes are an impressive attack on the possibility of arriving at any soundly based understanding of the hidden natures of things. As such, they are obviously of a piece with, and complement, the rest of Aenesidemus's skeptical argumentation. The last three *Pyrrhonian Discourses* dealt with ethical issues, with Aenesidemus arguing that the lack of philosophical agreement regarding good and bad, choice and avoidance, virtues, and finally the end, preclude the possibility of arriving at any secure judgments about them.

All of the evidence so far reviewed makes Aenesidemus a consistent and powerful skeptic. However, a number of passages in Sextus portray him in a much more Dogmatic light, as holding various views about the intellect (M 7.350), and endorsing the view that there are two types of change (M 10.38). Elsewhere he is said to be in agreement with Heraclitus, whom Sextus explicitly describes as a Dogmatist. These discrepancies are too widespread simply to be brushed aside. But there is as yet no scholarly agreement as to what to do about them.

See also Ancient Skepticism; Antiochus of Ascalon; Philo of Larissa; Pyrrho; Sextus Empiricus.

Bibliography

Annas, J., and J. Barnes. *The Modes of Scepticism*. Cambridge, U.K.: Cambridge University Press, 1985.

Hankinson, R. J. *The Skeptics*. London: Routledge, 1995.

Long, A. A, and D. N. Sedley. *The Hellenistic Philosophers*. Cambridge, U.K.: Cambridge University Press, 1987.

Rist, J. "The Heracliteanism of Aenesidemus." *Phoenix* 24 1970: 309–319.

Tarrant, H. *Skepticism or Platonism?* Cambridge, U.K.: Cambridge University Press, 1985.

R. J. Hankinson (2005)

AESTHETIC EXPERIENCE

An aesthetic experience arises in response to works of art or other aesthetic objects. Although the term *aesthetic* itself was not introduced until the eighteenth century, it is clear that what are identified in contemporary discussions as "aesthetic experiences" were "felt" by individuals long before this: for example, when Plato worried about excessively emotional reactions to recitations of poetry or when Aristotle described the positive effects of attending the theater. Nevertheless, the exact nature of aesthetic experience—even the idea that there is such a unique form of experience—remains a matter of controversy.

WHAT AESTHETIC EXPERIENCES FEEL LIKE

One area of contention concerns what it feels like to have an aesthetic experience—that is, whether there is some special emotion or attitude or other internal sign that enables one to recognize that what one is having is an aesthetic experience and not some other kind. Immanuel Kant, one of the first philosophers to have addressed these kinds of questions, characterizes aesthetic experiences as those pleasures associated with occasions when one judges something to be beautiful. He asserts that one recognizes that this pleasure does not result from a realization that an object is useful or agreeable to one because of special things about oneself. Instead the pleasure arises simply because the form of the object is delightful and could and should be enjoyed by anyone. Kant makes a sharp distinction between responding positively in this manner and responding positively for moral or scientific reasons. Although several theorists have disagreed with Kant's argument, most theorists agree that aesthetic experiences are identified as such at least partly because of an emotional involvement of the experiencer. One feels good (or bad) when one responds aesthetically to a beautiful sunset or elegant poem (or to a messy waste dump or plodding verse).

But it is more than just a feeling of pleasure (or pain) that characterizes aesthetic experiences, according to many theorists. John Dewey (1958), for example, argues that aesthetic experiences are the most complete, the richest, and the highest experiences possible. One is actively engaged and conscious of the world's effect on one but at the same time appreciative of one's possibilities for acting on the world. One senses an organization, coherence, and satisfaction as well as an integration of the past, present, and future that ordinary nonaesthetic experiences lack.

More recently, Nelson Goodman (1976) has warned that too much emphasis on the pleasurable aspects of aesthetic experiences deprives them of much of their importance. What he derisively calls "tingle-immersion" theories overlook the crucial role of intellect, he cautions. In aesthetic experiences, the emotions function cognitively, he says; one "feels" a heightened operation of both cognition and emotion operating together.

WHAT AESTHETIC EXPERIENCES FOCUS ON

Another area of debate is the object of aesthetic experience. Many philosophers have insisted that the pleasurable (or painful) responses associated with an aesthetic experience must be connected with something special about some objects and events—properties that nonaesthetic or nonartistic objects and events lack—for clearly we do not have aesthetic experiences with regard to just any old thing.

Aristotle believed that the pleasure unique to dramatic tragedies consisted in a catharsis of the painful emotions of pity and fear and that this could occur only if a play had certain properties—the right sort of plot and characters. Kant, we saw above, thought that aesthetic experiences were pleasant when objects were such that mere apprehension of their form alone evoked delight. In general, theorists and critics described as "formalists" insist that in an aesthetic experience attention is directed solely to immediately perceivable properties of objects and events—shape, colors, tones, sounds, and patterns. Monroe Beardsley (1958), for instance, characterizes the focus of aesthetic experiences as formal unity and the intensity of regional quality. Clive Bell (1914) claims that emotional responses to objects exhibiting "significant form" can be so intense that one does not care at all about the content of some artworks; what matters is always form and not content. Jerome Stolnitz (1960) argues that

one takes up a special attitude, distinterestedness, when one has an aesthetic experience. Ordinary everyday concerns or purposes are put aside, and one focuses on the form of an object for its sake alone, he believed.

An increasing number of theorists disagree with the formalist position that when one has an aesthetic experience one focuses solely on an object's formal properties and that one's scientific, moral, religious and other beliefs or concerns are put aside. For one thing, some insist, the expression of certain ideas plays a key role in some works of art, and surely thinking about these ideas (content) is an appropriate and important aspect of the aesthetic experiences of them. Even if focus on form is necessary to aesthetic experiences, it may be that content and context are also legitimate matters for aesthetic attention.

WHAT HAVING AN AESTHETIC EXPERIENCE REQUIRES

Even if one grants that aesthetic experiences arise only in the presence of objects that exhibit a form that pleases, many theorists have insisted that more than a formally pleasing object and passive viewer are required. Just as not every object gives rise to an aesthetic experience, so not all individuals have aesthetic experiences in reaction to the same objects. David Hume (1987) in the eighteenth century and, more recently, Frank Sibley (1959) in the twentieth, have insisted that only persons who have taste or special sensitivities are capable of responding aesthetically. Not all people are equally competent judges, Hume claims. Only people who are sensitive, attentive, open-minded, perceptive, clear-headed, trained, and experienced can tell a good poem from a bad poem. In the absence of sensitivity, one will be left completely cold by objects that enthrall a more acute and receptive observer.

Formalists, we saw above, insist that aesthetic experience requires an appropriate amount of distance—one must put aside beliefs or purposes and give oneself up entirely to the object. But others argue that precisely the opposite is the case. Contextualists insist that, before one can have an aesthetic response (or at least an appropriate or full one), one's intellect and moral beliefs must be engaged. Noel Carroll (2000), for example, argues that moral concerns may block or enhance aesthetic experiences. Kendall Walton (1970) asserts that one cannot interpret and otherwise respond to a work of art unless one is versed in the genre it represents. One cannot judge whether a sonnet is good or bad unless one knows that it is in fact a sonnet and not a haiku, for example. Allen Carlson (2000) points out that an aesthetic appreciation of nature requires an awareness that what one is appreciating is nature (not a painted landscape, for instance). This in turn demands an understanding of how nature works. The person who brings a fair degree of scientific knowledge to a particular environmental system will have a much fuller, richer aesthetic experience of that environment. What is required by or, at the very least, relevant to aesthetic experience may be whatever directs one's attention as fully as possible to the potentially pleasurable formal properties of an object or event.

WHERE OR WHEN AESTHETIC EXPERIENCES OCCUR

The nature of aesthetic experience may not be fully accounted for even if one knows everything important about objects that occasion them—the context or circumstances attending an individual's response may prove critical. Some philosophers call attention to the viewing conditions: for example, whether a concert is live or recorded or whether a poem is read to oneself or recited aloud. Others focus on the political, economic, or social conditions of an experience. To what extent are aesthetic experiences socially constructed? Is responding pleasurably to the color of a flower, for instance, "natural" (in the way that hunger or sexual arousal is), is it taught (in the way that acquired tastes are), or is there some mix of innate and learned response? Herein lies another set of issues that philosophers and others (for example psychologists, sociologists, and economists) debate.

AESTHETIC VERSUS ARTISTIC EXPERIENCE

Art objects are examples of aesthetic objects. But not all aesthetic objects are artworks—for example, sunsets or mountain vistas. Whether there is a difference between aesthetic experience and artistic experience is still another question that theorists address. Kant notes that in appreciating art objects one is aware of the fact that a human created it (and, in the case of great Art, that someone of genius was responsible for it). Thus artistic experiences lack the "purity" associated with those disinterested pleasures that arise from form alone.

Arthur Danto (1986) has argued that developments in the history of Art (such as the appearance of rather odd artifacts in museums) mean that one cannot tell if something is a work of art or not in the absence of a theory of art. This is not the case for aesthetic objects, it would seem. One does not need a theory of the aesthetic in order to have an aesthetic response, for one can have such a response to anything at all. It may be that some experiences of art are not aesthetic at all. If one is prima-

rily concerned with the history of an object or its economic or religious value, then one may not care about or may even completely ignore the formal properties of that object.

THE NEED FOR THE CONCEPT OF AESTHETIC EXPERIENCE

Finally it must be pointed out that not everyone believes that it is possible or necessary to distinguish aesthetic from other kinds of experiences. The whole notion is too vague and abstract, some philosophers argue. Reporting that one has had an aesthetic experience is no more informative than claiming that one has had an "economic experience" or an "automotive experience," according to some. One describes one's experience far better by saying things like "I bought some junk bonds yesterday" or "I had an exciting ride in a Porsche this morning" than by saying "I had an economic experience" or "I had an automotive experience." Similarly, one might do away completely with talk about aesthetic experiences and rely instead on discussions of reading particular poems or listening to pieces of music or birdsongs or looking at specific paintings or landscapes or drinking particular wines.

Nevertheless, people do talk about aesthetic experiences, and there might be good reason to try to articulate what they involve. If one goal of education is to improve the quality of life through aesthetic experiences, then it will be important to determine what such experiences feel like, focus on, and require. Moreover, if one fears that significant properties of objects or events will be overlooked if one confuses moral or scientific perspectives with aesthetic ones, then it may be necessary to distinguish the last from the former two.

See also Aesthetic Judgment; Aesthetic Qualities; Art, Interpretation of.

Bibliography

Beardsley, Monroe. *Aesthetics*. New York: Harcourt Brace, 1958.

Bell, Clive. *Art*. London: Chatto & Windus, 1914.

Carlson, Allen. *Aesthetics and the Environment*. London and New York: Routledge, 2000.

Carroll, Noel. *Theories of Art Today*. Madison: University of Wisconsin Press, 2000.

Danto, Arthur. *The Transformation of the Commonplace*. New York: Columbia University Press, 1986.

Dewey, John. *Art as Experience*. New York: Putnam's Sons, 1958.

Eaton, Marcia Muelder. *Merit, Aesthetic and Ethical*. New York: Oxford University Press, 2000.

Goodman, Nelson. *Languages of Art*. Indianapolis, IN: Hackett, 1976.

Hume, David. "Of a Standard of Taste" (1759). In *Essays Moral, Political and Literary*, edited by Eugene F. Miller. Indianapolis, IN: Liberty Fund, 1987.

Kant, Immanuel, *The Critique of Judgment* (1790). Translated by Werner S. Pluhar. Indianapolis, IN: Hackett, 1987.

Sibley, Frank. "Aesthetic Concepts." *Philosophical Review* 68 (1959): 421–450.

Stolnitz, Jerome. *Aesthetics and the Philosophy of Art Criticism*. New York: Houghton Mifflin, 1960.

Walton, Kendall. "Categories of Art." *Philosophical Review* 79 (1970): 334–367.

Marcia Mueder Eaton (2005)

AESTHETIC JUDGMENT

In recent analytic aesthetics, there have been two prominent questions about aesthetic judgments. One is how to distinguish aesthetic judgments from other judgments. Answering this question seems particularly urgent when an aesthetic judgment and a nonaesthetic judgment about the same object are incongruent. In such a case it seems that an object might be judged to have aesthetic value but also to be negatively judged, say ethically or in terms of its practical use. A corollary question is whether the negative value of a nonaesthetic judgment should affect the allegedly purely aesthetic judgment.

The other prominent question, a question present at least since the eighteenth century, is actually two questions: first, whether aesthetic judgments are objective or subjective, and second, whether aesthetic judgments can be verified or otherwise substantiated. Somewhat curiously, perhaps, some philosophers have thought that even though such judgments are subjective, they are still capable of being supported. David Hume is an example. In contrast, other philosophers have thought that even though such judgments are genuinely objective, they are nonetheless incapable of being verified by customary procedures. Frank Sibley has been the leading exponent of this opinion. A more obvious thesis is Immanuel Kant's, namely that aesthetic judgments are both subjective and impossible to support by any interpersonal means.

Hume (1987) believed that it is possible to identify certain judges as having especially reliable taste and then to take their subjective responses to objects as a standard in evaluating the objects. When such judges deliver what Hume called "a joint verdict," meaning, presumably, that they concur in taking pleasure in an object, taking pleasure in the object is then established as correct, in a sense, with at least customary probability, and any judge who fails to realize this pleasure is defective in his taste.

Kant, in contrast, thought that no corroboration of one's judgment is possible because a concurrence with or difference from the responses of other judges is logically irrelevant.

The idea of something explicitly called an aesthetic judgment seems first to have appeared in the eighteenth century and was formulated in detail by Kant (2000). By "aesthetic judgment" Kant meant a judgment based on a feeling. He was especially concerned to describe those feeling-based judgments in which an object is found beautiful, and then to show that we are entitled to make such judgments despite being unable to verify them. In his conviction that these judgments are essentially subjective (that is, derived from or based on the subject's feeling), Kant is in line with an earlier tradition. The most notable exponent of this tradition was Hume, though it remains unsettled just how much, if any, of Hume's writings on this topic were known to Kant. Yet Kant probably did know the earlier work of Francis Hutcheson, work in the spirit of Hume even if less compelling philosophically. In later developments of the idea of an aesthetic judgment, however, this feeling-based subjectivity has been less important than Kant's description of how an aesthetic judge attends to the object of his judgment.

The subjective character of judgments of beauty seemed obvious in the eighteenth century, especially to Hume and Kant, so obvious that neither of them argued for this notion but simply assumed it. Indeed, the etymology of the word "aesthetic" indicates that an aesthetic judgment must be essentially related to a feeling. The Greek term refers to sense perception, usually, but it has now come to refer to feelings in general, and in particular to feelings of pleasure. Hume does not use the term "aesthetic," and he speaks only of the exercise of taste in the discernment of beauty, but like Kant he takes it for granted that all judgments of beauty arise from feelings of pleasure experienced by the judge.

According to Hume, the term "beauty" does not correspond to any objective property of things, and so judgments of beauty cannot be correct or incorrect in any straightforward manner. Yet such judgments can be vindicated, he thought, by agreement with the judgments of especially well suited judges of the object. These exemplars of taste (whose responses, he said, constitute a "standard of taste") are identified by their stellar discernment, without prejudice, of all the properties of the objects being judged. There is no way to inspect an object for its beauty, Hume thought, because "beauty" does not mark any property of an object, but it is possible, as a matter of empirical investigation, to determine whether any particular judge is an exemplary judge.

Kant, in describing what he calls "a pure judgment of taste," had a different idea. He thought that the judge must pay no attention to any use to which the object might be put, to any concept that applies to the object, or to any interest that the judge might have in the object. The judgment must thus be entirely disinterested and free of any thought that relates the object to anything else. It is a judgment about the object purely and simply in itself.

Kant first described aesthetic judgments made about natural objects (his leading example being a beautiful rose), and then extended such judgments to works of art. He thus effectively regarded successful works of art (which for him meant artificial beautiful objects) as loci for such judgments.

The idea that aesthetic judgment requires a detached state of mind has sometimes been developed as the idea that aesthetic judgments require an aesthetic attitude, a distinct mode of addressing objects. An early exponent of this idea was Arthur Schopenhauer, although he does not use the term "aesthetic attitude." Pursuing a line different from Kant's, Schopenhauer thought that contemplation of works of art was an activity in which one could escape the usual constraints on one's will.

In the early twentieth century, the idea of an aesthetic attitude was developed further, given this particular name, and given more detailed treatment, though it eventually became a problematic notion. An early formulation is Edward Bullough's (1957), although his interests were somewhat more psychological than philosophical. A later, more sophisticated treatment is to be found in the works of Jerome Stolnitz (1978). A useful canvass of the idea is in George Dickie's "The Myth of the Aesthetic Attitude" (1964), where Dickie seeks to do away with the idea.

Although continuing conceptions of aesthetic judgment in many respects derive from the early work of Hume and Kant, these conceptions have taken at least two noteworthy turns. In philosophy at the beginning of the twenty-first century, the term "aesthetics" has become a virtual synonym for "philosophy of art." This assimilation sometimes draws attention to a question, but at other times tends to cover it up—the question of which is basic, the idea of art or the idea of the aesthetic. In Kant and many of his followers, the idea of the aesthetic is basic, and the idea of art is, so to speak, constructed out of the idea of the aesthetic. Kant thus first characterizes aesthetic judgments and then essentially describes works of

fine art as objects about which such judgments can be made. Richard Wollheim (1980), in contrast, reverses this dependence, declaring that to make an aesthetic judgment is to regard something as a work of art.

A radically different thesis is that of Frank Sibley (1959, 1965). Sibley takes aesthetic judgments to be judgments that apply aesthetic concepts to objects through the use of aesthetic terms. Rather than understand taste as Hume and Kant did, as the ability to take pleasure in the judgment of objects, Sibley takes taste to be the ability to use aesthetic terms and concepts. Furthermore, in view of his conviction that aesthetic judgments are objective, Sibley treats the term "beautiful" quite differently from his eighteenth-century predecessors. For Hume and Kant, the term "beauty" has very little semantic content, it indicating only that the object produces a particular feeling of pleasure in the judge. Sibley, in contrast, insists that the term refers to a property of the object being judged. Thus, for Sibley, "beautiful," "elegant," "graceful," and other terms indicated mainly by example are all aesthetic terms, and as such they all refer to objective properties, although only judges exercising what Sibley calls "taste" can detect these properties and hence correctly apply the terms. Thus, quite apart from the tradition of Hume and Kant, Sibley's thesis is that aesthetic judgments are perfectly objective, meaning that their terms refer to properties objectively present in the objects being judged. Yet Sibley's thesis, at least in one respect, is more like Hume's and Kant's than it is like Wollheim's. For Wollheim, to regard an object aesthetically is to regard it as a work of art. For Hume, Kant, and Sibley, aesthetic judgments are freely made of works of art but also of other objects, and in the latter case there is no need to treat these objects as works of art.

Even among those who regard the concept of art as more basic than the concept of the aesthetic, many such thinkers continue to insist, with Kant, that an aesthetic judgment must be disinterested and must not attend to anything besides the object itself. Those who believe aesthetic judgments to be a unique kind of judgment have been eager to distinguish aesthetic judgments from ethical judgments, in particular, and also from practical concerns. Others have wondered whether it is possible to make such a clear logical separation. When the question of design is raised, it becomes increasingly difficult to suppose that an aesthetic judgment about an object is entirely divorced from other considerations—an issue that is perhaps most acute in the case of architecture. If a building is beautiful to behold but ill suited to whatever activities it is meant to house, can one keep the building's evident disutility from contaminating one's sense of the aesthetic value of the building? The same question arises, obviously, in many other cases of artistic design, ranging from automobiles to writing instruments to time-keeping devices. It seems clear that a genuinely ugly object might be a perfectly serviceable automobile or watch. It is less clear that that a poorly performing object can still be beautiful. On this matter, Kant's opinion is clear. He thought that it is one thing to judge a watch, say, to be a good watch because of its perspicuous time display and reliable time keeping, this being to judge the watch in terms relying on the concept of a watch; it is another thing to offer a pure judgment of taste. To other authors, this is not obvious, because for them, questions of utility are difficult to separate from questions of the aesthetic value of an object.

Recently much attention has been given to the separation of ethical concerns from aesthetic concerns (Levinson 2001), and in 2005 it is a much debated question whether the dubious moral character of an art work can be kept separate from its artistic or aesthetic value. There has thus been a renewal of interest in the question of the relations of ethics and aesthetics to one another.

See also Aesthetic Experience; Aesthetic Qualities; Aesthetics, History of; Art, Interpretation of; Beauty; Sublime, The; Ugliness.

Bibliography

Brady, Emily, and Jerrold Levinson, eds. *Aesthetic Concepts: Essays after Sibley*. New York: Oxford University Press, 2001.

Bullough, Edward. *Æsthetics: Lectures and Essays* Stanford, CA: Stanford University Press, 1957.

Dickie, George. "The Myth of the Aesthetic Attitude." *American Philosophical Quarterly* 1 (1) (1964): 56–65.

Guyer, Paul. "History of Modern Aesthetics." In *The Oxford Handbook of Aesthetics*, edited by Jerrold Levinson. New York: Oxford University Press, 2003.

Guyer, Paul. "The Origins of Modern Aesthetics: 1711–35." In *The Blackwell Guide to Aesthetics*, edited by Peter Kivy. Oxford: Blackwell, 2004.

Hume, David. *Essays, Moral, Political, and Literary*. Rev. ed. Indianapolis, IN: Liberty Fund, 1987.

Kant, Immanuel. *Critique of the Power of Judgment*. Translated by Paul Guyer and Eric Matthews. New York: Cambridge University Press, 2000.

Levinson, Jerrold. *Aesthetics and Ethics: Essays at the Intersection*. New York: Cambridge University Press, 2001.

Schopenhauer, Arthur. *The World as Will and Representation*. Translated by E. F. J. Payne. Indian Hills, CO: Falcon's Wing Press, 1958.

Sibley, Frank. "Aesthetic and Non-aesthetic." *Philosophical Review* 74 (1965): 135–159.

Sibley, Frank. "Aesthetic Concepts." *Philosophical Review* 68 (1959): 421–450.

Stolnitz, Jerome. " "The 'Aesthetic Attitude'" in the Rise of Modern Aesthetics." *Journal of Aesthetics and Art Criticism* 36 (1978): 409–422.

Townsend, Dabney, ed. *Eighteenth-Century British Aesthetics*. Amityville, NY: Baywood, 1998.

Wollheim, Richard. *Art and Its Objects*. 2nd ed. New York: Cambridge University Press, 1980.

Ted Cohen (2005)

AESTHETIC QUALITIES

It is generally, although not universally, agreed among philosophers that there is an important distinction to be drawn between the aesthetic qualities of objects, especially art objects, and their nonaesthetic qualities: between being serene, stunning, or grating, and being square, in the key of A-minor, or weighing seven pounds. The concept of an aesthetic quality is a philosophical one, not in general use, but aestheticians appeal to it in clarifying the practice of art criticism, justifying aesthetic judgments, and evaluating artworks.

HISTORICAL BACKGROUND

Both David Hume (1963) and Immanuel Kant (1966) set the stage for this modern distinction in their discussions of aesthetic judgments, judgments regarding the beauty of objects. Both argued that such judgments differ in kind from judgments regarding ordinary perceptual properties. Both held that aesthetic judgments depend on subjective feelings of pleasure and affective responses, but both also sought a universal ground for such judgments. Unlike Francis Hutcheson (1971) before them, they did not find this ground in an objective property (for Hutcheson, unity in variety) that always gives rise to this pleasurable response in qualified observers. Instead, recognizing the normative force of ascriptions of beauty, the demand for agreement in one's ascriptions of this property, they sought a standard in universal subjective grounds of the judgments of qualified critics.

Hume emphasized that only the judgments of fully competent or ideal critics indicate the presence of beauty or aesthetic merit. The property of beauty is similar in this respect to secondary qualities like colors, as analyzed by John Locke. For Locke, the color red is a power in objects, based on objective properties of their surfaces, to cause red sensations in normal observers in normal conditions. For Hume, beauty is similarly a relation between various objective properties and subjective responses, differences being that, as noted, there is no single objective property to be found here, and that qualified observers are rarer and more difficult to define. Such observers must have developed tastes, be knowledgeable of the type of work they are judging and of the historical tradition with which to compare the work, and be sensitive to the sorts of subtle relations on which the beauty of the work might depend. In the end, even such qualified critics might disagree in their comparative aesthetic judgments, Hume recognized.

Kant was both more emphatic than Hume that there are no universal objective grounds for ascriptions of beauty, and was more confident that such judgments should nevertheless be universally shared. For him, there are no principles that connect objective properties with correct ascriptions of beauty. Nevertheless, the pleasure derived from the disinterested perception of form should be universally felt, since common human faculties are involved in such perception. The perception of formal properties elicits a value-laden (pleasurable) response that is common to all disinterested observers and expressed in ascriptions of beauty. Since there is no objective property common to all beautiful objects (no objective concept of beauty), one cannot tell from a description of an object whether it is beautiful. One must experience the pleasure from perception of the object. But in judging an object to be beautiful, one demands the agreement of other observers, unlike in judging mere agreeableness.

THE NATURE OF AESTHETIC QUALITIES: REALISM

The contemporary discussion of aesthetic qualities began with Frank Sibley (1959). He first expanded the list of aesthetic qualities from beauty and sublimity to include emotion qualities like being sad or serene, evocative qualities like being powerful or dull, behavioral qualities like being jaunty or sluggish, formal-evaluative qualities like being graceful or tightly knit, and second-order perceptual qualities like being vivid or steely. A major philosophical question resulted from this expansion. What do these qualities have in common that distinguishes them from nonaesthetic qualities? Other questions remain from the discussions of Hume and Kant. What is the nature of these qualities, and how are they related to the nonaesthetic qualities of their objects?

In regard to the first question, some of the properties listed may be ascribed to artworks only metaphorically, but others are ascribed literally. If "sad" here can mean expressive of sadness, and "powerful" can refer to the power to evoke a strong response, then these two properties fall into the latter category.

According to Sibley, perceiving aesthetic properties requires taste. If taste is a special quasi-perceptual faculty different from the ordinary five senses, as his usage sometimes suggests, then its existence and operation becomes mysterious, as do the aesthetic qualities it alone can grasp. If taste refers simply to sensitivity to aesthetic properties, then there is a tight circularity in the definitions that needs to be removed. But appeal to taste here can have two other more plausible functions. First, it can indicate that the perception of all the relevant nonaesthetic properties of an object is not sufficient for the perception of its aesthetic properties. One must perceive nonaesthetic properties to perceive aesthetic qualities, but not vice versa.

Second, since "taste" in one of its senses refers to dispositions to evaluate in certain ways, appeal to taste here can indicate that ascribing aesthetic properties to artworks is always relevant to their evaluation. We justify aesthetic evaluations by pointing to the aesthetic properties of objects. Some of these properties, like being graceful or tightly knit, are typically value-laden in themselves. Others, like being sad, seem not to be. But if artworks not only have such properties, but, as Nelson Goodman (1969) claims, exemplify them, that is, refer to them and tell us something of their nature, then this is of some value. And experiencing such qualities can also be of value by being part of an overall response to an artwork that engages not only the emotions, but the perceptual, imaginative, and cognitive faculties as well.

Thus, we can define aesthetic qualities as those that contribute directly to an object's aesthetic value, positive or negative. Again, there is a circularity here, but it can be removed by defining aesthetic value without appealing to aesthetic qualities, perhaps in terms of the overall engagement of our mental faculties just alluded to. What has aesthetic value, according to this concept, simultaneously challenges and exercises all our mental capacities—perceptual, imaginative, affective, and cognitive. If the concept of art itself is in turn evaluative, if having aesthetic value in the sense indicated is both necessary and sufficient for being a (fine) artwork, then aesthetic qualities are also definitive of (fine) artworks. Taken in this sense, however, the concept of aesthetic properties has not only been broadened from the initial reference to beauty; it has also been narrowed to the domain of artworks, at least in its primary use.

In regard to the second question on the nature of aesthetic qualities, it is clear that they are relational properties, as Hume and Kant held, involving appreciative responses to the objective or base qualities of objects. These base qualities include structural properties of tones, shapes, and colors; syntactic and semantic properties of literary texts; and relations between these and similar properties in other works. Appeal to these base properties justifies ascriptions of aesthetic qualities, and appeal to these aesthetic qualities in turn justifies overall aesthetic evaluations.

That aesthetic qualities involve subjective responses does not imply that these qualities are not real. Real properties are those that are instantiated independently of observers' beliefs about them and of how they appear to particular observers. Secondary qualities like colors are real in this sense because, even though particular observers can disagree and even though colors can appear other than they are, normal observers in normal conditions can achieve consensus on colors. Such consensus among qualified observers is essential to the reality of such relational properties. A crucial question is whether we would find agreement in the ascription of aesthetic qualities among fully qualified art critics.

THE RELATION TO BASE PROPERTIES: RELATIVISM

Kant held that there are no principles linking objective properties to beauty, and Sibley held that nonaesthetic properties are never sufficient conditions for aesthetic properties. The lack of such principles is due to the fact that aesthetic qualities are not only relational, but relative in several different senses. First, they are relative to the contexts of the particular objects that instantiate them. A graceful passage in a Mozart piece would not be graceful at all in a piece by Charles Ives. Second, they are relative to differing interpretations of the same work. Iago's "Credo" aria in Giuseppe Verdi's *Otello* can be interpreted as boisterous and defiant or as sinister and brooding. Third, they are relative to historical context and change with changing historical contexts. The works of Antonio Salieri were heard as graceful before Mozart but as somewhat stilted and awkward after Mozart. Finally, as Hume in the end affirmed but Kant denied, they are relative to differing tastes of different critics. What is poignant to one is maudlin to another; what is striking and powerful to one is garish and grating to another.

That the latter disagreements occur at all levels of actual competence and sophistication indicates that even ideal critics would fail to reach consensus in ascribing aesthetic properties. For every such property, there would be some disagreements among fully qualified critics as to whether some objects had the property in question. And this would occur not only in borderline cases, indicating only vagueness in the concepts of such properties. A paradigm of poignancy for some critics, for example, a Tchaikovsky symphony or Puccini aria, is a paradigm of maudlin sentimentality for others.

It seems, therefore, that we must relativize ascriptions of aesthetic properties to both tastes and contexts (including work, historical, and interpretive contexts). The main problem with doing so is that it then becomes problematic to see opposed ascriptions as really in disagreement and difficult to explain why opposing critics argue for their interpretations and evaluations. Genuine disagreement and argument about the presence of an aesthetic property seem to assume a right answer to the question of whether or not the property is present. But if an artwork is powerful to one critic and not to another, then what are they disagreeing about? In short, the problem for the relativist is to account for the normative force of judgments regarding aesthetic qualities. Even if Kant was too strong in his claim that we demand universal agreement in our aesthetic judgments, surely the practice of critical argument reflects some demand for agreement.

To maintain a realist account of aesthetic qualities in the face of disagreement among fully qualified critics, one might say that an object really has an aesthetic quality only if the quality is experienced by all qualified critics, or, alternatively, that it really has the quality even if it is experienced only by some qualified critics. But the first response leaves artworks with too few aesthetic qualities and makes almost all aesthetic judgments false, while the second response ascribes too many aesthetic qualities, even incompatible ones, to the same objects. Another possibility for the realist is to hold that when critics disagree about the evaluative aesthetic properties they ascribe, there are nevertheless real nonevaluative aesthetic properties that they agree on in perceiving. When, for example, one critic sees a painting as elegant and another as insipid, they nevertheless see the same aesthetic quality underlying these opposed evaluative qualities. But the problem with this response is, first, that it splits the account of aesthetic qualities in two and, second, that it fails to specify what the underlying aesthetic quality might be. The critics seem to react to the base, nonaesthetic formal properties of the painting with different responses.

The relativist account therefore seems preferable. In addition, it explains why we cannot know from an objective description of an object whether it has a given aesthetic quality. We can infer that it does from testimony only if we are certain that the testifier shares our taste. But the relativist must still account for the normativity of aesthetic judgments and how they are justified.

THE JUSTIFICATION OF ASCRIPTIONS OF AESTHETIC QUALITIES

Objective base properties justify ascriptions of aesthetic qualities, and these justify overall evaluations. But there are no principles at either level. On the second level, elegance, for example, usually contributes to a positive evaluation. But prose or painting styles can be too elegant for their subject matters, lessening the overall impact of their works. In view of the lack of principles and the relativity of aesthetic qualities to different tastes, how do these justifications work?

Ascriptions of aesthetic qualities are unjustified when based on inattention, bias, lack of knowledge of the formal properties of a work or its historical context, or an unacceptable interpretation. In asserting that an object has an aesthetic quality, one makes an implicit claim that one's judgment is not based on any of these disqualifying factors. This is equivalent to the claim that a fully competent or ideal critic who shares one's taste would respond to the object in the same way, would ascribe the same property to it. Thus, the relation between objective nonaesthetic properties and aesthetic qualities is simply that the former cause fully competent critics with certain tastes to respond in ways expressed by ascriptions of the aesthetic qualities.

Arguments over the presence of aesthetic qualities proceed until it is clear that both parties are fully competent in the circumstances to make the aesthetic judgments they make. Typically, critics proceed by pointing to the objective properties in the given historical context that elicit the responses expressed in their judgments, under the assumption that the other party has for one reason or another missed the relevance of the underlying base properties. But once the relevant base properties have been noted and interpretations agreed on, argument will cease, and the parties will have to accept ultimate differences in taste.

If aesthetic qualities are instantiated relative not only to contexts but, more significantly, to tastes of qualified critics, then two main questions remain. First, when do fully qualified critics share tastes? Can those who do share tastes nevertheless disagree about particular ascriptions of aesthetic qualities? Second, why should the judgments of such critics have normative force for others? If fully qualified or ideal critics who share tastes can disagree in their ascriptions of aesthetic qualities, and if objects have the relational properties that these critics ascribe, then the same problem that relativizing was intended to solve, the ascription of incompatible qualities to the same objects, reappears. When such critics disagree, they therefore have slightly different tastes. But if an ordinary observer who shares tastes with an ideal critic in all other aesthetic judgments disagrees in a particular case, this is a strong (but not infallible) indication that the observer is not making a sound aesthetic judgment, that he is mistaken in ascribing the aesthetic quality to the object. Clarifying argument is then in order. Only when all relevant base properties have been noted and acceptable interpretations agreed on can disagreements be explained away as reflecting different tastes. The object will then be asserted to have the disputed aesthetic qualities only relative to these different tastes.

To turn to the second question, when an ordinary observer disagrees with a fully competent critic who shares his taste, why should he accept the judgment of the critic as correct or normative for him? The answer can only be that such critics experience works more deeply—on cognitive, emotional, imaginative, and perceptual levels simultaneously. The works and their aesthetic qualities, when so appreciated, offer lasting satisfaction.

See also Aesthetic Experience; Aesthetic Judgment; Art, Interpretation of.

Bibliography

Beardsley, Monroe. "The Descriptivist Account of Aesthetic Attributions." *Revue internationale de philosophie* 28 (1974): 336–352.

Beardsley, Monroe. "What Is an Aesthetic Quality?" *Theoria* 39 (1973): 50–70.

Bender, John. "Realism, Supervenience, and Irresoluble Aesthetic Disputes." *Journal of Aesthetics and Art Criticism* 54 (1996): 371–381.

Budd, Malcolm. "Aesthetic Judgments, Aesthetic Principles, and Aesthetic Properties." *European Journal of Philosophy* 7 (1999): 295–311.

Cohen, Ted. "Aesthetic/Non-aesthetic and the Concept of Taste." *Theoria* 39 (1973): 113–152.

Currie, Gregory. "Supervenience, Essentialism, and Aesthetic Properties." *Philosophical Studies* 58 (1990): 243–257.

De Clercq, Rafael. "The Concept of an Aesthetic Property." *Journal of Aesthetics and Art Criticism* 60 (2002): 167–176.

Eaton, Marcia. "The Intrinsic, Non-supervenient Nature of Aesthetic Properties." *Journal of Aesthetics and Art Criticism* 52 (1994): 383–397.

Goldman, Alan. *Aesthetic Value.* Boulder, CO: Westview Press, 1995.

Goodman, Nelson. *Languages of Art.* Oxford, U.K.: Oxford University Press, 1969.

Hermeren, Goran. *The Nature of Aesthetic Qualities*. Lund, Sweden: Lund University Press, 1988.

Hume, David. "Of the Standard of Taste." In his *Essays, Moral, Political, and Literary*. Oxford, U.K.: Oxford University Press, 1963.

Hutcheson, Francis. *An Inquiry into the Original of Our Ideas of Beauty and Virtue*. New York: Garland, 1971.

Isenberg, Arnold. "Critical Communication." *Philosophical Review* 58 (1949): 330–344.

Kant, Immanuel. *Critique of Judgment*. Translated by J. H. Bernard. New York: Hafner, 1966.

Kivy, Peter. "Aesthetic Appraisals and Aesthetic Qualities." *Journal of Philosophy* 65 (1968): 85–93.

Levinson, Jerrold. "Aesthetic Properties, Evaluative Force, and Differences in Sensibility." In *Aesthetic Concepts: Essays after Sibley*, edited by Emily Brady and Jerrold Levinson. Oxford, U.K.: Oxford University Press, 2001.

Mitias, Michael, ed. *Aesthetic Quality and Aesthetic Experience*. Amsterdam: Rodolpi, 1988.

Sibley, Frank. "A Contemporary Theory of Aesthetic Qualities: Aesthetic Concepts." *Philosophical Review* 68 (1959): 421–450.

Walton, Kendall. "Categories of Art." *Philosophical Review* 79 (1970): 334–367.

Zangwill, Nick. *The Metaphysics of Beauty*. Ithaca, NY: Cornell University Press, 2001.

Zemach, Eddy. *Real Beauty*. University Park: Pennsylvania State University Press, 1997.

Alan H. Goldman (2005)

AESTHETICS

The Encyclopedia features two very detailed survey entries, *Aesthetics, History of*, and *Aesthetics, Problems of*, as well as the following entries: *Beauty*; *Humor*; *Metaphor*; *Tragedy*; and *Ugliness*.

AESTHETICS, HISTORY OF

In the West, the history of systematic philosophizing about the arts begins with Plato. But his great achievement was preceded, and prepared for, by certain developments in the preceding two hundred years, of which we know or can guess only a little. Thus, the famous aesthetic judgment—if such it was—of the picture on Achilles' shield, "That was a marvellous piece of work" (*Iliad* XVIII 548), hints at the beginning of wonder about imitation, i.e., the relation between representation and object, or appearance and reality. Plato shows the aesthetic consequences of the thinking on this problem by Democritus and Parmenides. Further, the elevation of Homer and Hesiod to the status of wise men and seers, and moral and religious teachers, led to a dispute over the truthfulness of

poetry when they were attacked by Xenophanes and Heraclitus for their philosophical ignorance and misrepresentation of the gods. Homer and Hesiod themselves raised the question of the source of the artist's inspiration, which they attributed to divine power (*Odyssey* VIII; *Theogony* 22 ff.). Pindar traced this gift to the gods but allowed that the poet's skill can be developed by his own effort. Pythagoras and his Order discovered the dependence of musical intervals on the ratios of the lengths of stretched strings, generalized this discovery into a theory about the elements of the material world (that they either are, or depend upon, numbers), and developed an elaborate ethical and therapeutic theory of music, which, according to them, is capable of strengthening or restoring the harmony of the individual soul—*harmonia* being the term for the primary interval, the octave.

PLATO

Nearly all of the fundamental aesthetic problems were broached, and some were deeply considered, by Plato. The questions he raised and the arguments he framed are astonishingly varied and deep. They are scattered throughout his dialogues, but the principal discussions are in (*a*) the *Ion, Symposium*, and *Republic*, belonging to Plato's early, pre-Academy period (roughly 399–387 BCE); (*b*) the *Sophist* and *Laws*, written at the end of his life (roughly 367–348/347 BCE); and (*c*) the *Phaedrus*, which lies between these periods. Though perhaps not Plato's, the *Greater Hippias* is very Platonic and may be drawn upon. (In this entry, no distinction will be attempted between Plato's views and those of Socrates.)

ART AND CRAFT. When today we speak of Plato's aesthetics, we mean his philosophical views about those fine arts that he discusses: visual arts (painting, sculpture, architecture), literary arts (epic, lyric, and dramatic poetry), and mixed musical arts (dance and song). Plato does not himself assign them a special name; for him they belong in the more general class of "craft" (*technē*), which includes all skills in making or doing, from woodcraft to statecraft. In the *Sophist* (265–266), crafts are divided into "acquisitive" and "productive," the latter being subdivided into (1) production of actual objects, which may be either human or divine (plants and elements by god, houses and knives by men), and (2) production of "images" (*idola*), which may also be human or divine (reflections and dreams by god; pictures by men). Images, which imitate their originals but cannot fulfill their function, are further subdivided; the imitator may produce (1) a genuine likeness (*eikon*), with the same properties as his model, or (2) an apparent likeness, or semblance (*phantasma*), which merely *looks* like the original (as when the architect makes his columns swell at the top so that they will not appear to diminish). There is thus false imitation, the making of deceptive semblances. Yet Plato finds this distinction troublesome to maintain, for it is essential to any imitation that in some way it falls short of its original; if it were perfect, it would not be an image (*eidolon*), but another example of the same thing, another bed or knife (*Cratylus* 432). So all imitation is in a sense both true and untrue, has both being and nonbeing (*Sophist* 240C).

IMITATION. The term "imitation" (*mimesis*) is one of the most troublesome in Plato's aesthetics, for its denotation constantly expands and contracts with the movement of the dialectic, along with that of its substitutes and near synonyms, *methexis* (participation), *homoiosis* (likeness), and *paraplesia* (resemblance).

If, in one sense, all created things are imitations of their eternal archetypes, or "forms," Plato seems also to regard paintings, dramatic poems, and songs as imitations in a narrower sense: They are images. It is this that places the arts at the second remove from the reality of the forms, on the lowest of the four levels of cognition, *eikasia* (imagining) (*Republic* 509–511). Some works of art, however—and Plato sometimes speaks as though he meant all of them—are imitative in the more pejorative sense, as deceptive semblances. In Book X of the *Republic*, the painter is said to represent the bed, not as it is but as it appears. It is this that puts him in the "tribe of imitators" (*Timaeus* 19D) and allies him with those pseudo craftsmen of the *Gorgias* (463–465) who do not possess a genuine craft, like medicine, but a pseudo craft, or knack (*tribē*), like cosmetics, which gives us the bloom of health rather than health itself.

BEAUTY. By this route, Plato approaches the question that is of great importance to him as a metaphysician: Do the arts contain, or convey, knowledge? Before coming to this question, there is another to be considered. If the architect, as a maker of semblances, changes reality to make it look better, why does he do this? He seeks those images that will appear beautiful (*Sophist* 236A). This is another basic fact about the arts, in Plato's view; they can embody in various degrees the quality of beauty (*to kalon*—a term that can branch out into more general senses of appropriateness or fitness to function but that often appears in a more strictly aesthetic sense). The beauty of concrete things may change or disappear, may appear to some but not to others (*Republic* 479A); but behind these temporal embodiments there is an eternal and absolute form of beauty. Its existence can be demonstrated dialectically, like that of the other forms; but direct acquaintance with it is to be sought, Plato says, via the partial and dimmer beauties open to the senses—and it is easier of access than the other forms (*Phaedrus* 249B–C).

The path to beauty is described most fully in the *Symposium* A man possessed by love (*eros*) of beauty is to progress from bodily beauty to beauty of mind, to beauty of institutions and laws and the sciences themselves, and finally to beauty in itself. It is noteworthy that Diotima of Mantineia, who presents this picture, does not assign to the arts any role in assisting this progress; that step was taken by Plato's successors.

It is also important to ask what beauty is, or, if that cannot be stated abstractly, what the conditions are under which beauty will be embodied in an object. The argument in the *Greater Hippias* takes up several possibilities, especially the possibility that the beautiful either is, or depends upon, what is beneficial or what pleases through the senses of hearing and sight. But in the *Philebus*, a careful discussion leads to the conclusion that beautiful things are made with care in the due proportion of part to part, by mathematical measurement (cf. *Timaeus* 87C–D; *Statesman* 284A). "The qualities of measure (*metron*) and proportion (*symmetron*) invariably … constitute beauty and excellence" (*Philebus* 64E, Hackforth translation). And because it is, or depends upon, measure, beauty is assigned a high place in the final list of goods (*Philebus* 66A–B; cf. *Sophist* 228B).

ART AND KNOWLEDGE. Knowledge (*episteme*), as distinct from mere opinion (*doxa*), is a grasp of the eternal forms; and Plato clearly denies it to the arts, as imitations of imitations (*Republic* 598–601). So the poet is placed on the sixth level of knowledge in the *Phaedrus* (248D), and Ion is said to interpret Homer not by "art or knowledge" (532C) but in an irrational way (cf. *Apology* 22), for he does not know what he is saying or why he might be right or wrong. On the other hand, a work of art that embodies beauty has some direct relation to one form. And if the artist inspired by the Muses is like a diviner in not knowing what he is doing (*Meno* 99C; *Timaeus* 71E–72A), he may have a kind of insight that goes beyond ordinary knowledge (cf. *Laws* 682A). His madness (*mania*) may be possession by a divinity that inspires him to truth (*Phaedrus* 245A; *Ion* 533E, 536B). Moreover, since the arts can give us genuine likenesses, not only of appearances but of actualities, and even imitate the ethical character of the human soul (*Republic* 400–401B; cf. Xenophon, *Memorabilia* III viii), it is possible, and indeed obligatory, to judge them by their truth, or their resemblance to actuality. The competent judge, especially of dance and song, must have "first, a knowledge of the nature of the original; next, a knowledge of the correctness of the copy; and thirdly, a knowledge of the excellence with which the copy is executed" (*Laws* 669A–B, Bury translation).

ART AND MORALITY. The supreme craft, for Plato, is the art of the legislator and educator, who must have the final say about the arts, for his task is to insure that they play their proper role in the life of the entire social order. The first problem is to discover what effects the arts have on people, and this problem has two aspects. First, there is the enjoyability of art. On the one hand, just insofar as it has beauty, the pleasures art gives are pure, unalloyed, and harmless (*Phaedrus* 51B–C), unlike the pleasure of scratching an itch, which is preceded and followed by discomfort. But, on the other hand, dramatic poetry involves the representation of unworthy characters behaving in undesirable ways (ranting and wailing) and tempts the audience into immoderate laughter or weeping. Therefore its pleasures are to be condemned for their unworthy effect on character. Second, when we consider this tendency of the arts to influence character and conduct, there are again two sides to the matter. In his *Republic* and *Laws*, Plato makes it quite clear that he thinks the literary imitation of evil conduct is an implicit invitation to imitate the conduct in one's life (*Laws* 665B). Thus the stories of gods and heroes who behave immorally have to be excluded from the education of the young guardians in the *Republic*, and stories in which the gods and heroes behave as they should must either be found or written (*Republic* 376E–411; cf. *Laws* 800–802, 664A). Music composed in enervating modes must also be replaced by a suitable kind (*Republic* 398E, 411A).

But this does not mean that the arts have no role to play in the cultural life and education of the citizens. Indeed, the fear of their power that underlies Plato's severe censorship and regulation is accompanied by an equally great respect. The measure that is so closely allied to beauty is, after all, closely allied to goodness and virtue too (*Laws* 655A; *Protagoras* 326A–B; *Republic* 432). Music and poetry and dancing are, at their best, indispensable means of character education, able to make men better and more virtuous (*Laws* 653–654, 664). The problem, as Plato in his role of legislator sees it, is to ensure the social responsibility of the creative artist by insisting that his own good, like that of every citizen, be subordinated and made conducive to the good of all.

ARISTOTLE

Our knowledge of Aristotle's aesthetic theory comes chiefly from the little collection of lecture notes that has come down to us as the *Poetics*, composed probably about 347–342 BCE and later added to. The text is corrupt, the argument condensed and puzzling. No work in the history of aesthetics has given rise to such vexatious problems of interpretation; no work has had so great an influence on the theory and practice of literary criticism.

THE ART OF POETRY. Aristotle's first task is to define the art of poetry (*poietike*), which is his subject. He assumes a distinction between three kinds of "thought," knowing (*theoria*), doing (*praxis*), and making (*poiesis*) (see *Metaphysics* E 1; *Topics* VI 6); but in the *Poetics*, "poiesis" is taken in a narrower sense. One kind of making is imitation, which Aristotle seems to take fairly straightforwardly as representation of objects or events. The imitative art divides into (1) the art of imitating visual appearances by means of color and drawing and (2) the art of poetry, the imitation of a human action (*praxis*) through verse, song, and dance (*Poetics*, Ch. 1). Thus the art of poetry is distinguished from painting by its medium (words, melody, rhythm) and from versified history or philosophy (the poem of Empedocles) by virtue of the object it imitates. Two of the species of the poetic art are of primary concern to Aristotle: drama (either tragic or comic) and epic poetry, distinguished from comedy by the gravity of the actions imitated (Chs. 2, 6).

What is of the first importance in Aristotle's treatise is his method of inquiry, for he aims to present a systematic theory of a particular literary genre. He asks: What is the nature of the tragic art? And this leads him to inquire not only into its material, formal, and efficient causes (many of his observations under these headings are of permanent value to literary theory) but also into its final cause or end (*telos*). What is a good tragedy, and what makes it good; what are "the causes of artistic excellence and the opposite" (Ch. 26, G. F. Else translation)? This function of tragedy, he thinks, must be to provide a certain kind of enjoyable experience—the "proper pleasure" (*oikeia he-done*) of tragedy (Chs. 14, 23, 26)—and if the nature of this pleasure can be determined it will then be possible to justify the criteria by means of which one can say that one tragedy is better than another.

THE PLEASURE OF IMITATION. Aristotle suggests briefly (Ch. 4) two motives that give rise to tragedy. The first is that imitation is natural; and the recognizing of imitation is naturally pleasurable to man because man finds learning pleasant, and recognizing, say, a picture of a dog, is a form of learning (cf. *Rhetoric* I xi). Since tragedy is an imitation of a special sort of object, namely fearful and pitiable events, its proper pleasure "is the pleasure that comes from pity and fear by means of imitation" (Ch. 4, Else translation). The problem that evidently arises is how we can derive pleasure from feeling emotions that are painful (cf. the definitions of "fear" and "pity" in *Rhetoric* II v, viii). Aristotle's nearest answer seems to be that though the object imitated may be in itself unpleasant to contemplate, the pleasure of seeing the imitation may overcome our distaste—as with skilled drawings of cadavers (see *De Partibus Animalium* I v; *Rhetoric* I xi). Here Aristotle is offering a partial answer to one of Plato's grounds for skepticism about art; he takes the basic aesthetic pleasure as a cognitive one, of the same genus as the philosopher's (though no doubt of a lower level).

THE PLEASURE OF BEAUTY. Tragedy also grows, Aristotle says (Ch. 4), out of our natural disposition to "melody and rhythm." He does not develop this point and may be postulating a kind of decorative impulse. But if we may think here of Plato's *Philebus*, our pleasure in melody and rhythm may be taken as pleasure in beauty in general. "A beautiful (*kalliste*) thing, either a living creature or any structure made of parts, must have not only an orderly arrangement of those parts, but a size which is not accidental" (Ch. 7). Thus a tragedy, or its plot, may be "beautiful," i.e., artistically excellent (Chs. 1, 13). And the "proper pleasure" of the epic, for example, depends on its unity, on being "like a single whole creature" (*zoon*) with a beginning, middle, and end (Ch. 23). This analogy echoes Plato's *Phaedrus* 264C. For the fineness of the object sensed or contemplated produces the highest degree of that pleasure that is proper to the organ sensing or mind contemplating (*Nicomachean Ethics* X iv).

THE UNIVERSAL. If the function of tragic poetry is to provide a certain species of enjoyment, we can then inquire into the features of a particular work that will promote or inhibit this enjoyment. Its concentration and coherence depend in large part upon the plot and the sense of inevitability in its development (Ch. 10). This is evidently achieved most fully when the characters act in accordance with their natures, when they do the "kinds of thing a certain kind of person will say or do in accordance with probability or necessity, which is what poetic composition aims at" (Ch. 9, Else translation). These sorts of behavior, i.e., behavior that is motivated in accordance with psychological laws, Aristotle calls "universal," contrasting them with the events in a historical chronicle, which he thinks of as a causally unconnected string of particular incidents ("what Alcibiades did or had done to him").

This famous passage has inspired many later theories about art imitating universals or essences, but the gist of it (for Aristotle) is that the poet must make his plot plausible by relying on general psychological truths. This important point adds another level to Aristotle's defense (against Plato) of the cognitive status of poetry, for the poet must at least understand human nature or he cannot even produce a good plot.

THE CATHARSIS. In Aristotle's definition of tragedy (Ch. 6) there is one phrase that has given rise to an enormous amount of interpretation: *di eleou kai phobou perainousa ten ton toiouton pathematon katharsin* (translated in the traditional way by Butcher: "through pity and fear effecting the proper purgation of these emotions"). Thus Aristotle is interpreted as having a further theory, not about the immediate pleasure of tragedy but about its deeper psychological effects. This phrase is the only basis for such an interpretation in the *Poetics*; but in the *Politics* (VIII 7), Aristotle clearly does propose a cathartic theory of music and even says he will explain catharsis further "when hereafter we speak of poetry"—a remark that possibly refers to the presumed lost parts of the *Poetics*. If tragedy produces a catharsis of the emotions, there are still other problems in deciding what Aristotle had in mind—whether, for example, he meant it in a medical sense (a purgation of the emotions, their elimination by mental physic) or in a religious and lustratory sense (a purification of emotions, their transformation into a less harmful form). Both senses had precedents. There is also the question whether Aristotle believed in a catharsis of pity and fear alone, or, through them, of all destructive emotions.

In any case, on this interpretation, Aristotle would be answering Plato's second objection to poetry in Book X of the *Republic*, by saying that poetry helps men to be rational. The traditional interpretation has been interestingly challenged in recent years by Professor Gerald F. Else, who argues that the catharsis is not an effect on the audience or reader but something accomplished in the play itself, a purification of the hero, a release from the "blood pollution" of his crime, through his recognition of it, his horror at it, and the discovery that it was due to a "serious mistake" (*hamartia*) on his part. This reading does not seem to fit some of the tragedies. If it is correct, Aristotle has no therapeutic theory of tragedy at all, but he may still be replying to Plato that the immoral effects of tragedy are not to be feared, since the finest ones, at least, will have to show a kind of moral progress if they are to be structurally capable of moving the spectator tragically.

THE LATER CLASSICAL PHILOSOPHERS

Aristotle's *Poetics* does not seem to have been available to his successors. His ideas had some influence via the works (now largely lost) of his favorite pupil, Theophrastus; and the *Tractatus Coislinianus* (Greek, probably first century BCE) shows an acquaintance with his work, for its definition of comedy parallels remarkably Aristotle's definition of tragedy. During the later classical period, Stoicism, Epicureanism, skepticism, and Neoplatonism flourished competitively, and each of these schools of thought had some contribution to make to the history of aesthetics.

STOICISM. The Stoics were much interested in poetry and in problems of semantics and logic. Zeno, Cleanthes, and Chrysippus wrote treatises on poetry, no longer extant. From Philodemus we know of a work on music by the Stoic Diogenes of Babylon, and from Cicero's *De Officiis* of a work on beauty by Panaetius. Both seem to have held that beauty depends on the arrangement of parts (*convenientia partium*, in Cicero's phrase). The delight in beauty was connected with the virtue that expresses itself in an ordered life, with decorum (*to prepon*). Thus not only irrational pleasure (*hedone*), but a rational elevation of the soul (*chara*), in keeping with the Stoic goal of tranquillity, was thought to be obtainable from poetry of the right sort. The Stoics emphasized the moral benefit of poetry as its chief justification and held that it might allegorize true philosophy (see Strabo, *Geography* I, i, 10; I, ii, 3).

EPICUREANISM. The Epicureans are said (by Sextus Empiricus, *Against the Professors* VI, 27) to have disapproved of music and its pleasure, but it appears that this is partly based on a misunderstanding of Epicurus's aversion to music *criticism* (see Plutarch, *That It Is Not Possible to Live Pleasurably According to the Doctrine of Epicurus* 13). Two important works by Philodemus of Gadara (first century BCE), parts of which have been unearthed at Herculaneum, give further evidence of Epicurean thinking about the arts. In his work *On Music* (*Peri Mousikes*), Philodemus strikes the earliest known blow for what later was called "formalism," by arguing (against the Pythagoreans, Plato, and Aristotle) that music by itself—apart from the words, whose effects are often confused with the music itself—is incapable either

of arousing emotions or of effecting ethical transformations of the soul. And in his work *On Poems* (*Peri Poematon*) he argued that specifically poetic goodness (*to poietikon agathon*) is not determined either by the moral-didactic aim (*didaskalia*), by the pleasure of technique and form (*psychagogia*), or by a mere addition of the two, but by a unity of form and content—his conception of which we do not now know.

The main lines of reflection about literature during the Roman period seem to have been practical and pedagogical. Two works were outstandingly influential (the second, however, not until its rediscovery in the modern period): the *Ars Poetica*, or *Epistle to the Pisos*, of Horace, which discusses many questions of style and form, and the work *On Elevation in Poetry* (*Peri Hypsous*, or *On the Sublime*), probably written during the first century CE, perhaps by a Greek named "Longinus." This lively and brilliant work defines the quality of great writing in affective terms, as that which transports the soul; and it investigates the stylistic and formal conditions of this effect.

PLOTINUS. The philosophical reflection that continued in the Platonic schools until the Academy at Athens was closed by Justinian I in CE, 529 culminated in the Neoplatonic system of Plotinus. Three of his fifty-four tractates, which make up the six *Enneads*, deal especially with aesthetic matters: "On Beauty" (I, vi); "On the Intellectual Beauty" (V, viii); and "How the Multiplicity of the Ideal-Forms Came into Being; and on the Good" (VI, vii).

Behind the visible world, in this view, stands "the one" (*to hen*), or "the first," which is ultimate reality in its first "hypostasis," or role, beyond all conception and knowledge. In its second hypostasis, reality is "intellect," or "mind" (*nous*), but also the Platonic forms that are known by mind. In its third hypostasis it is the "all-soul" (*psyche*), or principle of creativity and life. Within his scheme—infinite gradations of being "emanating" from the central "light"—Plotinus develops a theory of beauty that is highly original, though inspired by the *Symposium* and other Platonic dialogues. The tractate "On Beauty" (MacKenna and Page translation) begins by noting that Beauty lies in things seen and heard, and also in good character and conduct (I, vi, 1); and the question is, "What … is it that gives comeliness to all these things?"

The first answer considered, and rejected, is that of the Stoics. Beauty is, or depends on, symmetry. Plotinus argues that simple sense qualities (colors and tones), and also moral qualities, can have beauty though they cannot be symmetrical; moreover, an object can lose some of its beauty (as when a person dies) without losing any symmetry (VI, vii, 22). Therefore, symmetry is neither a necessary nor sufficient condition of beauty. It is not beauty but participation in ideal-form, that is, embodiment of Platonic ideas, that marks the difference in a stone before and after the sculptor carves it; for he gives it form. Where ideal-form enters, he says, confusion has been "rallied … into co-operation" (I, vi, 2): when an object becomes unified, "Beauty enthrones itself." A homogeneous thing, like a patch of color, is already unified by similarity throughout; a heterogeneous thing, like a house or ship, is unified by the dominance of the form, which is a divine thought (I, vi, 2). In the experience of beauty, the soul finds joy in recognizing in the object an "affinity" to itself; for in this affinity it becomes aware of its own participation in ideal-form and its divinity. Here is the historical source of mysticism and romanticism in aesthetics.

Love, in Plotinus's system, is always the love of beauty (III, v, 1) and of absolute and ultimate beauty through its lesser and dimmer manifestations in nature or in the work of the artist-craftsman (I, vi, 7; VI, ii, 18; V, viii, 8–10). Something of Plato's ambivalence toward art reappears in Plotinus's account at this point, though muted and closer to being overcome in the basic monism of the system. We ascend from the contemplation of sensuous beauty to delight in beautiful deeds, to moral beauty and the beauty of institutions, and thence to absolute beauty (I, vi, 8–9; II, ix, 16). Plotinus distinguishes three ways to truth, that of the musician, the lover, and the metaphysician (I, iii, 1–2); and he speaks of nature as offering a loveliness that cannot help but lead the admiring contemplator to thought of the higher beauties that are reflected there (II, ix, 7; V, viii, 2–3). Nor are the arts to be neglected, on the ground that they are mere imitations (here he comes closest to correcting the *Republic*, Book X), for both the painting and the object it copies are, after all, both imitations of the ideal-form; moreover, the painter may be able to imitate form all the more truly, to "add where nature is lacking" (V, viii, 1; cf. V, ix, 11). Yet, in his more religious mood, Plotinus reminds us that earthly and visible beauty may distract us from the infinite (V, v, 12), that "authentic beauty," or "beyond-beauty," is invisible (VI, vii, 33); and he who has *become* beautiful, and hence divine, no longer sees or needs it (V, vii, 11). The ladder, to use once more a too-familiar similitude, is kicked away by the philosophic mystic once he reaches home.

THE MIDDLE AGES

The early church Fathers were somewhat doubtful of beauty and the arts: They feared that a keen interest in earthly things might endanger the soul, whose true vocation lies elsewhere—especially since the literature, drama, and visual art they were acquainted with was closely associated with the pagan cultures of Greece and Rome. But despite the danger of idolatry, sculpture and painting became accepted as legitimate aids to piety, and literature became accepted as part of education in the liberal arts. Concern with aesthetic problems was not a prominent part of medieval philosophy, but some important lines of thought can be observed in the works of the two greatest thinkers.

ST. AUGUSTINE. In his *Confessions* (IV, xiii), Augustine tells a little of his lost early work, *De Pulchro et Apto* ("On the Beautiful and Fitting"), in which he distinguished a beauty that belongs to things in virtue of their forming a whole and a beauty that belongs to things in virtue of their fitting in with something else or being part of a whole. It is not possible to be sure, from his brief description, of the exact nature of this distinction. His later thoughts on beauty are scattered throughout his works, and especially in *De Ordine* ("Concerning Order," CE 386), *De Vera Religione* ("Concerning True Religion," CE 390), and *De Musica* (CE 388–391), a treatise on meter.

The key concepts in Augustine's theory are unity, number, equality, proportion, and order; and unity is the basic notion, not only in art (*De Ordine* II, xv, 42) but in reality. The existence of individual things as units, and the possibility of comparing them with respect to equality or likeness, gives rise to proportion, measure, and number (*De Musica* VI, xiv, 44; xvii, 56; *De Libero Arbitrio* II, viii, 22). Number, he emphasizes in various places, is fundamental both to being and to beauty—"Examine the beauty of bodily form, and you will find that everything is in its place by number" (*De Libero Arbitrio* II, xvi, 42, Burleigh translation). Number gives rise to order, the arrangement of equal and unequal parts into an integrated complex in accordance with an end. And from order comes a second-level kind of unity, the emergent unity of heterogeneous wholes, harmonized or made symmetrical through internal relations of likeness between the parts (*De Vera Religione* xxx, 55; xxxii, 59; *De Musica* VI, xvii, 58).

An important feature of Augustine's theory is that the perception of beauty involves a normative judgment. We perceive the ordered object as being what it ought to be, the disordered object as falling short; hence the painter can correct as he goes along and the critic can judge (*De Vera Religione* xxxii, 60). But this rightness or wrongness cannot be merely sensed (*De Musica* VI, xii,

34); the spectator must bring with him a concept of ideal order, given to him by a "divine illumination." It follows that judgment of beauty is objectively valid; there can be no relativity in it (*De Trinitate* IX, vi, 10; *De Libero Arbitrio* II, xvi, 41).

Augustine also wrestled with the problem of literary truth, and in his *Soliloquies* (CE 387) he proposed a rather sophisticated distinction between different sorts of lying or deception. In the perceptual illusion, the straight oar pretends to be bent, and could be bent, but the statue could not be a man and therefore is not "mendacious." So, too, the fictional character could not be real and does not pretend to be real by his own will, but only follows the will of the poet (II, ix, 16; x, 18; cf. *Confessions* III, vi).

ST. THOMAS AQUINAS. Thomas's account of beauty is given tersely, almost casually, in a few key passages that have become justly famous for their rich implications. Goodness is one of the "transcendentals" in his metaphysics, being predicable of every being and cutting across the Aristotelian categories; it is Being considered in relation to desire (*Summa Theologica* I, q. 5, art. 1). The pleasant, or delightful, is one of the divisions of goodness—"that which terminates the movement of appetite in the form of rest in the thing desired, is called the *pleasant*" (*S.T.* I, q. 5, art. 6, Dominican Fathers translation). And beauty is what pleases on being seen (*Pulchra enim dicuntur quae visa placent*, *S.T.* I, q. 5, art. 4).

Here, of course, "seeing" extends to all cognitive grasp; the perception of beauty is a kind of knowing (this explains why it does not occur in the lower senses of smell and taste, *S.T.* I–II, q. 27, art. 1). Since cognition consists in abstracting the form that makes an object what it is, beauty depends on the form. Thomas's best-known statement about beauty occurs in the course of a discussion of Augustine's attempt to identify the persons of the Trinity with some of his key concepts, the Father with unity, etc. Beauty, he says, "includes three conditions" (*S.T.* I, q. 39, art. 8). First, there is "integrity or perfection" (*integritas sive perfectio*)—broken or injured objects, incomplete objects, are ugly. Second, there is "due proportion or harmony" (*debita proportio sive consonantia*), which may refer partly to the relations between parts of the object itself but mainly refers to a relation between the object and the perceiver: that the eminently visible object, for example, is proportioned to the sight. Third, there is "brightness or clarity" (*claritas*), or brilliance (see also *S.T.* II–II, q. 145, art 2; q. 180, art. 2). The third condition has been variously explicated; it is connected with the medieval Neoplatonic tradition in which light is a symbol

of divine beauty and truth (see the pseudo-Dionysius on the *Divine Names*, Ch. 4; Robert Grosseteste, *De Luce*, and his commentary on the *Hexaëmeron*). Clarity is that "splendor of form [*resplendentia formae*] shining on the proportioned parts of matter" in the opusculum *De Pulchro et Bono* (I, vi, 2), written either by the young Thomas or his teacher Albertus Magnus. The conditions of beauty can be stated univocally, but beauty, being a part of goodness, is an analogical term (that is, has different senses when applied to different sorts of things). It signifies a whole family of qualities, for each thing is beautiful in its own way (Aquinas, *Commentary on the Psalms*, Psalm xliv, 2; cf. *Commentary on the Divine Names* iv, 5).

THE THEORY OF INTERPRETATION. The consuming tasks of the early Fathers, clarifying, reconciling, and systematizing Biblical texts in order to defend Christianity against external enemies and heretical deviations, required a method of exegetical interpretation. The Greek tradition of allegorizing Homer and Hesiod and the Rabbinical tradition of allegorical exposition of Jewish scriptures had been brought together and elaborately refined by Philo of Alexandria. His methods were adopted by Origen, who distinguished three levels of meaning in scripture: the literal, the moral, and the spiritual or mystical (see *De Principiis* IV, i, 16, 18, 20). This method was taken into the West by Hilary of Poitiers and Ambrose, bishop of Milan, and further developed by John Cassian, whose formulation and examples became standard throughout the medieval period up to the time of Dante (see Dante's letter to Can Grande, 1319, the Preface to the *Paradiso*).

In Cassian's example (*Collationes* xiv, 8), Jerusalem, in the Old Testament, is, "literally" or "historically," the city of the Jews; on the "allegorical," or what came to be called the "typical," level, it refers prophetically to the later church of Christ; on the "tropological," or moral, level, to the individual soul; on the "anagogical" level, to the heavenly City of God. The last three levels together are sometimes called the "allegorical," or (as by St. Thomas) the "spiritual," meaning. As Thomas also indicates (*Summa Theologica* I, q. 1, art 10), the "literal" meaning also includes metaphorical statements.

Origen insisted that all Biblical texts must have the highest level of meaning, the "spiritual," though they may lack a moral sense and may even fail to make sense on the literal level, if too great an absurdity would be entailed by taking them that way. In this he was followed by St. Augustine (*De Doctrina Christiana* III, x, 14; xv, 23) but not by Hugh of St. Victor (*De Scripturis*, v; *Eruditiones*

Didascalicon VI, iv, viii–xi), who held that the second-level meanings are a function of the first level, and a first-level meaning can always be found if metaphor is included in it.

Because Christianity taught that the world was created *ex nihilo* by God, rather than generated or molded out of something else, Christian thinkers tended, in the Middle Ages, to hold that nature itself must carry the marks or signs of its origin and be a symbolic embodiment of the Word; in this respect, like Holy Scripture, God's other creation, it can be subjected to interpretation. Thus, nature becomes an allegory, and every natural object a symbol of something beyond. This view reaches its fullest development in John Scotus Erigena (*De Divisione Naturae* I, iii) and St. Bonaventure (*Collationes in Hexaëmeron* II, 27).

Though these reflections were primarily theological, rather than aesthetic, they were of great significance to the later history of aesthetics: They raised important questions about the nature of metaphor and symbol, in literature as well as in theology; they initiated reflection on the general problem of interpreting works of art; and they showed the possibility of a broad philosophy of symbolic forms, in which all art might be understood as a kind of symbolism.

THE RENAISSANCE

The most interesting philosophical development in the fifteenth and sixteenth centuries was the revival, by a number of thinkers, of Platonism and the creation of a vigorous Neoplatonism. Of these thinkers, Marsilio Ficino, translator of Plato and Plotinus and founder of the new Academy (1462), was the greatest. In *De Amore* (his commentary on the *Symposium*, written 1474–1475) and in his principal work, the *Theologia Platonica*, Ficino took over a number of the leading aesthetic notions of the Greeks and of St. Augustine, and to them he added one of his most original ideas, a theory of contemplation based on Plato's *Phaedo*. In contemplation, he held, the soul withdraws to some extent from the body into a purely rational consciousness of the Platonic forms. This inward concentration is required for artistic creation, which involves detachment from the real, to anticipate what does not yet exist, and also is required for the experience of beauty (this explains why beauty can be grasped only by the intellectual faculties—sight, hearing, and thinking—and not by the lower senses).

More significant for the future, however, were the changes taking place in basic assumptions about the arts and in attitudes toward them. The most significant works on the fine arts were the three books on painting, sculpture, and architecture by Leon Battista Alberti, the large collection of notes toward a systematic treatise on painting by Leonardo da Vinci, and surviving memoranda and the two books, on geometry and perspective and on human proportions by Albrecht Dürer.

One of the most serious endeavors of these artists and others was to establish a status for painting within the liberal arts, separating it from the other manual crafts among which it had been classified throughout the medieval period. The painter, Alberti argued (in his *Della pittura*, 1436), requires a special talent and skill; he needs a liberal education and a knowledge of human affairs and human nature; he must be a scientist, in order to follow the laws of nature and produce accurate representations of natural events and human actions. His scientific knowledge, indeed, must be basically mathematical, for the theory of proportions and the theory of linear perspective (which preoccupied Renaissance theorists, and especially Dürer) are mathematical studies; and they provide the principles in terms of which paintings can be unified and made beautiful, but at the same time made to depict correctly. Leonardo's argument for the superiority of painting to poetry and music (and also, in some degree, to sculpture) followed similar lines (see the first part of the *Treatise on Painting*).

The concern for faithfulness of representation that is fundamental to Renaissance fine arts theory is also found in the developing theory of music. The music theorists, aiming to secure the place of music as a humanistic discipline, sought for a vocal music that would attain the powerful emotional and ethical effects attributed to Greek music. They stressed the importance of making the music follow the text, to intensify the meanings of the words. These ideas were defended, for example, by Gioseffe Zarlino, in his *Istitutioni Armoniche* (1558) and by Vincenzo Galilei, in his *Dialogo della musica antica e della moderna* (1581).

Renaissance poetics was dominated by Aristotle (especially the concept of poetry as imitation of human action) and Horace (the thesis that poetry aims to delight and instruct—though this dualism was rejected by one of the major theorists, Lodovico Castelvetro, in his commentary on Aristotle's *Poetics*, 1570). The concept of imitation was variously interpreted and criticized by the Italian theorists. Among the chief points of disagreement and contention was the question whether poetry must belong to fixed genres and obey rigid rules, such as the dramatic "unities" adopted so adamantly by Julius Caesar Scaliger in his *Poetics* (1561), and the question (as discussed, for example, in Sidney's *Defense of Poesie*, 1595) whether the poet is guilty of telling lies and of leading his readers into immorality. In these discussions, the Aristotelian *katharsis* and Plato's condemnation of the poets were central and recurrent topics.

THE ENLIGHTENMENT: CARTESIAN RATIONALISM

Though Descartes had no aesthetic theory, and indeed wrote nothing about the arts apart from his early *Compendium Musicae* (1618), his epistemological method and conclusions were decisive in the development of neoclassical aesthetics. As in other areas, the search for clarity of concept, rigor of deduction, and intuitive certainty of basic principles penetrated the realm of critical theory, and its effects can be traced in numerous works, for example, in Nicolas Boileau-Despréaux's *L'art poétique* (1674); in Alexander Pope's *Essay on Criticism* (1711); in Charles Du Fresnoy's *De Arte Graphica* (translated into French by Roger de Piles, 1668, into English by Dryden, 1695); and in Jean Philippe Rameau's *Traité de l'harmonie réduite à ses principes naturels* (1722). Cartesian and Aristotelian elements combined in the richly polysemous concepts of reason and nature, which became central to all theories of the arts. To follow nature and to follow rules of reason were identified in counsel to the creative artist as well as in critical judgment.

In the sixteenth century, the rules for making and for judging works of art were generally (but not always) supported by authority, either the supposed authority of Aristotle or the models provided by classical writers. The new rationalism in aesthetics was the hope that these rules could be given a more solid, a priori, foundation by deduction from a basic self-evident axiom, such as the principle that art is imitation of nature—where nature comprised the universal, the normal, the essential, the characteristic, the ideal. So, in Samuel Johnson (*Preface to Shakespeare*, 1765), "just representations of general Nature" become the end of art; the painter "is to examine, not the individual, but the species" (*Rasselas*, 1759, Ch. 10). And in the *Discourses* (1778) of Sir Joshua Reynolds, the painter is advised to "consider nature in the abstract, and represent in every one of his figures the character of its species" (III).

THE PROBLEM OF THE RULES. The controversy over the authority and infallibility of the rules reflected a conflict between reason and experience, between less and more empirical approaches to art. For example, Corneille, in his three *Discourses* (1660), admitted the necessity of observing unity of space, time, and action in dramatic construction but confessed also that he was by no means their "slave" and sometimes had to break or modify them for the sake of dramatic effect or the audience's enjoyment. Molière, in his *Critique de l'école des femmes* (1663), was even more outspoken in making experiment the test. However, other theorists held the line in France, for example, George de Scudéry and Charles de Saint-Évremond. Dryden, in his *Defense of an Essay of Dramatic Poesy* (1668), suggested that if drama has a function or end, there must be rules, but the rules themselves are only probable and rest in part upon experience. In this spirit, Johnson criticized the pseudo-Aristotelian rules of time and place.

In music, the conflict between reason and experience appeared in controversies over harmony and consonance, as well as over the absoluteness of rules, such as the avoidance of parallel fifths. The followers of Zarlino insisted on a mathematical basis for acceptable chords; the followers of Vincenzo Galilei were more willing to let the ear be the judge. A kind of reconciliation of these views appears in Leibniz's theory (*Principles of Nature and of Grace*, 1714, § 17) that, like all sensations, musical tones are confused mélanges of infinite sets of *petites perceptions* that at every moment are in pre-established harmony with the perceptions of all other monads; in hearing a chord, the soul unconsciously counts the beats and compares the mathematical ratio which, when simple, produces concord.

TOWARD A UNIFIED AESTHETICS. The Cartesian theory of knowledge led to a more systematic attempt at a metaphysics of art in the *Meditationes Philosophicae de Nonnullis ad Poema Pertinentibus* (1735) of Alexander Gottlieb Baumgarten. Baumgarten, who coined the term "aesthetics," aimed to provide an account of poetry (and indirectly of all art) as involving a particular form, or level, of cognition—"sensory cognition." He began with Descartes's distinctions (*Principles of Philosophy* I, xlv–xlvi), elaborated by Leibniz (*Discourse on Metaphysics*, xxiv), between clear and obscure ideas, and between distinct and confused ideas. Sense data are clear but confused, and poetry is "sensate discourse," that is, discourse in which such clear–confused ideas are linked together into a structure. The "extensive clarity" of a poem consists in the number of clear ideas combined in it, and the rules for making or judging poetry have to do with ways in which the extensive clarity of a poem may be increased or diminished.

Baumgarten's book is remarkably concise, and its formalized deductive manner, with definitions and derivations, goes out of its way to declare the possibility of dealing in an acceptably rigorous Cartesian way with matters apparently so little suited for rigorous treatment. Though he did not finish his *Aesthetics*, which would have generalized his study of poetry, the makings of a general theory are present in the *Meditations*. Its basic principle is still the imitation of nature—the principle that is also fundamental to the influential work of the Abbé Charles Batteux, *Les beaux arts réduits à un même principe* (1746), and to the important classification of the fine arts in d'Alembert's *Discours préliminaire* to the *Encyclopédie* (1751).

The importance of Lessing's *Laokoon oder über die Grenzen der Malerei und Poesie* (1766) is that, though he did not reject the possibility of a system that will relate all the arts, he attacked superficial and deadening analogies (many of them based on the Horatian formula, *ut pictura poesis*, torn from its context). He looked for the specific individual potentialities and values of painting and poetry in their own distinctive mediums. The medium of an art is, he says, the "signs" (*Zeichen*) it uses for imitation; and painting and poetry, when carefully examined for their capacities to imitate, turn out to be radically different. Consisting of shapes and colors, side by side, painting is best at picturing objects and visible properties, and can only indirectly suggest actions; poetry is just the opposite. When a secondary power of an art is made primary, it cannot do its best work. By the clarity and vigor of his argument and his sharp criticism of prevailing assumptions, Lessing gave a new turn to aesthetics.

THE ENLIGHTENMENT: EMPIRICISM

Contemporaneous with the development of neoclassical critical theory was the divergent line of aesthetic inquiry pursued principally, though not exclusively, by British theorists in the Baconian tradition of empiricism. They were greatly interested in the psychology of art (though they were not merely psychologists), especially the creative process and the effects of art upon the beholder.

THE IMAGINATION. That the imagination (or "fancy") plays a central, if mysterious, role in artistic creation had long been acknowledged. Its mode of operation—the secret of inventiveness and originality—was not systematically investigated before the empiricists of the seventeenth century. Among the rationalists, the imagination, considered as an image-registering faculty or as an image-combining faculty, played little or no role in knowledge. (See Descartes's Rule III of the *Regulae* ["the blundering constructions of imagination"]; *Principles* I, lxxi–lxxiii;

and *Meditation* VI.) But Bacon's *Advancement of Learning* (1605) placed the imagination as a faculty alongside memory and reason and assigned poetry to it, as history and philosophy (including, of course, both moral and natural philosophy) were assigned to the other faculties.

Thomas Hobbes, in the first chapters of his *Leviathan* (1651), undertook to give the first analysis of imagination, which he defined as "decaying sense" (I, ii), the phantasms, or images, that remain when the physiological motions of sensation cease. But besides this "simple imagination," which is passive, there is also "compound imagination," which creates novel images by rearranging old ones. Hobbes stated that the mind's "trains" of thought are guided by a general principle of association (I, iii), but he did not work it out very fully. Nor did Locke develop this idea very far in the famous chapter "Of the Association of Ideas" (II, xxxiii) that he added to the fourth edition (1700) of his *Essay concerning Human Understanding* (1690). The tendency of ideas that have accompanied each other to stick together and pull each other into the mind was noted by Locke as a pathological feature of the understanding: It explains various sorts of error and the difficulty of eradicating them (cf. *Conduct of the Understanding*, §41). The work of fancy is best seen, according to Locke, in the tendency of poetic language to become figurative. As long as we are interested in pleasure, we cannot be troubled by such ornaments of style; but metaphors and similes are "perfect cheats" when we are interested in truth (III, x, 34; cf. *Conduct of Understanding*, §§32–42). Locke here reflects a widespread distrust of imagination in the later seventeenth century. It is shown in a famous passage from Sprat's *History of the Royal Society* (1702), in which Sprat describes the "close, naked, natural way of speaking," in clearly defined words, required for scientific discourse, and contrasts it with the "specious tropes and figures" of poetry.

The theory of the association of ideas was developed into a systematic psychology by Hume, in his *Treatise of Human Nature* (1739–1740), and Hartley, in his *Observations on Man* (1749). In Hume, the tendency of ideas to consort with one another because of similarity, propinquity, or causal connection became a powerful principle for explaining many mental operations; and Hartley carried the method further. Despite attacks upon it, associationism played a crucial role in several eighteenth-century attempts to explain the pleasures of art.

THE PROBLEM OF TASTE. The investigation of the psychological effects of art and of the aesthetic experience (in modern terms) developed along two distinct, but occasionally intersecting, paths: (1) the search for an adequate analysis and explanation of certain basic aesthetic qualities (the beautiful, the sublime) or (2) an inquiry into the nature and justification of critical judgment, the problem of "taste." Without trying to keep these completely separate, let us first consider those philosophers in the early part of the eighteenth century in whose thinking the second problem was uppermost.

One phase of aesthetic thinking was launched by the very influential writings of the third earl of Shaftesbury (see especially his *Moralists*, 1709, III; *Inquiry concerning Virtue or Merit*, 1699, I; and *Characteristics*, 1711). Shaftesbury's philosophy was basically Neoplatonic, but to emphasize the immediacy of our impression of beauty, and also to underline his view that the harmony perceived as beauty is also perceived as virtue, Shaftesbury gave the name "moral sense" to that "inward eye" that grasps harmony in both its aesthetic and ethical forms. The concept of a special faculty of aesthetic apprehension was one form of the theory of taste. Shaftesbury's other contributions to the development of aesthetics are his description of disinterestedness as a characteristic of the aesthetic attitude (*Moralists* III) and his appreciation (along with his contemporaries John Dennis and Thomas Burnet) of wild, fearful, and irregular forms of nature—a taste that helped bring into prominence, in the eighteenth century, the concept of the sublime as an aesthetic quality distinct from beauty.

Joseph Addison's *Spectator* papers on aesthetic enjoyment (1712, Nos. 409, 411–421) conceived taste as simply the capacity to discern those three qualities that give rise to "the pleasures of the imagination," greatness (that is, sublimity), uncommonness (novelty), and beauty. Addison made some attempt to explain why it is that the perception of these qualities is attended by so much pleasure of so special a sort, but he did not go far; his service (earning the appreciation he received from succeeding thinkers) was the lively and provocative way in which he raised many of the basic questions.

The first real treatise on aesthetics in the modern world was Francis Hutcheson's *Inquiry concerning Beauty, Order, Harmony, and Design*, the first part of *An Inquiry into the Original of our Ideas of Beauty and Virtue* (1725). From Shaftesbury, Hutcheson took the idea of an inner sense; the "sense of beauty" is the power to frame the idea of beauty when confronted with those qualities of objects suited to raise it. The sense of beauty does not depend on judgment or reflection; it does not respond to intellectual or utilitarian features of the world, nor does it depend on

association of ideas. His analysis showed that we sense beauty in an object when it presents "a compound ratio of uniformity and variety" (2d ed., p. 17), so that beauty varies with either of these, if the other is held constant. A basis is thus laid for a nonrelativistic standard of judgment, and variations in actual preference are explained away as due to different expectations with which the beautiful object, in art or nature, is approached.

The question of a standard of taste was the chief concern of David Hume's thinking on aesthetic matters. In his *Treatise* (II, i, 8), he suggested that "beauty is such an order and construction of parts, as either by the *primary constitution* of our nature, by *custom*, or by *caprice*, is fitted to give a pleasure and satisfaction to the soul," thus allowing, like Hutcheson, who influenced him considerably, an immediate delight in beauty, but allowing also for a transfer of this delight by association. For example, the appearance (not necessarily the actuality) of convenience or utility explains why many objects are esteemed beautiful (III, iii, 1). Some types of beauty, then, are simply seen or missed; judgments of them cannot be corrected. But in other cases, especially in art, argument and reflection can correct judgment (see *Enquiry concerning the Principles of Morals*, 1751, Sec. 1). This problem is discussed most carefully in the essay "Of the Standard of Taste" (in *Four Dissertations*, 1757). Hume argued that it is natural to seek for a standard of taste, by which aesthetic preferences can be called correct or incorrect, especially as there are clear cases of error ("Bunyan is a better writer than Addison"). The rules, or criteria, of judgment are to be established by inductive inquiry into those features of works of art that enable them to please most highly a qualified perceiver, that is, one who is experienced, calm, unprejudiced. But there will always be areas within which preference is due to temperament, age, culture, and similar factors unchangeable by argument; there is no objective standard by which such differences can be rationally resolved.

THE AESTHETIC QUALITIES. The search for necessary and sufficient conditions of beauty and other aesthetic qualities (the concept of the "picturesque" was added late in the century) was continued enthusiastically in the latter half of the eighteenth century. In this debate, an important part was played by Edmund Burke's youthful work, *A Philosophical Enquiry into the Origin of Our Ideas of the Sublime and Beautiful* (1757). Its argument develops on two levels, phenomenological and physiological. The first task is to explain by what qualities objects excite in us the feelings of beauty ("love" without desire) and sublimity ("astonishment" without actual danger). The feeling of the sublime, to begin with, involves a degree of horror—controlled horror—the mind being held and filled by what it contemplates (II, 1). Thus, any object that can excite the ideas of pain and danger, or is associated with such objects, or has qualities that can operate in a similar way, can be sublime (I, 7).

Burke then goes on to argue that obscurity, power, privation and emptiness, vastness approaching infinity, etc. contribute to sublimity (II, 3–8). Beauty is analogously treated: The paradigm emotion is response to female beauty, minus lust; and objects that are small, smooth, gently varying, delicate, etc. can give the feeling of beauty (III, 1–16). The same scene can be both beautiful and sublime, but because of the opposition in several of their conditions it cannot be very intensely either if it is both.

Burke then moves to his second level of explanation (IV, 1, 5). He asks what enables the perceptual qualities to evoke the feelings of beauty and sublimity, and he answers that they do so by producing physiological effects like those of actual love and terror. "Beauty acts by relaxing the solids of the whole system" (IV, 19)—this is one of Burke's celebrated hypotheses, a pioneering attempt at physiological aesthetics.

In this very fertile period of aesthetic investigation, many other writers, of various degrees of sophistication, contributed to the theory of beauty and sublimity and to the foundations of taste. Among the most important works, still worth reading for some of their suggestions, are Alexander Gerard's *Essay on Taste* (written by 1756, published 1759; see also his *Essay on Genius*, 1774), which made much use of association in explaining our pleasure in beauty, novelty, sublimity, imitation, harmony, ridicule, and virtue; Henry Home's (Lord Kames) *Elements of Criticism* (1762); Hugh Blair's *Lectures on Rhetoric and Belles Lettres* (given from 1759 on, published 1783); Thomas Reid's essay on Taste in his *Essays on the Intellectual Powers of Man* (1785). On the Continent, the question whether there is a special aesthetic sense was discussed, along with many other problems, by Jean-Pierre de Crousaz, *Traité du beau* (1714), and the Abbé Dubos, *Réflexions critiques sur la poésie et sur la peinture* (1719). Noteworthy also are Voltaire's *Temple du goût* (1733), Yves-Marie André's *Essai sur le beau* (1741), and especially the article on beauty that Diderot wrote for the *Encyclopédie* (1751), in which the experience of beauty is analyzed as the perception of "relationships" (*rapports*).

In general, the later development of empiricist aesthetics involved increasingly ambitious attempts to explain aesthetic phenomena by means of association; a further broadening of the acknowledged aesthetic qualities, away from a limited concept of beauty; further reflection on the nature of "genius," the capacity to "snatch a grace beyond the reach of art"; and a growing conviction that critical principles have to be justified, if they can be justified at all, in terms of empirical knowledge of the characteristic effects of art. The achievements and the high level of discussion reached by the empiricist movement can be seen very well in a later treatise by Archibald Alison, his *Essays on the Nature and Principles of Taste* (1790; rev. ed., which became highly influential, 1811). Alison abandoned the hope for simple formulas of beauty and resolved the pleasure of taste into the enjoyment of following a train of imaginations, in which some of the ideas produce emotions and in which the entire train is connected by a dominant emotion. No special sense is required; the principles of association explain everything. And the arguments by which Alison supported his main theses, the careful inductions at all points, are models of one kind of aesthetics. For example, he showed, by experimental comparisons, that particular qualities of objects, or of Hogarth's "line of beauty" (II, iv, 1, Part II), do not produce aesthetic pleasure unless they become "expressive," or take on the character of signs, by being able to initiate a train of associations; and it is the same, he said, with colors: "Purple, for instance, has acquired a character of Dignity, from its accidental connection with the Dress of Kings" (II, iii, 1).

GERMAN IDEALISM

By assigning to the problems of aesthetic judgment the major part of his third *Critique* (*The Critique of Judgment*, 1790), Kant became the first modern philosopher to make his aesthetic theory an integral part of a philosophic system. For in this volume he aimed to link the worlds of nature and freedom, which the first two *Critiques* had distinguished and separated.

KANT'S ANALYSIS OF JUDGMENTS OF TASTE. Kant recast the problems of eighteenth-century aesthetic thought, with which he was thoroughly familiar, in the characteristic form of the critical philosophy: How are judgments of the beautiful and the sublime possible? That is, in view of their evident subjectivity, how is their implicit claim to general validity to be vindicated? That such judgments claim general validity and yet are also subjective is argued by Kant, in careful detail, in the "Analytic of the Beautiful" and the "Analytic of the Sublime."

Judgments of beauty (also called "judgments of taste") are analyzed in terms of the four "moments" of the table of categories: relation, quantity, quality, and modality. First, the judgment of taste does not (like ordinary judgments) subsume a representation under a concept, but states a relation between the representation and a special disinterested satisfaction, that is, a satisfaction independent of desire and interest (§5). Second, the judgment of taste, though singular in logical form ("This rose is beautiful"), lays title to universal acceptance, unlike a report of mere sensuous pleasure, which imposes no obligation to agree. Yet, paradoxically, it does not claim to be supportable by reasons, for no arguments can constrain anyone to agree with a judgment of taste (§9; cf. §33). Third, aesthetic satisfaction is evoked by an object that is purposive in its form, though in fact it has no purpose or function: because of a certain wholeness, it looks as though it were somehow made to be understood (§10; cf. §65 and Introduction): it has "purposiveness without purpose" (*Zweckmässigkeit ohne Zweck*). Fourth, the beautiful is claimed by the judgment of taste to have a necessary reference to aesthetic satisfaction (§18): not that when we find ourselves moved in this way by an object we can guarantee that all others will be similarly moved, but that they *ought* to take the same satisfaction we do in it.

THE PROBLEM OF VALIDATION. It is the above four aspects of the judgment of beauty that give rise to the philosophical problem of validation, which Kant formulates as he had the parallel problems in the earlier *Critiques*: How can their claim to necessity (and subjective universality) be legitimized? This can only be done, he argues, if it can be shown that the conditions presupposed in such a judgment are not confined to the individual who makes it, but may reasonably be ascribed to all rational beings. A minor clue is offered by the disinterestedness of aesthetic sansfaction; for if our satisfaction is in no way dependent on individual interests, it takes on a kind of intersubjectivity (§6). But the validation of the synthetic a priori judgment of taste requires something more searching, namely, a transcendental deduction.

The gist of this argument is as follows: Empirical knowledge is possible because the faculty of judgment can bring together general concepts and particular sense-intuitions prepared for it in the imagination. These cases of *determinate* judgment presuppose, however, a general harmony between the imagination, in its freedom as synthesizer of representations, and the understanding, in its a priori lawfulness. The formal purposiveness of an object as experienced can induce what Kant calls "a free play of the imagination," an intense disinterested pleasure

that depends not on any particular knowledge but just on consciousness of the harmony of the two cognitive powers, imagination and understanding (§9). This is the pleasure we affirm in the judgment of taste. Since the general possibility of sharing knowledge with each other, which may be taken for granted, presupposes that in each of us there *is* a cooperation of imagination and understanding, it follows that every rational being has the *capacity* to feel, under appropriate perceptual conditions, this harmony of the cognitive powers. Therefore a true judgment of taste can legitimately claim to be true for all (§9; cf. §§35–39).

Kant's system requires that there be a dialectic of taste with an antinomy to be dissolved on the principles of critical philosophy. This is a paradox about the role of concepts in the judgment of taste: If the judgment involves concepts, it must be rationally disputable, and provable by reasons (which it is not); if it does not involve concepts, it cannot even be the subject of disagreement (which it is). The solution is that no determinate concept is involved in such judgments, but only the indeterminate concept of the supersensible, or thing-in-itself that underlies the object as well as the judging subject (§§56–57).

KANT ON THE SUBLIME. Kant's analysis of the sublime proceeds on quite different grounds. Essentially, he explains this species of satisfaction as a feeling of the grandeur of reason itself and of humankind's moral destiny, which arises in two ways: (1) When we are confronted in nature with the extremely vast (the mathematical sublime), our imagination falters in the task of comprehending it and we become aware of the supremacy of reason, whose ideas reach toward infinite totality. (2) When we are confronted with the overwhelmingly powerful (the dynamical sublime), the weakness of our empirical selves makes us aware (again by contrast) of our worth as moral beings (see the "Analytic of the Sublime"). In this analysis, and again in his final remarks on beauty in nature, Kant goes some way toward re-establishing on one level a connection between realms whose autonomy he has fought for on a different level. As he had done earlier with the a priori concepts of the understanding and the sphere of morality, he has here tried to show that the aesthetic stands on its own feet, independent of desire and interest, of knowledge or morality. Yet because the experience of beauty depends upon seeing natural objects as though they were somehow the artifacts of a cosmic reason bent on being intelligible to us, and because the experience of the sublime makes use of natural formlessness and fearfulness to celebrate reason itself, these aesthetic values in the last analysis serve a moral purpose and a moral need, exalting and ennobling the human spirit.

SCHILLER. Kant's aesthetic theories were first made use of by the dramatic poet Friedrich Schiller, who found in them the key to a number of profound problems about culture and freedom that he had been meditating. In several essays and poems, and principally in the remarkable *Briefe über die ästhetische Erzieung des Menschen* ("Letters on the Aesthetic Education of Man," 1793–1795), he developed a neo-Kantian view of art and beauty as the medium through which humanity (and the human individual) advances from a sensuous to a rational, and therefore fully human, stage of existence. Schiller distinguishes (Letters 12–13) two basic drives in man, the sensuous impulse (*Stofftrieb*) and the formal impulse (*Formtrieb*), and argues that they are synthesized and lifted to a higher plane in what he calls the play impulse (*Spieltrieb*), which responds to the living shape (*Lebensform*) or beauty of the world (Letter 15). Play, in his sense, is a more concrete version of Kant's harmony of imagination and understanding; it involves that special combination of freedom and necessity that comes in voluntary submission to rules for the sake of the game. By appealing to the play impulse, and freeing man's higher self from dominance by his sensuous nature, art renders man human and gives him a social character (Letters 26–27); it is therefore the necessary condition of any social order that is based not upon totalitarian compulsion but upon rational freedom.

SCHELLING. Friedrich Wilhelm von Schelling was the first philosopher to claim to have discovered an "absolute standpoint" from which the dualisms and dichotomies of Kant's epistemology could be overcome, or overridden; and he was the first since Plotinus to make art and beauty the capstone of a system. In his *System of Transcendental Idealism* (1800), he attempted a reconciliation of all oppositions between the self and nature through the idea of art. In the artistic intuition, he says, the self is both conscious and unconscious at once; there is both deliberation, *Kunst*, and inspiration, *Poesie*. This harmony of freedom and necessity crystallizes and makes manifest the underlying harmony that exists between the self and nature. There is at work an unseen creative drive that is, on the unconsciousness level, the same as conscious artistic activity. In Schelling's lectures on the *Philosophy of Art* (given 1802–1803, but not published until 1859), transcendental idealism becomes "absolute idealism" and art becomes the medium through which the infinite "ideas," which are the expressions of the various "potencies"

involved in the ultimate absolute self-identity, become embodied in finite form, and therefore the medium through which the absolute is most fully revealed. This same general position underlies the famous work *Über das Verhältniss der bildenden Künste zu der Natur (On the Relation Between the Plastic Arts and Nature*, 1807).

HEGEL. The most fully articulated idealistic system of aesthetics was that of George Friedrich Wilhelm Hegel, in his lectures between 1820 and 1829, the notes for which were published (1835) as his *Philosophy of Fine Art*. In art, he says, the "idea" (the notion at its highest stage of dialectical development) becomes embodied in sensuous form. This is beauty. Man thereby renders explicit to himself what he is and can be (see *Philosophy of Fine Art*, Osmaston translation, I, 41). When the sensuous is spiritualized in art (I, 53), there is both a cognitive revelation of truth, and also a reinvigoration of the beholder. Natural beauty is capable of embodying the idea to some degree, but in human art the highest embodiment takes place (see I, 39, 10–11, 208–214).

Hegel also worked out, in great detail, a theory of the dialectical development of art in the history of human culture, from Oriental "symbolic" art, in which the idea is overwhelmed by the medium; through its antithesis, classical art, in which the idea and the medium are in perfect equilibrium; to the synthesis, romantic art, in which the idea dominates the medium and spiritualization is complete (see Vols. III, IV). These categories were to prove very influential in nineteenth-century German aesthetic thought, in which the Hegelian tradition was dominant, despite attacks by the "formalists" (such as J. F. Herbart), who rejected the analysis of beauty in terms of ideas as an overintellectualization of the aesthetic and a slighting of the formal conditions of beauty.

ROMANTICISM

Without attempting to trace its roots and early stages, we may say that the romantic revolution in feeling and taste was fully under way in Schelling's philosophy of nature and in the new forms of literary creation explored by the German and English poets from about 1890 to 1910. From the start, these developments were accompanied by reflection on the nature of the arts themselves, and they led in time to fundamental changes in prevailing views about the arts.

EMOTIONAL EXPRESSION. The romantics generally conceived of art as essentially the expression of the artist's personal emotions. This view is central to such basic documents as Wordsworth's 1800 Preface to *Lyrical Ballads*, Shelley's *Defense of Poetry* (written 1819) Mill's "What is Poetry?" (1833), and the writings of the German and French romantics. The poet himself, his personality as seen through the "window" of the poem (Carlyle's term in "The Hero as Poet," 1841), becomes the center of interest, and sincerity (in Wordsworth, Carlyle, Arnold) becomes one of the leading criteria of criticism.

IMAGINATION. A new version of the cognitive view of art becomes dominant in the concept of the imagination as a faculty of immediate insight into truth, distinct from, and perhaps superior to, reason and understanding—the artist's special gift. The imagination is both creator and revealer of nature and what lies behind it—a romanticized version of Kant's transcendental idealism, ascribing the form of experience to the shaping power of the mind, and of Fichte's Ego "positing" the non-Ego. A. W. Schlegel, Blake, Shelley, Hazlitt, Baudelaire, and many others spoke of the imagination in these terms. Coleridge, with his famous distinction between imagination and fancy, provided one of the fullest formulations: The fancy is a "mode of memory," operating associatively to recombine the elementary data of sense; the imagination is the "coadunating faculty" that dissolves and transforms the data and creates novelty and emergent quality. The distinction (based on Schelling) between the "primary" and "secondary" imagination is between the unconscious creativity involved both in natural processes and in all perception and the conscious and deliberate expression of this in the artist's creating (see Chs. 13 and 14 of Coleridge's *Biographia Literaria*, 1817). Through most of Coleridge's work there runs his unfinished task of supplying a new theory of mind and of artistic creation that would replace the current associationism, which he had at first enthusiastically adopted and then, under the influence of Plotinus and the German idealists, came to reject.

ORGANISM. Another important, and related, aspect of Coleridge's critical theory was his distinction (derived essentially from A. W. Schlegel's Vienna *Lectures on Dramatic Art*, 1809–1811) between mechanical and organic form and his conception of a work of art as an organic whole, bound together by deeper and more subtle unity than that explicated in the neoclassic rules and having a vitality that grows from within (see his Shakespearean criticism for examples). The concept of nature as organic, and of art as growing out of nature like a living being, had already been developed by Johann Gottfried Herder (see, for example, his *Vom Erkennen und Empfinden der Menschlichen Seele*, 1778), and by Goethe, in some of his essays (e.g., "Vom Deutscher Baukunst," 1772; "Über Wahrheit und Wahrscheinlichkeit der Kunstwerke," 1797).

SYMBOLISM. The idea of the work of art as being, in some sense (in some one of many possible senses), a symbol, a sensuous embodiment of a spiritual meaning, though old in essence, as we have seen, came into a new prominence in the romantic period. Goethe distinguished allegory, a mechanical combination of universal and particular, and symbol, as a concrete unity (see "Über die Gegenstände der bildenden Kunst," 1797); and Friedrich and August Wilhelm Schlegel followed with a new interest in myth and metaphor in poetry. The English Romantic poets (notably Wordsworth) evolved a new lyric poetry in which the visible landscape took on the attributes of human experience. And in France, later in the century, the symbolist movement, launched by Jean Moréas in 1885, and the practice of such poets as Baudelaire, Rimbaud, and Mallarmé emphasized concrete symbolic objects as the heart of poetry.

SCHOPENHAUER. Though first written in the climate of post-Kantian idealism, and, in that context, largely ignored, Arthur Schopenhauer's *Die Welt als Wille und Vorstellung* ("World as Will and Idea," 1819; 2d ed. enlarged, 1844) came into its deserved fame in the second half of the century. Its romantic pessimism and intuitionism and, more particularly, the central position it assigned to the arts (especially music) made it one of the most important aesthetic documents of the century. Schopenhauer's solution of the basic Kantian dualism was to interpret the thing in itself, or noumenal world, as the "Will to Live" and the phenomenal world as the objectification, or expression, of that primal will. The objects of the phenomenal world fall into a hierarchy of types, or grades, that embody, according to Schopenhauer, certain universals or Platonic ideas, and it is these ideas that are presented to us for contemplation by works of art. Since the idea is timeless, the contemplation of it (as, for example, some general character of human nature in a poem or painting) frees us from subjection to the "principle of sufficient reason," which dominates our ordinary practical and cognitive consciousness, and hence from the constant pressure of the will. In this "pure will-less state," we lose individuality and pain.

Schopenhauer has much to say about the various arts and the forms of ideas suited to them; the uniqueness of music in this scheme is that it embodies not ideas but the will itself in its striving and urging and enables us to contemplate its awfulness directly, without involvement.

Schopenhauer's theory of music was one of his most important contributions to aesthetic theory and influenced not only those theorists, such as Richard Wagner (see his essay on Beethoven, 1870), who emphasized the representative character of music, but also those critical of this view, such as Eduard Hanslick in *Vom Musikalisch-Schönen* ("The Beautiful in Music," 1854).

NIETZSCHE. Friedrich Nietzsche repudiated romantic art as escapist, but his own aesthetic views, briefly sketched in the notes published posthumously as *The Will to Power* (1901), are best understood in relation to those of Schopenhauer. Nietzsche's early work, *The Birth of Tragedy from the Spirit of Music* (1872), presented a theory of tragedy as arising from the conjunction of two fundamental impulses, which Nietzsche called the Dionysian and Apollonian spirits: the one a joyful acceptance of experience, the other a need for order and proportion. In Nietzsche's later thinking about art, it is the former that becomes dominant; he insists, for example, as opposed to Schopenhauer, that tragedy exists not to inculcate resignation and a Buddhist negation of life, by showing the inevitability of suffering, but to affirm life in all its pain, to express the artist's overabundance of will to power. Art, he says, is a "tonic," a great "yea-sayer" to life.

THE ARTIST AND SOCIETY

Political, economic, and social changes in the nineteenth century, in the wake of the French Revolution and the rise of modern industry, raised in a new form the Platonic problem of the artists' relation to their society, their possibly conflicting obligations to their craft and to their fellow human beings. In the nineteenth century, an important part of aesthetic thinking was concerned with this problem.

ART FOR ART'S SAKE. One solution to the problem was to think of the artist as a person with a calling of his own, whose whole, or at least primary, obligation is to perfect his work, especially its formal beauty, whatever society may expect. Perhaps the artist, because of his superiority, or higher sensitivity, or the demands of his art, must be alienated from society, and, though perhaps doomed to be destroyed by it, can carry his curse as a pride. This notion stems from the German romantics, from Wilhelm Wacken-Roder, Johann Ludwig Tieck, and others. From 1820–1830 it became the doctrine of "art for art's sake," the center of continuing controversy in France and, later, in England. In its extreme forms, as reflected, for example, in Oscar Wilde (*Intentions*, 1891) and J. A. M. Whistler ("Ten O'Clock" lecture, 1885), it was sometimes a claim that art is more important than anything else and sometimes a flaunting of the artist's freedom from responsibility. More thoughtfully and fundamentally, as in Théophile Gautier (Preface to *Mademoiselle de Maupin*, 1835) and throughout Flaubert's correspondence with Louise Colet and others, *l'art pour l'art* was a declaration of artistic independence and a kind of professional code of dedication. In that respect, it owed much to the work of Kant in carving out an autonomous domain for art.

REALISM. The theory of realism (or, in Zola's sense, naturalism) arose as a broadened conviction of the cognitive duty of literature, a desire to give it an empirical, and even experimental status (in Zola's essay on "The Experimental Novel," 1880), as exhibitor of human nature and social conditions. In Flaubert and Zola, realism called for the cool, analytical eye of the novelist, treating virtue and vice, in Hippolyte Taine's words, as "products like vitriol and sugar"; see the Introduction to his *History of English Literature* (1863), in which Taine set forth his program for explaining art deterministically in terms of race, context, and epoch (*race, milieu, moment*). Among the Russian literary theorists, Vissarion G. Belinsky, Nikolai G. Chernyshevski ("The Aesthetic Relation of Art to Reality," 1855), and Dmitri I. Pisarev ("The Destruction of Aesthetics," 1865), all art was given a similar treatment—as a reproduction of factual reality (sometimes an aid in explaining it, which may have value as a substitute, like a photograph, says Chernyshevski) or as the bearer of social ideas (Pisarev).

SOCIAL RESPONSIBILITY. The theory that art is primarily a social force and that the artist has a social responsibility was first fully worked out by the French socialist sociologists. Claude Saint-Simon (*Du système industriel*, 1821), Auguste Comte (*Discours sur l'ensemble du positivisme*, 1848, Ch. 5), Charles Fourier (*Cités ouvrières*, 1849), and Pierre Joseph Proudhon (*Du principe de l'art et de sa destination sociale*, 1865) attacked the idea that art can be an end in itself and projected visions of future social orders free of violence and exploitation, in which beauty and use would be fruitfully combined and for which art will help prepare. In England, John Ruskin and William Morris were the great critics of Victorian society from an aesthetic point of view. They pointed to the degradation of the worker into a machine, unfree to express himself, the loss of good taste, the destruction of natural beauty, and the trivialization of art. Ruskin's essay on "The Nature of Gothic" (*Stones of Venice*, 1851) and many other lectures (for example those in *The Two Paths*,

1859; *Lectures on Art*, 1870) insisted on the social conditions and effects of art. Morris, in his lectures and pamphlets (see, for example, "Art under Plutocracy," 1883; "The Aims of Art," 1887; "Art and Socialism," 1884), argued that radical changes were needed in the social and economic order to make art what it should be: "… the expression of man's happiness in his labor … made by the people, and for the people, as a happiness to the maker and the user" ("The Art of the People," 1879).

The functionalist tendencies of Ruskin and Morris also turned up, even earlier, in the United States, in the trenchant views of Horatio Greenough ("American Architecture," 1843) and in some essays of Ralph Waldo Emerson ("Thoughts on Art," 1841; "Beauty," *Conduct of Life*, 1860; "Art," *Essays, First Series*, 1841).

TOLSTOY. It was, however, Leo Tolstoy who drove the social view of art to its farthest point in the nineteenth century and issued the most fundamental challenge to art's right to exist. In *What Is Art?* (first uncensored edition, 1898, in English), he asked whether all the social costs of art could be rationally justified. If, as he argued, art is essentially a form of communication—the transmission of emotion—then certain consequences can be deduced. Unless the emotion is one that can actually be shared by men in general—is simple and human—there is either bad art or pseudo art: this criterion rules out most of the supposedly great works of music and literature, including Tolstoy's own major novels. A work must be judged, in the end, by the highest religious criteria of the age; and in Tolstoy's age that meant, he said, its contribution to the sense of human brotherhood. Great art is that which transmits either simple feelings, drawing men together, or the feeling of brotherhood itself (*Uncle Tom's Cabin*). In no other way can it claim genuine social value (apart from the adventitious value of jewelry, etc.); and where it falls short of this high task (as it usually does), it can only be a social evil, dividing people into cliques by catering to sensuality, pride, and patriotism.

CONTEMPORARY DEVELOPMENTS

Aesthetics has never been so actively and diversely cultivated as in the twentieth century. Certain major figures and certain lines of work stand out.

METAPHYSICAL THEORIES. Though he later proposed two important changes in his central doctrine of intuition, the early aesthetic theory of Benedetto Croce has remained the most pervasively influential aesthetics of the twentieth century. The fullest exposition was given in the *Estetica come scienza dell'espressione e linguistica generale* ("Aesthetic as Science of Expression and General Linguistic," 1902), which is part of his *Filosofia dello spirito*. Aesthetics, in this context, is the "science" of images, or intuitive knowledge, as logic is knowledge of concepts—both being distinguished from "practical knowledge." At the lower limit of consciousness, says Croce, are raw sense data, or "impressions," which, when they clarify themselves, are intuitions, are also said to be "expressed." To express, in this subjective sense, apart from any external physical activity, is to create art. Hence, his celebrated formula, "intuition = expression," on which many principles of his aesthetics are based. For example, he argued that in artistic failure, or "unsuccessful expression," the trouble is not that a fully formed intuition has not been fully expressed but that an impression has not been fully intuited. R. G. Collingwood, in his *Principles of Art* (1938), has extended and clarified Croce's basic point of view.

The theory of intuition presented by Henri Bergson is quite different but has also been eagerly accepted by many aestheticians. In his view, it is intuition (or instinct become self-conscious) that enables us to penetrate to the *durée*, or *élan vital*—the ultimate reality which our "spatializing" intellects inevitably distort. The general view is explained in his "Introduction à la métaphysique" (1903) and in *L'évolution créatrice* (1907) and applied with great ingenuity and subtlety to the problem of the comic in *Le rire* (1900).

NATURALISM. Philosophers working within the tradition of American naturalism, or contextualism, have emphasized the continuity of the aesthetic with the rest of life and culture. George Santayana, for example, in his *Reason in Art* (1903; Vol. IV of *The Life of Reason*), argues against a sharp separation of "fine" from "useful" arts and gives a strong justification of fine art as both a model and an essential constituent of the life of reason. His earlier book, *The Sense of Beauty* (1896), was an essay in introspective psychology that did much to restimulate an empirical approach to art through its famous doctrine that beauty is "objectified pleasure."

The fullest and most vigorous expression of naturalistic aesthetics is *Art as Experience* (1934), by John Dewey. In *Experience and Nature* (1925), Dewey had already begun to reflect upon the "consummatory" aspect of experience (as well as the instrumental aspects, which had previously occupied most of his attention) and had treated art as the "culmination of nature," to which scientific discovery is a handmaiden (see Ch. 9). *Art as Experi-*

ence, a book that has had incalculable influence on contemporary aesthetic thinking, develops this basic point of view. When experience rounds itself off into more or less complete and coherent strands of doing and undergoing, we have, he says, "*an* experience"; and such an experience is aesthetic to the degree in which attention is fixed on pervasive quality. Art is expression, in the sense that in expressive objects there is a "fusion" of "meaning" in the present quality; ends and means, separated for practical purposes, are reunited, to produce not only experience enjoyable in itself but, at its best, a celebration and commemoration of qualities ideal to the culture or society in which the art plays its part.

A number of other writers have worked with valuable results along similar lines, for example, D. W. Prall, *Aesthetic Judgment* (1929) and *Aesthetic Analysis* (1936); C. I. Lewis, *An Analysis of Knowledge and Valuation* (1946, Chs. 14, 15); and Stephen C. Pepper, *Aesthetic Quality* (1937), *The Basis of Criticism in the Arts* (1945), *The Work of Art* (1955).

SEMIOTIC APPROACHES. Since semiotics in a broad sense has undoubtedly been one of the central preoccupations of contemporary philosophy, as well as many other fields of thought, it is to be expected that philosophers working along this line would consider applying their results to the problems of aesthetics. The pioneering work of C. K. Ogden and I. A. Richards, *The Meaning of Meaning* (1923), stressed the authors' distinction between the "referential" and the "emotive" function of language. And they suggested two aesthetic implications that were widely followed: first, that the long-sought distinction between poetic and scientific discourse was to be found here, poetry being considered essentially emotive language; second, that judgments of beauty and other judgments of aesthetic value could be construed as purely emotive. This work, and later books of Richards, have been joined by a number of aesthetic studies in the general theory of (artistic) interpretation, for example, John Hospers, *Meaning and Truth in the Arts* (1946); Charles L. Stevenson, "Interpretation and Evaluation in Aesthetics" (1950); Morris Weitz, *Philosophy of the Arts* (1950); and Isabel C. Hungerland, *Poetic Discourse* (1958).

Meanwhile, anthropological interest in classical and primitive mythology, which became scientific in the nineteenth century, led to another semiotical way of looking at art, particularly literature. Under the influence of Sir James G. Frazer's *The Golden Bough* (1890–1915), a group of British classical scholars developed new theories about the relations between Greek tragedy, Greek mythology,

and religious rite. Jane Ellen Harrison's *Themis: A Study of the Social Origins of Greek Religion* (1912) argued that Greek myth and drama grew out of ritual. This field of inquiry was further opened up, or out, by C. G. Jung, in his paper "On the Relation of Analytical Psychology to Poetic Art" (1922; see *Contributions to Analytical Psychology*, 1928) and in other works. Jung suggested that the basic symbolic elements of all literature are "primordial images" or "archetypes" that emerge from the "collective unconscious" of man. In recent years the search for "archetypal patterns" in all literature, to help explain its power, has been carried on by many critics and has become an accepted part of literary criticism.

The most ambitious attempt to bring together these and other lines of inquiry to make a general theory of human culture ("philosophical anthropology") is that of Ernst Cassirer. In his *Philosophie der Symbolischen Formen* (3 vols., 1923, 1925, 1929), the central doctrines of which are also explained in *Sprache und Mythos* (1925) and in *An Essay on Man* (1944), he put forward a neo-Kantian theory of the great "symbolic forms" of culture—language, myth, art, religion, and science. In this view, man's world is determined, in fundamental ways, by the very symbolic forms in which he represents it to himself; so, for example, the primitive world of myth is necessarily different from that of science or art. Cassirer's philosophy exerted a strong influence upon two American philosophers especially: Wilbur Marshall Urban (*Language and Reality*, 1939) argued that "aesthetic symbols" are "insight symbols" of a specially revelatory sort; and Susanne K. Langer has developed in detail a theory of art as a "presentational symbol," or "semblance." In *Philosophy in a New Key* (1942), she argued that music is not self-expression or evocation but symbolizes the morphology of human sentience and hence articulates the emotional life of man. In *Feeling and Form* (1953) and in various essays (*Problems of Art*, 1957), she applied the theory to various basic arts.

Charles W. Morris presented a closely parallel view in 1939, in two articles that (like Mrs. Langer's books) have been much discussed: "Esthetics and the Theory of Signs" (*Journal of Unified Science* [*Erkenntnis*], VIII, 1939–1940) and "Science, Art and Technology" (*Kenyon Review*, I, 1939; see also *Signs, Language and Behavior*, 1946). Taking a term from Charles Peirce, he treats works of art as "iconic signs" (i.e., signs that signify a property in virtue of exhibiting it) of "value properties" (e.g., regional properties like the menacing, the sublime, the gay).

MARXISM–LENINISM. The philosophy of dialectical materialism formulated by Karl Marx and Friedrich Engels contained, at the start, only the basic principle of an aesthetics, whose implications have been drawn out and developed by Marxist theoreticians over more than half a century. This principle is that art, like all higher activities, belongs to the cultural "superstructure" and is determined by sociohistorical conditions, especially economic conditions. From this it is argued that a connection can always be traced—and must be traced, for full understanding—between a work of art and its sociohistorical matrix. In some sense, art is a "reflection of social reality," but the exact nature and limits of this sense has remained one of the fundamental and persistent problems of Marxist aesthetics. Marx himself, in his *Contribution to the Critique of Political Economy* (1859), pointed out that there is no simple one-to-one correspondence between the character of a society and its art.

In the period before the October Revolution of 1917, Georgi V. Plekhanov (*Art and Social Life*, 1912) developed dialectical materialist aesthetics through attacks on the doctrine of art for art and the separation of artist from society, either in theory or in practice. After the Revolution, there ensued a period of vigorous and free debate in Russia among various groups of Marxists and others (e.g., the formalists, see below). It was questioned whether art can be understood entirely in sociohistorical terms or has its own "peculiar laws" (as Trotsky remarked in *Literature and Revolution*, 1924) and whether art is primarily a weapon in the class struggle or a resultant whose reformation awaits the full realization of a socialist society. The debate was closed in Russia by official fiat, when the party established control over the arts at the First All-Union Congress of Soviet Writers (1934). Socialist realism, as a theory of what art ought to be and as a guide to practice, was given a stricter definition by Andrei Zhdanov, who along with Gorki became the official theoretician of art. But the central idea had already been stated by Engels (letter to Margaret Harkness, April 1888): the artist is to reveal the moving social forces and portray his characters as expressions of these forces (this is what the Marxist means by a "typical" character), and in so doing he is to forward the revolutionary developments themselves. (See also Ralph Fox, *The Novel and the People*, 1937; Christopher Caudwell, *Illusion and Reality*, 1937, and other works.)

Indications of recent growth in dialectical materialist aesthetics, and of a resumption of the dialogue with other systems, can be seen in the important work of the Hungarian Marxist Georg Lukács (see, for example, *The Meaning of Contemporary Realism*, translated, 1962, from *Wider den missverstandenen Realismus*, 1958) and in the writings of the Polish Marxist, Stefan Morawski (see "Vicissitudes in the Theory of Socialist Realism," *Diogenes*, 1962).

PHENOMENOLOGY AND EXISTENTIALISM. Among many critics and critical theorists, there has been, in the twentieth century, a strong emphasis on the autonomy of the work of art, its objective qualities as an object in itself, independent of both its creator and its perceivers. This attitude was forcefully stated by Eduard Hanslick in *The Beautiful in Music* (1854); it was reflected in the work of Clive Bell (*Art*, 1914) and Roger Fry (*Vision and Design*, 1920); and it appeared especially in two literary movements. The first, Russian "formalism" (also present in Poland and Czechoslovakia), flourished from 1915 until suppressed about 1930. Its leaders were Roman Jakobson, Victor Shklovsky, Boris Eichenbaum, and Boris Tomashevsky (*Theory of Literature*, 1925). The second, American and British "New Criticism," was inaugurated by I. A. Richards (*Practical Criticism*, 1929), William Empson (*Seven Types of Ambiguity*, 1930), and others (see René Wellek and Austin Warren, *Theory of Literature*, 1949).

This emphasis on the autonomy of the work of art has been supported by Gestalt psychology, with its emphasis on the phenomenal objectivity of Gestalt qualities, and also phenomenology, the philosophical movement first developed by Edmund Husserl. Two outstanding works in phenomenological aesthetics have appeared. Working on Husserl's foundations, Roman Ingarden (*Das Literarische Kunstwerk*, 1930) has studied the mode of existence of the literary work as an intentional object and has distinguished four "strata" in literature: sound, meaning, the "world of the work," and its "schematized aspects," or implicit perspectives. Mikel Dufrenne (*Phenomenologie de l'expérience esthétique*, 2 vols., 1953), closer to the phenomenology of Maurice Merleau-Ponty and Jean-Paul Sartre, has analyzed the differences between aesthetic objects and other things in the world. He finds that the basic difference lies in the "expressed world" of each aesthetic object, its own personality, which combines the "being in itself" (*en-soi*) of a presentation with the "being for itself" (*pour-soi*) of consciousness and contains measureless depths that speak to the depths of ourselves as persons.

The "existential phenomenalism" of Heidegger and Sartre suggests possibilities for an existentialist philosophy of art, in the central concept of "authentic existence," which art might be said to further. These possibilities have only begun to be worked out, for example, in Heidegger's paper "Der Ursprung des Kunstwerkes" (in *Holzwege*, 1950) and in a recent book by Arturo B. Fallico, *Art and Existentialism* (1962).

EMPIRICISM. The contemporary empiricist makes a cardinal point of attacking the traditional problems of philosophy by resolving them into two distinct types of questions: questions about matters of fact, to be answered by empirical science (and, in the case of aesthetics, psychology in particular), and questions about concepts and methods, to be answered by philosophical analysis.

Some empiricists emphasize the first type of question and have called for a "scientific aesthetics" to state aesthetic problems in such a way that the results of psychological inquiry can be brought to bear upon them. Max Dessoir, Charles Lalo, Étienne Souriau, and (in America) Thomas Munro have formulated this program (see, especially, Munro's *Scientific Method in Philosophy*, 1928, and later essays). The actual results of work in psychology, over the period since Fechner inaugurated experimental aesthetics (*Vorschule der Ästhetik*, 1876) to replace "aesthetics from above" by an "aesthetics from below," are too varied to summarize easily (see Bibliography). But two lines of inquiry have had an important effect on the way in which twentieth-century philosophers think about art. The first is Gestalt psychology, whose studies of perceptual phenomena and the laws of Gestalt perception have illuminated the nature and value of form in art (see, for example, Kurt Koffka's "Problems in the Psychology of Art," in *Art: A Bryn Mawr Symposium*, 1940; Rudolf Arnheim, *Art and Visual Perception*, 1954; Leonard Meyer, *Emotion and Meaning in Music*, 1956). The second is Freudian psychology, beginning with Freud's interpretation of Hamlet (*Interpretation of Dreams*, 1900) and his studies of Leonardo (1910) and Dostoyevsky (1928), which have illuminated the nature of art creation and appreciation. Description of aesthetic experience, in terms of concepts like "empathy" (Theodor Lipps), "psychical distance" (Edward Bullough), and "synaesthesis" (I. A. Richards), has also been investigated by introspective methods.

Analytical aesthetics, in both its "reconstructionist" and "ordinary language" forms, is more recent. This school considers the task of philosophical aesthetics to consist in the analysis of the language and reasoning of critics (including all talk about art), to clarify language, to resolve puzzles due to misapprehensions about language, and to understand its special functions, methods, and justifications (see M. C. Beardsley, *Aesthetics: Problems in the Philosophy of Criticism*, 1958; Jerome Stolnitz, *Aesthetics and Philosophy of Art Criticism*, 1960; William Elton, ed., *Aesthetics and Language*, 1954; Joseph Margolis, ed., *Philosophy Looks at the Arts*, 1962).

See also Addison, Joseph; Aesthetic Qualities; Albert the Great; Alembert, Jean Le Rond d'; Analysis, Philosophical; Aristotle; Arnold, Matthew; Art, Value in; Augustine, St.; Baumgarten, Alexander Gottlieb; Beauty; Belinskii, Vissarion Grigor'evich; Bergson, Henri; Blake, William; Burke, Edmund; Carlyle, Thomas; Cartesianism; Cassirer, Ernst; Chernyshevskii, Nikolai Gavrilovich; Chrysippus; Cicero, Marcus Tullius; Cleanthes; Coleridge, Samuel Taylor; Collingwood, Robin George; Comte, Auguste; Croce, Benedetto; Descartes, René; Dewey, John; Dialectical Materialism; Diderot, Denis; Dostoevsky, Fyodor Mikhailovich; Emerson, Ralph Waldo; Empiricism; Engels, Friedrich; Enlightenment; Epicureanism and the Epicurean School; Epicurus; Erigena, John Scotus; Existentialism; Fechner, Gustav Theodor; Fichte, Johann Gottlieb; Ficino, Marsilio; Fourier, François Marie Charles; Freud, Sigmund; Gestalt Theory; Goethe, Johann Wolfgang von; Greek Academy; Grosseteste, Robert; Hazlitt, William; Hegel, Georg Wilhelm Friedrich; Heidegger, Martin; Herbart, Johann Friedrich; Herder, Johann Gottfried; Hobbes, Thomas; Home, Henry; Homer; Hume, David; Husserl, Edmund; Hutcheson, Francis; Idealism; Imagination; Johnson, Samuel; Jung, Carl Gustav; Kant, Immanuel; Koffka, Kurt; Langer, Susanne K.; Leibniz, Gottfried Wilhelm; Lessing, Gotthold Ephraim; Leucippus and Democritus; Lewis, Clarence Irving; Locke, John; Lukács, Georg; Marx, Karl; Marxist Philosophy; Merleau-Ponty, Maurice; Mill, John Stuart; Naturalism; Neo-Kantianism; Neoplatonism; Nietzsche, Friedrich; Origen; Parmenides of Elea; Peirce, Charles Sanders; Phenomenology; Philodemus; Philo Judaeus; Pisarev, Dmitri Ivanovich; Plato; Platonism and the Platonic Tradition; Plekhanov, Georgii Valentinovich; Plotinus; Pope, Alexander; Proudhon, Pierre-Joseph; Pythagoras and Pythagoreanism; Rationalism; Realism; Reid, Thomas; Renaissance; Romanticism; Ruskin, John; Saint-Simon, Claude-Henri de Rouvroy, Comte de; Santayana, George; Sartre, Jean-Paul; Schelling, Friedrich Wilhelm Joseph von; Schiller, Friedrich; Schlegel, Friedrich von; Schopenhauer, Arthur; Sextus Empiricus; Shaftesbury, Third Earl of (Anthony Ashley Cooper); Shelley, Percy Bysshe; Skepticism; Socrates; Stevenson, Charles L.; Stoicism; Taine, Hippolyte-Adolphe; Theophrastus; Thomas Aquinas, St.; Tolstoy, Lev (Leo) Nikolaevich; Wilde, Oscar Fingal O'Flahertie Wills; Xenophanes of Colophon; Zeno of Citium.

Bibliography

CLASSICAL GREEK PHILOSOPHERS

See J. W. H. Atkins, *Literary Criticism in Antiquity*, Vol. 1 (Cambridge, 1934), Chs. 1, 2; G. F. Else, "'Imitation' in the Fifth Century," in *Classical Philology*, Vol. 53, No. 2 (1958), 73–90; T. B. L. Webster, "Greek Theories of Art and Literature down to 400 BC" in *Classical Quarterly*, Vol. 33, Nos. 3, 4 (1939), 166–179; Alice Sperduti, "The Divine Nature of Poetry in Antiquity," in *Transactions and Proceedings, American Philological Association*, Vol. 81 (1950), 209–240.

Plato

See Raphael Demos, *The Philosophy of Plato* (New York, 1939), Chs. 11–13; Rupert C. Lodge, *Plato's Theory of Art* (London, 1953), G. M. A. Grube, "Plato's Theory of Beauty," in *Monist*, Vol. 37, No. 2 (1927), 269–288; J. Tate, "Plato and 'Imitation,'" in *Classical Quarterly*, Vol. 26, Nos. 3, 4 (1932), 161–169.

Aristotle

See G. F. Else, *Aristotle's Poetics: The Argument* (Cambridge, 1957); S. H. Butcher, *Aristotle's Theory of Poetry and Fine Art*, 4th ed. (London, 1923); Ingram Bywater, *Aristotle on the Art of Poetry* (Oxford, 1909); G. F. Else, "Aristotle on the Beauty of Tragedy," in *Harvard Studies in Classical Philology*, Vol. 49 (1938); Roman Ingarden, "A Marginal Commentary on Aristotle's Poetics," in *Journal of Aesthetics and Art Criticism*, Vol. 20, No. 2 (Winter, 1961), 163–173; *Ibid.*, No. 3 (Spring, 1962), 273–285; Richard McKeon, "Literary Criticism and the Concept of Imitation in Antiquity," in R. S. Crane, ed., *Critics and Criticism* (Chicago, 1952).

LATER CLASSICAL PHILOSOPHERS

See Phillip De Lacy, "Stoic Views of Poetry," in *American Journal of Philology*, Vol. 49, No. 275 (1948), 241–271; L. P. Wilkinson, "Philodemus and Poetry," in *Greece and Rome*, Vol. 2, No. 6 (1932–1933), 144–151; L. P. Wilkinson, "Philodemus on *Ethos* in Music," in *Classical Quarterly*, Vol. 32, Nos. 3, 4 (1938), 174–181; Craig La Drière, "Horace and the Theory of Imitation," in *American Journal of Philology*, Vol. 60, No. 239 (1939), 288–300; Philippus V. Pistorius, *Plotinus and Neoplatonism* (Cambridge, U.K., 1952), Ch. 7.

THE MIDDLE AGES

See Edgar de Bruyne, *Etudes d'esthétique médiévale*, 3 vols. (Brugge, 1946); Edgar de Bruyne, "Esthétique païenne, esthétique chrétienne," in *Revue Internationale de Philosophie*, No. 31 (1955), 130–144; Emmanuel Chapman, *Saint Augustine's Philosophy of Beauty* (New York, 1939); K. Svoboda, *L'esthétique de Saint Augustin et ses sources* (Brno, 1933); Jacques Maritain, *Art and Scholasticism*, translated by J. F. Scanlan (London, 1930), esp. Ch. 5; Maurice de Wulf, *Études historiques sur l'esthétique de S. Thomas d'Aquin* (Louvain, 1896); Leonard Callahan, *A Theory of Esthetic According to the Principles of St. Thomas Aquinas* (Washington, DC, 1927); Bernard F. Huppé, *Doctrine and Poetry* (Albany, NY, 1959), Chs. 1, 2; H. Flanders Dunbar, *Symbolism in Medieval Thought* (New Haven, CT, 1929); Murray Wright Bundy, *The Theory of Imagination in Classical and Medieval Thought*, in University of Illinois Studies in Language and Literature (Urbana, 1927), Chs. 8–12.

THE RENAISSANCE

See Nesca A. Robb, *Neoplatonism of the Italian Renaissance* (London, 1935), Ch. 7; Erwin Panofsky, *Idea*, 2nd ed. (Berlin, 1960); Erwin Panofsky, *The Codex Huygens and Leonardo da Vinci's Art Theory* (London, 1940); Erwin Panofsky, *The Life and Art of Albrecht Dürer*, 4th ed. (Princeton, NJ, 1955), Ch. 8; Rensselaer W. Lee, "*Ut Pictura Poesis*: The Humanistic Theory of Painting," in *Art Bulletin*, Vol. 22, No. 4 (1940), 197–269; Anthony Blunt, *Artistic Theory in Italy, 1450–1600* (Oxford, 1940); Edward E. Lowinsky, "Music in the Culture of the Renaissance," in *Journal of the History of Ideas*, Vol. 15, No. 4 (1954), 509–553; D. P. Walker, "Musical Humanism in the 16th and Early 17th Centuries," in *Music Review*, Vol. 2, No. 1 (1941), 1–13; *Ibid.*, No. 2, 111–121; *Ibid.*, No. 3, 220–227; *Ibid.*, No. 4, 288–308; Vol. 3, No. 1 (1942), 55–71; Bernard Weinberg, *A History of Literary Criticism in the Italian Renaissance*, 2 vols. (Chicago, 1961); Baxter Hathaway, *The Age of Criticism: The Late Renaissance in Italy* (Ithaca, NY, 1962).

THE ENLIGHTENMENT

Cartesian Rationalism

See Émile Krantz, *Essai sur l'esthétique de Descartes* (Paris, 1882); Brewster Rogerson, "The Art of Painting the Passions," in *Journal of the History of Ideas*, Vol. 14, No. 1 (1953), 68–94; Scott Elledge, "The Background and Development in English Criticism of the Theories of Generality and Particularity," in *PMLA*, Vol. 62, No. 1 (1947), 147–182; A. O. Lovejoy, "'Nature' as Aesthetic Norm," in *Modern Language Notes*, Vol. 42, No. 7 (1927), 444–450; Hoyt Trowbridge, "The Place of Rules in Dryden's Criticism," in *Modern Philology*, Vol. 44, No. 2 (1946–1947), 84–96; Meyer H. Abrams, *The Mirror and the Lamp* (Oxford, 1953), Chs. 1, 2; Samuel H. Monk, *The Sublime*, rev. ed. (Ann Arbor, MI, 1960), Ch. 9; Claude V. Palisca, "Scientific Empiricism in Musical Thought," in H. H. Rhys, ed., *Seventeenth Century Science and the Arts* (Princeton, NJ, 1961); Louis I. Bredvold, "The Tendency toward Platonism in Neo-classical Esthetics," in *ELH: A Journal of English Literary History*, Vol. 1, No. 2 (1934), 91–119; Cicely Davis, "Ut pictura poesis," *Modern Language Review*, Vol. 30, No. 2 (1935), 159–169; P. O. Kristeller, "The Modern System of the Arts," in *Journal of the History of Ideas*, Vol. 12, No. 4 (1951), 496–527; *Ibid.*, Vol. 13, No. 1 (1952), 17–46; Ernst Cassirer, *The Philosophy of the Enlightenment*, translated by Koelln and Pettegrove (Princeton, NJ, 1951), Ch. 7.

Empiricism

See Clarence DeWitt Thorpe, *The Aesthetic Theory of Thomas Hobbes* (Ann Arbor, MI, 1940); Donald F. Bond, "The Neo-classical Psychology of the Imagination," in *ELH: A Journal of English Literary History*, Vol. 4, No. 4 (1937), 245–264; Martin Kallich, "The Association of Ideas and Critical Theory: Hobbes, Locke, and Addison," in *ELH: A Journal of English Literary History*, Vol. 12, No. 4 (1945), 290–315; R. L. Brett, *The Third Earl of Shaftesbury* (London, 1951); Jerome Stolnitz, "On the Significance of Lord Shaftesbury in Modern Aesthetic Theory," in *Philosophical Quarterly*, Vol. 11, No. 43 (1961), 97–113; Clarence D. Thorpe, "Addison and Hutcheson on the Imagination," in *ELH: A Journal of English Literary History*, Vol. 2, No. 3 (1935), 215–234; Martin Kallich, "The Argument against the Association of Ideas in Eighteenth-Century Aesthetics," in *Modern*

Language Quarterly, Vol. 15, No. 2 (1954), 125–136;
Margaret Gilman, *The Idea of Poetry in France from Houdar de la Motte to Baudelaire* (Cambridge, MA, 1958), Ch. 2; Wladyslaw Folkierski, *Entre le classicisme et le romantisme* (Krakow and Paris, 1925); Walter Jackson Bate, *From Classic to Romantic* (Cambridge, Mass., 1946); Ernest Lee Tuveson, *The Imagination as a Means to Grace* (Berkeley, CA, 1960); Jerome Stolnitz, "'Beauty': Some Stages in the History of an Idea," in *Journal of the History of Ideas*, Vol. 22, No. 2 (1961) 185–204; Walter John Hippie, Jr., *The Beautiful, The Sublime, and the Picturesque in Eighteenth-Century British Aesthetic Theory* (Carbondale, IL, 1957); Samuel H. Monk, *The Sublime*, rev. ed. (Ann Arbor, 1960).

GERMAN IDEALISM

See H. W. Cassirer, *A Commentary on Kant's Critique of Judgment* (London, 1938); James C. Meredith, *Kant's Critique of Aesthetic Judgement* (Oxford, 1911); Hermann Cohen, *Kant's Begründung der Ästhetik* (Berlin, 1889); Victor Basch, *Essai critique sur l'esthétique de Kant*, 2d ed. (Paris, 1927); Humayun Kabir, *Immanuel Kant on Philosophy in General*, essays on the first Introduction to the *Critique of Judgment* (Calcutta, 1935); G. T. Whitney and D. F. Bowers, eds., *The Heritage of Kant* (Princeton, NJ, 1939); Robert L. Zimmerman, "Kant: The Aesthetic Judgment," in *Journal of Aesthetics and Art Criticism*, Vol. 21, No. 3 (Spring, 1963), 333–344; Frederic Will, *Intelligible Beauty in Aesthetic Thought from Winckelmann to Victor Cousin* (Tubingen, 1958); S. S. Kerry, "The Artist's Intuition in Schiller's Aesthetic Philosophy," in *Publications of the English Goethe Society*, New Series 28 (Leeds, 1959); Elizabeth E. Bohning, "Goethe's and Schiller's Interpretation of Beauty," in *German Quarterly*, Vol. 22, No. 4 1949), 185–194; Jean Gibelin, *L'esthétique de Schelling d'après la philosophie de l'art* (Paris, 1934); E. L. Fackenheim, "Schelling's Philosophy of the Literary Arts," in *Philosophical Quarterly*, Vol. 4, No. 17 (1954), 310–326; H. M. Schueller, "Schelling's Theory of the Metaphysics of Music," *Journal of Aesthetics and Art Criticism*, Vol. 15, No. 4 (June, 1957), 461–476; W. T. Stace, *The Philosophy of Hegel* (London, 1924), Part IV, Third Div., Ch. 1; Israel Knox, *The Aesthetic Theories of Kant, Hegel, and Schopenhauer* (New York, 1936).

ROMANTICISM

See René Wellek, *A History of Modern Criticism: 1750–1950*, Vol. 2 (New Haven, 1955); M. H. Abrams, *The Mirror and the Lamp: Romantic Theory and the Critical Tradition* (Oxford 1953); W. J. Bate, *From Classic to Romantic* (Cambridge, MA, 1949), Chs. 5, 6; Paul Reiff, *Die Ästhetik der deutschen Frühromantik* in University of Illinois Studies in Language and Literature, Vol. 31 (Urbana, 1946); M. Z. Shroder, *Icarus: The Image of the Artist in French Romanticism* (Cambridge, MA, 1961); A. G. Lehmann, *The Symbolist Movement in France, 1885–1895* (Oxford, 1950); Joseph Ciari, *Symbolism from Poe to Mallarmé: The Growth of a Myth* (London, 1956); John M. Bullitt, "Hazlitt and the Romantic Conception of the Imagination," in *Philological Quarterly*, Vol. 24, No. 4 (1945), 343–361; J. B. Baker, *The Sacred River: Coleridge's Theory of the Imagination* (Baton Rouge, LA, 1957); James Benziger, "Organic Unity: Leibniz to Coleridge," in *PMLA*, Vol. 66, No. 2 (1951), 24–48; John Stokes Adams, *The Aesthetics of Pessimism* (Philadelphia, 1940); J. M. Stein, *Richard Wagner and the Synthesis of the Arts* (Detroit, 1960); E. A. Lippman, "The Esthetic Theories of Richard Wagner," in *Musical Quarterly*, Vol. 44 (1958), 209–220.

THE ARTIST AND SOCIETY

See R. F. Egan, "The Genesis of the Theory of 'Art for Art's Sake' in Germany and in England," in *Smith College Studies in Modern Languages*, Vols. 2, 5; Albert Cassagne, *La théorie de l'art pour l'art en France* (Paris, 1906); Irving Singer, "The Aesthetics of 'Art for Art's Sake,'" *Journal of Aesthetics and Art Criticism*, Vol. 12, No. 3 (March, 1954), 343–359; H. A. Needham, *La développement de l'esthétique sociologique en France et en Angleterre au XIXe siècle* (Paris, 1926); Bernard Weinberg, *French Realism: The Critical Reaction 1830–1870* (New York, 1937); H. M. Kallen, *Art and Freedom*, 2 vols. (New York, 1942); René Wellek, "Social and Aesthetic Values in Russian Nineteenth-Century Literary Criticism," in E. J. Simmons, ed., *Continuity and Change in Russian and Soviet Thought* (Cambridge, MA, 1955); F. D. Curtin, "Aesthetics in English Social Reform: Ruskin and his Followers," in Herbert Davis et al., eds., *Nineteenth-Century Studies* (Ithaca, NY, 1940).

CONTEMPORARY DEVELOPMENTS

Metaphysical Theories

See G. N. G. Orsini, *Benedetto Croce: Philosopher of Art and Literary Critic* (Carbondale, IL, 1961); John Hospers, "The Croce–Collingwood Theory of Art," in *Philosophy*, Vol. 31, No. 119 (1956), 291–308; Alan Donegan, "The Croce–Collingwood Theory of Art," in *Philosophy*, Vol. 33, No. 125 (1958), 162–167; T. E. Hulme, "Bergson's Theory of Art," in Herbert Read, ed., *Speculations* (New York and London, 1924); Arthur Szathmary, *The Aesthetic Theory of Bergson* (Cambridge, MA, 1937).

Naturalism

See W. E. Arnett, *Santayana and the Sense of Beauty* (Bloomington, IN, 1955); Jack Kaminsky, "Dewey's Concept of *An* Experience," in *Philosophy and Phenomenological Research*, Vol. 17, No. 3 (March 1957), 316–330; E. A. Shearer, "Dewey's Aesthetic Theory," *Journal of Philosophy*, Vol. 32, Nos. 23, 24 (1935), 617–627, 650–664; Sidney Zink, "The Concept of Continuity in Dewey's Theory of Esthetics," *Philosophical Review*, Vol. 52, No. 4 (1943), 392–400; S. C. Pepper, "The Concept of Fusion in Dewey's Aesthetic Theory," in *Journal of Aesthetics and Art Criticism*, Vol. 12, No. 2 (December, 1953), 169–176.

Semiotics

See Richard Rudner, "On Semiotic Aesthetics," in *Journal of Aesthetics and Art Criticism*, Vol. 10, No. 1 (September, 1951), 67–77; E. G. Ballard, "In Defense of Semiotic Aesthetics," in *Journal of Aesthetics and Art Criticism*, Vol. 12, No. 1 (September, 1953), 38–43; Max Rieser, "The Semantic Theory of Art in America," *Journal of Aesthetics and Art Criticism*, Vol. 15, No. 1 (September, 1956), 12–26.

Marxism-Leninism

See Karl Marx and Friedrich Engels, *Literature and Art: Selections from Their Writings* (New York, 1947); Victor Erlich, "Social and Aesthetic Criteria in Soviet Russian Criticism," R. M. Hankin, "Main Premises of the Communist Party in the Theory of Soviet Literary Controls," and E. J. Simmons, "Review," in Simmons, ed.,

Continuity and Change in Russian and Soviet Thought (Cambridge, MA, 1955); Max Rieser, "The Aesthetic Theory of Socialist Realism," in *Journal of Aesthetics and Art Criticism*, Vol. 16, No. 2 (December, 1957), 237–248; Ernst Fischer, *Von der Notwendigkeit der Kunst* (Dresden, 1959). Translated by Anna Bostock as *The Necessity of Art, A Marxist Approach* (Baltimore, 1963).

Phenomenology and Existentialism

See Herbert Spiegelberg, *The Phenomenological Movement: A Historical Introduction*, 2 vols. (The Hague, 1960); Fritz Kaufmann, "Art and Phenomenology," in Marvin Farber, ed., *Philosophical Essays in Memory of Edmund Husserl* (Cambridge, MA, 1940); Anna-Teresa Tymieniecka, *Phenomenology and Science in Contemporary European Thought* (New York, 1961); J.-Claude Piguet, "Esthétique et Phénomenologie" (discussion review of Dufrenne), in *Kantstudien* (1955–1956), 192–208; E. F. Kaelin, *An Existentialist Aesthetic: The Theories of Sartre and Merleau-Ponty* (Madison, WI, 1962).

Empiricism

See Douglas Morgan, "Psychology and Art: a Summary and Critique," in *Journal of Aesthetics and Art Criticism*, Vol. 9, No. 2 (December, 1950), 81–96; Douglas Morgan, "Creativity Today," in *Journal of Aesthetics and Art Criticism*, Vol. 12, No. 1 (September, 1953), 1–24; A. R. Chandler, *Beauty and Human Nature* (New York, 1934); C. W. Valentine, *The Experimental Psychology of Beauty* (London, 1962); Edward Bullough, in Elizabeth Wilkinson, ed., *Aesthetics: Lectures and Essays* (London, 1957); William Phillips, ed., *Art and Psychoanalysis* (New York, 1957); D. E. Schneider, *The Psychoanalyst and the Artist* (New York, 1950).

Bibliographies

For further bibliographies on contemporary aesthetics, see M. C. Beardsley, *Aesthetics* (New York, 1958); Guido Morpurgo-Tagliabue, *L'esthétique contemporaine* (Milan, 1960).

GENERAL HISTORIES

See the following general histories of aesthetics: Katherine Gilbert and Helmut Kuhn, *A History of Aesthetics* (New York, 1939; Bloomington, IN, 1954); M. C. Beardsley, *Aesthetics from Ancient Greece to the Present* (New York, 1965); Bernard Bosanquet, *A History of Aesthetic* (London, 1892; New York, 1957).

Monroe C. Beardsley (1967)

AESTHETICS, HISTORY OF [ADDENDUM]

TWENTIETH-CENTURY AESTHETICS

Aesthetics continued to be intensively cultivated in all the main schools of twentieth-century philosophy. The following survey emphasizes work that continues to be of interest at the beginning of the twenty-first century. It will focus first on the Anglo-American tradition, including continental work that has fed into it, and then will consider other work in the continental tradition.

ANGLO-AMERICAN AESTHETICS.

Naturalism, organicism, pragmatism. One main line of twentieth-century aesthetics begins with George Santayana's *The Sense of Beauty* of 1896. Santayana's book was a renewal of the empiricism and naturalism of the eighteenth century undertaken in opposition to the incorporation of aesthetics into speculative metaphysics by philosophers such as Schelling, Schopenhauer, and Hegel. Santayana held that beauty is "value positive, intrinsic, and objectified": a pleasurable emotion that is "pure gain" and that we regard as if it were a property of its object even though it depends upon our own response. The idea that beauty is objectified pleasure is found in writers from Hutcheson to Kant, but Santayana departed from the reductionism characteristic of many eighteenth-century authors by refusing to restrict the sources of such pleasure to a single category. He instead showed how such pleasure can arise from the materials of works of art, from their forms, and from their expression, which he defined broadly to include our emotional associations with objects. Santayana also rejected the attempt to justify the human interest in beauty, especially the often costly interest in artistic beauty, by claiming that it contributes to morality; for Santayana, morality is concerned with the removal of the evils of life, and thus exists only to facilitate the wider enjoyment of the positive pleasures of life, epitomized by beauty. In his second main work on aesthetics, *Reason in Art*, the fourth volume of his 1905–1906 *Life of Reason*, Santayana added that by the ability to adopt an aesthetic attitude and thus find beauty almost anywhere in nature, on the one hand, and by the ability to create art, on the other, we can augment our positive pleasure in life. In this work he also emphasized that the various arts have all arisen from the ordinary and natural activities of human beings, thus adding a pragmatist element to his naturalism and preparing the way for the later work of John Dewey.

Santayana's thesis that morality exists to remove the evils that stand in the way of the enjoyment of the positive pleasure of beauty anticipates the famous statement of G. E. Moore's *Principia Ethica* (1903) that "the most valuable things, which we can know or imagine, are … the pleasures of human intercourse and the enjoyment of beautiful objects" (Moore 1903, p.237), which would become the creed of the Bloomsbury group of artists and intellectuals. Moore treated "aesthetic appreciation" as an "organic whole" consisting of consciousness of both the beautiful qualities of an object and the feeling of its beauty, an idea that is related to Santayana's notion of beauty as objectified pleasure; but Moore also held that beautiful objects are themselves organic unities, in the sense that the contemplation of the individual parts may have no value, but the contemplation of the whole loses value without the contemplation of those parts. Moore thus adopted a more restrictive analysis of the objects of aesthetic pleasure than had Santayana.

Moore influenced the critic Clive Bell, who in his 1914 book *Art* postulated a special aesthetic emotion in response to "significant form" in works of art. Edward Bullough, a professor of literature who in 1907 gave the first course on aesthetics at Cambridge, has also been considered a follower of Moore, but his theory is different from Bell's; according to Bullough's famous 1912 paper "'Psychical Distance' as a Factor in Art and an Aesthetic Principle," distancing oneself from the most obvious emotions that might be aroused by some object, such as the emotion of fear in response to a fog at sea, does not allow one to enjoy some special aesthetic emotion, but rather opens oneself up to a whole range of other feelings and emotions that can be aroused by the very same object, thereby increasing the richness and intensity of one's emotional experience of life as a whole. Instead of being closely associated with Moore and Bell, Bullough might thus be better placed on a line of thought leading from Santayana to Dewey.

Dewey's *Art as Experience* (1934) came late in his lengthy career, but remains his most widely read book as well as one of the still most widely read books of twentieth-century aesthetics. He anticipated its central idea of "consummatory experience" in his 1925 *Experience and Nature*. A consummatory experience is a moment felt as one of repose and equilibrium in the constant flow of energy, in stimulus and response, that constitutes human life, and it is paradigmatically produced by the experience of art. As Dewey put it in 1925, "art is the solvent union of the generic, recurrent, ordered, established phase of nature with its phase that is incomplete, going on, and hence still uncertain, contingent, novel, particular" (Dewey 1925, p.301), or as he said in 1934, "Art is the living and concrete proof that man is capable of restoring consciously, and thus on the plane of meaning, the union of sense, need, impulse and action characteristic of the live creature" (Dewey 1934, p. 25).

But in the later work Dewey also argued that art has a special role in the expression of emotion, not merely projecting our emotions onto objects but clarifying them by presenting the contexts in which they arise. Here Dewey's thought comes into contact with the next stream of aesthetic thought to be considered here, which makes the expression of emotion the core of aesthetic experi-

ence. But Dewey's pragmatism reveals itself in his insistence that the aesthetic "is the clarified and intensified development of traits that belong to every normally complete experience," and even more so with his argument that while the term *aesthetic* connotes the "consumer's rather than the producer's standpoint" and the term *art* "denotes a process of doing and making," there is a strong element of each in the other: The audience for art must take an active and imaginative role in appreciating it, while the artist must also adopt the standpoint of his audience to gauge the effect of his work—hence Dewey's title *Art as Experience*, blurring the line between the production and the reception of art (Dewey 1934, p.47). This is a theme that would also be stressed by the British philosopher R.G. Collingwood a few years later, who though not considered a pragmatist came out of a Hegelian background with affinities to that of Dewey.

Before we turn to the tradition with which Collingwood is associated, we may note that Monroe C. Beardsley, the author of the first part of this article, was himself the most important heir to Dewey's aesthetics in the period after World War II. Although there are certainly other influences at work, the central claim of Beardsley's 1958 *Aesthetics* was clearly Deweyan. Beardsley wrote that an experience has a marked "aesthetic character" when it includes "attention firmly fixed on a perceptual or intentional object; a feeling of freedom from concerns about matters outside that object; notable affect that is detached from practical ends; the sense of exercising powers of discovery; and the integration of the self and of its experiences" (Beardsley 1981, p. lxii). The most recent heir to Dewey and Beardsley, Richard Shusterman, has particularly stressed the experience of one's own body as part of the complete aesthetic experience (*Pragmatist Aesthetics*, 1992).

Expression. A second main line of twentieth-century aesthetics identifies the chief goal of art as the expression of emotion, a feature that was only one facet of Dewey's notion of aesthetic experience. This theory is often thought of as an alternative to the idea that beauty is the essence of art, but at least in its early stages the successful expression of emotion in art was intended as an explanation of its beauty. This is evident in the 1892 *History of Æsthetic* by Bernard Bosanquet and in the 1902 work by Benedetto Croce, *Estetica come scienze dell'espressione e linguistica generale* (The aesthetic as the science of expression and of the linguistic in general). Bosanquet argued that art operates "through that expansion of self which comes in utterance," that is, that content acquires beauty by passing through the crucible of an individual sensibility and style—even though this means that it may take others time to appreciate the beauty of a distinctive style of expression (Bosanquet 1904, p. 453). Croce wrote that the beautiful is "successful expression, or better, … expression *simpliciter*, since expression, when it is not successful, is not expression (Croce 1992, p. 87). Ten years after Croce, the neo-Kantian Hermann Cohen based an elaborate *Ästhetick des reinen Gefühls* (Aesthetics of pure feeling) on the premise that human feelings have their own distinctive forms, which are most clearly revealed by art.

The fullest development of the expression theory, however, is found in the 1938 *Principles of Art* by the Oxford philosopher (and archaeologist) R. G. Collingwood. Collingwood is often thought of as a follower of Croce, but his theory is more fully developed than Croce's, and it also overcomes the supposition that successful expression must be perceived as beautiful in some traditional sense. Collingwood begins by distinguishing art from craft, arguing that in the latter there is always a clear distinction between means and end, but that there is never such a distinction in the case of art proper. This leads to two important claims: that art is never intended merely to arouse emotions for the sake of magic or propaganda or to discharge them for the sake of amusement; and that the element of craft that is typically part of art, namely the production of a physical object, is not essential to the true work of art at all, which thus appears to exist complete in the mind of the artist without any physical expression.

The latter claim, however, is clearly modified over the rest of Collingwood's book. The second part of the book argues that there is an affective or emotional aspect of all perception and thought, and that the special function of art is to clarify that dimension of our experience so that we can understand and gain control over it. In the third part of his work, Collingwood then argues that the clarification of emotion takes place through the artist's interaction with a physical medium and an audience. So Collingwood's initial claim that the work of art exists complete in the mind of the artist turns out to be an overstatement of the claim that the effort in art is aimed at the clarification of emotion rather than at the production of a physical object for its own sake. Writing at a tense moment in the 1930s, Collingwood concludes by stressing that art proper is necessary for the survival of civilization precisely because it allows us to gain control over our own emotions rather than having our emotions controlled by the propaganda of others.

Art and language. Expression theorists such as Croce and Collingwood suggested that all art, whether in verbal media or not, can be regarded as using or creating languages for the expression of emotion. Beginning in the 1930s, many other varieties of aesthetic theory focused on linguistic aspects of the arts and of critical discourse about art. One important movement was logical positivism, represented above all by A. J. Ayer's 1936 *Language, Truth, and Logic*, which argued that aesthetic discourse does not consist of verifiable, descriptive propositions about its objects at all, but only expresses the response of the speaker to such objects, to which a prescriptive rather than descriptive recommendation of the object to others might also be added. This doctrine, which applied to ethical as well as aesthetic discourse, became known as "emotivism" and enjoyed considerable currency after its further development in C. L. Stevenson's *Ethics and Language* (1944). It would become one of the sources for hostility to traditional aesthetic theory during the heyday of "analytical" philosophy in the 1950s and 1960s.

A different strand of thought can be traced back to Ernst Cassirer's *Philosophie der symbolischen Formen*, published in German from 1923 to 1929 and translated into English (*Philosophy of Symbolic Forms*) only in 1953, but preceded by Cassirer's English-language summary of his position, *An Essay on Man* of 1944. Cassirer, a student of Hermann Cohen, held that human beings represent and deal with their environment through a variety of symbolic systems, including natural language, mathematical and scientific language, mythology, and the arts, each of which has its distinctive uses and none of which can simply be subordinated to the others.

Cassirer was a major influence on the American philosopher Susanne K. Langer, who interpreted human thought as using a variety of symbol-systems in her 1942 *Philosophy in a New Key* and dedicated her major work in aesthetics, the 1953 *Feeling and Form*, to the memory of Cassirer. She held that the arts do not employ "discursive" symbol-systems to analyze experience but instead use non-discursive symbols to capture the felt quality of experience itself. Using music as an example, she argued that the symbol-systems of the arts do not use "syntactical terms with fixed connotations, and syntactical rules for deriving complex connections," like ordinary and scientific language, but instead "present emotive experience through global forms that are as indivisible as the elements of chiaroscuro" (Langer 1942, p. 232). Her position thus looks back to Alexander Baumgarten's original distinction between logic and aesthetics, but also looks forward to the 1968 *Languages of Art* of Nelson Goodman, who acknowledged affinities between his own approach and that of Langer as well as of Cassirer, Charles Sanders Pierce, and the semiotician C. W. Morris.

Goodman abjured any interest in the traditional topics of beauty and pleasure in the arts, and instead offered analyses of fictional and metaphorical depiction and of expression within the framework of an austerely nominalistic theory of language. But his affinity with Langer and indeed with Baumgarten became clear when he argued that symbols or uses of language are symptomatic of the aesthetic if they are syntactically and semantically dense rather than discrete, if they are replete, with many features of the symbol contributing to its meaning, and if they exemplify qualities metaphorically as well as literally. And while maintaining his emphasis on the cognitive rather than emotional or affective dimension of aesthetic experience, he also wrote about its dynamic rather than static character, its "restless, searching, testing" attitude, its creation and re-creation, in a way that ultimately makes clear the pleasurable character of the aesthetic form of cognition. At its deepest level, Goodman's aesthetics thus falls within the Kantian tradition.

A third major influence on modern thought about aesthetics and language was of course the philosophy of Ludwig Wittgenstein. Through the influence of his 1921 *Tractatus Logico-Philosophicus* on the so-called Vienna Circle, he was in the background of Ayer's *Language, Truth, and Logic*. In 1938 (thus the same year as the publication of Collingwood's *Principles of Art* in Oxford), he lectured on aesthetics in Cambridge. One central theme of these lectures, presumably directed against such nineteenth-century German psychologists as Hermann von Helmholtz and Gustav Theodor Fechner, was that aesthetics cannot be made into a science causally connecting measurable responses to measurable qualities of objects. Here Wittgenstein was in fact only reminding his auditors of an argument made long before by Hume and Kant. More influential themes of his lectures were, first, that aesthetic discourse does not typically work by using a general predicate like "beautiful" but instead uses more particular words and gestures to focus attention on particular aspects of objects that in their particular context look right or satisfying, and, second, that aesthetic response often involves imaginatively seeing an aspect or interpretation in an object.

Although these lectures were not published until 1967, the first of these themes was influential before that date. Thus Frank Sibley (himself a student of Gilbert Ryle) argued in 1959 that aesthetic concepts are not "con-

dition-governed" but are instead highly context-sensitive; this theme was further developed in Peter Kivy's 1973 *Speaking of Art*. The second theme, which Wittgenstein would develop further in the major work of his late philosophy, the *Philosophical Investigations*, posthumously translated and published in 1953, was carried on in Roger Scruton's *Art and Imagination* (1974) and in Richard Wollheim's theory of "seeing-in" in his A. W. Mellon Lectures on the Fine Arts, *Painting as an Art* (1987).

The greatest influence of the *Philosophical Investigations*, however, came from its view that many concepts, including the concept of language itself, are not defined by a determinate set of necessary and sufficient conditions, but by a looser network of "family resemblances." Wittgenstein argued that a concept like that of games could only be understood in this way, and that the abstraction of "language" likewise consists of a loosely interconnected network of "language-games." In a famous paper of 1956, Morris Weitz argued that this model applied to the arts as well, thus that the concept of art is an "open concept" for which there could be no determinate definition of art of the kind to which traditional aesthetics had aspired. In an equally important paper of 1965, Maurice Mandelbaum replied that a determinate definition of an abstract concept like art is compatible with diversity and constant change at the level of the particular objects of art. This interchange as well as the history of developments in twentieth-century art, from the "readymades" of Marcel Duchamp through Dada to the Pop Art of Andy Warhol and Robert Rauschenberg, launched a debate about the possibility of a definition of art that was a central topic of analytical aesthetics from the 1960s into the 1980s.

In a 1964 paper on "The Artworld," Arthur C. Danto used the cases of artworks that are perceptually indiscernible either from other artworks or from ordinary objects that are not artworks at all to argue that an artwork is never identical to a physical object, but is rather a physical object embedded in a world of artistic theory. In his 1974 *Art and the Aesthetic*, George Dickie was inspired by Danto's concept of the "artworld" to offer a definition of a work of art as an artifact offered as a candidate for appreciation by an agent of the artworld, where he understood the latter in sociological terms as the social system of artists, dealers, curators, critics, and so on.

Danto's 1981 *Transfiguration of the Commonplace* made it clear that this was not what Danto had meant by an artworld, but that by this concept he instead meant the complex of meaning, metaphor, and style within which an artist intended his work to be received, a view that he has refined in subsequent work, including his 2003 book *The Abuse of Beauty*, into the definition of art as "embodied meaning." Dickie acknowledged this basic difference in the understanding of the concept of an artworld in his 1984 book *The Art Circle: A Theory of Art*, and redefined an artworld as a set of artistic conventions rather than a sociological formation.

Jerrold Levinson and Noël Carroll subsequently developed historicized versions of Dickie's approach, arguing that a work of art is an object made within a historical tradition of art making. But from Danto's point of view, all such appeals to artistic conventions, histories, or traditions are circular without some definition of what makes the latter conventions, histories, or traditions of *art* in the first place. However, in his 1997 *Philosophies of Arts*, Peter Kivy argued against the assumption that all art has semantic meaning, which underlies Danto's definition of art, by appeal to "absolute" music and the decorative arts, which are not "about" anything.

The return of beauty. Danto's earlier work was very much under the influence of Marcel Duchamp's attack upon beauty as a mere "retinal flutter" inessential to the real character of art, and Goodman likewise dismissed beauty from the cognitive core of art. However, not all philosophers have been convinced of the inessentiality of beauty, and two important works of the 1980s offered detailed analyses of beauty while defending its centrality in the experience of art. In *The Test of Time* (1982), Anthony Savile argued that we find an object beautiful when we see it as a successful solution to its underlying problem or problems within its own style, that we are able to recognize a successful solution to a problem even when the problem is not our own, and that being beautiful in this sense, along with being deep—that is, revealing fundamental and general principles— and suggestive about the possibilities for successful forms of human life, is one of the things that enables a work of art to withstand the test of time.

Two years later, Mary Mothersill's *Beauty Restored* reached back to Hume and Kant and beyond them to Thomas Aquinas to argue that beauty is a disposition actualized when a person is pleased by the apprehension of the aesthetic qualities of objects, where the latter are precisely what distinguish an object from all others, and that beauty so understood is central to the ambitions of art. More recently, Alexander Nehamas has interpreted the traditional conception of beauty as a "promise of happiness" (a phrase that comes from Baudelaire) to mean that we find an object beautiful when it draws us into an ongoing engagement with itself and an open-ended network of related objects, and that this is essential to our experience of art, although he emphasizes that these networks are personal and that there is no reason to expect "universal validity" in responses to beauty. Art critics and literary theorists such as Dave Hickey, Elaine Scarry, and Wendy Steiner have also recently defended the importance of beauty in art.

Aesthetics and morality. One of the most significant developments in recent aesthetics is renewed interest in the relations between aesthetic experience and morality, one of the two issues initially raised by Plato's attack upon popular arts in the education of his guardians but one that had been largely neglected during the heyday of "analytical" aesthetics, when indeed traditional modes of theorizing in both aesthetics and ethics were under attack. Both Plato's original attack upon popular arts and contemporary versions thereof have themselves been subjects of recent investigations. Alexander Nehamas has examined parallels between the ancient and modern attacks in papers collected in his *Virtues of Authenticity* (1999), while in *A Philosophy of Mass Art* (1998), Noël Carroll has shown in detail how many forms of "mass" art engage their audiences in ways both cognitive and emotional that are no different from the ways in which "high" arts engage their audiences. This work may be considered as a rejoinder to the critique of the "culture industry" as necessarily a form of mass manipulation that was offered by Max Horkheimer and Theodor W. Adorno in their famous *Dialectic of Enlightenment*, first published in 1947 as *Dialektic der Aufklärung* (see below).

Most of the recent debates about aesthetics and morality, however, have focused on two distinguishable issues. The first concerns the value of the experience of art, especially literature, in moral education. One view here holds that the moral truths expressed in works of art are so obvious and general that there is no need to turn to art to learn them, thus that their role in moral education can hardly be central to the value we place on art. The opposing view concedes that it may be unnecessary to turn to art to learn general moral *principles*, but that we can learn a great deal from narrative art, particularly literature and cinema, about the emotions of both agents and patients in morally significant situations, and indeed that narrative art may well be the primary means by which we learn to be attentive to the details of the kinds of situations in which we will ultimately have to apply our general moral principles. This view has been defended in numerous works by Martha C. Nussbaum and Noël Carroll.

The current debate could be enriched by a return to its roots in the eighteenth century, where Kant recognized that the artistic presentation of examples of virtuous conduct are essential in teaching children not so much the content as the importance of aesthetic principles, while Schiller later argued that aesthetic experience sharpens our sensitivity to both general principles and particular situations in his letters *On the Aesthetic Education of Man* (1967). Another voice that needs to be incorporated into this debate is that of Stanley Cavell, who has argued in both his philosophical work such as *The Claim of Reason* (1979) and his critical work such as his 1969 essay "The Avoidance of Love" on Shakespeare's *King Lear* that a central lesson we learn from art concerns the epistemology of conduct itself, that is, our need to act upon trust in both ourselves and others in the face of our always imperfect knowledge of self and others rather than being destroyed by fantasies about the perfection of knowledge and love that are beyond human powers.

The other recent debate has been about what has come to be called "ethical criticism" of the arts. Here the issue is whether what may be perceived as ethical defects of works of art, that is, defects in the moral views that may be expressed by works of art, are necessarily also aesthetic defects in those works, or whether our appreciation of the aesthetic merits of a work can be independent of any such ethical defects. The latter position, called "autonomism," has been defended by Daniel Jacobson and others; "moderate moralism," the position that ethical defects are at least *pro tanto* aesthetic defects in a work of art, although they may be outweighed by other aesthetic merits of the work, has been defended by Noël Carroll and Berys Gaut. Carroll has argued that some moral defects may prevent imaginative "uptake" of a work while others may not, that is, that some ethical defects may be sufficient to prevent an audience from identifying with the characters and standpoints of a work in the way necessary for it to accomplish its aesthetic goals, while others may not. The conditions under which "uptake" of a work may be facilitated or blocked would seem to be a subject for psychological investigation, and thus one of the points at which aesthetics can intersect with contemporary cognitive science.

Fictionality. Another area of contemporary debate where aesthetic theory can intersect with cognitive science is the recent discussion of the emotional impact of fictions. This debate too has roots in antiquity, namely the paradox of tragedy. One side of this paradox is related to the issue just discussed, namely, how we can take pleasure in the depiction of events that, were they real, we should surely abhor. But there is also an epistemological and psychological question here, namely, how we can have emotional responses to fictions that are anything like the emotional responses we would have to the depicted events if they were real, when we know that they are not?

In his 1990 book *Mimesis as Make-Believe*, Kendall Walton has argued that we use works of art as props in games of make-believe, that it is fictional rather than actual that we respond to the work with the emotions that the objects they depict would induce in ordinary life, for example, that we respond with fear to events depicted in a horror movie, and therefore that there is no paradox in either how we can like or how we can fear fictions, because we do not in fact have the same emotional responses to fictions that we do to reality. This leads to an interpretation of the experience of fiction as "simulation" that is also investigated in contemporary cognitive science. An alternative position holds that to experience a fiction is like entertaining but not asserting a thought, and that we can have the same emotional response to an unasserted as to an asserted thought. This position has been developed by Noël Carroll and Peter Lamarque, among others. It too seems suitable for investigation by cognitive scientists.

CONTINENTAL AESTHETICS. Just as the division between "analytical" and "continental" aesthetics is less than clear-cut, so any rigid division of the continental tradition into separate lines of development will also be misleading. Nevertheless, the present discussion will be organized around a division between Marxist, phenomenological, and post-structuralist aesthetics.

Marxist aesthetics. Both Marx and Engels included the arts among the cultural superstructure of societies, which is determined by their economic substructure, but neither provided an extended treatment of aesthetics. That awaited twentieth-century Marxism. In the early days of Bolshevism and Russian communism, both Lenin and Trotsky addressed the role of the arts at length. Lenin treated art as a category of "intellectual work" that, like any other form of labor, could be used for or against the revolution. He expected art to serve the political education of the proletariat and therefore to remain accessible through the use of conventional forms.

This line of thought led to the official adoption of the style of "Socialist realism," defined by Andrei Zhdanov, at the First All-Union Congress of Soviet Writers in 1934. By that time, Leon Trotsky, a less conventional thinker, had already been exiled from the Soviet Union.

Trotsky, who had published *Literatura i revoliutsiia* (Literature and revolution) in 1924, also argued that art should serve as a "hammer" for building the new society, but recognized that art also needed to be a "mirror" of existing society in order to reveal what needed to be corrected or rejected in it. Trotsky also kept in mind that the ultimate point of the revolution was supposed to be the extension of the enjoyment of freedom from an elite to the masses, and therefore held that art was not merely instrumental in value, but should enjoy some freedom of its own. In this regard Trotsky actually remained closer to the mainstream of modern Western aesthetics.

Trotsky's recognition that traditional forms of art could be used as a mirror for the flaws of existing society was developed by the Hungarian György Lukács. His first books, *Die Seele und die Formen* (The soul and the forms; 1910) and *The Theory of the Novel* (1916), (Die Theorie des Romans" [1916]), were written in neo-Kantian and Hegelian veins respectively, but after World War I, Lukács became a major communist theorist with *Geschichte und Klassenbewusstsein* (History and class consciousness) in 1923. He then devoted the rest of his career to aesthetics, culminating in his massive and untranslated *Die Eigenart des Ästhetischen* (The uniqueness of the aesthetic) in 1963.

Lukács held that every society is a complex whole in which all aspects of life reflect its underlying economics and politics; that individual psychologies form types that reflect the roles that are possible within their society; and that art, especially the novel, should represent the types of psychologies possible within the society that it depicts. Lukács became hostile to modernists such as Joyce and Kafka, whom he saw as expressing their own, individual psychologies without regard for the larger society of which they were a part. He recognized that all art involves some abstraction, but rejected abstraction as an end in art. This led him into debates with Ernst Bloch and Bertolt Brecht, who held that abstract and unconventional means of presentation might work more effectively than traditional forms of mimesis to expose the contradictions within society and to agitate for change.

A figure who was much less influential when he was alive but who gained prominence in later decades is the literary critic Walter Benjamin. Benjamin failed to make an academic career in the 1920s with his work on the German baroque and romanticism, but had more of an impact with his work on modernist literature and life: He spent much of the last part of his life working on a Marxist-inspired study of modern sensibility through the lens of the twentieth-century shopping mall and its mass-produced goods, his so-called "Arcades Project." Among aestheticians, however, his most influential work was his 1936 essay on "The Work of Art in the Age of its Mechanical Reproducibility," in which he argued that the "aura" of traditional art derived from its original cultic role and then from the restriction of its accessibility to elites, conditions that could not be maintained with contemporary mass arts such as cinema. But Benjamin's essay left it open whether the mass rather than cultic accessibility of modern media makes them instruments for even greater domination, now by commercial rather than religious elites, or creates increased room for individual autonomy in the exercise of taste and choice of pursuits.

The most influential neo-Marxist aesthetician working after World War II was Theodor W. Adorno. Adorno was a student of composition under Alban Berg in Vienna as well as a student of philosophy in Frankfurt, where he became an associate of the "Frankfurt school" of critical theory before the war and eventually, after his return from his wartime exile in Oxford and Los Angeles, its postwar leader. Adorno wrote in many areas, from sociology (he coauthored *The Authoritarian Personality* in 1950), literary criticism (*Noten zur Literatur* [Notes to literature]; 1958–1965), and music theory (*Philosophie der neuen Musik* [Philosophy of modern music]; 1949). With Max Horkheimer, the original director of the Frankfurt school, he coauthored the *Dialektik der Aufklärung* (Dialectic of enlightenment; 1947), which argued that, contrary to its intention, the European Enlightenment was actually an extension of the traditional drive to dominate the individual by mythology, and then that the contemporary "culture industry" continues the mass manipulation of the individual. Horkheimer and Adorno thus disambiguated Benjamin's ambivalent attitude toward modern media in favor of the more pessimistic interpretation.

Adorno's largest works were his *Negativ Dialektic* (Negative dialectics) of 1966 and the posthumous *Ästhetische Theorie* (Aesthetic theory) of 1970. In the latter, a more optimistic work than the *Dialektik der Aufklärung*, Adorno emphasized that even though art is always located in a historical context and therefore "refuses definition," it has always "turned against the status quo and what merely exists just as much as it has come to its aid by giving form to its elements" (Adorno 1997, p.2). On his account, art both reveals the contradictions of existing society and yet can make us aware of the possibility of something better. Art shows both the fissures in current society and the possibility of a non-coercive integration beyond those fissures. In spite of the length of the book, much of Adorno's view remains programmatic. One distinctive feature often missing from other modern and especially Marxist aesthetics, however, is Adorno's reflection on the relation between artistic and natural beauty: He argues that natural beauty offers a model of integration or reconciliation that is often missing from the man-made, and thus that art often seeks to bring nature within its scope, but at the same time that we may easily be seduced by nature into thinking that reconciliation of social fissures will come automatically instead of by our own, intentional efforts.

The Frankfurt theorist who remained in America, Herbert Marcuse, drew on Freud to criticize orthodox Marxism in much of his late work, first in *Eros and Civilization* (1955), which as its title suggests argued for the necessity of Eros as well as social justice, and then in his last work, *The Aesthetic Dimension* (1978), which argued that art unequivocally reflects the human wish for life rather than death, that "Aesthetic form, autonomy, and truth… each *transcends* the socio-historical arena," and that art "challenges the monopoly of the established reality to determine what is 'real,' and it does so by creating a fictitious world which is nevertheless 'more real than reality itself'" (Marcuse 1978, p. 22). Marcuse's conviction that the resistance to the forces of Eros come primarily from politics rather than from the natural conditions of human life are regarded as naive by contemporary psychoanalysis.

The British literary theorist Terry Eagleton returned to more traditional Marxist-inspired critique of ideology in his 1990 *The Ideology of the Aesthetic*, arguing that the classical modern theory of the autonomy and universal validity of taste, which was developed simultaneously with the bourgeois domination of the economics and politics of European society beginning in the eighteenth century, was in fact a mask for that increasing domination.

The phenomenological tradition. The other main German-influenced line in twentieth-century aesthetics is the phenomenological tradition. This has its sources in both Wilhelm Dilthey and Edmund Husserl. Dilthey was a historian, biographer, and literary critic as well as a theorist of history, the arts, and the human sciences generally. He adopted the idea of hermeneutics from Friedrich Schleiermacher, the subject of one of his major studies, and introduced it into twentieth-century thought. He held that every society and period has a distinctive "worldview" (*Weltanschauung*), but that the modern worldview (since the Renaissance) has grown so complex that it can only be represented artistically, in virtue of art's powers of isolation or abstraction, concentration, and integration. In his view, hermeneutics is the method for interpreting the larger worldview expressed by a work of art.

Husserl, by contrast, started off as a technical philosopher of logic and mathematics, and then argued for a distinctive power of apprehending the essential structures of logical, mathematical, and scientific concepts, of ordinary objects, and of the social world that is independent of ordinary empirical investigation—what he called *Wesensschau*, or the intuition of essence. From such a premise, it would be natural to see art as a form of *Wesensschau*, especially in the pioneering period of abstract art. Husserl himself did not apply his phenomenology to the case of art, but the Pole Roman Ingarden did in *Literarische Kunstwerk* (The literary work of art; 1931). Ingarden employed Husserl's approach in seeing a work of literature (and by extension other works of art) as containing complex layers of intentionality, including meaningful words, meaningful combinations of words and elements, represented objects, and "schematized aspects" or implicit perspectives that need to be developed in the thought of the reader rather than the writer. In this regard Ingarden's works can be seen as a forerunner of the "reception aesthetics" of Wolfgang Iser (*The Act of Reading*, 1978; originally published as *Der Act des Lesens*, 1976) and Hans Robert Jauss (*Aesthetic Experience and Literary Hermeneutics*, 1982; originally published as *Äesthetische Erfahrung und literarische Hermeneutik*, 1977).

Martin Heidegger, however, was influenced by Wilhelm Dilthey as well as by Husserl, and it could be argued that in his case the influence of the former gradually overtook that of the latter: for Heidegger, art reveals more *Weltanschauung* than *Wesensschau*. Heidegger's magnum opus, *Being and Time* (1927) (*Sein und Zeit*) argues for the priority of the human experience (*Dasein*) of the world as an arena for agency with tools and instruments over the objectivist standpoint of science and traditional philosophy, which treats humans as more passive knowers of independent realities. Heidegger did not discuss art in this work, but it has proven tremendously influential on writers from Jean-Paul Sartre and Maurice Merleau-Ponty to the present, all of whom treat art as the special vehicle for the expression of the point of view of *Dasein* rather than objectifying science.

During the 1930s, as the style of his philosophy became more mythic (some would argue that this was a reflection of his allegiance to National Socialism), Heidegger lectured explicitly on aesthetics, culminating in the essay on *The Origin of the Work of Art* (Der Ursprung des Kunstwerks [1950]) that was written in 1935–1936 but not published until 1950. Here Heidegger describes art as revealing both "world" and "earth," the former the complex of beliefs, practices, and feelings that characterizes a human way of life and the latter the chthonic domain and forces from which the human world emerges. One striking feature of this essay is that it begins by stressing that art is a form of work, thus a product of human activity, but ends with a theory of truth in which truth is *revealed* to the artist who knows chiefly how not to get in its way (an approach that goes back to Schopenhauer's interpretation of genius). The essay thus ends up with a peculiarly passive view of artistic creation and, by implication, reception; it is thus very much opposed to the model of artistic creation and reception to be found in such writers as Collingwood, Dewey, Ingarden, and the "reception" theorists.

Heidegger's most influential student in the arena of aesthetics was Hans-Georg Gadamer, whose major work was *Wahrheit und Methode* (Truth and method; 1960). Gadamer was also influenced directly by Dilthey, and was the major proponent of hermeneutics in the second half of the twentieth century. *Wahrheit und Methode* is a general theory of hermeneutics as the means, though not a formal method, for understanding oneself and others. But it begins with an attack upon traditional aesthetics, especially Kant's, for "subjectivizing" aesthetic experience, or for seeing art as a means to producing an experience in the subject (the audience), which might be shared with other subjects because a *sensus communis* is presupposed, but not as a means for building a *sensus communis* or intersubjective understanding in the first place. Gadamer calls the first, narrowly subjective kind of experience *Erlebnis*, but the fuller experience that is essentially intersubjective *Erfahrung*. On his account, while we always already understand ourselves and others from within some conceptual framework, art is a fundamental means for us to revise and expand our understanding of self and others, and thus to make the transition from *Erlebnis* to *Erfahrung*.

Jean-Paul Sartre never wrote a treatise on aesthetics, although a large part of his enormous oeuvre consists of books and essays on particular artists such as Flaubert, Baudelaire, Jean Genet, and Mallarmé. His early work *Imaginaire; psychologie* (The psychology of imagination; 1940), under the influence of Husserl, stressed the role of forming images in imagining, although his own creative as well as critical output was in the field of literature rather than the visual arts. Like Adorno and Marcuse

later, he stressed the potential of art for non-alienating communication, in which the artist's expression of freedom invites the audience to experience their own freedom of imagination as well. In this regard, his view falls into the Kantian rather than Heideggerian tradition. Merleau-Ponty's emphasis on the primacy of perception over scientific understanding in his main work, *Phénoménologie de la perception* (The phenomenology of perception; 1945), is certainly influenced by the Heidegger of *Being and Time* as well as by Husserl's late emphasis on the *Lebenswelt* ("lifeworld"), but his three seminal essays on aesthetics, especially "Cézanne's Doubt," also stress the freedom and individuality of artistic vision.

Post-structuralism. Main voices in the French "post-structuralist" or "post-modernist" movement, which has had its primary influence on literary theory rather than philosophical aesthetics, include among others Roland Barthes, Michel Foucault, Jacques Derrida, Paul de Man, Jean-François Lyotard, and the sociologist Pierre Bourdieu. (An independent form of "post-modernism," and the term itself, originated within the precincts of architecture and architectural theory, beginning with the works of Robert Venturi and his widely read books *Complexity and Contradiction in Architecture* [1966] and *Learning from Las Vegas* [1972].)

With the exception of de Man, a literary critic who published only a few volumes of papers, all of these authors published a flood of works on a wide range of topics, and aesthetics in the traditional sense concerns only a small number of their works. Barthes's works in aesthetics touch on topics including criticism, fashion, and photography (*Camera Lucida*, 1980). Foucault's works, beginning with *Mots et les choses* (1966), translated as *The Order of Things* (1970), focused on the "archaeology of knowledge," an historicist analysis of cognitive systems and of the power relations underlying such systems. But both Barthes and Foucault were known particularly for the thesis of the "death of the author," which held that it is primarily the reader (or auditor or viewer) rather than the author who constitutes the meaning of a work of art, and thus of course that works of art do not have determinate meanings, since they may have many different audiences. This is an extreme version of what had been one aspect of aesthetic theory since Dewey and Collingwood, and a hyperbolic statement of the reception aesthetics developed in Germany by Iser and Jauss.

Derrida and de Man were the leaders of the movement called "deconstructionism," which pervaded literary studies in the last decades of the twentieth century. The central idea of this approach is that a text never has a "transcendental" meaning outside of itself, but only an endless deferral of meaning from one sign to another both within itself and intertextually, that is, in other texts but not in some reality beyond texts altogether, and further that texts, especially philosophical texts, are typically built upon unsustainable distinctions that inevitably collapse. A classic example of deconstructionist analysis is Derrida's argument in *La vérité en peinture* (1978), translated as *The Truth in Painting* (1987), that Kant's distinction between a painting and its frame (its *parerga*) collapses because sometimes one cannot tell the difference between the painting and the frame, and therefore the distinction between art and non-art collapses as well. This is a misreading of Kant, who introduced the concept of the *parerga* only to show that even in the frame or drapery around a work of art we respond primarily to formal properties, as with the work itself, and not to define the difference between art and non-art; and it ignores the fact that in the vast majority of cases we can perfectly well tell the difference between the painting and its frame, even if in a small number of cases we cannot. Most of our empirical concepts have a penumbra of borderline cases, and yet we successfully use them in all sorts of contexts.

Lyotard extended Derrida's attack on the determinacy of language by arguing that figural or visual imagery often brings us closer to our real desires (*Discours, figure* [Discourse, figure]; 1971), and among other works also published lectures on Kant's concept of the sublime (1991) that manifest deconstructionism's fascination with the sublime as purported evidence of the ultimate ineffability of meaning. Finally, in his widely influential *Distinction: Critique sociale du jugement* (Distinction: A social critique of the judgment of taste; 1979), Bourdieu argued against the existence of any universal validity in matters of taste, thereby rejecting the ambitions of traditional aesthetics.

As the creation and reception of art in many different forms remain fundamental features of human life in many different cultures throughout the world, it can be expected that aesthetics will remain a central branch of philosophy in the twenty-first century as in centuries past.

See also Adorno, Theodor Wiesengrund; Aesthetic Experience; Ayer, Alfred Jules; Barthes, Roland; Baumgarten, Alexander Gottlieb; Beardsley, Monroe C.; Benjamin, Walter; Bloch, Ernst; Bosanquet, Bernard; Cassirer, Ernst; Cavell, Stanley; Cohen, Hermann; Collingwood, Robin George; Croce, Benedetto; Danto, Arthur; Derrida, Jacques; Dewey, John; Dilthey, Wilhelm; Engels, Friedrich; Enlightenment; Fechner, Gustav Theodor; Foucault, Michel; Gadamer, Hans-Georg; Goodman, Nelson; Hegel, Georg Wilhelm Friedrich; Hegelianism; Heidegger, Martin; Helmholtz, Hermann von; Hermeneutics; Horkheimer, Max; Hume, David; Husserl, Edmund; Hutcheson, Francis; Ingarden, Roman; Kafka, Franz; Kant, Immanuel; Langer, Susanne K.; Lenin, Vladimir Il'ich; Lukács, Georg; Lyotard, Jean-François; Marx, Karl; Merleau-Ponty, Maurice; Moore, George Edward; Neo-Kantianism; Nussbaum, Martha; Peirce, Charles Sanders; Plato; Ryle, Gilbert; Santayana, George; Sartre, Jean-Paul; Schelling, Friedrich Wilhelm Joseph von; Schiller, Friedrich; Schleiermacher, Friedrich Daniel Ernst; Schopenhauer, Arthur; Stevenson, Charles L. ; Structuralism and Post-structuralism; Thomas Aquinas, St.; Wittgenstein, Ludwig Josef Johann.

Bibliography

Adorno, Theodore W. *Aesthetic Theory* (1970), edited by Gretel Adorno and Rolf Tiedemann. Translated by Robert Hullot-Kenter. Minneapolis: University of Minnesota Press, 1997.

Beardsley, Monroe C. *Aesthetics: Problems in the Philosophy of Criticism.* 2nd ed. Indianapolis: Hackett, 1981. 1st ed., New York: Harcourt, Brace & World, 1958.

Bosanquet, Bernard. *A History of Æsthetic.* 2nd ed. London: George Allen & Unwin, 1904.

Croce, Benedetto. *The Aesthetic as the Science of Expression and of the Linguistic in General.* Translated by Colin Lyas. Cambridge, U.K.: Cambridge University Press, 1992.

Dewey, John. *Art as Experience.* New York: G. P. Putnam's Sons, 1934.

Dewey, John. *Experience and Nature* (1925). 2nd ed., Chicago and LaSalle Open Court, 1929.

Langer, Suzanne K. *Philosophy in a New Key: A Study in the Symbolism of Reason, Rite, and Art.* Cambridge, MA: Harvard University Press, 1942.

Marcuse, Herbert. *The Aesthetic Dimension: Toward a Critique of Marxist Aesthetics.* Boston: Beacon Press, 1978.

Moore G[eorge] E[dward]. *Principia Ethica* (1903). 2nd ed., with other papers, edited by Thomas Baldwin. Cambridge, U.K.: Cambridge University Press, 1993.

Paul Guyer (2005)

AESTHETICS, PROBLEMS OF

The philosophical discipline of aesthetics deals with conceptual problems arising out of the critical examination of art and the aesthetic. Monroe Beardsley subtitled his 1958 book on general aesthetics *Problems in the Philosophy of Criticism*, implying that aesthetics is about philosophical concepts that are used—often unthinkingly—by critics of the arts, when they say that a work of art such as a painting is *beautiful* or has *aesthetic* value, that it *represents* some subject matter, has a well-composed *form*, is in a particular *style*, and *expresses* some emotion. But aesthetics also deals more broadly with the aesthetics of nature (Budd 1996, Carlson 2000) and gardens (Ross 1998), and with the aesthetic appreciation of objects and activities in everyday life (Dewey 1934). And even when focused on the arts, philosophical aesthetics is concerned with the philosophical problems that arise from the artist's point of view as well as the critic's. Thus creativity, expression, representation, form, and style are problems that can be addressed from the artist's point of view as well as the spectator's. Moreover, "the philosophy of criticism" does not do justice to the breadth of concerns addressed by philosophical aesthetics today. Some of the thorniest issues in aesthetics relate directly to problems in general philosophy: What is aesthetic value? Do the arts provide knowledge? Is there a special kind of aesthetic experience or aesthetic perception?

Most of the questions that come up in theorizing about particular art forms—the philosophy of literature, the theory of the visual arts, the philosophy of music, the philosophy of film, environmental arts and so on—are general questions having implications for other art forms. Some theorists, however, think that the individual arts come with their own unique sets of philosophical problems (Kivy 1997). The problem of the experience and value of absolute music, for example, does not have a clear parallel in any of the other arts, including the other abstract arts (Kivy 1990). Authenticity is a particular problem in the performing arts such as dance and music. But for the most part, questions in the philosophy of art have general application across the arts. Thus the problem of the nature of fictional characters has usually been taken to be a problem about literature, but representational works of visual art also contain fictional people, objects and events (Walton 1990). Similarly, the question as to why people get emotionally involved with fictional characters may seem to be unique to films and novels (Carroll 1990, Currie 1990, Feagin 1996, Lamarque 1996), but it applies equally to fictions in works of visual art. Again, the question why people enjoy tragedies is not peculiar to tragedies: It is the same kind of question as the question why do people listen to sad music if it makes them feel sad (Davies 1994, Levinson 1990)?

This brief overview first discusses the aesthetic in general and then turns to problems peculiar to the arts. It ends with some general remarks about how aesthetics connects to more general questions about knowledge, emotion, and value. Some effort has been made to point out how the most important concepts of aesthetics came to be considered important. The tendency of late-twentieth-century philosophy—especially analytic philosophy—has been to treat the problems of aesthetics as timeless problems having correct answers that will be true of all art works and aesthetic experiences no matter where or when they occur. But if one approaches aesthetics with an eye to the historical background from which its characteristic problems emerged, one will have a better sense not only of what those problems are but also of the different ways they have been conceptualized and why.

THE AESTHETIC

What is the realm of the aesthetic? Should it be thought of as a special kind of pleasure, or, more broadly, as a special kind of experience, as a special type of judgment, as a special type of attitude toward the world, or as a special type of quality? All these options have been pursued. The term "aesthetics" derives from the Greek word *aesthesis*, meaning "perception." The German rationalist philosopher Alexander Baumgarten coined the term in 1735 to mean the science of "sensory perception," which was designed to contrast with logic, the science of "intellect" (Baumgarten 1954), and ever since, the term "aesthetic" has kept its connotation as having an essential connection to the perceptually discriminable.

Although German rationalism gave the field of aesthetics its name and a rationale, it was the British empiricists who established aesthetics as a philosophical discipline and who set the agenda for its subsequent development. The problem that chiefly exercised the eighteenth century thinkers in aesthetics was the nature of aesthetic pleasure and of aesthetic judgment, the judgment of "taste." If aesthetics were to be a serious philosophical discipline, then presumably there must be principles that would justify aesthetic judgments, and distinguish them from mere assertions of liking or disliking. At the same time it was taken for granted by the empiricists that aesthetic judgments depend on subjective feelings of pleasure. For Hutcheson (1973), Hume, and their successors, the aesthetic judgment was primarily a judgment that something is beautiful. So the challenge was to figure out if there was a special kind of pleasure that was the proper response to beauty or a special kind of judgment that was being made when one judged an object beautiful.

BEAUTY

The concept of beauty was an heirloom of ancient and Medieval philosophy. For Plato (1953), only the Idea of Beauty is really beautiful, since everything else is only beautiful in one respect or at one time rather than another or by comparison with one thing and not another. Beautiful people and things can only approach the Form of Beauty. The Medievals, under the influence of the Neoplatonist Plotinus, thought of beauty, the good, and other perfections, as true in the strictest sense only of the highest level of reality. Christianity echoed this idea in the doctrine that beauty is one of God's perfections. In this framework the beauty of the world is derivative from "an image and reflection of Ideal Beauty" (Eco 1986, p. 17). Augustine, for example, believed that a person possesses beauty of body or soul only to the degree that he or she approximates God's perfect beauty. Such a conception of beauty is a far cry from the way it has come to be thought about in modern aesthetics.

Since the Enlightenment, beauty has by and large no longer been regarded as having or being an ethical or religious value. Instead, the eighteenth-century empiricists thought of it simply as the capacity of an object to produce a particular kind of pleasurable experience. The judgment that something is beautiful was the paradigm of what they called the aesthetic judgment or judgment of taste. If, however, the judgment that something is beautiful is not to be a mere statement of liking or preference, then there must be a standard of taste, a principle of justification for claims that something is beautiful which nevertheless preserves the insight that judgments of the beautiful are based on subjective feelings of pleasure. It is this formulation of the problem of beauty and the aesthetic that has come down to us and which continues to exercise theorists.

THE AESTHETIC JUDGMENT

The empiricists rejected the idea that there are universal standards of beauty: The great variety of beautiful things suggests that there are no general canons or rules of beauty as assumed by some classical writers in the Renaissance. Hutcheson thought that the classical idea of "unity in variety" is the one property that reliably evokes aesthetic pleasure (Hutcheson 1973), but whether something has the right degree of unity or variety is itself problematic. Hume famously solved the dilemma by arguing that we are all so constituted as to be pleased by the same sorts of objects in nature and works of art but that we do not all have the same background of experience, delicacy of taste, good sense, ability to make comparisons and lack of prejudice that we ideally could and should have (Hume 1985). Those who have these abilities in the highest degree are the "ideal critics" to whom the rest of us should defer about what is beautiful, and in theory these ideal critics will all agree with one another. Even Hume himself, however, suspected that this would not do entirely, pointing out that younger people have different tastes from older, and that people from one culture might take no pleasure in the art of another if the values it assumes and promotes are sufficiently alien. Today, Marxist critics, reader-response theorists and feminist critics have all emphasized the difficulty of generalizing about the responses of perceptive critics with different background assumptions and points of view.

KANT AND FORMALISM

After Hume, Kant (2000) gave an equally famous *a priori* argument that judgments of taste, though based on subjective feelings of pleasure, lay claim to universality because the pleasure in question is neither pleasure in the sensuously pleasing nor pleasure in the useful, but a disinterested pleasure that arises from the harmonious free play of imagination and understanding, which are cognitive faculties common to all rational human beings. Since it derives from these shared abilities, this pleasure is itself shareable and communicable. Kant thought that an aesthetic judgment is disinterested because it is not addressed to anything in which we have an interest or personal stake but instead is a judgment about the form of an object. The object of aesthetic judgment is "purposiveness without purpose," the appearance something has of having being harmoniously put together for some end even though it lacks any specific end. Kant's examples of aesthetic judgment are drawn primarily from the beauties of nature such as the shape and sweetness of the rose, but his ideas were influential in fixing attention on the formal aspects of art works as well. Kant himself emphasized the role of art works in producing "aesthetic ideas," but critics who focus exclusively on the early part of the *Critique of Judgment* have found there a justification for the view that with respect to both nature and art, the aesthetic judgment or judgment of taste is directed exclusively to formal qualities. This idea no doubt ultimately derives from the classical notion that measure and symmetry are important or even definitive of beauty.

At any rate, Kant has, perhaps unjustly, been seen as the main source of formalism, the idea that the most or only important features of a work of art are its formal qualities. To twentieth-century critics of painting such as Clive Bell and Clement Greenberg, this means that only color, line, and shape, and their inter-relations are of aesthetic importance and that content is aesthetically irrelevant. In music it is the doctrine that only structure is important. In literature, formalists have emphasized the structures of plots in narratives and the use of imagery and other rhetorical devices in poetry. There is something to be said for formalism—it draws people's attention to what is truly artistic in a work of art, the "art" with which it is put together—but it assumes a distinction between form and content that is very difficult—perhaps impossible—to make out.

Bell (1914) thought art could be defined as "significant form," suggesting that two paintings can imitate or represent the very same thing—the Virgin, say, or a field full of cows—yet one can be art and the other not, because of the way the artist has rendered the form of the work. Bell was part of the Art for Art's Sake movement that swept England in the late nineteenth and early twentieth century. The emphasis on form is congenial to critics of the abstract arts such as architecture and instrumental music, but it is far less plausible for such arts as literature and photography. Moreover, as has often been pointed out, Bell seems to be defining good art rather than art *simpliciter*, and in defining good art, he is attributing to it his own favored criterion of value.

AESTHETIC QUALITIES, AESTHETIC EXPERIENCE, AESTHETIC ATTITUDE

In the early eighteenth century the paradigm of an aesthetic judgment was taken to be the judgment that something is beautiful; and the beautiful was explained in terms of pleasure. In the later part of the century, however, the notion of aesthetic judgment was expanded to include judgments of the picturesque and the sublime, but the judgment of the sublime is no longer wholly pleasurable. Burke described the source of the feeling of the sublime as "whatever is fitted in any sort to excite the ideas of pain and danger" such as vastness, power and obscurity (Burke 1909, p. 36).

Once aesthetic judgments were no longer directed solely at the beautiful, the way was clear for thinking of the aesthetic not as one particular kind of pleasure or as one particular kind of judgment, but rather as a certain kind of quality of an object. Beauty and sublimity might then be merely two among a much broader class of aesthetic qualities, such as "dainty," "garish," "delicate," "insipid," and so on. One question raised by expanding the range of aesthetic qualities is whether all aesthetic qualities are correctly describable as formal qualities. Frank Sibley, who initiated the modern discussion of aes-

thetic qualities, includes on his list of examples not only clear-cut examples of formal qualities, such as "graceful" and "garish," but also qualities such as "melancholy," which are usually thought of as *expressive* properties, a special subset of aesthetic qualities (Sibley 1959).

Interestingly, very similar questions arise in connection with aesthetic qualities as formerly arose about beauty: Are they intrinsic or mind-dependent qualities? And if they are mind-dependent, do they behave like colors which are perceived similarly by everybody with properly functioning eyes, or are they more like the taste of curry or cilantro, which is perceived as delicious and piquant by some and disgusting by others? Is there a set of ideal critics, as Hume proposed, whose faculties are keener than those of the rest of us and who should be the true judges of aesthetic qualities? These are questions that are still being hotly debated.

The notion of a special aesthetic pleasure or aesthetic perception has also broadened since the eighteenth century into the more general concept of *aesthetic experience*. John Dewey is partly responsible for this change in emphasis. He wanted to stress the importance of having "experiences" in daily life that have the same wholeness, richness, and sense of integration that are characteristic of our encounters with works of art. Other theorists (for example, Schopenhauer [1958] and Stolnitz [1960]) have insisted that what marks out the aesthetic is a special kind of attitude, that should be taken to works of art but that can in theory be taken to anything whatsoever. It turns out that the aesthetic attitude has many of the features of an aesthetic judgment: It is a special kind of disinterested contemplation, often taking the form of an object or art work as the focus of attention.

THE THEORY OF THE ARTS: IMITATION AND REPRESENTATION

The idea that poetry and painting are arts of imitation derives from Plato, who likened imitations to shadows and reflections, and as such, he thought, led away from rather than toward the truth. Aristotle, too, thought that the arts of poetry and painting were imitations of reality, but, unlike Plato, he thought that we learn from imitations and that we take pleasure in doing so. Plato and Aristotle were the first in the western tradition to theorize about poetry and painting as arts of imitation, but they did not think of them as a special category of "fine arts" or Art with a capital "A." The Ancient Greeks had no concept of "the aesthetic" (Sparshott 1982). The arts of painting and sculpture were varieties of technē or craft. The word "art" derives from the Latinized form of the Greek *technē*, meaning a "corpus of knowledge and skills organized for the production of changes of a specific kind in matter of a specific kind," like the arts of cobbling or leatherwork (Sparshott 1982, p. 26). The art of poetry had a more important educational role as a source of moral education but it too is an art of imitation. In the Renaissance and the Enlightenment under the influence of Aristotle and his descendants in the classical period, it became a commonplace that poems and paintings imitated or represented the world.

The first attempt to systematize the fine arts came in 1746 when the abbé Batteux grouped together poetry, painting, sculpture, dance and music under the rubric of the imitation of beautiful nature. This was a revolutionary idea in that it categorized together craftsmen such as sculptors and painters with the more highly educated poets, and implied that all the practitioners of the fine arts provided representations of the world that were potential sources of knowledge (Kristeller 1951–1952). Once the idea of the fine arts was established, it was possible to search for traits that they all have in common, and the search for a definition of the fine arts and eventually of "Art" was born.

From the beginning, the search for a definition has been challenged by the multiplicity of the arts. Thus the idea that the arts imitate or represent beautiful nature may have seemed plausible in the age of Pheidias and Praxiteles who made realistic but highly idealized sculptures of the human body, and similarly in the High Renaissance when the beautiful paintings of Raphael and Leonardo imitated the beautiful female form in their paintings of the Virgin, but the arts of "pure" music and dance are not obviously imitating anything. Architecture, too, is only exceptionally an art of imitation. In the eighteenth-century synthesis of the fine arts as arts of the imitation of beautiful nature, we see an attempt to fit together two different conceptual traditions, on the one hand the new empiricist concern with aesthetic judgment, the judgment of beauty, and on the other hand the classical idea—derived from Plato and Aristotle—that the fine arts are arts of imitation. Although buildings, dances and music do not fit very well under the description of arts of imitation, they can certainly be beautiful by satisfying the formal demand for "unity within variety." We see here the beginnings of a clash which lasts to our own day, roughly speaking, the clash between thinking of the arts as aspiring to beauty of form or as seeking to show us the way things are in the world.

The idea that the arts are all arts of imitation has seemed more and more far-fetched in the contemporary world, where a tendency toward abstraction is the rule in the visual arts, and even literature has drawn attention to its formal aspects rather than the story it tells. Perhaps in some very broad sense the arts are "about" the world, but even this has been denied by some defenders of "absolute music" who see it rather as a means of escape from the world (Kivy 1990).

At the same time the notion of "imitation" has come under attack as an account of representation. Many works of art, such as representational paintings, photographs, films, and sculptures represent the world, but it does not seem right to say that they *imitate* it. The role of convention and style is too important in all these genres to make a comparison with a mirror image plausible. Widely discussed theories of pictorial representation include Ernst Gombrich's view that the history of realistic painting is a history of "making and matching" (Gombrich 1960), and Richard Wollheim's theory that pictorial representation rests upon a prior capacity people have for "seeing in" (Wollheim 1987). In literature, a distinction has been made between literary narratives that talk about the world in some sense but arguably do not *represent* it and literary dramas that do represent the world, but perhaps not in quite the same sense that pictures do. Kendall Walton thinks that representations in general should be analyzed in terms of the concept of what a work prescribes us to imagine (Walton 1990). When, for example, we encounter a pictorial representation of a water mill, we imagine of our act of seeing that it is a seeing of a watermill. His controversial theory of photography holds that, in contrast to paintings, we do not merely imagine but *really see* the object photographed that appears in the picture (Walton 1984).

EXPRESSION

In the Romantic period, artists and writers began to describe themselves not as merely imitating an inert reality but as expressing their own emotional perspectives on the world. Poetry, wrote Wordsworth in a famous phrase, is the "spontaneous overflow of powerful feelings" that are "recollected in tranquility" (Wordsworth 1963, p. 260). After the imitation theory, the next great attempt to define Art was the theory of art as expression. Kant had stressed the role of imagination in art, and the role of the genius that "gives the rule to art" (Kant 2000, p. 187), i.e. who makes up his own rules rather than obeys conventional canons. The Platonic notion of the craftsman who knew how to craft sculptures or poems and who was creative only insofar as he was inspired by the gods, gave way to the idea of the artist who used his creative imagination to come up with novel expressions of novel ideas and emotions.

Kant's notion that the mark of genius is to come up with "aesthetic ideas" was taken up by Hegel, who argued that art is one of the modes of consciousness whereby man reaches knowledge of Absolute Spirit; specifically it is that mode of consciousness whereby ideas are embodied in some sensuous form. For Hegel, then, art was an important means to knowledge, but it was a special kind of knowledge that could not be detached from the medium in which it is conveyed. The theorists of expression, including the idealist R. G. Collingwood and the pragmatist John Dewey, echoed some of these ideas, insisting that artistic expression is a *cognitive* activity, a matter of elucidating and articulating emotions (Collingwood 1938, Dewey 1934). Like Hegel, they seemed to think that the emotional attitude embodied in a poem or painting was unique to that poem or painting: Any change in color or line in a painting, any change in imagery or rhythm in a poem would change the emotion expressed. Some theorists stressed not so much personal expression as the communication of emotion from one person to another (Tolstoy 1960).

Just as the definition of art as the imitation of reality fits well with eighteenth-century poems and paintings, so the theory of art as expression fits best with Romantic and Expressionist poetry, music, sculpture and painting. Once again architecture is a problem: Most buildings do not seem to express the personal emotions and attitudes of their makers.

The concept of expression has proved malleable, however. More recent theories include Goodman's view that expression is metaphorical exemplification (Goodman 1976). In this sense a work of architecture can express some of its aesthetic properties, its gracefulness, its minatory look, its wit, and it can literally exemplify its mass, its solidity, and perhaps its style. Likewise, a piece of music can metaphorically exemplify its melancholy or jovial character. Other theorists have argued that expression is nothing but the *possession* of a certain sort of aesthetic property (Hospers 1954–1955), namely expressive properties such as "melancholy," "jovial," "witty," and "lively," and have disputed about whether these properties are possessed metaphorically or literally (Davies 1994). In this discussion, too, we see a clash of different conceptual traditions. The idea that art is expression is far removed from the notion that art has a special set of aesthetic properties called "expressive" properties.

The idea that art has expressive properties is not a very surprising revelation, but it does have the advantage of being true across a wide range of art works. By contrast the Romantic, idealist theory of art as expression fits poorly with most of the works made before the end of the eighteenth century. And although twentieth century modernist artists thought of themselves as "embodying" ideas and emotions in a medium just as Collingwood recommended, in the postmodern world artists seem to want to convey their ideas by any means possible rather than "embodying" them in a carefully constructed work of Collingwoodian expression. At the same time, however, many artists continue to talk about *expressing* themselves in their work.

THE INSTITUTIONAL THEORY OF ART

The imitation theory, the theory of art as form, and the expression theory all seem incapable of providing a definition of art that covers all those things that people in Western societies generally want to count as art. Consequently, some have despaired of the possibility of defining art at all, and have retreated to the position that "art" is a "family resemblance" concept in Wittgenstein's sense (Weitz 1956). The more popular move, however, has been to look for a definition which does not appeal to "exhibited" properties such as the form of a work, its representational content or its expressive qualities, but rather to historical or contextual features of the work. Arthur Danto has proposed that we count something as art if there is an artistic theory behind it that links it to the history of art (Danto 1964, 1981). Just as the theory of art as imitation had its origins in the classical world and the theory of art as expression in the Romantic period, so Danto's theory is a response to the conceptual art of the late twentieth century, art that does not necessarily *embody* or exemplify its meaning but which needs to be decoded by those who have an understanding of "the artworld"—an "atmosphere of artistic theory, a knowledge of the history of art"—in virtue of which the work counts as art (Danto 1964, p. 580). Again, the theory is most appropriate to works of "high" art that are made within and in recognition of the contemporary institutions of art. Work of folk art—such as the tattoos and walrus tusk carvings of the ancient Inuit—do not fit very easily into this definition, because folk cultures often do not have a concept of "Art" as was developed in the West in the eighteenth century.

George Dickie has taken the concept of the artworld to refer not to a body of theory but to a particular group of people—artists, curators, art critics, museum-goers—and has argued that, roughly speaking, something is art if it is the sort of thing that is designed to be presented to members of the artworld (Dickie 1984). But if we understand the artworld is this way, then once again the theory will not happily apply in cultures where there are no curators, critics or museums, and nothing approaching an "artworld." Modern attempts to surmount this problem (Levinson 1990, 1996; Carroll 2001) have emphasized the historical dimension of art and art appreciation: Perhaps we can define art in terms of the kinds of intention with which art works have traditionally been made or by the kinds of responses they have traditionally invited.

MEANING AND INTERPRETATION

In insisting that art works require an artistic theory to justify them, Danto is emphasizing that all art works have artistic meaning and require *interpretation*: One cannot just contemplate the beauty of an artwork; one needs to grasp the ideas that lie behind it, ideas that may not even be manifest in the aesthetic surface, at least until the artist or her surrogate has pointed them out. In Goodman's *Languages of Art*, art works are conceived of, by analogy with language, as symbols in different kinds of symbol system. As in Danto's theory, art is meant to be interpreted and understood, rather than merely contemplated and appreciated. The idea that works require interpretation fits well with the ethos of modernism. Modernist works are often difficult—one thinks of *The Wasteland* or the works of Schoenberg—and they *need* to be interpreted. Postmodern works may sometimes be more playful but often they too are mystifying unless you know the theory behind them, for example the stories of Italo Calvino or the late works of architecture by Peter Eisenman.

But what is it to interpret a work of art? In the late twentieth century there developed a sharp divide between the approach taken by analytic philosophers of literature who tend to stress the importance of understanding the author's probable intentions in constructing a work (Levinson 1996, Stecker 2003) and the various approaches taken by continental thinkers. German reception theory saw interpretation as primarily determined by readers' responses rather than the artist's intentions (Iser 1978). Thinkers in the structuralist and poststructuralist tradition emphasize the importance of how readers or viewers decode or deconstruct art works, thereby uncovering an abundance of possible meanings permitted by the interweaving structures of a text as well as by their interactions with further texts (Barthes 1974, Derrida 1974). Marxist, Freudian, and feminist theorists have reinterpreted works from the past from the perspective of

the contemporary reader's assumptions, that might well not have been shared by the author of the work. In both analytic and continental traditions, however, the importance of taking account of the cultural context of artist and reader has been stressed.

The rage for interpretation has even reached the aesthetics of nature. Instead of just contemplating the beauties of a waterfall, a flower or a mountain, it has been argued that we should base our appreciation on scientific knowledge about what we are looking at (Carlson 2000) and that the more we know about it the more aesthetically pleased we will become. To others this seems doubtful about much of our experience of nature (Budd 1996). They could argue that the Romantics who first fostered interest in the wilder aspects of nature were no experts in the sciences of botany or geology, but were deeply moved by nature all the same.

ONTOLOGY

The question of interpretation is closely bound up with the ontological status of art works. What is it that we are interpreting when we interpret a work of art? On the face of it, paintings and sculptures and works of architecture are individual physical objects, whereas novels, symphonies, etchings and digital art works are types or abstract objects of some kind (Wollheim 1980). In addition, some arts are performing arts, requiring a performance in order to be experienced (Davies 2001). Performance arts such as dance and music raise additional questions about the authenticity of modern performances of older works. If performance practice has changed radically from when a piece was composed, are we really experiencing the work itself, a modified version of the work, or a wholly new work bearing some resemblance to the old?

Goodman distinguished allographic from autographic art forms, the former being identifiable as a structure or sequence of symbols, such as a novel, and the latter being identifiable only by means of the history of production of the artwork (Goodman 1976). One problem with this distinction is that even allographic art works may need to be distinguished by their history of production (Levinson 1990): if Smith in 2005 composes what we identify as Beethoven's Fifth in total ignorance of the "original" Beethoven's Fifth, he would on Goodman's view have composed the very same symphony. But if we take seriously the idea that a work of art is partly identified by when, where, and by whom it was made, then it would seem that Smith's "Fifth" is a different work. Confirming this conclusion is the fact that Smith's Fifth has different artistic and aesthetic qualities from Beethoven's, being conventional and derivative, predictable and old-fashioned.

Works of art are cultural objects, objects with cultural significance, so they cannot be treated simply as individuals like tables and chairs on the one hand or like abstract types such as the standard meter on the other. Whether a work of art is an individual or a type, it has to be identified partly by means of the cultural context that spawned it, hence the importance of the artist's intentions and the historical, geographical, and intellectual context in which the artist operated (Margolis 1999). From this point of view, interpretation is necessarily bound up with ontology. Not everyone agrees, of course. But those who think that ontological questions should be kept separate from questions about interpretation have some difficulty in explaining how this is to be accomplished.

ART AND KNOWLEDGE

If art works are symbols that need to be pored over in order to release their meanings, then it is reasonable to expect them to advance our cognitive skills and to reveal truths about the world. This claim, however, has been controversial ever since Plato, who famously rejected the claims of poetry to knowledge, arguing that shadows and reflections lead away from rather than toward the truth. Aristotle, on the other hand, argued that poetry is more philosophical than history, because it is about universals rather than particulars, the probable rather than the actual (Janko 1987).

In the classical period, when the arts were thought of as arts of imitation, art works could be a means to knowledge in a very straightforward way: If a painting of Napoleon's Coronation is an imitation or representation of the coronation, then it can inform the world at large that Napoleon has been crowned emperor, what the event looked like, and how important it was. The absolute Idealists, however, made far weightier claims for art: For them it was a mode of knowledge of absolute Spirit. Shorn of its idealist underpinnings this idea can be seen to be a variety of a very old idea: that the artist is a special person with special insight into reality. In the Romantic period, when the arts were thought of as expressions of the artist's attitudes and emotions, the knowledge art works could be expected to provide was knowledge of the emotions, both the artist's and our own. The artist worked out his emotions for us in such a way that we can recreate them in imagination and thereby arrive at self-knowledge.

Current theories about the cognitive value of art are less ambitious. The tendency is to emphasize that works of art are not the best conduits for propositional scientific knowledge, but that they can teach us in other ways. Goodman stressed how paintings, sculptures, films and the other visual arts can teach us to become more adept at making perceptual discriminations of various kinds (Goodman 1976). Literary works in particular have often been thought to provide us with moral knowledge, knowledge of moral truths that can be expressed in propositional terms, as well as knowledge of how to live, how to balance different goods, how to treat one's friends and how to make moral decisions. Novels, films, plays and short stories are thought to be tailor-made to educate our emotions and teach us moral values (Nussbaum 1990, Robinson 2005). On the other hand, if we try to abstract what moral truths are taught by a great work of literature, the best we can often come up with is some banality that may not even be true: *King Lear* teaches us that love is exhibited in deeds, not words, *Anna Karenina* that misery ensues if you abandon your husband and children.

ART AND EMOTION

Goodman has suggested that in our appreciation of art works, the emotions function cognitively. This is an idea first found in Aristotle, who argues that the goal of tragedy is to evoke a catharsis of pity and fear. Although the meaning of "catharsis" has been much debated, nowadays it is usually thought to imply that the evocation of pity and fear is an aid to understanding, not just a fortuitous accompaniment of the tragedy. Aristotle is replying to Plato's denunciation of the art of tragedy as evoking emotions that weaken the moral fiber.

Goodman's idea is more general than Aristotle's. It suggests that understanding any kind of art work may be accomplished in part by having our emotions aroused. For example, feeling surprised, bewildered, and finally relieved by the way the themes and harmonies behave in a piece of music may alert us to the form or structure of the piece (Meyer 1956). Having our emotions aroused by the gradual unfolding of the plot of a novel may draw our attention to important structural high points. But in the literary case our emotions may also help us to understand not just the works of art themselves but also something of life itself. In responding sympathetically to how the characters are feeling and responding and what the significance of their various situations is, we learn what it is like to be in various unfamiliar situations. Responding sympathetically to characters in a novel can give us practice in understanding other people in real life (Feagin 1996, Carroll 2001). More generally, imaginative engagement with works of literature, film, painting and so on can broaden our imaginative horizons.

The Expression Theory insists that art works do not merely arouse emotions in audiences but also express emotions themselves. This means that an art work can contain a point of view or attitude that gets articulated in the work (Robinson 2005), as, for example, Wordsworth's famous poem articulates the emotions of a stranger, a wanderer, who feels "lonely as a cloud," but becomes happy when he comes across a joyous crowd of daffodils. Paintings too can contain such emotional points of view, for example Monet's *The Seine in Thaw*, painted after the death of his wife Camille, which Wollheim sees as an expression of mourning (Wollheim 1987).

ART AND VALUE

Views about the value of art vary depending on what the essential features of art are taken to be (Budd 1995). For formalists, the value of art is likely to be purely aesthetic, the provision of aesthetic pleasure or aesthetic emotion (Bell 1914). Expression theorists value the arts for their ability to articulate the artist's emotions (Collingwood 1938, Dewey 1934) or to communicate emotions from one person to another (Tolstoy 1960). Cognitive theories of art stressing the meaning and interpretation of art works stress the cognitive values of art, its ability to improve our perceptual and emotional awareness of the world (Goodman 1976, Langer 1953). Of these kinds of value, aesthetic value seems to be a genuinely intrinsic value and a value intrinsic to art. Increased understanding and improved communication among people are no doubt intrinsic goods also, but they are not unique to the arts. By contrast, theories of art that define art in terms of its cultural context or the institutions that surround it do not seem to explain why art has value.

One problem that has been much discussed returns us to the origins of aesthetic theory in the eighteenth century. The question is whether the aesthetic value of the arts includes other sorts of value. Most thinkers on the subject have rejected the idea that monetary value has any bearing on aesthetic value, and most have also distinguished between the aesthetic value of an artwork and its value as a historical or archeological document. But there is no clear consensus on whether the value of art includes moral value, or whether we should keep a sharp divide between the realms of the moral and the aesthetic (Lamarque and Olsen 1994, Gaut 1998). Those who think that art works are primarily designed to provide aesthetic

experiences (Beardsley 1958, Iseminger 2004), are more likely to think that moral value is irrelevant to aesthetic value. But to those who think that the arts are rich repositories of values of all sorts, including cognitive and emotional values (Goldman 1995), moral value will be just one more source of artistic value in a work.

See also Aesthetic Experience; Aesthetic Judgment; Aesthetic Qualities; Aesthetics, History of; Aristotle; Art, Value in; Batteux, Abbe Charles; Baumgarten, Alexander Gottlieb; Beardsley, Monroe C.; Beauty; Collingwood, Robin George; Continental Philosophy; Danto, Arthur; Dewey, John; Empiricism; Enlightenment; Feminist Aesthetics and Criticism; Goodman, Nelson; Hegel, Georg Wilhelm Friedrich; Hume, David; Hutcheson, Francis; Kant, Immanuel; Neoplatonism; Plato; Plotinus; Rationalism; Renaissance; Romanticism; Schopenhauer, Arthur; Sibley, Frank; Wittgenstein, Ludwig Josef Johann; Wollheim, Richard.

Bibliography

Barthes, Roland. *S/Z*. Translated by Richard Miller. New York: Farrar, Straus and Giroux, 1974.

Batteux, Abbé Charles. *Les Beaux-Arts réduits à un même principe* (1746). Geneva: Slatkine Reprints, 1969.

Baumgarten, Alexander. *Meditationes philosophicae de nonnulis ad poema pertinentilous*. Halle, 1735. Translated by K. Aschenbrenner and W. Holther as *Reflections on Poetry*. Berkeley: University of California Press, 1954.

Beardsley, Monroe C. *Problems in the Philosophy of Criticism*. New York: Harcourt, Brace, 1958.

Bell, Clive. *Art*. London: Chatto and Windus, 1914.

Budd, Malcolm. "The Aesthetics of Nature." *Proceedings of the Aristotelian Society* 100 (1996): 137–157.

Budd, Malcolm. *Values of Art: Painting, Poetry, and Music*. London: Penguin, 1995.

Burke, Edmund. *On the Sublime and Beautiful*, edited by Charles W. Eliot. New York: P.F. Collier, 1909.

Carlson, Allen. *The Aesthetics of the Environment: The Appreciation of Nature, Art and Architecture*. London: Routledge, 2000.

Carroll, Noël. *Beyond Aesthetics: Philosophical Essays*. Cambridge, U.K.: Cambridge University Press, 2001.

Carroll, Noël. *The Philosophy of Horror, or Paradoxes of the Heart*. New York: Routledge, 1990.

Collingwood, R. G. *The Principles of Art*. Oxford: Oxford University Press, 1938.

Currie, Gregory. *The Nature of Fiction*. Cambridge, U.K.: Cambridge University Press, 1990.

Danto, Arthur. "The Artworld." *Journal of Philosophy* 61 (1964): 571–584.

Danto, Arthur. *The Transfiguration of the Commonplace*. Cambridge, MA: Harvard University Press, 1981.

Davies, Stephen. *Musical Meaning and Expression*. Ithaca, NY: Cornell University Press, 1994.

Davies, Stephen. *Musical Works and Performances: A Philosophical Exploration*. Oxford: Oxford University Press, 2001.

Derrida, Jacques. *Of Grammatology*. Translated by Gayatri Chavrakorty Spivak. Baltimore: Johns Hopkins University Press, 1974.

Dewey, John. *Art as Experience*. New York: Putnam, 1934.

Dickie, George. *The Art Circle*. New York: Haven, 1984.

Eco, Umberto. *Art and Beauty in the Middle Ages*. Translated by Hugh Bredin. New Haven, CT: Yale University Press, 1986.

Feagin, Susan. *Reading with Feeling*. Ithaca, NY: Cornell University Press, 1996.

Gaut, Berys. "The Ethical Criticism of Art." In *Aesthetics and Ethics: Essays at the Intersection*, edited by Jerrold Levinson, 182–203. Cambridge, U.K.: Cambridge University Press, 1998.

Goldman, Alan H. *Aesthetic Value*. Boulder, CO: Westview, 1995.

Gombrich, Ernst. *Art and Illusion*. London: Phaidon, 1960.

Goodman, Nelson. *Languages of Art*. Indianapolis, IN: Hackett, 1976.

Greenberg, Clement. *The Collected Essays and Criticism*. 2 vols. Chicago: University of Chicago Press, 1986.

Hegel, G.W. F. *Vorlesungen über die Ästhetik*. Berlin: 1835. Translated by T. M. Knox as *Lectures on Fine Art*. 2 vols. Oxford: Oxford University Press, 1975.

Hospers, John. "The Concept of Artistic Expression." *Proceedings of the Aristotelian Society* 55 (1954–1955): 313–344.

Hume, David. *Essays, Moral, Political, and Literary*, edited by Eugene F. Miller. Indianapolis: Liberty Classics, 1985.

Hutcheson, Francis. *An Inquiry concerning Beauty, Order, Harmony, Design*, edited by Peter Kivy. The Hague: Martinus Nijhoff, 1973.

Iseminger, Gary. *The Aesthetic Function of Art*. Ithaca, NY: Cornell University Press, 2004.

Iser, Wolfgang. *The Act of Reading: A Theory of Aesthetic Response*. London: Routledge and Kegan Paul, 1978.

Janko, R. *Aristotle: Poetics* Indianapolis, IN: Hackett, 1987.

Kant, Immanuel. *Critique of the Power of Judgment*, edited by P. Guyer. Translated by P. Guyer and E. Matthews. Cambridge, U.K.: Cambridge University Press, 2000.

Kivy, Peter. *Music Alone*. Ithaca, NY: Cornell University Press, 1990.

Kivy, Peter. *Philosophies of Arts: An Essay in Differences*. Cambridge, U.K.: Cambridge University Press, 1997.

Kristeller, Paul. "The Modern System of the Arts." *Journal of the History of Ideas* 12 (1951–1952): 496–527; *Journal of the History of Ideas* 13 (1951–1952): 17–46.

Lamarque, Peter. *Fictional Points of View*. Ithaca, NY: Cornell University Press, 1996.

Lamarque, Peter, and Stein Haugom Olsen. *Truth, Fiction, and Literature*. Oxford: Clarendon, 1994.

Levinson, Jerrold. *Music, Art, and Metaphysics*. Ithaca, NY: Cornell University Press, 1990.

Levinson, Jerrold. *The Pleasures of Aesthetics*. Ithaca, NY: Cornell University Press, 1996.

Margolis, Joseph. *What, After All, Is a Work of Art?* University Park: Pennsylvania State University Press, 1999.

Meyer, Leonard B. *Emotion and Meaning in Music*. Chicago: University of Chicago Press, 1956.

Nussbaum, Martha. *Love's Knowledge*. Oxford: Oxford University Press, 1990.

Plato. *Dialogues*. Translated by B. Jowett. Oxford: Clarendon, 1953.

Robinson, Jenefer. *Deeper than Reason: Emotion and its Role in Literature, Music, and Art*. Oxford: Oxford University Press, 2005.

Ross, Stephanie. *What Gardens Mean*. Chicago: University of Chicago Press, 1998.

Schopenhauer, Arthur. *The World as Will and Representation*. Translated by E. F. J. Payne. Indian Hills, CO: Falcon's Wing Press, 1958.

Sibley, Frank. "Aesthetic Concepts." *Philosophical Review* 68 (1959): 421–450.

Sparshott, Francis. *The Theory of the Arts*. Princeton, NJ: Princeton University Press, 1982.

Stecker, Robert. *Interpretation and Construction: Art, Speech, and the Law*. Oxford: Blackwell, 2003.

Stolnitz, Jerome. *Aesthetics and the Philosophy of Criticism*. Boston: Houghton Mifflin, 1960.

Tolstoy, Leo. *What Is Art?* Translated by Almyer Maude. Indianapolis: Bobbs-Merrill, 1960.

Walton, Kendall. *Mimesis as Make-Believe*. Cambridge, MA: Harvard University Press, 1990.

Walton, Kendall. "Transparent Pictures: On the Nature of Photographic Realism." *Critical Inquiry* 11 (1984): 246–277.

Weitz, Morris. "The Role of Theory in Aesthetics." *Journal of Aesthetics and Art Criticism* 15 (1956): 27–35.

Wollheim, Richard. *Art and Its Objects*. 2nd ed. Cambridge, U.K.: Cambridge University Press, 1980.

Wollheim, Richard. *Painting as an Art*. Princeton, NJ: Princeton University Press, 1987.

Wordsworth, William. Preface to *Lyrical Ballads*, edited by R. L. Brett and A. R. Jones. London: Methuen, 1963.

Jenefer Robinson (2005)

AFFIRMATIVE ACTION

Affirmative action is a policy applied in the United States and other countries that aims to enhance educational and career opportunities for minorities and women by granting them preferences in college and graduate school admissions, promotions, and contract awards. Its detractors argue that a policy of favoring some races and ethnic groups over others not only fosters resentments and unrest but also compromises educational and professional standards by considering race or ethnicity ahead of objective criteria of achievement and qualifications. But supporters of affirmative action maintain that it necessary to redress past injustices—in their view created in part by traditional forms of de facto affirmative action (such as university "legacy" admissions) that have benefited only privileged elites.

In the United States, the term "affirmative action" originally referred to a court order requiring companies that had engaged in illegal racial or sexual discrimination to compensate those they had wronged and to show that they planned to avoid future illegal discrimination. Although this ruling suggested that affirmative action was compensation for unjust discrimination, it could not explain why the main beneficiaries of affirmative action were young women and young African Americans who had not been discriminated against by the companies required to hire and promote them. Some defenders of affirmative action responded that women and African Americans were the victims of a generalized prejudice compounded by a legacy of slavery. But critics pointed out that it hardly followed that companies that had refrained from participating in the pervasive discrimination and prejudice were required to compensate its victims; these critics contended that although the slaves deserved compensation from their masters, it did not follow that the descendants of the slaves deserved compensation from the descendants of the masters.

The debate on these issues was lively, but it was never completely settled because affirmative action began to refer to policies that took race and sex into account in order to increase the number of women and racial minorities in universities and businesses, with no implication that the policies were justified because the universities and businesses had practiced illegal discrimination. The defense of affirmative action therefore came to emphasize future results as much as past injustices. One early argument was that affirmative action would reduce inequality; critics countered that although it might increase the number of blacks in the middle and upper classes, it might do little to reduce overall inequality.

The most popular current defense of affirmative action in higher education centers on the educational and cultural advantages of a racially and ethnically diverse student body; this rationale was introduced by Justice Lewis Powell in the 1978 *Regents of the University of California v. Bakke* decision. Writing for the majority, Justice Sandra Day O'Connor appealed to this argument in the *Grutter v. Bollinger* decision of 2003, but critics objected that the principle of strict scrutiny forbids the state from giving racial preference unless it demonstrates that they serve a compelling state interest, which, in their view, had not been demonstrated in these cases. Defenders of these decisions countered that states do indeed have an obvious and compelling interest in eliminating the racial subordination that would likely persist without some form of affirmative action. If these observers are right, the diversity argument for affirmative action may require supplementation with evidence that affirmative action is necessary to reduce racial subordination.

See also Racism; Social and Political Philosophy.

Bibliography

Anderson, Terry H. *The Pursuit of Fairness: A History of Affirmative Action.* Oxford: Oxford University Press, 2004.

Boxill, B. "The Morality of Preferential Hiring." *Philosophy and Public Affairs* 7 (1978): 248–263.

Boxill, B. "Affirmative Action in Higher Education." In *A Companion to the Philosophy of Education*, edited by Randall Curren, 593–604. Oxford, Blackwell Publishers, 2003.

Bowen, W., and D. Bok. *The Shape of The River.* Princeton: Princeton University Press, 1998.

Cohen, C., and James Sterba. *Affirmative Action and Racial Preference.* Oxford: Oxford University Press, 2003.

Dworkin, R. *Sovereign Virtue.* Cambridge, MA: Harvard University Press, 2000.

Ezorsky, G. *Racism and Justice: The Case for Affirmative Action.* Ithaca, NY: Cornell University Press, 1991.

Fullinwider R. *The Reverse Discrimination Controversy.* Lanham, MD: Rowman and Littlefield, 1980.

Hill, T. E., Jr. "The Message of Affirmative Action." *Social Philosophy and Policy* 8 (1991): 108–129.

Kershnar, S. "Are the Descendants of Slaves Owed Compensation For Slavery?" *Journal of Applied Philosophy* 16 (1999): 95–101.

McGary, H. *Race and Social Justice.* Malden, MA: Blackwell, 1999.

Mosley, A., and N. Capaldi. *Affirmative Action: Social Justice or Unfair Preference.* Lanham, MD: Rowman and Littlefield, 1996.

Nickel, J. 1975. "Preferential Policies in Hiring and Admissions: A Jurisprudential Approach." *Columbia Law Review* 75, 534–558

Roberts, R. "Why Have the Injustices Perpetrated against Blacks in America Not Been Rectified?" *Journal of Social Philosophy* 32 (2001): 357–373.

Sowell, Thomas. *Affirmative Action around the World: An Empirical Study.* New Haven: Yale University Press, 2004.

Thomson, J. "Preferential Hiring." *Philosophy and Public Affairs* 2 (1973): 364–384.

Thomas, L. "What Good Am I?" In *Affirmative Action and the University*, edited by S. Kahn, 125–131. Philadelphia: Temple University Press, 1993.

Wasserstrom, R. "The University and the Case for Preferential Treatment." *American Philosophical Quarterly* 13 (1976): 165–170.

Bernard R. Boxill (2005)

AFRICAN PHILOSOPHY

Many of the greatest thinkers of the modern era, including David Hume, Immanuel Kant, and Thomas Jefferson, considered Africans and their descendants to be so intellectually handicapped as to make them philosophical invalids, incapable of moral and scientific reasoning. Thus, prior to the twentieth century, the idea of African Philosophy was, for most educated Europeans and Americans, an oxymoron (Eze 1997, pp. 4–5).

Moreover, the notion of African philosophy was provocative (in a way that the notion of British or French or German or Chinese philosophy was not) because the cultures of sub-Sahara Africa had no indigenous written languages in which issues were traditionally discussed and examined. Other than the Egyptians and Ethiopians, most African cultures developed a written script only in response to Islamic and European influences. Following the model of European and North American philosophy, one group of contemporary African philosophers has contended that philosophy requires a tradition of written communication, and that African cultures must evolve beyond traditional conceptions expressed in oral forms if they are to develop the levels of critical exchange required for sophisticated scientific and philosophical activities (Wiredu in Mosley 1995, pp. 160–169; Hountoundji 1983, p. 106). But others have argued that African philosophy should be sought in the values, categories, and assumptions that are implicit in the language, rituals, and beliefs of traditional African cultures. In this view, African philosophy is a form of ethnophilosophy—such as ethnobiology and ethnopharmacology—one of the many subject areas of ethnology.

AFRICAN PHILOSOPHY AS ETHNOPHILOSOPHY

One of the principal sources of African ethnophilosophy was the French philosopher Lucien Levy-Bruhl (1857–1939). Levy-Bruhl taught at the Sorbonne from 1896 to 1927 and was one of the leading ethnologists of his era. He argued that the primary concepts, causal relationships, and modes of reasoning used by non-European people were not the result of scripts developed through academic exercises to conform to the laws of Aristotelian logic. Rather, they were "collective representations" inculcated during rites and rituals as a result of intense affective and psychomotor experiences. The concepts of non-European people were felt rather than understood, mystical rather intellectual, and mediated relationships between both physical and nonphysical modes of being. Every event had not only a physical but a "mystical" significance, and the connections between physical and mystical realities were governed by "laws of participation" that transcended the laws of logic that structured thought

in European cultures. In contrast to the law of the excluded middle and the law of noncontradiction, these "laws of participation" allowed things to be both themselves and something else, to be "here" and not here, and to exist both in the present and in the future. Medicine, magic, witchcraft, divination, and communication with the dead were made possible through mystical forces apprehended through "laws of participation" that could not be reduced to "rational explanations" structured by the laws of logic.

In *Bantu Philosophy* (1945), Father Placide Tempels proposed to articulate the structure of reality implicit in traditional African culture. For Tempels, the basic difference between European and African views of reality was ontological. Whereas the basic constituents of reality in European civilization tended to be things with fixed natures (atoms, minds, bodies), the basic constituents of reality in traditional African cultures were dynamic forces. These forces were organized hierarchically into divine, celestial, terrestrial, animal, plant, mineral (including fire, water, and air), and human forces. Good and evil were made manifest in the use of these forces to amplify or diminish the vitality of human beings. Through medicine, witchcraft, sorcery, and divination, certain individuals were able to manipulate these forces to the benefit or detriment of their communities.

Temple's analysis reflected in many respects the Sapir-Whorf thesis that the structure of a culture's language shapes the way that culture structures reality. In his book Whorf argued that the structure of Native-American languages such as Hopi gave rise to an ontology of fields and forces, whereas the structure of Indo-European languages gave rise to an ontology of discrete things. From this point of view, philosophical principles were implicit in the structure of the language, beliefs, and practices of a culture, whether or not they were stated explicitly by any member of that culture. Tempel's analysis was extended and refined by Father Alexis Kagame of Rwanda and by the Belgian ethnographer Jahnhein Janz.

In his influential book, *African Religions and Philosophy* (1969), Professor John Mbiti elaborated the view that implicit in African cultures were different concepts of causality, time, and personhood. Every event had both a physical and a spiritual cause, traceable to the influence of a continuum of spiritual beings (consisting of the living, the ancestral dead, deities, and God). Key to understanding this African metaphysic was a concept of time that consisted of an endless past (the *Zamani*), a living present (the *Sasa*), and a truncated future that returned to the past. Those who had recently died continue to interact with the living for as long as they were remembered, and then they too returned to the *Zamani*.

One of the major expressions of philosophy as ethnology was *negritude*, a principal exponent of which was Leopold Senghor. Senghor argued that Africans have a distinctive approach to reality in which knowledge is based on emotion rather than logic, where the arts are privileged over the sciences, and where sensual participation is encouraged over cerebral analysis. For Senghor, the European analyzes reality from an objective distance whereas the African embraces reality by participating in it aesthetically and spiritually. This difference between African and European cultures was, for Senghor, physiologically based and inherited (Senghor 1962). However, for Aime Cesaire, the other principal exponent of negritude, though the differences between African and European cultures were real, they resulted primarily from historical circumstances rather than biological differences (Arnold 1981, p. 37).

Whether biologically, culturally, or historically determined, many have claimed that the African contribution to civilization was invaluable because it was unique and peculiar to Africans. Nationalists in Africa and in the diaspora—Edward Blyden, Martin Delany, Alexander Crummell, Ndabaningi Sithole, Kwame Nkrumah, Alex Quaison-Sackey, and Leopold Senghor—denied that the African was a degenerate form of the European, and instead held that Africans as a race embodied capacities and potentialities that were different from but equal to those of Europeans. Pan-African nationalists typically held that abolition of the slave trade, slavery, colonialism, and the return of Africans in the diaspora to Africa would reverse the paralyzing effect of European imperialism and make it possible for Africans to develop their peculiar contributions to the evolution of civilization. Africans who chose to remain in the diaspora nonetheless had an obligation to focus inward to develop their peculiar talents so as to address their peculiar problems, rather than looking to Europe for ideas and solutions. From a nationalist perspective, African philosophy should be concerned with articulating those factors that distinguish the African worldview. This orientation rejects the European Enlightenment focus on universal standards of reason, religion, and political development, relative to which every other culture was to be measured. Among European philosophers, it drew its support from Johann Herder, who championed a kind of cultural pluralism that encouraged each race or ethnic group to develop a national character that reflected its peculiar linguistic, historical, and cultural heritage.

CRITICISMS OF AFRICAN ETHNOPHILOSOPHY

Many critics of ethnophilosophy deny that the basis of African philosophy should be sought in the structure of traditional African culture, and tend to favor the more universalist outlook of the European Enlightenment. For Kwasi Wiredu, the development of philosophy in Africa should parallel the development of philosophy in Europe, and traditional African thought should not be considered the principal source of contemporary African philosophy any more than traditional European thought (of the Celtic and Nordic variety) is considered the primary source of contemporary European philosophy. Wiredu is critical of the tendency to preserve traditional beliefs and practices even when they have little rational justification or practical utility. He stresses the need to develop written modes of communication, arguing that literacy is a necessary condition of the transition from a prescientific to a scientific world view. In his view, it is likely that literacy will have as great an impact on the oral cultures of Africa as it had on the oral cultures of premodern Europe.

The fight against colonialism in Africa gave rise to many activists—such as Julius Nyerere, Kenneth Kaunda, Sekou Toure, and Leopold Senghor—who used philosophy for political purposes. But for the critics of ethnophilosophy, postcolonial philosophy in Africa is the era of the professional philosopher, whose interests have been formatively shaped by training in the European philosophical tradition. For the professional philosopher, just because something may have developed by Europeans is no argument against its proving useful for Africans. African philosophers have a pivotal responsibility to domesticate the products of European thought into materials usable by Africans both on the continent and in the diaspora.

But defenders of the professionalization of contemporary African philosophy are also critical of the tendency to automatically reject traditional African institutions and beliefs in favor of modern European ones. A central function of postcolonial African philosophy should be "conceptual decolonization," which means avoiding or reversing the unexamined assimilation of European ideas by African people. The necessity of a decolonization of the African mind derives from the imposition on Africa of foreign conceptual schemes through the mediums of language, religion, and politics. Wiredu, along with Kwame Gyekye (1995, 1997), Marcien Towa, and others, stress that the professional African philosopher must be prepared to utilize indigenous sources of wisdom when they offer viable insights and options. Only by the critical assessment of both modern and traditional sources will Africa develop cultural variants that are not the result of the indiscriminate acceptance of either.

Thus, Wiredu defends professional African philosophers from the charge of inauthenticity, and challenges them with two important responsibilities: domesticating European ideas and adapting them to African needs; and reconstructing traditional African ideas so they are relevant to contemporary problems. With his colleague, Kwame Gyekye, the procedure he suggests for domesticating European ideas is that of translating European ideas into an indigenous African language. If an issue addressed in European languages (e.g., the mind-body problem) makes no sense when translated into one's indigenous African language, then it is likely to be an issue that is peculiar to its European origins, and may produce more problems than it solves when applied within the African context. But one must recognize that this test of relevancy is problematic. For given the multiplicity of languages in Africa, even within a single modern nation state, it is questionable whether what does not make sense in one African language (e.g., Akan, Ga) will also not make sense in other African languages (e.g., Xhosa, Zulu). And what of Africans in the diaspora, whose indigenous language is English or French or Portuguese?

UNAMISM

One of the chief criticisms of the ethnophilosophical approach to African Philosophy is its tendency to treat African cultures as if they all must have some essential feature in common. Paulin Hountoundji (1983, 2002) rejects the contention that there is some unarticulated collective philosophy imbedded within folk beliefs that all Africans adhere to, a view he calls "unamism." Too often, he argues, ethnophilosophers intentionally or unintentionally reconstruct traditional beliefs according to categories provided by Europeans to advance European interests. Thus, Hountoundji claims, Tempels' analysis was made in order to help European colonialists devise better ways to rule the Bantu people. The intent was to benefit not Africans, but Europeans. Likewise, it was European racists who characterized Africans as being ruled by their emotions, incapable of logical thought or the ability to effectively plan for the future. Valorizing these traits as definitive of traditional African cultures simply plays into the hands of the racists. In contrast, Hountoundji argues that African philosophy must be a

critical literature produced by Africans for Africans. And philosophy, like science, must be a process of continual self-examination and critical reflection that requires a tradition of literacy. Only if ideas are recorded can energy be focused on assessing them rather than merely recalling them (Hountoundji 1983).

APPROACHES TO AFRICAN PHILOSOPHY

Whereas Wiredu and Hountoundji construe literacy as essential to the practice of African philosophy, others such as Odera Oruka (1990), Kwame Gyekye, and J. O. Sodipo insist that active engagement in critical reflection on the beliefs and practices of one's culture is a requirement sufficient for that culture to have a tradition of philosophy. From their perspective, African sages that critically reflect on the assumptions of their culture are just as much philosophers as was Socrates. Thus, one may legitimately consider proverbs to be the result of critical reflection in traditional African thought, their purpose being to provide, not a scripted system of abstract rules, but a situational model to guide concrete action. If one follows the orientation of traditional thought, Godwin Sogolo argues, the point of African philosophy would be more to guide people in how they should interact with the world rather than to provide them with a true understanding of it. Odera Oruka's conversations with Luo sages, Hallen and Sodipo's (1986) conversations with Yoruba Babalawo, and Marcel Griaule's conversations with Ogotemmeli show them to be individuals with levels of critical wisdom comparable to that of Socrates.

THE NATIONALIST-IDEOLOGICAL APPROACH. Another approach to African philosophy may be characterized as nationalist-ideological, hermeneutical, or liberationist. Its exponents would include Tsenay Serequeberhan, Franz Fanon, Kwame Nkrumah, Julius Nyerere, Amical Cabral, W. E. B. Dubois, Chubba Okadigbo, and Wamba Dia Wamba. In this approach, philosophy takes the lived experience of African people as its starting point, and the lived experience of most Africans revolves around a struggle to cope with the omnipresent effects of European colonialism and neo-colonialism. As such, the principle objective of African philosophy must be how to achieve liberation from the injuries imposed by European imperialism. Traditional beliefs are not valuable in themselves, but have merit in modern Africa only to the extent that they contribute to this end. A focus on the past as the source of authenticity diverts attention from the regressive nature of many beliefs and practices, and detracts from a critical posture that evaluates all practices, both traditional and modern, of both African and European origin, relative to their contribution to the liberation of Africa. African philosophy must address the fact that many traditional leaders were installed by European imperialists as mere mouthpieces of colonial rule, and many contemporary African leaders have remained neocolonial puppets, even as they have appropriated the symbols of traditional Africa with the power of the modern state.

In addressing the question of liberation, a central question for many African philosophers is the relative importance of race versus class. Many see race to be as or more important than class in the struggle for African liberation, and they doubt whether the white proletariat will abandon the privileges of white supremacy in order to form a united front with people of color. A case in point is the apartheid regime of South Africans, where poor whites who considered themselves Africans nonetheless insisted on privileges over black Africans. Even when race is secondary, the effects of colonial rule continue to divide Africans along tribal lines. Thus where Africans have replaced Europeans in neocolonial states, it is often tribal differences among Africans that is a source of current problems. As Kwame Gyekye (1997) points out, loyalty to family and tribal affiliations tends to breed nepotism, graft, and corruption when fostered by neocolonial ties. For Franz Fanon, racism was simply a way of justifying oppression by insisting on the inferiority of the oppressed. Africans would gain a sense of agency, he argued, only when, through struggle, they overcame the false separations of race and tribe introduced by colonialism. Africans must devise, through their own initiative, the means to liberate themselves (Fanon 1963). Cabral argued that this would require urban intellectuals to "return to the source" and form alliances with the agricultural peasantry in the fight for freedom from colonialism and neocolonialism. (Cabral 1979)

AFROCENTRISM. Afrocentricism is built around the claim that Black Africa's contributions to world culture have been denied in order to further a racist agenda. Afrocentrists take as their patron Cheik Anta Diop, who argued that Egypt was an African culture, and its achievements in science, mathematics, architecture, and philosophy were the basis for the flowering of classical Greek civilization. That the ancient Egyptians were black Africans was freely acknowledged in the ancient world but was denied and misrepresented by modern Europeans in order to justify racism, slavery, and colonialism. Diop uses language, rituals, and practices to trace the ori-

gins of the major sub-Saharan African cultures to ancient Egyptian civilization. As such, he denies that Africans are "naturally" more oriented towards the arts than to science and technology. Rather, he claims that European imperialism in the modern era impoverished Africa's resources and stifled it's scientific, technological, and political development. The imposition by Europe of a patriarchal ethical and social structure on an African orientation that was traditionally matriarchal further distorted Africa's social and political development.

THE PROBLEM WITH RACE. Kwame Appiah has mounted a sustained attack on the view that African philosophy should express the peculiar orientation of the African race. He argues in *In My Father's House* (1992) that, before their contact with Europeans beginning in the fifteenth century, people on the African continent did not view themselves as members of the same race. The notion of the African race was invented by Europeans to justify a generic form of continental oppression. Moreover, Appiah has argued that people should reject the notion of race because there is no biological or cultural basis for dividing humankind into races: there is more variation, he claims, both biologically and culturally, among those characterized as Africans than there is between the average African and European. Thus, the Pan-African ideal of uniting all members of the African race, both on the continent and in the diaspora, is flawed and is itself a form of "intrinsic racism." (Appiah 1992, p. 17) Attempts to identify some set of traits as the essence of the African race are misguided, whether the intent is to denigrate or valorize.

Appiah's views reflect a trend, since the end of WWII, of rejecting racism by rejecting the existence of races. However, within biology and anthropology this orientation is highly contentious. Many, including Diop, reject racial essentialism and racism but insist nonetheless that there are legitimate grounds for recognizing the existence of races. That Africa is the source of all humankind is one explanation for the huge range of variation among its people, who are moreover united by a history of super exploitation and denigration.

THE FEMINIST PERSPECTIVE European philosophy has typically assumed that the interest of males represents the interest of the species, just as it has assumed that European philosophy is the standard for judging all other attempts to do philosophy. Thus, given similar histories of struggling against domination, many feminist philosophers have shared with Africans and African Americans an interest in deconstructing traditional philosophical methods and assumptions so as to expose implicit agendas of domination. Ifa Amadiume (1997) has elaborated Diop's contention that precolonial Africa was primarily matriarchal, but moves beyond Diop to stress the advantages of small political units such as the family and village over large political units such as nations and empires. Other African feminists not only deny that traditional African societies followed the European paradigm of privileging men over women but also consider patriarchy and matriarchy to be European categories imposed to configure Africa on a European standard.

Africa has had its biggest cultural impact on the direction of contemporary European culture, not in the sciences, but in the arts. African sculpture, painting, music, and dance have radically influenced the development of modern European art forms and aesthetic values. But traditional African art forms have differed from modern European art forms in several important respects. Modern art is often displayed in museums as objects to be viewed, not touched. But traditional African art played functional roles in addressing practical realities, and Beauty resided as much in what something did as in how it looked. Music and dance were activities to be participated in, not simply perceived from a distance, and they provided individuals with a model of how to situate themselves in a world in which they played an active role in creating.

The American feminist Sandra Harding has stressed the similarity between the struggle of Africans and the struggle of women against European male hegemony. Other American feminists have argued that values implicit in Africa's practice of the arts may help to develop a better appreciation of the ingredients of the ethical life and reinforce orientations that enhance people's ability to live together. In much of the European philosophical tradition, ethics involves the attempt to articulate principles that should guide and justify the choices one makes. But Cynthia Willett (1995) and Kathleen Higgins (1991) have attempted to ground ethical relationships in the music and dance traditions of the African aesthetic rather than in principles deriving from rational choice or compassionate care. In a similar vein stressing the importance of the aesthetic orientation in African philosophy, Richard Bell (2002) proposes that African philosophy should be conceived as embodied in narrative icons rather than verbal texts. These developments show how African philosophy should not be considered the exclusive domain of men, that it need not take science as its principal exemplar, and that one need not be African in order to address issues of central importance in African philosophy.

The domination of African states by repressive regimes of colonial and neocolonial tyrants has institutionalized violence throughout Africa and its diaspora. The Truth and Reconciliation tribunals of South Africa have provided a novel process for achieving justice. This approach recognizes that the purpose of seeking the truth concerning violence against the people is to seek atonement and reconciliation; and that this is something that is as much needed in dealing with crimes of Africans against Africans as in crimes of Europeans against Africans.

See also Aristotelianism; Enlightenment; Feminist Philosophy; Harding, Sandra; Herder, Johann Gottfried; Hermeneutics; Hume, David; Jefferson, Thomas; Kant, Immanuel; Lévy-Bruhl, Lucien; Mind-Body Problem; Multiculturalism; Racism; Socrates.

Bibliography

Amadiume, Ifa. *Reinventing Africa: Matriarchy, Religion, & Culture.* London: Zed Books, 1997.

Appiah, Kwame Anthony. *In My Father's House: Africa in the Philosophy of Culture.* New York: Oxford University Press, 1992.

Arnold, A. James. *Modernism and Negritude – The Poetry and Poetics of Aime Cesaire.* Cambridge, MA.: Harvard University Press, 1981.

Bell, Richard. *Understanding African Philosophy.* New York: Routledge, 2002.

Cabral, Amilcar. *Unity and Struggle.* New York: Monthly Review Press, 1979.

Diop, Cheikh Anta. *Civilization or Barbarism: An Authentic Anthropology.* Translated by Yaa-Lengi Meema Ngemi. Brooklyn, NY: Lawrence Hill Books, 1991.

English, Parker, and Kibujjo Kalumba, eds. *African Philosophy: A Classical Approach.* Englewood Cliffs, NJ: Prentice Hall, 1996.

Eze, Emmanuel Chukwudi, ed. *Postcolonial African Philosophy: A Critical Reader.* Cambridge, MA: Blackwell, 1997.

Eze, Emmanuel Chukwudi, ed. *Race and the Enlightment: A Reader.* Cambridge, MA: Blackwell Publishers, 1997.

Fanon, Franz. *The Wretched Of The Earth.* New York: Grove Press, 1963.

Gyekye, Kwame. *An Essay on African Philosophical Thought.* Philadelphia: Temple University Press, 1995.

Gyekye, Kwame. *Tradition and Modernity* Oxford: Oxford University Press, 1997.

Hallen, Barry, and J. O. Sodipo. *Knowledge, Belief, and Witchcraft.* London: Ethnographica Press, 1986.

Higgins, Kathleen. *The Music of Our Lives.* Philadelphia: Temple University Press, 1991.

Hountoundji, Paulin. *African Philosophy: Myth and Reality.* Bloomington: Indiana University Press, 1983.

Hountoundji, Paulin. *The Struggle for Meaning: Reflections on Philosophy, Culture, and Democracy in Africa*. Athens: Ohio University Press, 2002.

Masolo, D. A. *African Philosophy in Search of Identity*. Bloomington: Indiana University Press, 1994.

Mbiti, John. *African Religions and Philosophy*. London: Praeger Publishers, 1969.

Mosley, Albert, ed. *African Philosophy: Selected Readings* Englewood Cliffs, NJ: Prentice Hall, 1995.

Mutiso, Gideon-Cyrus, and S. W. Rohio. *Readings in African Political Thought*. London: Heinemann Educational Books, 1975.

Nkrumah, Kwame. *Neo-Colonialism: The Last Stage of Imperialism*. London: Nelson, 1965, 1965.

Nkrumah, Kwame. *Consciencism*. New York: Monthly Review Press, 1970.

Onyewumi, Oyeronke. *The Invention of Women*. Minneapolis: University of Minnesota Press, 1997.

Oruka, Henry Odera. *Sage Philosophy*. Leiden, Netherlands: Brill, 1990.

Senghor, Leopold, "On Negrohood: Psychology of the African Negro," *Diogenes*, Spring (1962), pp. 1–15.

Serequeberhan, Tsenay, ed. *African Philosophy: The Essential Readings*. New York: Paragon House, 1991.

Serequeberhan, Tsenay. *The Hermeneutics of African Philosophy*. New York: Routledge, 1994.

Tempels, Placide. *La philosophie bantoue* (Bantu philosophy). Elisabethville: Lovania, 1945. Paris: Presence Africaine, 1959.

Willett, Cynthia. *Maternal Ethics and Other Slave Moralities*. New York: Routledge, 1995.

Wiredu, Kwasi. *Conceptual Decolonization in African Philosophy: Four Essays*. Selected and Introduced by Olusegun Oladipo. Ibadan, Nigeria: Hope Publications, 1995.

Wiredu, Kwasi. "How Not to Compare African Thought with Western Thought." In *African Philosophy: Selected Readings*, edited by Albert Mosley. Englewood Cliffs, NJ: Prentice Hall, 1995.

Albert Mosley (2005)

AGAPE

See *Love*

AGENT CAUSATION

The concept of an agent's causing some event seems distinct from that of an event's causing another event, and this apparent distinctness has been exploited by some philosophers of action—agent causationists—to defend an incompatibilist and libertarian account of free will. Agent causationism is associated historically with, among others, the philosophers Francisco Suárez and Thomas Reid, and in more recent times has been defended by Richard Taylor and Roderick Chisholm.

AGENT CAUSATION AND EVENT CAUSATION

What is indisputable is that causal statements come in at least two forms, one in which a term denoting a person or persisting object is the subject of the verb *cause* and one in which a term denoting a particular event occupies this role. Compare, for example, "The bomb caused the collapse of the bridge" and "The explosion of the bomb caused the collapse of the bridge." Here it seems plausible to contend that the first of these statements is elliptical, meaning something such as "Some event involving the bomb caused the collapse of the bridge," and more generally that the causation of events by inanimate objects is always reducible to the causation of those events by other events involving those objects. However, it is less evident that this sort of analysis applies in cases in which a person or other intelligent agent is said to cause some event. Sentences containing transitive verbs of action generate many such cases, because an action sentence such as "John raised his arm" clearly entails a corresponding agent-causal sentence, "John caused a rising of his arm." What seems less clear is that the latter sentence entails an event-causal sentence, "Some event involving John caused a rising of his arm," at least on the assumption that John raised his arm as a so-called basic action.

A basic action is standardly taken to be one that is not done by doing anything else. An action such as closing a door is nonbasic, because one can only close a door by doing something to it, such as pushing it. It is possible to raise one's arm as a nonbasic action—for example, by pulling on a rope attached to the arm, using one's other arm. But, it seems, there is nothing one needs to do in order to raise one's arm when one raises it in the normal way. This appears to generate a difference between the case of the bomb's causing the collapse of the bridge and that of John's causing the rising of his arm: the bomb caused the collapse by exploding, but John, it seems, did not cause the rising by doing anything else. Consequently, it is not evident that there was any event involving John that could be said to have caused the rising in the way that the explosion of the bomb can be said to have caused the collapse of the bridge. In this case it appears that a statement of agent causation is not reducible to one of event causation.

Philosophers who favor a volitionist theory of action may dispute this suggestion. They may urge that there is in fact something that John did, and by doing this he raised his arm—on the assumption, at least, that he did so voluntarily. Namely, John willed to raise his arm. It was by willing to raise his arm that he did raise it, and so it might be said that the agent-causal statement, "John caused the rising of his arm," is true only in virtue of the truth of the event-causal statement, "John's willing to raise his arm caused the rising of his arm." However, volitionism is now a minority position in the philosophy of action—in contrast with its heyday in the seventeenth and eighteenth centuries—because many philosophers are skeptical about the existence of volitions as a supposedly distinctive class of mental events. Proponents of the irreducibility of agent causation to event causation may take comfort in this fact, although they still have to face another and more prevalent kind of critic: the proponents of mainstream causal theories of action. These critics contend that intentional actions have mental causes of another sort—the onsets of states of belief and desire. While these philosophers may concede that there is no action by doing which John caused his arm to rise, they still contend that there was an event involving John that caused the rising of his arm—to wit, the onset of his desire to raise it and, perhaps, his belief that by raising it he could achieve some further desired end. This event was not an action of John's, to be sure, but it was nonetheless an event involving him that, like the exploding of the bomb, seems to explain how the effect he caused was brought about.

AGENT CAUSATIONISM AND FREE WILL

Agent causationists—that is, philosophers who maintain the irreducibility of agent causation to event causation—are opposed to mainstream causal theories of action, not least because the latter seem inhospitable to libertarianism (the doctrine that free actions lack determining causes in the form of antecedent events which causally necessitate their occurrence). Proponents of such mainstream theories are typically compatibilists concerning the relationship between free will and determinism. Agent causationists, in contrast, standardly hold that certain events caused by agents are not caused by any antecedent events, or at least that these certain events lack sufficient causes in the form of antecedent events. Some agent causationists maintain that the events in question are bodily movements—such as the rising of an arm—when these are the products of basic actions. Others maintain, perhaps more plausibly, that the events in question are certain neural events that are the causal precursors of bodily movements. Yet others seek to combine

agent causationism with a form of volitionism by contending that what agents cause directly are their own volitions, choices, or endeavors. Thus, agent causationism is not necessarily opposed to volitionism, only to certain versions of it.

Common to all standard forms of agent causationism, however, is the doctrine that at least some cases of an agent A's causing an event e do not consist in e's being caused by any antecedent event involving A. This doctrine seems to help the case for libertarianism in the following way. The libertarian wants to say that in a case of free action, an event e occurs that lacks a sufficient cause in the form of antecedent events. But this prompts the objection that e would then be a mere chance event—such as the spontaneous decay of a radium atom—and as such would not exhibit the kind of freedom associated with an action for which an agent may be held morally responsible. The agent causationist may respond by urging that there is a significant difference between the decay of a radium atom and a case of free action because in the latter an event e occurs that, while lacking a sufficient cause in the form of antecedent events, still has a cause in the form of the agent whose action it is. A radium atom does not cause itself to decay, but a free human agent may cause him or herself to act in a certain way, according to agent causationism. Free agents, according to this conception, are unmoved movers or ultimate initiators of certain trains of events. And it is in having this capacity for initiation that their freedom allegedly lies, for it supposedly enables free agents to intervene in and affect the ongoing stream of events in which natural physical processes consist. Free agents' capacity for initiation is conceived to be a "two-way power"—a power either to cause or to refrain from causing an initial event of an appropriate kind.

OBJECTIONS TO AGENT CAUSATIONISM

Not surprisingly, agent causationism is subject to many criticisms—in particular from philosophers who advertise their own position as being "naturalistic"—and is charged with being mysterious and incompatible with the modern scientific worldview as revealed by physics and biology. More specifically, one popular objection is that agent causationism is committed to some form of substance dualism in the philosophy of mind, which in the eyes of most naturalistic philosophers would be enough to condemn it. However, whereas many agent causationists may in fact be substance dualists, it is not clear that their agent causationism requires them to be.

A more cogent objection to agent causationism, forcibly expressed by C. D. Broad, is that the agent causationist cannot explain why an event supposedly caused irreducibly by an agent should occur when it does (since agent-causes, unlike event-causes, are not datable items). The collapse of the bridge occurred when it did because the explosion, which was its cause, occurred when it did. But why should the many different events supposedly caused by a single agent during his or her lifetime have occurred when they did? One possible answer is that these events also have contributory causes in the form of antecedent events occurring at different times, even though each of them additionally requires causation by the agent for its occurrence. Another possible response, consistent with the first, is to appeal to temporal factors included in the agent's reasons for causing the various different events in question. (Agent causationists typically repudiate the doctrine that reasons are causes, and distinguish between reasons-explanations and causal explanations—or at least they deny that an agent's reasons, in the form of certain beliefs and desires of the agent, are part of a sufficient event-cause of the agent's action.)

Others may object that agent causationism does not really assist the case for libertarianism in the way it is alleged to for the following reason. Suppose, for the sake of argument, that instances of irreducible agent causation really do occur, and that sometimes it is the case that an agent A causes an event e in this irreducible fashion, while e lacks a sufficient cause in the form of antecedent events. It was suggested earlier that this still allows us to say that e was not just a chance event, because it was caused by A. However, what about the event of A's causing e? It would seem that this event must either possess or lack a sufficient cause in the form of antecedent events. If the former, then it is hard to see how libertarianism is saved. If the latter, then it would seem that A's causing e is itself just a chance event and so once again provides the wrong sort of freedom for moral responsibility.

Once more, various replies are available. One is simply to deny that A's causing e qualifies as an event and as such is something eligible to possess a cause. After all, it seems odd to think of one event's causing another as itself being an event, just as it may be deemed equally odd to think of an agent's causing an event as itself being an event. Another possible reply is that when there is an instance of agent causation—A's causing e—the agent A is not only the agent-cause of e but is also, by virtue of that fact, the agent-cause of this instance of agent causation. If this is the case, then the instance of agent causa-

tion is excluded from being a mere chance event for the same reason that the event e is thus excluded.

It does not appear, on close inspection, that there is anything incoherent in the notion of irreducible agent causation, but whether it really helps to solve the problem of free will and whether it is consistent with current scientific theories in physics and biology are questions that still remain open to further debate.

See also Action; Causation: Metaphysical Issues; Causation: Philosophy of Science; Chisholm, Roderick; Determinism and Freedom; Freedom; Libertarianism; Reid, Thomas; Suárez, Francisco.

Bibliography

Broad, C. D. "Determinism, Indeterminism, and Libertarianism." In *Ethics and the History of Philosophy: Selected Essays*. London: Routledge, 1952.

Chisholm, Roderick M. *Person and Object*. La Salle, IL: Open Court, 1976.

Clarke, Randolph. "Toward a Credible Agent-Causal Account of Free Will." *Noûs* 27 (1993): 191–203.

Danto, Arthur C. *Analytical Philosophy of Action*. Cambridge, U.K.: Cambridge University Press, 1973.

Kane, Robert, ed. *The Oxford Handbook of Free Will*. New York: Oxford University Press, 2002.

Lowe, E. J. "Personal Agency." In *Minds and Persons*, edited by Anthony O'Hear. Cambridge, U.K.: Cambridge University Press, 2003.

O'Connor, Timothy, ed. *Agents, Causes, and Events: Essays on Indeterminism and Free Will*. New York: Oxford University Press, 1995.

O'Connor, Timothy. *Persons and Causes: The Metaphysics of Free Will*. New York: Oxford University Press, 2000.

Reid, Thomas. *Essays on the Active Powers of the Human Mind*, edited by Baruch A. Brody. Cambridge, MA: MIT Press, 1969.

Suárez, Francisco. *On Efficient Causality: Metaphysical Disputations 17, 18, and 19*. Translated by Alfred J. Freddoso. New Haven, CT: Yale University Press, 1994.

Taylor, Richard. *Action and Purpose*. Englewood Cliffs, NJ: Prentice Hall, 1966.

Watson, Gary, ed. *Free Will*, 2nd ed. New York: Oxford University Press, 2003.

E. J. Lowe

AGENT INTELLECT, THE

In his *On the Soul*, iii 4–5, Aristotle wrote that there is one intellect that becomes all things and another that makes all things, just as light makes colors visible. It is separate, impassible, unmixed, and in essence activity; it alone is immortal and eternal. Those few statements are the basis of the theory of the agent intellect.

Aristotle was studied with intense and sometimes imaginative care by ancient and medieval scholars, and his ideas were developed to the extent of dominating thought about human thinking. Our concept arose in Greek but was developed in Arabic and flowered in medieval Latin; "agent intellect" is the English rendering of the Latin *intellectus agens*, but behind that lie a number of other terms. Furthermore, English writers have sometimes used active instead of agent.

The field falls into three parts: the Greek commentators on Aristotle, the Arabic philosophers who developed his views, and the medieval Europeans who built on the rest. Aristotle himself was sparing with technical terms, and the text of *On the Soul*, iii 4 and 5. is in a poor state that raises several questions. Later thinkers brought in material from earlier parts of *On the Soul* (i 4, ii 2); part of *On the Generation of Animals* (ii 3) in which Aristotle says that in humans the intellect (unqualified) comes into the fetus from outside (*thurathen*); passages from his ethics and his metaphysics, in which the intellect is regarded as in some sense divine; and the end of his *Posterior Analytics* (ii 19). The result is far from anything Aristotle can have held.

Aristotle's student Theophrastus raised pertinent questions about the agent intellect, reported, perhaps unreliably, by Themistius (c. 317–88), who himself studied Aristotle with care and ingenuity. He reports one early view—that the agent intellect was the body of premises and deductions that form knowledge—but dismisses it, as he does the view of Alexander of Aphrodisias (c. 200 CE), who held that the productive or active or agent *nous* (now identified with the *nous thurathen* that for Aristotle was a biological concept) was identical with the First God or the unmoved mover of *Metaphysics* XII 8. It is clear that there had been much discussion about this already, and already we see a tendency to the hypostatization of various intellects.

Themistius and Alexander together influenced Arabic thinkers. Most important are Avicenna (980–1047) and Averroes (1126–98). Avicenna had a theory of celestial intellects, derived from Neoplatonist views as well as Aristotle's metaphysics and psychology; for him the agent intellect was the tenth and lowest of a chain descending from the First Intellect, far removed from the human soul. More accessible was Averroes's view, which started from Aristotle's distinction between intellect as potential and as active or agent but went on to argue that the agent intellect was one and the same in all men, leading on to the question whether the potential intellect was also one and the same in all men. The Arabic philosophers were also interested in this intellect as the source of prophecy, and in the possible conjunction with it of the human reason.

Arabic works were translated into Latin by Western medieval scholars, so that Europe became aware of much of Aristotle and of his Arabic interpreters at almost the same time; in the thirteenth century it was taken for granted that the words *intellectus agens* stood for something definite, but there remained many questions about it. Albert the Great (c.1200–1280) introduced the Latin expression *intellectus agens*. He got to know the Arabic evidence and dealt with the fourfold distinction of agent, possible, acquired, and speculative intellects, which became the basis for later discussion.

In his time there was an Averroist school of thought, particularly in Padua, which troubled more orthodox thinkers; even Thomas Aquinas (1225–1274) wrote against them. In his extensive writings he worked out a theory aimed at satisfying both Aristotelians and Christian theologians. He quoted Aristotle to disprove his opponents' views, using the *Physics*, *On the Soul*, and Themistius, Avicenna, and others. He was primarily concerned with whether there was but a single intellect for all men and the subsidiary question about the agent and the receptive intellects. In his *Summa* he concentrates on the internal features of the intellect, and the agent is that which by its light abstracts species from images.

A single agent intellect would not secure individual immortality as required by Christianity, and when many Averroist doctrines were condemned by the Church in 1277, a number were about the Agent Intellect. An anonymous work from the early fourteenth century covers sixteen supposed views about the agent intellect from Plato (who is said to have denied its existence) through the Arabs to a number of others; the writer favors Thomas Aquinas. An array of arguments, partly from Aristotle but partly independent, is deployed. There are questions about the existence of the agent intellect, and again about whether there is one in each person or only one for all, as there is one light source illuminating all illuminated objects.

Even in the Renaissance the concept is found in the Averroism of Pomponazzi (1462–1525): in his *On the Immortality of the Soul* he doubted immortality, but, opposed by the Church, argued that philosophy could not prove anything in this area. Zabarella (1533–1589), a logician, also still spoke of the agent intellect as playing a part in induction. Finally, Aristotle's dominance came to an end, and his account of the intellect has been described recently as a museum piece. Instead of his metaphysical approach, a scientific psychology slowly developed, which was not interested in analyzing his actual words.

See also Aristotle; Averroes; Pomponazzi, Pietro; Thomas Aquinas, St.

Bibliography

Davidson, H Alfarabi. *Avicenna and Averroes on Intellect.* Oxford: Oxford University Press 1992.

Huby, P. M. "Stages in the Development of Language about Aristotle's Nous." In Blumenthal and Robinson, *Aristotle and the Later Tradition.* OSAP suppl. vol.. Oxford: Oxford University Press 1991, 129–143.

Kuksewicz, Z. "The Potential and the Agent Intellect." In *Cambridge History of Later Medieval Philosophy.* Cambridge, U.K.: Cambridge University Press, 1982.

Kurfess, H. *Zur Geschichte der Erklärung der Aristotelischen Lehre vom sog. NOUS POIHTIKOS und PAQHTIKOS.* Tübingen, 1911. Reprinted in *Aristotle and His Influence,* edited by L. Taran. New York and London: Garland, 1987.

Pamela M. Huby (2005)

AGNOSTICISM

In the most general use of the term, "agnosticism" is the view that we do not know whether there is a God or not. Although the history of agnosticism, in this general sense, is continuous with that of skepticism (thus reaching back to the ancients), the term itself was coined by T. H. Huxley and its distinctive philosophical bearings emerged in the course of the nineteenth-century debate on religious belief. Participants in that debate often used the word in a strong and specific sense: To be an agnostic was to hold that knowledge of God is impossible because of the inherent, insuperable limitations of the human mind. To assert confidently either the existence or the nonexistence of a deity with definite and intelligible attributes was to transgress these limits.

This consciousness of limitation is classically expressed in the "Transcendental Dialectic" of Immanuel Kant's *Critique of Pure Reason* (1781). There is a continual temptation, Kant stated, to raise questions about the totality of things; but these questions, he argued, are demonstrably unanswerable. Contradictions are encountered, for instance, whether it is assumed that the world is finite in space and time or infinite in space and time. Or, in another instance, one event may properly be called the cause of another event, but such a concept cannot be used to assert that something (a First Cause) is the cause of the

universe as a whole. Of this "whole" one has, and can have, no experience. The main line of agnostic argument in the nineteenth century followed Kant closely in his criticism of cosmological reasoning, although many agnostic writers were not thoroughgoing Kantians. Nor did they have to be Humeans to have their metaphysical assurance called in question by David Hume's famous (or notorious) criticism of speculation in *An Enquiry concerning Human Understanding* (1748): "If we take in our hand any volume; of divinity or school metaphysics, for instance; let us ask, *Does it contain any abstract reasoning concerning quantity or number?* No. *Does it contain any experimental reasoning concerning matter of fact and existence?* No. Commit it then to the flames: for it can contain nothing but sophistry and illusion."

A person who calls himself agnostic commonly judges that he cannot have both agnosticism and, say, Christian belief. Yet the main positions of nineteenth-century agnosticism were in fact worked out and held by "religious agnostics," writers who argued that a very high degree of ignorance concerning the deity was nonetheless compatible with a religious commitment of some kind. In fact, if not in name, this view was also found in the twentieth century; it is essentially the view of those who disclaim metaphysical knowledge of God, but yet stake all upon "faith," "authority," or Christianity as a practical way of life. Kant may again provide the archetypal model: Having denied that theoretical reasoning could furnish arguments for the existence of God, he nevertheless claimed that God had to be "postulated" in order to make sense of moral experience.

In his most influential article, "Philosophy of the Unconditioned" (*Edinburgh Review,* 1829), Sir William Hamilton tersely introduced themes that were to be developed, refined, and repudiated by writer after writer to the end of the century and well beyond. "The mind," he wrote, "can … know only the *limited, and the conditionally limited.*" To attempt to think the unconditioned or absolute is to think away "those very conditions under which thought itself is realized." "Loath to admit that our science is at best the reflection of a reality we cannot know, we strive to penetrate to existence in itself; … But, like Ixion, we embrace a cloud for a divinity."

H. L. Mansel, in his Bampton Lectures, *The Limits of Religious Thought* (1858), tried to show in detail that alleged knowledge of the Absolute is self-contradictory at many points. One attributes personal qualities to God, for instance, and yet one cannot think through the notion of personality without the idea of limitation; thought must be distinguished from thinker, and so on. But limitation is incompatible with infinite and absolute deity. The conclusion, however, is not a total religious skepticism. For although speculation about the divine nature is a vain attempt to escape the inescapable conditions of human thought, yet through the "feeling of dependence" and in moral conviction faith may still operate where speculative reason cannot.

Herbert Spencer in his *First Principles* (1862) accepted this picture of a limited human reason, aware of its limits and yet (in his view) aware also that those limits are decidedly not the limits of the real. Science and religion could, in fact, be reconciled by realizing that each of them testifies to a mystery, to an inscrutable Absolute, quite beyond the frontiers of knowledge or conception but yet not mere negation or nothingness.

The sources of nineteenth-century agnosticism—particularly the agnosticism of those who abandoned organized religion—were, however, more numerous and complex than has been indicated so far. It is rare indeed that a single line of philosophical argument produces by itself either religious conviction or disillusionment. At least three additional sources should be mentioned.

First, a growing mass of data and theory supplied by the physical sciences was prima facie at variance with biblical history and cosmology. There was the new time scale of geology, the impersonal and amoral Darwinian evolutionary theory, and the radical textual, historical criticism of the Bible itself.

Second, once the strong initial resistance to systematic and searching criticism of Christian teaching had been overcome, it was possible to express openly a good many moral misgivings about the Christian conception of God and his governance of the world. J. S. Mill declared it was impossible for a thoughtful person to ascribe "absolute perfection to the author and ruler of so clumsily made and capriciously governed a creation as this planet" (*Three Essays on Religion,* 1874). He found "moral difficulties" also in "the recognition … of the object of highest worship, in a being who could make a Hell" and create creatures whom he foreknew to be destined to suffer in it eternally. No less morally repugnant to many writers was the insistence of the orthodox that their dogmas required sheer unswerving acceptance, and that breakdowns in argument or intelligibility were simply occasions for the exercise of an intensified faith. T. H. Huxley was forthright. In "Agnosticism and Christianity" (1889) he wrote, "I, and many other Agnostics, believe that faith, in this sense, is an abomination." In "Agnosticism" (1889) he said, "I verily believe that the great good which has been effected … by Christianity has been

largely counteracted by the pestilent doctrine … that honest disbelief in their more or less astonishing creeds is a moral offence, indeed a sin of the deepest dye."

Third, the same authors were vehemently critical of the standards of evidence and reasoning normal in theology, and contrasted them with the severe, rigorous, and dispassionate criteria of the sciences. To Mill, "The whole of the prevalent metaphysics of the present century is one tissue of suborned evidence in favour of religion." If one considers the nature of the world as one actually observes it, the very most one could dare to hazard is the existence of a good but finite deity; and Mill put forward even this possibility with a characteristically agnostic tentativeness. For Huxley agnosticism was "not a creed but a method, the essence of which lies in the rigorous application of a single principle": Reason should be followed "as far as it can take you," but undemonstrable conclusions should not be treated as if they were certain. "One may suspect," he said, "that a little more critical discrimination would have enlarged the Apocrypha not inconsiderably." In a similar vein, Leslie Stephen protested against theologians who ventured to define "the nature of God Almighty with an accuracy from which modest naturalists would shrink in describing the genesis of a black beetle" (*An Agnostic's Apology,* 1893).

It is not the purpose here to estimate how far theologians remedied, or could ever remedy, the deficiencies in their arguments that offended their agnostic critics. Some permanently valuable lessons can be learned, however, from the course of the controversies. An obvious one is the odd instability or ambiguity of certain agnostic positions. Let us suppose—as did many of the writers just quoted—that one ceases to find convincing the arguments for the existence of a deity. Experience, one now judges, is limited to the observable world; and reason, although it may lay bare the conditions and presuppositions of that experience, cannot extend our experience of what is. A religiously minded person, in this situation, is tempted to divide reality into the knowable and the unknowable and to attribute to the latter many of the lineaments of deity. Thus, "negative theology" and a religiously toned agnosticism can be the closest of relatives. No sweeping philosophical criticism can demonstrate that all such positions are untenable or involve a cryptotheism; each case must be scrutinized individually. Certain religious attitudes toward the unknown or unknowable—attitudes, for example, of wonderment and awe—can be perfectly appropriate and invulnerable to criticism, whereas others—such as the expectation of personal encounter with the unknown—are obviously most vulnerable. One can turn to history for some examples.

In 1896 James Ward delivered his Gifford Lectures, *Naturalism and Agnosticism* (published in 1899), at Aberdeen University. These contained a vigorous attack on the basic presuppositions of the Hamilton-Mansel-Spencer approach. The sciences, Ward said, do not form a whole that floats in a surrounding "nescience." The world we know does not consist of "appearance" concealing an "ultimate reality" that lies behind or beyond it. In any case, nescience is nescience. "Where nescience is absolute, nothing can be said; neither that there is more to know nor that there is not." Spencer and like-minded writers had, however, said a good many mysterious things about their Absolute, things that, by their own account, were strictly unsayable.

R. Flint (*Agnosticism,* Croall lectures, 1887–1888, published in 1903) also denounced the equivocations (as he saw them) of a religious agnosticism. "All that the mind can do on the side of the Unknowable is to play at make-believe, to feign faith, to worship nothingness." "Call your doubts mysteries," said Stephen, satirizing the complacent, "and they won't disturb you any longer."

Is it possible for a reflective person to be an agnostic in the present time? Logical positivists have answered "No." In *Language, Truth and Logic* (1936), A. J. Ayer claimed that since "all utterances about the nature of God are nonsensical," the agnostic's statements about God are no less nonsensical than the theist's. Both assume, wrongly, that "the question whether a transcendent God exists is a genuine question." According to positivism and postpositivist logical analysis, the theological problem is not a problem of evidence and argument, but a problem of meaningfulness. If "God" is a meaningless word, the sentence "Perhaps God does not exist" is also meaningless.

In stating the situation thus, positivism was dramatically drawing attention to what it believed to be distinctive in its approach, but it simultaneously obscured some important lines of continuity with the earlier debate on agnosticism. Before the nineteenth century had ended, Flint had written, in criticism of Hamilton, "*Credo quia absurdum* can be the only appropriate motto of a philosopher who holds that we may believe in a God the very idea of whom we can perceive to be self-contradictory." The possibility of internal illogicality in the very notion of deity, the risk of the absurd and nonsensical, were well enough recognized. Spencer, wrestling with the problems of the world's origin and beginning, said that the questions here are not questions of credibility but of *conceiv-*

ability. Notions such as self-existence and creation by an external agency "involve symbolic conceptions of the illegitimate and illusive kind." The logical positivist tethered his theory of meaning to the demands for observational verification and falsification of our claims about existents. Compare Spencer once more, writing in 1899: "Intellect being framed simply by and for converse with phenomena, involves us in nonsense when we try to use it for anything beyond phenomena." It must, of course, be added that the positivists and later analysts carried out their austere program with far greater thoroughness and consistency than did their predecessors. But the lines of continuity are there; and they are—once more—those same lines that reach back to Kant's "Transcendental Dialectic" and to David Hume. They justify the use of "atheist" to describe one who rejects the performances and attitudes of religion on the grounds that talk about God is unverifiable talk, or that the concept *God* contains inner illogicalities.

But is there still room for agnosticism as undogmatic dubiety or ignorance about the existence of God? A case for saying that there is still room can be made on the following lines. Where one gives an account of an expression in our language, and where that expression is one that refers to an existent of some kind, one needs to provide not only a set of rules for the use of the expression, but also an indication of how the referring is to be done— through direct pointing, perhaps, or through giving instructions for an indirect method of identifying the entity. Can this be done in the case of God? Pointing, clearly, is inappropriate, God being no finite object in the world. The theologian may suggest a number of options at this point. He may say: God can be identified as that being upon whom the world can be felt as utterly dependent, who is the completion of its incompletenesses, whose presence is faintly adumbrated in experience of the awesome and the numinous. Clear direction-giving has here broken down; the theologian may well admit that his language is less descriptive or argumentative than obliquely evocative. Does this language succeed in establishing that statements about God have a reference? To persons susceptible to religious experience but at the same time logically and critically alert, it may seem just barely to succeed, or it may seem just barely to fail. Some may even oscillate uneasily between these alternatives without finding a definite procedure of decision to help them discriminate once for all. A person in this last category is surely an agnostic. His agnosticism takes full account of current linguistic criticisms of religion; it is in the course of his reflections upon meaning that he sees the necessity of relating the linguistic to the extralinguistic, and his answers to this problem, the problem of reference, plunge him into the deepest uncertainty.

The temper of mind just outlined, with all its inner turbulence and anxiety, is probably the most creatively fruitful of the many varieties of agnosticism. Where there is no temptation to believe, there can be little philosophical interest in not believing. Where there has been little or no religious experience, no sense of the haunting strangeness that makes the believer wittingly violate language and logic to express it, there can be little incentive to explore minutely the possible interpretations—theistic, pantheistic, naturalistic—of that experience. As a matter of history, agnostics of this temper are to be found far more rarely today than at the height of the agnosticism controversy a century ago. For the great writers of that controversy were in most cases brought up within the Christian faith, had identified themselves with it, and subsequently suffered a bewildering disorientation. Yet, if one is to take seriously today the problems of philosophical theology, there must be some suspension of disbelief, at least an imaginative venture, in order to see why the believer feels compelled to use the extraordinary language he does use. He knows well enough that it is extraordinary; but he deems that it is ordinary language that is found wanting, and not his experiences and the interpretations he puts upon them. The agnostic knows that sometimes ordinary language needs to be violated, as a poet often violates it. He knows also that to disturb our linguistic apparatus in so radical a way can obscure some movements of thought of a very questionable (or downright invalid) logic. Has this happened in the particular case of theism? Searching in this obscurity, the agnostic reports that he cannot tell. For the health of philosophy and theology, it is well that he should continue to search.

See also Ayer, Alfred Jules; Empiricism; Hamilton, William; Hume, David; Huxley, Thomas Henry; Kant, Immanuel; Mansel, Henry Longueville; Mill, John Stuart; Skepticism, Contemporary; Skepticism, History of; Stephen, Leslie.

Bibliography

HUME AND KANT

Hume, David. *Dialogues concerning Natural Religion.* London: Robinson, 1779.

Hume, David. *Enquiry concerning Human Understanding.* London: A. Millar, 1748. Especially sections X and XI.

Kant, Immanuel. *Kritik der reinen Vernunft* (1781). In Berlin Academy, *Complete Works.* Berlin, 1902–1955.

See also the entries Empiricism; Skepticism, Contemporary; and Skepticism, History of.

NINETEENTH-CENTURY DOCUMENTS

Flint, R. *Agnosticism.* Edinburgh and London, 1903.

Hamilton, Sir William. "Philosophy of the Unconditioned." *Edinburgh Review* (October 1829).

Huxley, T. H. "Agnosticism and Christianity" (1889). In his *Collected Essays,* Vol. V. London: Macmillan, 1894. Entire volume is relevant.

Mansel, H. L. *The Limits of Religious Thought.* London, 1858.

Mill, J. S. *Three Essays on Religion.* London: Longmans, Green, Reader, and Dyer, 1874.

Spencer, Herbert. *First Principles.* London: Williams and Norgate, 1862.

Stephen, Leslie. *An Agnostic's Apology.* London: Smith Elder, 1893. First published as an essay in 1876.

Ward, James. *Naturalism and Agnosticism.* London: Macmillan, 1899; 2nd ed., with alterations, 1903.

SECONDARY SOURCES

Armstrong, R. A. *Agnosticism and Theism in the Nineteenth Century.* London: Green, 1905.

Britton, K. *John Stuart Mill.* London: Penguin, 1953.

Burtt, E. A. *Types of Religious Philosophy.* New York: Harper, 1951.

Collins, J. *God in Modern Philosophy.* Chicago: Regnery, 1959.

Garrigou-Lagrange, R. *Dieu, son existence et sa nature; solution thomiste des antinomies agnostiques.* Paris, 1915.

Hájek, Alan. "Agnosticism Meets Bayesianism." *Analysis* 58 (3) (1998): 199–206.

Kenny, Anthony. *Faith and Reason.* New York: Columbia University Press, 1983.

Lightman, Bernard. *The Origins of Agnosticism: Victorian Unbelief and the Limits of Knowledge.* Baltimore: Johns Hopkins University Press, 1987.

Marty, Martin E. *Varieties of Unbelief.* New York: Holt Rinehart Winston, 1964.

McGrath, P. J. "Atheism or Agnosticism." *Analysis* 47 (1987): 54–57.

Morris, Thomas. "Agnosticism." *Analysis* 45 (1985): 219–224.

Oppy, Graham. "Weak Agnosticism Defended." *International Journal for Philosophy of Religion* 36 (1994): 147–167.

Packe, M. St. John. *John Stuart Mill.* London: Secker & Warburg, 1954. Biography.

Passmore, J. *A Hundred Years of Philosophy.* London: Duckworth, 1957. Especially Ch. 2.

Pyle, Andrew, ed. *Agnosticism: Contemporary Responses to Spencer and Huxley.* Bristol, U.K.: Thoemmes, 1995.

Stephen, Leslie. *English Thought in the Eighteenth Century.* London: Smith, Elder & Company, 1876.

van Fraassen, Bas C. "The Agnostic Subtly Probabilified." *Analysis* 58 (3) (1998): 212–220.

Willey, Basil. *Nineteenth Century Studies.* New York: Columbia University Press, 1949.

Ronald W. Hepburn (1967)

Bibliography updated by Christian B. Miller (2005)

AGRIPPA
(c. 50 BCE–c. 150 CE)

Agrippa is known by way of one citation in Diogenes Laertius's *Lives of the Philosophers* (*DL* 9.88). Nothing is known of his life, and little of his dates (he lived between the mid-first century BCE and the second century CE). Yet Agrippa is indisputably a figure of the highest importance in the history of skepticism, indeed of epistemology in general. The citation attributes to him the invention (or at least the codification) of five "Modes," or argument patterns, which represent a new methodological rigor and self-consciousness in the development of Pyrrhonian skepticism. Earlier skeptics such as Aenesidemus had presented certain aspects of skeptical procedure in a more or less organized fashion; but the Ten Modes attributed to him are arranged according to the subject matter of the considerations appealed to. By contrast, the Modes of Agrippa seek to categorize skeptical practice according to the type and function of the argument patterns involved.

The Five Modes are summarized in two sources; in addition to Diogenes's brief notice (*DL* 9.88–89), a somewhat longer treatment survives (although without mentioning Agrippa by name) in Sextus Empiricus's *Outlines of Pyrrhonism* (*PH* 1.164–177). Taken together, they offer a general strategy for inducing doubt (and suspension of judgement, *epochē*) on every contentious issue. Two of the Modes, the First and the Third, may be described as material. The First Mode notes, in standard Pyrrhonian fashion, that most important issues are matters of dispute (*diaphōnia*) and if they are not, the skeptic will make them so. Sextus Empiricus describes skepticism as "a capacity for opposing appearances to appearances and judgments to judgments in whatever manner, so that we are brought … first to *epochē* and then to tranquility" (*PH* 1.8). Thus "we find an irresoluble conflict both among lay people and philosophers," which leads to these conditions "since we are unable either to assent or deny" (*PH* 1.165, cf. *DL* 9.88). The disputes are said to be "irresoluble" (*PH* 1.98, 212), because (skeptics allege) no independent criterion of judgment is available for them. Unpacking this claim involves invoking the other three, formal, Modes. This is because, as the Third Mode from Relativity holds, things are never apprehended in themselves and unalloyed, but only "along with something else" (*DL* 9.89): "the underlying object appears thus and so in relation to the one judging and concomitant circumstances, so we suspend judgment as to its real nature" (*PH* 1.167). Such considerations form the material for the Ten Modes of Aenesidemus, and via René Descartes and others came to dominate the landscape of epistemological scepticism (e.g., lights seem bright in the dark but dim in sunlight; oars seem straight in air, but bent in water: *PH* 1.119). Thus people can say how things appear to them but they have no grounds for any pronouncements as to how things really are.

But it is in the exposition and deployment of the three formal Modes that the power and originality of Agrippan skepticism becomes manifest. The Second is that from Regress: "what is adduced as confirmation for what is posited itself requires further confirmation, and that another, and so on *ad infinitum*" (*PH* 1.166). The Fourth is the Mode of Hypothesis, which the *Dogmatists* (Sextus's generic term for his nonskeptical opponents) resort to "when being forced to regress *ad infinitum*, take as an axiom something which they have not established, but see fit to assume as agreed without demonstration" (*PH* 1.168). This is hopeless, as Diogenes points out, because there is as a matter of fact no such agreement (*DL* 9.89). Finally the Fifth Mode, of Circularity, claims that "what ought to support the matter under investigation itself requires confirmation from that very matter" (*PH* 1.169). Diogenes adds an example: "as for instance someone seeking to confirm the existence of pores [in the skin] on the grounds of the emanations should establish the latter on the basis of the former" (*DL* 9.89).

The Modes lend themselves to use in combination. Take any dogmatic proposition *p*: one may ask what it is supposed to rest on. If the answer is "nothing," then it is a mere hypothesis, unworthy of credence by the Fourth Mode. If it is alleged to rest on *q*, one may ask the same question of *q*. If one gets the same answer, the same response applies. If *q* is said to rest on *p*, then the Mode of Circularity comes in; or else the process goes on, potentially *ad infinitum* in line with the Second Mode (*PH* 169–174). Credit for seeing the force of such objections is not due to Agrippa. Aristotle was aware of them (*Posterior Analytics* 1.3 [Barnes, ed. 1984]), and realized that any foundationalist epistemology requires its basic propositions to be more than mere assumptions. But how that is to be done—if it is to be done at all—is still a matter of dispute, apparently undecidable. Agrippa fashioned a powerful and elegant arsenal of skepticism, and all modern nonskeptical epistemologies sooner or later must confront them, and the challenge they pose, in one form or another.

See also Aenesidemus; Ancient Skepticism; Sextus Empiricus.

Bibliography

Annas, Julia, and Jonathan Barnes, eds. *Outline of Scepticism.* Translation of Sextus Empiricus's *Outlines of Pyrrhonism.* Cambridge, U.K.: Cambridge University Press, 1994.

Barnes, Jonathan. *The Toils of Scepticism.* Cambridge, U.K.: Cambridge University Press, 1989.

Barnes, Jonathan, ed. *The Complete Works of Aristotle.* 2 vols. Princeton, NJ: Princeton University Press, 1984.

Hankinson, R. J. *The Skeptics.* London: Routledge, 1995.

Hicks, R. D., ed. and trans. *Diogenes Laertius: Lives of the Eminent Philosophers.* 2 vols. Cambridge MA: Harvard University Press, 1925.

R. J. Hankinson (2005)

AGRIPPA VON NETTESHEIM, HENRICUS CORNELIUS
(1486–1535)

Henricus Cornelius Agrippa von Nettesheim, a colorful Renaissance figure—a diplomat, a military adventurer, a kabbalist, an expert on occult science, a medical doctor, a lawyer, a theologian, an early Reformer, as well as a troublesome and troubled intellectual—was born of minor nobility in or near Cologne. His first official position was that of a court secretary of the Holy Roman emperor. He was sent to Paris in 1506 and there joined a secret group of theosophists. He next became involved in a revolutionary plot in Catalonia. In 1509 he gave lectures at the University of Dôle, on Johannes Reuchlin's kabbalistic *De Verbo Mirifico.* He learned Hebrew and immersed himself in kabbalistic, Gnostic, and hermeneutic writings. This research culminated in three volumes on occult science, *De Occulta Philosophia,* written in 1509–1510 but not published until 1531–1533 in Cologne (trans. by J. F., London, 1651). At Dôle he also wrote on the superiority and nobility of women and entered into his first marriage. These early unpublished writings touched off a fight between Agrippa and certain conservative monks, who accused him, along with Reuchlin, Desiderius Erasmus, and the French humanist–Reformer Jacques Lefèvre d'Etaples, of being Judaizers and heretics.

In 1510 Agrippa was sent to London, where he lived with Erasmus's friend John Colet, who interested Agrippa in St. Paul's epistles. Next, Agrippa lectured on theology in Cologne. From 1511 to 1513 he fought in various Italian campaigns and engaged in theological battles, even with the pope. In 1515 he taught occult science at the University of Pavia. Three years later Agrippa became public advocate and orator of Metz and was soon embroiled again in theological battles and in defending a peasant woman accused of sorcery. The opposition of the inquisitor of Metz forced him to leave. Agrippa's wife died soon after, and he retired to Geneva. In 1522 he remarried and became a medical practitioner. He was appointed physician to the queen mother of France and became involved in a demoralizing struggle to collect his salary and to fulfill his duties. At the queen mother's orders he was stranded in Lyons from 1524 to 1526 without funds and without permission to leave. Agrippa wrote many bellicose letters to the court, antagonizing numerous people but settling nothing. His only official duty was the drawing up of horoscopes (which he knew were useless and fraudulent). In this period Agrippa wrote his major work, *De Incertitudine et Vanitate de Scientiarum et Artium* (Antwerp, 1530; trans, by James Sandford as *Of the Vanitie and uncertaintie of artes and sciences,* London, 1569), attacking every type of intellectual endeavor and art, as well as courtiers, princes, and monks. Even kabbalistic and occult researches were disowned as superstitious rhapsodies. Only pious Bible study remained worthwhile.

Agrippa abandoned hope of regaining court favor or receiving his salary and in 1528 went to Antwerp, where he had a brief flurry of success. He was appointed historiographer to Charles V, achieved success as a medical doctor, and finally published his works. This happy phase was soon followed by catastrophes. His second wife died of the plague. The publication of his *Vanity of the Sciences* outraged Charles V. Agrippa was jailed and branded a heretic. A disastrous marriage left him financially ruined and miserable. He returned to Germany, battled with the inquisitor of Cologne, and was banished in 1535. Having fled to France, he was arrested for having criticized the queen mother, was released, and died in Grenoble.

Agrippa was notorious as a magician and as a stormy opponent of the monks and the "establishment." He made his main intellectual contributions as an expositor of kabbalism and occult science, as a critic of all intellectual activities, and as a Reformer within Catholicism. His *De Occulta Philosophia* tried to explain the universe in terms of kabbalistic analyses of Hebrew letters and their relations to natural phenomena and divine understanding; in terms of the Pythagorean numerological symbols; and of the Christian interpretation of kabbalism and Pythagoreanism. *De Occulta Philosophia* played a major role in Renaissance magical and kabbalistic studies.

Agrippa's *Vanity of the Sciences* was one of the first contributions to the Renaissance revival of skepticism, but its weapons were denunciation and ridicule, not philosophical analysis. It is more a bitter version of Erasmus's *In Praise of Folly* than a serious epistemological examination of whether knowledge can be gained by human means. Its final appeal is to a type of fundamentalistic anti-intellectualism. The work represents a stage in Agrippa's journey from occult studies to a simple biblical faith opposed to late medieval Scholasticism. Agrippa, although he did not revolt against Catholicism, lacked Erasmus's patience and calm and became almost a Catholic Martin Luther, violently denouncing monks, Scholastic theologians, and others. In the end he rejected occult studies—and all others—as a way of penetrating the divine mysteries, and he proclaimed: "It is better therefore and more profitable to be idiots and know nothing, to believe by Faith and Charity, and to become next unto God, than being lofty and proud through the subtilties of sciences to fall into the possession of the Serpent."

See also Colet, John; Erasmus, Desiderius; Gnosticism; Hermeneutics; Kabbalah; Luther, Martin; Medieval Philosophy; Pythagoras and Pythagoreanism; Renaissance; Skepticism, History of.

Bibliography

WORKS BY AGRIPPA

Die Eitelkeit und Unsicherheit der Wissenschaften und die Verteidigungschrift, edited by Fritz Mauthner. Munich: Müller, 1913.

De occulta philosophia, edited by Karl Anton Nowotny. (Faksimile des ältesten Kölner Druckes, 1533.) Graz, Akademische Druck u. Verlagsanstalt, 1967.

Opera. Hildesheim, NY: G. Olms, 1970.

Three Books of Occult Philosophy or Magic. Book One: Natural Magic which Includes the Early Life of Agrippa, His Seventy-four Chapters on Natural Magic, New Notes, Illustrations, Index, and Other Original and Selected Matter. New York: S. Weiser, 1971.

Of the Vanitie and Uncertaintie of Artes and Sciences. Northridge: California State University, 1974.

Declamatio de nobilitate et praecellentia foeminei sexus edited by Elisabeth Gössmann. München: Iudicium. 2nd ed., überarbeitete und erw. Aufl., 1996.

WORKS ON AGRIPPA

Bayle, Pierre. "Agrippa." In *Dictionnaire historique et critique.* 2 vols. Rotterdam, 1695–1697.

Blau, Joseph. *The Christian Interpretation of the Cabala in the Renaissance.* New York: Columbia University Press, 1944.

Morley, Henry. *The Life of Henry Cornelius von Nettesheim.* 2 vols. London, 1856.

Nauert, Charles G. *Agrippa and the Crisis of Renaissance Thought.* Urbana: University of Illinois Press, 1965.

Nauert, Charles G. "Magic and Skepticism in Agrippa's Thought." *Journal of the History of Ideas* 18 (1957): 161–182.

Popkin, R. H. *History of Scepticism from Erasmus to Descartes.* Assen, 1960; New York: Humanities Press, 1964.

Prost, Auguste. *Les Sciences et les arts occultes au XVIe siècle: Corneille Agrippa, sa vie et ses oeuvres.* 2 vols. Paris: Champion, 1881–1882.

Walker, D. P. *Spiritual and Demonic Magic from Ficino to Campanella.* London: Warburg Institute, University of London, 1958.

Yates, Frances A. *Giordano Bruno and the Hermetic Tradition.* London, 1964.

Zarathustra, Frater. *Index to Agrippa's Occult Philosophy or Magic. Book 1, Natural magic.* Fremont, CA: Technology Group, 1993.

Richard H. Popkin (1967)
Bibliography updated by Michael J. Farmer (2005)

AILLY, PIERRE D'
(1350–1421)

Pierre d'Ailly, the Ockhamist philosopher, was born at Compiègne in France. He studied at the Navarre College in Paris in 1372, receiving his doctoral degree in 1380 and becoming chancellor of the university in 1389. He was made bishop of Puy in 1395 and bishop of Cambrai in 1396 and cardinal in 1411. He took a leading part in the Council of Constance (1414–1418), where he asserted the superiority of a general council of the church over the pope. He died as papal legate at Avignon.

D'Ailly's literary output was vast and wide-ranging. It comprehended philosophy, theology, scientific theory, political theory, canon law, and ecclesiastical politics and touched on mysticism. Among his more important writings were the treatise *De Anima*, commentaries on Boethius's *Consolation of Philosophy* and the four books of the *Sentences*, two studies of mysticism and asceticism, three works on different aspects of church government, and a series of works on logic, astronomy, and geography.

In his philosophical outlook d'Ailly seems to have been sympathetic to Ockhamism. Like so many fourteenth-century thinkers he postulated different degrees of certainty. The main distinction d'Ailly made was between what he called "natural light" and reason. Natural light corresponded to knowledge that was indubitable—namely, that which could be reduced to the principle of contradiction or immediate intuition of the existence of the self, in the manner of John of Mirecourt. Reason, on the other hand, was only relative in its certainty and was confined to the natural order. Included within it were the traditional arguments for God's existence, which d'Ailly treated as merely probable. The influence of William of Ockham is also apparent in d'Ailly's treatment of God's omnipotence; since it was independent of the natural order, God was in no way bound to follow nature's laws. Accordingly, God could create the illusion that something existed when in fact it did not; this was one of the most insistent Ockhamist arguments against the infallibility of experiential knowledge. At the same time d'Ailly was careful to distinguish the realm of God's absolute power (*potentia absoluta*) from the realm subject to his ordained power (*potentia ordinata*). Whereas the first realm referred to God's omnipotence as such, the latter constituted the specific application of his omnipotence to this world; it provided the laws by which creation was regulated, and among them d'Ailly included the laws of physics. They therefore operated constantly and with certainty.

D'Ailly's debt to Ockham and John of Mirecourt is also to be seen in his views on essences. There was no inherent reason why hot was hot or cold cold other than God's willing it. The same applied to the moral order, where good and bad were such because of God's voluntary decree: "Nothing is good or bad of itself such that God must love or hate it." Similarly, a man was just not from possessing the intrinsic property of justice but because God accepted him as just. Here was the same absence of a constant scale of values that had proved so destructive of the traditional teachings in the time of Ockham and the first generation of his followers, who included Robert Holkot, Adam of Woodham, and John of Mirecourt. D'Ailly further emphasized the uncertain nature of natural experience by his acceptance of the so-called *complexe significabile*, by which an expression such as "sin" did not denote a specific object but was a description or statement that referred to an action. As employed by Nicolas of Autrecourt, it had denied the reality of a wide range of expressions. Thus the word *God* stood not for a specific being but for a verbal expression: supreme or highest being. As such it lacked correspondence to anything but a grouping of words. At the same time, in keeping at the natural level, d'Ailly granted a correspondingly wider area of jurisdiction to faith. Thus evidence for God's existence could be held only as a matter of belief.

See also Holkot, Robert; John of Mirecourt; Nicolas of Autrecourt; Ockhamism; William of Ockham; Wodeham, Adam.

Bibliography

WORKS BY D'AILLY

Tractatus Exponibilium Magistri Petri de Allyaco. Paris, 1494.

Quaestiones Super Primum, Tertium et Quartum Sententiarum. Venice, 1500.

De Anima. Paris, 1501.

Tractatus et Sermones. Douai, France, 1639. Includes *De Anima.*

Destructiones Modorum Significandi. Conceptus et Insolubilia Secundum Viam Nominalium Magistri Petri de Allyaco. (No date.)

WORKS ON D'AILLY

Dictionnaire de théologie catholique. Vol. I, 642–654. Paris, 1903–1951.

Gandillac, M. P. de. "Usage et valeur des arguments probables chez Pierre d'Ailly." *Archives d'histoire doctrinale et littéraire* 8 (1933): 43–91.

Gordon Leff (1967)

AITIA

The Greek word *aitia* (or *aition*) derives from the adjective *aitios*, meaning "responsible," and functions as such as early as the Homeric poems. It was originally applied to agents, and only later does it come to qualify nonsentient items—although owing to the fragmentary nature of earlier sources, it is by no means clear when this transition takes place. But certainly by the latter part of the fifth century BCE, Hippocratic doctors were using the term, as were the historians Herodotus and Thucydides. It is in the latter, as well as in some of the Hippocratic texts, that the beginnings of the distinction of causal terminology can be found. Similar fine distinctions are also beginning to appear in the forensic and rhetorical traditions. In his discussion of the plague at Athens (*Peloponnesian War* 2.47–54), Thucydides disavows any knowledge of its origins or "what causes (*aitiai*) may be adduced adequate to explain its powerful natural effects" (2.48), and notes that "in some cases there seemed to be no *prophasis*" (2.49). A *prophasis* is an external cause, or occasion, or antecedent event correlated with an outcome. This word, as well, has Homeric roots, but it also has a legal (and more general) sense of pretext. Hippocratic texts also contrast *prophaseis* with *aitiai*, and in the same general way: *Prophaseis* are the observable antecedent signs, *aitiai* the inferred inner, structural facts causally responsible for the outcome. *Aitiai* are now closely linked with the notion of *phusis* or nature, the primary matter of pre-Socratic inquiry. If things have natures—internal structures—then those natures will explain how and why things behave the way they do.

Plato was the first philosopher to subject the concept of an *aitia* to detailed examination. Whereas generally an *aition* is "that because of which something comes to be"

(*Cratylus* 413a), and "the cause and the productive may rightly be said to be identical" (*Philebus* 26e), Plato treats these characterizations generally—they do not restrict causation to efficient causation. Indeed, at *Phaedo* 95e–103b, he takes the pre-Socratics to task for concentrating on mechanical causation at the expense of teleology: It is only if you know why things are for the best that you understand them. Moreover, Plato elaborates a thesis of necessity and sufficiency with regard to cause and effect (or *explanans* and *explanandum*): If *F*'s cause *G*'s, then there is no *F* without a *G*, and vice versa.

Aristotle followed Plato in espousing teleological explanations, and referring to them in the language of *aitiai*. Final causes are one of his four causal (or explanatory) types, along with material, efficient, and formal (*Physics* 2.3). But unlike Plato, Aristotle's final causes in nature presuppose no agency. Where Plato spoke of the Craftsman who designed everything for the best (*Timaeus*), Aristotle makes finality an irreducible component of nature itself. Nature is goal-directed, and no adequate account of natural processes can ignore that fact (as those of the atomists and other mechanists do). As Plato had before him, Aristotle thinks explanatory resources available to pure mechanism are inadequate to give a satisfying explanation of the order and regularity of the cosmos. The four causes are designed primarily to account for substances, and only derivatively for events and processes. Thus one might ask what makes an oak tree what it is. Firstly, its efficient cause—namely its parent tree, which supplies the formal model from which it derives. Secondly, its material cause: There could be no oak tree without a suitable supply of matter for the form to mold. Thirdly, there is the form itself, deriving from the efficient cause—yet from the moment the seed is created (or at least begins to germinate) it is an independent structural principle. And finally there is the end—or completely expressed form—toward which the process of maturation is directed and in which it will culminate if all other (material) factors equal.

Aristotle seeks to apply this model, with varying success, to all cases of coming to be (although he allows that coincidences lack final causes: *Physics* 2.4–6); and that all of the factors involved may equally be called *aitiai*. Moreover, he believes that even abstract objects have formal causes (the formal cause of the octave is the ratio 2:1). Plato's Stoic successors, however, reserved the term *aition* for a physical productive cause—a body that brought about in another body an incorporeal effect, a predicate's coming to be true of it. They allowed matter a role in overall explanation, yet being passive by definition it could not be a cause; neither could it be disembodied goals or ends. These Stoic successors, or their contemporaries in the medical schools, turned to making further fine distinctions within the notion even more restricted, distinguishing between "perfect" or "sustaining" causes on the one hand and "antecedent" causes on the other. "Perfect" or "sustaining" causes were sufficient, necessary, and coterminous with their effects—and functionally correlated with them—in that any increase or decrease in intensity in the one is matched by a similar change in the other, "antecedent" causes answered roughly to the earlier *prophaseis*: prior events that set a causal process in train but are not sufficient for it (since they require suitably constituted bodies upon which to act).

Skeptics were to argue that causes could not both precede and be coterminous with their effects; and that because cause and effect are relative terms, they cannot be conceived independently, as they must be if one is to explain the other. This and other such attacks in turn prompted doctors and philosophers such as Galen to even further conceptual refinements that continued at least until the third century CE, whereas Neoplatonists like Proclus would later insist that, properly speaking, all causes were immaterial (being the action of soul).

See also Aristotle; Causation; Plato; Stoicism.

Bibliography

Barnes, J., ed. *The Complete Works of Aristotle*. 2 vols. Princeton, NJ: Princeton UIniversity Press, 1984.

Cooper, J. M., ed. *Plato: Complete Works*. Indianapolis: Hackett, 1997.

Hankinson, R. J. *Cause and Explanation in the Ancient Greek World*. Oxford: Oxford University Press, 1998.

Warner, R. *Thucydides: History of the Peloponnesian War*. Harmondsworth, U.K.: Penguin Books, 1953.

R. J. Hankinson (2005)

ALBERT OF SAXONY
(c. 1316–1390)

Sometimes nicknamed Albertucius to distinguish him from Albert the Great, Albert of Saxony was born in Rickensdorf in the region of Helmstedt (Lower Saxony), in present-day Germany. He did his early studies in his native region, then most likely took a trip to Elfurt. He later went to Prague and Paris, where he earned his master of arts degree in 1351. He was rector of the university in 1353. He taught the arts there for a decade, while studying theology at the Sorbonne, apparently without earning a degree. After a few years as a diplomat mediating between Pope Urban VI and the Duke of Austria, he was called on to found the University of Vienna, becoming its first rector in 1365. He was appointed canon of Hildesheim in 1366 and became bishop of Halberstadt the same year. He served in that capacity until his death on July 8, 1390.

Albert of Saxony left behind no theological writings and is known primarily for his works in logic and natural philosophy. He also composed commentaries on Aristotle's *Nicomachean Ethics* and *Economics*, as well as a short mathematical treatise on the squaring of the circle.

In logic, his masterwork is a summa titled *Perutilis logica* (Very useful logic). He also composed a voluminous collection, the *Sophismata* (Sophisms), in which he examined many statements that raise difficulties of interpretation because they contain syncategoremes. In addition, he wrote *Commentarius in Posteriora Aristotelis* (Commentary on Aristotle's *Posterior Analytics*) and a collection of twenty-five questions (*Quaestiones circa logicam*) relating to semantic problems or the status of logic. He also commented on Aristotle's writings in logic. During Albert of Saxony's career, Jean Buridan enjoyed great renown at the faculty of arts in Paris. Albert's writings, however, attest to the influence exerted in Paris by English ideas. His *Very Useful Logic*, while developing treatises on obligations, insolubles, and consequences—topics that were becoming increasingly important during the period—was modeled after William of Ockham's *Summa logicae* (Summa of logic). Albert of Saxony adopted the Ockhamist conception of the sign and based signification on a referential relationship to a unique thing. He also subordinated the oral sign to the conceptual sign. He was an Ockhamist in his conception of the universal and, for the most part, in his theory of the supposition. In particular, he retained the notion of the simple supposition—that is, the reference of a term to a concept to which it is subordinated, even though it signifies an extra-mental thing. Finally, he was Ockhamist in his theory of categories. Unlike Jean Buridan, he refused to consider quantity an absolute reality and relegated it to a disposition of the substance and the quality.

On a few points, however, Albert departed from William of Ockham. Hence he rejected the idea that an ambiguous proposition ought to be assigned multiple meanings. Such a proposition can only be conceded, rejected, or called into doubt. In the *Sophisms*, William Heytesbury often served as his guide (for example, in the analysis of epistemic verbs and the study of the infinite). He grants the proposition a literal meaning, which is not

that of its terms. Like the syncategoreme, the proposition signifies a "mode of being." Nevertheless, Albert of Saxony avoided accounting for these "modes of being" and, in the last analysis, transferred them to relationships between the things to which the terms referred. But he used the idea of a proposition's meaning to define truth and to deal with "insolubles," that is, semantic paradoxes. By virtue of its form, every proposition signifies that it is true; for that reason, the insoluble is false, since it signifies both that it is true and that it is false.

This analysis of language was combined with a gnoseological realism that stemmed in part from an analysis of the void. It is possible to imagine that the void exists by divine omnipotence, but no science of nature can integrate the existence of the void as a hypothesis. Albert refused to extend the referent of physics terms to supernatural possibilities. For him, physics cannot develop into a study of imaginary cases, despite what was being done at Oxford at the time. It must account for the natural course of things.

In addition to commentaries on Aristotle's *Physica* (Physics), Albert composed a commentary on Johannes de Sacrobosco's *De sphaera* (On the sphere) and a treatise on relationships inspired by Thomas Bradwardine. In pursuing the work of the Oxford Calculators and of Nicole d'Oresme in Paris, he created a compendium setting out the elements of the theory of relationships and their application to different motions, adopting the rule elaborated by Bradwardine on the relationship between powers of propulsion and resistance. In his physics texts, he also displayed a curiosity for many natural phenomena, taking an interest in motions of the earth, tides, and geology.

It was undoubtedly in the field of dynamics, however, that Albert's role was most important. To account for the motion of projectiles and the acceleration of falling objects, he adopted the Buridanian theory of impetus, a quality acquired by the body. He drew clearly the consequences of extending that notion to celestial movements, rejected the notion of a propulsive intelligence, and followed the same principles in studying celestial bodies and earthly bodies. His commentary on Aristotle's *De caelo* (On the sky) exerted a great influence in northern Italy. Albert of Saxony thus played a role in developing a vision of the cosmos that departed from conceptions inherited from Greco-Arab Peripateticism.

See also Bradwardine, Thomas; Buridan, Jean; Heytesbury, William; Impetus; Oresme, Nicholas; William of Ockham.

Bibliography

WORKS BY ALBERT OF SAXONY

Perutilis logica. Maracaibo: Universidad del Zulia, 1988. Based on the incunabulum Venice edition of 1522. Critical edition with Spanish translation by Angel Muñoz García.

Perutilis logica, Tractatus II (De proprietatibus terminorum). Leiden: E. J. Brill, 1993.

Quaestiones in artem veterem. Maracaibo: Universidad del Zulia, 1988. Critical edition with Spanish translation by Angel Muñoz García.

"Quaestiones circa logicam." In *Albert of Saxony's Twenty-Five Disputed Questions on Logic, a Critical Edition of His "Quaestiones circa logicam,"* edited by Michael Fitzgerald. Leyden: E. J. Brill, 2002.

Expositio et Quaestiones in Aristotelis Physicam ad Albertum de Saxonia attributae, edited by Benoît Patar. 3 vols. "Philosophes médiévaux" 39–41. Louvain-la-Neuve: Peeters, 1999.

WORKS ABOUT ALBERT OF SAXONY

Biard, Joël. "Albert de Saxe et les sophismes de l'infini." In *Sophisms in Medieval Logic and Grammar*, edited by Stephen Read, 288–303. Dordrecht: Kluwer, 1993.

Biard, Joël. "Les sophismes du savoir: Albert de Saxe entre Jean Buridan et Guillaume Heytesbury." *Vivarium* 27 (1989): 36–50.

Gonzales, A. "The Theory of Assertoric Consequences in Albert of Saxony." *Franciscan Studies* 18 (1958): 290–354; 19: 13–114.

Heidingsfelder, Georg. *Albert von Sachsen. Sein Lebensgang und sein Kommentar zur Nikomachischen Ethik des Aristoteles.* "Beiträge zur Geschichte der Philosophie des Mittelalters" 22, 3–4. Münster: Aschendorff, 1927. The biographical part is now dated, but the study on ethics remains valid.

Kann, Christoph. *Die Eigenschaften der Termini. Eine Untersuchung zur "Perutilis Logica" des Alberts von Sachsen.* Leiden: E. J. Brill, 1993.

Sarnowsky, Jürgen. "Place and Space in Albert of Saxony's Commentaries on the *Physics.*" *Arabic Sciences and Philosophy* 9 (1999): 25–45.

Joël Biard (2005)

ALBERT THE GREAT

See Appendix, Vol. 10

ALBINUS

See *Alcinous*

ALBO, JOSEPH
(*c. 1380–c. 1444*)

The Spanish-Jewish preacher and philosopher Joseph Albo was the last major figure of the philosophical surge in medieval Jewry. Little is known about his early life; he was probably born at Monreal, in the kingdom of Aragon, and he asserted that Hasdai Crescas was his teacher. Albo was one of the principal apologists for the Jews at the Colloquium of Tortosa (February 7, 1413–November 3, 1414); his activities as apologist and preacher are reflected in the style of his philosophic classic, *Sefer ha-'Ikkarim* (*The Book of Roots*).

Albo's acknowledged and unacknowledged borrowings from other writers are so extensive that he was accused of plagiarism in his own age, as well as in more recent and more sensitive times. We must recognize, however, that Albo's purpose was to systematize and thus to defend the dogmas of Judaism rather than to produce an original philosophic work. Clarity and lucidity, systematic and easily remembered organization of materials, and simple and uninvolved style of presentation have made Albo's *The Book of Roots* one of the most popular works of medieval Hebrew literature. Indeed, it was one of the earliest printed Hebrew books, the first edition having been issued at Soncino, Italy, in 1485. Albo's occasional use of medical materials to illustrate his thought has suggested to critics that he may have been trained as a physician. He was well trained in Jewish philosophy, and in addition he knew, probably at second hand, the works of the Arabic Aristotelians.

Albo asserted that there are three essential dogmas ("roots") of Judaism: the existence of God, revelation, and reward and punishment. Seven secondary principles were derived from these three. The existence of God yields four: his unity, his incorporeality, his timelessness, and his perfection. From the dogma of revelation Albo derived two secondary principles: the prophets were the medium of revelation, and the Mosaic law will have binding force until another law is proclaimed with equal publicity; that is, before 600,000 men. God's providential knowledge in the matter of retribution was, for Albo, the sole secondary derivative from the doctrine of reward and punishment. Beyond these primary and secondary roots are other logically derived "branches" that every professing Jew must believe or be guilty of heresy, among them the doctrine of the Messiah.

It may be presumed that Albo removed the doctrine of the Messiah from the center of the Jewish faith as an important part of his polemic against Christianity, a recurrent feature of *The Book of Roots*. As an aspect of this polemic, Book III, Chapter 25 contains an actual summary of a disputation between a Jew and a non-Jew (omitted in some editions).

See also Crescas, Hasdai; Jewish Philosophy.

Bibliography

BILINGUAL EDITION

Husik, Isaac. *Sefer ha-'Ikkarim*, 5 vols. Philadelphia: Jewish Publication Society, 1929–1930. Critical edition of the Hebrew text, with facing English translation.

DISCUSSIONS

Agus, Jacob B. *The Evolution of Jewish Thought*. London and New York: Abelard-Schuman, 1959.

Blau, Joseph L. *The Story of Jewish Philosophy*. New York: Random House, 1962.

Guttmann, Julius. *Philosophies of Judaism*. Translated by D. W. Silverman. New York: Holt, Rinehart and Winston, 1964.

Husik, Isaac. *History of Mediaeval Jewish Philosophy*. New York: Macmillan, 1916.

J. L. Blau (1967)

ALBO, JOSEPH [ADDENDUM]

Albo remains one of the lesser-studied philosophers of the medieval period, in part because his main work more apologetic than philosophical in nature. No full-length monograph has been written on him; rather, he is the subject of scattered articles on diverse topics. Not surprisingly, the most systematic work has been done on his dogmatics, with the place of dogma in Judaism generally arousing a measure of philosophical interest in the late twentieth and early twenty-first centuries. Albo follows Simeon ben Tzemach Duran (1361–1444) in reducing Maimonides's thirteen principles of faith to three—with eight, not seven, derivative principles: revelation yielding (1) God's knowledge; (2) prophecy; and (3) the authenticity of the divine messenger. Menachem M. Kellner, however, has argued that in his portrayal of Torah as having the axiomatic structure of a deductive science, Albo is the first to present the commandments rather than metaphysics as embodying this scientific structure. Support for this view may be found in Albo's account of the six nonessential beliefs, or branches, particular to Jewish dogmatics, which are not strictly entailed by the earlier fundamental or derivative principles, even though their denial constitutes heresy.

A further significant strand in Albo's thought in which this emphasis on practice can also be found is the shift from the intellectualism of the Aristotelians—for whom intellectual apprehension was the path to perfection—to an act-based theology in which acts are even at one point referred to as knowledge.

The particular scientific topic of time has been subject to detailed analysis by Warren Zev Harvey. Whereas Albo follows his teacher Crescas in asserting that time is independent of motion and therefore of the physical world, Harvey argues that Albo is the first to state that time is an imagined duration rather than one that is intellectually cognized. This is significant for Albo as a foundation for one of his derivative principles—that God is independent of time—though Harvey argues that the links here are not demonstrated. As with all of the above, Albo's remarks here are suggestive, but left underdeveloped.

See also Aristotelianism; Crescas, Hasdai; Dogma; Jewish Philosophy; Maimonides.

Bibliography

Harvey, Warren Zev. "Albo's Discussion of Time." *The Jewish Quarterly Review* 70 (4) (1980): 210–238.

Kellner, Menachem M. "The Conception of the Torah as a Deductive Science in Medieval Jewish Thought." *Revue des etudes juives* 146 (1987): 265–279.

Manekin, Charles H. "Hebrew Philosophy in the Fourteenth and Fifteenth Centuries: An Overview." In *History of Jewish Philosophy*, edited by Daniel H. Frank and Oliver Leaman. New York: Routledge, 1997.

Shatz, David. "Freedom, Responsibility and Hardening of the Hearts: Albo *vs* Maimonides." *Faith and Philosophy* 14 (4) (1997): 478–509.

Sirat, Colette. *A History of Jewish Philosophy in the Middle Ages*, 374–381. Cambridge, U.K.: Cambridge University Press, 1985.

Daniel Rynhold (2005)

ALCINOUS
(fl. c. 150 CE)

Alcinous is the name that has come down to us in the manuscript tradition as the author of a handbook of Platonic doctrine, *Didaskalikos tôn Platonos dogmatôn*, probably from the second century CE. Following an 1879 suggestion by the German scholar Jacob Freudenthal, this figure was identified for more than a hundred years with the Middle Platonist philosopher known as Albinus, but this is now recognized to have been based on unsound assumptions, and the work has been returned to its shadowy author. The *Didaskalikos* has much in common with another second-century handbook of Platonism, the *De Platone et eius dogmate* of Apuleius, but the similarities are not close enough to indicate that they emanate from the same school.

The *Didaskalikos* is an introduction to Platonism as it was understood in the first and second centuries CE, which means that it exhibits an amalgam of Platonic, Aristotelian, and Stoic formulations and doctrines, presented as clarifications and amplifications of Plato's views. Aristotelian influence is particularly to be seen in the sphere of logic, where the whole system of syllogistic is claimed for Plato; Stoic influence may be seen chiefly in ethics, in relation to the doctrine that virtue is sufficient for happiness. In either case the assumption is that Aristotle and the Stoics are only expounding Platonic doctrine.

The work is divided as follows. After three introductory chapters, concerned with the definition of philosophy and the distinction of its "parts"—physics, ethics, and logic—Alcinous proceeds to take these three topics in order, beginning with logic (chaps. 4–6), then turning to "physics" (chaps. 7–26), comprising both an account of first principles, Matter, Form, and God (chaps. 7–11), and then of the physical world, largely based on Plato's *Timaeus*, but also including discussions of the immortality of the soul, and of fate and free will (chaps. 12–26); and finally ethics, covering such topics as the virtues, happiness, the purpose of life (*telos*)—which he characterizes as "likeness to God"—the emotions, and political theory (chaps. 27–34). The work ends with a disquisition on the difference between the philosopher and the Sophist (chap. 35), and a brief conclusion (chap. 36).

While the *Didaskalikos* is not securely datable, there is nothing in it that cannot be seen as "Middle Platonist" in doctrine. Even the discussion of God in chapter 10, which has many intriguing aspects, including a distinction between a supreme God, a cosmic Intellect and a World Soul, can be accommodated within Middle Platonist parameters.

See also Aristotle; Plato; Stoicism.

Bibliography

Dillon, John M. *The Middle Platonists: A Study of Platonism, 80 B.C. to A.D. 220*. London: Duckworth, 1977. Rev. ed. Ithaca, NY: Cornell University Press, 1996.

Dillon, John M., trans. *Alcinous: The Handbook of Platonism*. Oxford, U.K.: Clarendon Press, 1993.

Giusta, M. *I dossografi di etica*. 2 vols. Turin: Giappichelli, 1967.

Whittaker, John. *Alcinoos: Enseignement des doctrines de Platon*. Budé ed. Paris: Belles lettres, 1990.

John Dillon (2005)

ALCMAEON OF CROTON
(c. 540–500 BCE)

Alcmaeon of Croton (a Greek city-state in southern Italy) was a pioneer in the study of human psychology and physiology. He published one book in the late sixth or first half of the fifth century BCE. Only two or three fragments of the book survive, but substantial reports of his views are preserved in authors such as Theophrastus. It is controversial whether Alcmaeon was primarily a physician and medical writer or whether he dealt with physiological issues as part of a typical pre-Socratic account of the cosmos. Beginning in the second century CE, some authors call him a Pythagorean, but the earliest sources do not. Aristotle appears to distinguish him from the Pythagoreans (*Metaph.* 986a22).

Alcmaeon is the earliest author to state the common ancient view that health depends on a balance of opposed powers in the body. Just as Anaximander used a political analogy to explain the workings of the cosmos, Alcmaeon said that "equality (*isonomia*) of powers (wet, dry, cold, hot, bitter, sweet, etc.) maintains health, but monarchy among them produces disease" (Fr. 4 Diels-Kranz). Alcmaeon may have excised an eyeball and observed passages (*poroi*—i.e., the optic nerve) leading from the eye toward the brain. Perhaps as a result of this observation, he was the first person in the Greek tradition to argue that the brain was the seat of thought. There is no evidence, however, that he used dissection to any further extent or that he practiced it systematically. He was the first to address a series of issues that would become standard in later writings on physiology, such as the causes of sleep, waking, and death. He argued that human seed came from the brain, that the brain was the first part of the embryo to develop and that both parents contributed seed in the production of children.

In contrast to the wealth of evidence for Alcmaeon's views on human physiology, the evidence for his cosmological views is sketchy. He may have believed that the cosmos, like the human body, arose from a balance of opposing powers. He also maintained that the sun was flat.

Alcmaeon argued that there was no human knowledge of what is not perceptible and that judgments about what is not perceptible can only be made on the basis of what is perceived. He was the first to make a clear distinction between animals, which only have sense perception, and human beings, who also have understanding. Alcmaeon may have originated the three-step empiricist epistemology found in both Plato (*Phaedo* 96a–b) and Aristotle (*Posterior Analytics* 100a3) that begins with sensations, which when collected become memories and opinions, which in turn become knowledge when they gain fixity. Finally, Alcmaeon gave the first argument for the immortality of the soul. The exact nature of Alcmaeon's argument is hard to reconstruct, because it was later developed by Plato in the *Phaedrus* (245c), but he appears to have argued that the soul was immortal because it was in constant motion.

See also Anaximander; Aristotle; Plato; Psychology; Pythagoras and Pythagoreanism; Theophrastus.

Bibliography

TEXTS AND COMMENTARIES

Diels, H., and W. Kranz. *Die Fragmente der Vorsokratiker.* 6th ed., vol. 1, 210–216. Dublin, Ireland: Weidmann, 1952. Contains the Greek texts with translations in German.

Wachtler, J. *De Alcmaeone Crotoniata.* Leipzig, Germany: Teubner, 1896. Contains Greek texts with commentary in Latin.

DISCUSSIONS

Lloyd, G. E. R. "Alcmeon and the Early History of Dissection." *Sudhoffs Archiv* 59 (1975): 113–147.

Mansfeld, J. "Alcmaeon: 'Physikos' or Physician." In *Kephalaion: Studies in Greek Philosophy and its continuation offered to Professor C. J. de Vogel,* edited by J. Mansfeld and L. M. de Rijk, 26–38. Assen, Netherlands: Van Gorcum, 1975.

Vlastos, Gregory. "Isonomia." *American Journal of Philology* 74 (4) (1953): 337–366.

Carl Huffman (2005)

ALEMBERT, JEAN LE ROND D'
(1717–1783)

The French mathematician and encyclopedist Jean Le Rond d'Alembert was the illegitimate son of Madame de Tencin and the artillery general Destouches-Canon. He was abandoned by his mother on the steps of the baptistry of Saint-Jean-Le-Rond in Paris, from which he received his name. Shortly afterward his father returned from the provinces, claimed the child, and placed him with Madame Rousseau, a glazier's wife, with whom d'Alembert remained until a severe illness in 1765 forced him to seek new quarters. Through the Destouches family, Jean Le Rond was placed in the exclusive Jansenist Collège de Mazarin and given the name of d'Aremberg, which he later changed to d'Alembert, no doubt for phonetic reasons. At the college an effort was made to win him over to the Jansenist cause, and he went so far as to write a commentary on St. Paul. The intense Jesuit-Jansenist controversy served only to disgust him with both sides, however, and he left the college with the degree of bachelor of arts and a profound distrust of, and aversion to, metaphysical disputes.

After attending law school for two years he changed to the study of medicine, which he soon abandoned for mathematics. His talent and fascination for mathematics were such that at an early age he had independently discovered many mathematical principles, only to find later that they were already known. In 1739 he submitted a *mémoire* on integral calculus to the Académie des Sciences, but it was his *Traité de dynamique* in 1743 that won him acclaim and paved the way for his entry into the academy that same year. The introduction to his treatise is significant as the first enunciation of d'Alembert's philosophy of science. He accepted the reality of truths rationally deduced from instinctive principles insofar as they are verifiable experimentally and therefore are not simply aprioristic deductions. Although admitting unproved axioms at the base of his principles of mechanics, thus revealing his debt to René Descartes, d'Alembert rejected metaphysical affirmations and the search for universals and expressed admiration for Bacon's experimental and inductive method.

The decade of the 1740s may be considered d'Alembert's mathematical period during which he made his most outstanding and fruitful contributions to that discipline. In addition to the *Traité de dynamique* he wrote *Mémoire sur la réfraction des corps solides* (1741); *Théorie de l'équilibre du mouvement des fluides* (1744 and 1751); *Réflexions sur la cause générale des vents*, which won him the prize of the Berlin Academy in 1746 as well as membership in that body; a *mémoire* on vibrating strings (*Recherches sur les cordes vibrantes*), written in 1747 for the Berlin Academy; *Recherches sur la précession des équinoxes et sur la nutation* (1749); *Réflexions sur la théorie de la résistance des fluides* (1752); *Recherches sur differents points importants du systéme du monde* (1754–1756), plus eight volumes of *Opuscules mathématiques* (1761–1780).

D'Alembert's first philosophical work, the *Discours préliminaire* to the *Encyclopédie,* appeared in 1751. As early as 1746 he, with Denis Diderot, had been on the publisher's payroll as translator, in connection with the projected French version of Chambers's *Cyclopaedia.* We may suppose that, like Diderot, he had already worked for the publishers as a translator of English works for French consumption, thus exposing himself to the writings of the English empiricists and supplementing the meager pension left him by his father. In any event, d'Alembert had read Bacon as early as 1741; and his *Discours préliminaire* revealed not only his debt to the Descartes of the *Regulae,* shorn of metaphysics, but his admiration for, and indebtedness to, Bacon for his experimental method; Isaac Newton, whom he admired for proving gravitational force without trying to explain its first cause; and John Locke, whose metaphysical method he adopted. While paying lip service to the traditional religious concepts of his time, d'Alembert used Lockian sensationalist theory to arrive at a naturalistic interpretation of nature. It is not through vague and arbitrary hypotheses that nature can be known, he asserted, but through a careful study of physical phenomena. He discounted metaphysical truths as inaccessible through reason. In the *Discours,* d'Alembert began by affirming his faith in the reliability of the evidence for an external world derived from the senses and dismissed the Berkeleian objections as metaphysical subtleties that are contrary to good sense. Asserting that all knowledge is derived from the senses, he traced the development of knowledge from the sense impressions of primitive man to their elaboration into more complex forms of expression. Language, music, and the arts communicate emotions and concepts derived from the senses and, as such, are imitations of nature. For example, d'Alembert believed that music that is not descriptive is simply noise. Since all knowledge can be reduced to its origin in sensations, and since these are approximately the same in all men, it follows that even the most limited mind can be taught any art or science. This was the basis for d'Alembert's great faith in the power of education to spread the principles of the Enlightenment.

In his desire to examine all domains of the human intellect, d'Alembert was representative of the encyclopedic eighteenth-century mind. He believed not only that humanity's physical needs are the basis of scientific and aesthetic pursuits, but also that morality too is pragmatically evolved from social necessity. This would seem to anticipate the thought of Auguste Comte, who also placed morality on a sociological basis, but it would be a mistake to regard d'Alembert as a Positivist in the manner of Comte. If d'Alembert was a Positivist, he was so through temporary necessity, based on his conviction that since ultimate principles cannot be readily attained, one must reluctantly be limited to fragmentary truths attained through observation and experimentation. He was a rationalist, however, in that he did not doubt that these ultimate principles exist. In the *Discours préliminaire* he expressed the belief that everything could be reduced to one first principle, the universe being "one great truth" if we could only see it in a broader perspective. Similarly, in the realm of morality and aesthetics, he sought to reduce moral and aesthetic norms to dogmatic absolutes, and this would seem to be in conflict with the pragmatic approach of pure sensationalist theories. He was forced, in such cases, to appeal to a sort of intuition or good sense that was more Cartesian than Lockian, but he did not attempt to reconcile his inconsistencies and rather sought to remain within the basic premises of sensationalism. D'Alembert's tendency to go beyond the tenets of his own theories, as he did, for example, in admitting that mathematical realities are a creation of the human intellect and do not correspond to physical reality, has led Ernst Cassirer to conclude that d'Alembert, despite his commitment to sensationalist theory, had an insight into its limitations.

During the early 1750s d'Alembert engaged actively in the polemics of the time, particularly in the defense of the *Encyclopédie* and the party it represented. Many of the articles he wrote for that publication, as well as his preface to Volume III (1753), were aimed at the enemies of the *Encyclopédie,* notably the Jesuits, who were among the first to attack it for its antireligious and republican orientation. In addition, he took part in the controversy over French versus Italian music, which was inflamed by Jean-Jacques Rousseau's attack on French music in "Lettre sur la musique française" (1753). D'Alembert had already published his *Éléments de musique* (1752), based on Jean-Philippe Rameau's theories on harmonics, and in 1754 he published anonymously his *Réflexions sur la musique en général et la musique française en particulier.*

D'Alembert's chief preoccupation at this period, however, was with philosophy and literature. His *Mélanges de littérature et de philosophie* appeared in 1753 in two volumes (expanded to four volumes in 1759, with a fifth volume added in 1767), and it is here that his skepticism concerning metaphysical problems is delineated. Proceeding on the premise that certainty in this field cannot be reached through reason alone, he considered the arguments for and against the existence of God and cautiously concluded in the affirmative, on the grounds that intelligence cannot be the product of brute matter. Like Newton, d'Alembert viewed the universe as a clock, which necessarily implies a clockmaker, but his final attitude is that expressed by Montaigne's "*Que sais-je?*" Humankind's uncertainty before this enigmatic universe is the basis of d'Alembert's plea for religious tolerance. He maintained his skeptical deism as an official, public position throughout his life, but there is evidence for believing that in the late 1760s, under the influence of Diderot (whose *Rêve de d'Alembert* appeared in 1769), d'Alembert was converted to Diderot's materialism. In private correspondence with intimate friends, d'Alembert revealed his commitment to an atheistic interpretation of the universe. He accepted intelligence as simply the result of a complex development of matter and not as evidence for a divine intelligence.

Aside from the publication of a polemical brochure, *Histoire de la destruction des Jésuites,* in 1765 (with two additional *Lettres* on the subject in 1767), d'Alembert spent the last two decades of his life in furthering the cause of the *philosophes* in the Académie Française—by writing his *Éloges,* which were read in the Académie (and published in 1779), and by fostering the election of candidates of his own choice. Mademoiselle de Lespinasse's salon, where d'Alembert presided, became, in the words of Frédéric Masson, the "obligatory antechamber of the Académie." In this period he became influential with young aspiring men of letters, whom he recruited for his party and whose careers he fostered. The most notable of his disciples was the Marquis de Condorcet. After years of ill health, d'Alembert died of a bladder ailment and was buried as an unbeliever in a common, unmarked grave.

See also Bacon, Roger; Cassirer, Ernst; Comte, Auguste; Condorcet, Marquis de; Descartes, René Diderot, Denis; Locke, John; Music, Philosophy of; Newton, Isaac; Rousseau, Jean-Jacques.

Bibliography

WORKS BY D'ALEMBERT

Oeuvres philosophiques et littéraires. Edited by J. F. Bastien. 18 vols. Paris, 1805. Not so complete as the Belin edition but contains letters to d'Alembert not included elsewhere. *Nouvelle édition augmentée.* Edited by A. Belin. 5 vols. Paris, 1821. The most complete edition to date.

Oeuvres et correspondance inédites de d'Alembert. Edited by Charles Henry. Paris, 1887. Contains important supplements to above editions in the fields of philosophy, literature, and music, as well as additional correspondence.

Discours préliminaire de l'Encyclopédie. Edited by P. Picavet. Paris, 1912. Standard critical edition.

For a fuller listing, see *A Critical Bibliography of French Literature.* Edited by D. C. Cabeen. Syracuse, NY: Syracuse University Press, 1947–1951. Vol. IV, pp. 136–138.

WORKS ON D'ALEMBERT

Bertrand, Joseph. *D'Alembert.* Paris: Librarie Hochette, 1889. Despite shortcomings and reliance on Condorcet's *Eloge de d'Alembert,* the most complete biography to date.

Grimsley, Ronald. *Jean d'Alembert.* Oxford: Clarendon Press, 1963. A good, comprehensive treatment of d'Alembert's philosophy and ideas. Less concerned with biography.

Kunz, Ludwig. "Die Erkenntnistheorie d'Alemberts," in *Archiv für Geschichte der Philosophie,* Vol. 20 (1907), 96–126. Considers relation between d'Alembert's metaphysics and English empiricists. Presents him as a link between empiricists and Comte.

Misch, Georg. *Zur Entstehung des französischen Positivismus.* Berlin, 1900. Influence of d'Alembert's empiricism and materialistic viewpoint on Comte's Positivism.

Muller, Maurice. *Essai sur la philosophie de Jean d'Alembert.* Paris, 1926. Most important and complete study of d'Alembert's general philosophy.

Pappas, John N. *Voltaire and d'Alembert.* Bloomington: Indiana University Press, 1962. Considers d'Alembert's position and method in spreading the ideals of the Enlightenment and his influence on Voltaire.

John N. Pappas (1967)

ALEXANDER, SAMUEL
(1859–1938)

The British realist metaphysician Samuel Alexander was born in Sydney, New South Wales, and was educated at Wesley College, Melbourne. He came to England in 1877 on a scholarship to Balliol College, Oxford, where he read mathematics, classics, and philosophy (*literae humaniores*). In 1882 he was elected to a fellowship at Lincoln College, Oxford, becoming the first Jew to be a fellow of an Oxford or Cambridge college. His earliest work, the Green Prize essay in moral philosophy, subsequently published as *Moral Order and Progress* (1889), shows the influence of the idealist ethics dominant in Oxford at the time. But he soon began moving toward an approach to philosophy that could be more closely related to the development of the empirical sciences, particularly biology and psychology. He gave up his fellowship and spent a year in Hugo Münsterberg's psychological laboratory at Freiburg, Germany, continuing in private study until his election to the chair of philosophy at Owens College (later the Victoria University of Manchester) in 1893. He held the chair until his retirement in 1924 and lived in Manchester until his death in 1938, a beloved, influential, and, indeed, legendary figure in both city and university.

EMPIRICAL METAPHYSICS

Alexander wrote occasional papers and a small book on John Locke, but it was not until 1920 that he published his major work, *Space, Time and Deity* (delivered as the Gifford Lectures in Glasgow in 1915). This was a comprehensive and constructive system, which he claimed was metaphysics following an "empirical method." By this he meant that he understood metaphysics to be a very inclusive kind of science, differing from the special sciences "not in its spirit, but only in its boundaries, dealing with certain comprehensive features of experience which lie outside the purview of the special sciences." Alexander called these features "categorial" and "a priori" but said that this must not be taken to mean that they are imposed or constructed by thought; they are discerned by reflective inspection as pervasive features of the world. As such he called them "nonempirical," reserving the term *empirical* for the variable features of the world. But the *study* of both, as a study of what is found in experience, he called "empirical." This could be considered an empirical way of thinking only in a much broader and more speculative sense than subsequent forms of empiricism, with their stricter notions of what constitutes tests in observation and experiment. Nevertheless, Alexander insisted that his system not only was a speculative world view but also took account of certain ways of thinking he believed were suggested by work in contemporary experimental science. Here his starting point was probably his interest in physiological psychology (he had introduced this study into the University of Manchester at a time when British universities were still slow to recognize it).

MIND. In contrast to idealistic or dualistic views, Alexander regarded mind as, in one sense, identical with an organized structure of physiological and neural processes, there being no animistic or purely "mental" factor over and above these. But in another sense, mind could be looked on as a new "emergent"—when neural processes are organized in a certain way, they manifest a new quality, consciousness, or awareness.

EMERGENTS. By *emergents* (a term generally ascribed to C. Lloyd Morgan, though its first use can be found in G. H. Lewes) Alexander designated certain organized patterns which, he held, produce new qualitative syntheses that could not have been predicted from knowledge of the constituent elements of the pattern before they were so organized. Emergents are thus what others have called gestalt properties of organized systems; Alexander thought of them particularly as characteristics of those syntheses where some strikingly new quality can be dis-

cerned. He generalized the idea that new qualities emerge from patterns of subvening elements of certain degrees of complexity, so as to look on the world as a hierarchy of qualities, a hierarchy in which those higher in the scale depend on the lower but manifest something genuinely new.

SPACE-TIME. At the basis of nature Alexander set *space-time* as a continuum of interrelated complexes of motion. These can be analyzed into relations between "point-instants," a point-instant being the limiting case of a motion. Sometimes he spoke of point-instants as if they were real elements, the smallest instances of spatiotemporal motions, sometimes as if they were ideal concepts, the bare notion of time at a point or space at an instant, while any actual motion has a spatiotemporal spread.

Space-time was also distinguished into "perspectives." A perspective defines how space-time can be ordered with reference to particular point-instants. It is a line of advance, or phase of a spatiotemporal process, seen in relation to some point-instant as its center of reference. Alexander used the illustration of a tree sawn across. For the carpenter the concentric rings are simultaneous, but this is to look on it as an artificial section. For the botanist they are of different dates, carrying with them the history of the tree. Thus, a perspective is a historical phase of the process of nature, ordered with reference to some event, *e*, as center and integrating other events related to the event from which the perspective is developed. These may be integrated as observably contemporaneous or as earlier and later stages in motions of which *e* is a stage.

The definition of a perspective thus depends on the notion of motions and their interrelation, and even on their causal relations. It is difficult to see how these notions can be derived purely from that of structures within space-time. Indeed, the notion of space-time itself as the fundamental stuff or matrix out of which things arise is certainly not one that it is natural to see as an "empirical" description of the most general features of the world as it discloses itself to an observing mind.

CATEGORIES. It might be more plausible if Alexander could be taken to have meant that the basic universal feature of all experience is its spatiotemporal character. He did indeed claim to follow Kant in holding that the world is apprehended first and foremost as a spatiotemporal manifold, under categories. Apart from the union of space and time in a four-dimensional continuum, his categories follow closely the Kantian ones of substance, cause, number, and relation. But Alexander insisted that these categories are discovered or discerned in the world and are not a conceptual framework imposed by the mind. Indeed, according to his realist theory of knowledge, thought does not construct or impose conceptual schemes. Knowledge is "contemplation" of an object where there is a relation of "compresence" between a mind and an object (except in the special case of a mind's knowledge of itself, for a mind cannot be compresent as an object to itself but is aware of itself as knowing and perceiving; Alexander calls this kind of knowing "enjoyment"). But it is surely difficult to understand why any mind compresent with the world of nature would see in it just these particular all-pervasive categorial features.

EMPIRICAL FEATURES OF REGIONS OF SPACE-TIME. Beside the categorial features, which Alexander called "nonempirical," meaning by this that they are invariable and all-pervasive, we discover "empirical" features, defined as variable qualities characterizing particular regions of space-time. "Universals" are discerned *in rebus*, as plans of configurations of motions in space-time showing persistent identities; Alexander called them "habits" of space-time. Within space-time arises the hierarchy of emergent qualities. The patterns of motions that differentiate it are in the first place bearers of the properties of extension and inertia that characterize "matter." These organized patterns of matter are bearers of the qualities found in physical structures and chemical syntheses. Some of these syntheses, in turn, are bearers of the quality of "life," and some living structures are bearers of mind or consciousness, which is the highest empirical quality known to us. There is no reason, however, to assume that this is the highest possible emergent quality. Alexander held that the structures that are bearers of "mind" may in their turn become productive of a new emergent quality, which he called "deity."

DEITY. The term *deity* does not here stand for a God who precedes the universe as its cause or creator. Alexander did not try to find in such terms an "explanation" of why the universe should exist. Existence, he held, should be accepted with "natural piety" (borrowing a phrase of William Wordsworth's), and its general character should then be described. This general character is first and foremost spatiotemporal. In addition, Alexander held that it exhibits a *nisus*, or creative tendency, toward the production of new qualitative syntheses. So in one sense God can be thought of as *Deus sive Natura*, the universe of space-time "pregnant" with emergent qualities. In another sense deity is "the next highest emergent quality which the uni-

verse is engaged in bringing to birth." This quality, Alexander suggested, may emerge in beings—we do not yet know what they would be like—who would be bearers of deity as we are of mind, and these in their turn might prepare the basis for a yet further emergent quality. Alexander held that the existence of religious sentiments and aspirations witnesses to an experience of the *nisus* toward the higher quality of deity in some of those who are already bearers of mind. Such religious feelings, he thought, are incipient aspirations toward a new level of development. It is toward this further stage of development, not toward an already existent object, that the religious sentiment is directed. Alexander claimed that he started from the empirical fact of this sentiment, rather than from a theory of its object, and asked what it suggests; the religious sentiment can be interpreted as the feelings of beings caught up in the *nisus* of a universe "pregnant" with the quality of deity.

TIME AS MIND. Is there any reason in the nature of space-time itself why there should be this *nisus*? Alexander sometimes spoke as though the mere fact of conjoining time with space in itself produces the possibility not only of a dynamic but even of a creative process. He summed this up in the saying "Time is the Mind of Space"—surely one of the most astonishing remarks ever made by a metaphysician. But it was not intended merely to shock. It should be read in connection with Alexander's interest in physiological psychology and the view of the body-mind relation that he derived from this and that he here extended in a daring analogy. Alexander reported that he reached his notion of perspectives in space-time by considering the unity of the self. There is no such thing as awareness of the self at an instant. The least moment of conscious experience is a "specious present" with a durational aspect and, as embodied, a spatialized aspect. Our consciousness of what we are thinking at any moment is linked with the memory of what we were thinking, for example, a fraction of a second ago, and it is directed in anticipation toward what we are going to think a fraction of a second from now. What we are, at any given stage, is partly constituted by memories of the past and anticipation of the future.

Hence, the unity of the self depends on events of different dates being brought into a perspective with reference to the self of "present" experience. Similarly, a physical perspective consists of all events that can be shown to be earlier or later stages in lines of development in which a given event, taken as center of reference, is a phase. A perspective thus describes a historical line of advance. The temporal aspect of this is said to be the analogue of its "mind" and the spatial aspect the analogue of its "body." This is because mental experience is partly constituted by memory of the past and anticipation of the future and, more specifically, because the "mind" aspect of anything is looked on as the *new* quality it may exhibit at its latest point of development, whereas the organized structure that is the bearer of this property and could be described beforehand as accomplished fact is looked on as its body. Time is not mind in the sense of consciousness or thought, which is the distinctive quality characteristic of the level we call mind proper. It is "mind" in an analogical sense, as whatever is the new property characteristic of a new qualitative synthesis. Thus, for example, to Alexander the defining qualities of matter are the primary qualities, such as extension and inertia. Secondary qualities, such as color, are emergents from organized complexes of matter and may, as such, be called their "mind." This is not to give them some rudimentary degree of consciousness; it is to say that on each level there is an element that can be called the analogue of mind, as introducing something new. But what is new appears sometimes to be not describable as an *element*, but rather as a new way of *functioning* released in some particular kind of ordered structure. When this happens, the new way of functioning dominates the lower levels that support it but does not transform them into something different. Physicochemical processes continue to be physicochemical processes, and neural processes to be a form of physicochemical processes. But where there is conscious thinking, although no separate animistic or mental factor may be present, the whole ordered structure becomes a vehicle for this new activity, and we say we are confronted by an "embodied mind."

TIME AS AN ATTRIBUTE OF REALITY. Alexander's view of a hierarchy of syntheses with new emergent qualities may be significant, but can time, as the pure notion of irreversible succession, be sufficient to account for their possibility? To say that there is a general tendency for complexes of one order to combine and form complexes of what will become a new order must surely presuppose some fundamental property or properties in the world besides those of space and time; Alexander, in fact, admits this when he speaks of a *nisus,* or creative tendency, in space-time. But is this a necessary property of an infinite four-dimensional continuum, unless one can assume that the mere fact of succession entails creative advance? Alexander may have been near enough to nineteenth-century ideas of inevitable evolutionary progress to be able implicitly to assume this. In agreement with these ideas, he insisted that philosophers must "take Time seri-

ously"; that is to say, they must incorporate a conception of time as an essential attribute of reality and not only as describing a way of experiencing or measuring a reality that is ultimately nontemporal. Alexander said that if Benedict (Baruch) de Spinoza could be rewritten with time as well as extension as an attribute of substance, this would represent the type of past philosophy most congenial to him; indeed, if someone were to write on his funerary urn "*Erravit cum Spinoza,*" he would be content.

REALITY AS PROCESS. Alexander's view of space-time as the final reality seems, however, open to two interpretations. On the one (perhaps the more Spinozistic) interpretation, space and time are the two necessary attributes of an infinite substance, distinguishable, it is true, into perspectives defined by reference to point-instants, but where "motions" (analogous to Spinoza's "modes") are simply the redistribution of spatiotemporal coefficients within the whole already existent space-time. In this view space-time is looked on as that out of which things come, and we can ask whether, as with the materialist's conception of matter, this is not to treat an abstraction as though it were a reality. In another sense Alexander was giving a view of reality as essentially a process, and as historical. There is an irreversible direction in it, defined by "time's arrow" (to use Arthur Stanley Eddington's expression). In this, nature is focused in lines of development whose "history" describes the successive levels of ordered structures they exhibit. At each stage in time, where there is a new emergent quality, this quality is the spearhead of a genuine creative advance. Yet if this new emergent quality at each stage is said to be analogous to mind, is it satisfactory to equate this with saying that it is analogous to time? It might be more plausible to say that it was Alexander's notion of the *nisus* in space-time that corresponds to the "mind" factor in those complexes whose extended patterns can be regarded as the analogue of the body. Or one might say that the "body" of anything is the external view of nature as unified in that particular perspective, while its "mind" is the "idea" of the distinctive internal quality of that particular perspective; this indeed suggests comparison with Spinoza's view of the body-mind relation.

VALUES

Alexander wrote no large work besides *Space, Time and Deity*. The volume *Beauty and the Other Forms of Value* (1933) is a collection of occasional papers and lectures on themes relating to aesthetics and ethics. The general notion underlying these is that of values as related to the satisfaction of impulses. Values are "tertiary qualities" (supervening on the primary and secondary qualities), characterizing complexes where one component is a mind capable of interest or appreciation. The higher values—beauty, truth, and goodness—are qualities that arise in the satisfaction of certain impulses where these have become contemplative and disengaged from their immediate practical ends. Thus aesthetic creation and enjoyment grow out of the impulse to construct things, which Alexander traced down to the animals ("impulse," he thought, was a less question-begging term than "instinct"). The impulse to construct something out of physical materials, including sounds, becomes a contemplative delight in the form so imposed on the material. Truth is a value analogous to beauty, as that which satisfies the impulse of curiosity when this too becomes contemplative rather than practical. Moral value is a quality created out of natural impulses by the introduction of another natural impulse that can bring form and harmony into the impulses that are its materials. This impulse Alexander called "gregariousness." His interpretation of this was close to Adam Smith's view of "sympathy" as fellow feeling with the feelings of others. Gregariousness, like Smith's sympathy, becomes disinterested and so is able to act as a harmonizing agent both among a person's other impulses and in producing "sociality." The impulse of "sociality" was also invoked in support of Alexander's view that we are directly aware of other minds in such experiences as friendly conversation or quarrels, which are completed as experiences through reciprocated responses. These are not, in Alexander's view, adequately described as merely responses to behavior; they are responses to behavior as expressing the mind of the other person.

A collection of occasional papers and addresses, *Philosophical and Literary Pieces* (1939), was published posthumously by John Laird, prefaced by a memoir that gives a sympathetic account of Alexander the man, including a number of the stories, true or apocryphal, that were told about him. Some of the pieces on nontechnical themes—on Dr. Johnson, for instance, or Jane Austen, or Blaise Pascal—show Alexander in his happiest vein.

Alexander was awarded the Order of Merit in 1930. His appearance was impressive; a bust by Jacob Epstein in the entrance hall of the Arts Building of the University of Manchester gives a good impression of his massive head and beard but misses his kindliness. The library of the University of Manchester contains a large collection of letters written to him by his contemporaries, including the philosophers F. H. Bradley, G. F. Stout, and T. Percy Nunn, the physiologists C. Lloyd Morgan and Sir Charles Scott Sherrington, and the Jewish leaders Chaim Weizmann and Claude Montefiore.

See also Bradley, Francis Herbert; Emergence; Empiricism; Kant, Immanuel; Locke, John; Morgan, C. Lloyd; Pascal, Blaise; Smith, Adam; Spinoza, Benedict (Baruch) de; Stout, George Frederick.

Bibliography

WORKS BY ALEXANDER

Books

Moral Order and Progress. London: Trübner, 1889.

Locke. London: Constable, 1908.

Space, Time and Deity. 2 vols. London: Macmillan, 1920.

Beauty and Other Forms of Value. London: Macmillan, 1933.

Philosophical and Literary Pieces. Edited by J. Laird. London: Macmillan, 1939.

The papers of particular philosophical interest appearing in this volume are "Art and Instinct," Herbert Spencer Lecture (1927); "Artistic Creation and Cosmic Creation," Annual Philosophical Lecture of the British Academy (1927); and "Spinoza and Time," Arthur Davis Memorial Lecture (1921). The book also contains a list of Alexander's published works, including reviews and contributions to journals.

Periodicals

"The Method of Metaphysics; and the Categories." *Mind,* n.s., 21 (1912): 1–20.

"On Relations" and, in particular, "The Cognitive Relation." *Mind,* n.s., 21 (1912): 305–328.

"Collective Willing and Truth." *Mind,* n.s., 22 (1913): 14–47 and 161–189.

"The Basis of Realism." In *Proceedings of the British Academy,* 1914. Republished in *Realism and the Background of Phenomenology,* edited by Roderick M. Chisholm. Glencoe, IL: Free Press, 1960. This lecture relates Alexander's views on the theory of knowledge to those of other philosophers of the time and presents his theory that mind and object are both empirically within nature, their relation being a particular form of a more general relation of "compresence."

"Sense-Perception: A Reply to Mr. Stout." *Mind,* n.s., 32 (1923): 1–11. Written in answer to criticisms by G. F. Stout, in *Mind,* n.s., 31 (1922): 385–412.

WORKS ON ALEXANDER

Broad, C. D. *The Mind and Its Place in Nature,* pp. 646–650. New York: Harcourt, Brace, 1925. Discusses Alexander's "emergence" theory of mind. See also two reviews by Broad of *Space, Time and Deity,* in *Mind,* n.s., 30 (1921): 25–39 and 129–150.

Devaux, P. *Le système d'Alexander.* Paris: J. Vrin, 1929.

McCarthy, J. W. *The Naturalism of Samuel Alexander.* New York: King's Crown, 1948.

Dorothy M. Emmet (1967)

ALEXANDER OF APHRODISIAS

Alexander of Aphrodisias, who was teaching at Athens in 200 CE, was recognized for centuries as the most authoritative exponent of Aristotle. His influence has probably been most far-reaching in the development of the theory of universals because he emphasized certain elements in Aristotle's not always unambiguous account. These were the unqualified priority of the particular substance and the existence of universals only as concepts, or "acts of intellect." The form was what made "this" matter (that is, an identifiable piece) what it was, but it was contingent whether the form was universal in the sense of generic. (Alexander does not notice that a class with only one member, like his case of the sun, is still a class.) What the form is as a subject remains unclear.

More famous is his doctrine about soul and intellect. A human being's intellectual faculty can exist in three conditions, described as three intellects: (1) the "material" intellect (*intellectus possibilis*), which is nothing actual but the bare potentiality (so Aristotelian matter) of the body to develop reason—the condition of babies; (2) the intellect (*intellectus in habitu*) that is the possession of, in fact, is identical with, concepts, or universals gained from sense experience—the condition of adults; (3) the "active" intellect (*intellectus agens*), which is exercising the thoughts that form the *intellectus in habitu* and is thus equivalent to the intellect as aware of itself.

What is distinctively Alexandrist is the identification he made, or seemingly made, of the "active" intellect both with the intellect that Aristotle said entered the body "from outside" and with the intellect eternally thinking of itself that Aristotle said was God. Intellect was, of course, the highest part or function of the soul, but since only the "active" intellect, as a "separate form," could exist without matter, it followed that there was no individual immortality for human beings. The exact relation of the "active" intellect to the individual soul or intellect is obscure in Alexander. He does not describe an active intellect acting directly like an efficient or even formal cause on a passive intellect but suggests rather the quasi-logical relationship which was fundamental to Neoplatonism and which made the less perfect instance of a kind entail the existence of the perfect. Thus, it is not at all certain that he meant thinking itself to go the way of immortality. In the fifteenth century Italian philosophers known as Alexandristi defended this interpretation of Aristotle's psychology against both Averroes's version and the theologically orthodox version of Themistius and Thomas Aquinas.

In other subjects we see Alexander less original but often attacking Stoic doctrine, notably in his tracts *On Fate* and *On Mixture*. But the exact understanding of him is colored always by the difficulty of knowing how far we can trust the writings attributed to him. The commentary on Books E (VI) to N (XIV) of Aristotle's *Metaphysics* and parts of Book II of his own *De Anima* are probably not his. The latter includes the section *On Intellect* which greatly influenced later Greek, Arab, and medieval philosophers. But both may well depend on and be closer to his thought than is allowed by a modern tradition that underestimates Neoplatonizing features of Aristotle as well as of Alexander.

See also Aristotle; Averroes; Neoplatonism; Themistius; Thomas Aquinas, St.; Universals, A Historical Survey.

Bibliography

Alexander's works, including dubious ones, are in *Commentaria in Aristotelem Graeca*, Vols. I–III, and *Supplementum Aristotelicum*, Vol. II (Berlin, 1883–1901). P. Moraux, *Alexandre a'Aphrodise, exégète de la noétique d'Aristote* (Paris, 1942), includes a French translation of *On Intellect*. See also F. E. Cranz, in *Catalogus Translationum et Commentariorum: Mediaeval and Renaissance Latin Translations and Commentaries*, Vol. I (Washington, DC: Catholic University of America Press, 1960), pp. 77–135; Ernst Cassirer, *Das Erkenntnisproblem*, 3rd ed., Part I, "Die Reform der aristotelischen Psychologie" (Berlin: Cassirer, 1922); and J. H. Randall Jr., *The School of Padua and the Emergence of Modern Science* (Padua, 1961).

A. C. Lloyd (1967)

ALEXANDER OF APHRODISIAS [ADDENDUM]

Alexander of Aphrodisias's influence on Islamic philosophy was far reaching. In fact, it could appear to be somewhat out of proportion with his real importance as a thinker. The reason for this is partly fortuitous in that a large number of his works were preserved long enough for them to reach Baghdad in the ninth century CE and be translated into Arabic. Among the most significant of these are the following:

(1) The fragments of the Commentary on Aristotle's Metaphysics, book lambda (*lam* in Arabic) preserved by Ibn Rushd in his own Great Commentary on the same work. The original text is lost in Greek.

(2) The short treatise *On the Principles of the Universe* describing the mechanics of the heavenly motions and the mode of their influence on the sublunary world. It could be defined as a free synthesis of the main themes of Aristotle's *Physics* and *Metaphysics*, with some borrowings from the *De Anima* and the *Nicomachean Ethics*.

(3) A treatise, *On Providence*, preserved in two fairly different translations. This last work was of particular importance to the Muslims in that it provides an Aristotelian answer to a question that is crucial in the context of a monotheistic religion, but was never treated as such by Aristotle himself.

The main features of the philosophical system set forth in these works can be summarized as follows. The heavenly motions are caused by the souls of the spheres (which carry the stars) in their desire to imitate the First Mover of the universe. The counterpart of this upward motion is the influence that the contrasting motions of the stars exert on the world of nature. This influence is as a matter of fact identified by Alexander with nature and providence. But this providence, although emanating from the heavens, is not willed by them, because Alexander postulates that the superior cannot care for the inferior without debasing itself.

Another Alexandrian tenet that exerted a profound influence on the Arab philosophers is his identification of the Active Intellect of Aristotle's *De Anima* with the Unmoved Mover of the *Metaphysics*. The intellectual processes of the human mind were thus directly connected with the divine.

Bibliography

Genequand, Charles. *Alexander of Aphrodisias on the Cosmos.* Leiden, Netherlands: Brill, 2001.

Thillet, Pierre. *Alexandre d'Aphrodise. Traité de la Providence.* Paris: Verdier, 2003.

Charles Genequand (2005)

ALEXANDER OF HALES
(c. 1185–1245)

Alexander of Hales, "Doctor Irrefragabilis," friar minor, was an English Scholastic at the University of Paris. He was born in Hales Owen, Shropshire, and died in Paris.

Alexander was a student at Paris about 1200 and received his M.A. before 1210. He joined the faculty of theology, becoming a master regent about 1220. After 1222 Alexander made an innovation in the university by using the *Book of Sentences* of Peter Lombard as the basic text for theological courses. His newly published *Glossa* (identified only in 1945) was the result of this work. At the height of his career, about 1236, he became a Franciscan, "edifying the world and giving new status to the Order" (in the words of Roger Bacon). After he was put in charge of the school at the Paris friary, he continued his teaching, especially through his *Disputed Questions,* and had some part to play in the "great Summa weighing more than a horse, which the friars out of reverence ascribed to him and called 'the Summa of Friar Alexander'" (R. Bacon). At the same time, he participated in the affairs of the order, attending the chapter that deposed Brother Elias in 1239, and was a coauthor of an *Exposition of the Rule of St. Francis*; he was also active in the affairs of the church, both in the university and in the First Council of Lyon (1244–1245). His sudden death after his return from Lyon apparently resulted from an epidemic current in Paris. An epitaph in the convent church saluted him as *Gloria doctorum, decus et flos philosophorum* (Glory of learned men, the honor and pride of philosophers).

TEACHINGS

Alexander's own doctrines are found in his *Glossa* and *Disputed Questions* (which are divided in the British Museum manuscript *Royal 9. E. 14.* into two series: those written before and those written after he became a friar); the *Summa* ascribed to him does not necessarily represent his opinions. Both the *Gloss* and the *Questions* labor under the disadvantage of being students' reportations (although some copies seem to have had a kind of official approval); both, however, justify the encomium of Bernard of Bessa: *maximus in theologia et philosophia magister* (greatest master in theology and philosophy). Alexander is both theologian and philosopher, masterfully handling a wide range of questions. Undoubtedly a traditionalist whose prime sources are Augustine, John of Damascus, and Pseudo-Dionysius, and whose thought is close to the scholastic traditions of his predecessors, Alexander nonetheless surpasses his contemporaries in the breadth and profundity of his questions and in the new problems and tracts he introduced into theology. To this extent he was an innovator who helped open the way for the scholastic renaissance of the mid-thirteenth century. In particular, as head of the friars' studium at Paris, he initiated a certain approach that came to characterize such representatives of the Franciscan school as Odo Rigaldus, Bonaventure, and Matthew of Aquasparta.

The problems of the distinction between philosophy and theology, and the nature of theology as a science, much discussed after 1240, are not treated explicitly (though it is possible that Alexander wrote a question on the subject; see below). These problems are implicitly considered in scattered remarks on the kinds of human knowledge and the validity of arguments, in the general organization of material into specific questions and problems, and in the principles used in the solution of the problems. For example, our knowledge of God arises both from authority and from reason; that is, either from faith, which "depends on hearing" (Romans 10.17), or from knowledge drawn from the things God has made. Proofs of God's existence are suggested rather than developed at length: one is derived from the transcendental attributes of truth, goodness, and unity found in things; others are argued from the changing to the Unchanged, from dependent being to the Highest Being, from participated and partial good to the *summum bonum* (*Glossa* I, pp. 39–41). In the tradition of Augustine, Alexander finds analogies of the triune God in all creatures, thus setting the pattern for the Franciscan school, which, with St. Francis, delights to make of creation a "ladder" to the Creator. At the same time, Alexander shows the simplicity of the divine being to be in marked contrast to the composite character of all created being (*Glossa* I, p. 254; *Quaestiones*, pp. 14, 19). The doctrine here, that of *quo est* (the substance) and *quo est* (essence), is derived ultimately from Boethius, not from Avicenna, who seems to have been unknown to Alexander. In contrast to the *Summa Fratris Alexandri* and to Bonaventure, Alexander vehemently rejects any composition of matter and form either in angels or in the human soul (*Glossa* II, p. 28; other texts are in V. Doucet, *Prolegomena*, pp. 237, 268, n. 2). Apart from a lengthy question on immortality (*Quaestiones*, pp. 556–565), only passing remarks embody his notion of the soul. His attention is drawn more to the problem of free will (Ibid., pp. 566–608, plus an unedited question). Here, Alexander teaches that man by his nature is free and that freedom of choice resides both in the intellect and in the will. The primary purpose for which man has been given this freedom is to choose that which is morally good. Alexander considers the moral life of man in such *Disputed Questions* as "On Ignorance," "On Scandal," "Love of Neighbor," "Fraternal Correction," "On Impediments to Reason," "On Lying," and "Conscience" (the last two as yet unpublished). To the last question must be joined his study of synderesis (*Glossa* II, pp. 380–385), which seems to make Alexander, not Philip the Chancellor, the creator of such a tract in Scholasticism.

LITERARY PROBLEMS OF THE "SUMMA FRATRIS ALEXANDRI"

Since the *Summa* attributed to Alexander was unfinished at his death, William of Militona, who became master regent in 1248, seems to have undertaken its completion, for in 1255 Pope Alexander IV charged the provincial of Paris to supply Militona with capable assistants who without delay would bring the work to a finish. The text as it now stands consists of four parts. Book I deals with the nature of theology, the existence and nature of God, the divine names, and the Trinity. Book II is divided into two sections: II–1, creation in general, the angels, the six days of creation, the soul, the body, and the human composite, and II–2, a lengthy study of moral theology—the nature of evil, definition and classification of sins, and original and actual sins. Book III considers the Incarnation and mysteries of Christ's life, law (eternal, natural, positive, the commandments), grace, and faith (tome IV). Book IV treats of man's reparation through the sacraments, the mass, prayer, fasting, and almsgiving; quite evidently a section on "Last Things" was to be included as the climax of the work.

Except in a few manuscripts and in the protest of Roger Bacon, however, the compilatory nature of the *Summa* was forgotten. All four books came to be attributed to Alexander, despite the manifest contradictions and conflicting opinions in the various parts. Only since the end of the nineteenth century, with the renewal of interest in medieval Scholasticism, has the question of authorship attracted attention. A few writers, it is true, have gone to an extreme in claiming that the whole *Summa* was a compilation of the last half of the thirteenth century, in basic dependence on Thomas Aquinas, Albert the Great, and Bonaventure. But more mature and solid scholarship has established that, if by and large the *Summa* is a compilation, it existed as a whole by 1257. The first three books were in existence before the death of Alexander, with three notable exceptions: The last tract of Book I was added between 1250 and 1253, while in Book II–1 the two sections "On the Human Body" and "The Human Composite" were composed after Bonaventure, almost certainly in 1255–1257, as was the last book. On the other hand, modern research is forced to agree with Roger Bacon that Alexander was not the author, in the strict sense, of the pre-1245 *Summa*. At most, it appears that he planned and organized the work, while the details were left to others. Internal criticism of style, language, and doctrine would show essentially two authors at work, neither of whom, by reason of doctrinal positions, can be Alexander. Books I and III were almost certainly the work of John of La Rochelle, although the presence of other collaborators may be detected. Both parts of Book II, on the other hand, were written or compiled by some unknown friar who possessed a keen philosophical mind and a greater spirit of independence.

DOCTRINES OF THE PRE-1245 "SUMMA." The work of the "Summists" was largely one of compilation, yet not without a certain new and fresh viewpoint. If they drew on earlier material, they did not hesitate to insert their own views or add fresh tracts written specifically for the *Summa*. Relatively new was the opening inquisition on the nature of theology, based on the tract in manuscript *Vatican Latin 782*, folio 184d–186d (which may be by Alexander himself); it bears witness to the growing influence of Aristotle's ideal of a science. This inquisition is followed by an original tract on natural theology, remarkable for its metaphysical doctrine of God and creatures. This doctrine holds that the very conditions of finite being demand the existence of a First Being, even as the positive perfections of finite things reflect and lead to the infinite. The unknown author of Book II does not hesitate to repeat some of this material in an interesting and well-balanced dissertation on Creator and creature; he examines in detail the meaning of the act of creation, the properties of created being that reflect the divine cause, and those properties peculiar to creatures: composition, changeableness, time and space, and the beauty and order of the universe. Several questions seem to have bearing on problems that arose in the early thirteenth century under the influence of the newly known Arabian philosophers.

The importance of the *Summa* lies chiefly, perhaps, in its presentation and defense of the so-called Augustinian traditions in theology and philosophy without neglecting whatever was solid in the new philosophical literature. It may rightly be called the *Summa Minorum*, embodying the fundamental doctrines of the Franciscan school of the early thirteenth century.

See also Albert the Great; Augustine, St.; Bacon, Roger; Bonaventure, St.; John of Damascus; John of La Rochelle; Matthew of Acquasparta; Peter Lombard; Pseudo-Dionysius; Thomas Aquinas, St.

Bibliography

For texts of Alexander, see *Glossa in Quattuor Libros Sententiarum Petri*, 4 vols. (Quaracchi, 1951–1957); *Quaestiones Disputatae "Antequam Esset Frater,"* 3 vols. (Quaracchi, 1960)—the series "after he became a friar" awaits publication at Quaracchi; *Expositio Quattuor Magistrorum Super Regulam Fratrum Minorum*, L. Oliger, ed. (Rome, 1950). The text of the *Summa* is *Doctoris Irrefragabilis Alexandri de Hales Summa Theologica*, 4 vols. (Quaracchi, 1924–1948), books I–III; Book IV is found in several early editions, such as Nuremberg, 1482, and Cologne, 1622.

With regard to studies of Alexander's works, writings previous to 1948 that are concerned with doctrinal problems rather than literary ones must be interpreted in the light of new discoveries. For literary and historical aspects, see V. Doucet, *Expositio Quattuor Magistrorum III Necnon in Libros I et II Summa Fratris Alexandri* (Quaracchi, 1948), partially translated in *Franciscan Studies*, Vol. 7 (1947): 26–41, 274–312; Ibid., Vol. 6 (1946): 403–417; and Doucet's introductions to the authentic *Glossa* and *Quaestiones*.

Doctrinal studies on the authentic Alexander are just beginning to appear: A. Fuerst, *A Historical Study of the Doctrine of the Omnipresence of God* (Washington, DC: Catholic University of America Press, 1951); E. Lio, *Determinatio "Superflui" in Doctrina Alexandri Halensis* (Rome: Apud Pontificium Athenaeum Antonianum, 1953); A. Hufnagel, "Die Wesensbestimmung der Person bei Alexander von Hales," in *Freiburger ZPT*, Vol. 4 (1957): 148–174; Bettoni, *Il problema della cognoscibilità di Dio nella scuola francescana* (Padua, 1950); see also *Franciscan Studies*, Vol. 10 (1950): 164–185, 286–312; Vol. 19 (1959): 334–383; Vol. 20 (1960): 96–148; Vol. 22 (1962): 32–149.

For earlier and somewhat outdated studies on Alexander as author of the *Summa*, see I. Herscher, "A Bibliography of Alexander of Hales," in *Franciscan Studies*, Vol. 5 (1945), 434–454; and P. Boehner, "The System of Metaphysics of Alexander of Hales," in Ibid., 366–414.

Ignatius Brady, O.F.M. (1967)

AL-FĀRĀBĪ
(c. 873–950)

Al-Fārābī, more fully Abū-Nasr Muhammad al-Fārābī, known in Latin as Alfarabius or Avennasar, was one of the greatest Muslim philosophers. He was widely known as "the second master," Aristotle being the first, and Ab-Ar-Rahman ibn-Khaldūn rates him above Avicenna and Averroes. He was of Turkish origin, and his name indicates that he came from the district of Fārāb, on the middle Jaxartes River (now Syr Darya).

One of al-Fārābī's teachers was the Nestorian Christian Yuhannā ibn-Haylān, who was noted as a logician; it is uncertain whether al-Fārābī studied with him in Merv (Persia) or Harran (Syria) or Baghdad. His principal teacher was Abū-Bishr Mattā ibn-Yūnus, the most prominent member of the school of Christian Aristotelians in Baghdad. Here al-Fārābī studied not merely the various branches of philosophy, but also physics, mathematics, astronomy, and music, even becoming a skilled musical performer. He spent the last few years of his life at the court of the ruler Sayf-ad-Dawla at Aleppo. He did not seem to have had any regular occupation by which to earn a livelihood and lived frugally, even ascetically, often in solitude.

Al-Fārābī's philosophy is based on the teachings of Plato and Aristotle as they were interpreted in the school of Baghdad in the tenth century. Like all writers in Arabic he assumed there were no essential differences between the two, but he preferred the metaphysics of Aristotle, as interpreted by Neoplatonists. Plato, however, he regarded as superior in practical matters, and he wrote commentaries on the *Republic* and the *Laws*. What is often regarded as his major work is reminiscent of these books; it has the clumsy title "On the Principles of the Views of the Inhabitants of the Excellent State," often shortened in practice to "Der Musterstaat," or "The Ideal City" (*al-madīna al-fadila*). The first third of this work sets out al-Fārābī's metaphysical system, the second third his psychology (largely Aristotelian), and the concluding third his views on the ideal state and various imperfect states.

To those familiar with the intellectual environment in which al-Fārābī lived, it is immediately apparent that he wrote in such a way as to commend his views to as many different groups of people as possible. It has been alleged that he supported the Shiʿite sect of Islam, and certainly his last patron Sayf-ad-Dawla was a Shiʿite; features of his "ideal city," such as the dependence of all on the head, resemble Shiʿite conceptions. Yet it is also clear that he wrote in such a way as not to offend the Sunnite majority; for example, by avoiding such a technical Shiʿite term as *imam*. Indeed, his view of the relation of philosophy and religion led him to attach positive value to the religions, although he regarded them as inferior to philosophy. Philosophy was the supreme exercise of human reason and therefore the primary requirement of an ideal city. By it, humanity came to know the one ultimate truth about the universe. To this ultimate philosophical truth the symbolic representations of it found in the several religions stand in varying degrees of proximity and remoteness. Al-Fārābī paid particular attention, of course, to the forms of the main Islamic states of his time and developed his conception of the ideal city in such a way that the actual states he knew were within measurable distance of the ideal.

His metaphysics, similarly, resembles that implicit in the Qurʾan (Koran) and Islamic theology. God is the One or the First from whom all existence proceeds; and in this sense he accepts the Islamic doctrine that God is the creator of the world, although he also holds the heretical view that the world is eternal. In the relation of existent things to God there is a hierarchical order. Similarly in the ideal city there is a head (*raʾīs*) who is the source of all authority and who assigns men to their appropriate grades. This head is also described as commanding but not obeying; all the intermediate grades obey those above and command those below, and the lowest grade only obeys.

Interest has been shown, especially in recent times, in al-Fārābī's theory of prophecy; that is, in particular, how it was possible for Muhammad to receive the Qurʾan from God. Philosophic knowledge, the highest of all, he regarded as coming to the passive intellect of the philosopher from the Active Intellect, an existent below God in rank. Prophetic revelations also come from the Active Intellect but are received by the imagination of the prophet. In this al-Fārābī was able to accept the Qurʾan as coming from God and yet to place philosophy above it.

See also Aristotle; Averroes; Avicenna; Islamic Philosophy; Kant, Immanuel; Plato.

Bibliography

WORKS BY AL-FĀRĀBĪ

The "Ideal City" has been translated as *Der Musterstaat von al-Fārābī* by Friedrich Dieterici (Leiden: Brill, 1900) and as *Idées des habitants de la cité vertueuse* by R. P. Jaussen, Youssef Karam, and J. Chlala (Cairo, 1949). A critical edition of the Arabic text and an English translation by Richard Walzer is in preparation.

See also *Al-Fārābī's Short Commentary on Aristotle's Prior Analytics,* translated by Nicholas Rescher (Pittsburgh: University of Pittsburgh Press, 1963); *Al-Fārābī's philosophische Abhandlungen,* short essays translated by Friedrich Dieterici (Leiden, 1892); and *The Fusul al-Madani: Aphorisms of the Statesman of al-Fārābī,* with an English translation, introduction, and notes by D. M. Dunlop, ed. (Cambridge: Cambridge University Press, 1961).

WORKS ON AL-FĀRĀBĪ

De Boer, Tjitze J. *The History of Philosophy in Islam.* London: Luzac & Co., 1903. See especially pp. 106–128.

Rescher, Nicholas. *Al-Fārābī: An Annotated Bibliography.* Pittsburgh: University of Pittsburgh Press, 1962.

Rescher, Nicholas. *Studies in the History of Arabic Logic.* Pittsburgh: University of Pittsburgh Press, 1964.

Quadri, G. *La philosophie arabe dans l'Europe médiévale.* Paris: Payot, 1947. See especially pp. 71–94.

Walzer, Richard. *Greek into Arabic.* Oxford: B. Cassirer, 1962. See especially pp. 18–23, 206–219.

W. Montgomery Watt (1967)

AL-FĀRĀBĪ [ADDENDUM]

Al-Fārābī was a key figure in establishing much of the problematic of Islamic philosophy in the peripatetic tradition. He built on the earlier attempt by Abū-Yūsuf Yaʿqūb ibn Isḥāq al-Kindī to establish a technical language of philosophy in Arabic and presented a vocabulary and a curriculum that came to dominate for many centuries after his death. Al-Fārābī's epistemology and political philosophy were particularly influential. Firmly neoplatonic in tone, he differentiated between diverse kinds of intellect to describe human thought and gave an interesting and influential account of how knowledge can be analyzed in terms of a range of degrees of abstraction. The active intellect became a controversial topic in Islamic philosophy; it represented the highest one could go in one's thoughts and was responsible for emanating form to the world in which one lived. The nature of this concept came to dominate much of Islamic philosophy for a long time after al-Fārābī's death. There was a great deal of debate on the precise role and nature of the active intellect and whether the hidden agenda of its use by the philosophers was to limit human knowledge to a relatively low level of impersonal thought.

Similarly, the distinctions he made in his political thought won attention as a result of their conceptual clarity. Following Plato he distinguished between different kinds of state, and he used the concept of happiness as the ultimate aim of government. Different kinds of government can be distinguished from each other by their varying links with happiness, with corrupt states being very poor at reaching happiness while the virtuous states achieve that end to a high degree. Not surprisingly, the idea that philosophers make the best rulers was rather attractive to philosophers, and in al-Fārābī's case the skills of the philosopher need to be blended with those of a religious leader if the state is to be well organized and led. As with his work on epistemology and metaphysics, his writings on political philosophy produced a lively debate in Islamic philosophy on the role of philosophy and philosophers in the state and on the nature of the state itself.

Bibliography

Al-Fārābī. "Al-Madīna al-Fāḍila" (The virtuous city). In Al-Farabi on the Perfect State: Abū Nasr al-Fārābī's Mabādiʾ Arāʾ Ahl al-Madīna al-Fāḍila. Translated by Richard Walzer. Oxford, U.K.: Clarendon Press, 1985.

Alon, Ilai. "Farabi's Funny Flora: Al-Nawabit as Opposition." Arabica 37 (1990): 56–90.

Black, Deborah. "Al-Fārābī." In History of Islamic Philosophy. 2 vols., edited by Seyyed Hossein Nasr and Oliver Leaman. London: Routledge, 1996.

Fakhry, Majid. Al-Farabi, Father of Islamic Neoplatonism: His Life, Works, and Influence. Oxford, U.K.: Oneworld, 2002.

Galston, Miriam. Politics and Excellence: The Political Philosophy of Alfarabi. Princeton, NJ: Princeton University Press, 1990.

Netton, Ian Richard. Al-Fārābī and His School. London: Routledge, 1992.

Netton, Ian Richard. Allāh Transcendent: Studies in the Structure and Semiotics of Islamic Philosophy, Theology, and Cosmology. London: Routledge, 1989.

Oliver Leaman (2005)

AL-GHAZĀLĪ, AḤMAD
(c. 1062–1126)

Aḥmad al-Ghazālī's reputation as an Islamic thinker has unfortunately been overshadowed by that of his more celebrated elder brother, Muḥammad al-Ghazālī, author of the famous *Revivification of the Sciences of Religion*. The former was in fact the foremost metaphysician of love in the Sufi tradition and the chief founder of the philosophy of love in mystical Islam, and his impact on the later Persian Sufi tradition was more profound than his brother the theologian.

He spent most of his life in his *khānaqāh* (Sufi cloister) in Qazvīn, where he was famed for his eloquence as a preacher, and died there in 1126. Al-Ghazālī was the teacher of Abūʾ l-Najīb al-Suhrawardī, who was in turn the master of his nephew Shihāb al-Dīn Yaḥyā Suhrawardī, founder of the Suhrawardī order, famed as the "mother of Sufi orders." He was also the master of the enigmatic mystical theologian ʿAyn al-Quḍāt al-Hamadhānī, who was executed in 1132 by fanatical Muslim clerics for his uncompromising Sufi beliefs. He features as a central figure in the initiatic chains of most of the great Islamic Sufi orders.

His fame derives mainly from his authorship of the first treatise on mystical love in Persian, the *Sawāniḥ al-ʿushshāq* (The lovers' experiences), a short work on the spiritual psychology of divine love couched in the terminology of human erotic relationships. The main subject of his philosophy is passionate love (*ʿishq*), which is not formally speaking "philosophy"—*Falsafa*—but rather comprises a sort of erotic theosophy apprehended by intuitive means (*dhawq*), based on contemplative experience rather than on rational meditations and deliberations. Expressing little of the same animosity to peripatetic philosophy manifested by his famous brother, almost all his teachings are set in the context of commentary on Qur'ānic verses and prophetic traditions. Al-Ghazālī deliberately abstained from using any overt philosophical vocabulary in the text, employing instead terminology from a number of other fields, ethics, erotic poetry, and psychology, and so on. He follows Manṣūr al-Ḥallāj in identifying love with the divine essence as well as with the divine spirit. He maintained that knowledge ('ilm) alone is unable to grasp love ('ishq), comparing knowledge to the shore of the sea and love to a pearl in an oyster buried in its lowest depths. Forever shore-bound in immanence, neither dry reason ('aql) nor barren knowledge ('ilm) can ever access or apprehend the transcendent truths of love's apophatic teachings. The summit of knowledge lies in a kind of drunken inapprehension that is nonetheless a kind of apprehension without any of the limitations of subjective consciousness. Al-Ghazālī paradoxically describes this understanding of love that is "beyond knowledge" as being a kind of surmise or conjecture. This conjectural wisdom is higher than certainty for it is only that surmise or conjecture that can swim love's ocean to dive under in pursuit of its pearl. Due to Sawāniḥ and the many works of imitations it spawned, al-Ghazālī has come to be generally regarded as the foremost metaphysician of love in the Sufi tradition and the founder of the literary topos and mystical persuasion known as the "religion of love" (madhhab-i 'ishq) in Islam.

See also al-Ghazālī, Muḥammad; Sufism.

Bibliography

al-Ghazālī, Ahmad. Sawāniḥ, edited by Helmut Ritter. Tehran, Iran: Tehran University Press, 1989.

Pūrjavādī, Nasr Allāh, trans. Sawāniḥ: Inspirations from the World of Pure Spirits: The Oldest Persian Sufi Treatise on Love. London: KPI, 1986.

Leonard Lewisohn (2005)

AL-GHAZĀLĪ, MUḤAMMAD
(450 or 451 AH [1058 or 1059 CE]–505 AH [1111 CE])

Muḥammad al-Ghazālī (in Persian, "Ghazālī"), the Islamic theologian known to medieval Scholastics as Algazel, was born in Ghazāleh, a village on the outskirts of Tūs, in Khorāsān, northeastern Iran. His name is the same as that of his birthplace, which should be transcribed as Ghazālī, not as Ghazzālī. He died at Tūs. He was undoubtedly one of the strongest spiritual personal-ities of Islam, one of those who strove most effectively for the establishment of an "orthodox" Sufism that would transcend the legalistic and superficial religion of the doctors of the Law. Al-Ghazālī was well known to the medieval Scholastics through a Latin translation of an unfortunately truncated work, Maqasīd al-Falāsifa ("The Intentions of Philosophers"). As a result the true meaning of his work was completely misunderstood, and he was thought to be a philosopher, whereas in fact he was the most ardent critic of philosophy.

At the age of thirty-six, al-Ghazālī experienced a profound crisis, provoked by the problem of intellectual certitude. He abandoned his professorship and his position as rector of Niẓāmīya University of Baghdad. During a period of ten years, clothed in the characteristic wool garment of the Sufis and completely absorbed in spiritual practices, he made solitary pilgrimages throughout the Muslim world, to Syria, Egypt, Mecca, and Medina. What he conveyed in his doctrines cannot be separated from this pathetic experience. He solved the problem of knowledge and certitude by affirming a degree of comprehension that left the heart no room for doubt, a comprehension that is the essential apprehension of things. The thinking soul becomes the focus of the universal Soul's irradiations, the mirror of intelligible forms received from the universal Soul. This theme dominates certain characteristic short treatises (the Monqidh, or "Preservative from Error," and the Risālat al-Ladonīya) as well as the great synthesis titled Ihyā' 'Ulūm ad-Dīn ("Revival of the Religious Sciences"). But this theme had already been treated, undoubtedly without his knowledge, by the Imāms of Shi'ism, and it does not differ essentially from the Ishrāq of Sohrawardī. This very theme led Sohrawardī to advance philosophy on a new basis rather than destroy the efforts of philosophers as such.

It is principally this aspect of al-Ghazālī's work, developed in his Tahāfut al-Falāsifa ("Autodestruction of the Philosophers") that Westerners have been inclined to emphasize. An attempt has even been made to read into it a more incisive and decisive critique or metaphysics than that of Immanuel Kant. In fact, al-Ghazālī strove vehemently to destroy the demonstrative range that philosophers, Avicennians as well as others, accorded to their arguments regarding the eternity of the world, the procession of the Intelligences, the existence of purely spiritual substances, and the idea of spiritual resurrection. In general al-Ghazālī strove to refute the idea of any causality, of any necessary connection. According to him all that can be experimentally affirmed is, for example, that combustion of cotton occurs *at the moment of* contact with fire; it cannot be shown that combustion takes place *because of* the contact between cotton and fire. Nor can it be shown that there is any cause whatsoever. From this bursts forth the paradox of a thinker who professes the inability of reason to attain certitude while maintaining the certitude of destroying, with massive doses of rational dialectic, the certitudes of the philosophers. Averroes clearly discerned this self-contradiction and replied to it with his celebrated *Tahāfut al-Tahāfut* ("Autodestruction of the Autodestruction").

The same paradox is apparent in al-Ghazālī's other polemical works; in the "Courteous Refutation of the Divinity of Jesus Christ according to the Gospel"; in his treatise in Persian against all sorts of "freethinkers," or heretical thinkers (*Ibāhīya*); and, finally, in the treatise against the Ismāʿīlites (the Bātinites, or "esoterics"). The last treatise was overly influenced by the fact that it had been commissioned for political reasons by the ʿAbbāsid caliph al-Mostazhir, and the savage *dialectic*, deployed against an essentially *hermeneutic* Shiʿite thought, rings false. The Ismāʿīlites met this attack in the twelfth century with a monumental response (a work of the fifth Yemenite Dāʿī, in 1,500 pages), which unfortunately, is still unedited.

In any case, these polemical works had but a limited echo; al-Ghazālī's influence made itself felt principally through the *Ihya*. Without doubt this influence was, and remains, considerable in Sunnite Islam. In Shiʿite Islam, notably in Iran, it was another matter. First of all, his effort did not respond to the same necessity, since the teaching of the Imāms of Shiʿism had already opened the way to spiritual Islam. But his effort was not ignored in Shiʿism, especially in the Ispahan School. Mohsen Fayż (d. 1091 AH/1680 CE), one of the most celebrated pupils of Mullā Sadrā Shīrāzi (d. 1050 AH/1640 CE), even went so far as to rewrite the whole *Ihya* with a Shiʿite interpretation. (Certain authors believe with him, assuming the authenticity of the book titled *Sirr al-ʿĀlamayn,* "Secret of the Two Universes," that al-Ghazālī would finally have rallied to Shiʿism.) In any case, in Iran no one ever thought or heard it said, as in the West, that the Ghazalian critique might have rendered impossible the continuation of philosophy in Islam and that Islamic philosophy was perhaps obliged to transport itself to Andalusia, where its last flames glowed with Ibn Bājja, Ibn Tufayl, and Averroes. Avicennianism, for example, enriched and modified by diverse contributions, continued to develop in Shiʿite Iran, not only during the Safavid epoch but also afterward, even to this day.

See also al-Ghazālī, Ahmad; Averroes; Ibn Bājja; Ibn Tufayl; Suhrawardī, Shihāb al-Dīn Yahyā.

Bibliography

For works by al-Ghazālī, see *Al-Ghazali's Tahafut al-Falasifah* (*Incoherence of the Philosophers*), translated by S. A. Kamali (Lahore, Pakistan: Philosophical Congress, 1963); *Al-Ghazali's Ihya' ʿUlūm al-Dīn, Book XX,* translated and annotated by L. Zolondek (Leiden: Brill, 1963); W. Montgomery Watt, *The Faith and Practice of al-Ghazali* (London: Allen and Unwin, 1951), which contains translations of the *Monqidh* under the title "Deliverance from Error" and of "The Beginning of Guidance"; Ignaz Goldziher, *Streitschrift des Ghazālī gegen die Bātinijja-Sekte* (Leiden: Brill, 1916; Neudruck, 1956), an abbreviated edition with introduction and summary of the work against the Ismāʿīlites; and *Réfutation excellente de la divinité de Jésus-Christ d'après les Évangiles,* a translation and commentary on the "Courteous Refutation," by R. Chidiac (Paris: Leroux, 1939). See also *Averroes' Tahafut al-Tahafut (The Incoherence of the Incoherence),* translated by Simon van den Bergh, 2 vols. (London: Luzac, 1954), which incorporates most of al-Ghazālī's *Tahāfut al-Falāsifah.*

For works on al-Ghazālī, see Henry Corbin, *Histoire de la philosophie islamique,* Vol. I (Paris: Gallimard, 1964), pp. 251–261, with a detailed bibliography on pp. 358–359. See pp. 278–283 for Ahmad al-Ghazālī. See also W. Montgomery Watt, *Islamic Philosophy and Theology,* pp. 114–124, which includes bibliography (Edinburgh: Edinburgh University Press, 1962); this is Vol. I of *Islamic Surveys.*

Henry Corbin (1967)

AL-GHAZĀLĪ, MUHAMMAD [ADDENDUM]

For comparisons with the western Christian tradition, Augustine comes more readily to mind than Aquinas, yet al-Ghazālī fulfills something of the role of each. He realized that understanding can be perfected in a faithful response to divine revelation, and that human reason can elucidate that response by showing the way through many pitfalls. Al-Ghazālī is aware of the deleterious effect of a simple reading of the scriptures, and so helps his readers to a sophisticated yet respectful grasp of the Word of God in the Qur'an, all the while insisting that variant readings need to be discerned by careful intellectual examination. He is acutely aware of the way in which ordinary philosophical categories need to be stretched to accommodate the "creator of heaven and earth," and so of the necessary negative moments in using the names which the Qur'an itself gives to God. Al-Ghazālī's recommended way to engage in that negative moment is via Sufi meditation, which can alert both mind and heart to their inadequacy as well as bolster both to continue the journey toward proximity with the divine. In this respect he can also be favorably compared with Moses Maimonides, who was probably cognizant of at least some of al-Ghazālī's writings.

See also al-Ghazālī, Ahmad.

Bibliography

RECENT TRANSLATIONS OF AL-GHAZĀLĪ

Aims of the Philosophers. Translated by David Burrell and Tony Street. Provo, UT: Brigham Young University Press, 2004.

Incoherence of the Philosophers. Translated by Michael Marmura. Provo, UT: Brigham Young University Press, 1997.

On the Boundaries of Theological Tolerance in Islam. Translated by Sherman Jackson. Oxford: Oxford University Press, 2002.

TRANSLATIONS OF KEY BOOKS FROM THE *IHYA'*

Deliverance from Error. Translated by R. J. McCarthy. Louisville, KY: Fons Vitae, 1999.

Disciplining the Soul and *Breaking the Two Desires.* Translated by T. J. Winter. Cambridge, U.K.: Islamic Texts Society, 1995.

Faith in Divine Unity and Trust in Divine Providence. Translated by David Burrell. Louisville, KY: Fons Vitae, 2001.

Invocations and Supplications. Translated by K. Nakamura. Cambridge, U.K.: Islamic Texts Society, 1990.

Niche of Lights. Translated by David Buchman. Provo, UT: Brigham Young University Press, 1998.

Ninety-nine Beautiful Names of God. Translated by David Burrell and Nazih Daher. Cambridge, U.K.: Islamic Texts Society, 1992.

Remembrance of Death and the Afterlife. Translated by T. J. Winter. Cambridge, U.K.: Islamic Texts Society, 1989.

COMMENTARIES

Frank, Richard. *Al-Ghazali and the Ash'arite School.* Durham, NC: Duke University Press, 1994.

Gianotti, Timothy. *Al-Ghazali's Unspeakable Doctrine of the Soul.* Leiden, Netherlands: Brill, 2001.

Shehadi, Fadlou. *Ghazali's Unique Unknowable God.* Leiden, Netherlands: Brill, 1964.

David Burrell (2005)

ALIENATION

The term *alienation* (estrangement) has many different meanings in everyday life, in science, and in philosophy; most of them can be regarded as modifications of one broad meaning which is suggested by the etymology and the morphology of the word—the meaning in which alienation (or estrangement) is the act, or result of the act, through which something, or somebody, becomes (or has become) alien (or strange) to something, or somebody, else.

In everyday usage alienation often means turning away or keeping away from former friends or associates. In law it usually refers to the transfer of property from one person to another, either by sale or as a gift. In psychiatry alienation usually means deviation from normality; that is, insanity. In contemporary psychology and sociology it is often used to name an individual's feeling of alienness toward society, nature, other people, or himself. For many sociologists and philosophers, alienation is the same as reification: the act (or result of the act) of transforming human properties, relations, and actions into properties and actions of things that are independent of man and that govern his life. For other philosophers, "alienation" means "self-alienation" (self-estrangement): the process, or result of the process, by which a "self" (God or man) through itself (through its own action) becomes alien (strange) to itself (to its own nature).

HISTORY OF THE CONCEPT

The concept of alienation was first philosophically elaborated by Georg Wilhelm Friedrich Hegel. Some writers have maintained that the Christian doctrine of original sin and redemption can be regarded as a first version of Hegel's doctrine of alienation and dealienation. According to others, the concept of alienation found its first expression in Western thought in the Old Testament concept of idolatry. Still others have maintained that the source for Hegel's view of nature as a self-alienated form of Absolute Mind can be found in Plato's view of the natural world as an imperfect picture of the sublime world of Ideas. As investigation continues, probably more forerunners of Hegel will be discovered. But it seems established that Hegel, Ludwig Feuerbach, and Karl Marx were the three thinkers who first gave an explicit elaboration of alienation and whose interpretation is the starting point for all discussions of alienation in present-day philosophy, sociology, and psychology.

HEGEL. It is a basic idea of Hegel's philosophy that whatever is, is, in the last analysis, Absolute Idea (Absolute Mind, Absolute Spirit, or, in popular language, God) and that Absolute Idea is neither a set of fixed things nor a sum of static properties but a dynamic Self, engaged in a circular process of alienation and dealienation. Nature is only a self-alienated (self-estranged) form of Absolute Mind, and man is the Absolute in the process of dealienation. The whole of human history is the constant growth of man's knowledge of the Absolute and, at the same time, the development of self-knowledge of the Absolute, who through finite mind becomes self-aware and "returns" to himself from his self-alienation in nature. Finite mind, however, also becomes alienated. It is an essential characteristic of finite mind (man) to produce things, to express itself in objects, to objectify itself in physical things, social institutions, and cultural products; and every objectification is, of necessity, an instance of alienation: the produced objects become alien to the producer. Alienation in this sense can be overcome only in the sense of being adequately known. Again, it is the vocation of man as man to serve as the organon of the self-knowledge of the Absolute. To the extent that he does not perform this function, he does not fulfill his human essence and is merely a self-alienated man.

FEUERBACH. Feuerbach accepted Hegel's view that man can be alienated from himself, but he rejected both the view that nature is a self-alienated form of Absolute Mind and the view that man is Absolute Mind in the process of dealienation. Man is not self-alienated God. On the contrary, God is self-alienated man; he is man's essence absolutized and estranged from man. And man is not alienated from himself when he refuses to recognize nature as a self-alienated form of God; man is alienated from himself when he creates and puts above himself an imagined alien higher being and bows before that being as a slave. The dealienation of man consists in the abolition of that estranged picture of man which is God.

MARX. Marx praised Hegel for having grasped that the self-creation of man is a process of alienation and dealienation. But he criticized Hegel for, among other things, having identified objectification with alienation and the suppression of alienation with the abolition of objectivity, for having regarded man as self-consciousness and the alienation of man as the alienation of his self-consciousness, and for having assumed that the suppression of objectification and alienation is possible only and merely in the medium of pure thought. Marx agreed with Feuerbach's criticism of religious alienation, but he stressed that the religious alienation of man is only one among many forms of man's self-alienation. Man not only alienates a part of himself in the form of God; he also alienates other products of his spiritual activity in the form of philosophy, common sense, art, morals, and so on. He alienates products of his economic activity in the form of commodities, money, capital, etc.; he alienates products of his social activity in the form of the state, law, and social institutions. Thus, there are many forms in which man alienates from himself the products of his own activity and makes of them a separate, independent, and powerful world of objects toward which he is related as a slave, powerless and dependent.

Nevertheless, man not only alienates his own products from himself; he also alienates himself from the very activity through which these products are produced, from the natural world in which he lives, and from other men. All these kinds of alienation are, in the last analysis, one; they are only different aspects of man's self-alienation, different forms of the alienation of man from his human "essence" or "nature," from his humanity. The self-alienated man is a man who is really not a man, a man who does not realize his historically created human possibilities. A nonalienated man would be a man who really is a man, a man who fulfills himself as a free, creative being of praxis.

The concepts of alienation and dealienation were elaborated by Marx in his early writings, especially in his *Economic and Philosophical Manuscripts*, written in 1844 and first published in 1932. In his later works the two concepts were basic, but they were used implicitly rather than explicitly. Their importance was therefore overlooked. In no exposition or interpretation of Marx's views written in the nineteenth century or in the first three decades of the twentieth did the concepts of alienation and dealienation play any important role. But since the publication of the *Manuscripts* and especially since World War II, they have become the object of passionate discussions, not only among Marxists but also among non-Marxists (especially existentialists and personalists), and not only among philosophers but also among psychologists (especially psychoanalysts), sociologists, literary critics, and writers.

CONTEMPORARY INTERPRETATIONS AND DEFINITIONS

Present-day writers who use the term *alienation* differ very much in the ways in which they understand and define it. Some authors think that the concept can be applied both to man and to nonhuman entities (to God, world, and nature, for instance); but most writers insist that it is applicable only to humans. Some of those who apply it only to humans insist that it can refer only to individuals and not to society as a whole. According to a number of such authors, the nonadjustment of the individual to the society in which he lives is a sign of his alienation. Others maintain that a society also can be alienated, or "sick," so that an individual who cannot adapt to the existing society is not, of necessity, alienated.

Many of those who regard alienation as applicable merely to individuals conceive it as a purely psychological concept referring to a feeling, or a state of mind. Others insist that alienation is not only a feeling but that it is also an objective fact, a way of being. Some of the writers who characterize alienation as a state of mind regard it as a fact or concept of psychopathology; others insist that although alienation is not good or desirable, it is not strictly pathological. They often add that one should distinguish alienation (a psychological state of the individual characterized by feelings of estrangement) both from anomie (relative normlessness in a social system) and from personal disorganization (disordered behavior arising from conflict within the individual).

Those who oppose characterizing alienation as a psychological concept usually say that it is also (or primarily) an economic, or political, or sociological, or ethical concept. Some insist that it is basically a concept of general philosophy, or a concept of ontology and philosophical anthropology.

According to Gwynn Nettler, alienation is a certain psychological state of a normal person, and an alienated person is "one who has been estranged from, made unfriendly toward, his society and the culture it carries" ("A Measure of Alienation," p. 672). For Murray Levin, "the essential characteristic of the alienated man is his belief that he is not able to fulfill what he believes is his rightful role in society" (*Man Alone*, p. 227). According to Eric and Mary Josephson, alienation is "an individual feeling or state of dissociation from self, from others, and from the world at large" (Introduction to *Man Alone*, p. 13). For Stanley Moore, the terms *alienation* and *estrangement* "refer to the characteristics of individual consciousness and social structure typical in societies whose members are controlled by, instead of controlling, the consequences of their collective activity" (*The Critique of Capitalist Democracy*, p. 125). According to Jean-Yves Calvez, alienation is "a general type of the situations of the absolutized subject who has given a world to himself, a formal world, refusing in this way the true concrete and its requirements" (*La pensée de Karl Marx*, p. 51); and according to Erich Fromm, "Alienation (or 'estrangement') means, for Marx, that man does *not* experience himself as the acting agent in his grasp of the world, but that the world (nature, others and he himself) remain alien to him. They stand above and against him as objects, even though they may be objects of his own creation. Alienation is essentially experiencing the world and oneself passively, receptively, as the subject separated from the object" (*Marx's Concept of Man*, p. 44).

With such a variety of definitions, it is difficult to say which is the best one. One may reserve the term for a specific phenomenon in which one is interested and, consequently, define it in such a narrow way as to make the majority of existing uses of "alienation" entirely inadmissible; or one may define it so broadly as to make as many as possible of the existing uses at least partly admissible and then distinguish between different forms of alienation in order to account for the variety of phenomena and to prevent possible confusions. The latter course seems more promising.

FORMS OF ALIENATION

All authors who have used the concept of alienation have distinguished between different forms of alienation; but not all of them have done so explicitly. Hegel attempted no explicit classification of the forms of alienation; but since, for him, the essence of all development was a process of alienation and dealienation, different stages in the development of the Absolute could be regarded as so many forms of alienation. It would be much more difficult to develop a similar classification for Feuerbach's works because the essence of his philosophy was negation of systematic philosophy. "Alienated Labor," a well-known fragment in Marx's *Economic and Philosophic Manuscripts*, seems to suggest that we should distinguish between four forms of man's alienation: the alienation of man the products of his own activity, the alienation of man from his productive activity itself, the alienation of man from his human essence, and the alienation of man from other men. But in other places Marx talked about other forms and subforms of alienation not mentioned in this fragment. The enumeration seems to be defective also in that it puts on the same level forms of alienation that should not be at the same level.

Twentieth-century writers differed greatly in their enumeration of the basic forms of alienation. Frederick A. Weiss distinguished three basic forms (self-anesthesia, self-elimination, and self-idealization); Ernest Schachtel distinguished four (the alienation of men from nature, from their fellow men, from the work of their hands and minds, and from themselves); Melvin Seeman, five (powerlessness, meaninglessness, social isolation, normlessness, and self-estrangement); and Lewis Feuer, six (the alienation of class society, of competitive society, of industrial society, of mass society, of race, and of generations).

In listing five different forms of alienation, Seeman tried to define them strictly. According to him, powerlessness is "the expectancy or probability held by the individual that his own behavior cannot determine the occurrence of the outcomes, or reinforcements, he seeks"; meaninglessness results "when the individual is unclear as to what he ought to believe—when the individual's minimal standards for clarity in decision-making are not met"; normlessness is the characteristic of a situation "in which there is a high expectancy that socially unapproved behaviors are required to achieve given goals"; isolation is characteristic of those who "assign low reward value to goals or beliefs that are typically highly valued in the given society"; and self-estrangement is "the degree of dependence of the given behavior upon anticipated future rewards, that is upon rewards that lie outside the activity itself" ("On the Meaning of Alienation," pp. 786, 788, 789, 790).

Instead of trying to enumerate all classifications of the forms of alienation that have been made so far, we shall only mention a few of the basic criteria according to which such classifications could be made and actually have been made.

(1) According to the nature of that which is alienated, we may distinguish between alienation of things and alienation of selves. And if we distinguish different types of things or selves, we may add further subdivisions. To those for whom the only self is man, alienation of self is only another name for the alienation of man. But they may distinguish between individual alienation and social alienation. We may classify as types of social alienation the alienation of societies as a whole (such as feudal societies and capitalist societies), the alienation of social groups (capitalists, workers, intellectuals, bureaucrats, producers, consumers, etc.), and the alienation of social institutions (such as the state, the church, and cultural institutions).

(2) According to the question, we can distinguish between alienation from something else or somebody else and alienation from oneself. The distinction is applicable only to alienation of selves; a thing cannot be alienated from itself. A self can be alienated either from something or somebody or from itself. According to the different kinds of "others" and according to the different aspects or sides of the self, further subdivisions can be added (for example, alienation from nature, alienation from fellow men, or alienation of the self from its body, its feelings, its needs, or its creative possibilities).

(3) According to whether that which is alienated is alienated through its own activity or through the activity of another, we could distinguish between alienation through others and alienation through oneself. Alienation of a thing can obviously be only an alienation

through others. There can be different kinds of alienation of things (stealing, giving, and buying and selling). Alienation of self can be either alienation through others or an alienation through oneself.

SELF-ALIENATION

The concept of self-alienation, found in Hegel and Marx and of the greatest interest for philosophy, is a result of applying a combination of the above three basic criteria. What Hegel and Marx called self-alienation is alienation *of* a self *from* itself *through* itself. They differ in that Marx recognized only one self-alienated self (man), while Hegel recognized two (man and God, or Absolute). Some writers hold that one could also speak about self-alienation of nature or of the world. In religious myths we find self-alienated angels (for example, Lucifer), and in children's stories and fables we find self-alienated animals (the cowardly lion, the naive fox) and even plants (a humpy fir tree, a stinking rose). But the concept of a self-alienated man is basic.

In what sense is it possible for a self (either an individual man or a society) to be alienated from itself? It seems plausible to say that to be self-alienated means to be internally divided, split into at least two parts that have become alien to each other. But in that case, why talk of self-alienation; why not, instead, simply refer to an internal division or split? The term *self-alienation* seems to suggest some or all of the following points. (1) The division of the self into two conflicting parts was not carried out from the outside but is the result of an action of the self. (2) The division into conflicting parts does not annihilate the unity of the self; despite the split, the self-alienated self is nevertheless a self. (3) Self-alienation is not simply a split into two parts that are equally related to the self as a whole; the implication is that one part of the self has more right to represent the self as a whole, so that by becoming alien to it, the other part becomes alien to the self as a whole.

One way to specify and clarify the inequality of the two parts into which a self-alienated self is split is to describe the self-alienation as a split between man's real "nature," or "essence," and his factual "properties," or "existence." The self-alienated man in such a case is a man who is not in fact what he is in essence: a man whose actual existence does not correspond to his human essence. Similarly a self-alienated society would be a society whose factual existence does not correspond to the real essence of human society.

How can the actual existence of man deviate from his real essence or nature? If one were to conceive man's essence as something shared by all men, then somebody alienated from man's essence could not be a man in fact. Accordingly, if alienation of man from his essence is possible, his essence must not be conceived as something that all men have in common.

One possible interpretation would be the conception of man's essence as an eternal or nontemporal idea of man toward which the real man ought to strive. This interpretation is full of difficulties and leads to unanswerable questions, such as Where and in what way does such an idea of man exist? What is the way or method to achieve an adequate knowledge of it? Why should a real man strive toward it?

Another interpretation would consist in conceiving man's essence as something actually belonging to men—not to all, but only to some men; for example, to the majority of all so-far-existing men or to the majority of future men. Whichever interpretation one chooses, new difficulties arise. Why should a majority be more representative of the nature of man than a minority? If we already allow the split into essence and existence, why should we not also allow the possibility of the split being present in the majority? And why should a future actuality have any advantage over the past and the present one?

The third, and perhaps the most promising, interpretation consists in saying that man's essence is neither an eternal idea nor a part of actuality, but the sum of historically created human possibilities. To say that a man alienates himself from his human essence would then mean that a man alienates himself from the realization of his historically created human possibilities. To say that a man is not alienated from himself would mean that a man stands on the level of his possibilities and that in realizing his possibilities he permanently creates new and higher ones. The third interpretation seems more plausible than the first two, but it too leads to difficulties. In what way do the possibilities exist, and how do we discover them? On what basis do we divide man's real possibilities into human and inhuman possibilities?

SELF-ALIENATION AND HISTORY

Another much-discussed question asks whether self-alienation is an essential, imperishable property of man as man or whether it is characteristic only of one historical stage in man's development. Some philosophers, especially existentialists, have maintained that alienation is a permanent structural moment of man's existence. Man as man is necessarily self-alienated; in addition to his authentic existence he leads a nonauthentic one, and it is an error to expect that he will one day live only authentically.

Opposed to this view is the view that the originally nonself-alienated man, in the course of development, alienated himself from himself, but that he will return to himself in the future. This view was held by Friedrich Engels and is accepted by many contemporary Marxists; Marx himself seems to have been inclined to think that man had always been self-alienated, but that in spite of this, he can and ought to overcome his self-alienation in the future. In this sense, Marx, in *Economic and Philosophical Manuscripts*, wrote about communism as the positive supersession of all alienation and the return of man from religion, family, state, etc., to his human (that is, social) existence. Such a conception of communism as a dealienation of human community formed the basis of all of Marx's other works.

ALIENATION IN PAST AND PRESENT. If we assume that the whole of history up to now has been a history of humanity's self-alienation, then it may be asked whether history has been characterized by the gradual elimination of alienation or by its permanent deepening. Those who believe in constant progress have maintained that alienation has always been diminishing. But many contemporary philosophers and sociologists have found that alienation has constantly increased, so that it is much deeper and more pervasive than ever before in contemporary capitalism and bureaucratic socialism. A third group of authors have maintained that alienation has diminished in some respects and increased in others. Some have insisted that the question cannot be answered simply in terms of more or less, that we should investigate different types of self-alienated individuals typical of different periods in human history. An interesting attempt in this direction was made by Erich Fromm, who distinguished four basic types of "nonproductive" (self-alienated) character orientations (the receptive, hoarding, exploitative, and marketing orientations), each typical of a successive stage of historical development. According to Fromm, all four are found in contemporary self-alienated society, but whereas the first three were inherited from earlier periods, the marketing orientation is "definitely a modern product," typical of twentieth-century capitalism (*Man for Himself*, pp. 62–81).

ALIENATION IN THE FUTURE. For those who regard alienation as a historical phenomenon, the question about a possible end of alienation (dealienation or disalienation) naturally arises. Two main answers have been given.

According to one group of thinkers, absolute dealienation is possible; all alienation, both social and individual, can be once and for all abolished. The most radical among this group have even maintained that all alienation has already in principle been eliminated in socialist countries, that it exists there only as a case of individual insanity or as an insignificant remnant of capitalism. More realistic representatives of this view have not denied facts showing that in countries considering themselves socialist, many old forms and even some new forms of alienation exist. But they have insisted that in more mature stages of socialism all these forms of alienation are destined to disappear.

According to a second group, only a relative dealienation is possible. It is impossible to eliminate alienation completely and finally because human nature is not something given and unchangeable that can be fulfilled once and for all. It is possible, however, to create a basically nonalienated society that would stimulate the development of nonalienated, really human individuals.

OVERCOMING ALIENATION. The means recommended for overcoming self-alienation differ according to one's view of the essence of self-alienation.

Those who regard self-alienation as a psychological fact, as a fact of the life of the individual human self, dispute the importance or even the relevance of any external changes in circumstances and suggest the individual's own moral effort, a revolution within the self, as the only cure. Those who regard self-alienation as a result of the neurotic process are quite consistent in offering a psychoanalytical medical treatment; they regard the new creative experience of acceptance and meeting in a warm, truly mutual and trusting doctor–patient relationship as the main therapeutic factor.

Diametrically opposed to this view are those philosophers and sociologists who, basing their ideas on a degenerate variant of Marxism called economic determinism, hold that individuals are the passive products of the social organization, that the whole of social organization is determined by the organization of economic life, and that all economic life is dependent on the question of whether the means of production are or are not private property. For economic determinists, the problem of dealienation is reduced to the problem of social transformation, and the problem of social transformation is reduced to the abolition of private property.

In criticizing "the materialist doctrine that men are products of circumstances and upbringing," Marx stressed that "it is men that change circumstances," so that "the coincidence of the changing of circumstances and of human activity can be conceived and rationally understood only as *revolutionizing practice* (Praxis)" (*Basic Writings on Politics and Philosophy*, with Engels, New York, 1959, p. 244).

Those who have tried to elaborate such a conception have insisted that dealienation of the society and dealienation of individuals are closely connected: One cannot be carried out without the other or reduced to the other. It is possible to create a social system that would enable and even stimulate the development of dealienated individuals, but it is impossible to organize a society that would automatically produce such individuals. A nonalienated individual is an individual who fulfills himself as a free and creative being of praxis, and free creativity is not something that can be given as a gift or forced upon anyone from outside. An individual can become free only through his own activity.

It is not simply that dealienation of individuals cannot be reduced to dealienation of society; the dealienation of society, in turn, cannot be conceived as a change in economic organization that will automatically be followed by change in all other fields and aspects of social life. Far from being an eternal fact of social life, the split of society into mutually independent and conflicting spheres and the predominance of the economic sphere is, according to Marx, a characteristic of a self-alienated society. Therefore, the dealienation of society is impossible without abolishing the alienation of the different human activities from each other.

Finally, the problem of dealienation of economic life cannot be solved by the abolition of private property. The transformation of private property into state property does not introduce an essential change in the situation of the working man, the producer. The dealienation of economic life also requires the abolition of state property, that is, its transformation into real social property; and this can be achieved only by organizing the whole of social life on the basis of the self-management of immediate producers.

See also Absolute, The; Engels, Friedrich; Feuerbach, Ludwig Andreas; Hegel, Georg Wilhelm Friedrich; Marx, Karl; Ontology; Philosophical Anthropology; Plato.

Bibliography

ANTHOLOGIES

Josephson, Eric, and Mary Josephson, eds. *Man Alone: Alienation in Modern Society*. New York: Dell, 1962.

Sykes, Gerald, ed. *Alienation: The Cultural Climate of Our Time*. 2 vols. New York: G. Braziller, 1964.

CLASSICAL WORKS

Feuerbach, Ludwig. *Das Wesen des Christentums*. Leipzig, 1841. Translated by Marian Evans as *The Essence of Christianity*, 2nd ed. London, 1882.

Hegel, G. W. F. *Encyclopädie der philosophischen Wissenschaften im Grundrisse*. Heidelberg, 1817.

Hegel, G. W. F. *Die Phänomenologie des Geistes*. Bamberg and Würzburg, 1807. Translated by J. B. Baillie as *Phenomenology of Mind*. London: S. Sonnenschein, and New York: Macmillan, 1910; 2nd ed., 1931.

Hegel, G. W. F. *Theologische Jugendschriften*, edited by H. Nohl. Tübingen: J.C.B. Mohr, 1907.

Marx, Karl. *Grundrisse der Kritik der politischen Ökonomie (Rohentwurf) 1857–1858*. 2 vols. Moscow: Verlag für Fremdsprachige Literatur, 1939–1941; 2nd ed., Berlin, 1953.

Marx, Karl. *Das Kapital*. 3 vols. Hamburg, 1867–1894. Translated by S. Moore, E. Aveling, and E. Untermann as *Capital*. 4 vols. London, 1887–1909. Especially Vol. I, Ch. 1, Sec. 4.

Marx, Karl. *Die oekonomisch-philosophischen Manuskripte aus dem Jahre 1844*. In *Historisch-kritische Gesamtausgabe*, edited by Karl Marx and Friedrich Engels. Berlin, 1932. Div. I, Vol. III. Translated by Martin Milligan as *Economic and Philosophical Manuscripts of 1844*. London, 1959.

Marx, Karl, and Friedrich Engels. *Die deutsche Ideologie* (1844–1845). In their *Historisch-kritische Gesamtausgabe*. Berlin, 1932. Div. I, Vol. III. Translated as *The German Ideology*, edited by R. Pascal. London: Lawrence and Wishart, 1938.

Works on Hegel, Marx, and Engels

Calvez, Jean-Yves. *La pensée de Karl Marx*. Paris: Éditions du Seuil, 1956.

Fromm, Erich. *Marx's Concept of Man*. New York: F. Ungar Publishing, 1961.

Hyppolite, Jean. *Études sur Marx et Hegel*. Paris: M. Rivière, 1955.

Kangrga, Milan. *Eticki Problem u Djelu Karla Marxa*. Zagreb, 1963.

Lukács, Georg. *Der junge Hegel und die Probleme der kapitalistischen Gesellschaft*. Zürich and Vienna: Aufbau-Verlag, 1948.

Marcuse, Herbert. *Reason and Revolution*. New York: Oxford University Press, 1941.

Oizerman, T. I. *Formirovanie Filosofii Marksizma*. Moscow: Izd-vo sotsial'no ekon lit-ry, 1962.

Popitz, Heinrich. *Der entfremdete Mensch. Zeitkritik und Geschichtsphilosophie des jungen Marx*. Basel: Verlag für Recht und Gesellschaft, 1953.

Tucker, Robert. *Philosophy and Myth in Karl Marx*. Cambridge, U.K.: Cambridge University Press, 1961.

RECENT STUDIES

Arendt, Hannah. *The Human Condition*. Chicago: University of Chicago Press, 1958.

Fromm, Erich. *Escape from Freedom*. New York: Farrar and Rinehart, 1941.

Fromm, Erich. *Man for Himself*. New York: Rinehart, 1947.

Fromm, Erich. *Sane Society*. New York: Rinehart, 1955.

Goldmann, Lucien. *Recherches dialectiques*, 3rd ed. Paris, 1959.

Lefebvre, Henri. *Critique de la vie quotidienne*. Paris: B. Grasset, 1947; 2nd ed., 1958.

Lefebvre, Henri. *Le matérialisme dialectique*. Paris: F. Alcan, 1939.

Levin, Murray B. *The Alienated Voter*. New York: Holt, Rinehart and Winston, 1960.

Lukács, Georg. *Geschichte und Klassenbewusstsein*. Berlin, 1923.

Mills, C. Wright. *White Collar*. New York: Oxford University Press, 1951.

Moore, Stanley. *The Critique of Capitalist Democracy*. New York: Paine-Whitman, 1957.

Naville, Pierre. *De l'aliénation à la jouissance*. Paris: M. Rivière, 1957.

Pappenheim, Fritz. *The Alienation of Modern Man: An Interpretation Based on Marx and Tönnies*. New York: Monthly Review Press, 1959.

Riesman, David, with Nathan Glazer and Reuel Denney. *The Lonely Crowd*. New Haven, CT: Yale University Press, 1950.

Whyte, William H., Jr. *The Organization Man*. New York: Simon and Schuster, 1956.

ARTICLES

Bell, Daniel. "The 'Rediscovery' of Alienation: Some Notes along the Quest for the Historical Marx." *Journal of Philosophy* 56 (1959): 933–957.

Braybrooke, David. "Diagnosis and Remedy in Marx's Doctrine of Alienation." *Social Research* 25 (1958): 325–345.

Cornu, Auguste. "L'idée d'aliénation chez Hegel, Feuerbach et K. Marx." *La pensée* no. 2 (1948): 65–75.

Dean, Dwight. "Alienation and Political Apathy." *Social Forces* 38 (1960).

Dean, Dwight. "Meaning and Measurement of Alienation." *American Sociological Review* 26 (1961): 753–758.

Duhrsen, Alfred. "Philosophic Alienation and the Problem of Other Minds." *Philosophic Review* 69 (1960): 211–220.

Easton, Loyd D. "Alienation and History in the Early Marx." *Philosophy and Phenomenological Research* 22 (1961): 193–205.

Feuer, Lewis. "What Is Alienation? The Career of a Concept." *New Politics* 1 (3) (1962): 116–134.

Garaudy, Roger. "O Ponjatii Otčuždenie." *Voprosi Filosofii* no. 8 (1959): 68–81.

Glazer, Nathan. "The Alienation of Modern Man." *Commentary* 3 (April 1947).

Kraft, Julius. "Die Selbstentfremdung des Menschen." *Geist und Tat* (March 1956).

Löwith, Karl. "Man's Self-Alienation in the Early Writings of Marx." *Social Research* 21 (1954): 204–230.

Nettler, Gwynn. "A Measure of Alienation." *American Sociological Review* 22 (1957): 670–677.

Petrović, Gajo. "Man as Economic Animal and Man as Praxis." *Inquiry* 6 (1963): 35–56.

Petrović, Gajo. "Marx's Theory of Alienation." *Philosophy and Phenomenological Research* 23 (1963): 419–426.

Rose, Arnold M. "Alienation and Participation: A Comparison of Group Leaders and the 'Mass.'" *American Sociological Review* 27 (6) (1962): 834–838.

Seeman, Melvin. "On the Meaning of Alienation." *American Sociological Review* 24 (1959): 783–791.

Sommer, Robert, and Hall, Robert. "Alienation and Mental Illness." *American Sociological Review* 23 (1958): 418–420.

"Symposium on Alienation and the Search for Identity." *American Journal of Psychoanalysis* 21 (2) (1961).

Vignaud, P. "L'aliénation selon Karl Marx." *La vie intellectuelle* (February 1937).

G. Petrović (1967)

ALIOTTA, ANTONIO
(1881–1964)

Antonio Aliotta, the Italian philosopher, was born in Palermo and taught at the universities of Padua and Naples. Moving from studies in experimental psychology, *La misura in psicologia sperimentale* (1905), Aliotta published in 1912 a vast critical analysis of contemporary philosophy titled *La reazione idealistica contro la scienza* (English translation, London, 1914) in which he defended a monadological spiritualism with a theistic tendency. When the shadow of the neo-Hegelianism of Benedetto Croce and Giovanni Gentile began to loom over Italy, Aliotta took sides with the opponents of this idealism and in his teaching and writings spread the news of other philosophical movements going on outside Italy, especially the philosophy of science, realism, and pragmatism.

From 1917 to 1936, in the mature phase of his thought, Aliotta's sympathies were above all with pragmatism, and his experimentalism suggests many points of similarity with the philosophies of William James and George Herbert Mead. Experimentation is the only means of establishing the truth of any knowledge whatever, even metaphysical and religious. By "experimentation," Aliotta does not mean simply the techniques of the laboratory but any kind of trial-and-error procedure in any field of human activity. History is a kind of grand laboratory in which people seek, through conflict, to attain more harmonious forms of life.

The success of the experiment, according to Aliotta, consists in the elimination of conflict and in the realization of a certain degree of harmony. "The quest for truth," he says in *Relativismo e idealismo*, "is the quest for a superior harmony of active human and non-human forces, operating in the universe of our experience." Obviously, the presupposition is that experience is not a single and continuous process, but is composed of a plurality of individual centers that meet and limit each other by stages and, through conflicts, try to realize a growing coordination. Common sense, science, and philosophy are the steps, or phases, of this coordination. The "thing" of common sense makes possible a certain degree of coordination between individual intuitions. The syntheses of science represent a superior degree of coordination, since they eliminate the disparity between the perspectives of common sense; and philosophical inquiry seeks to collect the remaining dissident elements, to correct the restricted vision of the particular sciences, and to achieve a more comprehensive view. The concept limit toward which this process tends is the coordination of all activities and their convergence to a single end, which is, in other terms, the Leibnizian monad of monads, or God.

Aliotta insists, however, on the social character, in Mead's sense, of all degrees of knowledge. He denies the absoluteness of truth and defends philosophical relativism, of which he sees implicit proof in the physics of Albert Einstein; and he holds that the measure of truth is in every case determined by the degree of coordination that is experimentally realized between the intuitions, the perspectives, and the individual points of view that constitute the rough fabric of experience.

In later writings, for example, *Il sacrificio come significato del mondo* (1943), Aliotta sought to extend this point of view to ethics with an inquiry into what he calls "the fundamental postulates of action." The indeterminacy of the world and its relative uniformity, the value of the human person and the transcendence of reality, and the plurality of persons and their tendency toward unity are among these postulates, but *the* fundamental postulate is that of the "perennial character of human-values" and of the existence of God, which guarantees this character. The spiritualistic and fideistic aspect prevails over the pragmatic and methodological aspect in this final phase of Aliotta's thought.

See also Croce, Benedetto; Gentile, Giovanni; Hegelianism; Idealism; James, William; Mead, George Herbert; Philosophy of Science, History of; Pragmatism; Realism.

Bibliography

WORKS BY ALIOTTA

La misura in psicologia sperimentale. Florence, 1905.

La reazione idealistica contro la scienza. Palermo, 1912. Translated by Agnes McCaskill as *The Idealistic Reaction against Science.* London: Macmillan, 1914.

La guerra eterna e il dramma dell'esistenza. Naples, 1917.

Relativismo e idealismo. Naples: Perrella, 1922.

La teoria di Einstein. Palermo, 1922.

L'esperimento nella scienza, nella filosofia, e nella religione. Naples, 1936.

Opere complete (Complete works). 7 vols. Rome, 1942–1954.

Il sacrificio come significato del mondo. Rome, 1947.

Evoluzionismo e spiritualismo. Naples: Libreria Scientifica, 1948.

Le origini dell'irrazionalismo contemporaneo. Naples, 1950.

Pensatori tedeschi della fine dell'800. Naples: Libreria Scientifica, 1950.

WORKS ON ALIOTTA

Carbonara, Cleto et al. *Lo sperimentalismo di Antonio Aliotta.* Naples, 1951. Essays on the occasion of Aliotta's 80th birthday.

Sciacca, M. F. *Il secolo XX*, 2nd ed., Vol. 1, 470–490. Milan, 1947.

Nicola Abbagnano (1967)
Translated by Nino Langiulli

ALISON, ARCHIBALD
(1757–1839)

Archibald Alison was born in Edinburgh, Scotland, and educated at Glasgow and Balliol College, Oxford. He was ordained in the Church of England and held positions in both England and Scotland. He married a daughter of John Gregory (1724–1773), who was a professor of philosophy and medicine at Aberdeen and an associate of Thomas Reid in the Aberdeen Philosophical Society. Alison preached at the Cowgate Chapel in Edinburgh from 1800 until his death. He published a volume of sermons, but is known primarily for his "Essays on the Nature and Principles of Taste," published in 1790 and reissued in 1810.

Alison's theory of taste breaks with earlier eighteenth-century theories in several respects while retaining other characteristic features. Like his predecessors, Alison regards beauty and sublimity as essentially emotional, hedonic experiences. Beauty is a form of pleasure, and as such it is found not in objects but in the mind. He accepts a faculty psychology that is essentially associative, and he regards what he is doing as a scientific investigation of the principles of human nature. In addition, Alison is the first theorist to clearly separate what he calls the emotions of taste—beauty, sublimity, and so on—from other kinds of pleasure. Although earlier theories speak of the pleasures of the imagination as special pleasures and sometimes suggest distinctions from other pleasures, it is Alison who first clearly appeals to a separate aesthetic pleasure that in his words is distinct from "every other emotion of pleasure" (1790/1999, p. 407).

Alison also argues that the ideas required to produce the emotions of taste must be complex. A simple idea, such as that of a color, which may be pleasant in itself, is only felt as beautiful when it enters into an associative complex. Thus, he rejects both the view that taste is an effect of an internal sense and the view that some single principle, such as relation, utility, or order and design, produces the emotions of taste. Alison believes that the emotion he seeks to describe is very much a product of an active mind. So he distinguishes two elements in complex emotions such as beauty. One is a simple idea and its accompanying emotion. Almost any simple emotion will do, including painful as well as pleasurable emotions. But the complex emotion of taste only appears when the simple emotion is acted on by the faculty of the imagination to produce "a consequent excitement. … The *peculiar* pleasure of the beautiful or the sublime is only felt when these two effects are conjoined, and the complex emotion produced" (1790/1999, p. 408).

Alison's theory of the imagination moves away from the earlier eighteenth-century theories of imagination according to which imagination is essentially a faculty that recombines preexisting ideas into new, artificial images—for example, a centaur is a combination of the ideas of horse and man. Alison still thinks of imagination as producing new ideas, but his emphasis is on its ability to detect resemblances, "trains of imagery" (1790/1999, p. 412), and expressive signs. So the faculty of imagination is essentially an active, associative faculty and the peculiar pleasure that it produces arises from the activity of the mind itself.

Alison draws a conclusion, which parallels Immanuel Kant's theories in many respects, that for the imagination to do its work it must be "free and unembarrassed" (1790/1999, p. 412)—that is, disinterested—"so little occupied by any private or particular object of thought, as to leave us open to all the impressions which the objects that are before us can produce" (p. 412). Whereas the earlier theories that suggest the need for disinterestedness understand it as a negative condition—a condition of good taste (Third Earl of Shaftesbury [Anthony Ashley Cooper]) or an avoidance of prejudice (David Hume) and thus a part of a theory of criticism, Alison treats it as a condition of experience. It is what allows the imagination to form the associations that are a necessary condition for the production of the complex emotion of beauty or sublimity. Alison goes so far as to describe a kind of free play of the imagination, which is opposed to attention. For Alison, however, these are competing mental habits and not Kantian epistemological principles.

Alison does draw the conclusion, common to some twentieth-century aesthetic attitude theories, that criticism is incompatible with the emotion of taste. Thus, taste ceases to be a form of critical judgment. He acknowledges that an active imagination does not necessarily produce good taste—the young are undiscriminating, for example—but he does not seem to recognize that on his theory taste has ceased to be what it had been since the Renaissance formation of the idea—a form of judgment with social implications.

Instead, Alison develops two essentially romantic theses: "matter is not beautiful in itself, but derives its beauty from the expression of mind" (1790/1999, p. 417) and the qualities of matter that are productive of beauty or sublimity are either themselves immediately expressive of mental qualities or powers—for example, the activity of creation in the arts or of the divine creator in nature; or they are signs of mental qualities—for example, the tone of voice. So Alison's theory combines three elements: imagination, association, and expression. He concludes, "[T]he beauty and sublimity which is felt in the various appearances of matter, are finally to be ascribed to their expression of mind; or to their being, either directly or indirectly, the signs of those qualities of mind which are fitted, by the constitution of our nature, to affect us with pleasing or interesting emotion" (p. 419).

Alison anticipates Kant and many of the features of romantic and twentieth-century aesthetics, therefore, without completely abandoning the tradition of theories of taste with which he is most closely associated—particularly those of Alexander Gerard and Reid. Although there are extensive references to the fine arts, Alison's theory of the arts remains a theory of imitation, not a theory of artistic creation or genius. Natural beauty provides the paradigm for beauty in the arts. The only creative mind is the divine mind; artists can only discover beauty, not create it. At the same time, however, imagination and expression are given a new scope. They are the necessary faculties for an artist. Artistic imitation is an active, not a passive mental operation.

Alison does not go far in formulating the epistemological requirements of his theory. He is not prepared to go as far as Samuel Taylor Coleridge and declare that the artist is a second creator. He takes for granted a theory of natural signs, found also in Reid and drawn from earlier theories, and he depends on a theory of association that is rapidly losing its grounding in the theory of ideas developed by John Locke and Hume. This produces some obscurity about what aesthetic qualities in objects are, a good deal of rhetorical excess, and an avoidance of the problems that exist for a theory of taste in which taste is no longer a form of judgment. But the new scope given to

the imagination makes Alison one of the first to formulate a full theory of aesthetics as expression.

See also Aesthetics, History of.

Bibliography

WORKS BY ALISON

"Essays on the Nature and Principles of Taste" (1790). In *Eighteenth-Century British Aesthetics*, edited by Dabney Townsend. Amityville, NY: Baywood, 1999.

WORKS ABOUT ALISON

Dickie, George. *The Century of Taste: The Philosophical Odyssey of Taste in the Eighteenth Century.* New York: Oxford University Press, 1996.

Hipple, Walter J. *The Beautiful, the Sublime, and the Picturesque in Eighteenth-Century British Aesthetic Theory.* Carbondale: Southern Illinois University Press, 1957.

Kivy, Peter. *The Seventh Sense: Francis Hutcheson and Eighteenth-Century British Aesthetics.* 2nd ed. New York: Oxford University Press, 2003.

McCosh, James. "Archibald Alison" (1875). In *The Scottish Philosophy, Biographical, Expository, Critical, from Hutcheson to Hamilton*. Hildesheim, Germany: Georg Olms, 1966.

Stolnitz, Jerome. "On the Origins of Aesthetic Disinterestedness." *Journal of Aesthetics and Art Criticism* 20 (2) (1961): 131–143.

Townsend, Dabney. "Archibald Alison: Aesthetic Experience and Emotion." *Journal of Aesthetics* 28 (2) (1988): 132–144.

Dabney Townsend (2005)

AL-JABIRI, ʿABD
(1935–)

Muḥammad ʿAbd al-Jabiri studied philosophy at Muḥammad V University in Rabat, Morocco, where he got his PhD in 1970. He had been a school teacher since 1957 and after successive promotions he became professor of philosophy at that university in 1971. Al-Jabiri has been involved in politics and journalism, and he is the main editor of the journal *Fikr wa-Naqd* (Thought and criticism) published in Rabat. His philosophy has to be understood in the context of the effort to modernize his country while at the same time preserving its cultural identity.

Al-Jabiri is a prolific writer; his large project, *The Critique of the Arab Mind*, is in three volumes: *Formation of the Arab Mind* (1984), *Structure of the Arab Mind* (1986), and *The Arab Political Mind* (1990). Al-Jabiri emphasizes the concept of cultural legacy (*turāth*) and analyses different readings of it. The fundamentalists (*al-salafīya*) search for the pristine Islam and they commit a grave mistake because they ignore the historical factor. The original "authentic" form of Islam was valid in its time, but the fundamentalists do not see it as subject to the course of history, they consider its initial form perpetually valid. The liberals and the Orientalists read cultural legacy from the Western standpoint. Arab liberals suffer under such cultural alienation that they cannot perceive their own identity. As for the Marxists they expect tradition to develop into revolution and the revolution to develop into tradition, and they cannot escape this vicious circle.

Al-Jabiri's reading is based on his criticism of Arab rationality, or mind ('aql). To this purpose he follows a methodology to liberate the reader-subject from being a hostage as the read-object, that is, Arabic language and Arabic tradition. After gaining objectivity, the reader rejoins the object, apprehends it by means of intuition (h?ads), and recognizes the historicity of reason. According to him Arab reason started as a political instrument. Two trends existed within the Umayyad regime: the one rationalist and reformist—Mu'tazilite—and the other traditional and conservative—Sunnite; the Sunnites were in power, and the Mu'tazilites in opposition. When the Abbasids overthrew the Umayyads, the Mu'tazilites moved to the governing side, and the Sunnites to the opposition. Nevertheless, since the Mu'tazilites were not strong enough to face the challenge of esoteric movements, the caliph [Abū] al-Ma'mūn (786–833) turned to the philosophy of Aristotle for help.

For al-Jabiri philosophy in the Islamic East is radically different from that in the West. Avicenna in the East wanted to create the "Oriental" philosophy by combining Platonic philosophy with the Aristotelian and integrating esoteric Gnostic doctrines and Mu'tazilite theology; it survived only in Iranian Gnosticism. By contrast, Averroes in the West succeeded in standing by Aristotle and abandoning the other doctrines and solved the long-lasting issue of the relationship between revealed religion and philosophy by proving their coherence and continuity. Thus, al-Jabiri asserts that the future of Arab philosophy lies in Averroes's philosophical method and his rationalism ('aqlānīya).

See also Aristotle; Averroes; Averroism in Modern Islamic Philosophy; Gnosticism; Islamic Philosophy; Marxist Philosophy; Rationalism; Rationality.

Bibliography

WORKS BY AL-JABIRI

Arabic-Islamic Philosophy: A Contemporary Critique. Translated by Aziz Abbassi. Austin: University of Texas Press, 1999.

WORKS ABOUT AL-JABIRI

Ábed Yabri, Mohamed. *El legado filosófico árabe: Alfarabi, Avicena, Avempace, Averroes, Abenjaldún: Lecturas contemporáneas.* Madrid, Spain: Editorial Trotta, 2001.

Josep Puig Montada (2005)

AL-KĪNDĪ, ABŪ-YŪSUF YA'QŪB IBN ISHĀQ
(ninth century)

Abū-Yūsuf Ya'qūb ibn Ishāq al-Kindī was the first outstanding Arabic-writing philosopher. He was born in the Mesopotamian city of Basra and later held a distinguished position at the caliph's court in Baghdad, where he died shortly after 870. For about a century he enjoyed a reputation as a great philosopher in the Aristotelian-Neoplatonic tradition. He appears to have been the first to introduce the late Greek syllabus of philosophical learning into the Muslim world. It was mainly, though not exclusively, based on the *Corpus Aristotelicum* and its Peripatetic and Neoplatonic commentators. Numerous competent Arabic versions of Greek philosophical texts were available then, and al-Kindī himself commissioned translations of Aristotle's *Metaphysics* and of the so-called *Theology of Aristotle* (in fact a paraphrase of Plotinus) which are extant and available in print.

Al-Kindī's fame, however, was eclipsed by such later philosophers as al-Fārābī and Ibn-Sīnā (Avicenna). Only a few of his numerous treatises reached the Latin Schoolmen, but one recently discovered Arabic manuscript contains twenty-four of his otherwise unknown philosophical writings.

Two basic tenets of al-Kindī's, concerning prophecy and the creation of the world, were not accepted by his more famous Muslim successors. First, knowledge acquired through revelation in the Scriptures and from divinely inspired prophets is unambiguously superior to any knowledge acquired through philosophical training. In many cases, religious tradition and speculative, dialectical theology (repudiated emphatically by al-Fārābī) lead one to the same conclusions as philosophy and natural theology, which al-Kindī very consciously and proudly introduced for the first time into the Muslim discussion. He maintained, however, that there are certain fundamental tenets of faith that are guaranteed by revelation alone and cannot be demonstrated by human reason.

Second, unlike the later Muslim philosophers, al-Kindī did not proclaim the eternity of the world and an eternal, emanating creation. Rather, he attempted to prove in philosophical terms that the world had been created from nothing, in time, through a divine creator, and that at some future date, according to divine dispensation, it would dissolve again into nothing. In doing this, he appears to use essentially the same arguments that were developed with more sophistication and subtlety by John Philoponus, the Christian Neoplatonic-Aristotelian philosopher, in sixth-century Alexandria. Al-Kindī also disagreed with the leading later thinkers by considering astrology to be a genuine branch of rational and methodical knowledge.

See also al-Fārābī; Aristotle; Avicenna; Islamic Philosophy; Philoponus, John; Plotinus.

Bibliography

WORKS BY AL-KINDĪ

An Arabic text is *Rasā'il al-Kindī al-falasafiyyah,* edited with an introduction by 'Abd al-Hādī Abū Rīdah, 2 vols. (Cairo: n.p., 1950–1953), in which 24 scientific and philosophical texts are printed for the first time. An Arabic text with Italian translation is *Studi su Al-Kindī*: Vol. I was translated by M. Guidi and R. Walzer (Rome, 1940), and Vol. II was translated by H. Ritter and R. Walzer (Rome, 1938). An Arabic text with German translation is "Al-Kindi als Astrolog," translated by O. Loth, in *Morgenländische Forschungen fuer H. L. Fleischer* (Leipzig: Brockhaus, 1875), pp. 261ff. A Latin text with French translation is *Antécédents gréco-arabes de la psychologie,* a translation of *De Rerum Gradibus* by L. Gauthier (Beirut, 1939). A Latin text is found in *Die philosophischen Abhandlungen des Ja'qūb ben Ishāg Al-Kindī,* edited by A. Nagy, which is Vol. II of C. Baeumker, ed., *Beiträge zur Geschichte der Philosophie des Mittelalters* (Münster: Aschendorff, 1897).

WORKS ON AL-KINDĪ

Works on al-Kindī are A. Altmann and S. M. Stern, *Isaac Israeli* (London: Oxford University Press, 1958), passim; F. Rosenthal, "Al-Kindī and Ptolemy," in *Studi orientalistici in onore di G. Levi della vida*, Vol. II (Rome: Istituto per l'Oriente, 1956), pp. 436ff.; and Richard Walzer, *Greek into Arabic* (Oxford: B. Cassirer, 1962), passim.

Richard Walzer (1967)

AL-KINDĪ, ABŪ-YŪSUF YA'QŪB IBN ISḤĀQ [ADDENDUM]

Al-Kindī is important as the individual who established the earliest vocabulary for philosophy in the Islamic world. He was unusual in tending to avoid religious issues. In particular, in his ethics he tended to steer clear of specifically religious issues altogether. In this respect he followed a broadly Stoic line by advocating the life of the mind and the futility of relying on physical things to bring happiness. Virtue is attained by adhering to the middle ground and avoiding extremes. Toward the end of his life al-Kindī came under sustained attack by the local ruler. All in all, he did place philosophy in the Islamic world on a firm footing, and his influential disciples continued to debate and write along the lines their teacher had demonstrated.

See also Happiness; Islamic Philosophy; Stoicism; Virtue and Vice.

Bibliography

WORKS BY AL-KINDĪ

Al-Kindī's Metaphysics: A Translation of Ya'qub ibn Ishāq al-Kindī's Treatise "On First Philosophy" (fi al-Falsafah al-ūlā), edited and translated by Alfred L. Ivry. Albany: State University of New York Press, 1974.

"Uno scritto morale inedito di al-Kindi," edited and translated by H. Ritter and R. Walzer. *Memorie della Reale Accademia nazionale dei Lincei* (Rome), series VI, 8 (1) (1938): 47–62. Originally published as *Risalah fi al-hilah li-daf' al-ahzan* (On the art of averting sorrows).

Fī ḥudūd al-ashyā' wa-rusūmihā (On the definitions of things and their descriptions), edited by M. A. Abu Ridah. In *Rasā'il al-Kindī al-falsafiya*. Cairo, 1953. Translated by D. Gimaret in *Cinq épîtres*. Paris: Centre national de la recherche scientifique, 1976.

WORKS ON AL-KINDĪ

Klein-Franke, Felix. "Al-Kindi." In *History of Islamic Philosophy,* edited by Seyyed Hossein Nasr and Oliver Leaman. London: Routledge, 1996. ch. 11, 165–177. I: 182–191

Oliver Leaman (2005)

AL-MUQAMMIṢ, DAVID BEN MERWAN

See *Muqammiṣ, David ben Merwan Al-*

ALSTON, WILLIAM P.
(1921–)

William P. Alston, an American philosopher, was born in Shreveport, Louisiana. He earned his Ph.D. from the University of Chicago (1951), and has taught at the University of Michigan (1949–1971), Rutgers University (1971–1976), the University of Illinois (1976–1980), and Syracuse University (1980–2000). Alston is a past president of the Central Division of the American Philosophical Association, the Society for Philosophy and Psychology, and the Society of Christian Philosophers as well as the founding editor of both *The Journal of Philosophical Research* and *Faith and Philosophy*. He is best known for his work in epistemology, the philosophy of religion, metaphysics, and the philosophy of language.

Alston made his early reputation in *Philosophy of Language* (1964), where he rejects the verifiability criterion of meaning and referential theories, and argues that the meaning of a sentence consists in its illocutionary act potential. He defends this view in his recent *Illocutionary Acts and Sentence Meaning* (2000), emphasizing the normative character of illocutionary acts. To illustrate, in uttering "Eat all of your vegetables," Trudy performs the illocutionary act of ordering the hearer to eat all of his vegetables only if she *takes responsibility* for the satisfaction of certain conditions, including: the hearer has some vegetables, it is possible for him to eat them, and Trudy has authority over him. So, Trudy performs the aforementioned illocutionary act only if she renders herself liable to censure in case these conditions are not satisfied—only if, Alston argues, she subjects her utterance to an illocutionary rule. Alston endorses a "Use Theory of Meaning," according to which a sentence's having a particular meaning consists in its being usable to play a particular role in communication. Because it is a sentence's illocutionary act potential that enables it to play this role, the meaning of a sentence consists in its usability to perform illocutionary acts of a particular type (in its being subject to a particular illocutionary rule).

Alston is also one of the leading proponents of realism about truth. In *A Realist Conception of Truth* (1996), he argues for alethic realism, the view that (1) truth is important and (2) a proposition is true if and only if what it claims to be the case *is* the case. Accordingly, the proposition that snow is white is true if and only if snow is white. Nothing else is necessary for the truth of that proposition. In opposition to epistemic conceptions of truth, a person need not be justified (rational, warranted) in believing that snow is white, nor must it be the case

that she or he would be justified in believing it in ideal epistemic circumstances. Snow must simply be white. This is a minimalist—but not a deflationist—account of the *concept* of truth because the *property* of truth may have features that go beyond this concept. Consequently, Alston's realist conception of truth is consistent with the correspondence theory, but does not entail it. His conception of truth is also consistent with different types of metaphysical antirealism, including idealism and Hilary Putnam's conceptual relativism. In *A Sensible Metaphysical Realism* (2001), Alston defends his own version of *metaphysical* realism, according to which large and important stretches of reality do not depend on conceptual schemes for their existence.

Alston's early work in the philosophy of religion, much of which is collected in *Divine Nature and Human Language* (1989), focuses on the nature and properties of God, the literal application of predicates (e.g. "knowing") to God, and divine action. While Alston's views on philosophical theology are crucial contributions to the field, his most pioneering work is thought to be *Perceiving God* (1991), in which he develops a "doxastic practice" approach to the epistemology of religious experience. He argues that putative experiences of God can provide prima facie justification for beliefs about God. This is because mystical perception (MP), in which beliefs about a religiously construed ultimate reality are based directly on putative experiences of it, is a basic doxastic practice—a family of socially established belief-forming dispositions or mechanisms. MP (which includes Christian mystical perception [CMP], Hindu mystical perception, etc.) is analogous to sense perception—the basic practice of forming perceptual beliefs about the physical environment on the basis of sensory experience. Alston argues here, and in *The Reliability of Sense Perception* (1993), that any attempt to *show* that basic doxastic practices are reliable will be infected with epistemic circularity. Still, it is practically rational to suppose that CMP is reliable, and hence that the beliefs it generates are prima facie justified. It is also rational for practitioners of CMP, and practitioners of other forms of MP, to continue to engage in their respective practices.

Alston has had a striking impact on epistemology. His early work is devoted to defending fallibilist foundationalism, delineating and evaluating different concepts of epistemic justification, and advocating an account of justification that combines a core externalism with minimal accessibility to grounds. Rejecting perspectival internalism and higher-level requirements, Alston distinguishes between the activity of showing that a belief is justified and a belief's being justified. In *Epistemic Justification* (1989), he argues that a belief's being prima facie justified consists in its being based on an adequate ground that is fairly readily accessible. The ground must *be* adequate—it must actually be sufficiently indicative of the truth of the belief. Because the subject need not have access to, or beliefs about, its adequacy, this is primarily an externalist, reliable-indicator account of justification. It anticipates the externalism of Alston's doxastic practice approach, according to which, for example, the socially established practice of sense perception must simply be reliable in order for a person's perceptual beliefs to be prima facie justified. In his recent work, he defends the Theory of Appearing as a superior alternative to sense-data and adverbial theories of the nature of perception. And, radically, in *Beyond "Justification": Dimensions of Epistemic Evaluation* (2005), he argues that there is no objective, epistemically crucial property of beliefs picked out by "justified." Consequently, epistemologists should dispense with the debate over justification, and instead investigate a plurality of epistemic desiderata, some of which are salvageable from it.

See also Epistemology; Metaphysics; Philosophy of Language; Philosophy of Religion.

Bibliography

PRIMARY WORKS

"Ontological Commitments." *Philosophical Studies* 9 (1958): 8–17.

Philosophy of Language. Englewood Cliffs, NJ: Prentice-Hall, 1964.

"The Deontological Conception of Epistemic Justification." In *Epistemic Justification: Essays in the Theory of Knowledge.* Ithaca, NY: Cornell University Press, 1989.

Divine Nature and Human Language: Essays in Philosophical Theology. Ithaca, NY: Cornell University Press, 1989.

Perceiving God: The Epistemology of Religious Experience. Ithaca, NY: Cornell University Press, 1991.

The Reliability of Sense Perception. Ithaca, NY: Cornell University Press, 1993.

A Realist Conception of Truth. Ithaca, NY: Cornell University Press, 1996.

"Belief, Acceptance, and Religious Faith." In *Faith, Freedom, and Rationality: Philosophy of Religion Today*, edited by Jeff Jordan and Daniel Howard-Snyder. Lanham, MD: Rowman & Littlefield, 1996.

"Back to the Theory of Appearing." In *Epistemology: Philosophical Perspectives, 13*, edited by James Tomberlin. Oxford: Blackwell, 1999.

Illocutionary Acts and Sentence Meaning. Ithaca, NY: Cornell University Press, 2000.

A Sensible Metaphysical Realism. Milwaukee: Marquette University Press, 2001.

"Doing Epistemology without Justification." *Philosophical Topics* 29 (2001): 1–18.

Beyond "Justification": Dimensions of Epistemic Evaluation. Ithaca, NY: Cornell University Press, 2005.

SECONDARY WORKS

Battaly, Heather D., and Michael P. Lynch, eds. *Perspectives on the Philosophy of William P. Alston.* Lanham, MD: Rowman & Littlefield, 2005.

Senor, Thomas D., ed. *The Rationality of Belief and the Plurality of Faith: Essays in Honor of William P. Alston.* Ithaca, NY: Cornell University Press, 1995.

Heather D. Battaly (2005)

ALTERITY

The term *alterity* derives from the Latin word *alter*, which means "other." In contemporary philosophy the question of the other is primarily that of the other human being, the Other (*Autrui*, in French), although some thinkers have raised the question of whether the human other should be privileged in this way. However, the central question governing philosophical discussions of alterity is not that of who the other is, but that of our access to alterity. So-called continental philosophy highlights the ontological dimension of this question rather than its epistemological dimension, which was the focus in English-speaking philosophy of what, since the nineteenth century, has been called the problem of other minds.

In his *Cartesian Meditations* (1960 [1931]) Edmund Husserl offers an account of how, by an analogy with my own body, I recognize another body as organic and, by a kind of alienation in which I make myself other that we call empathy, constitute an other as an alter ego. Martin Heidegger in *Being and Time* (1996 [1927]) dismisses this approach as based on René Descartes's inadequate understanding of the human being as an isolated subject. Heidegger displaces the epistemological problem of alterity by issuing the ontological claim that the other possesses the kind of being that he calls *Mitsein* (literally "with-being"). Nevertheless, the problem of the other reappears in Jean-Paul Sartre's *Being and Nothingness* (1956 [1943]), where, in part under the impact of Georg Wilhelm Friedrich Hegel's account of the master-slave dialectic, the relation with the Other is presented as conflictual.

LEVINAS, DERRIDA, AND THE ABSOLUTE OTHER

In *Totality and Infinity* (1969 [1961]) Emmanuel Levinas radicalizes the problem of alterity by thinking of the other not as another subject like me, but as radically Other, the one who puts me in question and calls me to my responsibility. This ethical relation is asymmetrical in the sense the Other is accessible only starting from an I. However, the Other is no longer defined by his or her differences from me, but by the way he or she exceeds this relation in absolute separation from me. Thus, Levinas's conception of the absolute Other self-consciously breaks with the way that the other has been thought in the West since Plato's *Sophist*. According to Plato the other is always relative to some other (*Sophist* 255d), a formulation usually understood to mean that the other is "other than the same."

When Jacques Derrida challenges Levinas's account of the absolute Other in "Violence and Metaphysics" (1978 [1964]), he explicitly evokes Plato's critique that renders such a conception unthinkable, impossible, and unsayable (*Sophist* 238e). Without underwriting the legitimacy of Husserl's account of intersubjectivity Derrida asks whether Husserl's notion of an alter ego does not better secure the ethical character of the radical alterity of the other than does Levinas's notion of the absolutely other. Derrida's point is that the Other cannot be the Other of the Same except by being itself the same, that is, an ego, but he himself subsequently embraces Levinas's language of alterity with the phrase *tout autre est tout autre* (every other is wholly other) (1995 [1990]), p. 82).

Meanwhile, and in part in response to Derrida's essay, Levinas developed the fundamental idea of his later thought: the substitution of the one for the other. To the question of how it is possible for the Other to call me into question, Levinas, in *Otherwise Than Being* (1981 [1974]), gives the answer that it is possible because I am already for-the-other, that is to say, because the other is in me in the midst of my self-identification. A parallel gesture by which alterity is relocated within the same can be found in psychoanalytic literature, for example, in Julia Kristeva's *Strangers to Ourselves* (1991 [1988]). However, it can be argued that the new kind of cosmopolitanism she promotes retains the division between "them" and "us" and that it seeks to overcome, insofar as the world is now divided between those who recognize that there are no foreigners and those who do not.

To address the difficulty of thinking substitution, Levinas has recourse to Arthur Rimbaud's impossible phrase *je est un autre* (I is an other). Levinas uses the very difficulty of thinking and saying alterity not only to challenge the priority of ontology and proclaim the primacy of ethics but also to mark an exit from Western philosophy as he inherits it. This shows how far the question of alterity has departed from the Husserlian problem of intersubjectivity, as a regional problem, to become the philosophical site for explorations of the limits of thought and language.

See also Deleuze, Gilles; Derrida, Jacques; Levinas, Emmanuel.

Bibliography

Derrida, Jacques. *The Gift of Death* (1990). Translated by David Wills. Chicago: University of Chicago Press, 1995.

Derrida, Jacques. "Violence and Metaphysics." In *Writing and Difference* (1967). Translated by Alan Bass. Chicago: University of Chicago Press, 1978.

Heidegger, Martin. *Being and Time* (1927). Translated by Joan Stambaugh. Albany: SUNY Press, 1996.

Husserl, Edmund. *Cartesian Meditations: An Introduction to Phenomenology* (1931). Translated by Dorian Cairns. The Hague: Nijhoff, 1960.

Kristeva, Julia. *Strangers to Ourselves* (1988). Translated by Leon S. Roudiez. New York: Columbia University Press, 1991.

Levinas, Emmanuel. *Otherwise Than Being, or, Beyond Essence* (1974). Translated by Alphonso Lingis. The Hague: Nijhoff, 1981.

Levinas, Emmanuel. *Totality and Infinity* (1961). Translated by Alphonso Lingis. Pittsburgh, PA: Duquesne University Press, 1969.

Sartre, Jean-Paul. *Being and Nothingness: An Essay on Phenomenological Ontology* (1943). Translated by Hazel E. Barnes. New York: Philosophical Library, 1956.

Theunissen, Michel. *The Other: Studies in the Social Ontology of Husserl, Heidegger, Sartre, and Buber* (1977). Translated by Christopher Macann. Cambridge: MIT Press, 1984.

Robert Bernasconi (2005)

ALTHUSIUS, JOHANNES
(1557–1638)

Johannes Althusius, the German legal and political philosopher, was born at Diedenshausen, a village of the county of Wittgenstein-Berleburg in the Westphalian Circle. He is thought to have been the son of a farmer, although all data of his early youth are quite unknown. By 1581 he was studying Aristotle in Cologne, and he later studied Roman law at Basel. His experience of the Swiss way of life gave him a predilection for municipal freedom and self-government and for republican constitutionalism. Although deeply influenced by Calvinist piety, he was eager to become a learned classical scholar. The forces of Christian faith, humanistic learning, and democratic feeling formed his character. He was both a man of strong will with a tendency to stubbornness and an austere moralist. It is, therefore, not surprising that he was a rigorous logical thinker and a systematic teacher as well as a realistic positivist with a desire to describe the empirical realities of social life.

Althusius passed his examination for the doctorate of civil and ecclesiastical law at Basel in 1586 with theses on the right of succession. In the same year he published a booklet, *Iurisprudentia Romana, vel Potius Iuris Romani Ars, 2 Libri, Comprehensa, et ad Leges Methodi Rameae Conformata* (Basel, 1586), that discussed fundamental questions of Roman law and that is also of philosophical interest. Through this work Althusius introduced into political science the systematic method of the French philosopher Petrus Ramus that contrasted with the prevailing humanistic method based on philological concerns. But although Ramus opposed the traditional Scholastic method of instruction, he had nevertheless retained the formalism of his predecessors insofar as he used the "method of dichotomy." This specific "ramistic" method divided every logical concept into two others, and each of them into two new concepts. This method of an endless, progressing, systematic presentation was applied by Althusius to all his later writings.

Soon after receiving his doctorate, Althusius became a lecturer in Roman law and in philosophy at Herborn, a newly established Calvinist college attended by students from many countries. In 1594 he became professor of law, and he was appointed rector of the college in 1597 and again in 1602. He also served as an advocate in the chancellery at Dillenburg. In this capacity he defended the rights of the college against the ambitions of the noblemen of the county. He was also involved in controversies with his colleague, the law professor Anton Matthäus (1564–1637), and with some of the Herborn theologians. In spite of these activities, he found time to write his most famous work, *Politica Methodice Digesta et Exemplis Sacris et Profanis Illustrata* (Politics methodically arranged and illustrated by holy and profane examples [Herborn, 1603; 2nd enlarged ed., Groningen, 1610; 3rd enlarged ed., Herborn, 1614]). This work was, as C. J. Friedrich wrote, "the culminating point of his life." The book clearly showed Althusius's systematic strength. He undertook to coordinate the diverse views of the Bible, Roman law, and the advocacy of the right to resist an unjust monarch of George Buchanan and the monarchomachs,

and, on this basis, to write a compendium of political science.

The book was a natural and rational system of sociology, involving all the contemporary discussions of the problematical questions of theology, ethics, and jurisprudence. Althusius's fundamental view was that "politics is the science of linking human beings to each other for a social life." The whole of humankind, living in natural cooperative groups, builds up a universal community of civil and private corporations. The members join each corporation by the force of their sympathetic emotions. In this respect Althusius resembled both Hugo Grotius and Jean-Jacques Rousseau. However, he was a strong opponent of Jean Bodin's doctrine of royal absolutism, believing that the constituent power belongs to the community and that sovereignty is an attribute of the organized people, not of the king. The people decide all fundamental political questions through the representative assembly, and the chief of state is only a commissioner of the people and may be deposed if he acts contrary to the contract between him and the community. The representative assembly must obey the commandments of God and observe the natural laws. The necessities of human nature are as much a source of social order as is God's will.

Thus, Althusius held a threefold conception of social order: as a biopsychological social phenomenon, as a historically conditioned reality, and as a divinely limited work of man.

The principal sources of Althusius's thought were faith, reason, and experience. A major work composed somewhat later, *Dicaiologicae Libri Tres Totum et Universum Ius, Quo Utimur, Methodice Complectentes* (Digest of jurisprudence [Herborn, 1617]), is based on these three elements. In this work Althusius discussed the fundamental principles, institutions, and concepts of public and private law as they were found in the Roman jurisprudence of his day. By presenting the law as the realization of the concept of law and of its component legal categories, Althusius became one of the most important forerunners of modern Continental "legal conceptualism."

Meanwhile, in 1604 Althusius had been called as a syndic to Emden, a Calvinist city in eastern Frisia. He was soon appointed to the council, and he played an important part in the struggles of the city with the count of Frisia. He also became a dominant figure in the consistory of the Reformed Church in Emden.

See also Aristotle; Bodin, Jean; Grotius, Hugo; Political Philosophy, History of; Ramus, Peter; Rousseau, Jean-Jacques.

Bibliography

PRIMARY WORKS

"Politica Methodice Digesta" of Johannes Althusius (Althaus). Edited by Carl J. Friedrich. Cambridge, MA: Harvard University Press, 1932.

The Politics of Johannes Althusius. Abridged and translated by Frederick S. Carney. Boston: Beacon Press, 1964.

Politica. Edited and translated by Frederick S. Carney. Indianapolis, IN: Liberty Fund, 1995.

SECONDARY WORKS

Friedrich, Carl S. *Johannes Althusius und sein Werk im Rahmen der Entwicklung der Theorie von der Politik.* Berlin: Duncker und Humblot, 1975.

Gierke, Otto von. *The Development of Political Theory.* Translated by Bernard Freyd. New York: Norton, 1939.

Hueglin, Thomas O. *Early Modern Concepts for a Late Modern World: Althusius on Community and Federalism.* Waterloo, ON: Wilfrid Laurier University Press, 1999.

Wolf, Erik. *Grosse Rechtsdenker der deutsche Geistesgeschichte,* 4th ed. Tübingen: Mohr, 1963.

Erik Wolf (1967)
Bibliography updated by Philip Reed (2005)

ALTRUISM

While benevolence, compassion, and humanity were not major virtues for the ancient philosophers, modern moral philosophers generally agree that altruism is important to morality, although they disagree about what it is, how to explain it, and what its scope should be. The nineteenth-century French theorist Auguste Comte, who first coined the term *altruism*, claimed that the way to end social conflict is by training people to "live for others," rather than themselves. In a popular sense, altruism means something like noble self-sacrifice. A more minimal understanding, one that many philosophers favor, is an acknowledgment that the interests of others make claims on us and limit what we may do.

Altruism made its way into moral theory when Christian philosophers added the theological virtues of faith, hope, and charity to the cardinal virtues of the Greeks. Charity, the greatest of the theological virtues, was thought to be an inner spiritual orientation toward others. Charity is characterized as disinterested, universal, and unconditional. It should be directed to everyone, saint and sinner alike, regardless of merit.

The eighteenth-century Scottish philosopher Francis Hutcheson followed the Christian philosophers, claiming that everyone is capable of Christian love—calm universal benevolence—that aims at the good of all sentient creatures. He also distinguished two other types of benevolence: love directed toward smaller groups or particular persons, such as parental affection and friendship, and particular feelings of pity, sympathy, and gratitude. Christian love is the best form of benevolence; the other two are good so long as they do not counteract it.

Hutcheson's view about how altruistic we should be is even more radical than the Christian view. Reducing virtue to benevolence, he argues that none of the four cardinal virtues of the Greeks—temperance, courage, prudence, justice—are virtues unless their practice is motivated by love. Temperance is not a virtue, unless motivated by a concern to make ourselves fit to serve others. Courage is mere craziness, unless we face dangers in order to defend the innocent or to right wrongs. Prudence is not a virtue if it aims only at promoting our own interests. Justice is not a virtue unless it has a regard for the good of humankind. Hutcheson derives the utility principle—maximizing happiness for the greatest number—from the idea that the morally best motive is calm, universal benevolence.

Later utilitarians made the utility principle central to their account of moral rightness, but detached it from Hutcheson's basis in Christian love. Many utilitarians have argued that our duties of benevolence are extreme, so their view about the scope of benevolence is radical in another way. As long as I have the power to benefit others without hurting myself so much that total utility is reduced, I am obligated to help them. On this view, giving aid to famine relief, for example, is not a matter of charity but a duty.

There are two other ways of understanding altruism. One way, adopted by David Hume in the eighteenth century and by Bernard Williams as well as some feminist thinkers in the twentieth, characterizes altruism in terms of particular benevolent dispositions, desires, or affections. According to this view, you help others because you love them. Hume denied that we have the universal love of humankind to which Hutcheson and the Christian philosophers appealed, but thought that such benevolent dispositions as parental love and friendship were morally important character traits essential for virtue. Hume also thought that we possess the capacity to act from sympathy. When you see someone in distress, sympathy leads you to feel distress, which in turn motivates you to alleviate your distress by alleviating theirs. Sympathy enables us to extend our love for particular individuals and smaller groups to larger groups of people.

Williams's view is similar to Hume's. Some of our particular benevolent desires are directed toward people we care about, for example, a daughter or friend, and are motivated by thoughts like "Mary needs help." Other benevolent desires are more general and impersonal concerns, motivated by thoughts like "someone needs help." Williams claims that the structure of the motivating thought in both cases is the same. Although altruism is not a rational requirement on action, Williams thinks that sympathetic reflection may move us from benevolent desires motivated by our love of particular individuals to more general altruistic dispositions.

Some feminist philosophers have argued that altruistic dispositions such as caring, compassion, and maternal love should be made the focus of morality. These philosophers claim that relationships should be at the heart of morality and that most of our relationships are not only intimate, but also involuntary. They argue that an ethics of care rather than an ethics of justice is appropriate for these types of relationships.

By contrast, philosophers in the Kantian tradition conceive of altruism as a rational requirement on action. They claim there is no need to postulate a benevolent desire to explain altruism. Kant's initial argument appeals to his requirement that we may only act on principles that we can will as universal laws. Willing a world in which everyone has a policy of not helping others, while knowing that you will need help, would be inconsistent, so we must will to help those who are in need. Kant also argues for a duty of beneficence on the basis of the requirement of treating humanity as an end in itself. He argues that you must treat the ends of others as you treat your own ends. You take your own ends to be good and worth pursuing, so consistency requires that you treat the ends of others as good and worth pursuing. This suggests that we have reason to help not only those in need, but anyone we are in a position to help.

Thomas Nagel follows Kant in thinking that the reasons of others directly provide us with reasons. Suppose someone wants you to stop tormenting him. How does that person's desire not to be treated that way give you a reason to stop? At an intuitive level, Nagel's argument appeals to the question: How would you like it if someone did that to you? You realize that if someone were tormenting you, you would not merely dislike what he was doing, you would resent it. Resentment is a response to the idea that someone has ignored a reason he has to not treat you badly. The reason in this case is your own desire

not to be tormented. You think your desire not to be tormented is a reason for your tormentor to stop. Since you think that your reasons provide direct reasons for others, you must also think that the reasons of others provide you with reasons. The argument turns on the idea that your reasons and the reasons of your victim are the same: they are the reasons of a person. According to Nagel, the argument works only because you have the capacity to view yourself as just one person among others. Although Humeans and Kantians disagree about whether to explain altruism in terms of particular desires or to view it as a rational requirement on action, they agree that the force of altruism springs from our common humanity.

See also Egoism and Altruism; Ethical Egoism; Friendship; Human Nature; Love; Sympathy and Empathy; Virtue and Vice.

Bibliography

Hume, David. *Enquiry concerning the Principles of Morals* (1751), edited by L. A. Selby-Bigge and P. H. Nidditch. Oxford: Clarendon Press, 1975.

Hume, David. *A Treatise of Human Nature* (1739–1740). 3 vols., edited by L. A. Selby-Bigge and P. H. Nidditch. Oxford: Clarendon Press, 1985.

Hutcheson, Francis. *An Essay on the Nature and Conduct of Passions and Affections with Illustrations upon the Moral Sense* (1728), edited by Aaron Garrett. Indianapolis, IN: Liberty Fund, 2002.

Kant, Immanuel. *Grounding for the Metaphysics of Morals.* Translated by James W. Ellington. Indianapolis, IN: Hackett, 1993. Originally published as *Grundlegung zur Metaphysik der Sitten* (Riga: J. F. Hartknoch, 1875).

Nagel, Thomas. *The Possibility of Altruism.* Oxford: Clarendon Press, 1970.

Williams, Bernard. *Problems of the Self.* Cambridge, U.K.: Cambridge University Press, 1973.

Charlotte R. Brown (2005)

AMPÈRE, ANDRÉ MARIE
(1775–1836)

André Marie Ampère was a French physicist and philosopher; his main achievement in physics was the foundation of electrodynamics. He correctly recognized that Hans Christian Ørsted's discovery, in 1819, of the effect of electric current on a magnetic needle was merely a special case of the general correlation of electricity in motion with the rise of a magnetic field. His explanation of magnetism in terms of molecular electric currents was a bold anticipation of one feature of the later electron theory.

Shortly after Ampère's death his *Essai sur la philosophie des sciences* appeared with a biographical note by Charles-Augustin Sainte-Beuve and a warm appraisal by Émile Littré. Its subtitle, *Exposition analytique de toutes les connaissances humaines,* indicated that the main topic was the classification of sciences, in which Ampère was as much interested as his contemporary Auguste Comte. Ampère's main division of sciences into "cosmological" and "noological" was inspired by Cartesian dualism. The details of the classification, which also included "applied sciences"—medicine, agriculture, etc.—are now of only historical interest.

Far more interesting is *La philosophie des deux Ampères,* edited by J. Barthelémy Saint-Hilaire. The title is misleading because the only contribution of Ampère's son Jean Jacques is an introduction to the philosophy of his father. Besides this, the book contains some unfinished philosophical manuscripts as well as Ampère's letters to Maine de Biran, with whom he remained in personal contact and in correspondence until Maine de Biran's death in 1824. Ampère accepted the central idea of Maine de Biran's voluntaristic idealism that the true nature of the self is revealed in the introspective experience of effort. But unlike Maine de Biran, Ampère more cautiously differentiated what he called *emesthèse* (that is, consciousness of personal activity) from the sensation of muscular effort that can be induced by some external agency.

This was not the only instance of Ampère's remarkable gift for introspective analysis. In dealing with the association of ideas he distinguished two cases. The first is *commémoration,* or ordinary recall, when two associated ideas remain unaffected by their contiguity. The second is *concrétion,* when two ideas merge, for example, when the present perception of an object seen before blends with the recollection of its previous perception. But the main difference between Ampère and Maine de Biran concerned the problem of knowledge of the external world. Maine de Biran, under the influence of Immanuel Kant, denied any possibility of knowing things-in-themselves; Ampère, under the influence of Isaac Newton, John Locke, and his own scientific interests, believed in the possibility of knowing inferentially the relations between things-in-themselves. These "noumenal relations" are similar to Locke's primary qualities; they can be known when the general spatial, temporal, and numerical relations are divorced from the qualitative content (Locke's secondary qualities) of sensory experience. But unlike Locke, Ampère interpreted the impenetrability of matter dynamically, as being a

result of inextensive resistances (*résistances inétendues*) of which there is an indefinite number in each body. This view of matter as being a product of inextensive dynamic centers is thus closer to the dynamism of Gottfried Wilhelm Leibniz, Roger Joseph Boscovich, and Michael Faraday than to the traditional atomism of Newton. On the other hand, Ampère remained a Newtonian in his insistence on the reality of absolute space and time, which he interpreted theologically, again like Newton, as attributes of God. Equally Newtonian was his rejection of the Cartesian plenum.

See also Boscovich, Roger Joseph; Cartesianism; Comte, Auguste; Faraday, Michael; Kant, Immanuel; Leibniz, Gottfried Wilhelm; Littré, Émile; Locke, John; Maine de Biran; Newton, Isaac.

Bibliography

WORKS BY AMPÈRE

Théorie mathématique des phénomènes électrodynamiques, uniquement déduite de l'expérience. Paris, 1827. Ampère's account of electrodynamics.

Essai sur la philosophie des sciences, 2 vols. Paris: Chez Bachelier, 1834–1843.

La philosophie des deux Ampères. Edited by J. Barthelémy Saint-Hilaire. Paris: Didier, 1866; 2nd ed., 1870.

WORKS ON AMPÈRE

Broglie, Louis de. *Continu et discontinu en physique moderne.* Paris: A. Michel, 1941. Pp. 241–266.

Cantor, Georg. "Über verschiedene Theoreme aus der Theorie der Punktmengen." *Acta Mathematica* 7 (1885): 105–124.

"Lettres de Maine de Biran à A.-M. Ampère." *Revue de metaphysique et de morale* 1 (1893): especially 553.

Lorentz, Borislav. *Die Philosophie André-Marie Ampère.* Berlin, 1908. Inaugural dissertation.

Milič Čapek (1967)

ANALOGY IN THEOLOGY

Religious discourse has been under scrutiny since ancient Greece when Anaxagoras said if oxen and dogs could paint, they would depict the gods in their own likenesses. The Jewish, Christian, and Muslim scriptures depict the divine being in vivid humanlike traits while conveying the divine otherness, mystery, immateriality, and eternity. Thus there are religious currents of anthropomorphism, of transcendentalism, of metaphor and symbolism, and of literalism about the being and nature of God. The Greek philosophical ancestry of Western culture presents the divine as immaterial, immutable, everlasting, perfect, and incomprehensible. Both the Platonic and Aristotelian metaphysicians developed theories of analogical predication that were later extended to theology, the study of the revealed divinity.

Theologians used a theory of analogy that had three parts: analogy of *being* (of reality between God and world, and among created realities, too); analogy of *meaning* (of words and concepts); and analogical thinking (of conception by proportionalities). The aim was to explain how words that apply to sensible things also adapt in meaning to apply literally, not only metaphysically, to the transcendent deity known only by inference, revelation, or mystical experience. Words applied to God—"wise" and "good," for example—are neither entirely equivocal (such as *bank*/savings; *bank*/river), nor merely metaphorical (*drop*/an argument), but rather, they are analogous; that is, they adjust in ways explained below to the context, just as words generally adjust to contrasting contexts, say, as "knows"/the way differs from "knows"/arithmetic, and as "exist" does in "*there exist* /trees/species/numbers/shapes." Metaphysics articulates *theoretical* truth-conditions for such statements and for ordinary religious beliefs—conditions not accessible without such metaphysics—the way science states the molecular structure for water.

1. SECULAR ORIGIN IN PLATO AND ARISTOTLE

The thesis that words fit in literal meaning to diverse verbal contexts that reflect differences of reality—the analogy theory—has its origin in secular philosophy. For Plato, things that share in the Forms are not said to exist in the same sense as the Forms (compare *Sophist*; *Parmenides*), and the Form "Human" is *what*-it-is-to-be-human, and thus is human, but not in the sense in which Callicles is human by participating in the Form. Further, Plato used the same names, such as the *courageous* man and the *courageous* act, *just*/state; *just*/man, for things related as cause to effect and sign to signified.

Aristotle used those distinctions, added more, and regarded *real*, entitative analogy, reflected in word-meaning, as central to his explanatory principles. (*Metaphysics* 1070a.31). Such predication is *literal*, as opposed to metaphorical (*Poet* 1457b)—for example, "the fields *smile* with the sunlight" (Aquinas called that *improper* proportionality [*Summa Theologiae* 1.13.3.ad 3]). Aristotle acknowledged analogy by *attribution* (relational naming: *healthy*/animal; *healthy*/diet), and by *proper proportionality* (e.g., genus is to species as body is to soul, namely, as *potency* is to *act*). The explanatory terms—for example, "act/potency"—apply to diverse things analogically (*Met*

1048b, 5–8). Aristotle further reasoned that qualities, such as color and shape, and other accidentals, are said *to be* derivatively (*pros hen*) to substances; and "analogically the same things are principles, i.e. actuality and potentiality; but they are not only different for different things, but also apply in different ways to them" (*Met* 1071a.5). Aristotle says the causes and principles of different things are analogous and are spoken of analogously (*Met* 1070a.31). Moreover, the contrast-dependent notions, "act/potency," "matter/form," "substance/accident," "cause/effect," are all *analogical* in meaning because the phenomena to which they apply are really, *de re*, analogous; for instance, body is matter for soul, and clay is matter for a statue.

2. TRANSITION TO THEOLOGY

The Arabic philosophers adopted Aristotle's views on analogy in their metaphysics and physics and in their discussion of the simplicity of God in the Qur'an. That made the first connections of Aristotelian analogy-theory to scriptural theology. Islamic religious believers differed on how to interpret the physical descriptions of God's face, eyes, hands, speaking, sitting, and so on, in the Qur'an, as well as the description of God's feelings—for example, wrath, satisfaction, and God's traits, such as cunning and patience—whether anthropomorphically, metaphorically, symbolically, and so on (compare Van Ess 1954). Al-Kindī (c. 850) thought a literal reading of the Qur'an on creation is coherent with Aristotelian concepts. In his treatise "On the One True Agent" he holds God is literally the only agent bringing being from (absolute) nonbeing, whereas humans are only metaphorically (analogically?) agents, bringing being from potentiality. Al-Fārābī (c. 900) in chapter 1 of "On the Perfect State" says "existing," "having intellect," "knowing," "being wise," "real," "true," "living," and the like, are said of God in senses different from what we say of creatures because the divine being is simple, without composition or distinct traits. And Avicenna (980–1037) used Aristotle's views about analogy of meaning and of reality directly in his metaphysics and in his physics, where "motion," for instance, is said (as Aristotle also said) to apply analogously, to augmentation, alteration, and locomotion, and the analogy of "being" within the ten categories is acknowledged.

Avicenna reasoned that being and essence are really the same in God, and indicated that a creature's being is not explained by "*what*-it-is" as is the divine; Aquinas would adopt this. Avicenna also formulated the principle that God's knowledge is the cause of things (later used by

Aquinas as *cognito dei causa rerum*, *ST* 1.14.8), whereas our knowledge is posterior to things known. The Arabic writers, including the Jewish Moses Maimonides, all hold that God is simple; he is not a body, without any plurality of attributes except by attribution from the divine effects, infinite and incomprehensible. It is from those Arabic, chiefly Islamic, sources, along with the corpus of Aristotle, that the analogy theory came into Latin theology, Avicenna being the most influential in metaphysics.

Maimonides (1135–1204) argued that the eternity of the world is not demonstrated, and that it is both created and has a temporal beginning. Like Avicenna, he affirmed the divine simplicity in a strong sense, so that: "either every attribute we predicate of Him is an attribute of action [and so named from the received effect], or, if the attribute is intended for the apprehension of His essence and not of his action, it signifies the negation of the privation of the attribute in question" (*Guide for the Perplexed*, 1, p. 58). Thus, saying, "God is all knowing" means "God is not unknowing of anything," and saying "God is simple" means "God is not composite," and saying "God is eternal" means "God is without beginning or end." That came to be known as "negative theology," with no positive ascriptions to God, except existence and creation and the metaphors provided by scripture.

Christians, from the earliest fathers of the church, developed explanatory analogies—that is, proportional comparisons, say, of the Trinity to the unity amidst distinction of the essence, power, and operation of the human soul, and an analogy of the relation of the Father to the Son as "light from light" (in *Nicene Creed*, and Augustine's *De Trinitate*). Such explanatory analogies, not part of the theory described here, were devised throughout the predominantly neoplatonic first millennium of Christian thinking, for instance in Augustine's *De Trinitate* (c. 410) and Boethius's *De Trinitate* (c. 510), the School of Chartres (twelfth century), and the School of St. Victor (twelfth century), and continued throughout the later history of theology (compare Chollet 1923–1967).

A neoplatonic writer historians call Pseudo-Dionysius (c. 500) was widely believed, but not by Aquinas, to have authority as a disciple of St. Paul. He proposed, in his *Divine Names*, that one first knows God by negation (*via negationis*), "not a body," "not with parts," and so on, then by inadequate affirmation as "wise," "good" "loving," qualified by "but not in the way of creatures," and then in a third stage by superlatives, such as "infinitely knowing" and "good beyond excellence" (*via eminentiae*). But in his *Mystical Theology* Pseudo-Diony-

sius is more restrictive, saying one starts *via remotionis* by denying of God the things most remote from him, such as "drunkenness and fury," then progressing by denial even through all the higher attributes of creatures until one reaches "the super-essential darkness," entering "the cloud of unknowing," mystically united to what is "wholly unknowable" (because of the limitations of the human mind). This work had a profound influence on the development of transcendentalism in medieval theology and even into the twenty-first century.

3. AQUINAS (1225–1274)

Aquinas combined the influences of Avicenna, Maimonides, and Pseudo-Dionysius, along with mastery of Aristotle and Plato. He held that God infinitely transcends every true description achieved by human philosophical efforts, but that, nevertheless, a great deal can be known and positively established about God; in fact, Aquinas believed, there can be both a philosophical science of God from unaided reason, and a *divine science* whose first principles are given by revelation (*ST*, 1.q.1.a.2). Furthermore, he absorbed Aristotle's notion of analogy of "being" (*pros hen*) for the ten Categories into his own wider theory of analogy between creatures and God by participation. Aquinas said "being can be essentially predicated of God alone, because to be divine is to be subsistent and absolute, whereas being is predicated of any creature by participation; for no creature *is* its own being, but is something having being," as the actuality (*esse*) of its potentiality (its essence), because creatures do not exist on account of *what* they are, but on account of God (*Quod*.2, q.2, 1.1). Further, *what* God is, essentially, is not naturally knowable to humans, though it is disclosed to the blessed by divine gift (*ST* 1.12.1).

Thus, Aquinas reasoned that our knowledge is not limited to what we can attribute negatively or only by metaphor, or merely by the *extrinsic* attribution that would make "God is good" mean merely "God is the *cause* of creaturely goodness" (*ST* 13. a.6) in the way that a person is called "captain" because of what he does. Many writers, influenced by Philo Judaeus (c. 20 BCE–40 CE) whose work came to the West through Clement of Alexandria and Origen, held that God is named only with names of his effects. Aquinas, however, says we can know that pure perfections (unmixed with limits, such as "educated") apply intrinsically to God by *explanatory priority* because the divine perfections are the cause and exemplar of all perfections in creatures, such as being, life, knowledge, freedom, and love. This position is variously developed in *Summa Theologiae* (q.13, a.4–5), and *Summa*

Contra Gentiles (1, chap. 34), and *Q. D. De Veritate* (q 2.a.1). Nevertheless, the names and concepts of pure perfections are acquired only through our perceptual experience with creatures (*ST* 1.q.13, a.6), even though their primary reality is in God. Thus the words "loves," "knows," "chooses," and so forth, used of God and of humans, have similar definitions but differing presuppositions that reflect the diverse manner of being of God and creatures, the perfections being prior and all the same as God's being, and finite, received, and really separable from one another in creatures.

So whatever is predicated positively of God is either by *attribution*, as God is called "creator" on account of what is made and "happy" because of his perfect enjoyment, or predicated by *proportionality* and priority, as God is said to be "knowing, loving, wise, excellent and beautiful," and so on, but in a manner explanatorily prior to the creature's imperfect and derived being and knowledge. Aquinas also acknowledged metaphorical predicates of God, too (*ST* 1.19.11), many sanctioned by scripture ("angry," "Prince of Peace"), and many useful negative ones ("not a body," "not in space," "not with parts or complexity," "not with a beginning or end").

The religiously and philosophically central attributes are predicated literally and intrinsically, with their presuppositions adjusted to religious discourse (e.g., "God chooses" but does not deliberate), and elaborated theoretically (e.g., God's attributes are all "really the same as the divine being, *esse*, differing from one another only in concepts"). They include "knowing," "loving," "good," "righteous," "just," "omnipotent," "omniscient," "immutable," and "present everywhere"—and every other unmixed perfection, too. They apply to God but are adjusted to the priority and perfection of divine being. Thus, God knows but does not find out; God loves but does not need. All creation participates in God's being, not as being divine in any way, but as being continuously *from and on account of* God, and thus, being said "to be" analogously. Created being is God's proper and continuous effect; the way setting-alight—igniting—is the *proper* effect of fire; and the illumination of the air is the *continuous* effect of the sun (*ST* 1, 8.1).

Aquinas thought the real analogy between divine subsistent being (*ipsum esse subsistens*) and creaturely, participated being is an adequate basis for demonstrative knowledge of the existence and of the many attributes of God by reasoning that he displayed in *Summa Contra Gentiles*.

Nevertheless, Aquinas emphasizes that because what is received is received in the manner of the recipient (*quidquid recipitur recipitur modo recipientis, ST* 1.75.5), God is disclosed through nature only as far as nature is capable, with all creatures falling infinitely short of the divine reality. And he holds that the divine biblical revelation, though vastly exceeding anything humans could discover or even conceive on their own, is proportioned to what is fitting for humankind, thus leaving the infinite divine mystery "wrapped in a mist" (*caligine absoluta, Const. Dei Filius* ch. 4, Vat. 1), with the essence of God beyond all natural understanding.

By the Reformation in the sixteenth century, a religious role for scholastic philosophy was largely rejected, and the reformers held the faith to be in no need of fragile and contested support from philosophy. Biblical authority was said to stand on its own, to be understood by the "analogy of Faith" (*analogia fidei*, based in Rom. 12.6, according to both Luther and Calvin). Thus the analogy discussions dried up, except among Catholic philosophers such as Cardinal Cajetan (1458–1564), Sylvester of Ferrara (1474–1528), and Francisco Suárez (1548–1617), and mostly stayed that way, apart from the historical scholarship that continues to the present.

David Hume (1711–1776) inaugurated modern noncognitivism, consigning metaphysics to the flames (*Enquiry*, 1748), asserting that all truths are grounded in sense impressions or relations of ideas, thus setting the framework for twentieth-century verificationism and the attack on the cognitive content of religious discourse.

4. CONTEMPORARY CONTEXT

In the twentieth century, positivist philosophers, seeking to be like scientists, questioned whether talk about God had any cognitive content at all. Alfred Jules Ayer argued that talk about God is without content because it is unverifiable. Some believers, such as Richard Bevan Braithwaite and Frank Plumpton, proposed empirical understandings of its content; others, such as John Hick, even propose eschatological verifiability. Philosophers such as D. Z. Phillips argued that religious discourse belongs to its own "language game"—a notion adopted from Ludwig Wittgenstein—with its own conditions for meaningfulness, and its own conditions of rational belief, analogous to mathematics and aesthetics. Mostly, however, the discussion of meaningfulness was unconnected to the historical positions on analogy in metaphysics and theology.

One twentieth-century adaptation of the classical accounts (Ross 1981) reasoned that analogy, as "fit of word-meaning to contrasting contexts," is a universal feature of natural languages within which the Aristotelian cases of relational and presuppositional adaptation are particular species, and that the cognitive content of utterances is a function of the family of statements and practices in which they are employed (and often craft-bound to specialized skills and tasks, such as medicine or sailing). Thus, analogy of meaning in religious contexts is a special case of the analogy phenomena found in all the neighborhoods of discourse, whether specialized or not. And Aquinas's metaphysical theory, say of participation and *esse subsistens*, was interpreted, on that account, as his articulating *theoretical* truth-conditions for the ordinary and analogous talk of divine existence, perfection, and action, the way a chemist might explain the atomic constitution of a commonly known metal such as lead.

Thus there are at least two additions to Aristotle's and Aquinas's work on analogy: first, that the linguistic phenomena involve differences of *discourse* commitment (e.g., "God decides," but does not deliberate), as well as the differing *theoretical* presuppositions articulated by metaphysicians, such as "all divine perfections are really *de re* the same"; and second, that analogous fit of meanings to diverse context is lawlike, universal, and dynamic in natural languages. But *lexical* meanings of words are not to be regarded as direct pairings of words to concepts (considered to be their meanings), but are relations of contrast-dependence within the language itself (compare Saussure 1915)—that is, relations of contrastive expressive *capacity*, so that *meanings* and the world are correlated in clouds or clusters of discourse, not simply item by item.

As Wittgenstein, Wilfrid Sellars, and others observed, the cognitive content of verbalized beliefs is a function of the community of social behavior in which they have a place in the giving of explanations, reasons, motivations for actions, and interpretations. Thus, although a lot of nonsense is easily formulated in religious talk—as in any other talk—expressed convictions that modify action and attitudes either reflect reality or fail to, and either do so poorly or well. They are thus suitable for epistemic attitudes such as belief and denial. Nevertheless, the truth or falsity of what is said by the religious may not be accessible from outside the practicing community, just as the truth of medical, musical, manufacturing, or scientific expert discourse is largely inaccessible from outside the community of expertise.

The late twentieth- and early twenty-first-century cognitivity issue for religion involved three challenges: (i) whether characteristic expressions (say "Jesus is my personal savior"; "There is one God in three Persons") have stable conditions of appropriate utterance, qualification, reasons, rejoinder, and so on, within a practicing (relatively narrow) religious community; (ii) whether the community practice is one of coherent stable conditions, positive or negative, for acceptable use and endorsement and reason-giving for such assertions; and, (iii) whether basic claims, say, about the existence and nature of God, or some of them (*praeambula fidei*), can be rationally accepted or rejected, as well, from outside the confessing community. The common core of Judeo-Christian-Islamic monotheism meets the challenges affirmatively, and many find it externally well supported, even demonstrated in part, though other competent assessors disagree.

Some participants, such as the Reformers, thought external assessment carries no weight or utility for religious faith, though it may have some value in defense of the faith (apologetics). Note also that, in general, the false may sometimes be rationally accepted and the true rationally rejected, as the history of medicine and physics illustrates. Nothing requires a body of convictions to be decidable entirely, or even at its heart, from outside the practice in which conviction is arrived at and sustained. Otherwise the fabric of science would be subject to nonscientific rejection, rather than just parts of it. The same holds for religion. Still, Augustine and Aquinas held that the scripture cannot mean literally what science has demonstrated to be false (*ST* 1.68.1).

Some recent writers talk as if words, including temporal ones, apply to God not only literally but univocally; for instance, Richard Swinburne, in *The Coherence of Theism* (1977) said he applies "good" to God in the "perfectly ordinary" sense in which he would say his grandmother was good, though the conditions differ (p. 71). That contrasts with those philosophers such as D. Cupitt or Bishop Robinson who regard talk about God as merely metaphorical. Perhaps, like Duns Scotus, Swinburne and others consider the meaning of the words to be unaffected by differences in the mode of a thing's being. Charles Hartshorne, a Whiteheadean "process metaphysician," came closer to anthropomorphic literalism when he said that God, in process of self-surpassing, can suffer, change, and have other temporal predicates. Analogy theory is often mistaken for a theory of *non*literal predication, when it is just the opposite: an account of the literal but not anthropomorphic.

Some theologians such as Karl Barth say the meanings of "God loves," "forgives," "redeems," and "commands" are determined by the *scriptural* context as understood by the church (the community of believers): "Language about God has the proper content, when it conforms to the essence of the Church, i.e., to Jesus Christ…. according to the analogy of faith, (Rom 12.6)" (*Church Dogmatics*). In accord with Luther and Calvin, he probably meant that nothing *more* than the *analogia fidei*, as understood by the Church, determines what a faithful Christian is to believe and mean. But to say there can be *no further* truth-conditions at all, say, for "Jesus is the Son of God," would conflict with simple logic. So, sciences might investigate such conditions. And whether extrascriptural theoretical content is sometimes required for faithful belief (say, Eucharistic consubstantiation vs. transubstantiation, vs. mystical presence) is a matter not settled by *sola scriptura* and *analogia fidei*, unless theological inquiry is included.

Thus the analogy theorists, historically and in the twenty-first century—like the Reformers—and Barth, the Evangelicals, and philosophers such as Swinburne and Alvin Plantinga, hold that talk about God is neither empty of intelligible content (noncognitivism), nor only metaphorical, poetic, or symbolic (Paul Tillich); nor only negative, except for God's existence (Maimonides); nor positive only in superlatives (Pseudo-Denis—*via eminentiae*). And they reject the principle that what is not observationally verifiable or falsifiable is meaningless. They agree that the scripture is the norm for what is to be said about God as Revealed. But analogy theorists additionally maintain (i) that analogous predication is literal and perfectly common in discourse generally, and characteristic of discourse about God, and (ii) that the metaphysical exploration of the divine, even of what is revealed, discloses theoretical truth-conditions, not otherwise accessible, for claims that God exists and has the divine perfections, just as science discloses microconditions for water that are not contained on the surface of the ordinary vocabulary.

So it seems that analogy theory both as linguistic theory and as metaphysical account of being has more innings to play in the history of theology.

See also al-Fārābī; Anaxagoras of Clazomenae; Aristotelianism; Aristotle; Augustine, St.; Avicenna; Ayer, Alfred Jules; Barth, Karl; Boethius, Anicius Manlius Severinus; Braithwaite, Richard Bevan; Cajetan, Cardinal; Calvin, John; Clement of Alexandria; Creation and Conservation, Religious Doctrine of; Duns Scotus, John; Hume, David; Infinity in Theology and Metaphysics; Luther, Martin; Maimonides; Origen; Philo Judaeus; Philosophy of Religion, History of; Plantinga, Alvin; Plato; Platonism and the Platonic Tradition; Pseudo-Dionysius; Ramsey, Frank Plumpton; Reformation; Saint Victor, School of; Sellars, Wilfrid; Suárez, Francisco; Sylvester of Ferrara, Francis; Thomas Aquinas, St.; Tillich, Paul; Wittgenstein, Ludwig Josef Johann.

Bibliography

Aquinas, Thomas. *Summa Theologiae*. Vol. 1, edited by Thomas Gilby. Garden City, NY: Image Books, 1969.

Aquinas, Thomas. *Summa Contra Gentiles*. Translated by A. Pegis. Notre Dame, IN: University of Notre Dame Press, 1975. Both contain easily accessible and brief accounts of ideas developed in many other places of his work. See Wippel, below, for a comprehensive exposition of Aquinas.

Barth, Karl. *Church Dogmatics*. Vol. 2, edited by G. W. Bromiley and T. F. Torrance. Translated by G. W. Bromiley. Edinburgh: T. & T. Clark, 1957.

Cajetan, Thomas De-Vio. *The Analogy of Names, and The Concept of Being*. 1498. Translated by E. Bushinski and H. Koren. Pittsburgh: Duquesne University Press, 1953. An influential, brief, systematization and interpretation of Aquinas's positions, much disputed by later scholars, but still useful and the source of some classifications such as "analogy of proper proportionality."

Chollet, A. "Analogie." In *Dictionnaire de Theologie Catholique*, edited by A. Vacant et al. Paris: Librairie Letouzey, 1923–1967. A scholarly survey of analogy in Roman Catholic natural and dogmatic theology.

Klubertanz, George. *St. Thomas Aquinas on Analogy: A Textual Analysis and Systematic Synthesis*. Chicago: Loyola University Press, 1960. With an appendix of the passages (in Latin) in which Aquinas discussed analogy.

Lyttkens, H. *The Analogy Between God and the World: An Investigation of its Background and Interpretation of its Use by Thomas of Aquino*. Uppsala, Sweden: Lundequistska bokhandeln, 1953. A published doctoral dissertation with historical sweep and a comprehensive study of the primary sources.

McInerny, Ralph. *Aquinas and Analogy*. Washington, DC: Catholic University of America Press, 1996.

Ross, James F. *Portraying Analogy*. Cambridge, U.K.: Cambridge University Press, 1981. Expands Aristotle and Aquinas into a new account of analogy of *meaning*, its role in philosophy, and in the debate about the cognitive content of religious discourse. It does not address the *analogia entis*, the metaphysics (see Wippel).

Saussure, Ferdinand de. *Cour de linguistique generale*. Paris, 1915. Translated by W. Baskin in *Course in General Linguistics*. New York: Philosophical Library, 1959. By the "father" of modern linguistics, in which the "linguistic meaning is contrast of meaning," idea is developed along with the notion of paradigmatic contrasts that map meaning relationships (employed in Ross, 1981).

Van Ess, J. "Tashbih wa-Tanzih." In *Encyclopaedia of Islam*, edited by H. A. R. Gibb et al., vol. 10, 341–344. Leiden, Netherlands: Brill, 1960. Reference courtesy of Dr. Jon McGinnis.

Wippel, John, F. *The Metaphysical Thought of Thomas Aquinas: From Finite Being to Uncreated Being*. Washington, DC: Catholic University of America Press, 2000. The most comprehensive and up-to-date exposition of the whole of

Aquinas's theory, its development, and its rationales, especially in chapters 3 and 13.

James F. Ross (2005)

ANALYSIS, PHILOSOPHICAL

Philosophical analysis is a term of art. At different times in the twentieth century, different authors have used it to mean different things. What is to be analyzed (e.g., words and sentences versus concepts and propositions), what counts as a successful analysis, and what philosophical fruits come from analysis are questions that have been vigorously debated since the dawn of analysis as a self-conscious philosophical approach. Often, different views of analysis have been linked to different views of the nature of philosophy, the sources of philosophical knowledge, the role of language in thought, the relationship between language and the world, and the nature of meaning—as well as to more focused questions about necessary and apriori truth. Indeed the variety of positions is so great as to make any attempt to extract a common denominator from the multiplicity of views sterile and not illuminating.

Nevertheless analytic philosophy—with its emphasis on what is called "philosophical analysis"—is a clear and recognizable tradition. Although the common core of doctrine uniting its practitioners scarcely exceeds the platitudinous, a pattern of historical influence is not hard to discern. The tradition begins with G. E. Moore, Bertrand Russell, and Ludwig Wittgenstein (as well as Gottlob Frege, whose initial influence was largely filtered through Russell and Wittgenstein). These philosophers set the agenda, first, for logical positivists such as Rudolf Carnap, Carl Hempel, and A. J. Ayer and then later for Wittgenstein, who in turn ushered in the ordinary language school led by Gilbert Ryle and J. L. Austin. More recently the second half of the twentieth century has seen a revival of Russellian and Carnapian themes in the work of W. V. Quine, Donald Davidson, and Saul Kripke. Analytic philosophy, with its changing views of philosophical analysis, is a trail of influence, the broad outlines of which we will trace here.

G. E. MOORE

We begin with George Edward Moore, whose influence, along with that of his Cambridge classmate Bertrand Russell, was felt from their student days in the last decade of the nineteenth century throughout the whole of the twentieth. As a student Moore, who was to become the great defender of the Common Sense view of the world, was fascinated and perplexed by what he took to be the dismissive attitude toward common sense adopted by some of his philosophical mentors. He was particularly puzzled about the doctrines of absolute idealism that time is unreal (and so our ordinary belief that some things happen before other things must, in some way, be mistaken), that only the absolute truly exists (and so our ordinary conception of a variety of independently existing objects is incorrect), and that the essence of all existence is spiritual (and so our ordinary, non-mentalistic view of material objects is erroneous). Moore was curious how proponents of such doctrines could think themselves capable of so thoroughly overturning our ordinary ways of looking at things. How could anyone by mere reflection arrive at doctrines the certainty of which was sufficient to refute our most fundamental pre-philosophical convictions?

Before long he came to believe one couldn't. On the contrary, one's justification for a general principle of philosophy could never outweigh one's justification for the most basic tenets of the Common Sense view of the world. In essence he held that philosophers have no special knowledge that is prior to, and more secure than, the best examples of what we all pre-theoretically take ourselves to know. The effect of this position was to turn the kind of philosophy done by some of his teachers on its head. According to Moore the job of philosophy is not to prove or refute the most basic propositions, those we have no choice but to accept. It is however a central task of philosophy to explain *how* we know them. The key to doing so, he thought, was to analyze precisely what these propositions state, and hence what we know, when we know them.

Moore turned his method of analysis on two major subjects—perceptual knowledge and ethics. Although he achieved important results in both, they didn't fulfill his hopes for analysis. For example despite making a persuasive case in "A Defense of Common Sense" (1925) and "Proof of an External World" (1939) that we do know such elementary truths as *I am perceiving this and this is a human hand*, he never succeeded in explaining how, precisely, perception guarantees their truth. Moreover his speculative explorations of different analyses of their contents—briefly canvassed in "A Defense of Common Sense"—didn't advance the case very far. The paucity of these results—in which analysis aims at theoretical reconstructions of the contents of ordinary propositions—

contrasts with the modest but much more successful conception of analysis that emerges from his painstaking philosophical practice in papers such as "The Refutation of Idealism" (1903). The burden of that piece is to show that idealists who hold that all of reality is spiritual have no good reason for their view. A crucial step is the isolation and analysis of a premise—roughly *For anything to exist, or be real, is for it to be experienced*—that Moore takes to be crucial to their argument. His point is that in order to play the role required by the argument, it must be a necessary truth. But, he thinks, the only plausible ground for believing it to be necessary lies in wrongly taking the concept of being experienced to be (analytically) included in the concept of an object existing, or being real—a mistake, he thinks, that is akin to wrongly identifying the sensation of yellow with that of which it is a sensation. Putting aside the accuracy of Moore's depiction of his opponents, or of his contentious views of the distinction between analytic and synthetic propositions, the paper is a beautiful example of the theoretically modest but philosophically illuminating practice of analysis at which Moore excelled—conceptual clarification, the drawing of clear distinctions, avoidance of equivocation, logical rigor, and attention to detail.

Much the same can be said about his use of philosophical analysis in ethics. On the one hand his enormously influential view that *good* is unanalyzable may be criticized for falling prey to a crippling dilemma. On any understanding of analyzability on which the unanalyzability of good would justify Moore's claim that conclusions about what is good are not derivable from, or supported by, premises that don't contain it, his "open question" argument does not show that good is unanalyzable; whereas on any understanding of analyzability on which his argument does establish that good is unanalyzable, this result does not justify the claim that conclusions about what is good can't be derived from or supported by premises that don't talk about goodness. In this sense his most famous ethical analysis was unsuccessful. Moreover this failure was connected to his official view of analysis, which conferred a privileged status on those necessary, apriori truths that reflect part-whole relations between concepts—roughly those propositions expressed by sentences that can be reduced to logical truths by putting synonyms for synonyms (where pairs of synonyms are thought to be easily recognizable by anyone who understands them)—as opposed to those necessary, apriori truths that do not fall into this category. Far from a source of strength, this theoretically-loaded conception of analysis was, arguably, Moore's Achilles heel.

On the other hand the decidedly more modest, theoretically uncontentious, conception of analysis that emerged from his exemplary analytic practice of unrelenting, conceptual clarification undeniably advanced the subject and served as a model for generations of analytic philosophers to come. It also produced, in the first paragraph of *Principia Ethica* (1903), what may be the best expression of the guiding spirit of analytic philosophy, and philosophical analysis, ever written.

It appears to me that in Ethics, as in all other philosophical studies, the difficulties and disagreements, of which its history is full, are mainly due to a very simple cause: namely to the attempt to answer questions, without first discovering precisely *what* question it is which you desire to answer. I do not know how far this source of error would be done away, if philosophers would *try* to discover what question they were asking, before they set about to answer it; for the work of analysis and distinction is often very difficult: we may often fail to make the necessary discovery, even though we make a definite attempt to do so. But I am inclined to think that in many cases a resolute attempt would be sufficient to ensure success; so that, if only this attempt were made, many of the most glaring difficulties and disagreements in philosophy would disappear. At all events, philosophers seem, in general, not to make the attempt, and, whether in consequence of this omission or not, they are constantly endeavoring to prove that that 'Yes' or 'No' will answer questions, to which *neither* answer is correct, owing to the fact that what they have before their minds is not one question, but several, to some of which the true answer is 'No', to others 'Yes.' (p. vii)

BERTRAND RUSSELL

Bertrand Russell's views on philosophical analysis are unique in two respects. They are more explicit, highly articulated, and theoretically fruitful than those of other leading figures; and their historical influence remains unsurpassed. The most well-known of his doctrines about philosophical analysis is his theory of descriptions presented in "On Denoting" (1905). The initial problem to be solved was an ontological one, posed by negative existentials—sentences of the form ⌜α doesn't exist⌝ in which α is a name or description. The puzzle posed by such a sentence is that if it is true then there would seem to be nothing named or described; but if α doesn't stand for anything then it is hard to see how the sentence can be meaningful at all, let alone true. According to Russell the problem arises from false ideas about meaning—(i) the idea that the meaning of α is the entity it names or describes, and (ii) the idea that the meaning of ⌜α doesn't exist⌝ is a proposition that predicates non-existence of that entity. At first blush these ideas seem doubly problematic since, on the one hand, if α doesn't stand for anything then there is nothing for non-existence to be predicated of, and on the other if there is an object with the property of non-existence, it would seem that there must exist an object that doesn't exist, which is a contradiction. Since Russell thought that (i) and (ii) led to these paradoxical results, he rejected both. His theory of descriptions is a proposal for replacing them with a conception of meaning that avoids such paradox.

Russell begins by distinguishing grammatically proper names (like the ordinary names of people and places) from logically proper names (*this* and *that*). Whereas the meaning of a logically proper name is its referent, the meaning of a grammatically proper name n for a speaker s is given by some singular definite description, ⌜the F⌝, that s associates with n. When it comes to singular definite descriptions, Russell's view is that they are incomplete symbols, which have no meaning in isolation. By this he means three things: (i) that the objects (if any) they denote are not their meanings, (ii) that the propositions expressed by sentences containing them do not contain constituents corresponding to them, and (iii) that their meanings can be given by rules that explain the systematic contributions they make to the meanings of sentences containing them.

Consider, for example, the negative existential ⌜The F doesn't exist⌝. To understand this sentence is to grasp the proposition it expresses. However since for Russell its grammatical form is not the same as the logical form of the proposition p it expresses, he found it useful to translate it into a formula of his logical system the syntactic structure of which did match the logical structure of p. (Russell later came to think that he could dispense with propositions themselves as real entities, and get by with his logico-linguistic structures alone, but that may be regarded as a never-fully-worked-out afterthought.) The logical form of ⌜The F doesn't exist⌝ was identified with that of of ⌜~∃ x ∀ y (Fy ↔ y = x)⌝—where the proposition expressed by this formula was seen as having three constituents: negation, the property expressed by '∃x', of being "sometimes true," and the propositional function f expressed by the sub formula ⌜∀ y (Fy ↔ y = x)⌝. This function assigns to any object o the proposition that says

of o that it is identical with any object y if and only if y has the property expressed by F. Since o is identical with itself and nothing else, this means that the proposition f assigns to o is one that is true if and only if o, and only o, has the property expressed by F. Finally to say of a propositional function that it "is sometimes true" is to say that in at least one case it assigns a true proposition to an object. Putting all this together we get the result that the negative existential ⌜The F doesn't exist⌝ expresses a proposition which is true if and only if there is no object which is such that it, and only it, has the property expressed by F. Since this proposition simply denies that a certain propositional function has a certain property, neither the truth nor the meaningfulness of the negative existential that expresses it requires there to be any object with the property of non-existence.

Negative existentials were, in Russell's view, special in that they contain the grammatical predicate *exist*, which, on his analysis, does not function logically as a predicate of individuals. However his theory was intended to cover all sentences containing descriptions. Whenever ⌜is G⌝ does function as a predicate, the analysis of ⌜The F is G⌝ is ⌜∃ x ∀ y (Fy ↔ y = x) & Gx⌝, which may be paraphrased *there is something such that it, and only it, is F, and it is also G*. In "On Denoting," Russell showed how this analysis could be used to solve several logico-linguistic puzzles, and many other applications have been found since then. With the exception of Gottlob Frege's invention of the logical quantifiers in his *Begriffsschrift* (1879), one would be hard pressed to identify any comparably fruitful idea in the history of philosophical analysis.

Russell's revival of Frege's logicist program of reducing arithmetic to logic—in *Principia Mathematic* with Whitehead (1910, 1912) and *Introduction to Mathematical Philosophy* (1919)—represented a different, more philosophically ambitious kind of analysis. The task of deriving the axioms of Peano arithmetic from what Russell took to be axioms of pure logic required defining the arithmetical primitives *zero*, *successor*, and *natural number* in purely logical terms. Russell's approach (which he shared with Frege) was both elegant and natural. Let zero be the set whose only member is the empty set; let the successor of a set x (of sets) be a set y (of sets) with the following property: For each member of y the result of removing a member leaves one with a member of x. It follows that the successor of zero (i.e., the number one) is the set of all single-membered sets, the successor of one (i.e. the number two) is the set of all pairs, and so on. Note how natural this is. What is the number two? It is that which all pairs have in common; more precisely, it is the set of which they, and only they, are members. Finally the set of natural numbers is defined as the smallest set containing zero and closed under the operation of successor.

With these definitions, together with Russell's proposed logical axioms (formulated within his theory of logical types, so as to avoid paradox), the axioms of Peano arithmetic can be derived as theorems. As a result, arithmetical sentences can be viewed as convenient abbreviations of the complex formulas associated with them by the Russellian definitions. Since the sentences of higher mathematics can themselves be viewed as abbreviations of complex arithmetical sentences, it seemed to many that Russell's reduction had succeeded in showing that all of mathematics can be regarded as an elaboration of pure logic and that all problems in the philosophy of mathematics could, in principle, be solved by a correct philosophical account of logic. Thus the reduction, in addition to being recognized as a substantial technical achievement, was viewed by many as a stunning demonstration of the extraordinary philosophical power of Russell's version of logico-linguistic analysis. No matter that his system of logic and theory of types was, in point of fact, epistemologically less secure than arithmetic itself; the program of attacking philosophical problems by associating the sentences that express them with hidden logical forms was considered to have taken a huge step forward.

Russell pushed the program further in *Our Knowledge of the External World* (1914), in which he applied his method of analysis to Moore's problem of the external world. The problem that perplexed Moore was that, although we know that there are material objects and although our evidence is perceptual, there seems to be a gap between this evidence and that which we know on the basis of it. Whereas material objects are public and independent of us, Moore had come to think of the data provided to us by our sensory impressions as logically private and dependent for their existence on the perceiver.

Russell set out to bridge this gap. His solution was to analyze material-object talk as talk about a system of interrelated private perspectives—a forerunner of the idea that material objects are logical constructions out of sense data. According to this view sentences that appear to be about material objects are really about the sense data of perceivers, and each material-object sentence is analyzable into a conjunction of categorical and hypothetical sentences about sense data. Apart from the obvious, Berkeleyan problems inherent in this view, its portents of the future of philosophical analysis were omi-

nous. Prior to this Russell's main examples of analysis—his theory of descriptions and logicist reduction—were precisely formulated and well worked out. By contrast the supposed analysis of material object statements was highly programmatic—neither Russell nor anyone else ever attempted to provide a fully explicit and complete analysis of any material-object statement. It was supposed to be enough to sketch the outlines that presumed analyses were supposed to take.

This programmatic approach also characterized Russell's position in his 1918 lectures "The Philosophy of Logical Atomism," in which he sketched the outlines of an ambitious philosophical system that posited a thoroughgoing parallelism between language and the world. The idea was to use the techniques of logical and linguistic analysis to reveal the ultimate structure of reality. Before, Russell had offered analyses piecemeal—to provide solutions to different philosophical problems as they came up. Now he sought to develop a systematic framework in which philosophy would, for all intents and purposes, be identified with logico-linguistic analysis. However it was his former student, Ludwig Wittgenstein, who pushed this idea the furthest.

EARLY WITTGENSTEIN

The *Tractatus* (1922) is an intricate, ingenious, and highly idiosyncratic philosophical system of the general sort Russell had imagined. In it Wittgenstein presents his conception of a logically perfect language, which, he believes, underlies all language and, presumably, all thought. Crucial to the construction of a theory of meaning for this language is the account of its relation to the world, which we are told in the opening two sentences is the totality of facts rather than things. The simplest—atomic—sentences of language correspond (when true) to simple—atomic—facts. The constituents of these facts are metaphysically simple objects and universals named by linguistically simple expressions—logically proper names and predicates. All meaningful sentences are said to be truth functions of atomic sentences, each of which is logically independent of all other atomic sentences. Since atomic facts are similarly independent, all and only the possible assignments of truth values to atomic sentences determine possible worlds, which are possible constellations of atomic facts. The actual world is the combination all existing atomic facts.

For Wittgenstein what a sentence says is identified with the information it provides about the location of the actual world within the logical space of possible worlds. If S is atomic then S represents the actual world as being one that contains the possible atomic fact the existence of which would make S true. If S is both meaningful and logically complex, then S is a truth function of a certain set A_s of atomic sentences, and S represents the actual world as containing a constellation of facts that corresponds to an assignment of truth values to A_s that would make S true. However, in the system of the *Tractatus*, P is a member of A_s only if there are situations in which the truth value of S is affected by which truth value is assigned to P—only if there are complete assignments of truth values to A_s which differ solely in what they assign to P that determine different truth values for S. Since, when S is a tautology, its truth does not depend on the truth values of any atomic sentence in this way, it follows that S isn't a truth function of any non-empty set of such sentences.

For Wittgenstein this means that tautologies don't provide any information about the world, and so, strictly speaking, don't say anything. In this sense tautologies are not fully meaningful, though we may regard them as meaningful in the degenerate sense of arising from meaningful atomic sentences by permitted applications of truth-functional operators. Thinking of them in this way we may take tautologies to be true, so long as we understand that they don't state or correspond to any facts. For Wittgenstein there are no necessary facts for necessary truths to correspond to. Rather their truth is an artifact of our linguistic system of representation. Because of this, he thought, they should be knowable apriori, simply by understanding them and recognizing their form.

Many philosophers found the strikingly simple Tractarian conception of necessity, apriority, and logical truth to be compelling. According to the *Tractatus* (i) all necessity is linguistic necessity, in the sense of being the result of our system of representing the world, rather than the world itself; (ii) all linguistic necessity is logical necessity, in that all necessary truths are tautologies; (iii) all tautologies are knowable apriori; and (iv) only necessary truths are apriori. In short the necessary, the apriori, and the logically true are one and the same. These truths make no claims about the world but instead constitute the domain of logic, broadly construed. All other truths are contingent and knowable only by empirical investigation. These truths do make claims about the world and constitute the domain of science.

There are no other meaningful sentences, save for the logically or contingently false. According to the *Tractatus*, all meaningful sentences are either tautologies, contradictions, or contingent, aposteriori statements which are truth functions of atomic sentences that describe possible combinations of the basic metaphysical simples that make up the world. Since virtually all of the traditional statements of ethics, philosophy, and religion seem to fall outside these categories, Wittgenstein concluded that these statements are nonsense. No aspect of his system was more fascinating to readers of the *Tractatus* than this consequence of his global criterion of intelligibility. Moreover his conclusion was not limited to language. If one assumes, as Wittgenstein clearly did, that all genuine thoughts are in principle expressible by meaningful sentences then his criterion not only fixes the limits of meaning but it also fixes the limits of thought. Since ethical, philosophical, and religious sentences are meaningless, they don't express propositions; since there are no such propositions for us to believe, we have no ethical, philosophical, or religious beliefs.

Where does this leave philosophy and philosophical analysis? The lesson of the *Tractatus* is that here are no meaningful philosophical claims and hence no genuine philosophical questions for philosophers to answer. What then is responsible for the persistence of the discipline and for the illusion that it is concerned with real problems for which solutions might be found? Linguistic confusion. As Wittgenstein saw it all the endless disputes in philosophy are due to this one source. If we could ever fully reveal the workings of language, our philosophical perplexities would vanish, and we would see the world correctly. Fortunately, philosophy can help. Although there are no new true propositions for philosophers to discover, they can clarify the propositions we already have. Like Russell, Wittgenstein believed that everyday language disguises thought by concealing true logical form. The proper aim of philosophy is to strip away the disguise and illuminate the form. In short, philosophy is a kind of linguistic analysis that doesn't solve problems but dissolves them. As he put it in his first post-*Tractatus* paper, "Some Remarks on Logical Form" (1929),

> The idea is to express in an appropriate symbolism what in ordinary language leads to endless misunderstandings. That is to say, where ordinary language disguises logical structure, where it allows the formation of pseudo-propositions, where it uses one term in an infinity of different meanings, we must replace it by a symbolism which gives a clear picture of the logical structure, excludes pseudo-propositions, and uses its terms unambiguously.

(P. 163)

Though the Wittgenstein of the *Tractatus* did not himself practice this form of analysis, the vision of analysis he articulated was one that later philosophers found attractive in its own right, quite apart from the doctrines that led him to it.

LOGICAL POSITIVISM

We now turn to something new—a self-conscious school of philosophy that arose through the collaborative efforts of several like-minded thinkers, including, most prominently, Rudolf Carnap, Moritz Schlick, Hans Reichenbach, A. J. Ayer, and Carl Hempel. The evolving creation of many minds, logical positivism was not monolithic; there was always plenty of disagreement on matters of detail, and even its central doctrines were never formulated in a way that commanded universal assent. The positivists did, however, share a common commitment to the development of certain themes inherited largely from Russell and Wittgenstein. From Russell they took the theory of descriptions as the paradigm of philosophical analysis (so characterized by F. P. Ramsey), the reduction of arithmetic to logic as the key to the nature of all mathematical truth (set out in Hempel's "On the Nature of Mathematical Truth," 1945), and the systematic, empiricist reconstruction of our knowledge of the external world—undertaken in Carnap's *The Logical Structure of the World* (1928). From Wittgenstein they took the idea of a test of intelligibility, the identification of necessary, apriori, and analytic truth, the bifurcation of all meaningful statements into the analytic versus empirical, the dismissal of whole domains of traditional philosophy as meaningless nonsense, and the goal of philosophy as the elimination of linguistic confusion by philosophical analysis.

The centerpiece of logical positivism was, of course, the empiricist criterion of meaning, which stated roughly that a non-analytic, non-contradictory sentence S is meaningful if and only if S is in principle verifiable or falsifiable—where verifiability and falsifiability are thought of as logical relations R_V and R_F between observation statements and S. Although the idea initially seemed simple, the devil proved to be in the details. One source of contention was the nature of observation statements. Initially Carnap, Schlick, and others construed them as reports of private sense data of observers. However the dangers of solipsism and phenomenalism soon forced a retreat to reports of (unaided) observation of everyday physical objects. Even then the theoretical / observational distinction proved elusive, with obvious strain on the clarity and plausibility of the criterion of meaning.

Defining the relations R_V and R_F that were to hold between meaningful (empirical) sentences and observa-

tion statements proved even more problematic. Initially it was hoped that the needed relations could be something quite strong—like the notion of being either conclusively verifiable (i.e., logically entailed by some finite, consistent set of observation statements) or conclusively falsifiable (i.e., something the negation of which is conclusively verifiable). However it soon became clear that when R_V and R_F are defined in this way, many obviously meaningful statements of science and everyday life are wrongly characterized as meaningless. This led to the attempt, illustrated by Ayer's proposal in the Introduction to the second edition of *Language, Truth and Logic* (1946), to define empirical meaningfulness in terms of a weak notion of verifiability—roughly that of being a statement which, when combined with an independently meaningful theory T, logically entailed one or more observation statements not entailed by T alone. However, as Alonzo Church demonstrated in his 1949 review of Ayer, this criterion was far too promiscuous, classifying no end of nonsense as meaningful.

There were of course other attempts to secure a workable empiricist theory of meaning, such as Carnap's criterion of translatability into an empiricist language, sketched in his 1936 essay "Testability and Meaning." But as Hempel showed in "Problems and Changes in the Empiricist Criterion of Meaning" (1950) this formulation runs into serious problems over theoretical terms in science. In Hempel's view the source of these problems is that sentences about theoretical entities are meaningful by virtue of being embedded in a network of hypotheses and observational statements, which as a whole makes testable predictions. As W. V. Quine emphasized even more forcefully in "Two Dogmas of Empiricism" (1951) these predictions are the product of all the different aspects of the system working together—in the sense that, given a set of observational predictions made by a theoretical system, one cannot in general match each prediction with a single discreet hypothesis, or small set of hypotheses.

Quine suggests that this is the crucial fact that makes it impossible to devise an adequate criterion of empirical meaningfulness for individual sentences. If for each sentence S we could isolate a set P of predictions made by S alone, and if P exhausted the contribution made by S to the predictions made by the theory as a whole then one could define S in terms of P. However the interdependence of S with other sentences in the system makes this impossible. Thus, Quine maintained, what we have to look for is not the empirical content of each statement taken in isolation, but rather its role in an articulated system that, as a whole, has empirical content. This point effectively marked the end of the positivists' version of verificationism.

QUINE

From the *Tractatus* through logical positivism and beyond, many analytic philosophers identified the apriori with the necessary and attempted to explain both by appealing to the analytic. As they saw it there simply is no explaining what necessity is, how we can know any truth to be necessary, or how we can know anything apriori, without appealing to statements that are, and are known to be, true by virtue of meaning. From this point of view necessary and apriori truths had better be analytic, since if they aren't one can give no intelligible account of them at all. Ironically this theoretical weight placed on analyticity left the doctrines about necessity, apriority, and analyticity advocated by positivists and others vulnerable to a potentially devastating criticism. If it could be shown that analyticity cannot play the explanatory role assigned to it, then their commitment to necessity, apriority, and perhaps even analyticity itself might be threatened. This was precisely Quine's strategy.

He launched his attack in "Truth by Convention" (1936), the target of which is the linguistic conception of the apriori. According to this view all apriori knowledge is knowledge of analytic truths, which in turn is explained as arising from knowledge of the linguistic conventions governing our words. This view was attractive because it provided a seemingly innocuous answer to the question of how any statement could be known without empirical confirmation: A statement can be known in this way only if it is devoid of factual content—that is, only if its truth is entirely due to its meaning. Surely, it was thought, there is no mystery in our knowing what we have decided our words are to mean. But then, it was concluded, there must be no mystery in the idea that the truth of a sentence may follow, and be known to follow, entirely from such decisions. Putting these two ideas together, proponents of the linguistic conception of the apriori thought that they had found a philosophical explanation of something that otherwise would have been problematic.

Quine argued that this is not so. As noted, the proposed explanation rests on two bits of knowledge taken to be unproblematic—(i) knowledge of what our words mean, and (ii) knowledge that the truth of certain sentences follows from our decisions about meaning. However there is a problem here, located in the words *follows from*. Clearly we don't stipulate the meanings of all the necessary / apriori / analytic truths individually. Rather, it

must be thought, we make some relatively small number of meaning stipulations and then draw out the consequences of these stipulations for the truth of an indefinitely large class of sentences. What is meant here by *consequences*? Not wild guesses or arbitrary inferences with no necessary connection to their premises. No, by *consequences* proponents of the linguistic apriori meant something like *logical consequences, knowable apriori to be true if their premises are true*. But now we have gone in a circle. According to these philosophers, all apriori knowledge of necessary truths—including apriori knowledge of logical truths—arises from our knowledge of the linguistic conventions we have adopted to give meanings to our words. However, in order to derive this apriori knowledge from our linguistic knowledge, one has to appeal to antecedent knowledge of logic itself. Either this logical knowledge is apriori or it isn't. If it is then some apriori knowledge is not explained linguistically; if it isn't then it is hard to see how any knowledge could qualify as apriori. Since neither alternative was acceptable to proponents of the linguistic apriori, Quine's attack was a telling one.

Fifteen years later, in "Two Dogmas of Empiricism" (1951), he renewed it. He agreed with the positivists' premise that there is no explaining necessity and apriority without appealing to analyticity. However he challenged the idea that any genuine distinction can be drawn between the analytic and the synthetic without presupposing the very notions they are supposed to explain—a point he sought to drive home by demonstrating the circularity of the most obvious attempts to define analyticity. Hence, he concluded, there is no way of explaining and legitimating necessity and apriority—or analyticity either. For him this meant that there is no genuine distinction to be drawn between the analytic and the synthetic, the necessary and the contingent, or the apriori and the aposteriori. The idea that any such distinctions exist was one of the two dogmas targeted in his article.

In assessing this argument it is important to remember that it was directed at a specific conception of analyticity, which was taken to be the source of necessity and apriority. Although this conception was widely held at the time Quine wrote, it is radically at variance with the post-Kripkean perspective according to which necessity and apriority are, respectively, metaphysical and epistemological notions that are non-coextensive and capable of standing on their own. From this perspective the attempt to explain necessity and apriority in terms of analyticity appears to be badly mistaken. Since Quine's circularity argument shares the problematic presupposition that all these notions are acceptable only if such an explanation can be given, it doesn't come off much better. For this reason Quine should not be seen as giving a general argument against analyticity. At most his argument succeeds in undermining one particular conception that enjoyed a long run among analytic philosophers in the middle fifty years of the twentieth century.

The second dogma attacked by Quine is *radical reductionism*, the view that every meaningful sentence is translatable into sentences about sense experience. Quine points out that the two dogmas—(i) that there is a genuine analytic / synthetic distinction, and (ii) radical reductionism—are linked in empiricist thinking by verificationism. Roughly speaking, verificationism holds that two sentences have the same meaning if and only if they would be confirmed or disconfirmed by the same experiences. Given this notion of synonymy, one could define analyticity as synonymy with a logical truth. Thus if verificationism were correct then the analytic / synthetic distinction would be safe. Similarly if verificationism, or at any rate a particularly simple version of verificationism, were correct then any empirical sentence would be translatable into the set of observation sentences that would confirm it, and radical reductionism would be saved. For these reasons, Quine concludes, if simple verificationism were correct then the two dogmas of empiricism would be corollaries of it.

By the time Quine wrote "Two Dogmas," verificationism, as a theory of meaning for individual sentences, was already dead, as was radical reductionism. Nevertheless he noted that some philosophers still maintained a modified version of the latter according to which each (synthetic) statement is, by virtue of its meaning, associated with a unique set of possible observations that would confirm it and another that would disconfirm it. Against this Quine argued that verification is holistic, by which he meant that most sentences don't have predictive content in isolation but are empirically significant only insofar as they contribute to the predictive power of larger empirical theories. Since he continued to assume, with the positivists, that meaning is verification, his position was one of holistic verificationism. According to this view the meaning of a theory is, roughly, the class of possible observations that would support it, and two theories have the same meaning if and only if they would be supported by the same possible observations. Since individual sentences don't have meanings on their own, any sentence can be held true in the face of any experience (by making necessary adjustments elsewhere in one's overall theory), and no sentence is immune from revision—since given a theory T incorporating S, Quine thought that one

could construct a different, but predictively equivalent, and hence synonymous, theory T incorporating the negation of S.

The resulting picture of philosophy and philosophical analysis that emerges from Quine's work is radically at variance with any we have seen. He rejects the doctrine that philosophical problems arise from confusion about the meanings of words or sentences, and with it the conception of philosophy as providing analyses of their meaning. He rejects these views because he rejects their presuppositions—that words and sentences have meanings in isolation and that we can separate out facts about meanings or linguistic conventions from the totality of all empirical facts. For Quine philosophy is continuous with science. It has no special subject matter of its own, and it is not concerned with the meanings of words in any special sense. Philosophical problems are simply problems of a more abstract and foundational sort than the ordinary problems of everyday science.

In later years Quine put less emphasis on holistic verificationism (which is itself beset with problems akin to earlier versions of verificationism), but he did not back away from his skepticism about our ordinary, pre-theoretic conception of meaning. Instead he deepened and extended his attack with his doctrine of the indeterminacy of translation in *Word and Object* (1960) and its corollary, the inscrutability of reference, in "Ontological Relativity" (1969). Since Quine, the naturalist, could find no place in nature for meaning and reference as ordinarily conceived, he repudiated both in favor of radically deflated, behaviorist substitutes. Thus it should not be surprising that there is no place in his brave new world for philosophical analysis as a distinctive intellectual activity. Nevertheless his actual philosophical practice is hard to discern from that of his analytic predecessors. Like them he does little, when arguing for his central doctrines, to delineate their alleged contributions to the observational predictions made by our overall theory of the world.

LATER WITTGENSTEIN

In *The Philosophical Investigations* (1953) Wittgenstein outlines a new, essentially social conception of meaning that contrasts sharply with the one presented in the *Tractatus*. In the earlier work language was viewed on the model of a logical calculus in which conceptual structure is identical with logical structure, and all meaningful sentences are truth-functions of atomic sentences that represent metaphysically simple objects standing in relations isomorphic to those in which logically proper names stand in the sentences themselves. In the *Investigations* the picture is quite different. Language is no longer seen as a calculus, derivability by formal logical techniques is accorded no special role in explaining conceptual connections among sentences, and naming is not taken to be the basis of meaning. Instead, meaning arises from socially conditioned agreement about the use of expressions to coordinate the activities and further the purposes of their users. For the later Wittgenstein, to know the meaning of an expression is not to know what it names or how to define it but to know how to use it in interacting with others.

According to this conception of meaning, understanding a word is not a psychological state but rather a disposition to apply it in the correct way over a wide range of cases; where by *the correct way* we do not mean the way determined by a rule the speaker has internalized. The problem, as Wittgenstein sees it, with appealing to such rules to explain our understanding of words is that rules are themselves made up of symbols that must be understood if they are to be of any use. Obviously this sort of explanation can't go on forever. In the end we are left with a large class of words or symbols that we understand and are able to apply correctly, despite the fact that what guides us and makes our applications correct are not further rules of any sort. When we reach rock bottom we are not guided by rules at all; we simply apply expressions unthinkingly to new cases.

What determines whether these new applications are correct? The mere fact that I am inclined to call something F can't guarantee that I am right. If my use of F is to be meaningful, there must be some independent standard that my application is required to live up to in order to be correct. Wittgenstein thinks this standard can't come from me alone. The reason it can't is that the same argument that shows that the standard of correctness cannot be determined by an internalized rule can be repeated to establish that it can't be determined by any belief, intention, or other contended mental state of mine. The problem, Wittgenstein thinks, is that in order to perform such a role, any such mental state must itself have gotten its content from somewhere. A regress argument can then be used to conclude that the contents of all my words and all my mental states must, in the end, rest on something other than my mental states. Thus, he suggests, the standard of correctness governing my use of F cannot rest on anything internal to me, but must somehow come from the outside. What more natural place to look for this than in the linguistic community of which I am a part? Hence, he suggests, for me to use F correctly is for me to apply it in conformity with the way it is applied by others. For Wittgenstein this, in turn, implies that F must be associated with public criteria by which someone else can, in principle, judge whether my use of it is correct. Language is essentially public; there can be no logically private language.

This conception of language leads Wittgenstein to a new conception of philosophy and philosophical analysis. He continues to believe that philosophical problems are linguistic, and that philosophical analysis is the analysis of language—but this analysis is no longer seen as a species of logical analysis. According to the new conception there is no such thing as the logical form of a sentence, and one should not imagine that sentences have unique analyses. According to Wittgenstein we do not give an analysis of a sentence because there is anything wrong with it that demands clarification. We give an analysis when something about it leads us into philosophical confusion. The same sentence might even receive different analyses, if people become confused about it in different ways. In such a case each analysis may clear up a particular confusion, even if no analysis clears them all up.

Accompanying this deflationary view of analysis is a highly deflationary conception of philosophy. According to the *Investigations* the philosophical analysis of language does not aim at, and cannot issue in, theories of any kind. Philosophy, as Wittgenstein says in section 109, "is a battle against the bewitchment of our intelligence by means of language." According to this view the task of philosophy is essentially therapeutic. It is the untangling of linguistic confusions, achieved by examining our words as they are ordinarily used, and contrasting that use with how they are misused in philosophical theories and explanations.

This deflationary conception arises naturally from Wittgenstein's new ideas about meaning, plus certain unquestioned philosophical presuppositions that he brings to the enterprise. These include his long-held convictions (i) that philosophical theses are not empirical, and hence must be necessary and apriori, and (ii) that the necessary, the apriori, and the analytic are one and the same. Because he takes (i) and (ii) for granted, he takes it for granted that if there are any philosophical truths, they must be analytic. To this he adds his new conception of meaning—with its rejection of abstract logical forms, its deflationary view of rule-following and algorithmic calculation, and its emphasis on social conditioning as generating agreement in our instinctive applications of words. Having jettisoned his old conception of meaning as something hidden and replaced it with a conception of meaning that sees it as arising from an unquestioning, socially-conditioned agreement, he has little room in his conceptual universe for surprising philosophical truths. Genuinely philosophical truths, if there are any, can only be necessary and apriori, which in turn are taken to be true in virtue of meaning.

But how are the analytic truths of interest to a philosopher to be established if they are not to be translated into the formulas of a logical calculus and demonstrated by being given rigorous but sometimes also innovative and insightful logical proofs? For the Wittgenstein of the *Investigations*, the answer is that they don't need to be established, since they are already implicitly recognized by competent language users. To be sure they may sometimes need to be brought into focus by assembling examples of ordinary use that illustrate the constitutive role they play in our language; but there is little room here for surprising philosophical discoveries. Such is the official view of the *Investigations*.

As with the *Tractatus*, there is an evident problem here. Wittgenstein's official view of philosophy is at variance with his own philosophical practice. His general theses about language and philosophy (to say nothing of his surprising and, arguably, revisionist views about sensation and other psychological language arising from the private language argument) are by no means obvious or already agreed upon; nor are they the sorts of things that one can just see to be true, once they are pointed out. On the contrary they require substantial explanation and argument, if they are to be accepted at all. As was so often the case throughout the twentieth century, the practice of philosophical analysis—understood as whatever it is that analytic philosophers do—eluded the official doctrines about analysis propounded by its leading practitioners.

THE ORDINARY LANGUAGE SCHOOL

This school, which received great impetus from the *Investigations*, was shaped by two leading ideas. The first was that since philosophical problems are due solely to the misuse of language, the job of the philosopher is not to construct elaborate theories to solve philosophical problems but to expose linguistic confusions that fooled us into thinking there were genuine problems to be solved in the first place. The second idea was that meaning itself—the key to progress in philosophy—is not to be studied from an abstract scientific or theoretical perspective. Rather philosophers were supposed to assemble observations about the ordinary use of words, and to show how misuse of certain words leads to philosophical perplexity. In retrospect this combination of views seems quite

remarkable: All of philosophy depends on a proper understanding of something that there is no systematic way of studying. Fortunately this anti-theoretical approach changed over time with much of the progress in the period being marked by significant retreats from it—including Austin's theory of performatives in *How to Do Things with Words* and Paul Grice's theory of conversational implicature in "Logic and Conversation" (both originally delivered as the William James Lectures at Harvard, in 1955 and 1967, respectively).

A good example of the standard, anti-theoretical approach is Ryle's *Dilemmas* (1953), in which he identifies the main aim of philosophy as that of resolving dilemmas. For Ryle a dilemma arises when obvious theories or platitudes appear to conflict with one another. In such cases a view that is unobjectionable in its own domain comes to seem incompatible with another view that is correct when confined to a different domain. When this happens we find ourselves in the uncomfortable position of seeming to be unable jointly to maintain a pair of views, each of which appears correct on its own. Ryle believes that in most cases the apparent conflict is an illusion to be dispelled by philosophical analysis. However, the needed analysis is not a matter of defining key concepts or uncovering hidden logical forms. Although analysis is conceptual what is wanted is never a sequence of definitions that could in principle be presented one by one. Instead Ryle compares the required analysis to the description of the position of wicket keeper in cricket. Just as one can't describe that position without describing how it fits in with all the other positions in cricket, so, Ryle thinks, one cannot usefully analyze a concept without tracing its intricate connections with all the members of the family of concepts of which it is a part.

His most important application of this method is to psychological language, in *The Concept of Mind* (1949). There he rejects what he calls the myth of "the Ghost in the Machine," according to which belief and desire are causally efficacious, mental states of which agents are non-inferentially aware. Ryle takes this view to be "entirely false" and to be the result of what he calls "a category-mistake," by which he means that it represents mental facts as belonging to one conceptual type, when they really belong to another. He illustrates this with the analogy of someone who visits different buildings and departments of a university and then asks "But where is the university?" Here the category mistake is that of taking the university to be a separate building or department alongside the others the visitor has seen, rather than being the way in which all the different buildings and departments are coordinated.

Similarly, Ryle maintains, someone who believes that the mind is something over and above the body fails to realize that the mind is not a separate thing, and that talk of the mental is really just talk about how an agent's actions are coordinated. According to this view, to attribute beliefs and desires to an agent is not to describe the internal causes of the agent's action but simply to describe the agent as one who would act in certain ways if certain conditions were fulfilled. This is rather surprising. According to Ryle's ordinary-language ideology, philosophy is not supposed to give us new theories but to untangle linguistic confusions—leaving us, presumably, with a less muddled version of what we pretheoretically thought. Here, however, his aim was to undermine a certain widely-held view of the mind and to provide what, arguably, amounts to a sweeping revision of our ordinary conception of the mental.

J. L. Austin was similarly ambitious. In his elegant classic *Sense and Sensibilia*, published in 1962 but delivered as lectures several times between 1947 and 1959, he attempted to dissolve, as linguistically confused, phenomenalism, skepticism about knowledge of the external world and the traditional sense-data analysis of perception. His goal was to show these positions to be incoherent by undermining the presupposition that our knowledge of the world always rests on conceptually prior evidence of how things perceptually appear. For this he employed two main strategies. One was to try to show that certain statements—such as, "there is a pig in front of me" in normal circumstances, with the animal in plain sight—are statements about which the claim that knowledge of them requires evidence of how things appear cannot be true. Austin drew this conclusion from the observation that it would be an abuse of language for the speaker in such a situation to say, "It appears that there is a pig in front of me," or "I have evidence that there is a pig in front of me." His other strategy was to argue that appearance statements themselves are parasitic on ordinary non-appearance statements and so cannot be regarded as conceptually prior to the latter.

Neither strategy was successful. The first was rebutted by Ayer in "Has Austin Refuted the Sense Datum Theory" (1967), in which he pointed out that the abuse that Austin spotted was, in effect, a matter of Gricean conversational implicature (*Don't make your conversational contribution too weak!*) from which no conclusion about the possibility of knowledge without evidence can be drawn. The general lesson here is that not all matters of language use (or misuse) are matters of meaning (or truth). Austin's second strategy, though not similarly rebutted, was not developed in enough detail to be compelling. In addition it faced the general difficulty (common to many ordinary-language attempts to undermine skepticism) of appealing to non-skeptical claims about meaning to refute the skeptic. Even if the view of meaning is correct, it may have little argumentative force against a determined skeptic.

By contrast the theory of performative utterances given in *How to Do Things with Words* (1962) has become an enduring fixture of the study of language. The idea, in its simplest form, is that utterances of sentences like "I promise to come" or "I name this ship The Ferdinand" are, in proper circumstances, not reports of actions but performances of them. Although there have been many disputes about how to develop this idea, there is no question that there is something to it. Austin himself was inclined to think that performative utterances of this sort were attempts, not to state facts, but to perform certain conventionally recognized speech acts.

For a time this idea generated considerable optimism about performative analyses of important philosophical concepts of the sort illustrated by Peter Strawson's 1949 paper, "Truth"—according to which ⌜It is true that S⌝ is analyzed as ⌜I concede / confirm / endorse that S⌝—and R. M. Hare's *The Language of Morals* (1952)—according to which ⌜That is a good N⌝ is assimilated to ⌜I commend that as an N⌝. However, these views, along with other ambitious attempts to use performative analyses to sweep away age-old philosophical problems, ran into serious difficulties. Chief among them was the point—made by Peter Geach in "Ascriptivism" (1960) and John Searle in "Meaning and Speech Acts" (1962)—that any analysis of the meaning of S must explain the contribution S makes to complex sentences of which it is a constituent. Since analyses that focus exclusively on the speech acts performed by utterances of S on its own don't—and often can't—do this, they cannot be taken to be correct accounts of meaning. This reinforced a message noted earlier; not all aspects of language use are aspects of meaning. As this point sunk in, the need for systematic theories to sort things out became clear, and the ordinary language era drew to a close.

LATER DEVELOPMENTS

Many philosophers found what they were looking for in Donald Davidson's attempt to construct, in the 1960s and 1970s, a theory of meaning for natural language modeled on Alfred Tarski's formal definition of truth for logic and mathematics. According to Davidson it is possible to construct finitely axiomatizable theories of truth for natural languages L that allow one to derive—from axioms specifying the referential properties of its words and phrases—a T-sentence, ⌜'S' is a true sentence of L if and only if p⌝, for each sentence S of L, which gives its truth conditions. Since such a theory gives the truth conditions of every sentence on the basis of its semantically significant structure, it is taken to count as a theory of meaning for L. The theory is empirically tested by comparing the situations in which speakers hold particular sentences to be true with the truth conditions it assigns to those sentences. According to Davidson's view the correct theory of meaning is, roughly, the theory T_M according to which the conditions in which speakers actually hold sentences to be true most closely matches the conditions in which T_M, plus our theory of the world, predicts the sentences to be true. Roughly put Davidson takes the correct theory to be the one according to which speakers of L turn out to be truth tellers more frequently than on any other interpretation of L.

This bold idea generated a large volume of critical comment, both pro and con, over the next two decades. One important cluster of problems centers around the fact that the T-sentences generated by Davidsonian theories are material biconditionals and so provide truth conditions of object-language sentences only in the very weak sense of pairing each such sentence with some metalanguage sentence or other that has the same truth value.

One popular way of countering this difficulty is to strengthen the theory of meaning by putting it in the form of a theory of truth relative to a context of utterance and a possible world-state. This approach, widely known as *possible worlds semantics*, was pioneered from the 1940s through the 1970s by Carnap, Saul Kripke, Richard Montague, David Lewis, and David Kaplan, among others. As commonly pursued it involves enriching the formal languages amenable to Tarski's techniques, so that they incorporate more and more of the concepts found in natural language—including modal concepts expressed by words like *actual*, *necessary*, *possible*, *could*, and *would*, temporal concepts expressed by natural-language tenses, and indexical expressions like *I*, *we*, *you*, *he*, *now*, and *today*. By the end of the century it had become possible to imagine the day in which natural languages would be treatable in something close to their entirety by the descendants of the logical techniques initiated by Tarski. Analyses of central philosophical concepts, formulated in terms of possible world-states, had also become commonplace, as illustrated by the highly influential treatment of counterfactual conditionals given by Robert Stalnaker and David Lewis as well as Lewis's related analysis of causation.

However the most important philosophical development in the last half of the century occurred in Princeton in January of 1970 when Saul Kripke, then twenty-nine years old, delivered the three lectures that became *Naming and Necessity*. Their impact was profound, immediate, and lasting. In the philosophy of language Kripke's work ranks with that of Frege in the late nineteenth century, and of Russell and Tarski in the first half of the twentieth. Beyond the philosophy of language, it fundamentally changed the way in which much philosophy is done. The most important aspects of the work are (i) a set of theses about the meaning and reference of proper names according to which neither their meanings nor reference-determining conditions are determined by descriptions associated with them by speakers; (ii) a corresponding set of theses about the meaning and reference of natural kind terms such as *heat*, *light*, *water*, and *tiger*; (iii) a compelling defense of the metaphysical concepts of necessity and possibility; (iv) a sharp distinction between necessity and apriority; (v) forceful arguments that some necessary truths are knowable only aposteriori and some apriori truths are contingent; and (vi) a persuasive defense of the view that objects have some of their properties essentially and others accidentally. In addition to these explicit aspects of the work, Kripke's discussion had far-reaching implications for what has come to be known as externalism about meaning and belief—roughly the view that the meanings of one's words, as well as the contents of one's beliefs, are partly constituted by facts outside oneself. Finally *Naming and Necessity* played a large role in the implicit but widespread rejection of the view—so popular among earlier analytic philosophers—that philosophy is nothing more than the analysis of language.

See also Analytic and Synthetic Statements; Analytic Feminism; Austin, John Langshaw; Ayer, Alfred Jules; Carnap, Rudolf; Common Sense; Davidson, Donald; Frege, Gottlob; Grice, Herbert Paul; Hare, Richard M.; Hempel, Carl Gustav; Idealism; Kaplan, David; Kripke, Saul; Lewis, David; Logical Positivism; Materialism; Montague, Richard; Moore, George Edward; Philosophy of Language; Presupposition; Quine, Willard Van Orman; Ramsey, Frank Plumpton; Reichenbach, Hans; Russell, Bertrand Arthur William; Ryle, Gilbert; Schlick, Moritz; Searle, John; Strawson, Peter Frederick; Tarski, Alfred; Whitehead, Alfred North; Wittgenstein, Ludwig Josef Johann.

Bibliography

Austin, John Langshaw. *How to Do Things with Words*. New York: Oxford University Press, 1962.

Austin, John Langshaw. *Sense and Sensibilia*. London: Oxford University Press, 1962.

Ayer, Alfred Jules. "Has Austin Refuted the Sense-Datum Theory?" *Synthese* 17(1967): 117–140.

Ayer, Alfred Jules. *Language, Truth and Logic*. New York: Dover, 1952.

Carnap, Rudolf. *The Logical Structure of the World* (1928). Berkeley: University of California Press, 1969.

Carnap, Rudolf. *Meaning and Necessity*. Chicago: University of Chicago, 1947.

Carnap, Rudolf. "Testability and Meaning." *Philosophy of Science* 3 (1936): 419–71, and 4 (1937): 1–40.

Church, Alonzo. *Review of Language, Truth and Logic*. 2nd ed. *Journal of Symbolic Logic* 14 (1949): 52–53.

Davidson, Donald. "Truth and Meaning." *Synthese* 17 (1967): 304–323.

Davidson, Donald. "Radical Interpretation." *Dialectica* 27 (1973): 313–328. Reprinted in *Inquiries into Truth and Interpretation*. Oxford: Clarendon, 2001.

Davies, Martin. *Meaning, Quantification, and Necessity*. London: Routledge & Kegan Paul, 1981.

Dummett, Michael. "What Is a Theory of Meaning?" In *Mind and Language*, edited by Samuel Guttenplan. Oxford: Clarendon Press, 1975.

Dummett, Michael. "What Is a Theory of Meaning? (II)." In *Truth and Meaning*, edited by Gareth Evans and John McDowell. Oxford: Clarendon Press, 1976.

Foster, John A. "Meaning and Truth Theory." In *Truth and Meaning*, edited by Gareth Evans and John McDowell. Oxford: Clarendon Press, 1976.

Frege, Gottlob. *Begriffsschrift*. Halle, AS: Louis Nebert, 1879.

Geach, Peter. "Ascriptivism." *Philosophical Review* 69 (1960): 221–225.

Grice, Paul. "Logic and Conversation." In *Studies in the Way of Words*. Cambridge, MA: Harvard University Press, 1989.

Hare, Richard. *The Language of Morals*. Oxford: Clarendon Press, 1952.

Hempel, Carl. "On the Nature of Mathematical Truth." *American Mathematical Monthly* 52 (1945): 543–556. Reprinted in *The Philosophy of Mathematics*. 2nd ed., edited by Paul Benacerraf and Hilary Putnam. Cambridge, U.K.: Cambridge University Press, 1983.

Hempel, Carl. "Problems and Changes in the Empiricist Criterion of Meaning." *Revue Internationale de Philosophie* 4 (1950): 41–63. Reprinted in *Logical Positivism*, edited by Alfred Jules Ayer. New York: The Free Press, 1959.

Kaplan, David. "Demonstratives." In *Themes from Kaplan*, edited by Joseph Almog, John Perry, and Howard Wettstein. New York: Oxford University Press, 1989.

Kripke, Saul. "A Completeness Theorem in Modal Logic." *Journal of Symbolic Logic* 24 (1959): 1–14.

Kripke, Saul. *Naming and Necessity*. Cambridge, MA: Harvard University Press, 1980. Originally published in *Semantics of Natural Languages*, edited by Donald Davidson and Gilbert Harman. Dordrecht: Reidel, 1972.

Kripke, Saul. "Semantical Considerations on Modal Logic." *Acta Philosophica Fennica* 16 (1963): 83–94. Reprinted in *Reference and Modality*, edited by Leonard Linsky. London: Oxford University Press, 1971.

Lewis, David, "Causation." *Journal of Philosophy* 70 (1973): 556–567.

Lewis, David. *Counterfactuals*. Cambridge, MA: Harvard University Press, 1973.

Montague, Richard. *Formal Philosophy*. New Haven: Yale University Press, 1974.

Moore, George Edward. *Principia Ethica*. London: Cambridge University Press, 1903.

Moore, George Edward. "The Refutation of Idealism." *Mind* 12 (1903): 433–453.

Moore, George Edward. "A Defense of Common Sense." In *Contemporary British Philosophy* (Second Series), edited by John Henry Muirhead. New York: Macmillan, 1925. Reprinted in *Philosophical Papers*. New York: Collier 1962.

Moore, George Edward. "Proof of an External World." *Proceedings of the British Academy* XXV (1939): 273–300.

Quine, Willard Van Orman. "Ontological Relativity." In *Ontological Relativity and Other Essays*. New York: Columbia University Press, 1969.

Quine, Willard Van Orman. "Truth by Convention." *Philosophical Essays for A. N. Whitehead*, edited by O. H. Lee. New York: Longmans, 1936. Reprinted in *Ways of Paradox*. New York: Random House, 1966.

Quine, Willard Van Orman. "Two Dogmas of Empiricism." *Philosophical Review* 60 (1951): 20–43.

Quine, Willard Van Orman. *Word and Object*. Cambridge, MA: MIT Press, 1960.

Ramsey, Frank. *The Foundations of Mathematics*. London: Routledge and Kegan Paul, 1931.

Russell, Bertrand. *Introduction to Mathematical Philosophy*. New York: Macmillan, 1919. Reprinted New York: Dover, 1993.

Russell, Bertrand. "Knowledge by Acquaintance and Knowledge by Description." *Proceedings of the Aristotelian Society* 11 (1910–1911): 108–128.

Russell, Bertrand. "On Denoting." *Mind* 14 (1905): 479–493.

Russell, Bertrand. *Our Knowledge of the External World*. Chicago and London: Open Court, 1914. Reprinted London: Routledge, 1993.

Russell, Bertrand. "The Philosophy of Logical Atomism." *The Monist* 28 (1918): 495–527; and 29 (1919): 33–63, 190–222, 344–80; reprinted La Salle, IL: Open Court, 1985.

Russell, Bertrand, and Alfred North Whitehead. *Principia Mathematica*. Vol. 1. London: Cambridge University Press, 1910.

Russell, Bertrand, and Alfred North Whitehead. *Principia Mathematica*. Vol. 2. London: Cambridge University Press, 1912.

Ryle, Gilbert. *The Concept of Mind*. New York: Barnes and Noble, 1949.

Ryle, Gilbert. *Dilemmas*. Cambridge, U.K.: Cambridge University Press, 1953.

Searle, John. "Meaning and Speech Acts." *Philosophical Review* 71 (1962): 423–432.

Soames, Scott. *Philosophical Analysis in the Twentieth Century*, Vol. 1: *The Dawn of Analysis*. Princeton, NJ: Princeton University Press, 2003.

Soames, Scott. *Philosophical Analysis in the Twentieth Century*, Vol. 2: *The Age of Meaning*. Princeton, NJ: Princeton University Press, 2003.

Soames, Scott. "Semantics and Semantic Competence." *Philosophical Perspectives* 3 (1989): 575–596.

Soames, Scott. "Truth, Meaning, and Understanding." *Philosophical Studies* 65 (1992): 17–35.

Stalnaker, Robert. "A Theory of Conditionals." In *Studies in Logical Theory*, American Philosophical Quarterly Monograph Series 2. Oxford: Blackwell, 1968. Reprinted in *Ifs*, edited by William Harper, Robert Stalnaker, and Glenn Pearce. Dordrecht: Reidel, 1980.

Tarski, Alfred. "The Concept of Truth in Formalized Languages." In *Logic, Semantics, and Metamathematics*, edited by John Corcoran. Indianapolis: Hackett, 1983.

Wittgenstein, Ludwig. *Philosophical Investigations*. Translated by G. E. M. Anscombe. Oxford: Blackwell, 1953.

Wittgenstein, Ludwig. "Some Remarks on Logical Form." Proceedings of the *Aristotelian Society* supp. Vol. 9 (1929): 162–171.

Wittgenstein, Ludwig. *Tractatus Logico-Philosophicus*. Translated by C. K. Ogden. London: Routledge & Kegan Paul, 1922.

Scott Soames (2005)

ANALYTIC FEMINISM

Analytic feminism applies analytic concepts and methods to feminist issues and applies feminist concepts and insights to issues that traditionally have been of interest to analytic philosophers. Analytic feminists, like analytic philosophers more generally, value clarity and precision in argument and use logical and linguistic analysis to help them achieve that clarity and precision. Unlike nonfeminists, they write against a background of recognition of sexism (practices that take women and feminine things to be inferior to men and masculine things) and androcentrism (practices that take males or men or men's life experiences to be the norm or the ideal for human life), and work with the aim of contesting both.

Analytic feminism holds that the best way for scholars to counter sexism and androcentrism in their work is through forming a clear conception of and pursuing truth, logical consistency, objectivity, rationality, justice, and the good, while recognizing that these notions have often been perverted by androcentrism throughout the history of philosophy. Analytic feminists engage the literature traditionally thought of as analytic philosophy, but also draw on other traditions in philosophy, as well as work by feminists working in other disciplines, especially the social and biological sciences.

Analytic feminists assert the sex/gender distinction, a distinction between the biological concept of sex and the socially constructed concept of gender (non-isomorphic to sex), though they may disagree widely on how this distinction is to be drawn and what moral or political implications it has. Although they share the conviction that the social constructions of gender create a fundamentally unjust imbalance in contemporary social and political arrangements, there is no other political thesis generally held by them. Analytic feminists who are political philosophers defend political views that reflect progressive positions found in contemporary nonfeminist political philosophy, from liberalism (Okin 1989, Nussbaum 1999) to republicanism (Phillips 2000) to socialism (MacKinnon 1989, Ferguson 1991). They also draw on views of previous generations of feminist political philosophers from John Stuart Mill and Mary Wollstonecraft to Friederich Engels, Emma Goldman, Charlotte Perkins Gilman, and Simone de Beauvoir. Analytic feminists, like nonanalytic feminists, have written much about social and political issues like abortion, pornography, prostitution, rape, sexual harassment, surrogacy, and violence against women. What characterizes analytic feminism here is the use of logical and conceptual analysis and, sometimes, decision theoretic analysis (see article by Cudd in Antony and Witt 2001).

Analytic feminists often defend traditional analytic methods and concepts against criticism from nonanalytic feminists. Many nonanalytic feminists charge (in various ways) that the notions of reason, truth, objectivity, or the methods of logical and linguistic analysis are hopelessly masculinist, and cannot be reclaimed for feminist purposes. They criticize canonical male philosophers, including Aristotle, Descartes, Kant, Rousseau, Frege, Quine, and Rawls, as sexist or at least androcentric, and at times suggest that these philosophers have nothing useful to say to women. These charges challenge feminist philosophers who have been trained in the analytic tradition and who find that tradition valuable. To reject philosophers on those grounds, they argue, would indict similarly almost the entire history of philosophy. The question analytic feminists ask is whether those androcentric or sexist writings can be corrected and rescued by an enlightened critical reader. Annette Baier's work on Hume in "Hume, the Women's Moral Theorist?" and "Hume, the Reflective Women's Epistemologist?" (Baier 1994), Marcia Homiak's work on Aristotle in "Feminism and Aristotle's Rational Ideal" (Antony and Witt 2001), Barbara Herman's work on Kant in "Could It Be Worth Thinking about Kant on Sex and Marriage?" (Antony and Witt 2001), and Peg O'Connor's work on Wittgenstein in *Oppression and*

Responsibility: A Wittgensteinian Approach to Social Practices and Moral Theory (2002) exemplify such attempts.

An important insight of feminism has been to expose the androcentric bias toward seeing human individuals as essentially isolated, epistemically, socially, and morally, from others. One early result of this insight was the ethics of care (Held 1995), which challenges the dominant tradition of ethical theory with the idea that caring for others is a central ethical activity. Eva Kittay developed the "dependency critique" (Kittay 1999) of Rawls's theory of justice, arguing that the capacity for caring for dependent others is one of the central moral powers, just as basic as the capacities to form a sense of the good and a sense of justice. Analytic feminists have joined other feminist theorists in focusing much of their recent attentions to questions of the self. In the anthology *Relational Autonomy: Feminist Perspectives on Automony, Agency, and the Social Self* (2000), several articles examine the notion of relational autonomy, which takes seriously the idea that humans must define their identities in relation to others in ways which challenge their ability to be completely autonomous in the traditional sense. These articles attempt to define a new notion of autonomy that incorporates that insight. Another important book on the self (Brison 2002) connects traditional theories of personal identity with recent research on trauma, arguing that the trauma arising from sexual violence, for example, challenges those theories.

Analytic feminism holds that many traditional philosophical notions are not only normatively compelling, but also in some ways empowering and liberating for women. While postmodern feminism rejects the universality of truth, justice, and objectivity and the univocality of "women," analytic feminism defends these notions. They recognize that to reject a view because it is false or oppressive to women, one needs some rational, objective ground from which we can argue that it is in fact false or oppressive. An important task for analytic feminism involves investigating the objectivity of science. Helen Longino's *Science as Social Knowledge* (1990) was the first such analytic feminist work. Elizabeth Anderson's "Feminist Epistemology: An Interpretation and a Defense" (Anderson 1995) shows how a carefully aimed feminist critique can improve the objectivity of science by distinguishing and illustrating four ways that feminist critiques have corrected the distorted lenses of masculinist science: through the critique of gendered structures in the social organization of science, through the analysis of gendered symbols in scientific models, through exposing sexism in scientific practices and focuses, and through revealing androcentrism in its concepts and theories.

Louise Antony, in "Quine as Feminist: The Radical Import of Naturalized Epistemology" (Antony and Witt 2001) presented what she called the *bias paradox*: Feminists (and others) want to criticize certain claims as false because they are biased, and yet feminism is also clearly a bias; in effect, a particular slant on the world. She locates a solution in naturalized epistemology. First we must see that what we can know necessarily comes through our particular human cognitive apparatus, which *biases* the content of our claims. Thus, bias *per se* is not the problem, but some biases lead us away from the truth. Her more recent work has emphasized the importance of embodiment generally in epistemology (Antony 2002), and she credits feminism in large part for this insight. Other analytic feminists (Grasswick and Webb 2002) have extended the naturalized epistemology analysis to argue for a social feminist epistemology, which asserts that socially induced sexist and androcentric biases can affect the content and justification of knowledge. In its analysis of traditional philosophical topics like objectivity and personal identity and new topics such as sexism in language (Vetterling-Braggin 1981), analytic feminism reveals the blurriness of the distinction between metaphysics, epistemology, and social/political philosophy.

See also Feminist Epistemology; Feminist Ethics; Feminist Metaphysics; Feminist Philosophy; Feminist Philosophy of Science.

Bibliography

Anderson, Elizabeth. "Feminist Epistemology: An Interpretation and a Defense." *Hypatia* 10 (1995): 50–84.

Antony, Louise M. "Embodiment and Epistemology." In *The Oxford Handbook of Epistemology*, edited by Paul K. Moser. New York: Oxford University Press, 2002.

Antony, Louise M., and Charlotte Witt, eds. *A Mind of One's Own: Feminist Essays on Reason and Objectivity*. 2nd ed. Boulder, CO: Westview, 2001.

Baier, Annette C. *Moral Prejudices*. Cambridge, MA: Harvard University Press, 1994.

Brison, Susan. *Aftermath: Violence and the Remaking of a Self*. Princeton, NJ: Princeton University Press, 2002.

Cudd, Ann E., and Virginia Klenk, eds. *Hypatia* 10 (1995). This is a special issue of the feminist philosophy journal devoted to analytic feminism.

Ferguson, Ann. *Sexual Democracy: Women, Oppression, and Revolution*. Boulder, CO: Westview, 1991.

Grasswick, Heidi E., and Mark Owen Webb. "Feminist Epistemology as Social Epistemology." *Social Epistemology* 16 (2002): 185–196.

Haslanger, Sally. "Gender and Race: (What) Are They? (What) Do We Want Them to Be?" *Nous* 34 (2000): 31–55.

Held, Virginia, ed. *Justice and Care: Essential Readings in Feminist Ethics*. Boulder, CO: Westview, 1995.

Kittay, Eva Feder. *Love's Labor: Essays on Women, Equality, and Dependency*. New York: Routledge, 1999.

Longino, Helen. *Science as Social Knowledge*. Princeton, NJ: Princeton University Press, 1990.

Mackenzie, Catriona, and Natalie Stoljar, eds. *Relational Autonomy: Feminist Perspectives on Autonomy, Agency, and the Social Self*. New York: Oxford University Press, 2000.

MacKinnon, Catharine A. *Toward a Feminist Theory of the State*. Cambridge, MA: Harvard University Press, 1989.

Nelson, Lynn Hankinson. *Who Knows: From Quine to a Feminist Empiricism*. Philadelphia, PA: Temple University Press, 1990.

Nussbaum, Martha. *Sex and Social Justice*. New York: Oxford University Press, 1999.

O'Connor, Peg. *Oppression and Responsibility: A Wittgensteinian Approach to Social Practices and Moral Theory*. University Park: Pennsylvania State University Press, 2002.

Okin, Susan Moller. *Justice, Gender, and the Family*. Boston: Basic Books, 1989.

Phillips, Anne. "Feminism and Republicanism: Is This a Plausible Alliance?" *Journal of Political Philosophy* 8 (2000): 279–293.

Vetterling-Braggin, Mary, ed. *Sexist Language: A Modern Philosophical Analysis*. Lanham, MD: Rowman and Littlefield, 1981.

Ann E. Cudd (1996, 2005)

ANALYTIC AND SYNTHETIC STATEMENTS

The distinction between analytic and synthetic judgments was first made by Immanuel Kant in the introduction to his *Critique of Pure Reason*. According to him, all judgments could be exhaustively divided into these two kinds. The subject of both kinds of judgment was taken to be some thing or things, not concepts. Synthetic judgments are informative; they tell something about the subject by connecting or synthesizing two different concepts under which the subject is subsumed. Analytic judgments are uninformative; they serve merely to elucidate or analyze the concept under which the subject falls. There is a prima facie difficulty as to how a judgment can be simultaneously about an object, uninformative in relation to it, and explicative of the concepts involved, but this question will be examined later.

Kant associated this distinction with the distinction between a priori and a posteriori judgments. The one distinction was taken to cut across the other, except that there are no analytic a posteriori judgments. The remaining three classifications were, in Kant's opinion, filled; there are analytic a priori judgments, synthetic a posteriori judgments, and synthetic a priori judgments. Since Kant there has been little argument concerning the first two of these, but considerable argument and opposition, chiefly from empiricists, about the last. Analytic a priori and synthetic a posteriori judgments correspond roughly to logically and empirically true or false judgments. In distinguishing them, Kant was following in the steps of Gottfried Wilhelm Leibniz and David Hume, both of whom had made a similar distinction, although in different terms. Leibniz had distinguished between truths of fact, guaranteed by the principle of sufficient reason, and truths of reason, guaranteed by the principle of contradiction. The latter were such that their denial involved a contradiction; they could indeed be reduced to identical propositions via chains of definitions of their terms. Hume had likewise distinguished between matters of fact and relations of ideas. The former were merely contingent, while the latter were necessary and such that their denial involved a contradiction. Kant's innovation was to connect this distinction with the two further distinctions between the analytic and the synthetic and the a priori and the a posteriori.

It should be noted that Kant's distinction between the analytic and the synthetic was made in terms of judgments and concepts. This gave it a psychological flavor for which it has been criticized by many modern philosophers. The notion of judgment is ambiguous between the act of judging and what is judged. One problem is how to extend what Kant said so that it applies only to what is judged or to propositions. Furthermore, an implication of Kant's formal account of the distinction was that it is limited in its application to subject-predicate judgments (although it was also one of Kant's doctrines that existential judgments are always synthetic).

KANT'S CRITERIA AND USE OF THE ANALYTIC/SYNTHETIC DISTINCTION

CRITERIA. Apart from the general distinction, Kant offered two criteria for it. According to the first criterion, an analytic judgment is one in which the concept of the predicate is contained (although covertly) in the concept of the subject, while in a synthetic judgment the concept of the predicate stands outside the concept of the subject. According to the second criterion, analytic judgments are such that their denial involves a contradiction, while this is not true of synthetic judgments of any kind. Kant was here following his predecessors, although, with Leibniz, he did not suggest that analytic truths can be reduced to simple identities. This criterion can scarcely be said to suffice as a definition of an analytic statement, although it may provide grounds for saying whether a judgment is analytic or not. It will do the latter if it can be assumed that all analytic judgments are logically necessary, since reference to the principle of contradiction may provide the basis of logical necessity.

The first criterion seems on firmer ground in this respect, since it offers what seems to be a formal characteristic of all analytic judgments. It specifies what we must be doing in making an analytic judgment, in terms of the relations between the concepts involved. It has been objected that the idea of one concept being contained in another is also a psychological one, but this was certainly not Kant's intention. The point may perhaps be expressed in terms of meaning. When we make an analytic judgment, what we mean when we invoke the predicate concept is already included in what we mean by the subject concept. Just as the notion of a judgment is ambiguous, so a concept can mean either the act of conceiving or what is conceived, and it is the latter which is relevant here. By this criterion, therefore, a judgment is analytic when, in judging about something, what we judge about it is already included in what is meant by the term under which we subsume the subject. Kant assumed that all judgments of this kind are a priori, presumably on the grounds that their truth can be ascertained merely by considering the concepts involved, without further reference to the facts of experience.

CHARACTERISTICS OF ANALYTIC STATEMENTS. Kant's criterion could be applied only to statements of subject-predicate form, and could not, therefore, be used to make an exhaustive distinction between all statements. If Kant's distinction is to be of use, however, it must be extended to cover propositions or statements and, moreover, statements of any form, not just those of subject-predicate form. If an analytic judgment is of an object, an analytic statement must similarly be about the object or objects referred to by the subject expression. Analytic statements cannot, therefore, be equated with definitions, for the latter are surely about words, not things. It has sometimes been said (for instance, by A. J. Ayer in his *Language, Truth and Logic*) that analytic statements make clear our determination to use words in a certain way. Apart from the fact that the use of words cannot be a simple matter of choice, what Ayer says cannot be the main function of analytic statements, since this would be to identify them with (possibly prescriptive) definitions. If we learn something about the use of words from analytic statements, this must at most be indirect.

Analyticity, a property of statements. We have seen that Kant's point of view might be represented as saying that only the meaning of the terms involved, the nature of the corresponding concepts, makes the judgment true. It might, therefore, seem feasible that an analytic statement could be characterized as a statement about something which says nothing about the thing but is such that the meanings of the words involved make it true. To be more exact, it would be the meanings of the words involved in a sentence—*any* sentence that expresses the statement— that make that statement true. It is important to stress the words "any sentence," for analytic truth can be a feature only of *statements*. It cannot be a feature of sentences per se, nor can it be limited to sentences in a given language (as Rudolf Carnap in effect supposes). Truth is a property of statements, not sentences, and the same must be the case with analytic truth. No account of analyticity which explains it in terms of what is the case with regard to sentences in any one language will do. If someone who says "All bodies are extended" makes an analytic statement, so will anyone who says the same thing in any other language.

Analyticity as a function of the meanings of words. What is meant by saying that the meanings of the terms involved *make a statement true*? Are analytic truths those which follow from the meanings of the words involved; that is, from their definitions? This cannot be so, since all that can follow from a definition is another definition, and how, in any case, can a statement about things follow directly from one about words? If analyticity is connected with meaning, it must be more indirectly. Friedrich Waismann has suggested that an analytic truth is one which is so *in virtue of* the meanings of the words involved. But the words "in virtue of" are themselves vague. It has been held by certain empiricists that "All bodies are extended" is analytic if and only if we use "body" in exactly the same way we use "extended thing"; that is, if we attach the same meaning to each expression. Nevertheless, the truth of "All bodies are extended" does not follow simply from the fact that the expressions "body" and "extended thing" have the same meaning, for the substitution of expressions equivalent in meaning leaves one with a statement corresponding in form to the law of identity. Hence, the original statement will be true only if the law of identity holds. In other words, an analytic statement will be one whose truth depends not only on the meanings of the words involved but also on the laws of logic. This raises the question of the status of these laws themselves. It is sometimes claimed that they, too, are analytic; but this cannot be so if a definition of analyticity involves reference to the laws of logic.

Analyticity as a function of the laws of logic. The necessity of referring to the laws of logic in any account of analyticity has been noted in modern times by many philosophers. Waismann, for example, eventually defines an analytic statement as one which reduces to a logical truism when substitution of definitional equivalents is carried out. Gottlob Frege had much earlier defined an analytic truth as one in whose *proof* one finds only "general logical laws and definitions," and he had sought to show that arithmetical propositions are analytic in this sense. Both of these accounts make reference to logical truisms or logical laws. Whatever the status of these, it certainly seems that analytic statements must depend for their validity not only on the meanings of the terms involved but also on the validity of the laws of logic; and these laws cannot themselves be analytic.

OBJECTIONS TO THE DISTINCTION

THE PROBLEM OF SYNONYMY. Nevertheless, objections to the notion of analyticity have been made, particularly by Willard Quine, on the basis of supposed difficulties about meaning itself, and not merely on those about the status of the truths of logic—although here, too, Quine has found difficulties. He distinguishes between two classes of analytic statements. There are, first, those which are logically true, such as "No unmarried man is married"; these are statements which are true and which remain true under all reinterpretations of their components other than the logical particles. Second, there are those, such as "No bachelor is married," which can be turned into logical truths by substituting synonyms for synonyms. It is the second kind of analytic statement that raises problems here, and these problems arise from the notion of synonymy or, to be precise, cognitive synonymy; that is, synonymy that depends on words having the same meaning for thought, as opposed to merely applying to the same things. The notion of definition which other philosophers have invoked in this connection rests, Quine maintains, on that of synonymy. How is this to be explained?

Quine's difficulties here are associated with general difficulties about synonymy raised by himself and Nelson Goodman in the effort to embrace a nominalism that does not involve the postulation of so-called meanings, and to push as far as possible the thesis that language is extensional; that is, such that it can be built up from variables and an indefinite set of one and many-place predicates, so that complex sentences are related to atomic sentences by truth-functional relationships and by quantification. In such a language, sameness of meaning might

be equivalent to extensional equivalence, such that any two extensionally equivalent expressions are interchangeable *salva veritate*; that is, leaving unchanged the truth value of the statements in which they occur, wherever the expressions occur. The outcome of Goodman's argument in this connection is that since there may always be some occurrence in which the two expressions are not interchangeable *salva veritate,* no two expressions are identical in meaning. Quine himself recognizes something of this and has explored the restrictions which must be put upon the general thesis.

In the present connection, Quine explores the possibility that synonymity might be explained by interchangeability *salva veritate* except within words. But the interchangeability of, say, "bachelor" and "unmarried man" in this way may be due to accidental factors, as is the case with "creature with a heart" and "creature with kidneys." If it is the case that all—and only—creatures with a heart are creatures with kidneys, this is due simply to the fact that, as it happens, the two expressions always apply to the same things and not to any sameness of meaning. How do we know that the situation is not the same with "bachelor" and "unmarried man"? It is impossible to reply that it is because of the truth of "Necessarily, all—and only—bachelors are unmarried men," for the use of "necessarily" presupposes a nonextensional language. Furthermore, a sense has already been given to the kind of necessity involved here: analyticity. Hence, while cognitive synonymy might be explained in terms of analyticity, to try to explain analyticity in terms of cognitive synonymy would involve something like circularity.

Quine argues that similar considerations apply to attempts, such as Carnap's, to deal with the matter in terms of a semantic rule. Quine then considers the further possibility that, given that the truth of statements in general rests upon a linguistic component and a factual component, an analytic statement might be one in which the factual component is null. This, while apparently reasonable, has not, he objects, been explained; and the attempt by positivists to do so by reference to the verification theory of meaning (with its assumption that there are basic propositions in which the factual component is all that matters and, on the other hand, that there are analytic propositions in which the linguistic component is all that matters) involves reductionism, an unjustified dogma.

Synonymy and meaning. A possible objection to Quine—one in effect made by H. P. Grice and P. F. Strawson—is that his difficulty over synonymy involves a refusal to understand. There is a family of terms that includes analyticity, necessity, and cognitive synonymy, and Quine will not accept, as explanations of any one of them, accounts that involve reference to other members of the family. On the other hand, to go outside the family in one's explanations, as is involved in having recourse to extensional equivalence, is necessarily an inadequate explanation. This is a situation that frequently occurs in philosophy, wherever one is confronted with families of terms between which and any other family there is a radical or categorical distinction. This is perhaps an oversimplification of the situation, true though it is. It must be remembered that Quine's basic urge is to do without meanings, so as not to introduce unnecessary entities into our ontology. The failure of this particular enterprise of defining synonymy is, however, in fact, a demonstration of its futility. Meaning is a notion which must be presupposed rather than explained away in this connection.

THE BOUNDARY BETWEEN ANALYTIC AND SYNTHETIC STATEMENTS. Quine also has a second thesis in connection with analyticity, a thesis that has been echoed in different forms by other philosophers. It is a quite general thesis, in the sense that it does not depend on considerations about synonymy and is not, therefore, restricted to statements whose truth turns on synonymy. This thesis states that even if a distinction could be drawn between analytic and synthetic statements or between logical and factual truth, it is impossible to draw a sharp boundary between them. The contrary supposal rests on the dogma of reductionism already referred to. On that thesis, there is clearly an absolute distinction to be made. The denial of the dogma entails that there can be, at the most, a relative distinction. Within any particular system it is possible to distinguish those statements, those of logic and mathematics, which we should be extremely reluctant to give up and those, on the other hand, which we should be ready to give up if required to do so. The former are entrenched because of their close connections with other elements of the system. It has often been pointed out that the giving up of some high-grade scientific statements would involve the giving up with them of whole scientific systems. On Quine's view, the situation is worse, but not intrinsically different, with logical statements. There are no statements that depend for their truth on a direct confrontation with experience. The best that can be produced in the way of a distinction between different kinds of statements is a relative distinction between those which are more or less entrenched. No absolute and sharp distinction between analytic and synthetic statements can be drawn. Quine's conventionalism here reflects pragmatist tendencies.

One possible reply to this thesis is that the rejection of the dogma of reductionism does not by itself dispose of an absolute distinction of this kind. Even if it is accepted that there are no statements in which the factual component is everything, it does not follow that there are no statements in which the linguistic component is everything. Despite what Quine says, the thesis that there is a distinction between analytic and synthetic statements is independent of that of reductionism. Grice and Strawson have also attempted to deal with the issue by making a distinction in terms of the responses to attempts to falsify a statement. Analytic statements are those that, in a falsifying situation, demand a revision in our concepts; synthetic statements are those that demand a revision in our view of the facts. It has frequently been pointed out that it is possible to preserve a scientific statement against falsifying circumstances by making it logically true and thus immune to falsification. In doing this, we revise our concepts but not our view of the facts. It is clear that Quine could not accept this suggestion as such, since it presupposes that an answer has been given to the first of his problems—the definition of analyticity—in terms of notions like those of a concept or meaning. But, given that Quine's thesis is untenable in this first respect, there is no reason for denying its untenability in the second.

STATEMENTS THAT ARE NEITHER ANALYTIC NOR SYNTHETIC. Other reasons for dissatisfaction with a sharp distinction between analytic and synthetic statements have been offered by other philosophers. Waismann, for example, has maintained that there are some statements which do not admit of a clear classification; for instance, "I see with my eyes." In this case there are reasons for saying that it is analytic, since whatever I see with might be called "eyes"; on the other hand, it might be said that it is a matter of fact that it is with my eyes that I see. Hence, Waismann maintains, such statements are neither analytic nor synthetic, properly speaking. The objection to this, as has been pointed out by W. H. Walsh, is that Waismann has failed to consider the contexts in which such statements are made. The sentence "I see with my eyes" may be used in one context to express an analytic statement and in another to express a synthetic one. The fact that the same sentence may have different uses and that the analyticity or syntheticity of a statement is a function of those uses (a statement is just the use of a sentence) shows nothing about the necessity of abandoning the analytic-synthetic distinction.

ARE THERE ANY ANALYTIC STATEMENTS? Emphasis of the point that analyticity is a function of use prompts the question of whether sentences which purport to express analytic statements have a use at all and whether, in consequence, there *are* any analytic statements. It has been emphasized from Kant onward that analytic statements are trivial, and similar things were said even before Kant—by John Locke, for instance. The truth of an analytic statement makes no difference to the world. It is, therefore, difficult to see why anyone should ever make an analytic statement. A possible reply is that such a statement might be made in order to clarify something about the concepts involved. If the statements in question are about concepts, however, rather than about the thing or things referred to by the subject expression, why are they not simply definitions? Definitions are not in themselves analytic statements, whatever their exact status. It could thus be argued that any statement which has a use either provides information about things or about the meanings of words, and in either case the statement would be synthetic, or at least not analytic. The only viable function remaining for the term *analytic* would be as a term of logical appraisal, not as a classificatory expression. That is to say, the use of the words "That is analytic" would not be to classify the statement in question, but to say, in effect, "You have not said anything."

Whether or not this is plausible in itself, the crucial question remains: How is it possible for a statement both to be about something and to elucidate the concepts involved? (The question is probably more crucial for judgments than for statements, since it might seem obvious what a judgment must be about, while the criteria of "aboutness" are less obvious in the case of statements.) The issues are simple. A statement is one use of a sentence, and an analytic statement is such a use that conforms to certain conditions—two of which are that it says nothing about its subject and that its truth depends at least in part on the meanings of the words involved. If this is so, it cannot be used to make clear those meanings. If an analytic statement does serve to make clear those meanings to someone, this must be an incidental and unintended consequence of its use, not an essential part of that use. On the other hand, if the triviality of analytic statements is accepted, there can be no argument to show that their use is impossible, for there is no reason why a statement, if it is to be about something, should also *say* something about that thing. The use of such statements would simply lack point.

A POSSIBLE WAY OF MAKING THE DISTINCTION

Ludwig Josef Johann Wittgenstein pointed out in the *Tractatus Logico-Philosophicus* (4.4611) that tautologies are senseless but not nonsense. By "senseless" he meant that they do not pick out any determinate state of affairs that makes a difference to our view of the world. They are, in effect, trivial. They are not nonsense, however, because they are part of our symbolism, just as "0" is part of the symbolism of arithmetic, although it is useless for counting. Given a system of symbolism, or a language, it must always be possible to construct sentences that could be used to assert analytic truths or falsehoods (contradictions), whether or not there would be any point in doing so. This possibility is a necessary consequence of the nature of language. A language, however, is not just a system of symbols; it is something whose function is, among other things, to state and communicate facts. Hence, it is possible to say that, given that these sentences have a use, the truth of their uses (or, in the case of contradictions, their falsity)—that is, the truth of the relevant statements—is a necessary condition of the employment of the language from which the corresponding sentences are drawn, or of any language in which there are sentences with the same meaning. More briefly, analytic statements will be those whose truth is necessary to the employment, as expressed in language, of the system of concepts on which they depend. Any statement of which this is not true will be synthetic. Of these other statements, many will be such that their truth is not necessary in any way, but there may be others whose truth is necessary in some way other than that of analytic statements—as Kant maintained about the synthetic a priori.

See also A Priori and A Posteriori; Ayer, Alfred Jules; Grice, Herbert Paul; Hume, David; Kant, Immanuel; Locke, John; Quine, Willard Van Orman; Strawson, Peter Frederick; Wittgenstein, Ludwig Josef Johann.

Bibliography

BOOKS

Ayer, A. J. *Language, Truth and Logic,* 2nd ed. London: V. Gollancz, 1946. Ch. 4.

Carnap, Rudolf. *Introduction to Semantics.* Cambridge, MA: Harvard University Press, 1942.

Frege, Gottlob. *Foundations of Arithmetic.* Translated by J. L. Austin. Oxford: Blackwell, 1950.

Hume, David. *Treatise of Human Nature.* Oxford: Clarendon Press, 1896. I.iii.1.

Kant, Immanuel. *Critique of Pure Reason.* Translated by Norman Kemp-Smith. London, 1953. Especially the introduction.

Leibniz, G. W., throughout his works. Especially *Monadology*, 31ff.

Pap, Arthur. *Semantics and Necessary Truth.* New Haven, CT: Yale University Press, 1958. Useful discussions of general issues.

Quine, W. V. *From a Logical Point of View.* Cambridge, MA, 1953. Ch. 2.

ARTICLES

Goodman, Nelson. "On Likeness of Meaning." *Analysis* 10 (1) (October 1949): 1–7.

Grice, H. P., and P. F. Strawson. "On Defence of a Dogma." *Philosophical Review* 65 (March 1956): 141–158.

Hamlyn, D. W. "Analytic Truths." *Mind,* n.s., 65 (259) (1956): 359–367.

Hamlyn, D. W. "On Necessary Truth." *Mind,* n.s., 70 (280) (1961): 514–525.

Putnam, Hilary. "The Analytic and the Synthetic" In *Minnesota Studies in the Philosophy of Science.* Minneapolis, 1962. Vol. III, pp. 358–397.

Waismann, Friedrich. "Analytic and Synthetic." *Analysis* 10, 11, and 13 (1949–1952). A series of articles.

Walsh, W. H. "Analytic and Synthetic." *PAS* 54 (1953/1954): 77–96.

White, M. "Analytic-Synthetic: An Untenable Dualism." In *John Dewey: Philosopher of Science and Freedom,* edited by Sydney Hook, pp. 316–330. New York, 1950.

D. W. Hamlyn (1967)

ANALYTIC AND SYNTHETIC STATEMENTS [ADDENDUM]

There are several major philosophical projects that having a viable analytic/synthetic distinction would advance. For example: Analytic (true) sentences are supposed to have their truth values solely in virtue of the meanings (together with the syntactic arrangement) of their constituents; in effect, their truth values are supposed to supervene on their linguistic properties alone (Quine 1953). So they are true in every possible world where they mean what they mean here. So they are necessarily true. So if there were a viable analytic/synthetic distinction, we would understand the necessity of at least some necessary truths. If, in particular, it were to turn out that the logical and/or the mathematical truths are analytic, we would understand why *they* are necessary (Gibson 1988, Quine 1998).

An account of necessity according to which necessary truths are analytic has special virtues. Necessity is not, of course, an epistemic notion. Still, suppose that the necessity of a sentence arises from the meanings of its parts. It is natural to assume that one of the things one knows in virtue of knowing one's language is what the expressions of the language mean (Boghossian 1994). A treatment of modality in terms of analyticity therefore connects the concept of necessity with the concept of knowledge; and knowledge *is*, of course, an epistemic property. So if there is a viable analytic/synthetic distinction, we could explain why the necessary truths, or at least some of the necessary truths, are knowable a priori by anybody who knows a language that can express them (Quine 1991). It bears emphasis that not every theory of necessity yields a corresponding treatment of apriority; doing so is a special virtue of connecting modality with meaning.

Many philosophers interested in the metaphysics of semantical properties find attractive the idea that the meaning of an expression supervenes on its conceptual/inferential role (Sellars 1954, Harman 1987, Block 1994 and references therein). It is, however, a plausible objection to conceptual role semantics that it courts a ruinous holism unless there is some way to distinguish meaning-constitutive inferences from the rest (Fodor and Lepore 1991, 1992). A tenable analytic/synthetic distinction might resolve this tension; the meaning constitutive-inferences could be identified with the analytic ones. In practice, it is pretty widely agreed that saving the analytic/synthetic distinction is a condition for saving conceptual role semantics (Block 1994, Peacocke 1992).

For many linguists, it is a main goal of "lexical semantics" to predict which sentences express them; typically, by "decomposing" the meanings of some words into their definitions. On this sort of view, intuitions of analyticity play much the role vis-à-vis theories of meaning that intuitions of grammaticality do vis-à-vis theories of syntax (Katz 1972).

For all of the aforementioned points, many philosophers have been persuaded (largely by considerations Quine raised) that there is no unquestion-begging way to formulate a serious analytic/synthetic distinction (Gibson 1988, Harman 1999, Lepore 1995). The moral might be that philosophy will have to do without it, even if, in consequence, notions like necessity, apriority and definition seem deeply mysterious.

Harman (following Quine) has famously offered an across-the-board argument that the notion of analyticity is untenable; namely, that the truth of analytic sentences is supposed somehow to be independent of "how the world is," but it is puzzling how the truth of anything could be independent of how the world is. How, for example, could a stipulation, or a linguistic convention (implicit or otherwise) make a proposition *true*? How could our undertaking to respect the inference from "bachelor" to "unmarried" make it true that bachelors are unmarried?

There is an obvious problem in understanding how the truth of a statement can be independent of the way the world is and depend entirely on the meaning of the statement. Why is it not a fact about the world that copper is a metal such that, if this were not a fact, the statement "copper is a metal" would not express a truth? And why doesn't the truth expressed by "copper is copper" depend in part on the general fact that everything is self-identical (Harman 1999)?

Boghossian (1996) holds that a sentence can be made true by stipulation; and that that stipulation determines which proposition the sentence expresses. Call the sentence S and the proposition P. Surely, if S is true, P is true, since it is a truism (assuming sentences have truth values at all) that each sentence has the same truth-value as the proposition it expresses. It is thus unclear why making a sentence true by stipulation is not *thereby* making the corresponding proposition true by stipulation.

Still, whatever the truth maker for a proposition is, the proposition is true just in case its truth maker is "in place." Now consider the proposition expressed by a sentence that is true by stipulation. Presumably, the truth maker for that proposition *must be* in place since the sentence that expresses it is true. If so, then, Harman can object as follows: "It's not obvious how a stipulation could make the world such that a certain sentence is true of it. But it's also, and equally, not obvious how a stipulation could guarantee that the truth maker of the proposition that a sentence expresses is 'in place.'" In fact, the second question is plausibly just the first one all over again.

See also Analysis, Philosophical; Analyticity; Meaning; Quine, Willard Van Orman; Synonymity.

Bibliography

Block, N. "Advertisement for a Semantics for Psychology." In *Mental Representation: A Reader*, edited by Stephen Stich and Ted A. Warfield. Cambridge, MA: Blackwell, 1994.

Boghossian, P. "Analyticity Reconsidered." *Nous* 30 (3) (1996): 360–391.

Boghossian, P. "The Transparency of Mental Content." *Philosophical Perspectives* 8 (1994): 33–50.

Fodor, J., and E. Lepore. *Holism: A Shopper's Guide*. Oxford: Basil Blackwell, 1992.

Fodor, J., and E. Lepore. "Why Meaning Probably Isn't Conceptual Role." *Mind and Language* 6 (4) (1991): 329–343. Reprinted in *The Compositionality Papers*, edited by J. Fodor and E. Lepore. Oxford and New York: Clarendon Press, 2002.

Gibson, Roger. *Enlightened Empiricism: An Examination of W. V. Quine's Theory of Knowledge*. Tampa: University of South Florida Press, 1988.

Harman, G. "The Death of Meaning." In *Reasoning, Meaning, and Mind*, edited by G. Harman, 119–137. Oxford: Clarendon Press, 1999.

Harman, G. "(Non-Solipsistic) Conceptual Role Semantics." In *New Directions in Semantics*, edited by E. Lepore. London: Academic Press, 1987.

Katz, Jerrold. *Semantic Theory*. New York: Harper and Row, 1972.

Lepore, Ernest. "Two Dogmas of Empiricism and the Generality Requirement." *Nous* 24 (1995): 468–480.

Peacocke, C. *A Study of Concepts*. Cambridge, MA: MIT Press, 1992.

Quine, W. V. O. "Reply to Roger F. Gibson, Jr." In *The Philosophy of W. V. Quine*, edited by Lewis Edwin Hahn and Paul A. Schilpp, 684–685. Chicago: Open Court, 1998.

Quine, W. V. O. "Two Dogmas in Retrospect." In *Dear Carnap, Dear Van: The Quine Carnap Correspondence and Related Work*, edited by Richard Creath. Berkeley: University of California Press, 1991.

Quine, W. V. O. "Two Dogmas of Empiricism." In *From a Logical Point of View*, 20–46. Cambridge, MA: Harvard University Press, 1953.

Sellars, W. "Some Reflections on Language Games." *Philosophy of Science* 21 (1954): 204–228.

Ernest Lepore (2005)

ANALYTICITY

The idea of "analyticity"—or truth by virtue of meaning—can be understood in two different ways. On the one hand, it might stand for an epistemic notion, for the idea that mere grasp of the meaning of a sentence suffices for knowledge that it is true. On the other hand, it might stand for a metaphysical notion, for the idea that a statement owes its truth value completely to its meaning, and not at all to "the facts." We may call the first notion "epistemic analyticity" and the second "metaphysical analyticity." On the face of it, these are distinct notions that subserve distinct philosophical programs. Willard Van Orman Quine, whose writings are largely responsible for the contemporary rejection of analyticity, failed to distinguish between them; as a result, many philosophers came to assume that the two notions stand or fall together. However, it is the moral of recent work in this area that this assumption is mistaken: epistemic analyticity can be defended even while its metaphysical cousin is rejected.

The metaphysical concept of analyticity is presupposed by the logical positivist program of reducing all necessity to linguistic necessity. Guided by both the fear that objective, language-independent necessary connections would be metaphysically odd, and that no empiricist epistemology could explain our knowledge of them, philosophers like Rudolf Carnap (1947) and A. J. Ayer (1946) attempted to show that all necessary truths are simply disguised decisions concerning the meanings of words. According to this view, there is no more to the truth of, say, "Either snow is white or it is not" than a decision concerning the meaning of the word "or." On this view, linguistic meaning by itself is supposed to generate necessary truth; a fortiori, linguistic meaning by itself is supposed to generate truth. Hence the play with the metaphysical notion of analyticity.

However, it is doubtful that this makes a lot of sense. What could it possibly mean to say that the truth of a statement is fixed exclusively by its meaning and not by the facts? Is it not in general true that for any statement **S**,

S is true if and only if (iff) for some **p**, **S** means that **p** and **p**?

How could the mere fact that **S** means that **p** make it the case that **S** is true? Doesn't it also have to be the case that **p** (see Harman, 1960)?

The proponent of the metaphysical notion does have a comeback, one that has perhaps not been sufficiently addressed. What he will say instead is that, in some appropriate sense, our meaning **p** by **S** makes it the case that **p**.

But this line is itself fraught with difficulty. For how are we to understand how our meaning something by a sentence can make something or other the case? It is easy to understand how the fact that we mean what we do by a sentence determines whether that sentence expresses something true or false. But as Quine (1951) points out, that is just the normal dependence of truth on meaning. What is not clear is how the truth of what the sentence expresses could depend on the fact that it is expressed by that sentence, so that we would be entitled to say that what is expressed would not have been true at all had it not been for the fact that it is expressed by that sentence. But are we really to suppose that, prior to our stipulating a meaning for the sentence

"Either snow is white or it is not"

it was not the case that either snow was white or it was not? Is it not overwhelmingly obvious that this claim was true *before* such an act of meaning, and that it would have been true even if no one had thought about it, or chosen it to be expressed by one of our sentences?

There is, then, very little to recommend the linguistic theory of necessity and, with it, the metaphysical notion of analyticity that is supposed to subserve it. Epistemic analyticity, by contrast, is not involved in that futile reductive enterprise. Its role, rather, is to provide a theory of a priori knowledge.

Intuitively speaking, it does seem that we can know certain statements—the truths of logic, mathematics, and conceptual analysis, most centrally—without recourse to empirical experience. The problem has always been to explain how.

The history of philosophy has known a number of answers to this question, among which the following has been very influential: We are equipped with a special evidence-gathering faculty of intuition, distinct from the standard five senses, that allows us to arrive at justified beliefs about the necessary properties of the world. By exercising this faculty, we are able to know a priori such truths as those of mathematics and logic.

The central impetus behind the analytic explanation of the a priori is to explain the possibility of a priori knowledge without having to postulate any such special faculty of "intuition," an idea that has never been adequately elaborated.

This is where the concept of epistemic analyticity comes in. If mere grasp of **S**'s meaning by **O** were to suffice for **O**'s being justified (with a strength sufficient for knowledge—henceforth, we will take this qualification to be understood) in holding **S** true, then **S**'s apriority would be explainable without appeal to a special faculty of intuition: the very fact that it means what it does for **O** would by itself explain why **O** is justified in holding it to be true.

How could mere grasp of a sentence's meaning justify someone in holding it true? Clearly, the answer to this question has to be semantical: something about the sentence's meaning, or about the way that meaning is fixed, must explain how its truth is knowable in this special way. What could this explanation be?

In the history of the subject, two different sorts of explanation have been especially important. Although these, too, have often been conflated, it is crucial to distinguish between them.

One idea was first formulated in full generality by Gottlob Frege (1884). According to this view, a statement's epistemic analyticity is to be explained by the fact that it is transformable into a logical truth by the substitution of synonyms for synonyms. We may call statements that satisfy this semantic condition "Frege-analytic."

Quine's enormously influential "Two Dogmas of Empiricism," (1951) complained that there could not be any Frege-analytic statements because there could not be any synonymies. But, as Herbert P. Grice and Peter F. Strawson showed (1956), the arguments for this claim are highly disputable. And Paul Boghossian (1995) has added to this by arguing that Quine's negative arguments cannot plausibly stop short of his radical thesis of the indeterminacy of meaning, a thesis that most philosophers continue to reject.

The real problem with Frege-analyticity is not that there are not any instances of it, but that it is limited in its ability to explain the full range of a priori statements. Two classes remain problematic: a priori statements that are not transformable into logical truths by the substitution of synonyms for synonyms, and a priori statements that are trivially so transformable.

An example of the first class is the sentence "Whatever is red all over is not blue." Because the ingredient descriptive terms do not decompose in the appropriate way, this sentence is not transformable into a logical truth by substitution of synonyms.

The second class of recalcitrant statements consists precisely of the truths of logic. These truths satisfy, of course, the conditions on Frege-analyticity. But they satisfy them trivially. And it seems obvious that we cannot hope to explain our entitlement to belief in the truths of logic by appealing to their analyticity in this sense: Knowledge of Frege-analyticity presupposes knowledge of logical truth and so cannot explain it.

How, then, is the epistemic analyticity of these recalcitrant truths to be explained? The solution proposed by Carnap (1947) and the middle Ludwig Wittgenstein (1974) turned on the suggestion that such statements are to be thought of as "implicit definitions" of their ingredient terms. Applied to the case of logic (a similar treatment is possible in the case of the other class of recalcitrant truths), this suggestion generates the semantical thesis we may call:

Implicit definition: It is by arbitrarily stipulating that certain sentences of logic are to be true, or that certain inferences are to be valid, that we attach a meaning to the logical constants. A particular constant means that logical object, if any, which makes valid a specified set of sentences and/or inferences involving it.

The transition from this sort of implicit definition account of grasp to an account of the apriority of logic can then seem immediate, and the following sort of argument would appear to be in place:

1. If logical constant **C** is to mean what it does, then argument-form **A** has to be valid, for **C** means whatever logical object in fact makes **A** valid.

2. **C** means what it does.

Therefore,

3. **A** is valid.

Quine's "Truth by Convention" (1936) and "Carnap and Logical Truth" (1976) raised several important objections against the thesis of implicit definition: first, that it leads to an implausible conventionalism about logical truth; second, that it results in a vicious regress; and third, that it is committed to a notion—that of a meaning-constituting sentence or inference—that cannot be made out.

Even the proponents of implicit definition seem to have agreed that some sort of conventionalism about logical truth follows from implicit definition. However, Nathan Salmon (1994) and Boghossian (1997) have argued that this is a mistake: No version of conventionalism follows from the semantical thesis of implicit definition, provided that a distinction is observed between a sentence and the claim that it expresses.

Quine's second objection is also problematic in relying on a defective conception of what it is for a person to adopt a certain rule with respect to an expression, according to which the adoption of a rule always involves explicitly stating in linguistic terms the rule that is being adopted. On the contrary, it seems far more plausible to construe **x**'s following rule **R** with respect to **e** as consisting in some sort of fact about **x**'s behavior with **e**.

In what would such a fact consist? Here there are at least two options of which the most influential is this: **O**'s following rule **R** with respect to **e** consists in **O**'s being disposed, under appropriate circumstances, to conform to rule **R** in his employment of **e**.

According to this view, then, the logical constants mean what they do by virtue of figuring in certain inferences and/or sentences involving them and not in others. If some expressions mean what they do by virtue of figuring in certain inferences and sentences, then some inferences and sentences are constitutive of an expression's meaning what it does, and others are not.

Quine's final objection to implicit definition is that there will be no way to specify systematically the meaning-constituting inferences, because there will be no way to distinguish systematically between a meaning constituting inference and one that is not meaning-constituting but simply obvious. However, although this is a serious challenge, and although it remains unmet, there is every reason for optimism (see, for example, Peacocke 1994 and Boghossian 1995).

Quine helped us see the vacuity of the metaphysical concept of analyticity and, with it, the futility of the project it was supposed to underwrite—the linguistic theory of necessity. But those arguments do not affect the epistemic notion of analyticity, the notion that is needed for the purposes of the theory of a priori knowledge. Indeed, the analytic theory of apriority seems to be a promising research program, given reasonable optimism about the prospects both for a conceptual role semantics and for the idea of Frege-analyticity.

See also Ayer, Alfred Jules; Carnap, Rudolf; Conventionalism; Frege, Gottlob; Grice, Herbert Paul; Knowledge, A Priori; Moral Epistemology; Quine, Willard Van Orman; Strawson, Peter Frederick; Wittgenstein, Ludwig Josef Johann.

Bibliography

Ayer, A. J. *Language, Truth and Logic.* London: Gollancz, 1946.

Boghossian, P. A. "Analyticity." In *A Companion to the Philosophy of Language,* edited by C. Wright and B. Hale. Cambridge, U.K.: Blackwell, 1997.

Carnap, R. *Meaning and Necessity.* Chicago: University of Chicago Press, 1947.

Dummett, M. *Frege: The Philosophy of Mathematics.* Cambridge, MA: Harvard University Press, 1991.

Frege, G. *Die Grundlagen der Arithmetik: eine logisch-mathematische Untersuchung uber den Begriff der Zahl* (1884). Translated by J. L. Austin as *The Foundations of Arithmetic.* Oxford: Blackwell, 1950.

Grice, H. P., and P. Strawson. "In Defense of a Dogma." *Philosophical Review* 65 (1956): 141–158.

Harman, G. "Quine on Meaning and Existence I." *Review of Metaphysics* 21 (1960): 124–151.

Pap, A. *Semantics and Necessary Truth.* New Haven, CT: Yale University Press, 1958.

Peacocke, C. "How Are A Priori Truths Possible?" *European Journal of Philosophy* 1 (1993): 175–199.

Peacocke, C. *A Study of Concepts.* Cambridge, MA: MIT Press, 1992.

Putnam, H. *Mind, Language and Reality—Philosophical Papers 2.* Cambridge: Cambridge University Press, 1975.

Quine, W. V. O. "Carnap and Logical Truth" (1954). Reprinted in *The Ways of Paradox,* Cambridge, MA: Harvard University Press, 1976.

Quine, W. V. O. "Truth by Convention." In *Philosophical Essays for A. N. Whitehead,* edited by O. H. Lee. New York: Longmans, Green, 1936. Reprinted in *The Ways of Paradox,* Cambridge, MA: Harvard University Press, 1976.

Quine, W. V. O. "Two Dogmas of Empiricism." *Philosophical Review* (1951). Reprinted in *From a Logical Point of View,* Cambridge, MA: Harvard University Press, 1953.

Quine, W. V. O. *Word and Object.* Cambridge, MA: MIT Press, 1960.

Salmon, N. "Analyticity and Apriority." *Philosophical Perspectives* (1994).

Wittgenstein, L. J. J. *Philosophical Grammar* (1932–1934). Berkeley: University of California Press, 1974.

Paul Artin Boghossian (1996)

ANALYTIC JURISPRUDENCE

Analytic jurisprudence divides into two related areas: substantive and methodological. Until the late 1980s most analytic jurisprudence had been substantive. It focused on producing theories of the nature of law, the relationship between laws (particular legal standards) and law (a system of governance by laws), and the relationship of law to morality and other institutions for regulating human affairs and actions.

Whereas these debates in substantive jurisprudence remain as lively and urgent as ever, analytic jurisprudence has taken a decidedly methodological turn. Jurisprudence is a philosophical theory of the nature of law, not a historical, economic, or sociological one. But how can philosophy shed light on law? The conventional answer is that philosophy aims to uncover the nature of law.

But how can philosophy help uncover the nature of law? Since H. L. A. Hart, at least, the most prominent answer has been that philosophical theories of law are theories of the concept of law, of concepts related to it (such as obligation and authority), and of the relationships among these concepts. The philosophical method of jurisprudence is conceptual analysis. Thus, analytic jurisprudence is on the same footing as analytic epistemology, metaphysics, and metaethics. Analytic jurisprudence is conceptual analysis of the concept of law, just as epistemology is conceptual analysis of the concepts of epistemic warrant and knowledge.

The standard view is that competent speakers share the concept of law, though each has an incomplete grasp of it. While we take ourselves to be employing the same concept—a concept that regulates our usage and enables us to communicate meaningfully—in fact few competent speakers have theories of the concept in all its particulars. Constructing such a theory is the task of the jurisprudent. Such a theory refines and regulates our use and aims to deepen our understanding. Constructing such a theory begins with ordinary use, which reflects a partial understanding, but does not end there. Nor is jurisprudence merely a descriptive activity reporting on common or shared understandings.

Since Hart, at least, this has been the dominant method for approaching the study of the nature of law. Of contemporary legal philosophers, Joseph Raz is perhaps the preeminent proponent of this way of understanding conceptual analysis as a distinctive philosophical approach to law.

The place of conceptual analysis within jurisprudence has recently come under sustained attack from several quarters. These attacks have been responsible for much of the current interest in the methods of analytic jurisprudence. The first line of attack raises doubts about conceptual analysis, not just in jurisprudence, but in philosophy more generally. This is the naturalist challenge. In its stronger forms, naturalized jurisprudence argues that conceptual analysis is a form of inquiry that proceeds by culling usage and then testing various refinements and revisions against intuitions about proper use, and that it turns philosophical inquiry into an irreducible battle among competing intuitions and is ultimately hopeless.

Naturalists invite us to understand law by taking our cues from the social-scientific theories that explore the role of law in our social lives. We revise or amend those accounts only insofar as the theories fail to deliver the requisite goods: to enable us to make our way through the social world.

Within law, naturalists, Brian Leiter in particular, have focused more narrowly on the theory of adjudication. If we take authoritative legal texts as inputs and judicial decisions as outputs, then a theory of adjudication is a set of norms that takes the set of relevant authoritative texts, together with pertinent factual premises, and generates correct judicial opinions from them. A theory of adjudication is an account of warranted or justified legal inferences or decisions. The naturalist rejects the view that the norms governing proper legal reasoning can be determined by a priori reflection on our practice. Instead of trying to determine the norms by which judges ought to decide cases, they urge that we study how judges in fact decide cases. In this way, the legal naturalist echoes the claim, often attributed to W. V. O. Quine, that properly understood, epistemology would be no more than a chapter in a psychology text book.

The second kind of objection does not reject the idea that jurisprudence aims to provide a theory of the concept of law. Rather, it focuses on the form of conceptual analysis that Hart and others have been committed to, according to which the goal of jurisprudence is to identify the rule or criteria for the proper use of the concept of law. There are several objections to this project. One worry is that the concept of law may not be governed by a rule for its proper use, at least not one that is fixed by the shared understandings and behavior of competent speakers. As some have put it, the concept of law may be an essentially contested concept, the criteria of its proper application being fundamentally and inevitably in dispute.

Ronald Dworkin, for one, views the concept of law as essentially contested. Because the criteria for its application are necessarily in dispute, the proper application of the concept cannot be determined by a rule, and certainly not one whose content is shared by competent speakers. The essentially contestable nature of the concept of law implies that a theory of it cannot be constructed from reports of common use and understandings, even suitably revised and refined. Instead, the method of conceptual analysis appropriate to law is "constructive interpretation." Such an interpretation requires first attributing a value or purpose to law. The purpose of law is introduced to explain why it would be rational for agents to participate in it, or in some other sense to legitimate the practice. The theory of the concept is constructed by imposing this value on the practice of law as a way of organizing it and determining which features of it are most important to explain. Most important, a constructive interpretation of the concept of law is a normative theory of law. The interpretation begins with a contestable claim about the value of law that can only be defended by appealing to substantive moral principles.

Interestingly, Dworkin shares more with the natural jurisprudent than one might think. Both feel that a descriptive account of our legal practice is best left to social scientists, not philosophers. The naturalist takes this to be reason enough to deny that philosophical jurisprudence is a distinctive endeavor. For Dworkin, it is reason to think that philosophical jurisprudence must be normative.

Interpretivism is one form of normative jurisprudence. Like the so-called descriptivists and Dworkin, and unlike the naturalists, Stephen Perry accepts that the project of jurisprudence is to analyze the concept of law. Like Dworkin, he thinks the descriptivists have gone awry by thinking that an analysis of the concept of law can be achieved by reflecting on ordinary use, that is, by culling data about use, then revising and refining accordingly.

Perry's argument for normative jurisprudence is very different than Dworkin's, however. His point of departure is the claim that every theory of law has embedded within it a range of normative premises—about the nature of human agency, the value of governance by law, and most important, the proper function of law. According to Perry, the best way to interpret Hart is as claiming that the function of law is to guide conduct by reasons. By the same token, the best way to understand Dworkin is as claiming that the function of law is to justify the application of coercive force in terms of the past political decisions of legal actors. For Perry, defending a theory of the concept of law requires defending one or another view about the proper function of law. Any such defense calls for arguments of political morality, not for reports of common use or understanding.

Finally, other philosophers of law, notably Jules Coleman and Ori Simchen, take issue with conceptual analysis as the method of jurisprudence in somewhat different terms. As they see it, there are at least two problems with conceptual analysis. The first is that it relies on an unsustainable formulation of the analytic/synthetic distinction, according to which theorizing about a subject has distinct conceptual and empirical dimensions. The role of philosophy is identified with the former; the rest is a matter of empirical science. This division of labor, they claim, relies on a way of distinguishing the analytic from the synthetic that is untenable. Those who identify philosophical inquiry with conceptual analysis believe that the role of philosophy is to explore the fundamental concepts of an area of study. Philosophy uncovers the nature of the things studied by uncovering the conditions for the proper application of the relevant concepts. But this again artificially constrains the role of philosophy. It may well be that we cannot study a subject without having a concept of it, but that does not mean that philosophical inquiry must be identified with determining the conditions for the proper application of the concept. There is no reason why philosophical inquiry into law cannot be a direct account of the significant features of legal practice itself, and not merely of the concepts used to refer to the practice of law.

To sum up, the methods of analytic jurisprudence are hotly contested. The partisans fall into two camps: those who identify the distinctive role of philosophical inquiry with traditional conceptual analysis and those who, in one way or another, reject this approach. Arguably, Raz falls into the first category, whereas Leiter, Dworkin, Perry, Coleman, and Simchen, among others, fall into the second. Those who reject traditional conceptual analysis do so for a variety of reasons. Some naturalists, such as Leiter, take the rejection of the analytic/synthetic distinction to mean in effect that there is no distinctive role for philosophy in jurisprudence. That is, they implicitly accept the view that what is distinctive of philosophy is conceptual analysis, but since conceptual analysis requires the analytic/synthetic distinction, rejecting the distinction implies abandoning a distinctive role for philosophy.

Defenders of normative jurisprudence, especially Dworkin, believe that if there is a role for philosophy in the wake of the rejection of the analytic/synthetic distinction, it must take the form of a normative theory of law. After all, if jurisprudence cannot be conceptual, and empirical inquiries are best left to the social scientists, all that remains for philosophy is to advance a speculative normative philosophy of law. Still others who reject the analytic/synthetic distinction, like Coleman and Simchen, are inclined to the view that abandoning the distinction means that philosophical inquiry into law can be an amalgam of the empirical and the conceptual.

See also Feminist Legal Theory; Legal Realism; Natural Law; Positivism.

Bibliography

Coleman, Jules. "Methodology." In *The Oxford Handbook of Jurisprudence and Philosophy of Law*, edited by Jules Coleman and Scott Shapiro, 311–351. Oxford, U.K.: Oxford University Press, 2002.

Coleman, Jules. *The Practice of Principle*. Oxford, U.K.: Oxford University Press, 2001.

Coleman, Jules and Simchen, Ori. "Law." *Legal Theory* 9 (2003): 1–41.

Dickson, Julie. *Evaluation and Legal Theory*. Oxford, U.K.: Hart Publishing, 2001.

Dickson, Julie. "Methodology in Jurisprudence." *Legal Theory* 10 (2004): 117–156.

Dworkin, Ronald. *Law's Empire*. Cambridge, MA: Harvard University Press, 1986.

Finnis, John. "Law and What I Truly Should Decide." *American Journal of Jurisprudence* 48 (2003): 107–129.

Finnis, John. *Natural Law and Natural Rights*. Oxford, U.K.: Oxford University Press, 1980.

Greenberg, Mark. "How Facts Make Law." *Legal Theory* 10 (2004): 157–198.

Hart, H. L. A. *The Concept of Law*. Oxford, U.K.: Clarendon Press, 1994.

Leiter, Brian. "Beyond the Hart/Dworkin Debate: The Methodology Problem in Jurisprudence." *American Journal of Jurisprudence* 48 (2003): 17–51.

Leiter, Brian. "Legal Realism, Hard Positivism, and the Limits of Conceptual Analysis." In *Hart's Postscript*, edited by Jules Coleman, 355–370. Oxford, U.K.: Oxford University Press, 2001.

Leiter, Brian. "Naturalism and Naturalized Jurisprudence." In *Analyzing Law: New Essays in Legal Theory*, edited by Brian Bix, 79–104. Oxford, U.K.: Clarendon Press, 1998.

Marmor, Andrei, ed. *Law and Interpretation*. Oxford, U.K.: Oxford University Press, 1995.

Perry, Stephen. "Hart's Methodological Positivism." In *Hart's Postscript*, edited by Jules Coleman, 311–354. Oxford, U.K.: Oxford University Press, 2001.

Perry, Stephen. "Holmes versus Hart: The Bad Man in Legal Theory." In *"The Path of Law" and Its Influence*, edited by Steven Burton, 158–169. Cambridge, U.K.: Cambridge University Press, 2000.

Perry, Stephen. "Interpretation and Methodology in Legal Theory." In *Law and Interpretation*, edited by Andrei Marmor, 97–136. Oxford, U.K.: Clarendon Press, 1995.

Postema, Gerald. "Jurisprudence as Practical Philosophy." *Legal Theory* 4 (1998): 329–357.

Raz, Joseph. "The Problem about the Nature of Law." In *Ethics in the Public Domain*, 179–193. Oxford, U.K.: Oxford University Press, 1994.

Raz, Joseph. "Two Views of the Nature of Law: A Partial Comparison." In *Hart's Postscript*, edited by Jules Coleman, 1–38. Oxford, U.K.: Oxford University Press, 2001.

Shapiro, Scott. "The Bad Man and the Internal Point of View." In *"The Path of Law" and Its Influence*, edited by Steven Burton, 197–210. Cambridge, U.K.: Cambridge University Press, 2000.

Stavropoulos, Nicos. "Hart's Semantics." In *Hart's Postscript*, edited by Jules Coleman. Oxford, U.K.: Oxford University Press, 2001.

Stavropoulos, Nicos. "Interpretivist Theories of Law." In *The Stanford Encyclopedia of Philosophy*, winter 2003 ed., edited by Edward N. Zalta. Available at http://plato.stanford.edu/archives/win2003/entries/law-interpretivist/.

Waldron, Jeremy. *Law and Disagreement*. Oxford, U.K.: Oxford University Press, 2001.

Jules L. Coleman (2005)

ANANKE

See *Moira/Tyche/Ananke*

ANAPHORA

The study of *anaphora* (from Greek, "carry back") is the study of the ways in which occurrences of certain expressions, particularly pronouns, depend for their interpretations upon the interpretations of occurrences of other expressions. Problems of anaphora are of interest to philosophy and logic because of their intersection with problems of ontology, quantification, and logical form.

REFERENTIAL ANAPHORA

Pronouns understood as anaphoric on referential noun phrases are plausibly viewed as referring to the same things as their antecedents. Sentences (1)–(3) permit such readings (coindexing will be used to indicate an intentional anaphoric connection):

(1) Jim_1 respects students who argue with him_1.

(2) Jim_1 loves his_1 mother.

(3) Jim_1 is here. He_1 arrived yesterday. I think he_1's asleep right now.

We might call these pronouns "referential anaphors."

It is sometimes suggested (see, e.g., Soames 1994) that anaphoric pronouns in such constructions can be understood in a second way. For example, although (2) might be understood as equivalent to "Jim loves Jim's mother," it might seem to admit of another interpretation that makes it equivalent to "Jim is a self's-mother-lover," the logical form of which is given by (2'):

(2') $\lambda x(x$ loves x's mother)Jim.

The contrast between the two readings emerges when (2) is embedded, as in

(4) Mary believes that Jim_1 loves his_1 mother.

Certainly, many of the traditional problems involved in interpreting proper names recur for pronouns anaphoric on names.

BOUND-VARIABLE ANAPHORA

Pronouns anaphoric on quantified noun phrases cannot be treated as straightforwardly referential. Consider the following:

(5) Every man_1 thinks he would be a good $president_1$.

(6) No man_1 respects his_1 brothers' friends.

There is no point inquiring into the referents of the pronouns in examples like these. Following W. V. Quine (1960) and P. Geach (1962), philosophers have tended to treat such pronouns as the natural-language analogs of the variables of quantification theory. Certainly, the logical forms of quantified sentences of the form "every F is G" and "some Fs and Gs" can be captured using the standard first-order quantifiers "∀" and "∃." But a comprehensive semantic theory must treat sentences containing noun phrases formed using "no," "the," "exactly one," "most," "few," and so on. This fact highlights two problems. Using the identity sign "=" and the negation sign "¬," it is possible to use "∀" and "∃" to represent sentences containing "no," "the," "exactly one," "exactly two," and so forth, but the resulting formulae obscure the relationship between the surface syntax of a sentence and its logical form. For example, if Bertrand Russell is right that "the F is G" is true if and only if every F is G and there is exactly one F, then the logical form of this sentence is as follows:

(7) $(\exists x)((\forall y)(Fy \equiv y = x) \,\&\, Gx)$.

A more serious problem is that there are sentences that cannot be dealt with in first-order logic—for instance, sentences of the form "most Fs are Gs."

Both of these problems are solved if quantification in natural language is viewed as *restricted*. The basic idea here is that determiners combine with their complements (noun complexes) to form restricted quantifiers. So, for example, "every," "some," "most," "the," and so on combine with simple nouns such as "pig" (or "pigs"), "man" (or "men"), and so forth (or complex nouns such as "man who owns a pig," etc.) to form restricted quantifiers such as "some man," "most men," "every man who owns a pig," and so forth. We can represent a restricted quantifier "every man" as "[every x: man x]." This quantifier may combine with a predicate phrase such as "is mortal" (which we can represent as "x is mortal") to form the sentence "every man is mortal," which we can represent as

(8) [every x: man x]x is mortal.

Now consider sentences (5) and (6) again. If we treat the anaphoric pronouns in these examples as bound variables, their logical forms will be (abstracting somewhat):

(5') [every x: man x](x thinks x would be a good president).

(6') [no x: man x](x respects x's brothers' friends).

VARIABLE BINDING AND SCOPE

G. Evans (1977) has argued that not all pronouns anaphoric on quantified noun phrases are bound variables. Consider the following examples.

(9) Jim bought some pigs and Harry vaccinated them.

(10) Just one man ate haggis and he was ill afterward.

A bound-variable treatment of the occurrence of "them" in (9) yields the wrong result. On such an account, the logical form of the sentence will be

(9') [some x: pigs x](Jim bought x & Harry vaccinated x).

But (9') can be true even if Harry did not vaccinate *all* of the pigs Jim bought, whereas (9) cannot. (If Jim bought ten pigs and Harry vaccinated only two of them, (9') would be true whereas (9) would not.) And if the pronoun "he" in (10) is treated as a bound variable, the logical form of the sentence will be

(10') [just one x: man x](x ate haggis and x was ill afterward).

This is also incorrect; if two men ate haggis and only one was ill afterward, (10') will be true whereas (10) will be false.

There is a plausible syntactic explanation of these facts. In both (9) and (10), the pronoun is located outside the smallest sentence containing the quantifier upon which it is anaphoric and hence lies outside its scope, according to the most promising syntactic characterization of this notion. The scope of an expression α in a sentence of a natural language appears to correspond to the first branching node dominating α at the syntactic level relevant to semantic interpretation. If this is correct, and contemporary syntactic theory suggests it is, then syntactic theory explains why the pronouns in (9) and (10) are not understood as bound variables. There seem to be, therefore, anaphoric pronouns that are neither bound nor straightforwardly referential.

UNBOUND ANAPHORA

A plausible paraphrase of (9) is (9"):

(9") Jim bought some pigs and Harry vaccinated the pigs Jim bought.

In view of this, Evans (1977) suggests that the pronoun "them" in (9) is understood in terms of the plural description "the pigs Jim bought," as what he calls an "E-type" pronoun. An E-type pronoun has its reference fixed by description (in Saul Kripke's sense) and is therefore a rigid designator. On this account, in (9) the pronoun "them" is taken to refer to those objects satisfying "pigs Jim bought."

Similarly where the antecedent is singular. A plausible paraphrase of (11) is (11'):

(11) Jim bought a pig and Harry vaccinated it.

(11') Jim bought a pig and Harry vaccinated the pig Jim bought.

According to Evans, the pronoun "it" in (11) refers to the unique object satisfying "pig Jim bought."

This idea forms the basis of Evans's general account of the semantic content of unbound anaphors. The pronoun "he" in (10) has its reference fixed by "the man who ate haggis"; and in (12) "they" has its reference fixed by "the philosophers who came":

(12) A few philosophers came. They drank far too much.

Evans's proposal can be summarized thus: if P is an unbound pronoun anaphoric on a quantified noun phrase "[DET x: ϕ]" occurring in a sentence "[DET x: ϕ]ψ," then the referent of P is fixed by the description "[the x: ϕ & ψ]."

Examination of more complex cases reveals weaknesses in Evans's theory (see below). The problems uncovered have tended to steer semanticists in one of two directions. First, there have been attempts to modify or refine Evans's framework (Davies 1981, Neale 1990). Second, there have been attempts to replace the entire framework with a uniform, discourse-based approach (Kamp 1981, Heim 1982). Both approaches will now be examined.

DESCRIPTIVE ANAPHORA

Evans rejected the view that unbound anaphors go proxy for descriptions (in favor of the view that they have their referents fixed by description) on the grounds that such pronouns, unlike overt descriptions, do not give rise to ambiguities of scope. But consider the following:

(14) A man murdered Smith, but Jim doesn't think he did it.

(15) A man murdered Smith. The police have reason to think he injured himself in the process.

If "he" goes proxy for "the man who murdered Smith," there will be two readings for each of the anaphor clauses in these examples—the so-called *de re* and *de dicto* readings—according as the description for which the pronoun goes proxy is given large or small scope:

(14a) [the x: man x & x murdered Smith] (Jim doesn't believe that x murdered Smith)

(14b) Jim doesn't believe that [the x: man x & x murdered Smith](x murdered Smith)

It is natural to interpret (14) as attributing to Jim a noncontradictory belief concerning the murderer to the effect that he is not the murderer. On the proxy view this is captured by the *de re* reading of the second conjunct. The *de dicto* reading is technically available to the proxy theorist but is obviously not the preferred interpretation. But with (15) the *de dicto* reading of the second sentence is actually the more natural; yet Evans's theory explicitly precludes its existence.

Further support for the proxy rather than reference-fixing approach comes from examples containing modal expressions:

(16) Mary wants to marry a rich man. He must be a banker.

The first sentence in (16) may be read either *de re* or *de dicto*. Moreover, the pronoun "he" can be anaphoric on "a rich man" on either reading. But as L. Karttunen (1976) points out, the modal expression has to be there for the anaphora to work if the antecedent sentence is to be interpreted *de dicto*. That is, in

(17) Mary wants to marry a rich man. He is a banker.

it is not possible to get the *de dicto* reading for the antecedent clause if "he" is anaphoric on "a rich man." This contrast between (16) and (17) is explicable on the assumption that the anaphoric pronoun in (16) goes proxy for the description "the man Mary marries" and may therefore take large or small scope with respect to the modal expression. On the *de dicto* reading of the antecedent clause, the *de re* reading of the anaphor clause is infelicitous because an implication of existence results from giving the description large scope. But the *de dicto* reading of the anaphor clause is fine because on such a reading the description is within the scope of the modal expression. In (17), on the other hand, since there is no modal operator with respect to which the pronoun can be understood with small scope, the sentence has no felicitous reading when the antecedent clause is read *de dicto*.

DONKEY ANAPHORA

H. Kamp (1981) and I. Heim (1982) have explored alternative approaches that aim to treat all anaphoric pronouns in a unitary fashion. One motivation is the problem of so called donkey anaphora, typified by sentences such as (18) and (19), originally discussed by Geach (1962):

(18) If a man buys a donkey he vaccinates it.

(19) Every man who buys a donkey vaccinates it.

Both Evans's theory and the simple proxy theory seem to fail here. For example, if the pronoun "it" in (19) is analyzed in terms of the singular description "the donkey he buys" (with "he" bound by "every man who buys a donkey") the sentence will be true just in case every man who buys a donkey vaccinates the unique donkey he buys. Consequently, it will be false if any man buys more than one donkey. But this is incorrect; the truth of (19) is quite compatible with some men owning more than one donkey, as long as every man who buys a donkey vaccinates *every* donkey he buys. It would appear, then, that the indefinite description "a donkey"—which can normally be treated as an existentially quantified phrase—has the force of a *universally* quantified phrase in (19). And in (18) both "man" and "a donkey" appear to have universal force.

A common explanation of the "universalization" of the indefinite descriptions in such examples has been proposed by Kamp. The idea (roughly) is that noun phrases introduce variables to which common nouns and predicates supply "conditions" within a "discourse representation" (DR). Typically, the variable is bound by an existential quantifier taking scope over the entire discourse. On this account, an indefinite description is not inherently quantificational; rather, it introduces a variable with conditions on it imposed by, among other things, the predicative material it contains. The DR for (18) might be represented as:

(18') [man(x) & donkey(y) & buys(x,y)] IFTHEN [vaccinates(x,y)].

Kamp proposes that (18') is true if and only if every assignment of values to x and y that makes the antecedent true also makes the consequent true. The apparent universalization of the indefinite descriptions "a man" and "a donkey" is thus explained as a consequence of a general analysis of conditionals.

In the light of the equivalence of (18) and (19), Kamp suggests that, although (18) is not actually a conditional, because the subject quantifier is universal we get a DR in which the indefinite "a donkey" has universal force. That is, the DR for (19) is given by

(19') [man(x) & donkey(y) & buys(x,y)] EVERY [vaccinates(x,y)].

Like (18'), (19') is true if and only if every assignment of values to x and y that makes "[man(x) & donkey(y) & buys(x,y)]" true, also makes "[vaccinates(x,y)]" true.

One problem with this proposal is that it does not predict that indefinite descriptions "universalize" when they are embedded in *other* quantifiers and thus leads to the so-called proportion problem. Consider

(20) Most men who buy a donkey vaccinate it.

By analogy with (18') and (19'), the DR for (20) will be

(20') [man(x) & donkey(y) & buys(x,y)] MOST [vaccinates(x,y)]

which is true just in case *most* assignments of values to x and y that make "[man(x) & donkey(y) & buys(x,y)]" true also make "[vaccinates(x,y)]" true. But on its most

natural reading, the truth of (20) requires that most men who buy a donkey vaccinate *every* donkey they buy, whereas (20') can be true as long as most of the donkeys that are bought by men are vaccinated by their respective buyers. Suppose Alan buys five donkeys, Bill buys one donkey, Clive buys one donkey, and no other man buys any donkeys. Sentence (20') will come out true if Alan vaccinates at least four of his donkeys, even if Bill and Clive do not vaccinate their respective donkeys; but in such a situation (20) would be false. (It has been suggested that there is another reading of (20), which requires that most men who buy at least one donkey vaccinate most of the donkeys they buy; but (20') does not capture this reading either.)

From this brief overview it should be clear that both the simple descriptive theory and the simple DR theory need to be refined if they are to do justice to the full range of antecedent/anaphor relations in natural language. For example, the descriptive approach needs to be modified if it is to handle donkey anaphora, perhaps allowing for the possibility of interpreting some donkey pronouns in terms of "all of the" rather than "the" (Davies 1981, Neale 1990). And the DR approach needs to be modified to avoid the proportion problem and also permit pronouns to be understood with various scopes. At the time of writing, more sophisticated versions of these theories are being developed, as are alternatives to both.

See also Kripke, Saul; Logical Form; Ontology; Philosophy of Language; Quine, Willard Van Orman; Russell, Bertrand Arthur William.

Bibliography

Davies, M. *Meaning, Quantification, Necessity.* London: Routledge and Kegan Paul, 1981.

Evans, G. *The Collected Papers.* Oxford: Clarendon Press, 1985.

Evans, G. "Pronouns." *Linguistic Inquiry* 11 (1980): 337–362. (Reprinted in Evans [1985], 214–248.)

Evans, G. "Pronouns, Quantifiers, and Relative Clauses (I)." *Canadian Journal of Philosophy* 7 (1977): 467–536. (Reprinted in Evans [1985], 76–152.)

Geach, P. *Reference and Generality.* Ithaca, NY: Cornell University Press, 1962.

Heim, I. *The Semantics of Definite and Indefinite Noun Phrases.* Ph.D diss. University of Massachusetts, Amherst, 1982.

Kamp, H. "A Theory of Truth and Semantic Interpretation." In *Formal Methods in the Study of Natural Language*, edited by J. Groenendijk et al. Amsterdam Centre, 1981.

Karttunen, L. "Discourse Referents." In *Syntax and Semantics* 7, *Notes from the Linguistic Underground*, edited by J. McCawley. New York: Academic Press, 1976.

Kripke, S. "Naming and Necessity." In *Semantics of Natural Language*, edited by D. Davidson and G. Harman. Dordrecht: Reidel, 1972.

Neale, S. *Descriptions.* Cambridge, MA: MIT Press, 1990.

Quine, W. V. O. *Word and Object.* Cambridge, MA: MIT Press, 1960.

Soames, S. "Attitudes and Anaphora." *Philosophical Perspectives* 8 (1994): 251–272.

Stephen Neale (1996)

ANAPHORA [ADDENDUM]

Most recent work on anaphora has tended to focus on cases in which a pronoun is anaphoric on what appears to be a quantifier phrase, where it cannot be understood as a variable bound by that quantifier phrase (as it is in 5 and 6 above). Two central cases of this sort, to which attention will be confined here, are as follows. First, there is *discourse anaphora* in which the anaphoric expression is in a different sentence from its antecedent (see also 12, and 15–17 above):

(21) Few cars are gasoline and electric hybrids. They are expensive;

(22) A woman is at the door. She is from Santa Monica.

There are at least two reasons for thinking that the pronouns in 21 and 22 are not variables bound by its quantifier antecedents. Garreth Evans (1977) appears to be the first to discuss both reasons. Focusing on 21, the first reason is that such a treatment gets the wrong truth conditions for an example like 21. If *they* is a bound variable in 21, the two sentences of 21 together should be equivalent to: 21a) Few cars: x (x is a gasoline and electric hybrid and x is expensive). But this is obviously incorrect because 21 entails that few cars are hybrids, whereas 21a does not.

Second, it is generally thought that the scope of a quantifier cannot extend beyond the sentence in which it occurs. If that is correct, then the pronoun in 21 falls outside the scope of its quantifier antecedent and so cannot be bound by it. So, though the pronoun in 21 has a quantified antecedent, it cannot be understood as a variable bound by it.

Another sort of case in which this occurs is that of *donkey anaphora*, which comes in two varieties as illustrated above by 18 and 19. Let us call the former *conditional donkey anaphora* and the latter *relative clause donkey anaphora.* In the case of 18, all independent evidence suggests that (what appears to be) the quantifier "a donkey" cannot take wide scope over the conditional and bind the pronoun in the consequent. When one attempts

to do this with other quantifiers, one cannot bind the pronoun, as is the case here:

(23) If John buys every donkey$_1$, he beats it$_1$.

And even if "a donkey" could somehow scope over the conditional and bind the pronoun in the consequent, assuming it is as usual an existential quantifier, we still wouldn't get the right truth conditions for 18, which intuitively require donkey-owning men to vaccinate every donkey they own. In the case of 19, again the independent evidence suggests that a quantifier occurring in a relative clause cannot bind a pronoun outside the relative clause:

(24) Every teacher who flunks every male student$_1$ hates him$_1$.

So both donkey anaphora and discourse anaphora require treating the anaphoric pronoun as something other than a bound variable. Thus both of these phenomena shall be grouped under the heading *unbound anaphora.* In addition to the descriptive and discourse representation approaches discussed above, there are at least two other attempts to treat unbound anaphora.

First, there are Dynamic Logic Accounts (DL), originally formulated by Jeroen Groenendijk and Martin Stokhof (1991). Other DL accounts have been suggested by Gennaro Chierchia (1995) and Makoto Kanazawa (1994a and 1994b). DL accounts, which are descended from DR accounts, characteristically claim that quantifiers can semantically bind pronouns even if those pronouns do not occur in their syntactic scopes. The pronouns in 18, 19, 21, and 22, then, are semantically (though not syntactically) bound by their quantifier antecedents even though they are beyond the syntactic scope of their antecedents. DL also provides new accounts of the semantics of conditionals and universal quantification in assigning to 18 and 19 the intuitively correct truth conditions.

The second other sort of approach to unbound anaphora (in addition to descriptive and DR approaches) is the Context Dependent Quantifier Approach (CDQ), which was first suggested by George Wilson (1984) and further articulated and defended by Jeffrey King (1987, 1991, 1994, 2005). The CDQ approach holds that in cases of unbound anaphora, the pronouns in question are quantifiers. The forces (universal or existential), restrictions (what the quantifiers range over—e.g., "every student" ranges over students), and relative scopes of these pronouns and quantifiers are determined by features of their linguistic contexts. Thus, according to CDQ, the anaphoric pronouns in cases of unbound anaphora are contextually sensitive devices of quantification.

The precise natures of the quantifications they express, the forces, restrictions, and relative scope of the quantifications, are determined by features of their linguistic contexts. In 22, CDQ holds that the pronoun expresses the existential quantifier normally expressed outside any context by the indefinite "a woman who is at the door." Similar remarks apply to 18 and 19, except that the semantics of the conditional interacts with the pronoun qua quantifier to get the proper reading of 18 (King 2005); and in 19 the pronoun qua quantifier takes narrow scope with respect to the universal quantifier "every man" (because its antecedent does as well).

See also Quantifiers in Natural Language; Reference; Syntax.

Bibliography

Chierchia, Gennaro. *Dynamics of Meaning: Anaphora, Presupposition, and the Theory of Grammar.* Chicago: University of Chicago Press, 1995.

Evans, Gareth. "Pronouns, Quantifiers, and Relative Clauses." *Canadian Journal of Philosophy* 8 (3) (1977): 467–536.

Groenendijk, J., and M. Stokhof. "Dynamic Predicate Logic." *Linguistics and Philosophy* 14 (1991): 39–100.

Kanazawa, Makoto, ed. "Dynamic Generalized Quantifiers and Montonicity." In *Dynamics, Polarity, and Quantification.* Stanford, CA: Center for the Study of Language and Information, 1994a.

Kanazawa, Makoto. "Weak vs. Strong Readings of Donkey Sentences in a Dynamic Setting." *Linguistics and Philosophy* 17 (2) (1994b): 109–158.

King, Jeffrey C. "Anaphora and Operators."*Philosophical Perspectives, Logic, and Language* 8 (1994).

King, Jeffrey C. "Context Dependent Quantifiers and Donkey Anaphora." *Canadian Journal of Philosophy* (2005).

King, Jeffrey C. "Instantial Terms, Anaphora, and Arbitrary Objects." *Philosophical Studies* 61 (1991): 239–265.

King, Jeffrey C. "Pronouns, Descriptions, and the Semantics of Discourse." *Philosophical Studies* 51 (1987): 341–363.

Wilson, George. "Pronouns and Pronominal Descriptions: A New Semantical 'Category.'" *Philosophical Studies* 45 (1984): 1–30.

Jeffrey C. King (2005)

ANARCHISM

"Anarchism" is a social philosophy that rejects authoritarian government and maintains that voluntary institutions are best suited to express man's natural social tendencies. Historically the word *anarchist,* which derives from the Greek *an archos,* meaning "no government," appears first to have been used pejoratively to indicate one who denies all law and wishes to promote chaos. It was used in this sense against the Levelers during the English Civil War and during the French Revolution by most parties in criticizing those who stood to the left of them along the political spectrum. The first use of the word as an approbatory description of a positive philosophy appears to have been by Pierre-Joseph Proudhon when, in his *Qu'est-ce-que la propriété?* (*What is property?*, Paris, 1840), he described himself as an anarchist because he believed that political organization based on authority should be replaced by social and economic organization based on voluntary contractual agreement.

Nevertheless, the two uses of the word have survived together and have caused confusion in discussing anarchism, which to some has appeared a doctrine of destruction and to others a benevolent doctrine based on a faith in the innate goodness of man. There has been further confusion through the association of anarchism with nihilism and terrorism. In fact, anarchism, which is based on faith in natural law and justice, stands at the opposite pole to nihilism, which denies all moral laws. Similarly, there is no necessary connection between anarchism, which is a social philosophy, and terrorism, which is a political means occasionally used by individual anarchists but also by actionists belonging to a wide variety of movements that have nothing in common with anarchism.

Anarchism aims at the utmost possible freedom compatible with social life, in the belief that voluntary cooperation by responsible individuals is not merely more just and equitable but is also, in the long run, more harmonious and ordered in its effects than authoritarian government. Anarchist philosophy has taken many forms, none of which can be defined as an orthodoxy, and its exponents have deliberately cultivated the idea that it is an open and mutable doctrine. However, all its variants combine a criticism of existing governmental societies, a vision of a future libertarian society that might replace them, and a projected way of attaining this society by means outside normal political practice. Anarchism in general rejects the state. It denies the value of democratic procedures because they are based on majority rule and on the delegation of the responsibility that the individual should retain. It criticizes utopian philosophies because they aim at a static "ideal" society. It inclines toward internationalism and federalism, and, while the views of anarchists on questions of economic organization vary greatly, it may be said that all of them reject what William Godwin called accumulated property.

Attempts have been made by anarchist apologists to trace the origins of their point of view in primitive non-governmental societies. There has also been a tendency to detect anarchist pioneers among a wide variety of teachers and writers who, for various religious or philosophical reasons, have criticized the institution of government, have rejected political activity, or have placed a great value on individual freedom. In this way such varied ancestors have been found as Laozi, Zeno, Spartacus, Étienne de La Boétie, Thomas Münzer, François Rabelais, François Fénelon, Denis Diderot, and Jonathan Swift; anarchist trends have also been detected in many religious groups aiming at a communalistic order, such as the Essenes, the early Christian apostles, the Anabaptists, and the Doukhobors. However, while it is true that some of the central libertarian ideas are to be found in varying degrees among these men and movements, the first forms of anarchism as a developed social philosophy appeared at the beginning of the modern era, when the medieval order had disintegrated, the Reformation had reached its radical, sectarian phase, and the rudimentary forms of modern political and economic organization had begun to appear. In other words, the emergence of the modern state and of capitalism is paralleled by the emergence of the philosophy that, in various forms, has opposed them most fundamentally.

WINSTANLEY

Although Proudhon was the first writer to call himself an anarchist, at least two predecessors outlined systems that contain all the basic elements of anarchism. The first was Gerrard Winstanley (1609–c. 1660), a linen draper who led the small movement of the Diggers during the Commonwealth. Winstanley and his followers protested in the name of a radical Christianity against the economic distress that followed the Civil War and against the inequality that the grandees of the New Model Army seemed intent on preserving. In 1649–1650 the Diggers squatted on stretches of common land in southern England and attempted to set up communities based on work on the land and the sharing of goods. The communities failed, but a series of pamphlets by Winstanley survived, of which The New Law of Righteousness (1649) was the most important. Advocating a rational Christianity, Winstanley equated Christ with "the universal liberty" and declared the universally corrupting nature of authority. He saw "an equal privilege to share in the blessing of liberty" and detected an intimate link between the institution of property and the lack of freedom. In the society he sketched, work would be done in common and the products shared

equally through a system of open storehouses, without commerce.

Like later libertarian philosophers, Winstanley saw crime as a product of economic inequality and maintained that the people should not put trust in rulers. Rather, they should act for themselves in order to end social injustice, so that the land should become a "common treasury" where free men could live in plenty. Winstanley died in obscurity and, outside the small and ephemeral group of Diggers, he appears to have wielded no influence, except possibly over the early Quakers.

GODWIN

A more elaborate sketch of anarchism, although still without the name, was provided by William Godwin in his Enquiry concerning Political Justice (1793). Godwin differed from most later anarchists in preferring to revolutionary action the gradual and, as it seemed to him, more natural process of discussion among men of good will, by which he hoped truth would eventually triumph through its own power. Godwin, who was influenced by the English tradition of Dissent and the French philosophy of the Enlightenment, put forward in a developed form the basic anarchist criticisms of the state, of accumulated property, and of the delegation of authority through democratic procedure. He believed in a "fixed and immutable morality," manifesting itself through "universal benevolence"; man, he thought, had no right "to act anything but virtue and to utter anything but truth," and his duty, therefore, was to act toward his fellow men in accordance with natural justice. Justice itself was based on immutable truths; human laws were fallible, and men should use their understandings to determine what is just and should act according to their own reasons rather than in obedience to the authority of "positive institutions," which always form barriers to enlightened progress. Godwin rejected all established institutions and all social relations that suggested inequality or the power of one man over another, including marriage and even the role of an orchestra conductor. For the present he put his faith in small groups of men seeking truth and justice; for the future, in a society of free individuals organized locally in parishes and linked loosely in a society without frontiers and with the minimum of organization. Every man should take part in the production of necessities and should share his produce with all in need, on the basis of free distribution. Godwin distrusted an excess of political or economic cooperation; on the other hand, he looked forward to a freer intercourse of individuals through the progressive breaking down of social and economic barriers. Here, conceived in the primitive form of a society of free landworkers and artisans, was the first sketch of an anarchist world. The logical completeness of *Political Justice,* and its astonishing anticipation of later libertarian arguments, make it, as Sir Alexander Gray said, "the sum and substance of anarchism."

NINETEENTH-CENTURY EUROPEAN ANARCHISM

Despite their similarities to later libertarian philosophies, however, the systems of Winstanley and Godwin had no perceptible influence on nineteenth-century European anarchism, which was an independent development and which derived mainly from the peculiar fusion of early French socialist thought and German neo-Hegelianism in the mind of Proudhon, the Besancon printer who has been called the father of anarchism. This tradition centered largely on a developing social revolutionary movement that attained mass dimensions in France, Italy, and Spain (where anarchism remained strong until the triumph of Franco in 1939), and to a lesser extent in French-speaking Switzerland, the Ukraine and Latin America. Apart from Proudhon, its main advocates were Michael Bakunin, Prince Peter Kropotkin, Errico Malatesta, Sebastien Faure, Gustav Landauer, Elisée Reclus, and Rudolf Rocker, with Max Stirner and Lev Tolstoy on the individualist and pacifist fringes, respectively. Also, there arose among nineteenth-century anarchists a mystique that action and even theory should emerge from the people. Libertarian attitudes, particularly in connection with the anarchosyndicalism of France and Spain, were influenced by the rationalization and even romanticization of the experience of social struggle; the writings of Fernand Pelloutier and Georges Sorel in particular emanate from this aspect of the anarchist movement. Nineteenth-century anarchism assumed a number of forms, and the points of variation between them lie in three main areas: the use of violence, the degree of cooperation compatible with individual liberty, and the form of economic organization appropriate to a libertarian society.

INDIVIDUALIST ANARCHISM. Individualist anarchism lies on the extreme and sometimes dubious fringe of the libertarian philosophies since, in seeking to assure the absolute independence of the person, it often seems to negate the social basis of true anarchism. This is particularly the case with Max Stirner, who specifically rejected society as well as the state and reduced organization to a union of egoists based on the mutual respect of "unique" individuals, each standing upon his "might." French anar-

chism during the 1890s was particularly inclined toward individualism, which expressed itself partly in a distrust of organization and partly in the actions of terrorists like "Ravachol" and Émile Henry, who alone or in tiny groups carried out assassinations of people over whom they had appointed themselves both judges and executioners. A milder form of individualist anarchism was that advocated by the American libertarian writer Benjamin Tucker (1854–1939), who rejected violence in favor of refusal to obey and who, like all individualists, opposed any form of economic communism. What he asked was that property should be distributed and equalized so that every man should have control over the product of his labor.

MUTUALISM. Mutualism, developed by Proudhon, differed from individualist anarchism in its stress on the social element in human behavior. It rejected both political action and revolutionary violence—some of Proudhon's disciples even objected to strikes as a form of coercion—in favor of the reform of society by the peaceful spread of workers' associations, devoted particularly to mutual credit between producers. A recurrent mutualist plan, never fulfilled, was that of the people's bank, which would arrange the exchange of goods on the basis of labor notes. The mutualists recognized that workers' syndicates might be necessary for the functioning of industry and public utilities, but they rejected large-scale collectivization as a danger to liberty and based their economic approach as far as possible on individual possession of the means of production by peasants and small craftsmen united in a framework of exchange and credit arrangements. The mutualists laid great stress on federalist organization from the local commune upward as a substitute for the national state. Mutualism had a wide following among French artisans during the 1860s. Its exponents were fervently internationalist and played a great part in the formation of the International Workingmen's Association in 1864; their influence diminished, however, with the rise of collectivism as an alternative libertarian philosophy.

COLLECTIVISM. Collectivism is the form of anarchism associated with Michael Bakunin. The collectivist philosophy was developed by Bakunin from 1864 onward, when he was forming the first international organizations of anarchists, the International Brotherhood and the International Alliance of Social Democracy. It was collectivist anarchism that formed the principal opposition to Marxism in the International Workingmen's Association and thus began the historic rivalry between libertarian and authoritarian views of socialism. Bakunin and the other collectivists agreed with the mutualists in their rejection of the state and of political methods, in their stress on federalism, and in their view that the worker should be rewarded according to his labor. On the other hand, they differed in stressing the need for revolutionary means to bring about the downfall of the state and the establishment of a libertarian society. Most important, they advocated the public ownership and the exploitation through workers' associations of the land and all services and means of production. While in mutualism the individual worker had been the basic unit, in collectivism it was the group of workers; Bakunin specifically rejected individualism of any kind and maintained that anarchism was a social doctrine and must be based on the acceptance of collective responsibilities.

ANARCHIST COMMUNISM. Collectivism survived as the dominant anarchist philosophy in Spain until the 1930s; elsewhere it was replaced during the 1870s by the anarchist communism that was associated particularly with Kropotkin, although it seems likely that Kropotkin was merely the most articulate exponent of a trend that grew out of discussions among anarchist intellectuals in Geneva during the years immediately after the Paris Commune of 1871. Through Kropotkin's literary efforts anarchist communism was much more elaborately worked out than either mutualism or collectivism; in such books as *La conquête du pain* (*The conquest of bread*, 1892) and *Fields, Factories and Workshops* (1899) Kropotkin elaborated the scheme of a semiutopian decentralized society based on an integration of agriculture and industry, of town life and country life, of education and apprenticeship. Kropotkin also linked his theories closely with current evolutionary theories in the fields of anthropology and biology; anarchism, he suggested in *Mutual Aid* (1902), was the final stage in the development of cooperation as a factor in evolution.

Anarchist communism differed from collectivism on only one fundamental point—the way in which the product of labor should be shared. In place of the collectivist and mutualist idea of remuneration according to hours of labor, the anarchist communists proclaimed the slogan "From each according to his means, to each according to his needs" and envisaged open warehouses from which any man could have what he wanted. They reasoned, first, that work was a natural need that men could be expected to fulfill without the threat of want and, second, that where no restriction was placed on available goods, there would be no temptation for any man to take more than he could use. The anarchist communists laid great stress on local communal organization and even on local economic self-sufficiency as a guarantee of independence.

ANARCHOSYNDICALISM. Anarchosyndicalism began to develop in the late 1880s, when many anarchists entered the French trade unions, or syndicates, which were just beginning to reemerge after the period of suppression that followed the Paris Commune. Later, anarchist militants moved into key positions in the Confédération Générale du Travail, founded in 1895, and worked out the theories of anarchosyndicalism. They shifted the basis of anarchism to the syndicates, which they saw as organizations that united the producers in common struggle as well as in common work. The common struggle should take the form of "direct action," primarily in industry, since there the workers could strike most sharply at their closest enemies, the capitalists; the highest form of direct action, the general strike, could end by paralyzing not merely capitalism but also the state.

When the state was paralyzed, the syndicates, which had been the organs of revolt, could be transformed into the basic units of the free society; the workers would take over the factories where they had been employees and would federate by industries. Anarchosyndicalism created a mystique of the working masses that ran counter to individualist trends; and the stress on the producers, as distinct from the consumers, disturbed the anarchist communists, who were haunted by the vision of massive trade unions ossifying into monolithic institutions. In France, Italy, and Spain, however, it was the syndicalist variant that brought anarchism its first and only mass following. The men who elaborated the philosophy of anarchosyndicalism included militants, such as Fernand Pelloutier, Georges Yvetot, and Émile Pouget, who among them created the vision of a movement arising from the genius of the working people. There were also intellectuals outside the movement who drew theoretical conclusions from anarchosyndicalist practice; the most important was Sorel, the author of *Réflexions sur la violence* (*Reflections on violence,* 1908), who saw the general strike as a saving "social myth" that would maintain society in a state of struggle and, therefore, of health.

PACIFIST ANARCHISM. Pacifist anarchism has taken two forms. That of Tolstoy attempted to give rational and concrete form to Christian ethics. Tolstoy rejected all violence; he advocated a moral revolution, its great tactic the refusal to obey. There was much, however, in Tolstoy's criticisms of contemporary society and his suggestions for the future that paralleled other forms of anarchism. He denounced the state, law, and property; he foresaw cooperative production and distribution according to need.

Later a pacifist trend appeared in the anarchist movement in western Europe; its chief exponent was the Dutch ex-socialist, Domela Nieuwenhuis. It differed from strict Tolstoyism by accepting syndicalist forms of struggle that stopped short of violence, particularly the millenarian general strike for the abolition of war.

Despite their differences, all these forms of anarchism were united not merely in their rejection of the state, of politics, and of accumulated property, but also in certain more elusive attitudes. In its avoidance of partisan organization and political practices, anarchism retained more of the moral element than did other movements of protest. This aspect was shown with particular sharpness in the desire of its exponents for the simplification of life, not merely in the sense of removing the complications of authority, but also in eschewing the perils of wealth and establishing a frugal sufficiency as the basis for life. Progress, in the sense of bringing to all men a steadily rising supply of material goods, has never appealed to the anarchists; indeed, it is doubtful if their philosophy is at all progressive in the ordinary sense. They reject the present, but they reject it in the name of a future of austere liberty that will resurrect the lost virtues of a more natural past, a future in which struggle will not be ended, but merely transformed within the dynamic equilibrium of a society that rejects utopia and knows neither absolutes nor perfections.

The main difference between the anarchists and the socialists, including the Marxists, lies in the fact that while the socialists maintain that the state must be taken over as the first step toward its dissolution, the anarchists argue that, since power corrupts, any seizure of the existing structure of authority can only lead to its perpetuation. Anarchosyndicalists, however, regard their unions as the skeleton of a new society growing up within the old.

The problem of reconciling social harmony with complete individual freedom is a recurrent one in anarchist thought. It has been argued that an authoritarian society produces antisocial reactions, which would vanish in freedom. It has also been suggested, by Godwin and Kropotkin particularly, that public opinion will suffice to deter those who abuse their liberty. George Orwell, however, has pointed out that the reliance on public opinion as a force replacing overt coercion might lead to a moral tyranny which, having no codified bounds, could in the end prove more oppressive than any system of laws.

See also Bakunin, Mikhail Aleksandrovich; Communism; Diderot, Denis; Fénelon, François de Salignac de la Mothe; Godwin, William; Kropotkin, Pëtr Alekseevich; Laozi; Pacifism; Proudhon, Pierre-Joseph; Sorel, Georges; Stirner, Max; Swift, Jonathan; Tolstoy, Lev (Leo) Nikolaevich.

Bibliography

Avrich, Paul. *Anarchist Portraits*. Princeton: Princeton University Press, 1988.

Bakunin, Michael. *Michael Bakunin: Statism and Anarach.* Translated and edited by Marshall S. Shatz. Cambridge U.K.: Cambridge University Press, 1990.

Crowder, George. *Classical Anarchism: The Political Thought of Godwin, Proudhon, Bakunin, and Kropotkin.* Oxford: Oxford University Press, 1991.

Eltzbacher, Paul. *Anarchism.* Translated by Steven T. Byington. New York: Tucker, 1908.

Gans, Chaim. *Philosophical Anarchism and Political Disobedience.* Cambridge, U.K.: Cambridge University Press, 1992.

Godwin, William. *Political and Philosophical Writings of William Godwin,* 7 vols. Edited by Mark Philp. London: Pickering, 1993.

Gray, Alexander. *The Socialist Tradition, Moses to Lenin.* London: Longmans, Green, 1946.

Guérin, Daniel. *Anarchism: From Theory to Practice.* Translated by Mary Klopper. New York: Monthly Review Press, 1970.

Joll, James. *The Anarchists.* London: Eyre and Spottiswoode, 1964.

May, Todd. *The Political Philosophy of Poststructuralist Anarchism.* University Park: Pennsylvania State University Press, 1994.

Miller, David. *Anarchism.* London: Dent, 1984.

Nettlau, Max. *Der Anarchismus von Proudhon zu Kropotkin.* Berlin: Syndikalist, 1927.

Nettlau, Max. *Anarchisten und Social-Revolutionäre.* Berlin: Syndikalist, 1931.

Nettlau, Max. *Der Vorfrühling der Anarchie.* Berlin: Syndikalist, 1925.

Ritter, Alan. *Anarchism: A Theoretical Analysis.* Cambridge, U.K.: Cambridge University Press, 1980.

Rocker, Rudolf. *Anarcho-Syndicalism.* London: Secker and Warburg, 1938.

Russell, Bertrand. "Bakunin and Anarchism." In *Proposed Roads to Freedom.* New York: Holt, 1919.

Wolff, Robert Paul. *In Defense of Anarchism.* New York: Harper and Row, 1970.

Woodcock, George. *Anarchism: A History of Libertarian Ideas and Movements.* Cleveland: World Publishing, 1962.

Zenker, E. V. *Anarchism.* London: Methuen, 1898.

George Woodcock (1967)
Bibliography updated by Philip Reed (2005)

ANAXAGORAS OF CLAZOMENAE
(c. 500–428 BCE)

One of the leading philosophers of the fifth century BCE, Anaxagoras continued the cosmological style of philosophy begun in Miletus in the preceding century. Born in Clazomenae in Asia Minor around 500, he came to Athens and spent thirty years there, enjoying access to intellectual circles through his friendship with Pericles. Two alternate accounts of his dates in Athens are available: either he came around 480 and stayed until 450, or he came around 460 and stayed until 430. Because his name is associated with a meteor that fell near Aegospotami around 467, and his theory of the Nile floods was known to Aeschylus (d. 456), it appears that his work was well known already in the 460s, supporting an early date at least for his philosophical activity. Anaxagoras is said to have fled Athens to avoid prosecution on a charge of impiety, and he finished his days in Lampsacus in northern Greece, where he died in 428. He wrote a book that was well-known in Athens in the late fifth century BCE and was available until the sixth century CE. About twenty fragments of the book survive, describing some key points of his theory. Although Anaxagoras wrote in simple Ionic prose, many details of his theory remain obscure and controversial.

Like most natural philosophers of his time, Anaxagoras tells how the world arose from a primeval chaos. Initially, all things (kinds of matter, presumably) were mixed together to such an extent that nothing was differentiated. But Mind (*Nous*) caused a whirling motion to start, which caused different materials to separate out, as in a centrifuge, leading to the articulation of the cosmos. At the center of the cosmos is a flat earth, surrounded by stony bodies in the heavens carried around by the cosmic vortex motion. The sun is a hot stone and the moon an earthy body. This cosmogony broadly follows the pattern set by Anaximander, and it shows the influence of Anaximenes in some details. In making the heavenly bodies spherical bodies, Anaxagoras may be following the pattern of Parmenides's cosmology.

ANAXAGORAS'S PRINCIPLES

What is innovative about Anaxagoras's theory is not the sequence of his cosmogony, but the principles on which he bases it. In the first place, he adheres to a principle of No Becoming—previously articulated by Parmenides—according to which nothing can come to be out of what is not. But whereas Parmenides seems to have meant this

principle as a grounds for ruling out cosmological theories, Anaxagoras uses it as a restriction on what kind of explanation is allowed. Second, Anaxagoras follows a principle of Universal Mixture, which he states repeatedly, to the effect that everything is mixed with everything. There has been much controversy among interpreters about what the domain of "everything," in its two occurrences, is. Whatever the precise interpretation, the principle clearly applies to the primeval chaos insofar as all stuffs seem to be thoroughly mixed; but Anaxagoras maintains that even when the separation process takes over, some quantity of every stuff remains mixed with any given stuff. Third, Anaxagoras holds to a principle of Infinite Divisibility, according to which there are no minimal particles of matter—no atoms. Finally, Anaxagoras accepts a principle of Predominance, such that any stretch of matter manifests the properties of whatever stuff it has the largest quantity. Thus, if there is more water than salt in a mixture, people perceive it to be water; if more salt than water, they then perceive it to be salt.

It is generally agreed that the point of Anaxagoras's principles is to account for change with the least allowance for novelty: When one thing seems to change into another thing, the second does not arise out of nothing, but was already present (if in a lower concentration). Thus there is change, but no radical coming to be out of what is not—a possibility forbidden by Parmenides. What is less clear is whether Anaxagoras succeeds in formulating a coherent account of change. Whether he succeeds depends in large measure on how one interprets the details of his theories of matter and change, which will be discussed briefly below.

CONTROVERSIES

A fifth principle that is often attributed to Anaxagoras is Homoiomereity, using a Greek term of Aristotle's that designates a stuff in which the parts are like the whole. Thus if one divides a quantity of water in half, one gets two (smaller) quantities of water; but if one divides a chair in half one does not get two chairs. The former sort of being is called *homoiomerous*. Aristotle calls Anaxagoras's basic stuffs homoiomeries, but it is not clear whether he intends to say of them that they have the property of homoiomereity; or whether he simply wishes to denote things that in Aristotle's own system are homoiomeries (e.g., flesh and bone), whatever their properties for Anaxagoras. In any case, neither the term nor the property is found in the fragments of Anaxagoras—except as the property is applied to Mind, which does not behave like a physical element.

Another controversy concerns the relationship between stuffs and contraries, or qualities in general. Anaxagoras mentions qualities such as hot and cold alongside stuffs such as earth (fr. 4) and maintains that contrary qualities cannot be cut off from each other (fr. 8). Does Anaxagoras recognize a strong categorial difference between stuffs and qualities, and if so, what is their relationship? According to one interpretation, the stuffs are composed of qualities, such that different amounts of hot, cold, wet, dry, and so on, combine to constitute different stuffs. Thus Universal Mixture signifies that every stuff is potentially in every stuff because by changing the ratios of qualities one can produce other results. On this view Anaxagoras is a reductionist who reduces stuffs to qualities. Defenders of this view have sometimes claimed that only on this interpretation can Anaxagoras's principles be rendered consistent. Yet, other interpreters have shown that his principles can be made consistent without reducing stuffs to qualities. Critics of the reductionist view see Anaxagoras's stuffs as elemental bodies. Qualities could be either stuffs in their own right, or simply properties that happen to describe certain stuffs.

Another controversial question is the meaning of the seeds Anaxagoras refers to in fr. 4 as being part of the original mixture. Are these biological seeds, as some interpreters hold, from which the first plants and animals grew? Or are they structural principles generally, to account for the presence of shapes and structures which emerge from the formless mixture (perhaps including, but not confined to, shapes of plants and animals)? Or are they small particles of a given stuff that are present as starting points for the growth of that given stuff? (A number of other hypotheses have also been advanced.) On many of these hypotheses, at least, no stretch of matter could be homoiomerous, for it would contain seeds having a different composition from the whole. Anaxagoras does not say enough about seeds to allow scholars to make a clear determination in favor of one of these hypotheses.

In another difficult saying in fr. 4, Anaxagoras talks about an alternative to "our"world. But is his statement merely counterfactual, or does he hold that there are other worlds, like the atomists; or worlds within worlds, as among Leibniz's monads; or repeating worlds, as does Empedocles? There is no more consensus on this question than on the other controversies mentioned.

MIND AND KNOWLEDGE

One of Anaxagoras's most interesting and innovative theories is his philosophy of mind. As has been shown, Anaxagoras makes mind responsible for the beginning of the cosmic vortex. He says that mind is "boundless, autonomous, and mixed with no object" (fr. 12). If it were not "by itself" it would be mixed with everything, by Universal Mixture, which would hinder it from ruling things. As it is, mind is "the finest of all objects and the purest, and it exercises complete oversight over everything and prevails above all" (fr. 12). Mind is present in some things, namely those things that have soul, but it does not mix with them. Thus mind is not immaterial, but it is not material in the same way as the stuffs are. It exercises control over the stuffs of the world and comprehends all things. Anaxagoras's theory suggests a dualism of mind and matter, though it is not nearly as radical as Descartes's dualism. In any case, Anaxagoras is the first philosopher to recognize mind as a distinct reality alongside physical entities. In cosmology, Anaxagoras is the first philosopher to support creationism—involving not a creation ex nihilo, to be sure, but an organization of preexisting elements by an intelligent agency distinct from those elements.

Anaxagoras accounts for sense perception as the effect of opposite qualities on opposites; thus one perceives hot by cold and wet by dry. He observes that because of the weakness of the senses people are not able to perceive the truth (fr. 21). But, on the positive side, "Appearances are a vision of the invisible" (fr. 21a). A serious philosophical problem for Anaxagoras is how humans can have knowledge at all. Because everything is mixed in everything, if I perceive something as water, I may infer that it is composed of water, and salt, and every other kind of stuff. But how can I say that I know the body before me as water if I have to analyze it as, among other things, water, and the water that I analyze it into is a theoretical entity I do not perceive? I seem to be involved in a regress that keeps me from knowing anything, except in a purely hypothetical way, in which everything has exactly the same components (all the stuffs there are), all of which are perceptually inaccessible to me.

Here, fr. 21a (just cited) provides a possible way out of the problem. People know by an inference to the best (or only possible) explanation that there are countless basic stuffs in the world. Further, they are acquainted with those stuffs by their manifestations to sense experience. Because when some stuff predominates, it gives its character to the whole body it predominates in, they can infer the character of, for instance, elemental water from the character of phenomenal water in bodies of water they encounter. Similarly, people can infer the character of all other basic stuffs from their appearances, because, by hypothesis, the basic stuffs are like their phenomenal counterparts. People cannot give an adequate verbal definition of water, but they can give an ostensive definition of it. Thus they know the structure of reality by theory, but the content of reality by experience. This same sort of strategy appears to have appealed to Democritus, who approved of Anaxagoras's statement in B21a and applied it to his atoms (for a limited range of properties).

PHYSICAL THEORY

Though in some ways conventional, Anaxagoras's physical theories made some important advances. Like most of his predecessors, Anaxagoras envisioned a flat earth at the center of the circling heavens; the earth is held in place by air pressure, and the solstices of the sun are caused by winds in the heavens. He explained the annual floods of the Nile as the result of melting snows in southern Africa (the Nile is in fact fed by melting snows, but the floods are caused by monsoon rains), a view cited by Aeschylus, Sophocles, and Euripides, and criticized by Herodotus. He gave an essentially correct explanation of hail. His view that the heavenly bodies are earthy or stony was probably novel, and he believed that invisible stones were also carried about aloft with the vortex—in effect, he posited asteroids. When a large meteor fell at Aegospotami, Anaxagoras was given credit for predicting it, and henceforth meteors were included among data to be explained by cosmological theories. He gave the first correct explanation of solar and lunar eclipses (perhaps inspired by Parmenides's recognition that the moon gets its light from the sun), a feat that Aristotle regarded as a paradigm of scientific discovery. He also correctly hypothesized that the moon had mountains and valleys on its surface. In his physical theory he was followed by Archelaus of Athens, and in his teleological tendencies by Diogenes of Apollonia.

After Anaxagoras, natural philosophers mostly accepted his theory of eclipses and his view of heavenly bodies as spherical solid bodies. Though his astronomy was influential among intellectuals, it clashed with popular religious views according to which the sun and moon were gods, and led to an indictment of impiety in Athens. It was the sort of theory that Plato criticized in the *Laws* as leading to atheism. Anaxagoras presumably would reply that his views offered grounds for a more enlightened religion than those based on worshiping forces of nature.

Plato saw one of Anaxagoras's views as offering a new approach to cosmology. If Mind ordered everything with a view to the best, then philosophers should be able to explain the structure of the cosmos on the basis not of how it arose from a primeval chaos, but how it manifests order and value. Plato reports that Anaxagoras's book was disappointing because it failed to exploit this insight, and Aristotle agrees. In fact, Anaxagoras used the same style of explanation as other pre-Socratics stressing the natural capacities of different kinds of matter. But Plato later used Anaxagoras's insight to construct the cosmos on teleological principles in his *Timaeus*. In a sense, then, Anaxagoras provided the impulse for the rational cosmologies of Plato and Aristotle that dominated ancient and medieval thought. He was the first philosopher to make his home in Athens, and also the first to offend the Athenian people. Through the Athenian philosophical tradition he had a lasting influence.

See also Anaximander; Aristotle; Atomism; Cosmology; Descartes, René; Diogenes of Apollonia; Dualism in the Philosophy of Mind; Empedocles; Leucippus and Democritus; Nous; Parmenides of Elea; Philosophy of Mind; Plato; Pre-Socratic Philosophy; Sensa.

Bibliography

Barnes, Jonathan. *The Presocratic Philosophers*. Revised edition. Chaps. 16, 19. London: Routledge, 1982.

Graham, Daniel W. "The Postulates of Anaxagoras." *Apeiron* 27 (1994): 77–121.

Graham, Daniel W. "Was Anaxagoras a Reductionist?" *Ancient Philosophy* 24 (2004): 1–18.

Kerferd, G. B. "Anaxagoras and the Concept of Matter before Aristotle." In *The Pre-Socratics: A Collection of Critical Essays*, edited by Alexander P. D. Mourelatos, 489–503. Garden City, NY: Doubleday, 1974.

Kirk, G. S., J. E. Raven, and M. Schofield. *The Presocratic Philosophers*. 2nd edition, chap. 12. Cambridge, U.K.: Cambridge University Press, 1983.

Lesher, James H. "Mind's Knowledge and Powers of Control in Anaxagoras DK B12." *Phronesis* 40 (1995): 125–142.

Schofield, Malcolm. *An Essay on Anaxagoras*. Cambridge, U.K.: Cambridge University Press, 1980.

Sider, David. *The Fragments of Anaxagoras*. Meisenheim am Glan, Germany: Verlag Anton Hain, 1981.

Taylor, C. C. W. "Anaxagoras and the Atomists." In *Routledge History of Philosophy*, vol. 1: *From the Beginning to Plato*, edited by C. C. W. Taylor, 208–243. London: Routledge, 1997.

Vlastos, Gregory. "The Physical Theory of Anaxagoras." *Philosophical Review* 59 (1950): 31–57. Reprint in Gregory Vlastos's *Studies in Greek Philosophy*, vol. 1, 303–327. Princeton, NJ: Princeton University Press, 1995.

Daniel W. Graham (2005)

ANAXIMANDER
(c. 610 BCE–after 546 BCE)

Anaximander is the first Greek scientist and philosopher whose thought is known to us in any detail. He was born in Miletus c. 610 BCE and died shortly after 546 BCE. He was thus in his twenties in 585 BCE, the year of the famous solar eclipse that Thales is said to have predicted. According to the ancient tradition, Anaximander was the "pupil and successor of Thales"; but in view of our ignorance of Thales' real achievements, it is perhaps Anaximander who should be considered the founder of Greek astronomy and natural philosophy. Nothing is known of his life except an unverifiable report that he led a Milesian colony to Apollonia, on the Black Sea. His lifetime corresponds with the great age of Miletus, when it was the richest and most powerful Greek city in Asia Minor.

His scientific achievements are said to include the first Greek world map, the first Greek star map or celestial globe, and the invention, or rather adaptation, of the gnomon (the vertical pointer of a sundial) for use in measuring the hours of the day and annual variations in the course of the sun. According to Pliny, he also traced the sun's annual path in the ecliptic and noted its inclination with regard to the celestial axis. This last discovery may really belong to a later age, but there is no doubt that Anaximander conceived (and almost certainly constructed) a spherical model for the heavens, in the center of which was placed Earth, as a disk or cylinder whose height was one-third its diameter. The ratio 1:3 seems also to have been used in the spacing of the celestial circles or rings assigned to stars, moon, and sun: The conjectural sizes for these rings are 9, 18, and 27 Earth diameters, respectively. (His strange error in assigning the lowest circle to the stars is unexplained. There is, unfortunately, no evidence to support J. Burnet's attractive suggestion that this circle corresponds not to the fixed stars but to bright planets such as Venus. If we could accept this, the fixed stars might then be assigned to their natural place at the periphery of the celestial sphere.)

Anaximander is thus the author of the first geometrical model of the universe, a model characterized not by vagueness and mystery but by visual clarity and rational proportion, and hence radically different in kind from all known "cosmologies" of earlier literature and myth. The highly rational character of the scheme (despite its factual errors) is best indicated by Anaximander's explanation of Earth's stable position in the center: It remains at rest because of its equal distance from all points of the celestial circumference, having no reason to move in one direction rather than in another. This argument from symmetry contrasts not only with all mythic views but also with the doctrine ascribed to Thales: that Earth floats on water. Here Anaximander is clearly the precursor of the mathematical approach to astronomy developed later by the Pythagoreans, Eudoxus, and Aristarchus.

The book of Anaximander, quoted later under the standard title *On the Nature of Things (peri physeôs)*, seems to have contained a description of his map and celestial model, as well as an account of how the natural world functions and how it reached its present form. Beginning from a first principle called the Boundless or Infinite (*to apeiron*: see below), he describes how "something capable of generating Hot and Cold was separated off … and a sphere of fire from this source grew around the air in the region of earth like bark around a tree. When this sphere was torn off and enclosed in certain rings, the sun and moon and stars came into existence" (Diels-Kranz, 12 A 10). These heavenly bodies are "wheel-like, compressed masses of air filled with fire, which exhale flames from an orifice at one point" (Diels-Kranz, 12 A 17a).

Eclipses and lunar phases are explained by obstruction of the orifices. The sea is what remains of the primeval moisture, the rest having been evaporated as air or dried up by the celestial fire to form Earth. Land, sea, air, and heavens are thus all explained by a continual process of separating off from the primeval pair of Hot (dry) and Cold (wet). Wind, rain, lightning, thunder, and related phenomena are explained by the interaction of these elemental principles (water, air, fire) and opposite powers (hot, cold; dry, moist; thick, thin; light, dark). The origin of living things is explained as part of the same process: They arose as aquatic beings in moisture and later transferred to dry land. The first examples of each species developed to maturity within a protective membrane. In an interesting anticipation of modern ideas, Anaximander remarked that the first human beings could never have survived as helpless infants, but must have been born "from living things of another kind, since the other animals are quickly able to look for their own food, while only man requires prolonged nursing" (Diels-Kranz, 12 A 10).

The one quotation from Anaximander's book that seems to have been preserved in very nearly the original wording is his famous statement on cosmic justice: "Out of those things whence is the generation of existing things, into them also does their destruction take place, as is right and due; for they make retribution and pay the penalty to one another for their offense [or "injustice," adikia], according to the ordering of time." The interpretation of this oldest surviving philosophic text has been a subject of much controversy. The earlier commentators (including Friedrich Nietzsche) interpreted the "injustice" as the separation of individual things from their infinite source and saw the eventual reabsorption of all things back into the *apeiron* as their only fitting atonement. This fails to explain how the things that perish can pay the penalty *to one another*, or why the source of generation is referred to in the plural. It is now generally agreed that offense and compensation must both refer to the strife of opposing principles (such as the hot and cold), and that the "ordering of time" stands primarily for periodic regularity in the daily and seasonal variation of heat, moisture, daylight, and the like. Whether there is also a reference here to a larger cycle in which the cosmos itself would perish into its source is more doubtful.

Anaximander's fame rests chiefly on his doctrine of the Boundless as the *arche*, the starting point and origin of the cosmic process. For him, the term *apeiron* meant "untraversable" or "limitless" rather than "infinite" in any precise mathematical sense. He described this principle with the Homeric epithets for divinity, calling it "ageless and immortal," and probably even "the divine" (*to theion*). This *apeiron* surrounds and embraces all things and apparently "steers" or governs them as well. It seems to have been conceived as ungenerated as well as imperishable, and thus contrasts in every respect with the limited, perishable world it engenders. Our sources refer to "worlds" (*kosmoi*) in the plural; a succession rather than a simultaneous plurality of worlds seems to be meant. The Boundless transcends this process of world creation, circumscribing each individual world in space, outlasting all of them in time, and providing the inexhaustible material source, the eternal motive power, the vital energy, and (presumably) the geometrical form and cyclical regularity for the cosmic process as a whole. In its archaic complexity, the *apeiron* is thus both a physical and a metaphysical or theological concept, and points the way not only to the infinite void of the atomists but also to the cosmic deity of Xenophanes, Aristotle, and the Stoics.

See also Thales of Miletus.

Bibliography

ANCIENT EVIDENCE

Conche, Marcel. *Anaximandre, fragments et témoignages: Texte grec, traduction, introduction & commentaire.* Paris: Presses Universitaire de France, 1991.

Diels, Hermann, and Walther Kranz. *Die Fragmente der Vorsokratiker.* 6th ed. Berlin: Weidmann, 1951. Vol. I, Ch. 12.

Kirk, Geoffrey S., John E. Raven, and Malcolm Schofield, Malcolm. *The Presocratic Philosophers.* 2nd ed. Cambridge, U.K.: Cambridge University Press, 1983, Ch. 3.

IMPORTANT SPECIAL STUDIES

Asmis, Elizabeth. "What Is Anaximander's *Apeiron?*" *Journal of the History of Philosophy* 19 (1981): 279–297.

Barnes, Jonathan. *The Presocratic Philosophers.* 2 vols. London: A & C. Black, 1979.

Burnet, J. *Early Greek Philosophy.* 3rd ed. London: A. and C. Black, 1920.

Classen, C. Joachim. "Anaximander and Anaximenes: The Earliest Greek Theories of Change." *Phronesis* 22 (1977): 89–102.

Couprie, Dirk L., Robert Hahn, and Gerard Robert. *Anaximander in Context: New Studies in the Origins of Greek Philosophy.* Albany: State University of New York Press, 2003.

Engmann, Joyce. "Cosmic Justice in Anaximander." *Phronesis* 36 (1991): 1–26.

Freudenthal, Gad. "The Theory of the Opposites and an Ordered Universe: Physics and Metaphysics in Anaximander." *Phronesis* 31 (1986): 197–228.

Hahn, Robert. *Anaximander and the Architects: The Contributions of Egyptian and Greek Architectural Technologies to the Origins of Greek Philosophy.* Albany: State University of New York Press, 2001.

Kahn, Charles H. *Anaximander and the Origins of Greek Cosmology.* New York: Columbia University Press, 1960. Reprint, Indianapolis, IN: Hackett, 1994.

McKirahan, Richard. "Anaximander's Infinite Worlds." In *Essays in Ancient Greek Philosophy VI: Before Plato*, edited by Anthony Preus, 49–65. Albany: State University of New York Press, 1989.

Robinson, J., "Anaximander and the Problem of the Earth's Immobility." In *Essays in Ancient Greek philosophy I*, edited by John P. Anton and George L. Kustas, 111–118. Albany: State University of New York Press, 1971.

Shelley, Cameron. "The Influence of Folk Meteorology in the Anaximander Fragment." *Journal for the History of Ideas* 61 (2000): 1–17.

Vlastos, Gregory. "Equality and Justice in the Early Greek Cosmogonies." *Classical Philology* 42 (1947): 156–178.

Charles H. Kahn (1967)
Bibliography updated by Christian Wildberg (2005)

ANAXIMENES
(6th century BCE)

Anaximenes was the third and last member (the others were Thales and Anaximander) of what is traditionally called the Milesian school of natural philosophers (*physiologoi*). The date of his death is estimated 528/526 BCE; it is probable that he "flourished" about 545 BCE. Although little is known about his life and work, fragments of ancient testimony credit him with studies under his older contemporary, Anaximander; with the writing of a book in "simple Ionic"; and with the doctrine that air is the underlying principle of the universe, changes in physical state being the result of its condensation and rarefaction. It is likely that Aristotle read Anaximenes' book and that Theophrastus had access to it. Several of the doxographers (Aëtius, Hippolytus, Diogenes Laertius) may have read later Hellenistic versions of the work.

On the strength of ancient testimony, historians of philosophy after Aristotle regarded Anaximenes' doctrine as a contribution to the Milesian debates on Nature. They assumed that from Thales to Anaximenes there was a continuous development in physical thought, and they insisted that this development was intelligible only in terms of the supposedly unique problem of the period: the birth and structure of the physical world. On this interpretation, Anaximenes' air was taken to be an *arche*, and his condensation-rarefaction doctrine was construed as a theory about physical transformations. The physical system reconstructed along these lines was then usually shown to be, in comparison with that of Anaximander, not as cogent; and whatever could not be accommodated within such a reconstruction was relegated to Anaximenes' "retrogressive astronomy."

Recent studies in mythical and early cosmogonic discourse (Hesiod) perhaps call for some revision of the traditional estimate. At a time when mechanical change and biological growth had not yet been distinguished from each other, when physical permanence was regarded as incomprehensible apart from "justice" between the warring Opposites, when inanimate continuity was mistaken for animal kinship, when experience was permitted only to illustrate but never to refute supposed insight, when meteorology served as the foundation for astrophysics— several of Anaximenes' ideas were pioneering. A schematic reconstruction of some of these ideas follows.

The fundamental and most pervasive thing in the world is air (*aer*), according to Anaximenes. Air is infinitely vast in extent but perfectly determinate in character: It is ordinary atmospheric air, invisible where most even in consistency, visible through the Hot and Cold and Damp and motion. It is from air that all the things that exist, have existed, or will exist come into being. This applies to gods and divine things and also to the rest of the world, inasmuch as the world is compounded out of the offspring of air. On this account, Anaximenes suggests, the primordial air is continually in motion, and this motion is the cause of alternating physical states. Condensation and rarefaction are the key manifestations of changing air: rarefied air generates fire; condensed air creates winds; condensed winds, clouds; condensed

clouds, water; condensed water, earth; earth, stones and the rest of the world.

Throughout the process of cosmic change, the Hot and the Cold are dominant states of physical activity, but in no way are they forces distinct from air. They never come out of air by "separating off" (*ekkrisis*); rather, they are "attributes" of air when it condenses through "felting" or is rarefied through "loosening up."

From the genesis of the universe at large, Anaximenes moves to the description of the shape of Earth and of the visible sky. Earth, according to him, is broad, flat, and shallow—tablelike. All the heavenly bodies are fires in the sky, caused by the moist exhalations of Earth. The heavenly bodies are nailed on a hemispherical diaphanous membrane and move around Earth like a cap that can be turned around one's head, and not under Earth. The stars do not produce any sensible heat because of their distance. When the sun, moon, and stars disappear, they are hidden by the distant elevations of Earth. The stars may also be likened to fiery leaves floating on the air.

Clouds, rain, hail, and snow—all these phenomena, too, are caused by condensed air. And the same is true of the violent breaks of the clouds that produce lightning and thunder.

With the elements of his cosmology worked out, Anaximenes seems to need a general natural law guaranteeing the regularity of the world. He observes that as our souls, being air (according to an ancient tradition), hold us together, so does the cosmic Air hold the world together by enclosing it. Presumably what Anaximenes meant by this was that the regularity of an animated world is reliable and intelligible, as is the regularity of an animated body, a body that is organically self-regulative and autonomous—a microcosm. For Anaximenes, lawlike regularities were inconceivable without access to the idea of cause. The notion of physical constraint was accordingly effected through containment. The divine Air, by encasing the world, successfully regulates it.

See also Anaximander; Aristotle; Diogenes Laertius; Pre-Socratic Philosophy; Thales of Miletus.

Bibliography

"Anaximenes." In Pauly-Wissowa, *Realenzyklopädie der altertums Wissenschaft*, Vol. I, p. 2086. Stuttgart, 1893.

Burnet, J. *Early Greek Philosophy*, 4th ed. London: Black, 1930. Pp. 72–79.

Coxon, A. H. "Anaximenes." In *Oxford Classical Dictionary*. London: Clarendon Press, 1949. P. 51.

Diels, Hermann, and Walther Kranz, eds. *Fragmente der Vorsokratiker,* 5th ed. Berlin: Weidmannsche Verlagbuchhandlung, 1954. Vol. I, pp. 90–96.

Guthrie, W. K. C. "Anaximenes and τὸ κρυσταλλοειδές." *Classical Quarterly* (1956): 40–44.

Guthrie, W. K. C. *A History of Greek Philosophy.* Cambridge, U.K.: Cambridge University Press, 1962. Vol. I, pp. 115–150.

Heidel, W. A. "The δίνη in Anaximenes and Anaximander." *Classical Philology* (1906): 279–282.

Kerferd, G. B. "The Date of Anaximenes." *Museum Helveticum* (1954): 117–121.

Kirk, G. S., and J. E. Raven. *The Presocratic Philosophers.* Cambridge, U.K.: Cambridge University Press, 1957. Pp. 143–162.

Tannery, P. "Un fragment d'Anaximene." *Memoires scientifiques* 8 (1925).

P. Diamandopoulos (1967)

ANCIENT AESTHETICS

In antiquity, aesthetics did not form a distinct branch of philosophy. Ancient philosophers discussed literature, music, and the visual arts and reflected on the nature of beauty in a variety of contexts. Since the Greek word for "beautiful" or "fine," *kalos*, is a very general value term that can also be used to describe what is morally admirable, ancient discussion of beauty is often embedded in wider-ranging discussion of values. Literature, music, and the visual arts are frequently considered in an educational and political context; at the same time, most ancient philosophers' views about the arts are strongly influenced by other aspects of their philosophy, in particular their metaphysics.

The earliest Greek philosophy does include some suggestive remarks on aesthetic topics, notably some comments by Gorgias in his *Encomium of Helen,* written in the fifth century BCE, about the power of speech. However, in aesthetics as elsewhere, it was Plato and Aristotle who set the philosophical agenda for all subsequent discussion. We shall therefore begin with Plato and Aristotle and shall trace the development of what we now call aesthetics through the Hellenistic and Roman periods into late antiquity.

PLATO

Plato raises questions about the arts, and about beauty, in a number of different dialogues. Poetry is the art to which he devotes the most discussion, but this entry will also discuss his attitude to rhetoric, his use of the visual arts to illustrate his arguments about both poetry and rhetoric, his comments on music, and finally his view of beauty.

Plato alludes to "an old quarrel" between philosophy and poetry (*Republic* 10.607B). He saw dangers in the widespread use of Homer in classical Greek education and in the role played by tragic drama in classical Athens, a role comparable to that of the mass media in modern society. He therefore argues in the *Ion* and in *Republic* 10 that poets, unlike philosophers, do not have knowledge, and in *Republic* 2 and 3 he places strict limits on the amount of Homer that the future guardians of his ideal state may read and on the type of dramatic performance in which they may take part. In *Republic* 3 he describes drama as imitation (*mimesis* in Greek) and regards both acting and viewing drama as dangerous, both because playing a variety of different roles can destabilize the personality and because imitation of evil characters may likewise make us evil. Since poets lack knowledge, their poetry, according to Plato, appeals not to reason but to the emotions. This point recurs in the *Ion,* in *Republic* 2 and 3, and in *Republic* 10, where it is made using the theory of three parts of the soul first set out in *Republic* 4.

Traditionally Greek poets claimed to be inspired by the Muses. Plato too regards poets as inspired, in the *Ion* and elsewhere, but since such inspiration is contrasted with knowledge, it may not be worth much. However, he does suggest at *Phaedrus* 245A that inspired poetry is more valuable than poetry produced by technical skill alone.

In *Republic* 10, Plato puts forward perhaps his most famous and influential argument to distinguish poetry from philosophy, using the metaphysics developed in the central books of the *Republic.* According to that metaphysics, the physical world is only an imitation (*mimesis,* again) of a world of transcendent Forms. In *Republic* 10, Plato suggests that painters simply copy objects in the physical world and are thus at two removes from the true reality of the world of Forms. The point is then immediately applied to poets, who are regarded as low-grade copyists of the same kind. The scope of *mimesis* is now much wider than in *Republic* 3, where it applied only to drama; here Plato treats virtually all poetry as mimetic and so banishes it from his ideal state.

Plato is as harshly critical of rhetoric as he is of poetry, and for similar reasons. In classical Athens, teachers of rhetoric were popular and rhetorical skill was widely seen as the passport to a successful political career. Many of the Sophists, such as Gorgias and Thrasymachus, taught rhetoric. Plato regularly sets up an opposition between the Sophists, as false teachers, and his own mentor, Socrates; in dialogues such as the *Gorgias,* he contrasts the persuasive power of rhetoric, aimed only at pleasing the audience, with philosophy, which aims for knowledge of the truth. Similarly, in the *Sophist*, at 235Bff., Plato defines the Sophist as a maker of images, comparing his techniques to those used by sculptors and painters. In the *Phaedrus*, however, although Socrates criticizes severely a speech said to be by the orator Lysias, he also raises the possibility that there could be an ideal kind of rhetoric, based on knowledge.

Plato makes occasional remarks about music and in *Republic* 3.398Cff. proposes to regulate the music to which the future guardians of the ideal state may listen, just as he regulates the poetry that they may study. He assumes that music, like poetry, affects the emotions, and he distinguishes between musical modes such as the Dorian and the Lydian on ethical grounds: the future guardians should listen to music that will make them brave and warlike, not to music that will encourage excessive indulgence in unmanly emotions such as grief.

When Plato discusses poetry, rhetoric, and music, sometimes using the visual arts to illustrate and support his argument, he says little or nothing about beauty. He considers beauty in a quite different context in *Symposium* 210ff. where Socrates, speaking in praise of Love (*Erōs* in Greek), reports what he says he was told by a wise woman, Diotima. This passage describes, in lyrical, poetic language, a progression from the love of physical beauty to the love of moral and intellectual beauty and finally to the Form of Beauty itself. Plato here makes no direct reference to the arts, but it is worth noting that in the *Phaedrus* too he recognizes love as a powerful but nonrational motive force in the human soul. The *Phaedrus* also contains a mythical account of how the human soul, before it entered the body, was able to see the Forms, including the Form of Beauty. As we have seen, the *Phaedrus* includes some favorable comments on inspired poetry and the suggestion that an ideal rhetoric, based on knowledge, could be devised. It is therefore tempting to suggest that the right kind of poetry and rhetoric could find a place among the moral and intellectual beauties mentioned in the *Symposium*. Yet we should note that even if this is correct, such beauties will still be left behind by the soul that ascends to the Forms, the ultimate object of philosophical inquiry.

ARISTOTLE

Whereas Plato always discusses poetry and the other arts within a broader context, Aristotle devotes the *Poetics* solely to an examination of poetry. In fact the scope of the *Poetics* as we have it is narrower still: after some introductory remarks about the nature of poetry in general, Aristotle concentrates on tragedy and epic; a lost second book was devoted to comedy. Although the *Poetics* is the main source for Aristotle's aesthetic thought, there is a brief but important discussion of music in the *Politics* that supplements the single allusion in the *Poetics* to *katharsis*, and his views on rhetoric, expounded in the *Rhetoric*, are also of interest.

Like Plato, Aristotle regards poetry as a form of *mimesis*, or "imitation," but since Aristotle's metaphysics differs radically from Plato's, his understanding of *mimesis* is also radically different. For Aristotle forms are immanent in matter, not transcendent. Poetry imitates the world around us, and Aristotle is happy to accept both that we enjoy recognizing such imitation and that we can learn from it. Tragedy, for Aristotle, is an imitation of an action, and Aristotle focuses not on the characters represented but on the plot. Although he does discuss what kind of tragic hero is best, for example, his concern is primarily with what makes a good play. For that reason he has often, with some justice, been regarded as the first formalist in literary theory. He stresses the importance of a unified plot, arguing, for instance, in 1459a that Homer's *Iliad* and *Odyssey* are superior to other epics such as the *Cypria* or the *Little Iliad* in being less episodic. He illustrates his argument with many examples from classical Greek plays, particularly Sophocles' *Oedipus Tyrannus*, which he admires as a supreme example of a well-constructed tragedy.

Yet Aristotle's approach to poetry is not purely formal. He regards the action and the characters of a tragedy as morally significant and believes that poetry can convey universal truths, claiming, at 1451b, that it is closer to philosophy than to history in that respect. Like Plato he recognizes that poetry has a powerful effect on the emotions and like Plato he holds that tragedy arouses both pity and fear. However, whereas Plato, in *Republic* 10 and elsewhere, argues that tragedy and other forms of poetry overstimulate these emotions, Aristotle has a more complex view. When he gives a definition of tragedy in *Poetics* 1449b, he describes it as bringing about a *katharsis* of pity and fear and in *Politics* 8. 1341bff., in a discussion of music, he mentions a similar *katharsis* effected by the healing use of music in certain religious rites. There has been much scholarly discussion of just what Aristotle means by *katharsis*. Arguably it is best understood in the light of Aristotle's ethics: Aristotle holds that in order to act virtuously we need to feel the right emotions at the right time, in the right way and toward the right objects; in some way that is not fully explained, our feeling pity and fear as we watch a good tragedy brings about the result that, when we leave the theater, we feel not too much pity and fear, as Plato supposed, but just the right amount that we need for ethical action.

The rest of Aristotle's discussion of music in *Politics* 8 assumes, as Plato did in the *Republic*, that music has a powerful effect on the emotions. He criticizes some details of Plato's argument in *Republic* 3.398Cff., and by introducing the notion of *katharsis*, Aristotle opens up the possibility that music can be used for therapeutic purposes.

A similar interest in the effect of art on the emotions can be seen in Aristotle's *Rhetoric*. Aristotle devotes much of *Rhetoric* 2 to a discussion of the emotions because the orator will need to understand his audience's emotional responses in order to persuade them effectively. The *Rhetoric* also contains important discussions of rhetorical reasoning and of prose style. Just as the *Poetics* is not a handbook for poets but a philosophical treatise on poetry based on close study of tragedy and epic, so the *Rhetoric* is not a handbook for orators but a philosophical treatise based on close study of rhetorical practice.

THE HELLENISTIC AND ROMAN PERIODS

After the death of Aristotle, Greek philosophy became increasingly diverse. While the Platonist and Aristotelian schools continued, the Epicureans and the Stoics developed new approaches to many issues. Aristotle's pupil, Theophrastus, was interested in the therapeutic powers of music and claimed that music could even cure bodily afflictions such as sciatica. Another pupil of Aristotle, Aristoxenus, studied music from an empirical point of view, opposing the mathematical approach that had been taken by the Pythagoreans.

The Stoics regarded both the order of the universe and moral virtue as beautiful, and their interest in the philosophy of language led them to discuss poetry and rhetoric. They thought poetry could express truth, as we can see from Cleanthes' choice of verse to convey his philosophy in the *Hymn to Zeus* and from the way in which critics such as Heraclitus and Cornutus used allegorical interpretation of poetry and mythology. By contrast, Epicurus appears to have rejected the idea that poetry could have any value as a means of instruction, although he was prepared to accept that it could be a source of pleasure.

In the first century BCE, Philodemus, an Epicurean, wrote his important works *On Poems* and *On Music*, which survive only in fragmentary form in papyrus scrolls found at Herculaneum. Much of Philodemus's

work took the form of attacks on other critics and theorists. His own view was that poetry, and music, do not give pleasure by their sound alone. Music at this time was normally an accompaniment to poetry, and Philodemus holds that the value of music comes from the poetry that is performed with it, and the value of that poetry comes from the thought that it expresses; he also holds that form and content go closely together and that a poem cannot be good in thought but bad in composition.

Although Philodemus influenced the Roman poets Virgil and Horace, Epicurean views remained outside the mainstream of thinking about the arts in the first century BCE and the first century CE. Many educated writers of this period combine together ideas from more than one philosophical school. In both Cicero (*Orator* 8) and Seneca (*Letters* 58 and 65) we find an important new idea about the metaphysical status of works of art. Both these writers suggest that rather than merely imitating objects in the physical world, which are themselves copies of transcendent Forms, the artist looks to ideas in his own mind, which are themselves reflections of the Platonic Forms, understood by the Platonists of this period as the thoughts of God. The Greek sculptor Phidias, famous for his statue of the supreme god, Zeus, is used as an example of an artist who worked in this way.

Throughout the Hellenistic and Roman periods there continued to be great interest in the moral effect of the arts and the role of the arts in education. Plutarch (c. 45–c. 120 CE) discusses poetry from a moral point of view in his *De audiendis poetis*, in a way that reflects the continuing influence of Plato's views. He is familiar with the idea that music can be used as psychological therapy and associates this with Pythagoreanism in *De Iside* 384A.

The Pythagoreans, as we saw earlier, were also credited with a mathematical approach to music. Ptolemy's *Harmonics*, written in the second century CE, contrasts Pythagorean and Aristoxenian views of music. Ptolemy agrees with the Pythagoreans that musical structures must be analyzed in mathematical terms but criticizes them for neglecting empirical, perceptual evidence.

Literary criticism in the Hellenistic and Roman periods was closely intertwined with the theory and practice of rhetoric. Writers such as Cicero and Quintilian discuss literary and aesthetic matters in the context of rhetorical education. The work *On the Sublime* attributed to Longinus, which probably dates from the first century CE, blends ideas drawn from the rhetorical tradition of literary criticism with ideas drawn from philosophy, particularly from Platonism. The work is unusual among surviving ancient works of literary criticism both because the author develops the view that the best works of literature have an essential quality of sublimity that explains their enduring appeal and because he illustrates his view with detailed discussion of examples in a way that combines technical analysis with judgment of literary value.

LATE ANTIQUITY

Plotinus, writing in the third century CE, regarded himself as a Platonist but is now labeled rather a "Neoplatonist" because he elaborated a more complex metaphysics than previous Platonists, postulating a transcendent One beyond the realm of the Platonic Forms. In aesthetics, Plotinus combined the suggestion that the artist uses ideas in his own mind that directly reflect the Forms, already found in Cicero and Seneca, with the account of the ascent to the Form of Beauty offered in Plato's *Symposium*. *Ennead* 1.6 begins by rejecting a Stoic account of beauty as symmetry of parts, arguing that incomposite things can also be beautiful and that they derive their beauty from a higher source. Plotinus then draws on Plato's *Symposium* and *Phaedrus* to describe an ascent from physical beauty through moral and intellectual beauty to the Form itself, and ultimately to the One beyond the Form of Beauty. *Ennead* 1.6 has often been regarded as presenting an aesthetic theory, but we must recognize, first, that Plotinus is not talking just about "beauty" in the modern sense and, second, that his theory implies that beauty in the physical world is to be valued only insofar as it leads us to a higher realm. As noted at the beginning of this entry, the Greek word *kalos*, standardly translated as "beautiful," is a very general value term. It would be a mistake to say that Plotinus is aestheticizing morality when, like the Stoics and Plato before him, he describes moral virtue as *kalos*; it would be more correct to say that, like most ancient thinkers, he makes no distinction between aesthetic and moral value. It is also important to recognize that for Plotinus our ultimate goal is union with the One; intellectual contemplation is the next best thing, and appreciation of beauty is only a means to achieving these goals, not something valued for its own sake.

Plotinus says little or nothing about art in *Ennead* 1.6, but in *Ennead* 5.8.1 he combines the view of beauty found in 1.6 with the suggestion that the artist can imitate the Forms directly, using principles in his own mind that derive from the Forms. He uses the standard example of Phidias's statue of Zeus and suggests, very politely, that Plato's argument in *Republic* 10 is mistaken in representing works of art as imitating only objects in nature. According to Plotinus's argument, art itself is superior to its products, and he moves on in the rest of 5.8 to discuss the intellectual beauty of the world of Forms.

Although Plotinus himself shows only limited interest in the arts, his view of beauty led to important developments in poetic and musical theory. His views were applied to poetry by the later Neoplatonist Proclus, in the fifth century CE. In his *Commentary on the Republic*, Proclus argues that much of Homer's poetry is not after all vulnerable to Plato's criticisms, since it is not mimetic but inspired. Just as Phidias's Zeus, for both Plotinus and Proclus, portrays the god, capturing something of divine beauty in the statue we see, so Homeric poetry conveys truths about the divine world of Neoplatonic metaphysics. In order to maintain this view of Homer, Proclus resorts to allegorical interpretation of episodes criticized by Plato, drawing on a long tradition of such interpretation by Stoics and others.

Proclus and other later Neoplatonists also devoted attention to music. On the one hand, they integrated traditional views about the effect of music on the emotions into their philosophical system. On the other, they regarded music as one of the mathematical sciences, following a Pythagorean rather than an Aristoxenian approach. They perceived the same mathematical patterns in music as in the physical universe, believing that the beauty of such perceptible order derived from the ordered structure of the intelligible world. The *Institutio musica* of Boethius (c. 480–c. 524 CE), written in Latin, draws heavily on these ideas.

See also Aesthetics, History of; Aristotle; Boethius; Anicius Manlius Severinus; Gorgias of Leontini; Kalon; Katharsis; Mimesis; Neoplatonism; Philodemus; Plato; Plotinus; Proclus.

Bibliography

TEXTS AND TRANSLATIONS

Aristotle. *Ars rhetorica*. Edited by Rudolf Kassel. Berlin and New York: de Gruyter, 1976.

Aristotle. *De arte poetica* (Oxford Classical Text). Edited by Rudolf Kassel. Oxford: Oxford University Press, 1965.

Aristotle. *On Rhetoric: A Theory of Civic Discourse*. Translated by George A. Kennedy. New York and Oxford: Oxford University Press, 1991.

Aristotle. *Poetics*. Translated by Malcolm Heath. London: Penguin, 1996.

Aristotle. *Politica* (Oxford Classical Text). Edited by W. D. Ross. Oxford: Oxford University Press, 1957.

Barker, Andrew D. *Greek Musical Writings*. 2 vols. Cambridge, U.K.: Cambridge University Press, 1984, 1989.

Boethius. *De institutione arithmetica; De institutione musica*. Edited by Gottfried Friedlein. Leipzig: Teubner, 1867.

Boethius. *Fundamentals of Music*. Translated by Calvin M. Bower. New Haven and London: Yale University Press, 1989.

Longinus. *On the Sublime*. Edited by Donald A. Russell. Oxford: Oxford University Press, 1968.

Philodemus. *On Poems Book One*. Edited by Richard Janko. Oxford: Oxford University Press, 2000.

Plato. *Complete Works* (in English translation). Edited by John M. Cooper. Indianapolis and Cambridge: Hackett, 1997.

Plato. *Opera* (Oxford Classical Text). Edited by John Burnet. Oxford: Oxford University Press, 1902–1906.

Plato. *Opera*, vol. 1 (Oxford Classical Text). Edited by E. A. Duke and others. Oxford: Oxford University Press, 1995.

Plato. *Republic* (Oxford Classical Text). Edited by Simon R. Slings. Oxford: Oxford University Press, 2003.

Plotinus. *Enneads* (Loeb Classical Library). Edited by A. Hilary Armstrong. Cambridge, MA, and London: Harvard University Press and Heinemann, 1966–1988.

Russell, Donald A., and Michael Winterbottom. *Ancient Literary Criticism: The Principal Texts in New Translations*. Oxford: Clarendon Press, 1972.

STUDIES

Chadwick, Henry. *Boethius. The Consolations of Music, Logic, Theology, and Philosophy*. Oxford: Clarendon Press, 1981.

Halliwell, Stephen. *The Aesthetics of Mimesis*. Princeton, NJ, and Oxford: Princeton University Press, 2002.

Halliwell, Stephen. *Aristotle's Poetics*. London: Duckworth, 1986.

Janaway, Christopher. *Images of Excellence: Plato's Critique of the Arts*. Oxford: Clarendon Press, 1998.

Janko, Richard. *Aristotle on Comedy: Towards a Reconstruction of Poetics II*. London: Duckworth, 1984.

Kennedy, George A., ed. *The Cambridge History of Literary Criticism*, Vol. 1. Cambridge, U.K.: Cambridge University Press, 1989.

Lamberton, Robert. *Homer the Theologian*. Berkeley and Los Angeles: University of California Press, 1986.

Moravcsik, Julius, and Philip Temko, eds. *Plato on Beauty, Wisdom and the Arts*. Totowa, NJ: Rowman and Littlefield, 1982.

Obbink, Dirk, ed. *Philodemus and Poetry: Poetic Theory and Practice in Lucretius, Philodemus, and Horace*. Oxford: Oxford University Press, 1995.

Russell, Donald A. *Criticism in Antiquity*. London: Duckworth, 1981.

Anne Sheppard (2005)

ANCIENT SKEPTICISM

Tradition recognizes two schools of ancient skepticism: the Academics and the Pyrrhonists. The ancient Greek term "skeptic" was used by the Pyrrhonists to describe themselves. They denied that it described the Academics, but this point could be and was disputed, and later in antiquity the word may have been used as a common designation for both schools. Our use of the term in this way goes back to the seventeenth century.

The term itself is derived from a verb in common use meaning "to inquire" or "to investigate"—hence the skeptic as inquirer. This is a surprise. We take skepticism, roughly speaking, to imply a denial of the possibility of knowledge. Yet Sextus Empiricus, the second-century CE Pyrrhonist—and the only member of the school whose works have survived intact and in bulk—is quite firm on this point. In the opening chapter of his *Outlines of Pyrrhonism*, he distinguishes three types of philosophers: those who take themselves to have discovered the truth, those who hold that it cannot be apprehended, and those who persist in inquiring. Philosophers of the first type he calls "dogmatists," members of the last group "skeptics," and those of the middle tendency "Academics."

This is unfair. Even Academics like Philo of Larissa, who did hold that nothing can be apprehended, did not conclude from this that inquiry was pointless. Though they held that certain knowledge was unobtainable, they believed that it was possible to identify views that enjoyed a high degree of probability or verisimilitude—among them, the view that nothing can be known for certain—and they regarded inquiry for the sake of such discoveries as eminently worthwhile. What is more, Academics like Carneades and Clitomachus were no more convinced that nothing can be known than the Pyrrhonists, and they and deserved to be described as inquirers at least as much.

These facts only add to the puzzle, however. If not only the Pyrrhonists but also many Academics were skeptics in Sextus's sense, why the persistent tendency, beginning with the ancient skeptics' own contemporaries, to equate skepticism with one of the positions that Sextus expressly opposes to it? And why should a dedication to inquiry set the skeptics apart from members of other schools? Philo of Alexandria, who was active in the first century CE, was able to use the term "skeptikos" (in the sense of "inquirer") of philosophers quite generally.

Sextus's idea seems to be this: Inquiry into a particular question comes to a natural end either when the question that set the inquiry in train is resolved or when it becomes plain that it cannot be resolved. Absent either outcome, further inquiry is indicated. Dogmatists take themselves to have brought many inquiries to a successful conclusion in the first way. Negative dogmatists, or dogmatic skeptics as we may also call them, have satisfied themselves that the questions are beyond resolution. By contrast, skeptics, properly so called, find that question after question remains open and hence calls for further inquiry. On their view, dogmatists of both the positive and negative variety were guilty of calling off their inquiries prematurely. And the fault about which ancient skeptics complain most frequently is rashness or precipitate judgment.

The condition in which skeptics find themselves regarding the questions they investigate resembles that of negative dogmatists or dogmatic skeptics in being one of not knowing. But those who saw Academics and Pyrrhonists as skeptics in the modern sense were not simply confusing the condition of the inquirer with the dogmatic rejection of the possibility of knowledge. They were reacting to the fact that skeptics of both schools devoted far more time and energy to the case that nothing can be known than to arguments bearing on any other question.

The reason for this seems to be the following: It is possible to pursue unresolved inquiries into all sorts of questions without ever doubting that knowledge is, at least sometimes, achievable. But it is also possible to make the nature and possibility of knowledge an object of inquiry. If questions about knowledge remain stubbornly open, one of the things that one will not know, and that will require further study, is whether one can know at all; and from this central epistemological question the skeptical condition will spread to other inquiries, which can be brought to a conclusion only by justified claims to knowledge that the skeptic cannot make with confidence about anything. The inquiry into the possibility of knowledge remains open because of the persistent lack of satisfactory answers to the powerful arguments that knowledge is impossible. And ancient skeptics pursued the inquiry into the nature and possibility of knowledge chiefly by confronting the best theories of knowledge with these arguments.

Because the ancient skeptics consistently declined to make knowledge claims and constantly argued that nothing can be known, it is hardly surprising that outsiders took them to hold the position that nothing can be known and to hold it because they were convinced by the arguments they advanced in support of it. But if, in deference to tradition, we call this position the skeptical position and arguments supporting it skeptical arguments, for most ancient skeptics, being a skeptic was not a matter of holding the skeptical position in this traditional sense, and their reason for arguing skeptically was not to establish or defend the skeptical position. Rather, their skepticism was a matter of being unable to terminate the inquiries in which they were engaged—chiefly about the possibility of knowledge, but about the other matters as well.

PRECURSORS

The history of ancient Greek philosophy before the emergence of the main skeptical schools contains many figures who expressed doubts about the possibility of knowledge. Some of these were collected by skeptical Academics in order to provide themselves with a distinguished lineage.

Already in the sixth century BCE, the pre-Socratic philosopher Xenophanes composed some verses about the impossibility of human beings ever knowing for sure whether they had hit upon the truth or not. Perhaps the most important pre-Socratic precursor of skepticism was Democritus, who observed that his theory of atomism, which he took to be based ultimately on the evidence of the senses, had the consequence that the senses were unreliable, since the colors and flavors with which they appear to put us in contact would have no real existence if he were correct. It was characteristic of Academic argument especially, but also of many Pyrrhonian arguments, to proceed in the same way by deducing consequences imperiling the possibility of knowledge from dogmatic theories about knowledge. Though we are not well informed about the details, it is clear that a tradition calling the possibility of knowledge into question arose among philosophers influenced by Democritus. They include Metrodorus of Chios (fourth century BCE), whose work on nature begins, "None of us knows anything, not even this, whether we know or do not know," and Pyrrho of Elis (circa 365–275 BCE), who is traditionally, though probably wrongly, viewed as the founder of the school which bears his name.

Unsurprisingly, skeptical Academics in search of illustrious antecedents appealed to the example of Socrates, who was the teacher of the Academy's founder, Plato, and well known for claiming that he knew nothing except perhaps that he knew nothing. This was Socrates' explanation for the pronouncement of the oracle in Delphi that he was the wisest man in Greece. The wisdom that set him apart from others, he conjectured, could only be his recognition that he lacked knowledge, whereas others, who were no more knowledgeable, deluded themselves and others into believing that they had knowledge.

Academic skeptics were inspired by at least two other characteristics of Socrates. First, though he set the highest possible value on knowledge and devoted his life to the pursuit of wisdom, Socrates lived an exemplary life without having attained it, thus providing the Academic skeptics with a model of the life they took themselves to be leading. Second, Socrates was a master of dialectic. A dialectical argument involves two parties: a questioner and an answerer. The answerer commits himself to a thesis, which it is his task to defend. The questioner aims to construct an argument to the contradictory of the answerer's thesis from grounds acceptable to the answerer, and he poses his questions with this end in view. When the questioner succeeds, it is through an argument all of whose premises have been conceded by the answerer. The answerer is thereby shown to lack the kind of understanding of the subject under discussion that Socrates' interlocutors typically claimed. The dialectical inquiry thus exposes problems inherent in the answerer's position or his defense of it or both. Since this kind of refutation can be accomplished by a questioner with no independent knowledge of the matters in contention, dialectical argument recommended itself to committed inquirers like Socrates, and it became the principal method of the Academic skeptics, who drew their inspiration from him.

Attempts were also made in the Academy to interpret Plato as a skeptic. The argument is based on his many expressions of caution and his manifest willingness in the dialogues to raise difficulties without resolving them. Whatever the merits of this claim, questions about the possibility of knowledge were not as prominent among Socrates' and Plato's concerns as they were among those of the Academics and Pyrrhonians.

Although book 9 of Diogenes Laertius's *Lives and Opinions of Eminent Philosophers* (the fullest treatment Pyrrhonism apart from Sextus Empiricus) includes a list of Pyrrhonists extending from Pyrrho to Sextus and beyond, the first part of it is almost certainly a construction. Pyrrho should probably not be viewed as the founder of a skeptical school. The modern scholarly consensus is that the Pyrrhonian school was founded in the first century BCE by Aenesidemus, who appears to have been an Academic dissatisfied with what he saw as the drift to dogmatism in the Academy of his time. He and his followers seem to have turned to Pyrrho in an effort to create an alternative history of skepticism that would make his school the legitimate heir of an older skeptical tradition.

Pyrrho wrote nothing but made a strong impression on his contemporaries, at least as much through his character as through his teachings. Figures with no sympathy for the positions he is thought to have held praised his imperturbability, lack of conceit, and tranquility. His views are elusive, however. Cicero seems to have known of him only as a moralist. He grouped Pyrrho together with figures like the heterodox Stoic Aristo of Chios (third century BCE). Such thinkers, he maintains, by making virtue the sole human good, fail to supply it with an object outside itself and so produce ethical theories incapable of furnishing practical guidance. The poet Timon of Phlius (c. 325–c. 238 BCE) became a follower of Pyrrho, whom he celebrated in a number of works that were probably the later Pyrrhonists' principal source of information about Pyrrho.

There was enough of an affinity between Pyrrho and Arcesilaus, the school leader of the Academy responsible for its skeptical turn, for their relationship to be the subject of a satirical verse by Aristo. Later on the characteristics of the Pyrrhonian school were imputed to Pyrrho. But whether and in what way Pyrrho was himself a skeptic remains subject to controversy. The most complete surviving account of his views is a late antique quotation of a first century CE citation of Timon. According to it, Pyrrho maintained that "things are equally indifferent, unmeasurable, and undecidable," and he went on to say that "neither our perceptions nor our opinions are true or false." According to one school of interpretation, the first claim is best viewed an epistemological thesis that Pyrrho deduced from the second, which, on this view, is an assertion about the apparent impossibility of distinguishing true from false beliefs. This interpretation would make him a skeptic, albeit probably a dogmatic one. But others have argued that the claim that "things are equally indifferent, unmeasurable, and undecidable" is a metaphysical thesis about the nature of reality from which Pyrrho inferred that perceptions and opinions cannot be true or false. In any case, he maintained that the proper response was to be without opinion, and he claimed that the result for those who attain this condition is tranquility.

ACADEMIC SKEPTICISM

Arcesilaus (316/15–241/40 BCE) became the fifth head of the Academy after Plato and was responsible for the school's turn to skepticism. To mark this change in outlook, later ancient writers speak of Arcesilaus as the founder of the New Academy as opposed to the Old Academy of Plato and his earliest successors; sometimes the Academy of Arcesilaus and his successors is called the Middle or Second Academy to distinguish it from the New or Third Academy of Carneades and his followers. (None of these distinctions corresponds to changes in the Academy as an institution.)

Like Socrates, Arcesilaus wrote nothing but was distinguished by his mastery of dialectic in face-to-face conversation. Rather than expound or defend views of his own, he would let his interlocutors put forward a view that he would then subject to dialectical examination. His decision to make Stoic epistemology the principal object of his inquiries exerted a decisive influence on the subsequent history of ancient skepticism.

The Stoics took wisdom to mean a firm grasp of the truth, entirely free from error. They maintained that, though exceedingly rare and difficult of attainment, wisdom was nevertheless within the power of human beings. The key concept in the Stoics' account of wisdom, what they called cognitive impressions—their criterion of truth—which they define as impressions "from what is, stamped and impressed in exact accordance with what is, and such as could not be from what is not." In the paradigm case of perceptual impressions, this means that cognitive impressions arise in a way that ensures that they capture their objects with perfect accuracy, thus guaranteeing their truth, and at the same time impart to them a character that human beings can discern.

Assent to a cognitive impression is a cognition or apprehension, and, if further conditions are satisfied, it will qualify as knowledge. Assent to anything but a cognitive impression is opinion, and, according to the Stoics, the wise avoid error by remaining entirely free of opinion. Arcesilaus began the long Academic tradition of arguing that there are no cognitive impressions, which in the context of Stoic epistemology amounts to arguing that knowledge is impossible. He did this by arguing for indiscernibility— that is, he held that the character purportedly peculiar to cognitive impressions could also belong to impressions that did not arise in the required truth-guaranteeing way and were in fact false. His arguments were based as much as possible on considerations that the Stoics would have to acknowledge, either because they were drawn from Stoic theory or could be rejected only at a high cost in plausibility.

The idea that there are no cognitive impressions ("inapprehensibility" for short) was the first skeptical proposition with which the Academy came to be associated. The second, that it is incumbent on the wise to suspend judgment on all matters, Arcesilaus deduced from the first, along with the Stoic doctrine that wisdom is incompatible with opinion. Together they make up what we might call a skeptical position.

On a strictly dialectical interpretation of Arcesilaus's arguments, the conclusions he drew need tell us nothing about what views, if any, he held. The propositions that make up the skeptical position follow in the context of arguments dominated by Stoic assumptions about what is to count as knowledge and about the incompatibility of wisdom with opinion; these issues raise problems for the Stoics to solve. To be sure, Arcesilaus responded to Stoic arguments that action was impossible without assent, and

assent senseless in the absence of cognitive impressions, by defending the possibility of a life in which all judgment is suspended. But this argument may only have shown that the Stoics were not in a position to easily escape the difficulties raised by his first set of arguments. And the fact that his response to the Stoics was based so closely on their theory of action as to have no force outside this debate lends support to this suggestion.

It is clear, however, that Academics after Arcesilaus interpreted him as endorsing the skeptical propositions in a certain way. This was their own view, and they may have been right about Arcesilaus. Thus a skeptical stance or outlook arose in the Academy as a result of a dialectical dispute with the Stoa that was expressed by means of the skeptical propositions. But the Academic followers of Arcesilaus seem not to have subscribed to the skeptical propositions in the ordinary way. Instead, their situation is akin to that of the skeptics described by Sextus: They were not in a position to conclude the inquiry into the nature and possibility of knowledge or other inquiries dependent on its resolution. And it is this condition that they described in terms borrowed from their debate with the Stoa—inapprehensibility and suspension of judgment—not the condition of being convinced by the arguments on their side of the debate.

We know little about Arcesilaus's successors before Carneades. Carneades was another exceptionally gifted dialectician and nonwriter. It is likely that he supplemented and refined the arguments against cognitive impressions that he inherited from his predecessors, but his most distinctive contribution was his response to the Stoics' argument that without cognitive impressions and assent, action and life are impossible. Whereas Arcesilaus's response stayed very close to Stoic theory, Carneades's did not. Instead he seems to have worked out a full-blown theory of so-called probable impressions (*probabilis* was Cicero's Latin translation of the Greek *pithanos*, meaning *persuasive*). And he appealed to them to explain how life, even a life of wisdom, was possible without the perfectly secure foundation provided by cognitive impressions.

As Arcesilaus had done before him, Carneades defended the possibility of acting without assent. There is, he argued, a way of using or following probable impressions that does not amount to assent but is adequate for action and inquiry. But he also sometimes conceded that assent was essential in order to argue that even this consession did not vindicate Stoic claims about the cognitive impression. For, he suggested, it was permissible for the wise to form opinions by assenting to noncognitive impressions, opinions held in the full consciousness that they were only opinions and might be wrong.

This line of argument is behind the view that Carneades relaxed or weakened the more militantly skeptical stance of Arcesilaus. But perhaps the new features of Carneades's arguments are part of a broadly dialectical form of argument. The Stoics believe their views should win acceptance not because they are theirs but because they do justice to common assumptions about human nature—its needs and the resources available to it—as no others can. The challenge that Carneades accepted, then, was to show that the ready availability of equally sound or even better alternatives ought to discourage a premature embrace of the Stoic position.

This posture makes it hard to know whether Carneades actually subscribed to any of the views he defended. And his students and successors interpreted him in different ways. Clitomachus, his student and eventual successor, held that one should suspend judgment and that this had been Carneades's view. Philo of Larissa, who succeeded Clitomachus, contended that Carneades believed that the wise were permitted to form opinions in the absence of cognitive impressions and that one of the probable views deserving assent was inapprehensibility. Philo was, then, a dogmatic skeptic, who championed one of the skeptical propositions simply because he was convinced by the arguments for it. There is an air of paradox about this position, but it must be remembered that he did not claim to know for certain that nothing can be known for certain, but rather that it was highly probable, which, if nothing can be known for certain, is the most that can be said for it.

PYRRHONISM

It seems to have been Philo of Larissa's dogmatic skepticism that moved Aenesidemus to found or revive a competing school of Pyrrhonian skepticism in the first century BCE. The Pyrrhonian school he founded existed past the time of Sextus Empiricus, who is usually thought to have been active in the latter part of the second century CE. Although none of Aenesidemus's works have survived, a summary of eight books of his Pyrrhonian Arguments by Photius (ninth century CE) has. From it we learn that Aenesidemus, who had been an Academcie himself, charged the Academics of his time with being little more than Stoics fighting Stoics, disagreeing only about cognitive impressions while agreeing about many other issues. Though the decision by Aenesidemus and his followers to call themselves "Pyrrhonists" does not imply a direct line of descent from Pyrrho, it is probable

that they were influenced by traditions about Pyrrho. Another important influence came from the Empirical school of medicine, with which Pyrrhonism maintained close ties and shared many members including Sextus Empiricus (whose name means "the Empiricist").

In view of the school's origins, it is not surprising to find many points of contact between it and Academic skepticism. The Pyrrhonists describe the skeptical condition with the aid of terms like "inapprehensibility" and "suspension of judgment," which have their origins in the epistemological debate between the Academy and the Stoa. They view this condition as the result of a standoff or impasse between their arguments and those of their dogmatic opponents, not as the result of being convinced by their own skeptical arguments. And they explain that they are able to act and to live despite suspending judgment on all questions. This argument hinges on a distinction between two senses of "belief" (Greek: dogma) that is indebted to Carneades's and Clitomachus's contrast between assenting to an impression and using or following it. In the former sense, the Pyrrhonists had no beliefs, but in the latter sense they did have beliefs, which were able to serve as a basis for action. The two works of Sextus that have come down to us, the *Outlines of Pyrrhonism* in three books and *Against the Mathematicians* in nine, are packed with arguments against dogmatic positions, many of which are of Academic origin.

There are, however, equally notable differences between the two schools, some of which may reflect other influences on Aenesidemus and his followers. The most striking and important of these is the positive value the Pyrrhonists seem to attach to the skeptical suspension of judgment about all matters. According to Sextus, Pyrrhonism has a telos, a supreme aim or goal in life: tranquility (and, where that is unattainable, moderation in one's emotions). Suspension of judgment is recommended because it gives rise to tranquility. This recommendation is not based on a theory of human nature that would explain why it finds fulfillment in tranquility. Rather the argument seems to presupposed that tranquility is humans' goal. This assumption commands greater credibility if viewed not as a claim about the essential nature of the best life for human beings, which would elicit vehement disagreement from some ancient philosophical schools, but as a weaker claim that such a life will somehow involve tranquility. And the Pyrrhonists do not pretend to be able to explain why suspension of judgment should give rise to tranquility; they claim to have made this discovery only by accident. Tranquility is supposed to arise in a manner exemplified by the famous story of

Apelles the painter, who, despairing of being able paint the foam on the neck of a racing horse, gave up and threw his sponge at the painting, thereby producing by chance what he had been unable to achieve deliberately.

The idea of a correlation between freedom from opinion and tranquility may have been the Pyrrhonian school's truest debt to Pyrrho. This idea sets it clearly apart from the Academy. The Academy attached the highest value to knowledge and regarded the skeptical condition as a stop-gap, albeit a surprisingly congenial one. As a we have seen, the Pyrrhonists were officially committed to the quest for knowledge. But the accounts of Pyrrhonism in Sextus and Diogenes Laertius give evidence of a positive attachment to suspending judgment as a means to tranquility. Arguments and argumentative strategies are recommended for their efficacy in bringing about equipollence, the condition in which arguments on either side of a question are of apparently equal force; and equipollence is cultivated not as a means to cognitive certainty but to the suspension of judgment that leads to tranquility. Thus there is a sense in which Academics like Arcesilaus and Carneades exemplified true "skepticism," in the sense of open-minded inquiry, more than the Pyrrhonists did.

There is also a difference in the kinds of arguments the two schools used. Sextus and our other sources give pride of place to the so-called modes or tropes of argument that bring about suspension of judgment. There is a set of ten such tropes, which seem to go back to Aenesidemus, and a later set of five ascribed to Agrippa, who may, however, be a fictional character in a Pyrrhonian work. (There is also a set of two tropes, and a further set of eight tropes concerning causal explanation, which is likewise credited to Aenesidemus). The ten tropes appear to be the oldest, and they draw on arguments and examples with a long history. Book Gamma of Aristotle's *Metaphysics* is already familiar, with arguments resembling those in the ten tropes. Most of the ten aim to demonstrate that there are undecidable conflicts between the appearances perceived by different species or different human beings or the different senses or by the same human being in different conditions or between the appearances presented by objects in different circumstances. The existence of such conflicts is illustrated by a wealth of examples, some of them fanciful. Left unclear are the exact arguments envisaged and how they relate to the official program, which calls for the production of equipollence by the balancing of arguments. The tropes seemingly aim to elicit from these conflicting appearances a thesis of undecidability that requires suspension of judgment. That is, it appears as though undecidability arises from an argument whose premises would command the assent of the skeptic. But perhaps the arguments for the undecidability of conflicts are meant to oppose arguments that they are decidable, and it is the equipollence between these arguments that is supposed to lead to suspension of judgment.

Even so, by comparison with Academic arguments, and with the arguments found elsewhere in Sextus, the trope-based arguments appear somewhat naive. Substantial assumptions about species, perceptual faculties, and the requisite conditions for the acceptance of an impression as true enter the argument without being marked as dialectical concessions or without comment of any kind about their status. Perhaps the material collected in the ten tropes arose from traditions of dogmatic skeptical thinking outside the Academy and maybe even from Pyrrho himself. There is a problem with the trope of relativity, which may suggest a similar conclusion about origins. According to this trope, since all things are relative, we must suspend judgment about their real natures. Though Sextus makes an attempt to correct for this, the conclusion of this argument is not, properly speaking, skeptical.

The five Agrippan modes are (i) disagreement, (ii) regress to infinity, (iii) relativity, (iv) hypothesis, and (v) circularity. Except for relativity, they form a system by means of which dogmatic attempts to justify a disputed claim can be counteracted. Any claim put forward invites disagreement. Further claims enlisted in support of it will lead to an infinite regress, by requiring justification themselves, unless the process is brought to an arbitrary halt with a hypothesis or the justification depends on the originally disputed claim. To judge from the enormous mass of arguments preserved by Sextus, neither set of tropes consistently guided the Pyrrhonists as they collected and composed arguments to further their skeptical purposes.

See also Aenesidemus; Agrippa; Aristo of Chios; Aristotle; Carneades; Cicero, Marcus Tullius; Diogenes Laertius; Dogma; Greek Academy; Leucippus and Democritus; Philo Judaeus; Philo of Larissa; Plato; Pyrrho; Sextus Empiricus; Skepticism, History of; Socrates; Stoicism; Timon of Phlius; Xenophanes of Colophon.

Bibliography

Algra, Keimpe, Jonathan Barnes, Jaap Mansfeld, and Malcolm Schofield, eds. *The Cambridge History of Hellenistic Philosophy*. Cambridge, U.K.: Cambridge University Press, 1999.

Allen, James. "Academic Probabilism and Stoic Epistemology." *Classical Quarterly* 44 (1994): 85–113.

Allen, James. "Pyrrhonism and Medical Empiricism: Sextus Empiricus on Evidence and Inference." *Aufstieg und Niedergang der Römischen* Welt II. 37.1, edited by Wolfgang Haase. Berlin: Walter de Gruyter. 646–90.

Annas, Julia. "Plato the Sceptic." *Oxford Studies in Ancient Philosophy*, suppl. vol. (1992): 43–72.

Bailey, Alan. *Sextus Empiricus and Pyrrhonean Skepticism.* Oxford: Oxford University Press, 2002.

Bett, Richard. *Pyrrho, His Antecedents and his Legacy.* Oxford: Oxford University Press, 2000.

Brittain, Charles. *Philo of Larissa: The Last of the Academic Sceptics.* Oxford: Oxford University Press, 2001.

Brochard, Victor. *Les sceptiques grecs.* 2nd ed. Paris: Vrin, 1887.

Brunschwig, Jacques. *Papers in Hellenistic Philosophy.* Cambridge, U.K.: Cambridge University Press, 1994.

Burnyeat, Myles, ed. *The Skeptical Tradition.* Berkeley: University of California Press, 1983.

Burnyeat, Myles, and Michael Frede, eds. *The Original Sceptics: A Controversy.* Indianapolis: Hackett, 1997.

Cicero. *De natura deorum, Academica.* Translated by H. Rackham. Cambridge, MA: Harvard University Press, 1933.

Diogenes Laertius. *Diogenes Laertius: Lives of Eminent Philosophers.* 2 vols. Translated by R. D. Hicks. Cambridge, MA: Harvard University Press, 1929.

Frede, Michael. *Essays in Ancient Philosophy.* Oxford: Oxford University Press, 1987.

Glucker, John. *Antiochus and the Late Academy Hypomnemata 56.* Göttingen: Vandenhoeck und Ruprecht, 1978.

Groarke, Leo. *Greek Scepticism: Anti-realist Trends in Ancient Thought.* Montreal: McGill–Queen's University Press, 1990.

Hankinson, R. James. *The Sceptics.* London: Routledge, 1995.

Inwood, Brad, and Jaap Mansfeld, eds. *Assent and Argument: Studies in Cicero's Academic Books.* Leiden: Brill, 1997.

Robin, Léon. *Pyrrhon et le scepticisme grec.* Paris: Presses Universitaires de France, 1944.

Schofield, Malcolm, Burnyeat, Myles, and Barnes, Jonathan,eds. *Doubt and Dogmatism: Studies in Hellenistic Epistemology.* Oxford: Oxford University Press, 1980.

Sextus Empiricus. *Outlines of Pyrrhonism, Against the Professors.* 4 vols. Translated by R. G. Bury. Cambridge, MA: Harvard University Press, 1955.

Sextus Empiricus. *Outlines of Scepticism.* Translated by Julia Annas and Jonathan Barnes. Cambridge, U.K.: Cambridge University Press, 1994.

Sextus Empiricus. *The Skeptic Way: Sextus Empiricus's Outlines of Pyrrhonism.* Translated by Benson Mates. New York: Oxford University Press, 1996.

Stough, Charlotte. *Greek Skepticism.* Berkeley: University of California Press, 1969.

Striker, Gisela. *Essays on Hellenistic Epistemology and Ethics.* Cambridge, U.K.: Cambridge University Press, 1996.

Tarrant, Harold. *Scepticism or Platonism? The Philosophy of the Fourth Academy.* Cambridge, U.K.: Cambridge University Press, 1985.

James Allen (2005)

ANDERSON, JOHN
(1893–1962)

John Anderson, the Scottish-born Australian philosopher, was the son of a politically radical headmaster. Born at Stonehouse, Lanarkshire, and educated at Hamilton Academy and at the University of Glasgow, which he entered in 1911, he was at first principally interested in mathematics and physics; he turned to philosophy partly under the influence of his brother William, then a lecturer at Glasgow and later professor of philosophy at Auckland University College, New Zealand. Anderson graduated with an M.A. in 1917, with first-class honors both in the school of philosophy and in the school of mathematics and natural philosophy (physics). He lectured at Cardiff (1918–1919), Glasgow (1919–1920), and Edinburgh (1920–1927) before accepting an appointment in 1927 as professor of philosophy at the University of Sydney, Australia. He remained there, except for a visit to Scotland and the United States in 1938, until his retirement in 1958. He had almost no personal contact with philosophers in England, a country he regarded with the suspicion characteristic of a Scottish radical.

Anderson's career as a professor was an unusually stormy one. He attacked whatever he took to encourage an attitude of servility—and this included such diversified enemies as Christianity, social welfare work, professional patriotism, censorship, educational reform of a utilitarian sort, and communism. For a time he was closely associated with the Communist Party, seeing in it the party of independence and enterprise, but he broke with it in the early 1930s. His passionate concern for independence and his rejection of any theory of "natural subordination" were characteristic of his whole outlook—political, logical, metaphysical, ethical, and scientific. Attempts were made to silence him and even to remove him from his professorship; he was subjected to legislative censure and clerical condemnation. In the debates that these attacks provoked, he spoke out forcibly and fearlessly in defense of free speech and university autonomy.

METAPHYSICS AND EPISTEMOLOGY

Anderson was trained at Glasgow as an Absolute Idealist. However, he soon abandoned Idealism, influenced by William James, whom he studied very closely, G. E. Moore, Bertrand Russell, the American "new realists," and, most significantly, Samuel Alexander, whose Gifford Lectures on *Space, Time and Deity* he attended in Glasgow in 1916–1918. James and Alexander taught him that it was possible to reject absolute idealism without, like Russell, reverting to a modified version of traditional British empiricism. Anderson set out to show that continuity, stressed by absolute idealists, and distinction, stressed by empiricists, are equally real and equally involved in every experience. In experience, he argued, we encounter neither an undifferentiated continuum nor isolated sense data; our experience is of complex states of affairs, or "propositions," understood not as sentences, but as what true utterances assert to be the case. These propositions do not mediate between ourselves and reality; to take that view, Anderson argued, is to leave us in a state of invincible ignorance about this supposed "reality." To be real simply is to be "propositional," that is, to be a thing of a certain description, or, in Anderson's view, a complex of activities in a spatiotemporal region.

Unlike many of his British contemporaries, Anderson was by no means opposed to the use of philosophical labels; he was prepared to describe himself as an empiricist, a realist, a pluralist, a determinist, a materialist, or a positivist—but always in a somewhat individual sense. For example, although he insisted that he was an empiricist, he rejected what is usually taken to be the most characteristic doctrine of empiricism—that our experience is of "impressions" or "sense data." For Anderson, empiricism consisted in the rejection of the view that there is anything "higher" or "lower" than complex states of affairs as we encounter them in everyday experience; he rejected ultimates of every sort, whether in the form of ultimate wholes, like Francis Herbert Bradley's Absolute, or ultimate units, such as "sense data" or "atomic propositions."

Similarly, although he agreed with positivists in their opposition to metaphysics, when it is understood as the revelation of realities "beyond facts," he shared neither the positivist hostility to traditional philosophy as such, nor its conception of experience as consisting in "having sensations," nor its interpretation of logic and mathematics as calculi. He was a realist, insofar as he argued that what we perceive exists independently of our perceiving it; but he forcibly criticized the phenomenalism characteristic of so many twentieth-century realists. He described himself as a pluralist, but whereas classical pluralism had defended the thesis that there is a plurality of ultimate simples, everything, for Anderson, is complex. No state of affairs is analyzable into just so many ingredients—whether in the form of sense data or of abstract qualities. Pluralities, in his view, consist of pluralities, not of simples. For the same reason he was not a determinist in the classical sense, because for him no description of a

situation was ever complete; his determinism consisted only in his holding that there are sufficient and necessary conditions for the occurrence of any state of affairs. Finally, his materialism did not incorporate the classical conception of matter; what is essential to his view is the idea that every state of affairs is describable in terms of physical laws—which does not exclude its also being describable in terms of biological, psychological, or sociological laws.

The arguments by which Anderson attempted to establish his philosophical conclusions were manifold and diverse. What was perhaps his fundamental argument can be put thus: As soon as we try to describe "ultimate" entities or offer any account of their relation to those "contingent" entities whose existence and behavior they are supposed to explain, we find ourselves obliged, by the very nature of the case, to treat the alleged "ultimates" as possessing such-and-such properties as a "mere matter-of-fact." The metaphysician either sees his ultimate entities vanish into emptiness—like John Locke's "substance"—or else he is forced to admit that they exhibit precisely the logical characteristics which were supposed to indicate that a thing is not ultimate.

The emptiness of ultimates, Anderson thought, is often disguised by the fact that they are defined in wholly relational terms—as when, for example, substance is defined as "that which underlies qualities," or a sense datum as "that which is an object of immediate perception." Anderson attacked this procedure as "relativism," that is, as the attempt to think of an entity or a quality as being wholly constituted by its relation to something else. To be related, Anderson argued, an entity must be qualitatively describable; relational definitions, it follows, cannot be used to avoid the conclusion that the "ultimate," if it exists at all, must itself be a thing of a certain description. According to Anderson, every state of affairs is "ultimate," in the sense that it is something we have to take account of; but it is contingent, too, in the sense that there are circumstances in which it might not have come about. There is nothing whose nature is such that it must exist, but there is nothing, either, whose nature is exhausted by its relation to other states of affairs.

Particularly in Anderson's lectures, through which his influence has been mainly exerted, such general considerations were supported by detailed analyses of specific philosophical theories. Although he was not, in a professional sense, a scholar, it was his habit both to develop his own views by way of a criticism of his predecessors and also to ascribe to those predecessors—especially perhaps to Heraclitus and to the Plato of the later dialogues—the views that he took to be correct.

LOGIC AND MATHEMATICS

Anderson's approach to philosophy was in some respects formal. He agreed with the Russell of *Our Knowledge of the External World* that logic is the essence of philosophy—if by this is meant that philosophical problems are to be settled by an analysis of propositions. But despite strong mathematical interests, he was only to a very limited degree influenced by Russell's mathematical logic. He worked out, and defended against Russell's criticisms, a reformulated version of the traditional formal logic, which he tried to show had a much greater range and power than its critics would allow to it. He related logic very closely to discussion: the conception of an "issue," of what is before a group for consideration, bulks very large in his logic. The issue, he thought, is always whether some kind of thing is of a certain description, and discussion consists in drawing attention to connections between such descriptions. Unless these connections actually hold, discussion falsifies unless it is actually the case, for example, that what one person brings forward as an objection is logically inconsistent with what another person has said. To point to logical relations, Anderson concluded, is to assert that something is the case, just as much as to draw attention to any other sort of relation.

He took a similar stand concerning mathematics, which, he argued, can be applied to the world only in virtue of the fact that it describes that world. "Application," in Anderson's view, consists in drawing conclusions from what is being applied. If mathematics offered no description of the world, no application of it could describe the world.

He did not, however, agree with John Stuart Mill that mathematical propositions are "inductions from experience." He was a vigorous critic of induction. If, as traditional empiricists had assumed, all our experience is of "pure particulars," then, according to Anderson we would not have the slightest ground for believing in—we could not even conceive the possibility of—general connections. But, in fact, the least we can be acquainted with is not a bare particular but a particular state of affairs; from the very beginning, generality is an ingredient of our experience. We can recognize directly that, say, fire burns, although we can be mistaken in this as in any other of our beliefs; for to "recognize" is nothing more or less than to hold a belief.

AESTHETICS, ETHICS, AND POLITICAL PHILOSOPHY

Although even in his aesthetic, ethical, and political writings, Anderson was constantly concerned to make formal points—as, for example, that the definition of good as "that whose nature it is to be an end" exhibits the vice of "relativism"—yet he was also a good deal influenced by, and deeply concerned with, the issues raised by economists like Alfred Marshall, social theorists like Karl Marx and Georges Sorel, critics like Matthew Arnold, psychologists like Sigmund Freud, and novelists like James Joyce and Fëdor Mikhailovich Dostoevsky. His aesthetic, ethical, and political writings conjoin the logical and the concrete; in virtue of this fact he has influenced many Australian intellectuals who would not accept his formal analyses.

In his aesthetics, Anderson argued that the beauty of works of art is independent of the observer; and similarly in ethics, that acts are good or bad in themselves. He was influenced by Moore's *Principia Ethica* but critical of Moore's attempt to treat "good" as being a simple and indefinable quality and at the same time to define it as "that which ought to be," and thus a quality. Anderson took "good" to be a predicate of certain forms of mental activity—the spirit of inquiry, love, courage, artistic creation, and appreciation—and tried to work out a theory of the connection and distinction between these different forms of activity.

In his political theory, Anderson attacked, on the one hand, the view that human society has a single "good" to which all activity ought to be subordinated, and, on the other hand, the doctrine that it is a set of contractual relations between individuals. Society, as he saw it, is a complex of complex institutions, of which the state is only one. A community flourishes when this fact is fully realized, when no attempt is made to enforce uniformity upon these diverse competing and cooperating types of institutions. The attempt to achieve absolute security by social planning, Anderson held, is doomed to failure and is stultifying in its effects in society.

INFLUENCE. Anderson's ideas were presented in a series of articles, mainly in the *Australasian Journal of Philosophy,* and in his influential lectures at the University of Sydney, where he founded what has been described as "the only indigenous school of philosophy in Australia." Among those philosophers who have, in varying degrees, felt his influence, the best known are D. M. Armstrong, A. J. Baker, Eugene Kamenka, J. L. Mackie, P. H. Partridge, and J. A. Passmore.

See also Aesthetics, History of; Alexander, Samuel; Armstrong, David M.; Bradley, Francis Herbert; Dostoevsky, Fyodor Mikhailovich; Freud, Sigmund; Heraclitus of Ephesus; Idealism; James, William; Locke, John; Mackie, John Leslie; Marx, Karl; Mill, John Stuart; Moore, George Edward; Plato; Positivism; Russell, Bertrand Arthur William; Sorel, Georges.

Bibliography

Anderson's principal contributions to periodicals, together with two previously unpublished papers, have been brought together as *Studies in Empirical Philosophy* (Sydney: Angus and Robertson, 1962), with an introduction by J. A. Passmore, which contains a full bibliography. For further information, see Gilbert Ryle, "Logic and Professor Anderson," in *Australian Journal of Philosophy* 28 (3) (1950): 137–153; J. L. Mackie, "The Philosophy of John Anderson," in *Australian Journal of Philosophy* 40 (3) (1962): 264–281; J. A. Passmore, "Philosophy in Australia," in *Australian Culture* (Ithaca, NY: Cornell University Press, 1963).

John Passmore (1967)

ANDŌ SHŌEKI

Andō Shōeki was a critical thinker in the Tokugawa period of Japan. All that is known of his life is that he was born in Akita toward the end of the seventeenth century and died in the second half of the eighteenth century, that his profession was medicine, and that he went to Nagasaki, the first Japanese port to receive Western trade, where he learned about conditions in foreign countries. He is described as a man of stern character who in his teaching never quoted, except to criticize, the Chinese classical books, meaning that he followed only his own ideas, a very unorthodox way of teaching for Tokugawa Confucianists. Very fond of the peasant class, he insisted that his pupils, and he had very few, should do manual work to be in contact with nature, the greatest master of all. Until recently he was virtually unknown, because of his nonconformist ideas, although nowadays he is overpraised. His manuscripts were found only in 1889, and only in part. They were published with difficulty. The better-known are *Shizen shin-eidō* (The way and activity of nature, written in 1755) and *Tōdō shinden* (A true account of the ruling of the way). They are the most devastating critique ever made of Tokugawa society and of every kind of Japanese ideology.

Andō's iconoclasm was directed first of all against Shintoism and Buddhism. He sharply attacked Shinto mythology and Prince Shōtoku (574–622) for his role in spreading Buddhism. Other rulers, too, and priests of all sects came under his critical scrutiny, which is too negative. Nor had he a better appreciation of the different schools of Confucianism, for he accused them of perverting the teaching of the old sages in their interpretation of nature.

Nature for Andō is an eternal *ki,* or material energy, in perpetual motion. Nature is not to be conquered but to be known; and in following nature man attains the ideal. More positive were his ideas about society; he was the only genuine equalitarian of Tokugawa Japan, arguing against the evils of a system which oppressed the peasant. He cannot be considered completely iconoclastic, since he was not against authority as such, nor was he an atheist, and even his alleged materialism has to be qualified.

See also Japanese Philosophy.

Bibliography

For a guide to primary sources, see bibliography in the Japanese Philosophy entry. See also E. H. Norman, "Andō Shōeki and the Anatomy of Japanese Feudalism," *Transactions of the Asiatic Society of Japan,* 3rd series, 2 (1949): 1–340; and Y. B. Radul-Zatulovskij, *Andō Shōeki, Filosof Materialist XVIII Veka* (Moscow, 1961).

Gino K. Piovesana, S.J. (1967)

ANIMAL MIND

Mind is considered in terms of contents or processes or both. The term usually includes both conscious and unconscious events. In the case of the term *animal mind,* there is intense scientific and philosophical disagreement as to whether animal minds are unconscious or can include conscious events as well. In particular, even among scientists who may accede to the possibility of animal consciousness, there is great reluctance to consider the issue as amenable to scientific study. Donald R. Griffin is a particularly notable exception, who has made the issue a focus of his scientific attention.

OVERVIEW OF PHILOSOPHICAL AND SCIENTIFIC HISTORY

Concerns that still strongly engage philosophers and psychologists to this day were raised by the opposing ideas of John Locke (1632–1704) and Rene Descartes (1596–1650). In Locke's accounting, the elements of mind are ideas. Ideas are written by experience onto the blank slate of the mind, the *tabula rasa* first proposed by Aristotle. Descartes claimed that ideas are innate.

Locke considered that human's ideas are created through sensations; furthermore human minds can reflect upon their ideas. According to Locke, an automatic process of association is an essential mechanism in the linkage between ideas. Descartes, too, proposed automatic, mechanistic connections to explain the mind and behavior of animals and much of humans'. Descartes emphasized automatic reflexes, which are connections between stimulating sensations of the external world and the organism's response to those sensations. For humans, Descartes proposed a mediating influence that could be exerted on reflexes by the soul operating through the brain. These views of Locke and Descartes strongly determined the field of experimental psychology; the reflex and the process of association formed the basis of the phenomenon of classical conditioning.

Both Locke's and Descartes's ideas impacted directly on the study of animal mind. Descartes had claimed that man has a soul, while animals do not; they are mere automata. Humans too have automatic processes, but humans are conscious, feel pain, and experience pleasure, while animals do not. Locke considered animals to have memory and to be capable of simple cognitive processes, including simple reasoning. They lack, however, the capacity to manipulate their ideas, to reflect upon them, as humans can. Essentially, "Brutes abstract not" (Locke 1690, website, p. 31).

With the advent of Charles Darwin's theory of evolution, the proposed continuity between humans and animals promoted a search for animal abilities that were precursors of human abilities. Darwin's *The Expression of Emotions in Man and Animals* (1872) not only proposed that animals experience emotions, but that, indeed, the expression of human emotion is in many ways similar to and derivative from that of certain other species, particularly nonhuman primates. At about that time, George Romanes (1882) compiled numerous examples of animal intelligence; the range of presumed capacities startled the public and scientists were criticized. The criticism, especially in later decades, decried the anecdotal nature of many observations and stressed the need for experimental verification. These issues continue to trouble the adequate documentation of observed instances of intelligent behavior, which would most plausibly be revealed in single, unique instances as an organism attempts to deal with a novel situation.

In the 1920s, Ivan Pavlov's study of digestion in dogs led him to discover that the dogs learned to anticipate the arrival of food via signals in the environment, such as his entry into the room. Evidence was the dogs salivating well before food was in their mouths. Pavlov's many subsequent detailed studies revealed underlying laws of classical conditioning.

The behavioristic approach was further espoused by James Watson and then by B. F. Skinner. They argued that private mental states cannot be the subject matter of science, only public events can be. Concentration was on learned behavior, reducible to stimulus-response units, which were subject to psychological laws. The laws of behavior were derivative of Locke's postulated process of association and, with the Pavlovian laws of classical conditioning, dominate experimental psychology even into the twenty-first century.

In a more cognitive approach, Edward Tolman's studies (1948) of rats learning their way through complicated mazes led him to propose that rats create a tentative, cognitive map indicating routes and environmental relationships, which determine the rats' responses. He struggled with the issue of behavioral indices of mental states. Of particular interest to him was specifying descriptive properties of a behavior to indicate that it is purposive. Tolman's views met with skepticism and interest in them faded until the concept of animals' cognitive maps was revived in an important book by John O'Keefe and Lynn Nadel (1978).

Griffin's influential book, *The Question of Animal Awareness* (1976), and his several subsequent books, reawakened both interest and controversy about animal awareness and thinking. His emphasis that animal awareness is an issue amenable to scientific study spurred investigations into animal cognitive capacities, both in the lab and the field.

Yet just what cognitive processes animal minds possess is controversial. Most contemporary experimental psychologists prefer to examine such processes without relevance to issues of consciousness. In an effort to create highly replicable experimental paradigms in controlled laboratory settings, the scientists can justifiably be strongly criticized for setting for their subjects very simplistic tasks, many of little or no relevance to the organism in its natural life, situating them in impoverished environments for rearing and testing (e.g. T- mazes or Skinner boxes/operant chambers) and for ignoring the contextual effects that are always part of the experimental conditions (e.g., as Pavlov had noted, the dogs in his study began salivating before his original digestion experiment had officially begun). Furthermore the subject of choice is most often the white rat, a genetically inbred docile animal, which may well have lost some of the cognitive and other traits essential to survival in the complex, treacherous world of the wild rat.

In addition to psychologists, ethologists, in particular cognitive ethologists, also study animal minds. Cognitive ethology is a field established by Griffin, being the study of animals' mental experiences, particularly in the course of their daily lives in their natural environment. Data are gathered either from observations or experiments in the field, initial observations often forming the basis for creating the experimental investigations. Likewise some laboratory work has become more naturalistic, employing larger spaces and other means to simulate the organism's niche. Philosophers of science and of mind have shown interest in the field of cognitive ethology, and some, such as Daniel Dennett and Colin Allen, have collaborated in varying degrees with ethologists. Other very relevant contributions have been made, such as Ruth Millikan's (1984, 1995) analysis of natural functions and both Jonathan Bennett's (1989)and John Searle's (2000) considerations of intentionality, belief-desire systems, and consciousness.

CAPACITIES OF ANIMAL MIND

The aspects of animal mind include cognitive, emotional, moral, and communicative capacities and consciousness.

COGNITIVE CAPACITIES. By defining cognition very broadly, one can include the simplest processes, for example, habituation, found in fairly simple creatures such as the sea slug, *Aplysia*, to processes of abstraction, inference, and deception, credited to some primates and selected other species. (Habituation is a process whereby an organism decreases responding to a repeated stimulus.) In most psychological analyses, investigators assume that processes found at the lowest evolutionary levels are similarly to be found in any and all higher organisms (insofar as a hierarchical notion of evolution is appropriate). This is the model of experimental psychologists who conduct laboratory studies of white rats and pigeons.

However neurophysiological studies of simple organisms such as *Aplysia* and the mollusk *Hermissenda* do note different biochemical and neural mechanisms that may underlie similar psychological processes (e.g., classical conditioning at the cellular level). Ethologists, too, are quick to note species specific and niche specific behavioral traits, which often depend upon specialized sensory receptors. Without the capacity to detect certain information, there is no opportunity to develop advanced cognitive capacities dependent upon such information.

Thus bats can echo-locate and, thereby, in the dark navigate through obstacles and catch minute insects; dogs can follow faint odor trails of individuals; humans can do neither.

Psychologists would argue that the same basic psychological laws can be applied to different sensory systems, but there is mounting evidence against this interpretation. Rather than the laws of classical conditioning applying equally to all stimuli, evidence shows, for example, a bias for associating stimuli that are involved with ingestive systems. Thus, in laboratory experiments, rats tend to associate taste with apparent nausea (induced by X-rays) while visual and auditory stimuli are readily associated with painful exteroceptive stimuli. The latter biases are usually interpreted as associations most relevant in predatory-prey interactions and in other dangerous environmental events, as seen in work by John Garcia and R. A. Koelling (1966). Pigeons are biased to associate visual cues with X-ray induced illness; for the pigeon, vision is most essential in detecting their appropriate foods, such as grains. Simply put, organisms have evolved to readily learn which food associated stimuli make them ill, and thus are better able to avoid such. And further they can associate the stimuli with an illness occurring several hours later, contrary to assumed need for temporal contiguity.

In brief, all animal species, including some insects that have been studied, and probably even some single-celled animals, have been shown to be capable of at least the following: habituation, classical conditioning, and operant conditioning. But since the 1960s, important constraints on those basic processes have been recognized. Classical conditioning most simply refers to the learning process whereby a previously neutral stimulus (the conditioned stimulus or CS), when paired with a noxious or positive stimulus (the unconditioned stimulus or US), comes to elicit a response preparatory for or similar to that elicited by the US.

Since the 1960s important constraints on the basic learning processes have been recognized. Lab experiments showed that necessary conditions for classical conditioning were not merely those of temporal association as indicated by Locke and Pavlov. In addition, the CS had to have predictive value; thus if the US occurred too frequently not preceded by the CS, the CS was no longer predictive and much reduced conditioning occurred, if any (Rescorla 1966, 1988). These matters become of special significance when interpreting the overall cognitive abilities of animals: Are many processes most properly interpreted as simple, automatic, stamping in of associations, or should they be considered as expectancies and predictions that organisms hold about their world?

The same issues arise in considering operant conditioning, the strengthening of responses which are followed by reinforcement, or colloquially, rewards. This is basically the question: How do organisms learn how to behave in the world? Are the laws governing response learning automatic, generally applicable processes? Can animals learn behaviors without responding at all? An example might be the ability to form a cognitive map simply from observation. An early experiment had cats towed about in carts through a maze, so they never made responses to be reinforced; nevertheless the cats later could walk correctly thorough the maze. This may not seem surprising to many readers, but to psychologists intent on establishing simple, noncognitive, stimulus-response laws; this was anathema.

Animals are capable of many advanced abilities; certainly Locke was wrong in proclaiming, "Brutes abstract not." Even lab pigeons can learn natural, humanmade or even arbitrary categories. Pigeons were trained to peck for food reward at various slides including: tree/non-trees, water/non-water, people/non-people, scenes with a particular person/scenes with other people or no people, the letter *A* in various fonts/other letters, fish/non-fish (a natural category but not one within a pigeon's usual experience) and a random selection of fish versus non-fish versus another random collection of the same types. The pigeons succeeded at all these discriminations as indicated by differential pecking rates and were able to generalize appropriately to novel instances. Interestingly the birds took far longer to learn the arbitrary sets. And they were capable of correctly categorizing together such examples of water as a droplet or a pond.

Precisely what the pigeons were learning is open to question and beyond the scope of this limited survey. It has not been definitively demonstrated that the birds had formed concepts of tree and non-tree; they could have pecked upon detecting leafiness or trunkness; they could have refrained from pecking at various sub-groupings rather than non-tree. Numerous other studies do not resolve the issue to the satisfaction of all, though at least some species, particularly ravens, parrots, and great apes, can form concepts to criteria acceptable by very many researchers.

COGNITIVE MAPS. The study of cognitive maps in animals has produced evidence of impressive abilities. After training, pigeons shown a photograph with objects and food in it can go correctly to that location in a lab room.

Pigeons that have flown around a campus can, from an aerial photograph, learn to go to designated locations, including untrained sites (Honig 1991). In bird species that cache food for the winter, numerous experiments indicate that birds not only recall the placement of hidden seeds, but they recall better those seeds which they have hidden themselves. Experiments involving displaced landmarks indicate that rats and avian species studied use geometric information from their stored representations. Chimpanzees hide stones for later use as tools, and retrieve them using near optimal paths to do so. Succinctly put, pigeons, rats, and other species have been shown, with experimental evidence, to form concepts and cognitive maps, though the precise definitions of those terms is debated.

Animal knowledge of time presents a challenge to investigating scientists. There are many reports of animals returning at appropriate times to access regularly occurring food arrivals; the most notable may be the return of bees just before tea time each afternoon to the garden tea table of the famous bee scientist Karl von Frisch. Laboratory studies indicate that rats and pigeons can learn complicated schedules of responding for food, and can estimate time durations on the order of seconds very accurately.

But there are other aspects to the knowledge of time. As the philosopher Ludwig Wittgenstein noted when discussing Locke's ideas, "We say a dog is afraid his master will beat him, but not, he is afraid his master will beat him tomorrow." (Wittgenstein 1963, vol.1, p. 650). Relevant to this concern is research with scrub jays, a species that caches food for use at a later time; the work indicates use of elapsed time information in a fairly subtle way. According to the work of Nicola Clayton and colleagues (2003), these birds can discriminate and preferentially retrieve, depending on time elapsed since storage, either a preferred food (larvae) with a shorter time until decay or a less preferred food (peanuts), which lasts longer. Some of the ape cognition and language studies do include reports by apes of past occurrences, but those data do not appropriately tackle the issue of animal knowledge of time past, present, and future. In summary, by the current two-system hypothesis, both simple, automatic learning processes and more sophisticated cognitive skills are characteristic of both animals and humans.

MOTIVATIONAL, EMOTIONAL, AND MORAL CAPACITIES OF ANIMALS. These capacities have received far less investigation than have the cognitive. Motives and emotions have been studied in the laboratory and occasionally in the field (Robert Sapolsky), particularly in reference to possible practical applications to humans. Thus theoretical and neurophysiogical/hormonal models have been proposed with regard to stress, addiction, learned helplessness, and depression. Experimental psychologists are in a dubious position, whereby some deny the possibility of animal consciousness or its scientific study, while others use animals as models for human emotions and motivations.

A possible evolutionary basis for morality reawakened research interest, beginning in the 1990s with neuroanatomical investigations and field studies. Apparent animal altruism has long intrigued scientists, resulting in theoretical models drawn, for example, from economic theorizing. Some suggest that the basis for human morality can be found in human's capacity for empathy, for understanding another's thoughts and feelings. Neurological studies confirm that merely viewing pictures of people injuring themselves, even stubbing their toes, activates some of the same brain regions that are engaged when people stub their own toes. Relevant animal research could be undertaken with potentially important results.

COMMUNICATION. Griffin suggests that animal communication may well serve as a window on animal minds, and thus provide evidence relevant to animal consciousness. Comparisons are frequently made to human linguistic communication, provoking agreement and controversy. To be discussed here are both natural and artificial communication systems.

Natural animal communication systems. Late-twentieth-century research has developed beyond the rigid stimulus-response model of classical ethology and the notion that at least some animal communication is merely a by-product of an internal state, what Griffin (1992) has termed the Groan of Pain (GOP) interpretation. Central issues now concern *what* is being communicated.

An important approach to communication by W. John Smith (1977) stresses an interactional, informational framework, which, however, has not received adequate attention. He notes that animals' signals by themselves do not provide sufficient information to enable recipients to choose appropriate responses. The context of the signal, including the roles of the specific interactants, their past history, and the environmental characteristics, all help determine meaning. This evaluation of information implies complex cognitive processes. In Smith's view, communication importantly allows

interactants to predict the other's behavior; he avoids use of intentional terms, but his analyses are indeed amenable to such.

Beginning with mere insects, one finds surprising complexity and versatility in the genetically based dance communication system of honeybees. It has been known since the time of von Frisch, from studies begun in the 1920s, that the figure eight shaped waggle dances that honeybees perform inside their darkened hive convey information about the distance, direction, and desirability of a food source, though many academic battles were fought until that information was accepted. Later research indicated the dances could convey the same information about a potential new hive location, even including site height. The dance itself seems able to persuade other dancers to change their steps, and sometimes a recipient will begin to dance about a new location, sight unseen.

Of particular interest in the continuing controversy about the distinctions between human and animal communication, is the fact that several investigations indicate that some species' signals appear to be referential, that is, the calls specify the type of predator that has been detected. The species include vervet monkeys that appear able to indicate their three major predator types: the martial eagle, the leopard or other large carnivore, and the python. Diana and Campbells monkeys likewise have two different alarm calls, one for each of their major aerial and ground predators. Even some lemurs, primitive primate-like creatures, have calls specific to raptors, as does a mongoose species.

Sometimes level of arousal is included in the information of these various species' calls. Prairie dog calls reputedly identify predator types, even conveying information about the intruder's color and size, but the research needs further verification. Note, however, that the term *alarm call* is controversial, for some scientists, such as Smith, emphasize the broader use of some such calls. Peter Marler and his colleagues (1986) have also investigated reference in alarm and other calls, emphasizing the role of the audience, both that present and that to which a call is directed, in determining if a signal is given and which signal is made. It is also the case that many scientists are very reluctant to accept referential use of a signal by a nonhuman animal.

Artificial communication systems. Scientists have also undertaken studies of communication in apes and other species using modified forms of human sign language, plastic chips, computerized geometric figures (lexigrams), and spoken words. It is beyond the scope of this entry to discuss these investigations fully, but it should be noted that some of the chimpanzees can respond to and produce strings of words similarly to the behaviors of a two-and-one-half-year-old human. That is not to say that the understandings of the humans and other species are the same. Whether the units should properly be termed words and whether the behavior should be termed language use is hotly debated (Terrace 1979); linguists are the strongest dissenters.

However both apes and African Grey parrots can use the communication units to indicate the color, number, and shape of items, and can accomplish cognitive tasks such as indicating same-different. Some of the apes understand and use artificial units, while also appropriately responding to some spoken English words. Apes have been reported to use the lexigrams to express simple thoughts and emotional feelings (Ristau and Robbins 1982, Ristau 1991, Savage-Rumbaugh 1998, and others).

ANIMAL CONSCIOUSNESS. To study consciousness, it is first necessary to delineate possible levels or kinds of consciousness, a task for both psychologists and philosophers. Since the topic is beyond the scope of this entry, note at least that consciousness can refer most simply to perceptual consciousness or awareness of sensations and pain and in more complex states to consciousness of self through past, present and anticipated future and to metacognition, or thoughts about one's thoughts and knowing *that* one knows. Yet even at a primitive level, it is difficult to imagine that a sensing creature, infant or animal, does not in some way distinguish between an external world and that which belongs to itself—such as its own paw.

Griffin has suggested the following as kinds of evidence for consciousness:

(1) An argument from evolution: Given that many other aspects of human structure and function are derived from those of other animal species, why should not consciousness likewise be part of the continuum?

(2) An argument from neurology: No Consciousness producing neurological structure or process can be found in humans, but absent from nonhuman animals. On the contrary, similar electrical brain waves are correlated to apparently similarly psychological functions in both humans and animals.

(3) As Griffin notes, "Appropriate responses to novel challenges for which the animal has not been prepared by genetic programming or previous experi-

ence provide suggestive evidence of animal consciousness because such versatility is most effectively organized by conscious thinking" (Griffin and Speck 2003, p. 5).

(4) Animal communication may well serve as a window to the minds of animals, revealing their subjective experiences, including intentions.

In his books and papers, Griffin (1976, 2001, 2003) reviews many experiments that provide evidence for consciousness. A few examples are noted. Beginning in the late 1970s, experiments examined the ability of chimpanzees to recognize themselves in a mirror (Gallup 1970). Children can do this after about eighteen months of age, but up to that time, they react socially to the mirror, interacting with their reflection as though it were another child. Chimpanzees also react socially, unless they have had extensive experience with mirrors. Results are mixed for other great apes, with controversial evidence from monkey species and no positive results from chickens and a myriad of other animals. Yet some monkey species, unable to recognize themselves by the mirror test, can nevertheless use a mirror to help them in a task with their otherwise unseen hand. Whatever the final evidence and interpretations, the mirror test can imply only some sense of the self as a body and not necessarily of the self as a mind, or as a self persisting from the past into the future.

A more limited claim, that rats can discriminate their own behaviors, derives from a task in which rats learned to push one of four different levers when a buzzer sounded, depending upon their own activity at the moment, for example, face washing, rearing, walking, or immobility (Beninger et al. 1974). Again interpretations of the results vary; for example, whether a rat is associating a particular lever with kinesthetic feedback from its behavior or whether a rat is indicating, " Now I am walking."

There is evidence that monkeys sometimes know what they know. As Griffin notes, "Consciously considering the contents of memory, in contrast to automatically using stored information, is a kind of metacognition, which many are still hesitant to infer in animals" (Griffin and Speck 2003, p. 13). Yet the ability to consciously consider uncertainties faced in nature is indeed an asset for an animal in a critical situation. In experiments investigating metacognition, monkeys had a choice of pressing one lever, thereby producing a less preferred food, or another lever requiring correct stimulus selection in order to receive a more preferred reward. Correct selection was difficult if monkeys had to delay their responding after seeing the stimulus they were to match. On such trials, the monkeys most often chose the less desirable reward, rather than take the test and quite likely get no reward. The author concludes that the monkeys can report the presence or absence of memory (Hampton 2001).

Creative tool making by crows, and indeed by other species, is another ability that strongly suggests conscious deliberation. There has long been considerable evidence of tool making by chimpanzees and orangutans, but less so for other species. New Caledonian crows studied in lab aviaries spontaneously used sticks to reach food in a clear cylinder, most often selecting sticks of the proper length. In other experiments, the crows selected a hooked wire, rather than a straight one to reach food most readily gained with a hook. When only a straight wire was available, the female crow, never having seen the process of wire bending, bent the wire herself to make a hook and thereby obtain the food.

Experiments have also been conducted in the field, suggesting purposeful, strategic behavior by the organisms involved. For example, Carolyn Ristau (1991) conducted experiments with piping plovers, birds that perform broken-wing or distraction displays at an intruder's approach to their nest/young. She suggested criteria for purposive behavior and found that the birds met such criteria. The plovers used the display correctly, so as to draw a human intruder away from the nest/young, positioning themselves in the intruder's front visual field. When plovers flew to reposition themselves before displaying, they went nearer the intruder and the center of the intruder's visual field. Plovers, even mid-display, monitored the intruders. Should the intruder not follow the birds' displays, the plovers modified their behaviors, re-approaching the intruder or increasing display intensity. Other experiments indicated the plovers' awareness of the direction of an intruder's attention, by becoming more aroused when a passing intruder looked toward their nest area in the dunes in contrast to looking towards the sea. Alexandra Horowitz (2002) has further developed Ristau's criteria for intentional behavior and has applied the ideas to dogs' interactive behavior.

In research by David Premack (1978, 1992), Daniel Povinelli (2000), Michael Tomasello (1997), and Frans de Waal (2003) and their colleagues, chimpanzees have been shown to be capable of complex problem solving and social understanding, sometimes interpreted as the ability to attribute and to understand other minds. Such abilities include determining the intentions of others, detecting, understanding and engaging in deception, and distinguishing between knowledge held by another in contrast to another's visual perception. Many aspects of these capacities seem reasonable evidence for consciousness.

In summary, though unresolved in the view of some, many behavioral scientists appear to be coming to agree that animals are conscious. The matter of proof of the content of mental states of any creature, human or otherwise, remains a philosophical problem. There simply are no incontrovertible means by which external behaviors, linguistic or otherwise, provide absolute proof of specific mental states. One can be certain only of one's own consciousness; this is the extreme version of the solipsistic position.

PHILOSOPHICAL IMPLICATIONS

The essential problem confronting the study of animal minds as conscious entities is that of solipsism. However, in order to survive in daily life, one cannot accept the solipsistic position. In science, one can at least recognize that to declare that animals are not conscious is not a neutral stance, but one that demands proof. As Griffin notes, the probability of awareness (pA) must be assumed to be 0.5, not 0.0. So the scientific task becomes one of accumulating evidence that shifts pA in either direction, noting that level of awareness for a particular task does not necessarily imply the organism's consciousness during another task.

PHILOSOPHICAL PROBLEMS. Several traditional philosophical lines of inquiry are to be considered in the study of animal mind, certainly the philosophy of science and of mind including the nature of scientific evidence, solipsism, nature of experience (e.g., *qualia*), intentionality and gradations of belief-desire systems, linguistic concerns, nature of a referent and of representation, nature of specific cognitive capacities, and defining levels of awareness/consciousness and at least suggestive evidence for each.

POTENTIAL ROLES FOR PHILOSOPHERS

In the past, philosophers were usually dismissive of the need for scientific data in pursuing philosophical problems. Fortunately, that attitude has changed. Philosophers cognizant of the data in their area of interest can play much needed roles in elucidating unidentified assumptions in scientists' work. They can suggest the kinds of data and experimental designs required to provide insight into mental states. Philosophical examinations of Kantian and other concepts of space and time as relevant to animal minds would likewise be helpful.

But philosophers also need to accept real-world constraints on their thinking, prime among them being temporal: Organisms act in a time-limited world and often the most dangerous situations they face require making very rapid decisions. Thus organisms often operate using default mechanisms as well as more time-consuming, deliberative, or trial-and-error methods. Organisms, both animal and human, are often overloaded with information; thus simple heuristics must often suffice. Aware of constraints such as these, as well as the need to communicate effectively to those in other fields, philosophers' contributions to the understanding of animal mind can be outstanding.

See also Animal Rights and Welfare; Aristotle; Bennett, Jonathan; Darwin, Charles Robert; Dennett, Daniel Clement; Descartes, René; Locke, John; Millikan, Ruth; Pavlov, Ivan Petrovich; Qualia; Searle, John; Skinner, B. F.; Speciesism; Wittgenstein, Ludwig Josef Johann.

Bibliography

Beninger, R. J., S. R. Kendall, and C. H. Vanderwolf, "The Ability of Rats to Discriminate Their Own Behavior." *Canadian Journal of Psychology* 28 (1974): 79–91.

Bennett, Jonathan Francis. *Rationality: An Essay towards an Analysis*. Indianapolis, IN: Hackett, 1989.

Clayton Nicola S, Kara Shirley Yu, and Anthony Dickinson. "Interacting Cache Memories: Evidence for Flexible Memory Use by Western Scrub-Jays (*Aphelocoma californica*)." *Journal of Experimental Psychology: Animal Behavior Processes* 29 (2003): 14–22.

Darwin, Charles R. *The Expression of the Emotions in Man and Animals*. London: Appleton, 1872.

Dennett, Daniel C. *Kinds of Minds*. New York: Basic Books, 1996.

Frisch, Karl von. *The Dance Language and Orientation of Bees*. Cambridge, MA: Harvard University Press, 1967.

Gallup, Gordon G. "Chimpanzees: Self-Recognition." *Science*. Vol. 167 (3914) (January 1970): 86–87.

Garcia, John, and R. A. Koelling. "Relation of Cue to Consequence in Avoidance Learning." *Science* 4 (1966): 123–124.

Griffin, Donald R. *Animal Minds, Beyond Cognition to Consciousness*. Chicago: University of Chicago Press, 2001.

Griffin, Donald R. *The Question of Animal Awareness*. New York: Rockefeller University Press, 1976.

Griffin, Donald R., and Gayle B. Speck. "New Evidence of Animal Consciousness." *Animal Cognition* 7 (1) (2003): 5–18.

Hampton, Robert Russell. "Rhesus Monkeys Know When They Remember." *Proceedings of the National Academy of Sciences USA* 98 (2001): 5359–5362.

Honig, Werner K. "Structure and Function in the Spatial Memory of Animals," edited by Wickliffe C. Abraham, Michael Corballis, et al. In *Memory Mechanisms: A Tribute to G. V. Goddard*, pp. 293–313. Hillsdale, NJ: Lawrence Erlbaum Associates, 1991.

Horowitz, Alexandra C. "The Behaviors of Theories of Mind and a Case Study of Dogs at Play." PhD diss., University of California, San Diego, 2002. Available from http://www.crl.ucsd.edu/~ahorowit/frontmatters.pdf.

Locke, John. *An Essay concerning Human Understanding* (1690). Printed by Elizabeth Holt for Thomas Basset. Reprinted by Pelagus Free Books. www.pelagus.org/books/AN_ESSAY_CONCERNING_HUMAN_ UNDERSTANDING,_by_John_Locke_31.html

Marler, Peter, Alan Dufty, and Roberta Pickert. "Vocal Communication in the Domestic Chicken: II. Is a Sender Sensitive to the Presence and Nature of a Receiver?" *Animal Behaviour* 34 (1986): 194–198.

Millikan, Ruth Garrett. *Language, Thought and Other Biological Categories*. Cambridge, MA: MIT Press, 1984.

Millikan, Ruth Garrett. *White Queen Psychology and Other Essays for Alice*. Cambridge, MA: MIT Press, 1995.

O'Keefe, John, and Lynn Nadel. *Hippocampus as a Cognitive Map*. Oxford: Clarendon Press, 1978.

Povinelli, Daniel J. *Folk Physics for Apes: The Chimpanzees' Theory of How the World Works*. New York: Oxford University Press, 2000.

Pepperberg, Irene M. "Evolution of Avian Intelligence, with an Emphasis on Grey Parrots (*Psittacus erithacus*)." In *The Evolution of Intelligence*, edited by R. S. Sternberg and J. C. Kaufman, 315–337. Mahwah, NJ: Lawrence Erlbaum, 2002.

Premack, David. "On the Origins of Domain-Specific Primitives." *Cognition: Conceptual and Methodological Issues*, edited by Herbert L Pick, Jr. and Paulus Willem van den Broek, 189–212. Washington, DC: American Psychological Association, 1992.

Premack, David, and G. Woodruff. "Does the Chimpanzee Have a Theory of Mind?" *Behavioral and Brain Sciences* 4 (1978): 515–526 and commentaries.

Rescorla, Robert A. "Pavlovian Conditioning: It's Not What You Think It Is." *American Psychologist* 43 (1988): 151–160.

Rescorla, Robert A. "Predictability and Number of Pairings in Pavlovian Fear Conditioning." *Psychonomic Society* 4 (1966): 383–384.

Ristau, Carolyn A. "Aspects of the Cognitive Ethology of an Injury-Feigning Bird, the Piping Plover." In *Cognitive Ethology: The Minds of Other Animals: Essays in Honor of Donald R. Griffin*, edited by Carolyn A. Ristau, 91–126. Hillsdale, NJ: Lawrence Erlbaum, 1991.

Ristau, Carolyn A., and Donald Robbins. "Language in the Great Apes: A Critical Review." In *Advances in the Study of Behavior*. Vol. 12, edited by J. S. Rosenblatt, et al., 142–255. New York: Academic Press, 1982.

Romanes, George J. *Animal Intelligence*. London: Kegan Paul, 1882.

Savage-Rumbaugh Sue, S. G. Shanker, and T. Taylor. *Apes, Language, and the Human Mind*. New York: Oxford University Press, 1998.

Searle, John R. "Consciousness." *Annual Review of Neuroscience* 23 (2000): 557–578.

Smith, W. John. *The Behavior of Communicating*. Cambridge, MA: Harvard University Press, 1977.

Terrace, H. S. *Nim*. New York: Knopf, 1979.

Tolman, Edwin C. "Cognitive Maps in Rats and Men." *Psychological Review* 55 (1948): 189–208.

Tomasello, Michael, and Josep Call. *Primate Cognition*. New York: Oxford University Press, 1997.

Waal, Frans B. M. de, and Peter L. Tyack. *Animal Social Complexity: Intelligence, Culture, and Individual Societies*. Cambridge, MA: Harvard University Press, 2003.

Wittgenstein, Ludwig. *Philosophical Investigations*. Oxford: Basil Blackwell, 1963.

Carolyn A. Ristau (2005)

ANIMAL RIGHTS AND WELFARE

Although all the major moral philosophers in the Western tradition have had something to say about the moral status of animals, they have commented infrequently and for the most part only in brief. This tradition of neglect changed dramatically during the last quarter of the twentieth century, when dozens of works in ethical theory, hundreds of professional essays, and more than a score of academic conferences were devoted to the moral foundations of human treatment of nonhuman animals.

Two main alternatives—animal welfare and animal rights—have come to be recognized. Animal welfarists accept the permissibility of human use of nonhuman animals as a food source and in biomedical research, for example, provided such use is carried out humanely. Animal rightists, by contrast, deny the permissibility of such use, however humanely it is done.

Differ though they do, both positions have much in common. For example, both reject Descartes's view that nonhuman animals are *automata*. Those animals raised for food and hunted in the wild have a subjective presence in the world; in addition to sharing sensory capacities with human beings, they experience pleasure and pain, satisfaction and frustration, and a variety of other mental states. There is a growing consensus that many nonhuman animals have a mind that, in Charles Darwin's words, differs from the human "in degree and not in kind."

Proponents of animal welfare and animal rights have different views about the moral significance of human psychological kinship with other animals. Animal welfarists have two options. First, they can argue that we ought to treat animals humanely because this will lead us to treat one another with greater kindness and less cru-elty. On this view we have no duties to animals, only duties involving them; and all those duties involving them turn out to be, as Kant wrote, "indirect duties to Mankind" (Immanuel Kant, "Duties to Animals," in Regan and Singer, 1991, p. 23). Theorists as diverse as Kant, St. Thomas Aquinas, and John Rawls favor an indirect-duty account of the moral status of nonhuman animals.

Second, animal welfarists can maintain that some of our duties are owed directly to animals. This is the alternative favored by utilitarians, beginning with Jeremy Bentham and John Stuart Mill and culminating in the work of Peter Singer (1990). Animal pain and pleasure count morally in their own right, not only indirectly through the filter of the human interest in having humans treated better. The duty not to cause animals to suffer unnecessarily is a duty owed directly to animals.

Of the two options the latter seems the more reasonable. It is difficult to understand why the suffering of animals should count morally only if it leads to human suffering in the future. Imagine that a man sadistically tortures a dog and dies of a heart attack as a result of his physical exertion; what he does seems clearly wrong even though he does not live long enough to mistreat a human being. If this is true, then we have at least some direct duties to animals.

Animal welfarists who are utilitarians (Singer is the most notable example) use utilitarian theory to criticize how animals are treated in contemporary industries (animal agriculture and biomedical research, for example). For in these industries animals are made to suffer and, Singer alleges, to suffer unnecessarily.

Other animal welfarists who are utilitarians disagree. Government and industry leaders agree that some animals sometimes suffer in the course of being raised for food or used in biomedical research; but they deny that they are made to suffer unnecessarily.

Consider organ transplant research. Research on animals in this quarter involves transplanting some internal organ from one healthy animal to another; the "donor" animal, who is under anesthetic, is killed, but the "receiver" animal is permitted to recover and doubtless experiences no small amount of postoperative pain before being humanely killed.

Is the pain unnecessary? In one sense it clearly is. For since the organ was not transplanted for the good of the recipient animal, all the pain that animal experienced was unnecessary. However, this is not the real question, given the utilitarian perspective. The pain caused to this particular animal is only one part of the overall calculation that needs to be carried out. One also needs to ask about the possible benefits for humans who are in need of organ transplants, the value of the skills surgeons acquire carrying out animal organ transplants, the value of knowledge for its own sake, and so on. After these questions have been answered and the overall benefits impartially calculated, then an informed judgment can be made about whether organ transplant research involving nonhuman animals does or does not cause unnecessary suffering.

As this example illustrates, animal welfarists who are utilitarians can disagree about when animals suffer unnecessarily. As such, these animal welfarists can differ in judging whether animals are being treated humanely and, if not, how much reform is called for.

Advocates of animal rights advance a position that avoids the always daunting, frequently divisive challenge of carrying out uncertain utilitarian calculations. Central to their view is the Kantian idea that animals are never to be treated merely as a means to human ends, however good these ends might be. The acquisition of knowledge, including biological knowledge, is surely a good end, as is the promotion of human health. But the goodness of these ends does not justify the utilization of nonhuman animals as means. Thus, even if animal-model organ transplant research can be justified on utilitarian grounds, animal rights advocates would judge it immoral.

Of the two main options—animal welfare and animal rights—it is the latter that attempts to offer a basis for a radical reassessment of how animals are treated. Animal welfare, provided the calculations work out a certain way, enables one to call for reforms in human institutions that routinely utilize nonhuman animals. But animal rights, independent of such calculations, enables one to call for the abolition of all forms of institutional exploitation.

However these matters are resolved, one should note the major contribution philosophers have made in placing the "animal question" before a wider audience. Despite their philosophical differences, none of the philosophers participating in the debate is satisfied with how animals are treated by the major animal user industries. This consensus has meant that those who manage these industries have had to respond to new forms of moral criticism. Collectively, these philosophers have been and will continue to be a powerful voice calling for better treatment of animals.

In addition, the interest philosophers have shown in the "animal question" has spilled over into other disci-

plines, including sociology, history, anthropology, and law. The latter is of particular interest. Whereas thirty years ago not a single law school in America offered courses on animals and the law, upwards of thirty do so today. The evidence suggests that a new field of inquiry, Human and Animal Studies, is in the offing.

See also Darwin, Charles Robert; Descartes, René; Speciesism; Utilitarianism.

Bibliography

Carruthers, Peter. *The Animals Issue*. Cambridge, U.K.: Cambridge University Press, 1992.

Clark, S. S. L. *The Moral Status of Animals*. Oxford: Oxford University Press, 1977.

Cohen, C. and T. Regan. *The Animal Rights Debate*. Lanham, MD: Rowman and Littlefield, 2001.

Favre, David. *Animals: Welfare, Interests, and Rights*. East Lansing, MI: Animal Legal & Historical Center, 2003.

Francione, G. *Animals, Property, and the Law*. Philadelphia: Temple University Press, 1995.

Frey, R. G. *Interests and Rights: The Case Against Animals*. Oxford: Oxford University Press, 1980.

Frey, R. G. *Rights, Killing, and Suffering*. Oxford: Basil Blackwell, 1983.

Leahy, M. *Against Liberation: Putting Animals in Perspective*. Lanham, MD: Rowman and Littlefield, 1991.

Machan, T. *Putting People First: Why Humans are Favored by Nature*. Lanham, MD: Rowman and Littlefield, 2004.

Midgley, M. *Animals and Why They Matter*. New York: Thompson-Shore, 1983.

Pluhar, Evelyn. *Beyond Prejudice: The Moral Significance of Human and Nonhuman Animals*. Durham: Duke University Press, 1995.

Rachels, J. *Created from Animals: The Moral Implications of Darwinism*. Oxford: Oxford University Press, 1990.

Regan, Tom. *Animal Rights, Human Wrongs: An Introduction to Moral Philosophy*. Lanham, MD: Rowman and Littlefield, 2004.

Regan, Tom. *The Case for Animal Rights*. 2nd ed. Berkeley: University of California Press, 2004.

Regan, Tom, and Peter Singer, eds. *Animal Rights and Human Obligations*. 2nd ed. Englewood Cliffs, NJ: Prentice-Hall, 1991.

Rollin, B. *Animal Rights and Human Morality*. Buffalo, NY: Prometheus Press, 1981.

Rowland, Mark. *Animal Rights: A Philosophical Defense*. New York: MacMillan, 1998.

Sapontzis, S. *Morals, Reason, and Animals*. Philadelphia: Temple University Press, 1981.

Scruton, R. *Animal Rights and Wrongs*. London: Metro Press, 2000.

Singer, Peter. *Animal Liberation*. 2nd ed. New York: New York Review of Books: Distributed by Randon House, 1990.

Singer, Peter, ed. *In Defense of Animals*. New York: Blackwell, 1985.

Wise, Steven M. *Rattling the Cage: Toward Legal Rights for Animals.* Cambridge, U.K.: Cambridge University Press, 2000.

Tom Regan (1996, 2005)

ANIMAL SOUL

See *Animal Mind*

ANIMISM

See *Macrocosm and Microcosm; Panpsychism*

ANNET, PETER
(1693–1769)

Peter Annet, an English freethinker and deist, was by profession a schoolmaster. He lost his employment in 1744 because of his outspoken attacks on certain Christian apologists. A debater at the Robin Hood Society (named after a public house where the meetings were held), he soon became a popular lecturer. The first published result was a pamphlet of 1739, titled *Judging for Ourselves: Or Free-Thinking, the Great Duty of Religion. Display'd in Two Lectures, deliver'd at Plaisterers-Hall,* "By P. A. Minister of the Gospel. With A Serious Poem address'd to the Reverend Mr. Whitefield." The tone of the work is indicated by the statement: "If the Scriptures are Truth, they will bear Examination; if they are not, let 'em go." This was followed by several tracts directly attacking Thomas Sherlock, bishop of London: *The Resurrection of Jesus Considered: In Answer To the Tryal of the Witnesses* "By a Moral Philosopher," which ran through three editions in 1744; *The Resurrection Reconsidered* (1744); *The Sequel of the Resurrection of Jesus Considered* (1745); and *The Resurrection Defenders stript of all Defence* (1745).

In *Social Bliss Considered* (1749) Annet, like John Milton before him, advocated the liberty of divorce. He answered Gilbert West's *Observations on the Resurrection of Jesus Christ* (1747) in *Supernaturals Examined* (1747) and George Lyttleton's *Observations on the Conversion and Apostleship of St. Paul in a Letter to Gilbert West* (1747) in *The History and Character of St. Paul Examined* (1748). Arguing that all miracles are incredible, Annet proceeded to attack Old Testament history in his journal, *The Free Enquirer* (9 numbers, October 17, 1761–December 12, 1761). For this work he was accused of blasphe-

mous libel before Lord Mansfield in the Court of King's Bench in the Michaelmas term of 1762. There is some evidence that Lord Mansfield, urged on by Bishop Warburton and others, used Annet as a scapegoat after a fruitless attempt had been made to suppress the publication of David Hume's *Four Dissertations* of 1757.

Annet pleaded guilty to the charge. "In consideration of which, and of his poverty, of his having confessed his errors in an affidavit, and of his being seventy years old, and some symptoms of wildness that appeared on his inspection in Court; the Court declared they had mitigated their intended sentence to the following, viz., to be imprisoned in Newgate for a month; to stand twice in the pillory [Charing Cross and the Royal Exchange] with a paper on his forehead, inscribed Blasphemy; to be sent to the house of correction [Bridewell] to hard labour for a year; to pay a fine of 6s.8d.; and to find security, himself to 100 £ and two sureties in 50 £. each, for his good behaviour during life." Having survived this "mitigated," charitable, and humane punishment based on the iniquitous Blasphemy Act of 1698, Annet returned to schoolmastering. Archbishop Secker is said to have so far relented as to afford aid to the culprit until his death in 1769. In 1766 Annet issued *A Collection of Tracts of a Certain Free Enquirer noted by his sufferings for his opinions,* a work containing all of the tracts mentioned above.

Annet was long thought to have been the author of *The History of the Man after God's Own Heart* (1761), in which the writer took exception to a parallel drawn by a divine between George II and King David. The anonymous writer argued that such a comparison was an insult to the late king. Recent scholarship has proved that the real author was John Noorthouck, a respected member of the Stationers' Company.

Among his accomplishments, Annet was the inventor of a system of shorthand. Unlike most of the leading English deists, Annet had relatively little formal education and spoke and wrote plainly and forcefully directly to the masses. He was the last to suffer physical punishment for his heterodox religious opinions.

See also Deism; Hume, David; Milton, John.

Bibliography

There is no collected edition of Annet's works, and the texts mentioned in the article are extremely rare. A useful article, however, regarding the authorship of *The History of the Man after God's Own Heart,* is the anonymous "John Noorthouck, 'The Man after God's Own Heart,'" in *Times Literary Supplement* (August 25, 1945): 408.

See also *The English Reports,* Vol. 96, King's Bench Division, XXV (Edinburgh and London), 1909; and E. C. Mossner, "Hume's *Four Dissertations*: An Essay in Biography and Bibliography," in *Modern Philology* 48 (1950): 37–57.

Ernest Campbell Mossner (1967)

ANOMALOUS MONISM

Originated by Donald Davidson, "anomalous monism" is a nonreductive, token physicalist position on the relation between the mental and the physical. According to it, each mental event is a physical event, although mental descriptions are neither reducible to nor nomologically correlated with physical ones. In terms that are ontologically more robust than those used by Davidson, the position asserts identities between individual mental and physical events while denying that mental types or properties are either identical with, or nomologically connected with, physical ones. The position specifically concerns intentional mental phenomena such as beliefs and desires, although it is arguable that it can be extended to cover other mental phenomena such as sensations.

Davidson's argument for this position results from an attempt to reconcile three apparently inconsistent principles, two of which he finds independently plausible and the third of which he defends at length. The first is the principle of causal interaction (PCI), which states that mental events cause physical events and vice versa, causality being understood as relating events in extension. The second is the principle of the nomological character of causality (PNCC), which states that events that are causally related have descriptions under which they instantiate strict causal laws. The third is the principle of the anomalism of the mental (PAM), which states that there are no strict laws in which mental terms figure. The principles appear to conflict in that the first two imply what the third seems to deny—namely that there are strict laws governing causal interactions between mental and physical events.

Davidson argues that the principles can be reconciled by adopting the thesis that each mental event has a physical description and so is a physical event. He further suggests that a sound argument can be constructed from these principles to this thesis. Suppose a mental event, *m*, causes a physical event, *p*. Then, by the PNCC, *m* and *p* have descriptions under which they instantiate a strict causal law. By PAM this cannot be mental in that it cannot contain mental terminology. Therefore *m* must have a physical description under which it instantiates a strict

causal law, which is to say that it is a physical event. Although the argument is formulated in terms of events and their descriptions, it can be formulated equally effectively in the terminology of events and their properties.

Davidson does not take PAM to be obvious. His defense of it involves the idea that laws bring together terms from the same or similar conceptual domains. Using this idea he argues that the constraints that govern the application of mental terms and their associated concepts to things are normative in nature, involving "constitutive" principles of rational coherence, deductive and inductive consistency, and the like. These principles constitute the distinctive rationalistic normativity that is the earmark of the intentional domain; and Davidson argues that they have no place in physical theory.

The argument for anomalous monism appears to work because of the extensionality of the causal relation and the intensionality of nomologicality. Events are causally related no matter how described; but they are governed by laws only as they are described one way rather than another. This opens up a conceptual space between causality and nomologicality that makes it possible to hold both that mental events that interact causally with physical ones are governed by laws and that there are no strict psychological or psychophysical laws.

Davidson's argument has had a profound effect on discussions of mental causation and token physicalism. Many have found either the PNCC or the PAM questionable and have taken issue with it. However, the main objection to the argument is that, on a certain conception of the relation between causality and laws, it leads either to inconsistency or to epiphenomenalism. According to this conception, laws link events causally by linking certain, but not all, of their descriptions or properties, the causally relevant ones. The question now arises, In virtue of which of their properties do mental events interact causally with physical ones? If the answer is the mental ones, then anomalous monism is threatened with inconsistency since this implies that there are laws in which mental descriptions/properties figure. If the answer is the physical ones, then anomalous monism is threatened with epiphenomenalism since it is in virtue of their physical properties that mental events are causally efficacious. Since PAM is a crucial premise in the argument for anomalous monism, it is the epiphenomenalism charge that poses the real threat to the position.

There is a general question of whether nonreductive token physicalist theories count as proper forms of physicalism since they recognize the existence of irreducibly mental properties. Davidson himself favors supplementing his position with some sort of supervenience thesis, according to which, necessarily, if things (events) are the same with regard to their physical descriptions/properties, then they are the same with regard to their mental descriptions/properties. The principal difficulty in formulating such a thesis is in specifying a dependency relation strong enough to ensure that physical properties determine mental ones without leading to reducibility and hence to type physicalism.

See also Davidson, Donald; Mental Causation; Philosophy of Mind; Physicalism; Supervenience.

Bibliography

Davidson, D. "Mental Events." In *Experience and Theory,* edited by L. Foster and J. W. Swanson. Amherst: University of Massachusetts Press, Reprinted in D. Davidson, *Essays on Actions and Events* (Oxford: Clarendon Press, 1980). The classic statement of the argument for anomalous monism.

Davidson, D. "Psychology as Philosophy." In *Philosophy of Psychology,* edited by S. C. Brown. London: Macmillan, 1974. Reprinted in D. Davidson, *Essays on Actions and Events* (Oxford: Clarendon Press, 1980). Discusses anomalous monism and the argument against psychophysical laws.

Davidson, D. "Thinking Causes." In *Mental Causation,* edited by J. Heil and A. Mele. Oxford: Clarendon Press, 1993. Responds to the charge that anomalous monism leads to the causal inefficacy of the mental.

Honderich, T. "The Argument for Anomalous Monism." *Analysis* 42 (1982). Classic statement of the inconsistency-or-epiphenomenalism objection to anomalous monism.

Kim, J. "The Myth of Nonreductive Materialism." *Proceedings of the American Philosophical Association* 63 (1989): 31–47. Argues that nonreductive materialism leads to epiphenomenalism.

Kim, J. "Psychophysical Laws." In *Actions and Events: Perspectives on the Philosophy of Donald Davidson,* edited by E. LePore and B. McLaughlin. Oxford: Blackwell, 1985. Discusses and defends an interpretation of Davidson's argument against psychophysical laws.

LePore, E., and B. Loewer. "Mind Matters." *Journal of Philosophy* 84 (1987): 630–641. Discusses the causal efficacy of the mental within the context of physicalism.

LePore, E., and B. McLaughlin, eds. *Actions and Events: Perspectives on the Philosophy of Donald Davidson.* Oxford: Blackwell, 1985. Articles on Davidson's argument for anomalous monism.

Macdonald, C. *Mind-Body Identity Theories.* London: Routledge, 1989. Surveys various type-type and token identity theories, and defends a version of nonreductive monism.

Macdonald, C., and G. Macdonald. "Mental Causes and Explanation of Action." *Philosophical Quarterly* 36 (1986): 145–158. Reprinted in *Mind, Causation, and Action,* edited by L. Stevenson, R. Squires, and J. Haldane (Oxford: Blackwell, 1986). Defends anomalous monism against the charge of epiphenomenalism.

McLaughlin, B. "Type Epiphenomenalism, Type Dualism, and the Causal Priority of the Physical." *Philosophical Perspectives* 3 (1989). Discusses the problem of mental causation for anomalous monism.

Cynthia Macdonald (1996)

ANSCOMBE, GERTRUDE ELIZABETH MARGARET
(1919–2001)

G. E. M. Anscombe, English philosopher, was educated at Sydenham High School and St. Hugh's College, Oxford, where she read *Literae Humaniores* (Greats). She went as a research student to the University of Cambridge, where she became a pupil of Ludwig Wittgenstein (1889–1951). He and Aristotle were the most important influences on her philosophical thought. Anscombe became a Roman Catholic while in her teens, and her Catholicism was also a shaping influence. She was a Fellow for many years of Somerville College, Oxford, and held the Chair of Philosophy at the University of Cambridge from 1970 until 1986. A philosopher of great range, she made important contributions to ethics, philosophy of mind and action, metaphysics, epistemology, philosophical logic, and philosophy of language. Much of her most interesting work was in the history of philosophy; her discussions of ancient, medieval, and modern philosophers combine illuminating accounts of challenging texts with penetrating treatment of the philosophical problems themselves. As one of Wittgenstein's literary executors, as an editor and translator of his writings, and as a writer and lecturer about Wittgenstein, she has done more than anyone else to make his work accessible. Her *Introduction to Wittgenstein's "Tractatus"* (1959) is a superb introduction to the central themes of that work, making clear the character of the problems (like that of negation) treated in it.

Long before it became fashionable in the 1970s for moral philosophers to concern themselves with practical problems, Anscombe was writing about them. Her first published essay, in 1939, shortly after the beginning of World War II, concerned the justice of that war. She discussed closely related topics in her protest against the honorary degree that Oxford University awarded Harry Truman in 1957 and in connection with the policy of nuclear deterrence. She wrote also on contraception, murder, and euthanasia. All her writings on such questions reflect her belief that the concepts of action and intention are important for ethics, especially in connection with questions about our responsibility for the consequences of our actions. She explained and defended the doctrine of double effect (it is sometimes permissible to cause, as a side effect, a merely foreseen harm that is forbidden if sought intentionally). She argued that denial of this doctrine "has been the corruption of non-Catholic thought and its abuse the corruption of Catholic thought" (1981, 3:54).

Anscombe's interest in war and in the concept of murder led her also to more general philosophical questions about political authority. "Modern Moral Philosophy" (1981, 2005) has been the most influential of her papers on ethics and was an important impetus for the development of virtue ethics (which emphasizes the character traits a human being needs in order to flourish). She defended three theses in the paper: that moral philosophy cannot be done until we have an adequate philosophical psychology; that the concepts of moral obligation, moral duty, and moral "ought" are survivals from a now largely abandoned conception of ethics, are incoherent outside that framework, and should therefore be abandoned if possible; and that English moral philosophers from Henry Sidgwick (1838–1900) on differ only in superficial ways. In explaining the third thesis, Anscombe introduced the term "consequentialism" for the common view that right and wrong are determined by consequences (including among consequences the promotion of intrinsic values), and she argued that consequentialism is a corrupt and shallow philosophy.

In her ground-breaking monograph *Intention* (1957), Anscombe raised and discussed questions about intention, action, and practical thought (practical reasoning and practical knowledge). Widely prevalent philosophical ideas about intention had treated it as some special kind of mental state or event. Departing radically from that tradition, Anscombe gave an account of intentional action in terms of the applicability to it of a kind of question asking for the agent's reason. This account enabled her to show how conceptions of good are important for practical thought. The questions with which Anscombe was concerned frequently straddled metaphysics, philosophy of logic, and philosophy of mind. For example, in "The First Person" (1981), she explained how we are led into confusion by misunderstandings of "I" on the model of a proper name. In "The Intentionality of Sensation: A Grammatical Feature" (1981) she drew on philosophy of language in explaining grammatical analogies between intention and sensation, and was able to give a very interesting and original account of what is right in sense-impression philosophy and of what is misleading in it.

Anscombe explored the topic of causation in several papers, questioning in them widely held assumptions. "Causality and Determination" (1981) begins by formulating two such assumptions: that causality is a necessary connection of some kind, and that it involves a universal generalization connecting events of two kinds. One or the other or both of the assumptions are accepted by virtually all writers on causation, but Anscombe questioned both, together with the related idea that if two courses of events appear similar but have different outcomes, there must be some further relevant difference. She argued that the root idea in all our causal notions is that of one thing deriving from another, and that this need not involve necessitation. In "Times, Beginnings, and Causes" (1981) she challenged two widely accepted views of Hume's: that causal relations are never logically necessary, and that logically something can begin to exist without being caused to do so. Questions about time figure centrally in other papers as well. For example, in "The Reality of the Past" (1981) she treats a problem raised by Parmenides (b. c. 515 BCE) and shows how attempts to explain the concept of the past by reference to memory must fail. This paper also contains one of the best short discussions of Wittgenstein's later approach to philosophy.

While Anscombe worked within the tradition of twentieth-century analytic philosophy, she challenged many of the assumptions of her contemporaries. Although her work, especially on intention and action, has exercised wide influence, much of her thought has not yet been assimilated, owing partly to the fact that she maintained a critical distance from the ideas of her contemporaries and partly to the fact that many of her later papers are not readily accessible.

See also Aristotle; Consequentialism; Euthanasia; Feminist Philosophy; Intention; Metaphysics, History of; Philosophy of Language; Philosophy of Mind; Sidgwick, Henry; Virtue Ethics; Wittgenstein, Ludwig Josef Johann; Women in the History of Philosophy.

Bibliography

WORKS BY ANSCOMBE

Intention. Oxford: Blackwell, 1957. 2nd ed., 1963.

An Introduction to Wittgenstein's "Tractatus." 3rd ed. London: Hutchinson, 1959, 1971.

With P. T. Geach. *Three Philosophers.* Oxford: Blackwell, 1963.

Collected Philosophical Papers. Vol. 1: *From Parmenides to Wittgenstein.* Vol. 2: *Metaphysics and the Philosophy of Mind.* Vol. 3: *Ethics, Religion, and Politics.* Oxford: Blackwell, 1981.

Human Life, Action and Ethics: Essays by G. E. M. Anscombe, edited by Mary Geach and Luke Gormally. Exeter: Imprint Academic, 2005.

WORKS ON ANSCOMBE

Diamond, Cora, and Jenny Teichman, eds. *Intention and Intentionality: Essays in Honour of G. E. M. Anscombe.* Brighton, U.K.: Harvester Press, 1979.

Gormally, Luke, ed. *Moral Truth and Moral Tradition: Essays in Honour of Peter Geach and Elizabeth Anscombe.* Dublin: Four Courts Press, 1994.

Haber, Joram Graf, ed. *Absolutism and Its Consequentialist Critics.* Lanham, MD: Rowman & Littlefield, 1994.

Müller, Anselm. "G. E. M. Anscombe (1919–2001)." In *A Companion to Analytic Philosophy,* edited by A. P. Martinich and David Sosa, 315–325. Oxford: Blackwell, 2001.

Teichman, Jenny. "Gertrude Elizabeth Margaret Anscombe, 1919–2001." *Proceedings of the British Academy* 115 (2001): 31–50.

Teichmann, Roger, ed. *Logic, Cause, and Action: Essays in Honour of Elizabeth Anscombe.* Cambridge, U.K.: Cambridge University Press, 2000.

Cora Diamond (1996, 2005)

ANSELM, ST.

(1033–1109)

The greatest philosopher of the eleventh century, Anselm of Canterbury was the author of some dozen works whose originality and subtlety earned him the title of "Father of Scholasticism." Best known in the modern era for his "Ontological Argument," designed to prove God's existence, Anselm made significant contributions to metaphysics, ethics, and philosophy of language.

Anselm was born in Aosta, in the Piedmont region of the kingdom of Burgundy, near the border with Lombardy. His family was noble but of declining fortunes. Anselm remained at home until he was twenty-three; after the death of his mother he quarreled irrevocably with his father and left home, wandering for some years before arriving at the Benedictine Abbey at Bec in Normandy. Impressed by the abbey's prior Lanfranc, who had a reputation as a scholar and teacher of dialectic, Anselm joined the monastery as a novice in 1060. Such was his ability that in 1063 he was elected prior and in 1078 abbot, a position he held until his elevation as archbishop of Canterbury in 1093. While at Bec, Anselm wrote his *Monologion, Proslogion,* and the four dialogues *De grammatico, De veritate, De libertate arbitrii,* and *De casu Diaboli.* While archbishop, Anselm wrote his *De incarnatione Verbi, Cur Deus homo, De conceptu virginali, De processione Spiritus Sancti,* and *De concordia.* Perhaps from this time also date his fragmentary notes on power, ability,

and possibility. Anselm's archepiscopate was marked by controversy with the English kings William Rufus and Henry I over royal privileges and jurisdiction; Anselm spent the years from 1097 to 1100 and from 1103 to 1107 in exile. After a brief illness, Anselm died on April 21, 1109, in Canterbury, where he is interred in the Cathedral.

METHOD

Most of Anselm's work systematically reflects on the content of Christian doctrine: Trinity, Incarnation, the procession of the Holy Spirit, original sin, the fall of Lucifer, redemption and atonement, virgin conception, grace and foreknowledge, the divine attributes, and the nature of sin. He called this reflective activity "meditation" and also, in a famous phrase, "faith in search of understanding" (*fides quaerens intellectum*). His search for understanding is of interest to philosophers for three reasons. First, he often addresses arguments to those who do not share his dogmatic commitments—that is, he offers proofs based only on natural reason. He begins the *Monologion,* for example, with the claim that a person who does not (initially) believe that there is a God with the traditional divine attributes "can at least persuade himself of most of these things by reason alone if he has even moderate ability." Likewise, the "Ontological Argument" of the *Proslogion,* and indeed the treatise as a whole, is addressed to the Biblical Fool, who denies the existence of God. This approach, later known as "natural theology," may be given in support of but does not depend upon particular points of doctrine.

Second, even when Anselm assumes certain dogmatic theses, his analysis is often directed to specifically philosophical issues in the case at hand, and thereby has broader implications. While discussing Lucifer's sin and subsequent fall in his *De casu Diaboli,* for instance, Anselm formulates a series of general theses about responsibility and motivation that hold not only of Lucifer's primal sin (or Adam's original sin), but which apply to ordinary cases of choice. Elsewhere he offers a defense of metaphysical realism (*De incarnatione Verbi*), a reconciliation of foreknowledge with the freedom of the will (*De concordia*), an account of sentential truth-conditions (*De veritate*), and so on.

Third, even when pursuing his doctrinal agenda, Anselm is always a philosopher's philosopher: Distinctions are drawn and defended, theories proposed, examples given to support theses, and tightly constructed arguments are the means by which he meditates on Christian themes. He uses the selfsame method when no doctrinal commitment is at stake, as in the semantic analysis of the *De grammatico*, the account of power and ability in his fragmentary notes, or the analysis of freedom of choice in *De libertate arbitrii*. For Anselm, understanding—the very understanding for which faith is searching—is a philosophical enterprise, and his treatment of even the knottiest doctrinal difficulties is clearly philosophical in character. Intellectual integrity, he held, demands it. (He further held that although a philosophical approach to matters of faith is necessary, it is not sufficient; hence, in addition to systematic treatises, Anselm also composed prayers and devotional works.)

METAPHYSICS

Following Augustine, Anselm is, broadly speaking, a platonist in metaphysics. A thing has a feature in virtue of its relation to something paradigmatically exhibiting that feature. Anselm begins the *Monologion*, for example, by noting the diversity of good things in the world, and argues that we should hold that "there is some one thing through which all goods whatsoever are good" and that that one thing "is itself a great good … and indeed supremely good" (chap. 1). He reasons that we can judge that some things are better or worse than others only if there is something, namely goodness, which is the same in each, though in different degrees—a claim sometimes dubbed "the Platonic Principle" for Plato's use of it in the case of equal sticks and stones in his *Phaedo*. To establish the uniqueness of this one thing, Anselm applies the Platonic Principle again and rules out an infinite regress. Furthermore, since the goodness of good things is derivative, and things might be good in any degree imaginable, it follows that the one thing through which all good things are good must be supremely good; it can be neither equaled nor excelled by the goodness of any good thing that is good through it. Note that the Supreme Good does not strictly speaking "have" goodness but rather *is* goodness itself, a quasi-substantial entity whose nature is goodness.

Much of Anselm's metaphysics is a sustained study of such relations of dependence and independence: things may be the way they are "through themselves" (*per se*) or "through another" (*per aliud*), Anselm holds, and roughly the same reasoning can be applied to features other than goodness. The later medieval tradition called such features "pure perfections," and their defining characteristic is that it is unqualifiedly better to have them than not. Just as the presence of goodness in things leads to the conclusion that there is some one thing that is paradigmatically good, through which all good things have their

goodness, Anselm argues that so too the bare fact of their existence leads to the conclusion that there is some one thing through which everything else exists. Moreover, this one thing "paradigmatically" exists, namely, it exists through itself and of necessity: it is existence itself, something whose nature is existence (chaps. 3–4).

Anselm drops from the Platonic Principle the requirement that things having a certain feature exhibit it in varying degrees; rather, the possession of the same feature by itself licenses the inference that there is something each thing has, something exemplifying the feature itself. Likewise, the key move in his argument that there is only one such thing that exists through itself, rather than a plurality of independent things each equally existing through itself, is to apply the Platonic Principle to the feature of *self-existence* itself; this entails that there is a unique self-existent nature. Furthermore, since it is better to exist through oneself than through another (independence is better than dependence), the Supreme Good must exist through itself, and hence is identical with the self-existent nature, the source of the existence and goodness of all else there is. Anselm concludes that "there is accordingly a certain nature (or substance or essence) that through itself is good and great, and through itself is what it is, and through which anything that exists is genuinely either good or great or anything at all" (chap. 4). In short order Anselm shows that this being is appropriately called "God," and the remainder of the *Monologion* is devoted to establishing that God has the full range of divine attributes: simplicity, unchangeableness, eternality, triune nature of persons, and the like.

The existence of God is therefore the most fundamental metaphysical truth. Anselm tells us that he sought to replace the chain of arguments outlined above with "a single argument that needed nothing but itself alone to prove its conclusion, and would be strong enough to establish that God truly exists and is the Supreme Good, depending on nothing else, but on whom all other things depend for their existence and well-being." In doing so, he devised one of the most-discussed arguments in the history of philosophy, presented in *Proslogion* 2 as follows:

> Therefore, Lord, You Who give understanding to faith, give me understanding to the extent You know to be appropriate: that You are as we believe, and You are that which we believe. And, indeed, we believe You to be something than which nothing greater can be thought. Or is there is not some such nature, then, since "The Fool hath said in his heart: There is no God" [Psalms 13:1]? But certainly that same Fool,

when he hears this very thing I say, 'something than which nothing greater can be thought', understands what he hears; and what he understands is in his understanding, even if he were not to understand that to be. It is one matter that a thing is in the understanding, another to understand a thing to be. For when the painter thinks beforehand what is going to be done, he has it in the understanding but does not yet understand to be what he does not yet make. Yet once he has painted, he both has it in the understanding and also understands to be what he now makes. Therefore, even the Fool is convinced that there is in the understanding even something than which nothing greater can be thought, since when he hears this he understands, and whatever is understood is in the understanding. And certainly that than which a greater cannot be thought cannot be in the understanding alone. If indeed it is even in the understanding only, it can be thought to be in reality, which is greater. Thus if that than which a greater cannot be thought is in the understanding alone, the very thing than which a greater cannot be thought is that than which a greater can be thought. But certainly this cannot be. Therefore, without a doubt something than which a greater is not able to be thought exists (*exsistit*), both in the understanding and in reality.

The logical analysis, validity, and soundness of this argument have been a matter of debate since Anselm came up with it. Yet its general drift is clear. God, Anselm tells us, is something than which nothing greater can be thought. (Note that he does not present this formula as a definition or part of the meaning of "God" but rather only as a claim that is true of God; the indirect negative formulation is important since we cannot adequately think of or conceive God as such.) So understood, the denial of God's existence leads to a contradiction, as follows. That than which a greater cannot be thought cannot itself be thought not to exist, since if it were, we could think of something greater than it, namely that than which nothing greater can be thought existing in reality. But it is logically impossible to think of something greater than that than which nothing greater can be thought. Thus the denial of God's existence must be rejected, and so God's existence affirmed. Hence Anselm's argument as a whole is *ad hominem*, directed against someone who accepts the claim that God is something than which nothing greater

can be thought; once accepted, Anselm offers a *reductio ad absurdum* of the denial of God's existence.

Anselm's argument (as it was known in the Middle Ages) attracted attention from the very first. When the *Proslogion* was initially circulated, Gaunilon, a monk of Marmoutiers, wrote a brief in defense of the Fool; Anselm wrote a gracious reply and directed that thereafter the treatise should be copied with their exchange.

In the *Monologion* and *Proslogion*, Anselm says that he is trying to establish the existence of a "nature" (or equally an essence or a substance). The divine nature is identical with the very qualities of which it is the paradigm, and furthermore is also a concrete particular: God is an individual, albeit a three-in-one individual. In addition to such an extraordinary nature, there are also common natures, such as human nature, which is present in each human being as his or her individual nature. Anselm holds that such common natures "become singular" when combined with a collection of distinctive properties (*proprietates*) that distinguish an individual from all others (*De incarnatione Verbi* 11). In the same work he inveighs against the extreme nominalism of Roscelin of Compiègne that anyone taking universals to be no more than vocal utterances deserves no hearing on theological matters; Roscelin cannot understand how a plurality of humans are one human in species, and cannot understand how anything is a human being if not an individual (chap. 1).

While the extent of Anselm's metaphysical realism is a matter of debate, remarks such as these make it clear that he countenanced some form of realism about universals. Whereas some form of platonic exemplarism works for features that are identical with the divine essence, a more traditional realism applies to nondivine natures in the mundane world of creatures. From Boethius, Anselm adopts the standard metaphysical framework of substances and accidents, sorted into the ten Aristotelian categories. In the case of substances, Anselm holds that common names designate common natures, while proper names designate individuals metaphysically composed of a nature combined with distinctive properties with further accidental qualities. In addition, there are nonsubstantial qualities such as whiteness, instances of which may be found in individuals. Anselm speaks occasionally of form and of matter, but does not have a developed hylomorphic theory.

ETHICS

Anselm's positive ethical theory is grounded on his theory of the will and free choice, one of his most striking and original contributions. The traditional account of free will holds that an agent is free when there are genuine alternatives open to her, so that she can do one or another of them as she pleases. This traditional account is sometimes called "bilateral" since the agent must have at least two possible courses of action in order to act freely. In his *De libertate arbitrii*, by contrast, Anselm defends a unilateral normative conception of freedom, according to which an agent is free when two conditions are jointly satisfied: (a) she has the ability to perform a given action; and (b) that action is the one she ought to perform, that is, it is objectively the right action and hence the one she ought to want to perform—roughly, that an agent is free when she can act as she ought, regardless of alternatives. (Anselm, like all medieval philosophers, holds that what an agent ought to do is an objective matter.)

Note that Anselm is careful to say that an agent is free when she *can* act as she ought, not that she *does* so act; we commit wrongdoing freely when the right course of action is open to us but we fail to pursue it. The crucial issue, of course, is when an agent has the ability to perform a given action. Anselm devotes most of his fragmentary notes on ability and power to investigating this issue. His analysis tracks connections among ascriptions of ability, responsibility, and the cause of an action, much in the spirit of contemporary philosophical reflections on tort law. Very roughly, Anselm thinks there are a variety of freedom-canceling conditions; some of these, such as compulsion, are extremely sensitive to the kind of ability at stake.

One case in particular attracts Anselm's attention in his *De libertate arbitrii*. Some abilities can be exercised by an agent more or less at will: lifting a book, thinking about Rome, deciding not to eat pork, playing the piano. Other abilities depend on external factors, which may include the actions and abilities of other agents. It takes two to tango, a multitude of musicians to play a symphony, other runners to have a race. These are all necessarily dependent abilities: They require other agents acting appropriately for their exercise. But consider a case in which an ability that could be exercised at will can no longer be so exercised, though the agent retains the ability. A ballerina tied to a chair cannot dance but still has the ability to do so. More exactly, Anselm holds, she does not have the opportunity to exercise the ability, though she retains the ability; were the constraint removed, she could exercise her ability at will. Anselm argues that the ballerina's ability to dance is what matters to her free choice, according to (a), not whether she currently has the opportunity to exercise her ability.

Now suppose that the ballerina, no longer tied to a chair, has through excessive dancing injured her legs so badly that she can dance only if a doctor operates on her legs. Here too, Anselm maintains, she has not lost the ability to dance but only the opportunity to exercise her ability, and can regain the opportunity only if a doctor helps her to do so. This is the situation in which Anselm finds the human race. Through the (wrongful) exercise of our free choice in original sin, we have lost the opportunity to freely do what is right, and can only recover it through the actions of another (namely through God's grace). We can legitimately be faulted for not doing what is right even now, despite the fact that we cannot do what is right at will, by our unaided efforts; we have the ability, and we lost the opportunity to exercise it through its improper use, but these facts do not stand in the way of our being free to act rightly; hence our culpability for failing to do so. Whether we agree with Anselm or not, his analysis is subtle and provocative, and represents a new level of sophistication in the analysis of free choice.

Following Augustine, Anselm argues that we abandon rectitude of will only by our own choice. Many things can happen against one's will, but it is impossible to will against one's will, since that would require both willing something and willing not to will it—but that can be done by simply not willing it in the first place. Not even God can take away our rectitude of will, Anselm maintains, since rectitude of will is doing what God wants; if God wanted to deprive our wills of rectitude, He would want us to not do what he wants, and whether we try to obey or to disobey, we wind up doing as He wants. Thus abandoning rectitude must be through our own choice, since it cannot happen against our will or by external (even divine) compulsion. The responsibility for wrongdoing rests squarely on our shoulders.

Anselm returns to these topics in his *De casu Diaboli*, perhaps returning to the traditional bilateral conception of freedom in the process. In Chapter 12 he puts forward a famous thought-experiment in which God creates an angel with free will, but without any motive for action whatsoever—a free being with no ends at all. Anselm argues that such a being would never act, since any action is motivated by pursuit of an end, and by hypothesis the angel has no ends. (Nor is an angel ever prompted by biological needs, and this is the point of using an angel rather than a human being in the example.) From this case Anselm and later philosophers drew the moral that at least some ultimate end has to be given to agents in order for there to be action at all, and hence the possibility of moral action. An agent must therefore have at least one ultimate end, an end she does not choose.

Yet one end is not enough for moral agency. Anselm argues that there must be two ultimate and incommensurable ends to make sense of moral choices, and specifically of moral dilemmas. He reasons as follows. If an agent had only a single end, she would always act in pursuit of that end, unless deceived or misled through ignorance. There would be no moral conflict; her motives and reasons for action would be transparently in the service of her single ultimate end. This is quite similar to the life of nonrational animals. A dog pursues only its apparent good, as defined by its nature (which establishes its ultimate end). Dogs naturally aim at their own "perfection," as Anselm puts it. But human beings are more complicated. We face choices in which each alternative serves a distinct end, the ends being ultimate and incommensurable. Anselm holds that this fact explains moral agency and the possibility of moral wrongdoing, for rational agents have two distinct ultimate ends: they seek their own happiness (through advantage or benefit) on the one hand, and they seek justice (rectitude of will) on the other hand.

This is the core of Anselm's so-called "two-will theory" of motivation. Moral conflicts and dilemmas arise when we are faced with the choice between happiness and justice, between individual self-interest and impersonal fairness. Each end is a genuine good to the individual agent, and the conflict between them is real. Morality demands that we favor justice over happiness in such conflicts; wrongdoing is explained as the choice of happiness over justice. A thief prefers his own advantage to following the laws. While we might not side with the thief, his choice is not inexplicable; indeed, we may even sympathize with him while deploring his actions. The possibility of an irreducible clash between ultimate ends that we cannot forgo gives us the ability to explain moral agency. To say that justice and happiness can conflict is of course not to say that they do; if we are lucky, we might avoid moral dilemmas. Nevertheless, our actions are free because of the pull between these ends, even if we consistently take one side or the other.

Human fulfillment for Anselm thus turns out to be surprisingly paradoxical. We do not deserve to be happy unless we are prepared on principle to forgo happiness for justice. Indeed, only by pursuing justice for its own sake can we attain the self-interested happiness we have scorned. The price of moral agency is that happiness is the reward for those who do not pursue it.

PHILOSOPHY OF LANGUAGE

Anselm adopts Augustine's view of language as a system of signs. This general category covers linguistic items, such as utterances, inscriptions, gestures, and at least some acts of thought; it also covers nonlinguistic items, such as icons, statues, smoke (a sign of fire), and even human actions, which Anselm says are signs that the agent thinks the action should be done. Roughly, a sign signifies something by bringing it to mind; this single semantic relation, founded on psychology, is the foundation of Anselm's semantics.

As noted above, common names—at least natural-kind terms—signify common natures, and proper names signify the common nature in combination with distinctive properties. Nondenoting terms are problematic; "nothing" seems to be significant only by signifying nothing, a paradox that perplexes Anselm in several treatises. Troublesome as they are, Anselm directs his most sustained inquiry into semantics not at empty names but at "denominative" terms, roughly what we call adjectives.

The difficulty he addresses in his *De grammatico* can be stated simply: "white" cannot signify whiteness ("whiteness" does that); nor can it signify what is white ("snow" does that); what then does it signify? Anselm's answer depends on several distinctions, the most important of which is between direct and indirect signification (*per se* and *per aliud* signification). A term signifies directly if it brings the proper and customary signification to mind; it signifies other things indirectly, perhaps things linked somehow to what the term directly signifies. As a first approximation, then, Anselm holds that 'whiteness' directly signifies whiteness, whereas 'white' directly signifies whiteness and indirectly signifies things that have whiteness (and is used to pick out the latter).

Verbs, for Anselm, signify actions or "doings" of some sort, broadly speaking, including even passive processes; that is their distinguishing feature. Names and subjects, respectively, signify subjects and their doings; when combined in a sentence, the truth of the sentence reflects the underlying metaphysical dependence of doings on doers, of actions on subjects. Now just as Anselm's theory of meaning applies to more than words, so too his theory of truth applies to more than statements. In the *De veritate*, Anselm puts forward an account that recognizes a wide variety of things to be capable of truth—statements, thoughts, volitions, actions, the senses, even the very being of things. Truth, for Anselm, is a normative notion: Something is true when it is as it ought to be. Thus truth is in the end a matter of correctness (*rectitudo*), the correctness appropriate in each instance (*De veritate* 11). For statements there are actually two forms of correctness: A given statement ought to signify what it was designed to express, and, if assertoric, it ought to signify the world the way it is. The first is a matter of the propositional content of an utterance, the second whether that propositional content is asserted (or denied). The statement "snow is white" does what it should do when it succeeds in signifying that snow is white; it also does what it should do when it succeeds in signifying that snow is white in the circumstances that snow really is white. The latter is the closest to our contemporary notion of truth for statements, but Anselm insists that the former is a kind of truth too (he calls it the "truth of signification"), and indeed can hold even if the world changes such that snow is no longer white.

See also Aristotle; Augustine, St.; Ontological Argument for the Existence of God; Plato; Roscelin.

Bibliography

Anselm's works have been critically edited by F. S. Schmitt, *S. Anselmi Cantuariensis Archiepiscopi opera omnia*, vols. 1–6 (Edinburgh: T. Nelson, 1946–1961), supplemented by fragments and miscellaneous materials in R. W. Southern and F. S. Schmitt, *Memorials of St. Anselm* (Auctores Britannici Medii Aevi 1), published for The British Academy by Oxford University Press, 1969. Complete translations of Anselm's major works may be found in Jasper Hopkins and Herbert Richardson, *Anselm of Canterbury*, vols. 1–3 (New York: Edwin Mellen Press, 1976), as well as in Brian Davies and Gillian R. Evans, eds., *The Major Works: Anselm of Canterbury* (Oxford and New York: Oxford University Press, 1998). The most thorough modern biography of Anselm is by R. W. Southern, *Saint Anselm: A Portrait in a Landscape* (Cambridge and New York: Cambridge University Press, 1990).

Overviews of Anselm's thought are given in Jasper Hopkins, *A Companion to the Study of St. Anselm* (Minneapolis: University of Minnesota Press, 1972); Gillian R. Evans, *Anselm* (London: Chapman, 1989); Brian Davies and Brian Leftow, eds., *The Cambridge Companion to Anselm* (Cambridge and New York: Cambridge University Press, 2004). On the Ontological Argument, see Alvin Plantinga, ed., *The Ontological Argument* (Garden City, NY: Anchor Books, 1965); John Hick and Arthur McGill, eds., *The Many-Faced Argument* (New York: Macmillan, 1967); David Lewis, "Anselm and Actuality," in *Nous* 4 (1970): 175–188; Jonathan Barnes, *The Ontological Argument* (London: Macmillan, 1972); Paul Oppenheimer and Edward Zalta, "On the Logic of the Ontological Argument," in *Philosophical Perspectives*, vol. 5, edited by James Tomberlin (Atascadero, CA: Ridgeview, 1991). Issues having to do with free choice are discussed in John O'Neill, "Anselm on Conflicting Oughts," in *Heythrop Journal* 35 (1994): 312–314; Calvin Normore, "Picking and Choosing: Anselm and Ockham on Choice" in *Vivarium* 36 (1998): 23–39;

Thomas Williams and Sandra Visser, "Anselm's Account of Freedom" in *Canadian Journal of Philosophy* 31 (2001): 221–244. Anselm's theory of action is analyzed in Eileen Serene, "Anselmian Agency in the Lambeth Fragments: A Medieval Perspective on the Theory of Action" in *Anselm Studies* 1 (1983): 143–156; Douglas Walton, "Anselm and the Logical Syntax of Agency" in *Franciscan Studies* 14 (1976): 298–312. On Anselm's philosophy of language see Desmond P. Henry, *The Logic of Saint Anselm* (Oxford: Clarendon Press, 1967); and Marilyn Adams, "Saint Anselm's Theory of Truth" in *Documenti e studi sulla tradizione filosofica medievale* 1 (1990): 353–372.

Peter King (2005)

ANTHROPIC PRINCIPLE, THE

The term *Anthropic Principle* (AP) was introduced by the physicist Brandon Carter, who stated that "what we can expect to observe must be restricted by the conditions necessary for our presence as observers" (Carter 1974, p. 292). The central idea of AP could be put as follows: We can observe only those states of affairs that are compatible with the existence of observers.

The term has subsequently been applied to all manner of claims, variously obscure and bizarre. This entry restricts its attention to the central and philosophically interesting idea. Carter distinguished what he called the weak version of the principle, according to which "our location in the universe is necessarily privileged to the extent of being compatible with our existence as observers" (Carter 1974, p. 293), and the strong version, which states that "the universe (and hence the fundamental parameters on which it depends) must be such as to admit the creation of observers within it at some stage" (p. 295). The distinction was meant merely to apply the simple insight of AP on the one hand to local conditions at places and times within the universe, and on the other to features of the universe as a whole. The unfortunate wording of Carter's strong principle has led many to misunderstand it as attributing necessity to the universe's fundamental parameters. Whatever appeal this idea has seems to derive from a simple scope confusion. AP tells that necessarily, if humans observe a universe, then it has the parameters that allow for the development of observers. It does not follow that if humans observe a universe then the conditions required for observers take hold necessarily.

APPLICATIONS WITHIN THE UNIVERSE

AP is obviously true, and may appear too obvious to be of any interest. It is said to play a crucial role in explanation and theorizing about the universe. But how could a seemingly trivial, necessary truth enter into scientific explanations and inferences at all?

One can begin to answer this question by recalling that failure to consider the limits on what can be observed often leads to errors in scientific reasoning. This is well illustrated by one of John Leslie's cases of selection bias in *Universes* (1989). If a person finds all of the fish he or she has caught to be more than five inches long, this person may be tempted to inductively infer that all fish in the lake are longer than five inches. But the strength of this inference is undermined by noting that the net used cannot hold smaller fish. One can understand this epistemic situation in terms of competing explanations. The hypothesis that all fish in the lake are more than five inches long may, in principle, explain the failure to observe any shorter fish: One has not seen short fish because there are none around to see (perhaps chemical waste has rendered the adult fish population infertile). But such an explanation becomes redundant when it is noted that the method of observation prevents one from seeing smaller fish, whether there are any in the lake or not. If this person had been fishing with a regular reel and bait, it would be remarkable that he or she would have failed to catch small fish, and the hypothesis that all the fish in the lake are longer should be taken more seriously. The inference to all fish being more than five inches long is undermined by eliminating its use as an explanatory hypothesis.

It pays to be clear on what is explained here and what is not. The observational limitation—using a net with large holes—does nothing to explain, for any particular fish, why that fish is longer than five inches. What is explained is the failure to observe anything but long fish.

In a similar way, AP can serve as a check on overly zealous use of what is known as the Copernican Principle in cosmology. Copernicus famously taught that the Earth is not central to the solar system, let alone the universe. Taking this lesson to heart, cosmologists have been wary of theories that attribute special characteristics to the Earth's spatio-temporal position. The Copernican Principle instructs, roughly, to proceed on the assumption that the conditions that take hold within one's observable neighborhood are more or less the same throughout space-time. As a guard against gratuitous biases about the human place in the universe, the Copernican Principle is appropriate. But it would be equally arbitrary to rule out the possibility that in the vastness of space-time, there are isolated pockets with strikingly unique features. And it is not out of the question that humans may happen to occupy one of these special regions. Indeed, if these rare conditions are necessary for the development of intelligent life, this is just where humans should expect to find themselves. It would be a mistake akin to that in the fishing story to extrapolate too eagerly from observations of local conditions to the wider universe if these locally observed features are a necessary condition of one's being here to observe anything. For in this case one can adequately explain the failure to observe any other features, even if most of the universe is different. (One of the earliest influential appeals to AP by the physicist R. H. Dicke, in "Dirac's Cosmology and Mach's Principle" [1961], uses this kind of strategy.)

One must be careful to distinguish this lesson from some more grandiose claims made on behalf of AP. Some incautious statements by physicists have been taken to suggest that human's existence and ability to observe the universe helps to explain why those observed features took hold. Clearly this explanation goes in the wrong direction. From human existence together with certain laws of nature, it may be possible to deduce that certain conditions took hold; this is not, however, sufficient for explanation. It is the required conditions that (partly) explain why humans are here, and not the other way round. Human observational limits no more explain why any observed conditions took hold than the use of a fishing net with large holes explains the length of any fish. In each case it is only one's failure to make contrary observations that is explained.

APPLICATIONS TO THE UNIVERSE'S FUNDAMENTAL PARAMETERS

According to contemporary cosmology, if the values of various fundamental parameters of the universe—such as force strengths and particle masses—differed ever so slightly from their actual values, life could not possibly have developed anywhere in the universe. And it appears that these parameters could easily have been different. It is as if the universe were the product of a machine with dozens of dials that determined its features. The vast majority of dial combinations result in a universe that collapses within seconds, or that contains nothing but hydrogen, or nothing but black holes. Only the most delicate adjustment of the dials will produce a stable universe, capable of supporting life at some time and place. Without the aid of deliberate adjustment, the odds of the big bang producing a life-permitting universe appear extremely low.

In the light of these data, that the universe meets the conditions for life has struck many scientists and philosophers as a striking fact that requires explanation (whether or not this attitude is appropriate may be questioned, but it is only on this initial assumption that uses of AP arise). Some have taken these facts as the basis of a new version of the argument from design. The remarkable coincidence of physical parameters required for life may be explained by the actions of a rational agent. Others have suggested that the solution may lie in a more fundamental theory, with laws constraining the range of values that crucial parameters can take. The application of AP is supposed to undermine the need for such hypotheses. The simplest anthropic-style response takes the form of a popular glib reply: "If the physical parameters hadn't been just so, then we wouldn't be here puzzling about the matter!" The inadequacy of this response is well illustrated by the following analogy from Leslie (1989). Standing before a firing squad, a dozen guns are fired your way, but not a single bullet hits you. Clearly you have grounds to be astonished and wonder why you have been so lucky. Did they all deliberately miss? Did they fill their guns with blanks? It is possible that their missing you is just a fluke, but this seems incredible. It becomes no more credible when one considers that if the gunmen had not all missed, you would not be here to puzzle about it. Given that people do observe a universe, it is no surprise that they see one that meets the conditions for observers to exist. But they may well still wonder how they, or anyone, are here to see anything at all.

MULTIPLE UNIVERSES

More serious uses of AP couple it with the suggestion that this universe is just one of an enormous variety of actually existing universes. (Here "universe" does not refer to the totality of what there is, but rather to a large, more or less isolated aggregate of matter in space-time.) Of course this strategy is viable only to the extent that reason exists to suppose that there are a great number of universes. This is highly controversial. One of the proposed universe-generating models is the inflationary theory in cosmology. The multiple-universe hypothesis is distinct from the many-worlds interpretation of quantum mechanics, but some have appealed to the latter as a way in which the required variety of universes might be generated (see Leslie 1989).

How could the existence of other universes help solve a puzzle about this universe? For any improbable outcome of an event, if you repeat the type of event enough times you can expect to get an outcome of that type eventually. To take the popular example, if a monkey types for long enough, or a large enough army of monkeys is put to work, it is all but certain that somewhere, at some time, a monkey will type a sonnet. Similarly, whereas it may be extremely unlikely that any particular universe meets the conditions for life, if there are a large enough number of them, it is to be expected that at least one of them will by chance be life-permitting. The vast majority of universes will be rather bland, containing no stars or planets, let alone life. There should be no room to wonder why humans have been lucky enough to see only one of the nice universes. They may note by AP that they could not possibly have found themselves in any other kind of universe, as those universes fail to meet the conditions for human existence.

The same explanatory strategy has been employed in areas of science as diverse as statistical mechanics and evolutionary biology. Ludwig Boltzman (1895) suggested a similar idea to account for the extremely low level of entropy (i.e., roughly, the high degree of order) in the observable neighborhood. Boltzman's speculation was that the universe is extremely large in space and time, with disorder on the large scale, but large, finite regions of order within. One can picture this view as like an infinite number of coins tossed on an infinite expanse. The big picture will almost certainly be a random, disordered mess. But with maximum probability there will also be enormous finite stretches of nothing but heads, and vast regions of beautiful and orderly patterns. Boltzman noted that it is only in regions of low entropy that living organisms such as humans can be found. So on this hypothesis, people should not be surprised to find that theirs is a low-entropy environment. Similar principles are applied in Darwinian explanations of the evolution of organisms. The tree of life consists of an enormous variety of branches produced by random mutations. Most of these are hidden from human view. It is only those that have the remarkable ability to sustain themselves and reproduce that people are able to observe.

As before, care needs to be taken in stating what has been explained and what has not. The plenitude of universes does not explain why this particular universe humans inhabit is life-permitting. The answer to the question "Why is this universe suitable for life?" is not "Because there are many other universes." The existence of many universes does not raise the probability that any particular one such as this can support living creatures. At most, what is to be expected is some universe will do this.

What the hypothesis of many universes may do, however, is remove the urgency of explanation regarding the particular universe in which humans find themselves. That this universe is life-permitting seems remarkable only insofar as it seemed remarkable that there was life at all. But if there are many universes, then it is not surprising that somewhere in some universe life can develop. The more specific question of why it is this universe and not another one appears less urgent, such as the question of why Jones won the lottery, or why the golf ball landed on this blade of grass. An adequate answer may be along the lines of "That's just how it turned out."

See also Cosmology; Many Worlds/Many Minds Interpretation of Quantum Mechanics; Philosophy of Statistical Mechanics.

Bibliography

Barrow, John, and Frank Tipler. *The Anthropic Cosmological Principle.* Oxford: Clarendon Press, 1986.

Boltzman, Ludwig. "On Certain Questions of the Theory of Gases." *Nature* 51 (1895): 413–415.

Carter, Brandon. "Large Number Coincidences and the Anthropic Principle in Cosmology." In *Confrontation of Cosmological Theories with Observational Data*, edited by M. Longair, 291–298. Dordrecht, Netherlands: D. Reidel, 1974. Reprinted in *Modern Cosmology and Philosophy*, 2nd edition, edited by John Leslie. New York: Prometheus, 1998.

Dicke, R. H. "Dirac's Cosmology and Mach's Principle." *Nature* 192 (1961): 440–441. Reprinted in *Modern Cosmology and Philosophy.* 2nd edition, edited by John Leslie, 127–130. New York: Prometheus, 1998.

Earman, John. "The SAP Also Rises: A Critical Examination of the Anthropic Principle." *American Philosophical Quarterly* 24 (4) (1987): 307–317.

Leslie, John, ed. *Modern Cosmology and Philosophy.* 2nd edition. New York: Prometheus, 1998.

Leslie, John. *Universes.* London: Routledge, 1989.

Roger White (2005)

ANTHROPOLOGY

See *Philosophical Anthropology*

ANTIOCHUS OF ASCALON
(130/120?–68/7 BCE)

Antiochus joined the Academy, the school founded by Plato, late in the second century BCE, when Philo of Larissa was its head. Philo was (at this time) a moderate Academic skeptic who had been convinced by the Academy's anti-Stoic arguments that nothing can be known for certain, but he did not embrace the other doctrine for which Academic skeptics argued—suspension of judgment. According to Philo, although certain knowledge is unobtainable, it is possible to identify highly probable impressions, and there is no reason not to accept them, provided that one realizes that one might be wrong. Prominent among them is the impression that nothing can be known.

After defending this view for many years, Antiochus became a dogmatist by accepting that knowledge is possible. His epistemological position was now essentially that of the Stoa. He responded to accusations that he had left the Academy for the Stoa by claiming that Zeno of Citium (335–263 BCE), the founder of Stoicism, had introduced a new vocabulary but was otherwise in essential agreement with the schools of Plato and Aristotle. Far from abandoning the Academy, Antiochus maintained, he had returned it to its true self. For this reason, he and his followers styled themselves the Old Academy. It is unclear what institutional status this group enjoyed or whether Antiochus ever officially succeeded Philo.

Antiochus regarded the criterion of truth and the goal of life as the most important concerns of philosophy, and his ethical theory is the other area about which we are well informed. In opposition to the Stoics, who maintained that virtue is the sole good and therefore sufficient for happiness, Antiochus held that there were also bodily and external goods. He rightly took this to be the view of Aristotle and the Old Academy, but the form in which he presented his theory owes a good deal to the Hellenistic schools. Thus Antiochus relied heavily on the so-called cradle argument, which takes the uncorrupted behavior of infants as its starting point. Antiochus combined evidence from this source about the objects of our first natural concern with the general principle that what accords with a creature's natural impulses is its good, to derive his account of the goal.

He was in broad agreement with the Stoics that our constitution and things that preserve and develop it are the first objects of our natural concern, and not pleasure as Epicurus supposed. But the Stoics take it that this natural concern is replaced by a unique attachment to virtue. Antiochus held that, as the perfection of reason, which is the most important part of our constitution, virtue is the chief good. But he also regarded the other objects of natural concern as goods, albeit lesser goods, and therefore a part of the goal.

Antiochus wanted to claim that, even so, virtue is sufficient for happiness. To this end, he distinguished between the happy life (*vita beata*), for which virtue was enough, and the entirely happy life (*vita beatissima*), which requires other goods as well.

None of Antiochus's books have survived, but he is known to have written a work about epistemology, the *Canonica*, and another epistemological work, the *Sosus* against Philo of Larissa's late views. A book in which he stressed the close relation between the Peripatos, Aristotle's school, and the Stoa is attested, and Cicero tells us that he wrote in many places about his views concerning happiness and virtue.

See also Ancient Skepticism; Cicero, Marcus Tullius; Philo of Larissa; Stoicism; Zeno of Citium.

Bibliography

Barnes, Jonathan. "Antiochus of Ascalon." In *Philosophia Togata: Essays on Philosophy*, edited by Jonathan Barnes and Miriam Griffin. Oxford, U.K.: Oxford University Press, 1989.

Glucker, John. *Antiochus and the Late Academy*. Hypomnemata 56. Göttingen: Vandenhoeck und Ruprecht, 1978.

Mette, H. J. "Philon von Larissa und Antiochos von Askalon." *Lustrum* 28–29 (1986–1987): 9–63.

Striker, Gisela. "Academics Fighting Academics." In *Assent and Argument: Studies in Cicero's Academic Books*, edited by Brad Inwood and Jaap Mansfeld. Leiden, Netherlands: Brill, 1997.

James Allen (2005)

ANTIPHON
(c. 480–411 BCE)

Antiphon was an Athenian sophist, author of *Truth*, *Concord*, and—if identical with the same person as Antiphon of Rhamnus—three *Tetralogies* and many court speeches. The identity of the sophist and the speechwriter remains uncertain but is increasingly accepted (see Gagarin 2002; for contra, Pendrick 2002). If the two are the same, Antiphon was an aristocratic Athenian, admired by Thucydides (*History of the Peloponnesian War* 8.68), who wrote sophistic works, taught, gave legal and political advice, and wrote speeches for litigants in court. He was a leader of an oligarchic coup in 411 BCE and was tried and executed after the coup quickly failed.

Antiphon's *Tetralogies*, probably his earliest works (450–430 BCE), were intended for intellectual stimulation and pleasure and perhaps for public performance. Each group of four speeches (two on each side) treats a hypothetical case of homicide. In the *First Tetralogy*, the identity of the killer is uncertain, and arguments are based on the likelihood (*eikos*) that the defendant is the

killer. The *Second* disputes whether a young man who threw a javelin that killed a boy is responsible for the death. The *Third* questions who is responsible for a man's death during a drunken fight. None of the *Tetralogies* has a conclusion or verdict. Their aim is to explore issues and forms of argument (likelihood vs. truth, fault and responsibility, cause and effect) with subtlety and cleverness. They also raise questions about the relationship of *logos* (speech, argument) to reality, and the relationship between opposed arguments when each claims, with some justification, to speak the truth.

Perhaps in the 420s BCE, Antiphon composed the sophistic works *Truth* and *Concord*—only fragments of which now remain—and the even more fragmentary *Politicus* and *Dream-Interpretations*. *Truth* explored a wide range of issues, including mathematics (squaring the circle), meteorology, and natural philosophy. The largest surviving fragments show Antiphon exploring the relationship between *nomos* (law, convention) and *physis* (nature), particularly with respect to law and justice. He may be saying that law is purely a matter of convention, and that a person may violate the law as long as no one else will know of it.

See also Sophists.

Bibliography

Antiphon. "Antiphon." Translated by J. S. Morrison. In *The Older Sophists*, edited by Rosamond K. Sprague, 106–240. Columbia: University of South Carolina Press, 1972. English translation of all surviving works, including fragments, and of the ancient testimony for Antiphon.

Gagarin, Michael. *Antiphon the Athenian: Oratory, Law and Justice in the Age of the Sophists*. Austin: University of Texas Press, 2002. Assumes a single Antiphon and analyzes all the works, including the three surviving court speeches.

Pendrick, Gerard J. *Antiphon the Sophist: The Fragments*. Cambridge, U.K.: Cambridge University Press, 2002. Introduction, Greek text with translation, and full scholarly commentary on *Truth*, *Concord*, and the other sophistic fragments.

Thucydides. *History of the Peloponnesian War*. Edited by Robert B. Strassler. New York: Free Press, 1996.

Michael Gagarin (2005)

ANTIREALISM

See *Realism*

ANTISTHENES

(ante 443 BCE–post 366 BCE)

Antisthenes, son of an Athenian father and Thracian mother, was a pupil of the rhetorician Gorgias and an intimate and admirer of Socrates. He taught professionally at Athens, maintaining his own interpretation of Socrates against other Socratics such as Plato and Aristippus. There is, however, only one reference in classical literature to Antistheneans (Aristotle, *Metaphysics* 1043b24); later antiquity saw him as a founder of Cynicism, a view that may have gained support through later historical systematization or from Stoics attempting to trace their philosophical pedigree to Socrates. Nevertheless, while the historical relationship between Antisthenes and Diogenes remains obscure, there were elements in Antisthenes' thought that heralded and may have given some impulse to Diogenes. His numerous works have not survived (a list of titles is found in Diogenes Laertius's *Lives*, 6.15–18); but he is characterized in Xenophon, and Diogenes preserves a doxographical and anecdotal account. Antisthenes had rhetorical and sophistic interests and was famed for his style and his myths as well as for his Socratic dialogues.

The influence of Socrates shaped Antisthenes' overriding interest in practical ethics. He held happiness to be dependent solely on moral virtue, which involved practical intelligence and so could be taught, partly from a study of the names of things and definitions. But the good man also required strength of mind and character; for by contrasting external goods with the inviolability of the "wealth of the soul," Antisthenes came to stress the importance of self-control by a hostility to luxury and sensual pleasure that went some way toward Cynic asceticism. Thus, the achievement of virtue necessitated a mental and physical effort to toil through opposing difficulties, suffering, and pain. Antisthenes glorified this struggle in the myths of Heracles; and for Cynics "toil" (*ponos*) became a technical good and Heracles a saint.

Antisthenes combined a moral interest in politics with a wariness of the dangers of participation, and attacked the rules of convention when they were in opposition to the laws of virtue. He denounced famous statesmen of previous generations and outlined his own ideal king, whose preeminence was due to his own moral self-mastery.

Most tantalizing is the brief glimpse Aristotle affords of Antisthenes' interest in the logic of predication and definition. He denied the possibility of contradiction (*Topics* 104b21), apparently because he believed (*Metaphysics* 1024b27 ff.) that each object could be spoken of only by its own peculiar verbal designation that said what it was; that is, words corresponded directly with reality, and since predication was confined to assigning names to things, or limited to formulas determining their real structure, any other predicative account must then refer to something different or to nothing at all, and contradiction did not arise. There was a similar difficulty with falsity. Elsewhere (*Metaphysics* 1043b23ff.) the Antistheneans are said to have denied the possibility of defining what a thing (like silver) was; one could only explain what sort of thing it was (for instance, "like tin"). Aristotle's context referred to simple substances that could not be analyzed but only named or described. Similar problems to these occur in Plato (as in *Sophist* 251A f.; *Theaetetus* 201C ff.; *Euthydemus* 283E ff.; *Cratylus* 429B ff.). It has been argued that in one or more of these passages Plato had Antisthenes in mind, but this is not at all certain. The problems were common to the period. Interesting similarities have been pointed out between Antisthenes' logic and the nominalism of Thomas Hobbes.

See also Aristotle; Cynics; Diogenes Laertius; Hobbes, Thomas; Plato; Socrates.

Bibliography

CLASSICAL

Antisthenis Fragmenta. Edited by A. W. Winkelmann. Zürich, 1842.

Diogenes Laertius. *Lives.* 6.1–19.

Xenophon. *Symposium* and *Memorabilia.*

MODERN

Dudley, D. R. *A History of Cynicism from Diogenes to the 6th Century.* London: Methuen, 1937.

Dümmler, F. *Antisthenica.* Halle, 1882.

Field, G. C. *Plato and His Contemporaries.* London: Methuen, 1930; 2nd ed., 1948.

Fritz, K. v. "Zur Antisthenischen Erkenntnistheorie und Logik." *Hermes* 62 (1927): 453–484.

Fritz, K. v. "Antisthenes und Sokrates in Xenophons Symposium." *Rheinisches Museum* n. F. 84 (1935): 19–45.

Gillespie, C. M. "The Logic of Antisthenes." *Archiv für Geschichte der Philosophie* 26 (1913): 479–500; 27 (1914): 17–38.

Höistad, R. *Cynic Hero and Cynic King.* Uppsala, Sweden: n.p., 1949.

Sayre, F. *The Greek Cynics.* Baltimore: Furst, 1948.

G. Kidd (1967)

APEIRON/PERAS

The Greek term *Apeiron,* meaning originally "boundless" rather than "infinite," was used by Anaximander for the ultimate source of his universe. He probably meant by it something spatially unbounded, but since out of it arose the primary opposite substances (such as the hot and the cold, the dry and the wet) it may have been regarded also as qualitatively indeterminate. Aristotle, summarizing the views of certain early Pythagoreans (*Metaphysics* A, 5), puts the pair *Peras* ("Limit") and *Apeiron* ("Unlimited") at the head of a list of ten opposites. *Peras* is equated with (numerical) oddness, unity, rest, goodness, and so on; *Apeiron* is equated with evenness, plurality, motion, badness. The two principles *Peras* and *Apeiron* constituted an ultimate dualism, being not merely attributes but also themselves the substance of the things of which they are predicated. From the Pythagoreans on, the opposition of *Peras* and *Apeiron* was a standard theme in Greek philosophy.

Parmenides (fr. 8, 42ff.) seems to have accepted Limit and rejected the Unlimited for his One Being. The later Pythagoreans removed unity from the list of identities with *Peras* and argued that unity was the product of the imposition of the *Peras* upon the *Apeiron,* or else it was the source of both of them. Plato in the *Philebus* regards *Peras* and *Apeiron* as contained in all things, and supposes that it is through limit that intelligibility and beauty are manifested in the realm of Becoming. Exactly how the Ideas fit into this scheme is controversial, but in the doctrine of ideal numbers which Aristotle attributes to him Plato seems finally to have identified a material principle with the *Apeiron* and a formal principle with the *Peras.* Both principles apply to the ideal as well as to the sensible world. This leads in due course to the doctrine in Proclus (*Elementa* 89–90) that true being is composed of *Peras* and *Apeiron,* and beyond being there is a first *Peras* and a first *Apeiron.* The Christian writer known as Dionysius the Areopagite identified this doubled First Principle with God.

INFINITY

The concept of infinity, for long wrongly regarded as contrary to the whole tenor of Greek classicism, was in fact a Greek discovery, and by the fifth century BCE the normal meaning of *Apeiron* was "infinite." Infinite spatial extension was implied in the doctrines of Anaximander, Anaximenes, and Xenophanes and was made explicit by the Pythagoreans (see Aristotle, *Physics* IV, 6). Denied by Parmenides, it was reasserted for the Eleatics by Melissus (frs. 3–4) and adopted by the Atomists. Plato, however (in the *Timaeus*), and Aristotle (*Physics* III) insisted upon a finite universe, and in this they were followed by the Stoics and most subsequent thinkers until the Renaissance. Aristotle had, however, admitted that infinity could occur in counting and he stated the concept clearly for the first time. He also accepted infinite divisibility (*Physics* VI), which had been "discovered" by Zeno and adopted wholeheartedly by Anaxagoras. It was rejected by the Atomists. Plato rejected it in the *Timaeus,* although he seems to have admitted it at the precosmic stage in *Parmenides* 158B–D, 164C–165C. Aristotle accepted infinite divisibility for movements, for magnitudes in space, and for time. The concept of a continuum so reached has been a basic concept in physical theory ever since. The mathematical concept of infinitesimal numbers associated with infinite divisibility and also with the doctrine of incommensurables remained important until the development of calculus in modern times.

See also Anaximander; Aristotle; Parmenides of Elea; Plato.

Bibliography

Mondolfo, R. *L'infinito nel pensiero dell'antichita,* 2nd ed. Florence, 1956.

Solmsen, Friedrich. *Aristotle's System of the Physical World.* Ithaca, NY: Cornell University Press, 1960. Ch. 8.

G. B. Kerferd (1967)

APEL, KARL-OTTO
(1922–)

Karl-Otto Apel (born in Düsseldorf) is an influential post–World War II German philosopher responsible for creatively introducing analytic linguistic philosophy to the German philosophical tradition. He fought in the German army on the eastern front and, in fact, began his university studies while a prisoner-of-war in France. He completed his doctoral dissertation on Martin Heidegger in Bonn in 1950, wrote his *Habilitation* ("The Idea of Language in the Tradition from Dante to Vico") in Mainz in 1960, and, after several years teaching at the Universities of Kiel and Saarbrücken, spent the rest of his academic career at the Goethe University in Frankfurt am Main (where Jürgen Habermas, whom he had known since his student years in Bonn, was his colleague). He is best known for his development of transcendental semiotics that, as a first philosophy distinct from both traditional metaphysics and a modern (e.g., Cartesian, Kantian, or Husserlian) philosophy of the subject, provides an ultimate foundation (*Letzbegründung*) for knowledge (1998, chapter 2).

His so-called transformation of philosophy represents an ambitious attempt to bring together in a systematic form analytic philosophy of language, American pragmatism (especially Charles Sanders Peirce), and philosophical hermeneutics (Heidegger and Hans-Georg Gadamer). According to Apel, in light of these innovative traditions, the transcendental philosophy of Immanuel Kant must be fundamentally reconceived. In particular, the conditions for intersubjectively valid knowledge cannot be explicated in terms of the structure of consciousness or the cognitive capacities of the individual knowing subject but only through a systematic investigation of language as the medium of symbolically mediated knowledge. The pragmatic turn, initiated by Peirce and Charles W. Morris (1901–1979) and continued in the early twenty-first century in speech act theory, further implies that an adequate explanation of how meaningful communication is possible cannot be achieved by a semantic theory alone. Rather, it must be supplemented by a pragmatic study of the relation between linguistic signs and the conditions of their use by speakers. Apel's strong thesis is that his transcendental semiotics yields a set of normative conditions and validity claims presupposed in any critical discussion or rational argumentation. Central among these is the presupposition that a participant in a genuine argument is at the same time a member of a counterfactual, ideal communication community that is in principle equally open to all speakers and that excludes all force except the force of the better argument. Any claim to intersubjectively valid knowledge (scientific or moral-practical) implicitly acknowledges this ideal communication community as a metainstitution of rational argumentation, to be its ultimate source of justification (1980).

Drawing on the Continental tradition, Apel argues that the most important contribution of philosophical hermeneutics, Gadamer's in particular, has been to show that interpretation is not another method of investigation in addition to the methods used within the hard sciences, but an unavoidable dimension of all understanding. Every empirical investigation of a domain of objects implies at the same time a relation to other subjects, to a community of interpreters. Thus, the attempt to study language from an exclusively objectivistic or naturalistic perspective involves an abstraction from the inquirer's own membership in a linguistic community. The

inquirer's verbal behavior must also be interpreted by the community of investigators and this interpretive moment can never itself be displaced by objectivistic investigation. In fact, such investigation itself presupposes a communication community. But Apel's transcendental hermeneutics departs from Gadamer's historicism in that successive interpretations not only purport to understand differently but also raise an implicit claim to truth or correctness that can be clarified, once again, with reference to the ideal communication community. Furthermore, like Habermas, Apel does not exclude the possibility of introducing causal or functional explanations to clarify systematic distortions to communication, so long as they are "considered to be capable of conversion into a reflexively heightened self-understanding of the communicating parties" (1980, p. 125). In a response to externalist approaches (such as the strong program in the sociology of knowledge) Apel proposes a principle of self-appropriation that further develops this internalist (or rationalist) theme (see Kettner 1996).

In an important critique of the critical rationalism of Karl Raimund Popper and his followers, Apel further clarifies the status of transcendental pragmatics. He suggests that their skepticism with regard to the possibility of ultimate philosophical grounding is based on an abstractive fallacy in which sentences are viewed in isolation from the pragmatic contexts of argumentation. The so-called Münchhausen trilemma—that is, that all attempts to discover ultimate foundations result in either logical circularity, infinite regress, or an arbitrary end to the process of justification—can be overcome by moving from the level of semantic analysis to the level of pragmatics and recognizing that some presuppositions are necessary for the very possibility of intersubjectively valid criticism and argumentation. Similarly, he argues, even the "principle of fallibilism" (which holds that any claim can, in principle, be doubted) is only meaningful within an "institution of argumentation," where some pragmatic rules and norms are not open to question. Thus, contrary to the claim of critical rationalism, the principle of fallibilism does not exclude the notion of philosophical foundations and, Apel argues, certainly could not replace it as the basic principle of rational discourse (1998, chapter 4).

In a series of essays and in *Diskurs und Verantwortung* (1988) Apel argues that transcendental pragmatics can be used to develop an ethics of communication or *Diskursethik* that closely parallels the moral theory of Habermas. Like other cognitivist approaches, this ethics rejects the claim that moral judgments are ultimately the expressions of subjective preferences or an arbitrary will and hence beyond the reach of rational justification. By elucidating its basic principle in relation to the pragmatic presuppositions of argumentation in general, Apel seeks a more secure foundation than Kant's appeal to a fact of reason or John Rawls's reflective equilibrium. According to the basic principle of his ethics of communication, only those norms are justified that could meet with the agreement of all concerned as participants in a practical discourse. However, in contrast to Habermas, to avoid an abstract utopianism, Apel (1988) maintains that this basic principle must be supplemented by a further principle of responsibility. Taken together, however, these two basic principles offer a secular foundation for a new global ethics.

See also Critical Theory.

Bibliography

WORKS BY APEL

Towards a Transformation of Philosophy. Translated Glyn Adey and David Frisby. London: Routledge and Kegan Paul, 1980.
Diskurs und Verantwortung: Das Problem des Übergangs zur postkonventionellen Moral. Frankfurt am Main, Germany: Suhrkamp, 1988.
From a Transcendental-Semiotic Point of View, edited by Marianna Papastephanou. New York: Manchester University Press, 1998.

WORKS ABOUT APEL

Kettner, Matthias. "Karl-Otto Apel's Contribution to Critical Theory." In *The Handbook of Critical Theory*, edited by David M. Rasmussen. Cambridge, MA: Blackwell, 1996.
Mendieta, Eduardo. *The Adventures of Transcendental Philosophy: Karl-Otto Apel's Semiotics and Discourse Ethics*. Lanham, MD: Rowman & Littlefield, 2002.

Kenneth Baynes (2005)

APOLOGISTS

"Apologists" is the term used historically in reference to Christian teachers from the second century to the fourth who wrote treatises defending their religion against charges of godlessness and immorality and usually ascribing these traits to their opponents. The way had been prepared for such writings in Hellenistic Judaism when Philo of Alexandria wrote an apologetic *Hypothetica* (now lost). All his extant writings can be regarded as attempts to set forth the nature of Judaism in a way comprehensible to a Greek audience. Josephus had explained away the revolt against Rome (*History of the Jewish War*), had rewritten the history of Israel (*Antiquities of the Jews*), and had provided an explicitly apologetic defense

of Judaism (*Against Apion*). In addition, fragments of apologetic sermons are preserved in the New Testament book of Acts (14.15–17; 17.22–31), and perhaps may be reflected in I Thessalonians 1.9, I Corinthians 12.2, and Romans 1.18–32. The earliest known Christian apologists, however, wrote early in the second century.

Quadratus apparently wrote at Athens in the reign of Hadrian (117–138), and the one extant fragment of his work contrasts "our Savior" with some other savior. He argues that Jesus' healings and revivifications were authentic because some of the beneficiaries survived until Quadratus' own time. The *Apology* of Aristides (second century) begins with a semi-Stoic definition of God and goes on to show that all the gods of popular cult and legend cannot be gods because their deeds or sufferings are not in harmony with the definition. Finally, Aristides provides rather faint praise of Jews and high commendation for Christians. These writings cannot have won much, if any, favor with the pagans who read them.

The principal Christian apologist of the second century was Justin (c. 100–c. 165), born in Samaria of Greek parents and converted to Christianity (c. 130) after a fruitless quest for truth that had led him to religious-minded Middle Platonism. His education, he says, had not included many of the liberal arts; and from his account of his conversion, it is evident that he knew little about philosophy. A Christian whom he met by chance used Peripatetic arguments to indicate inconsistencies in Platonism. Justin, seeking new authority, was given the Old Testament prophecies. He had already admired the constancy of Christian martyrs; he soon became a Christian himself and instructed others, first in Asia Minor, later at Rome. He was martyred there between 163 and 167. Three of his works have survived: his *Apology*, written about 150 to show that Christians are not immoral and that Christ's life was foretold in the Old Testament; the *Dialogue with Trypho*, written about 160, developing this argument from the Old Testament; and an appendix to the *Apology*, also written about 160. His writings reflect a combination of Middle Platonism with Stoic terminology; he speaks of the divine Logos ("Word" for earlier Christians, "Reason" for Philo and the apologists), which was seminally present in some Greek philosophers but was incarnate in Christ. By working out some of the implications of this identification, Justin produced the first semiphilosophical Christian theology. It is possible that he knew something about Philo, but he cannot have understood his writings.

Justin's disciple Tatian (born c. 120), who later left the church, knew little about philosophy except for odd details from philosophers' biographies, although like Justin he discussed the Logos as God's agent in creation and criticized the Stoic doctrine of fate. From Alexandria, perhaps, came the *Plea for the Christians* by Athenagoras (second century). He is the first Christian writer to reflect knowledge of the compendium of philosophical opinions apparently used in school teaching, especially by Skeptics. On the basis of earlier arguments in the schools, Athenagoras constructed a defense of the unity of God; and his later work *On Resurrection* contains a similar rearrangement of arguments from the schools to prove that God is able and willing to raise corpses, and will do so because man is a unity of soul and body. The last Greek apologist of the second century was Theophilus, bishop of Antioch, whose work in three books, *To Antolycus,* is concerned with the works of the invisible God (Philonic-Platonic arguments), God's revelation to the prophets and his six-day work of creation, and Christian ethics and the antiquity of the Jewish-Christian revelation. Theophilus used handbooks for much of his information about philosophy, but he may have read some works by Plato.

Generally speaking, the second-century apologists knew something about Platonism (that is, Middle Platonism) and Stoicism (largely the older Stoics) and made use of philosophy at points where it supported—or could be made to support—their own ideas of revelation, creation, providence, free will, divine punishment, and resurrection. They reinterpreted the Johannine "Word" as the divine Reason, instrumental in creation and revelation alike; Justin, unlike the others, used this Reason to explain how it was that some Greeks possessed inklings of the truth. The apologists also stressed the disputes among various schools in order to show how wrong the Greek philosophers usually were and how subjective their knowledge was.

At the very end of the second century an ex-lawyer named Tertullian produced two apologies in Latin. The first, *Ad Nationes,* is not very original, since much of it is derived from Varro's critique of Roman religion; the second, the *Apologeticum,* is a completely rewritten, and much more brilliant, revision of the first. Either before or after these works were published, another Latin apology, the *Octavius* of Minucius Felix, appropriated much of Cicero's treatise *De Natura Deorum* to Christian use. Both Tertullian and Minucius also made use of their Greek predecessors' writings.

Greek apologetic continued to be produced in the third century; examples include the anonymous booklet *To Diognetus,* the *Protrepticus* by Clement of Alexandria,

and the highly important work *Against Celsus* by Origen, in which the author often makes use of philosophical topoi (commonplaces) in his argument (for instance, Platonic discussions of the divine nature; Stoic arguments in favor of providence) and reveals that he shares many presuppositions with Celsus himself. Apparently some of the writings later ascribed to Justin, such as the *Cohortatio* and the *Oration,* also come from the third century. In them we find extensive use of handbooks and a little first-hand knowledge of philosophical writings.

Stimulus for the production of further apologies was provided about 260, when the Neoplatonist Porphyry produced a work in fifteen books, *Against the Christians.* Now lost because it was later proscribed, this work criticized the Old and New Testament, the apostles, and the life and thought of the church. The *Praeparatio Evangelica* of Eusebius is primarily a reply to it and to the similar work by Hierocles. In the fourth century the emperor Julian composed a work in three books, *Against the Galileans*; this was answered by Theodoret and Cyril of Alexandria, among others. Among the later Latin apologists we should mention Arnobius (d. c. 330, vaguely acquainted with Neoplatonism), Lactantius (c. 240–c. 320, who relied extensively on Cicero), and—above all—Augustine, whose *City of God* contains much from Varro and sets forth a Christian philosophy of history in response to Porphyry and other critics.

The significance of the apologists lies not so much in what they actually wrote (their works seem to have been read chiefly within the church) but in the influence their effort had on one another's thought and on the thought of later theologians. Their criticisms of Greco-Roman philosophy compelled them not only to learn something about it but also to employ its modes of discourse and some of its axioms in expounding the nature of Christianity. It was through the apologists that philosophical theology entered, and to some measure shaped, Christian thought. To be sure, later theologians could not accept the apologists' rather naive theologies (Irenaeus, for example, learned from the apologists but also corrected some of their statements); but impetus for philosophical study was given in the apologists' works and by the school of Alexandria, whose members were more at home in philosophy, especially Platonism.

All the early apologists, and most of the later ones, admired Plato and were influenced by Middle Platonism; the work they valued most highly was the *Timaeus,* in which they found intimations of Christianity (sometimes explained as derived from the Old Testament). They usually employed traditional Stoic arguments in defense of providence and anti-Stoic arguments in opposition to fate. When they dealt with pagan mythology, they often employed the arguments of Skeptics. Their approach, then, was eclectic; and the famous statement of Justin, "Whatever has been well spoken by anyone belongs to us," had been made by eclectic philosophers. At the same time, the apologists were aware of the difference between all philosophies and their own cardinal doctrines of God (*Creator ex ouk ontōn,* "wrathful against sin"), the Incarnation, and the future corporeal resurrection. Even those apologists who were most eager to express their doctrines in philosophical modes of discourse were usually aware that the basic beliefs could not be so expressed. Theophilus, for example, defines *pistis* (faith) in a manner strongly reminiscent of the probabilism of Carneades and then provides analogies to the resurrection of the body that are based on Stoic arguments for the cosmic cycle. He admits, however, that only faith is ultimately convincing.

See also Augustine, St.; Cicero, Marcus Tullius; Clement of Alexandria; Eusebius; Origen; Platonism and the Platonic Tradition; Porphyry; Tertullian, Quintus Septimius Florens.

Bibliography

Amand, David. *Fatalisme et liberté.* Louvain: Bibliothèque de l'Université, 1945.

Becker, Carl. *Tertullians Apologeticum.* Munich: Kösel-Verlag, 1954.

Canivet, Pierre. *Histoire d'une enterprise apologétique au Ve siècle.* Paris: Bloud and Gay, 1957.

Daniélou, Jean. *Message évangélique et culture hellénistique.* Tournai: Desclée, 1961.

Geffcken, Johannes. *Zwei griechische Apologeten.* Leipzig: B.G. Teubner, 1907.

Pellegrino, Michele. *Gli apologeti.* Rome: Anonima Veritas, 1947.

Puech, Aimé. *Les apologistes grecs.* Paris: Hachette, 1912.

Robert M. Grant (1967)

APPEARANCE AND REALITY

In *The Problems of Philosophy* Bertrand Russell referred to the distinction between appearance and reality as "one of the distinctions that cause most trouble in philosophy." Why it should cause trouble in philosophy, however, when it causes little or no trouble outside of philosophy, Russell did not say. The distinction has played an important part in the thinking of many philosophers, and some of them, including Russell, have employed it in curious ways to support odd and seemingly paradoxical claims. It may be this last fact that Russell had in mind when he spoke of trouble.

Before turning to some of its troublesome uses in philosophy, let us consider some of its relatively untroublesome uses in everyday discourse.

LOOKS AND APPEARANCES

There is a potentially troublemaking ambiguity in the term *to appear* and its cognates. (This ambiguity is not peculiar to English but is also to be found, for example, in the Greek verb *phainesthai* and its cognates.) Contrary to Russell's suggestion, the distinction between appearance and reality is not simply the distinction "between what things seem to be and what they are," more precisely, the distinction between what things seem to be and what they are is not a simple distinction. There are at least two groups of appearance idioms—what might be called "seeming idioms" and "looking idioms." The first group typically includes such expressions as "appears to be," "seems to be," "gives the appearance of being"; the second, such expressions as "appears," "looks," "feels," "tastes," "sounds."

The two groups are not always as obviously distinct as these examples make them appear to be. The same expression, particularly one from the second group (notoriously, "appears," but also such expressions as "looks as if"), may be used either as a seeming expression or as a looking expression. For example, "The oar appears bent" may mean either "The oar looks bent" or "The oar appears to be bent." These are by no means the same. I may say that the oar appears to be bent *because* it looks bent, and this is not to say that the oar appears to be bent because it appears to be bent or that it looks bent because it looks bent. Nor is there any necessary connection between the two statements—or, generally, between statements employing seeming idioms and those employing looking idioms. "The oar looks bent" does not imply or entail "The oar appears to be bent"; for the oar may look bent—immersed in water, it naturally does—without appearing to be bent. As St. Augustine put it in a striking passage in *Contra Academicos* (III, xi, 26): "'Is that true, then, which the eyes see in the case of the oar in water?' 'Quite true. For since there is a special reason for the oar's looking (*videretur*) that way, I should rather accuse my eyes of playing me false if the oar looked straight (*rectus appareret*) when dipped in water; for in that case my eyes would not be seeing what, under the circumstances, ought to be seen.'" (Compare J. L. Austin, *Sense and Sensibilia,* p. 26.) The oar's looking bent in water is not an illusion, something that appears to be the case but is not; but this does not mean that the oar does not look bent. Conversely, "The oar appears to be bent" does not imply "The oar looks bent"; for the oar may appear to be bent without its looking bent; there may be reasons for saying that it appears to be bent (evidence that suggests that it is bent) other than its looking bent. (On this distinction, compare C. D. Broad, *Scientific Thought,* pp. 236–237.)

An example of the troublemaking neglect—or at least apparent neglect—of this distinction is to be found in Russell (op. cit.): "Although I believe that the table is 'really' of the same colour all over, the parts that reflect the light look much brighter than the other parts, and some parts look white because of reflected light. I know that, if I move, the parts that reflect the light will be different, so that the apparent distribution of colours on the table will change." But further on he wrote: "To return to the table. It is evident from what we have found, that there is no colour which pre-eminently appears to be *the* colour of the table, or even of any one particular part of the table—it appears to be of different colours from different points of view, and there is no reason for regarding some of these as more really its colour than others." But if all we have found is that the parts of the table that reflect the light *look* brighter than the others, it is by no means "evident" that there is no color which *appears to be* the color of the table.

SEEMING IDIOMS. Seeming idioms have nothing strictly to do with the senses; looking idioms characteristically do. From the evidence at hand, it may *appear,* or *look as if,* there will be an economic recession within the year. The characteristic uses of seeming idioms are to express what one believes is probably the case, to refrain from committing oneself, or to express hesitancy about what *is* the case. (Compare G. J. Warnock, *Berkeley,* p. 186: "The essential function of the language of 'seeming' is that it is noncommittal as to the actual facts.") Hence, "I know that *X* is *Y,* but it appears (to me) that it is not *Y*" is odd or paradoxical in much the same way as is "I know that *X* is *Y,* but it may not be the case that it is." From "*X* appears to be *Y*" (though *not* "merely appears to be *Y*"), I cannot validly infer either "*X* is *Y*" or "*X* is not *Y.*" But "*X* appears to be *Y*" entails that it is possible that *X* is *Y* and possible that *X* is not *Y.*

The same is not true of looking idioms, except in so far as they double as seeming idioms. No oddity or paradox is involved in saying such things as "I know that the two lines in Müller-Lyer's drawing *are* the same length, but one of them still *looks* longer than the other."

LOOKING IDIOMS. Looking idioms have a number of uses or senses that must be kept distinct.

Noticing resemblances. To notice that an inkblot has the appearance of (looks like) a face or that Alfredo's voice sounds like Caruso's is to note a visible resemblance between the inkblot and a face or an audible resemblance between Alfredo's voice and Caruso's. Here appearance does not normally contrast with what is possibly reality; rather it is a reality. "Alfredo's voice sounds like Caruso's" does not mean either "Alfredo's voice appears to be Caruso's" or "Alfredo's voice (merely) sounds like Caruso's, but it isn't Caruso's voice." To be sure, in certain circumstances one might be misled by appearances. For instance, by the audible resemblance between Alfredo's voice and Caruso's one might suppose that he was hearing Caruso's voice. Compare, however, "At a distance (in this light, at a quick glance) that looks like blood (a dollar bill), but it's really just red paint (a soap coupon)."

Describing. To describe something's appearance may merely be to describe its perceptible (visible, audible, tactile) features, and as such it is to describe how something *is,* not how it looks or appears as possibly *opposed* to how it is. Here the *apparent* qualities of something are the *real* perceptible qualities of it. To describe a man's appearance, as opposed, say, to his character, is to describe those features of him (his "looks") that he can be seen to possess. Appearances in this sense are what are most often referred to as phenomena in the nonphilosophical use of the latter term, in such phrases as "biological phenomena."

"Looks" and "merely looks." The phrase "mere appearance" ("merely looks, sounds") shows that there is a sense of "appears" as a looking idiom which is neutral with respect to how things are. "*X* merely looks red (to me, or under such-and-such conditions)" implies that *X* is not (really) red. But simply from "*X* looks red (to me, or under such-and-such conditions)" I cannot validly infer either that *X* (really) is red or that *X* (really) is not red. If it is possible, however, for *X* to look (sound, feel, taste) *Y,* it must at least be possible for *X* (really) to be *Y.* This logical feature of looking idioms, which—in this sense—they share with seeming idioms, may be the source of some confusion between them.

PROTAGOREAN RELATIVISM

According to Plato (*Theaetetus,* 152; Cornford trans.), Protagoras held that "man is the measure of all things—alike of the being of things that are and of the non-being of things that are not." And by this he meant that "any given thing is to me such as it appears to me, and is to you such as it appears to you." This statement can be read in two different ways, depending on whether "appears" is construed as a seeming idiom or a looking idiom. In either interpretation, however, it is a paradox or else a tautology.

Expressions such as "is for me" and "is for you" are distinctly odd, and one is puzzled to know what to make of them. If they are construed to mean the same as "is," Protagoras' statement then becomes manifestly paradoxical. For if "X appears to me to be Y (or looks Y to me)" and "X appears to you to be Z (or looks Z to you)" are equivalent respectively to "X is Y" and "X is Z," where Y and Z represent logically incompatible predicates, then the joint affirmation of two (possibly) true propositions, "X looks Y to me" and "X looks Z to you," would be equivalent to the necessarily false proposition that X is both Y and Z.

On the other hand, if we interpret "is for me" to mean the same as "appears to me" and "is for you" as "appears to you," Protagoras' dictum reduces to a tautology. For if "X appears to me to be Y" and "X appears to you to be Z" are equivalent respectively to "X is Y for me" and "X is Z for you," then, even if Y and Z represent logically incompatible predicates, the equivalent statements can be substituted for one another. In that case, Protagoras' dictum, generalized, reduces to either "Everything is for any given person such as it is for that person" or "Everything appears to any given person such as it appears to that person." But since the two statements are themselves equivalent, the effect of Protagoras' dictum is to obliterate any possible distinction between appearance and reality, or to claim what is clearly false, that there is no such distinction.

Protagoras' statement can be read in yet another way, but read in that way it is also a truism. The Greek verb *phainesthai*, especially with the participle, was used to state, not that something (merely) appears to be so, but that something manifestly is so. Read in this way, Protagoras' claim that appearance is reality is simply the claim that what is manifestly the case is the case. This innocent truism may have been intended to remind those of Protagoras' contemporaries who contemned the common run of men for living by appearances, which they equated with error, that what is reliably observed to be the case is justifiably said to be the case.

THE ARGUMENT FROM ILLUSION

What has been called the "argument from illusion" has been used by many philosophers (for example, George Berkeley in *Three Dialogues, I,* and A. J. Ayer in *Founda-*

tions of Empirical Knowledge, pp. 3–5) to justify some form of phenomenalism or subjective idealism. The argument rests on the fact that things sometimes appear (for example, look) different to different observers or to the same observer in different circumstances. This fact is supposed to show that sensible qualities, such as colors or odors, are not really "in" things. For if things can, say, look one color when they are (supposedly) really another, then we can never say what color they really are, what color really "inheres" in them. For all sensible qualities, as Berkeley put it, "are equally apparent"; he seems to have meant that for every putatively veridical perception there is a possible corresponding illusory one (or wherever it is possible that "X is Y" is true, it is equally possible that "X merely looks Y" is true). Hence, given any perception, P, it is possible that P is veridical and possible that P is illusory. But since there is no apparent or observable difference between a veridical P and an illusory P, we cannot in principle tell which it is. We cannot, for example, say what colors things *are*; we can only say what colors they *look*.

The consequence of this argument is the same as that of Protagoras' dictum, namely, to obliterate in principle any distinction between "is" and "(merely) looks or sounds." But this is a distinction on which the argument itself rests: if the distinction cannot, in principle, be made, then the argument cannot get off the ground; but if the distinction can, in principle, be made, the conclusion of the argument cannot be true.

"IS Y" AS A FUNCTION OF "APPEARS Y." Many philosophers who have used the argument from illusion have attempted to resist the consequence that there is then no distinction between "is" and "(merely) looks." Berkeley, for example, protested that "the distinction between realities and chimeras retains its full force" (*Principles of Human Knowledge,* §34). He was able to suppose that it does because he supposed that "X is Y" is a logical function of "X appears (appears to be *or,* for example, looks) Y": when the appearances of X are not only "lively" but "steady," "orderly," and "coherent," we say that X *is* (really) Y and not that it merely *appears* Y. Being is orderly and coherent appearing (*Principles,* §29).

But if this is so, the distinction between realities and chimeras does not retain its full force. "X appears Y consistently (steadily, in an orderly and coherent way)" neither is equivalent to, nor does it entail, "X is Y"; for it is possible that the former is true while the latter is false. The truth of the former may be *evidence for* the truth of the latter, but the latter is not a logical function of the former. (Compare Warnock, op. cit., pp. 180–182.) The same holds for such claims as that of G. E. Moore (*Commonplace Book,* p. 145) that "'This book is blue' = This book looks (or *would* look) blue to normal people … who look at it by *good* daylight at *normal distances,* i.e. not too far off or too near."

PHENOMENA AND THINGS-IN-THEMSELVES

One of the foundation stones of Immanuel Kant's philosophy is the claim that "we can know objects only as they *appear* to us (to our senses), not as they may be in themselves" (*Prolegomena,* §10.) Read in one way, Kant's claim is tautologous. If by "an appearance" we mean a possible object of knowledge and by "a thing-in-itself" something that can be "thought" but cannot be known, the claim reduces to "What we can know, we can know; and what we cannot know, we cannot know." As such, this tells us nothing about the limits of knowledge, about what we can know, any more than "God can do everything that it is possible for God to do" tells us anything about the extent of God's powers.

Kant may, however, have meant the following: I can know that X is Y only if X can appear (to be) Y; if, in principle, X cannot appear (to be) Y, then I cannot know that X is Y. This, too, is a truism. But it does not follow from this that "the things we intuit are not in themselves what we intuit them as being. … As appearances, they cannot exist in themselves, but only in us" (*Critique of Pure Reason,* A42; Kemp Smith trans.). That is, it does not follow that X as it appears is not what it is apart from how it appears; nor does it follow that what X is apart from how it appears is different from how it appears. To allow Kant's inference is implicitly to endorse a paradox or to adopt a new use of "appears" to which no sense has been given. For if something appears (to be) so, it must be *possible* for it to *be* so "in itself"; and this is precisely the possibility which Kant does not allow.

APPEARANCES OF THE IMPOSSIBLE. Closely related to Kant's distinction between appearances and things-in-themselves is the notion of appearances of the impossible. According to Parmenides and Zeno, multiplicity and motion, empty space and time, are impossible; yet things appear to be many, some of them appear to move, and so on. Similarly, for Gottfried Wilhelm Leibniz bodies with their qualities, such as colors, are well-founded appearances (*phaenomena bene fundata*), mere appearances "grounded" in monads and their perceptions; in reality there can be no such things as colored bodies. And according to F. H. Bradley in *Appearance and Reality,*

space, time, motion and change, causation, things, and the self are "unreal as such" because they "contradict themselves"; hence, they are "mere appearances" or "contradictory appearances."

Taken at face value, this view is blatantly paradoxical: If for something to appear (to be) the case it must be *possible* for it "really" to be the case, then if it is *impossible* for it to be the case, it is impossible for it to appear (to be) the case. (Compare Morris Lazerowitz, *The Structure of Metaphysics,* pp. 208–209.) The metaphysician of "contradictory appearances," however, may mean that for certain kinds of things, t, it is *never* permissible to say "There are t's," but only "There appear to be t's." But this, as Lazerowitz has pointed out (op. cit., esp. p. 225), has the consequence of obliterating the distinction between "is" and "appears" and hence of depriving "appears" of its meaning. For if "There are t's" is in principle disallowed, "There appear to be t's" loses its sense.

See also Augustine, St.; Austin, John Langshaw; Ayer, Alfred Jules; Berkeley, George; Bradley, Francis Herbert; Illusions; Kant, Immanuel; Moore, George Edward; Plato; Russell, Bertrand Arthur William.

Bibliography

Augustine, St. *Contra Academicos.* Translated by John J. O'Meara as *Against the Academics.* Westminster, MD: Newman Press, 1951.

Austin, J. L. *Sense and Sensibilia.* Oxford: Clarendon Press, 1962.

Ayer, A. J. *The Foundations of Empirical Knowledge.* London: Macmillan, 1940.

Berkeley, George. *A Treatise concerning the Principles of Human Knowledge.* Dublin: A. Rhames for J. Pepyat, 1710.

Berkeley, George. *Three Dialogues between Hylas and Philonous.* London: Henry Clements, 1713.

Bradley, F. H. *Appearance and Reality,* 2nd ed. Oxford: Clarendon Press, 1897.

Bradley, F. H. *Essays on Truth and Reality.* Oxford: Clarendon Press, 1914. Ch. 9.

Broad, C. D. *Perception, Physics and Reality.* Cambridge, U.K.: Cambridge University Press, 1914. Ch. 2.

Broad, C. D. *Scientific Thought.* London: K. Paul, Trench, Trubner, 1923. Part 2.

Chisholm, R. M. *Perceiving: A Philosophical Study.* Ithaca, NY: Cornell University Press, 1957.

Chisholm, R. M. "The Theory of Appearing." In *Philosophical Analysis,* edited by Max Black, pp. 102–118. Ithaca, NY: Cornell University Press, 1950.

Chisholm, R. M. "Theory of Knowledge." In his *Philosophy,* pp. 233–344. Humanistic Scholarship in America, The Princeton Studies. Englewood Cliffs, NJ: Prentice-Hall, 1964.

Kant, Immanuel. *Critique of Pure Reason.* Translated by Norman Kemp Smith. London, 1919.

Lazerowitz, Morris. "Appearance and Reality." In his *The Structure of Metaphysics*. London: Routledge and Paul, 1955. Ch. 10.

Lean, Martin. *Sense-Perception and Matter*. London: Routledge and Paul, 1953.

Moore, G. E. *The Commonplace Book 1919–1953*. London: Allen and Unwin, 1962. Passim.

Moore, G. E. "The Conception of Reality." In his *Philosophical Studies*. London: K. Paul, Trench, Trubner, 1922. Ch. 6.

Plato. *Theaetetus*. Translated by F. M. Cornford as *Plato's Theory of Knowledge*. London: K. Paul, Trench, Trubner, 1935.

Price, H. H. "Appearing and Appearances." *American Philosophical Quarterly* 1 (1964): 3–19.

Price, H. H. *Perception*. London: Methuen, 1932.

Prichard, H. A. "Appearances and Reality." *Mind* 15 (1906): 223–229.

Russell, Bertrand. *The Problems of Philosophy*. New York: Henry Holt, 1912. Ch. 1.

Ryle, Gilbert. *The Concept of Mind*. London: Hutchinson's University Library, 1949. Ch. 7.

Sibley, Frank. "Aesthetics and the Looks of Things." *Journal of Philosophy* 16 (1959): 905–915.

Taylor, A. E. *Elements of Metaphysics*. London: Methuen, 1903. Bk. 2, Ch. 3.

Warnock, G. J. *Berkeley*. London: Penguin, 1953. Ch. 9.

Wollheim, Richard. *F. H. Bradley*. Harmondsworth, U.K.: Penguin, 1959. Ch. 5.

W. E. Kennick (1967)

APPERCEPTION

Apperception is usually defined as the mental process that raises subconscious or indistinct impressions to the level of attention and at the same time arranges them into a coherent intellectual order. The term *apperception*, however, has been used ambiguously, sometimes to mean merely consciousness or awareness, at other times to mean the acts of concentration and assimilation. Inevitably, a process of such significance has implicitly and explicitly been dealt with by philosophers ever since they first concerned themselves with the cognitive process. Aristotle, the Church Fathers, and the Scholastics all distinguished between vague notions and feelings on the one hand, and conceptions brought about by an act of intellectual willing on the other.

DESCARTES

The concept of apperception (in the form of the verb *apercevoir*) appears in René Descartes's *Traité des passions*.

Later writers generally use the term *perception* for denoting a state of dim awareness. So John Locke believes that perception is "the first step and degree towards knowledge, and the inlet of all materials of it." It "is in some degree in all sorts of animals" (*Essay concerning Human Understanding*, Book II, Ch. 9). On the other hand, apperception denotes a state of conscious or reflecting awareness.

In contrast, Descartes makes no distinction between the two. But he stresses the volitional element (which he calls passion) in the cognitive process: "For it is certain that we would not even know how to will something, unless we had apperceived it by the same medium by which we will. And just as one can say with regard to our soul that willing is a form of action, so one can also say that there is in the soul an element ["passion"] by which it apperceives that which it wills" (*Traité des passions*).

LEIBNIZ

It was Gottfried Wilhelm Leibniz who introduced the concept of apperception into the more technical philosophical tradition. In his *Principes de la nature fondés en raison et de la grâce* he says: "One should distinguish between *perception*, which is an inner state of the monad reflecting the outer world, and *apperception*, which is our conscious reflection of the inner state of the monad."

For the understanding of Leibniz's ideas about perception and apperception, one should also refer to his *Nouveaux essais sur l'entendement humain*, which contain a discussion of Locke's *Essay concerning Human Understanding*. There Leibniz objects to Locke's *tabula rasa* theory, according to which "there are no innate principles in the mind" (Book I, Ch. 2). Leibniz's insistence on innate mental powers had a decisive influence on the idealism of Immanuel Kant and Johann Friedrich Herbart.

KANT

The concept of apperception was taken up by Kant in his *Critique of Pure Reason*. There he distinguished between empirical apperception, the person's awareness of himself which depends on the changing conditions of his consciousness, and transcendental apperception, or "pure reason," the inner, unchangeable fundamental, and therefore "transcendental" unity of consciousness. This transcendental unity of consciousness precedes all data of perception and makes possible their inner order and meaning ("Transcendental Logic," Para. 12). It consists of the ideas of space and time, which are not objects of perception but modes of perceiving, and a number of categories which Kant orders under the headings of quantity, quality, relation, and modality. Kant's attempt to organize these categories and their subcategories according to a symmetrical scheme has been generally rejected as artificial. Kant's rejection of the opinion, however, that our conscious reasoning about the world reflects the world as it really is remains as one of the great epistemological problems in his concept of apperception.

IDEALISTS

The self-critical quality in Kant's philosophy was not heeded by romantic idealists impatient to achieve a complete insight into the essence of all existence. Thus Johann Gottlieb Fichte turned Kant's self-critical concept of apperception into the absolute self; Hegel developed logical idealism; and Friedrich Wilhelm Joseph von Schelling maintained in his philosophy of identity that the evolution of mind or consciousness is nothing but the evolution of ultimate reality from its prerational and groping state of willing toward self-consciousness and self-direction, toward the discovery of its inherent and universal laws. Whatever we think about Schelling's lofty speculation, it led its author to the understanding of myth. For in myth, so Schelling concluded, the human mind in its prerational state creates its first perceptions of reality in the form of artistic intuition and imagery. Myth, so we could say with Schelling, is not untruth but pretruth. About half a century later, following Schelling's lead, Wilhelm Wundt became one of the foremost interpreters of prerational or mythical thinking.

HERBART

In contrast with the romanticists, Kant's successor, Johann Friedrich Herbart, insisted on a less romantic and more empirical interpretation of the transcendentalist position. In the second part of his *Psychologie als Wissenschaft*, however, Herbart characterizes the gift of apperception as one—though not the only one—of the qualities that distinguish man from animal because it gives him the power of reflection. In the human soul, so Herbart says, there are operating series of presentations, combinations, and whole masses of perceptions that are sometimes completely and sometimes incompletely interwoven, in part conforming and in part opposed to each other. It is the function of apperception to assimilate the various and often divergent ideas. In this process the older apperceptive mass, consisting of concepts, judgments, and maxims, will tend to assimilate more recent and less settled impressions. No one, however, can measure how strong the older apperceptive mass must be in order to fulfill effectively the function of assimilation.

Obviously, the power of apperception as conceived by Herbart is closely related to a person's inner stability, self-consciousness, and self-identity. Apperception requires will and attention in order to function adequately. A mentally sick person will be unable to perform it.

Inevitably, the concept of apperception plays a decisive role in Herbart's pedagogical theory. In his *Allgemeine Pädagogik aus dem Zweck der Erziehung Abgeleitet*, Herbart emphasizes the obligation of the teacher to arrange the course of instruction in such a way that the new material can be properly integrated with the already available store of knowledge. If the two fall apart, the learner cannot assimilate the new experience and will feel frustrated.

WUNDT

The qualities of will and attention, which from Descartes to Herbart were emphasized as inherent in the apperceptive process, are still more accentuated by Wilhelm Wundt. In his *Grundriss der Psychologie*, Wundt distinguishes between passive apperception, in which the consciousness simply accepts impressions, and active apperception, in which the new impression is met by an emotional state of tension followed by a sense of satisfaction. Furthermore, in all apperception a personifying element is at work in that the apperceived objects are colored by the mode of the apperceiving subject. This is the reason why we tend to identify apperceived objects with our own form of existence. The most obvious historical example of this tendency is myth, in which, for example, animals, the forces of nature, and the gods appear in anthropomorphic transfiguration.

Entirely in the spirit of Wundt is the following (freely translated) passage from the well-known *Grundriss der Geschichte der Philosophie seit Beginn des neunzehnten Jahrhunderts*:

> There is nothing inside and outside of man which he could call totally his own but his will. … Hence, looking for the terminus of individual psychological regression, we discover the *inner will* or the *pure apperception*, which is not in a state of quiet, but in a state of never resting activity. The apperceptive will is not an a-posteriori conception, but an a-priori, postulated by reason, a transcendental quality of the soul, postulated by empirical psychology as the ultimate source of all mental processes, yet at the same time beyond the competence of the empirical psychologist.

THE DEEPER UNITY

In quoting the foregoing passage (omitted in later editions of Ueberweg-Heinze) we have already indicated the deeper unity that in spite of all differences underlies the apperception theories of Leibniz, Kant, Herbart, and Wundt. They predicate a transcendental element, or an inherent logos, in the human process of cognition because they are convinced that there is no other explanation for its uniting and ordering capacity. They belong, in the wide sense of the term, to the "idealistic" tradition of the *philosophia perennis*, although they are in no way opposed to painstaking empirical and statistical inquiry, as the examples of Herbart and Wundt prove.

In postulating a transempirical factor as the condition of experience, however, they expose themselves to the reproach of mysticism by the empiricist. And there can be no doubt that the modern experimental, associationist, and behaviorist schools have made us more critical of psychological concept. Nevertheless, it still seems to many contemporary philosophers and psychologists that a purely empirical account of knowledge is inadequate and that in order to achieve a defensible position it is necessary to have recourse to nonempirical factors such as apperception.

See also Aristotle; Descartes, René; Fichte, Johann Gottlieb; Herbart, Johann Friedrich; Idealism; Kant, Immanuel; Leibniz, Gottfried Wilhelm; Locke, John; Patristic Philosophy; Schelling, Friedrich Wilhelm Joseph von; Wundt, Wilhelm.

Bibliography

In addition to the works cited in the text, the following may be consulted: Benno Erdmann, "Zur Theorie der Apperzeption," in *Vierteljahrsschrift für wissenschaftliche Philosophie* 10 (1886): 307ff.; Karl Lange, *Ueber Apperception*, 6th rev. ed. (Leipzig, 1899), translated by E. E. Brown (Boston, 1893); L. H. Lüdtke, "Kritische Geschichte der Apperzeptionsbegriffs," in *Zeitschrift für Philosophie* (1911); Hugo Münsterberg, *Grundzüge der Psychologie* (Leipzig: J.A. Barth, 1900), pp. 436–457; G. F Stout, "Apperception and the Movement of Attention," in *Mind* 16 (1891): 23–53, and *Analytic Psychology* (London, 1896); and Friedrich Ueberweg, *Grundriss der Geschichte der Philosophie seit Beginn des neunzehnten Jahrhunderts*, 10th ed., edited by Max Heinze. (Berlin: Mittler, 1902).

OTHER RECOMMENDED TITLES

Allison, Henry E. "Apperception and Analyticity in the B-Deduction." *Grazer Philosophische Studien* 44 (1993): 233–252.

BonJour, Laurence, and Ernest Sosa. *Epistemic Justification.* Oxford: Blackwell, 2003.

Brandom, Robert, B. "Leibniz and Degrees of Perception." *Journal of the History of Philosophy* 19 (1981): 447–479.

Castañeda, Hector-Neri. "The Role of Apperception in Kant's Transcendental Deduction of the Categories." *Nous* 24 (1) (1990): 147–157.

Howell, Robert. "Apperception and the 1787 Transcendental Deduction." *Synthese* 47 (1981): 385–448.

Kitcher, Patricia. *Apperception and Epistemic Responsibility in Central Themes in Early Modern Philosophy.* Indianapolis, IN: Hackett, 1990.

Kulstad, Mark. *Leibniz on Apperception, Consciousness and Reflection.* Germany: Philosophia, 1990.

Robert Ulich (1967)
Bibliography updated by Benjamin Fiedor (2005)

APPLIED ETHICS

Moral philosophers have traditionally aspired to normative theories of what is right or wrong that are set out in the most general terms. But a practical price is paid for generality in ethical theory: It is often unclear whether and, if so, how theory is to be applied in specific cases and contexts. The terms applied ethics and practical ethics came in vogue in the 1970s, when philosophical ethics began to address issues in professional ethics as well as social problems such as capital punishment, abortion, environmental responsibility, and affirmative action. Philosophers interested in applying their training to such problems share with persons from numerous other fields the conviction that decision making in these areas is fundamentally moral and of the highest social importance.

Philosophers working in applied ethics sometimes do more than teach and publish articles about applications of ethical theory. Their work involves actual applications. They serve as consultants to government agencies, hospitals, law firms, physician groups, business corporations, and engineering firms. Branching out further, they serve as advisers on ethics to radio and educational television, serve on national and state commissions on ethics and policy, and give testimony to legislative bodies. Occasionally, they draft public policy documents, some with the force of law.

Controversies have arisen about whether philosophers have an ethical expertise suited to such work and also about whether the work is philosophical in any interesting sense. Enthusiasm about applied ethics is mixed in academic philosophy. It has been criticized as lacking in serious scholarship, and many philosophers regard it as reducing ethics to engineering—a mere device of problem solving. Some philosophers are not convinced that philosophical theories have a significant role to play in the analysis of cases or in policy and professional contexts, and others are skeptical that philosophical theories have direct practical implications.

DEFINITIONAL PROBLEMS

"Applied ethics" has proved difficult to define, but the following is a widely accepted account: Applied ethics is the application of general ethical theories to moral problems with the objective of solving the problems. However, this definition is so narrow that many will not recognize is as reflecting their understanding of either the appropriate method or content. "Applied ethics" is also used more broadly to refer to any use of philosophical methods critically to examine practical moral decisions and to treat moral problems, practices, and policies in the professions, technology, government, and the like. This broader usage permits a range of philosophical methods (including conceptual analysis, reflective equilibrium, phenomenology, etc.) and does not insist on problem solving as the objective.

Biomedical ethics, political ethics, journalistic ethics, legal ethics, environmental ethics, and business ethics are fertile areas for such philosophical investigation. However, "applied ethics" is not synonymous with "professional ethics" (a category from which business ethics is often excluded). Problems such as the allocation of scarce social resources, just wars, abortion, conflicts of interest in surrogate decision making, whistleblowing, the entrapment of public officials, research on animals, and the confidentiality of tax information extend beyond professional conduct, but all are in the domain of applied ethics. Likewise, professional ethics should not be viewed as a part of the wider domain of applied ethics. The latter is usually understood as the province of philosophy, the former as reaching well beyond philosophy and into the professions themselves.

HISTORY

Philosophers from Socrates to the present have been attracted to topics in applied ethics such as civil disobedience, suicide, and free speech; and philosophers have written in detail about practical reasoning. Nonetheless, it is arguably the case that there never has been a genuine practical program of applied philosophy in the history of philosophy (the casuists possibly qualifying as an exception). Philosophers have traditionally tried to account for and justify morality, to clarify concepts, to examine how moral judgments and arguments are made, and to array basic principles—not to use either morality or theories to solve practical problems.

This traditional set of commitments began to undergo modification about the time the *Encyclopedia of Philosophy* was first published in 1967. Many hypotheses can be invoked to explain why. The most plausible explanation is that law, ethics, and many of the professions—including medicine, business, engineering, and scientific research—were profoundly affected by issues and concerns in the wider society regarding individual liberties, social equality, and various forms of abuse and injustice. The issues raised by civil rights, women's rights, the consumer movement, the environmental movement, and the rights of prisoners and the mentally ill often included ethical issues that stimulated the imagination of philosophers and came to be regarded by many as essentially philosophical problems. Teaching in the philosophy classroom was influenced by these and other social concerns, most noticeably about unjust wars, dramatic ethical lapses in institutions, domestic violence, and international terrorism. Increases in the number of working women, affirmative action programs, escalation in international business competition, and a host of other factors heightened awareness. Classroom successes propelled the new applied ethics in philosophy throughout the 1970s, when few philosophers were working in the area but public interest was increasing.

It is difficult to identify landmark events that stimulated philosophers prior to *Roe v. Wade* (the U.S. Supreme Court decision on abortion in 1973), which deeply affected applied philosophical thinking. But at least one other landmark deserves mention. Research ethics had been poorly developed and almost universally ignored in all disciplines prior to the Nuremberg Trials. This apathy was shaken when the Nuremberg Military Tribunals unambiguously condemned the sinister political motivation and moral failures of Nazi physicians. The ten principles constituting the "Nuremberg Code" served as a model for many professional and governmental codes formulated in the 1950s and 1960s and eventually influenced philosophers as well.

In the late 1960s and early 1970s there emerged a rich and complex interplay of scholarly publications, journalism, public outrage, legislation, and case law. The 1970s and 1980s saw the publication of several books devoted to philosophical treatments of various subjects in applied ethics, concentrating first on biomedical ethics and second on business ethics. Virtually every book published in these applied fields prior to 1979 was organized topically; none was developed explicitly in terms of moral principles or ethical theory. Philosophers had by this time been working in areas of applied ethics for several years with an interest in the connection between theory, principles, practical decision making, and policy. However, in retrospect, it appears that these connections and their problems were not well understood prior to the mid-1980s.

MODELS OF APPLICATION, REASONING, AND JUSTIFICATION

When applied ethics began to receive acceptance in philosophy, it was widely presumed that the "applied" part involves the application of basic moral principles or theories to particular moral problems or cases. This vision suggests that ethical theory develops general principles, rules, and the like, whereas applied ethics treats particular contexts through less general, derived principles, rules, judgments, and the like. From this perspective applied ethics is old morality or old ethical theory applied to new areas. New, derived precepts emerge, but they receive their moral content from the old precepts. Applied work need not, then, generate novel ethical content. Applied ethics requires only a detailed knowledge of the areas to which the ethical theory is being applied (medicine, engineering, journalism, business, public policy, court cases, etc.).

Many philosophers reject this account because it reduces applied ethics to a form of deductivism in which justified moral judgments must be deduced from a preexisting theoretical structure of normative precepts that cover the judgment. This model is inspired by justification in disciplines such as mathematics, in which a claim is shown to follow logically (deductively) from credible premises. In ethics the parallel idea is that justification occurs if and only if general principles or rules, together with the relevant facts of a situation (in the fields to which the theory is being applied) support an inference to the correct or justified judgment(s). In short, the method of reasoning at work is the application of a norm to a clear case falling under the norm.

This deductive model is sometimes said to be a top-down "application" of precepts. The deductive form in the application of a rule is the following:

1. Every act of description A is obligatory. (rule)

2. Act b is of description A. (fact)

Therefore,

3. Act b is obligatory. (applied moral conclusion)

This structure directs attention from particular judgments to a covering level of generality (rules and principles that cover and justify particular judgments) and then to the level of ethical theory (which covers and warrants rules and principles).

This model functions smoothly whenever a fact circumstance can be subsumed directly under a general precept, but it does not adequately capture how moral reasoning and justification proceed in complicated cases. The failure to explain complex moral decision making and innovative moral judgment has led to a widespread rejection of deductivism as an appropriate model for applied ethics. Among the replacements for deductivism as a model of application, two have been widely discussed in the literature: case-based reasoning and reflective equilibrium.

CASE-BASED REASONING (A FORM OF CASUISTRY). This approach focuses on practical decision making about particular cases, where judgments cannot simply be brought under general norms. Proponents are skeptical of principles, rules, rights, and theory divorced from history, circumstances, and experience: One can make successful moral judgments of agents and actions, they say, only when one has an intimate understanding of particular situations and an appreciation of the record of similar situations. They cite the use of narratives, paradigm cases, analogies, models, classification schemes, and even immediate intuition and discerning insight.

An analogy to the authority operative in case law is sometimes noted: When the decision of a majority of judges becomes authoritative in a case, their judgments are positioned to become authoritative for other courts hearing cases with similar facts. This is the doctrine of precedent. Defenders of case-based reasoning see moral authority similarly: Social ethics develops from a social consensus formed around cases, which can then be extended to new cases without loss of the accumulated moral wisdom. As a history of similar cases and similar judgments mounts, a society becomes more confident in its moral judgments, and the stable elements crystallize in the form of tentative principles; but these principles are derivative, not foundational.

In addition to having a history dating from medieval casuistry, the case method, as it is often called, has long been used in law schools and business schools. Training in the case method is widely believed to sharpen skills of legal and business reasoning as well as moral reasoning. One can tear a case apart and then construct a better way of treating similar situations. In the thrust-and-parry classroom setting, teacher and student alike reach conclusions about rights, wrongs, and best outcomes in cases. The objective is to develop a capacity to grasp problems and to find novel solutions that work in the context: Knowing how to reason and act is more prized then knowing that something is the case on the basis of a foundational rule.

The case method in law has come to be understood as a way of learning to assemble facts and judge the weight of evidence—enabling the transfer of that weight to new cases. This task is accomplished by generalizing and mastering the principles that control the transfer, usually principles at work in the reasoning of judges. Use of the case method in business schools springs from an ideal of education that puts the student in the decision-making role after an initial immersion in the facts of a complex situation. Here the essence of the case method is to present a situation replete with the facts, opinions, and prejudices that one might encounter and to find a way of making appropriate decisions in such an environment.

REFLECTIVE EQUILIBRIUM (A FORM OF COHERENCE THEORY). Many now insist that the relationship between general norms and the particulars of experience is bilateral (not unilateral). Moral beliefs arise both by generalization from the particulars of experience (cases) and by making judgments in particular circumstances by appeal to general precepts. John Rawls's celebrated account of "reflective equilibrium" has been the most influential model of this sort. In developing and maintaining a system of ethics, he argues, it is appropriate to start with the broadest possible set of considered judgments about a subject and to erect a provisional set of principles that reflects them. Reflective equilibrium views investigation in ethics (and theory construction) as a reflective testing of moral principles, theoretical postulates, and other relevant moral beliefs to make them as coherent as possible. Starting with paradigms of what is morally proper or morally improper, one then searches for principles that are consistent with these paradigms as well as one another. Widely accepted principles of right action and considered judgments are taken, as Rawls puts it, "provisionally as fixed points" but also as "liable to revision."

"Considered judgments" is a technical term referring to judgments in which moral beliefs and capacities are most likely to be presented without a distorting bias. Examples are judgments about the wrongness of racial discrimination, religious intolerance, and political conflict of interest. By contrast, judgments in which one's confidence level is low or in which one is influenced by the possibility of personal gain are excluded from consideration. The goal is to match, prune, and adjust considered judgments so that they coincide and are rendered coherent with the premises of theory. That is, one starts with paradigm judgments of moral rightness and wrongness and then constructs a more general theory that is consistent with these paradigm judgments (rendering them as coherent as possible); any loopholes are closed, as are all forms of incoherence that are detected. The resultant action guides are tested to see if they too yield incoherent results. If so, they are readjusted or given up, and the process is renewed, because one can never assume a completely stable equilibrium. The pruning and adjusting occur by reflection and dialectical adjustment, in view of the perpetual goal of achieving reflective equilibrium.

This model demands the best approximation to full coherence under the assumption of a never-ending search for defects of coherence, for counterexamples to beliefs, and for unanticipated situations. From this perspective moral thinking is analogous to hypotheses in science that are tested, modified, or rejected through experience and experimental thinking. Justification is neither purely deductivist (giving general action guides preeminent status), nor purely inductivist (giving experience and analogy preeminent status). Many different considerations provide reciprocal support in the attempt to fit moral beliefs into a coherent unit. This is how we test, revise, and further specify moral beliefs. This outlook is very different from deductivism, because it holds that ethical theories are never complete, always stand to be informed by practical contexts, and must be tested for adequacy by their practical implications.

METHOD AND CONTENT: DEPARTURES FROM TRADITIONAL ETHICAL THEORY

In light of the differences in the models just explored and the enormously diverse literature in applied philosophy it is questionable whether applied ethics has a special philosophical method. Applied philosophers appear to do what philosophers have always done: They analyze concepts, examine the hidden presuppositions of moral opinions and theories, offer criticism and constructive accounts of the moral phenomena in question, and criticize strategies that are used to justify beliefs, policies, and actions. They seek a reasoned defense of a moral viewpoint, and they use proposed moral frameworks to distinguish justified moral claims from unjustified ones. They try to stimulate the moral imagination, promote analytical skills, and weed out prejudice, emotion, misappropriated data, false authority, and the like.

Differences between ethical theory and applied ethics are as apparent over content as over method. Instead of analyzing general terms such as "good", "rationality", "ideals", and "virtues", philosophers interested in applied ethics attend to the analysis of concepts such as confidentiality, trade secrets, environmental responsibility, euthanasia, authority, undue influence, free press, privacy, and entrapment. If normative guidelines are proposed, they are usually specific and directive. Principles in ethical theory are typically general guides that leave considerable room for judgment in specific cases, but in applied ethics proponents tend either to reject principles and rules altogether or to advance precise action guides that instruct persons how to act in ways that allow for less interpretation and discretion. Examples are found in literature that proposes rules of informed consent, confidentiality, conflict of interest, access to information, and employee drug testing.

However, in philosophy journals that publish both applied and theoretical work no sharp line of demarcation is apparent between the concepts and norms of ethical theory and applied ethics. There is not even a discernible continuum from theoretical to applied concepts or principles. The applied/theoretical distinction therefore needs to be used with great caution.

COMPETING THEORIES AND PROBLEMS OF SPECIFICITY

One reason theory and application are merged in the literature is that several different types of ethical theories have been employed in attempts to address practical problems. At least the following types of theories have been explicitly invoked: (1) utilitarianism, (2) Kantianism, (3) rights theory, (4) contract theory, (5) virtue theory, (6) communitarianism, (7) casuistry, and (8) pragmatism. Many proponents of these theories would agree that specific policy and practical guidelines cannot be squeezed from appeals to these philosophical ethical theories and that some additional content is always necessary.

Ethical theories have rarely been able to raise or answer the social and policy questions commonplace in applied ethics. General theories are ill suited for this work, because they address philosophical problems and are not by their nature practical or policy oriented. The content of a philosophical theory, as traditionally understood, is not of the right sort. Philosophical theories are about morality, but they are primarily attempts to explain, unify, or justify morality, not attempts to specify the practical commitments of moral principles in public

policy or in particular cases. In applied ethics, ethical theory is often far less important than moral insight and the defense and development of appropriate guidelines suited to a complex circumstance.

Every general ethical norm contains an indeterminacy requiring further development and enrichment to make it applicable in a complex circumstance. To have sufficient content, general theories and principles must be made specific for contexts; otherwise, they will be empty and ineffectual. Factors such as efficiency, institutional rules, law, and clientele acceptance must be taken into account to make them more specific. An ethics useful for public and institutional policies needs to prove a practical strategy that incorporates political procedures, legal constraints, uncertainty about risk, and the like. Progressive specification of norms will be required to handle the variety of problems that arise, gradually reducing dilemmas, policy options, and contingent conflicts that abstract theory and principle are unable to handle.

Some philosophers view this strategy of specification as heavily dependent upon preexistent practices. They maintain that major contributions in philosophical ethics have run from "applied" contexts to "general" theory rather than the reverse. In examining case law and institutional practices, they say, philosophers have learned about morality in ways that require rethinking and modifying general norms of truth telling, consenting, confidentiality, justice, and so forth. To the extent that sophisticated philosophical treatments of such notions are now emerging, they move, not from theory application (including specification), but from practice to theory. Traditional ethical theory, from this perspective, has no privileged position and has more to learn from "applied contexts" than the other way around.

Nonetheless, there are problems with attempts to base applied ethics entirely in practice standards. A practice standard often does not exist within the relevant field, group, or profession. If current standards are low, they could not legitimately determine what the appropriate standards should be. Most moral problems present issues that have to be thought through, not issues to which good answers have already been provided, which explains why many in the professions have turned to philosophers for help in developing professional ethics. Applied philosophers are often most useful to those with whom they collaborate in other fields when practice standards are defective or deficient and a vacuum needs filling by reflection on, criticism of, and reformulation of moral viewpoints or standards.

See also Abortion; Affirmative Action; Business Ethics; Communitarianism; Deontological Ethics; Environmental Ethics; Justice; Metaethics; Pragmatism; Rawls, John; Rights; Utilitarianism; Virtue Ethics.

Bibliography

Beauchamp, T. L. "On Eliminating the Distinction between Applied Ethics and Ethical Theory." *The Monist* 67 (1984): 514–31.

Brock, D. W. "Truth or Consequences: The Role of Philosophers in Policy-Making." *Ethics* 97 (1987): 786–791.

Caplan, A. L. "Ethical Engineers Need Not Apply: The State of Applied Ethics Today." *Science, Technology, and Human Values* 6 (Fall 1980): 24–32.

DeGrazia, D. "Moving Forward in Bioethical Theory: Theories, Cases, and Specified Principlism." *Journal of Medicine and Philosophy* 17 (1992): 511–539.

Feinberg, J. *The Moral Limits of the Criminal Law.* 4 vols. New York: Oxford University Press, 1984–1987.

Fullinwider, R. K. "Against Theory, or: Applied Philosophy—A Cautionary Tale." *Metaphilosophy* 20 (1989): 222–234.

Gert, B. "Licensing Professions." *Business and Professional Ethics Journal* 1 (1982): 51–60.

Gert, B. "Moral Theory and Applied Ethics." *The Monist* 67 (1984): 532–548.

Jonsen, A., and S. Toulmin. *The Abuse of Casuistry: A History of Moral Reasoning.* Berkeley: University of California Press, 1988.

MacIntyre, A. "Does Applied Ethics Rest on a Mistake?" *The Monist* 67 (1984): 498–513.

MacIntyre, A. "What Has Ethics to Learn from Medical Ethics?" *Philosophic Exchange* 2 (1978): 37–47.

Noble, C. "Ethics and Experts." *Hastings Center Report* 12 (June 1982): 7–10, with responses by four critics.

Professional Ethics 1, 1–2 (Spring–Summer 1992). Special issue on applied ethics.

Rawls, J. *A Theory of Justice.* Cambridge, MA: Harvard University Press, 1971.

Regan, T., ed. *Matters of Life and Death.* 3rd ed. New York: McGraw-Hill, 1993.

Reich, Warren, ed. *Encyclopedia of Bioethics.* 2nd ed. New York: Macmillan, 1995.

Richardson, H. "Specifying Norms as a Way to Resolve Concrete Ethical Problems." *Philosophy and Public Affairs* 19 (1990): 279–310.

Singer, P. *Practical Ethics.* 2nd ed. New York: Cambridge University Press, 1993.

Winkler, E. R., and J. R. Coombs, eds. *Applied Ethics: A Reader.* Oxford: Blackwell, 1993.

Tom L. Beauchamp (1996)

A PRIORI AND A POSTERIORI

The distinction between the a priori and the a posteriori has always been an epistemological one; that is to say, it has always had something to do with knowledge. The terms *a priori* and *a posteriori* are Scholastic terms that have their origin in certain ideas of Aristotle; but their use has been considerably extended in the course of history, and their present use stems from the meaning given to them by Immanuel Kant. The terms literally mean "from what is prior" and "from what is posterior." According to Aristotle, *A* is prior to *B* in nature if and only if *B* could not exist without *A; A* is prior to *B* in knowledge if and only if we cannot know *B* without knowing *A.* It is possible for these two senses of "prior" to have an application in common; substance, for example, is prior to other things in both of these senses and in others. It follows that to know something from what is prior is to know what is, in some sense, its cause. Aristotle believed that it is possible to demonstrate a causal relationship by means of a syllogism in which the term for the cause is the middle term. Hence, to know something in terms of what is prior is to know it in terms of a demonstrable causal relationship. To know something from what is posterior, on the other hand, can involve no such demonstration, since the knowledge will be inductive in form.

The transition to Kant's conception of the matter is evident in Gottfried Wilhelm Leibniz. According to the latter, to know reality a posteriori is to know it from what is actually found in the world, that is, by the senses, by the effects of reality in experience; to know reality a priori is to know it "by exposing the cause or the possible generation of the definite thing" (*Nouveaux Essais*, Bk. III, Ch. 3). It is also possible to speak of a priori proofs. As a general consequence of this, Leibniz could distinguish between "truths a posteriori, or of fact," and "truths a priori, or of reason" (ibid., Bk. IV, Ch. 9); for a priori truths can be demonstrated in terms of their being based on identical propositions, while a posteriori truths can be seen to be true only from experience. Thus the distinction between the a posteriori and the a priori comes to be a distinction between what is derived from experience and what is not, whether or not the notion of the a priori also has the notion of demonstration in terms of cause or reason associated with it. Such is the distinction in Kant, and it has remained roughly the same ever since. Since in Kant there is no simple opposition between sense experience and reason (there being also the understanding), it is not possible to express the distinction he laid down as one between what is derived from experience and what is derived from reason.

The distinction, then, is roughly equivalent to that between the empirical and the nonempirical. Kant also connected it with the distinction between the necessary and the contingent, a priori truths being necessary and a posteriori truths contingent. But to assume without further argument that the two distinctions coincide in their application is to assume too much. The same is true of the distinction between the analytic and the synthetic; this too cannot be assimilated without argument to that between the a priori and a posteriori. Whether or not these distinctions coincide in their applications, they certainly cannot have the same meaning. The distinction between the a priori and a posteriori is an epistemological one; it is certainly not evident that the others are.

THE DISTINCTION APPLIED TO CONCEPTS

The distinction between the a priori and the a posteriori has been drawn not only in connection with truths or propositions but also in connection with concepts. Indeed, some truths are doubly a priori; not only is their truth knowable independently of experience but the concepts that they involve are similarly independent of experience. The distinction between a posteriori and a priori concepts may seem a perspicuous one, for it may be thought to be a distinction between concepts that we derive from experience by building them up therefrom and concepts that we have independently of experience. It has sometimes been said also that the latter concepts are innate ideas, with which we are born, so that we have no need to acquire them. But the question whether ideas are innate or acquired seems to be one of psychology, as is the question how we acquire ideas if we do. The distinction under consideration, being an epistemological one, has no direct connection with psychology. A concept that is independent of experience may or may not be innate; and although it cannot be acquired directly from experience, it may still be that experience is in some way a necessary condition of our having the concept. What then does it mean to say that a concept is independent of experience? The answer must be in terms of the validation of the concept.

It may be assumed for present purposes that a concept is what is meant by the corresponding term (although this may not be a fully adequate view and bypasses the question whether concepts are independent of words). To have a concept will thus at least be to understand the corresponding term. Perhaps, then, an a poste-

riori concept is one expressed by a term understandable purely in terms of experience, and an a priori concept one that does not satisfy this condition. The point has sometimes been made by saying that an a posteriori, or empirical, concept or term is one that is cashable in terms of sense experience. This is of course a metaphor, and what it means is that the meaning of empirical terms can be given by definitions that must ultimately depend on ostensive definitions only. Ostensive definitions are those which provide the definition of a term by a direct confrontation with experience. To define a term ostensively it is necessary only to repeat the expression together with some form of pointing to the object or phenomenon in question. It is highly questionable, however, whether any performance of this kind could ever constitute definition as such. For the meaning of a word to be taught in this way there would have to be (as Ludwig Wittgenstein in effect pointed out at the beginning of his *Philosophical Investigations*) a previous understanding that the noise made was a word in a language and in a language of a definite sort. Furthermore, it would have to be understood what sort of term was being defined—whether it was descriptive and, if so, what range of phenomena it was being used to describe. If all this must be understood, it can scarcely be said that the term in question is defined purely by reference to sense experience.

Nevertheless, there is some distinction to be made here. Even if such terms as "red" cannot be defined purely by reference to experience, they could not be understood fully without experience, for example, by someone who does not possess and never has possessed sight. There is a sense in which the blind *can*, up to a point, understand terms such as "red," in that they can know that red is a color and even a color of a certain sort related to other colors in certain ways. But since they cannot know when to apply the term in fact, there is an obvious sense in which they do not have a full understanding of it—and the same applies to the notion of color itself. A posteriori terms and concepts may thus be defined as those that directly require our having experience in order for us to apply them or those that can only be fully understood by reference to terms that directly require our having experience to apply them. Whether or not a creature without experience could ever come to have a concept such as, for example, validity, it is clear that being able to apply the concept does not directly require experience. This may afford the basis of a distinction between a posteriori and a priori concepts. There may be various views about a priori concepts, concerning, for example, whether they are to be restricted to concepts of, or concepts involved in, mental operations on a posteriori concepts. Empiricists have in general held that the only a priori concepts are those that express relations of ideas. The field is thus restricted to the concepts of logic and mathematics.

THE DISTINCTION APPLIED TO PROPOSITIONS

In a sense, the distinction between concepts presupposes the distinction between propositions, since concepts can be applied only in propositions. According to the rough criteria already mentioned, an a priori proposition will be one whose truth is knowable independently of experience. It may be questioned, however, whether there are any truths that can be known if the subject has no experiences whatever. Hence, the matter is better put in terms of the validation of the proposition in question, in terms of its verification or falsification. It has sometimes been suggested that a proposition is a priori if its truth is ascertainable by examination of it alone or if it is deducible from such propositions. An a priori proposition would thus be one that provides its own verification; it is true in itself. This account is too restrictive, since there may be propositions whose truth is ascertainable by argument that makes no reference to empirical matters of fact, but that may not be deducible from any propositions of the kind previously mentioned. That is to say, there may be circumstances in which it is possible to validate propositions by argument that makes no reference to matters of fact discoverable by experience. Empiricists have generally denied this, but the possibility of what Kant called "transcendental arguments" cannot be so lightly dismissed. Aristotle's argument for the truth of the principle of contradiction would be a case in point, namely, that a denial of it already presupposes it.

On the other hand, to say simply that a priori propositions are those whose truth can be discovered without reference to experience is too wide a definition. For it may be argued that the terms in which many such propositions are expressed could only be fully understood by reference to experience. A proposition may be a priori without its involving terms that are without exception a priori. It was for this reason that Kant distinguished between a priori and *pure* a priori judgments; only in the latter are all the terms a priori. In view of this, an a priori proposition may be defined as one whose truth, given an understanding of the terms involved, is ascertainable by a procedure that makes no reference to experience. The validation of a posteriori truths, on the other hand, necessitates a procedure that does make reference to experience.

CAN ANALYTIC PROPOSITIONS BE A POSTERIORI? It has already been mentioned that Kant superimposed upon the a priori–a posteriori distinction the distinction between the analytic and the synthetic. There are difficulties involved in defining this latter distinction, but for present purposes it is necessary to note that Kant assumed it impossible for analytic judgments to be a posteriori. He does this presumably on the grounds that the truth of an analytic judgment depends upon the relations between the concepts involved and is ascertainable by determining whether the denial of the judgment gives rise to a contradiction. This latter procedure is surely one that makes no reference to experience. Kant is clearly right in this. As already seen, it is not relevant to object that since analytic judgments, propositions, or statements need not involve purely a priori terms, evaluation of the truth of some analytic propositions will involve reference to experience; for in determining whether a proposition is a priori, it is necessary to take as already determined the status of the terms involved. It is similarly irrelevant to maintain that it is sometimes possible to come to see the truth of an analytic proposition through empirical means. It may be possible, for example, for a man to realize the truth of "All bachelors are unmarried men" as an analytic proposition as a consequence of direct experience with bachelors. But this consequence will be an extrinsic one. That is to say that while the man may attain this insight in this way, it will be quite accidental; the validity of the insight does not depend upon the method by which it is acquired. That is why the definition of an a priori proposition or statement involves the idea that its truth must be ascertainable without reference to experience. As long as a nonempirical procedure of validation exists, the proposition in question will be a priori, whether or not its truth is always ascertained by this procedure. It is quite impossible, on the other hand, for an a posteriori proposition to be validated by pure argument alone.

MUST A POSTERIORI PROPOSITIONS BE CONTINGENT? Given that all analytic propositions are a priori, it is a further question whether all synthetic propositions must be a posteriori. This is a hotly debated question, with empiricists maintaining that they must be. But first it is necessary to consider the relation between the a priori–a posteriori dichotomy and the necessary–contingent one.

Kant certainly associated the a priori with the necessary, and there is a prima facie case for the view that if a proposition is known a posteriori, its truth must be contingent. For how can experience alone tell us that something must be so? On the other hand, it might be maintained that we can learn inductively that a connection between characteristics of things holds as a matter of necessity. Some philosophers maintain that natural laws represent necessary truths, and they do not all think this incompatible with the view that natural laws can be arrived at through experience. What is sometimes called intuitive induction—a notion originating in Aristotle—is also something of this kind; we see by experience that something is essentially so and so. An even greater number of philosophers would be willing to assert that, in *some* sense of the word "must," experience can show us that something must be the case. Certainly the "must" in question is not a logical "must," and empiricists have tended to maintain that all necessity is logical necessity. This, however, is just a dogma. It seems plausible to assert that an unsupported body must in normal circumstances fall to the ground.

Yet it must be admitted that the normal philosophical conception of necessity is more refined than this, and to say that an unsupported body must in normal circumstances fall to the ground need not be taken as incompatible with saying that this is a contingent matter. Similarly, there is an important sense in which natural laws are contingent; they are about matters of fact. If we also think of them as necessary, the necessity in question stems from the conceptual framework into which we fit them. It is possible to conceive of empirical connections in such a way that, within the framework of concepts in which we place them, they are treated as holding necessarily. It is still a contingent matter whether the whole conceptual framework has an application. If propositions expressing such connections are a priori, it is only in a relative sense.

MUST A PRIORI PROPOSITIONS BE NECESSARY? It seems at first sight that there is no necessity for nonempirical propositions to be necessary, or rather that it is possible to construct propositions which, if true, must be true a priori, while they apparently remain contingent. These are propositions that are doubly general. They may be formalized in such a way as to contain both a universal and an existential quantifier, for example, $(x) \cdot \exists y \cdot \phi xy$. Such propositions have been called by J. W. N. Watkins (following Karl Popper) "all and some propositions." Because they have this kind of double generality, they are both unverifiable and unfalsifiable. The element corresponding to the universal quantifier makes them unverifiable; that corresponding to the existential quantifier makes them unfalsifiable. Under the circumstances they can hardly be said to be empirical. An example of this kind of proposition is the principle of universal causality,

"Every event has a cause," which is equivalent to "For every event there is some other event with which it is causally connected." It has been claimed by some philosophers, for instance, G. J. Warnock, that this proposition is vacuous, since no state of affairs will falsify it. But the most that can be claimed in this respect is that no *particular* state of affairs *which can be observed* will falsify it. It is clearly not compatible with any state of affairs whatever, since it is incompatible with the state of affairs in which there is an event with no cause. It remains true that it is impossible to verify that an event has no cause.

Watkins does not claim that the proposition is necessary, although the principle of causality has been held by many, for instance, Kant, to be an example of a necessary truth, and it could no doubt be viewed as such. But it is also possible to treat it as a contingent truth, one that holds only in the contingency of every event being causally determined. How we could know that such a contingency held is a further question. It is clear that nothing that we could observe would provide such knowledge. Such propositions certainly could not be *known* a posteriori; if true, they must be known a priori if they are to be known at all. The difficulty is just this— how *are* they to be known at all? Thus, it may be better to distinguish between a priori propositions and nonempirical propositions of this kind. A priori propositions are those which can be known to be true and whose truth is ascertainable by a procedure that makes no reference to experience; nonempirical propositions of the kind in question are not like this, for their truth is, strictly speaking, not ascertainable at all. If we accept them, it must be as mere postulates or as principles whose force is regulative in some sense.

This does not exclude the possibility that there are other propositions whose truth can be ascertained by a nonempirical procedure but that are less than necessary. It has been argued by J. N. Findlay that there are certain propositions asserting connections between concepts that are only probable, as opposed to the commonly held view that all connections existing among concepts are necessary. He maintains that our conceptual systems may be such that there are connections between their members that are by no means analytic; the connections do not amount to entailments. Perhaps something like the Hegelian dialectic is the prototype of this. Findlay argues, for example, that if one has likings, there is the presumption that one will like likings of this sort; on this sort of basis one could move toward the notion of a community of ends. It is difficult to speak more than tentatively here. Given, however, that the propositions stating these conceptual connections are, if true, then true a priori (as they surely must be), it is not clear that it is necessary to claim only that what one knows in relation to them is probable. Certainly the connections do not constitute entailments; but this of itself does not mean that what one knows is only probable. The fact that the argument for a certain position is not a strictly deductive one does not mean that the position cannot be expressed by truths that are necessary and can be known to be so. For the argument may justify the claim to such knowledge in spite of the fact that the argument is not deductively valid in the strict sense. If such a necessary proposition does not seem to have universal application, this may be due to the fact that it holds under certain conditions and that its necessity is relative to these conditions. This was Kant's position over the principle of universal causality. He held that the principle that every event has a cause is necessary only in relation to experience. If propositions of this sort lack absolute necessity, they need not lack necessity altogether. The tentative conclusion of this section is that while some propositions may in a certain sense be both nonempirical and contingent, it nevertheless remains true that if a proposition is known a priori, it must be necessarily true in some sense or other.

MUST A PRIORI PROPOSITIONS BE ANALYTIC? It has been suggested in the previous section that there may be a priori propositions that are not analytic. They depend for their validation on a priori argument but cannot be given a deductive proof from logical truths. The question of the synthetic a priori is one of the most hotly debated topics in philosophy and has, indeed, been so ever since Kant first stated the issues explicitly. Empiricists have always vehemently denied the possibility of such truths and have even tried to show that a proposition that is a priori must be analytic by definition. Most attempts of this sort rest on misconceptions of what is meant by these terms.

Kant's synthetic a priori. Kant claimed that synthetic a priori truths were to be found in two fields—mathematics and the presuppositions of experience or science—although he denied that there was a place for them in dogmatic metaphysics. He maintained that although mathematics did contain some analytic truths (since there were propositions which summed up purely deductive steps), the main bulk of mathematical truths were synthetic a priori; they were informative, nonempirical, and necessary, but not such that their denial gave rise to a contradiction. These characteristics were in large part due to the fact that mathematical knowledge involved intuitions of time (in the case of arithmetic) and space (in the

case of geometry). Kant's conception of arithmetic has not found much support, and his view of geometry has often been considered to have been undermined by the discovery of non-Euclidean geometries. It is doubtful, however, whether the situation is quite so simple as this, for what Kant maintained was that an intuition of space corresponding to Euclidean geometry was necessary at any rate *for creatures with sensibility like ours.* That is to say, what we perceive of the world must conform to Euclidean geometry, whether or not it can be conceived differently in abstraction from the conditions of perception. Whether or not this is true, it is not obviously false.

The main attack on the Kantian view of arithmetic, and thereafter on that view of other branches of mathematics, came from Gottlob Frege and from Bertrand Russell and Alfred North Whitehead. Frege defined an analytic proposition as one in the proof of which one comes to general logical laws and definitions only; and he attempted to show that arithmetical propositions are analytic in this sense. The crucial step in this program is Frege's definition of "number" roughly in terms of what Russell called one-to-one relations. (Russell himself gave a parallel definition in terms of similarity of classes.) Given Frege's definition of number, arithmetical operations had to be expressed in terms of the original definition. It is at least an open question whether this attempt was successful. The definition has been accused of being circular and/or insufficient. This being so, the most that can be claimed is that arithmetic, while not reducible to logic, has a similar structure. Nevertheless, Gödel's proof that it is impossible to produce a system of the whole of formal arithmetic that is both consistent and complete may be taken to cast doubt even on this claim. At all events, the exact status of arithmetical truths remains arguable.

Other synthetic a priori truths claimed by Kant were the presuppositions of objective experience. He tried to demonstrate that the truth of such propositions as "Every event has a cause" is necessary to objective experience. These propositions indeed express the necessary conditions of possible experience and of empirical science. As such, their validity is limited to experience, and they can have no application to anything outside experience, to what Kant called "things-in-themselves." According to Kant, these principles—which are of two kinds, constitutive or regulative in relation to experience—are ultimately derived from a list of a priori concepts or categories, which he claims to derive in turn from the traditional logical classification of judgments. These principles, in a form directly applicable to empirical phenomena, are also established by transcendental arguments. In the "Second Analogy" of the *Critique of Pure Reason*, for example, Kant sought to show that unless objective phenomena were irreversible in time, and therefore subject to rule, and therefore due to causes, it would be impossible to distinguish them from merely subjective phenomena. Causality is therefore a condition of distinguishing phenomena as objective at all. The cogency of this position depends upon the acceptability of the arguments, and it is impossible to examine them here. It is to be noted, however, that what the arguments seek to show is that certain necessary connections between concepts must be accepted if we are to give those concepts any application. The connection between the concepts of "objective event" and "cause" is not an analytic one, but it is a connection that must be taken as obtaining if the concepts are to have any application to empirical phenomena.

Another instance of this kind of situation, perhaps more trivial, can be seen in such a proposition as "Nothing can be red and green all over at the same time in the same respect." This proposition has sometimes been classified as empirical, sometimes as analytic; but it has been thought by empiricists a more plausible candidate for synthetic a priori truth than any of Kant's examples. There is clearly some kind of necessity about this proposition. It may be possible for something to *appear* red and green all over, but to suggest that something might *be* red and green all over or that one might produce examples of such a thing has little plausibility; for in some sense red excludes green. The question is, In what sense? Since "red" does not mean "not-green" and cannot be reduced to this (for terms such as "red" and "green" do not seem capable of analysis), the proposition under consideration cannot, strictly speaking, be analytic. How can red and green exclude each other without this being a logical or analytic exclusion? It is not merely a contingent exclusion, since it is clearly impossible to produce something that is red and green all over (shot silk, for example, although it appears so, does not conform to the conditions of being two-colored all over), and we cannot imagine what such a thing would be like.

It may be suggested that red and green are different determinates of the same determinable—color. We distinguish colors and use different terms in order to do so. To allow, then, that something might be described by two such terms at the same time would be to frustrate the purposes for which our system of color classification was devised. However, this may sound too arbitrary. After all, given two colors that do in fact shade into each other, we

might be less reluctant to allow that something might be both of them at once. It is no accident that we distinguish colors as we do. For creatures of our kind of sensibility, as Kant would put it, colors have a definite structure; it is natural to see them in certain ways and to conceive of them accordingly. We then fit them to a conceptual scheme that reflects those distinctions. If we will not allow that something may be red and green all over, it is because the mutual exclusion of red and green is a necessary feature of our scheme of color concepts. Yet the whole scheme has application to the world only because we see colors as we do.

THE RELATIVE AND ABSOLUTE A PRIORI. Because of the empirical preconditions for our scheme of color concepts, if we maintain that we can know a priori that something cannot be red and green all over, it cannot be absolutely a priori. For the truth that something that is red cannot also be green at the same time and in the same respect can scarcely be said to be ascertainable without any reference whatever to experience. The same is true of the principle of universal causality discussed earlier. It might be maintained that the truth that every event has a cause is necessary because "cause" and "event" are so definable that there is an analytic connection between them (implausible as this may be in fact). In that case the proposition in question would be true in all possible worlds (to use a Leibnizian phrase), since its truth would not depend on what is. In a world in which no events occurred, it would be true, in this view, that every event (if there were any) would have a cause. We can know the truth of this proposition absolutely a priori. However, if the principle is not analytic (and it is clearly not, in its ordinary interpretation) but is still thought to be necessary, this can be so only because the connection between cause and event is necessary to our conception of the world as we see it. Similarly, the mutual exclusion of red and green is necessary to our conception of colors as we see them. These propositions are not true in all possible worlds, and while their truth can be known a priori, it is not known absolutely a priori.

On the other hand, the so-called laws of thought, such as the principle of contradiction, while not analytic, must again be known absolutely a priori, whatever the kind of necessity they possess. The truth of the principle of contradiction is necessary to the possibility of thought in general, including the thought of the principle itself. It is not possible even to deny the principle without presupposing it. It cannot be maintained that its truth is in any way ascertainable by a procedure that makes reference to experience. Its truth is a necessity of thought, not of experience, and is not relative to experience. Hence it may be said to be known absolutely a priori.

Of those propositions that are absolutely a priori there are two kinds—analytic truths and the principles of logic themselves. (It is perhaps not surprising that these have sometimes been classified together, even if wrongly so.) On the other hand, there are some truths that are necessary but known only relatively a priori—truths such as the principle of causality and the principle of the incompatibility of colors. Finally, of course, there is that large class of truths which can only be known a posteriori. But for philosophers these are naturally much less interesting than truths of the first two kinds—those which are a priori in some sense or other. And over these there is still much argument.

See also Analytic and Synthetic Statements; Aristotle; Empiricism; Frege, Gottlob; Gödel, Kurt; Gödel's Theorem; Hegelianism; Innate Ideas; Kant, Immanuel; Knowledge, A Priori; Laws of Thought; Leibniz, Gottfried Wilhelm; Logic, History of; Mathematics, Foundations of; Popper, Karl Raimund; Propositions; Russell, Bertrand Arthur William; Whitehead, Alfred North; Wittgenstein, Ludwig Josef Johann.

Bibliography

For Kant's distinction between a priori and a posteriori, see the Norman Kemp Smith translation of the *Critique of Pure Reason* (London, 1953), especially the introduction but also the chapters on the aesthetic and the analytic of principles. For the precedents to Kant's distinction, see Aristotle, *Posterior Analytics*, especially Bk. I.2; Gottfried Leibniz, *Nouveaux Essais*, translated by A. G. Langley as *New Essays concerning Human Understanding* (Chicago: Macmillan, 1916), especially III.3 and IV.9. See also Arthur Pap, *Semantics and Necessary Truth* (New Haven, CT: Yale University Press, 1958), Pt. 1.

For the application of the distinction to concepts or terms, see H. H. Price, *Thinking and Experience* (London: Hutchinson, 1953); for criticisms of the notion of ostensive definition, see the opening sections of Ludwig Wittgenstein, *Philosophical Investigations* (Oxford: Blackwell, 1953); and Peter Geach, *Mental Acts* (London: Routledge and Paul, 1957), especially sections 6–11; and for discussion of the a priori in relation to analyticity, see G. H. Bird, "Analytic and Synthetic," *Philosophical Quarterly* 11 (1961): 227–237; L. J. Cohen, *The Diversity of Meaning* (London: Methuen, 1962), Chs. 6 and 10; and Ch. 5 of the work by Arthur Pap cited above.

For discussion of nonempirical propositions that are not necessary, see J. N. Findlay, *Values and Intentions* (London: Allen and Unwin, 1961); two articles by J. W. N. Watkins: "Between Analytic and Empirical," *Philosophy* 32 (1957): 112–131, and "Confirmable and Influential Metaphysics," *Mind* 67 (1958): 344–365; and compare G. J. Warnock, "Every Event Has a Cause," in *Logic and Language* (Oxford: Blackwell, 1953), Vol. II.

For Kant's views on the possibility of the synthetic a priori, see the Kemp Smith translation cited above. For discussions of examples, see: D. W. Hamlyn, "On Necessary Truth," *Mind* 70 (1961): 514–525; S. N. Hampshire, "Identification and Existence," in *Contemporary British Philosophers* (3d Series) (London, 1956); D. J. O'Connor, "Incompatible Properties," *Analysis* 15 (1955): 109–117; D. F. Pears, "Incompatibility of Colours," in *Logic and Language* (Oxford: Blackwell, 1953), Vol. II; and compare Aristotle's discussion of the principle of contradiction in *Metaphysics* IV.4.

OTHER RECOMMENDED TITLES

Boghossian, P., and C. Peacocke, eds. *New Essays on the A Priori*. Oxford: Clarendon Press, 2000.

BonJour, L. *In Defense of Pure Reason: A Rationalist Account of A Priori Justification*. Cambridge, U.K.: Cambridge University Press, 1998.

Casullo, Albert. *A Priori Justification*. New York: Oxford University Press, 2003.

Casullo, Albert, ed. *A Priori Knowledge*. Aldershot, U.K.: Ashgate, 1999.

Coffa, J. A. *The Semantic Tradition from Kant to Carnap*. Cambridge, U.K.: Cambridge University Press, 1991.

DePaul, M. R., and W. Ramsey, eds. *Rethinking Intuition: The Psychology of Intuition and Its Role in Philosophical Inquiry*. Lanham, MD: Rowman & Littlefield, 1998.

Foley, Richard. *A Theory of Epistemic Rationality*. Cambridge, MA: Harvard University Press, 1987.

Foley, Richard. *Working without a Net*. New York: Oxford University Press, 1993.

Fumerton, Richard. "A Priori Philosophy after an A Posteriori Turn." *Midwest Studies in Philosophy* 23 (1999): 21–33.

Gendler, T. S., and J. Hawthorne, eds. *Conceivability and Possibility*. Oxford: Oxford University Press, 2002.

Goldman, Alvin. *Epistemology and Cognition*. Cambridge, MA: Harvard University Press, 1986.

Hanson, P., and B. Hunter, eds. *Return of the A Priori*. Calgary, AB: University of Calgary Press, 1992.

Hawthorne, John P. "Deeply Contingent A Priori Knowledge." *Philosophy and Phenomenological Research* (September 2002): 247–269.

Kitcher, Philip. *The Nature of Mathematical Knowledge*. New York: Oxford University Press, 1983.

Kripke, Saul A. "Identity and Necessity." In *Naming, Necessity, and Natural Kinds*, edited by S. P. Schwartz, 66–101. Ithaca, NY: Cornell University Press, 1977.

Kripke, Saul A. *Naming and Necessity*. Cambridge, MA: Harvard University Press, 1980.

Kripke, Saul A. *Wittgenstein on Rules and Private Language*. Cambridge, MA: Harvard University Press, 1982.

Moser, Paul, ed. *A Priori Knowledge*. Oxford: Oxford University Press, 1987.

Moser, Paul. *Knowledge and Evidence*. Cambridge, U.K.: Cambridge University Press, 1989.

D. W. Hamlyn (1967)
Bibliography updated by Benjamin Fiedor (2005)

A PRIORI KNOWLEDGE

See *A Priori and A Posteriori; Innate Ideas; Knowledge, A Priori; Rationalism*

AQUINAS, ST. THOMAS

See *Thomas Aquinas, St.*

ARABIC PHILOSOPHY

See *Islamic Philosophy*

ARCESILAUS

(316/315–241/240 BCE)

Arcesilaus was born in Pitane, a Greek city on the coast of Asia Minor. In Athens, after a period of study with Theophrastus—Aristotle's successor as head of the Peripatos—he joined the Academy, Plato's school, which was then dominated by Crantor, Polemon, and Crates. Arcesilaus succeeded Crates, Polemon's successor, as head of the Academy and was responsible for the school's turn to skepticism. From this point, the skeptical examination of other schools' theories replaced the elaboration of its own positive doctrines as the Academy's principal occupation. This change in the Academy's direction is recognized in the ancient tradition that credits Arcesilaus with founding the second or Middle Academy, which replaced the first or Old Academy and gave way in turn to the third or New Academy of Carneades.

Like Socrates before him and Carneades after him, Arcesilaus wrote nothing, but made his mark in face to face philosophical argument. His practice was not to present views of his own, but instead to invite his interlocutors to put forward their views, which he then subjected to rigorous scrutiny. His method was dialectical: He put questions to his interlocutors from the answers to which he aimed to deduce conclusions at odds with their positions. The effect was to uncover difficulties internal to the interlocutors' positions without committing him to a position of his own. These arguments were conceived by Arcesilaus and his Academic followers as their contribution to argument on both sides of the question, which they regarded as the best way to discover the truth—their ultimate aim. The resemblance to Socrates is unmistakable and was much emphasized by the Academics.

Their principal target was Stoic epistemology. According to Zeno of Citium, the founder of Stoicism and an older contemporary of Arcesilaus's, it is possible for human beings to free themselves entirely from opinion—that is, false or insecure belief—and to attain the kind of knowledge that qualifies as wisdom. In the Socratic tradition, Zeno held that wisdom was identical with virtue and as such the one necessary and sufficient condition for happiness. A necessary condition for knowledge on the Stoic view was the existence of cognitive impressions (*kataleptikai phantasiai*). Each of these is a perceptual impression that arises in conditions which both ensure that, by capturing its objects with perfect accuracy, it is true while at the same time imparting to it a character that belongs only to impressions that arise in this way and which human beings can discriminate. According to Stoic epistemology, all knowledge depends in one way or another on cognitive impressions, which is why the cognitive impression is the school's criterion of truth. By restricting one's assent (in the sphere of perception) to impressions with this character, one can avoid ever assenting to a false perceptual impression. If further conditions are satisfied, one can avoid error altogether.

Arcesilaus and the Academics argued that, on any plausible account of it, the character allegedly proper to cognitive impressions was not in fact confined to impressions produced in the specified truth-guaranteeing way, but also belonged to false impressions. As a result, the former, though true, are indistinguishable from the latter and therefore unable to serve as a criterion. It follows on Stoic assumptions about knowledge that nothing can be known. This is the first of the two propositions most closely associated with ancient skepticism. The second—that one ought to suspend judgment—Arcesilaus deduced from the first, together with the Stoic insistence that wisdom is incompatible with mere opinion. Assent to a noncognitive impression (or an impression that does not stand in the proper relation to cognitive impressions), automatically results in opinion, so that, in the absence of cognitive impressions, a wise person can avoid opinion only by suspending judgment entirely.

On a strictly dialectical interpretation of his arguments, Arcesilaus did nothing more than present his Stoic opponents with a set of difficulties. On this view, it was their task either to resolve the difficulties or to abandon or modify the position that had given rise to them. Some ancient authorities held that Arcesilaus's arguments against the possibility of knowledge and in favor of suspension of judgment had implications only for the Stoa and did not prevent him from espousing a form of dogmatic Platonism within the Academy. But according to another, better-founded tradition in the Academy itself, Arcesilaus agreed with Zeno that opinion is utterly alien to wisdom and that it is a grave failing—indeed a sin—to allow assent to run ahead of knowledge. But, according to this tradition, the lesson he drew from the difficulties that he had uncovered in the Stoic position among others, was that he and his opponents were not, or not yet, in a position to assent, secure in the conviction that they were in possession of the truth. In these conditions, suspension of judgment and continued open-minded inquiry were indicated. The skepticism characterized by this attitude was a matter of intellectual honesty and prudence, rather than convinced adherence to the skeptical proposition that nothing can be known. And Arcesilaus, it is told, was careful to maintain that one could not even know that one could not know anything.

The Stoics responded to Arcesilaus by arguing that, if nothing can be known and people are therefore obliged to withhold assent, life becomes impossible, as there can no basis for judgment without a criterion nor any possibility of action without assent. Arcesilaus's answer appears to have been an extension of his first dialectical arguments, for it aimed to show that Stoic epistemology and moral psychology had the resources to explain how a human being may proceed in the absence of cognitive impressions and act without assent. In these conditions, one will be guided by what is reasonable, the notion that the Stoics had used to explain how the wise will act when certainty is not available. It will, for instance, be reasonable to expect a successful voyage if the weather is fair, the crew skilled and so on. Action, on the other hand, requires only that an impression elicit an impulse, which the Stoics used to explain the behavior of nonrational animals and human children, who lack the power of assent.

Arcesilaus's explanation of how action is possible without assent, at least in the form in which it has survived, is sketchy, and it is not clear that it can do justice to the concerns that moved the Stoics and other philosophers to develop their theories in the first place. It plainly does not have the independent appeal of Carneades's theory of probability or his suggestion that assent, as the Stoics conceived it, could be replaced either by qualified assent or a way of following or using impressions that did not entail assent. Nonetheless Arcesilaus's proposals marked the beginning of a long tradition of defending the skepticism as a way of life, of which Carneades's probabilism and Pyrrhonism were later examples.

The example of Arcesilaus continued to inspire members of the Academy until the end of the school's history and thereafter Pyrrhonists, who regarded New Academics such as Carneades as apostates from the true skeptical way but acknowledged a kinship with Arcesilaus.

See also Ancient Skepticism; Carneades; Stoicism; Zeno of Citium.

Bibliography

WORKS GIVING TEXTS OF ARCESILAUS

Long, A. A., and D. N. Sedley, eds. *The Hellenistic Philosophers.* 2 vols. Chapters 68–70. Cambridge, U.K.: Cambridge University Press, 1987.

Mette, H. J. "Zwei Akademiker heute: Krantor von Soloi und Arkesilaos von Pitane." *Lustrum* 26 (1984): 7–94.

STUDIES OF ARCESILAUS

Cooper, John. "Arcesilaus: Socratic and Skeptic." in *Knowledge, Nature and the Good*, by John Cooper. Princeton, NJ: Princeton University Press, 2004.

Couissin, P. "L'Origine et l'evolution de l'epoche." *Revue des études grecques* 42 (1929): 373–397.

Couissin, P. "The Stoicism of the New Academy." In *The Skeptical Tradition*, edited by Myles Burnyeat, 31–63. Berkeley: University of California Press, 1983.

Long, A. A. "Diogenes Laertius, Life of Arcesilaus." *Elenchos* 7 (1986): 429–449.

Schofield, Malcolm. "Academic Epistemology." In *The Cambridge History of Hellenistic Philosophy*, edited by Keimpe Algra, Jonathan Barnes, Jaap Mansfeld, and Malcolm Schofield. Cambridge, U.K.: Cambridge University Press, 1999.

Striker, Gisela. "Sceptical Strategies." In *Doubt and Dogmatism: Studies in Hellenistic Epistemology*, edited by Malcolm Schofield, Myles Burnyeat, and Jonathan Barnes. Oxford: Oxford University Press, 1980.

James Allen (2005)

ARCHĒ

The Greek term *archē* refers to the original stuff from which the world came to be, according to pre-Socratic philosophers. In his *Metaphysics* Aristotle explains:

> Of the first philosophers, the majority thought the sources [*archai*, plural] of all things were found only in the class of matter. For that of which all existing things consist, and that from which they come to be first and into which they perish last—the substance continuing but changing in its attributes—*this*, they say, is the element and this the source [*archē*] of existing

things. Accordingly they do not think anything either comes to be or perishes, inasmuch as that nature is always preserved. ... For a certain nature always exists, either one or more than one, from which everything else comes to be while this is preserved. All, however, do not agree on the number and character of this source, but Thales, the originator of this kind of theory, says it is water....

(METAPHYSICS 983B 6–21)

Aristotle seems to use the term *archē* to refer to several different notions that he holds are all part of the pre-Socratics' conception: (1) a primeval chaos in which only one element (or one set of elements) exists; (2) the primeval element that constituted the primitive state, from which all the bodies of the present world were formed; (3) that same fundamental element insofar as it even now constitutes the world; (4) the principle of explanation, or explanatory source (identified with the primeval element), that logically and causally accounts for the phenomena of the world.

According to Aristotle, the pre-Socratic philosophers with cosmological theories agreed in explaining all phenomena as deriving from a single stuff or set of stuffs (sense 4). They disagreed about whether there was only one stuff or several. Those who held that there was only one stuff (monists) disagreed as to what it was: Thales said water; Anaximander said the Boundless; Anaximenes said air; and Heraclitus said fire. Those who held there were several stuffs or elements (pluralists) disagreed among themselves as to what those were: Empedocles said earth, water, air, and fire; Anaxagoras said an unlimited number of homogeneous stuffs including flesh, gold, wood; the atomists said an infinite number of atomic particles of differing shapes.

Aristotle's account, partly through the writings of his colleague Theophrastus on the history of philosophical opinions, dominated ancient and then modern interpretations. Unfortunately, there are a number of problems with his account. First, it seems to conflate two different types of theory, that of the alleged monists, and that of the pluralists, which may operate on different principles. Second, it ignores theories that posit a stable cosmology (in which the world does not arise out of a primeval chaos), such as those of Xenophanes and Heraclitus. Third, it seems to project back onto cosmologists of the sixth century BCE the theory of changeless being that Parmenides invented in the early fifth century BCE.

Fourth, it assumes a sophisticated theory of matter in which a subject is distinguished from attributes or properties, which seems to arise only in the fourth century BCE. Fifth, it embodies a tendentious interpretation of how the pre-Socratics understood causal explanation.

The term *archē* itself in the sense of "beginning, starting point" might have been used by early pre-Socratics such as Anaximander, but there are no extant quotations to verify this. In the late fifth century Diogenes of Apollonia used the term to mean something like "starting point," with a possible implication of being an explanatory principle. (fr. 1). But the term only seems to become a philosophically important one when one considers that Plato described an archē as a principle to which nothing is prior (Republic 511b, Phaedrus 245c-d), in effect as supplying a metaphysical ground and a logical axiom. Aristotle himself distinguished six senses of the term, only the last of which is a technical philosophical one, reflecting Plato's use (Metaphysics V.1). Aristotle's account of the archē as a principle of explanation among the pre-Socratics is highly suggestive but should not be accepted uncritically.

Most of the pre-Socratics were interested in explaining how the present world arose out of a primeval chaos, and also in identifying the basic realities from which the world arose. In those two senses, they sought through their studies and writings to elucidate the sources, the archai, of the world. Whether, or in what sense, their basic realities were material, and whether they were changeless, are controversial questions scholars still wrestle with.

See also Aristotle; Pre-Socratic Philosophy.

Bibliography

Algra, Keimpe. "The Beginnings of Cosmology." In *The Cambridge Companion to Early Greek Philosophy*, edited by A. A. Long. Cambridge, U.K.: Cambridge University Press, 1999.

Alt, Karin. "Zum Satz des Anaximenes über die Seele: Untersuchung von Aetios *Peri archōn*." *Hermes* 101 (1973): 129–164.

Barnes, Jonathan. *The Presocratic Philosophers*. Rev. ed. London: Routledge, 1982.

Guthrie, W. K. C. *A History of Greek Philosophy*. Vol. 1: *The Earlier Presocratics and the Pythagoreans*. Cambridge, U.K.: Cambridge University Press, 1962.

Stokes, Michael C. *One and Many in Presocratic Philosophy*. Washington: Center for Hellenic Studies, 1971.

Daniel W. Graham (2005)

ARCHYTAS OF TARENTUM

(c. 425 BCE—c. 350 BCE)

Archytas of Tarentum was active in the first half of the fourth century BCE as a mathematician and a philosopher in the Pythagorean tradition. He is famous for having sent a ship in 361 BCE to rescue Plato from Dionysius II, tyrant of Syracuse. Archytas is unique among ancient philosophers for his success in the political sphere—he was elected general seven consecutive times in a democratically governed Tarentum (at the time one of the most important Greek city-states in southern Italy).

More texts have been preserved in Archytas's name than in that of any other Pythagorean, but the majority of these texts are spurious. The pseudo-Pythagorean treatises of the first century BCE and later were often written in his name, considering him the latest of the three great early Pythagoreans (following Pythagoras himself and Philolaus). The spurious works on categories in Archytas's name were regarded as genuine by the commentators on Aristotle's *Categories* and were frequently cited. Four fragments survive from Archytas's genuine works, of which *Harmonics* was the most important, and there is a relatively rich set of testimonia.

Archytas provided the first solution to one of the most celebrated problems in ancient mathematics, the duplication of the cube. One romantic version of the problem reports that the inhabitants of the island of Delos were commanded by the god to build an altar double the size of the current altar, which had the shape of a cube. The problem was thus to determine the length of the side on which to build a cube of double the volume. Archytas's solution is a masterpiece of mathematical imagination, requiring one to envision the intersection of two lines drawn on the surface of a semicylinder—one by a rotating semicircle and one by a rotating triangle. In later antiquity, a story arose that Plato was critical of Archytas for using mechanical instruments to find the solution and thus perverting the true function of mathematics—that is, to direct the soul to the intelligible realm. This story was probably invented to explain the separation of the science of mechanics from philosophy. No physical instruments are employed in Archytas's solution, and it was criticized by some ancient authors as too abstract and of little practical application. Although Plato's complaints about the state of solid geometry in his day (*Rep.* 528b–d) may be directed at Archytas, they focus not on the use of instruments but rather on the failure of its practitioners to develop a coherent science of solid geometry.

Fr. 1, the beginning of Archytas's *Harmonics*, is the earliest text to identify a quadrivium of four sciences (the science of number, geometry, astronomy, and music). Archytas praises the sciences for beginning by distinguishing the universal concepts relevant to the specific science, but he regards their ultimate goal as an account of individual things in the world in terms of number, thus building on Philolaus's insight that all things are known through number. Archytas's own *Harmonics* begins by distinguishing important general conceptions in acoustics. His mistaken view that pitch depends on the speed with which a sound travels—it depends, in fact, on the frequency of impacts in a given period—was adopted with modifications by both Plato and Aristotle and was the most common view in antiquity. Archytas provided an important proof that the basic musical intervals such as the octave, which correspond to ratios of the form $(n+1)/1$, cannot be divided in half.

The goal of Archytas's harmonics, however, was the description of a particular set of phenomena—in this case the musical scales in use in his day—in terms of specific numerical ratios. Plato complained that such a science of harmonics sought numbers in the sensible world rather than ascending to more abstract problems, which were independent of the phenomena (*Rep.* 531c). For Archytas, however, there was no split between the intelligible and sensible world. Logistic, the science of number and proportion, was the master science for Archytas, because all other sciences ultimately rely on number to provide knowledge of individual things (Fr. 4). Just as his science aimed at mathematical description of concrete phenomena, so Archytas also developed a theory of definition that earned Aristotle's praise (*Metaph.* 1043a14–26) for taking into account not just the limiting (formal) aspect of the definiendum but also the unlimited (material) aspect.

Archytas argued that number was crucial in the political and ethical sphere as well. The stability of the state is based on the widely held human ability to calculate, which convinces the rich and the poor that they have their fair share (Fr. 3). Archytas regarded bodily pleasure as inimical to the rational calculation that should guide one's life, because, he believed, someone in the throes of the most intense pleasure (e.g. sexual orgasm) is manifestly unable to calculate.

There is little evidence for Archytas's cosmology, but he developed the most powerful ancient argument for the infinity of the universe. Archytas assumes that, if the universe is limited, it has an edge (modern science would question this assumption) and asks whether or not someone standing at the edge would be able to extend his or her hand beyond the edge. Normal assumptions about space suggest that it would be paradoxical if the person could not extend a hand beyond the edge. Archytas can ask the same question about any supposed limit, and hence the universe will not have a limit and will extend indefinitely. Versions of this argument were adopted by the Epicureans, Stoics, Locke, and Newton—although both Plato and Aristotle rejected it. Aristotle wrote three books—now lost—on Archytas and presents him favorably. Plato was impressed with Archytas's work in mathematics, but the two philosophers disagreed sharply on important philosophical issues.

See also Philolaus of Croton; Pythagoras and Pythagoreanism.

Bibliography

TEXTS AND COMMENTARIES

Huffman, Carl A. *Archytas of Tarentum: Pythagorean, Philosopher and Mathematician King.* Cambridge, U.K.: Cambridge University Press, 2005.

DISCUSSIONS

Barker, Andrew D. *Greek Musical Writings, Vol. II: Harmonic and Acoustic Theory.* New York: Cambridge University Press, 1989.

Huffman, Carl A. "The Authenticity of Archytas Fr. 1." *Classical Quarterly* 35 (2) (1985): 344–348.

Knorr, Wilbur Richard. *The Ancient Tradition of Geometric Problems.* New York: Dover, 1993.

Lloyd, G. E. R. "Plato and Archytas in the Seventh Letter." *Phronesis* 35 (2) (1990): 159–174.

Winnington-Ingram, R. P. "Aristoxenus and the Intervals of Greek Music." *Classical Quarterly* 26 (1932): 195–208.

Carl A. Huffman (2005)

ARDIGÒ, ROBERTO
(1828–1920)

Roberto Ardigò, the principal figure in Italian positivism, was born in Casteldidone in Cremona. He became a Catholic priest, but left the priesthood when, at the age of forty-three, he found it no longer compatible with his beliefs, particularly his conviction that human knowledge originates in sensation—a conviction that came to him suddenly, as he recounted it, while staring at the red color of a rose (*Opere*, Vol. III, p. 368). From 1881 to 1909 he taught history of philosophy at the University of Padua. He spent the last years of his life defending and illustrating his fundamental ideas and debating with the prevailing idealism, which had supplanted positivism as the dominant viewpoint within and without the Italian universities during the last three decades of the nineteenth century. He died in Padua after two attempts at suicide.

The basic interests of Ardigò's positivism were not historical and social, as were Auguste Comte's, but scientific and naturalistic, like Herbert Spencer's. From Comte, Ardigò accepted the principle that facts are the only reality and that the only knowledge possible is the knowledge of facts, which consists in placing one fact in relation to others either immediately or by means of those mental formations that constitute ideas, categories, and principles. When these relations are established, the fact is "explained." Science, therefore, is the only kind of knowledge possible; and philosophy itself is a science that, like all other sciences, uses induction and does not have at its disposal privileged principles or procedures. Metaphysics, which claims to start from principles independent of facts and to use deduction, is a fictitious science. Yet philosophy is not just a "synthetic" discipline in Spencer's sense of the unifier of the general results of the individual sciences. On the one hand, it is a complex of special disciplines that is left after the natural sciences have gone their way. As such, it encompasses the disciplines that are concerned with the "phenomena of thought" and finds articulation in two spheres: psychology, which includes logic, "gnosis" (epistemology), and aesthetics; and sociology, which includes ethics, *dikeika* (doctrine of justice or of law), and economics. On the other hand, to philosophy belongs the field of the *indistinct*, which lies outside the realm of the distinct, which constitutes the object of the individual sciences (matter, for physics; life, for biology; society, for sociology; mind, for psychology, etc.). This realm of the indistinct constitutes the unique and common origin of all the realms of the distinct, and it is the object of philosophy as *peratology* (*Opere*, Vol. X, p. 10).

The indistinct in the philosophy of Ardigò had the same function as the unknowable in Spencer. Ardigò distinguished it from the unknowable in that the indistinct is not that which is not known but that which is not yet known distinctly. It is a relative concept, because the distinct that emerges from some knowledge is in its turn indistinct with respect to further knowledge insofar as it is that which produces, solicits, and explains that knowledge (*Opere*, Vol. II, p. 350). The indistinct-distinct relationship was, moreover, used by Ardigò—in a manner analogous to the way Spencer used the homogeneous-heterogeneous relation—to explain "the natural formation" of every known reality. Every natural formation, in the solar system as well as in the human spirit, is a passage from the indistinct to the distinct. This passage occurs necessarily and incessantly, regulated by a constant rhythm, that is, by an immutable order. But the distinct never exhausts the indistinct, which both underlies and transcends it; and since the distinct is the finite, then we must admit that, beyond the finite, lies the infinite as indistinct. Ardigò conceived the infinite as a progressive development without beginning or end (the analogue to Spencer's evolution), denying that such a development leads to a transcendent cause or principle (*Opere,* Vol. II, p. 129; Vol. III, p. 293; Vol. X, p. 519). All natural formations, including thought, which is a kind of "meteor" in the life of the universe, emerge from and return to this infinite (*Opere,* Vol. II, p. 189).

In the domain of psychology, Ardigò held that the I (self) and natural things are constituted by neutral elements, that is, sensations. The self and things differ, therefore, only by the nature of the synthesis, that is, by the connections that are established among the sensations. Those sensations that refer to an internal organ and have the character of continuity are associated in the "autosynthesis," or the self. Those sensations that refer to an external organ and are discontinuous are associated in the "heterosynthesis" that gives rise to things (*Opere,* Vol. IV, p. 529 ff.). This doctrine, propounded by Ardigò in his very first work, *La psicologia come scienza positiva* (Mantua, 1870), is similar to that later propounded by Ernst Mach in *Die Analyse der Empfindungen* (Jena, 1886).

In the moral domain Ardigò carried on a polemic against every kind of religious and rationalistic ethic. It is a fact, according to Ardigò, that humans are capable of disinterested or altruistic actions, but such actions can be explained by recourse to natural and social factors. The ideals and the prescriptive maxims that determine them derive from the reactions of society to acts that either preserve or damage it—reactions that impress the individual and become fixed in his conscience as norms or moral imperatives. That which is called "conscience," therefore, is the progressive interiorization accomplished by the repeated and constant experience of the external sanctions that the antisocial act encounters in society (*Opere,* Vol. III, p. 425; Vol. X, p. 279).

Finally, Ardigò tried to mitigate the rigorous determinism found in all forms of positivism by giving some emphasis to the notion of chance. Chance consists in the intersecting of various causal series that, taken together, constitute the order of the universe. These intersections are unpredictable, though the events that constitute every individual series are not unpredictable. So-called human "freedom" is an effect of the plurality of the psychical series, that is, of the multiplicity of the possible combinations of various causal orderings that constitute man's psychical life (*Opere,* Vol. III, p. 122).

See also Comte, Auguste; Determinism and Freedom; Idealism; Mach, Ernst; Positivism.

Bibliography

WORKS BY ARDIGÒ
Opere, 12 vols. Padua, 1882–1912.
La scienza dell'educazione. Padua, 1893; 2nd ed., 1903. Not included in the *Opere.*

WORKS ON ARDIGÒ
Amerio, F. *Ardigò.* Milan, 1957. With bibliography.
Bluwstein, J. *Die Weltanschauung Roberto Ardigòs.* Leipzig: Eckardt, 1911.
Marchesiani, G., and A. Groppali, eds. *Nel 70o anniversario di Roberto Ardigò.* Turin, 1898.
Marchesiani, G. *La vita e il pensiero di Roberto Ardigò.* Milan, 1907.
Marchesiani, G. *Lo spirito evangelico di Roberto Ardigò.* Bologna, 1919.
Marchesiani, G. *Roberto Ardigò, l'uomo e l'umanista.* Florence, 1922.

Nicola Abbagnano (1967)
Translated by Nino F. Langiulli

ARENDT, HANNAH
(1906–1975)

Hannah Arendt, American philosopher and political scientist, was born in Hanover, Germany. In 1928 she completed her PhD under Karl Jaspers at the University of Heidelberg, having previously studied with Martin Heidegger at the University of Marburg. Upon immigrating to the United States in 1941, she became director of several Jewish organizations and served as chief editor of Schocken Books before being appointed to the Committee on Social Thought at the University of Chicago in 1963. She taught at the New School for Social Research in New York from 1967 until her death.

THE INFLUENCE OF HEIDEGGER AND PHENOMENOLOGY

Despite sharing Jaspers's views about the existential importance of communication, Arendt's philosophy mainly bears the imprint of Heidegger's phenomenology. Following Edmund Husserl, Heidegger argued that the scientific worldview conceals the genuine appearances of things as they are directly presented within lived experience. By abstracting from, and thereby concealing, the primal experience of meaning and value, this worldview provokes a crisis of nihilism, the practical upshot of which—foreshadowed in Friedrich Nietzsche's thought—is a technological "will to power" that reduces all of being to the status of a predictable and useful object. Because modern science is but the culmination of a metaphysical tradition dating back to Plato, Heidegger turned to the pre-Socratics and the archaic language and life of the ancient Greek *polis* for disclosing a more original experience of things. Arendt followed him in this respect, but with different results. Heidegger's supreme estimation of the revelatory power of the lone thinker/poet/artist to open up a new experience of community and world—coupled with his contempt for the indecisiveness of public opinion and democratic political debate—led him to embrace the resolve of a Nazi führer who embodied the will of the German people. In Arendt's judgment, Heidegger's politics betrayed his own critique of European metaphysics as an elitist form of idealism that conceals the common roots of meaning and value in democratic action.

FREEDOM AND POLITICAL ACTION

Action is part of a triad of comportments that together make up the active life definitive of the human condition. As the quintessential appearance of human freedom, political action, Arendt argued, must be distinguished from both work and cultural fabrication. Laboring to procure life's necessities is unfree; and the freedom of artistic creation is at best hidden and derivative. As distinct from the solitary application of means in pursuit of ends, true freedom must be communicated publicly, in political deeds and words. For this there must be a public space—exemplified by the Greek *polis* and such modern-day equivalents as the worker council and town hall meeting—wherein equals representing diverse opinions meet and deliberate together.

Arendt often invoked Augustine's comment on the miracle of birth, or what she called *natality*, in capturing the distinctive capacity of political action to initiate new beginnings. The concept owes much to Arendt's lifelong obsession with modernity and political revolutions, although she traces it back to ancient Greek and early Christian notions of freedom. In discussing the archaic Greek notion of freedom (*archein* = to begin or initiate), Arendt stresses the utter unpredictability of actions that draw their meaning and identity from the distinctiveness of the individual actors whose personality they express. Early Christian thinkers such as Paul and Augustine

develop this idea further in discussing religious conversion as spiritual rebirth. The existential pathos of continually breaking with the past and remaking oneself also informs modern revolutionary thought, which appeals to free consent rather than traditional authority as the principal underlying political life.

THE TENSION BETWEEN FREEDOM AND SOCIAL EQUALITY

Although modern revolutions exemplify political freedom, Arendt thought that their failure to distinguish this end from the social struggle for equality conflated the imperatives of political action with those of economic production and consumption. The subsequent substitution of efficient administration for political action is especially apparent in the revolutionary movement inaugurated by the French Revolution and brought to completion in twentieth-century communist and fascist revolutions. Here, freedom is reduced to the sovereign legislation of a unified will that seeks to administer the general welfare of all citizens with the ultimate aim of remaking them into a single, harmonious body. In Arendt's opinion, the American Revolution evolved differently, partly because it was not faced with the same social problems, and partly because it was nourished on Protestant individualism rather than Catholic paternalism. It was not driven by economic need and class struggle, and the remnants of feudalism—mainly concentrated in the slave economy of the South—had already been eclipsed by the modern commercial economies of the North. Yet according to Arendt, the individualistic spirit of commercial life that compelled the Founding Fathers to adopt limited and divided forms of governance would also prove to be the undoing of their revolution. As Americans became more preoccupied with their private economic pursuits and problems of class developed within industrial capitalism, political life receded in importance and a paternalistic welfare state eventually emerged.

POWER, VIOLENCE, AND LEGITIMACY

Arendt's distinction between political power and political violence builds upon her critique of the welfare state. Contrary to the dominant view held by the Weberian school, political power is not equivalent to wielding a monopoly of instruments that can be brought to bear in top-down fashion by governmental elites in coercively defending and administering a state. On the contrary, political power consists in popular consent and public opinion nourished in open discussion. As such, its vitality depends on multiplying resistances rather than by concentrating forces, a condition that is best promoted by encouraging the flourishing of open debate. Following Baron de Montesquieu, Arendt held that policies that preserve this discursive plurality by separating or dividing governmental powers and instituting a system of checks and balances are more powerful and enduring than ones that do not. Totalitarian regimes that dispense with the rule of law and concentrate all power in the hands of a single leader are notoriously unstable and weak because they deprive their own citizens of the public space necessary for taking independent initiative and uniting politically.

According to Arendt, the violence exercised by totalitarian regimes against their own citizens is but the reverse side of their impotence. Arendt equates violence with any coercive, instrumental action that lacks prior popular consent. Although it can never be legitimate, or politically justified, violence may sometimes be morally justified as a necessary means for avoiding great evil. Emergencies of state sometimes call for violent measures, but as Arendt notes, liberal democracies often use this pretext to suppress political action unjustly, and indeed any unilateral governmental intervention, however bureaucratically routine, bears traces of violence.

THE DECLINE OF AUTHORITY AND THE CRISIS IN CULTURE

Many of Arendt's studies—on totalitarianism, evil, revolution, and the Jewish question—document the political impact wrought by the decline of traditional authority and the crisis of culture. Although she did not blame secular Enlightenment and its revolutionary offspring for this decline, she nonetheless believed that the destruction of the old Roman trinity of religion, tradition, and authority contributed to a crisis of culture that undermined essential differences—between public and private, political and economic, action and work—on which the survival of a public political space depended. Transcendent authority anchored the autonomy of the public realm as a space for manifesting immortal deeds in beautiful words; the waning of authority diminishes that autonomy, thereby enabling the assimilation of both culture and politics to economic life.

Arendt's diagnosis of the crisis in culture bears directly on her political concerns. She appealed to the Greek ideal of culture as a religious memorialization of political community. In the absence of traditional religious authority, culture can provide those standards of judgment so essential for maintaining a common space

for action. Political life is thus jeopardized whenever culture loses its normative authority—that is to say, whenever it is monopolized by elites, manipulated by government for purposes of propaganda, or is degraded to the mundane level of mass consumption and entertainment.

TOTALITARIANISM AND RADICAL EVIL

According to Arendt, the crisis of culture is symptomatic of all mass societies, or societies wherein individuals—isolated from one another in the lonely pursuit of familial and vocational aims—cease to engage in political action; and it is therefore one of the main conditions paving the way for modern totalitarianism. Under these conditions, it is the state, not politically engaged individuals, that assumes responsibility for integrating the masses, even when doing so renders individuality and life itself superfluous.

By engendering a system in which life is made superfluous, totalitarianism represents the epitome of evil. Contrary to popular opinion, such evil is seldom if ever motivated by diabolical intentions. Adolph Eichmann's evil, Arendt observed, simply consisted in his banal "thoughtlessness." Like most persons living in mass society, he confused moral duty with the duty to obey authority. However, Arendt also believed that the "absolute goodness" and violence born of idealism (as personified in Melville's Billy Budd) are as pernicious as the radical evil and destructiveness born of any workmanlike devotion to order. In both instances, the critical check provided by consulting the opinion of others who comprise an enlarged public sphere is totally absent.

JUDGMENT AND POLITICAL ACTION

Arendt's appeal to an enlarged public sphere touches upon the importance of judgment in sustaining political action. In the classical tradition of Aristotle and Aquinas, the judgment that guides action is intimately connected to a practical wisdom (*phronesis*), or prudential art, cultivated by experience and habituation in customary modes of behavior. In modern times, beginning with Immanuel Kant, judgment acquires an altogether different sense, one based on an impartial consideration of possible points of view. These two senses of judgment—the former typically associated with the standpoint of the political or moral actor faced with practical decision, the latter with the historical or aesthetic spectator who understands, interprets, and narrates action retrospectively and disinterestedly—intersect in Arendt's thought.

Prior to *The Life of the Mind* (1978), Arendt still affirmed the intimate connection between "a judgment of the intellect" and knowledge of the rightness and wrongness of practical aims (1968, p. 152). Indeed, she insisted that moral and political agents living in modern conditions are especially obligated to judge the laws, opinions, and actions of their society from the common—if not universal—standpoint of "all those who happen to be present" (p. 221).

Arendt's late lectures on Kant's political philosophy revise this connection between action and judgment. With the deterioration of public spaces requisite for exercising practical judgment, judgment ceases to be linked with the two faculties of practical reasoning—knowing and willing—and instead takes on the function of retrospective interpretation. As a vicarious form of action, historical spectatorship preserves the memory of those all-too-rare and tragically ill-fated moments of political action—such as the Paris Commune of 1871, the resistance of the Warsaw Ghetto, and the Hungarian revolt of 1956—by judging their universal, exemplary validity. Rescuing these unprecedented displays of spontaneous self-determination from the oblivion of history, judgment dignifies what otherwise appears to be an unbearable, arbitrary, compulsive—in short, utterly contingent and irresponsible—act of freedom.

Jürgen Habermas and others have rightly criticized Arendt for dissociating the common sense guiding judgment from any relationship to truth or justice. Her earlier work, for example, links the cultivation of common sense to the agonal exchange of opinions. Because this communication is constrained by the real effects of social domination, it remains prejudiced by ideological distortions. By contrast, her later work (following Kant) links historical judgment to an ideal *sensus communis*, or hypothetical community of taste (feeling). Here judgment achieves impartiality by imaginatively representing the standpoints of other persons as they may have been communicated had these persons been free from domination and constraint. No doubt, an accurate account of responsible judging lies somewhere between these extremes of realism and idealism, as even Arendt herself suggests; for judging, it seems, bears witness to rationality only when tempered by the real—mutual and impartial—criticism that obtains between actors who aspire to ideal freedom and equality.

See also Aristotle; Augustine, St.; Evil, The Problem of; Freedom; Habermas, Jürgen; Heidegger, Martin; Jaspers, Karl; Kant, Immanuel; Rousseau, Jean-Jacques; Thomas Aquinas, St.

Bibliography

WORKS BY ARENDT

The Human Condition. Chicago: University of Chicago Press, 1958.

The Origins of Totalitarianism. Enlarged edition. New York: Harcourt Brace & Co., 1958.

On Revolution. New York: Viking, 1963.

Eichmann in Jerusalem: A Report on the Banality of Evil. New York: Viking, 1965.

Men in Dark Times. New York: Harvest Books, 1968.

On Violence. New York: Harcourt Brace & World, 1970.

Crisis of the Republic. New York: Harcourt Brace & Jovanovich, 1972.

Rahel Varnhagen: The Life of a Jewish Woman. New York: Harcourt, 1974.

Between Past and Future: Eight Exercises in Political Thought. New York: Viking Press, 1978.

The Jew as Pariah: Jewish Identity and Politics in the Modern Age, edited by Ron Feldman. New York: Grove Press, 1978.

The Life of the Mind. 2 vols., edited by Mary McCarthy. New York: Harcourt Brace & Jovanovich, 1978.

Lectures on Kant's Political Philosophy, edited by R. Beiner. Chicago: University of Chicago Press, 1982.

Correspondence: 1926–1969: Hannah Arendt/Karl Jaspers, edited by Lotte Kohler and H. Saner. New York: Harcourt, Brace & Co., 1992.

Essays in Understanding: 1930–1954, edited by J. Kohn. New York: Harcourt, Brace & Co., 1994.

Love and Saint Augustine, edited by Joanna Scott & Judith Stark. Chicago: University of Chicago Press, 1996.

Responsibility and Judgment, edited by J. Kohn. New York: Schocken, 2003.

Letters: 1925–1975: Hannah Arendt/Martin Heidegger, edited by Ursula Ludz. New York: Harcourt Inc., 2004.

WORKS ON ARENDT

Benhabib, S. *The Reluctant Modernism of Hannah Arendt*. Beverly Hills, CA: Sage, 1996.

Bernauer, J., ed. *Amor Mundi: Explorations in the Faith and Thought of Hannah Arendt*. Dordrecht, Netherlands: Martinus Nijhoff, 1987.

Bernstein, R. *Hannah Arendt and the Jewish Question*. London: Polity, 1996.

Bowen-Moore, P. *Hannah Arendt's Philosophy of Natality*. New York: St. Martin's Press, 1989.

Bradshaw, L. *Acting and Thinking: The Political Thought of Hannah Arendt*. Toronto: University of Toronto Press, 1989.

Carnovan, M. *Hannah Arendt: A Reinterpretation of Her Thought*. New York: Cambridge University Press, 1992.

Disch, L. *Hannah Arendt and the Limits of Philosophy*. Ithaca, NY: Cornell University Press, 1994.

Garner, R., ed. *In the Realm of Humanitas: Responses to the Writings of Hannah Arendt*. New York: Peter Lang, 1990.

Gottsegen, M. G. *The Political Thought of Hannah Arendt*. Albany, NY: State University of New York, 1994.

Hill, M. A., ed. *Hannah Arendt: Recovery of the Public World*. New York: St. Martin's Press, 1979.

Hinchman, L. P., and K. Sandra, eds. *Hannah Arendt: Critical Essays*. Albany: State University of New York, 1994. Contains essays by Arendt.

Honig, B., ed. *Feminist Interpretations of Hannah Arendt.* Philadelphia: Pennsylvania State University, 1995.

Kateb, G. *Hannah Arendt: Politics, Conscience, Evil.* Totowa, NJ: Rowman & Allanheld, 1984.

Kohn, J., and L. May. *Hannah Arendt: Twenty Years Later.* Cambridge, MA: MIT Press, 1996.

Parekh, B. C. *Hannah Arendt and the Search for a New Political Philosophy.* Atlantic Highlands, NJ: Humanities Press, 1981.

Pitkin, H. F. *The Attack of the Blob: Hannah Arendt's Concept of the Social.* Chicago: University of Chicago, 1998.

Villa, D. *Arendt, Heidegger, and the Fate of the Political.* Princeton, NJ: Princeton University Press, 1996.

Villa, D., ed. *The Cambridge Companion to Hannah Arendt.* Cambridge, U.K.: Cambridge University Press, 2000.

Watson, D. *Hannah Arendt.* London: Fotaten Press, 1992.

Young-Bruehl, E. *Hannah Arendt: For Love of the World.* New Haven, CT: Yale University Press, 1982. Contains a bibliography.

David Ingram (1996, 2005)

ARETĒ /AGATHON/KAKON

Aretē, meaning "excellence" or "virtue," is central to ancient Greek ethics, from the early poets through Plato and Aristotle to the Stoics. It is a quality necessary for success, and the *aretai* for moral success are moral virtues. *Agathon,* meaning "good," implies virtue when used to describe human beings, as does *kalon* (meaning "noble" or "beautiful"), the adjective most closely associated with aretē and nearly synonymous with agathon. *Kakon* implies the lack of virtue. In Hesiod and Solon the moral use of these terms is well established, and it is clearly prefigured in Homer. Virtue, to such poets, no less than to Plato, is long lasting and independent of wealth and power. The principal virtues under discussion before Socrates were shame (*aidos*), reverence (*hosion*), and justice (*dike*). Protagoras evidently considered shame and justice to be essential to a stable society.

Socrates and Plato taught that virtue is to the soul as health is to the body. In addition to reverence and justice, they treated wisdom, courage, and sound-mindedness (or temperance; in Greek, *sôphrosunê*) as virtues. Plato represents Socrates in the early dialogues as unsuccessfully seeking definitions for the virtues, while hypothesizing that they are in some way identical with each other. Socrates is often thought to have held an intellectualist account of arête.

In the *Republic* Plato works out a theory of virtue from his account of health in the soul: Justice is the quality that allows the parts of the soul to work together in harmony, and the other virtues depend on that harmony.

In a related context Plato somewhat mysteriously compares the form of the good to the sun; what the sun does to illuminate and nourish the world humans can merely see with their senses, and what the good does for the world humans can investigate with their intellect.

Aristotle's ethics begins from the hypothesis that all things aim at the good (agathon). The good for human beings, he says, is flourishing or happiness (*eudaimonia*), and the qualities that enable people to reach these goals he calls virtues (aretai). His account of virtues has been fundamental to all subsequent discussion of the subject in the European tradition. Moral and intellectual virtues are both necessary for human flourishing, and for each other. Moral virtues temper the soul to enjoy what is good, rather than what is bad, and consist in a disposition to experience emotions that lie on a mean between excess and defect. Courage, for example, belongs to a soul that is neither too rash nor too timid. In Stoic theory, nothing is entirely good but virtue, and this consists mainly in the ability to resist powerful emotion.

Some early Greek authors distinguish aristocrats as *agathoi* from common people as *kakoi*. The scholar A. W. H. Adkins identified the virtues that marked this class difference as competitive (as opposed to moral) virtues; he argued that in the time of Socrates and Plato, Greek thought about virtue underwent a major shift, and the philosophers brought the first usage of these terms that is moral in human sense. Hugh Lloyd-Jones and Bernard Williams contested Adkins's arguments, and the emerging consensus among scholars favors a more unified account of these terms.

See also Aristotle; Eudaimonia; Plato; Socrates.

Bibliography

Adkins, A. W. H. *Merit and Responsibility: A Study in Greek Values.* Chicago: University of Chicago Press, 1975.

Annas, Julia. *The Morality of Happiness.* New York: Oxford University Press, 1993.

Cooper, John. *Reason and Human Good in Aristotle.* Cambridge, MA: Harvard University Press, 1975.

Irwin, Terence. *Plato's Ethics.* New York: Oxford University Press, 1995.

Lloyd-Jones, Hugh. *Sather Classical Lectures.* Vol. 41: *The Justice of Zeus.* Berkeley, CA: University of California Press, 1983.

Williams, Bernard. *Sather Classical Lectures.* Vol. 57: *Shame and Necessity.* 2nd ed. Berkeley: University of California Press, 1993.

Paul Woodruff (2005)

ARISTIPPUS OF CYRENE
(c. 435–c. 356 BCE)

Aristippus of Cyrene, founder of the Cyrenaic school of philosophy, was born in the Greek North African port city of Cyrene (now Shahhat, Libya). Attracted to Athens by the fame of Socrates, he became a member of the Socratic circle and probably associated with Protagoras and Gorgias as well.

Like Socrates, Aristippus concentrated on ethics, conceived as endeavoring to determine the good life for the individual, and rejected the study of nature as both uncertain and useless for furthering the good. He gave a simple answer to the question of the goal of life: It is pleasure and nothing else. The wise man will arrange his life so that, as far as possible, one pleasure follows another and pains are kept to a minimum. He will not forgo a present pleasure for the sake of one to come, for the future is uncertain. But he will be master of his pleasures, as Socrates was, unperturbed when they must be done without.

Pleasures are individual episodes of internal feeling, not mere absence of pain but positive bodily sensations as experienced in eating, drinking, and sex. All pleasures, considered as pleasures, are equal, he declared, though they may differ in intensity, which is why those of the body take precedence over those of the mind. They are still pleasures even if produced by activities convention-ally regarded as shameful. Virtues and friendships are goods only insofar as they are productive of pleasures. He found proof that pleasure is the goal of life in the (alleged) fact that all animals, as well as uninstructed human beings, pursue it by nature.

Aristippus taught his philosophy in the marketplace (unlike Plato, who taught in his gated Academy) and charged substantial fees. Like a modern psychiatrist, he regarded his services as therapy: liberation from superstitions and irrational conventions; and the fees, illustrating (so he claimed) the proper use of money, were part of the treatment. He also showed his pupils how to get along with anybody in any situation.

Many stories illustrate how Aristippus lived by his own principles, such as they were. Notorious for his involvement with the famous and expensive prostitute Lais, he insisted, "I have her, she doesn't have me." (As Cicero remarked, this sounds better in Greek.) And, he averred, having sex with one who has sex with many is no different from voyaging on a ship that carries other passengers. He perfumed himself. Sojourning in Syracuse at the court of Dionysius, he dressed in women's clothing for a party at the tyrant's behest. (Plato, there at the same time, refused.) When a client protested the high price he asked for educating his son, saying that for the same amount of money he could buy a slave, Aristippus told him to go ahead and buy the slave: Then he would have *two* slaves, the one he bought and his own son.

Traveling widely, Aristippus was pleased to be "everywhere a stranger," freeloading the advantages of city life without incurring the burdens of citizenship. Freedom, he held, consists not only in not being ruled but also in not ruling, for the ruler is the slave of those he rules.

See also Cyrenaics; Socrates.

Bibliography

Döring, Klaus. *Der Sokratesschüler Aristipp und die Kyrenaiker.* Mainz, Germany: Akademie der Wissenschaften und der Literatur; Stuttgart, Germany: F. Steiner Verlag Wiesbaden, 1988.

Mannebach, Erich, ed. *Aristippi et Cyrenaicorum fragmenta.* Leiden, Netherlands: E. J. Brill, 1961.

Wallace Matson (2005)

ARISTO OF CHIOS
(third century BCE)

Aristo of Chios was a disciple of Zeno of Citium, the founder of Stoicism. The scant biographical information that exists, from Diogenes Laertius (VII 160–64), describes him as an unorthodox Stoic, who later abandoned the school to found one of his own. There is some question in Diogenes' sources as to whether works ascribed to him are genuine or belong to the peripatetic Aristo of Ceos. But there are difficulties about his views as well. Like Zeno, he accepted the Socratic and cynic principle that virtue was sufficient for happiness. But whereas Zeno identified this with "living consistently," Aristo understood it as an internal consistency, where one behaved indifferently toward anything that was not virtue or vice (*adiaphoria*). At the core of his philosophy is the view that moral values are absolute: Only virtue is good and only vice bad; everything else intermediate between these is absolutely indifferent and equal. The third head of the school, Chrysippus, who polemicized against Aristo, was successful in establishing his own interpretation of Zeno's thought as the orthodox Stoic position, thus leading to Aristo's marginalization. But Aristo was held in high esteem by his contemporaries: Eratosthenes of Cyrene (c. 276–c. 194 BCE) maintained that Aristo's philosophy, along with that of the skeptic Arcesilaus, was the most important of his time.

The confusion with Aristo of Ceos makes it difficult to attribute fragments that do not specify the author's origin. The most important is the summary given by Philodemus (*PHerc.* 1008, columns 10–23 Jensen), which has been attributed by Wehrli (1952), to the peripatetic Aristo of Ceos, but a study of the language and philosophical terminology reveals similarities with the surviving fragments of the Stoic Aristo. (Although this is included by Wehrli in the fragments of the peripatetic Aristo, a study of the language and philosophical terminology reveals similarities with the surviving fragments of the Stoic Aristo.)

See also Chrysippus; Stoicism; Zeno of Citium.

Bibliography

Arnim, Hans Friedrich August von. *Stoicorum Veterum Fragment: Collegit Ioannes ab Arnim.* Vol. 1 (1905). Stuttgart: B. G. Teubneri, 1968.

Ioppolo, Anna Maria. *Aristone di Chio e lo Stoicismo antico.* Naples, Italy: Bibliopolis, 1980.

Ioppolo, Anna Maria. "Una polemica antiscettica in Filodemo?" In *Epicureismo greco e romano.* Vol. II, edited by Gabriele Giannantoni and Marcello Gigante, 715–734. Naples, Italy: Bibliopolis, 1996.

Porter, James. "The Philosophy of Aristo of Chios." In *The Cynics: The Cynic Movement in Antiquity and Its Legacy,* edited by R. Bracht Branham and Marie-Odile Goulet-Cazé, 156–189. Berkeley: University of California Press, 1996.

Wehrli, Fritz. *Die Schule des Aristoteles, Texte und Kommentar, herausgegeben von Fritz Wehrli.* Vol. VI. Basel: Benno Schwabe, 1952.

Anna Maria Ioppolo (2005)

ARISTOTELIANISM

The question of what it means to be an Aristotelian—whether this requires adherence to a specific set of doctrines, a certain methodological approach, or the fulfilment of some other set of conditions—is a vexed one and has exercised the minds of self-professed Aristotelians and anti-Aristotelians alike over the course of twenty centuries. Like many problems of definition, it is best approached indirectly (as indeed Aristotle would likely have approached it). This historical overview starts from the broad assumption that one may consider Aristotelian all those thinkers who have either (a) considered Aristotle's texts a suitable point of departure for an enquiry into a given subject, or (b) thought themselves to be extending a peripatetic approach to a subject not covered by Aristotle himself. This assumption will have the consequence of making Aristotelians out of many whom modern reckoning would not readily count as philosophers. The result is not untoward because Aristotle's own enterprise extended far beyond philosophy thus narrowly defined.

THE FIRST *PERIPATOS*

Upon returning to Athens in 335 BCE, Aristotle founded a school in a grove consecrated to Apollo Lyceus. Hence the school was termed the Lyceum, yet it became forever known as the Peripatos for its covered colonnade. Indeed, in the annals references to "Peripatetics" greatly outnumber those made to "Aristotelians."

Aristotle's school was both a teaching and a research institution, with scholars pursuing interests ranging from musicology and the cataloguing of Greek forms of government to public lectures on popular subjects. The school survived Aristotle's departure from Athens and subsequent death in 322 BCE: Indeed, it flourished under Aristotle's successor and close collaborator, Theophrastus (372–287 BCE), who is reported to have presided over some 2,000 students.

Theophrastus expanded upon Aristotle's philosophical and scientific program. Theophrastus's botanical studies are pioneering works; the ancients especially valued his contributions to the categorical and hypothetical syllogistic. Theophrastus adheres to an aporetic methodology in the philosophical treatises while amassing observations in the scientific; this commitment to a peripatetic approach even leads Theophrastus to criticize Aristotle's *Metaphysics* Lambda in his own work on first philosophy. Theophrastus questions the extent to which teleological language, central to Aristotle's explanation of living nature, is applicable in a cosmic context: In effect, Theophrastus questions whether Aristotle is Aristotelian enough.

The Lyceum's independent spirit is further manifested in how its third head, Strato of Lampsacus (d. 269), departed from Aristotle on several important points, notably in natural philosophy. The diffuse activities and conflicting viewpoints countenanced within the Peripatos may have worked to its detriment in an age of intensifying competition between the philosophical schools. Strato's stewardship coincided with a decline in the school's fortunes, and within two generations it had all but disappeared from view.

THE IMPERIAL AGE

The nascent Hellenistic schools found elements to their liking in Aristotle's now-lost dialogues, praised for their style by Cicero and plundered for their edifying materials. Through criticism and creative appropriation, the Stoa in particular remained indebted to the peripatetics, who in the second century enjoyed a measure of resurgence under Critolaus. Still, self-professed peripatetics are hard to come by before Andronicus of Rhodes presented the ancient world with his authoritative collection of Aristotle's school works c. 50 BCE. Thereafter appear figures such as the Augustan intellectual Nicholas of Damascus, whose self-portrait is a model of Aristotelian virtue and who is credited with writing a compendium of Aristotelian philosophy, and Alexander of Aigai, teacher to Nero.

Andronicus's epoch-making edition is as important for the organization of its materials as for its contents, which quickly became canon. Immediately the impression is one of a full-fledged curriculum: The acquisition of methodological tools—the *Organon* of reasoned argument—is followed by an account of natural principles and natural bodies. After this comes living nature, then first philosophy (now dubbed "metaphysics"), and then the practical and productive sciences. Aristotle's widely varied investigations take on the appearance of a system here and retained it thereafter.

In Andronicus's wake there are two signal developments. First, propounding Aristotelian doctrine comes to be viewed as involving the writing of commentaries, starting with the *Categories* and *On Interpretation*. Second, in the first century BCE the Academician Antiochus thinks to present Aristotle as belonging essentially to the Platonic tradition. This classification set the tone for much of the imperial period. The fundamental continuity of Plato's and Aristotle's projects was correctly ascertained by late ancient thinkers and seized upon with momentous consequences.

The most important late ancient philosopher of purely peripatetic persuasion was Alexander of Aphrodisias. Around 200 CE Alexander was appointed to Athens's imperial chair in Aristotelian philosophy: He expounded his master's teaching in a series of magisterial commentaries *ad litteram*. Alexander's commentaries remain unsurpassed for erudition and insight, taking on all comers in a spirited defence of the Aristotelian worldview. Alexander's sharp, down-to-earth observations—for instance his unflinching admission that Aristotelian psychology makes no provisions for an immortal soul—provided a sobering reminder to later commentators who approached Aristotle's texts with loftier aspirations and syncretistic leanings. Though Alexander's Aristotle is undeniably a system-builder—it is with Alexander that the Aristotelian program of "saving the appearances" becomes a desire to explain each Aristotelian sentence by reference to another—he occasionally advances different interpretations without feeling the need to come down on one side. Alexander also wrote new treatises where he felt a lacuna existed in the extant corpus; and from his circle derives the peripatetic genre of disputed questions.

A different approach to Aristotle's texts is offered by Themistius, a late-fourth-century senator and proconsul of Constantinople. Themistius wrote paraphrases rather than commentaries; aporias and scholarly disputes take a back seat to a clear exposition of the main points. Yet Themistius positions himself as a peripatetic: his works and Alexander's provided a touchstone for later scholars who sought a genuine understanding of Aristotle's meaning.H

THE LATE ANCIENT SYNTHESIS

Plotinus (d. 270) is credited with an impressive dismantling of Aristotle's criticisms of Plato, and with the subsequent triumph of (neo-)Platonism in antiquity. But in the process, Plotinus also consolidated the assimilation of central Aristotelian concepts into a Platonic framework: for example, the potentiality-actuality distinction and the notion of pure contemplation as self-reflective. Plotinus's pupil Porphyry (d. 309) went further, attempting to show how nothing in Aristotle's virulently anti-Platonic categorical scheme in fact speaks against the primacy of separate Forms. The *Categories*, in its own words, purports to detail how things are spoken of: its universals are those abstracted from sense-particulars. The suggestion, embedded in Porphyry's enormously influential introduction (*Eisagôgê*) to Aristotle's *Organon*, is that Aristotelian science deals with substances prior to us, not with those prior by nature. This move made Aristotelian logic, and by extension natural philosophy, innocuous to ancient Platonists. It also set up the protracted Latin debate concerning the universals.

The Platonist appropriation of Aristotle was made complete in the fifth-century revival of the Athenian and Alexandrian schools. Aristotle was considered a largely reliable guide to the workings of the sensible cosmos: His works became positioned between those Platonic dialogues that were considered propaedeutic in character and those that disclosed the higher realities that Aristotle either failed to mention or knew nothing about. Though committed to the supremacy of the "divine" Plato over the "daemonic" Aristotle, late ancient Platonists were thus Aristotelians, too, in their fashion. The voluminous commentaries on Aristotle's logic and natural philosophy testify to the care and attention devoted to subtle points of argument and doctrine. In negotiating tensions between Aristotle's treatises and Plato's dialogues, notably the *Timaeus* (a prime target of Aristotle's but a treatise that the Platonists ranked high), both reconciliation and taking Plato's side could produce philosophically interesting work, as the examples of Simplicius (*fl.* in the 530s) and Proclus (d. 485) show. So could an unorthodox mindset coupled with a healthy self-image and a nascent Christian agenda, as witnessed by the groundbreaking work of John Philoponus (d. 574).

Opinion varied about how far harmony extended in the direction of Plato's supernal principles. Iamblichus (d. 325) came under fire for suggesting that Aristotle would have subscribed to Plato's Forms, while Ammonius's (d. 517/526) equally hyperbolic claim that Aristotle's Prime Mover was intended as a divine creative force was broadly accepted. Ammonius's project of harmonizing Aristotle with Plato thus made Aristotle more acceptable to monotheists both in the Arabic-speaking East and, eventually, the Latin Christian West.

As for the Eastern Roman Empire, after the decline of Alexandria, the next high point for Aristotelian studies came with the Aristotelian circle assembled by Princess Anna Comnena in early-twelfth-century Constantinople. This activity resulted in commentaries by Eustratius and Michael of Ephesus and helped secure the transmission of Aristotelian materials to the Latin world.

ARISTOTELES ARABUS

Legend depicts Greek wisdom as passing from Alexandria to Baghdad: Although the chain of transmission is not as ironclad as Arabic-speaking Hellenophiles liked to pretend, the story contains a kernel of truth. The philosophy the Islamic world inherited, in particular, was Alexandrian and hence broadly Aristotelian. Aristotle's works were translated mostly through Syriac, by Christians. Many went through several recensions because the audience's growing scholarly acuity demanded progressively more exacting translations. By 950, all of Aristotle except for the *Politics* was available in Arabic (Plato's *Republic* replacing the latter), along with a host of commentaries. Creative reflection was underway among Muslims, Christians, and Jews alike, all of who wrote in Arabic.

A reliance on Alexandrian learning, which for the most part accepted the "lower" calling of explaining Aristotle, had the effect of making of Aristotle the preeminent

sage of old. In the Arabic understanding, Aristotle had perfected, but also corrected, the views of other ancient thinkers, including his teacher Plato: The well-known adage of Aristotle considering "truth a truer friend" is traceable to al-Ghazālī (1058–1111), who can thus mockingly position himself as a peripatetic in spirit even when questioning the cogency of the Muslim *falâsifah*. But the Arabic Aristotle also manifested Platonic traits. This was due partly to the pseudonymous *Theology of Aristotle* and *Epistle concerning the Pure Good* (really Plotinus and Proclus in disguise), and mostly to a comfortable familiarity with the synthesis effected in late antiquity. The Peripateticism taught in the wake of al-Kindī (d. ca. 873) and al-Fārābī (d. 950) was both theist and emanationist.

The most powerful synthetic mind in Arabic philosophy, and the man responsible for tying the disparate threads of Aristotelianisms past into the service of a singular vision, was also the philosopher who eclipsed Aristotle in the East. Ibn Sīnā (the Latin Avicenna, 980–1037) progressed from traditional commentary to comprehensive philosophical encyclopaedias "presented in the manner of the peripatetics" to free-form expositions of his own views. Too Platonizing to be considered purely peripatetic, altogether too Aristotelian to be mistaken for a Platonist, lifting materials from the Muslim dialectical theologians as needed, Ibn Sīnā's philosophy constitutes an original achievement, one whose success is measured by the fact that in the East his works supplanted Aristotle's as the basis for study and philosophical reflection. It is thanks to Ibn Sīnā that mainstream Islamic philosophy to this day retains a broadly peripatetic vocabulary and orientation. Yet his substantial revisions to Aristotelian metaphysics, psychology, and logic, among other areas, were presented in such an attractive package that later philosophers rarely paused to consider whether Ibn Sīnā's philosophy faithfully reflected that of Aristotle. More important was that it conveyed truth. The subsequent period is consequently more rightfully called Avicennian than Aristotelian.

From this perspective, Ibn Rushd (Averroes, 1126–1198) appears a man out of place. Following upon al-Ghazālī's criticisms of Ibn Sīnā, Ibn Rushd advocated a return to an undiluted Aristotle, undertaking a massive commentary project worthy of Alexander or Themistius, both of whom he used extensively. This Cordovan commentator regarded Aristotle as a model of human perfection (*In De anima* III, comm. 14). For him, this faith in Aristotle's exemplary rationality and consistency held the key to settling any outstanding scholarly dispute. Sidelined in Islamic philosophy, Ibn Rushd became fabulously influential among Jews and Christians, who viewed him as *the* Commentator (in antiquity, Alexander was similarly honoured).

ARISTOTELES LATINUS

The story of the Latin Aristotle begins with Boethius's (d. 525) stated intention of translating all of Aristotle's works. The project only got so far as the logical treatises; until the mid-twelfth century, of these only the *Categories* and *On Interpretation* circulated, making of Aristotle primarily a logician, and a curious one at that. A slow dissemination of the "new logic" (the full *Organon*) occurred in the twelfth century: acquaintance with Arabic philosophy—above all, Avicenna's *De anima* and *Metaphysics*—helped raise interest in Aristotle's natural philosophy and metaphysics, which were then translated in short order, often concurrently from the Greek and the Arabic in a race to get to the heart of the matter.

The theologically suspect aspects of Aristotelian teaching, which the Arabic tradition helpfully pointed out, promptly resulted in the 1210 and 1215 bans in Paris, then the most prestigious of the rising universities. This did little to stem the tide. By mid-century, studying the entire range of Aristotle's works—often coupled with Averroes's commentaries—was commonplace in the arts faculties. Aristotle himself was so ubiquitous that writers could refer to him simply as "the Philosopher."

Thereafter, Aristotle dominated philosophical teaching in the Christian West for three centuries. Hundreds upon hundreds of commentaries were produced at the height of scholasticism; the list of the major commentators was a roll call of the best and brightest of the schoolmen: Albertus Magnus, Thomas Aquinas, John Duns Scotus, William Ockham, Jean Buridan, and so on—for every major figure, there was a score more. As in ancient scholasticism, considerable philosophical ingenuity and innovation went on under a nominal exposition of the text (the *quaestiones* providing an even more congenial setting).

Especially going into the nominalist phase, the question arises: To what extent are some of these thinkers to be considered Aristotelian at all? Clearly, greater liberties were being taken; but this freedom would be expected following a period of assimilation. Moreover, adherence to a tradition need not stifle creative thought. The fallout from the famous condemnations of 1270–1277 spotlights the complex dynamic. For the most part, the condemnations were directed against the allegedly heterodox teachings of the so-called "Latin Averroists." But just because their radicalism was so resolutely Aristotelian—upholding the world's eternity and the unity of the intellect, and so on—the condemnations could be interpreted as an invitation to read Aristotle more creatively. And could the resultant bold conceptual and scientific inquiry not be considered more authentically Aristotelian than a single-minded adherence to the master's letter? "Radical" Aristotelians and radical "Aristotelians" were similarly drawn to the spirit of Aristotle's texts, in equal parts confident and intellectually curious. They merely took their admiration of the master in different directions.

THE MODERN AGE

The Renaissance humanists' newfound appreciation for the breadth of ancient culture put an end to Aristotle's supremacy. With the intellectual scene splintering into multiple incommensurable paradigms, Aristotle was effectively demoted to the headmastership of one school once more after long representing Greek wisdom in its entirety. As the quality of texts and translations came under scrutiny, the very state of Aristotle's preserved writings was found wanting. What to make of this was less evident. The Ciceronian Mario Nizilio could claim that wrinkles in expression signaled confusion in thought, whereas others blamed Andronicus's editorializing. Yet others took refuge in the ancient tradition, so that by the sixteenth century any configuration of Alexandrine, Themistian, Averroist, and even neo-Platonist tenets could be combined in an attempted rehabilitation of Aristotle, as exemplified by the works of philosophers such as Nicoletto Vernia (1442–1499) Agostino Nifo (d. 1538), and Pietro Pomponazzi (1462–1525). The textual drive had other unforeseen consequences. Elegant new translations of works such as the zoological and elemental treatises excited new scholarship, and Aristotle's *Poetics* at last found an appreciative audience among the literati.

With the Reformation, new complications emerged. Martin Luther's attitude towards Aristotle was ambivalent, but Melanchton enthusiastically endorsed the teaching of solid scholarly materials (excepting the *Metaphysics*). The Counter-Reformation likewise gravitated towards neoscholasticism. The late sixteenth and early seventeenth centuries thus saw a resurgence in the fortunes of Aristotle's works, which for a time were studied with equal intensity in the Protestant north and the Catholic south. Of particular note are the efforts of Francisco Suarez (1548–1617) and the Coimbra commentators.

By comparison, the seventeenth to nineteenth centuries represent a true dry spell for Aristotelian philosophy. One may ask why; a tentative answer, if necessarily incomplete and hesitant, may yet tell us something about Aristotelianism as a historical force. Part of Aristotle's attraction had been the promise of a comprehensive, largely unified worldview, with pressure points doubling as the main locus for scientific advancement (discrepancies calling for new solutions). With the new sciences wresting fields of inquiry from the philosophers' hands, discipline by discipline, what appeared to be left of Aristotle was the barest husk of a system—in effect its extremities, logic and moral education. And of these, the nineteenth century threatened to supplant Aristotle's logic, long regarded as his lasting achievement. Antiquarian interest, it seems, could not of itself make Aristotelianism thrive. It could, however, help keep it alive, at least for a time.

THE NEW ARISTOTLE

The post-Enlightenment rise in Classical scholarship eventually brought about a renewed interest in ancient philosophy. But the philological and historical orientation of the new generation meant that Aristotle (along with Plato) returned with a difference. Instead of unity, the new scholarship sought signs of discrepancy, editorial interference, and intellectual development. Werner Jaeger's (1888–1961) studies mark a watershed, representing the culmination of a century's worth of textual work but also providing the launching point for countless philosophical studies sharing the same problem-oriented, if not aporetic, approach to Aristotle's works. An alternative to the genetic method would be to treat individual treatises as essentially closed units, examined closely but in splendid isolation. Twentieth-century analytic philosophy produced many such Aristotelian essays, while thinkers such as Brentano, Husserl, and Heidegger took more general inspiration from the Stagirite's writings.

Within the Catholic Church's sphere of influence, the nineteenth century witnessed the ascendancy of neoscholasticism, culminating in Leo III's 1879 encyclical officially endorsing Aquinas. Pius X further singled out twenty-four Thomist tenets to be taught in all Catholic institutions. This development injected a more systematic impulse into Aristotelian studies because Aquinas's Aristotle was the undisputed "master of those who know." Still, questions about Aristotle's perennial wisdom—as opposed to his historically conditioned contributions—persisted. The Thomist revival undoubtedly perpetuated a medieval understanding of Aristotle. But it also represented an important moment in the recovery of the medieval Aristotelian tradition as a whole.

Late-twentieth-century philosophers discovered in Aristotle new things again. As virtue ethics flourished, some proponents declared themselves neo-Aristotelians (Alasdair Macintyre, Martha Nussbaum), while others were so labeled. Philosophers of mind and biology found intriguing formulations in Aristotle's studies on living nature; even Aristotle's notoriously problematic modal syllogistic has garnered newfound respect as a philosophically sophisticated formalization of an essentialist metaphysics. In each case many have determined that Aristotle is best approached through an analytic engagement with his commentators—itself an ancient strategy.

This interplay of historical and systematic concerns prompts one final observation. Aristotle's works have been said to present a system *in potentia*. One possible history of Aristotelianism would accordingly unfold as a series of attempts by different thinkers in different ages to map out and explore the conceptual possibilities and limitations embedded in the texts received as Aristotle's. Such a story would span the history of Western thought, because no other philosopher has enjoyed such sustained attention (admittedly, Plato comes close). A welcome corollary is that the contemporary student has at her disposal a kaleidoscope of "Aristotelianisms" to aid in further understanding and exploration.

See also Alexander of Aphrodisias; al-Fārābī; Aristotle; Averroes; Avicenna; Brentano, Franz; Buridan, Jean; Duns Scotus, John; Heidegger, Martin; Husserl, Edmund; Luther, Martin; Metaphysics; Philoponus, John; Plato; Plotinus; Pomponazzi, Pietro; Simplicius; Suàrez, Francisco; Substance and Attribute; Themistius; Theophrastus; Thomas Acquinas, St.; Universals, A Historical Survey; Virtue Ethics; William of Ockham.

Bibliography

Barnes, Jonathan, and Miriam Griffin, eds. *Philosophia Togata II. Plato and Aristotle at Rome*. Oxford: Clarendon Press, 1997.

Blackwell, C., and S. Kusukawa, eds. *Philosophy in the Sixteenth and Seventeenth Centuries: Conversations with Aristotle*. Aldershot: Ashgate, 1999.

Commentaria in Aristotelem Graeca. 23 vols. and 2 supplementary vols. Berlin: G. Reimer: 1882–1907.

Des Chene, Dennis. *Physiologia. Natural Philosophy in Late Aristotelian and Cartesian Thought*. Ithaca: Cornell University Press, 1996.

Düring, Ingemar. *Aristotle in the Ancient Biographical Tradition*. Gothenburg: Institute of Classical Studies, 1957.

Gutas, Dimitri. *Avicenna and the Aristotelian Tradition*. Leiden: E. J. Brill, 1988.

Kessler, Eckhard, Charles H. Lohr, and Walter Sparn, eds. *Aristotelismus und Renaissance*. Wiesbaden: Otto Harrassowitz, 1988.

Kraye, Jill, W. F. Ryan, and Charles B. Schmitt, eds. *Pseudo-Aristotle in the Middle Ages: The Theology and other Texts*. London: The Warburg Institute, 1986.

Kretzmann, Norman, Anthony Kenny, and Jan Pinborg, eds. *The Cambridge History of Later Medieval Philosophy*. Cambridge, U.K.: Cambridge University Press, 1982.

Lohr, Charles. *Latin Aristotle Commentaries*. 2 vols. Florence: L. S. Olschki, 1988.

Moraux, Paul. *Der Aristotelismus bei den Griechen*. 3 vols. Berlin: Walter De Gruyter, 1973–2001.

Olivieri, Luigi, ed. *Aristotelismo veneto e scienza moderna*. 2 vols. Padua: Editrice Antenore, 1983.

Pade, Marianne, ed. *Renaissance Readings of the* Corpus Aristotelicum. Copenhagen: Museum Tusculanum Press, 2001.

Peters, Francis E. *Aristoteles Arabus*. Leiden: E. J. Brill, 1968.

Sandbach, F. H. *Aristotle and the Stoics*. Cambridge, U.K.: Proceedings of the Cambridge Philological Society, Supplement 10, 1985.

Schmitt, Charles B. *Aristotle and the Renaissance*. Cambridge, MA: Harvard University Press, 1983.

Schmitt, Charles B. *The Aristotelian Tradition and Renaissance Universities*. London: Variorum Reprints, 1984.

Sharples, Robert W. "The Peripatetic School." *Routledge History of Philosophy. Vol. II: From Aristotle to Augustine*, edited by David Furley. London and New York: Routledge, 1999.

Sharples, Robert W., ed. *Whose Aristotle? Which Aristotelianism?* Aldershot: Ashgate, 2001.

Sorabji, Richard, ed. *Aristotle Transformed: The Ancient Commentators and their Influence*. London: Duckworth, 1990.

Wardy, Robert. *Aristotle in China: Language, Categories, and Translation*. Cambridge, U.K.: Cambridge University Press, 2000.

Wisnovsky, Robert. *Avicenna's Metaphysics in Context*. Ithaca: Cornell University Press, 2003.

Taneli Kukkonen (2005)

ARISTOTLE
(384 BCE–322 BCE)

Aristotle was born in Stagira, a Greek colony in Macedonia. His father was physician to the Macedonian king, and the family had both a tradition of learning and connections to the Macedonian elite. At the age of seventeen Aristotle came to Athens to study in Plato's Academy (he may also have briefly studied rhetoric under Isocrates). The community of the Academy included some people who would stay for a few years to learn some philosophy before pursuing political careers in their native cities, and others for whom philosophy was an end in itself, and who might spend their entire lives in the Academy. Aristotle

was one of the latter, and stayed in the Academy for twenty years, until Plato's death in 348, when Plato's nephew Speusippus succeeded him as head of the Academy, while the other most prominent Academics, Aristotle and Xenocrates, went to Assos in Asia Minor. There they seem to have formed a kind of local branch of the Academic community under the patronage of the tyrant Hermias of Atarneus, whose niece (and adopted daughter) Aristotle married.

Aristotle spent thirteen years around the north and east Aegean: in Assos; on Lesbos, where he did biological research; in Macedonia, as tutor to the future Alexander the Great; and in Stagira, where he is said to have given laws when it was rebuilt after the Macedonians burned it. He returned to Athens only in 335 (after the Macedonians had attained supremacy over Greece in 338, and after Alexander had succeeded his father in 336), not to the Academy, where Xenocrates had succeeded Speusippus, but to found his own school in the Lyceum, later called the Peripatetic school. He taught there until, after Alexander's death in 323, the Athenians revolted against Macedonia, and Aristotle was charged with impiety for a poem he had written that was held to have given divine honors to Hermias. He left Athens for family property in Stagira's mother-city, Chalcis on Euboia, where he died the following year.

With Aristotle, much more than with Plato, most of the preserved writings are closely connected with his teaching activity. Many of Aristotle's writings bear titles which remain the names of disciplines today (*Physics*, *Politics*, etc.), and much of Aristotle's work was either to introduce these disciplines into the Academy and its daughter communities, or to turn them from less systematic practices into systematically teachable disciplines. "Philosophy" in fifth–fourth century Athens meant simply "higher education," that is, whatever disciplines, beyond elementary education in gymnastics and "grammar" and "music" (including poetry), might be needed for someone who wishes to live well and to rule his city (or even his own household) well. For different teachers, this would cover different disciplines. For Isocrates, "philosophy" meant rhetoric. For Plato, to judge from the ideal curriculum of *Republic* VII, it meant mathematics (arithmetic, plane and solid geometry, astronomy, and "harmonics" or music theory) and dialectic (an art of regimented discussion, in which a respondent defends some thesis, typically a definition, and a questioner tries to refute it by yes-no questions leading to a contradiction); these are the means that will lead to knowledge of what really and eternally *is*, and ultimately of divine things (the Forms and the Good).

Plato conspicuously leaves out rhetoric, which deals with mere opinions rather than with how things really are. He also leaves out pre-Socratic–style "physics" or "natural history," which he thinks is approximate and probable rather than precise and certain, and which explains things by placing them in a grand cosmogonic narrative of how things come to be, rather than (like mathematics and dialectic) by defining and demonstrating what things eternally are. Aristotle teaches all of these disciplines, without claiming that they are all equally scientific; he introduces a hierarchy of disciplines, from those accessible even to an aspiring politician with no great patience for philosophy, up through more strictly scientific disciplines, to the most demanding but most intrinsically rewarding philosophical wisdom.

Aristotle's introduction of rhetoric (probably already in the Academy) should be seen in the context of the conflict between the Academy and the school of Isocrates. Plato draws a sharp contrast between dialectic and rhetoric: that is, between using question and answer to refute a single respondent on a universal question and using long speeches to persuade a group about such particular questions as are discussed in meetings of a citizen assembly (deliberative rhetoric) or a jury (forensic rhetoric). Plato thinks that only dialectic is worthy of the philosopher. But rhetoric is the path to political success, and so students flock to Isocrates instead. Aristotle thinks that, however narrowly practical many students are, "we Academics," with our philosophical knowledge, ought to be able to educate them better than Isocrates can. (Aristotle is said to have justified his teaching of rhetoric by saying "it were shameful to keep silence and let Isocrates speak," varying a line of tragedy, "it were shameful to keep silence and let barbarians speak.")

This might be merely a practical compromise. More shocking to a Platonist is Aristotle's claim that "rhetoric is the counterpart of dialectic"—they are both, not sciences of any one subject matter, but sub-scientific abilities to discover and arrange and express arguments, applicable equally to any subject. Rhetoric also requires rudimentary knowledge of ethics and politics, because these are the subjects about which we must persuade, and because we must know how to project a given character or emotional state, and how an audience of given character and political background will react; the focus remains on argument.

Plato thinks that dialectic, by allowing us to arrive at definitions, gives us a scientific knowledge of eternal Forms existing apart from the sensible world. Aristotle, who has participated in the same dialectical practice as Plato, thinks this claim about its status is spurious. Dialectic is not scientific knowledge of eternal separate Forms, since there are no such Forms. Aristotle is willing to speak of forms present within sensible things (a form is whatever is the object of scientific definition), but dialectic is not scientific knowledge of these forms either, since scientific definition of (say) lunar eclipse depends on specific knowledge of the cause of lunar eclipse, which the dialectician, as a generalist, does not have; it is not the dialectician but the physicist who grasps forms of physical things. Dialectic remains a valuable preliminary training because, by showing what can be refuted, it rules out wrong definitions and helps us find the right ones, and because, by allowing us to find arguments on both sides, it sets out puzzles that science must solve, but it is not itself science or philosophy. And while Plato speaks not of *teaching* in dialectic, but only of a communal *practice* of questioning and answering, Aristotle demystifies the practice, and claims in his *Topics* to teach rules for discovering dialectical arguments, just as his *Rhetoric* teaches rules for discovering rhetorical arguments.

The average practically minded student will probably study only rhetoric and not dialectic, but Aristotle hopes to lure the better students on further to more scientific disciplines. In the first place, this means ethics and politics, which are philosophical, that is, scientific or causal discussions of what is good for individuals and cities, based on an understanding of what human beings and cities are. But Aristotle distinguishes these "practical sciences" from the "theoretical sciences," that is, kinds of knowledge valued purely for the sake of knowing them, which are capable of greater precision and are more intrinsically worth knowing, though less useful. Against Plato, physics or natural science (in the broadest sense, including biology and psychology) is a theoretical science: when done correctly, it grasps forms of natural things, and proceeds by definition and demonstration, but the forms it grasps are inseparable from matter and motion, and many of its results hold only "for the most part," or *ceteris paribus*, rather than universally.

Aristotle agrees with Plato that the highest wisdom, the knowledge most intrinsically worth knowing, must be a science of things existing eternally apart from matter, and ultimately of the Good. But neither dialectic nor physics is such a wisdom (nor is mathematics, which is not about separately existing objects, but about ordinary objects hypothetically idealized), and so Aristotle announces, beyond dialectic and physics, a new discipline of "first philosophy" (what commentators of Aristotle since antiquity have called "metaphysics"), which will provide the theoretical wisdom that he thinks both Plato and the pre-Socratics have failed to deliver.

WRITINGS

We can broadly divide Aristotle's writings into three classes:

"Exoteric," or "published" writings, were intended for circulation outside the circle of philosophers, elegantly written and sometimes in dialogue form (also the poem for Hermias and a similar poem for Plato). All such writings are lost, but there are substantial fragments; we have perhaps as much as half of Aristotle's *Protrepticus*, or *Exhortation to Philosophy*, addressed to a royal patron, which remains an excellent introduction to Aristotelian philosophy. (Aristotle's will is also preserved, in Diogenes Laertius.)

Collections of data, classified but not written up with any literary pretensions, were intended as raw material to be further used in philosophical research and writing and teaching. These texts may have been "loose-leaf," with new material constantly added, some of it perhaps by members of the school other than Aristotle. Extant writings of this type are the *History of Animals*, the *Constitution of Athens* (discovered in a papyrus in 1890 and not quite complete, a fragment of a vast series of 158 *Constitutions* of different cities), and the *Physical Problems*.

"Acroamatic" writings, that is, writings related to Aristotle's lectures, form the bulk of the surviving corpus. This does not mean that the texts are verbatim identical with the lectures; while Aristotle sometimes speaks as if addressing a live audience, that is compatible with the texts being notes written beforehand as a basis for lectures, or a later revision retaining the lecture style (as in published Gifford or Sather lectures), and the treatises contain many passages which no student then or now could endure if read verbatim as a lecture. The problem is not special to Aristotle; most Greek literature was intended for oral performance, and in every case it is difficult to determine how close the transmitted text is to any given performance. Performances would vary, and the written text is not a transcript of any one occasion but a model for varying expanded or abridged oral performances. In Aristotle's case, while usually only one written version survives for each lecture series, occasionally (as in the *Ethics*) we can compare two and gain a sense of the range of variation.

The transmitted texts of the acroamatic writings vary greatly in style. Some passages are highly literary (often marked by avoidance of "hiatus"—the juxtaposition of a vowel at the end of a word with a vowel at the beginning of the next—as in Isocrates and in Plato's late dialogues), whether because they have been more thoroughly revised toward eventual publication, or because Aristotle delivered some pieces (especially the beginnings of works) in more elaborate form, or because they are excerpted from Aristotle's exoteric works. Other passages are long strings of brutally truncated arguments for the same conclusion, connected merely by "also"; in performance Aristotle would have selected only some arguments, and filled them out and connected them better.

The transmitted texts contain many references to "what we have said previously/elsewhere" or "what we will say," sometimes with a title "in the [writings or lectures] on *x*." (It is possible, but should not be the default assumption, that some of these cross-references were added by later editors.) While we can often supply a plausible page reference, we should beware of assuming that Aristotle's references are to texts now extant, or else to lost parallel texts: They are not necessarily to fixed texts at all, but to earlier and later parts of an idealized curriculum, each part of which would be repeatedly given (with variations) as a lecture, and also written down and occasionally updated, even if no actual student ever heard the whole series in order. "We have said" and "we will say" refer not to order of composition but to order in the curriculum; however, while Aristotle is *mostly* consistent about the ideal order, there are contradictions that may indicate that he changed his mind on the appropriate sequence of the psychological-zoological writings. There is no real contradiction in the fact that Aristotle (and his followers) cite the same work under different titles; the curriculum may be subdivided more or less finely, and the same title may be used generically for a large section or specifically for a smaller subsection: "physics" or "on nature" may refer to the entire physical-biological corpus or to something as narrow as *Physics* I–IV (with *Physics* V–VIII cited contrastively as "on motion").

Some ancient catalogs list Aristotle's works by shorter units and some by longer units (the catalogs may also contain duplications, and some catalogs refer to works not available to other catalogs, or to us). Andronicus of Rhodes in the first century BCE attempted to introduce order by determining the correct titles and sequence, generally opting for longer "works," and it is probably roughly his decisions that won out. (But the story that Andronicus, drawing on a rediscovery of Aristotle's library, made the acroamatic works available for the first time and so touched off a renaissance of Aristotelianism, is mostly or wholly fiction.) Following a Stoic division of philosophy, Andronicus organized the corpus into first "logical" writings, then "physical" (or more broadly "theoretical" writings, to include the *Metaphysics*, concerned with nonphysical things), then "ethical" writings (or more broadly "practical," to include the *Politics*).

Many of the texts are now lost. As with the rest of Greek literature, what survived was generally only what was used and copied for educational purposes, which explains why the "exoteric" works are lost and why usually only one version of each "acroamatic" text survives. The surviving texts have been edited many times since the invention of printing, often in complete editions that generally try to follow Aristotle's and other ancient indications of the correct sequence of the corpus (although these are not fully consistent and, for example, give no hint how to order the three surviving ethical works, which all fill the same place in the curriculum).

Immanuel Bekker's nineteenth-century edition has become standard. Modern editions and translations give "Bekker pages" in the margins (e.g., "1042b5," where "a" or "b" is a column of a double-columned page), and Aristotle is always cited in this form where possible; editions that aspire to completeness print the texts in Bekker's sequence. The editions divide Aristotle's treatises into books and chapters; the book divisions have (not always undisputed) ancient authority and may in some cases go back to Aristotle himself, but the chapter divisions are modern artifacts and deserve no deference (medieval authors use a different division into "lectiones"). Ancient writers cite the books of multibook treatises by Greek letter-names; modern writers generally use numbers, but prefer letters in the *Metaphysics*, where the presence of two books alpha (conventionally designated A and α) disrupts the usual letter-number conversion.

The following list presents the texts in Bekker's sequence, leaving out texts currently agreed to be spurious, and marking with an asterisk texts whose authenticity is currently controversial. The traditional Latin titles are added where these sound significantly different from the English.

Logical writings (*Organon*): *Categories* (the title is controversial), *On Interpretation, Prior Analytics, Posterior Analytics, Topics, On Sophistical Refutations* (*De sophisticis elenchis*).

Theoretical writings: *Physics, On the Heaven* (*De caelo*), *On Generation and Corruption, Meteorology, On the Soul* (*De anima*), *Parva naturalia* (including *On Sense and Sensibilia, On Memory, On Sleep* [*De somno*], *On Dreams* [*De insomniis*], *On Divination in Sleep, On Length and Shortness of Life*, and *On Youth, Old Age, Life, Death and Respiration* [*De juventute* for short]), *History of Animals, Parts of Animals, Movement of Animals, Progression of Animals* (*De incessu animalium*), *Generation of Animals, *Physical Problems, Metaphysics*.

Practical writings: *Nicomachean Ethics* (abbreviated "NE" or "EN"), **Magna Moralia, Eudemian Ethics* ("EE"), *Politics*. (In a peculiar situation, three central books are identical: NE V–VII = EE IV–VI. These books are usually printed with the NE, but most modern scholars agree that they were originally written with the EE instead.)

Bekker puts at the end the *Rhetoric* and *Poetics*, under the head of "productive philosophy" (i.e., philosophy to guide production, in this case of speeches or poems); their place is controversial, and they had sometimes been put at the end of the *Organon*. The **Constitution of Athens* and other texts not printed by Bekker (fragments discovered on papyrus or in later ancient citations or translations) are often placed at the end.

With Aristotle, as with Plato, there have been attempts to determine the order of composition of the works, distinguishing "early," "middle," and "late." Sometimes stylometric tests are applied. Some scholars, like Jaeger, assume that Aristotle moved from an early Platonism, to a critical revision of Platonism, to an independent mature philosophy. Such "developmental" studies have had the merit of bringing out tensions in Aristotle's work, and calling attention to works (often fragmentary, like the *Protrepticus*) that had been ignored or deemed spurious because they seemed embarrassingly close to Plato. Some chronological results have won widespread assent, notably that the *Protrepticus* is early, and the EE earlier than the NE. But dating has not generally been successful, and for a good reason, namely that Aristotle regularly revised his work, so that a single text may show both "early" and "late" features and thus resist easy classification. Aristotle was trying to present his treatises as parts of a synchronic system, ordered by pedagogical role; tensions remain, and while sometimes these tensions are best explained diachronically, this is not always the case. In what follows, the most important texts will be discussed, not in Bekker's order or in a presumed chronological order, but in roughly the order of increasing difficulty:

probably many of Aristotle's students dropped out early in this sequence, and only a few remained until the end.

ETHICS AND POLITICS

Aristotle conceives ethics as a part of political philosophy: We cannot understand and evaluate different political structures unless we understand individual character, and conversely, we cannot fully describe the best life for an individual without reference to the city in which he lives and is educated. Many comments in the ethical works assume that the reader or hearer is (or wants to be) a *politikos*, or statesman, and Aristotle assumes that the best life for an individual and the best *politeia* or constitution for a city, whatever they turn out to be, will be analogous. The ethical works, then, emerge from popular lectures to aspiring *politikoi*, who have come to hear lectures by a philosopher in the hope that it will make them happier and more successful *politikoi*, but who do not intend to spend their lives on philosophy.

Aristotle can be seen as trying to repair the damage that Plato did in his lecture on the Good, where an audience who had come expecting to hear about "health or wealth or some marvelous happiness" were surprised to find that the lecture was about numbers and that its conclusion was that the Good was the One, with the result that some of the audience gave up on philosophy altogether, while others presumably turned to the more practical philosophy of teachers like Isocrates (see Aristoxenus, *Elements of Harmonics* II,1, and cf. EE I,8). Aristotle is in part rejecting Plato's conclusions (he thinks mathematics has nothing to do with goodness), in part simply rejecting his method of presentation: we must start with what the audience antecedently believes and values, get them to see the difficulties, and so introduce philosophical doctrines (including any doctrine of a higher good) as solutions to those difficulties. But in ethics, as in rhetoric, he thinks that the Academics should be able to educate them better than Isocrates can.

Anyone who can choose how to live, and who wants to approach the question rationally, must first clarify what he is aiming at—what is the chief good of human life. Everyone agrees that the aim is *eudaimonia*—usually translated as "happiness," but perhaps best neutrally as "success"; it need not be introspectible, must be evaluated over a lifetime rather than at one moment, and can be said of cities as well as of individuals—but they disagree about what *eudaimonia* consists in. The three plausible contenders for the best way of life—the pleasure-seeking life, the active or political life, and the contemplative or philosophical life (Aristotle thinks the money-making life

is chosen only from necessity)—go with different contenders for the human good. The pleasure seekers think it is pleasure; the *politikoi* may think it is fame or honor or, more appropriately, that it is *aretê*, virtue, or excellence (what *deserves* honor).

Among the philosophers, Socrates thinks that virtue (consisting in some kind of knowledge) is necessary and sufficient for happiness, and Plato talks about the Form of the Good or about the One. Aristotle creates an aporia by using these views against each other and raising objections against each, in order to motivate his own account of happiness, and the conceptual distinction on which it is based, as a solution to the aporia. Happiness or success in life is not virtue, which is a stable *hexis* ("habit" or acquired state) persisting even when it is not exercised, but rather the *energeia* (exercise or activity) of virtue throughout a complete lifespan. We can thus avoid the paradox of saying that the good person is happy even when poor, sick, and unjustly despised by his fellow citizens; in such a condition he remains virtuous but cannot exercise his virtue, or is greatly hampered in exercising it. The happy life will *involve* virtue, and it will also involve wealth if the virtues (say, generosity) need wealth to be exercised, and these facts explain the temptation to identify happiness with virtue or even wealth. Likewise, the happy life is pleasant, since Aristotle analyzes pleasure as being (or following upon) the exercise of a natural state, but its pleasantness is not what *makes* it happy or worthy of choice. (This is against the view of some Academics that pleasure is always a process, the *restoration* of a natural state, and that the happiest life is a steady natural state without deficiency or restoration. Aristotle avoids the paradox that the happiest life is without activity or pleasure by arguing that there are *energeiai* that are not processes.)

Aristotle applies the same method of setting out competing beliefs and arguments, resolving the aporia through a distinction, and showing how justice can be done to all sides, to resolve Socrates' paradoxical argument that incontinence is impossible: I can do something wrong if I have *hexis*-knowledge that this type of action is wrong, but not if I am applying the *hexis* and have *energeia*-knowledge that this particular action is wrong. It must be stressed that this is a *teaching* method, designed to motivate Aristotle's doctrines and conceptual distinctions for his audience and to make softened versions of Socratic or Platonic paradoxes more palatable. We do not know that this is how Aristotle himself arrived at his conclusions.

Aristotle also tries to show what is right in the Socratic and Platonic conclusions that virtue and happiness consist in knowledge, perhaps knowledge of a transcendent Good. The work or task or function (*ergon*) of a human being is rational activity, and a virtue is a condition that disposes to such activity. But there are two kinds of virtues: "intellectual virtues," or virtues of the rational soul, and "moral virtues," conditions of an irrational part of the soul, according to which it is disposed to act as reason would require.

Genuine moral virtue is not simply habituation to desire the right amount, but involves choice, which involves deliberation or means-end reasoning: so moral virtue is not possible without the intellectual virtue of *phronêsis* ("prudence," "practical wisdom") or deliberative ability. (Nor, conversely, is *phronêsis* possible without moral virtue, since uncontrolled passions will warp our deliberations.) But *phronêsis* is not identical with the highest intellectual virtue, *sophia* ("wisdom"), knowledge of the divine things that are intrinsically most worth knowing. *Sophia* is exercised only in contemplation (*theôria*) and not in action: we cannot deduce, from these necessary eternal things, knowledge of the contingent temporal objects of practical choice. But *sophia* gives a starting point for deliberative reasoning in another way, because contemplation is itself the exercise of the highest virtue, and is therefore the highest happiness we can try to achieve. (It is the only exercise of virtue we can attribute to the gods, who can hardly be courageous or temperate.) So while happiness is possible with only moral virtue and practical intelligence, the highest happiness needs theoretical intelligence as well.

When Aristotle says that maximizing contemplation is the highest goal of human planning, he means not only planning an individual life, but also a statesman's planning for the city. (The statesman may have only *phronêsis*, but needs proper respect for *sophia*.) Happiness, for cities as for individuals, is an exercise of virtue, and while this may require material conditions (prosperity and external peace), the statesman's main concern should be making the city virtuous. And, for cities as for individuals, some virtues are more worth exercising than others: courage and military solidarity are virtues we would rather not have occasion to exercise. While a city must be able to defend itself, its highest goal is the exercise of the virtues of peaceful leisure. This is *theôria*, not only in its metaphorical sense (the philosopher's contemplation of nature or of incorporeal divine things), but also in its ordinary sense: attendance at civic religious festivals, including the musical-poetic contests (of tragedies,

comedies, etc.), which may be occasions for private or communal moral and political reflection. (The *Poetics* defends the value of such musical-poetic performances, and inquires how it comes about; it thus elaborates an important point too briefly treated in the *Politics*.)

Aristotle's main goal in the *Politics* is the construction of an ideal *politeia* (constitution or collective mode of life and governance), a critical revision of Plato's *Republic* and *Laws*. But he also discusses less ideal *politeiai*, how they are preserved by proper legislation, and how they are corrupted, leading to revolution; the trained *politikos* will be useful even to a non-ideal *politeia*, helping to preserve it by moderating and improving it. (And Aristotle's 158 collected *Politeiai* will help give an empirical base.) The central thesis of the *Politics* is the distinction between genuinely political rule (rule over free fellow citizens, in the interest of the ruled) and despotic rule (rule as of a master over slaves, in the interest of the ruler). While *Politics* I is notorious for defending slavery, Aristotle's main interest is to make clear the differences between despotic rule (legitimate only within the household) and political rule. (He thus also defuses the Socratic paradox that there is only one art of ruling, depending on philosophical knowledge of the good: to the Athenian bourgeois, this suggests that the Academics are claiming the right to rule over their fellow citizens, while not allowing ordinary citizens even to give orders to their servants.)

Within the city, not only tyranny but also oligarchy and democracy are despotic: even when they are ruled by law, their laws express the economic and political interests of a ruling individual or group (the rich few in an oligarchy, the poor majority in a democracy). But rather than conclude, with Thrasymachus, that all rule is despotic, Aristotle argues, with Plato, that genuinely political rule is possible. Officially (like Plato's *Statesman*) Aristotle has a two-by-three grid of constitutions: corresponding to tyranny, oligarchy, and democracy are three good constitutions, kingship, aristocracy, and (what Aristotle calls in a narrower sense) *politeia*, which are the rule of the one, the few, or the many in the interest of the whole city. But actually Aristotle treats kingship and aristocracy as an ideal constitution run by morally and practically virtuous people and aiming at the development and exercise of virtue; *politeia* is a more attainable ideal, a "mixed constitution" between democracy and oligarchy, as the moral virtues lie between vices of excess and deficiency. *Politeia*, though a "virtuous" constitution, does not aim at virtue in the citizens and does not choose officials for their virtue, but at least its laws, balancing the interests of different groups and designed to preserve peace between them, do not impose a partisan "justice" that would conflict with genuine moral virtue in the individual.

DIALECTIC AND ANALYTICS

Aristotle's logical treatises are usually grouped as the *Organon*, or "instrument"; against the Stoics, who make logic a part of philosophy alongside physics and ethics, the Peripatetics say that logic is a mere instrument of philosophy, valuable neither intrinsically nor as guiding action, but only as guiding reasoning in other fields. Also ancient is the arrangement of the *Organon*: first the *Categories*, dealing with single terms and the simple objects (substances, quantities, qualities, relations, actions, passions, "where," "when," positions [e.g., standing], states [e.g., armed]) that they signify; then the *De interpretatione*, dealing with propositions composed of two terms linked by a copula (affirmative or negative, universal or particular, assertoric or modal); then the *Prior Analytics*, dealing with syllogisms, valid arguments composed of three propositions sharing three terms (e.g., "A belongs to no B, C belongs to all B, therefore A does not belong to all C," valid since Aristotle rejects empty terms).

Then come treatises dealing with different types of syllogism: the *Posterior Analytics*, with scientific or demonstrative syllogism, where the premises must be true and causally explanatory of the conclusion; the *Topics*, with dialectical syllogism, where the premises need only be plausible; the *Sophistical Refutations*, with sophistical or pseudo-dialectical syllogisms, which are only apparently valid or have only apparently plausible premises; some ancient writers add "rhetorical" and even "poetic" syllogisms. At the end of the *Sophistical Refutations*, Aristotle says that while he has perfected earlier teaching of rhetoric, in the case of the syllogism there had been no such teaching before him; Aristotle has been taken as here summing up the *Organon* and reflecting on his crucial discovery, the syllogism.

However, Aristotle has no conception of "logic," but of two different disciplines, analytics (*Prior* and *Posterior*), and dialectic (the *Topics*, taken as including the *Sophistical Refutations*); the *Categories* and *De Interpretatione* seem designed to support the *Topics* rather than the *Analytics*. We have spoken above of dialectic, the practice of regimented discussion in which a questioner seeks to refute a respondent's thesis by a series of yes-no questions. The end of the *Sophistical Refutations* is summing up not the entire *Organon* but only the *Topics*, which has for the first time made dialectic a teachable art and has

shown how to discover syllogisms to deduce the contradictory of the respondent's thesis.

These arguments, unlike rhetorical arguments, can proceed only from premises the respondent will grant, and by steps he must accept as valid. Dialectic must proceed from plausible (*endoxa*) premises, since these are just those premises that a respondent will concede (if he does not see that they favor or hurt his thesis). It is a mistake to turn dialectic into "argument from prereflective intuitions," detached from the context of refutation, and to give it a foundational role in philosophy. Aristotle does say that dialectic gives a path to the principles of the sciences, but these principles are, especially, definitions, and, as in Socratic dialogue, dialectic is chiefly devoted to testing and refuting proposed definitions. The structure of the *Topics* brings this out: successive books give rules for testing claims that *P* belongs to *S*, that *P* is or contains the genus of *S*, and that *P* is proper (*idion*) to *S* (i.e., belongs to every *S* and no non-*S*), which are necessary but insufficient conditions for *P* to be the definition of *S*, and then give special rules for testing claims of definition. Aristotle also gives advice on how to order your questions, how to proceed as respondent, and background knowledge the dialectician should have.

The *Categories* and *De interpretatione*, as well as *Topics* I, seem to give such background knowledge; the most recent edition of the *Categories* prefers the alternative ancient title *The Before the Topics*, in part because the text is not just about categories. First, Aristotle distinguishes simple from complex expressions; then, what is signified by a simple expression is signified either synonymously (univocally) or homonymously (equivocally) or paronymously (denominatively). Two things are synonymous if they are signified by the same name and according to the same definition; homonymous if signified by the same name according to two different definitions (bank and bank, but also *mousikê*, the art of music, and *mousikê*, a female musician); paronymous if one name is derived from the other ("just" is paronymous or derived from "justice," not because the word "justice" is older, but because something is called "just" *because* there is justice in it).

Only synonymous things, not homonymous or paronymous, can be given genus-differentia definitions ("just" is neither a species of animal nor a species of virtue). Synonymous things that are in a subject (like justice) fall under one of the nine categories of accidents; synonymous things that are not in a subject are substances. (Substances can be "said of" something, but cannot be "in" something: horse is said of Bucephalus, since

Bucephalus is said to be a horse, but there is not a horse *in* Bucephalus. "Primary substances," like Bucephalus, are neither in anything nor said of anything.) Aristotle gives tests for when a thing falls under each category, which are needed to apply the rules of the *Topics* (thus if *P* is the genus of *S*, *S* and *P* must belong to the same category, but we need tests to determine to which category they belong). Likewise, after the categories proper, Aristotle gives accounts of the different kinds of opposition, priority and simultaneity, motion and having, which serve similar functions in dialectic.

Sometimes a dialectical questioner poses a series of questions that appear to necessitate the contradictory of the respondent's thesis, but which contain some hidden fallacy; the respondent must avoid assenting to what does not follow, and must be able to explain *why* it does not follow, in order to avoid appearing, to the spectators and perhaps even to himself, to have been refuted. The *Sophistical Refutations*, which may be considered as a final book of the *Topics*, is devoted to classifying such "sophisms," or "sophistical refutations," explaining how each type arises, and advising the respondent on how to recognize and to "solve" or "resolve" each such sophism as it comes at him in questioning.

Sophisms are not intrinsically dishonest: They are puzzles demanding solution. We should imagine, not an arms race between sophists devising offensive weapons and philosophers improving defenses, but a single intellectual community exploring sophisms and discussing the merits of different possible solutions. Often the most philosophically interesting sophisms are "sophisms of figure of speech," arising when the grammatical form of a term misrepresents its logical form: these include the family of sophisms concluding that "there is a third man" beyond mortal individuals and the Platonic Form, which turn on treating "man" as "signifying some this." Aristotle himself, in the fragmentary *On Ideas*, constructs a series of such philosophically serious sophisms, giving for each Platonic argument for the Forms a parallel argument to an unacceptable conclusion, such as the third man. Each sophism challenges the Platonists: "dismantle my sophistical argument without at the same time dismantling your own allegedly probative arguments for the Forms." The *Categories* helps solve sophisms of figure of speech by testing what category each term signifies, and its distinction between primary and secondary substances can solve many third man sophisms; but if Platonists accept these solutions, they risk undermining their own favorite arguments and conclusions.

A syllogism or deduction is "a discourse in which, some things being supposed, something different results of necessity through their being so." Syllogisms are as old as thought and language, and Aristotle does not claim to have invented them. What the *Analytics* invents is a method for *analyzing* them: that is, for classifying them and then, by giving a few primitive argument forms and derivation rules for generating more complicated forms, explaining why syllogism comes about. In every case, syllogism depends on two premises sharing a common term (the syllogism will be in different "figures," depending on whether the shared term is subject of one premise and predicate of the other, predicate of both, or subject of both; some "moods" will be valid and others not, depending on whether the premises are affirmative or negative, particular or universal, assertoric or modal). Aristotle's analysis depends on the realization that the necessity or validity of an argument, once all premises are made explicit, depends only on its form, so that the same analysis applies whether the premises are true or false; this realization presumably arose from the deliberate exploration, in dialectic, of the consequences of false hypotheses.

But Aristotle sharply distinguishes dialectical from scientific or causal reasoning, and he devotes the *Posterior Analytics* to analyzing "demonstrations" or *scientific* syllogisms, arguments that give their possessors knowledge or science (*epistêmê*) of some object; here *epistêmê* is a cognitive state that not only grasps an object as it is, without the possibility of falsehood, but also understands *why* the object is as it is. It seems surprising that mere arguments, without direct contact with the object, can give such knowledge, and Aristotle tries to analyze the conditions under which this can happen. The premises must be true, necessary, and better known than the conclusion; they must also express the causes that explain why the conclusion is true. We can of course come to know an object by reasoning from effects to causes, but properly scientific and explanatory knowledge must reason from causes to effects; the logical structure of the argument will mirror the causal structure of the world.

On pain of circularity or regress, the first principles of demonstrations must be known by some means other than demonstration (Aristotle calls the nondemonstrative grasp of first principles *nous* rather than *epistêmê*). Apart from some topic-neutral principles of reasoning ("axioms"), these will be either "hypotheses" that the objects of each science exist, or "definitions" of those objects; we accept without demonstration both the existence and definitions of the simple objects of the science (e.g., for geometry, point and straight line) and pre-

ENCYCLOPEDIA OF PHILOSOPHY
2nd edition

liminary definitions of the complex objects (e.g., regular pentagon), but we demonstrate the existence of complex objects satisfying those definitions. Dialectic can reach these preliminary definitions, but we can give properly scientific definitions of complex objects only once we demonstrate their existence from simple causes (thus not "thunder is noise in the clouds" but "thunder is noise of extinction of fire in the clouds"). We cannot give justificatory explanations of how we know the first principles of the sciences, but only causal explanations of how the human mind, primed by experience, comes to grasp them by *nous*; Aristotle's account is compressed enough that it has been read both as an empiricist account of induction and as a friendly revision of Plato's theory of recollection.

Aristotle's account of science is clearly modeled on geometry. But he tries to show that physics too can be a science, beginning from a grasp of the forms of natural things.

PHYSICS AND COSMOLOGY

Aristotle's project in physics is a response to Platonic challenges both to the narrative method and to the content of pre-Socratic physics. Anaxagoras's physics—to take a typical pre-Socratic example—narrates the origin of everything from a cosmogonic vortex, whose rotation and centrifugal force explain the separation of heaven from earth, the rotation of the heavens, the motion of heavy bodies down and light bodies up and the sorting of like bodies to like, and then the formation of the first plants and animals and humans out of seeds present in the precosmic mixture. Plato thinks such narrative can never be scientific; science must be concerned not with how things come to be but with what they are, beginning from their forms as grasped by definitions, and proceeding to demonstration.

Plato also complains that pre-Socratics explain the emergence of the cosmos by reference not to a rational plan or to some good to be accomplished, but through violence; if things are where they are because of a vortex (i.e., through being shoved by other bodies that are shoved into them) rather than because it is best for them to be there, then there will be no explanation of the goodness and orderliness of the universe, as manifested in the mathematically precise motions of the planets. In the *Timaeus*, Plato addresses the second objection by sketching an alternative teleological physics; but this too follows a narrative method, and even a reformed physics cannot be science but only a likely story.

Aristotle tries to address both objections and to produce a genuinely scientific physics, explaining the physi-

cists' traditional explananda (rotating heavens, fall of heavy bodies, lightning, earthquakes, animals ...) not in a narrative sequence but in a causal or explanatory sequence, beginning from the form or nature of each body, which is the object of a properly physical definition. Aristotle broadly accepts the *Timaeus*'s picture of the cosmos: a spherical earth is at rest at the center of a single spherical cosmos. The cosmos is made of earth, water, air, and fire intertransformed and combined, teleologically organized to support living things, and surrounded by heavenly bodies that are themselves living and divine; these move in several uniform circular motions, which combine to produce complex astronomical phenomena, and they are ultimately governed by an incorporeal god or gods. But Aristotle's method contrasts with the *Timaeus*, and leads him to challenge particular claims of the *Timaeus* as well as of the pre-Socratics.

Aristotle's particular physical treatises—the *De caelo*, *On Generation and Corruption*, *Meteorology*, and psychological-zoological writings—follow roughly what had been the traditional narrative sequence of the explananda. Thus the *De caelo* treats the rotation of the heavens and the motions of heavy and light bodies, traditionally explained through a cosmogonic vortex. But Aristotle rejects explanations through vortices or any other violent cause. What happens to a thing violently, contrary to its own nature, cannot happen always or for the most part, but only as a temporary interruption of a thing's natural behavior (e.g., a stone being thrown upward). Physics, as a science, seeks to explain what happens always or for the most part, and must therefore start by grasping the nature of each thing, where "nature" means "principle of natural motion"; so the nature of heavy bodies is to move toward the center of the cosmos, and thus teleology is built into each nature. (Thus physical definitions necessarily involve motion, and the forms they describe cannot exist separately from matter, as the Form described by a Platonic dialectical definition is supposed to. And fire and so on must be defined physically by their motions, rather than mathematically by their shapes as in Democritus and the *Timaeus*.)

Aristotle draws the conclusion that the heavens cannot be made of the four standard elements; since these naturally move in straight lines toward or away from the center, the heavens would have to be constrained to circular motion by violence (whether by a vortex or by a providential soul as in the *Timaeus*), and such motion could not be regular or permanent. Consequently, the heavens are made out of a fifth element (sometimes called "aether") whose natural motion is around the center. The aether is free of the accidents that obstruct natural motion in the sublunar world, so it rotates eternally without interruption or irregularity. Because this motion arises eternally from the nature of the thing, Aristotle rejects the claim of the pre-Socratics and the *Timaeus* that the rotation of the heavens and the separation of the elements into an ordered cosmos arose (by what could only be a violent process) from a precosmic chaos; the ordered world and its more-or-less regular phenomena have always existed, and a narrative explanation is excluded, since there is no precosmic situation from which a narrative could begin. Rather, the phenomena must be explained by the influence of the naturally rotating heavens on naturally moving sublunar elements.

The *On Generation and Corruption* and *Meteorology* continue this program. If it were not for the rotation of the heavens, the four sublunar elements would separate out into concentric spheres of heavier and lighter elements, with no intertransformation or combination, and therefore no living things. But the regular daily rotation of the heavens, combined with the regular rotation of the sun through the inclined circle of the ecliptic, bring it about that the sun is above the horizon more of the time in the summer than in the winter, causing regular cycles of heating and cooling, and thus of evaporation and condensation.

Aristotle sees evaporation as a genuine transformation of water into air, and likewise of earth into fire; when a heavy element is transformed into a light element, it begins to rise (and when a light element is condensed, it falls), and this cycle keeps the elements from separating and gives rise to combinations. But properly the light elements are not "air" and "fire" but "moist exhalation" and "dry exhalation"; air is a mixture of both, and the portion of the dry exhalation that gathers above the air and beneath the sphere of the moon is not actually fire, but is a fuel that easily becomes inflamed, as it does in comets and shooting stars.

Since Tycho Brahe proved that comets and novae are supralunar, Aristotle's account has been regarded as a desperate attempt to save his theory of immutable heavens by moving all changes in the heavens to a fictional sublunar fire-sphere governed by a fantastic exhalation process. Historically this is the wrong attitude. Aristotle's explanation of comets is among the most traditional parts of his physics: Heraclitus explains even the sun through a continuous process of exhalations rising from the sea and becoming inflamed. Aristotle's innovation is to separate out from meteorological phenomena genuinely astronomical things like the sun, which are not

dependent on the sublunar world but are governed only by themselves and by unchangeable incorporeal things, and therefore have eternally constant motions and can be objects of precise mathematical science; it is only because these things are perfectly regular that they can impose even an approximate regularity on the sublunar world.

The *Physics* in the narrower sense is a deliberately non-cosmological prolegomenon to the physical works, describing the principles from which all natural things arise and the necessary conditions (above all, motion) for anything to arise from these principles, and using a definition of "nature" to delimit the physicist's domain and methods and the causes or explanations that he must invoke in tracing natural things back to their principles. Aristotle begins, traditionally enough, with the *archai*, the principles or starting points of natural things—whatever must exist before each natural thing comes to be, and can be used in explaining it. (For narrative physics these would be whatever existed before the cosmos, e.g., for Empedocles the four elements and love and strife, for the *Timaeus* the Forms and receptacle and demiurge; but Aristotle's *archai* do not exist before the cosmos, since his cosmos never came to be.) We will infer to the *archai* by analyzing the characteristic effect that arises from them, which is, most generally, motion or change—not only change of place (locomotion) but also change of quality (alteration), change of quantity (growth and diminution), and the coming to be and passing away of substances (generation and corruption).

Aristotle argues that whenever some new *F* comes to be, in any category, there must be some persisting substratum that was not *F* and comes to be *F*; this analysis shifts *F* to predicate position. The subject that persists through even substantial change is one *archê*, the matter. This echoes the *Timaeus*'s argument that the apparent substantial change of (say) water into air shows that the real *archê* is not water or air, but the receptacle, the persisting substratum that appears now watery, now airy. But the *Timaeus* seems to infer that the change is not really substantial, that all sensible things are just accidental modifications of this single persisting substance. Aristotle argues that there is real substantial change, that the substance of a natural thing is not the matter that persists through the thing's generation and corruption, but the form that comes to be in the matter. Both form and matter are *archai* of natural things, and while the matter is *potentially* this or that substance, the form, as what makes each substance *actually* that substance, is substance in a stronger sense. (Plato would reply that while form as well as matter is an *archê* and a substance, the real Form is eternal and separate, and what comes to be in the matter is a nonsubstantial image of the Form.)

How do we tell when a form acquired through change is a new substance, and when it is merely a new accident of a persisting substance? The shape of an artifact is merely an accident, but the *nature* of a natural thing, that is, the distinctive "principle of motion and rest" within it that is responsible for its carrying out its characteristic activities, is a substance. *Physics* II argues that the nature of a natural thing is more properly its form than its matter, and therefore that the physicist must study form as well as matter; thus, as we have seen, physics must define and not merely narrate, giving definitions that, unlike Platonic dialectical definitions, are inseparable from motion and thus from matter—natures are like "snubness," which is neither the matter "nose" nor the form "concave," but a form that cannot be defined without reference to its appropriate matter, the nose. A natural thing acts *for the sake of* actualizing the characteristic potentialities of its nature, and so the physicist will give explanations not only through the material and formal causes and through the mover or efficient cause, but also through the final cause. Aristotle thus, like Plato in *Laws* X, argues against many pre-Socratic physicists that purposive activity is prior to chance and violence, but he does this while preserving what is specific to nature, and without reducing natural things to artifacts of a designing soul.

Nothing will arise from matter and form without motion; motion depends on time and place and (some people think) on void; also a motion, to be a single motion, must be continuous, and continuity implies infinite divisibility. All these concepts are problematic, and Aristotle tries to define, and to resolve *aporiai* about, motion, place, and time, and to show that the infinite and the void do not exist (except in specially qualified senses). He then turns to the "*On Motion,*" *Physics* V–VIII (*Physics* VII seems to interrupt the argument, and may be a survivor of an earlier stage of Aristotle's work). *Physics* V–VI give non-causal considerations that would apply equally to natural and violent motion, notably about when a motion is a single motion, about when two motions or a motion and a rest are contrary, and about the continuity of motion, place, and time; they seem to be there chiefly to supply premises for the causal argument of *Physics* VIII. *Physics* VIII, relying only on the abstract concepts of the *Physics* and not on empirical cosmology, gives an elaborate argument from the natural motions of corruptible things, first to the eternity of motion as such, then to self-moved movers (empirically, animals) and unmoved

movers (their souls), then to an eternally continuous motion (the motion of the heavens), and finally to an eternally unmoved cause outside the cosmos. This bravura display reaches beyond physics to metaphysics or theology, and Aristotle relies crucially on it in *Metaphysics* Λ, discussed below.

PSYCHOLOGY AND ZOOLOGY

Narrative physics typically ends with the production of plants and of animals, including humans, before turning to human societies and conventions, which Aristotle treats under practical philosophy. Aristotle devotes a large part of his writing to animals, complemented by Theophrastus's studies of plants. But his program of denarrativizing physics, and of physical teleology and physical definition, entail major differences from earlier accounts of animals; Aristotle also integrates an account of soul into his study of animals, though not as fully as we might expect. The crucial methodological texts are *Parts of Animals* Book I, which serves as an introduction to the zoological works generally, and *De anima* I,1.

A narrative physicist believes he has accounted for the elephant once he has taken the cosmogonic narrative far enough to generate the first elephant. This means that he puts his "Generation of Animals" before his "Parts of Animals." (The parts of an elephant are simply whatever results from the prior generative process: Thus the Hippocratic *On Fleshes* gives a cosmogonic account of the generation of each tissue, with no regard to how the tissues are arranged in the animal, what animal they are parts of, or what functions they have.) Such a physicist will also be more concerned with the hard problem of the "spontaneous" (nonsexual) generation of the first elephant than with the easier problem of how to get more elephants out of the elephants there already are.

For Aristotle, however, the whole cosmos with all its species has existed from eternity, so there is no reason to believe elephants were ever generated spontaneously. We never see elephants generated spontaneously anymore, and while nature might have had greater generative force at some past time when it was undergoing more violent motions (see *Physical Problems* X,13), when we understand the extremely complex arrangement of parts required for a functioning, self-sustaining elephant, it becomes incredible that the crude natural powers of the pre-elephantine era could have combined to produce it. (Plato might say that God intervened to produce the first elephant, but Aristotle thinks that God acted no more or less then than now, and that his activity simply sustains the regular activities of natures. While Aristotle is now notorious for defending spontaneous generation, he actually allows less scope to spontaneous generation than any other Greek philosopher, restricting it to lower life-forms.)

Thus when Aristotle studies the generation of living things, he is chiefly studying their generation out of already existing members of the same species. And we can understand this process not in narrative sequence but only backward, starting from the arrangement of parts that the generative process is for the sake of producing; so methodologically the *Parts of Animals* must precede the *Generation of Animals*. And the parts themselves must be explained teleologically, not through the generative process but through their function in the animal. Different species of animals will have different strategies for survival and reproduction, thus different characteristic activities, requiring different characteristic parts; the scientist will define each animal species by describing its characteristic parts, defining each part as an "organ" or instrument of some activity and deducing its shape and matter from its function.

Aristotle describes the parts, and the whole animal, as organs of the *soul*, that is, instruments through which the soul's powers are exercised. Because they cannot be defined without reference to the soul, it belongs to the natural scientist to study soul, or at least those powers of soul that are exercised through bodily instruments—all powers except, possibly, intellect (*nous*). Aristotle is trying here both to reform physics by making it include the soul, and also to make the study of soul scientific by bringing it under physics. However, he also makes the study of soul *further* from physics as usually conceived, by denying that the soul is moved, either in moving the body or in sensing and thinking. In *De anima* I he says that earlier philosophers have approached the soul either from its capacity to originate motion in the body, concluding that it is a self-moving source of motion; or from its ability to represent all things, concluding that it is composed of the elementary constituents of all knowable objects; or from its "bodilessness," identifying it either with fire or air or with something entirely incorporeal.

The *Timaeus* combines all of these approaches but, Aristotle thinks, in a mistaken way, representing the soul as a magical quasi-body interwoven with visible bodies, moved in the same way that bodies are, and moving bodies and being moved by them in the same way that bodies move each other. In *De anima* II, Aristotle instead defines the soul by its relation to its *energeiai*, the activities it carries out through the body. Soul is the *dunamis* (power, potentiality, capacity) for these *energeiai*, or it is that

which, added to a potentially living thing (a seed or embryo), makes it an actually living thing, where to be an actually living thing is to have the potentiality to carry out an appropriate range of the vital activities (nourishment, growth, reproduction, sensation, memory, imagination, desire, locomotion, intellection). In Aristotle's formula, soul is "the first actuality [*entelecheia*] of a potentially living body," the second actuality being the vital activities; soul stands to these activities as a *hexis* of science stands to the exercise of that science in contemplation, or as a productive art stands to its exercise in production.

Aristotle spells out his definition by saying that soul is "the first actuality of a natural organic body." Modern connotations of "organic" are misleading here: an organic body is an *instrumental* body, as is, for example, a hammer; the living body is the instrument of the soul as the hammer is an instrument of the art of carpentry. But the hammer is an *artificial* organic body, while the living body is a *natural* one, meaning (by the definition of the *Physics*) that it has an internal principle of motion and rest. So while the art of carpentry moves the hammer from outside (by inhabiting the body of the carpenter), the soul is a *nature* moving the body in a quasi-artistic way from inside, in producing and maintaining its natural instrument (nutrition, growth, reproduction) and in further using that instrument (sensation and the higher activities). The arts give us a model for how the soul can move its body without itself being moved (unlike a body pushing or pulling another body): though the carpenter's hand is moved when he moves the hammer, his art of carpentry is not. The arts also give a model for the cognitive powers, since an art contains the "formula," the definition or perhaps recipe, of its objects, without containing their matter; and arts can recognize individual objects through cognitive instruments (the art of measuring might use scales), as well as moving them through instruments of action.

The vegetative powers (powers shared even by plants) and the sensitive powers (powers shared by irrational animals) are "not without" their appropriate bodily instruments, as snubness is "not without" nose. So souls of plants and irrational animals cannot exist when separated from their bodies. The question whether any soul can so exist, and thus whether any soul is immortal (besides the souls of the heavens, which have immortal bodies), depends on whether all psychic powers are similarly dependent on bodily instruments. Sensation is not without its instruments, and imagination is not without sensation, so these are inseparable.

Some passages in *De anima* III suggest that intellection is not without imagination, so that it too is inseparable; other passages suggest that a special kind of intellection, of special matterless objects, is separable. (Fragments of Aristotle's "exoteric" works also argue that soul is immortal; perhaps Aristotle changed his mind from these early texts to the *De anima*, perhaps the texts can be reconciled, or perhaps the "exoteric" texts should be regarded as a popular approximation to a more precise truth.) *De anima* III,5 says that "the passive *nous* is corruptible," and that only the active or productive *nous* is immortal. But what is this productive *nous* and what does it do? Since it is eternally and essentially intellectually cognizing, it seems that it must not be a part of the human soul, but rather a separate immaterial divine thing that acts on the "passive *nous*" in the soul. This recalls Platonic texts on *nous* (here best translated as "reason" or "rationality") as a separately existing virtue in which souls participate, the *nous* apparently personified as the divine craftsman of the *Timaeus*. Aristotle rejects all other separately existing virtues, because they are "not without" the irrational soul and the conditions of the body, but he has no reason to reject this one; and he too in *Metaphysics* Λ will identify such a *nous* with a world-governing divine *archê*.

For Aristotle, we can fully understand soul only by understanding its specific powers, their activities, and the objects and instruments of those activities; the *De anima* gives a general abstract account, which is filled in by the *Parva naturalia*, which treats of the actions and passions "common to soul and body"—and almost all the soul's actions and passions are in common with the body—and by the accounts of the instruments and activities of different animal species in the zoological works. But the neat sequence of "psychological works" (*De anima* and *Parva naturalia*) followed by "zoological" or "biological" works (the *History*, *Parts*, *Movement*, *Progression*, and *Generation of Animals*), as presented in Bekker and other modern editions, is probably an illusion. The texts themselves frequently refer to what has preceded or what will follow, but they seem to indicate two different sequences. Some texts, especially the *Parts* and *Generation of Animals*, imply a sequence in which the *Parts* would lead immediately into the *Generation* (both presupposing the *History*, as giving the facts for which they will supply the causes); the *De anima* and *Parva naturalia* would be a separate sequence, if anything more likely to come after than before (Aristotle refers to a lost part of the *Parva naturalia*, on the principles of health and disease, as the end point of natural philosophy).

But other texts imply a different order. Call "*Parva naturalia* Group I" the treatises connected with sensation, the *On Sensation*, *On Memory*, *On Sleep*, *On Dreams*, and *On Divination in Sleep*; "*Parva naturalia* Group II" would be the *On Length and Shortness of Life*, *On Youth, Old Age, Life, Death and Respiration*, and the lost treatise on health. There are many indications for a sequence *Parts of Animals*, *Progression of Animals*, *De anima*, *Parva naturalia* Group I, *Motion of Animals*, *Generation of Animals*, *Parva naturalia* Group II, and perhaps a treatise on plants. It seems most likely that Aristotle began with the *Parts-Generation* sequence, and later inserted the other texts between the *Parts* and *Generation*, treating reproduction, like sensation and breathing, as an activity involving soul as well as body. No evidence supports putting the *De anima* before the *Parts of Animals*; one option is to regard biology as beginning with the body, turning to the soul, and then exploring how they act together.

METAPHYSICS

Sophia as an intellectual virtue—"*epistêmê* and *nous* of what is most noble by nature"—had been discussed in the *Ethics*. In the *Metaphysics*, Aristotle tries to provide a new discipline to bring us to this virtue, because he thinks that the existing disciplines with a claim to yield theoretical wisdom—physics, mathematics, and dialectic—are insufficient. The awkward title, literally "The [books or things] after the physical [books or things]," first attested in Nicolaus of Damascus (1st century CE), reflects the difficulty of fitting the treatise into the standard scheme of disciplines: it belongs to theoretical philosophy, and draws on physics, but does not belong to physics, because the divine things it considers (unlike the heavens, also divine) exist separately from matter and motion.

The unity of the treatise is problematic. It is clear that Aristotle intended to write a long treatise on *sophia*, and that most of the books of the *Metaphysics* were intended as materials for such a treatise. But it is also clear (from almost verbatim duplication between A9 and M4–5, verbatim duplication between the latter part of K and parts of the *Physics*, looser duplication between the former part of K and ΒΓΕ, and the coexistence of two books called alpha [now distinguished as A and α]) that Aristotle never finished the treatise to his satisfaction. Perhaps he would have discarded some parts of the *Metaphysics*, and perhaps some were never intended for the treatise; and there are grounds for suspecting that K is a student's reworking of Aristotle's lectures. In what follows, it will be assumed that all the books except α and K were intended to belong to the treatise, but many scholars have doubted this for Δ and (less plausibly) Λ. (There is nothing to support the view, popular among nonspecialists, that the *Metaphysics* consists of fourteen independent books assembled by later Peripatetic editors; there are many forward and backward references between the books, including Δ and Λ.)

Aristotle says different things in different parts of the *Metaphysics* about the object of wisdom (or "first philosophy," as he says when distinguishing it from physics; once he calls it "theology"). Jaeger took these as evidence of different chronological strata: Aristotle would first have conceived the project of wisdom as searching for divine substances to replace the Platonic Forms, then reconceived it as a general study of being. But usually, and rightly, Aristotle's descriptions of wisdom are thought to be compatible. They are best taken as part of a developing strategy in the *Metaphysics* to narrow down and finally to acquire *sophia*.

It is perhaps most often thought that Aristotle aims at a universal science; that this project faces a difficulty, because "being" is said in different ways of things in different categories; that Aristotle proposes to solve this by discovering things that *are* in the primary way (these things, whatever they are, will be called substances, and once we understand their mode of being, we can understand the derivative modes of being of other things); that there are different and sometimes conflicting criteria for something to *be* in the primary way; that forms meet these different criteria better than matter or matter-form composites, but that the forms of corruptible things do so only imperfectly (because they are not separable except by reason); and that Aristotle therefore turns to divine forms (forms existing separately from matter), which will allow us to understand the derivative modes of being of other forms, other substances, and non-substances. This would explain why Aristotle can say that wisdom is about being, that it is about substance, and that it is about divine things.

However, the *Metaphysics* does not actually follow this program, and Aristotle nowhere calls divine things "forms," and nowhere says that they are beings or substances in any stronger sense than ordinary form-matter composites are (still less does he use them to understand the inferior modes of being of other things). Instead, Aristotle begins with an ethical characterization of wisdom, infers that wisdom will be a science of the *archai* (the "principles," or first of all things) and of first causes, then specifies these as causes of *being*, then reaches an account of divine things as *archai* and first causes of being, not as instances of a special sense of being. Theol-

ogy is not a means to ontology; rather, ontology is a means to theology, or more precisely to "archeology" (knowledge of the *archai* might still count as wisdom even if there were nothing divine to know).

Metaphysics A begins by characterizing wisdom as the kind of knowledge intrinsically most worth having, setting aside practical consequences; Aristotle then argues that this is knowledge of the *archai*, and that these *archai* will be first causes of all things. Indeed, all philosophers who believe in theoretical wisdom claim knowledge of some *archai*; for pre-Socratic physicists, these are whatever existed from eternity before the ordered world arose out of them; for Platonic dialecticians, the Forms, especially maximally universal forms like being and unity; for Pythagorizing mathematicians, the one and the two or the infinite. We cannot directly observe any of these claimed *archai*, but must infer them as causes of more manifest things. Aristotle asks how each philosopher uses his *archai* as causes—that is, how the things he posits at the beginning of his account function in explaining the things he describes as arising later.

The best earlier philosophers, Anaxagoras and Empedocles and Plato, agree that among the *archai* is a Good and cause of goodness to the world. But, Aristotle claims, Anaxagoras and Empedocles cite only material and efficient causes (using *nous* or Love, their good *archai*, as efficient causes), and Plato cites only material and formal causes (using the one, his good *archê*, as a formal cause). Aristotle's main point is not that earlier philosophers have been discovering the four causes of his *Physics*, but that no one has yet used the Good as a *final* cause, thus no one has made it a cause whose *goodness* is explanatory. Aristotle thus motivates a new search for *archai* which will lead, in Λ, to a good *archê* as a final cause. He thus hopes to vindicate a key aspiration of Platonism, which Plato had undermined in his lecture on the Good by reinterpreting the Good as mathematical unity. Aristotle's rival Speusippus had concluded that the *archê* is One but not good; Aristotle makes the opposite decision, to discard the mathematics and save goodness. (Aristotle gives detailed objections against Academic accounts of Forms and numbers and their *archai* in *Metaphysics* MN.)

Metaphysics B raises a series of *aporiai*, some about how the science of *archai* should proceed, some about the *archai* themselves, some about what things exist "by themselves" or as substances. If some *X* (a genus or a number, or being or unity) is not a substance, but is merely an attribute of some other underlying nature, then *X* is posterior to that nature and cannot be among the *archai* that wisdom seeks. Now while we know that the *archai* will be first causes, this does not tell us how to find them, since there are different kinds of causes, and different effects we might seek to explain.

Metaphysics Γ proposes to find the highest causes as causes of the most universal effects: "there is a science of being, inasmuch as it is being, and its *per se* attributes"—a science that knows the causes to all things of the facts that they *are*, that they are each *one*, are severally *many*, and so on. It is sufficient to study the causes of being to *substances*, since the being of accidents is dependent on that of substances. (Γ argues that this science will also give explanatory understanding of the principles of noncontradiction and excluded middle.)

Metaphysics Δ distinguishes different senses of "*archê*," "cause," "one," "being," and other terms necessary for the investigation. Δ7 argues that "being" is said in several ways: being in different senses will have different kinds of cause, and confusion will result if we look for causes of being without drawing the necessary distinctions.

Metaphysics EZHΘ investigate causes of being in these different senses. E1 sets out the program of looking for the *archai* as causes of being, and specifically for *archai* which will be eternally unmoved and exist separately (not as attributes of something else); physics fails to reach unmoved *archai*, and mathematics fails to reach separately existing *archai*, and a new discipline of first philosophy or "theology" is needed. This might be dialectic, if Plato were right that the formal causes of things were eternal and separate, but he is not; E1 argues that physics, not first philosophy, understands the formal causes of natural things. E2–3 investigate the causes of "being *per accidens*," and E4 the causes of "being as truth," both concluding that no science (and certainly not wisdom) deals with these causes; the serious possibilities are "being as said of the categories," primarily of substance and derivatively of accidents, treated in ZH, and "being as actuality and potentiality," treated in Θ. *Metaphysics* I ("Iota") deals with causes of *per se* attributes of being such as unity, difference, and contrariety, arguing that these do not lead to a separately existing one-itself or first pair of contraries, but only to a unit or a contrariety within each genus.

Metaphysics Z examines the causes of being as said of substances and accidents, but quickly restricts itself to the primary case, causes of substance. Aristotle speaks interchangeably of "the cause of substance to *X*" and "the substance of *X*." The conventional translation "substance" for *ousia* (the nominalization of the verb "to be") obscures the point that the *ousia* of *X* is whatever answers the question "what is *X*?".

There are several ways we might answer this question, notably by giving the *subject* of *X* (i.e., a *Y* such that *Y* is *X*: "what is Socrates?" "this flesh and these bones"), or by giving the *essence* of *X* (i.e., a *Y* such that *X* is *Y*, or such that for *X* to be is for it to be *Y*: "what is man?" "wingless biped animal"), or by giving some part of the essence of *X*, such as a universal or genus under which *X* falls. The *ousia* of *X* taken the first way is its material cause; the *ousia* of *X* taken the second way is its formal cause. A philosopher might hope to reach *archai*, eternal and prior to sensible things, by starting with some sensible substance and asking "what is it?" repeatedly, in one of these ways, until some ultimate answer is reached: this might be, as a material cause, atoms and the void, or earth, water, air, and fire, or the "receptacle" of the *Timaeus*; or, as a formal cause, Platonic Forms, especially the genera and being and unity.

Z devotes much ingenuity to showing that these projects do not succeed; what a sensible substance *is* is most properly its form, not a separate eternal form but one that does not exist prior to the form-matter composite. Plato might argue that, if the composite *X* came to be, there must already have been a form or essence of *X* for the process of coming-to-be to aim at; Aristotle agrees, but argues that this is not a separate eternal form, but a form existing in a generator of the same species (e.g., for an animal, the father) or in the soul of the artisan who produced *X*. Aristotle also argues that if the parts of the essence mentioned in the definition of *X* (like three lines in the definition of triangle, or like the four elements in Empedocles' definition of blood as "earth, water, air, and fire in equal proportions," or like animal and biped in the definition of man) were *archai* existing in actuality prior to *X*, *X* would not be one thing but many things (thus, as a *reductio ad absurdum* of Plato, there would not be one Form, Man, but two Forms, Animal and Biped). This argument might seem to make definition impossible, since the *definientia* are supposed to be prior to the *definiendum*; but Aristotle argues that they can be definitionally prior without being capable of separate existence. There is no Animal that is just animal, prior to the differentiae of animals: an actual animal is always a biped animal or a quadruped animal or the like, and the genus "animal" is merely a potentiality for these differentiae. Likewise, actual matter is always hot or cold, wet or dry, and the common matter that underlies all sensible changes is only a potentiality, not something actually existing prior to all sensible things. *Metaphysics* ZH thus give rules for definition, with implications for understanding the relations between genus and differentia, universal and particular, form and matter; but the *archai* of these definitions are not the eternal, separately existing first things sought by wisdom (whether pre-Socratic physics or Platonic dialectic or Aristotelian first philosophy); prior in definition but not in separate existence, they are objects of Aristotelian physics.

Metaphysics Θ examines causes of being as actuality and as potentiality. A power or potentiality (*dunamis*), whether an active power to produce *X* or a passive power to undergo or become *X*, is a cause of *X*'s existing potentially (*dunamei*). Most of the *archai* of the physicists would be potentialities or potential causes. Thus the "seeds" in Anaxagoras's precosmic mixture *can become* plants and animals and their functional parts; Anaxagoras's *nous*, or the demiurge of the *Timaeus*, prior to the cosmos, *can act* to produce order, but are not yet doing so. But such causes explain only the potential existence of the cosmos, and give no sufficient reason why the active *archê* should begin to act on the passive *archê*. That the effect exists *actually* (*energeiâ[i]*) requires an *activity* (*energeia*) or an actual cause ("housebuilder" is a potential efficient cause, "housebuilder housebuilding" an actual efficient cause). Aristotle tries, both to extract general concepts of *dunamis* and *energeia*, and to argue that *energeia* is prior to *dunamis*: seeds are not prior to mature living things (since a seed exists dependently on a previous mature member of the species), and the *archai* in the strict sense, the first of all things, are not *dunameis* or potential causes, but *energeiai* or actual causes. Thus against (say) Anaxagoras's conception of the *archai* as temporally and narratively prior to the cosmos, the *archai* must from all eternity have been acting to produce the cosmos, so the cosmos too must have existed from eternity.

Metaphysics Λ pulls together the threads of ZHΘ and draws conclusions for what causal chains lead up from changing sensible things to separate eternal *archai*. There is no single separately existing matter of all changeable things, nor a single form even for all things in the same species. While the form of a natural composite substance does not exist before the composite, its generator, a previous mature member of the same species, does exist before; but this chain of efficient causes goes back *ad infinitum*, without leading to a separate eternal *archê*. But Aristotle argues (drawing on *Physics* VIII) that the eternal continuance and approximate periodicity of sublunar generation require a further cause: not simply the sublunar generators, but something eternal and perfectly regular—namely, the rotations of the heavens—that sets the

precise time lengths that sublunar cycles aim to approximate. Especially the daily and yearly motions of the sun, yielding the cycle of the seasons, serve to regulate cycles of generation.

Furthermore, these eternally unchanging motions require eternally unchanging substances as their efficient causes. Aristotle accepts Anaxagoras's and Plato's description of the mover of at least the first motion, the daily rotation of the whole heaven, as *nous*. But, using the premise that the *archê* must be pure *energeia*, he critically examines earlier philosophers' descriptions of *nous*'s causality, rejecting anything that would imply *dunamis* or changeability. Notably, *nous* must always move the heavens in the same way, and it must not move them in such a way as to be reciprocally affected by them. "Purifying" the Anaxagorean and Platonic accounts in this way, Aristotle concludes that *nous* moves the heaven only by causing the heaven to know and desire it: *Nous* is an efficient cause only by being a final cause. (When the heaven desires its mover, what does it desire to do, and how does this explain its motion? It should, like humans, order its actions toward contemplating God; and presumably its eternally unchanging motion is the best available imitation of God's eternally unchanging *energeia*.)

The premise that this *nous* is pure *energeia* also allows Aristotle (drawing on *De anima* III on "active *nous*") to "purify" earlier accounts of how it thinks and what it thinks. It is not a cognitive ability that could be applied to many objects, but a single eternal act of cognition of a single eternal object—the best object, or "good-itself." If this object were outside *nous*, *nous* would depend on something external to complete its act of cognition, and would of its own essence be merely potential *nous*; Aristotle concludes that *nous* is identical with the good-itself that it contemplates. This result allows Aristotle to fulfill various promises about wisdom from *Metaphysics* A, showing how the good is a cause, *qua* good (as a final cause), and not just as an efficient or formal cause. He vindicates Plato's promise of a single first good *archê* against Speusippus's criticism, but only by giving up on talk of the One, and finding a causal route up to the *archê* from physics rather than from mathematics.

INFLUENCE

Aristotle's immediate influence came through the Peripatetic school, led after Aristotle's death by his student Theophrastus; other important students were Eudemus, Aristoxenus, and Dicaearchus. The Peripatetic Demetrius of Phalerum governed Athens, backed by Macedonian power, from 317 to 307 BCE. But the Peripatetic school declined after this (perhaps in part because of the reaction against Demetrius at Athens); for most of the Hellenistic period (323–30 BCE), the dominant schools were the Academics, Stoics, and Epicureans. Peripatetics turn up more at Alexandria than at Athens, and more in biography and literary scholarship than in scientific philosophy.

However, there was a revival of Aristotle, as well as of Plato, in the first centuries BCE–CE, and attention turned from the "exoteric" texts to the "acroamatic" texts as offering a systematic teaching in all philosophical disciplines. Teaching would take place, by oral exposition of the texts of Aristotle, in whatever was thought to be the correct sequence, accompanied by refutations of more recent schools and solutions to new *aporiai*. This oral teaching is reflected in written commentaries, of which the most important are those of Alexander of Aphrodisias (c. 200 CE); we also have paraphrases of several Aristotelian treatises by Themistius (fourth century CE).

Besides the Peripatetics, late ancient Platonists make use of Aristotelian concepts in trying to extract a systematically teachable technical philosophy out of Plato's dialogues, and often wind up incorporating Aristotelian doctrines. In particular, they share Aristotle's concern to avoid inappropriately assimilating soul or *nous* or other divine realities to lower things, notably by attributing to them extension or change or *dunamis*. (Aristotle is here seen as an ally especially against Stoic corporealism.) Where Plato describes intelligible forms as conspecific with sensible things, the demiurge as acting after a period of inactivity, or thinking as a circular motion of soul, the Platonists use Aristotle's arguments, together with a principle of charity, to argue that Plato must have intended these comparisons to sensible things to be understood allegorically; they say either that Aristotle's criticisms of Plato are misunderstandings, or that Aristotle intended to criticize not Plato, but only disciples who took Plato's metaphors literally. At the same time, they reinterpret Platonic forms as a plurality of sciences in God, weakening Aristotle's insistence on the singleness of God's knowledge. Thus fifth- and sixth-century commentaries both on Plato and on Aristotle harmonize the two authors to some extent. This is taken furthest by Simplicius; by contrast, John Philoponus, for Christian reasons, defends some specifically Platonic doctrines, including creation in time, against Aristotle.

After the mid-sixth century, the teaching of philosophy collapses, beyond introductions to philosophy and lectures on Porphyry's *Introduction* (*Isagoge*) to the *Organon* and Aristotle's *Categories*, *De interpretatione*, and the elementary part of the *Prior Analytics*. The recovery of the rest of Aristotle's work as a basis for systematic philosophical instruction occurred first in the Islamic world; key figures are al-Fārābī and Avicenna (Ibn Sīnā). These thinkers accept the guidance of late ancient commentators, and thus share to some extent in the harmonizing of Aristotle and Plato; by contrast, Averroes (Ibn Rushd) champions Alexander of Aphrodisias against harmonistic commentators, and tries to defend "scientific" Aristotelian philosophy against what he sees as unscientific Platonist contamination. Versions of Avicennian philosophy are taught in Iran to the present day.

In Greece, Michael Psellus revived late ancient Platonic-Aristotelian philosophy, which remained vital until the fall of the Byzantine Empire. In the Latin West, knowledge of Aristotelian philosophy survived in the translations and commentaries on the *Organon* by Boethius; Abelard and his twelfth century contemporaries began a renaissance of Aristotelian philosophy based almost wholly on the logic. Around 1200, translations of the whole Aristotelian corpus became available (first from Arabic, along with Arabic commentaries and treatises, then directly from Greek), and a systematic teaching of Aristotelian philosophy ("scholasticism") became the basis for university instruction, and a prerequisite for the study of Christian theology; different solutions were proposed to the conflicts between Aristotle and biblical revelation (key figures are Thomas Aquinas, John Duns Scotus, and William of Ockham).

While scholastic Aristotelianism flourished in the Renaissance (key figures are Pietro Pomponazzi in Italy, Francisco Suárez in Spain and Portugal), there is also much Renaissance polemic against Aristotle. The charge may be that he is irreligious (he makes the causal connection of God with the world too thin, and seems to deny providence over the sublunar world and the immortality of human souls; he certainly denies miracles such as creation in time or resurrection); that his claims of scientific knowledge cannot overcome skeptical challenges; or that his explanations are tautologous, multiplying words without practical consequences either technical or moral. These criticisms are taken up by the mechanical philosophers of the seventeenth century (notably Descartes, Gassendi, Hobbes), who aim to give a systematic replacement for Aristotelian physics, doing without forms or qualities superadded to matter (except possibly the human rational soul), abolishing the distinction between heavenly and earthly matter, and deriving phenomena from a natural tendency of bodies to persist in rectilinear motion, and from the results of collisions between bodies. Since the successes of this new physics (culminating in Newton), no systematic revival of Aristotelian philosophy has been possible; likewise, modern mathematical logic has permanently eclipsed Aristotelian syllogistic. Kantians often accuse Aristotle of uncritical realism in epistemology.

But Aristotle continues to be central in philosophical education, and to be a source of inspiration, chiefly in practical philosophy, metaphysics, and the philosophy of mind. Often philosophers have turned back to Aristotle for a description of phenomena of ordinary experience and language, careful attention to which (it is claimed) would undermine the appeal of oversimple modern reductionist theories (utilitarianism, associationism, materialism), without positing anything radically beyond ordinary experience (categorical imperatives of pure reason, intellectual intuitions, incorporeal substances). Neo-Aristotelians prefer intensional to extensional distinctions: a soul is not a substance other than the living body, but is the body itself *qua* living and not merely *qua* body. And these intensional differences are discerned, not by intellectual intuition, or by Kantian *a priori* synthesis, but by ordinary perception disciplined to recognize things *as* what they are. (Thus the practical rationality required for virtue is neither means-end reasoning nor a Kantian faculty of rules, but a sensitivity to morally salient features of situations.) Aristotle is seen as seeking a "middle way," for example, between pre-Socratic materialism and Platonic metaphysics, that could be a model for modern philosophers. Such interpretations tend to understate the commitments that Aristotle shares with Plato, and his internal criticisms and refinements of the Platonic philosophical (and theological) project; the use of Aristotle for inspiration in contemporary philosophy should be balanced by an awareness of the risks of removing Aristotle from his context and reducing him to what seems usable for current philosophical problems.

See also Anaxagoras of Clazomenae; Ancient Aesthetics; Aristotelianism; Logic, History of: Ancient Logic; Neoplatonism; Plato; Theophrastus.

Bibliography

There is an excellent annotated bibliography in Jonathan Barnes, ed., *The Cambridge Companion to Aristotle* (Cambridge, U.K.: Cambridge University Press, 1995); there are also comprehensive bibliographies in Hellmut Flashar, ed., *Grundriss der Geschichte der Philosophie* ("Ueberweg"), *Die Philosophie der Antike*, Vol. 3, pp. 407–492 (Basel: Schwabe, 2004), and, for the *Metaphysics*, in Robero Radice and Richard Davies, *Aristotle's Metaphysics: Annotated*

Bibliography of the Twentieth-Century Literature (Leiden: Brill, 1997). Only primary sources, indispensable scholarly tools, and starting points for entering into scholarly discussions, including some particularly important publications that have appeared since Barnes, will be listed here. All the transmitted works and many fragments are translated in Jonathan Barnes, ed., *The Complete Works of Aristotle*, 2 vols. (Princeton, NJ: Princeton University Press, 1984); the translations are not uniform, and some are better than others. Many works have been well translated, with useful notes, in the Clarendon Aristotle series from Oxford University Press (thus far: *Categories and De interpretatione*, translated by J. L. Ackrill, 1962; *Posterior Analytics*, translated by Jonathan Barnes, 2nd ed., 1994; *Topics* I and VIII, translated by Robin Smith, 1994; *Physics* I–II, translated by William Charlton, 1980; *Physics* III–IV, translated by Edward Hussey, 1983; *Physics* VIII, translated by Daniel Graham, 1999; *De generatione et corruptione*, translated by C. J. F. Williams, 1982; *De anima* II–III, translated by D. W. Hamlyn, 2nd ed., 1993; *De partibus animalium* I and *De generatione animalium* I, translated by David Balme, 2nd ed., 1993; *De partibus animalium*, translated by James Lennox, 2001; *Metaphysics* B, translated by Arthur Madigan, 1999; *Metaphysics* ΓΔE, translated by Christopher Kirwan, 2nd ed., 1993; *Metaphysics* ZH, translated by David Bostock, 1994; *Metaphysics* MN, translated by Julia Annas, 1977; *Eudemian Ethics* I, II, and VIII, translated by Michael Woods, 2nd ed., 1992; *Nicomachean Ethics* VIII–IX, translated by Michael Pakaluk, 1998; *Politics* I–II, translated by Trevor Saunders, 1996; *Politics* III–IV, translated by Richard Robinson, 1962; *Politics* V–VI, translated by David Keyt, 1999; *Politics* VII–VIII, translated by Richard Kraut, 1997). The editions and translations in the Loeb Classical Library are usually less good. Hackett has published good annotated translations of the *Prior Analytics* (translated by Robin Smith, 1989), *Nicomachean Ethics* (translated by Terence Irwin, 1985), *Politics* (translated by C. D. C. Reeve, 1998), and *Poetics* (translated by Richard Janko, 1987), all Indianapolis, IN: Hackett. Also useful is George Kennedy's annotated translation of the *Rhetoric*, *On Rhetoric: A Theory of Civic Discourse*, New York: Oxford University Press, 1991. Many works are also available in the Budé series, from Editions Les Belles Lettres, Paris: Presses Universitaires de France, Greek text with facing French translation, and in the Oxford Classical Texts (Greek only, many of them edited by W. D. Ross) and the Teubner series (Greek text only; previously Leipzig: Teubner or Stuttgart: Teubner, now Munich: Saur). W. D. Ross's *editiones maiores* (Greek text with English introduction and commentary) of the *Metaphysics* (2 vols., 1924), *Physics* (1946), *Analytics* (1955), *De anima* (1961) and *Parva naturalia* (1955), and Harold Joachim's *editio maior* of the *On Generation and Corruption* (1922), all Oxford: Oxford University Press, are extremely useful. However, on the *Metaphysics* and *De anima*, it is advisable to compare Werner Jaeger's Oxford Classical Text (1957) and Antonio Jannone and Edmond Barbotin's Budé (1966), respectively; with Joachim compare Marwan Rashed's Budé (2005). The Budé texts are generally more prudent and reliable than Ross's; some have very useful introduction and notes, others are only sparsely annotated. For the *Categories*, compare the Oxford Classical Text of Lorenzo Minio-Paluello (also including the *De interpretatione*, 1949) with Richard Bodéüs' Budé (2001), which puts "[*Catégories*]" in brackets on the title page and then switches to *Les Avant les Lieux* ("The Before the Topics"). Jacques Brunschwig's Budé *Topiques* (Vol. 1, 1967; Vol. 2, forthcoming) particularly stands out. For the *Rhetoric*, the standard text is Rudolfus Kassel, *Aristotelis Ars rhetorica*, Berlin: De Gruyter, 1976. For the *De motu animalium*, see Martha Nussbaum, *Aristotle's De motu animalium*, Princeton, NJ: Princeton University Press, 1978; for the *Historia animalium*, see David Balme, *Aristotle: Historia animalium*, Cambridge, U.K.: Cambridge University Press (Vol. 1, 2002; Vol. 2, forthcoming). For the fragmentary *Protrepticus*, compare Ingemar Düring, *Aristotle's Protrepticus: An Attempt at Reconstruction*, Göteborg: Acta Universitatis Gothoburgensis, 1961 (including an edition of the fragments with English translation) with the forthcoming translation by Douglas Hutchinson and Monte Johnson (expected Indianapolis: Hackett). For the fragmentary *On Ideas*, see Gail Fine, *On Ideas*, Oxford: Oxford University Press, 1993, and Walter Leszl, *Il "De ideis" di Aristotele e la teoria platonica delle idee*, Florence: Olschki, 1975 (including a critical edition by Dieter Harlfinger). An extremely useful tool for studying concepts across the Aristotelian corpus (unfortunately presupposing Latin as well as Greek, and using a reference system that takes some getting used to) is Hermann Bonitz, *Index Aristotelicus*, Berlin: Reimer, 1870.

The most important secondary literature on Aristotle remains the late ancient commentaries collected in *Commentaria in Aristotelem Graeca*, 23 vols., Berlin: Reimer, 1882–1909, especially those of Alexander of Aphrodisias and Simplicius. Many of these volumes have been translated into English in the series *Ancient Commentators on Aristotle*, edited by Richard Sorabji, London: Duckworth, and Ithaca, NY: Cornell University Press. On the Greek commentators see Richard Sorabji, ed., *Aristotle Transformed*, London: Duckworth, 1990, and Richard Sorabji, ed., *Philoponus and the Rejection of Aristotelian Science*, London: Duckworth, 1987. For the earlier Greek reception of Aristotle, see Paul Moraux, *Der Aristotelismus bei den Griechen*, 2 vols., Berlin: De Gruyter, 1973–1984. For the availability of medieval Arabic and Latin commentaries on Aristotle, see the articles on, especially, al-Fārābī, Averroes (Ibn Rushd), and Thomas Aquinas.

Articles on Aristotle, edited by Jonathan Barnes, Malcolm Schofield, and Richard Sorabji, 4 vols., London: Duckworth, 1975–1979, is a good cross section of modern scholarship up to its time, with non-English articles translated. There are also excellent collections of articles, usually on a particular work of Aristotle, often arranged so as to form a collective commentary, in the proceedings of the triennial Symposia Aristotelica, including thus far: Ingemar Düring and G. E. L. Owen, eds., *Aristotle and Plato in Mid-Fourth Century*, Göteborg: Acta Universitatis Gothoburgensis, 1960; Suzanne Mansion, ed., *Aristote et les problèmes de méthode*, Louvain: Publications universitaires, 1961; G. E. L. Owen, ed., *Aristotle on Dialectic: The Topics*, Oxford: Oxford University Press, 1968; Ingemar Düring, ed., *Naturphilosophie bei Aristoteles und Theophrast*, Heidelberg: Stiehm, 1969; Paul Moraux, ed., *Untersuchungen zur Eudemischen Ethik*, Berlin: De Gruyter, 1971; Pierre Aubenque, ed., *Etudes sur la Métaphysique d'Aristote*, Paris:

Vrin, 1979; G. E. R. Lloyd and G. E. L. Owen, eds., *Aristotle on Mind and the Senses*, Cambridge, U.K.: Cambridge University Press, 1978; Enrico Berti, ed., *Aristotle on Science: the Posterior Analytics*, Padova: Editrice Antenore, 1981; Paul Moraux and Jürgen Wiesner, eds., *Zweifelhaftes im Corpus Aristotelicum*, Berlin: De Gruyter, 1983; Andreas Graeser, ed., *Mathematics and Metaphysics in Aristotle* (= *Metaphysics* MN), Bern: Haupt, 1987; Günther Patzig, ed., *Aristoteles' Politik*, Göttingen, 1990; David Furley and Alexander Nehamas, eds., *Philosophical Aspects of Aristotle's Rhetoric*, Princeton, NJ: Princeton University Press, 1994; Michael Frede and David Charles, eds., *Aristotle's Metaphysics Lambda*, Oxford: Oxford University Press, 2000; and Frans de Haas and Jaap Mansfeld, eds., *Aristotle's On Generation and Corruption I*, Oxford: Oxford University Press, 2004.

The classic attempt to write Aristotle's intellectual biography is Werner Jaeger, *Aristotle: Fundamentals of the History of his Development*, translated by Richard Robinson, Oxford: Oxford University Press, second edition, 1948. For a survey of the *status quaestionis* on Aristotle's development, see William Wians, ed., *Aristotle's Philosophical Development*, Lanham, MD: Rowman and Littlefield, 1996. The ancient sources on Aristotle's life are collected by Ingemar Düring, *Aristotle in the Ancient Biographical Tradition*, Göteborg: Acta Universitatis Gothoburgensis, 1957. On the titles and histories of Aristotle's writings, see Paul Moraux, *Les listes anciennes des ouvrages d'Aristote*, Louvain: Editions universitaires de Louvain, 1951; on stories about the rediscovery of the texts and on the possible role of Andronicus of Rhodes in editing and ordering Aristotle's texts, compare the treatment of Paul Moraux, *Der Aristotelismus bei den Griechen* (cited above) with that of Jonathan Barnes, "Roman Aristotle," in *Philosophia Togata* II, edited by Jonathan Barnes and Miriam Griffin, pp. 1–69, Oxford: Oxford University Press, 1997; and see Stephen Menn, "The Editors of the *Metaphysics*," in *Phronesis* 40, no. 2 (July 1995): 202–208. On Aristotle's treatment of his predecessors, the classic (but highly controversial) works are Harold Cherniss, *Aristotle's Criticism of Presocratic Philosophy*, Baltimore, MD: Johns Hopkins Press, 1935, and *Aristotle's Criticism of Plato and the Academy*, Vol. 1 (Vol. 2 was never published), Baltimore, MD: Johns Hopkins Press, 1944.

On the *Nicomachean Ethics*, starting points are R. A. Gauthier and J. Y. Jolif, *L'Ethique à Nicomaque*, introduction, traduction et commentaire, 2 vols. in 3, Louvain: Publications universitaires de Louvain, 1958–1959; W. F. R. Hardie, *Aristotle's Ethical Theory*, 2nd ed., Oxford: Oxford University Press, 1980; Sarah Broadie, *Ethics with Aristotle*, Oxford: Oxford University Press, 1991; and Amélie Rorty, ed., *Essays on Aristotle's Ethics*, Berkeley: University of California Press, 1980. On the relation between the different ethical works, starting points are (besides Michael Woods's Clarendon *Eudemian Ethics* I, II, and VIII) Anthony Kenny, *The Aristotelian Ethics*, Oxford: Oxford University Press, 1978 (although Kenny's claim that the *Nicomachean Ethics* is earlier than the *Eudemian* is idiosyncratic); and John Cooper, "The *Magna Moralia* and Aristotle's Moral Philosophy," in his *Reason and Emotion*, pp. 195–211, Princeton, NJ: Princeton University Press, 1999. On the *Politics*, besides the introductory volume and the essays and notes of the classic W. L. Newman, *The Politics of Aristotle*, 4 vols., Oxford: Oxford University Press, 1887–1902, see now Richard Kraut, *Aristotle: Political Philosophy*, Oxford: Oxford University Press, 2002; and, for the context of political debate, Josiah Ober, *Political Dissent in Democratic Athens*, Princeton, NJ: Princeton University Press, 1998. On the *Constitution of the Athenians*, see P. J. Rhodes, *A Commentary on Aristotle's Athênaiôn Politeia*, Oxford: Oxford University Press, 1981; and John Keaney, *The Composition of Aristotle's Athênaiôn Politeia*, New York: Oxford University Press, 1992.

On dialectic, besides Robin Smith's Clarendon *Topics* I and VIII, the introduction to Jacques Brunschwig's Budé *Topiques*, and G. E. L. Owen's Symposium Aristotelicum volume, all cited above, see the introduction to Eleonore Stump, *Boethius De differentiis topicis*, Ithaca, NY: Cornell University Press, 1978; and Robin Smith, "Aristotle on the Uses of Dialectic," in *Synthese* 96 (1993): 335–358. The majority of English-language literature on dialectic is really about the use of pre-reflective intuitions or ordinary language in argument, and has little to do with what Aristotle calls dialectic. On the *Categories*, see Michael Frede, "Title, Unity and Authenticity of the Aristotelian *Categories*," in his *Essays on Ancient Philosophy*, pp. 11–28, Oxford: Oxford University Press, 1987; and Stephen Menn, "Metaphysics, Dialectic, and the Categories," in *Revue de Métaphysique et de Morale* 100, no. 3 (July–September 1995): 311–337; on the *On Interpretation*, see C. W. A. Whittaker, *Aristotle's De interpretatione: Contradiction and Dialectic*, Oxford: Oxford University Press, 1996; on the *Sophistical Refutations*, see Louis-André Dorion, Aristote, *Les refutations sophistiques, introduction, traduction et commentaire*, Paris: Vrin, 1995. On Aristotle's syllogistic, besides Robin Smith's introduction to his Hackett *Prior Analytics*, see Jan Łukasiewicz, *Aristotle's Syllogistic*, 2nd ed., Oxford: Oxford University Press, 1957; Günther Patzig, *Aristotle's Theory of the Syllogism*, Dordrecht: Reidel, 1968; and Paul Thom, *The Syllogism*, Munich: Philosophia, 1981; on demonstration, see Enrico Berti's Symposium Aristotelicum volume (*Aristotle on Science*) and Jonathan Barnes' Clarendon *Posterior Analytics*. On the *Rhetoric*, the Symposium Aristotelicum volume (D. Furley and A. Nehamas, *Aristotle's Rhetoric*) gives one approach, and George Kennedy's translation (mentioned above), and his *The Art of Persuasion in Greece*, Princeton, NJ: Princeton University Press, 1963, give another. On the *Poetics*, good starting points are Richard Janko's Hackett and Amélie Rorty, ed., *Essays on Aristotle's Poetics*, Princeton, NJ: Princeton University Press, 1982.

On physics and cosmology, there is unfortunately not much to recommend, beyond the *editiones maiores* and Symposium Aristotelicum volumes noted above; still useful is Friedrich Solmsen, *Aristotle's System of the Physical World*, Ithaca, NY: Cornell University Press, 1960; on Aristotle on causality see Richard Sorabji, *Necessity, Cause and Blame*, London: Duckworth, 1980; and for the issues of Greek cosmology, see David Furley, *The Greek Cosmologists*, Vol. 1, Cambridge, U.K.: Cambridge University Press, 1987 (the promised Vol. 2 has not yet appeared), and his collection of articles *Cosmic Problems*, Cambridge, U.K.: Cambridge University Press, 1989. By contrast, there is a large literature on Aristotle's psychology and zoology. For orientation to the literature on the psychology, see Martha Nussbaum and Amélie Rorty, eds., *Essays on Aristotle's De anima*, 2nd ed., Oxford: Oxford

University Press, 1995; and see Stephen Menn, "Aristotle's Definition of Soul and the Programme of the *De anima*," in *Oxford Studies in Ancient Philosophy*, 22 (Summer 2002): 83–139. On Aristotle's ordering and reordering of the psychological-physiological-zoological corpus, see Marwan Rashed, "Agrégat de parties ou *vinculum substantiale*? Sur une hésitation conceptuelle et textuelle du *corpus aristotélicien*," in André Laks and Marwan Rashed, eds., *Aristote et le mouvement des animaux: dix études sur le De motu animalium*, pp. 185–202, Lille: Presses universitaires du Septentrion, 2004. On zoology, besides the translations and commentaries of Lennox, Balme, and Nussbaum, cited above, the best starting point is Alan Gotthelf and James Lennox, eds., *Philosophical Perspectives on Aristotle's Biology*, Cambridge, U.K.: Cambridge University Press, 1985.

For the *Metaphysics*, it is always helpful to compare Theophrastus's *Metaphysics*, for which see the Budé by André Laks and Glenn Most, 1993; for an English translation, see W. D. Ross and F. H. Fobes, eds., Theophrastus, *Metaphysics*, Oxford: Oxford University Press, 1929. Modern landmark studies on the *Metaphysics* are Werner Jaeger, *Studien zur Entstehungsgeschichte der aristotelischen Metaphysik*, Berlin: Weidmann, 1912; Pierre Aubenque, *Le problème de l'être chez Aristote*, Paris: Presses universitaires de France, 1966; Joseph Owens, *The Doctrine of Being in the Aristotelian Metaphysics*, Toronto: Pontifical Institute of Medieval Studies, 3rd ed., 1978; Günther Patzig, "Theology and Ontology in Aristotle's *Metaphysics*" in *Articles on Aristotle* (cited above), Vol. 3, pp. 33–49; Vianney Décarie, *L'objet de la métaphysique selon Aristote*, Paris: Vrin, 1961; Giovanni Reale, *The Concept of First Philosophy and the Unity of the Metaphysics of Aristotle*, translated by John Catan, Albany: SUNY Press, 1980; Michael Frede, "The Unity of General and Special Metaphysics: Aristotle's Conception of Metaphysics," in his *Essays on Ancient Philosophy* (cited above), pp. 81–95; Michael Frede and Günther Patzig, *Aristoteles: Metaphysik Z: Text, Übersetzung, Kommentar*, Munich: Beck, 1988; and Myles Burnyeat, *A Map of Metaphysics Zeta*, Pittsburgh: Mathesis Publications, 2001.

Stephen Menn (2005)

ARITHMETIC

See *Mathematics, Foundations of; Number*

ARIUS AND ARIANISM

Arius was a controversial fourth-century Christian thinker in Alexandria, Egypt, who was condemned by the first ecumenical council at Nicaea in 325. Because most of his writings were destroyed as heretical and "Arianism" as a movement developed only after his death, historians continue to debate both the content and the purpose of his teaching. Theological debate continued for a century within Christianity, prompting a number of councils and creeds as well as a voluminous literature exploring the definition of God as Trinity, the origin of the divine Son, and the nature of salvation. From these events "Arianism" has been traditionally defined in theological polemic as a denial of the essential divinity of the Son and therefore of both the orthodox doctrines of Incarnation and Trinity.

ARIUS AND THE COUNCIL OF NICAEA

As a Christian presbyter in Alexandria, Arius claimed a connection to a famous martyr and theologian, Lucian of Antioch. Philosophically educated as well as an exegete of scripture, he criticized Bishop Alexander of Alexandria for using language of eternity and nature with regard to the generation of the Son from the Father; this defended a common shared divinity, but muddled their separate personal identities. Arius argued that the Father, defined as the creator of all existence, could not share his uncaused nature or being with the Son. To speak of a shared divine nature would compromise biblical monotheism as well as contradict the definition of the creator as unbegun by nature, therefore opposing the first principle of all existence. The Son had to be of a separate nature because he was created or generated at some point as the offspring of the Father.

Contrary to earlier theologians, Arius argued that the Son could not be eternally begotten or he would be a coexistent principle. Instead, the Son possessed divinity from his direct creation by the Father and preexistence before all creation, but this was a separate and secondary divinity. Early authors had also interpreted the title of Word from the Gospel of John or Wisdom from Proverbs to show the Son's eternal presence with the Father as a mental attribute. By contrast, Arius accepted the traditional titles, but denied the eternal presence; he also denied that the Son knew the Father apart from what knowledge the Father had bestowed upon him. The secondarily divine Son remained the revealer of the Father, the agent of creation, and the mediator of the divine will and salvation through Incarnation.

The origins and motivations of Arius's views remain controversial, and no single interpretation has yet to persuade all scholars. Only three of his documents remain, and his opponent, Athanasius, preserved fragments of his theological poem, *Thalia*. All historians emphasize his indebtedness to earlier theologians, such as Origen, who described the Son as Word, and ascribed a lesser and derivative nature to the Son. This hierarchical model echoed both the philosophy of Numenius and Philo, in which the Logos was the mediator between transcendent

reality and the material world, as well as biblical accounts of the Son's obedience to the Father. However, by contrast, Arius denied any communication or participation of essence between the Father and the Son; apophatic theology became central to his thought. This highly significant shift may well reflect changes in contemporary Platonism, such as the increased transcendence of Plotinus's thought, but the parallels are not entirely conclusive.

Arius may also be defending the theology of Lucian of Antioch, which emphasized the will of God and the agency of the Son. The emphasis on the distinct nature of the Son may have been to portray him as a moral exemplar and mediator, in line with the New Testament model of the obedient Christ in Luke; the evidence for this interpretation, however, remains contested. Finally, Arius's rejection of coexistent principles could also be linked to the growing presence of Manichees in Egypt, who taught two eternal principles of good and evil. Clearly, Arius was a creative and powerful thinker who was revising traditional categories to clarify the singularity of the Father and the mediation of the Son.

After local councils did not succeed in reconciling or suppressing the controversy, Emperor Constantine convened a council of bishops from the East and West at Nicaea in 325. The accounts of the council show the difficulty of using scriptural language that, insofar as it was metaphorical, did not solve analytical difficulties concerning causality or nature. *Homoousios*, or "of the same nature," was adopted as a definition of the relation of the Father and Son, less as a positive definition than as a term rejected by Arius and others. However, the creed was not readily adopted by the larger church, and other councils were held over the next five decades to find more acceptable language. Constantine accepted a later statement by Arius that avoided discussing the nature of the Father and Son, if affirming the priority of the Father. Arius died in 336 before being accepted back into communion with the church, perhaps by poisoning.

"ARIANISM" AFTER ARIUS

The issues of divine causality and saving knowledge raised by the Arian controversy and the Nicene definition were strenuously debated for several decades. We may best speak of these shifting alliances as "non-Nicenes" rather than use the older categories of "Arians" or "Semi-Arians" to describe all those who for various reasons rejected the authority of the creed of Nicaea. Many were content to avoid substance language or affirm a "like substance" (*homoiousios*) between the Father and the Son, maintaining a traditional hierarchy of being and action. Aetius and Eunomius, often called "Neo-Arians," were the most strenuous opponents of Nicene theology; they argued that the Father and Son must be dissimilar in nature since the divine essence was "unbegun," and insisted this description was fully revelatory of God. These varied opponents of Nicaea thinkers did not describe themselves as followers of Arius; rather, they were tagged with his condemnation by opponents, such as Athanasius and Marcellus of Ancyra, in order to discredit their theological positions.

The separation of divine nature between the Father and the Son also had implications for salvation and incarnation. The author of the Latin *Opus imperfectum* insisted that the created Son was able to suffer authentically on the cross; he criticized the Christology of the orthodox of Docetism, since they claimed only the body suffered and not the eternal Word. A series of legislative acts curtailed the activities of the non-Nicenes after the council of Constantinople in 381.

LATER ARIANISM

The Christianization of the Goths occurred during this theological turmoil, and they were baptized as "Arians." The destruction of the Visigothic library in medieval Spain erased documents that might have provided significant clues to Gothic theology. In the seventeenth century "Arianism" was embraced by a number of English theologians, including Isaac Newton and William Whiston, who questioned the logic of the Trinity and the biblical authority of creeds.

See also Christianity; Newton, Isaac; Platonism and the Platonic Tradition; Plotinus.

Bibliography

Barnes, Michel R., and Daniel H. Williams. *Arianism after Arius: Essays on the Development of the Fourth Century Trinitarian Conflicts.* Edinburgh: T. & T. Clark, 1993.

Gregg, Robert, and Dennis Groh. *Early Arianism: A View of Salvation.* New York: Fortress Press, 1981.

Hanson, Richard P. C. *The Search for the Christian Doctrine of God.* Edinburgh: T. & T. Clark, 1988.

Kopecek, Thomas. *A History of Neo-Arianism.* 2 vols. Cambridge, MA: Philadelphia Patristic Foundation, 1979.

Vaggione, Richard P. "'Arius, Heresy and Tradition' by Rowan Williams: A Review Article." *Toronto Journal of Theology* 5 (1989): 63–87.

Vaggione, Richard P. *Eunomius of Cyzicus and the Nicene Revolution.* Oxford: Oxford University Press, 2000.

Wiles, Maurice. *Archetypal Heresy: Arianism through the Centuries.* Oxford: Oxford University Press, 1996.

Williams, Daniel. *Ambrose of Milan and the End of the Nicene-Arian Conflicts.* Oxford: Oxford University Press, 1995.

Williams, Rowan. *Arius: Heresy and Tradition.* 2nd ed. Grand Rapids. MI: Wm. Erdman's, 2001.

J. Rebecca Lyman (2005)

ARKOUN, MOHAMMED
(1928–)

Mohammed Arkoun was born in Kabylia, Algeria, and spent much of his career at the Sorbonne in Paris. His early work in philosophy was in the history of Islamic philosophy, and in particular the thought of the Persian philosopher Miskawayh. Like so many modern Arab philosophers, Arkoun is part both of the Islamic world and of the secular European world, and how to reconcile those two worlds has been a continuing issue for those philosophers. It has been a continuing issue of interest to them how to reconcile these two worlds. Arkoun, on the one hand, has in general been supportive of *laïcité*, the determined secularism of France that he argues preserves the freedom of all to follow their religions. On the other hand, he has roundly criticized the ways in which the Islamic and the non-Islamic worlds have cast each other in the role of the Other. He outlines in his work how a tradition creates a world of discourse, but at the same time also cuts people off from other forms of discourse. Thus traditions, and in particular religious traditions, can be seen to have both positive and negative features. Arkoun suggests that it is not acceptable for a tradition to rule out some ways of thinking, because in order to understand the whole range of alternatives that are available, people first need to contemplate a wide range of options.

But does this not contravene the idea that a tradition establishes rules about what can and cannot be thought? Here Arkoun broadens his analysis to suggest that traditions are not pure, and so do not have fixed boundaries. Traditions need to be applied to the world of experience; in turn, experiences will affect traditions on a piecemeal basis, and followers of a tradition will have to inevitably consider their responses to those experiences and the affect they had on the tradition. This brings out the problem with traditions that see the different approaches as representing the Other, because the distinctions between the tradition and the Other are often slight and difficult to determine. It follows that a program of secularism is not in opposition to religion, but should be seen as providing space for religions, and their opposites, to flourish and think through their foundations. He also argues that Islam's renaissance in the nineteenth century is incomplete, that Muslims should radically examine the roots of their faith and establish it in line with contemporary forms of reality. If there is a theme in Arkoun's work it is the significance of history. History shows that doctrines such as Islam are never finished and complete, but continue to develop. History also shows that the antagonisms and conflicts between different ways of looking at the world are variable. An investigation of history allows people to ground their understanding of significant ideas within a particular context and thus acquire a critical understanding of them. There is a tension in this thesis—which owes much to the thought of Foucault—and the transcendent role that any religion seeks to establish for itself. Much of Arkoun's work tries to reconcile the clash between these two intellectual positions.

See also Enlightenment, Islamic; Foucault, Michel; Islamic Philosophy; Thinking; Traditionalism.

Bibliography

Arkoun, Muhammad. *Rethinking Islam: Common Questions, Uncommon Answers.* Boulder, CO: Westview Press, 1994.

Arkoun, Muhammad. *The Unthought in Contemporary Islamic Thought.* London: Saqi, 2002.

Oliver Leaman (2005)

ARMINIUS AND ARMINIANISM

Jacobus Arminius (Jacob Harmanszoon, 1560–1609), who gave his name to a variant of Reformed belief, was born in Oudewater, Holland. After his father's early death, the boy was protected in turn by a minister, who converted him to Protestantism; by Rudolphus Snel van Rooijen the mathematician; and by Pieter Bertius of Rotterdam. With Pieter Bertius Jr., later important in the great Arminian disputes, Arminius studied at Leiden under the French Protestant Lambertus Danaeus. Later Arminius studied under Theodorus Beza in Geneva, where he met Johannes Uytenbogaert (Wtenbogaert), the chief proponent of Arminian doctrines after the death of Arminius.

Soon after his ordination (1588), Arminius was called upon by the ecclesiastical court of Amsterdam to refute the arguments of the Dutch "libertine" theologian Dirck Volckertszoon Coornhert, an exercise that undermined Arminius' orthodox Calvinism. He came to doubt the deterministic doctrine of damnation, and believed that election, dependent in part on man's free will, was not arbitrary but arose from God's pity for fallen men. Arminius was consistently attacked by orthodox clergymen (notably Petrus Plancius and Franciscus Gomarus) for his alleged Pelagianism; in spite of all opposition, however, he was made professor of theology at Leiden in 1603 and thereafter exercised great influence upon the next generation of divines. He died just prior to the national schism brought about by his beliefs.

ARMINIANISM

In 1610 the Arminian clergy published their Great Remonstrance, a codification of Arminius' creed. This work dealt with five doctrinal points: It rejected the doctrine of election and predestination, both supralapsarian and sublapsarian. It rejected the idea that Christ died for the elect alone and belief in irresistible grace. It asserted belief in the sufficient power of saints, rejecting the idea that saints could fall from grace.

To the orthodox, these were Romish heresies; for eight years the battle of the pulpits raged, with Uytenbogaert, Bertius, and Hugo Grotius the great defenders of the Remonstrance. A theological question of this magnitude necessarily involved political theory and practice: the Remonstrants developed several versions of a theory by which, to protect consciences, the magistrate, rather than the Dutch Reformed Church, was given final say in matters of religion. Naturally, since such a theory favored republican administration, Arminianism gained support in the town governments and in the States-General, particularly in the figure of the pensionary of Holland, Jan van Olden Barneveldt.

In 1618 a synod was called to rule on Remonstrant doctrine, with the open support of the *stadholder*, Prince Maurice of Orange, who realized that the theological controversy might be used to curb the power of the States-General. For the hearing at Dordrecht (Dort), Arminian tenets were slightly modified by Uytenbogaert. Election was interpreted as God's grace to true believers; but this grace was not irresistible, and salvation still depended on the cooperation of the human will, which was sufficiently strong to overcome the temptations of evil. By the time the sessions began, the leading Arminian laymen had been arrested for treason: Olden Barneveldt was sentenced to be beheaded in The Hague; Grotius and Rombout Hogerbeets were imprisoned in Loevestein Castle.

The Synod was international: Representatives from Germany, Geneva, and England took part in the hearings, but the Remonstrants were barely allowed to be heard.

Their five tenets were declared inadmissible, or heretical, and orthodox Calvinism was upheld. Remonstrants were given the choice of recantation or exile.

Most chose exile—in France, Geneva, or England. Until the death of Prince Maurice in 1625, Arminianism was persecuted in Holland; but with the accession to the *stadholderate* of the tolerant Frederick Henry, Arminians began to return, particularly to the great cities of Amsterdam and Rotterdam. In 1630 a church was organized in Amsterdam, to which in 1632 an academy was attached, to train Remonstrant clergymen and the sons of Remonstrants barred from studying at the universities.

Dutch Arminianism was closely allied with advanced secular learning, both philosophical and scientific. The Remonstrant "Illustre School" (later the nucleus of the University of Amsterdam) was distinguished for its mathematical and medical, as well as its theological and philosophical, faculties. Whatever the philosophical implications of Arminius' humanistic doctrine, in the seventeenth century it was coupled with broad learning: An Arminian professor translated René Descartes's *Discourse upon Method* into Latin for the general use of the learned world; Arminian professors contributed to the periodicals of the republic of letters; and John Locke found a home among the Arminians during his exile from England.

See also Determinism and Freedom; Grotius, Hugo; Locke, John; Pelagius and Pelagianism.

Bibliography

PRIMARY SOURCES

Arminius, Jacobus. *Disputationes XXIV.* Leiden, 1609.

Arminius, Jacobus. *The Works.* Translated and edited by James Nichols, 3 vols. London, 1825–1875.

Brandt, Gerard. *The History of the Reformation and Other Ecclesiastical Transactions in the Low Countries,* 4 vols. London: Timothy Childe, 1720–1723.

Limborch, Philippus van, and Christiaan Hartsoeker. *Praestantium ac Eruditorum Virorum Epistolae Ecclesiasticae et Theologicae.* Amsterdam, 1684. Letters of Uytenbogaert, Arminius, Grotius, et al.

Triglandius, Jacobus. *Kerckelycke Geschiedenissen, Begrypende de Swaere Ende Bekommerlijke Geschillen, in de Vereenigde Nederlanden Voor-gevallen, met Derselver Beslissinge.* Leiden: Ghedruckt by A. Wyngaerden, 1650.

Uytenbogaert, Johannes van. *Kerckelycke Historie.* Rotterdam, 1647.

SECONDARY SOURCES

Colie, R. L. *Light and Enlightenment: A Study of the Cambridge Platonists and the Dutch Arminians.* Cambridge, U.K.: Cambridge University Press, 1957.

Davies, Godfrey. "Arminian versus Puritan in England, c. 1620–1650" *Huntington Library Bulletin* 5 (1934).

Harrison, A. W. *Arminianism.* London: Duckworth, 1937.

Harrison, A. W. *The Beginnings of Arminianism.* London: University of London Press, 1926.

Itterzoon, G. P. van. "Koning Jacobus I en de Synode van Dordrecht." *Nederlandsch Archief voor Kerkgeschiedenis* 24 (1932).

Nobbs, Douglas. *Theocracy and Toleration. A Study in the Disputes in Dutch Calvinism from 1600 to 1650.* Cambridge: Cambridge University Press, 1938.

Rogge, H. C. *Johannes Wtenbogaert en Zijn Tijd,* 2 vols. Amsterdam, 1874–1876.

Tideman, Johannes. *De Remonstrantie en het Remonstrantisme.* Amsterdam, 1851.

R. L. Colie (1967)

ARMSTRONG, DAVID M.
(1926–)

David Malet Armstrong was born in Melbourne, Australia. He received his first degree at the University of Sydney where John Anderson held the Challis chair of philosophy. He then completed the bachelor of philosophy at Oxford (in 1954), being one of the first of the many Australian philosophers in the 1950s and 1960s to take that degree. After a short spell at Birkbeck College, London, he accepted a position at the University of Melbourne. In 1964 he took up the Challis chair in Sydney where he stayed until his retirement in 1991.

Armstrong has made influential contributions to a remarkable range of major topics in epistemology and metaphysics, including perception, materialism, bodily sensations, belief and knowledge, laws, universals, and the metaphysics of possibility. Recurrent themes have been the need to reconcile what the philosopher says with the teachings of science, a preference for realist over instrumentalist theories, and an interest in the fundamental elements of being. A feature of his work is his ability to write about difficult issues with directness and clarity without sacrificing rigor.

Armstrong's *A Materialist Theory of the Mind* (1968) is a seminal and comprehensive presentation of the mind-brain identity theory, the view that mental states are states of the brain. Armstrong argues that for each mental state, there is a distinctive functional role. For each mental state, we can specify what it does by way of mediating between inputs, outputs, and other mental states. For example, pain is typically caused by bodily injury and typically causes behavior that tends to alleviate it; thirst is typically caused by lack of water and typically gives rise to behavior that leads to drinking water, provided there is water knowingly available to the subject. This means, Armstrong argues, that the question of the identity of a given mental state is nothing more than the question of the identity of that which plays the functional role distinctive of that state: Thirst is that which plays the role just described. It is then a question for science what state in fact plays that role, and that it will in fact be some state of the brain. Thus, Armstrong derives the mind-brain identity theory from a view about the distinctive roles played by mental states, combined with a view about what kinds of states—namely brain states—play those roles.

In the philosophy of perception he was one of the first to argue that we must move away from the tradition that thinks of perception as acquaintance with a special, mental item sometimes called a "sense datum." Instead, we should adopt an account that analyses perception as the acquisition of putative belief about our world—an account that has the signal advantage of making sense of the role of perception in our traffic with the world. Armstrong saw bodily sensations as being a special kind of perception—in the case of pain, a perception of putative damage in a part of one's body, accompanied by a desire that it cease. His work on sensations and perception may be seen as a precursor to currently much discussed representationalist accounts that analyze an experience in terms of how the experience represents things as being.

Armstrong revived interest in F. P. Ramsey's view that belief is like a map by which we steer, in opposition to approaches that think of belief as a kind of "saying to oneself." His account of knowledge is a version of reliabilism: S's true belief that P is knowledge if it is an empirically reliable sign that P.

Armstrong is a realist about universals: they exist, they are not reducible to sets of particulars (squareness is not the set of square things), and although they serve as the truth makers for predication, there is no simple one-to-one correspondence between predicates and universals. But there are no uninstantiated universals, so Armstrong is not a realist in Plato's sense. Armstrong deploys his realism about universals to deliver an account of laws of nature and of possibility. Laws are to be understood in terms of relations of nomic necessitation between universals: Roughly "Every F is G" is a fundamental law if being F necessitates being G. Armstrong's account of possibility is a combinatorial one. The various possibilities are the various combinations and recombinations of particulars (individuals) and universals that obey the right combinatorial rules (for example, combin-

ing being square with not being square does *not* deliver a possibility).

Armstrong's overall position in analytic ontology—that part of metaphysics that seeks to inventory at the most fundamental level what there is—is given in *A World of States of Affairs* (1997), where states of affairs are the basis on which accounts of properties, relations, numbers, necessity, dispositions, classes, causes, and laws are constructed.

See also Anderson, John; Being; Functionalism; Laws of Nature; Pain; Perception; Plato; Ramsey, Frank Plumpton; Realism; Reliabilism; Universals, A Historical Survey.

Bibliography

ARMSTRONG'S MAJOR WORKS

Berkeley's Theory of Vision. Melbourne: Melbourne University Press, 1960.

Perception and the Physical World. London: Routledge, 1961.

Bodily Sensations. London: Routledge, 1962.

A Materialist Theory of the Mind. London: Routledge, 1968.

Belief, Truth and Knowledge. Cambridge, U.K.: Cambridge University Press, 1973.

Universals and Scientific Realism. 2 vols. Cambridge, U.K.: Cambridge University Press, 1973.

What Is a Law of Nature? Cambridge, U.K.: Cambridge University Press, 1983.

With Norman Malcolm. *Consciousness and Causality: A Debate on the Nature of Mind.* Oxford: Basil Blackwell, 1984.

A Combinatorial Theory of Possibility. Cambridge, U.K.: Cambridge University Press, 1989.

Universals: An Opinionated Introduction. Boulder, CO: Westview Press, 1989.

A World of States of Affairs. Cambridge, U.K.: Cambridge University Press, 1997.

The Mind-Body Problem: An Opinionated Introduction. Boulder, CO: Westview Press, 1999.

Frank Jackson (1996, 2005)

ARNAULD, ANTOINE
(1612–1694)

Antoine Arnauld, a Jansenist theologian and Cartesian philosopher, was one of the most skilled philosophical and theological controversialists of the seventeenth century. His reputation was such that he was known in the early modern period as *le grand Arnauld*. Arnauld was born in Paris on February 8, 1612, the last of twenty children of Catherine Marion de Druy and the elder Antoine Arnauld. Arnauld's father served as an attorney for Queen

Catherine de Médicis, and at the beginning of the seventeenth century he successfully argued the case in the Parlement de Paris for the expulsion of the Jesuits from France. Arnauld's sister, Mère Angélique Arnauld, was installed as abbess of Port-Royal des Champs at the age of thirteen and became a prominent member of the convent. Though Arnauld initially intended to follow in his father's footsteps by becoming a lawyer, he later changed his mind and began to study theology in 1633. He received his baccalaureate in theology in 1635, and soon thereafter came under the influence of Jean Duvergier de Hauranne, the abbé de Saint-Cyran, who was then closely linked to Port-Royal. Because Saint-Cyran was also a political opponent of Cardinal Richelieu, Arnauld was prevented from receiving a doctorate from the Sorbonne during Richelieu's life. Soon after Richelieu's death, however, Arnauld received his doctorate in 1641 and became a member of the Sorbonne.

In 1641 Arnauld also wrote a critically sharp yet sympathetic set of objections to René Descartes's *Meditations*, an event that marks the start of his lifelong association with Cartesianism. In 1643 he published *De la fréquente communion*, an attack on the penitential theology of the Jesuits that earned him the enmity of members of that order. At the urging of Saint-Cyran, Arnauld also responded that same year to the criticisms of the theological account of grace and sin in the *Augustinus* (1640) by Cornelius Jansen, the bishop of Ypres, against the criticisms of Isaac Habert, a Paris theologian. In particular Arnauld insisted that Jansenius's views were in line with the criticisms in St. Augustine of the heretical Pelagian view that salvation depends on one's free will rather than on the workings of grace.

After 1648 Arnauld lived near Port-Royal as one of the solitaires associated with the convent. He was forced to go into hiding during this time because his opposition to the campaign against the *Augustinus* brought him into conflict with Cardinal Mazarin, the French first minister. This opposition also set Arnauld against the decision in Rome to condemn five propositions purportedly drawn from the *Augustinus* in 1653 and to attribute those propositions to Jansenius's text in 1656. Arnauld criticized those who refused absolution to the Duc de Liancourt because of his failure to assert that Jansenius affirmed these propositions. For his efforts, Arnauld was excluded from the Sorbonne in 1656, after a celebrated trial. In defense of Arnauld, the Port-Royal solitaire Blaise Pascal wrote a series of *Lettres provinciales* (1656–1657) attacking the moral theology of the Jesuits. In further response to the 1656 papal bull attributing the condemned propositions to the *Augustinus*, Arnauld argued that, though the pope's word is definitive with respect to the *question de droit* regarding the unacceptability of the propositions, it is not authoritative with respect to the *question de fait* concerning the presence of the propositions in Jansenius. He advocated a "respectful silence" in response to the pope's opinion on the latter question.

LATER CAREER. After 1661, when Louis XIV took sole control of the government following the death of Mazarin, considerable pressure was placed on those associated with Port-Royal to bring them into conformity with the official church rejection of Jansenism. This pressure involved the closing of the *petite écoles* at Port-Royal, but the instruction there informed two books that Arnauld coauthored with fellow Port-Royalists, the *Grammaire generale et raisonée*, which he authored with Claude Lancelot in 1660, and the *Logique ou l'art de penser*, which he authored with Pierre Nicole in 1662. Noam Chomsky (1966) emphasizes the importance of the view in the former work that there is an innate "universal grammar" responsible for language (compare Arnauld and Lancelot 1975). The latter work served as a popular Cartesian alternative to scholastic texts on logic, and indeed the University of Paris formally adopted it in 1720 for use with Descartes's *Meditations*.

In 1669 the campaign against Jansenism was brought to a temporary end by the Peace of the Church that Pope Clement IX established in concert with Louis XIV. During this temporary truce, which allowed for the respectful silence concerning the heretical nature of the *Augustinus*, Arnauld turned his attention to his work with Nicole on the three-volume *Perpétuité de la foi* (1669–1674), which attacked the Eucharistic theology of the Calvinists. In 1672 Arnauld met the German intellectual Gottfried Wilhelm Leibniz during the latter's visit to Paris, and in 1679 he met his fellow Cartesian, Nicolas Malebranche. Both of these meetings set the stage for important later exchanges on philosophical and theological matters.

In 1679 Louis XIV forced Arnauld to leave France, bringing to an end the Clementine Peace. Arnauld took up residence in the Spanish Netherlands, where he lived the rest of his life. In 1683 he composed a critique of Malebranche's *Recherche de la vérité*, which triggered a long and increasingly bitter dispute with Malebranche over issues concerning the nature of ideas and of grace and divine providence. In 1686 Arnauld began a brief but important correspondence with Leibniz on a summary of Leibniz's *Discourse on the Metaphysics and the Monadology*. This correspondence addressed issues concerning the nature of divine freedom and creation as well as the tenability of a Cartesian conception of the material world.

In 1690 Arnauld succeeded in his campaign to have certain works of Malebranche placed on the Roman *Index of Prohibited Books*. During this same time he engaged in disputes with Nicole over general grace and one's knowledge of moral truth. Arnauld was also involved in several disputes with the Jesuits in the Spanish Netherlands. He died in Brussels on August 8, 1694, and was buried in the Church of St. Catherine in that city. His heart was buried in Port-Royal, and after the destruction of the latter in 1710 it was moved to the Church de Palaiseau.

FAITH AND FREEDOM

Arnauld was fond of the Augustinian slogan that "what we know, we owe to reason; what we believe, to authority" (1964–1967, p. 38:94). This slogan reflects Arnauld's own view that philosophy and theology are distinct disciplines with their own standards. Philosophical questions are to be resolved through the use of reason, and he took issue with scholastics who attempted to settle such questions by means of an appeal to the authority of Aristotle. In contrast, Arnauld insisted that questions pertaining to religious belief, and in particular to the content of the Catholic faith, are to be decided by an appeal to the authority of Scripture, interpreted in light of the church tradition. Here, he took issue with Jesuit critics who attempted to use their Aristotelian philosophy to explicate the mysteries of the faith.

Arnauld did recognize a distinction between "sacred theology" concerning Catholic doctrine and "natural theology" concerning theological truths accessible to reason. Indeed, one of the reasons he defended Cartesian philosophy so vigorously, even in the face of opposition from his fellow Port-Royalists, was that he took it to provide compelling arguments for the existence of a transcendent God and for the real distinction of the human soul from body. For Arnauld, Descartes's theistic and dualistic system complemented perfectly a theology based on the authority of Augustine.

Arnauld began by defending the particular version of Augustinian theology in Jansen's work. In particular, he was concerned to argue with Jansenius for the view that meritorious action is the result of grace that is "efficacious in itself," that is, that brings about the relevant action. This position conflicted with the Jesuit insistence on one's ability to freely reject the divine grace that is offered. In the last decade of his life, however, Arnauld rejected Jansen's account of grace in terms of a prevenient state of delight that causes the meritorious action. He claimed to find in St. Thomas Aquinas the alternative view that efficacious grace is simply the meritorious act of will that God produces in each person. His final position did not bring him closer to the Jesuits, however, and is in fact similar to the view of the Dominican Domingo Bañez, which the Jesuits had opposed, that God causally determines free human action.

EUCHARISTIC THEOLOGY

The other theological issue of most importance to Arnauld concerned the Catholic doctrine of the Eucharist. According to the Council of Trent there is in this sacrament a "marvelous and unique change of the whole substance of the bread into the body [of Christ], and of the whole substance of the wine into the blood, while only the appearances [*species*] of bread and wine remain." Arnauld and Nicole composed *Perpétuité de la foi*, in which they defended the Tridentine doctrine against the Calvinist position that Christ has a merely "spiritual presence" in this sacrament. In 1680 Arnauld wrote in defense of the compatibility of Descartes's view with Catholic teachings on the Eucharist to silence critics, including some Port-Royalists, who charged that Cartesianism has heretical implications. His "Examen" considers a text in which it is argued that since Christ's body must be present in the sacrament without its extension, it cannot be the case, as the Cartesian doctrine, that extension constitutes the essence of body. Arnauld countered that Catholic teaching requires only that Christ's body is present without the impenetrability by means of which it is enclosed in a place.

Though Arnauld thought of himself primarily as a theologian, his writings on both human freedom and the Eucharist reflect his ability to grapple with the subtle philosophical issues pertaining to theological topics. This facility with philosophical discourse is revealed as well in his interaction with three of his great philosophical contemporaries: Descartes, Malebranche, and Leibniz.

ARNAULD AND RENÉ DESCARTES

MEDITATIONS AND CORRESPONDENCE. Arnauld's set of objections to the *Meditations* prompted Descartes to comment that he could not have asked for a more perceptive critic. Arnauld was particularly sympathetic to those aspects of the *Meditations* that he took to be in line with Augustinian views of the soul and God. The first two sections of Arnauld's Fourth Objections are in fact devoted to these two topics. He offered penetrating objections in these sections to Descartes's arguments for mind-body distinctness and for the existence of God, as well as mentioning difficulties concerning Descartes's denial of the souls of nonhuman animals, his discussion of the "material falsity" of sensations, and the circularity of his defense of the truth of clear and distinct perceptions. Still, Arnauld also emphasized the Augustinian nature of Descartes's insistence that the intellect is distinct from and epistemically superior to the senses, and he showed himself to be sympathetic throughout to the central conclusions of the *Meditations*.

In a final section, "Points Which May Cause Difficulty to Theologians," Arnauld insisted that Descartes's principle that proper assent is governed by clear and distinct perception be restricted to intellectual matters to allow for the Augustinian conclusion that one's religious beliefs are grounded in one's acceptance of religious authority. He further noted that what is "likely to give the greatest offense to theologians" is the appearance that Descartes's view that bodily modes are inseparable from the substance they modify conflicts with the Catholic doctrine that in the Eucharist the sensible species of the bread and wine remain without inhering in any substance.

In 1648 Arnauld renewed contact with Descartes while in hiding because of the political controversies in France involving Jansenism. Arnauld asked for clarification on several issues pertaining to the nature of memory, the relation of particular thoughts to the attribute of thought, the duration of mind as a thinking thing, and Descartes's argument for the impossibility of a vacuum. In responding to questions concerning this argument, Descartes cited his view that all truths depend on God's omnipotence in warning against the claim that God cannot create a vacuum. Neither in this correspondence nor in his later exchanges with Malebranche and Leibniz, where this view was broached, did Arnauld take a firm position on Descartes's doctrine that all truths depend on God's will. However, Arnauld did profess himself satisfied with Descartes's responses to his questions concerning the nature of mind and its relation to body, concluding that "what you wrote concerning the distinction between the mind and the body seems to me very clear, evident, and divinely inspired" (1964–1967, vol. 5, p. 186).

QUALIFICATIONS OF CARTESIANISM. In his correspondence with Descartes Arnauld professed satisfaction with Descartes's solution to the problem concerning the Eucharist raised in the Fourth Objections. However, he mentioned as a further difficulty that Descartes's identification of the extension of a body with its quantity seems to conflict with the Catholic teaching that Christ's body is present in this sacrament without local extension. Descartes did not respond to this difficulty, even though in earlier correspondence with the Jesuit Denis Mesland he had proposed that the physical presence of Christ in the Eucharist is explained by the union of His soul with the matter of the elements. This proposal provided the basis for a Cartesian account of the Eucharist in the *Considérations sur l'état present* (1671) by the French Benedictine Robert Desgabets. Louis XIV's confessor declared the *Considérations* to be heretical, and Louis had his archbishop of Paris condemn it. When called before the archbishop, Arnauld and Nicole denounced the work, in part to disassociate it from their own account of the Eucharist in their writings against the Calvinists. In his later 1680 "Examen" Arnauld did offer his own version of a Cartesian account of the Eucharist. However, his version deviates from Descartes's own views insofar as it requires the possibility of the existence of the extension of Christ's body apart from the quantity by means of which it occupies a place.

Arnauld also departed from Descartes's views on human freedom. Although he approved of the account that Descartes provided in the Fourth Meditation, he was less happy with later correspondence in which Descartes attempted to accommodate the Jesuit position that free action involves an indifference that explains the power of the agent to act otherwise. Indeed, in response to Desgabets's claim that Descartes is "exceedingly enlightened in matters of religion," Arnauld responded that Descartes's "letters are full of Pelagianism and, outside of the points which he was convinced by his philosophy—like the existence of God and the immortality of the soul—all that can be said of him to his greatest advantage is that he always seemed to submit himself to the Church" (1964–1967, vol. 1, p. 671). Therefore, Arnauld's theological commitments placed clear constraints on what he could accept from Descartes's own writings.

ARNAULD AND NICOLAS MALEBRANCHE

THE *SEARCH* AND *IDEAS*. During the early 1670s Arnauld was on friendly terms with his younger Cartesian colleague, Malebranche. He also had an initially positive view of Malebranche's masterwork, the *Search after Truth* (first published 1674–1675). After seeing an initial draft of Malebranche's *Treatise on Nature and Grace* (1680), however, Arnauld had a more negative view. In a meeting with Malebranche in 1679, just before he left France for good, Arnauld took exception to the claim in that work that though God wills that all be saved, his wisdom requires that he distribute grace by means of a "general will" that allows for the salvation of only a few. Arnauld objected that this emphasis on the role of the general will is a novelty that is out of line with the view, deriving from the work of the church fathers, that God exhibits a "particular providence" in distributing grace to those whom he has predestined for salvation.

After Malebranche decided to publish his *Treatise* in 1680, Arnauld decided to go public with his criticisms of Malebranche. The public debate began with the publication in 1683 of Arnauld's *On True and False Ideas*, and it lasted until Arnauld's death in 1694. During his lifetime Arnauld published eight critiques of Malebranche and Malebranche published seven responses. A further text from Arnauld was published after his death, and Malebranche published three further responses to Arnauld, with the last appearing in 1709. The debate ranged over several topics, the most well known being the nature of ideas, but included as well the relation of "intelligible extension" to God, the relation of pleasure to happiness, the nature of causation, miracles, the efficacy of grace, divine providence, and divine freedom.

The issue of ideas is prominent at the start of the debate, for Arnauld's *On True and False Ideas* focuses on the doctrine in the *Search after Truth* that "we see all things in God," and more specifically, that one perceives bodies by means of ideas that exist in the divine intellect. For Arnauld, such a doctrine has the "bizarre" consequence that "we see God when we see bodies, the sun, a horse, or a tree" (1964–1967, p. 38:236). Still, Arnauld objected not only to the placement of ideas of material objects in God but also, and more basically, to the reification of the ideas. As an alternative to Malebranche's claim that the ideas one perceives are "representative beings" distinct from one's perceptions, he offered the position, which he claimed to find in Descartes's Third Meditation, that such ideas are merely the "objective reality" of perceptions, that internal feature of the perceptions in virtue of which they represent particular objects. Malebranche sometimes offered a different reading of this text, on which the objective reality of an idea is something distinct from the perception as a modification of mind. However, he typically appealed not to Descartes but to the view, which he claimed to find in Augustine, that "archetypes" in the divine intellect serve as the principle of one's knowledge of objects. In response, Arnauld insisted that it was never Augustine's intention to hold that one apprehends features of God's essence in perceiving objects.

GOD AND GENERAL WILL. The debate over the nature of ideas held the attention of the early modern intellectual community, with philosophers as diverse as John Locke, Leibniz, Pierre Bayle, and Pierre-Sylvain Regis offering commentaries on it. Indeed, Arnauld's friend, Nicole, claimed that the preoccupation with the topic of ideas served to divert attention from more important theological issues. Even so, most of the exchanges between Arnauld and Malebranche concerned just such issues. As discussed earlier, Arnauld's initial concerns with Malebranche's system derived from the claim in Malebranche that God distributes grace by means of His "general will." But Arnauld also objected that the stress on the generality of God's action undermined the belief in miraculous exceptions to the natural order. Most fundamentally, Arnauld was worried that the introduction of Malebranche's impersonal "God of the philosophers" would displace the "God of Abraham, Isaac, and Jacob," a God who takes a personal interest in the welfare of His creatures. Arnauld held that the latter sort of God governs by means of particular volitions, even in the case where He acts in accord with general laws.

Arnauld further protested against the suggestion in Malebranche that God cannot act to correct certain deficiencies in creation since He is constrained to act by means of His general will. For Arnauld, such a suggestion involves an unacceptable limitation of God's freedom. On this point Arnauld showed some sympathy for considerations that led Descartes to affirm that God is not constrained by the eternal truths since they derive from his free will. Even so, he never did explicitly affirm this doctrine in his exchange with Malebranche. One can speculate that Arnauld was reluctant to endorse this philosophical position due to his uncertainty about its implications for theology. This would at least be in keeping with his concern, evident in his long debate with Malebranche, to purify theology of various novelties deriving from philosophy.

FREEDOM AND CAUSATION. Arnauld's lifelong preoccupation with theological issues involving Jansenism is reflected in his objections to the view in Malebranche that meritorious action involves one's free and undetermined "consent" to the promptings of divine grace. Arnauld commented that he did not think that "Pelagius ever said anything more pelagian" (1964–1967, p. 37:648f). Though Arnauld later retracted his original endorsement of the view in Jansenius that this consent is determined by a psychological state of delight deriving from grace, he consistently held that such consent must be determined by God's action. It is interesting, however, that Arnauld at the same time took exception to the occasionalist position in Malebranche that God is the only real cause and that creatures serve merely as inefficacious "occasional causes" for the exercise of divine power. Since Arnauld held that mind is "more noble than" body, and since he accepted the Augustinian dictum that the less noble cannot act on the more noble, he allowed that bodily events can be only occasional causes of changes in mental states. He apparently saw no difficulty in allowing for the action of bodies on each other or the action of mind on body.

ARNAULD AND GOTTFRIED WILHELM LEIBNIZ

FATALISM AND ACTUALISM. On February 11, 1686, in the midst of Arnauld's polemical exchanges with Malebranche, Leibniz sent a request to the Landgrave Ernst von Hessen-Rheinfels to pass along to Arnauld "a short discourse" on "questions of grace, the concourse of God and creatures, the nature of miracles, the cause of sin, the origin of evil, the immortality of the soul, ideas, etc." (Mason 1967, p. 3). This discourse was simply a list of the titles of the thirty-seven articles of what became Leibniz's *Discourse on Metaphysics*. Arnauld engaged somewhat reluctantly with Leibniz on the content of some of these articles. In the end the two exchanged through Hessen-Rheinfels some dozen letters before Arnauld, preoccupied with other matters, failed to respond to Leibniz's letter to him of October 9, 1687. Leibniz attempted to reengage the correspondence in 1688 and 1690 letters to Arnauld, but without success.

In his initial response to Leibniz, Arnauld took exception to the claim in the title to article thirteen of Leibniz's discourse that "since the individual concept of each person contains once for all everything that will ever happen to him, one sees in it the a priori proofs or reasons for the truth of each event, or why the event has occurred rather than another," even though such truths "are nevertheless contingent, being based on the freewill of God and creatures" (Mason 1967, p. 5). He held that this claim is "shocking" since it seems to imply that everything that happens is obliged to do so "through a more than fatal necessity" (p. 9). In particular, God would have no choice, having decided to create Adam, to create all the features of the world that Adam actually inhabits.

After Leibniz bitterly rejected the charge of fatalism and some further letters were exchanged, Arnauld withdrew his charge in a letter of September 28, 1686. His willingness to do so was prompted by Leibniz's insistence that certain truths that are present in the individual concept of a person are present there only contingently. Even

so, Arnauld mentioned in this letter that he still had qualms about Leibniz's conception of God as "having chosen the universe amongst an infinite number of other possible universes which he saw but did not wish to create." A hint concerning the source of these qualms is provided by Arnauld's insistence in an earlier letter that God's omnipotence, being a "pure act," does "not permit the existence in it of any possibility" (Mason 1967, p. 31f). On Arnauld's view here, possibilities pertain only to the substances that God has freely created. On the basis of such a view, one commentator claims to find in Arnauld an "actualism" that contrasts with a "possibilism" in Leibniz that allows for possibilities founded in nothing external to the divine intellect (Nelson 1993). A further development of this sort of actualism may have led Arnauld to endorse some version of Descartes's doctrine of the creation of the eternal truths. As in the case of his debate with Malebranche, however, Arnauld failed in his correspondence with Leibniz to take any explicit stand on this doctrine.

CONCOMITANCE AND CARTESIANISM. In contrast to his treatment of Leibniz's critique of the eternal truths doctrine, Arnauld did engage both Leibniz's "hypothesis of concomitance or agreement between substances" and his claim that the reality of material objects depends on their possession of a "substantial form." Arnauld urged that the hypothesis of concomitance is not distinct in the end from the occasionalist position that God brings about the harmony among various substances by means of an eternal act of will. Moreover, he objected to Leibniz's claim that the soul expresses everything in its body on the Cartesian grounds that the soul must have some thought or knowledge to express anything. Since the soul has no more thought or knowledge "of the movements of lymph in the lymphatic vessels than of the movements of Saturn's satellites" (Mason 1967, p. 132), it cannot intelligibly be said to express this aspect of its body. Arnauld's Cartesianism is also evident in his response to Leibniz's position that to be substantial, material objects must have a unity conferred on them by an immaterial and indivisible substantial form. Assuming the Cartesian identification of matter with extension, Arnauld held that all material objects are mere composites and that their unity derives not from Leibniz's substantial form but from the functional interrelation of their parts.

In the note to Hessen-Rheinfels accompanying his final letter to Leibniz, Arnauld expressed the opinion that it would be "preferable" if Leibniz, a lifelong Protestant, "gave up, at least for a time, this sort of speculation, and applied himself to the greatest business he can have, the choice of the true religion" (Mason 1967, p. 138). This opinion indicates Arnauld's own preference for theology over philosophical speculation. Even so, his philosophically rich exchanges with Descartes, Malebranche, and Leibniz provide reason for philosophers to be grateful that he did not give up philosophical speculation entirely in the interests of furthering acceptance of the Catholic faith.

See also Aristotle; Augustine, St.; Augustinianism; Bayle, Pierre; Cartesianism; Descartes, René; Desgabets, Robert; Jansenism; Leibniz, Gottfried Wilhelm; Locke, John; Logic, History of; Malebranche, Nicolas; Nicole, Pierre; Pascal, Blaise; Pelagius and Pelagianism; Thomas Aquinas, St.

Bibliography

Arnauld, Antoine, and Claude Lancelot. *The Port-Royal Grammar: General and Rational Grammar*. Translated and edited by Jacques Rieux and Bernard E. Rollin. The Hague: Mouton, 1975.

Arnauld, Antoine, and Pierre Nicole. *Logic, or, The Art of Thinking*. 5th ed. Translated by Jill Vance Buroker. New York: Cambridge University Press, 1996.

WORKS BY ARNAULD

Oeuvres de Messire Arnauld. 42 vols. Brussels: Culture et Civilisation, 1964–1967.

On True and False Ideas, New Objections of Descartes' Meditations and Descartes' Replies. Translated by Elmar J. Kremer. Lewiston, NY: Mellen Press, 1990.

Textes philosophiques. Translated by Denis Moreau. Paris: Presses Universitaires de France, 2001.

WORKS ON ARNAULD

"Antoine Arnauld (1612–1694)." *Philosophe, Écrivain, Théologien, Chroniques de Port-Royal* (Paris) 44 (1995).

Chomsky, Noam. *Cartesian Linguistics: A Chapter in the History of Rationalist Thought*. New York: Harper and Row, 1966.

Kilcullen, John. *Sincerity and Truth: Essays on Arnauld, Bayle, and Toleration*. New York: Oxford University Press, 1988.

Kremer, Elmar J., ed. *The Great Arnauld and Some of His Philosophical Correspondents*. Toronto: University of Toronto Press, 1994.

Kremer, Elmar J., ed. *Interpreting Arnauld*. Toronto: University of Toronto Press, 1996.

Laporte, Jean. *La doctrine de Port-Royal*. 2 vols. Paris: Presses Universitaires de France, 1923.

Mason, H. T., ed. and trans. *The Leibniz-Arnauld Correspondence*. Manchester, U.K.: Manchester University Press, 1967.

Moreau, Denis. *Deux Cartésiens, La Polemique entre Antoine Arnauld et Nicolas Malebranche*. Paris: J. Vrin, 1999.

Nadler, Steven M. *Arnauld and the Cartesian Philosophy of Ideas*. Princeton, NJ: Princeton University Press, 1989.

Ndiaye, Aloyse Raymond. *La Philosophie d'Antoine Arnauld*. Paris: J. Vrin, 1991.

Nelson, Alan. "Cartesian Actualism in the Leibniz-Arnauld Correspondence." *Canadian Journal of Philosophy* 23 (4) (1993): 675–694.

Pariente, Jean-Claude. *L'analyse du langue à Port-Royal: Six études logico-grammaticales*. Paris: Les Éditions de Minuit, 1985.

Sleigh, R. C., Jr. *Leibniz and Arnauld: A Commentary on Their Correspondence*. New Haven, CT: Yale University Press, 1990.

Yolton, John W. *Perceptual Acquaintance: From Descartes to Reid*. Minneapolis: University of Minnesota Press, 1984.

Tad M. Schmaltz (2005)

ARNOLD, MATTHEW
(1822–1888)

Matthew Arnold, the English poet and social and literary critic, was the son of Dr. Thomas Arnold, headmaster of Rugby. Matthew Arnold was educated at Winchester and Rugby and entered Balliol College, Oxford, in 1841. In 1847 he became private secretary to Lord Lansdowne, who in 1851 appointed Arnold inspector of schools, a position he held until 1886. In 1857 he was elected professor of poetry at Oxford.

As a critic, Arnold ranged over a broad spectrum from literary criticism through educational theory to politics, social thought, and religion.

Arnold's most important contribution to nineteenth-century thought was his discussion of the significance of culture as a social ideal. His related discussion of the function of criticism has been widely influential. He also contributed to the dispute over the relation between the Christian Scriptures and belief.

In *Culture and Anarchy* (London, 1869), Arnold defined "culture" as "a pursuit of our total perfection by means of getting to know, on all the matters which most concern us, the best which has been thought and said in the world; and, through this knowledge, turning a stream of fresh and free thought upon our stock notions and habits." Culture is thus a process of learning, which can refine individuals and reform societies. Arnold often attacked the kind of reforming or progressive spirit that is not governed by this humane reference. At the same time, he made it clear that the object of the learning and refining process was indeed reform. He laid great stress on the development of the individual through the right use of literature and knowledge, but the pursuit of total perfection was still the ultimate objective. He argued that culture taught men "to conceive of true human perfection as a *harmonious* process, developing all sides of our humanity; and as a *general* perfection, developing all parts of our society." Perfection, although an "*internal* condition," is nevertheless "not possible while the individual remains isolated. The individual is required, under pain of being stunted and enfeebled in his own development if he disobeys, to carry others along with him in his march towards perfection, to be continually doing all he can to enlarge and increase the volume of the human stream sweeping thitherwards."

This position illuminates some of the apparent paradoxes of Arnold's thinking. In one sense, he was clearly a liberal thinker, stressing the criticism of institutions and beliefs by thought and knowledge and placing central emphasis on the development of the individual toward a possible perfection. In other respects Arnold was a notable critic of much of the liberal thought of his time. He criticized the "stock notions" of nineteenth-century liberalism and was a particularly firm advocate of increased social intervention by the state. He criticized the common liberal conception that progress is merely mechanical and the liberals' preoccupation with material and external improvement, which not only ignored the human results of its materialist emphasis, but also failed to advance any conception of humanity toward the realization of which material progress might be a means. His criticism of the "stock notions" of industry and production as major social ends is of this character. He similarly criticized the standard conception of freedom—"a very good horse to ride, but to ride somewhere." It is the way men use freedom, not merely their abstract possession of it, that for Arnold is really important.

Most liberal thought in his time opposed the state in the name of just this kind of abstract freedom. Arnold argued that the state was simply "the representative acting-power of the nation." To deny its right to act was to deny the possibility of any general action on behalf of the nation as a whole and to reserve the power of action to particular interests and classes. In the England of his time, he distinguished three classes—the aristocracy ("Barbarians"), the middle classes ("Philistines"), and the working class (the "Populace"). Social action by any one of these interests alone merely led to the clash of men's "worst selves." This disorder, or the resultant breakdown of effective government, would be "anarchy." But there existed, within each of these classes, "persons who are mainly led, not by their class spirit, but by a general *humane* spirit, by the love of human perfection." Each member of this human "remnant," maintaining his own "best self" by the process of culture and seeking to awake in others the "best self" now obscured by the "stock notions" and habits of the group, represented the "best self" of society as a whole. It was this "best self" that the state must represent and express.

Arnold never translated these ideas into a coherent political philosophy, but his liberal critique of liberalism was of considerable historical importance. The state, he felt, had to become a "centre of authority and light"; yet it must do this through the existing struggle, or deadlock, between limited interests and classes. Arnold's arguments, at this point, were sometimes vague. In line with his definition of culture as a learning process and with his career as inspector of schools, he stressed not politics, but education. It was in education that the state most needed to intervene, and Arnold acted as a tireless propagandist for a new system of humane state education.

Arnold saw the study of literature as a principal agency of the learning process, that is, of culture. At times, his definitions of criticism and of culture were virtually identical. Criticism was the central way of learning "the *best* that is known and thought in the world." Poetry in particular offered standards for the development of the best life of man.

In the same vein, in *Literature and Dogma* (London, 1873) Arnold offered to "reassure those who feel attachment to Christianity, to the Bible, but who recognise the growing discredit befalling miracles and the supernatural." For any adequate reading of the Bible, after the effects of the Higher Criticism and the scientific controversies, the spirit of culture was indispensable. Only by this approach could the Christian ethic, and its intense expression in the Scriptures as read undogmatically, be preserved in a time of inevitable change. In particular, it was necessary to understand that "the language of the Bible is fluid, passing and literary, not rigid, fixed, and scientific"; its truth had to be verified through reading, rather than merely assumed. The Christian ethic so verified would be stronger than the dogmatic theology that had made the Bible into what it evidently was not.

See also Belief; Literature, Philosophy of; Perfection.

Bibliography

WORKS BY ARNOLD

Poetical Works. Edited by C. B. Tinker and H. F. Lowry. Oxford: Oxford University Press, 1950.

Essays in Criticism. London: Macmillan, 1865.

God and the Bible. London: Smith, Elder, 1875.

Mixed Essays. New York: Macmillan, 1879.

Passages from the Prose Writings of Matthew Arnold, Selected by the Author. London, 1880. Edited by W. E. Buckler. New York: New York University Press, 1963.

Discourses in America. London: Macmillan, 1885.

Essays in Criticism, Second Series. London: Macmillan, 1889.

WORKS ON ARNOLD

Bonnerot, Louis. *Matthew Arnold, Poète.* Paris: Didier, 1947.

Brown, E. K. *Matthew Arnold.* Toronto, 1948.

Eliot, T. S. "Matthew Arnold," in *The Use of Poetry and the Use of Criticism.* Cambridge, MA, 1932.

Trilling, Lionel. *Matthew Arnold.* New York: Norton, 1939.

Raymond Williams (1967)

AROUET, FRANÇOIS-MARIE

See *Voltaire, François-Marie Arouet de*

ART, AUTHENTICITY IN

In the main sense of the term an artwork is "authentic" if it is the artwork it is thought to be—if it has the history of production it is represented as having or gives the impression of having, if it was created where, when, how, and by whom it is supposed or appears to have been created. Thus, a work may be inauthentic in virtue of being a forgery, or a misattribution, or a replica not identified as such. A reproduction (e.g., in an art book) is inauthentic only in a weaker sense: Though not the artwork it reproduces, it does not purport to be and runs no danger of being confused with it.

The chief issue concerning the authenticity of artworks has been the extent to which a work's aesthetic properties, artistic value, and proper appreciation legitimately depend on questions of authenticity in the above sense. The issue is often framed in terms of a challenge: What is wrong with a forgery? or What privileges an original artistically?

Broadly speaking, there are two opposed views on this issue. On one view an artwork is merely a perceivable structure—for example, a constellation of colors and shapes, a set of notes, a string of words, or the like. Furthermore, this structure is the entire source of its aesthetic and artistic properties and is the only thing relevant to its appreciation and evaluation as art. Thus, anything preserving the artwork's perceivable structure, so as to be perceptually indiscernible from it, is equivalent to it artistically and even ontologically. Such a view underlies the formalism of Clive Bell and Roger Fry, the literary stance of the New Critics, and to some extent the aesthetics of Monroe Beardsley. By these lights there is nothing much wrong with a forgery—provided, of course, that it is a perfect one, not detectably different from the original.

On the other view perceivable structure is not the sole determinant of a work's aesthetic complexion or its artistic character. Rather, a work's context of origination, including the problematic from which it issues, partly determines how the work is rightly apprehended and experienced and thus its aesthetic and artistic properties. Aspects of the context or manner of creation arguably enter even into the identity of the work of art, as essential to its being the particular work it is. By these lights there is quite a lot wrong with a forgery. It differs from the original in numerous respects, both aesthetic and artistic, and as a human product—a making, an achievement, an utterance—it is of an entirely different order, however similar it appears on superficial examination.

If the second view sketched above is sound, then any artwork, *pace* Nelson Goodman, can be forged—that is, represented as having a provenance and history other than its own, though how this will be effected differs from art form to art form, especially when one crosses from particular arts (such as painting) to type arts in which structure may be notationally determined (such as music). And this is because, in all art forms, the identity of a work is partly a matter of the historical circumstances of its emergence.

Goodman famously argued, against the aesthetic equivalence of an original painting and an ostensibly perfect forgery, that the possibility of discovering a perceptual difference between the former and the latter constitutes an aesthetic difference between them. Unfortunately, this argument seems to trade on conflating an aesthetic difference and an aesthetically relevant difference between two objects. As suggested above, however, the aesthetic and artistic differences between originals and forgeries, which are ample, rest securely on quite other grounds.

AUTHENTICITY OF ARTWORK INSTANCE

In cases of multiple or type arts an instance of a work—a copy, impression, casting, performance, staging, screening, and so forth—may be denominated authentic or inauthentic insofar as it is or is not a correct or faithful instance of the work. And this, according to different accounts, is a matter of its adequately instantiating and representing the structure thought definitive of the work in question, a matter of its having the right sort of causal or intentional relations to the work in question or of being produced in a certain manner, a matter of its conveying the aesthetic or artistic properties believed crucial to the work—or some combination of these.

AUTHENTICITY OF ARTIST

Finally, authenticity is sometimes considered a predicate of the artist, describing laudatorily the artist's characteristic mode of creating or the relation between the artist and the content of the works the artist creates. An authentic artist is one thought, variously, to be sincere in expression, pure in motivation, true to self, honest about medium, rooted in a tradition, resistant to ideology yet reflective of society—or all of these. There seems to be only a passing relation between authenticity in this sense and the authenticity of work or instance canvassed above.

See also Aesthetics, History of; Aesthetics, Problems of; Art, Truth in; Art, Value in; Beardsley, Monroe; Goodman, Nelson.

Bibliography

Bailey, G. "Amateurs Imitate, Professionals Steal." *Journal of Aesthetics and Art Criticism* 47 (1989): 221–228.

Baugh, B. "Authenticity Revisited." *Journal of Aesthetics and Art Criticism* 46 (1988): 477–487.

Currie, G. *An Ontology of Art.* New York: St. Martin's Press, 1989.

Danto, A. *Transfiguration of the Commonplace.* Cambridge, MA: Harvard University Press, 1981.

Davies, S. "Authenticity in Musical Performance." *British Journal of Aesthetics* 27 (1987): 39–50.

Davies, S. "The Ontology of Musical Works and the Authenticity of Their Performances." *Noûs* 25 (1991): 21–41.

Dutton, D., ed. *The Forger's Art.* Berkeley: University of California Press, 1983.

Godlovitch, S. "Authentic Performance." *Monist* 71 (1988): 258–277.

Goodman, N. *Languages of Art,* 2nd ed. Indianapolis: Bobbs Merrill, 1976.

Goodman, N. *Of Mind and Other Matters.* Cambridge, MA: Harvard University Press, 1984. Chap. 4.

Kennick, W. E. "Art and Inauthenticity." *Journal of Aesthetics and Art Criticism* 44 (1985): 3–12.

Levinson, J. "Art, Work of." In *The Dictionary of Art.* London, 1995.

Levinson, J. *Music, Art, and Metaphysics.* Ithaca, NY: Cornell University Press, 1990.

Sagoff, M. "Historical Authenticity." *Erkenntnis* 12 (1978): 83–93.

Sagoff, M. "On Restoring and Reproducing Art." *Journal of Philosophy* 75 (1978): 453–470.

Sartwell, C. "Aesthetics of the Spurious." *British Journal of Aesthetics* 28 (1988): 360–367.

Savile, A. "The Rationale of Restoration." *Journal of Aesthetics and Art Criticism* 51 (1993): 463–474.

Thom, P. *For an Audience: A Philosophy of the Performing Arts.* Philadelphia: Temple University Press, 1993.

Walton, K. "Categories of Art." *Philosophical Review* 79 (1970): 334–367.

Wollheim, R. *Art and Its Objects,* 2nd ed. Cambridge, U.K.: Cambridge University Press, 1980.

Jerrold Levinson (1996)

ART, DEFINITIONS OF

A range of related topics are gathered together under the title "The Definition of Art." These include: (1) metaphysical questions, such as "Is there a set of necessary properties whose possession is conjointly sufficient for a candidate to qualify as an artwork?" and, if so, "What are they?"; and (2) the epistemological issue of how we go about establishing that a candidate is an artwork. Traditionally the default assumption among many philosophers has been that there are necessary and sufficient conditions for classifying things as artworks; that these conditions can be assembled into a real or essential definition of art; and that the application of the aforesaid definition provides us with the means to establish that this or that candidate is an artwork. The trick with this approach is to specify, successfully, the pertinent necessary and sufficient conditions.

Needless to say, this enterprise has turned out to be more challenging than one might have anticipated. And the difficulties encountered in successive attempts to carry off this endeavor have left some philosophers either skeptical or agnostic regarding the prospects of the metaphysical project of defining art. Instead, they have tried more modestly merely to identify the epistemological grounds for classifying candidates as artworks without resorting to real definitions.

The search for a definition of art was not something that taxed ancient philosophers like Plato and Aristotle. For Aristotle, art was skill with respect to any practice or craft. There was an art of poetry and an art of painting, but also the art of medicine, navigation, warfare, and so on. Though Plato, Aristotle, and Horace compared poetry and painting, they did not presume an overarching framework that groups certain arts (in their sense) together in the category that we now call the fine arts or beaux arts, or maybe more simply just Art with a capital A—roughly, poetry (literature), painting, sculpture, music, theater, dance, architecture, and, nowadays, photography, film, and video.

The system of the arts was not stably consolidated until the eighteenth century (Kristeller 1992). Thus, it comes as no surprise that Aristotle felt no inclination toward defining the conditions for membership in the category, though he did analyze the nature of some of the things—like tragedy—that would later be subsumed under the concept of (fine) art. For the ancients, there were arts that were tied to certain functions—quite often religious, political, or otherwise social ones—and these art forms were defined and evaluated in light of that function. For example, Aristotle maintained that the function of tragedy was to educate the emotions by eliciting the catharsis or clarification of pity and fear.

When Aristotle and Plato single out mimesis or imitation as a necessary feature of drama—both tragedy and comedy—and painting respectively, it is immensely unlikely that they were attempting to isolate the essence of art in our sense of fine art. It is more plausible to suppose that they were merely singling out a necessary condition of the relevant art forms that is particularly revelatory of the point and purpose of these practices. If one wants to understand what poetry and painting are about, or wants to know what is appropriate to expect from them, the concept of imitation is central. However, when Plato speaks of mimesis in poetry and painting, he is not offering an analysis or definition of what we mean by (fine) art or even a real or essential definition of poetry or painting. Rather, he is merely pointing to a general feature of these art forms that is especially useful to have in mind, if one hopes to comprehend them and gauge their value.

The pressure to define Art (with a capital *A*) does not arrive on the scene, until the subset of arts mentioned above are separated from the rest and treated as an exclusive confraternity. Perhaps the reason for the emergence of this grouping has to do with the rise of the bourgeoisie who, with leisure time on their hands, turned to these particular arts to fill their hours and days. But, of course, once this grouping took hold, a question arises concerning what property or properties a prospective member needs in order to join the category.

At least initially, it seems that the first gambit for answering this question was that a candidate for membership in the fine arts had, harkening back to Plato and Aristotle, to be an imitation, but, more specifically, an imitation of the beautiful in nature. This view is explicitly advanced in Abbé Charles Batteux's 1746 treatise *The Fine Arts Reduced to the Same Principle* in which the eponymous principle is none other than the imitation of beautiful nature (Beardsley 1966). For something to count as art, then, in the relevant sense of that which the eighteenth century called the fine arts or the beaux arts (and what we now simply call Art with a capital *A*), something

had to be the imitation of the beautiful, though it seems that sometimes this requirement was slackened to no more than that the art form in question had to be representational. If the art form in question was representational, then a work made in accordance with this propensity of the pertinent art form was an artwork. That is, a painting that is a picture is, all things being equal, a work of art.

This definition of art—often called the representational theory of art (Carroll 1999, Chap. 1)—was certainly ill-suited for the developments in the arts to come, for example: An abstract expressionist painting is not a representation of anything and especially not an imitation of something beautiful in nature (Carroll 1999). So the definition was fated to be incessantly accosted by counterexamples in the future. But, perhaps more to the point, the representational theory of art was not even viable in its own day.

Dance, for instance, belonged to the system of the fine arts; it had its own muse, Terpsichore. However, not all dance, even in the eighteenth century, was representational. Much dance involved no more than cadenced steps, gracefully executed. In fact, in order to legitimatize a place for dance in the newly anointed system of the arts, choreographers, like Georges Noverre, had to invent the *ballet d'action*—the ballet that told a story. But in cases like this, the definition of art as a matter of representation, in fact, functioned prescriptively rather than descriptively.

But an even greater embarrassment for the representational theory of art than dance was the emergence of absolute music—that is to say, pure orchestral music. When opera and song were the dominant forms of music, music could be counted as implicated in representation because the words that accompanied the notes referred. But once absolute music took pride of place in the order of Calliope, it became very strained to think of the imitation of nature as the essence of art status. Indeed, as absolute music came in the nineteenth century to be praised for its possession of a condition to which all the other arts aspired, it became less and less credible that imitation was a necessary condition for entry into the citadel of art. Though some swatches of Beethoven's *Pastorale* symphony are imitative, most of the rest of his purely musical oeuvre is not. If for no other reason than the ascendancy of absolute music, the representational theory or definition of art was clearly inadequate. Another approach was needed.

Consonant with the reigning artistic movement of the day, Romanticism, one alternative approach to the representational theory of art was the expression theory—the view that something is an artwork only if it is the expression of an emotion or a feeling (Carroll 1999). Variations of this view have been defended by figures such as Leo Tolstoy (Tolstoy 1996), and R. G. Collingwood (Collingwood 1938).

If the representational theory of art emphasized the representation of the outer world, the expression theory of art stressed art as the presentation of the inner world of the affective life. William Wordsworth asserted that poetry is "the spontaneous overflow of powerful feelings," and this was also thought to be applicable to the other arts. It certainly appeared to fit the absolute music that is now called Romantic. Is that not why it is called Romantic? Moreover, the expression theory seemed to resist counterexamples insofar as it might be supposed that any human artifact would unavoidably carry an expressive trace of the affects of its maker.

Nevertheless, counterexamples appeared in droves starting in the early twentieth century. One source of these counterexamples were various sorts of aleatoric art; the Dadaist Tristan Tzara composed poems by cutting out words from a newspaper, placing them in a hat, and drawing them out randomly—thus thwarting the possibility of any causal connection with what he was feeling. Related chance techniques were mobilized by the surrealists and artists like John Cage and Merce Cunningham. Another kind of counterexample to the expression theory derived from found artworks an ordinary comb presented as an artwork by the likes of Marcel Duchamp, which projects no expressive properties, let alone the trace of anything felt by Duchamp.

Nor could these counterexamples be blocked by appealing to the idea that every human product bears an emotive residue from its maker, for the preceding strategies incontrovertibly sever the emotional link between the artist and the art object. Moreover, the expression theory of art would not only be challenged by the artists of the twentieth century. The theory was undermined by certain forms of art already in existence in the heyday of Romanticism, including art that aspired simply to beauty, as in the case of decorative art, perhaps some absolute music, and art that aimed only to represent the look of the world objectively.

Defenders of the expression theory might attempt to fend off these examples by invoking the claim that there is an inevitable and manifest emotive tie between any artifact and its creator. However, not only does this appear controversial, but if it were so, then the theory would be far too broad to be a satisfactory definition of art because it would fail to differentiate an artwork from any other artifact.

Around the same time that expression theories begin to make their appearance, so, too, do two alternative accounts of art derived from Immanuel Kant's *Critique of Judgment*. These theories can respectively be called the formalist theory of art and the aesthetic theory of art (Carroll 1999). Formalism, as presented by someone such as Clive Bell (1914), maintains that something is an artwork if and only if it is designed primarily to possess a formal design (called significant form) that is worthy of contemplation for its own sake. That is, the form of the work is intended, first and foremost, to afford an aesthetic experience, (which is sometimes called an experience of disinterested pleasure pursuant to contemplating the work's design).

The aesthetic theory of art (Beardsley 1983) is like formalism except that it leaves the object of experience unspecified by making no reference to the form of the work. On this view, something is an artwork if, and only if, it is made primarily with the intention to support an appreciable amount of aesthetic experience (in other words, experience valued for its own sake). Both the formalist theory of art and the aesthetic theory of art make essential reference to intentions in order to differentiate artworks from natural scenes that might give rise to aesthetic experience. With their emphasis on experiences valued for their own sake, both these views may actually articulate the motive behind the modern category of art as a grouping of the things suitable for leisured contemplation and/or diversion.

Neither formalism nor the aesthetic theory of art provides necessary conditions for classifying candidates as artworks. For it is implausible to suppose that most religious artworks were created with the primary intention of abetting experiences valuable for their own sake. Rather, like so many other premodern artworks, they were produced to perform a function. They were created with the primary intention of advancing religious purposes. Paintings of Christ's crucifixion were intended to instill reverence; they were not meant to be occasions for intrinsically valuable experiences of painterly form. And the designs on the shields of the Sepik warriors of New Guinea were not drawn in order to engender experiences valued for their own sake, but with the instrumental aim of frightening the enemy. Nor is experience valued for its own sake a sufficient condition for art status. Games of chess may be said to promote experiences valued for their own sake, but games of chess are not artworks, not even performance artworks.

The successive failures of attempts to define art disposed many philosophers to skepticism about the very venture itself. By the mid-twentieth century, the suspicion, generally encouraged by the writings of Ludwig Wittgenstein, that art could not be defined became popular. Philosophers like Morris Weitz (1956) argued that because art making is an arena in which experimentation, innovation, and novelty are prized, the notion of defining art is incompatible with the practice of art making. For to define art in terms of necessary and sufficient conditions would putatively somehow shackle the essential openness of art to invention and creativity. Philosophers of this ilk, often called neo-Wittgensteinians, maintained that to define art was to contradict the concept of art as that which contained the permanent possibility of art to expand its horizons in new directions. Consequently, neo-Wittgensteinians rejected the metaphysical project of identifying for artworks a set of necessary conditions that were conjointly sufficient. Moreover, with respect to the epistemological question of how it is established that something is an artwork, they suggested that it was a matter of family resemblance; something A is an artwork when it resembles artwork B in some respects, artwork C in other respects, and so on for further paradigmatic artworks.

Though initially quite influential, the spell of the neo-Wittgensteinian brief began to wane by the 1970s. On the one hand, the argument that specifying the conditions according to which a candidate counted as an artwork is inconsistent with the innovative nature of art could be seen to rest on an equivocation. For even if the practice of art is always, in principle, open to innovation and, therefore, supposedly inhospitable to definition, it is not clear why this would stand in the way of defining the concept of an artwork because individual artworks are not typically open to the permanent possibility of change. It just does not follow that if art (in the sense of the practice of art) is an open concept, then art (in the sense of an individual artwork) is an open concept. Moreover, this open concept argument, as it was called, was also challenged by the appearance of definitions of art by people like Arthur Danto (1981) and especially George Dickie (1974), which, though stated in terms of necessary conditions, provided more than ample room for artistic invention, accommodating the entire gallery of works of Dada and its legacy.

Finally, the epistemological wing of neo-Wittgensteinianism also came under fire. Because it relied upon similarity to establish art status and because everything is like everything else in some respect, by means of the family resemblance method one could in fairly short order establish that any candidate is an artwork. For example, Auguste Rodin's *Gate of Hell* and an I-beam about to be shipped from a steel mill are both physical objects, metallic, shaped by human designs, weigh more than 100 pounds, over two feet long, and so on. But all these similarities and more are not enough to warrant calling the I-beam an artwork. Though it may be that in the wake of the found artwork anything can be art, it is not the case that everything *is* art. Nevertheless, the family resemblance method for classifying artworks would appear to force us to conclude that everything is art now.

A common failing of the theories of art as representation, as expression, as form, as well as the family resemblance model for identifying art is that, in each case, art status rests upon some discernible or manifest feature of the object—such as the possession of anthropomorphic or expressive properties, significant form, or similarities with antecedently acknowledged artworks. Perhaps, it was suggested, by Danto and others, that art status rested in some property of art that the eye could not descry. Duchamp's *In Advance of a Broken Arm* and an ordinary snow shovel are putatively indiscernible. Thus, a theory of art that relies on discernible features of artworks cannot hope to cut the difference between them. Rather, the property (or properties) that are constitutive of art status is something perceptually indiscernible.

For Danto (2000), like G. W. F. Hegel, the relevant feature here is *aboutness* in a double sense. Something will be an artwork, on this account, only if: (1) It is about something; and (2) its mode of presentation says something about, makes some comment upon, or advances a point of view concerning whatever it is about. However, this formula is, on the one hand, too exclusive—there are artworks that may be about nothing, but which are simply beautiful or delightful to the senses. On the other hand, Danto's theory may be too inclusive. Though Danto means it to tell us the difference between Andy Warhol's artwork *Brillo Box* and an allegedly indiscernible, though inartistic, one from Proctor and Gamble, surely the ordinary soap pad container in the grocery store meets both of the conditions of Danto's theory of art.

Like Danto, George Dickie is impressed by the thought that the defining features of art might be perceptually indiscernible. This has disposed him to look toward the context that surrounds and frames the work for clues about its status as a work of art. That is, the work does not wear its artistic status on its face; rather, its position in a social framework or institution is the source of its pedigree. This insight has motivated Dickie (1984) to develop a series of what have been referred to as institutional theories of art, the latest version of which he has christened *The Art Circle*. According to Dickie, our concept of art can be captured by five interlocking definitions:

> 1) An artist is a person who participates with understanding in the making of a work of art.

> 2) A work of art is of a kind created to be presented to an art world public.

> 3) An art world public is a set of persons the members of which are prepared in some degree to understand an object which is presented to them.

> 4) The art world is the totality of all art world systems.

> 5) An art world system is a framework for the presentation of a work of art by an artist to an art world public.

Even a cursory examination of the preceding set of definitions reveals that it is circular. One needs the concept of an art world to define what counts as a work of art but the concept of a work of art figures in the definition of an art world system, which, in turn, is an element in the definition of an art world. Dickie is aware of this circularity but claims that it is not problematic. Yet it appears to leave the crucial notion of art undefined, though a definition of art was that at which Dickie was aiming.

Dickie's framework does articulate the structure of any communicative practice with its emphasis on mutual understanding. However, what makes art the very communicative practice it is rather than some other, such as philosophy, has not been clarified by Dickie's analysis. Moreover, some, such as Jerrold Levinson, suspect that the model does not even offer a set of necessary conditions for art status because it does not allow for art made by a solitary artist for himself—for example, some Neolithic wanderer who arranges a pile of colored stones in front of his fire because they are delightful to look at as the flames illuminate them variously (Levinson 1979).

Instead of social context, Levinson locates the defining feature of art in the intention of the artist. On Levinson's view, a candidate is an artwork if, and only if, it is created by a person: (1) who has a proprietary right over the work in question; and (2) who nonpassingly intends the work for regard as a work of art (i.e., in one or more of the ways that artworks have been correctly regarded historically [Levinson 1979]). Like Danto and Dickie, Levinson deploys a non-manifest property of the work—a certain kind of intention—as the crux of his definition.

Because this intention must be linked to the history of art, Levinson titles his approach *defining art historically*.

It is not clear why Levinson feels compelled to require that artists must have a proprietary right over the work in dispute. Surely if Brancusi constructed a sculpture out of stolen materials, there would be no question that he had created a work of art, even if the ownership of the object was in question. Moreover, the second condition of Levinson's definition is also fraught with difficulties. Though it is called a historical definition, it is historically insensitive. It overlooks the possibility that some historical art regards may become obsolete. For example, appreciating the verisimilitude of a picture was an art regard for centuries, but it is arguably no longer decisive, lest many ordinary family snapshots made with the intention to be appreciated integrally and nonpassingly for their accuracy would, counterintuitively, count as artworks. Unfortunately, Levinson makes no provision for anachronistic art regards.

Like Levinson, Robert Stecker (1997) appeals to history in order to define art. He labels his view *historical functionalism*. It is a disjunctive definition of art. Stecker claims that something is an artwork if, and only if, it is in a central art form at time *t* and it is made with the intention of fulfilling functions standardly or correctly recognized for that form, or it is an artifact that achieves excellence in fulfilling one of the functions of the central art forms at *t*.

This definition seems far too inclusive. According to Pierre Bourdieu, one of the functions of our art form is to produce social capital, or status, or identity. Thus, a Cadillac convertible would be a work of art in virtue of the second disjunct in Stecker's formula. The problem here is that Stecker has not limited the functions he countenances to exclusively artistic functions, but, of course, it is not evident that he can do that readily without inviting circularity.

Historical functionalism is also too exclusive. It cannot assimilate as artworks the initial avant-garde entries of radical art movements, for these works may not belong to a central form of art and they may be designed expressly to repudiate the recognized functions of art at time *t*. Consider the cases of found objects (Duchamp), found music (Cage), and found movement (Yvonne Rainer and Steve Paxton) when they first emerged. They were not obvious examples of a central form and, in any event, they repudiated the functions correctly associated with the forms to which they were related adversarially. Yet certainly any definition of art at this late date must accommodate works such as these.

Perhaps the historical functionalist will attempt to negotiate this shortfall in the theory by saying that once art movements like Postmodern Dance are successful they become—say at time *t+1*—central forms of art with correctly recognized functions; thus, in virtue of the second disjunct of the theory, the originating works of the movement from time *t* can be reclaimed as art. Yet this gambit comes with costs because it has the avant-garde works in question only becoming artworks due to our appreciation of them long after their creators produced them. But surely a dance such as *Satisfyin' Lover* or a composition such as *4'33"* were artworks from the very moment of their inception. And it is their actual creators who imbued them with art status and not some other folks at time *t+1*.

Due to the recurring difficulty with constructing an adequate conceptual analysis of art, some contemporary philosophers are agnostic about the metaphysical prospects of discovering a set of necessary properties that are conjointly sufficient for identifying artworks. Instead they focus their energies upon articulating epistemically satisfactory methods for identifying candidates as artworks which methods are not real definitions. Berys Gaut (2000), mining Wittgenstein again for inspiration, resurrects the notion of a cluster concept, arguing that it is sufficient for classifying a candidate as an artwork that the candidate scores well against the following ten criteria:

1) It possesses positive aesthetic properties.

2) It expresses emotion.

3) It is intellectually challenging.

4) It is complex and coherent.

5) It has the capacity to express complex meanings.

6) It exhibits an individual point of view.

7) It is an original exercise of the imagination.

8) It is the product of skill.

9) It belongs to an established form of art.

10) It is made with the intention to be a work of art.

This is not a real or essential definition of art because none of these properties are necessary conditions for art status. Anything that is a work of art will have at least one of these features; a work that has more and more of these features provides us with more and more reasons to categorize it as an artwork. On this view, a cluster account of a concept is true of that concept just in case it isolates properties whose possession by the work in question necessarily counts toward its belonging to that category.

However, though Gaut provides this list of the components of the cluster concept, he does not believe that the cluster concept approach to identifying art stands or falls with his particular sketch of it. He asserts that even if problematic cases for his formulation exist, that should not lead us to distrust in general the cluster concept approach to identifying artworks.

But is Gaut's assertion here convincing? Clearly, there are problem cases with respect to his dissection of the putative cluster concept. I see no reason why a delicious meal made by a master chef to express his devotion to his beloved and to recall their life together by means of culinary references could not instantiate every component of Gaut's list save obviously (9). Indeed, since the preparation of food occasionally figures in certain theatrical works, and especially in examples of performance art, maybe a case could even be made that it satisfies (9), generously construed. It should, therefore, count as a work of art, though this is certainly at least a very controversial case and, for many, a decisive counterexample to Gaut's proposal. But if Gaut's proposal is defeated, why believe that there is some other model of the cluster concept of art that will do the job? If it is inadmissible to maintain that the definitional approach to the concept of art will succeed despite the lack of evidence so far, why should one have faith in the cluster concept approach, when the best version of it so far misses the mark?

Another non-definitional approach to answering the epistemic question of how we might establish that a candidate is an artwork is that we do so by employing historical narratives (Carroll 1993 and 2001). According to what we may call narrativism, establishing that a candidate is an artwork involves telling a certain kind of story about the work in question, namely an accurate historical narrative about the way in which the candidate came to be produced as an intelligible response to an antecedently acknowledged art-historical situation. That is, in order to corroborate the claim that something is an artwork, one standardly mobilizes a narrative explanation of how the work emerged coherently from recognized artistic modes of thinking, acting, composing, decision-making, and so forth already familiar to the practice.

Usually the pressure to establish that something is an artwork arises when there is some dispute over its art status, as frequently occurs with works of the avant-garde. The narrativist observes that these imbroglios are typically managed by recounting art historical narratives that demonstrate the connection between the disputed work and some earlier artworks whose membership in the order of art is uncontested.

If, for example, the distorted figuration of German Expressionist painting is rejected as art properly so-called on the grounds that it departs from the canons of accurate pictorial representation, the narrativist traces its lineal descent from styles of art, such as that of the medieval artist Matthias Grunewald, where distortion was a strategy for signaling the sentiment of the artist toward his subject. Even if German Expressionist art repudiated prevailing styles of realism, the narrativist argues that there is still reason to count the works in question as art because they harken back to earlier forms of art making, discharging functions, such as the expression of feelings, that are abroad, alive, and acknowledged in their contemporary art world.

One objection to narrativism is that it is circular. However, though circularity is a defect in definitions, it is not clear that it raises any problems for narratives. It is also charged that narrativism confronts the same problem that perplexed the family resemblance approach to identifying art. But this is not the case because narrativists do not merely cite similarities between earlier and later works, but also seek to establish a network of causal relations between them. It is not merely that German Expressionist paintings resemble some medieval art that supports their art status; it is also the case that German Expressionist painting was influenced and inspired by the antecedently recognized medieval art.

Insofar as the narrative approach relies upon tracing lines of descent within historically situated artistic practices, the question arises as to how the narrativist intends to identify artworks in alien traditions. A first response is: by tracing the emergence of later works in that tradition from earlier works. But how can the narrativist identify the first works in alien traditions of art—something he needs to do in order to establish the bona fide origin of subsequent artworks from genuine precedents? Here, the narrativist needs to concede that narrativism is not the only way in which artworks may be identified.

With works in alternative traditions of art making, we frequently need to fix the earliest instances of art in those practices by isolating the works that in that culture are meant to perform the same functions—such as representation, expression, symbolization, decoration, signification, and so forth—that the earliest, already recognized artworks execute in our own culture. This, of course, admits that narration is not the only means of identifying candidates as artworks; sometimes we must depend on functional considerations. Moreover, though historical narration may be sufficient for establishing that a candidate is an artwork, it is not a necessary condition for art

status, if only because with certain cases of art, notably from ancient and remote civilizations, it may not be possible to retrieve a narrative account of their provenance.

See also Art, Expression in; Art, Ontology of; Art; Representation in.

Bibliography

Beardsley, Monroe. "An Aesthetic Definition of Art." In *What Is Art?*, edited by Hugh Curtler. New York: Haven, 1983.

Beardsley, Monroe. *Aesthetics: from Classical Greece to The Present.* New York: MacMillan, 1966.

Bell, Clive. *Art.* London: Chatto and Windus, 1914.

Carroll, Noël. *Beyond Aesthetics.* Cambridge, MA: Cambridge University Press, 2001.

Carroll, Noël. "Historical Narratives and The Philosophy of Art." *Journal of Aesthetics and Art Criticism* 51 (1993): 313–326.

Carroll, Noël. *Philosophy of Art: A Contemporary Introduction.* London: Routledge, 1999.

Collingwood, R.G. *Principles of Art.* Oxford: Clarendon Press, 1938.

Danto, Arthur. "Art and Meaning." In *Theories of Art Today*, edited by Noël Carroll. Madison: University of Wisconsin Press, 2000.

Danto, Arthur. *The Transfiguration of The Commonplace.* Cambridge, MA: Harvard University Press, 1981.

Davies, Stephen. *Definitions of Art.* Ithaca, NY: Cornell University Press, 1991.

Dickie, George. *Art and The Aesthetic.* Ithaca, NY: Cornell University Press, 1974.

Dickie, George. *The Art Circle.* New York: Havens Press, 1984.

Gaut, Berys. "Art as a Cluster Concept." *Theories of Art Today*, edited by Noël Carroll. Madison: University of Wisconsin Press, 2000.

Kristeller, Paul Oskar. "The Modern System of The Arts." In *Essays on the History of Aesthetics*, edited by Peter Kivy. Rochester, NY: University of Rochester Press, 1992.

Levinson, Jerrold. "Defining Art Historically." *British Journal of Aesthetics* 19 (1979): 232–250.

Stecker, Robert. *Artworks.* University Park, PA: Pennsylvania University Press, 1997.

Tolstoy, Leo. *What Is Art?*. Translated by Almyer Maude. Indianapolis, In.: Hackett, 1996.

Weitz, Morris. "The Role of Theory in Aesthetics." *Journal of Aesthetics and Art Criticism* 15 (1956): 27–35.

Noël Carroll (2005)

ART, EXPRESSION IN

Art is an expressive business, few would deny, but this assertion has meant quite different things to the large number of thinkers who have contemplated the concept of aesthetic expression over the centuries. Certainly, the fact that art has the power to evoke potent emotions has been noticed since ancient times. Thus Plato, although perhaps more centrally concerned with the imitative or mimetic dimensions of art, worried famously about the power of poetry and tragedy to subvert the control of reason by the arousal of intense emotions (*Republic* 10.605c, *Ion* 535, *Philebus* 47e–50b). Rather more positively, Aristotle argued that one of the beneficial functions of tragic drama is to provide a catharsis of pity and fear in an audience that is emotionally engaged with tragic personae (*Poetics*, Book VIII).

THE AROUSAL THEORY

The power of art to evoke emotional responses is the basis of the "arousal" theory of expression. The core idea is that an artwork expresses *x* if it has the capacity to arouse a feeling or sensation of *x* in the viewer or listener. Sad music, for example, is music that stirs sadness in the listener. The arousal theory has had many proponents, from Francis Hutcheson (1725) to Colin Radford (1989). The British associationist Archibald Alison, as early as 1790, characterized aesthetic experience in general as the employment of the imagination in the creation of a train of ideas that must be "productive of emotions."

Problems arise immediately for this thesis, however. Some writers with "formalist" inclinations flatly reject it. Eduard Hanslick, for example, in his 1891 work, *On the Musically Beautiful*, denied both that the purpose of music is to arouse emotions and that feelings are in any sense the "content" of music. Moreover, it has often been observed that the reactive emotions of the audience are not always those it is most appropriate to say the work expresses. A tragedy expressive of love, jealousy, and hatred may, as Aristotle said, cause feelings of pity and fear in its viewers. Furthermore, it seems possible to recognize the expressive content of a work without undergoing that very emotion or feeling. A sad or elegant artwork need not make the perceiver sad or elegant.

By contrast, Jerrold Levinson (1990) and Aaron Ridley (1995) have argued that music can arouse a truncated version of the emotions it expresses; the emotions or feelings aroused by music lack their usual contexts and intentional objects. Jenefer Robinson (1994) has pointed out that, although the emotions expressed by music are not always identical with what is aroused in the listener, certain "primitive" emotions can be directly aroused by music expressing those same emotions; music that disturbs us, makes us tense, or calms us down *is* disturbing, tense, or calm. However, music, as an extended composition, also expresses more complex emotions, for example, unrequited passion, which are not aroused in us, but

which we attribute as true of the piece partly on the basis of the clues given by the more basic emotions aroused in us.

EXPRESSION AND NINETEENTH-CENTURY IDEALISM

Much grander claims for the expressive power of art were made during the period of German idealism, when art was seen as a manifestation of Spirit. Schelling held that art can show what philosophical concepts cannot: the Absolute, the organic unity of the knower and the known. Schopenhauer called music a copy of the will itself—a direct presentation of the will, expressing the essential nature of emotion types. For Hegel, art provides an irreducible form of self-reflection, conveying knowledge of Spirit through a natural sensuous medium. Along with religion and philosophy, art expresses "the Divine, the deepest interests of mankind, the most all-embracing truths of Spirit" (Hegel 1835–1838, vol. I, p. 21).

In his earlier writings, especially *Die Geburt der Tragödie* (1872, later translated as *The Birth of Tragedy*), Friedrich Nietzsche saw art, especially tragedy and music, as expressing the conjunction or synthesis of two strong human impulses, the "Apollonian," a love of order, measure, and formal beauty, and the "Dionysian," the spirit that glories in a state of elation and joyful acceptance of the excitements and pains of life. Later, Nietzsche allied art more closely with the Dionysian solution to the problem of living, presenting the Dionysian in art as an expression of the basic human drive called the "will to power."

THE EXPRESSION THEORY

Romanticism, with its general emphasis on the emotions and its shift away from classicism, embraced and fostered the view that art is a form of expression in the sense of self-reflection or self-discovery. This theory, labeled by Alan Tormey (1971) the "expression theory of art," is a rival to both high-flown idealism and the arousal theory. According to the expression theory, artworks are expressions of the emotional states experienced by the artist during the creative process. In one variation or another, this view has been endorsed in the nineteenth and twentieth centuries by thinkers such as Eugène Véron, Benedetto Croce, R. G. Collingwood, John Dewey, L. A. Reid, and C. J. Ducasse.

Expression theorists see expressive art as a means of articulating the artist's inner life. In fact, the view can perhaps be thought of as romanticism's alternative to the arousal theory. Very early in the period, Samuel Coleridge observed that "in *Paradise Lost*—indeed in every one of his poems—it is Milton himself whom you see" (1833, p. 250). A systematic development of expression theory can be found in Véron's influential *L'Esthetique* of 1879, but the view reached its zenith in the early twentieth century in the writings of Italian philosopher Benedetto Croce.

Strongly influenced by Hegelian thought as well as by romanticism, Croce proposed that intuition is a kind of nonconceptual awareness of a mental image, and expression is the forming of "artistic intuitions," which are always infused with intense feeling. Artists express these initially inchoate feelings in the process of forming artistic, or "lyrical," intuitions. Indeed, famously and problematically, Croce identified intuition and expression, and defined art in terms of this mental process. "Intuition is truly such because it expresses intense feeling. ... Not idea but intense feeling is what confers upon art the ethereal lightness of the symbol" (1965 [1913], p. 25).

Clearly indebted to Croce, R. G. Collingwood took all art to be an expression of individual and unique emotions, but the process is not the mere exhibiting of the symptoms of the emotion. ("The artist never rants"; 1938, p. 22). Rather, expression is the lucid transformation of sensuous-emotional experience by the artist's imagination into an image or idea. True art, unlike the physical crafts accompanying the various arts, is made in the imagination of the artist.

The idealist tendencies seen in Croce and Collingwood are not shared by all expression theorists, perhaps for good reason. If expression is a purely mental or imaginative process, the artist's manipulation of the medium of his or her art appears to be wrongly undervalued. Although agreeing with Croce and Collingwood that expression always involves the artist's "inner" emotions in need of clarification and transformation, American pragmatist John Dewey emphasized that expression is an "outgoing activity" of interaction with the environment, involving the controlled working of a medium (1934, p. 62). In aesthetic expressiveness we find "meanings and values extracted from prior experiences and funded in such a way that they fuse with the qualities directly presented in a work of art" (p. 98).

Perhaps, then, expression theory can be rescued from the common objection that it makes art and the expressive process overly mentalistic, but it is unclear that it can be saved from another, which charges it with committing the "genetic fallacy" of mistaking judgments about the artist, the source of the art, for judgments about the art itself. The presence of expressive properties in an artwork does not entail the occurrence of prior acts of expression, any more than a cruel expression on a face entails that the owner of the face has acted cruelly.

The expression theory is correctly characterized as a theory of expression emphasizing the emotive processes undergone by the artist, but it would be misleading to think that the arousal of emotions in the viewer or audience is not at least acknowledged by most expression theorists. Dewey remarked, "Because the objects of art are expressive, they communicate. I do not say that communication to others is the intent of an artist. But it is the consequence of his work ..." (1934, p. 104). He and Collingwood claim that the emotional reaction of the viewer should mirror or reconstruct the artist's expressive process. When elements of the expression and arousal views are conjoined, the result is a kind of "communication" theory of the sort offered by Leo Tolstoy. In *What Is Art?* (*Chto takoe iskusstvo?*) Tolstoy wrote, "To evoke in oneself a feeling one has experienced, and having evoked it in oneself by means of movements, lines, colors, sounds or forms expressed in works, so to transmit that feeling that others experience the same feeling—this is the activity of art" (1960 [1898], p. 55). For Tolstoy, it is essential to the "sincerity" of the art that the artist feel the emotion communicated, and a condition of "success" of the art that the audience is "infected" with the same feeling.

Of course, a theory conjoining the arousal and expression theses inherits the problems of both views. And it does seem quite possible both that an artist can create a passionate artwork without himself being in a passionate state, and that the audience can recognize that the work is passionate without being made to feel passionate themselves. Composer Richard Strauss said, "I work very coldly, without agitation, without emotion, even" (Osborne 1955, p. 162).

Guy Sircello (1972) champions the romantic view that the mind does not merely mirror or represent nonmental reality but is an original source of some of the features of art, and that it thereby infuses art with intentional or anthropomorphic properties. Although Sircello admits a variety of sources for art's expressive properties, he emphasizes that many of the expressive features that we attribute to artworks are true of them because of the "artistic acts" in which the artist is engaged as he or she creates a work. Pieter Brueghel the Elder's painting *Peasant Wedding Dance* (1566) is ironic, Sircello says, because Brueghel views a happy scene ironically. Nicolas Poussin's *Rape of the Sabine Women* (c. 1635–1637) is aloof and detached, even though the scene

ENCYCLOPEDIA OF PHILOSOPHY
2nd edition

is one of violence, because Poussin observes calmly and paints in a detached fashion.

THE EMBODIMENT THEORY

The "embodiment" theory of expression is a reaction to both the expression and arousal theories, and asserts that expressive properties are rightly said to be possessed by, or true of, the artwork itself either in virtue of its form or composition, or as properties that "emerge" in the work due to broader contextual considerations of a cultural, artistic, interpretational, or psychological sort. Whereas the arousal theory focuses on the effects of expressive art, and whereas the expression theory is a theory of the source of art's expressiveness, the embodiment theory is a cognitivist view of our awareness of the expressive properties that are in, or are possessed by, an artwork. A work can be expressive of x even if the artist was not experiencing x in creating the work, and the audience does not necessarily feel x when they appreciate it.

It is worthy of note that American pragmatist George Santayana, although fitting no category very exactly, is closer to the embodiment theory than to the expression theory with which he is sometimes associated. Santayana wrote quite generally about a sense of expressive beauty and did not focus on the artistic process, nor exclusively on art *per se*. His position may be closer to the earlier British "taste" and associationist theories such as those of Archibald Alison and Joseph Addison: A thought or mental image becomes expressive, according to Santayana, when feelings, meanings, or emotive "tones," proper to some past experience, color and reverberate in our present consciousness, indeed become "incorporated" into it (1988 [1896], pp. 121–124).

Although embodiment theories of various sorts gained currency in the second half of the twentieth century, its most common variant, the "resemblance" thesis, has precursors in the eighteenth century. Johann Mattheson (1739), for example, asserted that by resembling the motion and structure of our vital spirits, music, in its structure, comes to bear a resemblance to the "emotive life," and the primary response of the listener is not to feel emotion but to perceive or recognize the emotive content present in the music. A contemporary version of this position can be found in Peter Kivy's theory of musical expressiveness. In most cases, we perceptually recognize music's expressive properties "in virtue of some perceived analogy" (Kivy 1989, p. 167) to the sound of a person's voice or the movements and gestures made by a person who is literally expressing some emotion. But the reason we animate our musical perceptions, so that we cannot

but hear the music as expressive, is, Kivy says, "a divine mystery" (p. 258). Stephen Davies (1994) has a similar view. Like Kivy, he says that music's expressive properties or "emotion characteristics in its appearance" depend mainly on a resemblance that we perceive between the dynamic character of the music and human movement, gait, bearing, or carriage. Both Kivy and Davies also allow that some cases of expression are to be explained by the fact that the musical work engages some wider social conventions surrounding the expression of emotions.

Some resemblance views conclude, on the basis of the resemblance, that an expressive artwork is a symbol of, or signifies, what it expresses. Semiotic theory is then seen as a tool for understanding the nature of expression in art. The best-known signification view based on resemblance is that of Susanne Langer. Art, especially music, is, for Langer, a "presentational symbol" of human feeling. Although feelings are not denoted by such symbols (because such symbols are non-discursive and in this respect unlike language), their form is presented to us in the artwork because there is a logical "isomorphism" between the structure of the work and the "morphology" of the feeling state. Artistic form is congruent with the dynamic forms of our direct sensuous, mental, and emotional life. According to Langer, "music is not the cause or the cure of feelings, but their logical expression." (1942, p. 218).

Other theories have also emphasized the semiotic functions of art in their treatment of expression, but have downplayed the resemblance theme. In his extremely influential book, *Languages of Art* (1968), Nelson Goodman, like Langer, treated artworks as symbols but, unlike Langer, defined expression in terms of the semantic relations of reference and denotation. A work expresses φ if and only if the predicate "φ" metaphorically denotes the work, and the artwork, in turn, "refers back" to that predicate. Less nominalistically stated, expression is a form of property exemplification for Goodman. A works exemplifies a property if it not only possesses but "highlights" that property, much as a tailor's swatch highlights the texture and design of the material because of the conventions surrounding its use. Expression, in this view, is the exemplification of properties that an artwork actually, though metaphorically, possesses. Artworks can express more than human emotions, for example, poised power or flashing action.

Although it is unclear whether Alan Tormey's embodiment theory is committed to the resemblance thesis, he does suggest that the relation between an artwork's nonexpressive and expressive properties is analogous to the relation between human behavior and the intentional states of which the behavior is partially constitutive. Tormey (1971) says that expressive properties are those properties of artworks whose names also designate the intentional states of persons. But, since artworks have no mental states, a work's set of nonexpressive properties is wholly constitutive of its expressive properties. In an interesting though puzzling turn, Tormey claims that expressive ambiguity is ineliminable in art, and therefore expressive properties, though wholly constituted by nonexpressive features, are ambiguously so constituted. Within a certain range of compatibility, there is no objective fact whether an artwork has one or another expressive property; only critical choice leads to a unique judgment as to whether Ravel's *Pavane*, for example, is tender, yearning, or nostalgic. The important question of how one comes to perceive the expressive features of art is left largely unanswered by this view.

OTHER VIEWS

Like all philosophical classifications, those of the arousal, expression, and embodiment theories need to be employed with an awareness of the shortcomings of pigeonholing. A case in point is the work of Richard Wollheim. Influenced by Ludwig Wittgenstein, psychoanalytic theory, and the celebrated work of psychologist E. H. Gombrich concerning the cognitive nature of our perception of art, Wollheim proposes that artistic expression involves "expressive perception," a kind of "seeing or hearing as," by which an artwork, because of how it looks or sounds, causes us to project an emotion or feeling onto that which we see or hear (1987, p. 138). Although the artwork does not simply arouse in us an emotion that we associate with its other features, it does arouse in us the process of projection. And, as in the embodiment theory, the expressive property is ascribed to the work, literally projected onto it, and the work is perceived as possessing it. Lastly, like the expression and communicative views, Wollheim's position suggests that correct expressive perception mirrors or recaptures the emotions that, either through direct experience or through contemplation of them, caused the artist to paint, write, or compose as he or she did.

Finally, a number of writers have introduced an imaginary or fictive element into the discussion of expression, especially regarding music. These theories suggest that artistic expression is often best described in terms of the imaginary occurrence of emotion in oneself or in a fictional persona. Bruce Vermazen (1986) thinks of the expressiveness of a musical passage in terms of an inferred ascription of a state of mind to an imagined utterer of the passage that would best explain the passage's features. Kendall Walton (1990) thinks that expressive music can induce listeners to imagine particular instances of properties expressed, such as instances of someone (perhaps oneself) or something's being exuberant, aggressive, uncertain, or resolved. Walton also claims that sometimes one is induced to imagine of one's own auditory experience that it is an expression of, say, anguish or exuberance (1994).

For Jerrold Levinson, the expressiveness of music derives from its "hearability" as a "sui generis" expression, by an imagined persona, of inner states through outer signs (Levinson 1990, 1996). What a passage of music expresses is what it can most readily and spontaneously be imagined to express by "suitably backgrounded" listeners. That is, music invites listeners to hear it, immediately and directly, as an alternate audible mode of behaviorally manifesting emotions by an imagined persona. Levinson argues against resemblance-based accounts, claiming that recognition of a similarity between music and some emotional behavior is not sufficient for hearing the music as expressive. Similarly, Gregory Karl and Jenefer Robinson (1995) claim that what a musical passage expresses can be the mental state ascribed to the imaginary protagonist of the passage that figures in the best overall interpretation of the work. Whether these "fiction-based" views are types of embodiment theory is somewhat difficult to say with confidence since, rather like expression theories, they emphasize the processes underlying expression in the arts rather than the logic and semantics involved in ascribing expressive properties to works of art.

See also Aesthetics, History of; Aesthetics, Problems of; Aristotle; Coleridge, Samuel Taylor; Collingwood, Robin George; Croce, Benedetto; Dewey, John; Ducasse, Curt John; Goodman, Nelson; Hegel, Georg Wilhelm Friedrich; Hutcheson, Francis; Idealism; Langer, Susanne K.; Music, Philosophy of; Nietzsche, Friedrich; Plato; Romanticism; Santayana, George; Schelling, Friedrich Wilhelm Joseph von; Schopenhauer, Arthur; Tolstoy, Lev (Leo) Nikolaevich; Wittgenstein, Ludwig Josef Johann; Wollheim, Richard.

Bibliography

Alison, Archibald. *Essays on the Nature and Principles of Taste* (1790). 6th ed. Edinburgh: A. Constable, 1825.

Aristotle. *Politics* (Book VIII). In *The Basic Works of Aristotle*, edited by Richard McKeon. New York: Random House, 1941.

Coleridge, Samuel T. *The Collected Works of Samuel Taylor Coleridge*. Vol. 14: *Table Talk* (1833). Princeton, NJ: Princeton University Press, 1990.

Collingwood, R. G. *The Principles of Art*. Oxford: Clarendon Press, 1938.

Croce, Benedetto. *Guide to Aesthetics* (*Breviario di estetica*, 1913). Translated by Patrick Romanell. Indianapolis: Bobbs-Merrill, 1965.

Davies, Stephen. *Musical Meaning and Expression*. Ithaca, NY: Cornell University Press, 1994.

Dewey, John. *Art As Experience*. New York: Minton, Balch, 1934.

Ducasse, C. J. *The Philosophy of Art*. New York: Dial, 1929.

Gombrich, E. H. *Art and Illusion*. 2nd ed. London: Phaidon, 1962.

Goodman, Nelson. *Languages of Art*. Indianapolis, IN: Bobbs-Merrill, 1968.

Hanslick, Eduard. *On the Musically Beautiful: A Contribution Towards the Revision of the Aesthetics of Music* (1891). 8th ed. Translated by Geoffrey Payzant. Indianapolis, IN: Hackett, 1986.

Hegel, G. W. F. *Philosophy of Fine Art* (*Äesthetik*, 1835–1838). 2 vols. Translated by T. M. Knox. Oxford: Oxford University Press, 1972.

Hutcheson, Francis. *An Inquiry concerning Beauty, Order, Harmony and Design* (1725). Rev. ed. The Hague: Martinus Nijhoff, 1973.

Karl, Gregory, and Jenefer Robinson. "Shostakovich's Tenth Symphony and the Musical Expression of Cognitively Complex Emotions." *Journal of Aesthetics and Art Criticism* 53 (4) (1995): 401–415. Reprinted in *Music and Meaning*, edited by Jenefer Robinson. Ithaca, NY: Cornell University Press, 1997.

Kivy, Peter. *Sound Sentiment*. Philadelphia: Temple University Press, 1989.

Langer, Susanne. *Philosophy in a New Key*. Cambridge, MA: Harvard University Press, 1942.

Levinson, Jerrold. "Hope in the Hebrides." In *Music, Art, and Metaphysics*, edited by Jerrold Levinson. Ithaca, NY: Cornell University Press, 1990.

Levinson, Jerrold. *The Pleasures of Aesthetics: Philosophical Essays*. Ithaca, NY: Cornell University Press, 1996.

Mattheson, Johann. *Der vollkommene Capellmeister*. Hamburg: C. Herold, 1739.

Nietzsche, Friedrich Wilhelm. *The Birth of Tragedy* (*Die Geburt der Tragödie*, 1872). Translated by W. Kaufmann. New York: Vintage Press, 1966.

Nietzsche, Friedrich Wilhelm. *The Will to Power: An Attempted Transvaluation of all Values* (*Wille zue Macht*, 1901). Translated by Anthony M. Lodovici. London: T. N. Foulis, 1914.

Osborne, Harold. *Aesthetics and Criticism*. London: Routledge and Kegan Paul, 1955.

Plato. *The Collected Dialogues*, edited by Edith Hamilton and Huntington Cairns. Princeton, NJ: Princeton University Press, 1961.

Radford, Colin. "Emotions and Music: A Reply to the Cognitivists." *Journal of Aesthetics and Art Criticism* 47 (1989): 69–76.

Ridley, Aaron. *Music, Value, and the Passions*. Ithaca, NY: Cornell University Press, 1995.

Robinson, Jenefer. "The Expression and Arousal of Emotion in Music." *Journal of Aesthetics and Art Criticism* 59 (1) (1994): 13–22.

Santayana, George. *The Sense of Beauty* (1896). Vol. 2 of *The Works of George Santayana*, edited by William Holzberger and Herman Saatkamp Jr. Cambridge, MA: MIT Press, 1988.

Schelling, Friedrich von. *System of Transcendental Idealism* (*System des transzendenalen Idealismus*, 1800). Translated by Albert Hofstadter in *Philosophies of Art and Beauty*, edited by Albert Hofstadter and Richard Kuhns. Chicago: University of Chicago Press, 1964.

Schopenhauer, Arthur. *The World as Will and Representation* (*Welt als Wille und Vorstellung*, 1818). Translated by E. F. J. Payne. New York: Dover, 1969.

Sircello, Guy. *Mind and Art: An Essay on the Varieties of Expression*. Princeton, NJ: Princeton University Press, 1972.

Tolstoy, Leo. *What Is Art?* (*Chto takoe iskusstvo?*, 1898). Translated by Almyer Maude. Indianapolis, IN: Bobbs-Merrill, 1960.

Tormey, Alan. *The Concept of Expression*. Princeton, NJ: Princeton University Press, 1971.

Vermazen, Bruce. "Expression as Expression." *Pacific Philosophical Quarterly* 67 (1986): 196–223.

Véron, Eugène. *Aesthetics* (*L'esthetique*, 1878). Translated by W. H. Armstrong. Philadelphia: J. B. Lippincott, 1879.

Walton, Kendall. "Listening with Imagination: Is Music Representational?" *Journal of Aesthetics and Art Criticism* 52 (1) (1994): 47–61.

Walton, Kendall. *Mimesis as Make-Believe*. Cambridge, MA: Harvard University Press, 1990.

Wollheim, Richard. *Art and Its Objects*. New York: Harper and Row, 1968.

Wollheim, Richard. *On Art and the Mind*. Cambridge, MA: Harvard University Press, 1974.

Wollheim, Richard. *Painting as an Art*. Princeton, NJ: Princeton University Press, 1987.

John Bender (1996, 2005)

ART, FORMALISM IN

The term *formalism* refers to a number of theses and programs in the philosophy of art and art criticism, all of which assign a priority to the formal elements of works of art.

The doctrine of formalism exists in a number of versions, not all of them compatible with one another, but in general it is a thesis that insists on the importance—either preeminent or exclusive—of the formal features of works of art in determining the value of those works. As such, it is both a topic for philosophical debate and a prescription for critical practice. This brief essay gives a description of the philosophical background of formalism, an indication of formalist commitments in criticism, and a statement of some logical problems besetting formalism.

PHILOSOPHICAL BACKGROUND

The philosophical basis of formalism is often, and typically, traced to Kant, and indeed Kant is a kind of formalist; but a much earlier formalist doctrine is to be found in Aristotle. A central thesis of Aristotle's *Poetics* is that plot is the most important part of tragedy. Aristotle says a tragedy customarily has six parts (plot, character, thought, diction, spectacle, and melody), and, in declaring plot the most important, he seems to be asserting that excellence of its plot contributes more to the overall excellence of a tragedy than does the excellence of any of its other parts.

Aristotle offers a number of arguments in support of his claim of the preeminent importance of plot. Two are of special interest here. One is the assertion that of all the parts, only plot is necessary to something's being a tragedy. The other is the claim that plot has more of a bearing than the other parts of a tragedy on the work's special and proper effect, namely the production of *catharsis*. Thus, although Aristotle himself does not speak in these terms, his arguments are close to a claim that plot is both a necessary and a sufficient condition of tragedy, and his thesis is a kind of essentialism. What makes this essentialism a formalism is Aristotle's conception of plot: a plot, he says, is the "arrangement of incidents." Although Aristotle sometimes uses the term *plot* in something like the modern sense, meaning roughly the "story," the more abstract conception (arrangement of incidents) suggests a structure—a formal entity. And indeed Aristotle identifies plot as the "formal cause" of a tragedy.

There have been attempts to generalize Aristotle's theory. The theory is offered by Aristotle specifically with reference to tragedy, and the obvious question is how to apply it to any other artistic form. Some interpreters have thought that Aristotle would regard the plot as the most important part of any artwork that has a plot, including, for example, an opera or ballet. But it might be a mistake to regard the plot as the most important element of, say, an opera. What an Aristotelian should be looking for is the necessary and sufficient condition of something's being an opera—opera's formal cause—and this may well be its music, as Joseph Kerman has argued in *Opera As Drama*. The incidents whose arrangement is vital will be musical incidents.

Whereas for Aristotle the centrality of form is a metaphysical or ontological matter, having to do with the nature of the objects themselves, for Kant the importance of form is grounded in a quasi-epistemological conviction. A Kantian judgment of taste requires exclusive attention to form because nothing else can underwrite such a judgment's claim to universality. Kant's reasons for thinking this are relatively clear, even if his argument is difficult to formulate.

According to Kant, a judgment of something's beauty is based on the judge's feeling of pleasure in the thing. It is distinguished from other so-called "aesthetic" judgments by its implicit claim to an intersubjective validity. The judgment is thus not parochial because it is in part to some extent a rational judgment, requiring the use of the faculty of concepts. In the exercise of such judgment, according to Kant, attention is restricted to the form of the object. The judge is entitled to suppose that any other judge would also experience pleasure in the object if he judged in the same way—taking pleasure in his contemplation of the mere form of the object. Why does Kant think that everyone judging in this way will experience pleasure? In answering this question, Kant seems to rely on what he claims to have proved in the *Critique of Pure Reason*—namely that states of mind are communicable because unless they were, objective knowledge of the world would not be possible, and he thinks that he demonstrated that such knowledge is possible.

The definition of form is much less clear in Kant than in Aristotle. Kant seems to be thinking of what we might roughly think of as shape, and that seems a reasonable way to understand one of Kant's leading examples, namely the judgment of the beauty of a rose. But it leaves it utterly unclear why Kant has such a low opinion of music, given the entirely plausible conviction that music may well display abstract form more conspicuously and typically than does any other art.

FORMALISM IN THE VARIOUS ARTS

In any art, formalism concentrates on the formal elements in the works it deals with. It is not always clear just which elements are formal, in these theories, and it is not uncommonly clearer which elements do not count as formal than it is how the formal elements are defined.

VISUAL ARTS. In the visual arts, formalism has insisted on a concentration on line and shape. Its early proponents were Clive Bell and Roger Fry, and perhaps its most conspicuous twentieth-century advocate was Clement Greenberg. In its more extreme formulations, formalism in the visual arts has insisted that the value in, say, a painting, is unrelated to its representational features and is due entirely to the its form, where that form is understood entirely as a generally abstract structure constituted by the lines, shape, and, perhaps, color of the painting.

MUSIC. Formalist theory and criticism of music almost always explicitly refuses to give attention to any "program" associated with the music or even to the sung text in vocal music. Formalism does not always refuse attention to the emotions that may be evoked by music, but it insists that these feelings arise from "music alone" and not from any representational or narrative features, no matter how closely these may be associated with the music. An early statement of this view is given by Eduard Hanslick, and recently one of its most sophisticated exponents has been Peter Kivy.

LITERATURE. Formalist literary theory is somewhat harder to describe than is formalism in the other arts. If formalism, in general, is thought to be a doctrine in which principal or exclusive attention is to be paid to the perceptual elements of a work and to the relations between these elements, then it would seem to require that literary formalists attend only to the shapes and sounds of words, and this requirement is surely incredible. Thus formalism in literature has to be understood more subtly. It is commonly taken to require attention exclusively to "the work itself," where this seems to mean eschewing references to considerations coming from "outside" the work. In particular, formalists have wished to deflect historical, biographical, and psychoanalytical interests, although, of course, even the most severe formalism may have to countenance some historical interests in so far as these are necessary to establish certain features of the work—for instance, the meanings of various words or the references of proper nouns. Furthermore, there have been different species of formalism because of different opinions about which formal features are most important.

PROBLEMS FOR FORMALISM

With it professed interest in works of art themselves, and not to any ancillary features, it is fair to say, with some qualification, that formalism does *not* want attention to representational or narrative features, or to any emotional evocations that result from those things. There are two main problems facing any advocate of formalism. One is to supply some argument in favor of the claim that a work's formal properties are either the only or the most important of its elements; but before that, there is a need to offer some criterion that distinguishes formal from nonformal elements. The latter problem may be more

bothersome than it first appears, especially when one asks what formalists mean by *formal*. A useful way of doing this is to ask, "Formal as opposed to what?" When that question is raised, quite different answers are given for various arts. Thus, some procedure or routine must be given that will answer, for any true statement about a work of art A, with the form A is F, whether the property F ascribed to A is a formal property. This is very difficult to do, and that difficulty often leads to something of a reduced insistence—namely that it be determined, given that F is a property of A, whether F is an *essential* property of A. This formulation tends to be more or less agreeable depending upon how favorably one looks at philosophical essentialism.

Supposing it is settled how to tell whether a property is a formal property; the formalist now needs an argument for dealing with this issue: Given that A has the property F, and also the property N, and that F is a formal property, whereas N is not a formal property, why is F a more important property of A than N, more critical to assessing A's value or importance? Even if it were true that F is an essential property, how does it follow that N is less important?

Whatever its defensibility as a philosophical thesis, and however vaguely it has to be stated, formalism retains one merit: it has recommended and insisted upon attention to those features of an art work that incontestably are features of the work itself—features often scanted in the assessments of antiformalists.

See also Aesthetic Qualities; Art, Definitions of; Pater, Walter Horatio; Wilde, Oscar Fingal O'Flahertie Wills.

Bibliography

Alperson, Philip. "The Philosophy of Music: Formalism and Beyond." In *The Blackwell Guide to Aesthetics*, edited by Peter Kivy. Oxford: Blackwell, 2004.

Aristotle. *Poetics.* Translated by James Hutton. New York: Norton, 1982.

Batkin, Norton. "Formalism in Analytic Aesthetics." In *Encyclopedia of Aesthetics*, edited by Michael Kelly. New York and Oxford: Oxford University Press, 1998.

Bell, Clive. *Art.* London: Chatto & Windus, 1916.

Davis, Whitney. "Formalism in Art History." In *Encyclopedia of Aesthetics*, edited by Michael Kelly. New York and Oxford: Oxford University Press, 1998.

Greenberg, Clement. *Art and Culture: Critical Essays.* Boston: Beacon Press, 1961).

Isenberg, Arnold. "Formalism." In *Aesthetics and the Theory of Criticism: Selected Essays of Arnold Isenberg*, edited by William Callaghan, et al. Chicago: University of Chicago Press, 1973.

Kant, Immanuel. *Critique of the Powqer of Judgment.* A translation of Kant's *Kritik der Urteilskraft* by Paul Guyer and Eric Matthews. Cambridge, U.K.: Cambridge University Press, 2000.

Kivy, Peter. *Music Alone: Philosophical Reflections on the Purely Musical Experience.* Ithaca, Cornell University Press, 1990.

Melville, Stephen. "Greenberg, Clement." In *Encyclopedia of Aesthetics*, edited by Michael Kelly. New York and Oxford: Oxford University Press, 1998.

Strier, Richard. "How Formalism Became a Dirty Word, and Why We Can't Do Without It." In *Renaissance Literature and its Formal Engagement*, edited by Mark David Rasmussen. New York: Palgrave, 2002.

Wollheim, Richard. "On Formalism and Its Kinds." In *On Formalism and Its Kinds/Sobre el formalism I els seus tipus*, edited by Fundacio Antoni Tapies. Barcelona, publisher unknown, 1995.

Ted Cohen (2005)

ART, INTERPRETATION OF

The concept of interpretation is key to our commerce with artworks. For if something is an artwork, then it falls into the category of things that are at least eligible for an interpretation. For example, all things being equal, an ordinary snow shovel is not a candidate for interpretation, but Marcel Duchamp's *In Advance of a Broken Arm* is, despite the fact that it is indiscernible from the other snow shovels produced at the same time, in the same factory.

However, not all the elements or combinations of elements in an artwork merit interpretation. Only those elements or combinations thereof are worthy of interpretation, which somehow mystify, perplex, or elude. The appropriate object of interpretation is that which goes beyond what is given or foregrounded (Barnes 1988).

An interpretation is a hypothesis that accounts for the presence of an element or combination of elements in an artwork where the presence of the relevant elements is not immediately obvious to the interpreter and/or to some target audience. The item may not be obvious in the sense of being unintelligible or enigmatic, or because it is symbolic or allegorical, or because it is understated, barely hinted at, only suggested, or it is in some other way recessive.

The purpose of an interpretation is to enhance our understanding of an artwork. There is something about the artwork that is obscure, ambiguous, apparently incoherent, anomalous, unexpected, inaccessible, perplexing, or latent that invites illumination. The aim of an interpretation is to elucidate the presence of the pertinent elements in the artwork by explaining the contribution they make to the unity, meaning, design, intended effect, and/or structure of the work. Consequently, the work of interpretation presupposes some target audience—to which the interpreter may or may not belong—for whom the significance of some part of the work, or even the artwork as a whole, is elusive, puzzling, obscure, nonmanifest, unfocused, symbolic, or otherwise not immediately apprehensible. The interpretation, then, ideally alleviates that perplexity or gap in the audience's understanding.

Not every element in an artwork calls for an interpretation. Where with respect to a painting such as El Greco's *The Adoration of the Shepherds*, everyone recognizes the subject to be a woman, a child, and two men, then the observation that "this painting represents a woman, a child and two men" is not an interpretation, but a description. Descriptions are nevertheless relevant to interpretations, since sound interpretations must rest upon accurate descriptions.

The literal meaning of many of the words and sentences in literary works are grasped by means of subpersonal routines of processing by literate readers in the language in which the work has been composed (Currie 2004). The literal meaning of the opening line of Kafka's *The Castle*—"It was late in the evening when K. arrived"—does not require an interpretation, insofar as it is obvious to the prepared reader. What might require an interpretation, on the other hand, is its place in the broader design of the novel. Interpretation only pertains to that which is not apparent to some audience. Thus, what is suggested, entailed, or implicated is grist for the interpreter's mill, though not what is spoken outright (although why an author chooses to speak directly rather than obliquely, in certain circumstances, may be a legitimate interpretive question).

That, in a movie, shots of waves pounding on the beach often symbolize intercourse when juxtaposed to shots of lovers may be obvious to the jaded film critic; however, making note of this cinematic figure counts as an interpretation, since there is a target audience for whom it is news. Likewise, a reading of the symbolism of the death's head in a *vanitas* painting is an interpretation, since most people, untutored in art history, are unaware of the association between it and the concept of mortality.

Interpretation is, in general, a holistic enterprise. It strives to isolate the point(s) or purpose(s) of an artwork in order to explain the ways in which the parts cohere or segue with the aims of the whole as contributions to the function and/or meaning of the artwork. The predominant tendency of interpretation is to show a work to be more and more unified in intent. Of course, in order to build up a conception of the whole, the interpreter must begin with the parts, conjecturing and then adjusting his hypotheses regarding their significance as they arrive before him. The interpreter moves from hypotheses about the part to hypotheses about the whole and then back to the part again. This is sometimes referred to as the *hermeneutic circle* (Gadamer 1975); it underscores the fact that interpretation is a continuous process of reflective equilibrium involving an iterative feedback loop from part to whole and then from whole to part.

The overall direction of interpretation is toward establishing the unity of intent, thought, or design in the artwork. Even an avant-garde work, like Luis Buñuel's *L'age d'or,* which is predicated upon insistently subverting our expectations by a series of what appear to be narrative *non sequiturs,* can be shown by an interpretation to exhibit a sort of second-order unity in virtue of its consistent choice for surrealist purposes of incoherent sequences of events. On the other hand, interpretation can also have a role to play in revealing the disunity in a work. After identifying the intended effect of a novel to provoke a sense of mystery in the audience, the interpreter may then go on to point out that that purpose was ill served by the ineptly transparent way in which the murderer was crudely marked as guilty from his first appearance onwards. Because of its overriding concern with the unity of the artwork, interpretation is intimately related to evaluation, often supplying premises for our judgments of the quality of artworks.

Since interpretation is so involved with exhibiting the unity of artworks, it is often connected to the discovery of meaning, especially in works of narrative, dramatic, and symbolic import. For meaning—in the sense of a theme, a thesis, or an overriding concept—is one of the most frequent ways in which such works may be unified. The theme of the inhumanity of war, for instance, governs *All Quiet on the Western Front.* The interpreter, contemplating the parts of the work, for example its various episodes, hypothesizes this theme and then goes on to show how this concept colligates or unifies Remarque's choice of the incidents he presents to the reader. That is, an interpretation like this isolates the principle of selection—in this case, a concept—that makes a coherent package of the collection of details assembled in the novel.

ANTI-INTENTIONALISM

Meaning of various sorts is so frequently associated with interpretation that many philosophers identify the excavation of meaning as the sole object of interpretation and, for that reason, propose linguistic meaning as the model for understanding interpretation. Linguistic meaning, of course, is highly structured in terms of conventions of semantics and syntax. So on this view, interpreting a work is a matter of discovering its meaning through the rules of the relevant art form. With respect to a poem, for example, it is said, one need only appeal to the public meanings of the words and the traditional practices of figuration; no recourse, for example, to authorial intention is necessary. Because of its reliance upon the conventional meanings of words to the exclusion of authorial intention, this view, which was ably defended by the late Monroe Beardsley, can be called anti-intentionalism.

To the extent that anti-intentionalism depends upon our understanding of linguistic meaning in terms of conventions as a model for the interpretation of works, it cannot, at the very least, be generalized across the arts. For most of the arts do not possess the highly structured meaning conventions that language does. The fact that a stage director chooses to incorporate a swimming pool into the set of her theatrical production of *A Midsummer Night's Dream* is certainly a decision worth pondering in an interpretation of the performance ("What might the director be symbolizing by this?"); but there is no fixed, public meaning attached to the appearance of swimming pools onstage.

And yet even with respect to the literary arts, many of the traditional objects of interpretation are inhospitable to the linguistic model. For example, interpreters often focus upon the significance of plot ellipses or they question why a character possesses a certain set of apparently conflicting attributes. But neither of these recurring objects of interpretation can be referred to pre-existing codes or conventions of decipherment.

Furthermore, literary works often mobilize irony and allusion. The conventions of language will be of no avail with radical cases of irony, since in these instances the author means to say exactly the opposite of what the rules of language entail, while there are no conventions to tell the difference between allusions, properly so called, and coincidental similarities of phrasing. Indeed, even in the case of metaphor, we have no laws to tell us how to proceed in unraveling them interpretively. So it is even controversial whether the anti-intentionalist or conventionalist stance can serve as a comprehensive account of the arts of language which, on the face of it, would appear to be its most welcoming field of application.

Perhaps an even deeper problem with the linguistic-model version of the conventionalist or anti-intentionalist stance is that it presumes that the object of interpretation is always something construable as a meaning—that is, either as a proposition, an utterance, or a concept. But often the object of interpretation is what the artist has done rather that what he has "said." For example, the art historian may explain to her class that the artist has placed the crucified Christ at the vanishing point of his painting in order to emphasize that it is Christ's death that is the subject of the painting and not, for instance, the Roman soldiers playing dice at the side of the cross. This is a rhetorical or dramaturgical effect that, inasmuch as it may not be apparent to many viewers until it is pointed out, is worthy of interpretive attention. However, it does not involve meaning, linguistically construed. It does not say, "look here"; rather it has the effect of tending to draw the eye of the normal viewer in that direction. Yet, explaining the function of this device in the design of the work as a whole is interpretative because it contributes to disclosing the unity of intent of the work—in effect, to explaining the way in which this strategy reinforces the plan, point, or purpose of the painting.

The limitations of the conventionalist model may encourage us to look elsewhere for a way of understanding interpretation. Moreover, we need not search far afield. For interpretation is not some strange phenomenon that we engage only with respect to rarefied objects like art objects; ordinary human life is shot through with interpretation.

INTENTIONALISM

Barely an hour goes by when most of us are not involved in interpreting the words and deeds, the sayings and doings of our conspecifics. The ability to read the minds of others is an indispensable part of social existence, and those who are extremely deficient at it, such as persons stricken by autism, are typically thought to be disabled. The interpretation of artworks appears simply to be a specialized extension of this natural capacity of the human frame, no different in kind than our interpretation of the behavior, verbal and otherwise, of the family, friends, strangers, and enemies who surround us daily.

Thus, our ordinary practices of interpretation may be expected to shed some light on the interpretation of artworks. In everyday life, interpretation is typically aimed at understanding the intentions of others. We scrutinize the speech and the behavior, often nonverbal, of conspecifics in order to make sense of it by inferring the intentions that gave rise to it. If the behavior takes place against the background of conventions, as speech does, we factor those conventions into our deliberations. However, arriving at our interpretation of an action, including a speech act, rarely involves applying conventional rules to behavior mechanically. We appeal to what we know about the agent, about her beliefs and her desires, about the context of her activity as well as what we know about pertinent conventions to arrive at our interpretations. Why not approach the interpretation of artworks in the same way that we interpret our conspecifics every day? Isn't it very likely that the interpretation of artworks is on a continuum with the interpretative propensities that appear to have been endowed innately by natural selection as a beneficial adaptation for social beings like ourselves?

If it is plausible to answer these questions affirmatively, then the narrow compass of linguistic meaning emphasized by the anti-intentionally disposed conventionalist may be exchanged for the broader notion of sense that is invoked when we speak of making sense of an action—where what makes sense or what renders an action comprehensible is the identification of the coherent intention that lies behind it. Why not suppose that making sense of an artwork is of a piece with making sense of an action? One advantage of this view, in contradistinction to the previous version of anti-intentionalism, is that art forms that are not governed by rules as strict as those of semantics and syntax are still readily interpretable under an intentionalist understanding of interpretation such as this one.

Artworks have a communicative dimension. Consequently, all things being equal, we should try engage them as we do the other communicative behaviors of our fellow humans—as sources of information regarding their intentions. Where interpretation comes into play, its point is arguably to discern the communicative intentions of the creator of the work. An interpretation is successful to the degree that it tracks the intentions of artists. This view, for obvious reasons, we may call intentionalism.

Intentionalism is often rejected because it is thought to force its proponents to the nonsensical position that the preferred interpretation of an artwork is that it has whatever meaning or function its creator says it does. So if a poet says the word "blue" in his poem means "red," then "blue" means "red." But this is absurd. Of course, in a case like this, we may suspect the poet is dissembling about what he truly intends. In the ordinary course of affairs, we do not allow our interlocutors the last word on their intentions. So it needs to be emphasized that intentionalism is not committed to the view that an artwork means whatever an author merely says it does. Rather, intentionalism is after the actual intention of the artist.

But let us imagine that in this case, we somehow are able to ascertain that the poet really does intend "blue" to mean "red." Surely, we will not accept that this is what the word means, and, moreover, the anti-intentionalist can say why—because it violates the rules of language.

This objection is fatal to the most radical variety of actual intentionalism (Knapp and Michaels 1982). However, there may be more modest forms of actual intentionalism that are capable of dodging this objection. One strategy in this respect is to regard the intentions of the creators of artworks as pertinent to the interpretation of artworks just in case the work itself—including, in this instance, the words and their conventional meanings—can support the putative intention of the artist (Hirsch 1967, Iseminger 1996, Carroll 1999). Where they cannot, isolating the artist's intention will not, the intentionalist concedes, promise a successful interpretation of the work. In this way, the modest actual intentionalist acknowledges the role of both conventional meaning as well as intention in interpretations (Stecker 2003).

Nevertheless, the modest actual intentionalist must surmount further challenges. One charge is that this approach misdirects the interpreter. Instead of focusing on the work, the interpreter is focused on something outside the work, in effect the artist's intention. However, the modest intentionalist notes that since the artwork is the primary source for our evidence about the artist's intention, intentionalism does not beckon us to turn away from the artwork, but to inspect it more closely. Furthermore, the intentionalist contends that it is not quite right to maintain that our interest is in the artwork as if it were an object in nature. Surely, since so many of the critical remarks we lavish on artworks presuppose the notion of *achievement*, our interest in the artwork is in the way intentions are realized in the work. But to appreciate that requires a grasp of the intentions that gave rise to the work.

The intentionalist argues that the interpretation of artworks is on a continuum with our everyday interpretation of our conspecifics. However, critics of intentionalism maintain that once we enter the realm of art, things change. Even if standardly we interpret in order to identify the intentions behind the words and deeds of others, art is not like that. It has purposes above and beyond the practical concern with gathering information from our conspecifics. An essential function of art is to afford aesthetic experience—experience valued for its own sake—by encouraging the imagination of the reader, listener, or viewer of the artwork in lively interpretive play. The claim that the proper aim of interpretation is to attempt to identify the intention of the artist may conflict with this putatively central function of art. Thus, in order to engage artworks appropriately, our normal inclination towards interpreting for intention should be suspended.

On the one hand, the view that a central function of art, one that trumps all the others, is to engender aesthetic experience by abetting the imaginative play of interpretation is, to say the least, controversial. Nor can it be bolstered, without begging the question, by suggesting that the authority of this viewpoint is manifest in the behavior of informed participants in the art world, since one finds that informed participants in the art world indulge in intentionalist interpretations with remarkable frequency.

On the other hand, it is difficult to gainsay that an artwork has at least a communicative dimension—that it is meant as the expression of a thought or a feeling or as a projection of a design for contemplation, or is meant to have some other intersubjectively detectable effect. Moreover, it may be argued, that once we enter a communicative relationship with another, including the creator of an artwork, then it would appear that we are bound by certain moral responsibilities.

That is, we must treat the communiqué of the other fairly, with charity, and with accuracy; we must engage our interlocutor justly and attempt to get at what she intends to communicate. Perhaps the best evidence for this moral commitment is the injustice we ourselves feel when we believe that others are "putting words in our mouths."

But if such moral considerations are germane to interpretation, then it does not seem that the supposed pursuit of aesthetic experience through the free, or, at least intentionalistically independent, play of interpretations trumps all of our other legitimate interests in artworks. Rather the range of acceptable interpretations will be morally constrained by our best hypotheses about what the creator of the artwork intended (Carroll 1991).

HYPOTHETICAL INTENTIONALISTS

Nevertheless, even if it is conceded that the work of interpretation aims at hypothesizing the intention of the creator of the artwork, there is a dispute among intentionalists over what should count as its preferred interpretation. One side—call them hypothetical intentionalists—claims that the preferred interpretation of the artwork is the one that would be conjectured by an idealized, fully informed audience member, availing herself of all the publicly accessible information surrounding the artwork (including knowledge about the rest of the creator's oeuvre, about the history and practice of the pertinent genre and style of the artwork, about the social context of the work, and even concerning whatever is in the public record of the author's life) (Levinson 1996). The other half of this debate—call them modest actual intentionalists—maintains that the preferred interpretation of the work is whatever the actual intention of the creator was so long as that is supported by the work itself.

Since both hypothetical and actual intentionalists will usually rely upon the same kinds of considerations to arrive at their interpretations—historical context, art history, the rest of the creator's oeuvre, and so forth—in practice the two positions are apt to converge generally on the same interpretations of the work. There is a point at which they clash, however. Since the goal of the modest actual intentionalist is the retrieval of the actual intention of the creator, she is willing to help herself to information—wheresoever it comes from—about what the author really intended, so long as what the creator is thought to intend is consistent with his creation. This includes being prepared to use clues from the private diaries, letters and notes of the creator as well as the reliable testimony of friends of the creator. In contrast, the hypothetical intentionalist believes that the interpreter must be limited in her hypotheses to just what can be found in the public record.

The hypothetical intentionalist defends his viewpoint, in part, by asserting that the aforesaid limitations on the kinds of evidence to which an interpreter has a genuine right are part and parcel of the principles underwriting art world practice. It is a violation of the rules of the game, in other words, to use the private papers of an artist to formulate the preferred interpretation However, it is not clear where the hypothetical intentionalist locates the basis of this alleged rule. It cannot be observed in the actual practice of interpretation, since many critics appear quite happy to use unpublished biographical confidences in their work. Perhaps they are in some violation of some rule, but, since the eclipse of the New Criticism, no one appears to call them on it anymore. Moreover, the notion that such a rule could govern the art world seems unlikely. For when we become interested in an artist and his artworks, we are happy to learn everything we can

about him and to incorporate it into our understanding, irrespective of from whence that information originates.

READER-RESPONSE THEORY

Because interpretation is so often involved with the identification of meaning, it is quite natural to suppose that it is connected to intentions. For, the meaning of an utterance—such as "The door is closed"—depends upon whether the speaker intends to be reporting a fact or asking a question (signaled, perhaps, by changing one's intonation at the end of the sentence). However, while agreeing that the meaning of an utterance requires an intention, some may question whether the pertinent intention needs to be that of the author or creator of the artwork. Might not the intention be supplied by the consumers of the work—the readers of the poem, for example?

On this view, which is a variant of reception theory or reader-response aesthetics (Tompkins 1980), the author of the poem supplies his readership with a text—a mere sequence of words whose meanings are to be imputed by the audience, albeit usually within the constraints of the possible dictionary senses of the relevant words and the rules of grammar. In this way, each reader may be thought to construct her own artwork, much as the interpretation of a score by a musician counts as a work of performing art in its own right. That is, in the inevitable process of filling-in the indeterminacies of the text (a sheer sequence of symbols sans fully determinate meaning), the reader putatively creates her own artwork.

Even if this view of interpretation suits some art forms, like literature, it is difficult to generalize across the arts. How exactly would it apply to architecture? It strains language violently to say that each spectator *constructs* his own building, and where, in any event, would those buildings be situated exactly? There would appear to be room for only one Notre Dame cathedral on its present site in Paris; or, Are all those imputed cathedrals immaterial? Surely, such thinking leads to a strange form of architecture.

Another problem with this way of talking is that it would seem to evaporate the relevant category of interpretation entirely. In ordinary language, we countenance at least two notions of interpretation—the notion of a critical interpretation (which has been the topic of this entry) and what might be called a performative interpretation—the sort of interpretation that a musician gives to a piece of music or that an actor gives to a role. These two kinds of interpretations may be related—the actor may produce or consult a critical interpretation of a play before creating his role through an interpretation/performance. But the two sorts of interpretation are usually thought to be distinct.

However, on the variation of reception aesthetics under discussion, the difference disappears. There is no artwork to be interpreted critically because the interpretation—the performative interpretation—by the reader just is the artwork. There is no conceptual space left over for the critical interpretation to inhabit. Or, in other words, the distinction between the artwork and its (critical) interpretation has disappeared.

Furthermore, if each interpretation, in the sense germane to the reception theorist, amounts to a different artwork, then it is not clear how we will go about comparing different interpretations. What will be the reference point in such comparisons? But we do compare interpretations. Consequently, a theory that makes this impossible is suspicious.

And finally, if audiences create artworks, what is it precisely that artists do? Is it that short-story writers produce texts—strings of symbols without intended meanings? This surely is not what writers think they do, nor does it seem humanly feasible for an author to produce a document on such a scale with no definite utterance meanings in mind. And how would we go about evaluating works constructed on this construal? Would the "text" that generated the most (or the least) reader-response artworks be the best and why? Or, would there be some other criteria.

At the very least, the reception-theory version of interpretation canvassed so far would call for a dramatic overhaul in the way in which we talk and think about art. Before embracing such a view of interpretation, we should require a fuller account of that alternative conceptual framework than any developed so far. On the other hand, it may be an added virtue of modest actual intentionalism that it fits our current interpretive practices as neatly as it does.

See also Hermeneutics; Literature, Philosophy of; Structuralism and Post-structuralism.

Bibliography

Barnes, Annette. *On Interpretation.* Oxford: Blackwell, 1988.

Beardsley, Monroe. *Aesthetics.* Indianapolis, IN: Hackett, 1981.

Carroll, Noël. "Art, Intention and Conversation." In *Intention and Interpretation*, edited by Gary Iseminger. Philadelphia: Temple University Press, 1991.

Carroll, Noël, "Interpretation and Intention: The Debate between Actual and Hypothetical Intentionalism." In *The Philosophy of Interpretation*, edited by Joseph Margolis and Tom Rockmore. Oxford: Blackwell, 1999.

Currie, Gregory. "Interpretation and Pragmatics." In *Arts and Minds.* Oxford: Oxford University Press, 2004.

Gadamer, Hans-Georg. *Truth and Method.* New York: Seabury Press, 1975.

Hirsch, E. D. *Validity in Interpretation.* New Haven, CT: Yale University Press, 1967.

Iseminger, Gary. "Actual Intentionalism versus Hypothetical Intentionalism." In *The Journal of Aesthetics and Art Criticism* 54 (1996): 319–326.

Knapp, Steven, and Walter Benn Michaels. "Against Theory." *Critical Inquiry* 8 (1982): 723–742.

Levinson, Jerrold. "Intention and Interpretation in Literature." In *The Pleasures of Aesthetics.* Ithaca, NY: Cornell University Press, 1996.

Stecker, Robert. *Interpretation and Construction.* Oxford: Blackwell, 2003.

Tompkins, Jane, ed. *Reader-Response Criticism: From Formalism to Post-Structuralism.* Baltimore, MD: Johns Hopkins University Press, 1980.

Noël Carroll (2005)

ART, ONTOLOGY OF

Ontology is concerned with what exists. So one may think the ontology of art is concerned with whether artworks exist. However, most people take the existence of artworks for granted. (See Dilworth 2004 for someone who does not.) The main issue for the ontology of art is what kind or kinds of objects artworks are. A second important issue is about the identity and individuation of works. Concerning both of these issues there is wide disagreement along a variety of parameters.

OBJECTS THAT ARE ARTWORKS

ONE KIND OR MANY. One parameter along which there is disagreement is whether all artworks belong to a single kind or whether they belong to irreducibly different kinds. The second view seems more plausible, at least initially. A painting, such as one made with oils or watercolors, is an entity that has physical properties, such as spatial dimensions, that exists in a single place at a single time, and, for these reasons, may be plausibly taken for a physical object. A novel could be said to exist in many places—wherever there is a copy—or in no place, because no copy or even the original manuscript is the novel. For this reason, novels could not be physical objects. One of a kind sculptures are more like paintings in the respects mentioned above, whereas many musical works are more like novels.

Nevertheless, there are a variety of attempts to argue that artworks belong to a single kind. One strategy for doing this is to argue that all works are types or kinds of some sort, thereby assimilating those, such as paintings, that appear to be physical objects to the category to which novels and musical works more obviously belong. One proposal is that all artworks are structural types. Musical works are sound-structures and literary works are linguistic structures (or possibly, in some instances, plot structures). Paintings also have a structure that could be defined in terms of patterns of colors and shapes, or defined in some other way. This structure is duplicated in a copy of the painting, perfectly duplicated in a perfect copy. Prints and sculpture produced from a model seem to fit this proposal better than paintings, because people currently recognize that prints and sculpture that share a common structure belong to a single work. Current practice does not do this for paintings, no matter how perfect the copy. One can imagine a future time when painters produce a work in two stages. First they paint something. Second, they authorize a certain number of mechanically produced copies to be housed in several different museums or galleries as instances of the work, just as there are now several authorized instances of Henry Moore's sculpture *King and Queen* on different sites in different parts of the world. However, the possibility of imagining this new practice does not show that paintings are really abstract structures. If anything it shows the opposite, because the imaginary practice stands in stark contrast with the actual one. This actual practice does not recognize copies as instances of the work, asserts that the work is deteriorating when the paint applied by artist to canvas deteriorates despite the existence of good copies, and so on. Because painting and some sculptures are not structural types, there are other works that also do not fit the proposal, even though they are not physical objects. Improvisations and happenings are nonrepeatable events. So the strategy of arguing that all artworks are abstract structural types fails.

These considerations also speak against a second proposal: that artworks are action-types (Currie 1988). The type is the discovering of an abstract structure in a specific way (a "heuristic path"). The proposal recognizes a consideration that is discussed at length below: a work's pattern or structure and the context of its making are distinct sources of important artistic properties. However, if the reasoning of the last paragraph is correct, the present proposal has a defect similar to the first proposal in misidentifying the sort of objects that paintings and uncast sculptures are. These are not types of achievement; rather, they are specific concrete objects that are appreciated only in part for what they achieve. Even genuinely abstract works seem to be objects brought about by a type of activity rather than that action-type itself.

A different strategy for arguing that all artworks belong to a single ontological category is to argue that they are all concrete objects of some sort rather than abstract objects. One proposal on the table that fits this approach claims that all artworks are action *tokens*, in particular, the creative activity of artists that bring into existence those objects normally thought of as works of art (D. Davies 2003). On this proposal, the actual work is uniformly the creative activity, the product of that activity being dubbed the work-vehicle and distinguished from the work itself. One may wonder what this accomplishes other than a renaming. Both the creative act and the object are recognized by everyone, and as such, no novel entity is involved in the act-token conception of artworks. So why depart from normal practice and assert that the artwork is not the object produced by the artist's activity, but is the activity itself? Simplifying a complicated argument, the main reason is the importance for art appreciation of reconstructing the artist's creative activity. The claim is that the only way to acknowledge this importance fully is to identify the work with the activity. This claim is unjustified. An object has many relational properties in virtue of its origin and recognizing these properties may be crucial to fully appreciating the object as an artwork. People can accord recognition to the artist's creative activity by understanding that it is in virtue of the creative act, and of the project that gives rise to it—that the work (object) has the relational properties crucial to appreciating it. There is no need to identify the work with the creative activity itself. Hence the renaming that the act-token view proposes is neither necessary nor desirable.

One may conclude that the heterodox view that artworks belong to irreducibly different kinds is not only more plausible initially, but more plausible after reflection as well. Taking this for granted, the next question is how to more sharply define these kinds.

THE ROLE OF INTENTIONS AND CONTEXT. According to the heterodox view, some artworks are abstract types or kinds, others are concrete objects with physical properties, and there are still others that are particular events or processes. One individuating feature of abstract artworks, such as novels, plays, and pieces of music, is that instances of each work share a common structure. Is this sharing of a structure sufficient to individuate a single work? It is clear that this is not always so. Consider the case of a sculpture that has multiple instances. The structural element here consists of a material such as bronze being shaped in a certain way. Wherever there is a piece of bronze so shaped there is an object that has a structure in common with the sculpture. But this is clearly not sufficient for the object to be an instance of the sculpture. Someone who produced pieces of bronze with shapes identical to those belonging to *King and Queen* would not thereby produce an instance of that sculpture. For the pieces to be such instances, they would have to be produced from the cast Moore supplied to a certain foundry chosen by the artist and be one of a specific number of instances as indicated by Moore. This much is obvious. Controversy arises when one asks why this is so and whether a common structure is equally insufficient to individuate musical and literary works.

One explanation of the insufficiency of structure to individuate works such as cast sculptures and prints appeals to a purported distinction between autographic and allographic works (Goodman 1968). The latter are those that, because they are made in a notational symbol system, are in fact individuated by a shared sequence or structure of symbols. A thought experiment suggesting that musical and literary works are allographic relies on the impossibility of forging a musical or literary work by copying the score of one or the sequence of words of the other. This simply would produce the score of the musical work or a copy of the novel rather than something to be passed off for one of these. If, however, someone copied a cast sculpture by creating a new cast that produced a piece of bronze identical in shape to the sculpture, that would be a forgery. To be the sculpture, even one that has multiple instances, each instance must derive in the right way from the hand of the artist. This is what makes sculpture an autographic art form.

One can accept a version of the autographic/allographic distinction that simply says that some works are made in notational symbol systems and others are not. What this version of the distinction does not imply is that if a work is made in a notational system, it is individuated entirely by notational structure. A different thought experiment suggests that even for works in notational systems, instances sharing a common structure are not necessarily the same work. The experiment revolves around structurally identical items from different periods or cultures. Because of the different historical contexts, the items will have different artistic properties despite sharing, say, the same sequence of words. A well-known version of this thought experiment is the often-cited story by Jorge Luis Borges, "Pierre Menard, Author of the Quixote" (1970). In this story, Borges imagines a late-nineteenth-century writer, Menard, who produces a manuscript word-for-word identical to some chapters of Cervantes' great novel. Borges plausibly proceeds to note the huge differences in style and meaning between the two works. Cervantes' style is colloquial, whereas Menard's is self-consciously archaic. The latter contains allusions to contemporary philosophic thought that the former could not possibly have. Hence even ignoring that Menard's text is identical to only a small part of Cervantes', the two are different works in virtue of different authorial intentions and contexts of creation.

Once one recognizes that intentions and context play roles in individuating works that have the ontological status of types or kinds—whether or not they are also "allographic" in the weak sense noted in the preceding paragraph—one can also recognize that intention and context play similar roles in the case of concrete works such as paintings and uncast sculptures. To recall another famous example from Arthur Danto's *The Transfiguration of the Commonplace* (1981) consider three pieces of canvas covered with red paint by the hand of three different, independent artists. Three "structurally identical" red canvases could form parts of a single work of art, a triptych, if produced with that intention by a single artist or a group working together. That three distinct physical objects are produced in isolation from each other, the product of three different "hands," implies that, if each red canvas is or constitutes a work of art, there are three distinct works. However, when does a red-paint-covered canvas constitute a work of art, and what sort of entity is the art object so constituted? The answer to the first question once again appeals to intentions and context. For a canvas uniformly covered with red paint to be a work of art—a painting—an art-historical context must be in place that permits certain intentions to count as art making ones. In eighteenth-century France such institutions were not present, whereas in twentieth-century America (or France) they were. Second, the art-making intentions must actually exist. If one canvas became red because the artist needed an empty spray paint can and got it by discharging the paint onto this canvas, there is no art-making intention and no artwork. If the canvas became red as the result of an intention to produce a work in the color-field genre, then there is an art-making intention, and thus an artwork.

The second, strictly ontological, question asked above is: What sort of entity is the art object? Is it the painting that results from covering the canvas with red paint? Is it identical to the paint-covered canvas or not?

To grasp the ontological puzzle here, it is easier to turn to a different example: a piece of clay shaped into a human figure. Is the sculpture identical to the lump of clay? Obviously not, because the lump existed before it was shaped to create the sculpture, but the sculpture itself did not exist. An alternative answer to this question is that the sculpture is the human-shaped lump. This entity came into existence when the sculpture did and could be regarded as a phase of the existence of the lump itself. However, even such a "phase" or "time-slice" could be understood as having its shape contingently. That is, if it is possible for it to continue existing as one and the same phase of the lump while radically changing in shape, the phase is not identical to the sculpture because the sculpture would not survive such a radical change in shape. Also, if it is possible for this entity to come into existence independently of any human intention, it could not be identical to the sculpture. A sculpture cannot come into existence exclusively through natural processes. These considerations imply that the entity identical to the sculpture is not simply a lump of material structured in a certain way but such a lump structured to fulfill an artistic function or intention typically made possible by certain institutions or practices. Exactly the same is true of the red painting. It is a canvas covered by red paint to in order fulfill an artistic function or intention made possible by certain institutions or practices (Levinson 1996).

ARE ALL ARTWORKS CREATED? Concrete artworks such as the red paintings and the clay sculpture just discussed are obviously created. Are the abstract works—the novels, musical pieces, and so on—also created? Some scholars, such as Jerrold Levinson (1980), have argued that it is a condition on a satisfactory ontology of art that the ontology accounts for the createdness of abstract artworks. Others, such as Peter Kivy (1993) and Julian Dodd (2000, 2002), have disputed this. Underlying these conflicting views are conflicting intuitions. One intuition is that novels, plays, and musical works are just as much the products of creative activity as are paintings. The other intuition is that abstract objects cannot be created because of the sort of objects that they are.

It may seem that the argument of the preceding section supports the claim that abstract artworks are created. It was argued that these works are not identical to abstract structures per se, but to structures tied to certain intentions and contexts. What could "tied to" mean but created with certain intentions in a certain context? But this raises an important question: What are these entities that are purportedly created? They are not pure abstract structures, because these are really uncreated and eternal,

and it has already been denied that they are the artworks. The best known proposal on this score is Levinson's. He claims that they are indicated structures "a structure-as-indicated-by-P-at-T-in-[art]-historical-context-C" (1996, p. 146). The dashes are intended to indicate that this is not a set-like ordered quadruple but something more "unified," a type that comes into existence with the act of musical or literary composition.

There are a variety of objections to Levinson's view. Stefano Predelli asserts that indicating does not in general create new entities (1980). If I point out my favorite house in the neighborhood, I haven't created a new entity: the-house-as-indicated-by-me. So it is implausible that indicating creates one when authors or composers indicate abstract structures. There are two ways of replying to this objection. One reply would be to claim that new entities are always created by indicatings, but people pay no attention to most of them because the indicatings are of no interest them. The house-as-indicated-by-me is an entity that has about as much interest as a scattered object such as a nose-tie consisting of Bill Clinton's nose and a tie he left in a hotel during a visit to Australia. Both nose-ties and indicated-buildings nevertheless exist. The other reply claims that some indicatings are special because they occur within institutions or practices that endow them with special properties and give them special recognition. Sentences can be regarded as abstract syntactic structures, which, when used (when *indicated* by a speaker or hearer) creates a new entity, which has semantic or pragmatic properties not possessed by the abstract sentence type. The ability to convey something distinct from the semantic meaning of the sentence type results from linguistic conventions combined with the intentions of language users and the context of use. Writers are just special cases of people who use (indicate) strings of sentence types to convey something through the creation of a complex literary object. Composers do something similar with abstract sound structures. The two replies are consistent with each other, though the second is available to those who would resist the first.

A second objection is that abstract entities, such as structural types, cannot be created because they cannot enter into causal relations. Being created means being caused to exist and, if an entity cannot enter into a causal relation, it cannot be caused to exist. This claim is said to apply to any abstract type whether it be of the pure unindicated variety or an indicated structural type. A related third objection should also be mentioned at this point. It could be said that even if there are indicated types, they are just as eternal and uncreated as any other abstract thing. Such types exist just in case a property corresponding to the type does, and all properties exist eternally. Hence the property of being a structure indicated by P at T in C exists eternally. Therefore the indicated structural type does too. Hence it is not created (Dodd 2000, 2002).

Both of these objections are too tendentious to be decisive. The issue of whether types can be caused to exist is not settled by their being abstract; they are abstract because they have instances or tokens. Someone could claim that a type does not exist until at least one token of it does, or instructions for creating a token are present. In either case causing the token (or the instructions for making tokens) to exist in effect causes the type to as well. There are many types that it is plausible to conceive in these terms. Consider artifact types, one example of which is an automobile model. It is plausible that automobile designers bring this type into existence when they create the design for a car model. This plausible claim is deniable. It could be consistently maintained that the type Volkswagen Beetle would exist even if intelligent life had never evolved anywhere in the universe. Though consistently maintainable, the claim is implausible. Saying it is tendentious is perhaps an understatement. If this is true for car models, it would be equally true for literary and musical works. So one may perhaps set aside the second and third objections to the idea that indicated structural types are a kind of entity that can be brought into existence.

INDIVIDUATING ARTWORKS

What has been demonstrated thus far is that indicated structures are distinguishable from unindicated ones, and that the idea that they come into existence—indeed, are brought into existence—is, at least, plausible. However, there is a final set of objections to them that question whether they individuate musical and literary works correctly. Are such works always essentially tied to the precise times they are created, to their creators, and to their context of creation? This is what is denied by the final set of objections.

Look first at authorship. It may be true that Cervantes and Menard (had there been such a person) could not possibly create the same work. But imagine two contemporary writers, composers, or even painters who belong to the same school working at the same time. There are two different scenarios to consider. One occurs when both produce identical works. Suppose Mozart and Haydn had produced, independently of each other, identical scores for a string quartet in the year 1787. Would

they both have independently composed the same work? An alternative scenario can be created by supposing a possible world in which Haydn instead of Mozart composed a score identical to the score for Mozart's G major quartet K.387 and in which Mozart produced no such score. Would Haydn have composed in this possible world the same quartet that Mozart composed in actuality? Some people would answer yes to both of these questions; but, if that answer is right for either one, the identity of the artist *may not* be essential to the identity of the work. The first scenario does not raise a problem when it comes to painting because two numerically distinct painted canvases from the hand of different artists are different paintings even if they are indistinguishable. The second scenario, however, raises the same question for painting as it does for music or literature. In a possible world in which Braque rather than Picasso had painted a portrait of Gertrude Stein exactly similar to Picasso's actual painting, would Braque be the artist responsible for the work Picasso actually made (Currie 1988, S. Davies 2001)?

Something similar can be said about the time at which the work is indicated or brought into existence. Is this always an essential property of artworks? Some works seem to be tightly tied to their time of production. Hemingway's fiction is closely tied to the World War I generation. Picasso's *Les demoiselles d'Avignon* seems even more tightly tied to its moment of production. But consider traditional African sculpture from a particular region, some forms of traditional Chinese painting, or the naive work of an amateur artist, all of which may remain unchanged in style over many years. In these cases, it may seem plausible that the same work could be produced many years apart in different possible worlds. However, it seems possible that even those works that seem most closely tied to a moment in time might have been produced at slightly different times or, in special circumstances, very different times. Consider a possible world that duplicates the history of European art, but in which that whole history begins two hundred years earlier than it in fact did. In that world, Picasso paints *Les demoiselles* in the early eighteenth century (D. Davies 2003).

The contextual variable is perhaps immune to considerations such as those just raised about artist and time of production. Works from different eras, traditions, styles, or works made with different intentions will not be the same no matter how superficially similar they appear. This is an important point of the Menard example. Nevertheless, a case may be made for the possibility of the same work in different contexts by appealing to the idea that slight differences in context in different possible worlds may still result in the same work. This is especially plausible if the specific difference in context would not make a difference to the creator of the work in question (D. Davies 2003).

This set of objections raises two broad concerns for the idea that musical and literary works are indicated structural types and that paintings are contextually identified physical objects. It raises objections to Levinson's specific proposal regarding the individuation of indicated structures, but it also questions whether any general formula appealing to any of the variables under discussion can individuate artworks correctly.

Before concluding that these concerns are correct, one needs to evaluate the objections on which they are based. Do the objections show what they set out to show? One problem with them is that they rely on uncertainties in human modal intuitions about artworks, which point more directly to epistemic rather than metaphysical possibilities. That is, in the face of the sorts of examples considered thus far, many individuals will be uncertain what to think, and so it will be epistemically possible, relative to their beliefs, that a certain principle of individuation is wrong. That, however, falls short of showing it is wrong.

Is there a way of sharpening intuitions to arrive at principles of individuation? Perhaps this can be done by getting clearer about what the Menard example and other similar examples reveal about structurally identical works. Cervantes and Menard had different artistic projects and, in pursuing these, each achieved (did) different things in their respective works. This pair of differences, concerning artistic project and artistic achievement, is crucial in individuating works and in identifying important artistic properties of them. In highlighting these differences, the analogy mentioned earlier between abstract sentence types and utterances—or, more broadly, sentences-in-use—is a helpful one to remember. The language user in question, along with the user's intentions, the time of utterance, and the context of use, all commonly contribute to fixing what the utterance conveys beyond or in distinction from the semantic content of the sentence. However, the precise role each of these items plays may vary in different uses of language. Further, it is possible for different utterances to convey precisely the same thing. Regarding artworks, something similar is true (Stecker 2003): They are individuated by being a specific abstract or concrete structure used by an artist in pursuing such and such a project and achieving so and so. Usually the three variables—identity of artist, time of creation, and artistic context—are crucial in constituting

projects and what they achieve, yet their exact role can vary in different art forms and different traditions, as well as for many other reasons. The emphasis on the artistic project and the artist's achievement recalls the idea that artworks are action types or tokens. However, those views identified the work with the wrong entity. As the indicated-structure view emphasizes, the artwork is the product that results from the project and embodies the achievement.

See also Aesthetics, History of; Aesthetics, Problems of; Art, Definitions of; Danto, Arthur; Existence; Ontology; Ontology, History of.

Bibliography

Borges, J. L. "Pierre Menard, Author of the Quixote." In *Labyrinthes*, translated by J. E. Irby, 62–71. London: Penguin, 1970.

Caplan, B., and C. Matheson. "Can Musical Works be Created?" *British Journal of Aesthetics* 44 (2004): 113–134.

Currie, G. *An Ontology of Art*. London: Macmillan, 1988.

Danto, A. *The Transfiguration of the Commonplace*. Cambridge, MA: Harvard University Press, 1981.

Davies, D. *Art as Performance*. Oxford: Blackwell, 2003.

Davies, S. *Musical Works and Performances*. Oxford: Oxford University Press, 2001.

Dilworth, J. *The Double Content of Art*. Amherst, NY: Prometheus Books, 2004.

Dodd, J. "Musical Works as Eternal Types." *British Journal of Aesthetics* 40 (2000): 424–440.

Dodd, J. "Defending Musical Platonism." *British Journal of Aesthetics* 42 (2002): 380–402.

Goodman, N. *Languages of Art*. New York: Bobbs-Merrill, 1968.

Howell, R. "Ontology and the Nature of Literary Works." *Journal of Aesthetics and Art Criticism* 60 (2002a): 67–79.

Howell, R. "Types, Indicated and Initiated." *British Journal of Aesthetics* 42 (2002a): 105–127.

Kivy, P. *The Fine Art of Repetition*. Cambridge, U.K.: Cambridge University Press, 1993.

Levinson, J. "What a Musical Work Is." *Journal of Philosophy* 77 (1980): 5–28.

Levinson, J. *The Pleasures of Aesthetics*. Ithaca, NY: Cornell University Press, 1996.

Predelli, S. "Musical Ontology and the Argument from Creation." *British Journal of Aesthetics* 41 (1980): 279–292.

Rohrbaugh, R. "Artworks as Historical Individuals." *European Journal of Philosophy* 11 (2003): 177–205.

Stecker, R. *Interpretation and Construction: Art, Speech, and the Law*. Oxford: Blackwell, 2003.

Wollheim, R. *Art and its Objects*. 2nd ed. Cambridge, U.K.: Cambridge University Press, 1980.

Wolterstorff, N. *Worlds and Works of Art*. Oxford: Clarendon Press, 1980.

Robert Stecker (2005)

ART, PERFORMANCE IN

Some philosophers hold that the creation of art always involves performance, and that artworks are more accurately defined as processes or actions than as objects or events. This entry will consider the more traditional view that only some art forms—drama, music, dance, opera or musical theater, and "performance art"—involve performance.

Performances can be freely improvised. In addition to being judged for their general interest and skill of execution, such performances are rated as well for elements of spontaneity and risk. The performers make and coordinate their activities in real time, without knowing how their performance will continue or end. Though drama can be extemporized, jazz takes improvisation to its highest level. In the paradigm case, however, performance involves the live presentation and interpretation of a previously specified work.

THE LIVE PRESENTATION OF WORKS

Works for performance are often specified through a form of notation, such as a musical score or a script. The notation is addressed to the performer and prescribes what must be done or achieved if the work is to be faithfully performed. It may also contain recommendations that are not work-determinative, and that need not be followed. Features crucial to the work's identity are not always mentioned in the notation, for instance, where they are dictated by practices and conventions that are taken for granted. The performer's first act of interpretation occurs in following and understanding what is instructed in the work's notation, if it has one, along with appreciating the background of performance practices and conventions that it assumes.

In oral traditions, works are transmitted verbally, not by notations. One or more suitably authorized performances are given the status of a model for further instances of the work. Just what in the model is work-specifying and what is merely optional is settled by reference to the work-and-performance traditions and genres within which the relevant piece is located. For example, although the melody in the exemplary performance is elaborately decorated, it might be understood that the manner of decoration is left to the performers' discretion, as long as they respect limits set by the appropriate style. Or it might be understood that the choreography of a sword fight need not be aped in subsequent performance, though appropriate fighting actions will be required.

The actor's, singer's, or dancer's medium is her body, along with costumes, props, and sets. For other musicians, their instruments are their media. When a work is designed for performance, its medium is usually crucial to its identity, since the medium affects and constrains what can be done by the performer. The artist's instructions usually indicate both what is to be achieved and the medium or manner in which this is to be done. To perform a violin concerto, one should play the violin. Merely generating the appropriate sounds on a synthesizer (or a record player) does not qualify as performing the work.

Some works call for media that are not standard. Electronic compositions for live performance involve the use of microphones, sound generators, and the like. One of John Cage's pieces was issued as a vinyl disk with instructions about how the settings of the hi-fi amplifier are to be modified as the disk plays. Hip-hop artists and sound appropriators take the recordings of others as source materials for their own works and, like Cage, turn the record player into an instrument of musical performance.

INTERPRETATION

Works that are for live performance are always ontologically thinner and more abstract than the concrete performances that instance them. If all the artist's work-determinative prescriptions are faithfully followed, many aspects of the performance's detail are not determined. The performer (or conductor/producer) resolves these uncertainties. The playwright might indicate that the actor is to say "Curse the gods," but the choice of facial expressions, gestures, and bodily attitude, along with the tone, inflection, pitch, and volume of the voice, are usually left to the actor. Whether through deliberation or not, the delivery of the line in an actual performance inevitably will display a particular version of all these features.

In adding flesh to the skeleton that is the work, and thereby creating a living performance, the performer interprets the work. It would be misleading, though, to say that interpretation is something added by the performer after he or she has satisfied the work-determinative prescriptions of the artist, or to suggest that interpretation fills the gap between the work's abstractness and its performance's concreteness. The delivery of the work is not prior to or apart from the interpretative contribution, which is crucial at every point or moment. The presentation of the words of a play or the notes of a symphony is not separable from the manner and inflection with which they are presented.

Some works for live performance can be very spare, ontologically speaking. Songs are so, when specified only as a melody, sequence of chords, and verse and chorus. Very different interpretations can be consistent with the faithful presentation of such works. The thinner the work, the more the performer becomes the focus of attention and the more the evaluation of the performance concerns the performer's creativity and vitality, rather than the faithful delivery of the work. But even where works are very detailed, as are Mahler's symphonies or Shaw's plays, the importance of the performer's interpretative contribution cannot be overlooked. Indeed, complex works offer the performer wonderful opportunities for displaying her talents, because their realization is unmistakably demanding and they allow for interpretations that are subtle, rich, and multilayered. Some works, such as instrumental concertos, are intended to draw attention to the virtuosic performances they require.

If all live performances embody interpretations of their works, so do thoughtless, unplanned performances and mechanical ones learned by rote. In the normal case, however, the interpretation is planned by the performer who delivers it and reveals a considered vision of the work. Some performers concentrate on the work's progression from moment to moment, leaving the artist's design to ensure that the whole is satisfying. Other performers structure their efforts in terms of a conception of the work's overall structure. Some performers can describe the ideas that inform their interpretations, while others have a more applied, unarticulated knowledge of what they do.

An interpretation, once mastered, can be repeated. Different performances of a production of a play usually present the same interpretation. Yet a given performer can have more than one way of interpreting a given work. A performer with a long career often adopts a fresh approach when she returns to works she performed previously.

AUTHENTICITY AND INTEGRITY CONDITIONS

The purpose of a performance of a work is to present the work along with an interpretation of it. Such performances therefore presuppose a commitment of faithfulness to the work, or authenticity. Deliberate departures from the work undermine the claims of a performance to be of that work. Accidental errors and slips in performances need not prove fatal to the attempt at performance, however. A performance can instance a work because of its intent, and the work can be recognized in what is produced, despite the imperfection of its representation of that work.

There is disagreement about what faithfulness requires when questions such as the following are debated: Is it necessary to use boys rather than women when performing Shakespeare? Should Scarlatti be performed on the harpsichord only, and can its jacks be made of plastic instead of quills? If an eighteenth-century playwright specifies that his work is set in the present, should we use period costume or the clothes and milieu of the twenty-first century?

Such disagreements can reflect deeper differences of opinion about the ontological character of the works in question. Someone who thinks a musical work is merely a pattern of notes will regard any presentation that reproduces that pattern as faithful, no matter what means are used to produce it. But another who believes the work's instrumentation is also central to its identity will conclude that authentic performances must use instruments of the kind known to and specified by its composer. Differences between their ontological theories lead philosophers to draw the line between performers' legitimate liberty and illegitimate license in contrasting places.

There is another reason for conflict, though. Some people think that authenticity can be traded for interpretative interest. In other words, they do not regard the pursuit of faithfulness to the work as a paramount virtue in performances. As supporting evidence, they may cite the free approach sometimes taken to the interpretation of Shakespeare and of the most famous musical works and operas. It might not be coincidental, however, that works approached in this manner are very familiar to the established audience and that there is a concern to maintain their relevance for future audiences. In other words, the free approach to interpretation in these cases is not necessarily indicative of indifference to or disrespect of the work as such. Provided that audiences are interested in the works being performed, authenticity in performance cannot be reduced merely to another interpretive option.

Stan Godlovitch (1998) specifies the following conditions for the integrity of performances: only one work is performed at a time; its proper sequence is respected, as is the indicated rate of delivery; the performance is continuous, without unjustified breaks; performers comply with the appropriate roles (and do not, for example, swap parts midway through). Also, the audience is in a position to receive the entire performance in its detail. Not all of these conditions are satisfied in all performances. Nevertheless, these conditions are normative in that they indicate what is expected from a performance.

Activities not directed to an audience—practicing, rehearsing, learning, doodling—do not result in performances, according to these conditions. (In many cases, such activities have the goal of preparing performers for performances, however.) Other performance-like activities violate other of the specified conditions and are not exemplary for that reason. Music-minus-one disks and karaoke (as well as new technology, allowing a person to speak one of the roles in a movie) are examples.

STUDIO PERFORMANCES

Not all performances are given live. Some take place in studios and result in recordings or films. Studio performances have their own integrity conditions. The work's segments can be recorded piecemeal and out of order. A single performer can take many different roles in the finished product, as a consequence of multitracking or filming. The performer's inputs can be electronically modified. The projected audience is not present to witness the studio performance.

We accept studio performances of pieces created originally for live performances, such as recordings of classical symphonies or movies of Elizabethan plays. They may use some of the studio's resources, such as the possibility in film of moving seamlessly between different indoor and outdoor locations. But in general, they simulate live performances, and the artists involved are capable of giving live performances.

Some works are designed for studio performances. Rock recordings that sculpt sounds electronically in a fashion that could not be achieved in real time are examples. These are works for performance, but not for live performance. The same song can be recorded by another group, and the result is a new (studio) performance of it, not a different but a derivative work.

Yet other works are not *for* performance of any kind, though they involve studio performances in their creation. Most films rely on the resources of the studios (slow motion, flashbacks, stunts, digital editing, and special effects) and result in works that are for screening, not performance. Similarly, purely electronic musical works are for playback, not for performance, though performers might supply material that is integrated into the work. "Directors' cuts" result in new versions of movies, not in new performances, while remakes result in new but derivative works.

PERFORMANCE ART

During the mid-twentieth century, artists began to challenge traditional conceptions of artworks and the separation of art from life by using their own bodies as the medium for their works. They posed in public or structured some aspect of their lives in terms of an aesthetic goal; they lived in cages or staged happenings. Different strands of the movement featured bodily mutilation, sexual orgies, and primitive rituals, often intended to deliver a political or socio-sexual message. Some feminist artists embraced performance art for its liberating energy, but were sensitive also to the need to subvert the objectifying equation of women with their bodies. Performance artists have often integrated video into their artworks. The works of the French feminist Orlan display many of these features; they are films of the surgical alteration of her face to give it the features of famous art-historical beauties.

See also Aesthetics, History of; Aesthetics, Problems of; Greek Drama; Music, Philosophy of; Tragedy.

Bibliography

Alperson, Philip. "On Musical Improvisation." *Journal of Aesthetics and Art Criticism* 43 (1984): 17–30.

Carlson, Marvin. *Theories of the Theatre: A Historical and Critical Survey from the Greeks to the Present.* Ithaca and London: Cornell University Press, 1984.

Carroll, Noël. "Interpretation, Theatrical Performance, and Ontology." *Journal of Aesthetics and Art Criticism* 59 (2001): 313–316.

Carroll, Noël. "Theater, Dance, and Theory: A Philosophical Narrative." *Dance Chronicle* 15 (1992): 317–331.

Copeland, Roger, and Marshall Cohen, eds. *What Is Dance?* New York: Oxford University Press, 1983.

Davies, David. *Art as Performance.* Oxford: Blackwell, 2003.

Davies, Stephen. *Musical Works and Performances.* Oxford: Clarendon Press, 2001.

Godlovitch, Stan. *Musical Performance: A Philosophical Study.* London: Routledge, 1998.

Hamilton, James R. "Theatrical Enactment." *Journal of Aesthetics and Art Criticism* 58 (2000): 23–35.

Hamilton, James R. "Theatrical Performance and Interpretation." *Journal of Aesthetics and Art Criticism* 59 (2001): 307–312.

Kemal, Salim, and Ivan Gaskell, eds. *Performance and Authenticity in the Arts.* New York: Cambridge University Press, 1999.

Kivy, Peter. *Authenticities: Philosophical Reflections on Musical Performance.* Ithaca: Cornell University Press, 1995.

Mark, Thomas Carson. "On Works of Virtuosity." *Journal of Philosophy* 77 (1980): 28–45.

Mark, Thomas Carson. "Philosophy of Piano Playing: Reflections on the Concept of Performance." *Philosophy and Phenomenological Research* 41 (1981): 299–324.

McFee, Graham. *Understanding Dance.* New York: Routledge, 1992.

Saltz, David. "How to Do Things on Stage." *Journal of Aesthetics and Art Criticism* 49 (1991): 31–45.

Sparshott, Francis. *A Measured Pace: Toward a Philosophical Understanding of the Arts of Dance.* Toronto: University of Toronto Press, 1995.

Sparshott, Francis. *Off the Ground: First Steps to a Philosophical Consideration of the Dance.* Princeton, NJ: Princeton University Press, 1988.

Thom, Paul. *For an Audience: A Philosophy of the Performing Arts.* Philadelphia: Temple University Press, 1993.

Stephen Davies (2005)

ART, REPRESENTATION IN

Pictures form a subset of the artifacts that serve to represent particular things or kinds of thing, real or imagined, in a broad inclusive sense of the term *represent*. Like some of their fellow representations, but unlike others, pictures go on to attribute properties to the things or kinds they represent—properties that thereby constitute their pictorial content. How does this work? What distinguishes the representing done by pictures—*depiction*—from the representing done by various other familiar kinds of representation?

PLATO AND PICTORIAL MIMESIS

Near the start of his case for banishing the poets from his ideally just city (Plato 1992, *Republic* X, 595a–598b), Plato urges that poetry and painting are analogous mimetic activities, structured so as to be able to imitate—approximately replicate—only a superficial and trivial part of the deep and serious things they profess to take as models. The argument employs a three-story metaphysics with Plato's Forms at the top, ordinary three-dimensional worldly particulars in the middle, and appearances (*eidola, phainomena, phantasmata*) at the bottom. Paradigm cases of appearances are shadows and reflections. Shifty, shimmery, and insubstantial, they owe such limited stability and stable apprehensibility as they to their owners, the three-dimensional worldly particulars from which they derive and to which they bear a real if limited resemblance. They therefore bear to worldly particulars many of the relations that worldly particulars are said to bear to the Forms.

The phrase "what S sees of X here and now" may be taken to refer to another appearance, another insubstantial something owing such limited stability and stable apprehensibility as it possesses to its three-dimensional owner X, the entity it manifests and imperfectly resembles. Such an appearance differs from a reflection or cast shadow in that it is attached to or embedded in its owner. In fact, it may be regarded as literally a part—albeit a dependent and ontologically inferior part—of that owner.

Now painters and poets are mimetic artists, renderers. Painters undertake to render three-dimensional arrangements of physical objects and to do so on a two-dimensional surface, using as their medium line and color. Tragic poets undertake to render human agents engaged in spontaneous morally significant action and to do so on a stage before an audience, using as their medium the rehearsed movements and speeches of actors. One may take these renderers at their word when they say that they are out to replicate important worldly originals to the full extent it is in their power to do so. Still, what extent is that? Given the materials he must work in and the way he must manipulate these materials to count as a painter or poet at all, the most such an imitator can ever accomplish by way of replicating his original is to produce a second worldly particular almost entirely unlike the first except for possessing an exactly similar appearance. His would-be traffic in second-rate entities (worldly particulars) comes to no more than a traffic in third-rate entities (appearances). "Imitation is far removed from the truth, for it touches only a small part of a thing and a part that is itself only an image" (598b).

Add that what meets the eye (or ear) about an important or valuable object seldom if ever includes what makes it behave as it does or what makes it a good or bad thing of its kind, and one will have powerful reason for suspecting that the theoretically and practically decisive aspects of worldly particulars lie beyond the reach of the senses, hence beyond the reach of the particular media that make painters painters and poets poets. Echoes of Plato's reasoning abound in texts as recent as Susan Sontag's *On Photography* (1977).

Thinkers who reject Plato's metaphysics and his deprecatory attitude toward painting nevertheless often agree that depiction consists in the partial replication in a new and alien medium of a certain superficial aspect of the depicted thing's nature, something inherently capable of meeting the eye, call it the depicted thing's outward appearance. Such thinkers have various ways of embracing Plato's account of depiction's workings while avoiding his negative conclusions about painting's value. Sometimes they insist that depictive success is one thing and artistic success is something different and deeper. Sometimes they insist with Oscar Wilde that there is nothing superficial about surfaces.

There have always been dissenters, of course. One is René Descartes, who insists that engravings successfully portray the things they depict as having lots of properties they could not possibly share with those things. Indeed, when it comes to objects standing at a great distance or whose accurate depiction requires foreshortening, "the perfection of an image often depends on its not resembling its object as much as it might" (Descartes 1985, *Optics*, Discourse IV, AT 113). Descartes thereby prepares his reader for the alarming thought that our most useful and reliable sense-based ideas resemble their originals as little as engravings do theirs.

GOMBRICH AND THE PURSUIT OF ILLUSION

A vast renewal of philosophical interest in depiction begins in the 1950s with the work of the art historian E. H. Gombrich. Like Hermann von Helmholtz, Karl R. Popper, R. L. Gregory, and others, Gombrich holds that the content of visual experience is produced in a kind of unconscious inference by the human visual system to the best available explanation of the available retinal stimuli. (The stimuli on which visual system inferences are ultimately based remain permanently out of introspective reach.) The conceptual resources a visual system may draw on in framing these hypotheses include any and all concepts available to its owner and the standards by means of which it assesses them are sensitive to the full range of beliefs, expectations, and practical priorities its owner brings to the task of seeing what is before his eyes. The beholder's share in determining the content of his own visual experience is therefore substantial indeed; there is no such thing as *the* appearance a thing can possess when accurately seen from a particular physical viewpoint.

Only one particular kind of image, the *naturalistic* kind, is out to replicate an appearance taken on by a particular object in a particular context for a particular sort of appropriately prepared spectator. Naturalistic image making catches on only in particular cultural traditions at particular times. Images more generally are best conceived as substitutes for the things they depict, standing in for them in various forms of ritual and imaginative activity and sharing with them only the handful of specific properties, visible and otherwise, required for this special purpose. (Think of how a hobby horse stands in for a real horse.) In this sense, *making* (the production of substitutes) comes before and is more generally prevalent than *matching* (the production of objects designed to visually match the things they depict under appropriate objective and subjective conditions).

Consider a naturalistic image maker, out to capture some particular appearance of the particular object she is about to depict. Just as there is no way for her to set aside the effects of past encounters with other objects when it comes to trying to see this one accurately, there is no way for her to set aside the effects of past efforts to depict other objects when it comes to trying to render her depiction of this one appropriately responsive to how she now sees it. Instead she must rely on habits, routines, and formulas inherited from past image-making practice to give her a skeletal generic image of an object of the right general kind, which she then works over in a trial-and-error manner until she finally achieves a convincing likeness of this particular object. Naturalistic image making is a process of *schema and correction*.

Such small-scale explorations contribute to the larger-scale explorations conducted in image-making communities as they invent, refine, and promulgate redeployable techniques for appearance-capturing techniques based on hard-won empirical insights into how the human visual system works. Foreshortening, tonal modeling, and the various perspective systems are major inventions of this sort, but there are countless smaller ones: Think of Rembrandt's readily imitated trick of suggesting the glint of gold braid with a few loose, broad dots and dashes of yellow paint. When and where the naturalistic project catches on in the first place, the history of art largely consists in the history of such progressive innovation. When and where it does not catch on, art may change over time, but not in ways that possess the large-scale narrative coherence historians demand.

> The history of art … may be described as the forging of master keys for opening the mysterious locks of our senses to which only nature herself originally held the key. … Like the burglar who tries to break a safe, the artist has no direct access to the inner mechanism. He can only feel his way with sensitive fingers, probing and adjusting his hook or wire when something gives way. Of course, once the door springs open, once the key is shaped, it is easy to repeat the performance. The next person needs no special insight—no more, that is, than is needed to copy his predecessor's master key (Gombrich 1961, pp. 359–360).

Gombrich's relation to Plato is complex. When properly experienced, a successful naturalistic image partially replicates an appearance the depicted object is capable of taking on. But this appearance is not a superficial part of the object; it is an effect of the object on a particular spectator made possible by the particular concepts and concerns he brings to the act of seeing. The artist devises her own means of achieving *some* of the effects the depicted object would have on a spectator's visual system if it were standing before him. But limitations inherent in her media—the restricted range of lights and darks available from her paints and inks, the manifest flatness of the surface on which she deposits these substances—ensure in advance that her replication of the object's appearance is partial at best. A depiction takes on the appearance the artist intends it to take on only if the spectator actively brings to his inspection of it the highly particular mental set the artist intends for him.

Still, and here Gombrich again sides with Plato, the experience the naturalistic image maker means to induce in the spectator is one in which it is for him as if he were seeing the depicted object face to face. This means he manages to neglect the lack of appropriate color (in drawings), the lack of appropriate binocular disparity (in full-color paintings of nearby objects), and so on. It also means that as the picture takes on its intended appearance for him, the content of his visual experience of the picture has less and less to do with the picture, and more and more to do with the thing depicted. He loses sight of the depiction in favor of the thing depicted, with the result that the specific devices by means of which the image maker induces the intended experience drop from visual awareness at the very moment they achieve their intended effect. Gombrich concludes that naturalistic image makers are inducers of illusion and that illusion obliterates its own conditions.

This illusion will be available to a given spectator only if he can approach the painting with its called-for mental set, hence only if he can readily identify this set and readily assume it without detailed instructions. Pictorial intelligibility is a special case of communicative intelligibility, depending on a rich, historically variable, culturally conditioned stock of expectations, assumptions, and conventions. In order to generate and disappear into an appropriate illusion, a set of marks must first be correctly interpreted as a communicative gesture on the part of the artist. Like Ferdinand de Saussure and Roman Jakobson before him, Gombrich olds that to understand any communicative gesture, one must view it as a choice from among a fixed range of available alternatives, owing its significance in part to the natural significance of certain dimensions of difference (darker tones are naturally taken to signal darker objects, more vigorous gestures to signal greater urgency), in part to the conventional fact that one is tacitly but publicly committed

to working within such and such a restricted set of choices (only these tones, only these gestures). To this extent, at any rate, art is a language, a system of signals resting on contingent and mutable conventions that must be internalized and respected by artists and audiences alike. All three main approaches to understanding depiction draw heavily on Gombrich's work, accepting some strands of it while rejecting others.

INTELLIGIBILITY ACCOUNTS

According to the intelligibility approach, pictures are distinctive in virtue of how one's ability as an audience member to make appropriate interpretive sense of them builds on and derives from one's ability as a perceiver to make appropriate visual sense of one's immediate physical surroundings.

J. J. Gibson (1971) holds that perceivers extract certain crucial elements of a picture's content (e.g., depicted recessions in depth) from features of the marked surface (e.g., texture gradients across that surface), using precisely the same methods they use to extract corresponding features of their real visual environment (e.g., actual recessions) from locally available features of the visual stimulus (e.g., texture gradients across one's visual field). Pictorial understanding is just routine environmental feature extraction applied to a special artificially contrived stimulus: a picture's marked surface. The proposal is closely bound up with Gibson's idiosyncratic account of ordinary visual perception, his environmental optics.

Flint Schier (1986) proposes that pictures exhibit a distinctive division of cognitive labor between the mastery of particular pictorial idioms and the ability to visually recognize a particular thing or kind when presented with it face to face. On the one hand, pictorial idioms possess *natural generativity*: every pictorial idiom is such as to make possible a picture so representative of the idiom as a whole that understanding this particular picture would suffice to confer a general competence with the entire idiom. On the other hand, the interpretation of any given picture P redeploys ordinary capacities for face-to-face visual recognition in such a manner that:

(1) a general competence with the idiom employed by P, and

(2) a capacity to recognize each of the particular things or kinds that P depicts (and each of the particular visually detectable properties and relations that figure in P's pictorial content)

are individually necessary and jointly sufficient for a given spectator to be able to understand P. As it stands,

Schier's proposal makes no allowance for the depiction of particular people that nobody could recognize on sight—Christ, for instance—nor does it allow for the large role collateral information plays in the correct interpretation of many pictures. Still, it feels like a first approximation to an important insight.

SEMIOTIC ACCOUNTS

According to the semiotic approach, pictures are conventional symbols in a richer sense than Gombrich allows. A *symbol system* involves syntactic rules that classify items as tokens of various permanently available symbol types, together with semantic rules determining what an object must be like if it is to *comply with*—be such that it could be accurately symbolized by—tokens of a given type. What differentiates pictures from other conventional symbols are distinctive structural features of the systems to which they belong and from which they derive their pictorial content—*pictorial* symbol systems.

Nelson Goodman (1976) never offers sufficient conditions for a system's being pictorial, but he declares that a system cannot be pictorial unless it is syntactically dense, semantically dense, and relatively replete. The effect of the first condition is to insist that there is no limit to how similar two pictorial symbol tokens can be while remaining tokens of distinct symbol types. The effect of the second is to insist that there is no limit to how similar two objects can be while remaining such that the accurate depiction of one and the accurate depiction of the other would require the deployment of two distinct symbol types, one for each. The effect of the third is to insist that a relatively large range of perceivable features of a given pictorial symbol token are relevant to determining its type. Yet depictions formed in the array of lights on a baseball scoreboard fail to exhibit any of Goodman's three features.

Commonly the most salient parts of a picture are depictions in their own right, depicting parts of the larger whole depicted by the bigger picture and arranged in a manner reflective of the arrangement in this larger whole of those depicted parts. This constitutes an interesting affinity between pictures and such manifestly conventional representations as maps and diagrams. Andrew Harrison (1991) infers from it that maps, diagrams, *and* pictures are conventional symbols, belonging to systems whose (compositional) syntax and semantics relate the part-whole structure of complex symbols to the part-whole structure of compliant objects in an especially simple and uniform manner. Yet while maps and diagrams often come equipped with keys explaining their simplest individual significant components, full-fledged pictures do not and apparently cannot come with anything comparable.

EXPERIENTIAL ACCOUNTS

According to the experiential approach, Gombrich is correct in thinking that pictures operate by inducing a distinctive kind of experience, with the thing depicted figuring in the content of that experience. But he is wrong to attribute an illusionist phenomenology to the experience. Instead we should conceive it as a unitary experience, visual at least in part, whose content involves both the depicted thing and various visible features of the depiction itself. There are three main stories about how this goes.

Experienced resemblance theorists (Peacocke 1987, Budd 1993, Hopkins 1998) hold that when one experiences a picture appropriately, one visually experiences it as resembling the thing or kind of thing it depicts with respect to certain of the visually detectable properties possessed by each. Hopkins's version of the theory centers on a highly relational property known as outline shape. Begin with the cone of rays connecting visible points on the object's facing surface to a given perceiver's point of view. Take the intersection of that cone with a plane perpendicular to the perceiver's line of sight. The shape of this intersection is the object's outline shape for the particular perceiver in question. Hopkins is at pains to argue that despite the arcane way outline shape is defined, people are ordinarily implicitly visually aware of the outline shapes of things around them. He contends that whenever one experiences portion D of marked surface P as depicting object O, one visually experiences the outline shape of P (as seen from where one actually stands) as resembling that of object O (as seen from an appropriate hypothetical place).

The most basic kind of pictorial content accruing to pictures in any given idiom consists of resemblances to parts of the picture surface itself with respect to some fixed list of visually detectable determinable properties renderable in that idiom. The list always includes outline shape; it sometimes includes such further properties as local color and texture. One can call the properties on such lists *visual field properties*. Hopkins maintains that portion D of picture P depicts object O if and only if we are meant to experience D (as seen from here) and O (as seen from some appropriate hypothetical place) as resembling one another with respect to the visual field properties renderable in P's idiom.

Hopkins's indebtedness to the optical approach to picturing running from figures like Euclid in the ancient world to figures like Leon Battista Alberti in the Renaissance is obvious enough. Yet when I inspect the portion of Pablo Picasso's *Guernica* depicting a lantern carrier, I am acutely aware that its outline shape resembles that of a teardrop. (It is by making me aware of this shape and this fact about it that Picasso suggests the haste and strain with which the lantern carrier peers into a scene of carnage from a position outside and behind it.) Still, I do not see the relevant portion of *Guernica* as depicting a teardrop, aware as I am and am meant to be of the just-mentioned resemblance in outline shape. Moreover, I do not experience the lantern carrier's neck and head as having an outline shape resembling that of the portion of *Guernica* by means of which they are depicted—to wit, one very much like that of a teardrop. To do so, I would need to experience the lantern carrier himself as having a flat face and a neck tapering off to nothing— and I do not.

Richard Wollheim (1987) begins by noticing cases in which one's experience of a differentiated flat surface (a muddy wall or a frosty windowpane) involves two distinct aspects:

(1) a *configurational* aspect, thanks to which one is visually aware (in a manner that is mostly veridical as far as it goes) of the surface itself and its variations in local color; and

(2) a *recognitional* aspect, thanks to which one is visually aware of various robustly three-dimensional things, things that are not and are not believed to be before one's eyes at the time of the experience (battling horsemen, dancers in gauzy dresses).

These two awarenesses are distinguishable but inseparable aspects of a single experience, an experience of *seeing-in: seeing* the relevant three-dimensional things *in* the relevant surface. The configurational aspect can be described on analogy with a veridical simple seeing of a differentiated surface, which it resembles both intrinsically and in its characteristic causal-psychological role. The recognitional aspect can be described on analogy with a face-to-face seeing *of* the things one in fact merely sees *in* the surface. However, one can be aware of a differentiated surface in the particular manner exhibited here only by using the surface to discern absent three-dimensional things, and one can be aware of discerned absent things in the particular manner exhibited here only by being aware of a differentiated surface whose features enable one to discern them in it. In at least this

respect, (1) and (2) are inseparable aspects of a single experience. And although they can be described on analogy with the simpler experiences just mentioned, there is a sense in which a detailed point-for-point comparison between them and such simpler experiences is out of the question: seeing-in and the simpler experiences to which it is in various ways analogous are "phenomenologically incommensurate" (1987) Such, Wollheim thinks, is the *twofoldness* involved in seeing-in. A painting depicts a given subject matter when one is inferably meant to see that subject matter in its surface and can indeed do so.

Michael Podro (1998) takes over from Wollheim's early *Art and Its Objects* (1980) the suggestion that a pictorial representation proposes a kind of simile or figurative comparison whose terms are the marked surface D and the subject O. And he adopts from I. A. Richards an interactionist view of figuration, on which any really deep comparison restructures one's thinking about both terms, reshaping one's thoughts about each on the model of one's thoughts about the other.

On the recognitional side of things, Podro insists that for depiction to occur, it is not enough that one's inspection of D activates one's capacity to recognize O in O's acknowledged absence; one must exploit one's recognition of X in a sustained, successful effort to visualize O. On the configurational side, he insists that one's awareness of D is never simply an awareness of how D is differentiated (lighter here, darker there; redder here, greener there); instead, it is framed in terms of how one takes the artist to have made her marks and handled her medium. There are at least two departures from Wollheim here. There is now a difference in kind between the configurational aspect of seeing a subject in a picture and the configurational aspect of seeing a dancer in a frosty windowpane. And configurational awareness is no longer largely veridical; the impressions a painter's marks generate about the manner of their making may be as designedly fanciful as the impressions a dancer's movements generate about the manner of their making. Configurational and recognitional awareness restructure each other repeatedly as one searches O (the represented subject) for real or merely fancied counterparts of what one has already discerned in D (the way the surface has been worked) and vice versa.

If Wollheim views depiction as one of several modes of pictorial meaning, Kendall Walton (1990) views it as lying at the heart of one of several related forms of make-believe pervading the cultural lives of children and adults alike. A *game of make-believe* is a form of individual or collective imaginative activity in which what players are to imagine comes under the sway of rules or norms of a certain special kind: given the rules of the game in question, what they are to imagine about themselves, the things around them, and reality at large (what is *fictional*) becomes a fixed function of what is actually and discernibly the case about them, the things around them, and reality at large (what is discernibly true). The rules of such games may be maddeningly difficult to state, yet people seem awfully good at playing them and awfully invested in doing so.

Walton proposes in effect that a depiction D of an object O is a prop in a game of make-believe whose role in the game to which it belongs has the following features:

(1) The player is to look at and thereby come to see the object D

(2) He is to imagine about his act of looking at D that it is instead an act of looking at O, and about his resulting experience of seeing D that it is instead an experience of seeing O

(3) He is to manage the foregoing lookings, seeings, and imaginings in such a manner that he imagines *looking at and thereby coming to see* O—and imagines it both (a) vividly and (b) from the inside

(4) The game leaves him free to look at D in any of a wide range of ways, tending to result in a correspondingly wide range of experiences of seeing D

(5) How he is to imagine himself looking at O depends in a richly detailed manner on how he actually ends up looking at D, and the nature and content of the experience of seeing O he is to imagine having as a result depends in a richly detailed manner on the nature and content of the experience of seeing D he actually ends up having

Even the most naturalistic images continue to function as Gombrichian substitutes. When such a game is played, the called-for imaginings are such that they could not take place in the absence of the called-for perceivings, since they are about those perceivings, take those perceivings as their objects. It is equally true that the called-for perceivings could not take place in the absence of the called-for imaginings, since the perceivings involved in the execution of any demanding exploratory project are colored by it, owe their phenomenal character to it, and contain thoughts specifying its goals. This suffices to account for our sense that a spectator's visual experience of a picture is a unitary experience with two different kinds of subject matter: the depicted thing on the one hand, the depiction itself on the other.

THE FUTURE OF DEPICTION THEORY

In the last years of the twentieth century, the perceptual hypothesis account of vision favored by Gombrich lost ground to the modular computational account advocated by David Marr (1982). Many now regard vision as the computation of an accurate spatial model of one's immediate physical surroundings, from raw data about intensity distributions across the visual field, via a fixed set of speedy unconscious algorithms that provably deliver the goods in all but a special and statistically rare set of working conditions—algorithms having no access to the higher recognitional capacities of the person who steers through the world with their help. The various mathematical representations computationalists must appeal to in dividing the task of vision into manageable subtasks turn out to bear striking structural affinities to various familiar kinds of picture. The work of Michael Baxandall (1995), John Willats (1997), and Patrick Maynard (2005) constitute the beginnings of an effort to make principled sense of the whole range of psychologically natural pictorial idioms (and the uses and limitations of each) in a manner informed by emerging computational accounts of vision. What impact these emerging accounts of how pictures differ will eventually have on the best philosophical accounts of how pictures are alike it is too soon to tell.

See also Aesthetics, History of; Aesthetics, Problems of; Art, Authenticity in; Descartes, René; Goodman, Nelson; Helmholtz, Hermann Ludwig von; Plato; Popper, Karl Raimund; Wollheim, Richard.

Bibliography

Baxandall, Michael. *Shadows and Enlightenment*. New Haven, CT: Yale University Press, 1995.

Budd, Malcolm. "How Pictures Look." In *Virtues and Taste: Essays on Politics, Ethics, and Aesthetics*, edited by Dudley Knowles and John Skorupski, 154–175. Oxford, U.K.: Blackwell, 1993.

Descartes, René. "Optics." In *The Philosophical Writings of Descartes*, Vol. 1. Translated by John Cottingham, Robert Stoothoff, and Dugald Murdoch, 152–176. Cambridge, U.K.: Cambridge University Press, 1985.

Feagin, Susan. "Presentation and Representation." *Journal of Aesthetics and Art Criticism* 56 (1998): 234–240.

Gibson, J. J. "The Information Available in Pictures." *Leonardo* 4 (1971): 27–35.

Gombrich, E. H. *Art and Illusion: A Study of the Psychology of Pictorial Representation*. 2nd ed. Princeton, NJ: Princeton University Press, 1961.

Gombrich, E. H. "Illusion and Art." In *Illusion in Nature and Art*, edited by R. L. Gregory and E. H. Gombrich, 192–243. New York: Scribner's, 1973.

Goodman, Nelson. *Languages of Art*. 2nd ed. Indianapolis, IN: Hackett, 1976.

Halliwell, Stephen. *The Aesthetics of Mimesis: Ancient Texts and Modern Problems.* Princeton, NJ: Princeton University Press, 2002.

Harrison, Andrew. "A Minimal Syntax for the Pictorial." In *The Language of Art History*, edited by Salim Kemal and Ivan Gaskell, 213–239. New York: Cambridge University Press, 1991.

Hopkins, Robert. *Picture, Image and Experience.* Cambridge, U.K.: Cambridge University Press, 1998.

Isenberg, Arnold. "Perception, Meaning, and the Subject Matter of Art." In *Aesthetics and the Theory of Criticism*, 36–52. Chicago: University of Chicago Press, 1973.

Kennedy, John M. *A Psychology of Picture Perception.* San Francisco: Jossey-Bass, 1974.

Lopes, Dominic. *Understanding Pictures.* Oxford, U.K.: Clarendon Press, 1996.

Marr, David. *Vision.* New York: Freeman, 1982.

Maynard, Patrick. "Depiction, Vision, and Convention." *American Philosophical Quarterly* 9 (1972): 243–250.

Maynard, Patrick. *Drawing Distinctions.* Ithaca, NY: Cornell University Press, 2005.

Merleau-Ponty, Maurice. *The Merleau-Ponty Aesthetics Reader: Philosophy and Painting*, edited by Galen A. Johnson. Evanston, IL: Northwestern University Press, 1993.

Peacocke, Christopher. "Depiction." *Philosophical Review* 96 (1987): 383–410.

Plato. *Republic.* Translated by G. M. A. Grube. Revised by C. D. C. Reeve. Indianapolis, IN: Hackett, 1992.

Podro, Michael. *Depiction.* New Haven, CT: Yale University Press, 1998.

Schier, Flint. *Deeper into Pictures: An Essay on Pictorial Representation.* New York: Cambridge University Press, 1986.

Walton, Kendall. *Mimesis as Make-Believe: On the Foundations of the Representational Arts.* Cambridge, MA: Harvard University Press, 1990.

Willats, John. *Art and Representation: New Principles in the Analysis of Pictures.* Princeton, NJ: Princeton University Press, 1997.

Wollheim, Richard. *Art and Its Objects.* 2nd ed. New York: Cambridge University Press, 1980.

Wollheim, Richard. *Painting as an Art.* Princeton, NJ: Princeton University Press, 1987.

David Hills (2005)

ART, STYLE AND GENRE IN

Style and genre are two distinct but related ways in which artworks can be grouped together in the interests of understanding and appreciation. Neither mode of classification is easy to characterize, and much of the philosophical discussion of both genre—predominantly by literary theorists—and style—predominantly by historians and philosophers of the visual arts—has been clarificatory in aim. In the case of genre, there is a tension between structural (e.g., ode, epic, and collage) and functional (e.g., tragedy, romance, and altarpiece) ways of categorizing artworks. But many genres seem to have more to do with subject matter (e.g., bildungsroman and still life)—at least in those art forms that are broadly representational. The diverse bases for generic classification of artworks are reflected in René Wellek and Austin Warren's proposed definition of a literary genre as "a grouping of literary works based, theoretically, upon both outer form (specific metre or structure) and also upon inner form (attitude, tone, purpose—more crudely, subject and audience)" (1949, p. 231).

A much discussed theme in contemporary discussions of literary genre is whether the latter is merely a taxonomic convenience, reflecting the classificatory interests of literary critics and historians, or whether it reflects real differences between works. Certainly, the ascription of a work to a genre sometimes plays a part in explaining puzzling features of that work. For example, the art historian Michael Baxandall (1985) accounts for puzzling features of a Renaissance painting in terms of its belonging to the genre altarpiece. This seems to require an objective basis for genre classification. One can explain features of a work by appeal to genre only if one takes the genre to which the work is ascribed to be causally implicated in its generation—presumably in virtue of the artist's creative activity being guided by a conception of relevant generic constraints.

While genre is predominantly a critic's term for which art historians sometimes have a use, style is traditionally a historian's categorization whose critical and appreciative relevance has been increasingly remarked. Originating etymologically in the Latin term for a writing instrument (*stilus*), and thus applying to styles of writing, the term came to prominence in the writings of eighteenth- and nineteenth-century German art historians such as Johann Joachim Winckelmann. Art historians seek to historically situate individual works in groupings that are open to analogous kinds of explanation and to explain how such works so grouped stand in historical relations to one another. Style serves the first purpose inasmuch as an artistic style is taken to be a manifest feature of works that provides evidence as to their provenance, and the second if one posits an internal or external dynamics to the development of style.

Perhaps the most enduring testament to this tradition in art history is Heinrich Wölfflin's (1950) account of how painting in the High Renaissance differs from Baroque art in its style of pictorial representation. He introduces certain binary distinctions that provide a framework within which one can define different ways in which one might articulate pictorial space. The most influential of these distinctions is between linear and painterly modes of representation and is defined in terms of a number of interrelated factors such as the way in which form is articulated (through outlines of masses or interplay between masses), the qualities of things through which they are represented (shape or texture), the manner in which relationships between objects are conveyed (atomistically or holistically), and the faculties through which pictorial articulation is primarily grasped (understanding and sensation).

Once one thinks of artworks as being groupable in terms of their styles, it is natural to ask why this is so and why such styles change over time—why, for example, late Renaissance and Baroque paintings differ in the cited ways. Wölfflin (1950) himself posits an internal logic underlying the historical development of artistic styles. His distinctions are taken to capture the various representational possibilities permitted by the artistic medium, and communities of artists are seen as pursuing their artistic goals within this framework of possibilities, which has within it its own dynamic. Wölfflin's account is interestingly but controversially extended to nonrepresentational painting by Clement Greenberg (1962), who sees an oscillation between linearity and painterliness in the postimpressionist tradition. A related idea is found in Arthur Danto's (1964) conception of the "style matrix." Alois Riegl's notion of *Kunstwollen* also manifests a commitment to an internal dynamic in the development of artistic style. On the contrary, James S. Ackerman (1962), reacting against the whiff of stylistic determinism in such accounts, offers an individualistic model where artistic styles change as a result of the attempts of artists to overcome problems arising in the activity of painting. Ernst Gombrich (1968) offers a more materialistic but still broadly individualistic model in which stylistic change is fueled by technological innovation and guided by the social structure of the art world.

As in the case of genre, some question whether the stylistic classifications employed by art historians reflect independent realities of the sort that both call for and furnish explanations, or whether they are taxonomic devices that reflect the culturally inflected interests and purposes of historians. A related concern is that, to the extent that style categories are viewed taxonomically, they are of questionable relevance for one's critical and appreciative engagement with particular artworks. In an influential paper, Richard Wollheim (1979) argues that the concept of style plays two importantly different roles in discussion about visual art. Wollheim distinguishes between general and individual style. The former, which

he subdivides into universal style, historical or period style, and school style, is indeed taxonomic in the manner just described. Individual style, however, is what is at issue when one talks of "the style of A" in reference to the work of a given painter A. Those painters whose works are objects of aesthetic interest have "a style of their own," which allows their works to be understood as expressive.

Furthermore, and crucially, individual style is to be understood in generative rather than taxonomical terms: a style description for a painter A picks out elements in A's work that depend on those "processes or operations characteristic of his acting as a painter" that Wollheim terms *style processes* (1979, p. 135). A style process is analyzable in terms of some subset of the pictorial resources available to a painter on which the painter is disposed to act in a rule-like manner. Individual style, so construed, has "psychological reality" in these dispositions of the artist and can be seen as causally operative in the production of the artist's works. Wollheim argues for this generative conception of individual style on the grounds that it is required to make sense of the role played by style descriptions in the explanation of the details of pictures and of the susceptibility of the works of a given artist to grouping in terms of a common style. While Wollheim explicitly restricts his account of individual style to painting, the notion has been extended to literary artworks and, by implication, to artworks in general in two articles by Jenefer Robinson (1984, 1985).

In extending Wollheim's analysis Robinson also insists, in line with an early paper by Kendall Walton (1979), that an artist's individual style is properly identified not with some set of manifest features of the products of the artist's "artistic acts" (Sircello 1975), but with features of those acts themselves, "[Pictorial] style ultimately cannot be defined as a list of pictorial elements but rather as a way of doing certain things, or manipulating pictorial elements" (Robinson 1981, p. 10). In the case of literary works, for example, the relevant artistic acts are "*describing* people, *portraying* landscape, *characterising* personal relationships, *manipulating* rhythms, *organising* patterns of imagery, and so forth" (Robinson 1984, p. 138). Furthermore, these ways of doing things, insofar as they constitute an artist's style, are taken to be characteristic expressions of the mind and personality that the artist appears to have. This agential conception of individual style accords with talk of style in nonartistic contexts and explains both the restriction of style predicates to human actions and their products and the explicitly expressive nature of many style predicates (e.g., a sentimental or witty style). As for those sets of elements proper to a given art form that are cited as constitutive of style by those who take the latter to reside in the products of artistic activity, Robinson maintains that they are grouped together as stylistic elements only in virtue of being the elements that the artist characteristically uses in performing the relevant artistic acts in a distinctive way.

Part of the significance of ascriptions of individual style for the critical appreciation of particular works of art is said to be their bearing on the expressive and other meaningful properties rightly ascribable to a work. Wollheim (1980), refining a suggestion by Gombrich (1960), argues that it is only through one's grasp of an artist's style that one can determine the precise expressive significance of a configuration of elements in the artist's work, and Robinson (1981) suggests that the same holds for at least some representational and formal properties. But both Walton (1979) and Robinson (1985) insist that what is expressed through the style of a work is not determined by facts about the actual artist, but by facts about the mind or personality of what Walton (1979) terms the *apparent artist*—the mentality or personality the artist appears to have given the stylistic features of the work. However, as Walton recognizes, to ascribe such a role to the apparent artist rather than to the actual artist is far from unproblematic, since what one sees in a configuration of elements in an artistic manifold may reflect ulterior knowledge about the actual artist. One therefore stands in clear need of a principle to delimit when such knowledge is rightly brought to bear in determining the expressivity embodied in the stylistic properties of an artwork.

Even if one thinks of individual styles as ways of doing, it is still through manifest features of the products of those ways of doing that one is able to recognize artists' styles. One question to which one would therefore expect an answer from an adequate philosophical account of style is whether artistic styles admit a univocal characterization in terms of the kinds of manifest features or elements that enter into their expressions. Both Walton (1979) and Robinson (1981, 1984) insist that there can be no checklist of stylistically relevant elements for a given art, since what makes an element part of the expression of an individual style is that it has been used in a particular way in an artistic act that is characteristic of the artist. This allows for all manner of different elements to enter into the styles of different artists and explains why only some elements that figure in an artist's works are mentioned in a style description, why a given element may figure in the style description of one artist but not in that of another who works in the same medium, and why a given

element may have different stylistic significance in the works of different artists (Robinson 1985).

Nelson Goodman (1978) also rejects any attempt to distinguish stylistic from nonstylistic elements in terms of such dichotomies as expressive versus nonexpressive, form versus content, intrinsic versus extrinsic, or "the 'how' versus the 'what' of what is said," and so on. A feature of style may be a feature of what a work says, what it expresses, or of its formal or configurational elements. But, according to Goodman, what makes any such feature stylistic is both its contribution to the symbolic functioning of the work and its linking works together in ways that serve to advance appreciation and understanding, "[T]he style consists of those features of the symbolic functioning of a work that are characteristic of author, period, place, or school" (p. 35).

This suggests a way of reconnecting the two conceptions of style distinguished by Wollheim (1979), since both general and individual style might be connected to symbolic functioning in this way. It also suggests how one might bring into dialogue the stylistic interests of the historian and the critic. Goodman (1978) argues that style, as he conceives it, is of interest not only to the historian, who seeks to correctly attribute a history of making to an artwork, but also to the critic, who can use the attributions of the historian to discover further and subtler shared elements of symbolic functioning in the resulting groupings of works. Walton (1979) and Robinson (1985), however, will insist that one's interest in the individual style of works necessarily refers one back to distinctive features of the artistic acts that seem to result in entities capable of so functioning and that the interest of critics, unlike the interest of historians, is in how things appear to have been made rather than in how they were made. The complex relationships between the stylistic concerns of the historian and of the critic have been commented on by Walton (1979) and discussed at some length by Robinson (1981).

See also Aesthetic Qualities; Art, Expression in; Art, Formalism in; Art, Interpretation of.

Bibliography

Ackerman, James S. "A Theory of Style." *Journal of Aesthetics and Art Criticism* 20 (1962): 227–237.

Baxandall, Michael. *Patterns of Intention: On the Historical Explanation of Pictures.* New Haven, CT: Yale University Press, 1985.

Carroll, Noel. "Danto, Style, and Intention." *Journal of Aesthetics and Art Criticism* 53 (3) (1995): 251–257.

Danto, Arthur. "The Artworld." *Journal of Philosophy* 61 (1964): 571–584.

Eck, Caroline van, James McAllister, and Renée van de Vall, eds. *The Question of Style in Philosophy and the Arts*. New York: Cambridge University Press, 1995.

Frye, Northrop. "Rhetorical Criticism: Theory of Genres." In *Anatomy of Criticism: Four Essays*, 243–326. Princeton, NJ: Princeton University Press, 1957.

Gombrich, Ernst. *Art and Illusion: A Study in the Psychology of Pictorial Representation*. New York: Pantheon, 1960.

Gombrich, Ernst. "Style." In *The International Encyclopedia of the Social Sciences*. Vol. 15, edited by David L. Sills, 352–361. New York: Macmillan, 1968.

Goodman, Nelson. *Ways of Worldmaking*. Indianapolis, IN: Hackett, 1978.

Greenberg, Clement. "After Abstract Expressionism." *Art International* 6 (8) (1962): 24–32.

Lang, Berel, ed. *The Concept of Style*. Philadelphia: University of Pennsylvania Press, 1979.

Robinson, Jenefer. "General and Individual Style in Literature." *Journal of Aesthetics and Art Criticism* 43 (1984): 147–158.

Robinson, Jenefer. "Style and Personality in the Literary Work." *Philosophical Review* 94 (2) (1985): 227–247.

Robinson, Jenefer. "Style and Significance in Art History and Art Criticism." *Journal of Aesthetics and Art Criticism* 40 (1) (1981): 5–14.

Sircello, Guy. *A New Theory of Beauty*. Princeton, NJ: Princeton University Press, 1975.

Walton, Kendall. "Style and the Products and Processes of Art." In *The Concept of Style*, edited by Berel Lang, 45–66. Philadelphia: University of Pennsylvania Press, 1979.

Wellek, René, and Austin Warren. *Theory of Literature*. New York: Harcourt, 1949.

Wölfflin, Heinrich. *Principles of Art History: The Problem of the Development of Style in Later Art*. New York: Dover, 1950.

Wollheim, Richard. *Art and Its Objects: With Six Supplementary Essays*. 2nd ed. New York: Cambridge University Press, 1980.

Wollheim, Richard. "Pictorial Style: Two Views." In *The Concept of Style*, edited by Berel Lang, 129–148. Philadelphia: University of Pennsylvania Press, 1979.

Wollheim, Richard. "Style in Painting." In *The Question of Style in Philosophy and the Arts*, edited by Caroline van Eck, James McAllister, and Renée van de Vall. New York: Cambridge University Press, 1995.

David Davies (2005)

ART, TRUTH IN

The question of artistic truth first arises with the ancients. In his *Republic*, Plato argues that fine art and poetry cannot impart truths because they do not give humankind access to the Forms. Just as a mirror can only deliver a reflection of the particulars that themselves are merely reflections of the Forms, so painting and poetry amount to little more than pale images of Platonic Ideas at a third remove. Aristotle, in contrast, defended poetry

as a means of obtaining general knowledge about probable courses of human events. One could learn from *Antigone*, for example, the likely turn of affairs when two strong-willed and unbending people, each convinced that he or she is in the right, disagree on matters of principle.

Though this topic is usually referred to in terms of "artistic truth," it is more precisely a concern with knowledge and the question of whether one can derive knowledge—or, even more broadly, cognitive value, from artworks. Truth, of course, comes into the picture, since it is one of the criteria of knowledge. Plato maintained that poets, like Homer, had no knowledge to teach and for that reason should not be esteemed as the educators of the Greeks. Aristotle, on the other hand, argued that poetry, especially tragedy, is akin to philosophy, since it has general truths about life to convey, namely universals about what is necessary or probable in the run of human events.

Throughout most of Western history, the view that art contributes to knowledge held sway. However, with the great advances of modern science and the empiricist philosophies that accompanied it, art began to look as though it had comparatively little, if anything, to offer by way of knowledge. Art, indeed, began to be treated by positivist philosophers as a primarily noncognitive enterprise.

Two types of arguments have been raised in order to challenge the cognitive credentials of art. The first group of arguments can be called epistemic. These allege that artworks cannot educate audiences because what artworks have to offer is not knowledge, properly so called; art is epistemically defective in various ways. The second group of arguments can be called aesthetic. They contend that it is inappropriate to expect artworks to function as sources of knowledge, even if for centuries in Western culture and others, art has been an object of respect for this very service.

EPISTEMIC ARGUMENTS

The epistemic arguments against the cognitive pretensions of art include: the banality argument, the no-evidence argument, and the no-argument argument. The banality argument takes a close look at the kinds of theses for which artworks are so often commended for teaching to their audiences. These are often truisms of the order of "crime doesn't pay" or "the prejudice of first impressions can be misleading." If this is knowledge, the skeptic observes, then it is nevertheless hardly something that we are taught by novels like *Crime and Punishment* or *Pride and Prejudice*. Rather, in order to understand such novels, we probably already need to have some version of these commonplaces in our cognitive stock. According to the banality argument, there may be truths embodied in artworks, but they are rather paltry, bland, and known by nearly everyone before they encounter the artworks in question. So we cannot be said to learn them from artworks. Indeed, having access to these bromides is often a condition for comprehending the very artworks that contain them. But in any event, these truisms are in no way as revelatory as scientific discoveries are; if they constitute knowledge at all, it is common knowledge.

Whereas the banality argument concedes that there may be knowledge, albeit of a threadbare sort, to be had from artworks, the next two arguments deny this possibility. Of course, one can derive beliefs from artworks; but skeptics charge that it is impossible to gain knowledge from artworks. For knowledge involves not only beliefs, or even true beliefs; those beliefs must also be based upon something—either evidence or argument. And artworks, as a matter of form, it is charged, typically lack these sorts of accompanying justifications.

The no-evidence argument shows the influence of empiricism most clearly. Since Aristotle, it has been claimed that artworks, notably literature, give us knowledge of general truths concerning human life. But, the skeptic retorts, most artworks trade in particulars and one cannot justify a general claim on the basis of a single case. It is not adequate evidence, even if the case is as arresting as that of Antigone versus Creon. Moreover, a very great many of the case studies that are supposed to carry these generalizations about human life are fictional. No claim, general or otherwise, can be supported by a made-up story. Furthermore, most of these fabricated stories are invented precisely to corroborate the point the author wishes to promulgate. So not only is the evidence insufficient; it looks like it is tainted to boot. Thus, the skeptic surmises, artworks cannot be said to afford the kind of general knowledge for which they are so often applauded just because they are evidentially defective.

Of course, not every general claim needs to be supported by empirical evidence. Many philosophical generalizations are not. And the knowledge in which much art is said to traffic is philosophical, concerned, for example, with issues like free will. Since no amount of evidence is going to sway the free will debate one way or the other, the fact that artists do not back up their perspectives on free will with empirical evidence makes them no worse off than philosophers. The no-evidence argument, that is, does not cut against philosophical artworks.

But, the skeptic replies, genuine philosophical theses, even if unaccompanied by a body of empirical evidence, are nevertheless advanced by means of argument and/or analysis. Yet that is something that artworks characteristically have not got. *Nausea* may assert that humans are free; the novel may even be said to illustrate the point. But there is *no argument* to that conclusion in the book. However, if there is no argument, then there is no philosophical knowledge to be had from the text. At best there is unsubstantiated belief.

Nor, the skeptic adds, do commentators on artworks—including even those commentators who speak as though artworks are involved in making philosophical knowledge claims—argue about the truth or falsity of the cognitive theses they excavate from artworks. This lack of concern with argumentation by critics, then, is thought to lend additional credence to the skeptical view that art is not in the knowledge business. If it were, there would be more explicit argumentation both inside the artworks and in the critical estate that surrounds them. The lack of argumentation implies that art is not about securing knowledge, and, be that as it may, sans argumentation it does not do so anyway.

AESTHETIC ARGUMENTS

The epistemic arguments against art propose that what artworks deliver is not worth being called knowledge—it is either too trivial or it is unjustified. As a matter of fact, art just is not a suitable vehicle for the communication of anything robust enough and defensible enough to be counted as knowledge. But another set of arguments worries that knowledge is just the wrong thing to expect from artworks. Even if some artworks could convey knowledge, knowledge is never something we should legitimately expect from artworks. These arguments may be regarded as aesthetic, rather than epistemic, in nature. Three of them are: the common denominator argument, the no-expertise argument, and the mistaken-belief argument.

The common denominator argument points out that even if some artworks appear to provide knowledge—as *Moby Dick* does concerning whaling—many other artworks, like a great many string quartets, do not. Therefore, the expectation that artworks afford knowledge or even that they suggest knowledge claims does not apply to all artworks. Knowledge is not a generic criterion of artistic excellence. Yet if something is a criterion of artistic excellence, it must be relevant to the evaluation of every artwork. Knowledge is not. Consequently, knowledge is an inappropriate expectation to bring to an artwork qua art.

Artists study their craft and the materials that comprise their art form. Painters learn perspective, poets master prosody, musicians scales, and so on. Their expertise is with the tools of their trade. They are not psychologists or political scientists or sociologists. They have no special expertise that entitles them to float generalizations about human life. How would a studio-arts education prepare one to discourse on human affairs? This is one of the earliest charges lodged against the attempt to enlist art as a producer of knowledge. Perhaps Plato holds the copyright on the no-expertise argument; Socrates used it to demolish Ion and, by extension, Homer.

Another argument striving to demonstrate the irrelevance of the pursuit of knowledge by art stresses that many artworks have been committed to beliefs that we now regard as obsolete and mistaken, and yet we still esteem the works in question. Indeed, many classic artworks are committed to beliefs that are contradicted by the beliefs recommended by other classic artworks and still, despite these contradictions, we are happy to embrace works on both side of the debate (say free will versus determinism) as canonical. But, it is conjectured, this would not be possible if we thought that truth and knowledge were appropriate standards for art. In that case, artworks associated with false beliefs would have to be demoted in our estimation. That they are not implies that knowledge is not an appropriate concern when it comes to art.

RESPONDING TO THE SKEPTICS

These arguments against the cognitive status of art are longstanding and serious. However, they can also be challenged in various ways. As a group, the epistemic arguments presuppose that if art is cognitive, then it will transmit knowledge to its audiences and this knowledge will take the form of general truths that can be stated in propositional form. Consequently, commentators often seek to outflank the epistemic objections by refusing this presupposition and locating the cognitive contribution of art primarily elsewhere than in the presentation of innovative general truths that can be articulated in propositions.

There are a number of different—nonexclusive and nonexhaustive—alternative candidates here and each suggests a way in which art may be said to make a contribution to cognition, broadly construed. Against the banality argument, it may be said that though artworks often deal in commonplaces, these are commonplaces that we are apt to forget. The cognitive function of art in this regard is to recall to mind the kinds of truths—such as the dangers of indulging a hasty prejudice or refusing to bend when one right is on a collision course with

another—that are well known but oft forgot. Artworks, like *Pride and Prejudice* and *Antigone*, are vivid reminders of what we already know, but that of which we are prone to lose sight.

Indeed, artworks—engaging as they do the senses, feelings, emotions, imaginations, and cognitions of their audiences—are especially efficacious instruments for educating peoples in the ethos of their culture, because by mobilizing so many powers of a person at once, artworks deeply embed the common knowledge of a society in its participants in a way that makes it readily accessible for retrieval and use. Arguably, the multidimensional address of the artwork suits it as a means for educating a populace in its ethos in a fashion unrivaled by any other mode of communication.

Epistemic arguments appear to suppose that the only relevant sort of knowledge is *knowing that*. But in addition to propositional knowledge, there is also knowledge by acquaintance. Thus, defenders of the educative power of art maintain that art can provide knowledge by affording the opportunity for audiences to learn about certain experiences from the inside—to acquire, perhaps by simulation or empathy in the process of watching a film, a sense of or a feel for what it would be like, for example, to be a slave.

Moreover, in addition to knowledge by acquaintance, there is also know-how. Artworks can contribute know-how in many ways. For example, many of our concepts of virtue, vice, and other character traits are rather abstract, as are our moral principles. In order to learn how to apply these extremely abstract concepts and maxims, we need practice. Artworks, especially fictions, can provide the opportunity to hone our powers of judgment by giving us particulars, often subtly drawn, that enable us to deepen our faculties of judgment and our skill in deploying them. That is, artworks may enhance cognition by putting it to work in assessing fictional characters and actions in terms of concepts and principles—moral and otherwise (e.g., psychological, political, social)—that we possess abstractly, but which we need to exercise concretely in order to acquire a genuine command over them. Furthermore, inasmuch as a refined sensitivity toward the relevant concepts, like true heroism, plays a role in eliciting appropriate emotional responses, artworks facilitate the education of the emotions.

In addition, artworks may serve the cognitive purpose of orientation; they may help us map our world. Novels present us with crystallizations of various character types—often newly emerging ones, like the radical empiricist in Turgenev's *Fathers and Sons* or the gallery of social tendencies inventoried in Balzac's *Comedie Humaine*, or the eponymous Sammy in *What Makes Sammy Run?* These character profiles—assembling a significant constellation of attributes—operate like concepts, supplying us with recognizable paradigms of social types which may even help us to navigate everyday life. Such paradigms are not true or false in the manner of a proposition, but apt or fitting. Nevertheless, aptness is as indispensable to cognition as propositional truth. Indeed, Nelson Goodman claims that the ultimate value of art is that it supplies us with apt models of the world.

Furthermore, art can tutor perception. Landscape painting and portraits can teach us how to look at the world. And Goodman has stressed the way in which even abstract paintings exercise and expand the viewer's ability to make fine perceptual distinctions.

One way to deal with the epistemic arguments, then, is to outflank them. But they can also be tackled head-on. Against the no-evidence argument, it is important to remind the skeptic that not all artworks are fictions and therefore cannot be uniformly dismissed as being evidentially empty for that reason. Nor is it only nonfiction literature with which the skeptic must contend. There is also photography, nonfiction motion pictures, and much installation art.

Moreover, even fictions can contain evidence. Thus, there is no grounds for summarily rejecting all fiction as incapable of proffering propositional knowledge. Michael Crichton's novel, *State of Fear*, about environmentalism, includes argumentative theses replete with footnotes to substantiate its case. Whether or not Crichton's book is correct is one question. Nevertheless, it is clear that a novel like it could be written that might succeed in proposing a series of true propositions supported by the appropriate documentary apparatus. This conjecture seems unobjectionable, furthermore, since, though many critics have complained about the quality of *State of Fear*, no one has denied that it is a novel.

Moreover, skeptics are wrong to contend that critics do not initiate charges of falsity accompanied by arguments against fictions. Presently secular humanists in the United States are waging a campaign against horror fictions for fostering superstitious beliefs. Likewise one can bet money that commentators sympathetic to the environmental movement will meet Crichton with the kinds of arguments they would unfurl against any scientist or politician who impugned their theories.

But we need not resort to Crichton to bridle at the no-evidence argument. We need only point out that it sets the bar for communicating knowledge too high. No one denies that the journalism on the op-ed pages of newspapers can convey knowledge. But the beliefs advanced there typically come to us without the kind of evidence it would take to vindicate them in the highest courts of reason. Rather, the author leaves it to the reader to reflect upon her assertions, encouraging us to weigh them against our own experience and to search out further proof of their accuracy. Likewise it may be argued that artists generally play by comparable rules. A novel like *Bonfire of the Vanities* provides a sketch of the 1980s that we are invited to substantiate on our own. Hence, if the aforesaid journalist is allowed into the knowledge game, so should a certain kind of novelist be. Indeed, doesn't the communication of knowledge usually leave some of the work of corroboration up to the reader? Consequently, that artworks encourage readers to test the hypotheses they suggest in what Peter Kivy thinks of as the laboratories of their minds is not an epistemic deficit. It is a recurring feature of the communication of knowledge across the board.

Similar reservations can be brought to bear on the no-argument argument. Not all theses are defended by means of empirical evidence. Most philosophical claims are not. A leading form of argument in defense of philosophical conjectures is the thought experiment—characteristically a narrative fiction predicated upon engaging the mind of the listener in a process of reflective equilibrium leading to a certain conclusion. But if philosophers are entitled to thought experiments as a mode of argument and/or analysis, why should artists be denied equal logical rights?

Many artworks are narrative fictions. Some at least are arguably thought experiments designed to encourage the embrace of certain discoveries, such as insight into the true nature of courage or compassion. That is, artworks may not only enable us through practice to apply concepts with finesse; they may also invite reflection upon the grammar of the concept in question—either by foregrounding a heretofore unappreciated essential criterion of the concept or by reminding us of the kinds of considerations it pays to remember whenever applying the concept. That is, a narrative artwork, functioning as a thought experiment, can engage the mind of the audience in a process of reflective equilibrium that results in propositional knowledge concerning the concept under scrutiny. Moreover, where the artwork is operating as a thought experiment, it is not without argument; the thought experiment, rather, stages the argument in the minds of the audience.

The aesthetic arguments against artistic claims to knowledge are not more decisive than the epistemic ones. The common denominator argument correctly observes that not *all* artworks are such that it is appropriate to evaluate them in terms of the knowledge they impart. They are not all vehicles for communicating knowledge; that is not the kind of thing they all are. So if aesthetic evaluation is keyed to the kind of thing a work is, then knowledge is not the sort of thing to employ in the assessment of, for example, most string quartets.

This much is true. However, the aesthete's argument here is more ambitious; it is that knowledge is never an appropriate measure of an artwork. However, some artworks, given the kinds of things they are essentially, are justifiably expected to bequeath knowledge, even propositional knowledge, to their audiences. This is not only the case with certain nonfiction examples. For instance, realist novels are committed, in virtue of their genre, to the production of various insights including social, psychological and political ones. Fledgling realist authors are instructed to become astute observers just because they are expected to inform readers about psychology and social mores. Moreover, since that is the kind of thing a realist novel is—i.e. B; in effect, the genre to which it belongs—it follows that in such cases disclosing truths figure in artistic evaluation. That the expectation of knowledge in inapposite with respect to many genres does not entail that it is out of bounds for every genre. It is not true that a criterion of artistic excellence must apply globally. Many art forms and genres may possess local standards of excellence given the kinds of artworks they are—the realist novel being a case in point.

The realist novel also indicates what is wrong with the no-expertise argument. Some artists—like realist novelists—are expected to sharpen their powers of psychological and social observation as part of their job description. Furthermore, with many of the things that realist authors have expertise in isolating and explaining—such as the ways of the heart or the claims of social justice—it is not really clear who the better experts are. And, in any event, given the power of artworks to engage simultaneously the whole person—feeling, imagination, memory, perception, cognition, and so forth—it is not evident that there is any more effective way of instilling these truths in recipients than artworks.

Lastly, the mistaken-belief argument is a non-starter. To maintain that knowledge may be a virtue in artworks does not imply that it is the only virtue. Thus, it may be the case that works that contain mistaken, perhaps outmoded, beliefs nevertheless have other merits that dis-

pose us to keep them in the canon. That is also why we may be happy to welcome classics that contradict each other into our pantheon. One virtue that they may possess is that they articulate compellingly the mistaken beliefs they uphold as a work from an archaic culture might. Here, the work gives us knowledge of the past, albeit inadvertently. But at the same time if the work is designed formally in such a way that its theses, however false, are given their best face, then we can appreciate the work aesthetically, despite its cognitive shortcomings. Thus, the fact that palpably false artworks continue to hold our interest does not show that truth and knowledge may not be pertinent to our respect for some other artworks. At best it shows that they are not our only desideratum.

See also Aesthetic Experience; Art, Value in.

Bibliography

Aristotle. *Poetics.* Translated by R. Janko. Indianapolis, IN: Hackett, 1984.

Beardsley, Monroe. *Aesthetics.* Indianapolis, IN: Hackett, 1981.

Carroll, Noël. "The Wheel of Virtue." *Journal of Aesthetics and Art Criticism* 60 (2002): 3–26.

Currie, Gregory. "The Moral Psychology of Fiction." *Australasian Journal of Philosophy* 73 (1995): 250–259.

Goodman, Nelson. *Languages of Art.* Indianapolis, IN: Bobbs-Merrill, 1968.

Hospers, John. *Meaning and Truth in the Arts.* Chapel Hill: University of North Carolina Press, 1949.

Johns, Eileen. "Reading Fiction and Conceptual Knowledge." *The Journal of Aesthetics and Art Criticism* 56 (1998): 331–348.

Kivy, Peter. "On the Banality of Literary Truths." *Philosophic Exchange* 28 (1997–1998): 16–27.

Lamarque, Peter, and Olsen Stein. *Truth, Fiction, and Literature.* Oxford: Clarendon, 1994.

Plato. *Republic.* In *The Dialogues of Plato.* Translated by Benjamin Jowett. Oxford: Oxford University Press, 1953.

Noël Carroll (2005)

ART, VALUE IN

The question of the nature of art, what art is, has been much more widely discussed in philosophy than the question of its value, why art matters. The two issues cannot be completely disentangled, of course, since any account of what makes art art will inevitably isolate features of special importance. In fact, all the main theories of the nature of art have an implicit explanation of its value, but since the question of the value of art has social as well as philosophical significance, it is useful to make these implicit accounts explicit, and thus expose them to critical scrutiny.

Four lines of thought have emerged as the principal ways in which philosophers and artists have explained the importance of art. These can be given convenient labels: hedonism, aestheticism, expressionism, and cognitivism. Briefly, the first holds that art is valuable for the pleasure derived from it; the second that art is valuable as a source of beauty; the third that art is valuable as a vehicle for expressing emotion; and the fourth that art is a source of knowledge and understanding equivalent to, but distinct from, science and philosophy.

Abstractly stated in this way, it unclear whether any of these theories construe the relationship between art and its value as intrinsic or instrumental. That is to say, is the value in question to be found in art itself, or is art simply a means to it? We might also wonder whether the value resides in the properties of art objects—books, sculptures, paintings, compositions, and so on—or in the experiences that these things give rise to in those who look or listen. These are issues that can be examined at a general level, but in fact the distinctions that they invoke—intrinsic/instrumental and object/experience— are more important in some explanations of the value of art than in others.

HEDONISM

The contention that art is valuable for the pleasure we derive from it is both longstanding and widespread. Indeed, most people, including those engaged in the arts, probably assume its truth without question. Yet as an explanation of the value and importance of art, it faces several difficulties. Before these can be considered directly, one point of clarification is required.

It is natural for people to describe their engagement with the arts in terms of enjoyment, and to express their artistic judgments in terms of liking and disliking. One result is that positive responses to art are usually construed as expressions of enjoyment obtained from encountering things we like. This then leads to the assumption that a favorable view of an artwork is an expression of pleasure. But in fact the conflation of pleasure and enjoyment is a mistake. Enjoyment can arise from other things besides pleasure. While the enjoyment of a good wine or a fine meal is largely, and sometimes exclusively, the result of gastronomic pleasure, a scientific lecture or a television documentary can be enjoyable for their intellectual content. They provide us with interesting material to think about, rather than a pleasurable experience to savor.

It might be replied that intellectual stimulation is a special kind of pleasure. The danger with this response is that it simply collapses the valuable into the pleasurable, and thus converts a substantial claim—that art is valuable *because* it is pleasurable—into an uninformative analytic claim—that to say art is valuable is *the same* as saying that it is pleasurable. In this way the claim about value and pleasure becomes true by definition. It follows that if hedonism about art is to be a substantial theory, we need to distinguish between enjoying something and getting pleasure from it. The fact that we derive pleasure from something is *one* reason for enjoying it and finding it valuable. But it is not the only possible reason.

In the light of this clarification we can now state the three main questions facing hedonism about art. First, is it generally true, as a matter of empirical fact, that the arts generate pleasurable experiences? Second, is it possible to discriminate between major and minor works of art in terms of pleasure? Third, if art is valuable because of the pleasure it gives us, would not other, better sources of pleasure make art redundant?

The first of these questions is a factual matter about which we have to be open-minded. Since probably the majority of people who philosophize about the value and importance of art are themselves art lovers, there is a tendency to assume that art does generally give pleasure. But the statistics of people attending classical concerts, reading serious literature, and making visits to art galleries do not bear this out. Considered solely in terms of the pleasure they give, soap operas, pop music, television shoot-'em-ups, and romantic pulp fiction almost certainly top grand opera, classical music, Shakespeare, and nineteenth-century Russian novels. Indeed, the position of the arts is worse than this. Far more people are bored by Shakespeare than are entertained by him, and to those same people, two hours of Bach or Beethoven is probably a dreadful prospect. Even artworks expressly created for entertaining can, with the passage to time, cease to provide much in the way of pleasure. For example, compared with modern television comedies like *Friends* or *Blackadder*, Restoration comedy is a very poor source of amusement.

The examples chosen to make this point can also be used to elaborate the second of the two difficulties outlined above. An enthusiast for classical music might insist that the principal value of concert going is indeed the pleasure we derive from it. While it is true that tastes differ, this pleasure, for those who find concert going pleasurable, is just as great or even greater than the pleasure of pop music, chiefly because high-quality music gives pleasure repeatedly. A similar claim might be made on the part of all the arts, but even if we concede that the arts give great pleasure to those who like them, this does not give us any reason to rank them higher than more mundane sources of pleasure, like crossword puzzles, jigsaw puzzles, or board games.

This issue was expressly addressed by the utilitarian philosopher Jeremy Bentham (1748–1832), who was willing to argue that since pleasure is the ultimate source of all value, pushpin (a kind of board game) is as good as poetry. What Bentham did not observe, however, is that subscribing to hedonism raises not only a question about the comparative value of the aesthetic and the nonaesthetic but also a problem within the realm of the aesthetic itself. If the value of an artwork is derived from the pleasure it gives, then major works of art must give more pleasure than minor ones. But have we any reason to believe this? Can pleasure be correlated with estimations of aesthetic merit? Is a piece of music by a major composer like Beethoven, for example, guaranteed to give more pleasure than one by a minor composer like Luigi Boccherini?

This raises a contentious philosophical topic: whether pleasure can be measured or not. But even if it can, it would be difficult to show that the relative amounts of pleasure given by different works of art can be mapped onto the relative artistic merits customarily accorded to them. One suggested solution to this second difficulty is to be found in Bentham's utilitarian successor, John Stuart Mill (1806–1873), who tried to draw a distinction between higher and lower pleasures, a distinction that might be called upon to distinguish the relative merits of poetry over those of pushpin and the merits of Beethoven over those of Boccherini.

How are we to differentiate between higher and lower pleasures? According to Mill, this can only be done in terms of quantity or quality. The former, he thought, will not serve the purpose, since if the only difference between higher and lower pleasures is quantity, then any lower pleasure can equal the value of a higher pleasure provided there is more of it. Lots of pushpin will be equivalent to a little poetry. So the difference between the two must be qualitative. How is this difference in quality to be assessed? Mill's answer is that we should entrust the assessment to a competent judge, defined as someone who has experience of both the pleasures in question. The problem with this proposal is that the deliverances of such a judge cannot in principle be distinguished from mere preferences. Perhaps someone who declares opera to be a higher pleasure than soap opera does indeed

detect differing qualities of pleasure arising from each of them. But it could be that there is no more to this "judgment" than a personal preference for opera. And we have no way of telling which is the case.

In any event, there is a further difficulty. If the value of art lies in the pleasure we get from it, and if, as seems obviously true, there are other good sources of pleasure, sports for example, it follows that a world without art would be no worse off than a world with art, provided that it had other sources from which equally pleasurable experiences could be generated. This objection relates to an important distinction drawn at the start, the instrumental versus the intrinsic. Hedonism attributes instrumental value, rather than intrinsic value, to art, and thereby implies that art has no value in and of itself. It is chiefly on this point that an alternative theory of the value of art, aestheticism, is built.

AESTHETICISM

The slogan "Art for art's sake" is a familiar one, and it is intended to capture the thought that art has value that cannot be accessed or realized in any other way. What could this intrinsic value be? One obvious contender is beauty. Since ancient times it has been believed that an important function of the arts is to make beautiful things—paintings, poems, music, buildings, and so on— and that these are to be savored for their beauty alone. Aestheticism holds that, though beautiful things are indeed pleasing, it is in their beauty, and not in the pleasure they give us, that their value lies. Since this beauty is an intrinsic property of the object, it cannot be replaced or substituted for without loss, as the extrinsic effect of giving us pleasure can be.

Now while it is undoubtedly true that many artworks are very beautiful, and valued in large part for this reason, it does not seem plausible to make beauty the ultimate explanation of their value, for two reasons. First, beauty is to be found elsewhere than in art. Second, not all art is, or aims to be, beautiful.

The first point is established by the existence of natural beauty. From the time of the ancient Greeks, human bodies and faces have not only been admired for their beauty, but regarded as templates and standards by which the beauty of pictures and statues is to be measured. Since the eighteenth century, landscapes, skies, and seascapes have also been held up as striking instances of the beautiful. All of these things are natural, not manufactured, and are therefore not works of art (the issue of divine creation aside). But if beauty is all around us in natural forms, a world without art would not be a world without beauty, and while this fact does not detract from artistic beauty, it does mean that beauty does not give art any special claim to value.

In any case, while some artworks are indeed beautiful, not all are. For some works of art, in fact, the concept of beauty seems hard to apply. There are beautiful speeches in Shakespeare's tragedies, but could *Lear* or *Othello* be called "beautiful" as a whole? Moreover, even in the visual arts and in music, many widely acclaimed works seem expressly to eschew beauty. In Picasso's famous painting *Les demoiselles d'Avignon*, the figures and faces are ugly—deliberately so, it seems. Many modern composers have written music that is harsh and disjointed rather than harmonious and melodic. The pre-Raphaelite painters and Romantic composers of the nineteenth century strove for visual and aural beauty, but the movements that followed them in the twentieth century strove equally vigorously to avoid it. In short, exclusive focus on beauty can at best explain the value only of some art, and even then not uniquely so.

EXPRESSIONISM

These two objections to aestheticism are overcome in a third theory: that the value of art lies in its being an expression of emotion. The difference between natural beauty and beauty in art is that the former is not an expression of anything, whereas the latter is. It is the expression of the artist's emotion or feeling. Conversely, though emotion can be expressed through beauty, it can be expressed in other ways too. What enables us to classify Titian and Picasso, Schubert and Schoenberg together under the label "art" is that these radically different styles are all equally modes of expression.

Expressionism as an explanation of the value of art is almost as widely held as hedonism. Among its best known advocates were the Italian philosopher Benedetto Croce (1866–1952) and the great Russian novelist Leo Tolstoy (1828–1910). But on closer inspection, it too encounters great difficulties. Three are specially important: Whose emotion is it that an artwork expresses? Why is the expression of emotion a good thing? What place does expressionism leave for imagination?

It might seem obvious to answer the first of these questions by saying that the emotion expressed is that of the creator (the author, painter, composer, and so on). But suppose we say of *Othello*, for example, that it is a dramatic expression of jealousy. What reason have we to say that it is *Shakespeare's* jealousy that is expressed? Since we know hardly anything about Shakespeare, still less about the circumstances in which he came to write this

play, we have no reason to say this. Something similar is true of a huge number of artworks. We do not know much, if anything, about the psychological or emotional history of their creators, and so we cannot say whether they ever felt the emotions expressed in their works.

An alternative would be to locate the emotion in the audience. Aristotle thought that dramatic works are "cathartic." That is to say, they become the vehicles by which audiences give vent to emotions that are often debilitating when discharged into ordinary life. His examples are fear and pity. By discharging these emotions on imaginary objects, we are less burdened by them in the business of day-to-day living. Aristotle only applied the theory of catharsis to drama, and it is unclear whether it could equally be applied to all the arts. But even if it can, there is this further question: What is so good about the expression of emotion as such? Imagine that a work enables those who watch, listen, or otherwise contemplate it, to give vent to ethnic feeling. Without the work, their racist emotions would never have had such clear definition or powerful expression. But why should that commend the work to us? It seems most plausible to hold that it is the powerful expression of *good* emotions that is to be valued, not the powerful expression of emotion per se. On the contrary, hurtful or destructive emotions ought not to be given powerful expression.

To identify the emotion expressed in a work of art as the audience's, then, carries no positive value; it could as easily be negative. To attribute it to the author means, in a very large number of cases, making unwarranted assumptions about the artist's psychological biography. But a further objection is that, by insisting that the origins of an artwork must lie in its creator's personal history, we seem thereby to deny any influence to the very faculty that seems central to artistic creativity, namely imagination. The great genius of such a major work of art as the novel *Middlemarch* lies in George Eliot's ability to rise above the confines of personal experience and imagine a world of people and events that the author never encountered. The most fundamental objection to expressionism is that it reduces acts of imagination to acts of reporting and recording.

COGNITIVISM

Some exponents of an expressionist account of art, notably R. G. Collingwood (1889–1943), have seen this difficulty and, in their efforts to avoid it, have effectively shifted the center of attention from feeling and expression to imagination and understanding. If there is any value in works that express or depict racist or other negative feelings, it lies not in the expression itself, but in the extent to which it gives us insight into the minds of those who have such feelings. This idea motivates the move from expressionism to cognitivism, the view that art should be valued as a form of understanding. On this view, the powerful expression of emotion we find in *Othello*, for example, should be valued for enabling us to understand and appreciate the mind of the intensely jealous. From this point of view, the play supplies its audience with material for thought rather than feeling, and it is of no consequence whether Shakespeare ever felt any of the same sort of rage as the character he invented. Indeed, it adds to the critical assessment of the play if he never did, since in that case the play stands as an even more impressive act of imagination.

Aesthetic cognitivism thus overcomes the most important objections to expressionism by construing artworks as acts of imagination rather than autobiography, and valuing them as such. By shifting the focus to imagination, it also circumvents some of the objections brought against aestheticism and hedonism. The products of the imagination can be beautiful, but this is not what makes them works of art. Artworks stand in contrast to natural beauty because natural beauty is not the outcome of imagination. The relative merits of major and minor works lie in the degree to which the understanding they offer us is more or less profound, and this is a judgment quite independent of the pleasure we do or do not derive from them. Relatively shallow works can be attractive and pleasing; much more profound ones rather taxing.

And yet aesthetic cognitivism faces difficulties of its own. First among these is the relation between imagination and reality. If we are to say that works of art enhance our understanding, this implies that they give us insight into the realities of human experience. But how can they do this if the people, places, and events that they depict are all products of the imagination? Must not understanding track how things really are, rather than how someone has imagined them to be? Second, while aesthetic cognitivism may seem plausible with respect to representative art, it seems more implausible when applied to abstract art. Great novels, films, and figurative paintings are easily thought of as giving us insight into life, but how can this be said of abstract painting, instrumental music, or architecture?

These are important questions, and it is by no means clear that they can be answered. But even if they can, there is a further issue. Does cognitivism about the arts not lead to their redundancy somewhat as hedonism

does? G. W. F. Hegel (1770–1831) was perhaps the greatest philosopher whose account of art can be broadly described as cognitivist, and he quite explicitly thought that because its value lies in its contribution to the development of human understanding, art must eventually be replaced by philosophy. Even at its best, we might say, art can only gesture toward the sort of understanding that philosophy makes explicit.

The most promising reply to this anxiety lies in stressing the sensuous nature of art, which enables it to enhance our felt experience. An artwork does not tell us about the nature of things, events, or people by formulating general statements about them. Rather, it depicts what has been called a "concrete universal," products of the imagination that give us a sense of what it is like to be present and to undergo the experience of things, people, and events from a particular perspective. In other words, art illuminates the things around us rather than providing us with information about them in the way that science, history, and philosophy do.

Whether this response is ultimately satisfactory is a large topic, but cognitivism's emphasis on the sensuous and on the imagination has the merit of being true to two central aspects of the arts. One further implication of cognitivism is that if the sensual is essential, the late-twentieth-century movement known as *conceptual* art may signal an acknowledgment of the end of art. This is an implication that some philosophers, notably Arthur C. Danto, have endorsed and even welcomed.

See also Aesthetic Experience; Aesthetic Qualities; Art, Interpretation of; Art, Truth in; Beauty; Ugliness.

Bibliography

Aristotle. *Poetics*. Translated by Malcolm Heath. London: Penguin, 1997.

Bell, Clive. *Art*. Oxford, U.K.: Oxford University Press, 1987.

Budd, Malcolm. *Values of Art*. London: Penguin, 1995.

Collingwood, R. G. *The Principles of Art*. Oxford, U.K.: Clarendon Press, 1938.

Croce, Benedetto. *Æsthetic as Science of Expression and General Linguistic*. Translated by Douglas Ainslie. London: Peter Owen, 1953.

Danto, Arthur C. *After the End of Art: Contemporary Art and the Pale of History*. Princeton, NJ: Princeton University Press, 1997.

Gadamer, Hans-Georg. *"The Relevance of the Beautiful" and Other Essays*. Translated by Nicholas Walker. Cambridge, U.K.: Cambridge University Press, 1986.

Goodman, Nelson. *Ways of Worldmaking*. Indianapolis, IN: Hackett. 1978.

Hegel, G. W. F. *Aesthetics*. Translated by T. M. Knox. Oxford, U.K.: Clarendon Press, 1975.

Hume, David. *Essays, Moral, Political, and Literary*. Oxford, U.K.: Oxford University Press, 1963.

Kant, Immanuel. *Critique of Judgment*. Translated by Werner S. Pluhar. Indianapolis, IN: Hackett, 1987.

Langer, Susanne K. *Feeling and Form*. London: Routledge and Kegan Paul, 1953.

Levinson, Jerrold. *The Pleasures of Aesthetics*. Ithaca, NY: Cornell University Press, 1996.

Mill, John Stuart. *Utilitarianism*. London: Fontana, 1985.

Nietzsche, Friedrich Wilhelm. *The Birth of Tragedy*. Translated by Shaun Whiteside. London: Penguin, 1993.

Schaper, Eva, ed. *Pleasure, Preference, and Value: Studies in Philosophical Aesthetics*. Cambridge, U.K.: Cambridge University Press, 1983.

Scruton, Roger. *Art and Imagination*. London: Methuen, 1974.

Tolstoy, Leo. *What Is Art?* Translated by Aylmer Maude. Oxford, U.K.: World Classics, 1955.

Walton, Kendall L. *Mimesis as Make-Believe*. Cambridge, MA: Harvard University Press, 1990.

Gordon Graham (2005)

ARTIFICIAL AND NATURAL LANGUAGES

The only natural languages we know of are human. In addition to such human languages as English, Spanish, Russian, and Chinese, with which we are all familiar, there are many less well-known languages, many of them spoken by hundreds of people. The more marginalized languages are dying out at an alarming rate. Owing to lack of evidence, our information about their origin is limited, but it seems likely that they evolved out of communication systems similar to those used by animals for communication. Living human languages are learned as first languages by infants and are used for face-to-face communication and many other purposes.

Natural languages are influenced by a mixture of unconscious evolutionary factors and conscious innovation and policy making. In most cases, the historical record does not allow us to tell what role these factors played in the development of a given feature, but the difficulty of consciously controlling the language used by a large population suggests that unconscious causes predominate.

The term "artificial language" is often used for humanlike languages that are created either for amusement (like J. R. R. Tolkien's Elvish) or for some practical purpose (Esperanto). Information on such projects can be found in Alan Libert's work (2000).

Artificial languages of a quite different sort are created for scientific and technological reasons, and the design of such languages is closely connected with logical theory. Logic originated with Aristotle in his *Prior Analytics*. Although Aristotle's syllogistic theory used symbols for terms (such as "some," "all," "not") that make up propositions, such symbols and the expressions made up out of them were not generally considered as part of a linguistic system until much later.

Modern logical theory and its connection with artificial languages owes much to the search for a universal language in the seventeenth century (Maat 1999). In Britain, George Dalgarno (1968 [1661]) and John Wilkins (2002 [1668]) promoted the idea of a philosophical language based on rational principles. In retrospect, their ideas seem to be more closely aligned with the goal of designing an improved human language than with the mainstream development of logic and were more concerned to facilitate clear expression of ideas than to serve as a framework for developing a theory of reasoning. Their projects stressed the need for basing a vocabulary on a rational ontology and are more closely connected with later attempts to develop taxonomies and thesauri than with logic per se.

At about the same time, however, G. W. Leibniz attempted to develop a "universal characteristic" based on several ideas central to the later development of logic and artificial-language design. In his "Dissertatio de Arte Combinatoria" (excerpts in Loemker 1956, pp. 117–133), written in 1666 when he was nineteen years old, Leibniz presents a logical program that, in its main proposals, informed his philosophy for the remainder of his life.

Like Dalgarno and Wilkins, Leibniz adopted the goal of a rationally ideal philosophical language, but he differs from them in the stress he lays on reasoning and in the degree to which his account of reasoning is inspired by mathematics. The leading ideas of his program—that truth can be discovered by analysis, or division of concepts into basic constituents; that such analytic reasoning is analogous to combinatory reasoning in mathematics; and that it is facilitated by a language with a clear syntactic structure reflecting the meanings of expressions—have furnished important insights for subsequent work in logic. The stress that Leibniz placed on calculation as part of the reasoning process gives him a well-deserved central place in the history of logic and computation.

The two weak points in Leibniz's program are (1) the assumption that once analysis was achieved in an ideally rational language, testing a proposition for truth should be a relatively trivial matter, and (2) the idea that analysis is appropriate and possible across the entire range of rational inquiry. The first of these weaknesses was corrected late in the nineteenth century, when Gottlob Frege developed a symbolic language for the representation of "pure" or mathematical thought. Frege's "Begriffsschrift," or conceptual calculus, achieves the goal prefigured by Leibniz of a language designed to facilitate reasoning by allowing the relations between concepts to be clearly and unambiguously displayed. And it conforms to the methodological ideal of being completely explicit more than any previous attempt to present an artificial language. Frege's presentation of the *Begriffsschrift* makes it possible to test each constellation of symbols to tell whether it is a well-formed formula (an expression that conforms to the syntactic rules of the system). Although part of proving such a formula in Frege's calculus is a matter of analysis, or the application of explicit definitions, the result of such analysis is a formula that must be proved using logical laws. These laws are explicitly formulated, so that it is also possible to tell whether or not a purported proof conforms to the rules of the system. But *whether there is a proof* of an analyzed proposition need not be a question that can be solved algorithmically. In fact, as the theory of the nature of reasoning systems has shown, we cannot in general expect to have an algorithmic criterion for whether a formula is provable.

The second weakness in Leibniz's program is more difficult to deal with decisively. But many years of experience indicate that we have no reliable methodology for isolating universal atoms of human thought. In many extended attempts to make the rules of reasoning in some domain explicit, it seems more useful to deal with many primitives that are conceptually related by axioms rather than by definitions.

Alonzo Church summarized the results of more than seventy-five years of philosophical and mathematical development of Frege's achievement in section 7, "The Logistic Method," of his *Introduction to Mathematical Logic* (1956). In that and the subsequent two sections, Church sets out the methods logicians had established in the first half of the twentieth century for constructing artificial logical languages (or, to use the usual current term, *formal languages*) and theorizing about them. These methods have changed slightly in the subsequent forty-eight years, the most significant changes having to do with interest in applications other than the explication of deductive reasoning and in the widespread use of formal languages in digital computing. In the beginning of the twenty-first century, it is not essential for formal languages to have a deductive component, and in some cases it may be important to associate implemented computational procedures with a formal language.

What are the essential features of a formal language? First, a formal language must have a *syntax*, a precise definition not only of the vocabulary of the language but also of the strings of vocabulary items that count as well-formed formulas. If other types of complex expressions than formulas are important, for each such *syntactic type* there must be a precise definition of the set of strings belonging to that type. These definitions must be not only precise but *effective*; that is, questions concerning membership in syntactic types must be algorithmically decidable. These syntactic definitions are usually presented as inductive definitions; for instance, the simplest formulas are defined directly, and rules are presented for building up complex formulas from simpler ones. The set of well-formed formulas is not only decidable but usually belongs to a known restricted class of efficiently computable sets of strings. The *context-free* sets of strings are heavily used in computational applications, and are also capable of standing in for large parts of human languages.

Second, if proofs are associated with the language, these too must be precisely defined. Whether or not a list of formulas is a proof must be algorithmically decidable.

Third, the formal language must have a semantic interpretation, which associates *semantic values* or *denotations* with the well-formed expressions of the language. The importance of a semantic component was recognized by Alfred Tarski, who also provided a methodology for placing semantics on a sound mathematical basis and applying it to the analysis of mathematical theories.

A version of Tarskian semantics due to Alonzo Church (1940) starts with a domain of individuals (the objects that the language deals with) and a domain of truth-values (the two values True and False) and constructs possible denotations by taking functions from domains to domains. Sentences, for instance, denote truth-values, and one-place predicates (verblike expressions taking just one argument) denote functions from individuals to truth-values.

In a semantics for deductive reasoning, truth-values are essential. Once the legitimate interpretations (or *models*) of a language are given, the validity of an inference (say of formula B from formula A) can be defined as follows: The inference is valid if every model that assigns A the value True also assigns B the value True.

The theory of any language (natural or artificial) has to be stated in some language. When one language serves as a vehicle for formulating and theorizing about another language, the first is called the *metalanguage* for the second, and the second is called an *object language* of the first. Nothing prevents a metalanguage itself from being formalized. When logicians wish to investigate theories of language, they may wish to formalize an object language and its metalanguage. The language in which the theory of both languages is stated would be a *meta-metalanguage*. Since formalization is a human endeavor, the whole enterprise is usually conducted in some human language (typically in some fairly regimented part of a human language, supplemented with mathematical notation), and this language serves as the metalanguage for all the languages developed in the course of the formalization project. In theory, a language can be its own metalanguage, but in such cases we have a situation that can easily lead to paradox.

The use of digital computers has led to the wholesale creation of special-purpose formal languages. Since computer scientists have borrowed the methods for presenting these languages from logic, computational formal languages usually conform to Church's recipe. Sometimes, however, a semantics is not provided. (For instance, mathematical tools for providing semantic interpretations for programming languages only became available years after such languages had been developed and used.) Often it is important to specify the crucial computational procedures associated with such a language. For example, a *query language*, intended to enable a user to present questions to a database, has to provide a procedure for computing an answer to each query that it allows. Sometimes a computational formal language is pointless unless procedures have been implemented to enable computers to process inputs formulated in the language. A programming language is useless without an implemented program that interprets it; a markup language like HTML (Hypertext Markup Language) is useless without browsers that implement procedures for displaying documents written in the language.

These are very natural additions to Church's logistic method. Even in 1956 a semantic interpretation was thought to be desirable but not essential. The methods developed by logicians in the first half of the twentieth century for formalizing languages have not changed greatly since then and are likely to be with us for a long time.

The distinction between natural and formal languages is not the same as the distinction between naturally occurring and artificial languages. Rather, it is the distinction between naturally occurring languages and languages that are formalized, or precisely characterized along the lines suggested by Church. As far as the distinc-

tion goes, what prevents a natural language from being formalized is the difficulty (or perhaps impossibility) of actually formalizing a language like English or Swahili. Can natural languages be formalized? Can the grammar of naturally occurring languages be articulated as clearly as the syntax of an artificially constructed language? In assigning denotations to the expressions of a natural language, do we encounter problems that do not arise with artificial languages designed to capture mathematical reasoning?

In fact, there are difficulties. But logical work on formal languages has served as one of the most important sources of inspiration for theories of natural-language syntax, and is by far the most important source of inspiration for semantic theories of natural language. Both types of theories are now primarily pursued by linguists.

The ideal of syntax stated by Church derives from earlier work by David Hilbert, Rudolf Carnap, and other logicians. The essential ideas are an utterly precise description of the syntactic patterns of a language and algorithmic rules specifying how complex expressions are built up out of simpler ones. In essentials, this ideal is also the one that Noam Chomsky proposed in 1957 for the syntax of natural language. It has persisted through the evolution of the theories that Chomsky and his students have created and is also accepted by most of the leading rival approaches. Although there are methodological difficulties associated with the paradigm, they are no worse than the difficulties encountered by other sciences. The idea that natural-language syntax resembles that of formal languages has proved to be a fruitful paradigm for almost fifty years of syntactic research.

Semantics presents a more difficult challenge. Tarski's program addressed the semantics of specialized mathematical languages, and its success seems to depend essentially on certain features of these languages that are not shared by natural human languages: (1) Mathematical notation is designed to be neither ambiguous nor vague, whereas natural languages are both vague and ambiguous. (2) Natural languages have many sorts of *indexical* or context-sensitive expressions, like "I" and "today," whereas mathematical notations tend to use only one kind of indexical expression, variables. (3) *Intensional* constructions like "believe" are not found in mathematics, and they create other difficulties. The verb "believe" does not act semantically on the truth-value of the sentence it modifies. If you know that "Sacramento is the capitol of California" is true, this does not tell you whether "Jack believes that Sacramento is the capitol of California" is true. There are practical difficulties as well as difficulties in principle. Natural languages are so complex that the task of formalizing them is open-ended and much too large for a single linguist or even for a single generation of linguists.

Richard Montague, a logician who taught at the University of California at Los Angeles until 1971, is primarily responsible for showing how to overcome obstacles that seemed to prevent a semantics for natural languages along the lines advocated by Tarski. His work began a program of research along these lines that is still being pursued. Montague's solution to the problem of ambiguity was to assign denotations to *disambiguated syntactic structures*. With a syntactic structure and a single reading for each word in a sentence, the sentence can have only one meaning. His solution to indexicality was to relativize interpretations to contexts. And his solution to the problem of intensionality, which followed earlier work by Rudolf Carnap, was systematically to assign linguistic phrases two denotations: an *intension* and an *extension*. Montague treated possible worlds as semantic primitives. Intensions, for him, were functions from possible worlds to appropriate extensions. The intension of a sentence, for instance, is a function from possible worlds to truth-values. Montague presented several formal "fragments" of English, the idea being to achieve rigor by focusing on a limited family of natural-language constructions. He also showed how to use higher-order logic to obtain a remarkably elegant and unified semantic interpretation.

This work on natural-language semantics leaves open a number of challenging questions concerning whether natural languages contain elements that somehow resist formalization. For one, Montague did not deal with vagueness, and there are difficulties with his accounts of intensionality and indexicality. These issues have been a major preoccupation of analytic philosophy since the 1970s. Although no philosopher has persuasively argued that the problems are unsolvable, they are certainly more difficult than many people imagined them to be in 1971. While the final question of whether natural languages can be completely formalized remains open, the assumption that this is possible has certainly inspired a fruitful paradigm of research.

See also Semantics; Syntactical and Semantic Categories.

Bibliography

Carnap, Rudolph. *Logische Syntax der Sprache Schriften zur wissenschaftlichen Weltauffassung.* Vienna: Verlag von Julius Springer, 1934.

Carnap, Rudolph. *Meaning and Necessity.* 2nd ed. Chicago: University of Chicago Press, 1956. First edition published in 1947.

Chomsky, Noam. *Syntactic Structures.* The Hague: Mouton, 1957.

Church, Alonzo. "A Formulation of the Simple Theory of Types." *Journal of Symbolic Logic* 5 (1) (1940): 56–68.

Church, Alonzo. *Introduction to Mathematical Logic.* Vol. 1. Princeton, NJ: Princeton University Press, 1956.

Dalgarno, George. *Ars Signorum, Vulgo Character Universalis et Lingua Philosophica* (1661). Menston, Yorkshire, U.K.: Scholar Press, 1968.

Frege, Gottlob. *Begriffsschrift: Eine der arithmetischen nachgebildete Formalsprache des reinen Denkens.* Halle, Germany: L. Nebert, 1879. Translated in *Frege and Gödel: Two Fundamental Texts in Mathematical Logic,* compiled by Jean van Heijenoort. Cambridge, MA: Harvard University Press, 1970.

Libert, Alan. *A Priori Artificial Languages.* Munich: Lincom Europa, 2000.

Loemker, Leroy E., ed. *Gottfried Wilhelm Leibniz: Philosophical Papers and Letters.* Vol. 2. Chicago: University of Chicago Press, 1956.

Maat, Jaap. "Philosophical Languages in the Seventeenth Century: Dalgarno, Wilkins, Leibniz." PhD diss., Institute for Logic, Language, and Computation, University of Amsterdam, Amsterdam, 1999.

Montague, Richard. *Formal Philosophy: Selected Papers of Richard Montague,* edited by Richmond H. Thomason. New Haven, CT: Yale University Press, 1974.

Tarski, Alfred. "The Concept of Truth in Formalized Languages" (1936). In his *Logic, Semantics, Metamathematics.* Oxford, U.K.: Clarendon Press, 1956.

Wilkins, John. *An Essay towards a Real Character and a Philosophical Language* (1668). Bristol, U.K.: Thoemmes, 2002.

Richmond H. Thomason (2005)

ARTIFICIAL INTELLIGENCE

Artificial Intelligence (AI) tries to enable computers to do the things that minds can do. These things include seeing pathways, picking things up, learning categories from experience, and using emotions to schedule one's actions—which many animals can do, too. Thus, human intelligence is not the sole focus of AI. Even terrestrial psychology is not the sole focus, because some people use AI to explore the range of all possible minds.

There are four major AI methodologies: symbolic AI, connectionism, situated robotics, and evolutionary programming (Russell and Norvig 2003). AI artifacts are correspondingly varied. They include both programs (including neural networks) and robots, each of which may be either designed in detail or largely evolved. The field is closely related to artificial life (A-Life), which aims to throw light on biology much as some AI aims to throw light on psychology.

AI researchers are inspired by two different intellectual motivations, and while some people have both, most favor one over the other. On the one hand, many AI researchers seek solutions to technological problems, not caring whether these resemble human (or animal) psychology. They often make use of ideas about how people do things. Programs designed to aid/replace human experts, for example, have been hugely influenced by knowledge engineering, in which programmers try to discover what, and how, human experts are thinking when they do the tasks being modeled. But if these technological AI workers can find a nonhuman method, or even a mere trick (a kludge) to increase the power of their program, they will gladly use it.

Technological AI has been hugely successful. It has entered administrative, financial, medical, and manufacturing practice at countless different points. It is largely invisible to the ordinary person, lying behind some deceptively simple human-computer interface or being hidden away inside a car or refrigerator. Many procedures taken for granted within current computer science were originated within AI (pattern-recognition and image-processing, for example).

On the other hand, AI researchers may have a scientific aim. They may want their programs or robots to help people understand how human (or animal) minds work. They may even ask how intelligence in general is possible, exploring the space of possible minds. The scientific approach—psychological AI—is the more relevant for philosophers (Boden 1990, Copeland 1993, Sloman 2002). It is also central to cognitive science, and to computationalism.

Considered as a whole, psychological AI has been less obviously successful than technological AI. This is partly because the tasks it tries to achieve are often more difficult. In addition, it is less clear—for philosophical as well as empirical reasons—what should be counted as success.

SYMBOLIC AI

Symbolic AI is also known as classical AI and as GOFAI—short for John Haugeland's label "Good Old-Fashioned AI" (1985). It models mental processes as the step-by-step information processing of digital computers. Thinking is seen as symbol-manipulation, as (formal) computation over (formal) representations. Some GOFAI programs are explicitly hierarchical, consisting of procedures and subroutines specified at different levels. These define a

hierarchically structured search-space, which may be astronomical in size. Rules of thumb, or heuristics, are typically provided to guide the search—by excluding certain areas of possibility, and leading the program to focus on others. The earliest AI programs were like this, but the later methodology of object-oriented programming is similar.

Certain symbolic programs, namely production systems, are implicitly hierarchical. These consist of sets of logically separate if-then (condition-action) rules, or productions, defining what actions should be taken in response to specific conditions. An action or condition may be unitary or complex, in the latter case being defined by a conjunction of several mini-actions or mini-conditions. And a production may function wholly within computer memory (to set a goal, for instance, or to record a partial parsing) or outside it (via input/output devices such as cameras or keyboards).

Another symbolic technique, widely used in natural language processing (NLP) programs, involves augmented transition networks, or ATNs. These avoid explicit backtracking by using guidance at each decision-point to decide which question to ask and/or which path to take.

GOFAI methodology is used for developing a wide variety of language-using programs and problem-solvers. The more precisely and explicitly a problem-domain can be defined, the more likely it is that a symbolic program can be used to good effect. Often, folk-psychological categories and/or specific propositions are explicitly represented in the system. This type of AI, and the forms of computational psychology based on it, is defended by the philosopher Jerry Fodor (1988).

GOFAI models (whether technological or scientific) include robots, planning programs, theorem-provers, learning programs, question-answerers, data-mining systems, machine translators, expert systems of many different kinds, chess players, semantic networks, and analogy machines. In addition, a host of software agents—specialist mini-programs that can aid a human being to solve a problem—are implemented in this way. And an increasingly important area of research is distributed AI, in which cooperation occurs between many relatively simple individuals—which may be GOFAI agents (or neural-network units, or situated robots).

The symbolic approach is used also in modeling creativity in various domains (Boden 2004, Holland et al. 1986). These include musical composition and expressive performance, analogical thinking, line-drawing, painting, architectural design, storytelling (rhetoric as well as plot), mathematics, and scientific discovery. In general, the relevant aesthetic/theoretical style must be specified clearly, so as to define a space of possibilities that can be fruitfully explored by the computer. To what extent the exploratory procedures can plausibly be seen as similar to those used by people varies from case to case.

CONNECTIONIST AI

Connectionist systems, which became widely visible in the mid-1980s, are different. They compute not by following step-by-step programs but by using large numbers of locally connected (associative) computational units, each one of which is simple. The processing is bottom-up rather than top-down.

Connectionism is sometimes said to be opposed to AI, although it has been part of AI since its beginnings in the 1940s (McCulloch and Pitts 1943, Pitts and McCulloch 1947). What connectionism is opposed to, rather, is symbolic AI. Yet even here, opposed is not quite the right word, since hybrid systems exist that combine both methodologies. Moreover, GOFAI devotees such as Fodor see connectionism as compatible with GOFAI, claiming that it concerns how symbolic computation can be implemented (Fodor and Pylyshyn 1988).

Two largely separate AI communities began to emerge in the late 1950s (Boden forthcoming). The symbolic school focused on logic and Turing-computation, whereas the connectionist school focused on associative, and often probabilistic, neural networks. (Most connectionist systems are connectionist virtual machines, implemented in von Neumann computers; only a few are built in dedicated connectionist hardware.) Many people remained sympathetic to both schools. But the two methodologies are so different in practice that most hands-on AI researchers use either one or the other.

There are different types of connectionist systems. Most philosophical interest, however, has focused on networks that do parallel distributed processing, or PDP (Clark 1989, Rumelhart and McClelland 1986). In essence, PDP systems are pattern recognizers. Unlike brittle GOFAI programs, which often produce nonsense if provided with incomplete or part-contradictory information, they show graceful degradation. That is, the input patterns can be recognized (up to a point) even if they are imperfect.

A PDP network is made up of subsymbolic units, whose semantic significance cannot easily be expressed in terms of familiar semantic content, still less propositions.

(Some GOFAI programs employ subsymbolic units, but most do not.) That is, no single unit codes for a recognizable concept, such as dog or cat. These concepts are represented, rather, by the pattern of activity distributed over the entire network.

Because the representation is not stored in a single unit but is distributed over the whole network, PDP systems can tolerate imperfect data. (Some GOFAI systems can do so too, but only if the imperfections are specifically foreseen and provided for by the programmer.) Moreover, a single subsymbolic unit may mean one thing in one input-context and another in another. What the network as a whole can represent depends on what significance the designer has decided to assign to the input-units. For instance, some input-units are sensitive to light (or to coded information about light), others to sound, others to triads of phonological categories … and so on.

Most PDP systems can learn. In such cases, the weights on the links of PDP units in the hidden layer (between the input-layer and the output-layer) can be altered by experience, so that the network can learn a pattern merely by being shown many examples of it. (A GOFAI learning-program, in effect, has to be told what to look for beforehand, and how.) Broadly, the weight on an excitatory link is increased by every coactivation of the two units concerned: cells that fire together, wire together.

These two AI approaches have complementary strengths and weaknesses. For instance, symbolic AI is better at modeling hierarchy and strong constraints, whereas connectionism copes better with pattern recognition, especially if many conflicting—and perhaps incomplete—constraints are relevant. Despite having fervent philosophical champions on both sides, neither methodology is adequate for all of the tasks dealt with by AI scientists. Indeed, much research in connectionism has aimed to restore the lost logical strengths of GOFAI to neural networks—with only limited success by the beginning of the twenty-first century.

SITUATED ROBOTICS

Another, and more recently popular, AI methodology is situated robotics (Brooks 1991). Like connectionism, this was first explored in the 1950s. Situated robots are described by their designers as autonomous systems embedded in their environment (Heidegger is sometimes cited). Instead of planning their actions, as classical robots do, situated robots react directly to environmental cues. One might say that they are embodied production systems, whose if-then rules are engineered rather than programmed, and whose conditions lie in the external environment, not inside computer memory. Although—unlike GOFAI robots—they contain no objective representations of the world, some of them do construct temporary, subject-centered (deictic) representations.

The main aim of situated roboticists in the mid-1980s, such as Rodney Brooks, was to solve/avoid the frame problem that had bedeviled GOFAI (Pylyshyn 1987). GOFAI planners and robots had to anticipate all possible contingencies, including the side effects of actions taken by the system itself, if they were not to be defeated by unexpected—perhaps seemingly irrelevant—events. This was one of the reasons given by Hubert Dreyfus (1992) in arguing that GOFAI could not possibly succeed: Intelligence, he said, is unformalizable. Several ways of implementing nonmonotonic logics in GOFAI were suggested, allowing a conclusion previously drawn by faultless reasoning to be negated by new evidence. But because the general nature of that new evidence had to be foreseen, the frame problem persisted.

Brooks argued that reasoning shouldn't be employed at all: the system should simply react appropriately, in a reflex fashion, to specific environmental cues. This, he said, is what insects do—and they are highly successful creatures. (Soon, situated robotics was being used, for instance, to model the six-legged movement of cockroaches.) Some people joked that AI stood for artificial insects, not artificial intelligence. But the joke carried a sting: Many argued that much human thinking needs objective representations, so the scope for situated robotics was strictly limited.

EVOLUTIONARY PROGRAMMING

In evolutionary programming, genetic algorithms (GAs) are used by a program to make random variations in its own rules. The initial rules, before evolution begins, either do not achieve the task in question or do so only inefficiently; sometimes, they are even chosen at random.

The variations allowed are broadly modeled on biological mutations and crossovers, although more unnatural types are sometimes employed. The most successful rules are automatically selected, and then varied again. This is more easily said than done: The breakthrough in GA methodology occurred when John Holland (1992) defined an automatic procedure for recognizing which rules, out of a large and simultaneously active set, were those most responsible for whatever level of success the evolving system had just achieved.

Selection is done by some specific fitness criterion, predefined in light of the task the programmer has in mind. Unlike GOFAI systems, a GA program contains no explicit representation of what it is required to do: its task is implicit in the fitness criterion. (Similarly, living things have evolved to do what they do without knowing what that is.) After many generations, the GA system may be well-adapted to its task. For certain types of tasks, it can even find the optimal solution.

This AI method is used to develop both symbolic and connectionist AI systems. And it is applied both to abstract problem-solving (mathematical optimization, for instance, or the synthesis of new pharmaceutical molecules) and to evolutionary robotics—wherein the brain and/or sensorimotor anatomy of robots evolve within a specific task-environment.

It is also used for artistic purposes, in the composition of music or the generation of new visual forms. In these cases, evolution is usually interactive. That is, the variation is done automatically but the selection is done by a human being—who does not need to (and usually could not) define, or even name, the aesthetic fitness criteria being applied.

ARTIFICIAL LIFE

AI is a close cousin of A-Life (Boden 1996). This is a form of mathematical biology, which employs computer simulation and situated robotics to study the emergence of complexity in self-organizing, self-reproducing, adaptive systems. (A caveat: much as some AI is purely technological in aim, so is some A-Life; the research of most interest to philosophers is the scientifically oriented type.)

The key concepts of A-Life date back to the early 1950s. They originated in theoretical work on self-organizing systems of various kinds, including diffusion equations and cellular automata (by Alan Turing and John von Neumann respectively), and in early self-equilibrating machines and situated robots (built by W. Ross Ashby and W. Grey Walter). But A-Life did not flourish until the late 1980s, when computing power at last sufficed to explore these theoretical ideas in practice.

Much A-Life work focuses on specific biological phenomena, such as flocking, cooperation in ant colonies, or morphogenesis—from cell-differentiation to the formation of leopard spots or tiger stripes. But A-Life also studies general principles of self-organization in biology: evolution and coevolution, reproduction, and metabolism. In addition, it explores the nature of life as such—life as it could be, not merely life as it is.

A-Life workers do not all use the same methodology, but they do eschew the top-down methods of GOFAI. Situated and evolutionary robotics, and GA-generated neural networks, too, are prominent approaches within the field. But not all A-Life systems are evolutionary. Some demonstrate how a small number of fixed, and simple, rules can lead to self-organization of an apparently complex kind.

Many A-Lifers take pains to distance themselves from AI. But besides their close historical connections, AI and A-Life are philosophically related in virtue of the linkage between life and mind. It is known that psychological properties arise in living things, and some people argue (or assume) that they can arise only in living things. Accordingly, the whole of AI could be regarded as a subarea of A-Life. Indeed, some people argue that success in AI (even in technological AI) must await, and build on, success in A-Life.

WHY AI IS A MISLEADING LABEL

Whichever of the two AI motivations—technological or psychological—is in question, the name of the field is misleading in three ways. First, the term *intelligence* is normally understood to cover only a subset of what AI workers are trying to do. Second, intelligence is often supposed to be distinct from emotion, so that AI is assumed to exclude work on that. And third, the name implies that a successful AI system would really be intelligent—a philosophically controversial claim that AI researchers do not have to endorse (though some do).

As for the first point, people do not normally regard vision or locomotion as examples of intelligence. Many people would say that speaking one's native language is not a case of intelligence either, except in comparison with nonhuman species; and common sense is sometimes contrasted with intelligence. The term is usually reserved for special cases of human thought that show exceptional creativity and subtlety, or which require many years of formal education. Medical diagnosis, scientific or legal reasoning, playing chess, and translating from one language to another are typically regarded as difficult, thus requiring intelligence. And these tasks were the main focus of research when AI began. Vision, for example, was assumed to be relatively straightforward—not least, because many nonhuman animals have it too. It gradually became clear, however, that everyday capacities such as vision and locomotion are vastly more complex than had been supposed. The early definition of AI as programming computers to do things that involve intelligence when done by people was recognized as misleading, and eventually dropped.

Similarly, intelligence is often opposed to emotion. Many people assume that AI could never model that. However, crude examples of such models existed in the early 1960s, and emotion was recognized by a high priest of AI, Herbert Simon, as being essential to any complex intelligence. Later, research in the computational philosophy (and modeling) of affect showed that emotions have evolved as scheduling mechanisms for systems with many different, and potentially conflicting, purposes (Minsky 1985, and Web site). When AI began, it was difficult enough to get a program to follow one goal (with its subgoals) intelligently—any more than that was essentially impossible. For this reason, among others, AI modeling of emotion was put on the back burner for about thirty years. By the 1990s, however, it had become a popular focus of AI research, and of neuroscience and philosophy too.

The third point raises the difficult question—which many AI practitioners leave open, or even ignore—of whether intentionality can properly be ascribed to any conceivable program/robot (Newell 1980, Dennett 1987, Harnad 1991).

AI AND INTENTIONALITY

Could some NLP programs really understand the sentences they parse and the words they translate? Or can a visuo-motor circuit evolved within a robot's neural-network brain truly be said to represent the environmental feature to which it responds? If a program, in practice, could pass the Turing Test, could it truly be said to think? More generally, does it even make sense to say that AI may one day achieve artificially produced (but nonetheless genuine) intelligence?

For the many people in the field who adopt some form of functionalism, the answer in each case is: In principle, yes. This applies for those who favor the physical symbol system hypothesis or intentional systems theory. Others adopt connectionist analyses of concepts, and of their development from nonconceptual content. Functionalism is criticized by many writers expert in neuroscience, who claim that its core thesis of multiple realizability is mistaken. Others criticize it at an even deeper level: a growing minority (especially in A-Life) reject neo-Cartesian approaches in favor of philosophies of embodiment, such as phenomenology or autopoiesis.

Part of the reason why such questions are so difficult is that philosophers disagree about what intentionality is, even in the human case. Practitioners of psychological AI generally believe that semantic content, or intentionality, can be naturalized. But they differ about how this can be done.

For instance, a few practitioners of AI regard computation and intentionality as metaphysically inseparable (Smith 1996). Others ascribe meaning only to computations with certain causal consequences and provenance, or grounding. John Searle argues that AI cannot capture intentionality, because—at base—it is concerned with the formal manipulation of formal symbols. And for those who accept some form of evolutionary semantics, only evolutionary robots could embody meaning (Searle, 1980).

See also Computationalism; Machine Intelligence.

Bibliography

Boden, Margaret A. *The Creative Mind: Myths and Mechanisms*. 2nd ed. London: Routledge, 2004.

Boden, Margaret A. *Mind as Machine: A History of Cognitive Science*. Oxford: Oxford University Press, forthcoming. See especially chapters 4, 7.i, 10–13, and 14.

Boden, Margaret A., ed. *The Philosophy of Artificial Intelligence*. Oxford: Oxford University Press, 1990.

Boden, Margaret A., ed. *The Philosophy of Artificial Life*. Oxford: Oxford University Press, 1996.

Brooks, Rodney A. "Intelligence without Representation." *Artificial Intelligence* 47 (1991): 139–159.

Clark, Andy J. *Microcognition: Philosophy, Cognitive Science, and Parallel Distributed Processing*. Cambridge, MA: MIT Press, 1989.

Copeland, B. Jack. *Artificial Intelligence: A Philosophical Introduction*. Oxford: Blackwell, 1993.

Dennett, Daniel C. *The Intentional Stance*. Cambridge, MA: MIT Press, 1987.

Dreyfus, Hubert L. *What Computers Still Can't Do: A Critique of Artificial Reason*. Cambridge, MA: MIT Press, 1992.

Fodor, Jerome A., and Zenon W. Pylyshyn. "Connectionism and Cognitive Architecture: A Critical Analysis." *Cognition* 28 (1988): 3–71.

Harnad, Stevan. "Other Bodies, Other Minds: A Machine Incarnation of an Old Philosophical Problem." *Minds and Machines* 1 (1991): 43–54.

Haugeland, John. *Artificial Intelligence: The Very Idea*. Cambridge, MA: MIT Press, 1985.

Holland, John H. *Adaptation in Natural and Artificial Systems: An Introductory Analysis with Applications to Biology, Control, and Artificial Intelligence*. Cambridge, MA: MIT Press, 1992.

Holland, John H., Keith J. Holyoak, Richard E. Nisbett, and Paul R. Thagard. *Induction: Processes of Inference, Learning, and Discovery*. Cambridge, MA: MIT Press, 1986.

McCulloch, Warren S., and Walter H. Pitts. "A Logical Calculus of the Ideas Immanent in Nervous Activity." In *The Philosoophy of Artificial Intelligence*, edited by Margaret A. Boden. Oxford: Oxford University Press, 1990. First published in 1943.

Minsky, Marvin L. *The Emotion Machine*. Available from http://web.media.mit.edu/~minsky/E1/eb1.html. Web site only.

Minsky, Marvin L. *The Society of Mind*. New York: Simon & Schuster, 1985.

Newell, Allen. "Physical Symbol Systems." *Cognitive Science* 4 (1980): 135–183.

Pitts, Walter H., and Warren S. McCulloch. "How We Know Universals: The Perception of Auditory and Visual Forms." In *Embodiments of Mind*, edited by Warren S. McCulloch. Cambridge, MA: MIT Press, 1965. First published in 1947.

Pylyshyn, Zenon W. *The Robot's Dilemma: The Frame Problem in Artificial Intelligence*. Norwood, NJ: Ablex, 1987.

Rumelhart, David E., and James L. McClelland, eds. *Parallel Distributed Processing: Explorations in the Microstructure of Cognition*. 2 vols. Cambridge, MA: MIT Press, 1986.

Russell, Stuart J., and Peter Norvig. *Artificial Intelligence: A Modern Approach*. 2nd ed. Upper Saddle River, NJ: Prentice-Hall, 2003.

Searle, John R. "Minds, Brains, and Programs," *The Behavioral and Brain Sciences* 3 (1980), 417–424. Reprinted in M. A. Boden, ed., *The Philosophy of Artificial Intelligence* (Oxford: Oxford University Press 1990), pp. 67–88.

Sloman, Aaron. "The Irrelevance of Turing Machines to Artificial Intelligence." In *Computationalism: New Directions*, edited by Matthias Scheutz. Cambridge, MA: MIT Press, 2002.

Smith, Brian C. *On the Origin of Objects*. Cambridge, MA: MIT Press, 1996.

Margaret A. Boden (1996, 2005)

ASCETICISM

There is a morbid fascination in any survey of the ascetic practices of humankind. Fasting, the virgin priestess, and the mutilation of the body are common features of ancient religions. In monastic Christianity the austere ideals of celibacy, obedience, and poverty have been both practiced and admired. Even today there are many who observe Lent and those for whom fasting and penance are seldom out of season. The most accomplished ascetics have been the wanderers (*sunnyasins*) of ancient India and the anchorites of fourth-century Egypt. One *sunnyasin* held his arms above his head with fists clenched until the muscles in his arms atrophied and the nails grew through his palms. It is said that the anchorite St. Simeon Stylites tied a rope tightly around himself until it ate into his body and his flesh became infested with worms. As the worms fell from his body he replaced them in his putrefied flesh, saying, "Eat what God has given you."

Behind such ascetic practices usually lies the philosophical theory of "asceticism," a theory that demands and justifies this unnatural way of life. Although the term *ascetic* was originally applied to any sort of moral discipline, it has since acquired a narrower and more negative meaning. Asceticism may now be defined as the theory that one ought on principle to deny one's desires. Asceticism may be partial or complete. Partial asceticism is the theory that one ought to deny one's "lower desires," which are usually identified as sensuous, bodily, or worldly and are contrasted with more virtuous or spiritual desires. Complete asceticism is the theory that one ought to deny all desires without exception. Asceticism may also be moderate or extreme. Moderate asceticism is the theory that one ought to repress one's desires as far as is compatible with the necessities of this life. Extreme asceticism is the theory that one ought to annihilate one's desires totally.

HISTORY

The belief that austerities (*tapas*) burn away sin was a product of the non-Aryan tradition of ancient India. This belief persisted, and austerities were recommended by the yogis and the Jains. All orthodox systems of Indian philosophy agreed that the goal of life is liberation (*moksa*) from this world of suffering, and most maintained that the renunciation of worldly desires is necessary for liberation. Although the Buddha tried and rejected austerities, his principle that the cause of suffering is craving led later Buddhists to advocate renunciation and even to practice austerities. The Jains held that liberation is possible only when one has annihilated all passion, because passion attracts karma, believed by this sect to be a subtle form of matter that holds the soul in bondage.

Asceticism seems to have entered Western philosophy from the mystery religions that influenced Pythagoreanism about the end of the sixth century BCE. Although Greek ethics was predominantly naturalistic, Plato sometimes argued that one ought to repress the bodily desires in order to free the soul in its search for knowledge. Some Cynics renounced worldly desires in order to pursue virtue in independence. The early Stoics defined emotion as irrational desire and held up the ideal of the apathetic man in whom all emotions had been annihilated. Plotinus emphasized the ascetic side of Plato's philosophy and claimed that matter is the source of all evil.

This undercurrent of asceticism rose to the surface in medieval philosophy with its emphasis on religious otherworldliness. The foundations of this asceticism were laid by such theologians as St. Athanasius, St. Gregory of Nyssa, St. Ambrose, and even St. Augustine. They believed that the desires of the flesh should be repressed in order to achieve moral virtue and the contemplation of God.

Their view molded the monastic institutions that were established in the fourth century. Virtually unchallenged, this asceticism remained a potent influence on religious life until the Renaissance.

Of modern philosophers, only Arthur Schopenhauer has been an important advocate of asceticism; he would have one completely annihilate the will to live in all its manifestations. Jeremy Bentham and Friedrich Nietzsche have each criticized asceticism from very different standpoints.

ARGUMENTS FOR ASCETICISM

The arguments for asceticism fall into three main classes. First, there are those that attempt a direct justification of self-denial. Although some of these arguments might justify a complete asceticism, they have traditionally been used to support only a partial asceticism. (1) We know by some authority that one ought to deny one's lower desires. One authority is the Bible, in which we find both express ascetic commandments and examples like those of the Virgin Mary and the celibate Christ. (2) The sacrament of penance requires the denial of worldly desires. Although one is cleansed of original sin by baptism, subsequent sins must be expiated by penance; the best way to make penance more than a formal ritual is to express repentance in a life of self-denial. (3) By undergoing the suffering of self-denial, one is taking up the cross of Christ. Since Jesus came into this world as a model for all men, all men ought to share in his redemptive suffering. (4) People ought to deny their lower desires to prove their virtue, for the ascetic life is a test of devotion to God, and those who pass the test will win a heavenly reward. (5) The suffering of self-denial is required by our guilt. Since every person has sinned, the retributive theory of punishment requires that every person suffer. By inflicting pain upon oneself, one balances the scales of justice and lifts the guilt from one's soul. (6) Self-denial is valuable because it develops certain character traits such as persistence and self-discipline, which are essential to living well.

The second class of arguments attempts to justify denial indirectly through a criticism of the lower desires. Since these criticisms are aimed only at certain desires, they can support only a partial asceticism. (1) The lower desires cost too much to satisfy. Gratification must be purchased with great effort, and perhaps these desires are insatiable, so that no expenditure of effort will gratify them. (2) The lower desires are misguided, for their objects are really evils or, at best, indifferent things. In either case, no genuine value is realized by fulfilling one's desires. (3) Although the objects of the lower desires are good, they are much less good than higher values like virtue, knowledge, or heaven. Since an individual's time and energy are limited, one ought not to allow these lower desires to distract from the pursuit of what really matters. (4) The lower desires are intrinsically evil. Since they turn people away from God and his commands toward earthly objects, they are infected with the sin of pride. (5) Although not sinful in themselves, the lower desires do motivate one to sinful actions. Thus greed may tempt a person to steal, and lust can lead to adultery. (6) These lower desires interfere with the pursuit of knowledge, which is essential for the good life. They interfere either by causing an agitation that destroys one's power of reasoning or by fixing one's attention on sensory objects that distract from the transcendent reality.

The third class of arguments also attempts to justify asceticism indirectly through a criticism of desire per se. Since these arguments are aimed at all desires, they support a complete asceticism. (1) Schopenhauer argued that desire, by its very nature, can yield nothing but suffering. Desire springs from a lack and consists in a dissatisfaction. When it meets with hindrances, it produces nothing but frustration, because it cannot attain its object; when it does attain its object, it produces nothing but boredom, because desire ceases with fulfillment and leaves one with an undesired object. Since desire necessarily involves dissatisfaction, frustration, and boredom, the only escape is by the annihilation of all desire. (2) The Buddhists and the Jains maintain that one ought to annihilate desire in order to achieve liberation from this world of pain. A person must destroy all desire because desire is the cause of rebirth into this world. For the Buddhist, desire causes rebirth because, being selfish, it causes selfish actions; these, by the moral law of karma, cause rebirth in painful forms. For the Jain, desire magnetizes the soul so that it attracts karmic matter which, by the physical laws of mechanics, weighs down the soul and causes it to be reborn into this lower world of pain.

ARGUMENTS AGAINST ASCETICISM

It is much harder to classify the traditional arguments against asceticism. Many of them attack some presupposition of the doctrine. (1) Many, but not all, forms of asceticism require a dualism of mind and body. The various philosophical difficulties with metaphysical dualism therefore tend to undercut asceticism. (2) Ascetic practices are often recommended as a means of freeing the soul from the body so that it can contemplate the truth. Actually these practices make knowledge in all its forms

impossible because self-denial produces frustration, uneasiness, and pain, which make clear thinking difficult, and self-mutilation destroys the bodily health that is the physiological basis of thought. (3) Asceticism usually assumes that desires are like little animals inside the self that grow when they are fed and wither when they are starved. Freudian psychology, however, reveals that one does not destroy a desire by suppressing it but that the desire continues to exist and to exert itself in new and usually devious ways. Hence ascetic practices may not be an effective means of annihilating or even of controlling desire. (4) Ascetic practices are often thought to be a means to, and even a guarantee of, moral goodness, but in fact they are no protection against vice. The ascetic may become complacent in his confidence in his ascetic practices; he may become proud of his ascetic achievements; and he may even despise others who are less accomplished in asceticism. (5) The religious arguments for asceticism frequently assume that God requires one to renounce available goods and even to inflict harm upon himself, but this is inconsistent with the benevolence of God. (6) There is also a religious argument against the view that bodily desires or worldly objects are essentially evil. Both this world and human nature must be good, because they are creatures of a Creator who is perfectly good.

Another group of arguments is pragmatic in nature. (1) As Bentham pointed out, asceticism cannot be consistently practiced because it runs counter to the basic motives in human nature. Since the function of morality is to guide conduct, asceticism is incapable of becoming a genuine moral standard. (2) To the limited extent that asceticism can be put into practice, its effects are harmful. It obviously increases the amount of suffering in the world. If Freudian psychology is correct, its attempt to suppress natural desires will result in various neuroses. Finally, it stultifies vitality, produces emotional excesses, and fosters the weakling at the expense of the strong man.

Then there are those arguments that attempt to refute asceticism by showing that it has unacceptable implications. (1) Asceticism condemns worldly concerns and natural impulses. This implies that one ought to abandon all social ties and mortify all family affection, which would be immoral. (2) If it is good for one to suffer, it should be better for everyone to suffer. This implies that a person has a duty to inflict pain on others, but not even the hardened ascetic will accept this. (3) If pleasure is really bad, it would seem that pain must be good. This implies the absurd conclusion that the best of all possible worlds would be the one with the least pleasure and the most pain.

Finally, there is Nietzsche's ad hominem argument. Those who are incapable of living well disguise their impotence and fear by inverting morality in order to excuse their own moral sickness and to restrain the strong men who appear dangerous. Although the ascetic priest condemns the will to power, he uses ascetic ideals as a means of maintaining his own power over the sick herd. Thus an analysis of the psychological origin of asceticism reveals that it is far from a worthy ideal.

Asceticism is the doctrine that one ought to deny his desires. In practice, denial means refraining from the fulfillment of desires and sometimes mortifying the desire by inflicting upon oneself the very opposite of what is desired. This involves abstinence from genuine goods, the frustration of unfulfilled desires, and even self-inflicted pain. Unless one is prepared to accept the view that abstinence, frustration, and pain are intrinsically good, the ascetic life can hardly be defended as an end in itself.

If ascetic practices are to be recommended, they must be a necessary evil, a means to something better. One might regard the ascetic life as a means to liberation from this world of suffering. It would be unrealistic to deny that we all suffer from time to time and that there are those for whom life is mostly suffering. It would be equally unrealistic, however, to deny that for most of us the evils we experience are more than balanced by the genuine values we enjoy. Granted the existence of evil, the obvious expedient is to improve our world rather than to make it even worse by adding the sufferings involved in ascetic practices. If escape were desirable, there is no guarantee that the ascetic life would actually lead to freedom.

One might advocate the ascetic life as a means of pleasing God and winning the eternal bliss of heaven. Asceticism seems most plausible within a religious context. But are its theological presuppositions themselves plausible? Is there really an immortal soul to be rewarded or a God to do the rewarding? Even the believer may reject asceticism on religious grounds. A benevolent deity would hardly have created us with natural desires and then commanded us to deny these very desires and to suffer the consequent evils of frustration and pain.

The ascetic life might be urged as a means to that knowledge which in turn brings the good life. Ascetic practices are supposed to help by freeing the soul from the body. Still, no empiricist would admit that the body, which is the source of all experience, is a hindrance to knowledge, and even a rationalist like Plato concedes that experience reminds reason of the truth. Unless reason is thought of as a disembodied spirit—in which case it is hard to see how the body hinders reason in the first place—it would seem that ascetic practices make one less, rather than more, capable of the clear and sustained reasoning that is required for attaining knowledge.

Finally, the ascetic life might be advanced as a means to virtue. It must be admitted that some desires sometimes cause one to act wickedly, but these same desires also cause one to act virtuously. The sexual desire that can lead to adultery more often leads to conjugal fidelity. Hence there is a double error in regarding sexual desire as evil. It does not always, or even usually, express itself in sinful action; and if adultery is a sin, that is because it does violence to the institution of marriage, which is itself an expression of sex. As this example shows, natural desires are in themselves morally neutral, and to deny desire is to forbid the virtuous act as well as the sin. Instead of being a means to virtue, self-denial is actually a vice. Virtue requires at least prudence and benevolence, but the ascetic is imprudent in abstaining from available goods and in even inflicting harm upon himself. By concentrating on the cultivation of his own soul through suffering, the ascetic tends to become callous toward the suffering of others and to ignore his obligation to work for their welfare.

The ascetic life is not good in itself, nor is it a means to liberation, divine reward, knowledge, or virtue. It does not follow that one must accept the advice of Callicles to attempt gratification of every desire without regard for temperance or justice. Self-discipline is a genuine virtue, but it denies desire only when this is necessary to achieve an inclusive and harmonious satisfaction. Asceticism goes beyond this point to advocate an unnecessary and pointless denial. The logical conclusion is that asceticism should be rejected.

See also Augustine, St.; Bentham, Jeremy; Buddhism; Christianity; Cynics; Gregory of Nyssa; Karma; Liberation in Indian Philosophy; Nietzsche, Friedrich; Pain; Plato; Plotinus; Punishment; Pythagoras and Pythagoreanism; Renaissance; Schopenhauer, Arthur; Stoicism.

Bibliography

Ambrose, St. "On Virgins." In *Ambrose*, translated by Boniface Ramsey. Early Church Fathers. New York: Routledge, 1997.

Ambrose, St. "Letter 59 [63]." In *Letters*, translated by Mary M. Beyenka. The Fathers of the Church, vol. 26. New York: Fathers of the Church, Inc., 1954. Both the treatise and the letter provide a justification of asceticism on primarily scriptural grounds.

Athanasius, St. "Life of Antony." In *Life of Antony and the Letter to Marcellinus*, translated by Robert C. Gregg. Classics of Western Spirituality. New York: Paulist Press, 1980. The biography of a model ascetic.

Augustine, St. *The City of God Against the Pagans*, edited and translated by Robert W. Dyson. Cambridge Texts in the History of Political Thought. New York: Cambridge University Press, 1998. An attack on the life of the flesh.

Bentham, Jeremy. "Of Principles Adverse to That of Utility." In *An Introduction to the Principles of Morals and Legislation*, edited by J. H. Burns and H. L. A. Hart. London: Athlone Press, 1970.

Blanshard, Brand. *Reason and Goodness*. New York: Macmillan, 1961. A brief, incisive criticism.

Buddhaghosa. "Chapter 17." In *The Path of Purity: Being a Translation of Buddhaghosa's Visuddhimagga*. 3 vols. (1923, 1929, 1931), translated by Pe Maung Tin. Reprint (3 vols. in 1). London: Pali Texts Society, 1975. A brief statement of the view that liberation requires annihilation of desire.

Davids, T. W. Rhys, and C. A. F. Rhys David. "Udumbarikā-Sīhanāda Suttanta." In *Dialogues of the Buddha, Part 3*. Sacred Books of the Buddhists, vol. 4, edited by T. W. Rhys Davids. 1921. Reprint. London: Pali Text Society, 1977. Criticism of austerities.

Diogenes Laërtius. "Diogenes" and "Zeno." In *Lives of Eminent Philosophers, Vol. 2, Books 6–10*. Loeb Classical Library. 1925. Limited but helpful information.

Gregory of Nyssa, St. "On Virginity." In *Ascetical Works*, translated by Virginia W. Callaban. The Fathers of the Church, vol. 58. Washington, DC: Catholic University of America Press, 1967. A defense of the ascetic life as means to virtue.

Lecky, William E.H. *History of European Morals from Augustus to Charlemagne, Vol. 2*, 107–148, 164–194. London: Longmans, Green, 1869. A critical history of the rise of Christian asceticism.

Nietzsche, Friedrich. *On the Genealogy of Morals: A Polemic*, translated by Douglas Smith. Oxford World's Classics (1996). Reprint. New York: Oxford University Press, 1998. Nietzsche's most sustained criticism of ascetic ideals.

Pantañjali. "Chapter II: Practices." In *The Yoga Sutras of Patañjali*, translated by Alfred Scheepers. Amsterdam: Olive Press, 2005. Especially Sutras 32 and 43, which give injunctions to practice austerities.

Plato. *Phaedo*, translated by David Gallop. Oxford World's Classics (1993). Reprint. New York: Oxford University Press, 1999. An important argument for freeing the soul from the body.

Plotinus. *The Enneads*, translated by Stephen Mackenna, abridged by John Dillon (1917–1930, 1956). Reprint. New York: Penguin Books, 1991. An influential condemnation of matter.

Reid, J. S. "Asceticism [Roman]." In *Encyclopedia of Religion and Ethics*, edited by James Hastings. New York: Charles Scribner's Sons, 1913. An informative survey.

Schopenhauer, Arthur. *The World as Will and Representation*. 2nd ed. 2 vols. Translated by E. F. J. Payne. New York: Dover, 1966. A wordy but interesting argument for the annihilation of the will.

Umasvati. *That Which Is: Tattvārtha Sūtra*, translated by Nathmal Tatia. The Sacred Literature Series, edited by Kerry Brown and Sima Sharma. San Francisco: HarperCollins, 1994. The basic document of the Jains.

OTHER WORKS OF INTEREST

Brown, Peter. *The Body and Society: Men, Women and Sexual Renunciation in Early Christianity*. New York: Columbia University Press, 1988. Magisterial survey of early Christian sexual renunciation.

Brown, Peter. "The Rise and Function of the Holy Man in Late Antiquity." *Journal of Roman Studies* 61 (1971):80–101. Explores the role and social function of the ascetic individual within society.

Clark, Elizabeth. *Reading Renunciation: Asceticism and Scripture in Early Christianity*. Princeton, NJ: Princeton University Press, 1999. Incisive study of early Christian asceticizing hermeneutic of scripture.

Dunn, Marilyn. *The Emergence of Monasticism: From the Desert Fathers to the Early Middle Ages*. Malden, MA: Blackwell, 2000. Useful survey of monastic development and transmission from fourth century Egypt to seventh century Europe.

Elm, Susanna. *Virgins of God: The Making of Asceticism in Late Antiquity*. Oxford: Clarendon Press, 1994. On the role of women in the development of ascetic traditions and institutions.

Flood, Gavin. *The Ascetic Self: Subjectivity, Memory and Tradition*. Cambridge, U.K.: Cambridge University Press, 2004. Comparative study of asceticism and identity formation across time and religious traditions.

Francis, James. *Subversive Virtue: Asceticism and Authority in the Second-Century Pagan World*. University Park: Pennsylvania State University Press, 1995. Analysis of the cultural perceptions of asceticism as "deviant" during the period from 121 CE to 217.

Harpham, Gregory Galt. *The Ascetic Imperative in Culture and Criticism*. Chicago: Chicago University Press, 1987. Important theoretical consideration of the implications of asceticism on language, text, and meaning

North, Helen. *Sophrosyne: Self-Knowledge and Self-Restraint in Greek Literature*. Ithaca: Cornell University Press, 1966. Follows the conceptual development of "self-control" from the Greek archaic period into the Patristic centuries.

Silbur, Ilana F. *Virtuosity, Charisma and the Social Order: a Comparative Sociological Study of Monasticism in Theravada Buddhism and Medieval Christianity*. Cambridge, U.K.: Cambridge University Press, 1995. Both a corrective and extension of Weber's pioneering work on religious [ascetic] virtuosi.

Theodoret of Cyhrrus, St. *History of the Monks of Syria*, translated by Richard M. Price. Cistercian Studies Series, no. 88. Kalamazoo, MI: Cistercian, 1985. Contemporary history of the peculiar ascetic behaviors of the early anchorites of Northern Syria.

Valantasis, Richard. "Constructions of Power in Asceticism." *Journal of the American Academy of Religion* 63 (1995): 775–821. On the reconstitution of subjectivity, social dynamics, and symbolic meaning through performative behaviors.

Wimbush, Vincent L., and Richard Valantasis, eds. *Asceticism* (1998). Reprint. Oxford: Oxford University Press, 2002. Very useful reference tool spanning periods, traditions, and religions.

Carl Wellman (1967)
Bibliography updated by Brent A. Smith (2005)

ASSOCIATIONISM

See *Psychology*

ASTELL, MARY

(1666–1731)

Mary Astell was born November 12, 1666, in Newcastle-upon-Tyne, into a family of coal merchants. This fact itself is interesting, since it means that she was a member of the comfortable middle class. Her circumstances became considerably less comfortable when her father died in 1678, when Astell was twelve, leaving her without a dowry, and hence, without prospects. Around 1684, and following the death of her mother, Astell took what seems to be a rather startling step: She transferred herself from Newcastle to London, away from what family she had left, apparently to live alone in a town without family. Scholars are tantalizingly ignorant of the circumstances that prompted this move and of Astell's prospects in London.

While things do not seem to have gone well for her initially, by 1695 she had established herself in Chelsea, enjoying the patronage of Lady Catherine Jones (1672–1740), and surrounded by a circle of intellectually minded women. By this time, moreover, Astell seems to have put herself in a position to make her living by her pen. Scholars are equally ignorant of the circumstances that gave Astell sufficient intellectual confidence to embark on a course such as this. She had, of course, no formal education. A clergyman uncle, Ralph Astell, is often credited with tutoring her, and, since he was known to have attended Emmanuel College, Cambridge during the heyday of the Cambridge Platonists, he is also often assumed to have shaped Astell's philosophical interests. But since he died soon after the death of Astell's father, when she herself was thirteen, her uncle's influence would have had to have been on a very precocious child. That he was removed from his pulpit for drunkenness raises further doubts about his effectiveness as an educator of a young girl.

Astell recently has attracted attention due to the undoubted feminist nature of at least some of her work, on the basis of which she has been hailed as an early feminist. In *A Serious Proposal to the Ladies* (1694), she argues that women's indubitable possession of rational faculties means that they deserve an education, one that would enable them to develop their rational, moral capabilities and so to live a life devoted to the care of their souls. In *Some Reflections upon Marriage Occasion'd by the Duke and Duchess of Mazarine's Case, Which Is Also Consider'd* (1700), Astell develops this theme, arguing that a well-trained mind will enable women to lead a virtuous life, even in the face of a bad marriage.

Astell's interests, however, extended into a number of other areas beyond the defense of her sex. She is the author of several political pamphlets, in which she took up and discussed issues of contemporary moment from a conservative perspective. Her *magnum opus* is a work of Christian theology, *The Christian Religion, as profess'd by a daughter of the Church of England* (1705). In this lengthy work, Astell, critically reacting to an anonymous work called *The Ladies' Religion*, lays out an extensive examination, first of natural, then of revealed religion, and concludes with an examination of Christian practice, including our duty to god, our neighbor and ourselves. There is some interesting philosophical material contained here, most especially in the discussion of the debate between John Locke and Edward Stillingfleet on the possibility of thinking matter. Astell's works that are most predominantly philosophical in nature, however, include her published correspondence with John Norris, *Letters concerning the Love of God* (1695) and *A Serious Proposal to the Ladies, Part II: Wherein a Method is Offer'd for the Improvement of Their Minds* (1697).

Letters concerning the Love of God contains some of the most interesting and tightly argued of Astell's writing. Her role in this correspondence, however, is that of a questioner and a critic. It is not entirely possible, therefore, to derive from the *Letters* an account of Astell's own position on the matters she discusses. She raises two issues with Norris. The first is how to understand God's causal role with respect to pain. If God, as Norris claims, is the sole object of our love as the cause of pleasure, is He not as well the sole object of our aversion, as the cause of pain? While she is prepared to admit that corporeal pain may have a purpose that is good, she is concerned to secure the possibility of a class of evils, that, as sinful, must be the object of aversion. Astell's second worry concerns the consequences for human social relations if God is the only object of our love. While she initially appears to accept Norris's distinction between loving creatures for our good but not as our good, in a final letter, she raises more substantive questions about Norris's occasionalism. She holds that if bodies are causally inefficacious and do not cause the sensations we have of them, then sensations are irrelevant and God must be said to have created in vain. It is not necessary to the thesis that God is the only object of our love, she points out, to suppose that God acts without instruments, for we never, when receiving a gift, feel gratitude towards the giver's instrument, rather than the giver.

In the second part of *A Serious Proposal*, Astell again adopts a position that reflects some of Norris's approach, while rejecting his occasionalism. The second part of *A Serious Proposal* has a somewhat different project than the first. By the time she wrote it, Astell, who had cherished hopes that she would receive funds to start the educational institution for which she had advocated, had come to realize that these funds would not be forthcoming. Therefore, the second part takes more of a self-help approach to the question of women's education, in which Astell outlines the methods by which a human understanding, as she describes it, may be improved. The argument in favor of improvement is the one she originally put forward, that human action, governed as it is by rationality, requires an informed understanding and a properly directed inclination.

In developing her account, Astell acknowledges a debt to Antoine Arnauld's *Art of Thinking* and to Rene Descartes's *Principles of Philosophy*. She argues that all human endeavor requires the application of right principles, and therefore that anyone, whether doctor or plowman, is concerned with knowledge and with the rules of right reason. These rules are to be induced from right practice, and are not a matter of formal structure. She takes the management of right inclination to be crucial to right conduct and follows Norris is holding that we ought to model our will on God's. She rejects his occasionalism, however, and instead insists that we need to recognize that our minds are united to our bodies. "For if we disregard the Body wholly," she writes, "we pretend to live like Angels whilst we are but Mortals and if we prefer or equal it to the Mind we degenerate into Brutes" (1997, p. 158). Our goal therefore is to harness the passions we feel to the proper goals for human happiness, as discovered by our rational nature, directed to eternal happiness.

See also Arnauld, Antoine; Cambridge Platonists; Descartes, René; Feminist Philosophy; Happiness; Locke, John; Norris, John; Stillingfleet, Edward; Women in the History of Philosophy.

Bibliography

WORKS BY ASTELL

Letters concerning the Love of God, between the Author of the Proposal to the Ladies and Mr. John Norris. Printed for Samuel Manship, 1695. Modern edition: Mary Astell and John Norris, *Letters concerning the Love of God* (Early Modern Englishwoman: A Facsimile Library of Essential Works), edited by Derek Taylor and Melvyn New. Ashgate, 2005.

A Serious Proposal to the Ladies for the Advancement of their True and Greatest Interest. London: printed for R. Wilkin, 1694.

A Serious Proposal to the Ladies, Part II, Wherein a Method Is Offer'd for the Improvement of their Minds. London: printed for Richard Wilkin, 1697. Modern edition: Mary Astell, *A Serious Proposal to the Ladies. Parts I and II*, edited with introduction and notes by Patricia Springborg. London: Pickering and Chatto, 1997.

Some Reflections upon Marriage Occasion'd by the Duke and Duchess of Mazarine's Case; Which is Also Consider'd. London: printed for John Nutt, 1700. Modern edition: (Third edition reproduced) in Astell, *Political Writings*, edited by Patricia Springborg. Cambridge, U.K.: Cambridge University Press, 1996.

The Christian Religion as Profess'd by a Daughter of the Church of England in a Letter to the Right Honorable T.L., C.I. London: printed by S. H. for R. Wilkin, 1705.

WORKS ABOUT ASTELL

Atherton, Margaret, "Cartesian Reason and Gendered Reason." In *A Mind of One's Own: Feminist Essays on Reason and Objectivity*, edited by Louise M. Antony and Charlotte Witt. Boulder, CO: Westview Press, 1993.

Broad, Jacqueline. "Mary Astell." In *Women Philosophers of the Seventeenth Century*, 90–113. New York: Cambridge University Press, 2002.

Perry, Ruth. *The Celebrated Mary Astell: An Early English Feminist*. Chicago: University of Chicago Press, 1986.

Smith, Florence M. *Mary Astell*. New York: Columbia University Press, 1916.

Springborg, Patricia. *Mary Astell: 1666–1731 Theorist of Freedom from Domination*. New York: Cambridge University Press, 2005.

Squadrito, Kathleen, "Mary Astell's Critique of Locke's View of Thinking Matter." *Journal of the History of Philosophy*, 25.3 (Sept 1987): 433–439.

Margaret Atherton (2005)

ATHEISM

The words *atheist* and *godless* are still frequently used as terms of abuse. Nevertheless, there are relatively few people nowadays in whom the thought of atheism and atheists arouses unspeakable horror. It seems to be agreed that an atheist can be a good person whose oaths and promises are no less trustworthy than those of other people, and in most civilized lands atheists have the same or nearly the same rights as anybody else. What is more, it appears to be generally realized that some of the world's foremost philosophers, scientists, and artists have been avowed atheists and that the increase in atheism has gone hand in hand with the spread of education. Even spokesmen of the most conservative religious groups in the mid-twentieth century conceded that atheism may well be a philosophical position that is adopted for the noblest of reasons. Thus, in "The Contemporary Status of Atheism" (1965), Jean-Marie Le Blond appealed to his fellow believers for a "truly human and mutually respectful dialogue" with atheists, insisting that a "life without God need not be … bestial, unintelligent, or immoral" and that atheism can be "serene and deeply human." In the previous year Pope Paul VI, in his encyclical *Ecclesiam Suam,* had observed that some atheists were undoubtedly inspired by "greathearted dreams of justice and progress" as well as by "impatience with the mediocrity and self-seeking of so many contemporary social settings."

HOSTILITY TO ATHEISM

It was otherwise in earlier ages. One could fill many volumes with the abuse and calumny contained in the writings of Christian apologists, learned no less than popular. The tenor of these writings is not simply that atheism is mistaken but also that only a depraved person could adopt so hideous a position and that the spread of atheism would be a horrifying catastrophe for the human race. "No atheist as such," wrote Richard Bentley in *Eight Sermons* (1724), "can be a true friend, an affectionate relation, or a loyal subject." In the preface to his *The True Intellectual System of the World* (1678), Ralph Cudworth made it clear that he was addressing himself not to "downright and professed atheists" but to "weak, staggering and sceptical theists." Downright atheists were beyond the pale, for they had "sunk into so great a degree of sottishness" that they evidently could not be reached. Writing almost exactly two centuries later, the Protestant theologian Robert Flint, who readily admitted that he had met atheists of great courage and integrity, nevertheless expressed his extreme concern over the "strenuous propagation" of atheism, especially in the "periodical press." "The prevalence of atheism in any land," he wrote, "must bring with it national decay and disaster." The triumph of atheism in England would "bring with it hopeless national ruin." If once the workers of the large cities became atheists, "utter anarchy would be inevitable" (*Anti-Theistic Theories,* pp. 36–37). All these quotations are from British Protestants. Very similar and frequently more virulent remarks could be quoted from German,

French, Italian, and American believers of the same periods.

In France until the Revolution and in most other countries until some time later, it was illegal to publish works in defense of atheism, and in fact real or alleged atheists were subject to dire persecution throughout the times of Christian domination. Some of the world's greatest philosophers were among those who advocated and in some instances actively promoted this persecution. The story antedates Christianity, and persecution of atheists was already advocated in Plato's *Laws.* Plato divided atheists into several groups, all of which must be punished; but whereas the members of some groups required no more than "admonition and imprisonment," those belonging to others deserved punishment exceeding "one death … or two." Thomas Aquinas (*Summa Theologiae,* II, 11, 3 and 4) had no doubt that unbelievers should be "shut off from the world by death." Such a course, he argued, is justified since it surely is "a much more serious matter to corrupt faith, through which comes the soul's life," than it is "to forge money, through which temporal life is afforded." If, as is just, forgers of money and other malefactors are straightaway put to death, it is all the more just that "heretics … be not only excommunicated but also put to death."

John Locke, one of the great pioneers of religious toleration, explicitly exempted Roman Catholics and atheists from the application of the principles he advocated. "Promises, covenants, and oaths, which are the bonds of human society," he wrote, "can have no hold upon an atheist." Moreover, since atheism is not a religion but, on the contrary, a position that is out to "undermine and destroy all religion," it cannot come under the privilege of the toleration that is justly claimed by bona fide religions (*A Letter concerning Toleration*). It may be assumed that Locke did not advocate that atheists be shut off from the world, but that he was merely opposed to the free advocacy of atheism in writing and speech.

After Locke's time, the "shutting off" approach became infrequent, but atheists continued to be the victims of persecution and discrimination in various forms. To give some interesting and far from untypical illustrations: Baron d'Holbach's *The System of Nature* was falsely attributed in its first edition to Jean-Baptiste de Mirabaud, a former secretary of the French Academy who had been dead for ten years. Very shortly after its publication in 1770, it was condemned to be burned by the public hangman after a trial in which the public prosecutor expressed his regret that he could not lay his hands on the unknown real author, adding that the corruption of morals evident in almost all sections of society was very probably due to the spread of ideas like those contained in the condemned book. When the poet Percy Bysshe Shelley was an undergraduate at Oxford, he published a short and very temperate pamphlet titled *The Necessity of Atheism*. This at once aroused a violent protest that resulted in the burning of all undistributed copies and in the expulsion of Shelley and his friend Thomas Hogg from the university. Some years later Shelley was judicially deprived of the custody of his children on the ground that he was "likely to inculcate the same [atheistic] principles upon them." As late as 1877 Annie Besant, the noted social reformer, was judged to be unfit to take care of her children on the same ground, although the judge admitted that she had been a careful and affectionate mother. Until the passing of the Evidence Amendment Act of 1869, unbelievers in Great Britain were considered incompetent to give evidence in a court of law. Atheists were thus in effect unable to sue when they were the victims of fraud or slander. Charles Bradlaugh, whose efforts were largely responsible for the Act of 1869, was also the main figure in a prolonged battle to secure the right of avowed atheists to sit in the House of Commons. After Bradlaugh was elected, he was found unfit to take his seat. He won the resulting by-election and was again declared unfit to sit in the House, and this merry-go-round continued for several years, until a Conservative speaker found a legal way of securing Bradlaugh's admission. In the United States there has not been similar legal discrimination against atheists, but there is perhaps to this day more de facto discrimination and prejudice than in any other Western country.

A comprehensive entry on atheism would, among other things, trace the history of the persecution of real and alleged atheists, of the changes in public attitudes, and of the gradual repeal of discriminatory legislation. It would also inquire into the psychological sources of the hatred of atheists that is sometimes found in otherwise apparently kindly and sensible men. Because of space limitations, the present entry will, however, be largely confined to what is undoubtedly the most interesting question for philosophers: Is atheism a logically tenable position? What are the arguments for it, what are the arguments against it, and how strong are these, respectively? It will not be possible to deal exhaustively even with these questions, but an attempt will be made to sketch the position of a philosophically sophisticated atheist and to explain why a view of this kind has appealed to many important thinkers in recent times.

DEFINITION OF *ATHEISM*

No definition of *atheism* could hope to be in accord with all uses of this term. However, it would be most confusing to adopt any of several definitions that can only be regarded as eccentric. These would result in classifying as believers many people who would not regard themselves as such (and who would not commonly be so regarded) and in classifying as atheists many people who have not usually been thought of in this way. Thus, Johann Gottlieb Fichte, in denying the charge of atheism, wrote in "Über den Grund unseres Glaubens an eine Göttliche Weltregierung" that the "true atheist" is the person who, instead of following the voice of conscience, always calculates consequences before acting in a moral situation. Friedrich Jodl, who was himself a positivist and an unbeliever, similarly remarked that "only the man without ideals is truly an atheist," implying, no doubt, that, although he did not believe in God, he was not a "true" atheist (*Vom Lebenswege*, 2 vols., Stuttgart and Berlin, 1916–1917, Vol. II, p. 370.). In the twentieth century Paul Tillich defined *atheism* as the view that "life has no depth, that it is shallow." Anybody who says this "in complete seriousness is an atheist"; otherwise, he is not (*Shaking of the Foundations*, New York, 1948, p. 63). Stephen Toulmin, in an article ("On Remaining an Agnostic," *Listener*, October 17, 1957) in which he championed agnosticism as he understood it, distinguishes his own position from that of both believers and atheists in that, unlike them, he does not "find personal attitudes of any sort in Nature-at-large." The believer, according to Toulmin, regards the Cosmic Powers as friendly to man, while the atheist regards the cosmos as indifferent or as "positively callous."

Whatever the point of the definitions just quoted, their paradoxical consequences make them useless in the present context. For our purposes, definitions of *atheism* and corresponding definitions of *God* will be serviceable only if they preserve, at least roughly, the traditional battle lines. Whatever their differences, Augustine, Thomas Aquinas, Locke, George Berkeley, William Paley, Henry Longueville Mansel, J. S. Mill, William James, Paul Tillich, and John Hick should continue to be classified as believers; T. H. Huxley, Leslie Stephen, and Clarence Darrow as agnostics; and Holbach, Ludwig Büchner, Ludwig Feuerbach, Karl Marx, Arthur Schopenhauer, Friedrich Nietzsche, and Jean-Paul Sartre as atheists. The definition proposed in the present entry will, in taking account of certain complexities of the situation, depart in a significant respect from the one that is most popular, but it will not involve reclassification of any of the great philosophers of the past. According to the most usual definition, an *atheist* is a person who maintains that there is no God, that is, that the sentence "God exists" expresses a false proposition. In contrast, an agnostic maintains that it is not known or cannot be known whether there is a God, that is, whether the sentence "God exists" expresses a true proposition. On our definition, an *atheist* is a person who rejects belief in God, regardless of whether or not the reason for the rejection is the claim that "God exists" expresses a false proposition. People frequently adopt an attitude of rejection toward a position for reasons other than that it is a false proposition. It is common among contemporary philosophers, and indeed it was not uncommon in earlier centuries, to reject positions on the ground that they are meaningless. Sometimes, too, a theory is rejected on such grounds as that it is sterile or redundant or capricious, and there are many other considerations that in certain contexts are generally agreed to constitute good grounds for rejecting an assertion. An atheist in the narrower, more popular sense, is ipso facto an atheist in our broader sense, but the converse does not hold.

THEISTIC POSITIONS. Before exploring the implications of our definition any further, something should be said about the different uses of the word *God* and the correspondingly different positions, all of which have been referred to as "belief in God." For our purposes, it will be sufficient to distinguish three of these. All the believers in question have characterized God as a supreme personal being who is the creator or the ground of the universe and who, whatever his other attributes may be, is at the very least immensely powerful, highly intelligent, and very good, loving, and just. While some of them would maintain that the predicates just mentioned—"powerful," "good," and the rest—are used in a literal sense when applied to God, other believers insist that when applied to God, these, and indeed all or almost all, predicates must be employed in "metaphorical," "symbolic," or "analogical" senses. Let us, without implying anything derogatory, refer to the belief that predicates can be applied literally to God as the "anthropomorphic" conception of God and to the belief that predicates can only be applied analogically to God as the "metaphysical" conception of God.

Among professional philosophers, belief in the metaphysical God has been much more common than belief in the anthropomorphic God. This metaphysical position is at least as old as Thomas (and, it may be plausibly argued, as old as Plato). In the early eighteenth century it was championed by Peter Browne, bishop of Cork, who was trying to answer difficulties raised by the infidel John

Toland. In the nineteenth century this position was defended by Mansel in his Bampton Lectures, and in the twentieth century it was a key feature of Tillich's philosophy. God, on Tillich's view, "infinitely transcends every finite being"; between the finite and the infinite there is "an absolute break, an 'infinite jump'"; there is here "no proportion and gradation." When we say, for example, "God is Love," or "God is Life," the words *love* and *life* are used symbolically, not literally. They were originally introduced in connection with "segments of finite experience," and when applied to God, they cannot have the same meaning that they have in ordinary human situations.

The anthropomorphic position is by no means confined to unsophisticated believers. It has commanded the support of several eminent philosophers, especially believers who were also empiricists or otherwise opposed to rationalism. Thus, Berkeley emphatically defended the anthropomorphic position against Bishop Browne. In *Alciphron* Berkeley attacked Browne's procedure on the ground that unless "wise" and "good" are used in the same sense for God and man, "it is evident that every syllogism brought to prove those attributes, or (which is the same thing) to prove the being of a God, will be found to consist of four terms, and consequently can conclude nothing." In the nineteenth century J. S. Mill championed anthropomorphic belief as opposed to the metaphysical theology of Hamilton and Mansel; more recently, Miguel de Unamuno y Jugo, who is perhaps best classified as a fideist, indicted the metaphysical God as a "Nothing-God" and a "dead thing." In *The Tragic Sense of Life in Men and in Peoples* he wrote that such a fleshless abstraction cannot be the answer to the cravings of the human heart. Only the anthropomorphic God can ever be "the loving God," the God to whom we come "by the way of love and of suffering."

Among those who believe in an anthropomorphic God, there are two positions to be distinguished. First, there is the more traditional position that allows no limitations upon the extent to which God possesses the various admirable characteristics—on this view, God is all-powerful, all-loving, infinitely good, perfectly just, and so on. Second, there is the somewhat heretical position of those who, while maintaining that God possesses these characteristics to a high degree, allow that he is limited at least in his power or in his goodness. Mill, who believed in such a finite anthropomorphic deity, claimed that regardless of the official pronouncements of the various religions, in actual practice most Western believers adhered to a theory like his own.

Creation. A few words must be said about the possible meanings of *creation* when God is referred to as the creator (or ground) of the universe. Thomas Aquinas, in his *On the Eternity of the World* and elsewhere, makes a distinction between the temporal sense in which God is supposed to have made the universe at a certain moment in time, prior to which it did not exist, and the more sophisticated sense in which it is asserted that the universe is absolutely dependent on God so that it would cease to exist if God were not sustaining it. Thomas himself believed in God's creation of the universe in both senses, but it was only in the second sense that he regarded the theory of divine creation as susceptible of logical proof. Both these senses must be distinguished from the creative activity ascribed to the demiurge of Plato's *Timaeus* or to Mill's God. Here the deity is not, strictly, a creator but merely an arranger of preexisting material. For the purposes of this entry, a person will count as a believer in the creation of the universe by God if he or she makes any of three claims just distinguished.

THE BROADER SENSE OF ATHEISM. Let us now return to our definition of *atheism.* A person is an atheist in our sense who adopts an attitude of rejection toward all three theistic positions previously stated—belief in a metaphysical God, in an infinite anthropomorphic God, and in a finite anthropomorphic God. He or she will count as a believer in God if maintaining that "God exists" expresses a true proposition, where "God" is employed in one of the three ways described. A person will be an agnostic who does not accept any of these three claims but at the same time suspends judgment concerning at least one of them. It will be observed that on our way of drawing the lines, agnosticism and atheism remain distinct positions, since suspension of judgment and rejection are different attitudes.

The broader definition here adopted enables us to classify together philosophers whose attitudes toward belief in God are exceedingly similar, although their detailed reasons may not always coincide. Rudolf Carnap, for example, regards metaphysical theology as meaningless, while treating belief in an infinite as well as a finite anthropomorphic God as "mythology," implying that both are false or probably false. In our sense, he can be classified as an atheist without further ado, and it is doubtful that believers would consider him less hostile than atheists in the narrower sense. It is also worth observing that our broader definition receives a good deal of backing from the actual writings of philosophers and others who regarded themselves as atheists. Many of them were by no means unaware of the fact that the word

God has a number of uses and that what may be a plausible justification for rejecting one kind of belief in God may be quite inappropriate in the case of another. Charles Bradlaugh, for example, made it very clear that in calling himself an atheist he did not simply maintain that there is no God. In his "Plea for Atheism," he wrote:

> The atheist does not say "there is no God," but he says "I know not what you mean by God; I am without idea of God; the word 'God' is to me a sound conveying no clear or distinct affirmation.… The Bible God I deny; the Christian God I disbelieve in; but I am not rash enough to say there is no God as long as you tell me you are unprepared to define God to me."

The writings of Jean Meslier, Holbach, and other eighteenth-century and nineteenth-century atheists, while certainly containing remarks to the effect that the sentence "God exists" expresses a false proposition, are also full of claims that once we critically examine the talk about a "pure spirit" that supposedly exists timelessly and without a body, we find that words have been used without any meaning. In any event, by using the word *atheism* in the broader sense, it will be possible to discuss certain antitheological considerations of great interest that would otherwise have to be excluded.

TRADITIONAL ATHEISTIC ARGUMENTS

In this section we shall discuss two of the arguments popular among atheistic writers of the eighteenth and nineteenth centuries. In later sections we shall present considerations commonly urged by Anglo-Saxon writers in more recent years. However, in a rudimentary form these more recent reflections are already present in the writings of earlier atheists, just as the older arguments continue to be pressed in current literature.

THE ETERNITY OF MATTER. The first of the two older atheistic arguments is based on the doctrine of the eternity of matter, or, to bring it more in accord with recent physical theory, the eternity of mass-energy. (As far as the basic issues here are concerned, it is not of any moment whether what is said to be eternal is matter or energy or mass-energy, and for the sake of convenience we shall speak only of the eternity of "matter.") There are two steps in this argument. It is claimed, first, either as something self-evident or as a proposition proved by science, that matter is eternal; second, it is asserted that this claim rules out a God conceived as the creator of the material universe. If the physical universe had been created by

God, it would follow that there was a time when the quantity of matter was less than it is now, when it was in fact zero. But physics proves or presupposes that the quantity of matter has always been the same.

Since most ordinary people include "creator of the material universe" in their concept of God, and since they mean by *creation* a temporal act of making something out of nothing, the appeal to the eternity of matter is effective as a popular argument for atheism. A little reflection shows, however, that by itself the argument is of very limited significance. To begin with, regardless of any scientific evidence, the doctrine of the eternity of matter, in all its forms, would be challenged by anybody who accepts any of the causal varieties of the Cosmological Argument. Such a person would presumably argue that while conservation principles may accurately describe a certain feature of the material universe *ever since it began existing*, the material universe itself requires a nonmaterial cause. Hence, any atheistic conclusion in the present context would have to be accompanied by a refutation of the causal forms of the Cosmological Argument. But granting for the moment that the eternity of matter is fully established, this is not incompatible with the theory of divine creation in the sense in which it has been put forward by its philosophically more sophisticated adherents. The eternity of matter is no doubt incompatible with the existence of a God who made the material universe out of nothing and with the kind of activity in which the demiurge is supposed to engage (since bringing order into previously chaotic materials requires the addition of energy); but it is not incompatible with creation in the second of the two senses distinguished by Thomas, in which *creation* means "absolute dependence" and does not refer to any datable act. There may indeed be some difficulty in the notion of a nonphysical entity nonphysically sustaining the universe, and it is tempting to think that this is an intelligible doctrine simply because the words *sustain* and *depend* immediately call up certain pictures in one's mind; but these difficulties raise rather different questions. Finally, in this connection it should be pointed out that the eternity of matter in all its forms is compatible with a belief in God or gods, like those of the Epicureans and Thomas Hobbes (if Hobbes was serious), who are physical beings, or in gods of any kind, as long as it is not claimed that these have created the universe or any aspect of it.

A few words should perhaps be added here about the claim of some writers that the doctrine of the eternity of matter in all its forms has now been refuted by physics and that physics even somehow proves the existence of God. In this connection it should be mentioned, first, that the great majority of scientifically informed philosophers agree that the findings of recent physics do not affect the issues dividing believers and unbelievers, and, second, that even if the doctrine of the eternity of matter were now untenable in all its forms, this would undermine one of the arguments for atheism, but not atheism itself. If there was a time when matter did not exist (assuming this to be a meaningful assertion), it does not automatically follow that matter was created by God. To show that matter was created by God, an appeal to the Cosmological Argument (and not to physics) would be as necessary as ever. As for the theory of continuous creation, advocated by some cosmologists, it does indeed imply that the principle of the conservation of mass-energy is false. However, the basic assumption behind the theory of continuous creation is the so-called perfect cosmological principle, which is in effect an endorsement of the eternity of matter. This principle asserts that the large-scale aspects of the universe are the same at all times and in all places; and this, more specifically, means that the stars and galaxies have always been about as evenly distributed as they are at the present time.

EVIL AND OTHER IMPERFECTIONS. Among the traditional atheistic arguments a second type has generally been regarded as more formidable and still enjoys an undiminished popularity. This type of argument points to some imperfection or defect in the universe and argues that the defect is incompatible with the existence of God insofar as God is defined as a perfect being.

Among the imperfections or alleged imperfections, emphasis has frequently been placed on the enormous waste in nature, especially in matters of reproduction, and on the trial-and-error "method" of evolution. Referring to the process of evolution, G. H. Lewes remarked that "nothing could be more unworthy of a supreme intelligence than this inability to construct an organism at once, without making several tentative efforts, undoing today what was so carefully done yesterday, and repeating for centuries the same tentatives and the same corrections in the same succession." And if the end of this entire process is man, it has been questioned whether it was worth all the pain and tribulations that preceded it. "If I were granted omnipotence, and millions of years to experiment in," writes Bertrand Russell, "I should not think Man much to boast of as the final result of my efforts" (*Religion and Science,* p. 222). Again, it has been suggested by several writers, and not at all facetiously, that if there were a God, then surely he would have provided human beings with clearer evidence of his own existence.

If an omniscient and omnipotent God did not take care that his intentions should be understood by his creatures, asked Nietzsche, "could he be a God of goodness?" Would he not, rather, be a cruel god if, "being himself in possession of the truth, he could calmly contemplate mankind, in a state of miserable torment, worrying its mind as to what was truth?" (*Morgenröte*, Aphorism 91). If a God exists, then, in the words of Charles Bradlaugh, "he could have so convinced all men of the fact of his existence that doubt, disagreement, or disbelief would be impossible."

The most widely discussed of all these arguments from the imperfections of the universe is the argument from evil, and it may be best to restrict our discussion to it. The following is a statement by Brand Blanshard:

> We are told that with God all things are possible. If so, it was possible for him to create a world in which the vast mass of suffering that is morally pointless—the pain and misery of animals, the cancer and blindness of little children, the humiliations of senility and insanity—were avoided. These are … apparently … inflictions of the Creator himself. If you admit that, you deny his goodness; if you say he could not have done otherwise, you deny that with him all things are possible. ("Irrationalism in Theology," in *Faith and the Philosophers*, edited by John Hick, London, 1964, p. 172)

It should be emphasized that the argument from evil, as here stated, is directed against the conclusion of the believer in an infinite anthropomorphic God and is not merely a criticism of his evidence. On occasions, for example in David Hume's *Dialogues concerning Natural Religion,* the argument has been used for the milder purpose of showing that the Design Argument cannot succeed in establishing a maker of the universe who is both omnipotent and perfectly good. It argues from the nature of the world to the nature of its cause, and since the world is a mixture of good and evil, it cannot be established in this way that its creator is perfectly good. The form in which we are concerned with the argument from evil— what we may call its stronger sense—maintains that the evil in the world shows the theological claim to be false. The argument may be construed as comparing the theological assertion to a falsified scientific hypothesis: If the theory that the universe is the work of an all-powerful and all-good being were true, then the universe would not exhibit certain features; experience shows that it does exhibit these features, and hence the theory is false.

The argument from evil has no logical force against belief in a finite God. The evil in the world is perfectly compatible with the existence of a God who is lacking either omnipotence or perfect goodness, or both. In fact, E. S. Brightman and the American personalists and other well-known champions of belief in a finite anthropomorphic God adopted their position precisely in order to reconcile belief in God with the existence of evil. There is also no obvious incompatibility between the existence of the metaphysical God and the evil in the world, since it is not claimed for the metaphysical God either that he is all-powerful or that he is perfectly good in the ordinary senses of these words. Mansel, for example, in *Limits of Religious Thought* openly acknowledged that in the light of the injustice and suffering we find in the world, the moral character of God cannot be represented "after the model of the highest human morality which we are capable of conceiving." His position, Mansel insisted, unlike the position of anthropomorphic believers, to whom Mansel referred as "vulgar Rationalists" in this context, was immune from difficulties like the problem of evil Substantially similar remarks are to be found in the writings of many other members of this tradition.

The most basic objections to metaphysical theology will be discussed in the next section, but perhaps it should be mentioned in passing that according to some critics, philosophers like Mansel have a tendency to revert to the view that God is good in the very same sense in which human beings are sometimes good and, more generally, to anthropomorphic theology. This is not at all surprising since, like other believers, they derive or wish to derive comfort and reassurance from their theology. Such comfort may be derivable from the view that the ultimate reality is good and just in the sense or one of the senses in which we use these terms when we praise good and just human beings. No comfort at all, on the other hand, seems derivable from the statement that God is good and just but that "the true nature and manner of all the divine operation of goodness," in the words of Bishop Browne, "is utterly incomprehensible" or that they differ from human justice and goodness, as Mansel put it, "in kind," not only in degree.

There is a long history of attempts by believers to show that the argument from evil does not really refute the assertion that an infinite anthropomorphic God exists. It has been maintained by some that evil is unreal; by others that, although real, it is of a "privative" rather than a "positive" character; that it is real and positive but that it is the consequence of man's abuse of his gift of free will and that a universe without evil and without free will would be worse than one with both; that the argument is based on a narrow hedonistic conception of good and evil and that, in any event, the theological position cannot be adequately judged unless it is viewed in conjunction with belief in an afterlife in which the wrongs of the present life will somehow be righted; and many more. Critics have come up with various answers to these rejoinders, and the discussion has been going on with unabated vigor in recent years. There would be little point in reviewing this debate here, but something should perhaps be said about two retorts by believers that have not been adequately discussed by the proponents of the argument from evil.

A Christian rejoinder. One rejoinder to the argument from evil seems to be of considerable value in showing that this argument does not by itself justify rejection of belief in an infinite anthropomorphic God. It has been argued (for example, by Arnold Lunn in his exchange of letters with C. E. M. Joad published in *Is Christianity True?*, London and Philadelphia, 1933) that although the existence of evil cannot be reconciled with the existence of an infinite anthropomorphic God, this is not too serious a problem in view of the powerful affirmative evidence for this position. In other areas too, Lunn reminds us, we do not abandon a well-supported theory just because we meet with some counterevidence. He is not in the least disturbed by "the fact that divine science, like natural science, brings us face to face with apparently insoluble contradictions." This hardly disposes of the argument from evil, as Lunn seems to think. The comparison between the difficulty that a believer faces from the facts of evil and the difficulties besetting a scientific theory for which there is otherwise strong evidence is somewhat tenuous. There are indeed cases answering to this description in science, but they are invariably resolved by further inquiry. Either we come to see that the difficulty or exception was merely apparent or else the original theory is modified or abandoned. In the theological case, several millennia of experience and debate do not seem to have brought us any nearer a resolution. But, assuming that Lunn's comparison fails as a defense of belief in an infinite anthropomorphic God, there can be no question that he would have made out a strong case in favor of agnosticism as opposed to atheism if there were in fact good evidence for the existence of the God in question. If, for example, the Cosmological Argument were, as far as we can judge, free from fallacious transitions, we would have a situation similar to the kind we frequently face in which there is significant and roughly equally impressive evidence both ways (for example, some apparently trustworthy witnesses implicating the defendant in a court case, while other equally trustworthy witnesses exonerate) and in which suspense of judgment is the

most rational attitude. The moral for our discussion is that an atheist cannot afford to neglect the arguments for the existence of God. Unless they can be demolished, the argument from evil will not by itself establish the atheist's case, even if none of the answers mentioned earlier are in fact successful.

A fideistic rejoinder. Another rejoinder to the argument from evil has become extremely popular in recent years among existentialist believers and all who maintain that arguments for or against the existence of God are, as it is put, radically beside the point. We are told that one simply either has faith or one has not, one is either "open" to the presence of God or one is not. If one has faith, proofs and reasoning are not needed; if one lacks faith, they are of no avail. A person who has faith is not shaken by absence of evidence or by counterevidence; a person who has no faith will never become a true believer even if intellectually convinced by the arguments of rationalistic theology.

Systematic defenses by those who adopt such a position are exceedingly rare, but in 1964 an article appeared by an existentialist philosopher who seems familiar with contemporary analytic philosophy and whose answer to the argument from evil is representative of this entire approach. In his "On the Eclipse of God" (*Commentary,* June 1964, pp. 55–60), Emil Fackenheim insists that the essential mark of the faith of a person who is "primordially open to God" is certainty, or, specifically, *"the believer's certainty of standing in relation to an unprovable and irrefutable God"* (Fackenheim's italics). It is this "irrefutability" of his faith that, Fackenheim believes, enables him to circumvent the problem of evil. No conceivable experience, he insists, can possibly upset the true biblical faith. If there is good fortune, it "reveals the hand of God." If the fortune is bad and if this cannot be explained as just punishment, the conclusion is that "God's ways are unintelligible, not that there *are* no ways of God." To put it "radically": *"Religious faith can be, and is, empirically verifiable; but nothing empirical can possibly refute it"* (Fackenheim's italics). Fackenheim cites the examples of Jeremiah, Job, and the Psalmist, all of whom encountered tragedy and disaster without losing their faith in the existence of God. Biblical faith, he observes in this connection, "is never destroyed by tragedy but only tested by it," and in the course of such a test, it "conquers" tragedy. To underline the invulnerability of this position, Fackenheim adds that no amount of scientific evidence can "affect" biblical belief any more than "historical tragedy" or "an empty heart" can.

What is to be said in reply to all this, especially to the remarkable claim, made in all seriousness, that although faith is empirically verifiable, nothing can possibly refute it? The answer is surely that there is a confusion here between logical and psychological issues. Fackenheim may well have given an accurate account of faith as a psychological phenomenon, but this is totally irrelevant to the question at issue among believers, agnostics, and atheists—namely, which position is favored by the evidence or lack of evidence. All the words—*destroy, test, conquer, affect,* and *refute*—are used ambiguously in this as in countless similar discussions. They refer on the one hand to certain psychological effects (or their absence) and on the other to the relation between facts and a proposition for or against which these facts are (or fail to be) evidence. If the question at issue were whether tragedy and injustice can produce loss of belief in a person who has the "biblical faith," the answer may well be in the negative, and Fackenheim's examples support such an answer. They have not the slightest bearing, however, on the question of whether the tragedies and the injustices in the world disprove or make improbable or are any kind of evidence against the statement that the world is the work of an all-powerful and all-good God—the statement in which the believers have faith. The first question may be of great psychological and human interest, and if Fackenheim is right, a person interested in dissuading "biblical" believers would be foolish even to try. It is the second question alone, however, that is of interest to philosophers, and it alone is at issue between believers and unbelievers. By telling his biblical stories, Fackenheim has done nothing whatsoever to circumvent the problem of evil or to show that what the believer has faith in is immune to criticism.

Before leaving this topic, a few words are in order about a certain concession, occasionally made by unbelievers, which does not appear to be warranted. Some atheists are willing to concede that whereas they can come to grips with rationalistic believers, they are powerless when faced with a fideist like Fackenheim. Thus, Ernest Nagel, in his "Defense of Atheism," remarks that such a position is "impregnable to rational argument." Now, if a proposition, *p*, is endorsed on the basis of faith and not on the basis of logical arguments, then indeed a critic cannot undermine any arguments supporting *p*, but may well be in a position to test (and falsify) *p* itself. If a fideist were to maintain, admitting from the outset that there is no evidence for the proposition and that it is based on faith alone, that the *New York Times* sells for 50 cents on weekdays, there is of course no evidence for the proposition that can be attacked, but this would not prevent us from disproving the assertion. Any plea by the fideist there is no evidence or that no evidence can ever move him or her will not have the slightest bearing on the soundness of the refutation. A proponent of the argument from evil would similarly maintain that the assertion of the existence of an infinite anthropomorphic deity has certain publicly testable consequences—that there is no evil in the world or at least not certain kinds of evil—and that experience shows these to be false. It would be to the point to argue either that the assertion of the existence of such a deity does not really have the consequences in question or that experience does not really falsify them; but it is totally beside the point to maintain either that faith in an infinite anthropomorphic God is not, in the case of a particular believer, based on any evidence or that the believer will not abandon his or her position, come what may.

REJECTION OF METAPHYSICAL THEOLOGY

In presenting the case against metaphysical theology, we shall concentrate on the views of Tillich and his disciple, Bishop J. A. T. Robinson, whose *Honest to God* created such a stir among theologians when it was published in 1963. No defender of this position had as much influence in the mid-twentieth century as Tillich. Moreover, his statement of the position is radical and uncompromising and is thus easier to discuss than more qualified versions. At the same time it may well be the case that some of these more qualified versions are not open to quite the same objections. In particular, it might be claimed that the Thomistic doctrine of analogy enables its proponents to escape both the difficulties of straightforward anthropomorphic theology and those besetting Tillich's position.

Tillich and Robinson entirely agree with atheists that belief in any anthropomorphic deity should be rejected. Traditional theism, Tillich writes, "has made God a heavenly, completely perfect person who resides above the world and mankind" (*Systematic Theology,* Vol. I, p. 271). Against such a highest person, he goes on, "the protest of atheism is correct." Elsewhere Tillich repeatedly pours scorn on what he terms "monarchic monotheism" and the theology of the "cosmic policeman." Following Tillich, Bishop Robinson tells us that we must now give up belief in God as somebody "out there," just as Copernican astronomy made people abandon "the old man in the sky." Most believers, he writes, are inclined to think of God as a kind of "visitor from outer space" (*Honest to God,* p. 50). Unlike the "old man in the sky" or the "visitor from outer space," the God of Tillich and Robinson is not another individual entity beside the familiar entities of experience, not even the "most powerful" or the "most perfect" one. He is "being-itself." As such, God is not contingent but necessary, and arguments for his existence are not required. The idea of God, writes Tillich, is not the idea of "something or someone who might or might not exist" (*Systematic Theology*, Vol. I, p. 205). "In making God an object besides other objects, the existence and nature of which are matters of argument, theology supports the escape to atheism.… The first step to atheism is always a theology which drags God down to the level of doubtful things" (*Shaking of the Foundations*, p. 52).

It should be mentioned in passing that to some readers of Tillich and Robinson there appears to be a radical ambiguity in their entire position, specifically in the reasons they give for rejecting the anthropomorphic theory of the God "out there." At times we are told that the old-fashioned believers are mistaken because God is really inside us—insofar as our lives have "depth," insofar as we live "agapeistically." This is what we may call the Feuerbachian tendency in Tillich and his followers. At other times anthropomorphic theology is denounced because God so radically transcends anything we ever experience that the picture of a glorified man cannot possibly do justice to the reality. In the former context, God must not be said to be "out there" because he is really "in here deep down," in the latter context, because he is too removed to be even out there. In the former context, theological sentences become a species of very special psychological statements, and in the latter they are clearly items of transcendent metaphysics. There seems to be a constant oscillation between these two positions, so that at times traditional theology is denounced for not being sufficiently this-worldly, while at other times it is condemned for being too close to the world. The former position is of no interest to us, since it may rightly be dismissed as not being in any accepted sense a theological position at all—it is clearly quite compatible with the most thoroughgoing positivism and atheism. Our discussion will therefore be confined to the latter position exclusively.

As already explained in a previous section, Tillich (that is, Tillich the transcendent metaphysician) regards God as so vastly transcending any finite, familiar entity that predicates taken from ordinary experience cannot be employed in their literal senses when applied to God but must be used symbolically or metaphorically. There is just one statement that we can make about God in which all words are used "directly and properly," namely, that "God as being-itself is the ground of the ontological

structure of being without being subject to the structure himself." Tillich expands this statement as follows: "God *is* that structure; that is, he has the power of determining the structure of everything that has being" (*Systematic Theology*, Vol. I, p. 239). If anything is said beyond this "bare assertion," Tillich insists it cannot be regarded any longer as a "direct and proper statement." Although all other predicates must be used symbolically when applied to God, certain symbols are justified or appropriate, while others are unjustified or inappropriate, since the former "point" to aspects of the ultimate reality, while the latter do not. Thus, we are justified in speaking of God, symbolically, as "King," "father," and "healing." These are "pointers to the "divine life."

UNINTELLIGIBILITY OF METAPHYSICAL THEOLOGY.

A philosophically sophisticated atheist would object to Tillich's theology not on the ground that it is false or not proven but on the very different ground that it is unintelligible—that it consists of sentences that may be rich in pictorial associations and in expressive meaning but that fail to make any genuine assertions. Tillich's position may indeed be immune to the difficulties of an anthropomorphic theology, but only at the expense of not saying anything about the world. This criticism would almost certainly be offered by anybody who accepts an empiricist criterion of meaning, but it is worth pointing out that it is an objection that has been endorsed, in substance if not in precisely these words, by numerous believers in an anthropomorphic God. Voltaire on occasion objected on such grounds to the theologians who claimed that we must not use words in their familiar senses when applying them to God, and it has already been mentioned that Unamuno dismissed the metaphysical God as a "Nothing" and a "dead thing." Similarly, William James objected to the emptiness of the "universalistic" theology of the Hegelians of his day, preferring what he called a particularistic belief.

Untranslatable metaphors. This criticism might be backed up in the following way: While recognizing that he constantly uses words symbolically or metaphorically, Tillich does not appreciate the difference between translatable and untranslatable metaphors, and he does not see that his own metaphors are untranslatable. Very frequently indeed, especially in ordinary life, when words are used metaphorically, the context or certain special conventions make it clear what is asserted. Thus, the editor of an encyclopedia, when asked why he or she looks so troubled, may reply, "Too many cares are weighing down on me—the pressure is too great." Obviously the words *weighing down* and *pressure* are here metaphorical, yet we all understand what is being said. Why? Because the metaphorical expressions are translatable—because we can eliminate them, because we can specify in non-metaphorical terms what the sentence is used to assert. If the metaphors could not be eliminated, we would not have succeeded in making any assertion.

A critic would proceed to argue that Tillich's metaphors are of the untranslatable variety and that when he has offered what seem to him translations, he has really only substituted one metaphor for another. Tillich believed that in his basic statement, quoted earlier, all words are used literally, or "properly." But this is open to question. The word *ground*, for example, is surely not used in any of its literal senses when being-itself is said to be the ground of the ontological structure of being. It can hardly be used in the physical sense in which the floor or the grass underneath our feet could be regarded as a "ground," or in the logical sense in which the premises of an argument may be the ground for endorsing the conclusion. Similar remarks apply to the use of *structure*, *power*, and *determine*. Hence, when we are told that "God is personal" (which is acknowledged to be metaphorical) means "God is the ground of everything personal," or that "God lives" (which is also acknowledged to be metaphorical) means "God is the ground of life," one set of metaphors is exchanged for another, and literal significance is not achieved. Tillich's God, it should be remembered, is so transcendent that not even mystical experience acquaints us with him. "The idea of God," he writes, "transcends both mysticism and the person-to-person encounter" (*The Courage To Be*, p. 178). Consequently, he does not have at his disposal any statements in which God is literally characterized and that could serve as the translations of the metaphorical utterances. The absence of such statements literally characterizing being-itself equally prevent Tillich from justifying the employment of his set of "symbols" as appropriate and the rejection of other symbols as inappropriate.

Unfalsifiability of metaphysical theology. We noted earlier that a metaphysical theology like Tillich's avoids the troublesome problem of evil because it does not maintain that God is perfectly good or, indeed, omnipotent in any of the ordinary or literal senses of these words. This very immunity would, however, be invoked by some critics as a decisive objection and they would, by a somewhat different route, reach the same conclusion—namely, that Tillich's theological sentences do not amount to genuine assertions. The point in question may perhaps be most forcefully presented by contrasting Tillich's position with that of anthropomorphic believers such as John

Hick or A. C. Ewing. Hick and Ewing are (theoretically) very much concerned with the problem of evil. They argue that given the nature of man and a world with dependable sequences (or causal laws), evil of certain kinds is unavoidable, and furthermore that (though they do not, of course, claim to be able to prove this) in the next life there will be appropriate rewards and compensations. They admit or imply that their belief would be logically weakened, perhaps fatally so, it if could be shown that there is no afterlife or that in the afterlife injustice and misery, far from vanishing, will be even more oppressive than in the present life, or that the evils which, given the nature of man and a world of dependable sequences, they thought to be unavoidable, could in fact have been prevented by an omnipotent Creator. Tillich, however, need not be (theoretically) concerned about any such contingencies. Even if things in this life became vastly more horrible than they already are, or even if we had conclusive evidence that in the afterlife things are so bad that by comparison, Auschwitz and Belsen were kingdoms of joy and justice, Tillich's theology would be totally unaffected. Being-itself, as Tillich put it, would still be "actual": It is not "something or someone who might or might not exist." God, as Bishop Robinson puts it, is not a "problematic" entity, which might conceivably not have been there." This is true of the anthropomorphic deity, but not of what Tillich in one place terms "the God above God" (*Listener*, August 1961, pp. 169ff.).

In other words, unlike the position of Hick and Ewing, Tillich's theology is compatible with anything whatsoever in this life as well as in the next one; and it is the opinion of many contemporary philosophers, believers as well as unbelievers, that if a putative statement is compatible with anything whatsoever, if it excludes no conceivable state of affairs, then it is not a genuine assertion (it should be noted that "state of affairs" is not used in a narrow way so that much that positivists exclude, for example, happiness or suffering in the next world, could count as conceivable states of affairs). This criterion may, of course, be questioned, but if it is accepted, then Tillich's theology, unlike that of anthropomorphic believers, would have to be condemned as devoid of any assertive force.

We have not here considered other variants of metaphysical theology, but those opposed to Tillich's system for the reasons here outlined would maintain that other forms of this general outlook are bound to be open to some of the same objections: In every case, words would have to be used in a metaphorical way in crucial places, and these metaphors would turn out to be untranslatable;

in every case it would be impossible to justify the employment of one set of metaphors or symbols in preference to another, and in every case the author of the system would be unable to specify what conceivable state of affairs is excluded by his sentences or, if he did do so, the exclusion could be shown to be arbitrary in a way that would not be true of the statements of anthropomorphic believers.

ATHEISM OR AGNOSTICISM?

It is time to discuss a very common challenge to atheists. The challenge is usually issued by agnostics, but it would in general also be endorsed by fideistic believers. "It is admittedly impossible," the critic would reason, "to prove the existence of God, but it is equally impossible to disprove his existence; hence, we must either suspend judgment or, if we embrace some position, we must do so on the basis of faith alone." To avoid misleading associations of the words *prove* and *disprove,* the same point may be expressed by saying that we have no evidence either for or against God's existence. Sometimes the reminder is added that the mere failure of the arguments for the existence of God does not show that there is no God. Anybody who supposed this would plainly be guilty of the fallacy of *argumentum ad ignorantiam.*

If certain of the considerations advanced by atheists that were discussed in previous sections are sound, this agnostic charge would be quite beside the point as far as belief in an infinite anthropomorphic or a metaphysical God is concerned. For in that event, the first theory can be shown to be false (with certain qualifications explained earlier), and the second can be rejected on the ground that it is unintelligible. In the case of an infinite anthropomorphic God, there is evidence against the position; in the case of a metaphysical God, we do not have a coherent position. However, when we turn to the question of a finite anthropomorphic God, the challenge does at first sight seem very plausible. As already pointed out, the argument from evil does not affect this position, and we may, at least provisionally, grant that belief in a finite anthropomorphic God is intelligible because the predicates used in expressing it are applied to this deity in their familiar senses. We shall see, before long, that there are difficulties in regard to the intelligibility of even this position, but waiving all considerations of this kind for the moment, let us inquire how an atheist could reply to this challenge. It is admitted by the challenger that there is no evidence for the existence of such a deity; where, he asks, is the evidence against its existence? If there is none, why should one be an atheist rather than an agnostic? Why is atheism justified if we cannot be sure that there is no God in the sense under discussion?

GROUNDS FOR THE REJECTION OF THEORIES. In justifying his position, an atheist should perhaps begin by calling attention to the fact that the agnostics who suspend judgment concerning God are not also agnostics in relation to the gods of the Greeks or in relation to the devil and witches. Like the majority of other educated people, most agnostics reject and do not suspend judgment concerning the Olympian gods or the devil or witches. Assuming that rejection is the appropriate attitude in these cases, what justifies this rejection?

It will be instructive to look at a concrete example of such a belief that is rejected by agnostics and atheists alike and, incidentally, by most believers in God. Billy Graham is one of the few Protestant ministers who still believe in the devil. The devil is introduced by Dr. Graham as the only plausible explanatory principle of a great many phenomena. He is brought in to explain the constant defeat of the efforts of constructive and well-meaning people, the perverse choices of men who so commonly prefer what is degrading to what is "rich and beautiful and ennobling," the speed with which lies and slander spread in all directions, and also the failure of the world's diplomats. "Could men of education, intelligence, and honest intent," asks Dr. Graham, "gather around a world conference table and fail so completely to understand each other's needs and goals if their thinking was not being deliberately clouded and corrupted?" All such failures are "the works of the devil" and they show that he "is a creature of vastly superior intelligence, a mighty and gifted spirit of infinite resourcefulness." The devil is no "bungling creature" but "a prince of lofty stature, of unlimited craft and cunning, able to take advantage of every opportunity that presents itself" (*Peace with God,* New York, 1954, pp. 59–63).

What reasons could or would be given for rejecting this explanation of diplomatic failures in terms of the devil's cunning ways? Aside from possibly questioning some of Dr. Graham's descriptions of what goes on in the world, that is, of the "facts" to be explained, our reasons would probably reduce to the following: First, we do not need to bring in the devil to explain the failure of diplomats to reach agreement on important international issues. We are confident, on the basis of past experience, that explanations of these failures in terms of human motives, in terms of human ignorance and miscalculation, are quite adequate, although in any particular case we may not be in the possession of such an explanation;

and, second, the devil hypothesis, granting it to be intelligible, is too vague to be of any use. It is hinted that the devil has a body, but what that body is like or where it lives and exactly how it operates, we are not told. If "devil" is construed on the analogy of the theoretical terms of the natural sciences, our complaint would be that no, or none but totally arbitrary, correspondence rules have been assigned to it.

It should be observed that the devil theory is rejected although it has not been tested and, hence, has not been falsified in the way in which certain exploded medical theories have been tested and falsified. There are, in other words, theories that we reject (and which agnostics, like others, believe they have good reason to reject), although they have not been falsified. It is important to distinguish here two very different reasons why a theory may not have been tested and, hence, why it cannot have been falsified. The theory may be sufficiently precise for us to know what would have to be done to test it, but we may be chronically or temporarily unable to carry out any of the relevant tests. This is to be sharply contrasted with the situation in which a theory is so vague that we do not know what we must do to subject it to a test. In the former case, suspension of judgment may well be the appropriate attitude; it does not follow that the same is true in the latter case, and in fact most of us regard rejection as the appropriate attitude in such a situation until and unless the theory is stated with more precision.

An atheist would maintain that we have just as good grounds for rejecting belief in a finite anthropomorphic deity of any sort as we have for rejecting belief in Zeus or in the devil or in witches. It should be noted that the believers in the finite anthropomorphic God usually advance their theory as a hypothesis that is the best available explanation of certain facts. Mill, for example, thought that the Design Argument, in the form in which he advocated it, affords "a large balance of probability in favor of creation by intelligence," although he conceded that new evidence for the Darwinian theory would alter this balance of probability (*Three Essays on Religion*, New York, 1874, p. 174). An atheist would argue that we do not need a finite God to account for any facts any more than we need the devil theory; and, more important, that the theory is too vague to be of any explanatory value. Mill, for example, talks of "creation by intelligence," but he does not tell us in any detail what the "Author of Nature" is like, where he can be found, how he works, and so on. Furthermore, because of its vagueness the theory is totally sterile. It does not lead to subsidiary hypotheses about celestial laboratories or factories in which eyes and ears and other organs are produced. Nor does it help us to interpret fossils or other remains here on earth. It is tempting, but it would be misleading, to say that the accumulation of evidence for the Darwinian theory (or some modified version of it) since Mill wrote on the subject has put the design theory "out of court." This would suggest that the theological explanation was at some time "in court," in the way in which a falsified scientific explanation may once have been a serious contender. It is true, of course, as a matter of history, that informed people cease to bring in God as an explanation for a given set of phenomena once a satisfactory scientific or naturalistic explanation is available. In a more important sense, however, the theological explanations were never serious rivals, just as the devil explanation of diplomatic failures is not a serious rival to psychological explanations. The theological explanations never were serious rivals because of their excessive vagueness and their consequent sterility. We do not at present have anything like a satisfactory scientific explanation of cancer, but no theological theory would be treated as a genuine alternative by a cancer researcher, even a devoutly religious one.

It should be added to all this that believers who, unlike Mill, do not treat their theology as a kind of hypothesis, are not affected by the above objections. Indeed, quite a number of them have strenuously opposed any kind of "God of the gaps." However, some of the very writers who insist that their theology must not be regarded as a scientific hypothesis elsewhere make statements that imply the opposite. They also frequently maintain that certain phenomena—for example, the universal hunger for God or the origin of life—can be explained only, or can be explained best, on the assumption that there is a God, and a God of a certain kind. Whatever they may say on other occasions, insofar as they propose their theology as the only possible, or as the best available, explanation of such phenomena, they are committed to the position that has been criticized in this section.

THE DEMAND FOR A COSMIC BRAIN

There was a good deal of discussion in the late nineteenth century of an antitheological argument that ought to be briefly mentioned here. To many persons, including unbelievers, the argument will seem to be merely grotesque; but in view of the revival in more recent years of several forms of extreme materialism, it deserves some discussion. Moreover, even if it is granted that the argument fails to prove its conclusion, the very grotesqueness of some of its formulations enables a more sophisticated contemporary atheist to state a challenge in a particularly forceful way.

The two writers chiefly associated with this argument were the German physiologist Emil Du Bois–Reymond and the English mathematician W. K. Clifford, both of whom wrote extensively on philosophical subjects. However, the argument is really much older, and versions of it are found in Meslier and Holbach. The remark attributed to Pierre Simon de Laplace that "in scanning the heavens with a telescope he found no God" may be regarded as an argument belonging to the same family. "Can we regard the universe," asked Clifford in his essay "Body and Mind," "or that part of it which immediately surrounds us, as a vast brain, and therefore the reality which underlies it as a conscious mind? This question has been considered by the great naturalist, Du Bois–Reymond, and has received from him that negative answer which I think we also must give." The student of nature, Du Bois–Reymond had written, before he can "allow a psychical principle to the universe," will demand to be shown "somewhere within it, embedded in neurine and fed with warm arterial blood under proper pressure, a convolution of ganglionic globules and nerve-tubes proportioned in size to the faculties of such a mind" (*Über die Grenzen des Naturerkennens,* p. 37). But, in fact, no such gigantic ganglionic globules or nerve-tubes are discoverable, and, hence, we should not allow a "psychical principle" to the universe. The following would be a more systematic statement of the argument: Experience shows that thinking, volition, and other psychological phenomena do not and cannot occur without a certain physiological basis—more specifically, without a brain and nervous system. Our observations appear to indicate, although this is not a matter of which one can be certain, that no cosmic brain or nervous system exists. Hence, it is probable that no cosmic consciousness exists either.

This argument has been criticized on the ground that it assumes a certain view (or a certain group of views) about the relationship between body and mind that is not self-evidently true and that many believers would deny. It assumes that consciousness can exist only in conjunction with a nervous system and a brain. However, the objector would maintain, the actual evidence on the subject does not warrant such a claim. It is true that within our experience, conscious processes are found only in connection with a highly developed brain, but this does not prove that consciousness may not occur in conjunction with other physical structures or without any physical "attachments" whatsoever. This is a big question about which nothing very useful can be said in a few words. Perhaps all

we can do here is point out that if materialism of some kind is true, then the demand to be shown the bodily foundation or aspect of the divine consciousness is not misplaced, while if the opposite view that consciousness can exist independently of a physical structure is correct, the Du Bois–Reymond argument would have no force.

Quite aside from this objection, the argument probably seems to many people, believers and unbelievers alike, to rest on a total, one is almost inclined to say a willful, misunderstanding of the theological position. James Martineau, who replied at some length to Du Bois–Reymond, protested that the "demand for organic centralization" was "strangely inappropriate," indeed quite irrelevant to the question at issue between the believer and the unbeliever. If Du Bois–Reymond himself, wrote Martineau, were "ever to alight on the portentous cerebrum which he imagines, I greatly doubt whether he would fulfill his promise and turn theist at the sight: that he had found the Cause of causes would be the last inference it would occur to him to draw: rather would he look round for some monstrous *creature,* some cosmic megatherium, born to float and pasture on the fields of space" (*Modern Materialism and Its Relation to Religion and Theology,* p. 184). Martineau then likened the argument to Laplace's remark, mentioned earlier, that in looking at the heavens with his telescope, he could nowhere see God and to statements by certain physiologists that in opening the brain, they could not discover a soul. All such pronouncements Martineau regarded as absurd. Although the physiologist finds no soul when he opens up the brain, "we positively know" (by introspection) the existence of conscious thought. Similarly, that "the telescope misses all but the bodies of the universe and their light" has no tendency to prove "the absence of a Living Mind through all." If you take the "wrong instruments" you will not find what you are looking for. "The test tube will not detect an insincerity," nor will "the microscope analyse a grief"; but insincerity and grief are real for all that. The organism of nature, Martineau concludes, "like that of the brain, lies open, in its external features, to the scrutiny of science; but, on the inner side, the life of both is reserved for other modes of apprehension, of which the base is self-consciousness and the crown is religion."

One is strongly inclined to agree with Martineau that there is something absurd in scanning the heavens for God. Étienne Borne, a French Catholic whose discussions are distinguished by fairness and sympathy for the opposition, refers to this approach as "a tritely positivist atheism" that "misses the point of the problem altogether" (*Modern Atheism,* p. 145). One must not expect to find

God or God's body in the heavens because God is not a huge man with huge arms, legs, arteries, nervous system, and brain. Only children think of God as a "king" sitting on his throne in Heaven. Educated grownups do not think of God in any such crude fashion. Du Bois–Reymond, Clifford, and Laplace are all guilty of an enormous ignoratio elenchi.

IS ANTHROPOMORPHIC THEOLOGY INTELLIGIBLE? Let us grant the force of Borne's objection. A critic may nevertheless raise the following questions: What is God like if he is not a grand consciousness tied to a grand body, if he is so completely nonphysical as to make any results of telescopic exploration antecedently irrelevant? If the telescope, as Martineau put it, is the "wrong instrument," what is the right instrument? More specifically, what does it mean to speak of a pure spirit, a disembodied mind, as infinitely (or finitely) powerful, wise, good, just, and all the rest? We can understand these words when they are applied to human beings who have bodies and whose behavior is publicly observable; we could undoubtedly understand these words when they are applied to some hypothetical superhuman beings who also have bodies and whose behavior is in principle observable; but what do they mean when they are applied to a pure spirit? Do they then mean anything at all? In recent years it has come to be widely questioned whether it makes any sense to talk about a disembodied consciousness. It is widely believed, in other words, that psychological predicates are logically tied to the behavior of organisms. This view, it should be pointed out, is not identical with reductive materialism. It does not, or at least does not necessarily, imply that the person is just a body, that there are no private experiences, or that feelings are simply ways of behaving. It makes the milder claim that however much more than a body a human being may be, one cannot sensibly talk about this "more" without presupposing (as part of what one means, and not as a mere contingent fact) a living organism. Anybody who has studied and felt the force of this thesis is not likely to dismiss as facetious or as "trite positivism" the question as to what words such as *wise, just,* and *powerful* can mean when they are applied to an entity that is supposedly devoid of a body. What would it be like to be, for example, just, without a body? To be just, a person has to act justly—to behave in certain ways. But how is it possible to perform these acts, to behave in the required ways, without a body? Similar remarks apply to the other divine attributes.

One may term this the "semantic" challenge to anthropomorphic theology, as distinct, for example, from arguments like the one from evil or from the eternity of matter, which assume the meaningfulness of the position attacked. A proponent of this challenge does not flatly maintain that anthropomorphic theology is unintelligible. For the point—that the predicates in question lose their meaning when applied to a supposedly disembodied entity—would be accompanied by the observation that in fact most anthropomorphic believers do, in an important sense of the word, believe in a god with a body, whatever they may say or agree to in certain "theoretical" moments. If we judge the content of their belief not by what they say during these "theoretical" moments but by the images in terms of which their thinking is conducted, then it seems clear that in this sense or to this extent they believe in a god with a body. It is true that the images of most Western adults are not those of a big king on his heavenly throne, but it nevertheless seems to be the case that, when they think about God unself-consciously (and this is, incidentally, true of most unbelievers also), they vaguely think of him as possessing some kind of rather large body. The moment they assert or deny or question such statements as "God created the universe" or "God will be a just judge when we come before him," they introduce a body into the background, if not into the foreground, of their mental pictures. The difference between children and adults, according to this account, is that children have more vivid and definite images than adults.

This entire point may perhaps be brought out more clearly by comparing it with a similar "semantic" criticism of belief in human survival after death. The semantic critic would maintain that while a believer in reincarnation or the resurrection of the body may be immune from this objection, those who claim that human beings will continue to exist as disembodied minds are really using words without meaning. They do not see this because of the mental pictures accompanying or (partly) constituting their thoughts on the subject. Or, alternatively, they do not see this because, in spite of what they say in certain "theoretical" contexts, in practice they believe in the survival of the familiar *em*bodied minds whom they know in this life. When they wonder whether their friends, enemies, certain historical personages, or, for that matter, anybody did or will go on existing after death, they think of them automatically in their familiar bodily "guises" or else in some ghostly "disguises," but still as bodily beings of some kind. If these images are eliminated on the ground that they are irrelevant or inappropriate because the subject of survival is a disembodied mind, it is not clear that an intelligible statement remains. What, for example, do such words as *love* and *hate* or *hap-*

piness and *misery* mean when they are predicated of a disembodied mind?

It will be seen from all this that the argument of Du Bois–Reymond and Clifford is not without some point. One may incorporate what is of value in their discussion into the following challenge to anthropomorphic theology: Insofar as the believer believes in a god with a body, what he or she says is intelligible; but in that case the available evidence indicates that there is no such body, and the remarks of Du Bois–Reymond and Clifford are to the point; if or insofar as God is declared to be a purely spiritual entity, the observations of Du Bois–Reymond and Clifford become irrelevant, but in that case the predicates applied to God have lost their meaning, and, hence, we no longer have an intelligible assertion.

SUMMARY OF THE ATHEIST'S POSITION. Let us summarize the atheist's case as it has here been presented. A philosophically sophisticated atheist would begin by distinguishing three types of belief in God—what we have called the metaphysical God, the infinite anthropomorphic God, and the finite anthropomorphic God. He will then claim that he can give grounds for rejecting all three, although he does not claim that he can prove all of them to be false. He will try to show that metaphysical theology is incoherent or unintelligible, and, if he can do this, he will certainly have given a good ground for rejecting it. He will also question the intelligibility of anthropomorphic theology insofar as God is here said to be a purely spiritual entity. If and insofar as belief in an infinite anthropomorphic God is intelligible, he will maintain that it is shown to be false by the existence of evil. In the sense in which he will allow the existence of a finite anthropomorphic God to be an intelligible hypothesis, he will argue that it should be rejected because it is not needed to account for any phenomena and, further, because it is too vague to be of any explanatory value. We saw that some of these justifications, even if sound as far as they go, would not establish the atheist's case unless they are accompanied by a demolition of the arguments for the existence of God.

SOME OBJECTIONS TO ATHEISM

If there were reason to believe that any of the arguments for the existence of God are sound or have at least some tendency to establish their conclusions, then they would of course constitute objections to atheism. Since these arguments are fully discussed elsewhere in this encyclopedia, we shall here confine ourselves to objections that are logically independent of them. Some of these objections have been put forward by writers who explicitly reject all the traditional proofs but nevertheless regard atheism as an untenable position.

THE MYSTERY OF THE UNIVERSE. It has been argued by several writers that whatever the objections to the different forms of theology may be, atheism is also unacceptable since it has no answer to the "ultimate question" about the origin of the universe. Thus, the nineteenth-century physicist John Tyndall, after endorsing a thoroughgoing naturalism, proceeded to reject atheism in favor of an agnostic position. In a paper titled "Force and Matter," he tells the story of how Napoleon turned to the unbelieving scientists who had accompanied him to Egypt and asked them, pointing to the stars, "Who, gentlemen, made all these?" "That question," Tyndall comments, "still remains unanswered, and science makes no attempt to answer it." Later he adds that "the real mystery of this universe lies unsolved, and, as far as we are concerned, is incapable of solution" (*Fragments of Science*, pp. 92–93). In much the same vein, the celebrated American freethinker and social reformer Clarence Darrow, after pointing out the weaknesses of the First Cause Argument, observed that the position of the atheist is just as vulnerable. If, he wrote, the atheist answers the question "What is the origin of it all?" by saying that the universe always existed, he has the same difficulty to contend with as the believer has when he is asked the question "Who made God?" To say that "the universe was here last year, or millions of years ago, does not explain its origin. This is still a mystery. As to the question of the origin of things, man can only wonder and doubt and guess" (*Verdicts out of Court*, pp. 430–431).

A philosophically acute atheist could offer a twofold answer to arguments of this kind. First, he would maintain that the question about the "origin of the universe" or the "origin of it all" is improper and rests on the mistaken or doubtful assumption that there is a thing called "the universe." It is tempting to suppose that there is such a thing because we have a tendency to think of the universe as a large container in which all things are located and, perhaps more important, because grammatically the expression functions analogously to expressions like "this dog" or "the Cathedral of Notre Dame," which do denote certain things. Upon reflection, however, it becomes clear, the rejoinder would continue, that "the universe" is not a thing-denoting expression or, putting the point differently, that there is not a universe over and above the different things within the universe. While it makes sense to ask for the origin of any particular thing, there is not a further thing left over, called "the universe" or "it all," into whose origin one can sensibly inquire. The origin of a great many things is of course unknown to us, but this is something very different from "the ultimate mystery" that figures in the argument under discussion; and there is no reason to suppose that questions about the origin of any individual thing fall in principle outside the domain of scientific investigation.

Furthermore, even if it is granted both that the question concerning the origin of the universe is proper and that we do not and cannot discover the true answer, this is not by itself an argument against atheism. It may well be possible to know that a certain suggested answer to a question is false (or meaningless) without knowing the true answer. All kinds of crimes have never been solved, but this does not prevent us from knowing that certain people did not commit them. An atheist can quite consistently maintain "I have no idea how the origin of the universe is to be explained, but the theological theory cannot be the right answer in view of such facts as the existence of evil." To support his position, the atheist must be able to justify his rejection of theological answers to the question "What is the origin of the universe?" He does not have to be able to answer that question.

ATHEISM PRESUPPOSES OMNISCIENCE. In the popular apologetic pronouncements of liberal believers, it is customary to contrast the agnostic, who is praised for his circumspection, with the atheist, who is accused of arrogant dogmatism and who, like the orthodox or conservative believer, claims to know what, from the nature of the case, no mere human being can possibly know. "The atheist," in the words of Dr. W. D. Kring, a twentieth-century Unitarian, "can be just as closed-minded as the man who knows everything. The atheist just knows everything in a negative direction" (New York Times, March 22, 1965).

Reasoning of this kind figured prominently in several influential works by nineteenth-century Protestant theologians. Their favorite argument was the following reductio ad absurdum: Atheism could be known to be true only if the atheist knew everything; but this is of course impossible; hence, atheism cannot be known to be true. For a man to deny God, wrote Thomas Chalmers, "he must be a God himself. He must arrogate the ubiquity and omniscience of the Godhead." Chalmers insists that the believer has a great initial polemical advantage over the atheist. For, he argues, some very limited segment of the universe may provide the believer with strong or even decisive evidence, with an "unequivocal token" of God's existence. The atheist, on the other hand, would have to "walk the whole expanse of infinity" to make out

his case (On Natural Theology, Vol. I, Book I, Ch. 2). By what miracle, asks John Foster, can an atheist acquire the "immense intelligence" required for this task? Unless he is "omnipresent—unless he is at this moment at every place in the universe—he cannot know but there may be in some place manifestations of a Deity by which even he would be overpowered." And what is true of space equally applies to "the immeasurable ages that are past" (Essays, 18th ed., p. 35). The atheist could not know that there is no God unless he had examined every part of the universe at every past moment to make sure that at no time was there a trace of divine activity.

According to Robert Flint, who endorsed and elaborated the arguments of Chalmers and Foster, the situation should be clear to anybody who reflects on the difficulty of "proving a negative." If a man landed on an unknown island, any number of traces in almost any spot would be sufficient to show that a living creature had been there, but he would have to "traverse the whole island, examine every nook and corner, every object and every inch of space in it, before he was entitled to affirm that no living creature had been there" (Anti-Theistic Theories, pp. 9–11). The larger the territory in question, the more difficult it would become to show that it had not a single animal inhabitant. If, then, it is "proverbially difficult to prove a negative," there can surely "be no negative so difficult to prove as that there is no God." This is plain if we reflect that "before we can be sure that nothing testifies to His existence, we must know all things." The territory in this case is "the universe in all its length and breadth." To know that there is no trace of God anywhere in eternal time and boundless space, a man would have had to examine and to comprehend every object that ever existed. This would indeed require omnipresence and omniscience, and Chalmers was there perfectly right when he maintained that the atheist's claim implies that "he is himself God."

Whatever its rhetorical force, this argument is so patently invalid that it can be disposed of in just a few words. We have in preceding sections of this entry presented several of the most widely used arguments and considerations that have been advanced in support of atheism. These may or may not be logically compelling, but none of them in any way imply that the atheist must be omniscient if he is right. To establish that the existence of evil is incompatible with the view that the universe is the work of an all-powerful and all-good Creator, to show that a given theory is too vague to be of any explanatory value, or to call attention to the fact that certain words have in a certain context lost their meaning—none of these require omniscience.

Writers like Chalmers, Foster, and Flint seem to labor under the impression that as far as its refutability is concerned, "God exists" is on par with a statement like "A hippogriff exists, existed, or will exist in some place at some time." It may be plausible to maintain that our not having found any hippogriffs on earth is no conclusive evidence that such an animal does not exist in some other part of the universe to which we have no access. The same does not at all apply to the question of whether one is or can be entitled to reject the claims of believers in God. For, unlike the hippogriff, God is by some declared to be the all-powerful and all-good Creator of the universe; he is said by most believers to be a mind without a body; and it is asserted by some that predicates taken from ordinary experience can never be applied to God in their literal senses. These features of theological claims may make it possible to justify their rejection although one has not explored every "nook and cranny" of the universe.

ATHEISM, ZEAL, AND GLOOM

In the opening section of this entry we referred to the view, common in previous centuries, that atheism is bound or, at any rate, very likely to lead to immorality, to national ruin, and to other disasters. This warning is no longer taken very seriously among reputable thinkers, but certain other statements about the baleful consequences of unbelief in general and atheism in particular continue to be widely discussed. Thus, it is frequently maintained that if atheism were true or justified, life would be deprived of all meaning and purpose. Again, it has been held that without God the universe becomes "terrifying" and man's life a lonely and gloomy affair. "Old age," wrote William James in his *Varieties of Religious Experience* (New York and London, 1902), "has the last word: a purely naturalistic look at life, however enthusiastically it may begin, is sure to end in sadness." Blaise Pascal, who was particularly concerned about the terror of a "silent universe" without God, observed in a similar vein that "the last act" is always tragic—"a little earth is thrown upon our head, and that is the end forever."

James and Pascal were believers, but very similar statements have frequently come from unbelievers themselves. "I am not ashamed to confess," wrote G. J. Romanes, a nineteenth-century biologist, at the end of his *A Candid Examination of Theism* (a work that was published anonymously in London in 1878 and which caused a commotion at the time), "that with this virtual

denial of God, the universe has lost to me its soul of loveliness."

More recently, the anthropologist Bronislaw Malinowski spoke of the state of mind of an unbeliever like himself as "tragic and shattering." Not only does the absence of God, in the opinion of these writers, make the universe "lonely," "soulless," and "tragic," but it also deprives it of love. Only when we have become accustomed to a "loveless" as well as a "Godless universe," in the words of Joseph Wood Krutch, shall "we realize what atheism really means."

Finally, it has been claimed that atheism is fatal to what William James called the capacity of the strenuous mood. James himself had no doubt that the unbeliever is prevented from "getting out of the game of existence its keenest possibilities of zest." Our attitude toward concrete evils, he asserted, "is entirely different in a world where we believe there are none but finite demanders, from what it is in one where we joyously face tragedy for an infinite demander's sake." Religious faith sets free every kind of energy, endurance, and courage in the believer and "on the battlefield of human history," religion will for this reason always "drive irreligion to the wall" (*The Will to Believe*, pp. 213ff.)

Some of these claims seem a great deal more impressive than others. It is not easy to deal with the charge that atheism deprives life of its meaning, chiefly because the word *meaning* in this connection is both ambiguous and extremely vague. However, if what is meant is that an atheist cannot be attached to certain goals that give direction to his life, then the charge is quite plainly false. If what is meant is that although the atheist may, like other men, pursue certain goals, he will not be able to justify any of his activities, then it should be pointed out that most human beings, even believers in God, do not justify the great majority of their acts by reference to God's will. Hence, the justification of these actions, if they ever are justified, could not be affected by the soundness of atheism. It is difficult to see how such activities as engaging in scientific research, assisting people who are in trouble, singing or dancing or making love or eating superb meals, if they ever were worthwhile, would cease to be so once belief in God is rejected. If what is meant by the charge is that the unbeliever will eventually have to fall back, in his justification, on one or more value judgments that he cannot justify by reference to anything more fundamental, this may be true, but it is not necessarily baleful, and it is not a consequence of atheism. Anybody who engages in the process of justifying anything will eventually reach a stage at which some proposition, principle, or judgment will simply have to be accepted and not referred back to anything else. The unbeliever may, in justifying his acts, regard as fundamental such judgments as "happiness is intrinsically worthwhile" or "the increase of knowledge is good for its own sake," whereas some believers may say that only service of God is intrinsically valuable. If it is a sign of irrationality, which in any normal sense of the word it is not, to accept a value judgment that is not based on another one, then the atheist is not one whit more irrational than the believer.

On the question of zest, it should be observed that neither James nor anybody else has ever offered empirical evidence for the assertion that unbelievers lead less active or strenuous lives than believers. What we know about human temperament suggests that the acceptance or rejection of a metaphysical position has, in the case of the vast majority of men, exceedingly little to do with whether they lead active or inactive lives. The Soviet cosmonauts, who were atheists (to take one relatively recent illustration), appeared to display the same courage and endurance as their American counterparts, who were believers. In general terms, a survey of the contributions of atheists and other unbelievers to science and social progress, often in conditions requiring unusual stamina and fortitude, would seem to indicate that James was in error. The a priori character of James's views on this subject remind one of Locke's conviction, mentioned earlier in this entry, that atheists, since they do not fear divine punishment, cannot be trusted to keep oaths and promises.

As for the "loveless universe" presented by atheism, it must of course be admitted that if there is no God who loves his creatures, there would be that much less love in the world. But this is perhaps all that an atheist would have to concede in this connection. Aside from certain mystics and their raptures, it may be questioned whether a biologically normal human being is capable of feeling any real or deep love for an unseen power; and it hardly seems credible to suppose that a person will cease to love other human beings and animals (if he ever loved them) just because he does not believe them to be the work of God. Perhaps one may hazard a guess that if more human beings grow up in an environment that is free from irrational taboos and repressions (and these, one may add, have not been altogether unconnected with religious belief in the past), there will be more, not less, love in the world—people will be more lovable and will also be more capable of giving love. As far as love is concerned, the record of theistic religions has not been particularly impressive.

The writers whose views we are discussing have probably been on stronger ground when they maintain that atheism is a gloomy or tragic philosophy, but here too some qualifications are in order. To begin with, if atheism implies that life is gloomy, it does so not by itself but in conjunction with the rejection of the belief in life after death. There have been atheists, of whom J. E. McTaggart is probably the most famous, who believed in immortality, and they would deny that their atheism had any gloomy implications. However, since the great majority of atheists undoubtedly reject any belief in survival, this does not go to the root of the matter. It cannot be denied that the thought of annihilation can be quite unendurable; but it may be questioned whether believers, whatever they may be expected to feel, do in fact find the thought of death any less distressing. In the opinion of some observers, this is due to the fact that regardless of his profession, the believer frequently does not really believe that death is the gate to an eternal life in the presence of God. "Almost inevitably some part of him," in the words of Russell, is aware that beliefs of this kind are "myths and that he believes them only because they are comforting" (*Human Society in Ethics and Politics,* p. 207). Russell and Sigmund Freud regard belief in God and immortality as illusions that usually do not work, but they are quick to add that anybody who refuses to be the victim of unworthy fears would dispense with such illusions even if they did work. "There is something feeble and a little contemptible," in Russell's words, "about a man who cannot face the perils of life without the help of comfortable myths." Some years earlier, in an essay titled "What I Believe," Russell had put the point very bluntly:

> I believe that when I die I shall rot, and nothing of my ego will survive. I am not young, and I love life. But I should scorn to shiver with terror at the thought of annihilation. Happiness is nonetheless true happiness because it must come to an end, nor do thought and love lose their value because they are not everlasting.... Even if the open windows of science at first make us shiver after the cozy indoor warmth of traditional humanizing myths, in the end the fresh air brings vigor, and the great spaces have a splendor of their own.

See also Agnosticism; Analogy in Theology; Augustine, St.; Berkeley, George; Blanshard, Brand; Brightman, Edgar Sheffield; Carnap, Rudolf; Clifford, William Kingdon; Cosmological Argument for the Existence of God; Cudworth, Ralph; Du Bois-Reymond, Emil; Epicureanism and the Epicurean School; Evil, The Problem of; Existentialism; Feuerbach, Ludwig Andreas; Fichte, Johann Gottlieb; Freud, Sigmund; Hamilton, William; Hobbes, Thomas; Holbach, Paul-Henri Thiry, Baron d'; Huxley, Thomas Henry; Immortality; James, William; Jodl, Friedrich; Laplace, Pierre Simon de; Locke, John; Mansel, Henry Longueville; Martineau, James; Marx, Karl; McTaggart, John McTaggart Ellis; Meslier, Jean; Mill, John Stuart; Nagel, Ernest; Nietzsche, Friedrich; Nihilism; Paley, William; Pascal, Blaise; Plato; Popular Arguments for the Existence of God; Russell, Bertrand Arthur William; Sartre, Jean-Paul; Schopenhauer, Arthur; Shelley, Percy Bysshe; Stephen, Leslie; Thomas Aquinas, St.; Tillich, Paul; Toleration; Unamuno y Jugo, Miguel de; Voltaire, François-Marie Arouet de.

Bibliography

The only full-length history of atheism in existence is Fritz Mauthner's four-volume work, *Der Atheismus und seine Geschichte im Abendlande* (Stuttgart: Deutsche Verlagsanstalt, 1920–1923). Although this work contains much interesting information that cannot easily be obtained elsewhere, it is marred by extreme repetitiousness and by a curiously broad use of the word *atheism,* which allows Mauthner to speak of agnostic and even deistic atheists. Probably of greater value are the various works on the history of free thought by J. M. Robertson, chiefly his *A Short History of Free Thought* (New York: Russell and Russell, 1899). Accounts of the struggles of atheists in England in the nineteenth century will be found in H. Bradlaugh Bonner, *Charles Bradlaugh: A Record of His Life and Work* (London: Unwin, 1895); G. J. Holyoake's two-volume *Sixty Years of an Agitator's Life* (London: Unwin, 1892); and A. H. Nethercot, *The First Five Lives of Annie Besant* (London, 1961).

An early defense of atheism is found in Vol. II of Holbach's two-volume *The System of Nature,* translated by H. D. Robinson (Boston: Mendum, 1853) and in his briefer work *Common Sense,* translated by A. Knoop (New York, 1920). Shelley defended atheism in his essays *The Necessity of Atheism* and *A Refutation of Deism,* and in one of the Notes to Canto VII of *Queen Mab,* titled "There is no God." All of these are included in *Shelley's Prose,* edited by D. L. Clark (Albuquerque: University of New Mexico Press, 1954). Charles Bradlaugh's "A Plea for Atheism" was first published in 1864 and reprinted in the Centenary Volume, *Charles Bradlaugh: Champion of Liberty* (London, 1933). Although he rarely used the term *atheism,* Schopenhauer is usually and quite properly classified as an atheist. His fullest discussion of the reasons for rejecting belief in God are found in his "The Christian System" and in his "Religion: A Dialogue." Both of these are available in a translation by T. B. Saunders in *Complete Essays of Schopenhauer* (New York: Willey, 1942). Another nineteenth-century work defending atheism is Ludwig Feuerbach, *The Essence of Christianity* (1841), translated by George Eliot, with an introduction by Karl Barth (New York: Harper, 1957). Of early critical

works, special mention should be made of Ralph Cudworth's two-volume *The True Intellectual System of the World* (London, 1678), which is an enormously detailed onslaught on all forms of atheism known to the author, and of Voltaire's article "Atheism" in his *Philosophical Dictionary,* translated by Peter Gay (New York: Basic, 1962). Part II of Voltaire's article is an extended critique of *The System of Nature.*

In more recent years, atheism has been championed in R. Robinson, *An Atheist's Values* (Oxford: Clarendon Press, 1964); in Ernest Nagel, "A Defence of Atheism," which is available in *A Modern Introduction to Philosophy,* edited by Paul Edwards and Arthur Pap (New York: Free Press, 1965), and in Michael Scriven, *Primary Philosophy* (New York: McGraw-Hill, 1966). Rudolf Carnap's position, which is briefly mentioned in the present entry, is presented in his "The Elimination of Metaphysics through Logical Analysis of Language," which is available in a translation by Arthur Pap in *Logical Positivism,* edited by A. J. Ayer (Glencoe, IL: Free Press, 1959). A somewhat similar position is defended by Antony Flew in "Theology and Falsification." This paper is available in various anthologies, perhaps most conveniently in *The Existence of God,* edited by John Hick (New York: Macmillan, 1964). An interesting and unusual defense of theology against contemporary criticisms like those of Carnap and Flew is found in I. M. Crombie's "The Possibility of Theological Statements," in *Faith and Logic,* edited by Basil Mitchell (London: Allen and Unwin, 1957). The comments in the present entry about the attempts of fideists to circumvent the argument from evil and other difficulties are elaborated in Paul Edwards, "Is Fideistic Theology Irrefutable?" in *Rationalist Annual* (1966).

There is a kind of "ontological" argument for atheism proposed by J. N. Findlay in "Can God's Existence Be Disproved?"; this, together with various rejoinders, is reprinted in *New Essays in Philosophical Theology,* edited by Antony Flew and Alasdair MacIntyre (London: SCM Press, 1955). The view that belief in God is not false but self-contradictory and that, hence, atheism is necessarily true is advocated by Jean-Paul Sartre in his *Being and Nothingness,* translated by Hazel Barnes (New York: Philosophical Library, 1956). Bertrand Russell wavered between calling himself an atheist and an agnostic. Many of his publications may plausibly be regarded as defenses of atheism. In this connection special mention should be made of *The Scientific Outlook* (New York: Norton, 1931), *Religion and Science* (New York: Holt, 1935), and *Why I Am Not a Christian and Other Essays on Related Subjects* (New York: Simon and Schuster, 1957), which includes "What I Believe."

What we have been calling metaphysical theology is defended by H. L. Mansel in *The Limits of Religious Thought* (London: Murray, 1858). Mansel's views were vigorously attacked by John Stuart Mill in his *An Examination of Sir William Hamilton's Philosophy* (4th ed., London, 1872); and Mill in turn was answered by Mansel in *The Philosophy of the Conditioned* (London: Strahan, 1866). The version of metaphysical theology on which we concentrated in the present entry is expounded by Paul Tillich in Vol. I of his three-volume *Systematic Theology* (Chicago: University of Chicago Press, 1951–1963), in his *The Courage to Be* (New Haven, CT: Yale University Press, 1952), and in J. A. T. Robinson, *Honest to God* (London, 1963). This position is criticized in great detail in Paul Edwards, "Professor Tillich's Confusions," in *Mind* 74 (1965): 192–214, and in Dorothy Emmet, "'The Ground of Being,'" in *Journal of Theological Studies* 15 (1964): 280–292. Various reactions to the views of Robinson are collected in *The Honest to God Debate,* edited by D. L. Edwards (London: SCM Press, 1963). The Thomistic doctrine of "analogical predication," which was not discussed in the present entry, is expounded in the *Summa Theologiae,* I, 13, 5, and in the work by Thomas Cajetan available in *On the Analogy of Names and the Concept of Being,* translated by E. A. Bushinski and H. J. Koren (Pittsburgh, 1953). Contemporary expositions of it may be found in G. H. Joyce, *The Principles of Natural Theology* (London: Longmans Green, 1923), and in E. L. Mascall, *Existence and Analogy* (London, 1949). The theory is criticized in Frederick Ferré, *Language, Logic and God* (New York: Harper, 1961), and in W. T. Blackstone, *The Problem of Religious Knowledge* (Englewood Cliffs, NJ: Prentice-Hall, 1963). There is an interesting attempt to state the doctrine with great precision by using the tools of contemporary logic in I. M. Bochenski, "On Analogy," in *Thomist* 11 (1948): 474–497. Tillich's theory, as well as the Thomistic theory, is criticized in Sidney Hook, *The Quest for Being* (New York: St. Martin's, 1960).

Thomas Aquinas's views on the nature of creation and the possibility of proving that the material universe has not always existed are given in *On the Eternity of the World,* translated by Cyril Vollert (Milwaukee: Marquette Univ. Press, 1964), which also contains relevant extracts from the *Summa Theologiae* and the *Summa contra Gentiles.* The argument for atheism based on the eternity of matter is stated in Ludwig Büchner, *Force and Matter* (4th English ed., London 1884; reprinted New York, 1950). The question of whether contemporary theories in physical cosmology have any bearing on the question of the existence of God is discussed in William Bonnor, *The Mystery of the Expanding Universe* (New York: Macmillan, 1964); M. K. Munitz, *Space, Time and Creation* (Glencoe, IL: Free Press, 1957); E. L. Mascall, *Christian Theology and Natural Science* (London: Longmans Green, 1956); and Antony Flew, "Cosmology and Creation," in *Humanist* 76 (May 1961): 34–35. All the writers just mentioned incline to the view that physical cosmology has no bearing on the question of the existence of God. The opposite position is supported by E. A. Milne in *Modern Cosmology and the Christian Idea of God* (Oxford: Clarendon Press, 1952).

The argument for atheism based on the premise that there is no "cosmic brain" is expounded in Emil Du Bois–Reymond, *Über die Grenzen des Naturerkennens* (Berlin, 1873), and by W. K. Clifford in an essay titled "Body and Mind," which is available in Vol. II of Clifford's two-volume *Lectures and Essays,* edited by F. Pollock (London and New York, 1879). It is criticized in James Martineau, *Modern Materialism and Its Relation to Religion and Theology* (London, 1876; New York, 1877). According to Mauthner, op. cit., Vol. III, pp. 439 ff., the remark that "in scanning the heavens with a telescope he found no God" has been falsely attributed to Laplace and occurs in fact in one of the writings of another distinguished astronomer of the same period, Joseph Jérôme de Lalande. Arguments by Indian philosophers, similar to those of Du Bois–Reymond and Clifford, are found in *Slovavartika,* Sec. I, verses 43–59, reprinted in *A Source Book*

in Indian Philosophy, edited by Sarvepalli Radhakrishnan and C. A. Moore (Princeton, NJ: Princeton University Press, 1957).

The essay by Tyndall in which he defends agnosticism in contrast to atheism is contained in his *Fragments of Science* (New York, 1871). A similar argument by Clarence Darrow occurs in his lecture "Why I Am an Agnostic," which was first delivered in 1929 and is now available in *Clarence Darrow—Verdicts out of Court,* edited by A. Weinberg and L. Weinberg (Chicago, 1963). Agnosticism is criticized from an atheistic viewpoint in several of the writings of Friedrich Engels. There is a useful collection of all the main discussions of religion by Marx and Engels in Karl Marx and Friedrich Engels, *On Religion* (Moscow, 1957; New York: Schocken, 1964).

The argument that atheism must be untenable since, if it were true, the atheist himself would have to be omniscient, is advanced in Thomas Chalmers's two-volume *On Natural Theology* (New York, 1836); in J. Foster, *Essays* (London, 1844); and in Robert Flint, *Anti-Theistic Theories* (London, 1878). There is a reply to Chalmers and Foster in G. J. Holyoake, *Trial of Theism* (London, 1858). A somewhat similar argument is contained in Paul Ziff, "About 'God,'" in *Religious Experience and Truth,* edited by Sidney Hook (New York: New York University Press, 1961). There is a reply to this in Paul Edwards, "Some Notes on Anthropomorphic Theology," in *Religious Experience and Truth.*

Pascal's horror of a universe without God is expressed in numerous passages in his *Pensées,* translated by W. E. Trotter, with an introduction by T. S. Eliot (New York: Dover, 2003). William James's claims that unbelief is fatal to "the strenuous mood" is contained in his essay "The Moral Philosopher and the Moral Life," which is reprinted in his *The Will to Believe* (New York: Longmans Green, 1897). The view that atheism makes the universe "loveless" is defended by J. W. Krutch in his *The Modern Temper* (New York: Harcourt, Brace, 1929). Malinowski's remarks about the "tragic" nature of life without God are found in his contribution to the BBC symposium *Science and Religion* (New York, 1931). The very different view that there is something liberating in the rejection of belief in God is advocated in J. M. Guyau, *The Non-Religion of the Future,* with an introduction from N. M. Glatzer (New York: Schocken, 1962); in Friedrich Nietzsche, *Die Fröhliche Wissenschaft,* in Vol. II of his three-volume *Werke,* edited by Karl Schlechta (Munich, 1954–1956); and in Sigmund Freud, *The Future of an Illusion,* translated by W. D. Robson-Scott (New York: Liveright, 1927).

In more recent years there have been numerous books and articles by religious thinkers in which the atheist's position is treated with a certain amount of sympathy. The following writings are especially worth mentioning in this connection: James Collins, *God in Modern Philosophy* (Chicago: Regnery, 1959); Henri de Lubac, *The Drama of Atheist Humanism,* translated by E. M. Riley (New York: Sheed and Ward, 1950); Étienne Borne, *Atheism,* translated by S. J. Tester (New York, 1961); Ignace Lepp, *Atheism in Our Time,* translated by Bernard Murchlord (New York: Macmillan, 1963); W. A. Luijpen, *Phenomenology and Atheism,* translated by W. van de Putte (Pittsburgh: Duquesne University Press, 1964); Jacques Maritain, "The Meaning of

Contemporary Atheism," in *Listener* (March 1950): 427–432; Gabriel Marcel, "Philosophical Atheism," in *International Philosophical Quarterly* 2 (1962): 501–514; and Jean-Marie Le Blond, "The Contemporary Status of Atheism," in *International Philosophical Quarterly* 5 (1965): 37–55.

Baggini, Julian. *Atheism: A Very Short Introduction.* Oxford: Oxford University Press, 2003.

Buckley, Michael. *At the Origins of Modern Atheism.* New Haven: Yale University Press, 1987.

Everitt, Nicholas. *The Non-Existence of God.* London: Routledge, 2004.

Flew, Antony. *The Presumption of Atheism, and other Philosophical Essays on God, Freedom and Immortality.* London: Pemberton, 1976.

Herrick, Jim. *Against the Faith: Essays on Deists, Skeptics, and Atheists.* Amherst, NY: Prometheus Books, 1985.

Hunter, Michael, and David Wootton, eds. *Atheism from the Reformation to the Enlightenment.* Oxford: Oxford University Press, 1992.

Le Poidevin, Robin. *Arguing for Atheism: An Introduction to the Philosophy of Religion.* New York: Routledge, 1996.

MacIntyre, Alasdair, and Paul Ricoeur. *The Religious Significance of Atheism.* New York: Columbia University Press, 1969.

Mackie, J. L. *The Miracle of Theism.* Oxford: Oxford University Press, 1982.

Martin, Michael. *Atheism: A Philosophical Analysis.* Philadelphia: Temple University Press, 1990.

McGrath, Alister E. *The Twilight of Atheism: The Rise and Fall of Disbelief in the Modern World.* New York: Doubleday, 2004.

Nielsen, Kai. *Philosophy and Atheism: In Defense of Atheism.* Amherst, NY: Prometheus Books, 1985.

Smart, J. J. C., and John Haldane. *Atheism and Theism,* 2nd ed. Oxford: Blackwell, 2003.

Smith, George H. *Why Atheism?* Amherst, NY: Prometheus Books, 2000.

Wallace, Stan, ed. *Does God Exist?: The Craig-Flew Debate.* Burlington, VT: Ashgate, 2003.

Paul Edwards (1967)
Bibliography updated by Christian B. Miller (2005)

ATHEISMUSSTREIT

Atheismusstreit, a famous controversy in Germany during the closing years of the eighteenth century, concerned the allegedly subversive philosophical views of Johann Gottlieb Fichte (1762–1814) and of the much less well-known Friedrich C. Forberg (1770–1848).

Fichte, who died as a pillar of respectability, had advanced various radical views in his earlier years, and on the nature and reality of God he never became fully orthodox. In 1793, while living as a private tutor in Zürich, Fichte published two political pamphlets titled "Reclamation of the Freedom of Thought from the Princes of Europe" and "Contributions Designed to Correct the Judgment of the Public on the French Revolution" in which he enthusiastically supported the basic principles of the French Revolution, arguing for free expression of opinion as an inalienable human right and subjecting the privileges of the nobility and the church to trenchant criticism. Fichte was at that time already famous, largely as a result of his Kantian work, *Versuch einer Kritik aller Offenbarung* (Essay toward a Critique of All Revelation), which had been published anonymously in Königsberg in 1792. Some reviewers attributed the essay to Immanuel Kant, who thereupon revealed Fichte as the true author, at the same time bestowing high praise on his gifts. In spite of Fichte's reputation as a political radical, he was appointed professor of philosophy at Jena in 1794.

For some time things went fairly smoothly at Jena. Fichte, who was a dynamic lecturer, made numerous converts among both his colleagues and the students, although there were some acrimonious exchanges with the psychologist C. C. E. Schmid and others distrustful of Fichte's speculative bent. There were two violent controversies before the *Atheismusstreit* broke out. One of these concerned a series of public lectures that Fichte had scheduled on Sundays from ten to eleven in the morning. Local clergymen were outraged, and the Over-Consistory (of which no less a man than Johann Gottfried Herder was a member) appealed to the government at Weimar to intervene. One local journal called attention to Fichte's revolutionary politics and asserted that he and his democratic followers were engaging in a deliberate attempt to substitute the worship of reason for the worship of God. The senate of the university and the government of Weimar decided in Fichte's favor, but it was agreed to give the lectures at three in the afternoon. The other controversy involved the university fraternities, which Fichte regarded as unethical and corrupt and whose abolition he publicly recommended. On New Year's Eve of 1795 students belonging to the fraternities attacked Fichte's house, breaking windows and heaping insults upon him and his wife. In the early months of 1795 Fichte felt his life to be in danger and found it necessary to reside outside of Jena until the tempers of the fraternity members had calmed down.

THE OFFENDING ARTICLES

The *Atheismusstreit* itself began in 1798 with the publication in the *Philosophisches Journal,* a periodical of which Fichte was coeditor, of an essay by Forberg titled "The Evolution of the Nature of Religion." Fichte's conservative

English biographer, Robert Adamson, dismisses Forberg's position as an "exaggeration of the dismal rationalism into which the weaker Kantians had drifted." In fact, however, Forberg's paper shows a powerful and independent thinker at work and does not seem dated even now. (Interestingly enough, Hans Vaihinger called attention to the philosophical merits of Forberg's work after almost total neglect for a century, citing him as an early positivistic fictionalist and praising his unusually fine appreciation of the more radical aspects of Kant's philosophy of religion.)

What, Forberg asks, is the foundation of the belief in a moral world order? There are three possible sources—experience, speculation, and conscience. Experience certainly lends no support to such a belief; if anything, it shows an evil deity in conflict with, and more often than not triumphing over, a good one. As for speculation, Forberg briefly and very clearly repeats Kant's objections to the ontological, cosmological, and teleological arguments, adding some critical observations of his own. Accordingly, the foundation of religion must be sought in our conscience. Religion is "purely and solely the fruit of a morally good heart …; it originates entirely from the wish of the good heart that the good in the world should triumph over the evil." To have "genuine religion" is not to have a belief in God; it is to be a partisan of the good, to act as if the kingdom of God, which for Forberg simply means a just and moral world, were attainable. Forberg himself evidently did not believe that such a world was attainable. This belief, however, is no more essential to true religion than is the belief in God. What is essential is the striving in the direction of a moral world whether or not one believes in its attainability. Forberg most emphatically insists that an atheist can be a religious person in his sense of religion. "Practical belief and theoretical unbelief on the one hand and theoretical belief and practical unbelief on the other may very well coexist."

At first sight this position may appear to be a kind of voluntaristic defense of traditional religion and an endorsement of Kant's moral argument, as this has frequently been interpreted. In fact, Forberg is very far removed from any such point of view. He is not saying that since there is no evidence either way, it is as well to believe in a just God or the attainability of a moral world. We are not, according to him, required to believe any such thing, and it does not really matter whether we do. We *are* required to *act as if we believed this*. Forberg was highly critical of the common interpretation of Kant's moral argument as providing cognitive support for belief in God. In his later defense of himself, *Friedrich Carl For-*

bergs Apologie seines angeblichen Atheismus (Gotha, 1799), he castigates the "usual, far too theoretical presentation of the notion of a practical belief," adding that it is "an unphilosophical conception which allows people to reintroduce through a back door every kind of nonsense of which theoretical philosophy has rid us with much effort."

In the same issue of the *Philosophisches Journal,* Fichte published an essay, "Concerning the Foundation of Our Belief in Divine Government of the World," which was intended to complement Forberg's paper. In a somewhat patronizing opening Fichte informs the reader that although he agrees with much in Forberg's piece, there are some important questions on which Forberg has not "quite reached" his, Fichte's, position and that since he had not previously had an opportunity to explain himself on these issues, he would do so now. Attempts to infer the existence of God from the world of sense objects, he proceeds, must inevitably fail. From the point of view of common sense and science, the world of sense objects is "absolute" and self-existing, and any attempt to go beyond it is "total nonsense." The assumption of a cosmic intelligence, moreover, would not explain anything, since it is quite unintelligible to talk about the creation of material things out of ideas. Considered from the transcendental viewpoint, the world of the senses is a "mere reflection of our own activity," and as a "nothing" it can hardly require an explanation outside itself.

Our belief in God can be grounded only in the supersensible world, which for Fichte is the only ultimately real world. This is the world of free moral agents, and unlike Forberg, Fichte teaches that the universe is, in fact, moral and just, that "every truly good act must succeed, that every evil one must surely fail, that for those who really love the good all things must turn out for the best." This does not mean that the good necessarily receive rewards in terms of pleasure but the world in which we experience pleasure is not the real world. The world of sense objects exists only as a "stage" on which free agents perform or fail to perform their duty. It has not "the slightest influence on morality or immorality, not the slightest power over our free nature." It is, in fact, nothing more than the "material objectification of our duty; our duty is what is ultimately real, what is the fundamental stuff of all phenomena."

God is identical with the moral world order. A person believes in God insofar as he does his duty "gaily and without concern," without doubts or fears about consequences. The "true atheist" is he who calculates the consequences instead of following the voice of his conscience; he "raises his own counsel above the counsel of God and thus raises himself to God's position." He who does evil in order to produce good is godless. "You must not lie," Fichte adds by way of illustration, "even if the world were to go to pieces as a consequence"; a moral agent knows, however, that the world could not go to pieces, since "the plan of its preservation could not possibly be based on a lie." Both here and elsewhere Fichte argued that all cognition is based on the existence of the moral world order. The existence of God, which here, of course, simply means the moral world order, is therefore more certain than anything else. It is presupposed in any piece of valid reasoning, and hence it cannot be, nor does it need to be, proved. "It is the ground of all other certainty and the only absolutely valid objective reality."

THE ANONYMOUS PAMPHLETS

Attention was drawn to these essays and their alleged subversion in a pamphlet published late in 1798 under the title "Letters from a Father to His Student-Son concerning the Atheism of Fichte and Forberg." The pamphlet was signed *G* and was at first attributed to D. Gabler, a respectable theologian teaching at Altdorf. Gabler vehemently denied any connection with the pamphlet, however, and publicly expressed his high regard for Fichte. Fichte himself attributed it to one of his enemies at Jena, Gruner, but the authorship remains uncertain. The main argument of the pamphlet followed a simple, popular line: Belief in an ever present "witness and judge" is essential to the moral behavior of human beings; if people were not afraid of punishment in the next world, they would be certain to do evil whenever they expected to escape the secular penalties. As a high school teacher, Forberg in particular is regarded as a most dangerous man. How could such a rector give a "thorough religious education" to the students under his charge? "To sow the seeds of immorality among young people and make belief in God suspect is not a permissible game." When compared to the protector of morality who hunted Bertrand Russell in New York City 150 years later, the attack was conducted with decorum and refinement; however, several later anonymous pamphlets were somewhat less refined. As usually happens in such cases, they contained slanderous comments about Fichte's private life and "sexual philosophy."

FICHTE'S DISMISSAL

The rest of the story does little credit to any of the parties except Fichte and Forberg. Moved by the "Father's Letter," the Saxon government, on November 19, 1798, published a Rescript ordering the universities of Leipzig and Wittenberg to confiscate all copies of the *Philosophisches Journal* because of the atheistic articles contained in it. This was followed by a request to the neighboring German governments to take similar steps. The dukes of Saxe-Weimar were informed that Saxon students would not be allowed to enroll in Jena unless there was an immediate investigation into the conduct of the two offenders. The grand duke of Weimar, a ruler with a genuine respect for scholarship, was free from any trace of religious fanaticism; however, any attempt he might have made to hush up the case was prevented by Fichte's public defenses of himself. In January 1799, Fichte wrote his "Appeal to the Public concerning the Accusation of the Expression of Atheistic Opinions," a copy of which was promptly sent to the grand duke. In March 1799 he wrote the "Juridical Defense against the Accusation of Atheism," which was primarily addressed to the university authorities but a copy of which was also forwarded to the grand duke. In these "defenses" Fichte contended, first, that his philosophical position, although far removed from the anthropomorphic popular religion, could not fairly be regarded as a form of atheism and was, in fact, "true Christianity" and, second, that any punishment inflicted on Forberg or himself would be a gross violation of academic freedom. The case, Fichte insisted, was one of great importance; since the accusation had been public, the verdict should also be public. Fichte's friends regarded this as a most imprudent demand, and rumors were soon current that the Weimar government was about to impose a public censure on Fichte. In the hope of preventing this, Fichte wrote a letter to Privy Councilor Voigt in which he declared that he would under no circumstances submit to censure. In such an event, he said, he would instantly resign. He added that several distinguished members of the Jena faculty shared his opinion that censure would constitute infringement of their academic rights and that they would resign with him. Voigt was told that he was free to show the letter to others, including, presumably, the Weimar authorities, who were about to reach their verdict.

This letter turned out to be Fichte's undoing at Jena. The Weimar government quite improperly treated it as a formal document. It avoided any censure of Fichte (or of his coeditor Niethammer) on the charge of atheism. Instead, both were rebuked in the mildest possible language for their "indiscretion" and advised to exercise greater caution in their selection of articles for the *Philosophisches Journal*. The journal itself was not proscribed, nor was there any mention of what teachers should or should not say in their classrooms. In a postscript, however, reference was made to Fichte's letter to Voigt, and his threatened resignation in case of censure was noted and accepted. In effect, this amounted to Fichte's dismissal, and two petitions on his behalf by the Jena student body to the duke were of no avail. Johann Wolfgang von Goethe, who a few years earlier had been largely instrumental in securing the Jena chair for Fichte, was one of those in the Weimar council who demanded Fichte's ouster. Fichte's support of the French Revolution was apparently a minor thing, but the language used in the letter to Voigt was unforgivable. "For my own part," Goethe wrote in a letter a few months later, "I declare that I would have voted against my own son if he had permitted himself such language against a government." Forberg was mildly censured by his superiors and did not return to any writings on religion until shortly before his death, when he published his autobiography, in which there is a very full account of the entire episode and a reaffirmation of all his earlier convictions.

THE CHARGE OF ATHEISM

In his "Appeal to the Public," Fichte had vehemently denied the charge of atheism. Using language which is very similar to that employed in the twentieth century by Paul Tillich and Bishop J. A. T. Robinson, he inveighed against the popular "idol-worship" of God as a "substance," as another entity *in* the world, and against the vulgar "eudaemonistic" morality that makes God a giver of "sensuous" rewards for good deeds and "sensuous" punishments for evil deeds. Such a conception—or, indeed, any attribution of personal characteristics to God—constitutes a lowering and limiting of the deity and has to be opposed in the interests of true religion. There is no need to question Fichte's sincerity, and in more senses than one it may be granted that he was a religious man.

At the same time the charge of atheism does not appear to have been totally unjustified. People do not usually mean by God simply the moral world order, and the denial of God as an entity over and above the more familiar objects of experience (including moral human agents) is precisely what is ordinarily meant by atheism. On all these points Fichte had been very explicit in the original essay. "There can be no doubt," he had written, "that the notion of God as a separate substance is impossible and contradictory, and it is permitted to say this plainly." Again, "We need no other god [than the moral world order], and we cannot comprehend another one. There is no rational justification for going beyond the moral world order to a separate entity as its cause."

Granting that there was some basis for the charge of atheism against Fichte, this in no way excuses the behavior of the Weimar authorities or of Fichte's and Forberg's other detractors. Not one distinguished voice was raised anywhere in Germany in defense of the accused men. Kant himself, who was still alive, was moved to a statement in the *Allgemeine Literaturzeitung* (1799, No. 109) in which he emphatically dissociated his philosophy from Fichte's system. "When I compare the state of the German republic of letters of this period with the Enlightenment literature of France a generation earlier, I am overcome with the deepest shame," was the apt comment of the historian Fritz Mauthner.

See also Fichte, Johann Gottlieb.

Bibliography

The main documents of the *Atheismusstreit* have been collected in *Fichte und Forberg. Die philosophischen Schriften zum Atheismusstreit,* edited by F. Medicus (Leipzig, 1910), and *Die Schriften zu J. G. Fichte's Atheismusstreit,* edited by H. Lindau (Munich, 1912).

Critical appraisals of the actions and writings of the participants are found in Vol. IV of Fritz Mauthner's *Der Atheismus und seine Geschichte im Abendlande* (Stuttgart: Deutsche Verlagsanstalt, 1923); F. Paulsen's "G. J. Fichte im Kampf um die Freiheit des philosophischen Denkens," in *Deutsche Rundschau* 99 (1899): 66–76; and H. Rickert's "Fichte's Atheismusstreit und die kantische Philosophie," in *Kant Studien* 4 (1899): 137–166.

There is a discussion of the originality of Forberg as well as of the evidence favoring a "left-wing" interpretation of Kant's moral argument for the existence of God in Appendix A and Appendix B of Hans Vaihinger, *Die Philosophie des Als Ob* (Berlin: Reuther and Reichard, 1911), translated by C. K. Ogden as *The Philosophy of "As If"* (New York: Harcourt Brace, 1924).

OTHER RECOMMENDED TITLES

Di Giovanni, George. "From Jacobi's Philosophical Novel to Fichte's Idealism: Some Comments on the 1798–99 Atheism Dispute." *Journal of the History of Philosophy* 27 (1989): 75–100.

Fabro, Cornelio. "Eine Unbekannte Schrift Zum Atheismusstreit." *Kant Studien* 58 (1967): 5–21.

Paul Edwards (1967)
Bibliography updated by Tamra Frei (2005)

ATOMIC THEORY IN INDIAN PHILOSOPHY

In classical Indian philosophy two Sanskrit words are used for the atom, the smallest impartite physical entity: "aṇu" and "paramāṇu." On the existence of such atoms, the classical Indian philosophers were divided. Among the orthodox Brahmanic schools, the Nyāya-Vaiśeṣika philosophers were the preeminent defenders of atomism, with the Mīmāṃsā philosophers as allies. On the opposite side, the Vedāntins denied atomism. Among the non-Brahmanic schools, the Jainas were clearly atomists, as were the Hinayana Buddhists. Yogācāra Buddhism, however, was strongly critical of atomism, and so too was Madhyamaka Buddhism.

The division of opinion on the issue thus cuts across the division between the Brahmanic and non-Brahmanic schools. Instead, the range of views about atomism more closely reflects the different schools' commitment to realism. After all, atomism is usually associated with a realist view of the world, in which atoms are taken to be objective, mind-independent entities. Predictably enough, then, we find espousing atomism such staunch philosophical realists as the Naiyāyikas and Mīmāṃsakas, as well as such heterodox realists as the Ābhidharmikas and the Jainas. In contrast, opposition to atomism is led by such antirealists as the Advaitins, the Mādhyamikas, and the Yogācārins.

ATOMISTS

The earliest Indian defenders of atomism may well be the Jainas, with texts defending atomism that date at least as far back as the third century CE. According to Jainism, everything in the world, save for souls and space, is produced from matter, and all matter consists of indivisible atoms (paramāṇu), each occupying a single point of space. Matter has two forms: a simple or atomic form and a compound (skandha) form. Perceivable material objects are compounds, composed of homogeneous atoms (there are no distinct kinds of atoms corresponding to the four kinds of elements). Impartite atoms are eternal, though this is obviously not true of the partite compounds. Indeed, atoms are supposed to be eternal precisely because they lack parts and are thus incapable of disintegration. But there is nonetheless a sense in which atoms, like compounds, are subject to qualitative change because, though all atoms are indistinguishable in substance, qualities present in an atom can be increased or decreased by many degrees.

To explain how atoms join as they do, the Jainas posit that some atoms are viscid and some dry, which permits aggregation of the two different kinds of atoms (much as particles of barley meal combine to form lumps when drops of water fall upon them). Moreover, they are viscid and dry in various degrees, with no aggregates combining

atoms with the lowest degrees of the two properties or equal degrees of the same property.

These Jaina speculations help to highlight three central questions for which the Indian philosophers expected atomic theories to provide answers: What evidence do we have for the existence of atoms? How is it possible for one atom to join with another? Why do atoms come together as they do?

With regard to the first question, the two main Indian arguments for the existence of atoms are both inferential. The first argument rests on the claim that there has to be a lower limit to the scale of diminishing minuteness. Gross objects clearly exist and are divisible. Yet the process of physical division must have a terminal point, and this terminal point to division must, by definition, be indivisible. The second argument attempts a reductio ad absurdum of the denial of such a terminal point: Unless the process of division comes to an end, everything must be equally composed of an infinite number of parts, and hence all comparative ascriptions of unequal magnitude to gross objects are undermined. The mountain and the mustard seed would have to be of equal size!

Of course, even if we are persuaded by these arguments that atoms do exist, any atomic theory still needs to address the second question and offer some explanation of how atoms combine to form partite entities. After all, atoms are supposedly impartite, and yet our only direct experience of conjunction involves partite things. But if we give up the thesis that atoms are truly impartite, we also have to give up one of the main arguments for the existence of atoms.

In reply, the Naiyāyikas utilize their distinctive mereological theory (theory of partition), according to which composite wholes are never reducible to their parts, though wholes inhere in parts. Hence a composite whole is a distinct entity, and not a mere collection of its conjoined parts. Moreover, since the whole is thus distinct from the sum of its parts, it can, unsurprisingly, have properties not possessed by any of its parts. This particular mereological theory, however, is unacceptable to both Buddhists and Advaitins, who object that the idea that wholes inhere in their parts would require a further relation to relate inherence to its relata, and so on ad infinitum. The Buddhists maintain instead that wholes are unreal, being mere conceptual constructions, and only parts are real. Thus for them, all conventional objects are mere aggregates of atoms. The Jaina response is different again: The composite whole is just the parts in a changed state.

Finally, even if we have reason to believe both that there are atoms and that they can combine, a viable atomic theory still needs to offer some sort of explanation of how atoms are brought together. The Jaina explanation in terms of a theory of varying degrees of viscidity and dryness builds on their view that all atoms are homogeneous, with the result that the division into the four elements is derived and secondary. The Nyāya-Vaiśeṣika school denies this, claiming instead that the four elements of earth, water, air, and fire involve four kinds of atoms sufficiently qualitatively different from each other so that the atoms of one element can give rise only to products of that element.

The elaborate Nyāya-Vaiśeṣika theory of how atoms combine to form compound entities seeks to address the issue of how atoms of infinitesimal magnitude can add together to produce a macroscopic object. Their explanation is that when two infinitesimal atoms combine into a dyad, there is a sort of quantum leap, and the new submolecule thus formed has a minute (*hrasva*) magnitude. Dyads then combine into perceptible molecules or triads (composed of three dyads), and there is another quantum leap in magnitude to a gross (*mahat*) quantum. The addition of gross quanta then straightforwardly accounts for the magnitude of macroscopic objects.

The point of this postulated double quantum jump from single atoms to dyads and then from dyads to triads is to insist that the finite magnitude of the triad arises from the infinitesimal atoms as a result of the *number* of the constituent atoms and not as a result of their magnitude, as in gross objects. Unsurprisingly, many Indian philosophers (both atomist and antiatomist) found this part of the Nyāya-Vaiśeṣika atomic theory unconvincing.

Moreover, all of this still leaves unexplained the initial conjunction of two atoms to produce a dyad. Later the Nyāya-Vaiśeṣika school invoked God's agency to help out here: Since all atoms are insentient, the process of combination must be guided by an intelligent divine agent. Other Indian philosophers disagreed, however, as to whether this amounts to a persuasive argument for the existence of God or to just an ad hoc addition to an already unsatisfactory atomic theory.

The Nyāya-Vaiśeṣika school took one advantage of its atomic theory to be that it can avoid the Buddhist theory of universal flux and can explain the identity of a substance through change in terms of the identity of unchanging, eternal atoms. A substance can undergo change without the constituent atoms changing because the qualities of a substance can change while the substance persists. However, consider what happens when we fire a clay pot so that it changes color. The Vaiśeṣikas claimed both that the unfired pot as a whole is replaced by a new pot as a whole, and that the application of heat causes a change of qualities to occur at the level of the individual atoms. But in admitting that change at the level of gross objects involves change at the atomic level, the Vaiśeṣika theory risks collapsing into the Buddhist theory of universal flux. Hence the Nyāya atomic theorists denied that change occurs at the level of the individual atoms, claiming instead that the whole remains intact while the change occurs.

Common to the different atomic theories of both Jainism and Nyāya-Vaiśeṣika are the claims that the atoms are genuinely indivisible, infinitesimal, and eternal. Other Indian atomists deny some of these claims. The Mīmāṃsā school, for instance, is willing to admit that whether entities are gross or minute is only relative. They thus accept as atoms the dust motes visible in a sunbeam (these are triads in the Nyāya-Vaiśeṣika system, the smallest perceivable particles). Although the Mīmāṃsakas do not entirely rule out the Nyāya-Vaiśeṣika conception of an atom as impossible, they criticize it as an overly speculative thesis. Even if the dust mote is theoretically divisible and hence apparently nonatomic, Mīmāṃsakas are only willing to accept such atoms as are established by common experience. There is no purpose served by assuming any atoms beyond these.

In contrast, the Ābhidharmika atomists affirm the existence of atoms smaller than dust motes but deny that they are eternal, since in Buddhism everything is taken to be impermanent. According to Buddhist atomic theory, although atoms are the smallest unit of matter, they never occur alone, but rather occur only as members of an aggregate of at least seven or eight atoms. Hence it is unsurprising that we do not experience individual atoms as separately perceptible. But we do nevertheless perceive the aggregates and, contrary to Nyāya-Vaiśeṣika claims, there are no aggregates distinct from the atoms themselves. Thus our perception that the atoms constituting an aggregate are gross is really an illusion due to the close and collective presence of a multitude of minute atoms.

ANTIATOMISTS

The Vedāntins and the Mahayana Buddhists were the chief representatives of Indian antiatomism, though their objections to atomism are frequently different and their own rival ontologies are significantly distinct. One specifically Vedāntin argument against atomism is that the Hindu scriptures nowhere affirm it. Clearly, this argument is not intended to persuade non-Brahmanic atomists, but it is interesting to note that most Brahmanic atomists too do not feel obliged to respond to it. The mere absence of a Vedic sanction is apparently thought to be obviously insufficient grounds for rejecting a philosophical theory. (A notable exception to this general trend of indifference is the Naiyāyika philosopher Udayana [eleventh century, CE], who goes out of his way to argue that there is indeed a scriptural warrant for atomism.)

The Advaita Vedāntins offered a more straightforwardly philosophical objection to the Nyāya-Vaiśeṣika theory of atomic composition. They argued that ontological parsimony ought to make us reject the Naiyāyikas' posit of dyads as unnecessary, for why can we not just say instead that three atoms directly combine to form a triad, the smallest visible substance. The gross magnitude of the triad will then be explicable not in terms of the magnitude or aggregation of atoms, but in terms of the *number* of atoms.

The main Indian argument that some form of atomism is rationally necessary is, of course, that it is required to explain the existence of gross material objects, which are indisputably partite. Again and again the atomists defended the controversial details of their theories with an argument to the best explanation: that since all agree that there are composite physical objects, one needs to posit atoms to best explain their existence and nature. But this strategy presupposes a common commitment to realism about the external world. The Indian antiatomists did not share this general commitment.

This is particularly obvious when we attend to the antiatomist arguments of the Yogācārin philosopher Vasubandhu (fourth or fifth century CE). Vasubandhu began by explicitly affirming the idealist thesis that everything is mind only. But realism, of course, denies this thesis. Vasubandhu responded by arguing that realism is false because realism implies atomism and atomism is incoherent.

Like the Ābhidharmikas, Vasubandhu rejected the Nyāya-Vaiśeṣika theory of organic wholes as unsupported by experience. But he also rejected the Abhidharma view that material wholes are mere aggregates of atoms, on the ground that for this to be so, the atoms would have to be joined. Such conjunction is either partial or total. If it is partial, the atoms must have parts in contact with one another; if it is total, all the atoms must collapse into the same atom-sized space. Either way, there cannot be a plurality of impartite atoms. Furthermore, an atom cannot be thought of as spatially extended without allowing that it has a front part different from its back part. But if

atoms are unextended, then aggregates of them cannot constitute extended gross objects. Thus atomism (and hence realism) is incoherent, and idealism is vindicated.

Yogācāra Buddhism is admittedly a rather peculiar kind of idealism, since it denies the existence of both the objects of consciousness and the subject of consciousness. Ultimately, all that exists is pure consciousness devoid of all subject/object duality. But whether or not Yogācāra thought is best classified as a variety of idealism, it is indubitably a variety of antirealism. Moreover, while other Indian antiatomists, such as the Mādhyamikas and the Advaitins, were certainly not idealists, they also in their various ways shared the Yogācāra thinkers' antirealist doubt of the commonsense assumption of an objective reality populated by ontologically independent entities. These Indian antiatomists are thus all equally unforgiving of the atomists' general strategy of attempting to excuse the anomalies in their various atomic theories by an appeal to atomism as the best explanation of gross external objects. In classical Indian philosophy, the avowed aim of philosophy is liberation (*mokṣa*). For the Indian antirealists, this goal is to be attained not by theorizing about the nature of a supposedly objective external world, but by transcending all such conceptions, including atomism and its presuppositions. In this sense, there is arguably a common antirealist motivation for Indian antiatomism, notwithstanding the very significant philosophical differences among the different antiatomist schools.

See also Causation in Indian Philosophy.

Bibliography

Gangopadhyaya, Mrinalkanti. *Indian Atomism: History and Sources*. Calcutta, India: K. P. Bagchi, 1980. A splendid anthology of Sanskrit primary sources together with annotated English translations. Also contains a very useful historical introduction.

Kapstein, Matthew T. *Reason's Traces*. Boston: Wisdom, 2001. Chapter 7 is an excellent philosophical study of Vasubandhu's arguments against atomism.

Potter, Karl H., ed. *Indian Metaphysics and Epistemology: The Tradition of Nyāya-Vaiśeṣika up to Gaṅgeśa*. Princeton, NJ: Princeton University Press, 1977. An extremely valuable survey of early Nyāya-Vaiśeṣika metaphysics.

Roy W. Perrett (2005)

ATOMISM

Atomism is a doctrine that has a long history in both philosophy and science. For this reason it is not easy to define its content in such a way as to comprehend all the historical variations and especially the historical development of the doctrine. In a very general sense, however, atomism may be defined as the doctrine that material reality is composed of simple and unchangeable minute particles, called atoms. It holds that all observable changes must be reduced to changes in the configuration of these particles. The multiplicity of visible forms in nature must likewise be based upon differences of configuration. The best way to discuss the variations of this general idea of atomism is to follow the historical development, which shows a gradual shift of emphasis from philosophical to scientific considerations. Consequently, the first part of this article, covering the period from the sixth century BCE to the seventeenth century, will be of a philosophical nature because in this period atomism was considered preponderantly from a philosophic point of view. The second part is concerned primarily with science, for it was in the period after the seventeenth century that atomism evolved in a scientific theory.

THE PHILOSOPHICAL PERIOD

In Greek philosophy we are already confronted with several types of atomism. Atomism in the strict sense, propounded by Leucippus and Democritus (fifth century BCE), should be looked upon as an attempt to reconcile the data of sense experience with Parmenides' thesis that matter is unchangeable. Parmenides rejected the possibility of change on rational grounds; change seemed to be unintelligible. He was convinced that reality must be one, that it must possess unity, and that, being *one* reality, it could not change. It may be remarked that this thesis of Parmenides is a presupposition for all rational science. Without fundamental unity, no universal laws are possible; without fundamental immutability, no laws covering past, present, and future can be valid. Yet, it is clear that Parmenides' approach is one-sided. Science may presuppose unity and immutability, but it also presupposes change. Only by studying changes is science able to discover the immutable laws of nature.

Democritus agreed with Parmenides on the unintelligibility and impossibility of qualitative change. He did not agree on the unintelligibility and impossibility of quantitative change. This type of change is subject to mathematical reasoning and therefore is possible. By the same token, Democritus denied qualitative multiplicity, but accepted multiplicity based on purely quantitative differences. Consequently, he accepted a numeric multitude of original beings, the atoms. These atoms did not differ qualitatively; only their sizes and figures differed.

The infinite variety of observable things could be explained by the different shapes and sizes of the atoms that constituted them and by the different ways in which the atoms were combined. Observable changes were based upon a change in combinations of the atoms. During such changes, however, the atoms themselves remained intrinsically unchanged. They did not change their nature, or even their size or figure; they were indivisible (hence their name ʹάτομος or indivisible).

Other forms of Greek atomism differed from that conceived by Democritus mainly in two points. First, they did not restrict the differences between the atoms to purely quantitative ones, but also accepted differences in quality. There was even a system that assumed as many qualitatively different atoms as there are different observable substances (Anaxagoras, fifth century BCE). Usually, however, only a few kinds of atoms were assumed, based upon the famous doctrine of the four elements: earth, water, air, and fire (Empedocles, fifth century BCE).

The second point of difference concerned the indivisibility of atoms. It is evident that a system that does not accept the indivisibility of atoms cannot properly be called atomism, but since such systems have played an important role in the history of atomism, we must mention them. For Democritus, the indivisibility of atoms was an absolute indivisibility, being the consequence of an absolute immutability. There were systems, however, that considered the indivisibility and immutability as only relative. The "atoms" could be divided, but they then became "atoms" of another substance; they changed their nature. (Here again an exception must be made for atoms as conceived of by Anaxagoras. These could be divided, but remained of the same kind. Hence they received the name of *homoiomerics*, possessing similar parts.) From the historical viewpoint, the most important system with qualitatively different atoms is that developed by the commentators on Aristotle—Alexander of Aphrodisias (second century CE), Themistius (fourth century) and John Philoponus (sixth century). In their system the atoms are called *elachista* (very small or smallest), the Greek equivalent of the Latin *minima*, which in medieval Latin writings indicates the smallest particles.

That these commentators on Aristotle combined the existence of "atoms" with the possibility of their changing their nature is not surprising. Aristotle was not satisfied by Democritus' atomism and was of the opinion that Democritus went only halfway. Atomism certainly opened up the possibility of explaining some changes that occur in nature, but not all. Nor did it account for all variety. Thus, the first task imposed upon Aristotle was a careful and critical reexamination of Parmenides' thesis. The result was his matter-form doctrine, stating that every material being is composed of *primary matter* and *form of being*. This composition, however, is not chemical or physical; it goes deeper. The possibility of change presupposes a certain fundamental nonsimplicity, for otherwise it is not possible to account for both aspects that are present in change: the aspect of a certain permanence (matter) and the aspect of something that is really new (form). Matter in the Aristotelian sense is not a substance, but the capacity to receive "forms."

To a certain extent, Democritus followed the same line of thought. Democritus, however, "substantialized" the permanent aspect (the atoms), thus narrowing the possibility of change. For Aristotle the "atoms" too should be subject to change and therefore "composed." Aristotle, however, did not propound a corpuscular theory of his own. Only a few remarks that could have been the starting point are found in a passus (*Physics* I 4, 187B18–34) in which he criticizes Anaxagoras' theory about the infinite divisibility of material things. Somewhere there must be a limit to divisibility. This limit depends on the specific nature of a thing. It was left to Aristotle's Hellenistic, Arabian, and medieval commentators to develop the casual remarks of their master into the *minima naturalia* theory, stating that each kind of substance has its specific *minima naturalia*.

In Greek philosophy there were also transitional theories between qualitative and quantitative forms of atomism. Plato (427–347 BCE), for example, adhered to the doctrine of the four elements; but the differences between the atoms of the respective elements were quantitative. An atom of fire had the form of a tetrahedron; that of air, an octahedron; that of water, an icosahedron; and that of earth, a cube.

When evaluating the importance of Greek atomism in the light of modern atomic theories, it should be borne in mind that in Greek thought philosophy and science still formed a unity. Greek atomism, therefore, was as much inspired by the desire to find a solution to the problem of mutability and plurality in general as by the desire to provide scientific explanations for specific phenomena. Although we meet with some ideas that can rightly be considered as precursors of classical physics and chemistry, the main importance of the old atomistic doctrines to modern science does not lie in these rather primitive scientific anticipations. The greatest achievement of Greek atomism was its general view of nature. The multitude of phenomena must be based upon some unity, and the ever-changing aspects of the phenomena are nevertheless aspects of a fundamentally unchanging world. To this view both the quantitative and the qualitative atomism have contributed—the latter by drawing attention to empirical aspects; the former, to the mathematical.

The history of the two forms of philosophical atomism until the birth of a scientific atomic theory has been rather different. This can easily be explained. Owing to the influence of Plato and Aristotle, Democritus' atomism did not gain preeminence in Greek, Arabian, and medieval thought. Yet that is not the only reason. Much more important is the fact that Democritus' atomism was more or less complete; and his followers, such as Epicurus (341–270 BCE) and the Latin poet Lucretius Carus (96–55 BCE), could confine themselves simply to taking over Democritus' doctrine.

The Aristotelian minima theory, however, existed only in an embryonic state. To Aristotle and his Hellenistic commentators the *minima naturalia* did not mean much more than a theoretical limit of divisibility; they were potentialities rather than actualities. With Averroes, however, we find an important development. According to him, the minima play an important role during chemical reactions. The Latin Averroists followed up this line of thought. Whereas most of the Latin commentators on Aristotle restricted themselves to a more or less systematic treatment of the minima as theoretical limits of divisibility, such Averroists as Agostino Nifo (1473–1538) attributed to the minima a kind of independent actual existence. The minima were considered as actual building stones of reality. The increase or decrease of a quantity of a substance amounts to the addition or subtraction of a certain number of minima. A chemical reaction takes place among the minima.

The fundamental importance of this view to science will be clear. Because the minima had acquired more physical reality, it became necessary to examine how their properties could be reconciled with the specific sensible properties of different substances. A first attempt to do so is found in Julius Caesar Scaliger (1484–1558). Some properties of matter, such as fineness and coarseness, depend on the minima themselves, while others depend on the manner in which the *minima* configurated. Rain, snow, and hail are composed of the same minima; but their densities are different because the minima of these three substances are at smaller or greater distances from one another. As to the chemical reaction, Scaliger remarked: "Chemical composition is the motion of the minima towards mutual contact so that union is effected" (*Exercitationes*, p. 345). Like Aristotle, he was convinced that Democritus was wrong. In a chemical compound the particles are not just lying close together; they form a real unity. Scaliger, however, was also convinced that the minima play a role in effecting the composition; and for that reason he was not satisfied with the Aristotelian definition of chemical composition as "the union of the reagents," in which the minima are not mentioned.

To sum up our survey of the development of the minima doctrine, and to prove that the opinions of Nifo and Scaliger were no exceptions, we may quote Francis Toletus (1532–1596), one of the best-known sixteenth-century commentators on Aristotle: "Concerning the manner of chemical composition, the opinions of authors vary, but they all agree in this: the reagent substances are divided into minima. In this division the separated minima of one substance come alongside the minima of the other and act upon each other till a third substance, having the substantial form of the compound is generated" (*De Generatione et corruptione* I, 10, 19).

THE SCIENTIFIC PERIOD

The seventeenth century is an important period in the history of atomism. Not only did atomism come to occupy a central position in philosophical discussion, but it also became an inspiring idea for the spiritual fathers of modern science. The philosophic differences between the atomic systems were soon pushed into the background, while the more scientific aspects that were held in common came to the foreground. Daniel Sennert (1572–1657) offers a clear example of this tendency. Basically, his corpuscular theories were derived from the doctrine of *minima naturalia,* but they also contain typically Democritean ideas. In a sense the same could be said of Scaliger; but the difference is that Scaliger discussed the philosophical controversies between Aristotle and Democritus, whereas Sennert showed a pronounced eclectic tendency. He was interested mainly in a chemical theory, and he found that from a chemical point of view the two theories really amount to the same thing. In order to support this opinion, Sennert refused to accept the interpretation that Democritus meant to deny the qualitative differences of atoms. As a chemist, Sennert was convinced that elementary atoms differ qualitatively. His main contribution to the corpuscular theory lies in the clear distinction that he made between elementary atoms and atoms of compounds (*prima mista*). This distinction forced itself upon Sennert through chemical experience. Each chemical substance, elementary or compound, must have its own atoms.

Contrary to Sennert, Pierre Gassendi (1592–1655) faithfully copied Epicurus and therefore Democritus as well. His own contribution consisted of a number of annotations designed to make the original atomic doctrine acceptable to his contemporaries. In order to effect this purpose, two things were necessary. First of all, the atomic system had to be divested of the materialistic interpretation with which it was hereditarily connected. Second, Gassendi had to "adapt" the original atomic theory to the science of his time. Science had reached the stage at which certain definite physical and chemical properties were attributed to the atoms—i.e., the atoms must possess definite natures; they could not be qualitatively equal. For this reason Gassendi stated that from the original atoms certain molecules were formed first; these differed from each other and were the seeds of different things.

While Gassendi's system is basically without any trace of originality, the corpuscular theory of René Descartes (1596–1650) is original in outline and execution. According to Descartes, matter and extension are identical. This thesis of course excludes the idea of indivisible atoms, but not of smallest particles. To the question of how such particles are separate and distinct from each other, Descartes answered that when a quantity of matter moves together, that quantity forms a unit, distinct from other units that have different motions. Along these lines, Descartes succeeded in devising a corpuscular theory in which the corpuscles were characterized by differences in mass, in amount of motion, and other properties that could be expressed in physical terms and treated mathematically. Descartes's corpuscles were endowed with exactly those properties that could be used in contemporaneous mechanics. As we have seen with Sennert, the seventeenth century was less interested in philosophical considerations than in scientifically fruitful ideas. Therefore, a corpuscular theory was judged, first of all, by this standard; and underlying philosophical discrepancies did not much interest the scientist. This explains why, to their contemporaries, Gassendi and Descartes could stand fraternally united as the renovators of the atomic theory.

Robert Boyle (1627–1691), for example, repeatedly confessed how much both Descartes and Gassendi had inspired him. On the other hand, Boyle was too much a chemist to be satisfied with a general idea of atoms or even with atoms endowed only with mechanical properties. Boyle looked for specific chemical properties. In contrast with mechanics, however, chemistry was not yet sufficiently developed to provide the theoretical framework necessary for a satisfactory chemical atomic theory. Boyle was keenly aware of this situation, as his *The Sceptical Chymist* (Oxford, 1661) proves. Neither the traditional theory of four elements nor the three-principle theory current among chemists could be of any use to him. Yet he was convinced that the distinction between elements and compounds was a sound one. This distinction therefore governed his own atomic theory. Theoretically, he adhered to the atoms of Democritus; practically, he did not use them. He was convinced that atoms were associated into so-called primary concretions, "which were not easily dissipable into such particles as composed them." Thus the primary concretions were corpuscles with definite qualities; they corresponded to the smallest particles of elements, and consequently Boyle treated them as such. The primary concretions could combine to form compounds of a higher order that may be compared with Sennert's *prima mista*. Although Sennert's corpuscular theory was based more on the minima theory and Boyle's theory more on the ideas of Gassendi and Descartes, in practice their theories were not very different. Both theories recognized atoms of compounds that are composed of atoms of elements. For Sennert the latter were elements, both theoretically and practically. For Boyle, theoretically they were not elements, but practically they were, because in chemical and physical processes primary concretions are not dissolved.

By combining the relative merits of the minima theory (qualitative atoms) and of Democritus' atomism (open to quantitative treatment), the seventeenth century laid the foundations for the scientific atomic theory of the nineteenth century. The further development of the seventeenth-century atomic theory, however, required better chemical insights, and especially a method of distinguishing elementary from compound substances. This method was found by Antoine Lavoisier (1743–1794), who postulated the conservation of weight as the guiding principle in chemical analysis. For the first time in history, a list of chemical elements could be given, based upon the results of chemical analysis.

The outstanding achievement of John Dalton (1766–1844) was that he connected these chemical results with the atomic theory. His atoms were no longer smallest particles with some general and rather vague physical properties, but atoms endowed with the properties of chemical elements. Dalton himself in *A New System of Chemical Philosophy* stressed the great importance of "ascertaining the relative weights of the ultimate particles, both of simple and compound bodies, the number of simple elementary particles which constitute one compound particle, and the number of less compound particles which enter into the formation of one more compound particle" (2nd ed., p. 213).

The fact that Dalton's theory is primarily a chemical theory does not mean that it has no philosophical implications. It is interesting to note that Dalton conceived the union of atoms in a compound as their simple juxtaposition without their undergoing any internal change. On this point the founder of the chemical atomic theory did not differ from the Democritean tradition. On another point, however, he followed the minima tradition. Dalton's atoms were specifically different for every kind of substance. He did not even think of building these atoms from particles without qualities, as Gassendi and Boyle had done.

After Dalton, the development of the atomic theory was very rapid. Jöns Jakob Berzelius (1779–1848) determined the relative atomic weights with surprising accuracy, guided by the hypothesis that under the same pressure and at the same temperature the number of atoms in all gaseous substances is the same. Since hydrogen and oxygen combine in the constant volume proportion of two to one, Berzelius concluded correctly that two atoms of hydrogen combine with one atom of oxygen. Berzelius also gave to chemistry its modern symbols. Amedeo Avogadro (1776–1856) completed the atomic theory by assuming that compound atoms, or molecules, do not necessarily have to be formed out of atoms of different elements; molecules of elements (H_2; O_2) also exist. According to Avogadro, the law that postulated an equal number of atoms in equal volumes of gas had to be understood as applying to an equal number of molecules. In a short time, the framework for classical chemistry was completed on the basis of Dalton's atomic theory. Chemical reactions were conceived of as a reshuffling of atoms and described by such chemical equations as $2 H_2 + O_2 \rightarrow 2 H_2O$.

An important contribution to the development of the atomic-molecular theory came from physics in the form of the kinetic theory of gases. With the aid of the calculus of probability, James Maxwell and Ludwig Boltzmann succeeded in deriving the behavior of gases, as described in the empirical laws of Boyle and Joseph-Louis Gay-Lussac, from the motions of the molecules.

The discovery of the electron, the electric atom, paved the way for a new theory about the nature of chemical compounds and chemical reactions. According to the new theory, a molecule such as NaCl did not consist of an Na atom and a Cl atom, but of an Na ion and a Cl ion; the Na ion was an Na atom minus an electron, and the Cl ion was a Cl atom plus an electron. Thus the so-called ionic theory revealed the nature of the forces of attraction between the various atoms of a molecule. The Na ion with its positive electric charge was attracted by the Cl ion with its negative charge. As a result of the connection that the theory of electricity established between physics and chemistry, theoretical and experimental materials were available at the beginning of the twentieth century. They led to a new development of the atomic theory that would endeavor to penetrate into the interior of Dalton's atoms.

The atomic model of Niels Bohr (1913) considered every atom as built of a positively charged nucleus around which circled, in fixed orbits as many electrons as were indicated by the charge of the nucleus. This charge corresponded to the place of the element in the periodic system. Bohr's model could explain not only the fundamental chemical properties of the elements, but also such physical properties as the spectrum that is characteristic of each element when it is emitting or absorbing light. Nevertheless, there were also serious difficulties with this model. According to electrodynamics, the moving electrons would ceaselessly emit electromagnetic waves. The atom would not be stable, but would always be losing energy. Hence, the motion of the electrons would gradually decrease and finally cease entirely. In order to save his model, Bohr postulated that emission of energy occurs only when an electron "jumps" from one orbit to another. In other words, the emission of energy is discontinuous. The emitted energy could be only a whole multiple of an elementary quantity of energy.

Thus, following the work of Max Planck, the idea of minima of energy was added to the idea of minima of matter, the traditional basis of atomism. Even light seemed to show an atomistic structure (photon theory). This would have meant a complete victory for the atomistic view if there had not been a complication. This complication was that the reasons which had formerly settled the dispute about the nature of light in favor of Christian Huygens's wave theory against Isaac Newton's corpuscular theory still retained their value. Light showed a dual character. In 1924, it occurred to Louis de Broglie that the same dualism might very well apply to the particles of matter. On the basis of this hypothesis, he could readily explain Bohr's postulate. This resulted in quantum mechanics, a new theory propounded by Erwin Schrödinger and Werner C. Heisenberg, which showed that both the atomic theory and the wave theory were only approximate models and not adequate representations of material reality.

The evolution of the atomic theory in the twentieth century was not limited to these rather startling new theoretical developments; it also gave rise to a new branch of physical science, nuclear physics, which studies the changes that the atomic nucleus is subject to. The first work in this area was in connection with the study of natural radioactivity. It had been observed that through radiation the nucleus of one element changes in charge and mass and thus becomes the nucleus of another element. In 1919 Ernest Rutherford succeeded in effecting an "artificial" transmutation; many others followed. The atoms of chemical elements appeared to be composed like the molecules of chemical compounds. Through nuclear processes a confusingly great number of new elementary particles has been discovered, all of which are subject to transformation under certain conditions. Particles can be changed into other particles and even into radiation. With such transmutations enormous amounts of energy are released.

Thus, twentieth-century science revolutionized many fundamental ideas of the nineteenth century; the atom is not only much more complex than Dalton thought; it is also much more dynamic. Yet Dalton is far from antiquated. Modern chemistry still works along the lines drawn by Dalton and his contemporaries. Can the same be said in relation to his forerunners in the philosophical period of atomism? The answer to this question can be found in the fact that the main mistake of Dalton and other advocates of essentially mechanistic theories lay in the conviction that atoms did not undergo any internal change. Science showed that this assumption was erroneous, but this should not be a de facto statement only. For if we think of the nature of science as experimental, then it is clear that unchangeable atoms would not offer any possibility of being investigated by experimental means. Without change, matter could not respond to experimental questions. Classical science could overlook this simple truth by assuming that it already knew all the relevant features of atoms. This assumption followed from the mechanistic doctrine that, from the seventeenth century onward, formed the philosophical background of the atomic theory and of classical science in general. The mechanistic doctrine points up the fact that classical science originated in a rationalistic climate. The idea of an unchangeable atom endowed with mechanical properties seemed to be in accordance with what an element should be. It satisfied both the imagination and the intellect. The program of science seemed to consist in explaining the forms of nature on the basis of component elements that were already known.

With the development of science, however, increasing knowledge of chemical compounds affected our understanding of elements. The elements, too, became the object of experimental investigation. From this it may be concluded that the mechanistic doctrine was not a real presupposition of the scientific method. In using the experimental method, science presupposed a much more fundamental mutability in nature than traditional mechanism could account for, and the scientific method implied a much more refined view of material reality than the mechanistic interpretations of science suggested. For this reason, the less orthodox forms of atomism were as important to the origin of the scientific atomic theory as were the orthodox. From the point of view of twentieth- and twenty-first-century science, the Greek philosophical discussions about the nature of change remain amazingly modern.

See also Alexander of Aphrodisias; Anaxagoras of Clazomenae; Aristotle; Averroes; Bohr, Niels; Boltzmann, Ludwig; Boyle, Robert; Chemistry, Philosophy of; Descartes, René; Empedocles; Epicurus; Gassendi, Pierre; Heisenberg, Werner; Lavoisier, Antoine; Leucippus and Democritus; Lucretius; Maxwell, James Clerk; Newton, Isaac; Parmenides of Elea; Philosophy of Science, History of; Planck, Max; Plato; Schrödinger, Erwin; Themistius; Toletus, Francis.

Bibliography

Dalton, John. *A New System of Chemical Philosophy.* London: Bickerstaff, 1808; 2nd ed., 1842.

Dijksterhuis, E. J. *The Mechanization of the World Picture.* Oxford: Clarendon Press, 1961. Excellent history of science from antiquity to the seventeenth century.

Hooykaas, R. "Elementenlehre und Atomistik im 17. Jahrhundert." In his *Die Entfaltung der Wissenschaft,* pp. 47–65. Hamburg: Augustin, 1957.

Lasswitz, K. *Geschichte der Atomistik vom Mittelalter bis Newton,* 2 vols. 2nd ed. Leipzig, 1926. A nineteenth-century classic.

Melsen, A. G. M. van. *From Atomos to Atom, the History of the Concept Atom,* 2nd ed. New York: Harper and Row, 1960. Includes references for the primary sources.

Nash, Leonard K. *The Atomic-Molecular Theory.* Cambridge, MA: Harvard University Press, 1950. Discusses the classical chemical theories.

Scaliger, J. C. *Exotericarum Exercitationum Libri XV de Subtilitate ad Hier.* Frankfurt, 1557; 2nd ed., 1607.

Whittaker, E. *History of the Theories of Aether and Electricity,* 2 vols. New York: Philosophical Library, 1951 and 1954. For readers with a good background in science.

Whyte, L. L. *Essay on Atomism: From Democritus to 1960.* Middletown, CT: Wesleyan University Press, 1961. A brief introduction to the idea of atomism and its history.

Yang, Chen Ning. *Elementary Particles, a Short History of Some Discoveries in Atomic Physics.* Princeton, NJ: Princeton University Press, 1962. Gives a general outline of the research done since 1900.

Andrew G. M. van Melsen (1967)

ATOMISM, LOGICAL

See *Analysis, Philosophical; Russell, Bertrand Arthur William; Wittgenstein, Ludwig Josef Johann*

ATTRIBUTE

See *Subject and Predicate; Universals, A Historical Survey*

AUGUSTINE, ST.
(354–430)

St. Augustine, also known as Aurelius Augustinus, was one of the key figures in the transition from classical antiquity to the Middle Ages. He was born at Thagaste, in north Africa, and died as the invading Vandals were closing in on his episcopal city, Hippo. He lived through nearly eighty years of the social transformation, political upheavals, and military disasters that are often referred to as the "decline of the Roman Empire." His life also spanned one of the most important phases in the transition from Roman paganism to Christianity. The old Roman pagan tradition was by no means dead, although the Roman emperors had been Christians since Constantine's conversion some forty years before Augustine was born. Augustine's youth saw the brief rule of Julian the Apostate as well as the last great pagan reaction in the empire, which broke out in the 390s. Nevertheless, it was during this period that the Roman state adopted Christianity as the official state religion. Medieval Europe began to take shape within the framework of the Roman Empire.

Augustine belonged to the world of late Roman antiquity, and its cultural and educational system had a decisive and lasting role in shaping his mind. His education, following the standard pattern of the time, was almost entirely literary, with great stress on rhetoric. Its aim was to enable its recipients to imitate the great literary masterpieces of the past. It tended, inevitably, to encourage a conservative literary antiquarianism. The culture it produced rarely rose above the level of the sterile cult of "polite letters" and generally had little contact with the deeper forces at work in contemporary society. There were many creative minds still at work; but even at their best, their thought was largely derivative. This is especially true of the philosophy of the period. Its stock of learning was in large part contained in compendia, though works of Cicero were still widely read, and those of the Neoplatonist thinkers gave inspiration to both pagans and Christians.

This culture and its educational system were the two sources that supplied the initial impulse for Augustine's thinking. His search for truth and wisdom began with his reading at the age of eighteen of a now lost dialogue by Cicero, the *Hortensius*. The work made an impact that Augustine could not forget and that he often mentions in his later writings. When he recounts the experience in the *Confessions* (III, 4, 7), written in his forties, he tells us that it was this work that changed his interests and gave his life a new direction and purpose: the search for wisdom. The search led him far afield; but looking back on it, Augustine could interpret its start as the beginning of the journey that was finally to bring him back to God.

PHILOSOPHY AND CHRISTIANITY

It was not until 386 that Augustine was converted to Christianity; he was baptized the following year. Meanwhile, his career as a teacher of rhetoric took him from his native Africa to Italy, first to Rome and then to Milan. During this period he was under the spell of the Manichaean religion. Its teachings appeared for a time to offer Augustine the wisdom for which he had been searching, but he became increasingly dissatisfied with it and finally broke with the sect through the influence of his new friends in Milan, Bishop Ambrose and the circle of Christian Neoplatonists around him. In Milan he learned the answers to the questions that had worried him about Manichaean doctrine, and there he encountered a more satisfying interpretation of Christianity than he had previously found in the simple, unintellectual faith of his mother, Monica. There was no deep gulf between the Christianity of these men and the atmosphere of Neoplatonic thought of the time. At this stage of his life Augustine saw no need to disentangle exactly what belonged to Christian and what to Neoplatonic teaching: What struck him most forcibly was how much the two bodies of thought had in common. The blend of Neoplatonism and Christian belief won his adherence, and the moral conflict recounted in his *Confessions* (Books VI–VIII) ended with his baptism.

Even in 400, when he wrote his *Confessions*, he spoke of the teachings of the "Platonists" as preparing his way to Christianity. In a famous passage (VIII, 9, 13–14) he describes Neoplatonism as containing the distinctive Christian doctrines about God and his Word, the creation of the world, and the presence of the divine light; all these he had encountered in the books of "the Platonists" before reading of them in the Scriptures. What he had failed to find anticipated in Neoplatonism were the beliefs in the Incarnation and the Gospel account of the life and death of Jesus Christ. Later in life Augustine came gradually to see a deeper cleavage between philosophy and Christian faith; but he never ceased to regard much of philosophy, especially that of the Neoplatonists, as containing a large measure of truth and hence as capable of serving as a preparation for Christianity.

From Milan he returned to north Africa and retired to live a kind of monastic life with like-minded friends until he was ordained, under popular pressure, to assist the aged bishop of Hippo as a priest. Within four years, in 395, he became bishop of Hippo. From the 390s onward, all of Augustine's work was devoted to the service of his church. Preaching, administration, travel, and an extensive correspondence took much of his time. He continued to lead a quasi-monastic life with his clergy, however, and the doctrinal conflicts with Manichaeans, Donatists, Pelagians, and even with paganism provoked an extensive literary output. Despite this multifarious activity, Augustine never ceased to be a thinker and scholar, but his gifts and accomplishments were turned increasingly to pastoral uses and to the service of his people. The Scriptures took a deeper hold on his mind, eclipsing the strong philosophical interests of the years immediately preceding and following his conversion.

Augustine did not, however, renounce his philosophical interests. He shared with all his contemporaries the belief that it was the business of philosophy to discover the way to wisdom and thereby to show people the way to happiness or blessedness (*beatitudo*). The chief difference between Christianity and the pagan philosophies was that Christianity considered this way as having been provided in Jesus Christ. Christianity could still be thought of as a philosophy, however, in that its aim was the same as that of other philosophic schools. The ultimate source of the saving truths taught by Christianity was the Scriptures, which for Augustine had supplanted the teachings of the philosophers as the gateway to truth. Hence, authority rather than reasoning, faith rather than understanding, came to be the emphasis of "Christian philosophy." For although the pagan philosophers had discovered much of the truth proclaimed by the Christian Gospel, what their abstract speculation had not, and could not have, reached was the kernel of the Christian faith: the belief in the contingent historical facts that constitute the history of salvation—the Gospel narrative of the earthly life, death, and resurrection of Jesus.

BELIEF AND UNDERSTANDING

Belief in the above facts was the essential first step along the way to saving truth and blessedness, but it was only a first step. Faith, while required of a Christian, was not in itself sufficient for a full realization of the potential rationality of man. For Augustine, an act of faith, or belief, was an act of rational thinking, but of an imperfect and rudimentary kind. In a late work he defined "to believe" as "to think with assent" (*De Praedest. Sanct.* 2, 5). The act of believing is, therefore, itself an act of thinking and part of a context of thought. What distinguishes it from understanding or knowledge is best brought out by Augustine in passages where he contrasts believing with "seeing." By "seeing" Augustine meant either vision, literally, or, metaphorically, the kind of knowledge to which its object is clear and transparent. This kind of knowledge could be acquired only through direct experience or through logical demonstration, such as is possible in mathematics and other forms of rigorous reasoning. Believing, though a necessary and ubiquitous state of mind without which everyday life would be impossible, is therefore a form of knowledge inferior to understanding. Its object remains distant and obscure to the mind, and it is not intellectually satisfying. Faith demands completion in understanding.

In this emphasis on the priority of belief and its incompleteness without understanding, we may see a reflection of Augustine's own intellectual pilgrimage. His tortuous quest for wisdom, with its false trails, had ultimately led him to consider the Christian faith as the object of his search. But this faith offered no resting place, for Augustine never lost his passion for further intellectual inquiry. His faith was only the first step on the way to understanding. He never ceased to regard mere faith as only a beginning; he often returned to one of his most characteristic exhortations: "Believe in order that you may understand; Unless you shall believe, you shall not understand." The understanding he had in mind could be fully achieved only in the vision of God face to face in the life of blessedness; but even in this life, faith could be—and had to be—intensified in the mind by seeking a deeper insight into it. Progress in understanding, founded on faith and proceeding within its framework,

was part of the growth of faith itself. After his conversion, then, reasoning and understanding were for Augustine no longer an independent, alternative route to faith. They still had their work, but now within a new setting and on a new foundation.

Some things, like contingent historical truths, could be the objects only of belief; others could be the objects of either belief or understanding (understanding means having an awareness of grounds and logical necessity). For instance, a mathematical theorem can be believed before it is understood. With understanding, however, belief inevitably follows. God, Augustine thought, belongs among the objects that are first believed and subsequently understood. In the process of gaining this understanding, the ordinary human endowments of rational thought, culture, and philosophy have a part to play. They form the equipment of which a Christian may avail himself in the work of seeking deeper insight into the meaning of his faith.

In his *De Doctrina Christiana* Augustine discusses the ways in which the various intellectual disciplines may serve to assist the Christian in understanding the faith he derives from scriptural sources. Philosophy, along with the other branches of learning, is here seen as subordinated to the service of a purpose outside it, that of nourishing and deepening faith; it is no longer to be pursued for its own sake, as an independent avenue to truth. It is also in *De Doctrina Christiana* that Augustine uses the image of the children of Israel, on their way to the Promised Land, spoiling the Egyptians of their treasures at God's bidding: In the same way, Christians are bidden to take from the pagans whatever is serviceable in understanding and preaching the Gospel. Again, we may see here a reflection of Augustine's narrowing of interests and the growing dominance of pastoral concerns in his mind. The theoretical statement of his subordination of secular learning and culture and their consecration to the service of preaching the Gospel (in its widest sense) is contained in the program laid down in the *De Doctrina Christiana*.

Therefore, Augustine is not interested in philosophy, in the modern sense of the word. Philosophical concepts and arguments play a subordinate role in his work; and where they occur, they are usually employed to help in the elucidation of some aspect of Christian doctrine. Typical examples are his use of Aristotle's *Categories* in an attempt to elucidate the notions of substance and relation in the context of Trinitarian theology, especially in his great work *De Trinitate*; his subtle inquiries into human knowledge and emotions, in the second half of the same work, with a view to discovering in man's mind an image of God's three-in-oneness; and his analysis of the temporal relations "before" and "after," undertaken to elucidate the nature of time in order to solve some of the puzzles presented by the scriptural doctrine of the creation of the world. In all these cases and many more, his purpose would be described today as theological. In Augustine's day the distinction between theology and philosophy did not exist, and "philosophy" could be—and often was—used in a sense so wide as to include what we should call theology.

To study Augustine's thought *as philosophy* is in a sense, to do violence to it: It is to isolate from their purpose and context what he would have regarded as mere techniques and instruments. To focus attention on what Augustine would have regarded as belonging to the sphere of means, however, allows us to see something more than a mere agglomeration of philosophical commonplaces derived, in large measure, from Neoplatonism. Augustine's originality lies not only in his determination to use his inherited philosophical equipment but also in the often slight, but sometimes profound, modification it underwent at his hands. And in the service of Augustine's purpose, many old ideas received new coherence and new power to move. Through his "spoiling of the Egyptians" much of the heritage of late antiquity received a new life in the European Middle Ages.

THE MIND AND KNOWLEDGE

At an early stage of Augustine's intellectual development, the skepticism of the Academic tradition of philosophy appears to have presented him with a serious challenge. His early philosophical dialogues, written in the period immediately after his conversion, are full of attempts to satisfy himself that there are at least some inescapable certainties in human knowledge on which we may absolutely rely. The basic facts of being alive, of thinking, or of simply existing are disclosed in one's immediate awareness of oneself. But Augustine did not limit the range of what was indubitably reliable in one's experience; nor did he seek to build an entire structure of indubitable knowledge on the basis of the absolute certainties of immediate awareness and its strict logical consequences, as René Descartes was to do. He tried instead to vindicate the whole range of human knowledge as being capable of arriving at truth, though also liable to err.

His vindication proceeds on two fronts, according to the fundamental duality of knowledge and of the objects corresponding to it. This duality, like much in his theory of knowledge, is of Platonic origin. Plato is the source of

his belief that "there are two worlds, an intelligible world where truth itself dwells, and this sensible world which we perceive by sight and touch" (*C. Acad.* III, 17, 37); and of its corollary, that things can be divided into those "which the mind knows through the bodily senses" and those "which it perceives through itself" (*De Trin.* XV, 12, 21). Although he never departed from this dualistic theory of knowledge, Augustine also always insisted that all knowledge, of either kind, is a function of the mind, or the soul.

He defines the soul as "a substance endowed with reason and fitted to rule a body" (*De Quant. Anim.* 13, 22). Augustine's use of the conceptual framework of the Platonic tradition made it difficult for him to treat man as a single, substantial whole. He did, nevertheless, attempt to stress the unity of body and soul in man as far as his inherited conceptual framework allowed. In a characteristically Platonic formula he defines man as "a rational soul using a mortal and material body" (*De Mor. Eccles.* I, 27, 52). The soul is one of two elements in the composite, but it is clearly the dominant partner: The relation between it and its body is conceived on the model of ruler and ruled, or of user and tool. This conception gave Augustine considerable trouble in his attempt to work out a theory of sense knowledge.

SENSE AND IMAGINATION. It was a basic axiom of Augustine's view of soul and body that while the soul can act on the body, the body cannot act on the soul. This is a consequence of the user-tool model in terms of which he understood their relation. The tool cannot wield its user; the inferior in nature has no power to effect or induce any modification in the higher. Augustine could not, therefore, elaborate a theory of sense knowledge in which the bodily affections would in any way cause or give rise to modifications in the soul; nevertheless, he insisted that even sense perception was a function of the soul, one that it carried out through the bodily sense organs. The mere modification of a sense organ is not in itself sense experience, unless it is in some way noticed by the mind. Augustine's problem was to explain this correlation between the mind's awareness and the modification of the organ without allowing the latter to cause or to give rise to the former.

In an early discussion of this problem, Augustine tried to explain the process of seeing as a kind of manipulation by the mind of its sense organs, much like a blind man's manipulation of a stick to explore the surface of an object (*De Quant. Anim.* 23, 41–32, 69). This is very much in line with his general conception of the relation of the body to the mind as that of an instrument to its user, but its inadequacy as an explanation of sense perception may have been apparent to Augustine. At any rate, he later came to prefer an account constructed in quite different terms. This account (elaborated in *De Genesi ad Litteram*, Book XII and generally underlying his later views, for instance, those stated in *De Trinitate*) is based on a distinction between "corporeal" and "spiritual" sight. Corporeal sight is the modification undergone by the eyes in the process of seeing and is the result of their encounter with the object seen. Spiritual sight is the mental process that accompanies corporeal sight, in the absence of which the physical process cannot be reckoned as sense experience (since all experience is a function of mind). Spiritual seeing is not, however, caused by corporeal seeing, since the body cannot affect the mind. Indeed, spiritual sight is a separate process that may take place in the mind spontaneously, in the absence of its corporeal counterpart—for instance, in dreaming or imagining. The mental processes involved in sight and in dreaming and imagination are identical; what is before the mind is, in all these cases, of the same nature. What the mind sees in each case is not the object outside it, but the image within it. The difference between sensation and imagination is that in sensation a process of corporeal seeing accompanies the mental process; this is absent in imagination.

Augustine never quite answers the question of how we may know the difference between perception and imagination. The part, however, which he attributes to attention in the process of sense perception is important and gives a clue: It is attention that directs the mind's gaze, and it appears that it is attention that checks the free play of imagery in the mind. Thus, perception and imagination can be distinguished in experience by adverting to the presence of attention; its presence immobilizes the creative imagination and ensures that the content of the mind has some sort of rapport with the bodily senses and their world. It is difficult to escape the impression that under the guise of "attention" Augustine has introduced what he had begun by excluding—mental process as responsive to bodily change. This is the peculiar difficulty that his two-level theory of man never quite allowed him to escape.

Augustine also speaks of a third kind of sight, one that he calls intellectual. This, the highest kind of sight, is the work of the mind whereby it interprets, judges, or corrects "messages" from the lower kinds of sight. The type of activity Augustine has in mind here is exemplified by any act of judgment on the content of sense perception; for instance, the judgment that an oar partly submerged in water is not actually bent, even though it looks bent. This activity of interpretation and judgment brings us to the second kind of knowledge, that which the mind has independently of sense experience.

REASON AND ILLUMINATION. In his account of sense knowledge, Augustine's Platonic inheritance was a source of difficulty. In the elaboration of his views on reason and intelligence, the reverse is the case: Augustine's account of these is largely an adaptation of the fundamental tenets of the Platonic tradition. Typical instances of knowledge that the mind has independently of sense experience are the truths of mathematics. Here Augustine discovered the universality, necessity, and immutability that he saw as the hallmarks of truth. Although he did not believe that knowledge obtained through the senses possessed these characteristics, Augustine widened the scope of truth considerably beyond the necessary truths of mathematics and logic. He thought that our moral judgments and judgments of value, at least of the more fundamental kind, also shared the character of truth. He did not, however, trace this universality and necessity of such propositions to their logical form or to the nature of the definitions and logical operations involved in them. (He wrote fourteen centuries before Immanuel Kant's distinction between analytic and synthetic judgments.)

Like all his predecessors and contemporaries, Augustine thought that this kind of knowledge was just as empirical as sense experience, and that it differed from the latter only in having objects that were themselves superior to the physical objects of sense experience by being immutable and eternal, and therefore capable of being known with superior clarity and certainty. The knowledge open to the mind without the mediation of the senses was conceived as analogous to sight; indeed, Augustine often speaks of it as sight, sometimes qualifying it as "intellectual sight." Its objects are public, "out there," and independent of the mind that knows them, just as are those of physical sight. In its knowing, the mind discovers the objects; it does not create them any more than the eyes create the physical objects seen by them. Together, the truths accessible to this kind of knowledge form a realm that Augustine, following the whole Platonic tradition of thought, often calls the intelligible world. This he identifies with the "Divine Mind" containing the archetypal ideas of all things. He was not, however, the first to take this step; this identification was the key to all forms of Christian Platonism.

Before Augustine, Plato had already used the analogy between sight and understanding. Its details are worked out in the analogy of the sun in the *Republic*. Here the intellectual "light" that belongs to the world of intelligible forms is analogous to the visible light of the material world. Like the latter, it renders "visible" the objects seen by illuminating both them and the organ of perception—in this case, the mind. All understanding is a function of illumination by this light. The intellectual light that illuminates the mind and thus brings about understanding is spoken of in various ways by Augustine. Since it is a part of the intelligible world, it is naturally conceived as a kind of emanation from the divine mind or as an illumination of the human mind by the divine. Augustine also refers to it as the human mind's participation in the Word of God, as God's interior presence to the mind, or even as Christ dwelling in the mind and teaching it from within.

Plato had tried to account for the mind's knowledge of the forms in the theory, expressed in the language of myth, that this knowledge was left behind in the mind as a memory of its life among the forms before it was enclosed in an earthly body. After some early flirtation with this theory of reminiscence, Augustine came to reject it; to hold that the mind's knowledge derived from a premundane existence would have raised serious theological difficulties. Therefore, instead of tracing this knowledge to a residue of a past experience, he accounted for it in terms of present experience; it was the result of continual discovery in the divine light always present to the mind. For this reason, too, his conception of *memoria* became so widened as to lose the reference to past experience that *memory* necessarily implies in English. Augustine's *memoria* included what we should call memory; in it, he thought, were preserved traces of past experience, as in a kind of storehouse or a stomach. But *memoria* included very much more than this. He speaks of our a priori mathematical ideas, numbers and their relations, as being contained in it; and in the course of the tenth book of the *Confessions,* in which he devotes a long discussion to the subject, the scope is so widened as to extend to our knowledge of moral and other values, of all truths of reason, of ourselves, and of God. It is, in effect, identified with all the latent potentialities of the mind for knowledge.

Memoria and divine illumination are alternative ways of expressing the basis of Augustine's theory of knowledge. The theory is, in its essence, the belief that God is always intimately present to the mind, whether this presence is acknowledged or not. His presence pervades everything and is operative in everything that happens. To this metaphysical principle the human mind is no exception. The only difference between the human mind, in respect to the divine presence within it, and

other things is that unlike these other things, the human mind is able to turn freely toward the light and to acknowledge its presence, or to turn away from it and to "forget" it. Whether the mind is present to the divine light or not, however, the light is present to the mind; on this presence is founded all the mind's ability to know.

The manner of operation of this illumination in the mind and what exactly it produces in the mind have been the subject of much debate. This uncertainty is due partly to the enormous variety of expressions used by Augustine to describe the divine light, but it is also partly the result of approaching Augustine's views with questions formulated in terms of concepts between which he would not have made a distinction. It is clear, at any rate, that Augustine did not think that the divine light in the mind gave the mind any kind of direct access to an immediate knowledge of God. This kind of knowledge was, to him, the result of understanding, a goal to be reached only at the end of a long process—and not this side of the grave. If, however, we ask further what exactly he thought illumination did reveal to the mind, the answer is more difficult. In particular, if we ask whether he conceived illumination primarily as a source of ideas in the mind or, alternatively, as providing the mind with its rules for judgment, the answer is not at all clear. He did not distinguish as sharply as one might wish between the making of judgments and the formation of concepts; he often speaks of both activities in the same breath or in similar contexts, or passes without the least hesitation from one to the other in the course of discussion. Sometimes he speaks of illumination as implanting in the mind an "impressed notion" (*notio impressa*), whether it be of number, unity, wisdom, blessedness, or goodness. Such passages suggest that Augustine thought of illumination primarily as a source of ideas, as providing "impressed notions." It is clear, however, that such "impressed notions" were also to serve as the yardsticks for judging all imperfect participations in individual instances of these notions. And in other passages, again, illumination is spoken of not as supplying any ideas or notions but simply as providing a criterion of the truth or falsity of our judgments.

It was very easy to pass from ideas to judgments in Augustine's way of speaking of illumination. In addition, Augustine's language when he speaks of the mind's judgment made in the light of divine illumination often has further overtones; the judgment he speaks of appears as a kind of foreshadowing of the ultimate divine judgment on all human life and action. The basic reason why Augustine had found Platonic metaphysics so congenial was that it harmonized so easily with the moral bearings of his own views; and its theories, especially in some of their more imaginative and dramatic expressions, allowed themselves to be exploited to serve Augustine's interests as a moralist. In his discussion of knowledge, as in his discussion of the relation of mind and body, ethical considerations very often play the major part. The central theories of Platonic thought buttressed views held by Augustine primarily on account of their moral bearings.

WILL, ACTION, AND VIRTUE

Morality lies at the center of Augustine's thought. There are many reasons for this, the most noteworthy being his conception of philosophy. As we have seen, philosophy was for Augustine far from being an exclusively theoretical study; and morality itself belonged to its substance more intimately than the discussion and analysis of moral concepts and judgments. Philosophy was a quest for wisdom, its aim being to achieve man's happiness; and this depended on right living as much as on true thinking. Hence the practical orientation of Augustine's thought—an orientation that it shared with most contemporary forms of thinking.

On human conduct and human destiny Augustine's thinking was, of course, molded very largely by the New Testament and by the Christian church's tradition in understanding its conceptions of divine law and commandment, of grace, of God's will, of sin, and of love. Much of this, being specifically theological in interest, lies outside the scope of this presentation of Augustine's thought. What is remarkable is the extent to which Augustine was prepared to read back the characteristic teaching of the Christian church into the works of the philosophers, Plato in particular. Thus he held that Plato had asserted that the supreme good, possession of which alone gives man blessedness, is God. "And therefore," Augustine concluded, Plato "thought that to be a philosopher is to be a lover of God" (*De Civ. Dei* VIII, 8). Rapprochements of this kind helped to reconcile the Christian and the Platonic teachings to each other; in Augustine's treatment of ethical topics the characteristically Christian themes and distinctively Platonic concepts are so closely interwoven that they are often inseparable.

Augustine is able, therefore, to define blessedness itself in terms that make no reference to any distinctively Christian teaching, for instance, when he says that man is blessed when all his actions are in harmony with reason and truth (*cum omnes motus eius rationi veritatique consentiunt—De Gen. C. Man.* I, 20, 31). Blessedness, according to this view, does not consist simply in the total

satisfaction of all desires. In another discussion Augustine makes this more explicit: While blessedness is incompatible with unsatisfied desires, the satisfaction of evil or perverse desires gives no ultimate happiness; hence blessedness cannot be identified simply with total satisfaction. "No one is happy unless he has all he wants and wants nothing that is evil" (*De Trin.* XIII, 5, 8; for the entire discussion, see ibid. XIII, 3, 6–9, 12). The only element in all this that is specifically Christian is the insistence that this happiness cannot be attained by man except with the aid of the way revealed by Christ and of God's grace given to men to enable them to follow it.

The dramatic account, given in his *Confessions,* of his own turning to God, though steeped in the language of the Bible and throbbing with the intensity of Augustine's feelings, is, at the same time, an illustration of a central theme in Greek metaphysics. The book opens with a powerful evocation of his coming to rest in God; it ends with a prayer for this rest, peace, and fulfillment. This central theme of longing and satisfaction is a commonplace of Greek thought from Plato's *Symposium* onward. Man, according to the cosmology implicit in this picture, illustrates in his being the forces that are at work in nature in general. Man, like everything else, is conceived as part of a vast nexus of interrelated things within an ordered hierarchy of beings that together form the cosmos. But it is an order in which the components are not stationary but are in dynamic rapport; they are all pursuing their own ends and come to rest only in attaining these ends. Their striving for rest, for completion or satisfaction, is the motive power that drives all things toward their purposes, just as weight, according to this image, causes things to move to the places proper to them in the cosmos—the heavy things downward, the light upward. Augustine thought of the forces that move men as analogous to weight and called them, collectively, love or loves. In a famous passage he wrote, "My weight is my love; by it am I carried wheresoever I am carried" (*... eo feror quocumque feror—Conf.* XIII, 9, 10).

LOVE, LAW, AND THE MORAL ORDER. Man, however, differs from other things in nature in that the forces that move him, his "loves," are very much more complex. Within him there are a great many desires and drives, impulses and inclinations—some of them conscious, others not. The satisfaction of some often involves the frustration of others, and the harmonious satisfaction that forms the goal of human activity appears to be a very distant and scarcely realizable purpose. The reason for this is not only the multiplicity of elements that go into the making of human nature; a further reason is the fact that these elements have been disordered and deprived of their original state of harmony. Augustine interpreted this aspect of the human condition as a consequence of the sin of Adam and the fall of man.

There is, however, a further respect in which man differs from other things in the way his activity is determined. This lies in the fact that even with his disordered impulses, he is not—at least not entirely—at the mercy of the conflicting forces within him. His activity is not, so to speak, a resultant of them: He is, in some degree, capable of selecting among them, deciding which to resist, which to follow. In this capacity for choice Augustine saw the possibility of what he called voluntary action as distinguished from natural or necessary behavior. He called this human capacity "will." It is a source of some confusion that he used the term *love,* or its plural, *loves,* to designate the sum total of forces that determine a man's actions, whether they are "natural" or "voluntary." As a collective name for natural impulses, "love" is therefore morally neutral; only insofar as the will endorses or approves love of this kind is love morally praiseworthy or blameworthy. Augustine expresses this graphically by distinguishing between loves that ought to be loved and loves that ought not to be loved; and he defines man's moral task in terms of sorting out these commendable and reprehensible loves in himself and putting his loves in their right order.

Augustine's favorite definition of virtue is "rightly ordered love" (as in *De Civ. Dei* XV, 22). This consists in setting things in their right order of priority, valuing them according to their true worth, and in following this right order of value in one's inclinations and actions. The idea of order is central to Augustine's reflections on morals. Before becoming a Christian, he had believed with the Manichaeans that the existence of good and of evil in the world was accounted for by their different origins, respectively from a good and an evil deity. The Neoplatonism of his Christian friends in Milan helped Augustine find an alternative explanation, one that was more in keeping with the Christian doctrine of one world created by one God. According to this theory, evil had no independent, substantial existence in its own right; it existed as a privation, as a distortion or damage within the good. All evil was thus in some sense a breach of the right relation of parts within a whole, a breach of order of some kind. Hence the great emphasis on order in Augustine's thought, from the time of his conversion to the writing of his last works.

Augustine calls the pattern to which human activity must conform "law." Law is, in the first place, the arche-typal order according to which people are required to shape their actions and by which their actions are to be judged. Augustine makes it clear that by "law" he means very much more than the actual legal enactments of public authorities. These "human laws" deal only with a part, greater or lesser, of human conduct; they vary from place to place and from time to time; they depend on the vagaries of individual legislators. The true "eternal law" by which all human behavior is judged leaves no aspect of man's life out of its purview; it is the same everywhere and at all times. It is not quite clear how Augustine conceived the relation between divine and human, eternal and temporal, law. His terminology is variable, and although he thought that human law ought to seek to approach the divine, or at least not to contradict it, he does not appear to have denied its claim to being law even when it failed to reflect the eternal law. Also, as we shall see, he appears to have changed his views on this matter in the course of his life.

The "eternal," or "divine," law is in effect the intelligible world or the divine mind (see discussion of reason and illumination above) insofar as it is considered as the pattern that should regulate activity. The language in which Augustine speaks about the divine law is the same as that which he uses in speaking of the eternal truth, and he believed that the achievement of wisdom consisted in pursuing this truth by understanding and then embodying in oneself the order understood. It is clear that there is no significant difference between "eternal law" and "eternal truth"; the two are identical: Eternal law is eternal truth considered under its aspect as a standard of moral judgment. Thus, the problem of how the eternal law is known to men is the same as the problem discussed above of how the eternal truth is known. Here, too, he speaks of the eternal law as being "transcribed" into the human mind or of its "notion" as being impressed on the mind. The deliverance of conscience or reason as manifested in moral judgment is thus no less and no more than the human mind's illumination by the eternal law, or its participation in it; Augustine describes conscience as "an interior law, written in the heart itself" (*lex intima, in ipso … corde conscripta—En. in Ps.* 57, 1). He refers to this law, inscribed in man's heart or known to him by reason, as "natural." He can thus speak of law (eternal or natural), reason, and order interchangeably when discussing the ordering of human action to bring about its virtuous disposition.

In defining this order of priority in value, the following of which constitutes virtue, Augustine makes a fundamental distinction between "use" and "enjoyment." These two forms of behavior correspond to the twofold classification of things according to whether they are valuable for their own sake or as means, for the sake of something else. Things valued for themselves are to be "enjoyed," things valued as means are to be "used"; the inversion of the relation between use and enjoyment is the fundamental perversion of the order of virtue. To seek to use what is to be enjoyed or to enjoy what is to be used is to confuse means with ends. The only object fit for enjoyment, in this sense, is God; he alone is to be loved for his own sake, and all other things are to be referred to this love. In elaborating this theory, Augustine was expressing the traditional view that it behooves people to journey through their lives on Earth as pilgrims and not to regard any earthly goal as a fit resting place. This did not, of course, imply, to Augustine's mind, that nothing but God was a fit object of love; on the contrary, it was a way of stressing the need to put loves in their right order and to love each thing with the kind and degree of love appropriate to it. Although he clearly conceived of love as capable of an endless series of gradations, Augustine is usually content to speak of two kinds of love, which he contrasts: charity (caritas) and cupidity (cupiditas). The basic distinction is between upright, well-ordered, and God-centered love and perverse, disordered, and self-centered love. A great deal of Augustine's thinking and writing hinges on this distinction.

The individual virtues interested Augustine less than the concept of love. He was content to take over the classical enumeration of the four cardinal virtues. But his own characteristic thoughts on the moral life are always developed in terms of love rather than of any of the virtues. Indeed, as we have seen, he defined virtue in terms of love; similarly, he liked to define the individual cardinal virtues as different aspects of the love of God. This tendency is one of the most important links between what we would distinguish as the theological and philosophical sides of his thought.

THE WORLD AND GOD

Order is a key idea in Augustine's reflections on the morality of human behavior. It also plays a large part in his reflection on the physical universe in its relation to God. The world of nature was not in itself an object of particular interest to Augustine. In cosmological thinking of the kind to be found in Aristotle's Physics, for instance, he had little interest. The physical world concerned him only insofar as it was related either to man or to God. Order, then, for Augustine was the expression of rationality. In human action this was something that men should

seek to embody in their conduct; in the world of physical and animate nature, which did not share the freedom of human activity, order expressed the divine rationality at work in all natural happenings. To human eyes, however, this order was often glimpsed only in isolated instances, while a great deal of disorder was manifest in the misery, disease, and suffering with which the world is shot through. In part these frustrations of order were held to be due, ultimately, to the initiative of human sin; in part they were held to be merely apparent and capable of being resolved within a perspective larger than that of finite human vision.

Behind the world order stands its author and sovereign ruler, God. All things testify to his presence; the world is full of his "traces" (vestigia). God's presence in and behind his creation was, for Augustine, not so much something to be established by argument as it was the premise, taken for granted, of a further argument. This argument, to which Augustine returned on a number of occasions, is particularly well expressed in a chapter of his Confessions (X, 6, 9, and 10). He there speaks of putting things to the question in order to allow them to reveal themselves as dependent on their creator. It is clear that what primarily interested Augustine was the questioner's moral attitude: The point of his argument is not so much that the order and beauty of things imply the existence of God, but rather that since God had created them, we must so discipline ourselves as to see things for what they are—his handiwork—and to value them at their true worth and worship only him, their creator—not his handiwork. Again, the moral concern is uppermost in Augustine's mind.

This is not the case with the discussion of the problem of time, in Book XI of the Confessions. The problem was forced on Augustine's attention by the scriptural doctrine of creation, but it is clear that it fascinated him and that he pursued it simply because he was interested in it. Manichaean objectors to the Christian doctrine of creation from nothing had raised difficulties about speaking of an absolute beginning. These critics had pointed out that in our ordinary language there is no room for an absolute beginning of the kind envisaged by adherents of the doctrine; we can always ask what happened before something else, even if this was the first of all happenings. Questions of this kind revealed the arbitrariness and absurdity of the belief that God made the world out of nothing: What was God doing before the creation? Why did he create the world when he did and not sooner, or later?

In answer to these difficulties Augustine in effect undertook a critique of the conception of time that underlay them. Such difficulties arise from the fact that time is thought of as having the same kind of being as the events and happenings going on in time; the question "What happened before time?" was thought to be of the same logical form as questions about what happened before any particular events. Augustine denied this assumed logical similarity behind the grammatical similarity of the questions. He pointed out that whereas it makes sense to ask what happened before any particular event, it does not make sense to ask what happened before all events, because time is the field of the relationships of temporal events, and there could ex hypothesi be nothing before the first temporal event. In this argument Augustine in effect rejected the conception of time according to which time has a substantial reality of its own, and he adopted a theory according to which time is the field of temporal relations between temporal events.

He did, however, go further in his reflections on time. Neoplatonic thought had always treated time in close relation to the soul, and Augustine could scarcely avoid discussing this topic. The reality of the past and of the future puzzled him: Can what is not yet but will be, and what is no longer but has been, be said to *be*? If not, then only the present has any reality. But if only the present is real, then reality shrinks to a dimensionless point at which the future is becoming the past. Augustine resolved the whole problem by locating time in the mind and adopting at the end of his discussion, though with hesitation, a definition of time as "extension [*distentio*], I am not sure of what, probably of the mind itself" (*Confessions* XI, 26, 33).

Another question that the doctrine of creation raised for Augustine concerns the natural activity, functioning, and development of creatures. This problem arose from the need to harmonize the story of the creation of the world in seven days or, according to an alternative version, at once, with the fact that some things came into existence only after the creation took place. Augustine's solution of this problem lay essentially in asserting that God created different things in different conditions; some left his hands complete and ready-made, others in a potential or latent state, awaiting the right conditions and environment for their full development. The latter are analogous to seeds, which are thought of as containing in themselves the fully developed plant in potency; and on this analogy, and using the traditional vocabulary, Augustine called these potentialities for later development "seminal reasons" (*rationes seminales,* or *causales*).

Apart from helping him to resolve the apparent contradiction between the belief in a primordial creation and the concept of continued development as a process of natural causality, this theory of "seminal reasons" also prompted Augustine at least to begin to feel his way toward some conception of nature and natural causality. At times, he comes very close to the later medieval distinction between the "First Cause" and the whole range of "second causes," the distinction according to which things depend in different senses both on God (the First Cause) and on their own immediate or distant created causes. Augustine, too, tried to endow the world of created causes with a specific reality of its own, one distinct from the causal activity of God in the world. In this he did not quite succeed. His failure becomes apparent in his treatment of miracles. He did not treat these—as the Scholastics later did as effects of the First Cause (God) produced without the instrumentality of second causes. He allowed the distinction between the two orders of causality (which he had never clearly formulated and which is hinted at, rather than stated, in his writings) to disintegrate during his discussion of miracles. In this context the very idea of "nature" is so widened as to include the miraculous within its scope. Miracles do not contradict the order of nature; they contradict only our idea of this order, an idea based on our restricted view and limited experience. They are not against nature, since nature is God's will; they are only against nature as it is known to us. The distinction between nature and miracle vanishes here, and in his well-known chapter in *The City of God* (X, 12) they become synonymous to the extent that nature itself and man, its crown, become the greatest miracles of all.

INDIVIDUALS IN SOCIETY

Society was not one of the subjects that loomed large in Augustine's earlier thought. Such hints as he gives us of his conception of society in his earlier works (those written before the mid-390s) suggest that he thought that organized human society and the state were part of the worldly dispensation whereby man is assisted to fulfill his destiny. A properly ordered society, like a properly ordered moral life, is a stage on the way to man's ultimate destination in eternity; and as far as Augustine's hints enable us to tell, he expected a properly ordered society to reflect, particularly by means of its legal institutions, the perfection of the eternal, intelligible world.

In step with his theological development, however, his views on human society underwent profound changes, and by the time that society became an important theme in his reflection, especially in his great work *The City of God* (written 413–427), these views had been radically transformed. An important factor in the course of this transformation was the increasing stress Augustine had come to lay on the power of sin in human life and in all earthly institutions, on man's need for redemption through Christ, and on his need for grace. In the most general terms Augustine came to see man's destiny and his realization of it more in terms of the scriptural pattern of a redemption-history and less in terms of the Neoplatonic theme of the ascent of the soul. Accordingly, human society came to be understood more in terms of its horizontal, historical relationships within the divine plan for men's salvation and less in terms of what we might call its vertical relationship to the intelligible world.

The first event in the course of the biblical redemption-history, man's fall from grace through Adam's sin, is of decisive importance for Augustine's changed attitude to organized human society. To live in society, according to Augustine, was natural to humans; without society they would not be able to realize fully their human potentialities, and the company of their fellow human beings was necessary to them. This, he held, was as true before man's fall as after; even in his state of primal innocence, in full possession of his nature prior to its distortion by sin, man was a social animal by nature; even the life of the blessed in heaven is a social life. But although Augustine believed that man's nature is social, he did not agree with Aristotle that it is also political. Politically organized society—the machinery of authority, government, and coercion—is, in Augustine's view, not natural to man. It was a useful and necessary arrangement for man in his fallen condition, and indeed the purpose of political society was to remedy at least some of the evils attendant upon man's fallen state. Its function was to check the social disorder and disintegration that followed from the general loss of order at the Fall. The institutions of government, the subjection of governed to government, and the coercive power of political authority over its subjects are thus but one instance of the subjection of man to man, and this was something that, Augustine held, did not exist in man's primal state of innocence. No slavery, servitude, or subjection could exist in that state of natural integrity; these things make sense only if understood as God's punishment for the sin that incurred the loss of integrity and, at the same time, as his dispensation for coping with the needs of man's condition in his new, fallen state.

Augustine used the traditional language of Christian theology to state his view of political society. For reasons to be considered below, he never drew out, at least not explicitly, the full implications of this view. In this view of society, however, the legitimate functions of the state are very much more restricted in scope than in theories according to which man is by nature a political animal. In Augustine's view, the state's sphere is confined to the requirements of social order and welfare; the individual's ultimate welfare and eternal destiny lie outside its realm of competence, whereas they are very much a part of the state's interest if the state is thought of as an ordinance of nature, as an indispensable means of man's realizing his ultimate destiny. In Augustine's estimate, the task of the state in the economy of salvation would be rather to establish the conditions in which men may work out their own salvation in relative peace and security than actively to promote their individual salvation through legislation and coercion.

The state was, for Augustine, synonymous with the Roman Empire; and having revised his ideas on the state in terms of the large categories of the scriptural redemption-history, he had inevitably to take the measure of the state he knew in this same perspective. Here his ideas make sense only if seen as a rejection of views of the empire generally current among Christians during the fourth century, after the adoption of Christianity by the emperors. The empire, represented as eternal ever since Vergil's day, was now widely regarded among Christians as an essential instrument of divine purpose in history, bound up with the possibility of salvation and destined to last until the end of time. It had been taken up into the dimension of the biblical redemption-history. The sack of Rome by the Visigoths in 410 gave a profound shock to this mentality. It led Augustine, whose mind had already moved a long way from the popular picture, to devote his greatest work, *The City of God,* to a reappraisal of the empire's place in the divine providential plan. The upshot was that the empire was no longer allowed an eternal destiny and was removed from the dimension of the redemption-history; the possibility of salvation was not necessarily bound up with it as a means of God's grace. It was simply one of a series of empirical, historic societies. The eternal categories of sin and holiness, of salvation and reprobation, did not apply to it or, indeed, to any other human assembly; they were embodied only in what Augustine called the earthly city and the heavenly city.

The two "cities" consist, respectively, of those predestined to eternal glory and those predestined to eternal torment or, as Augustine also defined them (clearly intending the various definitions to be equivalent), of those who live according to God and those who live according to man, of the altruistic and the selfish, of those whose love is upright and those whose love is perverse, and so forth. In none of these senses, however, have the two "cities" any discernible reality as communities until their final separation at the Last Judgment. In all discernible human communities they are inextricably intertwined. Here again we may see Augustine's modest estimate of the state's function, for when he discusses it in this context, the realm of the state is identified with the sphere in which the concerns of the two cities overlap. Its task is to secure the temporal peace: the order, security, and material welfare that both the wicked and the righteous cities require during their earthly careers. Its concern is with specifically communal, public matters affecting all its members. Citizens of the heavenly city will not, of course, be content with the welfare and peace thus secured: They will use these things but refer their use to the ultimate enjoyment of a peace beyond the terrestrial.

The general tendency of these views of Augustine's was to undermine the extremely close links that had come to exist between the empire and the Christian church, especially during his own lifetime. He was clearly ill at ease with the current representations of this relationship; but there were considerable pressures working on the minds of his contemporaries to keep them active, and Augustine himself was not exempt from their operation. In the course of the struggle with the Donatist movement in north Africa, a dissenting movement increasingly repressed by the imperial authorities, he came gradually and reluctantly to give his consent to the coercive measures that were being brought into use against the movement. His endorsement of these means of repression ran counter to the most fundamental direction of his thought. Although his endorsement must be regarded as a development in his practical, pastoral, and political attitudes rather than as a reversal of his basic views on the nature of political society, it left deep marks on those views. In later centuries his use of the Gospel phrase "Compel them to come in" (*Coge intrare*—Luke 19:23) and its consecration of repression, persecution, and coercion paved the way to much tragedy. It also helped to obscure the most profound and most original of his contributions to Christian political thinking.

See also Neoplatonism.

Bibliography

The most complete and generally reliable Latin edition of Augustine's works is the edition by the Benedictines of Saint-Maur (1679–1700). It supersedes all earlier editions and was reprinted in J. P. Migne's *Patrologia Latina*, Vols. 32–46 (Paris, 1841–1842), with some unfortunate variants and errors. It is also the basis of the texts of the works now being published in *Bibliothèque augustinienne* (with French translation and useful notes). Modern critical editions of many works exist, mainly in *Corpus Scriptorum Ecclesiasticorum Latinorum* (Vienna) and *Corpus Christianorum*. Details are in E. Dekkers, "Clavis Patrum Latinorum," in *Sacris Eruditi* 3 (1962).

English translations of many works appear in various series, such as Loeb Classical Library, Library of the Fathers, Select Library of Nicene and Post-Nicene Fathers of the Christian Church, Library of Christian Classics, The Fathers of the Church, Ancient Christian Writers, and the Catholic University of America Patristic Studies. A detailed, convenient, and fairly up-to-date list of translations is included in the bibliography by J. J. O'Meara appended to Marrou's *Saint Augustine*.

Of short introductory works, the best is H. I. Marrou, *Saint Augustine* (London: Longmans, 1957), translated from the French in the series Men of Wisdom. It contains a brief biography and a discerning characterization of Augustine's thought by a great scholar, as well as a selection of illustrative texts in translation. R. W. Battenhouse et al., *A Companion to the Study of St. Augustine* (New York: Oxford University Press, 1955), has been superseded by G. Bonner, *St. Augustine of Hippo: Life and Controversies* (London: SCM Press, 1963), as a survey and guide to Augustine's career and literary output. An essential to understanding Augustine in the setting of contemporary education and culture is H. I. Marrou, *Saint Augustine et la fin de la culture antique* (Paris, 1938), completed by his *Retractatio* (Paris, 1949). On Augustine as a bishop, see F. van der Meer, *Augustine the Bishop* (London: Sheed and Ward, 1962).

Among the many books on Augustine's intellectual development and his conversion, P. Alfaric, *L'évolution intellectuelle de saint Augustin* (Paris: Nourry, 1918), stands behind much of the subsequent controversy; C. Boyer, *Christianisme et néo-Platonisme dans la formation de saint Augustin* (Paris: Beauchesne, 1920), is one of the best-balanced replies provoked by it. P. Courcelle, *Recherches sur les Confessions de Saint Augustin* (Paris, 1950), has put the problem on new footing altogether; it is further pursued, with qualifications, by J. J. O'Meara, *The Young Augustine* (London: Longmans Green, 1954).

Of the philosophical aspects of Augustine's thought, the best general account is E. Gilson, *The Christian Philosophy of Saint Augustine*, translated by L. E. M. Lynch (New York: Random House, 1960). See also the survey by R. A. Markus in *Critical History of Western Philosophy*, edited by D. J. O'Connor (New York: Free Press of Glencoe, 1964).

On particular aspects, see C. Boyer, *L'idée de vérité dans la philosophie de saint Augustin* (Paris, 1941); J. Guitton, *Le temps et l'éternité chez Plotin et saint Augustin*, 2nd ed. (Paris, 1955); and E. Dinkler, *Die Anthropologie Augustins* (Stuttgart, 1934), on the topics named in their titles. M. Schmaus, *Die psychologische Trinitätslehre des heiligen Augustinus* (Münster, 1907), is the classic work on Augustine's theory of mind and the Trinitarian speculations based on it. Also valuable on his theory of knowledge are J. Hessen, *Augustins Metaphysik der Erkenntnis*, 2nd printing (Berlin, 1960), and R. Jolivet, *Dieu soleil des esprits* (Paris: Desclée, de Brouwer, 1934).

On ethical topics, see J. Mausbach, *Die Ethik des heiligen Augustins* (Freiburg, 1909); T. Deman, *Le traitement scientifique de la morale chrétienne selon saint Augustin* (Paris, 1957); J. Burnaby, *Amor Dei* (London: Hodder and Stoughton, 1938); and R. Holte, *Béatitude et sagesse: Saint Augustin et le problème de la fin de l'homme dans la philosophie ancienne* (Paris, 1962). On the state and society the least unsatisfactory accounts are Herbert A. Deane, *The Political and Social Ideas of Saint Augustine* (New York: Columbia University Press, 1963) and the short treatment by N. H. Baynes, *The Political Ideas of St. Augustine's De Civitate Dei* (London: G. Bell, 1936).

Many of the most important recent articles on Augustine are to be found in one of the following collections: *Augustinus Magister: Communications et actes du Congrès international augustinien* (Paris: Études Augustiniennes, 1954); *Recherches augustiniennes,* Vols. I and II (Paris: Études Augustiniennes, 1958–1963); *Studia Patristica,* Vol. VI, edited by F. L. Cross; *Texte und Untersuchungen zur Geschichte der altchristlichen Literatur* 81 (1962); and in the quarterly journal *Revue des études augustiniennes.*

The most up-to-date and best-selected bibliography is *Bibliographia Augustiniana,* appended to C. Andresen, ed., *Zum Augustin-Gespräch der Gegenwart* (Darmstadt, 1962), which is Vol. V in the series *Wege der Forschung.* Gilson's book (see above), in which the classified selection of the original is replaced by an alphabetical list in the English translation; B. Altaner, *Patrologie,* 5th printing (1958); and O. Bardenhewer, *Geschichte der altchristlichen Literatur,* Vol. IV (Freiburg, 1924; reprinted 1962), also have good bibliographies. Current literature is surveyed in the bibliographical supplements to *Revue des études augustiniennes.*

R. A. Markus (1967)

AUGUSTINE, ST. [ADDENDUM 1]

St. Augustine continues to elicit scholarly discussions of theological issues, but there is an ever-growing number of studies devoted to historical and philosophical issues in their own right. Recent philosophical work has concentrated on deepening our understanding of his arguments, assessing the adequacy of his positions, and contextualizing them in a historically informed way.

P. Brown, *Augustine of Hippo: A Biography* (London: Faber, 1967), is a masterful work that situates Augustine in his social and historical surroundings. Accessible overviews of Augustine's life and thought are provided in J. J. O'Donnell, *Augustine* (Boston, 1985), and H. Chadwick, *Augustine* (Oxford: Oxford University Press, 1986). Our understanding of Augustine's autobiography has been greatly advanced by the fine commentary given in J.

J. O'Donnell, *Augustine: Confessions* (3 vols., Oxford, 1992).

Augustine is seen against the background of classical philosophy in J. Rist, *Augustine: Ancient Thought Baptized* (Cambridge, U.K.: Cambridge University Press., 1994), which provides a guide to Augustine's philosophical views. Another introduction to Augustine as a philosopher is C. Kirwan, *Augustine* (London: Routledge, 1989), which takes up selected topics in detail. The bibliographies of both these works should be consulted as a guide to the literature. Articles on a variety of topics are usefully collected in R. A. Markus (ed.), *Augustine: A Collection of Critical Essays* (London, 1972); there has been no anthology for philosophers as of this writing.

Turning now to particular aspects of Augustine's philosophy, G. J. P. O'Daly, *Augustine's Philosophy of Mind* (London, 1987), and G. Matthews, *Thought's Ego in Augustine and Descartes* (Ithaca, NY: Cornell University Press, 1992), deal with his philosophical psychology. Epistemology and the theory of illumination are the primary focus of R. H. Nash, *The Light of the Mind: St. Augustine's Theory of Knowledge* (Lexington: University Press of Kentucky, 1969); B. Bubacz, *St. Augustine's Theory of Knowledge: A Contemporary Analysis* (New York: E. Mellen Press, 1981); U. Wienbruch, *Erleuchtete Einsicht: Zur Erkenntnislehre Augustins* (Bonn: Bouvier, 1989). Metaphysical problems as well as the issue of Augustine's indebtedness to Plotinus are treated in R. J. O'Connell, *The Origin of the Soul in St. Augustine's Later Works* (New York: Fordham University Press, 1987). Augustine's account of time is analyzed in R. Sorabji, *Time, Creation, and the Continuum* (Ithaca, NY: Cornell University Press, 1983), and subjected to a wide-ranging examination in J. Pelikan, *The Mystery of Continuity: Time and History, Memory and Eternity in the Thought of Saint Augustine* (Charlottesville: University Press of Virginia, 1986). Philosophy of language is discussed by M. Burnyeat, "Wittgenstein and Augustine *de Magistro,*" in *Proceedings of the Aristotelian Society* (1987, supp. vol.). Augustine's ethical theory is the subject of J. Wetzel, *Augustine and the Limits of Virtue* (Cambridge, U.K.: Cambridge University Press, 1992), and discussed in G. R. Evans, *Augustine on Evil* (Cambridge, U.K.: Cambridge University Press, 1982). A recent philosophical study of Augustine's views on freedom, weakness of will, and voluntary action is T. Chappell, *Aristotle and Augustine on Freedom* (New York: St. Martin's Press, 1995). R. Coles, *Self/Power/Other: Political Theory and Dialogical Ethics* (Ithaca, NY: Cornell University Press, 1992), offers a Foucaultian account of Augustine's political philosophy.

A bibliography of works through 1970 is provided in C. Andresen, *Bibliographia Augustiniana* (Darmstadt: Wissenschaftliche Buchgesellschaft, 1973); the next decade of Augustinian studies is covered in T. Miethe, *Augustinian Bibliography, 1970–1980* (Westport, CT: Greenwood Press, 1982).

See also Determinism and Freedom; Metaethics; Philosophy of Language; Plotinus; Time; Time, Being, and Becoming.

Peter King (1996)

AUGUSTINE, ST. [ADDENDUM2]

Augustine thought that what pleases people in beauty is design: "And in design, dimensions; and in dimensions, number" (*De Ordine* ch. 15). Beauty is ultimately a matter of numerical proportion. Rhythm, too, is based on numerical proportions (*De Musica* Book 6). Augustine sees numeric proportions as eternal and divine, yet at the same time he hints that the soul itself may be "the very number by which all things are numbered" (*De Ordine* ch. 15). If so, then he locates the source of all Beauty within the human soul, and this inner Beauty could be one of God's traces in the world.

See also Aesthetic Judgment; Beauty; Number.

Bibliography

Beardsley, Monroe C. *Aesthetics from Classical Greece to the Present: A Short History.* New York: Macmillan, 1966.

Paul Thom (2005)

AUGUSTINIANISM

"Augustinianism" may be described as that complex of philosophical ideas that reflected to a greater or lesser degree the philosophy of Augustine. Many of the philosophers who came after Augustine not only restated his leading ideas but also frequently modified them with their own interpretations. Such interpretations were often the result of the impact of other schools of thought, notably the Avicennian and the Aristotelian. Occasionally doctrines that were only implicit in Augustine—for instance, the plurality of forms and universal hylomorphism—were made explicit and assumed considerable importance. Thus there originated in the medieval period

what has been termed the Augustinian tradition, which in the later years of its development was closely identified with the Franciscan order. Such a tradition dominated medieval thought to the time of Thomas Aquinas. After Thomas it gradually disintegrated owing to the impact of Thomism and a resurgent Aristotelianism, and no longer represented a distinctive school or tradition. It continued, however, to be influential to the extent that it inspired or characterized in varying degrees later medieval and modern philosophers. The principal theses of Augustinianism will be discussed under seven headings.

FAITH AND UNDERSTANDING

The relationship between faith and understanding (or reason), with the implications of such a relationship for philosophy and theology, and the conception of Christian wisdom and Christian mysticism are central in the structure of Augustinian philosophy. One of the most influential and significant expressions of the relation between faith and understanding in Augustinian thought is summarized in the famous maxim of Anselm: *Credo ut intelligam* (I believe in order to understand). Peter Abelard similarly expressed the idea of the primacy of faith over understanding in his comments on the function of philosophy: "I do not want to be a philosopher if it is necessary to deny Paul. I do not want to be Aristotle if it is necessary to be separated from Christ. 'For there is no other name under heaven given to men, whereby we must be saved.'" With Roger Bacon the relationship of philosophy and theology is profoundly Augustinian. A conservative theologian despite his enthusiasm for scientific method and experimentation, he was convinced that the highest wisdom is found in Scripture and that philosophy exists only to explicate that wisdom. A similar theme is developed by Bonaventure in his *De Reductione Artium ad Theologiam.* He declared that all the sciences and philosophy should be subordinated to theology, which in turn must be subordinated to faith and the love of God; for faith alone enables man to avoid error and attain a union with God. Other philosophers of the Middle Ages who accepted this primacy of faith over reason and the complete subordination of philosophy to theology were Alexander of Hales, John of La Rochelle, Matthew of Aquasparta, and Roger Marston.

PSYCHOLOGY

The Augustinian psychology is characterized by the definition of man as a soul using a body and the implication of this definition for the relation of soul and body. The soul is regarded as an image of the Trinity and is said to have a direct knowledge of itself. Hugh of St. Victor is notably Augustinian, not only in his mysticism but also in his identification of the soul with man and his belief that we have a direct knowledge of the soul and its spirituality. The union of soul and body he described as one of "apposition" rather than composition. Similarly, William of Auvergne is Augustinian in his account of man as a soul using the body, his affirmation of the presence of the soul in all parts of the body, and his statement that: "No knowledge is more natural to the soul than the knowledge of its own self." The mysticism of Bonaventure is characterized by the notion of the journey of the soul to God, the presence of the Trinity in the soul of man, and the direct knowledge the soul has of itself. This principle that the soul has a direct knowledge of itself is characteristic of both the Augustinian psychology and the Augustinian theory of knowledge. It has been termed the "principle of interiorization." Augustine expressed it: "For what is so present to knowledge as that which is present to mind? Or what is so present to the mind as the mind itself?" In modern philosophy the principle of interiority was to have significant influence upon writers like René Descartes, Blaise Pascal, Tommaso Campanella, and Maurice Blondel.

EPISTEMOLOGY

The Augustinian theory of knowledge had an extensive influence upon medieval philosophers, but it was frequently compromised with Aristotelianism. This was particularly true with respect to the Augustinian theory that sensation is essentially an act of the soul. However, the theory of the divine illumination, in conjunction with the doctrine of exemplary ideas, and the concept of truth as identified with God and present to, but superior to, all minds had a much stronger influence; but it, too, was often qualified with an Aristotelian theory of knowledge. Anselm held that truth is based on the Divine Ideas that are one with God. William of Auvergne accepted the doctrine of divine illumination but interpreted it as giving us an intuitive knowledge of the intelligible forms. Robert Grosseteste combined the Augustinian theory of the divine illumination with an empirical approach in science; he regarded truth as the conformity of a thing with its divine exemplar. Roger Bacon considered divine illumination as an inspiration, and he compared the divine action in illumination to that of the active intellect. Alexander of Hales combined the theory of divine illumination with an Aristotelian theory of abstraction. John of La Rochelle also combined the two theories of knowledge, especially the notion of the active intellect and the

divine illumination. Bonaventure and Matthew of Aquasparta also modified the Augustinian theory of knowledge. The former accepted an Aristotelian account of sense knowledge and abstraction, of the existence of a possible and an active intellect, as well as the Augustinian concept of the necessity of the divine illumination for the attainment of truth. Matthew modified the Augustinian theory of sensation. On the other hand, Roger Marston and Peter Olivi followed closely Augustine's theory of knowledge. Among modern philosophers, the Augustinian doctrine of divine illumination was particularly influential with such philosophers as Nicolas Malebranche, Antonio Rosmini-Serbati, and Vincenzo Gioberti.

RATIONES SEMINALES

The conception of the *rationes seminales* (physical powers or "seeds") that Augustine postulated as potentially present in matter in order to explain the origin of creatures after the creation of the six days reappeared most markedly in the philosophical systems of the Augustinians of the thirteenth century.

HYLOMORPHISM AND PLURALITY OF FORMS

Hylomorphism and plurality of forms were doctrines that were developed from the thought of Augustine. The latter is said to have appeared first in Grosseteste's metaphysics of light and his analysis of bodies as possessing a number of different forms—for instance, the forms of elements, plants, animals. The highest form possessed by any body he held to be light, which was designated as the "form of corporeity." This notion of a plurality of forms was widely accepted by Augustinians after Grosseteste and is particularly prominent in the philosophies of Bonaventure, Raymond Lull, and John Duns Scotus. Generally it appears with its corollary universal hylomorphism, which states that all creatures are composed of matter and form. Thus angelic beings and human souls were said to be composed of a form and a spiritual matter. These doctrines enabled philosophers like Bonaventure and Duns Scotus to maintain more effectively their conception of the completeness of the substantial character of the human soul apart from the body. The Franciscan school strongly supported both doctrines. Robert Kilwardby and John Peckham in particular appealed to the plurality of forms in their vigorous opposition to the Thomistic doctrine of the oneness of man's substantial form.

THE MEANING OF HISTORY

Augustine rejected emphatically the cyclical conception of history as expressed in the Christian revelation and the doctrines of the Incarnation and salvation. History is a part of the divine plan and providence, and reflects the presence of the divine reason. The divine dispensation of grace gives hope to humankind and makes it possible for him to attain his eternal beatitude in the City of God after his pilgrimage in the earthly city. Few medieval philosophers escaped the influence of this Augustinian conception. It is particularly noticeable in the work of Dante Alighieri and in Roger Bacon's idea of a Christian republic. It influenced such later philosophers as Campanella, Jacques Bossuet, and Gottfried Wilhelm Leibniz. And it is indirectly represented in modern secularized versions of the idea of progress and social utopias.

ETHICS OF CHARITY AND SUPERIORITY OF THE WILL

The ethics of charity and the principle of the superiority of the will over the intellect in man as formulated by Augustine were important in the development of religious thought. The former, with its correlative doctrines of grace, election, and predestination, is essentially a religious ethic. It found universal acceptance within the Franciscan school and exerted considerable influence on all medieval theology and ethics. It affected such later thinkers as Martin Luther and John Calvin. The principle of the primacy of the will is reflected in Bonaventure insistence upon the need for moral as well as intellectual illumination. Richard of Middleton held that the will is a faculty that determines itself without being determined by any other faculty. Duns Scotus asserted that the will is free, whereas the intellect is determined by that which is known. The will is the nobler of the two faculties and commands the intellect.

See also Augustine, St.

Bibliography

Cary, Phillip. *Augustine's Invention of the Inner Self.* Oxford: Oxford University Press, 2000.

Cayré, F. "Augustinisme (développement de l')," *Note complémentaire, "Tables générales," Dictionnaire de théologie catholique,* Vol. 2, cols. 317–324. Paris, 1953.

Congrès international augustinien, *Augustinus Magister.* 3 vols. Paris, 1954.

Copleston, F. *History of Philosophy.* Vols. 2 and 3. London: Burns, Oates, and Washbourne, 1950.

Fitzgerald, Alan D. *Augustine through the Ages: An Encyclopedia.* Grand Rapids, MI: Eerdmans, 1999.

Gilson, E. *The Christian Philosophy of St. Augustine.* New York: Random House, 1960.

Gilson, E. *History of Christian Philosophy in the Middle Ages.* New York: Random House, 1955.

Kirwan, Christopher. *Augustine.* London: Routledge, 1989.

Marrou, Henri. *St. Augustine and His Influence through the Ages.* New York, 1958.

Matthews, Gareth B. *Augustine.* Oxford: Blackwell, 2005.

Matthews, Gareth B., ed. *The Augustinian Tradition.* Berkeley: California Press, 1999.

Matthews, Gareth B. *Thought's Ego in Augustine and Descartes.* Ithaca, NY: Cornell University Press, 1992.

Menn, Stephen. *Descartes and Augustine.* Cambridge, U.K.: Cambridge University Press, 1998.

Miscellanea agostiniana: testi e studii. Rome, 1930.

O'Daly, Gerard. *Augustine's Philosophy of Mind.* London: Duckworth, 1987.

Portalié, E. *A Guide to the Thought of St. Augustine.* Chicago: Regnery, 1960.

Rist, John M. *Augustine: Ancient Thought Baptized.* Cambridge, U.K.: Cambridge University Press, 1994.

Rondet, H. *Saint Augustine parmi nous.* Paris, 1954.

Rottmanner, O. *Der Augustinismus.* Munich, 1892.

Stump, Eleonore, and Norman Kretzmann, eds. *The Cambridge Companion to Augustine.* Cambridge, U.K.: Cambridge University Press, 2001.

Wetzel, James. *Augustine and the Limits of Virtue.* Cambridge, U.K.: Cambridge University Press, 1992.

John A. Mourant (1967)
Bibliography updated by Gareth Matthews (2005)

AUREOL, PETER

See *Peter Aureol*

AUSTIN, JOHN
(1790–1859)

John Austin, the most influential English legal philosopher of the analytical school, was born in London; at the age of sixteen he enlisted in the army and served five years, resigning his commission to study law. He was called to the bar in 1818. The following year he married Sarah Taylor, a woman of great intelligence and beauty, to whom many distinguished men of the age were deeply devoted.

The Austins became neighbors of Jeremy Bentham and the Millses and for twelve years remained closely associated with individuals in the Benthamite circle. The practice of law held little appeal for Austin, whose interests were primarily scholarly and theoretical; and after seven years he gave it up. In 1826, on the founding of the

University of London by the Benthamites with whom he had been closely associated for years, he was offered its chair in jurisprudence. He accepted with enthusiasm and immediately began to prepare himself by establishing his family in Bonn, where he taught himself German and studied the newly discovered *Institutes* of Gaius; the *Pandects*; and the works of Gustav Hugo, Anton Friedrich Justus Thibaut, and Friedrich Karl von Savigny. Some of the finest young minds in England—John Stuart Mill, George Cornewall Lewis, Sir John Romilly, and Sir William Erie among them—attended the first series of lectures at London. *The Province of Jurisprudence Determined,* published in 1832, is an expanded version of the first part of these lectures. Apart from this work, Austin published in his lifetime only two articles and a pamphlet attacking reform, *A Plea for the Constitution.* Austin, who once remarked, "I was born out of my time and place—I ought to have been a schoolman of the twelfth century—or a German professor," never again reached the high point of his first year at London. Student interest declined, and the chair, which had been supported by student fees, was given up by Austin in 1832 for financial reasons. His wife tells us that this was "the real and irremediable calamity of his life—the blow from which he never recovered." Plagued by illness and self-distrust, he served a brief and frustrating period, beginning in 1833, on the Criminal Law Commission; and later, with more satisfaction, he served as royal commissioner of Malta. During his remaining twenty years Austin spent some time on the Continent and a final period in Weybridge, not far from London, which proved to be the quietest and most contented part of his life. The second edition of the *The Province* was published in 1861, two years after his death. The first complete edition of *The Lectures on Jurisprudence or The Philosophy of Positive Law,* reconstructed from his notes by his wife, was published in 1863.

Both the nature and the results of Austin's inquiry deserve attention. What are the characteristics of his inquiry? First, his aim was to keep rigorously separate two questions that had formerly been confused, with much practical harm resulting: What is law? And what ought the law to be? Austin wished to lay a solid foundation for answering the second question by clarifying the first. His answer to the second question was along strictly utilitarian lines. Second, his inquiry was analytical rather than empirical. He was concerned with the analysis of concepts, not, for example, with historical or sociological questions. Finally, connected with the preceding analysis, he hoped to provide a general theory of law—"General jurisprudence"—whose concepts would permit us to grasp the essential features of any legal system without describing any particular system; this task of description was reserved for "particular jurisprudence."

What were the results of Austin's inquiry into the nature of law? The province of jurisprudence, the subject matter selected for study, is law "strictly so-called," or positive law, as contrasted, for example, with divine law (related to it by analogy) or physical laws of nature (related to it by metaphor). Positive law is a rule set for subjects by a sovereign in a politically independent society. A major part of *The Province* consists of analyses of the concepts in this explanatory definition. A rule is a species of command; it is a command that obliges the performance of a class of actions. A command is an expression or intimation of a wish that another do or forbear from doing some act, coupled with the ability and intention to inflict harm in case of noncompliance. The command concept, the key to the science of jurisprudence for Austin, encompasses the concept of a sanction (the evil that will probably be incurred in case of noncompliance), the concept of superiority (the power of forcing compliance with one's wishes), and the concept of obligation or duty (sometimes, for Austin, one is "obliged" because one fears the sanction, sometimes when one is "liable" to the sanction). A sovereign is that person or group of persons receiving habitual obedience from most members of a given society but not in turn having a like habit of obedience to a superior. An independent political society is one in which most members of the society have a habit of obedience to some person or group of persons who have no such habit of obedience to another.

Austin addressed his first class at London in these words: "Frankness is the highest compliment … I therefore entreat you, as the greatest favour you can do me, to demand explanation and ply me with objections—turn me inside out." Legal philosophers have paid him this compliment. His method and his results have come in for severe and often valid criticism. The inadequacies of Austin's theory result mainly from his selecting as basic tools of analysis the concepts of a command and habitual obedience. The former cannot account for certain commonly accepted features of law. It fails, first, to explain the varied content of laws, for if we view all law as an order or command backed by threats, we neglect those many laws that do not impose duties but, rather, function in a variety of ways. It also fails to account for the range of persons to whom laws are normally applicable, for orders are addressed to others, whereas most laws bind those who have enacted them as well as those who have not. Next, orders are deliberate datable events; only with much stretching of meaning and introduction of fictions (the sovereign commands what he permits) can they account for the legal status of customary law and the decisions of the courts. Finally, the concept of a command leads Austin to the erroneous claim that one has a legal obligation because one fears the sanction.

The peculiar deficiency of a concept that links the law to habitual obedience is that serious difficulties are encountered in accounting for either the continuity of legal authority or the persistence of law. With the concept of habitual obedience alone, we should be unable to explain the common legal phenomena of one person's succeeding another in the authority to legislate or of laws that remain obligatory long after the legislator and those who habitually obeyed him are dead. Finally, focusing on coercion as the essence of law prevented Austin from developing sufficiently the connections that law has with morality, connections that make understandable one's moral obligation to obey the law.

In addition to these criticisms, Austin has been charged with lack of originality, even in his fundamental mistakes, for identical views may be found in Thomas Hobbes and Bentham. Bryce commented, "Bentham … drops plenty of good things as he goes along. Austin is barren." It is understandable that we should wonder at Austin's great influence, and his reputation as a great legal philosopher.

First, Austin's positivism, his insistence on separating questions of fact and value, has made legal philosophers sensitive to how easily these questions may be confused and how we may, as a result, delude ourselves into thinking we have answered one of these questions when we have, in fact, answered the other. Even more important, Austin's failures, all associated in some way with his imperativism, have been helpful. He was not alone in feeling the grip of a certain idea, the idea that law is simply the impressing of the will of the stronger upon the weaker. Austin's chief virtue was that he systematically developed, defended, and refined this idea, stripping it of excess philosophical baggage. In doing this he enabled us to focus with greater precision on those features of law that connect it with coercion. More than this, his model presses us to remark upon its limitations, the respects in which viewing law as coercion obscures its complicated role in our lives. After Austin, we understand better what there is in law that connects it with coercion and what there is in law that does not. This is his principal legacy. He provides one more instance in philosophy of our

gaining something from a false statement that we might not have gained from a true one.

See also Bentham, Jeremy; Hobbes, Thomas; Legal Positivism; Mill, John Stuart; Philosophy of Law, Problems of; Savigny, Friedrich Karl von.

Bibliography

WORKS BY AUSTIN

Lectures on Jurisprudence, 5th ed., 2 vols. London: Murray, 1885.

The Province of Jurisprudence Determined. Introduction by H. L. A. Hart. London: Weidenfeld and Nicolson, 1954.

WORKS ON AUSTIN

Brown, Jethro. *The Austinian Theory of Law.* London: Murray, 1906.

Bryce, James. *Studies in History and Jurisprudence,* Vol. II. Oxford: Clarendon Press, 1901.

Hart, H. L. A. *The Concept of Law.* Oxford: Clarendon Press, 1961.

Maine, Henry. *Early History of Institutions.* London: Murray, 1875, Chs. XII and XIII.

Mill, J. S. *Dissertations and Discussions,* Vol. III. London: Longmans, 1867.

Morison, W. L. "Some Myths about Positivism." *Yale Law Journal* 68 (1958): 212–233.

Morris, Herbert. "Verbal Disputes and the Legal Philosophy of John Austin." *UCLA Law Review* 7 (1960): 27–56.

Herbert Morris (1967)
Bibliography updated by Philip Reed (2005)

AUSTIN, JOHN LANGSHAW
(1911–1960)

John Langshaw Austin was White's professor of moral philosophy at Oxford from 1952 until his death in 1960. Educated at Shrewsbury School and Balliol College, Oxford, he became a fellow of All Souls College in 1933; in 1935 he moved to Magdalen College, where he taught with conspicuous success until elected to the White's chair. During World War II he served with distinction in the British Intelligence Corps; he attained the rank of lieutenant-colonel and was awarded the OBE and the Croix de Guerre, as well as being made an officer of the Legion of Merit.

In the years before the war Austin devoted a great deal of his time and energy to philosophical scholarship. He made himself an expert in the philosophy of Gottfried Wilhelm Leibniz and also did much work on Greek philosophy, especially Aristotle's ethical works. At this period his own thought, although notably acute and already distinctive in style, was largely critical and altogether lacked the positive approach that distinguished his postwar work. His one published paper belonging to this early period, "Are There *A Priori* Concepts?" very fairly represents the astringent style and outlook that gave him the reputation of being a rather terrifying person. According to Austin's own statements, it was not until the beginning of the war that he began to develop the outlook on philosophy and method of philosophizing that marked his mature work, and it is of this work alone that an account will be given.

AIMS AND METHODS

The practical exigencies of lecturing and the traditions of paper reading (especially in symposia, to which some of his important papers were contributions) prevented some of the most characteristic features of Austin's preferred methods and aims from being clearly and fully exemplified in his written work. Lecturing is essentially a solo effort, whereas Austin believed that the best way of doing philosophy was in a group, and papers, especially in symposia, are almost inevitably on topics of traditional philosophical interest, whereas Austin preferred to keep the traditional problems of philosophy in the background. We shall therefore start by giving some account of the method and aims that Austin always advocated and practiced, most notably in meetings held regularly on Saturday mornings in the Oxford term with a group of like-minded Oxford philosophers.

LANGUAGE. Austin did not present his aims and methods as the only proper ones for a philosopher; whatever one or two uncautious remarks in his British Academy lecture "Ifs and Cans" may suggest to the contrary, he did not claim more than that his procedures led to definite results and were a necessary preliminary for anyone who wished to undertake other kinds of philosophical investigation. But he certainly considered them so valuable and interesting in their results, and so suited to his own linguistically trained capabilities and tastes, that he never felt it necessary to investigate for himself what else a philosopher might usefully do. What he conceived of as the central task, the careful elucidation of the forms and concepts of ordinary language (as opposed to the language of philosophers, not to that of poets, scientists, or preachers) was, as Austin himself was well aware, not new but characteristic of countless philosophers from Socrates to G. E. Moore. Nor were the grounds for this activity especially novel. First, he claimed, it was only common prudence for anyone embarking on any kind of philosophical investigation, even one that might eventu-

ally involve the creation of a special technical vocabulary, to begin with an examination of the resources of the terminology already at one's disposal; clarification of ordinary language was thus the "begin-all," if not the "end-all," of any philosophical investigation. Second, he thought that the institution of language was in itself of sufficient interest to make it worthy of the closest study. Third, he believed that in general a clear insight into the many subtle distinctions that are enshrined in ordinary language and have survived in a lengthy struggle for existence with competing distinctions could hardly fail to be also an insight into important distinctions to be observed in the world around us—distinctions of an interest unlikely to be shared by any we might think up on our own unaided initiative in our professional armchairs.

It is not too soon to remove at this stage some common misconceptions about Austin's aims and methods. First, although he was not concerned with studying the technical terminology of philosophers, he had no objection in principle to such terms; he thought that many such technical terms had been introduced inappropriately and uncritically, as is clear from his discussion, in *Sense and Sensibilia,* of the sense-datum terminology, but he used much of the traditional technical vocabulary of philosophy and added many technical terms of his own invention—as almost any page of *How to Do Things with Words* will bear witness. Second, Austin did not think that ordinary language was sacrosanct; he certainly thought it unlikely that hopelessly muddled uses of languages would survive very long and felt that they were more likely to occur in rather specialized and infrequently used areas of our vocabulary, but there was never any suggestion that language as we found it was incapable of improvement; all he asked was that we be clear about what it is like before we try to improve it.

TECHNIQUE. We have seen that there was nothing essentially novel in Austin's philosophical aims; what was new was the skill, the rigor, and the patience with which he pursued these aims. Here we are dealing with Austin's own personal gifts, which cannot be philosophically dissected. Nor did Austin have any theory of philosophical method; what he had was a systematic way of setting to work, something on a par with a laboratory technique rather than with a scientific methodology. This technique, unlike the skill with which he followed it, was quite public and one that he was willing and eager to employ in joint investigations with others, so we can easily give an account of it.

A philosopher or, preferably, a group of philosophers using this technique begins by choosing an area of discourse in which it is interested, often one germane to some great philosophical issue. The vocabulary of this area of discourse is then collected, first by thinking of and listing all the words belonging to it that one can—not just the most discussed words or those that at first sight seem most important—then by looking up synonyms and synonyms of synonyms in dictionaries, by reading the nonphilosophical literature of the field, and so on. Alongside the activity of collecting the vocabulary one notes expressions within which the vocabulary can legitimately occur and, still more important, expressions including the vocabulary that seem to be a priori plausible but that can nonetheless be recognized as unusable.

The next stage is to make up "stories" in which the legitimate words and phrases occur; in particular, one makes up stories in which it is clear that one can appropriately use one dictionary "synonym" but not another; such stories can also be found ready made in documents. In the light of these data one can then proceed to attempt to give some account of the meaning of the terms and their interrelationships that will explain the data. A particularly crucial point, which is a touchstone of success, is whether one's account of the matter will adequately explain why we cannot say the things that we have noted as "plausible" yet that in fact we would not say. At this stage, but not earlier, it becomes profitable to examine what other philosophers and grammarians have said about the same region of discourse. Throughout (and this is why Austin so much preferred to work in a group) the test to be employed of what can and what cannot be said is a reasonable consensus among the participants that this is so. Such a consensus, Austin found, could be obtained in an open-minded group most of the time; where such agreement cannot be obtained the fact should be noted as of possible significance. Austin regarded this method as empirical and scientific, one that could lead to definitely established results, but he admitted that "like most sciences, it is an art," and that a suitably fertile imagination was all important for success.

It was the lack of thoroughness, of sufficient research before generalization, in previous investigations of language, whether by those who called themselves grammarians or by those who called themselves philosophers, that Austin most deplored. He seriously hoped that a new science might emerge from the kind of investigations he undertook, a new kind of linguistics incorporating workers from both the existing linguistic and the philosophical fields. He pointed to other "new" sciences, such as

logic and psychology, both formerly parts of philosophy, as analogues and was indifferent about whether what he was doing "was really philosophy."

So much must suffice as an account of the method of work that Austin advocated. It has been based on a set of notes for an informal talk, characteristically titled "Something about One Way of Possibly Doing One Part of Philosophy." As Austin admitted in those notes, he had said most of this in his papers "A Plea for Excuses" and "Ifs and Cans," and to all who worked with him it was familiar from his practice. Although inevitably, as we have noted, this method could not be followed in writings (it is in any case a method of discovery and not of presentation), its use underlies and can be discerned in his published work. Thus, before writing "Words and Deeds" or *How to Do Things with Words* he went right through the dictionary making a list, which still survives, of all verbs that might be classed as "performative" in his terminology. The art of telling "your story" is amusingly illustrated over and over again in his paper "Pretending" and, indeed, in all his other published writings. His insistence that it is a mistake to dwell only on a few well-examined notions in a field of discourse is illustrated by his concentration on such notions as "mistake," "accident," and "inadvertence" (in "A Plea for Excuses") and on the use of "I can if I choose" (in "Ifs and Cans"), rather than on "responsibility" and "freedom," in his papers that have a bearing on the free-will problem. Similarly, when his Saturday morning group turned its attention to aesthetics Austin betrayed far more interest in the notions of dainty and dumpy milk jugs than in that of a beautiful picture.

WORK

It is not possible to give a systematic account of Austin's "philosophy," for he had none. His technique lent itself rather to a set of quite independent inquiries, the conclusions of none of which could serve as premises for a further inquiry; his discussions of the language of perception (in *Sense and Sensibilia*), the concept of pretending, the notion of truth, and the terminology of excuses were all based on the study of speech in those fields and not on any general principles or theories. Nor would it serve any useful purpose to attempt to summarize his various investigations one by one, since they depend so much for their interest and force on the detailed observations about language that they contain. It will be more useful to discuss, first, what he thought of as his main constructive work—the doctrine of illocutionary forces that arose out of his earlier distinction of performative and constative utterances, contained in *How to*

Do Things with Words—and, second, the application of his technique to the criticism of some traditional theories about perception as found in his *Sense and Sensibilia*.

THEORY OF ILLOCUTIONARY FORCES. Austin's theory of illocutionary forces arose from his observation that a considerable number of utterances, even those in the indicative mood, were such that in at least some contexts it would be impossible to characterize them as being true or false. Examples are "I name this ship the Saucy Sue" (which is part of the christening of a ship, and not a statement about the christening of a ship), "I promise to meet you at two o'clock" (which is the making of a promise and not the report of a promise or a statement about what will happen), and "I guarantee these eggs to be new-laid" (which is the giving of a guarantee and not a report of a guarantee). These utterances Austin called "performative," to indicate that they are the performance of some act and not the report of its performance; he did not speak as some do who purport to discuss his views, of "performative *verbs*," for the verb *promise* can well occur in reports—for example, "I promised to meet him." To provide the necessary contrast, Austin coined the technical term *constative* to apply to all those utterances that are naturally called true or false; he thought that *statement* and similar words often used by philosophers roughly as he used *constative* had in ordinary use too narrow a meaning to serve the purpose.

For a time Austin appears to have been fairly satisfied with this distinction, which he gave in print in his "Other Minds" article in 1946, using it to illuminate some features of utterances beginning "I know...." But although the distinction is clearly useful at a certain level, Austin began to doubt whether it was ultimately satisfactory. He found it impossible to give satisfactory criteria for distinguishing the performative from other utterances. The first person of the present indicative, which occurs in the three examples given above, is clearly not a necessary feature; "Passengers are warned to cross the tracks only by the bridge" is an act of warning as much as "I warn you to cross...." Further, in a suitable context "Don't cross the tracks except by the bridge" may also be an act of warning (as in another context it might be an act of commanding); this makes it necessary to distinguish the primative performative from the explicit performative, the latter, but not the former, making clear what act was being performed in its formulation.

Still more important, the constative seemed to collapse into the performative. Let us consider the four utterances "I warn you that a train is coming," "I guess that a train is coming," "I state that a train is coming," and "A train is coming." The first of these is an act of warning, the second is surely one of guessing, the third apparently one of stating, while the fourth may be any of these as determined by context. Thus, the various forms of constatives—stating, reporting, asserting, and the rest—seem to be merely a subgroup of performatives. It might seem that still one crucial difference remains, that while performative utterances may be in various ways unhappy (I may say "I promise to give you my watch" when I have not got a watch, or am speaking to an animal, or have no intention of handing the watch over), the characteristic and distinctive happiness or unhappiness of constatives is truth and falsehood, to which the other performatives are not liable.

In a brilliant, if not always immediately convincing, discussion (Lecture XI of *How to Do Things with Words*) Austin tried to break down even this distinction. First, we cannot contrast doing with saying, since (in addition to the trivial point that in stating one is performing the act of uttering words or the like) in constative utterances one is stating, describing, affirming, etc., and these acts are on a par with warning, promising, and so on. Second, all constatives are liable to all those kinds of infelicity that have been taken to be characteristic of performatives. Just as I should not promise to do something if I do not intend to do it, so I should not state that something is the case unless I believe it to be so; just as my act of selling an object is null and void if I do not possess it, so my act of stating that the king of France is bald is null and void if there is no king of France; just as I cannot order you to do something unless I am in a position to do so, so I cannot state what I am not in a position to state (I cannot *state*, though I can hazard a guess about, what you will do next year). Further, even if we grant that "true" and "false" are assessments specific to constatives, is not their truth and falsity closely parallel to the rightness and wrongness of estimates, the correctness and incorrectness of findings, and so on? Is the rightness of a verdict very different from the truth of a statement? Further, to speak of inferring *validly*, arguing *soundly*, or judging *fairly*, is to make an assessment belonging to the same class as truth and falsehood. Moreover, it is only a legend that "true" and "false" can always be appropriately predicated of constatives; "France is hexagonal" is a rough description of France, not a true or false one, and "Lord Raglan won the battle of Alma" (since Alma was a soldiers' battle in which Lord Raglan's orders were not properly transmitted) is exaggerated—it is pointless to ask whether it is true or false. It was on the basis of such considerations as these that

Austin felt himself obliged to abandon the distinction between the performative and the constative.

To replace the unsatisfactory distinction of performatives and constatives Austin introduced the theory of illocutionary forces. Whenever someone says anything he performs a number of distinguishable acts, for example, the *phonetic* act of making certain noises and the *phatic* act of uttering words in conformity with grammar. Austin went on to distinguish three other kinds of acts that we may perform when we say something: First, the *locutionary* act of using an utterance with a more or less definite sense and reference, for example, saying "The door is open" as an English sentence with reference to a particular door; second, the *illocutionary* act, which is the act I may perform in performing the locutionary act; third, the *perlocutionary* act, which is the act I may succeed in performing by means of my illocutionary act. Thus, in performing the locutionary act of saying that a door is open I may be performing an illocutionary act of stating, or hinting, or exclaiming; by performing the illocutionary act of hinting I may succeed in performing the perlocutionary act of getting you to shut it. In the same way, by performing the locutionary act of saying "Down with the monarchy" I may succeed in the perlocutionary act of bringing about a revolution, whereas in performing the locutionary act I would be inciting to revolution (successfully or unsuccessfully).

We now see that the constatives, along with performatives, can be construed as members of one particular subclass of illocutionary forces. Thus, in his provisional classification of illocutionary forces Austin had a subclass of *expositives*, which included the "constative" acts. In performing a locutionary act we may be affirming, denying, stating, describing, reporting, agreeing, testifying, rejoining, etc., but in performing a locutionary act we may also perform an act with *commissive* force, as when we promise, bet, vow, adopt, or consent; with *verdictive* force, as when we acquit, assess, or diagnose; with *exercitive* force, as when we appoint, demote, sentence, or veto; or with *behabitive* force, as when we apologize, thank, or curse.

Such is the crude outline of Austin's theory of illocutionary forces. Though his own exposition is of course much more full and rewarding, he said of it (*How to Do Things with Words,* p. 163): "I have purposely not embroiled the general theory with philosophical problems (some of which are complex enough almost to merit their celebrity); this should not be taken to mean that I am unaware of them." We may be permitted to illustrate the philosophical importance of bearing in mind the distinctions Austin made with one example of our own. Very often in recent years philosophers have set out to explain the meaning of the word *good* or of sentences containing the word *good.* Some of them have done so by saying that in such sentences the speaker expresses his own feelings (attitudes) and evokes similar feelings (attitudes in others). It might well seem that here they have set out to give an account relevant to locutionary force and that they have instead given one possible illocutionary force ("In saying that it was good I was expressing my favorable attitude toward it") and, alongside it, one possible perlocutionary force ("By saying that it was good I evoked in him a favorable attitude"). It should be clear in the light of Austin's work that such an account will not do. But Austin said very little about locutionary force in detail, and one of the most pressing general questions that arise from his work is that of the relationship between illocutionary force and locutionary force; while recognizing that they are different, and that locutionary force is in some way prior, can we, for example, conclude that the locutionary force of utterances containing the word *promise* can be explained without reference to the typical illocutionary force of "I promise"? This is far from clear.

CRITICISM OF TRADITIONAL PHILOSOPHY. We have examined in outline an example of Austin's work on a piece of clarification of language without any reference, save incidental, to the traditional problems of philosophy. We shall now turn to *Sense and Sensibilia,* which is emphatically a polemical discussion of one of the central problems of epistemology. But we shall find the essential features of Austin's method still present, the presentation only being different. Austin had recommended that when the method is used as one of inquiry the vocabulary and phrases, natural and odd, that occur to us should be studied and conclusions drawn *before* the conclusions of traditional philosophy are compared with them. Here, however, when he presents results he at each stage presents first the traditional philosophical theses and then shows their errors by confronting them with the actual facts, linguistic and otherwise.

In *Sense and Sensibilia,* Austin examines the doctrine that we never directly perceive material things but only sense data (or ideas, or sense contents, etc.), insofar as that doctrine is based upon the so-called argument from illusion. He maintains that it is largely based on an obsession with a few words "the uses of which are oversimplified, not really understood or carefully studied or correctly described" (*Sense and Sensibilia,* p. 3). With special reference to A. J. Ayer and Price, he shows how illusions are traditionally confused with delusions, are defined in terms of belief that one sees a material thing when in fact one does not (whereas some illusions, such as one hatched line appearing to be longer than another of equal length, involve nothing of the sort), and are taken to include such phenomena as sticks looking bent in water, which are not illusions at all. A portion of the argument that clearly exhibits his method at work is where he contrasts the actual complexities and differences in our use of "looks," "appears," and "seems" with the traditional confusion of these terms in traditional philosophy. Especially interesting is the discussion of the traditional accounts of "reality"; these he contrasts with the multifarious uses of the word *real*, which takes its significance only from the implied contrast in context with *artificial, fake, bogus, toy, synthetic,* and so on, as well as with *illusory* and *apparent.*

But it is perhaps more important now for us to notice another element in the argument that is very characteristic but that we have as yet given little notice, which is Austin's care to avoid oversimplification and hasty generalization of nonlinguistic, as well as linguistic, fact. The ordinary man does not, as is so often stated or implied in accounts of the argument from illusion, believe that he always sees material things; he knows perfectly well that he sees shadows, mirror images, rainbows, and the like. The number of kinds of things that we see is large and to be settled by scientific investigation, not by philosophy; the question whether the invariable object of perception is a material thing or a sense datum is thus absurd. Again, it is not true that a straight stick in water normally looks like a bent stick out of water, for we can see the water; an afterimage does not look like a colored patch on a wall; a dream is distinguished by the dreamlike quality that occasionally, but only occasionally, we attribute to some waking experience. Again, he points out that situations in which our perception is queer may arise because of defects in sense organs or peculiarities of the medium or because we put a wrong construction on what we (quite normally) see, and it is a mistake to attempt to give a single account of all perceptual error. None of these are linguistic points, and Austin had no purist, theoretical notion that he was prohibited as a philosopher from any attention to nonconceptual issues; he thought that philosophical error did arise from empirical error.

Once again, it would be pointless to attempt to reconstruct the whole argument of *Sense and Sensibilia* here; we must be content with noticing the few points made that perhaps have some bearing on a general understanding of his general position. But it should perhaps be stressed that Austin in these lectures discussed only one theory of perception as based on one particular kind of argument; although one may expect to get help from it in study of other problems in the field of perception, it would be a mistake to suppose that the book contains a full study of all problems of perception or to criticize it because it leaves many difficult problems unanswered.

It is hardly imaginable that anyone would ever deny that Austin displayed a very great talent in the kind of work he chose to do. Some have criticized him on the ground that there are more important things for philosophers to do than this; on that point Austin always refused to argue, simply saying that those who preferred to work otherwise should do so and asking only that they not do what he did in the traditional slipshod way. To those who said that philosophers should work with an improved scientific language he replied flatly that the distinctions of ordinary language were of interest in their own right and that one should not modify what one does not fully understand, but he offered no theoretical objections to such projects. He was content to work in a way which he felt he understood and found rewarding. As for the assertion sometimes made, that Austin's kind of work is private to his own peculiar gifts and that it was therefore a mistake for him to recommend the method to others, time alone can decide.

A final word should be said about Austin's relation to other philosophers. He greatly admired G. E. Moore, but it is a mistake to view his work as an offshoot of Cambridge philosophy. Moore, like Austin and unlike most Cambridge philosophers, had a linguistic and classical background rather than a scientific one. Austin owed no special debt to Bertrand Russell and was far more unlike Wittgenstein than is sometimes recognized. For Ludwig Wittgenstein an understanding of ordinary language was important because he believed that the traditional problems of philosophy arose from misunderstandings of it, but Wittgenstein had in mind gross category mistakes, and he wished to study ordinary language only so far as was essential for eliminating these. Austin was interested in fine distinctions for their own sake and saw the application of his results to the traditional problems of philosophy as only a by-product. He was uninterested in the party conflicts of philosophy, following always his individual bent.

See also Aristotle; Ayer, Alfred Jules; Language; Leibniz, Gottfried Wilhelm; Moore, George Edward.

Bibliography

PRIMARY WORKS

For brevity, first publication of individual papers (collected in *Philosophical Papers*) is omitted.

Foundations of Arithmetic. Oxford: Blackwell, 1950. Translation of Frege's *Grundlagen der Arithmetik.*

Critical notice of J. Łukasiewicz's *Aristotle's Syllogistic: From the Standpoint of Modern Formal Logic Mind* 61 (1952).

"Performatif-constatif" and contributions to discussion in *La philosophie analytique.* Paris: Minuit, 1962.

How to Do Things with Words, 2nd ed. Edited by J. O. Urmson and Marina Sbisà. Cambridge: Harvard University Press, 1975.

Sense and Sensibilia. Edited by Geoffrey J. Warnock. London: Oxford University Press, 1975.

Philosophical Papers, 3rd ed. Edited by J. O. Urmson and Geoffrey J. Warnock. Oxford: Oxford University Press, 1979.

SECONDARY WORKS

Berlin, Isaiah, et al. *Essays on J. L. Austin.* Oxford: Clarendon Press, 1973.

Cavell, Stanley. *Philosophical Passages: Wittgenstein, Emerson, Austin, Derrida.* Bucknell Lectures in Literary Theory, 12. Oxford: Blackwell, 1995.

Di Giovanna, Joseph J. *Linguistic Phenomenology: Philosophical Method in J. L. Austin.* American University Studies. Series V, Philosophy, Vol. 63. New York: Lang, 1989.

Fann, K. T., ed. *Symposium on J. L. Austin.* New York: Humanities Press, 1969.

Furberg, Mats. *Saying and Meaning: A Main Theme in J. L. Austin's Philosophy.* Totowa, NJ: Rowman and Littlefield, 1971.

Graham, Keith. *J. L. Austin.* Atlantic Highlands, NJ: Humanities Press, 1977.

Holdcraft, David. *Words and Deeds.* Oxford: Oxford University Press, 1978.

Rorty, Richard, ed. *The Linguistic Turn: Recent Essays in Philosophical Method.* Chicago: University of Chicago Press, 1967.

Searle, John. *Expression and Meaning: Essays in the Theory of Speech Acts.* Cambridge, U.K.: Cambridge University Press, 1979.

Searle, John. *Speech Acts: An Essay in the Philosophy of Language.* Cambridge, U.K.: Cambridge University Press, 1969.

Warnock, Geoffrey J. *J. L. Austin.* London: Routledge, 1989.

J. O. Urmson (1967)
Bibliography updated by Philip Reed (2005)

AUTHENTICITY REGARDING THE ARTIST AND THE ARTWORK

See Art, Authenticity in

AUTHORITY

Three topics have dominated philosophical discussion of authority: the *nature* of authority, the *point* of authority, and the *sources* of authority.

THE NATURE OF AUTHORITY

In providing an account of the nature of authority, the focus in this entry will be on de jure practical authority, though the differences between de facto and de jure authority and between theoretical and practical authority will also be briefly considered at the end of this section.

What is authority? Authority is a relational matter: A has authority over B with respect to some domain D. What follows is first a consideration of items A, B, and D that enter into this relationship, and then of the nature of the relationship among them.

With respect to A: while A need not be a person, it must be something that can have a say-so—that is, it must be the sort of thing about which one can truly assert "A says that B must φ." So, A can be a natural person, or a corporate person, or an institution, or a text. With respect to B: while B need not be a natural person, B must be the sort of thing that exhibits agency. B must, that is, be able to act on reasons: B must be capable of φ-ing because B has good reason to φ. In a relationship of practical authority, then, the authority-bearer must be a speaker, and the person under authority must be an agent.

With respect to D: Authority relationships are characteristically limited to a specific context and are characteristically limited by certain constraints within that context. An employer may have authority over an employee with respect to job-related matters, but may have no authority at all outside that context. And, further, it is not as if an employer has unlimited authority over an employee within the domain of job-related matters: if the employer told the employee to work until the employee dies of exhaustion, one would not take that to be within the range of the employer's authority. With each purported authority relationship there is assumed a domain for that authority, even though that domain is often poorly defined.

What, then, is the relationship between speaker A and agent B that makes for practical authority within a given domain D? Surely it is at least that the speaker has some control over the agent's reasons for action, and control of a specific kind: A's say-so makes a difference to the reasons that the agent B has by giving B a good reason to act a certain way. This good reason is, either in whole or in part, A's say-so—A's say-so produces a reason for action for B not merely causally but constitutively. So if A has authority over B, then A's telling B to ϕ is itself a reason for B to ϕ. If, for example, parents have authority over their children with respect to household chores, then a parent's telling the child to clean his or her room is itself a reason for the child to clean the room. By telling the child to clean the room, the parent has added to the child's reasons to clean the room; aside from the fact that the current condition of the room may be aesthetically displeasing—and even a health risk to the child—one reason for the child to clean the room is that the parent told him or her to do so.

In de jure practical authority a speaker has constitutive control over an agent's reasons for action. But it is not enough for authority simply that the speaker's say-so constitutes a reason for action for the agent; the speaker's say-so must constitute a particular kind of reason. Reasons of authority play a certain role in the proper decision making of the agent under authority: where there is practical authority, and in the domain in which that authority is effective, the authority's say-so is decisive with respect to the agent's rational action. Authoritative dictates have the function of bringing deliberation to a close by fixing the action selected by the authoritative dictate as the reasonable choice to make.

One prominent way of expressing this idea has been offered by Joseph Raz, whose work has been the most important in explicating the nature and justification of authority. Raz says that the way that authoritative norms fulfill this function is by providing what he calls "protected reasons" (Raz 1979, p. 29). A protected reason to ϕ is both a reason to ϕ and a reason to disregard reasons not to ϕ. Raz claims that the way that authoritative norms fulfill their function of decisively terminating deliberation is not by providing enormously weighty reasons, reasons that compete with and always best any reasons that militate in favor of rival options; rather, authoritative dictates fulfill their function by giving reasons that insulate a course of action from competition. When an authority tells one to ϕ, that is a reason not only to ϕ but also to disregard in deliberation courses of action that preclude ϕ-ing. One might dispute Raz's claim that authoritative norms are always protected reasons, but the more fundamental point is that where there is authority, there is a speaker whose say-so the agent has reason to treat as setting the rationally preferable course of action within some domain.

In sum: if A is a genuine practical authority over B in some domain, then in that domain A's telling B to ϕ is a decisive reason for B to ϕ. Whereas in *practical* authority, speakers have authority over what agents do, in *theoretical* authority, speakers have authority over what agents believe. There are, nonetheless, striking similarities between genuine practical authority and genuine theoretical authority. If A has theoretical authority over B in some domain, then A must be a speaker and B must be one who can believe things for reasons; and if A tells B that it is the case that p, then A's telling B that it is the case that p is a reason to B to believe that p, a reason that is decisive from B's point of view. If an accomplished chef tells a novice that this is not the best way to make a roux, then the novice has decisive reason to believe that this is not the best way to make a roux. Practical authority, being concerned with reasons for action, is an object of investigation within the province of moral philosophy (and political and legal philosophy as well); theoretical authority, being concerned with reasons for belief, is an object of investigation within the province of epistemology.

One can also distinguish between de facto and de jure authority. People often ascribe authority (practical and theoretical) to speakers even without holding that their assertions or commands are reasons for believing or doing anything. Authority is sometimes used as a term of classification and explanation in both the social sciences and in everyday talk without any attempt to evaluate the claims of these putative authorities to give reasons for action. Authority in this sense is de facto, as opposed to de jure, authority. But there is nevertheless a tight connection between them: no speaker can be correctly described as a de facto authority without that speaker's either claiming to be or being widely regarded as a de jure authority.

Here is why. Suppose that one wants to argue that A is a de facto authority over some group simply because as a matter of observable behavior, if A tells members of that group to ϕ, then members of that group, by and large, ϕ. But that would surely be an insufficient basis for ascribing de facto authority; if it were a mere accident that the behavior of the group fell in line with the commands issued by A, one would not say that A bears de facto authority. One might try to complete the case for de facto authority by adding a causal condition: that it is A's commanding the members of that group to ϕ that results in those members' ϕ-ing. But this addition would be insufficient; if it were simply a quirky feature of the individual psychologies of the group's members that believing that A told them to ϕ caused them to ϕ, then one would ascribe a nervous disorder to the group members rather than de facto authority to A. The moral here is that if one wants to appeal to agents' responses to a speaker to establish that the speaker is a de facto authority, one will have to argue that those agents act in accordance with A's say-so because they take A's say-so to be a reason for them to comply—that is, because they believe A to be a de jure authority.

One can make a similar argument from the side of the speaker: it is not sufficient to treat a speaker as a de facto authority that the speaker can (for example) have people locked up if they fail to obey. What makes the difference between effective kidnappers and de facto state authorities is, inter alia, that only the latter claim that their commands are binding standards, the violation of which justify locking people up—that is, that they are de jure practical authorities. Although there is no doubt a difference between de jure and de facto practical authority, de facto practical authority must be understood in terms of de jure practical authority.

The remainder of the entry will focus on genuine, de jure practical authority. Under what circumstances is it desirable for authority relationships of this sort of exist? And how are such authority relationships to be explained?

THE POINT OF AUTHORITY

What is the point of authority? Is there anything of value realized through such relationships?

Raz has written that the normal way of justifying authority is to show that those subject to it act better on their other reasons for action under authority than they would in the absence of authority. He calls this the "normal justification thesis." Practical authority provides a service—that is, the service of enabling persons to act more reasonably (Raz 1986).

There are several distinct contexts in which practical authority might provide this service. Practical authority might enable one to act more in accordance with what reason—prior to and apart from any authoritative imposition—determinately requires. It may be that a certain regimen of drug treatment is necessary for a person to regain her health. This is just a fact about the world, and given the value of this person's health, it would be unreasonable for her not to follow that regimen. But even if it is perfectly clear to her that this is the regimen to follow—because her doctor prescribes it, and her doctor's views are in line with the consensus of the medical community—she may fail to be motivated adequately by the doctor's theoretical authority alone. She might do better in acting in accordance with what reason requires if she had further reason to go along with the doctor's prescrip-

tion—perhaps by placing herself under the doctor's authority. Some people do this sort of thing with personal trainers (or career mentors, or spiritual directors): they treat the trainer's (or mentor's or director's) prescriptions not as pieces of advice but as authoritative dictates, and they better reach their health- (or career-, or sanctification-) related goals by having trainers (or mentors or directors) that are not merely dispensers of advice but practical authorities.

Another context in which practical authorities can help persons to act on their other reasons for action is that in which their reasons for action require actions that are, to a significant degree, vague or otherwise indeterminate. The most pressing of such cases are those in which persons need to act in a coordinated way. The standard example is the rule of the road: While there is strong reason for persons to drive on the same side of the road, it is indeterminate which side they should drive on. Although a solution may be reached through trial and error, it would be helpful if there were a party that could set the rule of the road in a clear and determinate way prior to the disasters that can occur on the way to a convention established by trial and error.

There are several ways in which such indeterminacy presents itself. In some cases, there are a number of instrumental means to a single well-defined goal—for example, keeping people from driving into each other—and practical authority's job is to select one such means as a common plan of action. In some cases, there are a number of ways to fill in a vague rule. For example: one should not drive an automobile if one is intoxicated. But: What counts as "intoxicated"? Is it to be fixed by actual level of impairment? By blood alcohol level? And, in either case, at what levels? This is a matter that can be resolved by authoritative imposition: a practical authority can set what counts as intoxication, thus helping persons act in a coordinated way both with respect to their driving behavior and with respect to the claims that they make on one another with respect to their driving behavior. For the rule about drunk driving matters not only when one is deciding whether to drive; it is also important both in deciding whether to make claims on another for the damages that the other has done while driving with alcohol in his or her system and in deciding whether to accept claims made on one by others for damages that one has done while driving with alcohol in one's system.

Raz's normal justification thesis brings out the points that practical authority calls for justification (and thus can fail with respect to this call) and that the usual way that practical authority is justified is by showing that our other reasons are better served by adding reasons of authority into the mix. Whereas this may indeed be the normal way of establishing the point of authority, it is not the only way. Here is another: Practical authority is not just an ability to change others' reasons for action, it is also a (typically) positive status. Because practical authority is a (typically) positive status, placing someone in a position of practical authority can be a way to honor that person, or a way to give that person what he or she deserves. So one justification for practical authority might make reference not to the ways in which those subject to authority are served by it but by reference to the way that the bearer of authority is appropriately honored or rewarded by it. There may, for example, be in some group no particularly pressing reason to institute structures of authority for decision making, but in light of the need to honor a person who has made great contributions to that group's aims, it would make sense to confer authority on that person.

There are also more tedious reasons for being in an authority relationship. Employers often have limited authority over their employees, and employees enter those authority relationships by contract. From the employer's point of view, the salient reason for the authority relationship is to bind the employee to performance of duties; from the employee's point of view, the salient reason for the authority relationship is that, unless he or she is willing to enter it, he or she will have no job, and no paycheck. This is a far cry from authority's helping an agent to act on his or her preexisting reasons or from authority's being conferred on someone in order to do him or her honor, but it cannot be denied that a number of more-or-less limited authority relationships in which people find themselves are justified in this way.

It is important to note, though, that practical authority has its drawbacks. Recall that what distinguishes the reasons of practical authority is their decisive role in deliberation. If reasons of authority are absent, then something else will have to fill the role that brings deliberation to its conclusion in these cases—often, the agent's own free, rationally underdetermined decision. If one takes the making of free, underdetermined decisions to be a good, then there is something lost by persons who are under practical authority (see Wolff 1970). So it is not as if practical authority is costless. And, furthermore, it should be noted that there may be bad psychological tendencies associated with certain sorts of otherwise worthwhile authority relationships, at least in certain classes of people. Even if practical authority is, properly circumscribed, necessary and valuable, there may be broad types

of person who tend to act worse when placed either in such positions of authority or under such authority (see Milgram 1974).

THE SOURCES OF AUTHORITY

Suppose that person X claims to have practical authority over person Y, and Y is rightly curious about the correctness of this claim. When Y challenges X, X's response is: "You are under my authority because I am I, and you are you. You are under my authority because I am X, and you are not." X's case is poor; not only is it unconvincing, but it borders on incoherent. It borders on incoherence because authority relationships are normative matters, and whether a normative fact obtains depends not on irreducibly particular facts but on general ones. So just as claims about one's duties and rights are correct not in virtue of the particular identity of the person to whom those duties and rights are ascribed but in virtue of the general properties instantiated by that person, claims about who holds authority depend on the general properties instantiated by that person. It might fundamentally matter with respect to the presence of authority whether one is a parent, or is morally good, or is powerful, or has a loud voice; it cannot fundamentally matter whether one is Bill Clinton, Bob Dylan, or Bozo the Clown.

How, then, does it come to be the case that one individual is a practical authority over another individual, given that it is not simply as that individual that one is an authority bearer or a person under authority? There are two ways to try to answer this question. The first is to begin with general practical principles, and to show that in certain circumstances those practical principles imply that one party has authority over another. It is crucial that one select a practical principle that stands a chance of generating the crucial features of authority, that is, that at least under some possible set of circumstances it implies that one party's say-so is in some domain a decisive reason for action for another party.

Here is one principle that has been invoked in a number of contexts to explain practical authority: the principle of promising. The principle of promising, stated loosely, is that if one promises to perform an act of ϕ-ing, then one is morally bound to ϕ. One's valid promise is, in standard cases, a reason for the promisor to perform the action promised, and it is a reason of a certain kind: that one validly promised to perform an action is characteristically decisive, again, at least in standard cases. But one can promise to act in accordance with another party's commands: one can promise to obey the personal trainer's commands with respect to one's exercise regimen, or to follow the policies of one's immediate superior in the performance of job duties, or to do the bidding of the king. If one has validly promised to act on another person's commands in some domain, then it seems that there is good reason to suppose that authority has been generated.

This way of accounting for practical authority can be called the "top-down" approach. It begins with practical principles of broader application and proceeds to show that in some circumstances the application of that general principle yields a relationship that bears all of the defining conditions of genuine authority. A rival approach, the "bottom-up" approach, takes authority relationships as basic, not to be explained as implications of other practical principles. The guiding idea of this way of proceeding is that relationships of practical authority are no less familiar than—and perhaps may be more familiar than—the general practical principles that users of the top-down approach have employed. The task for the user of the bottom-up approach is simply to describe the general features of the various relationships of genuine practical authority with which we are familiar, and so far as possible to exhibit the unity among them (either the precise features they share, or analogies between them). So, the bottom-up theorist might note (for example) that people commonsensically accept that parents have authority over children, and thus take his or her task to be to define more precisely what counts as the parent/child relationship in which authority exists (is it biological? social? legal? some combination of these?) and what defines the scope of the parent's practical authority (is it over all domestic matters? does it extend beyond that? does the size of its domain remain constant, or not?). He or she may wish to answer similar questions about the authority of the state and of God, and to draw the appropriate connections and disanalogies between these cases of authority.

There are potential drawbacks to both of these approaches. The bottom-up approach seems to be extremely deferential to de facto authorities, offering them the presumption of de jure status. As such, employment of the bottom-up approach is unable to ease the suspicions of the authority skeptic, who is concerned either in particular cases or in a more global way about the existence of de jure practical authority. The top-down approach, by contrast, runs the real risk of failing to hook up with de facto authority relationships in any straightforward way. If there is a clear lesson to be drawn from the history of uses of the top-down approach in investigating questions of practical authority—most attention

has been paid to parental, political, and divine authority—it is that it is extraordinarily difficult to generate plausible accounts of the de jure authority of common social institutions from standard applications of widely held general practical principles.

PARENTAL AUTHORITY It is commonly thought, especially among parents, that parents are practical authorities over their children. But employing the top-down approach to explain parents' status as authorities over their children has proven to be a difficult undertaking.

A preliminary difficulty for this undertaking is specifying the window in which this authority is supposed to obtain: at what age does a parent's authority over children begin (babies are not under authority, as they cannot yet act for reasons), and at what age does it cease? Suppose, though, that the time frame in which parents are to be authoritative over children is settled; how is one to explain why parents are authoritative during this stretch of time? A child's requirement of obedience to his or her parents cannot be a matter of voluntary undertaking, as Hobbes erroneously (and even inconsistently with his own view) supposed it to be (Hobbes 1651, ch. 20). So no principles of moral obligation founded on consent or voluntary acceptance of benefits will do. One might appeal to the requirements of gratitude, but this suggestion is rife with difficulties: Why does gratitude, which typically does not require obedience, generate such a requirement in this case? If it is a parent's duty to care for children, why is gratitude owed as a consequence of a mere doing of one's duty? Isn't gratitude characteristically conditioned on free acceptance of benefits, whereas children are typically not free to refuse such benefits from their parents or to seek the benefits elsewhere?

Locke argues, plausibly, that a parent's authority over children is due to the child's deficiencies in reason and choice, and it is only so long as those deficiencies remain that the parent has authority, for it is as a help to remedying those deficiencies that the parent has authority (Locke 1690, §55). These claims seem to be true, but this argument concerns the point, or value, of parental authority, not the explanation of how parents come to be authoritative over children. These are distinct questions. Even those who grant the value of parental authority can find its existence and explanation mysterious indeed. Little progress has been made in providing a top-down account of the authority of parents over their children.

POLITICAL AUTHORITY Political authority—its desirability, its scope, and its explanation—is one of the few truly perennial problems of political philosophy. The most familiar explanation for political authority is the consent account. On this view, most fully elaborated during the early modern period, citizens characteristically make an agreement, either explicitly or tacitly (Hobbes 1651, ch. 18; Locke 1690, §119; Rousseau 1762, bk. 4, ch. 2), to obey their rulers. It is in virtue of this original agreement that subjects are duty-bound to obey their political authorities. Whereas this view has been tremendously popular, it is subject to overwhelming objections, which are catalogued in David Hume's influential "Of the Original Contract" (1753). Hume convincingly argues that there is little evidence that explicit agreements have generally taken place, and that the tacit agreements that consent theorists find themselves forced to posit to explain state authority are in fact no more than a myth.

Hume's recommended account of political authority is a utilitarian one—that is, that it is simply in virtue of the public benefit brought about by having a political authority in place that the de jure authority of the state is established. As Hume puts it, public authority is necessary for the public good, and public authority cannot be sustained unless subjects pay "exact obedience" to their rulers. But this is unpersuasive: states maintain de facto authority in the face of quite a bit of disobedience, and so Hume has not explained why the need for de facto authority yields the conclusion that states have de jure authority over their subjects.

During the latter half of the twentieth century there was a revival of attempts to provide an account of state authority. Some were attempts to retrieve the old consent view, offering new accounts of the tacit consent that was necessary to bind that vast majority of persons who never explicitly consent. Some were attempts to revive Hume's utilitarian-style argument. H. L. A. Hart (1955) and John Rawls (1964) offered arguments from fairness, holding that the authority of law is based on the fact that those who accept the benefits of legally ordered cooperation would be unfairly free riding on the efforts of others were they not to obey as well. Others appealed to an argument that appears as early as Plato's *Crito*—the idea that citizens owe a debt of gratitude to their political authorities for the goods that they receive through them, and this debt is to be repaid through obedience.

Despite the ingenuity of writers attempting to provide top-down accounts of political authority, the most important writers on political authority at the end of the twentieth century were "philosophical anarchists"—they held, that is, that none of these attempts to account for genuine, de jure political authority is successful, and thus

people have reason to reject the view that modern states are genuinely authoritative. Some of these writers, such as Robert Paul Wolff (1970), hold that this is a necessary truth: there cannot be a genuinely authoritative state. But most of them—most prominently, A. John Simmons (1979), Joseph Raz (1979), and Leslie Green (1990)—argue simply that under current political conditions no state holds the wide-ranging authority that it claims for itself.

DIVINE AUTHORITY Recent scholarship employing the top-down approach has had difficulty exhibiting the sources of authority of the two likeliest bearers of wide-ranging authority: parents and political institutions. One might think that even if such human institutions were bound to fall short in this respect, surely divine authority would be an easier matter. After all, whereas God's existence remains a philosophically controverted matter, it is widely accepted by both theists and nontheists that if there is such a being as God then that being is practically authoritative over human beings.

It turns out that accounting for divine authority using a top-down approach raises difficulties that are just as pressing as the difficulties that attend accounting for parental or political authority in the top-down way. One might think that being a practical authority is a logical consequence of traditional divine attributes, such as omniscience, omnipotence, or perfect moral goodness, but this is wrong: omniscience and perfect moral goodness give us reasons only to think of God as a theoretical authority, not a practical authority; and whereas omnipotence of course enables God to control the circumstances in which our reasons for action have application, it does not of itself entail that God's commands constitute reasons for action for humans. One might think that traditional moral principles concerning gratitude for benefits or property in what one has created would yield a moral obligation to obey God, but it turns out that there are severe difficulties in demonstrating that the conditions of application for these principles generate such an obligation of obedience (Murphy 2002). The top-down approach has fared no better in the case of divine authority than in the cases of parental and political authority.

It is unclear what moral should be drawn from the failure of top-down philosophical investigation to generate plausible accounts of parental, political, and divine authority. On the one hand, one might take it simply to be an indication that, given the nature of authority, it is bound to be hard to show that one party has genuine authority over another in nonstylized contexts—that is, contexts that are not created for the purpose of generating authority relationships (e.g., employer-employee contracts). On the other hand, one might take it to be a reductio ad absurdum of reliance on the top-down approach. One might claim that among people's sturdiest considered moral judgments are the judgments that these authority relationships are genuine. To the extent that distinct general moral principles fail to illuminate the authority present there, this failure gives people reason not to jettison the view that these authority relationships are genuine but only to insist on a bottom-up approach, taking practical authority as a basic feature of the moral world.

See also Civil Disobedience; Cosmopolitanism; Postcolonialism; Republicanism.

Bibliography

For considerations of the nature and justification of authority, see Joseph Raz, *The Authority of Law* (Oxford, U.K.: Oxford University Press, 1979) and *The Morality of Freedom* (Oxford, U.K.: Oxford University Press, 1986). Several important discussions are collected in *Authority*, edited by Joseph Raz (Oxford, U.K.: Blackwell, 1990). For philosophical skepticism concerning the possibility of de jure authority, see Robert Paul Wolff, *In Defense of Anarchism* (New York: Harper & Row, 1970). For some discussion of the deleterious effects of submission to authority, see Stanley Milgram, *Obedience to Authority: An Experimental View* (New York: Harper & Row, 1974).

There is a vast literature on the sources of de jure authority, almost all of it focused on political authority. The classic contract account may be found in Hobbes, *Leviathan*, edited by Edwin Curley (Indianapolis, IN: Hackett, 1994; first published 1651), John Locke, *Second Treatise of Government* (1690), reprinted in *Two Treatises of Government*, edited by Peter Laslett (Cambridge, U.K.; Cambridge University Press, 1988), and Jean-Jacques Rousseau, *On the Social Contract*, in The *Basic Political Writings*, translated by Donald Cress (Indianapolis, IN: Hackett, 1987; first published 1762). David Hume's skeptical treatment of contract views may be found in his "Of the Original Contract" (1753), reprinted in *Political Essays*, and edited by Knud Haakonssen (Cambridge, U.K.: Cambridge University Press, 1994). Accounts justifying political authority in terms of fair distribution of the benefits and burdens of rule following are to be found in H. L. A. Hart, "Are There Any Natural Rights?" (*Philosophical Review* 64 (1955): 175–191), and John Rawls, "Legal Obligation and the Duty of Fair Play," in *Law and Philosophy*, edited by Sidney Hook (New York: New York University Press, 1964). A gratitude view is suggested in Plato's *Crito*, in *The Trial and Death of Socrates*, translated by G. M. A. Grube (Indianapolis, IN: Hackett, 1975). Recent accounts skeptical of all extant theories of political authority may be found in A. John Simmons, *Moral Principles and Political Obligations* (Princeton, NJ: Princeton University Press, 1979), Raz's *The Authority of Law* and Leslie Green, *The Authority of the State* (Oxford, U.K.: Oxford University

Press, 1990). There has been less recent work on parental and divine authority. For a discussion of parental authority, see Michael Slote, "Obedience and Illusions," in *Having Children*, edited by Onora O'Neill and William Ruddick (New York: Oxford University Press, 1979); for a discussion of divine authority, see Mark C. Murphy, *An Essay on Divine Authority* (Ithaca, NY: Cornell University Press, 2002).

Mark C. Murphy (2005)

AVEMPACE

See *Ibn Bājja*

AVENARIUS, RICHARD
(1843–1896)

Richard Avenarius, the German positivist philosopher, was born in Paris. He studied at the University of Leipzig, where he became a *Privatdozent* in philosophy in 1876. The following year he was appointed professor of philosophy at Zürich, where he taught until his death. His most influential work was the two-volume *Kritik der reinen Erfahrung* (1888–1890), which won him such followers as Joseph Petzoldt and such opponents as Vladimir Il'ich Lenin.

Avenarius was the founder of empiriocriticism, an epistemological theory according to which the task of philosophy is to develop a "natural concept of the world" based on "pure experience." To obtain such a coherent, consistent view of the world requires a positivistic restriction to that which is directly given by pure perception, together with the elimination of all metaphysical ingredients which man, through introjection, imports into experience in the act of knowing.

There is a close kinship between the ideas of Avenarius and those of Ernst Mach, especially as set forth in Mach's *Analyse der Empfindungen*. The two men never became personally acquainted, and they developed their points of view quite independently of one another; hence, it was only gradually that they became convinced of the profound agreement of their basic conceptions. They held the same fundamental view on the relationship between physical and mental phenomena, as well as on the significance of the principle of the "economy of thought." Above all, both were persuaded that pure experience must be recognized as the sole admissible—and thoroughly adequate—source of knowledge. Thus, the elimination of introjection by Avenarius is only a special form of that total elimination of the metaphysical which Mach sought.

In addition to Petzoldt and Lenin, others who dealt at length with the philosophy of Avenarius were Wilhelm Schuppe and Wilhelm Wundt. While Schuppe, the philosopher of immanence, agreed with Avenarius on essential points, Wundt criticized the scholastic character of Avenarius's expositions and sought to point out internal contradictions in his doctrines.

COGNITION

The two presuppositions of empiriocriticism are the empiriocritical axiom of the contents of cognition and the axiom of the forms of cognition. The first axiom states that the cognitive contents of all philosophical views of the world are merely modifications of the original assumption that every human being initially assumes himself to be confronted with an environment and with other human beings who make assertions and are dependent on the environment. The second axiom holds that scientific knowledge does not possess any forms and means essentially different from those of prescientific knowledge and that all the forms and means of knowledge in the special sciences are extensions of the prescientific (*Kritik der reinen Erfahrung*, Vol. I, Preface).

Especially characteristic of Avenarius' theory of human cognition was his biological approach. From this biological point of view, every process of knowledge is to be interpreted as a vital function, and only as such can it be understood. Avenarius' interest was directed chiefly to the pervasive relations of dependency between individuals and their surroundings, and he described these relations in an original terminology involving many symbols.

The point of departure for his investigations was the "natural" assumption of a "principal coordination" between self and environment, in consequence of which each individual finds himself facing both an environment with various component parts and other individuals who make assertions about this environment which also express a "finding." The initial principal coordination thus consists in the existence of a "central term" (the individual) and "opposite terms" about which he makes assertions. The encountering individual is represented and centralized in system C (the central nervous system, the cerebrum), the basic biological processes of which are nourishment and work.

System C is exposed to change in two ways; changes in it are dependent on two "partial-systematic factors": variations in the environment (R) or stimuli from the external world (whatever can, as a stimulus, excite a nerve), and fluctuations in metabolism (S), or absorption of food (whatever in the environment of system C conditions and constitutes its metabolism). System C constantly strives for a vital maximum conservation of its strength (V), a state of rest in which the mutually opposed processes $f(R)$ and $f(S)$—that is, the variations of system C as functions of R and S—cancel each other out, and the two variations maintain an equilibrium ($f(R) + f(S) = 0$, or $\Sigma f(R) + \Sigma f(S) = 0$). If $f(R) + f(S) > 0$, then there arises in the state of rest or equilibrium state of system C a disturbance, a relationship of tension, "a vital difference." The system strives to diminish or cancel out and equalize this disturbance by passing over spontaneously to secondary reactions in order to reestablish its original state (the conservation maximum, or V). These secondary reactions to deviations from V or to physiological fluctuations in system C are the so-called independent vital sequences (the vital functions in system C, the physiological processes in the brain), which run their course in three phases: the initial segment (appearance of the vital difference), the middle segment, and the final segment (reappearance of the earlier state). The canceling out of a vital difference is possible, of course, only in the manner and to the extent that system C exhibits a readiness for it. Among the changes preparatory to achieving readiness are hereditary dispositions, developmental factors, pathological variations, practice or exercise, and the like. The "dependent vital sequences" (experiences, or E-values) are functionally conditioned by the independent vital sequences. The dependent vital sequences, which, like the independent, proceed in three stages (pressure, work, release), are the conscious processes and cognitions ("assertions about contents"). For example, an instance of knowledge is present if in the initial segment the characterization reads "unknown" and in the final segment it reads "known."

Avenarius sought to explain the rise and disappearance of problems in general as follows. A disparity can arise between the stimulation from the environment and the energy at the disposal of the individual either (*a*) because the stimulation is strengthened as a result of the individual's having found anomalies, exceptions, or contradictions in the given, or (*b*) because an excess of energy is present. In the first case, problems arise that can, under favorable circumstances, be solved by knowledge; in the second case, practical-idealist goals arise. The latter are the positing of ideals and values (for example, ethical or aesthetic ideals and values), the testing of them (that is, the forming of new ones), and through them the alteration of the given.

The *E*-values, which depend on the fluctuations in the energy of system *C,* fall into two classes. The first are "elements," or simple contents of assertions—contents of sensation, such as green, hot, and sour, which depend on the objects of sensation or stimuli (whereby the "things" of experience are understood as nothing more than "complexes of elements"). The second are "characters," the subjective reactions to sensations, or the feelinglike modes of apprehension. Three groups of basic characters (kinds of awareness) are distinguished: the "affective," the "adaptive," and the "prevailing." Among the affective characters are the feelings proper (the "affectional," pleasure and aversion) and the feelings in a figurative sense (the "coaffectional," such as anxiety and relief, and the "virtual," such as feelings of movement). The adaptive characters include the "identical" (sameness or "tautote," difference or "heterote"); that is, the "fidential," the "existential" (being, appearance, nonbeing), the "secural" (certainty, uncertainty), and the "notal" (the being known, the being unknown), together with many modifications of these. For example, modifications of the "idential" include, among others, generality, law, whole, and part.

PURE EXPERIENCE AND THE WORLD

Avenarius constructed the concept of pure experience and related it to his theory of the natural concept of the world on the basis of his views on the biology and psychology of knowledge. The ideal of a natural concept of the world of pure experience is fulfilled in the complete elimination of metaphysical categories and of dualistic interpretations of reality, by means of his exclusion of introjection. The basic prerequisite for this is first to acknowledge the fundamental equivalence of everything that is encountered and that can be grasped, regardless of whether it is given through external or internal experience. As a consequence of the empiriocritical principal coordination between self and environment, individuals and environment are encountered in the same fashion, without distinction. "With respect to givenness, I and the environment are on completely the same footing. I come to know the environment in exactly the same sense that I come to know myself—as members of a single experience; and in every experience that is realized the two experience-values, the self and the environment, are in principle coordinated to each other and equivalent" (*Der menschliche Weltbegriff*).

Likewise, the difference between *R*-values and *E*-values is conditional upon the mode of apprehension. Both values are equally accessible to description. They differ only in that the former are interpreted as constituents of the environment, while the latter are conceived of as the content of an assertion of another human individual. In the same way, there is no ontological distinction between the mental and the physical; rather, there is a logical functional relation between them. A process is mental insofar as it is dependent on a change in system *C* and has more than mechanical significance, that is, insofar as it signifies an experience. Psychology has no separate subject matter at its disposal; it is nothing other than the study of experience insofar as experience is dependent on system *C*. Avenarius rejected the usual interpretation of and distinction between mind and body. He recognized neither the mental nor the physical but only a single kind of being.

ECONOMY OF THOUGHT

Of particular importance for the realization of the cognitive ideal of pure experience and for the notion of the natural concept of the world is the principle of the economy of thought. In the same way that thinking in conformity with the principle of least exertion is the root of the theoretical process of abstraction, so knowledge generally orients itself by the degree of exertion required to fulfill experience. Hence, one should exclude all elements of the mental image that are not contained in the given, in order to think about that which is encountered in experience with the least possible expenditure of energy, and thus to arrive at a pure experience. Experience, "cleansed of all adulterating additions," contains nothing but constituents of experience that presuppose constituents of the environment only. Whatever is not pure experience, and thus is not the content of an assertion (an *E*-value) subject to the environment itself, is to be eliminated. What we term "experience" (or "existing things") stands in a certain relationship of dependence to system *C* and to the environment; and experience is pure when it is cleansed of all those contents of assertions that do not depend on the environment.

A world concept relates to the "sum total of the constituents of the environment" and is dependent on the final character of the *C*-system. It is natural if it avoids the error of introjection and is not falsified by animistic "insertions." Introjection transfers the perceptual object into the perceiving person. It splits our natural world into inner and outer, subject and object, mind and matter. This is the origin of metaphysical problems (like immortality and the mind-body problem) and metaphysical categories (like substance). All of these must therefore be eliminated. Introjection, with its unwarranted duplication of reality, must be replaced by the empiriocritical principal coordination and the natural concept of the world that rests on it. Thus, at the end of its development the world concept returns to that natural form with which it began: a purely descriptive comprehension of the world, with the least expenditure of energy.

See also Cognitive Science; Experience; Lenin, Vladimir Il'ich; Mach, Ernst; Petzoldt, Joseph; Schuppe, Ernst Julius Wilhelm; Wundt, Wilhelm.

Bibliography

WORKS BY AVENARIUS

Philosophie als Denken der Welt gemäss dem Prinzip des kleinsten Kraftmasses. Prolegomena zu einer Kritik der reinen Erfahrung ("Philosophy as Thinking of the World in Accordance with the Principle of the Least Amount of Energy. Prolegomena to a Critique of Pure Experience"). Leipzig: R. Reisland, 1876.

Kritik der reinen Erfahrung ("Critique of Pure Experience"), 2 vols. Leipzig: R. Reisland, 1888–1890.

Der menschliche Weltbegriff ("The Human Concept of the World"). Leipzig: R. Reisland, 1891.

WORKS ON AVENARIUS

Ewald, Oskar. *Richard Avenarius als Begründer des Empiriokritizimus.* Berlin, 1905.

Lenin, V. I. *Materializm i Empiriokritizism.* Moscow, 1909. Translated as *Materialism and Empirio-criticism.* New York: International Publishers, 1927.

Raab, Friedrich. *Die Philosophie von Richard Avenarius.* Leipzig: Meiner, 1912.

Schuppe, Wilhelm. "Die Bestätigung des naiven Realismus." *Vierteljahrsschrift für wissenschaftliche Philosophie* 17 (1893): 364–388.

Suter, Jules. *Die Philosophie von Richard Avenarius.* Zürich, 1910.

Wundt, Wilhelm. "Über naiven und kritischen Realismus." *Philosophische Studien* 12 (1896): 307–408, and 13 (1897): 1–105 and 323–433.

Franz Austeda (1967)
Translated by Albert E. Blumberg

AVERROES
(c. 1126–c. 1198)

Averroes, or ibn Rushd, was the foremost figure in Islamic philosophy's period of highest development (700–1200). His preeminence is due to his own immense philosophical acuity and power and to his enormous influence in certain phases of Latin thought from 1200 to 1650.

Averroes ("ibn Rushd" is a more exact transliteration of the Arabic, while "Averroes" is the medieval Latin version) was born in Córdoba into a family of prominent judges and lawyers; his grandfather, bearing the same name, served as the chief *qāḍī* (judge) of Córdoba, and there is a tradition that his father carried out the same duties. (In Muslim society a *qāḍī*'s professional concepts and practical duties were simultaneously civil and religious. Thus, a "lawyer" had expert knowledge of divine law.)

There are, however, few other specific details about his life and career. Ernest Renan and Salomon Munk mention that he studied under the most learned teachers in theology and law (in the Muslim world the two disciplines are effectively the same). It has been suggested that he studied with such scientists and philosophers as ibn Ṭufayl (d. 1185) and ibn Bajja (or Avempace, d. 1138), but the tenuous evidence would indicate that he became acquainted with the former only when he was past forty and that the death of the latter occurred when Averroes was only eleven or twelve years of age. Thus, significant pedagogical influence by these personalities upon Averroes is doubtful.

There remain, nevertheless, scattered pieces of evidence and suggestions of dates delineating his career. Averroes himself mentions that he was in Marrakech in 1153, on which occasion he observed the star Canope, not visible in Spain at that time. This sighting confirmed for him the truth of Aristotle's claim that the world was round. Some years later he seems to have been associated with the family of the Ibn Zuhr, traditionally physicians and scholars of medicine. He is reported to have been well acquainted with Abū Marwān ibn-Zuhr, perhaps the most outstanding member of the family, and when Averroes composed his medical handbook titled *Kulliyat* (literally, "generalities," which became latinized to *Colliget*), he encouraged Abū Marwān to write a companion text concerned with the details of specific ailments.

Tradition next reports that Averroes came into the favor of the sultan of Marrakech, a notable patron of scholarship and research, through the personal recommendation of his friend and presumed mentor, ibn Ṭufayl. His ready intelligence seems to have pleased the *cālīf*, who, according to a student of Averroes, subsequently encouraged the vast series of commentaries on Aristotle that became known in the West around 1200. It is generally conjectured that the association among ibn Ṭufayl, the *cālīf*, and Averroes can be dated between 1153 and 1169.

Through the *cālīf*'s offices, Averroes was appointed *qāḍī* of Seville in 1169, and he began his array of commentaries on Aristotle about that time. In 1171 he returned to Córdoba, probably as *qāḍī*, and eventually became chief *qāḍī*. He was, however, continually traveling to Seville and to Marrakech, as the colophons of various of his writings attest. In 1182 he became physician to the *cālīf* of Marrakech, continuing as a court favorite until about 1195. At that time he is supposed to have retired, possibly under a cloud as the result of religious controversy, or perhaps to be protected from conservative theologians, to a village outside Seville; details are not available. In any case, he soon returned to Marrakech, where he died.

His death coincided with the virtual disappearance of the dynamic speculative tradition evidenced in Arabic thinking for the several centuries after 700. Interestingly, it also coincided with the bursting forth of a similarly active tradition in the Latin West, which was greatly stimulated by the translations of Aristotle and Greek science from Arabic and Hebrew manuscripts. All these events—the death of Averroes, the abrupt decline of Arab intellectual dynamism, the translation into Latin of Aristotle (notably the *Metaphysics* and *De Anima* about 1200), and the exponential acceleration of Western philosophizing—occurred virtually within two decades. These are perhaps neither radically causative nor dependent events, but their close association is historically remarkable.

WRITINGS

During the course of his active professional life as *qāḍī*, physician, scientist, and philosopher, Averroes found time to compose an impressive number of scientific, philosophical, and religious writings. It is possible that some of his appointments may have been, in part, preferments for the purpose of sustaining scholarship. Certainly in the medieval Latin West, many a Sorbonne scholar formally designated "canon of Rheims," for example, could rarely be found at Rheims fulfilling his canonic responsibilities.

Most of Averroes's writings that can be dated fall between 1159 and 1195. There is the medical encyclopedia *Kulliyat* (composed before 1162), along with expositions of and commentaries on such medical writers as the Greek Galen and the Eastern Islamic ibn Sīnā (normally latinized as Avicenna). There are writings on astronomy. In religious philosophy there is the famous reply to the philosopher Muhammad al-Ghazālī's attack on the pretensions of rationalism in matters of divine law (*The Incoherence of the Philosophers*); Averroes's response is titled *The Incoherence of the Incoherence,* in which he strongly affirms the solid adequacy of natural reason in all domains of intellectual investigation. There are many lesser writings, on problems of divine law, on logic, on natural philosophy, and on medicine. Finally, there is the massive set of commentaries on the Aristotelian corpus, which profoundly affected medieval Latin thought—sometimes with official ecclesiastical approbation, sometimes not.

COMMENTARIES ON ARISTOTLE. The commentaries on Aristotle are of three kinds: short, often called paraphrases or epitomes; intermediate; and long, usually meticulous and detailed explications. These different versions may well correspond to stages in the educational curriculum.

The commentaries survive in many forms. For some writings of Aristotle, all three commentaries are available, for some two, and for some only one. Since Aristotle's *Politics* was not accessible to him, Averroes wrote a commentary on Plato's *Republic,* under the assumption that Greek thought constituted a coherent philosophical whole. He believed that the *Republic* contributed to this total philosophical construction. In still a further attempt to complete the presumed integrity of all Greek natural philosophy, Averroes supplemented Aristotle's *Physics* and *De Caelo* with a treatise of his own titled *De Substantia Orbis.*

In supplementing Aristotle in this fashion, Averroes did violence to the original methodology of the Stagirite. For Aristotle the *Physics* and *De Caelo* investigated motions and processes according to two different perspectives—*Physics,* motion as such; *De Caelo,* motion in the particular context of the activities of the heavenly bodies. These investigations were not conceived as standing in any hierarchical order, reflecting any vertical order of being or reality; they were simply different investigations and must not be taken, as did many ancient and medieval commentators, in terms of category and subcategory. Averroes, with methodological dispositions akin to the Platonic, did take them in this way, and thus eventually he found it necessary to provide an all-comprehensive celestial physics—hence, the *De Substantia Orbis.*

TEXTUAL TRADITION. The actual textual tradition of Averroes's works is extremely complex. Some of the commentaries remain in Arabic versions, some in Hebrew translations from the Arabic, some in Arabic texts recorded in Hebrew script, and many in Latin translations. These categories are not mutually exclusive. Beginning in 1472 there appeared numerous printed editions of some, but by no means all, of the commentaries; the format usually consists of a paragraph of Aristotelian text followed immediately by Averroes's comments on and interpretation of that text. This was no doubt an apparatus designed for the practical needs of the teaching of natural philosophy in the Western Latin universities, for it is clear that Averroes's analyses had become influential by the first quarter of the thirteenth century, accompanying as they did the translations of Aristotle, and they remained influential in the traditions of the universities well into the seventeenth century.

AVERROES'S PHILOSOPHY

Averroes's own philosophical position can best be characterized as Aristotle warped onto a Platonic frame. He inherited Greek thought as a literary corpus and, like his Islamic philosophical predecessors, viewed this corpus as an intellectually integrated totality. Aristotle, his commentators (such as Alexander of Aphrodisias and Simplicius) and such thinkers as Plotinus and Proclus were all understood as parts dovetailing into a single coherent philosophical system. Al-Fārābī (d. c. 950) is an eminent example of this syncretism: he composed a work titled *The Harmony between Plato and Aristotle,* and Averroes himself, lacking Aristotle's *Politics,* found little difficulty in incorporating Plato's *Republic* within his compass of speculation.

RELIANCE ON NEOPLATONISM. The doctrinal positions of Greek and Alexandrian thinkers were, in fact, often quite divergent and even incompatible, and to complete the final union of their philosophies into a single intellectual system the Arab philosophers made use of a writing called the *Theology.* Late ancient tradition attributed this treatise to Aristotle, but modern scholarship has established that the *Theology* is fundamentally a compendium based on Plotinus's writings. This work was taken uncritically by Arabic philosophers as the capstone of all Greek speculative thought and, as such, was employed by them to effect the unity of ancient philosophy.

"Mystical" knowledge. There were at least two reasons for the eager Islamic approval of the *Theology.* First, it strongly reflected the Neoplatonic emphasis especially evident in Plotinus' *Enneads,* on the culminating "mystical" experience at the apex of human knowledge. This experience involved a passing from a condition of ordinary logical ratiocination over into a condition of nondiscursive (although quasi-rational) grasp of ultimate reality. Such an attitude is strongly sympathetic to the Islamic conception of ultimate religious experience, in which there is an analogous passing from individuality into an impersonal fusion with a Whole or Divine Essence.

Hierarchy of reality. Correlative to its reflection of Neoplatonic "mystical" knowledge, the *Theology* reflected the Neoplatonic methodological conception that is ordered in an organic hierarchy, with interlocking levels indicating superordinate and subordinate dependency. Such relationships involve levels of being and, concomitantly, sources and receivers of being. Such an intellectual structure might be visualized as a series of pyramids successively superimposed, with the preeminent pyramid pointing to an ultimate One that simultaneously comprehends being as such and is the culmination of human reflective experience. This structure is, moreover, dynamic and not static, with a continuing flow of creativity downward and a continuing activity of noetic discovery upward.

ANALYSIS OF THE SOUL. The general methodology described above is evident in many specific places in Averroes's philosophy. In his analysis of the soul, for example, Aristotle's original doctrine undergoes a transformation. Whereas Aristotle's insistence on the physical principle that every form separate from matter is one in species leads to a presumption against the possibility of individual immortality, Averroes takes the obverse: Separate forms or substances can subsist in the general hierarchy of being, and thus immortality, in a purely impersonal sense, is possible.

SCIENTIFIC KNOWLEDGE. The case in natural science is similar to that of the soul. In Aristotle the various sciences are diverse and not necessarily reducible to one another in any formal sense: the *Physics* views natural behavior from one perspective and in accordance with one set of working principles, while the *De Caelo,* in contrast, uses another perspective and another set of principles. Aristotle's natural sciences are irrefragably diversified. In the *Metaphysics* he goes so far as to say that similar terminology is employed in the several sciences; however, this apparent unity of the sciences is qualified by his insistence that the use of the most general metaphysical language is, in disparate domains, only analogous and not semantically equivalent. The particular subject matter that a science encompasses controls the precise significance of the terms and logic used in the analysis and description of that science; the term "being" as it is used in the *Physics* does not possess the same meaning as "being" used in *De Anima.*

For Averroes, however, such differentiations among the sciences were not the case. "Being" had a univocal significance, not equivocal, as it had for Aristotle; and Averroes viewed nature and reality as exhibiting a single coordinated and coherent structure, proceeding in orderly hierarchical fashion from levels that are lesser (both metaphysically and noetically) to greater and richer levels of being. Aristotle's horizontal and discrete conglomeration of sciences became a harmonious order of vertically structured science with dependent and causative relationships.

ACTIVE AND PASSIVE INTELLECTS. From Aristotle, Averroes understood that the knowing process in man comprised a passive aspect—adumbrant concepts capable of being fully activated—and an active aspect—a power of dynamically activating such concepts. This power, termed during the medieval period the "active intellect," was taken to operate against a "passive intellect" to actualize concepts and thus constituted the thinking activity; and the resulting fusion of function was termed the "acquired intellect." This terminology applicable to the noetic process was based on Aristotle's *De Anima,* and appears, with minor variations, in Greek and Arabic thought down to the time of Averroes. God, as the First Intelligence, provides through the next subordinate level of intelligences—the celestial bodies, upon which he exercises immediate control—activating power for the active intellect controlling man's thought.

The active intellect is not personalized, however, because it is Aristotelian form, and each such form is a species and never an individual. Nor is the passive intellect, in its nonnoetic status apart from participation in the acquired intellect—a further pressing of Aristotle impelled by Platonic dispositions. In Averroes's philosophy, consonant with Muslim theology, it is thus a domain of reality that looks upward to God for its sustaining power and with which individual souls strive to fuse impersonally, in knowledge and ultimately in immortality. Thus Averroes, and certainly his medieval interpreters, believed in the unlikelihood of individual immortality—the active intellect with which man hopes to unite at death being a single undifferentiated form—and the soul, as individuated in this life, cannot subsist without the body.

METAPHYSICS, NATURAL PHILOSOPHY, SCIENCE. Averroes's metaphysics, natural philosophy, and science can be classified as a moderate Platonism, tempered with a profound appreciation of Aristotle. Unlike many of his Islamic predecessors, Averroes accepted Aristotle's rigorous rationalism wholeheartedly, although at various crucial points his renderings of Aristotle's laconic texts are governed by his own Platonic methodological predispositions. Against the latter, he held the principle of the uni-

vocality of being, flowing downward from a Supreme Principle. God's existence is established from the *Physics,* in that the eternity of motion demands an unmoved mover, which is in itself pure form. In addition to being the source of motion, such pure form is also Intelligence as such, operating not only as the source of the celestial bodies and all subordinate motions but also as the creative originator and sustaining force behind all lesser intelligences.

THEOLOGY AND NATURAL PHILOSOPHY. In the Christian intellectual environment of the thirteenth century, apparent conflicts between argumentation in natural philosophy and argumentation in matters of theological doctrine became exceptionally acute. The newly introduced writings from the ancients—Greek philosophy and science, accompanied by Arabic and Hebrew commentary—rigorously set forth propositions alien to fundamental dicta of Christian faith: for example, the eternity of the world, the impossibility of individual immortality, and the radical noncontingency of existence as such. Averroes's rendering of the Aristotelian writings contributed heavily to these conflicts. Aristotle was read in the medieval faculties of arts as the staple of natural philosophy and science, and Averroes was read as his primary interpretive adjunct. In fact, in later medieval writings Averroes is merely referred to as "the Commentator." Thus, since he put forward analyses understanding Aristotle to deny the creation of the world in time, personal immortality, and the contingency of existence, such views attained wide currency among masters of arts.

The response from the theological side was early and direct. "Arabic" commentary was forbidden to be read in 1210 and 1215, and permitted only with censoring in 1231, at the University of Paris. Albert the Great published a treatise, *Contra Averroistas,* and Thomas Aquinas wrote about 1269, at a time of great intellectual controversy at Paris, a *Tractatus de Unitate Intellectus Contra Averroistas.*

"Double-truth" doctrine. The replies to Averroes were reasoned and moderate, but they seem to have been accompanied by many contemporary declarations that the "Averroists" were actually maintaining a doctrine of "double truth," according to which conclusions in natural philosophy were said to be true, while simultaneously conclusions affirming the contrary in theological argument were held true—presumably an intolerable intellectual situation. Thus there were official condemnations of "unorthodox" doctrines at the University of Paris in 1270 and 1277, including specific injunctions against two stan-

dards of truth. It is not, however, clear that any philosophers in the thirteenth century explicitly held such a theory of "double truth"; in the writings that survive, philosophers faced with these conflicts take great pains to concede truth itself to the declarations of faith and say of Aristotelian writings only that they have been properly arrived at according to Aristotle's methods.

Averroes himself composed the short treatise *On the Harmony between Religion and Philosophy*; his main effort in this work was to establish that there is but one truth to which there are several modes of access—the rhetorical, open to any man through the persuasions of teachers; the dialectical, available for some to explore the probability of truths of divine law; and the philosophical, to be used only by those few capable of exercising pure ratiocination with the fullest competence. Such a variety of methods ensures for each man, depending on his individual capability, the possibility of grasping ultimate realities. The fact that in this work Averroes distinguishes between such modes of access to truth has, by many historians, been taken to adumbrate the theory of the "double truth," as attributed to many thinkers in the thirteenth century, but this is not probable. First, this work of Averroes was not available to medieval Latin scholars and thus obviously cannot have been directly influential; second, the doctrine of alternative modes of access to truth is hardly the same as that of maintaining incompatible truths in disparate domains.

Thus, the attribution of a doctrine of "double truth" to medievals cannot be sustained by any writings of Aristotle accompanied by Averroistic commentaries, nor can it be justified explicitly from any Christian medieval master. The oppositions between Aristotelian-Averroist argument and basic Christian doctrine constituted a fundamental intellectual dilemma within Christian speculation—one never resolved by the masters of arts in an explicit proclamation of a logical contradiction between two domains of reflection but always by an absolute accession of truth to faith. Averroes did not contribute specifically to the discussion arising from this dilemma, except insofar as his rigorous analysis of Aristotle made necessary certain conclusions in natural philosophy.

Averroes stands as a philosopher in his own right, but his influence was felt essentially in Western Latin philosophy from 1200 to 1650. His commentaries on Aristotle, an integral part of the educational curriculum in the faculties of arts of western European universities, shaped several centuries of Latin philosophy and science. Despite institutional criticism and even formal condemnation, his powerful statements of Aristotelian doctrine were sus-

tained among Latin scholars and thinkers well into the mid-seventeenth century.

See also Albert the Great; Aristotelianism; Aristotle; Averroism; Averroism in Modern Islamic Philosophy; Ibn Bājja Ibn Ṭufayl; Jewish Averroism; Neoplatonism; Plato; Platonism and the Platonic Tradition; Plotinus; Thomas Aquinas, St.

Bibliography

The most important general references are Ernest Renan, *Averroès et l'averroisme* (Paris: A. Durand, 1852; modern ed., Paris, 1949); Salomon Munk, *Mélanges de philosophie juive et arabe* (Paris: A. Franck, 1859), pp. 418–458; Léon Gauthier, *Ibn Rochd* (Paris: Presses universitaires de France, 1948); and G. Quadri, *La philosophie arabe dans l'Europe médiévale* (Paris: Payot, 1947), pp. 198–340. The last two of these studies depend heavily on the first two, which are the unsuperseded (except in occasional detail) classics in the literature on Averroes, although Gauthier properly views some of the indirect traditions with caution. For Averroes's predecessors, mentors, and contemporaries, see George Sarton, *Introduction to the History of Science*, Vol. I (Baltimore: Carnegie Institution of Washington, Williams and Wilkins, 1927) and Vol. II (Baltimore: Carnegie Institution of Washington, Williams and Wilkins, 1931), *passim*. Significant recent interpretations, with varying emphases, can be found in Étienne Gilson, *History of Christian Philosophy in the Middle Ages* (New York: Random House, 1955); A. A. Maurer, *Medieval Philosophy* (New York: Random House, 1962); and D. Knowles, *Evolution of Medieval Thought* (Baltimore: Helicon Press, 1962).

For a detailed catalog of Averroes's writings, see George Sarton, *Introduction to the History of Science*, Vol. II, Part 2, pp. 356–360. Also see Léon Gauthier, *Ibn Rochd*, pp. 12–16, and M. Bouyges, *Notes sur les philosophes arabes connus de Latins au moyen âge*, Vol. IV, *Inventaires des textes arabes d'Averroès* (Beirut, 1922). The latter, a monograph, is in the *Mélanges de l'Université Saint-Joseph* (Beirut: Catholique, 1922), Vol. VIII, Fascicle 1. H. A. Wolfson has meticulously stated the ambitious program for preparing and publishing modern editions of the Aristotelian commentaries in "Plan for the Publication of a Corpus Commentariorum Averrois in Aristotelem," in *Speculum* 6 (1931): 412–427, and "Revised Plan for the Publication of a Corpus Commentariorum Averrois in Aristotelem," in *Speculum* 38 (1963): 88–104. The latter article provides the most reliable listing of the surviving writings. There are other modern editions and translations of some works: for instance, E. I. J. Rosenthal, *Averroës' Commentary on Plato's Republic* (Cambridge, U.K.: Cambridge University Press, 1966); G. F. Hourani, *Averroës on the Harmony of Religion and Philosophy* (London: Luzac, 1961); and Simon Van den Bergh's translation of *The Incoherence of the Incoherence* (London: Luzac, 1954).

Stuart MacClintock (1967)

AVERROES [ADDENDUM]

At the time that Ibn Rushd was working, the philosophical curriculum was largely Neoplatonic, and this is because the Greek tradition of philosophy was transmitted to the Islamic world via the Neoplatonic tradition. But some thinkers like Ibn Rushd were perceptive enough to realize that there were discrepancies between Aristotle—very much his hero—and the Neoplatonists, who were represented at the time by the thought of Ibn Sīnā. In his defense of philosophy in the *Tahāfut al-Tahāfut*, for instance, Ibn Rushd not only seeks to refute al-Ghazālī's attack on philosophy, but he also tries to argue with Ibn Sīnā's particular Neoplatonic philosophy. In fact, he manages to link al-Ghazālī, the critic of philosophy, with Ibn Sīnā, its main representative. Al-Ghazālī argues that causality is nothing more than the way in which people interpret God's bringing things into existence, and therefore they should not think of causal connections as being necessary. Ibn Sīnā does identify necessity and causality, but also, for him, something has to actualize essences. Ibn Rushd criticizes both of these views; he argued that existence is linked with essence—that is, what is meant by cotton is something that bursts into flames when it is touched by fire (other things being equal). The properties of cotton are not just an incidental feature of the cotton; they are an essential aspect of it.

The views of Ibn Rushd came to have a radicalizing influence on European thought when they were translated into Hebrew and Latin. They were often taken to imply that philosophical and religious truths could be in opposition to each other, and yet still both be true. This is not what Ibn Rushd himself argued; he was too good of a thinker to believe that contradictory propositions could both be true. However, he did argue that there are different routes to the truth—routes that are appropriate to different audiences. For those capable of understanding rigorous logical arguments there is philosophy, and for those disinclined or unable to appreciate such arguments there are argument forms of lesser rigor. Ibn Rushd sees the syllogism as being the basis of all uses of language. Thus while the philosopher employs the demonstrative syllogism, the politician will use rhetoric and sophistry, the prophet sometimes uses poetry, and the theologian dialectic. All of these are reasoning processes, but only demonstration—according to Ibn Rushd—reaches the highest standards of reason.

That does not mean, however, that there is anything wrong with the other methods of reasoning; they simply are not so secure as demonstration. The other methods may, nonetheless, be able to express what philosophers can discover through demonstration in ways that are accessible to more people. Because God made everyone different, Ibn Rushd believes it is appropriate that God make everyone capable of understanding some method of argument—although not everyone should be expected to employ the same method.

It is worth pointing to the radical nature of this doctrine. For one thing, Ibn Rushd's doctrine suggests that the philosophers as a group are the best able to understand the language of any text, even difficult scriptural passages. After all, philosophers can operate at the level of demonstration and so are skilled in working with the highest levels of reason. The theologians and lawyers are only used to dialectic, in which they start with propositions that are generally accepted as true, but might not be. Ibn Rushd disparages their efforts as compared with those of the philosophers. Ordinary people are in an even worse position. On the one hand they have to rely on language and on arguments that rely on imagery and persuasion, and thus they are a long way from demonstrative rigor. On the other hand, what they believe is perfectly valid because there is a demonstrative proof for it, but not a proof they themselves can grasp. They do not believe anything false, but they do not appreciate the entire basis of their beliefs. Ibn Rushd gives the analogy of going to a physician or a lawyer with a problem. He suggests that if a person had the expertise of the lawyer and the physician, there would be no need to consult them (even though when lawyer and physician are consulted, what they suggest may not be understood by client or patient). If the advice were understood, there would be no need for the doctor or lawyer in the first place. And yet, there is nothing wrong with people's reliance upon doctors and lawyers because it is assumed that they understand why they make the suggestions they do—and thus if people are wise they will accept and follow those suggestions.

This approach is not a doctrine of double truth, but it is a radical doctrine that relegates religion to a relatively lowly role in the hierarchy of human pursuits. Religion is certainly inferior to reason as a way of finding out truth, because religious language is to be understood primarily by examining it philosophically. One of the features of Ibn Rushd's thought that differentiates him from other Islamic philosophers is his supreme indifference to mysticism. Mysticism, or *taṣawwuf*, was of overriding significance for most of his contemporaries and predecessors—and indeed successors—but not for him. For Ibn Rushd, the meaning of the world is firmly in the world, and not something behind it. In this way he sought to establish a purified form of Aristotelianism shorn as far as possible from its Neoplatonic accessories and excesses.

It is not surprising that Averroism came to be regarded as a challenging doctrine in the Middle Ages and beyond, and it may well have played a role in displacing traditional religion from its established role in intellectual and social life. Within the Islamic world, Ibn Rushd's views largely disappeared until the Islamic Renaissance, when they reemerged to argue for a division between religious and rational language. In modern times, Averroism has once again been used in the Arab world to argue for a new and enhanced respect for reason as compared with religion. It still appears to be a philosophy for the intellectual elite rather than the religious masses.

See also Averroism; Averroism in Modern Islamic Philosophy; Jewish Averroism.

Bibliography

Some of Ibn Rushd's works now only exist in Hebrew or Latin, and some not at all. The most useful bibliography is "Ibn Rushd: A Catalogue of Editions and Scholarly Writings from 1821 onwards," edited by Phillip Rosemann, *Bulletin de philosophie médiévale* 30 (1988): 153–215.

WORKS BY AVERROES

"Long Commentary on Aristotle's Metaphysics." In *Ibn Rushd's Metaphysics*, edited by Charles Genequand. Leiden, Netherlands: Brill, 1984.

"Tahāfut al-Tahāfut" (The incoherence of the incoherence). In *Averroes' Tahafut al-Tahafut*, edited and translated by S. Van den Bergh. London: Luzac, 1978.

WORKS ABOUT AVERROES

Fakhry, Majid. *Islamic Occasionalism and Its Critique by Averroes and Aquinas.* London: Allen and Unwin, 1958.

Hourani, G., tr. *Averroes on the Harmony of Religion and Philosophy.* London: Luzac, 1976.

Kogan, Barry. *Averroes and the Metaphysics of Causation.* Albany: State University of New York Press, 1985.

Leaman, Oliver. "Averroes." In *Klassiker der Religionsphilosophie*, edited by F. Niewöhner. Munich: C.H. Beck, 1995.

Leaman, Oliver. *Averroes and His Philosophy.* Richmond, Surrey, U.K.: Curzon, 1998.

Leaman, Oliver. "Averroes and the West." In *Averroes and the Enlightenment*, edited by M. Wahba and M. Abousenna. New York: Prometheus, 1996.

Leaman, Oliver. *A Brief Introduction to Islamic Philosophy.* Malden, MA: Blackwell, 2000. Contains material on his philosophical arguments.

Leaman, Oliver. *An Introduction to Classical Islamic Philosophy.* Cambridge, U.K.: Cambridge University Press, 2001. Contains material on his philosophical arguments.

Leaman, Oliver. "Was Averroes an Averroist?" In *Averroismus im Mittelalter und in der Renaissance*, edited by F. Niewöhner and L. Sturlese. Zurich: Spur Verlag, 1994.

Urvoy, Dominique. "Ibn Rushd." In *History of Islamic Philosophy*, edited by S. Nasr and O. Leaman. London: Routledge, 1996.

Urvoy, Dominique. *Ibn Rushd (Averroes).* Translated by O. Stewart. London: Routledge, 1991.

Oliver Leaman (2005)

AVERROISM

As a designation applicable to a tradition or mode of philosophizing, "Averroism" cannot be used in any account of Arabic thought after the death of Averroes (c. 1198). After that, in a most unusual intellectual situation, Averroes's influence is to be found not in Muslim thought but in Western Latin philosophy between 1200 and 1650, for the dynamic speculative activity vital for five centuries in the Arabic tradition, which was founded in large part on Greek writings in philosophy and science (Aristotle's in particular), disappears after 1200, reappearing almost immediately in Western Latin thought. Throughout the century 1150–1250 a vast number of translations of most of Greek and Alexandrian philosophy and science were made from Arabic and Hebrew into Latin. This literary corpus, which had made its way around the Mediterranean littoral translated from Greek into Syriac and thence into Arabic and Hebrew, caught the attention of Latin scholars and such patrons of scholarship as King Frederick II of Sicily and Archbishop Raymond of Toledo. As a consequence, by about 1200 the indefatigable efforts of many translators working in many locations had made Greek thought, especially that of Aristotle, available to Latin thinkers. The impact of this solid and integrated corpus of natural science on the Western intellectual world was enormous, coming as it did into a climate where for centuries scholars eager for knowledge had had to content themselves with thirdhand encyclopedic compilations of inadequately developed science and scientific methodology.

AVERROES'S COMMENTARIES

The translations of the Greek writings were normally accompanied by many Greek and Arabic commentaries. Commentaries by Alexander of Aphrodisias and by Simplicius were frequent, but those by the Arab Averroes on the Aristotelian works were ultimately the most influential. During a long and varied career as judge, teacher, philosophical and medical adviser to several Muslim rulers, Averroes found time to compose a series of glosses and commentaries on Aristotle's works. These fall into three categories—short (often called epitomes), intermediate or middle, and long, a differentiation which probably corresponds to stages in the academic curriculum. The particular argumentation of certain passages of Aristotle presented by Averroes in the mass of commentary had strong appeal for many Western Latin thinkers, and the reflection of his interpretations in their own philosophical analyses gave rise to attitudes which were first termed (by Christian scholars suspicious of their novelties) Arabic and later more specifically called Averroist.

INITIAL IMPACT IN THE WEST. Upon translation the Greek writings, with their attendant commentaries, were rather quickly absorbed into Western Latin scholarship, but not without some formal opposition. These writings were banned at the University of Paris in 1210 and 1215, deemed usable only if corrected in 1231, and not officially introduced into the curriculum until 1255. This literature was nevertheless being intensively read during these years; the philosophical writings of Albertus Magnus (active at least as early as 1230), William of Auvergne (d. 1249), and Alexander of Hales (d. 1245), to name only three prominent examples, reveal an intimate acquaintance with the recently acquired corpus of Greek science. Similarly, in England the philosophy of Robert Grosseteste (bishop of Lincoln, died 1253) shows strong influences derived directly from the newly inherited Greek literature. In Italy, too, the Greek tradition was rapidly assimilated into the scholarly milieu, but the Italian intellectual atmosphere was either medical, as it had been at the University of Salerno for several centuries, or else legal, as at Bologna. There do not appear proscriptions by Italian ecclesiastical authorities as stringent as those made at the University of Paris throughout the thirteenth century, and the possible intellectual conflicts raised by the introduction of these writings into a context of Christian philosophy do not seem to have been seriously felt.

Intellectual conflicts became extremely explicit, however, when the Aristotelian writings were conceived to be in direct confrontation with doctrines of Christian faith. Aristotle asserted, for example, the eternity of the world, the unlikelihood of individual immortality, the possibility of man's attaining ethical perfection in this life, and other theses incompatible with tenets of Christian belief. The appearance of such philosophical conclusions, apparently well reasoned and buttressed by Arabic commentary, occasioned some severe crises for Western Christian philosophy.

The chief agents presenting these, as well as other, renderings of Aristotle were the commentaries of Averroes. For centuries he was called simply the "Commentator" in Latin writings, and his expositions of the Aristotelian corpus were read into the seventeenth century. Cesare Cremonini (d. 1631), the last of the self-proclaimed Averroists, used these commentaries, and even at that late date he was considered unorthodox enough to be included in an array of formal proceedings along with Galileo Galilei himself. Unorthodoxy makes strange bedfellows when the resolute claimant of Aristotelianism and the architect of a scientific rupture with Aristotelian Scholasticism are included in the same condemnatory document.

LATIN AVERROISM

Historically, *Averroism* is a designation applied to certain interpretations of Aristotelian doctrine by Western Latin thinkers. (There are medieval Jewish philosophers holding positions close to these, but the epithet itself does not seem to have been applied to them.) It was originally a term of opprobrium; no one called himself Averroist until possibly John of Jandun (c. 1286–c. 1328), who was followed by Urban of Bologna (fl. 1334) and Paul of Venice (d. 1428). During the thirteenth century Averroists were the object of violent philosophical attack and severe authoritarian action.

Averroes insisted upon, and many scholars in the Western faculties of arts concurred in, the reliable logic of Aristotle's argumentation. Thus, there was clearly the necessity of the purely rational acceptance, given Aristotle's premises, of such "unorthodox" conclusions as have been mentioned. Acceptance is, however, intolerable for serious Christian thinkers, and so such conclusions were taken to be erroneous and thus subversive when pronounced in the schools. When thirteenth-century arts masters taught Aristotle in this fashion, they were awarded (by their opponents) the pejorative title Averroist, and official action often resulted. Siger of Brabant, Boethius of Dacia, and Bernier of Nivelles, masters in the faculty of arts at Paris, were all named in condemnations of the 1270s. This special mention seems to have had limited effectiveness; although these particular masters disappeared from the intellectual scene, countless commentaries on Aristotle dating from the last quarter of the thirteenth century offer similar interpretations and similar caveats as to the logical validity, if not truth, of these interpretations. No recorded disapprovals have been found.

Incidentally, this represents another aspect of the history of intellectual conflict. Explicit authoritarian condemnations were more often the result of a refusal to accept organizational discipline than of a genuine philosophical error or ideological heresy. This can be illustrated in the careers of Gottschalk (d. c. 868), Peter Abelard (1079–1142), and Roger Bacon (c. 1214/1220–1292), all of whom were subjected to ecclesiastical punishment although little of their thinking was drastically at variance with established or recommended philosophical systems.

THE "DOUBLE TRUTH" PROBLEM

Every exposition of Averroism must examine the problem, arising in the thirteenth century, of the "double truth." The masters of arts, reading Aristotle and following his rigorous logic to conclusions incompatible with certain propositions held by faith, tried to resolve apparent contradictions by including in their commentaries reservations of this nature: "Although this conclusion has been reached according to the method of Aristotle and the Commentator, nevertheless faith and truth declare otherwise." While proclaiming logical rigor and precise validity for Aristotelian arguments, they conceded the final determination of truth itself to the Christian faith.

In this historical context it has often been maintained, both in the thirteenth century and in contemporary scholarship, that such thinkers were actually practicing a system of "double truth," in which a proposition can be true in natural philosophy but contradict a proposition true in theology and conversely. But, as Étienne Gilson and other scholars have convincingly pointed out, no master of arts has yet been found explicitly holding such a radical position. Regardless of the apparent persuasiveness of Aristotelian argument, the truth itself was always the dominant prerogative of Christian faith. In the face of such overwhelming requirements, the limitations and inadequacies of natural reason were recognized by the arts masters.

ATTEMPTED SOLUTIONS

Thus, an intellectual crisis of the first magnitude appeared in Western scholarship in the early thirteenth century. The attempts to deal with this conflict between important arguments in Greco-Arab philosophies and Christian-oriented intellectual systems fall into several main categories.

REASON NOT APODICTIC. First, the masters of arts, whose primary professional obligation was teaching natural philosophy, the core of which was Aristotle and his commentators, resorted to the attitude that although such science was orderly and rigorous, the unreliability of reason and the merely probable nature of its results suggested that conclusions based on such unaided reason must always yield, with respect to truth, to the apodictic proclamations of the faith. Such masters never claimed "truth" for a proposition of natural philosophy in conflict with a proposition of faith; they insisted on its logical validity, however, and conceded the determination of truth-value to faith. In this manner they endeavored to handle an intractable intellectual dilemma and at the same time to avoid subjecting themselves to overt charges of intellectual and ideological inconsistency.

AUGUSTINIANS. Second, masters of theology—for example, Bonaventure, Peter John Olivi, and, in the first decade of the fourteenth century, John Duns Scotus—employed a methodology often termed Augustinian. Their attempt to resolve the difficulties entailed, essentially, an assimilation of Aristotelian natural philosophy into a hierarchical scheme of knowledge. Such a resolution provided a coherent and orderly vertical relation among the several sciences, proceeding from the less perfect to the more perfect, from the less well known to the more surely known, from the less exact to the more exact. Such a structure, culminating in God himself, the ultimate source of perfection, knowledge, and precision, could be coherent and consistent and could accommodate both Christian doctrine and a qualified, because essentially incomplete, natural philosophy. But the achievement of this coherence was purchased at the cost of Aristotle himself, for his scheme of the sciences does not envisage a vertical, or hierarchical, ordering, whereby lesser sciences derive their logic, meaning, and reality from superior sciences. His sciences are basically ordered horizontally, diversified methodologically, and irreducible to any single set of common and univocally meaningful fundamental principles.

THOMAS AQUINAS. Third, the preeminent theologian St. Thomas Aquinas (1224?–1274) attempted a massive resolution maintaining the logical integrity and autonomy of Aristotelian natural philosophy while setting forth a supplementary and compatible structure of Christian theology. The two disciplines run in parallel courses, with differences based on distinctive premises and arguments, but there are many points where the propositions in each discipline are the same and are concluded to be true in both domains. These points were taken by Thomas to ensure the compatibility of Aristotelian natural philosophy and Christian theology, and by this means Thomas sought to sustain a consistent intellectual whole comprehending Greek philosophy and Christian truth.

The carefully poised system of Thomas was not, however, influential in his own time, and most of his immediate successors in the theological faculties preferred to continue in the Augustinian methodology. By the early fourteenth century, moreover, both approaches—the Augustinian assimilative technique and Thomas's sophisticated and delicately poised structure of complementary systems—were abandoned. This becomes explicit in the philosophy of William of Ockham, in whose thought natural science and systematic theology are totally independent domains.

Insofar, then, as the masters of arts, reading Averroes in close conjunction with Aristotle, tended to bring forward the incompatibilities between the two systems, it is possible to affirm the judgment of Gilson that "the rupture of Christianity is from this moment an accomplished fact."

ITALIAN AVERROISM

As a designation Averroism disappeared in the intellectual history of the University of Paris after the first quarter of the fourteenth century, although there are many manuscripts making explicit these crucial difficulties; however, their overt dependence on and acknowledgment of Averroes's commentaries diminish. From about 1300 to 1650 the term *Averroism*—assumed favorably by some thinkers and in a derogatory fashion by others—is found associated with philosophical activity in the Italian universities, Bologna and especially Padua.

Renan wished to establish a dichotomy between Averroist and Alexandrist Aristotelianism in Italy at this time. This distinction was based on alternative interpretations of Aristotle's *De Anima*. The Averroist view emphasized that personal, individual immortality could not be established in Aristotle's writings. In this interpretation the soul, when separated from the body, loses all individuality—a conception congenial to the Muslim doctrine of complete impersonal fusion at the apex of noetic experience. In purely Aristotelian terminology this is known as the theory of the unity of the active intellect—that is, that any form distinct from matter is one in species and never individuated. The Alexandrist analysis likewise denied the possibility of individual immortality but argued against the separate subsistence of the soul under any conditions whatsoever; when the soul-body composite dissolves, nothing remains.

This distinction is an oversimplification of the complexities of Italian Aristotelianism between 1300 and 1650, but it was employed by the scholars themselves and may thus be used with appropriate reservations. However, whether or not these thinkers were designated Averroist or Alexandrist, they all did agree in affirming the logical integrity of Aristotelian natural philosophy, even though some conclusions reached in this philosophy appeared in radical contradiction to dicta of Christian faith.

Although it would be misleading to speak crudely of an Alexandrist tradition in the later Middle Ages, there were eminent philosophers who, though thoroughly convinced of the logical autonomy of Aristotelian thought as such, did not adhere to the letter of Averroes's rather Platonic or Augustinian interpretation. Jean Buridan (d. c. 1358) at Paris and Pietro Pomponazzi (d. 1525) and Jacopo Zabarella (d. 1589), both at Padua, can be taken to fall within the non-Averroist but still naturalistic method of Aristotelian natural philosophy.

Averroism as a term designating a tradition, type, or method of philosophizing is difficult to make precise. Thinkers of varied methodological persuasions—for instance, Siger of Brabant and John of Jandun—have been called Averroist. Averroism can, however, be solidly connected with Latin Aristotelianism where Latin Aristotelianism is taken to include philosophies that agree on the logical rigor and systematic autonomy of natural philosophy as exemplified in Aristotle's writings. Since such arguments appear to lead to conclusions inconsistent with truths of Christian faith, Averroism in its earliest usage was pejoratively employed. But the demands of reason, working with the Aristotelian corpus, were insistent, and by the middle of the fourteenth century philosophers began to proclaim themselves openly Averroist. Gilson has suggested that Averroism was essentially conservative and sterile, but it is clear that it was an integral part of the tradition of Aristotelian scholasticism and that its disappearance in the seventeenth century coincided with the demise of medieval Scholasticism itself.

See also Augustinianism; Averroes; Averroism in Modern Islamic Philosophy; Thomas Aquinas, St.

Bibliography

LATIN AVERROISM

Ernest Renan's pioneering work on Averroism, *Averroès et l'averroïsme*, rev. ed. by H. Psichari (Paris, 1949), originally published in Paris, 1852, is now out of date. See rather *Averroes and the Aristotelian Tradition. Sources. Constitution and Reception of the Philosophy of Ibn Rushd (1126–1198)*, edited by G. Endress and J. A. Aertsen (Leyden-Boston-Köln: Brill, 1999); *Averroismus im Mittelalter und in der Renaissance*, edited by F. Niewöhner, L. Sturlese (Zürich: Spur Verlag, 1994); and *L'Averroismo in Italia, Atti dei* convegni Lincei, 40 (Rome: Accademia nazionale dei Lincei, 1979). For new manuscript evidences on Hebrew and Latin translations of Averroes's commentaries and their impact in the West, see Carlos Steel and Marc Geoffroy, La béatitude de l'âme (Paris: Vrin, 2001); Colette Sirat and Marc Geoffroy, L'Original arabe du Grand Commentaire d'Averroès au De Anima d'Aristote (Paris: Vrin, 2005). On Boethius of Dacia, Siger of Brabant, and the "double-truth" problem, see Luca Bianchi, Censure et Liberté intellectuelle à l'université de Paris (Paris: Les Belles Lettres, 1999); J. F. Wippel, "The Condemnations of 1270 and 1277 at Paris," Journal of Mediaeval and Renaissance Studies 7 (1977): 169–201. On Aquinas, see Aquinas against the Averroists, on there being only one intellect, translated by R. MacInerny (West Lafayette, IN: Purdue University Press, 1993).

JEWISH AVERROISM

Leaman, Oliver. "Jewish Averroism." In History of Islamic Philosophy, edited by S. H. Nasr and O. Leaman. London: Routledge, 1996.

Zonta, Mauro. La filosofia ebraica medievale. Storia e testi. Roma-Bari: Editori Laterza, 2002.

ARABIC ARISTOTELIANISM

The major figures of Arabic Aristotelianism are al-Kīndī (d. 873), al-Farābī (d. 950), ibn-Sīnā (Latinized Avicenna, d. 1037), and Ibn-Bajja (Latinized Avempace, d. 1138). See The Cambridge Companion to Arabic Philosophy, edited by Peter Adamson and Richard C. Taylor (Cambridge: CUP, 2005); Storia della filosofia nell'Islam medievale, edited by Cristina D'Ancona Costa (Torino: Einaudi, 2005). These important works provide references to many other valuable and supplementary studies. For a reader, see Medieval Islamic Philosophical Writings, edited by Muhammad Ali Khalidi (Cambridge: CUP, 2005). For al-Ghazzali's Incoherence of the Philosophers see The Incoherence of the Philosophers: English Translation of Imam Ghazali's Tahafut al-Falasifa, translated by Michael E. Marmura (Brigham Young University's Islamic Translation Series), (Brigham Young University Press: 2000). For Averroes' reply, see his Incoherence of the Incoherence, translated by Simon Van Den Bergh (Gibb Memorial Trust, 1978). In this debate the term philosophers is a translation of the Arabic falasifa, which is in turn a transliteration of the Greek philosophoi. Falasifa thus has the special meaning of "thinkers following the Greek tradition" and not the general sense of philosophers as such.

TRANSMISSION OF GREEK AND ARABIC PHILOSOPHY

Rencontres de cultures dans la philosophie médiévale: traductions et traducteurs de l'antiquité tardive au XIVe siècle, edited by J. Hamesse and M. Fattori. Louvain: Brepols, 1990.

The Introduction of Arabic Philosophy into Europe, edited by C. E. Butterworth and B. A. Kessel. Leiden: Brill, 1994.

Stuart MacClintock (1967)
Bibliography updated by Alain de Libera (2005)

AVERROISM IN MODERN ISLAMIC PHILOSOPHY

Averroes (Ibn Rushd) largely disappeared from the Islamic world after his death in 1198, but returned through the influence of Ernest Renan, who in the nineteenth century presented Averroes as a hero of rationalism and antireligious skepticism. Many Arab intellectuals were educated in France and came into contact with Renan's views, and they played a large part in the Islamic renaissance movement (al-Nahḍa). This was designed to combine adherence to religion with a commitment to reason, something that Ibn Rushd was regarded as exemplifying in his life and work. His work has been used to oppose the forces of conservatism and traditionalism in the Arab world. Averroes was in his life also opposed by the local religious authorities, as are his modern supporters in the Arab world.

The tanwīr—or enlightenment movement—is more radical than the Nahḍa because it often is highly critical of the influence of established religion. Its central text is Falsafat Ibn Rushd by Faruḥ Antūn, as well as the books of al-ʿĀṭif al-ʿIrāqī on Averroes. Although of limited influence in the Arab world as a whole, and even in Egypt where it has some presence in the universities of Cairo, this movement has created considerable intellectual discussion among Arab philosophers. Its critics regard it as too aligned with the West and too antagonistic to Islam, but proponents of the tanwīr movement argue that only a radical separation of faith and politics can initiate an appropriate degree of modernity into the Arab world.

See also Averroes; Averroism; Islamic Philosophy.

Bibliography

Antun, Faruh. Falsafat Ibn Rushd. Beirut, Lebanon: Dar al-Farabi, 1988.

Wahba, Mourad, and Mona Abousenna, eds. Averroes and the Enlightenment Movement. New York: Prometheus, 1996.

Oliver Leaman (2005)

AVERROISM, JEWISH

See Jewish Averroism

AVICEBRON

See Ibn Gabirol, Solomon ben Judah

AVICENNA
(980–1037)

Avicenna, whose full name was Abū ʿAlī al-Ḥusayn ibn ʿAbd-Allāh ibn Sīnā, was the most renowned and influential philosopher of medieval Islam. He was a Persian, born near Bukhara, then the capital of the Persian Samānid dynasty. His father was a partisan of the heterodox Ismāʿīlī sect, whose theology drew on current popularized Neoplatonism. As a boy, Avicenna was exposed to Ismāʿīlī doctrine but found it intellectually lacking. He received some of the basic Islamic religious education, then studied logic, mathematics, the natural sciences, philosophy, and medicine, mastering these subjects by the age of eighteen. A certain al-Nātilī introduced him to logic, geometry, and astronomy, but Avicenna was largely self-taught. He records that he was able to fathom Aristotle's *Metaphysics* only after a chance discovery of a commentary on it by al-Fārābī (Alfarabi). Appointed physician at the Samānid court, he intensified his studies at its excellent library. Thereafter, he states, he added little to his stock of learning but deepened his understanding of what he had acquired.

In 999 Samānid rule disintegrated with the onslaught of the Turkish Ghaznawid dynasty. Avicenna left Bukhara to roam the cities of Transoxania and Iran, serving local warring princes. Between 1015 and 1022 he acted as both vizier and physician to the ruler of Hamadan; after the latter's death he was imprisoned but was released four months later when ʿAlā al-Dawla, the ruler of Isfahan, temporarily occupied the city. Soon afterward, disguised as a dervish, Avicenna left Hamadan for Isfahan, where he spent the rest of his life as physician to ʿAlā al-Dawla. This was a relatively peaceful period of his life, during which he undertook astronomical investigations. A serious interruption occurred in 1030, when the Ghaznawids sacked Isfahan and some of Avicenna's works were pillaged and lost. He died in Hamadan while accompanying his patron on a campaign against that city.

Over a hundred of Avicenna's works have survived, ranging from encyclopedic treatments to short treatises and covering, apart from philosophy and science, religious, linguistic, and literary matters. He wrote some works in Persian, of which the *Dānishnāma-yi ʿAlāʾī* ("The Book of Science Dedicated to ʿAlā al-Dawla") is the most important. Most of his works, however, are in Arabic. His chief medical work is *al-Qanūn fi al-Tibb* ("The Canon of Medicine"), a synthesis of Greek and Arabic medicine which also includes his own clinical observations and views on scientific method. The most detailed philosophical work is the voluminous *al-Shifāʾ* ("The Healing"). *Al-Najāt* ("The Deliverance") is largely a summary of *al-Shifāʾ*, although there are some deviations. *Al-Ishārāt wa al-Tanbīhāt* ("The Directives and Remarks") gives the quintessence of Avicenna's philosophy, sometimes in an aphoristic style, and concludes with an expression of his mystical esoteric views, a part that relates to certain symbolic narratives which he also wrote.

PHILOSOPHY

Avicenna forged a comprehensive philosophical system that owed a great deal to Aristotle, but his system cannot be strictly called Aristotelian. In both his epistemology and his metaphysics he adopted Neoplatonic doctrines but formulated them in his own special way. There were other Greek influences: Plato on his political philosophy; Galen on his psychology; the Stoics on his logic. Nearer home was the influence of Islamic theology and philosophy. The theologians had stressed the contingent nature of things, subjecting Aristotelian causal theory to severe logical and empirical criticism. Avicenna undertook to meet this criticism and attacked the theologians' formulation of the notion of contingency, but he nonetheless was influenced by it. The Islamic philosopher who influenced him most was al-Fārābī; Avicenna adopted al-Fārābī's concept of the identity of divine essence and existence, and developed his dyadic emanative system into a triadic scheme. As both metaphysician and political thinker, Avicenna interpreted the Islamic religion in terms of his own system. Whether this religion remains "Islamic" when so interpreted is a debatable point, but it conditioned the way Avicenna formulated his philosophy.

METAPHYSICS. Although Avicenna's system rests on his conception of the Necessary Existent, God, he held that the subject matter of metaphysics is broader than theology. As distinct from physics, which considers moving things "inasmuch as they move," metaphysics is concerned with the existent "inasmuch as it exists." We arrive at the Necessary Existent by first examining the attributes of the existents. Avicenna undertook such examination in detail, drawing those distinctions which greatly influenced Latin scholastic thought. One such distinction is that between a universal like "horse," by definition predicable of many instances, and a universal like "horseness," in itself outside the category of such predication; considered in itself, horseness is simply horseness, neither one nor many. Related to this is the fundamental distinction between essence and existence.

If we examine any existing species, we find nothing in its essence to account for its existence. In itself, such an existent is only possible: it can exist or not exist. From *what* it is, we cannot infer *that* it exists, although in fact it exists. Something has "specified" it with existence; and this something, argued Avicenna, must be its necessitating cause. If it were not—if it were a cause that may or may not produce its effect—we would have to suppose another cause; and if this cause were not necessitating, yet another; and so on ad infinitum. But an infinity of such causes—even if allowed—would not specify the possible with existence. Hence, such an existent must be necessitated by another, by which Avicenna meant that its existence is the consequence of the essence of another existent. The theory involved here is that of essential causality, where causal action is a necessary attribute of a thing's essential nature and where cause and effect coexist. Existents form a chain of such essential causes; and since these coexist, the chain must be finite. Otherwise it would constitute an actual infinite, which Avicenna deemed impossible. The chain must proceed from an existing essence that does not derive its existence externally. This is God, the Necessary Existent, who, Avicenna attempted to demonstrate, must be eternal, one, and simple, devoid of all multiplicity. Since God, the necessitating cause of all the existents, is eternal, his effect, the world, is necessarily eternal.

The world emanates from God as the consequence of his self-knowledge. Self-knowledge, however, does not imply multiplicity in the knower; nor does multiplicity proceed from God directly. God's act of self-knowledge necessitates the existence of one intellect. Multiplicity proceeds from this intellect which undergoes three acts of awareness, corresponding to the three facts of existence it encounters: (1) God's existence as necessary in itself; (2) the intellect's own existence as necessitated; (3) the intellect's own existence as only possible in itself. These three acts of awareness necessitate the existence of three things—another intellect, a soul, and the first heaven, respectively. The second intellect, in turn, undergoes a similar cognitive process, necessitating another triad; the third intellect, yet another; and so on down to the sphere of the moon. The last intellect thus generated is the Active Intelligence, whose acts of cognition necessitate the world of generation and corruption.

Avicenna's cosmology was oriented toward the Ptolemaic system as modified by some of the Islamic astronomers, who, in order to explain the precession of the equinoxes, added another heavenly sphere beyond that of the fixed stars, and Avicenna inclined toward regarding the number of intellects as ten. He was not dogmatic on this point, however, leaving the question of the number of intellects adjustable to changes in astronomical and cosmological theory. What he insisted on was that the number of intellects should be at least equal to the number of heavens.

In this scheme Avicenna attempted to make precise the relation of the celestial intellects to God, something left uncertain in Aristotle. According to Avicenna, the intellects derive their existence from God and are arranged in an ontological and normative hierarchy corresponding to their proximity to God. God, for him, is not only the prime mover but also the cause of existence. The celestial intellects, in turn, although deriving their existence from God, cause other existents and act as teleological causes. Thus, in each of the triads the heavenly body is moved by its soul through the soul's desire for the intellect. The souls differ from the intellects in that they have a material aspect enabling them to have direct influence over the particulars in the sublunar world and to know them in their particularity. Neither God nor the celestial intellects have this direct influence and know these particulars only "in a universal way."

THE HUMAN SOUL. According to Avicenna, both the human soul and the rational knowledge it acquires are emanations from the Active Intelligence. As such, the body "receives" the soul and the soul "receives" rational knowledge. Certain combinations of formed matter induce the reception from the Active Intelligence of the vegetative soul. Other combinations induce, in addition to this, the reception of the animal soul; and others, in addition to these two, induce the reception of the rational soul, with its practical and theoretical aspects. The human rational soul is an individual, indivisible, and immaterial substance that does not exist as an individual prior to the body—Avicenna denied the theory of transmigration. Further, it is created *with* the body, not "imprinted" on it. The body is no more than the soul's instrument, which the soul must use for perfecting itself through the attainment of theoretical knowledge; this involves complete control of the animal passions. Souls inherently incapable of attaining theoretical knowledge can still control the body and live pure lives by adhering to the commands of the revealed law. With the body's corruption (death), the soul separates to exist eternally as an individual. Souls that have led pure lives and have actualized their potentialities continue in eternal bliss, contemplating the celestial principles. The imperfect souls, tarnished by the body, continue in eternal torment, vainly seeking their bodies, which once were the instruments of their perfection.

Avicenna denied bodily resurrection but insisted on the Soul's individual immortality. To begin with, he held that the immaterial is incorruptible. Moreover, he was convinced not only of the soul's immateriality but also of its individuality. He argued for both these points simultaneously: When one refers to himself as "I," this cannot be a reference to his body. If a man were to come into being fully mature and rational but suspended in space so that he was totally unaware of his physical circumstances, he would still be certain of one thing—his own existence as an individual self.

Theoretical knowledge consists in the reception of the intelligibles from the Active Intelligence. The primary intelligibles, the self-evident logical truths, are received by men directly, without the need of the soul's preparatory activities on the sensory level. The secondary intelligibles, concepts and logical inferences, whose reception is limited to people capable of demonstrative knowledge, normally require preparatory activities involving the external and internal senses—sensation, memory, imagination, estimation, and cogitation, or imaged thinking. Avicenna assigned special faculties and physiological places to these activities. The human intellect undergoes various stages in its acquisition of the intelligibles. At first it is a material intellect, a pure potentiality analogous to prime matter, ready for the reception of the intelligibles. With the reception of the first intelligibles it becomes the intellect with positive disposition. When it is *in the act* of receiving the secondary intelligibles, it becomes the acquired intellect. When an intellect that receives the secondary intelligibles is not engaged in the act of reception, it is termed "the actual intellect."

POLITICAL AND RELIGIOUS PHILOSOPHY. Avicenna followed al-Fārābī in holding that revealed religion gives the same truths as philosophy but in the symbolic, particular, imaged language that the masses can understand. According to Avicenna, some prophets receive this particular symbolic knowledge directly from the celestial souls. Such reception involves the prophet's imaginative faculty. In a higher form of prophecy that is intellectual, the prophet receives from the celestial intellects not only the first intelligibles, without the need of the soul's preparatory activities, but also the second. Prophetic reception of knowledge thus differs from the philosophical "in manner." It also differs "in quantity." Avicenna suggested that the prophet receives all or most of the intelligibles from the Active Intelligence "all at once." This intellectual reve-

lation is then translated into the language of imagery and divulged to the public. It includes the basic commands of the revealed law, without which man as a political animal cannot survive. Hence, divine goodness must reveal the law at certain moments of discussion through prophets. Prophecy is thus necessary in the sense that it is required for the survival of civilized society and in the sense that it is necessitated by the divine nature. Having argued for the necessity of prophecy, Avicenna proceeded to accommodate Islamic institutions within his philosophical framework.

The high point of Avicenna's religious philosophy is his discussion of mysticism in the *Ishārāt*. In this work he adopted the language of Islamic mysticism (*sufism*) to describe the mystic's spiritual journey to God: Beginning with faith and motivated by desire and love, the mystic undertakes spiritual exercises that first bring him to interrupted glimmerings "of the light of the Truth." These experiences become progressively more frequent and durable until the stage of "arrival" is reached, in which the mystic has a direct and an uninterrupted vision of God. According to Avicenna, there are further stages beyond this, but he declined to discuss them. He also ascribed some of the prophetic qualities to mystics, without implying that all mystics are law-revealing prophets. On the other hand, his language suggests that he held that all prophets are mystics.

LOGIC AND DEMONSTRATIVE METHOD. Avicenna inherited the Aristotelian and Stoic logical tradition as expounded by al-Fārābī and the Baghdadi school of logicians but treated his subject more independently. He found the then current classification of syllogisms into "attributive" (categorical) and "conditional" too narrow. Instead, he classified them as "connective" and "exceptive." Connective syllogisms have the *form* of the categorical, but their premises may consist of combinations of attributive and conditional statements. Similarly, exceptive syllogisms have the form of one of the two types of conditional syllogisms—the conjunctive, corresponding to the *modus ponens* and the *modus tollens,* and the disjunctive in which the logical relation is exclusive—but their premises may consist of attributive statements conditionally related, or combinations of conditional and attributive statements. He attempted the quantification of both conjunctive and disjunctive premises, discussed the temporal aspects of quantification in general, and treated the modality of premises and arguments at length.

Although Avicenna held logic to be merely a tool of knowledge and strove to treat it as distinct from philosophy, his discussion of the epistemic status of premises (which carried him considerably beyond anything in Aristotle) rendered his logic philosophically committed; his discussion of demonstrative premises was committed to his epistemology and metaphysics of causality. He followed Aristotle in his treatment of demonstrative inference, distinguishing between demonstrations that give the reasoned fact and those that give the fact. The former involve inference from cause to effect; the latter, inference from effect to cause. He also included in the latter class inferences from one effect to another. This is possible when it has been established that a single cause necessitates two effects; Avicenna gave a medical example of a disease that has two symptoms.

Avicenna's endorsement of the *Posterior Analytics* extended to much of the *Physics*. He rejected, however, Aristotle's account of falling bodies, substituting for it a theory of acquired force that was a forerunner of the theory of momentum.

Although some Jewish and Islamic philosophers (Maimonides, ibn Bājja [Avempace], Averroes) showed a preference for al-Fārābī, Avicenna's influence overshadowed the latter's in the Islamic world. The mystical side of his philosophy was elaborated in the illuminationist thought of the philosophers of Persia. The orthodox Ash'arite theologians who condemned his metaphysics adopted his logic, and his medical works continued to dominate the Islamic world until the emergence of the modern university.

In the Latin West his emanative metaphysics and epistemology blended with the Augustinianism of the Franciscan schools as a basic ingredient of their thought. His influence on Thomas Aquinas was considerable, notwithstanding Thomas's rejection of many Avicennian doctrines. He also greatly influenced the development of logic and science, his *Canon of Medicine* remaining an authoritative medical text into the seventeenth century.

See also al-Fārābī; Averroes; Cosmology; Ibn Bājja; Islamic Philosophy; Maimonides; Neoplatonism; Plato; Sufism; Thomas Aquinas, St.

Bibliography

There is no collected edition of Avicenna's works in the original. The closest thing to a collection of Persian works consists of Volumes X–XXV of the series *Silsila-i Intishārāt-i Anjuman-i Āthāri Millī* (Publications of the Society of National Monuments). These volumes, published by the University of Teheran, appeared in 1951 on the occasion of Avicenna's millenary.

Critical editions of parts of the *al-Shifā'*, in the original Arabic have been appearing in a series sponsored by the Egyptian ministry of education and supervised by Dr. Ibrahīm Madkūr. The following volumes have appeared: *Al-Madkhal* ("Isagoge," Cairo, 1952); *Al-Khaṭaba* ("Rhetoric," Cairo, 1954); *Al-Burhān* ("Demonstration," Cairo, 1955); *Jawami 'ilm al-Mūsīqā* ("Music," Cairo, 1956); *Al-Safsata* ("Sophistic," Cairo, 1958); *Al-Maqūlāt* ("Categories," Cairo, 1959); *Al-Ilāhīyāt* ("Metaphysics," 2 vols., Cairo, 1960); and *Al-Qiyās* ("Syllogism," Cairo, 1964).

Translations of Avicenna's works include *Avicenna on Theology,* translated by A. J. Arberry (London, 1951); *A Treatise on the Canon of Medicine,* translated by O. Cameron Gruner (London: Luzac, 1930); *Avicennae de Congelatione et Conglutinatione Lapidum,* translated by E. J. Holmyard and D. C. Mandeville (Paris: P. Guethner, 1927); *Die Metaphysik Avicennas,* translated by Max Horten (New York: R. Haupt, 1907); *La métaphysique du Shifā',* translated by M. M. Anawati, mimeographed ed. (Quebec, 1952); *Le livre de science,* translated by Mohammad Achena and Henri Massé, 2 vols. (Paris: Société d'édition "Les Belles Lettres," 1955); *Le livre des directives et remarques,* translated by A. M. Goichon (Paris, 1955); *Psychologie d'Ibn Sînā (Avicenne) d'après son oeuvre Aš-šifa',* edited and translated by Jan Bakoš (Prague: Editions de l'Académie tchécoslovaque des Sciences, 1956); Ralph Lerner and Muhsin Mahdi, eds., *Medieval Political Philosophy: A Source Book* (New York: Free Press of Glencoe, 1963), pp. 95–121; and *Avicenna's Psychology,* translated by Fazlur Rahman (London: Oxford University Press, 1952).

Studies include S. M. Afnan, *Avicenna, His Life and Works* (London: Allen and Unwin, 1958); M.-T. d'Alverny, "Anniya-Anitas," in *Mélanges offerts à Étienne Gilson* (Paris: J. Vrin, 1959), pp. 59–91; E. G. Browne, *Arabian Medicine* (Cambridge: Cambridge University Press, 1921); Henri Corbin, *Avicenna and the Visionary Recital,* translated by W. R. Trask (New York: Pantheon, 1960); M. Cruz Hernandes, *La metafísica de Avicena* (Granada: University of Granada, 1949); Louis Gardet, *La penséd religieuse d'Avicenne (Ibn Sīnā)* (Paris, 1951); Étienne Gilson, "Les sources gréco-arabes de l'augustinism avicennisant," in *Archives d'histoire doctrinale et littéraire du moyen âge* 4 (1929): 5–149; A. M. Goichon, *La distinction de l'essence et de l'existence d'après Ibn Sīnā (Avicenne)* (Paris: Desclée, de Brouwer, 1937), *Lexique de la langue philosophique d'Ibn Sīnā (Avicenne)* (Paris, 1938), *La philosophie d'Avicenne et son influence en Europe médiévale* (Paris: Adrien-Maisonneuve, 1944), and *Vocabulaires comparés d'Aristote et d'Ibn Sīnā* (Paris, 1939).

See also M. E. Marmura, "Avicenna's Theory of Prophecy in the Light of ash 'arite Theology," in W. S. McCullough, ed., *The Seed of Wisdom* (Toronto: University of Toronto Press, 1964), pp. 159–178, and "Some Aspects of Avicenna's Theory of God's Knowledge of Particulars," in *American Journal of Oriental Studies* 82 (3) (1962): 299–312; S. H. Nasr, *Islamic Cosmological Doctrines* (Cambridge, MA, 1964), pp. 177–281; Shlomo Pines, "La 'philosophie orientale' d'Avicenne et sa polémique contre les Bagdadiens," in *Archives d'histoire doctrinale et littéraire du moyen âge* 27 (1952): 5–37; Nicholas Rescher, *Studies in the History of Arabic Logic* (Pittsburgh: University of Pittsburgh Press, 1963), pp. 76–86 and 91–105; Djamil Saliba, *Étude sur la métaphysique d'Avicenne* (Paris, 1926); and G. M.

Wickens, ed., *Avicenna: Scientist and Philosopher; A Millenary Symposium* (London: Luzac, 1952).

Bibliographies include G. C. Anawati, *Essai de bibliographie avicennienne* (Cairo: Dar al-Mar'arf, 1950), and Yahya Mehdawi, *Bibliographie d'Ibn Sīnā* (Teheran, 1954).

Michael E. Marmura (1967)

AVICENNA [ADDENDUM]

Avicenna played an important role in Islamic aesthetics. Poetry relies on imagination, he argues, but that does not mean it is entirely without logical structure. On the contrary, one can only understand poetry if it is analyzed in terms of the syllogism. The premises of such a reasoning are statements produced by writers to bring about emotional states in the reader or hearer. This only works if there is some reason to connect the use of words with the emotion, and that reason has precisely to be a logical reason. The conclusion is the pleasure one feels at the bold and striking use of language, and because one is not the only person who can enjoy that use of language, the conclusion is also available to others. It then becomes a general conclusion rather like the conclusion of a strictly demonstrative syllogism. Avicenna follows a similar strategy in discussing music, in that at the end of the reasoning process one undergoes when listening to it, a conclusion is drawn in terms of a pleasure that one can expect others to share.

See also Aesthetics, History of; Logic, Traditional; Music, Philosophy of; Philosophy of Language.

Bibliography

Fakhry, Majid. *Ethical Theories in Islam*. 2nd ed. Leiden, Netherlands: Brill, 1994.

Goodman, Lenn E. *Avicenna*. London: Routledge, 1992.

Gutas, Dimitri. *Avicenna and the Aristotelian Tradition: Introduction to Reading Avicenna's Philosophical Works*. Leiden, Netherlands: Brill, 1988.

Inati, Shams. "Ibn Sina." In *History of Islamic Philosophy*. 2 vols., edited by Seyyed Hossein Nasr and Oliver Leaman. London: Routledge, 1996.

Kemal, Salim. *The Poetics of Alfarabi and Avicenna*. Leiden, Netherlands: Brill, 1991.

Nasr, Seyyed Hossein. "Ibn Sina's Oriental Philosophy." In *History of Islamic Philosophy*. 2 vols., edited by Seyyed Hossein Nasr and Oliver Leaman. London: Routledge, 1996.

Oliver Leaman (2005)

AXIOLOGY

See *Value and Valuation*

AXIOM AND AXIOMATIC METHOD

See *Logical Terms, Glossary of*

AYER, ALFRED JULES
(1910–1989)

Alfred Jules Ayer, the British philosopher, received his education at Eton, where he was a king's scholar, and at Christ Church, Oxford. After graduating in 1932, he spent some time at the University of Vienna familiarizing himself with the logical positivist movement, then little known among English-speaking philosophers. He returned to Oxford in 1933 as a lecturer in philosophy at Christ Church and in 1935 became a research fellow of the college. Army service in World War II kept him from philosophy until 1945, when he went back to university teaching as fellow and dean of Wadham College, Oxford. In the following year he became Grote professor of the philosophy of mind and logic at University College, London, where he remained until his return to Oxford as Wykeham professor of logic in 1959.

Ayer's first book, *Language, Truth and Logic*, was published in 1936. Its combination of lucidity, elegance, and vigor with an uncompromisingly revolutionary position has made it one of the most influential philosophical books of the century. As Ayer explains in the preface, the views he advocates derive from Bertrand Russell and Ludwig Wittgenstein among modern philosophers and from the earlier empiricism of George Berkeley and David Hume and have much in common with the logical positivism of the Vienna circle. But he accepts none of these influences uncritically and clearly puts his own stamp on the position he outlines. He adopts Hume's division of genuine statements into logical and empirical, together with a principle of verification that requires that an empirical statement shall not be counted as meaningful unless some observation is relevant to its truth or falsity. This starting point has drastic and far-reaching results. Metaphysical statements, since they purport to express neither logical truths nor empirical hypotheses, must accordingly be reckoned to be without meaning. Theology is a special case of metaphysics; affirmations of divine existence are not even false, they are without sense. For the same reason, value statements in ethics or aesthetics fail to attain the status of genuine statements and are exposed as expressions of emotion with imperative overtones. The a priori statements of logic and mathematics are empty of factual content and are true in virtue of the conventions that govern the use of the words that compose them. The tasks left for philosophy after this withdrawal from its traditional boundaries are those of solving by clarification the problems left untouched by the advance of the sciences. Philosophy is an activity of analysis and is seen, in the end, to be identical with the logic of science.

The second edition of the book (1946) contains an introduction that modifies, though it does not retract, the main theses of the first edition. Ayer's attention here is directed chiefly to giving a precise formulation of the principle of verification. His original version is replaced by a much more elaborate and carefully worded formula. Both versions have, however, been shown to be faulty in admitting as meaningful metaphysical statements of precisely the kind that the principle is designed to outlaw. Indeed, there seems to be a weakness of the principle in that, it appears plausible only when its expression is left uncomfortably vague.

The Foundations of Empirical Knowledge (1940) is concerned with two groups of problems, those of perception and those of "the ego-centric predicament" (privacy and publicity in language and in sense experience and the problem of other minds). The most interesting and original feature of the book is Ayer's treatment of the terminology of sense data as a language in which the problems of perception can be most appropriately dealt with rather than as a thesis embodying a discovery about the facts of sense experience. *Thinking and Meaning* (1947) was Ayer's inaugural lecture in the University of London. It is a trenchant application of Ockham's razor to the problems of intentionality and the relations between minds, thinking objects, words, and meaning. This short, powerful essay has so far received less than its due of critical attention. *Philosophical Essays* (1954) is a collection of papers ranging over philosophical logic, the theory of knowledge, and moral philosophy. Half the papers are carefully argued treatments of problems raised in Ayer's first two books; in particular, "The Analysis of Moral Judgements" is a moderate and persuasive restatement of the hints on ethics thrown out in *Language, Truth and Logic*.

In 1956 Ayer published *The Problem of Knowledge*, his most important book since his first was published in

1936. It is a sympathetic and constructive treatment of the various problems of philosophical skepticism. After a short discussion of philosophical method and the nature of knowledge, he discusses at length the pattern of skeptical arguments. He then examines three problems familiar from his earlier work—perception, memory, and other minds—as instances of skepticism at work. It may be that no statement is immune from doubt, but this does not entail that no statement can be known to be true. Where statements cannot, even in principle, be justified, we may conclude not that they are to be rejected but rather that no justification is called for.

The Concept of a Person (1963) is a collection of essays. The most striking, the one that gives the book its title, is a notable survey of some aspects of the problems of body, mind, and personal identity. The outcome can be roughly summarized as follows: To say that I own a mental state M is to say that there is a physical body B by which I am identified and that a state of B causes M.

Ayer's Shearman Lectures at the University of London in 1964 were on induction and probability. This was a new field of interest for Ayer, although it was foreshadowed in two papers in *The Concept of a Person*.

Ayer's work is very much of a piece, both in style and attitude. He became more catholic in interest and more cautious and temperate in expression than in his earlier writings. But his arguments were informed by the same principles and set out with the same grace and clarity. He leaned perhaps too heavily on Hume's dichotomy of statements into logical and factual, and he has not so far set himself seriously to meet contemporary criticisms (particularly those of W. V. O. Quine) that have been made of this famous distinction. This is at once a weakness of his present position and, perhaps, a presage of its future development.

Ayer died on June 29, 1989. He was professionally active virtually until the time of his death. In recognition of his accomplishments and public service, Ayer was Knighted in 1968. The following year he published both *Metaphysics and Common Sense*, a set of essays on diverse topics, and also *The Origins of Pragmatism*, an account of the philosophies of William James and Charles Sanders Peirce. In 1970 Ayer presented the William James lectures at Harvard in which he discussed the thought of G. E. Moore and Bertrand Russell. In that same year he gave the John Dewey lectures at Columbia University in which he revisited induction and probability, the topic of his 1964 Shearman lectures at the University of London. Ayer's *The Central Questions of Philosophy* (1974) is regarded by some as a new and refined version of his classic work *Language, Truth and Logic*. After serving for almost twenty years as Wykeham professor of logic at Oxford, Ayer retired from the position in 1978. Shortly thereafter a festschrift *Perception and Identity* was published in his honor, which contained essays by prominent thinkers and Ayer's replies to them. In 1982 Ayer offered his *Philosophy in the Twentieth Century* as a possible sequel to Bertrand Russell's *History of Western Philosophy*. He published interpretations of Ludwig Wittgenstein in 1985, Voltaire in 1986, and Thomas Paine in 1988. He also wrote two autobiographical volumes: *Part of My Life* (1977) and *More of My Life* (1984). His rather lengthy obituary in *The Times* of London concludes with these words: "Ayer was not a major philosopher like Russell or Wittgenstein, or even, perhaps like Popper and Ryle. But he was a very able philosopher indeed, endowed with particularly sparkling intellectual gifts, an admirable if slightly chilly prose style and unflagging energy. As a philosophical teacher and influence there is no one to compare with him since Russell and Moore."

See also Analytic and Synthetic Statements; Basic Statements; Berkeley, George;Ethics, History of; Hume, David; Logical Positivism; Other Minds; Personal Identity; Private Language Problem; Quine, Willard Van Orman; Russell, Bertrand Arthur William; Skepticism, History of; Verifiability Principle; William of Ockham; Wittgenstein, Ludwig Josef Johann.

Bibliography

WORKS BY AYER

Books

Language, Truth and Logic. London: Gollancz, 1936; 2nd ed., 1946.
The Foundations of Empirical Knowledge. London: Macmillan, 1940.
Thinking and Meaning. London: Athlone Press, 1947.
Philosophical Essays. London: Macmillan, 1954.
The Problem of Knowledge. London: Macmillan, 1956.
The Concept of a Person. London: Macmillan, 1963.
The Origins of Pragmatism. London: Macmillan, 1968.
Metaphysics and Common Sense. London: Macmillan, 1969.
Russell and Moore: The Analytical Heritage. London: Macmillan, 1971.
Probability and Evidence. London: Macmillan, 1972.
Bertrand Russell. London: Fontana, 1972.
The Central Questions of Philosophy. London: Weidenfeld, 1973.
Part of My Life. London: Collins, 1977.
Hume. Oxford: Oxford University Press, 1980.
Philosophy in the Twentieth Century. London: Weidenfeld, 1982.
Freedom and Morality and Other Essays. Oxford: Clarendon Press, 1984.
More of My Life. London: Collins, 1984.
Ludwig Wittgenstein. London: Penguin, 1986.

Articles and Symposium Pieces

"Jean-Paul Sartre." *Horizon* (1945).
"Albert Camus." *Horizon* (1945).
"Some Aspects of Existentialism." *Rationalist Annual* (1948).
"Logical Positivism—A Debate." Delivered on the BBC June 13, 1949. The participants were Ayer and F. C. Copleston. Published in *A Modern Introduction to Philosophy*, edited by P. Edwards and A. Pap (Glencoe, IL: Free Press, 1957).
"Professor Malcolm on Dreaming." *Journal of Philosophy* (1960): 517–535. Malcolm's reply, with Ayer's rejoinder, *Journal of Philosophy* (1961), 294–299.

WORKS ON AYER

For critical discussion of Ayer, see John Wisdom, "Note on the New Edition of Professor Ayer's *Language, Truth and Logic*," *Mind* 57 (228) (1948): 401–419, reprinted in Wisdom's *Philosophy and Psycho-analysis* (Oxford: Blackwell, 1953); H. H. Price, "Critical Notice of A. J. Ayer's *The Foundations of Empirical Knowledge*," *Mind* 50 (199) (1941): 280–293; H. H. Price, "Discussion: Professor Ayer's Essays," *Philosophical Quarterly* (1955); D. J. O'Connor, "Some Consequences of Professor A. J. Ayer's Verification Principle," *Analysis* (1949–1950); W. V. O. Quine, "Two Dogmas of Empiricism," in *From a Logical Point of View* (Cambridge, MA: Harvard University Press, 1953); M. Lazerowitz, "Strong and Weak Verification I," *Mind* (1939) and "Strong and Weak Verification II," *Mind* (1950), reprinted in Lazerowitz's *The Structure of Metaphysics* (London: Routledge and Paul, 1955).
Austin, J. L. *Sense and Sensibilia*. Oxford: Clarendon Press, 1962.
Church, A. "Review of *Language, Truth, and Logic*." *Journal of Symbolic Logic* (1949): 14:52–53.
Foster, J. *A. J. Ayer*. London: Routledge & Kegan Paul, 1985.
Griffiths, A. P. *A. J. Ayer Memorial Essays*. Cambridge, U.K.: Cambridge University Press, 1991.
Hahn, L. E. *The Philosophy of A. J. Ayer*. La Salle, IL: Open Court, 1992.
Hanfling, O. *Ayer*. London: Routledge, 1999.
Honderich, T. *Essays on A. J. Ayer*. Cambridge, U.K.: Cambridge University Press, 1991.
Macdonald, G., ed. *Perception and Identity*. London: Macmillan, 1979.
Macdonald, Graham, and C. Wright, eds. *Fact, Science, and Morality*. Oxford: Blackwell, 1986.
Martin, R. *On Ayer*. Belmont, CA: Wadsworth, 2000.
Rogers, Ben. *A. J. Ayer: A Life*. London: Grove Press, 2002.

D. J. O'Connor (1967)
Donald M. Borchert (2005)
Bibliography updated by Michael J. Farmer (2005)

BAADER, FRANZ XAVIER VON
(1765–1841)

Franz Xavier von Baader, the German philosopher and theologian, was born in Munich. He studied medicine at Ingolstadt and Vienna and practiced for a short time, but soon abandoned this career. While he was in England from 1792 to 1796 studying mineralogy and engineering, he became interested in philosophy and theology. On his return to Germany he formed friendships with Friedrich Heinrich Jacobi and Friedrich Wilhelm Joseph von Schelling. Although Baader later broke with Schelling, the three philosophers continued to exert strong influence on one another. Baader was appointed superintendent of the Bavarian mines and won a prize from the Austrian government for inventing a new method of glass manufacture. He retired in 1820 to devote himself to philosophy.

Baader's two major works are *Fermenta Cognitionis* (Vols. I–IV, Berlin, 1822–1824; Vol. V, Munich, 1825) and *Spekulative Dogmatik* (5 fascicles, Munich, 1827–1828). He was appointed professor of philosophy and speculative theology at the new University of Munich in 1826. He stopped lecturing on theology in 1838, when the Catholic bishop banned the public discussion of theology by lay-

men, but he continued to lecture on philosophy until his death.

Baader's philosophy is couched in aphorisms, symbols, and analogies, and it is therefore difficult to summarize. He detested David Hume's empiricism, William Godwin's radicalism, and Immanuel Kant's rationalism. He turned the critical method he had learned from Kant against criticism itself, calling for a return to the mystical tradition of Jakob Boehme, Paracelsus, Meister Eckhart, the Cabala, the Neoplatonists, and the Gnostics. He believed that since God is in all things, all knowledge is partly knowledge of God. God is not an abstract being but an eternal process, eternally becoming. As God creates himself, he comes to know himself. The relation between his will and his self-consciousness is the Holy Spirit. The Trinity is an eternal possibility in God and only becomes actual in nature, which is the principle of selfhood eternally produced by God. Nature is God alienated from himself—his shadow, his desire, his want. The purpose of the existence of nature is to afford an opportunity for the redemption of humanity.

Morality is not a matter of inner law, as Kant believed, but apprehension of, and obedience to, God's will. Salvation depends on prayer, faith, and the sacraments as well as on morality and good works. Humans are social beings under the law of the state, and the subjects owe total subservience to their ruler. But the state is under the law of the church. Any departure from this divinely ordained order leads to the twin modern evils of despotism and liberalism.

Baader sought a theistic, Catholic philosophy reconciling nature and spirit, science and religion, the individual and society. He believed that philosophy had to go back to its sources, from which it had been separated since the time of Descartes. Baader was thus a precursor of the neoscholastic revival, but his own teachings, close to heresy, have no important place in the movement.

See also Boehme, Jakob; Eckhart, Meister; Gnosticism; Godwin, William; Hume, David; Jacobi, Friedrich Heinrich; Kabbalah; Kant, Immanuel; Neoplatonism; Paracelsus; Schelling, Friedrich Wilhelm Joseph von.

Bibliography

The collected works of Franz von Baader were published as *Sämmtliche Werke,* 16 vols. (Leipzig: H. Bethmann, 1851–1860). Vol. XV contains a biography; Vol. XVI, a systematic exposition of Baader's ideas.

Works on Baader are D. Baumgardt, *Franz von Baader und die philosophische Romantik* (Halle: Salle, M. Niemeyer, 1927); J. Claasen, *Franz von Baaders Leben und theosophische Werke,* 2 vols. (Stuttgart, 1886–1887), and *Franz von Baaders Gedanken über Staat und Gesellschaft* (Gütersloh, Germany, 1890); and Kuno Fischer, *Zur hundert jährigen Geburtstagsfeier Baaders* (Erlangen, Germany, 1865).

Adam Margoshes (1967)

BACHELARD, GASTON
(1884–1962)

Gaston Bachelard, the French epistemologist and philosopher of science, was born at Bar-sur-Aube. He was a postal employee until 1913, when he gained his *licence* in mathematics and science and became a teacher of physics and chemistry at the Collège of Bar-sur-Aube. In 1927 he received his doctorate of letters and in 1930 became professor of philosophy at the University of Dijon. From 1940 to 1954 he held the chair of history and philosophy of science at the University of Paris.

Bachelard expounded a dialectical rationalism, or "dialogue" between reason and experience. His philosophy was a departure from the view of rational discovery as a process whereby new knowledge is assimilated into a system that changes only insofar as it grows. He rejected the Cartesian conception of scientific truths as immutable elements of a total truth that is in process of being put together like a jigsaw puzzle.

According to Bachelard, experiment and mathematical formulation are mutually complementary. Mathematics is not merely a means of expressing physical laws, nor is it a static realm of ideas; it is "committed." In this context Bachelard talked of "applied rationalism." Bachelard held that the empirical world is not utterly discontinuous and absurd; the confrontation of an isolated, rational human mind with an indifferent and meaningless world postulated by some existentialists is naive. Scientific hypotheses, and even scientific facts, do not present themselves passively to the patient investigator but are created by him. The investigator's reasoning and the natural world on which it operates together constitute a second nature over and above the crudely empirical one.

Bachelard described his conception of this two-way process in which rational organization and experiment are in constant cooperation as a "philosophy of saying no" (*philosophie du non*). It involves negation because the scientific attitude is necessarily "open" or "available" (*disponible*), and the scientist may be obliged at any time to recast his formulation of reality by facts which fail to fit into the old formulation. Since it is frequently mathematical, the reformulation may not necessarily involve the adoption of a new model, but it will often be analogous to a change of structure. At the same time, there will be no jettisoning of truths: The *philosophie du non* destroys nothing, Bachelard held; it consolidates what it supersedes. The framework may be recast and the picture of reality transformed, but only in such a way that the new phenomenon might have been foreseen.

Bachelard did not confine himself to an exclusively rationalist philosophy of science. He saw both technological and imaginative thinking as issuing from reverie and emotion into practical expression. His works on the psychological significance of the four elements, earth, air, fire, and water, illustrate this. He rejected, for example, the common account of the discovery of fire in the rubbing together of two sticks, seeing it rather as the outcome of a kind of symbolical representation of sexual intercourse. Thus passion is no more metaphorical fire than fire is metaphorical passion. Our science and our poetry have a common origin accessible only to psychoanalysis. There is a unity in Bachelard's studies on reason and imagination. In both cases he stressed the projective or creative role of the mind; in art "the subject projects his dream upon things," and in modern science, "above the *subject,* beyond the immediate object ... is the *project.*"

See also Epistemology; Philosophy of Science, History of; Rationalism.

Bibliography

WORKS BY BACHELARD

L'intuition de l'instant. Paris: Stock, Delamain and Boutelleau, 1932.

Le pluralisme cohérent de la chimie moderne. Paris: J. Vrin, 1932.

La dialectique de la durée. Paris, 1933.

Le nouvel Esprit scientifique. Paris: Presses universitaires de France, 1934.

La formation de l'esprit scientifique. Paris: J. Vrin, 1938.

La psychanalyse du feu. Paris: Gallimard, 1938.

Lautréamont. Paris: J. Corti, 1939.

La philosophie du non. Paris: Presses universitaires de France, 1940.

L'eau et les rêves. Paris: J. Corti, 1942.

L'air et les songes. Paris: J. Corti, 1943.

La terre et les rêveries de la volonté. Paris, 1945.

La terre et les rêveries du repos. Paris, 1945.

Le rationalisme appliqué. Paris: Presses universitaires de France, 1949.

La poétique de l'espace. Paris: Presses universitaires de France, 1957.

La poétique de la rêverie. Paris: Presses universitaires de France, 1960.

La flamme d'une chandelle. Paris: Presses universitaires de France, 1961.

WORKS ON BACHELARD

For a complete bibliography of Bachelard's works and for articles on him, see the "Bachelard" issue of the *Revue internationale de philosophie* 19 (1964). See also Jean Hyppolite's article, "Gaston Bachelard ou le romantisme de l'intelligence," *Revue philosophique de la France et de l'étranger* 144 (1954): 85–96.

Colin Smith (1967)

BACHOFEN, JOHANN JAKOB
(1815–1887)

Johann Jakob Bachofen, Swiss jurist, cultural anthropologist, and philosopher of history, studied philology, history, and law at the universities of Basel, Berlin (under Friedrich Karl von Savigny), and Göttingen. After taking his doctorate in 1839 in Roman law, he spent two years at the universities of Oxford, Cambridge, and Paris. In 1841, Bachofen was offered the chair in Roman law at the University of Basel, and a year later he was appointed a judge of the criminal court at Basel. In 1844 he resigned his professorship to devote himself to legal and anthropological research. In 1866 he also gave up his position as a judge. He traveled widely and lived for long periods in Greece, Italy, and Spain.

Bachofen's major works were in the fields of ancient Roman law and Greek antiquity. The work for which he is best known is *Das Mutterrecht. Eine Untersuchung über die Gynaikokratie der alten Welt nach ihrer religiösen und rechtlichen Natur* (Stuttgart, 1861). Following up Herodotus's description of a matriarchal system among the Lycians, Bachofen investigated diverse ancient myths and concluded that both matrilineal descent and matriarchal rule developed out of a state of unregulated promiscuity (*Hetärismus*) by virtue of the difficulty of ascertaining paternity under such conditions. He maintained that the dominant role of the mother in both the economic and political spheres was a phenomenon common to all primitive societies and that this role was inseparably linked to religious beliefs that established the secular primacy of woman on the basis of the cult of a female deity.

There is no element of evolution in Bachofen's theory. His main interest lay in tracing the transmission of social cultures, not in the biological characteristics attending heredity. Bachofen likewise rejected interpretations of myths in terms of individual psychology. The elements that constituted for him the essential ingredients of historical traditions—myths, cults and rituals, customs, law, and folklore—were *shared* characteristics and hence, in his view, objective factors. They embodied a people's collective "spirit," or *Volksgeist,* which, though a persistent continuum in social development, nonetheless operated at a nonrational and subconscious level. According to Bachofen it was the function of the woman and mother to preserve and uphold these nonrational historical forces and thus to exercise a uniting influence, whereas man, representing the progressive and rational forces, exercised a dividing influence over the development of humankind. The historical process consisted in a continuous striving for reconciliation between these opposing tendencies.

Das Mutterrecht encountered considerable skepticism, if not hostility, among contemporary anthropologists. Bachofen was charged with introducing rather fanciful and value-loaded notions into his theory and with confusing matrilineal descent with a matriarchate. But even though some of his theses have been disproved and others continue to be challenged, many of his suggestions have led to fruitful further research into the family customs of primitive peoples. Increasingly, too, Bachofen's works have been appraised as a major contribution to the philosophy of history.

Bachofen stressed the continuity of historical sequences and, above all, the close interpenetration of myth and history. In opposition to Georg Wilhelm Friedrich Hegel, Bachofen attached decisive importance to myths and symbols in the shaping of human history, since he accorded to them a far greater and more lasting emotive power than he did to rational concepts. In his stress on the irrational elements in history, as also in his insistence on regarding history as a continuous organic growth, Bachofen shared some of the basic premises of romantic thought. Yet, like Johann Gottfried Herder, the great precursor of romanticism, he never regarded himself as a romantic. Indeed, he explicitly repudiated the nostalgic sentimentality with which a number of romantics approached the study of the past.

Bachofen's political views show an undeniable affinity for the conservatism of the political romantics, but here also he was more directly influenced by Edmund Burke, whom he had assiduously studied during his stay in England. Paradoxically enough, Bachofen has often been associated with L. H. Morgan as one of the founders of a socialist philosophy of history. Bachofen did stipulate a "communist" origin of humankind in that he denied the existence of private property among primitive communities. He also prophesied an ultimate return to communism, understood in this sense. But he viewed such a return as a regression, not as "progress." Bachofen saw in socialism and democracy portents of social and political decay, for he held them to be inherently inimical to harmonious community life. Social and political harmony presupposed, in his view, the willing acceptance of the principle of subordination, for he regarded this principle as the prime source of a naturally and divinely ordered historical process.

Bachofen may have gone too far in the political application of his tradition-centered historicism, just as he probably overstated the role of woman in the development of religion, morals, law, and customs. But he did advance a functional conception of social development, in which social structures are seen as elements of a historical continuum and as constituents of an "idea-system" of nonrational and nonlogical beliefs and symbols, and in so doing he substantially contributed to the understanding of both ancient communities and societies of the modern world.

See also Burke, Edmund; Hegel, Georg Wilhelm Friedrich; Herder, Johann Gottfried; Morgan, Lewis Henry; Philosophy of History; Philosophy of Social Sciences; Savigny, Friedrich Karl von.

Bibliography

WORKS BY BACHOFEN

Collections

J. J. Bachofens gesammelte Werk. Edited by Karl Meuli. 10 vols. Basel: B. Schwabe, 1943–.

Der Mythus von Orient und Occident. Edited by Manfred Schroeter. 2nd ed. Munich: Beck, 1956. Contains a selection of Bachofen's works, with an introduction by Alfred Baeumler and a bibliography of Bachofen's published works.

Individual Works

Das Naturrecht und das geschichtliche Recht in ihren Gegensätzen. Basel, 1841.

Das römische Pfandrecht. Basel: Schweighauser, 1847.

Ausgewählte Lehren des römischen Civilrechts. Bonn: A. Marcus, 1848.

Versuch über die Gräbersymbolik der Alten. Basel, 1859; 2nd ed., Basel: Helbing and Lichtenhahn, 1925.

Das Mutterrecht. Stuttgart: Krais and Hoffmann, 1861.

Die Unsterblichkeitslehre der orphischen Theologie. Basel, 1867.

Die Sage von Tanaquil. Heidelberg: J.C.B. Mohr, 1870.

Antiquarische Briefe, 2 vols. Strassburg: K.J. Trübner, 1880, 1886.

Römische Grablampen. Basel, 1890.

WORKS ON BACHOFEN

Bernoulli, C. A. *J. J. Bachofen als Religionsforscher.* Leipzig, 1924.

Bernoulli, C. A. *J. J. Bachofen und das Natursymbol.* Basel: B. Schwabe, 1924.

Burckhardt, Max. *J. J. Bachofen und die Politik.* Basel, 1943.

Kerenyi, K. *Bachofen und die Zukunft des Humanismus.* Zürich: Rascher, 1945.

Klages, Ludwig, *Der Kosmogonischen Eros.* Munich, 1922.

Wolf, Erik, article on Bachofen. In *Neue Deutsche Biographie,* Vol. 1, pp. 502–503. Berlin: Duncker and Humblot, 1953. Also contains a detailed bibliography of secondary literature.

Frederick M. Barnard (1967)

BACON, FRANCIS
(1561–1626)

Francis Bacon, Baron Veralum, Viscount St. Albans, gained renown both as an English statesman and a natural philosopher. Bacon was instrumental in the replacement of Aristotelian natural philosophy, effecting a major shift to thinking about the natural world in exclusively empirical and experimental terms, although he remained entrenched in Aristotelian thought to a significant degree. His achievement was twofold: First, he transformed the discipline of philosophy from something contemplative that focused above all on moral questions into something practical that focused centrally on questions in natural philosophy (what is now called science). Second, his work in the natural sciences resulted in the formulation of precepts that are now regarded as foundation stones of the inductive modern scientific method: moving inferentially from observable effects to deeper underlying causes and eliminating various possible explanations by testing their consequences against experiment or observation.

LIFE

Bacon was born on January, 22, 1561, the eldest son of Sir Nicholas Bacon, lord keeper of the Great Seal, and Ann, second daughter of Sir Anthony Coke, known for her strong Protestant sympathies. Bacon attended Trinity College, Cambridge, from 1573 to 1575, but moved to Gray's Inn in 1575, traveling to France—where he came into contact with Italian republican ideas—in 1576 and remaining there until his father's death in 1579. From that time onward he began a career in law and politics that took him from his first parliamentary seat (1581), admission to the bar (1582), deputy chief steward of the Duchy of Lancaster (1594), solicitor general (1607), attorney general (1613), member of the Privy Council (1616), lord keeper of the Great Seal (1617), to his being created viscount of St. Albans in 1621. In that same year he was impeached and spent the rest of his life in comparative isolation from the court society he had enjoyed for the previous fifteen years. He died on April 9, 1626. His death has traditionally been attributed to his contracting pneumonia as a result of leaving his carriage to test the preserving effects of cold on a chicken, but it is more likely that he died of an overdose of inhaled niter or opiates, self-prescribed to cure a long-running illness.

His intellectual career falls into three stages. From 1592 to 1602, his main concern was the reform of English law. From 1602 to around 1620, he worked on a very ambitious project in natural philosophy, advocating a form of atomism and setting out a new method of inquiry in natural philosophy, as well as investigating a huge number of topics in natural history. Around 1620 he began to publish parts of his grand scheme on a systematic basis, although Bacon could never be called a systematic philosopher. His plans for the reform of natural philosophy were not taken seriously by his English contemporaries during his lifetime, but within a few years of

his death, critics of contemporary natural philosophy and founders of scientific academies in Italy, France, and England took him as their model, and by the beginning of the eighteenth century his name was linked with Newton's among the founders of modern science.

LAW AND RHETORIC

Bacon's first attempts at reform were in the area of law rather than natural philosophy. The law offered guidance on three questions that would subsequently make it a model for his proposed reform of natural philosophy: the reliability of testimony, what should be concluded from particular testimonies, and how one decided the relevance of particular laws to the case. It was the third of these that he saw most in need of reform, and he set out to investigate how the law might be systematized, how regular records and reviews of legal decisions might be provided, and whether some firm foundations for legal practice might be discovered. What is at issue here is what was referred to as the "discovery" of law. It was a shared premise that the law was structured in accord with reason and that this structure enabled one, in cases where the laws did not give a clear indication of infringements, to appeal to the implicit message of the common law. On the assumption that the law covered every eventuality, the task was to find one's way through its rational structure. The questions to which Bacon directed himself particularly were whether there was an optimal procedure by which to discover that rational structure and what the ultimate source of authority was in the case of dispute.

Bacon's emphasis on the role for discovery in the legal thinking reflects a concern with rhetoric, which plays a crucial role in both his proposed reform of the law and that of natural philosophy. The task of rhetoric was the formulation, organization, and expression of one's ideas in a coherent and compelling way. It was designed to help one find one's way around the comprehensive body of learning built up from antiquity, to recognize where appropriate evidence and arguments might be found, and to provide models that were designed to give one a sense of what was needed if a particular question was to be investigated, or a particular position defended, models that would be shared with those to whom one was expounding or defending one's case. Rhetoric, in Bacon's view, should help to focus the mental powers, to organize one's thoughts in the most economical fashion, and even (in writers like Quintilian) to provide vivid images or representations of situations that enabled one to convince oneself of a case (important especially in acting and in legal argument). It was designed to provide models to show one how particular kinds of case were best defended, depending on such facts as the availability of and complexity of the evidence and the knowledge, opinions, or prejudices of the audience toward which one was directing one's arguments.

At a general level, rhetoric was deemed to be indifferent to subject matter because comprehensive procedures were recommended that would aid a case or investigation, scientific or a legal, although there would be similarities or analogies (as regards the standing of various kinds of evidence, for example) and dissimilarities (as regards the means of evidence collection, for example) between legal cases and those in natural philosophy. The law, taken in a broad sense, was seen as a paradigm case for rhetorical writers: Rhetorical treatises were often explicitly directed toward lawyers and legislators, and examples were geared to the kinds of problems that arose in law. In light of this, it is only to be expected that using a rhetorical model for knowledge—that is, a model that gives direction on how to collect and assess evidence for a view, how to make a judgment on the basis of that evidence, and how to establish the correctness of judgment, using precepts derived from the study of rhetoric—is in many respects using a legal model.

Rhetoric provided a theoretical foundation for the law, something which, at a practical level, worked with elaborate procedures for the gathering, assessing, and testing of evidence. This was exactly the kind of thing that Bacon had in mind for natural philosophy. What was unusual about his application of precepts learned from rhetoric and law to natural philosophy was that he used them to propose a fundamental reform of philosophy. While Bacon started from a consideration of the law, however, law did not act as a model in its own right. Its importance arose from the fact that (especially once it had been reformed along Baconian lines) it exemplified a rhetorically motivated account of discovery. This holds the key to Bacon's enterprise.

The best way to understand this reform is in terms of the pervasive Renaissance contrast, often drawn in classical terms, between the life of contemplation (*otium*) and the life of practical, productive activity (*negotium*). There had been a decisive shift in favor of the latter in sixteenth-century England. In particular, there was a stress on practical questions and the practical uses of learning; and philosophy—above all Scholastic philosophy—was widely regarded as a useless discipline that fostered argument for its own sake, never getting anywhere and never producing anything of value. Moreover, morality was widely seen as the key philosophical topic (following the

Ciceronian model current in Renaissance Europe), and a number of Elizabethan thinkers, most notably the poet Sir Philip Sidney, were arguing that poetry was superior to philosophy because philosophy could only discourse on the nature of goodness, whereas poetry could actually move people to goodness, which was the point of the exercise.

Bacon did two things: He shifted philosophy from *otium* to *negotium*, and he made natural philosophy replace moral philosophy as the center of the philosophical enterprise. The combination of these two (and they are intimately connected) is a radical move that marks a decisive break not only with earlier conceptions of philosophy but also with earlier understandings of the task of the philosopher.

Natural philosophy existed in a number of forms in the sixteenth and seventeenth centuries, and there were two extreme forms. The first was exemplified by alchemy, an esoteric but practical discipline that had little connection with traditional philosophical practice and that suffered, in Bacon's view, from a lack of structure that produced few results, with most of that paucity attributable to chance. At the other extreme was Scholastic natural philosophy, an intensely theoretical discipline that, in Bacon's view, produced nothing at all; despite its great sophistication, it turned out to be almost exclusively verbal.

Bacon wanted something that could deliver the advantages of each of these without any of the disadvantages. He wanted something that would provide a detailed theoretical overview of the natural realm such that natural processes could not only be understood but, more importantly, also transformed on the basis of this understanding; this is the context of his famous dictum "knowledge is power." The ultimate aim was to transform natural processes for the common good (to be decided by the sovereign, on Bacon's view), and it was this, rather than some contemplative understanding of nature, that provided the rationale for natural philosophy and, by extension, philosophy per se.

Bacon himself formulated his project in terms of a politico-religious restoration of human dominion over the natural world, something lost with Adam's expulsion from Eden. Natural philosophy thereby gained a religious imperative, albeit one with little connection with traditional theology.

THE DOCTRINE OF IDOLS

If rhetoric is the first ingredient in Bacon's account of method, the second is a distinctive understanding of why the need for method arises. Here Bacon's stress on a psychological dimension of knowledge is important: Questions of presentation of knowledge are not only recognized to be important but also have to be understood, where such an understanding is not supplementary to epistemology but actually part of it. At one level, there is nothing new in this, for it is simply part of a long tradition that begins in earnest with the Roman rhetoricians; but although it borrows from Greek writers, it is rather different from the approach to epistemological questions that we find in the classical Greek and Hellenistic philosophers. When one thinks of Bacon's general project in this context, it becomes clear that there is something novel here. For natural philosophy had generally been the preserve of Greek philosophy and had been pursued in a similar way by Scholastic philosophers. The Roman tradition, with the exception of Lucretius, had typically not concerned itself with speculative natural-philosophical questions, dealing instead with practical moral, political, and legal questions. In thinking of persuasion in terms of a psychological theory, of psychological theory as part of epistemology, and of epistemology as being directed primarily toward natural philosophy, Bacon was able to provide himself with some of the resources to recast natural philosophy not as a speculative but as a practical discipline.

This psychological dimension of epistemology is brought out fully in Bacon's doctrine of the "idols of the mind." These idols "do not deceive in particulars, as the others do, by clouding and snaring the judgment; but by a corrupt and ill-ordered predisposition of the mind, which as it were perverts and infects all the anticipations of the intellect." The second part of the "Great Instauration," which aims at the renewal of learning, is devoted to the "invention of knowledge" and has two components, one aiming to rid the mind of preconceptions, the other to guide the mind in a productive direction. These components are interconnected, for until we understand the nature of the mind's preconceptions, we do not know in what direction we need to lead its thinking. In other words, various natural inclinations of the mind must be purged before the new procedure can be set in place. Bacon's approach here is genuinely different from that of his predecessors, as he realizes. Logic or method in themselves cannot simply be introduced to replace bad habits of thought because it is not simply a question of replacement. The simple application of logic to one's mental processes is insufficient.

In his doctrine of the four idols of the mind, Bacon provides an account of the systematic forms of error to which the mind is subject, and this is a crucial part of his epistemology. It is in his treatment of internal impediments, the "idols," that the question is raised of what psychological or cognitive state we must be in to be able to pursue natural philosophy in the first place. Bacon believes an understanding of nature of a kind that had never been achieved since the Fall is possible in his own time because the distinctive obstacles that have held up all previous attempts have been identified, in what is in many respects a novel theory of what might traditionally have been treated under a theory of the passions, one directed specifically at natural-philosophical practice.

The "idols of the tribe" derive from human nature itself, above all from "the homogeneity of the substance of the human mind, or from its preoccupation, or from its narrowness, or from its restless motion, or from an infusion of the affections, or from the incompetence of the senses, or from the mode of impression." (*Works* 1857–1874, vol. 4, p. 58–59). The idols of the tribe affect everyone equally and are manifested in an eagerness to suppose that there is more order and regularity in nature than there actually is; in the tendency to neglect or ignore counterexamples to one's theories; in the tendency to extrapolate from striking cases with which one is familiar to all other cases; in the restlessness of the human mind, which means it is not satisfied with perfectly good fundamental explanations, mistakenly and constantly seeking some more fundamental cause ad infinitum; and in the tendency to believe true what one would like to be true.

The "idols of the cave," we are told, "take their rise in the peculiar constitution, mental or bodily, of each individual; and also in education, habit, and accident" (*Works* 1857–1874, vol. 4, p. 59). They include fascination with a particular subject, which leads to overhasty generalization; the readiness of some minds to focus on differences, and some to focus on similarities and resemblances, while a balance is difficult to attain naturally; and the fact that some minds are overly attracted to antiquity and some to novelty. Finally, there are those who are concerned wholly with material constitution at the expense of structure (the ancient atomists) and those who are concerned wholly with structure at the expense of material constitution.

These examples bring to light a very significant difference between the idols of the tribe and idols of the cave. There seems to be a set of routine procedures one can go through to remedy the situation in the latter case, procedures provided by the positive part of Bacon's doctrine—eliminative induction—whereas the case of idols of the tribe is, in most cases, much more difficult to remedy.

The third kind of idols, those of the marketplace derive from the fact that we have to express and communicate our thoughts by means of language, which contains systematic deficiencies. One kind of problem with language lies in the fact that words "are commonly framed and applied according to the capacity of the vulgar, and follow those lines of division which are most obvious to the vulgar understanding. And whenever an understanding of greater acuteness or a more diligent observation would alter those lines to suit the true divisions of nature, words stand in the way and resist the change" (*Works* 1857–1874, vol. 4, p. 61). This leads to two kinds of linguistically induced deficiencies. First, language provides names that refer to things that do not exist, such as "Fortune, Prime Mover, Planetary Orbits, Element of Fire, and like fictions that owe their origin to false and idle theories" (*Works* 1857–1874, vol. 4, p. 61). The solution here is simply to get rid of the theories that give rise to these fictitious entities.

The second kind of case is not so straightforward. It arises because words have multiple and/or ill-defined meanings, and this is especially so in the case of terms such as *humid* that have been abstracted from observation. Bacon discerns a gradation in the "degrees of distortion and error" (*Works* 1857–1874, vol. 4, p. 62) of terms, beginning with names of substances, where the degree of distortion is low, proceeding through the names of actions, and finally reaching the names of qualities—he gives the examples of "heavy, light, rare, dense" (*Works* 1857–1874, vol. 4, p. 62)—where the degree of distortion is high.

Finally, the fourth kinds of impediment, the idols of the theater, are innate neither in the mind nor in language but are acquired from a corrupt philosophical culture and its perverse rules of demonstration. Here a general remedy is available, namely following Bacon's positive methodological prescriptions: "The course I propose for the discovery of sciences is such as leaves but little to the acuteness and strength of wits, but places all wits and understandings nearly on a level. For as in the drawing of a straight lines or a perfect circle, much depends on the steadiness and practice of the hand, but if with the aid of a rule or compass, little or nothing; so is it exactly with my plan" (*Works* 1857–1874, vol. 4, p. 62–63).

One of the great values of Bacon's account of the idols is that it allows him to make the case for method in a particularly compelling way. Indeed, never has the need for method been set out more forcefully, for Bacon's advocacy of method is not simply an aid to discovery. He argues that we pursue natural philosophy with seriously deficient natural faculties, we operate with a severely inadequate means of communication, and we rely on a hopelessly corrupt philosophical culture. In many respects, these are beyond remedy. The practitioners of natural philosophy certainly need to reform their behavior, overcome their natural inclinations and passions, but not so that, in doing this, they might aspire to a natural, prelapsarian state in which they might know things as they are with an unmediated knowledge. This they will never achieve. Rather, the reform of behavior is a discipline to which they must subject themselves if they are to be able to follow a procedure which is, in many respects, quite contrary to their natural inclinations, which is at odds with traditional conceptions of the natural philosopher, and which is indeed subversive of their individuality.

ELIMINATIVE INDUCTION

What Bacon is seeking from a method of discovery is something that modern philosophers would deem impossibly strong: the discovery of causes that are both necessary and sufficient for their effects. Why place such strong constraints on causation, so that we call something a cause only when the effect always occurs in the presence of this thing and never in its absence? What Bacon (like Aristotle before him) is after are the ultimate explanations of things, and it is natural to assume that ultimate explanations are unique. Bacon's method is designed to provide a route to such explanations, and the route takes us through a number of proposed causal accounts, which are refined at each stage. The procedure he elaborates, eliminative induction, is one in which various possibly contributory factors are isolated and examined in turn, to see whether they do in fact make a contribution to the effect. Those that do not are rejected, and the result is a convergence on those factors that are truly relevant. The kind of "relevance" that Bacon is after is, in effect, a set of necessary conditions: the procedure is supposed to enable us to weed out those factors that are not necessary for the production of the effect, so that we are left only with those that are necessary.

Bacon provides an example of how the method works in the case of color. We take, as our starting point, some combination of substances that produces whiteness—that is, we start with what are sufficient conditions for the production of whiteness, and then we remove from these anything not necessary for the color. First, we note that if air and water are mixed together in small portions, the result is white, as in snow or waves. Here we have the sufficient conditions for whiteness, but not the necessary conditions, so next we increase the scope, substituting any transparent uncolored substance for water, whence we find that glass or crystal, on being ground, become white, and albumen, which is initially a watery transparent substance, on having air beaten into it, becomes white. Third, we further increase the scope and ask what happens in the case of colored substances. Amber and sapphire become white on being ground, and wine and beer become white when brought to a froth.

The substances considered up to this stage have all been "more grossly transparent than air." Bacon next considers flame, which is less grossly transparent than air, and argues that the mixture of the fire and air makes the flame whiter. The upshot of this is that water is sufficient for whiteness but not necessary for it. He continues in the same vein, asking next whether air is necessary for whiteness. He notes that a mixture of water and oil is white, even when the air has been evaporated from it, so air is not necessary for whiteness; but is a transparent substance necessary? Bacon does not continue with the chain of questions after this point but sets out some conclusions, namely that bodies whose parts are unequal but in simple proportion are white, those whose parts are in equal proportions are transparent, those whose parts are proportionately unequal are colors, and those whose parts are absolutely unequal are black. In other words, this is the conclusion that might be expected of the method of sifting out what is necessary for the phenomenon and what is not, although Bacon himself does not provide the route to this conclusion here.

This being the case, one can ask what his confidence in his conclusion derives from if he has not been able to complete the "induction" himself. The answer is that it derives from the consequences he can draw from his account. There are two ways in which the justification for the conclusions can be assessed: by the procedure of eliminative induction that he has just set out and by the consequences of those conclusions generated by it. In other words, there is a two-way process, from empirical phenomena to first principles, and then from first principles to empirical phenomena. This is a classic Aristotelian procedure. Where Bacon's version of it differs is in how the first step is carried out, and the difference turns on the use of eliminative induction.

Bacon's treatment of heat in *Novum Organum* follows essentially the same route, albeit in a more elaborate way. The first thing to do, he tells us, is to list "instances agreeing in the nature of heat," that is, a list of those cases in which heat is present: the rays of the sun, reflected rays, meteors, thunderbolts, volcanic eruptions, flame, burning solids, natural warm-baths, boiling liquids, hot vapors and fumes, fine cloudless days, air confined underground, wool and down, bodies held near a fire, sparks, rubbed bodies, confined vegetable matter, quick lime sprinkled with water, metals dissolved in acids or alkalis, the insides of animals, horse dung, strong oil of sulfur and of vitriol (i.e. sulphuric acid), oil of marjoram, rectified spirit of wine, aromatic herbs (which are hot to the palate), strong vinegar and acids (which burn those parts of the body where there is no epidermis, such as the surface of the eye), and, finally, intense cold, which can produce a burning effect (*Works* 1857–1874, vol. 4, p. 127–129).

The list makes no claims to completeness, of course, but presumably it does aim to give us some idea of the range of phenomena we have to deal with. Because, on Bacon's view, a cause should not only be present when the effect is present but also absent when the effect is absent, the next step ideally would be to list those cases where the effect was absent, but this is clearly an impossible task, for the list would be infinite. So what Bacon does is to list, in some detail, counterinstances to the items of the first list: cases when heat is absent or at least where there is some doubt. So, for example, the rays of the sun are hot, but those of the moon and the stars are not; the reflections of the sun's rays are usually hot but not in the polar regions; the presence of comets (counting these as a type of meteor) does not result in warmer weather; and so on. The point of this exercise is not simply to record known counterinstances, however, but also to suggest experiments that need to be carried out to discover whether there are counterinstances—for example, in the case of lenses and "burning mirrors," in connection with which he makes several suggestions.

Instances and counterinstances of heat are absolute questions, but we can also discover something of the nature of heat by comparative means, by making a comparison either of its increase and decrease in the same subject, or of its amount in different subjects, as compared one with another. For since the Form of a thing is the very thing itself, and the thing does not differ from the Form except in the way that the apparent differs from the real, or the external from the internal, or the thing in reference to man from the thing in reference to the universe, it necessarily follows that no nature can be taken as the true Form unless it always decreases when the nature in question decreases, and in like manner always increases when the nature in question increases. (*Works* 1857–1874, vol. 4, p. 137)

This procedure for discovery requires the compilation of a "table of degrees or comparison," in which the instances previously listed are examined in respect of changes in heat. Putrefaction always "contains" heat, for example; inanimate things are not hot to the touch; the heat of lower animals such as insects is barely perceptible, but higher animals are hot to the touch; the heat in animals increases as a result of motion; the heat of celestial bodies is never sufficient to set fire to things on Earth; the sun and the planets give more heat in perigee than in apogee; and so on.

It is at this point that induction comes into play. The various instances must be reviewed with a view to eliminating those natures that can be absent while heat is still found, those natures that are present even though heat is absent, and those where the heat increases or decreases without a corresponding increase or decrease in the nature. Examples of the exclusions are as follows: Because the rays of the sun sometimes warm and sometimes do not, reject the nature of the elements as the explanation for heat; because of ordinary fire and subterranean fires, reject the nature of celestial bodies; because of boiling water, reject light or brightness; and so on. This process is less reliable than it might seem, for the exclusion of some simple natures and the narrowing down to others presupposes that we know what simple natures are, whereas in fact we do not know this; but the procedures followed this far, Bacon believes, do allow us to advance finally to the interpretation of nature, or at least to the first version of that interpretation, which he refers to as "the first vintage."

It is a premise of Bacon's account that the Form that causes an effect must be present in every instance and absent in every counterinstance, but he also points out that it is more evident in some instances than in others. This is particularly so in the case of heat: The tables show that hot things—such as flames and boiling water—are characteristically in rapid motion and that compression puts out a fire. The tables of results show, moreover, that bodies are destroyed or changed radically by heat, indicating that heat causes a change in the internal parts of the body and perceptibly causes its dissolution. Bacon concludes that heat is a species of the general genus of motion, but before examining what marks it out from other species of motion, he removes some ambiguities from the idea of heat. Sensible heat, for example, which is relative to individuals, not to the universe, is not heat properly speaking but the effect of heat upon the animal

spirits. Moreover, the communication of heat from one body to another is not to be confused with the Form of heat, for heat itself and the action of heating are two different things. Nor is fire to be confused with the Form of heat, for fire is a combination of heat and brightness.

Having removed these ambiguities, Bacon turns to heat proper. A number of things mark it out as a distinctive species of motion. First, heat is a motion that causes bodies to expand or dilate "towards the circumference"— that is, in all directions—as is evident in the case of vapors or air, liquids such as boiling water, and metals such as iron, which expand when heated. Cold has the opposite effect in all cases. The second distinctive feature is that heat, aside from being a motion to the circumference, is also a motion upward. To determine whether the contrary holds in the case of cold, Bacon proposes an experiment in which a sponge soaked with cold water is placed at the bottom of one heated rod and at the top of another to determine whether one cools faster than the other. He further suggests that the one with the sponge at the top will cool the other end of the rod more quickly.

The third characteristic is that heat comprises a variety of nonuniform motion, whereby small parts of a body are moved in different ways, some motions being checked and others proceeding freely, with the result that the body experiences a constantly subsiding quivering and swelling motion. This third characteristic is evident in flames and in boiling water. Moreover, where the motion is of the whole, such as a gas escaping from confinement at great pressure, we find no heat. Bacon maintains that cooling proceeds like heating, in a nonuniform way, although the absence of great cold on the Earth makes this phenomenon less evident. Finally, the fourth characteristic of heat as a species of motion is that it acts rapidly, for comparison with the effects of age or time on the corruption of bodies shows a similar result, corruption or dissolution of bodies, and the difference must lie in the rate at which the parts of the body are penetrated. The case of cold is not mentioned here, and, unlike the first three characteristics, it is not clear just what Bacon would want to establish in the case of cold. He sums up by drawing two kinds of conclusions from this "first vintage:"

> The Form or true definition of heat … [is that] heat is a motion, expansive, restrained, and acting in its strife upon the smaller particles of bodies. But the expansion is thus modified; while it expands all ways, it has at the same time an inclination upwards. And the struggle in the particles is modified also; it is not sluggish, but hurried and with violence. Viewed with refer-

ence to operation it is the same thing. For the direction is this: If in any natural body you can excite a dilating or expanding motion, and can so repress this motion and turn it back upon itself, so that the dilation does not proceed equably, but can have its way in one part and is counteracted in another, you will undoubtedly generate heat. (*Works* 1857–1874, vol. 4, p. 155)

This process is only the first stage in induction for Bacon, but it is the one that is both most novel and most problematic. In particular, it is appropriate to ask just how far the process of eliminative induction gets us. After all, to go back to the case of color, it is giant leap, indeed a qualitative leap, from noting that a mixture of oil and water is white to the conclusion that Bacon seeks, namely that those bodies whose parts are in simple proportion are white. Is it plausible to suppose that the continuation of the procedure would in fact get us to the conclusion? More particularly, the "directions" that have been followed to this stage remain wholly at the macroscopic level, yet their continued application is supposed to guide us to the particular microcorpuscular internal structure of a body that makes that body white. This issue prompts two questions: whether eliminative induction generates explanations and whether it genuinely involves a process that converges to a single cause or explanation.

On the first question Aristotelians would have resisted the demand that, in seeking an explanation for a physical phenomenon, they sift through all the possibilities until they have found *the* cause. The question turns on the relation between explanations and causes. Although the Greeks generally did not separate questions of causality and explanation, disputes did arise about which should be given priority. Cause would be given priority if one were seeking to determine or ascribe responsibility for something. Explanation would be given priority if one were trying to provide an account of all the relevant factors concerning how something came about, without necessarily wishing to apportion blame or responsibility. It makes a considerable difference which of these views we take. The Stoics, for example, maintained that the most important thing was to determine responsibility and, as a consequence, they viewed causes as being necessarily active. This view was supported by an analogy with the law, where the person deemed responsible for an offense is the person who had done whatever it was that resulted in the offense being committed.

The physical analogue here is a body: a cause is a body that does something to affect another body in some way. On this construal, an explanation is simply a state-

ment of a cause: cause is prior to explanation. The alternative is to make explanation prior to cause, in which case we might say that a cause is whatever figures in the explanation of an event. Take the legal analogy: if we were seeking an explanation of why an offense occurred rather than simply trying to find out who was to blame, we might look at all kinds of factors, such as the conditions under which offenses of this kind usually occur, whether preventive measures had been taken, what kinds of things motivated people to commit offenses of this kind, and so on. In natural philosophy, Aristotle makes explanations prior to causes. His famous "four causes" are, in fact, four kinds of explanation, the combination of which is designed to yield a complete understanding of the phenomenon. If we know what something is, what it is made from, how it was made, and for what end it was made, we have a complete understanding of the phenomenon. To restrict oneself effectively to efficient causes, as Bacon does, will not yield such an understanding. So Aristotelians might well resist the notion that Bacon's procedure is going to lead to explanations.

Someone who is committed to making explanations prior to causes will argue that there are as many causes of something as there are explanations of that thing, for what will count as a cause will be determined by the kind of explanation one is seeking. Bacon has little in reply to this kind of move. In *Valerius Terminus*, he sets out the error of seeking the causes of particular things, which are "infinite and transitory," as opposed to "abstract natures, which are few and pertinent." Such criticism seems most appropriately leveled against alchemists and others, whom Bacon criticizes for their piecemeal approach, rather than Scholastic natural philosophers, who would agree with his stricture here. But, in fact, Bacon has the Scholastics in mind, telling us that, despite appearances, on closer examination they do not seek abstract natures. This somewhat surprising criticism is possible only because of the very restrictive interpretation he places on "abstract natures," which he compares to "the alphabet or simple letters, whereof the variety of things consisteth; or as the colors mingled in the painter's shell, wherewith he is able to make infinite variety of faces or shapes" (*Works* 1857–1874, vol. 3, p. 243). Clearly, what he really wants is an atomist account of the "abstract natures" of things, something that can be only defended on substantive natural-philosophical grounds. The kind of explanation he is seeking, namely an atomist/corpuscularian one, is without doubt guiding what is going to count as a satisfactory argument here.

This issue brings us to the second question. Is eliminative induction suitable as a method of discovering efficient causes? It is hard to see how it could not help in such a process, but it is far from clear that in itself it could generate an account of such causes. Indeed, it is impossible to see how Bacon's examples of whiteness and heat can be pursued further by eliminative induction to generate a conclusion of the kind he wants. One might admit some degree of convergence, but there is nothing like convergence to a point: things become squared off well before that stage.

TRUTH

Closely tied up with Bacon's account of method is his treatment of the question of truth. Bacon goes through a number of what he considers to be inadequate criteria that have been used to establish truth. He rejects criteria depending on antiquity or authority, those deriving from commonly held views, and those relying upon the internal consistency or the capacity for internal reduction of theories, presumably on the grounds that such criteria do not bear on the question of whether there is any correspondence between the theory and reality. He also rejects "inductions without instances contradictory" that is, inductions that restrict themselves to confirming a theory, as well as "the report of the senses." None of these, he tells us, are "absolute and infallible evidence of truth, and bring no security sufficient for effects and operations." That he ties in evidence for the truth of a theory and its usefulness here is no accident, for these are intimately connected, telling us in *Valerius Terminus* that

> That the discovery of new works and active directions not known before, is the only trial to be accepted of; and yet not that neither, in case where one particular giveth light to another; but where particulars induce an axiom or observation, which axiom found out discovereth and designeth new particulars. That the nature of this trial is not only upon the point, whether the knowledge be profitable or no; not because you may always conclude that the Axiom which discovereth new instances be true, but contrariwise you may safely conclude that if it discover not any new instance it is in vain and untrue. (*Works*, vol. 3, p. 242)

It is unclear here whether Bacon is providing a gloss on truth, maintaining that it has been misconstrued, or saying that something is true, in the ordinary accepted sense, only if it is useful. Whichever, it is a very strong claim on Bacon's part. For there are certainly useless truths, just as there are falsehoods that have practical applications. It is not simply that false premises may lead to true conclusions, but there are cases where approximations, although false, may have more practical value than the truths of which they are the approximation.

The solution becomes clear when we consider that, since antiquity, debates on methods of generating truths had hinged on the question of generating informative truths, the aim being to discover something we did not already know. In particular, there was a concern among Aristotle and his Renaissance followers to show that formal modes of reasoning such as the syllogism were not trivial or circular because, at the start of the inferential process, we have knowledge *that* something is the case, whereas at the end of it we have knowledge *why* it is the case. In particular what they sought to show was that the kind of knowledge of an observed phenomenon we have through sensation is qualitatively different from and inferior to the kind of knowledge we have of that phenomenon when we grasp it in terms of its causes.

This latter kind of knowledge is also what Bacon was seeking. If we think in terms of "informative truths," Bacon's position makes more sense. He is saying that the only way in which we can judge whether something is informatively true is to determine whether it is productive, whether it yields something tangible and useful. And if something does consistently yield something tangible and useful, then it is informatively true. The case of approximations can perhaps be dealt with by saying that these derive their usefulness not from their falsity but from their proximity to the truth, although the cases where the approximation is more useful than the true account cannot be handled so easily.

The question of the practicality of truth turns on how informative it is, but there is another dimension to this question that, although not explicitly mentioned by Bacon, is of importance in understanding his general orientation. In the humanist thought that makes up the source from which Bacon derives much of his inspiration, moral philosophy figures prominently. Now in this philosophy, being virtuous and acting virtuously are the same thing: There is no separate practical dimension to morality. This is all the more interesting because moral philosophy is a cognitive enterprise, one in which the practical outcome is constitutive of the discipline, a point Bacon stresses the *Advancement of Learning*. If moral philosophy is the model for natural philosophy, a natural enough conclusion for a humanist and one that is reinforced in the shift from *otium* to *negotium*, then we may be able to make a little more sense of the idea that truth is not truth unless it is informative and productive.

If we think of Bacon's project as transforming moral philosophers into natural philosophers, then we might expect some carryover from conceptions of the moral philosopher. Notions that were quite appropriate in moral philosophy but not (at least outside Epicureanism) in natural philosophy remain in the transformation process. And this is exactly what we do find, most strikingly in the idea of truth as productive and informative. For Bacon, the truth of natural philosophy hinges as much on its being informative and productive of works as does the truth of moral philosophy in its way. "In religion," he tells us in *Redargutio Philosophiarum*, "we are warned that faith is to be shown by works" (*Works*, vol. 3, p. 576). And he proposes that the same test that is applied in religion be applied in philosophy: if it produces nothing at all, or, worse, if, "instead of the fruits of the grape or olive, it bear the thistles and thorns of disputes and contentions," then we can reject it.

BACON'S LEGACY

In the early modern era, there emerged in the West a style of doing natural philosophy, a way of thinking about the place of natural philosophy in culture generally, and a way of thinking about oneself as a natural philosopher. Bacon played a key role in this development. He inaugurated the transformation of philosophy into science, for even though the ideas of "science" and "scientist" in their modern sense were only really established in the nineteenth century, their genealogy goes back to Bacon's attempt to effect a fundamental reform of philosophy from a contemplative discipline, exemplified in the individual persona of the moral philosopher, to a communal, if centrally directed, enterprise exemplified in the persona of the experimental natural philosopher. Thanks in large measure to Bacon's exertions, observation and experiment were lifted out of the purview of the arcane and the esoteric and planted firmly in the public realm. As a result, science was transformed: Its tradition of irregular fits of progress alternating with long periods of stagnation gave way to the uninterrupted and cumulative growth that has characterized Western science since then.

In defending natural philosophy, Bacon reshaped it; his establishment of its autonomy, legitimacy, and central cultural role are on a par with Plato's defense of the autonomy and centrality of the "quiet" virtues, such as justice and moderation. Both irreversibly changed the cultures in which they lived and those that followed— above all our own.

See also Aristotelianism; Aristotle; Cicero, Marcus Tullius; Epicureanism and the Epicurean School; Ethics, History of; History and Historiography of Philosophy; Induction; Logic, History of; Lucretius; Naturalized Philosophy of Science; Newton, Isaac; Philosophy of Law, History of; Philosophy of Mind; Philosophy of Science, History of; Philosophy of Science, Problems of; Plato; Psychology; Renaissance; Scientific Method; Semantics, History of; Stoicism.

Bibliography

WORKS BY BACON

The Oxford Francis Bacon, edited by Graham Rees and Lisa Jardine. Oxford: Oxford University Press, 1996 onwards. This will eventually replace the Spedding and Ellis edition, as the volumes appear.

The Works of Francis Bacon. 14 vols, edited by James Spedding, Robert Leslie Ellis, and Douglas Denon Heath. London: Longmans, 1857–1874.

WORKS ABOUT BACON

Anderson, Fulton H. *The Philosophy of Francis Bacon*. New York: Octogan Books, 1971. A comprehensive treatment of Bacon's natural philosophy.

Gaukroger, Stephen. *Francis Bacon and the Transformation of Early-Modern Philosophy*. Cambridge, U.K.: Cambridge University Press, 2001. Looks at the connection between Bacon's natural philosophy and his account of method, and at his account of the shaping of the natural philosopher.

Jardine, Lisa. *Francis Bacon: Discovery and the Art of Discourse*. Cambridge, U.K.: Cambridge University Press, 1974. Deals with those issues in theories of rhetoric and logic that were the key ones in Bacon's formative years and shows their influence on his thinking.

Jardine, Lisa, and Alan Stewart. *Hostage to Fortune: The Troubled Life of Francis Bacon, 1561–1626*. London: Victor Gollancz, 1998. The most comprehensive and up-to-date biography.

Martin, Julian. *Francis Bacon, the State, and the Reform of Natural Philosophy*. Cambridge, U.K.: Cambridge University Press, 1992. The best available treatment of Bacon's thought on legal questions.

Peltonen, Markku, ed. *The Cambridge Companion to Bacon*. Cambridge, U.K.: Cambridge University Press, 1996. General collection of articles on all aspects of Bacon's thought.

Pérez-Ramos, Antonio. *Francis Bacon's Idea of Science and the Maker's Knowledge Tradition*. Oxford: Oxford University Press, 1988. Concentrates on the role of rhetoric in Bacon's work.

Rossi, Paolo. *Francis Bacon: From Magic to Science*. Chicago: University of Chicago Press, 1968. Deals with Bacon's natural philosophy.

Urbach, Peter. *Francis Bacon's Philosophy of Science: An Account and Reappraisal*. La Salle, IL: Open Court, 1987. Provides a comprehensive discussion of Bacon's account of method, with regular comparisons with Popper.

Webster, Charles. *The Great Instauration: Science, Medicine and Reform, 1626–1660*. London: Duckworth, 1975. The best available treatment of the influence of Bacon between the time of his death and the founding of the Royal Society.

Zagorin, Perez. *Francis Bacon*. Princeton, NJ: Princeton University Press, 1998. A general overview of Bacon's thought.

Stephen Gaukroger (2005)

BACON, ROGER
(between 1214 and 1220?–1292)

Roger Bacon, English philosopher and scientist, known as *Doctor Mirabilis*, was probably born between 1214 and 1220 and died in 1292, probably at Oxford. Bacon wrote in 1267 that he had learned the alphabet some forty years before and that his once wealthy brother had been ruined by his support of King Henry III during the barons' revolt. He studied arts at Oxford and then at Paris, where as regent master (c. 1237) he was among the first to lecture on the forbidden books of Aristotle when the ban was lifted. Here he wrote his *Summa Grammatica, Summulae Dialectices, Summa de Sophismatibus et Distinctionibus*, his *Quaestiones* on Aristotle's *Physics, Metaphysics*, and *De Sensu et Sensibili*, and on the pseudo-Aristotelian *De Plantis* and *Liber de Causis*; he also wrote commentaries, now lost, on *De Anima, De Generatione et Corruptione, De Caelo et Mundo*, and *De Animalibus.*

These early lectures reveal a philosopher, immature but of unusual ability, conversant with the new literature of Aristotle and his Arabic commentators. They are of some historical interest, since Bacon was representative of the new breed of masters at Paris who prided themselves on being pure Aristotelians. In fact, however, like Avicenna and Gundissalinus before them, they were still strongly influenced by other traditions (especially Neoplatonism) that dominated such apocryphal works as the *Liber de Causis* and, in Bacon's case, the popular *Secret of Secrets*. This latter work, thought to be Aristotle's esoteric instructions to Alexander the Great, is a study in kingcraft which, in addition to advocating a sound, practical philosophy, gives much astrological advice and hints at the magical virtues of herbs and gems and the occult properties of numbers. From his glosses on the book, it seems that Bacon was most impressed by its vision of a universal science of great practical import that included all the secrets of nature. This unified science, revealed by God to the Hebrews, who passed it on through the Chaldeans and Egyptians to Aristotle, was concealed in figurative and enigmatic language but might be rediscovered by one morally worthy and mentally qualified to receive it. Where the pagans failed, Bacon held, a Christian might succeed. Therefore, around 1247 he left Paris, where he had been pursuing a mastership in theology, and returned to Oxford, where Adam Marsh, Robert Grosseteste's Franciscan associate, introduced him to that great man's work. For two decades, Bacon writes, he studied languages and the sciences, training assistants, cultivating the fellowship of savants, and spending more than £2,000 on "secret books," instruments, and tables.

Sometime during the latter half of this period he must have joined the Franciscans, to whom Grosseteste bequeathed his library. Neither his impoverished brother nor the mendicant friars could provide the experimental equipment Bacon longed to have; nor did the majority of the friars share his views on the importance of his work. Resenting the preference shown to the more orthodox theologians, Bacon became embittered and vented his spite in cutting and often unjust criticisms of some of the best minds of the age. Worse, his childlike credulity with regard to the apocalyptic literature of the times led him to side with the extremist followers of Joachim of Floris. This made his views suspect; he was sent to Paris and forbidden to circulate his writings outside the order. But Pope Clement IV, learning of Bacon's proposed encyclopedia of unified science in the service of theology and unaware that the work was largely in the planning stage, wrote for a secret copy on June 22, 1266. Hoping for papal aid to complete the project, Bacon, in the short space of eighteen months, composed as a preliminary draft his *Opus Maius* (synopsized and implemented by the *Opus Minus* and *Opus Tertium*, the latter rich in biographical detail). With the *Opus Maius*, Bacon sent the pope a copy of his *Multiplicatio Specierum*, a concave lens "made at great expense," and "a precious map of the world." Unfortunately, Clement died in November 1268, before the last of the *opera* arrived.

Bacon probably returned to Oxford; he completed his *Communia Mathematica* and *Communia Naturalium* (two of his most mature works) and wrote Greek and Hebrew grammars and his *Compendium Studii Philosophiae*. The last, intended as a general introduction to his principal writings, degenerated into an emotional diatribe against the evils of the age; these were, according to Bacon, especially manifest in the universities where the two teaching orders (Dominicans and Franciscans) were neglecting his favorite subjects. It also revealed a revival of Joachite interests (Bacon referred to the ridicule his "logical proof" of the imminence of the Antichrist provoked among the friars).

According to the *Chronicle of the Twenty-four Generals*, written in 1370, the Franciscan minister general, Jerome of Ascoli (later Pope Nicholas IV), imprisoned him for "suspected novelties." This account has been questioned, primarily because nothing could be found in Bacon's scientific or astrological views that had not been endorsed by many reputable theologians of the day, such as Albertus Magnus. More likely, it was a political move to silence the irascible friar, whose caustic views on the morals of the secular masters would do little to ease the strained relations between them and the friars (whose orthodoxy had been seriously compromised by the fanatical Joachite fringe). At any rate, Bacon's confinement could hardly have been rigorous or long enough to inhibit his penchant for frank expression; in 1292 he was writing in the *Compendium Studii Theologiae* on his favorite topics with all his old verve and biting invective. He died, however, before this work was completed.

THOUGHT

The strength and the weakness of Bacon's erratic genius are nowhere more apparent than in the *Opus Maius,* his most characteristic and distinctive work. Both a plea and a plan for educational reform along the study lines pursued by Bacon himself, it is divided into seven parts—the causes of error, philosophy, the study of languages, mathematics, optics, experimental science, and moral philosophy. The first part descries four barriers blocking the road to truth: submission to unworthy authority (for example, crediting living theologians with a prestige due only to the Church Fathers or the Scriptures), the influence of custom, popular prejudice, and concealment of one's ignorance with a technical show of wisdom. Although by far the greatest portion of the book is devoted to mathematics, optics, and moral philosophy (to which, Bacon claimed, all speculative science should be ordered), Bacon's fame until recently rested on this first part and the relatively short section on experimental science. The belief that experimental science was the keystone of Bacon's reform was in part based on the misleading evidence of Samuel Jebb's 1733 edition of the *Opus Maius,* which omitted Part VII. By *scientia experimentalis,* however, Bacon meant any knowledge through experience as opposed to inferential or reasoned knowledge. When he said that nothing can be known with certainty without experience, his use of the term *experience* was twofold. One aspect of experience is based on sense perception and is called human or philosophical; the other aspect is

interior and is derived from an illumination of the mind by God (whom Bacon identified with Aristotle's agent intellect). Thus, although sense perception is necessary to knowledge, certainty cannot be attained without divine illumination. Interior experience admits of seven degrees, beginning with that required for certitude in mathematics or the natural sciences and culminating in such mystical or ecstatic states as St. Paul's vision of heaven.

Bacon devoted the most attention, however, to what humans can know about the wonders of nature by sense perception and the first degree of illumination. From the examples cited in Part VI and throughout the work, Bacon seems to have been less an original experimenter and more a propagandist for scientists such as Peter of Maricourt. His contributions to scientific theory, like his empirical research, were confined largely to optics. With the aid of new source material from Alhazen and Abū-Yūsuf Yaʿqūb ibn Ishāq al-Kindī, he was able to develop significantly many of Grosseteste's views concerning the tides, heat, and double refraction and to give the most mature expression to Grosseteste's theory that light (and all physical force generally) is transmitted in pulses like sound waves. Since this "multiplication of species" requires a medium, Bacon argued, the transmission cannot be instantaneous, even though the time interval is imperceptible. His application of the theory to vision and the working of the eye was one of the most important studies done on this subject during the Middle Ages and became the point of departure for developments in the seventeenth century. Bacon seems to have surpassed his teachers both in his knowledge of convex lenses and parabolic mirrors and in his ability to foresee such applications of science as automobiles, motorboats, and aircraft.

If, by continuing the Oxford tradition begun by Grosseteste, Bacon was in advance of his contemporaries, he was also incredibly naive in some of his other views. His uncritical acceptance of what others claimed to have observed is often in violation of his own canons for avoiding error. Much of his stress on the importance of language studies came from his conviction that all knowledge can be found in the Scriptures and "secret books," whose full meaning God reveals by interior illumination only to those whose lives are pure. He held that because of men's sins, God's scientific revelations were obscured by errors—which is one reason for testing empirically what the ancient sages say. Bacon seems to have had little use for abstract reasoning or speculation for its own sake. His interest in mathematics and logic, like his interest in astrology and alchemy, was purely practical. If all physical force, like light, is propagated rectilinearly, it is subject to geometric analysis. This, together with his conviction that the movement of the planets influences all terrestrial events except free will itself, was his reason for thinking that mathematics is the key to all natural sciences.

Not only was his faith in astrology unwarranted, but his ideas of theology belonged to a bygone age. Even prior to 1250, the Paris Franciscans, impressed by the Euclidean-Aristotelian ideal of a deductive science, were exploring how far the concepts of theology might be analyzed with greater logical rigor and theological propositions formalized in terms of axioms (first principles of reason and philosophy), postulates (the articles of faith), and theses (theological conclusions). Despite his sporadic attendance at theological lectures, Bacon seems to have had no comprehension of what the avant-garde theologians were doing. Perhaps this, more than any insistence on scientific values or the need for experimentation, brought him into conflict with his educated confreres, who apparently considered him, for all his flashes of brilliance and his scientific lore, something of a crank.

See also Albert the Great; Aristotle; Avicenna; Ethics, History of; Grosseteste, Robert; Joachim of Fiore; Neoplatonism.

Bibliography

Fr. Rogeri Bacon Opera Quaedam Hactenus Inedita, edited by J. S. Brewer (London: Longman, Green, Longman and Roberts, 1859), contains *Opus Tertium, Opus Minus, Compendium Studii Philosophiae,* and *Epistola de Secretis Operibus et de Nullitate Magiae.* For supplements to *Opus Tertium,* see Pierre Duhem, *Un Fragment inédit de l'Opus tertium de R. Bacon* (Quaracchi: Ad Claras Aquas, 1909), and A. G. Little, *Part of the Opus Tertium of Roger Bacon* (Aberdeen: University Press, 1912). Also see J. H. Bridges, ed., *Opus Majus,* 3 vols. (Oxford: Clarendon Press, 1897–1900; reprinted Frankfurt am Main: Minerva, 1964), Vol. II of which contains *Multiplicatio Specierum* as an appendix. For the complete text of Part VII, which is incomplete in Bridges, see F. Delorme and E. Massa, *Rogeri Baconis Moralis Philosophia* (Zürich, 1953).

Other writings by Bacon may be found in F. A. Gasquet, "An Unpublished Fragment of a Work by Roger Bacon," in *English Historical Review* 12 (1897): 494–517, a prefatory letter to the *Opus Maius* or *Opus Minus* or both; E. Nolan and S. A. Hirsch, *The Greek Grammar of Roger Bacon and a Fragment of His Hebrew Grammar* (Cambridge, U.K.: Cambridge University Press, 1902); and H. Rashdall, ed., *Fratris Rogeri Bacon Compendium Studii Theologiae* (Aberdeen: Typis Academicis, 1911). Most of Bacon's remaining works have been published by R. Steele (with individual volumes by F. M. Delorme, A. G. Little, and E. Withington) in *Opera Hactenus Inedita Fratris Rogeri Baconis,* 16 fascicles (Oxford: Clarendon Press, 1905–1940). The *Compotus* (Fasc. 6), ascribed to Bacon, is, however, the work of Giles of Lessines. See also S. H. Thomson, "An Unnoticed Treatise by Roger Bacon on Time and Motion," in *Isis* 27 (1937): 219–224, and F. M. Delorme, "Le Prologue de R. Bacon à son traité De influentiis agentium," in *Antonianum* 18 (1943): 81–90.

English translations of Bacon's work are R. B. Burke, *The "Opus Majus" of Roger Bacon,* 2 vols. (Philadelphia: University of Pennsylvania Press, 1928; reprinted, New York, 1962), and T. L. Davis, *Roger Bacon's Letter concerning the Marvelous Power of Art and Nature and concerning the Nullity of Magic* (Easton, PA: Chemical Publishing, 1923). For a bibliography of Bacon's works, see F. Alessio, "Un seculo di studi su Ruggero Bacone (1848–1957)," in *Rivista critica di storia della filosofia* 14 (1959): 81–108.

A discussion of the life and works of Roger Bacon appears in the introduction and appendix of A. G. Little, *Roger Bacon Essays, Contributed by Various Authors on the Occasion of the Commemoration of the Seventh Centenary of His Birth* (Oxford: Clarendon Press, 1914). Also see S. C. Easton, *Roger Bacon and His Search for a Universal Science* (New York: Columbia University Press, 1952), which contains an extensive and annotated bibliography. For a discussion of Bacon's philosophy, see T. Crowley, *Roger Bacon, the Problem of the Soul in His Philosophical Commentaries* (Louvain and Dublin: Éditions de l'Institut supérieur de philosophie, 1950), a good account of hylomorphic theory; D. Sharp, *Franciscan Philosophy at Oxford* (Oxford: Oxford University Press, 1930); and E. Heck, *Roger Bacon. Ein mittelalterlicher Versuch einer historischen und systematischen Religionswissenschaft* (Bonn, 1957). For Bacon's contributions to science, see Lynn Thorndike, *A History of Magic and Experimental Science* (New York: Macmillan, 1929), Vol. II, pp. 616–691, which minimizes Bacon's contributions (a reaction to earlier exaggerations); and A. C. Crombie, *Robert Grosseteste and the Origins of Experimental Science 1100–1700* (Oxford: Clarendon Press, 1953), pp. 139–162, a more balanced account.

Allan B. Wolter, O.F.M. (1967)

BACON, ROGER [ADDENDUM]

Twentieth-century research on Roger Bacon requires some changes to the account above. It is clear that Richard Rufus, and not Bacon, was the first to lecture on the new Aristotle at Paris circa 1235. Bacon responded to the ideas of Rufus in his Parisian *Quaestiones* (c. 1240s). He returned to these topics in his last work *Compendium of the Study of Theology* (1292).

Sometime around 1247, Bacon departed from his teaching at the University of Paris. For the next twenty years he devoted his time to a study of the following works: Ibn al-Haytham *Optics,* the Pseudo-Aristotelian *Secretum secretorum* on statecraft, the *Centiloquium,* the *Commentary on the Centiloquium,* and numerous works on astrology. Most important here was the work of Abu'-

mashar (Albumassar). The *Communia mathematica*, the *Communia naturalium*, and the *Compendium studii philosophiae* were most probably written in Paris.

Research on Bacon since the mid-twentieth century has yielded the following results:

1) Bacon plays a significant role in the history of logic, semantics, and semiotics. Bacon's originality stands out in regard to semiotics, philosophical grammar, quantification, theory of natural sense, univocity, and supposition.

2) The new editions of the *De multiplicatione specierum* (1266) and the *Perspectiva* (1266) have placed these two texts in their proper context as important works in natural philosophy and philosophy of mind.

3) Scholars have gained a greater understanding of Bacon's aims in his knowledge of mathematics, astronomy-astrology, music, experimental science, alchemy, and medicine. Bacon presents himself as an advocate for the experimental science of others such as Petrus Peregrinus of Maricourt. Nevertheless, his account of *Perspectiva* as a model of an "experimental science" is fundamentally important for the later development of optics, perspective, and philosophy of mind, and for methodology in science.

4) Bacon's treatise on *Moralis philosohpia* develops proto-humanist concerns. Overall, in his later post-1266 philosophy, Bacon subordinates his earlier Aristotelianism to a Stoic division of philosophy and to mainly Platonic concerns.

See also Aristotelianism; Aristotle; Logic, History of; Philosophy of Mind; Platonism and the Platonic Tradition; Semantics; Stoicism.

Bibliography

WORKS BY ROGER BACON

Fredborg, Karen Margarita, Lauge Nielsen, and Jan Pinborg, eds. "An Unpublished Fragment of a Work by Roger Bacon." *Traditio* 34 (1978): 75–136.

Lindberg, David C. *Roger Bacon and the Origins of Perspectiva in the Middle Ages: A Critical Edition of the "Perspectiva," with English Translation, Introduction, and Notes.* New York: Oxford University Press, 1995.

Lindberg, David C. *Roger Bacon's Philosophy of Nature: A Critical Edition, with English Translation, Introduction, and Notes, of "De Multiplicatione specierum" and "De speculis comburentibus."* Oxford, U.K.: Clarendon Press, 1983.

Linden, Stanton J. *The Mirror of Alchimy*. New York: Garland, 1997.

Maloney, Thomas S. *Compendium of the Study of Theology*. Leiden: Brill, 1988.

Maloney, Thomas S. *Three Treatments of Universals*. Binghamton: MARTS, 1989.

Molland, George. "Roger Bacon's *Geometria speculative*." In *Vestigia Mathematica: Studies in Medieval and Early Modern Mathematics in Honor of H.H.L. Busard*, edited by M. Folkerts and J. P. Hogendijk. Amsterdam and Atlanta: Editions Rodopi, 1993.

WORKS ABOUT ROGER BACON

Hackett, Jeremiah, ed. *Roger Bacon and The Sciences: Commemorative Essays*. Leiden: Brill, 1997. This volume introduced new work on languages and the natural sciences.

Hackett, Jeremiah, ed. *Vivarium: An International Journal for the Philosophy and Intellectual Life of the Middle Ages and Renaissance* Leiden: Brill, Vol. XXXV, N. 2 (September, 1997). This volume introduces new work on language, physics, metaphysics, and philosophy of mind. It also includes a bibliography.

Rosier-Catach, Irene. *La parole comme acte: Sur la grammaire et la semantique au XIIIe siecle*. Paris: Vrin, 1994. In this work, the author situates Bacon in the context of philosophy of language in the thirteenth century.

Jeremiah Hackett (2005)

BAD FAITH

The most common form of inauthenticity in the existentialism of Jean-Paul Sartre, "bad faith" is paradoxically a lie to oneself. For such self-deception to be possible, the human being must be divided against itself, one level or aspect concealing from the other what it in some sense "knows." The paradox arises from the condition that this operation occurs within the unity of a single consciousness.

The root of Sartrean bad faith is a twofold dividedness of the human being, psychological and ontological. As conscious, humans are prereflectively aware of what they may not reflectively know. Such prereflective awareness or "comprehension," as he will later call it, functions in Sartre's psychology in a manner similar to Sigmund Freud's unconscious, a concept that Sartre notoriously rejected. The project of bad faith—to keep oneself in the dark about certain matters—is itself in bad faith since prereflective consciousness "chooses" not to acknowledge on reflection what it is concealing from reflective consciousness.

There can be an entire Weltanschauung of bad faith: the habits, practices, objects, and institutions that one employs to maintain oneself in a state of "perpetual distraction." Sartre's analysis of Second Empire French society in his work on Gustave Flaubert is a study in collective bad faith. But the root of the moral responsibility that this term carries lies in the self-translucency of prereflective consciousness: individuals, alone or together, are pre-reflectively aware of more than they reflectively allow themselves to know.

The ontological basis of bad faith is the dividedness of the human situation. Every human exists in-situation. Situation is an ambiguous mix of facticity (the given) and transcendence (the surpassing of the given by our projects). Bad faith is our way of fleeing the anguish that this ambiguity causes either by collapsing our transcendence into facticity (as in various forms of determinism) or by volatilizing our facticity into transcendence (like the dreamer who refuses to acknowledge the facts of his or her life). Though the details of bad faith are as singular as our self-defining choices, its moral significance is the same in each instance. Bad faith is basically flight from our freedom-in-situation.

As Sartre's concept of situation expanded to include and even place a premium on socioeconomic conditions, the relation between bad faith and class struggle became more pronounced. He later argued that good faith, which in *Being and Nothingness* he dismissed as a form of bad faith, was fostered by socioeconomic equality and that scarcity of material goods made bad faith almost inevitable. The anti-Semite was in bad faith, but so too was his or her liberal assimilationist defender; likewise the neocolonialist and the industrial capitalist, both of whom fled their responsibility for subscribing to and sustaining a system that made exploitation of others "necessary."

Only in his posthumously published *Notebooks for an Ethics* does Sartre discuss the nature and possibility of good faith at any length. This presumes a "conversion" in which one chooses to live one's anguished dividedness while fostering via generous cooperation a situation that enables others to do likewise.

See also Determinism, A Historical Survey; Existentialism; Existential Psychoanalysis; Freud, Sigmund; Sartre, Jean-Paul; Unconscious.

Bibliography

Beauvoir, S. de. *Pour une morale de l'ambiguité.* Paris: Gallimard, 1947. Translated by B. Frechtman as *The Ethics of Ambiguity.* New York: Philosophical Library, 1948.

Fingarette, H. *Self-Deception.* London: Routledge and Kegan Paul, 1969.

Martin, M. W. *Self-Deception and Morality.* Lawrence: University Press of Kansas, 1986.

Mirvish, A. "Bad Faith, Good Faith, and the Faith of Faith." In *Sartre Alive,* edited by R. Aronson and A. van den Hoven. Detroit: Wayne State University Press, 1991.

Morris, P. "Self-Deception: Sartre's Resolution of the Paradox." In *Jean-Paul Sartre: Contemporary Approaches to His Philosophy,* edited by H. J. Silverman and F. A. Elliston. Pittsburgh: Duquesne University Press, 1980.

Santoni, R. E. *Bad Faith, Good Faith and Authenticity in Sartre's Early Philosophy.* Philadelphia: Temple University Press, 1995.

Sartre, J.-P. *Cahiers pour une morale.* Paris, 1983. Translated by D. Pellauer as *Notebooks for an Ethics.* Chicago: University of Chicago Press, 1992.

Sartre, J.-P. *L'etre et le néant.* Paris: Gallimard, 1943. Translated by H. E. Barnes as *Being and Nothingness.* New York: Philosophical Library, 1956.

Thomas R. Flynn (1996)

BAHRDT, CARL FRIEDRICH
(1740 or 1741–1792)

Carl Friedrich Bahrdt, probably the most widely read German theologian except for Martin Luther, was born in Bischofswerda in the electorate of Saxony. He held professorships and lectureships of theology, biblical studies, Christian ethics, classical languages, and many other subjects at the universities of Leipzig, Erfurt, Giessen, and Halle. He was the headmaster of a boys school, or *Philanthropinum,* in Marschlins in Switzerland and established his own *Philanthropinum* in Heidesheim while he was at the same time *Superintendent* (the highest ecclesiastical official) in the domains of Count Carl of Leiningen-Dachsburg. In his last years, he was an innkeeper near Halle. He died at Halle.

Bahrdt was always at the center of a controversy. In his early days he wrote in a fiery orthodox vein, but very soon he seems to have been started on the road to "enlightenment" by suddenly learning that the language of I John 5:7, did not, when subjected to philological scrutiny, constitute proof of the doctrine of the Trinity. He was still further dismayed to learn that the passage was considered by some excellent scholars to be an interpolation. Bahrdt then set out to find undoubted philological support for the orthodox Lutheran system of theology, and instead found that his doubts continued to increase, until by the end of his life he had arrived at a fully rationalistic concept of natural religion.

The high points in Bahrdt's "Rationalist's Progress" are his four-volume paraphrase of the New Testament, *Neueste Offenbarungen Gottes* (Riga, 1773–1774), his confession of faith, *Glaubensbekenntnis, veranlasst durch ein Kaiserliches Reichshofratsconclusum* (1779), and his fictionalized life of Jesus, *Briefe über die Bibel im Volkston* (Halle, 1782–1783) and *Ausführung des Plans und Zweckes Jesu* (Berlin, 1783–1785). Bahrdt's New Testament paraphrase was up-to-date, intelligible, fluent, and coherent, but it was also a propagandistic vehicle for his heretical views. His enemies were thus enabled to secure, in 1778, a decree barring him from all ecclesiastical offices in the Holy Roman Empire and adjuring him to recant. Bahrdt immediately published his confession of faith, stating in clear and succinct language what he did and did not believe. Through discarding beliefs that he felt could not endure the acid test of rational examination, Bahrdt was left with a Jesus who was a mere product of his life and time. In this almost completely naturalistic view, the teasing question was, "In what way did Jesus obtain his amazing wisdom?" In order to give a hypothetical answer to this question, Bahrdt produced his fictional life of Jesus, the culmination of his development and the first work of its kind. It took the form of a series of weekly letters about the Bible, written in a popular vein, and tried to demonstrate how Jesus might have learned and built up his teachings from the writings of Greek sages, which Providence could have put into his hands through his association with Hellenistic Jews. These first letters were continued in a series on the execution of Jesus' plan and purpose, in which Bahrdt advanced the theory that Jesus founded a kind of Freemasonry to aid him in his purpose to destroy superstition, eliminate all positive religion, restore reason to its rightful rule, and unite people in a rational faith in God, Providence, and Immortality.

See also Luther, Martin; Rationalism.

Bibliography

Bahrdt, C. F. *Dr. Carl Friedrich Bahrdts Geschichte seines Lebens, seiner Meinungen und Schicksale.* Berlin: Bei Friedrich Vieweg, dem Älteren, 1790–1791.

Brewer, John T. *"Gesunde Vernunft" and the New Testament: A Study of C. F. Bahrdt's* Die neuesten Offenbarungen Gottes. PhD diss., University of Texas at Austin, 1962.

Flygt, S. G. *The Notorious Dr. Bahrdt.* Nashville, TN: Vanderbilt, 1963.

Schweitzer, Albert. *Geschichte der Leben-Jesu-Forschung.* Tübingen: J.C.B. Mohr, 1913.

Sten G. Flygt (1967)

BAHYĀ BEN JOSEPH IBN PAQŪDA
(fl. 11th century)

Bahyā ben Joseph ibn Paqūda, the Jewish Neoplatonist, was the author of the first systematic philosophic work on ethics in the Jewish tradition. Beyond the fact that he served as a judge (*dayyan*) of the rabbinical court in Saragossa, details of his life are unknown. About 1040 he wrote in Arabic *Al-Hidaja ila Faraid al-Qulub* (Guide to the duties of the heart). This work, as translated into Hebrew about 1160 by Judah ibn Tibbon, under the title *Hoboth Ha-Lebaboth (Duties of the Heart)*, has achieved great popularity, both in full text and in abridged versions.

Bahyā's work cites Arabic as well as Jewish philosophers and contains many fine quotations from Arabic literature. There are considerable similarities between his general philosophic orientation and that of the Arabic school of encyclopedists known as the Brothers of Purity. If this relationship is accepted, there is no need to search further for the sources of the somewhat mystical, somewhat ascetic Neoplatonism that moderates the generally Aristotelian character of his position. It has also been suggested that Bahyā fell under the influence of the Sufi mystics of Islam, chiefly because of his emphasis on the cultivation of self-renunciation and indifference to the goods of the world in the last three books of *Duties of the Heart.*

The distinction between outward and inward obligation, "duties of the limbs" and "duties of the heart," which accounts for the title of the treatise, is a familiar distinction in both Arabic and Hindu religious literature. Bahyā used the theme to suggest that the rabbis, the leaders of the Jewish community, were overly concerned with the external obligations of men, rather than with the duties of the heart, and that, because of the rabbis' insistence on the duties of the limbs, the masses of the Jewish people remained totally unconcerned about all religious obligations. He tried to correct this deficiency by presenting Judaism as a message of great spiritual vitality and force, directed to the human heart and resting on the threefold base of reason, revelation, and tradition. The fundamental principle upon which the whole structure of Bahyā's work is based is the wholehearted conviction of God's existence and unity, the subject of the first book of *Duties of the Heart.* From this, he moves to the necessity for apprehending the wisdom, power, and goodness of God by careful study of the larger world in which we live and the smaller world of our own human nature. In this latter study there emerge the duties of the heart: service of God, trust in God, wholehearted devotion to God, humility in God's presence, repentance, self-communion, and renunciation. In this way, humanity reaches the height of the religious life, the love of God. Despite the superficially rational structure of the book, Baḥyā was not truly a rationalist; rather, he used the techniques of reason to subserve the ends of a contemplative view of life whose method was moral intuition, and whose goal was piety.

An Arabic treatise, *Maʿani al-Nafs* (The attributes of the soul), known only in manuscript until its publication in the early twentieth century, bears the name of Baḥyā on its title page, but this is now generally conceded not to be his work. No other works of Baḥyā are known.

See also Jewish Philosophy; Neoplatonism.

Bibliography

For Baḥyā's work, see *Torath Hoboth Ha-Lebaboth,* 5 vols. (New York: Bloch, 1925–1947). This contains Judah ibn Tibbon's Hebrew translation plus a facing English translation and an introduction by Moses Hyamson.

For discussions of Baḥyā, see Isaac Husik, *A History of Mediaeval Jewish Philosophy* (New York: Macmillan, 1916); Jacob B. Agus, *The Evolution of Jewish Thought* (London and New York: Abelard-Schuman, 1959); and Joseph L. Blau, *The Story of Jewish Philosophy* (New York: Random House, 1962). See G. Vajda, *La théologie ascétique de Bahja ibn Paquda* (Paris: Nationale, 1947), for a comparison of Baḥya's doctrines with Islamic ascetic literature.

J. L. Blau (1967)

BAḤYĀ BEN JOSEPH IBN PAQŪDA [ADDENDUM]

Although Baḥyā ben Joseph ibn Paqūda follows the major categories of Sufism in his exploration of human motivation, he also manages to find a social justification for many aspects of Judaism. For example, one of the virtues he discusses is restraint or abstemiousness, the need to resist our desires. He argues that we can pursue this socially by our attitude to others by acquiring a cheerful and calm attitude toward others. A means of being disposed to act thus is the Torah and its laws, for these have the effect of training ourselves to restrain our desires and bring them under the rule of law. For Baḥyā the very private and personal moral rules that we adopt to bring us closer to God have a significant public element. The highest virtue is love of God, and to acquire this we need to practice personal asceticism, together with justice, good

manners, and justice. Although the aim of his book on the duties of the heart is to show that Judaism is not only about external actions but has an inner spiritual dimension as well, he does not go to the extreme of denying the significance of law and prayer. On the contrary, he argues that the private and the public aspects of religion complement each other. His book also provides a detailed account of how that works in the case of Judaism.

See also Asceticism; Jewish Philosophy; Justice; Moral Rules and Principles; Sufism.

Bibliography

Fenton, Paul B. "Judaism and Sufism." In *Cambridge Companion to Medieval Jewish Philosophy*, edited by Daniel H. Frank and Oliver Leaman, 201–217. New York: Cambridge University Press, 2003.

Rudavsky, Tamar. "Medieval Jewish Neoplatonism." In *History of Jewish Philosophy*, edited by Daniel H. Frank and Oliver Leaman. London: Routledge, 1997.

WORKS BY BAḤYĀ

Al-Hidāya ilā faraʾiḍ al-Qulūb (The book of direction to the duties of the heart). Translated by Menahem Mansoor. London: Routledge, 1973.

"Prayer and Faith." In *Jewish Philosophy Reader*, edited by Daniel H. Frank, Oliver Leaman, and Charles H. Manekin. London: Routledge, 2000.

WORKS ON BAḤYĀ

Fenton, Paul B. "Judaism and Sufism." In *History of Islamic Philosophy*. 2 vols., edited by Seyyed Hossein Nasr and Oliver Leaman. London: Routledge, 1996.

Goodman, Lenn E. "Bahya on the Antinomy of Free Will and Predestination." *Journal of the History of Ideas* 44 (1) (1983): 115–130.

Oliver Leaman (2005)

BAIER, ANNETTE
(1929–)

Annette Baier was born in New Zealand in 1929. She received her bachelor of arts and master of arts degrees from the University of Otago, and, in 1954, her bachelor of philosophy degree from Oxford, writing a thesis on precision in poetry under J. L. Austin. After teaching in the United Kingdom, New Zealand, and Australia, Baier moved to the United States, teaching first at Carnegie Mellon and then at the University of Pittsburgh from 1973 until her retirement as Distinguished Service Professor in 1997.

Baier's primary commitment is to naturalism: Human beings are evolved animals and we must understand our capacities, both intellectual and moral, in the light of this natural history. Baier finds philosophers guilty of a kind of willful forgetting of the facts of our embodied existence. We are social animals who experience long periods of dependency in infancy and childhood, and even the more or less symmetric dependencies of maturity are liable to become asymmetric with age or, in some cases, illness. Baier's work charts the implications of our interdependency for epistemology, ethics, and action theory.

Epistemology is a social enterprise. In David Hume, Baier finds the resources to develop a feminist epistemology that recognizes the positive contribution of emotions to knowledge, and that recognizes that all inquiry is fallible and situated, beginning, as it must, from the "prejudices" of tradition and custom. Beliefs, attitudes, and practices that withstand reflective scrutiny merit continued allegiance; those that do not must be abandoned. Baier's account of reflection is distinctive for both its anti-intellectualism and anti-individualism. Reflection is carried out by a *community* of inquirers embracing many differing perspectives and, rather than being the sole province of intellect, reflection uses *all* the capacities of the human mind, including affective capacities such as sympathy. These capacities are capable of being turned on themselves and on our habits and customs and we can come to achieve "reflective self-acceptance, agreement with ourselves" (1994b, p. 277). Reflection reveals the importance of *judgment*. Rules are of limited use in guiding either practical or theoretical judgment; hence Baier's anti-theory stance. In ethics, this anti-theory stance takes the form of suspicion about the possibility of capturing morality in a set of rules. Such systemizing drives are to be replaced by careful exploration of the capacities that enable virtuous action.

In keeping with her emphasis on reflection, Baier proposes a reflective test for evaluating moralities: "a decent morality will *not* depend for its stability on forces to which it gives no moral recognition. Its account books should be open to scrutiny and there should be no unpaid debts, no loans with no prospect of repayment" (1994a, p. 8). Baier argues that liberal morality, with its focus on contractual relations and voluntarily assumed obligations, takes as paradigmatic the interactions between equals or near-equals and so is unable to pass this test. It depends on the unacknowledged moral labor of those producing future moral agents, a labor it cannot itself theorize. Had ethical theory begun from the perspective of those, chiefly women, engaged in such labor, relations between unequals would have come into focus, thus revealing the importance of trust.

Baier's work is largely responsible for the recent upsurge of interest in trust, not just among philosophers, but also among social scientists. She finds trust to bridge the traditional divisions between the cognitive, affective and conative: Trust has a distinctive feel, typically involves a tacit belief in the other's goodwill and competence, and explains the truster's willingness to let others get dangerously near things she cares about. According to Baier, trust, though instrumental to many human goods and a constitutive part of others (for example, friendship), is not a virtue. Nor is untrustworthiness always a vice: Misplaced trust enables exploitation and abuse and sometimes trust is best responded to with judicious betrayals of trust.

Our interdependence also has implications for our understanding of persons and their actions. We are inducted into the "arts of personhood" by others: "Persons essentially are *second* persons who grow up with other persons" (1985, p. 84). It is through being addressed and addressing other second persons—through, that is, coming to master the pronoun "you"—that we come to have self-consciousness. Baier rejects as reductive moves to identify bodily movements or volitions as "basic actions" (actions that are directly done rather than done by doing anything else) and argues that actions can be identified as intentional only given background assumptions of culturally dependent competences. She finds accounts of personhood that focus on a narrow range of properties such as autonomy, dignity, and the capacity to make evaluative judgments guilty of wilfully forgetting our biological nature. She substitutes in their stead a conception of ourselves as "intelligent, talkative, playful mammals" (1991, p. 13) whose personhood comprises many capacities, both cognitive and affective. All these capacities are to be recruited in doing philosophy, which, following Hume, is to use "*all* the capacities of the human mind: memory, passion and sentiment as well as a chastened intellect" (1994b, p. 1). Her own writing style, with its rich use of anecdote, association, playfulness, and irony, enacts as well as argues for a philosophy informed by passion and experience.

See also Analytic Feminism; Austin, John Langshaw; Emotion; Feminist Epistemology; Hume, David; Metaethics; Naturalism; Women in the History of Philosophy.

Bibliography

WORKS BY ANNETTE BAIER

Postures of the Mind: Essays on Mind and Morals. Minneapolis: University of Minnesota Press, 1985.

"A Naturalist View of Persons." Presidential Address Delivered before the Eighty-Seventh Annual Eastern Division Meeting of the American Philosophical Association in Boston, MA. *Proceedings and Addresses of the American Philosophical Association* 65 (1991): 5–17.

Moral Prejudices. Cambridge, MA: Harvard University Press, 1994a.

A Progress of Sentiments: Reflections on Hume's Treatise. Cambridge, MA: Harvard University Press, 1994b.

The Commons of the Mind: Carus Lectures 19. Chicago: Open Court, 1997.

WORKS ABOUT ANNETTE BAIER

Jenkins, Joyce, Jennifer Whiting, and Christopher Williams, eds. *Persons and Passions: Essays in Honor of Annette Baier.* Notre Dame, IN: University of Notre Dame Press, 2005.

Karen Jones (2005)

BAIER, KURT
(1917–)

Kurt Baier was born in Vienna, Austria, in 1917. He had to abandon his law studies at the University of Vienna in 1938, when he went as a refugee to Britain. There he was interned as a "friendly enemy alien" and sent to Australia. He began his study of philosophy in earnest in the internment camp and continued after the war ended. He received his BA (1944) and MA (1947) from the University of Melbourne, and his DPhil (1952) from Oxford University. He taught at the University of Melbourne, the Australian National University, and the University of Pittsburgh. He was a visiting professor at Cornell University, the University of Illinois, the University of Florida, and the University of Otago (New Zealand). He was president of the Eastern Division and chairman of the National Board of Officers of the American Philosophical Association. Annette Baier, whom he married in 1958, was also president of the Eastern Division. After they retired, they moved to New Zealand, which is Annette's native country. They may be the most distinguished philosophical couple in American philosophy, although neither was born in America. Both gave the Paul Carus Lectures, and both were invited to be members of the American Academy of Arts and Sciences. In 2001 Kurt was awarded an Honorary Doctorate of Jurisprudence from the Karl Franzen University of Graz, at a ceremony hosted by the University of Otago.

Baier was one of the most influential philosophers in the field of moral philosophy in the second half of the twentieth century. He is one of the philosophers primarily responsible for returning the field of moral philosophy from an obsession with the language of moral judgments to its traditional concern with describing and justifying guides to moral behavior.

Baier claims that moral rules are meant for everybody. They must be universally teachable, that is, they cannot involve beliefs or concepts not known to all normal adult humans. They cannot be self-frustrating, self-defeating, or morally impossible, that is, impossible or pointless if universally taught. Many moral philosophers after Baier have used these features as necessary conditions for a guide to conduct to count as a morality.

Baier recognizes that these features are merely formal and that moral rules must also have a particular kind of content. Baier describes this content by saying that moral rules must be for the good of everyone alike. However, when he gives examples of these rules (e.g., rules prohibiting killing, cruelty, inflicting pain, maiming, torturing, deceiving, cheating, rape, and adultery), it is quite clear that he means that these rules prohibit causing harm to anyone. He was prescient in recognizing, against both deontologists and utilitarians, that morality does not require doing the optimific act (the act having the best consequences), no matter how one determines what that optimific act is.

Like Thomas Hobbes, whom he acknowledges as a strong influence on his views, Baier put forward the principle of reversibility (a negative version of the Golden Rule), "Do not do unto others as you would not have them do unto you," as summarizing the moral guide to life. Although he does not use the language of natural-law theories, Baier also follows Hobbes in holding that morality has to be known by all those who are held morally responsible for their behavior, that is, moral rules apply to all who can understand the rules and can guide their behavior accordingly.

Baier argues, "It is the very meaning of 'a morality' that it should contain a body of moral convictions which can be true or false, that is, a body of rules or precepts for which there are certain tests" (Baier 1965, p. 89). Baier claims that these tests must involve what he calls "the moral point of view." Although Baier's description of this point of view is not universally accepted, it is acknowledged by all that moral rules must stem from a point of view based on universally shared beliefs and desires.

In addition to providing a plausible and influential account of morality, Baier also put forward an account of rationality that is more acceptable than the standard instrumentalist accounts. He recognizes that it is irrational "when, for no reason at all, we set our hands on fire or cut off our toes one by one" (Baier 1965, p. 158). Unlike many contemporary philosophers, he is aware that there are irrational desires, and hence that it cannot be correct to define a rational action as one that maximizes the satisfaction of a person's desires.

Baier's attempt to use his analyses of the concepts of rationality and morality to arrive at substantive moral conclusions marked the end, in ethics, of a concern with the language of morals that claimed to be morally neutral. By making a distinction between moral judgments and other value judgments, he showed that the terms "right," "ought," "good," and "bad" are primarily related to values, not morality. Recognizing that we offer reasons for choosing and doing many things in addition to those related to morality, Baier convinced many that concentrating on the use of these terms is not likely to be of much help in determining what morality is. Although many contemporary moral philosophers, especially consequentialists, continue to talk of good and bad, right and wrong, it is now generally recognized that these concepts are not identical to the concepts of morally good and morally bad, morally right and morally wrong.

Throughout his work Baier has attempted to show that reason supports acting morally. In his earlier work he distinguished between self-interested reasons, altruistic reasons, and moral reasons; and argued that although self-interested reasons were stronger than altruistic reasons, moral reasons were stronger than self-interested reasons. He showed that anyone picking worlds to live in would pick a world that had this ordering. In his later work, he distinguished between self-interested reasons, self-anchored reasons, and society-anchored reasons, and showed that if a society is to function, its members must accept that society-anchored reasons, particularly moral reasons, overrule both self-interested and self-anchored reasons. Although there is considerable doubt about whether Baier has shown that reason supports morality as he argues for it, his arguments for this view contain many valuable points. Failure to appreciate his distinction between altruistic reasons and moral reasons explains why some people find it difficult to accept that lying to protect a guilty colleague is immoral.

Largely because of Baier's work, moral philosophy no longer is dominated by concerns about the language of ethics. At the beginning of the twenty-first century, moral philosophers are now more likely to put forward substantive ethical views, be they Hobbesian, Kantian, or utilitarian, than they are to view their accounts of morality as having no normative implications. The distinction between concern with analyzing the terms or concepts involved in moral discourse and concern with substantive moral problems has largely disappeared. Even those concerned with analyses of ethical concepts now hold that analyses of these moral concepts may yield substantive moral conclusions. Baier is also primarily responsible for the fact that the central problem of moral philosophy is now showing the relationship between rationality and morality. The mark of a great philosopher is generally thought to lie not in the answers he gives but in the questions he raises. There is no question that on this view Kurt Baier is a great philosopher.

See also Baier, Annette; Ethics, History of; Hobbes, Thomas; Rationalism in Ethics (Practical-Reason Approaches).

Bibliography

WORKS BY BAIER

The Moral Point of View. Ithaca, NY: Cornell University Press, 1958.

The Moral Point of View. Abridged and rev. ed. New York: Random House, 1965.

Values and the Future, edited with Nicholas Rescher. New York: Free Press, 1969.

The Rational and the Moral Order. Chicago: Open Court, 1995.

Reason, Ethics, and Society: Themes from Kurt Baier, with His Responses, edited by J. B. Schneewind. Chicago: Open Court, 1996. Contains a complete bibliography of Baier's publications up until 1995.

Problems of Life and Death: A Humanist Perspective. Amherst, NY: Prometheus Books, 1997.

Bernard Gert (2005)

BAIN, ALEXANDER
(1818–1903)

Alexander Bain, the Scottish philosopher and psychologist, was the son of a weaver. He was mainly self-educated but managed to attend Marischal College, in his native city of Aberdeen. After graduating he assisted the philosophy professor there from 1841 to 1844. A confirmed radical, Bain established close contacts with utilitarian circles in London, helping John Stuart Mill in the revisions of his unpublished *System of Logic* in 1842 and helping Edwin Chadwick with his sanitation reforms from 1848 to 1850. During the next decade, supporting himself by journalism, he produced his magnum opus in two installments, titled *The Senses and the Intellect* (London, 1855) and *The Emotions and the Will* (London, 1859). Appointed professor of logic and rhetoric at Aberdeen in 1860, he published his *Manual of Rhetoric* (London, 1864) and his *Logic, Deductive and Inductive* (London and New York, 1870). On the proceeds of these and other textbooks he founded *Mind* in 1876, choosing his disciple George Croome Robertson as editor. After Bain's death his *Autobiography* (London, 1904), which gives his personal background and a useful criticism of his own books, was published.

CRITICISM OF ASSOCIATIONISM

Bain was not simply a pedestrian disciple of the two Mills. Fundamentally loyal to associationism, he was as discontented as J. S. Mill with its tenets but more systematic in his criticisms of them. What apparently made Bain uneasy was the narrow combination of introspection and emphasis on facts that characterized the associationistic science of mind. He was attracted by the physiologists' contemporary program of studying mind by a method uniting emphasis on facts with observation rather than introspection. At the same time Bain was interested in the recent efforts of the epistemologists to found a science that, while still introspective, was concerned not with empirical facts but with necessary truths. He had contacts with William Sharpey among the physiologists and James Ferrier among the epistemologists. Physiology and epistemology were interests alien to Mill.

THE WILL

The fusion of diverse tendencies in Bain's philosophy is best seen in the final section of his chief work—the discussion of the will—and especially its last hundred pages, which contain Bain's spirited defense of determinism, his justly famous theory of belief, and his equally interesting, though less known, analysis of consciousness. For Bain the central problem of the will apparently is the question of how I exercise voluntary control over my limbs. From the traditionalist standpoint it seemed an insoluble mystery how the mind knows just what motor nerves to activate when, for instance, expecting a blinding light to be switched on, it causes the eyes to close in advance. Bain's theory swept aside the traditional analogy with the case of first getting information about what is ahead and then operating a lever. The limbs are not inert like levers but possess an inherent spontaneity, and this spontaneity means that the expectation of the painful glare is inseparably associated with preparations to close the eye. The

idea is that theory and practice are one. This doctrine of spontaneity, a direct ancestor of pragmatism, Bain rightly considered to be his most original contribution to philosophy, and he both discussed it effectively at the animal level and struggled honestly, in his discussion of effort, with the difficulty of applying it at the human level.

BELIEF

Bain's doctrine of belief arose in the context of his view of will. When he spoke of belief as being inseparable from "a preparation to act," he was envisaging as basic a situation in which one seriously expects alleviation of a present pain from something that is visible but out of reach. In the ensuing action of trying to grasp this thing, the belief is inevitably put to the test: "We believe first and prove or disprove afterwards." The essence of the human situation was thus for Bain a kind of circle of activity in which we inevitably acquire new nonrational beliefs as a direct consequence of practically and experimentally testing those we start with. The point is apparently that our actions have unforeseen consequences.

CONSCIOUSNESS

By an ingenious turn Bain used the pragmatist analysis of belief as a basis for a theory of consciousness inspired by William Hamilton's doctrine of the inverse ratio of sensation and perception. In Bain's version of the theory, a sharp contrast is drawn between the emotive pole of consciousness, where absorption in one's pains or pleasures prevents the objective assessment of one's situation, and the cognitive pole, where pleasures and pains are forgotten in the business of mapping one's world and where emotion appears only in the shock of scientific discovery, as a feeling that, like boredom, is outside the pleasure-pain sphere. The movement from feeling to knowledge in consciousness is linked with the same facts that give human life the character of a passage from belief to self-criticism.

But what, then, is this consciousness that underlies both the emotional side and the intellectual? Inspired by Hamilton and Ferrier, Bain made two points. First, we are unconscious of the undifferentiated. "A constant impression is to the mind a blank"—if temperature were unvarying we would not notice it. Second, we are conscious of the constant only in the midst of variety and difference. The essence of consciousness is thus to be discriminative, and Bain pointed out that of the discriminations involved in consciousness, the most liable to be misunderstood is that implicit in the problem of the external world. Bain argued that although Berkeley was right in denouncing as meaningless the notion of material objects independent of experience, he overlooked an important point—that a distinction can be drawn within experience between the person sensing and the sensation sensed. Thus Bain, unlike J. S. Mill, conveyed a profound sense of the complexity of the problem of the external world.

Bain was aware that his philosophy was far removed from ordinary associationism. Above all, in the important Note F to the third edition of *The Senses and the Intellect*, he made it clear that for him association presupposed disassociation.

Bain progressively broke away from the heritage of the Mills, in logic as well as in psychology (he ultimately gave up Mill's view of logic for Augustus De Morgan's). At the same time there always survived in him certain tracts of unredeemed associationism. Thus, he retained to the last Mill's peculiar doctrine about the dependence of sight on muscular sense. So, too, his discussions of sympathy and of our knowledge of other minds are very crude examples of associationism.

These weaknesses in Bain have been too much stressed by his critics to the neglect of his merits. Thus, in dealing with the emotions the important role he gave to pure malice, or sadism, as a human motive contrasts refreshingly with the more commonplace views of such critics as Francis Herbert Bradley. Nevertheless, the only part of Bain's work that has been justly appreciated in our time is not his philosophy but his contribution to rhetoric.

See also Berkeley, George; Bradley, Francis Herbert; De Morgan, Augustus; Determinism, A Historical Survey; Ferrier, James Frederick; General Will, The; Hamilton, William; Introspection; Knowledge and Belief; Mill, James; Mill, John Stuart; Psychology; Utilitarianism.

Bibliography

Mental and Moral Science (London: Longmans, Green, 1868) is an abridgment of *The Senses and the Intellect* and *The Emotions and the Will*.

For works on Bain, see W. L. Davidson, "Professor Bain's Philosophy," in *Mind*, n.s., 13 (1904): 161–179; and Howard C. Warren, *A History of the Association Psychology* (New York: Scribners, 1921), pp. 104–117. For Bain's contributions to rhetoric, see Stephen Potter, *The Muse in Chains* (London: J. Cape, 1937).

George E. Davie (1967)

BAKER, LYNNE RUDDER
(1944–)

Lynne Rudder Baker was born in Atlanta, Georgia, received her PhD in philosophy from Vanderbilt University in 1972, and teaches at the University of Massachusetts at Amherst.

Her philosophical work provides a powerful critique of reductive accounts of minds, persons, and artifacts. Her writings in the philosophy of mind are directed against three distinct but related views. The first is that one's meaning something specific by a symbol can be naturalized, that is, reductively explained, in terms of some set of nonsemantic, nonmental, causal properties lawfully instantiated in nature. The second view is that folk psychology is, at best, a second-class prototheory of human behavior that only has instrumental value or, at worst, a discredited theory whose mental posits do not exist. The third view, what Baker calls "the Standard View," shared by dualists, materialists, and functionalists, says that beliefs are states of some proper part of persons, be it material (the brain) or immaterial (the soul).

All three views share two themes. First, we think of ourselves as sentient, sapient agents endowed with states that have referential content and causal efficacy. Second, if this conception is to be correct, it must reductively fit with our best scientific theories of nature, which have the right story (or much of it, at any rate) about things; otherwise, it must be rejected as false or treated as a useful but quaint myth. Baker accepts the first claim but rejects the second in *Saving Belief* (1987) and in *Explaining Attitudes* (1995). In the latter work, she defends practical realism, the view that beliefs are global states of a whole person, not of any proper part of the person. Although beliefs are not entities, they are real (contra eliminative materialists), since they make a genuine causal difference in the world in virtue of their contents (contra epiphenomenalists). Beliefs have an explanatory role, but not in virtue of their being identical to, constituted by, or supervening on brain states, since beliefs do not stand in those relations to any brain state. Rather, their explanatory role is grounded in our shared practice of causally explaining and rationalizing our actions. Baker's practical realism places her squarely in the company of American pragmatists (from William James to Hilary Putnam) and neo-Wittgensteinians.

Baker's third book, *Persons and Bodies* (2000), connects her early writings in the philosophy of mind with her more recent work in metaphysics. In that book she defends the constitution view of human persons, the view that a human person is a person in virtue of having a first-person perspective and is human in virtue of being constituted by a human body. To have the first-person perspective is to have the ability to think of oneself as oneself in an irreducibly direct way without the mediation of any name or description. Constitution, in turn, is a ubiquitous relation that holds whenever new kinds of things come into existence (e.g., statues, persons), with new causal powers in virtue of other kinds of things (e.g., slabs of marble, human bodies), existing in certain types of circumstances (e.g., the art world, social institutions, and social practices). The things that constitute and the things they constitute have different persistence conditions and natures; hence, they are numerically distinct. Both share many of the same properties and causal powers, although the source of their shared properties and powers may lie with the thing that constitutes and not with the constituted thing, or vice versa. Thus, contrary to immaterialism, human persons are material beings, because they are constituted by their human bodies. However, contrary to animalism, human persons are not identical to the bodies that constitute them.

On Baker's view, although persons are constituted by their bodies and cannot exist without being materially constituted in some way, their identity over time does not depend on the particular bodies that constitute them. Nor does personal identity depend on soul identity, brain identity, or (nonbranching) psychological continuity. Rather, it depends solely on one's having a first-person perspective over time. Facts about one's first-person perspective are not reducible to any nonpersonal fact. Thus, for Baker, one's identity over time is a simple irreducible fact about oneself.

See also Identity; Mental Causation; Personal Identity; Philosophy of Mind.

Bibliography

Baker, Lynne Rudder. *Explaining Attitudes: A Practical Approach to the Mind.* New York: Cambridge University Press, 1995.

Baker, Lynne Rudder. *Persons and Bodies: A Constitution View.* New York: Cambridge University Press, 2000.

Baker, Lynne Rudder. *Saving Belief: A Critique of Physicalism.* Princeton, NJ: Princeton University Press, 1987.

Meijers, Anthonie, ed. *Explaining Beliefs: Lynne Rudder Baker and Her Critics.* Stanford, CA: CSLI Publications, 2001.

Reinaldo Elugardo (2005)

BAKHTIN, MIKHAIL MIKHAILOVICH
(1895–1975)

Mikhail Mikhailovich Bakhtin was a Russian philosopher, philologist, and historian of culture. In opposition to rationalism and, in general, to the modern European (monologic) epistemology, he grounded a personalistic understanding of being as the co-being (event) of interrelations of "I" and the "other" (thou) and developed a corresponding dialogic (and/or polyphonic) approach in the capacity of the uniquely adequate method of the particular humanitarian sciences and—more broadly—of philosophical thought.

THE WORKS

Bakhtin wrote his main works in the period from the 1920s to the beginning of the 1950s, but because of the political conditions of the time, biographical reasons, and the peculiarities of the texts themselves (some of them consisting of unfinished archival manuscripts), they were published (except in one case) either in the final years of the author's life or after his death.

Bakhtin was born in Orel, south of Moscow, and in the second decade of the twentieth century he studied at the historico-philological and philosophy departments first at Novorossisk University and then at Petersburg University. After the Communist Revolution of 1917 he lived in Nevel and Vitebsk, where a circle of like-minded intellectuals was formed (M. I. Kagan, L. V. Pumpiansky, V. N. Voloshinov, P. N. Medvedev et al.). Here, at the beginning of the 1920s, Bakhtin wrote early drafts of philosophical works that remained unfinished, including "*K filosofii postupka*" (Toward a philosophy of the act), first published in 1986, and "*Avtor i geroi v esteticheskoi deiatel'nosti*" (The author and the hero in aesthetic activity), first published in 1979. In 1924 Bakhtin returned to Leningrad, and that same year he wrote the antiformalist essay "*K voprosam metodologii estetiki slovesnogo tvorchestva*" ("On Questions of the methodology of the aesthetics of verbal creation"), first published in 1975.

Bakhtin's first published book (and until the beginning of the 1960s it remained his only published book) was *Problemy tvorchestva Dostoevskogo* (Problems of Dostoevsky's creative works), which appeared in 1929. There exists the assumption (not shared by all scholars or not shared by scholars to an equal degree) that certain other books and essays published in the 1920s and attributed to other authors were to some degree written by Bakhtin. These works include *Freidizm: Kriticheskii ocherk* (Freud-ism: A critical essay), published in 1927, and *Marksizm i filosofiia iazyka* (Marxism and the philosophy of language), published in 1929, both attributed to V. N. Voloshinov, as well as P. N. Medvedev's *Formal'ni method v literaturovedenii* (Formal method in the study of literature), 1928.

In 1928 Bakhtin was arrested in connection with the affair of the illegal religious organization "Voskresenie." He was sentenced to five years in a concentration camp, but owing to the state of his health this sentence was replaced by a five-year exile in Kazakhstan. (Bakhtin suffered from chronic osteomyelitis, which in 1938 necessitated the amputation of one of his legs.) In accordance with this sentence, after returning from exile, he was prohibited from residing in large cities; and he was thus compelled to move from place to place. In 1945 he obtained a position in Saransk, at the Mordovia Pedagogical Institute, where he first worked as an instructor and then as department chairman. In the 1930s and 1940s he wrote a large study of Rabelais (which in 1946 he defended as his doctoral dissertation). In those years he also wrote a large cycle of works, published only in the 1970s, on the specific characteristics and genesis of the genre of the novel.

Bakhtin retired in 1961. By the middle of the 1960s his name could again be found in official scholarly publications. The second, revised edition of his book on Dostoevsky, *Problemy poetiki Dostoevskogo* (Problems of Dostoevsky's poetics) appeared in 1963; and the book based on his dissertation, *Tvorchestvo Fransua Rable i narodnaia kul'tura srednevekov'ia i Renessansa* (The work of Francois Rabelais and folk culture of the Middle Ages and Rennaissance), appeared in 1965. Bakhtin's ideas become known, particularly in Europe and the United States—first primarily among structuralists, and then, as the archive was published, among scholars with diverse philosophical and philological orientations. At the end of the 1960s Bakhtin moved first to a suburb of Moscow, and then at the beginning of the 1970s to Moscow itself, where he resided until his death.

THE INFLUENCE OF BAKHTIN

Bakhtin was initially subject to the diverse influences, on the one hand, of the development of the problem of the interrelations of "I" and the "other" in German philosophy (Feuerbach, Kierkegaard, Nietzsche, the neo-Kantians Cohen and Natorp) and on the other hand of Russian symbolism (in the version favored by Viacheslav Ivanov, who interpreted the interrelation of "I" and the "other" as a reduced transformation of the interrelations of "I" and "Thou" in the religious mysticism of commun-

ion with God). From the status of significant but particular problems of transcendental ethics and aesthetics or positivistic psychology and sociology, Bakhtin translated the interrelation between "I" and the "other" into a fundamental ontological structure of universal character, which determines both the forms of life's being and the forms of thought, language, and cultural meaning as such. In parallel with the legitimate goal, given such an approach, of identifying the universal archetypal forms of the interrelation of "I" and the "other," Bakhtin also posed the problem of exposing the various kinds of distortions of these archetypal forms in the historical types of culture.

Bakhtin did not leave an integral and consistently developed conception. Instead, he formulated several particular theories that are linked by a single personalistic-dialogic teleology but which are sometimes divergent in their outer conceptual contours (in particular, the conceptions of polyphony and carnival). In his early unfinished work "Toward a Philosophy of the Act," Bakhtin sketches out the project of a moral philosophy in which he grounds the constitutive role of the interrelations of "I" and the "other" for the structure of being. (Being is understood here as the co-being of two personal consciousnesses—as the minimum of the "co-being of being"; in order to accomplish the true co-being of the being of "I," which admits the validity of the ethical imperative, one must, according to this project, subject oneself to absolute self-exclusion from the values of the currently given being in favor of imparting these values to the "other.")

In "The Author and the Hero in Aesthetic Activity," Bakhtin gives a typology of different historical forms of the interrelations between author and hero, interpreted as aesthetic transformations of life-interrelations between "I" and the "other" (the author suppresses the hero and the hero suppresses the author; the crisis of the author, the revolt of the hero, etc.). In analyzing the historical types of culture, Bakhtin sees in the majority of them diverse forms of mutual overcoming and suppression of "I" and the "other," which replace their simultaneous mutual outside-locatedness and connectedness in one co-being by surrogates either of their illusory mutual isolation or of their just as illusory unity (physiological, psychological, ideological, national, social). Bakhtin attributed the disharmony of the interrelations between "I" and the "other" to the predominant orientation of the corresponding types of culture toward a unified and universal consciousness (the rationalistic gnoseologism, or monologism, of the modern period). The crisis of the position of the author shaping the aesthetic co-being of being is advanced as the central aesthetic problem.

In *Problems of Dostoevsky's Poetics*, Bakhtin develops a theory of polyphony as a particular variant (created by Dostoevsky) of the genre of the novel with a specific authorial position that overcomes the crisis, a position that presupposes polyphonic dialogic intersections of the voices of the characters in the absence of the domination of the author's voice (including the narrator and all his other functional variants), which enters into fully equal dialogic relations with the voices of the characters. In the cycle of essays about the novel written in the 1930s and 1940s, Bakhtin complements the polyphonic conception with a general theory of the language of the novel as based on a word with two voices (on the intersection of two personal voices in a formally single utterance); he expounds the theory of the chronotope: the ambivalent relation of the temporal and spatial characteristics of meaning as the inalienable premise of its artistic representation and reception. When united with the spatial-temporal characteristics of the axiological dimension, the chronotope grows for Bakhtin into the analogue of any (not only artistic) point of view concerning meaning in the capacity of a position determined with respect to co-being and person.

In the essay *"Problema rechevykh zhanrov"* (Problem of speech genres) and in the second, revised edition of the book on Dostoevsky, Bakhtin develops a conception of metalinguistics, extending the theory of two voices beyond the word of the novel into the entire sphere of the life of language. In the book on Rabelais, he develops the conception of carnival as a reflection of the ambivalence of the archetypal foundation of folk-comic culture (the fusion without mutual neutralization of serious and comic myths) and, genetically connected with this conception, the conception of cultural meaning that is always constituted by antinomic or, in one respect or another, opposed relations, including dialogic ones.

Bakhtin's fundamental works have been translated into many European and Oriental languages. International conferences devoted to Bakhtin are held regularly, and monographs, collections of articles, and issues of journals devoted to his work are regularly published. Bakhtin's ideas generate much discussion and controversy.

See also Bakhtin Circle, The; Cohen, Hermann; Dostoevsky, Fyodor Mikhailovich; Feuerbach, Ludwig Andreas; Ivanov, Viacheslav Ivanovich; Kierkegaard, Søren Aabye; Natorp, Paul; Neo-Kantianism; Nietzsche, Friedrich; Rationalism; Russian Philosophy.

Bibliography

WORKS ABOUT BAKHTIN

Clark, Katerina, and Michael Holquist. *Mikhail Bakhtin.* Cambridge, MA: Belknap Press of Harvard University Press, 1984.

Dialog. Karnaval. Khronotop [Dialogue. Carnival. Chronotope]. Vitebsk, Belarus, 1992–2004. A periodical quaterly devoted to Bakhtin.

Emerson, Caryl. *The First Hundred Years of Mikhail Bakhtin.* Princeton, NJ: Princeton University Press, 1997.

Gogotishvili, L. A., and P. S. Gurevich, eds. *M. M. Bakhtin kak filosof* [M. M. Bakhtin as philosopher]. Moscow: Nauka, 1992. A collection of articles.

Isupov, K. G. *Mikhail Bakhtin: Pro et contra.* Anthology in two volumes. St. Petersburg: Russian Christian Institute for the Humanities, 2001, 2002.

WORKS BY BAKHTIN

Avtor i geroi v esteticheskoi deiatel'nosti [Author and hero in aesthetic activity]. In *Sobranie sochinenii v 7 tomakh* [Collected works in 7 volumes], 1996–. Moscow: Russkie slovari, 2003. Translated by Vadim Liapunov as *Author and Hero in Aesthetic Activity.* In *Art and Answerability: Early Philosophical Essays by M. M. Bakhtin,* edited by Michael Holquist and Vadim Liapunov (Austin: University of Texas Press, 1990).

"Formy vremeni i khronotopa v romane" [Forms of time and chronotope in the novel]. In *Voprosy literatury i estetiki* [Questions of literature and aesthetics]. Moscow: Khudozhestvennaia literatura, 1975, pp. 234–407. Translated by Caryl Emerson as *Forms of Time and the Chronotope in the Novel.* In *The Dialogic Imagination,* edited by Michael Holquist (Austin: University of Texas Press, 1981).

K filosofii postupka [Toward a philosophy of the act]. In *Sobranie sochinenii v 7 tomakh* [Collected works in 7 volumes], 1996–. vol. 1. Moscow: Russkie slovari, 2003. Translated by Vadim Liapunov as *Toward a Philosophy of the Act,* edited by Michael Holquist and Vadim Liapunov (Austin: University of Texas Press, 1993).

Problemy poetiki Dostoevskogo [Problems of Dostoevsky's poetics]. In *Sobranie sochinenii v 7 tomakh* [Collected works in 7 volumes], 1996–. Moscow: Russkie slovari, 2002. Translated and edited by Caryl Emerson as *Problems of Dostoevsky's Poetics* (Minneapolis: University of Minnesota Press, 1984).

Tvorchestvo Fransua Rable i narodnaia kul'tura srednevekov'ia i Renessansa [The work of François Rabelais and the popular culture of the Middle Ages and the Renaissance]. Moscow: Khudozhestvennaia literatura, 1965. Translated by Hélène Iswolsky as *The Work of Francois Rabelais and Popular Culture of the Middle Ages.* In *Rabelais and His World* (Cambridge, MA: MIT Press, 1968).

Ludmila Gogotishvili (2005)
Translated by Boris Jakim

BAKHTIN, MIKHAIL MIKHAILOVICH [ADDENDUM]

By the time his boom and cult had passed, Mikhail Bakhtin had become a twentieth-century classic and the beneficiary of a huge research industry. Accordingly, the most exciting work shifted from literary or political applications of his famous terms—dialogue, carnival, chronotope—and toward the finer, and far more interesting, arts of historical recuperation: Bakhtin's intellectual debts, and his social and philosophical contexts (see Brandist 2002). For Bakhtin Studies, 1990 was something of a watershed year. It marked, of course, the beginning of the end of Soviet Communism, which made it possible for Russians to pursue pluralistic and de-ideologized scholarship throughout the humanities. For English speakers it was also the year that Bakhtin's writings from the 1920s (combining Kantianism and phenomenology in a distinctive moral philosophy) were published in the excellent Liapunov annotated translations.

It took several years for these difficult early texts to be assimilated, for the received image of Bakhtin in the 1970s and 1980s could not easily be fit back into them. That image, based on several widely (and quickly) translated texts from his middle-to-late period, was polarized between those who wished to see in Bakhtin a pragmatic, systems-shunning liberal humanist and those who preferred a more radical and subversive message. Neither variant had firm documentation (the liberal least of all). The question of Bakhtin's Marxism and his authorship of the "disputed texts" had ended in a draw. Left-wing cultural theorists were faulting "dialogism" for its fascination with process at the expense of justice and for its indifference to power. Bakhtinian ideas permeated every possible discipline (sociology, cultural studies, therapeutic psychoanalysis, history of science, theories of education) but as yet we lacked the luminous renderings of Bakhtin as a spiritual thinker and aesthetician. The biography was still awash in rumor, and influences on him largely conjectural.

By the mid-1990s several Bakhtin scholars, most prominently in Britain and Russia, began to suspect that Bakhtin's ideas were so shockingly famous because we had forgotten, or too thinly investigated, the richness of the historical period of which they were an organic part: the German and then Russian philosophical debates of the 1910s and 1920s. With the appearance of the first volumes of the collected works, *M. M. Bakhtin: Sobranie sochinenii* (Moscow, 1996–) and, in English, of the work

of Galin Tihanov, Brian Poole, Ken Hirschkop, David Shepherd, and especially Craig Brandist (2002), it became clear that the "trademark" concepts, painstakingly restored to their appropriate contexts, would have to be retranslated and critically rethought.

To be sure, these concepts had been under revision for some time. *Dialogue*, which insists upon the addressivity, reciprocity, and open-endedness of all relations, had long been reproached for political naiveté, for flattening the epic, for undervaluing poetry (with its tolerance for repetition, symmetry, and formal constraints), and for denying a stable core to the self. Novelistic *polyphony*, which Bakhtin saw exemplified in Dostoevsky, was also controversial. The idea (of surprising appeal to primary authors) that created characters that can act and speak alongside their creators as "equally weighted" consciousnesses has been dismissed by drier and more disciplined critics as a fantasy, as an illusion of the author—or of the readers—who project their own ideas and words on to the text.

Carnival was the term most indiscriminately applied. It had come to mean little more than sassiness, rebellion, or transgression, and as such was applied to every social practice, text, or body that revealed a disruptive, subversive, inverting, or comically grotesque aspect. Sobriety set in here too. Not only was Bakhtin's sunny carnivalesque shown to bear little relation to real, drunken, violent carnival rituals and bodies, but the literary masterwork Bakhtin used to illustrate his theory, Rabelais's *Gargantua et Pantagruel*, was served only partially and rather poorly by so crudely binary and folkloric a filter. Trivially oppositional readings of dialogue and of carnival reinforced each other: The double-voiced word was deployed more often to subvert a perspective than to supplement or enrich it. Of all Bakhtin's famous terms, the *chronotope* proved to be the least contentious. It was also the most "philosophical" of Bakhtin's constructs, a creative extension to narrative of the Kantian time-space matrix.

Thus the age of "applied Bakhtin" gave way to a study of "Bakhtin the philosopher." Problems remained, but they became deeper and more productive. Researchers took seriously Bakhtin's claim that his life's work aimed to present an integrated philosophical worldview rather than to further a strictly "philological" enterprise—that is, a series of literary readings designed to explicate or serve the interests of their respective literary authors. The starting point was Kant and his successors among the German Romantics, a powerful collage of thinkers united by their inquiry into the possibility of human freedom. The end point, arrived at with ample help from Ernst

Cassirer, Max Scheler, Matvei Kagan (1889–1937), and Bakhtin's peer intellectuals of his own circle, was an understanding of freedom not as agency or as initiated deed but as *response*: individuated, concrete, identity-bestowing, and in principle unfinalizable. This mandate applied not only to human responsibility but to thought itself. As Bakhtin's mentor Matvei Kagan wrote in his fragment "Philosophy and Life" (1918–1920), philosophy is a sort of immortal organism, not mechanically logical but also not subject to the constraints of "biologism." Most importantly, philosophy was not obliged to begin with nonbeing. It was always materialized and concrete. "The world is not dying, not being annihilated," Kagan wrote, astonishingly, at the end of the Great War; "*it has not yet completely come to life, but is doing so*." There is no absolute nonbeing, only not-yet-Being, and this "incomplete being is on a constant path of new becoming" (Kagan 2004, p. 311).

This philosophical reorientation promises further shifts and revised shapes for Bakhtin's ideas. The dialogic novel has already begun to be seen as the model site for the "relational self"— cocreated, but not for that reason any less coherent, unified, and authentic (de Peuter in Bell and Gardiner 1998, pp. 30–48). Inspiration for carnival and the grotesque body is being sought in areas as diverse as Ivan Kanaev's research on the regenerative capabilities of the freshwater polyp (Taylor in *The Bakhtin Circle* 2004, pp. 150–166) and in Trinitarian paradigms of Russian Orthodox thought (Mihailovic 1997). Bakhtin's ideas of genre and chronotope, and more recently of "answerability," have been immensely influential on the vast industry of college-level pedagogy in the United States, specifically on the theory of teaching English composition (Halasek 1999, Farmer 2001). And finally, attention is being paid to Bakhtin's fragmentary, somewhat dated, but still robust thoughts on the humanities as the realm of depth and reciprocity over time rather than of scientific precision, the realm of experience rather than experiment. As communication is increasingly pressured to default to the values of speed, here, now, and simultaneity without reflection, the historical embeddedness of Bakhtin's ideas will provide a welcome corrective and relief.

See also Philosophical Anthropology; Russian Philosophy.

Bibliography

WORKS BY BAKHTIN

Art and Answerability: Early Philosophical Essays, edited by Michael Holquist and Vadim Liapunov. Austin: University of Texas Press, 1990.

The Dialogic Imagination: Four Essays by M. M. Bakhtin, edited by Michael Holquist; translated by Caryl Emerson and Michael Holquist. Austin: University of Texas Press, 1981.

Problems of Dostoevsky's Poetics, edited and translated by Caryl Emerson. Minneapolis: University of Minnesota Press, 1984.

Rabelais and His World. Translated by Hélène Iswolsky. Cambridge, MA: MIT Press, 1968. First Midland book edition, Bloomington: Indiana University Press, 1984.

Speech Genres and Other Late Essays, edited by Caryl Emerson and Michael Holquist. Translated by Vern W. McGee. Austin: University of Texas Press, 1986.

M. M. Bakhtin: Besedy V. D. Duvakinym [1973–1974]. Moscow: Soglasie, 2002.

WORKS ABOUT BAKHTIN

Bell, Michael Mayerfeld, and Michael Gardiner, eds. *Bakhtin and the Human Sciences: No Last Words*. Thousand Oaks, CA: Sage, 1998.

Brandist, Craig. *The Bakhtin Circle: Philosophy, Culture and Politics*. Sterling, VA: Pluto, 2002.

Brandist, Craig, David Shepherd, and Galin Tihanov, eds. *The Bakhtin Circle: In the Master's Absence*. Manchester, U.K.: Manchester University Press, 2004.

Clark, Katerina, and Michael Holquist. *Mikhail Bakhtin*. Cambridge, MA: Harvard University Press, 1984.

Coates, Ruth. *Christianity in Bakhtin: God and the Exiled Author*. Cambridge, U.K.: Cambridge University Press, 1998.

Emerson, Caryl. *The First Hundred Years of Mikhail Bakhtin*. Princeton, NJ: Princeton University Press, 1997.

Farmer, Frank. *Saying and Silence. Listening to Composition with Bakhtin*. Logan: Utah State University Press, 2001.

Felch, Susan M., and Paul Contino, eds. *Bakhtin and Religion: A Feeling for Faith*. Evanston, IL: Northwestern University Press, 2001.

Halasek, Kay. *A Pedagogy of Possibility: Bakhtinian Perspectives on Composition Studies*. Carbondale: Southern Illinois University Press, 1999.

Haynes, Deborah J. *Bakhtin and the Visual Arts*. Cambridge, U.K.: Cambridge University Press, 1995.

Hirschkop, Ken. *Mikhail Bakhtin: An Aesthetic for Democracy*. Oxford, U.K.: Oxford University Press, 1999.

Hirschkop, Ken, and David Shepherd, eds. *Bakhtin and Cultural Theory*. 2nd ed. Manchester, U.K.: Manchester University Press, 2001.

Holquist, Michael. *Dialogism: Bakhtin and His World*. London: Routledge, 1990.

Kagan, M. I. *O khode istorii* (Collected writings), edited by V. L. Makhlin. Moscow, 2004.

Mihailovic, Alexandar. *Corporeal Words: Mikhail Bakhtin's Theology of Discourse*. Evanston, IL: Northwestern University Press, 1997.

Morson, Gary Saul, and Caryl Emerson. *Mikhail Bakhtin: Creation of a Prosaics*. Stanford, CA: Stanford University Press, 1990.

Poole, Brian. "Bakhtin and Cassirer: The Philosophical Origins of Bakhtin's Carnival Messianism." *South Atlantic Quarterly* 97 (3/4) (1998): 537–578.

Shepherd, David, ed, *The Contexts of Bakhtin: Philosophy, Authorship, Aesthetics*. London: Harwood, 1998.

Tihanov, Galin. *The Master and the Slave: Lukács, Bakhtin, and the Ideas of Their Time*. Oxford, U.K.: Clarendon Press, 2000.

Caryl Emerson (2005)

BAKHTIN CIRCLE, THE

The Bakhtin Circle was a group of Soviet scholars, including the cultural theorist Mikhail Mikhailovich Bakhtin (1895–1975), the linguist Valentin Nikolaevich Voloshinov (1895–1936), and the literary scholar Pavel Nikolaevich Medvedev (1891–1938). Drawing on a variety of philosophical positions, the group developed a philosophy of the human sciences, language, literary production, and history, and a wide-ranging cultural theory. The group's work combined, in various ways, the neo-Kantianism of the Marburg School (especially Ernst Cassirer), phenomenology (especially Max Scheler and Karl Bühler), Russian Formalism (especially Lev Iakubinskii), Hegelianism, and various types of Marxism current within Soviet scholarship (especially Georg Lukács and "Marrism").

In *K filosofii postupka* (Toward a philosophy of the act; 1993 [written in the mid-1920s]), Bakhtin combines a neo-Kantian idealism, in which ethics is the foundation of the human sciences and jurisprudence its "mathematics," with the phenomenological notion of intentionality to develop an ethics based on the acts of the responsible subject. *Avtor i geroi v esteticheskoi deiatel'nosti* (Author and hero in aesthetic activity; 1990 [written in the mid- to late-1920s]) is a phenomenological investigation into relations between author and hero in narrative fiction based to a considerable extent on the account of intersubjectivity found in Scheler's *The Nature and Forms of Sympathy* (Poole 2001).

Medvedev and Voloshinov had meanwhile been working on developing a sociological approach to poetics and discursive interaction, respectively. Both sought to bring about a meeting of contemporary philosophical trends with the sociological ideas championed by Russian Marxists at the time, particularly Nikolai Bukharin. In his essay *Formal'nyi metod v literaturovedenii* (The formal method in literary scholarship; 1978 [1928]), Medvedev argues that sociological factors shape literature from within and without and that exploration of the category of genre should precede analyses of individual literary devices. In *Marksizm i filosofiia iazyka* (Marxism and the philosophy of language; 1973 [1929]), Voloshinov contends that language is a product of social interaction, emerging in and through dialogue, and, following Bühler, that the utterance constitutes the primary unit of language *in actu*. This phenomenology of social interaction in language is given a sociological form, so that specific styles of language use are the discursive embodiments of the worldviews of specific social groups. Modalities of authorship are also reworked into an analysis of various forms of reported speech in literature whereas literary and extraliterary forms of discourse are all held to have generic characteristics. Bakhtin himself accepted this reworking in his now famous *Problemy tvorchestva Dostoevskogo* (Problems of Dostoevsky's poetics; 1984 [1929, 1963]), where the novelist is held to have produced a "polyphonic" form in which all languages, including that of the narrator, interact on an equal and, indeed, democratic basis.

Whereas the Circle ceased to function as a group after Joseph Stalin's consolidation of power at the end of the 1920s, Bakhtin's own most important work was produced in subsequent years. In a series of essays written in the 1930s and 1940s, Bakhtin drew on the work of, among others, Cassirer and Lukács to develop a radical re-reading of literary history and the place of the novel therein. Recasting Cassirer's idealist dialectic of mythical and critical symbolic forms, Bakhtin argues that the novel has roots in popular and skeptical discursive forms that exploit the social stratification of language (heteroglossia) to undermine the truth claims of official, poetic discourse. This skepticism operates through laughter that, following Cassirer and Henri Bergson, Bakhtin sees as deflating discursive pretension and revealing that knowledge of the empirical world is impossible. In a typically Hegelian move, Bakhtin argues that it is in and through the novel that culture, the totality of discursively embodied perspectives (heteroglossia), becomes aware of itself as its own object. The dogmatic and authoritarian attitude toward another's discourse is termed "monologic" whereas a critical and democratic attitude is termed "dialogic." These essays began to be published in the 1970s and appeared in English under the title *The Dialogic Imagination* (1981).

At the end of the 1930s, Bakhtin develops a theory that the rise of the critical forces of culture represents the reappearance of semantic forms that have survived from preclass society. This theory builds on the theory of "semantic paleontology" developed by the now discredited Soviet archaeologist and linguist Nikolai Marr, who argued that all languages develop from a primordial gesture language in primitive communism. Marr's position had been reworked and applied to literary material by the classicist Ol'ga Freidenberg, who identified certain primordial "semantic clusters" that reappear in various ways throughout cultural history. In Bakhtin's hands this model became the now-famous theory of carnival, in which forms associated with the popular culture of laughter come to permeate and structure literary works. Symbolic inversions, collective festivity, and mockery relativize the dominant culture, parading its conventionality, pomposity, and claims to discursive adequacy. Carnival on the streets is a licensed and limited rebellion against the ruling symbolic order, but once its features enter "great literature," the critical spirit that motivates it restructures the relationship between official and popular culture, democratizing the former and breaking the isolation of the latter. Bakhtin finds such features throughout the literature of the Renaissance, but he gives special attention to the work of the French novelist François Rabelais in *Tvorchestvo Fransua Rable i narodnaia kul'tura srednevekov'ia i Renessansa* (Rabelais and his world; 1984 [1965]) written at the end of the 1930s. This work was originally Bakhtin's doctoral (*kandidatskaia*) dissertation.

As part of his project dealing with the rise of modern critical culture, Bakhtin also writes important articles on the spatiotemporal characteristics of particular genres, or *chronotopes*, and a special work on the generic features of Johann Goethe's *Bildungsroman* the surviving part of which is known as *Roman vospitaniia vistorii realizma* (The Bildungsroman and its significance in the history of realism, written in the late 1930s). Bakhtin argues that it is in the work of the polymath Goethe that the Renaissance *demythification* of the world reaches its highest point. Following Stalin's denunciation of Marr in 1950, Bakhtin also sought to distinguish between a *human* science of discursive or speech (*rechevoi*) genres and a *natural* science of linguistic structures. In Bakhtin's posthumously published final works, translated as *Speech Genres and Other Late Essays* (1986), this neo-Kantian concern with demarcating the natural and human sciences becomes his central focus. The natural sciences, which adopt a *monologic* approach to their *voiceless* object, deal with questions of causality and determination whereas the human sciences, eschewing all such considerations, are based on a *dialogic* methodology and pursue an ethics of intersubjectivity.

See also Bakhtin, Mikhail Mikhailovich; Bergson, Henri; Cassirer, Ernst; Goethe, Johann Wolfgang von; Hegelianism; Idealism; Intentionality; Lukács, Georg; Marxist Philosophy; Neo-Kantianism; Phenomenology; Russian Philosophy; Scheler, Max.

Bibliography

WORKS

Bakhtin, M. M. *The Dialogic Imagination: Four essays* (*Voprosy literatury i estetiki*). Translated by Caryl Emerson and Michael Holquist; edited by Michael Holquist. Austin: University of Texas Press, 1981.

Bakhtin, M. M. *K filosofii postupka* (c. 1925) (Toward a philosophy of the act). Translation and notes by Vadim Liapunov; edited by Michael Holquist and Vadim Liapunov. 1st ed. Austin: University of Texas Press, 1993.

Bakhtin, M. M. *Problemy tvorchestva Dostoevskogo* (1929) (Problems of Dostoevsky's poetics), edited and translated by Caryl Emerson, 1984.

Bakhtin, M. M. *Rabelais and His World* (*Tvorchestvo Fransua Rable i narodnaia kul'tura srednevekov'ia i Renessansa*). Translated by Hélène Iswolsky. Bloomington: Indiana University Press, 1984.

Bakhtin, M. M. *Speech Genres and Other Late Essays* (*Estetika slovesnogo tvorchestva*). Translated by Vern W. McGee; edited by Caryl Emerson and Michael Holquist. 1st ed. Austin: University of Texas Press, 1986.

Medvedev, P. N. *The Formal Method in Literary Scholarship: A Critical Introduction to Sociological Poetics* (*Formal'nyi metod v literaturovedenii*) (1928).Translated by Albert J. Wehrle. Baltimore, MD: Johns Hopkins University Press, 1978.

Voloshinov, V. N. *Marksizm i filosofiia iazyka* (1929) (Marxism and the philosophy of Language). Translated by Ladislav Matejka and I. R. Titunik. New York: Seminar Press, 1973.

STUDIES

Brandist, Craig. *The Bakhtin Circle: Philosophy, Culture, and Politics*. London: Pluto, 2002.

Brandist, Craig, David Shepherd, and Galin Tihanov, eds. *The Bakhtin Circle: In the Master's Absence*. Manchester: Manchester University Press, 2004.

Hirschkop, Ken. *Mikhail Bakhtin: An Aesthetic for Democracy*. Oxford: Oxford University Press, 1999.

Poole, Brian. "From Phenomenology to Dialogue: Max Scheler's Phenomenological Tradition and Mikhail Bakhtin's Development from 'Toward a Philosophy of the Act' to His Study of Dostoevsky." In *Bakhtin and Cultural Theory*, edited by Ken Hirschkop and David Shepherd. Manchester: Manchester University Press, 2001.

Tihanov, Galin. *The Master and the Slave: Lukács, Bakhtin, and the Ideas of Their Time*. Oxford: Oxford University Press 2000.

Craig Brandist (2005)

BAKUNIN, MICHAEL

See Bakunin, Mikhail Aleksandrovich

BAKUNIN, MIKHAIL ALEKSANDROVICH
(1814–1876)

Mikhail Aleksandrovich Bakunin, the anarchist writer and revolutionary leader, was born on the estate of Premukhino in the Russian province of Tver'. His family were hereditary noblemen of liberal political inclinations. His father had been in Paris during the French Revolution and had taken his doctorate of philosophy at Padua. His mother was a member of the Murav'av family; three of her cousins were involved in the earliest Russian revolution, the December rising of constitutionalists in 1825. Bakunin was carefully educated under the supervision of his father, who regarded himself as a disciple of Jean-Jacques Rousseau; later he was sent to the Artillery School in St. Petersburg. He received his commission and went on garrison duty in Lithuania. An awakening taste for literature made him discontent with military life, and in 1835 he obtained his discharge from the army and went to Moscow to study philosophy. There he joined the discussion circle centered on Nicolai Stankevich, which concentrated on contemporary German philosophy.

HEGELIANISM AND REVOLUTION

Bakunin was first influenced by Johann Gottlieb Fichte; his earliest literary task was the translation of that philosopher's writings for Vissarion Belinskii's periodical, the *Teleskop* (The Telescope). Later he transferred his allegiance to G. W. F. Hegel, and he advocated the Hegelian doctrine in its most conservative form with such enthusiasm that when Stankevich left for western Europe, Bakunin became the leader of the Hegelian school in Moscow and challenged the liberalism of the rival group associated with Alexander Herzen, who propagated the ideas of Charles Fourier, Comte de Saint-Simon, and Pierre-Joseph Proudhon.

Bakunin left Russia in 1840 to study German philosophy in Berlin. He still wished to become a professor of philosophy, and assiduously attended the lectures for some time; in his leisure hours he frequented the literary salons in the company of Ivan Turgenev, who used him as a model for the hero of his first novel, *Rudin*.

In 1842 Bakunin moved to Dresden, an intellectual as well as a physical journey. He had made the acquaintance of Arnold Ruge, leader of the Young Hegelians, whose contention that Hegel's dialectical method could be used more convincingly to support revolution than reaction was to influence almost every school of socialist philosophy in mid-nineteenth-century Europe. Bakunin's meeting with Ruge, combined with his reading of Lorenz von Stein's writings on Fourier and Proudhon, effected a change of his viewpoint that had all the strength of religious conversion.

The first manifestation of this change was the essay "Reaction in Germany—A Fragment by a Frenchman," which Bakunin published under the nom de plume of Jules Elysard in Ruge's *Deutsche Jahrbücher für Wissenschaft und Kunst* (October 1842). It puts forward a Young Hegelian view of revolution; before it succeeds, revolution is a negative force, but when it triumphs, it will, by a dialectical miracle, immediately become positive. However, the most striking feature of the essay is the apocalyptic tone in which Bakunin introduces the theme—recurrent in his writings—of destruction as a necessary element in the process of social transformation. "Let us put our trust in the eternal spirit which destroys and annihilates only because it is the unsearchable and eternally creative source of all life. The urge to destroy is also a creative urge."

"Reaction in Germany," with its glorification of the idea of perpetual revolt, was the first step toward Bakunin's later anarchism, but he went through many stages before he reached that destination. At first, in Switzerland, he associated with the German revolutionary communist, Wilhelm Weitling. This drew the attention of the Russian authorities to Bakunin's awakening radicalism, and he was condemned in absentia to indefinite exile with hard labor in Siberia.

PAN-SLAVISM

Meanwhile, Bakunin moved to Paris, where he associated with Karl Marx, Robert de Lamennais, George Sand, and, most important, Proudhon. Only in later years did these discussions bear fruit, when Bakunin became Marx's great enemy and Proudhon's great disciple; for the time being, he was concerned with the liberation of the Poles and other Slav peoples. For his speeches against the Russian government he was expelled to Belgium; he returned to Paris with the February Revolution of 1848. The years of the revolutions in Europe—1848–1849—were the most dramatic period of Bakunin's life. He was an enthusiastic partisan of the uprising in France; later in 1848 he fought on the barricades of Prague, and in March 1849, he took a leading part, with Richard Wagner, in the Dresden revolution. He was captured there and, after periods in Saxon and Austrian prisons and twice being sentenced to death and reprieved, he was handed over to the Russian authorities, who imprisoned him in the Peter and Paul Fortress. Six years there ruined his health. In 1857 he was sent to exile in Siberia, and in 1861 he escaped, via Japan and the United States, to western Europe.

During the years of action and imprisonment Bakunin produced two important works, the *Appeal to the Slavs*, written in the interval between the Prague and Dresden revolutions, and the *Confession*, which he wrote in prison at the request of Tsar Nicholas II and which was published after the Russian Revolution. The *Appeal to the Slavs* is much more than a statement of Bakunin's Pan-Slavism; in many ways it anticipates his later anarchist attitudes. The social revolution, he declares, must take precedence over the political revolution and, on moral grounds, he claims that the social revolution must be total. "We must first of all purify our atmosphere and transform completely the surroundings in which we live, for they corrupt our instincts and our wills…. Therefore the social question appears first of all as the overthrow of society," by which Bakunin evidently means the overthrow of the contemporary social order. Bakunin further maintains that liberty is indivisible and thus implies the rejection of individualism in favor of the collectivism that becomes explicit in the later development of his anarchist doctrine. The *Confession* is important principally for its account of the early development of Bakunin's revolutionary philosophy.

After his escape to western Europe in 1861, Bakunin resumed the course of Pan-Slavism he had been forced to abandon in 1849 but, after taking part in an abortive Polish attempt to invade Lithuania in 1863, he went to Italy.

ANARCHISM

In 1865 Bakunin founded the International Brotherhood in Naples. Its program—embodied in Bakunin's *Revolutionary Catechism*—was anarchism without the name; it rejected the state and organized religion, advocated communal autonomy within a federal structure, and maintained that labor "must be the sole base of human right and of the economic organization of the state." In keeping with the cult of violence that was part of the romantic revolutionary tradition, Bakunin insisted that the social revolution could not be achieved by peaceful means.

The International Brotherhood was a conspiratorial organization, for Bakunin never outlived his taste for the dark and the secret. Nevertheless, in 1867 he emerged into public life as a figurehead of the short-lived League for Peace and Freedom. This was mainly a body of pacifistic liberals, within which Bakunin led the left wing.

Bakunin was not a systematic writer. He admitted that he had no sense of "literary architecture" and saw himself primarily as a man of action, although his action was rarely successful and his life was punctuated by abortive revolutions. His writings were intended to provoke action; they were topical in inspiration, if not always in content, and it is in pamphlets on current events and in reports written for congresses and organizations that his opinions are scattered. One such report, prepared for the benefit of the central committee of the League for Peace and Freedom, was eventually published as *Federalism, Socialism and Anti-Theologism*. More than any other work, it contains the gist of Bakunin's anarchism.

Bakunin was not a great theoretical originator. The influences in his writings are obvious—Hegel, Auguste Comte, Proudhon, Ruge, Charles Darwin, and even Marx. Original in Bakunin are his insight into contemporary events (he prophesied with uncanny exactitude the way in which a Marxist state would operate) and his power to create a synthesis of borrowed ideas around which the early anarchist movement could crystallize. In *Federalism, Socialism and Anti-Theologism* the view of the structure of a desirable society is almost completely derived from Proudhon's federalism. In one vital respect, however, Bakunin's view differs from Proudhon's: While he follows Proudhon in measuring the consumer's right to goods by the quantity of his labor, he also advocates the collectivization of the means of production under public ownership; Proudhon and his mutualist followers wished to retain individual possession of land and tools by peasants and artisans as far as possible, in order to create a guarantee of personal independence. This difference was regarded as so important that Bakunin's followers were actually described as "collectivists" and did not assume the name of "anarchists" until the 1870s.

In 1868 Bakunin left the League for Peace and Freedom to found the International Alliance of Social Democracy, which was dissolved when he and his followers entered the International Workingmen's Association in 1869. Within the International, Bakunin and the southern European federations challenged the power of Marx. The dispute centered on disagreement over political methods. Marx and his followers held that socialists must seize the state and usher in a transitional dictatorship of the proletariat. Bakunin argued that power seized by workers was no less evil than power in other hands, and a communist state would magnify the evil of other states; he called for the earliest possible destruction of the state and the avoidance of political means toward that end. The workers must win their own liberation by economic and insurrectional means. The dispute came to a head at The Hague Congress of the International in 1872, when Bakunin was expelled. The southern federations and those of the Low Countries seceded to form their own federation, and Marx's remnant faded away.

Meanwhile, Bakunin's health declined rapidly. He took part in the Lyons rebellion of 1870 and in the abortive Bologna uprising of 1874. He died, exhausted, two years later at Bern. After his death, the anarchist communism of Pëtr Alekseevich Kropotkin superseded his collectivist anarchism, except in Spain, where the large anarchist movement held his ideas in their purity until 1939.

See also Anarchism; Belinskii, Vissarion Grigor'evich; Comte, Auguste; Darwin, Charles Robert; Fichte, Johann Gottlieb; Fourier, François Marie Charles; Hegel, Georg Wilhelm Friedrich; Hegelianism; Herzen, Aleksandr Ivanovich; Kropotkin, Pëtr Alekseevich; Lamennais, Hugues Félicité Robert de; Marx, Karl; Political Philosophy, History of; Proudhon, Pierre-Joseph; Rousseau, Jean-Jacques; Russian Philosophy; Saint-Simon, Claude-Henri de Rouvroy, Comte de.

Bibliography

WORKS BY BAKUNIN

The Confession of Mikhail Bakunin: With the Marginal Comments of Tsar Nicholas I. Translated by R. C. Howes. Ithaca, NY: Cornell University Press, 1977.

Statism and Anarchy. Translated by M. S. Shatz. Cambridge, U.K., and New York: Cambridge University Press, 1990.

The Basic Bakunin: Writings, 1869–1871. Translated by R. M. Cutler. Amherst, NY: Prometheus, 1992.

Political Thought, edited by M. Rosen and J. Wolff, with the assistance of C. McKinnon. Oxford and New York: Oxford University Press, 1999.

WORKS ON BAKUNIN

Aldred, G. A. *Bakunin.* New York: Haskell House, 1971.

Kelly, A. *Mikhail Bakunin: A Study in the Psychology and Politics of Utopianism.* Oxford: Clarendon Press; New York: Oxford University Press, 1982.

Maximoff, G. P., editor. *The Political Philosophy of Bakunin: Scientific Anarchism.* New York: The Free Press; London: Collier Macmillan, 1953.

McLaughlin, P. *Mikhail Bakunin: The Philosophical Basis of His Theory of Anarchism.* New York: Algora, 2002.

Mendel, A. P. *Michael Bakunin: Roots of Apocalypse.* New York: Praeger, 1981.

Saltman, R. B. *The Social and Political Thought of Michael Bakunin.* Westport, CT: Greenwood Press, 1983.

George Woodcock (1967)
Bibliography updated by Vladimir Marchenkov (2005)

BALFOUR, ARTHUR JAMES
(1848–1930)

Arthur James Balfour, the first earl of Balfour, was born at Whittingehame, Haddington, East Lothian. He was the son of a Scottish landowning family and was connected, through his mother, with the aristocratic house of Cecil. After an education at Eton and Trinity College, Cambridge, where he came under the influence of Henry Sidgwick (later his brother-in-law), he became a Conservative M.P. in 1874 and, despite an early reputation for indolence and frivolity, soon rose, by a combination of influence and ability, to ministerial rank. Having made his name as a courageous and enlightened chief secretary for Ireland during the turbulent period from 1887 to 1891, he became leader of the House of Commons in 1891 and in 1902 succeeded his uncle, Lord Salisbury, as prime minister. Beset by dissensions over tariff reform, his administration fell in 1905; but he remained leader of the Opposition until 1911. He resumed office in the wartime coalition as first lord of the admiralty, later becoming foreign secretary and lord president of the council. In these capacities he played a major part in the postwar negotiations at Versailles and Washington and, by the Balfour Declaration of 1917, in the eventual establishment of the state of Israel. He received the Order of Merit in 1916 and a Garter knighthood, followed by an earldom, in 1922. Among many other distinctions, he was chancellor of both Cambridge and Edinburgh universities, fellow of the Royal Society, president of the British Academy, the British Association, and the Aristotelian Society, and one of the founders of the Scots Philosophical Club. As an elder statesman whose disinterested sagacity was equally valued by both parties, Balfour in his later years enjoyed a unique position in British political life. He died, unmarried, at Woking.

Balfour's intelligence, versatility, and charm were at the service of many causes besides politics. Science and education were among his keenest interests; with his sister, Mrs. Sidgwick, he was a leading figure in the Society for Psychical Research. His leisure was divided equally between the arts and society, on the one hand, and tennis and golf on the other. Philosophy, however, was his main pursuit in private life, and in this sphere also—like his fellow statesman Richard Burton Haldane—he made a definite, if temporary, mark. Aside from having considerable literary merits, his writings are chiefly notable as a vigorous and independent contribution to the literature of the perennial conflict between science and religion.

Balfour had a strong distaste for the evolutionary naturalism of his younger days, and made repeated attempts to expose its pretensions as a prelude to stating the case for a "higher Reason" and the acceptance of Christian belief. To this end he employs skeptical weapons of a type forged by George Berkeley and David Hume and subsequently wielded by Henry Longueville Mansel, while his own defenses owe more than a little to Edmund Burke. If the would-be scientific answers to the problems of knowledge and human existence turn out, on examination, to be at once ungrounded and inconsistent, they supersede neither the time-honored beliefs of common sense nor the equally cherished, albeit unprovable, convictions of religion. Balfour's first book, *A Defence of Philosophic Doubt* (London, 1879), argues derisively against the claims of any prevailing system of thought to justify, let alone criticize, the natural and "inevitable" beliefs in the external world, in the uniformity of nature and, to a lesser extent, in theism. His second book, the widely read *Foundations of Belief* (London, 1895), renews the polemic against John Stuart Mill and Herbert Spencer, dwelling on their inability to account either for the facts of perception or for the appearance of natural law, and still less for the data of ethical and aesthetic experience. So far from being rational, they degrade reason to the status of an evolutionary by-product and ignore the importance of belief. The latter, it is argued in a famous chapter, is founded, not on induction, but on the more enduring basis of "authority"—the climate of traditional opinion, by which all reasonable men live. Where nothing is certain and everything rests on belief, science not only cannot dictate to religion, but even presupposes theism as the basis for its own claims to rationality.

If Balfour's strictures on naturalism were not infrequently mistaken by his opponents for a Tory attack upon science, his defense of the faith tended equally to unnerve the faithful who distrusted its appearances of skepticism. So far as these misunderstandings resulted from his own rather casual employment of such terms as *naturalism, rationalism, theism, reason, authority,* and the like, they were clarified, in part, by his two sets of Gifford Lectures, *Theism and Humanism* (London, 1915) and *Theism and Thought* (London, 1923). These works, however, though readable enough as a restatement of his position, are essentially products of a bygone phase of controversy and have little to add that is new.

See also Berkeley, George; Burke, Edmund; Hume, David; Mansel, Henry Longueville; Mill, John Stuart; Naturalism; Sidgwick, Henry.

Bibliography

Balfour's minor writings are represented in *Essays and Addresses* (London, 1905) and *Essays, Speculative and Political* (London: Hodder and Stoughton, 1920). See also an anthology by his secretary, W. M. Short, *A. J. Balfour as Philosopher and Thinker* (London: Longmans, Green, 1912).

The leading biographies are Mrs. Dugdale (his niece), *Arthur James Balfour,* 2 vols. (London: Hutchinson, 1936), and K. Young, *Arthur James Balfour* (London: G. Bell, 1963). The former has an appraisal of his philosophy by A. Seth Pringle-Pattison, an old friend, whose *Man's Place in the Cosmos* (London: Blackwood, 1897) also contains a useful appreciation of Balfour's earlier point of view.

P. L. Heath (1967)

BALGUY, JOHN
(1686–1748)

John Balguy, the English theologian and moral philosopher, was born in Sheffield and educated at the Sheffield grammar school and at St. John's College, Cambridge. He was admitted to the B.A. in 1706, ordained in the established church in 1710, and granted the living of Lamesley and Tanfield in Durham in 1711. Later he was made a prebendary of Salisbury (1727) and finally vicar of Northallerton, York (1729). He was an associate of Bishop Benjamin Hoadley and was the bishop's defender in the Bangorian controversy. Hoadley was the close friend of Samuel Clarke.

Balguy's first piece of moral philosophy was an attack on the philosophy of Shaftesbury, titled *A Letter to a Deist concerning the Beauty and Excellency of Moral Virtue, and the Support Which It Receives from the Christian Religion* (London, 1726). His most important work was *The Foundation of Moral Goodness* (Part I first published in London in 1728, Part II in 1729). Part I is a criticism of the moral philosophy of Francis Hutcheson and an exposition of Balguy's own views, much influenced by Samuel Clarke. Part II is a set of critical queries with Balguy's answers. A Lord Darcy, an admirer of Hutcheson's philosophy, is said to have proposed the queries.

Hutcheson claimed that we distinguish between virtue and vice by means of the perceptions of a moral sense. These perceptions are kinds of pleasure and uneasiness, and they are invoked to account for our approval of virtue and our abhorrence of vice, as well as our obligation to behave virtuously and to avoid viciousness. Hutcheson believed that our moral sense has been determined by God to operate as it does and that we are naturally endowed with a benevolence toward our fellow creatures.

Balguy agreed that God has endowed our minds with benevolent affections toward others, but these affections are only helps or incentives to virtue and not the true ground or foundation of it. By making virtuous behavior flow from divinely founded instincts, Hutcheson had made virtue arbitrary. It is compatible with Hutcheson's view that God might have made us different from what we are, even inverting virtue and vice if he pleased. What is more, if God had not given us an instinct for benevolence, it appears that we should be altogether incapable of virtue; and this would be so even if we were possessed of reason and liberty.

Balguy argued that there is something in actions absolutely good (or bad) that is antecedent to both affections and laws. If this were not so, no reason could be given for God's preferring us to act benevolently and disposing us accordingly. For an action to be virtuous, there must be a perception or a consciousness of its reasonableness, or we would have to admit that beasts can be virtuous. Genuine goodness consists in our being determined to do a good action merely by the reason and the right of the thing. This is the purest and most perfect virtue of which any agent is capable. The obligation to perform a virtuous act is to be found in its reasonableness, and for a rational creature to refuse to be reasonable is unthinkable.

Balguy's elucidation of "reasonable" is found in his account of our knowledge of virtue. He argued that our understanding is altogether sufficient for the perception of virtue. Virtue is the conformity of our moral actions to the reasons of things; vice is the contrary. Moral actions are actions directed toward some intelligent being, and Balguy called them moral to distinguish them from other kinds of action. By a moral action's conformity to reason, Balguy meant the agreeableness of the action to the nature and circumstances of the persons concerned and the relations existing between them. Gratitude is an example of what he meant by conformity to reason: "We find … that some actions are agreeable, others disagreeable, to the nature and circumstances of the agent and the object, and the relations interceding between them. Thus, for instance, we find an agreement between the gratitude of A and the kindness of B; and a disagreement between the ingratitude of C and the bounty of D. These agreements and disagreements are visible to every intelligent observer, who attends to the several ideas" (*The Foundation of Moral Goodness*). He likens our perception of such an agreement to our perception of the agreement between the three angles of a triangle and two right ones, or our perception of the agreement between twice three and six. Since we do not require an intellectual sense superadded to our understanding in order to perceive these mathematical agreements, then clearly we do not require a moral sense to perceive the agreement of A's gratitude and B's kindness.

There are difficulties in Balguy's account of virtue as conformity to reason. The agreement between twice three and six is an equality, which is logically necessary. But the agreement of A's gratitude and B's kindness is not a defined equality. How, then, does the agreement come about? One of Balguy's synonyms for "agreement" is "fitting," and it appears to let the proponents of the moral sense in at the back door. For why is gratitude a fitting response to kindness and a lack of gratitude unfitting? What can we say but that we feel gratitude to be fitting and the lack of gratitude unfitting? "Fitting" and "unfitting" are normative terms, and while one can learn such a rule as "Gratitude is the fitting response to kindness," the rule must originally have been given life by someone's feeling that gratitude is the fitting response to kindness. Balguy would treat the rule as an end in itself, because he believed it exhibits some inherent self-consistency. The proponents of the moral sense would argue that the consistency of gratitude and kindness lies not in them but in us who find them to be consistent.

Balguy would agree, of course, that it is we who find gratitude to be the fitting response to kindness. The dispute is only over how we find it to be fitting, and we find it so not by a moral sense as by using our reason or understanding. The final defense for this contention is Balguy's assessment of reason as the noblest of our faculties, superior to any sense. Therefore, reason must be the arbiter of virtue and vice. The question of what faculty assesses the relative superiority of our faculties is never asked.

Balguy also wrote *Divine Rectitude: or a Brief Inquiry concerning the Moral Perfections of the Deity, Particularly in Respect of Creation and Providence* (London, 1730). He argued that God's goodness follows from a regard for a real and absolute order, beauty, and harmony.

See also Clarke, Samuel; Ethics, History of; Hutcheson, Francis; Moral Sense; Shaftesbury, Third Earl of (Anthony Ashley Cooper); Virtue and Vice.

Bibliography

L. A. Selby-Bigge, ed., *The British Moralists* (Oxford: Clarendon Press, 1897), Vol. II, reproduces Part I of *The Foundation of Moral Goodness* and representative selections from Part II.

For critical discussion, see B. Peach, "John Balguy," in *Encyclopedia of Morals,* edited by V. Ferm. (New York: Greenwood, 1956).

Elmer Sprague (1967)

BÁÑEZ, DOMINIC
(1528–1604)

Dominic Báñez, the Spanish theologian, was born at Valladolid and died at Medina del Campo. He studied at the University of Salamanca, where he entered the Dominican order. He first taught courses in philosophy and theology in various houses of study of his order in Spain (Salamanca, Ávila, Alcalá de Henares, Valladolid) and then became a professor at the University of Salamanca, teaching philosophy from 1577 and theology from 1581. He was noted for his role as the spiritual director of St. Teresa of Ávila and for his bitter controversy with the Jesuit Luis de Molina concerning divine grace. Báñez's view on grace and human liberty is called "physical predetermination," which means that man's will is unable to act unless empowered and applied to action by an ultimate principal cause, which is God. Apart from a commentary on Aristotle's treatise *On Generation and Corruption* (1585), Báñez's philosophy is found in his theological work *Scholastica Commentaria in Primam Partem Angelici Doctoris* (Commentary on the first part of the summa of theology; 2 vols., Salamanca, 1584–1588). As a philosopher, Báñez was at his best in interpreting the metaphysics of St. Thomas. Unlike most of his contemporaries, he saw the importance of the act of being (*esse*) as constituting every nature in existence (see L. Urbano, ed., *Scholastica Commentaria,* I, p. 141). In this he anticipated the existential view of Thomistic metaphysics now favored by such thinkers as Jacques Maritain and Étienne Gilson. On the other hand, Báñez interpreted the real distinction of essence and existence as the difference between two individual things (*res*) and then rejected this notion. Moreover, he regarded the limitation of the act of existing by the essence that receives it as an indication that essence may, in this sense, be more noble than existence.

See also Aristotle; Being; Essence and Existence; Gilson, Étienne Henry; Maritain, Jacques; Molina, Luis de; Teresa of Ávila, St.; Thomas Aquinas, St.

Bibliography

Works by Báñez include *Scholastica Commentaria,* newly edited by L. Urbano (Madrid and Valencia, 1934). A later section of the same *Commentary* has also been published as *Commentaria in Primam Secundae,* edited by B. de Heredia, 2 vols. (Madrid, 1942–1944).

For works on Báñez see W. R. O'Connor, "Molina and Báñez as Interpreters of Thomas Aquinas," in *New Scholasticism* 21 (1947): 243–259; and L. Gutiérrez-Vega, "Báñez filósofo existencial," in *Estudios Filosóficos* 3 (1954): 83–114.

Vernon J. Bourke (1967)

BANFI, ANTONIO
(1886–1957)

Antonio Banfi, the Italian philosopher, was born in Milan and studied at the Academy of Science and Letters there and at the University of Berlin. Banfi enjoyed a long acquaintance with Edmund Husserl, who influenced Banfi's thought along with the Marburg Neo-Kantians. Banfi taught at the universities of Florence, Genoa, and Milan. In 1940 he founded the review *Studi filosofici,* which played an important part in the Italian revolt against idealism. Banfi participated actively in political life. In 1925 he adhered to the manifesto of the antifascist intellectuals prepared by Benedetto Croce. After World War II he sat in the Italian Senate as a Communist.

German rather than Italian influences are apparent in Banfi's major work, *Principi di una teoria della ragione* (Principles of a theory of reason; Milan, 1926). According to Banfi philosophical inquiry does not spring from an immediate spontaneity of thought but arises as critical reflection on the cultural heritage of the speculative tradition. By studying the structures of knowledge, reflection grasps the function of reason. Reason is to be understood neither in a psychological sense nor in the metaphysical sense of Hegelianism. Reason, according to Banfi, is the indefinite law of the process of organization or of coordination of experience.

The task of science, Banfi held, is to study experience and resolve it into functional relations or laws. Philosophy continues the work of science in its own manner. It clarifies experience in terms of dialectical antitheses (reality and appearance, matter and form, necessity and liberty, and so on); it resolves the opposition of the antitheses in the unity of an idea; and in the phenomenological conclusion it discloses the rational structure progressively attained in the ordering of experience.

In subsequent works Banfi sought to emphasize the problematic nature of reason as an open system and as the self-ordering of experience. He saw in dialectical materialism the elimination of the mythical moment of knowledge, the affirmation of the unending development of reason, and the liberative function of reason.

See also Croce, Benedetto; Dialectical Materialism; Experience; Hegelianism; Husserl, Edmund; Idealism; Neo-Kantianism; Reason.

Bibliography

Banfi's *L'uomo copernicano* was published in Milan in 1950. His two-volume *La ricerca della realtà* was published in Florence in 1959.

For literature on Banfi, see Giovanni Maria Bertin, *L'idea pedagogica e il principio di ragione in Antonio Banfi* (Rome: A. Armando, 1961); and Fulvio Papi, *Il pensiero di Antonio Banfi* (Florence, 1961).

Eugenio Garin (1967)
Translated by Robert M. Connolly

BARTH, KARL
(1886–1968)

Karl Barth, the Swiss theologian, was born in Basel in 1886. He held professorships at Göttingen, Münster, Bonn, and Basel. His impact on the theological world dates from 1921, with the substantially revised second edition of his *Der Römerbrief* (the first edition was published in 1919). Herein he attacked the prevalent "subjectivism" of Protestant theology, in which he perceived the attempt to fit the Christian revelation into the mold of human preconceptions. After that, though Barth changed and developed many of his ideas, a single main concern ran through all his writings: namely, how to prevent theology from becoming an ideology, that is, a creation of human culture. This was the reason for his early violent attacks on the then fashionable liberal theology, as expounded, for instance, by Adolf von Harnack. According to Barth, the danger of such attempts to formulate a "reasonable" Christianity is threefold: intellectual, ethical, and soteriological. First, there is the danger of identifying human conclusions with the Word of God and thus of destroying the validity of the concept of revelation, which is God's self-manifestation and owes nothing to human initiatives. Second, there is the danger that the church will simply reflect the social and cultural situation, thus losing its power of criticism and its prophetic function. Barth was deeply disturbed by the support given to the kaiser by

a number of his liberal theologian teachers in 1914. It is notable that, while at Bonn, he threw his support behind the Confessing church in its opposition to the Nazis, an action that cost him his chair. Third, salvation comes from God alone, and the attempt to identify a human Weltanschauung with God's Word is an instance of the refusal to accept that the only justification is by grace. As Barth wrote: "This secret identification of ourselves with God carries with it our isolation from him."

The principle that theological exposition should be basically independent of human speculations (except insofar as historical and linguistic investigations, etc. are a necessary part of understanding Scripture) was reinforced by Barth's interpretation of the Fall. Not only is the human will vitiated by the Fall, but reason also, in such a way that it is impossible for men to discover the truth about God through their own efforts. Only if God manifests himself can there be any revelation. Thus Barth rejected the whole of natural theology as expounded by, for instance, Aquinas, and in particular its basis in the doctrine of the analogy of being (*analogia entis*), on the ground that it implies some similarity between creatures and God. A strong motif in Barth's theology, therefore, is the transcendence of God (in the sense of his distance from creatures—"the great Calvinist distance between heaven and earth"). Methodologically, all this implies that interpretation of the Bible should not betray the genuine meaning of the text by explaining away or avoiding those hard sayings that are supposedly scandals to modern thought. Nevertheless, Barth is no fundamentalist: The Word of God is not to be identified with the witness to it found in the Bible, and there is no question of using the latter as a "paper pope."

Der Römerbrief was critical rather than constructive, and during the 1920s Barth's theology had the character of being dialectical (to use a term that he later came to reject), that is, it called in question human preconceptions about God, often by denying them in the sharpest terms; but since theology is designed to proclaim what is God-given, it is always necessary to reach out beyond such denials. In this way, there is a constant dialectic between grace and man's religion. The concept that religion itself is under divine judgment, and is a human rather than strictly a divine phenomenon, has had great influence, culminating in Dietrich Bonhoeffer's idea of a "religionless Christianity."

In the late 1920s Barth started on the second main phase of his theological writing, and after what he called his "well-known false start," with the *Prolegomena to a Christian Dogmatics* (*Christliche Dogmatik im Entwurf,*

1927), he began on his many-volumed *Church Dogmatics* (*Die kirkliche Dogmatik,* 1932 and onward). Herein he was influenced by his study of Anselm (expressed in *Fides Quaerens Intellectum,* 1931). The heart of the Ontological Argument is the recognition that theology does not need any metaphysical substructure; it contains within itself its own rationale, namely the unfolding of the inner form of God's Word. Thus dogmatics is systematic in that it presents the material in an orderly way and in that it aims exhaustively to touch on all areas of human concern, but it is not a deduction from some principle or set of principles.

The *Church Dogmatics* is a rich work, though not altogether a consistent one, since Barth's thought was developing in the course of his writing. Its main emphasis is Christocentric. God's revelation is essentially seen in the Christ-event, and Christ is God's Word. However, the God so revealed is trinitarian: "the work of the Son of God includes the work of the Father as its presupposition and the work of the Holy Spirit as its consequence." The first article, the work of the Father, is "to a certain extent the source, the third article, the work of the Holy Spirit, the goal of our path. But the second article, the work of the Son, is the Way upon which we find ourselves in faith. From that vantage we may review the entire fullness of the acts of God." Consequently, such doctrines as creation must be seen from this perspective. The Bible presents no cosmology, but it does contain an anthropology; and thus God's relation to the natural world can only be understood by analogy with his saving revelation to human beings. Notions of a First Cause and Necessary Being, as explaining the existence of the cosmos, are thus beside the point, for they make no use of the concepts of grace and personality as ascribed to God. By contrast, the biblical saga of creation makes it continuous with God's covenant relationship with Israel.

Barth's exposition is controlled throughout by two considerations. First, dogmatics is necessarily church dogmatics, that is, it is an activity that must be carried on within the church, as the place where the preaching or proclamation of the Word occurs. Thus the theologian's continuous concern is to test the doctrine and preaching of the church, which, because it is carried on through human beings, is liable to go astray. Second, the standpoint from which the proclamation is tested is that of Scripture, which is "the document of the manifestation of the Word in Jesus Christ." Dogmatics would become irrelevant if it sacrificed this standard.

The implications of Barth's thesis for the relationship between philosophy and theology are clear. Insofar as philosophy is metaphysical, in the sense of saying something about God or some such substitute as the Absolute, it collides with theology; and it is the theologian's proper task to show how metaphysics has here gone beyond its legitimate limits. Philosophy, as logic, philosophy of science, and so on, is a proper inquiry, but one that is quite separate from theology. Barth does, however, allow (in his *Fides Quaerens Intellectum* and elsewhere) that philosophical concepts may be used in exegesis, so long as they are kept strictly subordinate to the Word of God. But Barth remains insistent that theologians should not make concessions to secular thought; indeed, he holds that such concessions are a principal reason for the contempt that many philosophers have had for "philosophical" theologians. Thus traditional forms of apologetic are ruled out.

Two issues arising from Barth's whole approach are crucial. First, how is one to know that the revelation in Christ is the true one? Or more particularly, how is one to know that the whole doctrine of God as expounded by Barth is true? Second, how can these propositions about God be meaningful if the similarity or analogy between God and human persons is denied? For Barth, the first question is one that virtually does not arise. The Bible, for instance, does not set out to prove God's existence or attributes, rather, it witnesses to his acts. The task of the preacher or theologian is to proclaim this revelation. Theology must be a rational inquiry that is appropriate to its subject matter, namely God's gracious self-revelation; and any attempt to establish the truth of doctrine upon grounds that are extraneous to its subject matter is both irrelevant and dangerous. Thus the Christian message is not to be seen as a religious teaching amid rival teachings, for all religious and metaphysical revelations and conclusions are projections of human wishes (here the influence of Ludwig Feuerbach is apparent). It by no means follows, however, that any particular statement of theology that is consistent with these presuppositions as to the nature of theological inquiry is correct. Barth holds that dogmatics is a continuing process within the church, and it is, of course, a human activity suffering from the defects of human reason. It is therefore necessary to consider the criteria of the worth of a system of dogmatics. These criteria are necessarily derived internally from God's self-revelation (by the former arguments). Barth singles out two. First, theological thinking must be humble: this is a practical test of whether it is refraining from establishing its own claim to truth, i.e., its being in effect an ideology. Second, it must express the doctrine of predestination, which encapsulates the whole of the revelational approach—what man "achieves" in relation to God is due to God. Because of the element of paradox in the first criterion (for the Thomist can be humble in his approach), Barth is at times inclined to speak in a syncretistic way. Imagining a conversation in heaven, he says: "Yes, dear Schleiermacher, I understand you now. You were right, except on some points!" (*Karl Barth's Table Talk*). Further, the notion that theology is dialectical, so that a statement can be balanced by affirming its apparent contradictory, has rendered Barth less rigid than many of the Barthians.

As to the problem of the meaning of theological utterances, Barth holds that revelation is a relational concept, and thus God does not, so to say, reveal himself independently of the human apprehension of his self-manifestation. Consequently, the knowledge of God is itself given by God, through grace. Thus, the *analogia entis* is replaced by the *analogia fidei* (the analogy of faith); faith gives us understanding of the nature of God and is God-given. Thus God is the cause of true theological assertions, as well as their ground.

Barth's influence has been great. This is partly because he has provided the outline of a theology that is powerfully biblical without being fundamentalist and, therefore, can escape the charge of being irrational by being nonrational. The most eminent Europeans who stand close to Barth are Emil Brunner and Oscar Cullmann. The former entered into controversy with Barth in the early 1930s over the question of the fallen character of human reason. Brunner held that in some areas this thesis was obviously false, for example, in the natural sciences; but, nevertheless, in relation to knowledge of God, men are capable of only the most shadowy awareness on their own. One of the most important attempts to apply Barth's theology has been Hendrik Kraemer's *The Christian Message in a Non-Christian World* (1938), which aims to show that all religions, including empirical Christianity, are under the judgment of the revelation in Christ. Thus there is no need to argue for Christianity as an empirical phenomenon as against other religions. But the question remains: If there is no correspondence between the Gospel and empirical Christianity, the church is a sham; and if there is, then the comparison and contrast between empirical Christianity and other faiths is possible, and apologetics unavoidable. This is one illustration of the central problem posed by Barth's theology.

See also Anselm, St.; Brunner, Emil; Creation and Conservation, Religious Doctrine of; Feuerbach, Ludwig Andreas; Harnack, Carl Gustav Adolf von; Ontological Argument for the Existence of God; Revelation; Thomas Aquinas, St.

Bibliography

There is a useful bibliography of Barth's works in T. F. Torrance's *Karl Barth, an Introduction to His Early Theology, 1910–1931* (London: SCM Press, 1962). The main works translated into English are *The Epistle to the Romans* (London: Oxford University Press, 1933); *Church Dogmatics,* edited by G. W. Bromiley and T. F. Torrance (London: T. and T. Clark, 1936; Edinburgh, 1956 onward), 4 vols., comprising 11 separately published sections, one of which is *Church Dogmatics: A Selection with Introduction,* edited by H. Gollwitzer and translated by G. W. Bromiley (Edinburgh: T. & T. Clark, 1961). An outline, by Barth himself, of the thought in this work is *Dogmatics in Outline* (London: Philosophical Library, 1949). Later works include *The Humanity of God* (Richmond, VA: John Knox Press, 1960); and *Anselm: Fides Quaerens Intellectum* (Richmond, VA: John Knox Press, 1960); and *Evangelical Theology: an Introduction* (New York: Holt, Rinehart and Winston, 1963). See also *Karl Barth's Table Talk,* recorded and edited by John D. Godsey (Edinburgh, 1963).

Works expressing related thought are E. Brunner, *Dogmatics,* 2 vols. (London, 1949; 1952); Oscar Cullmann, *Christ and Time* (London, 1951); and H. Kraemer, *The Christian Message in a Non-Christian World* (London: Edinburgh House Press for the International Missionary Council, 1938). Philosophical criticisms of Barth's position can be found in H. D. Lewis, *Morals and Revelation* (London: Allen and Unwin, 1951) and Ronald W. Hepburn, *Christianity and Paradox* (London: Watts, 1958), Ch. 5.

Ninian Smart (1967)

BARTH, KARL [ADDENDUM]

Since his death in 1968, time and distance have provided scholars with space to understand Karl Barth in a larger intellectual and cultural context. He has emerged as one of the most important Christian theologians of the twentieth century—perhaps the most important—while his massive theological oeuvre and the changing shape of his thought have generated a host of alternative interpretations, notably in respect to his understanding of and relationship to Western philosophy. Contemporary theologians have sought to appropriate Barth in several directions, exploring his thought in connection with various postmodern positions.

Barth consistently held that philosophy should not hold sway over theology. In a 1960 essay written in honor of his brother, who was a philosopher, Barth allows that theology and philosophy can coexist in harmony, but he also spells out the important differences between these disciplines. The Christian theologian must be held captive to the Word of God, he contends, for only God's revelation in Christ provides us with the key to understanding divinity; biblical theology, not philosophical reasoning, is the basis for Christian theology.

At the same time, Barth's thinking was influenced by European philosophers. The influence of existentialist thinkers (especially Kiekegaard) on Barth has long been acknowledged, even by Barth himself. Barth also read and responded to Heidegger in his own way. In recent years the importance of the Marburg school of Neo-Kantian philosophy has become more clear, especially in Barth's early development. Thus Barth's appreciation for philosophy is more expansive than had been acknowledged in earlier scholarship.

Contemporary scholarship has fruitfully engaged Barth's thought with larger philosophical concerns, bringing him into a larger orbit. Much of this research has brought to light Barth's critique of modernity and his ambivalence toward language as a vehicle for theology. Several so-called postliberal theologians have appropriated Barth as a narrative theologian who sought to read the rest of the world in terms of the biblical story. Here Barth is sometime brought into conversation with the later Wittgenstein, both in terms of an understanding of language and a critique of enlightenment rationalism. Most recently scholars have developed some of the parallels between Barth and postmodern philosophers, especially Derrida. This school seeks to appropriate Barth for postmodern theology, a move roundly criticized by more traditional Barth experts. Thus Barth remains at the center of contemporary theological debate.

See also Derrida, Jacques; Enlightenment; Heidegger, Martin; Kierkegaard, Søren Aabye; Neo-Kantianism; Rationalism; Wittgenstein, Ludwig Josef Johann.

Bibliography

Bush, E. *Karl Barth*. London: SCM, 1976.

Fisher, Simon. *Revelatory Positivism? Barth's Earliest Theology and the Marburg School*. Oxford: Oxford University Press, 1988.

Ford, David. *Barth and God's Story*. Frankfurt: P. Lang, 1981.

Frei, Hans. *Types of Christian Theology*. New Haven, CT: Yale University Press, 1992.

Johnson, W. Stacy. *The Mystery of God*.Louisville: Westminster John Knox, 1997.

MacDonald, Niel B. *Karl Barth and the Strange New World within the Bible*. Carlisle, U.K.: Paternoster, 2000.

Lowe, Walter. *Theology and Difference*. Bloomington: Indiana University Press, 1993.

McCormack, Bruce. *Karl Barth's Critically Realistic Dialectical Theology*. Oxford: Oxford University Press, 1995.

Ward, Graham. *Barth, Derrida and the Language of Theology*. Cambridge, U.K.: Cambridge University Press, 1995.

Alan G. Padgett (2005)

BARTHES, ROLAND
(1915–1980)

Ronald Barthes was a French writer most widely known for declaring "the death of the author." It is ironic, then, in a way Barthes would surely appreciate, that his *Œuvres completes* fill nearly 6,000 pages with the unmistakable observations, distinct voice, and style that shaped the form and content of what came to be known as "cultural studies." He was sixty-five years old in 1980 when a laundry truck struck him down in a street in front of the College de France. He died of his injuries four weeks later.

Barthes was born in November 1915, in Cherbourg. His father died before his first birthday, and he was raised by his mother and paternal grandparents in coastal Bayonne. Normal progress to a university degree was blocked by the onset of tuberculosis. Over the course of ten years convalescing in and out of sanatoria, Barthes earned advanced degrees in Greek and Latin, performed in the Ancient Theater Group, and taught French in Romania and in Egypt where A. J. Greimas introduced him to linguistics. He gained his first regular academic post at the *Écoles practique des haute etudes* in 1962 on the basis of his publications *Le degré zéro de l'écriture* (1953), *Michelet par lui-même* (1954), and *Mythologies* (1957). He gained wider public notice with the publication of *Le plaisir du texte* (1973), a critical erotics of reading pleasures, and *Roland Barthes par Roland Barthes* (1975), an autobiography prefaced, as it were, on the page ordinarily reserved for a dedication with the handwritten remark, "It must all be considered as if spoken by a character in a novel." He was appointed Chair of Literary Semiotics at the College de France in 1976 where he lectured until his death.

Barthes's contributions to philosophy fall under four headings defined, in each case, by pairs of opposed terms: mythology (nature/culture), semeiology (*langue/parole*), structuralism (reading/writing), and hedonism (*plaisir/jouissance*).

MYTHOLOGY

Myth today, according to Barthes, is found in a conflation of nature and culture or, more specifically, in the production and consumption of culture as nature. In his most famous example, it is no accident that the scurrilous competitor in a professional wrestling match is bested by the fair play of his adversary: his foul play (as the "fairness" of the victor) is fabricated to stage the "natural" and inevitable triumph of "good" over "evil." Again, in Parisian striptease, the *artiste* sheds layers of patently cultural trappings—feathers, furs, and exotic costumes—to reveal her naked body as the "natural" state of woman unnaturally desexualized, in this act, to forgive the voyeur and the culture that condones his voyeurism for their sins. In modern myths, an apparently natural meaning contains the form of a cultural signification whose content discloses the artifice of what is "natural" in appearance only. "Demythologization" was the name given to the critical practice of exposing these myths.

SEMEIOLOGY

Barthes's literary semeiology follows Ferdinand de Saussure's distinction between *la langue*, the syntactic and semantic paradigms that define the language one learns, and *parole*, the series of signifying acts that compose the language one speaks. On this model, meaning is the product of a system of distinctions and conventions, found in *la langue*, which anchor otherwise unruly syntagms of signifying units, articulated as *parole*. The meaning of this sentence, for example, depends on identifying the parts of speech in it and the rules governing their use that define the linguistic system in which the sentence is uttered. Reversing Saussure, semeiology was, for Barthes, a subset of linguistics, a science of the signifying function of language. In his studies of advertising, gastronomy, fashion and Japan, Barthes consistently emphasized the multiplicity and variability of the signifier over the system that governed its significations.

STRUCTURALISM

As Barthes defined it, structuralism studies the rules, norms, and organizing structures that make meaning possible. These structures are the products of cultural practices, which the structuralist uncovers beneath the singular meaning attributed to an image, an artifact, or a text. It is Author who could authorize a Single meaning (the capital letters standing for the "theological" authority supposed by such a concept of signification) who dies in Barthes's analysis of the rules, norms, and organizing structures, of the narrative and social and moral codes that govern the writing (literal and figurative) of a text or any other cultural artifact. In addition, this writing is governed by the rules, norms and structures of reading. So that writing, *écriture*, arranges a meeting of the structures and codes that have formed a writer and a reader and

stages the multiplication of meanings sustained by the text a writer and reader share. Barthes calls a text "writerly" which invites the reader to write meanings into it and "readerly" when the text insists on a single authorial intention.

HEDONISM

Our pleasures, in Barthes's writing, are divided along the same lines. There is, on the one hand, *plaisir*, the warmth of sensation that opposes cold abstraction, the contentment, euphoria and delectation that relieve the method, commitment and science of the intellect. It is found in texts of and on pleasure (Gustave Flaubert and Marquis de Sade, for example) and connected to a reading practice that is comfortable and continuous with the culture of the reader and the text. There is, on the other hand, the ecstatic pleasure of *jouissance*, a feeling of enjoyment characterized by a state of loss. It is not centered in the heart (as opposed to the head) but spread sensuously across the entire surface of the body. *Jouissance* is found in a reading practice that "cruises" the text, skipping passages anticipated as "boring," looking up distractedly to consider ideas associated with the body and dissociated from the culture of the reader or the text. *Jouissance* is found in distinctly "writerly" readings and texts that multiply meanings for the sheer pleasure of it.

There is, finally, a distinctive normative orientation in Barthes's writings. While he did not author or advocate an alternative, single meaning of culture, Barthes did license and exhort readers to take ecstatic pleasure in multiplying the meanings of culture and in rewriting the authority of its hegemonic codes.

See also Hedonism; Language; Myth; Structuralism and Post-structuralism.

Bibliography

WORKS BY ROLAND BARTHES

Le degré zéro de l'écriture. Paris, 1953. Translated by Annette Lavers and Colin Smith as *Writing Degree Zero* (New York: Hill and Wang, 1968).

Michelet par lui-même. Paris: Éditions du Seuil, 1954. Translated by Richard Howard as *Michelet* (Berkeley: University of California Press, 1992).

Mythologies. Paris, 1957. Selected translation by Annette Lavers as *Mythologies* (London: Paladan Books, 1973). Translation of remaining essays by Richard Howard as *The Eiffel Tower and Other Mythologies* (New York: Hill and Wang, 1979).

Sur Racine. Paris, 1963. Translated by Richard Howard as *On Racine* (New York: Octagon Books, 1977).

Essais critiques. Paris, 1964. Translated by Richard Howard as *Critical Essays* (Evanston: Northwestern University Press, 1972).

Éléments de sémiologie in Le degré zéro de l'écriture, suivi de: Éléments de sémiologie. Paris, 1965. Translated by Annette Lavers and Colin Smith as *Elements of Semiology* (New York: Hill and Wang, 1968).

Critique et verité. Paris, 1966. Translated by Katrine Kueneman as *Criticism and Truth* (Minneapolis: University of Minnesota Press, 1987).

Système de la mode. Paris, 1967. Translated by Matthew Ward and Richard Howard as *The Fashion System* (New York: Hill and Wang, 1983).

L'empire des signes. Geneva, 1970. Translated by Richard Howard as *Empire of Signs* (New York: Noonday Press, 1989).

S/Z. Paris: Éditions du Seuil, 1970. Translated by Richard Miller as *S/Z* (London: Cape, 1975).

Sade, Fourier, Loyola. Paris: Éditions du Seuil, 1971. Translated by Richard Miller as *Sade, Fourier, Loyola* (Baltimore: Johns Hopkins University Press, 1997).

Nouveaux essais critiques in Le degré zéro de l'écriture suivi de: Nouveaux essais critiques. Paris, 1972. Translated by Richard Howard as *New Critical Essays* (New York: Hill and Wang, 1980).

Le plaisir du texte. Paris, 1973. Translated by Richard Miller as *The Pleasure of the Text* (New York: Hill and Wang, 1975).

Roland Barthes par Roland Barthes. Paris, 1975. Translated by Richard Howard as *Roland Barthes by Roland Barthes* (Berkeley: University of California Press, 1994).

Et la Chine? Paris, 1976.

Fragments d'un discours amoureaux. Paris, 1977. Translated by Richard Howard as *A Lover's Discourse: Fragments* (New York: Hill and Wang, 1978).

Image, Music, Text. Essays selected and translated by Stephen Heath. New York: Hill and Wang, 1977.

Sollers ecrivain. Paris, 1979. Translated by Philip Thody as *Sollers Writer* (London: Athlone, 1987).

La chambre claire: note sur la photographie. Paris, 1980. Translated by Richard Howard as *Camera Lucida: Reflections on Photography* (New York: Hill and Wang, 1981).

Le grain de la voix: entretiens 1962–1980. Paris, 1981. Translated by Linda Coverdale as *The Grain of the Voice: Interviews 1962–1980* (New York: Hill and Wang, 1985).

A Barthes Reader. Edited and with an Introduction by Susan Sontag. New York: Hill and Wang, 1982.

L'obvie et l'obtus. Paris, 1982. Translated by Richard Howard as *The Responsibility of Forms: Critical Essays on Music, Art, and Representation* (New York: Hill and Wang, 1985).

Le bruissement de la langue. Paris, 1984. Translated by Richard Howard as *The Rustle of Language* (New York: Hill and Wang, 1986).

L'aventure sémiologique. Paris, 1985. Translated by Richard Howard as *The Semiotic Challenge* (New York: Hill and Wang, 1988).

Incidents. Paris, 1987. Translated by Richard Howard as *Incidents* (Berkeley: University of California Press, 1992).

Œuvres completes. 5 vols. New, revised, and corrected ed. Paris: Seuil, 2002.

WORKS ABOUT ROLAND BARTHES

Culler, Jonathan. *Barthes: A Very Short Introduction.* Oxford: Oxford University Press, 2002.

Heath, Stephen. *Vertige du déplacement: Lecture de Barthes.* Paris: Fayard, 1974.

Lavers, Annette. *Roland Barthes: Structuralism and After.* Cambridge, MA: Harvard University Press, 1982.

Miller, D. A. *Bringing Out Roland Barthes.* Berkeley: University of California Press, 1992.

John Carvalho (2005)

BASEDOW, JOHANN BERNHARD
(1724–1790)

Johann Bernhard Basedow, the German philosopher, theologian, and educational theorist, was born in Hamburg into the family of a poor wigmaker, whose name, more properly, was Bassedau. A benefactor financed his studies, first at Hamburg under H. S. Reimarus. In 1746 he entered the faculty of theology at Leipzig University, where he studied philosophy under the Pietist philosopher C. A. Crusius. In 1749 he became a private tutor in the family of Herr von Quaalen in Holstein. His experiences as a tutor turned his attention to educational problems, which were the subject of his master's thesis at Kiel University in 1752. On Friedrich Gottlieb Klopstock's recommendation, he was appointed professor of philosophy and rhetoric at the Knightly Academy at Soro, Denmark. A heterodox work, *Praktische Philosophie für alle Stände* (Practical philosophy for all states; Copenhagen, 1758), led to his dismissal. In 1761 he moved to the gymnasium at Altona, but again lost his position, and his writings were prohibited. He left theology and, supported by his benefactor, published his *Vorstellung an Menschenfreunde für Schulen, nebst dem Plan eines Elementarbuchs der menschlichen Erkenntnisse* (Appeal to the friends of mankind about schools, with a plan for an elementary book on human knowledge; Hamburg, 1768), his first significant work on education, which met with a tremendous response. With financial help from several influential people, he published during the following years several textbooks, the most important being his *Methodenbuch für Väter und Mütter der Familien und Völker* (Methodology for fathers and mothers of families and nations; Leipzig, 1770; edited by T. Fritzsch, Leipzig, 1913). Prince Franz Leopold Friedrich of Dessau invited him to organize an experimental school in Dessau. Basedow accepted, and the school, called the *Philanthropin,* opened in 1774.

It was soon imitated by a number of similar institutions in Germany and Switzerland.

By 1776 Basedow had returned to theology, living in Dessau, Leipzig, Halle, and Magdeburg. During this period he published his *Examen in der alten natürlichsten Religion* (Examination of the old most natural religion), which he considered his masterpiece. Basedow's theological ideas, inspired by the English and French deists, aimed at a natural religion, rational and practical, refraining from dogmas and rejecting every kind of orthodox Christianity.

Basedow was one of the "popular philosophers" (*Popularphilosophen*), but his importance as a theoretical philosopher has been underrated by modern historians. His work on theory of knowledge and metaphysics, *Philalethie* (Lübeck, 1764), inspired by Crusius, David Hume, and the French *philosophes*, was one of the most significant books on methodology of its time and influenced Immanuel Kant, Johann Nicolaus Tetens, and others. He supported a moderate skepticism based on common sense and denied the possibility of reaching absolute demonstrative truth in natural philosophy (out of skepticism concerning causation), in rational psychology, or in theology.

Basedow's chief importance lies in his educational theories, which are based on John Amos Comenius, John Locke, and Jean-Jacques Rousseau. He claimed that education should be cosmopolitan, free from any confessional imprint, equal for all classes, and aimed at enabling men to live useful and happy lives as good citizens. Instruction should appeal to the child's sensibility rather than to his understanding and should be encouraged by games and colloquial intercourse. Images (*Zeichen*) are more effective than words.

See also Comenius, John Amos; Crusius, Christian August; Deism; German Philosophy; Hume, David; Kant, Immanuel; Locke, John; Reimarus, Hermann Samuel; Rousseau, Jean-Jacques; Skepticism, History of; Tetens, Johann Nicolaus.

Bibliography

WORKS BY BASEDOW

Ausgewählte Schriften. Edited by Hugo Göring. Langensalza, 1880.

WORKS ON BASEDOW

Basedow, Armin. "Johann Bernhard Basedow." *Friedrich Manns pädagogisches Magazin* 995 (1924).

Diestelmann, Richard. *Johann Bernhard Basedow.* Leipzig, 1897.

Meyer, J. C. *Leben, Charakter und Schriften Basedows,* 2 vols. Hamburg, 1791–1792.

Rammelt, Johannes. *J. B. Basedow, der Philanthropinismus und das Dessauer Philanthropin.* Dessau, 1929.

Rathmann, H. *Beiträge zur Lebensgeschichte Basedows.* Magdeburg, 1791.

Surakoff, K. D. *Der Einfluss der zeitgenössischen Philosophie auf Basedows Pädagogik.* Giessen: Brühl, 1898.

Zimmermann, Hans. *Die Pädagogik Basedows vom Standpunkte moderner Geschichtsauffassung.* Langensalza, 1912.

Giorgio Tonelli (1967)

BASIC STATEMENTS

Any statement of fact is true or false in virtue of some existing state of affairs in the world. In many cases the truth-value of a statement is determined by appealing to the truth-values of certain other statements, but this process must terminate somewhere if the truth-value of any statement of fact is to be assessed at all. An epistemological view according to which the process of verification or falsification terminates with statements of a logically distinct kind is a view to the effect that there is a distinct class of *basic statements*. The principal questions that have been considered are (1) Is there such a class of statements? (2) If there is, what is the relation between these statements and certain nonverbal occurrences called experiences? (3) Are basic statements descriptions of the private experiences of the speaker or of publicly observable events? (4) Are these statements either incorrigible (that is, of such a character that they cannot be false, or cannot be shown to be false) or indubitable (that is, such that they cannot rationally be doubted)? These questions have been much discussed by modern empiricists, especially in connection with the verifiability criterion of meaning. The problems concerning basic statements are not, however, essentially confined to empiricist theories of meaning and truth; they are fundamental in any theory of knowledge.

WITTGENSTEIN

The thesis that there is a class of basic or elementary propositions is powerfully presented in Ludwig Wittgenstein's *Tractatus Logico-Philosophicus* (1921; first English translation, 1922). Wittgenstein argues that if a proposition contains expressions standing for complexes, the sense of the proposition will depend upon the truth of other propositions describing those complexes. This will again be the case if any one of those other propositions contains expressions standing for complexes. Thus, the determinateness of the sense of the original proposition requires that its analysis should terminate in elementary propositions consisting only of names of simple things (see 2.0211–2.0212, 3.23). An elementary proposition is an arrangement of names that represents a possible arrangement of simple things; it is a logical picture of an elementary state of affairs. Wittgenstein gave no explicit interpretation of "simple things," "names," or "elementary propositions." He is reported as saying that at the time he wrote the *Tractatus* he thought it was not his business, as a logician, to give examples of simple things, this being a purely empirical matter; the *Tractatus* view is that the application of logic decides what elementary propositions there are (5.557).

SCHLICK

Moritz Schlick and some other members of the Vienna circle gave an empiricist interpretation to Wittgenstein's theory. In "Über das Fundament der Erkenntnis" (1934) and other articles, Schlick inquired whether there is a class of statements which provide an "unshakeable, indubitable foundation" of all knowledge. This kind of incorrigibility, he argued (against Otto Neurath and Rudolf Carnap), cannot depend simply upon the coherence of a statement with the existing system of science, nor simply upon someone's decision to accept a statement as true. It is possessed only by the statements a person makes about his own experiences. Schlick called such statements *Konstatierungen* "confirmations" and contrasted these with the "protocol sentences" described by Neurath and Carnap.

Konstatierungen have the following characteristics: (1) They have the form "here, now, so and so"; examples are "here two black points coincide," "Here yellow borders on blue," "Here now pain." (2) In the case of other synthetic statements, understanding their meaning is quite distinct from the actual process of verifying them, and their meaning does not determine their truth-value; but in the case of a *Konstatierung* (since "'this here' has meaning only in connection with a gesture … one must somehow point to reality"), the occasion of understanding it is the same as that of verifying it. Therefore a (significant) *Konstatierung* cannot be false. (3) Unlike "protocol sentences," these statements cannot be written down or recorded at all because of the fleeting reference of the demonstratives that occur in them; but they provide the occasions for the formation of protocol sentences. (4) They are the only empirical statements that are not hypotheses. (5) They are not the starting points of science in either a temporal or a logical sense, but simply the momentary consummations of the scientific process; they are the means by which all scientific hypotheses are confirmed.

The first and most obvious objection to the view that there are *Konstatierungen* (in Schlick's sense) is that it results immediately in a radical form of solipsism. It may also be objected that *Konstatierungen* are either genuine contingent statements, in which case they cannot be of such a nature that they cannot be false, or they are purely demonstrative, in which case they are not statements. Following Wittgenstein's later work, many philosophers would deny the possibility of the essentially private use of demonstratives and descriptions that are supposed to occur in *Konstatierungen*. Further, no adequate account is given of the relation between these private statements and the public protocol sentences to which they give rise. Moreover, if the *Konstatierungen* are meaningful only at the moment at which they are verified, they cannot occur in predictions, and hence it cannot be through them that scientific hypotheses are confirmed.

CARNAP

Rudolf Carnap, in "Die physikalische Sprache als Universalsprache der Wissenschaft" (1931; translated as *The Unity of Science*, 1934) and elsewhere, had at first held that science is a system of statements based upon sentences describing the experiences of scientific observers. These "primitive protocol sentences," Carnap supposed, contain no inferential or theoretical additions; they describe only what is directly given, and hence they stand in no need of any further justification. At this time Carnap left it an open question whether protocol sentences describe the simplest sensations and feelings of the observer (for example, "here now red," "joy now"), or partial or complete gestalts of single sensory fields (for example, "red circle now"), or the total experience of the observer during an instant, or macroscopic material things (for example, "A red cube is on the table"). Later, however, in *Logische Syntax der Sprache* (1934) and other publications, due mainly to the criticisms of Neurath, Carnap held that the question of what protocol sentences describe is not a factual but a linguistic question and that we are free to choose whatever form of language is most convenient for reporting observations in science.

NEURATH

Otto Neurath, in "Soziologie im Physikalismus" (1931/1932; English translation, 1959) and other articles, had argued that sentences cannot be compared with the private experiences of the observer, nor with public material things, but only with other sentences. Some sentences are reports of acts of observation, in the sense of being behavioral responses to those acts, and such protocol sentences may have whatever form we find most convenient. In "Protokollsätze" (1932/1933), Neurath maintained that for the purposes of science it must be possible to incorporate the protocol sentences expressed at one time in those expressed at another time, and that comparison of protocols, even with one's own past protocols, requires an intersubjective language. Neurath remarks, "*every* language *as such* is inter-subjective." Carnap later agreed that if protocol sentences were regarded as describing the observer's private experiences, they could be understood, if at all, only solipsistically. Neurath suggested that a convenient form for protocol sentences would be one which contained a name or description of an observer and some words recording an act of observation; he gives as an example "Otto's protocol at 3:17 o'clock [Otto's word-thought at 3:16: (In the room at 3:15 was a table perceived by Otto)]." In this example, it is supposed that the entire sentence is written down by Otto at 3:17, simply as an overt verbal response; the sentence in brackets is Otto's response at 3:16, and the sentence in parentheses is his response at 3:15. The word "Otto" is repeated, instead of using "my" and "me," in order that the components of the protocol may be independently tested, for example, by being found in the protocols of other observers. The protocols of different observers or of the same observer may conflict, and when this happens, one or more of them is to be rejected.

According to Neurath, Carnap, and also Carl Gustav Hempel in "On The Logical Positivists' Theory of Truth" (1934/1935) it is a matter of convenience and decision which of the conflicting protocols should be rejected; hence, no protocol is incorrigible. The aim of science is to build up a coherent system of sentences, but no sentence at any level is sacrosanct; every sentence in science is in the end accepted or rejected by a decision made in the interests of coherence and utility. This view was strenuously opposed—by Schlick, Bertrand Russell, and A. J. Ayer, among others, who argued that (1) on this account protocol sentences are distinguished from others only in respect of their syntactical form; (2) a purely syntactical criterion of truth cannot do the work required of it; and (3) the Neurath–Carnap doctrine is a complete abandonment of empiricism.

RUSSELL

According to Bertrand Russell's early doctrine of knowledge by acquaintance and knowledge by description,

"every proposition we can understand must be composed wholly of constituents with which we are acquainted." A person is acquainted with those objects that are directly presented to his mind, and Russell held that sense data and universals are so presented. Later, in *The Analysis of Mind* (1921), Russell maintained that it is not possible to make a distinction between sensation and sense datum and that a sensation is not itself a cognition, although it is a cause of cognitions. This view led to the account of basic propositions that Russell gives in *An Inquiry into Meaning and Truth* (1940). In epistemology, he says, we can arrange our propositions about matters of fact in a certain order such that those that come later are known, if they are known, because of those that come earlier. At the beginning of such an ordering there will be "basic propositions"—those which "on reflection appear credible independently of any argument in their favour."

A basic proposition is one whose utterance is caused as immediately as possible by a perceptual experience. It is known independently of inference but not independently of evidence, since the perceptual experience that causes it to be expressed also gives the reason for believing it. The perceptual experience in question provides the strongest possible evidence for the basic proposition; no previous or subsequent occurrence and no experiences of others can prove that the proposition is false. Nevertheless, according to Russell, a basic proposition is not incorrigible; it cannot be disproved, but it may be false. Since one of the aims of epistemology is to show that all empirical knowledge is based upon these propositions, it is desirable that they should be given a logical form which makes contradiction between them impossible. Russell therefore defines a basic proposition as one "which arises on the occasion of a perception, which is the evidence for its truth, and ... has a form such that no two propositions having this form can be mutually inconsistent if derived from different percepts" (*Inquiry into Meaning and Truth*, p. 139). Examples are "there is a canoid (shaped) patch of color," "I am hot," "that is red." Alternatively, "we can consider the whole body of empirical knowledge and define 'basic propositions' as those of its logically indemonstrable propositions which are themselves empirical" (ibid.). Russell believes that this logical definition is extensionally equivalent to his epistemological definition.

AYER

Whether basic propositions are incorrigible or indubitable, and if so in what sense, has been considered at length by A. J. Ayer. In "Basic Propositions" (1950) he defends the view that if a sentence is a direct description of a private experience, it may be verbally incorrect, but it cannot express a proposition about which the speaker can be factually mistaken. He explains this in the following way. Many descriptive sentences, for example, "That is a table," may be used correctly (that is, in accordance with the rules of the language and on occasions generally agreed to be appropriate for their use), and yet the propositions they express may turn out to be false. But in the case of a sentence which directly describes a present experience, if the sentence is used correctly (that is, in accordance with the speaker's rules), the proposition it expresses cannot turn out to be false. Thus, "the sense in which statements like 'This is green,' 'I feel a headache,' 'I seem to remember——' can be said to be indubitable is that, when they are understood to refer only to some immediate experience, their truth or falsehood is conclusively determined by a meaning rule of the language in which they are expressed" ("Basic Propositions," p. 72).

Later, in *The Problem of Knowledge* (1956) and elsewhere, Ayer argues that language rules may be essentially private and that basic statements may be expressed in a sense-datum terminology, provided that this terminology is translatable into a terminology of seeming. Incorrigibility is not a property belonging to statements as such; "the sentences 'He has a headache,' when used by someone else to refer to me, 'I shall have a headache,' used by me in the past with reference to this moment, and 'I have a headache' all express the same statement; but the third of these sentences alone is used in such conditions as make it reasonable for me to claim that the statement is incorrigibly known" (*The Problem of Knowledge*, p. 58). But Ayer here allows that if he were asked, regarding two lines in his visual field, which looked to him to be the longer, he might very well be uncertain how to answer; and this uncertainty would not be about the meaning of the expression "looks longer than" but about a matter of fact. If anyone can have doubt about such matters of fact, he can presumably come to the wrong decision, that is, he can judge that one of the lines looks to him longer than the other when in fact it does not. No direct test of such a mistake is possible, but there may be various kinds of indirect evidence to show that it has occurred; hence, Ayer concludes, there is no class of descriptive statements which are incorrigible.

POPPER

The requirements made upon basic statements are very often governed by the general nature of the theory of knowledge held by a philosopher. Thus, according to Karl Popper, our experiences cannot justify or establish the truth of any statement; the question for epistemology is not "on what does our *knowledge* rest? … or more exactly, how can I, having had the *experience* S, justify my description of it and defend it against doubt," but rather "how do we test scientific statements by their deductive consequences … *what kind* of consequences can we select for this purpose if they in their turn are to be intersubjectively testable?" (*The Logic of Scientific Discovery*, p. 98). Popper requires a class of basic statements by reference to which it can be decided whether a theory or hypothesis in science is falsifiable. Evidently a theory can be falsified by a basic statement only if the negation of the latter is derivable from the theory. Popper finds that his requirements are met by taking singular existential statements of the form "There is a so-and-so in space-time region k" as basic. It follows that the negation of a basic statement is not itself a basic statement (Popper allows some simple exceptions to this in *Conjectures and Refutations*, Addenda, p. 386); it also follows that any conjunction of basic statements which is not a logical contradiction is a basic statement and that the conjunction of a nonbasic and a basic statement may be a basic statement (for example, the conjunction of "There is no pointer in motion at k" with "There is a pointer at k," which is equivalent to "There is a pointer at rest at k". Given a theory t conjoined with a statement of initial conditions r, from which a prediction p can be derived, it follows that $r \cdot \sim p$ will be a falsifier of t and a basic statement—since if $(t \cdot r) \rightarrow p$, then $t \rightarrow (r \rightarrow p)$, that is, $t \rightarrow \sim (r \cdot \sim p)$.

Popper also stipulates that the event referred to in a basic statement should be observable, that is, a basic statement must be intersubjectively testable by observation. He claims that the concept of an observable event can be elucidated either in terms of the experiences of an observer or in terms of macroscopic physical bodies, and hence that his account is neutral regarding the issue between psychologism and physicalism. In Popper's theory, the expression "observable event" is introduced "as an undefined term which becomes sufficiently precise in use: as a primitive concept whose use the epistemologist has to learn." According to Popper, "a science needs points of view and theoretical problems"; hence, in the practice of science we should not accept stray basic statements but only those which occur in the course of testing theories. Every test of a theory must terminate with some basic statement, but every basic statement can itself be subjected to further tests. There are no logical grounds for stopping at any particular basic statement. It is a matter for agreement and decision among those engaged in testing a theory; the process of corroboration or falsification terminates at the point at which they are satisfied for the time being.

From the preceding selection of views, held by recent and contemporary philosophers, it will be seen that there is no consensus concerning basic statements. The questions listed at the beginning of this article can be answered only in relation to a more general semantic and epistemological theory. Many such theories allow that there is a distinct class of basic statements. It seems that the relation between these statements and certain "experiences" of the speakers who express them must be partly semantic, and perhaps also partly causal, but the correct analysis of this relation is a matter of great difficulty. Many philosophers at the present time deny that there can be a class of statements that describe the *private* experiences of the speaker, on the grounds that there cannot be a language that is essentially private; but this latter view is also strongly contested. Finally, although on some views basic statements are indubitable, it seems that these statements cannot be incorrigible, at least in any sense that implies that they cannot be false. For if basic statements are to play the role assigned to them—namely, of being the terminating points of empirical verification—they must be genuine contingent statements; and a contingent statement is one whose negation is significant and could, as far as logic is concerned, be true.

See also Ayer, Alfred Jules; Carnap, Rudolf; Empiricism; Hempel, Carl Gustav; Knowledge and Belief; Neurath, Otto; Popper, Karl Raimund; Propositions; Russell, Bertrand Arthur William; Schlick, Moritz; Verifiability Principle; Wittgenstein, Ludwig Josef Johann.

Bibliography

Wittgenstein's view in the *Tractatus Logico-Philosophicus* (London: K. Paul, Trench, Trubner, 1922) is the object of his own criticism in *Philosophical Investigations* (Oxford: Blackwell, 1953), especially in Part I, Secs. 1–64.

Schlick's "Über das Fundament der Erkenntnis," in *Erkenntnis* 4 (1934), has been translated by David Rynin in *Logical Positivism*, edited by A. J. Ayer (Glencoe, IL: Free Press, 1959), pp. 209–227. The same volume also contains English translations by Morton Magnus and Ralph Raico of Otto Neurath's "Soziologie im Physikalismus" (which originally appeared in *Erkenntnis* 2 [1931/1932]) on pp. 282–317, and by Frederic Schlick of Neurath's "Protokollsätze" (which originally appeared in *Erkenntnis* 3 [1932/1933]) on pp. 199–208.

For Carnap's views, see "Die physische Sprache als Universalsprache der Wissenschaft," in *Erkenntnis* 2 [1931/1932]), translated by Max Black as *The Unity of Science* (London: K. Paul, Trench, Trubner, 1934), and *Logische Syntax der Sprache* (Vienna: Springer, 1934), translated by Amethe Smeaton as *The Logical Syntax of Language* (London: K. Paul, Trench, Trubner, 1937).

The views of Hempel may be found in "On the Logical Positivists' Theory of Truth," in *Analysis* 2 (4) (1934/1935).

Russell's views on basic statements can be found in *The Analysis of Mind* (London: Allen and Unwin, 1921) and *An Inquiry into Meaning and Truth* (London, 1940).

Ayer's contributions to this topic include the following: *Language, Truth and Logic* (London: Gollancz, 1936; 2nd ed., 1946), Ch. 5 and Sec. 1 of introduction to 2nd ed.; "Verification and Experience," in *PAS* 37; *Foundations of Empirical Knowledge* (London: Macmillan, 1940), Ch. 2; "Basic Propositions," in *Philosophical Analysis*, edited by Max Black (Ithaca, NY: Cornell University Press, 1950), reprinted in *Philosophical Essays* (London: Macmillan, 1954); and *The Problem of Knowledge* (London: Macmillan, 1956).

Relevant works by Karl Popper are *The Logic of Scientific Discovery* (New York: Basic, 1959), especially Ch. 5, and *Conjectures and Refutations* (New York: Basic, 1962).

Further discussion of Quine's views may be found in "Two Dogmas of Empiricism," in *Philosophical Review* (1951), reprinted in *From a Logical Point of View* (Cambridge, MA: Harvard University Press, 1953); *Methods of Logic* (London: Routledge and Paul, 1952), introduction; and *Word and Object* (New York: Wiley, 1960), Secs. 8–10.

OTHER RECOMMENDED TITLES

Alston, William. *The Reliability of Sense Perception*. Ithaca, NY: Cornell University Press, 1993.

Audi, Robert. *The Structure of Justification*. Cambridge, U.K.: Cambridge University Press, 1993.

BonJour, Laurence. *The Structure of Empirical Knowledge*. Cambridge, MA: Harvard University Press, 1985.

Chisholm, Roderick. *The Foundations of Knowing*. Minneapolis: University of Minnesota Press, 1982.

Chisholm, Roderick. *Theory of Knowledge*. Englewood Cliffs, NJ: Prentice-Hall, 1966; 2nd ed., 1977; 3rd ed., 1989.

DePaul, Michael, ed. *Resurrecting Old-Fashioned Foundationalism*. Lanham, MD: Rowman & Littlefield, 2001.

Foley, Richard. *The Theory of Epistemic Rationality*. Cambridge, MA: Harvard University Press, 1987.

Fumerton, Richard. *Metaphysical and Epistemological Problems of Perception*. Lincoln: University of Nebraska Press, 1985.

Haack, Susan. *Evidence and Inquiry: Towards Reconstruction in Epistemology*. Oxford: Blackwell, 1993.

Moser, Paul K. *Knowledge and Evidence*. New York: Cambridge Unversity Press, 1989.

Putnam, Hilary. "'Two Dogmas' Revisited." In *Realism and Reason, Philosophical Papers*. Vol. 3. Cambridge, U.K.: Cambridge University Press, 1983.

Sellars, Wilfrid. "Givenness and Explanatory Coherence." *Journal of Philosophy* 70 (1973): 612–624.

Sosa, Ernest. *Knowledge in Perspective: Selected Essays in Epistemology*. Cambridge, U.K.: Cambridge University Press, 1991.

Van Cleve, James. "Foundationalism, Epistemic Principles, and the Cartesian Circle." *Philosophical Review* 88 (1979): 55–91.

Wittgenstein, Ludwig. *On Certainty,* edited by G. E. M. Anscombe and G. H. von Wright. Oxford: Blackwell, 1969.

R. W. Ashby (1967)
Bibliography updated by Benjamin Fiedor (2005)

BATAILLE, GEORGES
(1897–1962)

Georges Bataille is a pivotal thinker in the history of twentieth-century thought, in a literal sense. His work serves as a pivot between any number of significant early twentieth-century trends, and later movements such as postmodernism and deconstruction.

The extremely eclectic Bataille was first, and perhaps most deeply, influenced by the Marquis de Sade. This scandalous thinker had an enormous impact on avant-garde French thought of the post-World War I period, most notably among the surrealists and their followers. Bataille, loosely associated with and against the surrealists, appropriated from Sade the notion of a violent, merciless natural order, and of man as a mimic of the destructive (and hence reconstructive) power of nature through the boundless expression of destructive sexual impulses. Bataille, like Sade, while a proclaimed atheist, nevertheless linked man's necessary violence to the blaspheming of God; in this way God, though denied, is in a strange way revived through the necessity of his transgression. (See early texts by Bataille, such as "The Solar Anus" [1927], and "The Use Value of D. A. F. de Sade [An Open Letter to My Current Comrades]" in *Visions of Excess* [1985]).

Bataille went on in the early 1930s to link Sade with the contemporary French anthropological theories of Marcel Mauss and Emile Durkheim. Both of these early twentieth-century thinkers hoped to find in primitive thought the kind of energy (social effervescence) whose absence led to the anomie, the rootlessness and pointlessness, of modern life. For Durkheim this energy was to be found in *mana,* the enthusiasm of crowds coming together; for Mauss, it was found in the rituals of gift-giving and ritualized destructions (such as the potlatch festivals of Northwest American Indians) of traditional societies. Both thinkers held that the basis for this social ritual was fundamentally rational: the energy of crowds and collective festivals was ultimately based on the peaceful tendency of people to recognize themselves as human. Mauss held that gift-giving, implemented as a major feature of modern economies, could counter the alienating tendencies of self-centered bourgeois economies. Bataille

took this model and radicalized it to the extent that he held that gift-giving, crowds, and ritual destruction were energizing to the extent that they were irrational: A person's fundamental tendency was to expend (*dépenser*), and this urge, while making possible the full social experience, nevertheless put in question the stability and comfort of human life, not to mention the sacred integrity of the human person (so beloved by Durkheim). Expenditure, in this sense, was the affirmation of life to the point of the risk of death, and the Sadean affirmation of a "general economy" based not on saving and reinvestment, but on the extravagant squandering of wealth. (See "The Notion of Expenditure" [1932] in *Visions of Excess*, and *The Accursed Share* [1949]).

Throughout the 1930s and 1940s Bataille was at the vanguard of the French reception of Friedrich Nietzsche and G. W. F. Hegel. From Nietzsche, Bataille took the assertion of the death of God as a radical embrace of death, an apocalyptic, erotic moment. Nietzsche for Bataille is a lighthearted leap into the moment when God affirms his own nonexistence: the point at which the sacred is an affirmation not of conservation and reuse (the eternity of divinity), but the night of sacrificial oblivion. Out of this "left-hand" sacred, Bataille evolves a practice of mystical meditation based not on a communion with an ever-present God, but on the ecstatic horror of his definitive absence. For Bataille, this mystical practice is inseparable from the impossible task of writing it: this results in such fragmentary works as *Inner Experience* (1943), *Guilty* (1944) and *On Nietzsche* (1945).

Bataille's reading of Hegel is similarly unusual and arguably mistaken: following and rewriting Alexandre Kojève's Hegel, Bataille's version posits the end of history as a moment in which absolute knowledge turns and tries to incorporate the radical negativity on which it depends (through exclusion) in order to be complete. Rational, recoverable negativity can only be determined as recoverable in opposition to a more fundamental negativity that refuses all use, all constructive effort, all knowledge. Yet to be truly posthistorical, this negativity must finally be (impossibly) appropriated. To be Hegel all the way, one must recognize a negativity that by definition is unrecognizable: what Bataille called "not-knowing." Without this gesture one has not fully attained the "end of History"; with it, one is condemned to a circular agitation in which one's knowledge is incessantly lost in the oblivion of not-knowing. Negativity now, at the end, is a toxic form of *dépense*; at the same time, Hegel is nevertheless maintained to the extent that his philosophy is followed through, mimed, and not so much negated as always-again affirmed in its loss, its madness (Bataille believed Hegel became mad at the moment he fully realized the consequences of the "end of History"). On this topic, see the "Hegel" section of *Inner Experience* (1943), and Bataille's short novel *Madame Edwarda* (1941).

Finally, in Bataille's writings on eroticism, he comes to see the expenditure of human limits in erotic contact; this "communication," as he called it, entails a community (of lovers) through the risk of the limits of the self. In this way Bataille revised the radical sexualized selfishness put forward by Sade: for Bataille "communication" is above all an act of generosity, if not a moral act. (See *Erotism*, 1957).

Bataille's eclectic rewriting of these major strands of French thought—moving in genres as diverse as sociological essays, mystical meditations, pornographic novels, and economic treatises—has had an enormous influence on French thought of the post-existentialist period. Two examples: Derrida's method of deconstruction, which involves not the refutation of a given work but rather the close following of that work and its steady disarticulation, all the while recognizing that the work of metaphysics cannot be escaped, but only endlessly repeated and deconstructed, owes much to the Bataillean reading of Hegel—indeed Derrida's reading of Bataille's Hegel may be seen as the model of the deconstructive project. Similarly, Foucault's affirmation of a "counter-discourse" in which a full, coherent discourse is destabilized by the discourse it must violently expel in order to constitute itself, clearly owes much to Bataille. Bataille, however, surpasses his recent avatars in his insistence on a political implementation of *dépense*; whereas Derrida, for example, is happy to rewrite Bataille's "general economy" as a "general writing"—thereby shifting the debate to an analysis of largely textual questions—Bataille insists on the need to rethink the future of society in ways that foresee a future economy based not on the profit motive but on the implementation of a global and orgiastic "spending without return."

See also Deconstruction; Derrida, Jacques; Durkheim, Émile; Foucault, Michel; Hegel, Georg Wilhelm Friedrich; Nietzsche, Friedrich; Postmodernism; Violence.

Bibliography

WORKS BY BATAILLE

Erotism. Translated by Mary Dalwood. New York: Marion Boyars, 1987.

Guilty. Translated by Bruce Boone. Introduction by Denis Hollier. Venice, CA: Lapis Press, 1988.

Inner Experience. Translated and introduced by Leslie Ann Boldt. Albany, NY: SUNY Press, 1988.

Madame Edwarda. Paris: Pauvert, 1966.

On Nietzsche. Translated by Bruce Boone. Introduction by Sylvère Lotringer. New York: Paragon House, 1994.

The Accursed Share. Translated by Robert Hurley. New York: Zone Books, 1988.

Visions of Excess: Selected Writings, 1927–1939, edited by Allan Stoekl. Translated by Allan Stoekl, with Carl Lovitt and Donald M. Leslie, Jr. Minneapolis: University of Minnesota Press, 1985.

WORKS ABOUT BATAILLE

Derrida, Jacques. "From Restricted to General Economy: A Hegelianism without Reserve." In *Writing and Difference*. Translated by Alan Bass, 251–277. Chicago: University of Chicago Press, 1978.

Foucault, Michel. "A Preface to Transgression." In *Language, Countermemory, Practice*, edited by Donald F. Bouchard. Translated by Sherry Simon, 29–52. Ithaca, NY: Cornell University Press, 1977.

Foucault, Michel. *The Order of Discourse*. Translated by Ian McLeod. In *Untying the Text: A Post-Structuralist Reader*, edited by Robert Young, 48–78. Boston: Routledge, 1981.

Gemerchak, Christopher M. *The Sunday of the Negative: Reading Bataille, Reading Hegel*. Albany, NY: SUNY Press, 2003.

Hegarty, Paul. *Georges Bataille: Core Cultural Theorist*. London: SAGE, 2000.

Allan Stoekl (2005)

BATTEUX, ABBÉ CHARLES
(1713–1780)

In the history of aesthetic ideas, the abbot Charles Batteux was less of an innovator than an apt synthesizer of prevailing ideas and a late defender of the classical theory of imitation in the new field of taste and aesthetic experience. Nonetheless, *Les beaux-arts réduits à un même principe* (The fine arts reduced to a single principle; 1746/1969) is generally thought to have provided the first modern classification of the fine arts. In all of his undertakings, Batteux sought to submit the fine arts—as opposed to the practical arts, which seek to fulfill various needs—to a single principle, "both simple and wide-reaching" (Foreword, *Les beaux-arts réduits à un même principe*), that could explain all varieties of art. In keeping with the classical theory of poetry and art, this principle is that art should imitate *la belle nature* (beautiful nature, including human actions and passions) to produce aesthetic pleasure. In other words, the *goal* of the fine arts is *pleasure*, their *essential characteristic* is *imitation*, and their *subject* is *la belle nature*. The *manner* in which this imitation is done makes for the *particular differences* of the various art forms: poetry, painting, sculpture, dance, and music. On this basis, Batteux divided the inquiry conducted in *Les beaux-arts* into three parts. First, he identified the nature of all art forms and their essential differences. Second, he examined the nature of taste as a way of evaluating *la belle nature*. Third, to verify his theory by practice, he proposed a detailed typology of the fine arts.

Batteux first tried to clarify what it means for the fine arts to imitate *la belle nature*. Three aspects of this process deserve to be highlighted: imitation as such, the process of idealization that presides over the production of *la belle nature* in art, and the function of genius in producing works of art. First, art, as the product of genius's activity, works by imitating. Yet all imitation finds its raison d'être and its limits in the model that goes before it. Poetic and artistic invention is therefore not creating per se but rather reproducing what already exists. The function of art is to re-present its subject in a medium. Imitations must nevertheless *appear* to be nature. Perfection in the arts being based on resemblance, falling back on the purely formal (or purely aesthetic) properties of the aesthetic medium seems inadmissible for Batteux.

Second, in the Aristotelian tradition to which Batteux was explicitly connected, what the fine arts imitate is not nature as it truly is, but *la belle nature*, or nature as it *should be* as a result of idealization. In contrast with history, which simply presents the facts and strives to speak the truth, the fine arts present the ideal and strive for verisimilitude. They aspire, through selective representation of the real, to the perfection of the type. Painting and poetry are born with history, but the invention that is their own aims at drawing human actions together in a new and more coherent totality that brings out their meaning.

Third, only an artist of genius in a state of enthusiasm can produce true imitation of *la belle nature*. Far from being an occult faculty, enthusiasm, for Batteux, complements the spirit of observation. It designates the moment when the artist's spirit warms up at the sight of a vivid representation stemming from his imagination.

Although his theory of the imitation of *la belle nature* anchors Batteux's thought in the classical tradition, his theory of taste tends to bring together newer aesthetic tendencies that were forming during his era. Artistic genius is subject not to predetermined rules but to taste, which he defined as the "faculty of appreciating the good, the bad, and the mediocre, and of distinguish-

ing among them" (Batteux [1746] 1969). Far from opposing the intelligence at work in the sciences, taste (which in its largest sense is essentially moral) always presupposes knowledge, to which feeling is added to motivate action or give rise to desire. In strictly artistic taste, sentiment, preceded by a knowledge of the qualities of an object, "tells us if the *la belle Nature* is well or poorly imitated" (Batteux [1746] 1969).

We can see to what extent ethics and aesthetics are intertwined: On the one hand, *la belle nature* that art imitates conforms to principles of taste to move individuals (in other words, it is directly connected with our general moral interests as human beings). On the other hand, it conforms to our cognitive nature, providing our minds with an exercise and movement that widens our sphere of ideas. Batteux considers the spectacle of human actions and human passions to be the primary subject of *la belle nature* represented, or rather engendered, by art. The ideal of artistic imitation associates the good (which corresponds with our universal moral interests), the beautiful (which satisfies our cognitive expectations of variety, uniformity, and novelty in the artistic representation), and the perfection of formal aspects of the work itself.

See also Aesthetics, History of; Aristotelianism; Art, Representation in; Pleasure.

Bibliography

WORKS BY BATTEUX

Les beaux-arts réduits à un même principe (1746). Geneva: Slatkine Reprints, 1969.
Principes de la littérature (5th ed., 1774). Geneva: Slatkine Reprints, 1967.

WORK ON BATTEUX

Saint-Girons, Baldine. *Esthétiques du 18e siècle: Le modèle français*. Paris: Philippe Sers, 1990.

Daniel Dumouchel (2005)

BAUDRILLARD, JEAN
(1929–)

Jean Baudrillard was born in the cathedral town of Reims, France. His grandparents were peasants, his parents became civil servants, and he was the first member of his family to pursue an advanced education. In 1956, he began working as a professor of secondary education in a French high school (Lyceé) and in the early 1960s did editorial work for the French publisher Seuil. Trained as a Germanist, Baudrillard translated German literary works—including Bertolt Brecht and Peter Weiss—

although he turned to the study of sociology and for some decades was a sociology professor at Nanterre.

Baudrillard became renowned for his theorizations of developments in contemporary society, including the trajectories of the consumer society, media and technology, cyberspace and the information society, and biotechnology. He claimed that cumulatively these forces had produced a postmodern rupture with modern culture and society. Whereas modern societies for Baudrillard were organized around production and political economy, postmodern societies were organized around technology and generated new forms of culture, experience, and subjectivities.

Baudrillard's work is extremely hard to categorize because he combines social theory, cultural and political commentary, philosophy, and literary stylistics in his work, crossing boundaries between academic disciplines and fields. Yet in an interview in *Forgetting Foucault* (1987, p. 84) he confessed: "Well, let's be frank here. If I ever dabbled in anything in my theoretical infancy, it was philosophy more than sociology. I don't think at all in those terms. My point of view is completely metaphysical. If anything, I'm a metaphysician, perhaps a moralist, but certainly not a sociologist. The only 'sociological' work I can claim is my effort to put an end to the social, to the concept of the social."

Indeed, beginning in the 1980s, more philosophical themes emerged in his work, although in a highly ironical and paradoxical form. Baudrillard's proliferating metaphysical speculations are evident in *Fatal Strategies* (1990), which can be seen as a turning to a sort of idiosyncratic philosophical musings. This text presented a bizarre metaphysical scenario concerning the triumph of objects over subjects within the obscene proliferation of an object world so completely out of control that it surpasses all attempts to understand, conceptualize, and control it. His scenario concerns the proliferation and growing supremacy of objects over subjects and the eventual triumph of the object.

For Baudrillard, the subject—the darling of modern philosophy—is defeated in his metaphysical scenario and the object triumphs, a stunning end to the dialectic of subject and object that had been the framework of modern philosophy. In *Fatal Strategies* and succeeding writings, Baudrillard seems to be taking theory into the realm of metaphysics, but it is a specific type of metaphysics deeply inspired by the pataphysics developed by Alfred Jarry in "What is Pataphysics" as "the science of the realm beyond metaphysics. ... It will study the laws which govern exceptions and will explain the universe supplemen-

tary to this one; or, less ambitiously, it will describe a universe which one can see—must see perhaps—instead of the traditional one. ..." (1963, p. 131ff.)

Like the universe in Jarry's play *Ubu Roi*, *The Gestures and Opinions of Doctor Faustroll*, and other literary texts, Baudrillard's is a totally absurd universe where objects rule in mysterious ways, and people and events are governed by absurd and ultimately unknowable interconnections and predestination. (The French playwright Eugene Ionesco is another good source of entry to this universe.) Like Jarry's pataphysics, Baudrillard's universe is ruled by surprise, reversal, hallucination, blasphemy, obscenity, and a desire to shock and outrage.

Thus, in view of the growing supremacy of the object, Baudrillard recommends abandoning the subject and siding with the object. Pataphysics aside, it seems that Baudrillard is trying to end the philosophy of subjectivity that has controlled French thought since Descartes by going over to the other side. Descartes's *malin genie*, his evil genius, was a ruse of the subject that tried to seduce him into accepting what was not clear and distinct, but over which he was ultimately able to prevail. Baudrillard's "evil genius" is the object itself that is much more malign than the merely epistemological deceptions of the subject faced by Descartes and which constitutes a "fatal destiny" that demands the end of the philosophy of subjectivity. Henceforth, for Baudrillard, people live in the era of the reign of the object.

Examples of the paradoxical and ironic style of Baudrillard's philosophical musings abound in *The Perfect Crime* (1996). Baudrillard claims that the negation of a higher and transcendent reality in the current media and technological society is a "perfect crime" that involves the destruction of the real. In a world of appearance, image, and illusion, Baudrillard suggests, reality disappears although its traces continue to nourish an illusion of the real. Driven toward virtualization in a high-tech society, all the imperfections of human life and the world are eliminated in virtual reality, but this is the elimination of reality itself, the Perfect Crime. This "post-critical" and "catastrophic" state of affairs render our previous conceptual world irrelevant, Baudrillard suggests, urging criticism to turn ironic and transform the demise of the real into an art form.

Baudrillard has entered a world of thought far from academic philosophy, one that puts in question traditional modes of thought and discourse. His search for new philosophical perspectives has won him a loyal global audience, but also criticism for his excessive irony, word play, and philosophical games. Yet his work stands as a provocation to traditional and contemporary philosophy that challenges thinkers to address old philosophical problems such as truth and reality in new ways in the contemporary world.

See also Structuralism and Post-structuralism.

Bibliography

Jarry, Alfred. *The Ubu Plays.* New York: Grove Press, 1969.
Jarry, Alfred. "What Is Pataphysics?" *Evergreen Review* 4 (13)(1963): 131–151.

WORKS BY BAUDRILLARD

Simulations. New York: Semiotext(e), 1983.
Forgetting Foucault. New York: Semiotext(e), 1987.
Fatal Strategies. New York: Semiotext(e), 1990.
Symbolic Exchange and Death. London: Sage, 1993.
The Perfect Crime. London: Verso, 1996.

WORKS ON BAUDRILLARD

Genosko, Gary. *Baudrillard and Signs.* London: Routledge, 1994.
Kellner, Douglas, ed. *Jean Baudrillard: A Critical Reader.* Oxford: Basil Blackwell, 1994.
Kellner, Douglas. *Jean Baudrillard: From Marxism to Postmodernism and Beyond.* Cambridge and Palo Alto: Polity Press and Stanford University Press, 1989.

Douglas Kellner (2005)

BAUER, BRUNO
(1809–1882)

Bruno Bauer, the German theologian and historian, studied theology under P. H. Marheineke in Berlin, at the height of Georg Wilhelm Friedrich Hegel's influence there. When Bauer became a docent at the University of Berlin in 1834, he joined Marheineke on the Hegelian right wing. When he transferred to the University of Bonn in 1839, however, he was already reacting theologically against right-wing Hegelianism. D. F. Strauss's *Life of Jesus* (1835–1836) rocked the theological world, but it seemed to Bauer not sufficiently critical, and helped to spur him on to his own investigations of the Gospels.

Bauer began with literary criticism of the Gospel texts themselves, without making any assumptions about the historical life of Jesus or the early church. The fourth Gospel was simply a work of reflective Christian art dominated by Philo's logos concept, impressive as such, but without historical basis (*Kritik der evangelischen Geschichte des Johannes,* Bremen, 1840). The situation was the same with regard to the Synoptic Gospels, except that they were based on the conception of the Messiah (*Kritik der evangelischen Geschichte der Synoptiker,* 3 vols. Leipzig, 1841–1842.) Bauer adopted the conclusion of C. H. Weisse and C. Wilke that only Mark's Gospel was original, but argued further that there was no reason to assume any historical tradition behind this single literary source. Incongruities in Mark's text suggested that Mark had invented the events he related. Mark's story was accepted because it answered the spiritual needs of his age. Jesus was the man in whose consciousness the antitheses between heaven and earth, God and man, were reconciled. His character evoked the Messiah concept, into which his life was absorbed by Mark. Bauer's view seemed to undercut the historical basis of Christianity so sharply that the theological faculties of the Prussian universities were polled (with mixed results) as to whether Bauer should be dismissed from Bonn. Bauer sealed his fate with the article "Theological Shamelessness" (1814), in which he denounced the Christian faith as the source of lies and servile hypocrisy; he was dismissed in March 1842. Ultimately, Bauer denied the historicity of Jesus altogether, holding that Christianity was an amalgam of Stoic and Gnostic ideas in Jewish dress.

Meanwhile, Bauer had written his anonymous *Die Posaune des jüngsten Gerichts über Hegel den Atheisten und Antichristen* (Trumpet of the last judgment on Hegel the atheist and Antichrist, Leipzig, 1841), ostensibly from the standpoint of faith, attempting to show that the real result of Hegelian philosophy was neither the pantheism of Strauss nor the humanism of Ludwig Feuerbach—much less a defense of the Gospel—but Bauer's own out-and-out atheism.

At that time living on a small estate in Rixdorf, near Berlin, Bauer gathered around himself a circle of "free spirits" (including his brother Edgar) who frequented Berlin cafes. Bauer wrote brilliantly ironical "critiques" of recent historical developments in which he announced the downfall of Western philosophy and culture. For a time he collaborated with Arnold Ruge and with other left-wing Hegelians. But Bauer was as contemptuous of their revolutionary programs as he was of the bourgeois establishment. He attacked the inconsistencies and misconceptions of both groups; special class interests, he argued, are blindly one-sided, and the masses are so much dead matter, and inimical to the spirit. Only criticism, without presupposition, reservation, or special pleading, can be pure, can replace blindness with true conceptions, and can bring about the fundamental change in human consciousness that would really be liberating. History will, by its own "logic," bring about the transformation which no deliberate program can institute: what criticism has destroyed in thought today, history will destroy in fact tomorrow. Bauer justified these views by means of a metaphysic of consciousness, according to which the world is the projection of the ego. Matter is the as yet unclarified aspect of the world; evil social conditions are the product of uncritical and self-alienated principles. Christianity, for example, freed the ego from its thralldom to the material world, but only through an alienation of spirit from matter that had in its turn created a new burden. But Bauer held that once Christianity's historical roots are exposed, its self-alienating power is broken; hence the importance of criticism. The same must be done with other forms of human bondage: revolutionary programs which do not reach to the roots of consciousness are futile.

Accordingly, Bauer attacked various reform movements as insufficiently radical. Jewish agitation for political rights, for example, was based on the separate religious identity of the Jew, and could never be defended on those grounds against those whose religious prejudices took a different form; the Jew could become free only by ceasing to be religious. Karl Marx answered this argument in his essay "On the Jewish Problem" (1844), and attacked Bauer as "St. Bruno" in *The Holy Family: Critique of the Critical Critic, against Bruno Bauer and Consorts* (1845). The real problem, according to Marx, was economic class behavior, and not the religious projections of that behavior. Bauer's view that social conditions could be changed by changing men's minds was a vestige of idealist-theological error, and the practical result of Bauer's theoretical radicalism would be political reactionism.

Bauer did in fact become a defender of Prussian conservatism, on the radical grounds that limited reform movements seemed to him to do more harm than good. But after 1850 his influence waned; though he continued to write prodigiously, his views were generally too eccentric to be relevant.

See also Conservatism; Feuerbach, Ludwig Andreas; Hegel, Georg Wilhelm Friedrich; Hegelianism; Marx, Karl; Philo Judaeus; Strauss, David Friedrich.

Bibliography

ADDITIONAL WORKS BY BAUER

Vollständige Geschichte der Parteikämpfe in Deutschland während der Jahre 1842–1846, 3 vols. Charlottenburg, Germany: E. Bauer, 1847.

Die bürgerliche Revolution in Deutschland seit dem Anfang der deutsche-katholischen Bewegung bis zur Gegenwart. Berlin: G. Hempel, 1849.
Russland und das Germanentum. Berlin: n.p., 1853.
Die Hegelsche Linke. Edited by Karl Löwith. Stuttgart and Bad Cannstatt: F. Frommann, 1962. Includes *Die Posaune* and selections from *Russland und das Germanentum*.
Christus und die Cäsaren, der Ursprung des Christentums aus dem römischen Griechentum. Berlin: E. Grosser, 1877.

WORKS ON BAUER

Hertz-Eichenrode, Dieter. *Der Junghegelianer Bruno Bauer im Vormärz*. Berlin: n.p., 1959.
Hook, Sidney. *From Hegel to Marx*. New York: Reynal and Hitchcock, 1936. Pp. 89–125.
Löwith, Karl. *Von Hegel zu Nietzsche*, 4th ed. Stuttgart, 1958. Pp. 120–125; 322–324; 366–374. For an extensive bibliography see pp. 432–433.
Schweitzer, Albert. *Geschichte des Leben-Jesu-Forschung*. Tübingen, 1926. Pp. 141–161. Translated from the first German edition, *Von Reimarus zu Wrede* (1906), by W. Montgomery under the title *The Quest of the Historical Jesus*. London, 1910. Pp. 137–160. Reprinted, New York: Macmillan, 1950.

Stephen D. Crites (1967)

BAUMGARTEN, ALEXANDER GOTTLIEB
(1714–1762)

Alexander Gottlieb Baumgarten, the German Wolffian philosopher and aesthetician, was born in Berlin. He was the son of an assistant to the Pietist theologian and pedagogue August Hermann Francke; his brother was the famous divine and church historian Sigmund Jakob. Baumgarten studied philosophy and theology at Halle. After receiving a master's degree in 1735, he was appointed a teacher at Halle and in 1738 became extraordinary professor. While teaching there, Baumgarten, in reaction against the Pietism dominant at Halle after the expulsion of Christian Wolff in 1723, reintroduced Wolffian philosophy. In 1740 he was appointed full professor at Frankfurt an der Oder, where he remained until his death.

Baumgarten's Latin handbooks on metaphysics, ethics, and practical philosophy were widely used in German universities both in his time and after his death, and his influence was extraordinary. Kant considered him to be one of the greatest metaphysicians of his time and adopted his *Metaphysics* and *Practical Philosophy* as textbooks for his own lectures at Königsberg. With the exception of his works on aesthetics, Baumgarten in general kept very close to Wolff's teachings, although he dissented from Wolff on several special points. For instance, he adopted a middle position in the controversy over the problem of the interaction of substances by reconciling Wolff's theory of the "preestablished harmony" of the soul and body with the theory of physical influence supported by the Pietists. Baumgarten, as a supporter of Leibnizian panpsychism, applied his solution to the connections among all substances. Wolff, to the contrary, distinguished very sharply between spiritual and material substances. Baumgarten was thus less Leibnizian than Wolff in accepting physical influence and more Leibnizian in his panpsychism.

Baumgarten made his most important contributions in the field of aesthetics, expanding a subject that had been summarily treated by Wolff and going far beyond Wolff in developing it. In this field he collaborated so closely with his pupil G. F. Meier (1718–1777) that it is difficult to establish the real authorship of many doctrines. There is a very close connection between Baumgarten's *Meditationes Philosophicae de Nonnullis ad Poema Pertinentibus* and his unfinished *Aesthetica* and Meier's *Anfangsgründe aller schönen Künste und Wissenschaften* (3 vols., Halle, 1748–1750). Baumgarten introduced the term *aesthetics* to designate that section of empirical psychology which treats of the inferior faculty, that is, the faculty of sensible knowledge. The problem of beauty was only one part of this subject. Even in Kant, *aesthetics* referred both to sensible knowledge in general and to knowledge of beauty and the sublime in particular. Only later was it restricted to the field of beauty and sublimity. Aesthetics and logic together composed, in Baumgarten's view, a science that he called *gnoseology*, or theory of knowledge.

According to Baumgarten, the foundations of poetry and the fine arts are "sensitive (*sensitivae*) representations," which are not simply "sensual" (*sensuales*), but are connected with feeling (and therefore are pertinent both to the faculty of knowledge and to that of will). A beautiful poem is a "perfect sensitive discourse," that is, a discourse that awakens a lively feeling. This requires a high degree of "extensive clarity," which is different from "intensive (or intellectual) clarity." This means that an aesthetic representation must have many "characteristics," that is, it must be characterized by many different traits or particular elements, rather than by a few well-differentiated characters. Beauty must be "confused" and, therefore, excludes "distinctness," the main property of intellectual representations. Distinctness is reached by rendering clearly each of the characteristics of the characteristics of a representation. Establishing these charac-

teristics presupposes intensive clarity and leads to a further abstraction of the concept of representations. This abstraction is obnoxious to aesthetic liveliness and leads to pedantry.

The artist is not an imitator of nature in the sense that he copies it: He must add feeling to reality, and thereby he imitates nature in the process of creating a world or a whole. This whole is unified by the artist through a coherent "theme," which is the focus of the representation.

This does not mean that the artist should prefer fiction to truth; on the contrary, knowledge of the beautiful is, at its best, sensible knowledge of truth made perfectly lively. This is a main point of divergence between Wolff and Baumgarten. Baumgarten held that, since rational knowledge of several orders of facts or of many facts in general is impossible, it must be replaced or supplemented by "beautiful knowledge," that is, reliable sensible knowledge of things that cannot be known rationally; such knowledge is as reliable as rational knowledge; typical aesthetic elements of the cognitive process are inductions and examples. By stressing the importance and relative independence of the inferior faculty (which Wolff held to be only an imperfect stage of knowledge, to be superseded by intellect and reason), Baumgarten foreshadowed Immanuel Kant's doctrine of the peculiar and independent function of sensibility in knowledge.

See also Aesthetics, History of; Aesthetics, Problems of; Kant, Immanuel; Leibniz, Gottfried Wilhelm; Meier, Georg Friedrich; Panpsychism; Pietism; Wolff, Christian.

Bibliography

WORKS BY BAUMGARTEN

Meditationes Philosophicae de Nonnullis ad Poema Pertinentibus. Halle, 1735. Translated by K. Aschenbrunner and W. B. Hoelther, eds., as *Reflections on Poetry.* Berkeley, CA, 1954.

Metaphysica. Halle, 1739.

Ethica Philosophica. Halle, 1740.

Aesthetica, 2 vols. Frankfurt an der Oder, 1750–1758.

Initia Philosophiae Practicae Primae. Halle, 1760.

Acroasis Logica. Halle, 1761.

Ius Naturae. Halle, 1765.

Sciagraphia Encyclopaediae Philosophicae. Edited by J. C. Förster. Halle, 1769.

Philosophia Generalis. Edited by J. C. Förster. Halle, 1769.

WORKS ON BAUMGARTEN

Abbt, Thomas. *A. G. Baumgartens Leben und Charakter.* Halle: C.H. Hemmerde, 1765.

Bergmann, Ernst. *Die Begründung der deutschen Aesthetik durch A. G. Baumgarten und G. F. Meier.* Leipzig, 1911.

Cassirer, Ernst. *Die Philosophie der Aufklärung.* Tübingen: Mohr, 1932. Translated by F. C. A. Koelln and James D. Pettegrove as *The Philosophy of the Enlightenment.* Princeton, NJ, 1954. Pp. 338–357.

Meier, G. F. *A. G. Baumgartens Leben und Schriften.* Halle, 1763.

Poppe, B. *A. G. Baumgarten, seine Bedeutung und seine Stellung in der Leibniz-Wolffschen Philosophie und seine Beziehung zu Kant.* Münster, 1907.

Riemann, A. *Die Ästhetik A. G. Baumgartens.* Halle: M. Niemeyer, 1928.

ON BAUMGARTEN'S RELATION TO KANT

Bäumler, A. *Kants Kritik der Urteilskraft.* Halle, 1923.

Tonelli, Giorgio. "Kant, dall'estetica metafisica all'estetica psicoempirica." *Memorie della Accademia delle Scienze di Torino* series 3, Vol. 3, Pt. 2.

Giorgio Tonelli (1967)

BAYES, BAYES' THEOREM, BAYESIAN APPROACH TO PHILOSOPHY OF SCIENCE

The posthumous publication, in 1763, of Thomas Bayes's "Essay Towards Solving a Problem in the Doctrine of Chances" inaugurated a revolution in the understanding of the confirmation of scientific hypotheses—two hundred years later. Such a long period of neglect, followed by such a sweeping revival, ensured that it was the inhabitants of the latter half of the twentieth century above all who determined what it was to take a "Bayesian approach" to scientific reasoning.

Like most confirmation theorists, Bayesians alternate between a descriptive and a prescriptive tone in their teachings: They aim both to describe how scientific evidence is assessed and to prescribe how it ought to be assessed. This double message will be made explicit at some points, but passed over quietly elsewhere.

SUBJECTIVE PROBABILITY

The first of the three fundamental tenets of Bayesianism is that the scientist's epistemic attitude to any scientifically significant proposition is, or ought to be, exhausted by the subjective probability the scientist assigns to the proposition. A subjective probability is a number between zero and one that reflects in some sense the scientist's confidence that the proposition is true. (Subjective probabilities are sometimes called degrees of belief or credences.)

A scientist's subjective probability for a proposition is then more a psychological fact about the scientist than an observer-independent fact about the proposition. Roughly, it is not a matter of how likely the truth of the proposition actually is, but about how likely the scientist thinks it to be. Thus *subjective*—though in hindsight, *psychological* might have been a better term.

Unlike every other approach to confirmation theory, Bayesianism has no use for the notion of theory acceptance: There is no amount of evidence sufficient to induce a qualitative shift in a Bayesian's epistemic attitude from not accepting to accepting a theory. Learning from the evidence is always a matter of a quantitative adjustment, of changing your subjective probability for a hypothesis to reflect the latest evidence. At any time, the most favored theories are simply those with the highest subjective probabilities.

To found its first tenet Bayesianism must establish that it is plausible to suppose or reasonable to require that scientists have a subjective probability for every proposition that figures in their inquiry. Ramsey proposed that to have a subjective probability for a proposition is to have a certain complex disposition to act, a disposition that can be measured at least tolerably well in many cases by assessing betting behavior, as follows. The higher your subjective probability for a proposition, the lower the odds, all other things being equal, you will be prepared to accept in betting on the truth of that proposition. To be precise, given a subjective probability p for the proposition, you will accept odds of up to $p:(1-p)$ on its truth—you will avoid just those bets, in other words, where you have to pay in more than p for every dollar you stand to win, so that for example if your subjective probability for the proposition is 0.3 then you will pay no more than \$3 to play per game in which you win \$10 just in case the proposition is true. Ramsey thought it likely that we have appropriately stable behavioral dispositions of this sort, accessible to measurement using the betting test, with respect to just about any proposition we understand, and so that we have subjective probabilities for all these propositions.

The Bayesian's principal tool is mathematical argument, and the mathematics in question is the probability calculus—the standard mathematics of probability—to which all subjective probabilities are assumed to conform. Conformance to the axioms is Bayesianism's second fundamental tenet.

Here the Bayesian argument tends to take a prescriptive turn. Having established that scientists have, as a matter of psychological fact, subjective probabilities for all propositions that matter, the next step is to show that scientists ought to—whether they do or not—arrange their probabilities so as to satisfy the axioms of the probability calculus.

Typically this is done by way of a Dutch Book argument, an argument that shows that, if you do not adhere to the calculus, there is a certain set of bets on the truth of various propositions that you are committed in principle to accepting, but that will lead to a certain loss however things turn out. The details of the argument are beyond the scope of this entry, but an example may help. The first axiom of the probability calculus requires that the probability of a proposition and that of its negation sum to one. Suppose you violate this axiom by assigning a probability of 0.8 both to a certain proposition h and to its negation. Then you are committed in principle to accepting odds of 4 : 1 on both h and $\neg h$, which means a commitment to playing, at the same time, two games, in one of which you pay $8 and win $10 (i.e., your original $8 plus $2 "profit") if h is true, and in one of which you pay $8 and win $10 if h is false. Whether h is true or false you pay $16 but win only $10—a certain loss. To play such a game is irrational; thus you should conform your subjective probabilities to the probability calculus. Objections to the Dutch Book argument typically turn on the vagueness of the idea that you are "committed in principle" to accepting the bets in question; replies to these objections attempt to make the nature of the commitment more precise without leavening its evident undesirability.

BAYESIAN CONDITIONALIZATION

The third of Bayesianism's three fundamental tenets is Bayes' conditionalization rule, which instructs you on how to update your subjective probabilities as the evidence arrives. There are four steps to Bayes' rule. The first step is to define prior and posterior subjective probability. These notions are relative to your receipt of a piece of evidence: Your prior probability for a hypothesis is your subjective probability for the hypothesis immediately before the evidence comes in; your posterior probability for the hypothesis is your subjective probability immediately after the evidence (and nothing else) comes in. Bayes' rule gives you a formula for calculating your posterior probabilities for every hypothesis given your prior probabilities and the nature of the evidence. In so doing it offers itself as the complete story as to how to take evidence into account. In what follows, prior subjective probabilities are written as $C(\cdot)$, and posterior subjective probabilities as $C^+(\cdot)$.

The second step towards Bayes' rule is the introduction of the notion of conditional probability, a standard notion in probability mathematics. An example of a conditional probability is the probability of obtaining a four on a die roll, given that an even number is obtained. This probability is ⅓, since there are three equally probable ways for a die roll to be even, one of which is a four. Formally the probability of a proposition h conditional on another proposition g is written $C(h|g)$; it is usually defined to be $C(hg)/C(g)$. (Alternatively conditional probability may be taken as a primitive, as explained in the entry on Probability and Chance.)

The third step is to make the following simple posit about conditionalization: when you receive a piece of evidence e, you should update your probability for any given hypothesis h so that it is equal to your prior probability for h given e. That is, on learning that e is true, you should set your posterior probability $C^+(h)$ equal to your prior probability $C(h|e)$. This is Bayes' rule in its simplest form, but one further step will produce a more familiar, and revealing, version of the rule.

The fourth and final step is to notice a simple mathematical consequence of the definition of conditional probability, confusingly called Bayes' theorem (confusing because Bayes' theorem and Bayes' rule are two quite different propositions). According to Bayes' theorem,

$$C(h|e) = \frac{C(e|h)}{C(e)}\, C(h).$$

Combine Bayes' theorem and the simple form of Bayes' rule and you obtain the more familiar version of Bayes' rule:

$$C^+(h) = \frac{C(e|h)}{C(e)}\, C(h).$$

The effect of the application of Bayes' rule then—or as philosophers usually say, the effect of Bayesian conditionalization—is, on receipt of e, to multiply the old probability for h by the factor $C(e|h)/C(e)$. Call this factor the Bayesian multiplier.

What justification can be offered for Bayesian conditionalization? Since the notion of conditional probability is introduced by definition, and Bayes' theorem is a simple consequence of the definition, this amounts to the question why you ought, on learning e, to set your posterior probability for a hypothesis h equal to the prior probability $C(h|e)$.

Various arguments for conditionalizing in this way exist in the literature, often based on Dutch book considerations that invoke the notion of a conditional bet. The consensus is that none is entirely convincing. It is important to note that mathematics alone cannot settle the question: The probability calculus relates only different probabilities that are part of the same overall distribution, whereas Bayes' rule relates probabilities from two quite different distributions, the prior and posterior distributions.

Two further remarks on Bayesian conditionalization. First Bayes' rule assumes that the subjective probability of the evidence e goes to one when it is acquired, therefore that when evidence arrives, its content is exhausted by a proposition that comes to be known for sure. A natural extension of the rule, called Jeffrey conditionalization, relaxes this assumption. Second you may wonder whether background knowledge must be taken into account when conditionalizing. In fact it is automatically taken into account: Background knowledge has subjective probability one, and for any proposition k with probability one, $C(h|k) = C(h)$; thus, your subjective probability distribution always has your background knowledge in every respect "built in."

Now to discuss the implications of Bayesianism for confirmation. (Further implications will be considered below.)

The impact of evidence e on a hypothesis h is determined, recall, by the Bayesian multiplier, $C(e|h)/C(e)$, which when multiplied by the prior for h yields its posterior. You do not need any great mathematical expertise to see that, when $C(e|h)$ is greater than $C(e)$, the probability of h will increase on receipt of e, while when it is $C(e)$ that is greater, the probability of h will decrease.

When the receipt of e causes the probability of h to increase, e is said to confirm h. When it causes the probability of h to decrease, it is said to disconfirm h. This may look like a definition, but it is in fact a substantive philosophical thesis: The Bayesian claims that the preexisting notions of confirmation and disconfirmation can be given a satisfactory Bayesian analysis. (Or at least the Bayesian usually makes this claim: They also have the option of interpreting their definition as a piece of revisionism, not intended to capture our actual notion of confirmation but to replace it with something better.)

Two remarks. First to say that a hypothesis is confirmed is only to say that its probability has received some kind of upward bump. The bump may be small, and the resulting posterior probability, though higher than that prior, may be almost as small. The term *confirmed* has, in philosophical usage, a different sense from a term such as *verified*.

Second since whether or not a piece of evidence confirms a hypothesis depends on a subjective probability distribution, confirmation is in the first instance a relative matter. More on this in The Subjectivity of Bayesian Confirmation below.

One further definition: The quantity $C(e|h)$ is called a likelihood, specifically the likelihood of h on e (not to be confused with the probability of h given e, though there is a close relationship between the two, spelled out by Bayes' theorem).

The significance of the Bayesian multiplier can now be stated in natural language: A piece of evidence confirms a hypothesis relative to a particular subjective probability distribution just in case the likelihood of the hypothesis on the evidence is greater than the subjective probability for the evidence.

Consider a special case, that in which a hypothesis h entails the evidence e. By a theorem of the probability calculus the likelihood of h on e, that is, $C(e|h)$, is in any such case equal to one. Suppose that e is observed to be true. Assuming that $C(e)$ is less than one (which will be true unless all viable hypotheses predict e), then the likelihood will be greater than $C(e)$, and so h will be confirmed. Ignoring the parenthetical qualification, a hypothesis is always confirmed by its predictions. Further the more surprising the prediction, in a sense—the lower the prior probability of e—the more h will be confirmed if e is in fact observed.

The significance of this observation is limited in two ways. First some hypotheses predict evidence only with a certain probability less than one. Second hypotheses tend to make observable predictions only in conjunction with other, "auxiliary" hypotheses. The Bayesian response will be considered in the next section.

THE BAYESIAN MACHINE

Suppose you want to know whether a certain coin is fair, that is, biased neither towards "heads" nor "tails." You toss the coin ten times, obtaining exactly five "heads" and five "tails." How to conditionalize on this evidence? You will need three subjective probabilities: The prior probability for the hypothesis h that the coin is fair, the prior probability for the evidence e, and the likelihood of h on e. A good Bayesian is committed to adopting definite values for these subjective probabilities one way or another. If necessary, they will be set "by hand," that is, by some sort of reflective process that is constrained only by the axioms of the probability calculus. But a great part of the appeal of Bayesianism is that the vast majority of subjective probabilities can be set "mechanically," that is, that they will have their values fully determined once a few special probabilities are set by hand. In the case of the coin, once the prior probability for h and its rivals is set by hand, a little philosophy and mathematics of probability will take care of everything else, mechanically fixing the likelihood and the probability for the evidence.

Begin with the likelihood, the probability of getting exactly five "heads" in ten tosses given that the coin is fair. Since the fairness of the coin entails (suppose) both a physical probability for "heads" of 0.5 and the independence of the tosses, the hypothesis that the coin is fair assigns a definite physical probability to your observed outcome of five "heads"—a probability of about 0.25, as it happens. Intuitively it seems right to take this as the likelihood— to set your subjective probability $C(e|h)$, that is, equal to the physical probability that h assigns to e. In its sophisticated form this intuition is what is sometimes known as Miller's Principle or the Principal Principle; call it the Probability Coordination Principle or PCP for short. Bayesians normally take PCP on board, thus relieving you of the effort of setting a value by hand for the likelihood in a case such as this.

Now consider the probability of the evidence. A theorem of the probability calculus, the total probability theorem, looks (in one of its forms) like this:

$$C(e) = C(e|h_1)C(h_1) + C(e|h_2)C(h_2) + \cdots.$$

where the hypotheses $h_1, h_2, \ldots$ form a mutually exclusive, exhaustive set, in the sense that one and only one of them must be true. In many cases the set of hypotheses among which you are trying, with the help of e, to decide form such a set (though see below). Thus if you have set values for the likelihoods $C(e|h_i)$ and prior probabilities $C(h_i)$ for all your rival hypotheses, the probability calculus gives you a unique correct subjective probability to assign to e.

To sum up: If your rival hypotheses assign definite physical probabilities to the evidence e and form a mutually exclusive, exhaustive set then by an independent principle of rationality, PCP, and a theorem of the probability calculus, total probability, the Bayesian multipliers for all of the hypotheses are completely determined once their prior probabilities are fixed.

As a consequence, you need only assign subjective probabilities by hand to a relatively small set of propositions, and only once in your life: At the beginning, before any evidence comes in, you will assign subjective proba-

bilities to every possible scientific hypothesis. These assignments made, everything you need for Bayesian conditionalization is decided for you by PCP and the probability axioms. In this sense, Bayesian confirmation runs like a well-conditioned machine: You flip the on switch, by assigning initial prior probabilities to the different hypotheses that interest you, and then sit back and enjoy the evidential ride. (Conditionalization is also machine-like without PCP and total probability, but in that case flipping the on switch involves assigning values to $C(e|h_i)$ and $C(e)$ for every possible piece of evidence e.)

There are two obstacles to the smooth functioning of the Bayesian machine. First it may be that some or all of the rival hypotheses do not, on their own, assign a determinate physical probability to the evidence. In such cases the likelihood must either be fixed by hand, without the help of PCP or (more usually in the quantitative sciences) by supplementing the hypothesis with an auxiliary hypothesis in conjunction with which it does fix a physical probability for the evidence. In the latter case, PCP can be applied but complications arise when, as is typical, the truth of the auxiliary hypothesis is itself not known for sure. The conjunction of original and auxiliary hypothesis may be confirmed or disconfirmed mechanically, but the implication for the original hypothesis on its own— whether it is confirmed, and if so by how much—will continue to depend on handcrafted likelihoods such as $C(e|h)$. This is the Bayesian's version of confirmation theory's QuineDuhem problem. Strevens offers a partial solution to the problem. (The application of PCP will also fall through if the evidence is "inadmissible.")

Second, even when the likelihoods are fixed mechanically, the theorem of total probability may not apply if the rival hypotheses are either not mutually exclusive or not exhaustive. Lack of exhaustiveness is the more pressing worry, as it would seem to be the norm: Exhaustiveness implies that you have thought of every possible theory that predicts e to any extent—an unlikely feat. A simple fix is to include a residual hypothesis in your set to the effect that none of the other hypotheses is correct. Such a hypothesis will not however determine a definite physical probability for the evidence, so its likelihood and therefore the probability for the evidence will after all have to be fixed by hand.

BAYESIANISM AND THE PROBLEM OF INDUCTION

Does the Bayesian theory of confirmation solve the problem of induction? The case for an affirmative answer: Adherence to the tenets of Bayesianism can be justified a priori (by Dutch book arguments and the like, or so some philosophers believe). And this adherence alone is sufficient to turn you into an inductive reasoner: Once you have settled on priors for all the hypotheses, the Bayesian machinery tells you what sort of things to expect in the future given your experience of the past.

Suppose for example that you wish to predict the color of the next raven. You have various theses about raven color: All ravens are blue; ravens are green with 50% probability, otherwise black; all ravens are black, and so on. In your life to date you have observed a number of ravens, all of them black. This evidence rules out altogether some of the raven color theses, such as the thesis that all ravens are blue. (The likelihood of the blue thesis on this evidence is zero, so the multiplier is zero: Observation of a black raven therefore causes your subjective probability for the blue thesis to drop to zero.)

Other theses have their probability shifted around by the evidence in other ways. The more they probabilify the evidence, the greater their likelihoods on the evidence and so the higher their Bayesian multipliers. Observing many black ravens has the effect then of moving your subjective probability away from hypotheses that do not probabilify blackness and towards theses that do. As a result, the observation of many black ravens in the past increases your subjective probability that the next raven will be black. Thus you have an a priori argument—the argument for accepting Bayesianism—that justifies inductive behavior.

The case for a negative answer as to whether Bayesianism solves the problem of induction can be made in two ways: By arguing that the a priori arguments for adopting the Bayesian apparatus fall through, or by arguing that Bayesianism does not, after all, underwrite inductive behavior. The second approach is the more illuminating.

Return to the ravens. The theses listed above have the uniformity of nature as a consequence: If any is true then the future will be, with respect to raven color, like the past. Once some non-uniform theses are thrown into the mix, everything changes. Consider for example the following thesis, reminiscent of Goodman's grue puzzle: All ravens observed until now are black, the rest green. The Bayesian multipliers for this thesis and the thesis that all ravens are black remain the same as long as all observed ravens are black, which is to say, up until this point in time. Just as probability has been flowing to the latter hypothesis, it will have been flowing to the former. It turns out then that the probability flow is not only towards theses that predict blackness for future ravens

but also toward many others. Since the multipliers for these theses have been the same until now, your predictions about the color of ravens will favor blackness only if your initial prior probabilities—the probabilities you assigned to the different theses before any evidence came in—already favored the thesis that all ravens are black over the grue-like thesis, which is to say, only if you yourself already favored uniformity over diversity.

Many Bayesians have made their peace with Bayesianism's open-minded policy on natural uniformity. Howson argues for example that the Bayesian approach should not be considered so much a positive theory of confirmation—of how evidence bears on hypotheses—as a framework for implementing any theory of confirmation you like.

THE SUBJECTIVITY OF BAYESIAN CONFIRMATION

Suppose that the Bayesian machine is in good working order: You choose your prior probabilities for the rival hypotheses and then let the evidence, in conjunction with PCP and the total probability theorem, do the rest. Even then, with your personal input limited to no more than an assessment of the initial plausibility of the rival hypotheses, there is an unsettling element of subjectivity to the process of Bayesian confirmation, which is perhaps best brought out by the following observation: Two scientists who agree on the physical probabilities that a hypothesis h assigns to evidence e, and who follow PCP, so assigning the same value to the likelihood $C(e|h)$, may disagree on whether e confirms or disconfirms h.

To see why: e confirms h if the Bayesian multiplier is greater than one, and disconfirms it if the multiplier is less than one. The question then is whether $C(e|h)$ is greater than or less than $C(e)$. The scientists agree on $C(e|h)$, but they may have different values for $C(e)$: A scientist who assigns higher prior probabilities to hypotheses that assign higher physical probabilities to e will have a higher value for $C(e)$. It is quite possible for the two scientists priors for e to fall on either side of $C(e|h)$, in which case one will take e to confirm, the other to disconfirm, h.

A radical personalist denies that this is a problem: Why should two scientists agree on the significance of the evidence when one was expecting the evidence much more than the other? In the extreme, personalism of this sort approaches the view that Bayesian confirmation theory provides no guidance at all on assessing the significance of evidence, other than by establishing a standard of consistency; see also the discussion of induction above.

There is some objectivity underlying Bayesianism's subjectivity, however. The two scientists above will, because they agree on the likelihoods, agree on the ordering of the Bayesian multipliers. That is they will agree on which of any two hypotheses has the higher Bayesian multiplier, even though they may disagree on the size of the multipliers.

An important consequence of this agreement is a result about the convergence of opinion. When hypotheses assign physical probabilities to the evidence, as assumed here, it can be shown that as time goes on, the subjective probability distributions of any two scientists will with very high physical probability converge on the truth, or rather to the class of hypotheses empirically equivalent to the truth. (Even when the likelihoods are purely subjective, or at least only as objective as the probability calculus requires, a convergence result, albeit more limited, can be proved.)

Many Bayesians regard this convergence as ameliorating, in every important way, the subjective aspect of Bayesianism, since any disagreements among Bayesian scientists are ephemeral, while agreement lasts forever. Indeed, that Bayesianism makes some, but not too much, room for scientific dissent may not unreasonably be seen as an advantage, in both a descriptive and a prescriptive light.

Now consider a contrary view: While dissent has its place in science, it has no place in scientific inference. It is fine for scientists to disagree, at least for a time, on the plausibility of various hypotheses, but it is not at all fine that they disagree on the impact of the evidence on the hypotheses—agreement on the import of the evidence being the *sine qua non* of science. In Bayesian terms scientists may disagree on the priors for the rival hypotheses, but they had better not disagree on the Bayesian multipliers. But this is, for a Bayesian, impossible: The priors help to determine the multipliers. The usual conclusion is that there is no acceptable Bayesian theory of confirmation.

A less usual conclusion is that Bayesianism is still viable, but only if some further principle of rationality is used to constrain the prior probabilities in such a way as to determine uniquely correct values for the Bayesian multipliers. This is objectivist Bayesianism. Just as PCP is used to determine definite, objective values for the likelihoods, the objectivists suggest, so another rule might be used to determine definite, objective values for the prior probabilities of the hypotheses themselves, that is, for the subjective probabilities $C(h)$.

What principle of rationality could possibly tell you, before you have any empirical evidence whatsoever, exactly how plausible you ought to find some given scientific hypothesis? Objectivists look to the principle of indifference for the answer. That principle, discussed more fully in the entry on Probability and Chance, is in one of its guises intended to specify a unique probability distribution over a set of propositions, such as hypotheses, that reflects complete ignorance as to which of the set is true. Thus the fact that you have no evidence is itself taken to commit you to a particular assignment of prior probabilities—typically, a probability distribution that is uniform in some sense. Jaynes (1983) has done the most to develop this view.

The objectivist envisages all Bayesian reasoners marching in lock-step: They start with precisely the same priors; they apply (thanks to PCP and total probability) precisely the same Bayesian multipliers; thus they have the same subjective probabilities at all times for everything.

There are various powerful objections to the most general forms of the principle of indifference. Even its most enthusiastic supporters would shy away from claiming that it determines a uniquely correct prior for absolutely any scientific hypothesis. Thus the lock-step picture of Bayesian inference is offered more as an ideal than as a realistic prospect. To be a modern objectivist is to argue that parts of science, at least, ought to come close to realizing the ideal.

THE PROBLEM OF OLD EVIDENCE

Among the many achievements of Newton's theory of gravitation was its prediction of the tides and their relation to the lunar orbit. Presumably the success of this prediction confirmed Newton's theory, or in Bayesian terms, the observable facts about the tides e raised the probability of Newton's theory h.

But the Bayesian it turns out can make no such claim. Because the facts about the tides were already known when Newton's theory was formulated, the probability for e was equal to one. It follows immediately that both $C(e)$ and $C(e|h)$ are equal to one (the latter for any choice of h). But then the Bayesian multiplier is also one, so Newton's theory does not receive any probability boost from its prediction of the tides. As either a description of actual scientific practice, or a prescription for ideal scientific practice, this is surely wrong.

The problem generalizes to any case of "old evidence": If the evidence e is received before a hypothesis h

is formulated then *e* is incapable of boosting the probability of *h* by way of conditionalization. As is often remarked, the problem of old evidence might just as well be called the problem of new theories, since there would be no difficulty if there were no new theories, that is, if all theories were on the table before the evidence began to arrive. Whatever you call it, the problem is now considered by most Bayesians to be in urgent need of a solution. A number of approaches have been suggested, none of them entirely satisfactory.

A recap of the problem: If a new theory is discovered midway through an inquiry, a prior must be assigned to that theory. You would think that, having assigned a prior on non-empirical grounds, you would then proceed to conditionalize on all the evidence received up until that point. But because old evidence has probability one, such conditionalization will have no effect. The Bayesian machinery is silent on the significance of the old evidence for the new theory.

The first and most conservative solution to the problem is to take the old evidence into account in setting your prior for the new theory. In doing this you are entirely on your own: You cannot use conditionalization or any other aspect of the Bayesian apparatus to weigh the evidence in a principled way. But because you are free to choose whatever prior you like, you are free to do so in part on the basis of the old evidence.

A second solution requires a radical revision of Bayesian conditionalization, so as to allow conditionalization using not the actual probability of the old evidence, but using a (now) counterfactual probability such as your prior for the evidence immediately before you learned it. This provides a natural way to use conditionalization to weigh the old evidence, but the difficulties involved in choosing an appropriate counterfactual prior and in justifying conditionalization on the false prior, rather than the actual prior, have not unreasonably scared most Bayesians away.

The third and perhaps most popular solution suggests that, although conditionalization on old evidence *e* has no effect on the prior probability of a new theory *h*, conditionalizing on the fact that *h* predicts *e* (for simplicity's sake, assume that it entails *e*) may have an effect. The idea: Until you formulate *h*, you do not know that it entails *e*. Once *h* is formulated and assigned a prior, you may conditionalize on the fact of the entailment; learning that *h* entails *e* will have much the same impact on the probability of *h*, it is supposed, as learning *e* would have had if it were not already known.

There are two difficulties with this suggestion. The first is that facts about entailment (either of *e* itself, or of a physical probability for *e*) are logical truths, which ought according to the probability calculus to be assigned probability one at all times—making the logical facts as "old" as the evidence itself. Proponents of the present approach to old evidence argue not unreasonably that a sophisticated Bayesianism ought to allow for logical learning, so that it is the requirement that subjective probabilities conform to the probability calculus in every respect that is at fault here, for imposing an unreasonably strict demand on flesh-and-blood inquirers.

The second (and related) difficulty is that the theory of conditionalization on logical facts is not nearly so nicely developed as the theory of orthodox Bayesian conditionalization. A case can be made that conditionalizing on *h*'s entailment of old evidence will increase the probability of *h*, but the details are complicated and controversial.

BAYESIANISM ACCESSORIZED

Two notable additions to the Bayesian apparatus are ever under consideration. First is a theory of acceptance, that is, a theory that dictates, given your subjective probabilities, which hypotheses you ought to "accept." Conventional Bayesianism has no need of acceptance: Your subjective probabilities are taken to exhaust your epistemic attitudes to the hypotheses, and also to determine, along with your preferences in the usual decision-theoretical way, the practical significance of these attitudes.

Some philosophers argue that there is, nevertheless, work for a notion of acceptance to do, and hold either a simple view on which hypotheses with high subjective probability are to be accepted, or a more sophisticated view on which not only probability but the consequences for science, good and bad, of acceptance must be taken into account.

Second is a theory of confirmational relevance, that is, a theory that dictates, given your subjective probabilities, to what degree a given piece of evidence confirms a given hypothesis. Conventional Bayesianism has no need of confirmational relevance: Your subjective probabilities are taken to exhaust your epistemic attitudes to the hypotheses, and so the dynamics of confirmation are exhausted by the facts about the way in which the subjective probabilities change, which are themselves fully determined, through conditionalization, by the values of the subjective probabilities themselves. Nothing is added to the dynamics of probability change—nothing could be added—by finding a standard by which to judge whether certain evidence has a "large" or "small" impact on the hypotheses; however you talk about probability change, it is the change that it is. (A pure-hearted Bayesian need not even define *confirms* and *disconfirms*.)

Many different measures of relevance have, nevertheless, been proposed. The simple difference measure equates the relevance of *e* to *h* with the difference between the prior and posterior probabilities of *h* after conditionalization on *e*, or equivalently, with $C(h|e) - C(h)$. The likelihood measure equates the relevance of *e* to *h* with $C(e|h)/C(e|\neg h)$. It should be noted that all popular Bayesian measures render relevance relative to background knowledge.

There is no doubt that scientists sometimes talk about accepting theories and about the strength of the evidence—and that they do not talk very much about subjective probability. The degree to which you see this as a problem for unadorned Bayesian confirmation theory itself measures, perhaps, your position on the spectrum between prescriptive and descriptive.

See also Confirmation Theory; Decision Theory; Goodman, Nelson; Induction; Newton, Isaac; Probability and Chance; Ramsey, Frank Plumpton; Rationality.

Bibliography

Earman, John. *Bayes or Bust?* Cambridge, MA: MIT Press, 1992.

Fitelson, Branden. "The Plurality of Bayesian Measures of Confirmation and the Problem of Measure Sensitivity." *Philosophy of Science* 66 (1999): S362–S378.

Glymour, Clark. *Theory and Evidence*. Princeton, NJ: Princeton University Press, 1980.

Howson, Colin. *Hume's Problem: Induction and the Justification of Belief*. Oxford: Oxford University Press, 2001.

Howson, Colin, and Peter Urbach. *Scientific Reasoning: The Bayesian Approach*. 2nd ed. Chicago: Open Court, 1993.

Jaynes, Edwin T. *Papers on Probability, Statistics, and Statistical Physics*, edited by Roger Rosenkrantz. Dordrecht: Reidel, 1983.

Jeffrey, Richard. *The Logic of Decision*. 2nd ed. Chicago: University of Chicago Press, 1983.

Levi, Isaac. *Gambling with the Truth*. Cambridge, MA: MIT Press, 1967.

Ramsey, Frank. "Truth and Probability." Reprinted in *Philosophical Papers*. Edited by D. H. Mellor. Cambridge, U.K.: Cambridge University Press, 1931.

Strevens, Michael. (2001). "The Bayesian Treatment of Auxiliary Hypotheses." *British Journal for the Philosophy of Science* 52 (2001): 515–538.

Michael Strevens (2005)

BAYLE, PIERRE
(1647–1706)

Pierre Bayle, the most important and most influential skeptic of the late seventeenth century, was born in Carla (now Carla-Bayle), a French village near the Spanish frontier, where his father was the Protestant pastor. He grew up during the religious persecutions under Louis XIV that culminated in the revocation of the Edict of Nantes (1685) and the outlawing of Protestantism in France. Bayle was sent first to a Calvinist school and then to a Jesuit college at Toulouse, where after studying the controversial literature and hearing the dialectical arguments of some of the professors, he converted to Catholicism. The intellectual considerations that led him to Catholicism, after further examination, soon led him back to Calvinism. He became technically a *relaps*, a person who has returned to heresy after having abjured it, and under French law he was therefore subject to severe penalties.

He left France for Geneva, where he completed his philosophical and theological studies. In 1674 he returned to France incognito and became a tutor in Paris and Rouen. The next year he obtained the philosophy professorship at the Protestant academy of Sedan as the protégé of Pierre Jurieu, a superorthodox theologian who was to become Bayle's greatest enemy. Bayle taught at Sedan until the school was closed in 1681. He and Jurieu went to Holland; they became members of the *École illustre* of Rotterdam and of the French Reformed church there. Bayle brought with him his first work, a letter concerning the comet of 1680, which he published under a pseudonym. This volume, like many of those to follow, attacked superstition, intolerance, and poor philosophy and history. The work was immediately successful and was soon followed by others, including an answer to Father Maimbourg's history of Calvinism and a collection of defenses of Cartesianism.

During these early years in Rotterdam, Bayle apparently made some fundamental personal decisions that affected the rest of his life. The first was not to marry but to devote himself to the solitary life of the dedicated scholar seeking truth. The second was to refuse any important professorship to carry on his work in Rotterdam (where he lived almost continuously for the rest of his life). Lastly, after his father and his brothers died in France as a result of the religious persecutions, Bayle apparently committed himself to both the cause of Calvinism and the cause of toleration.

From 1684 until 1687 he edited the *Nouvelles de la république des lettres*, one of the first learned journals of modern times, in which he reviewed works in many fields. His critical appraisals soon made him a major figure in the learned world and brought him in contact with the leading lights of his day, among them Antoine Arnauld, Robert Boyle, Gottfried Wilhelm Leibniz, John Locke, and Nicolas Malebranche.

TOLERATION

In 1686 Bayle published in Amsterdam his *Commentaire philosophique sur ces paroles de Jésus-Christ "Constrains-les d'entrer"* (Philosophical commentary on the words of Jesus "constrain them to come in"), a brilliant argument for complete religious toleration. Starting with the problem raised by Louis XIV's persecutions, Bayle developed a defense of toleration for Jews, Moslems, Socinians (Unitarians), Catholics, and even atheists, extending its scope far beyond Locke's not yet published *Essay on Toleration*.

Enmity had begun to develop between Bayle and Jurieu, who conceived of himself as the chief spokesman for Calvinist orthodoxy, opposed all kinds of deviation as heresy and atheism, and advocated political victory over Louis XIV. As Jurieu became a violent political radical and religious bigot, Bayle drifted away from the views and company of his former mentor. According to Jurieu the disaffection reached the breaking point with the publication of Bayle's "Philosophical Commentary." Bayle had tried to hide his authorship, but Jurieu soon guessed the truth and realized that they disagreed completely about almost everything. He saw his colleague as a menace to true religion and a secret atheist. Bayle intensified the quarrel by ridiculing Jurieu, attacking his intolerance and his political plans. Throughout the quarrel, Bayle insisted that he was a true follower of John Calvin and that he had imbibed his orthodoxy from Jurieu's antirational theology.

When Bayle began to publish his views, the Protestant liberals thought that he was on their side. But Bayle quickly employed his dialectical and critical skill to decimate their contentions and to show that there was no way of making the rational and scientific world compatible with the basic claims of Christianity, as they in part believed it to be. As a result, various liberal Protestants spent years defending themselves against Bayle's sharp criticisms, while Bayle alternately joined them in attacking Jurieu and Jurieu in attacking them.

Between 1690 and 1692 the argument between Bayle and Jurieu reached fever pitch, especially concerning whether or not Bayle was the author of the notorious "Advice to the French Refugees," a work criticizing the romantic optimism and hopes of the Protestant exiles. (Bayle so confused the evidence that even present-day scholars are unwilling to state positively that he did write it.) These controversies with Jurieu led in 1693 to Bayle's dismissal from his teaching post, an event that allowed him time to carry on his many controversies and to complete his great *Dictionnaire historique et critique* (A general dictionary, historical and critical; first published in two volumes in Rotterdam in 1695 and 1697), a work in which Jurieu is constantly attacked.

HISTORY AND COMPOSITION OF THE DICTIONARY

Bayle had conceived the basic idea of the *Dictionary* long before its composition. For many years he had been assembling collections of errors uncovered in various historical works. As early as 1675, Bayle's letters show, he was actively interested in skeptical thought. In the lectures Bayle gave at Rotterdam he criticized every possible theory. The *Dictionary* brought his critical and skeptical sides together. Originally, Bayle planned only to write a dictionary that would list the mistakes in all other dictionaries and in particular the one by Louis Moréri. A sample portion of this project was printed in 1692 to test public interest. The negative reaction led to a change of plan; the dictionary became a historical and critical one, dealing principally with persons and mainly with those who were not treated fully or at all (usually because of their obscurity or insignificance) in Moréri's opus. The result was two folio volumes full of articles on little-known or totally unknown figures, omitting significant figures like Plato, Michel Eyquem de Montaigne, and Cardinal Richelieu.

The *Dictionary* was composed in Talmudic style. Relatively brief biographical articles appeared at the top of the page, while all sorts of digressive notes on factual, philosophical, religious, or other matters appeared below, with notes on notes appearing in the margins. The biography of some extremely little-known personage, like Rorarius, would provide the stage for profound discussions of the nature of man and beasts, the mind-body problem, and the new metaphysical theory of Leibniz. Other subjects would provide forums for discussing the problem of evil; the immorality of great figures, especially Old Testament ones; the irrationality of Christianity; the problems of Locke's, Isaac Newton's, Malebranche's, Aristotle's, or anyone else's philosophy; or some salacious tale about a famous theologian, Catholic or Protestant, or a famous political figure of almost any age. There was little relation between the official subject of an article and its real content. But there were several major themes and threads that ran through many or most of the articles, themes that amounted to a massive onslaught against almost any religious, philosophical, moral, scientific, or historical view that anyone held. (Once Bayle explained that he was a Protestant in the true sense of the term and that he opposed everything that was said and everything that was done.)

The *Dictionary* was an instant success and immediately led to criticism and condemnation, both by the French Reformed church of Rotterdam and by the French Catholic church. The latter group banned the work, while the former demanded that the author revise or explain his views about the good moral character of atheists, the inability of Christians to answer the Manichaean views about the nature of evil, the strength of Pyrrhonian skepticism, the immoral character of King David, and why so many obscenities appeared in the work.

Bayle promised the congregation of the French Reformed church that he would revise the article "David" and would offer explanations of the other matters. Almost as soon as the first edition of the *Dictionary* appeared, he began work on the second, revising the article "David" and adding many additional articles, plus a set of clarifications. This final edition appeared in Rotterdam in 1702 and consisted of 7 to 8 million words. After this monumental effort, the rest of Bayle's career was devoted to carrying on various controversies, defending some of the claims in the *Dictionary*, and fighting a growing list of opponents. He died on December 28, 1706, while completing his *Entretiens de Maxime et de Thémiste* (Conversations between Maxime and Themiste; Rotterdam, 1707), a final reply to the liberal Protestants.

Replies to Bayle kept appearing, written by such figures as Leibniz, Bishop William King, and Jean-Pierre Crousaz; and the avant-garde spirits of the Enlightenment found much ammunition in Bayle's folio columns with which to attack the ideological and theological ancien régime. François-Marie Arouet de Voltaire, David Hume, Edward Gibbon, Denis Diderot, and many others found intellectual nutrition in Bayle's skeptical and critical efforts. Thomas Jefferson recommended the *Dictionary* as one of the hundred basic books with which to start the Congressional Library. Poets and writers of fiction like Alexander Pope, Henry Fielding, and Herman Melville found inspiration and plots in some of Bayle's spicy tales. Ludwig Feuerbach (1967), in the nineteenth century, saw Bayle as a major figure in the rise of modern thought and devoted a whole volume to him.

The *Dictionary* was enormously influential during the eighteenth century, both for its spirit and for its wealth of information. Though it was written in the form of a reference work, its lopsided contents, overloaded with lives of obscure theologians and figures of French political history, made it difficult for the *Dictionary* to maintain its character as a guide to research and scholarship. Efforts to improve it by adding and updating articles were only temporarily successful. The editors of the 1734–1741 English edition put in hundreds of articles on English and Arab figures, plus some "correctives" to what they regarded as outlandish in Bayle's original. In 1740 Jacques-Georges de Chaufepié translated many of the English articles into French, adding a great many more on Bayle's opponents, and put out a four-volume folio supplement. However, the type of critical and careful research Bayle had fostered gave birth to projects that would forever make his *Dictionary* obsolete as a reference work. *La Grande Encyclopédie* and the *Encyclopaedia Britannica*, which replaced it, were continuing team efforts, rather than one man's appraisal of the whole intellectual world. Thus, Bayle's work became a victim of its own offspring. It gradually disappeared as an important element in the intellectual world and was superseded by the works of leaders of the Enlightenment who had imbibed at least part of Bayle's spirit.

PHILOSOPHICAL ASPECTS OF THE DICTIONARY

The discussions in the *Dictionary* that had the greatest philosophical impact were those dealing with the problem of evil, with the independence of morality from religion, and with the unintelligible nature of the physical and mental world, especially when analyzed in terms of the categories of the "new science" and the "new philosophy." With a dialectical skill unknown to earlier skeptics Bayle dissected every theory and showed that it was unsatisfactory. Instead of merely utilizing the classical epistemological arguments of Sextus Empiricus, slightly modernized by the Montaignians, Bayle employed primarily the method of one of his heroes, the "subtle Arriaga" (Roderigo Arriaga, the last of the Spanish scholastics, who died in 1667), a method that Bayle had probably learned from the Jesuits at Toulouse.

The technique consisted in exposing the weakness of every rational attempt to make sense of some aspect of human experience. Bayle, like Arriaga before him, repeatedly exhibited man's sorry intellectual plight. All human rational efforts are always their own undoing and terminate in theories that are "big with contradiction and absurdity." Bayle concentrated on a few shocking illustrations of this thesis. In a series of articles, "Manichaeans," "Marcionites," "Pauilicians," and "Rufinus," he contended that the Manichaean or dualistic theory of two gods, one good and one evil, could not be refuted by orthodox Christian theology, that it was a better explanation of human experience of evil, but that it was ultimately repugnant to sound reasoning. (Leibniz's *Theodicy* was largely an attempt to refute Bayle on Manichaeanism and the problem of evil.)

RELIGION AND MORALITY

Throughout his writings, from his letter on the comet to the *Dictionary* and its various defenses, Bayle argued the then scandalous thesis that a society of atheists could be moral and a society of Christians immoral. He tried to show that people's moral behavior is not a consequence of their beliefs but is rather the result of many irrational factors, such as education, custom, passion, ignorance, and the trace of God. In the article "Jupiter" he pointed out that Greek mythology was absurd and immoral, but the Greeks lived moral lives nonetheless. In his "Clarification on Atheism" he stated that he could find no case of a classical atheist, or a modern one like Benedict (Baruch) de Spinoza, who lived a wretched, morally degenerate life. Instead, the cases he found all seemed to be ones of highly moral people, who also happened to be atheists.

Additionally, Bayle knew of myriad cases—from a biblical one to leading Catholic and Protestant clergy of his day—of religious heroes who were immoral and whose behavior seemed to have been influenced by the most irreligious factors. Among many articles dealing with the sexual aberrations of different religious fanatics, early reformers, and Renaissance popes, the long one on "David" brought this point out most forcefully. David was introduced as the most holy figure in the Old Testament, and a series of notes outlined and analyzed his immoral conduct. This massive assault on any alleged rational or necessary connection between religious belief and moral behavior greatly influenced the Third Earl of Shaftesbury (Anthony Ashley Cooper; who lived and argued with Bayle for a while), and Bernard Mandeville (who was apparently one of Bayle's students at Rotterdam), and through them many of the eighteenth-century British moralists.

METAPHYSICS

In metaphysics Bayle employed his dialectical skill to show that theories about the nature of matter, space, time, motion, mind, and mind-body relationships, when thoroughly analyzed, are contradictory, inadequate, and absurd. Starting with Zeno of Elea's paradoxes and the sections in Sextus against metaphysics, Bayle attacked all sorts of ancient and modern forms of atomism, Platonism, and Aristotelianism, as well as the modern substitutes offered by René Descartes, Thomas Hobbes, Spinoza, Malebranche, Leibniz, Locke, Newton, and many others. He showed the weird, incredible conclusions that would follow from each of these theories. (Bayle's article "Rorarius" was the first public examination of, and attack on, Leibniz's theories of preestablished harmony and of monads.) In the articles "Pyrrho" and "Zeno of Elea" (which greatly influence George Berkeley and Hume) Bayle brilliantly challenged the distinction between primary and secondary qualities, so fundamental in the theories about reality of all the "new philosophers."

SKEPTICISM

Bayle repeatedly showed that the many attempts by human beings to explain or understand their world were all just "highroads to Pyrrhonism," since they only made every supposition more perplexing, absurd, and dubious. Rational activity, no matter what problem it is directed at, leads to complete skepticism, since reason invariably leads one astray. In the article "Acosta" Bayle compared reason to a corrosive powder that first eats up errors, but then goes on to eat up truths, "When it is left on its own, it goes so far that it no longer knows where it is, and can find no stopping place."

FAITH

Each time Bayle reached this point he would proclaim that in view of the inability of reason to arrive at any complete and adequate conclusion about anything, man should abandon the rational world and seek a different guide: faith. This claim was forcefully stated in the articles "Bunel, Pierre," "Charron," "Manichaeans," "Pomponazzi," "Pyrrho," and the "Clarification on the Pyrrhonians." Bayle's dwelling on the theme that reason makes men perplexed and so requires that they look for another guide suggests, perhaps, that his purpose was something like that of Maimonides in *The Guide of the Perplexed*, one of Bayle's favorite works.

REVELATION

In various discussions (such as the articles "Pyrrho," "Simonides," and the "Clarification on the Pyrrhonians") Bayle insisted that the rational and the revealed worlds are in complete conflict, because the latter is based on claims that are in direct opposition to the principles that appear most evident to reason. Starting with the first line of Genesis, the world of faith contains claims that are rationally unintelligible and unacceptable. According to Bayle the principle that reason finds the most evident and certain is that nothing comes from nothing, whereas faith reveals that God created the world *ex nihilo*. Similarly, the most acceptable rational moral principles are at complete variance with the revealed accounts of the behavior of the heroes of the faith, the leading figures of the Old Testament. In this total opposition between reason and revelation, faith is man's only refuge. Bayle insisted that his irrational fideism was the traditional orthodox position from St. Paul and Quintus Septimius Florens Tertullian down to Calvin and Jurieu. (In fact, some passages of Bayle sound like Søren Aabye Kierkegaard and other more fideistic theologians.)

BAYLE'S RELIGIOUS POSITION

No matter how often Bayle claimed that he was advocating the faith and was merely restating what orthodox Christians had always said, his opponents, especially Jurieu and some of the liberals, insisted that Bayle was actually an unbeliever trying to destroy the faith by making it sound as ridiculous and irrational as possible. Certainly, some of Bayle's passages have such a ring. And none of his statements of the fideistic message have the anguish of Blaise Pascal or Kierkegaard, or even the despair of the truth seeker unable to find satisfaction in either the rational world or in revealed truths.

However, this may not necessarily be a sign that Bayle was insincere. Bayle himself offered an alternative possibility in a discussion in the longest article in the *Dictionary*, that on Spinoza. In note M Bayle described two kinds of people, those who have religion in their minds, but not in their hearts, and those who have religion in their hearts, but not in their minds. The first kind are convinced of the truth of religion, but their consciences are not affected by the love of God. The second kind lose sight of religion when they seek it by rational means and are lost in the wilderness of the pros and cons; but when they listen only to their feelings, conscience, or education, they find that they are convinced of religion and regulate their lives accordingly, within the limits of human frailties. If Bayle had religion in the heart in this sense (rather than Pascal's), it was an emotionless religion, which became confused and perplexing whenever he tried to explain or comprehend it. When he abandoned the attempt to be rational about it, then it became a calm guide for a life of pious study.

In the article "Bunel, Pierre" Bayle presented this fervorless religion as almost a testimonial of faith. Bunel, an obscure Renaissance pedant from Toulouse (who accidentally had an enormous influence on the development of modern skepticism by giving Raimond Sebond's *Natural Theology* to Montaigne's father) is one of the few genuine heroes of Bayle's *Dictionary*. He was pictured as a perfect Christian, in contrast to myriad imperfect ones (including Jurieu), because he rejected all worldly goals and devoted himself solely to the life of the pure scholar, harming no one and seeking truth. Bayle's own life was much like Bunel's. Beyond this, Bayle's religion seems to have had little or no content, though he always claimed to be a Calvinist Christian.

The lack of content in Bayle's religion may account for his important doctrine of toleration of the rights of the erring conscience. In many works Bayle insisted that man's ultimate appeal for justification of his beliefs and actions was his own conscience and that man had no further ultimate standard to employ to determine if his conscience was correct. Therefore, each man could act only as he saw fit, and no one was justified in trying to compel another to act contrary to the dictates of his conscience, erring or otherwise.

Though Bayle continually presented his appeal to faith, and his own faith, in tranquil and colorless terms, a fundamental problem remains of determining what Bayle did in fact believe and what his arsenal of doubts was intended to achieve. Shaftesbury, who knew Bayle well, called him "one of the best of Christians." Jurieu was sure he was an atheist. The Enlightenment leaders saw him as one of them, perhaps a deist, but definitely a scoffer at all historical religions. The biographical data would suggest that, barring some strange private joke, Bayle was committed to some aspects of the French Reformed church. He persisted in belonging to it, attending it, and proclaiming his sincere adherence to it, no matter how much he was abused by Jurieu and others. He could have lived and prospered in Holland either in a more liberal church or as a complete independent. In tolerant Holland it was extremely unlikely that he would have been punished or have had his works censored, no matter what he said or believed.

Coming from a family that suffered inordinately from persecution for its Calvinism, Bayle may have felt a need and desire to maintain his original tradition. His last message to a friend as he knew his life was ending was, "I am dying as a Christian philosopher, convinced of and pierced by the bounties and mercy of God, and I wish you a perfect happiness." Elisabeth Labrousse (1963) points out that this is a most minimal Christian testament, since Jesus is not mentioned, nor any Christian doctrine, nor anything about Bayle's church. In his writings Bayle rarely discussed religion without making Manichaeanism or Judaism seem either more plausible or more significant than Christianity; and he occasionally (as in the article "Takiddim") even called Judaism the true religion. Bayle may have been either a Christian in his own sense or actually a Manichaean or Judaizer or both, working out an enormous defense of his cause by undermining the rational and moral foundations of other possibilities.

Until it is possible to ascertain Bayle's actual beliefs, it will remain extremely difficult to determine his aims and whether the impact he had was the intended one. Bayle undermined all the philosophical positions of the great seventeenth-century metaphysicians and posed basic problems that Berkeley, Hume, Voltaire, and others were to use to establish other approaches and alternatives. He provided an enormous amount of argument and ridicule for the Enlightenment to use in destroying the intellectual ancien régime and in launching the Age of Reason. But even Voltaire and Hume were aware that Bayle was much more given to doubt and destructive criticism than they considered themselves to be. At times, they believed they had found new ways of overcoming Bayle's doubts. Perhaps they were both too far removed from Bayle's calm religious haven to be able to entertain his complete doubt about everything without utter dismay and horror.

Bayle seems to have lived in a different world from that of the Enlightenment that he helped produce. Though he may not have been "the greatest master of the art of reasoning," as Voltaire called him, he was one of the best. He was a genius at seeing how to attack and destroy theories about almost anything and a master at determining what the facts in the case were. Bayle would turn his attacks against everyone and everything, modern, ancient, scientific, rationalistic, or religious. He did not, apparently, see a new and better world emerging from his critique, nor see the need for one. The havoc he was wreaking seemed to leave him completely tranquil. It was for subsequent generations to discover the problem of living in a world in which all is in doubt and in which the solution proffered by Bayle seems meaningless or unattainable.

Some scholarship focuses on Bayle's last writings after the *Dictionary*. Gianluca Mori (1999) and others believe that they have found that Bayle was evolving more positive views in his last few years.

See also Aristotelianism; Aristotle; Arnauld, Antoine; Berkeley, George; Boyle, Robert; Calvin, John; Cartesianism; Descartes, René; Diderot, Denis; Enlightenment; Feuerbach, Ludwig Andreas; Fideism; Gibbon, Edward; Hobbes, Thomas; Hume, David; Jefferson, Thomas; Kierkegaard, Søren Aabye; Leibniz, Gottfried Wilhelm; Locke, John; Maimonides; Malebranche, Nicolas; Mandeville, Bernard; Mani and Manichaeism; Montaigne, Michel Eyquem de; Newton, Isaac; Pascal, Blaise; Plato; Pope, Alexander; Religion and Morality; Renaissance; Sextus Empiricus; Shaftesbury, Third Earl of (Anthony Ashley Cooper); Skepticism, History of; Spinoza, Benedict (Baruch) de; Tertullian, Quintus Septimius Florens; Voltaire, François-Marie Arouet de; Zeno of Elea.

Bibliography

WORKS BY BAYLE

Oeuvres diverses. 4 vols. The Hague: n.p., 1727. A collection of Bayle's writings other than the *Dictionary*.

A General Dictionary, Historical and Critical. 10 vol. Translated by John Peter Bernard, Thomas Birch, and John Lockman. London: J. Bettenham, 1734–1741. This was published in French under the title *Dictionnaire historique et critique* in 1740.

Historical and Critical Dictionary, Selections. Translated by Richard H. Popkin, with Craig Brush. Indianapolis, IN: Bobbs-Merrill, 1965. Contains selections from forty articles, plus Bayle's clarifications.

Correspondance de Pierre Bayle, edited and annotated by Elisabeth Labrousse et al. Oxford, U.K.: Voltaire Foundation, 1999–2004.

Bayle: Political Writings, edited by Sally L. Jenkinson. New York: Cambridge University Press, 2000.

WORKS ON BAYLE

Barber, W. H. "Bayle: Faith and Reason." In *The French Mind: Studies in Honour of Gustav Rudler*, edited by Will Moore, Rhoda Sutherland, and Enid Starkie, 109–125. Oxford, U.K.: Clarendon Press, 1952. Suggests that Bayle was sincerely religious.

Bracken, Harry M. "Bayle Not a Sceptic?" *Journal of the History of Ideas* 25 (1964): 169–180. Attempts to clarify the sense in which Bayle was a skeptic and a fideist.

Bracken, Harry M. "Pierre Jurieu: The Politics of Prophecy." In *Millenarianism and Messianism in Early Modern European Culture. Vol. 4: Continental Millenarians: Protestants, Catholics, Heretics*, edited by John Christian Laursen and Richard H. Popkin, 85–94. Boston: Kluwer Academic, 2001.

Courtines, Léo. *Bayle's Relation with England and the English*. New York: Columbia University Press, 1938. Deals with Bayle's contacts with and influence on English philosophers, theologians, and writers, including Berkeley and Hume.

Dibon, Paul, ed. *Pierre Bayle, le philosophe de Rotterdam*. Amsterdam: Elsevier, 1959. An important collection of articles in French and English reevaluating Bayle's views.

Feuerbach, Ludwig. *Pierre Bayle: Ein Beitrag zur Geschichte der Philosophie und Menschheit.* Berlin: Akademie-Verlag, 1967. Bayle seen as caught between rationalism and the irrationality of Christianity.

Hasse, Erich. *Einführung in die Literatur des Refuge.* Berlin: 1959. A monumental study of the French Protestant refugees. Places Bayle in the context of this group.

Hazard, Paul. *The European Mind, 1680–1715.* Translated by J. Lewis May. London: Hollis and Carter, 1953. Originally published in French under the title *La Crise de la conscience européenne, 1680–1715* in 1935. The intellectual climate of Bayle's time.

James, E. D. "Scepticism and Fideism in Bayle's Dictionnaire." *French Studies* 16 (1962): 307–324. Challenges the views of Popkin and others regarding Bayle's religious views.

Kemp Smith, Norman. *The Philosophy of David Hume: A Critical Study of Its Origins and Central Doctrines.* London: Macmillan, 1941. Contains analyses of sections in Bayle that influenced Hume, especially in his *Treatise of Human Nature.*

Labrousse, Elisabeth. *Pierre Bayle. Vol. 1: Du pays de foix à la cité d'Erasme.* The Hague: Nijhoff, 1963. First biography of Bayle in recent times, based on monumental researches.

Labrousse, Elisabeth. *Pierre Bayle. Vol. 2: Hétérodoxie et rigorisme.* The Hague: Nijhoff, 1964. A study of Bayle's theology by the leading authority today. Contains a massive bibliography.

Laursen, John Christian. "Bayle's Anti-millenarianism: The Dangers of Those Who Claim to Know the Future." In *Millenarianism and Messianism in Early Modern European Culture. Vol. 4: Continental Millenarians: Protestants, Catholics, Heretics,* edited by John Christian Laursen and Richard H. Popkin, 95–106. Boston: Kluwer Academic, 2001.

Mason, H. T. *Pierre Bayle and Voltaire.* London: Oxford University Press, 1963. A comparison, with an attempt to assess what Voltaire borrowed from Bayle.

Mason, H. T. "Pierre Bayle's Religious Views." *French Studies* 17 (1963): 205–217. Defends interpretation of Bayle as an irreligious thinker.

Mori, Gianluca. *Bayle philosophe.* Paris: Champion, 1999.

Norton, David. "Leibniz and Bayle: Manicheism and Dialectic." *Journal of the History of Philosophy* 2 (1964): 23–36. An attempt to see how Bayle might have dealt with Leibniz's *Theodicy* and a new analysis of Bayle's dialectic.

Paganini, Gianni, ed. *The Return of Scepticism from Hobbes and Descartes to Bayle.* Dordrecht, Netherlands: Kluwer Academic, 2003. Includes several articles on Bayle and eighteenth-century skepticism.

Popkin, Richard H. *The High Road to Pyrrhonism* edited by Richard A. Watson and James E. Force. San Diego, CA: Austin Hill Press, 1980. Contains articles on Bayle in the context of the late seventeenth century and on his legacy for the eighteenth century.

Rétat, Pierre. *Le "Dictionnaire" de Bayle et la lutte philosophique au XVIIIe siècle.* Paris: Les Belles Lettres, 1971.

Rex, Walter. *Essays on Pierre Bayle and Religious Controversy.* The Hague: Nijhoff, 1965.

Sandberg, K. C. "Pierre Bayle's Sincerity in His Views on Faith and Reason." *Studies in Philology* 61 (1) (1964): 74–84. Interprets Bayle as a sincere Calvinist. Shows Bayle had no need to fear censorship.

Whalen, Ruth. *The Anatomy of Superstition: A Study of the Historical Theory and Practice of Pierre Bayle.* Oxford, U.K.: Voltaire Foundation, 1989.

Richard Popkin (1967, 2005)

BEARDSLEY, MONROE
(1915–1985)

Monroe C. Beardsley published in several areas of philosophy but is best known as an aesthetician. He is arguably the most important figure of twentieth-century analytic aesthetics. His *Aesthetics: Problems in the Philosophy of Criticism* (1958) was a watershed book, furnishing an organization aesthetics had lacked. Beardsley's careful discussions of almost all of the field's questions provided an aesthetic education for his and succeeding generations.

Two ideas shaped all Beardsley's work: his view of the philosophy of art criticism (called "metacriticism") and his aestheticism. Metacriticism's task is the analysis of art criticism's central concepts. Aestheticism is the view that aesthetic characteristics (e.g., unity, delicacy) alone are the proper objects of art criticism; thus, aesthetic features become the sole focus of criticism and the basis for artistic value. Beardsley acknowledged that artwork can have nonaesthetic, referential characteristics, and he does not deny that these features are important. He does, however, deny that referential features are relevant to aesthetic experience and, thus, to artistic value.

Aesthetics begins with the metacritical task of discussing objects of criticism, designating them "*aesthetic objects*"; a hard-and-fast connection is, thus, forged at the book's beginning between metacriticism and aestheticism with the contents of the objects of criticism identified as aesthetic features. This identification sets the stage for Beardsley's view of artistic value. He claims that artworks are instrumentally valuable because their aesthetic characteristics can produce (valuable) aesthetic experience. Aesthetic experience, as he conceives of it, is the foundational notion of Beardsley's book.

John Dewey is the primary source of Beardsley's notion of aesthetic experience. Dewey conceived of aesthetic experience as an experience that coheres to such an extent that it is set off, although not detached, from the flow of experience. Beardsley, however, was also influenced by aesthetic-attitude theorists. Consequently, unlike Dewey, he claimed aesthetic experience is detached from ordinary experience. But whereas the aesthetic-attitude theorists claim various mental mechanisms—

such as "psychical distancing"—detach aesthetic experience from ordinary life, Beardsley maintained that aesthetic experience's internal coherence detaches it from the flow of experience. And it is the detachedness of aesthetic experience that blocks artworks' referential characteristics (names, descriptions, portrayals, etc.) from referring to anything outside of ongoing aesthetic experience of artworks. On his view, only aesthetic, nonreferential characteristics of an artwork can cause aesthetic experience and, thereby, be the focus of artistic criticism and the basis for artistic value.

Beardsley argued that artistic value is an instrumental value (an objective value) because it can cause valuable aesthetic experience. To provide an objective basis for the value of aesthetic experience, Beardsley contended that aesthetic experience is in turn instrumentally valuable, being productive of human welfare. As an aspect of his account of artistic value, Beardsley argued that there are principles of art criticism involving the potential of three aesthetic features (unity, intensity, and complexity) for producing aesthetic experience, thus, opposing the conventional wisdom that there are no such principles. Present-day accounts of critical principles have their beginnings in Beardsley's work.

Throughout his career Beardsley continued to defend aestheticism and the inherent detachment of the aesthetic from ordinary life. In 1978 he argued against Nelson Goodman's view that artworks' referential features produce artistic value. In the second edition of *Aesthetics*, Beardsley wrote, "I think distance or detachment—withdrawal from practical engagement—in some form … is a factor in aesthetic character" (1981, p. lxii).

The only major question not discussed in *Aesthetics* is the nature of art. Finally in 1979, responding to the art theories that developed in the wake of Arthur Danto's "The Artworld" (1964), Beardsley sketched a theory of art in the midst of discussing aesthetic value; he wrote, "… an artwork can be usefully defined as an intentional arrangement of conditions for affording experiences with marked aesthetic character" (1979, p. 729). Beardsley's theory of art was determined by his aestheticism.

In 1946 Beardsley and William Wimsatt had co-authored "The Intentional Fallacy" and initiated a polarizing debate by arguing that artists' intentions are irrelevant to the interpretation and evaluation of their artworks. Beardsley also defended anti-intentionalism in *Aesthetics*, "The Authority of the Text" in *The Possibility of Criticism* (1970), and "Intentions and Interpretations: A Fallacy Revived" in *The Aesthetic Point of View* (1982). On his anti-intentionalist account, artworks are severed from their creators' actions when they are objects of criticism and of aesthetic experience. According to both his anti-intentionalism and his aestheticism, artworks as objects of aesthetic experience and criticism are detached—on the one hand, from their creators and, on the other, from their referents. Thus, in an aesthetic experience, audiences and critics savor only the aesthetic features of artworks.

Anti-intentionalism has been debated on grounds other than those used in *Aesthetics*, making use of arguments from the philosophy of language. Beardsley himself participated in this later controversy and produced additional arguments against intentionalism in "The Authority of the Text" and in "Intentions and Interpretations: A Fallacy Revived." In the first article, he argued that three different kinds of texts created without any authorial intent have specific meanings, namely, some randomly generated computer texts, some poetic lines with a word that has come to have a different meaning than it had at the time it was composed, and texts that reveal meanings of which their authors were unconscious. Unfortunately, Beardsley's argument merely contradicts the intentionalists' claim that such texts cannot have meaning and, therefore, will not persuade them.

In the second article, Beardsley applies J. L. Austin's distinction between locutionary and illocutionary acts to fictional discourse, claiming that illocutionary acts in fiction are *representations* of illocutionary acts and thus not actual illocutionary action of the text's author. Unfortunately, this argument is limited to fiction and the dispute is about texts generally, not just fiction. Furthermore, the dispute is really about locutionary meaning rather than illuctionary meaning.

The controversy over intentionalism continues.

See also Aesthetics, History of.

Bibliography

WORKS BY MONROE BEARDSLEY

Aesthetics: Problems in the Philosophy of Criticism (1958). Indianapolis: Hackett, 1981.

"The Authority of the Text." In *The Possibility of Criticism*, 16–37. Detroit: Wayne State University Press, 1970.

"In Defense of Aesthetic Value." *Proceedings and Addresses of the American Philosophical Association* 52 (1979): 723–749.

"Intentions and Interpretations: Fallacy Revived." In *The Aesthetic Point of View*, edited by Michael C. Wreen and Donald M. Callen, 188–207. Ithaca, NY: Cornell University Press, 1982.

WORKS ABOUT MONROE BEARDSLEY

Dewey, John. *Art as Experience*. New York: Minton, Balch, 1934.

Dickie, George, and W. Kent Wilson. "The Intentional Fallacy: Defending Beardsley." *The Journal of Aesthetics and Art Criticism* 53 (1995): 233–250.

George Dickie (2005)

BEATTIE, JAMES
(1735–1803)

James Beattie was born in Laurencekirk, Scotland, on October 25, 1735. He received an MA at Marischal College, Aberdeen, in 1753, became schoolmaster at the Fordoun Parish Church, and in 1760 was appointed Professor of Moral Philosophy and Logic at Marischal College. He was a member of the Aberdeen Philosophical Society with Thomas Reid and other notable Scottish writers. Beattie was known internationally as both a philosopher and poet. His principal philosophical contribution is *An Essay on the Nature and Immutability of Truth* (1770), for which he was awarded a yearly pension of £200 by King George III. His relentless attacks on David Hume in that work sparked a controversy that permanently linked his name with Hume's. He was ill much of his life and endured the progressive insanity of his wife and the early death of his children. He died on August 18, 1803.

Beattie's *Essay* is an interesting critique of modern metaphysics as well as an important assault on Hume. The crux of his position is this: Truth is that which common sense "determines me to believe," and skeptical metaphysicians have erred by ignoring commonsense intuitions. He discusses eight types of human reasoning that are grounded in common sense: mathematics, external sensation, internal sensation such as moral approval and personal identity, memory, causality, induction, analogy, and testimony. He acknowledges that merely having a commonsense belief does not guarantee that such a belief is true, since one can never be in a privileged position to compare one's commonsense beliefs to absolute reality. Like René Descartes, though, Beattie argues that one can trust that God has not deceived one in giving one faulty commonsense intuitions (2000). He argues further that denying the truth of common sense leads to absurd consequences.

Beattie takes issue with the skeptical trend of modern philosophers since Descartes who begin, he holds, with a few presumably factual general principles and deduce from these a range of noncommonsensical conclusions that call into doubt one's senses, the external world, free will, memory, and any of the previously mentioned eight types of reasoning. Skeptical metaphysics, he argues, is loathsome and harmful to normal affairs of life. About one-fourth of the *Essay* is a criticism of Hume's views of personal identity, ideas and impressions, necessary connection, the broad scope of the virtues, the natural inferiority of blacks, and other issues. His rhetoric against Hume is harsh, and in a 1771 postscript to the *Essay* he states that this treatment is necessary for placing the absurdity of skeptics' views in perspective and to combat the danger that skeptics pose to morality. He writes, "Let opinions then be combated by reason, and let ridicule be employed to expose nonsense."

In addition to his polemical *Essay* Beattie published *Dissertations Moral and Critical* (1783) on the subjects of memory, imagination, and language, *Evidences of the Christian Religion* (1786), and a collection of his philosophy lectures titled *Elements of Moral Science* (1790–1793). One of his more provocative pieces is the allegorical short story "The Castle of Scepticism," which he circulated among friends but that remained unpublished for almost 200 years. It describes how, after falling asleep, he was led on a journey to a surreal land of skeptics who defied commonsense beliefs. During and shortly after his life, Beattie's *Essay* was defended by Thomas Blacklock (1720–1791) and Dugald Stewart, and criticized by Joseph Priestley, James Steuart (1712–1790), and Thomas Cogan (1736–1818), in writings all of which are reprinted in *Early Responses to Reid, Oswald, Beattie, and Stewart* (2000).

See also Common Sense.

Bibliography

WORKS BY BEATTIE

The Works of James Beattie. 10 vols., edited by Roger J. Robinson. Bristol, U.K.: Routledge/Thoemmes Press, 1996.

An Essay on the Nature and Immutability of Truth, in Opposition to Sophistry and Scepticism, edited by James Fieser. Bristol, U.K.: Thoemmes Press, 2000.

"The Castle of Scepticism." In *Early Responses to Hume's Life and Reputation*. 2 vols., edited by James Fieser. Bristol, U.K.: Thoemmes Press, 2003.

WORKS ABOUT BEATTIE

Fieser, James, ed. *Early Responses to Reid, Oswald, Beattie, and Stewart*. Bristol, U.K.: Thoemmes Press, 2000.

Forbes, Margaret. *Beattie and His Friends*. Westminster, U.K.: Archibald Constable, 1904.

Forbes, William. *An Account of the Life and Writings of James Beattie: Including Many of His Original Letters*. 2 vols. Edinburgh, Scotland: Archibald Constable, 1806.

Robinson, Roger J., ed. *The Correspondence of James Beattie*. 4 vols. Bristol, U.K.: Thoemmes Continuum, 2004.

James Fieser (2005)

BEAUTY

Until the eighteenth century, "beauty" was the single most important idea in the history of aesthetics. One of the earliest works in the literature of aesthetics, the *Hippias Major* (probably by Plato), was addressed to the question, "What is beauty?" Around this question most of later thought revolves. The treatment of the other major concept, *art,* when it is not ancillary to that of beauty, lacks comparable generality, for it is often restricted to a single artistic form or genre, or its theoretical status is equivocal, because art is taken as identical with craft or skill. The modern notion of the *fine arts* did not appear until the eighteenth century and, more important, it was then too that the concept of *aesthetic experience* was first formulated systematically. As a consequence, beauty lost its traditional centrality in aesthetic theory and has never since regained it.

Our survey of these historical developments will be selective. Specific theories will be singled out because they are paradigms of the major kinds of theory of beauty. Thus, where beauty is taken to be a property, we will be less concerned with what, on some particular proposal, this property is, more with the logical relations of beauty, so construed, to the other properties of beautiful things and to the conditions of its apprehension. Where it is not so construed, the chief alternative meanings for beauty will be illustrated. *Beautiful* is used to esteem or commend and therefore to make a claim that is honored in the processes of criticism. Throughout this article, accordingly, the implications of the major kinds of theory for evaluation of the object will be traced.

CLASSICAL AESTHETICS

The concluding section of Plato's *Philebus* is the prototype of the dominant ways of thinking about beauty prior to the eighteenth century. This will be shown by unpacking its major theses, which, whether they were taken over or whether they became the focuses of dispute, made up the framework of classical theory and defined its preoccupations.

The discussion of beauty in the *Philebus,* as in other dialogues, arises in the course of discussion of a larger question not itself aesthetic, namely, whether pleasure or knowledge is the supreme good for humankind. Socrates wished to distinguish "pure" from "mixed" pleasures, and among the examples that he gives of the former are the pleasures evoked by objects that are "beautiful intrinsically." He cited simple geometrical shapes, single colors, and musical notes (50E–52B).

The first thing to see is that Plato took beauty to be a property ingredient in things. It is nonrelational twice over, for its existence is not dependent upon, or affected by, perceiving it; and whereas "relative" beauty exists only by virtue of comparison with things that are of a lesser degree of beauty or simply ugly, "intrinsic" beauty does not. This view can be specified in two different ways, both of which appear to be suggested by Plato: Either the property of beauty is identified with, and defined by, certain properties of the object, here the determinate ordering or "measure" of the whole (64E), or beauty is itself indefinable, but supervenes upon a further, distinct property, the internal unity of the parts, which is the condition of its existence (66B).

On the former theory, whether a thing is beautiful is decided just by finding whether it does or does not possess the salient property. In the *Philebus,* the success of such inquiry, even on Plato's rigorous conception of knowledge, is assured by the markedly intellectualist character of measure. It is a formal or structural property and therefore cognate with the nature of intelligence (59B–C, 65D), unlike matter which is opaque to mind. It is no accident that, having illustrated intrinsic beauty by objects produced by the "carpenter's rule and square," Socrates later eulogized carpentering for its cognitive exactness (55D–56E). This insistence on the clarity and knowability of beauty (shared by Aristotle in *Metaphysics* 1078b) is also reflected in the choice of sight and hearing, the senses most appropriate to rational cognition, as the sole avenues of the perception of beauty (cf. *Phaedrus* 250D).

The nondefinist theory is, for the reasons to be cited in later philosophers, more plausible but considerably more complicated. This theory is that, given unity in variety in a thing, beauty is also necessarily present. It will still be true that whether a thing is beautiful can be decided by showing that it possesses internal unity if—but this proviso is crucial—we can be certain that the two properties do, in all instances, exist together. Hence we must be able to apprehend beauty in its own right. Yet to say that beauty is indefinable is to say that what it is cannot be identified conceptually and therefore in commonly understandable terms. The cognitive assurance and stability of definist theory may be lost as a result. Plato was amply aware of the possibility of uncertainty and disagreement among judgments of beauty (*Laws* Bk. II). The account of intrinsic beauty in the *Philebus* guards against these dangers. Things are beautiful intrinsically precisely because they are "always beautiful in their very nature" (51C–D). Though the objects cited by Socrates are empirical—"the surfaces and solids which a lathe, or a carpenter's rule and square, produces from the straight and the round"—they nevertheless enjoy the self-identity, unaffected by adventitious or contextual factors, that is also characteristic of the Platonic Ideas. Unlike objects of relative beauty, they resemble the ideal beauty described in the *Symposium* (211–212), which cannot be "fair in one point of view and foul in another" (cf. *Republic* 479). Socrates held that they will necessarily arouse in the beholder a kind of pleasure that is peculiar to intrinsic beauty (51D). That the apprehension of such beauty will be veridical is further assured in the *Philebus* by the notion of "pure" pleasures, that is, those unmixed with pain. Pain warps or falsifies judgment (36C et seq.), but it is never present in the appreciation of intrinsic beauty. The related concepts of the *intrinsic* and the *pure* are used to guarantee the stability of the experience of beauty. They lead, however, to a severe delimitation of the class of beautiful objects. Paintings and living creatures are excluded as relative, tragedy and comedy (50A–B) because they are impure. Human significances are hostile to beauty because they encourage error and diversity in our responses to it.

In its analysis of the concrete phenomena of beauty, the *Philebus* is distinguished from the mythic and metaphysical approaches of the *Phaedrus* and *Symposium* and the social moralism of the *Republic* and *Laws*. Even here, however, the beautiful does not constitute a distinct and autonomous subject matter. It is treated as a "form" or mode of goodness in general, and the term *beautiful* is used, as it was by the Greeks generally, interchangeably with *excellent, perfect,* and *satisfying.* It is also worthy of note that the concept of art enters in hardly at all. Painting and literature are mentioned only so that they may be excluded. By contrast, Aristotle's *Poetics* devotes itself to a single art form, tragedy, making only a casual reference to beauty —measure is a necessary condition (VII). Later treatments of beauty and art are even less congenial to our modern conception of aesthetics, which led the historian Bernard Bosanquet to speak of a centuries-long "intermission" in aesthetics between the Greco-Roman and the modern eras. The metaphysic of Plotinus, which derived from Plato, is spiritualist and Idealist; and here, as in later philosophy, the bias of such thought is to encourage regard for, and insight into, the experience of beauty. The soul is said to strive toward beauty, which is a mani-

festation of the spiritual force that animates all of reality. It is just because of the vitality and moving appeal of beauty that Plotinus rejected the identification of beauty with a merely formal property. The living face and the dead face are equally symmetrical, but only the former stirs us. Hence "beauty is that which irradiates symmetry rather than symmetry itself" (*Enneads* VI; VII, 22). Further, some simple, sensory objects lacking internal structure are beautiful, and, finally, symmetry is present in some ugly things as well (I; VI, 1). Plotinus's critique of formalism effectively made the larger point that beauty cannot be identified with any single element of the object, form or any other. It is the total object, the whole of form and expressiveness and what the form is of, that possesses beauty. If, on the other hand, beauty is thought to be a global quality that "irradiates" this object and moves us, it is difficult or impossible, in a definition, to specify conceptually the nature of this quality. Moreover, Plotinus's argument cast doubt on the possibility of finding even the conditions of beauty. A formal property such as symmetry is the most likely candidate, because it can be shared by objects that are otherwise highly diverse, artistic or natural, abstract or representational, sensory or mathematical. Yet if the negative instances cited by Plotinus show that this property is not even a universal concomitant of beauty, then a fortiori it cannot be the necessitating ground of beauty.

Still, the effort to enunciate a set of conditions for beauty is persistent in Western thought, because it answers to the desire for a criticism whose verdicts will be certifiable and authoritative. The high noon of such criticism was the neoclassical period, particularly the sixteenth and seventeenth centuries, when the conditions were detailed and formalized, and endowed with the institutional sanctions of the new "Academies." A multiplicity of treatises were devoted to particular arts or genres, each of which was taken to be subject to "rules," inherent in its specific nature and function, which can be rationally known (e.g., Castelvetro, Palladio). The treatises borrowed heavily from their Greek and Roman antecedents—Aristotle, Horace, Vitruvius. The "lawmakers of Parnassus" thereby invested their claims to speak on behalf of "reason" and "nature" with the authority of antiquity. Given that beauty is an objective property, attainable artistically and knowable critically, by reference to the rules, the question of the percipient's response to it was scanted. As in the *Philebus*, beauty can be expected to arouse the appropriate response, which was referred to briefly and loosely as "pleasure," or "delight."

THE EIGHTEENTH CENTURY

The rebellion against the rules, in the name of the spectator's felt response—"the taste is not to conform to the art, but the art to the taste" (Addison)—intimates, in art criticism, the larger and more profound reconstruction of thought that took place in aesthetic theory. In the eighteenth century, indeed, aesthetics first established itself as an autonomous philosophical discipline. It defined a subject matter that is not explicable in terms of any of the other disciplines and is therefore taken out of the metaphysical and moral context of much traditional aesthetics, to be studied in its own right. The pioneer work is to be found in the prolific and assiduous writings of the British who, throughout the century, carried out the inquiry that Addison, at its beginning, justly described as "entirely new."

The century was a Copernican revolution, for instead of looking outward to the properties of beauty or the art object, it first examined the experience of the percipient, to determine the conditions under which beauty and art are appreciated. The decisive condition is disinterestedness, that is, perception directed upon an object without, as in practical or cognitive activity, any purpose ulterior to the act of perception itself. In aesthetic theory so conceived, beauty is no longer the central concept. It now stands for just one kind of aesthetic experience among others, and it can be defined and analyzed only by reference to the logically more basic concept of *aesthetic perception.*

The introspective examination of our "ideas," stimulated by John Locke's *Essay,* discloses experiences that differ significantly, in their felt quality, from that of beauty. This century distinguished a great many other "species" of aesthetic response, but the most important was that of sublimity. Sublimity is profoundly unlike beauty, for whereas the latter arouses "joy" and "cheerfulness," the feeling of the sublime is "amazement" and awe. Still, most of the British hold that the two can coexist and that the experience of both is pleasurable. The most drastic distinction was drawn by Edmund Burke (1757), who argued that beauty and sublimity are, conceptually, mutually exclusive and, existentially, antithetical. He at the same time limited the range of beauty severely and pushed back the boundaries of the aesthetic to include a radically different kind of experience, which cannot be accommodated in the traditional category. Indeed Burke clearly considered the experience of sublimity to be the more valuable of the two. Both Moses Mendelssohn and Immanuel Kant read Burke and were greatly affected by him, and through their influence Burke's critique of beauty made a lasting impression on Continental thought.

Burke granted that a beautiful object arouses pleasure, but he argued that a sublime object, that is, one that is "terrible," even though it is apprehended disinterestedly, arouses "some degree of horror." Beauty "relaxes," but the experience of sublimity is of great emotional intensity. The two experiences are therefore incompatible with each other. Moreover, the properties that Burke attributed to sublime objects are just the opposites of those that the *Philebus* had enshrined in the classical conception of aesthetic value. Against clarity and lucidity, Burke urged that we are moved most greatly by what is "dark, uncertain, confused." In place of formal ordering, Burke eulogized what is "vast" and "infinite." The sublime therefore renders beauty "dead and unoperative." When beauty had been taken as the sole value category, ugliness, its contradictory, had necessarily been excluded from aesthetic value. Burke went so far as to suggest that even the ugly can be an object of aesthetic appreciation. In all this, he is pointing the way to the nineteenth-century and twentieth-century concept of *expression,* which, more catholic by far than classical beauty, admits a limitless diversity of subject matter, treatment, and form, if only the work of art be moving and powerful.

A comparable challenge to the classical values of order and serenity came from another direction. The historical study of art, pioneered by Johann Joachim Winckelmann (1764), disclosed that these values are found only in relatively limited epochs and styles, even, indeed, of Greek art itself. Later research emboldened the protest against the once unchallenged arbiters of classical and neoclassical criticism that they had identified selected stylistic properties of Greek and High Renaissance art with what is beautiful "naturally" and universally.

In the eighteenth century, also, the "logic" of beauty underwent a profound sea change. Francis Hutcheson (1725) announced a new locus for beauty: "Let it be observed, that in the following papers, the word *beauty* is taken for *the idea raised in us.*" It follows that any object whatever that does in fact excite this idea must be judged to be beautiful. But this invites the possibility of diverse and conflicting judgments that, if subjective response is the sole and decisive test, must all be accepted as equally valid. Are there, however, any properties peculiar to beautiful objects, which can be pointed to, to legitimate certain judgments and whose absence will show others to be mistaken? Hutcheson thought that there was—the classical property of "uniformity in variety." Yet to be consistent with the definition of beauty with which he began, he had to guarantee that things possessing this property would uniquely and universally arouse the appropriate idea. It can be said summarily that he failed to do so, and his failure is instructive. It points up the tension between the old and the new ways of thinking, between taking beauty to be an inherent, nonrelational property and using *beauty* to refer to the capacity of things to evoke a certain experience. A capacity is not, however, an observable property in things like uniformity. It must be interpreted as either a very different sort of property or else it is not a property at all. David Hume drew out the radical implications of Hutcheson's initial meaning for beauty with the acute remark that Euclid described all of the properties of a circle, but beauty is not among them ("The Sceptic").

In general, the later British aestheticians did not take *beautiful* to denote a property. Necessarily, therefore, the logical status of the properties that they attribute to beautiful objects—proportion, utility, and so on—is correspondingly altered. Such properties are no longer, as in the *Philebus*, either identical with, or the conditions of, a property of beauty. They are, rather, causes of the experience of beauty. Even so considered, however, the traditional formulas of beauty were brought under fire throughout the eighteenth century. Since the attribution of causes can be justified only by the evidence of their effects in experience, the British, arguing from the things that people do in fact find beautiful, showed that none of these properties are shared by all these things. There was also the more subtle and damning criticism that the traditional formula of "unity in variety" is simply devoid of meaning, because it applies indiscriminately to any object whatever. By the close of the century, Alison (1790) concluded that any attempt to find properties common and peculiar to beautiful objects is "altogether impossible." Finally it was suggested that "beautiful" is just "a general term of approbation" (Payne Knight, 1805).

The British thereby generated the problem that is central to Kant's *Critique of Judgment* (1790): How, if the aesthetic judgment arises from subjective feeling and predicates nothing of the object, can it claim to be more than an autobiographical report and can, indeed, claim to be universally binding?

THE NINETEENTH AND TWENTIETH CENTURIES

The most novel development in this period has been the attempt at a scientific approach to aesthetics. This has taken two forms, generally, and the status of beauty in each is worth noting. Psychological aesthetics applies experimental methods to aesthetic experience in an effort to work out "laws" of appreciation. These are to be derived from the consensus of pleasure and displeasure reported by the laboratory subject in the face of various objects. When beauty is used at all in speaking of these objects, as it was by Gustav Theodor Fechner (1876), it is a loose, omnium-gatherum term. The objectivist-formalist connotations of the word have made it increasingly unsatisfactory to later psychologists. Either they have stipulated that it refers to certain psychological responses (e.g., O. Külpe, 1921), or they have abandoned it in favor of the more apt "liberal and comprehensive" (E. Bullough, 1907) concept of "aesthetic value." The last decades of the nineteenth century also saw the rise of *Kunstwissenschaft*, which may be rendered as "the sciences of art," for it comprises historical, anthropological, and other empirical studies of art as a cultural product. One of the impulses to the development of this field was a pervasive dissatisfaction with beauty, either because it is too limited, if interpreted on the classical model, and cannot therefore encompass, for example, primitive art, or too vague, if it is not. Art, by contrast, is a concrete, institutional phenomenon that is tractable to science. Thus *Kunstwissenschaft*, which is at present one of the most thriving and fruitful branches of aesthetics, defines itself by opposition to the concept of beauty.

The distinction between the meaning of beauty when it is synonymous with aesthetic value generally and when it stands for one class or kind of such value has been commonly remarked in recent aesthetics. In the former sense, it is often used to signalize the characteristic excellence of a work of art or an aesthetic object. Thus *beautiful* does not denote a property such as symmetry but also it is more than just a "term of approbation." It makes a claim on behalf of the object, which must be supported by appealing to the relevant value criteria. These criteria need not, however, be the same for two different artistic media or even for two works in the same medium. They are, perhaps indefinitely, plural; they are of different weight in different cases, and no one of them can be said to be a necessary condition for the use of *beautiful*. Their relevance is determined by the unique character of each work. In its second meaning, *beauty* generally connotes a relatively high degree of value, in contrast to, for example, the *pretty*, a fairly orthodox style or genre, pleasure unmixed with pain and the absence of bizarre or discordant elements. But this is just why so much of recent aesthetics and ordinary discourse finds the word awkward or even irrelevant for evaluation. It will do for Wolfgang Amadeus Mozart, but not the later Ludwig van Beethoven, for Raphael, but not Francisco de Goya. In the

Philebus, Socrates had, for his own purposes, narrowed the range of beauty severely, but it was just this narrowness that made it impossible for later thought to preserve *beauty* as the sole, or perhaps even the major, concept of aesthetic value.

See also Addison, Joseph; Aesthetic Experience; Aesthetic Judgment; Aesthetic Qualities; Aesthetics, History of; Aesthetics, Problems of; Aristotle; Art, Value in; Burke, Edmund; Fechner, Gustav Theodor; Feminist Aesthetics and Criticism; Hume, David; Hutcheson, Francis; Kant, Immanuel; Locke, John; Mendelssohn, Moses; Plato; Plotinus; Properties; Tragedy; Ugliness; Winckelmann, Johann Joachim.

Bibliography

Bosanquet, Bernard. *A History of Aesthetic.* New York: Meridian, 1957. Fairly difficult but thoughtful and acute; sees the history of aesthetics as a movement from the concept of "unity in variety" to "significance, expressiveness."

Bullough, Edward. "The Modern Conception of Aesthetics." In *Aesthetics,* edited by E. Wilkinson. Stanford, CA: Stanford University Press, 1957. A vigorous polemic, by an able psychologist-philosopher, against the "sterile" effort to find a definition of "beauty"; the "modern conception" is the "study of aesthetic consciousness."

Carritt, E. F. *The Theory of Beauty.* London, 1931. A readable account, by a leading Crocean, of many of the major historical theories.

Kainz, Friedrich. *Vorlesungen über Ästhetik.* Vienna, 1948. Translated by Herbert Schueller as *Aesthetics the Science.* Detroit: Wayne State University Press, 1962. A valuable conspectus of the major tendencies in more recent Continental aesthetics; examines the relation between beauty and the aesthetic attitude.

Morpurgo-Tagliabue, Guido. *L'esthétique contemporaine.* Milan, 1960. An extremely comprehensive and well-documented study of aesthetics since 1800, weighted heavily on the twentieth century. Stresses the distinction between the theories of art and beauty.

Osborne, H. *Theory of Beauty: An Introduction to Ethics.* New York: Philosophical Library, 1953. Lucid and informed criticism of some of the major historical theories.

Stolnitz, Jerome. "'Beauty': Some Stages in the History of an Idea." *Journal of the History of Ideas* 22 (2) (April–June 1961): 185–204. An analysis of the history of the concept in eighteenth-century British aesthetics. An extensive bibliography includes works by authors referred to above.

OTHER RECOMMENDED WORKS

Brand, Peg Zeglin, ed. *Beauty Matters.* Bloomington: Indiana University Press, 2000.

Danto, Arthur C. *The Abuse of Beauty: Aesthetics and the Concept of Art* (Paul Carus Lectures). Chicago and LaSalle: Open Court, 2002.

Devereaux, Mary. "Beauty and Evil: The Case of Leni Riefenstahl's 'Triumph of the Will.'" In *Aesthetics and Ethics: Essays at the Intersection,* edited by Jerrold Levinson. Cambridge, U.K.: Cambridge University Press, 1998, pp. 227–256.

Donoghue, Denis. *Speaking of Beauty.* New Haven, CT: Yale University Press, 2004.

Eco, Umberto, et al. *History of Beauty.* Rizzoli International, 2004.

Guyer, Paul. *Values of Beauty: Historical Essays in Aesthetics.* Cambridge, U.K.: Cambridge University Press, 2005.

Hickey, Dave. *The Invisible Dragon: Four Essays on Beauty.* Los Angeles: Art Issues Press, 1993.

"Beauty" (several entries). In *Encyclopedia of Aesthetics,* edited by Michael Kelly. Oxford: Oxford University Press, 1998, pp. 237–251.

Kieran, Matthew. *Revealing Art.* New York: Routledge, 2004.

Lorand, Ruth. *Aesthetic Theory,* Vol. 5: *A Philosophy of Beauty and Art.* New York: Routledge 2000.

Mattick, Paul. "Beautiful and Sublime: 'Gender Totemism" in the Constitution of Art." In *Feminism and Tradition in Aesthetics,* edited by Peggy Zeglin Brand and Carolyn Korsmeyer. University Park: Pennsylvania State University Press, 1995, pp. 27–48.

Mothersill, Mary. *Beauty Restored.* Oxford: Clarendon Press, 1984.

Prettejohn, Elizabeth. *Beauty and Art.* New York: Oxford University Press, 2005.

Sartwell, Crispin. *Six Names of Beauty.* New York: Routledge 2004.

Scarry, Elaine. *On Beauty and Being Just.* Princeton, NJ: Princeton University Press, 1999.

Zangwell, Nick. "Beauty." In *The Oxford Handbook of Aesthetics,* edited by Jerrold Levinson. Oxford: Oxford University Press, 2003, pp. 323–343.

Jerome Stolnitz (1967)
Bibliography updated by Mary Devereaux (2005)

BEAUVOIR, SIMONE DE
(1908–1986)

Simone de Beauvoir, French existentialist feminist, was born in Paris in 1908 and died in 1986, after a prolific career as a philosopher, essayist, novelist, and political activist. Her writings were, by her own accounts, heavily influenced by the philosophy of Jean-Paul Sartre, her intellectual companion for half a century—a fact that led some critics to dismiss her as philosophically unoriginal. Even de Beauvoir, in a 1979 interview, said that she did not consider herself to be a philosopher. In her view, however, "a philosopher is someone like Spinoza, Hegel, or like Sartre, someone who builds a grand system" (quoted in Simons, 1986, p. 168), a definition that would exclude most contemporary professional philosophers. Furthermore, as several recent commentators have argued, de Beauvoir seems to have underestimated her influence on philosophy in general and on Sartre in particular. While she incorporated Sartre's ideas, such as his existentialist conception of freedom, in her ethical and political writings, her critiques of Sartre's work in progress also helped shape his philosophy, which she then extended and transformed in significant ways.

In *The Ethics of Ambiguity* (1948), de Beauvoir attempted to develop an existentialist ethics out of the ontological categories in Sartre's *Being and Nothingness*. In Sartre's view, there is no God and therefore no God-given human nature. Nor is human nature determined by biological, psychological, economic, cultural, or other factors. People are "condemned to be free," and in the course of existing and making choices, they construct their own natures (which are continually revisable). Although human consciousness is being-for-itself (the being of free and transcendent subjects), it vainly tries to turn itself into being-in-itself (the being of objects, things trapped in their immanence). De Beauvoir called this doomed attempt to synthesize the for-itself and the in-itself the "ambiguity" of the human condition, and she argued that ethics is both possible and required because of this inability of human beings to "coincide with" themselves. She attempted to ground ethics in individual freedom, asserting, "To will oneself free is also to will others free" (1948, p. 73), but her defense of this claim appears to slip Kantian and Hegelian presuppositions about human nature into a philosophy that denies that there is such a thing as human nature.

In *The Ethics of Ambiguity*, de Beauvoir moved beyond Sartrean existentialism in acknowledging certain constraints on freedom, including political oppression and early socialization, that Sartre did not recognize until much later. In her memoirs (1962), de Beauvoir recalled conversations she had with Sartre in 1940 about his account of freedom as an active transcendence of one's situation. She maintained that not every situation offered the same scope for freedom: "What sort of transcendence could a woman shut up in a harem achieve?" Sartre had insisted that even such a limiting situation could be lived in a variety of ways, but de Beauvoir was not persuaded. To defend her view, though, she would "have had to abandon the plane of individual, and therefore idealistic, morality," from which Sartre and de Beauvoir developed their philosophies (1962, p. 346).

In *The Second Sex* (1953) de Beauvoir continued to move away from a purely metaphysical view of freedom in developing an account of how the oppression of women limits their freedom. In arguing, "One is not born, but rather becomes, a woman," de Beauvoir applied the existentialist tenet that "existence precedes essence" to the situation of women, but she was also influenced by Marxist accounts of the material constraints on our freedom to create ourselves. In addition, she described how the socialization of girls and the cultural representations of women perpetuate the view of woman as other, thereby limiting women's potential for transcendence.

Critics of de Beauvoir's feminism have pointed out tensions between her existentialist premises and her account of the relation between embodiment and oppression. Although, according to existentialism, anatomy is not destiny (nor is anything else), de Beauvoir's discussion of female sexuality at times suggests that women's reproductive capacities are less conducive than men's to achieving transcendence. De Beauvoir has also been criticized for advocating in 1949 (1953) that women assume men's place in society, although in interviews in the 1970s and 1980s she urged a transformation of both men's and women's roles.

Even de Beauvoir's critics acknowledge her enormous impact on contemporary feminism. Her analysis of what has become known as the sex/gender distinction set the stage for all subsequent discussions. In drawing on philosophy, psychology, sociology, biology, history, and literature in *The Second Sex* and other essays, she anticipated the interdisciplinary field of women's studies. Her concern with autobiography, with self-revelation as "illuminating the lives of others" (1962, p. 8), prefigured the preoccupation of feminism with the personal as political. She also drew on a philosophical tradition as old as Socrates; her relentless scrutiny of herself and others exemplified, to an extent unmatched by any other twentieth-century philosopher, the maxim that "the unexamined life is not worth living."

In her fiction as well as in her essays and memoirs, de Beauvoir discussed numerous philosophical themes—for example, freedom, choice, responsibility, and the other—and she also explored the political issues and conflicts of the day, so much so that she has been described as "witness to a century." But she was more than a mere chronicler of events; she was a powerful social critic and an internationally known "public intellectual," whose influence will continue to be felt for a long time.

See also Existentialism; Sartre, Jean-Paul.

Bibliography

Francis, Claude, and Fernande Gontier. *Les écrits de Simone de Beauvoir*. Paris, 1979. A comprehensive bibliography of the publications of de Beauvoir from 1943 to 1977.

WORKS BY DE BEAUVOIR

Essays

Pyrrhus et Cinéas. Paris: Gallimard, 1944.

The Ethics of Ambiguity. Translated by Bernard Frechtman. New York: Philosophical Library, 1948. Originally published as *Pour une morale de l'ambiguïté.* Paris: Gallimard, 1947.

The Second Sex. Translated by Howard M. Parshley. New York: Knopf, 1953. Originally published as *Le deuxième sexe.* Paris: Gallimard, 1949.

The Coming of Age. Translated by Patrick O'Brien. New York: Putnam, 1972. Originally published as *La vieillesse.* Paris: Gallimard, 1970.

Fiction

She Came to Stay. New York: Norton, 1954. Translated by Yvonne Moyse and Roger Senhouse. Originally published as *L'invitée.* Paris: Gallimard, 1943.

The Mandarins. Translated by Leonard M. Friedman. New York: Norton, 1956. Originally published as *Les Mandarins.* Paris: Gallimard, 1954.

Memoirs

Memoirs of a Dutiful Daughter. Translated by James Kirkup. New York: Harper and Row, 1959. Originally published as *Mémoires d'une jeune fille rangée.* Paris: Gallimard, 1958.

The Prime of Life. Translated by Peter Green. New York; Paragon, 1962. Originally published as *La force de l'âge.* Paris: Gallimard, 1960.

Force of Circumstance. Translated by Richard Howard. New York: Putnam, 1965. Originally published as *La force des choses.* Paris: Gallimard, 1963.

All Said and Done. Translated by Patrick O'Brien. New York: Putnam, 1974. Originally published as *Tout compte fait.* Paris: Gallimard, 1972.

WORKS ON DE BEAUVOIR

Bauer, Nancy. *Simone de Beauvoir, Philosophy, and Feminism.* New York: Columbia University Press, 2001.

Brosman, Catharine Savage. *Simone de Beauvoir Revisited.* Boston: Twayne Publishers, 1991.

Card, Claudia. *The Cambridge Companion to Simone de Beauvoir.* Cambridge, U.K.: Cambridge University Press, 2003.

Dietz, Mary G. "Introduction: Debating Simone de Beauvoir." *Signs* 18 (1992): 74–88.

Gatens, Moira. "Woman as Other." In her *Feminism and Philosophy.* Cambridge, U.K.: Polity, 1991.

Le Doeuff, Michèle. "Simone de Beauvoir and Existentialism." Translated by Colin Gordon. *Feminist Studies* 6 (1980): 277–289.

Mackenzie, Catriona. "Simone de Beauvoir: Philosophy and/or the Female Body." In *Feminist Challenges: Social and Political Theory*, edited by Carole Pateman and Elizabeth Gross. Boston: Northeastern University Press, 1986.

McCall, Dorothy Kaufmann. "Simone de Beauvoir, *The Second Sex*, and Jean-Paul Sartre." *Signs* 5 (1979): 209–223.

Simons, Margaret A. "Beauvoir and Sartre: The Philosophical Relationship." *Yale French Studies* 72 (1986): 165–179.

Tong, Rosemarie. "Existentialist Feminism." In her *Feminist Thought.* Boulder, CO: Westview Press, 1989.

Whitmarsh, Anne. *Simone de Beauvoir and the Limits of Commitment.* Cambridge, U.K.: Cambridge University Press, 1981.

Susan J. Brison (1996, 2005)

BECCARIA, CESARE BONESANA
(1738–1794)

Cesare Bonesana Beccaria, the Italian criminologist and economist, was born in Milan of aristocratic parents. His formal education began at the Jesuit college in Parma and ended with his graduation from the University of Pavia in 1758. After graduation Beccaria came under the intellectual influence of two brothers, Pietro and Alessandro Verri, who had gathered around themselves the young Milanese intelligentsia to form a society known as the "academy of fists," committed to promoting reforms in political, economic, and administrative affairs.

Beccaria was prompted by Pietro Verri to read the then prominent philosophies of the Baron de Montesquieu, Claude-Adrian Helvétius, Denis Diderot, David Hume, and the Comte de Buffon. At the suggestion of his friends, Beccaria wrote and published his first treatise, *Del disordine e de' rimedi delle monete nello Stato di Milano nell'anno 1762* (Lucca, 1762). It was also through the encouragement of the Verri brothers that Beccaria composed his most important work, *Dei delitti e delle pene* (translated by H. Paolucci as *On Crimes and Punishments,* New York, 1963). Through Alessandro Verri, who was an official of the prison in Milan, Beccaria visited that institution and saw the conditions that furnished information and moral stimulus for his writing. Pietro, who had already begun writing a history of torture, in many conversations on the errors of criminal law and administration provided Beccaria with new arguments and insights for the treatise. In the end, the work was almost a collaboration by the three men, for Beccaria until that time had been relatively uninformed about crime and punishment. Begun in March 1763 and completed in January 1764, the book was published anonymously at Livorno out of fear of reprisals because of its devastating attack on the legal and judicial system then in operation. But anonymity was soon dropped when it became clear that the Milanese authorities were receptive and when the essay drew the attention and respect of the Parisian intelligentsia.

Beccaria held a chair in political economy in the Palatine School of Milan from 1768 to 1770, and his lectures during this period were published posthumously in 1804 under the title *Elementi di economia pubblica.* His economic ideas on the division of labor and the determination of wages have been compared to those of Adam Smith (who wrote the *Wealth of Nations* seven years after publication of Beccaria's economic views). In economics Beccaria espoused a form of mercantilism based on some of the ideas of the physiocrats, expressed the belief that agriculture was the most productive enterprise, advocated commercial freedom within a nation and the abolition of guilds, and displayed a Malthusian concern with the relation of population growth to the means of subsistence. He also held a series of minor public offices through which he aided his friends in securing reforms in taxation, currency, and the corn trade.

On Crimes and Punishments was a protest against the use of torture to obtain confessions, secret accusations, the arbitrary discretionary power of judges, the inconsistency and inequality of sentencing, the influence of power and status in obtaining leniency, the lack of distinction in treatment of the accused and the convicted, and the use of capital punishment for serious and even minor offenses.

The concepts that Beccaria employed—rationalism, the social contract, utility, and hedonism—were current among the intellectuals of his time. The application of these ideas to crime and punishment, and the style of writing, were his own. Building upon Rousseau's social-contract philosophy, he argued that each person willingly sacrifices to the political community only so much of his liberty as "suffices to induce others to defend it." Laws are only the necessary conditions of this contract, and punishments under the law should have no other purpose than to defend the sum of these sacrificed shares of liberty "against private usurpations by individuals." Punishments for any other reason are unnecessary and unjust.

Beccaria declared that the law should be clear in defining crimes and that judges should not interpret the law but simply ascertain whether a person has or has not violated the law. He also held that punishment should be adjusted in severity to the seriousness of the crime. The primary purpose of punishment, Beccaria argued, is to ensure the existence of society, and the seriousness of the crime, therefore, varies according to the degree to which the transgressor's act endangers that existence. Treason and other acts against the state are most harmful, followed by injuries to the security of person and property and finally, by acts which are disruptive of public harmony and peace, such as rioting or inciting to disorder.

To ensure the continuance of society, punishment should aim at deterrence, that is, at preventing offenders from doing additional harm and others from committing crimes. To be effective as a deterrent to crime, punishment should be swift and certain; it is the certainty rather than the severity of punishment that deters. Life imprisonment is sufficient to deter: The death penalty is not necessary, nor is it legitimate, for individuals did not under the social contract relinquish the right to their lives. Corporal punishment is bad, and torture as part of a criminal investigation makes the suffering of pain rather than evidence the test of truth. Crimes against property should be punished by fines or, when fines cannot be paid, by imprisonment.

Beccaria's classic conclusion—the principles of which were adopted almost in their entirety by the revolutionary National Assembly of France in 1789 as Article VIII of the "Declaration of the Rights of Man and of the Citizen"—read in part as follows: "In order for punishment not to be, in every instance, an act of violence of one or of many against a private citizen, it must be essentially public, prompt, necessary, the least possible in the given circumstances, proportionate to the crimes, dictated by the laws."

Beccaria's essay became famous almost overnight. It was translated into French in 1766 by the Abbé Morellet, passed through six editions within eighteen months, one of which was embellished by a laudatory comment by Voltaire, and was thereafter translated into every important language. The Church of Rome placed the treatise on the Index in 1766, but the Austrian government, which controlled Milan, defended and honored Beccaria. Maria Theresa of Austria, Leopold II, grand duke of Tuscany, and Catherine the Great of Russia announced their intentions to be guided by Beccaria's principle in the reformation of their laws. The essay both paved the way for, and was the guiding force in, the major penal reforms that took place for two centuries afterward.

See also Buffon, Georges-Louis Leclerc, Comte de; Diderot, Denis; Hedonism; Helvétius, Claude-Adrien; Hume, David; Montesquieu, Baron de; Philosophy of Law, History of; Rationalism; Smith, Adam; Social Contract; Voltaire, François-Marie Arouet de.

Bibliography

WORKS BY BECCARIA

Opere. Edited by Pasquale Villari. Florence, 1854. A more recent edition was edited by S. Romagnoli, 2 vols. (Florence, 1958), with a bibliography, Vol. 2, pp. 917–918.

Scritti e lettere inediti raccolti ed illustrati da Eugenio Landry. Edited by Eugenio Landry. Milan, 1910.

WORKS ON BECCARIA

Cantù, C. *Beccaria e il diretto penale.* Florence: G. Barbèra, 1862.

Monachesi, E. "Cesare Beccaria." In *Pioneers in Criminology,* edited by H. Mannheim. London: Stevens, 1960. Pp. 36–50.

Paolucci, Henry. "Introduction" to his translation of Cesare Beccaria, *On Crimes and Punishments.* New York, 1963. Pp. ix–xxiii.

Phillipson, Coleman. *Three Criminal Law Reformers: Beccaria, Bentham, Romilly.* London: Dent, 1923.

Schumpeter, J. A. *History of Economic Analysis.* New York: Oxford University Press, 1954.

Marvin E. Wolfgang (1967)

BECK, JAKOB SIGISMUND
(1761–1840)

Jakob Sigismund Beck, the German Kantian philosopher, was born in Marienburg. He studied mathematics and philosophy in Königsberg with P. Krause and Immanuel Kant, completing his studies in 1783. In 1791 he became a teacher at the gymnasium in Halle and, in 1796, extraordinary professor of philosophy at Halle University. He was called to Rostock as professor of metaphysics in 1799 and remained there until his death.

Purporting to defend the "true" Kantian position against "dogmatic" misinterpretations, Beck called attention to problems concerning the role of the thing-in-itself in Kant's theory of perception. Beck rejected any positive role for the thing-in-itself and argued that the object affecting our senses must be phenomenal. Kant's theory of affection is to be understood not in the transcendent sense, as the working of an unknowable thing-in-itself on an unobservable "I"-in-itself, but only in the empirical sense: A phenomenal body in phenomenal space affects the "I" of inner sense.

But this "I" and this body, according to Beck, are themselves the products of an original activity of the understanding. The synthetic activity of "representing" (*vorstellen*) is presupposed by our viewing sense data as given *by* something objectively outside ourselves. Beck therefore objected to Kant's definition of sensibility as an immediate relation to an affecting object. The intuitions of sense say nothing about their own objectivity or source. Not until they are subjected to the categories of the understanding do they become objective, for only then can we invoke the notion of external objects and speak of intuitions as given to our senses by such objects.

The order of exposition of the *Critique of Pure Reason* is therefore misleading. One ought not to begin with sensibility, but with the synthetic unity or "original activity" (*ursprüngliche Beilegung*) of the understanding, the unique a priori act of combination (*Zusammensetzung*).

In philosophy of religion, Beck held that God is a symbol created by man, a symbol of man's ethical conscience. Piety consists simply in obedience to the commands of conscience.

In letters to Beck (1792) Kant complimented him for investigating "what is just the hardest thing in the *Critique*," approved Beck's reorganization of the Critical Philosophy, and said that he himself planned to write a work on metaphysics that would utilize the order of exposition that Beck had suggested. Kant's *Opus Postumum* shows the extent of Beck's influence, particularly in Kant's manuscript on the progress of metaphysics since Gottfried Wilhelm Leibniz and Christian Wolff.

Some of Kant's followers classed Beck with Johann Gottlieb Fichte and accused Beck of making the understanding the creator of objects. Beck did write: "Reality is itself the original act of representing, from which the concept of objects subsequently derives." But although he spoke of the original act as object-generating, he told Kant that he did not mean that the understanding *creates* objects. Beck granted the existence and importance of the given in knowledge while he attempted to bridge the dualism of sense and intellect and to insist that neither the given nor the notion of "things" could be taken as epistemologically primary.

See also Kant, Immanuel.

Bibliography

WORKS BY BECK

Erlaüternder Auszug aus den kritischen Schriften des Herrn Prof. Kant, auf Anrathen desselben. Riga, 1793–1796. Volume III of this work, *Einzig möglicher Standpunkt aus welchem die kritische Philosophie beurteilt werden muss* (Only possible standpoint from which the critical philosophy must be judged), contains Beck's most important ideas.

Grundriss der kritischen Philosophie. Halle, 1796.

Kommentar über Kants Metaphysik der Sitten. Halle, 1798.

Lehrbuch der Logik. Rostock, 1820.

Lehrbuch des Naturrechts. Jena, Germany, 1820.

WORKS ON BECK

Dilthey, Wilhelm. "Die Rostocker Kanthandschriften." *Archiv für Geschichte der Philosophie* II (1889): 592–650. Discusses Beck's place among Kant's disciples and critics.

Durante, G. *Gli epigoni di Kant.* Florence: Sansoni, 1943.

Meyer, Thomas L. "Das Problems Eines Höchsten Grundsatzes der Philosophie bei Jacob Sigismund Beck." *Analogia Filosofica* 5 (2) (1991): 205–208.

Potschel, W. *J. S. Beck und Kant.* Breslau, 1910.

Vleeschauwer, H. J. de. *L'evolution de la pensée kantienne.* Paris, 1939. Translated by A. R. C. Duncan as *The Development of Kantian Thought.* London: Nelson, 1962. Discusses Beck's influence on Kant's last reworking of the *Critique of Pure Reason.*

Arnulf Zweig (1967)
Bibliography updated by Tamra Frei (2005)

BEHAVIORISM

Traditional notions of the mind have tended to treat mental states as "private" and "subjective," not accessible to the public and objective methods of science. With the failure of an "introspectionist" psychology in the early twentieth century, the only recourse seemed to be either to deny that mental states had any role to play in any serious science, or to try to find a way to understand talk of mental states that was entirely objective. The first option is called the "eliminativist" strategy, and *Radical behaviorism* was a monumental effort to realize it. The eliminativist strategy proposed to explain all human and animal behavior in terms of physically specified stimuli, responses, and reinforcements. It is to be distinguished from the second, "reductionist" strategy, which attempts not to *eliminate* mental phenomena, but rather to *save* mental phenomena by identifying them with some or other existing physical phenomena. *Analytical behaviorism* was the specific reductionist view that mental phenomena could be identified in one way or another with dispositions to overt behavior. Both Radical behaviorism and Analytical behaviorism dominated Anglo-American philosophy, and especially psychology, from roughly 1920 through 1970.

Although the two views are similarly motivated, they are independent. As will be seen in section one, Radical behaviorism is a specific scientific hypothesis, to be assessed according to the usual scientific criteria of how well it predicts and explains its intended range of phenomena. Analytical behaviorism is essentially a semantic, or philosophical hypothesis, to be assessed according to how well it captures the mental notions it purports to analyze (sec. 2). A person could subscribe to one and reject the other: Strict radical behaviorists might be skeptical of semantic proposals of analytical behaviorists; and many analytical behaviorists might reject the scientific proposals of Radical behaviorism.

There is also a third view, *methodological behaviorism*, according to which the only *evidence* for any mental phenomena must be behavioral. As a claim about evidence, this is actually independent of both the other views, although it often accompanied them. Indeed, one of the lasting positive contributions of the entire behaviorist movement was a much higher standard of evidence than had been observed previously, discouraging the kind of reliance on empathic intuitions that was characteristic, for example, of clinical psychotherapeutic claims. Unlike Radical behaviorism and Analytical behaviorism, methodological behaviorism survives in some quarters to this day, although some problems for methodological behaviorism are raised at the conclusion of section three.

RADICAL BEHAVIORISM

THE LAW OF EFFECT. Since this is a philosophical encyclopedia, the treatment of Radical behaviorism will perforce be brief (for a more thorough discussion in which references can be found to the experiments cited here see Gleitman et al. 2004, Gallistel 1990, and Rey 1997). However, the treatment of Radical behaviorism is not philosophically irrelevant since a substantial number of twentieth-century philosophical views often relied on it, most famously those of the American philosopher W. V. Quine.

Radical behaviorism emerged from the work of the Edward Thorndike (1874–1949), John Watson (1878–1958), and Ivan Pavlov (1849–1936), receiving its most energetic development in the work of B. F. Skinner (1904–1990) and attaining considerable precision in the work of Clark Hull (1884–1952). It has its source in traditional empiricist theories of the mind, according to which the mind at birth is a tabula rasa, or blank tablet on which experience forms sensory impressions. Ideas are derived from experience and are welded together to form complex ideas by a process of association, which closely tracks the presentation of those experiences in reality. Thus, certain sights, sounds, and tactile sensations become associated in experience to form the idea of a material object, and certain associations of "contiguity, succession and constant conjunction" form the idea of causation (Hume 1734).

This traditional suggestion, though regarded by radical behaviorists as right in spirit, suffered from a major defect—namely, a reliance upon peculiar private entities, ideas, and impressions, which did not seem to radical behaviorists to be proper objects of scientific inquiry. To remedy this situation, they proposed studying not associations among ideas but among physically characterizable stimuli to sense organs and responses of the motor system. The specific law that linked stimuli and responses was Thorndike's Law of Effect, which for purposes of this entry may be stated thus:

> The Law of Effect: *The probability of a response R following a stimulus S is increased/decreased if pairs ⟨R,S⟩ have been followed by positive/negative reinforcements, F, in certain patterns (e.g., intermittently) in the past.*

For example, should a particular movement like pressing a paw on a lever (=R) when a light is on (=S) be followed intermittently by the presentation to a hungry animal of a food pellet (=F), then the probability of the animal pressing its paw on the lever when the light is on in the future will be increased. Such are rewards. Negative reinforcements are either the absence of positive reinforcements, or actual punishments, which also reinforce, but in the opposite direction: the probability of the R given S is reduced if pairs of S and R have been followed by punishment in the past. Radical behaviorism is essentially the bold hypothesis that all intelligent human and animal behavior can be explained by the Law of Effect.

As Skinner frequently stressed, the Law of Effect is nearly the biological principle of natural selection, extended now beyond the persistence of traits that are genetically inherited to the persistence of acquired behaviors in individual animals. Just as from a random generation of genetic mutations certain ones are selected by virtue of meeting an environmental test of "survival of the fittest," so from an essentially random generation of responses in an animal certain ones are selected by virtue of being reinforced when they occur after certain stimuli. The responses that are selected in this way Skinner (1938) called "operants," since they involved ways that an animal "operated" on an environment that secured reinforcement. This process of "operant conditioning" was Skinner's distinctive contribution over "classical conditioning," where the response was *elicited* (e.g., salivation by hunger in Pavlov's dogs), rather than being spontaneously *emitted*.

How could such a simple law as the Law of Effect possibly stand a chance of explaining the full range of animal behavior? The central idea was an extension of the associationist strategy of building complex ideas from simpler ones, only now it was a matter of building not complex ideas, but complex responses. These could be built up out of simpler responses by "response chaining," whereby stimuli associated with a reward themselves become ("secondary") reinforcers, and so available for the conditioning of further responses. Thus, a pigeon conditioned to peck a lever on hearing a bell could now be conditioned by the sound of the bell itself to produce further responses given further stimuli, say, doing a little dance on seeing a red light, which is then followed by the bell, which is then followed by food if the pigeon pecks again at the lever. Discrimination of complex stimuli would similarly be built from discrimination of simpler stimuli, through either a chain of discriminations of simpler stimuli, or by "stimulus generalization," whereby novel stimuli are treated as "of the same kind" as earlier ones.

The Law of Effect is likely true of some animal behavior. Skinner achieved remarkable successes using it to train animals to engage in all manner of curious behavior: for example, rats to run mazes, pigeons to play Ping-Pong, and pigs to push shopping carts around supermarkets. And the Law of Effect seems to play a role in explaining a variety of persistent behavioral patterns, such as gambling and drug addiction, as well as in extinguishing them, as in "behavior modification therapy." For the purposes of this entry, the issue is not whether such applications occur or are a good idea, but whether they offer a theoretically adequate paradigm for understanding the full range of intelligent animal behavior.

INADEQUACIES OF THE LAW OF EFFECT. Problems with the Law of Effect emerge in the first instance from the radical behaviorist experiments themselves. Contrary to popular belief, it is not only human behavior that resists radical behavioristic explanation; the theory does not even really work for the rats. The main problem is that the probability of a response can be increased in ways other than by the Law of Effect. There are at least four classes of phenomena that the law has trouble explaining: latent learning, passive learning, spontaneous alteration, and improvisation.

Latent learning occurs when an animal learns without reinforcement. Rats that were well sated with, for example, food and water were allowed to run around in a maze for ten days without any reward, sometimes being placed in the maze at arbitrarily different points. Subsequently, when they were hungry again they were introduced into the maze and were able to find the food much faster than rats not previously exposed. Similarly, Harry Harlow showed that monkeys presented with a complex hinge, requiring the undoing of several pins and bolts to free it, learned to undo it with no special reward other than "the fun of it." Further, indigo buntings learn something about the position of the stars while still in the nest, despite not using this information for navigation (and so, *a fortiori*, not for any reward) until they are much older. In all of these cases the probability of the animal producing the appropriate response was greater than that of animals that had not been previously exposed to such stimuli, but without any history of reinforcement. In a related vein, passive learning occurs when an animal learns without antecedently producing the requisite response. Thus, rats can learn a maze merely by being pulled through it in a transparent trolley car, not executing anything like the responses that will take them through the maze when they are tested later.

Not only can rats learn without reinforcement or response, they can sometimes respond in ways that defy their conditioning history. In "spontaneous alteration," an animal actually avoids emitting the response that has recently been reinforced. After having found food at a particular location, for example, hummingbirds will go somewhere else to find more food. Rats presented with a number of paths of equal length to a goal will vary their routes, although invariably in ways that advance their approach to the goal. The phenomenon is most dramatically displayed by rats in a "radial maze," consisting of eight pathways radiating out in all directions from a central location, with baits placed at the end of each arm. The Law of Effect should predict that the rats should return to an arm in which they have found food. What they do instead, however, is to *avoid* an arm they have already visited until they had—at random—visited all the others. That is (as we might put it mentalistically), they seem not to be matching responses to stimuli, but "keeping track" of "where the baits are," and, knowing they had consumed one, no longer "expected" it to be there. The Law of Effect seems not only inadequate to account for such cases; it actually seems to be disconfirmed by them

Animals also produce appropriate behaviors that have not even previously been produced, much less reinforced. Thus, rats trained to take a circuitous route to a goal box will immediately take a shortcut if it is made available. Indeed, animals apparently refuse to be tied to specific physical responses: Rats will swim a flooded maze after being taught to run it, and—moving to the wild, outside the confines of a structured maze—desert ants will forage in a winding path up to one hundred meters from their nests, and then, once they find food, will take a beeline home.

Passing beyond issues of navigation, it has been noted with regard to latent learning that monkeys presented with a novel, complex hinge, figure out how to undo several pins and bolts to free it. Köhler demonstrated even more remarkable improvisation in chimpanzees: They would use sticks as rakes to secure food that was outside a fence; they would then use these sticks as poles, which they would climb up in order to snatch food that was out of reach, grasping the food just as the stick toppled over. In all of these cases, the responses—that is, the sequence of muscular motions required to execute the acts—are by no means physically type-identical between prior and test trials. So the animals must have learned something other than merely to repeat certain physically typed responses.

Of course, these inadequacies with the Law of Effect become even more glaring in the human case. Picking up on an example of Skinner's (1957, p. 38), Daniel Dennett (1975) provides an apt and amusing discussion of the difficulties besetting a radical behaviorist attempting to explain why someone mugged in New York hands over his wallet: Why doesn't the person instead do any number of things that were more likely to have been previously reinforced with the stimulus "Your money or your life," such as giggling, or yawning? Of course, it is not impossible that there is a story of prior threat stimuli and responses of the requisite sort. But the burden is squarely on the radical behaviorist to supply it.

Radical behaviorists, of course, did not take challenges to the inadequacies of the Law of Effect lying down. They often made ingenious replies to them involving elaborate emendations of the theory—for example, by Clark Hull (1943). But these emendations were then subject to further tests, showing animals to be more ingenious than the Law of Effect allowed. A consensus began to emerge that what animals learn is not any mere sequence of responses to stimuli, but rather to the development of what Edward Tolman called an "internal map" (1948). Such talk of "insight" and "maps" of course, begins to imperil any eliminativist ambitions of Radical behaviorism: such a map would be an inner representation, involving an internal mental state.

STRUCTURED RESPONSES AND LANGUAGE. An important problem in principle for Radical behaviorism was raised by Karl Lashley (1951): Serial responses like those involved in tying shoes or riding a bicycle seemed to be *structured* in a way that it did not seem possible to explain by local response-chaining alone. A domain of behavior that exhibits particularly striking structure is *language*. Skinner (1957) tried to sketch an account of linguistic behavior, but it was soon subject to a devastating review by the then young linguist Noam Chomsky (1964). Among other things, he pointed out:

(i) along lines indicated by Lashley, language is *structured* in units that cannot be captured by response chaining. For example, a sentence of the form "Either ... or ... ," or "If ... then ... " can involve waiting indefinitely for novel items to be inserted in the blanks;

(ii) language is *creative*: most of the sentences people encounter and produce are constantly *novel*—it is why people bother to converse, read, and write— all contrary to the Law of Effect's commitment to a prior history with the stimuli and responses;

(iii) language is *productive*: in grasping a grammar, even small children know how to produce a potential infinity of novel, structured sentences, as in "This is the house that Jack built," "This is the rat that lived in the house ... ," "This is the cat that chased the rat ... ," without any history of conditioning each component in this way; indeed:

(iv) the complex set of rules that constitute the grammar is acquired effortlessly by practically all human children by the age of three, without (and sometimes despite) any efforts at explicit instruction.

(For more detailed discussion see Chomsky 1972 and Pinker 1994).

Although Chomsky's review was (to many minds) a definitive blow by itself, what really led to the end of Radical behaviorism was the spectacular positive research program that he and others (e.g., Fodor 1968, 1975) had begun to develop, what has come to be called the *cognitive revolution*, associated with computational-representational theories of mental processes.

Often recognizing the difficulty of avoiding mentalisms in the explanation of animal behavior, radical behaviorists sometimes allowed mentalisms to creep into their explanations, postulating "exploratory" and "curiosity" drives, or "drives to perceive" or "know." Of course, if the theory was to remain true to its goal to avoid reference to subjective mental states that it regarded as unscientific, it would be obliged to define these postulations in terms of overt behavior. It was in this way that Radical behaviorism invited Analytical behaviorism, to which we now turn.

ANALYTICAL BEHAVIORISM

Analytical behaviorism was motivated by two related philosophical trends of the twentieth century that persist into the twenty-first century: the well-known *verifiability*

theory of meaning (or *verificationism*) and the less well-known doctrine that might be called *irreferentialism*. Because the latter serves as something of a background for the former, it will be considered first.

IRREFERENTIALISM. Irreferentialism is a novel suggestion that arose from Bertrand Russell's (1905) famous theory of definite descriptions, according to which expressions like "the present king of France" should not be construed as *referring* to any (in this case) nonexistent entity, but as rather shorthand for some logically complex expression, only some of the most basic parts of which manage to refer. Perhaps the most obvious deployment of such a strategy is the in the case of a sentence such as "The average American family has 2.5 children," which, of course, does not entail that there is some family somewhere in America that has a half of a child. A proper analysis of the grammar of the claim reveals that it is simply a way of expressing the ratio between American families and their children.

The view begins to be applied as a claim about mental expressions in the work of the later Wittgenstein (1953) and Gilbert Ryle (1949). They argued that philosophers too often think about the phenomena that people introspect in their "inner mental worlds" on the model of the objects in the familiar "outer" one. The temptation to this analogy arose, Wittgenstein and Ryle claimed, from an excessively referential conception of the functioning of the human mental vocabulary, treating words like "belief," "thought," and "sensation" as referring to "inner," "private" objects, in the way that words like "cat" and "rock" refer to outer, public ones. It is not that, like "Zeus," they do not *happen* to refer to anything; rather, like "the average American," they do not even *purport* to refer to anything. The view is perhaps best known from Ryle's attack on the idea of the "ghost in the machine": A mind is not some sort of *thing* that *could* be a ghost, or any other *thing*. Not surprisingly, this irreferentialism was often associated with an antipathy one finds in Wittgenstein (1953) and Ryle (1949) toward a psychology that suggests a "promise of hidden discoveries yet to be made of the hidden causes of our actions and reactions" (Ryle 1949, p. 325).

Irreferentialism is an essentially negative thesis about the analysis of mental terms. Understandably, many people might want to hear something more positive: if the analysis of mental terms does not involve the postulation of mental entities, what does it involve? For Wittgenstein and his followers, in particular, this question (like, in their view, most philosophical questions) was the wrong one to ask: it exhibited a somehow inappropriate "craving for generality" about the nature of thought and language. That may in the end be so, but many wanted to see a greater effort made toward some systematic account than he and his followers provided. The use of mental language does not seem entirely capricious and chaotic, and, if it is not, then it is not unreasonable at least to ask what the principles might be that guide its use.

VERIFICATIONISM. According to verificationism, the meaning of a claim consists in the method by which it could be tested (see Ayer 1952 for a classic statement). For example, claims about something's being an acid might be defined in terms of its turning litmus paper red. Or claims about the existence of material objects might be analyzed as logical construction of claims about those sense experiences that people ordinarily take to confirm such claims (e.g., that people would have certain experiences of color, shape, and resistance to touch). Hypotheses such as those of the possibility of human lives being a dream, or other people having radically different mental lives were to be ruled out as "meaningless" if there really were in fact no evidence in principle that could make a difference to their truth or falsity.

There are myriad problems with verificationism: It is by no means obvious how to apply it to the claims of logic, mathematics, ethics, or aesthetics, or even to itself (what is the test for assessing where it is true?). Even in the supposed parade cases of natural science verificationism did not fare well: Scientists often do not know how to seriously test a hypothesis (as in contemporary string theory in physics) and often change their tests as their theories evolve (as new tests are devised for a disease). But the most serious problem is *confirmation holism*, or the fairly obvious observation that claims are not tested by experiment individually, but only as parts of whole theories (see Quine 1960). As will be seen, Analytical behaviorism offered a vivid case in point.

ANALYTICAL BEHAVIORIST PROPOSALS. Analytical behaviorism was largely motivated by verificationism and the observation that the vast majority of human mentalistic claims are tested by observing overt behavior (of course, this does not seem to be true in the case of first-person reports, which were always a problem for Analytical behaviorism, although these represented a small minority of claims). Moreover, it did seem that those ascriptions were by and large indifferent discoveries that might be made about the actual physical aetiology of mental life. If one were to open up the heads of familiar people and discover that they were empty or full of saw-

dust, one would not conclude that these familiar people did not have the mental states that seem to be constituted by the familiar behavior observed. Consequently, it seemed reasonable to suppose that mental claims should be understood as equivalent to various sorts of dispositional or conditional claims about how an agent would behave if she were in such and such circumstances. One particular model that impressed behaviorists was that of *dispositional* claims that arise elsewhere: "Salt is soluble" presumably means something like, "If salt is put into water in certain normal conditions, then it dissolves"; "Glass is fragile," something like, "If struck in normal circumstances, it breaks." Analogously, *wanting* something should be taken to mean something like "*trying to get it, if the occasion were to arise.*"

Successfully spelling out the appropriate dispositions in the case of mental terms turned out, however, to be none too easy. Ryle was never precise, but he offered a strategy, exemplified by the following characterization of belief:

> To believe that the ice is dangerously thin is to be unhesitant in telling oneself and others that it is thin, in acquiescing in other people's assertions to that effect, in objecting to statements to the contrary, in drawing consequences from the original proposition, and so forth. (Ryle 1949, 134–135)

ACTION VS. "COLORLESS MOVEMENT." A formidable problem arises, however, as soon as one considers the "behavior" on which people normally rely, namely of distinguishing *actions* from *mere movement*: To take a famous example from Wittgenstein, it is the difference between raising one's arm and one's arm rising. The rising of an arm might occur as a result of, say, some machine moving the arm up and down; it is only the raising of an arm if it was the result of the person whose arm it is *intending* to raise it. Ryle may think that he is describing mere behavior in talking about someone being "unhesitant" and "acquiescing," "objecting" to certain "assertions," but a moment's reflection reveals these as only slightly covert mentalisms: *hesitation, acquiescence,* and the possible involvement of any of an indefinite variety of bodily movements (or none); all that is crucial is that whatever the agent does or does not do is a result of a certain psychological attitude.

This point was often most seriously missed by the radical behaviorists who, as has been noted already, often resorted to mentalisms to deal with the apparent counterexamples to their Law of Effect. Thus, Skinner wrote:

ENCYCLOPEDIA OF PHILOSOPHY
2nd edition

The artist ... is reinforced by the effects his works have upon ... others ... [his] verbal behavior ... reach[ing] over centuries or to thousands of listeners or readers at the same time. The writer may not be reinforced often or immediately, but the reinforcement may be great. (Skinner 1957, pp. 206, 224)

But, as Chomsky (1964) noted, the term *reinforcement* here has degenerated to only a ritual function, being used as a cover term for "X wants Y," "X likes Y," "and X wishes that Y were the case."

INSUPERABLE PROBLEMS. For every thought experiment arguing for Analytical behaviorism there are compelling ones against it as well. Consider not only people with sawdust heads, but people who turn out to be robots cleverly controlled by radio waves produced by some ingenious scientists at MIT: Such creatures would seem to have no more of a mental life than do marionettes. Or consider a race of "Super-Spartans" who, as matter of training and principle, refuse to flinch or complain in response to even the most excruciating pain and are inarticulate about an enormous range of their psychological repertoire (Putnam 1975). Surely it is possible that these Super-Spartans have by and large the full range of psychological states of the more expressive and articulate.

All of these objections become more evident when one considers an underlying technical difficulty noticed by Roderick Chisholm (1957): Every effort to define most mental states by behavior seems to require citation of other mental states. Typically, any particular mental state causes a particular behavior only in conjunction with (an often large number of) other mental states. Beliefs, hopes, and expectations issue in behavior only in conjunction with (at least) desires; desires issue in behavior only in conjunction (at least) with beliefs and expectations. To take a proposed example from Tolman, suppose a person tried to define a rat's expectation that there is food at L in terms of the rat's moving toward L: This only if the rat *wants* food; and the rat's *wanting* food can be defined in terms of its moving toward L only if it *expects* there is food at L. Insofar as this is true, the prospects of a definition of a single informational or single directional state in terms of behavior seem dim. This problem is an instance of the aforementioned confirmation holism emphasized by Quine. Indeed, a philosophically influential (and disconcerting) way of understanding this and related difficulties with Analytical behaviorism is provided by Quine's (1960, ch. 2) "thesis of the indeterminacy of translation," according to which there is no fact of the

matter about the content of mental states, a thesis that has influenced later philosophers such as Donald Davidson, David Lewis, and Dennett.

METHODOLOGICAL BEHAVIORISM

In the twenty-first century few, if any, philosophers or psychologists would be prepared to defend either Radical behaviorism or Analytical behaviorism. However, there is a weaker view that survives, called "methodological behaviorism," according to which the only permissible evidence for a psychological claim can be behavioral. It is not, like Radical behaviorism, an explanatory scientific hypothesis, but neither does it, like Analytical behaviorism, offer analyses of mental terms, although it is motivated by vaguely verificationist concerns like those that motivated Analytical behaviorism. Methodological behaviorism is perhaps best expressed by Wittgenstein's famous dictum, "An inner process stands in need of outward criteria," (1953, sec. 580) but without any of the analytical behaviorist commitment to defining an inner process in terms of some specific criteria. It has most recently been defended by Dennett (1993), who describes its motivation as not a "village" but an "urbane verificationism" that is merely trying to avoid "epiphenomenalism, zombies, conscious teddy bears, [and] self-conscious spiders" (1993, p. 461). Indeed he "unhesitatingly endorse[s] the claim that necessarily, if two organisms are behaviorally exactly alike, they are psychologically exactly alike" (1993, p. 922).

For all methodological behaviorism's urbanity, however, it is hard to find a convincing argument for it. Why shouldn't psychologists avail themselves of evidence that may go beyond ordinary overt behavior, as they indeed seem increasingly to do when they investigate the finer structure of the brain? Consider, for example, the nice case Dennett (1991, pp. 395–396) discusses of the familiar plight of the adult beer-drinker who wonders whether in coming to like it since childhood, it is his *experiences* or his *preferences* that have changed. It can seem obscure what further considerations should settle the matter, and it is not implausible to suppose that current behavioral discriminations or even introspection would not suffice. Dennett concludes that that there is in such a case "no fact of the matter" about "the way the beer tastes" to such a person.

But suppose it turns out that children have more taste buds than adults. One might have independent evidence that both children and adults have the same preferences for bitter titillation, but that consequently children reach a painful threshold sooner with the same quantity of a bitter substance. It tastes differently because, arguably, more intense sensation is caused by their tongues and/or gustation subsystems. However, such cases would clearly transcend mere behavioral evidence.

So, in the end, even methodological behaviorism seems problematic given the increasingly rich conceptual and evidential resources of cognitive science, and especially of a computational/representational theory of thought. Behaviorism in all its forms seems a heroic theory that was ultimately defeated by the high standards of theory and experimentation that it encouraged. Eliminativist strategies survive in ambitions to replace mental talk by neurophysiological descriptions, and reductionist strategies abound, along either neurophysiological lines or computational ones. But the effort to replace mental talk with behavioral talk, or reduce it to it, can safely be said to have passed with the twentieth century, in which it first appeared.

See also Chomsky, Noam; Fodor, Jerry A.; Functionalism; Mind-Body Problem; Physicalism; Quine, Willard Van Orman; Reductionism in the Philosophy of Mind; Verifiability Principle.

Bibliography

Ayer, A. *Language, Truth and Logic*. New York: Dover, 1952. A classic statement of the "Verificationist Theory of Meaning," which provided the general semantic view underlying Analytical behaviorism.

Chisholm, R. *Perceiving: A Philosophical Study*. Ithaca, NY: Cornell University Press, 1957.

Chomsky, N. *Language and Mind*. New York: Harcourt Brace Jovanovich, 1972. Chomsky's earliest and most accessible statement of the relation of his theory of grammar to theories of the mind generally.

Chomsky, N. "Review of Skinner's *Verbal Behavior*." In *The Structure of Language: Readings in the Philosophy of Language*, edited by J. Fodor and J. Katz, 547–578. Englewood Cliffs, NJ: Prentice Hall, 1964. The devastating review of Skinner's effort to incorporate linguistic behavior into Radical behaviorism.

Dennett, D. *Brainstorms*. Cambridge, MA: MIT Press, 1975. Several essays ("Skinner Skinner," "Why the Law of Effect Won't Go Away") provide excellent discussions of the attractions and limitations of Radical behaviorism.

Dennett, D. *Consciousness Explained*. New York: Little Brown, 1993. A recent defense of methodological behaviorism (which he calls "urbane verificationism").

Fodor, J. *The Language of Thought*. New York: Crowell, 1975. The classic statement of the computational/representational theory of thought that, he argues, is presupposed by virtually all work in cognitive and perceptual psychology.

Fodor, J. *The Modularity of Mind: An Essay on Faculty Psychology*. Cambridge, MA: MIT Press, 1983. The classic statement of the now highly influential view of perception and language processing as consisting of computational "modules."

Fodor, J. *Psychological Explanation: An Introduction to the Philosophy of Psychology*. New York: Random House, 1968. An early, powerful philosophical critique of both Radical behaviorism and Analytical behaviorism.

Gallistel, C. *The Organization of Learning*. Cambridge, MA: MIT Press, 1990. An important non-behaviorist, computational theory of animal navigation, bringing together extensive studies of animals in the wild.

Gleitman, H., A. Fridlund, and D. Riesberg. *Psychology*. 6th ed. New York: Norton, 2004. An excellent, up-to-date text in psychology. Chapter four provides a detailed account of Radical behaviorism.

Hull, C. *Principles of Behavior: An Introduction to Behavior Theory*. New York: Appleton-Century-Crofts, 1943. A serious, concerted effort to state the laws of behavior in terms of "colorless movement" in ways designed to accommodate many of the experimental problems Radical behaviorism faced.

Hume, D. *A Treatise of Human Nature*, (1739), edited by L. A. Selby-Bigge. 2nd edition revised by P. H. Nidditch. Oxford: Clarendon Press, 1975. The classic statement of an associationist psychology, of which Radical behaviorism was an instance.

Lashley, K. S. "The Problem of Serial Order in Behavior." In *Cerebral Mechanisms in Behavior*, edited by L. A. Jeffress, 112–136. New York: Wiley, 1951. Widely regarded as raising a crucial problem for Radical behaviorism by calling attention to highly structured behaviors that could not be the result of mere response chaining.

Pinker, S. *The Language Instinct: How the Mind Creates Language*. New York: Harper and Row, 1994.

Putnam, H. "Brains And Behavior." In *Mind, Language And Reality: Philosophical Papers*. Vol. 2. Cambridge, U.K., and New York: Cambridge University Press, 1975, 325–341.

Quine, W. V. *Word and Object*. Cambridge, MA: MIT Press, 1960. Chapter two presents his influential discussion of the "indeterminacy of translation," which he draws as an interesting consequence of Radical behaviorism.

Rey, G. *Contemporary Philosophy of Mind: A Contentiously Classical Approach*. Oxford: Blackwell, 1997. Chapters four and five present detailed discussions of Radical behaviorism and Analytical behaviorism along lines of the present article. Chapters seven and ten present arguments against methodological behaviorism (called "superficialism" there).

Russell, B. "On Denoting" *Mind* 14 (1905): 479–493.

Ryle, G. *The Concept Of Mind*. London: Hutcheson, 1949.

Skinner, B. F. *The Behavior of Organisms: An Experimental Analysis*. New York, Appleton-Crofts, 1938. The official statement of Skinner's famous version of Radical behaviorism.

Skinner, B. F. *Verbal Behavior*. New York: Appleton-Century-Crofts, 1957. Skinner's effort to provide a radical behaviorist framework for understanding language.

Tolman, E. "Cognitive Maps in Rats and Men." *Psychological Review* 55 (1948): 189–208.

Georges Rey (2005)

BEING

Philosophy proceeds in part by the asking of large, imprecise, and overgeneral questions. In the attempt to answer them, the questions themselves come to be reformulated with greater clarity, and one large question often comes to be replaced by several smaller ones. The history of pre-Socratic philosophy is the best example of this process, and Being first appeared on the philosophical scene as part of it. To the question "What is Being?" the Parmenidean answer that there is Being and nothing else besides Being appears to have the merit of truth, even if it is tautological truth. What is, is; and what is not, is not. But what Parmenides' question in fact contains is a non-tautological demand for the characteristics of what is, to which the answer that Being is one, unchanging, and eternal is appropriate. Since the objects we perceive are many, changing, and transient, they do not belong to the realm of Being. Parmenides thus fathered in broad outline a doctrine of Being from which philosophers as diverse as Aristotle, Georg Wilhelm Friedrich Hegel, and John Dewey have tried to rescue us. This is the doctrine that Being is a name.

"BEING" AS A NAME

"Being" may be thought to name a property possessed by everything that is. Or it may be thought to name an object or a realm beyond, above, or behind the objects of the physical world; in this case, physical objects somehow exist by virtue of their relationship to "Being." Or again, "Being" may be the name of the genus to which everything that is belongs in virtue of the possession of the property of Being or of standing in relation to Being. The doctrine that "Being" is a name implies some kind of dualism, according to which the realm of Being is contrasted with that of the merely phenomenal. Variations on this doctrine are general enough to be put to a number of different uses in the attempt to solve quite different problems. Nevertheless, the basic doctrine is founded on a false assumption, for it obscures the facts that the verb "to be" has a number of different uses and that in its central and commonest use it does not ascribe a property, a relation, or class membership in any way. "Being" is normally a participle, not a noun. To break with normal usage without special justification is to be gratuitously liable to confusion. We can investigate the type of confusion generated by the acceptance of "Being" as a name, and also the type of clarification that came to be needed, by considering what Plato and Aristotle make of Being.

PLATO AND ARISTOTLE

Plato was anxious to mark the distinction between properties and objects that possess properties. He located the former in the realm of Being and the latter in the realm of the transient. One reason for this distinction was that Plato accepted the identification of Being with the unchanging (in this case, the unchanging meanings of predicate, the Forms). As a consequence, he was forced to deny that physical objects "are"—they belong to a stage intermediate between Being and Not-Being, that of becoming. This is not the only paradox in Plato's analysis of the subject: The Form of the Good, which exists at a higher level than that of the other Forms, cannot just "be," either; it must exist "beyond being."

Thus, we can see in Plato one of the characteristic results of treating Being as either a special kind of object or a special kind of attribute, namely, that all sorts of ordinary uses of the verb "to be" must be qualified or rewritten. The outcome of the attempt to make what is mystifying clear is to make what was clear mystifying. The author who first attacked this kind of mystification was, of course, Plato himself. In the *Sophist,* the problem of negative judgment is handled in such a way that it is no longer possible to make Parmenides' mistake of supposing that when one speaks of what is not, one is speaking of what does not exist. Moreover, it is scarcely proper to speak casually of confusion and mistake at this stage in the development of philosophy. The first steps toward producing a logical grammar of the verb "to be" perhaps necessarily involved assimilating the different senses and uses of the words, and of consequently becoming caught up in paradox and learning how to free oneself. When Aristotle, in Book I of the *Metaphysics,* clarified earlier errors, he was able to do so only because he had learned from the efforts and missteps of Parmenides and Plato.

Aristotle made three crucial points about the study of Being as Being. The first is that the special sciences may make use of the concept of Being and of other similar fundamental concepts, but these concepts are not the objects of their inquiries—only philosophy has such fundamental concepts as the proper object of its studies. The second point is that to inquire about Being as Being is to attempt to isolate the unifying strand of meaning in the multifarious senses in which the word "is" is used. The third point is that this inquiry can be carried on only as an inquiry into a whole range of closely related fundamental concepts, in which the different species of cause and the notions of unity and plurality are foremost.

Aristotle recognized that we use "is" to deny as well as to affirm, and to ascribe properties as well as to ascribe existence; and in various passages he makes use of these distinctions to clarify conceptual points. He recognized, as did the Scholastics, that in ascribing properties to a subject we sometimes imply the existence of that subject and we sometimes do not. But in his willingness to recognize the diversity of uses of "is," Aristotle almost too easily accepted the view that we can speak of abstract entities as well as of physical objects without allowing the former "separate" existence. Aristotle said very little, in fact, about the common thread that binds together the various uses of "is."

SCHOLASTIC PHILOSOPHERS

The non-Aristotelian medieval writers who insisted on a single meaning for "is" unintentionally provided a reductio ad absurdum proof of the correctness of the Aristotelian approach. Both nominalists and realists, at least in their extreme and consistent versions, asserted that properties and objects exist in the same way: properties for the nominalists were merely collections of objects, and objects for the realists were merely properties of properties. For the nominalist Eric of Auxerre, "Being" was simply the collective name of all the individuals that exist taken together and was logically equivalent to "this and this and this …," while for the realist Odo of Tournai, individuals were accidents of properties that are substances, and the realm of Being was a realm only of properties.

Abelard to some extent reasserted the Aristotelian distinctions (and suggested some new ones of his own), but it was Thomas Aquinas who returned to the pure Aristotelian tradition. Thomas refuted once again the view that Being can be either a genus or a property.

In his Commentary on Aristotle's *Metaphysics*, Thomas diagnosed Parmenides' mistake and applied his conceptual insights to related problems, notably in his refutation of Anselm's Ontological Argument. But Thomas's position necessarily has a complexity lacking in some other writers who have been equally careful, for although he could not accept Anselm's view that to know what God is is to know that he is, he also could not reject the identification of God's Being with his essence. According to Thomas, with all finite creatures it is the case that what they are—their essence—is one thing, and that they are—their existence—is another. But God simply is Being—*Esse Ipsum Subsistens*. Because this is so, Thomas was obliged to agree with Anselm that *if* God exists, he exists necessarily. But from this it does not follow that God does exist. That there is such a being, who *is* Being, is shown, according to Thomas, by a posteriori proofs. And of course in Thomist terms it is improper to think of God as just *a* being, one entity among others. The difficulty here, however, is derived from difficulties that are implicit in the notion of the God of monotheism and not from difficulties in the notion of Being itself.

CENTRAL QUESTIONS

We are now in a position to discriminate different kinds of questions about Being raised by the Greeks and the Scholastics.

IS EXISTENCE A PREDICATE? How should we characterize the difference between ascribing existence to a subject and ascribing a property to a subject? Is "is" ever a predicate? If it is, what sort of predicate? Later writers who have discussed this problem include René Descartes, in his version of the Ontological Proof; Gottlob Frege, with his clarification of the nature of predicates; G. E. Moore, with his argument that "existence" is not a predicate because we cannot, for example, significantly replace "growl" with "exist" in all the quantified and negated forms of "Tame tigers growl"; and W. V. Quine, with his analysis of Being as "to be is to be the value of a variable." This list of names points up the fact that these questions are susceptible of solution only within the philosophy of logic, and the solution depends upon an adequate characterization of names, predicates, variables, functions, and so on. It is also clear that it is of primary importance to discriminate the metaphysically noncommittal "is," formalizable by means of the existential quantifier, from other uses of the verb "to be" that are far more committed in their implications. Noncommittal uses of the verb appear in ordinary language in such expressions as "There is a prime number between six and eight," "There are three basic colors," "There is a mountain more than 29,000 feet high." Other uses of the verb "to be," however, are far more committed. For example, in the statement "Rachel wept for her children because they were not," "to be" is equivalent to "to be alive." Clearly, however, if I say "There is such-and-such a prime number," there is no such implication; hence, this sense of "there is" must be different.

One finds that all analyses of existential assertions that treat them as predicative are generally unsatisfactory. Briefly, the reason for this is that predicates refer to properties, and properties are what discriminate individuals from each other and enable us to pick out similarities and dissimilarities, and hence to classify. But Being cannot be a property in this sense, for it is not something that it is logically possible for two objects either to have or not to have in common. Two objects cannot be said to resemble each other in virtue of their both being, and since existence is not a shared property, it cannot characterize a class of objects. For this reason, Being can be neither a property nor a genus.

Of course some philosophers—Gottfried Wilhelm Leibniz, for example—have talked as though Being were a property shared by actual objects but not possessed by *possibilia*. There is no objection to talking like this, provided that it is noticed that the word *property* is not now being used to refer to distinguishable characteristics of real things. Hence, the assertion by such philosophers that Being is a property is not compatible with the Thomas Aquinas–Moore view that it is not, given the two different senses in which the word is used.

ABSTRACT ENTITIES. How do we characterize the status of abstract entities, numbers, possibilities, fictions? These are all different problems, each of them complex. They are envisaged as part of the problem of Being, partly because of our ordinary use of "There is/are" in, for example, "There are two possibilities" or "There is a prime number between six and eight," and partly because of a misunderstanding involved in describing certain possibilities by such terms as "real." When we apply the adjective "real" both to possible states of affairs and to actual states, we suggest that there is a realm of reality wider than the merely existent. This is one source of the belief that there is a genus Being, of which the existent and the nonexistent (such as the possible) are species. Everything called real belongs to the realm of Being. The mistake lies in not seeing the difference between the way in which "real" functions as an adjective and the way in which "reality" functions as a noun. If I call a dollar bill real, I contrast "real" with "counterfeit." If I call a painting "a real Vermeer," I contrast it with a copy. But I do not ascribe to dollar bill and painting the common property of "being real," in virtue of which they belong to the same realm, that of "reality." To say that there is a kind of Being in which both what exists and what does not exist can share is obviously to commit the same mistake. But at this point we have returned to the question of whether Existence and Being can be properties, which belongs to our first group of questions.

THE CHARACTERIZATION OF BEING-AS-SUCH. Can we find any characteristic that belongs to everything that is and that may therefore be said to characterize Being-as-such, rather than individual objects? Here again, one must distinguish two kinds of questions. Aristotle pointed out that of any object whose existence I affirm, I shall also be able to say that it is *one*, that it is *an* object. That is, by picking out something for the purpose of saying that it is, or that it is such and such, I pick it out as an individual. But just because this is so, individuality or unity is not something that it is logically possible for a given object to possess or not to possess any more than existence is; hence, they are not properties any more than existence is. The Aristotelian question of what concepts must be applicable to anything that exists must not, therefore, be identified with the question of whether there are any properties that belong to everything that exists.

There might, of course, have been some property that belonged to everything that existed just as a matter of contingent fact. The world might have been such that everything was green or cubic, or made of blancmange. But this would be philosophically uninteresting (quite apart from the fact that in most such worlds there would be no philosophers). It has been held, however, that it is necessary on, for example, metaphysically epistemological grounds that everything that is shall be of a certain character. Hence Plato's view in his middle period that only Forms exist, and hence Leibniz's view that there are only monads, and George Berkeley's view that to be is always either to be percipient or to be perceived.

ABSOLUTE BEING. Is there a being who exists without the limitations of finite beings and who may therefore just be said to be? This is the question of God's existence.

REALM OF BEING-AS-SUCH. Is there—beyond, over, and above the being of individual objects—a realm of Being-as-such? If so, what is its character? The belief that there is such a realm has always haunted metaphysics. The notion that Aristotle held such a belief has pervaded the history of metaphysics. This misinterpretation of Aristotle has similarly been foisted upon Thomas, and a neo-Thomist myth of the history of philosophy has been constructed in which the four questions that have already been distinguished, all of which are genuine questions, are merged into this fifth question, whose character is much more dubious. It then becomes possible to suggest that there is a single problem: "What is Being?" to which different philosophers have given rival answers. The kind of metaphysics to which reference is being made can be found in Jacques Maritain's *Preface to Metaphysics,* where Maritain is ostensibly expounding Thomas. In order to treat Being as a subject matter, however, Maritain invokes what he calls the intuition of Being, a notion that cannot be found anywhere in Thomas. Thomas, as we have already seen, never treated "Being" as the name of an independent subject matter and thus had no reason to suggest any means of becoming aware of the existence of such a subject matter.

The kind of history of metaphysics to which reference is being made can be found in D. A. Drennan's *A Modern Introduction to Metaphysics,* which asserts that to the question "What is Being?" Parmenides replied that it was One; Plato, that it was One and Many; Aristotle, that it was Substance; Descartes, that it was Substance in the modes of thought and extension; and so on. Nevertheless, an awareness of the nonexistence of the single question of Being rids us of the misleading idea that we have here a set of competing answers to a single question.

The temptation to see the history of metaphysics in this light seems often to be provoked by an espousal of the metaphysics that makes "Being" a name. We can illustrate this point by considering two sequences in the history of modern philosophy. Hegel argued that Being is the most fundamental of concepts because the most elementary forms of judgment must involve some assertion of existence, no matter how bare. But, he continued, the notion of Being by itself is the emptiest of all notions. Merely to say of something that it is, is to say nothing at all about it; hence, the notion of Being merges into that of its apparent opposite, Nothing. It is not necessary to follow through the Hegelian scheme of categories to see that Hegel is, in fact, extremely cautious at this point. His extreme antidualism always led him to assert that there is nothing else beyond what we confront in experience. The Hegelian Absolute is the rational culmination of historical experience, not a power beyond and outside it. Similarly, for Hegel, Being is a concept expressed in our judgments of experience at a certain level, not the name of a realm beyond all judgments about experience.

In Nicolai Hartmann's philosophy, however, we find a misreading of Hegel parallel to the neo-Scholastic misreading of Thomas and Aristotle. In *Grundzüge einer Metaphysik der Erkenntnis,* Hartmann begins by stating a set of antinomies between, for example, the nature of consciousness as consciousness of what is other than itself and the nature of consciousness as self-contained, so that whatever consciousness is aware of is part of consciousness. That is, Hartmann describes consciousness in two ways that appear incompatible and then inquires how he may reconcile these two descriptions. Instead of asking whether the incompatibility is perhaps only apparent, however, he suggests that the problem arises, and is soluble, because both the knowing, conscious subject and the known object exemplify modes of Being, although different modes. Clearly, it is true that both

knower and known *are,* but equally clearly—for reasons given earlier—this is not a property that is open to further study and that has strange characteristics that enable us to resolve antinomies. This, however, was Hartmann's conclusion, and he attributed it to Hegel. He merged Hegel's classification of different subject matters and his scheme of concepts in order to read him as a metaphysician who understood Being as having different grades and modes.

Just as Maritain misreads Thomas and Hartmann misreads Hegel, so Martin Heidegger has misread the pre-Socratics. Heidegger's own views have a mixed ancestry. Søren Kierkegaard, one of the important influences on him, in the *Concept of Dread* writes of dread as an experience whose object is Nothing. Usually in Kierkegaard this sort of statement appears to be a dramatically effective and logically innocent way of characterizing dread as objectless, but at times it seems as if Kierkegaard is no longer saying that dread has no object. Rather, he gives it a particular object whose name is "Nothing," thus making—but not as a joke—the mistake of the Red King in *Through the Looking-Glass,* who thought that if Nobody had passed the messenger on the road, Nobody should have arrived first. To treat "Nothing" as a name is like treating "Something" as a name and easily becomes a counterpart to treating "Being" as a name, as it does with Heidegger. Heidegger takes up Leibniz's question, "Why is there something rather than nothing?" He objects that this question does not take seriously the fact that Being and Nothing necessarily exist together as contrasted and opposed powers. Heidegger allows that he is using "Being" and "Nothing" as names and is therefore involved in treating "Nothing" as if it were the name of something. He even allows that this is "unscientific," but he concludes that this is so much the worse for science and so much the better for philosophy and poetry. Being and Nothing are not objects, and Being is indeed sharply contrasted with beings. Logic presupposes Being and Nothing, but they lie beyond the grasp of logic. Heidegger treats what others have written of the indeterminateness of the concepts as evidence of the elusiveness of Being and Nothing.

Heidegger extends his metaphysics into the history of philosophy by finding his views anticipated in the thought of Heraclitus and Parmenides. The evidence for this claim depends partly on a set of unreliable etymologies that Heidegger thinks he has found for key Greek words, but even when Heidegger is plausible in his interpretation at the linguistic level, he is at the least anachronistic in his view of the kind of problem the pre-Socratics confronted. They progressively recognized as paradoxical, and therefore as needing reformulation, those very forms of utterance that to Heidegger are and remain fundamental.

If the philosophy of Being has bred not merely rival doctrines but rival views of the history of philosophy, it has also bred rival diagnoses of the errors involved in treating "Being" as a noun. A. J. Ayer has suggested that a misuse of the verb "to be" is the root of the error. This would imply, however, that standard forms of grammar embodied in ordinary usage are somehow philosophically normative—and this appears to get matters upside down. Linguistic distortion is certainly liable to breed confusion, but there is, in fact, nothing grammatically wrong with forming a verbal noun such as "Being" as an analogy with, for example, "riding." "Riding" is used as the name of an activity; why, then, should "Being" not be made into a name? It is surely because of the logical and metaphysical confusion involved that we want to criticize the linguistic construction and not because the linguistic construction itself is an error.

John Dewey diagnosed a twofold root of errors about Being. They are partly a survival from religious modes of thought, the retention of belief in a realm free from change and decay and separate from the realm of sense perception. This is explained by the fact that although mythological thought has been discredited, the impulses behind it still need satisfaction. Also, belief in changeless Being is a consequence of man's habit of abstracting truths from the contexts of practice and activity in which they were acquired (and where alone they have meaning) and treating them instead as belonging to a timeless realm in which they wait upon our apprehension. Dewey's diagnosis, however, while it may explain how we come to hold and retain confused views of Being, does not embody an explanation of why the views are confused, except perhaps to those who are already convinced in general of the truth of Dewey's pragmatism.

In order to clarify the issue, we must, in fact, make the sort of analysis of concepts that Aristotle used in the *Metaphysics*. We may expect any analysis of the concept of Being to vary with the general framework of concepts within which it is considered. Aristotelians, Hegelians, and Quineans will not all agree, but any analysis that fails to discriminate the different questions involved, and that fails to identify the confusion that results from merging them into a single question, will be doomed to conceptual error and very likely to a misreading of the history of philosophy as well.

See also Absolute, The; Anselm, St.; Aristotle; Ayer, Alfred Jules; Descartes, René; Dewey, John; Existence; Frege, Gottlob; Hartmann, Nicolai; Hegel, Georg Wilhelm Friedrich; Heidegger, Martin; Heraclitus of Ephesus; Kierkegaard, Søren Aabye; Maritain, Jacques; Medieval Philosophy; Moore, George Edward; Nothing; Ontological Argument for the Existence of God; Ontology; Parmenides of Elea; Plato; Quine, Willard Van Orman; Time, Being, and Becoming; Universals, A Historical Survey; Thomas Aquinas, St.

Bibliography

TEXTS

Aristotle. *Metaphysics.* Translated by H. Tredennick. Cambridge, MA, 1945.

Aristotle. *Metaphysics.* Edited by W. D. Ross. Oxford translation. Oxford, 1948.

Cajetan. *Commentaria in De Ente et Essentia.* Edited by M. H. Laurent. Turin, 1934.

Cornford, F. M. *Plato and Parmenides.* London, 1935; New York: Liberal Arts Press, 1957. A translation of the *Parmenides.*

Dewey, John. *The Quest for Certainty.* New York: Minton, Balch, 1929.

Duns Scotus. *Opera Omnia,* 12 vols. Paris, 1891–1895. Vol. III, *Quaestiones Subtillissimae Super Libros Metaphysicorum Aristotelis.*

Hartmann, Nicolai. *Grundzüge einer Metaphysik der Erkenntnis.* Berlin: de Gruyter, 1925.

Hegel, G. W. F. *The Science of Logic.* Translated by W. H. Johnston and L. G. Struthers. New York, 1929.

Heidegger, Martin. *Existence and Being.* Translated by D. Scott, R. Hall, and A. Crick. Chicago: H. Regnery, 1949. Includes various works.

Kant, Immanuel. *Critique of Pure Reason.* Translated by Norman Kemp Smith. London: Macmillan, 1934.

Kirk, G. S., and J. E. Raven, eds. *The Presocratic Philosophers.* Cambridge, 1960. Ch. 10, Parmenides texts. Also contains translation and commentary.

Plato. *Platonis Opera.* Edited by J. Burnet. Oxford, 1899–1906. The *Theaetetus* and the *Sophist.* Translated by F. M. Cornford as *Plato's Theory of Knowledge.* London: K. Paul, Trench, Trubner, 1935; New York: Liberal Arts Press, 1957.

Quine, W. V. *From a Logical Point of View.* Cambridge, MA, 1953.

Thomas Aquinas. *De Ente et Essentia.* Edited by M. D. Roland-Gosselin. Le Saulchoir, 1926. Translated by Armand Maurer as *On Being and Essence.* Toronto, 1949.

Thomas Aquinas. *In Metaphysicorum Aristotelis Commentaria.* Edited by M. R. Cathala. Turin, 1935.

Thomas Aquinas. *Summa Theologica.* Ottawa, 1941–1945. Translated by the Dominican Fathers of the English Province, 3 vols. New York: Benziger, 1947.

Wolff, Christian von. *Philosophia Prima Sive Ontologia.* Frankfurt and Leipzig: Officina libraria Rengeriana, 1736.

DISCUSSIONS OF TEXTS

Gilson, Étienne. *L'Être et l'essence.* Paris: J. Vrin, 1947.

Gilson, Étienne. *Being and Some Philosophers.* Toronto: Pontifical Institute of Mediaeval Studies, 1949.

Martin, Gottfried. *Immanuel Kant: Ontologie und Wissenschaftstheorie.* Cologne: University of Cologne, 1951. Translated by P. G. Lucas as *Kant's Metaphysics and Theory of Science.* Manchester, U.K.: Manchester University Press, 1955.

Owens, Joseph. *The Doctrine of Being in the Aristotelian Metaphysics.* Toronto: Pontifical Institute of Mediaeval Studies, 1951.

ARTICLES

Geach, P. T. "Form and Existence." *PAS* 55 (1954/1955): 251–272.

Geach, P. T., A. J. Ayer, and W. V. Quine. "Symposium: On What There Is." *Aristotelian Society Supplement* 25 (1951): 125–160.

Moore, G. E. "Is Existence a Predicate?" *Aristotelian Society Supplement* 15 (1936): 175–188.

Quine, W. V. "On What There Is." *Review of Metaphysics* 2 (1948–1949): 21–38.

Weiss, P. "Being, Essence and Existence." *Review of Metaphysics* 1 (1947–1948): 69–92.

Alasdair MacIntyre (1967)

BELIEF

Beliefs are a species of propositional attitude distinguished by their having the mind-to-world direction of fit.

Propositional attitudes are psychological states characterized by a psychological mode, Ψ, and a propositional content, P, schematically: $\Psi(P)$. My belief that the earth moves has *belief* as its psychological mode, and *that the earth moves* as its propositional content. A desire that the earth move has the same propositional content, but a different psychological mode, *desire*. Within a psychological mode, propositional attitudes are distinguished by their contents. I could not have two beliefs with the content that the earth moves. Many, though not all, propositional attitudes admit of a bivalent evaluation. Beliefs are true or false. Desires are satisfied or unsatisfied. Intentions are carried out or not carried out. Propositional attitudes with a bivalent evaluation have either the mind-to-world direction of fit or the world-to-mind direction of fit (Searle 1983, chapter 1). Its direction of fit expresses the basic function of a propositional attitude in our mental economy. Beliefs aim to represent how the world is independently. They aim at truth. The belief that Solomon was wise is true if and only if (iff) its content matches the world, that is, iff Solomon was wise. Belief's aim to repre-

sent how the world is independently is reflected in its being irrational to retain a belief when one sees that it does not match the world. Thus, beliefs have the mind-to-world direction of fit. A desire, in contrast, seeks not to match how the world is independently, but for the world to come to match its content. Desires seek satisfaction. The desire that a toothache go away is satisfied iff the world comes to match its content, that is, iff the toothache goes away. It is not irrational to retain desires known to be unsatisfied, for seeking satisfaction gives them their point. Desires thus have the world-to-mind direction of fit. Beliefs and desires, in virtue of their opposite directions of fit, have an interlocking role in the production and explanation of action.

BELIEF, SENSATION, EXPERIENCE, AND CONCEPT

Beliefs (and other propositional attitudes) must be distinguished from sensations, sensory images, and experience, on the one hand, and concepts, on the other. The classical British empiricists of the seventeenth and eighteenth centuries—John Locke (1632–1704), George Berkeley (1685–1753), and David Hume (1711–1776)—were unable to provide an adequate account of belief because they assimilated all of these to sensations or sensory images, like the taste of apple or a toothache. But sensations are not an adequate model for belief, or for other propositional attitudes. Sensations are not true or false, or satisfied or unsatisfied. They do not admit of a bivalent evaluation, as propositional attitudes do. They do not have propositional contents. Their differences are differences of qualitative feel. These differences are not variations in psychological function, as are the psychological modes of belief and desire. In particular, propositional contents are required to make sense of the logical relations that obtain between beliefs, and which are crucial to understanding the role of beliefs in reasoning and action. For example, understanding the validity of the inference from the belief that gold is a metal, and the belief that this ring is gold, to the belief that this ring is metal, requires seeing the logical connections between the propositional contents of the first two beliefs and the last, and their shared elements. Similarly, as explained below, the logical relations between the contents of belief and desire are crucial to understanding rational action (see the discussion of the practical syllogism below). Since sensations lack propositional contents, treating beliefs as a subclass of sensations obliterates distinctions needed to understand the role of beliefs in thought and action.

Perceptual experiences, unlike sensations, can be veridical or nonveridical. A hallucination of a rhinoceros on the sofa is a nonveridical perceptual experience. It represents what is not so. Perceptual experiences are like beliefs in admitting of bivalent evaluation and having the mind-to-world direction of fit. But though many beliefs are based on perceptual experience, they are a different coin. Perceptual experience is a fieldlike representational medium and makes use of the qualitative features of modes of consciousness associated with different sensory modalities (visual, auditory, tactile, etc.) to represent how things are around us. Beliefs, in contrast, do not in the same way make use of qualitative features of modes of consciousness to represent. Their mode of representation is purely propositional. Beliefs are to perceptual experiences as statements are to maps. Perceptual beliefs, those based directly on perceptual experience, in effect abstract from the richer representational content of perceptual experience.

Just as beliefs, sensations, and experiences must be distinguished from each other, they must also be distinguished from the shared elements, concepts, in different attitude contents. The concept of gold, for example, is shared between the belief that gold is a metal and the belief that this ring is gold. It is a constituent of both contents. Concepts are neither true nor false, though they apply or fail to apply to things. Sensations neither have such constituents nor are identical with them, for belief contents do not have sensations or images as constituents. Experiences involve concepts, much as beliefs do. A visual experience *as of* a baseball represents a spherical object as a baseball. The experience is distinct from the concept of a baseball, but represents something visually presented as falling under the concept. Without the concept, there could be no such visual experience.

Someone who believes that gold is a metal *possesses* the concept of gold and the concept of metal. Possessing a concept requires having beliefs expressing the simplest conceptual connections that the concept enters into. For example, someone who possesses the concept of a gun must believe that guns are weapons, that they are physical objects, that they can be aimed, and the like. Perhaps no precise set of beliefs is required, but if a person lacks a network of beliefs articulating the connections of a concept with other concepts, he does not possess the concept. This shows that we can make sense of attributing a belief to someone only by locating it in a pattern of beliefs, and that the other propositional attitudes and perceptual experience presuppose belief.

BELIEFS AND THE EXPLANATION OF ACTIONS

Beliefs, because they aim at truth, play a central role in theoretical reasoning (reasoning about what is so), and hence in practical reasoning (reasoning about what to do).

Theoretical reasoning is central to practical reasoning because we get what we want by doing something that promotes it. We therefore need to know what we can do, and how what we can do is related to what we want. When seeking knowledge of these things, we seek true beliefs about them. Thus, what we do is conditioned by what we believe, whether our aim at truth hits the mark or not. Accordingly, when one explains an action, it is not enough to cite a desire that the action satisfies. One must also cite a belief that the action increased the likelihood of satisfying the desire. If I want my rival to come to grief and an idle comment of mine leads to his downfall, my desire that he come to grief does not help explain my bringing about his downfall if I did not think that my idle comment would have that as a consequence.

An action explanation provides the materials for a practical syllogism that justifies the action from the point of view of the agent. Suppose that I lifted my finger because I wanted to signal you and believed that my lifting my finger, F, would constitute signaling you. One can construct the following argument in favor of this action, drawing the evaluative premise from the desire and the factual premise from the belief:

My signaling you is desirable (has a desirable aspect).
F, being lifting of my finger, is a signaling of you.

F is desirable (has a desirable aspect).

This does not show that the action is desirable all things considered, but only that it has a desirable aspect. Actions have many consequences and properties, some of which one may want and others of which one may not. In deciding all things considered what to do, the agent must rank his desires and take into account his degrees of confidence in desired outcomes attending certain actions, or, in a common phrase, his degrees of belief in outcomes, given the actions. Candidate actions are evaluated on the basis of the value of their results and one's degree of confidence in their having those results. If the chance is low but the value great, the undertaking may still be judged best overall. The notion of degree of belief in a proposition is often treated as a generalization of the ordinary notion of belief. Typically, on buying a ticket, one does not believe that one will win the lottery, though one does have a nonzero degree of belief that one will. However, it may be that degrees of belief in a proposition can be assimilated to beliefs about its probability.

BEHAVIORIST THEORIES OF BELIEF

Logical behaviorism, a form of materialism, holds that ascribing beliefs and desires and other mental states to an agent is just a compendious way of describing a complex pattern of his actual and potential behavior. On this view, there are no inner mental states or events—no "ghost in the machine," in Gilbert Ryle's memorable phrase. If logical behaviorism is true, action explanation is not causal explanation, but rather functions by locating some particular behavior in a broader pattern of behavior. Logical behaviorism was championed by the logical positivists of the 1930s (see Ayer), and in more subtle forms by Ryle and Ludwig Wittgenstein in the 1940s and 1950s. A central motivation for the logical positivists was their verificationist criterion of meaning, according to which the meaning of a statement should be sought in the conditions that verify or falsify it.

Logical behaviorism fell from fashion after the Second World War (Block). One reason was disenchantment with the verificationist criterion of meaning. A second was the failure to provide necessary or sufficient conditions for attributing psychological states in purely behavioral terms. This failure is connected with the interlocking roles of belief and desire in explaining behavior, and carries an important lesson about the relation of belief (and other propositional attitudes) to behavior.

Let us try to say what behavior is characteristic of the belief that there is an apple pie in the pantry. It is clear that what behavior we expect will depend on what the agent wants and what else she believes. If she is not hungry, we expect no tendency to investigate the pantry. If she likes apple pie but wants to save it for the guests more than to indulge herself, we expect a delayed advance on the pantry. If she believes it is poisoned, we expect her to dispose of it. And so on. The important point is that the behavior we expect from someone who has a particular attitude is conditioned by the other psychological states that we think he has. This makes it impossible to state, in purely behavioral terms, what it is to believe, for example, that there is a pie in the pantry.

Once one understands the role of desire, in particular, in action, one can see that it will play the spoiler for any behaviorist program. For desires can be about behavior usually taken to be a sign of a given sort of psychological state. In particular, one may want to exhibit misleading behavior. One can pretend to believe or want things one does not, and one can suppress behavior that expresses what one wants. It seems plausible, as Hilary Putnam argued in "Brains and Behavior," that the limited deceptions with which we are familiar could take forms that would preclude any behavioral expression of some of an agent's psychological states throughout his life.

BELIEFS AS CAUSES OF BEHAVIOR

The moral is that beliefs issue in behavior only in conjunction with appropriate other propositional attitudes. Desires motivate behavior, but beliefs guide it. Each is impotent without the other. To vary a phrase of Kant's, desire without belief is blind; belief without desire is empty. We cannot read back from behavior to the motivating belief and desire, because any given behavior may issue from different sets of beliefs and desires. Behavior is related to belief and desire as symptoms to a disease. The symptoms may be expressed in the absence of the disease, and the disease may be present without being expressed by any symptoms, or by the usual symptoms. The reason is that the disease is a cause of the symptoms. Its giving rise to the usual symptoms depends on the usual background conditions being present. This analogy suggests that, as with disease and background conditions, beliefs and desires are interlocking causes of behavior. This would explain the failure of the behaviorist programs, since, as Putnam put it, "*causes* are not logical constructions out of their *effects*" (p. 27).

This conclusion is bolstered by an argument by Donald Davidson in his seminal paper "Actions, Reasons, and Causes." We sometimes have multiple reasons (belief and desire pairs that potentially explain an action) for doing something, but we act on only one of them. I may believe that if I do not obey the speed limit when driving, I will likely receive a ticket, and I may wish to avoid receiving a ticket. I may believe also that obeying the speed limit is the right thing to do, and wish to do the right thing. I may obey the speed limit for the first reason rather than the second, or for the second rather than the first. In either case, each reason would justify what I do, but only one would explain it. We can make sense of this being so if we hold that the reasons for which I act are those that cause my action.

VOLUNTARISM ABOUT BELIEF

Beliefs play a role in guiding and explaining action, but can they be the products of actions? Can one come to believe something by choosing or deciding to believe it? According to voluntarism about belief, the answer is yes.

René Descartes (1596–1650), "the father of modern philosophy," apparently endorsed belief voluntarism. In his explanation in the *Meditations* (pp. 37–43) of how we fall into error despite God's supreme benevolence, he assumed that when one lacks adequate evidence one can choose to believe something and hence fall into error through the exercise of free will, and thereby absolve God of responsibility for the error. With his famous wager in *Pensées* (pp. 151–153), Blaise Pascal (1623–1662) argued that the infinite utility that attaches to believing truly that God exists means that no matter how small the probability, one is rationally compelled to belief. This argument likewise seems to assume belief voluntarism. In "The Will to Believe," William James (1842–1910), like Pascal, argued that it is not only possible but sometimes rationally required that we make decisions about belief when evidence underdetermines choice.

One may, of course, bring oneself to believe something indirectly. I may pay another to brainwash me. I may adopt the outer forms of religious faith in the hope that inner conviction will follow. But the issue is not whether I can bring myself to believe something by doing something else that brings it about, but whether I can do this without doing anything else to bring it about.

This seems not to be something that is typically within our power. I cannot just decide now to believe that I do not have hands or a head, or that I am flying, or fabulously wealthy. Religious belief, which is less engaged with the practical, is a more difficult case and has historically been the focus of the debate about belief voluntarism. One can try to inculcate religious belief indirectly, but can one simply decide to believe that God exists, while also believing one lacks adequate evidence? One might answer yes because it can be reasonable to continue to believe that God exists in the face of doubts. But this falls short of what is required. For this is not deciding to believe, but rather deciding not to give up a belief one already has.

Still, we are sometimes faced with an unavoidable practical choice where evidence bearing on a crucial fact leaves the fact, and hence the choice, undetermined. Must we not then make a choice about what to believe despite not having reasons to believe one way or the other? No. We must make the practical choice about what to do. But this does not imply belief. When some action is better than none, we take a chance and hope for the best, without belief.

Is the situation arguably different when a belief itself has a practical value? It is dubious that a belief itself having a practical value makes it easier to conceive of choosing to believe. If someone were to offer me a million dollars to believe that there is life on the Sun, I might wish to do so, but I would be baffled about how to comply.

The purpose of belief is to represent the world accurately. Therefore, belief serves its role only if the formation, retention, and revision of belief are sensitive to what one takes to be one's evidence. This does not mean that we always believe in proportion to our evidence. We make mistakes of assessment and reasoning; we are lazy; we fail to attend to evidence we have. Nor does it mean that what we take to be evidence is evidence, or that all our opinions were entrenched with the spade of reason. Further, it does not mean that belief is never influenced by desire. Otherwise, wishful thinking—believing what one wants to be true—would not be possible. Rather, it means that belief, by its nature, aims at truth, that its function is undermined if one lets belief formation be sensitive to anything other than what one takes to be evidence. Where there is uncertainty, one may be conservative and persist in a belief. But not to give up a belief in the face of strong contrary evidence is irrational. Worse still is to believe where no evidence bears, as in the case of wishful thinking. Even when belief has a practical benefit—as when believing one will win a race increases one's chances, but not enough to warrant the belief—rationality is at best at war with itself. Belief voluntarism thus seems to be something that can occur, at best, only on the fringes of rationality—in the shadow regions of self-deception.

See also Action; Ayer, Alfred Jules; Behaviorism; Berkeley, George; Davidson, Donald; Descartes, René; Hume, David; James, William; Locke, John; Materialism; Pascal, Blaise; Propositional Attitudes: Issues in Philosophy of Mind and Psychology; Ryle, Gilbert; Sensa; Voluntarism; Wittgenstein, Ludwig Josef Johann.

Bibliography

Ayer, Alfred Jules, ed. *Logical Positivism*. New York: Free Press, 1959.

Block, Ned. "Psychologism and Behaviorism." *Philosophical Review* 90 (1) (1981): 5–43.

Davidson, Donald. "Actions, Reasons, and Causes" (1963). In his *Essays on Actions and Events*. New York: Clarendon Press, 2001.

Descartes, René. "Meditations on First Philosophy" (1641). In *The Philosophical Writings of Descartes*. Cambridge, U.K.: Cambridge University Press, 1984.

James, William. "The Will to Believe" (1897). In his *The Will to Believe and Other Essays in Popular Philosophy*. Cambridge, MA: Harvard University Press, 1979.

Pascal, Blaise. *Pensées* (1670). Harmondsworth, U.K.: Penguin, 1966.

Price, H. H. *Belief: The Gifford Lectures Delivered at the University of Aberdeen in 1960*. London: Allen and Unwin, 1969.

Putnam, Hilary. "Brains and Behavior." In *Readings in Philosophy of Psychology*, Vol. 1, edited by N. Block. Cambridge, MA: Harvard University Press, 1980.

Ryle, Gilbert. *The Concept of Mind*. New York: Barnes and Noble, 1969.

Searle, John. *Intentionality: An Essay*. Cambridge, U.K.: Cambridge University Press, 1983.

James, William. "The Will to Believe" (1896). In his *The Will to Believe and Other Essays in Popular Philosophy*. Cambridge, MA: Harvard University Press, 1979.

Kirk Ludwig (2005)

BELIEF ATTRIBUTIONS

"Belief attributions" are uses of sentences of the form *N* believes that *s* (where *N* is a noun phrase, *s* a sentence). Their semantic and logical properties have been debated under the assumption that an account of "believes" will carry over to other propositional attitudes such as desire, knowledge, and fear. Most of the debate focuses on two issues: Does "believe" pick out a relation, and how do so-called *de re* and *de dicto* attributions differ?

IS "BELIEVES" RELATIONAL?

The obvious hypothesis is that in

(1) Maggie believes that Twain lives.

"believes" has the semantic status of a transitive verb, picking out a relation between a believer and something (a proposition) provided by the verb's complement,

(2) that Twain lives.

Grammatical evidence suggests this: "believes" can be followed by names and demonstratives ("I believe Church's thesis," "she believes that") as well as expressions that behave like (nominal) variables ("whenever the pope says something I believe it").

Gottlob Frege and Bertrand Russell, whose work inspires most subsequent debate about belief attribution, agreed on the obvious hypothesis. Frege held that expressions embedded within "believes that" shift their reference to a way of thinking, or sense, of what they refer to unembedded. Russell held that no such semantic shift occurs; the proposition "that *s*" is determined by what *s*'s parts pick out when used unembedded.

Since "Twain" and "Clemens" refer to the same author, the Russellian approach seems committed to the identity of the propositions, that Twain lives and that Clemens does, and thus to (1)'s implying

(3) Maggie believes that Clemens lives.

Russell would avoid this by saying that "Twain" and "Clemens" typically function as truncated definite descriptions. This last suggestion is widely thought to have been discredited by Saul Kripke.

One problem Fregean views face is that sense is idiosyncratic: Different people associate with a name different ways of thinking of the referent. It is implausible that when I utter (1) I speak truly only if Maggie thinks of Twain as do I. But if (2) in (1) named Maggie's sense for "Twain lives," the argument "Maggie believes that Twain lives; Seth believes what Maggie does; so Seth believes that Twain lives" would be invalid.

Contemporary Russellians such as Nathan Salmon and Scott Soames hold that to believe a proposition involves grasping or representing it and its constituents; thus, belief is a three-place relation among a believer, a Russellian content, and a representation. Salmon and Soames nonetheless hold that (1) tells us only that Maggie believes ("under some representation") the Russellian proposition that Twain lives; the appearance that (1) and (3) may disagree in truth value results from mistaking a conversational or pragmatic implicature, about the representation under which a belief is held, for part of what a belief attribution, strictly speaking, says.

John Perry and Mark Crimmins have suggested that a belief attribution involves implicit reference to the Russellian's representations or modes of grasping: the complement of "believes" determines a Russellian proposition, but the verb has an "implicit argument place" for representations. A use of (1) makes a claim along the lines of "Maggie believes the Russellian proposition that Twain lives under representation *r*," with the representation referred to differing across occasions of use. A problem with this view is that it renders the argument mentioned two paragraphs above invalid.

Some think belief attributions implicitly quotational. The simplest version of such a view sees *that s* as a quotation name of *s*, "believes" naming a relation to sentence types. To this it may be objected that different uses of "Seth thinks I am sad" may have different truth values. Another view sees a "that" clause as picking out a fusion of linguistic items with their interpretations—for example, the result of combining a sentence with the semantic values of its expressions.

Mark Richard's version of this view has *that s* pick out a fusion of the sentence *s* and its Russellian content.

In belief attribution, such fusions are offered as "translations" of the believer's thoughts, where a thought is the result of combining a representation that realizes a belief with its Russellian content: (1) is true if the "that" clause provides a translation of a thought of Maggie's. Standards of translation shift from context to context: "Twain" may represent a representation of Maggie's in some but not all contexts. Thus, on this view, the truth of (1) does not demand that of (3).

Donald Davidson denies that (2) is a semantically significant part of (1). "Believes" is a predicate whose second argument is the demonstrative "that"; its referent is the ensuing utterance of "Twain lives." The overall force of (1) is roughly some belief state of Maggie's agrees in content with that utterance. (Davidson made such a proposal for "says" but clearly intended to generalize.) Yet more radical views deny that "believes" is a predicate. Arthur N. Prior took "believes" to combine with a name and sentence to form a more complex sentence; W. V. O. Quine has entertained the idea that "believes that Twain lives" is a predicate without semantically significant structure. A problem for Quine is to explain how infinitely many (semantically unstructured) belief predicates acquire their meanings; Prior thought little useful could be said on such issues.

DE RE AND DE DICTO

There seem to be two ways of interpreting such sentences as

(4) Sam believes that Melinda's husband is unmarried. Sam believes that some Frenchman is not French.

One interpretation attributes to Sam necessarily false beliefs; the other, suggested by

(4') Of Melinda's husband, Sam believes he is unmarried.

Of some Frenchman, Sam believes he is not French, does not. Note that (4') ascribes to Sam beliefs in some sense about particular individuals, while this is not true of the interpretation of (4).

The interpretations seem to correspond to different scopes that may be assigned to the quantifier phrases "Melinda's husband" and "some Frenchman." In a *de re* attribution, an expression functioning as a variable within the scope of "believes" is bound by a quantifier outside its scope (and the scopes of other verbs of propositional attitudes). Interpreting the sentences in (4) as in (4') is *de re* attribution: "he" and "she" are bound to

"Melinda's husband" and "some women," which are not in the scope of "believes." An attribution that is not *de re* is *de dicto*. If we accept a relational account of "believes," we will say that a *de dicto* interpretation of "N believes that s" attributes to N a belief in the proposition expressed by s. (An attribution might also count as *de re* if it has a term anaphoric on a name outside of the attribution, as in the natural understanding of

(5) Twain was an author, but Seth believes that he was president.)

Not everyone would characterize the *de re–de dicto* distinction as above. Quine held that it is impossible for a quantifier to bind a variable that occurs opaquely—that is, inside a construction, like "believes," which causes failures to substitutivity. If Quine were correct, some other account of the two understandings of (4) is needed. (Quine himself suggested that "believes" is ambiguous.) Quine's view is not widely shared. (See Kaplan, 1986, for discussion.)

The relations between *de re* and *de dicto* attributions are of interest in good part because *de re* attributions are anomalous on some views. A *de re* attribution identifies a belief in terms of the objects it is about, not in terms of how those objects are conceptualized. For a Russellian this is the norm: All there is to belief attribution is identifying the state of affairs believed to obtain. For a Fregean, (4') is at best an aberration, lacking information about sense, which belief attribution is supposed to convey. *De re* belief attributions provide a focus for the debates among Russellians, Fregeans, and others.

See also Causal or Conditional or Explanatory-Relation Accounts; Content, Mental; Davidson, Donald; Epistemology; Frege, Gottlob; Knowledge and Belief; Kripke, Saul; Prior, Arthur Norman; Quine, Willard Van Orman; Russell, Bertrand Arthur William.

Bibliography

Crimmins, M. *Talk about Beliefs*. Cambridge, MA: MIT Press, 1992.

Davidson, D. "On Saying That." In *Inquiries into Truth and Interpretation*. Oxford: Clarendon Press, 1984.

Frege, G. "Uber Sinn und Bedeutung." *Zeitschrift fur Philosophie and Philosophische Kritik* 100 (1892): 25–50. Translated by P. Geach and M. Black as "On Sense and Reference," in *Translations from the Philosophical Writings of Gottlob Frege*, edited by Geach and Black. New York: Philosophical Library, 1952.

Higginbotham, J. "Belief and Logical Form." *Mind and Language* 6 (1991): 344–369.

Kaplan, D. "Opacity." In *The Philosophy of W. V. Quine*, edited by L. Hahn and P. Schilpp. La Salle, IL: Open Court, 1986.

Kaplan, D. "Quantifying In." In *Words and Objections,* edited by D. Davidson and G. Harman. Dordrecht: Reidel, 1969.

Kripke, S. "A Puzzle about Belief." In *Meaning and Use,* edited by A. Margalit. Dordrecht, 1979. Also in Salmon and Soames, 1988.

Perry, J., and M. Crimmins. "The Prince and the Phone Booth." *Journal of Philosophy* 86 (1989): 685–711.

Prior, A. N. *Objects of Thought.* Oxford: Clarendon Press, 1971.

Quine, W. V. O. "Quantifiers and Propositional Attitudes." *Journal of Philosophy* 53 (1956): 177–187.

Quine, W. V. O. *Word and Object.* Cambridge, MA: MIT Press, 1960.

Richard, M. *Propositional Attitudes.* Cambridge, U.K.: Cambridge University Press, 1990.

Salmon, N. *Frege's Puzzle.* Cambridge, MA: MIT Press, 1986.

Salmon, N., and S. Soames, eds. *Propositions and Attitudes.* Oxford: Oxford University Press, 1988.

Mark Richard (1996)

BELINSKII, VISSARION GRIGOR'EVICH

(1811–1848)

Vissarion Grigor'evich BelinskiI (Belinsky), the Russian literary critic, was an early leader of the Russian intelligentsia and a major representative of German Absolute Idealism, as well as of the subsequent reaction against it, in nineteenth-century Russian philosophy.

Belinskii was born in Sveaborg, Russia (now Finland), the son of a provincial physician. He entered the University of Moscow in 1829 but was expelled after three years, perhaps for the radical criticism of serfdom in a romantic drama he wrote; his subsequent education was self-acquired. He began a journalistic career in 1833 and soon became the chief critic for a succession of literary journals in Moscow and (after 1839) in St. Petersburg, principally *Otechestvennyye Zapiski* (Annals of the Fatherland). His brilliant, philosophically oriented critical essays, including perceptive early appreciations of Nikolay Gogol, Mikhail Lermontov, and Feödor Dostoevsky, won him great renown but little material reward; he died in St. Petersburg after a short life filled with poverty and illness.

Belinskii's intellectual development typifies that of the early Russian "Westernizers," or admirers of Western progressive ideas and institutions, whose leader he became: He passed from the romantic extremes of German Absolute Idealism through G. W. F. Hegel to a mature position representing the influence of the French socialists and Ludwig Feuerbach. In Belinskii's case, the doctrinal changes were magnified and accelerated by a mercurial personality, while their expression was often clouded by the pressures of journalistic writing under tsarist censorship. Belinskii published no systematic theoretical works, and his voluminous critical essays and private correspondence leave room for divergent interpretations of his views.

Belinskii's earliest writings (1831–1836) show the clear influence of Friedrich Schiller and Friedrich von Schelling. Basing his views on Schelling's nature philosophy and philosophy of art, Belinskii glorified art and the creative process, and emphasized man's inner aesthetic and moral experience in rising above empirical reality to the "eternal Idea."

In 1837, after a brief enthusiasm for Johann Gottlieb Fichte, Belinskii was introduced by his friend and mentor, Mikhail Bakunin, to the thought of Hegel. Belinskii found in the Hegelian formula "all that is real is rational" a summons to a "reconciliation with reality" that turned his attention from man's subjective world to the objective reality around him and led him to praise Russian autocracy, to view the state as sacred, and to regard society as metaphysically and ethically superior to the individual. He expressed a Hegelian conception of art as "thinking in images" and as reproducing rational reality.

Belinskii's Hegelianism, however, did not extinguish the regard for human individuality that in some degree had always marked his thinking and had been manifested most explicitly during his brief Fichtean period. By 1841 he repudiated Hegel's subordination of the individual and thenceforth turned from Absolute Idealism to an ethical personalism that emphasized the supreme value of the individual personality. At the same time, he abandoned the attempt to show the rationality of the tsarist order: He became acquainted with the writings of Comte de Saint-Simon and other French socialists, and called increasingly for radical social reforms in the direction of democracy and socialism. His mature view of art stressed art's moral and political functions in expressing socially progressive ideas, for which reason he is generally regarded as the founder of the dominant tradition of social or "civic" criticism in Russia.

Belinskii's socialism remained individualistic in inspiration, and there is evidence that toward the end of his life he moved to a more moderate liberal position, advocating the development of a middle class in Russia. His reformist enthusiasm and generally enlightened outlook were well expressed in a famous "Letter to Gogol" (1847), which set a moral tone for the Russian intelligentsia for generations. The "Letter" illustrates the antiecclesiasticism and positivist leanings of Belinskii's final period, if not the outright atheism and materialism attributed to him by Soviet interpreters.

See also Hegel, Georg Wilhelm Friedrich; Hegelianism; Russian Philosophy.

Bibliography

WORKS BY BELINSKII

Polnoye Sobraniye Sochineni (Complete Works). 13 vols. Moscow, 1953–1959.
Selected Philosophical Works. Westport, CT: Hyperion, 1981.
Russian Philosophy. Vol. 1, edited by James Edie, et al. Knoxville: The University of Tennessee Press, 1987, pp. 281–320.

WORKS ON BELINSKII

Bowman, Herbert E. *Vissarion Belinski, 1811–1848: A Study in the Origins of Social Criticism in Russia*. Cambridge, MA: Harvard University Press, 1954.
Ranall, F. B. *Vissarion Belinskii*. Newtonville, MA: Oriental Research Partners, 1987.
Terras, V. *Belinksij and Russian Literary Criticism: The Heritage of Organic Aesthetics*. Madison: University of Wisconsin Press, 1974.
Zenkovskii, V. V. *A History of Russian Philosophy*. 2 vols. Translated by G. Kline. New York and London: Routledge, 2003.

James P. Scanlan (1967)
Bibliography updated by Vladimir Marchenkov (2005)

BELL, JOHN, AND BELL'S THEOREM

John Stewart Bell (1928–1990), a truly deep and serious thinker, was one of the leading physicists of the twentieth century. He became famous for his discovery that quantum mechanics implies that nature is nonlocal, that is, that there are physical influences between events that propagate faster than light.

From 1960 until his death Bell worked at the Conseil Européen pour la Recherche Nucléaire (CERN; European Laboratory for Particle Physics) in Geneva, Switzerland, on the physics of particle accelerators, making a number of important contributions to high-energy physics and quantum field theory. Noteworthy was his discovery in 1969, together with Roman W. Jackiw, of the so-called "Bell-Jackiw-Adler" anomaly (discovered independently by Stephen Adler), a mechanism explaining physical effects such as neutral pion decay (which are unexplainable on the basis of the symmetries of the classical field Lagrangian), in terms of an "anomalous" term arising from the renormalization of quantum field theory. Since

then this mechanism has become an important cornerstone of quantum field theory. Another important contribution was the argument he gave in 1967 for why weak interactions should be described using a gauge theory.

John Bell was one of the leading experts—perhaps *the* leading expert—on the foundations of quantum mechanics. The book collecting his articles on this subject, *Speakable and Unspeakable in Quantum Mechanics* (1987), is unsurpassed for clarity and depth and it is still the best reference for whoever wishes to learn about the field.

Bell strongly opposed the "Copenhagen interpretation" of quantum physics, according to which macroscopic objects, such as chairs and planets, do exist out there, but electrons and other microscopic particles do not. According to the Copenhagen view, the world is divided into two realms, macro and micro, "classical" and "quantum," logical and contradictory—or, as Bell put it in one of his essays, into "speakable" and "unspeakable." Along with Albert Einstein, Erwin Schrödinger, Louis de Broglie, and David Bohm, Bell was one of the few physicists compelled by his conscience to reject the Copenhagen interpretation.

Bell emphasized that the empirical facts of quantum physics do not at all force us to renounce realism. There is, in fact, a realist theory (Bohmian mechanics, also known as the de Broglie–Bohm theory) that accounts—insofar as the nonrelativistic theory is concerned—for all of these facts in a most elegant way. This theory describes a world in which electrons, quarks, and the like are point particles, always having positions that move in a manner dictated by the wave function. It should be taught to students, Bell insisted, as a legitimate alternative to the prevailing orthodoxy. After GianCarlo Ghirardi, Alberto Rimini, and Tullio Weber succeeded in formulating in 1986 a second kind of realist theory, Bell encouraged the further development of this theory as well (1987). He thought that such a theory contained the seeds of a reconciliation of quantum mechanics with fundamental Lorentz invariance, and thus a resolution of the tension between quantum mechanics and relativity that arose from his own work on quantum nonlocality.

In 1964, Bell proved that any serious version of quantum theory (regardless of whether or not it is based on microscopic realism) must violate locality. He showed that if nature is governed by the predictions of quantum theory, the "locality principle," precluding any sort of instantaneous (or superluminal) action-at-a-distance, is simply wrong, and the world is nonlocal. The theoretical analysis leading to such a conclusion is commonly known as *Bell's theorem*.

Bell's theorem involves two parts. The first part is the Einstein-Podolsky-Rosen (1935) argument applied to the simplified version considered by David Bohm (1951), the EPRB experiment: a pair of spin one-half particles, prepared in a spin-singlet state, are moving freely in opposite directions. Measurements are made, say by Stern-Gerlach magnets, on selected components of the spins of the two particles. The spin-singlet state has the following property: whenever the component of the spin σ_1 in any direction α is measured for one of the two particles, a measurement of the same component of the spin σ_2 of the other particle will give with certainty the opposite value. For such a state the assumption of locality implies the existence of what are often called noncontextual hidden variables. More precisely, it implies, for the spin-singlet state, the existence of random variables $Z_\alpha^i (= Z_{\alpha \cdot \sigma_i})$, $i = 1, 2$, which can be regarded as corresponding to preexisting values of all possible spin components of the two particles. In particular, focusing on components in only three directions a, b, and c for each particle, locality implies the existence of six random variables Z_α^i, $i = 1, 2$, $\alpha = a, b, c$ such that

$$\textbf{(1)} \qquad Z_\alpha^i = \pm 1$$

$$\textbf{(2)} \qquad Z_\alpha^1 = -Z_\alpha^2$$

and, more generally,

$$\textbf{(3)} \qquad \text{Prob}(Z_\alpha^1 \neq Z_\beta^2) = q_{\alpha\beta},$$

where the $q_{\alpha\beta} = (1 + \alpha \cdot \beta)/2 = \cos^2(\theta/2)$ are the corresponding quantum mechanical probabilities, with θ the angle between α and β.

The argument for this conclusion can be expressed as follows: The existence of such random variables amounts to the idea that measurements of the spin components reveal preexisting values (the Z_α^i). Assuming locality, this is implied by the perfect quantum mechanical anticorrelations:

> Now we make the hypothesis, and it seems one at least worth considering, that if the two measurements are made at places remote from one another the orientation of one magnet does not influence the result obtained with the other. Since we can predict in advance the result of measuring any chosen component of σ_2, by previously measuring the same component of σ_1, it follows that the result of any such measurement

must actually be predetermined. (Bell 1964, p. 195; reprinted in Bell 1987, p. 14)

Otherwise, the result would have, at least in part, been produced by the remote measurement, just the sort of influence that Bell's locality hypothesis precludes. One may also note that if the results had not been predetermined, the widely separated correlated residual innovations thereby implied would be an instance of nonlocality.

Observe that, given locality, the existence of such variables is a consequence rather than an assumption of Bell's analysis. In his writing, Bell repeatedly stressed this point (by determinism Bell here means the existence of the preexisting values that would determine the results of the corresponding measurements):

> It is important to note that to the limited degree to which *determinism* plays a role in the EPR argument, it is not assumed but *inferred*. What is held sacred is the principle of "local causality"—or "no action at a distance." …
>
> It is remarkably difficult to get this point across, that determinism is not a *presupposition* of the analysis (1987, p. 143).

and

> Despite my insistence that the determinism was inferred rather than assumed, you might still suspect somehow that it is a preoccupation with determinism that creates the problem. Note well then that the following argument makes no mention whatever of determinism…. Finally you might suspect that the very notion of particle, and particle orbit … has somehow led us astray. … So the following argument will not mention particles, nor indeed fields, nor any other particular picture of what goes on at the microscopic level. Nor will it involve any use of the words "quantum mechanical system," which can have an unfortunate effect on the discussion. The difficulty is not created by any such picture or any such terminology. It is created by the predictions about the correlations in the visible outputs of certain conceivable experimental set-ups (1987, p. 150).

The second part of the analysis, which unfolds the "difficulty … created by the … correlations," involves only very elementary mathematics. Clearly,

$$\text{Prob}(\{Z_a^1 = Z_b^1\} \cup \{Z_b^1 = Z_c^1\} \cup \{Z_c^1 = Z_a^1\}) = 1$$

since at least two of the three (2-valued) variables Z_α^1 must have the same value. Hence, by elementary probability theory,

$$\text{Prob}(Z_a^1 = Z_b^1) + \text{Prob}(Z_b^1 = Z_c^1) + \text{Prob}(Z_c^1 = Z_a^1) \geq 1,$$

and using the perfect anticorrelations (2) one has that

(4)

$$\text{Prob}(Z_a^1 = -Z_b^2) + \text{Prob}(Z_b^1 = -Z_c^2) + \text{Prob}(Z_c^1 = -Z_a^2) \geq 1.$$

(4) is equivalent to the celebrated *Bell's inequality*. It is incompatible with (3). For example, when the angles between *a*, *b*, and *c* are 120°, the three relevant quantum correlations $q_{\alpha\beta}$ are all ¼, implying a value of ¾ for the left hand side of (4).

Let P be the hypothesis of the existence of noncontextual hidden variables for the EPRB experiment, that is, of preexisting values Z_α^i for the spin components relevant to this experiment. Then Bell's nonlocality argument, just described, has the following structure:

(5)   Part 1: quantum mechanics + locality ⇒ P

(6)   Part 2: quantum mechanics ⇒ not P

(7) Conclusion: quantum mechanics ⇒ not locality

For this argument, what is relevant about "quantum mechanics" is merely the predictions concerning experimental outcomes corresponding to (1–3) (with Part 1 using in fact only (2)). To fully grasp the argument it is important to appreciate that the content of P—what it actually expresses, namely the existence of the noncontextual hidden variables—is of little substantive importance for the argument. What is important is the fact that P is incompatible with the predictions of quantum theory.

The content of P is, however, of great historical significance: It is responsible for the misconception that Bell proved that (i) hidden variables are impossible, a belief until recently almost universally shared by physicists, and, more recently, for the view that Bell proved that (ii) hidden variables, while perhaps possible, must be nonlocal. Statement (i) is plainly wrong, since a hidden-variables theory exists and works, as mentioned earlier. Statement (ii) is correct, significant, but nonetheless rather misleading. It follows from (5) and (6) that *any* account of quantum phenomena must be nonlocal, not just any hidden-variables account. Bell's argument shows that nonlocality is implied by the predictions of standard quantum theory itself. Thus, if nature is governed by these predictions, then *nature is nonlocal*. (That nature is so governed, even in the crucial EPRB-correlation experiments, has by now been established by a great many experiments, the most conclusive of which is perhaps that of Alain Aspect, Jean Dalibard, and Gérard Roger [1982].)

Concerning the wrongness of statement (i), some historical facts should be recalled. John von Neumann, one of the greatest mathematicians of the twentieth century, claimed to have mathematically proven that Einstein's dream, of a deterministic completion or reinterpretation of quantum theory (i.e., a hidden-variables theory), was mathematically impossible. Von Neumann's claim was almost universally accepted among physicists and philosophers of science. But Bohmian mechanics is a counterexample, so something had to be wrong with von Neumann's argument. Precisely what was wrong was elucidated by Bell in 1966. Nonetheless, many physicists continued to rely on von Neumann's proof and in recent years more commonly on Bell's inequality to support their rejection of the possibility of hidden variables.

The following is how Bell himself reacted upon learning of Bohmian mechanics:

> But in 1952 I saw the impossible done. It was in papers by David Bohm. Bohm showed explicitly how parameters could indeed be introduced, into nonrelativistic wave mechanics, with the help of which the indeterministic description could be transformed into a deterministic one. More importantly, in my opinion, the subjectivity of the orthodox version, the necessary reference to the "observer," could be eliminated. …
>
> But why then had Born not told me of this "pilot wave"? If only to point out what was wrong with it? Why did von Neumann not consider it? More extraordinarily, why did people go on producing "impossibility" proofs, after 1952, and as recently as 1978? … Why is the pilot wave picture ignored in textbooks? Should it not be taught, not as the only way, but as an antidote to the prevailing complacency? To show us that vagueness, subjectivity, and indeterminism, are not forced on us by experimental facts, but by deliberate theoretical choice? (1987, p. 160)

In fact, Bell's examination of Bohmian mechanics led him to his nonlocality analysis. In the course of his investigation of Bohmian mechanics, he observed that

> … in this theory an explicit causal mechanism exists whereby the disposition of one piece of

apparatus affects the results obtained with a distant piece. ...

Bohm of course was well aware of these features of his scheme, and has given them much attention. However, it must be stressed that, to the present writer's knowledge, there is no *proof* that *any* hidden variable account of quantum mechanics *must* have this extraordinary character. It would therefore be interesting, perhaps, to pursue some further "impossibility proofs," replacing the arbitrary axioms objected to above by some condition of locality, or of separability of distant systems. (1966, p. 452; reprinted in Bell 1987, p. 11)

In a footnote, Bell added that "Since the completion of this paper such a proof has been found." This proof was presented in his 1964 EPR-nonlocality paper discussed here. (The 1966 paper was in fact written before the 1964 paper, but its publication was delayed.)

Physicists' misconceptions notwithstanding, Bell did not establish the impossibility of a deterministic reformulation of quantum theory, nor did he ever claim to have done so. On the contrary, over the course of several decades, until his untimely death in 1990, Bell was the prime proponent, for a good part of this period almost the sole proponent, of the very theory, Bohmian mechanics, that he is supposed to have demolished.

See also Bohm, David; Bohmian Mechanics; Einstein, Albert; Neumann, John von; Philosophy of Physics; Quantum Mechanics; Realism; Relativity Theory; Schrödinger, Erwin.

Bibliography

Aspect, Alain, Jean Dalibard, and Gérard Roger. "Experimental Test of Bell's Inequalities Using Time-Varying Analyzers." *Physical Review Letters* 49 (25) (1982): 1804–1807.

Bell, John Stewart. "On the Einstein-Podolsky-Rosen Paradox." *Physics* 1 (3) (1964): 195–200. Reprinted in Bell 1987.

Bell, John Stewart. "On the Problem of Hidden Variables in Quantum Mechanics." *Reviews of Modern Physics* 38 (3) (1966): 447–452. Reprinted in Bell 1987.

Bell, John Stewart. *Speakable and Unspeakable in Quantum Mechanics.* New York: Cambridge University Press, 1987.

Bohm, David. *Quantum Theory.* Englewood Cliffs, NJ: Prentice-Hall, 1951.

Einstein, Albert, Boris Podolsky, and Nathan Rosen. "Can Quantum-Mechanical Description of Physical Reality Be Considered Complete?" *Physical Review* 47 (1935): 777–780.

Detlef Dürr, Sheldon Goldstein,
Roderich Tumulka, and Nino Zanghì (2005)

BELLARMINE, ST. ROBERT
(1542–1621)

St. Robert Bellarmine, an Italian cardinal and controversialist, was born at Montepulciano in Tuscany and died at Rome. Educated in the Jesuit order, of which he became a member, he taught philosophy and theology at the University of Louvain (1570–1576), then at the Roman (Jesuit) College, where he later served as rector. After Bellarmine was created a cardinal in 1599, much of his time was devoted to the administrative and diplomatic affairs of the Roman Catholic Church, in which he is now venerated as a saint. His chief published work is the *Disputations on Controversial Matters (Disputationes de Controversiis),* in which Book III (*De Laicis*) treats questions of political and social philosophy. Another treatise in political philosophy is the *Defense of His Reply to King James I of England (Apologia Bellarmini pro Responsione Sua ad Librum Jacobi Magnae Britanniae Regis,* reprinted in Giacon's *Scritti politici*), concerning the theory of the divine right of kings.

In general, Bellarmine's philosophic thought is Thomistic. His lectures at Louvain covered all of Thomas Aquinas's *Summa Theologiae* and are now preserved in the Vatican Archives, though they have not been printed. As a result, little is known of his metaphysical and psychological views, except for occasional explanations given in his more practical writings. It is assumed that he had a very sound understanding of the speculative thought of Thomas Aquinas, however, and the publication of the Louvaine lectures is a desideratum. In ethics and philosophy of law, Bellarmine is a strong opponent of the view that the source of justice is the will of God; instead, he argues that man's awareness of moral law derives from his understanding of the nature of man and his environment, and that ultimately the command (*imperium*) of God's law is intellectual, stemming from the divine wisdom. Thus, he is opposed to voluntarism and defends intellectualism in morals and jurisprudence.

Bellarmine's political theories developed in part from opposition to King James's claim that both spiritual and temporal power belong to the civil monarch. In defending the autonomy of ecclesiastical authority, Bellarmine strongly supported the distinction and separation of the powers of church and state. In chapter 13 of the *Apologia*, he argued that, though the ultimate source of both powers is divine, the civil power is conferred on rulers, *mediately*, through the people as a medium. Thus, with Francisco Suárez, Bellarmine is one of the most prominent Catholic advocates of the "translation theory" of political sovereignty.

Bellarmine was firmly convinced of the importance of the individual citizen and the dignity of every person. His social and political thinking is reminiscent of the fourteenth-century views of Marsilius of Padua. There is a possibility that Bellarmine's arguments influenced British antimonarchist thinking and, through John Locke, the founders of American democracy. He also recognized something of the investment value of money and helped to modify the older Catholic theory that all taking of interest on loans was to be condemned as usury. In a treatise on the power of the pope (*De Summo Pontifice,* I, 9), Bellarmine favored the idea of a world state but admitted that a plurality of national states regulated by international law might be more practical.

About Bellarmine's role in the prosecution of Galileo Galilei it is hard to be precise; in 1616 he seems to have warned Galileo to discuss the Copernican theory merely as a "mathematical supposition," but he almost certainly did not enjoin him from "teaching or discussing Copernicanism in any way," as was charged after Bellarmine's death. Galileo's publication of the *Dialogue of the Two Chief World Systems,* in 1632, caused him to be prosecuted for heresy on the grounds that he had thereby violated the supposed stricter warning.

See also Thomism.

Bibliography

WORKS BY BELLARMINE

Disputationes de Controversiis Christianae Fidei Adversus Huius Temporis Haereticos. 3 vols. Ingolstadt: Ex Officina Typographica Davidis Sartorii, 1586–1593. Venice, 1596 (4 vols.). The Venice edition is the definitive Latin text.

Opera Omnia, edited by J. Fèvre. 12 vols. Paris, 1870–1874.

De Laicis or the Treatise on Civil Government. Translated by K. E. Murphy. New York: Fordham University Press, 1928.

Scritti politici, edited by C. Giacon. Bologna: Zanichelli, 1950. Selected politico-social writings in Latin.

WORKS ON BELLARMINE

Brodrick, J. *Robert Bellarmine: Saint and Scholar.* Westminster, MD: Newman Press, 1961.

Davitt, T. *The Nature of Law,* 195–218. St. Louis: B. Herder, 1951.

Kuntz, Paul G. "The Hierarchical Vision of St. Roberto Bellarmine." In *Jacob's Ladder and the Tree of Life,* edited by Marion Leathers. New York: Peter Lang, 1987.

Pera, Marcello. "The God of Theologians and the God of Astronomers: An Apology of Bellarmine." In *The Cambridge Companion to Galileo,* edited by Peter Machamer. New York: Cambridge University Press, 1998.

Riedl, J. "Bellarmine and the Dignity of Man." In *Jesuit Thinkers of the Renaissance,* edited by G. Smith, 193–226. Milwaukee: Marquette University Press, 1939.

Springborg, Patricia. "Thomas Hobbes and Cardinal Bellarmine: Leviathan and the 'Ghost of the Roman Empire.'" *History of Political Thought* 16 (4) (1995): 503–531.

Vernon J. Bourke (1967)
Bibliography updated by Tamra Frei (2005)

BENEKE, FRIEDRICH EDUARD
(1798–1854)

Friedrich Eduard Beneke, the German philosopher and psychologist, was born in Berlin and after his gymnasium education studied theology and philosophy, first at Halle and then at Berlin. He became university lecturer (*Privatdozent*) at the University of Berlin in 1820 and, despite Georg Wilhelm Friedrich Hegel's power and official connections, managed to have a considerable number of students.

His first books were *Erkenntnislehre nach dem Bewusstsein der reinen Vernunft* (Theory of knowledge according to the consciousness of pure reason) and *Erfahrungsseelenlehre als Grundlage alles Wissens* (Experiential theory of the soul as foundation of all knowledge). Both were published in Jena in 1820. Two years later, he published in Berlin *Grundlegung zur Physik der Sitten* (Foundations of the physics of morals), a work that found disfavor among the entrenched Absolute Idealists and resulted in his being forbidden to lecture. Beneke was accused of Epicureanism, although the objections given by Minister von Altenstein, a Hegelian who opposed Beneke's attempted application of science to ethics, were that the book was not so much wrong on particular points as that it was *unphilosophisch* in its totality because it did not attempt to derive everything from the Absolute. Beneke's anti-Hegelian position led to further difficulties. An offer of a position at the University of Jena was overruled by the authorities in Berlin, who managed to find a state law to support this move. Beneke moved to Göttingen, where his reception was more cordial, and remained there until 1827, when he received permission to resume his lectures in Berlin. After Hegel's death, Beneke managed to advance to the rank of "extraordinary professor." Although he was active in teaching and writing, his later years were plagued by illness. In 1854, under unexplained circumstances, his body was found in a Berlin canal.

Along with Johann Friedrich Herbart and some others, Beneke represented a reaction against the Fichte-Schelling-Hegel phase of German philosophy. He insisted that psychology, which ought to be established inductively, is the necessary presupposition of all disciplines in philosophy. Logic, ethics, metaphysics, and especially the philosophy of religion should be based on it. Beneke's psychology is a form of associationism, and shows the influence of both Immanuel Kant and the British empiricists, especially John Locke, whose disciple Beneke claimed to be. The senses give us only a mediated knowledge of the external world and of ourselves. Nevertheless, we can obtain an immediate, fully adequate knowledge of our own mental acts by means of inner perception. Starting from this perception, we infer the inner nature of other beings by analogy with our own. The result of this inference is a picture of reality as containing an uninterrupted series of minds or "faculties of representation" (*Vorstellungsfähigkeit*), extending downward from man. The soul consists of a system of powers or forces; it is a "bundle" but, contrary to Hume, not a bundle of perceptions.

Beneke used the language of faculty psychology, although he did not intend "powers" or "faculties" to be viewed as hypostatized concepts. All psychological processes, he claimed, can be traced back to four basic ones: (1) the process of stimulus appropriation (*Reizaneignung*), in which the mind creates sensations and perceptions out of externally caused impressions; (2) the process of formation of new "elementary faculties" (*Urvermögen*) by means of the assimilation of received stimuli; (3) the process of transmission (*Übertragung*) and equalization (*Ausgleichung*) of stimuli and powers, whereby a systematic connection is formed between our becoming conscious of one idea and our becoming unconscious of another idea; (4) the process of mutual attraction and "blending" (*Verschmelzung*) of ideas of the same sort.

Beneke's attempt to explain the mind's activities in terms of their genesis is reminiscent of Herbart. Unlike the latter, however, he assumed that philosophy must proceed from what is immediately given in consciousness. We have no alternative to this starting with inner experience, he believed, because our own soul is the only thing that we know as it is in itself. We recognize it as a nonspatial and therefore an immaterial entity. At least we have no reason to suppose it to be material, since it is not perceived through outer sense. The soul, however, cannot be simple, as Herbart had maintained. It has, as we have noted, specific powers or capacities for receiving and organizing stimuli; these powers must be underivative, since stimuli of different kinds can be received even at the outset of our experience. Each of our senses is supposed to include several of these *Urvermögen*. But the soul must also be capable of forming new *Urvermögen*, in order to be receptive to new sorts of stimuli.

Beneke thus conceived the mental life as compounded of active impulses (*Triebe*) that are activated by external stimuli. The seemingly substantial unity of mind is explained by the persistence of traces (*Spuren*) of ideas that have become unconscious and by the mutual adjustment of faculties that produce new impulses.

See also Empiricism; Epicureanism and the Epicurean School; Hegel, Georg Wilhelm Friedrich; Herbart, Johann Friedrich; Hume, David; Kant, Immanuel; Locke, John; Psychologism; Psychology.

Bibliography

ADDITIONAL WORKS BY BENEKE

Neue Grundlegung zur Metaphysik. Berlin, 1822.

Psychologische Skizzen, 2 vols. Göttingen: Vandenhoeck and Ruprecht, 1825–1827.

Das Verhältniss von Seele und Leib. Göttingen: Vandenhoeck and Ruprecht, 1826.

Kant und die Philosophische Aufgabe unserer Zeit. Berlin, 1832.

Lehrbuch der Psychologie als Naturwissenschaft. Berlin, 1833.

Die Philosophie in ihrem Verhältnisse zur Erfahrung zur Spekulation und zum Leben. Berlin, 1833.

Grundlinien des näturlichen Systems der praktischen Philosophie. Berlin, 1837. Beneke regarded the last part of the *Grundlinien*, which contains his theory of morals, as his best work.

Metaphysik und Philosophie der Religion. Berlin, 1840.

WORKS ON BENEKE

Benner, H. *Benekes Erkenntnistheorie.* Halle: Druck von Wischan and Wettengel, 1902.

Gargano, V. *L'Etica di Beneke.* Catania, Sicily, 1912.

Gramzow, O. *Benekes Leben und Philosophie.* Bern: Buchdr. Steiger, 1899.

Murtfeld, R. "Vergeblicher Kampf gegen den Idealismus: Friedrich Eduard Beneke." In *Zeitschrift für Geschichte der Erziehung und des Unterrichts,* pp. 1–48. Berlin: Weidmannsche, 1923.

Samuel, E. *Die Realität des Psychischen bei Beneke.* Berlin, 1907.

Wandschneider, A. *Die Metaphysik Benekes.* Berlin, 1903.

Arnulf Zweig (1967)

BEN GERSHON, LEVI

See *Gersonides*

BENJAMIN, WALTER
(1892–1940)

Walter Benjamin, philosopher, literary and social critic, and aesthetic theorist of the modernist period, was born to a liberal, middle-class Jewish family on July 15, 1892, in Berlin. He died in 1940 by suicide, having failed to cross the border from France to Spain. Many of his writings were published posthumously. He lived mainly in Germany, but spent his last years in exile in Paris barely surviving as an independent writer. Although close friends such as Gershom Scholem and Theodor W. Adorno encouraged him to move to Israel or to New York, he chose fatefully to stay in Europe.

Benjamin had a seminal impact, especially after the 1960s, on critical theory, art history, and aesthetics; on political philosophy and the philosophy of language and history (in the continental vein); on linguistics, literature, and criticism; on communications, technology, and mass media; even, later, on anthropology, cultural studies, and postcolonial and feminist theory.

Benjamin developed his central concept of *critique* from his extensive reading in philosophy, poetry, and literature, especially of Immanuel Kant, Johann von Goethe, Friedrich Hölderlin, and Friedrich Schlegel. Critique was a concept or, better, a philosophical approach to establishing the parameters of knowledge and experience (*Erfahrung*). Lifelong, Benjamin attempted to move beyond the limits that he saw the neo-Kantians to have imposed far more dogmatically than Kant himself. He saw in the Enlightenment concept of experience the gradual movement toward "scientism" and with this toward an ever more severe limitation and impoverishment of its promise. Experience, he argued, ought not to be reduced to the "object realm" of science.

His earliest work on educational reform was influenced by Gustav Wyneken's Youth Movement. Again, as that movement became more dogmatic, the more Benjamin distanced himself from it. He resisted partisan thinking all his life, given his unwillingness to compromise either "the life of the spirit" or the claims of the early Karl Marx's historical materialism. Similarly, though instructed by well-known professors, he showed himself to be as anti-academic and anti-programmatic as he was anti-partisan. He was wary of any well-trodden path or anything that smacked of matter-of-factness.

Benjamin became not only a philosophical thinker but also a writer who would sharply oppose those who aimed in thought and language simply to stipulate the principles of method. He wondered how a writer could release the truth in a world that acts as if it would rather have a "higher," "absolute," or "certain" truth imposed upon it. He thought about how one writes "against the grain" or how one writes oneself out of restrictions by which one, as a writer, is historically and socially conditioned. He wrote against the dominant positivist idea or myth of progress which, he maintained, far more concealed than brought truth to appearance.

Benjamin was wary of traditional forms of philosophical argument. He used literary and visual images to develop a language he regarded as more appropriate or truthful for modern times. He wrote sometimes in fragments, sometimes with quotations or aphorisms, in part to demonstrate his interest in what he called constellations or dialectical images. He experimented with both the long and the short form of the (literary) essay. He was particularly interested in story-telling as still historically able to transmit genuine experience.

In his "On Language as Such and on the Language of Mankind" (1916), he argued against the idea that writing was either transparent or merely a vehicle for the communication of an independently existing meaning. Meaning was, rather, contained and usually concealed within language, a view that necessitated entirely rethinking the task of translation. Given a secularized Messianic myth of the fall of humanity and of humanity's entry into history, Benjamin maintained that the more a society misuses its language the more the language (like society) falls into decay. The aim of critique was double-sided: to describe language's decay or the loss of meaning under present social or historical conditions at the same time that one seeks to bring that meaning back to presence. Critique as retrieval was no straightforward matter: It demanded different modes of extreme and explosive, but also fragile and experimental, thought.

Although influenced both by classicism and early romanticism, he explored in modernist terms the complex relations between the truth and deception of language, sign, and image. Between 1919 and 1920 he completed his doctorate in Switzerland with "The Concept of Criticism in German Romanticism." In 1928 the University of Frankfurt refused him his *Habilitation* for his *Origin of German Tragic Drama*. This dissertation, written largely through quotation and focused on a distinction between allegory and symbol, explored the modern form of tragedy. Benjamin often described modernity in terms of ruins: to modernity he liked to attach the terms of meaninglessness, mortification, and fragmentation. Allegory, as one critic has put it, was "a poetic response to the degradation that language undergoes in the instrumental conception that modernity gives to it" (Rochlitz 1996, p. 99). However, though Benjamin so described modernity, he did not engage merely in a conservative lament about how the world once was. Instead, through allegory, he sought the redemptory, and at times also the revolutionary, promise of the new languages, images, and cultural forms as given from the temporal perspective of the "here and now." Benjamin's work on allegory later proved most influential on the thinking of Jacques Derrida and Paul de Man.

Benjamin refused to treat works of art, literature, or philosophy as if one were attending a funeral, as if the works were situated merely in the monumentalized context of a dead past. As he argued in his "Theses" on the philosophy of history, so he argued in his work on literary criticism, that the critic should aim to keep works alive by showing how their meaning, described as belonging to the past, was still present or available to us albeit in enigmatic or allegorical form.

In his writing on history, he argued against the dominant teleological, progressivist and perfectibility visions which saw the world as ordered, rational, and, purposive. He rather presented a view of the past as radically fragmented and of history as something that narrates a story far less of victory and inclusion and far more of failure and exclusion. Inspired by a painting of Paul Klee, he pictured the historian as an angel (the "angel of history") who, though propelled by progressive forces toward the future, would prefer rather to look backward. He described the historian as a guardian of the past, as one who desires to subvert future catastrophe by awakening the dead in an attempt to make whole again what has been destroyed.

Comparably, in his literary criticism, he argued that meaning does not reside in works as if fixed, saturated, or completed; it exists rather as possibility or as a suggestion still flickering in the flames of the coherence the world once had. To retrieve the meaning present in a work is to retrieve that which critics of antiquarian tendency have allowed to fall into oblivion. For Benjamin, art cannot do without this act of retrieval, as he demonstrated in his early mammoth essay on Goethe's *Elective Affinities*. Here, Benjamin distinguished critique from commentary. Whereas the latter focuses on *material content*, the realities more immediately apparent to the eye, the former focuses on the concealed, but historically gradually to be revealed, *ideal- or truth-content* of the work; his point was always to demonstrate the intricate relation between the two.

Increasingly influenced by Baudelaire, Benjamin exposed the contradictory or antagonistic structures of modernist, urban, bourgeois or capitalist life in the metropolis: Berlin, Moscow, Paris. In his late and unfinished *Arcades Project*, he traced the allegorical significance of advertising slogans and neon signs attached to the aging architectural structures of the Parisian Arcades. He looked at the postures of prostitutes, mannequins, and gamblers, and at the movements of the trains and the stock exchange. He looked at the speed of pedestrian traffic and at the exhibition in the shoppers of their boredom, idleness, desire, and satisfaction. Stamps, toys, newspaper headlines revealed the city in its smallest details. No detail and no commodity were treated as trivial or insignificant.

Influenced by the Parisian surrealists, he described fantasies and dreams as collective forms of social experience; he experimented with opium to gain access to new forms of experience. He wrote about dialectical images, which, while structured by capitalist relations of production, nonetheless contained a redemptory potential that would appear to the viewer in momentary or disoriented experiences. He investigated the psychical processes (influenced by art, writing, and drugs) that would crack habitual forms of life or break through the apparent fixity of social forms. To interpret the world was to reorder (change) the world through profane illumination. With André Breton, it was to release the world from its chains or to allow the uncanny dimensions of experience, suppressed under the social construction of ordered appearance, to emerge.

Benjamin's work is often distinguished by earlier and later periods, by decisive transitions from his more esoteric and elitist interest, inspired by Jewish Messianic thought, to his late, often Bertold Brecht–inspired, more revolutionary work in (Marxist) historical materialism. As, however, his last writings on history and art show, there are significant continuities across these transitions. In perhaps his best-known essay, "The Work of Art in the Age of its Technological Reproducibility," he argued that how we receive or view art is changed not only by radical alteration in conditions of production, but also, more esoterically, by how the art, in its experimentation, may surrealise (transform or shatter through creative disorientation) how we think and feel. He showed how the mediation in art between aesthetic concepts and technological conditions matters both for the sake of art and for that of politics.

Crudely, to speak of the "aestheticization of the political" was to speak with the Fascists or the totalitarian thinkers, of how new forms of technology were being regressively employed to sustain outdated aesthetic concepts. He described how concepts of aura and aesthetic absorption had come increasingly to be employed to produce political rather than merely artistic forms, hence, the use of aesthetic concepts and artistic techniques in modern war and propaganda. Contrarily, to speak of the "politicization of art" encouraged a production of art that would more truthfully adapt to currently existing conditions, a production that would rather help liberate a people, so Benjamin argued at his most committed revolutionary moment, than be used to promote knowingly false political illusions.

Benjamin juxtaposed his concrete and diverse reflections on mass art, film, photography, epic theater, and spectatorship with reflections on violence, war, and militarism. In turn, his reflections on violence and fragility were inseparable from his own thinking and writing on the modern condition and possibility of experience.

See also Adorno, Theodor Wiesengrund; Aesthetics, History of; Critical Theory; Derrida, Jacques; Enlightenment; Goethe, Johann Wolfgang von; Historical Materialism; Hölderlin, Johann Christian Friedrich; Kant, Immanuel; Marx, Karl; Neo-Kantianism; Political Philosophy, History of; Schlegel, Friedrich von.

Bibliography

WORKS BY WALTER BENJAMIN

Illuminations. Translated by Harry Zohn; edited and with an introduction by Hannah Arendt. New York: Schocken Books, 1969.

The Origin of German Tragic Drama. Translated by John Osborne. Introduction by George Steiner. London: New Left Books, 1977.

Charles Baudelaire: A Lyric Poet in the Era of High Capitalism. Translated by Harry Zohn. London: New Left Books (Verso), 1983.

Understanding Brecht. Translated by A. Bostock. London: New Left Books (Verso), 1983.

The Arcades Project. Translated by Howard Eiland and Kevin McLaughlin. Cambridge, MA: Harvard University Press, 1999.

Selected Writings. 4 vols edited by Michael W. Jennings and Howard Eiland. Cambridge, MA: Harvard University Press, 2002.

WORKS ABOUT WALTER BENJAMIN

Benjamin, Andrew, ed. *Walter Benjamin and Art*. London and New York: Continuum, 2005.

Bolz, Norbert, and Willem Van Reijen. *Walter Benjamin*. Translated by L. Mazzarins. Atlantic Highlands, NJ: Humanities Press, 1996.

Buck-Morss, Susan. *The Dialectics of Seeing: Walter Benjamin and the Arcades Project*. Cambridge, MA: MIT Press, 1989.

Hanssen, Beatrice, and Andrew Benjamin, eds. *Walter Benjamin and Romanticism*. New York and London: Continuum, 2002.

Jennings, Michael W. *Dialectical Images: Walter Benjamin's Theory of Literary Criticism*. Ithaca, NY, and London: Cornell University Press, 1987.

McCole, John. *Walter Benjamin and the Antinomies of Tradition*. Ithaca, NY, and London: Cornell University Press, 1993.

Richter, Gerhard, ed. *Benjamin's Ghosts: Interventions in Contemporary Literary and Cultural Theory*. Stanford, CA: Stanford University Press, 2002.

Rochlitz, Rainer. *The Disenchantment of Art: The Philosophy of Walter Benjamin*. Translated by Jane Marie Todd. New York and London: The Guilford Press, 1996.

Smith, Gary, ed. *Benjamin: Philosophy, Aesthetics, History*. Chicago: University of Chicago Press, 1989.

Smith, Gary, ed. *On Walter Benjamin: Critical Essays and Recollections*. Cambridge, MA: MIT Press, 1991.

The Walter Benjamin Research Syndicate. Available from http://www.wbenjamin.org.

Wolin, Richard. *Walter Benjamin: An Aesthetic of Redemption*. Berkeley, CA: University of California Press, 1994.

Lydia Goehr (2005)

BENN, GOTTFRIED
(1886–1956)

Gottfried Benn, the German poet and critic, was born in Mansfeld in Westprignitz, of mixed Prussian and Swiss-French parentage. After studying philosophy and philology at the universities of Marburg and Berlin, he received a military scholarship to the Kaiser Wilhelm Academy of Berlin, from which he was graduated as doctor of medicine in 1912. Commissioned as a medical officer in the German Imperial Army, he served briefly in 1912 and then again after the outbreak of the war in 1914. A close friendship with the poet Else Lasker-Schüler ended in 1913, and in July 1914 he married the actress Eva Brandt. From 1917 to 1935 he practiced in Berlin as a specialist in venereal and skin diseases. After his wife's sudden death in 1922, he befriended Ellen Overgaard, a Danish woman, who adopted his daughter.

Benn collaborated with Paul Hindemith on the oratorio *Das Unaufhörliche*, which was performed in 1931. Extensive contact with representative writers of the Weimar Republic led to his election, in 1932, into the German Academy of Arts (whose president, Heinrich Mann, the brother of Thomas, Benn had eulogized in an essay in 1931). A somewhat sordid period of jockeying for positions in the new Reich ended in 1935 with Benn's losing the post of municipal medical specialist, and in 1938 all his writings were banned. He rejoined the army in 1935, coining for this move the much-publicized term *innere Emigration,* in contrast to the actual emigration of his former friends. In 1938 he married his secretary, Herte von Wedemeyer; she committed suicide in 1945, when the Russian armies were approaching the village to which she had been evacuated. After the war Benn's writings were banned, but the publication of *Statische Gedichte* in Switzerland (1948) marked the beginning of a new creative phase. In 1946 he married Ilse Kaul, a young dentist. Benn gave up his medical practice in 1953. Through his decision to remain in Berlin, he became something of a spokesman for the intelligentsia of the city. At his death he was hailed as the greatest German poet since Rainer Maria Rilke; his influence on the styles and themes of contemporary German poetry, certainly, is second to none.

Benn always insisted on the hermetic nature of his poetry and prose; nevertheless, his work faithfully reflects both the historical events and the intellectual turmoil of his age. His first collection of poems, *Morgue* (1912), achieved notoriety and success because of its ruthless exploitation of the phenomena of physical decay and disease. The stark naturalism of such a poem as "Man and Woman Walking through a Cancer Ward" lies both in its rhythmically weak form and in the direction of its argument, typical of much of Benn's later work: the poem attempts to designate some bedrock of "reality" that will withstand contemporary skepticism. The "reality" that emerges from behind the clinical details is a representation of life as impersonal, merely physical or biological, and bereft of all spirit.

The major German poets of the twentieth century have expressed an acute consciousness of their historical situation, a consciousness that derives from Friedrich Nietzsche's critique of the historical imagination and from Oswald Spengler's *Decline of the West.* Benn, in the wake of these works, described the age after the defeat of 1918 as "postnihilistic." In the face of national collapse he set out to formulate an "absolute aesthetic," the aim of which was to "transcend" the actual situation by means of the idea of a "pure poem," the poem of "absolute expressiveness" (as opposed to the poem of communication or opinion with didactic intent). In Benn's poetry, however, there are elements of self-disclosure that seem not to be consistent with his concept of the "pure poem." And his doctrine that art should be exclusively concerned with "style, not truth," raises more questions than it answers.

Benn's ideas on the role of art in life varied. He was able to speak of art as "historically ineffective, without practical consequences," but also to define it (in the wake of Nietzsche) as "the only valid vindication of life." The "biologism" of Benn's earlier poetry had been morally indifferent, and he had nothing but contempt for every form of social organization and democratic politics, especially those of the Weimar Republic. It is therefore not surprising that after March 1933 he emerged as the most important of those German poets who convinced themselves that national socialism offered an answer to their search for a valid artistic ideology—or, rather, for valid poetic symbols. Benn discerned in Adolf Hitler's regime the rule of "a new biological type … [and] the victory of the national idea, the victory of genuine human values, in perfect harmony with the logic of history." His courtship with national socialism was brief, yet even in 1950 (in his embarrassing autobiographical apologia, *Doppelleben*) his main criticism of the Hitler regime was that it "lacked style." "Style" was for Benn the product and the justification of an image-making faculty that conforms to certain "absolute" laws; these laws are "autonomous" in the sense of being indifferent to the demands of personal experience and social reality alike. Questions of personal expediency apart, Benn's astonishing expectations for Hitler's regime seem to have sprung from that contemptuous disregard of political realities that had been characteristic of an important section of the German cultural scene for many years. He saw no contradiction in asserting the hermetic nature of poetry while claiming that the heroic virtues of the new regime would be more propitious for its creation. The historicism he cultivated served Benn (as it did Martin Heidegger in 1933) as justification for his collaboration, but it did not lead him to a clear understanding of the total claim of Hitler's dictatorship.

Benn is the only major German poet who felt, albeit briefly, that his vision was realized in the National Socialist ideology, even though his poems soon proved to be incompatible with the party line in art. The elements that form his best poems derive from the cosmopolitan expressionist school that flourished in Germany in the 1920s as much as from French and Italian imagism; even his invocation of chthonic and instinctual values (in his praise of "Quaternary man" and his values) has its parallels in Ezra Pound, T. E. Hulme, and Julian Benda. His poetic style is clipped, paratactic, full of laconic allusions to the natural sciences. Memories are imaged by means of strong and complex sense perceptions; striking physical details are selected, often for their sound values; all mention of "you" and "we" is rhetorical, the solipsistic circle hardly ever being breached; and the situations invoked are almost always related to a self whose isolation is, if anything, underlined by an appeal to primordial memories.

See also Heidegger, Martin; Hermeticism; Historicism; Nietzsche, Friedrich; Rilke, Rainer Maria (René).

Bibliography

WORKS BY BENN

Gesammelte Werke. Wiesbaden: Limes, 1958–1961. The most important aesthetic statements are to be found in "Züchtung I" and "Züchtung II," Vol. I; "Roman des Phänotyps" and "Der Ptolemäer," Vol. II; "Doppelleben" and "Ausdruckswelt," Vol. III; and "Autobiographische und vermischte Schriften," Vol. IV.

Statische Gedichte. Zürich: Arche, 1948. These two volumes contain representative selections of Benn's poetry.

Trunkene Flut, 2nd ed. Wiesbaden: Limes, 1952.

WORKS ON BENN

Hamburger, M. *Reason and Energy.* London: Routledge and Paul, 1957.

Holthusen, H. E. *Das Schöne und das Wahre.* Munich: R. Piper, 1958.

Jens, W. *Statt einer Literaturgeschichte.* Tübingen, 1958.

Lohner, E. *Gottfried Benn.* Wiesbaden: Limes, 1958. Bibliography.

Loose, G. *Die Ästhetik Gottfried Benns.* Frankfurt, 1961.

Wellershoff, D. *Gottfried Benn: Phänotyp dieser Stunde.* Cologne: Kiepenheuer and Witsch, 1958.

Wodtke, F. W. *Gottfried Benn.* Stuttgart: J. B. Metzler, 1962. Biography.

J. P. Stern (1967)

BENNETT, JONATHAN
(1930–)

Born in 1930 and educated in New Zealand and at the University of Oxford, Jonathan Bennett taught philosophy at the University of Cambridge for twelve years before taking up professorial positions in Canada (at the University of British Columbia) and the United States (at Syracuse University). He is a Fellow of the American Academy of Arts and Sciences and of the British Academy. Now retired, he continues to write from his home on an island near Vancouver, British Columbia.

Bennett's work covers a wide range of issues in analytic philosophy and the history of philosophy, especially the early modern period. His first book, *Rationality* (1964), explored the differences between human intelligence and the intellectual capacities of other animals, and the role of language in these differences. Subsequently influenced by Paul Grice's seminal work on meaning and communicative intentions, he significantly modified his views about such matters in a later book, *Linguistic Behaviour* (1976), which incorporates an account of convention building on but also differs in certain respects from David Lewis's ground-breaking theory.

Bennett's interest in the nature of intentional behavior connects his work in philosophical psychology and the philosophy of language with his work in the metaphysics of actions and events. His major contribution to the latter topic is *Events and their Names* (1988), in which he explores the distinction between events and facts through an examination of the semantics of everyday language, focusing on the differences between two kinds of sentence nominals, exemplified by the pair *Quisling's betrayal of Norway/Quisling's betraying Norway*. In this book Bennett addresses the important question of whether facts or events should properly be regarded as the things related by causal relations; he contends that both may be but that fact-causation statements and event-causation statements require different kinds of analysis, whether in terms of counterfactual conditionals or in terms of causal laws. Bennett concludes, however, that the language of event-causation, though useful, is impoverished compared with that of fact-causation and that the former must be analysed in terms of the latter. He also offers an analysis of the "by" locution employed in action sentences of the form S *did such-and-such* by *doing so-and-so*.

In a later book on the theme of agency, *The Act Itself* (1995), Bennett discusses in depth the moral dimension of human action, including the thorny question of whether a morally significant distinction can be drawn between doing something and letting something happen: for example, between killing someone and letting someone die. He makes it clear, early in the book, that he is a moral nonrealist, denying that moral judgements are answerable to independent moral facts and hence denying that they have, in that sense, truth values.

Closely connected with Bennett's work on actions and events is his important contribution, over a period of more than thirty years, to philosophical debate on the semantics of conditional statements. This work culminated in his book *A Philosophical Guide to Conditionals* (2003), perhaps the most comprehensive and authoritative treatment of the subject available. On a number of key issues in this debate, Bennett has shifted his position over the years, notably on the question of whether there is a significant distinction to be drawn between counterfactual and indicative conditionals. Reversing his earlier opinion, formed under the influence of the work of V. H. Dudman, he now thinks that there is and that these two classes of conditionals demand radically different analyses: the former a possible-worlds analysis along the lines proposed by David Lewis and the latter a probabilistic analysis of the sort pioneered by Ernest Adams. As a consequence, he holds that indicative conditionals, unlike counterfactuals, lack truth conditions and hence truth values. At the same time, he tries to explain why, despite their radically different analyses, there are close similarities between the logics of the two kinds of conditionals and why it is often correct to move from asserting an indicative conditional at one time to asserting a corresponding counterfactual at a later time.

Bennett's work in the history of philosophy has centred on the core texts of the British Empiricists—Locke, Berkeley and Hume—and those of certain eminent continental philosophers of the seventeenth and eighteenth centuries, especially Spinoza and Kant. *Kant's Analytic* (1966) was followed eight years later by its sequel, *Kant's Dialectic* (1974), with *Locke, Berkeley, Hume: Central Themes* (1971) appearing in between. Bennett's next major project of this kind was *A Study of Spinoza's Ethics* (1984); at about the same time he collaborated with Peter Remnant to produce an important new edition and translation of *Leibniz's New Essays on Human Understanding* (1981).

The culminating synthesis of Bennett's thoughts about the major philosophers of the early modern period is provided by his magisterial two-volume magnum opus, *Learning from Six Philosophers* (2001). The first volume treats Descartes, Spinoza, and Leibniz and the second Locke, Berkeley, and Hume. Bennett has always been clear about his own approach to the writings of the great philosophers of the past: although he does not ignore their historical context, he is concerned chiefly with the ideas and arguments to be found in them—not merely as illustrative of the philosophical thought of their times, but for their own sake and for the light that they can shed on present-day philosophical debate. Inevitably, this sort of approach has attracted criticism from certain quarters, especially from historians of philosophy who are skeptical about the very notion of *philosophia perennis*—the idea that there are perennial philosophical problems and arguments that transcend cultural and historical boundaries. But whatever the rights and wrongs of this dispute might be, it is manifest that Bennett's approach is motivated not least by his concern, as a teacher of philosophy,

to keep the seminal texts of past philosophers alive for succeeding generations of students.

See also Berkeley, George; Conditionals; Counterfactuals; Descartes, René; Empiricism; Event Theory; Grice, Herbert Paul; History and Historiography of Philosophy; Hume, David; Kant, Immanuel; Leibniz, Gottfried Wilhelm; Lewis, David; Locke, John; Ontology; Spinoza, Benedict (Baruch) de.

Bibliography

WORKS BY BENNETT

Rationality: An Essay Towards Analysis. London: Routledge & Kegan Paul, 1964.

Kant's Analytic. Cambridge, U.K.: Cambridge University Press, 1966.

Locke, Berkeley, Hume: Central Themes. Oxford: Clarendon Press, 1971.

Kant's Dialectic. Cambridge, U.K.: Cambridge University Press, 1974.

Linguistic Behaviour. Cambridge: Cambridge University Press, 1976.

A Study of Spinoza's Ethics. Cambridge, U.K.: Cambridge University Press, 1984.

Events and their Names. Oxford: Clarendon Press, 1988.

The Act Itself. Oxford: Clarendon Press, 1995.

Learning from Six Philosophers. Oxford: Clarendon Press, 2001.

A Philosophical Guide to Conditionals. Oxford: Clarendon Press, 2003.

E. J. Lowe (2005)

BENTHAM, JEREMY
(1748–1832)

Jeremy Bentham, English philosopher and reformer, was born in Houndsditch, London, on February 15, 1748. His father was a solicitor, with wealthy and important clients in the City of London. Of his siblings, only one younger brother, Samuel (1757–1831), survived into adulthood, becoming a prominent naval architect and engineer. His mother died on January 6, 1759. In 1760 his father entered him, at the age of twelve, into the University of Oxford, where he attended the lectures of William Blackstone (later published as *Commentaries on the Laws of England*, 1765–1769). He graduated in 1764, having been obliged to subscribe to the Thirty-nine Articles of the Church of England, the statement of its dogma and discipline.

Having entered Lincoln's Inn in 1763, he was admitted to the bar in 1769. He did not, as his father wished, practice law, but decided instead to devote himself to its reform. Bentham thought of himself as "the Newton of legislation" (Milne 1981, p. 169); just as Isaac Newton (1642–1727) had brought order to the physical sciences, so would he to the moral sciences. Bentham adopted the principle of utility (an action was judged to be morally right to the extent that that it promoted the greatest happiness of the greatest number) as a critical standard by which to test the value of existing practices, laws, and institutions, and to suggest reform and improvement. He set about composing a comprehensive penal code, to which his best-known work, *An Introduction to the Principles of Morals and Legislation* (abbreviated as *IPML*), which was printed in 1780 and published in 1789, was intended to form a preface.

After returning from a visit to his brother in Russia from 1785 to 1788, his career was dominated by his attempt to build a panopticon prison in London. When the scheme effectively collapsed in 1803 Bentham was left embittered by what he regarded as the bad faith of successive ministries, and he became increasingly committed to political radicalism. In 1809 he began to write on parliamentary reform, and in 1822 he embarked on *Constitutional Code*, in which he advocated the establishment of a representative democracy. Having lived in Lincoln's Inn from 1769 to 1792, he had then inherited his father's home in Queen's Square Place, Westminster, where he died on June 6, 1832.

Bentham's contemporary reputation was founded on the five recensions of his works produced in elegant French between 1802 and 1828 by his Genevan translator and editor, Étienne Dumont (1759–1829). Bentham met Dumont in or around 1788, when both were members of the Bowood Circle that gathered at the country house of William Petty (1737–1805), second Earl of Shelburne and first Marquis of Lansdowne. Dumont's recensions were not literal translations of Bentham's writings, but lucid distillations of his central ideas. The first and most influential was *Traités de législation civile et pénale* (The Theory of Legislation; 1802). To those who wished to introduce political and legal reform, but who faced resistance from entrenched interests such as the privileged nobility and the church, the rational, secular, reforming programme offered by Bentham carried great appeal. While profoundly critical of the legal institutions and practices that he found in existence, he was at the same time optimistic about what could be achieved by law. As he had announced in *IPML*, his enterprise was "to rear the fabric of felicity by the hands of reason and of law" (Burns 1970. p. 11). Bentham's vision of the law as an instrument of reform and improvement had considerable impact in an age that viewed ignorance, prejudice, and superstition as the main barrier to human progress.

BENTHAM'S ACHIEVEMENTS

Bentham's achievements, only some of which are noticed in detail here, were immense. He was the founder of classical utilitarianism, which inspired the movement known as philosophic radicalism in which the young John Stuart Mill (1806–1873) played a leading role, and which has remained one of the most influential doctrines in political philosophy. His method of calculating the potential utility of actions forms the basis of cost benefit analysis in economics. Distinguishing sharply between law as it is and law as it ought to be, he inspired the proponents of the doctrine of legal positivism. In his extensive and detailed writings on judicial procedure, he produced the most comprehensive theory of evidence in the Anglo-American tradition. He developed a theory of punishment and reward which emphasized deterrence, proportionality, and rehabilitation of the offender, and which went far beyond, in terms of rigor and coherence, that associated with Cesare Beccaria (1738–1794).

In politics he produced, in 1789, the earliest utilitarian defense of political equality (at one point even advocating women's suffrage), and later, in *Constitutional Code*, produced a sophisticated and detailed blueprint for representative democracy. His essay on *Political Tactics* was the first systematic treatise on the organization of a political assembly. He put forward a scheme to promote peace between nations, advocating an international court of arbitration and a proportional reduction of armed forces. Indeed, the word "international" was coined by Bentham. His proposals for dealing with poverty provided the intellectual basis for the Poor Law Amendment Act of 1834, and for the welfare state more generally. His educational ideas, based on "useful learning" and access for all regardless of religion or gender (in contrast to the Universities of Oxford and Cambridge, where students had to be Anglican and male) inspired the founders of the University of London in the mid-1820s.

LANGUAGE

The starting point for Bentham's thought was his understanding of the way in which the human mind perceived the physical world, and the way in which language was used to describe that world. The fundamental distinction in language was between the names of real entities, which represented objects existing in the physical world (e.g., an apple), and the names of fictitious entities, objects that were spoken about as if they did exist, and about which it made sense to talk as though they existed, but to which it was not intended to ascribe physical existence (e.g., the property of a physical object, such as the sweetness of an apple, or an abstraction, such as a law). In order to make sense, language had to refer, either directly or indirectly, to physical objects. The difficulty lay in finding a method by which the names of fictitious entities could be related to their "real source" in the physical world. The names of fictitious entities were not capable of exposition by means of representation, where a specific object was produced and its assigned name pronounced, for there was no such object to produce. Nor was it possible to define a fictitious entity by means of the Aristotelian method of definition *per genus et differentiam*. Definition by this means was possible where the object belonged to a nest of aggregates, and was not the highest object in the nest, but was not possible where the word had no superior genus.

Bentham's solution consisted in the complementary techniques of paraphrasis and phraseoplerosis. The operation of phraseoplerosis, the filling up of the phrase, was logically prior to that of paraphrasis. Discourse often contained ellipses, which needed to be "filled in" by inserting the omitted words. Thereupon, the operation of paraphrasis could be undertaken, whereby a sentence in which the name of the fictitious entity appeared was translated into another sentence in which the words were either real entities, or were more nearly related to real entities. Take the word "duty." A person (X) had a legal duty when someone else (Y) had a right to have him (X) made to perform it, in which case X had a duty toward Y, and Y a right against X; what Y had a legal right to have X be made to do was that for which X was legally liable, upon a requisition made on Y's behalf, to be punished for not doing. The definition or exposition had "resolved" the notion of duty into its simple, or more simple, elements: namely the prospect of suffering a punishment (a term which itself would require further exposition), upon the forbearance to perform some action, when required to do so by the person invested with the corresponding right. However, if an exposition by paraphrasis proved to be impossible, then the fictitious entity in question belonged to the class of nonentities, the noun substantive by which it was represented was merely a sound, and any proposition in which it occurred was nonsensical.

PRINCIPLE OF UTILITY

Bentham's critical standard, the principle of utility, was a fictitious entity, and had to be expounded by relating it to the physical entities that formed its "real source." As Bentham explained in *IPML*, the "real source" in question consisted in the sensations of pain and pleasure: "Nature has placed mankind under the governance of two sovereign masters, *pain* and *pleasure*. It is for them alone to point out what we ought to do, as well as to determine what we shall do." The "sovereign masters" of pain and pleasure not only accounted for human motivation, "govern[ing] us in all we do, in all we say, in all we think," but also provided "the standard of right and wrong" (p. 11). Psychology and ethics were both founded on, and therefore linked by, their relation to pleasure and pain.

In relation to psychology, the desire for pleasure and the aversion to pain formed the basis for all motivation, both in humans and sentient creatures generally. An individual had a motive to perform an action—or put another way, had an interest in performing an action—if he or she expected to gain some pleasure or avert some pain from doing so; and the greater or more valuable the pleasure experienced or pain averted, the stronger the motive or greater the interest. The value of a pleasure or pain was determined by its quantity, which, in the case of a single individual, was a product of its intensity, duration, certainty or uncertainty, and propinquity or remoteness. Where the value of a pleasure or pain was considered in relation to more than one person, then in addition to these circumstances, the circumstance of extent, that is the number of persons affected by it, had also to be taken into account. At this point, a statement of psychological fact has become a statement of moral science. An act was morally good if, after calculating all the pains or pleasures produced in the instance of every individual affected, the balance was on the side of pleasure, and morally evil if on the side of pain. Bentham's method of determining the value of pleasure and pain is known as the "felicific calculus," though this was not a phrase that he appears to have used himself.

An adherent of the principle of utility would approve of any action that increased the overall happiness (understood in terms of a balance of pleasure over pain) of all the individuals affected by the action in question, where more than one individual was affected. An adherent of the principle of utility would likewise approve of any action that increased the happiness of a particular individual where no other individual was affected by the action in question. In the former instance the extent was equal to the total number of individuals in question, and in the latter instance to one. It was only when extent was taken into account that an action could be judged to be ethically right or wrong. The question of right and wrong was a question of fact—an account of the value, understood in terms of quantity, of the pleasures and pains that had been brought into existence by the act in question. In order for the utilitarian legislator to accomplish his objective of promoting the greatest happiness of the greatest number, he had to use sanctions (punishments and rewards), themselves composed of pain and pleasure, to discourage actions detrimental to the happiness of the community, and (to a lesser extent) to encourage those that were beneficial.

NATURAL LAW

Bentham's adoption of the principle of utility—with its "real source" in the feelings of pain and pleasure experienced by sentient creatures—as a critical standard of morality led him to distinguish between "law as it is" and "law as it ought to be." This distinction provided the basis both for his strategy of reform, and for his attack on natural law. In *A Fragment on Government* (1776), which took Blackstone's *Commentaries* for its target, Bentham distinguished two approaches that the legal commentator might adopt: the first was that of the expositor, whose task was to describe what had been done by legislators and judges (law as it is); the second was that of the censor, whose task to show what they ought to do in future (law as it ought to be).

Blackstone, by not only describing but also attempting to justify the laws of England, had confounded the two approaches. He had, moreover, failed to adopt the principle of utility as his standard of morality, but had appealed to the doctrine of natural law, claiming that human (positive) law was valid insofar as it did not contradict the natural law. Bentham condemned Blackstone both for linking the validity of positive law to a particular substantive content, and for thinking that the natural law could supply the content in question. The natural law did not exist (it was a nonentity), hence any appeal to the law of nature in order to validate a positive law was nonsense, and in practice reflected the mere subjective approval of the supporter of the positive law in question. Blackstone had stated that where there was law, there was some superior who made it. Bentham drew out the corollary: if there was no maker, there was no law. The same problem of nonexistence bedevilled a further device adopted by Blackstone, the original contract. Having accepted the criticisms of the doctrine made by David Hume (1711–1776), Bentham went on to argue that, even if one assumed its historical existence, the original contract, like any promise, had binding force only if adherence to it would promote utility. The original contract was, therefore, superfluous, since the question as to whether to obey or resist government should be based directly on considerations of utility.

NATURAL RIGHTS

Bentham deployed similar arguments against a doctrine closely related to that of natural law, namely the doctrine of natural rights. In the French Declaration of Rights of 1789 it was asserted that the end of every political association was the preservation of the natural and imprescriptible rights of man, and that these natural rights could not be abrogated by government. The purpose of establishing government was to protect preexisting natural rights, and any government that failed to do so lacked legitimacy. In "Nonsense upon Stilts" (known as "Anarchical Fallacies" until the publication of the authoritative text in *Rights, Representation, and Reform* [Schofield, Pease-Watkin, and Cyprian Blamires 2002, pp. 317–401]) Bentham argued that there were "no such things as natural rights—no such things as rights anterior to the establishment of government—no such things as natural rights opposed to, in contradistinction to, legal" (p. 329). The notion of a state of nature, where men lived without government, was perfectly comprehensible, but in such a state there were no rights, and consequently no property and no security. Such rights might be desirable, but it was fallacious to assume that because a certain thing was desirable, that the thing in question existed. Furthermore, if natural rights did not exist, they could not be abrogated. To say that they were imprescriptible was to mount one nonsensical statement upon another: "Natural rights is simple nonsense: natural and imprescriptible rights, rhetorical nonsense, nonsense upon stilts" (p. 330). The purpose of declaring the existence of imprescriptible rights was to incite resistance to law and insurrection against government. To claim that no government could abrogate natural rights was "Terrorist language," whereas those who spoke the "language of reason and plain sense" judged whether a right should or should not be established or abrogated on the basis of whether or not it was for the advantage of society to do so (p. 330).

In *A Fragment on Government* Bentham's concern was with the distinction between the censor and the expositor, while in "Nonsense upon Stilts" it was with that between the censor and the anarchist. The anarchy that Bentham associated with the French Revolution was closely related to the conservatism he associated with Blackstone. The latter had claimed to be describing the laws of England, but had attempted to justify those laws on no other ground than that they existed. His approach confused what existed with what ought to exist. A similar confusion characterized the anarchist, who, in claiming to describe natural rights, was making prescriptions. The difference was that while Blackstone assumed that existing law was consistent with the natural law, and therefore valid, the anarchist assumed that existing law was inconsistent with natural rights, and therefore invalid. To the extent that both were appealing to a nonexistent standard in justification of their respective claims, both were talking nonsense.

In Bentham's view, only the principle of utility provided any rational ground for resolving moral, political, and legal disputes, while talk of justice, right reason, natural rights, or moral sense was merely a cover to give respectability to, or to endow with persuasive force, the likes and dislikes of the speaker. The doctrines of natural law and natural rights were grounded on the delusive properties of language, and in particular the confusion involved in taking the name of a fictitious entity to be the name of a real entity. The use of the noun-substantive "rights" had given rise to the opinion that rights as such did actually exist. Now to talk of rights established by law did make sense, since they might be shown to have their "real source" in the will of a sovereign legislature. To talk of natural rights, with their source in natural law or a supernatural being, was to talk nonsense. The techniques of exposition that Bentham had developed in his theory of language were at the root of his attacks on natural law and natural rights.

CODIFICATION OF THE LAW

In the early 1780s Bentham concluded that the most effective means of promoting the happiness of the community would be through the introduction of a complete code of laws, or a "pannomion." Bentham's commitment to codification arose from a profound dissatisfaction with the English common law, which he characterized as corrupt, unknowable, incomplete, and arbitrary. It could not perform the minimum purpose for which law was instituted, namely to guide conduct. Still less was it able to afford protection to those basic interests of the individual—his person, property, reputation, and condition in life—which constituted his security, and hence a major component of his well-being. Security was closely related to the notion of expectations, for it involved both the present possession and the future expectation of possessing the property or other subject-matter in question. Without security, and thus the confidence to project oneself and one's plans into the future, there could be no civilized life. Security was a product of law, resulting from the imposition of rules on conduct. To an extent it did

not matter which set of rules were imposed, so long as some set of rules were imposed, and these rules were known and certain. The crux of the problem with the common law was that those subject to it did not, and could not, know what it ordained, and this created insecurity. Expectations could either not be formed or were constantly liable to be disappointed.

The solution lay in codification. In his writings on the subject in the 1810s and 1820s Bentham explained that the pannomion should be "all-comprehensive" and "rationalized." This meant that the law would be logically complete, in that all legal terms would be defined consistently and related to some superior genus (where one existed), and that each provision would be followed by the reasons that justified it. At the apex of the pannomion was the civil code, concerned with the distribution of rights and duties. The purpose of the civil law was to maximize the four sub-ends of utility—namely subsistence, abundance, security, and equality. The purpose of the penal law was to give effect to the civil law, by means of attaching punishment to certain actions which, on account of their tendency to diminish the greatest happiness, were classified as offenses.

The constitutional code was also, at least in part, distributive in character, being concerned with the powers, rights, and duties of public officials, and their modes of appointment and dismissal. As with the civil law, the penal law would give effect to the relevant parts of the constitutional law. The penal, civil, and constitutional law together formed the substantive law, which was itself given effect by the adjective law, or the law of judicial procedure. The chain was completed by the law of the judicial establishment, the purpose of which was to give effect to the adjective law, and thence to the substantive law. In other words, the civil code, and to some extent the constitutional code, would contain the "directive rules" by which rights and duties were distributed, while the penal code would contain the sanctions which would enforce observance. For instance, the penal code would forbid and sanction interference with property without title, while the civil code would explain what events constituted a valid claim to title.

Bentham offered his services as a codifier to a variety of countries, including Scotland in 1808, the United States in 1811, and Russia in 1814. In April 1822 he received the invitation for which he had been longing: the Portuguese Cortes formally accepted his offer to draw up civil, penal, and constitutional codes. He immediately began to compose *Constitutional Code*, but long before even the first volume of this work had been printed in

1827, the liberal regime that had accepted Bentham's offer had been swept away. In the 1820s Bentham also devoted time and attention to Spain, Tripoli, Greece, and the emerging states of Latin America, as well as becoming fully involved in the movement to reform and codify English law. By this time he enjoyed an international reputation as the doyen of liberal legal philosophers and political reformers. José del Valle (1776–1834), for instance, the Guatemalan lawyer, economist, and politician, wrote to Bentham hailing him as "the legislator of the world."

PANOPTICON

The panopticon design was the brainchild of Bentham's brother Samuel, when employed in the 1780s on the estates of Prince Grigoriy Aleksandrovich Potemkin (1724–1791) at Krichev, in Russia. He found that by organizing his workforce in a circular building, with himself at the center, he could supervise its activities more effectively. Visiting his brother and seeing the design, Bentham immediately appreciated its potential. Enshrining the principle of inspection, the design was applicable to mental asylums, hospitals, schools, poor houses, factories, and, of course, prisons.

The prison building would be circular, with the cells, occupying several stories one above the other, placed around the circumference. At the center of the building would be the inspector's lodge, with an open space between the lodge and the cells. Each cell would have a window to the outside of the building, which would, from the perspective of the lodge, backlight the cell in daytime, while lamps, placed outside the lodge with a reflector behind them, would light the cells at night. The lodge would be so constructed, with appropriate partitions and blinds, that the inspector would always be capable of seeing into the cells, while the prisoners would be unable to see whether they were being watched. The activities of the prisoners would be transparent to the inspector; his actions, insofar as the prisoners were concerned, were hid behind a veil of secrecy. On the other hand, it was a cardinal feature of the design that the activities of the inspector and his officials should be laid open to the general scrutiny of the public, who would be encouraged to visit the prison. Bentham did not succeed in building a panopticon in London, despite gaining parliamentary approval in 1794, and the scheme was effectively quashed in 1803 (a half-hearted attempt to revive it in 1811–1812 failed). Several so-called panopticons have since been built, but none which has been particularly faithful to Bentham's own vision.

Michel Foucault in *Discipline and Punish* (1977) has described Bentham's panopticon as a paradigm of the modern state, hence placing Bentham at the center of debates about what it means to be modern. What Foucault overlooked in Bentham's case (whatever might be the case with the modern state) is that Bentham was concerned not only with the ability of officials to gain knowledge of the community subject to them (which was, of course, critical if they were to rule well), but also with the ability of the people to monitor the conduct of their rulers. The panopticon prison would be open to inspection from the public at large, just as the actions of officials would be under *Constitutional Code*. Publicity was the means of securing responsibility, and the most effective antidote against corruption.

POLITICAL REFORM

By the 1820s Bentham was convinced that the only regime with an interest in enacting good legislation was a representative democracy. Scholars disagree over precisely when Bentham committed himself to political radicalism. One view is that Bentham was a political radical from the time of the French Revolution, when, for a short period in late 1789, he advocated democracy for France. Another view, which is based on a coincidence of dates, is that Bentham became a political radical in 1808–1809, having come into contact with James Mill (1773–1836). The most plausible view, however, is that the crucial development took place around 1804 with the emergence in Bentham's thought of the notion of sinister interests, that is the systematic development of the insight that rulers wished to promote not the happiness of the community, but their own happiness. There was no point in showing rulers what the best course of legislation might be unless they had an interest in adopting it. Only a legislature elected by a democratic suffrage had such an interest.

If the key episode is the emergence of sinister interests, then the panopticon prison becomes significant. Bentham devoted many years of his life, large sums of his money (which he eventually recovered in a compensation settlement), and considerable energy, on the scheme. He was never so bitter or so despondent as when the plan was quashed in 1803. He became convinced that nothing worthwhile could be achieved through the existing political structure in Britain, or through similar regimes elsewhere. Having concentrated on questions of law reform from 1803, he was in the summer of 1809 prompted to compose material on political reform, eventually bearing fruit in *Plan of Parliamentary Reform* (1817).

In this work Bentham called for universal manhood suffrage (subject to a literacy test), annual parliaments, equal electoral districts, payment of members of parliament, and the secret ballot. Bentham then went a stage further and drew up a blueprint for representative democracy that would have abolished the monarchy, the House of Lords and any other second chamber, and all artificial titles of honor, and would have rendered government entirely open and, he hoped, fully accountable. These proposals were developed in astonishing detail in the magisterial *Constitutional Code*, the work he began in 1822 upon learning that the Portugueze Cortes had accepted his codification offer.

For Bentham the key principle of constitutional design was to ensure the dependence of rulers on subjects. Instead of the traditional theory of the separation of powers, he proposed lines of subordination, based on the ability of the superior to appoint and dismiss (in Bentham's terminology to locate and dislocate) the inferior, and to subject the inferior to punishment and other forms of vexation. The supreme power or sovereignty in the state would be vested in the people, who held the constitutive power. Immediately subordinate to the people would be the legislature, elected by universal manhood suffrage, and subordinate to the legislature would be the administrative (i.e., the executive) and judicial powers. The system of representative democracy was not an end in itself—the end was the greatest happiness—but was an indispensable means to that end, in that it was only under such a constitution that effective measures could be implemented to secure the good behavior (appropriate aptitude) of officials and minimize the expense of government. The securities for official aptitude, otherwise termed securities against misrule, included the exclusion of factitious dignities (titles of honor), the economical auction (whereby officials made bids for the salary attached to the office), subjection to punishment at the hands of the legal tribunals of the state, the requirement to pass an examination, and, most importantly, publicity.

Bentham went to great lengths to ensure that government would be open to public scrutiny, and thence subject to the force of the moral or popular sanction operating through the public opinion tribunal, which consisted in all those who commented on political matters, and of whom newspaper editors were the most important. Bentham saw the freedom of the press as a vital bulwark against misrule: hence his proposal to encourage the diffusion of literacy by making the suffrage dependent on a literacy test. These measures were intended to ensure that rulers would be so situated that the only way they could promote their own interest was by promoting the interest of the community.

RELIGION

Bentham offered a secular vision of society, where the standard of rectitude would be founded not on theology, or natural law, or right reason, or precedent, or sheer prejudice, but on observation and experience. Knowledge of society (and of the individuals who composed it) enshrined in a "political science" (for Bentham's use of the term see, for instance, *Official Aptitude Maximized* [Schofield 1993, p. 191]) would be the basis for the art of legislation, the practical measures that an enlightened legislator would introduce in order to promote the greatest happiness of the community. Bentham was committed to freedom of expression in religion, as in other areas. While it may be too quick to conclude that he was an atheist, he did ally himself from an early period in his life with those who were sceptical, if not of religious belief, certainly of organized religion, and he never wavered in his outright opposition to religious establishments. As early as the mid-1770s, he drew attention to the potential mischiefs associated with what he termed the religious sanction. The expectation of a future state amounted to the expectation of the distribution of pains and pleasures, but did not in itself entail any rules specifying in what way such pains and pleasures would be distributed. If this distribution was to be random, then the expectation of them could not have any influence in encouraging good conduct or restraining bad. Given that the idea of God might provide motives, but could not provide direction, it was better that the moralist and legislator had nothing to do with it.

In the 1810s Bentham launched a sustained attack against established religion. He argued that religious belief was used to further the particular and sinister interest of the priesthood and those linked with it. The Anglican Church was an instrument in the hands of rulers to oppress and extort resources from subjects. It extracted large sums of money from the population generally, in order to provide income for rulers, without providing any useful service in return. The state supported the Church with its coercive force, while the Church manufactured delusive arguments in support of the state. Indeed, the scale of abuse in the Church was not only greater than that in the political and legal establishments, but acted as a bulwark against reform elsewhere. Bentham was particularly critical of the role of the Church in education, both in schools and in the Universities of Oxford and Cambridge. In relation to the poor, its policy was to exclude from the benefits of education those unwilling to declare their belief in Anglican doctrine, and to pervert the morals and intellects of those who were willing.

Bentham's resentment at being forced to subscribe to the Thirty-nine Articles while at Oxford led him to insist that the provision of education should be divorced from the profession of belief. He recommended the "euthanasia" of the Anglican Church, whereby, as livings and other offices became vacant, they would be abolished. The present possessors would retain their incomes and thereby not suffer the pain of disappointment, while the expense of the religious establishment to the state, and thus to the people generally, would gradually diminish, and the additional income derived would be used to reduce taxation. Those people who wished to receive religious instruction could continue to do so at their own expense.

AUTO-ICON

Bentham was not buried, but his body transformed into what he termed an auto-icon. He had left instructions in his will that his body should be used in a series of anatomical lectures, and thereafter his skeleton "put together in such manner as that the whole figure may be seated in a Chair usually occupied by me when living in the attitude in which I am sitting when engaged in thought" (Crimmins 2002, p. 8). The operation was entrusted to Bentham's surgeon, Thomas Southwood Smith (1788–1861), who created the auto-icon—the combination of skeleton, wax head, clothes, and stuffing—which now resides in University College London.

See also Aristotelianism; Beccaria, Cesare Bonesana; Democracy; Foucault, Michel; Hume, David; Legal Positivism; Mill, James; Mill, John Stuart; Newton, Isaac; Pleasure; Property; Punishment; Utilitarianism.

Bibliography

WORKS BY JEREMY BENTHAM

The Bentham Project, University College London, is preparing a new authoritative edition of *The Collected Works of Jeremy Bentham*, which, it is estimated, will run to sixty-eight volumes. The twenty-fifth appeared in March 2002. The new edition is based on two main sources: first, texts printed during Bentham's lifetime; and second, Bentham's original manuscripts, of which around 55,000 folios are deposited in University College London Library, and around 10,000 in the British Library. Of the volumes in *The Collected Works*, the following have been most extensively drawn on for the entry above, and in-text citations correspond to these editions:

An Introduction to the Principles of Morals and Legislation, edited by J. H. Burns and H. L. A. Hart. London: Athlone Press, 1970.

A Comment on the Commentaries and A Fragment on Government, edited by J. H. Burns and H. L. A. Hart. London: Athlone Press, 1977.

Constitutional Code, Vol., edited by F. Rosen and J. H. Burns. Oxford: Clarendon Press, 1983.

The Correspondence of Jeremy Bentham. Vol. 4, *October 1788 to December 1793* edited by A. T. Milne. London: Athelone Press, 1981.

First Principles Preparatory to Constitutional Code, edited by Philip Schofield. Oxford: Clarendon Press, 1989.

Official Aptitude Maximized; Expense Minimized, edited by Philip Schofield. Oxford: Clarendon Press, 1993.

"Legislator of the World": Writings on Codification, Law, and Education, edited by Philip Schofield and Jonathan Harris. Oxford: Clarendon Press, 1998.

Rights, Representation, and Reform. Nonsense upon Stilts and Other Writings on the French Revolution, edited by Philip Schofield, Catherine Pease-Watkin, and Cyprian Blamires. Oxford: Clarendon Press, 2002.

Where works have not appeared in *The Collected Works*, the standard source is the so-called Bowring edition: *The Works of Jeremy Bentham*, published under the superintendence of his executor, John Bowring. 11 vols. Edinburgh: William Tait, 1843. For Bentham's economic thought see *Jeremy Bentham's Economic Writings*. 3 vols., edited by Werner Stark. London: George Allen & Unwin, 1952–1954.

There are two convenient collections of essays on Bentham: *Jeremy Bentham: Critical Assessments*. 4 vols., edited by Bhikhu Parekh. London: Routledge, 1993; and *Bentham: Moral, Political, and Legal Philosophy*. 2 vols., edited by Gerald J. Postema. Aldershot: Ashgate, 2002.

WORKS ABOUT JEREMY BENTHAM

Bahmueller, Charles F. *The National Charity Company: Jeremy Bentham's Silent Revolution*. Berkeley: University of California Press, 1981.

Ben Dor, Oren. *Constitutional Limits and the Public Sphere: A Critical Study of Bentham's Constitutionalism*. Oxford: Hart Publishing, 2000.

Boralevi, Lea Campos. *Bentham and the Oppressed*. Berlin: Walter de Gruyter, 1984.

Crimmins, James E. *Bentham's Auto-Icon and Related Writings*. Bristol: Thoemmes Press, 2002.

Crimmins, James E. *Secular Utilitarianism: Social Science and the Critique of Religion in the Thought of Jeremy Bentham*. Oxford: Clarendon Press, 1990.

Dinwiddy, John. *Bentham: Selected Writings of John Dinwiddy*, edited by William Twining. Stanford, CA: Stanford University Press, 2004.

Engelmann, Stephen G. "Imagining Interest." *Utilitas* 13 (3) (2001): 289–322.

Foucault, Michel. *Discipline and Punish: The Birth of the Prison*. Translated by Alan Sheridan. Harmondsworth: Allen Lane, 1977.

Halévy, Elie. *The Growth of Philosophic Radicalism*. Translated by Mary Morris. London: Faber & Faber, 1928.

Harrison, Ross. *Bentham*. London: Routledge & Kegan Paul, 1983.

Hart, H. L. A. *Essays on Bentham: Jurisprudence and Political Theory*. Oxford: Clarendon Press, 1982.

Hume, L. J. *Bentham and Bureaucracy*. Cambridge, U.K.: Cambridge University Press, 1981.

Kelly, P. J. *Utilitarianism and Distributive Justice: Jeremy Bentham and the Civil Law*. Oxford: Clarendon Press, 1990.

Lieberman, David. "Economy and Polity in Bentham's Science of Legislation." In *Economy, Polity, and Society: British Intellectual History, 1750–1950*, edited by Stefan Collini, Richard Whatmore, and Brian Young. Cambridge, U.K.: Cambridge University Press, 2000.

Lieberman, David. *The Province of Legislation Determined: Legal Theory in Eighteenth-Century Britain*. Cambridge, U.K.: Cambridge University Press, 1989.

Lobban, Michael. *The Common Law and English Jurisprudence 1760–1850*. Oxford: Clarendon Press, 1991.

Long, Douglas G. *Bentham on Liberty: Jeremy Bentham's Idea of Liberty in Relation to His Utilitarianism*. Toronto: University of Toronto Press, 1977.

Lyons, David. *In the Interest of the Governed: A Study in Bentham's Philosophy of Utility and Law*. Rev. ed. Oxford: Clarendon Press, 1991.

Mack, Mary P. *Jeremy Bentham: An Odyssey of Ideas 1748–1792*. London: Heinemann, 1962.

Pitts, Jennifer. "Legislator of the World? A Rereading of Bentham on Colonies." *Political Theory* 31 (2) (2003): 200–234.

Postema, Gerald J. *Bentham and the Common Law Tradition*. Oxford: Clarendon Press, 1986.

Postema, Gerald J. "Fact, Fictions, and Law: Bentham on the Foundations of Evidence." In *Facts in Law*, edited by William Twining. Wiesbaden: Franz Steiner Verlag, 1983.

Rosen, Frederick. *Bentham, Byron, and Greece: Constitutionalism, Nationalism, and Early Liberal Political Thought*. Oxford: Clarendon Press, 1992.

Rosen, Frederick. *Classical Utilitarianism from Hume to Mill*. London: Routledge, 2003.

Rosen, Frederick. *Jeremy Bentham and Representative Democracy: A Study of the Constitutional Code*. Oxford: Clarendon Press, 1983.

Schofield, Philip. "Jeremy Bentham's 'Nonsense upon Stilts.'" *Utilitas* 15 (1) (2003): 1–26.

Schofield, Philip. "Jeremy Bentham, the French Revolution and Political Radicalism." *History of European Ideas* 30 (2004): 381–401.

Schofield, Philip. "Jeremy Bentham, the Principle of Utility, and Legal Positivism." In *Current Legal Problems 2003*. Vol. 56, edited by M. D. A. Freeman. Oxford: Oxford University Press, 2004.

Semple, Janet. *Bentham's Prison: A Study of the Panopticon Penitentiary*. Oxford: Clarendon Press, 1993.

Twining, William. "Imagining Bentham: A Celebration." In *Current Legal Problems 1998*. Vol. 51: *Legal theory at the End of the Millennium*, edited by M. D. A. Freeman. Oxford: Oxford University Press, 1998.

Twining, William. *Theories of Evidence: Bentham and Wigmore*. London: Weidenfeld & Nicolson, 1985.

Warke, Tom. "Multi-Dimensional Utility and the Index Number Problem: Jeremy Bentham, J. S. Mill, and Qualitative Hedonism." *Utilitas* 12 (2) (2000): 176–203.

Philip Schofield (2005)

BERDYAEV, NIKOLAI ALEKSANDROVICH
(1874–1948)

Nikolai Aleksandrovich Berdyaev, a Russian religious philosopher, was born in Kiev in a family of the old nobility. He attended the Kiev military school. In 1894 he enrolled in St. Vladimir's University of Kiev as a natural sciences student, but after a year transferred to the department of law. Infatuation with Marxism and participation in the social-democratic movement led to his arrest, exclusion from the university (in 1898), and a three-year exile to Vologda. This represented a break with the aristocratic environment to which he had been accustomed, a break that he later called a fundamental fact of his biography, not only of his external biography but also of his inner one.

Berdyaev's Marxist period did not last long; in a short period of time he underwent an evolution that was characteristic for many Russian thinkers of the beginning of the twentieth century—from Marxism to idealism to the search for God. Berdyaev was one of the initiators of three collections of essays that became famous and provoked much heated argument: *Problemy idealizma* (Problems of idealism; 1902), *Vekhi* (Landmarks; 1909), and *Iz glubiny* (De Profundis, Out of the depths; 1918). Berdyaev greeted the fall of the monarchy in February 1917 with great enthusiasm, but he assessed the October Revolution differently—as the triumph of the destructive principle in the Russian revolution. He participated in the work of the Vladimir Sergeevich Solov'ëv (Solovyov) Religious-Philosophical Society and was the founder of the Free Academy of Spiritual Culture (1918–1922), which became a non-Marxist spiritual center and continued the traditions of the Russian Silver Age after the Bolshevik coup. In 1919 Berdyaev was elected as a professor of Moscow University. Despite the fact that Berdyaev was remote from actual political struggle, in 1922 he and other outstanding figures of Russian culture were forcibly deported from Soviet Russia to Germany.

In 1922 Berdyaev founded the Religious-Philosophical Academy in Berlin, and in 1923 he became the dean of the Russian Scholarly Institute, established in Berlin to educate the Russian émigré youth. Also in 1923 he became a member of the council of the Russian Student Christian Movement, in which he participated until 1936. In 1924 he moved to France, where he edited the religious-philosophical journal *Put'* (The way; 1925–1940). The Religious-Philosophical Academy that he had founded also moved to Paris, and there he read lecture courses on "The Problems of Christianity," "The Fate of Culture," "Man, the World, and God," and so on. Berdyaev was one of the few Russian émigré thinkers who did not confine himself in the émigré milieu. During his lifetime he wrote a great many books that were published not only in Russian but also in other languages. His religious existentialism found a response among a number of West European thinkers; his philosophical ideas were esteemed highly by such figures as Jacques Maritain, Gabriel Marcel, Ernst Bloch, and Karl Barth. Berdyaev had a particular influence on the philosophical circles gathered around the journal *Esprit*, which was founded by Emmanuel Mounier in 1932 and inaugurated French personalism. In 1947 Cambridge University awarded Berdyaev the title "Honoris causa." Berdyaev died in 1948 in a suburb of Paris.

METAPHYSICS OF FREEDOM

Berdyaev's religious-philosophical doctrine was greatly influenced by the ideas of Solov'ëv, Immanuel Kant, Fëdor Mikhailovich Dostoevsky, and the seventeen-century German mystic Jakob Boehme. According to Berdyaev the distinguishing characteristic of philosophy consists in the fact that it is not reducible to a system of concepts, but that it rather represents a knowledge that speaks in the language of symbols and myths. In his own philosophy the central role belonged to freedom and creativity. Berdyaev (like Boehme) bestowed an ontological status on freedom; he believed that freedom has primacy in relation to natural and human being and that it is independent of God's being. Berdyaev often used Boehme's term *Ungrund* (groundlessness or bottomlessness) to describe such pre-ontic freedom. God expresses only the light or radiant side of this freedom, and the world created by him could also be radiant and good. But God cannot compel the world to be good, and one's free choice is not always in favor of the good (such was Berdyaev's interpretation of the biblical myth of the fall of man). That is how evil arises in the world. One has difficulty understanding why God did not create a world without sin, sicknesses, children's tears, and suffering. The answer is simple: Such a world would not have freedom, which lies at the foundation of the universe and which God does wish to limit and cannot limit.

Berdyaev traced the paradoxical and tragic dialectic of the good and freedom: on the one hand, it is obvious that one cannot be compelled to be good, but on the other hand, the freedom of the good also presupposes the freedom of evil in the world. Like Dostoevsky, Berdyaev rebelled against compulsory harmony imposed on human beings from outside. Without the freedom of sin, evil, trial, and suffering, one cannot understand harmony or the kingdom of God. Because of this tragic dialectic the world has to undergo the "trial by freedom" so that its choice in favor of the good will be free; and the fate of the world coincides, in the final analysis, with the fate of freedom in the world. The thesis that freedom has an uncreated and pre-ontic character is foundational for Berdyaev's philosophy, for if one supposes that freedom was created character, then God himself would turn out to be responsible for the evil of the world. However, for Berdyaev, God is revealed to humans, and humans, through their freely followed destiny, are revealed to God; and Revelation is thus a mutual process.

Berdyaev's Christianity was tragic and not fully orthodox. He had an acute sense of the presence of evil in the world and the substantiality of evil. This led him to pose the problem of theodicy, to attempt to understand the causes why evil is permitted in the world. If the first stage of Berdyaev's spiritual evolution was Marxist and the second idealistic in character, the third stage begins precisely with posing the problem of theodicy. It can be described as Berdyaev's Christian period.

PERSONALISM

In Berdyaev's worldview freedom and spirit are opposed to unfreedom and necessity, to the material "world of objects." For him these are two kinds of realities, interacting with each other. The world in which one lives is fallen precisely because it is dominated not by freedom but by necessity. In the reality that surrounds one, all things are regulated by law and unfree. (Here, Berdyaev's position converges with that of the other existentialists.) Reason and rational knowledge cannot help one free oneself from the necessity externally imposed on one, since reason and rational knowledge signify only adaptation to the world of objects.

Free people find themselves in a world dominated by necessity. And naturally they strive to escape from the power of the lower reality, where all things are regulated by law and are predictable. But they can escape only through creative activity, which is always a free expression of their selves. In a creative act people once again feel themselves to be a godlike being, not constrained by the laws of the material world. People are called to creative activity, to the continuation of the creation of the world, for the world is fundamentally unfinished. The primacy of freedom over being also determines the meaning of human life: the goal of people is not salvation, but creative activity; the creative act has intrinsic value.

Berdyaev proclaimed that the purpose of creative activity is not to accumulate cultural values, but to bring to an end the fallen world of necessity. For Berdyaev the social reality is only an objectification (symbolization or materialization) of the subjective personal spirit. He reinterprets Kant in his own manner, concurring with Kant's recognition of another reality that is more profound and hidden behind the objectified world.

For Berdyaev, social problems (e.g., hunger, poverty, and inequality) are secondary in comparison with spiritual problems. The elimination of hunger and poverty will not liberate people from the mystery of death, love, and creative activity. Furthermore, the conflicts between the individual and society, humans and the cosmos, history and eternity are only made more acute in the case of a more rationally ordered society. People are called to creative activity, but all creative activity is inevitably a failure, since the results of such activity are objectified and participate in the enslavement of man. "The ardent creative spirit" cannot recognize itself in works of art, books, or theories—in its products. The results of creative activity are alienated from the creator. According to Berdyaev creative activity is "ascent out of the world," but a total break with the world is impossible; and this constitutes the tragic character of human existence.

HISTORIOSOPHY

According to Berdyaev every person lives not in one time, but in at least three times: Since people are simultaneously natural, social, and spiritual beings, there also exist three times for them: cosmic, historical, and existential. Berdyaev uses geometrical figures to describe these three times: the circle, the line, and the point. Cosmic time follows the natural and regular logic of circular motion; this time operates not with days and years but with epochs and millennia. By contrast, historical time follows a straight line and operates with smaller temporal categories. However, the most significant events occur in existential time; it is precisely in the latter that creative acts and free choice take place. For existential time the duration of an event is relative: sometimes for a person a day is longer and more significant than a decade, whereas sometimes a year slips

by imperceptibly. A person's earthly time itself is only a phase, a period within eternity; it is rooted in eternity. The eternal is made incarnate in time; it invades time (just as heavenly history invades earthly history), and history becomes the history of the battle of the eternal against the temporal. But the forces are not equal. The eternal will triumph over all that is corruptible and fleeting: The objectified world will perish. All creative activity represents an escape from the chain of cause and effect, which is why every creative act shakes the foundations of cosmic necessity. Berdyaev's vantage point is an eschatological one; he believes that the meaning of history is in its end, in the triumph of the free spirit over objectification. Earthly history is the path to the other world; this history is too narrow and limited for the incarnation of the ideal; the problem of history can be solved only beyond the limits of earthly history, in eternity.

In trying to understand the tragic experience of the Russian revolution and the tendencies of European development, Berdyaev proclaimed that the areligious, humanistic epoch had reached its completion and that humankind had entered the sacral epoch of new Middle Ages, characterized by a religious renaissance and religious conflicts. Berdyaev claimed that, in the twentieth century, all significant ideas inevitably acquired a religious meaning. This goes also for communist ideology: using Soviet Russia as an example, he showed that this country had entered the epoch of new Middle Ages, for he considered Russian Marxism to be a type of religious faith with its savior (the proletariat), prophets (Marx, Friedrich Engels, and Vladimir Il'ich Lenin), "doctrine of man's fall" (the history of the emergence of private property), paradise (communism), and so on. Russia was at the leading edge of the historical process, as it were; and after the revolution the Russian idea had acquired a universal significance.

Berdyaev identified six fundamental stages of world history. The first stage was that of antiquity, when people were submerged in the depths of natural necessity. Berdyaev associated the second stage with the fate of the Jewish nation, with its messianic consciousness, thanks to which the static ancient was replaced by the historical approach to reality. The third stage was that of the overcoming of the two preceding stages by Christianity, which introduced the idea of eschatology into the human consciousness. The fourth stage was the epoch of the Renaissance, when humanism was born and people's falling away from God began. The reaction to this was the Reformation, the fifth stage, when, in counterweight to the Renaissance spirit, people's independence was denied and their total dependence on divine providence was proclaimed. The sixth stage, according to Berdyaev's conception, was associated with socialism, with the attempt to realize the kingdom of God on earth.

By the will of the fates, Russia, without having experienced some of these historical stages, became humanity's testing ground for the realization of the totalitarian-socialistic ideal. But, in Berdyaev's opinion, Russian socialism also became the sign of the transition to the seventh stage, to the new Middle Ages, a period of religious-social synthesis. Berdyaev proposed his own version of socialism, which resembled its Marxist counterpart in only one thing: a fundamental antibourgeois attitude. For Berdyaev, socialism has a dual nature: it can create either a new free society or a new slavery. Berdyaev himself was a proponent of personalistic Christian socialism.

See also Barth, Karl; Bloch, Ernst; Boehme, Jakob; Communism; Dostoevsky, Fyodor Mikhailovich; Engels, Friedrich; Evil; Existentialism; Humanism; Idealism; Kant, Immanuel; Lenin, Vladimir Il'ich; Marcel, Gabriel; Maritain, Jacques; Marxist Philosophy; Marx, Karl; Personalism; Reformation; Renaissance; Russian Philosophy; Socialism; Solov'ëv (Solovyov), Vladimir Sergeevich.

Bibliography

WORKS BY BERDYAEV

The Meaning of History. Translated by George Reavey. London: G. Bles, 1936.

The Origin of Russian Communism. Translated by R. M. French. London: G. Bles, 1937.

The Russian Idea. Translated by R. M. French. London: G. Bles, 1947.

The Meaning of the Creative Act. Translated by Donald A. Lowrie. London: V. Gollancz, 1955.

WORKS ABOUT BERDYAEV

Lowrie, Donald Alexander. *Rebellious Prophet: A Life of Nicolai Berdyaev.* New York: Harper, 1960.

Vallon, Michel Alexander. *An Apostle of Freedom: Life and Teachings of Nicolas Berdyaev.* New York: Philosophical Library, 1960.

Olga Volkogonova (2005)
Translated by Boris Jakim

BERGERAC, CYRANO DE

See *Cyrano de Bergerac, Savinien de*

BERGMANN, GUSTAV
(1906–1987)

Gustav Bergmann came to the United States in 1938 from Vienna, Austria, where he had earned a JD and a PhD in mathematics. He had also been a junior member of the Vienna Circle.

In 1939 he became a faculty member at the University of Iowa, retiring in 1976. He held a joint appointment in the Departments of Philosophy and Psychology. He regularly taught a course on the history and philosophy of psychology. Bergmann became well known as an apologist for behaviorism. Significantly, he distinguished between methodological and metaphysical behaviorism, embracing the former and rejecting the latter. Bergmann never wavered in his ontological commitment to the mental.

Bergmann also published in mathematics, the philosophy of physics, the history of philosophy, and the philosophy of law. His *Philosophy of Science* (1957) is an elegant and still useful work. He was, however, first and foremost a philosopher, an ontologist to be exact. The central question is what exists. His method for answering that question, the ideal-language method, was to design a formalism into which one could transcribe all empirical statements of the natural language and which formalism could be used to account for the difference between the necessary and the contingent statements of the natural language. The ontology of the world would be revealed by the difference in the kinds of basic, undefined sign of the formalism.

The necessary-contingent distinction was relatively easy to handle. What is necessary and contingent is a given. One needs merely to transcribe the necessary statements into sentences of the formalism, the truth values of which sentences are a matter of form, and the contingent ones to sentences the truth values of which are not a matter of form. The idea is a classical one; the only difference being that the classical philosophers spoke of thoughts as truth bearers whereas the ideal-language philosophers spoke of sentences of the formal language as truth bearers. Relatedly, for the classical philosophers the truth makers were either features of the thought or of something beyond, the thought, whereas for the formalist the truth bearers were either features of sentences or something beyond the sentence.

Determining what kinds of signs are basic was difficult to handle. Bergmann began as a positivist: The only existents were the entities stood for by the subjects and predicates of atomic sentences, entities with which one had to be acquainted. He was, then, a phenomenalist. In time, he acknowledged that the operators were not eliminable; they had to stand for entities that had ontological status. A distinction was thus made between existents and subsistents. Logical entities subsist; empirical, sensuous ones exist. The latter presented their own problems. Each entity was of a kind, particular or universal. Thus, a simple entity was a complex of sorts, a form and a content. Unlike the early Ludwig Josef Johann Wittgenstein, Bergmann insisted on according the forms ontological status. Forms subsist. That put pressure on the use of the Principle of Acquaintance, sufficient pressure to force Bergmann to replace it with a Principle of Presentation, a principle that cast a wide net indeed.

In his last phase Bergmann became sensitive to the criticism that he was a mere formalist and that all his ontological claims were transcendental ones, his talk of acquaintance and presentation being mere talk. His last work, *New Foundations of Ontology* (1992), published posthumously, is rich in talk about "phenomenological bedrock." Bergmann's fate was a curious one. His commitment to particulars, universals, forms, and whatever else was dictated by the needs of the formalism and by his conception of the difference between eliminable and ineliminable terms rather than by the need to solve such problems as that of individuation and universals. The issue of whether the basic entities are "experienced" was an afterthought, a most nettlesome one.

Bergmann's devotion to the method was never shaken; and in the context of the method he made two brilliant moves. First, in the mid-1950s he found a way to render in the formalism an analysis of mental acts. As act was a particular with two properties, one for the kind of act it was (a remembering, a doubting, or whatever) the other for the content of the act (that the moon is blue, that the ball is red, or whatever). (One would benefit from comparing Bergmann's analysis with René Descartes's third-meditation discussion of the use of the term *idea*.) Regarding the content-carrying property, Bergmann ran into a problem. He wanted it to be simple but had to have it complex, the reason being that the property had to serve as a truth bearer and for that need to be satisfied the property had to have within it a mark that would indicate the truth maker for it. The alternative would be to introduce an objectionable state of affairs that would show that the content property was related to a possibility that itself would contain a mark of its truth maker. The move, brilliant though it was, failed; but its failure provides one with something deeply instructive about the "make true" talk.

Second, ontology is about the kinds of entity that exist. Most formalisms need to give significance to the order of the signs in a relational sentence. There is an important difference between, say, Othello loving Desdemona and Desdemona loving Othello. The order of the terms flanking the relation sign contributes to the meaning of the sentences. Bergmann's last work was in part an attempt, as he liked to express it, to delinearize the language. He introduced dyads, a dyad being a pair of entities combined by a nexus that is other than exemplification, the tie that tied, say, two particulars and a relation into a fact. Accordingly, "aRb" was replaced by "aR{ab}," and "bRa" by "bR{ab}." Order makes no difference. The two relational facts are different in virtue of different entities. The disposing of order comes with a heavy price: nonsimple entities that are not facts require a tie, cannot exist independently of facts, and are treated by the syntax as if they were simple terms. Again, a brilliant move fails; and for a reason rather like the reason for the first failure. A nonfact complex is needed where one wants desperately to have a simple one.

Notwithstanding the failures, Bergmann's philosophical work is deep and probing and unfailingly illuminating. It has much to teach about not only the use of formalisms in doing ontology but also about the classical tradition.

See also Behaviorism; Descartes, René; Logical Positivism; Ontology, History of; Wittgenstein, Ludwig Josef Johann.

Bibliography

WORKS BY BERGMANN

The Metaphysics of Logical Positivism. New York: Longmans, Green, 1954.

The Philosophy of Science. Madison: University of Wisconsin Press, 1957.

Meaning and Existence. Madison: University of Wisconsin Press, 1959.

Logic and Reality. Madison: University of Wisconsin Press, 1964.

Realism: A Critique of Brentano and Meinong. Madison: University of Wisconsin Press, 1967.

New Foundations on Ontology, edited by William Heald. Madison: University of Wisconsin Press, 1992.

Collected Works, edited by Erwin Tegtmeier. Ontos Verlag, 2003–2004.

WORKS ABOUT BERGMANN

Gram, M. S., and E. D. Klemke, eds. *The Ontological Turn: Studies in the Philosophy of Gustav Bergmann*. Iowa City: University of Iowa Press, 1974.

Hochberg, Herbert. *The Positivist and the Ontologist: Bergmann, Carnap, and Logical Realism*. Amsterdam, Netherlands: Rodopi, 2001.

Edwin Allaire (2005)

BERGSON, HENRI

(1859–1941)

Henri Bergson, the French philosopher of evolution, was born in Paris of Anglo-Polish parentage. During a lifetime of teaching, lecturing, and writing, he gained an international reputation as the author of a new and distinctive philosophical outlook presented in a succession of books whose fluent, nontechnical style gave them a wide appeal. In 1900 Bergson became professor of philosophy at the Collège de France, a post he held until 1921, when ill health obliged him to retire. He received many honors, including election to the French Academy and in 1927 the Nobel Prize for literature. After World War I, Bergson devoted much attention to international affairs, in the hope of promoting peace and cooperation among nations. But World War II had begun and France had been occupied by the armies of Nazi Germany at the time of his death.

Despite the novelty of his outlook, Bergson owed much to his predecessors in the European, and especially in the French, philosophical tradition, primarily to thinkers whose ideas supported his opposition to materialism and mechanism; he was convinced that neither of these doctrines is philosophically tenable. Thus, he was influenced by the idea of Maine de Biran that we sense the "flow" of life as a primary inner experience; by the contentions of Felix Ravaisson that philosophic thought should be focused on the directly intuited, concrete individual, and that mechanism is the external form of an inner spiritual activity; by the contention of Alfred Fouillée that there is an intrinsic freedom in human action; and by the teaching of Émile Boutroux that there exists a radical contingency in nature. His obligation to ancient thought was chiefly to Plotinus, whose mysticism became increasingly congenial to Bergson in the later years of his life. The theory of biological evolution, in both Charles Darwin's scientific formulation and Herbert Spencer's speculative formulation deeply influenced him. He was once "very much attached to the philosophy of Spencer" (*The Creative Mind*, p. 93), but broke away because of its unsatisfactory treatment of evolution and of time.

TWO KINDS OF TIME

Of central importance in Bergson's outlook is his distinction between the time that occurs in the theories of natural science and the time that we directly experience. Scientific time is a mathematical conception, symbolized in physical theory by the letter t and measured by clocks and chronometers. Because these measuring instruments are spatial bodies, scientific time is represented as an extended, homogeneous medium, composed of standard units (years, hours, seconds). Most of man's practical life in society is dominated by these units. But time thus represented neither "flows" nor "acts." It exists passively, like a line drawn on a surface. When we turn to our direct experience, Bergson urged, we find nothing that corresponds to this mathematical conception. What we find, on the contrary, is a flowing, irreversible succession of states that melt into each other to form an indivisible process. This process is not homogeneous but heterogeneous. It is not abstract but concrete. In short, it is "pure time" or "real duration" (*durée reelle*), something immediately experienced as active and ongoing. If we try to represent it by a spatial image, such as a line, we only generate abstract, mathematical time, which is at bottom an illusion. The great weakness of mechanistic modes of thought is that they consider this illusion to be a reality.

DETERMINISM AND FREEDOM

In *Time and Free Will* Bergson undertook to show that the recognition of real duration provides a basis for vindicating human freedom and disposing of determinism. The determinist, according to Bergson, holds that freedom of choice does not exist. He supports his view by picturing the situation in which one confronts an ostensible choice as being like arriving at a point on a line where a branching occurs, and taking one of the branches. The determinist then contends that the particular branch taken could not *not* have been taken. He further holds that, given full knowledge of the antecedent states of mind of the agent, the branch taken could have been predicted beforehand.

The force of this argument, according to Bergson, derives from misrepresenting the situation of choice by using an abstract, spatialized conception of time. At best the determinist's image of the line symbolizes the choice already made, not the choice in the making. In acting we do not move along a path through time. Deliberating about a choice is not like being at a point on a line and oscillating in space between various courses confronting us. Deliberation and choice are temporal, not spatial, acts. Moreover, the determinist makes the associationist's mistake of supposing that the mind of the agent consists of a succession of atomic states that determine how he will act. The associationist's mechanistic interpretation of the mind produced a fallacious picture upon which determinism was superimposed.

Freedom of action, according to Bergson, is something directly experienced. Man feels himself to be free as he acts, even though he may be unable to explain the nature of his freedom. Nevertheless, we are free only when our act springs spontaneously from our *whole* personality as it has evolved up to the moment of action. If this spontaneity is absent, our actions will be simply stereotyped or mechanical responses. In such cases we behave like automata. Hence, freedom is far from being absolute. Indeed, for most people free acts are the exception, not the rule. To this extent the determinists are right.

BODY AND MIND

Direct experience not only establishes the reality of time and of freedom; it also testifies that each of us is a body, subject to the same laws as all other bits of matter. Bergson's dualism emerges clearly in *Matter and Memory*. Bodies are there interpreted as "images"; that is, objects perceived in space. Among these images is one that I know from the outside by perception and from the inside by sensation or affection. This is my own body, which I also know to be a center of action.

What is the relation between the body and the mind? Materialism holds that mind, or consciousness, is either identical with brain activity or existentially dependent on brain activity. Bergson rejected both positions because, he claimed, there is vastly more in a given occasion of consciousness than in the corresponding brain state. The attempt to substantiate this claim led him to reject the doctrine that a parallelism exists between the series of conscious states and the series of brain states. The considerations to which he appealed came mainly from an examination of memory.

TWO KINDS OF MEMORY

Living organisms, unlike nonliving objects, retain their past in the present. This phenomenon is manifested, according to Bergson, in two kinds of memory. One kind consists of sensory-motor mechanisms or "habits" fixed in the body of the organism and designed to ensure adaptation to a present situation. When an appropriate stimulus arises, one of these mechanisms "unwinds" as a response. The other kind of memory, which humans alone possess, records in the form of memory images all the events of daily life as they occur in time. These images

provide the content of occasions of recalling. This is "pure" memory, which is wholly spiritual. "Consciousness signifies, before everything, memory."

To defend his view of pure memory, Bergson argued against any correlation of memory images with hypothetical memory traces stored in the brain. Physiologically, the brain consists of a vast number of neurons, synapsing with each other and with afferent and efferent nerves. It resembles a telephone exchange, not a storage device. There is no evidence that memories are located spatially within it. Moreover, if a visual recollection of an object were dependent on a brain trace, there would have to be thousands of traces, corresponding to all the variations due to different points of view from which the object has been perceived. But what we actually have in each case is one practically invariable memory image of an object, not a large class of different images. This, Bergson thought, constitutes proof that something quite distinct from mechanical registration is involved. Finally, there are facts associated with loss of word memory and its restoration which point to the conclusion that the recollective process is independent of brain traces. It follows that materialism and psychoneural parallelism are untenable doctrines.

How, then, is pure memory related to the brain? Bergson's answer is derived from his contention that pure memory retains the whole of our past. If this is the case, something must prevent all our memories from being simultaneously present to consciousness, since we do in fact recall only one or two things at a time. The brain must therefore act as a filter for our memories, allowing only those that are practically useful to emerge on a given occasion. In other words, the brain is a mechanism invented by nature to canalize and direct our attention toward what is about to happen, in order to assist our actions. It is designed not so much to promote remembering as to promote forgetting. By bringing pure memory into contact with practical actions, it also establishes a link with habit memory, since most of our everyday actions tend to be habitual and routine. In this way the two kinds of memory are united.

Although he would not countenance the idea that memory traces are stored in the brain, Bergson allowed for the storage of images in pure memory. He asserted that pure memory retains all our conscious states "in the order in which they occur." This view led him to accept the conclusion that part of the mind is unconscious or subconscious. It is erroneous to suppose that the existence of psychical states depends on their apprehension by consciousness. To suppose this is to vitiate the concept of mind by casting an artificial obscurity over the idea of the unconscious. The significance of pure memory can be understood only by supposing that past psychological states have a real, though unconscious, existence.

It is now possible to explain the relation between the body and the mind. Here, as elsewhere, there has been a strong temptation to think in spatial terms, envisaging two separate substances that have to be connected. But the relation between body and mind must be understood in temporal, not spatial, terms. The point becomes clear when we unite the insight derived from our consciousness of real duration with the recognition that the body is a center of action, for on an occasion of action, body and mind are related by a convergence in time. No spatial representation of this convergence can be adequate. It can be grasped only by noting what takes place whenever we act. A familiar example is our perception of the external world.

PERCEPTION AND THE EXTERNAL WORLD

The discussion of this question forms an integral part of *Matter and Memory*. In considering perception, traditional realism and idealism have, according to Bergson, made two unjustified assumptions. First, they have assumed that perception is a kind of photographic process that yields a picture of what is perceived. The mind is envisaged as a *camera obscura* inside which images are generated. Second, they have regarded perception as a cognitive function whose aim is to provide pure knowledge. Bergson contended that perception cannot possibly be a photographic process, for images are not inside the mind but are part of the spatially extended world. Moreover, perception does not generate images, but selects those images that have a possible bearing on actions. Nothing remotely akin to pure knowledge is involved at the perceptual level. Once these assumptions are discarded, the dispute between realism and idealism can be resolved.

In supporting this idea Bergson used biological considerations. Biologists are agreed that there has been an evolution of the structure and the functions of the central nervous system in living organisms. This evolution has proceeded from relatively simple types of organization toward greater and greater complexity, through a series of minute, adaptively significant changes. In simple organisms the rudiments of perception are to be found in mechanical responses to external stimulation. Direct contact with bodies, such as we experience in tactile perception, belongs to this stage. The role of the rudimentary

nervous system is to facilitate action. What occurs is a reflex activity, not a "representation" of things. The sole difference between this stage and much later ones is that voluntary action became possible as a result of the evolution of the higher brain centers. But the difference is not one of kind, but only one of complication. Accordingly, since the nervous system is constructed from one end of the evolutionary scale to the other as a utilitarian device, we must conclude that perception, whose evolution is regulated by the evolution of the nervous system, is also directed toward action, not toward knowledge.

If that is so, why is human perception a conscious process, and why does everything happen as if consciousness were a product of brain activity? The reason is that human perception is normally "impregnated with memory images." It is possible to form a metaphysical concept of "pure perception" free from any admixture of memory. It is even possible, Bergson thought, to have such a pure perception, which he spoke of as an "intuition." But most of the time our perceptions are interlaced with memories; conversely, a memory becomes actual by being embodied in some perception. The convergence that takes place accounts for the fact that perceptual images (objects perceived) have a "subjectivity." We become conscious of them. This phenomenon has a biological significance, for in humans, and in higher organisms generally, perception is predominantly directed toward distant objects spread over a wide field. These objects have a great many potential effects on action. One way an organism has of adapting to this situation is to anticipate the effects by "reflecting" possible lines of action from its body to the distant objects. This gives the organism a biological advantage by putting it in a position where it can select a course of action that will serve its needs. Thus the world is consciously perceived by us; but it is not a different world from the one that antedated our perception. It is the same world related to our needs and intentions.

Body and mind, then, are united in the selective act of perception. The body contributes perceptive centers that respond to the influences of environing bodies. The mind contributes appropriate memory images that give to what is perceived a completed, meaningful form. There is no "constructing" of the external world out of subjective impressions; no "inferring" of the existence of that world from ideas in the mind; no positing of things in themselves that are beyond the limits of possible experience. By interpreting physical things as images, Bergson was able to regard the material world as directly perceivable. Traditional idealism was therefore repudiated. Yet a partial concession to idealism was made by calling things "images." This term implies a rejection of the realist's view that things consist only of material particles, or of primary qualities, or of some hidden substance. Things have all the qualities they are perceived to have. A partial concession to realism was made by admitting that the totality of perceived things, past, present and future, must always be a small fragment of material reality. The upshot is a doctrine, intermediate between idealism and realism, that combines, Bergson contends, what is sound in each and discards what is unsound.

Body and mind are above all united in real duration, for perception is an event in the concrete present, and the present is no geometrical point or "knife edge" separating past from future. It is a continuous flowing, an "invisible progress of the past gnawing into the future." Perceptual acts are intrinsically temporal and dynamic. Yet the world we come to know by means of them is not a flux. It has a relative stability. Our concepts often refer to things that remain much the same for long periods. These things may have fixed position, sharp outlines, and clearly marked qualities. In view of what has been said about perception, how are such facts accounted for? The reply involves Bergson's conception of the intellect and its functioning.

THE INTELLECT AND THINGS

The evolution of the human species gave rise to the capacity for conceptual or rational thought. This capacity is traditionally referred to as the intellect. Its origin, Bergson contended, was conditioned by several circumstances. First, man is one of the social animals, and effective action in human societies requires some use of rational thought. Second, man is a tool-using and tool-making animal. These activities could not advance far without fostering conceptualization. Third, man is an animal who invents and uses language. This powerful instrument of communication stimulated the development of intellect, and was in turn profoundly influenced by it. Here again the aim was to promote community of action. Thus, both in origin and in function, the intellect is a practical capacity. It is no more speculative than is perception.

By using his intellect, civilized man has produced a vast body of knowledge about the world. Is not much of this knowledge speculative, in the sense of being a cognitive reflection of the world as it really is? Bergson held that this is not so. Since the intellect is practical, its products must be instrumental to action, not mirrorlike reflections. Concepts, even when they belong to advanced theories in the sciences, are still pragmatic devices. For scientific knowledge is directed toward prediction and control of events, being in this respect an extension of commonsense knowledge. The technological triumphs of modern man provide the clue to the proper understanding of his intellectual powers.

Because of its practical orientation, the intellect functions in a characteristic way. It treats whatever it deals with in spatial terms, as if the latter were a three-dimensional body. Ordinary language is pervaded by spatial metaphors; and scientific theories, especially those of physics, make great use of geometrical models. The operations of our intellect, especially in science, "tend to geometry, as to the goal where they find their perfect fulfilment" (*Creative Mind*, Introduction II). Again, the intellect has an inherent tendency to break up whatever it deals with into homogeneous units. A whole can be understood only by analyzing it in terms of uniform parts. This tendency is reflected in the predominance of measuring operations and instruments, such as clocks, scales, and yardsticks, in civilized societies. Furthermore, the intellect is at home only when dealing with what is static, fixed, immobile.

Hence, in seeking to understand the phenomenon of motion, the intellect has recourse to immobile units, such as points of space or instants of time, out of which motion is reconstructed. Bergson spoke of "the cinematographical method" of the intellect, likening it to a movie camera that translates motion into a series of static "frames." An important consequence of this is that the intellect is committed to the use of formal logic and mathematics, both of which supply unchanging structures for thought. Finally, when something comes into existence or ceases to exist, the intellect interprets what happens as a rearranging of constituent elements. This means that the arising of something absolutely new, the creation of novelty, cannot be admitted by rational thought. Even growth and evolution must be understood as new arrangements of old parts.

It is now possible to explain why the world external to us consists of relatively stable, discrete things. The intellect, functioning in its characteristic way, is responsible. It "breaks up," "cuts up," or "carves up" matter into distinct and separate objects so as to promote the interests of action. Presumably, the operation requires the collaboration of perception, although Bergson did not make the point clear. He also failed to make clear whether the intellect is perfectly free in carving out individual things, or whether it has to follow certain lines of cleavage in the intrinsic structure of matter. Sometimes he talked as if the external world of things had been "fabricated" by the intellect's imposing form on a featureless, material flux. At other times, he implied that the intellect "carves nature at the joints," following "the lines which mark out the boundaries of real bodies or of their real elements." In one place he even stated that "matter is primarily what brings division and precision" into things; but this can hardly be construed as an acceptance of the doctrine that matter is the principle of individuation. Despite these obscurities, Bergson's position entails that the intellect is necessary, if not sufficient, for the "individuating" of things in space.

This requirement is relevant, of course, only to things of which we have conceptual knowledge. What is its bearing on the knowledge each of us has of his own body? Here a further obscurity arises. Bergson declared that we know our body in two ways, externally by perception and internally by affection. But since at the level of affection the intellect is not involved, it would appear to follow that the object known cannot be a separate, individual thing. Nevertheless, Bergson did speak of the central image, "distinct from all others," that each of us identifies as his body. What determines its distinct individuality? In *Matter and Memory* he remarked that "our needs … carve out, within this continuity [of the perceptible world], a body which is to be their own." This is a puzzling remark, because often the body is what has the needs, and hence it can scarcely be "carved out" by them. It may be that the living human body, unlike inanimate bodies, has an individuality that does not depend on the functioning of the intellect. Or it may be that the obscurity here originates in Bergson's doctrine about what the intellect knows and what can be known only by intuition.

INTUITION AND INTELLECT

Alongside the capacity for conceptual thought, there exists in humans a capacity that Bergson called "intuition." Both capacities are the result of evolution, but the second is derived from instinct, the type of biological activity most elaborately manifested in the social insects. Instinctive activity has consciousness "slumbering" within it, and evolution has awakened the consciousness in humankind. Intuition for Bergson is "instinct that has become disinterested, self-conscious, capable of reflecting upon its object and of enlarging it indefinitely." Since it is disinterested, the capacity is detached from the demands of action and of social life. It is like a painter's power of seeing the world just as it is presented to him in pure perception. But instead of yielding an aesthetic experience, intuition yields knowledge. Hence, it is of profound importance for the philosopher.

In his *Introduction to Metaphysics*, Bergson emphasized the immediate, nonconceptual character of intuition, envisaging it as a direct participation in, or identification with, what is intuited. In the case of the external world, intuition is an act "by which one is transported into the interior of an object in order to coincide with what there is unique and consequently inexpressible about it." In the case of the self, intuition is an immersion in the indivisible flow of consciousness, a grasping of pure becoming and real duration. The result is "knowledge which is contact and even coincidence." Unlike the intellect, which remains outside what it knows, requires symbols, and produces knowledge that is always relative to some viewpoint, intuition enters into what it knows, dispenses with symbols, and produces knowledge that is absolute.

Bergson subsequently modified this doctrine in certain respects. He came to emphasize the cogitative character of intuition instead of its immediacy, and even spoke of it as a mode of thinking. As such, it is not a spontaneous flash of insight but an act that is engendered by mental effort. To achieve an intuition, we must turn our attention away from its natural concern with action. This act demands concentration of thought. Even when we are successful, the results are impermanent. Yet the intellect can effect a partial communication of the results by using "concrete ideas," supplemented by images. "Comparisons and metaphors will here suggest what cannot be expressed." Consequently, the knowledge attained by intuition is not altogether ineffable. Nor is it, in the strict sense, absolute, for intuition is a progressive activity that can widen and deepen its scope indefinitely. Its limits cannot be fixed a priori. These modifications were related to changes in Bergson's conception of the roles of metaphysics and the natural sciences.

THE NATURAL SCIENCES AND METAPHYSICS

The natural sciences are for Bergson a typical achievement of the intellect, and they therefore reflect a limitation in the intellect's functioning. This limitation emerges when the sciences form their conceptions of time and motion. In each case a static abstraction is produced. Time is conceived as what clocks measure in spatially discrete units. Motion is conceived as a succession of fixed positions on a linear path. Both abstractions are practically useful, but they falsify the nature of time and motion as concretely experienced by ignoring the crucial element of becoming. This falsification is inherent in the intellect's way of working. By its very nature, the intellect is equipped to handle only what is repetitive and routine; real becoming baffles it. Hence the sciences have a severe disability built into them. Moreover, as the ancient philosopher Zeno of Elea first pointed out, conceptual thought runs into contradictions or "paradoxes" whenever it tries to give a thorough analysis of motion. These paradoxes, although designed by Zeno for a different purpose, show, according to Bergson, that the scientific concept of motion is basically incoherent. The conclusion must be that the sciences can never provide a complete and adequate account of the universe. They need to be supplemented by some other discipline.

An obvious choice would seem to be metaphysics, but classical metaphysics is equally a creation of the intellect and suffers from the same disability as the sciences. Metaphysicians, with a few exceptions like Heraclitus, have misconstrued change and failed to give it the priority it actually has in the world. They have regarded being as ultimate, and becoming as derivative. Accordingly, metaphysical theories have been based on such concepts as the indestructible atoms of Democritus, the eternal forms of Plato, or the fixed categories of Immanuel Kant. These concepts illustrate the intellect's addiction to unchanging units that are mechanically combined or separated according to the rules of logic. Neither time nor change can be understood when so approached. The constructions of metaphysics are as inadequate here as those of science, without the latter's usefulness.

Classical metaphysics has also mistakenly supposed that an all-embracing "system" can be constructed, bringing within its scope not only what is actual but also what is possible. This idea rests on a fallacious assumption that there is a "realm of possibility" over and above the realm of actuality. The belief in possibles that would be realized by acquiring existence is an illusion of the intellect, designed to exclude the notion of absolute novelty. "Let us have done," Bergson urged, "with great metaphysical systems embracing all the possible and sometimes even the impossible!"

By following this course, we shall automatically get rid of a number of pseudo problems that classical metaphysicians have generated. They have asked, for instance, why something exists rather than nothing. This has seemed a sensible question because they could always add, "There could be nothing." Bergson replied that the sentence "There could be nothing" has no meaning. "'Nothing' is a term in ordinary language which can only have meaning in the sphere proper to man, of action and fabrication." The term designates the absence of what we are seeking in the world around us. It can be properly used only because many things already exist. To oppose "nothing" in an absolute sense to existence is to embrace a pseudo idea and engender pseudo problems.

These criticisms do not imply that metaphysics is to be rejected, for Bergson proposed to redefine metaphysics and provide it with a new method. Instead of employing the intellect, it is to employ intuition. This is the theme of the *Introduction to Metaphysics*. In elaborating it, Bergson sometimes seemed to be saying that since intuition alone provides knowledge of the real, the intellect is restricted to knowledge of appearances. It would follow from this that metaphysics is a discipline superior to the natural sciences. Indeed, from a philosophical standpoint the sciences are cognitively worthless because they can say nothing about reality. The impression was thus created that Bergson's outlook was "antiscientific." In later writings he endeavored to correct this impression by urging that metaphysics and the sciences must be coordinate and equal in value. Both are concerned with the real, the sciences with the domain of matter, metaphysics with the domain of spirit. Moreover, the knowledge that each gains is capable of indefinite expansion, and can approach completeness as an ideal limit. It was in this connection that Bergson seems to have revised his doctrine of intuition, closing the gap between it and the intellect without obliterating the distinction between the two. His objective was to formulate a philosophy that would submit to the control of science and that could in turn enable science to progress. The disciplines would then have a common frontier. In adopting the method of intuition, metaphysics is able to supplement the sciences by giving a true account of duration, of becoming, and even of evolution.

MECHANISTIC AND CREATIVE EVOLUTION

Bergson was born in the same year that *The Origin of Species* was published, and the revolutionary implications of this work permanently affected his thought. He accepted the historical reality of evolution, but rejected attempts to explain it in mechanistic or materialistic terms. Hence he criticized Darwin's explanation, and also the less influential explanations of the Chevalier de Lamarck, Theodor Eimer, and Spencer. In place of them he advanced a doctrine that owed much to the tradition of European and especially French vitalism, and at the same time drew inspiration from Plotinus. The result was a vision of the cosmos going far beyond the facts of biology, though purportedly based on them. These matters were presented in *Creative Evolution*, Bergson's most famous book.

Darwin explained the evolutionary process by supposing that in every population of organisms there occur random variations that have different degrees of adaptive value. The variations having maximum value for the survival and reproduction of the organisms are "naturally selected"; that is, they are preserved and transmitted to subsequent generations, while the other variations are eliminated.

Bergson argued that this explanation failed to account for a number of facts. A multicellular animal, or an organ like the vertebrate eye, is a functional whole made up of coordinated parts. If just one or a few of the parts happened to vary independently of the rest, the functioning of the whole would be impaired. Since evolution has occurred, we must suppose that at each stage all the parts of an animal and of its complex organs have varied contemporaneously so that effective functioning was preserved. But it is utterly implausible to suppose, as Darwin did, that such coadapted variations could have been random, for then their coadaptation would remain a mystery. Some agency other than natural selection must have been at work to maintain continuity of functioning through successive alterations of form.

Another fact that Darwinism failed to explain is why living things have evolved in the direction of greater and greater complexity. The earliest living things were simple in character and well adapted to their environments. Why did the evolutionary process not stop at this stage? Why did life continue to complicate itself "more and more dangerously"? To appeal to the mechanism of selection for an answer was, Bergson thought, insufficient. Something must have driven life on to higher and higher levels of organization, despite the risks involved.

Darwin's predecessor Lamarck avoided the idea of random variations by supposing that variations were caused by the "effort" exerted by individuals in adapting to the environment. Bergson considered this a more adequate explanation than the Darwinian. Yet it involved accepting the principle that acquired characteristics are transmitted from one generation to the next, and empirical evidence is heavily against this. Furthermore, the Lamarckian notion of a conscious "effort" is too limited to serve as an explanatory device. It could perhaps operate in the case of animals but hardly in the case of plants or microorganisms. To make the notion work, it must be broadened and deepened. Similarly, Eimer's appeal to orthogenesis; that is, to an inner principle that directs the course of evolution, has merit if interpreted nonmecha-

nistically, but not if interpreted, as Eimer did, in physicochemical terms.

The synthetic philosophy of Spencer also had merit in so far as it sought to extend the evolutionary conception to the universe at large. Yet because Spencer relied exclusively on the intellect, and because he subscribed to the false idea that philosophy can be a super science, Spencer failed to do justice to real duration and to the creation of novelty. He held that evolution is due to combinations of matter and motion. This makes his philosophy a thinly disguised version of mechanical materialism, which reconstructs evolution "with fragments of the evolved."

To obtain a true understanding of the evolutionary process, the findings of biology must be supplemented, Bergson thought, by the findings of metaphysics. The chief clue is found in what intuition reveals of our own inner nature as living beings; we are typical constituents of the universe, and the forces that work in us also work in all things. When we focus upon what intuition discloses of ourselves, we find not only continuous becoming and real duration, but also a consciousness of a vital impetus (*élan vital*), of our own evolution in time. We are thus led to the idea of "an *original impetus* of life" (*un élan original de la vie*) that pervades the whole evolutionary process and accounts for its dominant features. Accordingly, the history of life is to be understood in creative, not mechanistic, terms.

THE VITAL IMPETUS AND EVOLUTION

Bergson's doctrine of the vital impetus is speculative, although often formulated as if it were a report of an established fact. The impetus is declared to be "a current of consciousness" that has penetrated matter, given rise to living bodies, and determined the course of their evolution. The current passes from one generation to the next by way of reproduction—in bisexual organisms, by way of the reproductive cells. The vital impetus is the cause of variations that accumulate and produce new species. It coordinates the appearance of variations so as to preserve continuity of functioning in evolving structures. And it carries life toward ever higher complexity of organization. Strictly speaking, the impetus does not generate energy of its own, over and above that already present in matter. What it does is "to engraft on to the necessity of physical forces the largest possible amount of indetermination." This indetermination is evident in the contingency and creativity that have characterized the history of life. At every stage the impetus has been limited by recalcitrant matter. Hence, it is always seeking to transcend the stage it has reached and always remains inadequate to what it tries to produce.

The earliest living things were physicochemical systems into which the vital impetus "insinuated itself." Its potentialities could be realized only minimally in these systems. Consequently, it divided so that life moved forward in several quite different directions. One direction was taken by the plants, another by the insects, and a third by the vertebrates. The three directions illustrate respectively the predominance of stability, instinct, and intelligence. No predetermined plan or purpose was involved in all this. Bergson expressed as much opposition to the doctrine of radical finalism as he did to mechanism. Both doctrines deny that there has been an unforeseeable creation of forms, that these forms involve discontinuous "leaps," and that real duration is a cumulative, irreversible flow. Yet although the vital impetus is not finalistic, it does engender progress. A perfecting of functions has occurred through successive stages. An increasing realization of consciousness has also occurred.

This last contention made it difficult for Bergson to maintain an opposition to finalism, for it is in man that consciousness has been most fully realized. Here the vital impetus has found its most adequate expression as intelligence. It has likewise achieved genuine freedom by at last making matter its instrument. There was in fact "a sudden leap from the animal to man." Hence in *Creative Evolution* Bergson said that man might be considered the reason for the existence of the entire organization of life on our planet. He immediately qualified this statement by adding that it is "only a manner of speaking." We should not think that humanity was "prefigured" in the evolutionary process from the beginning.

By the time he wrote the essay that became the "Second Introduction" to *The Creative Mind*, Bergson was more forthright. He there stated categorically that the appearance of humans is the *raison d'être* of life on the earth. In *The Two Sources of Morality and Religion* he also contended that it is humankind, "or some other being of like significance, which is the purpose of the entire process of evolution." This contention seems very close to finalism. Nevertheless, Bergson continued to insist that the appearance of man was in no sense predetermined, though "it was not accidental, either." Terrestrial evolution might have produced some other being "of the same essence." Such beings have doubtless arisen elsewhere, for Bergson thought that the vital impetus animates innumerable planets in the universe. The impetus is thus not limited to the earth; creative evolution is a cosmic process.

This contention is not argued for in any detail. As so often in his writings, Bergson tried to make the contention acceptable by means of analogies. He likened the vital impetus to steam escaping at high pressure through the cracks in a container. Jets gush out unceasingly, the steam condenses into drops of water, and the drops fall back to the source. Each jet and its drops represent a world of matter animated by life. A small part of the jet remains uncondensed for an instant, and makes an effort to raise the drops that are falling. But it succeeds at most in retarding their fall. So the vital impetus achieves a moment of freedom at its highest point, in humans. It might be inferred from this analogy that matter is not something sui generis, but is rather the lowest form assumed by the outpouring of spirit. Matter and spirit, however, were repeatedly described by Bergson as coexistent and interdependent.

GOD AND THE MYSTICS

The religious aspect of Bergson's outlook became increasingly pronounced toward the close of his life. Even in *Creative Evolution* he had spoken of the vital impetus as a "supra-consciousness" to which the name "God" might be attached. But this is very different from the conception of traditional Western theology. For if God is identical with the vital impetus, then he is pure activity, limited by the material world in which he is struggling to manifest himself. He is neither omnipotent nor omniscient. God "has nothing of the already made," but is ceaselessly changing. In *The Two Sources of Morality and Religion*, Bergson moved somewhat closer to the Christian position; he affirmed that God is love and the object of love. There is also a divine purpose in the evolutionary process. Evolution is nothing less than God's "undertaking to create creators, that He may have, besides Himself, beings worthy of His love."

The discovery of this purpose and of the reality of God cannot be made by the intellect. It can be made only by the sort of intuition that is the mystical experience. For the vital impetus, Bergson contended, is communicated "in its entirety" to exceptional persons. These are the mystics who achieve contact and partial coincidence with the creative effort that "is of God, if it is not God Himself." This experience does not terminate in passivity, but leads to intense activity. The mystics participate in God's love for humankind. They are therefore impelled to advance the divine purpose by helping to complete the development of man. They want to make of humanity what it would straightway have become if humanity had been able to reach its final form without the aid of humans themselves. The spirit of the mystics must become universal in order to ensure man's future evolution.

Bergson acknowledged that the biggest obstacle to the spread of the mystical spirit is the ceaseless struggle that most people must wage against the material conditions of life. Yet he did not believe that these conditions could be ameliorated by programs of political and economic reform devised by the intellect. Consequently, the most we can hope for at present is that the spirit of the mystics will be kept alive by small groups of privileged souls, "until such time as a profound change in the material conditions imposed on humanity by nature should permit, in spiritual matters, of a profound transformation." The mystics, through their experience of love, will keep open a trail along which the whole of humanity can eventually pass.

CLOSED AND OPEN SOCIETIES

Since man is a social animal, his future evolution will be accelerated or retarded by the sort of group in which he lives. Bergson discussed this question in *The Two Sources of Morality and Religion*, where he drew a distinction between a society that is "closed" and one that is "open," describing in each case corresponding types of religion and of morality.

A closed society is one dominated by the routine and mechanical. It is resistant to change, conservative, and authoritarian. Its stability is achieved by increasing its self-centeredness. Hence, conflict with other self-centered groups, often involving war, is a condition of its preservation. Internal cohesiveness is secured by a closed morality and a closed religion. Bergson's analysis was influenced by the sociological doctrines of Émile Durkheim. Closed morality is static and absolutistic; closed religion is ritualistic and dogmatic. Both institutions exert pressure on individuals to accept the standard practices of the community. Spontaneity and freedom are reduced to a minimum. Conformity becomes the prime duty of the citizen. There is an obvious analogy between such a society and the repetitive mechanisms dealt with by the intellect. Indeed, Bergson regarded closed societies as in large measure the intellect's products.

The existence of a multiplicity of closed societies on the earth is an obstacle to human evolution. Accordingly, the next development in humankind requires the establishment of an open society. Instead of being limited, it will embrace all humankind; instead of being static, it will be progressive; instead of demanding conformity, it will encourage the maximum diversity among individuals. Its moral and religious beliefs will be equally flexible and subject to growth. Religion will replace the stereotyped dogmas elaborated by the intellect with the intuition and illumination now achieved by the mystics. The spread of the mystical spirit must ultimately create an open society whose freedom and spontaneity will express the divine élan which pervades the universe.

Bergson's outlook had a marked influence on the thought and literature of Europe. His gifts as a writer, his ingenuity in constructing vivid analogies, and his flair for describing the subtleties of immediate experience—"true empiricism," as he called it—contributed to the popularity of his work, as did the impressive use that he made of the biological and psychological ideas of his time. On the other hand, critics have contended that many of his doctrines are vague and ill-supported by arguments. Too often, it is said, rhapsodic formulations are offered where there ought to be sustained logical analysis. There is, for instance, no clear statement of how real duration, the flow of consciousness, and the vital impetus are related. Are these separate processes, or just distinguishable aspects of one process? Does matter have an independent status, or is it simply a "devitalized" form of the *élan vital*? Such questions are difficult, if not impossible, to answer. Many critics have also deplored the encouragement that Bergson's doctrine of the intellect gave to the advocates of irrationalism and the cruder versions of pragmatism. Yet when all these criticisms have been made, the Bergsonian heritage remains an important element in twenty-first-century philosophy.

See also Aesthetic Experience; Continuity; Darwin, Charles Robert; Darwinism; Determinism and Freedom; Durkheim, Émile; Evolutionary Theory; Fouillée, Alfred; Idealism; Intuition; Irrationalism; Kant, Immanuel; Lamarck, Chevalier de; Leucippus and Democritus; Maine de Biran; Materialism; Memory; Metaphysics, History of; Mind-Body Problem; Mysticism, History of; Nothing; Philosophy of Language; Philosophy of Science, History of; Plato; Plotinus; Ravaisson-Mollien, Jean Gaspard Félix; Realism; Time; Vitalism; Zeno of Elea.

Bibliography

WORKS BY BERGSON

Quid Aristoteles de Loco Senserit. Paris: F. Alcan, 1889. Bergson's doctoral thesis. Translated by Robert Mossé-Bastide as "L'Idée de lieu chez Aristote," in *Les Études bergsoniennes*. Paris: A. Michel, 1949. Vol. II.

Essai sur les donnés immédiates de la conscience. Paris, 1889. Translated by F. L. Pogson as *Time and Free Will: An Essay on the Immediate Data of Consciousness*. New York: Macmillan, 1910.

Matière et mémoire. Paris, 1896. Translated by Nancy Margaret Paul and W. Scott Palmer [pseud.] as *Matter and Memory.* New York: Macmillan, 1912.

Le rire. Paris, 1900. Translated by Cloudesley Brereton and Fred Rothwell as *Laughter. An Essay on the Meaning of the Comic.* New York: Macmillan, 1911.

"Introduction à la métaphysique." *Revue de la métaphysique et de morale* 11 (January 1903): 1–36. Translated by T. E. Hulme as *Introduction to Metaphysics.* New York: Putnam, 1912.

L'évolution créatrice. Paris: F. Alcan, 1909. Translated by Arthur Mitchell as *Creative Evolution.* New York: Henry Holt, 1911.

L'énergie spirituelle. Paris: F. Alcan, 1919. Translated by H. Wildon Carr as *Mind-Energy.* New York: Henry Holt, 1920. A collection of essays.

Durée et simultanéité. Paris: F. Alcan, 1922; 2nd ed. with 3 appendices, 1923. On aspects of the theory of relativity; not included in centenary edition of Bergson's works.

Les deux sources de la morale et de la religion. Paris: F. Alcan, 1932. Translated by R. A. Audra and Cloudesley Brereton as *The Two Sources of Morality and Religion.* New York: Henry Holt, 1935.

La pensée et le mouvant. Paris: F. Alcan, 1934. Translated by Mabelle L. Andison as *The Creative Mind.* New York: Philosophical Library, 1946. A collection of essays.

Écrits et paroles. Edited by R. M. Mossé-Bastide. 3 vols. Paris, 1957–1959. Preface by Édouard LeRoy.

Oeuvres. Édition du centenaire. Paris: Presses universitaires de France, 1959. Annotated by André Robinet, introduction by Henri Gouhier.

WORKS ON BERGSON

English

Carr, Herbert Wildon. *The Philosophy of Change.* New York, 1912.

Chevalier, Jacques. *Henri Bergson.* New York: Macmillan, 1928.

Hanna, Thomas, ed. *The Bergsonian Heritage.* New York: Columbia University Press, 1962. Articles on Bergson's thought by various scholars.

Höffding, Harald. *Henri Bergson's Filosofi. Karacteristik ag Kritik.* Copenhagen, 1914. Translated by Alfred C. Mason in *Modern Philosophers and Lectures on Bergson.* London, 1915.

Huxley, Julian. *Essays in Popular Science.* New York: Knopf, 1927. Claims that Bergson's vitalism was based on dubious factual material.

LeRoy, Édouard. *Une Philosophie nouvelle: Henri Bergson.* Paris, 1912. Translated by Vincent Benson as *The New Philosophy of Henri Bergson.* New York: Henry Holt, 1913.

Lindsay, A. D. *The Philosophy of Henri Bergson.* London, 1911.

Ruhe, Algot, and Nancy Margaret Paul. *Henri Bergson.* London: Macmillan, 1914.

Russell, Bertrand. *Our Knowledge of the External World.* London, 1914. Ch. 1. Highly critical.

Russell, Bertrand. *The Philosophy of Bergson.* Cambridge, U.K.: Bowes and Bowes, 1914. Highly critical.

Santayana, George. *Winds of Doctrine.* New York: Scribners, 1913. Highly critical.

Scharfstein, Ben-Ami. *Roots of Bergson's Philosophy.* New York: Columbia University Press, 1943.

Stephen, Karin. *The Misuse of Mind.* London: K. Paul, Trench, Trubner, 1922.

Stewart, J. McK. *A Critical Exposition of Bergson's Philosophy.* London: Macmillan, 1911.

French

Delhomme, Jeanne. *Vie et conscience de la vie: Essai sur Bergson.* Paris, 1954.

Les études bergsoniennes. Paris: A. Michel, 1948–1959. Vols. I–V.

Husson, Léon. *L'intellectualisme de Bergson.* Paris: Presses universitaires de France, 1947.

Jankélévitch, Vladimir. *Henri Bergson.* Paris, 1959.

Marietti, Angèle. *Les formes du mouvement chez Bergson.* Paris, 1957.

Maritain, Jacques. *La philosophie bergsonienne.* Paris: M. Rivière, 1930.

OTHER WORKS OF INTEREST

Ansell-Pearson, Keith. *Philosophy and the Adventure of the Virtual: Bergson and the Time of Life.* London; New York: Routledge, 2002.

Bergson, Henri. *Durée et simultanéité.* 7th ed. Paris: Presses universitaires de France, 1968.

Bergson, Henri. *An Introduction to Metaphysics: The Creative Mind.* Totowa, NY: Littlefield, Adams, 1975.

Bergson, Henri. *Mind-Energy: Lectures and Essays.* Westport, CT: Greenwood Press, 1975,.

Bergson, Henri. *The Two Sources of Morality and Religion.* Westport, CT: Greenwood Press, 1974.

Bergson, Henri, and André Robinet. *Correspondances.* Paris: Presses universitaires de France, 2002.

Bergson, Henri, and André Robinet. *OEuvres.* 5th ed. Paris: Presses universitaires de France, 1991.

Capek, Milic. *Bergson and Modern Physics. A Reinterpretation and Re-evaluation.* Dordrecht: Reidel, 1971.

Deleuze, Gilles. *Bergsonism.* New York: Zone Books, 1988.

Fink, Hilary L. *Bergson and Russian Modernism, 1900–1930.* Evanston, IL: Northwestern University Press, 1999.

Gallagher, Idella J. *Morality in Evolution: The Moral Philosophy of Henri Bergson.* The Hague: Nijhoff, 1970.

Gunter, P. A. Y., comp. *Bergson and The Evolution of Physics.* Knoxville: University of Tennessee Press, 1969.

Gunter, P. A. Y. *Henri Bergson: A Bibliography.* 2nd rev. ed. Bowling Green, OH: Philosophy Documentation Center, Bowling Green State University, 1986.

Kolakowski, Leszek. *Bergson.* Oxford, Oxfordshire; New York: Oxford University Press, 1985.

Lacey, A. R. *Bergson.* London; New York: Routledge, 1989.

Maritain, Jacques. *Bergsonian Philosophy and Thomism.* New York: Greenwood Press, 1955, 1968.

Mullarkey, John. *Bergson and Philosophy.* Notre Dame, IN: University of Notre Dame Press, 2000.

Mullarkey, John. *The New Bergson.* Manchester; New York: Manchester University Press, 1999.

Pilkington, Anthony Edward. *Bergson and His Influence: A Reassessment.* Cambridge; New York: Cambridge University Press, 1976.

T. A. Goudge (1967)
Bibliography updated by Michael J. Farmer (2005)

BERKELEY, GEORGE
(1685–1753)

George Berkeley, the Irish philosopher of English ancestry, and Anglican bishop of Cloyne, was born at Kilkenny, Ireland. He entered Trinity College, Dublin in 1700 and became a fellow in 1707. In 1709 he published his first important book, *An Essay towards a New Theory of Vision.* This was well received, and a second edition appeared in the same year. The following year *A Treatise concerning the Principles of Human Knowledge,* Part 1, was published. This is the work in which Berkeley first published his immaterialist philosophy, and although it made him known to some of the foremost writers of the day, its conclusions were not taken very seriously by them. In 1713 Berkeley went to London and there published the *Three Dialogues between Hylas and Philonous,* a more popular statement of the doctrines of the *Principles.* While in London, Berkeley became acquainted with Joseph Addison, Jonathan Swift, Alexander Pope, and Richard Steele and contributed articles to Steele's *Guardian,* attacking the theories of the freethinkers. He traveled on the Continent in 1713–1714 (when he probably met and conversed with Nicolas Malebranche) and again from 1716 to 1720. During this tour he lost the manuscript of the second part of the *Principles,* which he never rewrote. Toward the end of the tour, he wrote a short essay, in Latin, titled *De Motu,* published in London in 1721, criticizing Isaac Newton's philosophy of nature and Gottfried Wilhelm Leibniz's theory of force. In 1724 Berkeley was made dean of Derry.

About this time, Berkeley began to prepare a project for establishing a college in Bermuda, at which not only the sons of American colonists but also Indians and Negroes were to receive a thorough education and be trained for the Christian ministry. Having obtained promises of subscriptions from many prominent people, Berkeley promoted a bill, which was passed by Parliament, providing for considerable financial help from the government. In 1728, before the money was forthcoming, Berkeley, who had just married, left for Rhode Island, where he intended to establish farms for supplying food for the college. He settled in Newport, but the grant never came; and in 1731, when it was clear that the government was diverting the money for other purposes, Berkeley had to return home. While in Newport, however, Berkeley had met and corresponded with the Samuel Johnson who later became the first president of King's College, New York (now Columbia University). Johnson was one of the few philosophers of the time to give close attention to Berkeley's philosophical views, and the correspondence between him and Berkeley is of considerable philosophical interest. While he was in Newport, Berkeley also wrote *Alciphron,* a series of dialogues in part developed from the articles he had written for the *Guardian,* directed against the "minute philosophers," or freethinkers. This was published in 1732.

Berkeley was in London from 1732 to 1734 and there wrote *The Analyst* (1734), a criticism of Newton's doctrine of fluxions and addressed to "an infidel mathematician." This and *A Defence of Free-Thinking in Mathematics* (1735) aimed at showing that the mathematicians so admired by freethinkers worked with concepts that could not withstand close scrutiny, so that the confidence given to them by "the philomathematical infidels of these times" was unjustified. It is not surprising that Berkeley was made bishop of Cloyne, Ireland, in 1734.

Berkeley carried out his episcopal duties with vigor and humanity. His diocese was in a remote and poor part of the country, and the problems he encountered there led him to reflect on economic problems. The result was *The Querist* (1735–1737), in which he made proposals for dealing with the prevailing idleness and poverty by means of public works and education. He also concerned himself with the health of the people and became convinced of the medicinal value of tar water. In 1744 he published *A Chain of Philosophical Reflexions and Inquiries concerning the Virtues of Tar-Water, and divers other Subjects connected together and arising from one another.* When the second edition appeared in the same year, the title *Siris,* by which the book is now known, was added. Much of the book is concerned with the merits of tar water, but Berkeley passed from this subject to the causes of physical phenomena, which, he held, cannot be discovered in the phenomena themselves but must be sought for in the Divine activity. This is in line with his earlier views, but some readers, on the basis of his admiring references to Plato and the Neoplatonists, have considered that by this time he had considerably modified his original system. The *Siris* was Berkeley's last philosophical work. He died suddenly in Oxford nine years later.

An account of Berkeley's life and writings would be inadequate without some reference to his *Philosophical Commentaries.* A. C. Fraser discovered a series of notes by Berkeley on all the main topics of Berkeley's philosophy and published them in 1871 in his edition of Berkeley's works, under the title of *Commonplace Book of Occasional Metaphysical Thoughts.* It was later noticed that these notes had been bound together in the wrong order, and it has now been shown that they were written by Berkeley, probably in 1707–1708, while he was thinking out his *New Theory of Vision* and *Principles.* This work makes it clear that Berkeley was already convinced of the truth of immaterialism before he published the *New Theory of Vision,* in which that view is not mentioned. The *Philosophical Commentaries* throw valuable light upon Berkeley's sources, bugbears, prejudices, and arguments.

MAIN THEMES OF BERKELEY'S PHILOSOPHY

Since the word *idealism* came into use in the eighteenth century, Berkeley has been known as a leading exponent of idealism, and even as its founder. He himself referred to his main view as "the immaterialist hypothesis," meaning by this that he denied the very possibility of inert, mindless, material substance. This description has some advantage over idealism in that it brings out Berkeley's radical opposition to materialism; whereas the opposite of idealism is realism, and there are grounds for doubting whether Berkeley intended to deny the realist contention that in perception people become directly aware of objects that persist unchanged when they cease to be perceived. Berkeley's fundamental view was that for something to exist it must either be perceived or else be the active being that does the perceiving. Things that are perceived he called "sensible things" or "sensible qualities," or, in the terminology he had borrowed from John Locke, "ideas." Sensible things or ideas, he held, cannot exist except as the passive objects of minds or spirits, active beings that perceive and will. As he put it in the *Philosophical Commentaries,* "Existence is *percipi* or *percipere,*" and he added "or *velle* i.e. *agere*"—existence is to be perceived or to perceive or to will, that is, to be active. Thus there can be nothing except active spirits on the one hand and passive sensible things on the other, and the latter cannot exist except as perceived by the former. This is Berkeley's idealism or immaterialism.

CRITICISM OF CONTEMPORARY SCIENCE. The above
account of Berkeley's writings emphasizes their apologetic intent, an intent that can be seen in the subtitles of his major writings—that of the *Principles* is typical: *Wherein the chief causes of error and difficulty in the sciences, with the grounds of scepticism, atheism and irreligion, are inquired into.* It will be seen that "the chief causes of difficulty in the sciences" are also prominent. Berkeley considered that in the mathematics and natural sciences of his day insufficient attention was given to what experience reveals to us. Apart from Newton, the mathematicians were, he wrote in the *Philosophical Commentaries,* "mere triflers, mere Nihilarians." For example, they conceived of lines as infinitely divisible, but this is not only

absurd, it could be maintained only by men who "despised sense." Thus Berkeley regarded himself as protesting against the excesses of uncontrolled rationalism. Hence he put forward a most antirationalistic view of geometry, although he never developed its implications very far. Similarly he thought that the natural philosophers deluded themselves with words when they tried to explain the physical world in terms of attractions, forces, and powers. Natural science, as he understood it, was descriptive rather than explanatory and was concerned with correlations rather than with causes. He thus sketched out a view of science that was revived and developed by nineteenth-century and twentieth-century positivists.

SENSIBLE QUALITIES ARE THE SIGNS OF GOD'S PURPOSE. Berkeley's positivism, however, was confined to his
account of natural science. The order of phenomena, he held, was willed by God for the good of created spirits. In deciphering the conjunctions and sequences of our sense experience we are learning what God has decreed. Thus sensible qualities are the language in which God speaks to us. In the third and fourth editions (1732) of the *New Theory of Vision* Berkeley said that the objects of sight are a divine visual language by which God teaches us what things are good for us and what things are harmful to us. In the *Alciphron,* published that same year, he argued that "the great Mover and Author of Nature constantly explaineth Himself to the eyes of men by the sensible intervention of arbitrary signs, which have no similitude or connexion with the things signified." We learn that certain visual ideas are signs of certain tactual ones, certain smells signs of certain colors, and so on. There is no necessity about this, any more than things necessarily have the names that convention assigns to them. Just as some sensible qualities are signs of others, so sensible qualities as a whole are signs of the purposes of God who "daily speaks to our senses in a manifest and clear dialect."

Thus, taken as a whole, Berkeley's philosophy is a form of immaterialism combined with an extreme antirationalist theory of science. The regularities between phenomena are regarded as evidence for, and as signs of, God's purposes. Just as a man's words reveal his thoughts and intentions by means of the conventional signs of language, so the sensible order reveals God's will in phenomena that could have been ordered quite differently if he had so decided.

THE NEW THEORY OF VISION

Although Berkeley did not mention his immaterialism in *An Essay towards a New Theory of Vision,* this work throws important light upon his quarrel with the mathematicians and his rejection of the rationalist point of view. It contains, too, an interesting statement of what Berkeley then thought about geometry. Furthermore, the *Essay* helps us to see, from what Berkeley said about the objects of vision, how he came to the view that sensible qualities cannot exist "without the mind." Among the main contentions of the book is the claim that distance or "outness" is not immediately perceived by sight; it is "suggested" in part by the sensations we get in moving our eyes but mainly by association with the ideas of touch. According to Berkeley, we see the distance (and size) of things only in the sense in which we see a man's shame and anger. We see his face, and the expression on it suggests to us how he is feeling. In themselves, shame and anger are invisible. Similarly, we see shapes and colors, which are signs of what we would touch if we were to stretch out our hands, but distance itself is no more seen than anger is. In expounding this view, Berkeley developed the thesis that the objects of sight and touch are utterly disparate, so that no feature of the one can have more than a contingent connection with any feature of the other.

DESCARTES'S THEORY OF THE PERCEPTION OF DISTANCE. Consideration should first be given to Berkeley's criticisms of an important geometrical account of how distance is perceived and assessed, the account given by René Descartes in his *Dioptrics* (1637). In this work Descartes referred to six "qualities we perceive in the objects of sight," namely, light, color, shape, distance, magnitude, and situation. Descartes argued that one of the ways in which men ascertain the distance of objects is by means of the angles formed by straight lines running from each of their eyes and converging at the object seen. He illustrated this by reference to a blind man with a stick (the length of which he does not know) held in each hand. When he brings the points of the sticks together at the object, he forms a triangle with one hand at each end of the base, and if he knows how far apart his hands are, and what angles the sticks make with his body, he can, "by a kind of geometry innate in all men" know how far away the object is. The same geometry would apply, Descartes argued, if the observer's eyes are regarded as ends of the base of a triangle, and straight lines from them are regarded as converging at the object. The more obtuse the base angles formed by the lines running from this base and converging at the object, the farther away the object

must be; the more acute these angles, the nearer the object must be. Berkeley put the matter somewhat differently from Descartes, pointing out that according to the latter's view the more acute the angle formed at the object by the lines converging from the eyes, the farther away it must be; the more obtuse this angle, the nearer the object must be. It is important to notice that this "must" is the "must" of mathematical necessity. From what Descartes said, it is necessarily the case that the more acute this angle is, the farther away the object is; the more obtuse the angle, the nearer the object. "Nearer" and "farther" logically depend upon the obtuseness or acuteness of the angle. In criticizing this view, therefore, Berkeley was criticizing the view that distance is known a priori by the principles of an innate geometry according to which we know that the distance of the object must vary in accordance with the angle made at the object by straight lines converging there from the eyes of the observer.

BERKELEY'S CRITICISM OF DESCARTES. Against Descartes's view Berkeley brought a complex argument that for purposes of exposition, is here broken up into three parts. The first is that people who know nothing of the geometry of the matter can nevertheless notice the relative distance of things from them. This is not very convincing, for Descartes obviously thought that the geometry he regarded as "innate in all men" might be employed by them without their having reflected on it. The second argument used by Berkeley is that the lines and angles referred to by Descartes "have no real existence in nature, being only an hypothesis framed by the mathematicians." This argument is of interest in showing how Berkeley thought that mathematicians were inclined to deal in fictitious entities, but it is unlikely that Descartes was deceived by them in this way.

Berkeley's third and main argument was based upon a theory that he expressed in the words, "distance, of itself and immediately, cannot be seen." William Molyneux, from whose *Dioptrics* (1692) Berkeley borrowed this theory, had supported it by the argument that since distance is a line or length directed endwise from the object seen to the eye, it can reach the eye at only one point, which must necessarily remain the same however near or far away the object is. If this argument is accepted, then distance could not possibly be seen, and could only be judged or, as Berkeley believed, "suggested."

DISTANCE IS SUGGESTED BY WHAT IS SEEN. What, then, according to Berkeley, is seen? The answer is not altogether clear, but it would seem that he thought that the immediate object of vision is two-dimensional, containing relations of above and below and of one side and the other, with no necessary connection with a third dimension. Hence the relation between what is immediately seen on the one hand and the distance of objects on the other must be contingent and cannot be necessary. Distance, then, must be ascertained by means of something that has only a contingent relationship with what is seen. Berkeley mentioned the sensations we have when we adjust our eyes, the greater confusedness of objects as they come very close to the eyes, and the sensations of strain as we try to see what is very near. But he mainly relied on the associations between what a man has touched and what he now sees. For example, when a man now sees something faint and dim, he may, from past experience, expect that if he approaches and touches it he will find it bright and hard. When he sees something at a distance, he is really seeing certain shapes and colors, which suggest to him what tangible ideas he would have if he were near enough to touch it. Just as one does not hear a man's thoughts, which are suggested by the sounds he makes, so one does not directly see distance, which is suggested by what is seen.

SIGHT AND TOUCH. Berkeley's view that distance is not immediately perceived by sight is rejected by some writers, for instance by H. H. Price, in his *Perception* (1932), on the ground that it is plainly contradicted by experience. We just do see visual depth, it is held, so that it is idle to deny this fact on the basis of an argument purporting to prove that we cannot. Again, some critics, such as T. K. Abbott in *Sight and Touch* (1864) have argued not only that we do get our idea of distance from sight, but also that touch is vague and uninformative by comparison with sight, and hence less effective in giving knowledge of the material world. This discussion need not be developed, however, since, although he said in the *Essay* that by touch we get knowledge of objects that exist "without the mind" (§55), Berkeley's real view was that no sensible thing could so exist. It cannot be denied that on occasion Berkeley's language was imprecise. A crucial example of this occurs in his discussion of the question of whether a man born blind would, on receiving his sight, see things at a distance from him. According to Berkeley, of course, he would not; but to such a man, the most distant objects "would all seem to be in his eye, or rather in his mind" and would appear "(as in truth they are) no other than a new set of thoughts or sensations, each whereof is as near to him as the perceptions of pain or pleasure, or the most inward passions of his soul" (*Essay*, §41). It will be noticed how readily Berkeley passed from "in his eye" to "in his mind," and how he assimilated such very different

things as sensations and thoughts. Indeed it is hard not to conclude that he thought that whatever was not seen at a distance must appear to be in the mind. If this is true, then one of the objects of the *Essay* was to show that the immediate objects of vision must be in the mind because they are not seen at a distance.

GEOMETRIES OF SIGHT AND OF TOUCH. As already seen, an extremely important thesis of the *Essay* is that the objects of sight and the objects of touch are radically different from one another. We see visible objects and we touch tangible objects, and it is absurd to suppose that we can touch what we see or see what we touch. According to Berkeley, it follows from this that tangible shape and visible shape have no necessary connection with one another. Geometers certainly supposed themselves to be concerned with shapes in abstraction from their being seen or touched, but Berkeley did not allow that this is possible. A purely visual geometry would necessarily be confined to two dimensions, so that the three-dimensional geometry that we have must be fundamentally a geometry of touch. He reinforced this strangely pragmatic view with the observation that a sighted but disembodied being that could not touch or manipulate things would be unable to understand even plane geometry, since without a body it would not understand the handling of rulers and compasses and the drawing of lines and the placing of shapes against one another.

ARGUMENTS FOR IMMATERIALISM

The arguments now to be considered are set out in the *Principles* and in the *Three Dialogues*. They are largely concerned with what Berkeley called "ideas," "ideas or sensations," "sensible things," or "sensible qualities." The very use of the word *idea* itself and, even more, its use in apposition with *sensation* had the purpose of indicating something that does not exist apart from the perception of it. Pains and itches are typical sensations, and no one supposes that they could exist apart from a being that experiences them. Rocks do not suffer, and water does not itch. When, therefore, sensible things such as colors, sounds, tangible shapes, tastes, and smells are called ideas, they are assimilated with sensations and hence relate to the perceiving beings that have them. It is now necessary, therefore, to examine the arguments with which Berkeley justified this.

SEVENTEENTH-CENTURY MATERIALISM. Berkeley's arguments for immaterialism can be understood only if we first consider the sort of view it was intended to refute. When Berkeley was forming his views, the natural sciences had been so far advanced by the work of such men as Galileo Galilei, Andreas Vesalius, William Harvey, Robert Boyle, and Newton as to have given rise to a scientific view of the world. Such a view had been elaborated, in its philosophical aspects, by Locke in his *Essay concerning Human Understanding* (1690). Space and time were, so to say, the containers within which material things were situated. The movements and relations of material things could be explored by experiments and characterized in mathematical formulae.

Explanation in terms of particles in motion. The features of the world, thus revealed as fundamental, were those of place, shape, size, movement, weight, and the like; and it was in terms of these that heat and cold and color and sound found their explanation. Heat was thought to be due to the rapid movement of atomic particles, color to the transmission of particles or to the spreading of waves, and sound to the movement of the air between the emitting object and the ear. Whereas solid, shaped, moving objects, and the air and space within which they existed, were regarded as basic features of nature, the colors we see, the heat we feel, and the sounds we hear were held to be the effects that substances possessing only the basic characteristics produced in creatures with sense organs. If all creatures with sense organs and consciousness were removed from the world, there would no longer be any experienced sounds, but only pulsations in the air; particles would increase or decrease their speed of movement, but no one would feel hot or cold; light would be radiated, but there would be no colors as we know them. In such a world colors and sounds, heat and cold, would exist, as Boyle put it, in his *Origins of Forms and Qualities* (Oxford, 1666), only "dispositively," that is, those primary things would be there that would have given rise to the secondary ones if creatures with the requisite sense organs and minds had been there too.

Primary and secondary qualities. In this way a distinction was made between the primary qualities of things, which are essential and absolute, and their secondary qualities, which are those among the primary ones that give or would give rise to heard sounds, seen colors, and felt heat. It was an important element of this view that nothing could be perceived unless it acted upon the sense organs of the percipient and produced in his mind an idea. What was immediately perceived was not the external object but an idea representative of it. Locke had made people familiar with this theory, and had maintained that whereas the ideas we have of heat and cold and of color and sound correspond to nothing like themselves in the external world; for all that exists in the external world are solid bodies at rest or in movement, the ideas we have of the solid, shaped, moving bodies, that is, our ideas of primary qualities are like their sources or archetypes outside us. According to the view, then, that Berkeley was considering, material objects are perceived mediately or indirectly by means of ideas, some of which, the ideas of primary qualities, are like their originals; others, the ideas of secondary qualities, are relative to percipients and are unlike anything that exists in the external world.

MATERIALISM LEADS TO SKEPTICISM. Berkeley had two objections to the view that material objects are perceived mediately by means of ideas. One is that since it is held that we never perceive material things directly, but only through the medium of ideas, then we can never know whether any of our ideas are like the qualities of material substances since we can never compare our ideas with them; for to do so we should require direct or immediate acquaintance with them (*Principles,* §18). Indeed, if we accept Locke's position, then the very existence of material substances is in doubt, and we are constantly under the threat of skepticism (*Principles,* §86). Thus Berkeley argued that Locke's theory was in fact, although not by intention, skeptical, and that it could be remedied only by the elimination of material substances that could never be directly apprehended.

DISTINCTION BETWEEN PRIMARY AND SECONDARY QUALITIES UNTENABLE. Berkeley's second objection is that there can be no distinction between ideas of primary qualities and ideas of secondary qualities such as to make secondary qualities relative to the mind in a way in which primary qualities are not. In the *Three Dialogues* Berkeley elaborated the arguments, already used by Locke, to show that the ideas we have of secondary qualities are relative to the percipient and are what they are by reason of his condition and constitution. Things have no color in the dark; the same water can feel hot or cold to different hands, one of which has been in cold water and the other in hot; heat and cold are inseparably bound up with pain and pleasure, which can only exist in perceiving beings; and so on. But Berkeley then went on to argue that just as heat, for example, is inseparably bound up with pleasure and pain, and can therefore, no more than they can, exist "without the mind," so extension is bound up with color, speed of movement with a standard of estimation, solidity with touch, and size and shape with position and point of view (*Principles,* §§10–15). Thus Berkeley's argument is that nothing can have the primary qualities without having the secondary qualities, so that if the latter cannot exist "without the mind," the former cannot so exist either.

ALL SENSIBLE QUALITIES MUST BE EITHER PERCEIVED OR PERCEPTIBLE.

The preceding argument, however, is only a hypothetical one to the effect that if secondary qualities cannot exist "without the mind," primary qualities are in like case. What must now be considered are the reasons for holding that secondary qualities and, indeed, all sensible qualities can exist only in the mind so that their being is to be perceived. Berkeley, as already indicated, stated and elaborated well-known arguments to show that heat and cold, tastes, sounds, and the rest are relative to the percipient. Perhaps the most persuasive of these are those that purport to establish an indissoluble connection between heat, taste, and smell on the one hand, and pain or pleasure or displeasure on the other. Since no one denies that pain and pleasure can exist only if felt, then this applies to heat so intense as to be painful and to lesser degrees of heat as well. But in the *Principles,* his systematic treatise on the subject, Berkeley did not make use of these arguments, but said that "an intuitive knowledge may be obtained of this, by any one that shall attend to what is meant by the term *exist* when applied to sensible things" (§3). His view here is that "sensible things" are by their very nature perceived or perceivable. He supported this by asserting that to say there was an odor is to say that it was smelled, to say that there was a sound is to say that it was heard, to say that there was a color or shape is to say that it was seen or touched. According to Berkeley, unsmelled odors, sounds unheard, colors unseen, and shapes unseen or untouched are absurdities or impossibilities; brown leaves could not rustle on a withered tree in a world where life was extinct and God was dead. The very notion is absurd or impossible. Can more light be shed on the matter than is provided by the assertion that we have "intuitive knowledge" of it?

It must be remembered, in the first place, that Berkeley was contrasting the sounds we hear, for example, with the movements in the air, which men of science sometimes call sounds. Sounds in the latter sense, he said, "may possibly be *seen* or *felt,* but never *heard*" (*Three Dialogues,* 1). From this it may be seen that Berkeley looked upon sensible qualities as each the object of its own mode of perception, so that sounds are heard but not seen or touched, colors seen but not heard, heat felt but not seen, and so on. Hence colors require a viewer, sounds a hearer, and heat someone who feels it; and this is one reason why the being of sensible things is held to be their being perceived. The various modalities of sense are distinguished from one another by the mode of perception peculiar to each one, and in making these distinctions it is implied that perception is essential to them all. It is well known, of course, that Berkeley's critics accuse him of failing to distinguish between the object perceived and the perceiving of it. The perceiving of it, they say, can only be an act of a percipient without whom it could not exist, but the perceived object, whether it be a sound or a color or a shape, is distinct from the perceiving and could conceivably exist apart from it.

Whatever may be thought of this argument, it should not be used against Berkeley as if he had not thought of it. In fact he put it into the mouth of Hylas in the first of the *Three Dialogues* and rejected it on the ground that in perception we are passive and so are not exerting an act or activity of any kind. It should also be noticed that when Berkeley discussed sensation in detail he stated that sensible things or sensible qualities are perceived *immediately,* that is, without suggestion, association, or inference. We say that we hear vehicles and that we hear sounds. According to Berkeley, we hear sounds immediately, but vehicles, if they are out of sight, are suggested by or inferred from what we do hear, and so are heard only mediately or by means of the sounds immediately heard. Thus the sound we hear immediately is neither suggested nor inferred, but is heard just as it is. For this to be so, it must be before the mind; for if it were not before the mind, it would have to be inferred or suggested. Thus sensible qualities, as immediately perceived, must be objects of perception; their being is to be perceived.

Inconceivability of a sensible object existing unperceived. A very famous argument is now to be considered: It is inconceivable that anything should exist apart from, or independent of, mind. This argument was put forward by Berkeley in similar terms both in the *Principles* (§§22, 23) and in the *Three Dialogues* (1) and takes the form of a challenge to the reader to conceive of something—e.g., a book or a tree—existing absolutely unperceived. Berkeley argued that the attempt is impossible of fulfillment, since in order to conceive of a tree existing unperceived we who conceive of it, by the very fact of doing so, bring it into relation to our conception and hence to ourselves. As Hylas admits, in recognizing the failure of his attempt, "It is a pleasant mistake enough. As I was thinking of a tree in a solitary place, where no one was present to see it, me-thought that was to conceive a tree as existing unperceived or unthought of, not considering that I myself conceived it all the while." This is an argument that was later accepted as fundamental by idealists of such different persuasions as Johann Gottlieb Fichte and Francis

Herbert Bradley, who held that it shows that mind or experience is essential to the universe.

Sensible objects are complex ideas. Berkeley's example of a tree makes it necessary to consider how trees and other things in nature are related to ideas, sensible qualities, sounds, colors, shapes, and so on. According to Berkeley, such things as trees, books, and mountains are groups of ideas or sensible qualities and are hence as much within the mind as the latter are. Indeed, in his view, books, trees, and mountains are ideas, though complex ones. He admitted (*Principles,* §38) that this use of the word *idea* for what is ordinarily called a *thing* is somewhat odd, but held that, the facts being as they are, *idea* is better than *thing.* A tree is a group of ideas touched, seen, and smelled; a cherry, a group of ideas touched, seen, smelled, and tasted. The sensible qualities or ideas, without which we should have no conception of a tree or cherry, do not belong to some unseen, untouched, untasted substance or substratum, for the very conception of such a "something I know not what" (as Locke had called it) is incoherent, and rests upon the false view that we can conceive something in complete abstraction from ideas of sense.

Sensible objects, as ideas, are perceived directly. Berkeley therefore concluded that it is his theory that conforms with common sense, not that of the materialists or the dualists. For according to Berkeley we perceive trees and cherries directly by seeing, touching, and tasting them, just as the plain man thinks we do, whereas his opponents regard them as perpetually hidden from us by a screen of intermediaries that may be always deceiving us. Berkeley considered that by this view he had refuted skepticism of the senses, for, according to his theory, the objects of the senses are the things in the world: the trees, houses, and mountains we live among. But trees, houses, and mountains, as compounded of sensible qualities or ideas, cannot exist "without the mind."

SENSIBLE OBJECTS NOT COPIES OF MATERIAL ARCHETYPES.

Berkeley's arguments showing that all sensible qualities or ideas exist only as perceived and that, therefore, things in nature, being groups of such ideas, cannot exist "without the mind" have now been expounded. It is now necessary to complete this account of Berkeley's arguments for immaterialism with his argument to show that not only must sensible qualities or ideas exist in the mind, but also that nothing like them can exist outside it. For anyone reluctant to accept immaterialism is likely to fall back on the view that our ideas, although in our minds, are copies of material archetypes.

Berkeley's objection to this in the *Principles* (§8) is that "an idea can be like nothing but an idea," which he illustrated by saying that a color or shape can only be like another color or shape. In the *Three Dialogues* (1) he expanded the argument in two ways. Ideas, he said, are regarded by some as the perceived representatives of imperceptible originals, but "Can a real thing in itself *invisible* be like a color; or a real thing which is not *audible,* be like a *sound?*" His other reason for holding that ideas cannot be like any supposed external originals is that ideas are "perpetually fleeting and variable," and "continually changing upon every alteration in the distance, medium or instruments of sensation," while their supposed originals are thought to remain fixed and constant throughout all changes in the percipient's organs and position. But something that is fleeting and relative cannot be like what is stable and absolute, any more than what is incapable of being perceived can be like what is essentially perceptible.

SUMMARY. The following are Berkeley's central arguments in favor of immaterialism. They arose out of his exposure of the weaknesses and inconsistencies in the then current scientific view of the world, with its distinction between primary and secondary qualities and its theory of representative perception. According to Berkeley, since primary qualities cannot exist apart from secondary qualities, and since secondary qualities, and indeed all sensible qualities, cannot exist "without the mind," the independent material world of the then current scientific view was a conceptual absurdity. This was supported by the argument that our ideas cannot be likenesses of an external material world, since there is nothing conceivable they could be likenesses of except mind-dependent existences of their own type. The theory of representative perception was held to be essentially skeptical, and Berkeley claimed that his own theory, according to which we directly perceive ideas and groups of ideas that exist only as perceived, eliminates skepticism and accords with common sense.

METAPHYSICS AND THEOLOGY

In section 3 of the *Principles,* where Berkeley stated that we have intuitive knowledge of the fact that for sensible qualities to exist they must be perceived, he also stated that when we say that the table is in the room that we have left we mean that if we were to return there we could perceive it "or that some other spirit actually does perceive it." This shows that Berkeley was concerned with the problem of giving an account, within the terms of his immaterialism, of the continued existence of things that are not being perceived by any human being. It also shows that he considered two ways of dealing with this problem. One way was to extend the doctrine that the existence of sensible things is their being perceived into the doctrine that the existence of sensible things is their being perceptible. The other way was to argue that when sensible things are not being perceived by human beings they must be perceived by "some other spirit."

BERKELEY NOT A PHENOMENALIST. The first way points in the direction of the modern theory of phenomenalism, the theory according to which, in John Stuart Mill's happily chosen words, material objects are "permanent possibilities of sensation." But might not anything, even material substances possessing only primary qualities, be perceptible, even if not actually being perceived? Some twentieth-century upholders of phenomenalism argued that the world was perceptible before there was any life or mind, in the sense that if there had been gods or human beings they would have perceived it. This could not be possible on Berkeley's theory, however, since, as we have seen, he held that only ideas or sensible things can be *like* ideas or sensible things, so that what is perceptible is limited by what is perceived.

PERCEPTIBLE OBJECTS PERCEIVED BY GOD. The perceptible, therefore, is limited to the mind-dependent, and, for Berkeley, the very notion of something that might be perceived, but is not, is unacceptable. Thus it seems that Berkeley was forced to supplement his phenomenalist account of unperceived objects with the view that whatever is not being actually perceived by human beings, but is only perceptible by them, must be an object of perception by "some other spirit." He used this same expression in section 48 of the *Principles,* where he denied that "bodies are annihilated and created every moment, or exist not at all during the intervals between our perception of them." In the *Three Dialogues* (2) he argued that since sensible things do not depend on the thought of human beings and exist independently of them "*there must be some other mind wherein they exist.*" This other mind is God; and thus, according to Berkeley, the existence of sensible things when not being perceived by finite spirits is a proof of the existence of an infinite spirit who perceives them always. Indeed, Berkeley considered it a merit of immaterialism that it enables this brief and, as he thought, conclusive proof to be formulated.

OUR IDEAS COME FROM GOD. In the *Principles* Berkeley put forward another proof of the existence of God, this time a proof based upon God as the cause of our ideas. As has been shown, Berkeley held that ideas are passive and that the only active beings are minds or spirits. Now some of our ideas, namely, ideas of imagination, we ourselves produce, but others, the ideas of sense, come to us without our willing them. "There is therefore some other will or spirit that produces them" (*Principles,* §29). That this is God may be concluded from the regular order in which these ideas come to us. The knowledge we have of God is analogous to the knowledge we have of other men. Since people are active spirits, we do not have ideas of them, but only of their expressions, words, and bodily movements. Through these we recognize them as possessors of minds and wills like those we know ourselves to have. Similarly, God reveals himself to us in the order of nature: "every thing we see, hear, feel, or in any wise perceive by sense, being a sign or effect of the Power of God."

ACTIVE SPIRITS AND PASSIVE IDEAS. These, then, are the elements of Berkeley's metaphysics. There are active spirits on the one hand and passive ideas on the other. The latter could not exist apart from the former, but the ideas in the minds of human beings are caused in them by God and sustained by him when they are not perceiving them. Regularly recurring groups of ideas are called bodies, and the ideas that form them are arbitrarily connected together and might have been connected quite differently. Thus there is no natural necessity or internal reason about the laws of nature, but the regular sequences of ideas reveal to us a single infinite being who orders things for our benefit. Active spirits and passive ideas are of different natures. The mind is not blue because the idea of blue is in it, nor is the mind extended because it has an idea of extension. Ideas are neither parts nor properties of minds. Berkeley seems to have thought that the relationship is sui generis, for he said that sensible qualities are in the mind "only as they are perceived by it, that is, not by way of *mode* or *attribute, but only by way of idea*" (*Principles,* §49).

GOD'S IDEAS AND OUR IDEAS. As already seen, Berkeley held that God was both the cause of the ideas in the minds of embodied finite spirits and also the Mind in which these ideas continued to exist when embodied finite spirits were not perceiving them. Berkeley was thus faced with the problem of how the ideas in finite minds are related to the ideas in God's mind. If we recall Berkeley's claim that he was on the side of common sense against the skeptics, then we should expect the ideas that continue to exist in God's mind to be identical with those that had been in the minds of the embodied finite spirits who had formerly perceived them.

However, he found that there were difficulties in this view. Humans perceive ideas of sense by means of sense organs, and their ideas vary in accordance with their position and condition, but God does not have sense organs. Furthermore, some ideas—for example, those of heat and cold, and sensations of smell and taste—are inseparable from sensations of pain and pleasure, but God is impassible, that is, not subject to feeling or emotion; hence he cannot be supposed to perceive ideas of this nature. In the *Three Dialogues* (3), therefore, Berkeley concluded that "God knows or hath ideas; but his ideas are not conveyed to Him by sense, as ours are." From this it is natural to conclude that the ideas that God perceives are not identical with the ideas that embodied finite spirits perceive. Berkeley was obviously thinking along these lines when, in the same *Dialogue,* he said that the things that one perceives, "they or their archetypes," must, since one does not cause them, have an existence outside one's mind. Elsewhere in this *Dialogue* he distinguished between what is "ectypal or natural" and what is "archetypal and eternal." Thus Berkeley's arguments and the language he used combine to suggest that the ideas in God's mind are not the same ideas as those in the minds of embodied percipients.

This point was taken up by the Samuel Johnson referred to earlier, in his correspondence with Berkeley. Johnson suggested that Berkeley's view is that "the real original and permanent existence of things is archetypal, being ideas *in mente Divina,* and that our ideas are copies of them." Johnson was too polite to press the point, but it follows that what we directly perceive are copies or representatives of divine originals, so that Berkeley's claim to have reinstated the direct, unmediated perception of common sense, in place of the representative and skeptical theory of the philosophers and scientists, cannot be substantiated. In his reply, Berkeley hardly met this point when he stated that material substance is an impossibility because it is held to exist apart from mind, whereas the archetypes in the divine mind are obviously inseparable from God's knowledge of them.

PHILOSOPHY OF NATURE

Berkeley carried on a persistent battle against the tendency to suppose that mere abstractions are real things. In the *New Theory of Vision* he denied the possibility of "extension in abstract," saying "A line or surface which is neither black, nor white, nor blue, nor yellow, etc., nor long, nor short, nor rough, nor smooth, nor square, nor round, etc., is perfectly incomprehensible" (§ 123). In the introduction to the *Principles,* his most explicit discus-

sion of the matter, he quoted Locke's account of the abstract idea of a triangle "which is neither oblique nor rectangle, neither equilateral, equicrural, nor scalenon, but all and none of these at once," and pointed out that any actual triangle must be one of these types and cannot possibly be "all and none" of them. What makes any idea general, he held, is not any abstract feature that may be alleged to belong to it, but rather its being used to represent all other ideas that are like it in the relevant respects. Thus if something that is true of a triangle of one of these types is not true of it because it is of that one type, then it is true of all triangles whatever. Nothing exists but what is particular, and particular ideas become general by being used as representatives of others like them. Generality, we might say, is a symbolic device, not a metaphysical status. Thus Berkeley's attack on abstractions is based on two principles: (1) that nothing exists but what is particular, and (2) that nothing can exist on its own except what can be sensed or imagined on its own. If we accept the first principle, then abstract objects and Platonic forms are rejected, and if we accept the second, then possibility is limited to the sensible or imaginable.

SPACE, TIME, AND MOTION. We have already seen how Berkeley applied the above two principles to the abstract conception of unperceived existence, and to the abstract conception of bodies with only the primary qualities. It must now be shown how he applied them to some of the other elements in the scientific worldview he was so intent on discrediting. Chief among these were the current conceptions of absolute space, absolute time, and absolute motion. According to Berkeley, all these are abstractions, not realities. It is impossible, he held, to form an idea of pure space apart from the bodies in it. We find that we are hindered from moving our bodies in some directions and can move them freely in others. Where there are hindrances to our movement there are other bodies to obstruct us, and where we can move unrestrictedly we say there is space. It follows that our idea of space is inseparable from our ideas of movement and of body (*Principles,* §116).

So too our conception of time is inseparable from the succession of ideas in our minds and from the "particular actions and ideas that diversify the day"; hence Newton's conception of absolute time flowing uniformly must be rejected (*Principles,* §§97, 98).

Newton had also upheld absolute motion, but this too, according to Berkeley, is a hypostatized abstraction. If there were only one body in existence there could be no idea of motion, for motion is the change of position of two bodies relative to one another. Thus sensible qualities, without which there could be no bodies, are essential to the very conception of movement. Furthermore, since sensible qualities are passive existences, and hence bodies are too, movement cannot have its source in body; and as we know what it is to move our own bodies, we know that the source of motion must be found in mind. Created spirits are responsible for only a small part of the movement in the world, and therefore God, the infinite spirit, must be its prime source. "And so natural philosophy either presupposes the knowledge of God or borrows it from some superior science" (*De Motu,* §34).

CAUSATION AND EXPLANATION. The thesis that God is the ultimate source of motion is a special case of the principle that the only real causes are spirits. This principle has the general consequence, of course, that inanimate bodies cannot act causally upon one another. Berkeley concluded from this that what are called natural causes are really signs of what follows them. Fire does not cause heat, but is so regularly followed by it that it is a reliable sign of it as long as "the Author of Nature always operates uniformly" (*Principles,* §107). Thus Berkeley held that natural laws describe but do not explain, for real explanations must be by reference to the aims and purposes of spirits, that is, in terms of final causes. For this reason, he maintained that mechanical explanations of movements in terms of attraction were misleading, unless it was recognized that they merely recorded the rates at which bodies in fact approach one another (*Principles,* §103). Similar arguments apply to gravity or to force when these are regarded as explanations of the movements of bodies (*De Motu,* §6). This is not to deny the importance of Newton's laws, for Newton did not regard gravity "as a true physical quality, but only as a mathematical hypothesis" (*De Motu,* §17). In general, explanations in terms of forces or attractions are mathematical hypotheses having no stable being in the nature of things but depending upon the definitions given to them (*De Motu,* §67). Their acceptability depends upon the extent to which they enable calculations to be made, resulting in conclusions that are borne out by what in fact occurs. According to Berkeley, forces and attractions are not found in nature but are useful constructions in the formulation of theories from which deductions can be made about what is found in nature, that is, sensible qualities or ideas (*De Motu,* §§34–41).

PHILOSOPHY OF MATHEMATICS

We have already seen that when he wrote the *New Theory of Vision,* Berkeley thought that geometry was primarily concerned with tangible extension, since visual extension does not have three dimensions, and visible shapes must be formed by hands that grasp and instruments that move. He later modified this view, an important feature of which has already been referred to in the account of Berkeley's discussion of Locke's account of the abstract idea of a triangle. A particular triangle, imagined or drawn, is regarded as representative of all other triangles, so that what is proved of it is proved of all others like it in the relevant respects. This, he pointed out later in the *Principles* (§126), applies particularly to size. If the length of the line is irrelevant to the proof, what is true of a line one inch long is true of a line one mile long. The line we use in our proof is a representative sign of all other lines. But it must have a finite number of parts, for if it is a visible line it must be divisible into visible parts, and these must be finite in length. A line one inch long cannot be divided into 10,000 parts because no such part could possibly be seen. But since a line one mile long can be divided into 10,000 parts, we imagine that the short line could be divided likewise. "After this manner the properties of the lines signified are (by a very usual figure) transferred to the sign, and thence through mistake thought to appertain to it considered in its own nature." Thus it was Berkeley's view that infinitesimals should be "pared off" from mathematics (*Principles,* §131). In the *Analyst* (1734), he brought these and other considerations to bear in refuting Newton's theory of fluxions. In this book Berkeley seemed to suggest that the object of geometry is "to measure finite assignable extension" (§50, Q.2).

Berkeley's account of arithmetic was even more revolutionary than his account of geometry. In geometry, he held, one particular shape is regarded as representative of all those like it, but in arithmetic we are concerned with purely arbitrary signs invented by men to help them in their operations of counting. Number, he said, is "entirely the creature of the mind" (*Principles,* §12). He argued, furthermore, that there are no units and no numbers in nature apart from the devices that men have invented to count and measure. The same length, for example, may be regarded as one yard, if it is measured in that unit, or three feet or thirty-six inches, if it is measured in those units. Arithmetic, he went on, is a language in which the names for the numbers from zero to nine play a part analogous to that of nouns in ordinary speech (*Principles,* §121). Berkeley did not develop this part of his theory. However, later in the eighteenth century, in various works, Étienne Bonnot de Condillac argued in detail for the thesis that mathematics is a language, and this view is, of course, widely held today.

CONCLUDING COMMENTS

Berkeley's immaterialism is a strange and unstable combination of theses that most other philosophers have thought do not belong together. Thus he upheld both extreme empiricism and idealism, both immaterialism and common sense, and both subjectivism (as it would seem) and epistemological realism (as it would also seem). Are these mere skillful polemical devices in the war against the freethinkers, or can they be regarded as elements in a distinctive and reasonably coherent metaphysics?

It is odd that Berkeley had so much to say about the relativity of each particular sense and so little to say about our perception of the physical world. He referred to perspectival distortions and the like in the course of defending his view that the existence of sensible qualities is their being perceived, but he did not seem to realize the difficulties they made for his view that perception is direct. Indeed, when, in the *Three Dialogues* (3) he mentioned the case of the oar that looks bent in the water when in fact it is straight, he said that we go wrong only if we mistakenly infer that it will look bent when out of the water. There is something seen to be straight, something else seen to be crooked, and something else again felt to be straight. We go wrong only when we expect that when we see something crooked we shall feel something crooked. But this implies that our perceptions of such things as oars, as distinct from our perceptions of colors and pressures, are not direct as common sense supposes. This reinforces the criticism we have already mentioned, that the ideas perceived by finite spirits with sense organs are different from, and representative of, the ideas in the mind of God. Berkeley was farther from common sense and closer to the views that he was criticizing than he was ready to admit.

It is obvious enough that Berkeley's immaterialism is not in accord with common sense. What place, then, must be given to his empiricism? He certainly rejected the Cartesian conception of a natural world that deceives the senses and is apprehended by the reason. He denied that mathematics reveals the ultimate necessities of things and anticipated to some extent the linguistic theory of mathematics. In arguing that causes are not to be found in nature, and in maintaining that the sciences of nature are primarily concerned with predicting human experiences, he formulated views that Ernst Mach and his modern-day followers have advocated. Furthermore, although he did not himself adopt it, he briefly formulated the theory of the physical world known as phenomenalism, the theory that consistent empiricists have adopted in order to avoid

postulating objects that transcend sense experience. But, in spite of all this, Berkeley was an idealist rather than an empiricist. He held that sensible qualities or ideas are not independent or substantial existences and that minds or spirits are. On this most important matter, he was in agreement with his great contemporary, Leibniz. Furthermore, Berkeley's antiabstractionism, as we may call it, was constantly leading him toward the conclusion that the universe is a concrete unity in which an infinite mind is manifesting itself. If we look at his writings as a continuing and developing critique of abstraction, then we shall see that the *Siris* is not an aberration or a recantation but, as Henri Bergson said in his lectures on Berkeley, 1908–1909, a natural continuation of Berkeley's earlier views (*Écrits et paroles*, 2, p. 309).

See also Touch.

Bibliography

LIFE AND PRINCIPAL EDITIONS OF WORKS

Fraser, A. C. *The Works of George Berkeley*. 4 vols. London: Clarendon Press, 1871. New (first complete) edition, 1901.

Luce, A. A. *The Life of George Berkeley, Bishop of Cloyne*. London: Nelson, 1949.

Luce, A. A., and T. E. Jessop, eds. *The Works of George Berkeley, Bishop of Cloyne*. 9 vols. London and New York: Nelson, 1948–1957. The introduction and notes in this definitive edition are of great value.

Rand, Benjamin. *Berkeley and Percival*. Cambridge, U.K.: Cambridge University Press, 1914.

MAIN THEMES OF BERKELEY'S PHILOSOPHY

Hicks, G. Dawes. *Berkeley*. London: Benn, 1932.

Leroy, A. L. *George Berkeley*. Paris, 1959.

Warnock, G. J. *Berkeley*. London, 1953.

Wild, John D. *George Berkeley: A Study of His Life and Philosophy*. New York: Russell and Russell, 1936, 1962.

THE NEW THEORY OF VISION

Abbott, T. K. *Sight and Touch*. London: Longman, 1864.

Armstrong, D. M. *Berkeley's Theory of Vision*. Melbourne: Melbourne University Press, 1960.

Bailey, S. *A Review of Berkeley's Theory of Vision*. London, 1842.

Turbayne, C. M. "Berkeley and Molyneux on Retinal Images." *Journal of the History of Ideas* 16 (1955).

Vesey, G. N. A. "Berkeley and the Man Born Blind." *PAS* 61 (1960–1961).

ARGUMENTS FOR IMMATERIALISM

Bracken, H. M. "Berkeley's Realism." *Philosophical Quarterly* 8 (1958).

Broad, C. D. "Berkeley's Denial of Material Substance." *Philosophical Review* 43 (1954).

Laird, J. "Berkeley's Realism." *Mind*, n.s., 25 (1916): 308ff.

Luce, A. A. "The Berkeleyan Idea of Sense." *PAS*, supp. 27 (1953).

Luce, A. A. "Berkeley's Existence in the Mind." *Mind,* n.s., 50 (1941): 258ff.

Mates, Benson. "Berkeley Was Right." In *George Berkeley, Lectures Delivered before the Philosophical Union of the University of California.* Berkeley: University of California Press, 1957.

Moore, G. E. "Refutation of Idealism." In his *Philosophical Studies.* London: Routledge, 1922.

Sullivan, Celestine J. "Berkeley's Attack on Matter." In *George Berkeley, Lectures Delivered before the Philosophical Union of the University of California.* Berkeley: University of California Press, 1957.

METAPHYSICS AND THEOLOGY

Bracken, H. M. "Berkeley on the Immortality of the Soul." *Modern Schoolman* 38 (1960–1961).

Davis, J. W. "Berkeley and Phenomenalism." *Dialogue. Canadian Philosophical Review* 1 (1962–1963): 67–80.

Fritz, Anita D. "Berkeley and the Immaterialism of Malebranche." *Review of Metaphysics* 3 (1949–1950).

Gueroult, M. *Berkeley. Quatre études sur la perception et sur Dieu.* Paris, 1956.

Luce, A. A. *Berkeley and Malebranche.* London: Oxford University Press, 1934.

Myerscough, Angelita. "Berkeley and the Proofs for the Existence of God." In *Philosophy and the History of Philosophy.* Vol. 1, edited by John K. Ryan. Washington, DC: Catholic University of America Press, 1961.

Sillem, E. A. *George Berkeley and the Proofs for the Existence of God.* London: Longmans Green, 1957.

PHILOSOPHY OF NATURE AND PHILOSOPHY OF MATHEMATICS

Mach, Ernst. *The Analysis of Sensations.* Chicago: Open Court, 1914.

Myhill, John. "Berkeley's *De Motu*—An Anticipation of Mach." In *George Berkeley, Lectures Delivered before the Philosophical Union of the University of California.* Berkeley: University of California Press, 1957.

Popper, K. R. "A Note on Berkeley as Precursor of Mach." *British Journal for the Philosophy of Science* 3 (1953–1954).

Strong, Edward W. "Mathematical Reasoning and Its Object." In *George Berkeley, Lectures Delivered before the Philosophical Union of the University of California.* Berkeley: University of California Press, 1957.

Whitrow, G. J. "Berkeley's Critique of the Newtonian Analysis of Motion." *Hermathena* 82 (1953).

Whitrow, G. J. "Berkeley's Philosophy of Motion." *British Journal for the Philosophy of Science* 3 (1953–1954).

Wisdom, J. O. "Berkeley's Criticism of the Infinitesimal." *British Journal for the Philosophy of Science* 3 (1953–1954).

H. B. Acton (1967)

BERKELEY, GEORGE [ADDENDUM]

George Berkeley believed that there are only minds and ideas. The existence of minds (or spirits or souls), Berkeley contended, consists in perceiving whereas the existence of ideas (including sensations) consists in being perceived. Minds, which are the only substances, are active, and ideas are passive. The existence of physical objects consists in their being perceived. This is so because such objects consist of their qualities, and qualities are sensations. Thus Berkeley endorsed the idealist view that the physical world is kept in existence by being perceived. It depends upon the mind and cannot exist apart from perception. Consequently there is no need to presuppose material substance. Indeed, the very concept of material substance is incoherent. God is the source of our sensations. Hence we are in intimate contact with God, and we ought therefore always to be assured of God's existence and to be thankful to God.

The foregoing claims are central to Berkeley's thought. However, questions remain about the meaning and implications of some of these claims and about other aspects of his philosophy.

IDEAS AND OBJECTS

Berkeley sometimes espouses the view that physical objects are just collections or families of sensations that are produced by God in the minds of finite perceivers. But he explains the continued existence of objects that are not currently perceived by us by appealing to God's perceptions and to God's volitions. In addition he says that the ideas we perceive exist apart from the minds of finite perceivers at all times at which they exist. But if physical objects can exist qua divine ideas or volitions, or if they have any sort of existence independent of our sense perception, then such objects are not just collections of sensations in our minds.

Further, God perceives a great deal more than we perceive. For example, God presumably perceives all perceivable objects. Perhaps God perceives all such objects from all angles at once and perceives the interiors of physical objects whose surfaces alone we can see. Moreover, whatever form God's perception may take, it is not limited to the few senses that are our lot. Hence, if objects consist of our ideas along with God's ideas, our ideas are in danger of being second-class counterparts of God's. Our sensations seem to be relatively insignificant constituents of the familiar objects of our experience. It would not follow that the real objects are solely in God's mind. What would follow is that each object is largely in God's mind.

Nor would it follow that our perception of objects is indirect or lacking in immediacy. If objects consist, or even partly consist, of ideas of sense, we can perceive them immediately and directly by perceiving our ideas ofsense that are among their constituents. We perceive physical objects byperceiving them in part.

THE EXISTENCE OF GOD

Berkeley thought that we can know that God exists because our sensations both come to us from an external source and display a coherence, beauty, scale, and variety that bespeak a wise and benevolent source. He also thought that because some physical objects continue to exist while unperceived by us, there must be some other mind that perceives them while we do not perceive them. And Berkeley also presents this line of thought as the basis of a case for God's existence. Further, he thought that either the ideas we perceive or their archetypes exist independent of our perception in some other mind that exhibits them to us. Hence there must be such a mind.

Does Berkeley intend to offer three distinct arguments for God's existence (one that appeals to the source of our ideas, a second that appeals to the continued existence of unperceived objects, and a third that appeals to the independent existence of our ideas or their archetypes) or are these best understood as three strands in a single argument? However he may have conceived of the connections among these lines of thought, a case can be made for regarding the appeal to continuity as subsidiary to the appeal to the independent existence of our ideas or their archetypes. For if, at all times at which they exist, the objects we perceive by sense exist in another mind, by whom they are exhibited to us, then the fact that they exist when we do not perceive them seems fairly incidental. That is, their existence at times when we are not perceiving them is just a function of the fact that they have an independent existence, an existence that they have both while we perceive them and at times at which we do not perceive them but during which they exist.

Yet another argument for God's existence derives from Berkeley's thought that visual sensations are a language—for example, they tell us what other sensations we may receive, and our sensations are often combined in complex patterns. The use of a language requires a mind.

MINDS AND BODIES

How did Berkeley conceive of the relationship between the mind and the body? A human body, like any other physical object, is—at least is in part—a set of sensations. If the sensations that constitute, or partly constitute, physical objects are bestowed on finite minds by God, then when, say, I perceive your arm moving, one set of ideas produced in me by God is followed by another such

set. Yet Berkeley says that we move our own limbs and that on this issue he differs from Malebranche. But how can he account for our moving our limbs or for our being able to move anything else by moving our limbs, or in any other way? Motion is always motion of some sensible body: it is inseparably united with other sensible qualities. There seems to be little room in Berkeley's theory for an account of motion without sensations. And if he is unable to account for our being able to move our limbs, on what basis does he think that one finite mind may reasonably conclude that there are other such minds?

Perhaps the claim that we are able to move our limbs is to be reduced to the view that certain volitions or nonsensory ideas that we produce serve as the occasion for God to grant us certain sensations. Or perhaps this claim is to be reduced to the view that certain sensations (such as those that constitute, or partially constitute, states of affairs that we wish to obtain) can be thought of as being produced by us, without any suggestion that this is indeed the case.

On these readings Berkeley would be "speaking with the vulgar and thinking with the learned" on the various occasions on which he says that we are able to move our limbs. However, he gives no indication that this is so. His treatment of this issue is quite different from that of physical causation. In the latter case, unlike the former, he is willing to say that fire heats and that all manner of causal connections obtain in the world even though, strictly speaking, he believes that this is not so.

One alternative reading is that we are able to produce some sensations. If God provides us with sensations on a great and wonderful scale, can we do so on a small scale? If the coherence, regularity, and so forth, of nature as a whole is good reason to conclude that God is its source, then perhaps the presence of discrete portions of the whole that manifest their own coherence and regularity is good reason to conclude that finite beings with limited powers are the sources of some of the sensations we receive.

If, in order to make a difference to the sensations you receive, I have to make a change in a mind-independent object, the suggestion that I should directly affect the sensations you receive without changing the world, including my body, seems absurd. If, on the other hand, as Berkeley avers, your sensations (and the sensations of all perceivers) constitute (or partly constitute) the physical world, to say that I can directly affect your sensations is just to say that I can make (or contribute to making) a change in the physical world.

IDEAS AND THE PERCEPTION OF IDEAS

How did Berkeley conceive of the relationship between ideas and their perception? Are there two things, an object and an act, that stand in a certain relationship to each other? Are there, at any rate, an object and a process in the mind to be related? For Berkeley says that in sense perception the mind is passive, which incidentally is a view that needs to be reconciled with his idea of the mind as an active, indivisible entity. Berkeley says that the existence of an idea is identical with its being perceived. His model for the relation between an idea and its perception is the relation between a pain and its perception. That relation is one of numerical identity. If an idea is identical with its being perceived, and if the perception of an idea is a private event in the mental life of an individual, it follows that an idea is something private to the mind in which it occurs.

At the same time it is natural to think of the qualities of objects, such as the redness of an apple, as something public that different people can perceive. Berkeley would want to preserve this commonsense belief. Yet if qualities are ideas, and an idea is identical with its being perceived, how can different perceivers perceive the same quality? Perhaps Berkeley should say that different people may perceive numerically the same quality even though they may not perceive numerically the same idea, thereby abandoning his identification of ideas and qualities.

ABSTRACTION

Berkeley devotes most of the Introduction of *A Treatise concerning the Principles of Human Knowledge*, Part 1, to a refutation of the Lockean belief in abstract ideas. Berkeley believed himself to have shown that abstract ideas are impossible. For any abstract idea would contain at least one inconsistency. Consider the abstract idea of man. This is supposed to contain only what is common to all men and to leave out what is distinctive of each. Yet, being the idea of a man, it must have some determinate human features. For example, it must be of a man with a particular size and shape. So an abstract idea of man must both lack and have such features. Again, since it must contain only what is common to all motion, the abstract idea of motion can't be of fast or slow, straight or curved motion. Yet being an idea of motion it must be of motion that is either fast or slow, either straight or curved. Therefore there can be no such idea.

Berkeley denies the possibility of a certain sort of precision or mental separation that allegedly gives rise to abstract ideas. He considers it to be impossible to separate mentally from our perception of an object that has color, extension, and motion an idea that consists of, say, extension alone or motion alone. Motion cannot exist except in something moving and we cannot separate mentally what can not exist separately. Moreover, he thought that, having noticed that particular motions have something in common, namely their motion, it is impossible for us to separate mentally what they have in common, thereby forming, once again, an idea that consists of motion alone.

In addition to being both incoherent and the alleged product of a process that actually is nonexistent, abstract ideas are quite unnecessary. General terms have meaning without signifying any such idea. For example, *triangle* has meaning in virtue of signifying indifferently a vast number of ideas of particular triangles.

ABSTRACTION AND IMMATERIALISM

Berkeley apparently understood his case against abstraction to be central to his case for thinking that physical objects cannot exist apart from perception. This is suggested by the fact that he devoted the introduction of what is probably his most important work to opposing abstract ideas. Indeed he says that the belief in abstraction has led to numerous errors and difficulties in nearly every area of inquiry, including the error of distinguishing the existence of sensible things from their being perceived. But it is not immediately obvious how he conceived of the connections between exposing the bogus character of abstract ideas and arguing that sensible objects can not exist unperceived.

One strand in his thinking may be this: It is impossible to believe to exist apart things that are incapable of existing apart. Physical objects are incapable of existing apart from perception. Hence it is impossible to believe them to do so. Or perhaps the point is that we cannot conceive of, or have an idea of, *a* and *b* as existing apart if *a* and *b* are incapable of existing apart; and since there cannot be existence apart from perception, we are unable to conceive of, or have an idea of, existence without perception.

On neither of these very similar readings does the case against abstraction contribute to the argument against mind-independent existence. Instead it has to be shown independently that there cannot be existence apart from perception. At most the case against abstraction illuminates the sort of error that is involved in believing that there are unperceived objects. Or at least it is a diagnosis of the sort of error involved in thinking that one is believing in mind-independent existence, because we are told that it is impossible to so believe. But that believing in mind-independent existence actually involves this error is something that has to be established independently. Indeed, if the idea of unperceived existence is contradictory, as Berkeley insists, then even if there were abstract ideas, we would still be incapable of conceiving of existence apart from perception, just as we would still be incapable of conceiving of married bachelors or round squares or any other manifestly contradictory concepts.

Perhaps the focus should instead be on the idea of a material substratum and on an argument along the following lines. The idea, or rather alleged idea, of a material substratum involves the idea of being in general. The idea of being in general would be an abstract idea. And because there are no abstract ideas, there is no idea of being in general. Hence the very idea of a material substratum is unthinkable.

BERKELEY'S PHILOSOPHY OF LANGUAGE

We have already mentioned the central aspect of how general terms get their meaning: They signify a range of particular ideas. Berkeley makes some additional comments that bear on this topic, but the connections between the various themes he pursues are not always clear.

One question concerns the relationship between, on the one hand, thinking that *triangle* may be used to signify indifferently any and every idea of a triangle and, on the other hand, having in mind when one talks of triangles the idea of a particular triangle that stands proxy for other triangles, the latter being another theme that Berkeley mentions. Berkeley says that ideas, like terms, become general while remaining particular by fulfilling a general function. The latter of the two themes just mentioned is a matter of a general term getting its meaning by signifying a general idea. But the former seems rather different.

Another question concerns the role of selective attention. Berkeley says that we can consider a triangle solely as a triangle, ignoring all of its other features. It is not clear exactly what this involves. For example, if I selectively attend to the color of the red apple before me, do I concentrate on its redness while also being aware of its other properties, or perhaps while merely being aware that it has other properties? Whatever exactly selective attention may amount to, it—or something like it—is presupposed by the idea of one particular standing proxy for others that resemble it. For there will be some crucial respect in which those other things resemble it, and the idea that stands proxy for those other things will emphasize or single out in some way that crucial aspect.

Berkeley's account of what is involved in meaningful use of language has additional aspects. Words, whether they are particular or general, are sometimes used without the ideas they signify being brought to mind. Once the meaning of a term has been fixed by habitual association with one or more ideas, we often use it meaningfully without bringing those ideas to mind. Thus we can talk meaningfully about triangles without having any idea of a triangle in mind. We also become habituated to the association between certain terms or expressions and the arousal of passions such as fear, love, hatred, or admiration. Originally this process of arousal required an intervening stage at which ideas would render the relevant use of language meaningful, with the ideas in turn giving rise to various passions. But when the path is well trodden and the connections have become familiar, the mediating stage is omitted. This point about arousing passions exemplifies an important theme for Berkeley, namely that language has a number of uses. It can be used to communicate ideas to others. It can also be used to influence others—for example, by causing them to feel a certain way or by leading them to behave in a certain way.

So in virtue of the prior establishment of a word-idea connection, language can come to be used meaningfully without our having the relevant ideas before our minds. This assumes that, at least initially, a word is rendered meaningful by signifying one or more ideas. Berkeley may have held that there are also uses of language that are meaningful in the complete absence of all word-idea connections. At the very least the connection with ideas is further weakened. He seems to have thought this to be so in theology, in science, and indeed in some everyday parlance.

There are scriptural passages that are largely beyond our grasp but that we must nevertheless accept on faith. And Christians ought to be believe in, value, and pursue eternal happiness in heaven even though they lack any determinate ideas of the pleasures of heaven. Theological terms such as *grace* and *original sin* derive much of their significance from their influence on our passions and conduct, perhaps eliciting in us hope or gratitude or charity and in turn the actions that bespeak these attitudes.

Likewise, scientific terms such as force and gravity are convenient theoretical fictions that can help us to make accurate predictions and hence have practical value even though we lack a distinctive idea in each case. And there are many everyday terms (*myself, will, memory, love,* and *hate*, for example) that we understand perfectly well but that do not suggest any distinct ideas to us. Also we talk meaningfully of minds even though these, being active, are not such that there could be an idea of them.

It is not clear in some of these cases whether Berkeley thought that we have no idea rather than no distinct and precise idea. If the latter were the case we might still have a vague and imprecise idea. Indeed, sometimes he seems to aim to show only that we have no relevant *abstract* idea.

See also Idealism; Ideas; Locke, John; Malebranche, Nicolas; Mind-Body Problem; Perception; Philosophy of Language; Sensa; Volition.

Bibliography

IDEAS AND OBJECTS

Foster, John. "Berkeley on the Physical World." In *Essays on Berkeley: A Tercentennial Celebration*, edited by John Foster and Howard Robinson. Oxford: Clarendon, 1985.

McKim, Robert. "Berkeley on Perceiving the Same Thing." In *Minds, Ideas, and Objects: Essays on the Theory of Representation in Modern Philosophy*, edited by Phillip D. Cummins and Guenter Zoeller. Atascadero, CA: Ridgeview, 1992.

THE EXISTENCE OF GOD

Ayers, M. R. "Divine Ideas and Berkeley's Proofs of God's Existence." In *Essays on the Philosophy of George Berkeley*, edited by Ernest Sosa. Dordrecht: D. Reidel, 1987.

Kline, A. David. "Berkeley's Divine Language Argument" In *Essays on the Philosophy of George Berkeley*, edited by Ernest Sosa. Dordrecht: D. Reidel, 1987.

MINDS AND BODIES

Taylor, C. C. W. "Action and Inaction in Berkeley." In *Essays on Berkeley: A Tercentennial Celebration*, edited by John Foster and Howard Robinson. Oxford: Clarendon, 1985.

Tipton, Ian. *Berkeley*. London: Methuen, 1974, 302 ff.

IDEAS AND THE PERCEPTION OF IDEAS

McCracken, Charles J. "Berkeley on the Relation of Ideas to the Mind." In *Minds, Ideas, and Objects: Essays on the Theory of Representation in Modern Philosophy*, edited by Phillip D. Cummins and Guenter Zoeller. Atascadero, CA: Ridgeview, 1992.

ABSTRACTION

Atherton, Margaret. "Berkeley's Anti-Abstractionism." In *Essays on the Philosophy of George Berkeley*, edited by Ernest Sosa. Dordrecht: D. Reidel, 1987.

Winkler, Kenneth. *Berkeley: An Interpretation* Oxford: Clarendon, 1989, Ch. 2.

ABSTRACTION AND IMMATERIALISM

Brandt Bolton, Martha. "Berkeley's Objection to Abstract Ideas and Unconceived Objects." In *Essays on the Philosophy of George Berkeley*, edited by Ernest Sosa. Dordrecht: D. Reidel, 1987.

Pappas, George S. "Abstract Ideas and the esse is percipi thesis." In *George Berkeley: Essays and Replies*, edited by David Berman. Dublin: Irish Academic Press, 1986.

PHILOSOPHY OF LANGUAGE

Pitcher, George. *Berkeley*. London; Boston: Routledge & Kegan Paul, 1977, pp. 78–90.

Warnock, G. J. *Berkeley* London: Penguin, 1953. Chapter 4.

OTHER WORKS

Atherton, Margaret. *Berkeley's Revolution in Vision*. Ithaca: Cornell University Press, 1990.

Berman, David. *George Berkeley: Idealism and the Man*. Oxford: Clarendon, 1994.

Dancy, Jonathan. *Berkeley: An Introduction*. Oxford: Basil Blackwell, 1987.

Grayling, A. C. *Berkeley: The Central Arguments*. La Salle, IL: Open Court, 1986.

Jesseph, Douglas. *Berkeley's Philosophy of Mathematics*. Chicago: University of Chicago Press, 1993.

Muehlmann, Robert. *Berkeley's Ontology*. Indianapolis: Hackett, 1992.

Muehlmann, Robert. *Berkeley's Metaphysics: Structural, Critical and Interpretive Essays*. University Park: Pennsylvania State University Press, 1995.

Turbayne, Colin M., ed. *A Treatise concerning the Principles of HumanKnowledge: George Berkeley with Critical Essays*. Indianapolis: Bobbs-Merrill, 1970.

Robert McKim (1996, 2005)

BERLIN, ISAIAH
(1909–1997)

Latvian born, English educated, and a cosmopolitan in the world of ideas, Isaiah Berlin was both a prolific public intellectual and a distinguished academic, concluding his career as Oxford University's Chichele Professor of Social and Political Theory. After publishing some early essays in analytical philosophy, Berlin soon turned to more historical studies. While favoring the essay form, he published an important book-length study of Marx (1939) that was critical of Marx's historical determinism in ways that anticipated his later critiques of theories of historical inevitability. During the Second World War, Berlin worked for the British government in the United States, after which he returned to teaching at Oxford University, with occasional sojourns in London and the United States. His practical political involvements lent a spirit of engagement to his writings, whatever the subject.

Berlin championed political theory at a time when it was distinctly unfashionable in professional philosophy. To dismiss political reflection because of its rough-hewn character, he maintained, is to misconstrue the nature of the subject and leave oneself at the mercy of uncriticized political prejudices. But Berlin's major importance as a political thinker rests in the vision of liberalism that he articulated in the post–World War II decades. In his seminal essay "Two Concepts of Liberty," he developed an influential distinction between negative freedom (to act without interference) and positive freedom (to be one's own master), and expressed special concern about the totalitarian dangers lurking in the latter.

While Berlin clearly privileged negative freedom over positive freedom, his distinction is more nuanced than is often acknowledged. He made no fetish of liberty, and reminded readers that communities in conditions of dire poverty cannot give much thought to formal freedoms. What he most bemoaned in positive freedom was the ideal of self mastery projected onto classes, peoples, or the whole of mankind. His championing the liberal commitment to rights, as demarcating individual spheres of autonomy, has had a deep impact on all subsequent liberal theory, including John Rawls's political liberalism and Richard Rorty's pragmatic liberalism. He wrote, "There are frontiers, not artificially drawn, within which men should be inviolable," frontiers so secure that their observance "enters into the very conception of what it means to be a human being" (1969, 165).

Berlin also argued for identifying liberalism with an ethic of pluralism, for which ultimate good as postulated by determinist views of historical development, does not exist. "To assume that all values can be graded on one scale ... seems to me to falsify our knowledge that men are free agents" (1969, p. 171). Liberal society is one in which values are always in conflict, and such conflicts cannot be resolved by metaphysical fiat but must instead be addressed by the arduous patient work of practical negotiation. Thus conceived, the liberal outlook is intrinsically opposed to the totalitarian impulse in all its forms. It rests on the acceptance of moral uncertainty as our epistemological fate, and tolerance as our political imperative.

Of his many contributions to the history of ideas, Berlin's studies of Giambattista Vico, Johann Gottfried Herder, Johann Georg Hamann, and Romanticism were of special importance to philosophy. His discussions of Romantic "expressivism" were instrumental to the English-language revival of studies in the philosophy of Georg Wilhelm Friedrich Hegel, starting in the 1970s. They helped shape the understanding of the Romantic background that Hegel both appropriated and criticized. Berlin's writings on Romanticism intertwined with his long interest in modern nationalism, which he regarded more sympathetically than many other post–World War

II liberals. Berlin also wrote widely on Russian novelists and thinking, translating Ivan Turgenev (1818–1883) and other classic writers into English.

Berlin wrote for popular as well as academic audiences and received much acclaim throughout his long life. He was awarded the Jerusalem Prize, the Erasmus Prize, the Angelli Prize, and the Lippincott Prize, among others. He was knighted in 1957 and received the Order of Merit in 1971. He died in Oxford, U.K., at the age of 88, having once remarked, "I don't mind death. ... but I find dying a nuisance" (*New York Times*, November 7, 1997).

See also Determinism in History; Hamann, Johann Georg; Hegel, Georg Wilhelm Friedrich; Herder, Johann Gottfried; Ideas; Liberalism; Marx, Karl; Pluralism; Rawls, John; Rights; Romanticism; Rorty, Richard; Vico, Giambattista.

Bibliography

WORKS BY BERLIN

Marx: His Life and Environment. London: T. Butterworth, 1939.
Four Essays on Liberty. London: Oxford University Press, 1969.
The Hedgehog and the Fox: An Essay on Tolstoy's View of History. New York: Simon and Schuster, 1970.
Russian Thinkers. New York: Viking Press, 1978.
Against the Current. New York: Viking Press, 1980.
The Crooked Timber of Humanity. London: John Murray, 1990.
The Proper Study of Mankind. London: Chatto and Windus, 1997.
The Roots of Romanticism. Princeton, NJ: Princeton University Press, 1999.
Vico and Herder: Two Studies in the History of Ideas. Princeton, NJ: Princeton University Press, 2000.

WORKS ON BERLIN

Gray, John. *Isaiah Berlin*. Princeton, NJ: Princeton University Press, 1996.
Ignatieff, Michael. *Isaiah Berlin: A Life*. New York: Metropolitan Books, 1998.
Ryan, Alan, ed. *The Idea of Freedom: Essays in Honour of Isaiah Berlin*. Oxford, U.K.: Oxford University Press, 1979.

Cheyney Ryan (2005)

BERNARD, CLAUDE
(1813–1878)

Claude Bernard, French physiologist, was born in Saint-Julien (Rhône). He received his M.D. in 1843 and became a professor at the Sorbonne in 1852, taking the new chair in physiology in 1854. The following year he was appointed professor of experimental medicine at the Collège de France and in 1868 became professor of general physiology at the Museum of Natural History in Paris. He was elected a member of the Academy of Sciences in 1854 and of the Académie Française in 1868; in 1869 he became a senator.

Bernard early gave up any idea of clinical practice in favor of experimental physiology. He made a number of important contributions in this field (on the chemistry of digestion, the production of sugar in animals, the nervous system, poisons, and anesthetics), many of which were awarded scientific prizes. After a period of ill health, while not ceasing laboratory work, he turned to more general and programmatic questions of scientific method and published, in particular, his famous *Introduction à l'étude de la médecine expérimentale* (Paris, 1865; translated by H. C. Green as *An Introduction to the Study of Experimental Medicine*, New York, 1927).

In the *Introduction*, Bernard based his conclusions as much as possible on his own scientific experiences, since he believed that proper procedure cannot be legislated for scientists from without but must be developed from the nature and needs of science itself. He distinguished the mature experimental method from empiricism, which is merely its first step. Bernard identified crude empiricism, which observes and experiments at random, not only with his own teacher, François Magendie, but also, mistakenly, with Francis Bacon, regarding himself rather in the tradition of Descartes, despite the fact that he insisted on constant laboratory experimentation and criticism and had a low opinion of the application of mathematics to biological problems. His hostility to the use of statistical methods in biology derived from the one article of faith he regarded as necessary to any scientist: belief in the operation of a determinism without exceptions, such that a set of conditions (a cause) will invariably produce the same phenomenon (an effect). This determinism he called an absolute principle, in contrast to theories and hypotheses, which are always provisional and subject to revision or abandonment because of the discovery of incompatible facts. But theories and hypotheses, the products of human reason, are on the other hand the necessary guides for rational experimentation.

Bernard saw no difference in principle between scientific method as applied to living beings and to inorganic matter, although results were more difficult to achieve in physiology because of the far greater complexity of the phenomena. He believed in a fundamental unity among all forms of life, the higher forms being distinguished by their greater independence of the external environment and a correspondingly greater dependence on their "internal environment" (above all, the blood). He also held that the phenomena taking place in living beings are ultimately reducible to physicochemical processes. Efforts to enlist Bernard in the cause of vitalism are wide of the mark. Equally mistaken is the attempt to affix a positivist label. He strenuously advocated scientific doubt and self-criticism, and was opposed to all philosophical systems, including the positivist, while not denying the usefulness of the work of philosophers in their own sphere. Bernard's critical method was closer to twentieth-century methods based on the principle of falsifiability, used by Karl Popper and others, than to those of many of his contemporaries.

See also Bacon, Francis; Descartes, René; Empiricism; Popper, Karl Raimund; Positivism; Scientific Method; Vitalism.

Bibliography

Bernard's general works also include *La science expérimentale* (Paris: J. B. Baillière, 1878) and *Principes de médecine expérimentale* (Paris: Presses universitaires de France, 1947).

For works on Bernard, consult J. M. D. Olmsted and E. H. Olmsted, *Claude Bernard and the Experimental Method in Medicine* (New York: H. Schuman, 1952); Robert Clarke, *Claude Bernard et la médecine expérimentale* (Paris, 1961); and Paul Foulquié, *Claude Bernard* (Paris: Éditions de l'école, 1954).

W. M. Simon (1967)

BERNARD OF CHARTRES
(died c. 1124–1130)

Bernard of Chartres, a Breton and elder brother of Theodoric of Chartres, was a master at Chartres at periods during the second and third decades of the twelfth century and became chancellor at least by 1119. He is no longer to be confused with Bernard Silvestris of Tours. To Bernard of Chartres belongs much of the credit for bringing the intellectual life of Chartres to its apogee, and his pupils included Gilbert of Poitiers, William of Conches, and Richard the Bishop. No complete writing by Bernard has survived, although he is known to have written philosophical verse and to have expounded Porphyry's *Isagoge*. Nevertheless, John of Salisbury learned of the character of Bernard's literary and philosophical teaching through William and Richard, and in John's writings we find a sympathetic portrait of Bernard as a real lover of learning and a leading grammarian, the most abounding spring of letters and the most finished Platonist of those days. John eulogizes the "old Chartrain" as an excellent teacher of Latin language and literature, whose aim was to produce well-lettered and well-spoken students by means of an unhurried, cultured, humanist education, firmly based upon a groundwork of grammar. Bernard's love of the ancients was expressed in a famous simile of the moderns as dwarfs who can see farther than the ancients because they are perched upon the shoulders of giants.

Bernard was a philosopher with a taste for speculative grammar and for Platonism. He held opinions that the more Aristotelian John did not entirely share. We know only one of Bernard's grammatical speculations, namely, that the relationship of a quality-word (e.g., whiteness) to its derivatives (e.g., to whiten, white) resembles the relationship of the Platonic Ideas to the things in which they participate. As a Platonist, Bernard held that true reality is found in the eternal Ideas, which are the models of all perishable things. Particular sensible things, being unstable and ephemeral, cannot properly be said to be. Bernard's contribution to the disputes of his time over the nature of universals was to equate universals with Ideas; hence universals, in his view, were real beings. Guided by Boethius, Bernard and his school also labored to reconcile the differences between Plato and Aristotle.

Under the influence of the ninth-century thinker John Scotus Erigena, Bernard also sought to reconcile the teaching of Plato's *Timaeus* with that of the Bible by reexamining the relationships between the three categories of true being: God, matter, and the Ideas. He adhered to patristic teaching in accepting the view that matter was created by God. He also held that the eternal Ideas are in some way posterior to God. The Ideas are assimilated with God's mind or the divine providence; but although they are immanent in the mind of God, they are also a created effect. They are eternal, but not, in Bernard's view, coeternal with God. Only the three persons of the Trinity are both coequal and coeternal.

On the other hand, Bernard also attempted to show that the Ideas were not directly mixed with sensible objects. He distinguished between Ideas that subsist in the mind of God and the copies of these Ideas that are concreated with matter. To the latter Ideas he gave, under Boethian influence, the name of native forms (*formae nativae*).

Essentially, Bernard sought to affirm the transcendence of God over the Ideas and to avoid pantheism by the theory of native forms, which allowed no confusion of God with creation. Insofar as we can judge his motives, Bernard was adapting the Platonism that he knew to

Christianity, just as he modified this Platonism in the light of Aristotelianism. His teaching was promoted by other Chartrains, especially by Gilbert of Poitiers.

See also Aristotelianism; Aristotle; Bernard of Tours; Boethius, Anicius Manlius Severinus; Chartres, School of; Erigena, John Scotus; Gilbert of Poitiers; Ideas; John of Salisbury; Plato; Platonism and the Platonic Tradition; Theodoric of Chartres; William of Conches.

Bibliography

PRIMARY SOURCES

John of Salisbury. *Metalogicon.* Edited by C. Webb. Oxford, 1929. I, v, xi, xxiv; II, xvii; III, ii; IV, xxv. Translated under the same title by D. D. McGarry, Berkeley: University of California Press, 1955.

John of Salisbury. *Policraticus.* Edited by C. Webb. Oxford, 1909. VII, 13.

Otto of Freising. *Gesta Friderici.* Edited by G. Waitz. 3rd ed. Hanover, 1912. I, xlvii; lii.

SECONDARY SOURCES

Clerval, A. *Les Écoles de Chartres au moyen âge.* Paris: A. Picard, 1895. Pp. 158–163.

Gilson, Étienne. *History of Christian Philosophy in the Middle Ages.* New York: Random House, 1951. Pp. 619–620.

Gilson, Étienne. "Le Platonisme de Bernard de Chartres." *Revue néo-scolastique de philosophie* 25 (1923): 5–19.

Gregory, T. *Anima Mundi. La filosofia di Guglielmo di Conches.* Florence: G. C. Sansoni, 1955. Pp. 76–79.

Parent, J. *La Doctrine de la création dans l'école de Chartres.* Paris: J. Vrin, 1938. Pp. 45–48, 84–85.

Poole, R. L. *Illustrations of the History of Medieval Thought,* 2nd ed. London: Society for Promoting Christian Knowledge, 1920. Pp. 100–107.

David Luscombe (1967)

BERNARD OF CLAIRVAUX, ST.
(1090–1153)

St. Bernard of Clairvaux, the monastic reformer and theologian, was born of a noble family at Fontaine, France, near Dijon. He became a Cistercian at Cîteaux in 1112 and founding abbot of Clairvaux in 1115. Throughout his life he was a tireless founder, reformer, preacher, and writer who, as friend or opponent, made contact with almost every notable in western Europe. His influence as a simple abbot on high ecclesiastical affairs is without parallel in the history of the Western church, and his spiritual teaching has been a living force to the present day. Though he was a professed enemy of secular culture (he "raided" the schools of Paris on a celebrated occasion in 1140) and was lacking in scholastic training, Bernard was a literary genius of the first order, and no mean theologian. His treatises *De Diligendo Deo* (On the love of God; 1126) and *De Gratia et Libero Arbitrio* (On grace and free will; 1127), though based on St. Augustine, also show the influence of Origen, Gregory of Nyssa, and the Pseudo-Dionysius, as do also some of his longer letters. In the history of thought he is remembered for his controversies with Peter Abelard and Gilbert de La Porrée. He distrusted contemporary dialectic, partly because of a justified apprehension of the dangers in the formulas of both his opponents, but most of all because his approach to theological truth was by way of meditation and intuitive penetration, whereas theirs was by way of logical expression and analysis. His influence restrained theological improvisation and methodical virtuosity, and left the field clear for the great scholastics of the next century.

His most valuable contribution to thought was in the realm of mystical theology. He was a medieval pioneer of the analysis and explanation of mystical experience. His teaching, ostensibly based on St. Augustine, was in many respects new, and was followed by that of the Victorines and others, though later rivaled and eclipsed by the Dionysian-Thomist school of Rhineland Dominicans. Bernard's mysticism was one of love. Man, by recognizing his own nothingness, turns to God with humility and love, and man's will, with divine help, can reach perfect accord with the divine will. The divine Word can then teach him (infused knowledge) and move him (infused love) in an intimate union sometimes momentarily experienced as ecstasy. Thus Bernard differs, in expression at least, from the intellectual mysticism of Neoplatonism reflected in both Augustine and Dionysius. In his *Sermons on the Canticle,* Bernard was also a pioneer in the clear description of his own mystical experience, which in many ways resembled that of St. Teresa of Ávila.

See also Abelard, Peter; Augustine, St.; Gregory of Nyssa; Love; Medieval Philosophy; Mysticism, History of; Neoplatonism; Origen; Pseudo-Dionysius; Teresa of Ávila, St.

Bibliography

Works by Bernard are to be found in *Patrologiae Cursus Completus, Series Latina.* Edited by J. P. Migne, Vols. 182–185 (Paris, 1844–1864).

For biography, see E. Vacandard, *Vie de saint Bernard,* 2 vols. (Paris, 1895), often reprinted. Also useful are articles on Bernard by E. Vacandard in *Dictionnaire de théologie catholique* (Paris, 1910) and by J. Canivez in *Dictionnaire d'histoire et de géographie écclesiastique* (Paris, 1935).

For Bernard's contribution to mystical theology, see Étienne Gilson, *Théologie mystique de saint Bernard* (Paris: J. Vrin, 1934), translated by A. H. C. Downes as *The Mystical Theology of Saint Bernard* (London: Sheed and Ward, 1940), C. Butler, *Western Mysticism: The Teaching of SS. Augustine, Gregory and Bernard on Contemplation and the Contemplative Life,* 2nd ed. (London: Constable, 1951). Dom J. Leclercq is preparing a critical edition of St. Bernard's works.

David Knowles (1967)

BERNARD OF TOURS
(d. after 1167)

Bernard of Tours was a humanist who taught at Tours and was known as Bernardus Silvestris. He is uncertainly identified with Bernard, chancellor of Chartres circa 1156 and bishop of Quimper from 1159 to 1167. Very little else is known of his life except that he taught the art of writing and wrote an *Ars Versificatoria,* which has not been found. He also wrote a moralizing allegorical commentary on part of Vergil's *Aeneid* that displays leanings toward a naturalistic ethic. He translated into Latin an Arabic treatise on geomancy, the *Experimentarius,* and, inspired by Quintilian, composed the *Mathematicus,* a poem about an astrological prediction.

His most famous work, dedicated to Theodoric of Chartres in about 1150, is the *De Mundi Universitate,* an allegory in prose and verse on the origin of the world and man. The theme is Nature's appeal to Nous (mind), the providence of God, to end the chaos of *hylē* (matter), the primordial matter of the megacosmos. In Nous exist the exemplary forms of creation. Nous separates four elements out of *hylē* and informs the world with a soul ("entelechy," the Aristotelian ἐντελέχια). Nous next sends Nature to find Urania and Physis. Urania, queen of the stars, and Physis, in the lower world, use the remains of the four elements, in collaboration with Nature, to form man (the microcosmos). The sources of Bernard's inspiration were the Latin version of Plato's *Timaeus* with the commentary of Chalcidius, and also Ovid, Claudian, Macrobius, Boethius, and Augustine. There is, in addition, a marked biblical and a Hermetic influence.

The humanism of this work is more profane than Christian; the world is that of the *Timaeus* rather than that of Genesis. But the paganism, even unorthodoxy, of Bernard should not be exaggerated. Thus, Bernard was silent about a divine creation of matter, but his concern was to depict the organization of matter into the universe. There is no consistent dualism of God and matter;

hylē is preexistent to the ordering work of Nous, but the problem of its eternity is not broached. One should not conclude from the emanation of a world soul from Nous that Bernard was a pantheist. We cannot, in fact, extract from this often nebulous work a unified view of Bernard's thought. Bernard's purpose was imaginative rather than strictly philosophical. Nonetheless, Bernard reflects the speculative interests of his time, particularly those of the Chartrains; he reflects their desire for a more rational explanation of the universe and of biblical cosmology with the aid of Greek ideas.

See also Augustine, St.; Boethius, Anicius Manlius Severinus; Chartres, School of; Hermeticism; Humanism; Medieval Philosophy; Nous; Plato; Theodoric of Chartres.

Bibliography

WORKS BY BERNARD OF TOURS

Commentum Super Sex Libros Eneidos. Edited by G. Riedel. Greifswald, 1924.

De Mundi Universitate. Edited by Carl Sigmund Barach and Johann Wrobel. Innsbruck: Wagner'schen Universitäts-Buchhandlung, 1876.

"Experimentarius." Edited by M. B. Savorelli. *Rivista critica di storia di filosofia* 14 (1959): 283–342.

Mathematicus. Edited by B. Hauréau. Paris, 1895.

WORKS ON BERNARD OF TOURS

Curtius, E. R. *European Literature and the Latin Middle Ages.* London, 1953. Pp. 108–113. Translated from the German edition of 1948 by W. R. Trask.

Faral, E. "Le manuscrit 511 du Hunterian Museum." *Studi medioevali,* n.s., 9 (1936): 69–88.

Gilson, E. "La cosmogonie de Bernardus Silvestris." *Archives d'histoire doctrinale et littéraire du moyen âge* 3 (1928): 5–24.

Gregory, T. *Anima Mundi. La filosofia di Guglielmo di Conches,* Florence: G. C. Sansoni, 1955. Pp. 64–67.

Silverstein, T. "The Fabulous Cosmogony of Bernardus Silvestris." *Modern Philology* 46 (1948/1949): 92–116.

Thorndike, Lynn. *A History of Magic and Experimental Science.* New York: Macmillan, 1929. Vol. II, pp. 99–123.

David Luscombe (1967)

BERTALANFFY, LUDWIG VON
(1901–1972)

Ludwig von Bertalanffy, one of the chief exponents of the "organismic" standpoint in theoretical biology, was born in Austria in 1901 and educated at the universities of Innsbruck and Vienna. Until 1948 he taught at the University of Vienna, first as an instructor and later as professor of biology in the medical school. He emigrated to Canada in 1949 and held academic posts at the University of Ottawa and the University of Alberta, where he was appointed professor of theoretical biology in 1962. Von Bertalanffy's writings are voluminous, amounting to more than two hundred items. These include scientific papers in such fields as animal growth, cell physiology, experimental embryology, and cancer research. His two best-known books on philosophical biology are *Kritische Theorie der Formbildung* (Berlin, 1928; translated by J. H. Woodger as *Modern Theories of Development,* London, 1933) and *Das biologische Weltbild* (Bern, 1949; translated by the author as *Problems of Life,* New York, 1960). Since 1950 he had been active in promoting an interdisciplinary field called "General System Theory." The society associated with this enterprise has issued several yearbooks.

Von Bertalanffy contended that neither classical mechanism nor vitalism provides an adequate model for understanding organic phenomena. Vitalism is intellectually sterile because it appeals to a mysterious élan vital, entelechy, or psychoid to account for the properties of living things. Mechanism, von Bertalanffy declared, involves three mistaken conceptions: (1) the "analytical and summative" conception, according to which the goal of biological inquiry is the analysis of organisms into fundamental units and the explaining of organic properties by a simple adding up of these units; (2) the "machine-theoretical" conception, which regards the basis of vital order as a set of preestablished structures or "mechanisms" of a physicochemical kind; and (3) the "reaction-theoretical" conception, according to which organisms are automata, reacting only when subjected to stimulation and otherwise quiescent. These conceptions, von Bertalanffy argued, cannot yield a well-grounded explanatory theory of life.

In place of them he proposed an organismic model on which such a theory can be built. The model represents organisms as wholes or systems that have unique system properties and conform to irreducible system laws. Organic structures result from a continuous flow of processes combining to produce patterns of immense intricacy. Far from being passive automata, living things are centers of activity with a high degree of autonomy. Biological systems are stratified. There is a hierarchy of levels of organization from living molecules to multicellular individuals and supraindividual aggregates. The whole of nature is "a tremendous architecture in which subordinate systems are united at successive levels into ever higher and larger systems."

Von Bertalanffy sought to show that this conception illuminates such matters as embryonic development, genetic processes, growth, self-regulation, metabolism, and evolution. Thus, in embryology it is no longer necessary to take sides in the old contest between preformationism and epigenesis, if we adopt the hypothesis that a fertilized ovum is a system whose development is determined by internal system conditions. Similarly, the ostensible purposefulness manifested by this development is an illustration of the unique property of "equifinality," which marks the behavior of organisms as "open" systems. These systems differ in important respects from the closed systems dealt with by physics. The thermodynamic principles that apply to the two cases are by no means the same. Nevertheless, von Bertalanffy believed that "there are general principles holding for all systems, irrespective of their component elements and of the relations or forces between them." These principles, he thought, can be studied through General System Theory, whose function is to bring about the unity of science.

The organismic conception of life is presented by its author as an intellectual breakthrough that "may well be set beside the great revolutions in human thought." Critics have found this claim extravagant in view of the sketchy and programmatic character of von Bertalanffy's presentation. They contend that the organismic conception has no right to be called "revolutionary" until its merits have been shown in detailed and extensive biological analysis. Nevertheless, von Bertalanffy has called attention to issues of major importance for the future of theoretical biology.

See also Organismic Biology; Philosophy of Biology; Vitalism.

Bibliography

ADDITIONAL WORKS BY BERTALANFFY

"An Outline of General System Theory." *British Journal for the Philosophy of Science* 1 (1950): 134–165.

"Problems of General System Theory." *Human Biology* 23 (1951): 302–311.

Bertalanffy, Ludwig von, and A. Rapoport, eds. *General Systems Yearbook.* Published yearly since 1956.

WORKS ON BERTALANFFY

Buck, R. C. "On the Logic of General Behavior Systems Theory." In *Minnesota Studies in the Philosophy of Science,* edited by H. Feigl and M. Scriven. Minneapolis: University of Minnesota Press, 1956. Vol. I, pp. 223–238.

Hempel, Carl G. "General System Theory and the Unity of Science." *Human Biology* 23 (1951): 313–327.

Jonas, Hans. "Comment on General System Theory." *Human Biology* 23 (1951): 328–335.

Medawar, P. B. Review of *Problems of Life. Mind,* 43 (1954): 105–108.

T. A. Goudge (1967)

BIBLIOGRAPHIES OF PHILOSOPHY

See "Philosophy Bibliographies" in Volume 10

BIEL, GABRIEL
(c. 1410–1495)

Gabriel Biel, the Ockhamist philosopher and theologian, was born at Speyer, Germany, and died at Einsiedel (Schönbuch). He studied philosophy and theology at Heidelberg and Erfurt, joined the Brethren of the Common Life, and became a professor of theology (1484) at the newly founded University of Tübingen, where he taught the "modern way," that is, according to the nominalist position of William of Ockham. Biel's "Commentary on the Sentences" (*Epithoma Pariter et Collectorium Circa IV Sententiarum Libros,* Tübingen, 1495) is a skillful summary of Ockham and a collection of the views of other medieval thinkers from Anselm to John Duns Scotus. Widely read in the German universities, Biel exerted a strong influence on Martin Luther (see P. Vignaux, *Luther, Commentateur des Sentences,* Paris, 1935).

As a philosopher, Biel was quite ready to criticize and to offer his own developments of Ockham's nominalism. Basically a theory of knowledge, his thought had some influence in ethics and political philosophy. For Biel formal logic displaced metaphysics because he considered universals to be but names (*nomina*) arbitrarily applied to classes; he considered all existents to be completely individual in character. Essence and existence are not really distinct principles in things but are merely distinguished in thought.

Biel's psychology was, like Ockham's, close to Augustinianism: the powers of the soul are not distinct faculties; intellect is the soul understanding, will is the soul desiring and loving. Biel was a psychological voluntarist; for him the most important psychic activity of man was willing. He taught that all man's conscious activities entailed some use of will. Man was viewed as a volitional rather than rational animal.

In practical philosophy, he considered moral goodness to consist in volitional conformity to God's will. The obligatory force of law has no basis in the nature of created things but is solely due to the fact that God has willed a certain action to be right. This is moral and legal voluntarism. "God could command that a man deceive another through a lie," wrote Biel, "and he would not sin" (*Epithoma*, II, 38, q. 1, G).

See also Anselm, St.; Augustinianism; Duns Scotus, John; Essence and Existence; Luther, Martin; Ockhamism; Psychology; Voluntarism; William of Ockham.

Bibliography

Bonke, E. *Doctrina Nominalistica de Fundamento Ordinis Moralis apud Guillelmum de Ockham et Gabriel Biel.* Rome, 1944. Pp. 57–83.

Davitt, T. *The Nature of Law.* St. Louis: B. Herder, 1951. Pp. 55–68.

Feckes, C. *Die Rechtfertigungslehre des Gabriel Biel und ihre Stellung innerhalb der nominalistischen Schule.* Münster, 1925.

Vernon J. Bourke (1967)

BILFINGER, GEORG BERNHARD
(1693–1750)

Georg Bernhard Bilfinger was the German philosopher who coined the expression Leibniz-Wolffian philosophy for the view he expounded. Bilfinger, whose family name was also spelled Buelffinger, was born in Kannstadt, Württemberg. He studied theology at Tübingen, and mathematics and philosophy at Halle under Christian Wolff. He was appointed extraordinary professor of philosophy at Tübingen in 1721, but after Wolff's expulsion from Halle in 1723, Bilfinger was accused of atheism and deprived of his positions. On Wolff's recommendation he was appointed professor of philosophy and academician in St. Petersburg. His growing reputation as a natural philosopher caused Duke Eberhard Ludwig of Württemberg to recall him to Tübingen as professor of theology. In 1735 the new Duke Karl Alexander of Württemberg called Bilfinger to his capital, Stuttgart, as a member of the privy council. Bilfinger became president of the Con-

sistorium, a council for ecclesiastical and educational affairs, and in this capacity permitted Pietism to be taught in Württemberg.

Although Bilfinger's doctrines are quite close to Wolff's, he showed a certain originality, discussing Wolff's doctrines critically and frequently accepting them only with reservations. In an early work he held, against John Locke, the view that there are innate ideas in the human mind, identifying them with axioms. In psychology he did not accept the distinction, introduced by Wolff, between empirical and rational psychology, but proceeded in a more traditional manner. In his later writings, Bilfinger referred less frequently to Wolff.

The most independent part of Bilfinger's system was his theory of possibility, expounded in his main work, *Dilucidationes Philosophicae de Deo, Anima Humana, Mundo et Generabilis Rerum Affectionibus* (Tübingen, 1725). He asserted that the notion of possibility is more fundamental than the principles of identity and contradiction. Possible things are not absolute beings in an independent realm of ideas, but they depend for their existence on God's understanding (not on his will). It is a part of God's essence to think possible things as they are, but they are, only insofar as God thinks them.

See also Leibniz, Gottfried Wilhelm; Wolff, Christian.

Bibliography

ADDITIONAL WORKS BY BILFINGER

De Harmonia Animi et Corporis Humani Maxime Praestabilita ex Mente Illustris Leibnitii, Commentario Hypothetica. Frankfurt and Leipzig, 1723.

"De Viribus Corpori Moto Insitis et Illarum Mensura." *Commentarii Academiae Petropolitanae*, Vol. 1 (1728). A famous essay on the measurement of forces.

Praecepta Logica, edited by C. F. Vellnagel. Jena, Germany, 1739.

Varia in Fasciculos Collecta. 3 vols. Stuttgart, 1743.

WORKS ON BILFINGER

Kapff, P. "G. B. Bilfinger als Philosoph." *Württembergischen Vierteljahrshefte für Landesgeschichte*, n.f. (1905).

Liebing, H. *Zwischen Orthodoxie und Aufklärung. Das philosophische und theologische Denken G. B. Bilfingers.* Tübingen: Mohr, 1961.

Wahl, Richard. "Professor Bilfingers Monadologie und prästabilirte Harmonie in ihrem Verhältniss zu Leibnitz und Wolff." *Zeitschrift für Philosophie und philosophische Kritik* 85 (1884): 66–92 and 202–231.

Giorgio Tonelli (1967)

BINET, ALFRED
(1857–1911)

Alfred Binet, the French psychologist, was born at Nice. The son of a doctor and an artist, Binet studied at the Sorbonne, qualifying in 1878 in both law and science. He embarked immediately on a doctorate under Edouard Balbiani, embryologist and professor at the Collège de France, whose daughter Binet married in 1884. In the same year he submitted an article on the fusion of images to *La revue philosophique*. The editor, Théodule Ribot, persuaded him in due course to devote his energies to psychology. Through Charles Féré, Binet came to work with Jean Charcot at the Salpêtrière hospital.

Binet is known mainly for his work, with his younger colleague Théodore Simon, in devising tests for assessing children's intelligence. The Binet-Simon scale, published in 1905 and revised in 1908 and 1911, constituted the first systematic, effective, and widely accepted attempt to devise sets of simple verbal and nonverbal tasks, performance on which could be quantified with a fair degree of objectivity, and on which norms for different age groups in the school population were carefully worked out. The principal American versions were produced, revised, and restandardized by L. M. Terman and his colleagues at Stanford University in 1916 and 1937. It was, however, Binet and Simon's careful studies that showed the necessity of valid data to ascertain the intellectual skills and concepts normally to be expected of children at each age before any assessment of a child's retardation can fairly be made. The revised tests are still employed for research and clinical purposes, although increasing use is now being made of the Wechsler tests.

Binet himself was well aware that cultural factors have a bearing on test performance and that interestingly different patterns of results on various subtests might be shown by children achieving similar overall scores. Hence, the conception of an intelligence quotient (IQ) as

$$\frac{\text{mental age}}{\text{chronological age}} \times 100$$

popularly linked with Binet's name, in fact runs counter to his stress on studying and appreciating individual differences.

The practical utility of the Binet-Simon scale has overshadowed to a large extent the rich background of inquiries from which the tests were developed. A man of wide theoretical and practical interests, Binet wrote in lucid and lively French a dozen books and some 250 articles, many of which appeared in *La revue philosophique* and in *L'année psychologique*, of which he was the editor. Seven of his books and a few articles appeared in English, which Binet wrote and spoke fluently. The *Psychologie des grands calculateurs et joueurs d'échec* (Paris, 1894), and *L'étude expérimentale de l'intelligence* (Paris, 1903), the latter reporting studies of his own children, remain neglected classics of French psychology. Both works provided evidence of individual differences in imagery and evidence that images could be less important in thinking than the associationists supposed. Furthermore, these studies, especially the former, showed that the subsequent line of thought was affected by the nature and presentation of the problem a thinker was asked to solve, by the mental set induced by that problem, and by his attitudes in other respects. The studies of his young daughters illustrate Binet's patient, systematic mode of inquiry into children's thought processes, and they enhance understanding of the developmental approach to psychology to which Jean Piaget was the heir.

Chronological scrutiny of his writing shows Binet's work on intelligence to have been the practical outcome of prolonged theoretical and experimental study of the nature of thought processes—subnormal, normal, outstanding, and abnormal. These investigations were carried out in hospitals, notably the Salpêtrière, in schools, and in the psychological laboratory at the Sorbonne, of which Binet became director. Influenced by Hippolyte Taine in France and by the British empirical tradition (including J. S. Mill, Alexander Bain, and Francis Galton), Binet had started as a narrowly orthodox associationist. His evidence for conceptual processes not involving visual imagery anticipated some of the Würzburg experimental findings on "imageless thought." This evidence and that found by Binet and his collaborators for central factors, for unconscious processes, and for attitudes influencing a train of thought led Binet slowly to change his standpoint. In doing so, he moved from treating thinking by analogy with visual inspection to emphasizing the affinities of thought and action and to stressing the importance of developmental studies. Such an approach has proved more acceptable in the 1960s than when Binet died, unfortunately leaving his own research and theory incomplete.

See also Bain, Alexander; Empiricism; Mill, John Stuart; Piaget, Jean; Psychology; Scientific Method; Taine, Hippolyte-Adolphe.

Bibliography

WORKS BY BINET

"Mental Imagery." *Fortnightly Review* 52 (1892): 95–104.

"The Mechanism of Thought." *Fortnightly Review* 55 (1894): 785–799. Except for this and the preceding reference, all of Binet's works are listed in the Varon monograph (see below).

"L'intelligence des imbéciles." *L'année psychologique* 15 (1909): 1–147. Written with Théodore Simon. This and the following article are of salient importance for understanding Binet's later treatment of thinking.

"Qu'est ce qu'une émotion? Qu'est ce qu'un acte intellectuel?" *L'année psychologique* 17 (1911): 1–47.

WORKS ON BINET

Bertrand, F. L. *Alfred Binet et son oeuvre*. Paris, 1930.

Groot, A. D. de. *Thought and Choice in Chess*. The Hague: Mouton, 1965.

Reeves, Joan Wynn. *Thinking about Thinking*. London, 1965. Ch. 7.

Varon, Edith J. *The Development of Alfred Binet's Psychology*. Psychological Monographs, Vol. 46 (No. 207). Princeton, NJ, and Albany, NY: Psychological Review, 1935. Includes a full bibliography of Binet's works except for the first two cited above.

Wolf, Theta A. "An Individual Who Made a Difference." *American Psychologist* 16 (5) (1961): 245–248.

Joan Wynn Reeves (1967)

BINSWANGER, LUDWIG
(1881–1966)

Ludwig Binswanger, the Swiss psychiatrist whose school of *Daseinsanalyse*, or existential analysis, is the most extensive attempt to relate the philosophies of Edmund Husserl and Martin Heidegger to the field of psychiatry, was born in Kreuzlingen, Thurgau, Switzerland, into a family line of eminent physicians and psychiatrists. After attending the universities of Lausanne, Heidelberg, and Zürich, he received his medical degree from Zürich in 1907. In 1910 he succeeded his father, Dr. Robert Binswanger, as chief medical director of the Sanitorium Bellevue, an institution founded by his grandfather at Kreuzlingen. He relinquished his directorship in 1956.

Daseinsanalyse is an original amalgam of phenomenology, Heideggerian existentialism, and psychoanalysis, the goal of which is to counter the tendency of scientific psychology to view man's being as solely that of a natural object. However, the school does not seek spheres of human existence that argue against the explanatory power of psychoanalysis. Binswanger complained of the overreductionism of natural science as applied to humankind, but in doing so he was not questioning science's ability to explain; he was, rather, urging that that which is being explained be kept in mind in its full phenomenal reality. Binswanger is a phenomenologist in that he demands a presuppositionless discipline in which the investigator can apprehend the world of the patient as it is experienced by the patient. To this end he limits his analysis to that which is actually present (or immanent) in the patient's consciousness. He seeks the essential structure of these phenomena without relying on reductive theory, his aim being to allow the phenomena to speak for themselves. As an existentialist he views the essential structures that the phenomena reveal on their own terms as "universals with power." That is, he sees them as the matrix within which the individual's world and self—his essence—are determined. He seeks in each patient a general context of meaning within which the patient exists. He calls this meaning-context the transcendental category of that patient's world design.

This notion of a general existential meaning-context must be understood as that which expresses with equal validity all aspects of the patient's life and world. The criterion of a complete expression is based on Heidegger's ontology of man and includes his orientation in space, his mode of being in time, his relation to his bodily life and to his fellow man, his way of thinking, and his fears and anxieties. For example, a universal such as continuity is equally understandable and expressive in reference to time (continuity of events versus the sudden and unexpected), space (contiguity), relationships with others (for example, oedipal ties or bonds), and the individual's own world ("inner" continuity, continuity of feelings or of affections). But such explanatory categories as aggression or libidinal energy emphasize one aspect of man's being as most real and are therefore rooted in a one-sided ontology of human existence.

What psychoanalysis takes as conditioning factors—such as instinct or childhood sensations—are regarded by Binswanger as already being representations of a basic world design. It is not that Binswanger wants to push back the causal chain beyond instincts or childhood sensations, but rather that the causal chain itself, as described in scientific depth analysis, must be viewed as a whole, without any a priori privileged reference point in terms of which all else is to be explained. Explanation in terms of a privileged reference point presupposes a theory, and a theory assumes a world outlook—in this case the world outlook of natural science. Binswanger does not, therefore, use the past to account for the present. He sees the past of a patient as existing in the present in that the entire world design—within which a particular event in the past "conditioned" a present neurosis—*is* the patient. Therefore, the present, or the conscious, or the manifest content of dreams and the manifest verbal expressions, all point to a unity or category(ies) that is the basis of the patient's world. In other words, because the self cannot experience a "pure" event outside of a meaning-context, even if the self be that of a child, it is that source meaning-context which Binswanger seeks to apprehend.

Binswanger does not offer his approach as a substitute for psychoanalysis; insofar as the goal of psychiatry is intervention in the patient's life—manipulation of or change in it—only a scientific approach, such as psychoanalysis or clinical psychiatry, is adequate. For Binswanger, phenomenology and reductive explanation are two complementary aspects of the *Geisteswissenschaften*, including psychology. Phenomenology can provide us with an essential description of the data, and phenomenological existentialism can provide a full dynamic understanding of the individual's life on his own terms. But if we are willing and find it necessary to transform and control phenomena, natural science is at present our major tool. However, whereas in the natural sciences we confer meanings, in the *Geisteswissenschaften* the phenomena under investigation are themselves meanings to a self, and it becomes necessary phenomenologically to receive these meanings on their own terms.

See also Heidegger, Martin; Husserl, Edmund.

Bibliography

PRINCIPAL WORKS BY BINSWANGER

Wandlungen in der Auffassung und Deutung des Traumes von der Griechen bis zur Gegenwart (Changes in understanding and interpretation of the dream from the Greeks to the present). Berlin: Springer, 1928.

Über Ideenflucht (On the flight of ideas). Zürich, 1933.

Einführung in die Probleme der allgemeinen Psychologie (Introduction to the problems of general psychology). Berlin, 1942.

Grundformen und Erkenntnis menschlichen Daseins (Basic forms and cognition of human existence). Zürich: Niehans, 1942; 2d rev. ed., Zürich, 1953.

Ausgewählte Vorträge und Aufsätze (Selected lectures and essays). 2 vols. Bern: Francke, 1947–1955.

Drei Formen Missglückten Daseins (Three forms of unsuccessful dasein). Tübingen: Niemeyer, 1956.

Schizophrenie. Pfullingen, 1957. Contains Binswanger's well-known clinical studies of Ilse, Ellen West, Jürg Zünd, Lola Voss, and Suzanne Urban.

Melancholie und Manie. Pfullingen: Neske, 1960.

Traum und Existenz (with an introduction by M. Foucault). Bern: Gachnang & Springer Verlag, 1992.

Ausgewählte Werke in vier Bänden. Heidelberg: R. Asanger Verlag, 2004.

ENGLISH TRANSLATIONS

May, Rollo, Ernest Angel, and Henri F. Ellenberger, eds. *Existence*. New York: Basic, 1958. This and the following work contain some of Binswanger's works in translation.

Needleman, Jacob. *Being-in-the-World*. New York: Basic, 1963.

WORKS ON BINSWANGER

Keen, E. *A Primer in Phenomenological Psychology*. New York: Holt, Reinhart & Winston, 1975.

Needleman, Jacob. *Being-in-the-World*. New York: Basic, 1963. A philosophical critique of Sigmund Freud and Binswanger, taking account of the background of Immanuel Kant and Heidegger.

Sonnemann, Ulrich. *Existence and Therapy*. New York: Grune and Stratton, 1954. Brilliant and unreadable.

Speigelberg, H. *Phenomenology in Psychology and Psychiatry*. Evanston: Northwestern University Press, 1992.

Van Den Berg, J. H. *The Phenomenological Approach to Psychiatry*. Springfield, IL: Thomas, 1955. Simple and clear.

Jacob Needleman (1967)
Bibliography updated by Thomas Nenon (2005)

BIOETHICS

Bioethics is an interdisciplinary field of study dealing with practical ethical issues roughly at the intersection of morality, medicine, and the life sciences. Within philosophy, bioethics is one of several different areas of applied ethics, a domain within general normative ethics. The term "bioethics" was coined in 1970, but the development of bioethics as a discipline may be dated to the late 1960s or early 1970s, depending on which historical markers are used.

The scope of bioethics as a discipline is not entirely fixed, it is important to note. At least three competing visions are available. On the most restricted view, bioethics simply reduces to biomedical ethics, which encompasses ethical issues relating to the practice of medicine broadly understood and the pursuit of medical research. Even on this restricted view of bioethics, the scope extends to the ethics of our use of nonhuman animals in biomedical research, for example. On the second understanding, bioethics encompasses, in addition to biomedical ethics, ethical issues related to the life sciences and technologies. On this understanding, also included is consideration of environmental issues, for example, issues such as genetic modification of plants or the use of cloning technologies to revive extinct species of animals or plants. According to the widest view, bioethics includes the biological aspects of environmental ethics, issues related to nonhuman-animal use, and biomedical ethics. On this understanding, the ethical dimensions of vegetarianism and how global warming affects biotic communities are also bioethical issues. Interestingly, this widest understanding of the term is closest to the meaning given by biochemist Van Rensselaer Potter, who originally coined the term. However, it also offers the least common understanding of the term within the discipline. The second sense probably offers the most common understanding within the discipline, while most people working in the field of bioethics work on issues in biomedical ethics, the first sense. This entry will explore issues related to all three senses of bioethics.

LOCATING BIOETHICS WITHIN PHILOSOPHICAL ETHICS

Ethics is the philosophical study of morality. It is to be distinguished from the empirical study of moral norms and practices. This second area of investigation is sometimes also called simply "ethics," but to distinguish it from philosophical ethics, it may more felicitously be called descriptive ethics. As a philosophical discipline, ethics may be further divided into metaethics, general normative ethics, and various areas of applied ethics. Metaethics is concerned primarily with reflections on ethics itself. Some issues within metaethics include the meaning of moral terms like "ought," "right," and "virtue"; the metaphysical status of moral norms; the proper grounds for justifying moral claims; and the nature of moral knowledge.

Normative ethics, by contrast is concerned in general with positive guidance to living morally. Normative ethics concerns questions about how to act, what kind of character to develop, and what values to live by. Within normative ethics generally, various ethical theories have been developed as guides in answering these questions. Normative moral theories lay out the structure for particular fundamental sources of normative moral value. Examples include utilitarianism (a type of consequence-based ethics), deontology (a duty-based ethics), and virtue ethics (a character-based ethics). However, normative ethics may also proceed without any particular theoretical structure and may engage directly with the various issues at stake in practical moral living.

Applied ethics is normative ethics at the level of engagement with various specific topics in practical moral life. As such, applied ethics may proceed by following some more general normative theory, by following some methodology or theory particular to the area of study, or without following any specific theoretical or methodological underpinning. The term "*applied* ethics" implies that general normative theories are simply interpreted in light of specific moral problems to generate practical moral answers; however, this is seldom actually the case. A better term might be "practical ethics."

Bioethics, then, is a type of practical ethics. It is on the same philosophical level as business ethics, environmental ethics generally (unless understood as a subset of bioethics), cyberethics, and a host of other specific fields dealing with particular areas of complex lived morality. The division into areas of practical ethics may not be particularly neat. As already discussed, bioethics may be understood as distinct from, or inclusive of, environmental ethics. Other areas of practical ethics, such as professional ethics, overlap with various other fields (for example, business ethics, legal ethics, and medical ethics).

HISTORY AND SOCIAL CONTEXT

Many of the specific issues addressed in bioethics have historical roots. The issue of physician-patient confidentiality was addressed in the Hippocratic oath. The bioethics of how we treat animals has roots in the work of such historical figures as Porphyry (232–309) in his treatise *On Abstinence from Animal Food* (discussed in Sorabji 1993). More recently, the requirement that human subjects voluntarily consent to medical research was spelled out in the Nuremberg Code (International Military Tribunal 1949), following the "doctors trial" for atrocities committed as part of the holocaust.

Despite these and multiple other sources of historical precedence, the discipline of bioethics coalesced only in the very late 1960s to early 1970s. The social forces behind this formation into a specific disciplinary field include a growing social awareness of issues of medical paternalism and some unethical practices in medical experimentation; the consumer, feminist, and civil rights movements; the increased institutionalization of health care and with it a growing concern for issues of allocation; advances in biotechnology and biomedicine; growing awareness of issues of sustainable economic growth and environmental impact; and rising awareness of the conditions of animals in newly evolving factory farms.

Since its inception, bioethics has taken deep root in academia, professional education, public policy, the law, and public deliberation. Bioethics courses are offered to undergraduates as part of humanities and science curricula and to medical and other health-professional students. A variety of centers for bioethics research have been established, and numerous government commissions dealing with bioethical issues have been formed and have had varying impact on public policy. A U.S. commission of high impact was the National Commission for the Protection of Human Subjects of Biomedical and

Behavioral Research, the source for the *Belmont Report* (1979), spelling out the ethical principles guiding experimentation on human subjects. Those working in bioethics have extensively scrutinized legal cases, such as the 1989 U.S. Supreme Court case regarding Nancy Beth Cruzan, whose parents sought to withdraw life support after Ms. Cruzan fell into a persistent vegetative state. The law has also been influenced by bioethical analysis, for example by the inclusion of those working in bioethics as expert witnesses in trials. Finally, as biomedical ethical issues and advances in the life sciences have received more attention by the mass media, public arenas for debate over these issues has also grown.

THE DISCIPLINE

Bioethics as a discipline crosses over other disciplinary boundaries, both within and outside of philosophy. Here the focus is on the philosophical aspects of the discipline. Nonetheless, some general remarks about the discipline as a whole are necessary in order to view the philosophical area of bioethics in context. This is important also because there is controversy within the field of bioethics, as has been seen, about what counts as bioethics, but also about the extent to which it is a unified discipline, and about exactly which general methodologies and areas of expertise are relevant.

It is uncontroversial that moral philosophy plays a central role within bioethics, and also that other areas of philosophical study are implicated by the topics relevant to bioethics. For example, political philosophy is central to issues of distributive justice in access to health care and to public-health measures affecting human health, as well as in adjudicating questions of public, institutional, and governmental decision-making about controversial bioethical issues such as use of stem cells and cloning of human somatic cells. In addition to addressing general issues of the relationship between the law and practical morality, philosophy of law is also relevant to determining how case law and legislative law relate to ethical decision making. Finally, although the connection is less widely recognized, philosophy of science is crucial to the investigation of some central conceptual issues in bioethics, for example, the nature of the scientific facts that often play a central role in practical ethical decisions and the meaning of the concept of human health often invoked in such ethical distinctions as that between using genetic technologies for enhancements versus using them therapeutically. Even the question of what counts as a biological kind or species is central in determining whether legitimate ethical distinctions can be made

between human beings and other nonhuman animals for how we treat them, and in dealing with ethical issues related to the transhuman movement for improved humans.

While philosophy is the right place to look for expertise in clarifying the issues involved in answering moral questions and for theoretical structures intended in part to answer those questions, it is not clear that philosophy is the right place to look for positive answers to specific practical moral questions. We might then delineate two kinds of ethics expert: academic and directive. The broader issue is whether expertise in academic bioethics provides any expertise in directive ethics. There is no clear consensus within the discipline on this issue.

Outside of philosophy, disciplines relevant to bioethics include the social sciences, law, and medicine, as well as those within what has been termed the medical humanities. With such a wide range of participants, it is not surprising that there are disagreements over the scope of bioethics, the relevance of different fields to the discipline, the training necessary to qualify as a member of the discipline, the kind of expertise that such members have, and the legitimacy of the very term "discipline" in describing this diverse range of fields, methodologies, and topics of interest. What is certain, however, is that enough overlapping consensus exists to create a discipline identifiable to its members and to the general public.

METHODS IN BIOETHICS

How do moral philosophers and others working in bioethics go about dealing with the complex moral issues at the heart of many bioethical issues? The answer to this question is quite complex. Three basic approaches are available. The first approach applies established general normative theories to particular issues in bioethics. The second embraces one or several methodologies specifically developed for bioethical issues. The third method either avoids or rejects outright specific methodologies outside of basic philosophical and critical-thinking skills. These methods will be discussed in turn.

GENERAL NORMATIVE THEORIES

Perhaps surprisingly, the least common approach to bioethics is the approach of applied ethics, that is, the application of general normative theories to specific moral problems in bioethics. Nevertheless, there is some substantial work in bioethics that proceeds roughly along these lines. Examples include Peter Singer's utilitarian approach to the ethics of how we treat animals (2002), Tom Regan's deontological approach to that same issue

(1983), and Rosalind Hursthouse's essay on abortion from a virtue-ethical perspective (1991). Of work that follows this general model, the most commonly appealed-to theories are the three just mentioned: utilitarianism, deontology, and virtue ethics. These theories are actually umbrella categories under which fall a number of specific theories.

Even the work in bioethics that falls into this first category is not really simply straightforward application of normative theories to particular bioethical problems. Rather, some particular vision of a general theoretical structure is rendered, and the bioethical problem is interpreted in light of that theoretical structure. This might involve, among other things, modifying the theory to fit the issue and arguing for some particular interpretation of the practical implications of the theory over others.

Some theories lend themselves more readily than others to application to specific moral problems. However, even the application of these theories requires extensive interpretation. For example, according to hedonistic act utilitarianism, the right action is the one that maximizes pleasure (or minimizes pain) for all those affected. In principle, then, the answer to the question "Which action is right?" is a matter of calculation of hedonistic utility output. Yet we still need to know which outcomes count as pleasures and pains, of what strength and type, and for what range of beings. (Does the calculation include sentient nonhuman animals? Future persons?)

Despite the term "applied ethics," then, normative moral theories are at a level of abstraction not conducive to straightforward application to particular moral problems. Making matters more difficult, normative theories conflict with one another, sometimes in ways that imply different practical recommendations. In such cases one has to decide which theoretical approach is the best before tackling the moral problem at hand. Moral theories are still helpful in making practical moral decisions, since they provide essential analysis of basic moral values, coherent frameworks for understanding moral issues, and general justificatory strategies for particular approaches to morality. Yet it is not even clear that a proper goal of normative moral theory is to generate specific moral directives. On a virtue-ethical view, for example, moral guidance in specific practical contexts flows from a virtuous character, not from abstract theoretical principles.

METHODS SPECIFIC TO BIOETHICS

In part because of the problems associated with the application of general normative theories of morality to prob-

lems in bioethics, a number of methodologies specific to bioethics have been developed since the inception of the discipline. It is important to note at the outset that these methods have been developed largely for biomedical ethics rather than for bioethics in the broader sense embraced in this entry. Among these methods, the most well known is the principles-based approach developed largely by Tom Beauchamp and James Childress in successive editions of *Principles of Biomedical Ethics* (2001) but also inspired by the more general approach to ethics favored by earlier philosophical figures such as W. D. Ross (1930). The principles approach relies on a variety of prima facie norms, the most prominent of which are four principles: beneficence, nonmaleficence, justice, and respect for autonomy. The source of these principles is supposedly common morality. No single principle is a trump principle, since each may be overridden by considerations deriving from the others in specific contexts. How the principles are spelled out in specific situations and which one(s) hold sway in case of conflict is determined by a process of specification and balancing.

Another influential approach is the casuistic approach revitalized from ancient and medieval roots by Albert Johnson and Stephen Toulmin in *The Abuse of Casuistry: A History of Moral Reasoning* (1988). For casuists, general ethical principles stem only from the analysis of paradigm cases. These paradigm cases offer clear moral outcomes and create a set of initial presumptions about how to resolve other cases. These presumptions hold sway unless we come across exceptional circumstances. When such exceptional circumstances arise, we must go through a process of analogical reasoning, which includes identifying the ethical values at issue, the alternate courses of action, the morally relevant ways in which cases of the sort at issue can differ (the casuistic factors), and the relevant paradigm case(s) (Strong 2000).

A third approach, narrative bioethics, is a relative newcomer but has close ties to antitheoretic trends in normative moral philosophy generally. Insofar as narrative bioethics is not a single approach, it is hard to specify exactly what it amounts to methodologically. However, a couple of themes can be drawn out to give a flavor for this type of approach. First is the ethical significance of the various narrative voices involved in ethically complex situations. In opposition to casuistry, which relies on some single paradigm case and thereby a neutral voice, narrative bioethics focuses on telling the story from the viewpoints of all the participants. In this way we can see that the neutral voice in the paradigm cases (the physicians, lawyers, and/or judges) may in fact be the most powerful voice. Further, narrative bioethics focuses not on principles as a way of solving ethical quandaries, but rather on the different ways of telling the story and the comparative choices supported by these ways. Thus the stories themselves have normative impact.

While none of these approaches offers a general normative theory for bioethics, the principles-based approach comes closest, whereas the narrative and casuist approaches offer methods to deal with bioethical issues but eschew theory. A final approach offers a general theory of practical morality with particular focus on bioethics issues. This is the theory offered by Bernard Gert, Charles Culver, and K. Danner Clouser in *Bioethics: A Return to Fundamentals* (1997). On their view, morality is a public system whose purpose is to minimize the amount of evil suffered by those protected by it. In opposition to the principles-based view of bioethics, this view has more specific moral rules as fundamental touchstones.

Despite the availability of these various methods, much work in bioethics actually proceeds without a specified method or by a piecemeal approach. This kind of no-method method can be criticized for its ad hoc nature and for its lack of any specific justificatory framework. Even without specific appeal to some particular methodological framework, bioethical analysis at its best avails itself of a number of useful tools in approaching areas of ethical conflict, including gathering and sifting through morally relevant factual information; providing conceptual clarity on the moral concepts at issue; engaging in casuistic reasoning (without necessarily embracing casuistry as a methodology); and offering analysis, critique, construction, and revision of moral arguments.

THEMES IN BIOETHICS

As already discussed, bioethics as understood here includes at least biomedical ethics and ethical issues related to advances in the life sciences and life-science technologies, but may be broadened to include environmental ethics and ethics related to our treatment of nonhuman animals generally. The specific topics in bioethics are numerous and change in character and focus over time as the field advances. Each anthology of bioethics lists and groups the topics somewhat differently. A small sampling of these topics from four well-known anthologies includes justice in access to health care, mother-fetus relations, research involving human subjects, reproductive technologies, eugenics, genetics, health-care policy, physician-assisted suicide and euthanasia, medical confidentiality, the physician-patient relationship, informed consent, research involving animal subjects, definitions of death, human cloning and stem-cell research, and organ donation. Most of these topics include subtopics and may also be subsumed under more general headings. Developing any additional list of specific topics in bioethics here would be unhelpful; more useful is to focus on a few general philosophical issues at the overlap of a variety of topics in bioethics.

MORAL STATUS

A key issue in several central topics in bioethics is the moral status of various animal species, the environment, and human beings in various life stages. The issue of moral status is in part a question about how far the moral community extends, that is, what the scope is of those entities considered to have direct moral value. An answer to the scope question does not resolve the issue entirely, since there may be different degrees of moral status. For example, we might think that both pigs and adult human beings have some direct moral status, but still that the adult human being has more moral status.

One way in which the issue of moral status has been addressed is through the concept of personhood. This concept introduces a normative category for those kinds of beings with full moral status, namely persons. In the philosophical debate, persons are not simply all and only human beings. Rather, it is normally assumed that some capacities are required to attain the status of a person. These capacities must be judged by their moral relevance, and not simply along species lines. Some morally relevant capacities might be the ability to feel pain and to have pleasure, the ability to engage emotionally with others, the ability to act intentionally, and the ability to make rational choices. If the level of capacity required for personhood is drawn at the more basic abilities, then the category of persons will include many animals and most human beings. Alternately, if the line is drawn at the higher abilities, for example at the capacity for autonomous actions and choices, then many human beings and most animals will not be persons.

Within biomedical ethics, the issue of moral status is of crucial significance for topics such as abortion and for issues at the beginning and end of life, for example, issues of the moral acceptability of discontinuing life support for severely impaired newborns or humans in persistent vegetative states. For those wanting to extend full moral status to fetuses and severely impaired postnatal human beings, a problem arises of how to ground that moral status. If it is grounded in the particular capacities or potential capacities of those beings, then a relevant question is whether the same moral status should also be extended to some nonhuman animals.

A central question in environmental ethics is the moral status of the environment in general and of particular ecosystems or other entities. Do two-hundred-year-old oak trees have sufficient moral status that it is wrong to cut them down independently of their effect on human beings or animals with moral status? Establishing the source of such moral status has been a source of difficulty within the field. Yet reflecting on questions like this may bring to light some of the limitations of a capacities-based approach to moral status. Moreover, even if oak trees, nonhuman animals, and human fetuses do not have individual moral status, it does not follow that we can ignore their well-being. Indeed, through such ethical resources as virtuous habits of character, the relationships of persons to other beings, and the effects of our treatment of such beings on other persons, we can establish a wide range of protections for nonpersons.

DISTRIBUTIVE JUSTICE

A very different core topic within bioethics focuses on questions of distributive justice, that is, what the proper distribution is of social resources and burdens. Looking more closely at this issue gives a sense of the different types of theoretical resources brought to bear in bioethics and also shows how the discipline has developed. Issues of distributive justice are usually approached not from the perspective of general normative moral theory, although they may be, but from theories in political philosophy. Examples of theories constructed to deal generally with issues of distributive justice are John Rawls's *A Theory of Justice* (1971) and the libertarian theory found in Robert Nozick's *Anarchy, State, and Utopia* (1974). However, as with normative moral theories, these general approaches to the distribution of social resources and burdens are often not well suited to the specific practical issues involved in bioethics.

To deal with issues of distributive justice at a level directly relevant to bioethics, a number of specific views have been developed. Many of these are varieties of egalitarianism, a general view in distributive justice focusing on the moral foundations for an equal distribution of social goods and resources. A major question for egalitarian theories in bioethics is what should be equally distributed: health care, health outcomes, satisfaction with health? Other views of the ethically proper way to allocate health care rely on formal mechanisms, such as cost-effectiveness analysis, which has theoretical roots in utilitarianism. The least common approach to issues of

distributive justice in bioethics is libertarianism, although this view has had some supporters.

The evolution of the particular topics involved in distributive justice in bioethics gives a sense of how the discipline has changed over time. Initially, there was little focus on issues of distributive justice except for the discussion of the just distribution of the burdens of research on human subjects. While the issue of research on human subjects has retained significance, with the growth of patient activism and the perception of promising new interventions the distributive focus shifted from protection from the burdens of research to assurance of equitable access to research protocols. As the ramifications of institutionally centered health care and various health-insurance mechanisms grew, issues of distributive justice in health care became focused on questions of access. Such questions as whether there is a right to health care came to the fore. These questions have remained significant, particularly in the United States, where the number of uninsured persons continues to rise along with the costs of health care.

To complicate matters further, an additional twist has been added into the mix, which is that health inequalities appear to be tied less to health-care access than to relative social and economic status. While providing equitable access to health care may retain moral significance as a matter of distributive justice, providing such access may make a relatively small dent in the problem of health inequality.

OTHER THEMES

In addition to the problem of moral status and topics in distributive justice, a number of other philosophical issues lie at the core of various specific topics in bioethics. While it is impossible to discuss all these topics here, several significant questions should be noted. One set of issues focuses on the science side of bioethics. First, what is the role of scientific facts in moral decision making? In this area, relevant questions might be, "How significant is an understanding of the biological developmental stages of human fetuses to the morality of abortion?" And, "What difference does it make to issues of distributive justice whether some genetic predispositions to disease significantly lower some persons' life expectancies?" Second, how do advances in the life sciences affect ethical issues? In this area the main issue is whether advances in the life sciences actually create the need for new ethical concepts and models or whether they simply create an opportunity to reinterpret established ethical debates. Fields where this question is especially relevant include human-somatic-cell cloning and assisted-reproduction technologies. A general underlying question with regard to these and other issues at the overlap of science and ethics is the moral relevance of naturalness.

Another set of core issues has to do with the development of role ethics as a way of understanding the specific obligations of physicians, other health-care workers, researchers, and scientists to particular populations. Here the main philosophical issue is whether individuals incur some obligations simply by occupying particular social roles or whether all obligations are versions of more general social obligations. The question is not whether physicians, for example, have a specific duty to protect the privacy of some medical information. All agree that this is the case, in addition to agreeing on a number of other specific duties that physicians have to their patients. The question is rather whether this duty is the product simply of occupying a specified social role or whether it is a duty that anyone with the requisite expertise in the particular relationship would also have. If there are obligations that are completely role dependent, then one can expect that some of these may conflict with other moral obligations, thus creating the potential for moral dilemmas. By contrast, if role obligations are contextual renderings of general moral obligations, then no such conflict can be expected.

Bioethics is a relatively young discipline that has already had a dramatic impact on academic curricula, public policy, public awareness of ethical issues, health care practices, and health sciences research. Continued advances in the life and health sciences on the one hand and continued disparities in health and health care on the other hand make it likely that bioethics as a discipline will continue both to grow as a field and to evolve in focus and methodology.

See also Environmental Ethics; Medical Ethics; Science, Research Ethics of.

Bibliography

Beauchamp, Tom L., and James F. Childress. *Principles of Biomedical Ethics*. 5th ed. New York: Oxford University Press, 2001.

Beauchamp, Tom L., and LeRoy Walters. *Contemporary Issues in Bioethics*. 6th ed. Belmont, CA: Wadsworth Press, 2003.

Buchanan, Allen E. "The Right to a Decent Minimum of Health Care." In *Securing Access to Health Care*, Vol. 2, by the President's Commission for the Study of Ethical Problems in Medicine and Biomedical and Behavioral Research. Washington, DC: U.S. Government Printing Office, 1983.

Casarett, David J., Frona Daskal, and John Lantos. "Experts in Ethics? The Authority of the Clinical Ethicist." *Hastings Center Report* 28 (6) (1998): 6–11.

Charon, Rita, and Martha Montello, eds. *Stories Matter: The Role of Narrative in Medical Ethics*. New York: Routledge Press, 2002.

Clarke, Stanley G., and Evan Simpson. *Anti-theory in Ethics and Moral Conservatism*. Albany, NY: SUNY Press, 1989.

Crosthwaite, Jan. "Moral Expertise: A Problem in the Professional Ethics of Professional Ethicists." *Bioethics* 9 (5) (1995): 361–379.

Daniels, Norman. "Equality of What: Welfare, Resources, or Capabilities?" *Philosophy and Phenomenological Research* 50, suppl. (1990): 273–296.

Daniels, Norman. *Just Health Care*. New York: Cambridge University Press, 1985.

DeGrazia, David. *Taking Animals Seriously: Mental Life and Moral Status*. New York: Cambridge University Press, 1996.

Engelhardt, H. Tristram, Jr. *The Foundations of Bioethics*. 2nd ed. New York: Oxford University Press, 1996.

Gert, Bernard, Charles M. Culver, and K. Danner Clouser. *Bioethics: A Return to Fundamentals*. New York: Oxford University Press, 1997.

Gruen, Lori, and Dale Jamieson, eds. *Reflecting on Nature: Readings in Environmental Philosophy*. New York: Oxford University Press, 1994.

Hargrove, Eugene C., ed. *The Animals Rights/Environmental Ethics Debate: The Environmental Perspective*. Albany, NY: SUNY Press, 1992.

Hursthouse, Rosalind. "Virtue Theory and Abortion." *Philosophy and Public Affairs* 20 (3) (1991): 223–246.

International Military Tribunal. "Permissible Military Experiments." In *Trials of War Criminals before the Nuremberg Military Tribunals under Control Council Law No. 10*, 2: 181–184. Washington, DC: U.S. Government Printing Office, 1949.

Johnson, Albert R., and Stephen Toulmin. *The Abuse of Casuistry: A History of Moral Reasoning*. Berkeley: University of California Press, 1988.

Kuhse, Helga, and Peter Singer, eds. *Bioethics: An Anthology*. Oxford, U.K.: Blackwell Publishers, 1999.

Mappes, Thomas A., and David DeGrazia, eds. *Biomedical Ethics*. 5th ed. Boston: McGraw-Hill, 2001.

Nelson, Hilde Lindemann, ed. *Stories and Their Limits: Narrative Approaches to Bioethics*. New York: Routledge Press, 1997.

Nozick, Robert. *Anarchy, State, and Utopia*. New York: Basic Books, 1974.

Potter, Van Rensselaer. "Bioethics: The Science of Survival." *Perspectives in Biology and Medicine* 14 (1970): 127–153.

Rawls, John. *A Theory of Justice*. Cambridge, MA: Harvard University Press, 1971.

Regan, Tom. *The Case for Animal Rights*. Berkeley: University of California Press, 1983.

Rhodes, Rosamond, Margaret P. Battin, and Anita Silvers, eds. *Medicine and Social Justice: Essays on the Distribution of Health Care*. New York: Oxford University Press, 2002.

Ross, William David. *The Right and the Good*. Oxford, U.K.: Oxford University Press, 1930.

Singer, Peter. *Animal Liberation*. New York: Ecco, 2002.

Sorabji, Richard. *Animal Minds and Human Morals: The Origins of the Western Debate*. Ithaca, NY: Cornell University Press, 1993.

Spielman, Bethany J., and Ben A. Rich, eds. *Expert Testimony: Bridging Bioethics and Evidence Law. Law, Medicine, and Ethics* 33 (2) (2005): 194–278.

Steinbock, Bonnie, John D. Arras, and Alex John London, eds. *Ethical Issues in Modern Medicine*. 6th ed. Boston: McGraw-Hill, 2003.

Strong, Carson. "Specified Principlism: What Is It, and Does It Really Resolve Cases Better Than Casuistry?" *Journal of Medicine an Philosophy* 25 (3) (2000): 323–341.

Rebecca L. Walker (2005)

BIOLOGY, PHILOSOPHY OF

See *Philosophy of Biology*

BLACK, MAX

(1909–1988)

The American analytic philosopher Max Black was born in Baku, Russia (now Baky, Azerbaijan). He read mathematics at Cambridge and, after he earned his BA in 1930, received a fellowship for research at Göttingen, Germany, where he wrote *The Nature of Mathematics* (1933). Returning to Britain, he was awarded a doctorate by the University of London for his dissertation *Theories of Logical Positivism* (1939) and held the position of lecturer and tutor in its Institute of Education from 1936 to 1940. After he emigrated to the United States in 1940, he was appointed to the faculty at the University of Illinois. In 1946 he moved to Cornell University, in Ithaca, New York, where, in 1954, he became Susan Linn Sage Professor and later helped found both the Society for the Humanities and the Program on Science, Technology, and Society. He was president of the Eastern Division of the American Philosophical Association; president of the International Institute of Philosophy; Tarner Lecturer at Trinity College (Cambridge), Guggenheim Fellow; Fulbright Fellow; and visiting fellow at Oxford, Cambridge, Princeton, Palo Alto, and Canberra. He also lectured on contemporary American philosophy in Japan (1957) and India (1962). He died in Ithaca in 1988.

Black's early years in Cambridge—where he attended classes of G. E. Moore, Frank Ramsey, Susan Stebbing, and Ludwig Wittgenstein—influenced his later teaching and writings. Along with his analytic orientation of C. D. Broad and Ramsey, Black retained a wide range of scientific and humanistic interests and a careful regard for the commonsensical approach that marked the writings of Moore and Stebbing; but the influence of Wittgenstein was the most profound. Black's first work, *The Nature of Mathematics*, was an exposition of the logicist, formalist, and intuitionist conceptions of mathematics; it paralleled Wittgenstein in declining to embrace any of the three theories or to propose a new one, and his subsequent doctoral study of logical positivism required coming to grips with Wittgenstein's *Tractatus*. His abiding interest in that work culminated in *A Companion to Wittgenstein's* Tractatus (Cambridge and Ithaca, 1964), a work some six times as long as the text it analyzed; it was posthumously reprinted, and admired—even imitated—for its astute and engaging combination of exegesis, explication of sources, and critical comment.

Black's commitment to philosophical analysis involved constructive work on small, well-defined problems with expository and critical discussion; hence the bulk of Black's contributions are essays rather than books. The exceptions are the two noteworthy books already mentioned and a logic text, *Critical Thinking* (1951). Other volumes were published, to be sure, but they are collections of essays rather than treatises. Black published some twenty books (including those edited and/or translated) and more than 200 essays and reviews.

Many of Black's essays take up problems or themes from Wittgenstein's later works, generally concentrating on the issues, especially meaning, rather than on Wittgenstein's texts. Black did not fret about the metaphysical status of meanings, since (as for the later Wittgenstein) explanations of meanings are explanations of how words are used, and it is a mistake to suppose that there are "such things as meanings to be categorized." One aspect of explanations of meaning involves formulating rules for the use of words, and Black (again following Wittgenstein) shows how seemingly necessary propositions often serve as surrogates for rule formulations. Black is aware that a certain vagueness or "looseness" pervades these rules governing ordinary usage, and he explores this dimension in several essays. One of his conclusions is that we normally presuppose that the looseness does not matter. This calling attention to presuppositions of linguistic acts is characteristic of Black. In other essays he calls attention to the contrasting presuppositions of definitions and assertions, and he gives a detailed comparison of presupposition and implication, with special reference to controversies about denoting phrases.

Black's conception of philosophy emphasizes the everyday practicality of linguistic analysis: "philosophical clarification of meaning is … as practical as slum clearance and as empirical as medicine"—hence the title essay of one of his last books: "The Prevalence of Humbug." This all-too-prevalent humbug consists not only in logical fallacies but also in overvaluing speculation, ignoring or minimizing induction, and, at times, misplaced logical rigor. Therefore Black deplores not only broad-brush dismissals of rationality and science but also the excesses of pettifogging rationalism and scientism; he lacks sympathy with Hume's criticism of induction and philosophical complaints about vagueness. Here we see Black's respect for common sense, which he learned in part from Moore. The vagueness of ordinary language works partly because normal usage has roots in truth: "To say that a word is correctly used in accordance with normal usage, in certain circumstances, is to say that a certain sentence containing the word is, in those circumstances, true." This remark works in defense of the much-criticized paradigm-case argument, because the circumstances envisaged will be a paradigm case for that word. In other essays, Black augments references to paradigm cases by discussing models and metaphors, both of which also occur in ordinary language but exemplify different sorts of justified vagueness. One later essay, "Reasoning with Loose Concepts," (1963) argues that we can be sure of clear cases without knowing at what point cases cease to be clear. Paradigm cases, however, do not provide a road from language to metaphysics: "The conception of language as a mirror of reality is radically mistaken."

As an undergraduate, Black heard Moore deliver the Tarner Lectures at Trinity College in 1929, so he was delighted to receive an invitation to deliver them in 1978. His topic, "Models of Rationality," conformed to his customary piecemeal pattern of output in yielding not in a book but a series of essays that were incorporated into several later publications. One theme running through the lectures is that models of rationality cannot eliminate the need for judgment; hence formal schemes, such as those employed by economists in decision theory and choice theory, are bound to remain heuristic rather than definitive.

Black's interests had an Enlightenment breadth; the topics of his essays range from formal logic to poetry. In the philosophy of science, he argued eloquently and persuasively for induction and commented on perception, cosmology, decision theory, aesthetics, and sociology, all while retaining his early interest in mathematics. His work in philosophy of language included reviews of the work of many of his contemporaries, including Russell, Dewey, Wittgenstein, Korzybski, Carnap, Tarski, Morris, Whorf, Chomsky, and Skinner. His writing is remarkably free of specialized terminology or jargon. The range and the freshness of his writing help to account, no doubt, for his continuing appeal and relevance.

See also Analysis, Philosophical; Broad, Charlie Dunbar; Carnap, Rudolf; Chomsky, Noam; Decision Theory; Dewey, John; Enlightenment; Induction; Logical Positivism; Metaphor; Moore, George Edward; Paradigm-Case Argument; Philosophy of Language; Ramsey, Frank Plumpton; Russell, Bertrand Arthur William; Skinner, B. F.; Stebbing, Lizzie Susan; Tarski, Alfred; Wittgenstein, Ludwig Josef Johann.

Bibliography

In addition to the works mentioned, Black's publications include eight volumes of essays: *Language and Philosophy* (Ithaca, NY: Cornell University Press, 1949), *Problems of Analysis* (Ithaca, NY: Cornell University Press, 1954), *Models and Metaphors* (Ithaca, NY: Cornell University Press, 1962), *Margins of Precision* (Ithaca, NY: Cornell University Press, 1970), *The Labyrinth of Language* (New York: Praeger, 1968), *Caveats and Critiques* (Ithaca, NY, 1975), *The Prevalence of Humbug and Other Essays* (Ithaca, NY: Cornell University Press, 1983), and *Perplexities* (Ithaca, NY: Cornell University Press, 1990).

Volumes translated or edited include *R. Carnap, The Unity of Science* (London, 1934), *Philosophical Analysis* (Ithaca, NY, 1950), *Translations from the Philosophical Writings of Gottlob Frege* (with P. T. Geach; Oxford, 1960), *The Social Theories of Talcott Parsons* (Englewood Cliffs, NJ: Prentice-Hall, 1961), *The Importance of Language* (Englewood Cliffs, NJ: Prentice-Hall, 1962), *Philosophy in America* (Ithaca, NY: Cornell University Press, 1965), *The Morality of Scholarship* (Ithaca, NY: Cornell University Press, 1967), and *Problems of Choice and Decision* (Ithaca, NY: The Program, 1975).

A reasonably complete bibliography to 1985 is appended to Black's autobiographical sketch in Volume 12 of *Philosophers on Their Own Work* (Bern/Frankfurt/New York: H. Lang, 1985), pp. 9–41.

Newton Garver (1967, 2005)

BLACK HOLES

A black hole (the term was coined by John Archibald Wheeler in 1967) is a closed surface through which gravity prevents light from propagating. Insofar as relativity prohibits anything from traveling faster than light, it follows that nothing can escape through the surface of a relativistic black hole. That said, in general relativity the notion of energy is problematic, and energy and hence mass can be extracted by classical and quantum processes. Classically the interior of a black hole contains a *singularity*: Along certain paths physical quantities become ill-behaved (e.g., the gravitational field may become infinite). While nothing can pass back through the surface of a black hole, it is possible in certain models to travel into other universes. All of these properties have philosophically disturbing implications that have strongly influenced the development of physics, especially since there are solid theoretical and experimental reasons to believe that black holes are not merely hypothetical, but actually exist.

HISTORY

Black holes (henceforth BHs) arise in the general theory of relativity (GTR). However something similar is possible in Newtonian physics. John Michell (1784) and Pierre Simon Laplace (1796) pointed out that, as a ball thrown upwards with insufficient speed will eventually fall back to Earth, if a star of a given mass were smaller than a certain size (in modern parlance, its *critical radius*) then even light corpuscles, emitted from the surface at the speed of light, would eventually be pulled back to its surface. If such a star were a sufficient distance away it would not be directly visible (though faster or accelerating bodies could escape).

Karl Schwarzschild discovered the first exact solution of GTR in 1916, before the Einstein field equations of the theory were cast in their final form. The model has a point mass M at its center and in radial co-ordinates (two angles, θ and Φ, giving the latitude and longitude of a point, its distance r from the center and time t) the line element (the distance between two infinitesimally separated points) is:

$$ds^2 = -(1 - 2GM/c^2 r)dt + \frac{dr^2}{1 - 2GM/c^2 r}$$

$$+ r^2(d\theta^2 + \sin^2\theta d\phi^2)$$

where G is Newton's gravitational constant and c the speed of light. The idea in GTR is that M determines ds^2, which determines the geometry of spacetime, which explains the effect of gravity. Inspection of the second and first terms reveals ds^2 diverges at $r = 2GM/c^2$—the "Schwarzschild radius"—and $r = 0$—the location of the point mass, respectively. The singularity at $r = 0$ is genuine, though one would suspect (wrongly) that it would not occur if it were not for the idealization of a point mass—see below. The divergence at $r = 2GM/c^2$ is not physical, but merely an artifact of the co-ordinates used to describe the solution, a point that was not properly appreciated until the late 1930s. By way of analogy, if we used $x'=1/(x-1)$, $y'=y$ as co-ordinates for the x-y plane,

then $ds^2 = dx'^2 x'^4 + dy'^2$. Along $x=1$ the plane is perfectly smooth but ds^2 is singular since $x'=\infty$, a reflection of the "poor" choice of co-ordinates.

In the Schwarzschild solution the singularity reflects not a geometric irregularity but the existence of a sphere of radius $2GM/c^2$ (named the "horizon" by Wolfgang Rindler in the 1950s) from which no light can escape (a point first made by Johannes Droste in 1916). Clearly if a body is smaller than $2GM/c^2$ then light cannot escape its horizon, so a star's Schwarzschild radius is its critical radius: The horizon forms a BH around any star smaller than its Schwartzschild radius. Other solutions for BHs were discovered by Hans Reissner (1916) and Gunnar Nordström (1918) for a charged BH, by Roy Kerr (1964) for a spinning BH, and by Ted Newman (1965) for a charged and spinning BH. It is important to emphasize that the nature of the horizon and hence of the BH (and hence of the early solutions) was not properly understood until the mid-1960s. Remarkably a so-called "No Hair Theorem" shows that the exterior (but not the interior) of any BH is completely characterized by its mass, charge, and spin and not on any other details of its composition or formation: The exterior of every possible BH is described by one of the four models mentioned here.

The Schwarzschild solution was quickly accepted as the description of gravity outside a (stationary) star, where the mass could be treated as located at the star's center—that is, providing that the star was larger than its Schwarzschild radius (18.5km for the Sun). The early pioneers of GTR did not properly understand the horizon (they worried about its possible singular nature and the fact that bodies approaching it would apparently take bodies an infinite time to reach it) and tried to argue that they could not occur in nature. However the question arose of what would happen to a star after it exhausted its fuel supply and began to cool and contract. By 1925 it was apparent that such stars could shrink under their own gravity to form *white dwarfs* 1,000s of times denser than the Sun, but in the early 1930s Subrahmanyan Chandrasekhar showed that white dwarfs of masses more than 1.5 the mass of the Sun ($M_\odot$) were not stable against gravity. In 1933 Walter Baade and Fritz Zwicky proposed that stars could further implode to form *neutron stars* as dense as atomic nuclei (the gravitational energy released by the implosion explaining supernovae), but in 1938 Robert Oppenheimer and George Volkoff argued that neutron stars heavier than a few times $M_\odot$ (the contemporary value is $2M_\odot$) would be unable to resist their own gravity, and in 1956 Wheeler and Masami Wakano demonstrated that there were no denser stable objects than neutron stars. In 1939 Oppenheimer and Hartland Snyder provided the first model of a star collapsing through its Schwarzschild radius, a model vindicated in the early 1960s by simulations based on hydrogen bomb research (subsequent models show that stars below around $20M_\odot$ will eject sufficient matter during implosion to avoid complete collapse). In other words, it became clear not only that BHs were quite possible but also that their formation was likely. One philosophically significant aspect of this scientific revolution is how it was affected by physicists' changing intuitions about what mathematical models were physically realistic.

In the first years of the twenty-first century the astronomical evidence for BHs was strong and rapidly evolving; as of this writing, there are some fifty known candidates, half of them strong candidates. One class of candidates occurs in binary systems in which a star orbits a heavy body that strips material from it. The speed of the star can be calculated from the Doppler shift of its emission spectrum and the mass of the heavy body derived from that: If it is above $2M_\odot$ it is too heavy to be a neutron star and is presumably a BH. Typical BHs of this type have $5-15M_\odot$. A second kind of BH candidate is the *supermassive* BH, thought to occur at the center of galaxies. For instance it is believed that a BH over $3 \times 10^6 M_\odot$ lies at the heart of our galaxy in the constellation Sagittarius. Observational work has been done to verify that these candidates are not some unknown, denser objects, for example by looking for nuclear reactions that can occur only on material surfaces and not on horizons.

BH INTERIOR

When objections to the physical possibility of a horizon were overcome, the question became whether real BHs, like the known solutions, contained singularities. According to Oppenheimer and Snyder's model, stellar matter collapses to a point to form a singularity, but their work was not definitive because it assumed an unrealistically symmetric distribution of collapsing matter. However in the late 1960s Roger Penrose and then Steven Hawking proved Singularity Theorems showing that singularities must arise under very general conditions, including those believed to hold in BH formation, while in 1969 Vladimir Belinsky, Isaac Khalatnikov, and Evgeny Lifshitz found a singularity that would form if stellar collapse was only approximately symmetric.

Ordinarily a singularity in a function means that it diverges somewhere in its domain. The situation is more complicated in GTR because space has no existence separately from the fields: GTR is the theory of the metric field (the coefficients of ds^2), which describes the geometry of space. Intuitively speaking, when the fields of GTR become singular the very notion of spatial points fails, and space can contain a singularity even though the fields do not diverge anywhere. Singularities potentially raise several philosophically interesting issues. One is that singularities are associated with failures of determinism: The problem is roughly analogous to that of calculating the propagation of an electromagnetic wave in a space with a hole removed. Another is that Physicists have thus postulated various forms of *Cosmic Censorship*: That singularities cause at most localized failures of determinism (e.g., only inside a BH).

One may be struck by the similar (mistaken) initial reaction to the horizon (also by the "transcendental" nature of this move—without censorship and determinism, physics of a certain kind is impossible), though censorship has been shown in a range of cases. If uncensored "naked singularities" are possible, then it would be possible to use them to complete "supertasks" in a finite time relative to a distant observer. Important to remember is that our discussion so far has been in the context of classical GTR (utilizing some quantum properties of matter), but around a singularity, quantum gravitational effects likely become important. Physicists generally expect that singularities will not occur in a quantized version of GTR. If so, classical singularities may offer no philosophically important lessons after all. However John Earman's *Bangs, Crunches, Whimpers, and Shrieks* argues that classical singularities may pose no physical problem, so physicists need not demand that quantum gravity banish them.

Everything that enters the Schwarzschild BH eventually reaches its singularity, but in the other models it is possible to avoid the singularity altogether and travel on to a flat region of spacetime: The other BHs contain "worm holes" or "Einstein-Rosen bridges" to a "new" universe or to a region of space far from the BH (in the latter case spacetime would contain "closed timelike curves," paths that allow one to travel to one's past). However even in classical GTR the models assume unrealistic symmetries, and so the interior parts cannot be trusted: As of this writing, while it has not been shown that more realistic classical BHs do not contain worm holes, it is widely assumed that they do not. The situation in quantum gravity is even less clear, though Lee Smolin (1992) has speculated that a new universe is created inside whenever a BH forms, with laws of nature that vary in a small, random way from their parent universe, so that all possible physics eventually comes into existence.

BLACKNESS

Consider what would happen as an astronaut entered the horizon of a BH while he was watched from the outside. It is useful to think of the region around the BH as analogous to a deep, sloped, hole in the ground: As one gets nearer the center, the distance up the walls and along the ground to the outside grows rapidly. Analogously, as the BH is approached, light has to travel up ever steeper "walls" of curved spacetime to escape: Since the speed of light is constant, it follows that light takes an increasingly long time to reach the outside. Just as showing movie frames at increasing intervals makes a scene appear to slow, so the astronaut will appear to decelerate. In a BH, however, the time for light to reach the outside becomes infinite at the horizon (though space there is perfectly smooth). The effect is that the astronaut appears to decelerate indefinitely and from the outside can never be seen to enter the BH, as if the movie were slowed until frozen on a single frame. It is crucial to appreciate that this phenomenon is entirely optical: The astronaut himself measures only a finite amount of time until he is inside the BH. (That a collapsed massive star would thus be seen frozen at its horizon was an impediment to understanding BH formation.)

Just as it would take light infinitely long to escape from the horizon of a BH, nothing localized inside the horizon can pass through it (ignoring subtleties concerning the speed of light as a cosmic speed limit): The BH is opaque to its exterior. However it is theoretically possible to extract energy and hence mass, via the relativistic equivalence of mass and energy, from a spinning BH by classical processes that slow the spin. It is rather surprising that this extraction is achieved by throwing matter into the hole, but not surprising that a BH stores energy in its rotation. In other words part of the BH's mass arises from its interaction with the spacetime outside it, so no energy has to leave the interior. More surprisingly, Hawking (1974) showed quantum effects mean that even a non-spinning BH would radiate energy (and mass) with a temperature inversely proportional to it mass.

This effect is philosophically important for two reasons. First it confirmed Jacob Bekenstein's (1972) speculation that BHs obeyed the laws of thermodynamics and hence possessed entropy; among other things BHs are relevant to an arrow time based on the Second Law of thermodynamics. Second what happens when the mass of the BH "evaporates" to zero? One issue is the possibility of a naked singularity. Another is the "loss of information paradox": Physical theories typically allow an earlier state to be retrodicted from a later one, so that no information

about the earlier state is lost over time. However, in Hawking's calculation, radiation carries no information about how a BH was formed, so that information remains inside the BH and is lost: Once a BH evaporates, retrodiction is impossible. For these reasons BH radiation became an important issue since theories of "quantum gravity" can be judged according to how they treat BH entropy and the loss of information paradox. In particular, BH entropy is connected to the powerful idea of "holography," which connects the physics of any region to the physics of the surface bounding it.

See also Earman, John; Laplace, Pierre Simon de; Philosophy of Physics; Quantum Mechanics; Space; Time.

Bibliography

Bekenstein, Jacob D. "Blackholes and Information Theory." *Contemporary Physics* 45 (2003): 31–43. Available from http://www.arXiv.org/abs/quant-ph/0311049.

Belot, Gordon, John Earman, and Laura Ruetsche. "The Hawking Information Loss Paradox: The Anatomy of a Controversy." *British Journal for the Philosophy of Science* 50 (1999): 189–229.

Carroll, Sean. *Spacetime and Geometry: An Introduction to General Relativity*. New York: Pearson Addison Wesley, 2003.

Earman, John. *Bangs, Crunches, Whimpers, and Shrieks: Singularities and Acausalities in Relativistic Spacetimes*. Oxford: Oxford University Press, 1995.

Israel, Werner. "Dark Stars: The Evolution of an Idea." In *Three Hundred Years of Gravitation*, edited by Steven S. Hawking and Werner Israel. Cambridge, U.K.: Cambridge University Press, 1987.

Smolin, Lee. *The Life of the Cosmos*. Oxford: Oxford University Press, 1997.

Taylor, Edwin F., and John Archibald Wheeler. *Exploring Black Holes: Introduction to General Relativity*. New York: Benjamin Cummins, 2000.

Thorne, Kip S. *Black Holes & Time Warps: Einstein's Outrageous Legacy*. New York: Norton, 1994.

Unruh, William. "Black Holes, Dumb Holes, and Entropy." In *Physics Meets Philosophy at the Planck Scale: Contemporary Theories in Quantum Gravity*, edited by Craig Callender and Nick Huggett. Cambridge, U.K.: Cambridge University Press, 2001.

Ziólkowski, Janusz. "Black Hole Candidates." arXiv.org e-print Archive. Available from http://www.arXiv.org/abs/astro-ph/0307307.

Nick Huggett (2005)

BLAKE, WILLIAM
(1757–1827)

William Blake was an English poet, painter, and engraver. He was born in London, the second of five children in the family of a retail hosier. His social status precluded university education, and he was apprenticed to an engraver. Apart from that training and a few months at the Royal Academy, Blake was self-educated. Most of his pictorial work took the form of illustrations for books, biblical subjects forming the largest group. His painting and engraving were thus primarily related to literature, and the interdependence of poetry and painting is a central principle of all his work. He lived in London nearly all his life, very frugally, sometimes in poverty, and constantly dependent on patrons. He met William Wordsworth, Samuel Taylor Coleridge, and Charles Lamb, and was admired by the last two; but he died practically unknown as a poet, although he had been writing poetry since the age of twelve. After one volume of juvenile verse (*Poetical Sketches,* 1783) was published through the efforts of friends, Blake determined to produce his poetry by engraving the text himself and accompanying it with illustrations. Practically all his later poetry, except what was left in manuscript, took the form of a text and designs etched on copper, stamped on paper, and then colored by hand. Most of his lyrics are in two collections: *Songs of Innocence* (first engraved in 1789) and *Songs of Experience* (1794). Others are longer poems, generally called prophecies, which are sequences of plates. The "prophecies" include *The Book of Thel* (1789), *The Marriage of Heaven and Hell* (1793), *America* (1793), *Europe* (1794), *Milton* (about 1808, in 50 plates) and *Jerusalem* (about 1818, in 100 plates).

THOUGHT

The prophecies are symbolic poems in which the characters are states or attitudes of human life. This means that these poems embody religious and philosophical concepts as well as poetic imagery. These concepts are mainly concerned with Blake's sense of the relevance and importance of the arts and of the creative faculty of man, and seem to have been derived mainly from a negative reaction to the British empirical tradition of thought. He tells us that he had read John Locke and Francis Bacon in his youth and had decided that they mocked inspiration and vision. Blake's attitude would be better understood if it were thought of as anti-Cartesian, although he is unlikely to have read René Descartes, and his attitude embodies many elements that would now be called existential.

IMAGINATION. According to Blake, man is a working or constructing imagination—the creative artist is normative man. In this context there is no difference between human essence and human existence, for the imagination is the human existence itself and is also essential human nature. Works of art are neither intellectual nor emotional, motivated neither by desire nor by reason, neither free nor compelled: all such antitheses become unities in them. Even more important, the imagination destroys the antithesis of subject and object. Man starts out as an isolated intelligence in an alien nature, but the imagination creates a world in its own image, the world of cities and gardens and human communities and domesticated animals.

INTERPRETATION OF THE BIBLE. For Blake, the Bible is a definitive parable of human existence, as it tells how man finds himself in an unsatisfactory world and tries to build a better one—one which eventually takes the form of a splendid golden city, the symbol of the imaginative and creative human community. God in Blake's work is the creative power in man (here Blake shows the influence of Emanuel Swedenborg, with his emphasis on the unity of divine and human natures in Jesus), and human power is divine because it is infinite and eternal. These two words do not mean endless in time and spaces; they mean the genuine experience of the central points of time and space, the now and the here. Many features of Blake's anti-Lockean position remind us of George Berkeley, especially his insistence that "mental things are alone real"; but this doctrine of God takes Blake far beyond the subjective idealism and nominalism of Berkeley.

In Blake's reading of the Bible, "the creation"—the alien and stupid nature that man now lives in—is part of "the fall" and is the world man struggles to transcend. The objective world is the anticreation, the enemy to be destroyed. Blake says that man has no body distinct from his soul. He does oppose mind and body, but as contrasting attitudes to nature, not as separate essential principles. The "corporeal understanding," or perverted human activity, contemplates nature as it is (as a vast, objective, subhuman body) and tries to overcome the alienation of the subject by identifying the subject with nature as it sees nature. Nature is controlled, apparently, by automatic laws like the law of gravitation and by a struggle to survive in which force and cunning are more important than love or intelligence. Perverted human life imitates nature by continually waging war and by maintaining a parasitic class. Perverted religion, or natural religion, as Blake calls it, invents harsh and tyrannical gods on the analogy of nature. Perverted thought exposes itself passively to impressions from the external world and then evolves abstract principles out of these impressions that attempt to formulate the general laws of nature. These are the operations known as sensation and reflection in Locke. The abstracting tendency is perverted because it is not a genuine effort to understand nature, but is a step toward imitating the automatism of nature by imposing a conforming morality on human life. The principle of this conformity is the acceptance of injustice and exploitation as inescapable elements of existence. The end of this perverted process is hatred and contempt of life, as expressed in the deliberate efforts at self-annihilation that Blake saw as beginning with the Napoleonic wars in his own time.

PROPHETIC BOOKS. The action in Blake's prophecies is concerned with the conflict of these creative and perverted states in human life. The sense of conservatism, of accepting things as they are, is symbolized by Urizen, who is associated with old age and the sky. When conservatism deepens into hatred of life itself, Urizen is replaced by Satan. The force that struggles against Urizen is the revolutionary impulse in man, called Orc or Luvah, who is associated with youth and sexual desire. Orc cannot achieve a permanent deliverance from Urizen; that is possible only for the creative power itself, called Los. The central theme of the prophecies is the effort of humanity, called Albion, to achieve through Los the kind of civilization that is symbolized in the Bible as Jerusalem and thus to reach the integration of human and divine powers represented in Christianity by Jesus.

See also Bacon, Francis; Berkeley, George; Coleridge, Samuel Taylor; Descartes, René; Existentialism; Imagination; Locke, John; Romanticism; Swedenborg, Emanuel.

Bibliography

The most convenient edition of Blake's literary work is the one-volume *The Poetry and Prose of William Blake,* edited by Geoffrey Keynes (London: Random House, 1927).

Works on Blake include Bernard Blackstone, *English Blake* (Cambridge, U.K.: Cambridge University Press, 1949); Foster S. Damon, *William Blake: His Philosophy and Symbols* (Boston: Houghton Mifflin, 1924); David V. Erdman, *Blake: Prophet against Empire* (Princeton, NJ: Princeton University Press, 1954); Northrop Frye, *Fearful Symmetry: A Study of William Blake* (Princeton, NJ: Princeton University Press, 1947); and Mark Schorer, *William Blake: The Politics of Vision* (New York: Henry Holt, 1946).

Northrop Frye (1967)

BLANCHOT, MAURICE
(1907–2003)

Maurice Blanchot was first and foremost a literary theorist, and his work included a number of essay collections, among them *The Space of Literature* (1982), *The Book to Come* (2003), and *Friendship* (1997). He also wrote powerful but rather hermetic novels such as *Thomas the Obscure* (1973), *Death Sentence* (1978), *Aminadab* (2002), and *The Most High* (1996), in addition to aphoristic works such as *The Writing of the Disaster* (1986). Blanchot's work has profound implications for the practice of philosophy. His influence therefore stretches from practitioners of the New Novel to philosophers such as Jacques Derrida and Michel Foucault.

Blanchot's strategy, which is meant to reconceive literature and to carry out a thoroughgoing critique of the possibility of language, is in major part derived from a critique of the Hegelian notion of the sign, by way of Martin Heidegger. In Blanchot's version of Hegel—as seen in his essays "The Experience of Mallarmé" and "Literature and the Right to Death"—the word, by isolating things and representing them in their absence, "gives me the being, but it gives it to me deprived of being"; or, put another way, the word makes the world appear and disappear in a moment (Blanchot, 1995, p. 322). The givenness of the thing (or person) in and through the word is also its radical removal, its distance from simple subjectivity or objectivity, its mortality. That one's words represent a thing that—or person who is—absent means that it or she or he can be absent (can be removed, destroyed, can be dead). The word thus represents things or persons in the act of constituting them and indicating their disappearance, their death. This is a negation that has nothing to do with the patient work of the dialectic; it is of the instant, an instant that cannot be recaptured in any constructive movement. Named things—people—are always already dead, and their life is an infinitely repetitious death. "Pure language," as Blanchot calls it, entails a nomination where this "neutral" action of language is recognized; this (impossible) recognition in turn characterizes true literature (Blanchot, 1995). Put another way, the world of work recognizes and uses the negating power of the word; true literature, however, recognizes this negation as so thorough that it penetrates and radically negates beings and things—including, of course, literature itself—in the moment of their constitution. Blanchot in fact compares literature to the Terror, where beings are called forth in a repetitious movement that both constitutes them as revolutionary subjects and kills them. Thus Blanchot can write, as he did in "The Experience of Mallarmé," that "the fulfillment [*accomplissement*] of language coincides with its disappearance" (1982). This fulfillment is literature.

This "neuter" (*le neutre*) of Blanchot bears an obvious connection with the Heideggerian *Dasein* or the Levinasian *Il y a*. But there are crucial differences. The work of death is so thorough for Blanchot that it is hard to see how any notion of authenticity or foundational ethics could be carried out through it. This incessant, unproductive constituting and destroying death erodes all philosophical systems, all coherent models of subjectivity (Descartes), all constructive movements of negation in time, and all doctrines based on force and power. As Gerald Bruns puts it, "The 'nocturnal' experience of words, in which the cognitive or speaking subjectivity is deprived of its sovereignty and its power, reduced to the passivity of its fascination, is one of the most important events in Blanchot's thinking" (1997, p. 77). One could add that the sovereignty of space and time are emptied out as well, because the subject moving in them and making the world is not making a coherent entity but rather is caught up in the emptying out of the possibility of all relation, all mediation between (dead) self and (dead) world.

Blanchot narrativizes this nocturnal relation in myths and fictions. "The Gaze of Orpheus" provides an excellent example: Orpheus would bring Eurydice from death to a realm of the disclosure of truth and beauty. But halfway through the journey he must see her as she is, as death, as radical concealment. This demand, to see and to speak "the most certain masterpiece," is inevitably fatal to Orpheus's aesthetic and philosophical hopes. Seeing constitutes, but it is also inseparable from, radical loss, "the movement of writing" (1982, pp. 103–104). Truth and beauty can be grasped, but only in the night in which such certainties are immediately and incessantly lost. The strangeness of the Heideggerian "thing" is rewritten as an impossible interpersonal relation, between man and woman, that is also an allegory of the necessity and impossibility of language at its limit (literature).

Many of Blanchot's fictions work out this interpersonal relation between man and woman, or self and other, in the mode of the radical death of both the subject and signification. The Blanchotian hero is thus a figure obsessed with a negativity that pervades all things, a personage for whom the only relation is a repetitive recognition of the impossibility of the recognition of a stable relation, as in *Death Sentence* and *The Most High*.

Blanchot's conception of language is literary in that its radicality is seen to characterize literature at the highest level. Blanchot, however, does not limit its implications exclusively to what is conventionally conceived as the literary realm. Language as understood by Blanchot invests philosophy, making its movement possible and at the same time undermining every one of its certainties. In this way Blanchot's version of literary language and of language in general clearly anticipates Jacques Derrida's analyses of writing. But language also conditions Blanchot's version of the community.

The problem of the enthusiastic community, so central to French social thought since (at least) the Revolution, is rewritten by Blanchot in *The Unavowable Community* as the fundamental relation of those who have "nothing in common," an inescapable and unmediated relation of reading in which nothing is knowable, nothing endures, a moment that constitutes nothing in a coherent movement of time. Similarly, in *The Writing of the Disaster*, the Holocaust is seen as a "disaster" in the Blanchotian sense. Not a "word, not the name of anything … but always an entire complex or simple sentence, where the infinitude of language … seeks … to fall outside language—without, however, ceasing to belong to it" (1986, p. 84). From writing on literature and literary language, then, Blanchot has moved to a larger conception of the word, and language. Essential language leads nowhere, guarantees nothing, and only has "its end in itself" ("The Experience of Mallarmé" 1982), yet its negativity is fundamental to an understanding of society and its limit term, the moment in which it grasps itself as the radically ungraspable: the Holocaust. "Literature," in Blanchot's sense, therefore resists any easy containment.

See also Death; Derrida, Jacques; Descartes, René; Foucault, Michel; Heidegger, Martin; Literature, Philosophy of; Philosophy of Language.

Bibliography

WORKS BY BLANCHOT

Essay Collections

The Space of Literature. Translated by Ann Smock. Lincoln: University of Nebraska Press, 1982. Includes the essays "The Gaze of Orpheus" and "The Experience of Mallarmé."

The Writing of the Disaster. Translated by Ann Smock. Lincoln: University of Nebraska Press, 1986.

The Unavowable Community. Translated by Pierre Joris. Barrytown, NY: Station Hill, 1988.

The Step Not Beyond. Translated by Lynette Nelson. Albany: State University of New York Press, 1992.

The Work of Fire. Translated by Charlotte Mandell. Stanford, CA: Stanford University Press, 1995. Includes the essay "Literature and the Right to Death."

Friendship. Translated by Elizabeth Rottenberg. Stanford, CA: Stanford University Press, 1997.

The Instant of My Death. With Jacques Derrida as *Demeure: Fiction and Testimony*. Translated by Elizabeth Rottenberg. Stanford, CA: Stanford University Press, 2000.

Faux pas. Translated by Charlotte Mandell. Stanford, CA: Stanford University Press, 2001.

The Book to Come. Translated by Charlotte Mandell. Stanford, CA: Stanford University Press, 2003.

Novels

Thomas the Obscure. Translated by Robert Lamberton. New York: D. Lewis, 1973.

Death Sentence. Translated by Lydia Davis. Barrytown, NY: Station Hill, 1978.

The Most High. Translated by Allan Stoekl. Lincoln: University of Nebraska Press, 1996.

Aminadab. Translated by Jeff Fort. Lincoln: University of Nebraska Press, 2002.

WORKS ABOUT BLANCHOT

Bruns, Gerald L. *Maurice Blanchot: The Refusal of Philosophy*. Baltimore: Johns Hopkins University Press, 1997.

Haase, Ullrich, and William Large. *Maurice Blanchot*. New York: Routledge, 2001.

Herr, Deborah. *Politics and Literature: The Case of Maurice Blanchot*. New York: Peter Lang, 1999.

Allan Stoekl (2005)

BLANSHARD, BRAND
(1892–1987)

Brand Blanshard was an American philosopher whose task is best described in his own words as the "vindication of reason against recent philosophical attacks." Blanshard was thus a critic—a critic of all those who, he alleged, reject rationality—but at the same time he tried to exhibit the credentials that reason can show in its own right.

Blanshard was educated at the University of Michigan, Columbia, Oxford, and Harvard—where he received his PhD. He taught at the University of Michigan, at Swarthmore College, and at Yale—where he was Sterling professor of philosophy and chairman of the department. The multitude of honors he received during his career precludes their enumeration here.

Blanshard's first major work was *The Nature of Thought* (London, 1939), in two volumes, each divided into two books. The first volume is largely concerned with a subject matter common to both philosophy and psychology. The stated goal is to discover a theory of perception (Book I) and a theory of ideas (Book II) that will simultaneously satisfy the psychologist, who views percepts and ideas as contents of the mind, and the philosopher, who views them as potential items of knowledge. Various theories are examined and rejected—most notably the traditional empiricist approach—and it is finally argued that only a theory along the lines developed by Francis Herbert Bradley, Bernard Bosanquet, and

Josiah Royce is able to meet this double demand. The universal, Blanshard maintained, is present in all thought, even in the most rudimentary forms of perception; and it is the presence of the universal that is the most important feature of thought. This conclusion exhibits a theme that recurs throughout both volumes: the use of doctrines drawn from the idealist tradition in dealing with contemporary problems.

In the second volume of *The Nature of Thought*, the subject matter becomes more specifically philosophical. The main task of Book III (titled "The Movement of Reflection") is to answer the epistemological problem: What is the test and the nature of truth? Once more, after examining and rejecting alternatives, Blanshard turns to the idealist tradition for his answer, adopting a version of the coherence theory of truth. His exposition of the coherence theory has a number of distinctive features. Foremost is the clarity, rigor, and persuasiveness of the presentation; in this respect Blanshard has only Royce as a rival. Furthermore, he develops the theory independently of metaphysical doctrines that are for the most part now repudiated. Finally, he develops the theory in full cognizance of contemporary criticisms and attempts to offer direct answer to them.

In Book IV (titled "The Goal of Thought") Blanshard moves from epistemology into metaphysics. Still operating within the framework of idealism, he accepts the connected notions of internal relations, concrete universality, and concrete necessity. But he does not, as do most idealists, give these doctrines a gratuitous theological turn, nor does he attempt to secure the foundation of the entire system through an a priori proof that the completed, fully articulated system must exist. He does introduce the conception of a transcendent end for thought, which he considers a necessary postulate for knowledge, but he admits that it is possible (though unlikely) that this postulate is mistaken.

Some two decades after the publication of *The Nature of Thought*, and upon retirement from Yale, Blanshard began a projected three-volume sequence that would bring together material originally presented in his Carus and Gifford lectures. *Reason and Analysis* (London, 1962), the second of the three volumes, is his most polemical work. It is in large measure a systematic and unremitting attack upon the analytic tradition as it emerged in various forms during the twentieth century. Some of the arguments presented are refinements of those used in *The Nature of Thought*, but *Reason and Analysis* is not a mere echo of the earlier work. On the constructive side, many of the earlier idealistic doctrines, although not silenced, seem decidedly muted. If philosophies are to bear labels, this later position might better be called rationalism than idealism.

The first work in the sequence, *Reason and Goodness* (London, 1961), introduces another aspect of Blanshard's thought. In this work he traces out the dialectical interplay between the demands of reason and the demands of feeling throughout the history of ethical theory. Not surprisingly, Blanshard rejects any theory that will not provide a place for reason in the account of human values, and he thus offers elaborate critiques of subjectivism, emotivism, and related theories.

In developing his own ethical position Blanshard does not turn, at least primarily, to the idealist tradition but rather to the works of Henry Sidgwick, G. E. Moore, H. A. Prichard, and W. D. Ross. Throughout his career Blanshard favored teleology in ethics, and for a time he was attracted by Moore's ideal utilitarianism. He came to reject this position largely because of the difficulties associated with Moore's conception of nonnatural properties. In *Reason and Goodness* Blanshard rejects Moore's critique of naturalism and argues that goodness is characterized by the joint properties of satisfaction and fulfillment. The idea of fulfillment is associated with the idealist tradition, but as Blanshard uses it, it carries no suggestion of loss of individuality and is thus quite different from the idea of fulfillment as employed by Bradley and most other idealists. By including both satisfaction and fulfillment in the definition of goodness, Blanshard hopes to provide for feeling on one hand and reason on the other and, in this way, to resolve the dialectical tension outlined earlier in the work.

Reason and Belief was not yet published as of this writing, but from Blanshard's lectures it may be assumed that in this work he will challenge the religious irrationalism that is currently fashionable in some quarters. What positive doctrines he will espouse is more a matter of speculation.

See also Bosanquet, Bernard; Bradley, Francis Herbert; Coherence Theory of Truth; Idealism; Relations, Internal and External; Moore, George Edward; Rationalism; Reason; Ross, William David; Royce, Josiah; Teleology.

Bibliography

Blanshard, Brand. *Reason and Belief*. New Haven, CT: Yale University Press, 1974.

Additional works by Blanshard are "Current Strictures on Reason," in *Philosophical Review* 54 (1945): 345–368, and *On Philosophical Style* (Bloomington: Indiana University Press, 1954).

A work on Blanshard is Ernest Nagel, "Sovereign Reason," in his *Sovereign Reason* (Glencoe, IL: Free Press, 1954), pp. 266–295.

Robert J. Fogelin (1967)

BLOCH, ERNST
(1885–1977)

Ernst Bloch, the German Marxist philosopher, was born at Ludwigshafen. Influenced by late German expressionism and by the atmosphere of Munich after World War I, Bloch's style and thought reveal contradictory and uncertain trends. He began his career at the University of Leipzig by publishing *Von Geist der Utopie* in 1918. This work was followed in 1922 by a study of Thomas Münzer in which mystical and eschatological ideas blend with dialectic elements of Marxist-Hegelian origin. *Spuren* followed in 1930 and *Erbschaft dieser Zeit* in 1933. In the latter work the various elements of Bloch's thoughts are for the first time clearly placed within a Marxist framework showing revisionist tendencies.

In 1933 Bloch left Germany, eventually reaching the United States, where he created his major work, *Das Prinzip Hoffnung*, a huge work that has been called "a monstrous essence of his thoughts." After World War II Bloch, like Bertolt Brecht, went to East Germany, where from 1948 until his retirement in 1957 he was professor at the University of Leipzig. At first, Bloch's political and intellectual influence in East Germany was limited, but nevertheless, he was never fully appreciated by party authorities. His winning the *Nationalpreis* of the German Democratic Republic in 1955 stirred controversy, and Bloch's views had changed considerably during his sojourn there. His ideas, which were carefully watched by party authorities, became the center of many discussions. In 1953, after the publication of *Subjekt-Objekt, Erläuterung zur Hegel* and *Avicenna und die Aristotelische Linke*, Bloch became editor of the *Deutsche Zeitschrift für Philosophie*. But the journal's comparative independence led to a series of arrests and trials of its collaborators and editors. Wolfgang Harich, Günther Zehm, and Manfred Hertwig were sentenced to prison, and Richard Lorenz and Gerhard Zwerenz fled to the Federal Republic. Although Bloch was only slightly involved, he was forbidden to publish, and in 1957 his works were officially condemned. When Bloch tardily made a declaration of loyalty, it was vague and noncommittal.

Although he was finally permitted to publish the third volume of his *Das Prinzip Hoffnung* in 1959, Bloch asked for political asylum during a visit to the Federal Republic in 1961, where he became a visiting professor at the University of Tübingen. Bloch is generally known in the West as a major Marxist philosopher, but he drew on a far wider heritage that includes classical German thought, Christian and Jewish mysticism, Neoplatonism, and even the esoteric speculation of the *Zohar*. His major work, *Das Prinzip Hoffnung*, gives the impression that Bloch, although claiming that the economic element is fundamental, relegates it to a secondary level and focuses his attention on what Marxist theory regards as only a superstructure, the problem of intellectual culture.

According to Bloch, all reality is "mediation," or the subject-object relation, a dynamic relation that tends ultimately toward the final goal (*Endziel*) of the reunion of subject and object. The *Urgrund*, the primordial stuff prior to the distinction between subject and object, matter and spirit, is moved by an obscure immediate cosmic impulse, which Bloch terms "hunger" and contrasts with Sigmund Freud's libido. After subject and object have been distinguished, Bloch claims, this hunger remains essential to both subject and object. Thus the reality of both subject and object is in the future, and the category of possibility comes to play a central role in his thought.

SUBJECT

In humans, the primordial hunger becomes desire, or hope. Hope presents itself as utopia, as a vision of a possibility that might be realized. Hope is tension toward the future, toward the new. It moves from a mere state of mind (*Stimmung*) to a representation, and then to knowledge. Although hope is founded on the will, in order to be hope that understands (*begriffene Hoffnung, docta spes*), it must draw strength from something real that will survive even when hope itself is completely satisfied. This residue makes hope something more than a project of reason and puts it in relation to what is objectively possible. The future possibility is not just a dream, even if it is heralded in dreams.

POSSIBILITY

The relations between subject, object, reality, and possibility are complex. The nature of the real is a tendency toward, or anticipation of, the future, and thus its reality is the reality of something in the future. But the future is already real as objective possibility. Bloch distinguishes between objective possibility, which (because the object as object is not real) is merely theoretical, and real possi-

bility, which is practically connected with the future. What is really possible is concretely connected with utopia. Reality always contains elements of possible change, possibilities not yet actually existing. Utopias are concerned with these possibilities and thus have an essential function in human consciousness. On the other hand, these possibilities must have a foundation in the object because thought can represent in imagination infinitely many possible objects in infinitely many relationships.

If an event were completely conditioned, it would be "unconditionally certain." Therefore, what can possibly come into existence is possible only insofar as it is not conditioned. What is objectively possible, therefore, is so only insofar as it is not constrained by predetermined conditions. Bloch distinguishes between two senses of objective possibility. One sense concerns the thing and is the thing's "behavior," or the appearance of the thing as an object of knowledge. The other sense concerns our knowledge of the thing. The objectivity (*Sachlichkeit*) of the thing concerns only our knowledge of it, while its factuality (*Sachhaftigkeit*) concerns only the object of knowledge.

MATTER

The distinction between objectivity and factuality leads Bloch to claim that Marxism is only a partial outlook on reality and needs completion, even though the reconciliation of the real and the possible is achieved in historical materialism, which retains, in its complete immanentism, an element akin to the doctrine of salvation of the great religions. According to Marxism, historical changes arise out of precise historical socioeconomic conditions, and physical movement arises out of contradiction, the clash of opposites. But just as Bloch supplements the claims of historical materialism with his concept of hope, so he supplements the claims of dialectical materialism. In the object, or matter, the primordial hunger becomes a motive force (*agens*). But even though Bloch affirms that this force is completely immanent in matter, it is doubtful whether his view is still materialistic. His hostility toward all forms of mechanism and his inclination toward organic solutions weaken the materialistic features of Marxism to the point of nonexistence. The innate drive that he ascribes to matter has meaning only from the point of view of the final goal. Matter is not predetermined, since it has the capacity not only to express itself in existence but also to do so in forms that are always new. Nevertheless, the teleological doctrine of a final goal for the entire world process is not an extension of a psychological category or historical principle to nature. Rather, it is the cosmic unity of the subject process and object process when being finally becomes thinking and thinking finally becomes being. The historical process of society is thus related to the world process and ultimately to matter.

Thus Bloch identifies dialectical matter with real possibility, but its being in process is not material and contradicts the fundamental Marxist tenet that matter is an independent reality that cannot enter into a relation with anything. Several critics have remarked that Bloch's conception of matter has its sources in the romantic *Naturphilosophie* of G. W. F. Hegel and Friedrich von Schelling; on this view, Bloch belongs among the idealist critics of natural science.

UTOPIA

The reconciliation of subject and object comes through utopia. In utopia, romantic *Sehnsucht*—the nostalgic regret that our dream of rationally conquering the world is blocked by a limit that we try unceasingly but perhaps vainly to overcome—is united with messianic expectancy. Utopia foresees the "kingdom of the children of God" of Thomas Münzer, the kingdom of freedom in which the exploitation of man by man ceases. At this time will come that unification, the identification of subject and object, which Bloch claims Karl Marx foresaw when he spoke of the future historicization of nature and naturalization of man. It is thus from man that the world expects its realization, and the realization of the world process coincides with the self-realization of humankind. The Marxist epistemological theory of reflection will no longer be needed, since knowledge itself will be overcome by hope and the object as object will disappear; it will no longer be the having-become (*Gewordenes*) but rather pure process, the becoming (*Werdendes*), the not-yet (*noch nicht*).

Block's thought is very far from Marx's historical outlook and perhaps not too far from the early views of Georg Lukács. In his conflict with the schematicism and dogmatism of orthodox Marxism, Bloch belongs with such idealist and existentialist revisionists as Lukács, Antonio Gramsci, and Jean-Paul Sartre. Bloch's attempt to save Marxist theory from ossifying has wider implications than their attempts, however, for it is related to the problem of how Marxism is to make use of a cultural heritage, especially the heritage of classical German philosophy and, at least for Bloch, the heritage of the great religions of salvation. Bloch's solution has been to develop one vast comprehensive vision of reality, combining the original intuitions of the Old Testament and apocalyptic literature with the dynamic and messianic elements in Marxism. Bloch's very language reveals this mixture of ancient and modern. Difficult and intense, it echoes both recent expressionism and the language of the Bible and of mystical literature. The past is for Bloch not something fixed in an unreachable dimension, its cultural wealth to be discarded in order to start anew, but a dynamic field of research still of use to man.

See also Marxist Philosophy.

Bibliography

WORKS BY BLOCH

Vom Geist der Utopie. Munich: Duncker and Humblot, 1918.
Thomas Münzer als Theologe der Revolution. Munich: Wolff, 1921.
Spuren. Berlin: Cassirer, 1930.
Erbschaft dieser Zeit. Zürich: Oprecht and Helbling, 1935.
Freiheit und Ordnung, Abriss der Sozial-Utopien. New York: Aurora, 1946.
Subjekt-Objekt: Erläuterung zur Hegel. Berlin: Aufbau, 1951.
Avicenna und die Aristotelische Linke. Berlin: Rütten and Loening, 1951.
Das Prinzip Hoffnung. 3 vols. Berlin: Aufbau, 1954–1959.
Gesamtausgabe, 17 vols. Frankfurt: Suhrkamp, 1959–1978.
Naturrecht und menschliche Würde. Frankfurt: Suhrkamp, 1960. Vol. VI of *Gesamtausgabe*.
Philosophische Grundfragen, zur Ontologie des Noch-Nicht-Seins. Frankfurt: Suhrkamp, 1961. Vol. I of *Gesamtausgabe*.
Fromm, Erich, ed. *Socialist Humanism: An International Symposium*. New York: Doubleday, 1965. Contains an essay by Bloch.
Ernst Bloch zu ehren; Beiträge zu seinem Werk. Edited by Siegfried Unseld. Frankfurt am Main: Suhrkamp Verlag, 1965.
Bildung und Konfessionalität;. Frankfurt am Main: M. Diesterweg, 1967.
Religion im Erbe. Eine Auswahl aus seinen religionsphilosophischen Schriften. Edited by Jürgen Moltmann. München u. Hamburg, Siebenstern-Taschenbuch-Verlag, 1967.
Widerstand und Friede; Aufsätze zur Politik. Frankfurt am Main: Suhrkamp, 1968.
Uber Karl Marx. Frankfurt am Main: Suhrkamp, 1968.
Atheismus in Christentum; zur Religion des Exodus und des Reichs. Frankfurt am Main: Suhrkamp, 1968.
"Man as Possibility." In *Hope: A Symposium*. West Nyack, NY: Cross Currents, 1968.
Christian Thomasius, ein deutscher Gelehrter ohne Misere. Frankfurt am Main: Suhrkamp, 1968.
Philosophische Aufsätze zur objektiven Phantasie. Frankfurt am Main: Suhrkamp, 1969.
Die Kunst, Schiller zu sprechen: Und andere literarische Aufsätze. Frankfurt am Main: Suhrkamp, 1969.
Karl Marx und die Menschlichkeit. Utopische Phantasie u. Weltveränderung. Reinbek b. Hamburg: Rowohlt, 1969.
Man on His Own; Essays in the Philosophy of Religion. New York: Herder and Herder, 1970.

Uber Methode und System bei Hegel. Frankfurt am Main: Suhrkamp, 1970.

A Philosophy of the Future. New York: Herder and Herder, 1970.

Bloch, Ernst. Frankfurt am Main: Suhrkamp, 1970.

Politische Messungen, Pestzeit, Vormärz. Frankfurt am Main: Suhrkamp, 1970.

Marx und die Revolution. Frankfurt am Main: Suhrkamp, 1970.

Das Materialismusproblem, seine Geschichte und Substanz. Frankfurt am Main: Suhrkamp, 1972.

Vorlesungen zur Philosophie der Renaissance. Frankfurt am Main: Suhrkamp -Taschenbuch-Verl., 1972.

Erbschaft dieser Zeit. Frankfurt am Main: Suhrkamp Verlag, 1973.

Ästhetik des Vor-Scheins. Frankfurt am Main: Suhrkamp, 1974.

Zur Philosophie der Musik. Frankfurt am Main: Suhrkamp, 1974.

Experimentum mundi: Frage, Kategorien d. Herausbringens, Praxis. Frankfurt am Main: Suhrkamp, 1975.

Ernst Bloch zum 90. Geburtstag: Es muss nicht immer Marmor sein: Erbschaft aus Ungleichzeitigkeit. Berlin: K. Wagenbach, 1975.

Zwischenwelten in der Philosophiegeschichte: Aus Leipziger Vorlesungen. Frankfurt am Main: Suhrkamp, 1976.

Aesthetics and Politics. London: NLB, 1977.

Literarische Aufsätze. Frankfurt am Main: Suhrkamp, 1977.

Experimentum mundi: Frage, Kategorien des Herausbringens, Praxis. Frankfurt am Main: Suhrkamp, 1977.

Tendenz, Latenz, Utopie. Frankfurt am Main: Suhrkamp, 1978.

Aesthetics and Politics. London: Verso, 1980.

"Denken heisst überschreiten": In Memoriam Ernst Bloch. Frankfurt: Ullstein, 1982, 1978.

Essays on the Philosophy of Music. Translated by Peter Palmer. Cambridge; New York; Cambridge University Press, 1985.

Werkausgabe. Frankfurt am Main: Suhrkamp, 1985, (c)1969.

Natural Law and Human Dignity. Cambridge, MA: MIT Press, 1986.

The Utopian Function of Art and Literature: Selected Essays. Cambridge, MA: MIT Press, 1988.

Heritage of Our Times. Cambridge, U.K.: Polity Press, 1991.

WORKS ON BLOCH

Baumgart, J. "E. Bloch, Erbschaft dieser Zeit." *Neue Rundschau* 2 (1963).

Buhr, M. "Der religiöse Ursprung und Charakter der Hoffnungsphilosophie." *Deutsche Zeitschrift für Philosophie* 6 (1958): 576–598.

Bütow, H. G. *Philosophie und Gesellschaft im Denken Ernst Blochs.* Wiesbaden, 1963.

Eucken-Erdsiek, E. "Prinzip ohne Hoffnung. Kritische Betrachtungen zum Hauptwerk von E. Bloch." *Philosophische Jahrbuch* 70 (1962): 147–156.

Holz, H. H. "Der Philosoph E. Bloch und sein Werk 'Das Prinzip Hoffnung.'" *Sinn und Form* 3 (1955).

Kurella, A. "Zur Theorie der Moral. Eine alte Polemik mit E. Bloch." *Deutsche Zeitschrift für Philosophie* 6 (1958): 599–621.

Ley, H. "Ernst Bloch und das Hegelsche System." *Einheit* 3 (1957).

Lorenz, K. "Hoffnung als Wissenschaft. Die Philosophie Ernst Blochs." *Deutsche Universitätszeitung* 22 (1957): 9–11.

Rühle, Jürgen, "Philosopher of Hope: Ernst Bloch." In *Revisionism,* edited by Leopold Labedz, 166–178. New York: Praeger, 1962.

Strolz, W. "Der Marxist und die Hoffnung. Einige Überlegungen zu dem Werke Ernst Blochs." *Wort und Wahrheit* (1960).

Tjaden, K. M. "Zur Naturrechts Interpretation Ernst Blochs." *Archiv für Rechts- und Sozialphilosophie* 56 (1962): 573–584.

Zehm, G. A. "Ernst Bloch." *Der Monat* 158 (1961).

See also *Ernst Bloch zum 70. Geburtstage; Festschrift* (Berlin: Deutscher Verlag der Wissenschaften, 1955); and *Ernst Blochs Revision des Marxismus* (Berlin, 1957), an anthology with an introduction by J. H. Horn.

Franco Lombardi (1967)
Bibliography updated by Michael J. Farmer (2005)

BLONDEL, MAURICE
(1861–1949)

Maurice Blondel is considered one of the foremost French Catholic philosophers of the twentieth century. Blondel was born at Dijon. He studied at the local *lycée,* and in 1881 entered the École Normale Supérieure, where he was taught by Léon Ollé-Laprune. Because of pragmatic tendencies in his thought, Blondel's name was associated for a time with the modernist movement. He was, however, essentially orthodox, and his work has been increasingly influential among those Catholic thinkers who look for an alternative to Thomism.

Through Ollé-Laprune, Blondel was influenced by John Henry Newman's theory that belief is a matter of will as well as of logical demonstration. Blondel was far from being a thoroughgoing pragmatist or vitalist and showed none of the naturalism of thinkers like Henri Bergson and James, yet he held that truth is to be reached not only through the intellect but through the whole range of experience, and to this extent he departed from the emphasis on rational demonstration found in traditional Catholic philosophy. Most of Blondel's teaching was done at the University of Aix-en-Provence, where he taught from 1896 until his death.

THOUGHT

An extended statement of Blondel's philosophy is found in the book *L'Action,* first published in 1893 and revised near the end of his life. This book should not be confused with another of the same title, published in 1937.

The claim of Blondel's early work is that philosophy must take its impetus from action rather than from pure thought. The expression "action" is used in a wide sense to refer to the whole of our life, thinking, feeling, willing. Blondel tells us that it is to the whole man in his concreteness that philosophy must look in its quest for truth. One must turn from abstract thought to actual experience in all its fullness and richness. It is indeed this experience itself that motivates the philosophical quest, for man by his nature must act, and then he cannot help questioning the meaning of his action. Blondel anticipated the ideas later developed in existentialism when he pointed out that although we have not chosen to live and know neither whence we come nor even who we are, we are continually taking action and engaging ourselves in chosen policies.

Blondel rejected any nihilistic attempt to set aside the question of the meaning of action, and he had an ingenious argument to show that we cannot be content to say that action has no meaning. He claimed that to affirm nothing is really to affirm being. The very idea of nothing can be formed only by conceiving something positive and then denying it. There is something positive and affirmative underlying the denials of the nihilist, and even from his pessimistic view of life he derives a certain satisfaction. Blondel argued that the nihilist's nothing is his all. The very extent of what he denies reveals the greatness of what he wishes, for he cannot prevent affirmative ideas and aspirations from asserting themselves in the midst of his denials. Therefore, Blondel claimed, the problem of action and of its meaning must have a positive solution.

This solution is to be sought by means of a kind of phenomenology of action, though a phenomenology that is meant to show that we must pass beyond the phenomena to the discovery of the "supraphenomenal." We are impelled to this solution by reason of an immanent dialectic in action itself, made clear by a phenomenological description.

The basis of the dialectic is the gap between action and its realization. Man cannot in his action equal what he himself demands, and so there is in life a permanent dissatisfaction set up by the contrast between action and the realization at which it aims. This impels man to further action, and in the effort to close the gap, Blondel visualized the expansion of action in terms of an ever-wider outreach. Self-regarding action passes over into various forms of social action, and these in turn come to their limit in the highest type of moral action—that which aims at the good of all humankind.

But although this process partially overcomes the contrast between action and its realization, it never does so completely, and the gap reappears at each stage. There is no immanent solution to the problem of action. But we have seen already that an affirmative solution is demanded, and Blondel claimed that the demands of action itself point us from the immanent to the transcendent or supraphenomenal. The Catholic dimensions of Blondel's philosophy become fully apparent at this point, for it is essentially a philosophy of grace. God is immanent within man, in the sense that human action is already directed beyond the phenomenal order. To will all that we do will is already to have the action of God within us. Yet this quest for realization would be a frustrating one were it not that God in turn moves toward us in his transcendence, and human action is supported and supplemented by divine grace.

Since action is concrete, the beliefs that arise out of action and the experience of acting are not abstract formulations. It is in action that we apprehend God, but if we try to imprison him in a proposition or prove his existence by a logical demonstration, he escapes us.

In *La pensée* and subsequent writings, Blondel gave a more prominent place to thought and modified some of the anti-intellectualist tendencies that characterized his earlier period. At the same time, he reduced the differences that had separated him from traditional Catholic philosophy. But it must not be supposed that he departed in any essential respect from his philosophy of action. Thought and action were never rival principles for Blondel, but were at all times to be taken together. Action is no blind drive, but always includes thought; thought can attain its philosophical goals only as it remains closely associated with action. Thus, in his later phase, when he reconsidered the rational proofs of theism, he claimed that these proofs are possible only on the basis of a prior affirmation of God that has arisen out of our experience as active beings.

See also Action; Bergson, Henri; Dialectic; Existentialism; James, William; Modernism; Newman, John Henry; Nothing; Thomism.

Bibliography

WORKS BY BLONDEL

L'action: Essai d'une critique de la vie et d'une science de la pratique. Paris, 1893; rev. ed., 1950.

La pensée, 2 vols. Paris, 1934.

L'être et les êtres. Paris: Presses universitaires de France, 1935.

L'action, 2 vols. Paris: F. Alcan, 1937.

La philosophie et l'esprit chrétien, 2 vols. Paris: Presses universitaires de France, 1944–1946.

Exigences philosophique du christianisme. Paris: Presses universitaires de France, 1950.

WORKS ON BLONDEL

Dumery, H. *Blondel et la religion.* Paris, 1954.

Dumery, H. *La philosophie de l'action.* Paris: Aubier, 1948.

Lefèvre, F. *L'itinéraire philosophique de Maurice Blondel.* Paris, 1928.

Taymans d'Eypernon, F. *Le Blondélisme.* Louvain, 1935.

Tresmontant, Claude. *Introduction à la métaphysique de Maurice Blondel.* Paris: Éditions du Seuil, 1963.

John Macquarrie (1967)

BLOUNT, CHARLES
(1654–1693)

Charles Blount was an English deist, freethinker, and controversial writer on religion and politics. He was born at Upper Holloway, and was educated under the supervision of his father, Sir Henry Blount, traveler and author of *Voyage to the Levant* (1636). A disciple of Lord Herbert of Cherbury ("father of English deism") and of Thomas Hobbes, Blount is commonly regarded as the second English deist. Although not particularly original, he was the first popularizer of deistic thought. By artful writing—associating himself not only with Lord Herbert and Hobbes but also with John Dryden, Dr. Thomas Sydenham, Bishop Thomas Burnet, and Sir Thomas Browne—and by family influence, Blount was able to steer clear of prosecution under the Licensing Act and the blasphemy laws.

In 1679 Blount began a career of publication with *Anima Mundi: or an Historical Narration of The Opinions of the Ancients concerning Man's Soul after this Life: According to Unenlightened Nature*, a collection from pagan writers concerning disbelief in immortality. This was shortly followed by *The Last Sayings, or Dying Legacy of Mr. Thomas Hobbs of Malmsbury, who departed this Life on Thursday, December 4th, 1679* (1680). This work is a compilation of some of Hobbes's rationalistic (deistic) passages on religion: For example, "To say he [man] speaks by supernatural inspiration, is to say he finds an ardent desire to speak, or some strong opinion of himself, for the which he can alledge no natural reason"; "He that believes a thing only because it may be so, may as well doubt of it, because it may be otherwise."

Also in 1680 Blount published an oblique attack on priestcraft in *Great Is Diana of the Ephesians, or the Original of Idolatry, Together with the Politick Institution of the Gentiles Sacrifices*. In the same year there appeared his ironic survey of a sham pagan miracle-maker in *The Two First Books of Philostratus concerning the Life of Apollonius Tyaneus, written originally in Greek, with philological notes upon each chapter*. In 1683 Blount published *Religio Laici*, "Written in a Letter to John Dryden, Esq.," whose poem of the same name had appeared the previous year. Blount's work, long supposed to have been derived from Lord Herbert's prose tract of 1645 also titled *Religio Laici*, is now known to be much more closely related to a similarly titled manuscript of Lord Herbert's, unpublished until 1933. In his tract, Blount, under the guise of defending universal or natural religion, attacked by indirection the whole concept of a particular revelation. Attributed to Blount (by Antony a Wood) was the free translation (1683) of Chapter VI of Benedict de Spinoza's *Tractatus Theologico-Politicus* (in Latin, 1670; in English, 1689), under the title of *Miracles No Violations of the Laws of Nature*, which emphasized the Spinozistic interpretation of biblical miracles as natural phenomena or metaphorical or exaggerated language.

The appearance of Bishop Thomas Burnet's *Archaeologiae Philosophicae* (Latin and English versions in 1692) gave Blount the welcome opportunity to "vindicate" the pseudoscientific and allegorical attempts of the writer to explain certain delicate problems in the early chapters of Genesis. Writing in the form of a letter to Charles Gildon, Blount cited the authority of Sir Thomas Browne that "there are in Scripture stories that do exceed the Fables of Poets" and proceeded to ridicule Burnet's amiable rendition of the conversation between Eve and the Serpent, and his handling of such questions as "how out of only one rib a woman's whole body could be built" and "what language Adam spoke in the first hour of his nativity in naming the animals." This work, edited by Gildon, appeared in 1693, the year of Blount's death, in *The Oracles of Reason*. Another letter in the same collection from Blount to Dr. Thomas Sydenham is prefixed to *A Summary Account of the Deist's Religion*, wherein the worship of God by means of images and sacrifices or through a mediator is impugned and worship by imitation of God's perfections is upheld.

Blount, a Whig, was also active on the political front. Derived from John Milton's *Areopagitica*, his *A Just Vindication of Learning, And the Liberty of the Press*, and *Reasons humbly offered for the Liberty of Unlicensed Printing* were published in 1693. A third work of the same year, written under the pseudonym "Junius Brutus," was a master stroke demonstrating the futility of licensing. It was titled *King William and Queen Mary Conquerors: Or, A Discourse Endeavouring to prove that their Majesties have on Their Side, against the Late King, the Principal Reasons that make Conquest a Good Title*, and Blount duped the Tory licenser, Edmund Bohun, into granting permission to publish. By order of the House of Commons the work was burnt by the common hangman, and Bohun was dismissed in disgrace (Thomas Macaulay makes much of the incident in Chapter 19 of his *History of England*).

In this year of triumph Blount let emotionalism get the better of rationalism and committed suicide over hopeless love for his deceased wife's sister, who would not agree to a marriage deemed illegal by the Church of England.

See also Deism.

Bibliography

The nearest approach to a collection of Blount's works is *Miscellaneous Works* (London, 1695), edited by Charles Gildon with a life of Blount and a justification of his suicide. But see J. S. L. Gilmour, "Some Uncollected Authors XVII: Charles Blount," in *Book Collector* 7 (1958): 182–187.

Modern studies of Blount include Harold R. Hutcheson, "Lord Herbert and the Deists," in *Journal of Philosophy* 43 (1946): 219–221; Eugene R. Purpus, "Some Notes on a Deistical Essay Attributed to Dryden," in *Philological Quarterly* 30 (1950): 342–349; George F. Sensabaugh, "Adaptations of *Areopagitica*," in *Huntington Library Quarterly* 13 (1950): 201–205; J. A. Redwood, "Charles Blount (1654–93), Deism, and English Free Thought." in *Journal of the History of Ideas* 35 (1974): 490–498.

See also the general bibliography under the *Deism* entry.

Ernest Campbell Mossner (1967)
Bibliography updated by Tamra Frei (2005)

BODIN, JEAN
(1530–1596)

Jean Bodin, the French philosopher, statesman, and early writer on economics, is known chiefly for four major systematic works: *Method for the Easy Comprehension of History* (*Methodus ad Facilem Historiarum Cognitionem*, Paris, 1566); *Six Books of the Republic* (*Six Livres de la république*, Paris, 1576); *Universae Naturae Theatrum* (The Theater of Nature; Lyons, 1596); and *Heptaplomeres Sive Colloquium de Abditus Rerum Sublimium Arcanus* (Dialogue of Seven Wise Men; Schwerin, 1857).

Although Bodin's life is only imperfectly known, he was probably born in Anjou into a Catholic family who sought social promotion through service to the king and in clerical charges. Through the help of his bishop, Bodin was admitted at an early age to the Carmelite friars of Angers, who sent him to their school in Paris. While in Paris he probably later studied under the *lecteurs royaux*

instituted by Francis I, who personified for Bodin the ideal sovereign. Bodin was probably imprisoned for some time, but later released, on charges of professing Lutheran views. He later studied in Toulouse and was an assistant in the faculty of law there. He participated enthusiastically in the Renaissance ferment at Toulouse, which at that time was a great center of international learning, in close contact with Germany, Switzerland, Italy, Spain, and the papacy at Avignon. Bodin kept in touch with all foreign publications on religion and history, which benefited his lectures on the *Pandects*. He envisaged for a short time the career of a humanist historian in the capacity of headmaster of the Collège de l'Esquille, to which idea we owe a superb discourse of 1559, *Oratio de Instituenda in Republica Juventate*. In addition to a panoramic picture of the French Renaissance inspired by Francis I, the discourse presents a complete humanist pedagogical system.

The failure of his local ambitions and the expectation that the approaching religious wars would engulf Toulouse induced Bodin to leave for Paris, where he found a position as advocate of the Parliament of Paris, a favorable post for receiving any nomination of significance in the king's service. In his work in parliament, Bodin found a type of practical law far superior to the exegesis of ancient texts. He broke with the writers of such exegeses in the preface to his first systematic work, the *Method of History*. The history of the title is the history of knowledge and is similar in conception to that which René Descartes later presented in the preface to his *Principles*. For Bodin the three main branches of knowledge are human history, or anthropology; natural history, or physics; and divine history—theology or religion. The *Method* is a general outline of Bodin's whole system; his other three major works are each devoted to one of the three branches. The *Method* itself, though it outlines the entire system, covers in detail only Bodin's anthropology and discusses nearly all of the topics of the later *Republic*.

SOCIAL THEORY

The *Republic* itself, though it partly owes its genesis to Bodin's entire scheme, is also an outcome of a serious French political crisis of the period, which engaged Bodin's attention for many years. The book is a defense of the theory of the French monarchy, as Bodin conceived it, against Machiavellians in the Court and against various rebellious groups. The book seeks to demonstrate that monarchy, and the French monarchy in particular, is the best of all possible regimes.

The state, the republic, is a lawful government of the several households comprising it. The state arises when each head of a household, each *pater familias*, acts in concert with the others. These men are the citizens of the republic. Private property is an inalienable right of the family. At the head of this group of households is the sovereign, the administrator of the republic, whose task is the proper government of the households composing the state.

SOVEREIGNTY. Bodin's whole political philosophy rests on the doctrine of sovereignty. Sovereignty is defined in the *Republic* as "the absolute and perpetual power of a Republic, that is to say the active form and personification of the great body of a modern State."

In Bodin's conception of sovereignty two different traditions, that of Roman law and that of French monarchy, converge. The former brought with it the notion of *majestas,* which gave supreme authority established above all magistrates, however important they might be, to an absolute power of which they were but a reflection. The tradition of French monarchy, in order to demonstrate the autonomy of the French king in relation to the emperor, had been concerned chiefly with cataloguing the privileges acknowledged as the king's by the pope; these were regarded as so many proofs of the king's sovereign authority. Of these *insignia pecularia,* one list contains no fewer than 208 items.

Bodin reinterprets this twofold juridical trend and attempts to synthesize it. In the *Method* he therefore retains only five marks of sovereignty: the power of appointing higher magistrates and delineating their offices, the power of promulgating or repealing laws, the power of declaring war and concluding peace, the power of judicial review, and the power of life or death even when the law requires death.

When he wrote the *Republic,* Bodin had realized that the essential mark of sovereignty was that of making and repealing laws and that the others were dependent on this right. This right of the sovereign cannot be restricted by custom; the sovereign sanctions customary law by allowing it to continue in force. "Thus, all the force of civil laws and custom lies in the power of the Sovereign Prince." All legislative and judicial power is concentrated in the sovereign, but the sovereign is conceived as the incarnation of a principle and cannot be regarded as having a personal will at variance with the interests of the state. Against the medieval theory, reaffirmed in France in Bodin's day, of the *Politie*—a state in which supreme authority was shared among the prince, an aristocracy based on birth and office, and the representatives of the people—Bodin contends that, if sovereignty is absolute, it

is therefore indivisible, wherever it resides. There can be monarchies, aristocracies, or democracies, but never a mixed state.

In a given system of government, different modes of rule are possible. An aristocracy may be governed monarchically, as in Germany, or more or less democratically, as in Venice. But a monarchy, in which the king guarantees all liberty, is the best of regimes.

The state that Bodin depicts—a complex of families and of corporations, classes, and heterogeneous provinces—is enriched by the differences and interactions of its components. They all obey the sovereign, their sole arbiter and the personification of a public weal that is also the weal of its parts. Thus the absolute power of the sovereign transcends that of the paterfamilias, but is conceived in the latter's image. Though the authority of the sovereign is absolute with respect to the other elements of the state, the source of this authority lies in social law, as is clear from the long history of the French state, with its hereditary monarchy subject to a higher law. Though sovereignty is not limited by custom, it is limited by the requirements of justice: Authority is acknowledged as belonging only to a just government—a regime that gives every person, even the wicked, his chance. Sovereignty is also limited externally through the recognition of the legitimacy of other sovereignties, even of conflicting types. The sovereign is further obliged to collaborate with neighboring countries, so that M. J. Basdevant was enabled to see in Bodin one of the founders of modern international law. Bodin's thought is very close to the concept of peaceful coexistence that today forms one of the norms of international law.

THE THEORY OF CLIMATES. Besides outlining the structure of his ideal republic, a monarchy, Bodin also examines the diversity of states offered by experience. On the one hand he follows the pattern of the Greek philosophers, tracing historically the degradation of this ideal prototype and the manner in which are successively engendered the various forms, sound and pathological, of political organization— tyranny, democracy, aristocracy, and so on. But Bodin also studies the modes of a state's adaptation to its territory. In this investigation, which is known as the theory of climates from a later similar exposition by Montesquieu, Bodin seeks to define more precisely the ways through which geography influences human societies: "the nature of Northern and Southern peoples as well as that of the Eastern and Western ones, then, the influence of the various places, either mountainous, marshy, windswept or sheltered" (*Method of His-*

tory, Ch. 5). He gives a rather circumstantial account agreeing in many respects with modern human geography and ethnic psychology. He describes northerners as unequaled in wars and industry and southerners as unequaled in the contemplative sciences, but the inhabitants of the median region are in a particularly fit position for the blossoming of arts and laws.

In the *Method*, Bodin uses anthropogeography as a critical weapon to detect errors committed by outstanding historians in their assessment of facts, and to build a solid framework relating human history to natural history. In the *Republic* his point of view becomes more dogmatic, though his individual observations are more perspicacious. And he makes the important observation that, whatever the ontological superiority of monarchy over other forms of government may be, for a given state the most appropriate regime is the one that answers best to the people and the geography of the place. "One of the greatest and perhaps the chief foundation of Republics is to adapt the state to the citizens' nature, and the edicts and ordinances to the character of places, persons, and times."

Bodin's defense of the French monarchy in the *Method* and his vast culture and philosophical wisdom won him the confidence of the royal family, and in 1571 he entered the service of the duke of Alençon, the brother of the future Henri III, who, after his coronation in 1574, befriended Bodin. But in 1576, at a meeting of the States-General, Bodin delivered a speech in which he succeeded in defeating the king's request for the financial means necessary to suppress the French Protestants. By this speech Bodin temporarily diverted the civil war, but lost the king's favor and was relegated to a humble post in Laon, where he took advantage of the relative calm to write in 1578 the Latin version of the *Republic* (published Paris, 1586) and the *Demonomanie des sorciers* (Paris, 1580). The latter work, which went through some ten editions, advocates the repression of witchcraft and contains as well a complete demonology, in great part taken from the Bible.

NATURAL HISTORY

Upon his return to Laon from trips to the Court of Queen Elizabeth I and to Belgium on missions with the duke of Alençon, Bodin returned to work on the second part of his system, his physics. The *Amphiteatrum Naturae* is in the form of a dialogue in which a "mystagogue" expounds to a "theoretician" a complex and obscure philosophy that attempts to reconcile Neoplatonic idealism with Aristotelian naturalism and also with important religious

attitudes derived from the Hebrew tradition. Living beings are explained in terms of Platonic forms, but the nature of the explanation and of the forms remains obscure. The soul is corporeal and is the form of the body. It is separable from the body both in life and at death. It possesses unity, and its function is to vivify the extended matter of the body. The powers of the soul, including sensation and appetite, are seen as modeled on the will: They act directly upon the body with no need of an intermediary. Angels, too, are material, and the human soul is inhabited not only by a good angel and a bad angel, but also by a large number of spirits, each in charge of a special gift. But Bodin is constrained from scrutinizing too closely the mysteries of nature by his awareness of the abyss that separates the Creator from the world of creatures. The *Amphiteatrum Naturae* thus fails, in the end, on a level where Bodin's contemporaries could not question its failure, the religious level.

THEOLOGY. A similar failure is evident in the *Heptaplomeres Sive Colloquium de Abditus Rerum Sublimium Arcanus,* a work composed during the last years of Bodin's life and published in part in 1841 and completely in 1857. This work is on the third of Bodin's three branches of knowledge, theology. The seven sages of the title represent three branches of Christianity, Judaism, Islam, natural religion, and skeptical materialism. Despite fertile discussion and a generous courtesy to one another, they cannot arrive at a common foundation for religious matters. In the progress of the discussion, it becomes apparent that in almost every instance the majority agrees with the doctrine of the Jews and that all might accept the Decalogue, looked upon as a spiritualization of the natural law and as embodying such fundamental principles. (Bodin had in an earlier work made a comparative study of the institutions of the most diverse countries, from the ancient empires to the recently discovered nations of Africa and America. From this study he had conceived the idea of replacing Roman law with a synthetic and universal law that allowed for different modes of application depending on the place, the era, and the geographic or economic conditions.)

But from the historical standpoint, which is so significant for Bodin, only the Christian faiths can contend for victory. Among these, the discussion goes badly for the Protestants, who cannot rationally justify their conservatism, their innovations, or their contradictions. The Catholic Church, since it possesses the most elaborate body of doctrine, is subjected to the most criticism; but the fact that the Catholic Church remains the religion of the state, and is relatively stable in the midst of uncertainty, is for Bodin to some degree a vindication of the faith of its partisans. The book proposes, therefore, that the church is to be believed, as the Catholic prelate has held successfully throughout the dialogue.

This justification of the Catholic Church is in line with Bodin's support of the Catholic League during his last years, a support that was not dictated simply by the instinct of self-preservation. But Bodin was not fully trusted by the members of the League and was more or less confined to his house, where he spent most of his time in contemplation and the education of children, for whom he wrote a catechism in the spirit of the *Amphiteatrum Naturae.* Bodin died as a Christian and was buried in the choir of a church.

Bodin's work enjoyed outstanding renown until the middle of the seventeenth century but was totally disregarded in the eighteenth, and without a famous article in Pierre Bayle's *Dictionary,* it would never have recovered from this neglect. Bodin's work was restored to favor in 1853 through Henri Baudrillart's *Jean Bodin et son temps,* and in the twentieth century he resumed his place among the acknowledged great political philosophers of all time. Bodin also merits consideration as one of the most representative spirits of the Renaissance, and one of the first to formulate historical laws in each of the three realms— divine, natural, and human—that he considered.

See also Aristotelianism; Bayle, Pierre; Descartes, René; Idealism; Naturalism; Neoplatonism; Philosophy of Law, History of; Renaissance; Sovereignty.

Bibliography

WORKS BY BODIN

Le théâtre de la nature. Translated by François de Fougerolles. Lyons, 1597.

The Six Books of a Commonweale. Translated by Richard Knolles. London, 1606. Modern edition, edited by K. D. McRae. Cambridge, MA, 1962.

Johannis Bodini Colloquium Heptaplomeres. Edited by L. Noack. Paris and London, 1857.

La réponse à M. de Malestroict, edited by Henri Hauser. Paris, 1932. One of Bodin's economic works.

La méthode de l'histoire. Translated by Pierre Mesnard. Algiers, 1941.

Method for the Easy Comprehension of History. Translated by Beatrice Reynolds. New York: Columbia University Press, 1945.

Oeuvres philosophiquès, edited by Pierre Mesnard. Paris: Presses Universitaires de France, 1951. Vol. I.

On Sovereignty: Four Chapters from "The Six Books of the Commonwealth," edited and translated by Julian H. Franklin. New York: Cambridge University Press, 1992.

Selected Writings on Philosophy, Religion, and Politics, edited by Paul L. Rose. Geneva: Librairie Droz, 1980.

WORKS ON BODIN

Blair, Ann. *The Theater of Nature: Jean Bodin and Renaissance Science.* Princeton, NJ: Princeton University Press, 1997.

Brown, L. S. *The Methodus ad Facilem Historiarum Cognitionem.* Washington, DC: Catholic University of America Press, 1939.

Chauvire, R. *Jean Bodin l'auteur de la République.* Paris, 1914.

Engster, Dan. "Jean Bodin, Scepticism and Absolute Sovereignty" *History of Political Thought* 17 (4) (1996): 469–499.

Franklin, Julian H. "Bodin and Locke on Consent to Taxation: A Note and Observation." *History of Political Thought* 7 (1986): 89–91.

Franklin, Julian H. *Jean Bodin and the Rise of Absolutist Theory.* London: Cambridge University Press, 1973.

Franklin, Julian H. *Jean Bodin and the Sixteenth-Century Revolution in the Methodology of Law and History.* New York: Columbia University Press, 1963.

Garosci, A. *Jean Bodin.* Milan: Corticelli, 1934.

Harding, Alan. "The Origins of the Concept of the State." *History of Political Thought* 15 (1) (1994): 57–72.

King, Preston. *The Ideology of Order: A Comparative Analysis of Jean Bodin and Thomas Hobbes.* New York: Barnes and Noble, 1974.

Kuntz, Marion D. "Harmony and the Heptaplomeres of Jean Bodin." *Journal of the History of Philosophy* 12 (1974): 31–41

Lloyd, Howell A. "Sovereignty: Bodin, Hobbes, Rousseau." *Revue Internationale de Philosophie* 45 (179) (1991): 353–379.

Mayer, Jacob P., ed. *Fundamental Studies on Jean Bodin.* New York: Arno Press, 1979.

Mesnard, Pierre. *L'essor de la philosophie politique au XVIème siècle.* 2nd ed. Paris: Vrin, 1952.

Mesnard, Pierre. *Jean Bodin en la historia del pensamiento.* Translated by José Antonio Maravall. Madrid: Instituto de Estudios Políticos, 1962.

Mesnard, Pierre. "The Psychology and Pneumatology of Jean Bodin." *International Philosophical Quarterly* 2 (May 1962).

Parker, David. "Law, Society and the State in the Thought of Jean Bodin." *History of Political Thought* 2 (1981): 253–285.

Reynolds, Beatrice B. *Proponents of Limited Monarchy in Sixteenth Century France: Francis Hotman and Jean Bodin.* New York: AMS Press, 1968.

Salmon, John Hearsey McMillan. "The Legacy of Jean Bodin: Absolutism, Populism or Constitutionalism?" *History of Political Thought* 17 (4) (1996): 500–522.

Smith, Constance I. "Jean Bodin and Comparative Law." *Journal of the History of Ideas* 25 (1964): 417–422.

Pierre Mesnard (1967)
Bibliography updated by Tamra Frei (2005)

BODY-MIND PROBLEM

See *Mind-Body Problem*

BOEHME, JAKOB
(1575–1624)

Jakob Boehme, the Lutheran contemplative, was born at Alt Seidelberg near Görlitz in Silesia and lived there nearly all his life, working chiefly as a cobbler. Among his mystical experiences, the seminal one occurred in 1600, when he glanced at a pewter dish that reflected the sunlight and in a rapt state saw "the Being of Beings, the Byss and the Abyss, the eternal generation of the Trinity, the origin and descent of this world, and of all creatures through the Divine Wisdom" (*Second Epistle*, §6). Though not formally educated, Boehme read rather widely and was influenced by, among others, Paracelsus (1493–1541) and Valentin Weigel (1538–1588), the Lutheran mystic. The above quotation, however, hints at most of the main features of Boehme's *Weltanschauung*, which he first expressed in his *Aurora, oder die Morgenröte im Aufgang* (1612) and then in other works (from 1618 onward—he did not write in the intervening period because of ecclesiastical pressure). The "Abyss" is God considered as the *Ungrund*—the undifferentiated Absolute that is ineffable and neither light nor darkness, neither love nor wrath. The "eternal generation of the Trinity" occurs because the *Ungrund* contains a will to self-intuition. This will (identified with the Father) finds itself as the "heart" (the Son). Emanating from these is the "moving life" (the Spirit). This eternal process toward self-knowledge and outgoing dynamic activity generates the inner spiritual world, which is the prototype of the visible universe. With differentiation, conflict of wills becomes possible; and Satan, in severing himself from the "heart," falls. Sometimes Boehme writes as if evil were necessary, at others as though it were a contingent spoiling of the cosmic harmony. Indeed, Boehme in general shifted his position, and no single metaphysical theory fits all his writings.

This was partly because, in addition to his doctrine of the Trinity considered in itself, Boehme also enunciated a theory of seven qualities or energies in nature; and the fluidity of his metaphysics results from different ways of coordinating these two main aspects of his thought. The seven qualities divide into two triads, a higher and a lower, between which there is the crucial energy he called "the flash" (*Blitz*). The lower triad is (1) contraction (whereby substances become individuated), (2) diffusion (whereby things gravitate to one another), and (3) rotation or oscillation (the tension produced by the interplay of the forces of contraction and diffusion). The higher triad is in effect the lower triad transformed: It is (1) love, (2) expression, and (3) eternal nature or the Kingdom of God, through which there is achieved a harmony between the material and spiritual worlds.

The meaning of this evolutionary scheme is that the Trinity considered in itself is merely formal or ideal. The abysmal will needs a real object to arouse self-knowledge. Thus the Father differentiates himself through the first (lower) triad into material nature. An obstacle is thereby created to the abysmal will, which can be overcome, not by abolition, but only by transformation. The flash is the collision, as it were, between the absolute will and nature. Herein the Spirit reveals in its light the higher triad, identified with the Son as the incarnation of spirit in matter. This is the goal of the divine operation, whereby the opposition is overcome and made into a harmony.

Psychologically, the flash reveals to man his choices. He can remain at the level of anguish implicit in the welter of sensation represented by the oscillation of nature; or he can "die" unto self, and identify himself with the abysmal will—which also has to negate itself in order to achieve victory. Thus the mystical life is an imitation of Christ's suffering and triumph.

Boehme's doctrines brought him into conflict with church authorities. He was critical of the bibliolatry he detected in contemporary Protestantism, of a formalistic doctrine of election, and of crude notions of heaven (for Boehme, heaven is not a place). In England, William Law and the Behmenists (Boehme's disciples), who merged with the Quakers, were strongly influenced by him. And German Romanticism owed something to him—especially Friedrich von Schelling, notably in his later writings.

See also Evil; Law, William; Mysticism, History of; Paracelsus; Romanticism; Schelling, Friedrich Wilhelm Joseph von.

Bibliography

WORKS BY BOEHME

The German edition of Boehme is *Jakob Böhmes sämmtliche werke*, 7 vols. (Leipzig: Barth, 1832–1860); translated by J. Ellistone and J. Sparrow as *The Works of Jacob Behmen*, 4 vols. (London, 1644–1662; reedited, London: Richardson, 1764–1781; reprinted, 1909–1924). *The Signature of All Things* and two other works are to be found in the Everyman edition, edited by Emert Rhys, introduction by Clifford Bax (London: Dent, 1912). See also W. S. Palmer, ed., *The Confessions of Jacob Boehme* (London: Methuen, 1920).

WORKS ON BOEHME

A good introduction is Rufus M. Jones, *Spiritual Reformers in the 16th and 17th Centuries* (London: Macmillan, 1914),

Chs. 9–11. See also H. H. Brinton, *The Mystic Will* (London: Allen and Unwin, 1931) and H. L. Martensen, *Jacob Boehme: His Life and Teaching,* translated by T. Rhys Evans (London: Hodder and Stoughton, 1885).

Other Recommended Titles

Brown, Robert F. *The Later Philosophy of Schelling: The Influence of Boehme on the Works of 1809–1815.* Lewisburg, PA: Bucknell University Press, 1977.

Dourley, John P. "Jacob Boehme and Paul Tillich on Trinity and God: Similarities and Differences." *Religious Studies* (4) (1995): 429–445.

Koenker, Ernest. "Potentiality in God: Jacob Boehme." *Philosophy Today* 15 (1971): 44–51.

O'Regan, Cyril. *Gnostic Apocalypse: Jacob Boehme's Haunted Narrative.* Albany: State University of New York Press, 2002.

Walsh, David. *The Mysticism of Innerworldly Fulfillment.* Gainesville: University Press of Florida, 1983.

Ninian Smart (1967)
Bibliography updated by Tamra Frei (2005)

BOETHIUS, ANICIUS MANLIUS SEVERINUS

(c. 480–524)

Anicius Manlius Severinus Boethius, late Roman statesman and philosopher, was born into the ancient Anician family in Rome, the son of a distinguished father who was consul in 487 and twice prefect of the city. Carefully educated in the liberal arts and philosophy—possibly in Athens—and precocious in genius, he entered public life at an early age under Theodoric the Ostrogoth, the Arian king of Italy from 493 to 526, who made use of Romans and the traditional administrative methods in his government.

Boethius became consul in 510 and for many years was Theodoric's principal minister (*magister officiorum*). In 522 his two sons became consuls; shortly thereafter Boethius was arrested on a charge of treason that cannot now be defined but that he denounced as a calumny. It has been suggested that he wished to exalt the Roman senate and to negotiate with Byzantium; it is also possible that as a Catholic he was distasteful to Theodoric. Condemned to exile and then to death, he was imprisoned for a year at Pavia and executed in 524. His father-in-law Symmachus and Pope John II were similarly put to death in 525 and 526.

Boethius's cult at Pavia, apparently resting on a confusion with Severinus of Cologne, won him popular canonization as a martyr. In recent centuries, however, his Christian allegiance has been questioned because of the absence of religious themes in his *De Consolatione* and the doubtful authenticity of his theological writings. The question was settled when definite proof of his authorship of these pieces was provided by H. Usener in 1877. Many readers have felt it strange that Boethius, faced with death, should have found his principal stay in Stoic and Neoplatonist philosophy, but such an attitude is not without parallels in the cultured circles of late Roman society. We may note that the readers of Boethius in the ages of faith seem to have felt no uneasiness on this count.

WRITINGS

The literary fecundity of Boethius is astonishing, especially in view of his family life and exacting official duties. He wrote on education, science, philosophy, and theology, but he was above all a logician, a translator, and a commentator. His *Elements of Arithmetic, Elements of Music,* and *Elements of Geometry* (written 500–510) all summarize existing works by Nicomachus of Gerasa and by Euclid. Of theological works attributed to him, four are now recognized as authentic: *On the Trinity* and *On the Person and Two Natures in Christ, Against Eutyches and Nestorius,* and two smaller tracts. The treatise *On the Catholic Faith* is of doubtful authenticity.

In philosophy Boethius set himself the task of translating and commenting upon all the works of Plato and Aristotle, with a view to a final harmonization of their teachings.

TRANSLATIONS. As part of his ambitious program, Boethius produced the following translations: the *Introduction* (*Isagoge*) of Porphyry and the *Categories* of Aristotle (the so-called old logic); the *Prior Analytics* and *Posterior Analytics,* the *Sophistic Arguments* and the *Topics* of Aristotle (the so-called new logic). It is questionable whether the Boethian translations are still extant among the various primitive translations that were supplanted by versions by Gerald of Cremona and others.

COMMENTARIES. Boethius produced two commentaries on the *Introduction* of Porphyry, one for beginners and the other, his chief philosophical work, for advanced students (composed 507–509); one on the *Categories* (510); on Victorinus's translation of the *Introduction* (before 505); and on the *Topics* of Cicero. In addition, he wrote several short treatises on logic.

Finally, there is Boethius's masterpiece, *On the Consolation of Philosophy,* written while he was in prison at Pavia, a dialogue in prose and verse between the writer and Philosophy personified, in which the just man unjustly suffering is confirmed in his conviction that happiness and fortitude may be found in adversity. The arguments used are in part Stoic and in part Neoplatonic, but the sentiment throughout is religious, though not explicitly Christian.

Boethius lived during a period of considerable intellectual activity in Rome. Cassiodorus was his colleague, and among his elder contemporaries were the great popes Gelasius I and Hormisdas, and the canonist and chronologist Denis the Little. By his early death he escaped the disasters that befell Italy during Justinian's attempt to recapture the peninsula for the Byzantine Empire and the ravages of the Goths.

The sack and evacuation of Rome in 546 may with some assurance be taken as the dividing line in Italy between the ancient and the medieval cultures. Standing thus at the very end of a civilization, Boethius may rightly be called an eminent founder of the Middle Ages and a figure of supreme importance in the history of Western thought. Himself one of the "last of the Romans," he was also the last Western thinker to whom the works of Plato and Aristotle were familiar in Greek and to whom ancient thought in all its fullness was still comprehensible. His translations and commentaries, though neglected for centuries, stimulated and fed the minds of those who brought about the revival of dialectic in the eleventh century, and gave to medieval speculation the dialectical bent and the Aristotelian color that it never lost. Moreover, his approach to theological issues, though consciously reflecting the procedure of Augustine, was in fact more technical and dialectical in method than that of any of his predecessors. He professedly used the human power of reasoning to penetrate and explain the dogmas of Christianity and regarded the effort of reason (*ratio*) to support and discuss authority (*auctoritas*) as a principal means in the elucidation of revealed truth. On the technical level of a translator he had a genius second only to that of Cicero for exact reproduction of terms of art in his native language. Many of these terms became current coin in the Middle Ages, and a number of his definitions—those of nature, substance, person, eternity, providence, and beatitude—were accepted and stereotyped by Aquinas and others.

Boethius's influence upon the thinkers of the early scholastic period (1000–1150) can scarcely be exaggerated. It was the Boethian age as surely as the next age was Aristotelian. It was his commentary on Porphyry, in which he gave the answers of Plato and Aristotle to the "problem of universals" that initiated the great controversy on universals in the eleventh century. The early Scholastics' concentration of interest upon logic gave to the whole fabric of medieval thought from Roscelin to William of Ockham, and to the form and content of academic teaching, that preoccupation with method rather than with matter which characterized Scholastic thought, giving it accuracy and subtlety but also tending to divorce it from life and to substitute logic for discovery.

THE "CONSOLATION"

In another realm, the *Consolation of Philosophy* was one of the two or three books of universal appeal throughout the Middle Ages. Philosophically it is notable for containing a long discussion of the eternity of God, defined as the full and perfect possession of endless life always present in its entirety, and the "aeviternity" of the created universe, without beginning or end but existing in the ever-changing succession of time. On the basis of this definition, Boethius tried to solve the problem raised by God's prevision of free human acts. God in eternity has a simultaneous *vision* of all temporal reality, and he sees free acts as free. Here Boethius also made the valuable and influential distinction between that which is (*id quod est*)—for instance, the totality of parts of an individual compound substance—and that by which a substance is what it is, its being (*quo est, esse*). He identified the latter with the "form" of the whole, an important metaphysical declaration rendered classical by Thomas Aquinas. Boethius, who was engaged in distinguishing God from all other things, went on to remark that in creatures the form (*esse*) is mentally separable from the substance (*id quod est*), whereas in God his being is identical with "that which is." This is not, as has sometimes been stated, a first enunciation of the celebrated Thomist distinction between essence and existence—it is, rather, the distinction between a substance and its metaphysical cause—but it was a step on the journey, inviting further progress. The mingled melancholy, resignation to divine providence, and sense of the supreme value of the good in life in the *Consolation* appealed powerfully to the experience of those confronting the risks and disasters of medieval life, and it was to them, rather than to monks or theologians, that the work of Boethius brought comfort. It was translated into Anglo-Saxon by King Alfred the Great (c. 890), into German by Notker (c. 1000), and into French by Jean de Meung (c. 1300). It was favorite reading of Dante Alighieri, Giovanni Boccaccio, and Geoffrey Chaucer, and inspired numerous imitators.

See also Aristotelianism; Aristotle; Augustine, St.; Cicero, Marcus Tullius; Dante Alighieri; Logic, History of; Medieval Philosophy; Neoplatonism; Plato; Porphyry;

Roscelin; Stoicism; Thomas Aquinas, St.; William of Ockham.

Bibliography

Critical editions of all of Boethius's translations and of his own treatise *De divisione* have now been published as well as new editions of his *Theological Treatises, Consolation of Philosophy, De differentiis topicis, De hypotheticis syllogismis,* and *De institutione arithmetica.*

WORKS BY BOETHIUS

Boethius's "De Topicis Differentiis." Translated by Eleonore Stump. Ithaca, NY: Cornell University Press, 1978.

Boethius's "In Ciceronis Topica." Translated by Eleonore Stump. Ithaca, NY: Cornell University Press, 1988.

The Consolation of Philosophy. Translated with an introduction and explanatory notes by P. G. Walsh. Oxford: Clarendon Press, 1999.

De divisione. Edited and translated by John Magee. Leiden: Brill, 1998

De hypotheticis syllogismis. Edited by Luca Obertello. Brescia: Paideia, 1969.

De topicis differentiis. In *De topicis differentiis kai hoi buzantines metafraseis tou Manouel Holobolou kai Prochorou Kudone,* edited by Dimitrios Nikitas. Athens: Academy of Athens, 1969.

Opuscula Sacra and *De consolatione Philosophiae.* Edited by Claudio Moreschini. Munich: K. G. Saur, 2000.

Porphyry's *Isagoge* and Aristotle's *Categories, de Interpretatione, Prior Analytics, Topics, Sophistical Refutations. Arisoteles Latinus.* Vols. I–III, V, VI. Brussels: Desclée De Brouwer; Paris: Leiden, 1961–1975.

The Theological Tractates. Translated by H. F. Stewart, E. K. Rand, and S. J. Tester. Cambridge, MA: Harvard University Press, 1973.

WORKS ABOUT BOETHIUS

Chadwick, Henry. *Boethius: The Consolations of Music, Logic, Theology, and Philosophy.* Oxford: Oxford University Press, 1981.

Courcelle, Pierre. *La Consolation de Philosophie dans la tradition littéraire.* Paris: Études Augustiniennes, 1967.

Magee, John. *Boethius on Signification and Mind.* London: Brill, 1989.

Marenbon, John. *Boethius.* New York: Oxford University Press, 2002.

Martin, Christopher J. "The Logic of Negation in Boethius." *Phronesis* 36 (1991): 277–304.

Martin, Christopher J. "Non-Reductive Arguments from Impossible Hypotheses in Boethius and Philoponus." *Oxford Studies in Ancient Philosophy* 17 (1999): 279–302.

Sorabji, Richard, ed. *Aristotle Transformed: The Ancient Commentators and Their Influence.* London; Duckworth, 1990.

Sorabji, Richard. *Time, Creation, and the Continuum.* London: Duckworth, 1983.

David Knowles (1967)
Bibliography updated by Christopher J. Martin (2005)

BOETHIUS, ANICIUS MANLIUS SEVERINUS [ADDENDUM]

Boethius's position in the history of philosophy is curious. He is at best a competent representative of the Neoplatonic commentary tradition of late antiquity. His decision, however, to make that tradition available in Latin led to his having a deep and lasting influence on the development of philosophy.

It was Boethius's answer to the question left open by Porphyry that provided the basic material for later disputes over universals. Boethius argues that no extramental thing can be present entire in each of many individuals. He offers, without apparently noticing a difference, two accounts of universal concepts that are not obviously compatible. In one he maintains that mind is able to separate, or abstract, from an individual that which makes it the kind of thing it is: its species. In the other, inductive, account, he claims that the mind collects "likenesses" from many individuals to obtain their species. On either account the result is a universal. Boethius concludes that species and genera are incorporeal things that are universal in the mind and singular in sensible individuals. He does not, however, explain how this multiplied singularity is to be reconciled with his own argument against an extramental unity common to many and so leaves open to medievals the full range of positions on universals from extreme antirealism to extreme realism.

In his commentary on Porphyry's *Isagoge*, Boethius develops a distinction made there between separable accidents, such as being asleep, which a subject can cease to have without ceasing to exist, and "inseparable" accidents such as the blackness of crows, which, he claims, can be mentally but not actually separated—we can conceive of a crow that is not black but one cannot exist.

A related distinction is made by Aristotle between numerical separability and separability in account, or definition. Features included in the definition of something are conceptually inseparable from it. Inseparable accidents and properties are conceptually but not actually separable. This distinction seems to be invoked by Boethius in *De hypotheticis syllogismis,* in which he allows that we may suppose to be so what is actually impossible in order to see what follows. An example of such a nonreductive hypothesizing of an impossibility is found in his theological treatise *Quomodo substantiae.* There Boethius posits the impossibility that god does not exist in order to explore the nature of the goodness of created things. Similar thought experiments are found in Philoponus and, through Boethius, were transmitted to the Middle Ages, during which they played a crucial role in theology and were formalized in logic textbooks as the *obligatio* of impossible *positio*.

In *Quomodo substantiae* Boethius proposes to derive his conclusion about the goodness of created beings from a set of principles that, he claims, are recognized as true by everyone or at least by the learned. These principles provided a terminology for the description of the ontological structure of created beings and God that became the standard one in Middle Ages. Boethius characterizes here as "*id quod est*" (that which is) what he refers to in his commentaries on Porphyry and Aristotle as a substance. That which makes a creature the kind of thing that it is, according to *Quomodo substantiae*, its *esse* (being). For creatures *id quod est* and *esse* are distinct, but for God they are one and the same.

In another of the *Theological Treatises*, *Contra Eutychen*, Boethius makes a different but historically equally important distinction. Here *esse* refers to any kind of being, that is to individuals and their species and genera in the Aristotelian category of substance or any of the accidental categories. Subsistences (*subsistentia*) are beings that are not accidents and do not require accidents in order to exist—that is to say, individuals and species from the category of substance. Finally substances are the individuals but not the species in this category because, according to Boethius, a substance is a being which is the subject of accidents.

Probably the most influential of Boethius's definitions, however, was that which he gave in *Contra Eutychen* of a person as an individual substance with a rational nature. The problem that Boethius began to tackle here and that exercised theologians for rest of the Middle Ages was that of showing how God may be three persons without at the same time being three distinct substances.

In *De hypotheticis syllogismis* Boethius distinguishes two sorts of conditional propositions. Accidental conditionals such has "*If fire is hot, then the heavens are spherical*" hold merely because it is impossible for the antecedent to be true when the consequent is false. The condition is also satisfied by natural conditionals, such as "*If something is human, then its an animal*," but in these there is a connection between the antecedent and consequent.

The distinction between two forms of conditional was identified in the twelfth century with that between actual inseparability and inseparability in account and for reasoning about impossibilities only the latter were allowed. It provided the basis for Peter Abaelard's development of a unified theory of inference from Boethius's remarks on topical inference in *De differentiis topicis* and on the conditional in *De hypotheticis syllogismis*.

Boethius's own account of the hypothetical syllogism did not survive long into the twelfth century because he had no understanding of propositional negation. He thus allows inferences such as "*If (if it's an A, it's a B), then it's a C, but its not a C; therefore if it's an A, then its not a B*," which later logicians, possessing the notion of propositional negation, were able to make little sense of.

The treatment of the reconciliation of divine foreknowledge and human freedom in Books 4 and 5 of the *Consolation of Philosophy* provided the Middle Ages with one of its standard solutions. Boethius makes a distinction between absolute necessity—such as that in virtue of which a human being is an animal—and conditioned necessity—the necessity, for example, that Socrates is sitting given that he is known to be sitting. This latter necessity, he claims, is compatible with Socrates freely having chosen to sit.

Boethius argues that God's knowledge of the past, present, and future history of the world determines it only with conditioned necessity and so is compatible with human freedom. What he does not offer, however, is an account of the possibility, corresponding to that of Socrates' not choosing to sit, of the history of the world being other than it will be. Rather, he maintains, it is the expression, as fate, of the divine providential plan. Again medieval thinkers were left with a problem as much as with a solution. Of Boethius's works on the quadrivium, only two—*De institutione arithmetica* and *de Institutione Musica*—survived into the twelfth century, but they became textbooks for the rest of the Middle Ages.

See also Logic, History of; Medieval (European) Logic.

Christopher J. Martin (2005)

BOETIUS OF DACIA
(c. 13th century)

Boetius of Dacia was an Aristotelian and Averroist philosopher of the thirteenth century, sometimes called Boetius of Sweden, after the country of his birth. Born during the first half of the century, he was probably a secular cleric and canon of the diocese of Linköping. He was an associate of Siger of Brabant as a teacher of philosophy in the faculty of arts at Paris and, as a leader of the Averroist movement, condemned in 1277 by Stephen Tempier, bishop of Paris. With Siger, Boetius fled the city after the condemnation and appealed to the pope. After detention at the pontifical curia at Orvieto, Boetius joined the Dominican order as a member of the province of Dacia. The date of his death is unknown.

Boetius wrote works on logic, natural philosophy, metaphysics, and ethics. Some of these are lost; only a few have been edited. A complete edition of his extant works is now in progress.

Boetius philosophized in a rationalistic spirit, defending his right as a philosopher to discuss any subject falling within the competence of reason and to come to whatever conclusions reason dictated, even though they might contradict Christian faith. He taught, for example, that philosophizing is the most excellent human activity, that philosophers alone are the wise men of this world, that creation ex nihilo is impossible, that the world and the human species are eternal, and that there can be no resurrection of the dead. His treatise *On the Highest Good, or On the Life of the Philosopher* contains one of the most glowing and optimistic descriptions of the life of pure reason written in the Middle Ages. Setting aside the teachings of faith, Boetius inquires what reason tells us about the ultimate purpose of human life. Following Aristotle, he defines man's supreme good as the philosophical contemplation of truth and virtuous living according to the norms of nature. The philosopher alone, he concludes, lives rightly and achieves the ultimate end of human life.

Despite his rationalism, Boetius did not abandon his Christian faith but sought an ultimate reconciliation with it. Philosophy, in his view, is the work of human reason investigating the natural causes and principles of the universe, whereas the Christian religion rests on supernatural revelation and miracles of God. Because the teachings of faith have a higher source than those of philosophy, in cases of conflict the latter must give way to the former. Human reason is fallible and often comes to only probable conclusions. Even when its conclusions seem necessary, if they are contrary to revealed doctrine they are not true. In these cases truth is on the side of revelation and not on the side of reason. For example, the philosophical conclusion that the world is eternal must give way to the revealed truth that the world was created in time.

Boetius was condemned for speaking as though there were a double truth, one of faith and another of philosophy. But he carefully avoided calling true a philosophical conclusion contrary to faith.

See also Aristotelianism; Averroism; Logic, History of; Medieval Philosophy; Rationalism; Siger of Brabant.

Bibliography

Doncoeur, P. "Notes sur les averroistes latins. Boèce le Dace." *Revue des sciences philosophiques et théologiques* 4 (1910): 500–511.

Gilson, Étienne. *History of Christian Philosophy in the Middle Ages.* New York: Random House, 1955.

Grabmann, M. "Die Opuscula De Summo Bono sive De Vita Philosophi und De Sompniis des Boetius von Dacien." *Archives d'histoire doctrinale et littéraire du moyen âge* 6 (1931): 287–317.

Grabmann, Martin. *Mittelalterliches Geistesleben,* 2nd ed. Munich, 1936. Vol. II.

Grabmann, Martin. *Neuaufgefundene Werke des Siger von Brabant und Boetius von Dacien.* Munich, 1924.

Mandonnet, P. "Note complémentaire sur Boèce de Dacie." *Revue des sciences philosophiques et théologiques* 22 (1933): 246–250.

Maurer, Armand A. *Medieval Philosophy.* New York: Random House, 1962.

Sajó, G. "Boèce de Dacie et les commentaires anonymes inédits de Munich sur la physique et sur la génération attribués à Siger de Brabant." *Archives d'histoire doctrinale et littéraire du moyen âge* 33 (1958): 21–58.

Sajó, G. "Boetius de Dacia und seine philosophische Bedeutung." In *Miscellania Mediaevalia, Vol. II, Die Metaphysik im Mittelalter.* Berlin: De Gruyter, 1963.

Sajó, G. *Tractatus de Aeternitate Mundi.* Berlin, 1964.

Armand A. Maurer (1967)

BOHM, DAVID
(1917–1992)

David Bohm was a major twentieth-century physicist, and one of the world's leading authorities on quantum theory and its conceptual foundations. He was born in Wilkes-Barre, Pennsylvania, on December 20, 1917, and died on October 27, 1992, in London.

A student of J. Robert Oppenheimer, Bohm received his doctorate from the University of California at Berkeley in 1943. While still a graduate student, he discovered a particular collective movement of electrons in a plasma, now called Bohm-diffusion. At Princeton University in 1950, he completed the first of his six scientific books, *Quantum Theory*, which became the definitive exposition of the orthodox (Copenhagen) interpretation of quantum mechanics, the development of which was led by the Danish physicist Niels Bohr between 1925 and 1930. Here

Bohm presented his reformulation of the paradox of Albert Einstein, Boris Podolsky, and Nathan Rosen (EPR) concerning the possibility of simultaneous values of position and momentum for a pair of separated particles.

Bohm's version of the EPR analysis, involving components of spin in place of position and momentum, has been the basis of the enormous expansion of research on the foundations of quantum theory, focusing on nonlocality and the possible incompleteness of the quantum description (the question of "hidden variables"), that has occurred during the past several decades. Bohm and Yakir Aharonov, in 1957, made the first major step in this research when they demonstrated the existence of a "rather strange kind of correlations in the properties of distant things" (p.1072). This work was a forerunner of the seminal work of John Bell on quantum nonlocality (Bell's theorem).

In 1951 Bohm accomplished what physicists at the time regarded as impossible: He constructed, as an alternative to the prevailing observer-oriented Copenhagen interpretation of quantum theory, an objective, fully deterministic account of nonrelativistic quantum phenomena in terms of a theory describing a motion of particles under an evolution choreographed by the wave function (Bohmian mechanics). The theory Bohm proposed was in fact a rediscovery of Louis de Broglie's 1927 pilot-wave model, of which Bohm had been unaware. However, unlike de Broglie, Bohm fully appreciated the significance of the model. In particular, he showed how the predictions of the quantum measurement formalism, involving a non-noncommutative algebra of operators as observables, could be entirely explained.

In 1959 at Bristol, England, Bohm again collaborated with Aharonov, this time on a paper concerned with a very different sort of nonlocality. The result was the Aharonov-Bohm effect: In quantum mechanics a magnetic field can influence the behavior of electrons confined far away from the field, a phenomenon incompatible not only with classical physics but with the spirit of the Copenhagen interpretation of quantum theory as well. The Aharonov-Bohm effect remains, some four decades after its discovery, a subject of intense research.

Bohm was a person of extraordinary commitment to principle, both moral and scientific. He refused in 1951 to testify against colleagues before the House Un-American Activities Committee, an act that led to his indictment for contempt of Congress and his banishment from Princeton and, indeed, from all of American academia. During most of his last forty years he was engaged in an often lonely pursuit of scientific truth, showing little regard for prevailing fashion or orthodoxy.

Bohm's interests were not confined to physics. In particular, he was profoundly concerned with philosophical issues, ranging from the philosophy of science and the philosophy of mind to ethics and moral philosophy. Late in his life he was also inspired by mysticism. He saw an all-encompassing unity in the world and thought that quantum physics was but a manifestation of a deeper underlying wholeness of nature, an idea that he developed in his 1980 book *Wholeness and the Implicate Order*.

Shortly after his death Bohm's last book, *The Undivided Universe*, was published. Written in collaboration with Basil J. Hiley, his long-time colleague at London's Birkbeck College, where Bohm had for three decades been a professor, the book provided an exposition of his 1951 pilot-wave theory, together with later developments including his thoughts on the implicate order.

Bohmian mechanics in the early twenty-first century is an area of increasingly active research. However, very few scientists working in this field see an operational connection between Bohmian mechanics and Bohm's ideas on the implicate order. Nonetheless, these ideas remain an inspiration for many others.

See also Bell, John, and Bell's Theorem; Bohmian Mechanics; Quantum Mechanics.

Bibliography

Bohm, David, and Yakir Aharonov. "Discussion of Experimental Proof for the Paradox of Einstein, Rosen, and Podolsky." *Physical Review* 108 (1957): 1070–1076.

Peat, F. David. *Infinite Potential: The Life and Times of David Bohm*. Reading, MA: Addison-Wesley, 1997.

Detlef Dürr, Sheldon Goldstein,
Roderich Tumulka, Nino Zanghì (2005)

BÖHME, JAKOB

See *Boehme, Jakob*

BOHMIAN MECHANICS

While quantum mechanics as presented in physics textbooks provides us with a formalism, it does not attempt to provide a description of reality. The formalism is a set of rules for computing the probability distribution of the outcome of essentially any experiment (within the realm of quantum mechanics). A description of reality, by contrast, would tell us what processes take place on the microscopic level that lead to the random outcomes that we observe and would thus explain the formalism. While the correctness of the formalism is almost universally agreed upon, the description of the reality behind the formalism is controversial. It has also been doubted whether a description of reality needs to conform to ordinary standards of logical consistency, and whether to have such a description is desirable at all. Indeed it has often been claimed that quantum theory forces us to reject the reality of an external world that exists objectively, independently of the human mind.

BOHMIAN MECHANICS AND QUANTUM MECHANICS

Bohmian mechanics, which is also called the de Broglie-Bohm theory, the pilot-wave model, and the causal interpretation of quantum mechanics, is a version of quantum theory discovered by Louis de Broglie in 1927 (de Broglie 1928) and rediscovered by David Bohm in 1951 (Bohm 1952). It is a theory providing a description of reality, compatible with all of the quantum formalism and all of ordinary logic. In Bohmian mechanics a system of particles is described in part by its wave function, evolving according to Schrödinger's equation, the central equation of quantum theory. However the wave function provides only a partial description of the system. This description is completed by the specification of the actual positions of the particles. The latter evolve according to the "guiding equation," which expresses the velocities of the particles in terms of the wave function. Thus in Bohmian mechanics the configuration of a system of particles evolves via a deterministic motion choreographed by the wave function. In particular, when a particle is sent into a two-slit apparatus, the slit through which it passes and where it later arrives on a screen are completely determined by its initial position and wave function.

As such, Bohmian mechanics is a counterexample to the claim that quantum theory is incompatible with the reality of an objective external world. It is a "realistic quantum theory," and, since its formulation makes no reference to observers, it is also a "quantum theory without observers." For historical reasons it has been called a "hidden-variables theory." The existence of Bohmian mechanics shows that many of the radical epistemological consequences usually drawn from quantum mechanics by physicists and philosophers alike are unfounded. It shows that there is no need for contradictory notions such as "complementarity," that there is no need to imag-

ine a particle as somehow being in two places at the same time or physical quantities as having unsharp values, and that there is no need to assume that human consciousness intervenes in physical processes (by, e.g., collapsing wave functions). Bohmian mechanics resolves all of the paradoxes of quantum mechanics, eliminating its weirdness and mystery.

THE MEASUREMENT PROBLEM

The most commonly cited of the conceptual difficulties that plague quantum mechanics is the measurement problem or, what amounts to more or less the same thing, the paradox of Schrödinger's cat. The problem is as follows: Suppose that the wave function of any individual system provides a complete description of that system. When we analyze the process of measurement in quantum mechanical terms we find that the after-measurement wave function for system and apparatus arising from Schrödinger's equation for the composite system typically involves a superposition over terms corresponding to what we would like to regard as the various possible results of the measurement—for example different pointer orientations. It is difficult to discern in this description of the after-measurement situation the actual result of the measurement—for example some specific pointer orientation. By contrast if, like Einstein, one regards the description provided by the wave function as incomplete, the measurement problem vanishes: With a theory or interpretation like Bohmian mechanics, in which the description of the after-measurement situation includes, in addition to the wave function, at least the values of the variables that register the result, there is no measurement problem. In Bohmian mechanics pointers always point.

THE EQUATIONS OF BOHMIAN MECHANICS

Bohmian mechanics is the minimal completion of Schrödinger's equation, for a nonrelativistic system of particles, to a theory describing a genuine motion of particles. For Bohmian mechanics the state of a system of N particles is described by its wave function $\psi = \psi(\mathbf{q}_1, \dots, \mathbf{q}_N) = \psi(q)$, a complex- (or spinor-) valued function on the space of possible configurations q of the system, together with its actual configuration Q defined by the actual positions $\mathbf{Q}_1, \dots, \mathbf{Q}_N$ of its particles. The theory is then defined by two evolution equations: *Schrödinger's equation*

$$i\hbar \frac{\partial \psi}{\partial t} = H\psi$$

for $\psi = \psi_t$, the wave function at time t, where H is the nonrelativistic (Schrödinger) Hamiltonian, containing the masses of the particles and a potential energy term, and a first-order evolution equation, *the guiding equation*

$$\frac{d\mathbf{Q}_j}{dt} = \frac{\hbar}{m_j} \mathrm{Im} \frac{\psi^* \nabla_j \psi}{\psi^* \psi} (\mathbf{Q}_1, \ldots, \mathbf{Q}_N),$$

for $Q = Q(t)$, the configuration at time t, the simplest first-order evolution equation for the positions of the particles that is compatible with the Galilean (and time-reversal) covariance of the Schrödinger evolution. Here $\hbar$ is Planck's constant divided by 2π, m_j is the mass of the j-th particle, and ∇_j is the gradient with respect to the coordinates of the j-th particle. If ψ is spinor-valued, the products in the numerator and denominator should be understood as scalar products. If external magnetic fields are present, the gradient should be understood as the covariant derivative, involving the vector potential. For an N-particle system these two equations (together with the detailed specification of the Hamiltonian, including all interactions contributing to the potential energy) completely define the Bohmian mechanics.

It is perhaps worth noting that the guiding equation is intimately connected with the de Broglie relation $\mathbf{p} = \hbar\mathbf{k}$, proposed by de Broglie in late 1923, the consideration of which quickly led Schrödinger to the discovery of his wave equation in late 1925 and early 1926. The de Broglie relation connects a particle property, momentum $\mathbf{p} = m\mathbf{v}$, to a wave property, the wave vector $\mathbf{k}$ of a plane wave $\psi(\mathbf{q}) = e^{i\mathbf{k}\cdot\mathbf{q}}$. From this one can easily guess the guiding equation as the simplest possibility for an equation of motion for Q for the case of a general wave function ψ.

Bohmian mechanics inherits and makes explicit the nonlocality implicit in the notion, common to just about all formulations and interpretations of quantum theory, of a wave function on the configuration space of a many-particle system. It accounts for all of the phenomena governed by nonrelativistic quantum mechanics, from spectral lines and scattering theory to superconductivity and quantum computing. In particular the usual measurement postulates of quantum theory, including collapse of the wave function, probabilities given by the absolute square of probability amplitudes constructed from the wave function, and the role of self-adjoint operators as observables emerge from an analysis of the two equations of motion—Schrödinger's equation and the guiding equation.

QUANTUM RANDOMNESS

The statistical significance of the wave function was first recognized in 1926 by Max Born, just after Schrödinger discovered his famous wave equation. Born postulated that the configuration Q of a quantum system is random, with probability distribution given by the density $|\psi(q)|^2$. Under the influence of the developing consensus in favor of the Copenhagen interpretation, $|\psi(q)|^2$ came to be regarded as giving the probability of *finding* the configuration Q were this to be measured, rather than of the configuration actually *being* Q, a notion that was supposed to be meaningless. In accord with these quantum probabilities, quantum measurements performed on a system with definite wave function ψ typically yield random results.

For Bohmian mechanics the $|\psi(q)|^2$-distribution has a particularly distinguished status. As an elementary consequence of Schrödinger's equation and the guiding equation, it is *equivariant*, in the sense that these equations are compatible with respect to the $|\psi(q)|^2$-distribution. More precisely this means that if, at some time t, the configuration $Q(t)$ of a Bohmian system were random, with distribution given by $|\psi_t(q)|^2$, then this would also be true for any other time. This distribution is thus called the *quantum equilibrium distribution*.

A Bohmian universe, though deterministic, evolves in such a manner that an *appearance* of randomness emerges, precisely as described by the quantum formalism. To understand how this comes about one must first appreciate that in a world governed by Bohmian mechanics, measurement apparatuses too are made of Bohmian particles. In a Bohmian universe tables, chairs, and other objects of our everyday experience are simply agglomerates of particles, described by their positions in physical space and whose evolution is governed by Bohmian mechanics.

Then, for the analysis of quantum measurements, the following observation is crucial: To the extent that the result of any quantum measurement is registered configurationally, at least potentially, the predictions of Bohmian mechanics for the result must agree with those of orthodox quantum theory (assuming the same Schrödinger equation for both) provided that the configuration Q (of the largest system required for the analysis of the measurement, with wave function ψ) is random, with probability density in fact given by the quantum equilibrium distribution, the quantum mechanical prediction for the distribution of Q.

To justify this quantum equilibrium hypothesis is a rather delicate matter, one that has been explored in considerable detail (Dürr, Goldstein, and Zanghì 1992). It can be shown that the probabilities for positions given by the quantum equilibrium distribution $|\psi(q)|^2$ emerge naturally from an analysis of "equilibrium" for the deterministic dynamical system defined by Bohmian mechanics, in much the same way that the Maxwellian velocity distribution emerges from an analysis of classical thermodynamic equilibrium.

TYPICALITY

Thus, with Bohmian mechanics, the statistical description in quantum theory indeed takes, as Einstein anticipated, "an approximately analogous position to the statistical mechanics within the framework of classical mechanics" (1949, p.672). A key ingredient for appreciating the status and origin of such a statistical description is the notion of *typicality*, a notion that, historically, goes back to Ludwig Boltzmann's mechanical analysis of the second law of thermodynamics. In Bohmian mechanics, a property P is typical if it holds true for the overwhelming majority of histories $Q(t)$ of a Bohmian universe. More precisely, suppose that Ψ_t is the wave function of a universe governed by Bohmian mechanics; a property P, which a solution $Q(t)$ of the guiding equation for the entire universe can have or not have, is called *typical* if the set $S_0(P)$ of all initial configurations $Q(0)$ leading to a history $Q(t)$ with the property P has size very close to one,

$$\int_{S_0(P)} |\Psi_0(q)|^2 dq = 1 - \varepsilon \qquad 0 \leq \varepsilon \ll 1,$$

with "size" understood relative to the $|\Psi_0|^2$ distribution on the configuration space of the universe. For instance, think of P as the property that a particular sequence of experiments yields results that look random (accepted by a suitable statistical test), governed by the appropriate quantum distribution. One can show, using the *law of large numbers*, that P is a typical property; see Dürr, Goldstein, and Zanghì (1992) for a thorough discussion.

OPERATORS AS OBSERVABLES

It would appear that because orthodox quantum theory supplies us with probabilities for a huge class of quantum observables and not merely for positions, it is a much richer theory than Bohmian mechanics, which seems exclusively concerned with positions. In this regard, as with so much else in the foundations of quantum mechanics, the crucial remark was made by Bell (1987 p. 666): "[I]n physics the only observations we must consider are position observations, if only the positions of instrument pointers. It is a great merit of the de Broglie-Bohm picture to force us to consider this fact. If you make axioms, rather than definitions and theorems, about the 'measurement' of anything else, then you commit redundancy and risk inconsistency."

In Bohmian mechanics, the standard quantum observables, represented by self-adjoint operators, indeed arise from an analysis of quantum experiments, as "definitions and theorems": For any quantum experiment, take as the relevant Bohmian system the combined system that includes the system upon which the experiment is performed as well as all the measuring instruments and other devices used in performing the experiment (together with all other systems with which these have significant interaction over the course of the experiment). The initial configuration is then transformed via the guiding equation for the big system into the final configuration at the conclusion of the experiment. With the quantum equilibrium hypothesis, that is, regarding the initial configuration of this big system as random in the usual quantum mechanical way, with distribution given by $|\psi|^2$, the final configuration of the big system, including in particular the orientation of instrument pointers, will be distributed according to $|\psi|^2$ at the final time.

If the experiment happens to be "measurement-like," and the outcomes of the experiment are calibrated by an assignment of numerical values to the different pointer orientations, then the induced probability distributions of these results will be given by the familiar quantum measurement postulates—that is, by the spectral measure, relative to the wave function of the system upon which the experiment is performed, of a self-adjoint operator A associated with the experiment (Dürr, Goldstein, and Zanghì 2004), in which case we speak, in orthodox quantum theory, of a "measurement of A."

The Stern-Gerlach experiment provides an illuminating example: By means of a suitable interaction (with a magnetic field), the parts of the wave function that lie in different eigenspaces of the relevant spin operator become spatially separated, and the result ("up" or "down") is thus a function of the final, detected position of the particle, concerning which we can only predict that it is random and distributed according to $|\psi|^2$ at the final time. By calibrating the outcomes of the experiment with numerical values, e.g., +1 for upper detection, and −1 for lower detection, it is not difficult to see that the probability distribution for these values can be conveniently expressed in terms of the quantum mechanical spin operators—for a spin-1/2 particle given by the Pauli spin matrices.

CONTEXTUALITY AND NAÏVE REALISM ABOUT OPERATORS

Since the result of a Stern-Gerlach experiment depends upon, not just the initial position and the initial wave function of the particle, but also on a choice among several magnetic fields that could be used to perform a Stern-Gerlach measurement of the same spin operator, this experiment is not a genuine measurement in the literal sense, that is, it does not reveal a preexisting value associated with the spin operator itself. In fact there is nothing the least bit mysterious or even nonclassical about the nonexistence of such values associated with operators. Thus the widespread idea that in a realistic quantum theory all quantum observables should possess actual values, which is in fact impossible by the Kochen-Specker theorem, was from the outset not as reasonable at it may have appeared but rather was based on taking operators as observables too seriously—an attitude, almost implicit in the word "observable," that can be called "naïve realism about operators."

Another consequence concerns *contextuality*, the notion that the result of an experiment depends not just on "what observable the experiment measures" but on more detailed information that conveys the "context" of the experiment. Contextuality is often regarded as deep, mysterious, and even close to Bohr's complementarity. However in Bohmian mechanics it boils down to the trivial insight that the result of an experiment depends on the experiment.

COLLAPSE OF THE WAVE FUNCTION

According to the quantum formalism, performing an ideal quantum measurement on a quantum system causes a random jump or "collapse" of its wave function into an eigenstate of the observable measured. But while in orthodox quantum theory the collapse is merely superimposed upon the unitary evolution of the wave function, without a precise specification of the circumstances under which it may legitimately be invoked—and this ambiguity is nothing but another facet of the measurement problem—Bohmian mechanics consistently embodies both the unitarity evolution and the collapse of the wave function as appropriate. Concerning the evolution of the wave function Bohmian mechanics is indeed formulated in terms of Schrödinger's equation alone. However, since observation implies interaction, a system under observation cannot be a closed system but rather must be a subsystem of a larger system that is closed, for example, the entire universe. And there is no reason a priori why a subsystem of a Bohmian universe should itself be a Bohmian system, even if the subsystem happens to be "closed." Indeed, it is not even clear a priori what should be meant by the wave function of a subsystem of a Bohmian universe.

The configuration Q of this larger system, this universe, naturally splits into X, the configuration of the subsystem, and Y, the configuration of its environment. Suppose the universe has wave function $\Psi = \Psi(q) = \Psi(x, y)$. According to Bohmian mechanics, this universe is then completely described by Ψ, evolving according to Schrödinger's equation, together with X and Y. Thus there is a rather obvious choice for what should be regarded as the wave function of the subsystem, namely the *conditional wave function* $\psi(x) = \Psi(x,Y)$, obtained by plugging the actual configuration of the environment into the wave function of the universe. Moreover, taking into account the way that the conditional wave function $\psi_t(x) = \Psi_t(x,Y(t))$ depends upon time, it is not difficult to see that it obeys Schrödinger's equation for the subsystem when that system is suitably decoupled from its environment and, using the quantum equilibrium hypothesis, that it randomly collapses according to the usual quantum mechanical rules under precisely those conditions on the interaction between the subsystem and its environment that define an ideal quantum measurement.

UNCERTAINTY

It follows from the quantum equilibrium hypothesis and the definition of the conditional wave function that when the (conditional) wave function of a subsystem is ψ, its configuration must be random, with distribution $|\psi(x)|^2$, even if its full microscopic environment Y—itself grossly more than what we could conceivably have access to—were taken into account. In other words, the (conditional) wave function ψ of a subsystem represents maximal information about its configuration X. Thus, in a universe governed by Bohmian mechanics there are sharp, precise, and irreducible limitations on the possibility of obtaining knowledge, limitations which can in no way be diminished through technological progress leading to better means of measurement. This *absolute uncertainty* is in precise agreement with Heisenberg's uncertainty principle. The fact that knowledge of the configuration of a system must be mediated by its (conditional) wave function may partially account, from a Bohmian perspective, for how orthodox physicists could identify the state of a quantum system—its complete description—with its (collapsed) wave function without encountering any practical difficulties.

OBJECTIONS

A great many objections have been and continue to be raised against Bohmian mechanics. Most of these objections have little or no merit. The most serious is that Bohmian mechanics does not account for phenomena such as pair creation and annihilation characteristic of quantum field theory. However this is not an objection to Bohmian mechanics per se but merely a recognition that quantum field theory explains a great deal more than does nonrelativistic quantum mechanics, whether in orthodox or Bohmian form. It does however underline the need to find an adequate, if not compelling, Bohmian version of quantum field theory, and of gauge theories in particular, a problem that is pretty much wide open.

A related objection is that Bohmian mechanics cannot be made Lorentz invariant, by which is presumably meant that no Bohmian theory—no theory that could be regarded somehow as a natural extension of Bohmian mechanics—can be found that is Lorentz invariant. The main reason for this belief is the manifest nonlocality of Bohmian mechanics. But nonlocality, as John Bell has argued and the experiments have shown, is a fact of nature. Moreover, concerning the widespread belief that standard quantum theories have no difficulty incorporating relativity while Bohmian mechanics does, there is much less here than meets the eye. On the one hand, one should keep in mind that the empirical import of orthodox quantum mechanics relies on both the unitary evolution of the state vector (or the equivalent unitary evolution of the operators in the Heisenberg representation) and the collapse or reduction of the state vector (or any other equivalent device that incorporates the effect of observation or measurement). But the Lorentz invariance of this part of the theory has rarely been considered in a serious way—most of the empirical import of standard relativistic quantum mechanics is in the so-called "scattering regime." But if this were done, arguably, the tension between Lorentz invariance and quantum nonlocality would soon become manifest. On the other hand, a variety of approaches to the construction of a Lorentz invariant Bohmian theory have in fact been proposed, and some toy models formulated.

WHAT IS A BOHMIAN THEORY?

Finding a satisfactory relativistic version of Bohmian mechanics and extending Bohmian mechanics to quantum field theory are topics of ongoing research and we shall not attempt to give an overview here. (Some remarks, however, are given in the next section.) Rather we shall briefly sketch what we consider to be the general traits of any theory that could be regarded as a natural extension of Bohmian mechanics. Three requirements seem essential to us: 1. The theory should be based upon a clear ontology, the *primitive ontology* representing what the theory is fundamentally about—the basic kinds of entities (such as the particles in Bohmian mechanics) that are to be the building blocks of everything else, including tables, chairs, and measurement apparatuses. 2. There should be a quantum state vector, a wave function, that evolves according to the unitary quantum evolution and whose role is to somehow generate the motion for the variables describing the primitive ontology. 3. The predictions should agree (at least approximately) with those of orthodox quantum theory—at least to the extent that the latter are unambiguous. Note that we do not regard as essential either the deterministic character of the dynamics of the primitive ontology or that the latter should be given by particles described by their positions in physical three-dimensional space—a field ontology, or a string ontology would do just as well.

In short a "Bohmian theory" is merely a quantum theory with a coherent ontology. But when the theory is regarded in these very general terms, an interesting philosophical lesson emerges: In the structure of a Bohmian theory one can recognize some general features that are indeed common to all "quantum theories without observers," that is, to all precise formulations of quantum theory not based on such vague and imprecise notions as "measurement" or "observer"—such as Ghirardi-Rimini-Weber-Pearle's "dynamical reduction" models or Gell-Mann and Hartle's "decoherent histories" approach. One essential feature is the primitive ontology of the theory—what the theory is fundamentally about. The other very general and crucial feature is the sort of explanation of physical phenomena the theory should provide: an *explanation based on typicality*. Not just for a Bohmian theory, but for any physical theory with probabilistic content, the physical import of the theory must arise from its provision of a notion of typical space-time histories, specified for example via a probability distribution on the set of all possible histories of the primitive ontology of the theory.

HISTORY AND PRESENT STATUS

In 1951 Bohm rediscovered de Broglie's 1927 pilot-wave model and showed that the quantum measurement formalism, based on non-commuting operators as observables, emerged from the basic principles of de Broglie's theory. Since then Bohmian mechanics has been developed and refined: Noteworthy are Bell's clarification of the axioms of the theory and the analysis of the status of probability and the role of typicality (Bell 1987; Dürr, Goldstein, and Zanghì 1992), as well as the investigations of quantum non-equilibrium (Valentini 2002). Several ways of extending Bohmian mechanics to quantum field theory have been proposed. One (Bohm 1952) for bosons (i.e., force fields) is based on an actual field configuration on physical three-dimensional space that is guided by a wave functional according to an infinite-dimensional analogue of the guiding equation (see also Bohm and Hiley 1993; Holland 1993). Another proposal (Dürr, Goldstein, Tumulka, and Zanghì 2004) relies on seminal work by Bell (1987 p. 173) and ascribes trajectories to the electrons or whatever sort of particles the quantum field theory is about; however, in contrast to the original Bohmian mechanics, this proposal involves a stochastic dynamics, according to which particles can be created and annihilated.

See also Bell, John, and Bell's Theorem; Bohm, David; Boltzmann, Ludwig; Einstein, Albert; Quantum Mechanics; Realism.

Bibliography

Bell, John. *Speakable and Unspeakable in Quantum Mechanics.* Cambridge, U.K.: Cambridge University Press, 1987.

Bohm, David. "A Suggested Interpretation of Quantum Theory in Terms of 'Hidden' Variables, Parts I and II." *Physical Review* 85 (1952): 166–193.

Bohm, David, and Basil Hiley. *The Undivided Universe: An Ontological Interpretation of Quantum Theory.* London: Routledge & Kegan Paul, 1993.

Broglie, Louis de. *Electrons et Photons: Rapports et Discussions du Cinquième Conseil de Physique tenu à Bruxelles du 24 au 29 Octobre 1927 sous les Auspices de l'Institut International de Physique Solvay.* Paris: Gauthier-Villars, 1928.

Dürr, Detlef, Sheldon Goldstein, Roderich Tumulka, and Nino Zanghì. "Bohmian Mechanics and Quantum Field Theory." *Physical Review Letters* 93 (2004): 090402.

Dürr, Detlef, Sheldon Goldstein, and Nino Zanghì. "Quantum Equilibrium and the Origin of Absolute Uncertainty." *Journal of Statistical Physics* 67 (1992): 843–907.

Dürr, Detlef, Sheldon Goldstein, and Nino Zanghì. "Quantum Equilibrium and the Role of Operators as Observables in Quantum Theory." *Journal of Statistical Physics* 116 (2004): 959–1055.

Einstein, Albert. "Reply to Criticisms." In *Albert Einstein, Philosopher-Scientist,* edited by Paul Arthur Schilpp. New York: Tudor, 1951.

Holland, Peter. *The Quantum Theory of Motion.* Cambridge, U.K.: Cambridge University Press, 1993.

Valentini, Antony. "Subquantum Information and Computation." *Pramana-Journal of Physics* 59 (2002): 269–277.

Detlef Dürr, Sheldon Goldstein, Roderich Tumulka, Nino Zanghì (2005)

BOHR, NIELS
(1885–1962)

Quantum physics is often credited with far-reaching metaphysical and epistemological implications, including the denial of causality and determinism and the existence of strict limits on what can be known about natural systems. One of the main figures whose work has been used—and often misused—in support of such conclusions is the Danish physicist Niels Bohr. Bohr is rightfully viewed as one of the major figures in the history of quantum physics and is widely known both for his extraordinary contributions to the development of quantum theory and for his philosophically oriented work, which focused on the task of interpreting the quantum mechanics. Bohr's interpretation centers on his notion of complementarity, which he developed in 1927, two years after the development of quantum mechanics by Heisenberg, Born, Jordan, and Schrödinger and shortly after the publication of Heisenberg's famous uncertainty paper.

Bohr's interpretive approach attracted many followers but also many critics. Most notable among the latter was Einstein, whose public critique of quantum mechanics and Bohr's interpretation began in 1927 and culminated with his 1935 "EPR" paper, written with Podolsky and Rosen. Bohr's response to Einstein's criticisms, and part of his general interpretive approach, was that quantum mechanics is a complete theory the statistical indeterminacies of which neither need be nor could be overcome with a more foundational theory.

While Bohr is most philosophical after the introduction of complementarity, the overarching theme of much of his earlier work was also associated with certain clear philosophical ideas about the nature of physical theories and the appropriate method for developing a theory in a new realm, and complementarity can be seen as an application of these ideas to the new quantum mechanical formalism.

QUANTUM THEORY

Bohr's famous 1913 model of the hydrogen atom, with which he explained the hydrogen spectrum, marks the beginning of the quantum theory of the atom. Because classical electrodynamics had dictated that the oscillation of electrons is accompanied by the emission of electromagnetic radiation, the theory could account neither for the stability of the atom nor for the discreteness of the spectrum of frequencies emitted by excited hydrogen gas. Bohr's model solved this puzzle by suggesting that the electron orbits the nucleus in stable stationary states and that the emission of radiation occurs not during that orbit but rather in sudden transitions between the states; the radiation carries the difference in energy between the states according to a quantum frequency rule (based on work by Planck and Einstein) that correlates energy with frequency. Bohr eventually presented the rationale for his model in terms of the quantization of angular momentum, and that is how it is often presented in texts. However, Bohr's original rationale, and arguably the one closest to his actual approach to physics in the years afterwards, is that he read the existence of independent stationary states off the Balmer formula of the hydrogen spectrum by interpreting the spectrum with the quantum-frequency rule. That is, the discrete stationary states were not hypothesized but rather were inferred from an empirical generalization.

THE CORRESPONDENCE PRINCIPLE

Bohr eventually expanded this general approach of inferring atomic properties from empirical generalizations or phenomena with the development of his correspondence principle. The principle, first implicitly used in a general form in 1918 and named as a specific principle by Bohr in 1920, is a claim about the relationship between classical and quantum theory, and in particular about classical descriptions of empirical evidence and quantum models of the atom. As Bohr sometimes stated it—the way in which it is most often quoted—the new quantum theory ought to recapture classical electrodynamics in some limit—that is, the old theory ought to be shown to be an approximation that in retrospect is roughly accurate in the realms where quantum effects are negligible. In the hydrogen atom, according to Bohr's principle, that will occur when the quantum number is high, where the difference in energy between stationary states becomes small in comparison with the energies of the states themselves.

While it is tempting to understand the correspondence principle as a requirement for the rationality of the progression of theories, that is at best only one aspect of Bohr's approach with the principle. For Bohr, the correspondence principle was an intratheory claim, not an intertheory one, and it was important because the developing quantum theory had no account of the relation between the motions of the electrons within their orbits and the empirical phenomena of the atomic spectra, whereas classical theory had had such an account. Bohr consistently insisted that we need a stable description of observations from which we can infer atomic properties, and he emphasized that generalizations about atomic spectra—about the frequencies of radiation emitted or absorbed by atoms—are essentially claims about wave phenomena, because measurements of radiation frequencies with spectroscopy equipment unavoidably assume wave theory. Thus, even though the quantum theory might seem to call into question the wave nature of electromagnetic radiation (at least according to the light-quantum concept implied by the photoelectric effect, and later by the Compton effect), scientists still must use wave electrodynamics to provide evidence about atomic properties, so a link or coordination between the theories is needed.

The agreement in the limit between the theories was therefore not the goal of the correspondence principle but only a means of allowing the linkage of claims within the new theory. In particular, it let Bohr relate periodic motion within the atom to periodic aspects of the radiation in the spectrum. This principle both gave empirical content to parts of the model that previously had had none and allowed the inference of properties of certain atomic processes—for example, selection rules for quantum transitions—for which there was no other method of determination. For Bohr the principle was a way to relate observable, empirical phenomena with the quantum mechanisms (such as they were) "behind" the empirical phenomena.

Two related aspects of the correspondence principle were very important for Bohr's work after the development of quantum mechanics. First, although Bohr had been able to apply it only imprecisely and often only qualitatively, it inspired Heisenberg's approach in developing what was to become quantum mechanics, and Bohr claimed that quantum mechanics embodied the correspondence principle. Second, the general approach of incorporating independent, classically based descriptions of empirical phenomena within quantum theory became the foundation for his own interpretation of that quantum mechanics.

COMPLEMENTARITY AND THE INTERPRETATION OF QUANTUM MECHANICS

Bohr's interpretation is notoriously difficult to pin down, but the core ideas are that our descriptions of the properties of quantum systems must be based on classical concepts, that these concepts are restricted in scope to a particular experimental context, that different concepts are appropriate for different contexts, that the different contexts make the use of certain pairs of mutually exclusive concepts, and that those concepts do not fully capture the nature of quantum systems. Bohr used the word "complementarity" to describe this complex of ideas that together were meant to address interpretive problems posed by quantum mechanics.

Quantum mechanics, especially in Heisenberg's formulation, had retained some aspects of the old quantum theory but had abandoned the definite electron orbits of that theory and had substituted abstract, formal methods for calculating "observable" properties. Heisenberg's uncertainty paper had given a further argument for thinking in these terms by deriving equations that described a reciprocal relationship between the precisions with which certain pairs of properties (for example, position and momentum) could be measured. Although there is some indication in Heisenberg's paper that he might have thought of the tradeoffs in precision in terms of disturbance (every measurement of one property disturbs a specific other one in a way that prevents us from knowing simultaneously both properties to arbitrary precision), Bohr associated the uncertainty relations with his notion of complementarity and claimed that the uncertainty or indeterminacy described by the relations reflect not merely a lack of knowledge of the values of metaphysically definite properties of a system, but rather a degree to which our concepts just do not and cannot be made to apply to the system. Complementarity claims that, although we cannot simultaneously give both normal space-time and causal descriptions of the same quantum phenomenon and although neither description fully captures the nature of the phenomenon, we nevertheless have no other way to describe phenomena besides through these causal and spatiotemporal pictures.

Although Bohr's philosophy is sometimes called the Copenhagen interpretation, there are important distinctions between Bohr's actual views and what is often meant by that name. The name is sometimes used to describe what might better be called the standard interpretation, which is perhaps inspired by Bohr but is really based on von Neumann's work and includes the collapse of the wave packet, which had no part in Bohr's philosophy. Otherwise, it is used to describe a set of views held by Bohr and a number of his former students and associates from Copenhagen, especially Heisenberg and Pauli, but there are disputes regarding how much their views really had in common.

Central to Bohr's interpretation is a sort of holism that we can now understand in terms of entanglement. This holism is clear in Bohr's work starting in 1929 and certainly by 1935. Bohr then explicitly states that it is misleading to think that observation disturbs properties because that would imply the existence of preexisting

complete sets of properties. Bohr emphasized that the novel and interpretively challenging aspect of quantum effects is not the discreteness of, say, the exchange of energy but rather the apparent mathematical and theoretical fact that quantum mechanical processes generally cannot be broken down in a way that allows us accurately to describe them in terms of an interaction between component systems such as a measuring instrument and a measured system. In order to describe or analyze an experiment, scientists nevertheless must treat measurement in this way, and the consequence is that descriptions of measured properties of subsystems of a larger whole system at best misconstrue the true quantum mechanical state or phenomenon. And it is precisely in this misconstrual that the statistical nature of quantum mechanical predictions arise.

Though not all interpreters of Bohr agree, this explicit emphasis in his later work did not represent a drastic change in his interpretation. Indeed, it is plausible to argue that complementarity is and was always for Bohr a conclusion based on his correspondence approach and the discovery of noncommutativity and the holism of entanglement. Bohr thought that although one can give an abstract mathematical representation of a quantum mechanical system independent of classical conceptualizations of the phenomena, the symbols used to represent quantum properties have empirical meaning only when they can be associated or put into correspondence with observable phenomena. Doing this requires first establishing independent theoretical descriptions of the observations, and for this it is necessary to use classical concepts to describe the measurement context. Complementarity is, then, an expression of the limitations that noncommutativity places on the degree to which different quantum symbols can be given empirical meaning.

Although Bohr was a realist about the entities described by quantum mechanics and he seems to have believed that quantum mechanics does describe the true nature of quantum-mechanical systems, the foregoing features of his work suggest certain antirealist aspects to his interpretation, especially with respect to the way the meaning and applicability of our concepts about quantum properties depend somehow on the context in which those properties are measured.

This tension is evident in Bohr's response to the EPR paper. That paper questioned the completeness of quantum mechanics precisely on the grounds of the quantum relations of entangled systems; EPR claimed that the ability to predict the properties of one of an entangled pair of particles after the measurement of the other, over distances and within times that preclude a causal interaction on relativistic grounds, indicates that quantum mechanics must assume that the prediction concerns a real, pre-existing property that is independent of the other measurement. Bohr's response does not explicitly deny realism but says that any descriptive account of quantum reality is good only within the conditions of applicability of the concepts used in measurement and prediction and that the effect on the distant particle is not a causal, physical one but rather an effect on those conditions; this suggests, perhaps, that disentanglement is only conceptual.

Although in later years Bohr began to discuss complementarity in increasingly broad terms and as applied to other fields, especially biology, it is his philosophical work closest to physics that has had the greatest impact in both philosophy and physics. In the early twenty-first century theorems about the impossibility of certain kinds of hidden variable theories can be seen as a vindication of many of the intuitions in that work, intuitions that remain evident in the pragmatic approach to quantum mechanics assumed by many working physicists.

See also Bell, John, and Bell's Theorem; Bohm, David; Copenhagen Interpretation; Einstein, Albert; Heisenberg, Werner; Quantum Mechanics.

Bibliography

GENERAL

Einstein, Albert, Boris Podolsky, and Nathan Rosen. "Can Quantum-Mechanical Description of Physical Reality Be Considered Complete?" *Physical Review* 47 (1935): 777–780. Reprinted in Wheeler and Zurek.

Heisenberg, Werner. "Über den ansclauchichen Inhalt der quantentheoretischen Kinematik und Mechanik." *Zeitschrift für Physik* 43 (1927): 172–198. Translated as "The Physical Content of Quantum Kinematics and Mechanics" in Wheeler and Zurek.

Wheeler, John Archibald, and Wojciech Hubert Zurek. *Quantum Theory and Measurement.* Princeton, NJ: Princeton University Press, 1983.

WORKS BY NIELS BOHR

"On the Constitution of Atoms and Molecules." *Philosophical Magazine* 26 (1913): 1–25, 476–502, 857–875.

"The Quantum Postulate and the Recent Development of Atomic Theory." *Nature* 121 (supplement) (1928): 580–590.

"Can Quantum-Mechanical Description of Physical Reality Be Considered Complete?" *Physical Review* 48 (1935): 696–702.

"Discussion with Einstein on Epistemological Problems in Atomic Physics." In *Albert Einstein: Philosopher-Scientist*, edited by P. A. Schilpp. Cambridge: Cambridge University Press, 1949. Reprinted in Wheeler and Zurek.

Atomic Theory and the Description of Nature, reprinted as *The Philosophical Writings of Niels Bohr.* Vol. 1. Woodbridge, CT: Ox Bow Press, 1934/1987.

Essays 1932–1957 on Atomic Physics and Human Knowledge. Reprinted as *The Philosophical Writings of Niels Bohr.* Vol. 2. Woodbridge, CT: Ox Bow Press, 1958/1987.

Essays 1958–1962 on Atomic Physics and Human Knowledge. Reprinted as *The Philosophical Writings of Niels Bohr.* Vol. 3. Woodbridge, CT: Ox Bow Press, 1963/1987.

Causality and Complementarity, edited by Jan Faye and Henry Folse as *The Philosophical Writings of Niels Bohr.* Vol. 4. Woodbridge, CT: Ox Bow Press, 1998.

WORKS ABOUT NIELS BOHR

Beller, Mara. *Quantum Dialogue: The Making of a Revolution.* Chicago: University of Chicago Press, 1999.

Faye, Jan. *Niels Bohr: His Heritage and Legacy: An Anti-Realist View of Quantum Mechanics.* Dordrecht: Kluwer Academic Publishers, 1991.

Faye, Jan, and Henry J. Folse, eds. *Niels Bohr and Contemporary Philosophy.* Boston Studies in the Philosophy of Science 153. Dordrecht: Kluwer Academic Publishers, 1994.

Folse, Henry J. *The Philosophy of Niels Bohr: The Framework of Complementarity.* Amsterdam: North-Holland, 1985.

Jammer, Max. *The Conceptual Development of Quantum Mechanics.* New York: McGraw-Hill, 1966.

Pais, Abraham. *Niels Bohr's Times: in Physics, Philosophy, and Polity.* Oxford: Clarendon Press, 1991.

Tanona, Scott. "Uncertainty in Bohr's Response to the Heisenberg Microscope." *Studies in History and Philosophy of Modern Physics* 35 (2004): 483–507.

Scott Tanona (2005)

BOILEAU, NICOLAS
(1636–1711)

Nicolas Boileau, also known as Boileau-Despréaux, has retrospectively been raised to the rank of emblematic figure of French classicism. He has been described as the "lawgiver of Parnassus" (a reference to his being an arbiter of taste), the champion of poetic rationalism, and a chief apologist for the ancients in their quarrel with the moderns. At the beginning of the twenty-first century, specialists of the era consider the truth about Boileau to be more nuanced. Boileau was first and foremost a poet engaged in the literary life of his time. After having written his *Satires*, a vigorous denunciation of the faults and mistakes commonly made in the literary world of his days, he attempted, in his *Art poétique* (1674), to determine the rules that should govern the creation and reception of art in most literary genres.

Published during the same year, his translation of Longinus's *Peri hypsous* (*On the Sublime*, first cent.) contributed to popularizing this work all over Europe. In 1677 he became, along with Jean Racine, the historiographer of Louis XIV. This noticeably slowed down his literary production. From 1687 on, as defender of the ancients, he was Charles Perrault's main adversary in the first of two disputes between the ancients and the moderns that divided the field of classical aesthetics in France. His nine *Réflexions critiques sur quelques passages du rhéteur Longin* (Critical reflections on several passages of the orator Longinus; 1694) are explicit arguments in favor of the advocates of the ancients.

Boileau's position was not simply the result of a general nostalgic or conservative attitude, but rather followed from his very strict conception of literature. His aim is to look at the ancients' masterworks in order to find examples of perfection to stimulate the creativity and imagination of contemporaries, and models to provide the distance necessary to avoid the relativist pitfalls, not to mention the conceit, that threatened modernist partisans. According to Boileau, the criterion by which one can attest to the merit of the great artworks of the past is that they have passed the test of time. Far from being an illegitimate prejudice, imitation of the ancients is the source of the true rules of art, which reason can use as its guide.

Two aspects of Boileau's thought are of interest to the historian of philosophical aesthetics. First, there is his formulation of classical doctrine, of which *Art poétique* provides a synthesis. Far from displaying the merely theoretical attitude of an arbiter, Boileau reflects the aesthetic consensus obtained during the decades from 1630 to 1670 on the basis of a precarious balance between reason and sentiment, freedom and norms. Second, there is his clarification of the role of the sublime in poetry. In discussing the sublime, Boileau tried to cast light on the causes of the legitimate and enduring admiration we have for authors of merit, whether ancient or modern.

Art poétique, where Boileau provided a synthesis of classical doctrine, explicitly draws from the tradition inherited from Aristotle and Horace. It is divided into four cantos written in verse. The first canto gives authors general advice on poetry. The second canto deals with minor genres: the eclogue, sonnet, ode, satire, elegy, epigram, and the like. The third canto tackles major genres: tragedy, comedy, and epic. The fourth canto gives rules for writing, insisting on the edifying function of poetry, on the writer's disinterestedness, and on the need for the writer to surround himself with friends whose sound judgment will help him improve himself.

In the course of the four cantos, Boileau simply reaffirmed, without ever analyzing, all the principles of classical aesthetics. If genius, as a natural gift, is necessary to write poetry, only art, polishing of the work under the guidance of reason and judgment, can lead to perfection. Thus, although it is not a source of inspiration, the light

of reason must nonetheless accompany the conception of thoughts, their arrangement, and their expression. As far as tragedy is concerned, Boileau reinforced the classical interpretation of the Aristotelian theory held by his contemporaries. Tragic art was said to provide an idealizing imitation of the terrifying in which pain is transformed into pleasure. The purpose of tragedy is to please and move the spectator by producing a "pleasant terror" and a "delightful pity." To produce such effects, however, reason must be respected.

Thus Boileau advocated absolute respect for the three unities of action, time, and place, even though Aristotle confined himself to the unity of action. Also, the representation ought to be submitted to the principle of *verisimilitude*, since what is historically true but not credible will not produce any emotion in the spectator. Verisimilitude also requires the writer to respect the rules of propriety (Horace's decorum), whether from an external point of view (agreement between the represented action and the public's expectations and customs) or from an internal one (internal coherence among characters and the language ascribed to them).

For Boileau, the sublime constitutes the supreme perfection of poetic discourse. He saw a nonrhetorical conception of the sublime at work in Longinus's treatise, one that makes possible the distinction between the really sublime (what "strikes us in a discourse, elevates, ravishes and transports us" (*On the Sublime*, first cent) and the sublime *style* (the lofty style that traditional rhetoric thought best adapted to the expression of noble ideas). The sublime can thus be found in a single thought or turn of phrase, an excellent example being God's command "Let there be light," in Genesis. The sublime reconciles grandeur and conciseness in accordance with the demands of simplicity and naturalness imposed by the aesthetics of classicism.

In his last three reflections on Longinus, published posthumously in 1713, Boileau added that the perfectly sublime—that which has the property of elevating the soul and making us participate in the greatness that we perceive—unites the grandeur of the thought with the nobility of the sentiment driving the person expressing it, the splendor of the words, and the harmony of the expression. The sublime is, paradoxically, the summit of Boileau's aesthetics. On the one hand, the "energic littleness of the words" (*Réflexions* X) manifests the sublime in the density of meaning sought by classicism. On the other hand, favoring the sublime introduces tension in a system of thought governed by the ideal of reason and clarity. The significant role of the sublime sufficiently demonstrates that classicism, far from being a sterile formalism, is in fact a constantly renewed demand for equilibrium between judgment and inspiration, lucidity and emotion, conciseness and grandeur.

See also Aesthetics, History of.

Bibliography

WORKS BY BOILEAU

Œuvres complètes, edited by Antoine Adam and Françoise Escal. Paris: Gallimard, 1966.

WORKS ON BOILEAU

Beugnot, Bernard, and Roger Zuber. *Boileau: Visages anciens, visages nouveaux, 1665–1970.* Montreal: Presses de l'Université de Montréal, 1973.

Brody, Jules. *Boileau and Longinus.* Geneva: Droz, 1958.

Génetiot, Alain. *Le classicisme.* Paris: Presses universitaires de France, 2005.

Pocock, Gordon. *Boileau and the Nature of Neo-classicism.* Cambridge, U.K.: Cambridge University Press, 1980.

Wood, Theodore E. B. *The Word "Sublime" and Its Context, 1650–1760.* The Hague: Mouton, 1972.

Daniel Dumouchel (2005)

BOLINGBROKE, HENRY ST. JOHN
(1678–1751)

Henry St. John Bolingbroke, the English Tory statesman, orator, man of letters, friend of the Augustan wits, libertine, and deist, was born at Battersea, the son of Sir Henry St. John and Lady Mary Rich, daughter of the second earl of Warwick. After early schooling by his paternal grandmother, he was educated at Eton and, putatively, at Christ Church, Oxford, for in 1702 he was made an honorary doctor of Oxford. He had made the customary dissipated grand tour, 1698–1699, but he also mastered several languages and studied the history and customs of the lands he visited. In 1701 he became M.P. for the family borough of Wootton Bassett in Wiltshire. His eloquence and brilliance soon made him a leader of the Tory party. With the help of Robert Harley, he became secretary at war in 1704, but resigned in protest over the dismissal of Harley in 1708. The growing unpopularity of the "Whiggish" War of the Spanish Succession brought Harley back into power in 1710, and Bolingbroke joined the new Tory ministry as secretary of state. Two years later he was created Viscount Bolingbroke and was one of the negotiators of the Treaty of Utrecht signed in 1713. Following the accession of George I in 1714, Bolingbroke and the other Tory ministers were dismissed from office. In 1715 he fled to France to take political asylum for alleged Jacobitism. In 1723 he was pardoned, and he spent the remainder of his life living variously in England and in France.

WORKS

Some of Bolingbroke's political writings appeared in the Tory periodical the *Craftsman* between 1726 and 1736; but most others, including the philosophical, were published posthumously in 1754 by David Mallet in an edition of five quarto volumes. This publication elicited Dr. Johnson's famous attack on this "blunderbuss against religion and morality." David Hume's reaction is less well known but more pertinent:

> Lord Bolingbroke's posthumous Productions have at last convinc'd the whole World, that he ow'd his Character chiefly to his being a man of Quality, & to the Prevalence of Faction. Never were so many Volumes, containing so little Variety & Instruction: so much Arrogance & Declamation. The Clergy are all enrag'd against him; but they have no Reason. Were they never attack'd by more forcible Weapons than his, they might for ever keep Possession of their Authority.

POLITICAL AND HISTORICAL WORKS. Bolingbroke's contributions to the *Craftsman* exhibit much vigorous political writing, including *Remarks on the History of England* and *Dissertation on Parties.* Other tracts, political and historical, are *On the True Use of Retirement and Study, On the Spirit of Patriotism,* and *Letters on the Study and Use of History,* the last of which made famous the maxim, "History is philosophy teaching by examples." *The Idea of a Patriot King* also became famous because of its use in the education of the future George III. Matthew Arnold was to lament that Bolingbroke's historical writings were unduly neglected. Unfortunately, the neglect of his philosophical writings is less to be regretted.

PHILOSOPHICAL WRITINGS. Bolingbroke made much of the antithesis between nature and art; that is, the alleged superiority of a pure state of nature over the evils of civil society. Edmund Burke, who wrote his *Vindication of Natural Society* (1756) as an imitation of Bolingbroke's style and as an ironic refutation of this antithesis, asked rhetorically in *Reflections on the Revolution in France* (1790): "Who now reads Bolingbroke? Who ever read him through?" The long-held myth of Voltaire's great indebtedness to Bolingbroke has been completely disproved by N. L. Torrey. A similar claim of Alexander

Pope's great indebtedness has been vigorously challenged by Maynard Mack, who presents evidence that Bolingbroke's *Fragments or Minutes of Essays* were composed later than the *Essay on Man.* There is, however, no question that Pope discussed many matters with his "Guide, Philosopher, and Friend." With the single exception of Peter Annet, Bolingbroke was the last of the distinguished group of English deists beginning with Lord Herbert of Cherbury; but he proves somewhat of a disappointment to students of the history of ideas. Scrappy and unsystematic in his presentations, he is replete with contradictions. Despite recent attempts, especially by D. G. James and W. McMerrill, to take Bolingbroke's philosophy more seriously than has been customary, candor demands the conclusion that, although his style is more eloquent than that of most other deists, he contributed little or nothing original to the movement. This is not, however, to accuse him of plagiarism; for his ideas were part and parcel of the Augustan climate of opinion.

Despite frequent use of the name of John Locke (a device used by many deists), Bolingbroke was an unmitigated but curiously inconsistent rationalist. At one moment he asserts that the existence of Deity can and must be proved empirically, and at the next he asserts that only Right Reason can demonstrate the existence of Deity. He wrote *Reflections concerning Innate Moral Principles* to prove that compassion or benevolence is founded on reason alone. Unlike many of the deists, he was a metaphysical optimist, explaining away the evils of the universe and arguing that it is for man the best of all possible worlds despite the sufferings of individuals. He did not, however, believe that immortality and a future state of rewards and punishments can be proved by reason; and, although he accepted God as spirit, he was a materialist insofar as man is concerned.

He believed that there is no separation between soul and body and that at death man is annihilated; even in life, there is no communication between divine spirit and human matter.

Bolingbroke's concept of Natural Religion was essentially the same as the Common Notions of Lord Herbert of Cherbury. Yet with all his insistence on a priori reason, he lamented time and again that reason is fallible and must be corrected by a return to the primitive religions, particularly those of China and Egypt. Like all the deists, he was contemptuous of priestcraft and, despite his rationalism, of metaphysics. His criticism of Christian revelation is much like Matthew Tindal's, and the insinuation is that any revelation that is not universal is unnecessary.

In sum, Bolingbroke was more the orator than the philosopher. There is, however, considerable truth in his statement that "There is no reason … to banish eloquence out of philosophy; and truth and reason are no enemies to the purity, nor to the ornaments of language." He considered Plato, Nicolas Malebranche, and George Berkeley as poets, not philosophers, and his own best defense is the eloquence he admired.

See also Annet, Peter; Arnold, Matthew; Berkeley, George; Burke, Edmund; Deism; Herbert of Cherbury; Hume, David; Johnson, Samuel; Locke, John; Malebranche, Nicolas; Plato; Pope, Alexander; Tindal, Matthew; Voltaire, François-Marie Arouet de.

Bibliography

PRIMARY WORKS

A Collection of Political Tracts, 2nd ed. London: B. Francklin, 1748.

Letters on the Study and Use of History. London: T. Cadell, 1770.

The Works of Lord Bolingbroke, 4 vols. New York: A. M. Kelley, 1967.

Political Writings. Edited by David Armitage. Cambridge, U.K.: Cambridge University Press, 1997.

SECONDARY WORKS

Dickinson, H. T. *Bolingbroke.* London: Constable, 1970.

Harkness, Sir Douglas. *Bolingbroke: The Man and His Career.* London: Staples Press, 1957.

James, D. G. *The Life of Reason: Hobbes, Locke, Bolingbroke.* London: Longmans, Green, 1949.

Kramnick, Isaac. *Bolingbroke and His Circle: The Politics of Nostalgia in the Age of Walpole.* Cambridge, MA: Harvard University Press, 1968.

Mansfield, Harvey C., Jr. *Statesmanship and Party Government: A Study of Burke and Bolingbroke.* Chicago: University of Chicago Press, 1965.

McMerrill, Walter. *From Statesman to Philosopher: A Study in Bolingbroke's Deism.* New York: Philosophical Library, 1949.

Nadel, George H. "New Light on Bolingbroke's *Letters on History.*" *Journal of the History of Ideas* 23 (1962): 550–557.

Petrie, Sir Charles. *Bolingbroke.* London: Collins, 1937.

Pope, Alexander. *An Essay on Man.* Edited by Maynard Mack. London: Methuen, 1951.

Sichel, Walter. *Bolingbroke and His Times,* 2 vols. London: J. Nisbet, 1901.

Torrey, Norman L. "Chubb and Bolingbroke: Minor Influences." In *Voltaire and the English Deists.* New Haven, CT: Yale University Press, 1930.

Ernest Campbell Mossner (1967)
Bibliography updated by Philip Reed (2005)

BOLTZMANN, LUDWIG
(1844–1906)

Ludwig Boltzmann was born in Vienna, where he received his education. Boltzmann's major contribution to physics and, indirectly, to philosophy, was his profound work in the theory that grounded the phenomenological theory of heat, temperature, and the transformations of internal energy at the macroscopic level—that is to say thermodynamics—in the theoretical description of the underlying mechanical behavior of the basic constituents of a system, such as the molecules of a gas. Boltzmann also contributed directly to the ongoing philosophical discussions about the nature of scientific theories as a member of the group of outstanding physicist-philosophers concerned with such issues in the latter half of the nineteenth century, a group including Pierre Duhem, Ernst Mach, Wilhelm Ostwald, and Heinrich Hertz. During his career he held chairs at Graz, Munich, and Vienna.

After a long career as distinguished researcher and teacher whose influence through popularizing works extended beyond the narrow confines of academic scientists, Boltzmann tragically fell into a terminal depression ending in his suicide.

PHILOSOPHY OF SCIENCE

It would probably be a mistake to seek for a single, coherent, and fully developed account of the nature of scientific theories in Boltzmann's work. One must extract his views from a large number of short discussions, marginal remarks, and views expressed in correspondence with his colleagues. Nonetheless, certain themes are constant and clear and one can gain some understanding of what Boltzmann was after when one considers the scientific and philosophical context in which his remarks on the nature of theories were made.

Boltzmann's central scientific work posits that a macroscopic piece of matter, such as the volume of gas in a box, is composed of innumerable components—the molecules of the gas—too small to be observed in any direct manner. Following a long development from John Bernoulli, John Herepath, John Waterston, August Krönig, and Rudolf Clausius, and working in parallel with James Clerk Maxwell, Botzmann developed the kinetic theory of heat in which the dynamics of molecules moving more or less independently of one another—except for collisions and short-range interactions with one another and with the walls of a confining box—was used to explain the well-known laws of macroscopic thermodynamics.

It is important to understand just how indirect the evidence was for the genuine existence of molecules at this time. Their existence had been hypothesized in a resurrection of ancient atomic theory by chemists such as John Dalton to explain the combining laws of weight and volume in chemistry. The partial success of kinetic theory also provided indirect evidence of their existence. But the kinds of rich and more direct evidence available now for this particulate view of matter was then nonexistent.

A kind of radical empiricism was popular among the physicist-philosophers with whom Boltzmann associated. Duhem, Mach, and Ostwald shared the view that the aim of science was the production of simple and elegant lawlike regularities among the observable features of matter. They also shared deep skepticism toward any science that hypothesized unobservable entities as real explanatory components of the world. This skepticism included a negative attitude toward any theory positing "unobservable" molecules or atoms. Naturally such a position would be uncongenial to Boltzmann.

Boltzmann sought a view about theories that would legitimate inference to the existence of molecules, but that would not fall prey to empiricist skepticism about any scientific belief that rests upon "mere hypothesis" and that leaps beyond the observable features of the world to the postulation of unobservable entities and properties. Boltzmann's position seems close to that adopted by Hertz.

Theoretical beliefs do, indeed, rest upon hypotheses. New concepts for describing the world arise out of the scientist's imagination and are not all presented to one's direct sensory experience. There is no certainty in theoretical beliefs; they are certainly not derivable by any a priori reasoning, nor can they be established by "induction" from experience. They are hypotheses, guesses, invoked by humans to explain the observable phenomena. Such explanations consist in deductions of the observable phenomena from the hypothesized theory.

Only theories built on such hypotheses and invoking the unobservable will provide truly useful explanations in science. There is no hope of reconstructing science as a set of regularities that range only over the directly observable features of the world. But one must always remember that such hypothesized theories are merely pictures (*Bilder*) constructed by humans to fit the observable order into a coherent, deductive scheme. And one must always contemplate the possibility that alternative schemes—alternative pictures—may be available. These may present a different picture of the unobservable world, but insofar as they are as empirically adequate as the theories people have adopted, they are equally satisfactory from a scientific point of view.

That the deepest theories rest upon idealization is another reason—in addition to the belief in these theories resting only upon hypothesis—for Boltzmann to retreat from a fully realist position with regard to fundamental physical theories.

Boltzmann's views may perhaps be best understood as a kind of instrumentalism and pragmatism with regard to theories, but with the insistence that physics could not do without such hypothesized theories in its attempts to account for the observable data. Although people must be wary of taking theoretical inferences too realistically, they must not put any of their hopes in a reconstructed physics that eschews the use of concepts and laws invoking the unobservable altogether.

THEORETICAL PHYSICS

Boltzmann's great contribution to physics was in kinetic theory and the beginnings of what later was called statistical mechanics. Here his work paralleled that of Maxwell. The two great scientists often came up with similar results independently, but each also found great inspiration in the work of the other.

Maxwell had found a velocity distribution for the molecules of a gas at equilibrium by a curious argument that utilized results from the theory of errors. Boltzmann generalized this distribution to allow for external forces acting on the molecules. In studying the problem of approach to equilibrium, Maxwell derived his so-called "transfer equations." Independently Boltzmann derived his kinetic equation of how the velocity distribution changes with molecular collisions, the famous Boltzmann Equation.

It was easy to show that the Maxwell-Boltzmann equilibrium distribution would be a stationary solution of this equation, hence appropriate for equilibrium that is an unchanging thermodynamic state. To show that this was the only possible such state, Boltzmann invented a quantity "H" as a function of the distribution. He showed that according to his equation this quantity must decrease unless the distribution is the standard equilibrium distribution. Hence the standard distribution is the only one possible for equilibrium.

Boltzmann developed a new method of thinking about the equilibrium as well. Divide a space in which points represent the position and momentum of a single molecule into boxes macroscopically small but in which one expects to find many molecular states. Boltzmann considered all of the ways in which molecules could be permuted among these boxes. He then showed that the combination (number of molecules in specific boxes) corresponding to the largest number of possible ways of permuting the molecules among the boxes (subject to conservation of total energy of the molecules) was that corresponding to the standard equilibrium distribution. One could then think of the numbers of permutations corresponding to a combination as the "probability" of that combination and argue that equilibrium was the overwhelmingly most probable state of the gas. And one could identify thermodynamic entropy as a measure of such probabilities.

Considerations of these results by Maxwell, Boltzmann, and such critics as Samuel Burbury, Edward Culverwell, and later Ernst Zermelo, led Boltzmann to a long process of reinterpretation of his work. Maxwell, considering the possibilities of mechanisms that would molecule-by-molecule subvert the approach to equilibrium (Maxwell's Demon) spoke of the kinetic equation as only describing probable changes in the gas. Considerations of the dynamical reversibility of the system at the molecular level, and of recurrence results for dynamical systems discovered by Henri Poincaré, also forced Boltzmann to modify the initial view of the equation as describing the inevitable behavior of a system.

Reflection revealed that in deriving his equation Boltzmann had used a time-asymmetric hypothesis about the numbers of collisions of molecules of specified kinds that would occur over a given time interval (the *Stosszahlansatz*). Both Maxwell and Boltzmann began to frequently invoke probabilistic language in their interpretations of their results. What were such "probabilities"? Boltzmann expressed the view that whereas Maxwell thought of them as frequencies with which states would occur in a large collection of similarly prepared systems, he, Boltzmann, thought of them as frequencies with which states would occur over long periods of time for an individual system.

Maxwell and Boltzmann also discovered another approach to calculating equilibrium values, in which these values could be calculated as average values of functions of the microscopic dynamical state of the system in question, where one used (1) a collection of all possible such microscopic states compatible with the macroscopic constraints, and (2) an easily discovered probability distribution over these states, to calculate the mean values.

Both Maxwell and Boltzmann introduced dynamical postulates (the Ergodic Hypotheses) to justify this method. The nature of this justification was made much clearer later by the work of Paul and Tatiana Ehrenfest. Although one can show the Ergodic Hypothesis in its Ehrenfest version false, this work led to later, sounder formulations of this approach by means of correct ergodic theorems and important work on the specific dynamics of idealized molecular systems.

Boltzmann, pushed by insightful criticism, realized that invoking probability by itself would not solve all his interpretive problems. His kinetic equation was time asymmetric, but the underlying dynamics was time symmetric. Because for each molecular motion going from nonequilibrium to equilibrium there was one going from equilibrium to nonequilibrium, it was hard to see how one could argue that the equation even characterized "most probable" evolutions of systems. (Although there are current interpretations of the Boltzmann equation that revert to this way of thinking.)

Boltzmann's later interpretation of the whole scheme resorted to cosmological considerations. One thinks of probabilities of states as given by Boltzmann's method. Equilibrium is then the overwhelmingly most probable state. Why is the world in nonequilibrium then? Boltzmann's assistant Dr. Schuetz suggested that maybe the cosmos is in equilibrium overall, but that humans live in a "small" part of it temporarily in a nonequilibrium fluctuational condition. Boltzmann added to this the "anthropic" argument that people must find themselves in such a region because equilibrium regions could not support life-forms. Finally Boltzmann added the argument that what is meant by the "future" direction of time is just the direction of time in which entropy is increasing in this local, nonequilibrium patch of the universe. He draws a deep analogy here with the fact that what people take as "down" is just the local spatial direction of the gravitational force. In equilibrium regions of the cosmos there would be two time directions, but neither could be thought of a "past" or as "future," just as in gravitation-free regions there is no "up" and no "down."

The Ehrenfests later provided a deep interpretation of the kinetic equation and its solutions consonant with this later Boltzmannian interpretation. The solutions to the equation describe neither the inevitable not the most probable behavior of a system, but rather the "concentration curve" that describes the state of most of the systems of a collective of systems started in common nonequilib-

rium at any later moment of time. But at different times different members of the original collection are making up this majority that is approaching equilibrium.

BOLTZMANN'S CONTINUED INFLUENCE

Boltzmann's methodological thoughts about theories remain provocative and worthy of reflection when one reflect's now on the still problematic status of foundational physical theories. His introduction of probabilistic reasoning into physics was seminal. His work on kinetic theory and statistical mechanics is a rich source of problems for the philosopher of physics interested in probabilistic explanation in physics and in the relationship between phenomenological macroscopic theories and their microscopic, atomistic underpinnings. Boltzmann's invocation of cosmology (still done in current theories of statistical mechanics but within an entirely different cosmological background) also opens up a wide range of important questions for methodologists concerned with how people can construct their fundamental physical explanations. And his views on the "direction of time" remain fundamental for anyone discussing the origin and nature of ideas of the asymmetric nature of past and future.

See also Philosophy of Statistical Mechanics.

Bibliography

Blackmore, John. *Ludwig Boltzmann His Later Life and Philosophy 1900–1906*. Dordrecht, Netherlands: Kluwer, 1995.

Broda, Englebert. *Ludwig Boltzmann: Man, Physicist, Philosopher*. Woodbridge, CT: Ox Bow Press, 1983.

Brush, Stephen. *The Kind of Motion We Call Heat*. Vol. 2: *Statistical Physics and Irreversible Processes*. Amsterdam: North-Holland, 1976.

Brush, Stephen. *Kinetic Theory*. Vol. 2: *Irreversible Processes*. Oxford: Pergamon Press, 1966.

Brush, Stephen. *Statistical Physics and the Atomic Theory of Matter, from Boyle and Newton to Landau and Onsager*. Princeton, NJ: Princeton University Press, 1983.

Ehrenfest, Paul and Tatiana. *The Conceptual Foundations of the Statistical Approach in Mechanics*. Ithaca, NY: Cornell University Press, 1959.

Sklar, Lawrence. *Physics and Chance: Philosophical Issues in the Foundations of Statistical Mechanics*. Cambridge, U.K.: Cambridge University Press, 1993.

Lawrence Sklar (2005)

BOLZANO, BERNARD

(1781–1848)

Bernard Bolzano, a philosopher, theologian, logician, and mathematician, was born in Prague, where his father, an Italian art dealer, had settled; his mother was a German merchant's daughter. Bolzano studied mathematics, philosophy, and theology in Prague and defended his doctor's thesis in mathematics in 1804; he was ordained a Roman Catholic priest the following year. Shortly thereafter he was appointed to a temporary professorship in the science of religion at Karlova University in Prague and two years later was given a newly established chair in this field. Some time later he was accused of religious and political heresy and was removed from his teaching position in December 1819. Bolzano spent much of his time thereafter with the family of his friend and benefactor, A. Hoffmann, at their estate in southern Bohemia. He had difficulty getting his later publications through the Metternich censorship. Some of his books were put on the Index, and many appeared only posthumously. Some manuscripts are yet to be published; the most important of these are in the National Museum and the University Library in Prague, others are in the Österreichische Nationalbibliothek in Vienna. In December 1848, Bolzano died of a respiratory disease from which he had suffered for most of his life.

MATHEMATICS

Bolzano's mathematical teachings were not quite understood by his contemporaries, and most of his deep insights into the foundations of mathematical analysis long remained unrecognized. A famous theorem in the early stages of a modern presentation of the calculus is known as the Bolzano-Weierstrass theorem, but another masterful anticipation (by more than forty years) of Karl Theodor Wilhelm Weierstrass's discovery that there exist functions that are everywhere continuous but nowhere differentiable remained buried in manuscripts until the 1920s. But perhaps more important than Bolzano's actual discoveries of new theorems was the meticulousness with which he endeavored to lay new foundations for the *Grössenlehre,* the science of quantity—which was how Bolzano, using a very broad interpretation of "quantity," designated mathematics. In particular, his insistence that no appeal to any intuition of space and time should be acknowledged for this purpose and that only "purely analytical" methods were to be recognized put him in opposition to the then current Kantian ways of thinking and back into the Leibnizian tradition.

Bolzano's most famous posthumously published work is *Paradoxien des Unendlichen* (F. Prihonsky, ed., Leipzig, 1851; translated by D. A. Steele as *The Paradoxes of the Infinite,* London, 1950), in which he anticipated certain basic ideas of set theory, developed only a generation later by Georg Cantor, who fully acknowledged his indebtedness to Bolzano in this respect. This anticipation should, however, not be overrated. Bolzano was not quite able to rid himself of all the prejudices of his time and was, therefore, unable to reach a clear and fruitful conception of equivalence between infinite sets.

ETHICS AND PHILOSOPHY OF RELIGION

Bolzano was, in his time, much more influential as a theologian and social moralist than as a mathematician. An advocate of the Bohemian Catholic enlightenment, he lectured on religion and moral philosophy with strong pacifistic and socialistic overtones. He used the pulpit to proclaim before hundreds of impressed students a kind of utopian socialism. In his sermons he tried to prove the essential equality of all human beings, attacked private property obtained without work, and exhorted his listeners to sacrifice everything in their struggle for human rights. These sermons served him as a preparation for what he regarded as his most important book, *Von dem besten Staate,* which he finished in 1837 but was unable to publish. It first appeared in Prague in 1932.

Bolzano's philosophy of religion is presented in the books *Athanasia oder Gründe für die Unsterblichkeit der Seele* (Sulzbach, 1827) and *Lehrbuch der Religionswissenschaft* (4 vols., Sulzbach, 1834), the latter being a revised version of his lectures at the Prague university. He tried to prove that Catholicism is in full harmony with common sense. To this end he either disregarded or interpreted allegorically all mystical elements of Catholicism.

Bolzano derived his utilitarian ethics from a "highest ethical principle": "Of all actions possible to you, choose always the one which, weighing all consequences, will most further the good of the totality, in all its parts" (*Lehrbuch der Religionswissenschaft,* Vol. I, Sec. 87). This reminds one, of course, of Jeremy Bentham. "The most important idea of mankind" Bolzano took to be the "essential" equality of all human beings, which he tried to prove from historical, rational, and ethical considerations.

LOGIC AND EPISTEMOLOGY

It is as logician, methodologist, and epistemologist that Bolzano, after a long period of neglect, regained philosophical attention in the twentieth century. Mainly in order to combat radical skepticism, he found it necessary to base his teachings in these fields on certain ontological conceptions. He was convinced that there exist truths-in-themselves (*Wahrheiten an sich*) prior to and independent of language and man. These truths he carefully distinguished from truths expressed in words and conceived truths. The set of truths-in-themselves is a subset of the set of propositions (in-themselves) (*Sätze an sich*), again to be distinguished from propositions expressed in words and conceived propositions. Propositions consist of terms (ideas-in-themselves, *Vorstellungen an sich*). These are likewise to be distinguished, on the one hand, from the words or word sequences by which they are denoted and, on the other, from subjective ideas that occur in our mind. Although linguistic entities and conceived entities exist concretely, terms, propositions, and truths do not. Terms were equally carefully distinguished from their objects, whether or not these objects themselves existed concretely. Though Bolzano was a Platonist (in the modern sense), his ontology was rather remote from that of Plato or, for that matter, from that of Immanuel Kant, in spite of the common *an sich* terminology.

Beyond these negative determinations, Bolzano had little positive to say on the ontological status of terms and propositions except that they are the matter (*Stoff*) or sense (*Sinn*) of their correlates in language and thought.

Terms can be either simple or complex and either empty (*gegenstandslos*) or nonempty (*gegenständlich*); if nonempty, they are either singular or general. Examples of empty terms are –1, 0, Nothing, Round Square, Green Virtue, and Golden Mountain; absolutely simple terms are Not, Some, Have, Be, and Ought, but Bolzano was uncertain about others. Simple, singular terms he called intuitions (*Anschauungen*).

Propositions are composed of terms and are perhaps best regarded as ordered sequences of terms, while the content (*Inhalt*) of a proposition is the (unordered) set of the simple terms out of which the terms constituting the proposition are composed. The content of a complex term is similarly defined. The terms 3^5 and 5^3 are different, though they have the same content. The terms 2^4 and 4^2 are different, though they have not only the same content but even the same object. With this conception of content, the traditional doctrine of the reciprocity between the extension of a term (the set of objects falling under it) and the content of a term can easily be seen to be invalid.

Among Bolzano's many idiosyncratic convictions, perhaps the most interesting, but also the most strange to the modern mind, was his belief that each branch of science has a unique, strictly scientific presentation, which for him meant not only a unique finite axiom system (a belief he shared with many) but also an essentially unique entailment (*Abfolge*) of each theorem of this science by the axioms, a belief which might well be unique to Bolzano.

This relationship of entailment, as presented by Bolzano, is very peculiar and obscure. Bolzano was never quite sure that he understood it himself, though he was convinced that there objectively must exist some such relationship, that each science must have its basic truths (*Grundwahrheiten*) to which all other truths of that science stand in the peculiar relation of consequence (*Folge*) to ground (*Grund*). Bolzano was constantly struggling to differentiate this relation of entailment from the relation of derivability (*Ableitbarkeit*), which was the basic relation of his logic. Though he did not succeed in putting his theory of entailment into consistent and fruitful shape—and could not possibly have done so, in view of the chimerical character of his goal—his acumen, mastery of the contemporary logical and methodological literature, intellectual honesty, and lifelong self-criticism more than made up for his numerous shortcomings. Bolzano remains a towering figure in the epistemology, logic, and methodology of the first half of the nineteenth century.

See also Bentham, Jeremy; Cantor, Georg; Kant, Immanuel; Logic, History of; Propositions, Judgments, Sentences, and Statements.

Bibliography

ADDITIONAL WORKS BY BOLZANO

Bolzano's masterwork is his *Wissenschaftslehre,* 4 vols. (Sulzbach, 1837; edited by Wolfgang Schultz, Leipzig: F. Meiner, 1929–1931). *Grundlegung der Logik* (Hamburg, 1964) is a very useful selection by Friedrich Kambartel from the first two volumes of the *Wissenschaftslehre,* with summaries of omitted portions, an excellent introduction, and a good index.

WORKS ON BOLZANO

Bolzano's philosophical work was virtually disregarded until Edmund Husserl called attention to it at the start of the twentieth century. Hugo Bergmann's monograph, *Das philosophische Werk Bernard Bolzanos* (Halle: M. Niemeyer, 1909), increased the revived interest in Bolzano's ideas. Heinrich Scholz's articles, especially "Die Wissenschaftslehre Bolzanos," in *Abhandlungen des Fries'schen Schule,* n.s, 6

(1937): 399–472, reprinted in *Mathesis Universalis*, pp. 219–267 (Basel: B. Schwabe, 1961), presented Bolzano's contributions to logic, semantics, and the methodology of the deductive sciences in a modernized form. The best recent study in English of Bolzano as a logician is J. Berg's *Bolzano's Logic* (Stockholm: Almqvist and Wiksell, 1962). D. A. Steele's historical introduction to his translation of Bolzano's *Paradoxien des Unendlichen* is useful. Among other secondary works the most important are Eduard Winter's *Bernard Bolzano und sein Kreis* (Leipzig: J. Hegner, 1933), Günter Buhl's *Ableitbarkeit und Abfolge in der Wissenschaftstheorie Bolzanos* (Cologne: Cologne University Press, 1961), and (from a Marxist viewpoint) A. Kolman's *Bernard Bolzano* (in Russian, Moscow, 1955; in Czech, Prague, 1957; and in German, Berlin, 1963).

Yehoshua Bar-Hillel (1967)

BONALD, LOUIS GABRIEL AMBROISE, VICOMTE DE
(1754–1840)

Louis Gabriel Ambroise, Vicomte de Bonald, the French publicist and philosopher, was born in the château of Le Monna, near Millau (Aveyron). He emigrated in 1791, during the Revolution, to Heidelberg, moving later to Constance, and joined the circle of royalist writers who in 1796 published a number of books attacking the Revolutionary Party and defending the monarchy. His own contribution to the propaganda was his famous *Théorie du pouvoir politique et religieux* (3 vols., Constance, 1796), the first of a long series of volumes expressing the ultramontane position, the political supremacy of the papacy, absolute monarchy, and traditionalism.

The basic premise of Bonald, as far as his philosophy was concerned, was the identity of thought and language. Against the usual eighteenth-century idea that language was a human invention, he revived Jean-Jacques Rousseau's argument that since an invention requires thought and thought is internal speech, language could not have been invented. Consequently, he argued, it must have been put into the soul of man at creation. By means of certain philological investigations, Bonald was able to convince himself that there was a basic identity in all languages, as indeed there is in the Indo-European.

But language is a social, not an individual, phenomenon. It binds individuals together into groups and expresses an interpersonal set of ideas. These ideas are tradition. The unity of tradition may be disrupted, as it was during the Revolution, but nevertheless humankind will have to return to it if they have any hope of regaining social health. When this return occurs, people will coop-erate in a single political system and a single set of religious beliefs. The former will be absolute monarchy, the latter Roman Catholicism, both having single and omnicompetent heads. Thus, just as the universe is created and governed by one God, so both the church and state must preserve administrative unity. But since the church is the direct channel of communication between God and his creatures, the state and its subjects must be governed in moral affairs by the church.

The ultramontanism of Bonald was as extreme as logically possible. He maintained that the arts, for instance, flourished only in an absolute monarchy, and hence saw nothing to praise in Greek art. In fact, he had nothing good to say about anything Greek, since Greece was given to democracy, though he made an exception of the Spartans. He was opposed to the legalization of divorce and to equal rights for women. He accepted capital punishment, since God would see to it that the innocent would not suffer in the afterlife. He supported general censorship and denounced freedom of the press. And since he was a man of Stoic morals, he did not worry much about human dissatisfaction or unhappiness.

Bonald was a philosopher who never changed his views. In each of his numerous works he repeated the same fundamental theses. His influence was restricted to men of the extreme right, in spite of his ingenuity in argument and logical rigor. His ideas survived in France in *L'action française* and even in the nonpolitical writings of Charles Maurras, through whom they passed in diluted form to T. S. Eliot.

See also Eliot, Thomas Stearns; Language and Thought; Rousseau, Jean-Jacques; Traditionalism.

Bibliography

The collected works of Bonald appeared as *Oeuvres complètes*, edited by Abbé Migne (Paris, 1859).

For works on Bonald, see G. Boas, *French Philosophies of the Romantic Period* (Baltimore: Johns Hopkins Press, 1925), ch. 3; Harold Laski, *Authority in the Modern State* (New Haven, CT: Yale University Press, 1919), which follows Moulinié; H. Moulinié, *De Bonald* (Paris: Alcan, 1916); C. Sainte-Beuve, *Causeries du lundi* (Paris: Garnier, 1851–1862), Vol. IV, 426; Émile Faguet, *Politiques et moralistes du dix-neuvième siècle*, 1ère série (Paris, 1890).

OTHER RECOMMENDED TITLES

Dejnozka, Jan. "Origins of the Private Language Argument." *Dialogos* 30 (66) (1995): 59–78.

Reedy, W. Jay. "Language, Counter-Revolution and the 'Two Cultures': Louis de Bonald's Traditionalist Scientism." *Journal of the History of Ideas* 44 (1983): 579–598.

Reedy, W. Jay. "The Traditionalist Critique of Individualism in Post-Revolutionary France: The Case of Louis de Bonald." *History of Political Thought* 16 (1) (1995): 49–75.

George Boas (1967)
Bibliography updated by Tamra Frei (2005)

BONATELLI, FRANCESCO
(1830–1911)

Francesco Bonatelli, an Italian spiritualist philosopher, was born in Iseo, Brescia. He studied at the University of Vienna and taught philosophy at the universities of Bologna (1861–1867) and Padua (1867–1911). Bonatelli belonged to the tradition of Catholic spiritualism. He was one of the principal editors of *Filosofia delle scuole italiane,* a review founded in 1870 by Terenzio Mamiani to defend a Platonizing position, but he resigned in 1874 when the Platonist Giovanni Maria Bertini published criticisms of Catholicism that Bonatelli considered too bold. Bonatelli introduced the analytic method of German psychological research into Italy.

Bonatelli attempted to distinguish consistently between the unity of the ego and the multiplicity of psychic events. In his first work, *Pensiero e conoscenza* (Thought and consciousness; Bologna, 1864), Bonatelli distinguished two ways of life for the soul, one that is subject to the laws of fate and another that, although it recognizes these laws, is able to rise above them and use them as tools.

The conscious subject can be aware of other things only if it is capable at one and the same time of being modified and of remaining identical with itself, or inalterable. The solution of this apparent contradiction might lie in distinguishing between consciousness, understood as thought or pure mentality, and sensibility. In his most important work, *La coscienza e il meccanismo interiore* (Consciousness and the internal mechanism; Padua, 1872), Bonatelli insisted that consciousness neither is changed by the object nor changes it. The act of consciousness detaches the psychic event from its matrix in reality and thinks its possible essence or its "possibility or quiddity or whatever you wish to call it." Bonatelli investigated both consciousness itself and the relation between the psychic mechanism external to consciousness and consciousness, between the existing object and the object thought in its "quiddity."

He regarded consciousness as thought turned back upon itself and almost creating itself, but also as freely accepting the "yoke of logic." If consciousness were not of this nature, it would be reduced to a "logical machine," whereas it is free reflection on itself, grasping itself by directing itself toward objects. However, although the distinctive essence of consciousness is its infinite turning back upon itself (*la riflexione infinita degli atti,* "the infinite reflection of acts"), this reflection is not an infinite succession in which consciousness would lose itself in an endless postponement but rather a completed penetration of self, the fullness and richness of the activity of thought.

See also Consciousness.

Bibliography

ADDITIONAL WORKS BY BONATELLI
La filosofia dell'inconscio di Edoardo von Hartmann. Rome, 1876.
Elementi di psicologia e logica. Padua, 1892.

WORKS ON BONATELLI
Alliney, Giulio. *Francesco Bonatelli.* Brescia, 1947.
Gentile, Giovanni. *Le origini della filosofia contemporanea in Italia.* Messina: G. Principato, 1917. Vol. I, pp. 220–227.
Scatturin, Umberto. "Francesco Bonatelli." *Filosofia* 3 (1952): 433–439.
Varisco, Bernardino. *Francesco Bonatelli.* Chieri, 1912.
See also "In onore di Francesco Bonatelli," by various authors. *La cultura filosofica* 4 (2) (1910). Contains a bibliography.

Eugenio Garin (1967)
Translated by Tessa Byck

BONAVENTURE, ST.
(c. 1217–1274)

St. Bonaventure, the Italian Scholastic philosopher, was known as the Seraphic Doctor. Bonaventure, whose real name was John of Fidanza, was born in Bagnorea, in Tuscany. After obtaining a master of arts degree at Paris, Bonaventure joined the Franciscan friars (probably in 1243) and studied theology under their masters, Alexander of Hales and John of La Rochelle. After their deaths in 1245, he continued his studies under Eudes Rigaud and William of Meliton. He also came under the influence of the Dominican Guerric of Saint-Quentin and the secular master Guiard of Laon. In 1248 as a bachelor of Scripture he began lecturing on the Gospel of St. Luke and then on other books of Scripture (not all of these commentaries have survived). His monumental "Commentary on the *Sentences* of Peter Lombard," perhaps the most perfect example of this form of medieval literature, was composed between 1250 and 1252.

In 1253 he was licensed by the chancellor of the University of Paris and functioned as regent master of theology until 1257. During this time he composed four sets of *Quaestiones Disputatae,* of which the *De Scientia Christi* (On Christ's knowledge) is important for his theory of illumination; *De Mysterio Trinitatis* (On the mystery of the Trinity) contains the best exposition of his proofs of God's existence; and *De Caritate et de Novissimis* (On charity and the last things) contains sections taken over literally by Thomas Aquinas.

Bonaventure's formal reception into the masters' guild was delayed until October 1257 by the controversy between the mendicant friars and the secular masters. By that time, however, he was no longer actively teaching; in February 1257 he had been elected minster general of the Franciscan order and had resigned his chair at the university to devote himself to the administration of that post. Although often absent on business for the order or church, he continued to make Paris his general headquarters and was largely responsible for the friars' being so active in academic pursuits. He himself preached frequently at the university, touching on many of the religious and philosophical troubles that disturbed faculty and students.

It was during these years that he composed the *Breviloquium* (1257), or brief compendium of speculative theology, which was a departure from the usual scholastic method of presentation; *De Reductione Artium ad Theologiam* (On the reduction of the arts to theology), whose exact date of composition is unknown; and *Itinerarium Mentis in Deum* (The journey of the mind to god; 1259). All of these are important for understanding his general system of thought and the particular role of philosophy in it. Even more important in this connection are the three sets of *Collationes*—a series of informal evening conferences given during Lent to the faculty members and students in the Paris friary—including *De Decem Praeceptis* (On the ten commandments; 1267), *De Septem Donis Spiritus Sancti* (On the seven gifts of the Holy Spirit; 1268), and *In Hexaemeron Sive Illuminationes Ecclesiae* (On the six Days of creation or enlightenments of the church; 1273). All of these reflect the Averroistic tendencies in the arts faculty and Bonaventure's reaction to them. The last of these *Collationes* was left unfinished when Bonaventure was called from Paris and made cardinal bishop of Albano by Pope Gregory X, with whom he worked in organizing the Second Ecumenical Council of Lyons. He died shortly before the council closed and was buried there in the presence of the pope.

SPIRIT OF BONAVENTUR'S PHILOSOPHY

Bonaventure's fame rests primarily on his reputation as a theologian rather than as a philosopher. In both Dante Alighieri's *Paradiso* and Raphael's "Disputà" he appears as the equal of St. Thomas, and in the field of mystical theology he has been considered without peer. It is more difficult, however, to isolate the philosophical components of his system. This is partly due to the fact that all Bonaventure's extant works postdate his entrance into the Franciscan order and the beginning of his career as a theologian and ascetical writer. The chief reason, however, for the prevalence of theological interests in all of his writings was his understandable reaction against the rationalism rampant in the arts faculty at Paris that threatened the very raison d'être of speculative theology and led to the condemnations of 1270 and 1277 by Stephen Tempier, bishop of Paris. Among the 219 items listed as theological errors in the second of these condemnations, for example, are such statements as

(a) The most exalted of all vocations is that of the philosopher.

(b) There is no subject he is not competent to discuss and settle.

(c) One gains nothing in the way of knowledge by knowing theology.

(d) Only the philosophers deserve to be called wise; the speech of the theologian is founded on fables.

In the face of such views, it is understandable why Bonaventure, who believed in the validity of Christian revelation, should have stressed the inability of philosophers in general and of Aristotle in particular to learn the full truth about man's existential situation. Conversely, Bonaventure tried to show the continuity between the aims of philosophy and those of theology. He maintained that philosophy has a genuine, albeit limited, autonomy; the knowledge it yields is a stage in the overall ascent of the human mind to true wisdom, the culmination of which in this life is found in quasi-experiential knowledge of God, achieved by such mystics as Francis of Assisi.

Part of the great literary charm of Bonaventure's style is his ability to play upon words. Throughout his later works, particularly his sermons and *Collationes,* he continually gives a deliberately theological twist to technical philosophic terms, with the result that he has frequently been unjustly accused of confusing theology with philosophy either in principle or in practice. The truth of the matter is that while he was eminently able to conduct a purely philosophical discussion and often did so in his university lectures, he preferred to limit himself to particular topics. He never formed a complete system from his philosophical analyses, but he put them into the service of his overall theological synthesis.

BONAVENTURE'S METAPHYSICS

Bonaventure's linguistic sophistication and his idea of the continuity between philosophy and theology are perhaps best represented in his discussion of metaphysics in the *In Hexaemeron.* Christ, the Son of God, not Aristotle, is the "metaphysician" par excellence.

> As the Son said: "I came forth from the Father and have come into the world; again I leave the world and go to the Father" [John 16:28], so anyone may say: "Lord, I came forth from you, the All High; I go to you, the All High, and by means of you, the All High." Here is the metaphysical medium leading us back. And this is the whole of our metaphysics: it concerns emanation, exemplarity, and consummation [that is, being illumined by spiritual rays and led back to the All High]. It is in this way you become a true metaphysician. (*Collatio* I, No. 17; in *Opera,* Vol. V, p. 332)

EMANATION. Bonaventure uses the term *emanation* to designate the general theory of how creation proceeds from God. With its Plotinian overtones, however, "emanation" suggested more specifically the thesis of al-Fārābī, Avicenna, and Averroes that all creatures, by an inevitable and eternal process, spring from the creative mind of God through a chain of intermediary causes of continually diminishing perfection. This thesis was designed to reconcile Aristotle's eternal world with the creation concept of the Qur'an. Bonaventure, however, wished to reconcile "emanation" with Christian theology. His counterthesis is summarized in the *Breviloquium:* "The whole of the cosmic machine was produced in time and from nothing, by one principle only who is supreme and whose power, though immense, still arranges all according to a certain weight, number and measure" (Book II, Part 1, in *Opera,* Vol. V, p. 219). It is to be noted that he rejects the concepts of the eternity of the world, of the eternity of matter, of a dual principle of good and evil, and of the existence of intermediary causes.

His description of the supreme principle implies that a perfect power must be free to create varying degrees of perfection, in contrast with the Arab belief that direct creation by a perfect power could only result in perfect effects. Also, the use of Augustine's triad of weight, number, and measure suggests the seal of the Blessed Trinity stamped on every creature. This becomes clearer if we consider the next and most characteristic feature of Bonaventure's metaphysics.

EXEMPLARISM. Emanation concerns natural philosophy as much as metaphysics. God, as final cause and ultimate goal of man's quest for happiness, is the concern of the moral philosopher as well as the metaphysician. But only the metaphysician can understand God as exemplar cause. And it is in analyzing this aspect of the science of causes and first principles that man is most truly a metaphysician.

Though this metaphysical pursuit begins with reason, it can be successfully terminated only by a person with faith. Comparing the two greatest pagan philosophers, Aristotle and Plato, Bonaventure maintained that Plato, the master of wisdom, erred in looking only upward to the realm of eternal values, of the immutable ideas, while Aristotle, the master of natural science, looked only earthward to the everyday sensible world that Plato neglected. But Aristotle's was the greater sin, for in rejecting the Platonic ideas in toto, he closed the door to a full understanding of the universe in terms of its causes. Bonaventure saw Augustine as the model of Christian wisdom because he combined the science of Aristotle with Plato's wisdom (*Christus Unus Omnium Magister,* Nos. 18–19, in *Opera,* Vol. V, p. 572). As a Christian he could complete what Plato could only begin. Not only did he demonstrate that Plato's archetypal Ideas are the exemplar causes or models that God used in creating the universe, a point that a philosopher alone could establish, but he also showed further that these Ideas are associated in a special way with the second person of the Trinity, an insight only divine revelation could help one discover. Bonaventure, following Augustine, explained that since the Father begets the Son by an eternal act of self-knowledge, the Son may also be called the wisdom of the Father and expresses in his person all of God's creative possibilities. As such, the Son is the Word or Logos adumbrated in the writings of the philosophers but fully revealed only at the beginning of the Gospel of John, where he appears as the one through whom all things are made (that is, as exemplar cause) and who "enlightens every man who comes into the world" (an allusion to Augustine's theory that only some illumination by divine ideas can account for man's knowing immutable truths). "From his [magisterial] chair in heaven Christ teaches us interiorly," wrote Bonaventure. "If as the Philosopher [Aristotle] says, the knowable qua knowable is eternal, nothing can be known except through that Truth which is unshaken, immutable and without limit" (*In Hexae-meron, Collatio* I, No. 13; in *Opera,* Vol. V, p. 331).

Averroes had written of Aristotle: "I believe this man to be nature's model, the exemplar which nature found to reveal the ultimate in human perfection" (*De Anima* III, 2). Bonaventure maintained that Christ, not Aristotle, is God's model for humanity. The Word is not only God but also a perfect man. He gives us "the power of becoming the sons of God," and he is the "one master of all the sciences" (*Sermo IV*; in *Opera,* Vol. V, p. 567); to know him fully is to know all that can be known.

Bonaventure held that Plato's theory of Ideas was a first philosophical approximation to this theological insight, and Aristotle's rejection of this view led to his errors about God. For if God lacked the exemplar ideas, he would know only himself and nothing of the world. He would be, as Aristotle claimed, related to the world only as final cause and not as creator. Moreover, in Aristotle's world, since chance clearly does not explain the cyclic changes of the cosmos, the universe must be ruled by determinism, as the Arabic commentators claim. But then man would no longer be a responsible agent; he would deserve neither reward nor punishment, and divine providence would be a myth.

With the recognition of exemplarism, on the other hand, the whole of creation takes on a sacramental character— that is, it becomes a material means of bringing the soul to God. Nature becomes the "mirror of God," reflecting his perfections in varying degrees. Although we see only a shadowy likeness (*umbra*) or trace (*vestigium*) of the creator in inorganic substances and the lower forms of life, the soul of man is God's image (*imago*) and the angel his similitude (*similitudo*).

The recognition of God in nature begins in philosophy, but it is continued and perfected in theology. In *De Mysterio Trinitatis* Bonaventure argued that philosophers know that secondary beings imply a first; dependent beings imply an independent being; contingent things imply some necessary being; the relative implies an absolute; the imperfect, something perfect; Plato's participated beings imply one unparticipated being; if there are potential beings, then pure act must also exist; composite things imply the existence of something simple; the changeable can only coexist with the unchangeable. Pagan philosophers, knowing that these ten self-evident conditionals have their antecedents verified in the corporeal world, learned much about God (*De Mysterio Trinitatis* I, 1; in *Opera,* Vol. V, pp. 46–47).

More can be learned, however, by the soul reflecting upon itself. In his other works Bonaventure went on to suggest that the soul, possessed of memory, intelligence, and will, is an image of God, not only mirroring his spiritual nature but adumbrating the Trinity itself. Memory, which creates its own thought objects, resembles the Father who begets the Son or Logos (intelligence) as an intellectual reflection of himself, and the two through their mutual love (will—the active principle of "spiration") breathe forth the Holy Spirit. But although a philosopher can discover a spiritual God as the ultimate object of the soul's search for truth and happiness, only a man of faith like Augustine can find the Trinity manifest throughout creation.

CONSUMMATION OR ENLIGHTENED RETURN. The third aspect of Bonaventure's metaphysics concerns a creature's fulfillment of its destiny by returning to God. This return (called technically a *reductio*) in the case of the lower creation is achieved in and through man (who praises God for and through subhuman creation). Man's return is made possible in turn by Christ. For man returns to God by living an upright life—that is, by being rightly aligned with God—and this can be accomplished only through the grace of Christ. Man's mind is right (*rectus*) when it has found truth, and above all, eternal truth. His will is right when it loves what is really good, his exercise of power is right when it is a continuation of God's ruling power. Through original sin or the Fall, man lost this triple righteousness. His intellect, lured by vain curiosity, has enmeshed itself in interminable doubts and futile controversies; his will is ruled by greed and concupiscence; in his exercise of power he seeks autonomy. But although man lost the state of original justice, he still hungers for it. This longing for the infinite good is revealed in his ceaseless quest for pleasures. Through faith and love (grace), man can find his way back.

Since knowledge is involved at every stage of the return, *reductio* is also a quest for wisdom and hence, in an extended theological sense, it is metaphysical. It is an enlightened return, because every branch of learning is a gift from above, from the "Father of lights" (Epistle of St. James, 1. 17), and can be put into the service of theology (this is the theme of Bonaventure's *De Reductione Artium*). Although man's return begins with the natural light of reason reflecting first on the external world and then turning inward in an analysis of the soul, it is perfected initially by a natural illumination of the divine ideas and then by varying additional degrees of supernatural illumination which culminate in the experiential cognition of God through mystical union (the theme of the *Itinerarium*). This experience is not the same as the clear vision of the blessed in heaven but is the "learned ignorance" referred to by the mystical writers—a union of the soul with God in darkness, granted to saints like Francis before death.

OTHER DOCTRINES

The elements of Bonaventure's philosophy are woven into his religiously oriented system. Like all the Parisian thinkers of this period, Bonaventure developed a basically Aristotelian philosophy, but he included a larger admixture of Neoplatonic and Augustinian elements than we find in St. Thomas, for instance, who studied Aristotle somewhat later and more thoroughly under Albert the Great.

THEORY OF KNOWLEDGE. Bonaventure believed that the mind has no innate ideas, not even in the sense postulated by the authors of the *Summa Theologica* (ascribed to Alexander of Hales), who argued that ideas are latent in the agent intellect but are actually acquired only when the light of the agent intellect illumines the possible intellect. Bonaventure rejected this, holding with Aristotle that the mind at birth is a tabula rasa. It needs sensory stimulation before it can acquire any notions about the external world of objects. However, Bonaventure did use the Augustinian theory of illumination to explain how the mind passes judgment on sensible things in terms of their values. For when the mind judges something to be, for example, good or beautiful, there must be an implicit awareness of what beauty and goodness are in themselves; and this requires that the human mind have some knowledge of the divine ideas. Obviously this is not a clear or intuitive knowledge of God such as the angels or the blessed in paradise possess. Yet just as one can see by sunlight without looking into the sun itself, so one can have knowledge of the divine ideas. At the same time, Bonaventure rejected the interpretation (also found in the *Summa* of Alexander) that we attain these ideas only in terms of the residual effects of the divine action—effects which remain in the soul like habitual or buried memories. Bonaventure claimed that in some mysterious way (which he called *contuition* but which he never fully explained), when we know a created object, our mind is simultaneously enlightened so that it is moved to judge correctly about the object and is hence in accord with God's own mind on the subject.

Although Bonaventure agreed with Aristotle that our knowledge of the external world is sense-dependent, he did not fully subscribe to Aristotle's principle that "noth-ing is in the intellect that was not first in the senses." He held that the intellect can turn inward, reflecting on the soul and its tendencies. In analyzing the precise nature of the object of these tendencies, the mind discovers God and itself as his image. The reasoning process involved is neither deductive nor inductive in the usual meaning of these terms, but is called technically a "reduction" and seems to resemble in some respects the "abduction" of Charles S. Peirce. Reasoning proceeds by progressively deepening insights into what the desire for truth and perfect happiness involve. If the reduction remains imperfect and does not go on to completion, God is not discovered and one may err about his nature or even his existence. Although at times Bonaventure, following the authority of John of Damascus, Ancius Manlius Severinus Boethius, or Augustine, spoke of the existence of God as a truth implanted by nature in the human mind, he meant this to be interpreted as referring immediately to man's natural desire for knowledge, truth, happiness, or goodness—all of which need explication before man realizes they have God as their ultimate object (*De Mysterio Trinitatis*, I, 1; in *Opera*, Vol. V, p. 49).

COSMOLOGY. In his analysis of material creation, Bonaventure introduced extraneous elements into Aristotle's theory of matter and form. Thus, for instance, he adopted Avicebron's theory of the hylomorphic composition of spiritual as well as corporeal creatures. The argument here is that since creatures have some measure of potentiality (only God is pure actuality), they must have some kind of matter, for according to Aristotle matter is the principle and source of potentiality. This spiritual matter, found both in the angel and in the human soul, is never separable from its spiritual form; hence, such spiritual substances are not subject to change—they cannot die or disintegrate like terrestrial bodies, nor can they be perfected by a hierarchy of forms, as can corporeal matter.

In *Breviloquium*, Book II, Bonaventure, in explaining the visible universe, made use of the theories of light developed by Robert Grosseteste and the Oxford school. He distinguished light (*lux*), luminosity (*lumen*), and color. The first is the most basic of substantial forms; it enables both terrestrial and celestial bodies to subsist and is the root source of whatever internal dynamism they possess. *Lumen* is the invisible radiation which has its origin especially in celestial bodies like the sun but exists in the intervening transparent medium. It is described by Bonaventure as being both an active power (*virtus activa*) and something substantial in itself but only accidentally related to the transmitting medium through which it flows continually and instantaneously by a self-generative process called multiplication. Being neither an accidental nor a substantial form properly speaking, it is not educed from the potentialities of matter as are other corporeal forms, with the exception of *lux*. Yet it requires some material medium or body and coexists with such without changing it substantially. Not only does it penetrate the bowels of the earth, where it governs the formation of minerals, but in virtue of its purity and similarity to the spiritual, this substantial radiation disposes bodies to receive the life form and acts as a sort of intermediary between soul and body. It is active in the reproduction of animals, functioning as one of the external agents that educes the higher forms from the matter where they exist as "seminal reasons."

This theory of seminal reasons was adopted on the authority of Augustine, but Bonaventure interpreted it within the framework of the general Aristotelian formula that forms are educed from the potency of matter. Unlike St. Thomas, Bonaventure interpreted these "potencies" as active powers rather than passive potentialities. They are really latent forms existing in matter in an inchoate or germinal state. External agents only cooperate with these powers, in much the way that a gardener cultivates a rosebush or a seedbed so that it bears flowers or germinates (*Commentarium in Librum II Sententiarum*, Dist. 7, in *Opera*, Vol. II, p. 198). All forms, except the primary light form and the human soul, which are directly created by God, arise through the cooperation of seminal powers and external agents, under the influence of light.

Bonaventure, unlike Thomas, believed that creation in time (in contrast with Aristotle's belief in the eternity of the world) is demonstrable from reason, using Aristotle's own principles (*Commentarium in Librum I Sententiarum*, Dist. 1, in *Opera*, Vol. II, pp. 20–22). His arguments, although interesting, are based on a medieval concept of number and infinity and on the presupposition that the immortality of the human soul is a purely rational truth.

As his name implies, Bonaventure's character seems to have represented all that the medieval Christian regarded as ideal. Born at a critical period in the history of his church, his order, and of speculative theology, he saw himself cast in a mediating role. As a bachelor of theology, trained in the arts, he sought to put the new philosophy into the service of theology. As a master of theology he tried not only to defend the new mendicant orders against the attacks of the secular masters but also to heal their differences. As minister general he took a middle position between the extreme factions of the Franciscan order, who differed on the subjects of evangelical poverty and the pursuit of studies. Bonaventure's works, such as *De Reductione Artium ad Theologiam* and *Itinerarium Mentis in Deum* were not only theoretical expressions of his gift for synthesis but also served the practical purpose of silencing the anti-intellectual friars who claimed that the academic life was incompatible with the ascetical aims of a follower of St. Francis. As cardinal, Bonaventure played a major role at the Council of Lyons in healing the rift between Greek and Latin Christendom. Under the aegis of Augustine, he consolidated theological opposition to the cult of Aristotle and Averroistic rationalism. Although this led eventually to the Parisian condemnations of 1270 and 1277, in which even theses of St. Thomas were included, it also bore fruit in a renewed interest in Augustine's contributions to philosophy by Matthew of Acquasparta, Roger Marston, John Peckham, and others of the Augustinian school.

See also Albert the Great; Alexander of Hales; al-Fārābī; Aristotle; Augustine, St.; Augustinianism; Averroes; Averroism; Avicenna; Boethius, Ancius Manlius Severinus; Dante Alighieri; Determinism, A Historical Survey; Grosseteste, Robert; Ibn Gabirol, Solomon ben Judah; John of Damascus; John of La Rochelle; Marston, Roger; Matthew of Acquasparta; Medieval Philosophy; Mysticism, History of; Peckham, John; Peter Lombard; Plato; Rationalism; Revelation; Thomas Aquinas, St.

Bibliography

The collected Latin works of St. Bonaventure were published as *S. Bonaventurae Opera Omnia.* 10 vols. (Quaracchi, 1882–1902). The two works not contained in that collection are *Questions disputées "De Caritate," "De Novissimis,"* edited by P. Glorieux (Paris, 1950), and a second redaction of *Collationes in Hexaemeron,* edited by F. Delorme (Quaracchi, 1934). *Commentary on the Sentences* has been reprinted in 4 vols. (Quaracchi, 1934–1949) without the critical notes. Also see *Tria Opuscula,* 5th ed. (Quaracchi, 1938), which includes *Breviloquium, Itinerarium Mentis in Deum,* and *De Reductione Artium ad Theologiam.*

English translations of Bonaventure's work include *St. Bonaventure's De Reductione Artium ad Theologiam,* translated by E. T. Healy (St. Bonaventure, NY, 1955), in Latin and English; *St. Bonaventure's Itinerarium Mentis in Deum,* translated by Philotheus Boehner (St. Bonaventure, NY, 1956), in Latin and English; *Breviloquium by St. Bonaventure,* translated by E. E. Nemmers (St. Louis and London: Herder, 1946); J. de Vinck, *The Work of Bonaventure* (Paterson, NJ: St. Anthony Guild Press, 1960–1970); and four questions from the "Commentary on the Sentences" in *Selections from Medieval Philosophers,* edited by Richard McKeon (New York: Scribners, 1930), Vol. II, pp. 118–148.

A Latin and Spanish translation is L. Amoros, B. Aperribay, M. Oromi, and M. Oltra, eds., *Obras de S. Buenaventura*, 6 vols. (Madrid, 1945–1949), Vol. I of which contains an extensive bibliography and new data on authentic works not in *Opera Omnia*.

General bibliographies for Bonaventure can be found in F. Ueberweg and B. Geyer, *Grundriss der Geschichte der Philosophie*, 12th ed. reprint (Basel, 1951), Vol. II, pp. 735–738, and Étienne Gilson, *History of Christian Philosophy in the Middle Ages* (New York: Random House, 1955), pp. 685–686. For studies after 1953, see the annotated *Bibliographia Franciscana* (Rome: Istituto Storico dei Cappuccini, 1962–), Vol. XI ff. The classic introduction to Bonaventure's thought is Étienne Gilson, *La philosophie de saint Bonaventure*. 2nd ed. (Paris, 1953; English translation of 1st ed., London: Sheed and Ward, 1938). Critical evaluations of this and alternate views are B. A. Gendreau, "The Quest for Certainty in St. Bonaventure," in *Franciscan Studies* 21 (1961): 104–227, and J. G. Bugerol, *Introduction à l'étude de S. Bonaventure* (Paris, 1961). Bonaventurean themes in Raphael are discussed in H. B. Gutman, "The Medieval Content of Raphael's 'School of Athens,'" in *Journal of the History of Ideas* 2 (1941): 420–429, and "Raphael's 'Disputà,'" in *Franciscan Studies* 2 (1942): 35–48. For Bonaventure's own theory of art, see E. J. M. Spargo, *The Category of the Aesthetic in the Philosophy of St. Bonaventure* (St. Bonaventure, NY, 1953). Also see R. P. Prentice, *The Psychology of Love according to St. Bonaventure*, 2nd ed. (St. Bonaventure, NY, 1957), which is a comparison of Bonaventure and Max Scheler, and A. Schaefer, "The Position and Function of Man in the Created World according to St. Bonaventure," in *Franciscan Studies* 20 (1960): 261–316; and 21 (1961): 233–382.

Allan B. Wolter, O.F.M. (1967)

BONHOEFFER, DIETRICH
(1906–1945)

Dietrich Bonhoeffer was a German theologian and religious leader during the period when National Socialism dominated. He was active in the resistance to Hitler; and his anti-Nazi activities led to his death in a concentration camp. The heroism of his end served to call attention to his life and thought, but by itself the drama of his life does not account for the continuing interest Bonhoeffer has aroused in twenty-first century theological circles. He has been read eagerly for the substance of his thought, his example of resistance to oppression, and his provocative portrayal of the secular settings that provide the context for much theological inquiry. The Nazi milieu prevented Bonhoeffer from making a sustained impact on the academic world during his lifetime; he was then recognized chiefly for his involvement in the nascent ecumenical movement, for his leadership of a clandestine seminary at Finkenwalde and, of course, for his part in the resistance to Hitler. (Thanks to the work of theologians such as John de Gruchy, Bonhoeffer's thought inspired much South African resistance to apartheid, and he has been invoked elsewhere by critics of oppressive political orders.)

PHILOSOPHY AND THEOLOGY

Only one of Bonhoeffer's works, *Akt und Sein*, is wholly devoted to formal questions concerning the relation of philosophy to theology. *Akt und Sein* was his inaugural dissertation, and it is marked by a certain pretentiousness and heavy-handed systematic theological concern. At times its jargon obscures the author's line of thought. It is doubtful whether the work possesses any great worth in isolation from Bonhoeffer's life. However, because it anticipates many of the themes that he later elaborated without explicit philosophical reference, it is of interest.

In *Akt und Sein* Bonhoeffer carried on a veiled polemic, on the one hand, against those who wished to reduce Christianity either to a philosophy of transcendence (*Akt*) or of being (*Sein*), and on the other hand against those who believed that Christian theology could be expressed independently of philosophical concerns. His own interests were in many ways synthetic. Critical of philosophical attempts to account for or exhaust the meaning of Christian revelation, Bonhoeffer admitted the general necessity of relating theology and philosophy. He appreciated the Kantian *Akt*-philosophy, which stresses the thinker or the knower "in relation to" the known, but he criticized its lack of interest in the problem of the known, as in the mundane world. He turned with some interest to the *Sein*-philosophies, which focus on God as the known but which may lack a proper corollary interest in the concrete historical events in which believers find God to be revealed. These philosophies Bonhoeffer categorized repeatedly throughout his career as "theologies of glory" that seek to explicate the nature of the Divine on a philosophical basis. He advocated mainly what in his Lutheran theological lineage has always been called "a theology of the Cross" because it accented an event in history, specifically in the crucifixion of Jesus Christ.

If the corpus of Bonhoeffer's most important literary work is to be related to philosophy, it must be categorized as a philosophy of history. In all his writings he shows an active and positive interest in the concrete character of Divine revelation. He often voiced an agnostic position on the possibility of making meaningful statements about God apart from revelation in Jesus Christ. In lectures on Christology delivered in 1932 and available in the form of published classroom notes, he concentrated consistently on the historical, concrete, and conditioned character of revelation in Jesus Christ and the church over against philosophies of transcendence.

ETHICS

Bonhoeffer's *Ethics* is his most systematic work (although it survives only in fragments from the concentration camp years). Whereas it profits from philosophical debate, *Ethics* is largely a rejection of philosophical ethics. In this book Bonhoeffer takes a negative view of Roman Catholic ontological ethics, which moves from general abstract ethical statements to specific Christian principles. He was more closely identified with existentialism, but he regarded that philosophy also as an abstraction from revelatory events in Jesus Christ. Bonhoeffer has been accused, along with his teacher Karl Barth, of presenting an overly Christological philosophy and ethic, a critique that would not have disturbed him at all.

LATER THOUGHT

During his final imprisonment before his execution, Bonhoeffer's thought took a surprising—some would say a radical—turn. Pondering the collapse of continental humanist traditions at the hands of Nazis and other totalitarians, he focused on the blithe ways many of his contemporaries shrugged off inherited traditions of piety, even though some remained Christian. In his eyes, they joined free-spirited nonbelievers as they left behind preoccupations with guilt and modes he associated with conventional religion. He has come to be best remembered for his interpretation of modern history, developed on the basis of these observations and his study of the Bible during his imprisonment. From the Christian point of view he regarded secularization as a largely positive process. In a celebrated historical analysis he perceived that the "god of explanation" was gradually disappearing from European history; and disappearing with it was what he called "the religious *a priori*" (Bonhoeffer 1953). By this term he referred to the idea that a person must adopt a specific metaphysics, a specialized view of transcendence, or a particular form of piety and churchly existence before becoming a Christian. All of these, Bonhoeffer claimed, belonged to the spiritual adolescence of humans.

Contemporary humans, Bonhoeffer thought, reckoned less and less with a transcendent and hypothetical deity located outside the circle of the empirical. He cherished those Biblical texts and those aspects of theological tradition that spoke of transcendence located in the center of human affairs, particularly in the history of Jesus Christ. In this historical context, Bonhoeffer pointed out, the role of philosophy had become increasingly secularized as it focused on human autonomy (Bonhoeffer 1953).

In his eyes, René Descartes had begun to see the world as a mechanism. Benedict de Spinoza was a pantheist. Immanuel Kant, in Bonhoeffer's view, was close to the deists in his reluctance to deal philosophically with God as the known, in his revelation in history. He commented on the ways in which Johann Gottlieb Fichte and Georg Hegel had also developed brands of pantheism that drew them away from the historical involvement of God with the secular world.

All of these developments, he claimed in letters he wrote from prison, revealed the "growing tendency to assert the autonomy of man and the world" (*Prisoner for God*, Bonhoeffer 1954, p. 163). He came to be seen as a forerunner of a school of antimetaphysical theologians who insisted that Christian life and language were most free when they were not based on a philosophy of being or the expression of transcendence. Some of their writings became best-sellers in the 1960s and 1970s, when elements of Bonhoeffer's thought appeared in the controversial *Honest to God* (1963) by Bishop John A. T. Robinson and in a number of radical theological works, some of them momentarily associated with the concept of "the death of God."

Subsequently, cultural changes in Europe, wherein non-Christians and many Christians came to rediscover the potency of myths and symbols, which Bonhoeffer had earlier come to minimize, found significant figures resorting to new languages touting spirituality. In this context, a later generation of those influenced by Bonhoeffer reexplored those sources in his thought that were not exhausted by his witness to a "world come of age" and to the existence of a Christian church that was engaged, in almost carefree ways, with secular philosophies.

Part of this reexploration led some theologians to revisit the long-overlooked influence of Martin Heidegger on the young Bonhoeffer who wrote *Akt und Sein*. In that work, only Martin Luther was referenced more frequently than Heidegger. The most elaborate statement of this engagement was written by the American Charles Marsh in *Reclaiming Dietrich Bonhoeffer* (1994). Recognizing that Heidegger, a devotee of National Socialism, and Bonhoeffer, who was to give his life opposing it, were poles apart in politics, and that Bonhoeffer seldom quoted Heidegger after that early work, Marsh did discern some revisitations of the themes of transcendence that showed the influence of the philosopher. In Marsh's terms: "In an attempt to shape reflection in a way that is not determined by the totality of the self-reflective subject but emerges from a source prior to and external to the individual, Bonhoeffer finds certain themes in Heidegger's fundamental ontology congenial to his theological purposes. Bonhoeffer subjects these themes to Christological redescription," and so does not stay with existential analysis (1994, p. 112). Nonetheless, Marsh argued, "Heidegger's notions of potentiality-for-being, authenticity, and being-with others push[ed] Bonhoeffer in his thinking about human selfhood and sociality to recognize specific social-ontological distinctions and concepts critical to his developing Christology" (Marsh 1994, p. 112).

Needless to say, such a view of connections and influence does not go unchallenged. Thus German theologian Ernst Feil presented anew what Marsh called "the conventional wisdom." In it, Heidegger's "concept of existence, derived from the human and not from revelation, was, for Bonhoeffer, theologically unusable" (1985, p. 31) agrees that Bonhoeffer finally did reject Heidegger's fundamental ontology on theological grounds, but awareness of this rejection "should not obscure Bonhoeffer's' admiration for Heidegger's *Being and Time's* attempt to 'destrue' or destructure the history of ontology," which captured Bonhoeffer's imagination in a decisive way (1994, p. 31). Yet even this self-described "reclamation" project by thinkers such as Marsh, while showing early dependence on Heidegger, does not serve to limit the imagination with which Bonhoeffer "revisited" Christological themes in a milieu he described as "a world come of age" (Bonhoeffer 1953, p. 327).

See also Barth, Karl; Descartes, René; Existentialism; Heidegger, Martin; Kant, Immanuel; Philosophy of History; Religion; Religious Language; Spinoza, Benedict (Baruch) de.

Bibliography

WORKS BY BONHOEFFER

Nachfolge. München: C. Kaiser, 1937. Translated by Reginald H. Fuller as *The Cost of Discipleship* (New York: Macmillan, 1959).

Ethik. München: C. Kaiser, 1949. Translated by Neville Horton Smith as *Ethics* (New York: Macmillan, 1955).

Widerstand und Ergebung, edited by Eberhard Bethge. München: C. Kaiser: 1951. Translated by Reginald H. Fuller as *Letters and Papers from Prison.* London: SCM Press, 1953 and New York: Macmillan, 1971; and as *Prisoner for God* (New York, Macmillan, 1954).

Gesammelte Schriften. 4 vols. Munich: C. Kaiser, 1958–1961.

Akt und Sein. Translated by Bernard Noble as *Act and Being* (New York: Harper, 1962).

Sanctorum Communio. Translated as *The Communion of Saints* (New York: Harper & Row, 1963).

WORKS ON BONHOEFFER

DeGruchy, John W. *Bonhoeffer and South Africa: Theology in Dialogue.* Grand Rapids, MI: Wm. B. Eerdmans, 1984.

Feil, Ernst. *The Theology of Dietrich Bonhoeffer.* Translated by Martin Rumscheidt. Philadelphia: Fortress, 1985.

Marsh, Charles. *Reclaiming Dietrich Bonhoeffer: The Promise of His Theology.* New York: Oxford, 1994.

Robinson, John A. T. *Honest to God.* London: SCM Press, 1963.

Martin E. Marty (1967, 2005)

BONNET, CHARLES
(1720–1793)

Charles Bonnet, the Swiss naturalist, "religious cosmologist," and philosopher, was born and died in Geneva. An original if eccentric thinker, Bonnet was widely read and influential. He was early attracted to natural history, and especially to entomology, by René Réaumur's work and by the Abbé Pluche's apologetic, *Spectacle de la nature* (1732). At the age of twenty, he discovered that the aphis can reproduce for several generations without mating, and that animals other than the "polyp" (hydra) can regenerate themselves. He treated these and other matters in his *Traité d'insectologie* (1745). When his eyesight became severely weakened from microscopic work, he turned to botany and philosophy. In *Recherches sur l'usage des feuilles dans les plantes* (1754), he outlined a vitalistic concept of plant behavior in relation to physical environment. In the *Essai de psychologie* (1754) and the *Essai analytique sur les facultés de l'âme* (1760), he followed Étienne Bonnot de Condillac by using the device of the imaginary statue to illustrate the genetic method of explaining the development of the personality. The personality arises from memory, which grows out of sensations. Especially concerned with the body-mind relation, Bonnet accepted David Hartley's theory of association of ideas. He defined freedom as the power of the soul to follow necessary motives; but in granting man a substantial mind, he denied mechanical determinism. He held that the relation between mind and body indicates that the mind must operate in a physical organism, but survives it—an idea that was to be developed in his cosmic speculations.

With the *Considérations sur les corps organisés* (1762) and the popular *Contemplation de la nature* (1764–1765), Bonnet approached the general problems that were crucial in the biology of his time. In the *Considérations* he espoused the preformation theory (which he also needed for his cosmological speculations), using the work of

Albrecht von Haller and Lazzaro Spallanzani. In the *Contemplation,* he developed the traditional idea of the chain of beings, temporalizing it as a process rather than as a static creation. Bonnet's cosmic philosophy received full development in his *Palingénésie philosophique, ou Idées sur l'état passé et sur l'état futur des êtres vivants* (1770), a work that Arthur O. Lovejoy termed "one of the most extraordinary speculative compounds to be found in the history of either science or philosophy." Bonnet looked to biology as a support for his religious beliefs, and used both biology and religion to build a view of cosmic evolution.

Bonnet's theory held, essentially, that the immortal soul ("the ethereal machine") is a "subtle matter" (as distinguished from "gross matter") in the pineal gland. The ethereal machine is the germ of the resurrected body. All possible beings, all individuals, were created at once, according to the principle of plenitude. They exist in germ until released by the death of other individual organisms. The lower souls of animals are perfectible, and the universe is one in which all things tend to perfection. The principal changes occur as the result of catastrophes. Earth has passed through a series of epochs, each terminated by a cataclysm that destroyed all organic life except the immortal germs, allowing the germs to take on different forms, all foreseen in the original creation and all ascending to higher levels. Ontogenesis is a proof of this. Thus, every germ will reappear in a succession of higher embodiments, the soul of each waiting until the proper state of Earth evokes its next and higher incarnation. The entire creation is moving upward; man will become angel, and apes and elephants will take man's place. There is also life on other worlds, more or less advanced in perfection than on Earth.

This theory cannot be called one of organic evolution (as is sometimes erroneously affirmed), since species, according to Bonnet, have no natural history within a single world epoch. Species do not evolve from lower forms in the way modern biology conceives this process; their history is predetermined and fully inscribed in the germ at the moment of the original creation. The germ bears the form of all it will ever be. Nevertheless, Bonnet's universe is self-differentiating arid progressive.

Bonnet considered finalism in organisms an incontrovertible argument against atheism. An optimist, he maintained there is greater good than evil in the universe, and that created things necessarily have a lesser degree of perfection than their creator. Man is superior to animals in his sensual apparatus, brain, and speech organs; but he is part of the general, unfolding order of nature. Man knows a Natural Law that is virtual in him but develops by experience; however, he is moved by self-love and by passions, which may be beneficent or may be destructive and cruel. In considering the inherited organization more determining than education (experience), Bonnet was closer to the "man-machine" school of Julien Offray de La Mettrie than to the sensationist theories of Claude-Adrien Helvétius.

See also Condillac, Étienne Bonnot de; Descartes, René; Fichte, Johann Gottlieb; Hartley, David; Hegel, Georg Wilhelm Friedrich; Helvétius, Claude-Adrien; La Mettrie, Julien Offray de; Lovejoy, Arthur Oncken; Mind-Body Problem; Organismic Biology; Philosophy of Biology; Psychology.

Bibliography

The best work on Bonnet is Max Offner, *Die Psychologie Charles Bonnets* (Leipzig, 1893). See also Georges Bonnet, *Charles Bonnet* (Lac, 1929); Edouard Claparède, *La psychologie animale de Charles Bonnet* (Geneva: Georg, 1909); Jacques Roger, *Les sciences de la vie dans la pensée française du XVIII siècle* (Paris, 1963). For further bibliographical information, see D. C. Cabeen, A *Critical Bibliography of Eighteenth Century French Literature* (Syracuse, NY: Syracuse University Press, 1951), pp. 294–296.

OTHER RECOMMENDED TITLES

Anderson, Lorin. *Charles Bonnet and the Order of the Known.* Boston: Kluwer, 1982.

Anderson, Lorin. "Charles Bonnet's Taxonomy and Chain of Being." *Journal of the History of Ideas* 37 (1976): 45–58.

Kaitaro, Timo. "Ideas in the Brain: The Localization of Memory Traces in the Eighteenth Century." *Journal of the History of Philosophy* 37 (2) (1999): 301–322.

O'Neal, John C. *The Authority of Experience: Sensationist Theory in the French Enlightenment.* University Park: Pennsylvania University Press, 1996.

L. G. Crocker (1967)
Bibliography updated by Tamra Frei (2005)

BOOLE, GEORGE
(1815–1864)

George Boole, an English mathematician and logician, is regarded by many logicians as the founder of mathematical logic. He could be called the Galileo of logic in that he definitively established the mathematical nature of logic—assuming that it was Galileo Galilei who did this for physics, rather than, say, Archimedes. He is considered to be among the five greatest logicians, the others being the Greek philosopher Aristotle, the German mathematician Gottlob Frege, the Austrian mathematician Kurt Gödel, and the Polish mathematician Alfred Tarski.

Like Aristotle, he never had the opportunity to take a course in logic. His parents' economic circumstances precluded the usual formal education. He never took a college course and, thus, never received a bachelor's degree. Nevertheless, he taught many college courses as a professor of mathematics and he received honorary doctoral degrees from such distinguished institutions as Trinity College of Dublin and Oxford University. These are among the many surprises, ironies, and paradoxes surrounding Boole's life and work.

His ambition, energy, originality, and dedication were evident even when he was a boy. By the age of twenty-six he had published the first of many articles in mathematics journals. By twenty-nine, for his 1844 article "On a General Method in Analysis," he had won the Royal Society's gold medal first prize recognizing "the most significant contribution to mathematics" submitted between 1840 and 1844. At thirty-four he was appointed Professor of Mathematics at Queen's University. In 1864, when he died tragically just before the age of fifty, he was one of the most celebrated figures on the British intellectual scene.

In his lifetime he was known almost exclusively for his work in mathematical analysis, a specialty that includes traditional algebra, differential equations, the calculus of finite differences, and, of course, differential and integral calculus. In this field he wrote several articles and two books, both still in print: *Treatise on Differential Equations* (1859) and *Treatise on the Calculus of Finite Differences* (1860). During his lifetime few knew his logic at all, and of them few appreciated it. Today, his work in mathematical analysis is largely unknown; his fame rests entirely on his logic. Boolean algebra, the branch of modern mathematics named in his honor, derives from Boole's logic, not from his other mathematics.

REVOLUTIONARY LOGICIAN WHO NEVER INTENDED TO REVOLUTIONIZE LOGIC

His work in logic still retains a vigor and freshness; it continues to be read and enjoyed by many people including professional mathematicians and logicians. In 2003 Prometheus Books brought out a new reprint edition of his most mature and influential book: *An Investigation of the Laws of Thought on Which Are Founded the Mathematical Theories of Logic and Probabilities*—better known by its shortened title *Laws of Thought*—which was origi-

nally published at his own expense in 1854. The non-mathematical passages in this book are lucid and unusually well written—a testament to Boole's humanistic learning, to his confidence in his own theories, and to his desire to contribute to the advancement of knowledge. Besides the logic, Boole's 1854 book applies logic to probability theory.

Unlike other revolutionary logical innovators, Boole's greatness as a logician was recognized almost immediately. In 1865, hardly a decade after his 1854 *Laws of Thought* and not even a year after his death, his logic was the subject of the Harvard University lecture "Boole's Calculus of Logic" by Charles Sanders Peirce, America's most creative native logician. Peirce opened his lecture with these prophetic words: "Perhaps the most extraordinary view of logic which has ever been developed with success is that of the late Professor Boole. His book … *Laws of Thought* … is destined to mark a great epoch in logic; it contains a conception which in point of fruitfulness will rival that of Aristotle's *Organon*" (Peirce, pp. 223f.).

Even though Boole is thought of today as the initiator of a radical revolution that conclusively and irrevocably overthrew the Aristotelian paradigm then reigning in the domain of logic, he never thought of himself as opposing Aristotle. He admired Aristotle's logic—as far as it went. He never criticized any of the positive features that Aristotle instituted; he accepted as valid every argument that was valid according to Aristotle—including those with "existential import," deducing existential conclusions from universal premises. On the contrary, Boole's goals included revealing the mathematical nature of Aristotle's logic, something that he felt Aristotle had failed to clarify, broadening Aristotle's logic by showing that it could be made to do much more than was envisaged by Aristotle's followers, and deepening it by penetrating beyond Aristotle's analysis to the "ultimate" fine structure of the reasoning process—thereby providing it with what he called a mathematical foundation and showing that it had much more in common with mathematics than had previously been thought and thus justifying it. From Boole's point of view Aristotle's faults were all faults of omission, not of commission. Ironically, Boole's unquestioning acceptance of certain details of Aristotle's system, for example, existential import, may have been one of the things that led to Boole's unfortunate mistaken implementation of his own sound ideas.

BOOLE'S FULLY SYMBOLIC LOGIC

In the process of extending and deepening Aristotle's logic Boole brought many radical ideas into logic. Where Aristotle had represented propositions by a kind of formalized phonetic Greek, Boole represented them by purely ideographic algebraic equations—giving rise to the first successful formalized language in the modern sense. Where Aristotle's propositions were limited to exactly two basic nonlogical elements, one being the "subject" and one the "predicate," Boole's propositions had no limitation of that kind—they could involve any finite number of basic elements, which Boole represented with the letters familiar from algebra: x, y, z, and so on. In fact, by introducing for the first time in history the two logical elements—1 for "everything" or the universe of discourse and 0 for "nothing" or the empty class—he was able to express propositions of pure logic that were devoid of nonlogical elements, another historical first. It was Boole who coined the expression "universe of discourse," which is ubiquitous in modern logic, and it was Boole who first suggested the possibility of reinterpreting a formal language by changing the universe of discourse and the meanings of the nonlogical symbols.

Where for Aristotle the elements were represented by the Greek words having fixed meanings—for *human, animal*, and other substantives, Boole's letters were reinterpretable. Each of Aristotle's formal sentences expressed exactly one proposition whether true or false, but for Boole any single formal sentence was capable of expressing indefinitely many propositions not necessarily all true (as $x(1-x) = 0$) or all false (as $x(1-x) = 1$). Those that expressed only truths he said were "true in virtue of form," perhaps coining this expression also. This innovation was eventually to play a crucial role in modern logic. For example, with the multiplication sign or juxtaposition representing "logical term-conjunction" (the Boolean "and"), with x for *human* and y for *animal*, Boole thought he had expressed Aristotle's "Every human is an animal" by $xy = x$.

SOLVING LOGICAL EQUATIONS, DISCOVERING PROPOSITIONAL LOGIC, TRANSFORMING AN ORGAN INTO AN AXIOMATIC SCIENCE

These innovations opened the way to Boole's most radical, totally unexpected and unprecedented insight: that a fully interpreted equation expressing a proposition, whether true or false, could be considered as an equation with one element regarded as an "unknown" to be solved for in terms of the others. Where Aristotle's focus in for-mal logic had been exclusively with determining logical validity and invalidity of premise-conclusion arguments, that is, with what has been called formal epistemology, Boole's broader focus included, besides a much expanded formal epistemology, several new concerns, two of which were his wholly new theory of logical equation-solving and his formal ontology concerned with axiomatizing logical truths, which he called by the expression "laws of thought." Moreover, Boole explicitly recognized, as Aristotle had not, that "class logic," even in its expanded form, could not treat the arguments now dealt with in truth-functional proposition logic. To meet this deficiency, he proposed an ingenious reinterpretation of his "class logic" that, in his view, transformed it into a propositional logic. In the process he discovered the key ideas now incorporated into laws of modern truth-function logic, establishing himself as the first modern figure in any history of propositional logic.

Before Boole, logic had been thought of as an *organon* or general instrument necessarily presupposed by any axiomatic science, not as an axiomatic science; Boole proposed regarding logic itself as subject to axiomatic treatment. Boole believed that his logic transcended, included, explained, and thus replaced Aristotle's in much the way that Isaac Newton's mechanics transcended, included, explained, and thus replaced Johannes Kepler's.

See also Aristotle; Frege, Gottlob; Galileo Galilei; Gödel, Kurt; Kepler, Johannes; Logic, History of: Modern Logic; Mathematics, Foundations of; Newton, Isaac; Peirce, Charles Sanders; Probability and Chance; Tarski, Alfred.

Bibliography

WORKS BY BOOLE

The Mathematical Analysis of Logic: Being an Essay Towards a Calculus of Deductive Reasoning. Cambridge, U.K.: Macmillan, Barclay, and Macmillan, 1847.

"The Calculus of Logic." *Cambridge and Dublin Mathematical Journal* 3 (1848): 183–198.

Laws of Thought (1854). Introduction by John Corcoran. Amherst, NY: Prometheus Books, 2003.

WORKS ABOUT BOOLE

Boole, Mary Everest. *Collected Works.* Vol. 1, edited by E. M. Cobham. London: C. W. Daniel, 1931. Originally published under the title "The Home Side of a Scientific Mind" in *The University Magazine* in 1878.

Corcoran, John. "Aristotle's *Prior Analytics* and Boole's *Laws of Thought.*" *History and Philosophy of Logic* 24 (2003): 261–288. This is an extensive, but incomplete, point-by-point comparison of Boole's logic with the Aristotelian system it was intended to perfect.

Gasser, James, ed. *A Boole Anthology: Recent and Classical Studies in the Logic of George Boole.* Dordrecht, Netherlands: Kluwer Academic, 2000.

Grattan-Guinness, Ivor, and Gérard Bornet, eds. *George Boole: Selected Manuscripts on Logic and Its Philosophy.* Boston: Birkhäuser Verlag, 1997.

Hailperin, Theodore. *Boole's Logic and Probability: A Critical Exposition from the Standpoint of Contemporary Algebra, Logic, and Probability Theory.* Amsterdam: North-Holland, 1976.

MacHale, Desmond. *George Boole: His Life and Work.* Dublin, Ireland: Boole Press, 1985. This includes a complete bibliography of Boole's publications.

Peirce, Charles. *Writings of Charles S. Peirce.* Vol. I. Bloomington: Indiana University Press, 1982.

Rhees, R., ed. *Studies in Logic and Probability.* London: Watts, 1952.

John Corcoran (2005)

BOSANQUET, BERNARD
(1848–1923)

Bernard Bosanquet, the English philosopher, was born at Altwick and educated at Harrow and at Balliol College, Oxford. He taught ancient history and some philosophy at Oxford from 1871 to 1881, when he left Oxford for London. In London he edited translations of Rudolf Hermann Lotze's *Logic* and *Metaphysics*, played an active part in the London Ethical Society, worked with the Charity Organisation Society, and did some teaching in the adult education movement. In 1895 he married Helen Dendy, who had been employed by the Charity Organisation Society and who later wrote much on social problems and became a member of the important Royal Commission on the Poor Law of 1909. From 1903 to 1908 he held the chair of moral philosophy at St. Andrews. He died in London.

Bosanquet's first important philosophical work is an essay titled "Logic as the Science of Knowledge" in *Essays in Philosophical Criticism* (A. Seth and R. B. Haldane, eds., London, 1883), a collection of papers in memory of T. H. Green. In *Knowledge and Reality* (London, 1885) he criticized F. H. Bradley's *Principles of Logic* for divergences from the central and, as Bosanquet thought, correct course charted in that book. In 1888 Bosanquet's *Logic or the Morphology of Knowledge* (2 vols., London) was published. Bosanquet had earlier translated the introduction to G. W. F. Hegel's *Philosophy of Fine Art* (London, 1886), and his own *History of Aesthetics* appeared in London and New York in 1892. His Gifford lectures were published as *The Principle of Individuality and Value* (London, 1912) and *The Value and Destiny of the Individual* (London, 1913). Bosanquet was a prolific writer who contributed to discussion in all branches of philosophy and also took part in some social controversy. He was two years younger than Bradley and, like him, came to the Idealist point of view partly through the influence of T. H. Green and partly through reading Hegel. Bradley's *Ethical Studies* influenced him, but Bradley, in his turn, learned from Bosanquet's writings, especially from those on logic. Although both were Idealists, and both were called Absolutists, Bosanquet was more Hegelian and less of a skeptic than Bradley.

LOGIC

In the essay "Logic as the Science of Knowledge," which appeared in the same year as Bradley's *Logic* and seems to be independent of it, Bosanquet set out the main lines of his 1888 *Logic*. In this preliminary essay he argued that truth is comprehensible only within systems of knowledge, and that although truth is correspondence with fact, such correspondence is conceivable only within systems because "the facts by which we test conclusions are not simply given from without," and they are not available for judgment until they are "organised into knowledge." He also argued that judgment and inference are not fundamentally distinct, but that judgment is inference not yet made explicit and inference is explicit judgment. A further feature of this striking essay is that in it the forms of judgment are not regarded as fixed and rigid but as "elastic" in their application, so that a form of sentence best suited to express one form of judgment can in fact be used to express many others.

In *Knowledge and Reality* Bosanquet suggested that Bradley had, in spite of his "essential and original conceptions" as to the general nature of judgment and inference and their connection with each other, fallen into some of the errors of "reactionary logic." Bradley said, for example, that categorical judgments state facts, whereas hypothetical judgments (and with them universal ones) do not. By an ingenious choice of examples, Bosanquet shows that such a contrast cannot be sustained and that there is no contrast between being a fact and being a universal. Bosanquet's method is to cite intermediate cases that make impossible the acceptance of sharp distinctions between forms of judgment. He thinks that Bradley was inclined to isolate his examples from their contexts and to lose sight of the subtleties and complexities of language. An instance of this part of Bosanquet's argument is his discussion of Bradley's example "the sea-serpent exists."

Bosanquet points out that it is far from clear what this means in the abstract and that "'exist' is a formal predicate which receives material interpretation from context."

In *Logic or the Morphology of Knowledge* these views are worked out in systematic form. The first volume is concerned with judgment and the second with inference, but the two parts are very closely linked. Bosanquet did not think that, in actual and advancing thought, form and subject matter could be separated. Thus he regarded formal logic not as the standard of thought but as a highly specialized and idealized, and somewhat subsidiary, type of thinking. The forms of judgment and inference with which he concerns himself, therefore, are those that he regards as operative in the actual advancement of knowledge. Judgment is concerned with truth, and mere interjections do not claim to be true; but there are rudimentary judgments of quasi-interjectional type, such as "How ugly!" or "Oh, horrible!" Such impersonal judgments as "It rains" take us still further along the road of developing thought, and demonstratives take us still further. "This" is always so by relation to "that," so that demonstratives lead on to comparison; and as comparison is made more exact, it leads on to proportion and measurement.

At this point, according to Bosanquet, the series diverges, one route being that taken by what he calls "the concrete or categorical series" and the other by what he calls "the abstract or hypothetical series." Along the first route there are singular judgments and those he calls generic judgments, in which a kind is regarded as real, as when we say "Man is mortal" or "Water boils at 212 degrees Fahrenheit." Along the second line of development there are the various types of abstract judgment, such as "Heat is a mode of motion" or "7 + 5 = 12," in which the emphasis is on necessary connection rather than on concreteness. The two series converge again in the hypothetical judgment, and the whole culminates in the disjunctive judgment, which Bosanquet regards as the most adequate form. His reason for this is that it combines the concreteness of the categorical series with the necessity of the hypothetical series. The various disjuncts, in this view, reveal a system in which every member has its distinct place.

Bosanquet illustrates this by such examples as "The triangle is either scalene, isosceles, or equilateral." In the *Essentials of Logic* (London and New York, 1895), he refers to functions within a social order of the sort which, if an individual exercises one of them he does not and cannot exercise any of the others: if a person is king, he is not subject; if he is judge, he is not prosecutor. In his account of inference, Bosanquet also lays great stress on intermediate and transitional forms. Furthermore, just as he minimizes the difference between judgment and inference, so he minimizes the difference between deduction and induction. He holds that knowledge advances neither by generalization from particulars nor by the elimination of hypotheses. Inference, in his view, depends upon the existence of systematic connections, and neither mere counting nor mere discarding can reveal these to us. What is needed is "depth and complexity of insight into a sub-system of the world," and the word "induction" is used when our points of contact with the real world are "isolated perceptions, occurrences or qualities." But the aim of all inquiry is to break down this isolation and to show how the elements of a system must be what they are. Thus, as knowledge advances, the aspect of contingency is less prominent, mere facts or mere observations play a vanishing part, and we come to see that things must be as they are.

METAPHYSICS

For Bosanquet, as for Hegel, there is no sharp division between logic on the one hand and epistemology and metaphysics on the other. Indeed, although logic is concerned with the forms of judgment and inference, the study of these forms leads to the conclusion that reality is systematic. If facts were distinct and isolated, it would be impossible to infer from one to another. Since inferences can be made, facts are not isolated but are "implicated" with one another and "transcend" themselves. The possibility of inference points to the metaphysical fact of "self-transcendence."

Bosanquet's metaphysical system is outlined in his *Principles of Individuality and Value* and given more detailed application in *The Value and Destiny of the Individual*. These titles indicate Bosanquet's concern with individuality and individuals. His view is that individuals are concrete universals. He contrasts (as Bradley had done) abstract universals, such as redness, with concrete universals, such as Julius Caesar. Abstract universality is the repetition of an identical quality in many instances, whereas concrete universality is the realization of the same individual in its various interrelated acts or manifestations. The many red things are extremely diverse, whereas the actions of an individual are more or less systematically connected with one another. According to Bosanquet, "there can be only one individual, and that, *the* individual, the Absolute." When people are called individuals, it is in a "secondary sense," insofar as they are regarded as relatively independent, stable, and unique.

But this uniqueness is not some internal, private, inaccessible feature of them. The "inwardness" of persons is not something private, not "the banishment of all that seems outward, but the solution of the outward in the circulation of the total life."

McTaggart complained that everything Bosanquet says about mind and body "might have been written by a complete materialist," and Bosanquet himself in *Knowledge and Reality* had written that "a consistent materialist and a thorough idealist hold positions that are distinguishable only in name." Bosanquet rejects both psychophysical interactionism and the view that mind is an effect of matter. He holds that mind is a perfection of the organism and that an organism possesses more or less of it as the organism selects from, and adapts itself to, the circumstances of its world. He rejects the possibility of a mind independent of matter, and draws ethical conclusions from this. Without things, he says, there would be no problems for men. If there were nothing but disembodied persons, there would be nothing to do.

In bringing these general principles to bear upon aspects of experience, Bosanquet comes to some surprising conclusions. His view of individuals as concrete universals might have been expected to lead to a respect for historical knowledge, as it has done with other Idealists. But, according to Bosanquet, history is "a hybrid form of experience," "the doubtful story of successive events." His view is that the spatiotemporal contingencies of human life must, as knowledge grows, become absorbed into a fuller understanding of society, art, philosophy, and religion. These, he says, are "concrete and necessary living worlds." Bosanquet also rejects the view, advocated by Thomas Carlyle, James Anthony Froude, and Bradley, that human conduct and discovery cannot be predicted. He argues that this thesis depends upon the false assumption that individuals cannot overlap, and he holds that such facts as "anticipatory" inventions that have to be "reinvented" are evidence to the contrary. Thus, in *The Value and Destiny of the Individual* he concluded that "intelligences must overlap" and stigmatized as "the pathos and bathos of sentimentalism" the view that selves are essentially withdrawn and alone.

SOCIAL PHILOSOPHY

From what has already been said about Bosanquet's metaphysics, it follows that societies are individuals to a fuller degree than individuals can be. In the *Philosophical Theory of the State*, he treats the relation between the individual and the state as that of microcosm to macrocosm. The individual world and the social world are held to be correlated with one another in such a way that for every element in the one there is some corresponding element in the other. Like Aristotle and Jean-Jacques Rousseau, he emphasizes the civilizing influence of the state on the individual. He rejects the commonsense, pluralistic metaphysics that he thinks misdirects the social philosophy of Jeremy Bentham and John Stuart Mill. "All individuals," he writes, "are continually reinforced and carried on, beyond their average immediate consciousness, by the knowledge, resources, and energy which surround them in the social order." "The common self or moral person of society," he holds, "is more real than the apparent individual."

Hence, like Rousseau, he regards coercion by the state as coercion exercised by the social aspect of the individual upon the recalcitrant and less real aspects of his being. According to classical liberalism, the individual is free when he is left alone to do what he wants. According to Bosanquet, this is a metaphysical as well as a practical impossibility, so he develops the conception of freedom as self-mastery. But since selves are not exclusive atoms, self-mastery, social control, and freedom are held to coincide. Bosanquet accepts T. H. Green's view that action under compulsion has less value than action freely willed, thus recognizing that state enforcement can lead to mere external conformity. But just as he regarded nature as the necessary complement of mind, so he regarded force, habit, and tradition as the necessary complements of creative choice. Thus, although punishment acts on the "lower self" by means of threats, it can also stimulate the "higher self" by producing a shock that forces attention to legitimate social demands. Still, the function of the state is forcibly to "hinder hindrances to the best life or common good," and the very notion of promoting morality by force is "an absolute self-contradiction."

Thus, although Bosanquet minimizes and even denies the reality of individual men, he does not advocate totalitarian or even socialistic measures. Indeed, just as Bastiat, the publicist of laissez-faire, considered that society as a whole was moved by an impersonal reason, so Bosanquet believed that intelligence is manifested in society to a greater degree than it ever could be in any particular person. He has been criticized for failing to distinguish between society and the state and for suggesting that the state can do no wrong. There is justice in the former criticism, even though we may agree that force is inevitable if developed societies are to continue in existence. As to the second, Bosanquet's main philosophical point was that theft, murder, and such are concepts that apply to people within a society, and that war, conquest, confiscation, and such are concepts of a different type, applying to beings of a different type.

Bosanquet's account of what makes them different types is very complex. He points out that many crimes committed on behalf of the state result from the desire of some individual agent of the state to take a short cut or to save trouble and hence are not imputable to it. Furthermore, the state cannot commit wrongs of the sort that are the consequences of individual selfishness or sensuality. On the other hand, a state that ordered the killing of a hostile statesman would rightly be criticized, not on the ground of murder but "by the degree of its failure to cope with the duties of a state." Bosanquet seems to mean that when a state is rightly criticized, it is compared with more adequate specimens of its own type but is not blamed or punished as are individuals who break the law. Bosanquet holds that states are morally responsible beings, but that they cannot do wrong in the way that individual persons can and do. States fall short rather than do wrong. Furthermore, he repudiates the idea that individuals are guilty of murder when a state wages war or of theft when it annexes or confiscates; any moral criticism, he holds, should be directed against the morally responsible agent, the state itself, and such criticism must relate to the general level of life it sustains and promotes. At the end of World War I Bosanquet opposed such popular appeals as "Hang the Kaiser" and "Punish the Germans," and although he said that the League of Nations was "the hope and refuge of mankind," he believed that individual members should no more submit themselves unreservedly to this organization than individual men should submit themselves unreservedly to their own governments.

See also Aristotle; Bentham, Jeremy; Bradley, Francis Herbert; Carlyle, Thomas; Green, Thomas Hill; Hegel, Georg Wilhelm Friedrich; Idealism; Knowledge and Belief; Logic, History of; Lotze, Rudolf Hermann; Macrocosm and Microcosm; McTaggart, John McTaggart Ellis; Mill, John Stuart; Punishment; Rousseau, Jean-Jacques; Society; State.

Bibliography

On Bosanquet's life, see Helen Bosanquet, *Bernard Bosanquet* (London: Macmillan, 1924) and J. H. Muirhead, ed., *Bernard Bosanquet and His Friends: Letters Illustrating the Sources and Development of His Philosophical Opinions* (London: Allen and Unwin, 1935).

Apart from the works mentioned in the text, Bosanquet's books include: *A Companion to Plato's Republic* (New York: Macmillan, 1895); *The Psychology of the Moral Self* (London and New York: Macmillan, 1897); *Three Lectures on Aesthetics* (London: Macmillan, 1915); *Some Suggestions in Ethics* (London: Macmillan, 1918); *Implication and Linear Inference* (London: Macmillan, 1920); *What Religion Is* (London: Macmillan, 1920); *The Meeting of Extremes in Contemporary Philosophy* (London, 1921); and other shorter works.

There are also the following collections of essays and lectures: *Essays and Addresses* (London, 1889); *The Civilisation of Christendom* (London S. Sonnenschein, 1893); *Social and International Ideals* (London: Macmillan, 1917); *Science and Philosophy and Other Essays* (London: Allen and Unwin, 1927).

For discussions of Bosanquet's views, see: J. M. E. McTaggart's critical notice of *The Principle of Individuality and Value* in *Mind*, n.s., 21 (1912): 416–427; H. B. Acton, "The Theory of Concrete Universals," in *Mind*, n.s., 45 (1936): 417–431 and n.s., 46 (1937): 1–13; and F. Houang, *Le Néo-Hégélianisme en Angleterre: la philosophie de Bernard Bosanquet* (Paris, 1954).

On Bosanquet's social philosophy, see: L. T. Hobhouse, *The Metaphysical Theory of the State* (London: Allen and Unwin, 1918) and A. J. M. Milne, *The Social Philosophy of English Idealism* (London: Allen and Unwin, 1962), Ch. VII.

OTHER RECOMMENDED WORKS

Bosanquet, Bernard, ed. *Aspects of the Social Problem*. New York: Kraus Reprint, 1968.

Bosanquet, Bernard. *Croce's Aesthetic* (1919). Folcroft, PA: Folcroft Library Editions, 1974.

Bosanquet, Bernard. *The Distinction between Mind and Its Objects* (1913). Bristol: Thoemmes, 1990.

Bosanquet, Bernard, tr. *The Education of the Young in The Republic of Plato* (1917). Folcroft, PA: Folcroft Library Editions, 1973.

Bosanquet, Bernard. *Three Chapters on the Nature of Mind* (1923). Edited by Helen Dendy Bosanquet. New York, Kraus Reprint, 1968, 1923.

H. B. Acton (1967)
Bibliography updated by Michael J. Farmer (2005)

BOSCOVICH, ROGER JOSEPH
(1711–1787)

Roger Joseph Boscovich (or Rudjer Josip Bošković) was a Jesuit scientist whose originality and advanced views have only recently been appreciated. A natural philosopher, mathematician, physicist, astronomer, geodesist, engineer, and poet, Boscovich was, in the words of the physicist John Henry Poynting, "amongst the boldest minds humanity has produced." Boscovich published about one hundred books and papers, most of them in Latin. These works display an unusual combination of enthusiasm and logic as well as a passionate conviction that simple fundamental assumptions and precise reasoning can lead to the understanding of natural phenomena. The French astronomer Joseph Jérôme Le Français de Lalande said that in each of these works there are ideas worthy of a man of genius.

Boscovich was born at Ragusa (now Dubrovnik, Croatia) of Serb and Italian parentage. He entered the novitiate of the Society of Jesus in Rome in 1725 and the Collegium Romanum in 1727. At the Collegium stress was laid on clear logical thought and on the development of a way of thinking that combined religious convictions with the results of science. Boscovich devoted himself chiefly to mathematics and physics and published his first scientific paper in 1736. He became professor of mathematics at the Collegium in 1740, and in 1744 he took his vows as a priest. Since his gifts were scientific, Boscovich was left free to apply himself to teaching, research, and tasks designated by the religious authorities. In 1734 Pope Benedict XIV appointed him, with others, as a technical adviser concerned with cracks in the dome of St. Peter's, and in 1750 commissioned him with Christopher Maire, an English Jesuit, to measure an arc of the meridian through Rome. Later, Boscovich was designated to arbitrate a dispute between the Republic of Lucca and Austrian Tuscany over the drainage of a lake. This task took him to Vienna, where he already enjoyed a high reputation as a scholar and a diplomat. From 1759 on, Boscovich was engaged in extensive travels as far away as Constantinople. In 1760 he met Benjamin Franklin and many other leading personalities in London and Cambridge, and he was elected a fellow of the Royal Society in 1761. He became professor of mathematics at Pavia in 1765, but his health was failing and he grew restless. A chair was created for him at Milan in 1769, and he pursued studies at the Brera observatory. In 1775 Boscovich was appointed director of naval optics for the French navy and went to Paris, where he was made a subject of France by Louis XV. He returned to Italy in 1783. During his last years he suffered from melancholia.

Despite these activities Boscovich continued to publish. Each of his numerous works in pure and applied mathematics presented either a new method for or a survey of some branch of mathematical inquiry. Among the topics he discussed were spherical trigonometry, the cycloid, conic sections, infinitely great and infinitely small quantities, the accuracy of astronomical observations, the telescope, sunspots, eclipses, the determination of the sun's rotation and of the orbits of planets and comets, the aurora borealis, the transit of Mercury, the shape of Earth, the variation of gravity, the center of gravity, and optical problems. His last major publication was a five-

volume work on optics and astronomy, *Opera Pertinentia ad Opticam et Astronomiam,* published at Venice in 1785.

Boscovich's masterpiece, and his work of greatest interest to philosophers, is *Philosophiae Naturalis Theoria Redacta ad Unicam Legem Virium in Natura Existentium* (A theory of natural philosophy reduced to a single law of the actions existing in nature), published in Vienna in 1758 and, in an improved edition, at Venice in 1763. In this work Boscovich presented an atomic theory on which he had been working for fifteen years. The importance of this theory was widely recognized, especially in Britain, where the *Encyclopaedia Britannica* devoted fourteen pages to it in 1801. Boscovich had been the first supporter in Italy of Isaac Newton's theory of gravitation, and the *Theoria* was looked upon in Britain as an interesting speculative extension of the Newtonian system.

Boscovich's atomic theory arose, as he himself stated, from an attempt to build a comprehensive physics based on the ideas of Newton and Gottfried Wilhelm Leibniz but going beyond both to obtain new results. Boscovich developed the idea that all phenomena arise from the spatial patterns of identical point particles (*puncta*) interacting in pairs according to an oscillatory law that determines their relative acceleration. This view of matter is akin to that of recent physics in that it is relational, structural, and kinematic. It contains three original features:

(1) Material permanence without spatial extension: Quasi-material point-centers of action are substituted for the rigid finite units of matter of earlier atomists.

(2) Spatial relations without absolute space: Internal spatial coordinates (the distances between the two members of pairs of *puncta*) are used instead of external coordinates.

(3) Kinematic action without Newtonian forces: In modern dimensional terms, Boscovich's theory is kinematic rather than dynamical. It uses only two-dimensional quantities (length and time) rather than the three (mass, length, and time) used by Newton. Since all particles are identical, the number of particles in a system, which is an integral pure number obtained by counting, is employed in place of Newtonian mass.

Although all of these features are of interest, the first is most important, for by it Boscovich helped emancipate physics from naive atomism's uncritical assumption that the ultimate units of matter are small, individual, rigid pieces possessing shape, size, weight, and other properties. The alternative point atomism assumes that the ultimate units are persistent quasi-material points, all identical, which form stable patterns or interact to produce changes of pattern and relative motion. Between 1710 and 1760 such other thinkers as Giambattista Vico, Leibniz (whose theory of monads and relational conception of space influenced Boscovich), Emanuel Swedenborg, John Michell, and Immanuel Kant had produced atomic theories based on points, but Boscovich was the first scientist to develop a general physical theory using point particles.

Boscovich preferred the concept of *puncta* to that of rigid pieces of matter because they were simpler and, since they avoided the awkward discontinuity at the surface of a piece of matter, were better adapted to mathematical treatment. His law of oscillatory change from attraction to repulsion enabled him to posit points of stable equilibrium at finite distances and thus to account for the finite extension of gross matter, as Kant did also. The complexity of the world, according to Boscovich, arises from two factors: the varied arrangement of different numbers of particles, and the parameters determining the law of oscillation.

To a modern reader, the impressive feature of the *Theoria* is Boscovich's interpretation of the universe as a three-dimensional structure of patterns in equilibrium or change determined by points and their mutual distances. There is no distinction between occupied and empty space, for space is only the relation between *puncta*. Space, time, and motion are all relative; the *puncta* form a vast variety of stable patterns; the laws of the universe are simple, but their consequences are complex; the laws contain several natural units of length, as do the laws of modern physics since the introduction of Planck's constant; there is a pervasive continuity in nature permitting inference from the macroworld to the microworld; geometry is in part a creation of the human mind and can to some extent be chosen at will; the ability of atomism to account for the forms and processes of the natural universe is unlimited, and even organic forms are easy to understand, because complex patterns of particles will adhere to one another in figures of certain shapes.

As a speculative vision of a universe of changing structure supported by an appropriate philosophy of physics, Boscovich's system is brilliant, but as a scientific theory it is incorrect because it does not allow for the highly complex properties of the wave-particles of present-day physics. No data concerning the atomic world were available to provide a quantitative basis for Boscovich's theory, and he was able to give only a qualitative description of simple mechanical and physical properties. The physical world is more complex than the world Boscovich created from his imagination. Nevertheless, his philosophy of physics was in some respects near the truth, for he predicted—a century and a half before the facts were known—that matter is penetrable by high-speed particles and that relative motion affects the measurement of space and time. Moreover, these predictions were necessary consequences of his mathematical conception of three-dimensional structure. Boscovich's standard of simplicity remains a challenge to physics, and only a future, fully unified, particle theory will be able to show precisely where his assumptions were mistaken. Boscovich postulated that there is only one fundamental particle; we do not yet know how many must be assumed. Modern conceptions of molecular structure have much in common with Boscovich's ideas, but since the development of the physical concept of a field, it can be seen that the Boscovichian particle is inadequate even to account for electromagnetic processes.

It is not certain how far the *Theoria* influenced the development of atomic theory. It was widely studied, and Michael Faraday, Sir William Hamilton, James Clerk Maxwell, and Lord Kelvin (to mention only English scientists) stressed the theoretical advantages of the Boscovichian atom over rigid atoms. In any case, Boscovich's work marked an important stage in the history of our ideas about the universe, and his system will remain the paradigm of the theory of point particles.

See also Faraday, Michael; Franklin, Benjamin; Hamilton, William; Kant, Immanuel; Laws, Scientific; Leibniz, Gottfried Wilhelm; Maxwell, James Clerk; Newton, Isaac; Philosophy of Physics; Swedenborg, Emanuel; Vico, Giambattista.

Bibliography

The second edition of the *Theoria* was republished in a Latin-English edition, with the English translation by J. M. Child, as *Theory of Natural Philosophy* (Chicago and London: Open Court, 1922).

For literature on Boscovich, see L. L. Whyte, ed., *Roger Joseph Boscovich, S.J., F.R.S., 1711–1787: Studies of His Life and Work on the 250th Anniversary of His Birth* (London: Allen and Unwin, 1961; New York: Fordham University Press, 1961), which contains a biographical essay by Hill and eight papers on aspects of Boscovich's work by English, American, and Yugoslav scholars. Its extensive bibliography of works by and about Boscovich does not, however, cover Yugoslav studies. See also H. V. Gill, *Roger Joseph Boscovich, S.J., 1711–1787: Forerunner of Modern Physical Theories* (Dublin, 1941), and L. Pearce Williams, *Michael Faraday* (New York: Basic, 1965).

Lancelot Law Whyte (1967)

BOSSUET, JACQUES BÉNIGNE

(1627–1704)

Jacques Bénigne Bossuet was born in Dijon, the son of a lawyer. At the age of thirteen he was a boy canon of Metz. After a period in Paris, where he became known in the salons and distinguished himself as a theologian, he was ordained priest in 1652 (having been prepared by Vincent de Paul) and began his ministry at Metz. Friends in high places secured his recall to Paris in 1659, and he soon established a reputation as preacher and spiritual director. Contemporaries agree that he had the ability, and presumably the desire, to please everyone; and his early reputation for moderation may reflect tactics more than convictions. Winning favor at Court, he was rewarded in 1669 with the see of Condom and was appointed tutor to the dauphin, Louis XIV's son, in 1670. He is most famous for the series of funeral orations he delivered as Court preacher (1666–1687), of which the last and finest commemorates the great Condé. Besides these set (and published) pieces, he preached numerous sermons for all occasions, often using the feast of a particular saint for an exposition of his own views on a contemporary question, such as the relations between church and state, lucidly discussed in the panegyric of St. Thomas of Canterbury (Becket). Some 200 sermons survive, mostly as notes on which he usually improvised, and it is easier to establish his main ideas than to reconstruct his mastery of the spoken word.

On completion of the tutorial task, he was transferred in 1681 to Meaux, conveniently near Paris, where he remained until his death. His influence at Court gave him more effective power than his hierarchical superiors, and in 1682 he composed and presented the Gallican Articles as spokesman for the whole French church. His last years were marred by quarrels, especially with his former protégé François Fénelon, whose condemnation for quietism he secured only by resorting to methods so ignoble that formal victory was bought at the cost of moral defeat. Despised at Court and broken in health, he ended his life among relatives of notoriously unedifying character.

All Bossuet's thinking was deeply influenced by St. Augustine and characterized by a peculiar emphasis on authority. In his eyes, obedience and discipline are the highest virtues. The supreme authority of the church and the divine right of kings are inseparable and constantly recurrent themes in his work. In the *Politique tirée de l'e-criture sainte* (Politics Drawn from Scripture), written for

the dauphin, he is heavily in favor of the absolute monarch, chosen by God and responsible to him alone (distinguished, however, from the arbitrary monarch, a tyrant who merely gratifies his own whims). The *Traité de la connaissance de Dieu et de soi-même* (Treatise concerning the Knowledge of God and Oneself) combines Thomist and other standard teaching with a marked sympathy for the reassuringly authoritarian side of Cartesianism, with its insistence on order and certainty, although Bossuet elsewhere denounced the dangers of encouraging individual reason and inquiry. The unfinished *Discours sur l'histoire universelle* (Discourse on Universal History) was intended to teach the dauphin not so much what had happened as why. Though later editions made some concessions to currently changing views on the chronology of ancient times, history was primarily interpreted as showing the ways of God to man, especially as revealed in the Bible. In tracing the fortunes of empires down to Charlemagne (and to Louis XIV, if he had completed his plan), Bossuet emphasized moral and religious development, regarding freedom as a prime cause of decadence.

Similarly, the *Histoire des variations des églises protestantes* (History of the Variations of the Protestant Churches) attributes to Protestant reliance on individual liberty of conscience a disunity amounting to near anarchy. Bossuet naturally regarded heresy and sedition as twinned evils; and in his orations on Henrietta Maria and Henrietta Anne (widow and daughter of Charles I), he adduces the recent revolution in England to prove his contention that social equality is an impious chimera. He was curiously ambivalent in his relations with Protestants, converting many individuals (including the vicomte de Turenne) and courteously corresponding with Gottfried Wilhelm Leibniz in an attempt to effect a reconciliation, while greeting the revocation of the Edict of Nantes, followed as it was by brutal persecution, with an embarrassingly effusive eulogy of Louis's piety.

Bossuet earns his place in history above all as a public figure, "the eagle of Meaux." In the *grand siècle* Bossuet was the church, just as Louis was the state.

See also Augustine, St.; Authority.

Bibliography

WORKS BY BOSSUET

Oeuvres complètes. 31 vols, edited by F. Lachat. Paris, 1862–1866.

Discourse on Universal History, edited by Orest Ranum; translated by Elborg Forster. Chicago: University of Chicago Press, 1976.

Politics Drawn from the Very Words of Holy Scripture, edited by Patrick Riley. New York: Cambridge University Press, 1990.

WORKS ON BOSSUET

Adam, A. *Histoire de la littérature française au XVIIe siècle*. Paris, 1956, Vol. V, Ch. 4.

Calvet, J. *Bossuet, l'homme et l'oeuvre*. Paris: Boivin, 1941.

Hazard, P. *La crise de la conscience européenne*. 2nd ed. Paris: Fayard, 1961. Translated by J. L. May as *The European Mind*. London: Hollis and Carter, 1953.

Kearns, Edward J. *Ideas in Seventeenth Century France*. New York: St. Martin's Press, 1979.

Lebarcq, J. *Histoire critique de la prédication de Bossuet*. Lille, 1888.

Rebelliau, A. *Bossuet*. Paris, 1900.

A. J. Krailsheimer (1967)
Bibliography updated by Tamra Frei (2005)

BOSTRÖM, CHRISTOPHER JACOB
(1797–1866)

Christopher Jacob Boström, an Swedish Idealist philosopher, studied and also taught at Uppsala University, where he was assistant professor of "practical philosophy" (the philosophy of morals, law, and religion) from 1828 to 1833. After an interlude as tutor to the royal princes in Stockholm from 1833 to 1837, he resumed his academic teaching, and from 1842 to 1863 he held the chair in practical philosophy. His "rational idealism" is a spiritualistic metaphysics, combining traits from Plato's theory of ideas, Gottfried Wilhelm Leibniz's monadology, and George Berkeley's immaterialism. With arguments, some of which are reminiscent of Berkeley's, he tried to show that nothing but minds and their perceptions exist.

Two of his more original, though hardly very convincing, arguments were these: (1) Truth means agreement between the perception and the perceived object. Perfect truth, therefore, is perfect agreement; and perfect agreement is the same as identity. Hence, the object of any perfectly true perception is identical with that perception; in other words, any object, when perceived with perfect truth, is itself a perception. (2) "Outside" has a meaning only when it refers to space. Since a mind is not in space, nothing can be outside a mind. Hence, everything exists inside a mind.

Particular minds and particular perceptions are forms of "self-consciousness," which can be likened to "a substance or stuff of which everything ultimately consists." With this spiritualistic position Boström combined the Leibnizian-Kantian distinction between a thing as it is in itself (essence) and a thing as it appears to us (phenomenon). The spatiotemporal world of experience is merely phenomenal. Or, more correctly, the spatiotemporal world of a person's experience is merely the way in which the things-in-themselves appear to that person because of the imperfection of his particular perceptive faculty. The things-in-themselves, which underlie the appearances, are purely rational minds whose existence is nonspatial and nontemporal. Boström usually called them "ideas," the word being borrowed from Plato rather than from British empiricism. These ideas form a series that, according to him, is similar to the series of natural numbers—except that it contains a maximal idea, God. In this series each idea contains and perceives all the preceding, but none of the succeeding, ones. On this point, however, he was apparently not quite consistent. Simultaneously he asserted that every idea perceives the entire system of ideas but with varying perfection and clarity. God alone has a perfect perception of the whole system. Because every idea that is not God perceives the system imperfectly, the system presents a phenomenal appearance to that idea.

Boström's system contains several other apparent inconsistencies. Although each mind is a purely rational, nonspatial, and nontemporal idea, Boström also taught that each mind other than God has a double existence. Besides existing as a rational idea, it also exists as a temporal mind with a mixed rational and sensual nature. Each mind even has a whole (temporal?) sequence of such mixed and temporal manifestations. (Boström himself points to the analogy between this doctrine and the Hindu belief in reincarnation.) He was thinking primarily of human beings in this context, but the doctrine of double existence is also supposed to apply to such "moral personalities" as the state, the "people," and each one of the four estates.

Boström was aware of the nonintellectual motives that attracted him to this view of the world and once asserted that no philosopher would ever embrace a system that was repugnant to his feelings. Simultaneously, however, he made excessive claims concerning the provability of his own doctrine, to which he attributed the same kind of certainty that has traditionally been ascribed to mathematics.

From the vantage point of his rather fantastic metaphysics, Boström took an active part in public debate in Sweden. In religious questions he was, on the whole, a liberal, vigorously attacking many of the dogmas of Lutheran orthodoxy, especially the dogma of eternal damnation. On political questions, on the other hand, he took an ultraconservative stand. He was one of the staunchest opponents of the parliamentary reform that took place in 1866, soon after his death, and that replaced the four estates by a two-chamber system. His metaphysics might seem to indicate a mystical strain, but his very systematic, precise, and dry mode of writing does not corroborate this impression. The dominant traits in his philosophic temperament would seem to be a strong, puritanical, moral pathos, an unorthodox but firm religious belief, a love of neat systematics, and a rather naive private dogmatism. Boström's philosophy represents the culmination of the idealistic tradition that dominated Swedish philosophy through the entire nineteenth century. In the 1860s, 1870s, and 1880s, Boströmianism and Hegelianism reigned supreme in Swedish academic philosophy. At the turn of the twentieth century a strong neo-Kantian current set in.

See also Berkeley, George; Hegelianism; Idealism; Leibniz, Gottfried Wilhelm; Plato.

Bibliography

WORKS BY BOSTRÖM

Skrifter av Christopher Jacob Boström. Edited by H. Edfeldte and J. G. Keijser. Vols. I and II, Uppsala, Sweden: V. Roos, 1883; Vol. III, Norrköping, Sweden, 1901. Collected works.

C. J. Boströms Förelasningar i Religionsfilosofi. Edited by S. Ribbing. Stockholm, 1885. Lectures on philosophy of religion.

Prof. C. J. Boströms Förelasningar i Etiken. Edited by S. Ribbing. Uppsala, Sweden, 1897. Lectures in ethics.

C. J. Boströms Förelasningar i Religionsfilosofi II. Edited by G. J. Keijser. Vol. I, Stockholm, 1906; Vol. II, Stockholm, 1910; Vol. III, Stockholm, 1913. Second series of lectures in the philosophy of religion.

Prof. C. J. Boströms Förelasningar i Etik Vårterminen 1861. Edited by G. Klingberg. Uppsala, Sweden: Akademiska bokhandeln, 1916. Boström's lectures in ethics of the spring term of 1861.

Translations

Grundlinien eines philosophischen Systems. Translated by R. Geijer and H. Gerloff. Leipzig, 1923. German translation of various writings.

Philosophy of Religion. Translated by Victor E. and Robert N. Beck. New Haven, CT: Yale University Press, 1962.

WORKS ON BOSTRÖM

Larsson, H. *Minnesteckning över C. J. Boström.* Stockholm, 1931. Memorial oration.

Morin, Harald. *Om Dualismen i Boströms Definitiva Filosofi.* Uppsala, Sweden: Almqvist and Wiksells, 1940. On the dualism in Boström's definitive philosophy.

Nyblaeus, A. *Den Filosofiska Forskningen i Sverige,* 4 vols. Lund, Sweden, 1873–1897.

Rodhe, S. E. *Boströms Religionsfilosofiska Åskådning.* Göteborg, Sweden: Elanders, 1950. Boström's views in the philosophy of religion.

Wedburg, A. *Den Logiska Strukturen hos Boströms Filosofi.* Uppsala, Sweden, 1937. Logical structure of Boström's philosophy.

GENERAL BACKGROUND

Ueberweg, F., and M. Heinze. *Grundriss der Geschichte der Philosophie,* 12th ed. Berlin, 1928. Vol. 5. Excellent survey of Swedish philosophy up to the beginning of the twentieth century.

A. Wedburg (1967)

BOULAINVILLIERS, HENRI, COMTE DE
(1658–1722)

The historian, philosopher, astrologer, and savant Henri, Comte de Boulainvilliers, or Henry, Comte de Boulainviller, as he preferred to spell his name, was born at Saint-Saire, Normandy. From 1669 to 1674 he was educated at the Oratorian school at the College of Juilly, where Richard Simon taught rhetoric and philosophy. Boulainvilliers took up military service, as befitted a member of an old aristocratic family, proud of his lineage. After leaving the army, he developed an interest in history, first studying his own family tree and then the social and political institutions of the Middle Ages. He approved of feudalism, which he envisaged as a kind of federal republic governed by distant and independent aristocratic families, whom he considered to be the inheritors of the Franks who had conquered the Gauls. He deplored the increase in the power of the central authority—the king—and in the liberties of the people as encroachments on the rights of the nobles. He favored a patriarchal society. Many of his reforms, submitted to the regent, recommended the fostering of trade, proportional taxation, the suppression of tax collectors, and the calling of the États Généraux. The count had access to Court circles; he was connected with d'Argenson, president of the council of finance, to whom it is thought he passed on a number of clandestine philosophical tracts. He also frequented the home of the maréchal, duc de Noailles, where he met César Dumarsais, a disciple of Bernard Le Bovier de Fontenelle, future author of articles for the *Encyclopédie* and probable author of *La religion chrétienne analysée* and *Examen de la religion*; Nicolas Fréret, a devotee of Pierre Bayle; and Jean-Baptiste de Mirabaud, the *secrétaire perpétuel* of the *Académie Française*.

For a time Boulainvilliers was the center of much intellectual activity, and in the history of free thought his coterie antedates by fifty years the better-known *côterie holbachique*. Voltaire in his *Dîner du comte de Boulainvilliers* (1767) has given us an insight into this milieu, which certainly disseminated a surprisingly large number of clandestine manuscripts and seems to have provided the only organized center for the compiling, copying, and distribution of philosophical tracts. Boulainvilliers is best known as the probable author of parts of the *Essai de métaphysique*, which was published in 1731 under the title *Réfutation des erreurs de Benoît de Spinoza*. He became interested in Benedict de Spinoza through reading the *Tractatus Theologico-Politicus*, which he annotated copiously, and also the *Ethics*, which he read in 1704. The first part, or *Vie de Spinoza*, of the *Essai de métaphysique* has been attributed to J. M. Lucas. The second part, or *Esprit de Spinoza*, has been attributed by I. O. Wade and others to Boulainvilliers. Both parts are commonly coupled together in the manuscripts and in the editions under the title *La vie et l'esprit de Spinoza*. Boulainvilliers correctly presents Spinoza's doctrine that God and the universality of things are one and the same, then proceeds to argue that Spinoza's "attributes" are in fact "modes"; that is, "modes" of something he terms existence.

In this work, he has evolved an original philosophy. Starting from the Cartesian principle that he knows himself to be a thinking being, he infers that other beings exist, some endowed with thought, others only with feeling, and others without feeling or thought. All beings, whether living or nonliving, thinking, feeling, or merely extended, have one property in common: existence. From such premises, he proceeds to a universal Idea or Being more all-embracing than matter. He stresses the degrees of being, and claims that sensations are the source of all experience. He concludes by asserting that at death the body returns to universal matter while the soul remains as an idea in the infinite mind and is, therefore, capable of being restored to the body. It is clear that Boulainvilliers's exposition of Spinoza is curiously based on the Cartesian assertions and incorporates ideas borrowed from John Locke.

He strove to harmonize the notion of a single substance with a sensationalist psychology and a naturalistic ethics. He believed in a "chain of being," in the capacity of animals to think, and in evidence (as opposed to judgment) as the only criterion of truth; he also helped to discredit Christian revelation. In an *Abrégé d'histoire ancienne* he expressed his belief in the primacy of natural laws, denying the possibility of miracles. These points were later taken up by Denis Diderot in the article "Certitude" of the *Encyclopédie*.

DE TRIBUS IMPOSTORIBUS

Figuring as part of the *Essai de métaphysique*, sometimes titled *L'esprit de Spinoza*, is to be found a treatise commonly known as the *Traité des trois imposteurs*, under which title it was published in 1719 (2nd ed., 1721; numerous others throughout the century). Since printed copies were commonly impounded and consequently hard to find, manuscript copies continued to circulate both before and after publication. Polemic and concise, it provided freethinkers with valuable ammunition. Its aggressive title helped to ensure its success and may have been chosen by the Dutch printers as the last and profitable stage of an elaborate hoax. It is an allusion to a lost treatise, *De Tribus Impostoribus* (1230), supposedly written by Frederick II for the edification of his friend Othon. Interest in this Latin work, evidenced in *Theophrastus Redivivus* (1659), had been revived at the close of the seventeenth century and the beginning of the eighteenth.

The author of the *Traité des trois imposteurs*, believed by Voltaire to be Boulainvilliers, launched a virulent attack on the prophets and apostles; he expressed his disbelief in heaven or hell, rewards or punishments, his faith in natural law as enshrined in the hearts of men, and in the soul as the expression of the principle of life. The system of religion is, according to him, the work of false legislators, among whom are Moses, Christ, and Muḥammad. Moses was nothing more than a magician and a charlatan; Christ, who may be likened to Genghis Khan, was a casuist in his discussions with the Philistines and in claiming to be the son of a god; his religion owes much to Greek mythology and his ethics compare unfavorably with those of Epictetus and Epicurus. Muḥammad differs from the other two impostors in having recourse to violence in the establishment of his kingdom. Voltaire, among others, seized on these points to bolster his polemics against the church. He, too, saw the advantage of an oblique attack on the church by an onslaught against Islamic fanaticism, coupled with the claim that all religions are equal. The treatise marks an early, if crude, attempt to consider religion from the comparative standpoint.

Boulainvilliers is best remembered as a confirmed "spinoziste," and his views on the subject of nature and matter, the relationship of matter and thought, and the origin and nature of government won him a place as a forerunner of the philosophes.

See also Clandestine Philosophical Literature in France; Spinozism.

Bibliography

WORKS BY BOULAINVILLIERS

État de la France, etc., avec des mémoires historiques sur l'ancien gouvernement de cette monarchie jusqu' à Hugues Capet .... 3 vols. London: T. Wood and S. Palmer; W. Roberts, 1727.

Histoire de l'ancien gouvernement de la France, avec 14 lettres historiques sur les parlements ou états généraux. 3 vols. The Hague and Amsterdam: Aux dépends de la compagnie, 1727.

Mémoires présentés au duc d'Orléans, régent de France, contenant les moyens de rendre ce royaume très puissant et d'augmenter considérablement les revenus du roi et du peuple. 2 vols. The Hague, 1727.

La vie de Mahomed. London: Humbert, 1730. Unfinished.

Essai de métaphysique dans les principes de Spinoza. Brussels, 1731. Published under the title *Réfutation des erreurs de Benoît de Spinosa,* par M. de Fenelon, par le P. Lami et par M. le Comte de Boullainvilliers, avec *La vie de Spinosa* écrite par M. Jean Colerus....

Histoire des Arabes. 2 vols. Amsterdam: Humbert, 1731.

Mémoire pour la construction d'un nobiliaire général and *Mémoire sur la noblesse* (1753). Both unpublished; Mss. at Angoulême.

WORKS ON BOULAINVILLIERS

Buranelli, V. "The Historical and Political Thought of Boulainvilliers." *Journal of the History of Ideas* 18 (4) (1957).

Dosher, Harry R. "Henri, Comte de Boulainvilliers, Historian of the French Aristocracy, 1658–1722." MA thesis. University of North Carolina, Chapel Hill, 1960.

Gargallo di Castel Lentini, Gioacchino. *Boulainvilliers e la storiografia dell'Illuminismo francese.* Giannini-Naples, 1954.

Levy, Neil. "History as Struggle: Foucault's Genealogy of Genealogy." *History of the Human Sciences* 11 (4) (1998): 159–170.

Simon, R. *Henry de Boulainviller, historien, politique, philosophe, astrologue.* Paris, 1939.

Spink, J. S. *French Free-Thought from Gassendi to Voltaire.* London: Athlone Press, 1960.

Torrey, N. L. "Boulainvilliers: The Man and the Mask." *Travaux sur Voltaire et le XVIIIe siècle* 1 (1955): 159–173.

Wade, I. O. *The Clandestine Organization and Diffusion of Philosophic Ideas in France from 1700 to 1750.* Princeton, NJ: Princeton University Press, 1938.

Robert Niklaus (1967)
Bibliography updated by Tamra Frei (2005)

BOWNE, BORDEN PARKER
(1847–1910)

Borden Parker Bowne, an American Personalist philosopher, spent his scholarly life, that is, from 1876 to 1910, at Boston University, where he taught in the liberal arts college and the school of theology, and where he became the first dean of the graduate school. In many articles and in seventeen books, Bowne expounded his Personalism, or Personalistic Idealism, which held that the Creator-Person, God, and created persons constitute the real.

Bowne was constantly concerned with taking full account of every dimension of human experience, be it the logical, the emotional, the moral, or the religious. Each dimension should be given full value and not be arbitrarily explained away by pontifical claims made in the name of such doctrines as Christian supernaturalism, psychological associationism and materialism, or ethical utilitarianism. For Bowne, reason is the criterion of truth. This means that for him reasoning discovers the real by interweaving and interpreting the different dimensions of experience.

The presupposition of thought and action is a unified, thinking self, or person. Were the person unable to will freely (granted limitations) and to choose in accordance with moral and intellectual ideals, there could be no trustworthy science or philosophy and no significance to moral and religious living. It is in the nature and experience of this self-identical, thinking, willing, and feeling person, who may not be reduced either to a mode of matter or to a mode of divinity, that Bowne finds his clue to, and his model of, reality.

Persons, however, do not create themselves, or each other. They could not communicate with each other were they not bound by the same laws of reason and subject to a common world. Each knower is bombarded by a flux of discontinuous sense impressions and responds as constructively as possible in accordance with his or her own dynamic categories, such as time, space, quality, quantity, cause, substance, and purpose. Thus the "common world" is the phenomenal world as organized by knowers who interact with, and ultimately depend upon, the structure of the real world independent of them. The phenomenal world is not a mask of the real world; it is the real world as related to the cognitive nature and purposes of finite knowers.

Bowne argues that the real world is neither nonmental nor independent of persons. For in knowing, and in interacting with an order other than itself, the mind must meet not only the conditions of its own nature but those of some agency or agencies independent of it. Since knowledge exists, and yet is not imported into a passive mind, the realist's contention that the real is unaffected by knowing is unintelligible. The fact must stand that minds, in following their own natures, can know with reasonable assurance the reality in which they live and can construct a common world of thought and action, even though they are not identical with the real in knowing.

Furthermore, minds in their theoretical and practical action are clearly alien neither to each other nor to the reality that is the source of their experiences. The world as known is the world persons construct, following the nature of their own theoretical interests, on the basis of the reality beyond their thought. Why, then, hold that any reality beyond finite things is nonmental if such cooperative interaction is possible?

Bowne granted that the case against nonmental "material being" is not proved beyond a shadow of a doubt. But he argued that what we do know about the relation of mind to nature is more economically explained if we think of nature as the energizing of a cosmic Person. Nature is God willing in accordance with rational principles, hence nature dependably supports the orderly common world our finite reasons construct in response to it. God, however, is not identical with the natural world. He is transcendent as well as immanent in relation to it. He is the unified, dynamic ground of nature, and he uses it for his purposes, inclusive of his interaction with finite persons.

How, then, are finite persons related to God? Finite persons are created by God and have relative, delegated autonomy. The real world, whose structure maintains and guides the constructive cognitive adjustments of persons, does not force their moral and appreciative responses. But when persons do not treat each other as persons in a realm that is morally purposeful, they fall short of what their own natures in God's world can be. God created man free, to work out the content of his freedom in a world order that at once limits and gives him opportunity for fulfillment. Human freedom could effect nothing in a world without order, for persons do not create the rational or moral principles by which they guide their thought and action in the given ultimate order.

For Bowne, then, the natural world as known by persons is the objectification of the orderly interaction between finite wills and cosmic Will. The ethical world is the objectification of the orderly, chosen, interaction among free, finite persons in the natural world God makes possible. Bowne's universe is not (like Benedict de Spinoza's) a unity with many finite modes. It is a realm of persons united both by God's purposive action in nature and by the further moral unity created as persons freely respond to the reason, will, and love of the cosmic Person.

See also Idealism; Personalism; Spinoza, Benedict (Baruch) de.

Bibliography

Among the most interesting philosophical works by Borden Parker Bowne are *The Theory of Thought and Knowledge* (New York: Harper, 1897); *Metaphysics* (New York: Harper, 1898); *Theism* (New York: American, 1902); and *Personalism* (Boston: Houghton, Mifflin, 1908).

Works about Bowne include E. S. Brightman, "Personalism and the Influence of Bowne," in *Proceedings of the Sixth International Congress of Philosophy,* edited by E. S. Brightman (New York: Longmans, Green, 1927); and A. C. Knudson, *The Philosophy of Personalism* (New York: Abingdon Press, 1927).

For bibliography, see F. J. McConnell, *Borden Parker Bowne* (New York: Abingdon Press, 1929).

Peter A. Bertocci (1967)

BOYLE, ROBERT
(1627–1691)

Robert Boyle, the English natural philosopher, was the fourteenth child of Richard Boyle, the first earl of Cork, who by judicious marriages and land purchases had made himself the most influential man in Ireland and the richest in England. The political and financial fortunes of the earl of Cork fluctuated considerably during his son's lifetime, but ultimately Robert Boyle inherited a considerable income, which greatly facilitated his scientific researches.

In October 1635, Boyle entered Eton, which with Sir Henry Wotton as provost was a notable center of culture and learning. As a result of a change of teachers, Boyle left Eton in 1638 to be privately tutored. In 1639 he went to Geneva, where he studied mathematics; his devotion to religion, so he tells us in his fragment of an autobiography, *An Account of Philaretus during His Minority,* dates from this same period. A visit to Florence in 1641–1642 introduced him to Galileo Galilei's ideas and confirmed him in his hostility to Roman Catholicism. His return to England was delayed by a crisis in his father's affairs. When Boyle was free to return to England in 1644, his father was dead and he had inherited the manor of Stalbridge in Dorsetshire.

Boyle stayed at first in London with his favorite sister, Lady Ranelagh, whose house was a center of intellectual life. There he met Samuel Hartlib (d. 1670?), an enthusiastic educator and intellectual middleman, through whom Boyle was brought in touch with the burgeoning scientific activities of London. In Boyle's correspondence with Hartlib there are several references to their membership in an "Invisible College"; this has generally been identified by biographers with the Gresham's

College group out of which the Royal Society was to develop. The "Invisible College" Boyle referred to, however, would seem rather to have been an independent group centering on Hartlib and having an interest in social and educational reform as well as in science.

From 1645 until 1652 Boyle lived in retirement at Stalbridge, remote from the political upheavals of the times. He was still essentially a dilettante, interesting himself— but not too seriously—in chemistry, writing theological tracts of a highly moral character, and composing what was perhaps the first religious novel, *Seraphic Love* (1648). In 1652–1653 he visited his Irish estates; unable to obtain materials for chemical experiments, he studied anatomy under William Petty. The interest in biological processes thus engendered remained with him. In bad health from early manhood, he was particularly interested in the application of chemical methods to the cure of disease and was a diligent collector of prescriptions.

The Commonwealth had appointed a number of London scientists to posts at Oxford; in 1654 Boyle accepted an invitation from John Wilkins to make his home there. Now his serious career as a scientist began. He built a laboratory and employed a number of research assistants, in particular Robert Hooke (1635–1703), later to be curator of experiments at the Royal Society. With Hooke's help, Boyle constructed a greatly improved air pump, experiments with which provided the groundwork for Boyle's first and most important scientific work: *New Experiments Physico-Mechanical touching the Spring of the Air and Its Effects* (1660). Following up the work of Galileo and Evangelista Torricelli, Boyle demonstrated that air has both weight and elasticity and that the phenomena that had traditionally been ascribed to an anthropomorphically conceived "horror of a vacuum" were, in fact, a product of the air's elasticity.

His conclusions created an immediate stir but were not universally accepted. Boyle was criticized on philosophical grounds by Thomas Hobbes, Henry More, and the Jesuit Franciscus Linus (1595–1675), to all of whom he replied in detail. In the course of his reply to Linus, Boyle formulated what is known as Boyle's law. (On the Continent it is called Mariotte's law, Mariotte having confirmed it in 1676.) In the years that followed, Boyle took part in the meetings of the embryonic Royal Society at Oxford, conducted and published a great many experiments, corresponded voluminously with most of the leading thinkers of Europe, studied Oriental languages, actively supported the distribution of the Bible in foreign parts—becoming for that purpose a governor of the Corporation for the Spread of the Gospel to New England

and a director of the East India Company—and wrote a considerable number of scientific, philosophic, and theological treatises. After the Restoration most of his scientific friends returned to London; Boyle left Oxford for London in 1668 and lived in Lady Ranelagh's household until her death. He died a week later.

SCIENCE AND PHILOSOPHY

Boyle was profoundly influenced by Francis Bacon's conception of science; much of his published work consists of what Bacon called "histories"—systematic accounts of such qualities as color, firmness, and coldness as they appear under a variety of circumstances. His *Spring of the Air* was the first scientific paper of the modern type. He encouraged scientists to write relatively brief experimental "essays" rather than general treatises. His *Animadversions upon Mr. Hobbes' Problemata de Vacuo* (published in Boyle's *Tracts*, 1674) emphasized the fruitlessness of a priori philosophical reasoning—what Boyle called "book philosophy"—about issues that could be settled only by experiment.

But it is wrong to suppose that Boyle was an opponent of theorizing. He discusses the place of theory in science in his proemial essay to *Certain Physiological Essays and other Tracts* (1661). Scientists, he says, should "set themselves diligently to make experiments and collect observations, without being over forward to establish principles and axioms." Theories ought never to be taken as final; they should be thought of as "the best we have but capable of improvement." Nevertheless, it is the scientist's task to develop theories that are as clear, as simple, and as comprehensive as possible—a point that particularly emerges in Boyle's essay "About the Grounds of the Mechanical Hypothesis" (published in *The Excellency of Theology*, 1674).

Indeed, it was Boyle's main object "to beget a good understanding between the chemists and the mechanical philosophers, who have hitherto been too little acquainted with each other's learning." The corpuscular theory, which Pierre Gassendi had revived, suffered, Boyle thought, in the eyes of practical chemical experimentalists because so little had been done to test it. Theorists had been accustomed to illustrate their theories rather than to test them. On the other side, the work of the chemists had been ignored by physical theorists, largely because it had been associated with theories of a totally inadequate kind.

DOCTRINE OF MATTER

Boyle's *The Sceptical Chemist* (1661) is mainly concerned with demonstrating the unsatisfactory character of the standard chemical theories. It is written in the form of a dialogue in which the main speaker, Carneades, attacks not only the traditional theory of elements but also the alchemical theories that had been proposed by Paracelsus and Jan van Helmont. None of these theories, Boyle argued, can be reconciled with experiment, unless they are interpreted in so vague and symbolic a manner as to make them scientifically worthless. As an alternative, he set up the corpuscular theory. It is sometimes said that he also so redefined "elements" as to prepare the way for the modern doctrine of elements; but that is a mistaken interpretation. Indeed, what his chemistry lacked was precisely this modern conception of elements. That is why he was still able to believe in the possibility of alchemical transmutations. In 1689 he secured the repeal of Henry IV's statute against "multiplying gold."

In a sense, however, Boyle's work was too advanced theoretically. Not enough was known about chemical substances to enable the corpuscular theory to be effectively applied in chemistry. Although, in trying to bring together physics and chemistry and chemistry and biology, Boyle anticipated the long-range development of science, the program that he laid down for chemistry was one that for the moment no one knew how to fulfill; the immediate effect may well have been to hold back the development of chemistry. Boyle conceded, it is true, that explanations referring to perceptible properties rather than to the behavior of corpuscles are, at a certain level, perfectly satisfactory; but the general effect of his work was to discourage explanations of the only sort that chemists were actually in a position to offer. His own writings abound in interesting theoretical suggestions—in his *General History of the Air* (1692), for example, he anticipated the kinetic theory of gases—but for a very long time they had to remain no more than suggestions. Although Boyle's actual contributions to science are very few in number, the range of his anticipations is remarkable. He had set out to make chemistry respectable; he had succeeded, many chemists thought, only at the cost of turning it into physics.

PRIMARY AND SECONDARY QUALITIES

Boyle exerted an important influence on philosophy by lending the authority of a practicing scientist to the corpuscular theory of matter and the associated doctrine of primary and secondary qualities. In *The Experimental History of Colours* (1663), Boyle sets out to demonstrate that color is a "secondary quality" (his own terminology). Objects give rise to sensations of color, he tries to show, not because they are themselves colored but because the structure of their corpuscles modifies light in a special way. The word *color* is most properly applied, he argues, to the modified light that "strikes upon the organ of sight and so causes that sensation we call colour"; if we say that bodies themselves are colored, this can mean no more than that, by virtue of "a certain disposition of the superficial particles," they are capable of refracting or reflecting light.

This thesis is generalized in *The Origin of Forms and Qualities according to the Corpuscular Philosophy* (1666), in which the theory of qualities, which John Locke was to rely upon in his *Essay concerning Human Understanding*, is set forth in detail and contrasted with the Scholastic doctrine of substantial forms. The qualities of a material object, Boyle argues, consist of "the size, shape and motion or rest of its component particles, together with that texture of the whole which results from their being so contrived as they are." These primary qualities of objects, operating upon the "peculiar texture" of a sensory organ, "occasion ideas in us."

SCIENCE AND RELIGION

The corpuscular philosophy had generally been associated with atheism. Boyle sets out to show that "by being addicted to experimental philosophy a man is rather assisted than indisposed to be a good Christian" (*The Christian Virtuoso*, 1690). His views about the relation between God and Nature, however, are by no means clear. In "An Hydrostatical Discourse Occasioned by Some Objections of Dr. Henry More," included in *Tracts* (1672), Boyle strongly opposes More's view that mechanical principles cannot explain the phenomena of pressure or any other physical phenomena. We do not need, he says, to have recourse to More's "incorporeal creatures"; mechanism is enough. Yet, at the same time, in *Forms and Qualities* he argues against René Descartes that we cannot account for the behavior of living organisms by supposing that they consist of particles on which God bestowed motion. We have to suppose, Boyle says, that the Creator not only set the world moving but also introduced into it "seminal seeds" that are responsible for the growth and propagation of animal organisms.

Again, in *A Disquisition about the Final Causes of Natural Things* (1688), he expresses his disagreement with those who would reject final causes completely, although he also argues that the scientist, in his day-today work, need pay no attention to anything except the size, shape, texture, and motion of particles. At times, indeed, as in *The Excellency of Theology, or the Pre-eminence of the Study of Divinity above That of Natural Philosophy,* Boyle's anxiety about the contemporary tendency to abandon theology in favor of scientific inquiries leads him into a skepticism about science. If theology has its obscurities, he argues, they are as nothing to the obscurities inherent in the scientific account of continuity or of the relation between mind and body. Revelation can tell us far more about the place of man in nature than can science. But the example of Boyle the scientist was more influential than the precepts of Boyle the theologian. His last gesture in favor of Christianity was to leave in his will a sum sufficient to endow lectures for the defense of Christianity against its opponents; his intellectual legacy, however, was the mechanical interpretation of the world that deism took as its starting point.

See also Atheism; Bacon, Francis; Carneades; Colors; Deism; Descartes, René; Galileo Galilei; Gassendi, Pierre; Hobbes, Thomas; Locke, John; Matter; More, Henry; Paracelsus; Physicotheology; Primary and Secondary Qualities; Scientific Method; Scientific Theories.

Bibliography

For a bibliography of Boyle's voluminous works, see John Farquhar Fulton, *A Bibliography of the Honourable Robert Boyle,* rev. 2nd ed. (Oxford: Clarendon Press, 1961). The only complete collected edition of Boyle's *Works,* edited by Thomas Birch, and with a still useful life by Birch that incorporates Boyle's *Account of Philaretus,* was published in London in five volumes in 1744 and in six volumes in 1772. *The Sceptical Chemist* is in the Everyman Library (London, 1911), and *The Weight and Spring of the Air* is in Vol. I of *Harvard Case Histories in Experimental Science* (Cambridge, MA: Harvard University Press, 1957), an anthology edited by James B. Conant.

For works on Boyle, see Edwin A. Burtt, *The Metaphysical Foundations of Modern Physical Science* (London: K. Paul, Trench, Trubner, 1925; rev. ed., 1932), Ch. 6, "Gilbert and Boyle"; Louis T. More, *The Life and Works of the Hon. Robert Boyle* (New York and London: Oxford University Press, 1944); Mitchell S. Fisher, *Robert Boyle, Devout Naturalist* (Philadelphia: Oshiver Studio Press, 1945); Marie Boas, *Robert Boyle and Seventeenth Century Chemistry* (Cambridge, U.K.: Cambridge University Press, 1958)—an excellent book; Richard S. Westfall, "Unpublished Boyle Papers relating to Scientific Method," in *Annals of Science* 12 (1) (March 1956): 63–73, and 12 (2) (June 1956): 103–117.

John Passmore (1967)

BRADLEY, FRANCIS HERBERT
(1846–1924)

The English idealist philosopher Francis Herbert Bradley was born in Clapham and educated at University College, Oxford; in 1870 he was elected to a fellowship at Merton College, Oxford, terminable on marriage. Since he never married and the terms of the fellowship did not require him to teach, he was able to devote himself entirely to philosophical writing. His first published work was a pamphlet titled *The Presuppositions of Critical History* (Oxford, 1874). There followed *Ethical Studies* (London, 1876), *Principles of Logic* (London, 1883), and *Appearance and Reality* (London, 1893), as well as many articles in philosophical journals, some of which were published in *Essays on Truth and Reality* (Oxford, 1914) and others in *Collected Essays* (Oxford, 1935).

Like Bernard Bosanquet, Bradley was influenced by T. H. Green. Like Bosanquet, too, he read and admired G. W. F. Hegel, but was less in sympathy with Hegelianism than Bosanquet was. Bosanquet was active in social reform, as Green had been, whereas Bradley was a Tory who hated liberalism and sometimes thought along the lines of Thomas Carlyle's later writings. Bradley was, and intended to be, a highly polemical writer. His *Ethical Studies* and *Principles of Logic* are a sustained attack on the utilitarianism and empiricism of John Stuart Mill and his followers and upon the positivist outlook of the times. Later in his career, Bradley crossed swords with William James (who, however, greatly influenced Bradley's views on existence and reality) and with Bertrand Russell. His views were at their maximum influence during the first decade of the twentieth century, and the philosophical analysis of Russell and G. E. Moore arose largely in the attempt to refute them. Bradley's literary style has been much admired, notably by T. S. Eliot, who, as a graduate student at Harvard, studied Bradley in detail and wrote a thesis about him. Few if any other works on logic have been written with the verve, eloquence, and exuberant clarity of Bradley's *Principles,* but *Appearance and Reality* is less varied, and, from a stylistic point of view, much less successful.

ETHICS

Bradley's *Ethical Studies* is the most Hegelian of his writings. There is much criticism in it of Mill and some criticism of Immanuel Kant. There are amusing skirmishes with Matthew Arnold and with Frederick Harrison, the English positivist. Running through the book is the idea that it is not for the moral philosopher to tell people what to do, but rather to dispel false views of the nature of morality and to provide an analysis of morality that can stand up to philosophical criticism. Thus he starts with an analysis of the moral concepts of the plain man, which, he holds, are not consistent with utilitarian views on punishment and responsibility. He goes on to criticize hedonism, largely on the ground that since pleasure is an "infinite perishing series," it cannot be the object of a rational pursuit. (The influence of Hegel's doctrine of the False Infinite is apparent here.) As to utilitarianism, Bradley holds that in the light of the Greatest Happiness Principle *any* course of conduct *might* conceivably be right, and "this is to make possible, to justify, and even to encourage, an incessant practical casuistry; and that, it need scarcely be added, is the death of morality."

Like Hegel, Bradley considered Kantian ethics to be formal and abstract, and, again like Hegel, he endeavored to supplement Kant's theories by a more concretely social view of ethics. In the study "My Station and its Duties" he developed the concept that Hegel had called "social morality" (*Sittlichkeit*). According to this view, duties are determined by the agent's place and functions in society. Bradley argued, furthermore, that men themselves are what they are because the society in which they are born and bred is what it is. The "individuals" of liberal and utilitarian social theory do not exist. The community is not, as the liberals assumed, a mere collection of individuals who are logically prior to it, but is a real being "and can be regarded (if we mean to keep to facts) only as the one in the many."

This language shows that Bradley regarded communities as both real and as concrete universals, and individual men as factually and logically dependent upon them, a view that was to achieve logical status in the *Principles of Logic*. Bradley wrote of morality as "self-realization," and some writers have therefore classed him as an ethical egoist. But the self that realizes itself is, according to Bradley, a socialized self that expresses and develops itself in making its contribution to the whole. It should be noted (and here again he is following Hegel) that Bradley did not regard "my station and its duties" as the culmination of morality. He held that on the basis of social morality other forms are developed. In pursuing science or in producing works of art, people are not confined to any particular station, and they also set themselves ideals that go beyond what mere duty would require of them. Perhaps humankind is the beneficiary in such cases, but humankind is not a being or community (this is in criticism of the positivists) in the way that a state or a nation

is. Thus, on the basis of "the objective world of my station and its duties" ideals of social and of nonsocial perfection are constituted. These various spheres and duties often clash with one another, but the moral philosopher cannot formulate rules (as the utilitarians thought they could) that would enable the clashes to be avoided or settled. Conflict and failure are inseparable from morality, which could not exist without them.

The *Ethical Studies* are impressive today by virtue of the anticipations in them of twentieth-century views on socialization and the formation of conscience. But Bradley's position is different from that of present-day sociologists in that he thought that the plain man's views on responsibility are superior to any utilitarian reformulation of them and that they presuppose a nonatomistic metaphysics. The facts of moral judgment and of moral action, he held, force the philosopher to a monistic view of social life and to a metaphysics of the self as a being that can be itself only by transcending itself.

LOGIC

In his *Principles of Logic*, Bradley endeavored to refute false views of the subject without going thoroughly into questions of epistemology and metaphysics. The main objects of his attack were: the traditional subject-predicate, syllogistic, formal logic; the inductive logic with which, since the appearance of Mill's *Logic*, this traditional logic had been supplemented; and the confusion he claimed to see in the current empiricist logic between logical and psychological problems.

Bradley thought that the traditional logic was inadequate and incomplete. For example, in treating all judgments as of the subject-predicate form it omitted relational judgments, and the doctrine of the syllogism failed to take account of relational arguments. He maintained, too, that universal affirmative judgments are not categorical but hypothetical, since they do not necessarily assert that there are members of the subject class. These are theses that subsequent logicians have accepted.

Bradley denied that the advance of knowledge was from particulars to universals, or from particulars to particulars as Mill had suggested. Hence he denied the existence of induction as understood by Mill and the writers of textbooks who followed him. The great mistake of the empiricists, Bradley argued, was to suppose that thought could possibly get started with knowledge of separate and independent particulars. Such particulars, in his view, could be known only after a preceding condition of vagueness, ambiguity, and generality. This, however, is a historical, not a logical, consideration. Bradley's main argument is that inference is possible only on the basis of universals and hence cannot be a procession from particulars to particulars or from particulars to universal. Inference presupposes judgments and ideal contents, and these, in their turn, presuppose generality and universality. It is only legitimate to argue from some to all if it is known or surmised that the particulars share some universal character. Bradley supported this by a detailed examination of Mill's inductive methods, an examination that owes something, as Bradley acknowledged, to William Whewell's criticism of them in his *Philosophy of Discovery*. The main point is that the facts or particulars from which the induction is alleged to start must already be ordered and defined in terms of some sort of theory, and hence in terms of a universal, if they are to give rise to an advance in knowledge. Both premises and conclusion must be organized around the central concept in a system of related concepts.

The empiricists subordinated logic to psychology. David Hume's account of thought was in terms of ideas that, by the very fact of being described as "fainter" than impressions, were regarded as a sort of mental image. Based on Hume's views, there had grown up a theory that knowledge advanced by the association of ideas. Bradley set out to refute this view, which today is known as psychologism. He argued that logicians are not concerned with ideas as psychical facts, but with ideas as meanings. As meanings, ideas do not have dates and histories, but are "ideal contents" and hence abstract. The real distinction between subject and predicate, he argued, is not to be found in the relation of one ideal content to another but in the relation of a complex ideal content to the reality to which it is referred.

In judgment, therefore, an ideal content is referred to a reality existing beyond the act of judgment. The real subject of a judgment is thus often quite different from the grammatical subject of the sentence, as can be seen in such an example as "A four-cornered circle is an impossibility," where the real subject is not a four-cornered circle, for there could be no such reality, but the nature of space. (This distinction between the grammatical form and the logical form was later to play an important part in analytic and linguistic philosophy.) If this view is accepted, then psychological accounts of inference fare no better than psychological accounts of judgment, since it is meanings, not psychical occurrences, that are relevant. There could not be any association between particular mental occurrences since they perish as they pass, and past ones would have somehow to be revived or re-created if they were to be associated with those existing in the present. Thus similarity and reproduction presuppose universals, just as inference itself does.

We have said that in his *Logic* Bradley tried to avoid being drawn into epistemological and metaphysical discussions. It is not surprising that he failed in this. Part of his attack on the "School of Experience" consisted in his bringing to light the untenable atomistic metaphysics that he regarded as basic to it. This is a parallel operation to his assault on utilitarianism. The claim that scientific knowledge is based on a prior knowledge of facts or particulars he rejected on the ground that from atomistic particulars no inference could be made. No inference could be valid apart from identities or universals linking one fact with another. It is clear, therefore, that Bradley thought that the fact of inference invalidated metaphysical pluralism, as the facts of morality went against it too. At this point Bradley has some important things to say about universals. He takes the view that what is essential to universality is identity in difference. Identity in difference can take two main forms. It can be abstract, as with such adjectives as "red" or "hard," which require substances in which to inhere. Or it can be concrete, as with an individual man, who is identical throughout his many actions, or a community, which persists through many generations of inhabitants. Abstract universals, therefore, are dependent, insubstantial, unreal, whereas concrete universals are (relatively) independent, substantial, and real. If what is real is individual, then concrete universals are individuals. Bradley ends this part of the discussion with the words: "It might be urged that if you press the enquiry, you will be left alone with but a single individual. An individual which is finite or relative turns out to be no individual; individual and infinite are inseparable characters." He does not pursue this in the *Logic*, but says that such a "revision" (an interesting choice of words) "must be left to metaphysics." So it is to his metaphysics that we now turn.

METAPHYSICS

Bradley's metaphysics, apart from the glimpses of it given in the *Ethical Studies* and the *Logic*, is set out in *Appearance and Reality* and in *Essays on Truth and Reality*. The main argument of *Appearance and Reality* is quite simple. It is divided into two books. The first and shorter one is titled "Appearance" and is about the contradictory character of mere appearances. Book II is titled "Reality" and is about the Absolute.

In Book I, certain commonsense concepts, such as relation, cause, space, time, thing, and self, and certain philosophical concepts, such as the thing-in-itself and the distinction between primary and secondary qualities, are declared to be self-contradictory and are in consequence "degraded to the rank of mere appearances." In Chapters 2 and 3 of Book I, titled, respectively, "Substantive and Adjective" and "Relation and Quality," Bradley argues that the very notion of a relation is self-contradictory and that this inconsistency is alone sufficient to condemn "the great mass of phenomena," since space, time, causation, the self, all imply relations.

In Chapter 2, in considering the suggestion that all things are groups of related attributes, Bradley argues that if *A* and *B* stand in relation to *C*, then *C* must be related to *A* and *B* by another relation *D*, and this by a third relation *E*, and so on indefinitely. In Chapter 3 he argues that if simple qualities are to be conceived, they must be conceived as related to one another; but if *A* is related to *B*, then there must be the independent aspect of *A* and the aspect in which it is related to *B*, and hence it cannot be simple; but if *A* is not simple, then the independent aspect and the aspect in which it is related to *B* must be related to one another, so that there is set up in each of them a further plurality of aspects generating what Bradley calls "a principle of fission which conducts us to no end."

In Book II, it is argued that if it is being self-contradictory that degrades mere appearances, then reality must at least be not self-contradictory, but consistent and harmonious. Furthermore, reality must also be of the nature of experience, for what is not experience cannot be conceived of without self-contradiction. Finally, it is clear that reality must be comprehensive and include all that is. If reality is a consistent and harmonious and all-inclusive experience, then it cannot be a plurality of independent reals, for whatever is related to anything else must be to some extent dependent on it. "Plurality and relatedness are but features and aspects of a unity." Furthermore, the sort of unity that reality or the Absolute must have may be understood by analogy with feeling or immediate experience, for here there is diversity without relatedness.

According to Bradley, our experience of related things arises out of a prior immediate experience in which there are felt differences but no distinct qualities, and therefore no conception of things with different qualities in relation with one another. In passing from the primitive harmonious vagueness to a knowledge of related things, we pass from what might be called the state of precognitive innocence to the flawed world of contradiction. Wherever there is thought, there is the distinction between the what and the that, between ideal content and reality, between adjective and substantive; and hence

wherever there is thought, there is contradiction. Thus reality, or the Absolute, must transcend thought, and thought always points beyond itself to something in which "mere thinking is absorbed." The Absolute must be conceived as analogous to immediate experience but transcending thought rather than falling short of it.

It is clear that contradiction, error, and evil are not harmonious and hence are not real, but it is equally clear that they are not nothing. How then must they be considered in the light of the Absolute? To this question Bradley gives a very interesting answer. He says that although error and evil are discordant and hence not real, it is possible that they contribute to the harmony of the whole, and if this is possible then we must conclude that it is so even though we do not know how it is possible. "For what is *possible*," he says, "and what a general principle compels us to say *must be*, that certainly *is*" (*Appearance and Reality*, Ch. 16). In this way, he protects himself against demands to show exactly how appearances are self-contradictory, unreal, not nothing, and yet are elements in the total harmony. Even so, he does make some attempts to show how all this is possible. In Book I, for example, time is condemned as self-contradictory, but in Book II Bradley says that although it is not real it nevertheless exists.

In explaining what he means by existence, he says it consists in being an event in time, in being a fact, in being directly perceived. In a later essay he says that what exists is what is continuous with our waking body. Existence, therefore, is the mode of being of the phenomenal world. But this would seem to bring us back to the point from which we started. Bradley also says that the real, the Absolute, must appear in what exists, that it cannot remain unmanifested. But he also attempts to mitigate the dualism between harmonious reality and self-contradictory appearance-existence by sketching a scheme in which reality permits of degrees. At the bottom of the scale, there are sheer contradictions and the abstract being of lifeless matter. Organic matter has more reality and is higher in the scale, and mind is higher still, for in mind the whole is immanent in its manifestations and the manifestations express the whole.

It is in mind that we see how the real must appear. But insofar as mind is thought, it suffers the disruption into the what and the that, which we have already considered. Perhaps, then, reality is to be found in mind as practical. This is rejected on the ground that practice essentially contains the distinction between reality as it is and reality as it will be when altered. Reality cannot be found in aesthetic experience either, for art entails pleasure, pleasure is an experience of selves, and selves, Bradley has argued, cannot be ultimately real. "The Absolute," Bradley concludes, "is not personal, nor is it moral, nor is it beautiful or true." Yet in spite of all this he ends *Appearance and Reality* with the words: "… the more that anything is spiritual, the more is it veritably real."

The weakest part of *Appearance and Reality* is Book I. The amount of space and care given in it to the task of discrediting the whole of common sense and much of the philosophy of the past is trifling compared with the magnitude of the desired result. Bradley seems almost to take the reader's agreement for granted and to hasten on to the more congenial, yet only slightly more constructive, task of showing what the Absolute must be. A good part of the argument of Book I assumes that predication is identity, in accordance with "the old puzzle how to justify the attributing to a subject something other than itself." After all, Bradley had refuted this view of predication in his *Logic*. Perhaps then he is arguing dialectically, in order to bring out the unhappy consequences of working with this "logic of identity." But if this were so, then relation, space, time, the self, etc. would only be self-contradictory if looked at in the light of a false logic, and might be reinstated if the true logic were brought to bear on them. The doctrine of degrees of reality goes some way towards meeting this difficulty. But in Book I there is no indication that the self is more real or less self-contradictory than space and time. As A. S. Pringle-Pattison put it in his review of *Appearance and Reality*: "Mr. Bradley has the aim of swallowing at a gulp in Book II what he had choked over in the successive chapters of Book I."

As to Book II there are two main defects. One is that the Absolute described in it seems to be without any definite features but is an amorphous refuge into which appearances are "fused," "transformed," "transmuted," or "dissolved." The other is that in the course of developing the doctrine of degrees of reality Bradley unwittingly reverts on occasion to the arguments of Book I, as when he says that aesthetic experience cannot be or reveal the Absolute since it involves pleasure and selves and selves are self-contradictory. Bradley here seems to be reverting to the logic of identity that in Book II he had been moderating. On the other hand, there is much excellent discussion of details. The account of time is particularly good. Bradley holds that we should not think in terms of one time series only, but in terms of several or many. Just as the events of one fiction are not temporally related to the events in another fiction, so there may be various time series in which what is past in one may be yet to come in another.

What Bradley said about time and about existence and reality greatly exercised G. E. Moore who, in various writings, notably "The Conception of Reality" (1917–1918), endeavored to make clear what it is to say that something exists. Moore argued that Bradley's view that time, although unreal, must exist, depended upon his assuming that whatever can be thought of must somehow exist in order to be thought of. But Moore rejected this assumption. Bradley, he thought, was deceived into making it because he did not notice that although "unicorns are objects of thought" is of the same *grammatical* form as "lions are objects of the chase," it is of quite a different *logical* form. Moore's reason for this was that if lions are to be hunted there must be lions, whereas unicorns can be thought of although there are no unicorns. Thus Moore used against Bradley the distinction between logical and grammatical form that Bradley had formulated in 1883. A weapon that Bradley had himself devised was employed against him by a philosopher who had improved its range and sophistication.

See also Absolute, The; Analysis, Philosophical; Appearance and Reality; Arnold, Matthew; Bosanquet, Bernard; Carlyle, Thomas; Eliot, Thomas Stearns; Ethics, History of; Green, Thomas Hill; Hegel, Georg Wilhelm Friedrich; Hegelianism; Hume, David; Idealism; James, William; Kantian Ethics; Kant, Immanuel; Logic, History of; Logic, Traditional; Mill, John Stuart; Moore, George Edward; Pringle-Pattison, Andrew Seth; Psychology; Russell, Bertrand Arthur William; Whewell, William.

Bibliography

Bradley's main writings and the dates of publication have been indicated in the body of the article. A second edition of *Ethical Studies* (Oxford: Clarendon Press, 1927) contains corrections and additional notes that Bradley left at his death. A second edition of *Principles of Logic* (London: Oxford University Press, 1922) contains the original unaltered text with an extensive commentary, which owes much to Bosanquet, at the end of each chapter and a set of "Terminal Essays" at the end of the book. The second edition of *Appearance and Reality* (London, 1897) contains an appendix occasioned by criticisms of the first edition. See also *Aphorisms* (Oxford: Clarendon Press, 1930), a few of which appeared in the preface to *Appearance and Reality*. Collections of his works include *Collected Essays* (Freeport, NY: Books for Libraries Press, 1967) and *Essays on Truth and Reality* (Oxford: Clarendon Press, 1968).

For a detailed critical study of Bradley's philosophy, see Richard Wollheim, *F. H. Bradley* (Harmondsworth, U.K.: Penguin, 1959). This contains further bibliographical references. See also C. A. Campbell, *Scepticism and Construction* (London: Allen and Unwin, 1931); R. W.

Church, *Bradley's Dialectic* (London: Allen and Unwin, 1942); and T. S. Eliot, *Knowledge and Experience in the Philosophy of F. H. Bradley* (New York: Farrar, Straus, 1964), the thesis mentioned above.

A. S. Pringle-Pattison, "A New Theory of the Absolute," reprinted in *Man's Place in the Cosmos* (Edinburgh and London: Blackwood, 1897, 1902), is probably the best criticism of Bradley's metaphysics. G. E. Moore, *Some Main Problems of Philosophy* (London: Allen and Unwin, 1953), Chs. 11, 12, 16, contains a detailed discussion of parts of Bradley's metaphysics.

Criticism of Bradley's view that the notion of relation is self-contradictory is contained in J. Cook Wilson, *Statement and Inference* (Oxford: Clarendon Press, 1926), Vol. I, p. 255, Vol. II, pp. 692–695. See also W. H. Walsh, "F. H. Bradley," in *A Critical History of Western Philosophy*, edited by D. J. O'Connor (New York: Free Press of Glencoe, 1964).

OTHER RECOMMENDED WORKS

Bradley, F. H. *Selected Correspondence, January 1905–June 1924*, edited by Carol A. Keene. Bristol, U.K.: Thoemmes Press, 1999.

Bradley, F. H. *Collected Works of F. H. Bradley*, edited by Carol A. Keene. Bristol, U.K.; Sterling, VA: Thoemmes Press, 1999.

Horstmann, Rolf-Peter. *Ontologie und Relationen: Hegel, Bradley, Russell und die Kontroverse über interne und externe Beziehungen*. Athenäum: Hain, 1984.

Ingardia, Richard. *Bradley: A Research Bibliography*. Bowling Green, OH: Philosophy Documentation Center, 1991.

Mander, W. J. *An Introduction to Bradley's Metaphysics*. Oxford: Clarendon Press; New York: Oxford University Press, 1994.

Mander, W. J. *Perspectives on the Logic and Metaphysics of F. H. Bradley*. Bristol: Thoemmes, 1996.

Manser, Anthony Richards. *Bradley's Logic*. Totowa, NJ: Barnes & Noble Books, 1983.

Manser, Anthony Richards, and Guy Stock. *The Philosophy of F.H. Bradley*. Oxford; New York: Clarendon Press, 1984.

Shrivastava, S. N. L. *Sámkara and Bradley: A Comparative and Critical Study*. Delhi: Motilal Banarsidass, 1968.

Sprigge, Timothy L. S. *James and Bradley: American Truth and British Reality*.Chicago, IL: Open Court, 1993.

H. B. Acton (1967)
Bibliography update by Michael J. Farmer (2005)

BRADWARDINE, THOMAS
(c. 1300–1349)

Thomas Bradwardine studied arts at Balliol College and theology at Merton College, Oxford. In September 1337, he was appointed chancellor of Saint Paul's in London. From 1346 to 1348, as a king's clerk, he enjoyed a prominent position in the household of Edward III. In June 1349 he was elected archbishop of Canterbury; soon afterwards, in October, he died of the Black Death.

Like many Mertonians, Bradwardine was a logician and a mathematician. He wrote a treatise *De insolubilibus* (an *insolubile*is a self-referential sentence, such as the "liar paradox"), a *Geometria speculativa*, and a treatise *De continuo*. In his *Tractatus de proportionibus velocitatum in motibus* (1328) he attempted to introduce mathematic functions into Aristotelician physics. His masterpiece, however, is a voluminous theological and philosophical work, *De causa Dei contra Pelagium*, divided into three books (1344). It originates from lectures he had given in Oxford and London and, more radically, from a deep spiritual change he had experienced in his youth: "When I was applying myself to philosophy … Pelagius's opinion seemed to me nearer to truth.… But afterwards (I was not yet a theological student) … I thought I saw from afar the grace of God preceeding all merits in time and in nature, in the same way that in all movements He is the first Mover." (bk. I, ch. 35, p. 308). This conversion induced Bradwardine to fight for God's cause against "the new Pelagians, " a group of post-ockhamists theologians that included Richard Fitzralph, Adam Wodeham, and Robert Holcot.

To these thinkers the issues of chief concern were grace and merit, future contingents, prescience, and predestination. On the first point, Bradwardine, as an ardent Augustinian, strongly reasserts that grace is a mere gift, not a retribution: in no way man can merit it, and, moreover, without God's special help man cannot act right.

Concerning future contingents, the new Pelagians' opinion stressed the contrast between the necessity—that is, the fixity—of the past and the contingency of the future. This view could hardly be reconciled with the idea of an immutable and truthful God: If God or a prophet were to reveal a future event, is it possible that it would not happen? If it is possible, then God can deceive and lie. Countering this opinion, which he had first rejected in his question, *De futuris contingentibus*, Bradwardine closely examines the notions of contingency and necessity; he argues they are founded on the power of the will. Aristotle wrote, "What is, necessarily is, when it is. (*De interpretation*, ch. 9). But Duns Scotus observed that when man wills *A* at time *t*, he has the power not to will *A*, not only before or after *t*, but also at time *t*. Therefore a kind of necessity, the "consequent" necessity of present, is compatible with contingency. Regarding God, Bradwardine extends this conclusion to all times: For God, past, present, and future are equally contingent and equally necessary. Consequently He can undo any past event (in an improper meaning of *undo*), not because He could alter it (this would be a contradiction), but because at each instant of time He is yet freely willing the past event. In this way, there is no longer antinomy between the necessity of the prophecy and the contingency of the future event.

The same argument about contingent causality clears up the most famous tenet of Bradwardine's teaching, the assertion of "antecedent necessity": Since God's will is the first cause of everything and cannot be thwarted, everything happens by necessity in relation to His will. That is the proper definition of theological determinism. But again, according to Bradwardine, when man is willing something, though his act is determined by God, he does not lose the power to do the opposite act at the same time. So it seems there is in Bradwardine's doctrine an original attempt to conciliate God's predetermination and human freedom of will.

See also Determinism and Freedom; Duns Scotus, John; Pelagius and Pelagianism; Precognition.

Bibliography

WORKS BY BRADWARDINE

De causa Dei contra Pelagium. Franfurt am Main: Minerva, 1964. This is a reprint of a work that was originally edited by Henry Savile in London and published in 1618.

De proportionibus velocitatum in motibus. In *Thomas of Bradwardine: His* Tractatus de Proportionibus—*Its Significance for the Development of Mathematical Physics,* edited by Lamar H. Crosby Jr. Madison: University of Wisconsin Press, 1955.

"Insolubilia." In "La problématique des propositions insolubles au xiiiesiècle et au début du xive, suivie de l'édition des traités de W. Shyreswood, W. Burleigh et Th. Bradwardine," edited by Marie-Louise Roure. *Archives d'histoire doctrinale et littéraire du moyen âge,* 37 (1970): 205–326.

"De futuris contingentibus." In "Le *De futuris contingentibus* de Thomas Bradwardine," edited by Jean-François Genest. *Revue des études augustiniennes,* 14 (1979): 249–336.

WORKS ON BRADWARDINE

Leff, Gordon. *Bradwardine and the Pelagians: A Study of His "De Causa Dei" and Its Opponents.* Cambridge, MA: Cambridge University Press, 1957.

Oberman, Heiko A. *Archbishop Thomas Bradwardine: "A Fourteenth Century Augustinian."* Utrecht: Kemink & Zoon, 1958.

Genest, Jean-François. *Prédétermination et liberté créée à Oxford au xive siècle. Buckingham contre Bradwardine.* Paris: J. Vrin, 1992.

Sylwanowicz, Michael. *Contingent Causality and the Foundations of Duns Scotus' Metaphysics.* Leiden: E. J. Brill, 1996.

Jean-François Genest (2005)

BRAHMAN

The origin and meaning of the term *brahman* are shrouded in mystery. Using the verbal root √*bṛh*, Western Indological scholars derive such meanings as "sacred magical power" (Hermann Oldenberg), "form, formulation" (Paul Thieme), "priestly utterance," "energy that is expressed in paradoxical terms" (Louis Renou), and "the live connection that holds the cosmos together" (Jan Hesterman) The meanings of *brahman* in the ancient "heard texts" (*śrutis*) and later Indian philosophical systems are not unrelated to these meanings. For example, the Vedic understanding of the *brahman* survives in Bhartrhari's concept of the "*śabda brahman*." Likewise, the ideas of power, energy, and cosmic unity among opposites are taken up in the Vedāntic notion of the *brahman* as absolute reality. The notion of the *brahman* as the sacred power within a priest may have contributed to an identification of the brahman with the inner spirit (*ātman*). This transformation of a much older notion into a discursively idealized philosophical concept resembles the way the concept of *logos* was transformed into "logic" "*Vernunft*," and "language."

Etymologically, the word *brahman* has two constituent components: the verbal root √*bṛh* and the suffix *matup*. The verbal root √*bṛh* means "to grow" and "the great," and together with the suffix provides two allied meanings: "the greatest" and "the root of all things." In the Vedic hymns the term *brahman* not only refers to the power contained in the words recited but also to the mysterious power present in the utterances of the Vedic hymns. Though the idea of *brahman* as the ground of all things is not entirely absent in the Vedas, the primary goal was to search for the power connecting the microcosm with the macrocosm.

BRAHMAN IN THE UPANIṢADS

This sense of power continues in the Upaniṣads (e.g., *Kaṭha Upaniṣad*), which say that the various *devas* (gods; literally, "the shining ones") each carry out their respective jobs for fear of the brahman (6.3); *Kena Upaniṣad* states that the various *devas* have no power outside the power of *brahman* residing in them. The *brahman* of the Upaniṣads is much more than a power; it is the cause of the origination, sustenance, and destruction of the world (*Taittīya Upaniṣad,* 3.1.1). In the *Bṛhadāraṇyaka Upaniṣad,* when Yājñavalkya is questioned about the number of gods, he initially responds by saying that 3,306 gods were simply manifestations of thirty-three gods, and then successively reduces the number to six, three, two, one and a half, and then one. This god is none other than the *brahman,* and all other gods of the Vedas, the senses, and the mind are said to be the various powers of *brahman* (*Bṛhadāraṇyaka Upaniṣad,* 3.9.1–10). The central question in the Upaniṣads is framed as follows: "What is that by knowing which all else becomes known?" (*Muṇḍaka Upaniṣad*, 1.13) The answer given is "*brahman*." If *brahman* is the source of everything, then *brahman* is also the core of each individual being, and this core is called *ātman*. In many places in the Upaniṣads the two terms *brahman* and *ātman* are used synonymously. The *Chāndogya Upaniṣad* asks: "What is *ātman*? What is *brahman*?" (5.11.1, *ko nu ātmā, kiṃ brahmeti?*) When the inquiry pertains to the source of the universe, the word *ātman* is used, and in other cases when the inquiry is regarding the true self of a human being the word *brahman* is used. To the Upaniṣadic seers the *brahman* and the ātman signified the same reality, one within, and the other without.

The Upaniṣads describe *brahman* both negatively and positively. It is described as neither gross, nor subtle, nor short, nor long, nor red, nor adhesive, without shadow, darkness, air, space, attachment, taste, smell, eyes, ears, speech, mind, light, breath, mouth, and measure, and without inside and outside (*Bṛhadāraṇyaka Upaniṣad*, 3.8.8), and that who consists of mind, whose body is life, whose form is light, whose conception is truth, whose soul is space, containing all works, desires, odors, and tastes, and encompassing the whole world, the speechless and the calm (*Chāndogya Upaniṣad*, 3.14.2).

BRAHMAN IN VEDĀNTA

The exegetical effort to construe these different groups of sentences to resolve any apparent contradiction shaped the understanding of *brahman* in the Upaniṣadic schools. Two hermeneutic principles were applied: accord priority and finality to the positive texts, or since negation implies a prior affirmation that is then negated, the final import of the Upaniṣads may be taken to be expressed in the negative texts, the positive ones simply preparing the ground for it. The latter hermeneutical principle is adopted by Śaṃkara, the most well-known exponent and defender of the school known as Advaita Vedānta (nondualistic Vedānta); and the former by Rāmānuja, the founder of Viśiṣṭādvaita (qualified nondualism), and Madhva in his Dvaita Vedānta.

ADVAITA VEDĀNTA

From the perspective of Śaṃkara's nondualistic Vedānta, *brahman* is one without a second; the world is false (*māyā*, in a rather technical sense of "presented appearance") and the finite individual and the *brahman* are nondifferent. The *brahman* can neither be comprehended by rational minds, nor be expressed or literally referred to in the language, nor be an object of knowledge. It does not have qualities (because all determination is negation), and so it cannot be described or defined. While using language to refer to *brahman* is natural, it does not achieve its goal. Language refers to an object either by its direct power of meaning (*abhidhā*), or as its suggested meaning (*lakṣaṇā*). Normally, the suggested meaning is sustained and supported by its relationship to the literal meanings, but in the case of language referring to the brahman, the meaning may be said to be "only the meaning function, but not an actual meaning" (Bhattacharyya 1930). There is a pointing, as one points to something with one's finger, toward a small, almost invisible star, accompanied by a series of descriptions each one of which is then canceled, leading the listener to identify, even in the absence of an identifying description of, what is being pointed at. *Brahman* is described as *saccidānanda*, that is, as *sat* (existence), *cit* (consciousness), and *ānanda* (bliss), with reference to its essence (*svaūpa lakṣaṇā*), whereas *brahman* as the cause, sustainer of the universe, and so on with reference to its accidental attributes (*taṭastha lakṣaṇā*).

It is important to keep in mind that from a strictly Advaita point of view no positive description can be intrinsic when the thing being described lacks any positively determining qualities. Nevertheless, Advaita Vedānta describes the *brahman* as existence, pure consciousness, and bliss. These three are not qualities or qualifying attributes of the *brahman*. Advaita Vedānta holds that these familiar terms must be understood in their negative implications, not as referring to what *brahman* is, but rather as pointing to what the *brahman* is not. *Sat* points to the fact that the *brahman* is not *asat* (nonexistent); cit suggests that the *brahman* is not *acit*, that is, *jaḍa* (insentient matter); and ānanda points to that, in the experience of the *brahman*, there is no *duḥkha*, no unsatisfied desire. The negative statements in this regard more closely approach the intrinsic nature of the *brahman*. In this light one can say that in Advaita Vedānta, Benedict (Baruch) de Spinoza's principle "all determination is negation" holds good of the infinite: no determination of it is possible. Underlying this account are a theory of meaning and a theory of language that are of particular importance, and, that possibly, found their first systematic exposition in the Buddhist theory of *apoha* (the negative theory of meaning).

The thesis of Advaita Vedānta is logically substantiated (1) by a critique of difference (*bheda nirodha*) and (2) hermeneutically by an exegesis of the *śrutis*. To these one may add (3) a phenomenological and experiential dimension that would consist in showing that in its search for freedom from all suffering, human subjectivity passes through levels of ordinary experience: the waking-bodily, the dreaming-psychic, and the dreamless sleep (the seemingly total inaction and quietude). Finally, there is the experience of the *brahman*, which goes beyond the distinction of the subject and the object and which is articulated in such famous *mahāvākyas* (great sentences) of the Upaniṣads as "I am he" and "thou art that." Knowing the *brahman*, according to the tradition of Advaita Vedānta, is to become the *brahman*. It is not knowing an object, however large and great in its dignity, that stands over against one as an other; rather, it is an experience in which all otherness is canceled, and one discovers that within oneself nothing else remains to be achieved. When there is no duality between the subject and the object, there is no duḥkha or fear. A modern account of the phenomenological stages of a path to freedom is found in Krishna Chandra Bhattacharyya's *The Subject as Freedom* (1930).

VIŚIṢṬĀDVAITA VEDĀNTA

In his Viśiṣṭādvaita, that is, "one reality (*brahman*) with qualifications," Rāmānuja holds that all knowledge necessarily involves distinctions and differentiations. It is impossible to know an object in its undifferentiated form; therefore, both pure identity and pure difference are false. The *brahman* as God possesses cit (matter) and acit (self); all three are real (*brahman*, cit, and acit). Though real, the last two are dependent on the *brahman*. Consciousness presupposes the self of which it is an essential attribute (*dharmabhuta jñāna*). Perhaps the most original aspect of Rāmānuja's philosophy is the rejection of the principle that to be real means to be independent. Although soul and matter are substances in themselves, in relation to the *brahman* they are attributes. They are God's body and he is their soul. The self is substance and quality, an organ and organism of the *brahman*. Rāmānuja's theory of *apṛthaksiddhi viśeṣaṇa*, that is, the adjectival theory of inseparability, explains this relation. Just as qualities are real and cannot exist apart from the substances in which they subsist, similarly matter and soul are parts of the brahman and cannot exist without the *brahman*.

Rāmānuja used the same Upaniṣadic texts that Śaṃkara used, but arrived at a different conception of the *brahman*. Rāmānuja holds that the Upaniṣadic texts such as *neha nānā asti kiṃcena* (there is no multiplicity here) do not really deny the multiplicity of objects, names, and forms, but asserts that these objects do not have any existence apart from the *brahman*. Thus, all negative texts of the Upaniṣads, which assert that none of this is the brahman, are construed to mean that none of it in its presumed independence is the *brahman*. However, the positive sentences, for example, "all this is the *brahman*," mean that everything belongs to the *brahman* as the ultimate totality. Whereas for Śaṃkara the *brahman* is pure consciousness devoid of any distinctions, a pure identity without any difference (*nirguṇa*), Rāmānuja's brahman is identity-in-difference. The *brahman* creates the world out of acit by an act of will, so creation is a real act of will. Ignorance (māyā or *avidyā*) in this system is no longer creative of illusory world, and the finite individuals are not illusory. It is indeed true, Rāmānuja concedes, that some Upaniṣadic texts articulate the *brahman* as wielder of a magical power (*māyā*). However, *māyā* for Rāmānuja properly understood is the unique power of God by which God creates the wonderful world of objects. He vehemently criticizes Śaṃkara's theory of the world as false appearance. The created world, for Rāmānuja, is as wonderful as the *brahman* himself.

If someone were to ask how the one contains the many, Rāmānuja would respond with the grammatical principle of *sāmānādhikaṇya* (coordination). According to this rule, the words in a sentence with different meanings can denote one and the same thing. Rāmānuja's interpretation of the classical text "this is that Devadattaḥ" explains this rule clearly. For Rāmānuja, Devadattaḥ of the past and the Devadattaḥ of the present cannot be entirely identical, because the person seen at the present and the person seen in the past are different, have different meanings, and yet both refer to the same person. Similarly, unity and diversity, the one and the many, can coexist; they are not contradictions and they can be reconciled in a synthetic unity. Thus, he does not deny the many: the many, on the contrary, characterizes the one. *Mokṣa* comes about with the knowledge of the *brahman* together with devotion (*bhakti*).

DVAITA VEDĀNTA

Madhva carries much further the protest against the nondualism of Śaṃkara than Rāmānuja. Whereas for Śaṃkara the texts teaching difference have a practical value in that they steer one in the right direction and lead one to the real teaching of the Upaniṣads, that is, the teaching of nondifference, for Madhva the texts teaching difference convey the true import of the Upaniṣads. Substance is one of the ten categories that Madhva accepts. Out of the twenty substances that Madhva enumerates, he accepts, like Rāmānuja, three as the most important: brahman or God, matter, and selves.

Bheda (difference) is the central category in Madhva's philosophy. This is another way of saying that each object is unique; each object possesses its own nature, which accounts for one object's difference from another object. The *brahman* or God is the only independent reality. God has a divine body and is transcendent. However, since God is the inner controller of all souls, he is also immanent. God creates the world by his will and brings into existence the world of objects and selves. Objects and selves, though real, eternal, and irreducible to each other, are dependent on the first. At the time of the dissolution of the world, God transforms material objects into undifferentiated matter and selves into disembodied intelligences. It is important to note in this context that even in the state of dissolution God, matter, and selves remain distinct. Unlike Rāmānuja, for Madhva no two souls are alike. Thus, whereas Rāmānuja advocates qualitative monism and quantitative pluralism of souls, Madhva advocates both qualitative and quantitative pluralism of souls. Since the immediate cause of bondage is ignorance of the real nature of the *brahman* or God, the soul must acquire the knowledge of the real nature of God to attain mokṣa. It is important to remember in this context that knowledge by itself does not and cannot remove ignorance; knowledge is only a qualification for release, which in the final analysis depends on God's will. No matter how hard an aspirant may try, he or she cannot gain such an immediate knowledge, unless God chooses to reveal himself to him or her.

ŚAIVISM

Finally, apart from the previously discussed classical understandings of the brahman, there is another nondualistic school known as Śaiva Siddhānta. Of its many representative schools and thinkers, Kāshmir Śaivism of Abhinavagupta is the most well known. In his nondualism Abhinavagupta argues that *brahman* alone *is*. He painstakingly attempts to bridge the gulf between the one and its many phenomenal differences by positing many levels of consciousness, descending from the one to the many. *Māyā* or *avidyā* is now construed as a *śakti* or the power of the *brahman*-consciousness; consciousness is not a mere *prakāśa* (illumination) but also *śakti* (force). Indeed, the two in their difference are also one. While, on the one hand, Abhinavagupta wishes to preserve both the one and the many in the being of brahman, he makes it a graded dynamic process instead of using a static set of categories like the part and the whole. The one *brahman*-consciousness or pure *cit* objectifies itself into "I," and this power of self-objectification is called *vimarṣa śakti* (the reflective power), from which arises the power of referring to intentional objects that lie concealed within it. This process yields a domain of seemingly independent objects. Kāshmir Śaivism has been a major influence in the shaping of the concept of the "integral *brahman*" of Sri Aurobindo's philosophy.

Other systems of Indian philosophy do not advance a concept of the *brahman*. Although Sāṃkhya-Yoga seems to have had a theistic form in addition to the better-known atheistic form, it does not develop a concept of the *brahman*, nor do the Nyāya-Vaiśeṣika schools. The latter systems come perhaps closest to such a project when they substantiate their concept of God as an infinite self, all knowing, omnipresent, which is called Iśavara in the school. Despite the fact that the authors may cite many texts of the Upaniṣads in support of their theism, one misses in these schools any attempt to take into account the *śruti* texts in their totality.

To sum up: The *brahman* is the absolute reality in the school of Vedānta. The relationships of the one with the many preoccupied its thinkers, leading them to postulate a fundamental category to explain the connection. These categories range from pure identity (*tādātmya* having that as its self), *apṛthakasiddhi* (the relation of no separate existence), pure difference, and a progressive self-differentiation through self-objectification and intentionality. In the nondualistic Vedānta, the *brahman*, in the words of Georg Wilhelm Friedrich Hegel, is (Spinozistic) "the substance becoming spirit," bringing together two different concepts of monism into one, resulting in the position that the only reality is the spirit. The following crucial issues remained: How does the one spirit become many? How to understand self-differentiation? Where to locate the power of creativity? Does it belong to the *cit* or consciousness as an inalienable aspect, or is it an "other" to consciousness? In the latter case, the basic otherness is not a product of ignorance. However, can one escape this problem by saying as nondualist Vedānta says, that ignorance is not a real other and not a nonreal other? Is not this nonreality itself a creation of ignorance? Thus, dialectic of one and many seems to have had an interminable hold on Indian metaphysical theories.

See also Causation in Indian Philosophy; God in Indian Philosophy; Mind and Mental States in Indian Philosophy; Self in Indian Philosophy.

Bibliography

Abhinavagupta. *Parātriśikā-vivarana: The Secret of Tantric Mysticism*. Translated by Jaidev Singh; edited by Bettina Bäumer. Delhi, India: Motilal Banarsidass, 1988.

Apte, V. M., tr. *Brahma-sūtra Shānkara-Bhāsya*. Bombay, India: Popular Book Depot, 1960.

Bhattacharyya, Krishna Chandra. *Studies in Vedantism*. Calcutta, India: Calcutta University Press, 1909.

Bhattacharyya, Krishna Chandra. *The Subject as Freedom*. Bombay, India: G.R. Malkani, 1930.

Carman, John Braisted. *Theology of Rāmānuja: An Essay in Interreligious Understanding*. New Haven, CT: Yale University Press, 1974.

Hesterman, J. "Brahmin, Ritual, and Renouncer." *Weiner Zeitschrift Deutschen Morgenländischen* 8 (1964): 1–31.

Hume, Robert Ernest, tr. *The Thirteen Principal Upaniṣads*. 2nd ed. Madras, India: Oxford University Press, 1965.

Mahadevan, T. M. P. *The Philosophy of Advaita, with special reference to Bhāratītīrtha-Vidyāranya*. New Delhi, India: Arnold-Heinemann, 1976.

Murti, T. R. V. "The Two Definitions of Brahman in the Advaita." In *Studies in Indian Thought: Collected Papers of Prof. T. R. V. Murti*, edited by Harold G. Coward. Delhi, India: Motilal Banarsidass, 1983.

Oldenberg, Hermann. *Der Religion des Veda*. Stuttgart, Germany: J. G. Cotta, 1923.

Ranade, R. D. *A Constructive Survey of Upaniṣadic Philosophy: Being an Introduction to the Thought of the Upaniṣads*. 2nd ed. Bombay, India: Bharatiya Vidya Bhavan, 1968.

Sharma, B. N. K. *A History of the Dvaita School of Vedānta and Its Literature: From the Earliest Beginnings to Our Own Time*. 2nd ed. Delhi, India: Motilal Banarsidass, 1981.

Sivaraman, Krishna. *Śaivism in Philosophical Perspective: A Study of the Formative Concepts, Problems, and Methods of Śaiva Siddhānta*. Delhi, India: Motilal Banarsidass, 1973.

Thibaut, George, tr. *The Vedānta-Sūtras: With the Commentary by Śankarākārya*. 3 vols. Oxford, U.K.: Clarendon Press, 1890–1904.

Bina Gupta (2005)

BRAITHWAITE, RICHARD BEVAN
(1900–1990)

Richard Bevan Braithwaite, an English philosopher, was educated at King's College, Cambridge, where he studied physics and mathematics before turning to philosophy. Braithwaite was Knightbridge Professor of Moral Philosophy at Cambridge University. He served as the president of the Mind Association (1946) and of the Aristotelian Society (1946–1947). In the philosophy of science he made significant contributions on the nature of scientific theories and explanation, theoretical terms, models, foundations of probability and statistics, the justification of induction, and teleological explanations. He also wrote on subjects in moral and religious philosophy.

SCIENTIFIC THEORIES

Braithwaite defended the view that a scientific theory consists of a set of initial hypotheses, with empirically testable generalizations that follow deductively. To explain a generalization is to show that it is implied by higher level generalizations in the theory. Often, especially in the physical sciences, the initial postulates will contain so-called theoretical terms, such as *electron* or *field*, that refer to items not directly observable. To understand the meaning of such terms, as well as the logical structure of the theory, one must begin by considering the theory as a formal calculus; that is, as a set of uninterpreted formulas. A calculus designed to represent a specific theory will have to be interpreted, but not all at once and not completely: Meanings are directly given only to those formulas representing the lower order empirical generalizations, rather than to initial formulas containing theoretical terms. The latter are indirectly and partially interpreted by the former.

Braithwaite's major contribution here consisted in the detailed attention he devoted to the nature of the initial or "theoretical" postulates. He divided these postulates into Campbellian hypotheses, which contain only theoretical terms, and dictionary axioms, which relate theoretical terms to observational ones. The latter include identificatory axioms, which identify single observational terms with theoretical terms—for example, a color word with expressions referring to wavelengths of light. Braithwaite argued that the advantage of systems containing theoretical terms over those whose initial postulates are entirely observational is that the former can more readily be extended to new situations than can the latter. However, Braithwaite held there is no special advantage to Campbellian hypotheses, because, at least for certain systems, the same testable consequences can be derived from identificatory axioms.

Scientific models are to be construed as alternative interpretations of a theory's calculus where the theoretical concepts in the original theory (such as molecules) are interpreted as designating more familiar and intelligible items (such as billiard balls). Accordingly, the theory and the model are to be distinguished; and while a model is not essential, it can sometimes be of help in extending a theory and clarifying its concepts.

PROBABILITY AND INDUCTION

Braithwaite proposed a novel finite-frequency theory of probability. Consider the statement (P), "The probability of a child being born a boy is 0.51," and the observed data that among 1,000 children 503 are boys. Such a situation is to be understood by imagining 1,000 sets of children, each containing 100 children of whom 51 are boys, and a selection of 1 child from each of the 1,000 sets, of whom 503 are boys. Since P is logically consistent with any observed data, the problem is to decide when to reject P. For this purpose it is necessary to have a rule specifying that a probability statement is to be rejected if the observed relative frequency differs from the probability postulated by more than a specified amount. This amount is determined by extralogical considerations involving the purpose for which the hypothesis is to be used and the value attached to possible consequences of its adoption. Such a rejection rule, Braithwaite claimed, is what gives empirical meaning to probability statements considered as constituents of theoretical systems. But suppose there are alternative probability hypotheses not rejected by the evidence in accordance with this rule. How is one to choose among them? Here again considerations of value must be invoked, and Braithwaite outlined a "prudential policy" of choosing the probability hypothesis that maximizes the minimum mathematical expectation of value.

Braithwaite also provided an original defense of Charles Sanders Peirce's solution to the problem of justifying induction. The problem was formulated by Braithwaite as follows: What warrant does one have for adopting the policy of accepting a hypothesis on the basis of many positive instances (the policy of "induction by simple enumeration")? The proposed answer consists of the following argument (where π is the principle of induction by simple enumeration): The policy of using π has been effective in many instances in the past; therefore (using π as the rule of inference) π will continue to be effective. Such an argument was traditionally dismissed as viciously circular, and Braithwaite undertook to prove this charge unjustified. The argument can be deemed valid and hence free from circularity, he claimed, because it enables one to pass from a mere belief in the general effectiveness of using π as a rule of inference, with a reasonable belief in π's past effectiveness, to a reasonable belief in π's general effectiveness. It would be viciously circular only if one were required to have an initial reasonable belief in π's general effectiveness. Since this requirement is unnecessary, the argument is not invalidated.

MORAL AND RELIGIOUS PHILOSOPHY

Many of the conclusions and techniques of the philosophy of science were applied by Braithwaite in areas of moral and religious philosophy. Thus, just as one can defend the adoption of a particular scientific hypothesis by appeal to an inductive policy, so one can justify a particular action, such as returning a book, by reference to a moral policy, such as promise-keeping. Both sorts of policies are in turn justified by reference to the ends they subserve. Braithwaite showed how the mathematical theory of games, which he invoked in his discussion of hypothesis selection, can also be used to shed light on such notions as prudence and justice in situations involving human choices and cooperation between individuals. Finally, just as a moral assertion is to be construed as an expression of an intention to act in accordance with a certain policy, so a religious assertion must be understood, according to Braithwaite, as a declaration of adherence to a system of moral principles governing "inner life" as well as external behavior. The major difference between religious and moral assertions is that the former, being associated with empirical narratives, have a propositional element lacking in the latter.

See also Explanation; Game Theory; Induction; Knowledge and Belief; Peirce, Charles Sanders; Philosophy of Science, History of; Teleology.

Bibliography

Black, Max. Review of *Theory of Games as a Tool for the Moral Philosopher*. *Philosophical Review* 66 (1957): 121–124.

Hirst, R. J. Review of *Scientific Explanation*. *Philosophical Quarterly* 4 (1954): 351–355.

Russell, L. J. Review of *Scientific Explanation*. *Philosophy* 20 (1954): 353–356.

WORKS BY BRAITHWAITE

"Propositions about Material Objects." *Proceedings of the Aristotelian Society* 38 (1937–1938): 269–290.

"Teleological Explanation." *Proceedings of the Aristotelian Society* 47 (1946–1947): 1–20.

"Moral Principles and Inductive Policies." *Proceedings of the British Academy* 36 (1950): 51–68.

Scientific Explanation: A Study of the Function of Theory, Probability, and Law in Science. Cambridge, U.K.: Cambridge University Press, 1953.

An Empiricist's View of the Nature of Religious Belief. Cambridge, U.K.: Cambridge University Press, 1955a.

Theory of Games as a Tool for the Moral Philosopher. Cambridge, U.K.: Cambridge University Press, 1955b.

"Probability and Induction." In *British Philosophy in the Mid-Century: A Cambridge Symposium*, edited by Cecil Alec Mace. London: Allen and Unwin, 1957.

"Axiomatizing a Scientific System by Axioms in the Form of Identifications." In *The Axiomatic Method with Special*

Reference to Geometry and Physics, edited by Leon Henkin, Patrick Suppes, and Alfred Tarski, 429–442. Amsterdam: North-Holland, 1959.

"Models in Empirical Science." In *Logic, Methodology, and Philosophy of Science*, edited by Ernest Nagel, Patrick Suppes, and Alfred Tarski, 224–231. Stanford, CA: Stanford University Press, 1962.

WORKS ABOUT BRAITHWAITE

Coburn, Robert C. "Braithwaite's Inductive Justification of Induction." *Philosophy of Science* 28 (1961): 65–71.

Nagel, Ernest. "A Budget of Problems in the Philosophy of Science." *Philosophical Review* 66 (1957): 205–225.

Peter Achinstein (1967, 2005)

BRANDT, R. B.
(1910–1997)

Richard Booker Brandt was born on October 17, 1910, in Wilmington, Ohio. He graduated from Denison University in 1930 and received a second BA from Trinity College in Cambridge, U.K. After receiving a PhD in philosophy at Yale University in 1936, Brandt taught at Swarthmore College and then at the University of Michigan, where he was named Roy Wood Sellars Distinguished College Professor of Philosophy. Brandt was a fellow of the Guggenheim Foundation and of the Center for Advanced Studies in the Behavioral Sciences at Stanford University; he was also a senior fellow of the National Endowment for the Humanities and a member of the American Academy of Arts and Sciences.

For more than fifty years, Brandt addressed a broad spectrum of theoretical and applied issues in ethics, drawing on the natural and social sciences to enrich our understanding of morality. His empiricist orientation displayed itself early on in his *Hopi Ethics* (1954), which recorded his own anthropological studies undertaken during three summers spent on a Hopi reservation in the 1940s. It found full expression in *A Theory of the Good and the Right* (1979), which presented his mature metaethical ideas and reflected his close study of work in behavioral psychology.

Brandt was a prominent exponent of utilitarianism, the view that morally correct action is action that maximizes utility. His ideas about what utility is changed over the years. In *Ethical Theory* (1959), he adopted a pluralistic view that included pleasure, knowledge, virtue, and equality of welfare as intrinsic values. Soon, however, he came to see happiness and desire-satisfaction theories as the real contenders. He briefly defended a desire theory,

but by the time he wrote *A Theory of the Good and the Right*, he had evidently come to favor a happiness theory.

Brandt's most important contribution to normative ethics was his formulation and defense of an ideal rule utilitarianism, or "ideal moral code" theory. According to ideal rule utilitarianism, an act is right if and only if it would not be prohibited by the ideal moral code for a society. By an "ideal moral code," Brandt meant a code, the currency of which in a society would produce at least as much welfare or good per person as that of any other code. A moral code has currency in a society when a high proportion of adults in that society subscribe to its rules and recognize that those rules are accepted. The rules an ideal code comprises must be ones that people can learn and apply, so they cannot be too complex or too numerous. And because any set of rules will exact costs—in training, in guilt for noncompliance, and in restrictions on freedom—the rules should pertain only to important matters. Brandt recognized that the institutional rules of a society can give rise to obligations, even when existing institutions are less than optimal, and so institutional setting partly determines which moral code would produce the most good in the long run.

Brandt argued that ideal rule utilitarianism was distinct from act utilitarianism, because it need contain no higher-order rule prescribing that people maximize utility when lower-level rules conflict. So the two theories will differ in at least some of their implications. He also argued that whereas act utilitarianism seemingly implies that various immoral acts, like murdering one's aged parent, would be permissible if they could be kept secret, a moral code that sanctioned secret murders, say, would not maximize utility. Finally, because an ideal moral code would contain rules akin to W. D. Ross's prima facie duties, ideal rule utilitarianism can capture the personal character of morality, which Ross alleged that act utilitarianism misses.

Critics have questioned whether Brandt's ideal rule utilitarianism escapes the standard problems for rule utilitarianism, among them, that it is internally inconsistent, that it collapses into act utilitarianism, and that it cannot handle cases where others are not behaving as they ought. Critics have also questioned whether Brandt's theory can allow for moral appraisal of unique situations not covered by the rules, and whether moral rules lacking actual currency can plausibly provide the criterion of right acts. But at least one defender of an ideal-code consequentialism, Brad Hooker (2000), argues that a properly formulated theory can withstand such objections.

Later in his career, Brandt famously worked to resuscitate the metaethical theory known as ethical naturalism. He advocated a "method of reforming definitions," which involves redefining our ordinary vague ethical words in terms sufficiently clear and precise to render the traditional questions of moral philosophy empirically tractable. Following his proposed method, Brandt defined "rational" to refer to desires, actions, and moral systems that would survive maximal criticism and correction by facts and logic. He defined "good" to mean rationally desired, treating rational desires as those that would survive or be produced by "cognitive psychotherapy," a process in which persons represent to themselves repeatedly, in an ideally vivid way and at the appropriate time, all available relevant information. He defined "morally wrong" and "morally right" relative to the idea of a moral code that all fully rational persons would tend to support for a society in which they expected to spend a lifetime. Brandt argued that fully rational persons would opt for a broadly welfare-maximizing moral code, and that fully rational persons, insofar as they are benevolent, would seek to maximize not desire satisfaction but net lifetime enjoyment or happiness.

Brandt's critics have argued that his definitions foreclose important normative questions, such as whether it is rational to smoke even when the desire to smoke survives cognitive psychotherapy. They have questioned the coherence and empirical adequacy of appeals to full information, though such appeals remain common. They have also argued that his method begs the question against moral realism, and that his theory, like earlier forms of ethical naturalism, fails to capture the normativity of ethics. Ethicists continue to debate whether naturalism and moral realism are tenable. Whatever one concludes about Brandt's own views, his work played a crucial part in the late-twentieth-century revival of metaethics.

See also Consequentialism; Ethical Naturalism; Hedonism; Metaethics; Utilitarianism.

Bibliography

WORKS BY BRANDT

Hopi Ethics. Chicago: University of Chicago Press, 1954.

Ethical Theory. Englewood Cliffs, NJ: Prentice-Hall, 1959.

"Toward a Credible Form of Utilitarianism." In *Morality and the Language of Conduct*, edited by Hector-Neri Castañeda and George Nakhnikian. Detroit, MI: Wayne State University Press, 1965.

"Some Merits of One Form of Rule-Utilitarianism." In *Readings in Contemporary Ethical Theory*, edited by Kenneth Pahel and Marvin Schiller. Englewood Cliffs, NJ: Prentice-Hall, 1970.

A Theory of the Good and the Right. Oxford, U.K.: Clarendon Press, 1979.

Morality, Utilitarianism, and Rights. Cambridge, U.K.: Cambridge University Press, 1992.

Facts, Values, and Morality. New York: Cambridge, 1996.

WORKS ON BRANDT

Diggs, B. J. "A Comment on 'Some Merits of One Form of Utilitarianism.'" In *Readings in Contemporary Ethical Theory*, edited by Kenneth Pahel and Marvin Schiller. Englewood Cliffs, NJ: Prentice-Hall, 1970.

Hooker, Brad. *Ideal Code, Real World: A Rule Consequentialist Theory of Morality*. Oxford, U.K.: Clarendon Press, 2000.

Hooker, Brad, ed. *Rationality, Rules, and Utility: New Essays on the Moral Philosophy of Richard B. Brandt*. Boulder, CO: Westview Press, 1993.

Loeb, Don. "Full-Information Theories of Individual Good." *Social Theory and Practice* 21 (1995): 1–30.

Rosati, Connie S. "Brandt's Notion of Therapeutic Agency." *Ethics* 110 (2000): 780–811.

Rosati, Connie S. "Persons, Perspectives, and Full-Information Accounts of the Good." *Ethics* 105 (1995): 296–325.

Sobel, David. "Full Information Accounts of Well-Being." *Ethics* 104 (1994): 784–810.

Sturgeon, Nicholas. "Brandt's Moral Empiricism." *Philosophical Review* 91 (1982): 389–422.

Velleman, J. David. "Brandt's Definition of *Good*." *Philosophical Review* 97 (1988): 353–371.

Connie S. Rosati (2005)

BRENTANO, FRANZ
(1838–1917)

Franz Brentano, a German philosopher and psychologist, was the nephew of the poet Clemens Brentano and of the author Bettina von Arnim. He taught at Würzburg and at the University of Vienna. As a teacher he exerted extraordinary influence upon his students, among whom were Alexius Meinong, Edmund Husserl, Kasimierz Twardowski, Carl Stumpf, Tomas Masaryk, Anton Marty, Christian Ehrenfels, and Franz Hillebrand. Brentano became a Roman Catholic priest in 1864, was involved in the controversy over the doctrine of papal infallibility, and left the church in 1873. At his death he left behind voluminous writings and dictation (he was blind during the last years of his life) on almost every philosophical subject. Some of this material has since been published.

The most important of Brentano's works published during his lifetime is *Psychologie vom empirischen Standpunkt* (Leipzig, 1874). The two-volume second edition (Leipzig, 1911) includes revisions and supplementary material; the third edition, edited by Oskar Kraus, was published in Leipzig in 1925. The second edition includes *Von der Klassifikation der psychischen Phänomene*, which had also been published separately (Leipzig, 1911). The posthumously published *Vom sinnlichen und noetischen Bewusstsein*, also edited by Kraus (Leipzig, 1928), is referred to as Volume III of the *Psychologie*.

OBJECTS OF MENTAL PHENOMENA

Brentano took the mental to comprise such phenomena as hearing, seeing, sensing, thinking, judging, inferring, loving, and hating. He held that what is common to mental phenomena and what distinguishes them from the physical is "intentional inexistence," which he also described as "reference to a content" and "direction upon an object." Mental phenomena, he said, may be defined as phenomena that "include an object intentionally within themselves." He did not mean to imply, however, that when, for example, a person thinks of a horse, there is a duplicate of the horse, a mental simulacrum, existing within the mind. The essential point, as he later emphasized, is that a person could think of a horse even if there were no horse. In the second edition of the *Psychologie*, he contrasted strict relations with mental relations. *A* and *B* cannot be related in the strict sense of the term *relation* unless *A* and *B* exist; if one tree is to the left of another, then both trees exist. "But in the case of psychical relations the situation is entirely different. If someone thinks of something, then, although there must be a thinker, the thing that he thinks about need not exist."

Reference or "direction upon something" (*Gerichtet-sein*) thus is common and peculiar to what is mental, and Brentano classified mental phenomena in terms of the different ways in which they may refer to, or be directed upon, their objects. There are three ways in which one may be "intentionally" related to any object *A*. (1) One may think of *A*, or, as we sometimes say, have it "before the mind" or "present to consciousness." (2) One may take an intellectual stand with respect to *A*; this stand will consist either of accepting *A* or of rejecting *A*. (3) One may take an emotional stand with respect to *A*: This is a matter of loving or hating *A*, in a very broad sense of these terms. It is a matter of pursuit or avoidance, or, as one might now say, a matter of having a "pro-emotion" or an "anti-emotion" with respect to *A*. Brentano identified these three types of phenomena with (1) *Vorstellungen* (ideas, thoughts, or presentations); (2) judgments; (3) "emotive phenomena," or "phenomena of love and hate," a category including both emotions and volitions.

Ideas, or thoughts, are basic in that the other two types of mental phenomena presuppose them. In judging

that there is food, or in wanting it, one has ipso facto the thought of food. Nevertheless, judging is not simply a matter of "combining ideas"; if we combine the idea of gold and the idea of a mountain, we obtain not a judgment but another idea—that of a golden mountain. The members of the third class of mental phenomena, the "phenomena of love and hate," are like judging—and unlike the mere having of an idea—in that they involve an "opposition of intentional relation." We adopt toward the object of our idea an attitude of liking or disliking, love or hate.

There is still another respect in which the third class of phenomena is like the second and unlike the first. This is stated in Brentano's *Ursprung sittlicher Erkenntnis* (The origin of our knowledge of right and wrong; 1889).

> Concerning acts of the first class, none can be called either correct [*richtig*] or incorrect. In the case of the second class, on the other hand, one of the two opposed modes of relation, affirmation and rejection, is correct and the other incorrect. The same naturally holds good of the third class. Of the two opposed modes of relation, love and hate, being pleased and being displeased, one of them in every case is correct and the other incorrect.

This significant thesis is basic to Brentano's theory of knowledge and to his moral philosophy.

To judge, then, is to take an intellectual stand with respect to an object, and the object of the judgment is the same as the object of the idea that the judgment presupposes. If one judges that there are horses, the object of one's judgment is simply the object *horse*, which one thereby accepts, affirms, or acknowledges (*erkennt*); if one denies that there are horses, the object of one's judgment is again the object *horse*, which this time one denies or rejects (*leugnet*). In neither case does the judgment take as its object either a proposition or state of affairs or the type of entity that other philosophers have attempted to designate by such phrases as "the being of horses," "the nonbeing of horses," and "that there are horses."

This nonpropositional theory of judgment, which is fundamental to Brentano's theory of truth and his theory of categories, may be put schematically, in slightly oversimplified form, as follows. To judge that there are *A*'s is to accept (or affirm) *A*'s. To judge that there are no *A*'s is to reject (or deny) *A*'s. To judge that some *A*'s are *B*'s is to accept *AB*'s (*A*'s that are *B*'s), and to judge that no *A*'s are *B*'s is to reject *AB*'s. To judge that some *A*'s are not *B*'s, therefore, is to accept *A*'s that are non-*B*'s, and to judge that all A's are B's is to reject them. (Brentano noted, however, that the sentence "All A's are B's" is normally used to express a twofold judgment: the acceptance of A's that are B's and the rejection of A's that are non-B's.)

Brentano attempted to extend his theory to apply to so-called compound judgments. "He judges that there are A's and B's" presents no difficulty, since, according to Brentano's theory of categories, if A is a concrete object and B is a concrete object, then the collective consisting of just A and B is also a concrete object. The object of this conjunctive judgment is simply A-and-B, which the judger is said to accept. Brentano suggests two interpretations of "He judges that if there are A's, then there are B's." According to the first interpretation, the judger is said simply to reject A's-without-B's. The second interpretation is more complex, making use of the terms *true* and *apodictic*. (The latter term designates a mode of judgment. To reject A "apodictically" is, in effect, to reject the possibility of A; but Brentano explicated "possibility" in terms of "apodictic rejection," and not conversely.) If by "a correct A-acceptor" we mean a man who accepts A truly, or correctly, then the hypothetical judgment becomes: "He apodictically rejects judgers who are both correct A-acceptors and correct B-rejectors." The disjunctive judgment "He judges that either there are A's or there are B's" could then become "He apodictically rejects judgers who are both correct A-rejectors and correct B-rejectors."

The philosophical consequences of this nonpropositional theory of judgment are far-reaching. One consequence is an interpretation of Immanuel Kant's dictum that "existence" is not a predicate. According to Brentano, when we say that A exists, "it is not the conjunction of an attribute of 'existence' with 'A,' but 'A' itself which we affirm." The word *exists* is a synsemantic term that is used to express the act of judgment.

All of the doctrines set forth above fall within the province of what Brentano called descriptive psychology. Unlike experimental psychology—including genetic and physiological psychology—descriptive psychology, according to Brentano, is an exact science, capable of arriving at laws that hold true universally and not merely "for the most part." It is the basis for all philosophy and is even capable of providing a *characteristica universalis* of the sort that Gottfried Wilhelm Leibniz had conceived. Descriptive psychology is closely related to what Husserl was to call phenomenology. Husserl had studied with Brentano in Vienna from 1884 to 1886, when Brentano used the expression *beschreibende Phänomenologie* (descriptive phenomenology) as an alternative name for descriptive psychology. (Husserl later wrote that without Brentano's doctrine of intentionality, "phenomenology could not have come into being at all.") Brentano's conception of psychology has led some of his critics to accuse him of what Gottlob Frege and Husserl called psychologism. This accusation, however, does not take into account Brentano's theory of evidence and his moral philosophy, both of which he took to be branches of descriptive psychology.

MORAL PHILOSOPHY

Brentano's ethical views are set forth in *Ursprung sittlicher Erkenntnis* (Leipzig, 1889; 3rd ed., edited by Oskar Kraus, 1934), translated by Cecil Hague as *The Origin of Our Knowledge of Right and Wrong* (London, 1902), and in *Grundlegung und Aufbau der Ethik* (The basis and structure of ethics; edited by F. Mayer-Hillebrand, Bern, 1952). Brentano based his ethics upon the assumption that the members of the third class of mental phenomena, loving and hating, may be said to be correct or incorrect, just as judgments may be said to be correct or incorrect. To say that something, A, is good is to say that it is impossible to love A incorrectly; that is, it is apodictically to reject incorrect lovers of A. Analogously, to say that A is bad is apodictically to reject incorrect haters of A.

The only way to grasp the concept of correct emotion, according to Brentano, is to contrast actual cases of emotions that are "qualified as correct" with cases of emotions that are not. This is analogous to the way in which we understand, for example, what it is to be red and what it is to be colored. Thus we learn that knowledge is good, joy is good (unless it is joy in what is bad), every enrichment within the realm of ideas is good, love of the good is good, love of the bad is bad, and the right end in life is to choose the best among all attainable ends.

The correctness of loving and hating, like that of judging, is objective in that it is impossible for anyone to love correctly what anyone else hates correctly or to love incorrectly what anyone else hates incorrectly. Ethics must make use of the comparative concept *better than*, for which there is no analogue in the theory of knowledge. "A is better than B," according to Brentano, means that it is correct to prefer A, as an end, to B.

EVIDENCE AND TRUTH

Brentano's views on evidence and truth may be found in the posthumously published *Wahrheit und Evidenz* (edited by Oskar Kraus, Leipzig, 1930). The distinction between judging on the basis of evidence and judging "blindly" is not to be described in terms of instinct, feelings, degree of conviction, or impulse to believe. We arrive at the general concept of being evident, according to Brentano, in the same way we arrive at the concept of a correct emotion: by contemplating actual instances of the concept, in this case actual instances of evident judgments and of blind judgments.

Every evident judgment is either directly or indirectly evident; if a judgment is indirectly evident, its evidence is conferred, ultimately, by judgments that are directly evident. Directly evident judgments are of two kinds. First, there are the judgments of "inner perception," such as the judgments that I am now judging in a certain way, that I seem to see such-and-such, that I think I remember so-and-so. Second, there are judgments of reason or insights (*Einsichten*), such as the judgments that two things are more than one thing; that that which is red is, as such, other than that which is green; that there cannot be a triangle with four sides; or that a whole cannot exist if its parts do not exist.

Every judgment that is evident is true, but not every judgment that is true is evident. Most judgments of "outer perception" (of the external world), Brentano believed, are true, but all of them are "blind"; they are not evident. He argued, however, that the hypothesis of a three-dimensional external world, with its familiar details concerning physical bodies, has an "infinitely greater probability" than any of its alternatives. Judgments based on memory, too, are "blind"; but many of them confirm each other, and they are worthy of our confidence.

In *Wahrheit und Evidenz* Brentano characterized truth by reference to evidence: "Truth pertains to the judgment of the person who judges correctly … hence it pertains to the judgment of one who asserts what the person who judges with evidence would assert" (p. 139). In addition, to say that *A* exists is to say that anyone who judged about *A* with evidence would accept *A*, and to say that *A* does not exist is to say that anyone who judged about *A* with evidence would reject *A*. The "measure of all things," then, is the man who judges with evidence.

These statements, however, relating truth to evidence, do not give us the whole of Brentano's theory of truth. "Evident" is said to be predicate in the strict sense of the term, but "true" and "exists" are not, being only synsemantic. This brings us to Brentano's theory of categories.

THEORY OF CATEGORIES

The basic theses of Brentano's theory of categories may be stated as (1) there is nothing other than concrete particular things, and (2) every judgment is either the acceptance or the rejection of some concrete particular thing. "Concrete" must be taken as the opposite of "abstract" and not as a synonym for "physical." Human souls and God, according to Brentano, are concrete things but not physical things.

Our language seems to make reference to a great variety of *irrealia*—entities that are not concrete things. In fact, however, "the objects of our thought are never anything other than concrete things," and therefore for every sentence that is true and that seems to mention some nonconcrete thing, "one can form an equivalent in which the subject and predicate are replaced by something referring to a real thing" (*Psychologie*, Vol. II, p. 163). For example, "There is a lack of gold" becomes "There is no gold" (a rejection of gold); "He believes that there are horses" becomes "He accepts (affirms) horses"; and "Red is a color" becomes "A red thing is, as such, a colored thing." This latter translation is more effective in German—*Das Rotes ist als solches ein Farbiges*—where adjectives are readily transformed into nouns.

Many philosophically troublesome words, such as "exists," "good," "impossible," and "true," are synsemantic; their linguistic function is not that of referring to concrete things. "Exists" in "God exists," as we have noted, is used to express acceptance of God; "does not exist," analogously, is used to express rejection. "*A* is good" expresses an apodictic rejection of incorrect lovers of *A*. "*A* is impossible" expresses an apodictic rejection of evident acceptors of *A*—of judgers who accept *A* with evidence.

A true judgment, according to Brentano, is a judgment that cannot contradict an evident judgment. Thus "true," in "It is true that God exists," may be used to express apodictic rejection of evident rejectors of God. "It is not both true and false that God exists" may express apodictic rejection of collectives consisting of evident acceptors and evident rejectors of God. (He also noted that "true" may be used to express agreement and that, at times, it is simply redundant.) Brentano could thus be said to have an expressive theory of truth, but one that involves an objective—and not merely expressive—theory of evidence. His theories of existence and of the nature of goodness may be similarly described. Brentano's theory of categories contains important material on substance and accident, wholes and parts, the theory of relations, causation, and time and space that cannot be summarized here.

LOGIC

Brentano proposed the following revision of the theory of the syllogism on the basis of his theory of judgment. He wrote "All S are P" (A) as "There is no S which is a non-P"; "No S are P" (E) as "There is no S which is a P"; "Some S are P" (I) as "There is an S which is a P"; and Some S are not P" (O) as "There is an S which is a non-P." Since in this account both A and E are denials, and both I and O affirmations, Brentano was able to say that no affirmative judgment is universal and no negative judgment is particular. Barbara is written as "There is no M which is a non-P; there is no S which is a non-M; hence there is no S which is a non-P." And Ferio is written as "There is no M which is a P; there is an S which is an M; hence there is an S which is a non-P." Brentano was then able to formulate the doctrine of the syllogism in three rules, which may be confirmed by the two examples just cited.

> (1) Every categorical syllogism contains *four* terms, two of which are opposed to each other and the other two of which occur twice. (2) If the conclusion is negative, then each premise is negative and has a term in common with the conclusion. (3) If the conclusion is affirmative, then one premise will share its quality and contain one of its terms, and the other premise will have the opposite quality and contain the opposite of one of its terms. (*Psychologie*, Vol. II, p. 78)

The so-called weakened and strengthened moods, according to this account, are invalid. The subaltern inferences from A to I and from E to O fail, but all four propositions, if written in Brentano's notation, may be simply converted.

OTHER WRITINGS

Vom Dasein Gottes (On the existence of God; edited by Alfred Kastil, Leipzig, 1929), is a systematic theodicy in which Brentano appealed to the fact of contingency and the principle of sufficient reason, a principle that he believed to be logically necessary, in order to prove that there is a Necessary Being. He appealed to the evidence of design in order to prove that this Being is intelligent and good. Here, and in *Religion und Philosophie* (edited by F. Mayer-Hillebrand, Bern, 1954), he attempted to show that the soul is both spiritual and immortal. The subject of consciousness is said to be a nonspatial substance, forming no part of the physical body but capable of acting upon and being affected by the brain; it is created ex nihilo at the time of the conception of the body. Brentano defended the concept of creation ex nihilo by noting that whenever one calls an image to mind, one creates ex nihilo.

In *Versuch über die Erkenntnis* (Inquiry into the nature of knowledge; edited by Alfred Kastil, Leipzig, 1925) and *Grundlegung und Aufbau der Ethik*, Brentano argued that the assumption that there can be absolute chance is self-contradictory and that the thesis of indeterminism is incompatible with the existence of human responsibility. But we have "freedom of the will" in that we are able to bring about some of the things we desire to bring about and are able to deliberate and then to decide accordingly. Moreover, we can "will to will" in that, at any given time, there are things we can do that will affect our volitions at some later time.

According to *Die vier Phasen der Philosophie* (edited by Oskar Kraus, Leipzig, 1926), those periods in which philosophy flourishes tend to be followed by three phases of decline: the first phase is characterized by a transfer of interest from the theoretical to the practical, the second by a tendency toward skepticism, and the third by a relapse into mysticism. This was the pattern of Greek philosophy; in modern philosophy the period of John Locke, René Descartes, and Leibniz was followed by the Enlightenment, then by the skepticism of David Hume, and finally, according to Brentano, by the obscurities of Kant and the idealists who followed him.

See also Descartes, René; Ehrenfels, Christian Freiherr von; Enlightenment; Ethics, History of; Existence; Frege, Gottlob; Hume, David; Husserl, Edmund; Idealism; Intentionality; Kant, Immanuel; Leibniz, Gottfried Wilhelm; Locke, John; Logical Terms, Glossary of; Marty, Anton; Masaryk, Tomáš Garrigue; Meinong, Alexius; Propositions; Psychology; Stumpf, Karl; Twardowski, Kazimierz.

Bibliography

Brentano's historical writings include the following works on Aristotle: *Von der mannigfachen Bedeutung des Seienden nach Aristoteles* (Freiburg, 1862; republished Darmstadt, 1960), an important work that is the source of much of Brentano's later thought; *Die Psychologie des Aristoteles* (Mainz: Kirchheim, 1867); *Aristoteles Lehre vom Ursprung des menschlichen Geistes* (Leipzig: Veit, 1911); and *Aristoteles und seine Weltanschauung* (Leipzig: Quelle and Meyer, 1911). His *Geschichte der griechischen Philosophie*, edited by F. Mayer-Hillebrand (Bern: Francke, 1963), is compiled from the notes for his university lectures.

Brentano's other writings include *Untersuchungen zur Sinnespsychologie* (Leipzig: Dunker and Humblot, 1907); *Die Lehre Jesu und ihre bleibende Bedeutung*, edited by Alfred Kastil (Leipzig, 1922); *Grundzüge der Ästhetik*, edited by F. Mayer-Hillebrand (Bern: Franck, 1959); and *Aenigmatias*, 5th ed. (Bern, 1962).

Certain portions of the *Psychologie* are translated in *Realism and the Background of Phenomenology*, edited by R. M.

Chisholm (Glencoe, IL: Free Press, 1960); other translations are being prepared.

The most informative works on Brentano are Alfred Kastil, *Die Philosophie Franz Brentanos: Eine Einführung in seine Lehre* (Bern: Francke, 1951) and Oskar Kraus, *Franz Brentano: Zur Kenntnis seines Lebens und seiner Lehre* (Munich: Beck, 1919). The latter contains "Erinnerungen an Franz Brentano," by Carl Stumpf and Edmund Husserl. See also G. E. Moore, "Review of Franz Brentano, *The Origin of the Knowledge of Right and Wrong*," in *International Journal of Ethics* 14 (1903): 115–123.

Works published since this original entry was written in 1967 include the following:

The True and the Evident. Edited by Oskar Kraus. English ed. edited by Roderick M. Chrisholm. Translated by Roderick M. Chrisholm, Ilse Politzer, and Kurt R. Fischer. London: Routledge & K. Paul; New York: Humanities Press, 1966.

Die vier Phasen der Philosophie und ihr augenblichlicher Stand, nebst Abhandlungen über Plotinus, Thomas con Aquin, Kant, Schopenhauer und Auguste Comte, mit Anmerkungen, edited by Oskar Kraus. Hamburg: Meiner, 1968.

Über die Zukunft Philosophie; nebst den Vorträgen: Über die Gründe der Entmutigung auf philosophischem Gebiet, Über Schellings System, sowie den 25 Habilitationsthesen, edited by Oskar Kraus and Paul Weingartner. Hamburg: F. Meiner, 1968.

Vom sinnlichen und noetischen Bewusstsein. Aussere und innere Wahrnehmung, Begriffe. 2nd ed., edited by Oskar Kraus. Hamburg: Felix Meiner, 1968.

Kategoriënlehre. Mit Einleitung und Anmerkungen hrsg. von Alfred Kastel, edited by Alfred Kastel. Hamburg: Meiner, 1968.

The Origin of our Knowledge of Right and Wrong, edited by Oskar Kraus. English ed. edited by Roderick M. Chisholm. Translated by Roderick M. Chisholm and Elizabeth H. Schneewind. New York: Humanities Press, 1969.

The Foundation and Construction of Ethics. Compiled from His lectures on Practical Philosophy, edited by Franziska Mayer-Hillebrand. English ed. edited and translated by Elizabeth Hughes Schneewind. London: Routledge and Kegan Paul, 1973.

Psychology from an Empirical Standpoint, edited by Oskar Kraus. Translated by Antos C. Rancurello, D. B. Terrell, and Linda L. McAlister. English ed. edited by Linda L. McAlister. London: Routledge and Kegan Paul; New York: Humanities Press, 1973.

The Philosophy of Brentano, edited by Linda L. McAlister. London: Duckworth, 1976.

Philosophische Untersuchungen zu Raum, Zeit und Kontinuum. Hamburg: Meiner, 1976.

The Psychology of Aristotle: In Particular His Doctrine of the Active Intellect: With an Appendix concerning the Activity of Aristotle's God. Berkeley: University of California Press, 1977.

Aristotle and His World View, edited and translated by Rolf George and Roderick M. Chisholm. Berkeley: University of California Press, 1978.

Die Philosophie Franz Brentanos: Beiträge zur Brentano-Konferenz Graz, 4-8. September 1977, edited by Rocerick M. Chisholm and Rudolf Haller. Amsterdam: Rodopi, 1978.

Aristoteles Lehre vom Ursprung des menschlichen Geistes, edited by Rolf George. Hamburg: Meiner, 1980.

Geschichte der mittelalterlichen Philosophie im christlichen Abendland, edited by Klaus Hedwig. Hamburg: F. Meiner, 1980.

Sensory and Noetic Consciousness: Psychology from an Empirical Standpoint III, edited by Oskar Kraus. English ed. edited by Linda L. McAlister. Translated by Margarete Schättle and Linda L. McAlister. London: Routledge & Kegan Paul; New York: Humanities Press, 1981.

The Theory of Categories. The Hague; Boston: Martinus Nijhoff, 1981.

Deskriptive Psychologie, edited by Roderick M. Chisholm and Wilhelm Baumgartner. Hamburg: Meiner, 1982.

Brentano and Meinong Studies. Atlantic Highlands, NJ: Humanities Press, 1982.

Brentano and Intrinsic Value. Cambridge, U.K; New York: Cambridge University Press, 1986.

On the Existence of God: Lectures Given at the Universities of Würzburg and Vienna, 1868–1891, edited by Susan F. Krantz. Dordrecht; Boston: M. Nijhoff, 1987.

Brentano Studien: Internationales Jahrbuch der Franz Brentano Forschung / Franz Brentano Forschung; Franz Brentano Foundation. Würzburg: Röll, 1988.

Grundzüge der Ästhetik. 2nd ed., edited by Franziska Mayer-Hillebrand. Hamburg: F. Meiner, 1988.

Über Ernst Machs "Erkenntnis und Irrtum": mit zwei Anhängen, Kleine Schriften über Enrst Mach, Der Brentano-Mach-Briefwechsel. Amsterdam: Rodopi, 1988.

Philosophical Investigations on Space, Time, and the Continuum. London: New York: Croom Helm, 1988.

Clemens Brentano: Briefe 1803–1807: Textedition und Kommentierung. München: s.n., 1989.

Descriptive Psychology, edited and translated by Benito Müller. London; New York: Routledge, 1995.

The Four Phases of Philosophy. Amsterdam; Atlanta, GA: Rodopi, 1998.

Roderick M. Chisholm (1967)
Bibliography updated by Michael J. Farmer (2005)

BRIDGMAN, PERCY WILLIAM

(1882–1962)

An American physicist and professor of mathematics and natural philosophy at Harvard, Percy William Bridgman was awarded the Nobel Prize for physics in 1946 for his work on the properties of matter under extremely high pressures. He wrote at length on the philosophical implications of the discoveries of modern physics, particularly Albert Einstein's revolutionary special theory of relativity, and on the analysis of scientific concepts. To Bridgman it seemed that Einstein's theory arose chiefly from the application of sound conceptual analysis based on what Bridgman called the "operational point of view." In his opinion, Einstein had not shown "something new about nature"—he was "merely bringing to light implications already contained in the physical operations used in measuring time." Bridgman held that analysis shows that there exists no answer to the question of what we should do, what operations we could perform, in order to determine whether or not two distant events occurred simultaneously. Therefore, it is meaningless to speak of the two events as having or not having occurred simultaneously.

According to Bridgman, then, Einstein's work dramatically highlighted an important feature of scientific methodology, the determination to link all scientific concepts to experimental procedures. From the operationalist views implicit in the practices of working scientists, we should learn to undertake a rigorous analysis of all scientific concepts, cleansing science of operationally undefinable elements.

Bridgman disclaimed all intention of founding a new philosophical school, yet his name has become linked inseparably with operationalism. Many scientists have hailed Bridgman's ideas as indispensable to the correct understanding of modern science, and some, particularly psychologists, have urged the inauguration of an extensive program of analysis of scientific concepts along the lines laid down by Bridgman. Others have regarded Bridgman's philosophy as not only wrong, but also harmful—if it were imposed on science, it could stifle creative inquiry. Bridgman later claimed that each concept need not be completely definable in terms of performable instrumental operations, but that it is sufficient that a concept should be one "indirectly making connection with instrumental operations."

The controversy over operationalism diverted attention from Bridgman's numerous other ideas, many of which are original and provocative. Perhaps the most interesting is his view that discoveries in physics may help us to deal with problems in quite different domains. In his opinion, the great achievements in physics are discoveries of new ways in which our minds can master problems, discoveries about our conceptual makeup.

Through relativity physics, we have learned how apparent contradictions may arise through inadvertently admitting into science meaningless propositions that cannot stand up to operational analysis. Similarly, in human affairs seemingly irreconcilable demands of different groups may be eliminated by showing that some of the basic tenets on which the demands rest are meaningless. The methodology of the social sciences no doubt can learn much from the methodology of physics, but Bridgman's suggestion as to how human conflicts may be

resolved will strike many as overly optimistic and somewhat naive.

See also Einstein, Albert; Operationalism; Philosophy of Physics; Relativity Theory.

Bibliography

WORKS BY BRIDGMAN

The Logic of Modern Physics. New York: Macmillan, 1927.

The Nature of Physical Theory. Princeton, NJ: Princeton University Press, 1936.

Reflections of a Physicist. New York: Philosophical Library, 1950.

The Nature of Some of Our Physical Concepts. New York: Philosophical Library, 1952.

SECONDARY SOURCES

Cornelius, B. A. *Operationalism.* Springfield, IL, 1955.

Frank, Philipp. *The Validation of Scientific Theories.* Boston: Beacon, 1957.

G. Schlesinger (1967)

BRIGHTMAN, EDGAR SHEFFIELD
(1884–1953)

Edgar Sheffield Brightman was the leading American advocate of personalism. At Boston University he studied under Borden Parker Bowne, the first philosopher in America to develop the personalistic position. Brightman taught at Nebraska Wesleyan University (1912–1915), Wesleyan University (1915–1919), and from 1919 at Boston University, occupying the chair of Borden Parker Bowne professor of philosophy from 1925 until his death. He was president of the Eastern Division of the American Philosophical Association in 1936.

Brightman conceived of personalism as a mediating position in philosophy. As such, it for him superseded William James's pragmatism and Josiah Royce's absolute idealism, to each of which, in turn, he had been attracted early in his career. Brightman also held that personalism could resolve the impasse between supernaturalism and naturalism. Furthermore, although he criticized positivism for being too restricted an empiricism and although he eschewed much in existentialism, Brightman's personalism can be understood as an attempt to combine the surface experience (sense) of positivism and the depth dimension (value) of existentialism in a concept of the total person.

EPISTEMOLOGY

Brightman held firmly to an epistemic dualism of the "shining present" (immediate experience) and "the illuminating absent" (the referent). Constantly emphasizing that all primary data were present experiences, he advocated a radically empirical method; that is, a method that considers whatever is, at any time, present in consciousness. Since knowledge involves reference, it is always hypothetical and tentative. Brightman accepted this as a healthy probabilism (and not a destructive skepticism), because he found in the principle of coherence an adequate test of reference (or criterion of truth). Deeply influenced by Hegelian dialectic, he viewed coherence not as formal consistency but as a principle for interpreting experience: a statement or a set of statements is true to the extent that it organizes and orders experience.

ONTOLOGY

The metaphysical perspective that emerges is a pluralistic idealism. Reality is a society of persons: the ultimate (uncreated) Person and finite (created) persons. Reality is thus not nature but history. The natural order does not have ontological identity "outside" the ultimate Person; rather, this order is his "behavior." The laws of logic do not have privileged priority; they are constitutive of the supreme mind. In philosophy of religion, this position is idealistic theism (not theological dualism). God is a conscious Person who creates finite persons and cooperates with them in the cosmic endeavor. A human person is a context of experience capable of self-consciousness, reason, and ideal values.

EVIL

Brightman is probably most widely known for his controversial treatment of the problem of evil. He argued that the power of God is limited by nonrational conditions (the Given) within the divine nature that God's will neither created nor approves. God maintains constant and growing, though never complete, control of the Given.

See also Bowne, Borden Parker; Evil, The Problem of; James, William; Personalism; Royce, Josiah.

Bibliography

Brightman's chief works are *Introduction to Philosophy* (New York: Henry Holt, 1925; revised editions, 1951 and 1963, the latter edited by Robert N. Beck); *The Problem of God* (New York: Abingdon Press, 1930); *The Finding of God* (New York: Abingdon Press, 1931); *Moral Laws* (New York: Abingdon Press, 1933); *A Philosophy of Religion* (New York: Prentice-Hall, 1940); *Nature and Values* (New York: Abingdon-Cokesbury Press, 1945); *Person and Reality* (edited by Peter A. Bertocci in collaboration with Jannette E. Newhall and Robert S. Brightman [New York: Ronald Press, 1958]). A selected bibliography of his philosophical writings, including some 200 monographs and articles in addition to books, may be found in *Person and Reality,* pp. 367–370, or in the Brightman Memorial issue of *Philosophical Forum* 12 (1954): 22–28.

For references to discussions of Brightman's influence, see Peter A. Bertocci, "Edgar S. Brightman—Ten Years Later," in *Philosophical Forum* 20 (1962/1963): 3–10.

John H. Lavely (1967)

BROAD, CHARLIE DUNBAR
(1887–1971)

Charlie Dunbar Broad, the English epistemologist, historian of philosophy, moral philosopher, philosopher of science, and writer on the philosophical aspects of psychical research, was born at Harlesden, now a suburb of London. The only child of middle-class parents in comfortable circumstances, he received a good education at Dulwich College. With his special interest and ability in science and mathematics he won, in 1905, a science scholarship to Trinity College, Cambridge, with which Broad's philosophical career was to be chiefly associated. Despite success in his work at Cambridge, he became convinced that he would never be outstanding as a scientist and turned to philosophy, in which he took first-class honors with special distinction in 1910. A year later he was elected to a fellowship at Trinity because of a dissertation that became his first book, *Perception, Physics, and Reality* (Cambridge, U.K., 1914).

From 1911 to 1920 Broad was at the University of St. Andrews, first as assistant to G. F. Stout, the professor of logic and metaphysics, then as a lecturer at Dundee. During World War I, he combined his lecturing duties with work for the Ministry of Munitions in a chemical laboratory. He followed C. Lloyd Morgan in the chair of philosophy at the University of Bristol in 1920, but after a few years he returned to Trinity College to succeed J. M. E. McTaggart as lecturer in moral science. In 1933 Broad somewhat reluctantly became Knightbridge professor of moral philosophy. Until his retirement in 1953, Broad had not traveled outside Great Britain except for periodic visits to Scandinavia, in particular to Sweden, a country whose people, life, and language had long attracted him. Broad's encouragement of Swedish philosophers and philosophy led to his being generously honored by the academicians of that country. In Britain his services to philosophy were recognized by bestowal of most of the honors available to a don so secluded from public activity.

At Cambridge, Broad was most influenced by his teachers, McTaggart and W. E. Johnson, and by Bertrand Russell and G. E. Moore. These four men, with the important additions of Stout and A. E. Taylor at St. Andrews, represent in the diversity of their thought something of the extraordinary range of Broad's own interests. Among British philosophers of this century, no one, including Russell, published so much on so many different philosophical topics. The largest part of Broad's writing falls within the theory of knowledge and the philosophy of science—provided that we assign some of the problems of traditional metaphysics to these two fields—although he also wrote extensively, if less systematically, on ethics and on the life and thought of such scattered figures as Francis Bacon, Isaac Newton, Butler, and Immanuel Kant.

The ample scope and scale of Broad's work were displayed early in his career. Within his first three years of serious publication, he had produced almost two dozen reviews of widely different books, essays on "The Doctrine of Consequences in Ethics" (*International Journal of Ethics* 24 [April 1914]: 293–320) and "Lord Hugh Cecil's 'Conservatism'" (*International Journal of Ethics,* 23 [July 1913]: 396–418), a critical notice of Meinong's *Über Annahmen* (*Mind*, n.s., 22 [January 1913]: 90–102), and his own first volume, which discussed the relation between causation and perception. This catholicity of interest remained apparent for the next fifty years, despite Broad's confession in the autobiographical chapter of *The Philosophy of C. D. Broad* that some time after his acceptance of the Knightbridge chair he gave up philosophy in all but title and routine: "I no longer believed in the importance of philosophy, I took little interest in its later developments, and I knew very well that I at least had shot my bolt and had nothing further of value to contribute."

The most curious feature of this confession is that it makes the development of ennui coincide with a period of considerable publication by Broad. The 800 pages of the second volume of his *Examination of McTaggart's Philosophy* (Cambridge, U.K., 1933–1938) were written at this time, as were his essays on John Locke (*Hibbert Journal* 31 [January 1933]: 249–267) and Henry Sidgwick (ibid., 37 [October 1938]: 25–43), his inaugural lecture on determinism, a number of papers given to the Aristotelian Society, and a spate of notes on psychical phenomena. Broad's changed attitudes and feelings toward his chosen field had little substantial effect on the work he contributed to it.

THEORY OF KNOWLEDGE

Broad's writings on perception and knowledge, like the rest of his work, form neither a system nor a set of unequivocal answers to a group of related questions. For every philosophical position there were always reasons pro and con; and on any given issue Broad often found it difficult to decide where the weightier reasons lay.

SENSE DATA. Thus, following Stout, and ultimately Locke, in distinguishing between the odors, noises, and colored patches that we sense and the physical objects like coins and books that we perceive, Broad gave rather cautious support to a version of the causal theory of perception. There are, he thought, two kinds of particulars involved in perception—persistent substances (bodies) with properties like shape, size, inertial mass, and spatial position; and the "sense-qualified occurrents" of which we are immediately aware in sensing, as when we see the upper surface of a dinner plate. Broad argued that visual sense data, or *sensa* as he called them, at least are never, in fact, identical with, or parts of, the surface of the physical object that is seen. If we recall that the sense data obtained by a given person in looking at the same surface from different positions and angles form a continuous series, and that the velocity of light is finite, it is reasonable to believe that at least some of the properties of sense data must be different from those of their correlated bodies, that a penny, for example, retains the same size and shape while our sense data of it change in these respects as we alter position. The greater the distance between our eyes and the body seen, the more obvious it is that the properties of the body and of our sense data must differ.

It is likewise reasonable that if this difference sometimes holds, it must always hold; for there is no gap in the continuity of conditions in which we obtain sense data of a particular surface that would allow us to identify only some of the sense data with that surface. As underpinning for this sharp distinction, Broad tried to establish that a sense datum must have all the properties that it is sensed as having, although it may also have unnoticed properties; that unsensed sense data can exist; and that the word *sensation* refers both to bodily feelings and to "genuine sensations," the former of which are not, although the latter are, analyzable into an act of sensing and its object, the sense datum.

In general, Broad treated these claims about the existence and properties of sense data as being empirical ones, and so was led to a similar treatment of such questions as: Are sensa qualitatively mind-dependent? Can two people sense the same sensum? How long can a sensum last? Do we infer from the properties of our sensa to the properties of physical objects? How much resemblance is there between the properties of sensa and the properties of physical objects? In his "Reply to Critics," written late in his career, Broad indicated that he did not feel the force of the view, made familiar by G. A. Paul and A. J. Ayer, that these questions can be answered only by decisions in particular cases or else are misconceived, since the sense-data theory is simply an elaborate terminological proposal for dealing with the argument from illusion. Nor did he recognize the radical criticism that this view offered of his own attempts to deal with sense data as private objects interposed between human observers and the unobservable physical world. The latter is the "remote causal ancestor" of our sensations, he thought, and the kind of isomorphism one must postulate between the properties of sense data and the properties of "the hypothetical system of physical things and events" he was "willing to leave to experts to decide."

THE MIND-BODY PROBLEM. In his discussion of the mind-body problem, Broad set out to produce a theory that would account for the apparent fact that brain events are a necessary condition of mental events, and also leave open the possibility that some mental events occur after the death of their associated bodies. He suggested that minds are the result of two components—a nervous system, and a "psychogenic factor," which is modified by experience and capable of persisting after bodily death. Since no other properties are assigned to the psychogenic factor, nor is its relation to the brain described, the factor remains unobservable, either directly or indirectly; and the parent theory is obviously ad hoc. Broad would have welcomed a theory that was more open to experimental testing; although he distinguished metaphysical from scientific theories by the latter's susceptibility to such testing. He was thus in the position of answering the philosophical question, How are bodies related to minds? with what was, by his own criteria, an inadequate scientific theory. Just as he took sense data to be private objects whose properties could be investigated by introspection, so he took the mind-body relation as being similar to the relation between a visible body and an invisible one—a relation open in theory, if not in practice, to empirical investigation.

GENERAL EXPLANATORY PRINCIPLES. Closely related to this treatment of philosophical problems was Broad's attempt, throughout his writings, to isolate a set of very general principles that would be both necessarily true and genuinely explanatory of the most pervasive and important features of the world. Broad was not convinced either that every necessarily true statement is analytic or that every synthetic statement is testable by means of perceptual experience. He thought that there might well be propositions, such as "The cause of any change contains a change as an essential factor," which are synthetic—informative about the world—but necessarily true. The denial of this proposition is not self-contradictory, so the proposition cannot be analytic; yet a counterexample is impossible to imagine, so the proposition, rather than being an ordinary empirical one, is self-evidently true. Propositions as general as this, Broad half suggested, are the appropriate axioms of metaphysical theories, theories whose results he compared unfavorably to the "beautiful and surprising consequences" deduced from the premises of geometry and such physical premises as the "entropy principle." Broad's pessimism about the utility of deductive metaphysics seems to have been the outcome of a desire to treat speculative philosophy as a suprascience, one that accounted for our most general concepts, such as cause, substance, potentiality, and actuality, in much the same way that physics accounted for such less general concepts as velocity, mass, simultaneity, and the atom.

A PRIORI CONCEPTS. This distinction between the concepts dealt with by the sciences and those more general ones dealt with by philosophy has its parallel, and perhaps its source, in the distinction drawn by Broad between empirical and a priori (nonempirical) concepts. He believed that the simplest empirical concepts, for example, the ideas of red or yellow, are formed by our contrasting and comparing many different red or yellow objects. Eventually, we abstract the required quality from all other qualities and from any particular substance in such a way that we are able to think of the quality in the absence of any instance or image of it. In thus accepting the traditional story of the genesis of empirical concepts, Broad hesitated between the two equally ancient views of how we form a priori concepts. The first view is that we have innate dispositions to form specific ideas like those of cause, substance, and rightness as the result of having certain kinds of experiences. The second is that we have "a general power of non-perceptual intuition," distinct from our ability to have sense perceptions and to introspect, which allows us to intuit such relations as causation and rightness whenever we have the appropriate kinds of experiences to stimulate the power.

A standard criticism of these theories of concept formation is that the story about abstraction is logically circular; and that the accounts of a priori concepts apply equally well or little to empirical ones, so that Broad's distinction between the two cannot be drawn. The abstraction story is circular because in order to compare and contrast one color with another we must already have the ability to recognize and distinguish those colors. Yellow objects that are to be compared must be seen as yellow before the suggested procedure can begin. Hence, we can rightly claim that innate ideas or nonempirical intuitions are needed for the concept of yellow as they are for concepts like that of substance.

However, thinking of an absent quality yellow is not the intellectual analogue of sensing a yellow patch, for thinking of yellow is not a matter of "contemplating the characteristic" yellow, as Broad once assumed it was. Noting the logically necessary relations between concepts, for example, that all yellow things must be colored, is not like having a sense datum and noting that in it a red patch borders on a yellow patch. Granting these two points, as Broad did in his "Reply to Critics," would make it less plausible to hold that some synthetic propositions may be necessarily true. For once we abandon the sense-datum picture of logical necessity, there is little temptation to appeal to self-evidence (the intellectual sensing of universal connections) in support of metaphysical principles.

PSYCHICAL RESEARCH

Broad often urged philosophers to take something of his own keen interest in psychical research. He claimed that no one could answer the question as to whether any person actually has the power of paranormal precognition without having made a careful study of the available evidence; but most philosophers obviously considered this to be a scientific task for psychologists. In the absence of any encouragement from scientists, few philosophers would join Broad in discussing the further question, which chiefly interested him, How does the existence of supernormal precognition affect such philosophical topics as causation, the mind-body problem, immortality, and sense perception? Suppose we took seriously the suggestion that each person has an extended but intangible and invisible body as well as his ordinary body and that the invisible body puts forth pseudopods that touch and affect external objects. The existence of such a body would certainly alter a number of our views on topics like causation and the mind-body problem. But exactly how they were altered would depend on such factors as the degree of control we could exert over our invisible bodies,

whether they survived our corporeal bodies, and what sort of knowledge we could have of our intangible bodies.

Thus until there is scientific agreement on what has been established concerning paranormal cognition, it is difficult to say how its existence would affect philosophical discussion. What can undoubtedly be done is to consider whether the notion of supernormal precognition is logically coherent. Broad thought that it is and tried to rebut arguments that it is self-contradictory to speak of precognizing something that does not yet exist as well as arguments that paranormal precognition makes an effect precede its cause—correctly guessing a card symbol would be influenced by what is to be known later about the card. However, showing that paranormality is logically possible does nothing to advance its claims over alternative hypotheses in the explanation of unlikely experimental data, data that may be unlikely because of selective sampling alone.

PROBABILITY AND INDUCTION

Although Broad's two papers titled "Induction and Probability" gave what will probably be a definitive expression to their point of view, they were overshadowed by the simultaneous appearance of J. M. Keynes's *A Treatise on Probability*. In much the same way, Broad's *Scientific Thought* (London, 1923)—perhaps his best book—was neglected after the publication, a few years later, of Russell's *The Analysis of Matter*. Broad argued that the degree of belief we give to well-established inductions cannot be justified "by any known principle of probability unless some further premise about the physical world be assumed." Yet this premise is notoriously difficult to state. If induction is to be a rational procedure, nature must consist of a few kinds of substances that combine in various lawlike ways and thus produce variety in a finite world. In brief, we need Keynes's principle of limitation of independent variety. Without such a principle we cannot make use of inductive analogies, for they assume that future cases will resemble past cases, or in other words, that no one object has an infinite number of independent qualities or is producible by an infinite number of different causes. In "The Principles of Problematic Induction" (*PAS*, n.s., 28 [1927–1928]: 1–46), Broad went on to consider, and answer affirmatively, the question whether we can know that nature has this desirable structure.

Thus, Broad held that the problem of justifying inductive inferences is a genuine one. He thought that the two questions, What is meant by calling this inductive belief well-supported? and What makes induction a valid procedure? have similar answers. Each question requires us to state the criteria by which we can distinguish sound from unsound inferences, and these criteria will enable us to provide the necessary and sufficient conditions for well-grounded inferences. Such conditions must in turn be based on fundamental principles that will serve as general premises in every sound inductive inference. This last step of Broad's claim has been much criticized as confusing two quite different issues. The first concerns the empirical statement, for which there is ample evidence, that nature is so organized that in the future at least some of our inductive beliefs will be correct. The second concerns the logically necessary truth that induction is a rational procedure; for we could not have an inductive policy that was both successful and irrational, that is, not supported by good evidence. What we mean by "rational inductive procedure" is one that is well supported by evidence. It is this support that "justifies" the policy in the only permissible sense of "justify." The structure of nature is known inductively and so cannot itself be referred to for support of the inductive procedure; nor is there any need to do so. The only justification we require is the success of the policy, and that we already have.

ETHICS

On the problems of ethics, Broad showed a cautious hesitancy to commit himself. Two of his late papers, "Some Reflections on Moral-Sense Theories in Ethics" (*PAS*, n.s., 45 [1944–1945]: 131–166) and "Some of the Main Problems of Ethics" (*Philosophy* 21 [July 1946]: 99–117), have been widely read; but they provide only hints as to Broad's own views. As in the early chapters of *Five Types of Ethical Theory* (London 1920), on such writers as Benedict de Spinoza and David Hume, Broad classified types of ethical theories, exposed their assumptions, and drew out their logical implications, without committing himself. For example, in his paper on moral-sense theories he distinguished three analyses of "That act is right": The sentence does not express the speaker's judgment, but his emotions or desires or commands; what is expressed is a judgment about "certain human experiences, certain sensations or emotions or desires," that is, a "moral feeling"; and a judgment is made that ascribes a property like "what it is fitting to approve" or "conducive to social stability," properties independent of the speaker's opinions, desires, or feelings.

In his "Reply to Critics" Broad said that theories of the second and third types must admit the existence both of nonempirical concepts of moral attributes and of synthetic a priori propositions like "any act of promise-breaking tends as such to be wrong." Since he was not convinced that there were no such concepts and propositions, he was able to sympathize with theories of these types, as well as with theories of the first type. But to the question, does "That act is right" express a judgment, a feeling, or a command? Broad could only reply, "I have no definite opinion." He was similarly undecided on the question whether ethical terms such as *wrong* and *duty* stand for properties, and if so, exactly what sort of properties these might be. His attitude here, as to many other philosophical problems, resembled that of a prudent scientist awaiting further evidence before coming to a decision.

Broad had no "philosophy" in the sense of a deeply original way of interpreting and dealing with the issues of his field. He was a scientist manqué who took up philosophical problems much as he found them, leaving them classified and more manageable but not transformed. His impressive ability to understand and recast the most difficult arguments, the elegance of his writing, his unrivaled thoroughness and lucidity, were placed at the service of other people's questions rather than his own.

See also Ayer, Alfred Jules; Bacon, Francis; Ethics, History of; Hume, David; Induction; Innate Ideas; Kant, Immanuel; Keynes, John Maynard; Locke, John; McTaggart, John McTaggart Ellis; Meinong, Alexius; Mind-Body Problem; Moore, George Edward; Newton, Isaac; Parapsychology; Precognition; Probability and Chance; Russell, Bertrand Arthur William; Sensa; Sidgwick, Henry; Spinoza, Benedict (Baruch) de; Stout, George Frederick; Taylor, Alfred Edward.

Bibliography

Broad's other books include *The Mind and Its Place in Nature* (London: Kegan Paul, 1925), his most characteristic work, and *Lectures on Psychical Research* (London: Routledge, 1963). Some of his essays have been collected in two volumes, *Ethics and the History of Philosophy* (London: Routledge, 1952) and *Religion, Philosophy, and Scientific Research* (London: Routledge, 1953). His two papers titled "Induction and Probability" appeared in *Mind* 27 (1918): 389–404 and 29 (1920): 11–45. There is a complete bibliography up to 1959 in *The Philosophy of C. D. Broad*, edited by P. A. Schilpp (New York: Tudor, 1959), which also contains 21 essays on his work by various philosophers, Broad's "Reply to Critics," and his "Autobiography." A critical examination of Broad's theory of perception is given in Martin Lean, *Sense Perception and Matter* (London: Routledge and Kegan Paul, 1953).

OTHER RECOMMENDED WORKS BY BROAD

The Nature of Existence (1921), edited by John McTaggart Ellis McTaggart. Northampton: John Dickens, 1968.

Induction, Probability, and Causation: Selected Papers. New York: Humanities, 1968.

Broad's Critical Essays in Moral Philosophy, edited by David Ross Cheney. London: Allen and Unwin; New York: Humanities Press, 1971.

Ethics. Edited by Casimir Lewy. Dordrecht; Boston: M. Nijhoff; Hingham, MA: Kluwer, 1985.

Robert Brown (1967)
Bibliography updated by Michael J. Farmer (2005)

BROUWER, LUITZEN EGBERTUS JAN
(1881–1966)

Luitzen Egbertus Jan Brouwer, the founder of mathematical intuitionism, was born in 1881 in Overschie, near Rotterdam, the Netherlands. After attending schools in Medemblik, Hoorn, and Haarlem, he studied mathematics at the Municipal University of Amsterdam. He obtained his doctorate in 1907 for his thesis, *Over de Grondslagen der Wiskunde* (Amsterdam and Leipzig, 1907). He became *privaat-docent* at Amsterdam in 1909 and served as professor there from 1912 until his retirement in 1955. In the year that he became a professor he was elected to the Royal Dutch Academy of Sciences.

Besides contributions to the foundations of mathematics, Brouwer made major contributions to other areas of mathematics, in particular to topology, in which his most important publications date from the period 1909–1913. Combinatorial or algebraic topology came into being through discoveries of Henri Poincaré in the 1890s. A fundamental technique of Poincaré was to analyze figures into combinations of simple figures and to represent the topological structure of the figures by algebraic properties of the combination. Brouwer extended and deepened this technique, particularly in relation to questions of the existence of mappings and fixed points. He proved such classic results as the topological invariance of dimension, which implies that there is no bicontinuous one-to-one mapping of Euclidean m-dimensional space onto Euclidean n-dimensional space, for $m \neq n$.

Although he was primarily a mathematician, Brouwer was always preoccupied with general philosophy and had elaborated a highly individual philosophical vision. Indeed, the most remarkable feature of Brouwer's work in the foundations of mathematics was the boldness and consistency with which, starting from his own philosophical position, he questioned the principles on which the mathematics he inherited was based, down to so elementary a principle as the law of excluded middle, and then proceeded to criticize these principles in detail and to begin to reconstruct mathematics on a basis he regarded as sound.

Although he later presented them more systematically, the essentials of Brouwer's philosophy were already present in his thesis of 1907 and, in certain respects, in *Leven, Kunst, en Mystiek* (Delft, 1905). These works antedate the decisive steps in the development of mathematical intuitionism. In effect, Brouwer argued in his thesis that logic is derivative from mathematics and dependent for its evidence on an essentially mathematical intuition that rests on a basis close to Immanuel Kant's notion of time as the "form of inner sense." Intellectual life begins with "temporal perception," in which the self separates experiences from each other and distinguishes itself from them. Brouwer describes this temporal perception as "the falling apart of a life moment into two qualitatively different things, of which the one withdraws before the other and nonetheless is held onto by memory" ("Weten, Willen, Spreken," 1933). This perception, however, belongs to an attitude (which Brouwer earlier termed "mathematical consideration") that the self adopts to preserve itself; the adoption of this attitude is an act of free will, in a broad sense that Brouwer probably derived from Arthur Schopenhauer. The fundamental intuition of mathematics is this structure of temporal perception "divested of all content"; in mathematics one sees that the process of division and synthesis can be iterated indefinitely, giving rise to the series of natural numbers. In the temporal order thus revealed, one can always imagine new elements inserted between the given ones, so that Brouwer could say that the theories of the natural numbers and of the continuum come from one intuition, an idea that, from his point of view, was made fuller and more precise by his theory of free choice sequences, although one might argue that it was made superfluous by that theory.

Brouwer's constructivism was developed in this context. His constructivism was probably motivated less by an insistence on absolute evidence and a rejection of hypotheses (which might have led to "finitism" in David Hilbert's sense of the term or even to a still narrower thesis) than by Brouwer's subjectivism and his insistence on the primacy of will over intellect. On these grounds, mathematics should consist in a constructive mental activity, and a mathematical statement should be an indication or report of such activity. Brouwer credited this way of looking at mathematics to the inspiration of his teacher, Gerrit Mannoury.

In his thesis Brouwer limited himself to criticizing alternative theories of the foundations mathematics and to criticizing Cantorian set theory, but in "De Onbetrouwbaarheid der Logische Principes" (1908), perhaps urged on by Mannoury, Brouwer raised doubts about the validity of the law of excluded middle, although he still regarded the question as open. In *Intuitionisme en Formalisme* (1912) Brouwer did not say flatly that the law of excluded middle is false, but he gave an instance of his standard argument, an example like that presented in the section on intuitionism in the entry titled "Mathematics, Foundations of," which also gives a fuller exposition of constructivism.

In a number of publications beginning in 1918 and extending through the 1920s, Brouwer developed intuitionist mathematics and worked out in detail his critique of classical mathematics, determining for different branches of mathematics which of their theorems are intuitionistically true. In "Begründung der Mengenlehre unabhängig vom logischen Satz vom ausgeschlossenen Dritten," Brouwer undertook to develop an intuitionist set theory, on which a theory of the continuum could be based. In this work he introduced his concept of set (*Menge*; later, in "Points and Spaces," 1954, he called it "spread") and therefore the idea of an arbitrary infinite sequence as generated by successive free choices. He also introduced the notion of species, which led to his own version of a predicative hierarchy of classes. The principle that the value of a function everywhere defined on a spread must, for a given sequence as argument, be determined by a sufficiently large finite number of its terms is already present in "Begründung der Mengenlehre." This "continuity axiom" is the first of the two distinctive principles of intuitionist analysis.

In "Beweis, dass jede volle Funktion gleichmässig stetig ist" (1924), Brouwer announced a proof that a function everywhere defined on the closed unit interval is uniformly continuous. In this proof Brouwer used two fundamental assertions about spreads, later called the bar and fan theorems. The bar theorem, or an equivalent assertion, constitutes the other distinctive principle of intuitionist analysis. Brouwer's proof was presented in full in "Über Definitionsbereiche von Funktionen" (1927) and reworked, in a more general setting, in "Points and Spaces."

After World War II Brouwer published a long series of short papers in which he developed a new type of counterexample to classical theorems, based on another new principle.

Brouwer's philosophy is not limited to what is relevant to the foundations of mathematics. Mathematical consideration has a second phase, which he called causal attention. In this phase "one identifies in imagination certain series of phenomena with one another," an operation by which one can pick out objects and postulate causal rules. (The relation between temporal perception and causal attention is analogous to that between Kant's mathematical and dynamical categories.) The whole point of mathematical consideration lies in the fact that it makes possible the use of means: One produces a phenomenon that will be followed in a certain repeatable series by a desired phenomenon that cannot be directly reproduced. This makes the pursuit of instinctual satisfaction more efficient.

Especially in *Leven, Kunst, en Mystiek* and in "Consciousness, Philosophy, and Mathematics" (1948), Brouwer regards this "mathematical action" as a kind of fall from grace, whose results are uncertain and ultimately disappointing. With this view he couples a pessimism about society. Society is based on communication, which is itself a form of mathematical action. What is ordinarily called communicating one's thoughts actually amounts to influencing the actions of another, although sometimes a deeper communication of souls is approached. Brouwer, however, was not always aloof from all efforts at social reform, as is shown by his participation, immediately after World War I, with the poet Frederik van Eeden, Mannoury, and others, in the Signific Circle, whose original goal, inspired by the abuses of propaganda during the war, was a far-reaching reform of language.

See also Hilbert, David; Intuitionism and Intuitionistic Logic; Kant, Immanuel; Mathematics, Foundations of; Number; Poincaré, Jules Henri; Schopenhauer, Arthur.

Bibliography

ADDITIONAL WORKS BY BROUWER

"De Onbetrouwbaarheid der Logische Principes." *Tijdschrift Voor Wijsbegeerte* 2 (1908): 152–158. Reprinted in *Wiskunde, Waarheid, Werkelijkheid.*

"Die Theorie der endlichen kontinuerlichen Gruppen." *Mathematische Annalen* 69 (1910): 181–202.

"Beweis der Invarianz der Dimensionenzahl." *Mathematische Annalen* 70 (1911): 161–165.

"Über Abbildung von Mannigfaltigkeiten." *Mathematische Annalen* 71 (1912): 97–115.

Intuitionisme en Formalisme. Amsterdam, 1912. Reprinted in *Wiskunde, Waarheid, Werkelijkheid.* Translated by A. Dresden as "Intuitionism and Formalism." *Bulletin of the American Mathematical Society* 20 (1913): 81–96. Reprinted, with other writings by Brouwer, in *Philosophy of Mathematics: Selected Readings,* edited by Paul Benacerraf and Hilary Putnam. Englewood Cliffs, NJ: Prentice-Hall, 1964.

"Über den naturlichen Dimensionsbegriff." *Journal für die reine und angewandte Mathematik* 142 (1913): 146–152.

"Begründung der Mengenlehre unabhängig vom logischen Satz vom ausgeschlossenen Dritten." *Verhandelingen der Koninklijke Nederlandse Akademie van Wetenschappen,* Series A, 12 (1918–1919), Nos. 5 and 7.

Wiskunde, Waarheid, Werkelijkheid. Groningen: P. N. Noordhoff, 1919.

"Besetzt jede reele Zahl eine Dezimalbruchentwicklung?" *Mathematische Annalen* 83 (1921): 201–210.

"Begründung der Funktionenlehre unabhängig vom logischen Satz ausgeschlossenen Dritten." *Verhandelingen der Koninklijke Nederlandse Akademie van Wetenschappen,* Series A, 13 (1923), No. 2.

"Über die Bedeutung des Satzes vom ausgeschlossenen Dritten in der Mathematik, insbesondere in der Funktionentheorie." *Journal für die reine und angewandte Mathematik* 154 (1924): 1–7. Translated in *From Frege to Gödel: A Source Book in Mathematical Logic, 1879–1931,* edited by John van Heijenoort. Cambridge, MA: Harvard University Press, 1965.

"Beweis, dass jede voile Funktion gleichmässig stetig ist." *Koninklijke Nederlandse Akademie van Wetenschappen, Proceedings.* Series A, 27 (1924): 189–194 (cf. the remarks in ibid., 644–646).

"Zur Begründung der intuitionistischen Mathematik." *Mathematische Annalen* 93 (1924): 244–257; 95 (1926): 453–473; 96 (1927): 451–489.

"Über definitionsbereiche von Funktionen." *Mathematische Annalen* 97 (1927): 60–75. Translated in van Heijenoort.

"Weten, Willen, Spreken." *Euclides* 9 (1933): 177–193.

"Synopsis of the Signific Movement in the Netherlands." *Synthese* 5 (1946): 201–208.

"Address to Prof. G. Mannoury." *Synthese* 6 (1947): 190–194.

"Consciousness, Philosophy, and Mathematics," in *Proceedings of the Tenth International Congress of Philosophy.* Amsterdam, 1949. Vol. II, pp. 1235–1249. Last section of this paper reprinted in Benacerraf and Putnam.

"Historical Background, Principles, and Methods of Intuitionism." *South African Journal of Science* 49 (1952): 139–146.

"Points and Spaces." *Canadian Journal of Mathematics* 6 (1954): 1–17.

WORKS ON BROUWER AND INTUITIONISM

Heyting, Arend. *Les Fondements des mathématiques. Intuitionnisme. Théorie de la démonstration.* Paris: Gauthier-Villars, 1955. Expanded version of German original, *Mathematische Grundlagenforschung. Intuitionismus. Beweistheorie.* Berlin: J. Springer, 1934.

Heyting, Arend. *Intuitionism: An Introduction.* Amsterdam: North-Holland, 1956. This work by Heyting, and the one

above, contain the most comprehensive bibliographies on intuitionism.

Charles Parsons (1967)

BROUWER, LUITZEN EGBERTUS JAN [ADDENDUM]

Luitzen Egbertus Jan Brouwer was one of the first to clearly distinguish between language and metalanguage, as well as to distinguish between mathematics and metamathematics. Published in his dissertation from 1907—written in Dutch—these ideas did not disseminate quickly, although they soon found fertile ground when Brouwer explained them to David Hilbert on the beach of Scheveningen, Holland, in 1909.

Brouwer also had conversations with Ludwig Wittgenstein (Vienna, 1928), Edmund Husserl (Amsterdam, 1928), and Kurt Gödel (Princeton, New Jersey, 1953). These conversations may equally have been of philosophical interest, but little seems to be known about their actual contents.

Throughout his life, Brouwer explored a deep interest in the history and practice of mysticism, yet this had no effect on the content of intuitionistic mathematics. In fact, in Brouwer's view, not to engage in even the simplest mathematics is a necessary condition for obtaining mystical insight, and the other way around. He reasoned that, whereas mathematics comes into being with the perception of a move of time, abolishing that perception is a necessary condition for the return of consciousness to its "deepest home" (Brouwer 1975, p. 480).

A note by Brouwer in the margin of an offprint (kept in the Brouwer archive, Utrecht, Holland) of his 1928 lecture "The Structure of the Continuum" (Brouwer 1975, pp. 429–440) shows that he held that the introduction of choice sequences did not make the intuitive continuum dispensable: "the continuum is still the result of the Ur-intuition." One can make do with just the choice sequences as far as the mathematical modeling of the continuum is concerned, but from a philosophical point of view, its intuitive givenness remains: Continuity and discreteness are mutually dependent and irreducible polarizations of the fundamental intuition of mathematics.

While from the beginning of his career Brouwer had combined mathematical and philosophical work, it was upon the theft of his mathematical notebook from a tram in Brussels, Belgium, in 1929, that he came to despair of the continuation of his mathematical research. Perhaps the difficulties he foresaw in reconstructing these notes made him want to concentrate on philosophy instead. However, there were two other setbacks around the time that, in the long run, proved so devastating to Brouwer as to thwart whatever career plans he may have had. One setback was his conflict with Hilbert over the German journal *Mathematische Annalen*, on the editorial board of which they both served. The direct outcome of this dispute was—as intended by Hilbert—Brouwer's expulsion from the journal's board. The other setback was Brouwer's priority conflict with Karl Menger over the correct definition of *dimension*. Through the emotional and mental toll these fights took from someone of Brouwer's constitution, his creative work was, for the most part, brought to a halt (he would resume his work after 1945).

See also Gödel, Kurt; Hilbert, David; Husserl, Edmund; Intuitionism and Intuitionistic Logic; Mathematics, Foundations of; Mysticism, History of; Wittgenstein, Ludwig Josef Johann.

Bibliography

The Brouwer Archive is kept at the Department of Philosophy at Utrecht University, the Netherlands.

WORKS BY BROUWER

Collected Works. Vol. 1: *Philosophy and Foundations of Mathematics*, edited by Arend Heyting. Amsterdam: North-Holland, 1975.

Collected Works. Vol. 2: *Geometry, Analysis, Topology and Mechanics*, edited by Hans Freudenthal. Amsterdam: North-Holland, 1976.

Brouwer's Cambridge Lectures on Intuitionism, edited by Dirk van Dalen. Cambridge, U.K.: Cambridge University Press, 1981.

Intuitionismus, edited by Dirk van Dalen. Mannheim, Germany: BI-Wissenschaftsverlag, 1992.

"Life, Art and Mysticism." Translated by Walter van Stigt. *Notre Dame Journal of Formal Logic* 37 (3) (1996): 389–429. Introduction, also by Walter van Stigt, pp. 381–387.

WORKS ON BROUWER AND INTUITIONISM

Dummett, Michael. *Elements of Intuitionism.* Oxford: Clarendon Press, 1977. 2nd, rev. edition, 2000.

Hesseling, Dennis. *Gnomes in the Fog. The Reception of Brouwer's Intuitionism in the 1920s.* Basel: Birkhäuser, 2003.

Heyting, Arend. *Intuitionism. An Introduction.* Amsterdam: North-Holland, 1956. 2nd, rev. edition, 1966. 3rd, rev. edition, 1971.

Heyting, Arend. *Mathematische Grundlagenforschung, Intuitionismus, Beweistheorie.* Berlin: Springer, 1934. Expanded French translation: *Les Fondements des mathématiques. Intuitionnisme. Théorie de la démonstration.* Paris: Gauthiers-Villars, 1955.

Largeault, Jean. *Intuition et Intuitionisme.* Paris: Vrin, 1993.

Mancosu, Paolo, ed. *From Hilbert to Brouwer: The Debate on the Foundations of Mathematics in the 1920s.* Oxford: Oxford University Press, 1998.

Placek, Tomasz. *Mathematical Intuitionism and Intersubjectivity: A Critical Exposition of Arguments for Intuitionism.* Dordrecht, Holland: Kluwer, 1999.

Tieszen, Richard. *Mathematical Intuition. Phenomenology and Mathematical Knowledge.* Dordrecht, Holland: Kluwer, 1989.

Tieszen, Richard, ed. *Perspectives on Intuitionism.* Special issue, *Philosophia Mathematica* 6 (2–3) (1998).

Tieszen, Richard, ed. *Phenomenology and Mathematics.* Special issue, *Philosophia Mathematica* 10 (2) (2002).

Troelstra, Anne. *Choice Sequences: A Chapter of Intuitionistic Mathematics.* Oxford: Clarendon Press, 1977.

van Atten, Mark. *On Brouwer.* Belmont, CA: Wadsworth, 2004.

van Dalen, Dirk. *Mystic, Geometer, and Intuitionist.* Oxford: Clarendon Press, 1999.

van Dalen, Dirk, and Anne Troelstra. *Constructivism in Mathematics.* 2 vols. Amsterdam: North-Holland, 1988.

van Stigt, Walter. *Brouwer's Intuitionism.* Amsterdam: North-Holland, 1990.

Mark van Atten (2005)

BROWN, THOMAS
(1778–1820)

Thomas Brown, a philosopher on the periphery of the common sense school, was born at Kirkmabreck in Scotland. Radically opposed eighteenth-century traditions met in him. He shared with the common sense school, which derived from Thomas Reid, a number of its metaphysical doctrines and its appeal to intuitive truths; and he was also Reid's tireless critic. Philosophy, for Brown, was very largely "analysis": analysis of what he regarded as darkened notions, designed to exhibit their character free from spurious mystery and complication; analysis of the genuinely complex into its elementary constituents and of the deceptively simple into its real complexity. He saw Reid as a great resister of analysis. In the procedure of analysis Brown was influenced by French empiricism in the line of descent from Étienne Bonnot de Condillac.

During the course of his studies at the University of Edinburgh, Brown attended the lectures given by Dugald Stewart, Reid's close adherent. He subsequently graduated in medicine. In 1798 he published a criticism of the *Zoonomia* of Erasmus Darwin and in 1804 a defense of David Hume's account of causal relations (enlarged in 1806 and again in 1818, when it appeared under the title *Inquiry into the Relation of Cause and Effect*). Brown was among the first of the contributors to the *Edinburgh Review* (he attacked Immanuel Kant in the second number of the *Review*). In 1810 he was appointed conjoint professor of moral philosophy with Stewart and took over the teaching duties of the chair. His lectures were a dazzling success; they were published after his death and went through many editions in a few years.

CAUSE AND EFFECT

Brown's views on causation typically combined an empiricist analysis with what he called a principle of intuitive belief. He defined a cause as "that which immediately precedes any change, and which, existing at any time in similar circumstances, has been always, and will be always, immediately followed by a similar change" (*Cause and Effect*, p. 13). Brown thought that if we reflect with sufficient patience and imagination, we can see that this definition exhausts the notion of a cause. To suppose that a cause is something more than the antecedent of an invariable consequent is to suppose that we might know all the unfailing regularities of nature and yet have no conception of a causal connection. Material and volitional agents, Brown argued in detail, do not differ in agency; all agency is the same. The omnipotence of God resides simply in the fact that whenever he wills anything, his will is "immediately and invariably *followed* by the existence of its object" (p. 103).

In tracing the sources of the complex illusion which, he thought, hangs over the relation of cause and effect, Brown emphasized the power of metaphor to mislead. Thus, things that are connected or bound together dependably go together; from this circumstance various figurative expressions enter the language and their figurative character is unnoticed. No bond or connection between causally connected events ever presents itself; yet unless we shift our attention from words to things, we shall easily suppose that it must be insensibly present. Experience (coupled with a kind of negative insight) enables us to see that the causal relation is merely one of sequence; but on what authority do we import the notion of invariableness into this sequence? Brown maintained that we are intuitively certain that the same antecedents will always be followed by the same consequents.

THE WILL

Under Brown's analysis, mystery vanished from the will: will is an amalgam of desire and the belief that one has it in one's power to realize the desire; there is no further, indefinable operator in our voluntary actions. Brown was not impressed by denials of the identity of will and desire

on the ground that there can be opposition between them—Reid had said, "We may desire what we do not will, and will what we do not desire." When the types of situation referred to are looked at more carefully, Brown said, the opposition is seen to lie between desire and desire, and to be terminated by the desire upon which action immediately depends.

CONSCIOUSNESS

The examination of consciousness that provides data for the philosophy of mind is not, in Brown's opinion, conducted by consciousness. Once again, he saw entities as having been multiplied beyond necessity and, in this case, beyond possibility. He maintained that consciousness is not, as some philosophers have supposed, a surveyor of the mind's various states as they occur; rather, it is constituted by them. To suppose that "the same indivisible mind" could exist at the same time in two different states, one of them an object to the other, is "a manifest absurdity" (*Philosophy of the Human Mind*, Lectures XI and XII). What is thought of as an introspective examination of mental phenomena is therefore, strictly speaking, retrospective.

Below the phenomena of the mind, analysis encounters metaphysical bedrock. Let us imagine, Brown said, a man born with fully matured powers and a completely blank mind. Let him now be allowed a single sensation. This will be his total consciousness. Let a second sensation be added and let him be made to recall the first. He will then come to a recognition of something different from either—of himself as their common subject. The conviction that we exist with an "absolute" identity through time is intuitive and irresistible; only the circumstances in which it arises afford matter for inquiry. This identity is the prerogative of our minds; "some sort of identity of the body" is associated with it in our ordinary ideas about "sameness of person" (Lecture XII).

PERCEPTION

Brown's most subtle analyses occur in his theory of perception. His general problems were to explain how we come to know of the existence of an external, physical world and to specify the precise content of this knowledge. He was very conscious of the danger of question-begging assumptions; he maintained that at every turn we take externality for granted, and that all our language implies it. ("There is no distinct vocabulary of scepticism." Lecture XXII). Brown considered that our original awareness of things in their externality—their independence of our perception—is brought about by means of sensations commonly but inaccurately ascribed to touch. The sensations belonging to other senses acquire an external reference by association with these.

Brown proceeded first to reductive simplification: the various tangible qualities were maintained to be various modifications of either extension or resistance. He then went on to disclose and systematize the complexity of sensations involved in our tactual relations with things. He argued that sensations of mere touch do not primitively inform us of extension and externality. We derive the notion of spatial extension from our repeated experience of the temporal succession of muscular feelings in the movements of arms and fingers. When a familiar series of these feelings is interrupted by feelings of resistance to muscular effort—as, for example, our fingers closed around an object—we become aware for the first time of something separate from ourselves and learn something of its dimensions. Physical objects were, for Brown, essentially extended, resisting objects; but before his argument has ended, extension and resistance seem to have become merely phenomenal and, in their unperceived existence, to have disappeared into their unknown causes.

MORAL THEORY

Brown's zeal for simplification is nowhere more conspicuous than in his moral theory. The distinctions, for example, between the obligatoriness, rectitude, and merit of an action are simply a matter of tense: contemplated before performance, the action is "obligatory"; in performance, it is "right"; and it is "meritorious" afterward. And what makes it so is the "emotion" of approval it arouses in us when we are in a fit state of mind to form a moral judgment—an emotion in no way arbitrary, for as morally definitive it proceeds from constitution of human nature. The strength and elevation of Brown's moral sentiments assisted his great, brief reputation.

See also Common Sense; Condillac, Étienne Bonnot de; Darwin, Erasmus; Hume, David; Kant, Immanuel; Reid, Thomas; Stewart, Dugald.

Bibliography

Principal works by Thomas Brown are *Inquiry into the Relation of Cause and Effect* (Edinburgh, 1818); and *Lectures on the Philosophy of the Human Mind* (Edinburgh, 1820).
Selections from Brown appear in Daniel Sommer Robinson, *The Story of Scottish Philosophy* (New York: Exposition Press, 1961).
For literature on Brown, see David Welsh, *Account of the Life and Writings of Thomas Brown* (Edinburgh: W. and C. Tait, 1825), and François Réthoré, *Critique de la philosophie de Thomas Brown* (Paris, 1863). Sir William Hamilton, *Discussions on Philosophy and Literature,* 2nd ed. (Edinburgh: Longman, Brown, Green and Longmans, 1853), pp. 39–99, attacks Brown in defense of Reid. Brown is defended against Hamilton by John Stuart Mill in *An Examination of Sir William Hamilton's Philosophy* (London: Longman, Green, Longman, Roberts and Green, 1865), Ch. 10.
There are chapters on Brown in James McCosh, *The Scottish Philosophy* (New York: R. Carter, 1875), and in Henry Laurie, *Scottish Philosophy in Its National Development* (Glasgow: J. Maclehose, 1902). An indication of Brown's influence in America can be found in Terence Martin, *The Instructed Vision* (Bloomington: Indiana University Press, 1961).

S. A. Grave (1967)

BROWNSON, ORESTES AUGUSTUS
(1803–1876)

Orestes Augustus Brownson, a Transcendentalist philosopher and journalist, was born in Stockbridge, Vermont. He had little formal education. Until 1822 he belonged to the Congregationalist Church; he then joined the Presbyterians but was quickly repelled by their depreciation of human reason and by the Calvinist doctrine of predestination. In 1824 he became a Universalist, being ordained a minister in 1826. Three years later he abandoned Christianity and joined the socialist sect of Robert Dale Owen and Fanny Wright; at this time he wrote in behalf of the Workingmen's Party. He was reconverted to the Christian religion in 1832, when he joined the Unitarians.

Brownson was introduced to philosophy in 1833, through the works of Victor Cousin, whose disciple he remained for ten years. Cousin was warm in his praise of Brownson as a philosopher. Though Brownson later criticized Cousin's philosophy for its eclecticism and psychologism, he always remained under its influence. His reading of Immanuel Kant and the Italian idealist Vincenzo Gioberti were major factors in shaping his mature philosophy. For a while he was a member of the Transcendentalist group that met in Boston and at Brook Farm, but he considered their thinking poorly grounded and undisciplined.

In 1838 he founded the *Boston Quarterly Review,* which in 1842 was merged with the *U.S. Magazine and Democratic Review of New York.* In 1844, he was received into the Catholic Church. The same year he founded *Brownson's Quarterly Review,* which he published, except for the years 1865–1872, until 1875. Most of Brownson's numerous articles and reviews appeared in this publication. His most important book was *The American Republic: Its Constitution, Tendencies, and Destiny.*

Although Brownson was a deeply religious thinker, he insisted that philosophy should begin not with authority or faith, but with data of reason. He criticized the notion of Christian philosophy proposed by the *Annales de philosophie chrétienne* for failing to do justice to the rational nature of philosophy.

Like Cousin, he made the starting point of philosophy the analysis of thought, stressing, in opposition to Cousin, its objective, rather than its subjective, side. All thought, he maintained, presupposes the presence of an object that can be analyzed into three elements: the ideal, the empirical, and the relationship between them. The ideal is the a priori element in all thought; it is that which makes any experience intelligible. The ideal is not a Kantian category, which Brownson interpreted to be a subjective form, but a necessary aspect of the object of knowledge. Since the object must be real in order to present itself to thought, its ideal, or content, must also be real. Further analysis revealed that this content includes both necessary and contingent "being," which Brownson identified respectively with God and creatures. God is a necessary and independent being; creatures are dependent existences, so called because they stand outside (*exstare*) their cause. Hence Brownson adopted the "ideal formula" of Gioberti: "Being creates existences" (*Ens creat existentias*). Accordingly, creative being is present to the mind in all its thinking; it alone makes thought possible.

Brownson defended himself against the charge of ontologism, which was condemned by Rome in 1861, on the ground that he did not teach that we have an immediate intuition of God, but only of being. Though being is God himself, we discover this only by rational analysis.

In his early days, Brownson believed in the divinity of humanity and the infallibility of the popular will. Political experience in later life convinced him of the absurdity of these notions. He rejected the idea that government and law have a purely human origin. Only in a qualified sense did he admit that governments derive their powers from the assent of the governed. All power ultimately comes from God; he alone has absolute sovereignty. Brownson thought the American constitution more nearly perfect than others because it recognizes the existence of the Creator and of God-given rights of individuals, which the government is bound to respect and protect.

See also Being; Cousin, Victor; Gioberti, Vincenzo; Kant, Immanuel; New England Transcendentalism.

Bibliography

WORKS BY BROWNSON

The Works of Orestes A. Brownson, 20 vols. Edited by H. F. Brownson. Detroit: T. Nourse, 1822–1907.

WORKS ON BROWNSON

Brownson, H. F. *Orestes A. Brownson's Early, Middle, and Latter Life,* 3 vols. Detroit: H. F. Brownson, 1898–1900.

Cook, T. I., and A. B. Leavelle. "Orestes A. Brownson's *The American Republic.*" *Review of Politics* 4 (1) (January 1942): 77–90; 4 (2) (April 1942): 173–193.

Farrell, Bertin. *Orestes Brownson's Approach to the Problem of God.* Washington, DC: Catholic University of America Press, 1950.

Fitzsimons, M. A. "Brownson's Search for the Kingdom of God: The Social Thought of an American Radical." *Review of Politics* 16 (1) (January 1954): 22–36.

Maynard, Theodore. *Orestes Brownson, Yankee, Radical, Catholic.* New York: Macmillan, 1943.

McMahon, F. E. "Orestes Brownson on Church and State." *Theological Studies* 15 (1954): 175–228.

Parry, S. J. "The Premises of Brownson's Political Theory." *Review of Politics* 16 (2) (April 1954): 194–211.

Raemers, Sydney A. *America's Foremost Philosopher.* Washington, DC: St. Anselm's Priory, 1931.

Schlesinger, A. M., Jr. *Orestes A. Brownson: A Pilgrim's Progress.* Boston: Little, Brown, 1939.

Armand A. Maurer (1967)

BRUNNER, EMIL
(1899–1966)

Emil Brunner was a Swiss theologian. He was educated in Switzerland and served in the Swiss army in 1914. Later he became a pastor and then professor of theology at Zürich. He participated extensively in the work of the World Council of Churches and also for a time in the Moral Re-Armament movement. He lectured on theology in many countries, notably in the United States, Japan, and Scotland.

Brunner's earliest theological positions were typical of Swiss and German Protestantism before 1914. He accepted the liberal theological emphasis on the social and ethical aspects of the Gospel, as well as its stress upon the rational alliance between philosophy and theology. Even in his earliest theological writings he exhibited his personal interest in philosophy in a well-informed discussion of Edmund Husserl, *Das Symbolische in der religiösen Erkenntnis* (Tübingen, 1914). But after World War I he embarked upon a critique of liberalism that at first seemed to make him the natural ally of Karl Barth. His *Die Mystik und das Wort* (Tübingen, 1924) is a hostile discussion of Friedrich Schleiermacher's attempt to find a basis for Christianity in the general form of religious experience. Against this, Brunner poses the distinctive claims of Christian revelation, a revelation that cannot be discovered or appropriated through the use of criteria derived from natural theology or private experience.

The adjective much used of Brunner's (and also Barth's) concept of revelation was "dialectical." Theology is dialectical in that its attempts to grasp revelation necessarily involve the use of concepts that in purely philosophical discourse would cancel each other out. So the contradictions that arise, for example, in combining belief in divine goodness and omnipotence with an acknowledgment of the occurrence of physical evil are taken by the dialectical theologian to be simply manifestations of the necessarily paradoxical character of theological concepts. Contradiction is not a sign of intellectual failure, but of the inadequacy of our intellects before the splendor of divine revelation. Thus, if we try to use our ordinary criteria of consistency, we shall fail to grasp revelation at all. The major reason for this is that we shall be at fault if we try to understand revelation as consisting in a set of propositions. When God reveals himself, he does so as a person. Revelation is the act of a person, not the setting out of a doctrine.

It is for this reason that philosophy must necessarily limit its aspirations. The god of whom philosophy speaks is not the God of Christian revelation for at least two reasons. First, he is an inferred entity; and second, he is an object. It is not always clear whether Brunner believes that what philosophy says about God is false or simply inadequate. At times it seems clear that it is the former, yet Brunner is unlike Barth in the stress he puts upon the positive contribution that philosophy can make to theological thinking. Philosophy's role is to be critical, in the Kantian sense. It is to exhibit the limitations of human reason, and so to prevent speculative reason from attempting to occupy territory that belongs by right to revelation.

In revelation, God encounters man as person to person; man cannot argue his way to God by philosophy or discover God apart from the biblical revelation, yet when God calls, man at least can answer. Even this minimal concession to human powers brought Brunner into conflict with Barth. Barth's position, which he outlined in the short, bitter pamphlet *Nein! Antwort an Emil Brunner*

(1934), is that man, totally corrupted by the Fall, cannot advance an inch toward God by means of his natural powers. Grace has to supply even the capacity of responding to God's initiative. Brunner, who always feared the depiction of men as mere puppets, laid great stress on the natural man's capacity for speech and for elementary rationality as a precondition of any response to God.

The contrast between Brunner's theology and both liberalism on the one hand and Barthianism on the other is most marked in Brunner's ethics and social philosophy. Unlike Barth, Brunner believes that the basis for a natural ethics, even if a very limited one, exists. He revives the idea, which is found in Luther, of orders of creation. An order of creation is a social institution or practice of ordinary human origin, not derived from revelation, but shown by biblical evidence to have divine authorization. So Christ blessed monogamy in his appearance at the wedding at Cana and in his utterances about marriage; so he expressed the divine source of the state's authority when he said, "Render unto Caesar …" These orders supply human beings with norms to whose validity revelation itself testifies, but for knowledge of which revelation is not necessary. Such norms have the negative function of restraining sin, rather than any positive role. Brunner differs from liberal theology in his belief that no secular morality can hope to provide a satisfactory way of life, but is bound to founder on the sinfulness of human nature.

The key way in which sin manifests itself in human life is in the failure of men, both in theory and in practice, to understand themselves as persons. (It should be noted that it is not clear how far Brunner uses the word *person* in the same sense when he speaks of God as a person and men as persons. He speaks of God as the "original" person and of men as "derivative" persons, and says that before the Fall men were persons as God is a person. Some analogy is intended, but we are not told how strong the analogy is.) Brunner makes the position of philosophy in respect to human beings parallel to that which he gives it in respect to the knowledge of God. Philosophy as philosophy cannot grasp men as persons, but only as objects and inferred entities. The ghost of the view of both God and the self as Kantian noumena haunts his thought at this point. But it is not only in philosophy that the secular view of man is inadequate. In practice, too, men continually reject their status as persons.

They do this by seeking to be autonomous. The will, as the center of man's rebellion against God, seeks continually to be its own master. The ideal of the self-sufficient individual is one human ideal that must be rejected.

Its counterpart, the concept of man in the mass—collective man—is equally subhuman. But secular thought provides us with no adequate basis for rejecting these alternatives. Only revelation can do this, for it is only in revelation that we discover not only God as a person but also ourselves as persons. This is where Brunner's doctrine of atonement finds its place. What Jesus Christ showed us in his life, death, and resurrection was a love that alone can break our rebellious self-will and that alone can provide us with a model for goodness. Secular ethics can at best exhibit the kind of goodness that can defeat depersonalization as a hypothetical possibility. The revelation of Christ alone makes it actual. Revelation, however, does not provide us with a code that we can then detach from its origin and live by. We must return continually to revelation for renewal. This is in part because of the character of human sin, but it is also in part because we must reassert the personal character of social life in new contexts.

According to Brunner, the depersonalization that is a consequence of technology is distinctive of the contemporary context. Men are degraded to the status of tools and means. The social incarnation of this process is the totalitarian state. For Brunner, totalitarianism is the category ultimately opposed to that of true community, and both Nazism and communism are forms of it. This political judgment took Brunner into further public argument with Karl Barth, on the grounds that Barth's theological views obliterate the moral differences between rival political systems by insisting on the sinfulness of human nature as such.

See also Barth, Karl; Human Nature; Husserl, Edmund; Revelation; Schleiermacher, Friedrich Daniel Ernst.

Bibliography

ADDITIONAL WORKS BY BRUNNER

"Religionsphilosophie evangelischer Theologie." In *Handbuch der Philosophie* (Munich: R. Oldenbourg, 1927). Translated by A. J. D. Farrer and B. L. Woolf as *Philosophy of Religion from the Point of View of Protestant Theology*. Edinburgh, 1937.

Der Mittler. Tübingen, 1927. Translated by Olive Wyon as *The Mediator*. New York: Macmillan, 1934.

Das Gebot und die Ordnungen. Tübingen, 1932. Translated by Olive Wyon as *The Divine Imperative*. London: Lutterworth Press, 1937.

Der Mensch im Widerspruch. Berlin: Furche, 1937. Translated by Olive Wyon as *Man in Revolt*. London: Scribners, 1939.

Christianity and Civilisation. London: Scribners, 1948–1949. Parts I and II.

CRITICAL STUDY

Kegley, Charles W., ed. *The Theology of Emil Brunner.* New York: Macmillan, 1962.

Alasdair MacIntyre (1967)

BRUNO, GIORDANO
(1548–1600)

Giordano Bruno, the most famous of the Italian philosophers of the Renaissance, was born at Nola, near Naples. At an early age he entered the Dominican order and became an inmate of the Dominican convent in Naples. In 1576 he was accused of heresy and fled, abandoning the Dominican habit. Thereafter he wandered through Europe. After visiting Geneva, and lecturing on the *Tractatus de Sphaera Mundi* of Sacrobosco at Toulouse, Bruno reached Paris in 1581. Here he gave public lectures that attracted the attention of King Henri III, and published two books on the art of memory that reveal him as greatly influenced by that textbook of Renaissance magic, the *De Occulta Philosophia* of Henry Cornelius Agrippa, from which he quotes lists of magic images of the stars, incantations, and other occult procedures. Bruno as a Renaissance magus, in line of descent from the learned philosophical magic inaugurated by Marsilio Ficino, is already present in these books. The title of one of them, *De Umbris Idearum* (Shadows of Ideas), is taken from the necromantic commentary on the *Sphere* of Sacrobosco by Cecco d'Ascoli, whom Bruno mentions admiringly in other works. It may be inferred that the lectures at Toulouse were probably based on this commentary.

Early in 1583 Bruno went to England with letters of recommendation from Henri III to the French ambassador in London. He lived in the French embassy during the two years he spent in England, and the ambassador protected him from the tumults aroused by his writings, which were clandestinely printed in London. These included the *Triginta Sigilli* (Thirty seals), an extremely obscure work on his magic art of memory; those who manage to reach the end of it find an advocacy of a new religion based on love, art, magic, and mathesis. It is dedicated to the vice-chancellor and doctors of the University of Oxford in high-sounding terms in which Bruno announces himself as "the waker of sleeping souls, tamer of presumptuous and recalcitrant ignorance, proclaimer of a general philanthropy."

In June 1583 the Polish prince Albert Alasco (Laski) visited Oxford and was entertained with public disputations. Bruno was in his train, and, according to a recently discovered account by George Abbot, afterward archbishop of Canterbury, Bruno returned to Oxford after the party had left and delivered, uninvited, lectures that were largely a repetition of Marsilio Ficino's work on astral magic, the *De Vita Coelitus Comparanda* (On drawing down the life of heaven), although he also maintained Nicolas Copernicus's opinion "that the earth did go round and the heavens did stand still." Abbot says that Bruno was induced to discontinue the lectures when the plagiarism from Ficino was pointed out to him.

While in England, Bruno published five dialogues in Italian. In *La cena de le ceneri* (The Ash Wednesday supper; 1584) he defends his version of the Copernican theory against Oxford "pedants," a reflection of his visit to Oxford. In *De la causa, principio e uno* (1584) he apologizes for the storms aroused by his attack on Oxford, but makes matters worse by defending the friars of pre-Reformation Oxford, whom he prefers to their Protestant successors. The *De l'infinito, universo e mondi* (1584) is an exposition of his vision of an infinite universe and innumerable worlds. The *Spaccio de la bestia trionfante* (The expulsion of the triumphant beast; 1584) envisages a universal moral and religious reform and is dedicated to Sir Philip Sidney. The *Cabala del cavallo pegaseo* (Cabal of the horse Pegasus; 1585) indicates Bruno's adaptation of the Jewish kabbalah. The *De gli eroici furori* (On heroic enthusiasms; 1585) also dedicated to Sidney, is in the form of a sonnet sequence with commentaries expounding the philosophical and mystical meanings of the poems. It is upon this series of most striking and brilliant works, in which Bruno appears as the propagator of a new philosophy and cosmology, a new ethic and religion, that his fame largely rests. They are all full of Hermetic influences and are bound up with a complex religious, or politico-religious, mission for which Bruno believed he had the support of Henri III, and which cannot have been uncongenial to the French ambassador, Michel de Castelnau de Mauvissière, to whom three of the books are dedicated. Sidney's reactions to Bruno are unknown.

Late in 1585 Bruno returned to Paris, where he delivered an address on his philosophy in the Collège de Cambrai, arousing strong opposition, and where he had a curious controversy with Fabrizio Mordente about the compass that Mordente had invented. Paris was in a disturbed state, on the eve of the wars of the League, and Bruno's activities added to the "tumults," from which he fled in 1586 and began his travels through Germany. He was favorably received at the University of Wittenberg, and during his stay there he wrote a number of works, particularly on the art of Ramón Lull, to which he

attached great importance and which he believed he understood better than Lull himself. From Wittenberg he went to Prague, where he tried to obtain the favor of Emperor Rudolph II with his *Articuli Adversus Mathematicos* (1588), in which he states that he is strongly against mathematics, which he regarded as a "pedantry" lacking in deep magical insight into nature. His objection to Copernicus as a "mere mathematician" had been on similar lines. The work is illustrated with magical diagrams, representing what he called his mathesis, and its preface outlines a movement of tolerance and general philanthropy that is to replace sectarian bitterness. He next spent some time at Helmstedt, where he enjoyed the favor of the reigning duke, Henry Julius of Brunswick-Wolfenbüttel, and made a speech in praise of the late duke in which he outlined his program of moral reform in language similar to that used in the *Spaccio de la bestia trionfante*. It was probably while at Helmstedt that Bruno wrote the *De Magia* and other works on magic unpublished in his lifetime.

With the money Henry Julius gave him for the oration, Bruno went to Frankfurt to have printed the Latin poems he had written during his wanderings. These were the *De Innumerabilibus, Immenso et Infigurabili*, the *De Triplici Minimo et Mensura*, and the *De Monade Numero et Figura*, all of which were printed by John Wechel in 1591. In these Latin poems, written in a style imitating Lucretius, Bruno expresses his philosophical and cosmological speculations in their final form. Like the Italian dialogues on these themes, the Latin poems are full of Hermetic influences, particularly of the mathesis, or magical numerology, which Bruno had been further developing during his travels. He also published the last of his books on his magical arts of memory at Frankfurt.

TRIAL AND DEATH

In August 1591, Bruno returned to Italy at the invitation of a Venetian nobleman who wished to learn the secrets of his art of memory. There can be little doubt that Bruno was encouraged to take this step by the hopes of greater religious toleration aroused by the conversion of Henri IV of France. Bruno had in his baggage the manuscript of a book he intended to dedicate to Pope Clement VIII. It is strange that one who had stated in his published works that Christ was a magus and that the magical religion of the Egyptians was better than Christianity should have felt that he could place himself with impunity within reach of the Inquisition. Bruno seems, however, always to have sincerely believed that his religious and moral reform could take place within a Catholic framework. He was arrested in Venice and thrown into the prisons of the Inquisition. At the end of the Venetian trial he recanted his heresies, but was sent to Rome for another trial. Here he remained in prison for eight years, at the end of which he was sentenced as a heretic (having refused, this time, to recant) and was burned alive on the Campo de' Fiori.

Although the actual *processo* stating on what grounds he was condemned is not extant, it seems most probable that Bruno was burned as a magician, as an "Egyptian" who had been propagating throughout Europe some movement the nature of which remains mysterious, although it may well be connected with the origins of Rosicrucianism and of Freemasonry. His philosophical views in themselves can have had little to do with the condemnation, unless insofar as they, too, were associated with the movement.

LATER INTERPRETATION

In the seventeenth century there was a conspiracy of silence about Bruno and his reputation. Where the silence was broken, he usually appeared in the character of a diabolical magician. It was rumored that he had made a speech in praise of the devil at Wittenberg (Pierre Bayle and Gottfried Wilhelm Leibniz heard this story). In the eighteenth century he was interpreted by John Toland as a deist. The nineteenth century rediscovered Bruno and read its own beliefs and attitudes into his works. It was then that he appeared as the martyr for modern science and the Copernican theory, and statues were erected in his honor by anticlericals in Italy. The crudity of this approach was modified in later philosophical studies of Bruno, but the attempt to isolate a philosophy or a metaphysics from his works and to discuss his thought in a context of straight history of philosophy meant that large areas in his writings must be disregarded as unimportant or unintelligible. Moreover, no coherent philosophical system could be extracted in this way, as Leonardo Olschki saw when he criticized Bruno as a confused thinker. But when Bruno is placed in the context of the Renaissance Hermetic tradition, his philosophy, his magic, and his religion can all be seen as forming part of an outlook on nature and on man which, however strange, is nevertheless perfectly coherent within its own premises.

HERMETIC PHILOSOPHY

The extraordinary prestige of the Hermetica in the Renaissance was encouraged by the belief that they were the writings of Hermes Trismegistus, an Egyptian sage who foretold Christianity and whose wisdom had inspired Plato and the Platonists. The Hermetic core in Renaissance Neoplatonism was an important factor in the revival of magic. Christian magi, like Ficino and Giovanni Pico della Mirandola, used some caution in their approach to the magical passages in the Hermetic *Asclepius,* which is the basis of the astral magic described by Ficino in his *De Vita Coelitus Comparanda.* These safeguards were largely abandoned by the magician Cornelius Agrippa and totally abandoned by Bruno, who adopted the position that the Hermetic magical religion was the true religion, the religion of nature in contact with its powers. The cure for the wars, persecutions, and miseries of contemporary Europe was a return to the magical religion of the Egyptians—hence the long quotations in the *Spaccio de la bestia trionfante* from the passages in the *Asclepius* describing the religious practices of the Hermetic pseudo Egyptians, ecstatically interpreted by Bruno as their worship of "God in things," and as a "profound magic" by which they were able to draw down cosmic powers into the statues of their gods. The lament for the Egyptian religion in the *Asclepius* was interpreted by Bruno as a lament for a better religion, destroyed by Christianity. Since Augustine had condemned these passages as referring to the wicked demon worship of the Egyptians, it is easy to see how Bruno's "demonic" reputation arose. Bruno's "Egyptian" religion included belief in metempsychosis, which he also derived from the Hermetic writings.

Bruno's views on religion are organically related to his philosophy, for the philosophy of the living Earth moving around the divine sun and of the innumerable worlds, moving like great animals with a life of their own in the infinite universe, is the animist philosophy of a magus who believes he can establish contact with the divine life of nature. The sun is frequently mentioned in the Hermetic writings as a god, and it is the chief of the astral gods worshiped in the religion described in the *Asclepius.* Ficino's use of the astral magic of the *Asclepius* was chiefly directed toward the sun, whose beneficent influences he sought to draw down through solar talismans and incantations.

BRUNO'S COPERNICANISM

That Bruno thought of the Copernican sun in the context of the magic of Ficino's *De Vita Coelitus Comparanda* is indicated in the report of his lectures at Oxford, in which he is said to have repeated the Ficinian text while also maintaining the opinion of Copernicus. This report fits in with passages in Bruno's works in which the sun appears in a magical context, and particularly with his defense of the Copernican opinion against the Oxford doctors in *La cena de le ceneri,* where he describes Copernicus as "only a mathematician" who has not seen the true meaning of his discovery as he, Bruno, has seen it. When a speaker in these dialogues asks what is the cause of Earth's movement around the sun, the reply is an almost verbatim quotation from *Corpus Hermeticum* XII, in which Hermes Trismegistus explains that the energy of life is movement and that therefore nothing in the living universe is immobile, not even Earth. Bruno applied these words as an explanation of the cause of Earth's movement around the sun. The Copernican opinion had, for him, confirmed the "Egyptian" philosophy of universal animation. He also repeated from the same Hermetic treatise one of his most characteristic doctrines: that there is no death in nature, only change.

Thus Bruno's acceptance of Copernican heliocentricity did not rest on Copernicus's mathematical arguments. On the contrary, Copernicus as a mere mathematician was despised by him as a superficial person who had not understood the true meaning of his discovery. Bruno was always "against" mathematics. Although he had some acquaintance with the scientific basis of the Copernican theory, it was not on mathematical grounds that Bruno defended Copernicanism from reactionary Aristotelians, but on animist and magical grounds. In fact, when the passages on the sun in the different works are compared, it becomes apparent that Copernican heliocentricity was for Bruno a kind of celestial portent of the approaching return of "Egyptian" philosophy and religion. "Aristotelianism" was for Bruno a symbol of all that is dead and dry—or, as he would say, "pedantic"—in philosophy and religion (the two were for him inseparable), compared with his own philosophy and religion—in contact, so he believed, with living, divine nature.

NEW VISION OF THE UNIVERSE

The essence of the Hermetic writings is that they give a religious impulse toward the world. It is within the setting of the universe, not through any divine mediator, that the Hermetic gnostic achieves his religious experience. The closest parallel to Bruno's imaginative leap upward through the spheres is the description in the Hermetic *Pimander* of how man "leant across the armature of the spheres, having broken through their envelopes." So did Bruno break through the spheres in his ecstatic ascent to his new vision of the universe. The immediate source of his vision of infinite space and innumerable inhabited worlds was Lucretius's poem *De Rerum Natura,* But Bruno transformed the Epicurean and Lucretian notions

by imparting animation to the innumerable worlds—a feature totally absent from Lucretius's universe—and by imparting the function of being an image of the infinite divinity to the infinite. The godless universe of Lucretius turns in the Brunian vision into a vast extension of Hermetic gnosis; in order to receive this within himself, man, that "great miracle," as he is defined in the *Asclepius,* must expand himself infinitely. The *magnum miraculum est homo* passage is quoted from Trismegistus near the beginning of the *De Immenso* as a preliminary to the new vision of the world to be revealed in the poem.

This infinitely extended All was nevertheless One. The unity of the All in the One is a basic theme of the Hermetic writings and also of Bruno's. The unity of the All in the One is for Bruno "a most solid foundation for the truths and secrets of nature. For you must know that it is by one and the same ladder that nature descends to the production of things and the intellect ascends to the knowledge of them; and that the one and the other proceeds from unity and returns to unity" (*De la causa, principio e uno,* in *Dialoghi italiani,* edited by Giovanni Aquilecchia, p. 329).

This is the philosophy conducive to magic—that the magus can depend on the ladders of occult sympathies running through all nature. When this philosophy is not only a magic but also a religion, it becomes the religion of the Hermetic pseudo Egyptians who, as Bruno says in the *Spaccio de la bestia triofante,* "with magic and divine rites … ascended to the height of the divinity by that same scale of nature by which the divinity descends to the smallest things by the communication of itself" (*Dialoghi italiani,* p. 777). Bruno's philosophy and religion are one and the same, and both are Hermetic. This accounts for the main aspects of his philosophy, his panpsychism and his monism, and also for the magic and the references to magical practices with which his books are filled.

Like all Renaissance magi, Bruno was a syncretist and drew from his vast reading many philosophies which had accreted to the Hermetic core. The pre-Socratics, Plato and the Platonists, the Scholastics (Bruno revered Thomas Aquinas as a great magus), Nicholas of Cusa—all were incorporated into the central theme. Bruno's chief textbook of magic was Agrippa's *De Occulta Philosophia*; he also used the conjuring books of Trithemius and admired, and perhaps practiced, the Paracelsian medicine.

ART OF MEMORY

The side of Bruno's work that he regarded as the most important was the intensive training of the imagination in his occult arts of memory. In this he was continuing a Renaissance tradition that also had its roots in the Hermetic revival, for the religious experience of the Hermetic gnostic consisted in reflecting the universe within his own mind or memory. The Hermeticist believed himself capable of this achievement because he believed that man's *mens* is in itself divine and therefore able to reflect the divine mind behind the universe. In Bruno, the cultivation of world-reflecting magic memory becomes the technique for achieving the personality of a magus, and of one who believes himself to be the leader of a religious movement. Strange though these beliefs and practices are, Bruno had some profound things to say in his books on memory concerning the imagination, which he made the sole cognitive power (sweeping away the divisions of the Aristotelian faculty psychology by a kind of inner anti-Aristotelianism), and on the mental image in relation to the psychology of the "inspired" personality. When the magical aspect (which includes such practices as the use of talismans or images of the stars as mental images) is discounted or allowed for, Bruno's bold explorations of the inner world may become important to the historian of psychology.

SIGNIFICANCE AND INFLUENCE

The emphasis on the Hermetic and magical side of Bruno's thinking does not discredit his significant contribution to the history of thought. He exemplifies the Hermetic religious impulse as a motive force behind the imaginative formulation of new cosmologies. From within his own frame of reference, this highly gifted man made guesses that may have given hints to seventeenth-century thinkers. A notable example is his transformation of the Democritean atoms, of which he read in Lucretius, into magically animated monads; this may well have been a stage leading to Leibniz's monadology, and there are other curious links between Bruno and Leibniz. Although Bruno was obviously not in the line leading to the mathematical advances, his extraordinary vision of an immensely expanded universe, ruled by the laws of magical animism, may be said to prefigure, on the Hermetic plane, the new cosmology of the seventeenth century. Drained of its animism, with the laws of inertia and gravity substituted for the psychic life of nature as the principle of movement, Bruno's universe would turn into something like the universe of Isaac Newton, moving under laws placed in it by a God who is not a magician but a mathematician and a mechanic. In the Hermetic phase of European thought, which was the immediate prelude to the seventeenth-century revolution, Bruno is

an outstanding figure. Regarding him in this light, the old legend of the martyrdom of the advanced thinker becomes almost true again, although not in the old sense.

See also Hermeticism.

Bibliography

Additional works by Bruno in Italian are *Dialoghi italiani,* edited by Giovanni Gentile and revised by Giovanni Aquilecchia (Florence, 1957), which contains all the Italian dialogues in one volume, and *Il candelaio,* a comedy, edited by Vincenzo Spampanato (Bari, 1923). In Latin, see *Opera Latine,* edited by Francisco Fiorentino, Vittorio Imbriani, C. M. Tallarigo, Felice Tocco, and Girolamo Vitelli, 3 vols. (Naples: Morano, 1879–1891), issued in eight parts; there is also a facsimile reprint (Naples and Florence, 1962).

Translations include *The Heroic Enthusiasts,* translated by L. Williams (London: Redway, 1887); *Des Fureurs héroïques,* translated by P.-H. Michel (Paris, 1954); *Giordano Bruno's The Heroic Frenzies,* translated by P. E. Memmo Jr. (Chapel Hill: University of North Carolina Press, 1964); *The Expulsion of the Triumphant Beast,* translated by A. D. Imerti (New Brunswick, NJ: Rutgers University Press, 1964); "On the Infinite Universe and Worlds," in D. W. Singer, *Giordano Bruno, His Life and Thought* (New York: Schuman, 1950), pp. 227ff.; and "Concerning the Cause, Principle and One," translated by D. W. Singer in S. Thomas Greenberg, *The Infinite in Giordano Bruno* (New York: King's Crown Press, 1950), pp. 77ff.

Documentary sources on Bruno's life are Vincenzo Spampanato, ed., *Documenti della vita di Giordano Bruno* (Florence, 1933), and Angelo Mercati, ed., *Il sommario del processo di Giordano Bruno* (Vatican City: Biblioteca Apostolica Vaticana, 1942). A biography is Vincenzo Spampanato, *Vita di Giordano Bruno* (Messina: Principato, 1921). On his trial, see Luigi Firpo, "Il processo di Giordano Bruno," in *Rivista storica italiana* 60 (1948): 542–597, and 61 (1949): 5–59.

For a bibliography of Bruno's works and of books and articles on him up to and including 1950, see Virgilio Salvestrini and Luigi Firpo, *Bibliografia di Giordano Bruno 1582–1950* (Florence, 1958).

Studies of Bruno include Felice Tocco, *Le opere latine di Giordano Bruno* (Florence: Sansoni, 1889), and *Le fonti più recenti del Bruno* (Rome, 1892); J. L. McIntyre, *Giordano Bruno* (London: Macmillan, 1903); Giovanni Gentile, *Giordano Bruno e il pensiero del Rinascimento* (Florence, 1920); Leonardo Olschki, *Giordano Bruno* (Halle, 1924), which has also been translated into Italian (Bari, 1927); Ernst Cassirer, *Individuum und Kosmos in der Philosophie der Renaissance* (Leipzig: Teubner, 1927), translated by Mario Domandi as *The Individual and the Cosmos in Renaissance Philosophy* (New York: Harper, 1963); Antonio Corsano, *Il pensiero di Giordano Bruno* (Florence: Sansoni, 1940); Eugenio Garin, *La filosofia* (Milan, 1947); Alexandre Koyré, *From the Closed World to the Infinite Universe* (Baltimore: Johns Hopkins Press, 1957); Paolo Rossi, *Clavis Universalis* (Milan, 1960); P.-H. Michel, *La cosmologie de G. Bruno* (Paris: Hermann, 1962); and Paul O. Kristeller, *Eight Philosophers of the Italian Renaissance* (Stanford, CA:

Stanford University Press, 1964). Also see Frances A. Yates, *The Art of Memory* (Chicago: University of Chicago Press, 1966).

OTHER RECOMMENDED TITLES

Byrum, Stephen C. "A Proposal for Considering Giordano Bruno's Influence on Descartes." *Philosophy Research Archives* 9 (1983): 303–336.

Calcagno, Antonio. *Giordano Bruno and the Logic of Coincidence: Unity and Multiplicity in the Philosophical Thought of Giordano Bruno.* New York: Peter Lang, 1998.

Decker, Kevin S. "The Open System and Its Enemies: Bruno, the Idea of Infinity, and Speculation in Early Modern Philosophy of Science." *American Catholic Philosophical Quarterly* 74 (4) (2000): 599–620.

Dynnik, M. A. "Man, Sun, and Cosmos in the Philosophy of Giordano Bruno." *Soviet Studies in Philosophy* 6 (1967): 14–21.

Gatti, Hilary. *Giordano Bruno and Renaissance Science.* Ithaca, NY: Cornell University Press, 1999.

Gatti, Hilary, ed. *Giordano Bruno: Philosopher of the Renaissance.* Aldershot, U.K.: Ashgate, 2002.

Gatti, Hilary. "The Natural Philosophy of Giordano Bruno." *Midwest Studies in Philosophy* 26 (2002): 111–123.

Granada, Miguel A. "Aristotle, Copernicus, Bruno: Centrality, the Principle of Movement and the Extension of the Universe." *Studies in History and Philosophy of Science* 35a (1) (2004): 91–114.

Maiorino, Giancarlo. "The Breaking of the Circle: Giordano Bruno and the Poetics of Immeasurable Abundance." *Journal of the History of Ideas* 38 (1977): 317–327.

Massa, Daniel. "Giordano Bruno's Ideas in Seventeenth-Century England." *Journal of the History of Ideas* 38 (1977): 227–242.

Paris, Paul-Henri. *The Cosmology of Giordano Bruno.* Translated by R. E. W. Maddison. Ithaca, NY: Cornell University Press, 1973.

Paterson, Antoinette Mann. *The Infinite Worlds of Giordano Bruno.* Springfield, IL: Thomas, 1970.

Voise, Waldemar. "Bruno on the Morality of the Inhabitants of the Infinite Universe and on the Cognitive Passion of Copernicus." *Dialectics and Humanism* 6 (1979): 115–123.

White, Michael. *The Pope and the Heretic: The True Story of Giordano Bruno, the Man Who Dared to Defy the Roman Inquisition.* New York: Morrow, 2002.

Yates, Frances A. *Giordano Bruno and the Hermetic Tradition.* New York: Routledge, 1999.

Frances A. Yates (1967)
Bibliography updated by Tamra Frei (2005)

BRUNSCHVICG, LÉON
(1869–1944)

Léon Brunschvicg, the French idealist philosopher, was born in Paris and educated at the Lycée Condorcet, where he won awards in science as well as in classics and philosophy. He received both the *licence ès lettres* and the *licence ès sciences* from l'École Normale Supérieure in 1891. During the following nine years he taught philosophy at lycées in Lorient, Tours, and Rouen. His doctoral thesis, *La modalité du jugement*, was presented to the Sorbonne in 1897, and published in Paris the same year. In 1900 he returned to Paris to teach at his old lycée, later moving to the Lycée Henri IV and l'École Normale de Sèvres. In 1909 he was named professor of general philosophy at the Sorbonne. Except for the period 1914–1918, when he served in the armed forces auxiliary and as adviser to the government on educational reform, Brunschvicg held various chairs at the Sorbonne until the German occupation of Paris in 1940. He then settled in Aix-en-Provence and finally in Aix-les-Bains until his death.

Brunschvicg was one of the founders of the *Revue de Métaphysique et de Morale* (1893) and of the Société française de Philosophie (1901). In 1919 he was elected to the Académie des Sciences morales et politiques, serving as president in 1932. A prolific writer, editor of Blaise Pascal, and well known for his studies of René Descartes and Benedict de Spinoza, Brunschvicg was a major figure in French intellectual life for nearly half a century.

The "critical idealism" of Brunschvicg primarily recalls Immanuel Kant's analysis of the conditions of knowledge, but Brunschvicg's method was historical rather than deductive: He wished to grasp the mind's activity as it has revealed itself in the history of mathematics, science, and philosophy. In general perspective, Brunschvicg may be seen as heir to two currents in nineteenth-century French philosophy: the tradition of epistemological idealism descending through Charles Renouvier from Kant and Antoine Cournot, and the metaphysical idealism of Maine de Biran, Félix Ravaisson, Jules Lachelier, and Jules Lagneau.

For Brunschvicg, the goal of philosophical reflection was to disclose intellectual activity tending toward self-consciousness as it progressively constitutes knowledge. He therefore frequently characterized history as "the progress of consciousness" (*le progrès de la conscience*). The double meaning of this expression—the progress of conscience as well as of consciousness—also suggests the moral dimension of Brunschvicg's monistic idealism. Viewed subjectively, the process is a conversion from naive acceptance of reality as external to an affirmation of the primacy of the mind as it provides intelligibility. Brunschvicg equated this with recognition of the supremacy of intelligence in a moral sense, which is to say that self-knowledge progresses toward refinement of conscience and moral autonomy. According to Brunschvicg, personal conversion reflects an absolute historical development undetermined in form but immanently oriented toward spiritual values (of which Unity is highest) and self-knowledge on the part of humanity as a whole.

The critique of this process, Brunschvicg insisted, cannot depend on a priori assumptions, nor can it hope to specify categories or functions of thought; such analysis would only falsify the mind's essential freedom and inventiveness. The emphasis on creative spontaneity suggests a relationship with Henri Bergson that Brunschvicg was proud to acknowledge, but not to the extent that he wished to embrace Bergson's intuitionism. Although Brunschvicg preferred the general terms *mind* and *intelligence* to *thought* and *reason*, this does not imply a commitment to nonintellectual modes of understanding. At the heart of his work lay studies in the history of science and of mathematics. Brunschvicg regarded scientific progress not only as a triumph of intellect but also as an exemplification of humankind's growing self-understanding. In this way, he defended a moral or "spiritual" conception of science as opposed to positivistic and conventionalistic theories. In his view, the truth of a theory essentially depends on the creative vitality of the mind as it assimilates what is given as nonmental, and as it judges, in turn, the adequacy of this synthesis.

In *La modalité du jugement*, Brunschvicg attempted to delineate the mind's developing accord with being or the real in a theory that classifies judgments according to the forms of "internality" and "externality." Brunschvicg took judgment, rather than the concept or category, as fundamental because he saw it as a synthesizing or unifying act, combining form and content. The form of "externality" was interpreted (evidently following Johann Gottlieb Fichte) as a restraining activity that the mind imposes dialectically on its own creative freedom or "internality."

In *Les étapes de la philosophie mathématique* (Paris, 1912), Brunschvicg examined the highest expression of "internality," mathematical judgment, which he regarded as uniquely appropriate to science because it is at once a free creation—not to be justified through physical interpretation—yet inseparable from experience in its origin and in its "collaborative" task of assimilating being to the understanding. Brunschvicg substantiated this theme in *L'expérience humaine et la causalité physique* (Paris, 1922), which further revealed an implicit dualism and a reluctance to employ categories or principles of analysis, however provisional.

Brunschvicg's last decade was marked by works of a religious nature, following a comprehensive history of philosophy, *Le progrès de la conscience dans la philosophie occidentale* (Paris, 1927), intended to bear witness to humanity's spiritual unification. "Our destiny is to tend toward unity." Religious value apparently attaches to a particular dimension of the "progress of consciousness": The assimilation of being to consciousness insofar as the process is regarded as immanently guided by the value of unity. In this assimilation, humankind moves toward self-identification through the communion of shared intelligence.

Although it appears likely that Brunschvicg felt a moral or spiritual ideal to be predominant in his career, he will perhaps be best remembered as an interpreter of the French philosophical tradition and as a leading spokesman for the life of reason and the value of science.

See also Bergson, Henri; Cournot, Antoine; Descartes, René; Fichte, Johann Gottlieb; Idealism; Kant, Immanuel; Lachelier, Jules; Maine de Biran; Ravaisson-Mollien, Jean Gaspard Félix; Renouvier, Charles Bernard; Spinoza, Benedict (Baruch) de.

Bibliography

ADDITIONAL WORKS BY BRUNSCHVICG

Introduction à la vie de l'esprit. Paris, 1920.

Spinoza et ses contemporains. Paris: Alcan, 1923.

Les âges de l'intelligence. Paris: Alcan, 1934.

La raison et la religion. Paris: Alcan, 1939.

Écrits philosophiques. 3 vols. Paris: Presses Universitaires de France, 1951, 1954, 1958.

WORKS ON BRUNSCHVICG

Boirel, R. *Brunschvicg, sa vie, son oeuvre avec un exposé de sa philosophie.* Paris: Presses Universitaires de France, 1964.

Cochet, M. A. *Commentaire sur la conversion spirituelle dans la philosophie de Léon Brunschvicg.* Brussels, 1937.

Dagognet, F. "Brunschvicg et Bachelard." *Revue de Métaphysique et de Morale* 70 (1965): 43–54.

Deschoux, Marcel. *La philosophie de Léon Brunschvicg.* Paris: Presses Universitaires de France, 1949. Contains a complete bibliography.

Gex, M. "L'idéalisme critique de Léon Brunschvicg." *Revue de Théologie et de Philosophie* 19 (1969): 145–164.

Messaut, J. *La philosophie de Léon Brunschvicg.* Paris: Presses Universitaires de France, 1938.

Bernard Elevitch (1967)
Bibliography updated by Thomas Nenon (2005)

BUBER, MARTIN
(1878–1965)

Martin Buber, the religious existentialist, was born in Vienna and spent his childhood in L'viv, Galicia, at the home of his grandfather Solomon Buber, a businessman and well-known scholar of rabbinic literature. From 1896 to 1900 he studied philosophy and art history at the universities of Vienna, Leipzig, Berlin, and Zürich. He was early active in the Zionist movement, especially in its cultural and religious aspects, and in 1901 he was appointed editor of the Zionist journal *Die Welt.* Instrumental in the founding of the publishing house Jüdischer Verlag in 1902, in 1916 he founded the German Jewish monthly *Der Jude,* which, until it ceased publication in 1924, was the most respected and literate voice of German Jewry. From 1924 until 1933 Buber was professor of the philosophy of Jewish religion and ethics at Frankfurt-am-Main University, the only chair in Jewish religion at any German university. In 1920 he and Franz Rosenzweig founded the Freies Jüdisches Lehrhaus, an institute for adult Jewish education; and with Adolf Hitler's coming to power Buber devoted his energy to strengthening the religious and spiritual resources of German Jewry in the face of the unprecedented challenge posed to it. Buber continued in the institute until 1938, when he left for Palestine, where he was appointed professor of sociology of religion at the Hebrew University. With Y. L. Magnes he led the Yihud movement, devoted to Arab-Jewish understanding and to the creation of a binational state. In 1952 and 1957 he traveled widely in the United States, lecturing at many universities and to diverse student groups. While his acceptance of various German awards in the postwar period led to criticism from some Jewish quarters, Buber remained steadfast in his encouragement of those German circles that realize the magnitude of the Nazi crimes against the Jews and seem genuinely repentant. He died in Jerusalem.

Buber's basic insight, an insight that runs through all of his work and that determines his approach to everything he touches, is the realization that there is a basic difference between relating to a thing or to an object that I observe, and to a person or a "Thou" that addresses me and to whose address I respond. In its simplest form, this is the difference between the way people usually relate to inanimate things on the one hand and to living persons on the other. Inanimate objects are watched, while persons are spoken to. However, the distinction cannot be drawn simply on this basis. A person as well as an inanimate thing can be viewed as a thing, or, in Buber's terminology, an "It." Whenever we take an "objective" attitude toward a person, whenever we view him as part of the world and caught in its causal chain, we are in an "I–It" relationship, even though the object happens to be a person. The "I–It" relationship is characterized by the fact that it is not a genuine relationship because it does not take place between the I and the It. When another person is an It to me, I am, first of all, perfectly alone. I gaze at him and view him from every possible direction, I observe his place in the scheme of things, and I find elements that he has in common with other persons and things and elements that distinguish him from them. All of this, however, takes place within me; *I* am judging and *I* am observing, and the external world is relevant only to the extent that it enters my being.

It is otherwise in the "I–Thou" relationship. Here the relationship is genuine because it is between me and the Thou that addresses me. This Thou is no longer one thing among other things of the universe; the whole universe is seen in the light of the Thou, and not the Thou in the light of the universe. In fact, it is not only the object in the "I–Thou" relationship that is different from that in the "I–It" situation; the very "I" is different in the two situations. There is no "I" that sometimes relates to a Thou and sometimes to an It. If that were the case, both the It and the Thou would be objects that float into the I's field of vision and then out of it, leaving the I essentially unaffected. Instead, Buber argues, the I of the I–It is a different I from that of the I–Thou because it is not the I as such that has preeminent reality, but the relations I–It and I–Thou. The I appears and is shaped only in the context of some relationship with either an It or a Thou and can never be viewed independently of such a relationship.

Buber further states that the I–It relationship is maintained with only part of ourselves in it. There is always a part of us that remains outside the relationship and views it from some vantage point. In the I–Thou relationship, on the other hand, our whole being must be involved. Should I attempt to hold back any part of myself, I will find myself in an I–It situation because there will be a part of me that is not participant but spectator, a sure sign of the I–It. This means that the I–Thou relationship carries with it much greater risk than the I–It, since there is no withholding of the self possible, as in the I–It. In the I–It situation the part of the self that remains outside the relationship cannot be injured by the other party because he cannot reach it. In the I–Thou relationship there is no such security because the Thou of the I is addressed with the whole of the I, and any response elicited necessarily pertains to this total I. In the I–Thou relationship, therefore, everything possible is risked without any defensive position being left to which the I can withdraw in case of need. However, this is not the only risk involved in the I–Thou situation. The Thou who is addressed cannot be viewed in the context of any causal, deterministic framework. He must be encountered in the full freedom of his otherness, an otherness that is addressed and that responds in the total unpredictability of human freedom. The moment the responses of the Thou are calculated, the moment the I asks itself what impression its speech and being will make on the Thou, it is relating to an It instead of to a Thou.

Because of this, Buber tells us, there is never a present for the I–It relationship, only a past. This is so because all objective knowledge about a human being is knowledge about his past, of what he has been rather than of what he is. If the present moment is to have genuine novelty, if it is not perfectly determined by the events of the past, then it must be possible for the present to produce a break with the past in the form of a response that could not have been calculated from a knowledge of the past. In the I–Thou relationship we are therefore genuinely living in the present because we are prepared for any and every response to our address, the expected as well as the unexpected—and it is this that constitutes genuine listening. The difference between a pseudo listening and a genuine listening is that while in the pseudo listening situation the listener pretends to listen, what he hears is determined by his past knowledge of the person he is listening to or by his theories concerning the nature of man. Genuine listening does not know ahead of time what it will hear; in the full uniqueness of the present it listens to the speech of the other without filtering what it hears through the screen of its own prejudgments. The purpose of genuine listening is therefore really to hear what the other is saying, constantly being aware that he is saying something that is new and not just a revelation of his nature, which the hearer has already identified and which is fixed as the other's "psychology."

It is in the religious context that the significance of Buber's distinctions emerges most clearly. In contrast to much of mysticism that aims at the obliteration of the abyss between the self and the Absolute in the ecstasy of mystical union, the essence of biblical religion, as conceived by Buber, is the dialogue between man and God in which each is the other's Thou. "The extended lines of relations meet in the eternal Thou," writes Buber in the opening sentence of the final portion of *I and Thou*. Life is an endless transition from the Thou to the It and back to the Thou. Sooner or later, the time comes when even the most cherished Thou recedes, when a spiritual tiredness overtakes the most authentic I–Thou relationship and turns it into the I–It. There is one Thou, argues Buber, who by his very nature cannot become an It. A man may hate God and curse him, he may turn away from him when the suffering of human destiny becomes unbearable; but no man can reduce God to the status of a thing who no longer addresses him and who becomes one object among others in the world for him. Much of traditional theology, for Buber, errs in dealing with God as if he could be turned into an It. Time and again, however, man turns from thinking about God to addressing him, and it is then that he communicates with the living God, as distinct from merely giving intellectual assent to the God of the philosophers. This is true even when the Absolute Thou addressed is not called God. "But when he, too, who abhors the name, and believes himself to be godless, gives his whole being to addressing the Thou of his life as a Thou that cannot be limited by another, he addresses God."

In the course of his long career Buber applied these basic ideas to a diversity of fields. In a number of works devoted to biblical interpretation, he developed in detail his view of the Bible as the record of Israel's dialogue with God. He wrote a definitive work on the relation between Christian and Jewish faith. In this work he distinguishes between the Jewish *emunah* and the Greek *pistis,* the former of which, according to Buber, is faith in the sense of trust while the latter is faith in the sense of belief in the truth of propositions. Jewish faith, as found in the Hebrew Bible, is Israel's trust in the faithfulness of God's word as that word is spoken in dialogue. The faith of the New Testament, particularly in its Pauline version, is heavily influenced by Greek philosophical elements that are reflected in the emphasis on salvation as resulting from belief in the truth of propositions concerning the divinity and resurrection of Jesus. In Paul, Buber thus sees a profound departure from the Hebrew biblical spirit, a departure that is no more than partial and implicit in the Gospels.

In his later years Buber's interest to some extent turned to psychotherapy, in which he emphasized the necessity for the therapist not to hide behind the teachings of his school and not to forget that psychotherapy is above all dialogue in which therapist and patient speak to each other. When seen in this light, the therapist encounters the patient for the individual he is and is ready for the unexpected that the theoretical categories of his discipline do not prepare him for. Similarly, in the field of social philosophy Buber contrasted Marxist socialism, with its centralized control and allegiance to impersonal and inevitable historical forces, with the socialism of the community in which the authenticity of the I–Thou relationship is the foundation on which the living community is built and to which it must return, again and again, for renewal. In the Israeli kibbutz Buber saw an exemplification of the communal or "Utopian" socialism for which he stands.

See also Absolute, The; Existentialism; Jewish Philosophy; Philosophical Anthropology; Rosenzweig, Franz.

Bibliography

Publication of the collected works of Buber in German, *Werke,* was begun in 1962 by Kösel Verlag in Munich. The first three volumes appeared by 1964.

Buber's most important work is *Ich und Du* (Berlin, 1922), translated by R. G. Smith as *I and Thou* (New York: Scribners, 1958). *Die Frage an den Einzelnen* (Berlin: Schocken, 1936), translated by R. G. Smith in *Between Man and Man* (Boston: Beacon, 1955), develops the basic themes in some detail. *Der Glaube der Propheten* (Zürich, 1950), translated from the Hebrew by C. Witton-Davies as *The Prophetic Faith* (New York: Macmillan, 1949), is one of Buber's best biblical studies. *Paths in Utopia,* translated by R. F. C. Hull (London: Routledge, 1949), is Buber's study of social philosophy; *Two Types of Faith,* translated by N. P. Goldhawk (London: Routledge and Paul, 1951) is his study of Judaism and Christianity.

Other writings that have been translated into English are *Eclipse of God; Studies in the Relation between Religion and Philosophy,* translated by Maurice Friedman et al. (New York: Harper, 1952) and *Bilder von Gut und Böse* (Cologne, 1952), translated by R. G. Smith and M. Bullock as *Good and Evil; Two Interpretations* (New York: Scribners, 1953); *Pointing the Way: Collected Essays,* translated and edited by Maurice Friedman (New York: Harper, 1957); and *Martin Buber, Writings,* a selection edited and introduced by Will Herberg (New York: Meridian, 1956).

Maurice Friedman's *Martin Buber: The Life of Dialogue* (Chicago: University of Chicago Press, 1955; New York: Harper, 1960) is a thorough secondary work with an extensive bibliography.

Edwards, Paul. *Buber and Buberism: A Critical Evaluation.* Lawrence: University of Kansas Press, 1970.

Friedman, Maurice. *Martin Buber's Life and Work: The Early Years, 1878–1923.* New York: Dutton, 1981.

Friedman, Maurice. *Martin Buber's Life and Work: The Middle Years, 1923–1945.* Reprint ed. Detroit: Wayne State University Press, 1988.

Friedman, Maurice. *Martin Buber's Life and Work: The Later Years, 1945–1965.* New York: Penguin, 1986.

Moonan, Willard. *Martin Buber and His Critics: An Annotated Bibliography of Writings in English through 1978.* New York: Garland Publishing, 1981.

Schilpp, Paul, and Maurice Friedman, eds. *The Library of Living Philosophers, Vol. 12: The Philosophy of Martin Buber.* La Salle, IL: Open Court, 1967.

Wood, Robert. *Martin Buber's Ontology.* Evanston, IL: Northwestern University Press, 1969.

Michael Wyschogrod (1967)
Bibliography updated by Christian B. Miller (2005)

BUCKLE, HENRY THOMAS
(1821–1862)

Henry Thomas Buckle, the English historian, was the son of a prosperous businessman who left him sufficient money to devote his life to private study and writing. In common with a number of other dominant thinkers of the Victorian age—such as J. S. Mill, Herbert Spencer, and T. H. Huxley—he was largely self-educated. As he was a delicate child, it was thought unwise for him to undertake work involving much intellectual effort or strain, with the consequence that he was (as he put it) "never much tormented with what is called Education, but allowed to pursue my own way undisturbed … whatever I may be supposed to know I taught myself." Thus he was taken from school, at his own request, at the age of fourteen, never went to a university, and conducted his subsequent reading and research (which by any standards were vast) in the absence of all external supervision or direction. Buckle expressed no regret at not having gone to Oxford or Cambridge, considering both universities to be in a contemptible condition and believing himself in any case to be equipped with natural aptitudes and talents that more than compensated for the lack of a rigorous academic training. Certainly his gifts were far from negligible. He had an excellent memory, he could express himself both in writing and in conversation with great fluency and eloquence, and he was a first-class linguist (by the age of thirty he could read eighteen foreign languages and speak six); he possessed, moreover, an immense capacity for methodical work, together with an intense intellectual curiosity and a meticulous eye for detail.

Buckle led a comparatively uneventful life, his energies being to a large extent absorbed by the ambitious project of writing a history of civilization, to which, from his early twenties, he had decided to dedicate his career. But though the preparation of this enormous enterprise always remained his chief concern, he was not without other interests. He was, for example, a brilliant chess player, achieving an international reputation; he traveled widely, in Europe and beyond; and by the end of his life he had established a wide circle of acquaintances, including William Makepeace Thackeray, Charles Kingsley, Charles Darwin, and John Stuart Mill. For Mill in particular he had the highest admiration, and in 1859 he wrote a long review in *Fraser's Magazine* praising Mill's essay "On Liberty"—a review that created considerable stir at the time, since in it Buckle drew public attention to the fantastic sentence of twenty-one months' imprisonment recently passed upon a man for inscribing on a gate words offensive to Christianity. Although Buckle never married, he liked feminine society and secretly kept a mistress; when, after his death, the truth ultimately leaked out, it caused consternation and dismay among some of his close friends and relatives.

SIGNIFICANCE OF THE *HISTORY*

Buckle died at the age of forty while touring the Middle East. Only two volumes of his *History of Civilisation in England* had appeared, and these represented no more than an introduction to the vast work he had envisaged writing. Yet they had been sufficient to achieve for their author sensational fame, not merely in his own country but also throughout Europe and in the United States; Darwin applauded the work's brilliance and originality; and an influential American writer, Theodore Parker, attributed to it an importance in the history of thought comparable to that of Francis Bacon's *Novum Organum.* Buckle's reputation has since suffered a heavy decline, and many of the claims made on behalf of his work at the time of its publication seem grotesquely exaggerated today. Even so, what he wrote represents (as Henry Sidgwick pointed out) the first major attempt on the part of a thinker versed in the tradition of British empiricism and inductivism to enter the treacherous field of historical speculation, and to offer a comprehensive and detailed theory of historical development of the type that previously only Continental philosophers had ventured to provide. For this reason alone it preserves a certain interest and is still worth studying.

BUCKLE'S INTENTIONS

Buckle was fully aware of what had been done by some of his predecessors in Germany and France; and references to their works, particularly to those of Johann Gottfried Herder and Auguste Comte, are to be found scattered among the footnotes that abound throughout his own volumes. Like Herder, he was eager to connect the facts of human history with the conditions imposed by different forms of natural and geographical environment; like Comte, he wished to present the course of history as exemplifying a fundamental pattern of progress and improvement. But he rejected the tendency to revere past ages, and to exalt imagination at the expense of rational and scientific modes of thinking, that often manifested itself in Herder's writings; and he equally distrusted the strain of aprioristic dogmatism and respect for authoritarian methods of social control that he detected in Comte's historical system, calling the latter's theory of government "monstrously and obviously impracticable."

Buckle's allegiance lay chiefly with the ideals set out by English radicals and Utilitarians early in the nineteenth century, and it was these that finally determined the valuations embodied in his conception of social and historical progress.

HUMAN ACTIONS SUBJECT TO LAWS

Early in his book Buckle raised the question, "Are the actions of men, and therefore of societies, governed by fixed laws, or are they the result either of chance or of supernatural interference?" He supposed these possibilities to represent exhaustive alternatives, and argued that either variety of the latter hypothesis was plainly unacceptable.

So far as the theory of supernatural interference was concerned, this, together with the associated theological doctrine of predestination, must remain a "barren hypothesis," since no conceivable experience could count for or against its truth. On the other hand, the view that what occurs in the realm of human affairs is the product of chance was demonstrably false; it had, however, been given an aura of spurious respectability by metaphysical philosophers who had carried the principle in question over into the sphere of individual human psychology. There it emerged as the famous doctrine of free will, according to which a mysterious, undetermined power of free choice is held to be directly vouched for by the evidence of the introspective consciousness. But in Buckle's opinion it is precisely such blind reliance upon the findings of individual introspection that has been the besetting sin of "metaphysicians," leading them to construct their impressive-looking, though nonetheless mutually incompatible, systems in accordance with a radically mistaken procedure.

By contrast, in order to achieve a realistic conception of the nature and workings of the human psyche it is necessary to adopt an external and general view of human behavior analogous to that taken by natural scientists in the investigation of nonhuman phenomena: From this altered standpoint it can indeed be seen that the actions of men are subject to regularities as strict and mathematically exact as those that operate in other spheres of scientific inquiry. As a conclusive demonstration of his thesis, Buckle cited the evidence afforded by large-scale statistical surveys concerning the numbers of marriages contracted, and of murders and suicides committed, in particular countries and towns during successive years; the relative uniformity of the results obtained would, he held, be unintelligible on any other assumption than that there are certain social laws capable of keeping the level constant.

When discussing this topic, Buckle on occasions fell into confusions; he did not, for example, always distinguish between the necessary and the sufficient conditions of an occurrence, and was prone to disregard the difference between causal laws and statistical frequencies. In consequence he sometimes interpreted the statistical data in a misleading way, suggesting that the sole effective determinant of individual actions was what he called "the general condition of society." He also spoke as if the mere existence of a proportional average, observed to hold over a period of time, necessitated, with a kind of irresistible momentum, the commission of a particular number of crimes in any given year. As a result, a picture is presented wherein human beings appear as the helpless victims of social forces over which they can exert no effective influence or control—a conclusion in no way entailed by the premises from which Buckle initially proceeded.

ORIGIN AND DEVELOPMENT OF CIVILIZATION

Be this as it may, it is noticeable that when Buckle approached his principal theme—the genesis and development of civilization—he made little further reference to precise numerical regularities or frequencies; although he still spoke of "laws," it was the broad, indeterminate, and sometimes very doubtful generalizations concerning the factors influencing the evolution of human societies that he chiefly appealed to in providing his explanations. Thus, the fundamental agents of social growth were deemed to be material or, to use his term, "physical," and were listed as being "Climate, Food, Soil, and the General Aspect of Nature." These—and not, as some previous theorists had alleged, innate racial characteristics or mysterious "national spirits"—originally determine the divergent forms of organization and progress achieved by different historical cultures.

FOOD SUPPLY AND CIVILIZATION. Buckle believed that the degree of civilization attained by a society depended upon its wealth and upon the manner in which this wealth was distributed; such factors were in turn dependent upon the population of the country concerned, and the size of the population was determined by its food supply. In countries where cheap food was plentiful, the population increased in a fashion that led to the labor market's becoming overstocked; as a consequence there was unemployment and also poverty, since there is an inevitable tendency in societies where there is a sur-

plus of labor for laborers to be underpaid and for immense economic inequalities to develop. He cited such examples as Egypt, Peru, Mexico, and India, where riches were concentrated in very few hands and where the vast majority of the inhabitants lived in a miserable and depressed condition: "Among nations subjected to these conditions, the people have counted for nothing, they have had no voice in the management of the state, no control over the wealth their own industry created."

EUROPEAN CONDITIONS IDEAL. Buckle, in fact, considered that the ideal conditions for the development of civilization were to be found in Europe. Here the food supply was not so abundant as to lead to overpopulation, nor was it so scanty as to make the accumulation of wealth and the enjoyment of leisure (on which intellectual progress depends) impossible. Here, also, the temperate climate was favorable to enterprise and the energetic exploitation of natural resources; moreover, the aspect that nature presented to human beings was of a less extreme and unpredictable character than in other parts of the world. Thus, men did not regard it with superstitious awe as a terrifying and insuperable power, but saw it instead as something that obeys regular laws and is therefore capable of being tamed and utilized for their purposes. It followed (he thought) that Europe could be distinguished from all other centers of human society by the circumstance that it was human rather than natural or physical factors that had determined the course taken by its history and progress. Man was here the master of nature, and consequently the key to the development of European culture lay in the influence exercised by "the laws of the human mind."

KNOWLEDGE DETERMINED DIRECTION OF CULTURE

It might be expected that Buckle would go on to state what these laws of the human mind were, using them to explain patterns of social change in European history in a fashion comparable to that suggested by Mill in Book VI of his *System of Logic* when he spoke of the possibility of deriving principles governing historical development from the "ultimate" laws of human psychology. Buckle can scarcely be said, however, to have adopted this procedure, perhaps because he believed that the psychological and historical data available at his time were insufficient to make it practicable. Instead, he contented himself mainly with trying to show that it was the advance and diffusion of knowledge, and particularly of scientific knowledge, that had in the last analysis given European history its characteristic overall direction—"the progress Europe has made from barbarism to civilization is entirely due to its intellectual activity."

Other factors were considered, but only to be ruled out. Thus Buckle claimed—as if (rather surprisingly) it were a self-evident truth—that men's moral opinions had remained essentially unaltered for thousands of years: How then could these have been responsible for the far-reaching transformations that had overtaken European nations like England and France in the course of their historical evolution? Likewise, he rejected the claims of religion, literature, and government to be "prime movers of human affairs." Acceptance of a particular religious creed is a symptom rather than a cause of the condition in which a given society finds itself. The literature of a country merely reflects and serves to fix the degree of civilization already attained; it does not initiate further achievement. So far as the influence of government is concerned, Buckle maintained that the rulers of a nation were only "creatures of the age, never its creators." Enlightened legislation occurs only as a consequence of the pressure exerted by changes in the climate of opinion, these being due in the first instance to the efforts of "bold and able thinkers" who belong to the intellectual, and not the governing, classes; nor will such legislation be effective unless the ground has been prepared for it and "the age is ripe."

POLITICAL THOUGHT

Writing very much as an exponent of the principles of laissez-faire radicalism, Buckle displayed an intense distrust of governmental interference and "protectionism," which tended to be identified in his mind with the suppression of free opinion and free trade. Accordingly, he argued that most beneficial legislation is negative in character, taking the form of repealing the bad enactments passed by earlier generations; and, generally speaking, he restricted the legitimate functions of government to such things as the maintenance of order and the preservation of public health. The moral drawn is that the ineluctable laws of historical development should be permitted to take their course freely and without impediment; unlike many other philosophers of history, Buckle did not try to combine a doctrine of historical inevitability with a comprehensive positive program of political action and social reconstruction.

BUCKLE'S SIGNIFICANCE

There is much that is intellectually naive in Buckle's theory of history, and it is easy to find inconsistencies and non sequiturs among his arguments; Leslie Stephen's gibe that Buckle's "mental fibre was always rather soft" is not wholly beside the mark. His uncritical use of vague abstractions like "intellectual progress" and the "spirit of a time" often led him into treating vacuous truisms as significant discoveries, and the collectivist conception of historical change that pervades much of his work contrasts oddly with the influence he ascribes to individual scientists and economists in promoting social advance. Nevertheless, the impact of his ideas upon his age was undeniably great, and his criticisms of previous and current historiography were not without important long-term effects. Like Karl Marx, though with far less insight and imagination, he helped to turn the eyes of historians away from the political surface of events, making them look more closely at the technological and economic realities of human life that lie beneath; at the same time, through his determinism, he provided a corrective to the tendency toward excessive moralizing that his contemporaries exhibited in their treatment of the past. And, by enlarging the perspective of historical study to include cultures and societies remote in time or space from his own, he made a definite, if limited, contribution to widening the horizons and counteracting the provincialism of future students of human affairs.

See also Bacon, Francis; Comte, Auguste; Darwin, Charles Robert; Herder, Johann Gottfried; Huxley, Thomas Henry; Marx, Karl; Mill, John Stuart; Parker, Theodore; Sidgwick, Henry; Spencer, Herbert; Utilitarianism.

Bibliography

PRIMARY SOURCES

Buckle, H. T. *The History of Civilisation in England,* 2 vols. London, 1857–1861.

Taylor, Helen, ed. *Miscellaneous and Posthumous Works of Henry Thomas Buckle,* 3 vols. London: Longmans, Green, 1872.

STUDIES AND COMMENTARIES

Huth, Alfred Henry. *Life and Writings of Henry Thomas Buckle,* 2 vols. London: S. Low, Marston, Searle, and Rivington, 1880.

Robertson, John M. *Buckle and His Critics.* London: n.p., 1897.

St. Aubyn, Giles. *A Victorian Eminence.* London: Barrie, 1958.

Stephen, Leslie. *The English Utilitarians,* Vol. III. London: Duckworth, 1900.

Patrick Gardiner (1967)

BUDDE, JOHANN FRANZ
(1667–1729)

The German philosopher, theologian, and historian Johann Franz Budde, or Buddeus, was born in Anklam, Pomerania. He entered the University of Wittenberg in 1685 and became an assistant there in 1689. Budde was appointed professor of moral philosophy at Halle in 1693, full professor of theology at Jena in 1705, and church councilor at Gotha in 1715. Although he insisted on his independence from all schools and considered himself an eclectic, he was close to Pietist thought and to the philosophy of Christian Thomasius, his colleague at Halle.

Budde's most significant work in theoretical philosophy was his *Institutiones Philosophiae Eclecticae* (2 Teile, Halle, 1703). In the first section, in which he expounded his logical doctrines and the intent was chiefly methodological, the influences of John Locke and Thomasius are apparent. Budde derived error from original sin and prescribed means for restoring the "good health" of the mind. He regarded ontology as a part of logic and as consisting in a simple explanation of basic metaphysical terms. According to Budde, these terms had a purely instrumental value because he refused to confer upon metaphysics the rank of independent and universal science. Rather, he interpreted it as the science of the most general nouns used in theology and philosophy.

In the second section of the *Institutiones,* Budde first discussed natural philosophy in a phenomenalistic manner, holding that we cannot know the real nature of things, but only their appearances and effects. He attempted to reconcile the physical animism or spiritualism typical of Pietist natural philosophy with mechanism. He frequently appealed to the Bible and gave an important place to final causes. At the end of this section he discussed spirits and God, whose existence he demonstrated by rational proofs.

In practical philosophy (*Elementae Philosophiae Practicae,* Halle, 1697) Budde followed Hugo Grotius, Samuel von Pufendorf, and Thomasius. He completely denied human freedom, referring the possibility of good actions to God's grace and restricting accountability to a narrow and extrinsic sphere of material liberty. He devoted much space to discussions of practical psychology and prudence, for he believed that such practical psychology was a better means than abstract instruction of healing the human will from sin. However, revelation is essential to this healing process.

As with the Pietists, practical philosophy is central to Budde's thought. He also agreed with the Pietists in stressing the will's independence of the intellect, in his emphasis on psychology in practical philosophy and on spiritualism in cosmology, and in the importance he placed on revelation. However, Budde was much more systematic than Thomasius, who was likewise very much influenced by Pietism. Budde joined the Pietists in their fight against Christian Wolff, and in 1723 he wrote a pamphlet attacking Wolff.

Although in practical philosophy Budde agreed with the Pietists, in theology he tried to reconcile the views of orthodoxy and Pietism. Because he held that man has an original religious impulse, he gave an important position to natural religion. He presented cosmological, physicotheological, and historical proofs of God's existence, and tried to refute atheism by argument.

Budde was one of the most learned men of his time. His writings on the history of Jewish philosophy (*Introductio ad Philosophiam Ebraeorum,* Halle, 1707), on general history of philosophy, and on the history of theology (*Historia Theologiae Dogmaticae et Moralis,* Frankfurt, 1725) were excellent in their time and are still valuable for the information they contain.

See also Determinism, A Historical Survey; Grotius, Hugo; Jewish Philosophy; Locke, John; Pietism; Pufendorf, Samuel von; Revelation; Thomasius, Christian; Wolff, Christian.

Bibliography

ADDITIONAL WORKS BY BUDDE
Selecta Iuris Naturae et Gentium. Halle, 1704.
Institutiones Theologiae Moralis. Leipzig, 1711.
Institutiones Theologiae Dogmaticae. Leipzig, 1723.

WORKS ON BUDDE
Hirsch, E. *Geschichte der neuren evangelischen Theologie.* Vol. II, 319–340. Gütersloh, 1960.
Stolzenburg, A. F. *Die Theologie des Joh. Fr. Buddeus und des Chr. Pfaff.* Berlin, 1926.
Wundt, Max. *Die deutsche Schulphilosophie im Zeitalter der Aufklärung,* 63–75, 242–243. Tübingen: Mohr, 1945.

Giorgio Tonelli (1967)

BUDDHISM

Buddhism derives its name from the Sanskrit word *buddha* (awakened, wise, or learned), which was one of the many epithets given to Siddhārtha Gautama (c. 563–c.

483 BCE), the founder of the set of theories and practices that are now called Buddhism. Traditional accounts of Gautama's life are more inspirational and hagiographical than historical in nature, and any attempt to extract a historical record from them is likely to prove frustrating, although the attempts of such authors as Hans Wolfgang Schumann (1989) and Michael Carrithers (1983) to find a credible story of Gautama's life are well worth reading.

According to traditional accounts Gautama left his wife and newborn child to seek his liberation from suffering and followed various teachers who ultimately failed to satisfy his needs. He then set out on his own and found the liberation he sought through meditation and self-discipline. At first disinclined to teach, because he felt his teachings would appeal to few people, he finally decided to tell others what he had discovered. Soon after his death, his disciples met and repeated all they could remember being taught by him, and these recollections were committed to memory. All the rules he had set down for the community of his disciples were collectively known as the *vinaya*. The collections of his other teachings on good character, contemplative exercises, and the theory behind them were known collectively as *sutras*. The vinaya and sutras supposedly collected shortly after Gautama's death became a closed canon for some Buddhists; other Buddhists eventually accepted as canonical a large corpus of other literature. Although there is a great deal of agreement between what is found in both the closed and extended canon, there is also a good deal of difference. In what follows, an attempt will be made to make note of where there is agreement and where there is divergence of opinion among Buddhists.

The epithet Buddha emphasizes Gautama's claim to have awakened, as if from a slumber, to seeing things as they really are. Another epithet commonly given to Gautama is *jina* (conqueror), which emphasizes his having overcome his internal enemies, the passions. In much of the Buddhist canonical literature Gautama refers to himself as *Tathāgata*, an epithet that has been explained in various ways by later Buddhists; one possible interpretation is that the Tathāgata knew the truth or understood things as they really are. Traditionally being a follower of Buddhism consists in going for refuge to the Buddha, the *dharma* (the goal of Buddhist practice), and the *sangha* (the community of virtuous people). In what follows, each of these terms will be discussed with reference to how understanding of them has changed down through the centuries.

THE BUDDHA

During the time when the Buddha Gautama was alive, going for refuge to him meant becoming his disciple and agreeing to follow his teachings and the rules of his community. After his death, however, the meaning of going for refuge to the Buddha changed. The action came to mean making an effort to cultivate in oneself the virtues associated with buddhas in general, for the claim attributed to Gautama was that he was the most recent in a series of buddhas, all of whom had taught the same thing to the people of their generation and all of whom had had the same set of virtues. The set of virtues associated with buddhas are called the factors of awakening. Canonical texts always talk about thirty-seven mental factors that are required for awakening. These factors are the sum of seven different lists of wholesome mental qualities. When all redundant terms are eliminated from these lists, however, there are just ten different factors: wisdom, courage, concentration, mindfulness, inner joy, mental and emotional flexibility, equanimity, faith, right resolve, and good moral habit.

Wisdom is explained as understanding and discrimination, and it includes awareness of one's own body and mind, reflections on the inevitability of death, and recognition that all complex beings change and therefore are not worth striving for. Wisdom also entails realizing that no one is fully in control of one's own body, mind, or personality and that therefore these things are not really one's self, and none of them really belongs to anyone; rather, everything that comes into being is an essentially impersonal event. Because the factors conditioning any one event are beyond reckoning, no one can be in control of all of them; since it is possible to alter some of the conditions in one's life, however, discipline and practice are not in vain, however difficult they may be.

Courage consists in having the resolve and energy to do virtuous and wholesome actions that benefit oneself and others. Concentration is defined as having a healthy mentality focused on a single topic at a time. Mindfulness is defined as good memory, and especially recalling the importance of virtue in all situations and remembering to cultivate it. Inner joy is described as zest and enthusiasm for being virtuous and helping others do the same. Flexibility is defined as workability and pliability of one's thoughts and emotions, which are the opposite of intellectual and emotional rigidity, obsessiveness, and the tendency to pass judgment on others. Equanimity means indifference to pleasure and pain, and impartiality with respect to people. Faith is described as conviction and trust in the teachings of the Buddha as a result of experiencing the initial benefits of practicing what he taught. Right resolve consists in the resolve to cultivate wholesome and to eliminate unwholesome mental states. Good moral habit includes thinking, speaking, and acting in ways that conduce to the well-being of oneself and others, and it manifests in earning one's livelihood in ways that minimize damage done to other living beings and to their environment.

Even though it was considered possible for a person to cultivate all these virtues while living an ordinary family life, it was said to be much easier to succeed if one first renounced family life and lived alone or in a community of like-minded friends. For this reason, the ideal setting for Buddhist practice has nearly always been seen to be a monastery.

For the first several centuries in the history of Buddhism, the Buddha was venerated as a man who had been born an ordinary man and who had struggled to discover and eliminate the root causes of rebirth and its inevitable difficulties. After a long life of teaching others how to eliminate their own causes of rebirth, he died a serene death, knowing that he had helped many others to become awakened and liberated from their suffering. He likened himself to a physician who had studied the symptoms of a disease, made a diagnosis, and prescribed a course of treatment. Like a physician, he could only encourage his patients to take the necessary course of treatment; he could not do their work for them. After some five or six centuries, however, this description of the Buddha's career lost its appeal to many people, and new movements evolved within Buddhism that portrayed buddhas in importantly different ways.

One of the most influential of these new portrayals of what a buddha is appeared in a Mahayana Buddhist text, probably written in the second or third century CE, known as the Sutra of the White Lotus of the True Doctrine, commonly referred to simply as the Lotus Sutra. This complex and highly polemical text repudiates the earlier Buddhist doctrine that the Buddha was born, lived, and died, never again to be reborn in any form anywhere. The Lotus Sutra puts forth the view that all particular buddhas, including Gautama, are but manifestations of an eternal entity known as Shakyamuni Buddha, who is omniscient, omnipotent, and perfectly compassionate but otherwise beyond human comprehension. Shakyamuni Buddha, being transcendent, can be known to human beings only by taking human form. All the buddhas of the past, present, and future should be known to be manifestations of this cosmic buddha.

Moreover, the most important teaching of all these manifestations of Shakyamuni Buddha is that every sentient being in the universe is destined to become a fully enlightened buddha, for all beings, and not just those who are known now to be buddhas, are essentially one with the enlightened mind called Shakyamuni Buddha. Announcing this message in various ways, the Lotus Sutra pronounces harsh condemnation of those who teach that the goal of Buddhism is to attain nirvana, if that is understood as the end of the cycle of rebirths. Monks who teach that Buddha Gautama was an ordinary human being who achieved extraordinary things and that he eventually died never to be reborn, are denounced in the Lotus Sutra as charlatans and pseudo-Buddhists whose teachings could prevent others from attaining perfect enlightenment. The immediate destiny of such monks is a long and painful stay in hell, but even they, assures the Lotus Sutra, will eventually realize full and perfect enlightenment.

A second sort of new portrayal of a buddha figure is found in a genre of literature that has come to be known as Pure Land sutras. The term *pure land* is a translation of a Chinese expression that is in turn an interpretation of a Sanskrit expression that means "a happy land" or "a land of ease." The principal innovation in this genre of sutras is the notion that there are buddhas who attained buddhahood only after amassing an incalculable amount of merit through austerities and good works. After attaining buddhahood these buddhas used their merit to create realms in which all the distractions posed by hardships are unknown so that inhabitants of these realms could devote all their energy to cultivating virtue and striving for nirvana. People from our burdensome world are said to be able to gain entry in one of these realms of ease simply by calling on the name of the buddha who created it.

By far the most popular of these buddhas was Amitābha, whose name means "he whose light is unmeasured." The invocation of Amitābha's name became one of the most common practices among Buddhists in East Asia. In some places, and especially in Japan, some followers of the Lotus Sutra held Amitābha (Amida in Japanese) practitioners in contempt because of the latter's reluctance to regard Amitābha as a manifestation of Shakyamuni. The various views that Buddhists have held on what exactly the nature of a buddha is have been described in detail and with considerable philosophical refinement by Paul J. Griffiths in *On Being Buddha: The Classical Doctrine of Buddhahood* (1994).

THE DHARMA

Those who followed the closed canon of Buddhist texts teach that the dharma to which a Buddhist goes for refuge is nirvana, which is seen as the ultimate goal of all Buddhist practice and theory. Ultimately, nirvana is defined as the cessation of rebirth after one's present life comes to an end, but the term also refers to the cessation of psychological afflictions while one is still alive. The principal afflictions discussed in Buddhist teachings are greed, hatred, and delusion. Greed is understood broadly as all craving for material possessions, physical and psychological comforts, physical and psychological pleasures, celebrity, approval, and anything that one regards as desirable. Hatred includes irritation, resistance, anger, and any sort of aversion or wish for dissociation from something. Delusion includes any sort of misunderstanding or misjudgment that could result in unsuccessful action.

These three root afflictions are said to be the principal causes of all distress and discontent. Eliminating them results in being content with whatever situation that may present itself. In many Buddhist texts it is said that contentment arises not merely from the absence of afflictions but from the presence of their opposites. Thus, when greed is replaced by generosity, hatred by love, and delusion by wisdom, then one is truly contented, and when these replacements are permanent, then one has attained liberation from suffering in this life.

While the dharma to which a Buddhist goes for refuge is nirvana, the term *dharma* also refers to virtue in general and to anything, such as teachings and practices, that help one to cultivate virtue. The most important of the virtues is wisdom, since it plays a role in the cultivation of all other virtues. Wisdom is said to arise in three stages. The first stage consists in learning what wise people have said and how they have acted. The second consists in reflecting on what one has learned through study. And the third consists in realizing in one's own life what the wise people of the past have discussed. This third stage includes a variety of contemplative exercises that have been designed to improve a person's mentality. For each of the virtues discussed earlier as those associated with buddhas, specific meditative exercises have been designed.

In canonical Buddhism the attainment of nirvana is usually described as incremental. The analogy most frequently used is that one's mentality is like gold ore, which is a mixture of precious metal and various unwanted minerals. Refining ore to get pure gold requires a gradual elimination of the unwanted minerals through various chemical and mechanical processes. Similarly, one's mentality is a mixture of wholesome and unwholesome habits that mute the effectiveness of the wholesome traits. Refining one's character requires the gradual elimination of bad habits through study, reflection, and cultivation, and the culmination of all this refinement is nirvana. In some forms of later Buddhism, however, a different conception of nirvana arose. In this new view nirvana, understood not as the mere absence of affliction but as the constant presence of tranquillity, lucidity, and bliss, is the fundamental nature of all things. Thus, all consciousness is fundamentally calm, lucid, and contented, and the so-called afflictions are temporary obscurations of that lucidity. The most common analogy for this view of nirvana is that of the sun, which shines all the time but is sometimes temporarily obscured by clouds. In this view of consciousness the condition of enlightenment is innate and permanent.

Nirvana, therefore, is not the cessation of existence but the realization that consciousness is beginningless and endless and constantly tranquil. In some forms of this doctrine it is said that ultimately there is only one mind, namely, the Buddha's; all apparently individual minds are but episodes of this one Buddha mind. Since the Buddha's mind can only be wholesome, it follows that all those who are apparently individuals are also wholesome, and all mental events, including those called unwholesome or vicious are in fact virtuous. Delusion, then consists in a failure to recognize the innate wholesomeness of all existence. In some formulations of this position delusion consists in thinking in terms of oppositions at all; thus, it is delusional to think in terms of the contrast between virtue and vice, wholesomeness and unwholesomeness, delusion and wisdom, liberation and bondage, buddha and ordinary person, and so forth.

THE SANGHA

The word *sangha* means "community." The community to which a Buddhist goes for refuge is the so-called noble (*ārya-sangha*) community, which comprises all those who have reached one of the four stages leading to and including nirvana. Since it is seen as nearly impossible for an individual to make the necessary refinements in character that lead to nirvana, it is considered almost essential for one to keep company with virtuous people who will understand and support one's resolve to cultivate virtue and attain nirvana. In the hopes of providing a community of people dedicated to virtue and thus providing a noble sangha, the Buddha Gautama founded a monastic community as well as a community of lay disciples. Ideally, these formal communities should include enough members of the noble community to be of benefit to the world as a whole, and so to help these visible communities not only to be virtuous but also to be seen to be virtuous, Gautama set forth various sets of precepts. Lay disciples are expected to refrain from five harmful activities: killing, stealing, sexual transgressions, lying, and intoxication. Novitiates seeking ordination into the monastic community are expected to refrain from ten harmful actions and thoughts: the first four of the five expected of the laity plus refraining from harsh speech, gossip, frivolous speech, attachment, anger, and false views. Monastics are expected to observe more than two hundred vows, depending on which monastic order they belong to. Four of those vows are considered so important that any person who breaks them is dismissed from the monastic order for the rest of his or her life; these four vows are refraining from killing a human being, from the theft of anything that human beings regard as property, from any kind of sexual intercourse with any other being living or dead, and from making false claims about one's spiritual attainments.

The study of the monastic rules (vinaya) suggests that the principal purposes of the monastic community were twofold: to provide an ideal environment for individuals to cultivate virtue and to serve as a visible community that demonstrated to the society at large that a life of material simplicity dedicated to the cultivation of virtue and self-contentment is far more satisfactory than a life of material acquisitiveness dedicated to seeking possessions and the approval of others. Taking monastic vows is not seen as necessary for the attainment of nirvana, but is seen rather as the taking on of responsibilities to be of service to society at large. Some scholastics favor the view, based on passages in canonical texts, that, while it is not necessary to be a monastic to attain nirvana, it is impossible for anyone who has attained nirvana to remain a lay person for more than one day. Others, however, take the view that renunciation is itself a kind of attachment and that a liberated person would be able to live a normal lay life without becoming either attached to or afraid of its pleasures. This latter attitude can be found in many Buddhist movements within East Asia, and especially Japan, and in some movements in Tibetan Buddhism.

The Buddha Gautama made several observations about statecraft. He made these observations by telling stories, which often had a satirical edge. One attitude that emerges in these stories is that government came into human society at a time when morality was breaking down, and, since government was devised by people living in morally broken down cultures, government is itself as likely to exacerbate the problem as alleviate it. That notwithstanding, those whose task is to provide governance can sometimes benefit by the counsel of wise people, although not all governments are equally willing to heed wise counsel.

In his own instructions to kings, Gautama urged them, above all else, to provide to all citizens the means to earn their own livelihoods. This could best be achieved by taxing the wealthy and distributing resources to the needy and by educating the unskilled. A king who fails to do these things, said Gautama, is most likely to bring about a society in which the poor have no means of living other than stealing from the wealthy, and the wealthy then hire guardians to protect their wealth. This situation in turn leads to both the thieves and the mercenary guardians arming themselves to protect themselves against one another, and it leads to the wealthy seeking ever stricter laws and more severe punishments, until nearly everyone is armed and afraid. As fear and suspicion grows, violence increases, and as violence increases, the life expectancy of people declines. Eventually, said Gautama, the decline will become so dramatic that most people will die only shortly after reaching the age of reproduction, and children will be left to raise themselves, and morality will become so rare that people will have forgotten even the word *virtue*, let alone know what it stands for. All this can be avoided by governments that are more interested in protecting the poor than in serving the wealthy, said Gautama, and such governments are more likely to occur if wise and learned men and women remain actively engaged in society. Even monks who have renounced the family life should take an interest in providing wise counsel to governments. The ideal of providing selfless service to one's society was particularly emphasized in some of the Mahayana sutras that came into prominence in the first several centuries CE.

The entire philosophy of Buddhism is traditionally summarized in a formula called the four noble truths: (1) all forms of existence involve some suffering, (2) suffering arises because of unrealistic expectations, (3) suffering can be eliminated by eliminating unrealistic expectations, and (4) there is a method to be followed to eliminate them. The method itself is summarized in the formula: "Do what is beneficial, avoid doing harm, and keep the mind pure."

See also Buddhism—Schools: Chan and Zen; Buddhism—Schools: Dge-lugs; Buddhism—Schools: Hua yan; Buddhism—Schools: Madhyamika; Buddhism—Schools: Yogacara; Buddhist Epistemology.

Bibliography

Carrithers, Michael. *The Buddha.* New York: Oxford University Press, 1983.

Conze, Edward, tr. *The Large Sutra on Perfect Wisdom, with the Divisions of the Abhisamayālankāra.* Berkeley: University of California Press, 1975.

Griffiths, Paul J. *On Being Buddha: The Classical Doctrine of Buddhahood.* Albany: SUNY Press, 1994.

Harvey, Peter. *An Introduction to Buddhism: Teachings, History, and Practices.* New York: Cambridge University Press, 1990.

Keown, Damien. *The Nature of Buddhist Ethics.* New York: St. Martin's Press, 1992.

Lopez, Donald S., ed. *Buddhist Scriptures.* London: Penguin, 2004.

Lopez, Donald S. *The Story of Buddhism: A Concise Guide to Its History and Teachings.* San Francisco: HarperSanFrancisco, 2001.

Schumann, Hans Wolfgang. *The Historical Buddha: The Times, Life, and Teachings of the Founder of Buddhism.* London: Arkana, 1989.

Sizemore, Russell F., and Donald K. Swearer, eds. *Ethics, Wealth, and Salvation: A Study in Buddhist Social Ethics.* Columbia: University of South Carolina Press, 1990.

Swearer, Donald K, ed. *Me and Mine: Selected Essays of Bhikkhu Buddhadāsa.* Albany: SUNY Press, 1989.

Richard P. Hayes (2005)

BUDDHISM—SCHOOLS

This composite entry is composed of the following subentries:

CHAN AND ZEN
DGE-LUGS
HUA YAN
MADHYMAKA
YOGĀCĀRA

CHAN AND ZEN

Zen is the latest Japanese development in a number of similar Buddhist traditions known as "Chan" in China, "Seon" in Korea, and "Thiên" in Vietnam, all supposedly having origins in India. It is an open question whether there is a sufficient degree of homogeneity to label this multifarious tradition "Chan" or "Zen." A safe alternative would be to treat each of the regional variations as distinct traditions, or even to handle the numerous subcategories in each of the East Asian regions as not necessarily connected with each other, at least not in the sense of a historical continuity.

One factor that makes these traditions especially complex is their emergence at various times and in various settings without being submitted to a central religious authority that would have defined their identity, their doctrine, and their structure as a religious unity. The multifarious nature of these traditions does not mean that Zen institutions did not participate in games of power; they certainly did. The vicissitudes of these lineages result from influences that cannot be reduced to institutional fates and orientations, or to their connections with political contingencies. This is because in most cases their self-proclaimed criterion for religious authority was spiritual realization.

ZEN AGENDAS

While there is no unified tradition, this presentation uses the word "Zen" to indicate the fuzzy field comprising all the traditions mentioned above. For the sake of simplicity it is convenient to adopt the widely used Japanese pronunciation, except when referring to a specific geographical area.

Since many Zen lineages and most Buddhist schools seek to disentangle the nexus of our projections even on sacred matters, awareness of our own hermeneutic circle is a necessary prerequisite for examining the possible confluence between traditional and philosophical approaches to Zen. One of the sources that have shaped the understanding of Zen is the agendas of those who first introduced it to Western audiences and readers. Fortunately, a growing array of sharp studies is now available to facilitate the deconstruction and subsequent understanding of how missionaries, apologists, and romantics contributed to fabricating a contemporary notion of Zen. These studies examine why, for instance, Daisetsu Suzuki (1870–1966) in his own time and context chose to present Zen as the finest product of "Japanese spirituality," and even to claim, "As I conceive it, Zen is the ultimate fact of all philosophy and religion" (1961, p. 268). Works by Faure, McRae, and Wright provide an insightful analysis of this crucial dimension and some of the necessary antidotes. One of their achievements is to reveal contradictions inherent in the discourse of apologists who denied their own historicity.

THE CONCEPT OF MEDITATION

"Zen," pronounced "Chan" in Chinese, has an interesting linguistic background. The Chinese compound "channa" was used to phonetically transcribe the Pali terms "jhāna" or "jhān," from which it derives. "Dhyāna" being the Sanskrit equivalent for the Pali "jhāna," popularizers often simplify this etymology by explaining "chan" as if it derived from "dhyāna." Eventually "chan," the first half of the compound, became a word in itself, retaining some of its original implications.

Indian Buddhists chiefly used the word "jhāna" as a generic term for meditation (singular) and as a technical term for particular meditative states (plural). For example, in the *Sutta-nipāta*, "jhāna" is always singular, and appears in contexts such as "One who possesses the strength of wisdom, born of the moral precepts and restraints, who is tranquil in mind and delights in *meditation*, who is mindful, free from attachment, free from fallowness of mind and the Intoxicants, is called a sage by the wise" (I.12, verse 212; Saddhātissa 1985, p. 22; italics added). Here "meditation" is apt, as long as the English word is understood in its pseudo-etymological sense of (*re*)*centering* the mind, an approximation for one of the definitions of "jhāna," the mind "focused on one point" (Skt., *ekagrātā*), and as long as the object of this concentration is understood as being nondiscursive.

The technical usage of "jhānas" in the plural refers to particular meditative states, often translated as "absorptions" or "enstasis." In the Buddhist canon the *jhānas* gradually were systematized to include four stages. An even more elaborate description of these stages in the canon mentions how the practitioner moves through these four successive absorptions, then enters the four "attainments" (*samāpattis*), which culminate in the ninth stage with cessation of perception and feeling (Pali, *saññāvedayitanirodha*), better known as the attainment of cessation (Skt., *nirodha-samāpatti*).

Despite the importance of these nine meditative states, no Indian Buddhist school ever focused exclusively on the practice of absorptions or the practice of meditation. Such developments in the Chinese cultural sphere constitute a huge semantic leap and a complete reinterpretation of the tradition. (See Griffiths [1993] on *jhānas*.)

THE EMERGENCE OF CHAN AS A DISTINCT MOVEMENT

Details of how Buddhism entered East Asia around the first century CE and gradually spread within the Chinese cultural sphere remain surprisingly ill defined. At a certain point after the end of this transmission process, in some circles, meditation ceased to be considered as only one of the three central methods of self-cultivation (morality, concentration, and insight), and groups of practitioners started identifying themselves as adepts of Chan, understood in the sense of "meditation."

When did Chan Buddhism emerge as a distinct movement, historically and geographically? Here again caution is required, because those seeing themselves as spokespersons for Chan largely defined their identity in contrast with other Buddhist schools prevalent at that time. If we adopt the scheme proposed by John McRae (2003), this phase began with proto-Chan around 500–600 CE, which coincides with the growing success of the rival Tiantai lineage. In the following stage,

> at the beginning of the eighth century the self-described successors to this community exploded on the national scene, and in the process they described themselves as an identifiable religious movement using the lineage model. No matter how diverse and multifaceted the Chan movement was at this point in time, no matter how fuzzy the boundaries were between it and other realms of Chinese religious life, from this point onward Chan had achieved a significant level of sectarian identity. (McRae, p. 121)

Yet in the Chinese context it would be inaccurate to speak of members of an organized "meditation school." Even in the ninth century, Guifeng Zongmi (780–841) included in his *Chan yuan zhu quanji duxu* (Preface to the collected writings on the source of Chan) a list of Chan teachers that included the Tiantai patriarch Zhiyi (538–597) (Gregory 1991). Put differently, "Chan" in the sense of meditation never exclusively belonged to the Chan School. For one, it was part of the Buddhist legacy and played a central role in the practice of other lineages, such as the Tiantai School. For another, as John McRae convincingly argues, the organization of Chinese Buddhism never implied a sectarian-centered administrative system. Despite a heavy bureaucratic apparatus and the government-sponsored system that emerged in the Song dynasty (960–1279), monasteries were mostly administrated in rotation by the different lineages, and in China sectarian borders never became as strictly delimited as in premodern and modern Japan.

Sectarian developments took a further turn in Japan during the Tokugawa period (1600–1867) and evolved into the present rigid structures at the beginning of the Meiji era (1868–1912). Yet even in Japan until at least the eighteenth century, the expression "Chanzong" (Jpn., *Zenshū*) meant the Chan lineage or the principle of Chan, and by no means referred to the Zen School or any institutionalized sect. The latter connotation emerged in Japan after the Meiji Restoration, when in 1872 the new Ministry of Doctrine created a single school labeled "Zen sect" including the Rinzai, Sōtō, and Ōbaku denominations. However, this forceful attempt to centralize Buddhist institutions met such strong clerical opposition that the government quickly stepped back. It recognized the independence of the Rinzai and Sōtō schools in 1874, then the autonomy of the Ōbaku School in 1876.

Geographically, where did Chan emerge? Saying that it emerged in the Chinese cultural sphere, rather than in China, aims at avoiding the easy assumption that China (understood as the modern nation) was the one and only cradle in which the Chan tradition grew up. This point is still controversial. Thich Nhât Hanh, a leading representative of the Vietnamese Thiên tradition, claims that the area of Jiaozhou, a colony of southern China from 111 BCE until 939 CE corresponding to present Thuan Thanh in northern Vietnam, saw the emergence of such a tradition at a much earlier time. He argues, "Buddhism was first introduced to Vietnam from India via the sea trade routes, beginning around the first century CE. Many people think that Buddhism came to Vietnam through China, but in fact it arrived first in Vietnam from India and was subsequently introduced to southern China from Vietnam" (2001, p. 4). This idea is appealing, especially to demonstrate that the Vietnamese Buddhist tradition is older than that of its former Chinese oppressor, but the additional suggestion that Buddhism was introduced to southern Vietnam (Cham at the time) from Jiaozhou seems difficult to support. Further, Nhât Hanh's presenting Kuong Tang Hôi (Chin., Kang Senghui; d. 280) as the first patriarch of Zen in Vietnam is questionable. Unfortunately, Nhât Hanh's ambiguous use of the word "Zen" and his agenda to demonstrate the antiquity of the Vietnamese tradition with a candidate who predates proto-Chan by more than two centuries undermine the reliability of his perspective. (For a balanced evaluation of the construction of Vietnamese orthodoxy, see Nguyen's [1997] study.)

THE PHILOSOPHICAL TURN

There are contemporary philosophers who seek inspiration in Zen or Buddhism, and there is a philosophical endeavor within the tradition itself. The former case stretches from intellectual curiosity to the commitment of Nishida Kitarō (1870–1945), whose Zen practice laid the basis for a major part of his philosophical work. Yet even Nishida claimed not to formulate a Zen philosophy,

but only to reflect about universal philosophical problems in the light of his personal understanding of Buddhism. In any case, Nishida and his philosophical project must be appreciated within the context of the Japanese industrial revolution. Japan was engaged in importing techniques and culture from the West at a high pitch. To compensate for the unbalance caused by this new situation, Japanese thinkers sought to highlight the unique aspects of Japanese culture. This desire found expression in efforts by Nishida and others to demonstrate the compatibility or superiority of the alleged intuitive thinking of the East with the newly imported Western rationality. (About Nishida, see Heisig 2001, Tremblay 2000, and Yusa 2002.)

The philosophical articulation of the tradition itself is a more difficult subject. The difficulty stems not from the alleged absence of rationality in the East Asian Buddhist tradition, a critique overcome by the dedicated work of a generation of scholars. Rather, it results from the absence of a clear demarcation between Zen philosophy and Buddhist philosophy. Kasulis observes that, despite a huge literary production, traditional Zen accounts fail to justify their distrust of verbal distinctions or dualistic formulations "simply because it has already been offered by traditions influential in the very emergence of Zen Buddhism" (1981, p. 15).

Here the term "Zen Buddhism" (an oddity coined by Daisetsu Suzuki that should be avoided in scholarly contexts) confirms the suspicion that philosophical questioning cannot be confined to Zen alone, insofar as it constitutes a subcategory of the Buddhist worldview. Past attempts to present Zen as special and unfathomable are now better understood for what they were: sectarian proselytism. This observation does not prevent one from asking whether, after all, the Zen traditions have a specific philosophical perspective to offer.

SPECIFIC FEATURES OF ZEN

The quest to discover the real self, with subtle nuances sometimes labeled as "awakening" or "seeing one's true nature," is not a uniquely Zen feature. No doubt it occupies a central place in the Zen traditions, but it equally belongs to all Buddhist schools, being precisely what makes them Buddhist. Yet each particular Buddhist approach definitely displays a different flavor. For instance, Pure Land practices favor more devotional attitudes, while the Tiantai or Huayan traditions tend to privilege a more intellectual apprehension of the Buddhist path. Specific features can be found in the style of teaching, in the emphasis on particular types of cultivation, in doctrinal formulations or textual records, in rituals, and in the interactions with distinctive sociohistorical contexts. The use of vernacular Chinese in the Chan literature to duplicate or imagine dialogical encounters also constitutes a new genre.

The special features of the various Zen lineages did not pop up from some transhistorical background. Scholars now unanimously agree that most of the above-mentioned features of Chan in the Chinese cultural sphere found some degree of standardization during the Song dynasty. This means that even philosophical investigations into the spiritual cultivation of past Zen practitioners must cope with a double-layered filter: the construction of various orthodoxies in the Song period and subsequent interpretations by proselytes, which often replicate or amplify the first filter. With this in mind, let us nevertheless examine an example of a Zen teaching device where the context appears sufficiently explicit.

CRITICAL VOICE OR RHETORICAL DEVICE

One of the literary monuments of the Song period is the *Blue Cliff Record* (*Biyan lu*), a Chan anthology with commentaries by Yuanwu Keqin (1063–1135). The following dialog is provided here as it stands as case 11 in the *Hundred Cases of Xuedou*, the older version containing only the cases selected by Xuedou Zhongxian (980–1052) without Yuanwu's commentary:

> Huangbo taught the Sangha saying: "All of you people are stuffing yourselves with wine lees! If you keep roaming this way, how could this [decisive] moment [ever] arrive? Are you aware of the *nonexistence* of Chan teachers in the whole Tang China?"
>
> At this point, a monk emerged [from the crowd] saying: "What about all those [like you] who help students and lead the Sangha?"
>
> Huangbo.—"I didn't say Chan is nonexistent, only teachers are nonexistent." (Taishō 48: 151b11–b16)

Previous translations used the expression "gobblers of dregs," which sounds good in English and has the advantage of evoking lowlifes, but remains unsatisfactory. The provocation at the beginning of the passage refers to wine lees to make listeners aware that just as eating wine lees leads to intoxication, so depending on teachers and repeating teachings without personal insight is delusive.

Another overlooked dimension of this passage is the allusion of this metaphor to the Buddhist canon. The *Nir-vana Sutra* tells an elaborate story about an ignorant king debating with a wise physician. The physician describes a marvelous medication that counteracts the effects of poison. This drug is actually a particular type of milk produced under strict conditions:

> If the cows don't eat *wine lees*, smooth grasses, or barley chaff, their calves will choose the good [path]. For grazing they will neither stay in the highlands nor come down to swamps. They will drink in limpid streams and won't be forced to run. They will not gather in herd with the bulls. Their drinking and eating will be adjusted; they will fit walk or immobility and find their place. Milk [produced] this way perfectly eliminates all ailments. (Taishō 12: 378c04–07)

Should this metaphor remain obscure, several commentators offer keys to understanding it. Huiyuan (523–592) of Jingying Temple provides a straightforward explanation: "If the cows represent the bodhisattvas … , *wine lees* represent ignorance, smooth grasses represent avidity, and barley chaff represents anger" (Taishō 37: 651a19–21).

In this light, the utterance attributed to Huangbo (d. c. 850) is far from simple rudeness to his audience or a dismissive critique of contemporary teachers. This teaching is a rhetorical device pointing at the auditors' fundamental ignorance and need to rediscover true autonomy. Whether Huangbo really uttered these words is best answered by Wright's careful statement: "The Huang Po texts available for our reading should be attributed not to any one creative individual or mind, but rather to the Zen tradition in China as it took shape over many centuries" (1998, p. 18).

The above excursion into the maze of intertextuality serves three purposes. First, it illustrates the immaturity of most Chan translations. Second, it shows the interdependence of Chan texts and Buddhist classics, and the need for further integration of the two fields. Third, it allows one to envision these dialogs in the context of monastic practice.

THE PRIORITY OF SOTERIOLOGICAL CONCERNS

If a common thread binds together the different Zen lineages, it may seem to be their uncompromising emphasis on awakening, based on the premise that the means and the end ultimately are not separate. In his characterization of Buddhism in general, Guy Bugault notes the primacy of the soteriological dimension over theoretical constructs, saying, "Accurately speaking, Buddhism at its original stage was neither a religion nor a philosophy, but a psychosomatic discipline including three elements: morality (*śīla*), concentration (*samādhi*), and intellectual discernment or *acies mentis* (*prajñā*). None of them can function without the other" (1994, p. 43, translated from the French).

As with the poisoned arrow representing existential dis–ease (Pali, *dukkha*), the most urgent task is to remove it, speculations about its nature or shape being no more than delusive thought. Acute intellectual discernment is required to remove the arrow. The subtle boundary separating concentration and intellectual discernment is itself a theme worthy of examination, from both the Zen and philosophical perspectives. If there is a philosophical aspect specific to the Zen traditions, it is not so much in their striving to remove the arrow than in their emphasis on going beyond it, aiming at removing all traces of the operation.

See also Buddhism; Buddhism—Schools: Hua yan; Dogen; Jinul.

Bibliography

Bugault, Guy. *L'inde pense-t-elle?* Paris: Presses universitaires de France, 1994.

Buswell, Robert E., Jr. *The Zen Monastic Experience: Buddhist Practice in Contemporary Korea.* Princeton, NJ: Princeton University Press, 1992.

Faure, Bernard. *Chan Insights and Oversights: An Epistemological Critique of the Chan Tradition.* Princeton, NJ: Princeton University Press, 1993.

Faure, Bernard. *Double Exposure: Cutting across Buddhist and Western Discourses.* Translated by Janet Lloyd. Stanford, CA: Stanford University Press, 2003.

Foulk, T. Griffith. "Myth, Ritual, and Monastic Practice in Sung Ch'an Buddhism." In *Religion and Society in T'ang and Sung China,* edited by Patricia Buckley Ebrey and Peter N. Gregory. Honolulu: University of Hawai'i Press, 1993.

Gregory, Peter N. *Tsung-mi and the Sinification of Buddhism.* Princeton, NJ: Princeton University Press, 1991.

Griffiths, Paul J. "Indian Buddhist Meditation." In *Buddhist Spirituality.* Vol. 1: *Indian, Southeast Asian, Tibetan, and Early Chinese,* edited by Yoshinori Takeuchi and Jan Van Bragt. New York: Crossroad, 1993.

Heine, Steven, and Dale S. Wright, eds. *The Kōan: Texts and Contexts in Zen Buddhism.* New York: Oxford University Press, 2000.

Heisig, James W. *Philosophers of Nothingness: An Essay on the Kyoto School.* Honolulu: University of Hawai'i Press, 2001.

Heisig, James W., and John C. Maraldo, eds. *Rude Awakenings: Zen, the Kyoto School, and the Question of Nationalism.* Honolulu: University of Hawai'i Press, 1994.

Hoffman, Frank J. *Rationality and Mind in Early Buddhism.* Delhi: Motilal Banarsidass, 1987.

Hori, Victor Sōgen. *Zen Sand: The Book of Capping Phrases for Kōan Practice.* Honolulu: University of Hawai'i Press, 2003.

Huiyuan of Jingying Temple. *Dapan niepanjing yiji.* Taishō 37 no. 1764, pp. 613–903.

Kasulis, Thomas P. "The Zen Philosopher: A Review Article on Dogen Scholarship in English." *Philosophy East and West* 28 (3) (1978): 353–373.

Kasulis, Thomas P. *Zen Action, Zen Person.* Honolulu: University Press of Hawaii, 1981.

Kirchner, Thomas Yūhō. *Entangling Vines: Zen Koans of the Shūmon Kattōshū.* Kyoto: Tenryu-ji Institute for Philosophy and Religion, 2004.

McRae, John R. *Seeing through Zen: Encounter, Transformation, and Genealogy in Chinese Chan Buddhism.* Berkeley: University of California Press, 2003.

Mohr, Michel. "Hakuin." In *Buddhist Spirituality,* Vol. 2: *Later China, Korea, Japan, and the Modern World,* edited by Yoshinori Takeuchi, J. W. Heisig, P. L. Swanson, and J. S. O'Leary. New York: Crossroad, 1999.

Mohr, Michel. "Emerging from Non-duality: Kōan Practice in the Rinzai Tradition since Hakuin." In *The Kōan: Texts and Contexts in Zen Buddhism,* edited by Steven Heine and Dale S. Wright. New York: Oxford University Press, 2000.

Mohr, Michel. "Imagining Indian Zen: Tōrei's Commentary on the *Damoduoluo chanjing* and the Rediscovery of Early Meditation Techniques during the Tokugawa." In *Zen Classics,* edited by Steven Heine and Dale S. Wright. New York: Oxford University Press, 2005.

Nguyen, Cuong Tu. *Zen in Medieval Vietnam: A Study and Translation of the Thien Uyen Tap Anh.* Honolulu: University of Hawai'i Press, 1997.

Nhât Hanh, Thich. *Master Tang Hôi: First Zen Teacher in Vietnam and China.* Berkeley, CA: Parallax Press, 2001.

Nirvana Sutra. Translation attributed to Dharmaksema, Taishō 12 No. 374 pp. 365–604.

Nishida Kitarō. *L'éveil à soi,* edited by Jacynthe Tremblay. Paris: CNRS éditions, 2003.

Saddhātissa. *The Sutta-Nipāta.* London: Curzon Press, 1985.

Sharf, Robert H. *Coming to Terms with Chinese Buddhism: A Reading of the Treasure Store Treatise.* Honolulu: University of Hawai'i Press, 2001.

Suzuki, Daisetz Teitaro. *Essays in Zen Buddhism.* First series (1927). New York: Grove Press, 1961.

Tremblay, Jacynthe. *Nishida Kitarô: Le jeu de l'individuel et de l'universel.* Paris: CNRS éditions, 2000.

Williams, Duncan Ryūken. *The Other Side of Zen: A Social History of Sōtō Zen Buddhism in Tokugawa Japan.* Princeton, NJ: Princeton University Press, 2005.

Wright, Dale S. *Philosophical Meditations on Zen Buddhism.* New York: Cambridge University Press, 1998.

Yusa, Michiko. *Zen and Philosophy: An Intellectual Biography of Nishida Kitarō.* Honolulu: University of Hawai'i Press, 2002.

Yuanwu Keqin. *The Blue Cliff Record.* Translated by Thomas Cleary. Berkeley, CA: Numata Center for Buddhist Translation and Research, 1998.

Yuanwu Keqin, and Xuedou, Zhongxian. *Biyan lu.* Taishō 48 no. 2003, pp. 139–225.

Michel Mohr (2005)

DGE-LUGS

The Dge-lugs (pronounced "geluk") tradition of Tibetan Buddhism, the tradition followed by the Dalai Lamas, traces its origins to the towering Tibetan philosopher and monastic reformer Tsong kha pa (1357–1419) and his two closest disciples, Rgyal-tshab (pronounced "gyelt-sap") (1364–1432) and Mkhas grub (pronounced "kay-drup") (1358–1438), whose views have come to represent orthodoxy for the tradition. According to traditional hagiographies, Tsong kha pa studied with more than sixty of the greatest scholars in Tibet during his early life and went on to compose numerous treatises and commentaries on the entire spectrum of Buddhist thought and practice, leaving a set of collected works that numbers nineteen volumes. His philosophical works address virtually all the major topics in Buddhist philosophical discourse, including issues of ontology, metaphysics, epistemology, logic, soteriology, and hermeneutics, among others. Aided by historical and political conditions Tsong kha pa's works, those of his disciples, and the monastic and educational systems he initiated made the Dge-lugs tradition the dominant philosophical tradition in Tibet. Indeed, Tsong kha pa was such a powerful intellectual force in Tibet that all subsequent philosophers, including those who disagreed with him, felt compelled to acknowledge and address Dge-lugs-type criticisms that they anticipated their views might incur.

While there is much in common among Dge-lugs philosophers in terms of their philosophical positions and methods, it would be misleading to suggest that the Dge-lugs tradition and its notable philosophers are univocal in their philosophical presentations. Many lively debates and polemic directed at fellow members of the Dge-lugs tradition can be found in the works of the great thinkers of the tradition, including Tsong kha pa's direct disciples Rgyal-tshab and Mkhas grub, as well as later thinkers such as 'Jamdbyangs bzhad pa (1648–1721), Rje btsun Chos kyi 'gyal mtshan (1469–1544), and Lcang skya rol baï rdo rje (1717–1786), among others. Despite this marked diversity of opinion, there is nonetheless a relatively standard Dge-lugs philosophical presentation that those in the tradition generally agree on. The intra-tradition debates tend to focus on lofty and quite subtle points, while the mainstream Dge-lugs philosophical worldview accepted across the tradition remains as the foundation for debates about such subtle points of contention.

Many significant features of Dge-lugs philosophy stand in contrast with other Buddhist traditions. Among the most significant is the marked emphasis Dge-lugs philosophers place on the study of the Indian Buddhist philosophical tradition they inherited and on what they understand to be the correct interpretation of that tradition. Thus any discussion of Dge-lugs philosophy must be approached through an examination of how the earliest Dge-lugs masters interpreted and represented Indian Buddhist philosophical history.

DGE-LUGS MADHYAMAKA

While the works of many Indian philosophers have impacted Dge-lugs philosophy, the Dge-lugs tradition traces its intellectual lineage most significantly through two important Indian philosophers: Nāgārjuna (c. first century C.E.) and Candrakīrti (c. 600–650). Nāgārjuna, author of the The Fundamental Wisdom of the Middle Way (Mūlamadhyamakakārika), among other texts, is considered the founder and systematizer of the school of Mahayana philosophical thought known as Madhyamaka or the Middle-Way School. Virtually all Tibetan Buddhist schools consider themselves to be Mādhyamikas, followers of Nāgārjuna's tradition in one form or another and the Dge-lugspas are no exceptions in this regard. The central idea that guides the thought of Nāgārjuna and the Madhyamaka School is the notion of emptiness (śūnyatā). When Mādhyamikas such as Tsong kha pa use the term "emptiness," they mean that an object lacks a fixed or unchanging nature. To say that a pot, for example, is empty (metaphysically empty) is to say that it lacks a permanent nature or essence, an independent, intrinsic identity.

The Dge-lugs presentation of the middle way owes much to their reading of the history of their Indian Madhyamaka predecessors. When Dge-lugs philosophers and scholars study the history of Indian Madhyamaka, they begin by recognizing that Nāgārjuna and his student Āryadeva are considered authoritative by all subsequent commentators and interpreters of Madhyamaka thought. According to Tsong kha pa's assessment of the history of Indian Madhyamaka, an important philosophical split occurred in Madhyamaka discourse several centuries after Nāgārjuna when Buddhapālita (c. 470–540?) wrote a commentary on Nāgārjuna's Fundamental Wisdom of the Middle Way. This was followed by a criticism of that treatise by Bhāvaviveka (c. 500–570?) and a subsequent defense by Candrakīrti of Buddhapālita's position against those criticisms leveled by Bhāvaviveka. Much of this debate in the Indian tradition revolved around the appropriate form of reasoning to be utilized by Madhyamaka philosophers. With this point in mind, later Tibetans such as Tsong kha pa distinguished subschools of Indian Madhyamaka philosophy, in part on the basis of the form of reasoning that their proponents utilize.

Buddhapālita's commentary, simply titled (in English) *Buddhapālita's Commentary on [Nāgārjuna's] "Fundamental Wisdom of the Middle Way"* is a lucid exposition of Nāgārjuna's text that utilizes a method known as consequentialist argument (*prasaṅga*). Much as in Nāgārjuna's text, Buddhapālita's form of argumentation examines the positions of philosophical rivals to reveal the absurd consequences of holding such positions. In other words, consequentialist arguments attempt to reduce the philosophical positions of opponents to absurdities. All philosophical opponents of Mādhyamikas maintain that some things are not empty, have a true nature or essence, and have independent, permanent existence. For all such contemporary opponents, Buddhapālita, like Nāgārjuna before him, attempted to reveal what he saw to be the absurd positions entailed by their various positions asserting true existence. Though the logical innovations of Dignāga (c. 480–540) were beginning to make headway into Mahayana discourse, Buddhapālita avoided these innovations in logic, such as the use of independent argument (*svatantrānumāna*), thus avoiding commitment to a counterposition when criticizing his opponents. Dge-lugspas have tended to presume that Buddhapālita was simply and faithfully following the method of Nāgārjuna.

Bhāvaviveka, in contrast, argued that Mādhyamikas must assert their own philosophical position. Simply to criticize others without establishing one's own position, the emptiness view, is inadequate. And to establish one's own position, Bhāvaviveka argued, one must use independent inferences. Thus, in *Prajñā-pradīpaḥ: A Commentary on the Madhyamaka Sūtra*, his commentary on Nāgārjuna's *Fundamental Wisdom of the Middle Way*, Bhāvaviveka offers a pointed criticism of Buddhapālita's failure to establish a Madhyamaka thesis, as well as an exposition of the need to use independent argument (*svatantrānumāna*) to fulfill that task. Accordingly, Dge-lugspas categorized Bhāvaviveka's particular brand of the middle way as Svātantrika-Madhyamaka. In contrast, Dge-lugs doxographers describe Buddhapālita and his defender Candrakīrti (described below) as Prāsaṅgika-Mādhyamikas, because they insist on primarily using consequentialist arguments (*prasaṅga*).

Candrakīrti (c. 600–650) is the third important figure in this Indian Madhyamaka debate, according to Dge-lugs authors. Candrakīrti composed several philosophical texts, two which are important to Dge-lugs philosophers on the central issue of the appropriate form of reasoning

for proponents of Madhyamaka views: his *Introduction to the Middle Way* (*Madhyamakāvatāra*) and *Lucid exposition of the middle way* (*Prasannapadā Madhyamakavrtti*. In these texts Candrakīrti philosophically defended Buddhapālita against the criticisms leveled by Bhāvaviveka. Candrakīrti argued not only that Buddhapālita was correct to use only consequentialist arguments, but also that using independent arguments are incompatible with Madhyamaka tenets.

In the Dge-lugs reading of this debate, there is a fundamental ontological problem with using independent arguments. Such usage implies acceptance of an inherent, absolute, or unchanging nature in phenomena, and this implication is utterly contrary to the most basic Madhyamaka tenet—that all phenomena are empty of just such a nature or essence. Dge-lugs philosophers such as Tsong kha pa argued that because one characteristic of an independent inference is a commonly appearing subject in the inference, the inference implies that the subject must have some sort of absolute existence. For example, in the independent inference "This book is impermanent because it is produced," the subject, this book, must appear in precisely the same way, in a way which is common to both the proponent and opponent of the argument. If it does not, then the two debaters are just talking past each other. If it does have a precise and common mode of appearance to both the proponent and opponent, then it must have some absolute mode of existence, some intrinsic identity, some sort of inherent nature.

Thus, the mere use of independent arguments runs utterly contrary to the Madhyamaka view, according to Tsong kha pa and his Dge-lugs followers. Although Tsong kha pa considered Buddhapālita to be a Prāsaṅgika-Mādhyamika from his views and method, he considered Candrakīrti to be the "founder" of the Prāsaṅgika-Madhyamaka view, since he was the first clearly to articulate the importance of using consequentialist arguments and the contradictions involved when Mādhyamikas use independent arguments.

An interesting feature of Tsong kha pa's middle way is that though he recognized the limits of language, he still insisted on rationality and the laws of logic in his investigations and conclusions concerning the ultimate. In this sense, notes Georges Dreyfus in *The Sound of Two Hands Clapping*, Tsong kha pa ought to be considered a realist. Śāntarakṣita, an eighth-century scholar who was a key figure in the early dissemination of Buddhism in Tibet, was a late Indian Mādhyamika who incorporated the logico-epistemological (*pramāṇavāda*) innovations of Dignāga and, more prominently, Dharmakīrti (seventh century) into his particular brand of the middle way. Though Śāntarakṣita was considered to be a Svātantrika-Mādhyamika with whom he took issue on several counts, Tsong kha pa nevertheless preserved, and even intensified, Śāntarakṣita's emphasis on the role of reason in his Madhyamaka method. The particularities of how Tsong kha pa integrated the logico-epistemological tradition into Madhyamaka analysis are central to the insights that made his thought unique.

To turn now to the Tibetan Madhyamaka tradition, for Dge-lugs philosophers, an issue central to all Madhyamaka philosophical analysis and inseparably tied to the issue of an appropriate logic is the issue of the two types of truth: ultimate truth (*don dam bden pa* [Tibetan], *paramārthasatya* [Sanskrit]) and conventional truth (*kun dzob bden pa*, *saṃvṛtisatya*). Truths in this context are objects of knowledge. Hence it makes sense to talk of truths existing. Since its earliest formulation in the works of Nāgārjuna, Madhyamaka thinkers have used a presentation of the two types of truths as a primary marker against which they have delineated their positions on central Buddhist topics in ontology and epistemology.

Dge-lugs philosophers illuminated the distinctions they drew between ultimate and conventional truths by contrasting their positions as Prāsaṅgika-Mādhyamikas with the position of their Madhyamaka rivals, the so-called Svātantrika-Mādhyamikas, such as Bhāvaviveka. This takes place in the treatises of Tsong kha pa and his direct disciples and also in a genre of philosophical literature prominent in monastic study and known as tenet-system texts or doxographies. In this literature, Dge-lugs authors present major systems of non-Buddhist and Buddhist philosophical thought in a hierarchically organized fashion. Each of the tenet systems (or at least the Buddhist systems) are presented in terms of a host of philosophical categories of analysis, such as the two truths, definitions of consciousness and objects of consciousness, delineation of the path, delineation of the fruits of the path, and so on. Consistency in analytic categories across the presentation of schools of thought facilitates easy comparisons between systems and usefully allows one easily to ascend a hierarchy of philosophical positions in a dialectical fashion by contrasting the present system with the less subtle and less accurate system just below it.

For example, one can easily compare all four Buddhist schools' definitions of ultimate truths, conventional truths, consciousness, and the like, by seeing that school *x* defines a conventional truth in one way, school *y* in another, and school *z* in yet another. Often the views presented in this literature do not precisely mirror those of

any single Indian author, but rather are amalgamations of the views of several presumably like-minded thinkers and of unstated positions considered to follow logically from other stated positions. As mentioned above, for Dge-lugs thinkers, the highest and most accurate Buddhist philosophical description of the nature of reality is the Prāsaṅgika-Madhyamaka. Just below that position in the hierarchy is the Svātantrika-Madhyamaka view. Thus, the Svātantrika view is most commonly contrasted with the Prāsaṅgika-Madhyamaka position to help illuminate the Dge-lugs-Prāsaṅgika view.

When Dge-lugs authors discuss the issue of the two types of truths, they employ a number of key technical terms. Jeffrey Hopkins mentions sixteen terms in his book *Meditation on Emptiness*, of which the six most commonly used are the following:

- Ultimately established existence (*don dam par grub pa*)
- Truly established existence (*den par grub pa*)
- Existence established in reality (*yang dag par grub pa*)
- Existence established by way of the intrinsic identity/characteristics of an object (*rang gi mtshan nyid kyis grub pa*)
- Existence established by way of the inherent nature of an object (*rang bzhing gyis grub pa*)
- Existence established from its own side (*rang ngos nas grub pa*)

According to Dge-lugs philosophers such as Tsong kha pa, all Mādhyamikas, including the Prāsaṅgikas and the Svātantrikas, held that the first three terms on the list accurately describe ultimate truths, since such truths lack (are empty of) ultimately established existence, truly established existence, and existence established in reality. An example of an ultimate truth for either a Svātantrika-Mādhyamika or a Prāsaṅgika-Mādhyamika would be the lack of any ultimately established existence or truly established existence in this book, for example. The lack of ultimately or truly established existence refers to the absence of any objective existence, any independent absolute mode of being, any fixed independent essence, within this book. Thus far, according to Dge-lugs thinkers, both subschools of Madhyamaka thought are in agreement.

The disagreement between the two subschools concerns their positions on the ontological status of conventional truths. According to Dge-lugs thinkers, while all Mādhyamikas, when presenting ultimate truths, argue that phenomena lack an ultimate nature, the Svātantrika-Mādhyamikas accept that conventional truths exist in the latter three ways listed above; that is, they exist by way of their own intrinsic identity, by way of inherent nature, and from their own side. This, according to Dge-lugspas, is how the Svātantrika-Mādhyamikas could view their position as maintaining a middle ground between absolute permanence and absolute nonexistence, or nihilism. They avoid the extreme of permanence by saying that phenomena ultimately lack true existence. They avoid the extreme of nihilism by claiming that phenomena conventionally exist by way of their own characteristics, by way of their intrinsic nature, or from their own side.

In relation to the logical issues discussed above, because phenomena conventionally exist from their own side or by way of their own intrinsic identity/characteristics, objects such as books and tables can serve as commonly appearing subjects in independent inferences. An inherent nature or intrinsic characteristics on the side of the book, for example, cause an ignorant, unenlightened consciousness to recognize that object and correctly impute the conventional designation "book" on the basis of a nondefective conventional cognition. Such an imputation has a referent as object, to which it correctly points with a conventional designation ("book").

Dge-lugspas found this position, which they attributed to Svātantrika-Mādhyamikas, highly problematic. They argued that all six technical terms mentioned above to describe the ontological status of things are coextensive. If an object can be described in one of the six ways, it can be described in all six ways. Dge-lugspas thus argued that ultimate truths *and* conventional truths do not exist in any of the ways described above. They argued that if objects are established by way of their own intrinsic identity, by way of some sort of inherent nature of their own, or from their own sides, even conventionally, then objects must have some sort of ultimate nature. Dge-lugspas would criticize their Madhyamaka opponents by arguing that although they claim that some objects exist only conventionally, if they assert that the objects inherently possess some nature of their own in any way, even conventionally, this is really just a masked way of continuing to cling to some independent essence or nature in the objects ultimately. For an object to cause a conventional consciousness to correctly recognize and label it, there must be something true or absolute in the object. Thus in the Prāsaṅgika-Madhyamaka position held by Dge-lugspas, both ultimate and conventional

truths lack all six criteria (sixteen as listed by Hopkins) of ultimate and conventional truths.

While Svātantrikas accept that conventional truths exist inherently, by way of their own characteristics, and from their own sides, Dge-lugspas, such as the Prāsaṅgikas, reject the idea that even conventional truths are established in this way. Conventional truths are actually falsities. There is nothing true about how minds under the sway of ignorance conceptualize these falsities. This is not to say that the world does not exist out there. It is just to say that we are utterly deluded when we engage with the world because we impose fixed essences in things when no such essences exist. And this is what Svātantrikas are doing when they claim that even mere conventional truths inherently exist. For Dge-lugspas, such as the Prāsaṅgika-Mādhyamikas, conventional truths are true only for a consciousness for which the actual nature of reality is obscured. They do not exist as they appear to a conventional consciousness. Dge-lugspas such as Tsong kha pa held that they avoided the extreme of nihilism by accepting the functionality of conventional phenomena despite the falsity of their appearances.

It is important to keep in mind that this is a standard Dge-lugs presentation of this history and these ideas. While Dge-lugs authors associated specific Indian Madhyamaka thinkers with these subschools of Madhyamaka thought, there does not appear to be evidence in Indian sources before the twelfth century of any explicitly named subschools of Madhyamaka thought. Prior to this time, the thinkers discussed here and labeled "Prāsaṅgika-Madhyamaka" or "Svātantrika-Madhyamaka" in the Dge-lugs literature identified their own views as simply Madhyamaka.

THE DGE-LUGS CURRICULUM AND SCHOLASTIC METHODS

Any discussion of Dge-lugs philosophy must move beyond ideas and also discuss the curriculum and methods employed in Dge-lugs institutions, which direct a significant amount of their focus to philosophical study. Tsong kha pa initiated a scholastic approach to Buddhism that, although presented to lesser degrees before him in Tibet, marked a significant departure from the mystical gnosis of individuals as sources of authority for the tradition before him. Tsong kha pa emphasized reasoning, which could be learned, in time, only in monastic universities, thus advancing a shift in authority from individuals to institutions and a wholesale reform of monastic culture, which he saw as deteriorating in Tibet during his time. As time went on and the monastic colleges grew, the degree of scholasticism grew with it. Key figures from the Dge-lugs monastic colleges began to compose textbooks (*yig cha*) as manuals for study in attempt to present coherent, consistent, totalizing systems of thought immune to critique, especially internal contradiction. This move toward scholasticism certainly reinforced institutional authority, but the importance of mystical gnosis of expert scholar-adepts was far from lost in the Dge-lugs tradition, though the reins on the careers of independent yogis were significantly tightened in this tradition.

The Dge-lugs tradition maintains a large monastic component that includes three major monastic seats—Sera, Drepung, and Ganden—and several colleges within those monastic seats. Traditionally, the monastic seats housed between 5,000 and 10,000 monks in each, with good portions of the monks engaged in the philosophical curriculum of one of the monastic colleges. Even in exile in south India, Sera and Drepung each had more than 5,000 monks in residence in 2005. The colleges of the three monastic seats all have a similar curriculum that culminates in a degree known as "geshe." A geshe degree is somewhat akin to a doctorate in Buddhist philosophy. It generally takes somewhere between fifteen and twenty-five years to complete the curriculum, which includes study and memorization of all the major philosophical texts of the tradition, extensive periods of debate (usually four to six hours a day, six days per week), and study of the major commentaries and textbooks of the college, which serve as the interpretive frame through which to engage the major treatises of the Indian and Dge-lugs traditions. Though most monks at Sera, Drepung, and Ganden begin the geshe training, only a small percentage successfully complete the degree because of the difficulty of the subject matter and the rigors of the curriculum, again, much like a doctoral program in the West.

Each of the monastic colleges cover the same basic subjects, though they use different monastic textbooks (*yig cha*), commentaries that present the interpretive frameworks of their particular colleges. Here in the monastic textbooks one begins to find differences in interpretation on subtle philosophical points between authors within the Dge-lugs tradition. Often scholars from the different monastic colleges will take great pride in the monastic textbooks of their particular colleges and the interpretive framework they employ for understanding the philosophical views of Tsong kha pa, Candrakīrti, and other great philosophers. Within the curriculum there are preliminary subjects covering the basics of topics such as the forms of reasoning and debate, soteriolog-

ical grounds, and paths; types of minds/consciousnesses according to the Buddhist tradition; the philosophical tenet systems of the four Indian Buddhist schools; and so on. Once these preliminary subjects are successfully completed, the Dge-lugs scholar progresses on to the five subjects of the geshe curriculum, which include the perfection of wisdom, maplike descriptions of states of consciousness as the practitioner removes obstacles to enlightenment and progresses along the Buddhist path, logic and epistemology, Madhyamaka philosophy, cosmology, and monastic ethics. These five subjects include topics on ethics, metaphysics, ontology, hermeneutics, karma, and personal identity among others. For each of these subjects, years are dedicated to primary philosophical texts, which are memorized and then studied intensively with a teacher, who gives the students informed oral explanation on the texts. Students then debate the ideas and fine-tune their understanding in the debate courtyards. Progress exams are given regularly, and the final exam includes a multi-day public debate with top scholars in the tradition.

Many of those who complete this geshe curriculum successfully go on for a sort of postdoc for one to three years at one of the two major tantric colleges, Gyume or Gyuto. Here they study the theory and practice of the major tantric meditational cycles in the Dge-lugs tradition. Completing all these requirements usually qualifies the student as a teacher. Thus, authority is granted primarily through institutions, though this curriculum ideally cultivates—and indeed, was constructed to cultivate—experiential/gnostic authority as well.

The Dge-lugs tradition of Tibetan Buddhism is perhaps the most scholarly and philosophical of all the world's Buddhist traditions. As a living Buddhist tradition, it makes for a fascinating area of investigation, not only for those interested in the history of Buddhist philosophy in general, but also and particularly for those interested in understanding the ideas and structure of a living Buddhist tradition, and understanding how philosophy and philosophical study are integrated with a larger human path.

See also Buddhism; Buddhism—Schools: Madhyamika; Buddhism—Schools: Yogācāra.

Bibliography

Blumenthal, James. *The Ornament of the Middle Way: A Study of the Madhyamaka Thought of Śāntarakṣita.* Ithaca: Snow Lion Publications, 2004.
Cabezón, José Ignacio. "The Canonization of Philosophy and the Rhetoric of Siddhānta in Tibetan Buddhism." In *Buddha*

Nature: A Festschrift in Honor of Minoru Kiyota, edited by Paul J. Griffiths and John P. Keenan. San Francisco: Buddhist Books International, 1990.

Cabezón, José Ignacio. *A Dose of Emptiness: An Annotated Translation of the sTong thun chen mo of mKhas grub dGe legs dpal bzang*. Albany, NY: SUNY Press, 1992.

Cabezón, José Ignacio. "The Prāsaṅgikas' Views on Logic: Tibetan Dge-lugs pa Exegesis on the Question of Svatantras." *Journal of Indian Philosophy* 16 (1988): 217–224.

Cozort, Daniel. *The Unique Tenets of the Middle Way Consequence School*. Ithaca, NY: Snow Lion, 1998.

Dreyfus, Georges. *The Sound of Two Hands Clapping: The Education of a Tibetan Buddhist Monk*. Berkeley: University of California Press, 2003.

Dreyfus, Georges. "Tibetan Scholastic Education and the Role of Soteriology." *Journal of the International Association of Buddhist Studies* 20 (1) (1997): 31–62.

Hopkins, Jeffrey. *Emptiness in the Mind-Only School of Buddhism*. Berkeley: University of California Press, 1999.

Hopkins, Jeffrey. *Maps of the Profound: Jam-yang-shay-ba's Great Exposition of Buddhist and Non-Buddhist Views on the Nature of Reality*. Ithaca, NY: Snow Lion Publications, 2003.

Hopkins, Jeffrey. *Meditation on Emptiness*. London: Wisdom Publications: 1983.

Hopkins, Jeffrey. *Reflections on Reality: The Three Natures and Non-natures in the Mind-Only School*. Berkeley: University of California Press, 2002.

Hopkins, Jeffrey. "The Tibetan Genre of Doxography: Structuring a Worldview." In *Tibetan Literature: Studies in Genre*, edited by José Ignacio Cabezón and Roger R. Jackson. Ithaca, NY: Snow Lion Publications, 1996.

Jinpa, Thupten. "Delineating Reason's Scope for Negation: Tsongkhapa's Contribution to Madhyamaka's Dialectical Method." *Journal of Indian Philosophy* 26: 275–308, 1988.

Jinpa, Thupten. *Self, Reality, and Reason in Tibetan Philosophy: Tsongkhapa's Quest for the Middle Way*. London: RoutledgeCurzon, 2002.

Klein, Anne. *The Path to the Middle: Oral Mādhyamika Philosophy in Tibet; The Spoken Scholarship of Kensur Yeshey Tupden*. Albany, NY: SUNY Press, 1994.

Lopez, Donald S. *A Study of Svātantrika*. Ithaca, NY: Snow Lion Publications, 1987.

Napper, Elizabeth. *Dependent Arising and Emptiness: A Tibetan Buddhist Interpretation of Mādhyamika Philosophy Emphasizing the Compatibility of Emptiness and Conventional Phenomena*. Boston: Wisdom Publications, 1989.

Ruegg, David Seyfort. *Two Prolegomena to Madhyamaka Philosophy*. Vienna: Arbeitskreis für Tibetische und Buddhistische Studien, Universität Wien, 2002.

James A. Blumenthal (2005)

HUA YAN

The Hua yan school of Buddhism developed in China between 600–1000 CE, flourishing at the end of the Tang dynasty. It relies for much of its doctrine on exegesis of the Mahayana Buddhist scripture known as the *Hua yan Jing*. The name *Hua yan* (Japanese: *Kegon*) is intended to be the Chinese translation of the Sanskrit *Avataṃsaka*, which means "flower garland." The term is ostensibly the title of a Sanskrit sutra, the *Mahāvaipulya Buddhāvataṃsaka Sūtra*. The Hua yan school developed a *panjiao* (system of classification of Buddhist doctrines), which takes the *Hua yan Jing* to be the most profound of all the Buddhist sutras. This is because it was, according to legend, spoken by the Buddha while in the throes of his awakening experience.

CENTRAL TEXTS

The term *vaipulya* in the title indicates that the text is a composite one, cobbled together from several other texts of various lengths and origins. Some parts of the text, for example the *Daśabhūmika* and the *Gandavyūha*, do exist in a Sanskrit original. In addition, some parts of the text are laden with Chinese phoneticizations of Sanskrit terms, which also indicate a likely Indian origin. The rest is more or less likely to be of indigenously Chinese origin, passed off as or uncritically taken to be translations of Sanskrit originals. For this reason, the origins of the Hua yan tradition are linked to the evolution of a fully sinicized Buddhism.

This is complicated by the fact that many of the key, pivotal translators and advocates of these materials were not indigenously Chinese but in fact were from Central Asia. China and India were kept culturally autonomous for a long time because of the daunting obstacle presented by the Himalayas, so early contact actually was more likely to take place in areas of easy access to the Silk Road. This complicated matters because of the cultural homogenization that also followed along with such developments. Since the latter part of the twentieth century, there has been much study about the extent to which the flow of ideas from many cultures along the Silk Road influenced the development of the uniquely Chinese forms of Buddhism.

There are two arguably complete versions, or translations, of the text in Chinese. The earliest consists of sixty chapters, produced by Buddhabhadra in about 420. Traditionally, this has been used by Hua yan writers as the standard text. In 699 a version in eighty chapters was produced by Śikṣānanda. The only complete English translation of the Hua yan sutra, in three volumes, was produced by Thomas Cleary in the late 1980s. For reasons he does not explain, Cleary translates Śikṣānanda's version, although it is not as historically important as Buddhabhadra's text.

In addition, there do exist various Chinese versions of parts of the sutra, such as the *Gandavyūha*, for which is there is a Sanskrit original.

Another text of crucial importance to the development of the Hua yan tradition is the *Dasheng Qixin Lun* (Mahayana awakening of faith). This text is also arguably an apocryphal text, written in Chinese but taken as a translation of a nonexistent Sanskrit text ostensibly titled *Mahayānaśraddhotpāda*. This text is cited by all the prominent Hua yan writers and is thus granted a substantial authority. This text has been linked to the ontologization of Buddhism as it developed in the Chinese context, perhaps due to Central Asian and Silk Road influences. Ideas that take shape in this text include such metaphysical notions as buddha nature and *tathāgatagarbha* (womb of buddhahood), which some scholars take to be countertheoretical to basic Indian Buddhist premises of the pointlessness of metaphysical assertions and speculations. In fact, within modern Japanese Zen traditions, there are those who suggest that East Asian Buddhism in general is not Buddhism. These critical Buddhists point precisely to the type of foundational *tathāgatagarbha* thinking that can be directly linked to the *Awakening of Faith* and its influence as topical, non-Buddhist elements that encroach on the central insights.

PATRIARCHAL LINEAGE

According to the retrospective view of Zongmi (780–841), there are four patriarchs or lineage figures in the Hua yan tradition, and he styles himself as the fifth patriarch. This comes to be seen as the orthodox lineage by the subsequent tradition. This standard list of patriarchs includes Dushun, Zhiyan, Fazang, Chengguan, and Zongmi. This is a retrospective lineage, which means that it is not at all clear that Dushun and Zhiyan saw themselves as members of a Hua yan school. This attribution is applied after the fact, as the tradition comes to consider the sources of its own emphases.

Dushun is said to have lived from 558 to 640. Although apparently prominent as an adept and miracle worker in his time, he is most influential as the purported author of a text known as the *Hua yan Fajie Guanmen* (Meditative approaches to the Hua yan Dharmadhātu). This text introduces the Four *Dharmadhātu* model that will be discussed later on, and thus provides a solid basis for the later developments in Hua yan thought.

Zhiyan (602–668), the second patriarch, is not as well known. His most prominent contribution to the discourse is the so-called Ten Mysteries. These are basically a series of metaphors for interpenetration and mutual causation, and many of them are in fact redundant. Regardless, this language persists in the work of Fazang, perhaps the grand systematizer of Hua yan thought.

Although attributed as the third patriarch, Fazang (643–712) may have been the first to think of himself as founding or joining a specific school of thought. Fazang's family was of Central Asian origin, in Samarqand, a prominent center on the Silk Road. A prolific writer, he wrote somewhere between sixty and one hundred works on various topics, the most important being commentaries on the *Hua yan Jing* and the *Mahayana Awakening of Faith*. He rose to prominence at the court of the empress Wu, after a series of performances in which he used such examples as a room of mirrors to demonstrate Hua yan principles of interpenetration and nonobstruction. Fazang's school stood in contrast to the school of Xuanzang, who had gone to India to learn Sanskrit and translate scores of Buddhist texts into Chinese. This conflict can be seen as being between the Indic and the sinicized forms of Buddhism. Ultimately, Fazang's view prevails, for a variety of philosophical, cultural, and political reasons. This may be an early and important stage in the sinicization of Buddhism.

Chengguan, the fourth patriarch, lived from 738 to 840. The lineage is somewhat obscure here, as Fazang's actual disciple, Huiyan, was understood by the later tradition to have corrupted the teaching. Chengguan, who was born after Fazang died, was nevertheless seen as the fourth patriarch in the sense that he is believed to have restored the integrity of Fazang's teachings. He did seem to have led a renewed interest in the school on the part of the ruling class and the scholars.

The last of the orthodox patriarchs is Zongmi (780–841). Zongmi is best known for his syncretic concerns, including his interest in sorting out the various schools of Buddhism, especially Chan Buddhism. Because of his interest in *panjiao*, his works are a treasure house of historical information about the schools of Buddhism active at his time. What is perhaps most significant about Zongmi is his concern with reconciling and synthesizing Hua yan and Chan Buddhism. In fact, Zongmi is sometimes attributed with lineage roles in both the Chan and Hua yan traditions, though these claims cannot be accepted uncritically. This leads to an oversimplification expounded by the famous Japanese Zen scholar Daisetz Suzuki, who argues that Hua yan is theoretical and establishes the principle behind Zen that is practical. However, this is too polemic a description of the situation, since Chan and Zen have a long textual and theoretical history, while Hua yan does provide practices of its own, for instance the meditation on the Four *Dharmad-hātus* discussed later in this entry.

Besides the so-called orthodox lineage just discussed, there are also a number of figures who belong to what might be called heterodox lineages in the sense that they follow exegetical lines of reasoning not adopted by the later traditions. These include, as mentioned, Fazang's student, Huiyuan, and the iconoclastic Li Tongxuan.

THE FOUR *DHARMADHĀTUS*

Perhaps the most fundamental concept in all of Hua yan Buddhist thinking is the synonymy of emptiness and dependent arising. Emptiness (Sanskrit: *śūnyatā*; Chinese: *kong*) is a traditional Buddhist notion that refers to the absence of self-being in all things and events. It does not mean that things do not exist—it means that all things that exist do so in dependence on other things, which is the meaning of dependent arising (Sanskrit: *pratītyasamutpāda*; Chinese: *yinyuan*). Hua yan, consistent with characteristic Chinese attitudes, placed focus on the positive side of this formulation, that even though empty, things actually do exist.

This is perhaps most clearly expressed in the model of the Four *Dharmadhātus* as initially formulated in Dushun's seminal text, *Meditative Approaches to the Hua yan Dharmadhātu*, and subsequently developed further by Chengguan. The term *dharmadhātu* is a way of referring to the realm of all *dharmas* (events). In other words, the *dharmadhātu* is the world in the most comprehensive sense. This model of the world is represented sometimes, especially in the work of Fazang, in terms of the metaphor of Indra's jeweled net. This net consists of many-faceted gems, each of which reflects every other gem, and reflects itself reflected in every other gem.

The formula of the Four *Dharmadhātus* is proposed as a support for meditation practices. Although they are often rendered in such a way as to suggest that there are four separate realms, they more properly represent four types or orders of perspectives on experience. The first is the tacit, uncritical commonsense lower-order perspective, and the others are higher-order or meditative perspectives. The goal seems to be a type of perspectival flexibility, which corrects the obsessive-compulsive tendency to identify with a single perspective by acknowledging the multiplicity of perspectives available and by adopting higher-order perspectives that reconcile the inconsistencies present between lower-order perspectives. This is like standing in a hallway with two people on either end. I can see one or the other, because of my limited perspective, but I cannot see both simultaneously. If

I were to stand above the hallway somehow and look down on it, I might be able to see both at once. Higher-order perspectives similarly circumscribe and sustain perspectives that appear incompatible at the surface level.

The first of these types of perspectives is termed *shi*, often rendered as "phenomenon" or "event." This is the tacit, ordinary, conventional perspective adopted and identified with by most people most of the time. It takes events at more or less face value—it does not raise questions about metaphysics or ontological or epistemological status. There is virtually an infinite set of possible perspectives at this level. Garma C. C. Chang, in *The Buddhist Teaching of Totality* (1971), offers the example of a glass of water. The water is seen by a chemist as H_2O, or a universal solvent. It is seen by a firefighter as something to extinguish flames. It is seen by a thirsty person as something to drink. It is in fact all these things, potentially, though at any given time it may function in one or another way. The problem with this perspective arises when it is universally applied, even in cases when other perspectives seem to conflict with it. Although admittedly a silly example, if a firefighter were dying of thirst but could only see the water as a means of extinguishing fires, then he might die of thirst before he would think to drink the water. An obstinate application of disjunctive perspectives is counterproductive and causes frustration or suffering, the elimination of which is the goal of Buddhism in general.

The second type of perspective is represented by the word *li*, which translates as "rule" or "underlying or abstract principle." In that general sense, *li* is what all *shi* have in common. To shift perspective to the *li* is to resolve all distinctions into some commonality. For example, one can either see coffee and tea as separate things, which would be the level of *shi*, or one can see them as all being water, which is the level of *li*. However, in the case of Hua yan metaphysics, the *li* is *śūnyatā* (emptiness). What all things have in common is that they all lack self-causation or causal autonomy. Everything depends on everything else. The Buddhist texts warn, however, not to ontologize emptiness and make it into a thing. It is the nature of things, which is not a thing in itself. So whereas in the first *dharmadhātu* things are seen as distinct things, in the second they are all seen as empty of self-being.

The third *dharmadhātu* is called *lishi wuai* (nonobstruction of *li* and *shi*). From this perspective, the emptiness of things does not interfere with the thingness of things. This would be experience things as in some sense distinguishable while simultaneously experiencing them as indistinguishably empty.

This does not, however, yet constitute full accomplishment. The final *dharmadhātu* is *shishi wuai* (nonobstruction between phenomena and other phenomena). By realizing that the emptiness of things does not interfere with the thingness of things, one is then able to realize that the specific nature of any one thing does not interfere with the specific nature of any other one thing. As Zongmi says in his commentary to Dushun's text, "all distinct phenomenal dharmas interfuse and penetrate in all ways" (Fox 1988, p. 299). In terms of the example used earlier in the description of the first dharmadhātu, the potability of the water does not interfere with the fire extinguishing properties of the water, which does not interfere with the solvency of water. All these manifestations are all potential manifestations of the same phenomenon. This is how the Buddha sees the world according to the Hua yan tradition, as omnipotentially present in a world of infinitely fractal possibilities. This is a liberation from the fixation on a single, lower-order perspective.

To put this model using modern concepts, one might look at a baseball as a baseball, intended for a certain use in a certain game according to certain rules. One would not be wrong in doing so, but one can also see the baseball as more basically composed of atoms. One would also not be wrong, of course. When one sees the baseball as a baseball, one sees what makes it different from everything else. When one sees the baseball as atoms, one sees what the baseball has in common with everything else, that is, one overlooks the distinctions between things. At the level of the third *dharmadhātu*, one is able to see that the phenomenal and atomic natures of the object do not interfere with each other. It is both atoms and a baseball. Meanwhile, the fourth level encourages one to see the baseball in either its phenomenal or atomic sense as overlapping with every other ostensible object in the universe. This is not far fetched. Phenomenally, one might point out that a baseball would not exist if there was not a game and a population to play it, and so is not entirely separable from those other events. Atomically, one notes that objects share ions with their environments in such a way as to constitute overlapping. It would not even make sense to suggest that an atom could exist in complete isolation, since in fact the atom is made of parts as well, which are made of parts, possibly ad infinitum, as modern string theorists suggest.

Fazang is particularly famous for a couple of metaphors used to demonstrate this principle of nonobstruction and mutual penetration. He is said to have made a huge impression on the empress Wu with these demonstrations, attracting much in the way of imperial support for his writing and translation projects. In one case he is said to have had constructed a room with mirrors on all four walls, as well as in the corners, floor, and ceiling. A torch and statue of the Buddha were placed in the center, and the result was reflections within reflections, each mirror reflecting the other mirrors reflecting itself. This suggested to Fazang a way of explaining how everything can simultaneously be the cause and the effect of everything else. As Chang notes in the *The Buddhist Teaching of Totality*, Fazang is said to have exclaimed that "[t]he principle of the simultaneous arising of different realms is so obvious here that no explanation is necessary" (1971, p. 24). Fazang is also known for using a golden statue of a lion to illustrate a similar principle. Although from one point of view the lion has distinguishable hairs and claws and limbs and teeth, from another point of view the lion is entirely and homogeneously gold.

It is worth pointing out that such an omnicausal model conflates the various types of causal relations that Aristotle, for example, distinguishes, such as efficient, material, final, contiguous, and other types of causal relations. By contrast, the purpose of the model is not to distinguish causal subtleties but to stimulate contextual and perspectival flexibility.

In general, the practice of Hua yan can be described as the attempt to deconstruct one's typically logocentric preoccupation with a fixed perspective, by engaging in a series of exercises that cultivate perspectival flexibility. This is seen to liberate one from the oppression of identifying with a single perspective, which leads to conflict and frustration.

There are many possible parallels between Hua yan thought and Western philosophers and philosophies. For instance, Alfred North Whitehead's process philosophy has been compared to Hua yan's emphasis on the actualization of events out of potentiality, an idea that is also present in modern quantum mechanics. Gestalt and other forms of cognitive psychologies share with Hua yan an emphasis on the importance of perspectival flexibility. In particular, contemporary phenomenological approaches have much in common with Hua yan's concern with the phenomenon qua phenomenon, and both share an emphasis on the importance of experience and perspective that renders metaphysical and absolute statements speculative and counterproductive.

See also Buddhism; Buddhism—Schools: Chan and Zen.

Bibliography

Chang, Garma C. C. *The Buddhist Teaching of Totality: The Philosophy of Hwa Yen Buddhism.* University Park: Pennsylvania State University Press, 1971.

Cleary, Thomas, tr. *Entry into the Inconceivable: An Introduction to Hua-yen Buddhism.* Honolulu: University of Hawaii Press, 1983.

Cleary, Thomas, tr. *Entry into the Realm of Reality: The Guide.* Boulder, CO: Shambhala, 1989.

Cleary, Thomas, tr. *The Flower Ornament Scripture.* 3 vols. Boulder, CO: Shambhala, 1984–1987.

Cook, Francis. *Hua-yen Buddhism: The Jewel Net of Indra.* University Park: Pennsylvania State University Press, 1981.

Fox, Alan. *Elements of Omnicontextual Thought in Chinese Buddhism: Annotated Translations of Gui Feng Zong Mi's Preface to Collection of Various Writings on the Chan Source and His Commentary on "Meditative Approaches to the Hua Yen Dharmadhatu."* Ann Arbor, MI: University Microfilms International, 1988.

Gimello, Robert. *Chih-yen and the Foundations of Hua-Yen Buddhism.* Ann Arbor, MI: University Microfilms International, 1976.

Gimello, Robert, and Peter Gregory, eds. *Studies in Ch'an and Hua-yen.* Honolulu: University of Hawaii Press, 1983.

Gregory, Peter. *Inquiry into the Origin of Humanity.* Honolulu, Hawaii: Kuroda Institute, 1995.

Gregory, Peter. *Tsung-mi and the Sinification of Buddhism.* Princeton, NJ: Princeton University Press, 1991.

Liu, Ming-wood. *The Teaching of Fa-tsang: An Examination of Buddhist Metaphysics.* Ann Arbor, MI: University Microfilms International, 1979.

Odin, Steve. *Process Metaphysics and Hua-Yen Buddhism: A Critical Study of Cumulative Penetration vs. Interpenetration.* Albany: SUNY Press, 1982.

Suzuki, Daisetz Teitaro. *Essays in Zen Buddhism, Third Series.* New York: Samuel Weiser, 1971.

Takakusu, Junjiro. *The Essentials of Buddhist Philosophy.* Delhi, India: Motilal Banarsidass, 1956.

Verdu, Alfonso. *Dialectical Aspects in Buddhist Thought: Studies in Sino-Japanese Mahayana Idealism.* Lawrence: Center for East Asian Studies, University of Kansas, 1974.

Wright, Dale. *Emptiness and Paradox in the Thought of Fa-Tsang.* Ann Arbor, MI: University Microfilms International, 1980.

Alan Fox (2005)

MADHYAMAKA

Madhyamaka is one of the two major schools of Mahāyāna Buddhist philosophy (the other being Yogācāra. It traces its origins to the work of the South Indian philosopher Nāgārjuna (c. 150 CE), who first gave systematic philosophical expression to insights articulated in the earliest Mahāyāna sūtras, the *Prajñāpāramitā* literature. Central to those texts was the claim that all things thought to be ultimately real are in fact "empty" or devoid of intrinsic nature. The Madhyamaka school arose out of efforts to defend this claim and explore its consequences. The Madhyamaka understanding of the concept of emptiness, and the dialectical strategies used to establish its validity, played central roles in the development of Mahāyāna thought in India and subsequently in Tibet and East Asia.

EMPTINESS AS LACK OF INTRINSIC NATURE

When the Mādhyamikas say that all things are empty (*śūnya*), what they mean is that nothing bears an intrinsic nature (*svabhāva*). To understand this claim, one must consider the concept of intrinsic nature as it was developed in the scholastic Abhidharma phase of Buddhist philosophy. It is a basic teaching of Buddhism that suffering is caused by one's ignorance of the truth of nonself: that one does not have a separately existing self and that what one thinks of as an enduring person just consists in a causal series of impermanent, impersonal physical and mental events. Philosophers of the Abhidharma schools sought to buttress this conclusion by arguing that all partite entities (wholes made up of parts) are conceptually constructed and thus not ultimately real. This would enable them to claim that the person is conceptually constructed out of the psychophysical elements making up a causal series and so is not itself objectively real.

The general argument is that a partite thing such as a chariot borrows all its properties from the properties of its parts: There is no fact about a chariot that cannot be explained strictly in terms of facts about its parts and their relations. This is taken to show that positing the chariot as an additional entity is superfluous, something one is inclined to do only because of facts about one's interests and cognitive limitations. Since this holds as well for the person, as a whole made up of the elements in a causal series, it follows that one's view of oneself as an enduring substance reflects a failure to distinguish between a mere useful fiction and what is ultimately or mind-independently real.

This reductionist line of thought in the Abhidharma rests on the assumption that there are entities that are ultimately real. To say that persons and other partite things are not ultimately real because they are conceptually constructed is to assume that there are those ultimately real things out of which partite things are constructed. Now conceptually constructed things were held to borrow their properties from the properties of their parts. So Abhidharma thinkers concluded that ultimately real things must have their natures intrinsically. Only that is ultimately real, they claimed, that "is found under analysis," that is conceptually irreducible. The Madhyamaka claim that all things are empty is meant to contest the Abhidharma view that there could be such things. Through a wide variety of arguments the Mādhyamikas seek to demonstrate the absurd consequences that would follow if it were held that there are entities with intrinsic nature.

THE ARGUMENT FROM CAUSATION

One such argument concerns the causal relation. It is a fact of one's experience that existing things are impermanent, and this would seem to hold for whatever is ultimately real. But it is also a fact of one's experience that things do not come into or go out of existence in an utterly random way. There seem instead to be patterns of regular succession. So an adequate account of the nature of reality seems to require that ultimately real things be said to arise and cease in accordance with causal laws. At this point the Mādhyamikas raise a simple question: Are cause and effect identical or distinct? Consider the first possibility. Certain Indian philosophers held that the effect is identical with the cause—that causation represents just the manifestation of what already exists in the cause in unmanifest form. But this view is readily dismissed. For it requires that there already exist something with the intrinsic nature of the effect before the effect is produced. And in that case one must wonder why one would set about trying to produce the effect. One might build a fire because one is cold and wants the heat of fire. But if the fire already existed in its cause, the fuel, then its heat should already be present there, so it would be pointless to build a fire.

If, on the contrary, cause and effect were distinct things, two difficulties would follow. First, if these are genuinely distinct things, some account must be given as to why things of the first sort regularly give rise to things of the second sort. Why should fuel give rise to fire and not, say, to cheese? The stock answer to this question is that fuel possesses the causal power to produce fire. But now it must be asked whether this causal power is a third thing that is distinct from both cause and effect or is rather identical with one or the other. If it is distinct from the cause, one may then ask why this sort of cause should be conjoined with just this sort of causal power. This quickly leads to an infinite regress: A second causal power will be required to account for the occurrence of the first, a third for that of the second, and so on. But if the causal power is identical with the cause, then no answer has been given to the original question, and likewise if the causal power is identical with the effect.

The second problem for the view that cause and effect are distinct things is that it is then unclear when the cause produces the effect. To call one thing the cause of another is to say that the first produces the second, so surely there must be some time when this productive activity takes place. There are three possibilities here: when the effect already exists, when the effect does not yet exist, and when the effect is coming into existence. The first is clearly ruled out, since production of something that already exists would be redundant. The second is likewise wrong, for something may be said to be productive only if there is some actually existing product. And with respect to things that are ultimately real, there could be no third time during which they are coming into existence. With respect to partite things like chariots it makes sense to speak of a process of assembly during which the entity is undergoing production. But this is possible only because the chariot is made of parts. Something impartite that bore its nature intrinsically could only be said to be either existent or nonexistent; a third intermediate time is ruled out for such a thing. The upshot of all this is that it appears impossible to account for the causal relations that should obtain among things with intrinsic natures.

THE ARGUMENT FROM THE PROPERTY-BEARER RELATION

A second Madhyamaka argument for emptiness involves examining the relation between an ultimately real thing and its intrinsic nature. Either these are distinct or they are identical. If they are distinct, a number of difficulties follow. First, there is the problem of saying what the entity itself is like apart from its intrinsic nature. Since the notion of a pure propertyless substrate seems incoherent, this problem is likely to prove intractable. But there is also the difficulty that then the entity's acquiring its nature will depend on causes and conditions. Such dependence seems incompatible with calling its nature intrinsic; it then seems more appropriate to say that the entity borrows its nature from other things.

Suppose then that the entity and its intrinsic nature are identical—that one's distinction between the thing and its nature merely reflects the concepts one uses. In that case an occurrence of what one calls fire is really just the occurrence of heat (the property of being hot). But then the question arises how fires are to be individuated. Suppose there are two distinct fires of equal intensity. Each fire is just its heat, and the two heats are identical in nature. Ordinarily, one would say that the two occurrences of heat are distinct because each occurs in a distinct particular (the fire whose heat it is). But on the hypothesis under scrutiny there are no particulars over and above the property of heat; the occurrence of what one judges to be a particular fire just is the occurrence of heat. One might then suppose that each fire is individuated in terms of the discrete space that it occupies. But then the question arises what makes two spaces discrete? Suppose the intrinsic nature of a space is its nonresistance. Since one is now supposing that the existence of a space just is the occurrence of a certain nonresistance, it is not clear what will make two spaces distinct, unless it is their being occupied by distinct entities, such as two fires. But now one has come full circle. So it looks as if the hypothesis that entity and intrinsic nature are identical does not hold up to critical scrutiny either. It appears that no adequate account can be given of how something could have an intrinsic nature.

MADHYAMAKA AS NIHILISM

A host of similar arguments against things with intrinsic nature was developed by Mādhyamika philosophers such as Nāgārjuna, Āryadeva (170–270), Buddhapālita (c. 500), Bhāvaviveka (500–570), and Candrakīrti (c. 600–650). Nāgārjuna's targets were chiefly views held by Ābhidharmikas, but Āryadeva extended the scope of Mādhyamika dialectics to include the views of non-Buddhist Indian philosophers, a practice that becomes systematic in Bhāvaviveka's *Tarkajvālā*. Suppose that these arguments succeed in showing that nothing could bear an intrinsic nature. Suppose also that the Ābhidharmikas were correct in concluding that only something with an intrinsic nature could be ultimately real. What would then follow? What should one make of the Mādhyamika doctrine of emptiness? Modern scholars have put forward a wide variety of interpretations, but there is also some difference of opinion among classical Indian authors. One modern reading, that of Thomas E. Wood (1994) and David Burton (1999), that is also the common view of the Mādhyamikas' ancient Indian critics is that the doctrine of emptiness is tantamount to metaphysical nihilism, the thesis that reality is ultimately devoid of existing things. The stock characterization of the Mādhyamikas that one finds in the writings of their classical opponents is that the Mādhyamikas believe nothing whatever exists.

Of course, the thesis of metaphysical nihilism is virtually self-refuting: If nothing whatever existed, the thought could not occur that it might be true. Still, attributing this thesis to the Mādhyamikas might not seem unfair. If there is reason to believe that only things with intrinsic nature could be ultimately real, then demonstrating the incoherence of the concept of a thing with intrinsic nature seems equivalent to showing that ultimately nothing whatever is real. One major difficulty with this interpretation, however, is that it is explicitly argued against by the Mādhyamikas. Thus, Nāgārjuna points out that to understand the thesis that no ultimately real things exist, one must first understand what it would mean for there to be ultimately real things. But an ultimately real thing would have to be something with intrinsic nature. Since the Mādhyamikas claim there can be no such things, they would say one cannot understand the thesis that ultimately nothing exists. So perhaps they should not be interpreted as seeking to establish metaphysical nihilism.

DO MĀDHYAMIKAS AFFIRM CONTRADICTIONS?

Of the remaining interpretations of emptiness found in the modern scholarship, only some find support in the original sources. (Of course, the lack of such support need not detract from the philosophical significance of an interpretation.) For instance, Graham Priest and Jay L. Garfield (2002) claim Nāgārjuna as perhaps the first exponent of dialetheism, the view that there are true contradictions that arise at the limits of thought. As evidence, they cite his assertion that it cannot be ultimately true that all things are empty (*Madhyamakakārikā* chapter 22, verse 11). The notion of ultimate truth at work here derives from the Abhidharma distinction between two kinds of truth: conventional and ultimate. Only statements concerning ultimately real things can be said to be ultimately true; statements concerning such mere conceptual fictions as chariots and persons can only be conventionally true. For Abhidharma, then, the set of ultimately true statements would give the complete account of all those things with intrinsic natures; it would be a complete description of the ultimate nature of reality.

Now the Mādhyamikas claim to have shown that the only statement that can truly be made about those things that are thought to be ultimately real is that they are empty. But in the verse in question Nāgārjuna says that this cannot be ultimately true. Indeed, he says it is not ultimately true that all things are empty, or that they are nonempty, or both or neither. The reason for this is that emptiness is itself a mere conceptual fiction. So any statement about emptiness could at best be conventionally true. Priest and Garfield take Nāgārjuna to be thereby asserting both that the ultimate truth cannot be characterized and that it can be characterized (namely as being uncharacterizable). But this is not how Mādhyamika commentators have understood the verse. Instead, they assimilate it to the Buddha's treatment of the so-called indeterminate questions (*avyākṛta*). When, for instance, the Buddha was asked whether the enlightened person survives death, does not survive death, both survives and does not survive, or neither survives nor does not survive death, the Buddha rejected all four possibilities. One can consistently do this, they explain, because all share an implicit presupposition—that there ultimately is such a thing as an enlightened person—and this presupposition should be rejected. By the same token, the commentators say, Nāgārjuna should be understood as rejecting the presupposition that there is such a thing as the ultimate truth. In that case he asserts neither that the ultimate truth is uncharacterizable nor that it can be characterized. He does not hold that a contradiction is true.

MADHYAMAKA AS SKEPTICISM

Other interpreters of the doctrine of emptiness, such as Thomas McEvilley (1982) and Bimal Krishna Matilal (1986), see it as a form of skepticism. This reading is suggested by the Mādhyamika response to objections coming from Indian epistemologists. The thrust of these objections is that since the Mādhyamikas hold all things to be empty, they must hold that all means of knowledge are empty. But in that case it cannot be known that all things are empty, so the Mādhyamika claim is a mere dogmatic assertion. Part of the Mādhyamika response involves calling into question the epistemologist's project of determining which are the means of knowledge. For instance, they argue that a given procedure can be known to be a means of knowledge—a reliable cause of veridical belief—only if one already possesses some means of knowing which beliefs are true. Thus, any attempt to determine which are the means of knowledge either is circular or else leads to an infinite regress.

An argument of this sort might be used to support the skeptic's claim that one can never know which, if any, of one's beliefs amount to knowledge. But this is not how the Mādhyamikas themselves see such arguments. For one thing, the skeptical conclusion requires the additional assumption that one can only know some statement p if one knows that one knows p—an assumption that neither the Mādhyamikas nor their opponents seem to have held. Second, nowhere do the Mādhyamikas appeal to the sorts of error possibilities that are the skeptic's stock in trade, such as perceptual illusions, hallucinations, dreams, and the like. Indeed, the Mādhyamikas do not deny that, conventionally, certain procedures can

count as means of knowledge. What they deny is just that anything could ultimately be a means of knowledge, that anything could have the intrinsic character of reliably causing veridical beliefs as part of its mind-independent essential nature. The Mādhyamika epistemological stance seems to be that something can be a means of knowledge only through its relations to other things that are themselves equally empty of intrinsic nature. The resulting view may have its affinities with some forms of skepticism (particularly Pyrrhonian skepticism). But its chief concern is not to call into question the possibility of knowledge, but to deflate the pretensions of a certain sort of epistemological realism.

THE MĀDHYAMIKAS AS MYSTICS OR AS QUIETISTS?

Two interpretations of emptiness seem more firmly grounded in the self-understanding of the Mādhyamika tradition. The first sees emptiness as leading to a kind of mystical silence. Mādhyamika arguments are said to demonstrate that no set of concepts can ever adequately represent the world. This realization is said to then usher in a nondiscursive grasping of the nature of reality (perhaps through a kind of intuition that is cultivated in meditation). On this interpretation, emptiness serves to point to an ultimate reality that lies beyond the reach of philosophical rationality. The second of the two, by contrast, sees emptiness not as pointing to an ineffable ultimate, but as indicating that the very idea of an ultimate nature of reality is incoherent. The exercise of philosophical rationality leads not to the silence of the beyond, but back to the conventional. For Mādhyamika dialectic reveals the error in the notion of an ultimate truth that represents how things are independently of all facts about the cognizer. This shows that truth can only be transactional, a matter of what facilitates interactions among creatures like us. The notion of a truth that potentially outstrips all our conceptual resources is revealed to be no more than a useful fiction.

The "mystical silence" reading of emptiness has been championed by T. R. V. Murti (1955) and David Seyfort Ruegg (1977) among others. The second reading is commonly called a quietist interpretation, since it grows out of the attempt by Frederick J. Streng (1967) to read elements of the later Ludwig Josef Johann Wittgenstein into Nāgārjuna. But as developed by Tom J. F. Tillemans (2002), it has clear affinities with both antirealist and minimalist conceptions of truth. Both readings may be seen as seeking to explicate the claim that insight into emptiness results in a kind of nondual awareness.

Mahāyāna Buddhist texts commonly claim that final liberation from suffering requires a kind of seeing that transcends all problematic dualities. On the mystical silence interpretation it is the dualism fostered by conceptualization that is to be overcome, for without concepts one cannot make such invidious distinctions as that between cognizing subject and object. On the quietist reading it is the dualism of ultimate and conventional truth that is erased through knowledge of emptiness. Presumably, this duality is problematic because the notion of ultimate truth as correspondence to mind-independent reality fosters a subtle form of belief in a self, namely that expressed through attachment to metaphysical theories.

Each reading is not without its own difficulties. For the mystical silence view, the chief problem is to explain how Madhyamaka then differs from other views that posit an ineffable ultimate, such as the absolute monisms of Advaita Vedānta and Parmenides of Elea. For the quietist there is the difficulty of explaining how there can be truth without there being such a thing as how the world is anyway. This problem is sometimes addressed by claiming that what emptiness really shows is just that no entity has a nature that is independent of its relations to other things. But to the extent that this addresses the problem of grounding truth in mind-independent reality, it contravenes the quietist claim to be showing a way out of the trap of metaphysical theories.

THE SVĀTANTRIKA-PRĀSAṄGIKA DISTINCTION

Modern studies of the Mādhyamikas have profited enormously from contact with the Tibetan tradition, a tradition for which Mādhyamika thought continues to play a crucial role. But there are cases in which reliance on Tibetan doxographical categories has led to distortion of the Indian Mādhyamika sources. A case in point is the alleged distinction between two schools of Madhyamaka: Svātantrika and Prāsaṅgika. This distinction was invented by Tibetan doxographers, and it is a matter of some dispute to what extent it reflects substantive differences in the views of the Indian thinkers covered by the classification. It is in any event clear that Indian Mādhyamikas did not see themselves as falling into two camps to which these labels could be applied.

Those who accept the distinction identify a dispute between Bhāvaviveka and Candrakīrti as its point of origin. The dispute concerns the proper methodology for a Mādhyamika. The arguments of Bhāvaviveka's Mādhyamika predecessors were usually expressed in the *reductio ad absurdum* (*prasaṅga*) style: The hypothesis to

be refuted (e.g., that something with intrinsic nature could be an effect) is considered and then shown to lead to some absurd result (e.g., that its intrinsic nature is actually extrinsic). Employing the methods of the Buddhist logician Diṅnāga, Bhāvaviveka sought to convert such *reductios* into independent arguments (*svatantra anumāna*). Thus, one would have:

> It is not the case that ultimately an entity arises from distinct causes and conditions.Because of depending on them for its nature.

Whatever depends on other things for its nature is not ultimately real, like the chariot. Candrakīrti disagrees, claiming that the Mādhyamikas may only use *reductios*. But since the two types of argument turn out to be formally equivalent once the *reductio* has been fully spelled out, it may not be clear what the dispute is actually about.

The difference Candrakīrti sees between them is this: In giving a *reductio* one need not assert anything to be the case oneself; the proponent merely shows the opponent the inconsistency in his or her view, thereby impelling the opponent to withdraw assent from his or her thesis. In the case of an independent argument, on the contrary, both the proponent and opponent must agree about such things as the subject (in this case, an entity), the pervasion (that what is dependently originated is not ultimately real), and the example (the chariot). But the Mādhyamika proponent holds that entities can only exist conventionally, while the opponent thinks some entities are ultimately real, so the two sides do not agree about the subject. And likewise for the other elements of the argument that require consensus. From the perspective of the Mādhyamikas, the opponent is simply, hopelessly wrong about everything. So there can be no common framework for resolving their disagreement. Instead, the Mādhyamikas should just give their opponents the rope with which to hang themselves.

SYNCRETISM IN MADHYAMAKA

One may wonder if the opponent will be so obliging toward a proponent who seems to speak a different (and perhaps unintelligible) language. But there may be a deeper point here. Those Tibetan commentators such as Tsong-kha-pa (1357–1419) who align themselves with the Prāsaṅgika allege that Svātantrikas have not fully realized emptiness, since they continue to posit intrinsic natures, albeit at just the conventional level. And it is true that those Mādhyamikas who are identified as Svātantrikas exhibit a tendency toward syncretism, seeking to incorporate the views of overtly metaphysical Buddhist schools within an overall Mādhyamika framework.

This tendency is especially clear in Śāntarakṣita (eighth century), who embraces Dharmakīrti's formulation of the Yogācāra school's subjective idealist ontology and epistemology. But it can already be seen in Bhāvaviveka, who champions the Sautrāntika school's realism about physical objects and its associated representationalist theory of sense perception. In neither case is the other school's view identified as anything more than the best way of representing conventional truth. As Mādhyamikas, Śāntarakṣita and Bhāvaviveka remain committed to the position that the only ultimate truth is that there is no ultimate truth (i.e., that all things, including emptiness, are empty). Still, they do take a position on the question whether external objects exist conventionally.

Candrakīrti does as well. He sides with Bhāvaviveka in rejecting the idealist view. But his reasons are different. Where Bhāvaviveka tries to answer Yogācāra arguments against the existence of physical objects, Candrakīrti simply dismisses the arguments. For him such arguments can only show that physical objects are ultimately empty—something a Mādhyamika already knows. But by the same token mental states (which the idealist thinks are real) are equally empty. So the availability of philosophical arguments against the conventional belief in external objects cannot show that they are not conventionally real. While Bhāvaviveka thinks the use of philosophical rationality can lead to improvements in one's conventional account of the world, Candrakīrti thinks it can only lead to the ultimate truth of emptiness. Conventional truth neither needs nor can it sustain either refinement or defense at the hands of philosophers. It is just simply that which is given through the everyday practices of ordinary people.

Given this difference in attitude, one can see why Svātantrikas might be described by their critics as positing conventionally real intrinsic natures. It is, after all, philosophical analysis that gives rise to the demand for things with intrinsic nature. So if philosophical rationality is allowed to play a role in shaping one's conventional worldview, the resulting theory will be committed to there being such things, the things at which analysis stops. And to Candrakīrti, Bhāvaviveka's demand that the Mādhyamikas give independent arguments and not mere reductios looks like a requirement that the Mādhyamikas construct a philosophically defensible version of the conventional truth. This will inevitably lead in the direction of syncretism, and with it the danger that the Mādhyamikas will become ensnared in metaphysical theories. The Prāsaṅgika side in this dispute is not without its dangers as well though. For on its account, conventional truth does not allow of progressive improvement, it can only be utterly overthrown. The result would seem to be a strong form of relativism about conventional truth. And an opponent could always use this to turn back the Prāsaṅgika's reductio arguments, in effect saying to the Mādhyamikas, "We simply disagree about whether there is an inconsistency in my position, and in such matters there is no right and wrong." What this dispute brings out, then, is a tension that seems inherent in the concept of truth, a tension that is also reflected in current debates between realists and antirealists.

Indian Madhyamaka came to an end in the late twelfth century, when all Buddhist philosophical activity ceased in India following the Turkish invasion. Madhyamaka has continued to play a prominent role in Tibetan Buddhism to this day. It also enjoyed some popularity among Chinese Buddhist philosophers, playing an important role in the development of the Huayan school. Perhaps a case might even be made for its having had a profound impact on Chan Buddhism. Chan formally eschews the study of precisely those sorts of doctrinal texts that form the core of Mādhyamika practice. But it does make extensive use of paradox in some of the methods it has devised for helping the adept attain enlightenment. Analysis of the structural features of those paradoxes and their uses might reveal more than merely superficial resemblances with the dialectical strategies of Madhyamaka.

See also Buddhism; Buddhism—Schools: Dge-lugs.

Bibliography

PRIMARY SOURCES AND TRANSLATIONS

Āryadeva. "Catuḥśataka." In *Āryadeva's Catuḥśataka*, edited and translated by Karen Lang. Copenhagen: Akademisk Vorlag, 1986.

Bhāvaviveka. *Madhyamakahṛdayakārikā Tarkajvālā*. In *Reason and Emptiness: A Study in Logic and Mysticism*. Translated by Iida Shōtarō. Tokyo. Hokuseido Press, 1980.

Nāgārjuna. "Mūlamadhyamakakārikā." In *Mūlamadhyamakakārikās (Mādhyamikasūtras) de Nāgārjuna avec la Prasannapadā, Commentaire de Candrakīrti*, edited by Louis de La Vallée Poussin. Osnabrück, Germany: Biblio Verlag, 1970. Also in *The Fundamental Wisdom of the Middle Way: Nāgārjuna Mūlamadhyamakakārikā*. Translated by Jay L. Garfield. New York: Oxford University Press, 1995.

Nāgārjuna. "Vigrahavyāvartanī." In *The Dialectical Method of Nāgārjuna: Vigrahavyāvartanī*. Translated by Kamaleswar Bhattacharya and edited by E. H. Johnston and Arnold Kunst. Delhi: Motilal Banarsidass, 1978.

Śāntarakṣita. "Tattvasaṅgraha." In *The Tattvasaṅgraha of Śāntarakṣita, with the Commentary of Kamalaśīla*, edited by Embar Krishnamacharya. Baroda, India: Oriental Institute,

1984. Also in *The Tattvasaṅgraha of Śāntarakṣita, with the Commentary of Kamalaśīla*. Translated by Ganganatha Jha. Delhi: Motilal Banarsidass, 1986.

Śāntideva. "Bodhicāryāvatāra." In *The Bodhicāryāvatāra of Ārya Śāntideva with the Commentary Pañjika of Śrī Prajñākaramati*, edited by Dwārikādās Śāstrī. Varanasi, India: Bauddha Bharati, 2001. Also in *The Bodhicaryāvatāra*. Translated by Kate Crosby and Andrew Skilton. New York: Oxford University Press, 1993.

SECONDARY LITERATURE

Burton, David. *Emptiness Appraised: A Critical Study of Nāgārjuna's Philosophy*. Richmond, U.K.: Curzon, 1999.

Dreyfus, Georges B. J., and Sara McClintock, eds. *The Svātantrika-Prāsaṅgika Distinction: What Difference Does a Difference Make?* Boston: Wisdom Publications, 2002.

Eckel, Malcolm David. *Jñānagarbha's Commentary on the Distinction between the Two Truths: An Eighth Century Handbook of Madhyamaka Philosophy*. Albany, NY: SUNY Press, 1987.

Hayes, Richard P. "Nāgārjuna's Appeal." *Journal of Indian Philosophy* 22 (1994): 299–378.

Huntington, C. W., Jr., with Geshé Namgyal Wangchen. *The Emptiness of Emptiness: An Introduction to Early Indian Mādhyamaka*. Honolulu: University of Hawaii Press, 1989.

Lopez, Donald S., Jr. *A Study of Svātantrika*. Ithaca, NY: Snow Lion, 1987.

Matilal, Bimal Krishna. *Perception: An Essay on Classical Indian Theories of Knowledge*. New York: Oxford University Press, 1986.

McEvilley, Thomas. "Pyrrhonism and Mādhyamika." *Philosophy East and West* 32 (1) (1982): 3–35.

Murti, T. R. V. *The Central Philosophy of Buddhism: A Study of the Mādhyamika System*. London: Allen and Unwin, 1955.

Oetke, Claus. "Remarks on the Interpretation of Nāgārjuna's Philosophy." *Journal of Indian Philosophy* 19 (3) (1991): 315–323.

Potter, Karl H., ed. *Encyclopedia of Indian Philosophies, Vol. 8: Buddhist Philosophy from 100 to 350 A.D.* Delhi: Motilal Banarsidass, 1999.

Potter, Karl H., ed. *Encyclopedia of Indian Philosophies, Vol. 9: Buddhist Philosophy from 350 to 600 A.D.* Delhi: Motilal Banarsidass, 2003.

Priest, Graham, and Jay L. Garfield. "Nāgārjuna and the Limits of Thought." In *Beyond the Limits of Thought*, edited by Graham Priest. New York: Oxford University Press, 2002.

Robinson, Richard H. *Early Mādhyamika in India and China*. Madison: University of Wisconsin Press, 1967.

Ruegg, David Seyfort. "The Uses of the Four Positions of the Catuṣkoṭi and the Problem of the Description of Reality in Mahāyāna Buddhism." *Journal of Indian Philosophy* 5 (1977): 1–71.

Ruegg, David Seyfort. *The Literature of the Madhyamaka School of Philosophy in India*. Wiesbaden, Germany: Harrassowitz, 1981.

Siderits, Mark. "The Madhyamaka Critique of Epistemology I." *Journal of Indian Philosophy* 8 (1980): 307–335.

Siderits, Mark. "Thinking on Empty: Madhyamaka Anti-realism and Canons of Rationality." In *Rationality in Question: On Eastern and Western Views of Rationality*, edited by Shlomo Biderman and Ben-Ami Scharfstein. Leiden, Netherlands: Brill, 1989

Streng, Frederick J. *Emptiness: A Study in Religious Meaning*. Nashville, T.N.: Abingdon Press, 1967.

Tillemans, Tom J. F. *Materials for the Study of Āryadeva, Dharmapāla, and Candrakīrti: The Catuḥśataka of Āryadeva, chapters XII and XIII, with the commentaries of Dharmapāla and Candrakīrti*. 2 vols. Vienna: Arbeitskreis für Tibetische und Buddhistische Studien Universität Wien, 1990.

Tillemans, Tom. "Metaphysics for Mādhyamikas." In *The Svātantrika-Prāsaṅgika Distinction: What Difference Does a Difference Make?* edited by Georges B. J. Dreyfus and Sara McClintock. Boston: Wisdom Publications, 2002.

Williams, Paul. "On the Interpretation of Madhyamaka Thought." *Journal of Indian Philosophy* 19 (1991): 191–218.

Wood, Thomas E. *Nāgārjunian Disputations: A Philosophical Journey through an Indian Looking-Glass*. Honolulu: University of Hawaii Press, 1994.

Mark Siderits (2005)

YOGĀCĀRA

The origins of Yogācāra Buddhism—one of the two mainstream schools of Indian Mahāyāna Buddhism (the other being Madhyamaka)—are obscure, but tradition credits its founding to two half-brothers, Asaṅga and Vasubandhu (c. fourth century). Many of Yogācāra's distinctive terms and models, such as eight consciousnesses, three self-natures, and *vijñapti-mātra* (explained later in this entry), had already appeared in certain Mahāyāna scriptures such as the *Saṅdhinirmocana Sūtra* (Sūtra elucidating the hidden connections), but the expansion of those ideas in the prolific writings of Asaṅga and Vasubandhu gave the school its foundation. Yogācāra attempted to absorb the full range of teachings and practices that had arisen over the centuries since the time of the Buddha—from the elaborate scholastic schemas of the Abhidharma schools to the reformulation of Buddhist doctrine in terms of emptiness (*śūnyatā*) posed by early Mahāyāna literature—to fashion a detailed, systematic, coherent, step-by-step path to unsurpassable complete awakening (*anuttarā-samyak-saṃbodhi*) and nirvāṇa.

Since Buddhism identified the root problem as ignorance, Yogācāra devised methods for uncovering and correcting the cognitive errors inherent in the way the mind works. Yogācāra's sustained attention to cognitive issues such as consciousness, perception, psycholinguistic conditioning, and epistemology, coupled with claims such as "external objects do not exist," has led some to misinterpret Yogācāra as a form of metaphysical idealism. For Yogācāra, however, consciousness is not an eternal substance or immutable substrate. Rather, individual consciousnesses arise and cease each moment because of everchanging causes and conditions, these discrete moments of consciousness linked in sequential causal chains, giving the illusion of a continuous self-identity or selfhood. Overcoming ignorance meant first eliminating this false view of self and subsequently seeing things as they truly are. Yogācāra developed perhaps the most sophisticated examination and description in all of Buddhism of how the mind works—in psychological, epistemological, logical, emotional, cognitive, meditative, developmental, and soteric modes.

HISTORICAL OVERVIEW

Though the historical details of the lives of the early Yogācāras have been obscured by later legends—some so unreliable that a few scholars swayed by miscues theorized that tradition had conflated two different Vasubandhus who lived at different times, a theory no longer accepted—enough of their prolific writings has survived (though not always in the original Sanskrit) for us to appreciate the depth and complexity of their thinking. Legend holds that Asaṅga, after years of fruitless meditation, was about to give up when the future Buddha, Maitreya, appeared to him, instructing him in hitherto unknown scriptures. Some of his writings are ascribed to Maitreya, others to Asaṅga himself (the Chinese and Tibetan traditions differ on which texts to ascribe to which). Most important among his works are the encyclopedic *Yogācārabhūmi* (Stages of yoga practice), *Mahāyānasaṃgraha* (Compendium on Mahāyāna), *Abhidharmasamuccaya* (Abhidharma compilation), and *Madhyānta-vibhāga* (Differentiating the middle from the extremes). Vasubandhu at first studied Vaibhāṣika Buddhism at its headquarters in Kashmir, composing a detailed summary of its doctrines titled *Abhidharmakośa* (Treasury of Abhidharma). Under Asaṅga's influence, Vasubandhu became a Yogācāra, adding a commentary to his *Kośa* that critiqued the Vaibhāṣika positions, incorporating ideas and phraseology found in Asaṅga's works. Along with many commentaries on Mahāyāna scriptures (most no longer extant), his most important works are his commentary on *Madhyānta-vibhāga*, *Triṃsikā* (Thirty verses), *Viṃśatikā* (Twenty verses), and four of the earliest Buddhist treatises on logic.

Yogācāra subsequently split into two wings: (1) an Abhidharmic wing primarily engaged in commentary writing and doctrinal exposition, its main figures being Sthiramati (sixth century), Dharmapāla (sixth century), and Xuanzang (seventh century); and (2) an epistemological-logic wing that for centuries became the vanguard of Indian epistemology and logic, its main figures including Dignāga (fifth century), Dharmakīrti (seventh century), and Ratnakīrti (c. eleventh century). By the seventh century Yogācāra dominated the leading Indian Buddhist centers at Nālandā and Vālabhī. Texts like the *Laṅkāvatāra Sūtra* blended Yogācāra with *tathāgatagarbha* (Buddhahood-potentiality) thought.

Translators introduced Yogācāra writings to China in the early fifth century, where it dominated for the following two centuries. It became influential in Korea and Japan in the seventh century, and though it eventually was overshadowed by other forms of East Asian Buddhism that themselves were offshoots of Yogācāra-*tathāgatagarbha* hybrids, periodically East Asians have renewed interest in Yogācāra. Yogācāra was also influential during the formative years of Tibetan Buddhism, and has remained part of the Tibetan Buddhist curriculum until the present.

VIJÑAPTI-MĀTRA

The core of Yogācāra doctrine is expressed by the term *vijñapti-mātra*, usually translated "consciousness-only" or "representation-only." Despite repeated strenuous denials in Yogācāra texts that *vijñapti-mātra* means that only consciousness exists or that consciousness alone is real, over the centuries many non-Yogācāras have interpreted it that way. Since consciousness (*vijñāna*) is the domain in which all contemplation, examination, theorization, and knowledge about reality occurs, its facticity is undeniable, though, for Yogācāra, consciousness is neither ultimate reality nor the solution to life's problems. Rather, consciousness itself is the problem. The grammatically causative term *vijñapti* means "what makes known," signifying that consciousness actively constructs the appearances it apprehends and appropriates. Since to appear within a perception or cognition means to appear within an act of consciousness, we are usually not directly aware of anything outside of consciousness. Whatever one is aware of or thinks about necessarily occurs to one only within consciousness. *Vijñapti-mātra* means that we confuse our imaginary projections for the world itself. Since this confusion pervades ordinary mental operations, it ends only when those operations cease.

Yogācāra explains that each individual is a distinct consciousness stream or mental continuum (*citta-santāna*) that, like a river, changes moment by moment in accord with causes and conditions, giving the illusion of a continuity of identity despite the perpetual reconfiguring of the water. It has no fixed, invariant identity or self.

The stream flows from moment to moment and from life to life. These distinct consciousness streams can affect and communicate with other streams, learning from and teaching each other, and mutually influencing each other. Hence, Yogācāra rejects both solipsism and the idea of an overarching universal mind. If, as solipsists claim, each mind is closed off from others, how could Buddhas and others teach anyone anything? If we cannot learn from others, then Buddhism itself becomes superfluous and untenable. If everything shares a single mind, then that mind would have to be either deluded or enlightened. If deluded, then enlightenment for individuals would be impossible; if enlightened, then either unenlightened individuals should be impossible, or else they are already enlightened just as they are, which again would render individual practice and Buddhism meaningless.

Vijñapti-mātra is not the denial of anything real outside an individual mind. Even *rūpa* (sensorial materiality) is accepted, since physicality is known through the senses and cognition; sensations should not be confused, however, with abstract concepts or theories about materiality. Sensation is real (Asaṅga calls the five senses pure); conceptualization is not real in the same way, especially when it imports notions of selfhood or substantialism, or posits appropriational entities. That would be the sort of error the term *vijñapti-mātra* is designed to caution against.

Everything we know, conceive, imagine, or are aware of, we know through cognition, including the notion that entities might exist independent of our cognition. Cognitive objects appear within acts consciousness; Yogācāra never denies that. By definition, they cannot appear elsewhere. What Yogācāra denies in the term *external object* is the concept of externality, not the object itself. Although the mind does not create the physical world, it generates the interpretative categories through which we know, classify, and interact with the physical world, and it does this so seamlessly that we mistake our interpretations for the world itself. Those interpretations—conditioned conventionalisms expressed as desires, preferences, and anxieties—become obstructions (*āvaraṇa*) that prevent us from seeing what is actually the case. In simple terms, we are blinded by our own self-interests, our own prejudices, our desires. We think like others because we have undergone similar conditioning and reinforce that conditioning by congregating with those who are like-minded. Such consensus is bred from tautology, not universality.

Unenlightened cognition is an appropriative act. Yogācāra texts do not speak about subjects and objects; instead, perception is analyzed in terms of sentient beings and cognitive fields, or, more often, graspers (*grāhaka*) and what is grasped (*grāhya*). The Buddhist notion of karma is intimately connected to the notion of appropriation (*upādāna*). As explained in the earliest Buddhist texts, suffering and ignorance are produced by karma. Karma is defined in Buddhism as any intentional activity of body, speech, or mind. Intention is the crucial factor, and, since intention is a cognitive condition, whatever is noncognitive must be also nonkarmic and nonintentional. Thus, by definition, whatever is noncognitive can have no karmic implications or consequences. Intention means to direct one's attention toward some thing or purpose, to desire something. Physically, linguistically, or mentally, we try to "get it."

Put another way, only cognitive acts can have karmic repercussions. Cognitive acts include meaningful bodily gestures that communicate intentions (such gestures are also called *vijñapti*). Thus, to overcome ignorance and suffering by eliminating karmic conditioning, Buddhists need only focus on what occurs within the domain of cognitive conditions (*citta-gocara*).

Categories such as external object and materiality (*rūpa*) are cognitive constructions. *Materiality* is a word for the colors, textures, sounds, and so on that we cognize in acts of perception, and it is only to the extent that they are perceptually apprehended and ideologically grasped, thereby becoming objects of attachment, that they have karmic significance. Materialism is not the problem. There is nothing intrinsically good or bad about gold, for example; rather, our ideas about gold's value and uses, which we project and then act upon, lead to good or bad consequences. The incessant propensity (*anuśaya*) to appropriate what consciousness projects is the problem. These projections are not just things, but moral qualities, status, ideals, religious and national doctrines and identities, the holding of opinions, whatever we can make our own, or make ourselves to be. For Buddhism, attachment to ideas and theories is much deeper and more problematic than attachment to physical things, since the latter is rooted in and merely an expression of the former.

A deceptive trick is built into the way consciousness operates at every moment. Consciousness constructs a cognitive object in such a way that it disowns its own creation, pretending the object is "out there," to render that object capable of being appropriated. Even while what we cognize is occurring within our act of cognition, we cognize it as if it were external to our consciousness. This is called *abhūta-parikalpa*, imagining something exists in a locus in which it is absent. Realizing *vijñapti-mātra* means exposing this trick at play in every act of consciousness, catching it in the act, as it were, and thereby eliminating it. Consciousness engages in this deceptive game of projection, dissociation, and appropriation because there is no self. The most deep-seated erroneous view to which sentient beings cling, according to Buddhism, is *ātmadṛṣṭi*, the view that a permanent, eternal, immutable, independent self exists. No such self exists, and deep down we know that. This makes us anxious, since it entails that no self or identity endures forever. To alleviate that anxiety, we attempt to construct a self, to fill the anxious void, to do or acquire something enduring. Projecting objects and ideas that one can appropriate and cling to is the way consciousness contributes to this project. If I own things (e.g., ideas, theories, identities, and material objects), then "I am." If there are eternal or universal objects that I can possess, then I, too, must be eternal or universal. To undermine this erroneous appropriative grasping, Yogācāra texts say: Negate the object, and the self is also negated (e.g., *Madhyānta-vibhāga*, 1:4, 8).

Intentional acts also have moral motives and consequences. Since effects are shaped by their causes, an act with a wholesome intent would tend to yield wholesome fruits, while unwholesome intentions produce unwholesome effects.

THREE NATURES

Yogācāra devised a model of three self-natures (*trisvabhāva*) to explain *vijñapti-mātra* more concisely. The pervasive mental constructions that obstruct our view of what truly is the case are called *parikalpita* (imaginative construction). The actual webs of causes and conditions at play are called *paratantra* (dependent on other [causes]). Other-dependence is so-called to emphasize that no thing exists independently, self-caused, eternal, invariant; everything arises dependent on causes and conditions other than itself, in the absence of which it ceases to be. Ordinarily, *paratantra* is infested with *parikalpita*. *Pariniṣpanna* (consummation) is the removal of *parikalpita* from *paratantra*, leaving only purified *paratantra*.

Since the notion of self-nature is itself a parikalpic idea that presumes selfhood, it, too, must be eliminated. Thus, the three self-natures are actually three nonself-natures (*tri-niḥsvabhāva*). *Parikalpita* is devoid of self-nature since it is unreal by definition. *Paratantra* lacks self-nature, since other-dependence precludes self-nature. *Pariniṣpanna*—the Yogācāra counterpart to the Madhyamaka notion of *śūnyatā* (emptiness), which signifies the lack of self-nature in everything—is defined as the absence of self-nature. Thus, the three self-natures are ultimately understood as three nonself-natures.

EIGHT CONSCIOUSNESSES

According to Buddhism, consciousness arises as a by-product of the contact of a sense organ with its corresponding sphere of sense objects. The eye contacting visibles (e.g., colors and shapes) produces visual consciousness; likewise for the remaining four senses (hearing, smell, taste, and touch). The mental organ, *manas*, operates similarly. Coming into contact with the sphere of mental objects (*mano-dhātu*), mental consciousness (*mano-vijñāna*) arises. Hence, there are six sense organs and six corresponding sense realms, which, combined with the six types of resultant consciousnesses, makes eighteen factors altogether. Yogācāra accepted these eighteen factors but found them inadequate to explain several issues that had become important for Buddhists, including the sense of selfhood, appropriative propensities, continuity of experience, and how projection worked. To address these issues, Yogācāra expanded the mental level, resulting in eight rather than six types of consciousness. *Mano-vijñāna* became the sixth sense organ, a kind of empirical consciousness that discerns mental objects as well as the activities of the five senses; *manas* became the seventh consciousness, responsible for appropriating experience as "mine" and thus infesting experience with a sense of selfhood (thus also called *kliṣṭa-manas*, "defiled mind"). The eighth consciousness, *ālaya-vijñāna*, was a novel innovation.

Yogācāra used a seed metaphor to describe the process of karmic conditioning. Experience engenders a seed that is planted out of sight (unconsciously retained in the *ālaya-vijñāna*), where it remains latent until catalytic conditions bring it to fruition (karmic result, *vipāka*), engendering new seeds of the same type. This was a powerful metaphor in agrarian societies. As a warehouse (*ālaya*) to these seeds, the *ālaya-vijñāna* was called the all-seeds consciousness (*sarva-bījāka-vijñāna*). Since it was the conduit and repository of their fruitions, it was also called *vipāka-vijñāna* (karmic requital consciousness). Since the *ālaya-vijñāna* always operates, even when the other seven consciousnesses temporarily cease (e.g., in deep sleep), it was also called foundational consciousness (*mūla-vijñāna*). Although it stores karmic seeds and engenders their projection, the *ālaya-vijñāna* is a karmically neutral mechanical process (*anivṛta*, *avyākṛta*). *Manas* appropriates the activities of the other consciousnesses, thinking they are "my" experience, and appropriates the *ālaya-vijñāna* as a "self."

Karmic continuity ceases by overturning the basis (*āśraya-parāvṛtti*), in which the *ālaya-vijñāna* and the other consciousnesses cease to function. The consciousnesses (vijñāna) lose their discriminative (vi-, compare the English prefix dis-) projective propensities and become direct cognitions (jñāna). Ālaya-vijñāna becomes the "great mirror cognition" (mahādarśa-jñāna), no longer appropriatively storing or engendering new seeds; instead, like a mirror, it reflects everything impartially without attachment. Manas loses its self-prejudicial nature and becomes the equalizing immediate cognition (samatājñāna), equalizing self and other. Mano-vijñāna, which discriminates cognitive objects, becomes immediate cognitive mastery (pratyavekṣamā-jñāna), and properly discerns the particular and general characteristics of things. The five sense consciousnesses, now unhindered by the mental obstructions of the sixth and seventh consciousness, become immediate cognitions that accomplish what must be done (kṛtyānuṣṭhāna-jñāna), thereby engaging the world effectively. Yogācāra texts differ on which overturning occurs at which stage of practice, but they agree that full enlightenment entails accomplishing all of them.

ASAṄGA ON LANGUAGE AND NONLINGUISTIC THINGS

In his texts—notably the Madhyānta-vibhāga and the tattvārtha ([relation of] referents and real things) chapter of the Yogācārabhūmi—Asaṅga challenges the Madhyamaka claim that emptiness (śūnyatā) is the ultimate and final position, the true Middle Way, not by denying the importance and validity of emptiness, but by taking the analysis one extra step. For Asaṅga, emptiness is a tool for eliminating false views, especially the false view of selfhood attributed to beings or things. But once these views are emptied, something remains, namely reality understood as emptied of false conceptualizations.

A quick summary of the tattvārtha chapter of Asaṅga's Yogācārabhūmi may illustrate how he refashioned rival teachings, in this case redefining emptiness (śūnyatā) and the Middle Way, while providing a useful summary of his philosophy. For Madhyamaka the Middle Way (madhyamā-pratipad, from which Madhyamaka derives its name) entails that all things are empty (śūnya)—meaning they are devoid of self-essence or own-being (svabhāva)—because they are dependently arisen from causes and conditions that are themselves empty. Thus, existent things are conventionally real but ultimately empty.

Asaṅga responds by describing four types of people, each experiencing a different phenomenological sphere of reals (tattva) and conceptual-linguistic referents (artha): (1) ordinary people, (2) philosophers, (3) Hīnayāna adepts, and (4) Mahāyāna adepts, the latter denoting accomplished Bodhisattvas and Buddhas. The first are naive realists, immersed in a cognitive field of compulsive presuppositions (niścitādhimukti-gocara), who accept things as established by convention. What appears to be real to an ordinary person has been conceptually and linguistically constructed from one's own discriminative imaginings (vikalpa) and remains unquestioned. Philosophers apply rational epistemological methods to logically investigate things and accept as real what has been logically proven by an articulate, discursive person. Hīnayāna adepts who have eliminated the affective obstructions (kleśāvaraṇa) realize there is no real referent corresponding to the notion self. They see a person as the five aggregates only (skandha-mātra; the five are form, hedonic tone, linguistic conceptualizing, embodied karmic conditioning, and consciousness), conditionally arisen, devoid of an imagined self.

By seeing that not only people, but all things lack selfhood, Mahāyāna adepts eliminate all obstructions to knowable realities (jñeyāvaraṇa). Asaṅga then enters a detailed discussion on the relation between the linguistic ideational sphere (nominal reality, prajñapti) and its cognitive basis (nonarticulable, nonconceptual things, vastu), providing numerous reasons for why they are not reducible to each other, nor entirely separable from each other. For Asaṅga emptiness signifies cleansing cognition of erroneous conditioning and views, so that reality is cognized nonerroneously. Emptiness is not a final state, but a purificatory, antidotal process that eliminates erroneous conceptualizations; once they are eliminated what remains is reality. Since this remainder is nonconceptual and therefore nonlinguistic, it cannot be adequately rendered in words without re-reducing it to the conceptual sphere.

Put simply, to perceive something blue is nonlinguistic (and hence indescribable to a blind person), though one can conceive of it as "something blue." The concept blue is neither the same nor different from the perception. Without vastus, referential articulations (abhilāpya) would have no basis; without such articulations, the nature of vastus could not be defined or intellectually understood. To think that vastus are merely nominal realities is more pernicious than believing in self, Asaṅga argues, since believing in self is to be mistaken about only one type of knowable, whereas to reject all vastus is to be mistaken about everything. Not holding the extreme views that (1) nonexistent things (like self) exist or (2) that all cognizables are nonexistent is, for Asaṅga, the true

Middle Way. Neither *prajñapti* nor *vastu* is rejected completely or accepted naïvely.

In his *Madhyānta-vibhāga*, implicitly deploying the theory of three natures to explain Buddhist practice, Asaṅga illustrates how emptiness and cultivating positive insight (*pariniṣpanna*) act as an antidote (*pratipakṣa*) to the pervasive false mental constructions (*parikalpita*) one projects as lived experience, resulting in reality being experienced just as it is (purified *paratantra*). In the *Mahāyānasaṃgraha* Asaṅga asserts that bondage and liberation cannot be explained coherently without reference to the *ālaya-vijñāna*, since it conveys the seeds and habits (*vāsanā*) that make bondage and liberation possible. Even brief contact with true Buddhist teachings (*saddharma*) may instill a propensity (*śruta-vāsanā*), outside one's conscious awareness, toward enlightenment and Buddhahood. Asaṅga claims this propensity, called *mano-jalpa* (mental murmuring), is utterly different from and irreducible to the *ālaya-vijñāna*; it gradually destroys the *ālaya-vijñāna* from within, like a germ infecting a host. Eliminating the *ālaya-vijñāna* results in Buddhahood. To label Asaṅga an idealist would be a gross mischaracterization.

VASUBANDHU'S *TWENTY VERSES*

In the *Viṃśatikā* (Twenty verses) Vasubandhu, following Asaṅga's lead, refutes the realism of naive and philosophical realists. The realists assert that the objects we perceive exist outside of consciousness, which is the reason that these objects remain stable through (1) time and (2) space; (3) different people can have differing perceptions of a thing and yet reach a consensus about it; and (4) the objective world operates by determinate causal principles, rather by than imaginary, ineffective fantasies.

Vasubandhu addresses each of these four claims with numerous counterarguments, including an analogy to dreams. In dreams seemingly external objects appear as if in time and space, even though no actual external object is present to cause them, thus proving that while consciousness is a necessary and sufficient condition for objects to appear in perception, the presence of actual external objects is neither necessary nor sufficient. For Vasubandhu, as for Asaṅga, the perceptions of ordinary people are like a dream, a mental projection based on conditioned predispositions. That different beings have differing perceptions of the purportedly same thing proves this. Updating Vasubandhu's example, that flies and humans perceive and react to excrement in radically different ways, demonstrates that what each perceives is a projection based on its own conditioning, or its own

mental seeds (*bījās*) acquired from past experiences (perhaps in past lives). Moreover, karma (action) is collective, in that we gravitate toward beings or types who perceive as we do, erroneously justifying the seeming universality of our group perspective.

Thus, the varying perception argument supports rather than undermines the Yogācāra position. Note that the dream example and the varying perception example not only neglect to disprove that something outside the activities of consciousness may play a role in its perceptions; on the contrary, both require that there be such a thing for the examples to make sense at all. The observation that dreams imitate waking perceptions minus the presence of actual objects requires that we appreciate the contrast; the object in contention between flies and humans is obviously not reducible to the perceptual projections of either.

Vasubandhu is not arguing for either a subjectivism or a metaphysical relativity, but he is pointing out that we mistake our imaginings for reality, obstructing our view of things as they are. Projective imaginings blocking our vision can have powerful karmic consequences, as Vasubandhu shows in his response to the realist's claim about causal efficacy. He uses the example of a wet dream. Though the erotic cognitive object is a mental construction, without an actual external or physical corresponding object present, the imaginative act causes actual seminal emission, a physical effect produced outside the dream and recognized as such on awakening. The monastic vow of celibacy treats wet dreams as an infraction of the monastic code. Even though dreams are only fantasies, they have real karmic consequences. The deluded mind produces real effects that can only be fully known after awakening, once delusion has ceased. Awakening means enlightenment—the term *bodhi* (awakening) can also mean "enlightenment"—the cessation of the deluded mind. Even though we act in a collective deluded world of our own construction, our actions have real causal consequences.

The realist objects that objects perceived while awake seem stable in time and space, whereas objects in dreams do not. Vasubandhu replies that objects and events seem less clear and consistent in dreams because one's mind is overcome by sleepiness so one is not "thinking clearly." Furthermore, one does not know that the objects in a dream are only dream-objects until one awakens. Vasubandhu's reply to the question of whether we can know other minds extends the dream analogy: Even our own minds are opaque to us since our mental capacities are dim and sleepy. However, one who is awakened (the literal meaning of *Buddha*) can know other minds more clearly than we know our own. Not only can we know other minds (if we awaken), but we constantly influence each other for better and for worse (though we may not notice that within our individual dreams). Thus, karma is intersubjective. Moreover, since the more awake one is the more causally effective one's mind becomes, sages and buddhas can exert powerful effects on the world, including devastating destruction, and even life and death.

THE FIVE STAGES

Precise details of the stages in which the mental stream is purified of pollutants (*āsrava*), filtering out karmically unwholesome seeds while nourishing and fortifying the wholesome ones, vary across different Yogācāra texts. A five-stage model is found in several foundational texts and has become the standard account:

(1) During the provisioning stage (*saṃbhārāvasthā*) one gathers and stocks up on "provisions" for the journey. The provisions consist of orienting oneself toward the pursuit of the path and developing the proper character, attitude, and resolve to accomplish it. This stage commences at the moment the aspiration for enlightenment (*bodhicitta*) arises.

(2) Next is the experimental stage (*prayogāvasthā*), in which one converts Buddhist theory into praxis. *Prayoga* also means "intensifying effort," or applying oneself with increasing vigilance. While increasing meditative abilities, one begins to suppress the grasper-grasped relation and commences on a careful and detailed study of the relation between things, language, and cognition.

(3) The next stage is deepening understanding (*prativedhāvasthā*), also called the Path of Corrective Vision (*darśana-mārga*). One works on realizing the emptiness of self and *dharmas* while reducing the obstructions (*kleśāvaraṇa* and *jñeyāvaraṇa*). This stage ends when one acquires some insight into nonconceptual cognition (*nirvikalpa-jñāna*), that is, cognition devoid of interpretive or imaginative overlay.

(4) In the Path of Cultivation (*bhāvanā-mārga*), nonconceptual cognition deepens. The grasper-grasped relation is utterly eliminated, as are all cognitive obstructions. This path culminates in the full Overturning of the Basis, or enlightenment.

(5) In the final stage (*niṣṭhāvasthā*) one abides in unsurpassable complete awakening and engages the world through the four immediate cognitions (mirror cognition and so on). All of one's activities and cognitions are postenlightenment (*pṛṣṭhalabdha*), and one compassionately endeavors to alleviate the suffering and ignorance of others.

See also Buddhism.

Bibliography

Anacker, Stefan, trans. and ed. *Seven Works of Vasubandhu: The Buddhist Psychological Doctor*. Delhi, India: Motilal Banarsidass, 1984.

Cook, Francis H., trans. *Three Texts on Consciousness Only*. Berkeley, CA: Numata Center, 1999.

Ganguly, Swati. *Treatise in Thirty Verses on Mere-Consciousness*. Delhi, India: Motilal Banarsidass, 1992.

Griffiths, Paul. *On Being Mindless: Buddhist Meditation and the Mind-Body Problem*. La Salle, IL: Open Court, 1986.

Griffiths, Paul, et al. *The Realm of Awakening: Chapter Ten of Asaṅga's Mahāyānasaṃgraha*. New York: Oxford University Press, 1989.

Hayes, Richard P. *Dignāga on the Interpretation of Signs*. Dordrecht, Netherlands: Kluwer Academic, 1988.

Hopkins, Jeffrey. *Reflections on Reality: The Three Natures and Non-natures in the Mind-Only School*. Berkeley: University of California Press, 2002.

Kochumuttom, Thomas. *A Buddhist Doctrine of Experience: A New Translation and Interpretation of the Works of Vasubandhu the Yogacarin*. Delhi, India: Motilal Banarsidass, 1982.

Lamotte, Étienne, trans. *Saṃdhinirmocana-sūtra*. Louvain, Belgium: Université de Louvain and Adrian Maisonneuve, 1935.

La Vallée Poussin, Louis de, trans. *Vijñaptimātratāsiddhi*. 2 vols. Paris: Geuthner, 1928.

Lusthaus, Dan. *Buddhist Phenomenology: A Philosophical Investigation of Yogācāra Buddhism and the Ch'eng wei-shih lun*. London: RoutledgeCurzon, 2002.

Nagao, Gadjin. *Mādhyamika and Yogācāra*. Translated by Leslie Kawamura. Albany: SUNY Press, 1991.

Powers, John. *Wisdom of the Buddha: The Saṃdhinirmocana Mahāyāna Sūtra*. Berkeley, CA: Dharma, 1995.

Powers, John. *The Yogācāra School of Buddhism: A Bibliography*. Metuchen, NJ: Scarecrow Press, 1991.

Rahula, Walpola, trans. *Le Compendium de la Super-Doctrine d'Asaṅga (Abhidharmasamuccaya)*. Paris: Publications de l'École Française d'Extrême Orient, 1971. Translated by Sara Webb-Boin as *Abhidharmasamuccaya: The Compendium of the Higher Teaching*. Freemont, CA: Asian Humanities Press, 2001.

Schmithausen, Lambert. *Ālayavijñāna*. Tokyo, Japan: International Institute for Buddhist Studies, 1987.

Shih, Heng-ching, and Dab Lusthaus, trans. *A Comprehensive Commentary on the Heart Sutra: Translated from the Chinese of K'uei-chi*. Berkeley, CA: Numata Center, 2001.

Sparham, Gareth, trans. *Ocean of Eloquence: Tsong kha pa's Commentary on the Yogācāra Doctrine of Mind*. Albany, NY: SUNY Press, 1993.

Tat, Wei, trans. *Ch'eng Wei-Shih Lun: The Doctrine of Mere Consciousness*. Hong Kong: Ch'eng Wei-Shih Lun Publication Committee, 1973.

Tatz, Mark. *Asaṅga's Chapter on Ethics with the Commentary of Tsong-kha-pa: The Basic Path to Awakening, the Complete Bodhisattva*. Lewiston, NY: Edwin Mellen, 1986.

Willis, Janice Dean. *On Knowing Reality: The Tattvārtha Chapter of Asaṅga's Bodhisattvabhūmi*. New York: Columbia University Press, 1979.

Dan Lusthaus (2005)

BUDDHIST EPISTEMOLOGY

For Buddhist thinkers philosophy should aid one in eliminating suffering and obtaining happiness. They maintain that to achieve those ends, one must eliminate ignorance (*avidyā*), a fundamental mental flaw that is suffering's basic cause. Although variously construed ignorance inevitably involves the mistaken belief that a fixed, unchanging personal essence, or *ātman*, lies at the core of each person's identity. Hence, to eliminate ignorance one must eradicate that belief, and to do so Buddhist philosophers stress the importance of seeing things as they are (*yathābhūtadarśana*), a corrective cognitive state through which one knows that persons necessarily lack essence. The need to give an account of such a state leads to a concern with epistemology in Buddhist thought from its earliest period (500 BCE–100 CE) in South Asia.

Although early Buddhism evinces a nascent epistemology, precise and sophisticated accounts of knowledge do not begin until adequate tools are developed by South Asian philosophers, primarily non-Buddhists, starting no later than the first century CE. The Buddhist theorist Vasubandhu initially appropriates these tools, but Dignāga first employs them in a manner that reflects all the issues addressed by later Buddhist epistemologists. Finally, Dharmakirti modifies and expands Dignāga's work in such a manner that all subsequent Buddhist epistemologists in India and Tibet cast their work as interpretations of Dharmakirti's philosophy. Hence, for the purposes of this entry, *Buddhist epistemology* refers to the thought of Dharmakirti and his subsequent interpreters in both India and Tibet, where epistemological works continue to be composed. In their voluminous writings Buddhist epistemologists express a variety of competing views developed in distinct historical contexts. Nevertheless, they largely agree on the following central theories and principles.

MODEL OF KNOWING

Buddhist epistemologists examine knowledge in terms of a knowledge-event or act of knowing (*pramiti*). Their account rests on the claim that the mind consists of a series of causally related, instantaneous mental moments, each of which is ontologically irreducible. Thus, as a mental event the act of knowing is ontologically identical to a mental moment. The act of knowing occurs when the mind comes into a direct or indirect causal relation with an object such that, with other conditions in place, the next mental moment contains an image (*ākāra*) of the object. Due to the ontological unity of a mental moment, the notion that the mental moment contains an image of the object is metaphorical; in fact, the image is ontologically identical to that mental moment itself. Nevertheless, from a phenomenal standpoint the act of knowing presents itself with two images, the aforementioned object-image (*grāhyākāra*) and a subject-image (*grāhakākāra*). The latter accounts for the sense of subjectivity in the act of knowing, whereas the former accounts for the content of the cognition.

On the Buddhist theory of mind all cognitions must have an object, which is to say that all cognitions have an object-image. Not every cognition, however, is an act of knowing. Instead, only two types of cognitions—perception (*pratyakṣa*) and inference (*anumāna*)—can be acts of knowing because only they can satisfy two criteria: they are reliable (*avisaṃvāda*) and they are motivators of action (*pravartaka*). Reliability concerns the justification of knowledge. The fact of being a motivator of action is a psychological feature that reflects teleological and ontological concerns.

RELIABILITY

For Buddhist epistemologists, an act of knowing—whether it be a perception or an inference—is reliable in that it directs one to an object with the desired telic efficacy (*arthakriyā*). On this criterion an act of knowledge is distinguished from an unreliable cognition in one of two ways: Either it directs one to an object that can fulfill a particular goal, or it presents itself as the fulfillment of that goal. Suppose, for example, that one is cold, and that one seeks to warm one's hands at a fire. Because the hearth contains a fire that is capable of fulfilling one's goal, the perception of a fire in the hearth is deemed reliable. When one reaches the hearth, the sensation of heat on one's hands is itself the fulfillment of one's goal. Thus, that cognition of heat is also reliable.

By grounding reliability in telic efficacy Buddhist thinkers seek to justify beliefs by interpreting them as descriptions of their objects' causal characteristics. Hence, the ultimate arbiter of a cognition's reliability is the way in which it presents its objects in causal terms. If it presents the object's causal characteristics such that the object is capable of functioning in the expected fashion, then the cognition is reliable; otherwise, it is not. In some cases the evidence for the desired functionality is given with the cognition itself: for example, the sensation of warmth requires no other cognition to verify that one is feeling warm. Such cognitions are said to be intrinsically (*svataḥ*) reliable, and this applies to all inferences and some perceptions. In other instances of perception another cognition must verify the cognition's content. One may only glimpse the fire from a corner of the room, and one must appeal to inferential evidence (such as smoke) or a subsequent perception to verify that one was indeed seeing fire. A perception that requires such confirmation is said to be extrinsically (*parataḥ*) reliable.

PURPOSE AND MOTIVATION

Arguments for a cognition's reliability generally serve to justify a belief. Thus, one's belief that "there is a fire in the hearth" is true inasmuch as the cognition that includes that belief reliably represents the causal characteristics of the object in question. For that cognition to be an act of knowing, however, that cognition must include other dispositions. Of prime importance is the desire to know (*jijñāsa*) without which the cognition could not arise: it may be true that "there is a fire in the hearth," but without some purpose one will not have a cognitive event in which that belief occurs. Thus, for Buddhists the account of knowledge as justified true belief is inadequate if that account ignores the role played by cognitive dispositions, especially those related to purpose.

In appealing to dispositions related to purpose Buddhist epistemologists hold that the reliability of a belief shifts according to the purpose to which it is tied. One might believe, for example, that the object on one's table is an unbreakable vase, although it is in fact fragile. Relative to the purpose of containing a bouquet, the cognition in which that belief occurs is reliable, since the vase can function so as to hold flowers. But relative to the aim of cracking a walnut's shell, a cognition in which that belief occurs would not be reliable, since the vase lacks the causal capacity to crack open a nut. By thus evaluating complex beliefs within various teleological contexts, Buddhist thinkers can accept some philosophical claims in one context, while rejecting them in another—a strategy that is central to Buddhist soteriology.

In relating reliability to purpose Buddhist epistemologists argue that an act of knowing must not only be reliable but must also be a motivator of purposeful action. Frequently, this assertion is formulated as a requirement for novelty, whereby an act of knowing reveals a previously unknown object (*ajñātārthaprakāśa*). On either version—motivation or novelty—this requirement points not only to the role of purpose but also to the notion that an act of knowing reduces doubt. That is, the cognition must pass a threshold whereby the person, usually idealized as judicious (*prekṣāvant*), is willing to act on a particular goal based on the content of that cognition. The early epistemologist Dignāga appears less concerned with the utter removal of doubt, but Dharmakīrti and most subsequent thinkers maintain that an act of knowing grants apodictic certainty, even if certainty must sometimes be supplied by a subsequent cognition.

Finally, the notion that an act of knowing must motivate action is also tied to ontological issues. The chief concern here is to eliminate the possibility that universals could be the objects of perception. As will be evident in the following text, the Buddhist strategy is to make perception the actual motivator of action, while relegating the determinate content of perception to a subsequent judgment, which is not strictly speaking the motivator.

PERCEPTION AND ILLUSION

As one of the two types of cognitions that are both reliable and motivate action, a perception is an act of knowledge. The Buddhist model of perception is causal and eidetic: an object interacts with a sense-organ such that, with other factors in place, the next moment of mind occurs with an image or simulacrum (*sādṛśya* or *sārūpya*) of the object. Unlike inference, in perception the image is produced directly by the object, and the reliability of perception is based on this direct causal relation.

As a mental moment, a perception is causally conditioned by the previous mental moment, including all the dispositions and physiological conditions that contribute to its occurrence. In a perception, however, not only the previous mental moment but also the perceived object is contributing causally to the occurrence of the perception. Hence, the causal character of the mental moment that is a perception is restrained (*niyata*) by the causal characteristics of the object to which it is in relation through the sense organ. Thus, a perception is reliable—it accurately reflects the object's causal characteristics—because the causal constraints imposed by the object on the perception's contents are indicative of that object's causal characteristics. To put it another way, the perception of blue is a reliable indicator of its object's causal characteristics because when that content—an image of blue—is the undistorted effect of an object, it can only be produced by an object with the causal capacity to produce a blue image.

This appeal to a causal relation between perceptual content and object compels Buddhist epistemologists to face the problem of illusion. A favorite Tibetan example is the "blue snow mountain": When one looks at a snowy Himalayan peak on a clear day, the snowcap appears blue because it reflects the sky's color. Here, the cognition is a spurious perception (*pratyakṣābhāsa*) because it lacks reliability, in that snow is not blue. But since the perceptual content—the image—is distorted by causal factors not given with the object, the content itself does not provide any basis for recognizing that distortion. Instead, some other perception or inference would need to reveal that distortion. Still, as noted earlier, some perceptions are alleged to be intrinsically reliable, such that they do not require confirmation by a subsequent act of knowing. What then would distinguish those perceptions such that, unlike the sight of "blue snow," they could never be spurious?

Buddhist epistemologists do not provide an easy answer to this question, but their theory of perceptual judgment provides a partial response. On their view perception itself is indeterminate in that it involves no conceptual or linguistic operation. A purely indeterminate cognitive event, however, cannot be either reliable or unreliable because it conveys no knowledge about the causal characteristics of its object in relation to one's goal. Hence, the reliability of a perception consists in that it leads to an immediately subsequent perceptual judgment (*tatpṛṣṭhalabdhaniścaya*) that does provide that knowledge. Strictly speaking, only the judgment is reliable or unreliable, in that it only describes the object in a determinate fashion. Nevertheless, since the form of that judgment is causally constrained by the image presented by indeterminate perception, the perception itself is considered reliable.

Returning, then, to the problem of illusion, the theory of perceptual judgment means that an uninterpreted perception could not itself be an act of knowing because, lacking any depiction of its object's causal characteristics, it could not be reliable. But when the subsequent judgment describes the object, it must do so in relation to a particular goal. One explicit outcome of this in theory is that a perception may only be partially reliable in that it can lead to correct judgments in regard to one goal, but not in regard to some other goal. For example, the perceptual content interpreted as "blue snow" might be unreliable in regard to one's need to identify a blue object, and yet it may still be reliable in regard to the need to identify snow. Although the implications of this claim are left covert, it seems likely that for Buddhist epistemologists one factor in the intrinsic reliability of some perceptions is that the goals in question are such that the perceptual content could never be erroneously interpreted. In other words the teleological context constrains the perceptual judgment such that incorrect interpretations of the perceptual content cannot occur in those cases.

PERCEPTUAL JUDGMENT AND ONTOLOGY

Besides its role in intrinsic reliability, the theory of perceptual judgment is also closely allied to Buddhist ontological concerns. For Buddhist epistemologists to exist is to be knowable (*jñeya*), and since knowledge is a causal process, an existent entity must therefore be causally efficient; likewise, any causally efficient entity must exist. The paradigmatic case of an entity's causal efficiency is its capacity to produce an image of itself in a perceiver's mind, and it is for this reason that Dharmakīrti remarks, "To exist is to be perceived" (*sattvam upalabdhir eva*). Moreover, since any object of perception must exist, Buddhists are careful to exclude the possibility of perceiving any metaphysically objectionable entity, such as a fixed personal essence. Largely because a personal essence is considered a special case of a universal, Buddhists likewise reject the existence—and hence the perception—of universals. Instead, only particulars (*svalakṣaṇa*) truly exist, and particulars alone are the objects of perception because only particulars are causally efficient.

Perception cannot include universals, and linguistic or conceptual cognitions must include universals. Hence, perception must be a sheer apprehension of an object that is not linguistic or conceptual in character. But as noted earlier, the criterion of reliability requires a determinate cognition, which is necessarily conceptual or linguistic in form. Hence, on the one hand, perception must be the immediate apprehension of a particular through a nonconceptual image in the mind and, on the other hand, to be reliable and to motivate action, that nonconceptual content must be interpreted by a determinate cognition. The solution is to relegate the determinate aspect of a perception to an immediately subsequent judgment, and in doing so Buddhists avoid the notion that linguistic or conceptual entities—that is, universals—are the objects of perception.

INFERENCE AND THE PROBLEM OF REFERENCE

Besides perception, inference is considered an act of knowing. As with perception, inference is a cognitive event in which an image of the object appears. Unlike perception, however, the image in an inference is not directly produced by the object. Instead, it bears an indirect causal relation to the object in two ways, namely, by way of the relations on which an inference relies and by way of the process of constructing universals.

The Buddhist approach to universals is central to their theory of inference because inferences are conceptual or linguistic acts of knowing. Moreover, their theory arises in response to the way their non-Buddhist rivals address the problem of reference. In short, these rivals claim that, for words to successfully refer to their proper referents, they must always have a relation to those referents and only to those referents. The word *cow*, for example, should refer only to a cow, and not to something different, such as a horse. Each individual cow, however, is different from every other cow. Hence, if the word *cow* were to stand in a direct relation to one individual cow, it should always refer only to that individual. Such would be the case because the word *cow* should never refer to something that is different from its proper referent, and if the proper referent of the word *cow* were a particular cow, then by referring to some other cow, the word *cow* would be referring to something different from its proper referent. And if the word *cow* can refer both to its proper referent and something other than its proper referent, why should it not refer to a horse?

Most South Asian thinkers solve this familiar problem in the philosophy of language by positing the existence of real universals (technical terms for which include *sāmānya*, *jāti*, and *ākṛti*). On this model, the word *cow* does not have a direct relation to any particular cow. Instead, it is directly related to the universal "cowness." Nevertheless, the word *cow* still refers successfully to each individual cow because the universal cowness is necessarily instantiated in each individual cow. A word such as *cow* thus refers to each particular cow by virtue of the universal cowness to which both the word and each particular are related. On this view one can thus say that all cows are the same not because each individual is identical, but because each individual instantiates that one universal cowness.

This model is problematic for Buddhists because it would justify the false belief in a personal essence. That is, just as cowness is present in each different cow in time and space, so, too, a personal essence would be present in

all the different spatiotemporal instances of what people consider to be one person. To avoid this outcome, Buddhist epistemologists therefore deny the ultimate reality of universals as things in the world. Thus, for them the universe is populated by spatiotemporally unique particulars, and nothing more. All cows are in fact unique; one only thinks that they are the same because one constructs a universal or sameness (*sāmānya*) for them. So too, each spatiotemporal instance of a person is actually unique. "John" at birth and "John" at forty-five are actually different. When one constructs a sameness that warrants one's use of the label "John," one falsely believes that the sameness is not constructed, but real.

THE EXCLUSION THEORY

Although Buddhist epistemologists deny the ultimate existence of universals, they nevertheless adopt their rivals' approach to reference. They are therefore obliged to formulate a theory that, while denying the ultimate reality of universals, accounts for the way that universals may be contingently constructed so that words may refer to their referents. Buddhists develop a model known as the exclusion theory (*apohavāda*), and to do so they once again resort to causality. In brief, the sameness required to construct the universal cowness is formulated by appealing to the causal characteristics of the individuals in question. More specifically, even though all individual cows are in fact utterly unique and distinct, one may ignore the differences among them and focus instead on the way they are different or excluded from all other entities. That difference or exclusion from other entities is a matter of causality: All cows are the same in that they are all equally different from those entities that are not capable of the causal functionality that one expects when one uses the word *cow*.

Here as well, the paradigmatic case for causal functionality is a perceptual image. Thus, all cows are the same in that they produce the same effect, namely, the same perceptual image in the mind. The problem, however, is that just as each cow is a unique individual, so, too, each perceptual image should also be a unique mental particular. Hence, Buddhist epistemologists must argue that all those images are the same, and to do so they use the same reason: Those images are the same because they all have the same effect, which in this case is a second-order determination of sameness (*ekapratyava-marśajñāna*). The obvious question here is: What warrants the sameness of all those determinations? If one again asserts that they all have the same effect, then the argument ends in an infinite regress. Well aware of this problem, Buddhist epistemologists follow Dharmakirti's argument: The sameness of those second-order determinations is not constituted by the fact that they all produce the same effect; rather, they are counted as the same because they are phenomenally presented in that fashion. In short, each instance of the judgment, "That is a cow," just seems the same.

Dharmakirti's answer to the problem of infinite regress may seem ad hoc, but it probably reflects a subtle approach to conventionality. In brief, Dharmakirti apparently holds that some conventions—including causality—are so stable that they may be treated as invariable when they are used in nomological arguments about the interpretation of perceptual content. Most Buddhist epistemologists, however, do not pursue this controversial aspect of Dharmakirti's thought and instead leave such concerns to philosophers of the *Madhyamika* or Middle Way school.

RELATIONS IN INFERENCE

The exclusion theory and the attendant problem of infinite regress may leave several questions unasked, but Buddhists seem satisfied with its use, perhaps because it so greatly simplifies the theory of inference. On their view, all inferences take this basic form: "S is P because S is E," where S is the subject of the proposition to be proven, P is the predicate, and E is the evidence. A common example would be: "The mountain is a locus of fire because it is a locus of smoke." The success of the inference depends on the pervasion (*vyāpti*), which by the time of Dharmakirti is understood as a necessary relationship between evidence and predicate. Dharmakirti formulates this relation as a necessary rule of unaccompanied nonarising (*avinābhāvaniyama*). In other words the evidence cannot occur if it is not accompanied by the proximate occurrence of the predicate, or to put it another way the predicate is necessarily predicable of any subject to which the evidence is correctly predicated.

Buddhist epistemologists describe this invariable relation between evidence and predicate as being of only two kinds: either the evidence is the effect of the predicate, or else the evidence stands in a relation of identity (*tādātmya*) to the predicate. The causal relation is operative in the inference of fire from smoke; the identity relation is operative in an inference such as, "This is a tree because it is an oak."

Both in the case of the causal relation and the identity relation the success of the Buddhist analysis of inference depends heavily on the exclusion theory of meaning and reference. For example, when one infers the presence of fire from seeing smoke, the inference succeeds precisely because of the meaning of the concept smoke. That is, an instance of smoke is excluded from all those other entities that do not have the causal characteristics of smoke. One of those characteristics is central to the inference: namely, that any entity properly called smoke is necessarily caused by an entity that can be properly described as fire. Hence, if one's perceptual content has been correctly interpreted, the identification of the object as smoke already gives one the information needed to infer the presence of fire. The same type of account holds true in the identity relation: the concept or term *oak* can only be properly applied to an entity that also has all the causal characteristics that make it suitable to be called a tree. In this way the inferential process is a matter of recognizing the relation between concepts, sometimes through the help of empirical examples.

The exclusion theory thus provides a seemingly analytical relation between the concepts employed in an inference, and inferences are therefore treated as intrinsically reliable. This suggests that inference is largely a matter of understanding the conventions that govern the use of concepts. The problem, however, is determining whether those conventions accurately depict the causal characteristics of real things. How does one determine, for example, that smoke is necessarily produced by fire? Here, one encounters the general problems of induction, and while Buddhist epistemologists propose various empirical means of overcoming such problems, it would be difficult to argue that they have fully succeeded.

See also Buddhism; Buddhism—Schools: Dge-lugs; Buddhism—Schools: Madhyamaka; Epistemology, History of; Illusions; Mind and Mental States in Buddhist Philosophy; Perception; Reference; Universals, A Historical Survey; Vasubandhu.

Bibliography

Dreyfus, Georges B. J. *Recognizing Reality: Dharmakīrti's Philosophy and Its Tibetan Interpretations.* Albany: SUNY Press, 1997.

Dunne, John D. *Foundations of Dharmakīrti's Philosophy.* Boston: Wisdom Publications, 2004.

Frauwallner, Erich. "Landmarks in the History of Indian Logic." *Wiener Zeitschrift für die Kunde Süd und Ostasiens* 5 (1961): 125–148.

Hayes, Richard P. *Dignāga on the Interpretation of Signs.* Dordrecht: D. Reidel, 1987.

Katsura, Shoryu. "Dharmakīrti's Theory of Truth." *Journal of Indian Philosophy* 12 (3) (1984): 215–235.

Matilal, Bimal Krishna. *Perception: An Essay on Classical Indian Theories of Knowledge.* Oxford, U.K.: Clarendon Press, 1986.

Siderits, Mark. "Apohavāda, Nominalism and Resemblance Theories." In *Dharmakīrti's Thought and Its Impact on Indian and Tibetan Philosophy: Proceedings of the Third International Dharmakīrti Conference, Hiroshima, November 4–6, 1997*, edited by Shoryu Katsura. Vienna: Verlag der Österreichische Akademie der Wissenschaften, 1999.

Siderits, Mark. "Deductive, Inductive, Both or Neither?" *Journal of Indian Philosophy* 31 (1–3) (2003): 302–321.

Steinkellner, Ernst. "Once More on Circles." *Journal of Indian Philosophy* 31 (1–3) (2003): 323–341.

Tillemans, Tom J. F. *Scripture, Logic, Language: Essays on Dharmakirti and His Tibetan Successors.* Boston: Wisdom Publications, 1999.

John D. Dunne (2005)

BUFFON, GEORGES-LOUIS LECLERC, COMTE DE
(1707–1788)

The French naturalist and author Georges-Louis Leclerc, Comte de Buffon, enjoyed international acclaim for the artistic expression of his own grandiose, often brilliant theories and for presenting in similar fashion the discoveries of leading contemporaries, particularly in the field of natural science.

LIFE

Born at Montbard, son of an upper middle-class magistrate, Buffon was first educated by the Jesuits of Dijon. Details about his personal life are sparse and uncertain. It is generally believed that, after studying law and despite a marked proclivity for mathematics, he went to Angers at the age of twenty-two to study medicine while indulging in botany and horsemanship. His stay ended abruptly when, presumably having killed an opponent in a duel for no verifiable reason, he set out on travels through France and Italy with the irresponsible young duke of Kingston. His mother's death in 1731 recalled him to Montbard where, as heir to her wealth, he turned the family manor into a château. Assuming the name of de Buffon, he adroitly enlarged his estates, which, in due course, were raised to an earldom.

The rest of his long life was divided between Montbard and Paris; no evidence has yet appeared supporting the belief that he also spent a year in England. When only twenty-six, he was, through influence in high places, elected to the Academy of Science after having presented a paper on mathematical probability. He was soon engaged in silviculture and publishing experiments on the means of preserving and strengthening wood, and his reputation as a scientist was further enhanced by a translation in 1735 of Stephen Hales's *Vegetable Staticks* and, five years later, of Isaac Newton's *Method of Fluxions,* for which he wrote a much admired preface on the history of calculus.

From 1739 until his death he was curator of the Jardin du Roi in Paris, which, under his direction, expanded greatly and became an important scientific center. By 1740 he had begun work on his monumental forty-four-volume *Histoire naturelle,* the most ambitious and comprehensive history of natural science until recent times. Buffon was aided in this enormous task by reports from correspondents scattered throughout the world and by a team of highly specialized collaborators at home.

The first three volumes of the *Natural History,* including *Theory of the Earth* and *History of Man,* appeared in 1749. Published by the royal press, they were exempt from censorship. Almost immediately, however, they incurred the wrath of the Sorbonne for the bold views that ran counter to the book of Genesis. Out of deference to religious authority, Buffon penned an act of submission, only to proceed serenely in the same audacious manner.

Along with the volumes on quadrupeds (1753–1767), birds (1770–1783), and minerals (1783–1788) were the so-called *Supplements* (1774–1779), which included his justly famous work on Earth's geological periods, *The Epochs of Nature* (1778). After Buffon's death the vast project was brought to a close by B. G. E. Lacépède, with eight volumes on oviparous quadrupeds, snakes, fish, and whales.

Buffon's *Discourse on Style,* delivered upon the occasion of his admission to the French Academy in 1753, remains the best known of his shorter pieces. It contains the celebrated dictum: "The style is the man himself," the meaning of which has often been simplified to the point of misinterpretation.

THOUGHT

Buffon's death in Paris shortly before the French Revolution was mourned by the leading journals of Europe as the passing of one of the great figures of the century. His place in the history of ideas has since been undergoing a gradual reassessment still far from settled; certain areas of agreement have, nevertheless, been established. It is generally accepted that while he often engaged in scientific investigation, either through personal observation or through wide reading, his true inclination was for generalization. Influenced especially by Bacon, Newton, Gottfried Wilhelm Leibniz, and John Locke, he held seminal views that frequently inspired others to push his inquiries to fruitful conclusions. He rejected the popular conception of God as the Great Clockmaker and, instead of final causes, he looked for natural causes to explain the world about him. He insisted, and the stand was unusual for the day, that religion and science should be strictly separated. Thus, he evolved the theory that our planetary system had resulted from the glancing blow of a comet against the sun's molten surface. Perhaps the most original contribution of Buffon's cosmogony to science was to have introduced a new concept of the vast expanses of geological time. His published calculation of Earth's age as some 80,000 years, rather than the traditional estimate of 6,000, was in itself a generous concession to the prevailing spirit of the day; in his unpublished manuscripts he deals with figures that run into the millions.

Not an evolutionist in the modern sense, he nevertheless persistently stressed change at least in varieties, if not in species, of animal life. This and similar propositions or speculations led Charles Darwin to acclaim Buffon as the first author in modern times to have treated transformism in a scientific spirit. Moreover, in biology he rightly opposed epigenesis to the more widely accepted preformation theory of generation, though his ideas on "inner molds," "organic molecules" and spontaneous generation have long since fallen into disrepute. "He may be said to have asked all the questions which were to be answered in the course of the succeeding century," the oft-quoted comment of Henry Fairchild Osborn, perhaps remains the best generalization to date on Buffon's contribution to posterity.

See also Bacon, Francis; Darwin, Charles Robert; Evolutionary Theory; Leibniz, Gottfried Wilhelm; Locke, John; Newton, Isaac; Scientific Method.

Bibliography

WORKS BY BUFFON

Histoire naturelle, générale et particulière. 44 vols. Paris, 1749–1804. Translated and edited by William Smellie as *Natural History, General and Particular.* 20 vols. London, 1812. More recent edition edited by Jean Piveteau. Paris, 1954.

Oeuvres complètes de Buffon, edited by J.-L. Lanessan. Vols. 13 and 14: *Correspondance inédite.* Paris, 1885.

WORKS ON BUFFON

Cherni, Amor. "Brute Matter and Organic Matter in Buffon." *Graduate Faculty Philosophy Journal* 22 (1) (2000): 87–106.

Duchesneau, François. "The Role of Hypotheses in Descartes's and Buffon's Theories of the Earth." In *Problems of Cartesianism,* edited by Thomas M. Lennon. Montreal: McGill Queen's, 1982.

Fellows, Otis. "Buffon's Place in the Enlightenment." *Studies on Voltaire and the Eighteenth Century* 25 (1963): 603–629.

Flourens, Pierre. *Des Manuscrits de Buffon.* Paris, 1860.

Gayon, Jean. "The Individuality of the Species: A Darwinian Theory?—From Buffon to Ghiselin and Back to Darwin." *Biology and Philosophy* 11 (2) (1996): 215–244.

Goodman, David. "Buffon's *Histoire Naturelle* as a Work of the Enlightenment." In *The Light of Nature,* edited by J. D. North and J. J. Roche. Dordrecht: Kluwer, 1985.

Heim, Roger et al. *Buffon.* Paris: Museum National d'Histoire Naturelle, 1952.

Wilkie, J. B. "The Idea of Evolution in the Writings of Buffon." *Annals of Science* 12 (1) (1956): 45–62; 12 (3) (1956): 212–227; 12 (4) (1956): 255–266.

Wohl, Robert. "Buffon and His Project for a New Science." *Isis* 51 (2) (1960): 186–199.

Otis Fellows (1967)
Bibliography updated by Tamra Frei (2005)

BULGAKOV, SERGEI NIKOLAEVICH
(1871–1944)

Sergei Nikolaevich Bulgakov, a Russian economist, philosopher, and theologian, was a leading twentieth-century religious philosopher in the tradition of Vladimir Solov'ëv. Bulgakov was born in Livny, Russia, the son of a priest. He attended a church school in Livny and spent four years in a theological seminary before enrolling in the faculty of law at the University of Moscow in 1890. He was graduated in 1894 and began teaching political economy at the Moscow Technical School in 1895. From 1898 to 1900 he traveled in western Europe and Great Britain, gathering material for his master's dissertation, *Kapitalizm i zemledelie* (Capitalism and agriculture; 2 vols., St. Petersburg, 1900). Through this and other writings on economic and social questions he soon acquired a national reputation. After teaching in Kiev for five years, he returned to Moscow in 1906 to become professor of political economy at the Moscow Institute of Commerce; in the same year he was elected to the second state Duma as a Constitutional Democrat. In 1912 he received a doctorate from the University of Moscow, and in 1917 he was named professor of political economy at that institution.

Although Bulgakov was a leading "legal Marxist" in the 1890s, he even then acknowledged the philosophical supremacy of Immanuel Kant and soon began to depart from orthodox Marxism on socioeconomic issues as well. In his master's dissertation he argued that Karl Marx's theory of the centralization of production is inapplicable to agriculture, where small-scale production is more stable and viable than large-scale. When, in the early years of the twentieth century, Bulgakov underwent a religious crisis, he abandoned Marxism completely, first for the idealistic position represented in his book of essays, *Ot Marksizma k idealizmu* (From Marxism to idealism; St. Petersburg, 1903), and subsequently for a mystical, "Sophiological" interpretation of the Russian Orthodox faith showing the direct and extensive influence of Solov'ëv and Pavel Florenskii and the ultimate influence of Plato and Friedrich Wilhelm Joseph von Schelling. In 1909 Bulgakov contributed to the celebrated miscellany, *Vekhi* (Landmarks), in which ex-Marxist Russian intellectuals, including Nikolai Berdiaev and Petr Struve, criticized the radical intelligentsia. Bulgakov first outlined his positive religious philosophy in his doctoral dissertation, *Filosofiia khoziaistva* (The philosophy of the economy; Moscow, 1912) and over the years 1911–1916 he composed the work in which this philosophy received its fullest expression, *Svet nevechernii* (The unfading light; Moscow, 1917).

During the same period Bulgakov studied for holy orders, and in 1918 he was ordained a priest in the Russian Orthodox Church. He moved to the Crimea, where he became professor of political economy and theology at the University of Simferopol', but in 1921 he lost this position because he was a member of the clergy. At the end of 1922 he was expelled from Russia along with many other non-Marxist scholars and writers. He settled first in Prague and lived from 1925 in Paris, where he took part in founding the Orthodox Theological Institute, serving as its dean and professor of dogmatic theology until his death. During these years Bulgakov wrote extensively on theological subjects and took an active part in ecclesiastical conferences in many countries, becoming an internationally known church figure. Some of his later theological works, particularly *Agnets Bozhii* (The lamb of God; Paris, 1933) and *Nevesta Agntsa* (The bride of the lamb; Paris, 1945) also carried further the development of his distinctive philosophical outlook.

Basic to this outlook is a cosmology that, although marked in its expression by obscurities and progressive modifications, centered consistently on the following themes: (1) The world, or cosmos, is an organic whole animated by a "world soul" or entelechy that is revealed in the structure, function, and connection of its parts. (2) God, or the Absolute, in creating the cosmos "out of nothing," created it not as something external or alien to him (for then it would limit the Absolute, which is impossible), but as an emanation of his own nature; the world is God as

becoming, the divine nature fused with nothingness. (3) Mediating between the Absolute and the cosmos, uniting them both within itself, is a "third being"—Sophia, the principle of divine wisdom. As the world of Platonic Ideas, Sophia is the ideal basis of the cosmos; as the object of divine love, purely receptive and conceiving everything within herself as the womb of being, Sophia is "eternal femininity"; as the principle of the Divine within the created, she is the "world soul," or entelechy; as a participant with the Trinity in the generation of the cosmos, she is a kind of "fourth hypostasis" in God. In his later works Bulgakov distinguished between the "divine Sophia" in God and the "created Sophia" in the cosmos, but he still emphasized their ultimate metaphysical identity and thus the consubstantiality of God and the cosmos.

Bulgakov resisted the pantheistic implications of his position, preferring to call it a form of panentheism, and strove to provide solutions to the chief philosophical problems it raised, such as the problems of evil and human freedom. He attributed evil to the nothingness or nonbeing that is the substratum of the cosmos: Through the willfulness of created beings, nothingness is actualized as a chaotic force erupting into the created world, which in itself is not evil but simply incomplete. He provided for human freedom through a doctrine of self-creation: man is free even in the act by which he comes into existence, for God allows man to collaborate in his own creation; at the same time, however, Bulgakov also asserted that Sophia guides history by a kind of necessity.

Like Florenskii, Bulgakov laid great stress on the antinomic character of rationality and looked to divine revelation through religious experience for knowledge of the highest truths, but his epistemological views in general received no thorough, original development or synthesis; the same is true of his scattered treatments of ethical questions and of his aesthetic reflections—the latter appearing principally in *Tikhie dumy* (Quiet meditations; Moscow, 1918). The work Bulgakov himself regarded as his most strictly philosophical product—*Filosofiia imeni* (Philosophy of the name)—was written in 1919 but first published posthumously in Paris in 1953. It is an exhaustive study of language, with particular application to theology, in which Bulgakov argued that words are not mere outward signs of meanings but are internally related to them as animate symbols.

Bulgakov's later works abounded in imaginative theological conceptions, including a doctrine of universal salvation and original treatments of the Incarnation and of the theological differences between Roman Catholicism and Orthodoxy. Some of his theological views, particularly his Sophiology, were severely censured in the early 1930s by the Moscow patriarchate, which affirmed that the doctrine of Sophia is incompatible with the Trinitarian nature of God and that it falsely introduces a distinction between masculine and feminine principles into the divine essence.

See also Absolute, The; Berdyaev, Nikolai Aleksandrovich; Florenskii, Pavel Aleksandrovich; Kant, Immanuel; Marxist Philosophy; Marx, Karl; Plato; Russian Philosophy; Schelling, Friedrich Wilhelm Joseph von; Solov'ëv (Solovyov), Vladimir Sergeevich; Sophia.

Bibliography

ADDITIONAL WORKS BY BULGAKOV

The Orthodox Church. Crestwood, NY: St. Vladimir Seminary Press, 1988.

Pain, J., and Nicholas Zernov, eds. *A Bulgakov Anthology.* Philadelphia: Westminster Press, 1976.

Philosophy of Economy: The World as Household. Translated by C. Evtuhov. New Haven, CT: Yale University Press, 2000.

Poole, R., ed. *Problems of Idealism: Essays in Russian Social Philosophy.* Translated by R. A. Poole. New Haven, CT: Yale University Press, 2003.

Sophia, the Wisdom of God: An Outline of Sophiology. Hudson, NY: Lindisfarne Press, 1993.

Williams, R., ed. *Sergii Bulgakov: Towards a Russian Political Theology.* Edinburgh: T&T Clark, 1999.

WORKS ON BULGAKOV

Evtuhov, C. *The Cross and the Sickle: Sergei Bulgakov and the Fate of Russian Religious Philosophy.* Ithaca, NY: Cornell University Press, 1997.

Kindersley, R., *The First Russian Revisionists: A Study of Legal Marxism in Russia.* Oxford: Clarendon, 1962.

Lossky, N. O., *History of Russian Philosophy,* Ch. 15. New York: International Universities Press, 1951.

Zenkovskii, *A History of Russian Philosophy.* 2 vols. Translated by G. Kline. New York and London: Routledge, 2003.

James P. Scanlan (1967)
Bibliography updated by Vladimir Marchenkov (2005)

BULLOUGH, EDWARD
(1880–1934)

Edward Bullough was a British aesthetician and literary scholar. He taught modern languages at Cambridge University, holding University lectureships in German and then Italia. He never held a philosophy fellowship or chair, but he gave the first lectures on aesthetics at Cambridge, beginning in 1907, and was widely read in aesthetics. He also conducted psychological research on aesthetic responses in collaboration with Cambridge psychologists.

Bullough is known in aesthetics primarily on the basis of a single article, "'Psychical Distance' as a Factor in Art and an Aesthetic Principle," originally published in *The British Journal of Psychology* in 1912, in which he maintains that aesthetic experience depends on a distancing from "our practical, actual self," thereby "permitting only such reactions on our part as emphasise the 'objective' features of the experience." By means of such distance, we can escape what is merely idiosyncratic but still experience a "*personal* relation, often highly emotionally coloured," to the object, whether work of art or nature.

Bullough's proposal stands in the long tradition of theories of disinterestedness dating back to Shaftesbury and Hutcheson and of the "aesthetic attitude" dating back to Schopenhauer. Bullough's innovation in this tradition is to treat aesthetic distance as a factor in both the creation and reception of art (it is obviously not involved in the creation of nature), and as a variable in the sense that different degrees of distance are appropriate for different kinds of objects, artists, and audiences. The experience of a particular object could thus suffer from either under-distancing or overdistancing. Bullough's emphasis on the variability of distance was suggested at least in part by his experiments on different aesthetic responses to colors, reported in a series of articles from 1907 to 1910, and led him to emphasize the variability rather than uniformity of indidual tastes. In this regard he distanced himself from the traditional theory of disinterestedness.

The 1912 article does not, however, fully explain the value of distancing oneself from objects. For Bullough's fuller account of the "aesthetic consciousness" that can be produced by the proper degree of distance from an object and its value to us, one must turn to his lectures on aesthetics, which were posthumously published in 1957. Here, after a thorough review of the problems of previous approaches to aesthetics, Bullough argues that "the aesthetic attitude is neither scientific nor ethical … neither explanatory nor final, but *contemplative*," giving "a plasticity and relief to objects and experiences which they inevitably lose" in ordinary scientific or practical contexts, an experience we obviously enjoy (Bullough 1957, p. 75). Here again Bullough stands in a long tradition, going back at least to Kant, but his view is distinguished by his emphasis on the availability of "aesthetic consciousness" in both quotidian and artistic contexts, and on its role in the creation and the reception of works of art. Bullough also stresses in a distinctive way in which "aesthetic consciousness" is a form of "objectivity," although it is distinct from both scientific objectivity and from the "egotistical *subjectivity* of practical consciousness."

Bullough's conceptions of aesthetic distance and aesthetic consciousness were harshly criticized by later analytical philosophers, such as George Dickie. But his use of these concepts to characterize a valued form of experience and to ground the possibility of a general "aesthetic culture" going beyond the specific realm of art save his reflections from the critique that these concepts cannot yield a satisfactory definition of art proper, which was not Bullough's goal.

See also Aesthetic Experience; Aesthetics, History of.

Bibliography

Bullough, Edward. *Æsthetics: Lectures and Essays*, edited with an introduction by Elizabeth M. Wilkinson. Palo Alto, CA: Stanford University Press, 1957.

Dickie, George. "Psychical Distance: In a Fog at Sea." *British Journal of Aesthetics* 13 (1973): 17–29.

Paul Guyer (2005)

BULTMANN, RUDOLF
(1884–1976)

Rudolf Bultmann, the biblical historian and theologian, was born in Wiefelsted, Oldenburg, Germany. He studied at Marburg, Tübingen, and Berlin and taught first at Marburg and then at Breslau and Giessen. In 1921 he became professor of New Testament studies at Marburg, where he remained until his retirement in 1951.

Bultmann's work and the controversies it has generated are of undoubted importance for the philosophy of religion. His ventures in "demythologizing" the New Testament and in reinterpreting its content "existentially" have raised (and have tried to answer) crucial questions about the logical status of religious language and the nature of Christian belief.

CHRISTIAN FAITH

Bultmann's thought was inspired by his keen sense of the remoteness and unacceptability of the thought forms of New Testament Christianity to most people of the twentieth and twenty-first centuries. We do not and cannot see our world as a theater of conflict between supernatural powers, the demonic seeking to possess and destroy us, and God intervening to secure our salvation. Moreover, miracle stories lie at the very heart of New Testament

belief: "If Christ be not raised, your faith is vain" (1 Corinthians 15:17). Thus, the critical question is: Must a man, in order to be a Christian, commit himself simultaneously to two mutually incompatible world pictures— that of twenty-first-century science and that of first-century prescientific speculation? According to Bultmann, to attempt this is to make Christian belief unnecessarily difficult. It is equally unrewarding to view Christianity as a strictly and objectively "historical" religion and anxiously to sift all the evidence for and against the recorded events of the life of Jesus. The evidence is substantial enough to show that Jesus indeed lived and that he made a quite extraordinary impact upon certain contemporaries. But if religious faith is to stand or fall with the historicity of, say, the birth stories or the Easter narratives, if its degree of assurance must rationally be tempered with the historical probabilities, the assurance will be pitifully uncertain, and faith will almost certainly fall.

To these perplexities Bultmann offers a bold remedy. The Christian may properly grant that a very large part of the New Testament message is couched in mythical language and does not record objective history. This mythical material is not, however, an embarrassment, and it need not be discarded. It can be interpreted as indirect description not of the cosmos but of the conditions and possibilities of human existence. Historical studies derive their real seriousness not from sheer factuality but from what they discover about viable ways of life and viable options for human decision. Among such options, the Christian gives preeminence to that displayed in the accounts of the cross and the resurrection. For it is through these that God makes available a distinctively "authentic" and free mode of existence to all humanity.

INFLUENCE OF HEIDEGGER

"Authentic" is Martin Heidegger's term. It is only one of Bultmann's many borrowings from *Sein und Zeit*. There is a prima-facie oddness here—a Christian theologian reinterpreting the New Testament teachings in terms of concepts drawn from atheist existentialism. Nevertheless, the concepts are undeniably relevant and, within limits, illuminating. There are clear and suggestive analogies between Heidegger's general picture of inauthenticity and the New Testament's accounts of life "in" and "after" the flesh, the life of the "natural man" who is alienated from God. In both views humans are uneasy, anxious, and guilty over their condition. If to Heidegger Angst reveals that man is "not at home" in the world, the New Testament affirms that here we have no continuing city but seek one to come. To both we are strangers and pilgrims.

On the "authentic" type of existence, there are both marked similarities and differences in the views of Heidegger and Bultmann. Heidegger's account centers upon a total acceptance of the fundamental conditions of our life. This involves, for any man, a realization of his own death, not as some vague, unpleasant, but indefinite future event, but as something whose constant presence, in possibility, should modify his sense of his own existence at every moment. Christianity, too, speaks of renouncing the world and a life entangled with the world, of "dying" to the life of self. It has, however—or ought to have—some very different things to say about life eternal.

Heidegger's authentic man sees and accepts the limitations on his freedom imposed by the given circumstances of his life as so far lived ("facticity"); he sees the present moment as the locus of decision, and it is in the future that he will work out those authentic possibilities of existence for which he decides. The Judeo-Christian tradition also has a dualism of facticity and freedom: It claims both that man was created "out of the dust of the ground," stressing the given factuality of human existence, and that God "breathed into his nostrils the breath of life," endowing him with freedom to pursue his diverse possibilities.

How can we discover our authentic possibilities? In answering this question both Heidegger and Bultmann point to the thoroughly temporal, historical nature of human life. History discloses human possibility. For Bultmann the Christian is he who, in R. G. Collingwood's term, "incorporates" the essentials of the New Testament story in his present thought and action.

Bultmann's account of the human situation is, therefore, an "existential" analysis, and to call it that is to contrast it both with the findings of empirical psychology and with a philosophical analysis of nonpersonal structures. Far from being based on empirical investigations, existential analysis tries to uncover the concepts that are, and have to be, employed in any such researches—the fundamental concepts of personal existence.

But there are complexities to be noted here. Although to Bultmann the New Testament has much to say about the general human predicament, we must not analyze its discourse exhaustively as delineating permanent and universal human possibilities. The authentic life, crucially, is available to a man only by virtue of divine grace and through his appropriating the Word revealed in Christ.

DEMYTHOLOGIZING

There is, however, an uneasy duality in Bultmann's thought. Almost everything in the New Testament is to be understood as describing modes of personal existence, but not so the central claim of the kerygma itself, the claim that God decisively acted in Christ. This contains a reference to God that cannot be eliminated. Yet it must be noted that although Bultmann refuses to "dekerygmatize," others (Fritz Buri, for instance) have tried to do just that. They have been unable to stop at what looks to them like a halfway house and have taken the kerygma too as material for existential analysis.

Other theologians have offered various arguments to show that Bultmann's position is too extreme. They claim that he has underestimated the importance of objective history, that he has made too many concessions to twentieth-century skepticism, that his existentialist concepts cannot express the full meaning, the nuances, the complex mesh of associations of the biblical writings, that the myth must be kept intact.

It is not surprising, therefore, that the controversy over demythologizing has been intense and involved. This entry shall single out for brief discussion only a few of the most crucial issues, beginning with the question of Bultmann's existentialism.

CRUCIAL ISSUES. (1) Without doubt, Heidegger's existential analysis has provided Bultmann with a valuable nonmythical vocabulary, able to express an important part of the New Testament message. However, there are certainly some points at which his analyses appear to clarify the Christian position but in fact tempt a theologian to distort it seriously. For example, if Christianity were no more than a philosophy of life, then matters of objective history would not be crucial to it. So long as we knew that someone had lived roughly the sort of life Jesus allegedly lived, we could at least take the "imitation of Christ" as an ideal for human living. "Possibility," in this rather weak sense, would be enough. But if we want to go beyond that (as Bultmann certainly does) and claim that God was actually imparting himself in a quite distinctive and decisive way in the events of Jesus' life, then it is a matter of immense seriousness to learn what these events were. We cannot have a historical religion, in that strong sense, without historical vulnerability. For all its subtlety (most likely because of its subtlety), the existential analysis of historicity deflects attention from this uncomfortable fact.

One should not conclude, however, that Bultmann has never stated a coherent and clear position on historicity and Christian belief. In *History and Eschatology* (1957) he expressed himself much more lucidly in alternative terms derived from Collingwood. But the link between his position in this book and traditional Christian theology has become very tenuous indeed. Whatever the impression we receive from other writings of Bultmann, in *History and Eschatology* the Gospel seems to be about human self-understanding from first to last; dependence on objective historicity has receded to the vanishing point.

(2) Several important and difficult New Testament concepts seem to yield very readily to existential analysis; yet these concepts remain philosophically problematic. The concept of "body" has clear existential meaning—related to Heidegger's concept of what it is to "exist-in-a-world." Likewise, "eternal life," in the New Testament, characterizes a manner, or quality, of living. Yet even if much of the meaning of these expressions is translatable into existentialist language, there surely remains a vital part that is not. The existential analysis by itself cannot answer such a question as "Does our existence end with our bodily death?" Nor does it help solve the problems of meaning and logic (particularly problems of personal identity) that arise over concepts like life after death and the resurrection of the dead.

(3) Because the life and personality of Jesus play so muted a part in this theology, and because the summons to authentic existence tends to be rather individualistic in its emphasis, it is very difficult to build up an adequate account of Christian discipleship and Christian love on Bultmann's foundations. The quality of the Christian ethical life has always been determined by the believer's response not simply to the bare proclamation that a new life has been made available to him, but to the concrete particularities of the life and teaching of Jesus. One guesses that a theology like Bultmann's can succeed in expressing this quality only through implicit dependence on a more conservative view of the New Testament that is still secretly operative in the religious imagination.

(4) From the philosopher's point of view, perhaps the most urgent need is for Bultmannian theology to construct a much more precise logical map of its key concepts, myth, mythology, and analogy. "Mythology," Bultmann wrote, "is the use of imagery to express the other worldly in terms of this world and the divine in terms of human life, the other side in terms of this side." But Bultmann does not want to conclude that discourse about God is always, and necessarily, mythological. To speak mythologically is to represent God as a kind of superentity, observably acting upon and interacting with

natural entities. However, Bultmann has claimed (in *Kerygma and Myth*) that it is possible to speak of God's "acts" analogically, and to do so with the help of concepts borrowed once again from the field of human personal existence.

Bultmann is here in pursuit of what may well be a valuable distinction, but it has not been at all clearly articulated. The different modes of discourse about God are not rigorously defined, and thus a good deal of uncertainty is left about appropriate tests for sense and nonsense, truth and falsity, in claims about God. It is by no means obvious, for instance, whether one can really think through those existential, "analogical" utterances about God without implicitly relying upon a mythological picture of God as a superperson and superentity. Further, since both mythological discourse and analogical discourse are indirect or oblique, we need to ask whether any direct, literal talk about God is possible, or whether it is necessarily all oblique. If it must all be oblique, the problem of how we can refer to God and relate the myths and analogies to him surely becomes unmanageable. If it is not all oblique, then we still need to discover what, and how much, can be affirmed directly and literally about God. The temptation is to resort to theological makeshifts—to analyze virtually all talk about God in terms of human self-understanding, but to rely, devotionally and pastorally, upon an unanalyzed transcendent remainder, of which, however, no clear account is given in a systematic theology.

All these puzzling instabilities in Bultmann's thought are not careless or stupid blunders of reasoning. They are illuminating, disturbing indications of how immensely hard it is to steer between, on the one hand, a wholly secularized Christianity, a humanism, and, on the other, a religion of the supernatural and the miraculous.

See also Christianity; Collingwood, Robin George; Existentialism; Heidegger, Martin; Philosophy of Religion; Philosophy of Religion, History of; Religious Language.

Bibliography

OTHER RECOMMENDED WORKS

Barth, Karl, Rudolf Karl Bultmann, and Bernd Jaspert. *Karl Barth-Rudolf Bultmann, Briefwechsel, 1922–1966.* Zürich: Theologischer Verlag, 1971.

Barth, Karl, Rudolf Karl Bultmann, Bernd Jaspert, and Beoffrey William Bromiley. *Karl Barth-Rudolf Bultmann Letters, 1922–1966.* Grand Rapids, MI: Eerdmans, 1981.

Bultmann, Rudolf Karl. *Das Evangelium des Johannes.* Gottingen, Vandenhoeck & Ruprecht, 1968.

Bultmann, Rudolf Karl. *Das Urchristentum in Rahmen der antiken Religionen.* Reinbek b. Hamburg: Rowohlt, 1969.

Bultmann, Rudolf Karl. *Das Verhältnis der urchristlichen Christusbotschaft zum historischen Jesus.* Heidelberg: C. Winter, 1965.

Bultmann, Rudolf Karl. *Der zweite Brief an die Korinther.* Göttingen: Vandenhoeck und Ruprecht, 1987.

Bultmann, Rudolf Karl. *Die drei Johannesbriefe* (1967). Göttingen: Vandenhoeck & Ruprecht, 1969.

Bultmann, Rudolf Karl. *Die Geschichte der synoptischen Tradition.* Göttingen: Vandenhoeck & Ruprecht, 1967.

Bultmann, Rudolf Karl. *Die zweite Brief an die Korinther.* Göttingen: Vandenhoeck & Ruprecht, 1976.

Bultmann, Rudolf Karl. *The Gospel of John; A Commentary.* Philadelphia: Westminster Press, 1971.

Bultmann, Rudolf Karl. *The History of the Synoptic Tradition* (1963). New York, Harper & Row, rev. ed. 1968.

Bultmann, Rudolf Karl. *The Johannine Epistles: A Commentary on the Johannine Epistles.* Philadelphia: Fortress Press, 1973.

Bultmann, Rudolf Karl. *Primitive Christianity in Its Contemporary Setting* (1956). New York: Meridian Books, 1965.

Bultmann, Rudolf Karl. *What Is Theology?.* Minneapolis: Fortress Press, 1997.

Bultmann, Rudolf Karl, and Erich Dinkler. *The Second Letter to the Corinthians.* Minneapolis: Augsburg, 1985.

Bultmann, Rudolf Karl, Friedrich Gogarten, and Hermann Götz Göckeritz. *Briefwechsel, 1921–1967.* Tübingen: Mohr Siebeck, 2002.

Bultmann, Rudolf Karl, Friedrich Gogarten, and Hermann Götz Göckeritz. *Rudolf Bultmann-Friedrich Gogarten: Briefwechsel, 1921–1967.* Tübingen: Mohr Siebeck, 2002.

Bultmann, Rudolf Karl, and Bernd Jaspert. *Rudolf Bultmanns Werk und Wirkung.* Darmstadt: Wissenschaftliche Buchgesellschaft, 1984.

Bultmann, Rudolf Karl, and Roger A. Johnson. *Rudolf Bultmann.* Collins, 1987.

Bultmann, Rudolf Karl, and Roger A. Johnson. *Rudolf Bultmann: Interpreting Faith for the Modern Era.* London; San Francisco, CA: Collins, 1987.

Bultmann, Rudolf Karl, Eberhard Jüngel, and Klaus W. Müller. *Theologische Enzyklopädie.* Tübingen: Mohr, 1984.

Bultmann, Rudolf Karl, Karlis Kundzins, and Frederick C. Grant, ed. and tr. *Form Criticism; Two Essays on New Testament Research. The Study of the Synoptic Gospels.* New York: Harper, 1966.

Bultmann, Rudolf Karl, and Andreas Lindemann. *Neues Testament und christliche Existenz: Theologische Aufsätze.* Tübingen: Mohr Siebeck, 2002.

Bultmann, Rudolf Karl, and James McConkey Robinson, ed. *The Future of Our Religious Past; Essays in Honour of Rudolf Bultmann.* New York, Harper & Row, 1971.

Bultmann, Rudolf Karl, Rudolf Zingel, and Otto Kaiser. *Gedenken an Rudolf Bultmann.* Tübingen: Mohr, 1977.

Malet, André, and Rudolf Karl Bultmann. *Bultmann et la mort de Dieu; Présentation, choix de textes, biographie, bibliographie.* Paris: Seghers, 1968.

Ronald W. Hepburn (1967)
Bibliography updated by Michael J. Farmer (2005)

BURCKHARDT, JAKOB
(1818–1897)

The Swiss cultural historian Jakob Burckhardt was born in Basel, the son of a Protestant minister. He began his university education as a theology student, but lost his faith in orthodox Christianity comparatively early and turned instead to history. He spent part of his formative years in liberal and freethinking circles in Germany; it was in Germany, too, that he discovered and worked under Leopold von Ranke, probably the most potent and lasting influence upon his future career as a historian. On his return to Switzerland in the 1840s, Burckhardt was at first attracted to the political and religious dissensions that he found there. The violence to which they subsequently led, however, was repulsive to his temperament; and he retired to Italy, having, in his own words, "given up political activity forever." Some time later he finally settled in Basel, dedicating himself, as professor of history and history of art, to the routine of teaching and lecturing that was to occupy him continuously up to the last years of his life.

Burckhardt's chief writings were all published before he was fifty: *The Age of Constantine the Great* (1852), *Cicerone* (1855), *The Renaissance in Italy* (1860), and *The History of the Renaissance* (1867). In addition to these major works, he also gave a number of lectures between 1868 and 1871 on the general study of history, the notes for which were preserved and eventually published posthumously under the title of *Weltgeschichtliche Betrachtungen* (Reflections on world history). These are remarkable, not only for the prophetic insight they display in their analysis of contemporary trends, but also for the many subtle and individual observations they contain concerning the purposes of historiography and the theoretical problems it poses. They were attended by Friedrich Nietzsche, who at the time was professor of classics at Basel and whose later essay, *The Use and Abuse of History,* bears the impress of some of Burckhardt's ideas.

Burckhardt did not regard his lectures as representing a contribution to "philosophy of history" in the then current sense. Indeed, he made it clear at the outset that he was profoundly suspicious of fashionable schemes and systems that attempted to exhibit the course of historical development as conforming to a rationally ordered pattern, and referred with special scorn to the Hegelian conception of history as the "inevitable march of the world spirit." For him such projects were the manifestation of a crude and vulgar "optimism"; they sprang from the arrogant and egotistical assumption that "our time is the consummation of all time" and tended to "justify" the crimes and disasters of previous ages as necessary to the promotion of what came afterward. Burckhardt thought that the role of moral judgment in history could not be spirited away in this complacent manner; but neither, on the other hand, should the historian allow his view of the past to be distorted by moral predilections peculiar to his own time and society. What was above all requisite for true historical understanding was a contemplative, disinterested sense of the abiding and tragic aspects of human existence. Only through such detachment from prevailing concerns and preoccupations could the historian transcend the barriers that separate the mental life of one age from that of another.

Burckhardt admired Arthur Schopenhauer, and he tended to extend to the historian a position in some ways similar to that which the German philosopher had reserved for the artist. It was not merely that works of art and culture provided the historian with his most fertile material for the interpretation of previous phases of human experience; history itself was (or should be) a form of art. The mechanical piling up of the results of specialized research, dear to so-called scientific historians, was not enough; there must also be "intuition," an imaginative ability to re-create the vision of life underlying the relics left by former times. To see the past in these terms was to see it as the expression of the inexhaustible creative power of the human mind—great individuals, great artistic achievements, great moments of civilization, all exemplified in different ways its potentialities. Scholarship, painstaking investigation, were indeed essential, but they must be properly used and directed. Only thus could a particular source or authority throw light on the character of a person, the significance of a style, the pervasive atmosphere of a period.

Ultimately, Burckhardt claimed, the subject of historical study was man himself, not the hypostatized abstractions of the philosophers of history. These philosophers, by implying that the historical process followed a fixed and predetermined course, betrayed a fundamental blindness to its most striking feature, the revelation of individual originality and creativity. Likewise, their "astrological impatience" to set limits to its future by talk of world plans and metaphysical goals was not only unwarranted; it failed to respect the very conditions of uncertainty and suspense that make human achievement possible. From this point of view, and insofar as the development of humankind is concerned, "a future known in advance is an absurdity."

Toward the close of the nineteenth century the tide of historical speculation began to recede. Philosophers, rather than continuing to offer sweeping interpretations of the human past, turned their attention toward examining the distinctive characteristics of historical thought and inquiry. In retrospect, Burckhardt can be seen to occupy an interesting position in this development. Though not a philosopher himself, he nonetheless anticipated in his own reflections on historical procedure some of the ideas that later found philosophical expression in the writings of Wilhelm Dilthey and Benedetto Croce.

See also Croce, Benedetto; Dilthey, Wilhelm; History and Historiography of Philosophy; Nietzsche, Friedrich; Renaissance; Schopenhauer, Arthur.

Bibliography

WORKS BY BURCKHARDT

Die Zeit Constantins des Grossens. Basel, 1852. Translated by Moses Hadas as *The Age of Constantine the Great.* New York: Pantheon, 1949.

Der Cicerone. Basel, 1855. Translated by Mrs. A. H. Clough as *Cicerone,* rev. ed. London: J. Murray, 1879.

Die Cultur der Renaissance in Italien. Basel: Schweighauser, 1860. Translated by S. G. C. Middlemore from 15th German ed. as *The Civilization of the Renaissance in Italy,* 2nd ed. London, 1890.

Geschichte der Renaissance in Italien. Stuttgart, 1867.

Weltgeschichtliche Betrachtungen. Edited by J. Deri, 2nd ed. Berlin, 1910. Translated by J. H. Nichols as *Force and Freedom: Reflections on History.* New York: Pantheon, 1943.

Gesammelte Werke, 7 vols. Basel, 1957.

WORKS ON BURCKHARDT

Duerr, E. *Freiheit und Macht bei Jacob Burckhardt.* Basel: Helbing and Lichtenhahn, 1918.

Heller, E. "Burckhardt and Nietzsche." In *The Disinherited Mind.* Cambridge, U.K.: Bowes and Bowes, 1952, Ch. 3.

Joel, K. *Jacob Burckhardt als Geschichtsphilosoph.* Basel, 1910.

Martin, A. W. O. von. *Burckhardt und Nietzsche philosophieren über Geschichte.* Krefeld, 1948.

Meinecke, F. "Ranke and Burckhardt." In *German History: Some New German Views,* edited by Hans Kohn. London: Allen and Unwin, 1954.

Trevor-Roper, H. R. "The Faustian Historian: Jacob Burckhardt," in *Men and Events.* New York: Harper, 1957, Ch. 40.

Patrick Gardiner (1967)

BURIDAN, JOHN
(c. 1300–1361)

John Buridan, or Johannes Buridanus, was a philosopher and arts master at the University of Paris. Little is known about his early life other than that he hailed from Picardy in the north of France, most likely from the town of Béthune. As a young man he studied at the Collège Lemoine in Paris, where he was awarded a benefice or stipend for needy students, and then at the University of Paris, where he earned the degree of master of arts and received his license to teach in the 1320s. He spent his entire academic career at the University of Paris, twice serving as its rector. He was a respected figure who was often asked to settle jurisdictional disputes and assist in other matters of academic governance.

Two features of Buridan's career are distinctive. The first is that he remained a teaching master in the faculty of arts without ever moving on to take a higher, doctoral degree in theology, which was the more typical career track for philosophers at the time. Why he decided not to join the more prestigious ranks of the theologians he does not say, but given his philosophical talent and stature at the University, it is safe to assume that he had his reasons for remaining where he was. One possibility, which is suggested by some of his remarks about the relation between philosophy and theology, is that he believed philosophy to be an essentially secular enterprise, which he would have to abandon if he became a theologian. Whether this represents an important first step in the direction of modernity awaits further investigation, but at the very least, Buridan was passionately committed to the autonomy of philosophy as a discipline proper to the faculty of arts, not theology.

The other distinctive feature of Buridan's academic career is that he remained a secular cleric rather than joining a religious order such as the Dominicans or Franciscans. The popularity of these orders in the thirteenth century had revitalized the study of theology, raising it to speculative heights it has not seen since. But as the larger orders began to institutionalize the training of their novices outside the university and develop their own intellectual traditions—with Thomas Aquinas being championed by the Dominicans and Bonaventure and John Duns Scotus by the Franciscans—serious disputes arose not only within religious orders but between them, a phenomenon that led to the development of different schools of philosophy: Thomistic, Scotistic, and so on (hence the term *Schoolmen*). As a secular cleric, Buridan could safely ride above these disputes, without being obliged to defend or explain the authorities of any particular tradition. This theoretical independence can be seen in the occasionally eclectic character of his remarks.

Most of Buridan's writings are in the form of commentaries on Aristotle, whose texts were the primary sub-ject of study in the medieval arts curriculum. These commentaries survive in two forms: *expositiones* or literal commentaries and *quaestiones* or question commentaries, both of which have their origins in the way Buridan actually taught. He would begin by giving his students a line-by-line exposition of a portion of Aristotle's text and follow this up with a problem or question raised by the passage although not explicitly discussed in it, such as whether the intellect has the capacity to recall previous thoughts, analogous to the power of memory in the sensitive part of the soul (see Aristotle, *De Anima* III.5, 430a24). Arguments for and against would be inventoried, after which Buridan would give his own—sometimes lengthy—resolution of the question, with responses to arguments on the opposite side. A similar method was used by Thomas Aquinas in composing the *Summa Theologiae*.

Buridan wrote commentaries on all of the major works of Aristotle. But because he lectured more than once on a given text over the course of his long career, some commentaries exist in more than one version, and the evolution in his thinking about a particular issue can occasionally be seen in these different versions. In addition to the commentaries, he wrote a massive logic textbook, the *Summulae de Dialectica* (Compendia of dialectics), as well as a number of shorter, independent treatises on controversial topics such as the *Tractatus de relationibus* (Treatise on relations)], *Tractatus de universalibus* (Treatise on universals), and *Tractatus de consequentiis* (Treatise on consequences). He was by any measure a prolific author.

Buridan's influence is immediately evident in the work of his younger contemporaries at Paris: Albert of Saxony, Marsilius of Inghen, and Nicole Oresme. But his commentaries and his *Summulae de Dialectica* continued to be read and commented on for several generations. Manuscripts and early printed editions of his writings were carried by his students and followers to the new universities in Heidelberg, Kraków, Prague, and Vienna, where they served as primary texts in courses on logic and Aristotelian philosophy. In this way, the *via Buridani* continued to influence European thought well into the early modern period.

LOGIC

Buridan's view of logic is best conveyed by the opening line of Peter of Spain's *Summulae Logicales* (Compendia of logics), the thirteenth-century textbook on the basis of which Buridan prepared his logical masterwork, the *Summulae de Dialectica*: "*Dialectica est ars artium, ad omnium methodorum principia viam habens* (Dialectic is the art of arts, having access to the principles of all other inquiries)." More than just a method, logic is the grammar of philosophical discourse, the discipline whose procedures govern rational inquiry in virtually every field investigated by the arts master, from metaphysics and cosmology to natural philosophy and ethics. Buridan composed the nine treatises of his *Summulae* so that they exhibit an orderly progression of teachings based on the proposition, beginning with propositions themselves (I), moving down to the significance and referential function of their component terms (II–IV), then back up to propositions again, considered as parts of more complex patterns of reasoning: syllogisms (V), topics (VI), fallacies (VII), and demonstrations (VIII). The work closes with a series of logical exercises (IX). The order of the *Summulae* reflects Buridan's assumptions about the semantic character of human understanding, which is in turn a reflection of the metaphysical structure of creation.

Buridan is usually classed as a terminist logician. The terminists (sometimes referred to as the *moderni* or *moderns*) were a diverse group of thirteenth- and fourteenth-century philosophers who regarded the semantic properties of terms (literally, the "ends [*termini*]," or subjects and predicates, of propositions) as the primary unit of logical analysis. His main contribution was to modernize and systematize the old logic of Aristotle and Boethius using the newer techniques of the terminists, though in the process he offered innovative solutions to traditional problems in the philosophy of logic. His solutions to logical paradoxes such as the liar are still being discussed today. Consider, for example, the sentence, "Every proposition is false," assuming "that all true propositions are annihilated while the false ones remain, and then Socrates propounds only this: 'Every proposition is false' " (*Summulae* 9.8, seventh sophism). Is Socrate' proposition true or false? Buridan argues that it is false, and his reasoning shows his mastery of the semantic nuances of the question. "Every proposition," he says, "virtually implies another proposition in which the predicate 'true' is affirmed of the subject that supposits for [the original proposition]" (*Summulae* 9.8, seventh sophism). Thus, for the truth of any proposition P, it is required not only (1) that the subject and predicate terms of P stand for the same thing or things, but also (2) that P imply another proposition, "P is true," which must also be true—otherwise there would be a true antecedent and a false consequent. Accordingly, the constituent terms in the proposition uttered by Socrates—"Every proposition" and "false"—stand for the same things, since in the

posited case, "all true propositions are annihilated and the false ones remain, and then Socrates propounds only this: 'Every proposition is false.'" So the first condition is satisfied. But the implied proposition, "P is true" (where P is the name of "Every proposition is false"), is false because its constituent terms, "Every proposition is false" and "true," do not stand for the same thing, since *ex hypothesi*, P stands for the antecedent proposition "Every proposition is false," not for things that are true. But this gives us a true antecedent and a false consequent, and so the consequence does not hold. Therefore, the sophism is false.

METAPHYSICS

Buridan viewed metaphysics as the highest form of philosophical inquiry, yet his *Questions on Aristotle's Metaphysics* is among the shortest of his commentaries. There appear to be two reasons for this. First, he is not optimistic about the possibility of humans coming to know the ultimate nature of reality in this life because he doubts whether people are ever in a position to be acquainted with the natures or essences of things as such. Most of the time one must make do with inferences based on sense, memory, and experience, and the latter experience shows that even the firmest empirical conviction is subject to revision. Second, Buridan is adamant that metaphysics belongs to philosophy, not to theology, and hence that it cannot take its principles or starting points from Scripture or religious doctrine: "metaphysics differs from theology in the fact that although each considers God and things that pertain to divinity, metaphysics considers them only as regards what can be proved and implied, or inductively inferred, by demonstrative reason. But theology has for its principles articles [of faith], which are believed quite apart from their evidentness, and further, considers whatever can be deduced from articles of this kind" (*Questions on Aristotle's Metaphysics*, I.2). This leads him to assert the autonomy of philosophers—and implicitly of the arts masters as well—in a rather striking way: metaphysics, or philosophical wisdom, cannot be ordained by theology because its methods, which are rooted in its principles, are different. Philosophy is accordingly not inferior to theology, just different. This was an important step toward the modern view of philosophy as a secular enterprise.

Buridan was also a nominalist, though it is better to think of late-medieval nominalism as a parsimonious way of doing philosophy than as a commitment to denying the existence of real or Platonic universals. The method in Buridan's metaphysics is his logic. He tries wherever possible to apply the *Summulae*'s analytical techniques to the interpretation of Aristotle, and his approach is critical in that it tends to view traditional questions in metaphysics as based on confusions of logic or language. Thus, when asked whether universals really exist outside the soul, he replies by clarifying the meaning of the common term *universal* with respect to its correlative terms, *individual*, *particular*, and *singular*. His rejection of realism is expressed in the same fashion: universal terms have no ultimate significate, nothing outside the soul they can make known as such. What such terms mean is other terms: the primary signification of *universal* is "predicable of many," which makes it a term of second intention, or a term of terms, since only terms are predicable. Likewise, when the term *universal* occurs in a proposition, it signifies not a *what* but a *how*, that is, how one conceives of something—in this case, that the term so designated is "indifferent to many supposits," or individuals.

Clearly, Buridan thinks that the careful and systematic analysis of language is the best way of dealing with such metaphysical problems. The trouble usually begins with untutored persons who think that each and every substantive term must correspond to a thing, or that true predication must involve the real inherence of attributes in subjects rather than making the more modest assumption that the subject and predicate terms simply stand for the same thing(s).

NATURAL PHILOSOPHY AND ETHICS

Buridan's natural philosophy and ethics are also shaped by the methods of the *Summulae*. Thus, his treatment of infinite magnitudes in his *Questions on Aristotle's Physics* focuses on clarifying the different senses of the term *infinite*: nothing is infinite if by that one means an actually existing infinite magnitude, although one can always imagine a magnitude greater than the one being considered, and do so without limit. The concept of infinity is thereby redeemed for natural science as a mode, or way of thinking.

Buridan also played a key role in the demise of the Aristotelian picture of the cosmos in the later Middle Ages. His major contribution was to develop and popularize the theory of impetus, or impressed force, to explain projectile motion. Rejecting the Aristotelian idea of *antiperistasis*—according to which the tendency of a moving projectile to continue moving (think of a ball after it has left the hand of a thrower) is due to a proximate but external moving cause (the air surrounding it, in this case)—Buridan argued that only an internal

motive force, transmitted from the mover to the projectile, could explain its continued motion. The theory did not originate with Buridan, but he is perhaps the first to have seen that a force of this kind need not be self-dissipating: "[A]fter leaving the arm of the thrower, the projectile would be moved by an impetus given to it by the thrower," he says, "and would continue to be moved as long as the impetus remained stronger than the resistance, and would be of infinite duration were it not diminished and corrupted by a contrary force resisting it or by something inclining it to a contrary motion" (*Questions on Aristotle's Metaphysics*, XII.9). This is a long way from Aristotle, and not all that far from Galileo.

Despite its revolutionary implications, Buridan did not use impetus to transform the science of mechanics. He remained unapologetically Aristotelian in other respects, continuing to hold, for example, that motion and rest are contrary states of bodies. He should instead be thought of as someone who tried hard to reshape Aristotelian physics in the face of an increasingly mechanistic worldview.

Buridan's method in natural science is empirical in the sense that it emphasizes the evidentness of appearances, the reliability of a posteriori modes of reasoning, and the application of naturalistic models of explanation—such as the concept of impetus—to natural phenomena. Purely theological considerations are dismissed as irrelevant: "[O]ne might assume that there are many more separate substances than there are celestial spheres and celestial motions, viz., great legions of angels [*magnae legiones angelorum*], but this cannot be proved by demonstrative arguments originating from sense perception" (*Questions on Aristotle's Metaphysics*, II.9). Buridan concedes that an omnipotent God could deceive people in ways they could never detect, but this is tempered by his confidence, for which he cites empirical evidence, that people's ordinary powers of perception and inference are sufficiently reliable to make "the comprehension of truth with certitude possible for us" (*Questions on Aristotle's Metaphysics*, II.1). He had little patience for skeptical arguments (such as those he believed were advanced by his Parisian contemporary, Nicholas of Autrecourt), objecting that it is absurd to demand that all knowledge be demonstrable by reduction to the principle of noncontradiction. Natural philosophy is about what happens for the most part, assuming the common course of nature.

Despite Buridan's prolific output, stellar reputation, and profound influence on later thinkers, most philosophers know of him only in connection with Buridan's

Ass, the traditional example in which a donkey starves to death because it has no reason to choose between two equidistant and equally tempting piles of hay. This is doubly unfortunate because this example is nowhere to be found in Buridan's writings, though there are versions of it going back at least to Aristotle (see *De Caelo* 295b32). The best explanation of its association with Buridan is that it began as a parody of his account of free choice by later critics, who found absurd his idea that the will's freedom could consist in inaction, or more specifically, in its ability to defer or send back for further consideration any practical judgment that is not absolutely certain. But Buridan's Ass, which is apparently possessed of reason, would have surely seen the good in ceasing to deliberate once his hunger or thirst became too acute, and would have permitted his sensory appetite to lead him to whichever appeared first.

See also Impetus; Logic, History of: Medieval (European) Logic; Universals, a Historical Survey.

Bibliography

WORKS BY JOHN BURIDAN

Iohannis Buridani Tractatus de consequentiis. Edited by Hubert Hubien. Louvain, Belgium: Publications universitaires, 1976.

John Buridan on Self-Reference: Chapter Eight of Buridan's Sophismata: An Edition and Translation with an Introduction and Philosophical Commentary. Edited and translated by G. E. Hughes. Cambridge, U.K.: Cambridge University Press, 1982.

Iohannes Buridanus Quaestiones in Praedicamenta. Edited by Johannes Schneider. Munich, Germany: Beck, 1983.

"Jan Buridan, Kommentarz do *Isagogi* Porfiriusza." Edited by Ryszard Tatarzyński. *Przeglad Tomistyczny* 2 (1986): 111–195.

"Johannis Buridani, Tractatus de differentia universalis ad individuum." Edited by Sławomir Szyller. *Przeglad Tomistyczny* 3 (1987): 137–178.

John Buridan's "Tractatus de Infinito". Edited by J. M. M. H. Thijssen. Nijmegen, Netherlands: Ingenium, 1991.

Le traité de l'âme de Jean Buridan [De prima lectura]. Edited by Benoît Patar. Louvain-la-Neuve, Belgium: Editions de l'Institut supérieur de philosophie; Longueuil, Quebec: Editions du Préambule, 1991.

Johannes Buridanus, Questiones Elencorum. Edited by Ria van der Lecq and H. A. G. Braakhuis. Nijmegen, Netherlands: Ingenium, 1994.

"Buridan, On Aristotle's *Ethics*, Book X." Edited by R. J. Kilcullen. Edition available online at: http://www.humanities.mq.edu.au/Ockham/ (1996).

Ioannis Buridani, Expositio et Quaestiones in Aristotelis "De Caelo". Edited by Benoît Patar. Louvain-la-Neuve, Belgium: Éditions de l'Institut supérieur de philosophie; Paris: Peeters, 1996.

Summulae de Dialectica. Translated by Gyula Klima. New Haven, CT: Yale University Press, 2001.

WORKS ABOUT JOHN BURIDAN

Biard, Joël. *Logique et théorie du signe au XIVᵉ siècle.* Paris: Vrin, 1989.

Klima, Gyula. "Buridan's Logic and the Ontology of Modes." In *Medieval Analyses in Language and Cognition*, edited by Sten Ebbesen and Russell L. Friedman, 473–495. Copenhagen: Royal Danish Academy of Sciences and Letters—C. A. Reitzels Forlag, 1999.

Thijssen, J. M. M. H., and Jack Zupko, eds. *The Metaphysics and Natural Philosophy of John Buridan.* Leiden-Boston-Köln: Brill, 2001.

Walsh, James J. "Buridan on the Connection of the Virtues." *Journal of the History of Philosophy* 24 (1986): 453–482.

Willing, A. "Buridan and Ockham: The Logic of Knowing." *Franciscan Studies* 45 (1985): 47–56.

Zupko, Jack. "John Buridan." In *The Stanford Encyclopedia of Philosophy*, edited by Edward N. Zalta. Winter 2003 Edition. Available from http://plato.stanford.edu/.

Zupko, Jack. *John Buridan: Portrait of a Fourteenth-Century Arts Master.* Notre Dame, IN: University of Notre Dame Press, 2003.

Zupko, Jack. "Substance and Soul: The Late Medieval Origins of Early Modern Psychology." In *Meeting of the Minds: The Relations between Medieval and Classical Modern European Philosophy*, edited by Stephen F. Brown, 121–139. Turnhout, Belgium: Brepols, 1999.

Jack Zupko (2005)

BURKE, EDMUND
(1729–1797)

Edmund Burke, the British statesman and political philosopher, was born in Ireland to a family of modest means. His mother's family was Catholic, his father's Protestant. He was raised a Protestant and educated at a Quaker school and at Trinity College, Dublin, where he took the equivalent of a first-class honors degree in classics. He went to London to read law but was never called to the bar. He devoted most of his time to authorship and literary journalism. Robert Dodsley, a leading London bookseller of the time, loyally backed him; by 1757, Dodsley had published two books by Burke, *A Vindication of Natural Society* (1756) and *Philosophical Inquiry into the Origin of Our Ideas on the Sublime and the Beautiful* (1756), had given him employment as editor of *The Annual Register,* and had contracted to pay him £300 for an *Abridgement of the History of England.*

A Vindication of Natural Society is a satire on the views of Henry St. John Bolingbroke. It claimed to be a recently discovered work by Bolingbroke and was designed to ridicule the idea that the rise of civilized society is attended by misery and suffering. The parody was written with such conviction, however, that many assumed it was in fact the work of Bolingbroke, and even when it was known that Burke was the author, some critics still thought it was a sincere expression of his true opinion.

Burke's book *On the Sublime and the Beautiful* is more important; indeed, it might well be said to signalize the point at which aesthetic taste in England changed from the classical formalism of the earlier years of the eighteenth century to the romanticism of the later years. Burke attacked the rationalist, classicist notion that clarity is an essential quality in great art. He argued, on the contrary, that what is greatest and noblest is the infinite, and that the infinite, having no bounds, cannot be clear and distinct. He argued that the imagination, moreover, is most strongly affected by what is suggested or hinted at and not by what is plainly stated. Burke also maintained that fear plays a large part in our enjoyment of the sublime. Such fear is diminished by knowledge, but sharpened by veiled intimations. Obscurity, not clarity, is the property of the most powerfully moving art; and, Burke added, "It is our ignorance of things that causes all our admiration and chiefly excites our passions."

Both of Burke's first two works were well received, but neither set him on the road to any further achievement. The *Annual Register* was a success, although Burke regarded it as mere hackwork. He never finished the projected *History of England*. Burke's growing interest in questions of ethics and politics provided him, in time, with an escape from the frustrations of Grub Street. He entered the House of Commons at the age of thirty-seven, and this new life brought him satisfactions he had never known in his earlier career. He became an outstanding parliamentarian; what distinguished him and made him a philosopher among politicians, however, was his capacity to look beyond the matters of the day and to articulate general principles in terms of which he believed the problems of the day should be judged.

A diligent study of Burke's letters and manuscripts brings home the extent to which his approach to politics was a religious one. What is often spoken of as his "empiricism" appears in this light to be better described as Christian pessimism. As a Christian, Burke believed that the world is imperfect; he regarded his "enlightened" contemporaries' faith in the perfectibility of man as atheistical as well as erroneous. Thus, whereas the fashionable intellectuals of his time looked for the progressive betterment of the world through the beneficent influence of Reason and Nature, Burke maintained that the moral order of the universe is unchanging. The first duty of rulers and legislators, he argued, is to the present, not to the future; their energies should be devoted to the correction of real ills, not to the promotion of an ideal order that exists only in the imagination.

Burke put great faith in the inherited wisdom of tradition. He held that the moral order of the temporal world must necessarily include some evil, by reason of original sin. Men ought not to reject what is good in tradition merely because there is some admixture of evil in it. In man's confused situation, advantages may often lie in balances and compromises between good and evil, even between one evil and another. It is an important part of wisdom to know how much evil should be tolerated. To search for too great a purity is only to produce fresh corruption. Burke was especially critical of revolutionary movements with noble humanitarian ends because he believed that people are simply not at liberty to destroy the state and its institutions in the hope of some contingent improvement. On the other hand, he insisted that people have a paramount duty to prevent the world from getting worse—a duty to guard and preserve their inherited liberties and privileges.

These considerations explain the so-called inconsistencies often attributed to Burke, who supported the movement for the independence of Ireland and the rebellion of the American colonists against the English government, but bitterly opposed the French Revolution. The reason for this seeming inconsistency was that Burke regarded the Irish movement and the American rebellion as actions on behalf of traditional rights and liberties that the English government had infringed on. The French Revolution was quite different, he argued, because it was designed to introduce a wholly new order based on a false rationalistic philosophy. Burke did not object to a resort to force as such; it was the aims of the French revolutionists to which he objected. Similarly, Burke approved of the English Revolution of 1688 because he saw it as designed to restore the rights of Englishmen and to secure the hereditary succession to the throne. The French Revolution, on the contrary, was intended to establish the so-called rights of man and the republican ideals of liberty, equality, and fraternity at the expense of personal property, religion, and the traditional class structure of a Christian kingdom.

In one of his most celebrated works, *Reflections on the Revolution in France* (1790), Burke attacked those of his contemporaries who made an abstraction of liberty, and who invited people to seek liberty without any real knowledge of what they meant by it. He claimed that he himself loved "a manly, moral, regulated liberty as well as any gentleman in France," but he would not "stand forward and give praise" to an "object stripped of all concrete relations" and standing "in all the solitude of a metaphysical idea." As for equality, Burke insisted that it was contrary to nature and therefore impossible to achieve; its advocates, moreover, did "great social harm," for by pretending that real differences were unreal, they inspired "false hopes and vain expectations in those destined to travel in the obscure walk of laborious life." Burke dismissed talk of fraternity as so much "cant and gibberish"; such splendid words were simply the pretexts of the French revolutionists; the causes of the French revolution, however, were "men's vices—pride, ambition, avarice, lust, sedition."

Burke's view of the ancien régime in France was in many ways a romantic one; he was certainly no less a "man of feeling" than was Jean-Jacques Rousseau, whom he detested. But Burke was essentially a religious man living in a rationalistic age. Although he often spoke the language understood by that age—the language of calculation, expediency, utility, and political rights—he had a mind that his contemporaries, and many others, could not readily comprehend. Burke was conscious, above all things, of the reality and unavoidability of evil, and was thus led to claim that the only hope for humankind was to cling to safeguards that had stood the test of time. His hopes for bliss lay in heaven; on earth, his policy was to defend the tolerable, and sometimes the bad, against the immeasurably worse.

Until recently Burke was considered too unsystematic, too empirical, too "unphilosophical," and too much of a theorist to deserve serious attention. His conservative views were uncongenial to left-wing historians, such as Harold J. Laski and Richard Wollheim, who found him inconsistent. In 1948, however, the Sheffield Public Library (Yorkshire, England) acquired the Wentworth Woodhouse manuscripts, and the largest known collection of Burke's private papers became available to scholars for the first time since the writer's death. The study of these papers did much to enhance Burke's reputation as a political philosopher of signal importance and originality.

See also Aesthetics, History of; Bolingbroke, Henry St. John; Political Philosophy, History of; Rousseau, Jean-Jacques; Social and Political Philosophy; Traditionalism.

Bibliography

WORKS BY BURKE

Works, 16 vols. Edited by F. Lawrence and W. King. London: F. C. and J. Rivington, 1803–1827.

Correspondence of Edmund Burke, 10 vols. Edited by Thomas W. Copeland et al. Chicago: University of Chicago Press, 1958–1978.

The Writings and Speeches of Edmund Burke, 12 vols. Edited by Paul Langford et al. Oxford: Clarendon Press, 1981–.

WORKS ON BURKE

Cobban, A. *Edmund Burke and the Revolt against the Eighteenth Century.* London: Allen and Unwin, 1929. Adds new thought on the resemblances between Burke's thought and that of Rousseau.

Cone, C. B. *Burke and the Nature of Politics.* Lexington: University of Kentucky Press, 1957. A valuable introductory study from a modern standpoint.

Copeland, T. W. *Our Eminent Friend, Edmund Burke: Six Essays.* New Haven, CT: Yale University Press, 1949. Essays by a literary historian and leading Burke scholar.

Lock, F. P. *Edmund Burke,* 2 vols. Oxford: Clarendon Press, 1998–.

MacCunn, J. *The Political Philosophy of Burke.* London: Arnold, 1913. A useful traditional reading of Burke's philosophy.

Magnus, P. *Edmund Burke.* London: Murray, 1939. A reliable short biography.

O'Brien, Conor Cruise. *The Great Melody: A Thematic Biography and Commented Anthology of Edmund Burke.* Chicago: University of Chicago Press, 1992.

Parkin, Charles. *The Moral Basis of Burke's Political Thought.* Cambridge, U.K.: Cambridge University Press, 1956. Stresses the importance of religion in Burke's political philosophy.

Stanlis, Peter J. *Edmund Burke: The Enlightenment and Revolution.* New Brunswick, NJ: Transaction, 1991.

Maurice Cranston (1967)
Bibliography updated by Philip Reed (2005)

BURLEY, WALTER
(c. 1274–c. 1345)

Walter Burley, renowned logician, natural philosopher and theologian, was born in 1274 or 1275, perhaps at Burley-in-Wharfedale or Burley, near Leeds, in Yorkshire, England. He studied and taught both at Oxford (c. 1294–c.1309) and at the University of Paris (c.1309–1327). Based in England from 1327–1341, he perhaps spent his last years in retirement in southern France and Italy (1341–1344).

OXFORD

Burley was a master of arts by 1301 and is mentioned as a fellow of Merton College in 1305. He appears to have heard John Duns Scotus lecture on the *Sentences*, probably in the academic year 1298–1299, and adopts some Scotistic positions in later works: that being *qua* being is the primary and adequate object of the intellect, and that the intellect understands the singular as singular. If Burley began to study theology at Oxford, he and William of Ockham, whose studies began c.1307–1308, may have been fellow students. Burley's writings from this period, as Jan Pinborg (1937–1982) has rightly observed, "comprise an almost complete course of logic," including *Quaestiones in librum Perihermeneias* and *Quaestiones super librum Posterior Analytics*, as well as treatments of specific topics, *De suppositionibus* and *De consequentiis*. There are commentaries on Aristotle's natural philosophy as well, including *Questions on the De anima of Aristotle*, Book 3.

PARIS

Burley's career in Paris, assuming some prior study of theology, could be reconstructed as follows. Between 1309 and 1314 he was an *auditor* of lectures on the scriptures and the *Sentences* of Peter Lombard, from 1314 to 1317 a *biblicus* (lecturer) on the scriptures, and from 1317 to 1318 a *sententiarius* although his lectures on the *Sentences* are lost. The *Tractatus Primus*, however, recounts a controversy on accidental form with his master, Thomas Wilton, which arose out of his *principium* on Book IV. Its argumentation exhibits a layering of logic and physics in a way that makes Burley a precursor of the Oxford *calculators*, such as Richard Swineshead and John Dumbleton (fourteenth century). In support of his claim that contrary forms, such as hot and cold, belong to the same ultimate species, he argues first *from logic* that things equidistant from an extreme are of the same species. Then, *from Aristotle in natural philosophy*, he argues that if a cooled body is immediately reheated, at some instant, B, preceding the first instant the body is cold, A, it will have a degree of heat, and at some instant, C, succeeding A, it will have a degree of cold, both of which degrees will be formally equidistant from maximum heat and thus in the same species. This argument also reflects contemporary debates over first, the *latitude* of forms, the intensive range of possible degrees that an instance of a species of quality may possess; and second, the *first and last instants* of change, the subject also of his *disputatio* at Toulouse, *De primo et ultimo instanti* of the same period.

In 1321, now a priest, he received his last leave of absence for two years of study and had completed his studies by the end of 1323 at the latest. He is referred to as *doctor of sacred theology* in 1324. His teaching career was short since he had left Paris by the beginning of 1327.

BURLEY AND OCKHAM

Perhaps in the same year (1317–1318) that Burley was lecturing on the *Sentences* at Paris, William Ockham was doing likewise at Oxford. It is clear that from his first exposure to Ockham's *Sentences* commentary, Burley found it necessary to oppose him on a number of important issues in logic and natural philosophy. It was not a one-sided engagement. Ockham borrows from Burley's *Tractatus primus* (before 1324) in his *Quaestiones* on the *Physics*, which Burley in turn uses and criticizes in his own final commentary on the *Physics*, the first six books of which were written after 1324–7. In the *Summa logicae* Ockham both uses and attacks Burley's *De suppositionibus*. Burley counterattacks in his second version (after 1323) of *De puritate artis logicae*. While Ockham's *Logic* is organized in the traditional way around terms, propositions, and arguments, Burley's is organized around the general rules of consequences, thus giving priority to propositional logic.

Burley's explanation of the supposition of terms differs from Ockham's, who holds that first, universals do not exist in re, and second, that they are not constitutive parts of the essence of individuals. On the contrary, Burley holds that universals do exist in re although not apart from singulars. Therefore, according to Burley, when the term *human* in a sentence has *simple supposition* or stands for what is common or universal, it stands for what it primarily signifies: the humanness in Socrates or Plato. For Ockham, however, when *human* has simple supposition, it stands for a common concept, humanness in the mind. The only thing a term can signify or refer to is the individual, for instance when *human* supposits *personally* for Socrates, Plato, and so on. Burley eventually ceded ground to Ockham on the issue of universals as constitutive parts, holding that the universal form merely discloses the individual's essence (for instance, human). Ockham's position that universals are only general concepts implies that science, which is of the universal, must be about spoken, written, and mental propositions while for Burley, science is founded on *real propositions*, that is, propositions whose subjects and predicates are real entities, either singular or universal, but whose copulas are purely mental.

As well as resisting Ockham's reduction of res to singular things, Burley objects to Ockham's reduction of Aristotle's categories to substance and quality. In his *De formis*, (c. 1324–1326), he holds that quantity is a form separate from the quantified body, and he also argues that motion is a form over and above the body in motion, increased and decreased by a succession of specifically distinct forms (*De intensione et remissione formarum*, written after 1323). This explanation, which can be calls a *succession* theory, extends to all changes in the degree of a quality a thing may possess: how the just person comes to have more justice, or that something cold becomes somewhat hot. Every increase in justice or heat, every acceleration of motion, results from the acquisition of a new, more perfect form and the loss of the old, less perfect form.

ENGLAND

Burley's departure from Paris was coincident with the coronation of Edward III (1312–1377), who sent him with a deputation in February 1327 to the papal court in Avignon and again in 1330, now as one of the king's *beloved clerks*, men in the royal service, usually of humble beginnings, who were often the king's agents on diplomatic missions. Again, from September 1338 until Easter 1339, Burley went "beyond the seas on the king's service" (*Calendar of Patent Rolls*, 1338–1340, p. 123).

Burley's academic career ended when he left Paris, and it seems that he had no significant scholarly projects in hand during the next seven years. However, some time after Richard Bury was enthroned as bishop at Durham in 1334, Burley became a member of his household. Bury's patronage and the intellectual energy of the circle he gathered around him would fuel Burley's renewed career as a scholar.

Between 1334 and 1337 Burley completed a commentary on Books 1–6 of the *Ethics*, added Books 7 and 8 to his final commentary on the *Physics*, and revised his commentary on the *Ars vetus*. He began to revise the commentary on *Ethics* 1–6 and add a commentary on 7–10 in 1338–1339. In the commentaries on the *Physics* and *Ars vetus* are found Burley's references to the *moderni*, those thinkers encountered first during his Paris years, who threaten the purity of the font of all philosophy: Aristotle. The doctrines that Burley identifies as being those of the *moderni* are not confined to any single philosophical discipline, and appear, by Burley's account, to form a systemic threat to philosophy itself. His commentary on Aristotle's *Politics*, begun in 1338–1339, is, along with his *Ethics* commentary, heavily dependent on Thomas Aquinas's expositions of those works (written between 1269–1272). Nevertheless, they contain doctrines original with Burley, for example, in the *Politics*, that of the "co-rulership" of kings with those who are "their friends and the friends of the government" (fol. 186r) and doctrinal divergences from Aquinas, for example, in the *Ethics*, the role of the speculative intellect in understanding the precepts of natural law (1500, fol. 103r).

Upon completion of the four expositions of Aristotle (c.1340), Burley, who was now in his mid-sixties, appears to have sought some disengagement from the rigors and antagonisms of scholarly life, which may have led to his journey to Italy, probably in 1341.

SOUTHERN FRANCE AND ITALY

In 1341 Burley engaged in a *disputatio de quolibet* in the arts faculty at Bologna, an event that has been connected with his supposed Averroism. Burley was not an Averroist, however, if this term implies someone who adopts positions contrary to the Christian faith on the authority of Averroes. This is clear from the beginning of his career in his questions on *De anima*, Book 3, where he concludes that "neither is the material intellect one in all, nor also the agent intellect" (3.44). Then in Paris, where his master was the Averroist Wilton, his short work *De potentiis animae* reiterates this position.

The *De vita et moribus philosophorum* was long thought to have been the fruit of Burley's retirement in southern Europe. However, large sections from it are found in a manuscript dated 1326, when Burley was in Paris, which, together with the claim that no attribution of the work to him is earlier than the fifteenth century, has led to a presumption against Burley's authorship of this immensely popular work. Nevertheless, this evidence is not conclusive, and given his habits of appropriating large amounts of text from other authors and frequently reworking his own texts, it is not impossible that the *De vita et moribus philosophorum* passed through Burley's hands at some point in its history.

On 23 November 1343, Burley was in Avignon to present a copy of his commentary on the *Politics* to his old Parisian acquaintance Pierre Roger, now Clement VI (1291–1352). This gift, complete with an elegant letter and a miniature showing the presentation, could have been both in appreciation and expectation of further patronage. Indeed, Burley obtained the rectory at Great Chart, Kent, on 19 June 1344, the last date he is known to have been alive.

Walter Burley exerted considerable influence both on his contemporaries and on philosophical thought into the sixteenth century, to which the number of early printed editions of his commentaries on Aristotle testify. This influence may be attributed, firstly, to the originality and the clarity of the positions he maintained in the controversies of his day, both in logic and natural philosophy. He contributed significantly to the debates concerning supposition theory, consequences, *obligationes*, and *sophismata*. In natural philosophy his theory of the *first and last instants* of change, which distinguishes between *permanent* and *successive* things or states, becomes a standard view, and the *succession* position, which he defends in his classic work, *On the Intension and Remission of Forms*, is frequently cited, being both opposed and defended, into the sixteenth century.

His skill at the traditional exercise of commentary on Aristotle was also acknowledged. In glossed Latin manuscripts of Aristotle and Averroes, he is one of the commentators most frequently cited, especially in connection with the *Ethics*, *Politics*, *Physics*, and logical works of Aristotle. In addition, manuscripts of Burley's commentaries on these works had a wide circulation. Early printed editions of an important collection of *auctoritates* of Aristotle and other philosophers carry his textual comments, along with those of Averroes, Robert Grosseteste, Albert the Great, and Thomas Aquinas. A revival of interest in Burley's thought, particularly his logic and natural philosophy, was underway by the 1960s, and earlier assessments of him as an unworthy opponent of Ockham have not survived a closer study of his work, which has revealed its originality and depth.

See also Albert the Great; Aristotle; Averroes; Averroism; Duns Scotus, John; Grosseteste, Robert; Peter Lombard; Swineshead, Richard; Thomas Aquinas, St.; William of Ockham.

Bibliography

WORKS BY BURLEY

De formis, edited by F. J. D. Scott. Bayerische Akademie der Wissenschaften, 1970.

Commentary on *Ethics*. Venice, 1481, 1500.

De intensione et remissione formarum. Venice, 1496.

Commentary on *Logica Vetus*. Venice, 1497.

Commentary on *Physics*. Venice, 1509, 1524.

De vita et moribus philosophorum, edited by H. Knust. Stuttgard: Tübingen, 1866.

De puritate artis logicae tractatus longior, with a revised edition of the *Tractatus brevior*, edited by P. Boehner. St. Bonaventure, NY: Franciscan Institute Publications, 1955.

De primo et ultimo instanti, edited by H. and C. Shapiro, *Archiv fur Geschichte der Philosophie* 47 (1965): 157–173.

De potentiis animae, edited by M. J. Kitchel. *Mediaeval Studies* 33 (1971): 85–113.

De suppositionibus, edited by S. F. Brown. *Franciscan Studies* 32 (1972): 15–64.

Quaestiones in librum Perihermeneias, edited by S. F. Brown. *Franciscan Studies* 34 (1974): 200–295.

De consequentiis, edited by N. J. Green-Pedersen. *Franciscan Studies* 40 (1980): 102–166.

Questions on the De anima of Aristotle, edited by E. A. Synan. Leiden: E. J. Brill, 1997.

On the purity of the Art of Logic: The Shorter and the Longer Treatises. Translated by P. V. Spade. New Haven, CT: Yale University Press, 2000.

Quaestiones super librum Posterior Analytics, edited by M. Sommers. Toronto: Pontifical Institute of Mediaeval Studies, 2000.

WORKS ON BURLEY

Conti, A. D. "Ontology in Walter Burley's Last Commentary on the *Ars vetus*." *Franciscan Studies* 50 (1990): 120–176.

De Rijk, L. M. "Burley's So-Called *Tractatus primus*, with an edition of the additional quaestio *Utrum contradictio sit maxima oppositio*." *Vivarium* 24 (1996): 61–91.

Krieger, Gerhard. "Studies on Walter Burley 1989–1997." *Vivarium* 37 (1) (1999): 94–100.

Martin, C. "Walter Burley." In *Oxford Studies Presented to Daniel Callus*, Oxford Historical Society, 194–230. Oxford: Clarendon Press, 1964.

Nederman, C. J. "Kings, Peers, and Parliament: Virtue and Corulership in Walter Burley's *Commentarius in VIII libros politicorum Aristotelis*." *Albion* 24 (3) (1992): 391–407.

Ottman, Jennifer, and Rega Wood. "Walter Burley: His Life and Works." *Vivarium* 37 (1) (1999): 1–23.

Pinborg, J. "Walter Burley on Exclusives." *English Logic and Semantics*, Acts of the 4th European Symposium on Medieval Logic and Semantics. Leiden: Nijmegen, 23–27 June 1979. Reprinted in J. Pinborg. *Medieval Semantics: Selected Studies on Medieval Logic and Grammar*. London: Variorum, 1984.

Sylla, E. D. "Infinite Indivisibles and Continuity in Fourteenth-Century Theories of Alteration." In *Infinity and Continuity in Ancient and Medieval Thought*, edited by N. Kretzmann, 231–257, 322–330. Ithaca: Cornell University Press, 1982.

Sylla, E. D. "Medieval Concepts of the Latitude of Forms: The Oxford Calculators." *Archives d'Histoire Doctrinale et Littéraire du Moyen Âge* 40 (1973): 223–283.

Sylla, E. D. "Ockham and the Mertonians." *History of the University of Oxford*. Vol. 1: *Early Oxford Schools*, edited by J. I. Catto, 607–558. Oxford: Clarendon Press, 1984–2000.

Sylla, E. D. "*Repertorium Mertonense*." *Mediaeval Studies* 31 (1969): 185–208.

Weisheipl, J. A. "Ockham and Some Mertonians." *Mediaeval Studies* 30 (1968): 174–188.

Wood, Rega. "Studies on Walter Burley, 1968–1988." *Bulletin de Philosophie Médiévale* 30 (1988): 233–250.

Mary Sommers (2005)

BURTHOGGE, RICHARD
(c. 1638–c. 1698)

Richard Burthogge, the English physician and idealist philosopher, was born in Plymouth. After taking an arts degree at Lincoln College, Oxford, he studied medicine at the University of Leiden and returned to his native country to practice near Totnes in Devonshire. Of pacific and conciliatory disposition, he seems to have wavered in the religious controversy between Catholicism and Puritanism, and in philosophy, between Lockean sensationalism and Cambridge Platonism. He distinguished between heresy and error, maintaining that the former "must be eradicated," but the latter tolerated for humanity's sake. His life is obscure, and little is known of it beyond that information revealed in his writings, which have a certain importance as anticipations of Immanuel Kant.

We know the world, according to Burthogge, only through our own ideas, and these do not give us its real nature. On the contrary, our ideas transform the nature of things into qualities that are purely subjective. Similarly, our values are our own; and such relative judgments as those involving categories of cause and effect, or whole and part, are arrived at through the constitution of our minds, not discovered embedded *in rerum natura*. The things themselves, though remaining unknowable, nevertheless cause ideas to arise in our minds. Here Burthogge foreshadowed Kant's paradox of the relation between *noumena* and *phenomena*. Burthogge's view that the human mind projects relations into the external world exemplifies his Neoplatonic streak. However, this strain was accompanied by a Lockean one which led him to assert that no confidence could be placed in an idea contradicted by sensation. Burthogge thus seems to have accepted John Locke's theory of two kinds of ideas, those of sensation and those of reflection.

For Burthogge, there were also two kinds of truth—metaphysical and logical. Metaphysical truth is found in the conformity between our ideas and those in the mind of God; logical truth, in the conformity between our ideas and the things of which they are ideas. We cannot apprehend the former kind of truth; but since the latter involves knowing the unknowable, logical truth is reduced to consistency. Burthogge would not accept the doctrine of innate ideas, because if we had such ideas, we would be able to discover truth through introspection alone. He asserted dogmatically that there is a coherent system of ideas, duplicating the system of things, even though no individual possesses it. This system, he maintained, exemplifies God's ideas.

In his treatise on the soul of the world, Burthogge supported the Neoplatonic concept of a plastic nature permeating the universe and accounting for its "harmony." This is breathed into things by God himself but is not to be identified with God. If nothing else, this treatise is valuable as an example of the philosophy of nature which was acceptable to learned men of the time.

Burthogge, in sum, is one of the anomalies of the history of philosophy. He advanced startlingly "modern" ideas, side by side with fantasies no longer taken seriously.

See also Cambridge Platonists; Error; Idealism; Ideas; Kant, Immanuel; Locke, John; Neoplatonism; Sensationalism.

Bibliography

WORKS BY BURTHOGGE

Organum Vetus et Novum. London, 1678.

An essay upon Reason, and the Nature of Spirits. London: Dunton, 1694.

Of the Soul of the World, and of Particular Souls. London, 1699.

Landes, Margaret W., ed. *The Philosophical Writings of Richard Burthogge.* Chicago and London: Open Court, 1921. Contains reprints of the three above works by Burthogge as well as a valuable introduction, notes, and bibliography.

WORKS ON BURTHOGGE

Boas, George. *Dominant Themes of Modern Philosophy*, pp. 253–259. New York: Ronald Press, 1957.

Cassirer, Ernst. *Das Erkenntnisproblem in der Philosophie und Wissenschaft der neueren Zeit.* Vol. 1, pp. 464–473. Berlin: Cassirer, 1906.

Grünbaum, Jacob. *Die Philosophie Richard Burthogges.* Unpublished PhD diss., Bern, 1939.

L[ee], S. L. "Burthogge, Richard." In *Dictionary of National Biography.* Vol. 7, p. 453. London: Smith Elder, 1885–1900.

Lovejoy, A. O. "Kant and the English Platonists." In *Essays Philosophical and Psychological in Honor of William James*, pp. 265–302. New York, 1908.

George Boas (1967)

BUSINESS ETHICS

Discussions of ethics and business trace back to the writings of Plato and Aristotle and persist in the modern philosophical writings of Karl Marx, John Rawls, and others. Although business ethics as a specialized field of study did not emerge until the 1970s, it has grown sharply since. Philosophers, political scientists, business academics, and social psychologists have written systematically about a variety of issues such as the moral status of the corporation, the ethical foundations of the market, fairness in advertising, bribery, corporate governance, human rights and multinational corporations, and business obligations to the environment. During that time, rival theories for interpreting business ethics have emerged and been debated.

Traditional philosophers such as Plato, Aristotle, Aquinas, and Kant discuss issues of the right and wrong in economic activity. They sometimes examine specific business ethics puzzles, including the ethics of the profit motive, just price in trade, usury in lending, and ethics in negotiation. Thomas Aquinas writes at length about the question raised first by Cicero of whether a grain merchant carrying grain to a community stricken by famine is obliged to reveal to the townspeople that other merchants behind him are bringing more grain. (Aquinas concludes that, contra Cicero, the merchant is not so obliged because no businessperson has an obligation to make a prediction which, if it turned out to be false, would rob him of a "just" price.) Moreover, questions about broad economic design are ubiquitous in the history of philosophy. For example, the issue of the communal ownership of property (in modern terms, communism and socialism) was first brought into sharp relief by Plato, was critiqued by Aristotle, and has been the subject of bitter controversy ever since.

For convenience, it is helpful to conceive business ethics as having three parts, where each part corresponds to the level of entity being analyzed: namely,

1. Individual businesspersons: including employees, entrepreneurs, investors, traders, and consumers

2. Business systems, including economic systems, cultural norms, and regulatory and judicial systems.

3. Business organizations, including corporations, trade associations, and international financial organizations such as the WTO, the World Bank, and the IMF.

Each of these three entities gives rise to both questions of right and wrong (normative issues) and to questions of fact (empirical issues). Because empirical issues are not, properly speaking, philosophical ones, and despite the fact that a large and important empirical literature now exists (authored by sociologists, economists, and business academics), this article will not attempt to analyze and explain that empirical literature.

INDIVIDUAL BUSINESSPERSONS

Philosophers have debated the issue of the individual's pursuit of money and profit for centuries. Plato famously denied top-status positions of ruler or guardian in his ideal state, the Republic, to business people (indeed to all owners of property) out of fear that their pursuit of wealth would corrupt their political virtue. It remained for the eighteenth-century philosopher, Adam Smith, author of the *Wealth of Nations*, to make the pursuit of profit at least moderately respectable: "It is not from the benevolence of the butcher, the brewer, or the baker that we expect our dinner, but from their regard of their own interest. We address ourselves not to their humanity, but to their self-love and never talk to them of our own necessities, but of their advantage." (p. 13.)

Smith meant to draw attention to the fact that efficient economic transactions frequently rely on self-interested or profit-oriented motives rather than more noble motives such as benevolence. In his view, then, our shared goal of achieving a healthy, efficient economy justifies a significant amount of profit-seeking and self-interested activity in business. His well known "invisible hand" provides a metaphor for explaining how free markets seem to direct the inevitable, if regrettable, self-interest of businesspersons toward the common good.

One's ethical evaluation of profit-seeking by businesspersons may be influenced by one's antecedent commitments to ethical theory. Smith's invisible hand relies heavily on consequential considerations: Individual acts and motives are judged ethically through their consequences. For Adam Smith, then, we should sometimes tolerate darker, self-interested motives in business so long as the consequences produce social benefits. Yet a nonconsequential approach to ethics—one placing more emphasis on the quality of the motive or the principle of the individual's action—lacks appeal directly to such a practical justification. A nonconsequential approach must justify profit-seeking, if at all, by nesting the profit motive under other, less selfish motives, such as attempting to benefit one's family, one's community, or society by way of pursuing profit.

Critics have objected to a broad, self-centered view of business because it appears to presume selfishness or, at the very least, psychological egoism. The focus in much of modern economics is upon developing increasingly sophisticated conceptual mechanisms to maximize the achievement of economic goods such as money, market share, or profits, all of which seem to exclude the pursuit of "higher" interests such as benevolence, social welfare, and environmental integrity. Even well-known economists such as Amartya Sen have asserted that the rational economic man, *homo economicus*, is dangerously close to being a "rational fool." Opposing economists respond, however, that the maximization of individual preferences can easily include the satisfaction of other-oriented preferences such as helping the poor or protecting the environment. A businessperson may simply prefer saving the environment to maximizing his income. Whether such other-oriented preferences can be subsumed comfortably within the mathematically inclined methods that dominate modern-day economics remains hotly debated.

BUSINESS SYSTEMS

Disputes are common about the extent to which self-interested motives are acceptable in economic behavior. These disputes overlap with others about the desirability of forms of business systems. Just as Adam Smith did, modern economists often stress the societal benefits of free, self-interested market activity. They note that markets free from government interference encourage free exchanges among individuals, and, in turn, business productivity. A realm of perfectly free exchanges, indeed, is often said to establish a condition called "Pareto Optimality": a state in which no one can be made better off without someone being made worse off.

Not surprisingly, then, debates in business ethics have frequently centered on the assumptions of traditional economic theory. Microeconomic theory (which constitutes a part of what is sometimes called neoclassical economic theory) views market participants as rational agents seeking to maximize their own utility. In more recent economic writings "utility" is interpreted to mean the maximal satisfaction of one's individual preferences.

Whether economic theory contains an embedded bias towards selfishness or not, most economists agree that market participants can encounter situations where a businessperson's rational self-interest collides with the social welfare. One of the most notable of these situations is the "prisoner's dilemma" discussed by game theorists, wherein rational self-interest leads each player to defect in certain contexts where cooperation is clearly the best long-term strategy for all. Because prisoner's-dilemma situations are believed to arise frequently in business transactions, it follows that even fully self-interested businesspersons should have an interest in developing techniques of cooperation, both for themselves and others. Indeed, some philosophers have even argued that nearly all morality can be derived from such rational pursuit of self-interest through cooperation.

Others theorists argue that business ethics is simply impossible so long as market freedom is the dominant value. They assert that, in addition to problems such as the prisoner's dilemma, persistent discrimination, sexual harassment, environmental pollution, false advertising, financial scandals, child labor, and bribery require a more of a "visible hand" (usually government's) than an "invisible" one.

Nonetheless, even defenders of heaver regulation of business grant that often law is relatively impotent in ensuring business ethics. For example, law tends to lag behind the knowledge emerging in an industry, so that it often comes too late to correct abuse. Scientists in the asbestos industry in the United States knew about the dangers of asbestos long before laws could be drafted to regulate asbestos harm. Moreover, laws tend to apply to the jurisdiction from which they emanate. Hence, U.S. or German law is nearly powerless to control multinational corporations operating in host countries. This point has special force in many developing host countries where laws are unsophisticated and poorly enforced.

Conflicting cultural values can frustrate ethical decisions. For example, in countries where "grease" payments are common, are businesspersons justified in paying customary bribes to government officials? Or consider issues of human rights. In countries where educational opportunities are inadequate, is it acceptable to hire a fourteen-year-old for full-time employment? Does it make a difference that, as sometimes happens, the majority opinion among adults in a given country holds that child labor is ethically acceptable? Business ethicists have proposed a variety of theories to help solve such dilemmas. Most deny that all employment conditions between the home and host countries of the corporations must be comparable; if that were true, it is argued, employees would, for example, receive exactly the same pay (or at least the same pay adjusted for cost-of-living differences) for the same work. But such wage parity would freeze out almost all foreign investment by multinational corporations in the developing world. Instead, the dominant approach has been to specify a floor of rights that apply to labor conditions and that all corporations must respect.

BUSINESS ORGANIZATIONS

Some disagree that a corporation can ever be "responsible" or "irresponsible." They note that corporations have exceedingly narrow personalities; they are chartered for the purpose of making money for their investors. They have, in the words an English jurist, "no pants to kick or soul to damn." Can such organizations be said to have a conscience or moral responsibility? A few theorists regard the corporation as analogous to a large bureaucratic machine and for this reason hold it to be misleading to speak of a corporate "conscience." In turn, they reject the very idea of corporate ethical responsibility. Only individual businesspersons, not corporations, are the true bearers of ethical responsibility. They thus deny moral agency to the corporation, denying that a corporation attains the status of an actor for which such moral predicates as "is responsible" and "is blameworthy" are appropriate. In contrast, theorists who see the corporation as either a large, abstract "person" (the corporation in most legal systems is regarded as a *persona ficta*, a fictional person) or an organization possessing a decision-making structure capable of rational deliberation are called moral-agency theorists. They believe that corporations *are* capable of behaving responsibly or irresponsibly.

Assuming, then, that the corporation is even the kind of thing that can behave responsibly or irresponsibly, the question next arises about what a corporation's "being responsible" means. Three major approaches to this question have been offered. These may be labeled: the Classical Framework, the Stakeholder Framework; and the Social Contract Framework.

THE CLASSICAL FRAMEWORK

The "classical" framework asserts that the moral responsibility of the corporation is nothing other than maximizing profits for its investors. This approach is associated with modern economic theory and writings of Frederich Hayek and Milton Friedman. The view holds that the sole moral responsibility of the corporation, and in turn of the managers who serve as agents for the shareholders, is to enhance the interests *only* of the owners of the corporation, the shareholders. The corporation is often seen by its classical defenders as a nexus of contracts among free-acting individuals whose peculiar advantage lies in its ability to reduce transaction costs among participants by, for example, offering organizational remedies in lieu of expensive, individual contracts among individuals.

Critics of the this approach are quick to point out that corporate executives are not publicly elected officials and as such are poor choices for shouldering decision-making promoting the common good. Indeed, often corporate executives have been associated with bad choices, as when large U.S. companies in Chile decades ago helped unseat the country's democratically elected president. Do we really want, these critics ask, to entrust corporate officials with the common good?

THE STAKEHOLDER FRAMEWORK

On the stakeholder theory, managers have obligations primarily to shareowners but also have certain ethical obligations to other groups called "stakeholders"—those who have a stake in the corporation's activity, including customers, stockholders, employees, and people who live in areas affected by the corporation. Disagreements exist about precisely who should be included as stakeholders, but almost all theorists agree that three principal groups of stakeholders are customers, employees, and stockholders. Hence, the stakeholder framework agrees with the classical framework in assigning special importance to the interests of stockholders. The difference between the stakeholder view and the classical view, however, is that stakeholder theorists do not limit the responsibilities of corporate managers entirely to satisfying stockholder interests. Managers, in turn, must make tradeoffs among the interests of the corporation's stakeholders if they are to manage well. Some stakeholder theorists argue that by working to enhance the interests of all stakeholders, the company will also maximize the long-run interests of the stockholders. But other theorists disagree, arguing that some stakeholders must inevitably receive less in order for the stockholder to achieve a maximum return on his investment.

THE SOCIAL CONTRACT/SOCIAL CONTRACTS FRAMEWORK

This view construes corporate and managerial obligations in terms of implicit "contracts" that exist in and among companies, industries, political units, and other relevant economic communities. For example, it has been argued that an implicit "social contract" exists between corporations and society requiring that corporations refrain from exploiting their workers or from destroying the environment; in return for the special favors it receives from society—unlimited longevity (because in most legal systems a corporation is a "persona ficta" or fictional person, it never dies) and limited liability (investors in corporations are responsible for the actions and debts of the corporation only up to the extent of their invested money). In a similar vein, it has been argued that an implicit social contract exists in most societies requiring that jobs and advancements allocated by a consideration of the qualifications of the applicant rather than his or her gender or race. Beginning in the 1990s, the idea of a social contract was extended by some to include the possibility of a multiplicity of social contracts, interpreted as the implicit set of agreements that exist within and among communities of economic actors, including corporations, trade associations, unions, industries, and professional associations.

Other business ethics issues arise for for-profit corporations. One of these is the factual question of whether a corporation that has better ethics will make more money in the long run than a corporation with worse ethics. Scores of empirical studies on this topic have been conducted, although the answer remains elusive. There is also the question of how a good corporation should be structured. What form of corporate governance should a corporation adopt? Should it include employees on its board of directors? Should employees participate in the management of the corporation, and should they perhaps be given automatic status as shareholders?

Lurking in the backdrop of many discussions of corporate ethics is the issue of what power, if any, managers should have in making ethical decisions. Suppose, for example, that competitive market forces eclipse any moral "space" that managers might have. In such an instance, the entire notion of "business ethics" seems irrelevant. If "ought implies can" and if business managers are captive to the dictates of the market, then how can one say that they "ought" to behave well? On this view, the only way to reform business behavior is to change the surrounding market or regulatory environment—that is, to force business to recognize that its self-interest lies in ethical behavior. Most business ethicists, however, agree that corporations have at least some discretionary space. The empirical debate centers on how much.

See also Applied Ethics; Aristotle; Cicero, Marcus Tullius; Engineering Ethics; Ethics and Economics; Kant, Immanuel; Marx, Karl; Philosophy of Economics; Plato; Rawls, John; Sen, Amartya K.; Smith, Adam; Thomas Aquinas, St.

Bibliography

Arrow, Kenneth J. "Social Responsibility and Economic Efficiency." *Public Policy* XXI.3 (1973).

Coase, R. H. "The Nature of the Firm." In *The Nature of the Firm: Origins, Evolution, and Development*, edited by Oliver E. Williamson and Sidney G. Winter, 18–33. New York: Oxford University Press, 1991.

Donaldson, Thomas. *The Ethics of International Business*. New York: Oxford University Press, 1989.

Donaldson, Thomas, and Thomas Dunfee. *Ties That Bind: A Social Contracts Approach to Business Ethics*. Cambridge, MA: Harvard Business School Press, 1999.

Frank, Robert H. "Can Socially Responsible Firms Survive in a Competitive Environment?" In *Codes of Conduct: Behavioral Research into Business Ethics*, edited by David M. Messick and Ann E. Tenbrunsel, 86–103. New York: Russell Sage Foundation, 1996.

Freeman, R. Edward. *Strategic Management: A Stakeholder Approach*. Pitman Series in Business and Public Policy. Boston: Pitman, 1984.

Jackall, Robert. *Moral Mazes: The World of Corporate Managers*. New York: Oxford University Press, 1988.

Mitchell, R. K., B. R Agle, and D. J. Wood. "Toward a Theory of Stakeholder Identification and Salience: Defining the Principle of Who and What Really Counts." *Academy of Management Review* 22 (1997): 853–886.

Preston, Lee E., and Duane Windsor. *The Rules of the Game in the Global Economy: Policy Regimes for International Business*. 2nd ed. Norwell, MA.: Kluwer Academic Publishers, 1997.

Sen, Amartya. "Does Business Ethics Make Economic Sense?" *Business Ethics Quarterly* 3 (1993): 45–54.

Sen, Amartya Kumar. *On Ethics and Economics*. New York: Blackwell, 1987.

Smith, Adam, and D. D. Raphael. *The Wealth of Nations*. New York: Knopf, 1991.

Solomon, Robert C. *Ethics and Excellence: Cooperation and Integrity in Business*. New York: Oxford University Press, 1992.

Trevino, L. K., and G. R. Weaver. "Business Ethics/Business Ethics: One Field or Two?" *Business Ethics Quarterly* 4 (1994): 13–128.

Thomas Donaldson (2005)

BUTLER, JOSEPH
(1692–1752)

Though he has not left us a complete philosophical system, Joseph Butler produced a moral philosophy that is still held in the highest esteem, and a philosophical theology of considerable long-term value. Butler was the eighth child of a prosperous draper. His father enrolled him in a dissenting academy, but he decided to join the established church and entered Oriel College, Oxford, in 1714. While still at school he had engaged in a philosophical correspondence with Samuel Clarke and at Oxford was befriended by Edward Talbot, son of the Bishop of Salisbury. Clarke and Talbot's father were instrumental in Butler's being appointed, after graduation, as Preacher at the Chapel of the Rolls. A selection of his sermons there was published in 1726 under the title *Fifteen Sermons Preached at the Rolls Chapel*. In 1729 a second edition appeared, with an important new preface. Bishop Talbot's patronage continued with Butler's entering the living of Haughton, and later that of Stanhope, in Talbot's later diocese of Durham. While at Stanhope Butler wrote his other major work, of which the full title is *The Analogy of Religion, Natural and Revealed, to the Constitution and Course of Nature*. This appeared in 1736, and appeared in a second edition in the same year. By then Butler had entered royal circles. His school friend Robert Secker had drawn him to the attention of Queen Caroline, who appointed him Clerk of the Closet in 1736, conversed with him frequently on theological and philosophical matters, and received the sacrament from him on her deathbed in 1737. The king promised her that he would advance Butler and made him Bishop of Bristol in 1738. There is an unsubstantiated story that he was offered the see of Canterbury in 1747 and declined it. In 1751 he became Bishop of Durham but was not destined to preside there for long because his health rapidly declined. He died in 1752, and was buried in Bristol. He never married.

BUTLER'S AIMS AND METHODS

Butler's personal history shows that he was, in C. D. Broad's words, "a thoroughly unworldly man whom the world treated very well." His integrity and intellectual prowess were widely recognized, and the patronage he received merely ensured that he did not suffer for them. His writings are often hard reading (and the sermons must often have been hard listening), not because they are unclear but because Butler aims at clarity exclusively and often sacrifices elegance in pursuit of it.

Butler is a Christian priest who seeks his readers' spiritual welfare. So, although his theoretical skills are considerable, they are wholly subordinated to his practical concern for the exercise of virtue and the proper consideration of the claims of religion. In urging these, however, he does not appeal to revelation. Nor does he use the a priori arguments in ethics and theology employed by Clarke, although he says he agrees with these. Butler's own methods are empirical ones. His ethical arguments are designed to show that the exercise of virtue is the expression of our true human nature and that vice violates it. His religious apologetic is based on the same appeal to probability that he thinks necessary for prudent conduct in everyday life. His famous attacks on selfish and hedonistic theories of human nature are designed to remove what he sees as the morally dangerous influence of faulty philosophy and are not intellectual explorations undertaken for their own sake.

ETHICS

In the Rolls Sermons, Butler seeks to encourage his worldly-wise hearers to practice virtue by arguing that to do so is to live in accordance with our nature. Virtue is the natural form of life for us, and vice is unnatural. He assumes, as his hearers would also have done, at least nominally, that the motives and capacities in our nature are placed there by God for our good, and he maintains that a realistic attention to those motives and capacities will show that living virtuously represents their natural exercise.

His argument has two main stages. The first stage is an account of the components of human nature, and the second is a claim about its structure and about the implications of that structure for our conduct. He argues that our nature is misrepresented by those (particularly Hobbes) who think that we are always selfish and by those who hold

that we are always motivated by the desire for pleasure. If either of these theories were true, genuinely virtuous action would be impossible. Butler holds instead that our nature contains within it several distinct principles. There are, first, the "particular passions, appetites, and affections" such as the desires for food or possessions, or the emotions like joy or anger. There is, next, the "general affection of self-love," which is the desire for one's own long-term interest or happiness (which Butler interprets as the proper satisfaction or expression of one's own particular passions). It is self-love that causes us to restrain our present appetites in the interest of our long-term health, for example; and Butler clearly thinks of it as requiring rational calculation. Thirdly, there is the "natural principle" of benevolence. Butler uses this term as a general name to include all those desires we have for the good of others. (Scholars disagree over whether he also thinks of it as a rational principle in the same way that self-love is.) He identifies it with the love of one's neighbor.

Finally, and most important, our nature includes conscience. He describes this as "a principle of reflection in men, by which they distinguish between, approve and disapprove their own actions." Its judgments pronounce actions and motives to be "in themselves just, right, good" or "evil, wrong, unjust," and when it makes such judgments it "magisterially exerts itself." So conscience judges actions and motives in an intuitive manner and judges them as being of certain kinds, not as having good or bad consequences.

In defending his account of the components of our nature, Butler appeals primarily to our common experience. He also produces classic arguments against Hobbesian and other theories that say our motives are always selfish or are always directed toward pleasure. Experience seems to show us many examples of actions done from benevolence, and only a priori commitment to theory can incline us to doubt that our motives are often as they seem. Furthermore, self-love is only the motive for some actions and not for all. And although we do indeed gain pleasure from the successful pursuit of objects we desire, it is these objects themselves, and not the pleasure we derive from them, that we are pursuing.

But our nature is not merely one in which all these principles are to be found. It is one in which they form a system or constitution in which there is a built-in order of superiority and subordination. When we act in accordance with this order, we act naturally and so virtuously; when we violate it, we act unnaturally and so viciously. Butler introduces this claim with reference to the natural superiority of self-love to particular desires. If an animal enters a baited trap in pursuit of food, it acts naturally because it follows the desire that is the strongest. But if a human knowingly satisfies a desire at the expense of his or her long-term good, then he or she acts unnaturally by ignoring the proper superiority of self-love to the ruinous desire. There is, therefore, a crucial distinction to be made in human nature between the strength of some motivating principle and its authority. In prudent behavior they coincide; in imprudent behaviour they clash.

Butler's key ethical doctrine is that of the natural supremacy not of self-love but of conscience. To live virtuously is to do what conscience approves and avoid what it disapproves. This does not mean that Butler identifies virtue with acting from duty (or conscientiousness); for conscience may well add its approval to actions that are already motivated by desire or by self-love. But when we are inclined to do something conscience rejects, or fail to desire what it enjoins, it may well have to supply its own motivating influence.

Butler thinks we usually have no difficulty in identifying right actions. He also thinks that these very largely coincide with the promptings of benevolence. But in the "Dissertation on Virtue" appended to the *Analogy*, he firmly rejects the utilitarian suggestion that virtue and benevolence can be identified. We lack the detailed knowledge of consequences for this to be true, so virtue consists rather in doing those acts that conscience approves—that is, acts of the right kind. That such acts will lead to the general good must be left to providence. He also thinks that providence must ensure that following conscience will not prove to be at odds with the demands of self-love and that benevolence (or love of neighbor) and self-love will also prove, in the end, to coincide.

Butler's case for the supremacy of conscience is therefore based on four related claims: that conscience has a natural authority, that is manifest in the way it makes its judgments; that to disregard it is to behave unnaturally; and that doing what conscience tells us is in the end for our good, even though we may not immediately discern this. These arguments are designed to persuade those who feel they know well enough what conscience tells them to do, but are still inclined to ask whether this is a compelling reason to do it. He tells them that if they recognized the place conscience has in their natures, they would see that it is.

The Rolls Sermons are notable for Butler's shrewdness, theoretical acumen, and wise moral psychology. They contain interesting and durable treatments of themes such as compassion, resentment, forgiveness, and self-deception.

PHILOSOPHICAL THEOLOGY

Butler's ethical sermons are still widely read, and their arguments have not dated. His religious apologetic has fared less well, even though it was better known in the century after his death. The reason for its present lack of influence is the fact that the debates to which it was intended to be a contribution have long since ceased. Butler's intent in the *Analogy of Religion* was to respond to the attacks on Christian orthodoxy made by the Deists. The Deists believed that the rational order of the cosmos revealed by science shows that our world had a creator, but they rejected Christian claims to revelation, maintaining that we only have need of "natural religion"—that is, the moral guidance of conscience and a vague general reverence for God. A deity who is rational in the way the design in nature shows God to be would have no need of special revelation, miracle, or priest craft to instruct us. Butler sees it as his task to restore the traditional connection between belief in God and openness to revelation in the face of this criticism.

Butler wants to encourage his readers, whom he assumes accept the reality of God, to pay close attention to the claims of Christianity and not dismiss them. He thinks that these claims have strong evidence in their favor; but his aim in the *Analogy* is less to show this than to persuade those who doubt it that they would still be prudent to examine them with care. He repeatedly stresses the importance of the claims that Christianity makes and the rashness of disregarding them. Probability, he tells us famously, is the guide of life. This assertion, though it is not accompanied by any philosophical analysis of the concept of probability, has two implications in Butler's thought. First, just as we have, in daily life, to base decisions on likelihoods rather than certainties, so in religious matters we must recognize our intellectual limitations and base our faith on what experience and reflection teach us is likely to be true rather than demand an unattainable certainty. Second, just as in life we often have to base decisions on the fact that there is a small chance of events that it would be foolish not to be prepared for, so in religious matters we should take the claims of revealed religion seriously as along as they have some degree of probability, even if it is a very modest one.

Butler opens the first part of the *Analogy*, on natural religion, with a case for a future life, a case that makes no appeal to providence. The key argument that he uses rests on a distinction between a person's possession of powers and the possession of means for their exercise. Although physical death clearly removes all sign of the capacity to exercise our powers, we cannot assume that it destroys those powers themselves; just as there are many examples in nature of radical transformation in the history of living creatures, so we can reasonably expect the continuance of human powers hereafter. (In a well-known appendix to the *Analogy*, "Of Personal Identity," he further argues that our consciousness reveals to us that we are identical beings in the "strict and philosophical" sense—that is, fundamentally unchanging spiritual substances.)

In the remainder of Part I, Butler draws an analogy between the early and mature stages of human life on the one hand and the present life and the future life taken together on the other. He argues that we can discern clear signs that God teaches us the value of prudent and moral behavior in the early years of life in order to equip us to make good choices in our adult years and that we can reasonably infer that the exercise of virtue in the present life should be viewed as a training that fits us to enter the next. We are, he says, in a state of moral probation—a concept that partially anticipates John Hick's "soul-making" theodicy of the mid-twentieth century. God's government of the world is a "scheme imperfectly comprehended"; our ignorance of it, which Butler repeatedly emphasizes, is nevertheless only partial.

Part II defends revealed religion against deist criticisms. There should be no general presumption against miracles, because occasional divine violations of natural law might still be manifestations of "general laws of wisdom" and thus teach us, even though we could not predict them; and even though biblical prophecies may not have involved foresight on the part of their writers, if one thinks of God as the ultimate author of the book in which they are recorded, they can still reveal a divine purpose. Butler's basic defense, however, is that the recognition of our limitations should deter us from supposing that we know enough of God's purposes to dismiss the claims of revelation without careful study and that the overwhelming importance of Christian claims, if they are true, makes it frivolous and imprudent not to consider them with care, even if their probability may not at first seem high. He insists that with our limitations we should not expect more certainty in religious matters than we do in comparable secular ones, where our knowledge is also often merely partial—a form of argument that anticipates later demands by Christian apologists for philosophers to accord intellectual parity to the claims of religion. He also tells us that the claims of Christianity should be considered as a whole rather than piecemeal and that the case for its acceptance must be a cumulative one.

Butler's theology suffers in retrospect because Hume has made us question whether we can properly draw the analogy between this life and another on which the arguments of Part I of the *Analogy* depend, because only one of the terms of this analogy has been an object of experience. It has also seemed dated because the assumption of divine government that Butler and the Deists shared are no longer current. But many features of his reasoning can be detached from these two handicaps. His emphasis on our intellectual limitations, his doctrine of probation, and his insistence that the case for Christianity is a cumulative and probable on, all have present-day counterparts, and his detailed defenses of revealed religion are easily detachable from their contexts.

See also Clarke, Samuel; Conscience; Deism; Egoism and Altruism; Ethical Egoism; Ethics, History of; Evil; Hobbes, Thomas; Hume, David; Moral Motivation; Revelation; Self-Interest.

Bibliography

There is no complete edition of Butler's works in print at present. The best available is *The Works of Joseph Butler*, edited by J. H. Bernard, 2 vols. London: Macmillan, 1900. Next best is *The Works of Bishop Butler*, edited by W. E. Gladstone, 2 vols., Oxford, 1897. (Gladstone breaks up Butler's paragraphs, which Bernard numbers but leaves intact; and Bernard's notes are often helpful.) Butler, Joseph, *Fifteen Sermons* and *Dissertation upon the Nature of Virtue*, edited by T. A. Roberts, London: S.P.C.K., 1970, is a good recent edition of the Rolls Sermons. The most accessible reprint of the sermons it contains, and of the Dissertation, is *Five Sermons Preached at the Rolls Chapel and a Dissertation upon the Nature of Virtue*, edited by Stephen L. Darwall, Indianapolis: Hackett, 1983. There is no extant edition of the *Analogy of Religion*, although libraries and bookstores often have nineteenth-century reprints of it because it was required reading for Anglican ordinands for many years. As of this writing, a new edition of Butler's sermons is expected from Oxford University Press (U.K.) in 2006, edited by David McNaughton.

There are two general books about Butler and his times that are valuable: W. A. Spooner, *Bishop Butler*, London: Methuen, 1901; and Ernest Campbell Mossner, *Bishop Butler and the Age of Reason*, New York: B. Blom, 1971. A recent collection that contains fine essays on all aspects of Butler's life and work is Christopher Cunliffe, ed., *Joseph Butler's Moral and Religious Thought: Tercentenary Essays*, Oxford: Clarendon Press, 1992. Terence Penelhum, *Butler*, London: Routledge, 1985, covers his ethical teachings and attempts to rescue his philosophical theology from undeserved neglect. Austin Duncan-Jones, *Butler's Moral Philosophy*, Harmondsworth: Penguin, 1952, is a high-quality treatment of the ethics.

There are many good essays and chapters about Butler. On the ethics, the best beginning is Chapter 3 of C. D. Broad's *Five Types of Ethical Theory*, London: Routledge, 1930. A severe critique of Butler that argues his doctine of the naturalness of virtue leads to incoherence is Nicholas L. Sturgeon, "Nature and Conscience in Butler's Ethics," *Philosophical Review* 85 (1976), 316–356. On this and the issue of the supremacy of conscience, see Stephen Darwall, "Conscience as Self-Authorizing in Butler's Ethics" in Cunliffe (1992), 209–242. The notion of the naturalness of virtue is explored with originality in Alan Millar, "Butler in God and Human Nature" in Cunliffe, 293–315. Another excellent essay is Jerome Schneewind, "The Divine Corporation and the History of Ethics," in *Philosophy in History*, edited by R. Rorty, J. B. Schneewind, and Q. Skinner, 173–192, Cambridge, U.K.: Cambridge University Press, 1984.

For a long time the only good treatment of Butler's theology was C. D. Broad, "Bishop Butler as Theologian," in C. D. Broad, *Religion, Philosophy, and Psychical Research*, London: Routledge, 1953, 202–219. The situation improved with Anders Jeffner's *Butler and Hume on Religion*, Stockholm: Diakonistyrelsens Bokforlag, 1966. Penelhum, *Butler* (above), carries the debate further. See also especially the essays by David Brown ("Butler and Deism," 7–28), Basil Mitchell ("Butler as a Christian Apologist," 977–1116), and T. A. Roberts ("Butler and Immortality," 169–188) in Cunliffe. The importance of Butler's thinking as a stimulus to Hume is explored in Paul Russell, "Butler's 'Future State' and Hume's 'Guide of Life,'" *Journal of the History of Philosophy* 42 (2004): 425–448. It is clear that Section 11 of Hume's *Enquiry concerning Human Understanding*, "Of a Particular Providence and Of a Future State," is for the most part an attempt to undercut the use of analogical reasoning found in Butler's *Analogy*. John Hick's "soul-making" theodicy is to be found in his *Evil and the God of Love*, London: Macmillan, 1966.

The best place to begin study of Butler's religious thought, however, is Sermon 15 of the Rolls Sermons, "Of the Ignorance of Man," which prefigures much of the prudential apologetic that the *Analogy* develops in detail.

Terence Penelhum (2005)

BUTLER, SAMUEL
(1835–1902)

The English writer and critic Samuel Butler was the author of the satirical novels *The Way of All Flesh*, *Erewhon*, and *Erewhon Revisited*, as well as several discussions of philosophical biology and the theory of evolution. He was the son of the Reverend Thomas Butler, whom he depicted as a domestic tyrant in *The Way of All Flesh*. Butler was sent to Cambridge by his father in the hope that he would become a clergyman, but after graduating he refused to take orders because of doubts about the Christian creed. In 1859 he emigrated to New Zealand, where he became a successful sheep farmer and for a time a convert to Darwinism. Returning to England in 1864 with enough money to live on, he began a career as an author, painter, and musician. The subject of evolution continued to occupy his mind for many years. It forms the substance of several essays and four books: *Life and Habit* (London, 1878), *Evolution, Old and New* (Lon-

don, 1879), *Unconscious Memory* (London, 1880), and *Luck or Cunning?* (London, 1887). These works reflect a mounting hostility to the ideas of Charles Darwin and a desire to champion those of Erasmus Darwin and the Chevalier de Lamarck. This hostility first made its appearance in *Erewhon* (London, 1872).

EVOLUTION

Butler was neither a scientist nor a philosopher. His discussions of evolution are the work of a literary man with strong intellectual interests but little capacity for exact thought. He was at his best when giving scientific and philosophical ideas an original twist that often put them in quite a new light. To many fellow Victorians he seemed an irreverent skeptic or even an atheist; but in fact, he wanted to retain religion while discarding the Christian creed and to discard Darwin while retaining evolution. This outlook pervades all his major writings.

The central weakness of Darwinism, according to Butler, was its failure to identify the cause of the variations on which selection was said to operate. They were described as random or accidental, which would mean that the course of evolution has been a matter of luck. The older evolutionists, such as Erasmus Darwin and Lamarck, were far sounder in their views, for they attributed the cause of variations to the activity of organisms and to the inherited effects of the use or disuse of their various functions. Not luck, they claimed, but cunning displayed by organisms in coping with their environment lies at the basis of evolution. Hence, the activity of organisms is profoundly purposive. The great mistake of Charles Darwin was to dismiss teleology from the domain of living things, for they then become indistinguishable from machines.

In an essay of 1865 Butler toyed with the idea that machines are adjuncts to organisms, like extra, though inferior, limbs, by means of which organisms have become more highly evolved. Hence, "a leg is only a much better wooden leg than anyone can manufacture." This led Butler to consider the problem of how living things have come to produce their natural organs and to equip themselves with adaptive habits. The answer, he asserted, is that the individual plant or animal must "know" at the start what to do. A fertilized ovum possesses the knowledge it needs to make itself into an embryo and subsequently into an adult organism. This knowledge is really a remembering of what its ancestors did in the past. Hence, we must postulate an "unconscious memory" at work in all living things, binding successive generations and providing the basis for the transmission of acquired characteristics.

Butler then leaped to two sweeping conclusions. First, consciousness and intelligence exist throughout the whole organic world. "For the embryo of the chicken, we claim exactly the same kind of reasoning power and contrivance which we claim for the amoeba, or for our own intelligent performances in later life." Second, since evolution involves a continuous process of derivation, there must be an "identity" between parents and offspring: the latter are not different individuals but *are* the parents at a later evolutionary stage. "Birth has been made too much of." A newborn infant is simply part of an unbroken biological process, not an utterly separate individual. Accordingly, there is a deep unity of all life, so that it constitutes "in reality, nothing but one single creature, of which the component members are but, as it were, blood corpuscles or individual cells."

With the aid of these conclusions, Butler sought to justify an idealistic and religious interpretation of evolution. In *Unconscious Memory* he contended that his earlier separation of the organic from the inorganic was unwarranted. "What we call the inorganic world must be regarded as up to a certain point living, and instinct with consciousness." Hence, "all space is at all times full of a stuff endowed with a mind," and "both stuff and mind are immaterial and imperceptible, so long as they are undisturbed, but the moment they are disturbed, the stuff becomes material and the mind perceptible." Evolution is therefore the life history of this primordial world stuff, "to which no name can be so fittingly applied as 'God.'"

Many of Butler's criticisms of Darwinism have been made irrelevant by the rise of the science of genetics. Yet he was justified in urging those criticisms at the time and in calling attention to vacillations in Darwin's thought on basic issues. If Butler had been more scrupulous in his own thinking and less facile with his pen, his works on philosophical biology might have had greater survival value.

THEOLOGY

Butler's rather unusual theology is set forth in three essays, posthumously published as *God the Known and God the Unknown* (London, 1909). He there contended that an adequate concept of God requires him to be a living person with a material body. To regard God as *merely* a spirit is tantamount to atheism. At first Butler held that the divine body is just the totality of life, the "one single creature" whose unconscious memory is part of the divine mind. When he rejected the distinction between the organic and the inorganic, his view shifted from a "panzoistic" conception of God to pantheism. He intended to rewrite his theology in the light of this shift,

but never managed to do so. One odd belief he expressed was that the grand design of the cosmos points to the existence of "some vaster Person who looms out behind our God, and who stands in the same relation to him as he to us. And behind this vaster and more unknown God there may be yet another, and another, and another." This pyramiding of deities was one of the many items with which Butler enlivened the Victorian scene.

SOCIAL THOUGHT

Despite the barbs he directed at the institutions of his day, Butler's social outlook was conservative. He took the position that those who are rich and successful are the highest types thus far produced in the evolutionary process. Poor men are biological misfits; hence, the sooner they disappear and leave room for those better able to take care of themselves, the better. In the imaginary society of Erewhon, "if a man has made a fortune of over £20,000, they exempt him from all taxation, considering him a work of art and too precious to be meddled with." Butler's account of this society is not so much a blueprint of utopia as a device for satirizing the beliefs and practices of middle-class Englishmen by inverting accepted values. Thus, in Erewhon bodily illness was considered a punishable crime, whereas moral failings deserved sympathy and were given therapeutic treatment. Instead of fostering machinery, the Erewhonians, after a long struggle, destroyed it when they realized that machines, like organisms, were evolving and would soon acquire a mastery over men. In *Erewhon Revisited* (London, 1901), Butler depicted a community showing signs of degeneration, as if to underline the conclusion that a social order is an impermanent evolutionary product and inevitably alters. Yet here again no consistent point of view was worked out.

See also Consciousness; Darwin, Charles Robert; Darwin, Erasmus; Darwinism; Evolutionary Theory; Lamarck, Chevalier de; Pantheism; Philosophy of Biology; Teleology.

Bibliography

Furbank, P. N. *Samuel Butler.* Cambridge, U.K., and New York: Cambridge University Press, 1948.

Jones, H. Festing. *Samuel Butler, Author of Erewhon (1835–1902): A Memoir,* 2 vols. London: Macmillan, 1919. The standard biography.

Kingsmill, Hugh. *After Puritanism.* London: Duckworth, 1929.

Muggeridge, Malcolm. *The Earnest Atheist: A Study of Samuel Butler.* London: Eyre and Spottiswoode, 1936.

Willey, Basil. *Darwin and Butler, Two Versions of Evolution.* New York: Harcourt, Brace, 1960.

T. A. Goudge (1967)

BYZANTINE PHILOSOPHY

The age of the Byzantine Empire stretches from the end of late antiquity to the fall of Constantinople in 1453. During Byzantine times scholars who copied and studied or even lectured on the texts of ancient philosophers are known and praised chiefly for their efforts to transmit and to keep alive the philosophical traditions of antiquity. To take the obvious case of Plato's and Aristotle's works, there are more than 260 Byzantine manuscripts of dialogues by Plato and at least 1,000 Aristotelian texts. This does not mean, however, that all Byzantine scholars should be regarded as mere copyists. There were among them important figures who, being philosophers themselves, not only carefully studied and commented on ancient philosophical works but also wrote their own treatises on central philosophical problems.

How did the Byzantines conceive of philosophy and of themselves as philosophers? John of Damascus (*Dialectica* 1:56), for instance, gives six complementary definitions of philosophy:

(1) the knowledge of beings as beings;

(2) the knowledge of things divine and human;

(3) a preparation for death;

(4) the assimilation of man to God as far as humanly possible;

(5) the art of arts and the science of sciences;

(6) the love of wisdom.

These six definitions, which were often cited by other Byzantine philosophers too, can also be found in the works of the Neoplatonists of the Alexandrian school (for example, David, *Prolegomena* 20.27–31). They are clearly derived from Aristotelian (1, 5), Stoic (2), and Platonic (3, 4) conceptions of philosophy, attesting thus to the Byzantines' solid knowledge and eclectic use of the different traditions in ancient philosophy.

However, the Byzantines were by no means unanimous about the importance of ancient philosophy, or of "the wisdom from without," as they called pagan philosophy in contrast to Christian theology, which they called "the wisdom from within." Some, under the influence of St. Paul and authors like Tatian, considered ancient philosophy useless and dangerous because it corrupts the Christian view of things and leads to heresies. Others, under the influence of Basil the Great and Gregory of Nyssa, claimed that ancient philosophy, if used in a cautious way, could be a preparation for the true faith, help

in its elucidation, and serve as a dialectical weapon against heresies. Moreover, Byzantine philosophers like John Italos and Barlaam of Calabria undertook the task, in some cases at high personal risk, of defending ancient philosophy in its own right, but also as a means for a better understanding of Christian dogma.

The term *philosophy* could also be used in Byzantium in a much wider sense to include encyclopedic knowledge, including mathematical sciences such as astronomy. Sometimes, following some of the Church Fathers, the term could be used to refer to a life of contemplation as exemplified by Christian monasticism. But that philosophy was partly understood as the Christian way of contemplative life does not necessarily mean that philosophy collapsed into theology. On the contrary, the borders between philosophy and theology were reasonably clearly defined in Byzantium.

The view expressed by some Church Fathers, for instance by Clement and by Origen, that philosophy is the handmaiden of theology (*philosophia theologiae ancilla*), was not the dominant position in the Byzantine East. Byzantine philosophy seems to have managed to preserve its autonomy. Even though many of the problems with which Byzantine philosophers were concerned, like that of divine providence, did indeed arise in the context of a Christian theological tradition, these problems nonetheless constitute genuine philosophical issues that would be of interest to any philosopher, even one who did not believe in Christian dogma. For example, the following are some of the issues that profoundly and systematically occupied many Byzantines philosophers: the creation or origin of the world, the existence of God, the ontological status of universals, the character of the perceptible world, the problem of evil and human free will, the relation between soul and body, the necessary requirements for a good life, the possibility of a just state, the connection between faith and reason, the skeptical challenge to knowledge.

But did the Byzantine philosophers express original views in discussing these issues? There is no doubt, of course, that Byzantine philosophical writings are quarries of information about earlier philosophical doctrines, which would have been otherwise completely lost or only meagerly documented. Besides, whatever attitude the Byzantines took towards ancient philosophy, it was impossible for them to escape altogether from its influence. It was ancient philosophy that clearly provided them with a well-articulated theoretical framework and with the philosophical language that served as the basis for their own philosophical discourse. At the same time, however, the Byzantine philosophers offered in their commentaries and treatises numerous clarifications, developments, criticisms, and modifications of ancient doctrines, some of which are philosophically interesting and remarkably subtle.

Even when they simply paraphrased or briefly commented on ancient philosophical texts, the Byzantines presented different degrees of independent thinking; sometimes they gave a slightly different argument to support an established position, sometimes they made a small but interesting addition to an ancient doctrine, and sometimes they considerably diverged from the view generally accepted in antiquity. But this should not be understood as suggesting that the Byzantine philosophers were interested in being original; like most of their late ancient predecessors they would have firmly rejected such a suggestion.

Nevertheless, Byzantine philosophy as a whole exhibits a distinctive character that differentiates it from the previous period in the history of philosophy. For it is clear that many of the views and doctrines presented by the Byzantines originated in their aim to reconcile their Christian tradition with ancient philosophy. For instance, they taught Aristotle's logic as generally useful, but mainly as a preparation for more theoretical studies; they disagreed, however, with his doctrine of the eternity of the world and his understanding of God as the first unmoved mover who moves the heavens but exerts no providence on the details of the sublunary world, including individual human beings. Instead, Byzantine philosophers considered Plato's metaphysics to be closer to the Christian worldview, especially on issues like the immortality of the soul and the creation of the world; still, for doctrinal reasons they could not accept the Platonic theory of metempsychosis and the separate existence of eternal ideas or forms.

Hence, Byzantine philosophers seem to have followed the eclectic tradition of late antiquity and combined aspects of Plato's and Aristotle's theories, although always strongly influenced by Neoplatonic philosophers like Proclus. The Byzantines also engaged in a limited dialogue with the other schools of ancient philosophy; for instance, they were interested in criticizing elements of Epicurean or Stoic doctrine, and they critically examined the implications of the Skeptics' views on the possibility of human knowledge. This is the picture at least up to the fifteenth century, when the leading intellectuals of the time, George Gemistos Pletho and George Scholarios Gennadios, started emphasizing the contrast between ancient philoso-

phers and believed that they should take sides, presenting themselves either as Platonists or as Aristotelians.

BYZANTINE PHILOSOPHERS

In Byzantium there were no institutions of higher education in which philosophers could be trained as philosophers. The main purpose of institutional higher studies was to train civil servants. The figure of the Byzantine philosopher, therefore, emerges as somewhat of a polymath and an erudite scholar, who, moreover, might make use of his knowledge and rhetorical skill to play an active role in the political life of his times. Philosophical instruction was mainly private, but it sometimes received support from the Emperor and the Church, as in the case of the so-called University of Constantinople, which was founded in 1045 by Constantine Monomachos. Such support, however, also meant occasional intervention by the secular or ecclesiastical authorities, as when John Italos was put on trial and condemned for advocating the systematic use of philosophical analysis in clarifying theological issues.

In general, the philosophical curriculum would start with Aristotle's logic, considered as the instrument of all sciences (Porphyry's *Isagoge*, Aristotle's *Categories*, *De interpretatione*, and *Prior Analytics* 1.1–7); then ethics, teaching a rationally ordered moral life of the soul as joined to the body; and finally, through physics and the *quadrivium* (arithmetic, geometry, astronomy, and harmonics), to Platonic or, more precisely, to Neoplatonic metaphysics, which is the highest philosophical science because it has to do with knowledge of first principles and brings the soul nearer to assimilation to the divine.

The genres of philosophical writing in Byzantium are quite diverse. For teaching purposes the Byzantine scholars produced marginal notes and explanatory paraphrases on ancient philosophical works, but also extended commentaries, sometimes in question-and-answer form, small handbooks, or large surveys of philosophy. They also wrote small treatises on specific topics or longer works, occasionally in dialogue form, with the aim of rebutting the views of their opponents and to explain and defend their own theories. To all these we should further add their letters and orations, which frequently made reference to philosophy.

The real starting point of Byzantine philosophy is usually placed in the ninth and tenth century, when the so-called Byzantine humanists, men like the Patriarch Photios, Arethas, or Leo the Mathematician, started again studiously to read, edit, and comment on the works of ancient philosophers. Having said that, however, the distinctive character of Byzantine philosophy undoubtedly owes a lot to the influence of the previous period, which was dominated by the thought of the Church Fathers such as Basil the Great, Gregory of Nyssa, Pseudo-Dionysius, Maximus the Confessor, and John of Damascus.

Photios (820–891), who is famous mainly for his *Bibliotheke*, a vast compilation of ancient Greek literature, also taught Aristotelian logic and wrote, for this purpose, comments on Aristotle's *Categories*. In addition, he composed a number of small treatises in which he criticized both Plato's and Aristotle's views, especially their theories on universals; he himself claimed that universals have no independent existence but are conceived by God and are instruments of God's will. Arethas (c. 850–944) also commented on Aristotle's *Categories* and Porphyry's *Isagoge*, but he is better known for having been instrumental in the transmission of ancient texts, in particular the Platonic corpus. He commissioned the transcription of a complete copy of Plato's works, to which he added marginal notes; the first part of his Plato text is extant as the famous Clarkianus 39 manuscript in the Bodleian Library of Oxford. Unfortunately, we know little about Leo the Mathematician (c.790–869), who seems to have taught philosophy at the so-called Magnaura School in Constantinople.

There is a significant development from the humanistic Photios and Arethas interests to the way the Byzantines in the eleventh and twelfth century, the period of the Comneni, viewed the philosopher as someone with a hard-earned and unsurpassed knowledge in all branches of learning, and especially as someone who formed his own views on the philosophical topics discussed by the ancients. Michael Psellos (1018–1078) was one of the most erudite and intriguing figures of the Byzantine Middle Ages. He was given the honorific title "first among the philosophers" and taught all branches of philosophy. He commented on Aristotle's logic (*Categories*, *De interpretatione*, *Prior Analytics*) and his physics, and he wrote a large number of short treatises discussing particular problems raised by his pupils; he also compiled a short encyclopaedia with the title *De omnifaria doctrina*. He was greatly influenced by Proclus, whom he considered as an authority among ancient authors. In his attempts to advance philosophical learning he was often attacked concerning his theological orthodoxy, so that he often had to be careful to distance himself from heretical doctrines, as in his writings on the *Chaldaean Oracles*.

John Italos (c.1025–1082), a pupil of Psellos, who was condemned by the Church of Constantinople for his extensive use of logical reasoning in theological matters,

wrote treatises discussing the Aristotelian categories and commented on Aristotle's logic (*De interpretatione*, *Topics*). Eustratios of Nicaea (c.1050–1120) and Michael of Ephesus (c.1050–1129) belonged to the intellectual circle around Anna Comnena and took part in her project to produce commentaries on Aristotle's works.

Eustratius wrote commentaries on Aristotle's *Posterior Analytics* and *Nicomachean Ethics*, whereas Michael of Ephesus commented on Aristotle's metaphysics, logic (*Sophistici elenchi*), ethics, and natural philosophy (*Parva naturalia*, *De partibus animalium*, *De generatione animalium*, *De motu animalium*, and *De incessu animalium*). Their work, in which they followed ancient commentaries (some of which are now lost) but also added their own insightful remarks, was instrumental in the transmission and revolutionary rediscovery of Aristotelian thought in the Latin West. Finally, Nicholas of Methone (d. 1165) wrote at the same time a detailed refutation of Proclus's *Elements of Theology*. During the short period after the Latin conquest of Constantinople in 1204, when the center of Byzantine intellectual life moved to Nicaea in Asia Minor, the main intellectual figure was Nikephoros Blemmydes (1197–1272), who wrote a much-used handbook of physics and logic that also was translated in Latin.

Lastly, the final centuries of the Byzantine empire, which are known as the Palaeologan period, saw a renewal of interest in the sciences, particularly in mathematics and astronomy. George Pachymeres (1242–1310) composed a summary of Aristotelian philosophy and wrote Neoplatonic commentaries, supplementing Proclus's commentary on Plato's *Parmenides*. Theodore Metochites (1270–1332) criticized Aristotelian physics and metaphysics in debate with Nikephoros Choumnos (c. 1250–1327), who in turn attacked the orthodoxy of Neoplatonic psychology. Sophonias and Leo Magentinos paraphrased works of Aristotle; Sophonias paraphrased Aristotle's *Categories*, *Sophistici elenchi*, and *De anima*, while Leo Magentinos paraphrased Aristotle's *De interpretatione*, *Prior Analytics*, and *Sophistici elenchi*.

Moreover, three important intellectuals of the fourteenth century, namely Nikephoros Gregoras (1290/3–1358/61), Barlaam of Calabria (c. 1290–1348), and Gregory Palamas (c.1296–1359), got involved in a fierce dispute over the use of logical reasoning in theology. Gregoras claimed that logical studies should be regarded as completely useless and should be therefore altogether dismissed, whereas Barlaam and Palamas adopted a more complex attitude toward logic. They both stressed that logic is indeed useful in defending Christian dogma against pagans and heretics, but they disagreed about the limits of the use of logical reasoning in clarifying or establishing the truth of Christian belief; whereas Barlaam argued that logical methods can be used to prove the Christian beliefs, Palamas insisted that logical arguments are of no help in our attempt to acquire knowledge of God and of his attributes. The controversy between Gregoras, Barlaam, and Palamas extended to a second stage, known as the Hesychast debate, which centered on the method of prayer and contemplation of the Byzantine monks, who claimed to be able to achieve communion with God through inner quietude and silence.

In the fifteenth century, around the time of the fall of Constantinople, a main focus of Byzantine philosophers was, as mentioned above, stressing the differences between Plato and Aristotle and determining the superiority of the one over the other. George Gemistos Plethon (c. 1360–c. 1453) is famous for his renewal of Proclus's Neoplatonism as a theological and political alternative to Christianity. In his treatise *De Platonis et Aristotelis philosophiae differentia* he argued for the superiority of Plato over Aristotle; in his *Laws* he presented an utopia based primarily upon Plato and the Neoplatonists. George Scholarios Gennadios (c. 1400–1424) thought that Pletho's utopia was heretical and should be consigned to the flames. He defended Aristotle's works and was more favourable to Latin scholasticism. He commented on Aristotle's logic (*Categories, De interpretatione*), natural philosophy (*Physics 1–3, Parva naturalia*), and Aristotle's *De anima*. He also translated part of Petrus Hispanus's *Summulae logicales* and works by Thomas Acquinas, for instance the *De fallaciis* and his commentary on the *Posterior Analytics*. Bessarion (1403–1472), who had studied under Pletho, tried to mediate the dispute between Pletho and Scholarios, and gave a sympathetic summary of Plato's philosophy, which he thought reconcilable with Aristotelianism. He, like Pletho, greatly helped to bring works of Plato and Aristotle to the attention of Italian humanists.

From the second half of the thirteenth century onward, there were translations into Greek of Western Latin texts, especially logical texts: Manuel Holobolos (fl. 1267) translated Boethius's *De topicis differentiis* and *De hypotheticis syllogismis*; Maximos Planudes (c. 1255–c. 1305) translated Boethius's *De consolatione philosophiae* and Augustine's *De trinitate*; Demetrios Kydones (c. 1324–97/8) and his brother Prochoros Kydones (c. 1333–69/70) translated Augustine, Anselm, and Thomas Aquinas. But it was only in the fifteenth century that Byzantine and Western philosophers actually began to talk to one another, to read one another's books, and to be influenced by others' traditions and views. Still, although the Byzantine scholars like John Argyropoulos—who went to Italy and worked there as teachers of Greek, editors of Greek texts and translators, and as teachers of philosophy—exerted a fertile influence on the West, Byzantium itself in general remained closed to Western scholasticism.

THE STUDY OF BYZANTINE PHILOSOPHY

Byzantine philosophy remains a little-explored field. Most of the writings of Byzantine philosophers are yet unpublished or are available only in old and often quite inadequate editions. The nineteenth-century Berlin series *Commentaria in Aristotelem Graeca*, which was supposed to include all commentaries on Aristotle's works, actually includes a very small selection of Byzantine commentaries. Translations of and commentaries on Byzantine philosophical works are hardly ever available. In addition, there are important unresolved issues about the authorship of many Byzantine philosophical texts, and we often have no reliable information concerning their sources. But even when we do have careful editions of the philosophical works of Byzantine thinkers, their philosophical contribution for the most part still needs to be critically assessed. Being regarded either as mere scholars or as religious thinkers, Byzantine philosophers have not been studied on their own merit, and their works have hardly been scrutinized as works of philosophy.

The interest of the scholars of the nineteenth and early twentieth century, who worked with great care on some Byzantine philosophical texts, was not primarily philosophical. Philosophers, on the other hand, understandably were discouraged both by the rhetorical style of the Byzantine writings and by the theological interests displayed in much of Byzantine philosophy. Therefore, although distinguished historians have in the past tried to reconstruct the intellectual life of the Byzantine period, we still lack even the beginnings of a systematic understanding of the philosophical works produced in Byzantium. It is particularly telling that there is no adequate recent monograph even on the most prominent Byzantine philosopher, Michael Psellos.

After World War II, however, we see significant changes in the study of Byzantine philosophy. These changes clearly are connected with the rediscovery and philosophical reappraisal of the Western medieval philosophical tradition and of certain areas in ancient philosophy, such as the works of the Neoplatonists and of the ancient commentators. Critical editions of texts are appearing regularly, in particular in the series *Corpus Philosophorum Medii Aevi—Philosophi Byzantini* (The Academy of Athens) and in the Bibliotheca Teubneriana. Moreover, books and articles are now being published that investigate the teaching of philosophy in Byzantium and the original philosophical contributions of Byzantine philosophers in a philosophically more adequate and serious way. Nevertheless, much more work is required to achieve a reliable overview of Byzantine thought. Following the rising interest of the last decades of the twentieth century, it now seems important to encourage further the systematic study and critical assessment of the individual works of Byzantine thinkers. Most importantly, we need to take their works seriously as philosophical writings; putting aside our prejudices and misconceptions, we need to make a renewed effort to reconstruct and to do justice to Byzantine philosophy.

See also Analysis, Philosophical; Anselm, St.; Aristotelianism; Aristotle; Augustine, St.; Boethius, Anicius Manlius Severinus; Clement of Alexandria; Determinism and Freedom; Evil, The Problem of; Gregory of Nyssa; John of Damascus; Medieval Philosophy; Neoplatonism; Origen; Patristic Philosophy; Plato; Platonism and the Platonic Tradition; Pletho, Giorgius Gemistus; Proclus; Pseudo-Dionysius; Stoicism; Thomas Aquinas, St.

Bibliography

Arethas of Caesarea. *Scholia on Porphyry's Isagoge and Aristotle's Categories.* Edited by M. Share. Athens: The Academy of Athens, 1994.

Gregoras, Nikephoros. *Antirrhetika I.* Edited by H.-V. Beyer. Vienna: Verl. d. Osterr. Akad. D. Wiss., 1976.

Gregoras, Nikephoros. *Fiorenzo o Intorno alla Sapienza.* Edited by P. Leone. Naples: University of Naples, 1975.

Italos, Joannes, and Leon Magentinos. *Byzantinische Kommentatoren der aristotelischen Topik.* Edited by Sofia Kotsabassi. Thessaloniki, Greece: Vanias, 1999.

John of Damascus. *Schriften.* Edited by B. Kotter. Berlin: De Gruyter, 1969.

Nicholas of Methone. *Refutation of Proclus' Elements of Theology.* Edited by A.A. Angelou. Athens: The Academy of Athens, 1984.

Pachymeres, George. *Commentary on Plato's Parmenides.* Edited by T. Gadra et al. Athens: The Academy of Athens, 1989.

Pachymeres, George. *Philosophia. Buch 10. Kommentar zur Metaphysik des Aristoteles.* Edited by Eleni Pappa Athens: The Academy of Athens, 2002.

Photios. *Epistulae et Amphilochia.* Edited by L. G. Westerink. Leipzig: Teubner, 1986.

Pletho, George Gemistos. *Contra Scholarii pro Aristotele objections.* Edited by E. V. Maltese. Leipzig: Teubner, 1988.

Pletho, George Gemistos. *Oracles Chaldaïques. Recension de Georges Gémiste Pléthon.* Edited by Brigitte Tambrun-Krasker. Athens: The Academy of Athens, 1995.

Pletho, George Gemistos. *Traité des vertus.* Edited by Brigitte Tambrun-Krasker. Athens: The Academy of Athens, 1987.

Psellos, Michael. *De omnifaria doctrina.* Edited by L. G. Westerink. Utrecht: J. L. Beuers N.V., 1948.

Psellos, Michael. *Philosophica minora I.* Edited by J. M. Duffy. Leipzig: Teubner, 1992.

Psellos, Michael. *Philosophica minora II.* Edited by D. J. O'Meara. Leipzig: Teubner, 1989.

Scholarios Gennadios, George. *Oeuvres complètes.* Edited by L. Petit, X. A. Sidéridès, and M. Jugie. Paris: Maison de la bonne presse, 1936.

SUGGESTED READING

Benakis, Linos. "Commentaries and Commentators on the Logical Works of Aristotle in Byzantium." In *Gedankenzeichen. Festschrift Klaus Oehler.* Edited by R. Clausen and R. Daube-Schackat. Tübingen, Germany: Stauffenburg, 1988: 3–12.

Benakis, Linos. "Bibliographie internationale sur la philosophie byzantine (1949–1990)." In *Bibliographie byzantine publiée à l'occasion du XVIIIe Congrès international d'Etudes byzantines.* Athens: Assoc. intern. D. Etud. Byz., 1991.

Benakis, Linos. "Commentaries and Commentators on the Works of Aristotle (Except the Logical Ones) in Byzantium." In *Historia philosophiae Medii Aevi. Festschrift Kurt Flasch.* Edited by B. Mojsisch and O. Pluta. Amsterdam: B. R. Grüner, 1991. Vol. I: 45–54.

Bydén, Börje. *Theodore Metochites' Stoicheiosis Astronomike and the Study of Natural Philosophy and Mathematics in Early Palaiologan Byzantium.* Göteborg, Sweden: Acta Universitatis Gothoburgensis, 2003.

Hunger, Herbert. *Die hochsprachliche profane Literatur der Byzantiner.* Munich: C.H. Beck, 1978. Vol. 1:3–62.

Ierodiakonou, Katerina, ed. *Byzantine Philosophy and Its Ancient Sources.* Oxford: Oxford University Press, 2002.

Kapriev, Georgi. *Philosophie in Byzanz.* Wurzburg, Germany: Konigshausen & Neumann, 2005.

Lemerle, Paul. *Le premier humanisme byzantin.* Paris: Presses Univeritaires de France, 1971.

Oehler, Klaus. *Antike Philosophie und byzantinische Mittelalter.* Munich: C. H. Beck, 1969.

Podskalsky, Gerhard. *Theologie und Philosophie in Byzanz.* Munich: C. H. Beck, 1969.

Ševčenko, Ihor. *Études sur la polémique entre Théodore Métochite et Nicéphore Choumnos.* Brussels: Byzantion, 1962.

Tatakis, Basil. *La philosophie byzantine.* Paris: Presses Univeritaires de France, 1949. (Modern Greek translation with bibliography for 1949–1976 by L. Benakis, Athens: Etaireia Spoudon, 1977; English translation by N. J. Moutafakis, Indianapolis/Cambridge: Hackett, 2003.)

Wilson, Nigel. *Scholars of Byzantium.* London: Duckworth, 1983.

Katerina Ierodiakonou (2005)